HOW TO USE THIS BOOK

1. ■ If you know the name of your plant, the problem it has, or the insect that is bothering it, look up that name in the index beginning on **PAGE 17.**

2. ■ If you don't know the name of your plant, turn to one of these sections:

Houseplants **PAGE 173**

Lawns **PAGE 249**

Groundcovers **PAGE 281**

Annuals, Perennials, and Bulbs **PAGE 303**

Trees, Shrubs, and Vines **PAGE 405**

Fruit and Nut Trees **PAGE 591**

Vegetables, Berries, and Grapes **PAGE 659**

3. ■ If you have a household pest and don't know its name, turn to **PAGE 785.**

4. ■ If you want to know more about a problem, turn to one of these pages:

Weeds **PAGE 811**

Plant Diseases **PAGE 847**

Insects **PAGE 863**

Animal Pests **PAGE 895**

Soil, Cultural, and Climate Problems **PAGE 903**

5. ■ For a complete description of ORTHO products and a list of the problems each solves, turn to **PAGE 929.**

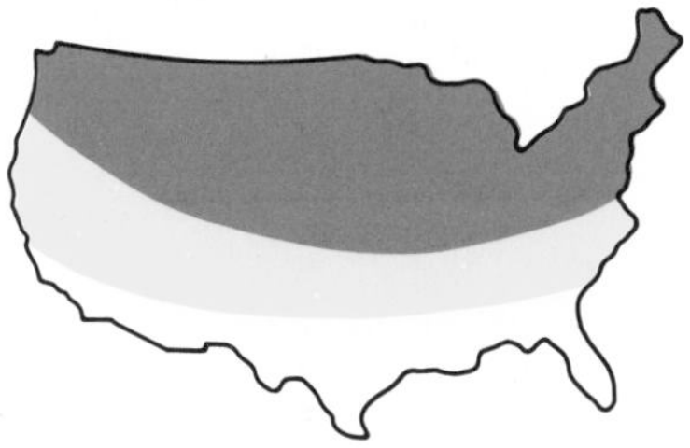

Each problem is accompanied by a map of the United States. In parts of the country that are colored red, the problem is severe or commonplace. In parts of the country that are yellow, the problem is secondary or occasional. In parts of the country that are white, the problem is rare or nonexistent.

THE ORTHO PROBLEM SOLVER

SECOND EDITION

THE ORTHO PROBLEM SOLVER

SECOND EDITION

Edited by Michael D. Smith

Ortho Information Services
San Francisco, California

Howard County Library
Big Spring, Texas

Project Editor:	Jim Beley
Editor:	Deni W. Stein
Associate Editors:	Julia W. Hall Alice E. Mace
Writers:	Clare A. Binko Gene Joyner Wayne S. Moore Robert D. Raabe Lauren B. Swezey
Illustrator:	Ellen Blonder
Photographic Editors:	Michael D. McKinley Pamela K. Peirce
Indexer:	Elinor Lindheimer
Copy Editors:	Teresa Castle Nancy Cooney Scott Lowe Jessie Wood
Research Assistants:	Jo Brownold Ann Tweed
Editorial Assistants:	Wade F. Anderson William Lawrence William F. Yusavage
System Manager:	Mark Zielinski
Production Managers:	Laurie Sheldon Ernest Tasaki
Designers:	John A. Williams Barbara Ziller
Publisher:	Robert L. Iacopi
Editorial Director:	Min S. Yee

First printing in September 1984

ISBN 0-89721-032-8

Library of Congress Catalog Card Number
84-061510

Chevron Chemical Company
575 Market Street, San Francisco, CA 94105

To the members of the Cooperative Extension Service, who have been solving America's garden problems since 1914.

PREFACE

We at Ortho, as publishers of gardening books and as manufacturers of a leading line of garden chemicals, have been very aware of the difficulty experienced by home gardeners in finding information about plant problems. This book is an attempt to make that information conveniently accessible to every gardener.

Our goal in writing *The Ortho Problem Solver* has been to help the reader:

1. Diagnose a problem correctly.
2. Understand what is causing it.
3. Find a solution.

We have avoided using terms that are known only to horticulturists or experienced gardeners, but if you want to know these terms, there is a glossary on page 168. We have tried to give you only the information that you need to solve your specific problem, but if you want to know more about it, we refer you to pages that give more information.

Our first step in writing *The Ortho Problem Solver* was to gather plant lists from more than 200 horticulturists in all parts of the country. These lists represented nearly all of the plants grown in the homes and gardens of each state. From this information, we compiled a list of the most popular house and garden plants.

Then we sent this list to professionals in the fields of plant problem-solving—entomologists, plant pathologists, and Cooperative Extension agents—and asked them to tell us about the most serious problems these plants had in their part of the country. From this information we compiled the plant problems included in *The Ortho Problem Solver*.

We gave the task of writing the houseplant section to an expert—Dr. Robert Raabe, Extension Plant Pathologist at the University of California, Berkeley, and a specialist in identifying and solving problems of houseplants.

Information about problems of garden plants and their solutions come from our own scientists at Ortho and from the Cooperative Extension services of each of the states. We consulted the Cooperative Extension because Extension scientists have had the opportunity to study the most severe problems in their state. Also, since Extension literature is constantly updated, we knew the information would be current.

Some of the most difficult information to locate concerned the range of each problem—the information on the small maps that accompany each problem. Although we feel it is important for a reader to know whether a certain problem is serious in his area, the range of most of these problems is tenuous and constantly changing. A problem may be severe in one county and nonexistent in the next. At best, these maps represent a generalization and an approximization. If a map needs to be adjusted for your area, please let us know. We will refine the maps in future editions so they reflect as accurately as possible constantly changing situations.

A word of explanation is needed about the solutions we offer. The "Solution" section of each problem assumes that you have seen the problem at the time when the symptoms first become obvious. Our solution begins by telling you what you can do right now to alleviate that problem. Then it tells you what changes you can make in the environment or in your gardening practices to prevent the return of that problem. In many cases, this involves a chemical spray as an immediate solution, and a cultural change or a resistant variety as a long-range solution.

We offer several solutions for most of the problems in this book. We leave it to your judgment to choose those most appropriate to your situation. For example, we tell you that you can protect your sycamore tree from anthracnose by spraying it with a fungicide in the spring. If your sycamore is 6 feet high, you might choose to spray it next spring. But if it is 40 feet high, you will find that hiring an arborist to spray it will be expensive. From our description of the problem, you know that anthracnose seldom does permanent harm to the tree, so you may choose to do nothing.

We recommend Ortho products by brand name in this book because we are a part of Chevron Chemical Company, which manufactures these products, and we can vouch for their quality and consistency. If Ortho does not make a product to solve a problem, we recommend chemical solutions by their generic names—the common name of the active ingredient. When we recommend chemicals by the names of their active ingredients, we say to apply a product "that contains" the active ingredient. This wording alerts you to the fact that you may not find a product by that name, but must look on the list of active ingredients on the product labels. Ask your garden center professional to help you select a product.

When we recommend an Ortho product, we know that it will do the job for which we recommend it, and that it will not harm your plant if you use it according to label directions. But when choosing products by a generic name—even if these are Ortho products—read the label carefully. Although all *malathion* is the same, all products containing it are not. Even though we know *malathion* will solve a particular problem and tell you so, some products that contain *malathion* may be manufactured for a different purpose, and may injure your plant. Be sure that the plant you wish to spray is listed on the product label.

Also, since we can't know the individual circumstances of your problem, the solutions we offer are not guaranteed. We offer the best general proposals we know for helping to solve common garden problems, but we do not and cannot assume liability for failure of our recommendations to solve any particular problem or for any injury that comes as a result of following these instructions. Always read pesticide labels carefully and follow the label directions to the letter.

Since you are the ultimate judge of how successful we have been in helping you to solve your garden problems, we invite you to tell us of any inaccuracy or omission you find in *The Ortho Problem Solver*. We hope, with your help, to make the book ever more useful to the home gardener. Please send your comments to:

The Ortho Problem Solver
Ortho Information Services
Chevron Chemical Company
P.O. Box 7144
San Francisco, CA 94120-7144

Consultants

This has been a vast project and we have received help from hundreds of people—members of the Cooperative Extension Service, horticulturists, nursery professionals, and knowledgeable amateur gardeners. The following names are those of major consultants—people who spent many hours checking manuscripts for accuracy and patiently answered our questions about fine points of obscure garden problems. The accuracy and validity of this book are due to the careful work of these people.

Dr. Jan Abernathie
Plant Pathologist
Chesapeake, VA

Dr. James Beutel
Extension Pomologist
University of California, Davis

Dr. Darrel R. Bienz
Professor of Horticulture
Washington State University

Dr. Eugene Brady
Professor of Entomology
Universiy of Georgia

Bartow H. Bridges, Jr.
Landscape Architect and
Horticulturist
Virginia Beach, VA

Dr. Jack Butler
Department of Horticulture
Colorado State University

Dr. Ralph S. Byther
Extension Plant Pathologist
Washington State University

Sharon J. Collman
County Extension Agent
Seattle, WA

Dr. Samuel D. Cotner
Extension Horticulturist
Texas A&M University

Dr. G. Douglas Crater
Extension Horticulturist,
Floriculture
University of Georgia

Dr. T. E. Crocker
Professor of Fruit Crops
University of Florida

Dr. J. A. Crozier
Chevron Chemical Company
San Francisco, CA

Dr. Spencer H. Davis, Jr.
Horticultural Consultant
North Brunswick, NJ

Dr. August De Hertogh
Department of Horticultural Science
North Carolina State University

Dr. Clyde Elmore
Extension Weed Scientist
University of California, Davis

Barbara H. Emerson
Senior Product Specialist
Union Carbide Agr. Products Co.
Research Triangle Park, NC

Dr. James R. Feucht
Extension Professor,
Department of Horticulture
Colorado State University

Dr. Ralph Garren, Jr.
Small Fruit Specialist
Cooperative Extension Service
Oregon State University

Dr. M. Ali Harivandi
Cooperative Extension
University of California, Berkeley

Duane Hatch
Cooperative Extension Service
Utah State University

PREFACE

Dr. Sammy Helmers
Area Extension Horticulturist
Stevenville, TX

Kermit Hildahl
Cooperative Extension
University of Missouri

Everett E. Janne
Landscape Horticulturist
Texas Agricultural Extension Service
College Station, TX

Dr. Ron Jones
Department of Plant Pathology
North Carolina State University

Caroline Klass
Senior Extension Associate
Department of Entomology
Cornell University

Dr. Charles Marr
Extension Horticulturist
Kansas State University

Bernard Moore
Extension Plant Diagnostician, Retired
Oregon State University

Lester P. Nichols, Professor
Emeritus of Plant Pathology
The Pennsylvania State University

Dr. Norman F. Oebker
Vegetables Specialist
Cooperative Extension Service
University of Arizona

Dr. Howard Ohr
Plant Pathologist
Cooperative Extension Service
University of California, Riverside

Dr. Albert O. Paulus
Plant Pathologist
University of California, Riverside

Dr. Charles C. Powell, Jr.
Department of Plant Pathology
Ohio State University

Dr. Robert D. Raabe
Plant Pathologist
University of California, Berkeley

Dr. Charles Sacamano
Professor of Horticulture
University of Arizona

Professor Donald Schuder
Extension Entomologist
Purdue University

Dr. Arden Sherf
Professor, Department of Pathology
Cornell University

Dr. Gary Simone
Extension Plant Pathologist
University of Florida

Dr. Walter Stevenson
Associate Professor of Plant Pathology
University of Wisconsin

Dr. O. Clifton Taylor
Statewide Air Pollution Research Center
University of California, Riverside

William Titus
County Coordinator
Cooperative Extension Service
Plainview, NY

Dr. John Tomkins
Associate Professor of Pomology
Cornell University

Carl A. Totemeier
Director
Old Westbury Gardens
Old Westbury, NY

John White
County Extension Agent—Horticulture
El Paso, TX

Dr. Gayle Worf
Extension Plant Pathologist
University of Wisconsin

SPECIAL CONSULTANTS

Many other gardening professionals and gifted amateurs have shared their experience and wisdom with us. The people on the following list are specialists in particular problems. They have often been able to supply answers when nobody else could, and we are deeply indebted to them for their contribution to *The Ortho Problem Solver*.

Dr. Maynard Cummings
Extension Wildlife Specialist
University of California, Davis

Phil Horne
Mosley Nurseries
Lake Worth, FL

Joseph R. Konwinski
Turfgrass Consultant
Lake Worth, FL

Dr. Lloyd A. Lider
Professor of Viticulture
University of California, Davis

Dr. Wayne S. Moore
Entomologist
Berkeley, CA

John Pehrson
Extension Agent
Parlier, CA

Warren G. Roberts
U.C. Davis Arboretum Superintendent
University of California, Davis

Donald Rosedale
Cooperative Extension Service
University of California, Riverside

Dr. Terrel P. Salmon
Extension Wildlife Specialist
University of California, Davis

Ross R. Sanborn
University of California
Farm Advisor
Contra Costa County, CA

Joseph Savage
Entomologist
Cooperative Extension Service
Cornell University

Arthur Slater
Senior Environmental Health and Safety Technologist
University of California, Berkeley

Richard Tassan
Staff Research Assistant
University of California, Berkeley

PHOTOGRAPHERS

In order to make *The Ortho Problem Solver* as useful as possible, we have published a color photograph of every problem in the book. Gathering this many photographs was a tremendous task. We relied extensively on college professors and county extension agents for photographic contributions. Many of the photographs were taken originally for use in teaching students or the public about plant problems. We wish to thank the following photographers for their invaluable assistance in supplying these photographs.

After each photographer's name, we have listed the pages on which their photographs appear. The letter that follows the page number shows the position of the photograph on the page, from left to right. A lower-case letter "i" refers to an insert photograph.

Ralph J. Adkins: 414C, 427B, 446C, 450A, 458B, 466B, 483C, 487C, 510A, 515A, 531A, 549B, 560A, 571C, 581C, 587A, 599C, 698Ai, 699B, 708B, 723C, 750C, 770B, 774A, 781B, 818C, 819C, 826A, 833B, 840B, 844C, 876C

Scott T. Adkins: 435C, 716A, 829B

Airrigation Engineering Co., Inc.: 428A

Roger D. Akre: 874A, 880C

William W. Allen: 613A, 613B, 651A

American Phytopathological Society: 210A, 771A
K. Hickey: 594B(also on cover)
Kirby: 706C
A.A. MacNab: 718Ci, 725Ci
J.R. McGrew: 732A
A.F. Sherf: 710C, 719C, 740A
T.B. Sutton: 608C, 642C
K. Yoder: 636B

Arthur L. Antonelli: 563C

William C. Aplin: 276B

Allan M. Armitage: 201C, 399A

Max E. Badgley: 181A, 261B, 586C, 598A, 614C(also on cover), 623A, 623Ai, 623B, 637C, 646Bi, 659, 664A, 664B, 675C, 711C, 728C, 748B, 751C, 768B, 777A, 787C, 789C, 795B, 797A, 802A, 803C, 805B, 807C, 817A, 872B, 874C, 876B, 878A, 881C, 888B, 889A, 890A, 890B, 891A, 891B, 892Bi, 893B

J.R. Baker: 461B, 507B, 546C, 572B

D.R. Bienz: 781A, 858C, 859A

Ray R. Bingham: 604B, 613C, 681B, 727C

Laurie Black: 566A, 566B

John Blaustein: 908A, 925A, 927C

Allen Boger: 208C, 250B, 251B, 254B, 259A, 260A, 272B, 272C, 275A, 284B, 285C, 310C, 311B, 408B, 419B, 421B, 423A, 429B, 434B, 435B, 436A, 438A, 439A, 439C, 447B, 449B, 455B, 469C, 472B, 473A, 474C, 474Ci, 484A, 488B, 488C, 490A, 495A, 512C, 519B, 519C, 533C, 541C, 562A, 576C, 582A, 593A, 595C, 597A, 600B, 661A, 662B, 662C, 663B, 665A, 667B, 668A, 668C, 682A, 684B, 684C, 686A, 688B, 693A, 715A, 726C, 729B, 733B, 746C, 759B, 764C, 765A, 773A, 773B, 779Ci, 780B, 852C, 853A, 896A, 898A, 904C, 906B, 907B, 909C, 919B, 923B

R. Harper Brame: 445C, 471B, 494A, 510B, 542C(also on cover), 549Bi, 550A, 559B, 588A, 648B, 669B, 684Ai, 712B, 723B, 775C, 777B, 843C, 843Ci

Bartow H. Bridges, Jr.: 263B, 270C, 294A, 408C, 421C, 428B, 431A, 433C, 458A, 459B, 461A, 482C, 501A, 501B, 516A, 533B, 856C, 910A, 927A

Jackie D. Butler: 256C, 265B, 269C

PREFACE

Ralph S. Byther: 190C, 224A, 246A, 255B, 293B, 310A, 311C, 370Ci, 376C, 377A, 397A, 397B, 405, 413C, 437B, 437C, 443A, 451Ci, 462A, 464B, 471C, 477C, 478C, 480C, 492A, 496A, 500B, 518C, 529C, 530B, 534C, 536A, 541A, 541Ai, 547C, 551C, 563A, 567A, 578A, 580A, 597Ci, 604C, 607B, 608B, 612B, 618C, 619B, 631A, 634C, 635B, 642A, 649A, 652B, 655C, 656A, 656Ai, 669A, 683C, 683Ci, 690B, 690C, 692B, 692C, 694C, 695A, 695B, 702C, 703A, 704B, 706A, 716C, 720B, 721B, 721C, 735B, 741A, 743C, 744A, 744B, 755A, 762C, 764B, 765C, 766C, 767A, 775A, 775B, 854C, 857C, 899B, 925C

Kristie Callan: 186C, 189B, 192C, 193A, 193C, 195B, 198A, 199B, 200B, 203B, 206C, 215C, 220B, 224C, 227A, 229C, 237A, 238A, 292C, 295A, 298A, 299B, 305B, 306A, 306B, 307B, 308B, 309B, 310B, 312B, 313A, 313B, 313C, 315C, 317C, 318A, 318B, 319B, 319C, 320C, 321A, 321B, 321C, 322B, 323C, 324A, 324B, 325A, 325C, 327B, 327C, 328A, 329A, 329B, 330B, 331A, 331B, 332B, 332C, 333C, 334C, 335A, 335C, 336A, 336B, 336C, 337A, 338A, 339A, 340A, 340C, 341A, 341B, 341C, 342B, 343A, 343C, 344A, 345B, 345C, 346A, 346B, 346C, 347A, 347B, 347C, 348A, 348B(also on cover), 349A, 349B, 349C, 350A, 351A, 351B, 351C, 352B, 353A, 353C, 354C, 355C, 356A, 356B, 356C, 357B, 357C, 358A, 358B, 361A, 361B, 361C, 362A, 362C, 364A, 365A, 365B, 365C, 366A, 366B, 367A, 367B, 369C, 370A, 370B, 371A, 371B, 372B, 373B, 373C, 374C, 375A, 376A, 376B, 377C, 379B, 381A, 383B, 383C, 384A, 384C, 385B, 386B, 386C, 387A, 387B, 388A, 388B, 389A, 389B, 389C, 390A, 390B(also on cover), 390C, 391B, 392C, 394A, 394B, 395A, 395C, 396A, 396B, 396C, 397C, 398C, 399C, 400C, 401A, 401B, 401C, 403A, 451A, 467C, 499B, 603B, 702B(also on cover), 734A, 734B,

Kristie Callan (continued): 734C, 742C, 767B, 917C

T.D. Canerday: 889B

Chevron Chemical Company: 265C, 278A, 498A, 526C, 564C, 637B, 672B, 841B, 905A, 912B, 913A, 913B, 914C, 918C, 920B, 922B

Dick Christman: 161, 678C, 787B, 929

Jack K. Clark: 286C, 328B, 430B, 600A, 625Ai, 626C, 629C, 653C, 653Ci, 654C, 729A, 731Ci, 754Bi, 787A, 793B, 796B, 804C, 805A, 806C, 884B, 892B, 895, 899A, 899C

Jack K. Clark, Bio-Tec Images: 375C, 730B, 650C, 796A

Clemson University: 712A, 791C

James S. Coartney: 179C, 480A, 561C, 591, 607A

Josephine Coatsworth: 907C, 915B, 924C

Sharon J. Collman: 180C, 260C, 270A, 288C, 303, 309A, 320A, 359A, 392A, 393A, 411C, 413A, 415B, 415C, 417B, 419C, 420C, 421A, 423C, 425B, 425C, 427A, 430C, 436B, 440B, 450B, 450C, 451C, 479A, 479C, 481C, 483B, 484C, 486A, 489A, 490B, 508A, 508Ai, 509C, 510C, 516B, 516C, 537C, 538C, 543C, 544A, 544Ai, 545C, 545Ci, 560B(also on cover), 563B, 564A, 566C, 568A, 569B, 570C, 573B, 577C, 580B, 595A, 674B, 743B, 772A, 772C, 776C, 816A, 823A, 856A, 894, 906A, 915A, 922A, 924B

Rollin E. Colville: 886B

Alan Copeland: 196B

David M. Coppert: 393C, 666B

Samuel Cotner: 323A, 673A, 696C, 697C, 699C, 700A, 704C, 708A, 710B, 717C, 718B, 724A, 724C, 735A, 753Bi, 755B, 760B, 761A, 780A

David J. Cross: 188A, 200A, 212B, 222C, 292A, 491C, 524B, 803B, 927B

J.A. Crozier: 186A, 186B, 187C, 191C, 268B, 269Ai, 271A, 273B, 273C, 275B, 277A, 278C, 283A, 289A, 289B, 289Bi, 289C, 290B, 290C, 291A, 307C, 322C, 382B, 382C, 413B, 480B, 491A, 499A, 501C, 540B, 567B, 569C, 594A(also on cover), 672C, 698A, 698B, 708C, 715B, 746A, 756B, 757B, 780C, 782C, 814A, 814C, 817C, 824C, 825C, 828C, 832A, 842A, 851B, 870C, 875B, 922C, 923A

Maynard W. Cummings: 267C, 595B, 628B, 792B, 793A, 794A, 794B, 896Ai, 896B, 896C, 897A, 897C, 901A

Margery Daughtrey: 298B, 339C, 352A, 381B, 505C

The Davey Tree Expert Company: 266B, 426A, 447A, 454B, 546A, 546Ai, 552A, 578B, 856B

Spencer H. Davis, Jr.: 177B, 194B, 207B, 213C, 234C, 263A, 296C, 326A, 355B, 359C, 374B, 378B, 398A, 425A, 434A, 440C, 448A, 448C, 466A, 468C, 470A, 472C, 479B, 499C, 500C, 508C, 509B, 530C, 532Ai, 532Bi, 534B, 557C, 558B, 559A, 559C, 575B

Jim DeFilippis: 411A(also on cover), 456A, 487B, 503A, 503B, 521C(also on cover), 568Ai, 598C, 623C, 770A, 869B, 878B, 888A, 888C, 888Ci

August A. De Hertogh: 373A

James F. Dill: 241B, 255C, 278Bi, 402B, 431B, 442C, 468B, 507C, 528A, 530A, 535B, 536C, 553B, 573C, 596C, 609B, 663C, 672A, 673C, 679C, 679Ci, 680C, 681C, 691A, 693C, 694A, 697A, 704A, 709A, 712Bi, 717B, 718C, 727B, 735Ci, 753C, 754A, 757A, 759C, 763A, 776A, 776B, 783A, 790A, 790B, 797B, 799C, 802B, 803A, 809A, 827B, 867C, 870Ai, 872C, 875C, 878C, 881B, 887A, 892A, 892C, 898C

Michael A. Dirr: 283C, 362B, 363A, 392B, 409B, 472A, 476B, 489B, 502A, 515C, 523C, 527B, 540C, 561A, 583C, 588B, 589A, 837C, 840A, 861A, 861C, 917B

Walter Ebeling: 790C, 796C, 798C, 799Ci, 800A, 805C, 808A

C.W. Ellett: 447C

C.L. Elmore: 271C, 273A, 816C, 818A, 830B, 830C, 831C, 832C, 833C, 834B, 834C, 835B, 836C, 837A, 838B, 839B

Barbara H. Emerson: 277C, 813B, 813C, 815A, 817B, 818B, 826B, 828B(also on cover), 829C, 830A, 838C, 840C, 842B, 843A

Frank Emerson: 916A

Arthur W. Engelhard: 357A, 849C

Entomological Society of America—Ries Memorial Slide Library: 445B, 874B, 879C

Derek Fell: 620A

James Feucht: 263Ci, 266C, 370C, 379A, 417C, 427C, 432B, 437A, 443B, 477B, 482A, 529Ai, 535A, 543B, 544B, 556A, 575C, 585A, 600C, 609Ci, 860B, 906C

Charles Marden Fitch: 180A, 180B, 185A, 194A, 205B, 217A(also on cover), 221B, 225A, 230B, 230C, 231A, 232C, 235A, 240C, 244A, 281, 287B, 316B, 319A, 326B, 344C, 367C, 369B, 385C, 410B, 410C, 460B, 460C, 486B, 552C, 554C, 556B, 569A, 570A, 571A, 618B, 675A, 718Bi, 732C(also on cover), 773C, 780Ai, 792C, 794C, 802C, 821A, 822A, 852A, 858A, 863, 869A, 870B(also on cover), 875A, 893A, 901B, 926C

W.E. Fletcher: 458C

Lee Foster: 886C, 900A

William J. French: 465A, 639A

Paul F. Frese: 378C

Mal Furniss: 533A, 865C

Raymond J. Gill: 181B, 187A, 187B, 199C, 219C, 452C

A.S. Greathead: 677C

Nelson Groffman: 898B, 900C

John E. Hafernik, Jr.: 789B, 870A, 882C, 883B, 884C, 887C

Dennis H. Hall: 679B, 688A, 720A, 720Ai, 740B, 760C, 768C, 769B, 769C, 778B

M. Ali Harivandi: 251C, 258A, 271B, 815C, 826C, 829A, 831A, 832B, 833A, 836A, 905C

Raymond F. Hasek: 182Bi, 216C, 245B

Duane L. Hatch: 464A, 474A, 634Ci, 661C, 670B, 673B, 674A, 693B, 697B, 701C, 705B, 725A, 738C

George R. Hawkes: 593B, 601A, 601B, 625B, 661B, 860A, 910C, 911A

Richard W. Henley: 210C, 211C, 212A, 220A, 221C, 223A, 225B, 226A, 231C, 237C, 494B

W. Richard Hildreth: 489C

R.K. Horst: 230A, 235B, 243C, 334A, 340B, 372A, 382A, 619A, 663A

Judy Howard: 797C, 801C, 867B, 882A

Tony Howarth: 920C

Angus J. Howitt: 605C, 605Ci, 610C, 616C

Robert L. Iacopi: 463A

E.E. Janne: 257B, 526B, 795C, 820B, 823C, 861B

R.A. Jaynes: 509A

A.L. Jones: 602B, 602C, 606B, 611C, 612A, 620B, 634B(also on cover), 635A, 636C, 638B, 639C, 648C, 649B, 652A, 851A

R.K. Jones: 211A, 380A, 380B, 460A, 646A, 766A

Gene Joyner: 259C, 259Ci, 264C(also on cover), 279B, 444B, 444C, 451B, 453B, 453C, 455C, 456B, 457A, 457B, 465B, 483A, 492B, 493C, 497B, 502B, 502C, 504A, 505A, 512B, 522B, 523B, 524C, 525B, 525C, 526A, 539C, 542B, 615A, 615B, 615Bi, 615C, 621A, 621B, 622A, 622B, 624B, 626A, 627C, 629A, 632C, 633A, 633Ai, 633B, 729C, 819B, 825B

M. Keith Kennedy: 182B, 194C, 214A, 223C, 226C, 232B, 256A, 264A, 287A, 294B, 297B, 312C, 322A, 342A, 359B, 412B, 430A, 446A, 455Ai, 476C, 477A, 478A, 486C, 519A, 520C, 528B, 529B, 529Bi, 570B, 574B, 617B, 641C, 655A, 670C, 777C, 868B, 877B

Marvin G. Kinsey: 788B

Alan Klehr: 297C, 354B, 531B, 765B

R.R. Kriner: 257C, 261A, 473B, 513C, 537B, 574A, 601C, 606Ai, 606C, 607C, 608A, 617A, 634A, 635C, 636A, 637A, 638A, 638C, 641A, 651C, 653A, 681A, 689B, 689C, 698C, 703B, 726A, 727A, 749B, 759Ai, 762A, 770C, 806Ai, 827C, 841C, 872A, 881Bi

F. Laemmlen: 318C, 434C, 435A, 717A, 747B

Susan M. Lammers: 364B

Michael Lamotte: 590

Michael Landis: 248, 784, 902, 912C, 913C, 914B, 915C, 917A, 925B, 926A, 926B

James H. LaRue: 616A, 647C

George D. Lepp, BIO-TEC Images: 896Ci

Peter Lindtner: 315B, 513A, 572A, 579C, 596A, 597B, 612C, 722A, 825A, 838A, 918B

Don Linzy: 260Ci

Kenneth Lorenzen: 802Ci

Fred Lyon: 250C

Robert E. Lyons: 181C, 190A

J.D. MacDonald: 296A, 296Ai

Phil Mayer: 793C

Steven L. Mayer: 731A

Arthur H. McCain: 284A, 293A, 368C, 470C

Charles A. McClurg: 709C, 713A, 854B

Dennis McFarland: 182A, 806B

J.R. McGrew: 728B, 731C

Michael McKinley: 172, 174, 175, 202A, 218A, 218B, 242B, 283B, 284C, 285A, 286A, 286B, 302, 393B, 409A, 420A, 420B, 424A, 429A, 429C, 513B, 664C, 814B, 885B, 905B, 909A, 918A, 919C, 924A

J.A. Menge: 627A

Richard W. Meritt: 804A, 804B

Jeffrey C. Miller: 443Bi, 868C, 871C

Richard L. Miller: 520B, 544C, 545A, 571B, 748C, 759A, 761B, 763B, 792A, 798B, 800B, 871A, 900B

R.H. Miller: 548A

Wayne S. Moore: 209B, 216A, 238B, 246B, 246C, 247B, 294C, 295C, 300A, 311A, 343B, 345A, 381C, 398B, 409C, 443C, 463B, 487A, 586Ci, 605B, 791B, 801A, 843B, 867A, 881A, 886A

Cooperative Extension Association of Nassau County, NY: 247C, 254C, 254Ci, 263C, 274C, 436C, 441A, 484B, 496C, 538B, 582B, 584A, 586B, 587B

Jean R. Natter: 178C, 279A(also on cover), 279C, 290A, 428C, 523A, 789A, 836B, 842C, 848C, 854A(also on cover), 857B, 859B, 873C

New York State Ag. Exp. Sta., Geneva, NY: 763Bi

New York State Turfgrass Association: 254A, 256Bi, 259B, 269A, 272A, 272Ai, 274A, 274B, 276C

Lester P. Nichols: 183C, 209C, 223B, 234A, 465C, 469B, 485B, 511A, 514B, 587C

R.A. Norton: 592C, 593C, 598B, 641B, 643B, 650B

J. M. Ogrodnick: 728A

Howard D. Ohr: 266A

Oregon State University—Dept. of Entomology: 762B

Oregon State University—Ken Gray Collection: 257Ci, 377B, 410A, 463C, 538A, 574C, 574Ci, 579A, 586A, 630B, 630C, 640C, 642B, 643A, 654A, 703C, 705C, 711B, 711Bi, 713C, 722B, 739A, 744C, 766B, 865A, 890C, 890Ci

J. Parker: 862

John W. Parrish: 267A, 493B

Jerry M. Parsons: 678B, 715C, 737B, 737C, 741B, 771C, 781C, 853B

John Pehrson: 622C, 626B

Pamela K. Peirce: 692A, 758A, 823B, 828A

Sandra Perry: 207A, 219A, 329C, 332A, 518A, 650A, 680A

The Plant Photo Library: 414A, 498C

Robert G. Platt: 627B

D.K. Pollet: 512A, 542A, 555B, 631C, 632A, 644B, 644C, 645A, 645B, 651B

C.C. Powell: 173, 189C, 217B, 237B, 240B, 241A, 261C, 285B, 288B, 291C, 297A, 300B, 330A, 330C, 338B, 339B, 353B, 355A, 372C, 380C, 414B, 448B, 449A, 466C, 467A, 482B, 517C, 518B, 532B, 533Ci, 549A, 551B, 562B, 669C, 849B

R.P. Puck: 676C(also on cover), 677A, 677B, 677Bi

Purdue University: 606A

Cecil B. Quirino: 192A, 196A, 211B, 307A, 316C, 491B, 713B, 718A, 785, 786C, 788A, 791A(also on cover), 807B, 808B, 808C, 824B, 882B, 883A, 883C, 884Ci, 889C, 921A, 921B, 921C

Robert D. Raabe: 178A, 183A, 183B, 184A, 184B, 184C, 185B, 185C, 188B, 188C, 189A, 190B, 191A, 191B, 195A, 195C, 196C, 197A, 197B, 197C, 198C, 199A, 200C, 201B, 202C, 203A, 203C, 204B, 204C, 205A, 205C, 207Bi, 207C, 208B, 209A, 210B, 213A, 213B, 214B, 214Bi, 214C, 215A, 216B, 219B, 222A, 224B, 225C, 226B, 227B, 228A, 228B, 228C, 229A, 232A, 233A, 233C, 235C, 236A, 236C, 238C, 239A, 239C, 241C, 242A, 242C, 243A, 243B, 244B, 245A, 247A, 291B, 295B, 305C, 309C, 327A, 333B, 338C, 342C, 344B, 350B, 354A, 360A, 369A, 388C, 402C, 415A, 440A, 462B, 462C, 497C, 503C, 506A, 506B, 524A, 548C, 558C, 567C, 572C, 603A, 611A, 621C, 629B, 654B, 660C, 683B, 730A, 756A, 774B, 779B, 847, 849A

Roscoe Randell: 514A, 514Ai

Ann F. Rhoads: 204A, 312A, 423B, 432A, 454C, 565C, 742A(also on cover), 855A

Paul A. Rogers: 525A, 525Ai, 554A, 557A, 912A

Barbara Rothenberger: 298C, 315A, 325B, 337B, 400B, 495B, 527A, 581A, 624C, 685C

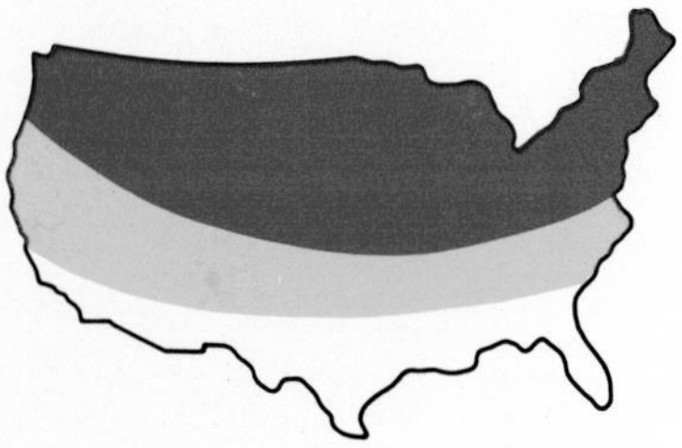

Each problem is accompanied by a map of the United States. In parts of the country that are colored red, the problem is severe or commonplace. In parts of the country that are yellow, the problem is secondary or occasional. In parts of the country that are white, the problem is rare or nonexistent.

HOW TO USE THIS BOOK

1. If you know the name of your plant, the problem it has, or the insect that is bothering it, look up that name in the index beginning on **PAGE 17.**

2. If you don't know the name of your plant, turn to one of these sections:

Houseplants **PAGE 173**

Lawns **PAGE 249**

Groundcovers **PAGE 281**

Annuals, Perennials, and Bulbs **PAGE 303**

Trees, Shrubs, and Vines **PAGE 405**

Fruit and Nut Trees **PAGE 591**

Vegetables, Berries, and Grapes **PAGE 659**

3. If you have a household pest and don't know its name, turn to **PAGE 785.**

4. If you want to know more about a problem, turn to one of these pages:

Weeds **PAGE 811**

Plant Diseases **PAGE 847**

Insects **PAGE 863**

Animal Pests **PAGE 895**

Soil, Cultural, and Climate Problems **PAGE 903**

5. For a complete description of ORTHO products and a list of the problems each solves, turn to **PAGE 929.**

TABLE OF CONTENTS

A

Note: *Italicized* page numbers refer to photographs.

in wheat, 272
Almond, 604
culture, 604
diseases of
bacterial blight, 1013
shothole fungus (coryneum blight; peach blight), *604*
fertilizing, 604, 934
flowering. *See Prunus*
ground squirrel damage to, *594*
harvesting, 604
insects on
filbertworms, 630
peach twig borers, *604*
poor fruiting on, *593*
***Alnus* (Alder)**
culture, 450
insects on
alder flea beetles, *450*
aphids, *450*
as powdery mildew susceptible, 1006
as wet soil tolerant, 1010, 450
***Alphitobius* species (Mealworms)**, 808
***Alsophila pometaria* (Fall cankerworm)**, 872
Alternaria blight
on Zinnia, *402*
Alternaria fruit rot
controlling, 977
Alternaria leaf spot
on *Brassaia*, *456*
on cabbage family, *700*
controlling, 962, 965, 968, 977
on lawns, 962, 965
on cucurbits, *735*
on *Dianthus*, 355
on *Pelargonium*, *381*
***Alternaria* species**
A. cucumerina
on cucurbits, 735
A. dauci
on carrots, 704
A. dianthi
on *Dianthus*, 355
A. porri
on onion family, 740
A. solani
on potatoes, 754
on tomatoes, 780
A. tenuis
on *Pelargonium*, 381
A. zinniae
on *Brassaia*, 456
on cabbage family, 700
on *Zinnia*, 402
***Althaea officinalis* (Marsh mallow)**
as wet soil tolerant, 1010
***Altica* species**
A. ambiens (Alder flea beetle), 450
A. chalybea (Grape flea beetle), 728
Aluminum
in acid soil, 908
Aluminum plant. *See Pilea*
Aluminum Sulfate. *See* ORTHO Aluminum Sulfate
Alumroot. *See Heuchera*
Alyssum, sweet. *See Lobularia*
Alyssum
as verticillium wilt resistant, 1006
***Amaranthus* (Amaranth)**
as cotton root rot resistant, 1007
flowering times for, 1004
germination of, 1004
pigweeds, 838
planting time for, 1004
as powdery mildew susceptible, 1006
Amaryllis. *See Hippeastrum*
Amber (*Hypericum perforatum*), 824
***Ambrosia* species. *See* Ragweed**
***Amelanchier* (Serviceberry)**
as acid soil tolerant, 1019
as crown gall resistant, 1013
as fireblight susceptible, 1016
insects on
gypsy moths, 1014
pear leaf blister mites, 475, 578
woolly aphids, 586
as quince rust susceptible, 1015
as shade tolerant, 1008
as wet soil tolerant, 1010
American cockroach (*Periplaneta americana*). *See* Cockroaches
Aminotriazole
for bitter nightshade, 841
for black nightshade, 841
for common cattail, 822
for hairy nightshade, 841
for Japanese honeysuckle, 843
for milkweed, 838
for mugwort, 838
for Virginia peppergrass, 823
Ammonia
as nitrogen source, 910
Ammoniacal nitrogen, 910
Ammoniated sawdust
for heavy soils, 904
Ammonium
as nitrogen source, 910
Ammonium sulfate
for blueberries, 689
for cotton root rot, 851
for cotton root rot
on fruit and nut trees, 602
on *Juniperus*, 506
on pecan, 646
on woody ornamentals, 440
ferrous
for mosses and liverworts, 823
on lawns, 279
for Ophiobolus patch on lawns, 255
***Amsinckia douglasiana* (Douglas fiddleneck)**, 842
***Anagasta kuehniella* (Flour moth)**, 808
***Anarsia lineatella*. *See* Peach twig borer**
***Anasa tristis* (Squash bug)**, 717
***Anastrepha suspense* (Caribbean fruit fly)**
on citrus, 622
***Ancylis comptana fragariae* (Strawberry leafroller)**, 763
Andromeda. *See Pieris*
Andromeda lacebug (*Stephanitis takeyai*), *531*
***Anemone* (Windflower)**
culture, 324, 1004
diseases of
aster yellows, 1005
leaf spot, *324*
tuber rot (Southern blight), *323*
flowering times for, 1004
insects on
ants, 324
aphids, *324*
leaf spot, *324*
tuber rot, *323*
as verticillium wilt resistant, 1006
watering, 324
Angoumois grain moths, *808*
Angular leaf spot
controlling, 965
on cucurbits, *719*
varieties resistant to, 1028
Anilazine, for alternaria leaf spot on cucurbits, 735
Animal pests
See also specific animals
in avocado, 615
bark-feeding, 594
in fruit and nut trees, 594, 595
in woody ornamentals, 432
birds, 899. *See also* Bird damage
in flowers, 320
cats, 898
deer, 897
in flowers, 320
in fruit and nut trees, 594
in woody ornamentals, 432, 897
dogs, 898
earthworms, 898
field mice. *See* mice
in fig, 628
in flowers, 320
birds, 320
deer, 320, 897
mice, 320, 896
moles, 320
pocket gophers, 320
rabbits, 320
raccoons, 320
squirrels, 320
tree squirrels, 899
woodchucks, 320, 901
in fruit and nut trees, 594, 595
birds, 595
deer, 594
ground squirrels, 900
mice, 594
rabbits, 594, 900
raccoons, 595, 900
skunks, 901
tree squirrels, 595, 899
gophers. *See* pocket gophers
in grapes, 731
ground squirrels, 900
groundhogs, 901
in households. *See* Household pests
in lawns
birds, 268
moles, 896
pocket gophers, 267
mice, 896
in flowers, 320
in fruit and nut trees, 594
in households, 792
in woody ornamentals, 432
moles, 896
in flowers, 320
pocket gophers
in flowers, 320
in lawns, 267
rabbits, 900
in flowers, 320
in fruit and nut trees, 594, 900
in woody ornamentals, 432
raccoons, 900
in flowers, 320
in fruit and nut trees, 595, 900
in *Ranunculus*, 388
rats, 794
sapsuckers, 899
in woody ornamentals, 1012, 423
skunks, 901
squirrels, 793, 899, 900
See also Ground squirrels; Tree squirrels
in flowers, 320
traps for, 897
house mice, 793
rats, 794
tree squirrels, 793
tree squirrels, 899
in flowers, 899
in fruit and nut trees, 595, 899
in households, 793
in woody ornamentals,

427
in vegetables
birds, 899
deer, 897
ground squirrels, 900
mice, 896
rabbits, 900
raccoons, 900
skunks, 901
woodchucks, 901
voles, 432
in *Wisteria*, 589
woodchucks, 901
in flowers, 320
in woody ornamentals
birds, 423, 899, 1012
deer, 432, 897
mice, 432, 896
rabbits, 432
squirrels, 432
tree squirrels, 427, 899
voles, 432
woodchucks, 901
Anise. ***See*** **Herbs**
Annual aster. ***See Callistephus***
Annual bluegrass. ***See*** **Bluegrass, annual**
Annual morning glory. ***See*** **Morning glory**
Annual speargrass. ***See*** **Bluegrass, annual**
Annuals, defined, 168. *See also* Flowers
Ant, Roach & Spider Killer. ***See*** **ORTHO Ant, Roach & Spider Killer**
Anthemis cotula **(Mayweed),** 827
Anthonomous signatus **(Strawberry weevil),** 763
Anthracnose
and twig blight, on *Ligustrum*, 512
on brambles, *695*, 1023
controlling, 962, 965, 968, 977
on cucurbits, 719
varieties resistant to, 1028, 1033
foxglove, 356
on grapes, *729*
on lawns, *253*
controlling, 962, 965
on *Ligustrum*, *512*
on mango, *633*
maple, *447*
on melon, *719*
oak, 551
on peppers, *747*
spot, on *Cornus*, 471
spots on beans, *682*
on tomato, 774
walnut, 656
Anthurium
culture, 184
insects on
mealybugs, *184*
spider mites, 184
leaf polish on, 938
root rot on, 185
Antirrhinum **(Snapdragon)**
in containers
watering, 324
as cotton root rot resistant, 1007
culture, 324, 1004
damping-off, *318*
diseases of
aster yellows, 1005
fungicides for, 956
fusarium wilt, 1005
gray mold, *326*
powdery mildew, 1006
root and stem rot, 325
rust, *325*
fertilizing, 324
iron deficiency and, 937
flowering times for, 1004
germination of, 1004
insects on
cyclamen mites, 764
insecticides for, 957
two-spotted spider mites, *325*
iron deficiency in, 937
planting, 324, 1004
directions for, 326
gray mold and, 326
root and stem rot and, 325
rust and, 325
root and stem rot, *325*
as smog tolerant, 1008
soil pH for, 324
watering, 324
gray mold and, 326
root and stem rot and, 325
rust and, 325
Antlions, 888
Ants, ***893***
on *Acer*, 445
on *Anemone*, 324
aphids and, 893
on *Acer*, 445
on *Anemone*, 324
on apple, 607
on *Aquilegia*, 326
on *Astilbe*, 328
on *Bambusa*, 452
on beans, 699
on *Betula*, 454
on cabbage family, 699
on *Camellia*, 463
on *Centaurea*, 337
on *Chrysanthemum*, 342
on citrus, 623
on *Cosmos*, 347
on *Crataegus*, 477
on currants; gooseberries, 722
on *Daphne*, 481
on *Digitalis*, 355
on eggplant, 724
on *Fagus*, 484
on *Fatshedera*, 485
on flowers, 316
on *Fraxinus*, 489
on *Freesia*, 357
on fruit and nut trees, 599, 598
on *Fuchsia*, 491
on *Gardenia*, 493
on *Gerbera*, 358
on grapes, 728
on groundcovers, 287
on *Hemerocallis*, 363
on *Hibiscus*, 498
on *Ixora*, 503
on *Juniperus*, 507
on *Laburnum*, 509
on *Lagerstroemia*, 510
on *Lilium*, 372
on *Liriodendron*, 513
on peach; nectarine, 637
on peas, 744
on *Philadelphus*, 526
on *Pinus*, 536
on *Pittosporum*, 539
on *Platanus*, 542
on *Quercus*, 555
on *Rhododendron*, 563
on *Rosa*, 569
on *Salix*, 574
on *Tropaeolum*, 393
on *Tulipa*, 397
on vegetables, 673
on walnut, 654
on woody ornamentals, 412, 430, 422
on apple, 607
on *Aquilegia*, 326
on *Astilbe*, 328
on *Bambusa*, 452
on *Bauhinia*, 453
on beans, 699
on *Betula*, 454
on cactus, 461
on *Camellia*, 463, 464
carpenter (*Camponotus* species)
in firewood, 801
in households, 799
on *Centaurea*, 337
on *Chrysanthemum*, 342
on citrus, 623
on *Coleus*, 344
on *Cosmos*, 347
cottony cushion scales and
on citrus, 623
cottony scales and
on bamboo, 453
on *Crataegus*, 477
on currants; gooseberries, 722
on *Daphne*, 481
on *Digitalis*, 355
on eggplant, 724
on euphorbia, *316*
on *Fagus*, 484
on *Fatshedera*, 485
feeding on mango, *598*
fire (*Solenopsis* species), 889
as household pests, 806
insecticides for, 950, 952, 961, 964
on lawns, 268
on flowers, 316
on *Fraxinus*, 489
on *Freesia*, 357
on fruit and nut trees, 599, 598
on *Fuchsia*, 491
on *Gardenia*, 493
on *Gerbera*, 358
on groundcovers, 287
harvester, 806
on lawns, 268
on *Hedera*, 294
on *Hemerocallis*, 363
on *Hibiscus*, 498
in households, 791
carpenter, 799
fire, 889
insecticides for, 946, 949, 951, 952, 961
as Hymenoptera, 880
insecticides for, 946, 949–954, 957, 959, 961, 963, 967, 973
on *Ixora*, 503
on *Juniperus*, 507
on *Laburnum*, 509
on *Lagerstroemia*, 510
on lawns, *268*
insecticides for, 949–952, 961, 963
on *Lilium*, 372
on *Liriodendron*, 513
on mango, 633
mealybugs and, 893
on cactus, outdoors, 461
on citrus, 623
on *Coleus*, 344
on flowers, 316
on fruit and nut trees, 598, 599
on peach; nectarine, 637
on peas, 744
on *Philadelphus*, 526
on *Pinus*, 536
on *Pittosporum*, 539
on *Platanus*, 542
on *Quercus*, 555
on *Rhododendron*, 563
on *Rosa*, 569
on *Salix*, 574
scales and, 893
on *Camellia*, 464
on citrus, 623
on flowers, 316
on fruit and nut trees, 598
on *Hedera*, 294
on mango, 633
snow scales and
on *Bauhinia*, 453
on *Tropaeolum*, 393
on *Tulipa*, 397
on vegetables, 673
on walnut, 654
whiteflies and, 893
on flowers, 316
on fruit and nut trees, 598, 599
on woody ornamentals, 412, 422, 430
Apanteles congregatus
as hornworm parasite, 893
Aphanomyces raphani
on radishes, 757

B

beet leafhoppers, curly top and, *685*
cutworms, 664

bean anthracnose and, 682
gray mold and, 683
mold and, 683
white mold and, 683
seedcorn maggots, *686*, 713
snakehead or baldhead from, *684*
southern root knot nematodes, varieties resistant to, 1026
spider mites, *681*
stink bugs, *737*, *776*
wireworms, 704
iron deficiency in, *666*
lima
harvesting time for, 680
planting dates for, 1025
mice in, 675
nematode-resistant varieties of, 1026
planting directions for, 680
seedcorn maggots and, 686
snakehead and baldhead and, 684
planting locations for, 680
bacterial blights and, 682
bean anthracnose and, 682
white mold and, 683
white or gray mold and, 683
planting times for, 1025
failure to set pods and, 682
seedcorn maggots and, 686
pole
mosaic-resistant variety of, 1027
potassium deficiency in, *911*
rabbits in, *675*
snails and slugs on, 684, 947
snakehead or baldhead in, 684
snap
germination of, 1025
harvesting time for, 680
planting dates for, 1025
soil pH for, 680
soybeans
harvesting time for, 680
as verticillium wilt resistant, 1006
watering, 680
bacterial blights and, 682
failure to set pods and, 682
root rot and, 685
rust and, 683
white or gray mold and, 683
wax bush
mosaic-resistant varieties of, 1027
Bear bind. ***See*** **Field bindweed**
Bearberry. ***See Arctostaphylos uva-ursi***
Beargrass. ***See*** **Sandbur**
Bedbugs (*Cimex lectularius*), ***796***
insecticide for, 972
Bedding
pests in
bedbugs, *796*
brown recluse spiders, *805*
clover mites, *792*
earwigs, *789*
Bedding plants
fertilizers for, 933
Bedstraw
in lawns
herbicides for, 981
Bee nettle. ***See*** **Henbit**
Beech. ***See Fagus***
Beech scale (*Cryptococcus fagisuga*), 485
Beefwood. See ***Casuarina***
Bees
bumble, 880
carpenter (*Xylocopa virginica*)
in households, *800*
on cucurbits
pollination by, 715
fireblight and
on *Crataegus*, 475
on *Eriobotrya*, 483
on pear, 640
on *Pyracantha*, 548
on *Sorbus*, 577
on woody ornamentals, 439
on fruit and nut trees
honeydew and, 599
pollination and, 593
fuchsia mites and, 491
in households, *802*
leafcutter (*Megachile* species)
on *Rosa*, *569*
plants attractive to, 1007
solitary,
on *Rosa*, 572
stings by, 802
in swimming pools, 788
on woody ornamentals
fireblight and, 439
honeydew and, 422
Beet armyworms
insecticide for, 961
Beet leafhopper (*Circulifer tenellus*)
on cucurbits, *714*
curly top and
on beans, 685
on beets, 688
on cucurbits, 714
on tomato, 781
damage to zucchini, *714*
Beet leafminer (*Pegomya hyoscyami*), ***687***
Beetles, 865
See also Borers; Curculios; Leafminers; Weevils
Asiatic
on lawns, 256
asparagus (*Crioceris asparagi*; *C. duodecimpunctata*), *679*
crooked spears and, 678
insecticide for, 971
bark. *See* Bark beetles
bean. *See* Bean beetles
bean leaf (*Cerotoma trifurcata*), *681*
insecticides for, 972, 973
black carpet
insecticide for, 957
blister (*Epicauta* species)
on eggplant, *723*
grasshoppers and, 723
insecticides for, 956, 963, 973, 976, 977,
on potatoes, *753*
as Cantharidae, 867
carpet
insecticides for, 957
on cherry, *618*
cigarette (*Lasioderma serricorne*)
in households, *809*
click, 783
on carrot, 704
plants susceptible to, 704
on potatoes, 751. *See also* Wireworms
Colorado potato (*Leptinotarsa decemlineata*)
on eggplant, *723*
insecticides for, 955, 972, 973, 976, 977
on potatoes, *753*
cottonwood leaf
insecticide for, 961
cucumber. *See* Cucumber beetles
darkling ground, 867
described, 317
diabrotica. *See* Cucumber beetles, spotted
diseases and, 879
dried fruit
insecticide for, 955
drugstore (*Stegobium paniceum*)
in households, 809
elm leaf, *586*
insecticides for, 961, 963, 964, 973, 956
fireflies, 868
flea. *See* Flea beetles
flour, 867
darkling grain beetles as, 867
flour
in households, *808*
on flowers, 315, 317
fruit tree bark
on cherry, *618*
ground, 867
ips engraver
on *Pinus*, *532*
Japanese. *See* Japanese beetle
June
on lawns, 256
Klamathweed (*Chrysolina quadrigemina*)
on *Hypericum*, 295
lady, *891*
larvae of. *See* Leafminers
leaf
Chrysomela specieson *Populus*, *544*
on *Salix*, *573*
strawberry, insecticide for, 958
willow, insecticide for, 961
lightning bugs, 868
long-horned, pine wilt nematodes carried by, 533
long-horned, *410*
masked chafer
on lawns, 256
May
on lawns, 256
Mexican bean (*Epilachna varivestis*), *680*
insecticides for, 955, 972, 973, 976, 977
as night-flying pests, 788
nocturnal
on flowers, 317
on vegetables, 670
on woody ornamentals, 418
potato. *See* Colorado potato
powderpost
in firewood, 801
in households, *798*
predaceous ground, 867
red flour
in households, *808*
on *Rosa*, 571, 572
sap-feeding
insecticides for, 972, 973
on *Platanus* canker stain disease and, 541
on *Quercus* oak wilt and, 556
sawtoothed grain
in households, 808
insecticide for, 957
sawyer (*Monochamus titillator*), pine wilt nematodes carried by, 533
shothole borer
on cherry, *618*
snout, 866. *See also* Curculios; Root weevils; Weevils
soldier, 867
spotted cucumber. *See* Cucumber beetles, spotted
strawberry leaf
insecticide for, 958
striped cucumber. *See* Cucumber beetles, striped
in swimming pools, 788
tule (*Agonum maculicolle*),

as household pest, 867
turpentine (*Dendroctonus* species), on *Pinus*, 533
twelve-spotted
insecticides for, 971, 976
on vegetables, 670
willow leaf
insecticide for, 961
wood-boring
on *Quercus*, 554
on woody ornamentals, 410, 418
Beets, 686
boron deficiency in, *687*
in containers
fertilizing, 686
culture, 686
diseases of
cercospora leaf spot, *687*
curly top, 685, *688*
damping-off, *688*
leaf spot, *687*
powdery mildew, 1006
root rot, boron deficiency and, 687
scab, 751
southern blight, 1007
verticillium wilt, 1025
fertilizing, 686, 941–943
boron deficiency and, 686, 687
damping-off and, 688
germination of, 1025
harvesting, 686
insects on
aphids, 545
beet leafhopper, scurly top and, 688
beet leafminers, *687*
celery leaftiers, 705
flea beetles, *686*
millipedes, *674*
seedcorn maggots, *686*
wireworms, 704, *714*, 783
misshapen roots on, 688
overcrowded, 688
planting directions for
damping-off and, 688
misshapen roots and, 688
planting locations for, 686
planting times for, 1025
beet leafminers and, 687
damping-off and, 688
round-rooted varieties of, 1027
snails and slugs on
baits for, 947
soil pH for, 686
boron deficiency and, 687
thinning
misshapen roots and, 688
varieties of
root development and, 688
root quality and, 1027
watering, 686
damping-off and, 688
leaf spot and, 687
Beggarweed
creeping
herbicides for, 983, 984
***Begonia*, indoors**
angelwing
insecticide for, 979
culture, 189
heat requirements for
powdery mildew and, *189*
insects on
cyclamen mites, 239
greenhouse whiteflies, *191*
insecticide for, 957
mealybugs, *190*
scales, *190*
spider mites, *190*
insufficient light for, *189*
powdery mildew on, *189*
propagating, 1001
***Begonia*, outdoors**
in containers
watering, 328
culture, 328, 1004
diseases of
bacterial leaf spot, *329*
fungal leaf spot, *329*
gray mold, *329*
powdery mildew, 1006, *330*
root and stem rot, *330*
fertilizing, 328, 936, 940
fibrous
culture, 328
flowering times for, 328, 1004
germination of, 1004
insects on
insecticides for, 957, 979
leaf nematodes, *330*
mealybugs, *331*
planting locations for, 328
root and stem rot and, 330
planting times for, 328, 1004
soil pH for, 328
strawberry
insecticide for, 979
transplant shock, *314*
tuberous
culture, 328
fertilizers for, 328, 932, 935, 940
as verticillium wilt resistant, 1006
watering, 328
bacterial leaf spot and, 329
gray mold and, 329
leaf nematodes and, 330
Bell peppers. *See* Peppers
Bellflower. *See Campanula*
***Bellis perennis* (English lawn daisy)**
as weed, 275
Beneficial insects
on avocado, 614
antlions, 888
aphid parasites, 893
assassin bugs, 874
bees. *See* Bees
butterflies, 868
caterpillar parasites, 893
cinnabar moth
tansy ragwort eaten by, 837
crickets, *882*
damsel bugs, 874
earwigs as, *673*
European winter moths controlled by, 871
fire ants, 806
fireflies or lightning bugs, 868
ground beetles, 867
hornworms, 724
hover or flower flies, 892
Hymenoptera, 880
Jerusalem crickets, 883
lacewings, *892*
lady beetles, *891*
leafcutter bees, 569
maggots, 883
minute pirate bugs, 874
moths, 868
parasitic wasps, 893
praying mantids, *892*
predaceous bugs, 874
predaceous ground beetles, 867
soldier beetles, 867
spiders, 787
tree crickets, 882
Trichogramma species, 893
whitefly parasites, 893
Benlate
for ash anthracnose, 488
for bulb rot
on *Lilium*, 372
for camellia flower blight, 462
for dieback
on *Rosa*, 572
for diplodia tip blight
on *Pinus*, 532
for *Euonymus*
powdery mildew on, 483
for *Fraxinus*
anthracnose on, 488
for fungal leaf spot
on *Rhododendron*, 560
for *Lilium*
root and bulb rot on, 372
for petal blight
on *Rhododendron*, 558
for *Pinus*
diplodia tip blight on, 532
for powdery mildew
on *Euonymus*, 483
on *Platanus*, 540
for *Rhododendron*
fungal leaf spot on, 560
petal blight on, 558
for root and bulb rot
on *Lilium*, 372
for *Rosa*
stem cankers and dieback on, 572
Benomyl
for anthracnose
on lawns, 253
walnut, 656
for *Antirrhinum*
gray mold on, 326
for apple
powdery mildew on, 609
for apricot
scab on, 612
for *Araucaria*
needle blight on, 451
for beans
white or gray mold on, 683
for *Begonia*
fungal leaf spot on, 329
gray mold on, 329
for black knot
on plum, 652
for blueberries
stem and blossom blight on, 690
for botrytis blight
on *Tulipa*, 397
for brambles
powdery mildew on, 695
for brown rot
on plum, 649
for bulb and stem rot
on *Tulipa*, 397
for *Buxus*
volutella canker and blight on, 459
for canker and dieback
on *Vinca*, 299
for canker wilt
on *Gleditsia*, 496
for celery
early blight on, 706
late blight on, 706
for *Chrysanthemum*
leaf spot on, 339
for *Cineraria*
powdery mildew on, 343
for citrus
greasy spot on, 626
for *Cornus*
flower and leaf blight on, 471
leaf spot on, 472
for *Cosmos*
powdery mildew on, 346
for cucurbits
powdery mildew on, 720
for *Delphinium*
powdery mildew on, 351
for *Dianthus*
gray mold on, 353
for didymellina leaf spot
on *Iris*, 368
for early blight
on celery, 706
for flower and leaf blight
on *Cornus*, 471
for fruit and nut trees
powdery mildew on, 599
for fungal leaf spot
on *Begonia*, outdoors, 329
on *Kalmia*, 509
on woody ornamentals, 414

See Cat flea; Dog flea
Cuban laurel. ***See Ficus***
Cuban laurel thrips (*Gynaikothrips ficorum*)
on *Ficus*, 487
insecticides for, 960, 961, 964, 974
Cuckold (*Bidens bipinnata*), 825
Cucumber. ***See*** **Cucurbits**
Cucumber, wild
mosaic virus harbored by, 720, 736
Cucumber beetles
on cucurbits, 717
angular leaf spot and, 719
anthracnose and, 719
bacterial wilt and, 718
mosaic virus and, 720
feeding on zinnia, *315*
insecticides for, 950, 955, 971–973, 977
spotted (*Diabrotica* species)
on *Coreopsis*, 345
on corn, bacterial wilt and, 710
on cucurbits, *717*
insecticide for, 974
on vegetables, 671
striped (*Acalymma* species)
on cucurbits, 717
insecticide for, 976
on vegetables, 671
twelve-spotted
insecticides for, 971, 976
Cucumber mosaic virus
on cucurbits, 720
varieties resistant to, 1028
on *Tolmiea*, 245
on tomato, 781
Cucurbits, 714
angular-leaf-spot-resistant varieties of, 719
bees on
pollination and, 715
beet leafhopper damage to, *714*
bitter cucumbers, *715*
calcium deficiency in
blossom-end rot and, 716
cantaloupe
See also melon; muskmelon
anthracnose on, 1028
cotton root rot on, 720
culture, 714
disease tolerant varieties of, 1028
downy mildew on, 1028
insecticide for, 950
as Japanese beetle resistant, 1009
Mediterranean fruit flies on, 1018
powdery mildew on, 720, 1006, 1028
as southern blight susceptible, 1007
as verticillium wilt susceptible, 1025
casaba melon
as verticillium wilt susceptible, 1025. *See also* melon
as cotton root rot resistant, 1007
crenshaw melon, as verticillium wilt susceptible, 1025. *See also* melon
cucumber
alternaria leaf spot on, 735
angular leaf spot on, 1028, 719
anthracnose on, 1028, 719
bacterial wilt on, 718
bitter taste to, 715
disease-resistant varieties of, 1028
downy mildew on, 1028, 720
fertilizers for, 941
as fusarium wilt susceptible, 1025
germination of, 1025
harvesting, 714
insecticide for, 972
as Japanese beetle resistant, 1009
Mediterranean fruit flies feed on, 1018
mice in, 675
misshapen and tough fruit on, 715
mosaic virus on, 1028, 720
mosaic-virus-resistant varieties of, 1028
pickleworms on, 716
pickling, scab-resistant varieties of, 716
planting dates for, 1025
planting directions for, 714
pollination problems in, 715
poor yield of, 715
powdery mildew on, 1028, 1006, 669, 720
scab on, 1028, 716
seedcorn maggots on, 686
snails and slugs on, baits for, 947
southern blight on, 1007
storing, 714
tough over maturity, 715
transplanting, 714
cultivating
blossom-end rot and, 716
culture, 714
diseases of
alternaria leaf spot, *735*
angular leaf spot, *719*, 1028
anthracnose, *719*, 1028, 1033
bacterial wilt, *671*, 717, *718*, *852*
blossom-end rot, 716
curly top, 688, 714
downy mildew, *720*, 1028, 1033
fungicide for, 977
mosaic virus, 717, *720*, 736, 1028
powdery mildew, 669, *720*, 1006, 1028, 1033
scab, *716*, 1028
varieties resistant to, 1028
verticillium wilt, susceptibility to, 1025
fertilizing, 714, 941, 943
bitter taste and, 714, 715
blossom-end rot and, 716
germination of, 1025
gourds
harvesting, 714
squash vine borers on, 718
harvesting, 714
fruit problems and, 715
healthy plants—no fruit, *715*
honeydew melon
as verticillium wilt susceptible, 1025. *See also* melon
insects on
aphids, mosaic virus and, 720
bees, pollination and, 715
beet leafhoppers, 714
cucumber beetles, 717, 719, 718, 720, 719
Mediterranean fruit flies, 1018
pickleworms, *716*
spider mites, *718*
spotted cucumber beetles, 717
squash bugs, 717
squash vine borers, *718*
striped cucumber beetles, 717
as Japanese beetle resistant, 1009
melon
see also specific melons
anthracnose on, 719
as cotton root rot resistant, 1007
curly top on, 688
fertilizers for, 941, 943
as fusarium wilt susceptible, 1025
germination of, 1025
insecticides for, 950 951, 972
as Japanese beetle resistant, 1009
planting dates for, 1025
poor yield on, 715
as powdery mildew susceptible, 1006
snails and slugs on, baits for, 947
as southern blight susceptible, 1007
spider mites on, 718
as verticillium wilt susceptible, 1025
misshapen and tough, *715*
muskmelon
see also cantaloupe; melon
alternaria leaf spot on, 735
anthracnose on, 1033, 719
bacterial wilt on, 718
downy mildew on, 1033, 720
harvesting, 714
millipedes and, 890
mosaic virus on, 720
pickleworms on, 716
planting dates for, 1025
planting directions for, 714
as pollution tolerant, 1008
powdery mildew on, 1033
scab on, 716
transplanting, 714
nitrogen excess in
blossom-end rot and, 716
Persian melon
as verticillium wilt susceptible, 1025. *See also* melon
planting directions for, 714
planting locations for, 714
blossom-end rot and, 716
scab and, 716
pollination of
poor fruit yield and, 715
powdery-mildew-resistant varieties of, 720
pumpkin
as aster yellows susceptible, 1005
as cotton root rot resistant, 1007
downy mildew on, 720
fertilizers for, 941, 943
harvesting, 714
as Japanese beetle resistant, 1009
Mediterranean fruit flies feed on, 1018
planting directions for, 714
squash bugs on, 717
storing, 714
transplanting, 714
as verticillium wilt susceptible, 1025
as raccoon repellent for corn, 675
soil pH for, 714
alternaria leaf spot and, 735
soil salts in
blossom-end rot and, 716
squash bugs, *717*
squash

D

E

E/Earwigs — Erysiphe Species

F

1002
red
characteristics of, 262, 1007
as shade tolerant, 263, 1007
tall
characteristics of, 262, 1007
mowing heights for, 250
weeds in
herbicides for, 982
as weed
herbicides for, 983, 984
***Festuca arundinacea.* See Fescue, tall**
***Festuca ovina glauca.* See Fescus, blue**
Fetid chamomile. *See* Mayweed
Feverfew. *See Chrysanthemum*
***Ficus, edible.* See Fig**
***Ficus* (Ornamental fig; Rubber plant), indoors,** 217
F. elastica (Rubber plant)
insecticides for, 979
leaf polishes for, 938, 939
low light tolerated by, 979
F. lyrata (Fiddle leaf fig)
low light tolerated by, 979
culture, 217
environmental stress in, leaf drop and, 218
fertilizing, 217
salt damage and, *218*
growing locations for, 217, 1001
leaf drop and, 218
light and, 1001
insects on
insecticides for, 948, 979
mealybugs, *219*
scales, *219*
leaf drop on, 218
leaf polishes for, 938, 939
light requirements for, 1001
leaf drop and, 218
oedema on, *219*
planting directions for, 217, 218
salt damage to, *218*, 1001
soil for, 217
transplant shock in, leaf drop and, 218
watering, 217
leaf drop and, 218
oedema and, 219
salt damage and, 218
weeping fig
insecticide for, 979
***Ficus* (Cuban laurel; Laurel fig; Ornamental fig), outdoors**
F. carica. See Fig
F. retusa (Laurel fig)
as paving tolerant, 436
Cuban laurel thrips on, *487*
culture, 487
Fiddle leaf fig. *See Ficus*, indoors
Fiddle leaf philodendron. *See Philodendron*
Fiddleneck, common
herbicides for, 983, 984
Fiddleneck, Douglas (*Amsinckia douglasiana*), 842
Field balm (*Glechoma hederacea*), 831
Field bindweed (*Convolvulus arvensis*), *840*, 983
See also Wild morning glory
Field crickets (*Gryllus assimilis*)
bait for, 964
in households, 788
Field daisy
aster yellows and, 854
Field dodder (*Cuscuta campestris*), *840*
Field garlic. *See Allium vineale*
Field kale (*Brassica kaber*), 824
Field mice. *See* Mice
Field pansies (*Viola* species)
as weeds, 831
Field sorrel (*Rumex acetosella*), 836. *See also* Red sorrel
Field thistle. *See* Thistles
Fields
weeds in
bitter nightshade, 841
black nightshade, 841
bracken, 823
bulrush, 821
Canada thistle, 834
carrot, 826
chicory, 835
common groundsel, 835
common lambsquarters, 839
common yarrow, 826
controlling, 815
cudweed, 826
dallisgrass, 817
Douglas fiddleneck, 842
fall panicum, 818
field dodder, 840
foxtails, 819
German velvetgrass, 816
goldenrod, 837
groundsel, 835
hairy nightshade, 841
horseweed, 836
iris, 820
Johnsongrass, 818
Klamath weed, 824
ladysthumb, 833
lambsquarters, 839
lettuce, prickly, 832
mallow, 832
mayweed, 827
milkweed, 838
morning glory, 840
mugwort, 838
mustard, 824
nightshades, 841
oats, 820
panicum, fall, 818
peppergrass, Virginia, 823
pigweeds, 838
pineappleweed, 827
prickly lettuce, 832
ragweed, 834
Russian thistle, 824
sandbur, 819
shepherds purse, 837
sowthistle, 836
Spanishneedles, 825
starthistle, 834
tansy ragwort, 837
thistles, yellow starthistle, 834
thistles Canada, 834
thistles Russian, 824
thistles sowthistle, 836
velvetgrass, German, 816
Virginia peppergrass, 823
wild carrot, 826
wild iris, 820
wild mustard, 824
wild oats, 820
yarrow, 826
yellow starthistle, 834
Fiery skippers
insecticides for, 961
Fig
See also Ficus, indoors and outdoors
bird damage to, *628*
Brown Turkey, 628, 1017
Celeste, 628, 1017
closed-eye varieties of, 628
culture, 628
as disease and insect resistant, 1012
diseases of
Botryosphaeria ribis, 1018
armillaria root rot, varieties resistant to, 1016
fig mosaic, 629
rust, *629*
souring, *628*
Eastern Brown Turkey, 1017
fertilizing, 628
Green Ischia, 1017, 628
harvesting, 628
bird damage and, 628
insects on
dried fruit beetles, souring and, 628
fig mites, mosaic and, 629
Mediterranean fruit flies, 1018
scales, 629
vinegar flies, souring and, 628
Kadota, 1016, 1017
King ('Desert King'), 1017
Latterula, 1017
Magnolia, 1017
Mission
as armillaria resistant, 1016
planting locations for, 1017
as souring resistant, 628
Mosaic, *629*
ornamental. *See Ficus*,
planting locations for, 628, 1017
pruning, 628
soil pH for, 628
as verticillium wilt resistant, 1006
watering, 628
weeping. *See* Weeping fig
Fig mite (*Eriophyes fici*), 629
Fig mosaic, *629*
Filaree
herbicides for, 984
redstem (*Erodium cicutarium*), 825
Filbert (Hazelnut), 630
culture, 630
diseases of
bacterial blight, 631
powdery mildew, 1006
fertilizers for, 934
insects on
European leafrollers, 630
filbert leafrollers, 630
filbertworms, *630*
Turkish
as disease and insect resistant, 1012
Filbert leafroller larvae (*Archips rosanus*), *630*
Filbertworm (*Melissopus latiferreanus*), *630*
Fill injury
trees susceptible to, 1011
Fingergrass. *See* Crabgrass
Fiorinia hemlock scales
on *Tsuga*, 584
Fir. *See Abies*
Douglas. *See Pseudotsuga*
Fire Ant Control. *See* ORTHO Fire Ant Control
Fire ants (*Solenopsis* species), *889*
as household pests, 806
insecticides for, 950, 952, 961
on lawns, 268
stings by, 806
Fireblight
on apple, *609*, 1016, 1021
on brambles, 1016, 1021
on *Chaenomeles*, 1016
on *Cotoneaster*, *474*, 1016
on *Crabapple*, *439*
on *Crataegus*, *475*, 1016
variety tolerant of, 1016
on *Eriobotrya*, *483*, 1016
fruit trees susceptible to,

mushrooms around base of, 602
neglect and, 603
nitrogen deficiency in, 601
pollination for
poor yield and, 593
premature fruit drop and, 592
powdery mildew, *599*
powdery mildew, *599*
pruning
after neglect, 603
broken branches, 916
cankers and, 596
dressings for, 969
failure to set fruit and, 593
limb breakage and, 595
poor fruit yield and, 593
small fruit and, 593
sunscald and, 597
purchasing, 924
root knot nematode damage, *602*
snail and slug bait for, 947
soil pH for
iron deficiency and, 600
nitrogen deficiency and, 601
root and crown rots and, 602
sooty mold on, 600
stunted growth or decline in
crown gall, 603
neglect, 603
nematodes, 602
root and crown rots, 602
sunscald on
cankers and, 596
thinning fruit on, 593
transplanting
sunscald and, 597
watering
fruit or nut flavor and, 594
leaf scorch and, 600
nitrogen deficiency and, 601
premature fruit drop and, 592
timing for, 917
wind damage to
leaf scorch and, 600

Fruit drop
on citrus, *621*
on persimmon, *647*

Fruit flies, 883
apple, 605
blueberry. *See* Blueberry maggot
Caribbean (*Anastrepha suspensa*)
on citrus, 622
cherry
insecticide for, 955
Mediterranean, 884
plants infested by, 1018

Fruit moths
oriental (*Grapholitha molesta*)
on apricot, 613
on cherry, 617
on peach; nectarine, 636
on plum, 651

Fruit rot
alternaria
controlling, 977
on brambles, *692*
on cherry, *619*
controlling, 977
leaf spot and
on eggplant, 725
on apricot, *611*
on peach and nectarine, *636*
on plum, *649*
rhizoctonia
controlling, 977

Fruit scab
on avocado, *615*

Fruit spot
Brooks, 958
controlling, 958, 965

Fruit tree bark beetle (*Scolytus rugulosus*)
on cherry, 618

Fruit tree leafroller (*Archips argyrospilus*)
on apple, *608*
insecticide for, 955
on pear, *643*

Fruiting body, defined, 169

Fruitworms
on blueberries, 689
cherry (*Grapholitha packardii*)
on blueberries, 689
insecticide for, 955
cranberry (*Acrobasis vaccinii*)
on blueberries, 689
insecticide for, 955
insecticides for, 956, 963, 973
raspberry (*Byturus* species)
on brambles, 692
insecticides for, 955, 977
tomato (*Heliothis zea*), 775
See also Corn earworm
insecticides for, 972, 973, 977

Fuchsia
birds on
fuchsia mites and, 491
in containers, 490
culture, 490
diseases of
rust, 492
fertilizing, 490, 935, 940
flowering times for, 490
insects on
ants, 491
aphids, 491
bees, 491
fuchsia mites, 491
greenhouse whiteflies, 491
insecticide for, 979
planting directions for, 492
rust and, 492
planting locations for, 490
pruning, 490
watering, 492
rust and, 492

Fuchsia mites (*Aculops fuchsiae*), ***491***

Fungal leaf or stem gall
on woody ornamentals, 415

Fungal leaf spot
See also Leaf spot
on *Acer, 447*
on *Begonia, 329*
controlling, 850
on flowers, 310
on *Hedera, 293*
on *Impatiens, 310*
on *Kalmia, 509*
on *Rhododendron, 560*
on rhubarb, *848*

Fungal mats
on *Quercus, 557*

Fungal wilt. *See* Wilt; *specific fungi*

Fungi, 848
See also Mushrooms
Albugo occidentalis
on spinach, 761
Alternaria
on cabbage family, 700
Alternaria cucumerina
on cucurbits, 735
Alternaria dauci
on carrots, 704
Alternaria dianthi
on *Dianthus*, 355
Alternaria porri
on onion family, 740
Alternaria solani
on potato, 754
on tomato, 780
Alternaria tenuis
on *Pelargonium*, 381
Alternaria zinniae
on *Zinnia*, 402
on *Shefflera*, 456
Aphanomyces raphani
on radishes, 757
Armillaria mellea, 851
on *Acacia*, 444
on fruit and nut trees, 602
on grapes, 730
on *Juniperus*, 506
plants resistant to, 1016
on *Quercus*, 557
on strawberries, 767
on woody ornamentals, 415, 440, 851
Botryosphaeria ribis
on *Cercis*, 469
plants susceptible to, 1018
Botrytis, 849
on *Ageratum*, 321
on *Dahlia*, 349
on *Petunia*, 383
on *Verbena*, 398
Botrytis allii
on onion family, 740
Botrytis cinerea
on *Antirrhinum*, 326
on beans, 683
on *Begonia*, outdoors, 329
on blueberries, 690
on brambles, 692
on *Cornus*, 471
on *Cymbidium*, 348
on *Dianthus*, 353
on *Dimorphotheca*, 356
on *Euphorbia*, 214
on *Gerbera*, 358
on *Paeonia*, 378
on *Pelargonium*, outdoors, 380
on strawberries, 762
on *Tagetes*, 393
on *Vinca*, 299
on *Zinnia*, 403
Botrytis paeoniae
on *Paeonia*, 378
Botrytis tulipa
on *Tulipa*, 397
Ceratocystis fagacearum
on *Quercus*, 556
Ceratocystis fimbriata
on sweet potato, 769
Ceratocystis ulmi
on *Ulmus*, 585
Cercospora apii
on celery, 706
Cercospora beticola
on beets, 687
Cercospora calendulae
on *Calendula*, 332
Cercospora capsici
on peppers, 749
Cercospora carotae
on carrots, 704
Cercospora citri-grisea
on citrus, 626
Cercospora purpurea
on avocado, outdoors, 615
Cerotelium fici
on fig, 629
Cladosporium carpophilum
on apricot, 612
on peach; nectarine, 634
Cladosporium cucumerinum
on cucurbits, 716
Clitocybe tabescens
on *Acacia*, 444
on *Quercus*, 557
on woody ornamentals, 851
Coccomyce hiemalis
on cherry, 620
Coleosporium solidaginis
on *Callistephus*, 333
Coleosporium
on *Pinus*, 536
Colletotrichum coccodes
on tomato, 774
Colletotrichum fuscum
on *Digitalis*, 356
Colletotrichum gloeosporioides
on mango, 633
Colletotrichum lagenarium
on cucurbits, 719
Colletotrichum

F/FUNGI — FUNGI

on cabbage family, 700
on cucurbits, 720
on grapes, 732
on *Lobularia*, 373
on onion family, 741
on spinach, 760
on *Dracaena*
fusarium leaf spot, 211
dry rot, 800
on *Gladiolus*, 361
Dutch elm disease, 585
elm bark beetles and, 587
ear rot
on corn, 709
early blight
on celery, 706
on potato, 754
on tomato, 780
eastern gall rust
on *Pinus*, 538
on eggplant
leaf spot and fruit rot, 725
phomopsis leaf spot, 725
verticillium wilt, 725
on *Elaeagnus*
canker, 482
verticillium wilt, 482
on *Erica*
root rot, 482
on *Euonymus*
powdery mildew, 483
on *Euphorbia*
botrytis, 214
root and stem rot, 357
eutypa dieback
on grapes, 729
fabraea leaf spot
on pear, 642
on *Fagus*
canker and dieback, 485
on ferns
root rot, 216
on fig
rust, 629
souring, 628
flower and leaf blight
on *Cornus*, 471
on flowers
blossom blight, 849
botrytis blight, 849
bud and flower blight, 849
collar rots, 849
crown rot, 849, 851
damping-off, 318, 319
fungal leaf spot, 310
fusarium wilt, 850, 1005
gray mold, 849
powdery mildew, 311, 1006
rust, 311
sclerotium root rot, 851
slow or no growth and, 308
southern blight or wilt, 851, 1007
stem and root rot, 813
verticillium wilt, 850, funit0880
water molds, 849
fly speck
on apple, 606
foot rot
on citrus, 627
on *Gerbera*, 357
on rhubarb, 758
foxglove anthracnose, 356
on *Fragaria*
leaf spot, 291
root rot, 292
on *Fraxinus*
ash anthracnose, 488
canker and dieback, 490
frog-eye leaf spot
on apple, 608
on peppers, 749
on fruit and nut trees
blossom blight, 849
botrytis blight, 849
bud and flower blight, 849
cankers, 596
cotton root rot, 602
gray mold, 849
gummosis, 596
mushroom root rot, 602
oak root fungus, 602
powdery mildew, 599
root and crown rots, 602
shoestring root rot, 602
Texas root rot, 602
verticillium wilt, 850
fruit rot
on apricot, 611
on brambles, 692
on cherry, 619
on eggplant, 725
fruit scab
on avocado, 615
on *Fuchsia*
rust, 492
fungal leaf or stem gall
on trees, 415
fungal leaf spot
see also leaf spot
on *Acer*, 447
on *Begonia*, 329
on flowers, 310
on *Kalmia*, 509
on *Rhododendron*, 560
fungal wilt. *See* wilt disease; *specific fungal wilts*
fungicides for, 923
types of, 923
fusarium basal rot
on onion family, 739
fusarium blight
on lawns, 254
fusarium bulb rot
on *Narcissus*, 377
fusarium leaf spot
on *Dracaena*, 211
fusarium patch
on lawns, 253
fusarium wilt, 665, 778
on asparagus, 679
on *Dianthus*, 353
on *Matthiola*, 374
on tomato, 665, 778
vegetables susceptible to, 1025
fusarium yellows
on *Gladiolus*, 360
gall rust, eastern or western
on *Pinus*, 538
galls from, 861
on *Gardenia*
sooty mold, 494
on *Gazania*
crown rot, 292
on *Gerbera*
foot rot, 357
gray mold, 358
on *Gladiolus*
dry rot, 361
fusarium yellows, 360
leaf spot, *359*
penicillium corm rot, 361
on *Gleditsia*
canker wilt, 496
gliocladium rot
on palms, indoors, 233
on grapes
anthracnose, 729
armillaria root rot, 730
bird's eye rot, 729
black rot, 726
downy mildew, 732
eutypa dieback, 729
powdery mildew, 730
gray mold, 849
See also Soft rot
on *Ageratum*, 321
on *Antirrhinum*, *326*
on beans, *683*
on *Begonia*, outdoors, 329
on *Cymbidium*, 348
on *Dianthus*, 353
on *Dimorphotheca*, 356
on *Gerbera*, 358
on *Pelargonium*, outdoors, 380
on *Petunia*, 383
on strawberries, 762
on *Tagetes*, *393*
on *Verbena*, 398
on *Vinca*, 299
on *Zinnia*, 403
greasy spot
on citrus, 626
on groundcovers
powdery mildew, 286
gummosis
on fruit and nut trees, 596
hawthorn rust, 476
on *Hedera*
leaf spot, 293
sooty mold, *294*
on *Helianthemum*
leaf spot, 385
on *Helianthus*
powdery mildew, *362*
verticillium wilt, 362
on *Helleborus*
black spot, *363*
crown rot, 362
on *Hemerocallis*
leaf spot, 363
on *Heuchera*
leaf spot, 364
on *Hippeastrum*
leaf scorch, *224*
honey mushroom
on woody ornamentals, 851
on *Hydrangea*
powdery mildew, 499
on *Hypericum*
leaf spot, 295
rust, 295
on *Iberis*
damping-off, 366
powdery mildew on, 355
on *Ilex*
leaf spot, 500
on *Impatiens*
leaf spot, 367
on *Iris*
crown rot, 369
leaf spots, 368
rust, 369
on *Jasminum*
sooty mold, 504
on *Juniperus*
cedar-apple rust, 508
root and crown rots, 506
twig blight, 505
on *Kalanchoe*
powdery mildew, 226
on *Kalmia*
leaf spots, 509
on *Lagerstroemia*
powdery mildew, 510
late blight
on celery, 706
on potato, 755
on tomato, 779
on *Lathyrus*
powdery mildew, 370
wilt disease, 371
on lawns
anthracnose, 253
brown patch, 254
collar rots, 849
crown rots, 849
damping-off, 257
dollar spot, 254
fusarium blight, 254
fusarium patch, 253
helminthosporium leaf spot, 263
melting out, 263
ophiobolus patch, 255
pink snow mold, 253
powdery mildew, 266
pythium blight, 256
red thread, 255
rust, 266
septoria leaf spot, 265
spring dead spot, *255*
stripe smut, 265
tip burn, 265
water molds, 849
leaf and stem blight
on *Pachysandra*, 297
leaf and stem rusts
on woody ornamentals, 413
leaf blight

twig and branch borers and, 730
planting time for, 726
poor fruiting on
armillaria root rot, 730
grape flea beetles, 728
grape phylloxera, 731
pruning, 729
after eutypa dieback, 729
snails and slugs on
baits for, 947
soil pH for, 726
watering, 726
***Grapholitha* species**
G. molesta. See Oriental fruit moth
G. packardii (Cherry fruitworm)
on blueberries, 689
insecticide for, 955
Grass seed. *See* Lawns, seed for
Grass webworms
tropical
insecticides for, 961
Grasses. *See* Lawns; Pastures; Weeds, grasslike
Grasshoppers, *881*
blister beetles and, 723
on corn, *711*
poor pollination and, 708
diseases and, 879
insecticides for, 952, 955, 961, 963, 964, 973
as Orthoptera, 883
on vegetables, 663, 672
Grasslike weeds. *See* Weeds, grasslike
Gravel
as mulch, 926
Gray leaf spot
controlling, 962, 965, 977
Gray mold, *See also* Soft rot
on *Ageratum*, *321*
on *Antirrhinum*, *326*
on beans, *683*
on *Begonia*, outdoors, *329*
botrytis
controlling, 977
on *Cymbidium*, *348*
on *Dianthus*, 353
on *Dimorphotheca*, *356*
on *Gerbera*, *358*
on *Paeonia*, *378*
on *Pelargonium*, *380*
on *Petunia*, *383*
on *Salvia*, *389*
on strawberries, 762
on *Tagetes*, *393*
on *Verbena*, *398*
on *Vinca*, 299
on *Zinnia*, *403*
Gray squirrel, *793*
Grease spot
on lawns, 256
Greasy spot
on citrus, *626*
Green beans. *See* Beans
Green bug, *261*
Green bunching onion. *See* Onion family
Green foxtail. *See* Foxtails
Green peach aphid (*Myzus persicae*), 875
on flowers, 875
on fruit and nut trees, 875
insecticide for, 976
on lettuce, 733
on peach; nectarine, 637
on potato, 756, 875
leaf roll virus and, 756
on spinach, 875
on vegetables, 875
virus diseases and, 875
weeds harbor, 875
on woody ornamentals, 875
Green scurf
on *Camellia*, 465
on *Magnolia*, 515
Green spruce aphid (*Cinara fornacula*)
on *Picea*, *529*
Green striped mapleworms
insecticide for, 964
Green vine. *See* Wild morning glory
Greenbug (*Schizaphis graminum*)
insecticide for, 964
on lawns, 261
Greenhouse thrips (*Heliothrips haemorrhoidalis*), 886
insecticides for, 886
Greenhouse whitefly (*Trialeurodes vaporariorum*)
See also Whiteflies
on *Ageratum*, *322*
on avocado, indoors, *188*
on *Begonia*, indoors, *191*
on *Browallia*, *331*
on *Capsicum*, *195*
on *Chrysanthemum*, indoors, *197*
on *Cineraria*, outdoors, 343
on *Clerondendrum*, *200*
on *Coleus*, indoors, *203*
on *Coleus*, outdoors, *344*
on eggplant, *724*
on flowers, 317
on *Fuchsia*, *491*
on *Gardenia*, *493*
on groundcovers, *287*
on *Hibiscus*, *497*
on houseplants, *181*
on *Lantana*, *370*
on *Pelargonium*, indoors, *234*
on *Pelargonium*, outdoors, *382*
on *Poinsettia*, *214*
on *Solanum*, 390
on *Tolmiea*, 246
on tomato, 777
on *Verbena*, *399*
Greenhouses
insects in
insecticides for, 978
snails and slugs in
bait for, 947
whitefly control in
parasitic wasps for, 893
Greenol Liquid Iron. *See* ORTHO Greenol Liquid Iron
***Grevillea* (Silk oak)**
as disease and insect resistant, 1012
sapsucker damage, 1012
Grimsel. *See* Groundsel
Ground bark
as soil amendment, 926
Ground beetles, 867
Ground burnut (*Tribulus terrestris*), 825
Ground ivy (*Glechoma hederacea*), *831*
in lawns, *276*
herbicides for, 980, 981, 986, 987
Ground squirrels. *See* Squirrels
Groundcovers, 282
See also specific groundcovers
in acid soil, 285
acid-tolerant varieties of, 285
bare spots in
compacted soil, 283
drought, 284
excess water, 284
insufficient light, 283
weeds in, 282
book about, 994
in compacted soil, 283
diseases of
compacted soil and, 283
powdery mildew, 286
drought damage to, 284
drought resistant, 1003
for erosion control, 905
fertilizing, 285
scorch and, 286
tools for, 992
heat scorch on, 286
insects on
ants, 287
aphids, 287
bait for, 974
cockroaches (wood roaches) 789
greenhouse whiteflies, 287
Japanese beetles, 1009
spider mites, 286
insufficient light for, 283, 284
invading other areas, *283*
iron deficiency in, 285
lack of nutrients in, 285
lawn pennywort as, 832
leaf problems on
acid soil, 285
aphids, 287
compacted soil, 283
drought, 284
excess water, 284
greenhouse whiteflies, 287
insufficient light, 283, 284
iron deficiency, 285
lack of nutrients, 285
powdery mildew, 286
scorch, 286
snails and slugs, 287
spider mites, 286
lippia as, 830
nutrients for, 285
planting directions for
weed control and, 282
planting locations for
compacted soil and, 283
insufficient light and, 283, 284
invasiveness and, 283
shady areas, 263, 283, 284, 1003
sunny areas, 1003
salt damage to, 286
for sandy soils, 1011
scorch on, 286
smog-tolerant varieties of, 1008
snails and slugs on, 287, 891
bait for, 974
soil compaction in, 283
drought and, 284
soil pH for, 285
iron deficiency and, 285
watering
drought and, 284
excessive, 284
scorch and, 286
as weeds, 276, 283, 832
weeds in, *282*
winter injury to, 286
Groundhogs. *See* Woodchucks
Groundsel, common (*Senecio vulgaris*), 835
herbicides for, 980, 984
near lettuce
mosaic virus and, 736
Growth cracks
on cabbage family, *696*
on sweet potatoes, 769
on tomatoes, 773
Growth regulators
as litter preventive, 409
Grubs
on lawns, 256, 268
insecticides for, 949, 951, 961
moles and, 896
of root weevils
on *Rhododendron*, 562
on woody ornamentals, 438
white
insecticides for, 949–951, 961
***Gryllus assimilis* (Field crickets)**
bait for, 964
in households, 788
Guava
Mediterranean fruit flies attracted by, 1018
***Guignardia* species**

362
See also Sunflower, edible-seeded
bees attracted by, 1007
culture, 362, 1004
diseases of
powdery mildew, 1006
verticillium wilt, 362, 1006
powdery mildew on, *362*
***Helichrysum* (Straw flower)**
as aster yellows susceptible, 1005
***Heliothis zea*. *See* Corn earworm; Tomato fruitworm**
***Heliothrips haemorrhoidalis* (Greenhouse thrips), 886**
Hellebore. *See Helleborus*
***Helleborus* (Christmas rose)**
crown rot on, *362*
culture, 362
diseases of
black spot, *363*
as verticillium wilt resistant, 1006
Helminthosporium leaf blight
controlling, 977
Helminthosporium leaf spot
on lawns, *263*
bluegrass varieties and, 1003
Helminthosporium melting out
controlling, 965
Helminthosporium species
on corn, 710
on lawns, 263
***Helxine* (Baby tears)**
as smog tolerant, 1008
***Hemerocallis* (Daylily)**
culture, 363, 1004
insects on
ants, 363
aphids, *363*
leaf spot on, 363
Hemispherical scales, *877*
Hemlock. *See Tsuga*
Hemlock rust mite (*Nalepella tsugifoliae*), 584
Henbit (*Lamium amplexicaule*), *842*
herbicides for, 980, 981, 983, 984, 986
in lawns, *275*
Herbaceous, defined, 169
Herbaceous perennials. *See* Flowers, perennial
Herbaceous plants
pinching, 927
Herbicides
See also ORTHO herbicides; *specific herbicides*
applying, 923
contact vs. systemic, 923
defined, 259
labeling law for, 989
pesticide burn and, 668
preemergent vs. postemergent, 923
selective vs. nonselective, 923
storing, 993
types of, 923
woody ornamentals damaged by, *417*
Herbs, 732
book about, 999
butterflies attracted by, 868
in containers
fertilizing, 732
culture, 732, 999
fertilizing, 732
harvesting, 732
by pinching, 927
insects on, *732*
pinching, 927
storing, 732
Heron's bill (*Erodium cicutarium*), 825
***Heuchera* (Alumroot; Coral bells)**
H. sanguinea (Coral bells)
as smog tolerant, 1008
culture, 364, 1004
diseases of
leaf spot, *364*
powdery mildew, 1006
as verticillium wilt resistant, 1006
Hi-Power Indoor Insect Fogger. *See* ORTHO Hi-Power Indoor Insect Fogger
***Hibiscus* (Rose-of-Sharon), 497**
as alkaline soil tolerant, 1019
as armillaria resistant, 1016
fertilizing, 932, 943
iron deficiency and, 937
insects on
ants, 498
cotton and cowpea aphids, *498*
greenhouse whiteflies, *497*
iron deficiency in
correcting, 937
leaf drop in, *497*
as phytophthora susceptible, 1013
soil moisture change in, 497
soil pH for, 1019
correcting, 932
temperature changes and, 497
watering
leaf drop and, 497
Hickory
as *Botryosphaeria ribis* susceptible, 1018
culture, 631
fertilizing, 631, 934
as fill injury susceptible, 1011
insects on
fall or spring cankerworms, 872
gypsy moths, 1014
hickory bark beetles, *632*
hickory shuckworms, *631*
pecan phylloxeras, 645
pecan weevils, 644
leaf scorch, *600*
planting locations for, 631
pruning, 631
shagbark
bark shedding on, 424
Hickory bark beetle (*Scolytus quadrispinosus*), *632*
Hickory shuckworm (*Laspeyresia caryana*)
on hickory, *631*
on pecan, *644*
***Hippeastrum* (Amaryllis)**
culture, 224
leaf scorch on, *224*
Hoary cress. *See* Whitetop
Hog brake (*Pteridium* species), 823
Hog's fennel. *See* Mayweed
Hogweed. *See* Horseweed; Ragweed
***Holcus mollis* (German velvetgrass), 816**
Hollow heart, in potatoes, 753
Holly. *See Ilex*
Holly bud moths
insecticide for, 950
Holly fern (*Cyrtomium falcatum*)
insecticide for, 979
as shade-tolerant groundcover, 1003
Holly grape. *See Mahonia*
Holly leafminers (*Phytomyza* species), *500*
insecticides for, 961, 975
Hollyhock (*Alcea*), 322
bees attracted by, 1007
culture, 1004, 322
diseases of
powdery mildew, 1006
rust, 322
southern blight, 1007
flowering times for, 1004
two-spotted spider mites on, 322
as verticillium wilt resistant, 1006
Hollyleaf cherry. *See Prunus*, evergreen forms of
***Homadaula anisocentra* (Mimosa webworm)**
on *Albizia*, 449
on *Gleditsia*, 495
***Homaledra sabalella* (Palm leaf skeletonizer)**
on palms, outdoors, 1012
Home & Garden Insect Killer. *See* ORTHO Home & Garden Insect Killer
Home Orchard Spray. *See* ORTHO Home Orchard Spray
Home Pest Insect Control. *See* ORTHO Home Pest Insect Control
***Homoeosoma electellum* (Sunflower moth)**
on edible-seeded sunflower, 768
insecticide for, 964
plants susceptible to, 768
Honey bees (*Apis mellifera*), 880
See also Bees
bumble bees vs., 880
as Hymenoptera, 880
in households, *802*
on pear
fireblight and, 640
stings by, 802
Honey locust. *See Gleditsia*
Honey mushroom. *See* Armillaria root rot; Mushroom root rot; Oak root fungus; Shoestring fungus
Honeydew
on *Abies*, 443
on *Acer*, 445
on *Aglaonema*, 184
on *Alnus*, 450
on *Anemone*, 324
on *Anthurium*, 184
ants and, *422*
on flowers, 316
on fruit and nut trees, 598
on woody ornamentals, *422*
on *Aphelandra*, 186
from aphids, 722
on *Acer*, 445
on *Alnus*, 450
on *Anemone*, 324
on apple, 607
on *Aquilegia*, 326
on *Astilbe*, 328
balsam twig, on *Abies*, 443
on bamboo, 452
bean, on *Tropaeolum*, 393
on beans, 699
on *Betula*, 454
on cabbage family, 699
on *Camellia*, 463
on *Capsicum*, 195
on *Centaurea*, 337
on *Chrysanthemum*, outdoors, 342
on *Cineraria*, 198
on citrus, outdoors, 623
on *Cosmos*, 347
crapemyrtle, 510
on *Crataegus*, 477
on *Crocus*, 347
on currants; gooseberries, 722
on cypress family, 480

leaf polishes for, 938, 939, 978
leaf problems on
aphids, 180
greenhouse whiteflies, 181
insufficient light, 179
iron deficiency, 179
mealybugs, 181
nitrogen deficiency, 178
oedema, 860
salt damage, 177
scales, 180
spider mites, 179
sunburn or bleaching, 178
too little water, 177
too much water or poor drainage, 178
light for
insufficient, 179
low, plants tolerant of, 1001
sunburn or bleaching and, 178
supplementary, *920*
nitrogen deficiency in, 178
oedema on, 860
pinching, 937
planting directions for, *924*
poor growth in
insufficient light, 179
iron deficiency, 178
mealybugs, 181
nitrogen deficiency, 178
sunburn or bleaching, 178
too little water, 177
too much water or poor drainage, 178
propagating, 994
by rooting cuttings, 921
root problems on
examining plant for, 921
fungus gnats, 182
too much water or poor drainage, 178
salt damage to, 177
plants susceptible to, 1001
seedling problems in
from fungus gnats, 182
soil mixtures for, 924
iron deficiency and, 178
for rooting cuttings, 921
soil pests on
springtails (collembola), 182
soil problems in
root mealybugs, 180
sunburn on, 178
watering, 919
bleaching and, 178
excessive, 178, 860
insufficient, 177
nitrogen deficiency and, 178
oedema and, 860
salt damage and, 177
springtails and, 182
sunburn and, 178

Hover flies, 883, 892
***How to Attract Birds* (ORTHO)**, 997
How to Build & Use Greenhouses (ORTHO), 997
How to Design & Build Decks & Patios (ORTHO), 997
***How to Design & Install Outdoor Lighting* (ORTHO)**, 998
How to Select, Use & Maintain Garden Equipment (ORTHO), 998
***How to Select & Care for Shrubs & Hedges* (ORTHO)**, 998
***Howea* (Kentia palm)**
insecticide for, 979
low light tolerated by, 1001
as salt sensitive, 1001
***Hoya* (Wax plant)**
culture, 225
insects on
aphids, *225*
insecticide for, 979
mealybugs, *226*
spider mites, *225*
insufficient light for, *225*
leaf polish for, 939
sunburn on, 225
watering, 225
light and, 225
Hubbard squash. *See* Cucurbits
Human flea (*Pulex irritans*), in households, 795
Human hair, as deer repellent, 675
Humidity
defined, 169
for ferns, indoors, *215*
Hummingbirds, fuchsia mites and, 491
Humus
from organic matter, 926
potassium and, 911
Hundred-legged worms. *See* Centipedes
Hungarian wax. *See* Peppers
***Hyacinthus* (Hyacinth)**, 364
bacterial soft rot on, 365
bulbs
diseased, *365*
precooling, 364
storing, bacterial soft rot and, 365
as cotton root rot resistant, 1007
culture, 364, 1004
planting locations for, 364
short stems on, *365*
***Hyadaphis tataricae* (Honeysuckle or Russian aphids)**
on *Lonicera, 514*
Hybrid, defined, 169

Hydrangea
cold injury to
failure to bloom and, 498
color of
acidifying soil and, 932
in containers
protecting from cold, 498
culture, 498
diseases of
powdery mildew, 499, 1006
southern blight, 1007
failure to bloom in, 498
fertilizing, 498, 932
iron deficiency and, 499
flowering times for, 498
iron deficiency in, 499
as Japanese beetle resistant, 1009
planting directions for
iron deficiency and, 499
sunburn and, 499
planting locations for, 498
failure to bloom and, 498
shady areas, 1008
sunburn and, 499
pruning, 498
failure to bloom and, 498
soil pH for, 498, 1019
color and, 932
correcting, 932
iron deficiency and, 499
sunburn on, 499
***Hydrocotyle* species. *See* Pennywort**
***Hydrophyllum virginianum* (Virginia waterleaf)**
as wet soil tolerant, 1010
***Hylemya* species**
See also Root maggots; Seedcorn maggots
H. antiqua (Onion maggot), 739
H. brassicae (Cabbage maggot), 699
Hymenoptera, 880
***Hypericum* (Aaron's beard; St. John's wort)**, 295
as armillaria resistant, 1016
culture, 295
diseases of
leaf spot, *295*
phytophthora rot, 1013
rust, *295*
as drought resistant, 1003
fertilizing, *295*
insects on
Klamathweed beetles, 295
planting locations for, 295
shady areas, 1003
sunny areas, 1003
watering, 295
rust and, 295
as weed, 824
herbicide for, 983
Hyperodes weevils
insecticide for, 951
***Hyphantria cunea* (Fall webworm)**
on fruit and nut trees, 599
insecticides for, 960, 961, 964
on woody ornamentals, 411
Hypoderma lethale
on *Pinus,* 532
Hyssop. *See* Herbs

I

***I. batatas. See* Sweet potato**
***Iberis* (Candytuft)**
as cotton root rot resistant, 1007
culture, 355, 1004
diseases of
damping-off, *366*
powdery mildew, 355, 1006
flowering times for, 1004
as Japanese beetle resistant, 1009
planting directions for
damping-off and, 366
as verticillium wilt resistant, 1006
Ice plant
Carpobrotus
as drought resistant, 1003
for sunny areas, 1003
Delosperma 'Alba' (White ice plant)
as saline soil tolerant, 1011
Drosanthemum (Rosea ice plant)
as saline soil tolerant, 1011
Lampranthus (Trailing ice plant)
as drought resistant, 1003
as saline soil tolerant, 1011
for sunny areas, 1003
Mesembryanthemum
as drought resistant, 1003
root rot on, 296
scales on, 296
for sunny areas, 1003
***Icerya purchasi* (Cottonycushion scale), on citrus**, 623
***Ilex* (Holly)**, 500
I. aquifolium (English holly)
as armillaria resistant, 1016
as pollution tolerant, 1008
I. cassine (Dahoon holly)
as wet soil tolerant, 1010
I. glabra (Gallberry)
as wet soil tolerant, 1010
I. opaca (American holly)
as pollution tolerant, 1008
as wet soil tolerant, 1010

J

973, 976, 977
on lawns, 256
on vegetables, 671
vegetables resistant to, 1009
on woody ornamentals, *411*
woody ornamentals resistant to, 1009
Japanese honeysuckle. *See Lonicera*
Japanese maple. *See Acer palmatum*
Japanese pagoda tree. *See Sophora japonica*
Japanese painted fern (*Athyrium goeringianum*)
as shade-tolerant groundcover, 1003
Japanese rose. *See Kerria*
Japanese spurge. *See* Pachysandra
Japanese zelkova. *See* Zelkova
Jasmine. *See Jasminum*
Jasmine, star. *See* Trachelospermum
***Jasminum* (Jasmine)**
culture, 503
insects on
scales, *503*, *504*
sooty mold and, 504
whiteflies, *503*, 504
sooty mold on, 504
Jerusalem artichokes
rust on, 768
Jerusalem cricket (*Stenopelmatus fuscus*), 883
Jerusalem thorn
fungicides for, 956
Jimson weed
near tomato
virus diseases and, 781. *See also* Nightshades
Joe-Pye weed (*Eupatorium maculatum*)
as wet soil tolerant, 1010
Johnsongrass (*Sorghum halepense*), *818*
herbicides for, 975, 983, 984
lesser corn stalk borers on, 975, 712
maize dwarf mosaic harbored by, 710
for unplanted areas, 985
Jonquil. *See Narcissus*
Judas tree. *See Cercis siliquastrum*
***Juglans. See* Walnut**
Juglone
walnut wilt on tomato from, 778
Jujube (*Zizyphus jujuba*)
as alkaline soil tolerant, 1019
Jumping plant lice. *See* Psyllids
Juneberry. *See* Amelanchier
Jungle rice
herbicide for, 975
Juniper scale (*Carulaspis juniperi*), *507*
Juniper twig girdler (*Periploca nigra*), *504*
Juniper webworm (*Dichomeris marginella*), *508*
***Juniperus* (Juniper), 504**
J. chinensis (Chinese juniper)
as cedar-apple rust resistant, 1015
as twig blight resistant, 1015
J. chinensis 'Pfitzerana' (Pfitzer's juniper)
as phytophthora resistant, 1013
J. communis (Common juniper)
as cedar-apple rust resistant, 1015
as quince rust susceptible, 1015
as twig blight resistant, 1015
J. horizontalis (Creeping juniper)
as groundcover for sunny areas, 1003
as twig blight resistant, 1015
J. sabina (Savin juniper)
as cedar-apple rust resistant, 1015
as phytophthora resistant, 1013
as twig blight resistant, 1015
J. scopulorum (Rocky Mountain juniper)
as cedar-apple rust susceptible, 1015
J. squamata 'Fargesi' (Singleseed juniper)
as cedar-apple rust resistant, 1015
J. squamata 'Meyeri' (Meyer juniper)
as phytophthora resistant, 1013
J. virginiana (Red cedar)
cedar-apple rust on, 518, 1015
hawthorn rust on, 476
as quince rust susceptible, 1015
J. virginiana var. *'Tripartita'* (Fountain red cedar)
as cedar-apple rust resistant, 1015
in alkaline soils
needle browning and, 505
culture, 504
diseases of
cedar-apple rust, 508, 518, 1015
cotton root rot, 506
hawthorn rust, 476
mushroom root rot, 506
oak root fungus, 506
phytophthora rot, 506, 1013
quince rust, 470, 577, 1015
root and crown rots, 506
shoestring root rot, 506
Texas root rot, 506
twig blight, 505, 1015
drought damage to, 505
twig blight compared with, 505
as drought tolerant, 1009
as drought-resistant groundcover, 1003
fertilizing, 504, 505, 932
salt burn and, 504, 505
as groundcover, 1003
herbicide application to, *923*
insects on
ants, *507*
aphids, *507*
bagworms, 412, *508*
insecticide for, 957
juniper scales, *507*
juniper twig girdlers, 504
juniper webworms, 508
leafminers and tip moths, 479, 506
spruce spider mites, *507*, 584
two-spotted spider mites, *507*
as Japanese beetle resistant, 998
mulching, 505
winter injury and, 505
mushrooms at base of
from root and crown rots, 506
natural leaf browning and shedding in, 505
in overfertilized soils, 505
planting directions for
root and crown rots and, *506*
planting locations for, 504, 1009
ash rust and, 577
cedar-apple rust and, 508
hawthorn rust and, 476
quince rust and, 470
salt burn and, 505
twig blight and, 505
winter injury and, 505
as pollution tolerant, 1008
pruning, 504
salt damage to, 505
soil pH for
root and crown rots and, 506
salt burn and, 505
as verticillium wilt resistant, 1006
watering, 504
dog urine damage and, 505
drought damage and, *505*
root and crown rots and, 506
salt burn and, 505
twig blight and, 505
wind damage and, 505
winter injury and, 505
weeds in
herbicide application to, *923*
wind damage to, 505
winter injury to, 505
Juvenile, defined, 169

K

Kaffir lily. *See Clivia*
***Kalanchoe* (Airplant; Felt plant; Maternity plant)**
culture, *226*
insects on
cyclamen mites, 240
insecticide for, 979
mealybugs, *227*
powdery mildew on, 226
Kale. *See* Cabbage family
***Kalmia* (Mountain laurel), 509**
as crown gall resistant, 1013
culture, 509
fertilizing, 509
iron deficiency and, 509
fungal leaf spots on, *509*
gypsy moths feed on, 1014
iron deficiency on, 509
as Japanese beetle resistant, 1009
planting directions, 509
as shade tolerant, 1008
soil pH for, 1019
***Kalopanax pictus* (Castor-aralia)**
as disease and insect resistant, 1012
Kangaroo ivy. *See Cissus*
Karathane
for *Platanus*
powdery mildew on, 540
Katsura tree (*Cercidiphyllum japonicum*)
as disease and insect resistant, 1012
Katydids
as Orthoptera, 883
Kedlock (*Brassica kaber*), 824
Kelthane. *See* Dicofol
Kentia. *See Howea*
Kentucky coffee-tree. *See Gymnocladus dioica*
***Kerria* (Japanese rose)**
as alkaline soil tolerant, 1019
as disease and insect resistant, 1006

chickweed, common, 274, 828
chickweed, mouseear, 274, 829
chicory, 835
clover, *273*
common chickweed, *274*, 828
common groundsel, 835
common yarrow, 826
in compacted soil, 272. *See also* compacted soil in
controlling, 813. *See also* herbicides for
couchgrass, 270
crabgrass, *270*, 817, 813
creeping charlie, *276*
creeping jenny, 276
creeping veronica, 828
cudweed, 826
curly dock, *277*, 833
dallisgrass, *271*, 813, 817
dandelion, *277*, 836
dead nettle, 275
dichondra, 830
Douglas fiddleneck, 842
English ivy (*Hedera helix*), 843
English lawn daisy, *275*
fairy rings, 842
fescue, tall, 271
field bindweed, 278, 840
field pansies (*Viola* species), 831
filaree, redstem, 825
Florida betony, 841
Florida pusley, 828
foxtails, 819
garlic, wild, 272, 821
German velvetgrass, 816
goosegrass, *270*, 818
grasslike. *See* grasslike weeds in
ground ivy, *276*, 831
groundsel, 835
hearts-ease (*Viola* species), 831
henbit, *275*, 842
herbicide application to, 969
herbicides for, 980–984, 986, 987
honeysuckle, 843
horsenettle, 839
horseweed, 836
iris, wild, 820
ivy, ground, 831
Japanese honeysuckle, 843
Johnsongrass, 818
Klamath weed, 824
knotweed. *See* prostrate knotweed
ladysthumb, 833
lambs-quarters, 987
lawn pennywort, 832
lettuce, prickly, 832
liverworts, 823
mallow, *278*, 832
mayweed, 827
milk purslane, 274
in moist areas. *See* moist areas on
moneywort, 276
morning glory, 278, 840
mosses, 279, 823
mouseear chickweed, *274*, 829
mugwort, 838
mushrooms, *279*, 842
mustard, wild, 824
nettles, stinging, 839
nimblewill, 817
nutsedge, *272*, 821
oak, poison, 986
oats, wild, 820
onion, wild, 272, 821
oxalis, *273*, 830
pennywort, lawn, 832
peppergrass, Virginia, 823
pigweeds, 838
pineappleweed, 827
plantain, 278, 833
prickly lettuce, 832
prostrate knotweed, *272*, 827
purslane, *275*, 829
pusley, Florida, 828
quackgrass, *270*, 816
ragweed, 834
red sorrel, 277, 835
redstem filaree, 825
Russian thistle, 824
sandbur, 819
in shady areas. *See* shady areas on
sheep sorrel, *277*
shepherds purse, 837
silver crabgrass, 270
sowthistle, 836
Spanishneedles, 825
speedwell, *276*
spotted spurge, *274*, 829
starthistle, yellow, 834
stinging nettles, 839
tall fescue, *271*
in thin areas. *See* thin areas on
thistle. *See* Canada thistle; Russian thistle; sowthistle; starthistle
velvetgrass, German, 816
violets (*Viola* species), 831
Virginia peppergrass, 823
watergrass, 271
wild carrot, 826
wild garlic, 272, 821
wild geranium, 820
wild morning glory, *278*, 840
wild mustard, 824
wild oats, 820
wild onion, 821
wild violets (*Viola* species), 831
wiregrass, 272
witchgrass, 270
yarrow, 826
yellow starthistle, 834
yellow woodsorrel, 273
white appearance to
annual bluegrass seedheads, 252, 269
brown patch, 254
dull lawn mower, 264
salt damage, 260
white grubs on, 256
billbugs, 259
wild garlic, *272*
wind damage to
fusarium blight and, 254
worms in, 268, 898
moles and, 896
yellowing. *See* pale or yellow areas on
Layered soils, 907
Leaching, defined, 169
Leader, defined, 169
Leaf and flower blight
on *Cornus*, 471
Leaf and flower spots
on flowers, 310
Leaf and stem blight
on *Pachysandra*, 297
on *Pelargonium*, indoors, 234
volutella
on *Buxus*, *459*
Leaf and stem rusts
on woody ornamentals, *413*
Leaf beetles
bean
insecticide for, 972
cottonwood
insecticide for, 961
elm (*Pyrrhalta luteola*), 586
insecticides for, 961
insecticides for, 956
on *Populus* (*Chrysomela* species), *544*
on *Salix*, *573*
insecticide for, 961
strawberry
insecticides for, 958
Leaf blight
on carrots, *704*
controlling, 977
on corn, *710*
varieties resistant to, 1027
flower blight and
on *Cornus*, 471
helminthosporium
controlling, 977
on *Pachysandra*, *297*
on pear, 642
stem blight and. *See* Leaf and stem blight
Leaf blister, oak, 552
Leaf blotch
on *Aesculus*, *448*
Leaf browning
on cedar, *479*
Leaf bugs, 873
fourlined
insecticides for, 963
Leaf burn, 857. *See also* Summer leaf scorch
Leaf curl
on peach; nectarine, *635*
Leaf curl aphids
on *Fraxinus*, 489
Leaf drop
on *Bucida*, *457*
on *Cornus*, *419*
on *Euphorbia*, *213*
on *Gardenia*, outdoors, *492*
on *Hibiscus*, *497*
on woody ornamentals, 433
Leaf gall aphid (*Tamalia coweni*)
on *Arctostaphylos*, *452*
Leaf gall psyllids
hackberry (*Pachypsylla* species), 469
on *Salix*, *415*
Leaf galls
on *Camellia*, *462*
from psyllids
on fruit and nut trees, 878
on vegetables, 878
on woody ornamentals, 878
on *Rhododendron*, *559*
on trees, *415*
Leaf margins, defined, 169
Leaf nematodes (*Aphelenchoides* species)
on *Begonia*, outdoors, *330*
on *Chrysanthemum*, outdoors, *339*
Leaf polish. *See* **ORTHO Leaf Polish (Aerosol or Pump)**
Leaf roll
on potato, 756
discolored tubers and, 752
on tomato, 780
sunscald and, 773
Leaf rusts
on woody ornamentals, 413
Leaf scar, defined, 169
Leaf scorch, 857
on *Acer*, *429*
on *Ajuga*, 288
on *Betula*, *429*
on fruit and nut trees, 600
on *Hedera*, 293
on Hickory, *600*
on *Hippeastrum*, 224
on *Lilium*, 373
on strawberries, 765
summer
on *Acer*, 447
on *Aesculus*, 449
on *Catalpa*, 467
on *Cornus*, 472
on *Euonymus*, 484
on *Magnolia*, *515*
on *Platanus*, 541
on *Quercus*, 551
on woody ornamentals, 429
Leaf spot, 850
alternaria
on *Brassaia*, 456
on cabbage family, 700
controlling, 962, 965, 968, 977

on cypress family, 479
damage to Arborvitae, *479*
damage to *Ilex, 500*
dipterous
insecticides for, 955
on flowers, 312
holly (*Phytomyza* species)
insecticides for, 961, 975
insecticides for, 950, 955, 960, 962–965, 973, 974
lilac (*Caloptilia syringella*), 580
insecticide for, 961
locust (*Odontota dorsalis*), 565
oak, 552
sawflies as, 881
on *Schefflera*, 456
spinach (*Pegomya hyoscyami*), 761
on swiss chard, 772
on Tagetes, *392*
tentiform
insecticide for, 955
tip moths and (*Argyresthia* species)
on *Juniperus*, *506*
trails, *885*
on vegetables, 667
on woody ornamentals, *418*
Leafrollers
Ancylis comptana fragariae
insecticides for, 955, 972, 973
on strawberries, 763
Archips argyrospilus
on apple, 608
insecticide for, 955
on pear, 643
Archips rosanus
on filbert, 630
Argyrotaenia velutinana
on grapes, 727
insecticide for, 963, 964
on blueberries, 691
European (*Archips rosanus*)
on filbert, 630
feeding on hickory leaf, *873*
fruit tree (*Archips argyrospilus*)
on apple, 608
insecticide for, 955
on pear, 643
on grapes, 727
insecticides for, 950, 956, 958, 961, 963, 970, 973
oblique-banded (*Choristoneura rosaceana*)
insecticide for, 964
omnivorous (*Platynota stultana*)
on grapes, 727
redbanded (*Argyrotaenia velutinana*)
on grapes, 727
insecticide for, 963
on *Rosa*, *569*
strawberry (*Ancylis comptana fragariae*), 763
insecticides for, 955, 972, 973
on woody ornamentals, *418*
Leafstalk, defined, 169
Leaftiers, 873
on blueberries, 691
celery (*Udea rubigalis*), 705
cherry laurel
insecticide for, 964
insecticides for, 974
omnivorous
insecticides for, 964, 977
Leafy mistletoe (*Phoradendron* species), *856*
on *Quercus*, *556*
on woody ornamentals, *416*
Leaves, as mulch, 926
Lecanium scale, *412*
Leeks. *See* Onion family
Leggy growth
in *Chrysanthemum*, *338*
Legumes. *See* Beans; Peas
Lemon. *See* Citrus
Lemon balm. *See* Herbs
Lemon cucumber. *See* Cucurbits
***Lepidium virginicum* (Virginia peppergrass),** 823
Lepidoptera, 868
***Lepidosaphes ulmi* (Oystershell scale)**
on *Fraxinus*, 490
***Lepisma* species (Silverfish)**
in households, 789
insecticides for, 946, 957
***Leptinotarsa decemlineata* (Colorado potato beetle)**
on eggplant, 723
insecticides for, 955, 972, 973, 976, 977
on potato, 753
***Leptocoris* species (Boxelder bug)**
on *Acer*, 445
in households, 791
insecticides for, 950, 963
Leptosphaeria coniothyrium
on brambles, 694
Lesion, defined, 169
Lespedeza
in lawns
herbicides for, 981
Lesser corn stalk borer (*Elasmopalpus lignosellus*), *712*
Lethal yellows disease
on palms, outdoors, *524*
susceptibility to, 1014
Lettuce, 733
animal pests in, 675
bitter taste to
aster yellows, 736
bolting, 733
bolting, *733*
butterhead
bolt-resistant varieties of, 733
in containers
fertilizing, 733
culture, 733
diseases of
aster yellows, *736*, 1005
bottom rot, *735*
mosaic virus, 733, *736*
powdery mildew, 1006
southern blight, 1007
watery soft rot, 735
white mold, 735
fertilizing, 733, 935, 941, 942
germination of, 733, 1025
harvesting, 733
aphids and, 733
head
bolt-resistant varieties of, 733
harvesting, 733
tip-burn-resistant varieties of, 735
insects on
aphids, 545, 733, 736
aster (six-spotted) leafhoppers, 734, 736
cabbage loopers, *734*
cabbage worms, 698
cutworms, *734*
green peach aphids, 733, 736
leafhopper, *734*
potato aphid, *733*
wireworms, 704
as Japanese beetle resistant, 1009
loose-leaf
bolt-resistant varieties of, 733
harvesting, 733
pan damage to, *855*
planting directions for, 733
bottom rot and, 735
planting locations for, 733
bottom rot and, 735
watery soft rot and, 735
planting times for, 1025
bolting and, 733
prickly (*Lactuca serriola*), 832
herbicides for, 981, 983
mosaic virus harbored by, 736
rabbits in, 675
snail and slug bait for, 947
soil pH for, 733
tip burn on, *735*
varieties resistant to, 1027
transplanting, 733
as verticillium wilt resistant, 1006
watering, 733
tip burn and, 735
watery soft rot and, *735*
weeds in
aster yellows and, 736
leafhoppers and, 736
mosaic virus and, 736
wild. *See* Lettuce, prickly
Lettuce mosaic virus, 736
green peach aphids and, 733
wild lettuce harbors, 736
Leucothoe
as crown gall resistant, 1013
culture, 511
leaf spots on, *511*
as shade tolerant, 1008
soil pH for, 511, 1019
***Libocedrus* (Incense cedar)**
as disease and insect resistant, 1012
diseases of
Chaenomeles and, 470
Sorbus and, 577
phytophthora rot, 1013
rust, 470, 577, 1015
juniper scales on, 507
witch's broom on
from rust, 470
Lice
jumping plant. *See* Psyllids
plant. *See* Aphids
on poultry
insecticide for, 972
Lichens
on woody ornamentals, *416*
Lighting
supplementary, 920
Lightning bugs, 868
soldier beetles vs., 867
Lightning injury
to palms, outdoors, *525*
to woody ornamentals, *425*
woody ornamentals susceptible to, 1012
***Ligustrum* (Privet)**
L. amurense (Amur privet), 512
L. ibota (Ibota privet), 512
L. lucidum (Glossy privet), 1012
litter problem from, 409
L. obtusifolium var. *regelianum* (Regal privet), 512
L. ovalifolium (California privet), 512
bees attracted by, 1007
culture, 511
diseases of
anthracnose and twig blight, *512*
powdery mildew, 1006
variety resistant to, 1012
fertilizing, 511, 932, 934
iron deficiency and, 937
insects on
lilac leafminers, 580
privet rust mites and privet mites, *511*
scales, *512*
variety resistant to, 1012
iron deficiency in
fertilizer for, 937
planting locations for, 511
shady areas, 1008
as pollution tolerant, 1008
Lilac. *See Syringa*
Lilac borers (*Podoseia*

syringae), *580*
insecticide for, 962
Lilac leafminers (*Caloptilia syringella*)
insecticide for, 961
on Syringa, *580*
***Lilium* (Lily)**
L. canadense (Canada lily)
as wet soil tolerant, 1010
in containers, watering, 371
culture, 371, 1004
diseases of
fleck, 372
mosaic virus, 372, 1004
root and bulb rot, 372
southern blight, 1007
viruses, 372, 398
fertilizing, 371
leaf scorch and, 373
flowering times for, 1004
insects on
ants, 372
aphids, *372*
leaf scorch on, 373
root and bulb rot, *372*
as smog tolerant, 1008
soil pH for, 373
leaf scorch and, 373
virus, *372*
Lily of the Nile. *See Agapanthus*
Lily turf. *See Liriope*
Lily-of-the-valley. *See Convallaria*
shrub. *See Pieris*
Lima beans. *See* Beans, lima
Limb breakage
caused by snow load, *426*
caused by weak fork, *426*
on fruit and nut trees, *595*
Lime. *See* Citrus
Lime sulfur, 552
for *Acer*
cottony scales and mealybugs on, 446
for anthracnose
on brambles, 695
on grapes, 729
for aphids
on *Picea*, 528
for apple scab
on *Malus*, 518
for beech scales, 485
for blister mites, pear leaf
on *Cotoneaster*, 475
on *Sorbus*, 578
for brambles
anthracnose on, 695
spider mites on, 694
for cooley spruce gall aphids
on *Picea*, 528
for *Cotoneaster*
pear leaf blister mites on, 475
for cottony maple leaf scales
on *Nyssa*, 523
for cottony scales and mealybugs
on *Acer*, 446
on *Morus*, 520
for currants; gooseberries
powdery mildew on, 721
for dieback, stem cankers and
on *Rosa*, 572
for *Fagus*
scales on, 485
as generic name, 1040
for grapes
anthracnose on, 729
for *Lagerstroemia*
powdery mildew on, 510
for *Malus*
apple scab on, 518
for mites
on *Cotoneaster*, 475
on pear, 641
on *Quercus*, 552
on *Sorbus*, 578
for *Morus*
cottony scales and mealybugs on, 520
for *Nyssa*
cottony maple leaf scales on, 523
for oak mites, 552
in ORTHO Dormant Disease Control, 951
in ORTHO Orthorix Spray, 967
for pear leaf blister mites
on *Cotoneaster*, 475
on *Sorbus*, 578
for pear rust mites, 641
for *Picea*
cooley spruce gall aphids on, 528
pine needle scales on, 530
for powdery mildew
on currants; gooseberries, 721
on *Lagerstroemia*, 510
for *Quercus*
oak mites on, 552
for *Rosa*
stem cankers and dieback on, 572
for scab
on *Malus*, 518
for scales
beech, 485
cottony maple leaf, on *Nyssa*, 523
on *Fagus*, 485
on *Picea*, 530
on *Pinus*, 535
for *Sorbus*
pear leaf blister mites on, 578
for spider mites
on brambles, 694
on pear, 641
for spruce gall aphids
on *Picea*, 528
for stem cankers and dieback
on *Rosa*, 572
for two-spotted spider mites
on pear, 641
Lime
applying, 908, 1019
dolomitic limestone
use of, 908, 1019
for groundcovers, 285
for growing transplants, 925
for *Hydrangea*, 498
for lawns, 251
for *Syringa*, 579
Lindane
for aphids
on *Pseudotsuga*, 547
for apricot
peachtree borers on, 613
for beetles
in households, 798
for *Betula*
borers on, 455
for borers
on apricot, 613
bronze birch, 455
on cherry, 618
on *Crataegus*, 477
on fruit and nut trees, 597
honeylocust, 496
on plum, 651
on *Quercus*, 553
on woody ornamentals, 424
for cherry
peachtree borers on, 618
shothole borers on, 618
for cooley spruce gall aphids
on *Pseudotsuga*, 547
for *Crataegus*
borers on, 477
for flowers
snout beetles on, 866
symphylans on, 890
weevils on, 866
for fruit and nut trees
borers on, 597
for garden centipedes, 890
as generic name, 1040
for *Gleditsia*
honeylocust borers on, 496
honeylocust pod gall midges on, 496
for nematodes
pine wilt, 533
in ORTHO Lindane Borer & Leaf Miner Spray, 962
for peachtree borers
on apricot, 613
on cherry, 618
on plum, 651
for pecan phylloxeras, 645
for *Pinus*
pine wilt nematodes protection for, 533
for plum
peachtree borers on, 651
for powderpost beetles
in households, 798
for *Pseudotsuga*
cooley spruce gall aphids on, 547
for *Quercus*, borers on, 553
for shothole borers
on cherry, 618
for snout beetles, 866
for symphylans, 890
for vegetables
snout beetles on, 866
weevils on, 866
for weevils, 866
for woody ornamentals
borers on, 424
pine wilt nematode protection for, 533
snout beetles on, 866
symphylans on, 890
weevils on, 866
Lindane Borer & Leaf Miner Spray. *See* ORTHO Lindane Borer & Leaf Miner Spray
Linden. *See Tilia*
Linden aphid (*Myzocallis tiliae*), *583*
Linuron
as generic name, 1040
for Virginia peppergrass, 823
Lion's tooth. *See* Dandelion
Lippia (*Phyla nodiflora*), 830
as groundcover, 830
drought-resistant, 1003
for sunny areas, 1003
as lawn, 830
as weed, *830*
herbicide for, 987
Lipstick plant. *See Aeschynanthus*
Liquid African Violet Food. *See* ORTHO Liquid African Violet Food
Liquid Iron. *See* ORTHO Greenol Liquid Iron
Liquid Lawn Disease Control. *See* ORTHO Liquid Lawn Disease Control
Liquid Plant Food. *See* ORTHO Ortho-Gro Liquid Plant Food
Liquid Sevin. *See* ORTHO Liquid Sevin
***Liquidambar* (Sweet gum)**
L. orientalis, 1016
L. styraciflua, 1016
as armillaria resistant, 1016
as *Botryosphaeria ribis* susceptible, 1018
as crown gall resistant, 1013
excess flowers or fruit from, 409
insects on
gypsy moths, 1014
redhumped caterpillars, 870
as Japanese beetle resistant, 1009
leaf spots on, *414*

litter problem from, 409
as verticillium wilt resistant, 1006
***Liriodendron* (Tuliptree)**
as armillaria resistant, 1016
brittle wood on, 1012
as crown gall resistant, 1013
culture, 513
diseases of
leaf spot, *850*
powdery mildew, 1006
sooty mold, 513
fertilizing, 513
summer leaf yellowing and, 512
as fill injury susceptible, 1011
as frost crack susceptible, 426
insects on
ants, 513
aphids, *513*
gypsy moths, 1014
mealybugs, 513
scales, *513*
whiteflies, 513
as lightning injury susceptible, 1012
sooty mold on, *513*
summer leaf yellowing on, *512*
watering, 513
summer leaf yellowing and, 512
***Liriope* (Lily turf)**
as shade-tolerant groundcover, 1003
***Listronotus oregonensis* (Carrot weevil), 703**
Litter
from excess flowers or fruits, 409
Little bittercress
herbicide for, 984
Little house fly (*Fannia canicularis*), 786
Liverworts, 823
Livestock
plants injurious to
rhubarb leaves, 759
weeds injurious to
Nerium, 523
horsenettle, 839
Klamath weed, 824
Klamath weed beetles and, 295
nightshades, 841
puncturevine, 825
yellow starthistle, 834
***Livistona chinensis*. See Palms, outdoors**
***Lixus concavus* (Rhubarb curculio), 759**
Loam
See also Clay loam; Sandy loam
correcting soil pH for, 1019
watering
measuring amount of, 912
***Lobelia* (Cardinal flower)**
as aster yellows susceptible, 1005
flowering times for, 1004
germination of, 1004
no flowers, *305*
planting times for, 1004
as wet soil tolerant, 1010
without flowers, *305*
***Lobularia* (Sweet alyssum), 373**
bees attracted by, 1007
as cotton root rot resistant, 1007
culture, 373, 1004
diseases of
downy mildew, *373*
powdery mildew, 1006
root and stem rot, *373*
fertilizing, 373
flowering times for, 1004
germination of, 1004
planting locations for, 373
planting times for, 1004
watering
downy mildew and, 373
Locust
black. *See Robinia*
honey. *See Gleditsia*
Locust borer (*Megacyllene robiniae*)
on *Robinia, 564*
Locust leafminer (*Odontota dorsalis*)
on *Robinia, 565*
Locusts. *See* Grasshoppers
17-year. *See* Periodical cicada
Loganberries. *See* Brambles
Lombardy poplar. *See Populus nigra cv.* 'Italica'
London plane-tree. *See Platanus*
London rocket
herbicides for, 983, 984
***Longistigma caryae*. See Giant bark aphid**
***Lonicera* (Honeysuckle)**
L. fragrantissima (Fragrant honeysuckle)
as alkaline soil tolerant, 1019
L. japonica (Japanese honeysuckle), 282
as vigorous groundcover, 282
as weed, *843*
L. nitida (Box honeysuckle)
as armillaria resistant, 1016
bees attracted by, 1007
culture, 514
insects on
honeysuckle (Russian) aphids, *514*
as Japanese beetle resistant, 1009
powdery mildew on, *514*, 1006
witch's broom on
aphids and, *514*
Loopers
See also Caterpillars
barberry (*Coryphista meadii*)
on *Mahonia*, 517
cabbage (*Trichoplusia ni*), 670
on cabbage family, 698
on *Calendula*, 332
insecticides for, 961, 964, 972
on lettuce, 734
on turnips, 783
on herbs, 732
leaf-feeding caterpillars, *4111*
on *Pelargonium*, outdoors, 382
on *Petunia*, 384
on vegetables, 670
Lophodermium pinastri
on *Pinus*, 532
Loquat. *See Eriobotrya*
Love lies bleeding. *See Amaranthus*
Lovegrass
herbicides for, 983
Lovers pride (*Polygonum persicaria*), 833
***Loxosceles reclusa* (Brown recluse spiders), 805**
Lumber
woodwasps in, 800
***Lupinus* (Lupine)**
as acid soil tolerant, 1019
as southern blight susceptible, 1007
***Lycopersicum esculentum*. See Tomato**
Lygus bugs, 873
insecticides for, 972, 973
***Lygus lineolaris* (Tarnished plant bug)**
on peach; nectarine, 637
***Lysimachia nummularia*. See Creeping charlie; Moneywort**

M

***Macronoctua onusta*. See Iris borers**
Macronutrients, defined, 169
***Macrosiphum* species**
M. liriodendri (Tuliptree aphid), 513
M. rhododendri (Rhododendron aphid), 563
M. rosae (Rose aphid), 569
***Macrosteles fascifrons*. See Aster leafhopper**
Madrone. *See Arbutus*
Maggots, 883
See also Flies
apple, 605
insecticides for, 955, 956, 973
blueberry (*Rhagoletis mendax*), 955
on blueberries, 689
insecticide for, 955
cherry fruitworms
insecticide for, 955
of hover or flower flies, 892
onion (*Hylemya antiqua*)
on onion family, 739
root (*Hylemya* species). *See* Root maggots
seedcorn (*Hylemya platura*)
on beans, 686
on corn, 713
on radish, 757
***Magicicada septendecim* (Periodical cicada), 879**
insecticides for, 956, 963, 973
Magnesium deficiency
acid soils and, 908. *See also* Minor nutrient deficiency
***Magnolia*, 514**
M. acuminata, 1012
M. grandiflora (Southern magnolia)
as armillaria resistant, 1016
brittle wood on, 1012
M. kobus borealis, 1012
M. salicifolia (Anise magnolia), 1012
M. soulangiana (Saucer magnolia)
as lawn tree, 1009
M. stellata (Star magnolia)
as disease and insect resistant, 1012
as lawn tree, 1009
M. virginiana (Sweetbay *magnolia*)
as wet soil tolerant, 1010
bird damage, 1012
as crown gall resistant, 1013
culture, 514
diseases of
algal spot, *515*
green scurf, 515
powdery mildew, 1006
varieties resistant to, 1012
fertilizing, 514, 932
iron deficiency and, 515
flowering times for, 514
insects on
gypsy moths, 1014
magnolia scales, *516*
tuliptree scales, 513
varieties resistant to, 1012
iron deficiency in, *515*
as Japanese beetle resistant, 1009
as lawn tree, 1009
planting locations for, 514
summer leaf scorch and,

M/MAGNOLIA — MALATHION

515
pruning, 514
sapsucker damage, 1012
soil pH for, 514, 1019
iron deficiency and, 515
summer leaf scorch on, 515
watering, 514
summer leaf scorch and, 515
Magnolia scale (*Neolecanium cornuparvum*), *516*
Mahogany, mountain. ***See* Cercocarpus**
***Mahonia* (Holly grape; Oregon grape),** 516
barberry or mahonia loopers on, *517*
as crown gall resistant, 1013
culture, 516
diseases of
armillaria root rot, 1016
rust, *516*
fertilizing, 516, 932
winter injury and, 516
planting locations for, 516
shady areas, 1008
winter injury to, *516*
Mahonia or barberry looper (*Coryphista meadii*), 517
Maiden cane
herbicides for, 984
Maidenhair fern (*Adiantum pedatum*)
as shade-tolerant groundcover, 1003
Maidenhair tree. ***See* Ginkgo**
Maize dwarf mosaic
on corn, *710*
varieties resistant to, 1027
***Malacosoma* species.** ***See* Tent caterpillar**
Malathion
for *Abies*
spruce budworms on, 442
for aphids
bean, on *Tropaeolum*, 393
on *Centaurea*, 337
cooley spruce gall, on *Picea*, 528
cotton and cowpea, on *Hibiscus*, 498
cowpea and bean, on *Laburnum*, 509
on currants; gooseberries, 722
on *Daphne*, 481
on *Dianthus*, 354
on *Digitalis*, 355
Eastern spruce gall, on *Picea*, 528
on *Fagus*, 484
on flowers, 316
on *Freesia*, 357
on fruit and nut trees, 598
on *Gerbera*, 358
on *Hemerocallis*, 363
on *Hibiscus*, 498
on *Iris*, 368
on *Ixora*, 503
on *Laburnum*, 509
on *Larix*, 510
on *Lilium*, 372
on *Liriodendron*, 513
on *Malus*, 518
on *Picea*, 528
on *Sorbus*, 578
on swiss chard, 771
on *Tropaeolum*, 393
tuliptree, 513
on vegetables, 673
woolly, on *Sorbus*, 578
woolly larch, 510
for apricot
peachtree borers on, 613
for *Aquilegia*
columbine leafminers on, 326
for *Araucaria*
mealybugs on, 187
scales on, 187
for aster leafhoppers
on flowers, 316
on vegetables, 672
for avocado, indoors
mealybugs on, 189
for bean aphids
on *Tropaeolum*, 393
for bedbugs, in households, 796
for beech scales, 485
for beet leafhoppers
on beets, 688
on tomato, 781
for beet leafminers, 687
for beetles
cigarette, in households, 809
drugstore, in households, 809
flour, in households, 808
on flowers, 315
sawtoothed grain, in households, 808
for beets
beet leafhoppers on, 688
beet leafminers on, 687
for *Begonia*, indoors,
mealybugs on, 190
for *Begonia*, outdoors
leaf nematodes on, 330
mealybugs on, 331
for blueberries
blueberry fruitflies on, 689
blueberry maggots on, 689
cherry fruitworms on, 689
cranberry fruitworms on, 689
leafrollers and leaftiers on, 691
plum curculios on, 690
for borers
on apricot, 613
on cherry, 618
on *Iris*, 369
on plum, 651
for boxelder bugs
in households, 791
for brambles
raspberry cane borers on, 693
red-necked cane borers on, 693
for *Browallia*
greenhouse whiteflies on, 331
for budworms, spruce, 528
for cactus, indoors
mealybugs on, 194
for cactus, outdoors
cactus scales on, 461
mealybugs on, 461
for *Callistephus*
leafhoppers on, 334
for caterpillars
on *Tropaeolum*, 394
for celery
celery leaftiers on, 705
leafhoppers on, 707
for *Centaurea*
aphids on, 337
for cherry
peachtree borers on, 618
for cherry fruitworms
on blueberries, 689
for *Chrysanthemum*, outdoors
leaf nematodes on, 339
leafhoppers on, 341
for cigarette beetles
in households, 809
for citrus
cottonycushion scales on, 623
mealybugs on, 623
for clover mites
in households, 792
for *Coleus*, outdoors
greenhouse whiteflies on, 344
mealybugs on, 344
for columbine leafminers, 326
for cooley spruce gall aphids
on *Picea*, 528
for cotton and cowpea aphids
on *Hibiscus*, 498
for cottony scales and mealybugs
on ferns, 486
on *Morus*, 520
for cottonycushion scales
on citrus, 623
for cowpea and bean aphids
on *Laburnum*, 509
for cranberry fruitworms
on blueberries, 689
for currants; gooseberries
aphids on, 722
for *Cycas*
scales on, 206
for cypress family
leafminers and tip moths on, 479
for *Daphne*
aphids on, 481
for *Dianthus*
aphids on, 354
for *Digitalis*
aphids on, 355
for drugstore beetles
in households, 809
for Eastern spruce gall aphids
on *Picea*, 528
for eggplant
spider mites on, 726
for *Fagus*
aphids on, 484
scales on, 485
for ferns
cottony scales and mealybugs on, 486
scales on, 486
for fig
scales on, 629
for flea beetles
on vegetables, 671
for flies
walnut husk, 654
for flour beetles, 808
for flowers
aphids on, 316
aster leafhoppers on, 316
beetles on, 315
greenhouse whiteflies on, 317
Japanese beetles on, 315
leafminers on, 312
mealybugs on, 316
scales on, 316
six-spotted leafhoppers on, 316
snout beetles on, 866
spittlebugs on, 317
treehoppers on, 878
weevils on, 866
whiteflies on, 316, 317
for *Freesia*
aphids on, 357
for fruit and nut trees
aphids on, 598
leafhoppers on, 598
mealybugs on, 598
psyllids on, 878
scales on, 597, 598
whiteflies on, 598
for fruitflies
on blueberries, 689
for fruitworms
on blueberries, 689
for gall aphids
cooley spruce, on *Picea*, 528
Eastern spruce, on *Picea*, 528
as generic name, 1040
for *Gerbera*
aphids on, 358
for *Gladiolus*
leafhoppers on, 360
thrips on, 359

fungal leaf spot on, 310
for *Fragaria*
leaf spot on, 291
for frog-eye leaf spot
on peppers, 749
for fruit and nut trees
botrytis blight on, 849
for fungal leaf or stem gall
on woody ornamentals, 415
for fungal leaf spot, 850
See also for leaf spot
on flowers, 310
on *Hedera*, outdoors, 293
on woody ornamentals, 414
as generic name, 1040
for *Gerbera*
gray mold on, 358
for *Gladiolus*
leaf spot on, 359
for gray mold, 849
on *Ageratum*, 321
on *Gerbera*, 358
on *Petunia*, 383
on *Tagetes*, 393
on *Verbena*, 398
on *Zinnia*, 403
for hawthorn rust, 476
for *Hedera*
outdoors, leaf spot on, 293
for *Hemerocallis*
leaf spot on, 363
for *Heuchera*
leaf spot on, 364
for *Hypericum*
leaf spot on, 295
for *Ilex*
leaf spot on, 500
for late blight
on celery, 706
for lawns
algae on, 279, 823
septoria leaf spot on, 265
for leaf and stem rusts
on woody ornamentals, 413
for leaf blight, flower blight and
on *Cornus*, 471
for leaf blister
on *Quercus*, 552
for leaf gall
on woody ornamentals, 415
for leaf rusts
on woody ornamentals, 430
for leaf spot, 850
See also for fungal leaf spot
alternaria. *See* for alternaria leaf spot
on *Calendula*, 332
on *Chrysanthemum*, outdoors, 339
on *Delphinium*, 351
on *Fragaria*, 291
on *Gladiolus*, 359
on *Hedera*, outdoors, 293
on *Hemerocallis*, 363
on *Heuchera*, 364
on *Hypericum*, 295
on *Ilex*, 500
on *Phlox*, 385
on vegetables, 668
on *Viola*, 400
for *Malus*
cedar-apple rust on, 518
for maple anthracnose, 447
for needle cast
on *Pinus*, 532
for oak leaf blister, 552
for onion family
downy mildew on, 741
purple blotch on, 740
for *Paeonia*
phytophthora blight in, 379
for *Pelargonium*, outdoors
rust on, 380
for peppers
cercospora leaf spot on, 749
for *Petunia*
gray mold on, 383
for *Phlox*
leaf spot on, 385
for phytophthora blight
on *Paeonia*, 379
for *Pinus*
needle cast on, 532
for *Platanus*
sycamore anthracnose on, 541
for *Potentilla*
rust on, 298
for purple blotch
on onion family, 740
for *Pyracantha*
scab on, 549
for *Quercus*
oak leaf blister on, 552
for *Rosa*
stem cankers and dieback on, 572
for rust
on *Alcea*, 322
on *Antirrhinum*, 325
on *Asparagus*, 680
hawthorn, 476
leaf, on woody ornamentals, 430
leaf and stem, on woody ornamentals, 413
on *Pelargonium*, outdoors, 380
on *Potentilla*, 298
on sunflower, 768
white, on spinach, 761
for *Salix*
willow scab on, 575
for scab
on *Pyracantha*, 549
on *Salix*, 575
willow, 575
for septoria leaf spot
on lawns, 265
for spinach
downy mildew on, 760
white rust on, 761
for stem cankers and dieback
on *Rosa*, 572
for stem gall
on woody ornamentals, 415
for sunflower
rust on, 768
for sycamore anthracnose
on *Platanus*, 541
for *Tagetes*
gray mold on, 393
for tomato
bacterial speck on, 774
bacterial spot on, 774
for vegetables
botrytis blight on, 849
leaf spot on, 668
for *Verbena*
gray mold on, 398
for *Viola*
leaf spot on, 400
for walnut anthracnose, 656
for white rust
on spinach, 761
for willow scab, 575
for woody ornamentals
botrytis blight on, 849
fungal leaf or stem gall on, 415
fungal leaf spot on, 414
leaf and stem rusts on, 413
leaf rusts on, 430
for *Zinnia*
gray mold on, 403
Manganese
in acid soils, 908
deficiency of, 860
alkaline soils and, 908
in palms, outdoors, 525
as minor nutrient, 911
Manganese sulfate
for palms, outdoors, frizzle top on, 525
***Mangifera indica. See* Mango**
Mango
culture, 632
diseases of
anthracnose, *633*
scab, *632*
fertilizing, 632
harvesting, 632
insects on
ants, *598*, 633
insecticide for, 978
scales, false oleander, *633*
Mantids, praying, 892
Manure
for heavy soils, 904
maggots feed on, 883
nitrogen supplied by, 910
salt damage and, 857, 926
as soil amendment, 926
sowbugs and pillbugs in, 857, 673
Manzanita. *See Arctostaphylos*
Manzate
for *Araucaria*
needle blight on, 451
for *Brassaia*
alternaria leaf spot on, 456
Maple. *See Acer*
Maple anthracnose, *447*
Maple shoot moths
insecticides for, 960, 961, 964,
***Maranta* (Prayer plant)**
culture, 227
insecticide for, 979
insects on
mealybugs, *228*
spider mites, *179*, *227*
propagating, 1001
salt damage to, *227*, 1001
Mare's tail. *See* Horseweed
Marguerites. *See Chrysanthemum*, indoors and outdoors
Marigold. *See Tagetes*
cape. *See Dimorphotheca*
Marigold, marsh (*Caltha palustris*)
as wet soil tolerant, 1010
Marjoram. *See* Herbs
Marsh mallow (*Althaea officinalis*)
as wet soil tolerant, 1010
Marsh marigold (*Caltha palustris*)
as wet soil tolerant, 1010
Mason wasps, 803
Mat lippia. *See* Lippia
Matchweed. *See* Lippia
Maternity plant. *See Kalanchoe*
Matgrass. *See* Lippia; Prostrate knotweed
***Matricaria matricarioides* (Pineappleweed), 827**
***Matthiola* (Stock), 374**
as cotton root rot resistant, 1007
culture, 374, 1004
diseases of
bacterial blight, 1013
bacterial wilt, *374*
fusarium wilt, 374, 1005
verticillium wilt, *374*
Mayflies, 888
Maytenus boaria
as armillaria resistant, 1016
Mayweed (*Anthemis cotula*), 827
See also Ragweed
herbicides for, 983, 984
MCPP
for curly dock, in lawns, 277
in ORTHO Chickweed & Clover Control, 980
in ORTHO Chickweed, Spurge & Oxalis Killer D, 981
in ORTHO Poison Ivy & Poison Oak Killer, 985
in ORTHO Weed-B-Gon for Southern Grasses, 986

M/MCPP — METHOXYCHLOR

in ORTHO Weed-B-Gon Jet Weeder, 986
in ORTHO Weed-B-Gon Lawn Weed Killer, 987
MDM. See Maize dwarf mosaic
Meadow garlic (*Allium canadense*), 821
Meadow rush (Bulrush), 821
Meadow spittlebug (*Philaenus spumarius*),
on strawberries, 762
Meadows. *See* Fields
Mealweed (*Chenopodium album*), 839
Mealworms (*Tenebrio* and *Alphitobius* species), 867
in households, *808*
Mealybugs, 876
Planococcus citri
on citrus, 623
on *Acer, 446*
on *Aglaonema, 184*
on *Anthurium, 184*
ants and, 893
on flowers, 316
on fruit and nut trees, 598
on *Aphelandra, 186*
on *Aralia, 186*
on *Araucaria*, 187
on *Asparagus, 188*
on avocado, indoors, *189*
bacterial gall and
on *Nerium*, 523
on bamboo, 453
on *Begonia*, indoors, *190*
on *Begonia*, outdoors, *331*
on *Brassaia, 191*
on *Bromeliads, 193*
on cactus, indoors, *194*
on cactus, outdoors, *461*
on *Camellia*, 463
on *Chrysanthemum*, indoors, *197*
on *Cissus, 198*
on citrus, *623*
on *Clivia, 200*
on *Codiaeum, 201*
on *Coleus*, indoors, *181*, *203*
on *Coleus*, outdoors, *181*, *344*
on *Columnea, 204*
cottony scales and
on bamboo, 453
on *Camellia*, 463
on ferns, 486
on fruit and nut trees, 598
on *Morus*, 520
on *Pittosporum*, 539
on *Populus*, 544
on woody ornamentals, 413
on *Dieffenbachia, 208*
diseases and, 879
on *Dizygotheca, 210*
on *Episcia, 212*
on *Euphorbia, 215*
on ferns, outdoors, *486*
on *Ficus, 219*
on *Fittonia, 220*
on flowers, ants and, 316
on fruit and nut trees, *598*
ants and, 598
honeydew and, 599
sooty mold and, 600
on *Gardenia*, outdoors
sooty mold and, 494
on *Gynura, 221*
on *Hedera*, indoors, *224*
honeydew from. *See* Honeydew
on houseplants, 979
insecticide for, 979
spraying, 921
hover flies as predators of, 892
on *Hoya, 226*
insecticide application to
spreader-stickers for, 922
insecticides for, 950, 955, 960, 961, 963, 964, 974, 978, 979,
on *Jasminum*
sooty mold and, 504
on *Kalanchoe, 227*
lacewings and, 892
on *Liriodendron*, 513
longtailed, *181*
on *Maranta, 228*
Mexican
insecticide for, 948
on *Monstera, 229*
on *Morus, 520*
on *Nerium*
bacterial gall and, 523
sooty mold and, 521
on Oleander, *876*
on orchids, *231*
on palms, indoors, *232*
on *Peperomia, 236*
on *Philodendron, 238*
on *Pilea*, 238
on *Pittosporum*, 539
on *Plectranthus, 239*
on *Populus, 544*
predators of, 892
hover fly larvae, 892
on *Pyracantha*
sooty mold and, 550
root, on houseplants, 180
on *Saintpaulia, 241*
sooty mold and
on fruit and nut trees, 600
on *Gardenia*, outdoors, 494
on *Jasminum*, 504
on *Liriodendron*, 513
on *Nerium*, 521
on *Pyracantha*, 550
on woody ornamentals, 414
on *Streptocarpus, 243*
on *Syngonium, 244*
on *Tolmiea*, 246
on *Tradescantia*, 247
on woody ornamentals, 413, 417
honeydew from, 413, 422
sooty mold and, 414
woolly aphids and, 598
on fruit and nut trees, 598
Mean's grass. *See* Johnsongrass
Measurements
metric conversion chart for, 1039
Mechanical injury
to flowers, wilting and, 314
leaf burn and, 857
leaf scorch and, 857
to woody ornamentals, 439
from fill, 1011
oozing sap and, 422
wilting and, 419
Mecoprop
for English lawn daisy, in lawns, 275
as generic name, 1040
for Japanese honeysuckle, 843
in ORTHO Poison Oak & Poison Ivy Killer, 985
in ORTHO Weed-B-Gon Jet Weeder, 986
Medflies. *See* Mediterranean fruit flies
Medic, black (*Medicago lupulina*), 831, 981, 984, 986, 987
herbicides for, 981, 984, 986, 987
in lawns, 273, 981
***Medicago lupulina*. *See* Black medic**
Mediterranean flour moth (*Anagasta kuehniella*), 808
Mediterranean fruit flies, *884*
larvae, *884*
plants infested by, 1018
***Megachile* species (Leafcutter bees)**
on *Rosa,* 569
***Megacyllene robiniae* (Locust borer)**
on *Robinia,* 564
***Megalopyge opercularis* (Puss caterpillar)**
as stinging insect, 803
***Melacosoma* species (Tent caterpillars)**
on *Malus*, 519
Melaleuca
brittle wood on, 1012
***Melanconis* species**
dieback from, on *Betula,* 455
Melanose
controlling, 968
***Melia azedarach* (Chinaberry)**
brittle wood on, 1012
***Melissopus latiferreanus* (Filbertworm),** 631
***Melittia satyrininformis*. *See* Squash vine borer**
***Meloidogyne incognita* (Southern root knot nematode)**
vegetables resistant to, 1026
Melons. *See* Cucurbits
Melonworms
insecticides for, 956, 963, 972, 973, 977
Melting out
controlling
See also Helminthosporium leaf spot, 962, 963, 965, 972, 973
***Mentha* (Mint)**
as wet soil tolerant, 1010
***Merodon equestris* (Narcissus bulb fly),** 377
as hover fly, 892
Mescal bean. *See Sophora*
***Mesembryanthemum* (Ice plant)**
as drought resistant, 1003
root rot on, *296*
scales on, *296*
for sunny areas, 1003
Mesospora hypericorum
on *Hypericum,* 295
Metaldehyde,
in ORTHO Bug-Geta Snail & Slug Pellets 947
for snails and slugs, on artichoke, 677
Metamorphosis
defined, 169
***Metaphalaria ilicis* (Yaupon psyllid),** 502
***Metasequoia glyptostroboides* (Dawn redwood)**
as armillaria resistant, 1016
as disease and insect resistant, 1012
Meteor cherry. *See* Cherry
Methidathion
for scales, on walnut, 655
Methiocarb
in ORTHO Slug-Geta Snail & Slug Bait, 974
Methoxychlor
for angoumois grain moths in households, 808
for aphids
on vegetables, 673
for aster leafhoppers
on vegetables, 672
for beets
flea beetles on, 686
for carpet beetles, 790
for caterpillars
on vegetables, 670
for clothes moths, 791
for curculios
on pear, 641
for elm bark beetles, 585
for flea beetles
on beets, 686
on radish, 757
on sweet potato, 770
on turnip, 783
for flour moths

Mottled willow borer (*Cryptorhynchus lapathi*), *575*
Mountain ash. *See Sorbus*
Mountain laurel. *See Kalmia*, 509
Mountain mahogany. *See Cercocarpus*
Mourning cloak butterfly (*Nymphalis antiopa*), 870
Mouseear chickweed. *See Cerastium vulgatum*
Mowing, *250*
guidelines, *250*
scalped spot, *258*
Mud daubers, 881
nest *803*
Mud swallows (*Petrochelidon pyrrhonota*), 801
Mugwort. *See Artemisia*
***Muhlenbergia schreberi* (Nimblewill), 817**
herbicides for, 983, 984
Mulberry. *See Morus*
Mulch, 926
cold damage and, 919
defined, 169
for erosion, 905
for frost protection, of asparagus, 679
materials for, 926
as potato tuberworm preventive, 751
in vegetable gardens, for weed control, 814
for *Vinca*, as scorch protection, 300
weeds in, herbicides for, 983
Mullein
common, herbicides for, 983
Multiplying onion. *See* Onion family
Mummy berry
on blueberries, *690*
Mums. *See Chrysanthemum*, indoors and outdoors
Mung beans. *See* Beans
***Mus musculus* (House mice), 793. *See also* Mice**
***Musca autumnalis* (Face flies)**
in households, 786
***Musca domestica. See* Houseflies**
Mushroom root rot, 851
See also Armillaria root rot
on *Acacia*, *444*
on fruit and nut trees, 602
on *Juniperus*, 506
on woody ornamentals, 415, 440, 851
Mushrooms, 415, 440, *842*
See also Fungi
on lawns, *279*
in fairy rings, 267
as weeds, 842
fungicides for, 279
on woody ornamentals, *415*
Musk plant. *See* Mallow
Muskmelon. *See* Cucurbits
Mustard, wild or field (*Brassica kaber*), 824
clubroot harbored by, 701
herbicides for, 980
tansy, herbicides for, 981
Mustard greens. *See* Cabbage family
Mycelium, defined, 169
Mycoplasmal diseases
aster yellows, 854
on *Callistephus*, 334
on carrots, 704
on celery, 707
on *Chrysanthemum*, outdoors, 341
on *Gladiolus*, 360
on lettuce, 736
on vegetables, 854
on weeds, 854
on woody ornamentals, 854
lethal yellowing, on palms, outdoors, 524
phloem necrosis, on *Ulmus*, 586
Mycosphaerella fragariae
on strawberries, 764
***Myosotis* (Forget-me-not)**
bees attracted by, 1007
culture, 375
powdery mildew on, 375
as powdery mildew susceptible, 1006
as wet soil tolerant, 1010
***Myrica* (Bayberry)**
M. pensylvanica (Bayberry), as armillaria resistant, 1016
as disease and insect resistant, 1012
as groundcover, 1003
Myrtle. *See Myrtus; Vinca*
***Myrtus* (Myrtle)**
bees attracted by, 1007
as phytophthora susceptible, 1013
***Myzocallis tiliae* (Linden aphid), 583**
***Myzus persicae* (Green peach aphid), 875**
on flowers, 875
on fruit and nut trees, 875
insecticide for, 976
on lettuce, 733
on peach; nectarine, 637
on potato, 875
leaf roll virus and, 756
on spinach, 875
on vegetables, 756
virus diseases and, 756
weeds harbor, 756
on woody ornamentals, 875

N

NAA (Napthalene acetic acid)
as litter preventive, 409
***Nalepella tsugifoliae* (Hemlock rust mite), 584**
***Nandina* (Heavenly bamboo; Sacred bamboo)**
as armillaria resistant, 1016
culture, 521
iron deficiency in, *521*
as shade tolerant, 1008
Nantucket pine tip moths, insecticides for, 961, 964
Nappa cabbage. *See* Cabbage family
Napthalene acetic acid (NAA), as litter preventive, 409
***Narcissus* (Daffodil; Jonquil; Narcissus)**
as cotton root rot resistant, 1007
culture, 375
diseases of
fusarium bulb rot, *377*
smoulder, *376*
southern blight, 1007
dividing, need for, 376
failure to bloom in, *376*
fertilizing, 375
insects on
narcissus bulb flies, 377
thrips, *375*
planting directions for, 375
narcissus bulb flies and, *377*
smoulder and, 376
planting locations for, 375
failure to bloom and, 376
planting time for, 375
as smog tolerant, 1008
soil pH for, 375
watering, 375
weak growth, *376*
Narcissus bulb fly (*Merodon equestris*), *377*
as hover fly, 892
Nasturtium. *See Tropaeolum*
Natal plum (*Carissa*)
culture, 465
root rot on, 465
as saline soil tolerant, 1011
Navy beans. *See* Beans
Neanthe bella palm, insecticide for, 979
Neck rot, on onion family, 740
Nectarine. *See* Peach, Nectarine
Needle blight
on *Araucaria*, *451*
on cypress family, 487
Needle cast, on *Pinus*, *532*
Needle point ivy, insecticide for, 979
Needle rust, on *Pinus*, *536*
Neglect, of fruit or nut trees, 603
Nemas. *See* Nematodes
Nematodes, *854*
pine wilt (*Bursaphelenchus xylophilus*), 533
southern root knot (*Meloidogyne incognita*)
vegetables resistant to, 1026
on sweet potato, 771
Nematodes
on *Asplenium*, 217
on broccoli, 697
on *Buxus*, *460*
on carrots, 702
on *Chrysanthemum*, outdoors, 339, *340*
on corn, 709
defined, 169
on flowers
slow or no growth and, 308
wilting and, 813
foliar, 854
Aphelenchoides fragariae, on *Asplenium*, 217
on fruit and nut trees, *602*
on *Gardenia*, outdoors, *494*
on lawns, *264*
leaf
Aphelenchoides olesistus, on *Begonia*, outdoors, 330
Aphelenchoides ritzema-bosi, on *Chrysanthemum*, outdoors, 339
on okra, *737*
on potato, 752
root, 854
on *Pinus*, 533
on woody ornamentals, 436
root rot fungi and, 854
on tomato, 779
varieties resistant to, 1026
on vegetables, 665
virus diseases and, 854
***Nemesia*, as verticillium wilt resistant, 1006**
***Nemophila* (Baby-blue-eyes), as verticillium wilt resistant, 1006**
***Neoceruraphis viburnicola* (Ash-gray snowball aphid), on *Viburnum*, 588**
***Neodiprion* species (Sawflies), on *Pinus*, 537**
***Neolecanium cornuparvum* (Magnolia scale), 516**
Nephthytis. *See Syngonium*
***Nerium* (Oleander), 521**
bees attracted by, 1007
culture, 523
diseases of
bacterial blight, 1013
bacterial gall, *523*

O

O/ORIENTAL FRUIT MOTH — ORTHO CITRUS INSECT SPRAY

for *Celastrus*
euonymus scale on, 468
for *Celtis*
psyllids on, 469
for *Codiaeum*
mealybugs on, 201
spider mites on, 201
for cottony scales
on *Camellia*, 463
on woody ornamentals, 413, 876
for *Crataegus*
aphids on, 477
for Cuban laurel thrips
on *Ficus*, 487
for cypress family
scales on, 481
for *Dieffenbachia*
mealybugs on, 208
for *Dizygotheca*
mealybugs on, 210
for elm leaf beetles, 586
for euonymus scales
on *Celastrus*, 468
on *Euonymus*, 483
for fall webworms
on fruit and nut trees, 599
on woody ornamentals, 411
for *Ficus*
Cuban laurel thrips on, 487
for fire ants, 806
for flower thrips, 885
on *Rosa*, 565
for flowers
sawflies on, 881
thrips on, 307, 885
for fruit and nut trees
fall webworms on, 599
tent caterpillars on, 599
for *Gardenia*, indoors
scales on, 221
for *Gardenia*, outdoors
greenhouse whiteflies on, 493
for giant bark aphids
on *Quercus*, 555
for *Gleditsia*
mimosa webworm on, 495
for grasses
flower thrips on, 885
for greenbugs
on lawns, 261
for greenhouse whiteflies, 877
on *Ageratum*, 322
on *Gardenia*, outdoors, 493
on *Lantana*, 370
for grubs
on woody ornamentals, 438
for gypsy moths
on woody ornamentals, 410, 869
for hackberry leaf gall psyllids, 469
for hawthorn lacebugs
on *Pyracantha*, 549
for *Hedera*, indoors
mealybugs on, 224
for honeylocust spider mites, 495
for honeysuckle aphids, 514
for *Ilex*
psyllids on, 502
scales on, 501
for irregular pine scales, 535
for *Juniperus*
bagworms on, 412, 508
for lacebugs, 874
hawthorn on *Pyracantha*, 549
on *Rhododendron*, 559
sycamore, on *Platanus*, 540
on woody ornamentals, 431
for *Lantana*
greenhouse whiteflies on, 370
for lawns
greenbugs on, 261
leafhoppers on, 260
for leaf beetles
elm, 586
on *Salix*, 573
for leaf-feeding caterpillars,
on *Salix*, 573
on woody ornamentals, 411
for leafhoppers
on lawns, 260
on woody ornamentals, 430
for leafminers, 885
birch, 454
oak, 552
on woody ornamentals, 418
for leafrollers, 873
on *Rosa*, 569
on woody ornamentals, 418
for leaftiers, 873
for *Lonicera*
aphids on, 514
for *Magnolia*
scales on, 516
for mealybugs
on *Brassaia*, 191
on *Camellia*, 463
on *Codiaeum*, 201
on *Dieffenbachia*, 208
on *Dizygotheca*, 210
on *Hedera*, indoors, 224
on *Philodendron*, 238
on *Pilea*, 238
on *Syngonium*, 244
on *Tradescantia*, 247
on woody ornamentals, 413
for midges
rose, 568
for mimosa webworms
on *Albizia*, 449
on *Gleditsia*, 495
for *Morus*
scales on, 520
for *Nerium*
black scales on, 522
for oak lacebugs, 553
for oak leafminers, 552
for oak webworms, 872
for *Philadelphus*
aphids on, 526
for *Philodendron*
mealybugs on, 238
for *Picea*
spruce needle miners on, 529
for *Pilea*
mealybugs on, 238
for *Pinus*
irregular pine scales on, 535
pine needle scales on, 535
pine tip or shoot moths on, 537
sawflies on, 537
for pit scales
on *Quercus*, 555
for *Pittosporum*
aphids on, 539
for *Platanus*
sycamore lacebugs on, 540
for *Podocarpus*
scales on, 542
for psyllids
hackberry leaf gall, 469
on *Ilex*, 502
on woody ornamentals, 878
yaupon, 502
for *Pyracantha*
aphids on, 550
hawthorn lacebugs on, 549
scales on, 549
for *Quercus*
giant bark aphids on, 555
oak lacebugs on, 553
oak leafminers on, 552
pit scales on, 555
webworms on, 872
for *Rhododendron*
lacebugs on, 559
root weevils on, 562
for root weevils
on *Rhododendron*, 562
on woody ornamentals, 438
on woody ornamentals, 866
for *Rosa*
caterpillars on, 570
flower thrips on, 565
leafrollers on, 569
rose aphids on, 569
rose midges on, 568
scales on, 571
for Russian aphids
on *Lonicera*, 514
for *Salix*
leaf beetles on, 573
leaf-feeding caterpillars on, 573
scales on, 574
for sawflies, 881
on *Pinus*, 537
for scales
armored, 877
on *Begonia*, indoors, 190
black, on *Nerium*, 522
on *Camellia*, 464
on cypress family, 481
euonymus, 483
on *Gardenia*, indoors, 221
on *Ilex*, 501
irregular pine, 535
magnolia, 516
on *Morus*, 520
pine needle, on *Pinus*, 535
on *Pinus*, 535
pit, on *Quercus*, 555
on *Podocarpus*, 542
on *Pyracantha*, 549
on *Rosa*, 571
on *Salix*, 574
soft, on woody ornamentals, 877
on *Syringa*, 580
on *Tsuga*, 584
on *Ulmus*, 587
wax, 876
on woody ornamentals, 412, 877
for shoot moths
on *Pinus*, 537
for soft scales
on woody ornamentals, 877
for spider mites
on *Codiaeum*, 201
for *Spiraea*
aphids on, 579
for spring cankerworms, 872
for sycamore lacebugs
on *Platanus*, 540
for *Syngonium*
mealybugs on, 244
for *Syringa*
scales on, 580
for *Taxus*
taxus weevils on, 582
for tent caterpillars
on fruit and nut trees, 599
on woody ornamentals, 411
for thrips
on flowers, 307, 885
on *Rosa*, 565
on woody ornamentals, 431
for tip moths
pine, 537
for *Tradescantia*
mealybugs on, 247
for *Tsuga*
scales on, 584
for *Tulipa*
aphids on, 397, 398

as alkaline soil tolerant, 1019
P. nigra cv. 'Italica' (Lombardy poplar)
as canker and dieback susceptible, 546
P. tremuloides (Quaking aspen)
as acid soil tolerant, 1019
gypsy moths feed on, 1014
birds damage, 1012
borer damage to, *545*
brittle wood on, 1012
culture, 543
dieback, *546*
diseases of
Botryosphaeria ribis, 1018
canker and dieback, 546
fungicide for, 956
powdery mildew, 1006
slime flux (Poplar), *421*
slime flux (wetwood), *543*
fertilizing, 543, 934
canker and dieback and, 546
as fill injury susceptible, 1011
insects on
aphids, 545
cottony scales and mealybugs, 544
gypsy moths, 1014
leaf beetles, damage to, *544*
leaf-feeding caterpillars, 543
mourning cloak or spiny elm caterpillars, 870
oystershell scale, *544*
poplar and willow borers, 545
poplar borers, *545*
poplar petiole gall aphids, 545
poplar scale, *544*
satin moth catepillars, *543*
scales, 544
leaf scorch, *857*
as lightning injury susceptible, 1012
planting locations for, 543
pruning, 543
sapsuckers damage, 1012
watering, 543
canker and dieback and, 546
Porthetria dispar (Gypsy moth), 869
See also Gypsy moth
food plant preferences of listed, 1014
Portulaca (Moss rose)
as cotton root rot resistant, 1007
as Japanese beetle resistant, 1009
as verticillium wilt resistant, 1006
wild (*P. oleracea*). *See* Purslane
Pot marigold. See Calendula
Potassium (K), 911
on fertilizer label, 911
role of, 911
for groundcovers, 285
Potassium deficiency, 860
in soybeans, *911*
in vegetables, 667
on walnut leaf, *860*
Potassium salts, for moss, liverwort, or algae control, 823
Potato, 751
bacterial ring rot, *752*
bacterial soft rot, *755*
Black leg, *755*
blister beetle, *753*
Colorado potato beetle, *753*
containers for, 753
culture, 750
green tubers and, 750
curing
bacterial soft rot and, 755
diseases of
aster yellows, 736, 1005
bacterial soft rot, 755
black leg, 755
common scab, 751
discolored tubers and, 752
early blight, *754*
fungicide for, 977
late blight, 755, 779
leaf roll, 752, 756
mosaic, discolored tubers and, 752
ring rot, 752
scab, 751, 1027
southern blight, 1007
verticillium wilt, 1025
viruses, 756, 752
fertilizing, 750, 941, 943
hollow heart and, 753
scab and, 751
flea beetle damage, *754*
frost damage to
discolored tubers, 752
green potato beetle, *750*
harvesting, 750
bacterial soft rot and, 755
early blight and, 754
late blight and, 755
hollow heart in, 753
insects on
aphids, 875
aphids, viruses and, 752, 756
blister beetles, 753
click beetles, 751
Colorado potato beetles, 753
European corn borers, 712
flea beetles, 754
green peach aphids, 875
green peach aphids, leaf roll virus and, 756
Jerusalem crickets, 883
millipedes, 674
nematodes, 752
potato bugs, 753
potato leafhoppers, 754
potato tuberworms, 751
wireworms, 704, 714, 751
internal discoloration, *752*
late blight, *755*
leaf problems on
black leg, 755
blister beetles, 753
Colorado potato beetles, 753
early blight, 754
flea beetles, 754
late blight, 755
leaf roll, 756
nematodes, 752
potato leafhoppers, 754
ring rot, 752
viruses, 756
leaf roll, *756*
leafhopper, *754*
manure for
scab and, 751
mulching
as potato tuberworm preventive, 751
planting dates for, 1025
planting directions for, 750
bacterial soft rot and, 755
black leg and, 755
potato tuberworms and, 751
ring rot and, 752
viruses and, 756, 752
planting locations for, 750
containers, 753
scab and, 751
verticillium wilt and, 725
as pollution tolerant, 1008
poor yield on
black leg, 755
potato leafhoppers, 754
root knot nematode damage, *752*
scab, *751*
scab-tolerant varieties of, 1027
snail and slug bait for, 947
soil pH for, 750
scab and, 751
storing, 750
green tubers and, 750
ring rot and, 752
tuber problems on, 750
bacterial soft rot, 755
black leg, 755
common scab, 751
early blight, 754
early frost, 752
excessive light, 750
excessive soil fertility or moisture, 753
hollow heart, 753
improper planting, 753
late blight, 755
leaf roll, 756
nematodes, 752
ring rot, 752
viruses, 752, 756
wireworms, 751
virus, *756*
watering, 754
black leg and, 755
discolored tubers and, 752
early blight and, 754
hollow heart and, 753
late blight and, 755
potato tuberworms and, 751
weeds near
viruses and, 756
wireworms, *751*
Potato beetle, Colorado (Leptinotarsa decemlineata)
on eggplant, 723
insecticides for, 955, 972, 973
on potato, 753
Potato bug (Stenopelmatus fuscus), 883
See Also potato beetle, Colorado
Potato leafhopper (Empoasca fabae)
on beans
hopperburn and, 684
insecticide for, 963
on potato, 754
Potato tuberworm (Phthorimaea operculella), 751
Potentilla (Cinquefoil), 298
P. fructicosa (Bush cinquefoil)
as alkaline soil tolerant, 1019
culture, 298
diseases of
leaf spot, *298*
powdery mildew, 1006
rust, *298*
as drought tolerant, 1009
as lawn weed
herbicides for, 986
for restricted root space, 1009
as verticillium wilt resistant, 1006
Pothos. See Scindapsus
Potted plants. See Containers, plants in; Houseplants
Potter wasps, 803
Potting soils, 920
Poultry
insecticide for, 972
Powderpost beetles
emergence holes, *798*
in firewood, 801
in households, *798*
Powdery mildew, 848
on *Achillea*, *320*
on apple, *609*
varieties susceptible or resistant to, 1021
on *Aquilegia*, *327*
on *Aster*, *328*

on beans, 683
on *Begonia*, indoors, *189*
on *Begonia*, outdoors, *330*
on brambles, *695*
varieties resistant to, 1023
on *Calendula*, *332*
on cherry, 620
on Chrysanthemum, *338*
on *Cineraria*, *343*
controlling, 951, 954, 956, 965, 967, 968, 970, 974, 977
on *Cosmos*, *346*
on cucurbits, *669*
cucumber, *669*
pumpkin, *720*
varieties resistant to, 1028, 1033
on currants; gooseberries, *721*
on *Dahlia*, *350*
on *Delphinium*, *351*
on *Euonymus*, *286*, 483
on flowers, *311*
fungi causing, 1006
on grapes, *730*
varieties resistant to, 1024
on groundcovers, 286
on *Helianthus*, *362*
on *Hydrangea*, *499*
on *Iberis*, *355*
on *Kalanchoe*, *226*
on *Lagerstroemia*, *510*
on *Lathyrus*, 370
on lawns, *266*
on *Lonicera*, *514*
on *Myosotis*, 375
on peas, *743*
on *Phlox*, *385*
plants susceptible to, 1006
on *Platanus*, *540*
on *Quercus*, *553*
on *Rosa*, *567*
varieties tolerant of, 1005
on *Saintpaulia*, *241*
on strawberries
variety resistant to, 1024
on sunflower, 768
on *Syringa*, *579*
on *Tolmiea*, *246*
on trees, *413*
on vegetables, 669
on *Verbena*, *398*
on *Viburnum*, *588*
on woody ornamentals, 413
on *Zinnia*, *402*
Prayer plant. *See Maranta*
Praying mantids, *892*
as Orthoptera, 883
Predaceous bugs, 874
of European winter moths, 871
painful bites by, 874
Predaceous ground beetles, 867
Predaceous insects
antlions, 888
fire ants, 806
fireflies or lightning buts, 868
ground beetles, 867
hover flies as, 892
Hymenoptera as, 880
Jerusalem crickets as, 883
soldier beetles, 867
Prickly glass wort. *See* Russian thistle
Prickly lettuce (*Lactuca serriola*), ***832***
herbicide for, 983
Primrose. *See Primula*
Primrose
evening (*Oenothera*)
herbicides for, 983, 984, 986
***Primula* (Primrose),** 386
P. japonica (Japanese primrose)
as wet soil tolerant, 1010
in containers
watering, 386
as cotton root rot resistant, 1007
culture, 386, 1004
damage from overwatering, *309*
diseases of
leaf spots from, 386
root and stem rot, 386
fertilizing, 386, 940
flowering times for, 1004
germination of, 1004
iron deficiency in, *387*
leaf and stem rot, *386*
leaf spot, *386*
minor nutrient deficiency in, 387
planting locations for, 386
planting times for, 386, 1004
slug damage, *387*
snails and slugs on, 387
soil pH for, 386
minor nutrient deficiency and, 387
as verticillium wilt resistant, 1006
watering, 386
leaf spot and, 386
Prince's feather. *See Amaranthus*
Privet. *See Ligustrum*
Privet mite (*Brevipalpus obovatus*), *511*
Privet rust mite (*Aculus ligustri*), *511*
***Prociphilus* species**
on *Fraxinus*, 489
***Procyon lotor. See* Raccoons**
Propagating plants, 921
easily-rooted cuttings, 1001
Propagation defined, 170
Propoxur
as generic name, 1040
for household pests
clover mites, 792
grain weevils, 809
granary weevils, 809
rice weevils, 809
scorpions, 806
in ORTHO Ant, Roach & Spider Killer, 946
in ORTHO Earwig, Roach & Sowbug Bait, 952
in ORTHO Hornet & Wasp Killer, 959
in ORTHO Mole Cricket Bait, 964
in ORTHO Pest-B-Gon Roach Bait, 968
Prostrate knotweed (*Polygonum aviculare*), 827, *827*
See also Knotweed
herbicide for, 983
in lawns, *272*
Prostrate pigweed
herbicide for, 983
Protectant, defined, 170
Pruning
Abies, 442
after transplanting, 924
almond, 604
apple, 605
black rot and, 608
apricot, 610
avocado trees, 614
Betula, 454
book about, 995
Camellia, 461
cherry, 616
citrus, 620
cold damage and, 858
Coleus, indoors, 202
Cornus, 471
Crataegus, 475
Dieffenbachia, 208
dressings for
ORTHO Pruning Seal, 969
ORTHO Pruning Sealer, 969
Euphorbia, 212
fig, 628
filbert, 630
flowers
perennial, 995
Fraxinus, 488
fruit and nut trees
cankers and, 596
limb breakage and, 595
after neglect, 603
small fruit and, 593
sunscald and, 597
Fuchsia, 490
Gleditsia, 494
Hedera, indoors, 222
hickory, 631
Hydrangea, 498
Ilex, 500
Ixora
cold damage and, 502
Juniperus, 504
Ligustrum, 511
Magnolia, 514
mango, 632
peach; nectarine, 633
flowering, 546
pear, 639
flowering, 550
pecan, 644
persimmon, 647
Picea, 527
Pinus, 531
Platanus, 540
plum, 648
Populus, 543
Prunus, 546
evergreen, 547
Pyracantha, 548
Pyrus, 550
Quercus, 551
quince, 652
Rhododendron, 558
Rosa, 565, 566
Salix, 573
shrubs, 995
Syringa, 579
Ulmus, 584
vines, 995
walnut, 653
Wisteria, 588
woody ornamentals, 995
borers and, 419
broken branches on, 916
failure to bloom and, 408
oozing sap and, 422
sunscald and, 425, 859
transplant shock and, 421
wounds and, 419
Pruning Seal. *See* ORTHO Pruning Seal
Pruning Sealer. *See* ORTHO Pruning Sealer
***Prunus* (Flowering almond; Flowering cherry; Flowering peach; Flowering plum)**
P. armeniaca. See Apricot
P. avium. See Cherry
P. domestica. See Plum
P. dulcis. See Almond
P. ersica. See Peach; Nectarine
P. salicina. See Plum
citrus whiteflies on, *546*
culture, 546, 547
diseases of, 1016
fireblight, 1016
powdery mildew, 1006
fertilizing, 546
flowering time for, 546
as frost crack susceptible, 426
insects on, 547
citrus whiteflies, 546
as lawn tree, 1009
as low-growing street tree, 1012
planting locations for, 546
watering, 546
***Prunus* (evergreen forms)**
P. caroliniana (Cherry laurel)
as armillaria resistant, 1016
P. ilicifolia (Hollyleaf cherry)
as armillaria resistant, 1016
P. lyonii (Catalina cherry)
as armillaria resistant, 1016
citrus whiteflies on, 546
culture, 547
diseases of
armillaria root rot, 1016
powdery mildew, 1006
leaf spot, *547*
fertilizing, 546, 547, 934, 936
flowering times for, 547
planting locations for, 547
leaf spot and, 547
***Pseudaletia unipuncta* (Armyworms)**

R

R/RANUNCULUS — RHODODENDRON

bird damage to, *388*
in containers
watering, 387
culture, 387, 1004
diseases of
powdery mildew, 1006
ranunculus mosaic, *388*
root rot, 388
fertilizing, 387
flowering times for, 1004
planting directions for, 387
bird damage and, 388
planting locations for, 387
root rot and, 388
wet soil, 1010
planting times for, 387, 1004
root rot, *388*
soil pH for, 387
as verticillium wilt resistant, 1006
watering, 387
root rot and, 388
Ranunculus mosaic, *388*
***Raphanus sativus.* *See* Radish**
***Raphiolepis* (India hawthorn)**
R. umbellata (Yedda hawthorn)
as armillaria resistant, 1016
bees attracted by, 1007
as powdery mildew susceptible, 1006
Ra-Pid-Gro Bloom Builder, 944
Ra-Pid-Gro Evergreen & Azalea Food, 944
Ra-Pid-Gro Fruit & Citrus Tree Food, 945
Ra-Pid-Gro House Plant Food, 945
Ra-Pid-Gro Plant Food, 946
Raspberries. ***See*** **Brambles**
Raspberry cane borer (*Oberea maculata*), 693
Raspberry crown borer (*Pennitsetia marginata*)
on brambles, *693*
Raspberry fruitworm (*Byturus* species)
on brambles, *692*
insecticides for, 955, 977
Raspberry root borer (*Pennitsetia marginata*)
on brambles, 693
Raspberry sawflies
insecticide for, 955
Rats, *794*
See also Rodents
on avocado, 615
Rattlesnakeweed. ***See*** **Florida betony**
Rattus* species.** ***See **Rats**
Rayless chamomile (*Matricaria matricarioides*), 827
Red berry trouble
controlling, 967
Red bugs. ***See*** **Chiggers**
Red cedar. ***See Juniperus virginiana***
Red dead nettle
herbicides for, 983
Red flour beetles, 808
Red mite, southern. ***See*** **Southern red mite**
Red root. ***See Amaranthus***
Red shanks (*Polygonum persicaria*), 833
Red sorrel (*Rumex acetosella*), 835, *835*
in lawns, 277
herbicides for, 981, 987
Red spider mites
insecticides for, 948, 954, 958, 963
on tomato
insecticide for, 954
Red stele
on strawberries, 766
varieties resistant to, 1024
Red thread
on lawns, 255
controlling, 962
varieties resistant to, 1003
Red-breasted sapsucker (*Sphyrapicus varius ruber*), 899
Red-necked cane borer (*Agrilus ruficollis*), 693
Redbanded leafroller (*Argyrotaenia velutinana*)
on blueberries, *691*
on grapes, *727*
Redbud. ***See Cercis***
Redheaded pine sawflies
insecticide for, 961
Redhumped caterpillar (*Schizura concinna*), 870
Redroot pigweed
herbicide for, 983
Redstem filaree (*Erodium cicutarium*), *825*
Redweed (*Rumex acetosella*), 835
Redwood. ***See Sequoia***
dawn. *See Metasequoia glyptostroboides*
Removing trees or shrubs, 918
Repellents
for night-flying insects, 788
Resistant plant, defined, 170
Resmethrin
for clover mites
in households, 792
as generic name, 1040
for greenhouse whiteflies
on *Cineraria*, outdoors, 343
on *Fuchsia*, 491
on *Hibiscus*, 497
in ORTHO Flea-B-Gon Flea Killer, 953
in ORTHO Flying & Crawling Insect Killer, 954
in ORTHO Fogging Insecticide, 955
in ORTHO Home & Garden Insect Killer, 957
in ORTHO House Plant Insect Killer, 960
in ORTHO Household Insect Killer, 959
in ORTHO Systemic Rose & Floral Spray, 974
in ORTHO Whitefly & Mealybug Killer, 979
***Rhagoletis* species**
R. mendax. (Blueberry maggot), 689
insecticide for, 955
cherry fruit flies, 616
insecticide for, 955
walnut husk fly, 654
***Rhamnus* (Buckthorn)**
as disease and insect resistant, 1012
***Rheum rhabarbarum.* *See* Rhubarb**
Rhizoctonia fruit rot
controlling, 977
***Rhizoctonia* species,** 850
R. solani
on *Ageratum*, 321
on *Aglaonema*, 183
on *Anthurium*, 183
on beans, 685
on *Dianthus*, 354
on *Gazania*, 292
on *Hedera*, outdoors, 294
on lawns, 254
on lettuce, 735
on *Peperomia*, 235
on *Syngonium*, 244
on *Coleus*, indoors, 202
on lawns, 254
newly seeded, 257
on *Lilium*, 372
on *Philodendron*, 237
on *Primula*, 386
on *Tulipa*, 397
Rhizoctonia stem rot
on *Dianthus*, *354*
Rhizome, defined, 170
Rhizopus nigricans
on brambles, 692
***Rhododendron* (Azalea; Rhododendron),** 558
R. arborescens (Smooth azalea)
as wet soil tolerant, 1010
R. molle (Chinese azalea)
as smog tolerant, 1008
R. mucronatum (Evergreen snow azalea)
azalea whiteflies on, 564
R. obtusum (Hiryu azalea)
as phytophthora resistant, 1013
R. vaseyi (Pink-shell azalea)
as wet soil tolerant, 1010
branches dying on
dieback, 562
rhododendron borers, 560
scales, 563
wilt and root rot, 562
culture, 558
diseases of
Botryosphaeria ribis, 1018
azalea petal blight, *558*
dieback, *562*
fungal leaf spot, 560
leaf gall, *559*
phytophthora root rot, 562, *849*, 1013
powdery mildew, 1006
pythium root rot, 562
rust, *669*
wilt and root rot, 419, 562
dying
dieback, 562
root weevil adults, 563
root weevil larvae, 562
scales, 563
wilt and root rot, 562
fertilizing, 558, 932, 935, 936, 940, 943
iron deficiency and, 558, 560, 932, 935, 937
salt burn and, 561
flower problems on
azalea petal blight, 558
leaf gall, 559
rhododendron aphids, 563
insects on
ants, rhododendron aphids and, 563
azalea whiteflies, 564
cyclamen mites, 240
insecticides for, 957, 962
lacebugs, *559*
rhododendron aphids, *563*
rhododendron borers, *560*
rhododendron whiteflies, *564*
root weevil adults, *563*
root weevil larvae, *562*
scales, *563*
spider mites, 558
iron deficiency in, *433*, *560*, 937
as Japanese beetle resistant, *433*, 1009
leaf problems on, 558
dieback, 562
fungal leaf spot, 560
iron deficiency, 560
lacebugs, 559
leaf gall, 559
rhododendron aphids, 563
rhododendron borers, 560
rhododendron whiteflies, 564
root weevil adults, 563
root weevil larvae, 562
rust, 669
salt burn, 561
scales, 563
spider mites, 558
sunburn, 561
wilt and root rot, 562
windburn or winter injury, 561
pinching, 937
planting locations for, 558
fungal leaf spot and, 560
lacebugs and, 559
leaf gall and, 559
shady areas, 1008
sunburn and, 561
wet soil, 1010
windburn and, 561
winter injury and, 561
pruning, 558
salt burn on, *561*
as shade tolerant, 1008

types of, pruning methods and, 566
watering, 565
black spot and, 566
weeds near
herbicides for, 975, 980
Rose. ***See Rosa***
Christmas. *See Helleborus*
Japanese *See Kerria*
moss. *See Portulaca*
rosin. *See Hypericum*
sun *See Helianthemum*
Rose & Floral Dust. *See* ORTHO Rose & Floral Dust
Rose & Flower Insect Killer. *See* ORTHO Rose & Flower Insect Killer
Rose aphid (*Macrosiphum rosae*), ***569***
Rose chafers
insecticides for, 958, 970
Rose curculio, ***866***
Rose Food. *See* ORTHO Rose Food
Rose leafhopper (*Edwardsiana rosae*), ***568***
insecticides for, 963, 970
Rose mallow. *See Hibiscus*
Rose midge (*Dasineura rhodophaga*), ***568***
insecticides for, 960, 964, 974
Rose-of-Sharon. *See Hibiscus*
Rosea iceplant. *See Drosanthemum*
Rosemary. *See* Herbs; *Rosmarinus*
Roseslugs, 570
insecticides for, 956, 963, 970, 973
on Rosa, *570*
Rosin rose. *See Hypericum*
Rosmarinus **(Rosemary)**
R. lockwoodii
as saline soil tolerant, 1011
R. officinalis'Prostratus' (Dwarf rosemary)
as drought resistant groundcover, 1003
for sunny areas, 1003
bees attracted by, 1007
as drought tolerant, 1003, 1009
planting locations for restricted root space, 1009
sunny areas, 1003
spittlebugs on, *879*
Rotenone
for brambles
raspberry cane borers on, 693
red-necked cane borers on, 693
as generic name, 1040
for household pests
boxelder bugs, 791
cigarette beetles, 809
drugstore beetles, 809
in ORTHO Rotenone Dust or Spray, 971
in ORTHO Tomato & Vegetable Insect Spray, 976
in ORTHO Tomato Vegetable Dust, 977
for raspberry cane borers, 693, 693
for red-necked cane borers, on brambles, 693
for vegetables
cucumber beetles on, 671
flea beetles on, 671
Rotenone Dust or Spray. *See* ORTHO Rotenone Dust or Spray
Round worms. *See* Nematodes
Roundheaded borers, 799
See also Borers
in firewood, 801
insecticide for, 962
Rubber plant. *See Ficus*, indoors
Rubber tree, hardy. *See Eucomia ulmoides*
as disease and insect resistant, 1012
Rubus **species. *See* Brambles; Wild blackberry**
Rudbeckia **(Black-eyed Susan; Coneflower; Gloriosa daisy)**
culture, 389, 1004
diseases of
aster yellows, 854
powdery mildew, 1006
southern blight, 1007
as weed
aster yellows and, 854
verticillium wilt, *389*
Rugby grass
as fusarium blight resistant, 1002
as helminthosporium leaf spot resistant, 1003
as mildew resistant, 266
as rust resistant, 1003
Rumex **species**
R. acetosella (Red sorrel), 835
herbicides for, 981, 987
in lawns, 277
R. crispus (Curly dock), 833
herbicides for, 981, 983, 987
in lawns, 277
rhubarb curculios and, 759
Runners, defined, 170
Rush nut. *See* Nutsedge
Russet mites
tomato (*Aculops lycopersici*), 777
insecticide for, 954
Russian aphids (*Hyadaphis tataricae*)
on *Lonicera*, *514*
Russian cactus. *See* Russian thistle
Russian olive. *See Elaeagnus*
Russian thistle (*Salsola kali* var. *tenuifolia*), ***824***
beet leafhoppers harbored by, 824
herbicide for, 975
Rust, 848
Puccinia species
on lawns, 266
on *Alcea*, *322*
on Antirrhinum, *325*
on apple, 609, 1015, 1021
on asparagus, 680
on beans, *683*
varieties resistant to, 1027
on bluegrass
controlling, 962
varieties resistant to, 1003
on brambles, 695
on *Callistephus*, *333*, 333
cedar-apple, 609, 848
on apple, 609, 1015, 1021
on *Juniperus*, 508, 1015
on *Malus*, 518
plants susceptible to, 1015
on *Chaenomeles*, *470*
on *Chrysanthemum*, *338*
cultivars resistant to, 1004
controlling, 951, 956, 965, 965, 968, 974, 977
on currants; gooseberries, 721
on *Duchesnea*, *291*
eastern gall
on *Pinus*, 538
on fig, *629*
on flowers, 311
on geranium, *311*, *848*
hawthorn, *311*
on *Crataegus*, 476
on Hypericum, *295*
on incense cedar, 470
on *Iris*, *369*
on *Juniperus*, 508
Chaenomeles and, 470
varieties susceptible to, 1015
on lawns, 266
controlling, 962
varieties resistant to, 1003
leaf
on woody ornamentals, 430
leaf and stem
on woody ornamentals, 413
on *Mahonia*, *516*
on mallow, 322
needle
on *Pinus*, 536
orange
on brambles, 695
on *Pelargonium*, outdoors, *380*
on *Pinus*, 534, 536, 538
on *Potentilla*, *298*
quince, 470
plants susceptible to, 1015
on *Rhododendron*, *669*
on *Rosa*, *567*
varieties tolerant of, 1005
on ryegrass, 266
on *Sorbus*, *577*
on spinach, 761
stem
on bluegrass, controlling, 962
on sunflower, 768
western gall
on *Pinus*, 538
white pine blister
on currants; gooseberries, 721
on *Pinus*, 534
white
on spinach, 761
on woody ornamentals, 413, 415
Rust fly
carrot (*Psila rosae*), 703
insecticide for, 951
Rust mites
hemlock (*Nalepella tsugifoliae*), 584
insecticide for, 967
pear
on fruit and nut trees, 601
plum
on fruit and nut trees, 601
Rutabaga
See also Turnip
as clubroot resistant, 701.
Ryegrass
diseases of
brown patch, varieties resistant to, 254
red thread, 255
rust, 266
as fusarium blight resistant, 254
herbicide for, 984
mowing heights for, 250
planting times for, 257

S

Sabal palmetto. *See* Palms, outdoors
Sabulodes caberata **(Omnivorous looper)**
on avocado, 614
Sacred bamboo. *See Nandina*
Saddleback caterpillar (*Sibine stimulea*)
as stinging insect, 803
Saddled prominent caterpillars
insecticide for, 961
Sage. *See* Herbs; *Salvia*
Sago palm. *See Cycas*
Saintpaulia **(African violet)**
See also African violet family
culture, 239
diseases of
powdery mildew, *241*
root and crown rot, *240*
failure to bloom in insufficient light, *239*

plants susceptible to, 1007
on *Sedum*, 390
on *Ajuga*, 288
on *Daphne*, 481
root rot of carrot, *851*
on *Tulipa*, 397
***Sclerotium*, defined**, 170
***Scolytus* species**
S. quadrispinosus (Hickory bark beetle), 632
S. rugulosus (Shothole borer)
on cherry, 618
Scorch
See also Heat damage; Sunburn; Sunscald
on *Ajuga*, *288*
on ferns, 487
on groundcovers, 286
on *Hedera*, outdoors, *293*
on *Pachysandra*, *296*
summer leaf
on *Aesculus*, 449
on *Catalpa*, 467
on *Cornus*, 472
on *Euonymus*, 484
on *Magnolia*, 515
on *Pachysandra*, 296
on *Platanus*, 541
on *Quercus*, 551
on *Tsuga*, *583*
on *Vinca*, *300*
winter
on groundcovers, 286
on *Pachysandra*, 296
Scorpions (*Centruroides* species)
as Arachnida, 887
in households, *806*
insecticide for, 950
Scram Dog & Cat Repellent. *See* ORTHO Scram Dog & Cat Repellent
Scurf
on sweet potatoes, 770
Scutchgrass. *See* Bermudagrass
***Scutigera coleoptrata* (House centipedes)**, 790
***Scutigerella immaculata*. *See* Garden symphylans**
Seasonal leaf drop
on trees, 433
Sedge. *See Cyperus*
***Sedum* (Stonecrop)**
culture, 390, 1004
as drought resistant, 1003
flowering times for, 1004
snails and slugs on, *390*
stem and root rot on, *390*
for sunny areas, 1003
Seed rot
controlling, 965
Seedcorn maggot (*Hylemya platura*)
on beans, *686*
on corn, *713*
Seedlings, *251*
cold damage to, 858, 919
feeding, 925
hardening off, 858, 919, 925
phosphorus deficiency in, 858, 859, 919
thinning, 925
transplanting, 925
vegetable. *See* Vegetables, seedling problems in
Seeds
starting indoors, 925
starting outdoors, 925
***Senecio* species**
S. jacobaea (Tansy ragwort), 837
S. vulgaris. *See* Groundsel
Sensitive mimosa
as lawn weed
herbicide for, 986
Septoria leaf spot
controlling, 965, 968, 977
on lawns, *265*, 780
on tomato
sunscald and, 773
***Septoria* species**
S. apiicola
on celery, 706
S. lycopersici
on tomato, 780
Sequoia
S. sempervirens (Coast redwood)
as armillaria resistant, 1016
brittle wood on, 1012
as phytophthora susceptible, 1013
as verticillium wilt resistant, 1006
Serviceberry. *See Amelanchier*
***Setaria* species (Foxtails)**, 819
herbicides for, 975, 980, 983, 983
Seventeen-year locust. *See* Periodical cicada
Sevin. *See* Carbaryl
Sevin 10 Dust. *See* ORTHO Sevin 10 Dust
Sevin 5 Dust. *See* ORTHO Sevin 5 Dust
Sevin Garden Dust. *See* ORTHO Sevin Garden Dust
Sevin Garden Spray. *See* ORTHO Sevin Garden Spray
Sewage sludge
as nitrogen source, 910
Sewer lines
tree roots plugging, 428
Shadblow. *See* Serviceberry
Shadbush. *See* Serviceberry
***Shade Gardening* (ORTHO)**, 998
Shade
lawn damaged by, *263*
Shade trees
on lawns
thin grass under, 263
varieties forlisted, 1009
Shady areas
groundcovers for, 1003, 263, 276
landscaping for, 998
trees and shrubs for, 1008
weeds in mosses, liverworts, or algae, 823
Shallots. *See* Onion family
Shallow soil, *905*
Shasta daisy. *See Chrysanthemum*
She-oak. *See Casuarina*
Sheep sorrel. *See* Red sorrel
Shellygrass. *See* Quackgrass
Shepherds purse (*Capsella bursa-pastoris*), *837*
clubroot harbored by, 701
herbicides for, 980, 981, 983, 984, 986, 987
Shepherds-bag. *See* Shepherds purse
Shoestring fungus. *See also* Armillaria root rot; Mushroom root rot; Oak root fungus; Shoestring root rot
on fruit and nut trees, 602
on grapes, 730
on *Juniperus*, 506
on *Quercus*, 557
on strawberries, 767
on woody ornamentals, 415, 440, 851
Shoot moths (*Rhyacionia* species)
on *Pinus*, *537*
Short stems
on *Hyacinthus*, *365*
on *Tulipa*, *395*
Shothole borer (*Scolytus rugulosus*)
on cherry, *618*
Shothole fungus
on almond, *604*
on apricot, *612*
on peach; nectarine, *634*
Shrub alcea. *See Hibiscus*
Shrubs. *See* Woody ornamentals; *specific shrubs*
***Sibine stimulea* (Saddleback caterpillar)**
as stinging insect,c 803
Sidewalks and driveways
pests on
woollybear caterpillars, 872
weeds in
See also Walkways
black medic, 831
crabgrass, 817
goosegrass, 818
herbicides for, 815, 983, 984, 985
mosses, liverworts, or algae, 823
prostrate knotweed, 827
purslane, 829
spotted spurge, 829
Siduron
as generic name, 1040
Silk oak. *See Grevillea*
Silk tree. *See Albizia*
Silkweed. *See* Milkweed
Silver crabgrass. *See* Goosegrass
Silver tree
insecticide for, 979
Silverberry. *See Elaeagnus*
Silverfish (*Lepisma* species), 887
in households, *789*
insecticides for, 946, 957
***Silybum marianum* (Milk thistle)**
near globe artichoke curly dwarf and, 677
Simazine
as generic name, 1040
for morning glory, 840
for Spanishneedles, 825
for wild oats, 820
Simson. *See* Groundsel
***Sinningia* (Gloxinia)**, 241
See also African violet family
culture, 242
failure to bloom
insufficient light, *241*
insects on
cyclamen mites, 240
insecticide for, 948
insufficient light for, 241
sunburn on, 241
water spots on, *242*
watering, 242
***Sisyrinchium californicum* (Golden-eyed grass)**
as wet soil tolerant, 1010
***Sitophilus* species (Grain weevil)**
in households, 809
Six-spotted leafhoppers (*Macrosteles fascifrons*)
on *Coreopsis*, 346
on flowers, 316
insecticide for, 972
on lettuce, 734
on vegetables, 672
Skeletonizers
grape leaf (*Harrisina* species)
on grapes, 727
palm leaf (*Homaledra sabalella*), on palms, outdoors, 525, 1012,
Skippers
fiery
insecticide for, 961
Skunks, *794*, *901*
Slender chess (*Bromus tectorum*), 820
Slime flux
on *Morus*, *519*
on *Populus*, *421*
on *Salix*, *576*
on *Ulmus*, *587*
on woody ornamentals, 421
Slime molds
on lawns, *266*
Slow-release fertilizers, defined, 170
Slug-Geta Snail & Slug Bait. *See* ORTHO Slug-Geta Snail & Slug Bait
Slugs. *See* Pearslugs; Roseslugs; Snails and slugs
Slugs
ground beetles feed on, 867
on Primula, *387*
snails and, 891
Smartweed, spotted. *See* Ladysthumb

U

V

grasshoppers, *663*
incorrect planting depth, *662*
millipedes, *674*
nocturnal pests, *670*
overwatering, *662*
rabbits, *663*
slow germination, *662*
snails and slugs, *663*
soil temperature and, *662*
weevils, *670*
wilting and dying, *671*, *662*
seedlings
thinning, 925
seeds
eaten, by millipedes, *674*
fail to sprout, *662*
germination of, 1025
starting outdoors, 925
watering, *662*, 925
shade tolerant, *661*
skunks in, 901
smog damage to, 688
smog-tolerant, 1008
snails and slugs on, *663*, *670*
bait for, *663*, 947
soil pests near
earwigs, *670*
garden symphylans, *674*
millipedes, 674
moles, *674*
nematodes, *665*
pocket gophers, 675
sowbugs and pillbugs, *673*
soil problems in, *661*, *666*
iron deficiency, *666*
minor nutrient deficiencies, *666*
nitrogen deficiency, *666*
nitrogen excess, *663*
pests. *See* soil pests near
pH and, *661*, *666*
phosphorus deficiency, *661*, 933
potassium deficiency, *667*
salt damage, *667*
sowbugs and pillbugs on, *673*
spray damage to, *668*
stem problems on
cucumber beetles, *671*
cutworms, 664
hail damage, *669*
nocturnal pests, *670*
storing
botrytis blight and, 849
stunted growth in
aphids, 673
cool weather, *661*
cucumber beetles, *671*
dehydration, 664
excess water, *661*
garden symphylans, *674*
incorrect soil pH, *661*
insufficient light, *661*
nematodes, *665*
nitrogen deficiency, *666*
phosphorus deficiency, *661*
poor soil, 660, *661*
root rot, *666*
salt damage, *667*
soil moisture and, *661*, 664
weeds and, 814
thinning, 925
transplanting
cutworms and, 664
watering, 912, 917
dehydration and, 664
nitrogen deficiency and, *666*
poor quality and, 660
root and stem rot and, *665*
root rot and, *661*, *666*
salt damage and, *667*
seed germination and, *662*
seedlings, *662*
stunted growth and, *661*, 664
timing for, 917
types of, 912
weeds and, 814
weeds near
annual bluegrass, 815
aster yellows and, 854
bitter nightshade, 841
black nightshade, 841
chickweed, mouseear, 829
chickweed, common, 828
crabgrass, 817
field bindweed, 840
goosegrass, 818
hairy nightshade, 841
herbicides for, 814, 983
lamb's-quarters, 839
leafhoppers and, *672*
milkweed, 838
nimblewill, 817
pigweeds, 838
prostrate knotweed, 827
purslane, 829
stinging nettles, 839
yarrow, 826
wildlife eating. *See* animal pests in
wilting
dehydration, 664
flea beetles, 671
moles, *674*
nematodes, 665
pocket gophers, 675
root and stem rot, 665
root rot, 666
wilt diseases, *665*
woodchucks in, *675*, 901
Vein clearing, defined, 170
Velvet leaf
in lawns
herbicides for, 981
Velvet plant. ***See Gynura***
Velvetbean caterpillars
insecticide for, 972
Velvetgrass
German (*Holcus mollis*), *816*
Velvetweed
herbicide for, 983
***Venturia* species**
V. inaequalis
on apple, 608
on *Malus*, 518
V. pyrina
on pear, 639
Verbena
V. peruviana (Peruvian verbena)
as drought-resistant groundcover, 1003
culture, 398
diseases of
bacterial wilt, *399*
gray mold, *398*
powdery mildew, *398*, 1006
insects on
greenhouse whiteflies, *399*
two-spotted spider mites, *399*
planting locations for, *399*
as verticillium wilt resistant, 1006
watering
gray mold and, *398*
Vermiculite
for growing transplants, 925
Vernalization, defined, 170
***Veronica filiformis* (Speedwell),** 828
in lawns, 276
herbicides for, 981, 987
***Verticillium* species,** 850
V. albo-atrum
on brambles, 693
on *Callistephus*, 333
on eggplant, 725
on *Helianthus*, 362
on *Rhus*, 564
on tomato, 779
V. dahliae, 349
on *Capsicum*, 336
on *Cinnamomum*, 470
on *Dahlia*, 349
on strawberries, 765
on *Acer*, 448
on *Ailanthus*, 449
on *Catalpa*, 467
on *Cercis*, 469
on *Chrysanthemum*, outdoors, 340
on *Cotinus*, 473
on *Elaeagnus*, 482
on *Lathyrus*, 371
on *Matthiola*, 374
on *Papaver*, 379
on *Pistacia*, 539
on *Rosa*, 572
on *Rudbeckia*, 389
on *Salvia*, 389
Verticillium wilt, 850
See also Wilt
on *Acer*, *448*
on *Ailanthus*, *449*
on brambles, 693
varieties resistant to, 1023
on *Capsicum*, *336*
on *Catalpa*, *467*
on *Cercis*, *469*
on *Chrysanthemum*, outdoors, *340*
on *Cinnamomum*, *470*
on *Cotinus*, *473*
on eggplant, *725*
on *Elaeagnus*, *482*
on *Helianthus*, *362*
on *Matthiola*, *374*
on *Papaver*, *379*
on *Pistacia*, *539*
plants resistant to, 1006
on Raspberry, *693*
on *Rosa*, *572*
on *Rudbeckia*, *389*
on *Salvia*, *389*
on strawberries, 765
varieties resistant to, 1024
on tomato, 779
sunscald and, 773
varieties resistant to, 1026
vegetables susceptible to, 1025
Verticutter
for dethatching lawns, 251
***Vespamima* species (Pitch moths), on *Pinus*,** 538
Vetch
crown (*Coronilla varia*)
as drought-resistant, 1003
as groundcover, 283
near peach; nectarine
insects harbored by, 637
Viburnum
V. davidii (David viburnum)
as shade tolerant, 1008
V. dentatum (Arrowwood)
as alkaline soil tolerant, 1019
V. dilatatum (Linden viburnum)
as alkaline soil tolerant, 1019
V. opulus (Snowball viburnum)
ash-gray snowball aphids on, 588
V. sieboldii (Siebold viburnum)
as disease and insect resistant, 1012
V. tinus (Laurestinus)
as shade tolerant, 1008
culture, 588
diseases of
phytophthora rot, 1013
powdery mildew, 1006, 588
fertilizing, 588, 932
insects on
aphids, *588*
ash-gray snowball aphids, *588*
insecticide for, 957
leaf thrips, *885*
overwatering damage, *432*
Vigor, defined, 170
***Vinca* (Periwinkle)**
culture, 299
diseases of
canker and dieback, *299*
gray mold, 299
leaf spot, *300*
powdery mildew, susceptibility to, 1006
root and stem rot, 299
fertilizing
scorch and, 300
mulching
as scorch protection, 300

scorch on, *300*
as shade tolerant, 263, 276, 283, 284, 1003, 1008
as verticillium wilt resistant, 263, 276, 1003, 1006
watering
gray mold and, 299
scorch and, 300
Vine rot
botrytis
controlling, 977
Vinegar flies (*Drosophila* species), *787*
on fig
souring and, 628
insecticides for, 951
Vines. *See* Woody ornamentals
***Viola* (Pansy; Viola; Violet),** 1003
V. blanda (Sweet white violet)
as wet soil tolerant, 1010
V. lanceolata (Lance-leaved violet)
as wet soil tolerant, 1010
V. odorata (Sweet violet)
as groundcover, 1003
as annual, 499
in containers
watering, 400
culture, 400
damage to
flower thrips, *885*
diseases of
leaf spot, *400*
powdery mildew, 1006
root and stem rot, *401*
southern blight, 1007
fertilizing, 400
field pansy
as weed, 831
hearts-ease
as weed, 831
as Japanese beetle resistant, 1009
poor flowering in, *499*
snails and slugs on, *401*
spindly growth in, *499*
as verticillium wilt resistant, 1006
violet
as weed, 831
watering, 400
root and stem rot and, *401*
wet-soil-tolerant varieties of, 1010
wild violets
as weed, 831
Violet. *See Viola*
African. *See* African violet family
flame. *See Episcia*
Virginia creeper. *See Parthenocissus*
Virginia peppergrass (*Lepidium virginicum*), *823*
in lawns
herbicide for, 981
Virginia waterleaf (*Hydrophyllum virginianum*)
as wet soil tolerant, 1010
Virus diseases
aphids and, 853, 875
on peas, 744
on *Tulipa*, 397
on vegetables, 673
on beans
curly top, 685
mosaic, 685
on beets, 688
blackline
on walnut, 656
camellia yellow mottle leaf, *462*
on *Chrysanthemum*, outdoors, 341
on citrus, outdoors
psorosis (scaly bark), 626
tristeza (quick decline), 626
cucumber beetles and, 671
cucumber mosaic, 781
cucumber varieties resistant to, 1028
on *Lilium*, 372
on *Tolmiea*, *245*
on tomato, 781
on cucurbits
curly top, beet leafhoppers and, 714
mosaic. *See* cucumber mosaic
curly dwarf
on globe artichoke, 677
curly top
on beans, 685
on beets, 688
on cucurbits, beet leafhoppers and, 714
on tomato, 781
on *Cymbidium*, 348
on *Dahlia*, 350
on fig, 629
fleck
on *Lilium*, 372
on flowers, 312
on flowers
green peach aphids and, 875
galls from, 861
on *Gladiolus*, *359*
on globe artichoke, 677
green peach aphids and, 875
on *Iris*, 368
killer vs. latent
on strawberries, 764
leaf roll
on potato, 756
on potato, discolored tubers and, 752
on lettuce, 736
on *Lilium*, *372*
maize dwarf mosaic (MDM)
on corn, 710
on mint, *853*
mosaic, 853
on beans, 685
on *Chrysanthemum*, outdoors, 341
cucumber. *See* cucumber mosaic
on cucurbits, 1028, 671, 720
on *Cymbidium*, 348
on *Dahlia*, 350
on fig, 629
on flowers, 312, 853
on *Iris*, 368
on lettuce, 736
on *Lilium*, 372
maize dwarf (MDM), on corn, 710
on peppers, 750
on potato, 756
on potato, 752
on *Ranunculus*, 388
squash, 671
squash, 853
tobacco (TMV), on tomato, 781, 775
on tomato, 781
yellow, on beans, 685
nematodes and, 854
on orchids, *230*
on peas, aphids and, 744
on peppers, 750
on potato
discolored tubers and, 752
leaf roll, 756
mosaic, 752
psorosis
on citrus, outdoors, 626
quick decline
on citrus, outdoors, 626
on *Ranunculus*, 388
ring-spot, 853
on flowers, 312
on *Rosa*, 568
scaly bark
on citrus, 626
squash mosaic, 853
on cucurbits, cucumber beetles and, 671
on strawberries, 764
varieties resistant to, 1024
stunts, 853
tobacco mosaic (TMV)
on peppers, 750
on tomato, 775, 781
on tomato
curly top, 781
mosaic, 781
tristeza
on citrus, outdoors, 626
on *Tulipa*, *398*
aphids and, 397
on vegetables
aphids and, 673
green peach aphids and, 875
on walnut, 656
yellow mottle leaf
on *Camellia*, 462
yellows
on flowers, 312
***Vitex agnus-castus* (Blue chaste tree)**
as armillaria resistant, 1016
***Vitis. See* Grapes**
Volck Oil Spray. *See* ORTHO Volck Oil Spray
Voles
in woody ornamentals, 432
Volutella blight
on *Pachysandra*, 297
Volutella buxi
on Buxus, 459
Volutella canker and blight
on Buxus, *459*
Volutella leaf and stem blight
on Buxus, *459*
VPM
as soil fumigant, 927

W

Walkgrass. *See* Bluegrass, annual
Walkingsticks, 882
as Orthoptera, 883
Walkways
pests on
woollybear caterpillars, 872
weeds in
See also Sidewalks and driveways
carpetweed, 841
Florida pusley, 828
German velvetgrass, 816
herbicides for, 815, 984, 985
ladysthumb, 833
mugwort, 838
prickly lettuce, 832
prostrate knotweed, 827
red stem filaree, 825
Virginia peppergrass, 823
Walnut, 653
as armillaria root rot resistant, 1016
black (*Juglans hindsii*)
as armillaria resistant, 1016
black (*Juglans nigra*)
gypsy moths on, 1014
walnut wilt and, 778
culture, 653
diseases of
blackline, *656*
crown rot, *656*
phytophthora rot, 1013
powdery mildew, 1006
walnut anthracnose, *656*
walnut blight, *654*
early-blooming varieties of
codling moths and, *653*
fertilizing, 653, 934
harvesting, 653
insects on
ants, 654
aphids, *654*
blister mite damage, *655*
codling moths, *653*
European dusky-veined walnut aphids, 654
Mediterranean fruit flies, 1018
oystershell scales, *655*
redhumped caterpillars, 870
scales, *655*
spider mites, 655
walnut aphids, *654*
walnut caterpillars, *655*

Wild oats (*Avena fatua*), *820*
Wild onion (*Allium canadense*), *821*
in lawns
herbicides for, 981, 986, 987
Wild opium. *See* Wild lettuce
Wild portulaca. *See* Purslane
Wild strawberry. *See Fragaria*
Wild tansy. *See* Ragweed
Wild tomato. *See* Horsenettle
Wild violets (*Viola* species), 831
Wildlife. *See* Animal pests; Rodents
Willow. *See Salix*
Willow borers
Cryptorhynchus lapathi
on *Populus*, 545
on *Salix*, 575
Saperda species, *574*
Willow leaf beetles, *574*on *Salix*,573
insecticides for, 961, 964
Willow scab, 575
Willowweed (*Polygonum persicaria*), 833
Wilt and root rot
on *Rhododendron*, *562*
Wilt and stem rot
on *Tagetes*, 392
Wilting
Hosta, *314*
Pincushion flowers, *813*
Snapdragons, *813*
Wilt
bacterial. *See* Bacterial wilt
on *Callistephus*, *333*
canker
on *Gleditsia*, 496
crown rot and
on *Aquilegia*, *327*
on *Dahlia*, *349*
on Dimorphotheca, *356*
fusarium. *See* Fusarium wilt
on *Lathyrus*, *371*
on *Rhus*, *564*
on tomato, 665, 778
on vegetables, 665
verticillium. *See* Verticillium wilt
walnut
on tomato, 778
Wind damage
leaf burn or leaf scorch and, 857
to asparagus
crooked spears from, 678
to brambles, 692
to flowers, 314
to fruit and nut trees, 600
to *Juniperus*, 505
to *Rhododendron*, 561
sandblasting
to asparagus, 678
to woody ornamentals
limb breakage and, 426
wilting and, 420
Wind witch. *See* Russian thistle
Windburn
on *Rhododendron*, *561*. *See also* Wind damage
Windflower. *See Anemone*
Winter burn
on *Vinca*, *300*
Winter creeper. *See Euonymus*
Winter injury, 858
See also Cold damage
to *Arborvitae*, *479*
to *Buxus*, *458*
to citrus, 627
to cypress family, 479
to groundcovers, 286
to *Juniperus*, 505
leaf burn or leaf scorch, 857
to *Mahonia*, *516*
to *Pachysandra*, 296
protecting plants from, 919
to *Rhododendron*, *561*
scorch
on *Vinca*, *300*
sunscald. *See* Sunscald
to woody ornamentals, 417
leaf scorch, 429
limb breakage and, 426
Winter sunscald. *See* Sunscald
Winterberry. *See Ilex verticillata*
Winterweed. *See* Chickweed
Wiregrass. *See* Bermudagrass; Prostrate knotweed
Wireworms
on carrot, 704
on corn, *714*
false, darkling beetles as, 867
insecticides for, 950, 951
plants susceptible to, 704, 783
on potatoes, 751
on turnip, 783
on vegetables
insecticide for, 951
Wisteria
W. sinensis (Chinese wisteria)
as armillaria resistant, 1016
bees attracted by, 1007
bird damage to, *589*
culture, 588
failure to bloom in, *589*
Witch hazel.*See Hamamelis*
Witch's broom, 861
aphids and
on *Lonicera*, *514*
on *Celtis*, *468*
on Hackberry, *861*
on *Libocedrus*, 470
on *Lonicera*, aphids and, *514*
on *Nerium*, *523*
on *Quercus*
from powdery mildew, 553
on woody ornamentals, *417*
Witch-hazel leaf gall aphid (*Hormaphis hamamelidis*), 497
Witchgrass. *See* Quackgrass
Wood ashes
for potassium deficiency in vegetables, 667
Wood chips
as mulch, 926
Wood fern (*Dryopteris*)
as shade-tolerant groundcover, 1003
Wood piles
cockroaches originating in, 789
insects in, 801
***Wood Projects for the Garden* (ORTHO),** 999
Wood roaches, 789
Wood-boring beetles
insecticide for, 962
on *Quercus*, 554
Woodchucks, *901*
diseases carried by, 901
in flowers, 320
in vegetables, 675
Wooded areas
weeds in
cudweed, 826
horsetail, 822
poison oak, 845
Spanishneedles, 825
Woodpeckers, 801
Woodruff, sweet (*Galium odoratum*)
as shade-tolerant groundcover, 1003
Woodsorrel, yellow. *See* Oxalis
Woodwasps
in firewood, 801
Woodwasps
in households, *800*
Woody ornamentals
See also specific trees, shrubs, and vines
acid soil tolerant, 1019
air pollution damage to, *432*
algae, lichens, and mosses on, *416*
alkaline soil tolerant, 1019
animal pests on, 432
birds, 899. *See also* sapsuckers
deer, 897
mice, 896
raccoons, 900
sapsuckers, 423, 899
tree squirrels, 427, 899
woodchucks, 901
balled and burlapped, 924
bare root, 924
bark shedding on, *424*
bird damage to, 423, 899
books about
All About Trees (ORTHO), 996
How to Select & Care for Shrubs & Hedges (ORTHO), 998
branch problems on
algae, lichens, and mosses on, *416*
aphids, *412*, 430
bacterial crown gall, 415
bagworms, 873
balled roots, *436*
bark beetles, *435*, 865
bark shedding, 424
bark-feeding animals, 432
beetles, *410*, *435*
borers, 419, 422, *424*, 439, 865
breakage, 427, *426*, *916*
cankers, 419, 422, *424*, 439, *917*
compacted soil, *434*
cottony scales, mealybugs, and woolly aphids, *413*
dieback, 439, 440
disease, 413, 422, 427, *439*, *440*
distorted growth, 417, 861
dog urine injury, *439*
dwarf mistletoe, *416*
dying, 412, 413,*415*, 424, *435*, 436–*439*, *440*
environmental stress, 422
fireblight, *439*
fluids or stickiness, 421, *422*
gall-forming insects, 415
galls or growths, *415*, *416*
girdling roots, *434*
grade change, 437
growths, 873
gummosis, 422
heart rot, 427
holes or cracks, *424*, 432
honeydew, *422*
insects, 410–413, 415, 419, 422, *424*, *430*, 436, 438, 439
leaf and stem rusts, 413
leafhoppers, *430*
leafy mistletoe, *416*
lightning damage, 425
mechanical injury, 419, 422, 435, 439
natural sap ooze, *422*
oozing sap, 421, *422*
overwatering, *438*
paving over roots, 436
powdery mildew, 413
root and crown rots, *440*
root nematodes, 436
root problems causing, 434, *435*, *436*, 437, 438, 440
scales, 412
shallow soil or hardpan, 434
slime flux, 421
snow and ice damage, 426
soil problems causing, 434, *434*
sudden limb drop, 426
tent caterpillars and fall webworms, *411*
trunk injury, 435
uglynest caterpillars, 872
weak forks, 426, *916*
webbing, 872
wind damage, 426
witch's broom, 416, 417,

X

Y

Z

SOLVING PLANT PROBLEMS

Diagnosing problems in landscape plants requires careful observation of the problem plants and their environment. The key to an accurate diagnosis is knowing *how* to look for clues to a problem and the *type* of clues to look for. The checklist on the next page gives a step-by-step procedure for gathering clues and diagnosing the problem. It will help you to develop a case history, eliminate unlikely causes of the problem, and find the real cause.

HOW TO OBSERVE

Begin your observations by examining the plant from a distance. Note its general condition. Is the entire plant affected, or only a few stems, branches, or leaves? If the entire plant shows symptoms, this indicates that the cause will probably be found on the trunk or roots, or in the soil. Look for patterns and relationships with other plants. Is the problem confined to the sunny side of the plant? Is only the young growth affected? Are there many sick plants in one spot? Locate a part of the plant that shows obvious symptoms and take a closer look. Mottled or discolored leaves may indicate an insect or disease problem. A 5 to 15-power hand lens will allow you to see insects or fungus spores that are not easily visible to the naked eye.

If the initial inspection does not reveal any obvious reason for the symptoms, developing a case history for the plant may lead you to a less conspicuous cause of the problem. What has the weather been like recently? Has the temperature been fluctuating drastically? What kind of winter was it? An unusually dry, cold winter can cause dieback on trees and shrubs that may not become apparent until new growth begins in spring. Study the recent care of the plant. Has it been watered or fertilized regularly? All plants require fertilizer. Without regular feeding, their leaves turn yellow and growth is poor. (For information about fertilizers, see page 910.) When you are observing the area around the plant, be aware of changes in the environment. Construction around established plants can be very damaging, although symptoms of decline may not appear for several years. Drastic changes in light, such as moving a houseplant from a sunny window to a dark corner, or pruning a fruit tree heavily, may cause problems that appear many days later.

It may be necessary to dig into the plant or the soil to find the cause of the problem. If there is a hole in a stem, cut into it. Or slice a piece of bark off a wilting branch to determine whether the wood is discolored or healthy. The only way to learn about the roots of a sick plant is to dig up a small plant, or to carefully dig a hole to examine the roots of a large plant. The key to a root problem may be the soil. Investigate the drainage

A magnifying glass is an important tool in diagnosing plant problems.

(see page 907), probe the soil with a soil auger to determine the soil depth and the type of soil, or test the pH of the soil with a pH kit. (For more information about testing the soil, see page 909.) Look at all sides of the question and explore each clue.

Particular types of plants are susceptible to typical problems at certain times of the year. For instance, cherries are usually plagued with fruit flies in the spring when the fruit is ripening, and snapdragons are likely to be infected with rust in spring and summer when the temperature is mild and moisture is present.

PUTTING IT ALL TOGETHER

When you're reading about a plant problem in *The Ortho Problem Solver*, read carefully. Every word and phrase is important for understanding the nature of the problem. "May" means that the symptom develops only sometimes. And certain phrases offer you clues about the problem, such as the time of year to expect it ("In spring to midsummer . . .") and where to look for the symptom (". . . on the undersides of the leaves").

Unfortunately, plants frequently develop more than one problem at a time. Plants have natural defenses against diseases and insects. But when the plant is weakened by one problem, its defenses are lowered and other problems are able to infect it. For instance, borers are often responsible for a tree's decline, but borers seldom are a serious problem on healthy trees. A borer problem may indicate another problem, such as a recent severe winter, or root rot.

When using *The Ortho Problem Solver*, look for the cause of your plant's problem under the listing for that plant, and under the general problem headings that begin each section. If you are not able to find the problem here, look through some of the Galleries near the end of the book; you may pick up a clue here that will indicate the general nature of your problem.

THE CHECKLIST

Use this checklist to develop a case history for the problem and to identify symptoms that will lead to an accurate diagnosis. Answer each question that pertains to your plant carefully and thoroughly. When looking for symptoms and answering questions about the condition of the plant, begin with the leaves, flowers, or fruit (unless it is apparent that the problem is elsewhere), because they are the easiest to examine. Once you've eliminated those possibilities, move down the plant to the stems, or branches and trunk. Inspect the roots after all other possibilities have been rejected.

INFORMATION ABOUT THE PLANT

LOOK AT THIS	WHAT TO LOOK FOR
Kind of plant	☐ What type of plant is it? ☐ Does it prefer moist or dry conditions? ☐ Can it tolerate cold or does it grow best in a warm climate? ☐ Does the plant grow best in acid or alkaline soil?
Age	☐ Is the plant young and tender, or old and in a state of decline?
Size	☐ Is the plant abnormally small for its age? ☐ How much has the plant grown in the last few years? ☐ Is the size of the trunk or stem in proportion to the number of branches?
Time in present site	☐ Was the plant recently transplanted? ☐ Has it had time to become established, or is it still in a state of shock from transplanting? ☐ Is the plant much older than the housing development or buildings nearby?
Symptom development	☐ When were the symptoms first noticed? ☐ Have symptoms been developing for a long period of time, or have they appeared suddenly?
Condition of plant	☐ Is the entire plant affected, is the problem found on only one side of the plant, or are symptoms scattered throughout the plant? ☐ What part or parts of the plant are affected? ☐ Are all of the leaves affected, or only the leaves on a few branches? ☐ Are the leaves abnormal in size, color, shape, or texture? ☐ Do the flowers and fruit show symptoms?
Condition of plant	☐ Are there any abnormal growths, discolorations, or injuries on the branches, stems, or trunk? ☐ Is there anything wrapped around and girdling the plant or nailed into the wood? ☐ Does the trunk have a normal flare at the base, or is it constricted or entering the ground straight like a pole? ☐ If the entire plant is affected, what do the roots look like? Are they white and healthy, or are they discolored? (Use a trowel to dig around the roots of large plants; pull up small, sick plants to investigate the roots; and examine roots of container plants by removing the container. For instructions on examining roots of container plants, see page 921.) Is the bark brown and decayed? ☐ Have the roots remained in the soil ball, or have they grown into the surrounding soil? (For information about balled roots, see page 436.) ☐ Are there insects on the plant, or is there evidence of insects, such as holes, droppings, sap, or sawdustlike material? ☐ What other symptoms are visible on the plant? ☐ Has the problem appeared in past years?

PLANT ENVIRONMENT

LOOK AT THIS	WHAT TO LOOK FOR
Location of property	☐ Is the property near a large body of fresh or salt water? ☐ Is the property located downwind from a factory, or is it in a large polluted urban area? ☐ Is the property part of a new housing development that was built on land fill?
Location of plant	☐ Is the plant growing next to a building? If so, is the location sunny or shady? Is the wall of the building light in color? How intense is the reflected light? ☐ Has there been any construction, trenching, or grade change nearby within the past several years? ☐ Have there been any natural disturbances? ☐ How close is the plant to a road? Is the road de-iced in the winter? ☐ Is the plant growing over or near a gas, water, or sewer line, or next to power lines? ☐ Is the ground sloping or level?
Relationship to other plants	☐ Are there large shade trees overhead? ☐ Is the plant growing in a lawn or groundcover? ☐ Are there plants growing nearby that are also affected? Do the same species show similar symptoms? Are unrelated plants affected? How close by are they?
Weather	☐ Have you had unusual weather conditions recently (cold, hot, dry, wet, windy, snowy, etc.), or in the past few years?
Microclimate	☐ What are the weather conditions in the immediate vicinity of the plant? ☐ Is the plant growing under something that prevents it from receiving moisture? ☐ How windy is the location? ☐ How much light is the plant receiving? Is it the optimum amount for the type of plant? (For information about supplying extra light to houseplants, **see page 920.**)
Soil conditions	☐ What kind of soil is the plant growing in? Is it clayey, sandy, or loamy? (For information about heavy, sandy, and rocky soil, **see pages 904 to 906.**) ☐ How deep is the soil? (For information about shallow soil, **see page 905.**) Is there a layer of rock or hardpan beneath the topsoil? (For information about hardpan, **see page 906.**) ☐ What is the pH of the soil? (For information about testing the soil for pH, see **page 909.**) ☐ Does the soil drain well, or does the water remain on the surface after a heavy rain or irrigation? (For information about drainage, **see page 907.**) Does the soil have a sour smell? ☐ Is the soil hard and compacted? (For information about compaction, see page **906.**) ☐ Has the soil eroded away from around the roots? (For information about erosion, **see page 905.**)
Soil coverings	☐ Is there asphalt, cement, or other solid surface covering the soil around the plant? (For information about paving over roots, **see page 436.**) How close is it to the base of the plant? How long has it been there? ☐ Has the soil surface been mulched or covered with crushed rock? ☐ Was the mulch obtained from a reputable dealer? ☐ Are weeds or grass growing around the base of the plant? How thickly?
Recent care	☐ Has the plant or surrounding plants been fertilized or watered recently? (For information about fertilizers and watering, **see pages 910 and 912.**) ☐ If fertilizer was used, was it applied according to label directions? (For information on how to read a fertilizer label, **see page 911.**) ☐ Has the plant or the area been treated with a fungicide or insecticide? (For information about how to spray and dust, **see page 922.**) ☐ Was the treatment for this problem or another one? ☐ Was the pesticide registered for use on the plant (is the plant listed on the product label)? ☐ Was the pesticide applied according to label directions? ☐ Did it rain right after spraying, so the spray was washed off? ☐ Did you repeat the spray if the label suggested it? ☐ Have weed killers (herbicides) or lawn weed and feeds been used in the area in the past year? How close by? (For information about applying herbicides, **see page 923.**) ☐ Did you spray on a windy day? ☐ Has the plant been pruned heavily, exposing shaded areas to full sun? ☐ Were stumps left after pruning, or was the bark damaged during the pruning process? (For information about pruning, see ORTHO's book *All About Pruning.*)

TRANSPORT (XYLEM)

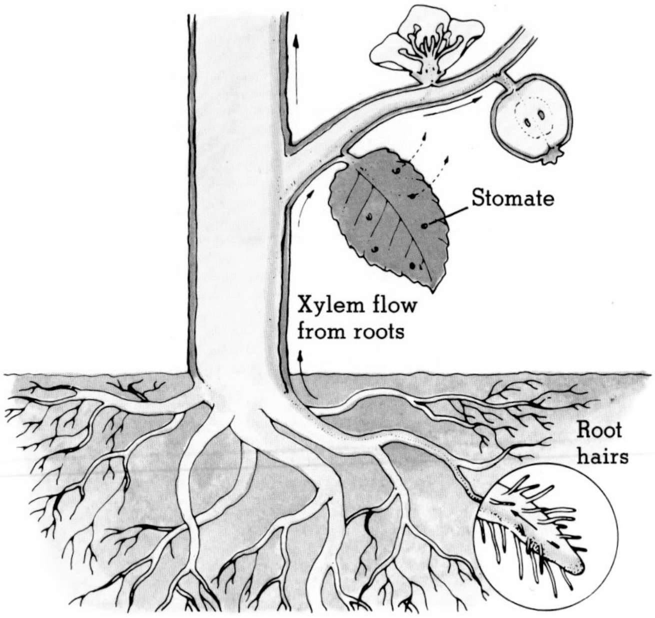

TRANSPORT (PHLOEM)

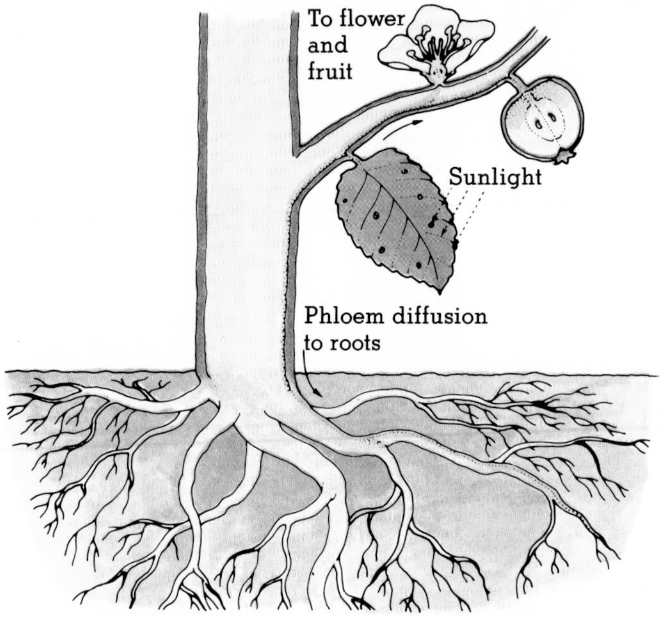

TRANSPORT

The transport system of a plant does many of the same jobs that the circulatory system does in a human being, but it is not called circulation because it does not go in a circle, as the human blood stream does. Plants have two transport systems, one carrying water and dissolved minerals from the roots to the top of the plant, and the other carrying sugars and other manufactured material from the leaves to all other parts of the plant.

Xylem flow: The part of a plant's transport system that carries water upward flows through a system of microscopic tubes called the *xylem* (pronounced ZYE-lem). In woody plants, the xylem is the outermost layer of wood. This wood, which is just under the bark, contains the xylem tubes. These tubes extend into the leaves and, through the leaf veins, into every part of the leaf. The xylem tubes end in the leaf tissue. Water leaves the xylem in the leaf tissue and evaporates through microscopic pores called *stomates* in the leaf surface.

Transpiration: This evaporation out of the stomates is called *transpiration*. Transpiration not only provides the power that moves water and nutrients into the top of the plant, but it also cools the leaf, just as evaporation cools a wet towel. Although the principles are different, you can think of transpiration as pulling water from the roots to the leaves just as soda is sucked through a drinking straw. Since plants can only transport nutrients that are dissolved in water, insoluble materials are not available to them.

Three main factors reduce xylem flow: dry soil, a sick root system, or a plugged or cut xylem system. Any of several diseases or injuries can cause these problems. If the xylem flow is reduced below a certain point, the leaves receive less nutrients than they need to sustain good health, and begin to show symptoms of nutrient deficiencies, usually by turning pale green or yellow, with the veins remaining green. If the xylem flow is reduced when the water demand is high — during hot weather — the leaves may wilt or scorch. This happens because the leaves lose water faster than it can be replaced.

Stomate control: Plants control transpiration by opening and closing their stomates. The stomates are shut at night. They open in the morning, but may shut down partially if the light is dim. Stomates also close if a leaf runs out of water. This usually happens before any sign of wilting is seen. If the weather is hot when the leaf runs out of water, and if the leaf is in the sun, it is very likely to overheat and burn. This is called *sunburn* or *scorch*, depending on the pattern of the burning.

Phloem flow: The part of the transport system that carries sugars and other manufactured material from the leaves to other parts of the plant is called the phloem (FLO-em). This system of tubes lies inside the bark. If you peel off some bark in the spring, the phloem is visible as the white part of the bark. Flow in the phloem is by diffusion, and is much slower than xylem flow. Sugars and other material manufactured in the leaves diffuse through the phloem to growing shoots, flowers, fruit, and roots. Since the roots are so large, most of the phloem flow in the trunk of a tree is downward.

PHOTOSYNTHESIS

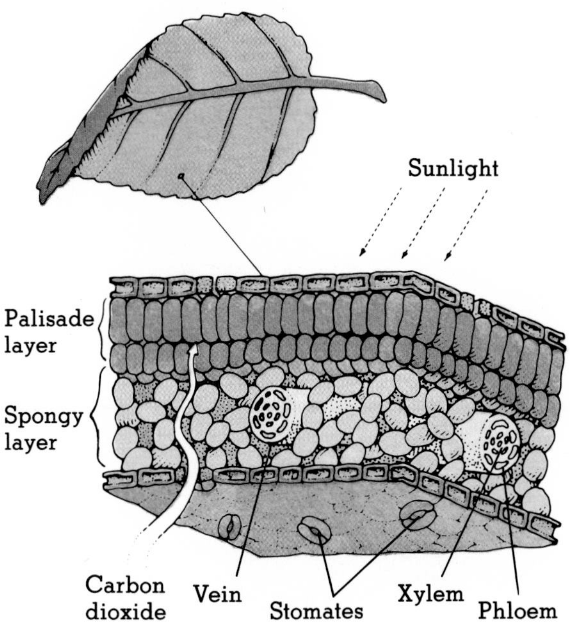

PHOTOSYNTHESIS

Photosynthesis is a chemical reaction that locks up the sun's energy in the form of a chemical so that it can be used to support life. This reaction takes carbon dioxide from the air and combines it with water from the soil to make sugars. Photosynthesis takes place in the green parts of plants. The green pigment is called *chlorophyll*. It is chlorophyll that collects and focuses the energy in light to make sugar. Most photosynthesis takes place in leaves, in a layer of cells, called the *palisade layer*, near the upper surface of the leaf. Carbon dioxide enters the leaf through the stomates in the lower surface and enters the palisade cells, where it is combined with water to make sugar. As a by-product of this reaction, oxygen is released to the air. The sugars are then transported through the phloem to all parts of the plant, where they are burned to release their energy. All animals and humans depend on both the sugars and the oxygen produced by plants, so all life on earth depends on photosynthesis.

Light: Light is the source of energy that combines carbon dioxide and water to make sugar. The more light a plant receives, the more sugar it makes, the faster it grows, and the more flowers and fruit it produces. In dim light, a plant makes barely enough sugar to maintain its life. But in bright light, it makes a surplus that it uses for growth and reproduction.

Water stress: Carbon dioxide enters the leaves through the stomates. Since most plants can't store carbon dioxide, photosynthesis can take place only when the stomates are open. If a plant does not have enough water, it closes its stomates to avoid losing water it can't afford to lose. But when the stomates are closed, photosynthesis stops. One of the first effects of water stress is that photosynthesis — and growth — stops.

TOP GROWTH

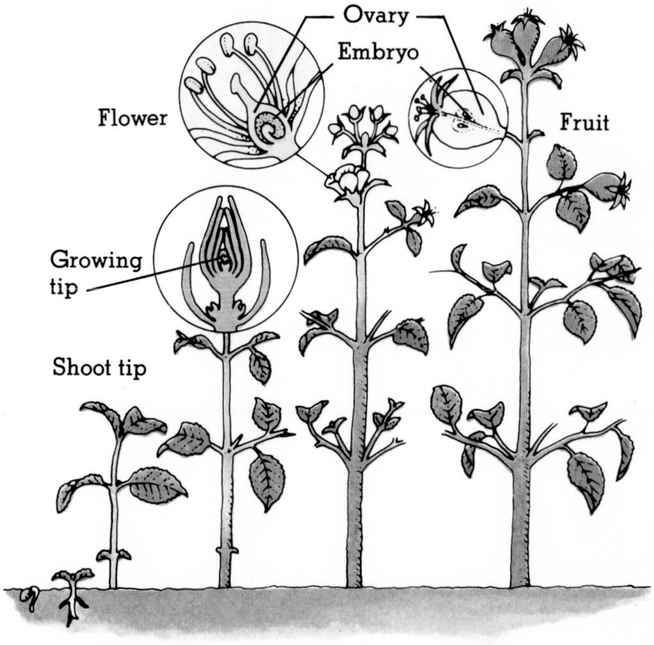

TOP GROWTH

Unlike human growth, which takes place in all parts of the body, plant growth occurs in only a few places, called the *growing points*. The growing points in a plant are in the tips of the roots and shoots, and just under the bark in woody plants.

Tip growth: The growing points in the tips of shoots and roots are composed of tiny bunches of cells that divide repeatedly, building the specialized organs of the plant but always remaining at the tip of the new growth. The new plant parts are tiny while they are in the growing point, but they are complete, with all the cells they will ever have. As the growing point moves beyond them, the new parts fill with water and swell, as a rubber raft does when it is blown up, until they reach their full size. But all the time they are expanding, no new cell division is taking place.

Buds: The growing point moves ahead, but a bud is left at the base of each leaf. A bud is a growing point that is, for the moment, dormant. On some plants, such as tomatoes, these *axillary buds* begin growing as soon as they are formed. Others, such as those on apple trees, remain dormant until the following spring. Then they all begin growing at once. Some of the buds never open by themselves, but can be made to open and begin growing by pinching off the growing point at the end of the branch they are on.

Stem growth: The other place a woody plant grows is under the bark. A sheet of cells, called the *cambium*, lies between the wood and the bark. These cells divide repeatedly just as those in the shoot and root tips do. As they divide, they produce xylem cells toward the center of the stem, and phloem cells toward the outside. When growth is fastest, in the spring, large xylem cells are made; as growth slows in the summer, smaller cells are made. The difference in the size of these cells makes up the annual rings visible in most wood.

Flowers and fruit: Flowers are produced by the growing point just as the leaves and stem are. Flowers begin as buds, which in some plants open immediately, and in others wait for the following spring. At the base of each flower is an *ovary*, an organ that will contain the seed, and in some plants, becomes the fruit.

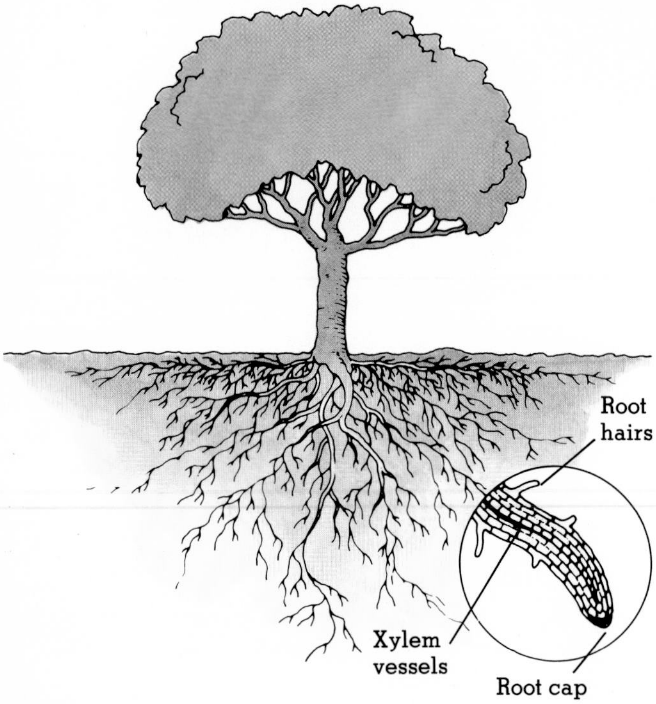

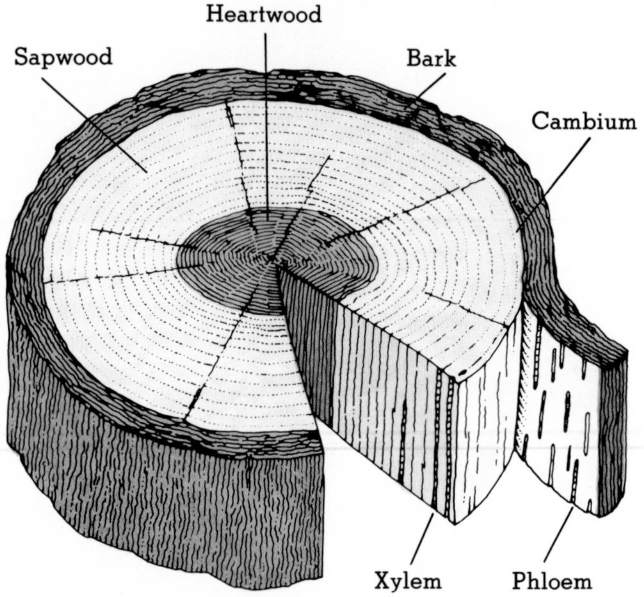

ROOT GROWTH

Plants live in two distinctly different environments: the air and the soil. The root system of a plant "mines" the soil for water and nutrients, the raw materials used by the plant. These raw materials are transported through the stems to the leaves, where they are combined with carbon dioxide to make sugars and complex chemicals. These processed chemicals are then transported through the stems back to the roots, where they are used for growth.

Root tips: As the growing point at the end of the root moves through the soil it leaves behind a soft, white, threadlike root tip. Downy *root hairs* grow from the tip. Most of the absorbing of water and nutrients is done by the root tips. As the root ages it becomes yellow, then brown, and the root hairs disintegrate. By the time the root turns brown, it no longer absorbs very much water from the soil.

The root system: Roots need three things for vigorous growth: oxygen, water, and nutrients. Of these three, oxygen is the one most frequently in short supply. Because plants cannot transport oxygen, each part of the plant must absorb it directly from the air. Oxygen diffuses through the spaces between soil particles to reach the roots. Where roots find an abundance of these three necessities, they proliferate.

The root system of a plant is often thought of as extending through the soil about as far as the top growth does above the ground. But plants vary greatly in the extent of their root systems. Trees may have roots that extend dozens or even hundreds of feet beyond their top growth, especially if the soil is frequently dry. Also, the root system is often not symmetrical, but is more dense on the side that more frequently receives food or water.

Although some plants have very deep root systems, garden plants get most of their nutrients from the top foot of soil. For this reason, plants are sensitive to the condition of the surface of the soil. If it is paved over, or becomes compacted, the roots near the surface receive less oxygen and water, and may die.

TRUNK GROWTH

Growth of tree trunks and expansion of the stems of woody plants take place in the *cambium*, a layer of dividing cells just under the bark. As each cell in the cambium divides, one of the two new cells becomes either a xylem cell or a phloem cell, and the other remains a cambium cell and divides again.

Wood: As the newest xylem cells expand, they push the cambium layer a little farther away from the center of the tree. The new cells live for only a year or two; then they die and only their woody cell wall remains. This cell wall continues to function as a xylem tube for another year or two, then it becomes plugged with the detritus of life and ceases to function. By this time, the cell is deep in the wood of the tree, and is heavily packed with a rigid material called *lignin*, the material that gives stiffness and rigidity to wood.

Bark: The phloem cells that form in the cambium are pushed to the outside of the tree by their expansion and the expansion of the new xylem cells. Like the xylem cells, they transport nutrients for a couple of years, then die and dry out to become the bark of the tree. However, the green bark on young stems is composed of a living layer of cells called the *epidermis*. As the twig ages and expands, this living bark is replaced by the dead phloem cells.

Girdling: If the phloem and xylem are cut through in a ring around the trunk of a tree, the flow of water to the top of the tree is stopped, the leaves wilt, and the top of the plant dies. The roots may die, or they may resprout and grow a new top. If only the bark is cut through — by root weevils, for instance — water can still reach the top of the tree, and it does not wilt. But the flow of sugars and nutrients from the leaves to the roots has been stopped, and the roots slowly starve. As they cease functioning, the top also starves, inevitably killing the tree.

Bark wounds: Any wound in the bark of a tree trunk interrupts the flow of water and nutrients through the tree. If a spot is repeatedly wounded, as frequently happens when a lawn tree is hit with a lawnmower, the growth of the plant is slowed and it becomes stunted.

FUNGI

HOW PLANTS SPREAD

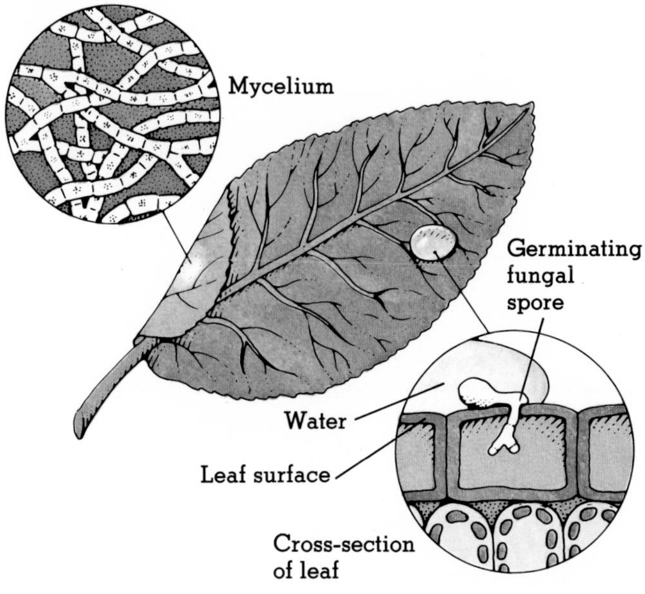

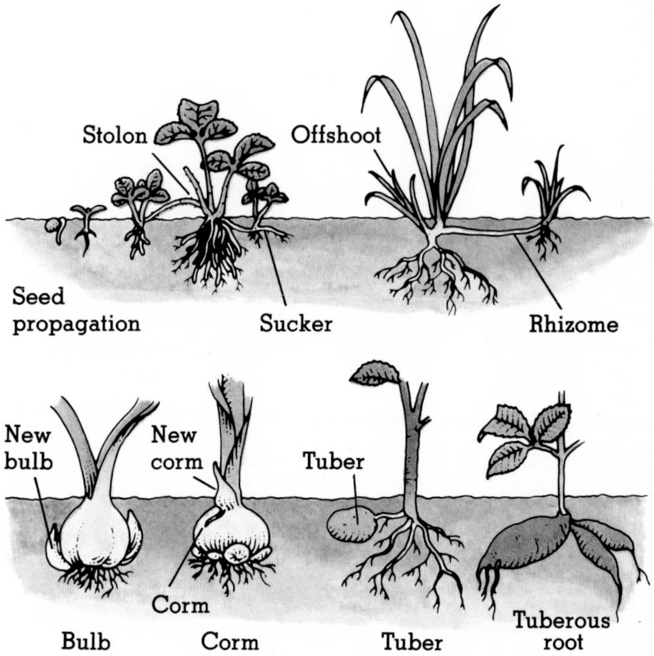

FUNGI

Fungi are primitive plants that do not contain chlorophyll and cannot make their own sugars as green plants do. Their structure is simple; most fungi are composed of a network of threads, which are sometimes bundled into cords. These threads and cords are called the *mycelium* (my-SEE-lee-um), and make up the body of the fungus. They are most easily seen as the fragile white threads that form under rotting leaves. Most fungi decompose dead plant matter into simpler chemicals. They are responsible for most of the decay of plant material in nature. But some fungi cause plant diseases by invading living plants. Fungus diseases spread in several ways, but three of these ways are most common: through the soil, by splashing water, and by the wind.

Soil-spread fungi: Fungi that live in the soil and attack plant roots are most commonly spread by moving soil or infected plants from one place to another. Soil-borne fungi are often brought to the garden initially on the roots of a transplant, then spread from one end of the garden to the other by irrigation water or cultivation.

Water-spread fungi: Other fungi depend on splashing water to spread their spores. Many of the fungi that cause leaf spots on trees and shrubs spend the winter as spores on the bark or on fallen leaves, then in the spring are washed to new leaves by splashing rain.

Wind-spread fungi: The third common way fungi spread is by dustlike spores that are carried by the wind to other plants. Many of these spores live for only a few hours or days after they are released into the air, so they must find suitable conditions for germination soon. For almost all such fungi, "suitable conditions" means a drop of water on a leaf surface. It takes a fungus spore from 4 to 8 hours to germinate and penetrate a leaf. If the drop of water in which it is growing dries out during this time, the spore dies. The notable exception to this need for a drop of water in which to germinate is powdery mildew (see page 413), the spores of which can germinate on a dry leaf. But even powdery mildew is more active in wet conditions.

HOW PLANTS SPREAD

Plants have two ways of propagating themselves: by seed, and by growing new plants from parts of the old one.

Seed propagation: Most plants make seeds, and some make vast numbers of them. Annual plants (those that live for only one growing season) depend on seeds to continue their species. They often put all their energy into ripening a crop of seeds. Annual weeds, such as crabgrass, usually make thousands of seeds per plant. It is important to kill these weeds before they make their seeds, or you will have the same job to do all over again the following year.

Offshoots: All other methods of propagation involve some form of growing new plants from parts of the old one. Offshoots are new plants that arise from the base of the old one. If allowed to continue, this will eventually lead to a dense bunch of plants. Offshoots can usually be broken or cut off and planted to make new plants.

Rhizomes and stolons: These horizontal stems form new plants at a distance from the mother plant. *Rhizomes* travel underground and form new plants where they near the surface. *Stolons* travel aboveground, and make new plants where they come in contact with the ground.

Suckers: The word *sucker* has two different but similar meanings. It refers to a stem that arises from the base of the trunk. It also refers to a plant that arises from the roots of the parent plant, often at some distance from the trunk. Plants that sucker freely, if left to their own devices, will form a thicket in a couple of years. The type of sucker that arises from a root is a whole plant, and can be removed and planted elsewhere.

Bulbs: Plants form a wide variety of underground food storage organs. Most of these organs remain dormant for part of the year, and then, because of the large amount of food stored in them, burst into vigorous growth. If the storage organ is formed from fleshy leaves, it is called a *bulb*. If it is formed from a vertical stem, it is called a *corm*. If it is formed from a rhizome, it is called a *tuber*. If it is formed from a root, it is called a *tuberous root*. When they are dormant, these organs can be moved to new locations, or stored before being replanted.

GLOSSARY

Abscission: A natural dropping of leaves, flowers, and other plant parts.

Acaricide: A chemical that kills spider mites and other types of mites. Acaricides are also known as miticides.

Acid soil: Soils with a pH below 7.0. Acid soils can cause problems when their pH is below 5.5. For more information about acid soils, **see page 908.**

Adventitious: Plant parts that form in unusual locations. For example, roots that grow from leaves or aboveground stems.

Aeration: To increase the amount of air space in the soil by tilling or otherwise loosening the soil.

Algae: Simple plants without visible structure that grow in wet locations. Some types of algae form a slippery black or green scum on wet soil, plants, walkways, and other surfaces.

Alkaline soil: Soil with a pH above 7.0. Alkaline soils slow the growth of many plants when their pH is above 8.0. For more information about alkaline soils, **see page 908.**

Annual plant: A plant that grows, flowers, produces seeds or fruit, and dies in a year or less. Many herbaceous flowers and vegetables are annual plants.

Axil: The location on a stem between the upper surface of a leaf or leafstalk and the stem from which is it growing.

Axillary buds: Buds that form in leaf axils.

Balled and burlapped plants: Trees and shrubs that are dug out of the ground with the intact soil ball surrounding the roots; the soil ball is then wrapped in burlap or plastic.

Bare-root plants: Trees and shrubs that are dug out of the ground and sold with their roots bare of soil. Roses and fruit trees are commonly sold in this manner. Bare-root plants are available in the winter.

Biennial plant: A plant that grows, flowers, produces seeds or fruit, and dies in two years. Some herbaceous flowers and vegetables are biennial. Most biennial plants produce foliage the first year and bloom the second year.

Bolting: Rapid development of flowers and seedheads in vegetables. Premature bolting may be stimulated by hot weather, drought, or lack of nutrients.

Bract: A modified leaf that is sometimes brightly colored, resembling a petal.

Bud: A condensed shoot consisting mainly of undeveloped tissue. Buds are often covered with scales, and develop into leaves, flowers, or both.

Callus: A mass of cells, often barklike in appearance, that forms over wounded plant tissue.

Cambium: A thin ring of tissue within the stem, branch, and trunk that continually forms nutrient and water-conducting vessels.

Canker: A discolored lesion that forms in stems, branches, or trunks as a result of infection. Cankers are often sunken, and may exude a thick sap. For more information about cankers, **see page 861.**

Chlorophyll: The green plant pigment that is necessary for photosynthesis.

Chlorosis: Yellowing of foliage due to a loss or breakdown of chlorophyll. Chlorosis may result from disease or infestation, poor growing conditions, or lack of nutrients.

Cold frame: A protective structure that uses the sun's energy to provide heat for plants. Plants may be grown in cold frames early in the spring before all danger of freezing is past.

Complete fertilizer: A fertilizer containing nitrogen, phosphorus, and potassium, the three nutrients in which plants are most commonly deficient.

Compost: Partially decomposed organic matter used to amend the soil. Compost is often made from grass clippings, leaves, and manure.

Conifers: Woody trees and shrubs that produce cones. Common conifers include pines, firs, spruces, junipers, redwood, and hemlocks.

Conks: Mushroomlike fruiting bodies of several different kinds of tree-decaying fungi.

Corm: A short, solid, enlarged, underground stem from which roots grow. Corms are food-storage organs. They contain one bud that will produce a new plant.

Dead-heading: The removal of old blossoms to encourage continued bloom or to improve the appearance of the plant.

Deciduous: Plants that shed all of their leaves annually, usually in the fall.

Defoliation: Leaf drop that often results from infection, infestation, or adverse environmental conditions.

Desiccation: Dehydration or loss of water.

Dormant: A state of rest and reduced metabolic activity in which plant tissues remain alive but do not grow.

Dormant oil: Oil sprayed on deciduous trees while they are dormant. Dormant oils are used to kill overwintering insects or insect eggs on plant bark.

Espalier: To train a plant (usually a tree or vine) along a railing or trellis so that the branches grow flat against the rail or trellis that supports them.

Evergreen: A plant that retains all or most of its foliage throughout the year.

Fasciation: An abnormal fusion of stems, leaves, or flowers, or the production of distorted growth.

Fertilizers: These substances contain plant nutrients. Fertilizers may be liquid or dry, and may be formulated in many different ways. For more information about fertilizers, **see page 911.**

Formulation: The form in which a compound may be produced. For example, a pesticide may be powdered, liquid, granular, or in an oil solution.

Frass: Sawdustlike insect excrement.

Fruiting body: A fungal structure that produces spores.

Fungicide: A chemical that kills fungi or prevents them from infecting healthy plant tissue.

Galls: Abnormal growths that form on plant roots, shoots, and leaves. Galls often result from infection or insect infestation. For more information about galls, **see page 861**.

Germination: The sprouting of seeds.

Girdle: Encircling of plant roots, stems, trunks, or branches resulting in a constriction of the plant part, or a reduction of water and nutrient flow through the girdled plant part.

Graft: To unite a stem or bud of one plant to a stem or root of another plant.

Gummosis: Oozing of plant sap, often from a plant wound or canker. Gummosis may occur as a result of infection or insect infestation.

Hardiness: The ability of a plant to withstand cold temperatures.

Hardening off: The process of plant adjustment to cold temperatures.

Heartwood: The inner core of wood inside a woody stem or trunk.

Herbaceous: Plants that are mainly soft and succulent, forming little or no woody tissue.

Herbicide: A chemical that kills or retards plant growth. Herbicides may kill the entire plant; or they may kill only the aboveground plant parts, leaving the roots alive.

Host: An organism that is parasitized by another organism, such as a plant that is infected by a fungus, or infested by an aphid.

Humidity: The amount of water vapor (moisture) in the air.

Hybrid: The offspring of two distinct plant species; a plant obtained by crossing two or more different species, subspecies, or varieties of plant. Hybrids are often made to produce a plant that has the best qualities of each parent.

Immune: A plant that is not susceptible to a disease or insect.

Infiltration (soil): The process by which water moves into the soil.

Insecticide: A chemical that kills insects.

Internode: The section of stem between two nodes.

Interveinal: Between the (leaf) veins. Interveinal yellowing, or *chlorosis*, refers to a discoloration occurring between the leaf veins.

Juvenile: An early growth phase differentiated from later growth by a distinctly different leaf shape, habit of growth, or other characteristics.

Larva: An immature stage through which some types of insects must pass before developing into adults. Caterpillars are the larvae of moths and butterflies, and grubs are the larvae of beetles. Larvae are typically wormlike in appearance.

Lateral bud: A bud forming along the side of a stem or branch rather than at the end.

Leaching: The removal of salts and soluble minerals from the soil by flushing the soil with water.

Leader: The main stems or trunk of a tree or shrub from which side stems or branches are produced.

Leaf margins: The edges of a leaf. Variations in the shape of leaf margins are used to help identify many plants and differentiate among them.

Leaf scar: The tiny scar left on a twig or stem after a leaf or leafstalk (petiole) drops off.

Leafstalk: A stalk that attaches a leaf to the stem; a petiole.

Lesion: A wound, discoloration, or scar caused by disease or injury.

Macronutrients: Nutrients required by plants for normal growth. Macronutrients such as nitrogen, phosphorus, and potassium are needed in large quantities by most plants.

Metamorphosis: Changes in body shape undergone by many insects as they develop from eggs into adults.

Microclimate: The environment immediately surrounding a plant; very localized climate conditions. Many different microclimates may occur at the same time in different areas of a garden.

Micronutrients: Nutrients required by plants for normal growth. Micronutrients (also called minor nutrients) such as iron, zinc, and manganese are needed in small quantities by most plants.

Mites: A group of tiny animals related to spiders, many of which feed on plants.

Mulch: A layer of organic or inorganic material on the soil surface. Mulches help to moderate the temperature of the soil surface, reduce loss of moisture from the soil, suppress weed growth, and reduce run-off. For more information about mulches, **see page 926**.

Mycelium: Microscopic fungal strands that form the major part of a fungal growth.

Nematode: Microscopic worms that live in the soil and feed on plant roots. Some nematodes feed on plant stems and leaves. For more information about nematodes, **see page 854**.

Node: The part of a stem where leaves and buds are attached.

Nymph: An immature stage through which some types of insects must pass before developing into adults. Nymphs usually resemble the adult form, but lack wings and cannot reproduce.

Oedema: Watery blisters or swellings that form on many herbaceous plants. These swellings may burst open, forming rust-colored lesions.

Organic matter: A substance derived from plant or animal material. For more information about organic matter, **see page 926**.

Ozone: A common air pollutant that may cause plant injury. For more information about ozone, **see page 855**.

Palisade cells: A layer of columnar cells located just beneath the upper surface of a leaf.

PAN (peroxyacetyl nitrate): A common air pollutant that may cause plant injury. For more information about PAN, **see page 855**.

Parasite: An organism that obtains its food from another living organism. Parasites live on or in their host.

Pathogen: An organism (such as a fungus, bacterium, or virus) capable of causing a disease.

Peat: Partially degraded vegetable matter found in marshy areas. Peat is commonly used as a soil amendment.

Perennial plant: A plant that lives for more than 2 years, often living for many years. Almost all woody plants and many herbaceous plants are perennials.

Permanent wilting point: The point of soil dryness at which plants can no longer obtain water from the soil. Once plants have reached the permanent wilting point they do not recover, even if they are supplied with water.

Pesticide: A chemical used to kill an organism considered a pest.

Petiole: A stalk that attaches the leaf to the stem; a leafstalk.

pH: A measure of the acidity or alkalinity of a substance; a measure of the relative concentration of hydrogen ions and hydroxyl ions. For more information about pH, **see page 908.**

Phloem: Nutrient-conducting vessels found throughout the plant. Phloem vessels transport nutrients produced in the foliage down through the stems, branches, or trunk to the roots.

Photosynthesis: The process by which plants use the sun's light to produce food (carbohydrates).

Plant disease: Any condition that impairs the normal functioning and metabolism of a plant. A plant disease may be caused by a fungus, bacterium, or virus, or by an environmental factor such as lack of nutrients or sunburn.

Propagation: Means of reproducing plants, such as by seeds, cuttings, budding, or grafting.

Protectant: A chemical that protects a plant from infection or infestation.

Pupa: An immature resting stage through which some types of insects must pass before becoming adults.

Resistant plant: A plant that can overcome the effects of a disease or insect infestation, or a plant that is not very susceptible to attack by a pathogen.

Rhizome: An underground stem from which roots grow. Rhizomes function as storage organs, and may be divided to produce new plants.

Rootstock: 1. The roots and crown, or roots, crown, and trunk of a plant upon which another plant is grafted. 2. The crown and roots of some types of perennial herbaceous plants, also known as *rhizomes.*

Root zone: The volume of soil that contains the roots of a plant.

Runners: Aboveground, trailing stems that form roots at their nodes when they make contact with moist soil.

Sapwood: The outer cylinder of wood in a trunk between the heartwood and the bark.

Saturated soil: Soil that is so wet that all the air pores in the soil are filled with water.

Sclerotium: A compact mass of fungal strands (mycelium) that functions as a resting stage for a fungus. Sclerotia are usually brown or black, and can usually withstand adverse conditions.

Slow-release fertilizers: Fertilizers that release their nutrients into the soil slowly and evenly, over a long period of time.

Soil heaving: Expansion and contraction of soil during periods of freezing and thawing. Plant roots may be sheared off, or plants may be lifted out of the ground during soil heaving.

Solubility: The degree to which a compound will dissolve in water. Compounds with high solubility will dissolve in water more readily than compounds with low solubility.

Soluble fertilizers: Fertilizers that dissolve easily in water and are immediately available for plant use.

Spore: A microscopic structure produced by fungi, mosses, and ferns that can germinate to form a new plant or a different stage of the same plant.

Spur: A short lateral branch bearing buds that will develop into flowers and then into fruit.

Stomates: Tiny pores located mainly on the undersides of leaves. Oxygen, carbon dioxide, water vapor, and other gasses move in and out of the leaf through these pores.

Sucker: A shoot or stem that grows from an underground plant part.

Surfactant: A substance added to a spray that increases its wetting and spreading properties. Surfactants are also called *wetting agents* or *spreader-stickers.*

Systemic pesticide: A pesticide that is absorbed into part or all of the plant tissue.

Tender plant: A plant that cannot tolerate freezing temperatures.

Terminal bud: A bud at the end of a stem or branch.

Toxin: A poisonous substance produced by a plant or an animal.

Translocation: The movement of a compound from one location in a plant to another.

Transpiration: Evaporation of water from plant tissue to the atmosphere. Transpiration occurs mainly through the stomates in the leaves.

Vascular system: The system of tissues (phloem and xylem) that conducts nutrients and water throughout the plant.

Vein clearing: A lightening or total loss of color of leaf veins. Vein clearing often results from plant infection or nutrient deficiency.

Vernalization: A cooling period required by many plants in order to germinate, grow, or flower properly.

Vigor: The health of a plant. A vigorous plant grows rapidly and produces healthy, normal amounts of foliage and flowers. A nonvigorous plant grows slowly, if at all, and produces stunted, sparse growth.

Wetting agent: A substance that changes the surface tension of water or other liquid, causing it to wet a repellent surface more thoroughly. Wetting agents are often used when spraying pesticides on waxy or fuzzy foliage.

Xylem: Water-conducting vessels found throughout the plant. Xylem vessels transport water and minerals from the roots upward through the plant.

THE ORTHO PROBLEM SOLVER SECOND EDITION

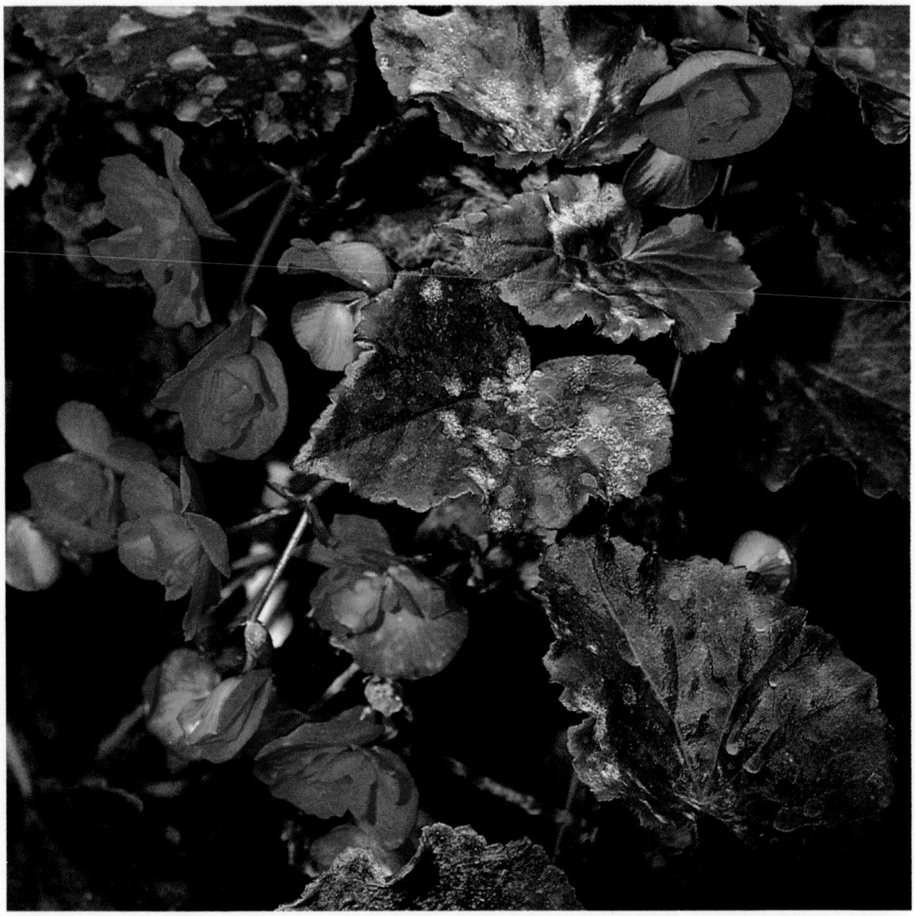

On the next 9 pages, you will find some of the most common problems of any houseplant. Look for your plant's problem on these pages. If you don't find it there, look up your plant in the alphabetical section beginning on page 182 where you will find some of the most common problems of specific houseplants. If you don't know the name of your houseplant, find it in the Houseplant Identifier on the next page.

PLANTS IN THE HOME

To us, our homes may be comfortable and inviting, but to our plants, they constitute harsh and uncomfortable environments. The pots we use to contain our plants limit root space. We often underwater and underfertilize—or overwater and overfertilize. And the light levels in our home vary from full sunlight to very dim light. A plant in the wrong place can burn from too much light or starve for lack of light. All these inhospitable conditions put stress on plants. Nevertheless, houseplants can be easy to grow; all you need is an understanding of these stress factors and the ability to minimize them or compensate for them.

Most problems with houseplants are probably caused by the fact that they are confined to containers. In nature, plant roots are free to range over a wide and deep area. If the surface layers of soil dry out, deep roots can still supply water to the plant. But plants in containers are at the mercy of their caretakers. If somebody doesn't water them, the plants may suffer frequently from lack of water.

Knowing when and how to water houseplants is a skill—an easily learned skill, but one that must be learned. For instructions for watering plants in containers, see page 919.

The second environmental stress suffered frequently by houseplants is caused by low levels of light. Each species of plant is adapted to a certain level of light. Most houseplants are adapted to tropical forests, where the light level is low, so they are able to tolerate the dim (for a plant) light in our homes. But most of the locations in our homes are too dim for any plant. Picking the right location in your house for each plant is part of the skill of raising houseplants. In general, plants raised for their foliage tolerate lower levels of light than plants raised for their flowers, and foliage plants with green leaves need less light than those with brightly colored leaves.

If the light is too bright for a plant, its leaves bleach to a gray or yellow color, and may burn. If the light is too dim, the plant grows very slowly, doesn't flower, and may lean toward the light. Move your plants around until you find the location that suits them best.

Although our houses create difficult environments for plants, they also protect them from extremes of weather and many of the diseases and insects that prey on outdoor plants. In the following pages, you will see that a few insects or diseases are repeated over and over. This is because insect and disease problems of houseplants are less varied and less severe than with outdoor plants—although you may not think so if you are fighting off an invasion of mealybugs. If you learn to recognize insect, disease, and environmental stress problems as soon as they appear, and deal with them immediately, your houseplants will reward you with beauty and health.

Above: Powdery mildew on a begonia. See page 189.
Left: A healthy episcia. See page 212.

HOUSEPLANT IDENTIFIER

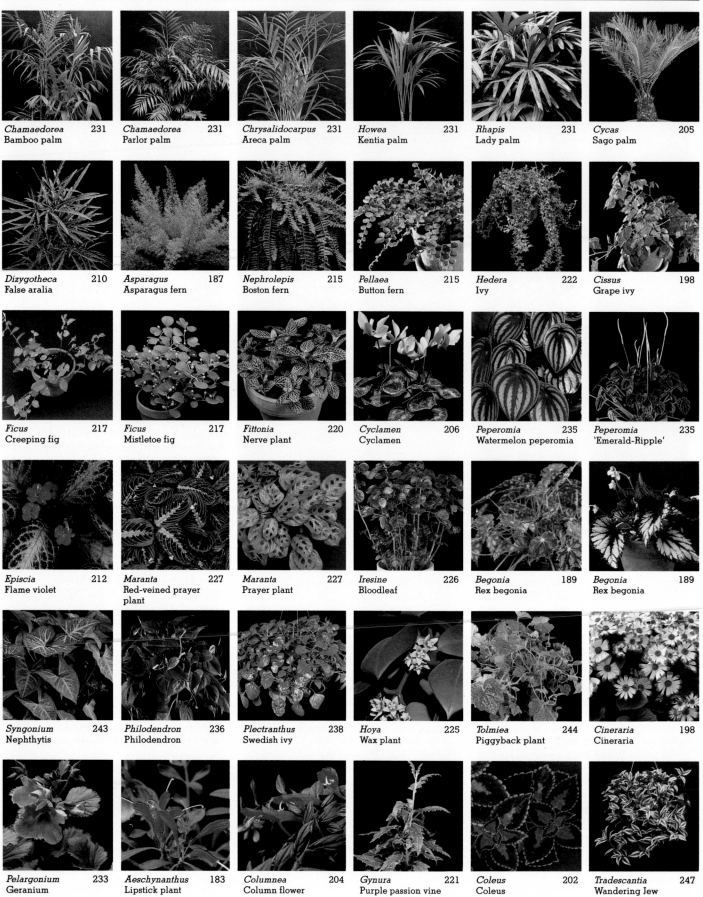

Chamaedorea 231
Bamboo palm

Chamaedorea 231
Parlor palm

Chrysalidocarpus 231
Areca palm

Howea 231
Kentia palm

Rhapis 231
Lady palm

Cycas 205
Sago palm

Dizygotheca 210
False aralia

Asparagus 187
Asparagus fern

Nephrolepis 215
Boston fern

Pellaea 215
Button fern

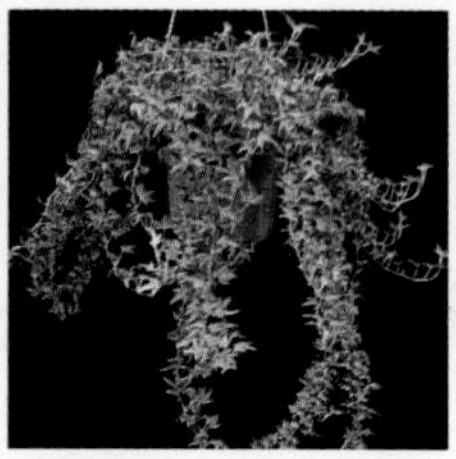
Hedera 222
Ivy

Cissus 198
Grape ivy

Ficus 217
Creeping fig

Ficus 217
Mistletoe fig

Fittonia 220
Nerve plant

Cyclamen 206
Cyclamen

Peperomia 235
Watermelon peperomia

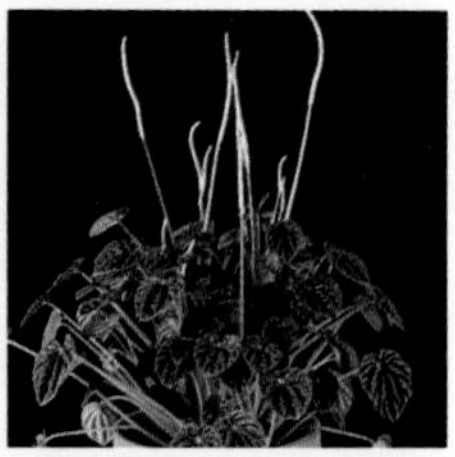
Peperomia 235
'Emerald-Ripple'

Episcia 212
Flame violet

Maranta 227
Red-veined prayer plant

Maranta 227
Prayer plant

Iresine 226
Bloodleaf

Begonia 189
Rex begonia

Begonia 189
Rex begonia

Syngonium 243
Nephthytis

Philodendron 236
Philodendron

Plectranthus 238
Swedish ivy

Hoya 225
Wax plant

Tolmiea 244
Piggyback plant

Cineraria 198
Cineraria

Pelargonium 233
Geranium

Aeschynanthus 183
Lipstick plant

Columnea 204
Column flower

Gynura 221
Purple passion vine

Coleus 202
Coleus

Tradescantia 247
Wandering Jew

Achimenes 183
Rainbow flower

Saintpaulia 239
African violet

Streptocarpus 242
Cape primrose

Sinningia 241
Gloxinia

Dracaena 211
Dracaena

Fatsia 186
Aralia

Ficus lyrata 217
Fiddle-leaf fig

Ficus elastica 217
Rubber plant

Brassaia 191
Schefflera

Monstera 228
Split-leaf philodendron

Asplenium 215
Bird's-nest fern

Spathiphyllum 242
Spathe flower

Anthurium 184
Anthurium

Aglaonema 183
Chinese evergreen

Dieffenbachia 208
Dumb cane

Aechmea 192
Bromeliad

Aphelandra 185
Zebra plant

Codiaeum 201
Croton

Polypodium 215
Rabbit's-foot fern

Platycerium 215
Staghorn fern

Ficus 217
Weeping fig

Araucaria 187
Norfolk Island pine

Kalanchoe 226
Kalanchoe

Zygocactus 247
Christmas cactus

Opuntia 193
Cactus

Haworthia 222
Haworthia

Chlorophytum 196
Spider plant

Chrysanthemum 196
Chrysanthemum

Euphorbia 212
Poinsettia

Cordyline 204
Ti plant

Clerodendrum 200
Glory-bower

Gardenia 220
Gardenia

Hippeastrum 224
Amaryllis

Paphiopedilum 229
Orchid

Capsicum 195
Ornamental pepper

Clivia 200
Kaffir lily

INDEX TO HOUSEPLANTS

PROBLEMS COMMON TO MANY HOUSEPLANTS

Dry poinsettia.

PROBLEM: Leaves are small, and plants fail to grow well and may be stunted. Plant parts or whole plants wilt. Margins of leaves or tips of leaves of narrow-leafed plants may dry and become brittle but still retain a dull green color. Bleached areas may occur between the veins. Such tissues may die and remain bleached, or turn tan or brown. Plants may die.

ANALYSIS: Too little water
Plants need water in order to grow. Besides making up most of the plant tissue, water is also the medium that carries nutrients into the plant, so a plant that is frequently short of water is also short of nutrients. Water also cools the leaves as it evaporates from them. If a leaf has no water to evaporate, it may overheat in the sun and burn. If plants wilt and then are given water, sometimes the margins or tips of the leaves will have completely wilted and will not recover. If this occurs, the margins or tips will die and become dry and brittle, but will retain a dull green color.

SOLUTION: Water plants immediately and thoroughly. If the soil is completely dry, add a bit of wetting agent (available at garden centers) or soak the entire pot in water for a couple of hours. Follow the watering guidelines given on page 923.

Salt damage to a spathiphyllum.

PROBLEM: The leaf margins of plants with broad leaves or the leaf tips of plants with long, narrow leaves turn brown and die. This browning occurs on the older leaves first, but when the condition is severe, new leaves may also be affected. On some plants, the older leaves may yellow and die.

ANALYSIS: Salt damage
Salt damage is a common problem on container-grown plants. Soluble salts are picked up by the roots and accumulate in the margins and tips of the leaves. When concentrations become high enough, the tissues are killed. Salts can accumulate from water or from the use of fertilizers; or they may be present in the soil used in potting. Salts accumulate faster and do more harm if plants are not watered thoroughly. Water that is high in lime does not cause as much salt damage as water that is high in other salts.

SOLUTION: Leach excess salts from the soil by flushing with water. Water thoroughly at least three times in a row, letting the water drain from the pot each time. This is most easily done if the pot is placed in the bathtub, a basin, or outside in the shade to drain. If you use a saucer to catch the water, empty the saucer after each watering. If the plant is too large to lift, empty the saucer with a turkey baster. Never let a plant stand in the drainage water. To prevent further salt accumulation, follow the watering instructions on page 923. For a list of plants sensitive to salts, see page 1001.

PROBLEMS COMMON TO MANY HOUSEPLANTS

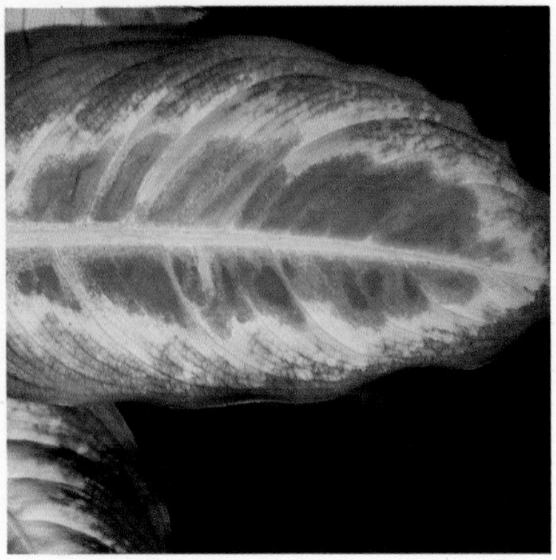

Sunburn on dieffenbachia.

PROBLEM: Dead tan or brown patches develop on leaves that are exposed to direct sunlight. Or leaf tissue may lighten or turn gray. In some cases, the plant remains green but growth is stunted. Damage is most severe when the plant is allowed to dry out.

ANALYSIS: Sunburn or bleaching
Sunburn or bleaching occurs when a plant is exposed to more intense sunlight than it can tolerate. Plants vary widely in their ability to tolerate direct sunlight; some plants can tolerate full sunlight, while others will burn or bleach if exposed to any direct sun. Bleaching occurs when light and heat break down chlorophyll (green plant pigment), causing a lightening or graying of the damaged leaf tissue. On more sensitive plants, or when light and heat increase in intensity, damage is more severe, and plant tissues die. Sometimes tissue inside the leaf is damaged, but outer symptoms do not develop. Instead, growth is stunted. Plants are more susceptible to bleaching and sunburn when they are allowed to dry out, because the normal cooling effect that results when water evaporates from leaves is reduced. Plants that are grown in low light conditions burn very easily if they are suddenly moved to a sunny location.

SOLUTION: Move plants that cannot tolerate direct sun to a shaded spot. Or cut down the light intensity by closing the curtains when the plant is exposed to direct sun. Prune off badly damaged leaves, or trim away damaged leaf areas to improve the plant's appearance. Keep plants well watered. For more information about watering, see page 923. For a list of indoor plants that will tolerate direct sunlight, see page 1001.

Overwatering damage to schefflera.

PROBLEM: Plants fail to grow and may wilt. Leaves lose their glossiness and may become light green or yellow. The roots are brown and soft, and do not have white tips. (For instructions on examining the rootball, see page 921.) The soil in the bottom of the pot may be very wet and have a foul odor. Plants may die.

ANALYSIS: Too much water or poor drainage
Although plants need water to live, the roots also need air. If the soil is kept too wet, the air spaces are filled with water, and the roots are weakened and may die. Weakened plants are more susceptible to root-rotting fungi, which wet soils favor. Plants with diseased roots do not absorb as much water as they did when they were healthy, so the soil remains wet. If roots are damaged or diseased, they cannot pick up water and nutrients needed for plant growth.

SOLUTION: Discard severely wilted plants and those without white root tips. Do not water less severely affected plants until the soil is barely moist. Then follow the instructions on watering given on page 923. Prevent the problem by using a light soil with good drainage.

Nitrogen-deficient Swedish ivy plant.

PROBLEM: The oldest leaves—usually the lower leaves—turn yellow and may drop. Yellowing starts at the leaf margins and progresses inward without producing a distinct pattern. The yellowing may progress upward until only the newest leaves remain green. Growth is slow, new leaves are small, and the whole plant may be stunted.

ANALYSIS: Nitrogen deficiency
Nitrogen is a nutrient that is used by the plant in many ways, including the production of chlorophyll (the green pigment in leaves and stems). Nitrogen is used in large amounts by the plant. When there is not enough nitrogen for the entire plant, it is taken from the older leaves for use in new growth. Nitrogen is easily leached from soil during regular watering. Of all the plant nutrients, it is the one most likely to be lacking in the soil.

SOLUTION: Spray the leaves with Ra-Pid-Gro Plant Food for a quick response. Fertilize houseplants with ORTHO House Plant Food, ORTHO Fish Emulsion Fertilizer, or ORTHO Ortho-Gro Liquid Plant Food. Add the fertilizer at regular intervals, as recommended on the label.

Iron-deficient piggyback plant.

PROBLEM: Newer leaves turn yellow at the margins. The yellowing progresses inward, so that in the advanced stages the last tissues to lose their green color are those immediately surrounding the veins. This condition may gradually work down the plant a short distance, but only rarely is the whole plant affected. The plant may be stunted.

ANALYSIS: Iron deficiency
This is a common problem with acid-loving plants, which grow best in soil with a pH between 5.5 and 6.5. (For more information on soil acidity, see page 908.) The yellowing is due to a deficiency of iron in the plant. The soil is seldom deficient in iron. However, when the soil pH is 7.0 or higher, iron is found in a less soluble form that is not available to some plants. Plants use iron in the formation of the green pigment (chlorophyll) in the leaves. When it is lacking, the new leaves become yellow.

SOLUTION: Spray the foliage with ORTHO Greenol Liquid Iron 6.13% and apply it to the soil in the pot to correct iron deficiency. Use acid-forming fertilizers, such as ORTHO Azalea, Camellia & Rhododendron Food. When planting or transplanting acid-loving plants, use an acidic soil mix that contains at least 50 percent peat moss. Use a minimum amount of lime or dolomite in the soil mix.

Leaf drop on zebra plant.

PROBLEM: Plants fail to grow well. Leaves may be lighter green and smaller than normal. Lobes and splits that are normal in leaves may fail to develop. Lower leaves may yellow and drop. Stems and leaf stalks may elongate and be spindly and weak. Plants grow toward a light source. Flowering plants fail to produce flowers, and plants with colorful foliage become pale. Variegated plants may lose their variegation and become green.

ANALYSIS: Insufficient light
Plants use light as a source of energy, and grow slowly in light that is too dim for their needs. If most of the available light is coming from one direction, stems and leaves bend in that direction. If the light is much too dim, plants grow poorly. Although foliage plants generally need less light than plants grown for their flowers or fruit, plants with colorful foliage need abundant light.

SOLUTION: Move the plant to a brighter location. The brightest spots in most homes are the sills of windows that face east, west, or south, or locations as close to a window as possible. To avoid sunburn on sensitive plants, close lightweight curtains when the sun shines directly on the plant. If not enough light is available, supply extra light. (For information about supplemental light for plant growth, see page 920.) Move plants from one location to another until you find a place where they grow well. For a list of plants that tolerate dim light, see page 990.

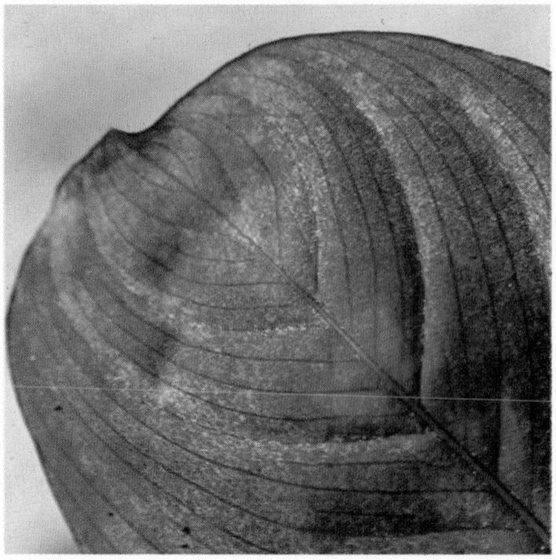

Spider mite damage to prayer plant.

PROBLEM: Leaves are stippled, yellowing, and dirty. Leaves may dry out and drop. There may be webbing over flower buds, between leaves, or on the lower surfaces of the leaves. To determine if a plant is infested wth mites, hold a sheet of white paper underneath an affected leaf and tap the leaf sharply. Minute green, red, or yellow specks the size of pepper grains will drop to the paper and begin to crawl around. The pests are easily seen against the white background.

ANALYSIS: Spider mites
These mites, related to spiders, are major pests of many houseplants. They cause damage by sucking sap from the undersides of the leaves. As a result of feeding, the green pigment disappears, producing the stippled appearance. Under warm, dry conditions, which favor mites, they can build up to tremendous numbers. For more information about spider mites, see page 887.

SOLUTION: Spray infested plants with ORTHO House Plant Insect Control, ORTHO House Plant Insect Killer, or ORTHO Whitefly & Mealybug Killer. (For instructions on spraying houseplants, see page 921.) Plants need to be sprayed weekly for several weeks to kill the mites as they hatch from the eggs. To avoid introducing mites into your house, inspect newly purchased plants carefully.

PROBLEMS COMMON TO MANY HOUSEPLANTS

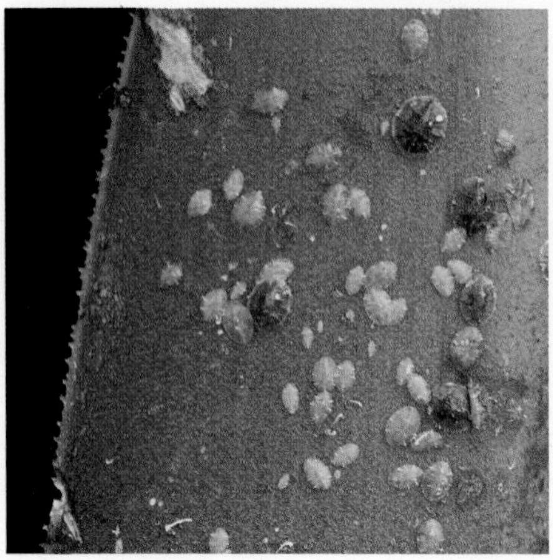
Scale on dracaena (life size).

PROBLEM: Nodes, stems, and leaves are covered with white, cottony, cushion-like masses or brown crusty bumps or clusters of somewhat flattened reddish, gray, or brown scaly bumps. The bumps can be scraped or picked off easily. Leaves turn yellow and may drop. A shiny or sticky material may cover the leaves.

ANALYSIS: Scale insects
Several different types of scale insects attack houseplants. Some types can infest many different plants. Scales hatch from eggs. The young, called *crawlers*, are small (about 1/10 inch), soft-bodied, and move about on the plant and to other plants. After moving about for a short time, they insert their mouthparts into the plant, withdrawing the sap. The legs usually atrophy, and the scales remain in the same area for the rest of their lives. Some develop a soft covering over their bodies, while others develop a hard covering. Some species of scales are unable to digest fully all the sugar in the plant sap, and excrete the excess in a fluid called honeydew, which may cover the leaves or drip onto surfaces below. For more information about scales, see pages 876 to 877.

SOLUTION: Spray with ORTHO Whitefly & Mealybug Killer, ORTHO House Plant Insect Killer, or ORTHO House Plant Insect Control. Spraying is more effective against the crawlers than against adults. Repeated applications may be necessary.

Aphids on ivy (half life size).

PROBLEM: Leaves are curling, discolored, and reduced in size. A shiny or sticky substance may coat the leaves. Tiny (1/8 inch) nonwinged, green soft-bodied insects cluster on the buds, young stems, and leaves.

ANALYSIS: Aphids
Aphids do little damage in small numbers. However, they are extremely prolific and populations can rapidly build up to damaging numbers on houseplants. Damage occurs when the aphid sucks the juices from the leaves. The aphid is unable to digest fully all the sugar in the plant sap and excretes the excess in a fluid called honeydew, which often drops onto leaves below. Any furniture below the plants may be coated with honeydew. For more information about aphids, see page 875.

SOLUTION: Use ORTHO House Plant Insect Control, ORTHO House Plant Insect Killer, or ORTHO Whitefly & Mealybug Killer. Check the labels for directions and for plants on which these products can be used. Spray houseplants according to directions given on page 921.

Root mealybugs (twice life size).

PROBLEM: White, cottony or waxy masses are found on the stem and roots at or just below the soil surface. Some of these masses may also be on the aboveground portions of the plant. Small (1/16 inch long), white insects that look like grains of rice may be in the soil around the roots and stem. The plant may grow slowly and wilt easily, and the leaves may turn yellow. Severely infested plants may die.

ANALYSIS: Root mealybugs
Several species of this common insect feed exclusively on plant roots, while others feed on leaves and aboveground stems as well. Root mealybugs feed on the fine root hairs and can go unnoticed for long periods. Root-feeding mealybugs weaken the plant, so when it is stressed from lack of water or fertilizer, it may readily decline and die. Root mealybugs infest African violets and many other houseplants.

SOLUTION: Drench infested plants with an insecticide containing *malathion*. Make sure your plant is listed on the product label. Place the insecticide solution in a pail and dip the pot and soil, as well as the stem and foliage if infested, in the solution. Keep the plant immersed for several minutes. Add a few drops of a spreader-sticker to the insecticide for better control. For more information about spreader-stickers, see page 922. Repeat the treatment in 2 weeks. Inspect the plant monthly and retreat if infestion recurs. (Follow the directions on page 181 for control of mealybugs on stems and foliage.)

Citrus mealybugs on coleus (twice life size).

Longtailed mealybugs (twice life size).

PROBLEM: White cottony or waxy insects are on the undersides of the leaves, on the stems, and particularly in the crotches or where leaves are attached. The insects tend to congregate, giving a cottony appearance. Cottony masses that contain eggs of the insects may also be present. A sticky substance may cover the leaves or drop onto surfaces below the plant. Infested plants are unsightly, do not grow well, and may die if severely infested.

ANALYSIS: Mealybugs

Mealybugs are one of the more serious problems of houseplants. There are many different types of mealybugs and virtually all houseplants are attacked by one or more of these insects. Female mealybugs have soft bodies that appear to have segments, and are covered with waxy secretions, giving them a cottony appearance. The female may produce live young or may deposit hundreds of yellow to orange eggs in white cottony egg sacs. The young insects, called *nymphs,* crawl about the same plant or to nearby plants. Males do no damage because they do not feed and are short-lived. Female mealybugs feed by sucking sap from the plant. They take in more than they can use, and excrete the excess in a sugary fluid called honeydew, which coats the leaves and may drop to surfaces below the plant. This fluid may mar finished furniture. For more information about mealybugs, see page 876.

SOLUTION: Control of mealybugs on houseplants is difficult. Spray with ORTHO Whitefly and Mealybug Killer, ORTHO House Plant Insect Killer, or ORTHO House Plant Insect Control. Make sure your plant is listed on the product label. For information on spraying houseplants, see page 921. Repeat applications at intervals of 2 weeks and continue for a little while after it appears that the mealybugs have been controlled. The waxy coverings on the insects and on the egg sacs, and the tendency of the insects to group together, protect them from insecticides. If only a few mealybugs are present, wipe them off with a damp cloth, or use cotton swabs dipped in rubbing alcohol. Carefully check all parts of the plant to make sure all insects are removed. Search for egg sacs under the rims or bottoms of pots, in cracks or on the undersides of shelves, and on brackets or hangers. Wipe off any sacs; they are a constant source of new insects. Discard severely infested plants, and avoid taking cuttings from such plants. The growing area should be thoroughly cleaned with soapy water before starting new plants. Be on a constant vigil for mealybugs, and start control measures immediately if they appear. Inspect new plants thoroughly before putting them in the house.

Greenhouse whiteflies (twice life size).

PROBLEM: Tiny, winged insects 1/12 inch long feed mainly on the undersides of the leaves. The insects are covered with white waxy powder. When the plant is touched, insects flutter rapidly around it. Leaves may be mottled and yellow.

ANALYSIS: Greenhouse whitefly

(*Trialeurodes vaporariorum*)

This insect is a common pest of many houseplants. The four-winged adult lays eggs on the undersides of leaves. The larvae are the size of a pinhead, flat, oval, and semitransparent, with white waxy filaments radiating from the body. They feed for about a month before changing to the adult form. Both the larval and adult forms suck sap from the leaves. The larvae are more damaging because they feed more heavily. Adults and larvae cannot fully digest all the sugar in the sap, and excrete the excess in a fluid called honeydew, which coats the leaves and may drop from the plant. For more information about whiteflies, see page 877.

SOLUTION: Spray with ORTHO Whitefly & Mealybug Killer, ORTHO House Plant Insect Killer, or ORTHO House Plant Insect Control. Make sure your plant is listed on the product label. For instructions on spraying houseplants, see page 921. Spray weekly as long as the problem continues. Remove heavily infested leaves.

PROBLEMS COMMON TO MANY HOUSEPLANTS

Springtails (3 times life size).

PROBLEM: Tiny white to gray or bluish gray insects less than ⅕ inch long are found in the soil of potted plants or in the saucer underneath. They may be seen crawling rapidly on the soil or hopping up to several inches in the air when disturbed.

ANALYSIS: Springtails *(Collembola)*
These creatures can build up to enormous numbers in soil, particularly if the soil is moist and has a high content of organic matter. They mainly feed on various kinds of decaying plant matter such as peat moss, compost and leaf mold. Springtails seldom damage mature houseplants, but do chew on seedlings and occasionally feed on other plant parts in close contact with the ground. Usually springtails are more of a curiosity, and a nuisance when numerous, than a cause for alarm. Springtails should not be confused with symphylans, centipedes, or millipedes which also may occur in soil. These other creatures have many legs and cannot jump. Springtails have only three pairs of legs.

SOLUTION: Springtails cannot live in dry soil. Water plants less often and drain the saucer below the plant to kill springtails. If springtails persist, take plants outside and treat the soil with an insecticide containing *diazinon.*

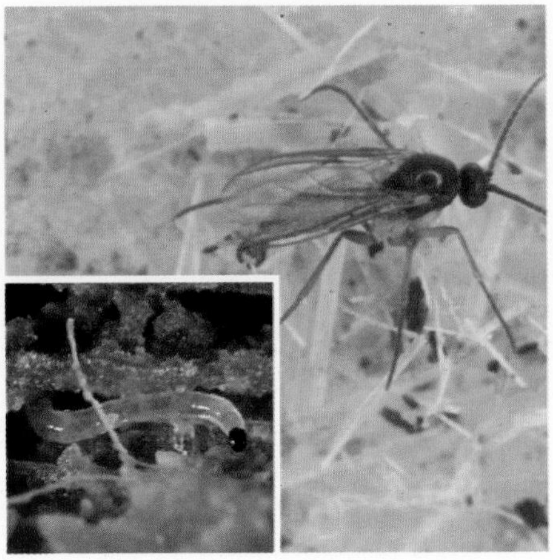

Fungus gnat. *Insert:* Larva (10 times life size).

PROBLEM: Small (up to ⅛ inch), slender, dark insects fly around when plants are disturbed. They frequently run across the foliage and soil, and may also be found on windows. Roots may be damaged, and seedlings may die.

ANALYSIS: Fungus gnats
These insects are small flies that do little damage but are unpleasant if present in large numbers. They lay their eggs in soil that contains organic material. After a week the eggs hatch, and the larvae crawl through the upper layer of the soil. The larvae are white, ¼ inch long, and have black heads. They feed on fungi that grow on organic matter. The larvae usually do not damage plants but, when present in large numbers, may feed on the roots of some plants, killing very young seedlings. The larvae feed for about 2 weeks before maturing into adults. There can be many generations in 1 year.

SOLUTION: Spray with an insecticide containing *diazinon* according to the instructions on page 921. Repeated applications may be necessary. Keep doors and windows closed to keep fungus gnats out.

PROBLEMS OF INDIVIDUAL HOUSEPLANTS

This section is arranged alphabetically by the botanical name of each plant. If you are not familiar with the botanical name of your plant, check the index on page 176.

ACHIMENES

Water spots.

PROBLEM: Small, light tan to reddish brown, somewhat angular spots appear on the upper surfaces of the leaves. These spots are scattered, and are found most frequently on the older leaves.

ANALYSIS: Water spots
Members of the African violet family, including achimenes, are very sensitive to rapid temperature changes. This most commonly occurs when cold tap water contacts the leaves during watering. If chilling occurs in the presence of light, the chlorophyll (the green pigment in plants) is broken down. In this plant family, all of the chlorophyll is found in a single layer of cells near the upper leaf surface. If the chlorophyll is broken down, the green color disappears. In achimenes, the leaf tissue of different varieties varies in color, but these colors are masked by the green chlorophyll. When the chlorophyll disappears, the underlying color of the tissue becomes apparent.

SOLUTION: The spots cannot be removed. Pick off unsightly leaves. Prevent new spots by being careful not to splash water on the leaves when watering. Or use tepid water, which will not spot the leaves.

Achimenes cultural information
Light: Needs bright light
Water: When the soil surface is moist but not wet

AESCHYNANTHUS (LIPSTICK PLANT)

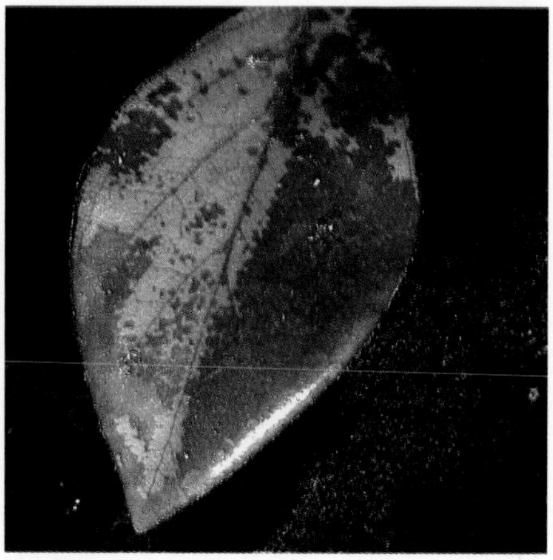

Water spots.

PROBLEM: Small tan to brown spots appear on the upper surfaces of the leaves. Spots are not found on the newest leaves.

ANALYSIS: Water spots
Members of the African violet family, including lipstick plant, are very sensitive to rapid temperature changes. Water spots occur most commonly when cold water is splashed on the leaves while the plant is being watered. If this happens in the presence of light, the green pigment (chlorophyll) is destroyed. In this plant family, all of the chlorophyll in the leaves is found in a single layer of cells near the upper surface. If the chlorophyll in that layer is broken down, the green color disappears and the color of the underlying leaf tissue is exposed.

SOLUTION: The spots cannot be removed. Pick off unsightly leaves. Prevent new spots by being careful not to splash water on the leaves when watering. Or use tepid water, which will not spot the leaves.

Aeschynanthus cultural information
Light: Needs bright light
Water: When the soil is moist but not wet

AGLAONEMA (CHINESE EVERGREEN)

Root rot.

PROBLEM: Plants fail to grow, and the lower leaves may turn yellow, wilt, and die. An area of dead tissue may be found on the main stem just at the soil line. Many of the roots are brown, mushy, and easily detached. For information on inspecting roots, see page 921. Infected plants may die.

ANALYSIS: Root and stem rot
This plant disease is caused by any of several soil-dwelling fungi, also known as *water molds* (see page 849 for more information about *water molds*). *Rhizoctonia solani* may attack portions of the main stem and form brown, sunken areas. The fungus may girdle the stem, causing the portion above to die. *Rhizoctonia* and *Pythium* species may attack the roots, turning them brown and mushy, with dark tips. If the roots are severely damaged or killed, they cannot supply the plant with moisture and nutrients.

SOLUTION: If the plant is only mildly affected, let the soil dry out between waterings. For more information on this technique, see page 919. If the soil mix is heavy, or the container does not drain well, transplant the plant into a container that drains freely. Use a well-drained soil mix. For information on soil mixes, see page 920. If stem or root rot occurs but the top of the plant is still vigorous, cut it off above the diseased area and root it according to instructions on 921. Discard severely infected plants and the soil in which they grew. Wash the pots thoroughly, and soak them in a mixture of 1 part household bleach to 9 parts water for 30 minutes. Rinse with plain water and dry thoroughly before reuse.

AGLAONEMA (CHINESE EVERGREEN) ■ ANTHURIUM

Mealybugs (half life size).

PROBLEM: Oval, white insects up to ¼ inch long cluster in white, cottony masses on leaves, stems, and in the crotches where branches or leaves are attached. A sticky material may coat the leaves. Leaves may be spotted or deformed. When the condition is severe, leaves and plants may wither and die.

ANALYSIS: Mealybugs
Several species of this common insect feed on Chinese evergreen. Mealybugs damage plants by sucking sap, causing leaf distortion and death. The adult female mealybug may produce live young, or may lay eggs in a white fluffy mass of wax. The immature mealybugs, called *nymphs*, crawl all over the plant and onto nearby plants. Soon after they begin to feed, they produce white waxy filaments that cover their bodies, giving them a cottony appearance. As they mature, they become less mobile. Mealybugs cannot digest all the sugar in the sap and excrete the excess in a fluid called honeydew, which coats the leaves and may drop onto furniture below the plant. For additional information on mealybugs, see page 181.

SOLUTION: Spray infested plants with an insecticide containing *diazinon*. For instructions on spraying houseplants, see page 921. Where practical, wipe mealybugs off the plant with a damp cloth or with cotton swabs dipped in alcohol. Avoid bringing mealybugs into the house by carefully inspecting new plants.

Aglaonema cultural information
Light: Tolerates dim light
Water: When the soil just below the surface is barely moist

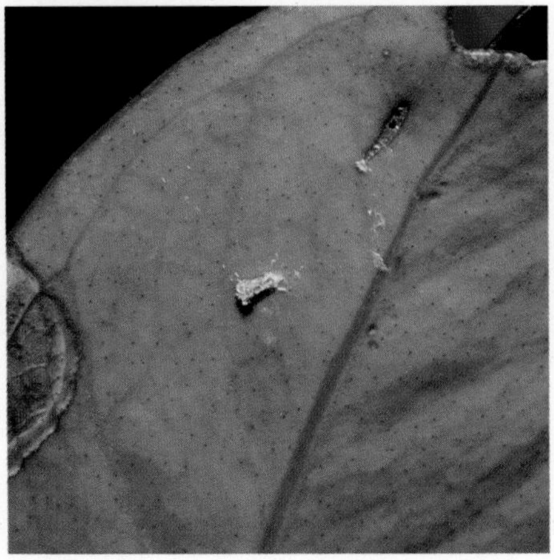
Mealybugs (twice life size).

PROBLEM: Oval, white insects up to ¼ inch long cluster in white, cottony masses on leaves, stems, and in the crotches where the leaves are attached. A sticky material may coat the leaves. Leaves may be spotted or deformed. When the condition is severe, leaves and plants may wither and die.

ANALYSIS: Mealybugs
Several species of this common insect feed on anthurium. Mealybugs damage plants by sucking sap, causing leaf distortion and death. The adult female mealybug may produce live young, or may lay eggs in a white fluffy mass of wax. The immature mealybugs, called *nymphs*, crawl all over the plant and onto nearby plants. Soon after they begin to feed, they produce white waxy filaments that cover their bodies, giving them a cottony appearance. As they mature, they become less mobile. Mealybugs cannot digest all the sugar in the sap and excrete the excess in a fluid called honeydew, which coats the leaves and may drop onto furniture below the plant. For additional information on mealybugs, see 181.

SOLUTION: Spray infested plants with an insecticide containing *diazinon*. (For instructions on spraying houseplants, see page 921.) Where practical, wipe mealybugs off the plant with a damp cloth or with cotton swabs dipped in alcohol. Inspect the pot, including the bottom, for mealybug egg masses. Wipe these off. Avoid bringing mealybugs into the house by carefully inspecting new plants.

Spider mites (life size).

PROBLEM: Leaves are stippled, yellow, and dirty; they may dry out and drop. There may be webbing between leaves or on the lower surfaces of the leaves. To determine if a plant is infested with mites, hold a sheet of white paper underneath an affected plant and tap the leaves sharply. Minute green, red, or yellow specks the size of pepper grains will drop to the paper and begin to crawl around. The pests are easily seen against the white background.

ANALYSIS: Spider mites
These mites, related to spiders, are major pests of many houseplants, including anthurium. They cause damage by sucking sap from the undersides of the leaves. As a result of this feeding the green pigment (chlorophyll) disappears, causing the stippled appearance. Under warm, dry conditions, which favor mites, they can build up to tremendous numbers. For more information about spider mites, see 887.

SOLUTION: Spray infested plants with ORTHO House Plant Insect Control. (For instructions on spraying houseplants, see page 921.) Plants need to be sprayed weekly for several weeks to kill the mites as they hatch. To avoid introducing mites, inspect new plants carefully.

Anthurium cultural information
Light: Needs bright light
Water: When the soil surface is moist but not wet

APHELANDRA (ZEBRA PLANT)

Root rot.

PROBLEM: Plants fail to grow. Leaves or the whole plant may wilt and die. Examination of the rootball (as described on page 921) shows the roots are brown and mushy. When the disease is severe, all of the roots are rotted, and the plant can be lifted easily from the soil.

ANALYSIS: Root rot
This plant disease is caused by any of several soil-dwelling fungi, also known as *water molds* (see 849 for more information about *water molds*). These fungi, including *Pythium* species or *Rhizoctonia solani*, are favored by wet, poorly drained soils. Anthuriums grow best with excellent drainage; although they need lots of water, the soil mix should drain quickly.

SOLUTION: If the plant is only mildly affected, let the soil dry out between waterings. For more information on this technique, see 849. If the soil mix is heavy, or the container does not drain well, transplant the plant into a container that drains freely. Use a well-drained soil mix. For information on soil mixes, see page 920. If stem or root rot occurs but the top of the plant is still vigorous, cut it off above the diseased area and root it according to instructions on page 921. Discard severely infected plants and the soil in which they grew. Wash the pots thoroughly, and soak them in a mixture of 1 part household bleach to 9 parts water for 30 minutes. Rinse with plain water and dry thoroughly before reuse. Or, pasteurize the pots according to the directions on page 920.

Sunburn.

PROBLEM: Leaves that are exposed to sunlight become yellow between the veins, and may die and turn brown. The brown areas may have a silver cast. If the condition is severe, the dead areas may coalesce and large areas may be affected.

ANALYSIS: Sunburn
Aphelandra grows best in very bright, indirect light. When exposed to direct sunlight, it may burn. Sunburn causes the affected tissues to lose their green color between the veins then die and turn brown. Plants that are allowed to dry out are more susceptible to sunburn than those that are given adequate water.

SOLUTION: Move the plant to a location that receives bright indirect light. Or cut down the light intensity by closing the curtains when the plant is exposed to direct sun. Prune off badly damaged leaves, or trim away damaged leaf areas to improve the plant's appearance. Keep plants well watered. For more information about watering, see page 919.

Aphelandra cultural information
Light: Needs bright light
Water: When the soil surface is moist but not wet

Salt damage.

PROBLEM: Margins of older leaves die and turn brown. The brown tissues are brittle. When the condition is severe, all leaves may have dead margins. Tissue adjacent to the dead margins of older leaves may turn yellow.

ANALYSIS: Salt damage
Aphelandra is sensitive to excess salts. Soluble salts are picked up by the roots and accumulate in the leaf margins, where concentrations may be high enough to kill the tissue. Salts can accumulate from water or from the use of fertilizers, or they may be present in the soil used in potting. Salts accumulate more rapidly and do more harm if the plant is not watered thoroughly.

SOLUTION: Leach excess salts from the soil by flushing with water. Water the plant at least three times, letting the water drain each time. This is done most easily in a bathtub or laundry sink, or outside. Always water aphelandra from the top of the pot. Enough water should be added at each watering that some of the water drains through the pot. Empty the saucer after the pot has finished draining. If the plant is too large to handle easily, use a turkey baster to remove the drainage water. For additional watering instructions, see page 919.

APHELANDRA (ZEBRA PLANT)

Mealybugs (half life size).

PROBLEM: Oval, white insects up to ¼ inch long cluster in white, cottony masses on leaves, stems, and in the crotches where the leaves are attached. A sticky material may coat the leaves. Leaves may be spotted or deformed. When the condition is severe, leaves and plants may wither and die.

ANALYSIS: Mealybugs
Several species of this common insect feed on zebra plants. Mealybugs damage plants by sucking sap, causing leaf distortion and death. The adult female mealybug may produce live young, or may lay eggs in a white fluffy mass of wax. The immature mealybugs, called *nymphs*, crawl all over the plant and onto nearby plants. Soon after they begin to feed, they produce white waxy filaments that cover their bodies, giving them a cottony appearance. As they mature, they become less mobile. Mealybugs cannot digest all the sugar in the sap and excrete the excess in a fluid called honeydew, which coats the leaves and may drop onto furniture below the plant. For additional information on mealybugs, see page 181.

SOLUTION: Spray infested plants with ORTHO Whitefly & Mealybug Killer, ORTHO House Plant Insect Killer, or ORTHO House Plant Insect Control. (For instructions on spraying houseplants, see page 921.) Where practical, wipe mealybugs off the plant with a damp cloth or with cotton swabs dipped in alcohol. Inspect the pot, including the bottom, for mealybug masses. Wipe these off. Avoid bringing mealybugs into the house by carefully inspecting new plants.

ARALIA (FATSIA)

Scale (half life size).

PROBLEM: Stems and leaves are covered with white, cottony, cushionlike masses or brown crusty bumps. The bumps can be scraped or picked off easily. Leaves turn yellow and may drop. A shiny or sticky material may cover leaves and stems.

ANALYSIS: Scale insects
Several different types of scale insects attack aralia. Scales hatch from eggs. The young, called *crawlers*, are small (about 1/10 inch), soft-bodied, and move about on the plant and onto other plants. After moving about for a short time, they insert their mouthparts into the plant, feeding on the sap. The legs disappear, and the scales remain in the same place for the rest of their lives. Some develop a soft covering, others a hard covering. Some species of scales are unable to digest fully all the sugar in the plant sap and excrete the excess in a fluid called honeydew, which may cover the leaves or drip onto surfaces below. For more information about scales, see page 876.

SOLUTION: Spray infested plants indoors with ORTHO Whitefly & Mealybug Killer, ORTHO House Plant Insect Killer, or ORTHO House Plant Insect Control; or take the plants outside and spray them with ORTHO Isotox Insect Killer according to the directions on the label. Repeated applications may be necessary. For additional information on spraying houseplants, see page 921.

Aralia cultural information
Light: Needs medium light
Water: When the soil just below the surface is barely moist

Mealybugs (half life size).

PROBLEM: Oval, white insects up to ¼ inch long cluster in white, cottony masses on leaves, stems, and in the crotches where branches or leaves are attached. A sticky material may coat the leaves. Leaves may be spotted or deformed. When the condition is severe, leaves and plants may wither and die.

ANALYSIS: Mealybugs
Several species of this common insect feed on aralia. Mealybugs damage plants by sucking sap, causing leaf distortion and death. The adult female mealybug may produce live young, or may lay eggs in a white fluffy mass of wax. The immature mealybugs, called *nymphs*, crawl all over the plant and onto nearby plants. Soon after they begin to feed, they produce white waxy filaments that cover their bodies, giving them a cottony appearance. As they mature, they become less mobile. Mealybugs cannot digest all the sugar in the sap and excrete the excess in a fluid called honeydew, which coats the leaves and may drop onto furniture below the plant. For additional information on mealybugs, see page 181.

SOLUTION: Spray infested plants indoors with ORTHO Whitefly & Mealybug Killer, ORTHO House Plant Insect Killer, or ORTHO House Plant Insect Control; or take the plants outside and spray them with ORTHO Isotox Insect Killer. (For instructions on spraying houseplants, see page 921.) Where practical, wipe mealybugs off the plant with a damp cloth or with cotton swabs dipped in alcohol. Inspect the pot, including the bottom, for mealybug egg masses. Wipe these off. Avoid bringing mealybugs into the house by carefully inspecting new plants.

ARAUCARIA (NORFOLK ISLAND PINE)

Scale (4 times life size).

Mealybug (twice life size).

PROBLEM: Stems and needles are covered with white, cottony, cushionlike masses or brown crusty bumps. The bumps can be scraped or picked off easily. Needles turn yellow and may drop. A shiny or sticky material may cover leaves and stems.

ANALYSIS: Scale insects
Several different types of scale insects attack Norfolk Island pine. Some types can infest many different plants. Scales hatch from eggs. The young, called *crawlers*, are small (about 1/10 inch), soft-bodied, and move about on the plant and onto other plants. After moving about for a short time, they insert their mouthparts into the plant, feeding on the sap. The legs disappear, and the scales remain in the same place for the rest of their lives. Some develop a soft covering, others a hard covering. Some species of scales are unable to digest fully all the sugar in the plant sap and excrete the excess in a fluid called honeydew, which may cover the leaves or drip onto surfaces below. For more information on scales, see page 876.

SOLUTION: Spray infested plants with an insecticide containing *malathion*. Spraying is more effective against the crawlers than against the adults. Repeated applications may be necessary. For additional information on spraying houseplants, see page 921.

Araucaria cultural information
Light: Tolerates dim light
Water: When the soil just below the surface is barely moist

PROBLEM: Oval, white insects up to 1/4 inch long cluster in white, cottony masses on needles, stems, and in the crotches where the branches are attached. A sticky material may coat the needles. Growth may be deformed. When the condition is severe, plants may die.

ANALYSIS: Mealybugs
Several species of this common insect feed on Norfolk Island pine. Mealybugs damage plants by sucking sap, causing leaf distortion and death. The adult female mealybug may produce live young, or may lay eggs in a white fluffy mass of wax. The immature mealybugs, called *nymphs*, crawl all over the plant and onto nearby plants. Soon after they begin to feed, they produce white waxy filaments that cover their bodies, giving them a cottony appearance. As they mature, they become less mobile. Mealybugs cannot digest all the sugar in the plant sap and excrete the excess in a fluid called honeydew, which coats the plant and may drop onto furniture below. For additional information on mealybugs, see page 181.

SOLUTION: Spray infested plants with an insecticide containing *malathion*. (For instructions on spraying houseplants, see page 921.) Where practical, wipe mealybugs off the plant with a damp cloth or with cotton swabs dipped in alcohol. Inspect the pot, including the bottom, for mealybug egg masses. Wipe these off. Avoid bringing mealybugs into the house by carefully inspecting new plants.

ASPARAGUS (ASPARAGUS FERN)

Weak stems.

PROBLEM: Leaves (which in asparagus are needlelike) turn pale green or yellow, beginning with the older leaves and progressing toward the tip of the stem. Yellow leaves may drop. Stems may be elongated and weak; sometimes they bend toward the light. Stems in the center of the plant may die and turn tan or brown.

ANALYSIS: Insufficient light
Plants use light as a source of energy, and grow slowly in light that is too dim for their needs. If most of the available light comes from one direction, the stems and leaves bend distinctly in that direction. If the light is much too dim, the plant has little energy and grows poorly. Although foliage plants generally need less light than plants grown for their flowers or fruit, asparagus fern has a relatively high need for light.

SOLUTION: Move the plant to a brighter location. Asparagus fern will tolerate direct sun if it is kept well watered. But if it is allowed to become dry while in direct sunlight, it will sunburn. (For more information on sunburn, see page 178.) If a brighter location is not available, provide supplemental lighting as described on page 920. If you wish to grow a houseplant in a dim location, select a plant that is tolerant of dim light from the list on page 990.

ASPARAGUS (ASPARAGUS FERN)

Scale (3 times life size).

PROBLEM: Stems and leaves are covered with white, cottony, cushionlike masses or brown crusty bumps. The bumps can be scraped or picked off easily. Leaves turn yellow and may drop. A shiny or sticky material may cover leaves and stems.

ANALYSIS: Scale insects
Several different types of scale insects attack asparagus fern. Some types can infest many different plants. Scales hatch from eggs. The young, called *crawlers*, are small (about 1/10 inch), soft-bodied, and move about on the plant and onto other plants. After moving about for a short time, they insert their mouthparts into the plant, feeding on the sap. The legs disappear, and the scales remain in the same place for the rest of their lives. Some develop a soft covering, others a hard covering. Some species of scales are unable to digest fully all the sugar in the plant sap and excrete the excess in a fluid called honeydew, which may cover the leaves or drip onto surfaces below. For more information about scales, see page 876.

SOLUTION: Spray with ORTHO Whitefly & Mealybug Killer, ORTHO House Plant Insect Killer, or ORTHO House Plant Insect Control. Spraying is more effective against the crawlers than against the adults. Repeated applications may be necessary. For additional information on spraying houseplants, see page 921.

Asparagus cultural information
Light: Needs bright light
Water: When the soil just below the surface is dry

Mealybugs (life size).

PROBLEM: Oval, white insects up to 1/4 inch long cluster in white, cottony masses on leaves, stems, and in the crotches where the leaves are attached. A sticky material may coat the leaves. Leaves may be spotted or deformed. When the condition is severe, leaves and plants may wither and die.

ANALYSIS: Mealybugs
Several species of this common insect feed on asparagus fern. Mealybugs damage plants by sucking sap, causing leaf distortion and death. The adult female mealybug may produce live young, or may lay eggs in a white fluffy mass of wax. The immature mealybugs, called *nymphs*, crawl all over the plant and onto nearby plants. Soon after they begin to feed, they produce white waxy filaments that cover their bodies, giving them a cottony appearance. As they mature, they become less mobile. Mealybugs cannot digest all the sugar in the sap and excrete the excess in a fluid called honeydew, which coats the leaves and may drop onto furniture below the plant. For additional information on mealybugs, see page 181.

SOLUTION: Spray infested plants with ORTHO Whitefly & Mealybug Killer, ORTHO House Plant Insect Killer, or ORTHO House Plant Insect Control. (For instructions on spraying houseplants, see page 921.) Where practical, wipe mealybugs off the plant with a damp cloth or with cotton swabs dipped in alcohol. Inspect the pot, including the bottom, for mealybug egg masses. Wipe these off. Avoid bringing mealybugs into the house by carefully inspecting new plants.

AVOCADO

Greenhouse whiteflies (life size).

PROBLEM: Tiny, winged insects 1/12 inch long feed on the undersides of the leaves. The insects are covered with white waxy powder. When the plant is touched, insects flutter rapidly around it. Leaves may be mottled and yellowing.

ANALYSIS: Greenhouse whitefly
(*Trialeurodes vaporariorum*)
This insect is a common pest of avocado. The four-winged adult lays eggs on the undersides of leaves. The larvae are the size of a pinhead, flat, oval, immobile, and semitransparent, with radiating white waxy filaments. In about a month, they change to the winged adult form. The larvae are more damaging because they suck more sap from the plants than do the adults. They cannot digest all the sugar in the sap they remove, and excrete the excess in a sugary material called honeydew, which coats the leaves and may drop from the plant onto furniture below.

SOLUTION: Spray with ORTHO House Plant Insect Control. Spray weekly as long as the problem continues. Remove heavily infested leaves. If only a few leaves are infested, wipe off larvae with a damp cloth.

BEGONIA

Mealybugs (half life size).

PROBLEM: Oval, white insects up to ¼ inch long cluster in white, cottony masses on leaves, stems, and in the crotches where branches or leaves are attached. A sticky material may coat the leaves. Leaves may be spotted or deformed. When the condition is severe, leaves and plants may wither and die.

ANALYSIS: Mealybugs
Several species of this common insect feed on avocado plants. Mealybugs damage plants by sucking sap, causing leaf distortion and death. The adult female mealybug may produce live young, or may lay eggs in a white fluffy mass of wax. The immature mealybugs, called *nymphs*, crawl all over the plant and onto nearby plants. Soon after they begin to feed, they produce white waxy filaments that cover their bodies, giving them a cottony appearance. As they mature, they become less mobile. Mealybugs cannot digest all the sugar in the sap and excrete the excess in a fluid called honeydew, which coats the leaves and may drop onto furniture below the plant. For additional information on mealybugs, see page 181.

SOLUTION: Spray infested plants with an insecticide containing *malathion*. Where practical, wipe mealybugs off the plant with a damp cloth or with cotton swabs dipped in alcohol. Inspect the pot, including the bottom, for mealybug egg masses. Wipe these off. Avoid bringing mealybugs into the house by carefully inspecting new plants.

Avocado cultural information
Light: Needs bright light
Water: When the soil just below the surface is barely moist

Sparse growth.

PROBLEM: Leaves fade to light green. In variegated varieties, the colors in the leaves become lighter and less intense. Stems become elongated and weak. Lower leaves may yellow and drop. Flowering varieties stop producing flowers.

ANALYSIS: Insufficient light
Plants use light as a source of energy, and grow slowly in light that is too dim for their needs. If most of the available light is coming from one direction, the stems and leaves bend distinctly in that direction. If the light is much too dim, the plant has little energy and grows poorly. Plants grown for their brightly colored leaves—or for their flowers—have a relatively high need for light.

SOLUTION: Move the plant to a brighter location, such as a lightly curtained sunny window. If a brighter location is not available, provide supplemental lighting as described on page 920. If you wish to grow a houseplant in a dim location, select a plant that is tolerant of dim light from the list on page 990.

Powdery mildew.

PROBLEM: White powdery patches appear on the leaves, stems, and flowers. Leaves may be covered with the powdery growth. This material usually appears first on older leaves and on the upper surfaces of the leaves. Tissue under the powdery growth may turn yellow or brown. Sometimes such leaves drop from the plant.

ANALYSIS: Powdery mildew
Powdery mildew on begonia is caused by a fungus (*Erysiphe cichoracearum*). The powdery patches on begonia are composed of fungus strands and spores. These spores are carried by air currents and are capable of infecting leaves, stems, and flowers of the same or nearby plants. The disease is favored by dim light and warm days with cool nights. Older leaves are more susceptible than new leaves. Plants in dry soil are more susceptible. Severe infections cause yellowing, browning, and leaf drop.

SOLUTION: Spray with a fungicide containing *dinocap*, *cycloheximide*, or *wettable sulfur*. For instructions on spraying houseplants, see page 915. Remove infected leaves. Move plants to locations with more light. Keep plants out of cool drafts and in rooms with temperatures as even as possible.

Begonia cultural information
Light: Needs bright light
Water: When the soil just below the surface is barely moist

BEGONIA

Mealybugs (half life size).

PROBLEM: Oval, white insects up to ¼ inch long cluster in white, cottony masses on leaves, stems, and in the crotches where the leaves are attached. A sticky material may coat the leaves. Leaves may be spotted or deformed. When the condition is severe, leaves and plants may wither and die.

ANALYSIS: Mealybugs
Several species of this common insect feed on begonias. Mealybugs damage plants by sucking sap, causing leaf distortion and death. The adult female mealybug may produce live young, or may lay eggs in a white fluffy mass of wax. The immature mealybugs, called *nymphs*, crawl all over the plant and onto nearby plants. Soon after they begin to feed, they produce white waxy filaments that cover their bodies, giving them a cottony appearance. As they mature, they become less mobile. Mealybugs cannot digest all the sugar in the sap and excrete the excess in a fluid called honeydew, which coats the leaves and may drop onto furniture below the plant. For additional information on mealybugs, see page 181.

SOLUTION: Spray infested plants with ORTHO Whitefly & Mealybug Killer, or ORTHO House Plant Insect Killer. Where practical, wipe mealybugs off the plant with a damp cloth or with cotton swabs dipped in alcohol. Inspect the pot, including the bottom, for mealybug egg masses. Wipe these off. Avoid bringing mealybugs into the house by carefully inspecting new plants.

Spider mite damage.

PROBLEM: Leaves are stippled, yellow, and dirty; they may dry out and drop. There may be webbing over flower buds, between leaves, or on the lower surfaces of the leaves. To determine if a plant is infested with mites, hold a sheet of white paper underneath an affected plant and tap the leaves sharply. Minute green, red, or yellow specks the size of pepper grains will drop to the paper and begin to crawl around. The pests are easily seen against the white background.

ANALYSIS: Spider mites
These mites, related to spiders, are major pests of many houseplants, including begonias. They cause damage by sucking sap from the undersides of the leaves. As a result of this feeding the green pigment (chlorophyll) disappears, causing the stippled appearance. Under warm, dry conditions, which favor mites, they can build up to tremendous numbers. For more information about spider mites, see page 887.

SOLUTION: Spray infested plants with ORTHO Whitefly & Mealybug Killer, ORTHO House Plant Insect Killer, or ORTHO House Plant Insect Control. (For instructions on spraying houseplants, see page 921.) Plants need to be sprayed weekly for several weeks to kill the mites as they hatch. To avoid introducing mites, inspect new plants carefully.

Scales (3 times life size).

PROBLEM: Stems and leaves are covered with white, cottony, cushionlike masses or brown crusty bumps. The bumps can be scraped or picked off easily. Leaves turn yellow and may drop. A shiny or sticky material may cover leaves and stems.

ANALYSIS: Scale insects
Several different types of scale insects attack begonias. Some types can infest many different plants. Scales hatch from eggs. The young, called *crawlers*, are small (about ⅒ inch), soft-bodied, and move about on the plant and onto other plants. After moving about for a short time, they insert their mouthparts into the plant, feeding on the sap. The legs disappear, and the scales remain in the same place for the rest of their lives. Some develop a soft covering, others a hard covering. Some species of scales are unable to digest fully all the sugar in the plant sap and excrete the excess in a fluid called honeydew, which may cover the leaves or drip onto surfaces below. For more information about scales, see page 876.

SOLUTION: Spray infested plants indoors with ORTHO Whitefly & Mealybug Killer or ORTHO House Plant Insect Killer, or take the plant outdoors and spray with ORTHO Orthene Systemic Insect Control. Spraying is more effective against the crawlers than against the adults. Repeated applications may be necessary. For additional information on spraying houseplants, see page 921.

BRASSAIA (SCHEFFLERA)

Whiteflies (life size).

PROBLEM: Tiny, winged insects 1⁄12 inch long feed on the undersides of the leaves. The insects are covered with white waxy powder. When the plant is touched, insects flutter rapidly around it. Leaves may be mottled and yellowing.

ANALYSIS: Greenhouse whitefly
(*Trialeurodes vaporariorum*)
This insect is a common pest of begonia. The four-winged adult lays eggs on the undersides of leaves. The larvae are the size of a pinhead, flat, oval, immobile, and semitransparent, with white waxy filaments radiating from the body. They feed for about a month before changing to the adult form. The larvae are more damaging because they suck more sap from the plants than do the adults. They cannot digest all the sugar in the sap they remove, and excrete the excess in a sugary material called honeydew, which coats the leaves and may drop from the plant.

SOLUTION: Spray with ORTHO Whitefly & Mealybug Killer or ORTHO House Plant Insect Killer. For instructions on spraying houseplants, see page 921. Spray weekly as long as the problem continues. Remove heavily infested leaves.

Root rot.

PROBLEM: Plants fail to grow. Lower leaves may turn yellow and drop. The roots are brown, soft, and mushy. When the condition is severe, no roots are found on the outside of the rootball, and plants may wilt and die. For information about examining the roots, see page 921.

ANALYSIS: Root and stem rot
This plant disease is caused by any of several soil-dwelling fungi (*Pythium* species) that are also known as *water molds*. (See page 849 for more information about *water molds.*) The fungi attack the roots, turning them brown and mushy with dark tips. The disease is usually an indication that the plant has been watered too frequently or that the soil mix is too heavy and does not drain well. The fungi are common in garden soils, but pasteurized soil or soilless potting mixes are free of them unless they are introduced on a plant or dirty pot, or transferred from another pot on dirty fingers. Root rot spreads quickly through a root system if the soil remains wet.

SOLUTION: If the plant is only mildly affected, let the soil dry out between waterings. For more information on this technique, see page 849. If the soil mix is heavy, or the container does not drain well, transplant the plant into a container that drains freely. Use a well-drained soil mix. For information on soil mixes, see page 920. Discard severely infected plants and the soil in which they grew. Wash the pots thoroughly, and soak them in a mixture of 1 part household bleach to 9 parts water for 30 minutes. Rinse with plain water and dry thoroughly before reuse. Or pasteurize the pots according to the directions on page 920.

Mealybugs (life size).

PROBLEM: Oval, white insects up to 1⁄4 inch long cluster in white, cottony masses on leaves, stems, and in the crotches where branches or leaves are attached. A sticky material may coat the leaves. Leaves may be spotted or deformed. When the condition is severe, leaves and plants may wither and die.

ANALYSIS: Mealybugs
Several species of this common insect feed on schefflera. Mealybugs damage plants by sucking sap, causing leaf distortion and death. The adult female mealybug may produce live young, or may lay eggs in a white fluffy mass of wax. The immature mealybugs, called *nymphs*, crawl all over the plant and onto nearby plants. Soon after they begin to feed, they produce white waxy filaments that cover their bodies, giving them a cottony appearance. As they mature, they become less mobile. Mealybugs cannot digest all the sugar in the sap and excrete the excess in a fluid called honeydew, which coats the leaves and may drop onto furniture below the plant. For additional information on mealybugs, see page 181.

SOLUTION: Spray infested plants indoors with ORTHO Whitefly & Mealybug Killer, ORTHO House Plant Insect Killer, or ORTHO House Plant Insect Control; or take the plants outside and spray them with ORTHO Orthene Systemic Insect Control or ORTHO Isotox Insect Killer. (For instructions on spraying houseplants, see page 921.) Where practical, wipe mealybugs off the plant with a damp cloth or with cotton swabs dipped in alcohol. Inspect the pot, including the bottom, for mealybug egg masses. Wipe these off. Avoid bringing mealybugs into the house by carefully inspecting new plants.

BRASSAIA (SCHEFFLERA)

Spider mite damage.

PROBLEM: Leaves are stippled, yellow, and dirty; they may dry out and drop. There may be webbing between leaves or on the lower surfaces of the leaves. To determine if a plant is infested with mites, hold a sheet of white paper underneath an affected plant and tap the leaves sharply. Minute green, red, or yellow specks the size of pepper grains will drop to the paper and begin to crawl around. The pests are easily seen against the white background.

ANALYSIS: Spider mites
These mites, related to spiders, are major pests of many houseplants, including schefflera. They cause damage by sucking sap from the undersides of the leaves. As a result of this feeding the green pigment (chlorophyll) disappears, causing the stippled appearance. Under warm, dry conditions, which favor mites, they can build up to tremendous numbers. For more information about spider mites, see page 887.

SOLUTION: Spray infested plants with ORTHO House Plant Insect Control, ORTHO Isotox Insect Killer, ORTHO House Plant Insect Killer, or ORTHO Whitefly & Mealybug Killer. (For instructions on spraying houseplants, see page 921.) Plants need to be sprayed weekly for several weeks to kill the mites as they hatch. To avoid introducing mites, inspect new plants carefully.

Brassaia cultural information
Light: Needs bright light
Water: When the soil just below the surface is dry

BROMELIADS

BROMELIADS

LIGHT: Bromeliads will tolerate considerable variation in light exposure. Because they are flowering plants, most do better in bright light. Some will tolerate dim light, and will flower under such conditions.

SOIL MIX: Plant in osmunda fiber, shredded fir bark, coarse sphagnum, lava rock, or any of these mixed with an equal amount of coarse sand.

FERTILIZER: Fertilize with ORTHO House Plant Food or ORTHO Ortho-Gro Liquid Plant Food once every 3 months. Fertilize plants growing in reduced light less frequently.

WATER:
How much: Add enough water so that some drains out the bottom of the pot. Most bromeliads have cupped leaves that form a vase and hold water. It is important to keep this vase filled. Flush out old water with fresh water.
How often: Water when the planting medium is dry. Do not let the pot stand in drainage water.

Overwatering damage.

PROBLEM: Plants fail to grow. Root development is poor and roots may rot. The whole plant can be lifted easily from the soil. The plant may die.

ANALYSIS: Heavy soil and overwatering
Most bromeliads that are grown as houseplants are epiphytes (plants that grow on other plants instead of in the ground). Because of this, their roots are usually exposed to the air and can't tolerate wet conditions for very long. If planted in heavy soil, or in soil that is too wet, water fills the spaces between the soil particles so that the roots can't get enough air and die.

SOLUTION: Grow bromeliads only in planting mixes that have exceptional drainage, such as coarse bark, lava rock, or osmunda fiber. Water the plants every day until the roots are established. After that, plants should be watered one or two times a week.

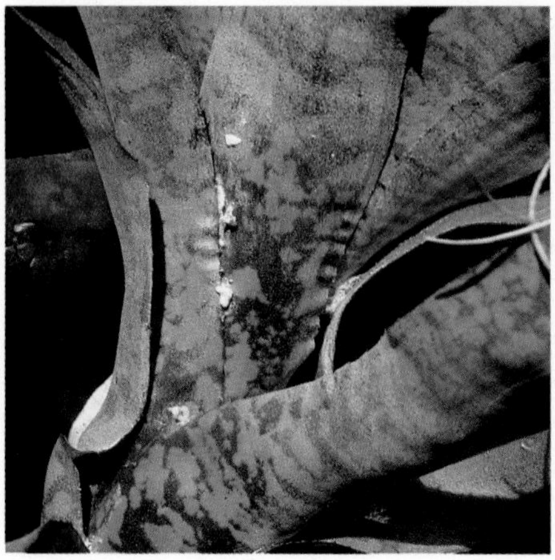
Mealybugs (⅓ life size).

PROBLEM: Oval, white insects up to ¼ inch long cluster in white, cottony masses on leaves, stems, and in the crotches where the leaves are attached. A sticky material may coat the leaves. Leaves may be spotted or deformed. When the condition is severe, leaves and plants may wither and die.

ANALYSIS: Mealybugs
Several species of this common insect feed on bromeliads. Mealybugs damage plants by sucking sap, causing leaf distortion and death. The adult female mealybug may produce live young, or may lay eggs in a white fluffy mass of wax. The immature mealybugs, called *nymphs*, crawl all over the plant and onto nearby plants. Soon after they begin to feed, they produce white waxy filaments that cover their bodies, giving them a cottony appearance. As they mature, they become less mobile. Mealybugs cannot digest all the sugar in the sap and excrete the excess in a fluid called honeydew, which coats the leaves and may drop onto furniture below the plant. For additional information on mealybugs, see page 181.

SOLUTION: Spray infested plants with an insecticide containing *diazinon*. (For instructions on spraying houseplants, see page 921.) Where practical, wipe mealybugs off the plant with a damp cloth or with cotton swabs dipped in alcohol. Inspect the pot, including the bottom, for mealybug egg masses. Wipe these off. Avoid bringing mealybugs into the house by carefully inspecting new plants.

CACTUS

FLOWERING TIME: Summer.

LIGHT: Most cacti thrive in bright sunny conditions. They should be grown in south or west-facing windows.

SOIL: Cacti should be planted in a sandy mix for good aeration and drainage. Use half regular potting mix and half semicoarse to coarse builder's sand. For more information on potting mixes, see page 924.

FERTILIZER: Fertilize once every 3 months during the growing season with ORTHO House Plant Food, ORTHO Fish Emulsion Fertilizer, or ORTHO Ortho-Gro Liquid Plant Food.

WATER:
How much: Add enough water so that some drains out of the bottom of the pot. Empty the saucer when the water has finished draining.
How often: Water when the surface soil is dry. In winter, the plants do not need to be watered as frequently as they do in the spring and early summer. For additional information on watering, see page 919.

TEMPERATURE: Place cacti in the warmest areas of the house during spring and summer.

Stem rot.

PROBLEM: Plants fail to grow well, and may die. Roots fail to grow, and may be dead and brown.

ANALYSIS: Overwatering
Most cacti are native to areas that are hot and dry, with very sandy soils. Such soils have large spaces between the particles and therefore have little ability to retain moisture. Because cacti need a lot of air around the roots, they do well in sandy soils. If deprived of air, the roots decay, and the plants fail to grow or die.

SOLUTION: Discard rotted plants. Repot mildly affected plants with a potting mix that is a very sandy or loose mix. (For a discussion of soil mixes, see page 920.) Cacti should be watered thoroughly and then allowed to dry out before watering again. But do not leave them completely dry in containers for very long, or they will die.

CACTUS

Bacterial soft rot.

PROBLEM: Soft, mushy, circular areas appear in the stems. As these areas enlarge, they become sunken and the tissues die. These cavities are frequently surrounded by tissue that appears to be water soaked. The whole stem may rot, and the plant may die.

ANALYSIS: Bacterial soft rot
This plant disease is caused by any of several bacteria (*Erwinia* species) that enter the cactus through a wound under wet conditions. Once established, the bacteria produce materials that dissolve the layers between the cells. As the cells die liquids are released from them, producing a soft, mushy rot. At high temperatures, the bacteria move through the tissue rapidly. The dead tissue dries, producing sunken cavities. The bacteria may invade the whole stem and kill the plant.

SOLUTION: Cut out the diseased area with a knife. Remove at least ½ inch of apparently healthy tissue around the diseased spot. The operation disfigures the plant, but the cactus may live and produce new portions that can be used to propagate more plants. Avoid wounding plants, and avoid getting water on them. Keep them separated enough so that good air circulation keeps them dry.

Scab.

PROBLEM: Irregular brown, corky, or leathery areas develop on the stems. These areas continue to enlarge until much of the plant may be covered. When these areas develop on younger tissue, they may cause sunken areas and deformities on the stem.

ANALYSIS: Scab
The cause of scab is unknown. It seems to be most prevalent on plants subjected to high humidity and low light. But sometimes it appears to spread, which suggests that it may be infectious.

SOLUTION: Grow cacti under conditions that are as close to ideal as possible: adequate light, and dry air and soil. Discard severely affected plants, and do not propagate from them. Isolate mildly affected plants from those not affected.

Mealybugs (life size).

PROBLEM: Oval, white insects up to ¼ inch long cluster in white, cottony masses on stems and in the crotches where the stems or branches are attached. A sticky material may coat the plant. When the condition is severe, plants may wither and die.

ANALYSIS: Mealybugs
Several species of this common insect feed on cacti. Mealybugs damage plants by sucking sap, causing plant distortion and death. The adult female mealybug may produce live young, or may lay eggs in a white fluffy mass of wax. The immature mealybugs, called *nymphs*, crawl all over the plant and onto nearby plants. Soon after they begin to feed, they produce white waxy filaments that cover their bodies, giving them a cottony appearance. As they mature, they become less mobile. Mealybugs cannot digest all the sugar in the sap and excrete the excess in a fluid called honeydew, which coats the stems and may drop onto furniture below the plant. For additional information on mealybugs, see page 181.

SOLUTION: Spray infested plants with an insecticide containing *malathion*. Some varieties of cactus are sensitive; test the spray on a small area before spraying the entire plant. (For instructions on spraying houseplants, see page 921.) Where practical, wipe mealybugs off the plant with a damp cloth or with cotton swabs dipped in alcohol. Inspect the pot, including the bottom, for mealybug egg masses. Wipe these off. Avoid bringing mealybugs into the house by carefully inspecting new plants.

CAPSICUM (ORNAMENTAL PEPPER)

Insufficient light.

PROBLEM: Plants stop producing flowers and fruit. Flowers may drop from the plant. Plants lose their deep green color and bushy habit. Older leaves may yellow and drop. Stems elongate and are weak.

ANALYSIS: Insufficient light
Plants use light as a source of energy, and grow slowly in light that is too dim for their needs. If most of the available light is coming from one direction, the stems and leaves bend in that direction. If the light is much too dim, the plant has little energy and grows poorly. Plants grown for their flowers or fruit, such as ornamental pepper, have a relatively high need for light.

SOLUTION: Move the plant to a brighter location. Ornamental pepper will tolerate direct sun if it is kept well watered. But if it is allowed to become dry while in direct sunlight, it will sunburn. (For more information on sunburn, see page 178.) If a brighter location is not available, provide supplemental lighting as described on page 920. If you wish to grow a houseplant in a dim location, select a plant that is tolerant of dim light from the list on page 990.

Aphids (half life size).

PROBLEM: New leaves are curled, discolored, and reduced in size. A shiny or sticky substance may coat the leaves. Tiny (1/8 inch), nonwinged, green, soft-bodied insects cluster on the buds, young stems, and leaves.

ANALYSIS: Aphids
Aphids do little damage in small numbers. However, they are extremely prolific and populations can rapidly build up to damaging numbers on ornamental peppers. Damage results when the aphids suck sap from the leaves and stems. Aphids are unable to digest fully all the sugar in the plant sap and excrete the excess in a fluid called honeydew, which often drops onto leaves or furniture below the plant. For more information about aphids, see page 875.

SOLUTION: Treat plants with ORTHO House Plant Insect Control. Spray thoroughly, being sure to cover the upper and lower surfaces of the leaves. For additional information on spraying houseplants, see page 921.

Capsicum cultural information
Light: Needs bright light
Water: When the soil just below the surface is dry

Whiteflies (twice life size).

PROBLEM: Tiny, winged insects 1/12 inch long feed on the undersides of the leaves. The insects are covered with white waxy powder. When the plant is touched, insects flutter rapidly around it. Leaves may be mottled and yellowing.

ANALYSIS: Greenhouse whitefly
(*Trialeurodes vaporariorum*)
This insect is a common pest of ornamental pepper. The four-winged adult lays eggs on the undersides of leaves. The larvae are the size of a pinhead, flat, oval, immobile, and semitransparent, with radiating white waxy filaments. In about a month, they change to the winged adult form. The larvae are more damaging because they suck more sap from the plants than do the adults. They cannot digest all the sugar in the sap they remove, and excrete the excess in a sugary material called honeydew, which coats the leaves and may drop from the plant onto furniture below.

SOLUTION: Spray with ORTHO House Plant Insect Control. For instructions on spraying houseplants, see page 921. Spray weekly as long as the problem continues. Remove heavily infested leaves.

CHLOROPHYTUM (SPIDER PLANT)

Dead leaf tips.

Salt damage.

PROBLEM: Tips of leaves turn brown or tan. The damaged area spreads slowly along the leaf. Older leaves are most severely affected.

ANALYSIS: Dead leaf tips
There are several reasons why spider plant leaf tips die. Frequently the problem is a combination of causes.
1. *Salt damage:* Salts accumulate in the soil from irrigation water or fertilizer. Excess salts are carried to the leaves and deposited in the tips of pointed leaves like those of spider plants. When enough salts accumulate there, the leaf tip dies. Salts accumulate most rapidly when the soil is dry.
2. *Too dry:* The leaf tip, being farthest from the roots, is the first part of the leaf to die when the plant is not getting enough water.
3. *Toxic salts:* Some chemicals, usually in the form of soluble salts, are damaging in very small amounts. They accumulate in leaf tips as other salts do, killing the tissue there. The most common of these chemicals are chloride and borate.

SOLUTION: Remove the dead tips by trimming the leaves to a point with a pair of scissors. The numbered solutions below correspond to the numbers in the analysis.
1. Leach excess salts from the soil by flushing with water. Water the plant at least 3 times, letting the water drain through each time. This is done most easily in a bathtub or laundry sink or outside. Always water spider plants from the top of the pot. Enough water should be added at each watering so that some drains through the pot. Empty the saucer after the pot has finished draining. If the plant is too large to handle easily, use a turkey baster to remove the drainage water. (For additional watering instructions, see page 923.) Do not overfertilize.
2. Water the plant regularly, following the directions on page 923.
3. There isn't much you can do about traces of toxic chemicals in the water, other than find another source of water. Distilled or deionized water is always free of chemicals.

Chlorophytum cultural information
Light: Needs medium light
Water: When the soil just below the surface is dry

CHRYSANTHEMUM

Weak growth.

PROBLEM: Soon after potted plants are brought inside, their leaves turn yellow, wilt, and fall off. The plants are located in dim light.

ANALYSIS: Insufficient light
Chrysanthemums are outdoor plants that need full sun, but they will tolerate household conditions for a few weeks if they are kept in a bright place and are well watered. Flowering mums from a florist have been grown in bright sun, and will not remain healthy in a location that does not allow them full sun for at least part of the day.

SOLUTION: Move the plants to a brighter location. However, if the leaves are very yellow they will not be able to tolerate direct sun until they become accustomed to higher light levels. Put the plants in a lightly curtained window for a week before exposing them to full sun. It is difficult to get satisfactory flowers from a forced mum a second time the same season. As soon as possible after the blossoms die, cut the flower stalks to the ground and plant the mums in the garden. They may not bloom that fall, but will probably bloom the following year.

Chrysanthemum cultural information
Light: Needs bright light
Water: When the soil surface is moist but not wet

Mealybugs (half life size).

PROBLEM: Oval, white insects up to 1/4 inch long cluster in white, cottony masses on leaves, stems, and in the crotches where the leaves are attached. A sticky material may coat the leaves. Leaves may be spotted or deformed. When the condition is severe, leaves and plants may wither and die.

ANALYSIS: Mealybugs
Several species of this common insect feed on chrysanthemums. Mealybugs damage plants by sucking sap, causing leaf distortion and death. The adult female mealybug may produce live young, or may lay eggs in a white fluffy mass of wax. The immature mealybugs, called *nymphs*, crawl all over the plant and onto nearby plants. Soon after they begin to feed, they produce white waxy filaments that cover their bodies, giving them a cottony appearance. As they mature, they become less mobile. Mealybugs cannot digest all the sugar in the sap and excrete the excess in a fluid called honeydew, which coats the leaves and may drop onto furniture below the plant. For additional information on mealybugs, see page 181.

SOLUTION: Spray infested plants indoors with ORTHO House Plant Insect Control, or take plants outside and spray them with ORTHO Diazinon Insect Spray. (For instructions on spraying houseplants, see page 921.) Where practical, wipe mealybugs off the plant with a damp cloth or with cotton swabs dipped in alcohol. Inspect the pot, including the bottom, for mealybug egg masses. Wipe these off. Avoid bringing mealybugs into the house by carefully inspecting new plants.

Spider mite damage.

PROBLEM: Leaves are stippled, yellow, and dirty; they may dry out and drop. There may be webbing over flower buds, between leaves, or on the lower surfaces of the leaves. To determine if a plant is infested with mites, hold a sheet of white paper underneath an affected plant and tap the leaves sharply. Minute green, red, or yellow specks the size of pepper grains will drop to the paper and begin to crawl around. Mites are easily seen against the white background.

ANALYSIS: Spider mites
These mites, related to spiders, are major pests of many houseplants, including chrysanthemums. They cause damage by sucking sap from the undersides of the leaves. As a result of feeding the green pigment (chlorophyll) disappears, causing the stippled appearance. Under warm, dry conditions, which favor mites, they can build up to tremendous numbers. For more information about spider mites, see page 887.

SOLUTION: Spray infested plants with ORTHO House Plant Insect Control. (For instructions on spraying houseplants, see page 921.) Plants need to be sprayed weekly for several weeks to kill the mites as they hatch. To avoid introducing mites, inspect new plants carefully.

Whiteflies (life size).

PROBLEM: Tiny, winged insects 1/12 inch long feed on the undersides of the leaves. The insects are covered with white waxy powder. When the plant is touched, insects flutter rapidly around it. Leaves may be mottled and yellowing.

ANALYSIS: Greenhouse whitefly
(*Trialeurodes vaporariorum*)
This insect is a common pest of chrysanthemum. The four-winged adult lays eggs on the undersides of leaves. The larvae are the size of a pinhead, flat, oval, immobile, and semitransparent, with radiating white waxy filaments. In about a month, they change to the winged adult form. The larvae are more damaging because they suck more sap from the plants than do the adults. They cannot digest all the sugar in the sap they remove, and excrete the excess in a sugary material called honeydew, which coats the leaves and may drop from the plant onto furniture below.

SOLUTION: Spray with ORTHO House Plant Insect Control or ORTHO Malathion 50 Insect Spray. For instructions on spraying houseplants, see page 921. Spray weekly as long as the problem continues. Remove heavily infested leaves.

CINERARIA

Aphids (life size).

PROBLEM: New leaves are curled, discolored, and reduced in size. A shiny or sticky substance may coat the leaves. Tiny (1/8 inch), nonwinged, green, soft-bodied insects cluster on the buds, young stems, and leaves.

ANALYSIS: Aphids
Aphids do little damage in small numbers. However, they are extremely prolific and populations can rapidly build up to damaging numbers on cineraria. Damage results when the aphids suck sap from the leaves and stems. Aphids are unable to digest fully all the sugar in the plant sap and excrete the excess in a fluid called honeydew, which often drops onto leaves or furniture below the plant. For more information about aphids, see page 875.

SOLUTION: Use ORTHO House Plant Insect Control. For additional information on spraying houseplants, see page 921.

Cineraria cultural information
Light: Needs bright light
Water: When the soil surface is moist but not wet

CISSUS (GRAPE IVY)

Salt damage.

PROBLEM: Margins of older leaves die and turn brown and brittle. In severe cases, all leaves may have dead margins. Tissues adjacent to the dead margins of older leaves may turn yellow. New leaves may be distorted.

ANALYSIS: Salt damage
Grape ivy and kangaroo ivy are sensitive to excess salts. Soluble salts are picked up by the roots and accumulate in the leaf margins, where concentrations may become high enough to kill the tissues. Salts can accumulate from water or the use of fertilizers; or they may be present in the soils used in potting. Salts accumulate more rapidly and do more harm if the plant is not watered thoroughly.

SOLUTION: If symptoms of salt damage occur, leach excess salts from the soil by flushing with water. Water the plant at least three times, letting the water drain each time. This is done most easily in a bathtub or laundry sink or outside. Always water grape ivy and kangaroo ivy from the top of the pot. Enough water should be added at each watering so that some drains through the pot. Empty the saucer after the pot has finished draining. If the plant is too large to handle easily, use a turkey baster to remove the drainage water. (For additional watering instructions, see page 923.) Do not overfertilize.

Cissus cultural information
Light: Needs medium light
Water: When the soil just below the surface is dry

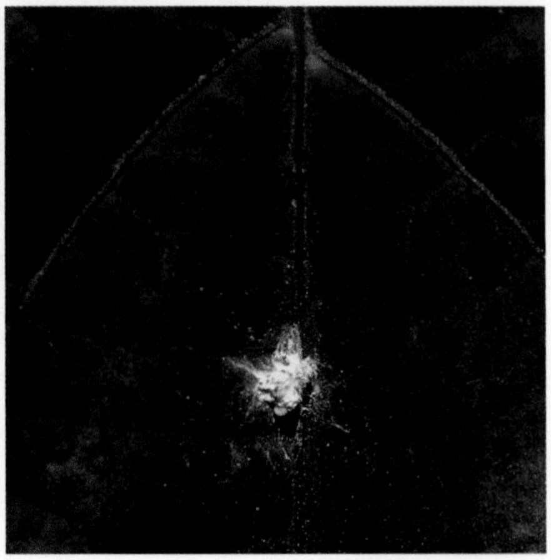

Mealybug (twice life size).

PROBLEM: Oval, white insects up to 1/4 inch long cluster in white, cottony masses on leaves, stems, and in the crotches where the leaves are attached. A sticky material may coat the leaves. Leaves may be spotted or deformed. When the condition is severe, leaves and plants may wither and die.

ANALYSIS: Mealybugs
Several species of this common insect feed on grape ivy. Mealybugs damage plants by sucking sap, causing leaf distortion and death. The adult female mealybug may produce live young, or may lay eggs in a white fluffy mass of wax. The immature mealybugs, called *nymphs*, crawl all over the plant and onto nearby plants. Soon after they begin to feed, they produce white waxy filaments that cover their bodies, giving them a cottony appearance. As they mature, they become less mobile. Mealybugs cannot digest all the sugar in the sap and excrete the excess in a fluid called honeydew, which coats the leaves and may drop onto furniture below the plant. For additional information on mealybugs, see page 181.

SOLUTION: Spray infested plants with ORTHO House Plant Insect Control. (For instructions on spraying houseplants, see page 921.) Where practical, wipe mealybugs off the plant with a damp cloth or with cotton swabs dipped in alcohol. Inspect the pot, including the bottom, for mealybug egg masses. Wipe these off. Avoid bringing mealybugs into the house by carefully inspecting new plants.

CITRUS

Iron-deficient leaves.

Yellowing caused by nitrogen deficiency.

PROBLEM: Older (lower) leaves start turning yellow at the margins; yellowing progresses inward on the leaves, and upward on the plant. Older leaves may drop, and the plant may wilt. Or yellowing may start on new growth, with the leaf margins losing their green color first and the areas surrounding the veins losing their color last.

ANALYSIS: Yellowing of leaves
Yellow leaves on citrus may be caused by any of several factors:

SOLUTION: The numbered solutions below correspond to the numbers in the analysis.

1. If the older leaves turn yellow but the new leaves remain green, the problem is probably nitrogen deficiency. Nitrogen is an essential plant nutrient. If it is deficient, the plant will withdraw nitrogen from the old leaves for the sake of the new growth. For more information about nitrogen deficiency, see page 178.

1. For a quick response, spray the leaves with Ra-Pid-Gro Plant Food. Feed citrus plants regularly with ORTHO House Plant Food.

2. Yellowing of older leaves may be associated with root rot, a plant disease caused by any of several fungi, also known as *water molds*. Examine the root system as explained on page 921. If the roots are brown, dead, and soft, without white tips, root rot is the problem. Rotted roots are unable to absorb nutrients and water needed by the plant. For more information about water molds, see page 849.

2. Avoid excess watering of soil in which citrus is growing. For instructions on watering container plants, see page 923. Plant citrus in a well-drained soil mix.

3. If only the new leaves are yellow, the plant is probably deficient in iron. This condition is caused by alkaline soil. In alkaline soil, iron is less available to the plant, and some plants cannot absorb all the iron they need. For information on acid and alkaline soils, see page 908.

3. Fertilize citrus with ORTHO Greenol Liquid Iron. Treat the soil with *ferrous sulfate* to increase acidity.

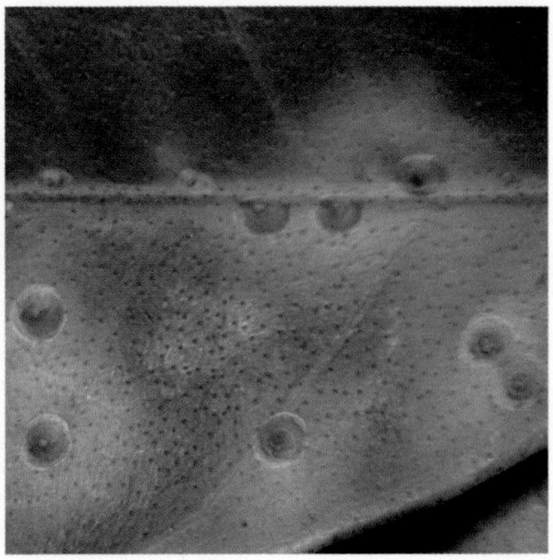

Scale (3 times life size).

PROBLEM: Stems and leaves are covered with white, cottony, cushionlike masses or brown crusty bumps. The bumps can be scraped or picked off easily. Leaves turn yellow and drop. A shiny or sticky material may cover leaves and stems.

ANALYSIS: Scale insects
Several different types of scale insects attack citrus plants. Some types can infest many different plants. Scales hatch from eggs. The young, called *crawlers*, are small (about 1/10 inch), soft-bodied, and move about on the plant and onto other plants. After moving about for a short time, they insert their mouthparts into the plant, feeding on the sap. The legs disappear, and the scales remain in the same place for the rest of their lives. Some develop a soft covering, others a hard covering. Some species of scales are unable to digest fully all the sugar in the plant sap and excrete the excess in a fluid called honeydew, which may cover the leaves or drip onto surfaces below. For more information about scales, see page 876.

SOLUTION: Take the infested plant outside and spray it with ORTHO Malathion 50 Insect Spray or ORTHO Citrus Insect Spray. Spraying is more effective against the crawlers than against the adults. Repeated applications may be necessary. For additional information on spraying houseplants, see page 921.

Citrus cultural information
Light: Needs bright light
Water: When the soil just below the surface is dry

CLERODENDRUM (GLORY-BOWER) ■ CLIVIA ■

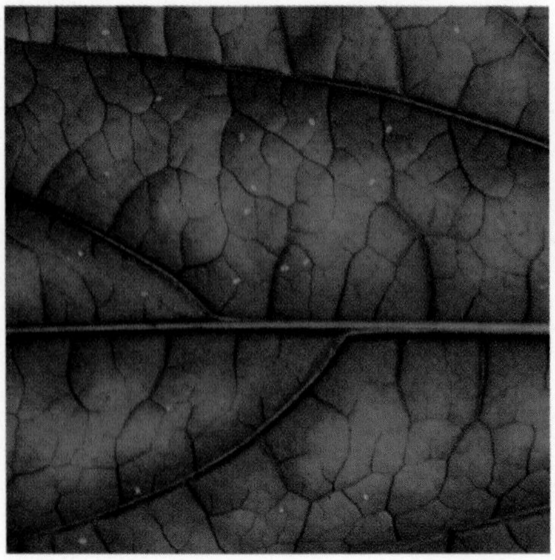
Whitefly larvae (twice life size).

PROBLEM: Tiny, winged insects 1/12 inch long feed on the undersides of the leaves. The insects are covered with white waxy powder. When the plant is touched, insects flutter rapidly around it. Leaves may be mottled and yellowing.

ANALYSIS: Greenhouse whitefly
(*Trialeurodes vaporariorum*)
This insect is a common pest of clerodendron. The four-winged adult lays eggs on the undersides of leaves. The larvae are the size of a pinhead, flat, oval, immobile, and semitransparent, with radiating white waxy filaments. In about a month, they change to the winged adult form. The larvae are more damaging because they suck more sap from the plants than do the adults. They cannot digest all the sugar in the sap they remove, and excrete the excess in a sugary material called honeydew, which coats the leaves and may drop from the plant onto furniture below.

SOLUTION: Spray with ORTHO House Plant Insect Control. Spray weekly as long as the problem continues. Remove heavily infested leaves.

Clerodendrum cultural information
Light: Needs bright light
Water: When the soil is moist but not wet

Mealybugs (1/4 life size).

PROBLEM: Oval, white insects up to 1/4 inch long cluster in white, cottony masses on leaves and in the crotches where the leaves are attached. A sticky material may coat the leaves. Leaves may be spotted or deformed. When the condition is severe, leaves and plants may wither and die.

ANALYSIS: Mealybugs
Several species of this common insect feed on clivia. Mealybugs damage plants by sucking sap, causing leaf distortion and death. The adult female mealybug may produce live young, or may lay eggs in a white fluffy mass of wax. The immature mealybugs, called *nymphs*, crawl all over the plant and onto nearby plants. Soon after they begin to feed, they produce white waxy filaments that cover their bodies, giving them a cottony appearance. As they mature, they become less mobile. Mealybugs cannot digest all the sugar in the sap and excrete the excess in a fluid called honeydew, which coats the leaves and may drop onto furniture below the plant. For additional information on mealybugs, see page 181.

SOLUTION: Spray infested plants with an insecticide containing *diazinon*. (For instructions on spraying houseplants, see page 921.) Where practical, wipe mealybugs off the plant with a damp cloth or with cotton swabs dipped in alcohol. Inspect the pot, including the bottom, for mealybug egg masses. Wipe these off. Avoid bringing mealybugs into the house by carefully inspecting new plants.

Leaf bleaching from too much light.

PROBLEM: Plants fail to flower. They are growing in dim light.

ANALYSIS: Incorrect light
Clivia is native to areas that receive filtered sunlight or bright, indirect light. Indoors, clivia requires very bright indirect light in order to produce blooms. However, it cannot tolerate much direct sun; it may burn if it receives more than 1 or 2 hours of direct sunlight.

SOLUTION: Grow clivia in an east-facing window or in a curtained south or west-facing window. During the summer, clivia can be grown outside in semishade.

Clivia cultural information
Light: Needs bright light
Water: When the soil just below the surface is barely moist

CODIAEUM (CROTON)

LIGHT: Grow crotons in bright light to maintain the brilliant leaf colors. If new leaves are green, move the plants to a brighter spot.

SOIL: Crotons can be grown in any of the standard soil mixes for houseplants. For more information about soil mixes, see page 924.

FERTILIZER: Feed once a month with ORTHO Fish Emulsion Fertilizer or ORTHO Ortho-Gro Liquid Plant Food.

WATER:
How much: Add enough water so that some drains out of the bottom of the pot. Empty the saucer when the water has finished draining.
How often: Water when the top inch of soil is barely moist. For additional information on watering houseplants, see page 919.

TEMPERATURE: Average house temperatures of 68° to 70°F are adequate.

Mealybugs (3 times life size).

PROBLEM: Oval, white insects up to ¼ inch long cluster in white, cottony masses on leaves, stems, and in the crotches where branches or leaves are attached. A sticky material may coat the leaves. Leaves may be spotted or deformed.

ANALYSIS: Mealybugs
Several species of this common insect feed on croton. Mealybugs damage plants by sucking sap, causing leaf distortion and death. The adult female mealybug may produce live young, or may lay eggs in a white fluffy mass of wax. The immature mealybugs, called *nymphs*, crawl all over the plant and onto nearby plants. Soon after they begin to feed, they produce white waxy filaments that cover their bodies, giving them a cottony appearance. As they mature, they become less mobile. Mealybugs cannot digest all the sugar in the sap and excrete the excess in a fluid called honeydew, which coats the leaves and may drop onto furniture below the plant. For additional information on mealybugs, see page 181.

SOLUTION: Spray infested plants indoors with ORTHO House Plant Insect Control, or take the plants outside and spray them with ORTHO Orthene Systemic Insect Control. (For instructions on spraying houseplants, see page 921.) Where practical, wipe mealybugs off the plant with a damp cloth or with cotton swabs dipped in alcohol. Inspect the pot, including the bottom, for mealybug egg masses. Wipe these off.

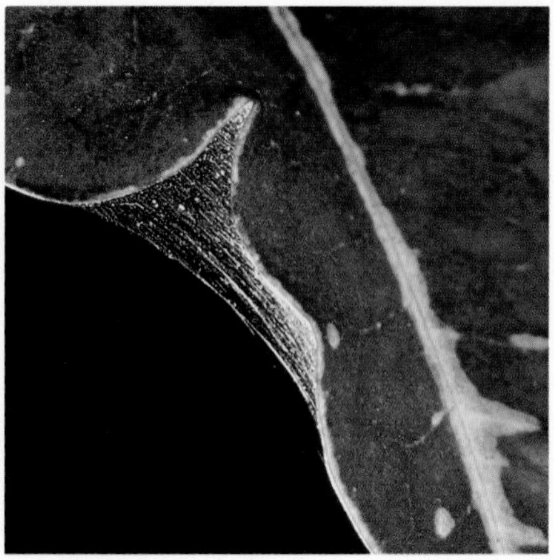

Spider mites and webs (life size).

PROBLEM: Leaves are stippled, yellowed, and dirty. Leaves may dry out and drop. There may be webbing between leaves or on the lower surfaces of the leaves. To determine if a plant is infested with mites, hold a sheet of white paper underneath an affected leaf and tap the leaf sharply. Minute green, red, or yellow specks the size of pepper grains will drop to the paper and begin to crawl around. The pests are easily seen against the white background.

ANALYSIS: Spider mites
These mites, related to spiders, are major pests of many houseplants, including croton. They cause damage by sucking sap from the undersides of leaves. As a result of feeding, the green pigment (chlorophyll) disappears, producing the stippled appearance. Under warm, dry conditions, which favor mites, they can build up to tremendous numbers. For more information about spider mites, see page 887.

SOLUTION: Spray infested plants with ORTHO House Plant Insect Control or ORTHO Isotox Insect Killer. (For instructions on spraying houseplants, see page 921.) Plants need to be sprayed weekly for 2 to 3 weeks to kill the mites as they hatch. To avoid introducing mites, inspect new plants carefully.

New leaves are green.

PROBLEM: New leaves are green, instead of brightly colored. Stems may be thin and bend toward a light source. The lower leaves may drop.

ANALYSIS: Insufficient light
Plants use light as a source of energy, and grow slowly in light that is too dim for their needs. If most of the available light is coming from one direction, the stems and leaves bend in that direction. Although foliage plants generally need less light than plants grown for their flowers or fruit, brightly colored plants like croton need fairly bright light in order to produce the pigments that color their leaves.

SOLUTION: Move the plant to a brighter location. A lightly curtained sunny window is ideal. If a brighter location is not available, provide supplemental lighting as described on page 920. Crotons may be grown outside in the summer. When moving them from indoors to outdoors, place the plants in light shade for at least 2 days before putting them in full sun. If you wish to grow a houseplant in a dim location, select a plant that is tolerant of dim light from the list on page 990.

COLEUS

FLOWERING TIME: Although coleus are not grown for their flowers, they frequently produce flowers. Flowering depends on the size of the plant; larger plants flower any time.

LIGHT: Grow coleus in as much light as possible to maintain the brilliant colors. If colors fade and stems elongate, move to a brighter spot.

SOIL: Coleus can be grown in any of the soil mixes for general houseplants. For additional information on soil mixes, see page 924.

FERTILIZER: Feed once a month with ORTHO Fish Emulsion Fertilizer, ORTHO House Plant Food, or ORTHO Ortho-Gro Liquid Plant Food.

WATER:
How much: Add enough water so that some drains out of the bottom of the pot.
How often: Water when the top inch of soil is barely moist. For additional information on watering houseplants, see page 919.

TEMPERATURE: Average house temperatures of 68° to 70°F are adequate for coleus.

SPECIAL CONDITIONS: Pinch stems to encourage branching. Cut off flower stems as they appear. Plants may be grown outside in partial shade in the summer.

Root rot.

PROBLEM: Lower leaves wilt or all of the leaves wilt. The plant may be stunted, and leaf colors fade. The lower portion of the main stem above the soil line may be darkened. Examination of the roots, as described on page 921, shows them to be brown, dead, and mushy, with no white tips. Severely infected plants may die.

ANALYSIS: Root rot
This plant disease is caused by any of several soil-dwelling fungi, also known as *water molds*, (see page 849 for more information about water molds). These fungi are favored by excessively wet soil and poor drainage. Plants weakened by poor light, inadequate fertilization, excess salts, or other adverse factors are more susceptible to root rot fungi. Damaged roots are unable to absorb water and nutrients.

SOLUTION: If the plant is only mildly affected, let the soil dry out between waterings. For more information on this technique, see page 849. If the soil mix is heavy, or the container does not drain well, transplant the plant into a container that drains freely. Use a well-drained soil mix. For information on soil mixes, see page 920. If stem or root rot occurs but the top of the plant is still vigorous, cut it off above the diseased area and root it according to the instructions on page 921. Discard severely infected plants and the soil in which they grew. Wash the pots thoroughly, and soak them in a mixture of 1 part household bleach to 9 parts water for 30 minutes. Rinse with plain water and dry thoroughly before reuse. Or, pasteurize the pots according to the directions on page 920.

Insufficient light.

PROBLEM: Old leaves drop off. Leaves fade and look bleached. Stems are long, with large spaces between the leaves. Young stems may be weak and unable to support themselves. Young stems tend to grow toward the light source. Brown patches may appear in the faded area.

ANALYSIS: Insufficient light
Plants use light as a source of energy, and grow slowly in light that is too dim for their needs. If most of the available light is coming from one direction, the stems and leaves bend in that direction. If the light is much too dim, the plant has little energy and grows poorly. Although foliage plants generally need less light than plants grown for their flowers or fruit, coleus has a relatively high need for light.

SOLUTION: Move the plant to a brighter location, such as a lightly curtained sunny window. If a brighter location is not available, provide supplemental lighting as described on page 920. If you wish to grow a houseplant in a dim location, select a plant that is tolerant of dim light from the list on page 990.

Mealybugs (half life size).

PROBLEM: Oval, white insects up to ¼ inch long cluster in white, cottony masses on leaves, stems, and in the crotches where the leaves are attached. A sticky material may coat the leaves. Leaves may be spotted or deformed. When the condition is severe, leaves and plants may wither and die.

ANALYSIS: Mealybugs
Several species of this common insect feed on coleus. Mealybugs damage plants by sucking sap, causing leaf distortion and death. The adult female mealybug may produce live young, or may lay eggs in a white fluffy mass of wax. The immature mealybugs, called *nymphs*, crawl all over the plant and onto nearby plants. Soon after they begin to feed, they produce white waxy filaments that cover their bodies, giving them a cottony appearance. As they mature, they become less mobile. Mealybugs cannot digest all the sugar in the sap and excrete the excess in a fluid called honeydew, which coats the leaves and may drop onto furniture below the plant. For additional information on mealybugs, see page 181.

SOLUTION: Spray infested plants with ORTHO Whitefly & Mealybug Killer, ORTHO Orthene Systemic Insect Control, ORTHO House Plant Insect Killer, or ORTHO House Plant Insect Control. (For instructions on spraying houseplants, see page 921.) Where practical, wipe mealybugs off the plant with a damp cloth or with cotton swabs dipped in alcohol. Inspect the pot, including the bottom, for mealybug egg masses. Wipe these off. Avoid bringing mealybugs into the house by carefully inspecting new plants.

Greenhouse whiteflies (life size).

PROBLEM: Tiny, winged insects 1/12 inch long feed on the undersides of the leaves. The insects are covered with white waxy powder. When the plant is touched, insects flutter rapidly around it. Leaves may be mottled and yellowing.

ANALYSIS: Greenhouse whitefly
(*Trialeurodes vaporariorum*)
This insect is a common pest of coleus. The four-winged adult lays eggs on the undersides of leaves. The larvae are the size of a pinhead, flat, oval, immobile, and semitransparent, with radiating white waxy filaments. In about a month, they change to the winged adult form. The larvae are more damaging because they suck more sap from the plants than do the adults. They cannot digest all the sugar in the sap they remove, and excrete the excess in a sugary material called honeydew, which coats the leaves and may drop from the plant onto furniture below.

SOLUTION: Spray with ORTHO Whitefly & Mealybug Killer, ORTHO House Plant Insect Killer, or ORTHO House Plant Insect Control. For instructions on spraying houseplants, see page 921. Spray weekly as long as the problem continues. Remove heavily infested leaves.

COLUMNEA

Water spots.

Mealybugs (half life size).

PROBLEM: Small, sunken white to tan spots are scattered on the upper surfaces of the leaves.

ANALYSIS: Water spots
Columnea water spots result from a rapid temperature change in the presence of light. This usually occurs when cold water is dropped on the foliage during watering. The green pigment (chlorophyll) in columnea leaves is found in a layer of cells near the upper surface of the leaf. A rapid temperature change in the presence of light destroys the chlorophyll, causing the loss of green color and allowing the color of the underlying tissue to show through.

SOLUTION: The spots are permanent. Remove unsightly leaves. When watering columnea plants, use tepid water and be careful not to get water on the foliage.

Columnea cultural information
Light: Needs bright light
Water: When the soil just below the surface is barely moist

PROBLEM: Oval, white insects up to ¼ inch long cluster in white, cottony masses on leaves, stems, and in the crotches where the leaves are attached. A sticky material may coat the leaves. Leaves may be spotted or deformed. When the condition is severe, leaves and plants may wither and die.

ANALYSIS: Mealybugs
Several species of this common insect feed on columnea. Mealybugs damage plants by sucking sap, causing leaf distortion and death. The adult female mealybug may produce live young, or may lay eggs in a white fluffy mass of wax. The immature mealybugs, called *nymphs*, crawl all over the plant and onto nearby plants. Soon after they begin to feed, they produce white waxy filaments that cover their bodies, giving them a cottony appearance. As they mature, they become less mobile. Mealybugs cannot digest all the sugar in the sap and excrete the excess in a fluid called honeydew, which coats the leaves and may drop onto furniture below the plant. For additional information on mealybugs, see page 181.

SOLUTION: Spray infested plants with an insecticide containing *diazinon*. (For instructions on spraying houseplants, see page 921.) Where practical, wipe mealybugs off the plant with a damp cloth or with cotton swabs dipped in alcohol. Inspect the pot, including the bottom, for mealybug egg masses. Wipe these off. Avoid bringing mealybugs into the house by carefully inspecting new plants.

CORDYLINE (TI PLANT)

Salt damage.

PROBLEM: Tips of older leaves die and turn brown and brittle. This condition progresses down the margins of the leaves. In severe cases, all leaves may have dead tips and margins. Tissues adjacent to the dead margins may turn yellow.

ANALYSIS: Salt damage
Cordylines are very sensitive to excess salts. Soluble salts are picked up by the roots and accumulate in the leaf tips, where concentrations may become high enough to kill the tissues. Salts can accumulate from water or the use of fertilizers; or they may be present in the soil used in potting. Salts accumulate more rapidly and do more harm if the plant is not watered thoroughly.

SOLUTION: Leach excess salts from the soil by flushing with water. Water the plant at least three times, letting the water drain through each time. This is done most easily in a bathtub or laundry sink or outside. Always water cordylines from the top of the pot. Enough water should be added at each watering so that some drains through the pot. Empty the saucer after the pot has finished draining. If the plant is too large to handle easily, use a turkey baster to remove the drainage water. (For additional watering instructions, see page 923.) Do not overfertilize. Dead tips can be trimmed off with scissors. If the leaves are trimmed to a point, the damage is less noticeable.

Cordyline cultural information
Light: Needs medium light
Water: When the soil just below the surface is barely moist

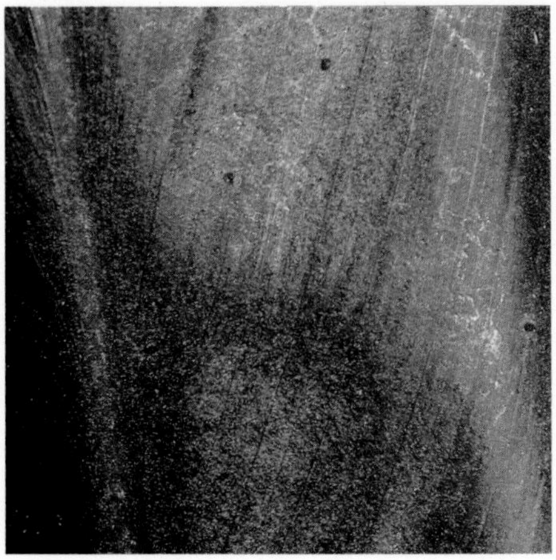

Spider mite damage.

PROBLEM: Leaves are stippled, yellow, and dirty; they may dry out and drop. There may be webbing between leaves or on the lower surfaces of the leaves. To determine if a plant is infested with mites, hold a sheet of white paper underneath an affected plant and tap the leaves sharply. Minute green, red, or yellow specks the size of pepper grains will drop to the paper and begin to crawl around. The pests are easily seen against the white background.

ANALYSIS: Spider mites
These mites, related to spiders, are major pests of many houseplants, including ti plants. They cause damage by sucking sap from the undersides of the leaves. As a result of feeding, the green pigment (chlorophyll) disappears, causing the stippled appearance. Under warm, dry conditions, which favor mites, they can build up to tremendous numbers. For more information about spider mites, see page 887.

SOLUTION: Spray infested plants with ORTHO House Plant Insect Control. (For instructions on spraying houseplants, see page 921.) Plants need to be sprayed weekly for several weeks to kill the mites as they hatch. To avoid introducing mites, inspect new plants carefully.

CRASSULA (JADE PLANT)

Root rot.

PROBLEM: The leaves and stems darken and turn soft and mushy, beginning with the lower leaves and stems. Leaves drop from the plant. Examination of the rootball (as described on page 921) show the roots to be brown and mushy. When the disease is severe, all the roots are rotted, and the plant can be lifted easily from the soil.

ANALYSIS: Root rot
This plant disease is caused by any of several fungi (*Pythium* species) that are favored by wet soil. These fungi decay plant roots. If the roots are severely damaged or killed, they cannot supply the plant with moisture and nutrients. The disease is an indication that the plant has been watered too frequently or that the soil mix is too heavy and does not drain well.

SOLUTION: Remove the plant from the pot and shake most of the soil from the roots. Let the plant dry for 1 or 2 days, or until the "mushy" leaves and stems have dried. Repot the plant in a light soil mix that drains well. For information on soil mixes, see page 920. Do not water again until the soil is almost dry.

Crassula cultural information
Light: Needs bright light
Water: When the soil just below the surface is dry

CYCAS (SAGO PALM)

Salt damage.

PROBLEM: Margins of older leaves die and turn brown, beginning at the base of the fronds and progressing outward. In severe cases, all fronds may have dead margins. Tissues adjacent to dead margins of older fronds may turn yellow.

ANALYSIS: Salt damage
Sago palms are sensitive to excess salts. Soluble salts are picked up by the roots and accumulate in the leaf margins, where concentrations may become high enough to kill the tissues. Salts can accumulate from water or the use of fertilizers; or they may be present in the soil used in potting. Salts accumulate more rapidly and do more harm if the plant is not watered thoroughly.

SOLUTION: Leach excess salts from the soil by flushing with water. Water the plant at least three times, letting the water drain each time. This is done most easily in a bathtub, or laundry sink or outside. Always water sago palms from the top of the pot. Enough water should be added at each watering so that some drains through the pot. Empty the saucer after the pot has finished draining. If the plant is too large to handle easily, use a turkey baster to remove the drainage water. (For additional watering instructions, see page 923.) Do not overfertilize.

Cycas cultural information
Light: Needs bright light
Water: When the soil just below the surface is barely moist

Scale (life size).

PROBLEM: Fronds and leaflets are covered with white, cottony, cushionlike masses or brown crusty bumps. The bumps can be scraped or picked off easily. Fronds turn yellow and may drop. A shiny or sticky material may cover the fronds.

ANALYSIS: Scale insects
Several different types of scale insects attack cycas. Some types can infest many different plants. Scales hatch from eggs. The young, called *crawlers*, are small (about 1/10 inch), soft-bodied, and move about on the plant and onto other plants. After moving about for a short time, they insert their mouthparts into the plant, feeding on the sap. The legs disappear, and the scales remain in the same place for the rest of their lives. Some develop a soft covering, others a hard covering. Some species of scales are unable to digest fully all the sugar in the plant sap and excrete the excess in a fluid called honeydew, which may cover the fronds or drip onto surfaces below. For more information about scales, see page 876.

SOLUTION: Spray with an insecticide containing *malathion*. Spraying is more effective against the crawlers than against the adults. Repeated applications may be necessary. For additional information on spraying houseplants, see page 921.

CYCLAMEN

LIGHT: Flowering plants need more light than foliage plants. To keep cyclamen plants in flower, place them in a south-facing window.

SOIL: Grow cyclamens in a loose, well-drained soil mix. For more information about soil mixes, see page 924.

FERTILIZER: Fertilize monthly with ORTHO Ortho-Gro Liquid Plant Food or ORTHO Evergreen & Azalea Food according to directions on the label.

WATER:
How much: Add enough water to the pot so that a little water drains from the bottom.
How often: Water whenever the top inch of soil is slightly moist. Do not let the soil get dry.

TEMPERATURE: Cyclamens will continue to flower when daytime temperatures are warm and nighttime temperatures are cool. In mild climates, put the plant outside at night. In areas with extremely cold winters, put the plant in a cool area but do not allow it to freeze. When days and nights are warm, the leaves will yellow and the plant will stop flowering.

SPECIAL CONDITIONS: Do not allow cyclamens to become dry. In bright light, plants that are dry will sunburn. Avoid overwatering. Cyclamens are very susceptible to root rots.

High temperature damage.

PROBLEM: Outer leaves turn yellow. Leaves may die and turn brown, and their stems become soft. Plants stop flowering.

ANALYSIS: High temperatures
Although cyclamen are cool weather plants, they will tolerate warm days as long as they have cool nights (below 55°F). Cool temperatures initiate flower buds. Constant high temperatures inhibit flower buds, and plants stop flowering. High temperatures also prevent the plant from growing well, causing leaves to lose their green color and die.

SOLUTION: Grow cyclamen plants in a cool room with as much light as possible. If a cool room is not available, put them near a window at night. If temperatures are not below freezing, put the plants outside at night. Under alternating temperatures, they will flower for long periods. Keep plants adequately watered and fertilized.

Cyclamen mite damage.

PROBLEM: Leaves become curled, wrinkled, and cupped in scattered areas. New leaves may be more severely affected, remain very small, have a bronze discoloration, and be severely misshapen. Flower buds are distorted, and may drop or fail to open.

ANALYSIS: Cyclamen mite
(*Steneotarsonemus pallidus*)
Cyclamen mite is a very small mite related to spiders. These mites attack a number of houseplants, and can be very damaging on cyclamen. Their feeding injures the plant tissues, causing the leaves and flower buds to be malformed and stunted. They infest the new growth most heavily, but will crawl to other parts of the plant or to other plants. Cyclamen mites reproduce rapidly.

SOLUTION: Spray plants with *dicofol* (KELTHANE®) at intervals of 2 weeks until new growth is no longer affected. Discard severely infested plants. Spray plants according to instructions given on page 921. Houseplants showing cyclamen mite damage should be isolated from other plants until the mites are under control. Nearby plants should be observed closely so that if symptoms appear, they can be sprayed. Avoid touching leaves of infested plants and then touching leaves of other plants.

Botrytis. *Insert:* Spotted petals.

PROBLEM: Leaves in the center of the plant turn yellow, wilt, and die. Leaf and flower stems in the center of the plant develop a soft rot near their base and collapse. Plants stop flowering. Much of the center of the plant may die. Plant tissues there may be covered with a gray to brown powdery fungal growth. Flower petals of colored varieties may have spots of deeper color.

ANALYSIS: Botrytis
This disease is caused by a fungus (*Botrytis* species) that is commonly found on dead and decaying plant materials. The spores of the fungus can invade dead or weak tissues and flowers, but not healthy stems and leaves. However, leaves and stems in contact with infected tissue can be invaded. The fungus is favored by moist conditions and temperatures below 65°F. Under very humid conditions, the infected tissues may be covered with a fuzzy gray or brown growth composed of the strands and spores of the fungus. The spores are spread by air currents and, in the presence of water, will invade dead leaves on old flowers in the center of cyclamen plants. On cyclamen flowers of colored varieties, the fungus may cause spots of deeper color.

SOLUTION: No chemical control is presently available for home use. Remove any dead plant materials, especially old flowers and leaves in the center of the plant. Avoid getting foliage and flowers wet when watering. Do not mist plants. Increase air circulation to keep humidity low.

Root rot.

PROBLEM: Older leaves turn yellow and may curl up at the margins. The leaf stems and flower stems may wilt. The plant may be stunted. All of the leaves may wilt, die, and turn brown. The roots are brown, dead, and soft, with no white tips. (For instructions on examining plant roots, see page 921.) All of the roots may be rotted, and the bulb may be lifted easily from the soil.

ANALYSIS: Root rot
This plant disease is caused by any of several soil-dwelling fungi, also known as *water molds*, (see page 849 for more information about water molds). These fungi are favored by wet soil and poor drainage. Plants weakened by other factors are more susceptible to attack by the fungi, which invade the roots and kill them, causing the plant to wilt. The fungi may invade so much of the root system that the plant dies.

SOLUTION: If the plant is only mildly affected, let the soil dry out between waterings. For more information on this technique, see page 849. If the soil mix is heavy, or the container does not drain well, transplant the plant into a container that drains freely. Use a well-drained soil mix. For information on soil mixes, see page 920. Discard severely infected plants and the soil in which they grew. Wash the pots thoroughly, and soak them in a mixture of 1 part household bleach to 9 parts water for 30 minutes. Rinse with plain water and dry thoroughly before reuse. Or, pasteurize the pots according to the directions on page 920.

DIEFFENBACHIA (DUMB CANE)

LIGHT: Dieffenbachia will tolerate considerable variations in light, and will grow in full sun to medium light, as in a north-facing window.

SOIL: Any standard potting mix. For information on potting mixes, see page 924.

FERTILIZER: Fertilize once a month during spring and summer with ORTHO Fish Emulsion Fertilizer, ORTHO House Plant Food, or ORTHO Ortho-Gro Liquid Plant Food.

WATER:
How much: Add enough water so that some drains out of the bottom of the pot. Empty the saucer when the water has finished draining.
How often: Water when the top inch of soil is barely moist. For additional information on watering houseplants, see page 919.

TEMPERATURE: Average house temperatures are adequate.

SPECIAL CONDITIONS: Plants may grow too tall and need to be cut back. This will force multiple stems and make the plant more attractive. For information on rooting the tops, see page 921. Because they are adaptable to low light conditions, dieffenbachia are sometimes grown in inadequate light, where they grow poorly. Variegated varieties with very white blotches may sunburn if grown in direct sunlight.

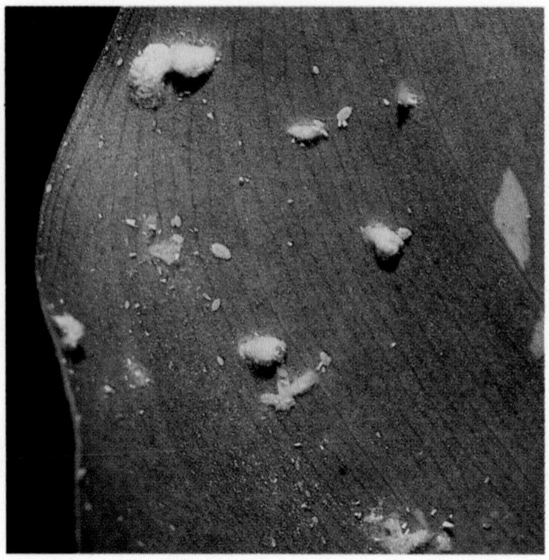
Mealybugs (half life size).

PROBLEM: Oval, white insects up to ¼ inch long cluster in white, cottony masses on leaves, stems, and in the crotches where the leaves are attached. A sticky material may coat the leaves. Leaves may be spotted or deformed. When the condition is severe, leaves and plants may wither and die.

ANALYSIS: Mealybugs
Several species of this common insect feed on dieffenbachia. Mealybugs damage plants by sucking sap, causing leaf distortion and death. The adult female mealybug may produce live young, or may lay eggs in a white fluffy mass of wax. The immature mealybugs, called *nymphs*, crawl all over the plant and onto nearby plants. Soon after they begin to feed, they produce white waxy filaments that cover their bodies, giving them a cottony appearance. As they mature, they become less mobile. Mealybugs cannot digest all the sugar in the sap and excrete the excess in a fluid called honeydew, which coats the leaves and may drop onto furniture below the plant. For additional information on mealybugs, see page 181.

SOLUTION: Spray infested plants indoors with ORTHO Whitefly & Mealybug Killer, ORTHO House Plant Insect Killer, or ORTHO House Plant Insect Control; or take the plants outside and spray them with ORTHO Orthene Systemic Insect Control. (For instructions on spraying houseplants, see page 921.) Where practical, wipe mealybugs off the plant with a damp cloth or with cotton swabs dipped in alcohol. Inspect the pot, including the bottom, for mealybug egg masses. Wipe these off. Avoid bringing mealybugs into the house by carefully inspecting new plants.

Spindly growth.

PROBLEM: Lower leaves turn yellow, starting at the margins. These leaves may wilt, die, and turn light brown. Dead leaves hang down and remain attached to the stem. This condition may progress up the stem until only a few green leaves are left at the top of the plant. Plants may become weak, and the remaining leaves may face toward the light.

ANALYSIS: Insufficient light
Plants use light as a source of energy, and grow slowly in light that is too dim for their needs. If most of the available light comes from one direction, the stems and leaves bend in that direction. If the light is much too dim, the plant has little energy and grows poorly. Although foliage plants generally need less light than plants grown for their flowers or fruit, dieffenbachia has a relatively high need for light.

SOLUTION: Move the plant to a brighter location. If it is allowed to become dry while in direct sunlight, it will sunburn. (For more information on sunburn, see page 178.) If a brighter location is not available, provide supplemental lighting as described on page 920. If you wish to grow a houseplant in a dim location, select a plant that is tolerant of dim light from the list on page 990. If your dieffenbachia has lost most of its lower leaves, reroot the top as described on page 921, cutting the stem back to two nodes. The stem will resprout.

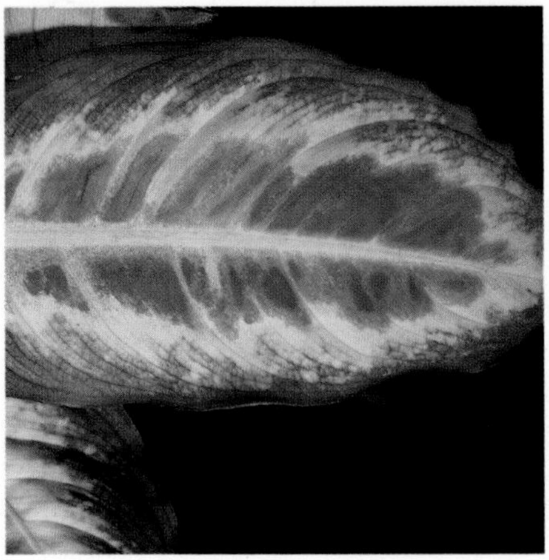

Sunburn.

PROBLEM: Areas between the veins near the margins of older leaves turn yellow, and then tan or light brown. Very light green or white tissues of variegated varieties turn brown between the veins.

ANALYSIS: Sunburn
Dieffenbachia is adaptable to varying amounts of light from bright to relatively dim. Leaf tissue that is deficient in green pigment (chlorophyll) is very susceptible to sunburn, so if variegated dieffenbachias are grown in very bright light, they may sunburn. Leaves on plants that dry out are also susceptible to sunburn. Older leaves are the first to be affected by sunburn when a plant dries out.

SOLUTION: Grow variegated dieffenbachias that have white areas in filtered light. Avoid letting dieffenbachias dry out. Follow watering directions as given on page 919. Avoid moving plants directly from very dim light to very bright light.

Salt damage.

PROBLEM: Tips of older leaves turn brown and brittle and die. Brownish spots and streaks may appear in both young and old leaves.

ANALYSIS: Salt damage
Dieffenbachia is very sensitive to excess salts. Soluble salts that are absorbed by the roots accumulate in the leaves, where concentrations become high enough to kill the tissues. Salts can accumulate from the use of fertilizers or they may be present in the soil used in potting. In some cases, chloride and other damaging salts may be present in tap water. An acidic soil mix (below pH 5.5) will increase the amount of spotting caused by some of these salts. Salts accumulate more rapidly and do more harm if the plant is not watered thoroughly.

SOLUTION: Leach excess salts from the soil by flushing with water. Do this at least three times in a row, letting the water drain through each time. This is done most easily in a bathtub or laundry sink, or outside. As part of normal care, always water dieffenbachia from the top of the pot. Enough water should be added at each watering so that some drains through the pot. Empty the saucer after the pot has finished draining. If the plant is too large to handle easily, use a turkey baster to remove the drainage water. Check the soil pH, and if it is too acidic, raise it to a pH of 6.0 to 7.0 by adding a mixture of ground dolomitic limestone in lukewarm water to the potting soil (use about 2 tablespoons per quart). Water thoroughly afterwards. Recheck the pH after 2 to 3 weeks. For more information about pH, see page 908.

Bacterial stem blight.

PROBLEM: Soft sunken areas with water-soaked margins appear on the stems. Cracks sometimes appear in the affected areas. Lower leaves may turn yellow and become severely wilted. They tend to hang on the stem even when collapsed. If the condition is severe, the stem may rot clear through so that the top of the plant breaks off. Brown streaks occur inside infected stems.

ANALYSIS: Bacterial stem blight
This plant disease is caused by a bacterium (*Erwinia chrysanthemi*). Under wet conditions, the bacteria gain entrance through wounds on the stem. Propagation pieces from infected plants may be infected. Inside the stems, the bacteria cause a soft rot of the tissue, resulting in sunken areas or complete collapse of the stem. Inner stem tissue is discolored brown. Cuttings from infected stems frequently produce infected plants; or they may not root.

SOLUTION: There is no cure for this disease. Discard severely infected plants. If some of the stems are still healthy, cut them off above the diseased area and reroot them according to the instructions on page 921. Do not use any stems if they have brown streaks in them.

DIEFFENBACHIA (DUMB CANE)

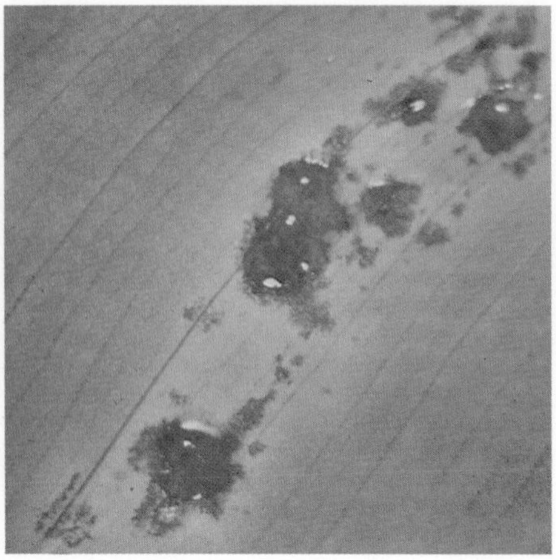

Bacterial leaf spot.

Spider mite damage.

PROBLEM: Small yellow spots with translucent centers appear on the leaves. The spots may enlarge to ¼ inch in diameter, and may become orange with clear centers. Under humid conditions, glistening mounds of bacteria may appear, first on the undersides and then on the upper sides of the spots. The spots may merge, causing larger areas to be affected. The spots are sometimes angular because they are bounded by the veins. If the spots are numerous, leaves have a speckled appearance. Infected leaves may turn yellow, wilt, and die.

ANALYSIS: Bacterial leaf spot
This disease is caused by a bacterium (*Xanthomonas dieffenbachiae*). Under humid conditions, the bacteria gain entrance through wounds or natural openings in the leaves of dieffenbachia. Inside the leaf the bacteria rot the tissue, causing the spots. Under very humid conditions, so many bacteria may be produced that they ooze out of the tissue in a mass. If many infections occur the leaf dies.

SOLUTION: Once leaves are infected, nothing can be done to control the spots already formed. Prevent the spread of the disease to other portions of the leaf or to other plants by keeping the leaves dry. Do not mist the plants. Keep the plants in a room where condensation does not form on the leaves. Remove and destroy severely infected leaves.

PROBLEM: Leaves are stippled, yellow, and dirty; they may dry out and drop. There may be webbing between leaves or on the lower surfaces of the leaves. To determine if a plant is infested with mites, hold a sheet of white paper underneath an affected plant and tap the leaves sharply. Minute green, red, or yellow specks the size of pepper grains will drop to the paper and begin to crawl around. The pests are easily seen against the white background.

ANALYSIS: Spider mites
These mites, related to spiders, are major pests of many houseplants, including dieffenbachia. They cause damage by sucking sap from the undersides of the leaves. As a result of this feeding the green pigment (chlorophyll) disappears, causing the stippled appearance. Under warm, dry conditions, which favor mites, they can build up to tremendous numbers. For more information about spider mites, see page 887.

SOLUTION: Spray infested plants with ORTHO House Plant Insect Control, ORTHO House Plant Insect Killer, or ORTHO Whitefly & Mealybug Killer. (For instructions on spraying houseplants, see page 921.) Plants need to be sprayed weekly for several weeks to kill the mites as they hatch. To avoid introducing mites, inspect new plants carefully.

DIZYGOTHECA (FALSE ARALIA)

Mealybugs (⅓ life size).

PROBLEM: Oval, white insects up to ¼ inch long cluster in cottony masses on leaves, stems, and in the crotches where branches or leaves are attached. A sticky material may coat the leaves.

ANALYSIS: Mealybugs
Several species of mealybugs feed on false aralia. The adult female mealybug may produce live young, or may lay eggs in a white fluffy mass of wax. The immature mealybugs, called *nymphs*, crawl all over the plant and onto nearby plants. Soon after they begin to feed, they produce white waxy filaments that cover their bodies, giving them a cottony appearance. Mealybugs cannot digest all the sugar in the sap and excrete the excess in a fluid called honeydew, which coats the leaves and may drop onto furniture below the plant. For additional information on mealybugs, see page 181.

SOLUTION: Spray infested plants indoors with ORTHO Whitefly & Mealybug Killer, ORTHO House Plant Insect Killer, or ORTHO House Plant Insect Control; or take the plants outside and spray them with ORTHO Orthene Systemic Insect Control or ORTHO Isotox Insect Killer. (For instructions on spraying houseplants, see page 921.) Where practical, wipe mealybugs off the plant with a damp cloth or with cotton swabs dipped in alcohol. Inspect the pot, including the bottom, for mealybug egg masses. Wipe these off.

Dizygotheca cultural information
Light: Needs bright light
Water: When the soil just below the surface is barely moist

DRACAENA

Fusarium leaf spot.

PROBLEM: Circular, reddish brown spots appear on the leaves. The spots are surrounded by a yellow margin. Several spots may join to form blotches. Badly spotted leaves may turn yellow and die.

ANALYSIS: Fusarium leaf spot
This plant disease is caused by a fungus (*Fusarium moniliforme*). Fungal spores are spread from plant to plant by splashing water. The spores germinate on a wet leaf surface within a matter of hours, causing a new spot. In most cases, spotting is unsightly but not harmful. However, if spotting is severe the leaf may weaken and die.

SOLUTION: Clip off badly spotted leaves. Keep the foliage dry to prevent the spread of the fungus. If spotting continues, spray the plant with a fungicide containing *chlorothalonil* (DACONIL 2787®).

Dracaena cultural information
Light: Tolerates dim light
Water: When the soil just below the surface is dry

Salt damage.

PROBLEM: Tips of older leaves die and turn brown and brittle. In severe cases, tips of new leaves may be dead and brown. Tissues adjacent to the dead tips on older leaves may be yellow.

ANALYSIS: Salt damage
Dracaena is very sensitive to excess salts. Soluble salts are picked up by the roots and accumulate in the leaf tips, where concentrations become high enough to kill the tissues. Salts can accumulate from water or the use of fertilizers; or they may be present in the soil used in potting. Salts accumulate more rapidly and do more harm if the plant is not watered thoroughly.

SOLUTION: Leach excess salts from the soil by flushing with water. Water the plant at least three times, letting the water drain each time. This is done most easily in a bathtub or laundry sink or outside. Always water dracaena from the top of the pot. Enough water should be added at each watering so that some drains through the pot. Empty the saucer after the pot has finished draining. If the plant is too large to handle easily, use a turkey baster to remove the drainage water. (For additional watering instructions, see page 923.) Trim the dead tips to a point with a pair of scissors. Do not overfertilize.

Spider mite damage.

PROBLEM: Leaves are stippled, yellow, and dirty; they may dry out and drop. There may be webbing between leaves or on the lower surfaces of the leaves. To determine if a plant is infested with mites, hold a sheet of white paper underneath an affected plant and tap the leaves sharply. Minute green, red, or yellow specks the size of pepper grains will drop to the paper and begin to crawl around. The pests are easily seen against the white background.

ANALYSIS: Spider mites
These mites, related to spiders, are major pests of many houseplants, including dracaena. They cause damage by sucking sap from the undersides of the leaves. As a result of this feeding the green pigment (chlorophyll) disappears, causing the stippled appearance. Under warm, dry conditions, which favor mites, they can build up to tremendous numbers. For more information about spider mites, see page 887.

SOLUTION: Spray infested plants indoors with ORTHO Whitefly & Mealybug Killer, ORTHO House Plant Insect Killer, or ORTHO House Plant Insect Control; or take the plants outdoors and spray them with ORTHO Isotox Insect Killer. (For instructions on spraying houseplants, see page 921.) Plants need to be sprayed weekly for several weeks to kill the mites as they hatch. To avoid introducing mites, inspect new plants carefully.

Water spots.

PROBLEM: Small pale yellow to brown spots appear on the upper surfaces of the leaves. Older leaves are affected more than young leaves.

ANALYSIS: Water spots
Members of the African violet family—including episcia—are very sensitive to rapid temperature changes. Water spots most commonly occur when cold water used in watering is allowed to get on the foliage. If the rapid temperature change occurs in the presence of light, the chlorophyll (green pigment) in the leaves is broken down. In the members of this plant family, all of the chlorophyll in the leaf is found in a single layer of cells near the upper surface. If the chlorophyll in that layer is broken down, the green color disappears, and the underlying leaf color shows through.

SOLUTION: Avoid getting cold water on the foliage when watering episcia plants. Or use water at room temperature. Spotted leaves will not recover. Pick off unsightly leaves.

Episcia cultural information
Light: Needs bright light
Water: When the soil surface is moist but not wet

Mealybugs (half life size).

PROBLEM: Oval, white insects up to ¼ inch long cluster in white, cottony masses on leaves, stems, and in the crotches where leaves are attached. A sticky material may coat the leaves. Leaves may be spotted or deformed. When the condition is severe, leaves and plants may wither and die.

ANALYSIS: Mealybugs
Several species of this common insect feed on episcia. Mealybugs damage plants by sucking sap, causing leaf distortion and death. The adult female mealybug may produce live young, or may lay eggs in a white fluffy mass of wax. The immature mealybugs, called *nymphs*, crawl all over the plant and onto nearby plants. Soon after they begin to feed, they produce white waxy filaments that cover their bodies, giving them a cottony appearance. As they mature, they become less mobile. Mealybugs cannot digest all the sugar in the sap and excrete the excess in a fluid called honeydew, which coats the leaves and may drop onto furniture below the plant. For additional information on mealybugs, see page 181.

SOLUTION: Spray infested plants indoors with an insecticide containing *diazinon.* (For instructions on spraying houseplants, see page 921.) Where practical, wipe mealybugs off the plant with a damp cloth or with cotton swabs dipped in alcohol. Inspect the pot, including the bottom, for mealybug egg masses. Wipe these off. Avoid bringing mealybugs into the house by carefully inspecting new plants.

EUPHORBIA (POINSETTIA)

LIGHT: Poinsettias need abundant light to grow well and flower; grow them in a south-facing window. They also need short days to set flower buds. Put plants in a closet for 13 hours a day for a period of 7 weeks starting around the middle of September, and no later than October 1. They can be brought into bloom any time of the year by giving the short-day treatment 10 weeks before flowering is desired.

SOIL: Any standard houseplant mix. For information on mixes, see page 924.

FERTILIZER: Fertilize monthly during the spring, summer, and fall with ORTHO Ortho-Gro Liquid Plant Food or ORTHO House Plant Food.

WATER:
How much: Add enough water so that some drains out of the bottom of the pot. Empty the saucer as soon as the water drains.
How often: Water when the top soil is barely moist. If allowed to dry out, poinsettias drop their leaves. For additional information on watering houseplants, see page 919.

TEMPERATURE: Poinsettias grow best at warm temperatures. Grow in warm rooms where the temperature does not fall below 60°F at night.

SPECIAL CONDITIONS: Poinsettias will get spindly if not pruned. Pinch regularly to shape plant until August. Do not prune after short-day treatment begins, or flower buds will be removed.

Sporadic flowering.

PROBLEM: Plants continue to produce new leaves, but fail to produce flower heads.

ANALYSIS: Failure to bloom
Poinsettias set flower buds in the fall when the days are less than 12 hours long. In order for flower buds to be produced, they need to be kept in total darkness for at least 13 hours a day for 7 weeks. If this does not occur, they will continue to grow and produce new leaves but not flower heads.

SOLUTION: Place poinsettias in a dark closet at night. Leave them in the closet overnight for at least 13 hours. Make sure that the plants are not exposed to any light while they are in the closet. During the day, place plants where they will receive direct sunlight. To get flowers by Christmas, it is best to begin this process by September 15, and no later than October 1. During the summer, you can grow poinsettias outside. Place them in partial shade for at least 2 days before moving them into direct sun outdoors to prevent sunburn. If poinsettia stems are weak and long, prune them back in July or August.

Leaf drop.

PROBLEM: Lower leaves turn yellow and drop. The leaf dropping progresses up the stem until only the colored bracts may be left on the plant.

ANALYSIS: Leaf drop
Leaf drop in poinsettia may be caused by any of several factors.
1. Root rot, which kills the roots, preventing the top from getting water.
2. Inadequate or irregular watering.
3. Too much water. Even in the absence of disease-producing organisms, too much water will result in lack of air to the roots, causing leaf drop.
4. Insufficient light.

SOLUTION: The numbered solutions below correspond to the numbers in the analysis.
1. Root rot is discussed on page 213.
2. and **3.** Keep plants adequately watered, as discussed on page 923.
4. Give poinsettia plants as much light as possible. Grow them in a sunny window. Supplemental light, as described on page 920, may be desirable.

Root rot of poinsettia.

PROBLEM: Starting at the bottom, leaves turn yellow and drop off. Other leaves may wilt. Eventually the stem has only the colored bracts at the top. Examination of the root system (as described on page 921) reveals dead roots that are brown and soft without white tips.

ANALYSIS: Root rot
Root rot in poinsettia is caused by any of several soil-dwelling fungi, also known as *water molds.* (For more information about water molds, see page 849). These fungi (*Pythium* species and *Thielaviopsis basicola*) invade the small roots, killing them. When the condition is extensive, the plant can no longer obtain water or nutrients, and the leaves drop. The disease is most severe in wet soil. Poinsettia plants retain their colored bracts for a long time after the roots have been killed.

SOLUTION: If the plant is only mildly affected, let the soil dry out between waterings. For more information on this technique, see page 849. If the soil mix is heavy, or the container does not drain well, transplant the plant into a container that drains freely. Use a well-drained soil mix. For information on soil mixes, see page 920. Discard severely infected plants and the soil in which they grew. Wash the pots thoroughly, and soak them in a mixture of 1 part household bleach to 9 parts water for 30 minutes. Rinse with plain water and dry thoroughly before reuse. Or, pasteurize the pots according to the directions on page 920.

EUPHORBIA (POINSETTIA)

Botrytis on poinsettia.

PROBLEM: Brown to purple spots appear on the petallike leaves (bracts) of the red varieties of poinsettia. Tan to brown spots appear on the bracts of the white or pink varieties. In all varieties, the spots tend to appear first at the margins of the bracts, but may appear anywhere on them. The spots may enlarge until a whole bract is destroyed. The flowers (the tiny upright structures in the center of the bracts) die and are covered with a gray to brown, powdery growth. A brown, slightly sunken, soft area may be found on the stem. If this girdles the stem, the portion above it dies.

ANALYSIS: Botrytis

This disease is caused by a fungus (*Botrytis cinerea*). The fungus is unable to directly attack actively growing plant material, but can attack weakened, dead, or inactive tissues. Flowers and bracts are inactive tissues. During periods of high moisture and low temperatures, botrytis will infect such tissues. Once they are invaded, the fungus can then grow into any adjacent healthy plant tissue, such as the stem or leaves. During periods of high humidity, the fungus produces many gray to brown spores borne on dark brown stalks. These spores are carried by air currents, and in the presence of moisture will invade susceptible tissues on the same or other plants.

SOLUTION: It is not necessary to spray to control this disease. Avoid getting water on the bracts or flowers. Keep poinsettia plants in a warm room (above 65°F). Remove and destroy infected parts. Do not keep poinsettias in an environment where the humidity is high.

Spider mites and webs (life size). *Insert:* Damage.

PROBLEM: Leaves are stippled, yellow, and dirty; they may dry out and drop. There may be webbing between leaves or on the lower surfaces of the leaves. To determine if a plant is infested with mites, hold a sheet of white paper underneath an affected plant and tap the leaves sharply. Minute green, red, or yellow specks the size of pepper grains will drop to the paper and begin to crawl around. The pests are easily seen against the white background.

ANALYSIS: Spider mites

These mites, related to spiders, are major pests of many houseplants, including poinsettia. They cause damage by sucking sap from the undersides of the leaves. As a result of feeding, the green pigment (chlorophyll) disappears, causing the stippled appearance. Under warm, dry conditions mites can build up to tremendous numbers. For more information about spider mites, see page 887.

SOLUTION: Spray infested plants indoors with ORTHO House Plant Insect Control, or take the plants outside and spray them with ORTHO Isotox Insect Killer. (For instructions on spraying houseplants, see page 921.) Plants need to be sprayed weekly for several weeks to kill the mites as they hatch. To avoid introducing mites, inspect new plants carefully.

Whiteflies (twice life size).

PROBLEM: Tiny, winged insects 1/12 inch long feed on the undersides of the leaves. The insects are covered with white waxy powder. When the plant is touched, insects flutter rapidly around it. Leaves may be mottled and yellowing.

ANALYSIS: Greenhouse whitefly

(*Trialeurodes vaporariorum*)

This insect is a common pest of poinsettia. The four-winged adult lays eggs on the undersides of leaves. The larvae are the size of a pinhead, flat, oval, immobile, and semitransparent, with radiating white waxy filaments. In about a month, they change to the winged adult form. The larvae are more damaging because they suck more sap from the plants than do the adults. They cannot digest all the sugar in the sap they remove, and excrete the excess in a sugary material called honeydew, which coats the leaves and may drop from the plant onto furniture below.

SOLUTION: Spray with ORTHO House Plant Insect Control or take the plant outside and spray with ORTHO Isotox Insect Killer. For instructions on spraying houseplants, see page 921. Spray weekly as long as the problem continues. Remove heavily infested leaves.

Mealybugs (life size).

PROBLEM: Oval, white insects up to ¼ inch long cluster in white, cottony masses on leaves, stems, and in the crotches where stems or leaves are attached. A sticky material may coat the leaves. Leaves may be spotted or deformed. When the condition is severe, leaves and plants may wither and die.

ANALYSIS: Mealybugs
Several species of this common insect feed on euphorbia. Mealybugs damage plants by sucking sap, causing leaf distortion and death. The adult female mealybug may produce live young, or may lay eggs in a white fluffy mass of wax. The immature mealybugs, called *nymphs*, crawl all over the plant and onto nearby plants. Soon after they begin to feed, they produce white waxy filaments that cover their bodies, giving them a cottony appearance. As they mature, they become less mobile. Mealybugs cannot digest all the sugar in the sap and excrete the excess in a fluid called honeydew, which coats the leaves and may drop onto furniture below the plant. For additional information on mealybugs, see page 181.

SOLUTION: Spray infested plants indoors with ORTHO House Plant Insect Control; or take the plants outside and spray them with ORTHO Isotox Insect Killer. (For instructions on spraying houseplants, see page 921.) Where practical, wipe mealybugs off the plant with a damp cloth or with cotton swabs dipped in alcohol. Inspect the pot, including the bottom, for mealybug egg masses. Wipe these off. Avoid bringing mealybugs into the house by carefully inspecting new plants.

FERNS

LIGHT: Ferns prefer bright, indirect light, but will usually adapt to moderate light. They will burn in direct sun.

SOIL: Use a standard potting mix and add an equal amount of peat moss. For information on potting mixes, see page 924.

FERTILIZER: Fertilize once a month during the growing season (early spring through late summer) with ORTHO Fish Emulsion Fertilizer or ORTHO Fern & Ivy Food.

WATER:
How much: Add enough water so that 10 percent of the water drains through the pot.
How often: Water when the top inch of soil is still moist, but not wet. For additional information on watering houseplants, see page 919.

TEMPERATURE: Ferns will do well in average house temperatures.

SPECIAL CONDITIONS: Ferns are sensitive to salts, and salts must be flushed from the soil with extra water. Do not let ferns stand in drainage water.

Dieback caused by low humidity.

PROBLEM: Leaves turn yellow and eventually die. Fronds may die from the tips down. The center parts of the plant are more severely affected than are the outer portions.

ANALYSIS: Low humidity
Most ferns need higher humidity than homes provide. The ferns used as houseplants are adapted to forest floors and creeksides, where the air is usually moist. In the winter, when homes are heated, the air can become as dry as desert air. Air is particularly dry near heater vents or radiators. The problem is made more severe if the soil in which the fern is growing is allowed to dry out.

SOLUTION: Move the fern to a more humid location, such as a well-lit bathroom. Misting does not help relieve stress on the fern. The mist only dampens the fronds for a few minutes at a time. Placing the plant in a tray of gravel in which some water is kept raises the humidity around the plant only if the damp air is not allowed to escape. If there is free movement of air around the plant, the practice is of little value. A portable humidifier will raise the humidity in the immediate vicinity while it is operating. Plant ferns in a potting mix that contains a high proportion of organic material, such as peat moss or ground bark, and which drains quickly. Never allow the potting mix to dry out.

FERNS

Insufficient light.

PROBLEM: The plant grows slowly or stops growing entirely. More fronds grow from the side of the pot nearest the light source. Some of the fronds may turn yellow or brown and die, beginning with the older frondlets and progressing toward the tip of the frond. Fronds may be weak and spindly.

ANALYSIS: Insufficient light
Ferns use light as a source of energy and grow slowly in dim light. If most of the available light is coming from one direction, the fronds grow mainly from that side. If the light is much too dim, the plant cannot support healthy, vigorous growth. Although foliage plants generally need less light than plants grown for their flowers or fruit, many ferns have a relatively high need for light.

SOLUTION: Move the plant to a brighter location, such as a lightly curtained sunny window. If a bright location is not available, provide supplemental lighting as described on page 920. If you wish to grow a houseplant in a dim location, select a plant that is tolerant of dim light from the list on page 1001.

Salt damage.

PROBLEM: Margins of older leaves die and turn brown, beginning at the base of the fronds and progressing outward. In severe cases, all fronds may have dead margins. Tissues adjacent to the dead margins of older fronds may turn yellow.

ANALYSIS: Salt damage
Ferns are sensitive to excess salts. Soluble salts are picked up by the roots and accumulate in the leaf margins, where concentrations may become high enough to kill the tissues. Salts accumulate from water or the use of fertilizers; or they may be present in the soil used in potting. Salts accumulate more rapidly and do more harm if the plant is not watered thoroughly.

SOLUTION: If symptoms of salt damage occur, leach excess salts from the soil by flushing with water. Water the plant at least three times, letting the water drain each time. This is done most easily in a bathtub or laundry sink or outside. Always water ferns from the top of the pot. Enough water should be added at each watering so that some drains through the pot. Empty the saucer after the pot has finished draining. If the plant is too large to handle easily, use a turkey baster to remove the drainage water. (For additional watering instructions, see page 923.) Do not overfertilize.

Root rot.

PROBLEM: Plants fail to grow and are stunted. Roots are soft and decayed. The outer portion of the roots slips off easily from the central portion. (For instructions on examining roots, see page 921.) The top of the plant may fall over or be lifted easily out of the soil. Infected plants may die.

ANALYSIS: Root rot
This plant disease is caused by soil-dwelling fungi (*Pythium* species), also known as *water molds.* (For more information about water molds, see page 849.) These fungi attack and rot the roots of many plants, including ferns. The fungi may invade only the smaller rootlets, stunting the plant; or they may invade the main root system and cause severe rotting. Fern roots are dark, so inspecting them may be difficult. Infected roots are unable to pick up enough moisture and nutrients to support the plant. The leaves of ferns are so stiff that they wilt only slightly. Plants in soil that is too wet are more susceptible.

SOLUTION: If the plant is only mildly affected, let the soil dry out between waterings. For more information on this technique, see page 849. If the soil mix is heavy, or the container does not drain well, transplant the plant into a container that drains freely. Use a well-drained soil mix. For information on soil mixes, see page 920. Discard severely infected plants and the soil in which they grew. Wash the pots thoroughly, and soak them in a mixture of 1 part household bleach to 9 parts water for 30 minutes. Rinse with plain water and dry thoroughly before reuse. Or, pasteurize the pots according to the directions on page 920.

Scale (twice life size).

PROBLEM: Stems and fronds are covered with white, cottony, cushionlike masses or brown crusty bumps. The bumps can be scraped or picked off easily. Fronds turn yellow and may drop. A shiny or sticky material may cover fronds and stems. The bumps are sometimes mistaken for reproductive spores produced by the fern. The round, flat, sometimes hairy spores are found only on the undersides of fronds, spaced at regular intervals. They are difficult to pick or scrape off.

ANALYSIS: Scale insects
Several different types of scale insects attack ferns. Some types can infest many different plants. Scales hatch from eggs. The young, called *crawlers*, are small (about 1/10 inch), soft-bodied, and move about on the plant and onto other plants. After moving about for a short time, they insert their mouthparts into the plant, feeding on the sap. The legs disappear, and the scales remain in the same place for the rest of their lives. Some develop a soft covering, others a hard covering. Some species of scales are unable to digest fully all the sugar in the plant sap and excrete the excess in a fluid called honeydew, which may cover the fronds or drip onto surfaces below. For more information about scales, see page 876.

SOLUTION: Spray infested plants with ORTHO Whitefly & Mealybug Killer, ORTHO House Plant Insect Killer, or ORTHO House Plant Insect Control. Spraying is more effective against the crawlers than against the adults. Repeated applications may be necessary. For additional information on spraying houseplants, see page 921.

Foliar nematode damage to bird's-nest fern.

PROBLEM: Brown spots appear first near the central vein at the bases of the fronds of bird's-nest fern. The spots spread outward between the parallel veins forming brown bands. Much of the leaf may become infected. Severely infected leaves or entire plants may die.

ANALYSIS: Foliar nematode
(*Aphelenchoides fragariae*)
This disease is caused by a nematode that infests the leaves. Nematodes are microscopic, clear worms that usually infect the roots of plants. This nematode, however, infects the foliage of a large number of plants, including bird's-nest fern. The nematodes enter the leaves through the breathing pores. Inside the leaves, they feed on the tissues, killing them, then spread into healthy tissue, extending the damage. The veins in the leaves act as barriers, resulting in the parallel bands. The nematodes reproduce rapidly in the infected leaves. They spread outside the leaves when the leaves are wet by swimming through the film of water. They may be splashed to other leaves or plants. When the condition is severe, leaves or plants may be killed.

SOLUTION: Cut off and destroy infested leaves. If plants are severely infested, destroy them. Avoid getting the leaves wet when watering. Do not spray or mist the foliage of bird's-nest fern. Keep plants in rooms warm enough so that dew does not form and the leaves do not exude water at their margins.

FICUS (ORNAMENTAL FIGS)

LIGHT: Most figs should be grown in the best light available. Fiddle leaf fig can tolerate somewhat lower light.

SOIL: Any standard houseplant mix. For information on soil mixes, see page 924.

FERTILIZER: Fertilize once a month with ORTHO Fish Emulsion Fertilizer, ORTHO House Plant Food, or ORTHO Ortho-Gro Liquid Plant Food. Plants in reduced light should be fertilized once every 2 months.

WATER:
How much: Add enough water so that some drains out of the bottom of the pot.
How often: Water when the soil under the surface is moist but not wet. *Ficus* must not be allowed to dry out. For additional information on watering houseplants, see page 919.

TEMPERATURE: Keep *Ficus* as warm as possible under house conditions.

SPECIAL CONDITIONS: Avoid moving *Ficus* to areas where light levels are different. Abrupt changes in light cause leaf yellowing and dropping on some species. If moving plants to different light intensities, move them several times so that the change in light is gradual.

FICUS (ORNAMENTAL FIGS)

Yellow leaves.

Leaf drop.

Salt damage to Java fig.

PROBLEM: Leaves of weeping fig drop. The leaf dropping may cause defoliation of many branches or, in severe cases, the entire plant. Dropping leaves may be green and healthy looking or yellow and discolored.

ANALYSIS: Leaf drop Weeping figs may drop their leaves in response to any of the following conditions.	**SOLUTION:** The numbered solutions below correspond to the numbers in the analysis.
1. *Overwatering:* When plants are watered too frequently or soil drainage is poor, the roots are susceptible to root-rotting fungi. Weak and decaying roots cannot provide enough water and nutrients for proper plant growth.	**1.** Allow the plant to dry out slightly between waterings. The soil just beneath the surface should be moist but not wet when you water. Empty the saucer after the pot has drained. If the pot is not draining well, transplant to a pot with a good drainage hole, and use a light, well-draining soil mix.
2. *Underwatering:* Weeping figs need constantly moist soil. If plants are not watered frequently enough, or the soil is not thoroughly soaked at each irrigation, they respond by dropping their leaves.	**2.** Check the soil periodically. Water when the soil just below the surface is still moist, but is no longer wet.
3. *Insufficient light:* Weeping figs need bright indirect light or direct sunlight for best growth. They may drop their leaves even in locations that are bright enough for most other foliage plants.	**3.** Move plants to a location in bright, indirect light or direct sunlight. If the plants have been growing in a dark area, first move them for 2 weeks to a location that receives bright, indirect light or only 1 to 2 hours of morning sun; then place them in direct sunlight.
4. *Transplant shock:* Transplanting always results in some disturbance to the rootball. Weeping figs are likely to drop some leaves even when the disturbance is minimal.	**4.** Transplant weeping figs carefully, so as not to disturb the rootball. Some leaf drop after transplanting is normal. The plant will stop dropping leaves after a few weeks if given proper care.
5. *Changes in enviornment:* Drafts and extreme fluctuations in temperature, light levels, and watering patterns are likely to cause leaf drop. When a greenhouse-grown plant is brought into a drier, darker, cooler home environment, it will often respond to the change by dropping many of it leaves.	**5.** Avoid drafty areas and sudden environmental changes. Place new plants where conditions are as similar as possible to those in which they were grown. Some leaf drop is normal for a few weeks until the plant becomes acclimated to its new location.

PROBLEM: Margins of older leaves die and turn brown and brittle. In severe cases, all leaves may have dead margins. Tissues adjacent to the dead margins of older leaves may turn yellow. Branches may die back.

ANALYSIS: Salt damage
Ficus is sensitive to excess salts. Soluble salts are picked up by the roots and accumulate in the leaf margins, where concentrations may become high enough to kill the tissues. Salts can accumulate from water or the use of fertilizers; or they may be present in the soil used in potting. Salts accumulate more rapidly and do more harm if the plant is not watered thoroughly.

SOLUTION: Leach excess salts from the soil by flushing with water. Water the plant at least three times, letting the water drain each time. This is done most easily in a bathtub or laundry sink or outside. Always water *Ficus* from the top of the pot. Enough water should be added at each watering so that some drains through the pot. Empty the saucer after the pot has finished draining. If the plant is too large to handle, use a turkey baster to remove the drainage water. (For additional watering instructions, see page 923.) Do not overfertilize.

Oedema on fiddleleaf fig.

PROBLEM: Small (up to 3⁄16 inch) yellow or brown spots appear on the upper surfaces of older leaves. On the undersides of the spots and sometimes on the veins are small, raised, corky areas, which may be lighter green or tan. These spots may have a dark brown center, and may be surrounded by a water-soaked area. If many spots occur, the lower leaves may turn yellow and drop.

ANALYSIS: Oedema
Oedema is a disease found on many plants. It is not caused by infection, but results from environmental factors. It is believed to be caused by excessive watering during periods of high humidity, but it also develops sometimes in plants that are kept dry and in low humidity. In *Ficus*, a milky juice may leak out of the corky spots. When this juice dries, it leaves a brown spot on the raised area. For more information about oedema, see page 860.

SOLUTION: Give *Ficus* adequate light and adequate moisture. Avoid keeping the soil too wet, especially during periods of cloudy, damp weather. Avoid letting plants dry out.

Mealybugs on mistletoe fig (life size).

PROBLEM: Oval, white insects up to 1⁄4 inch long cluster in white, cottony masses on leaves, stems, and in the crotches where branches or leaves are attached. A sticky material may coat the leaves. Leaves may be spotted or deformed. When the condition is severe, leaves and plants may wither and die.

ANALYSIS: Mealybugs
Several species of this common insect feed on *Ficus*. Mealybugs damage plants by sucking sap, causing leaf distortion and death. The adult female mealybug may produce live young, or may lay eggs in a white fluffy mass of wax. The immature mealybugs, called *nymphs*, crawl all over the plant and onto nearby plants. Soon after they begin to feed, they produce white waxy filaments that cover their bodies, giving them a cottony appearance. As they mature, they become less mobile. Mealybugs cannot digest all the sugar in the sap and excrete the excess in a fluid called honeydew, which coats the leaves and may drop onto furniture below the plant. For additional information on mealybugs, see page 181.

SOLUTION: Spray infested plants with ORTHO Whitefly & Mealybug Killer, ORTHO House Plant Insect Killer, or ORTHO House Plant Insect Control. (For instructions on spraying houseplants, see page 921.) Where practical, wipe mealybugs off the plant with a damp cloth or with cotton swabs dipped in alcohol. Inspect the pot, including the bottom, for mealybug egg masses. Wipe these off. Avoid bringing mealybugs into the house by carefully inspecting new plants.

Florida wax scale (twice life size).

PROBLEM: Stems and leaves are covered with white, cottony, cushionlike masses or brown crusty bumps. The bumps can be scraped or picked off easily. Leaves turn yellow and may drop. A shiny or sticky material may cover leaves and stems.

ANALYSIS: Scale insects
Several different types of scale insects attack *Ficus*. Some types can infest many different plants. Scales hatch from eggs. The young, called *crawlers*, are small (about 1⁄10 inch), soft-bodied, and move about on the plant and onto other plants. After moving about for a short time, they insert their mouthparts into the plant, feeding on the sap. The legs disappear, and the scales remain in the same place for the rest of their lives. Some develop a soft covering, others a hard covering. Some species of scales are unable to digest fully all the sugar in the plant sap and excrete the excess in a fluid called honeydew, which may cover the leaves or drip onto surfaces below. For more information about scales, see page 876.

SOLUTION: Spray infested plants with ORTHO Whitefly & Mealybug Killer, ORTHO House Plant Insect Killer, or ORTHO House Plant Insect Control. Spraying is more effective against the crawlers than against the adults. Repeated applications may be necessary. For additional information on spraying houseplants, see page 921.

FITTONIA (NERVE PLANT)

Mealybugs (half life size).

PROBLEM: Oval, white insects up to 1/4 inch long cluster in white, cottony masses on leaves, stems, and in the crotches where the leaves are attached. A sticky material may coat the leaves. Leaves may be spotted or deformed. When the condition is severe, leaves and plants may wither and die.

ANALYSIS: Mealybugs
Several species of this common insect feed on nerve plant. Mealybugs damage plants by sucking sap, causing leaf distortion and death. The adult female mealybug may produce live young, or may lay eggs in a white fluffy mass of wax. The immature mealybugs, called *nymphs*, crawl all over the plant and onto nearby plants. Soon after they begin to feed, they produce white waxy filaments that cover their bodies, giving them a cottony appearance. Mealybugs cannot digest all the sugar in the sap and excrete the excess in a fluid called honeydew, which coats the leaves and may drop onto furniture below the plant. For additional information on mealybugs, see page 181.

SOLUTION: Spray infested plants with an insecticide containing *diazinon*. (For instructions on spraying houseplants, see page 921.) Where practical, wipe mealybugs off the plant with a damp cloth or with cotton swabs dipped in alcohol. Inspect the pot, including the bottom, for mealybug egg masses. Avoid bringing mealybugs into the house by carefully inspecting new plants.

Fittonia cultural information
Light: Needs bright light
Water: When the soil surface is moist but not wet

GARDENIA

Cold damage.

PROBLEM: Plants fail to produce flowers. If buds are produced, they drop from the plant without opening. Foliage may be light green; plants may be stunted.

ANALYSIS: Too cold
Gardenia plants are native to warm areas. If they do not receive enough heat, they cannot manufacture enough food to grow well, and they stop producing flowers. If too cold, the plants will be stunted and not as much green pigment (chlorophyll) will be produced.

SOLUTION: Grow gardenia plants in the warmest location with the most light possible. If the room is cool at night, move the plant to a warm room. In the summer, the plant can be grown outside in light shade.

Gardenia cultural information
Light: Needs bright light
Water: When the soil just below the surface is barely moist

Iron deficiency.

PROBLEM: The newest leaves turn yellow at the margins. As the leaves become more yellow, the veins remain green. In severe cases, the entire leaf is yellow and small. The plant may be stunted.

ANALYSIS: Iron deficiency
This is a common problem with acid-loving plants like gardenia, which grow best in soil with a pH between 5.5 and 6.5. (For more information on soil acidity, see page 908.) The leaf yellowing is due to a deficiency of iron and other minor nutrients in the plant. The soil is seldom deficient in iron. However, iron is often found in an insoluble form that is not available to gardenias, especially when the soil pH is too high. Plants use iron in the formation of the green pigment (chlorophyll) in the leaves.

SOLUTION: Spray the foliage with ORTHO Greenol Liquid Iron, and apply it to the soil in the pot to correct iron deficiency. Use only acid-forming fertilizers like ORTHO Azalea, Camellia & Rhododendron Food. When potting or transplanting gardenias, use an acidic soil mix that has about 50 percent peat moss. Use a minimum amount of lime or dolomite in the soil mix.

GYNURA (PURPLE PASSION VINE)

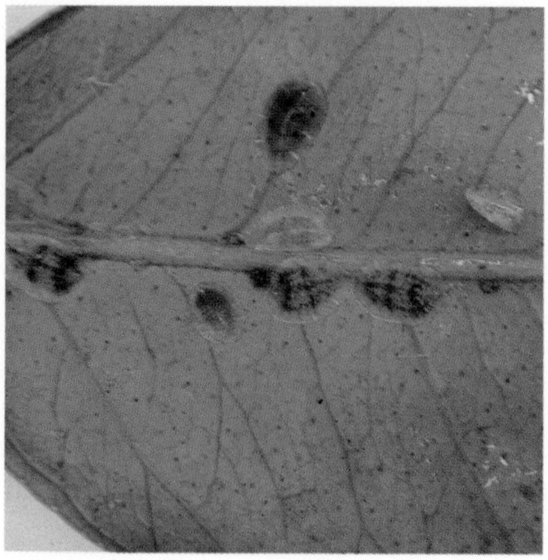

Brown soft scale (twice life size).

PROBLEM: Stems and leaves are covered with white, cottony, cushionlike masses or brown crusty bumps. The bumps can be scraped or picked off easily. Leaves turn yellow and may drop. A shiny or sticky material may cover leaves and stems.

ANALYSIS: Scale insects
Several different types of scale insects attack gardenias. Some types can infest many different plants. Scales hatch from eggs. The young, called *crawlers*, are small (about 1/10 inch), soft-bodied, and move about on the plant and onto other plants. After moving about for a short time, they insert their mouthparts into the plant, feeding on the sap. The legs disappear, and the scales remain in the same place for the rest of their lives. Some develop a soft covering, others a hard covering. Some species of scales are unable to digest fully all the sugar in the plant sap and excrete the excess in a fluid called honeydew, which may cover the leaves or drip onto surfaces below. For more information about scales, see page 876.

SOLUTION: Spray infested plants indoors with ORTHO House Plant Insect Control; or take the plants outside and spray them with ORTHO Malathion 50 Insect Spray, ORTHO Orthene Systemic Insect Control, or ORTHO Isotox Insect Killer, according to the directions on the label. Spraying is more effective against the crawlers than against the adults. Repeated applications may be necessary. For additional information on spraying houseplants, see page 921.

Aphids (life size).

PROBLEM: New leaves are curled, discolored, and reduced in size. A shiny or sticky substance may coat the leaves. Tiny (1/8 inch), nonwinged, green, soft-bodied insects cluster on the buds, young stems, and leaves.

ANALYSIS: Aphids
Aphids do little damage in small numbers. However, they are extremely prolific and populations can rapidly build up to damaging numbers on purple passion vines. Damage results when the aphids suck sap from the leaves and stems. Aphids are unable to digest fully all the sugar in the plant sap and excrete the excess in a fluid called honeydew, which often drops onto leaves or furniture below the plant. For more information about aphids, see page 875.

SOLUTION: Use ORTHO House Plant Insect Control, ORTHO House Plant Insect Killer, or ORTHO Whitefly & Mealybug Killer. For additional information on spraying houseplants, see page 921.

Gynura cultural information
Light: Needs bright light
Water: When the soil just below the surface is barely moist

Mealybugs (1/3 life size).

PROBLEM: Oval, white insects up to 1/4 inch long cluster in white, cottony masses on leaves, stems, and in the crotches where the leaves are attached. A sticky material may coat the leaves. Leaves may be spotted or deformed. When the condition is severe, leaves and plants may wither and die.

ANALYSIS: Mealybugs
Several species of this common insect feed on purple passion vine. Mealybugs damage plants by sucking sap, causing leaf distortion and death. The adult female mealybug may produce live young, or may lay eggs in a white fluffy mass of wax. The immature mealybugs, called *nymphs*, crawl all over the plant and onto nearby plants. Soon after they begin to feed, they produce white waxy filaments that cover their bodies, giving them a cottony appearance. As they mature, they become less mobile. Mealybugs cannot digest all the sugar in the sap and excrete the excess in a fluid called honeydew, which coats the leaves and may drop onto furniture below the plant. For additional information on mealybugs, see page 181.

SOLUTION: Spray infested plants indoors with ORTHO Whitefly & Mealybug Killer, ORTHO House Plant Insect Killer, or ORTHO House Plant Insect Control. Or take the plants outside and spray them with ORTHO Isotox Insect Killer. (For instructions on spraying houseplants, see page 921.) Where practical, wipe mealybugs off the plant with a damp cloth or with cotton swabs dipped in alcohol. Inspect the pot, including the bottom, for mealybug egg masses. Wipe these off. Avoid bringing mealybugs into the house by carefully inspecting new plants.

HAWORTHIA ■ HEDERA (IVY)

Salt damage.

PROBLEM: Tips of older leaves die and turn brown. In severe cases, the tips of all leaves may be dead.

ANALYSIS: Salt damage
Haworthia is sensitive to excess salts. Soluble salts are picked up by the roots and accumulate in the leaf tips, where concentrations may become high enough to kill the tissues. Salts can accumulate from water or the use of fertilizers; or they may be present in the soil used in potting. Salts accumulate more rapidly and do more harm if the plant is not watered thoroughly.

SOLUTION: Leach excess salts from the soil by flushing with water. Water the plant at least three times, letting the water drain each time. This is done most easily in a bathtub or laundry sink or outside. Always water haworthia from the top of the pot. Enough water should be added at each watering so that some drains through the pot. Empty the saucer after the pot has finished draining. (For additional watering instructions, see page 923.) Do not overfertilize.

Haworthia cultural information
Light: Needs bright light
Water: When the soil just below the surface is dry

HEDERA (IVY)

LIGHT: Ivy adapts to various levels of light. It will grow in bright light, but will also grow in relatively dim light, as in a north-facing window.

SOIL: Use any of the standard potting mixes. For information on soil mixes, see page 920.

FERTILIZER: For best growth, fertilize once a month with ORTHO Fish Emulsion Fertilizer or ORTHO Fern & Ivy Food. If less growth is desired, fertilize every other month.

WATER:
How much: Add enough water so that some drains through the pot.
How often: Water when the top layer of soil begins to get dry. Ivy is very tolerant of dry conditions if it is not in direct sun. For additional information on watering houseplants, see page 919.

TEMPERATURE: Average house temperatures are suitable.

SPECIAL CONDITIONS: Do not let ivy plants stand in drainage water. Excessive moisture will favor oedema (see page 223). Fertilizing and watering less frequently will result in slower growth and more compact plants. Plants can be cut back to induce compactness.

Sunburn.

PROBLEM: Pale green to yellow blotches appear between the leaf veins. These blotches may become bleached white or tan as the tissue between the veins dies. Whole sections between veins may be affected. Spots may merge, affecting larger areas.

ANALYSIS: Sunburn
Excessive sunlight causes the green pigment (chlorophyll) to disappear in ivy leaves. This happens most easily if the plant is allowed to dry out. Once the tissues have lost their chlorophyll, the sunlight kills the tissues between the veins. The underlying color of different ivy species determines the color of the dead tissues. Plants moved from inside to direct sunlight will sunburn very severely.

SOLUTION: Keep ivy plants well watered so they do not dry out, particularly if they are in direct sunlight. If you are moving plants from inside to outside, place them in the shade for several days before putting them in direct sunlight.

Salt damage.

PROBLEM: Margins of older leaves die and turn brown and brittle. In severe cases, all leaves may have dead margins. Tissues adjacent to the dead margins of older leaves may turn yellow.

ANALYSIS: Salt damage
Ivy is sensitive to excess salts. Soluble salts are picked up by the roots and accumulate in the leaf margins, where concentrations may become high enough to kill the tissues. Salts can accumulate from water or the use of fertilizers; or they may be present in the soil used in potting. Salts accumulate more rapidly and do more harm if the plant is not watered thoroughly.

SOLUTION: Leach excess salts from the soil by flushing with water. Water the plant at least three times, letting the water drain each time. This is done most easily in a bathtub or laundry sink or outside. Always water ivy from the top of the pot. Enough water should be added at each watering so that some drains through the pot. Empty the saucer after the pot has finished draining. If the plant is too large to handle easily, use a turkey baster to remove the drainage water. (For additional watering instructions, see page 923.) Do not overfertilize.

Oedema.

PROBLEM: Small (3/16 inch), red to black spots appear on the upper surfaces of the leaves. On the undersides of these spots are raised corky areas that first appear light green and water-soaked. Eventually they become dark brown or black. In severe cases, leaves may become yellow.

ANALYSIS: Oedema
Oedema is a disease found on many plants. It is not infectious but results from unfavorable environmental factors. It is believed to be due to excessive watering during periods of high humidity. However, it occasionally occurs with low humidity and on ivy plants that have been kept dry. For more information about oedema, see page 860.

SOLUTION: Grow ivy with adequate moisture and fertilizer. Avoid keeping soil too wet or too dry. (For additional watering instructions, see page 919.) Avoid overcrowding plants.

Brown soft scale (twice life size).

PROBLEM: Stems and leaves are covered with white, cottony, cushion-like masses or brown crusty bumps or clusters of somewhat flattened, reddish, gray or brown scaly bumps. The bumps can be scraped off or picked off easily. Leaves turn yellow and may drop. A shiny or sticky material may cover leaves and stems.

ANALYSIS: Scale insects
Several different types of scale insects attack ivy. Some types can infest many different plants. Scales hatch from eggs. The young, called *crawlers*, are small (about 1/10 inch), soft-bodied, and move about on the plant and onto other plants. After moving about for a short time, they insert their mouthparts into the plant, feeding on the sap. The legs atrophy, and the scales remain in the same place for the rest of their lives. Some develop a soft covering, others a hard covering. Some species of scales are unable to digest fully all the sugar in the plant sap and excrete the excess in a fluid called honeydew, which may cover the leaves or drip onto surfaces below. For more information about scales, see page 876.

SOLUTION: Spray infested plants with ORTHO Whitefly & Mealybug Killer, ORTHO House Plant Insect Killer, or ORTHO House Plant Insect Control according to the directions on the label. Spraying is more effective against the crawlers than against the adults. Repeated applications may be necessary. For additional information on spraying houseplants, see page 921.

HEDERA (IVY)

Spider mites (twice life size) and webs.

PROBLEM: Leaves are stippled, yellow, and dirty; they may dry out and drop. There may be webbing between leaves or on the lower surfaces of the leaves. To determine if a plant is infested with mites, hold a sheet of white paper underneath an affected plant and tap the leaves sharply. Minute green, red, or yellow specks the size of pepper grains will drop to the paper and begin to crawl around. The pests are easily seen against the white background.

ANALYSIS: Spider mites
These mites, related to spiders, are major pests of many houseplants, including ivy. They cause damage by sucking sap from the undersides of the leaves. As a result of this feeding, the green pigment (chlorophyll) disappears, causing the stippled appearance. Under warm, dry conditions, which favor mites, they can build up to tremendous numbers. For more information about spider mites, see page 887.

SOLUTION: Spray infested plants with ORTHO House Plant Insect Control, ORTHO House Plant Insect Killer, or ORTHO Whitefly & Mealybug Killer. (For instructions on spraying houseplants, see page 921.) Plants need to be sprayed weekly for several weeks to kill the mites as they hatch. To avoid introducing mites, inspect new plants carefully.

Mealybugs (life size).

PROBLEM: Oval, white insects up to ¼ inch long cluster in white, cottony masses on leaves, stems, and in the crotches where the leaves are attached. A sticky material may coat the leaves. Leaves may be spotted or deformed. When the condition is severe, leaves and plants may wither and die.

ANALYSIS: Mealybugs
Several species of this common insect feed on ivy. Mealybugs damage plants by sucking sap, causing leaf distortion and death. The adult female mealybug may produce live young, or may lay eggs in a white fluffy mass of wax. The immature mealybugs, called *nymphs*, crawl all over the plant and onto nearby plants. Soon after they begin to feed, they produce white waxy filaments that cover their bodies, giving them a cottony appearance. As they mature, they become less mobile. Mealybugs cannot digest all the sugar in the sap and excrete the excess in a fluid called honeydew, which coats the leaves and may drop onto furniture below the plant. For additional information on mealybugs, see page 181.

SOLUTION: Spray infested plants indoors with ORTHO Whitefly & Mealybug Killer or ORTHO House Plant Insect Killer; or take the plants outside and spray them with ORTHO Orthene Systemic Insect Control or ORTHO Isotox Insect Killer. (For instructions on spraying houseplants, see page 921.) Where practical, wipe mealybugs off the plant with a damp cloth or with cotton swabs dipped in alcohol. Inspect the pot, including the bottom, for mealybug egg masses. Wipe these off. Avoid bringing mealybugs into the house by carefully inspecting new plants.

HIPPEASTRUM (AMARYLLIS)

Leaf scorch.

PROBLEM: Red spots and lesions appear on the flower stalk, leaves, and petals. The spots may elongate to several inches in length. Reddish brown, sunken lesions (cankers) with bright red borders may develop on the flower stalks. Flower stalks may be stunted, distorted, and growing at an angle. Severely infected flower stalks fail to bloom.

ANALYSIS: Leaf scorch
This plant disease is caused by a fungus (*Stagonospora curtisii*) that attacks both growing plants and bulbs in storage. Soon after infected bulbs produce growth, fungal spores are splashed and blown to the stems and leaves. The spores germinate and infect the tissue, causing spots and cankers to form. The disease is spread by contaminated bulbs, and is most severe in moist conditions.

SOLUTION: Discard severely infected plants. Infection may be controlled on mildly infected plants by keeping them in a dry location and spraying with a fungicide containing *ferbam* or *zineb* every 2 weeks until they bloom. Check all bulbs before planting, and discard infected bulbs.

Hippeastrum cultural information
Light: Needs bright light
Water: When the soil surface is moist but not wet

HOYA (WAX PLANT)

Aphids (twice life size).

PROBLEM: New leaves are curled, discolored, and reduced in size. A shiny or sticky substance may coat the leaves. Tiny (1/8 inch), nonwinged, green, soft-bodied insects cluster on the buds, young stems, and leaves.

ANALYSIS: Aphids
Aphids do little damage in small numbers. However, they are extremely prolific and populations can rapidly build up to damaging numbers on hoya. Damage results when the aphids suck sap from the leaves and stems. Aphids are unable to digest fully all the sugar in the plant sap and excrete the excess in a fluid called honeydew, which often drops onto leaves or furniture below the plant. For more information about aphids, see page 875.

SOLUTION: Use ORTHO House Plant Insect Control. For additional information on spraying houseplants, see page 921.

Hoya cultural information
Light: Needs bright light
Water: When the soil just below the surface is barely moist

Spider mite damage.

PROBLEM: Leaves are stippled, yellow, and dirty; they may dry out and drop. There may be webbing over flower buds, between leaves, or on the lower surfaces of the leaves. To determine if a plant is infested with mites, hold a sheet of white paper underneath an affected plant and tap the leaves sharply. Minute green, red, or yellow specks the size of pepper grains will drop to the paper and begin to crawl around. The pests are easily seen against the white background.

ANALYSIS: Spider mites
These mites, related to spiders, are major pests of many houseplants, including wax plant. They cause damage by sucking sap from the undersides of the leaves. As a result of this feeding, the green pigment (chlorophyll) disappears, causing the stippled appearance. Under warm, dry conditions, which favor mites, they can build up to tremendous numbers. For more information about spider mites, see page 887.

SOLUTION: Spray infested plants with ORTHO Whitefly & Mealybug Killer, or ORTHO House Plant Insect Killer. (For instructions on spraying houseplants, see page 921.) Plants need to be sprayed weekly for several weeks to kill the mites as they hatch. To avoid introducing mites, inspect new plants carefully.

Failure to flower.

PROBLEM: Plants fail to flower. Vines tend to grow toward a light source. Leaves are produced far apart on the stems.

ANALYSIS: Insufficient light
Plants use light as a source of energy. If there is only enough light for leaf and vine growth, hoya will not bloom. It must have bright light in order to make flowers. If the light is too dim for optimum growth, the plant not only will not bloom, but growth is slowed, and the vines grow toward a light source. Leaves will be small and far apart on the vines.

SOLUTION: Move the plant to a brighter location. Hoya will tolerate direct sun if it is kept well watered. But if it is allowed to become dry while in direct sunlight, it will sunburn. (For more information on sunburn, see page 178.) If a brighter location is not available, provide supplemental lighting as described on page 920. If you wish to grow a houseplant in a dim location, select a plant that is tolerant of dim light from the list on page 1001.

HOYA (WAX PLANT)

Mealybugs (half life size).

PROBLEM: Oval, white insects up to 1/4 inch long cluster in white, cottony masses on leaves, stems, and in the crotches where the leaves are attached. A sticky material may coat the leaves. Leaves may be spotted or deformed. When the condition is severe, leaves and plants may wither and die.

ANALYSIS: Mealybugs
Several species of this common insect feed on wax plant. Mealybugs damage plants by sucking sap, causing leaf distortion and death. The adult female mealybug may produce live young, or may lay eggs in a white fluffy mass of wax. The immature mealybugs, called *nymphs*, crawl all over the plant and onto nearby plants. Soon after they begin to feed, they produce white waxy filaments that cover their bodies, giving them a cottony appearance. As they mature, they become less mobile. Mealybugs cannot digest all the sugar in the sap and excrete the excess in a fluid called honeydew, which coats the leaves and may drop onto furniture below the plant. For additional information on mealybugs, see page 181.

SOLUTION: Spray infested plants indoors with ORTHO Whitefly & Mealybug Killer, or ORTHO House Plant Insect Killer. (For instructions on spraying houseplants, see page 921.) Where practical, wipe mealybugs off the plant with a damp cloth or with cotton swabs dipped in alcohol. Inspect the pot, including the bottom, for mealybug egg masses. Wipe these off. Avoid bringing mealybugs into the house by carefully inspecting new plants.

IRESINE (BLOOD LEAF)

Weak stems.

PROBLEM: Leaves fade from deep red to very light red. Stems elongate, and leaves are produced farther apart on the stems. Stems become weak.

ANALYSIS: Insufficient light
Plants use light as a source of energy, and grow slowly in light that is too dim for their needs. If most of the available light comes from one direction, the stems and leaves bend in that direction. If the light is much too dim for them, the plant has little energy and grows poorly. Plants with brightly colored leaves, such as blood leaf, need bright light to develop the color fully.

SOLUTION: Move the plant to a brighter location, such as a lightly curtained sunny window. If a brighter location is not available, provide supplemental lighting as described on page 920. If you wish to grow a houseplant in a dim location, select a plant that is tolerant of dim light from the list on page 1001.

Iresine cultural information
Light: Needs bright light
Water: When the soil just below the surface is barely moist

KALANCHOE

Powdery mildew.

PROBLEM: White to light tan powdery patches appear on the leaves and stems. Severely infected leaves may turn yellow, wither, and fall.

ANALYSIS: Powdery mildew
This plant disease is caused by a fungus (*Sphaerotheca humuli* var. *fuliginea*). It grows on the surface of the leaves and stems, producing white strands and spores that make powdery patches. The spores are carried by air currents to other plants. If the fungus is abundant, leaves are weakened, turn yellow, and die. Powdery mildew is favored by reduced light.

SOLUTION: Spray with a fungicide containing *dinocap* or *cycloheximide.* (For instructions on spraying houseplants, see page 921.) Remove severely infected leaves. Move any infected kalanchoe plants away from healthy ones. Grow kalanchoe in a sunny window.

Kalanchoe cultural information
Light: Needs bright light
Water: When the soil just below the surface is dry

MARANTA (PRAYER PLANT)

Mealybugs (¼ life size).

PROBLEM: Oval, white insects up to ¼ inch long cluster in white, cottony masses on leaves, stems, and in the crotches where the leaves are attached. A sticky material may coat the leaves. Leaves may be spotted or deformed. When the condition is severe, leaves and plants may wither and die.

ANALYSIS: Mealybugs
Several species of this common insect feed on kalanchoe. Mealybugs damage plants by sucking sap, causing leaf distortion and death. The adult female mealybug may produce live young, or may lay eggs in a white fluffy mass of wax. The immature mealybugs, called *nymphs*, crawl all over the plant and onto nearby plants. Soon after they begin to feed, they produce white waxy filaments that cover their bodies, giving them a cottony appearance. As they mature, they become less mobile. Mealybugs cannot digest all the sugar in the sap and excrete the excess in a fluid called honeydew, which coats the leaves and may drop onto furniture below the plant. For additional information on mealybugs, see page 181.

SOLUTION: Spray infested plants indoors with ORTHO Whitefly & Mealybug Killer; ORTHO House Plant Insect Killer, or ORTHO House Plant Insect Control; or take the plants outside and spray them with ORTHO Isotox Insect Killer. (For instructions on spraying houseplants, see page 921.) Where practical, wipe mealybugs off the plant with a damp cloth or with cotton swabs dipped in alcohol. Inspect the pot, including the bottom, for mealybug egg masses. Wipe these off. Avoid bringing mealybugs into the house by carefully inspecting new plants.

Salt damage.

PROBLEM: Margins of older leaves die and turn brown and brittle. In severe cases, all leaves may have dead margins. Tissues adjacent to the dead margins of older leaves may turn yellow.

ANALYSIS: Salt damage
Prayer plant is very sensitive to excess salts. Soluble salts are picked up by the roots and accumulate in the leaf margins, where concentrations may become high enough to kill the tissues. Salts can accumulate from water or the use of fertilizers; or they may be present in the soil used in potting. Salts accumulate more rapidly and do more harm if the plant is not watered thoroughly.

SOLUTION: Leach excess salts from the soil by flushing with water. Water the plant at least three times, letting the water drain each time. This is done most easily in a bathtub or laundry sink or outside. Always water prayer plant from the top of the pot. Enough water should be added at each watering so that some drains through the pot. Empty the saucer after the pot has finished draining. If the plant is too large to handle easily, use a turkey baster to remove the drainage water. (For additional watering instructions, see page 923.) Do not overfertilize.

Maranta cultural information
Light: Needs medium light
Water: When the soil just below the surface is barely moist

Spider mite damage.

PROBLEM: Leaves are stippled, yellow, and dirty; they may dry out and drop. There may be webbing between leaves or on the lower surfaces of the leaves. To determine if a plant is infested with mites, hold a sheet of white paper underneath an affected plant and tap the leaves sharply. Minute green, red, or yellow specks the size of pepper grains will drop to the paper and begin to crawl around. The pests are easily seen against the white background.

ANALYSIS: Spider mites
These mites, related to spiders, are major pests of many houseplants, including prayer plants. They cause damage by sucking sap from the undersides of the leaves. As a result of this feeding, the green pigment (chlorophyll) disappears, causing the stippled appearance. Under warm, dry conditions, which favor mites, they can build up to tremendous numbers. For more information about spider mites, see page 887.

SOLUTION: Spray infested plants indoors with ORTHO House Plant Insect Control, ORTHO House Plant Insect Killer, or ORTHO Whitefly & Mealybug Killer; or take the plants outside and spray them with ORTHO Isotox Insect Spray. (For instructions on spraying houseplants, see page 921.) Plants need to be sprayed weekly for several weeks to kill the mites as they hatch. To avoid introducing mites, inspect new plants carefully.

MARANTA (PRAYER PLANT) ■ MONSTERA (SPLIT-LEAF PHILODENDRON)

Mealybugs (life size)

PROBLEM: Oval, white insects up to ¼ inch long cluster in white, cottony masses on leaves, stems, and in the crotches where the leaves are attached. A sticky material may coat the leaves. Leaves may be spotted or deformed. When the condition is severe, leaves and plants may wither and die.

ANALYSIS: Mealybugs
Several species of this common insect feed on prayer plants. Mealybugs damage plants by sucking sap, causing leaf distortion and death. The adult female mealybug may produce live young, or may lay eggs in a white fluffy mass of wax. The immature mealybugs, called *nymphs*, crawl all over the plant and onto nearby plants. Soon after they begin to feed, they produce white waxy filaments that cover their bodies, giving them a cottony appearance. As they mature, they become less mobile. Mealybugs cannot digest all the sugar in the sap and excrete the excess in a fluid called honeydew, which coats the leaves and may drop onto furniture below the plant. For additional information on mealybugs, see page 181.

SOLUTION: Spray infested plants indoors with ORTHO Whitefly & Mealybug Killer, ORTHO House Plant Insect Killer, or ORTHO House Plant Insect Control; or take the plants outside and spray them with ORTHO Isotox Insect Killer. (For instructions on spraying houseplants, see page 921.) Where practical, wipe mealybugs off the plant with a damp cloth or with cotton swabs dipped in alcohol. Inspect the pot, including the bottom, for mealybug egg masses. Wipe these off. Avoid bringing mealybugs into the house by carefully inspecting new plants.

Failure to split.

PROBLEM: New leaves do not grow as large as older leaves. New leaves are darker green, and have fewer or no splits in them. The stem is elongated, with more space between the new leaves. The leaves turn toward the light. Older leaves may turn yellow.

ANALYSIS: Insufficient light
Split-leaf philodendrons need a lot of light to grow correctly. The large split leaves for which they are known are the mature form of the plant. In dim locations, the plant reverts to an immature form, which has smaller leaves that do not split.

SOLUTION: Give split-leaf philodendrons enough light so that normal splitting of the leaves occurs. If leaves do not split, move the plant to a brighter area. Although they will tolerate somewhat reduced levels of light, split-leaf philodendrons grow best in a curtained south, east, or west-facing window.

Monstera cultural information
Light: Needs medium light
Water: When the soil just below the surface is barely moist

Salt damage.

PROBLEM: Margins of older leaves die and turn brown and brittle. In severe cases, all leaves may have dead margins. Tissues adjacent to the dead margins of older leaves may turn yellow.

ANALYSIS: Salt damage
Split-leaf philodendron is sensitive to excess salts. Soluble salts are picked up by the roots and accumulate in the leaf margins, where concentrations may become high enough to kill the tissues. Salts can accumulate from water or the use of fertilizers; or they may be present in the soil used in potting. Salts accumulate more rapidly and do more harm if the plant is not watered thoroughly.

SOLUTION: Leach excess salts from the soil by flushing with water. Water the plant at least three times, letting the water drain each time. This is done most easily in a bathtub or laundry sink or outside. Always water split-leaf philodendron from the top of the pot. Enough water should be added at each watering so that some drains through the pot. Empty the saucer after the pot has finished draining. If the plant is too large to handle easily, use a turkey baster to remove the drainage water. (For additional watering instructions, see page 923.) Do not overfertilize.

Mealybug (life size).

PROBLEM: Oval, white insects up to ¼ inch long cluster in white, cottony masses on leaves, stems, and in the crotches where the leaves are attached. A sticky material may coat the leaves. Leaves may be spotted or deformed.

ANALYSIS: Mealybugs
Several species of this common insect feed on split-leaf philodendron. Mealybugs damage plants by sucking sap, causing leaf distortion and death. The adult female mealybug may produce live young, or may lay eggs in a white fluffy mass of wax. The immature mealybugs, called *nymphs,* crawl all over the plant and onto nearby plants. Soon after they begin to feed, they produce white waxy filaments that cover their bodies, giving them a cottony appearance. As they mature, they become less mobile. Mealybugs cannot digest all the sugar in the sap and excrete the excess in a fluid called honeydew, which coats the leaves and may drop onto furniture below the plant. For additional information on mealybugs, see page 181.

SOLUTION: Spray infested plants with ORTHO Whitefly & Mealybug Killer, or ORTHO House Plant Insect Killer. Where practical, wipe mealybugs off the plant with a damp cloth or with cotton swabs dipped in alcohol. Inspect the pot, including the bottom, for mealybug egg masses. Wipe these off. Avoid bringing mealybugs into the house by carefully inspecting new plants.

ORCHIDS

LIGHT: Many orchids like abundant light, and grow best in bright light. Some may need filtered light during the hottest part of the day, and some may need filtered light all day.

FERTILIZER: Fertilize with half-strength ORTHO Ortho-Gro Liquid Plant Food once every 2 weeks during the growing and blooming season. The rest of the year, fertilize every other month.

WATER:
How much: Orchids should be watered until water runs out the bottom of the pot.
How often: Orchids in osmunda fiber, shredded tree fern, or fir bark should be watered once a week during the growing and blooming season, and less often during the winter months. Orchids in soil mixes should be watered when the soil at the top is barely moist.

SOLUTION: Grow epiphytic orchids (*Cattleya, Laelia, Miltonia, Oncidium, Phalaenopsis, Vanda*) in osmunda fiber, shredded tree fern, or fir bark. If using bark, orchids with large roots should be planted in coarse bark; those with smaller roots should be planted in medium-sized bark; those with small roots should be planted in fine bark. Epiphytic orchids may also be grown on pieces of tree fern to which sphagnum moss has been tied. *Cymbidium, Epidendrum, and Paphiopedilum* should be grown in an orchid mix or a mix containing 5 parts fine fir bark to 1 part standard orchid mix.

Failure to bloom.

PROBLEM: Plants do not bloom. The leaves are a deep green.

ANALYSIS: Insufficient light
Plants use light as a source of energy, and will not bloom unless they have enough light to fulfill their needs for growth, and some surplus. Although orchids are adapted to blooming in shaded locations, they still need relatively bright light, compared to houseplants that are grown for their foliage.

SOLUTION: Move the plants to a brighter location, but do not put them in direct sun. If the light is too bright, the leaves will turn yellow and burn. A lightly curtained window that receives more than 4 hours of sun a day is an ideal location for orchids. If a brighter location is not available, provide supplementary lighting as described on page 920. For a list of plants that will tolerate dim light, see page 1004.

ORCHIDS

Virus.

PROBLEM: Leaves are mottled with yellow blotches. Or they have yellow streaks or flecks that later turn dark brown or black. Leaves may have partial, complete, or concentric rings of dark-colored tissue. New leaves may be stunted and cupped. Flowers may be mottled and the colors broken. They may be moderately or severely distorted, and may have brown flecks or streaks in them. Affected flowers do not last long.

ANALYSIS: Viruses
Several viruses infect orchids. Some infect many different types of orchids, and others infect only a few. Viruses cause a plant to manufacture new viruses from its protein. In the process, the metabolism of the plant is upset. Different symptoms appear, depending upon the orchid and the virus present. Viruses are easily transmitted on tools used in cutting orchid plants.

SOLUTION: Observe the effects of viruses on the plants. If flowers are badly malformed or discolored, discard the plants. Keep plants that are virus-free separate from those showing virus symptoms, because the viruses are easily transmitted. Sterilize cutting tools by dipping them in rubbing alcohol when moving from one plant to another. Do not purchase plants that show such symptoms.

Spider mite damage.

PROBLEM: Leaves are stippled, yellow, and dirty; they may dry out and drop. There may be webbing over flower buds, between leaves, or on the lower surfaces of the leaves. To determine if a plant is infested with mites, hold a sheet of white paper underneath an affected plant and tap the leaves sharply. Minute green, red, or yellow specks the size of pepper grains will drop to the paper and begin to crawl around. The pests are easily seen against the white background.

ANALYSIS: Spider mites
These mites, related to spiders, are major pests of many houseplants, including orchids. They cause damage by sucking sap from the undersides of the leaves. As a result of feeding, the green pigment (chlorophyll) disappears, causing the stippled appearance. Under warm, dry conditions, which favor mites, they can build up to tremendous numbers. For more information about spider mites, see page 887.

SOLUTION: Spray infested plants with ORTHO House Plant Insect Control. (For instructions on spraying houseplants, see page 921.) Plants need to be sprayed weekly for several weeks to kill the mites as they hatch. To avoid introducing mites, inspect new plants carefully.

Orchid scale (half life size).

PROBLEM: Stems and leaves are covered with white, cottony, cushionlike masses or brown crusty bumps. The bumps can be scraped or picked off easily. Leaves turn yellow and may drop. A shiny or sticky material may cover leaves and stems.

ANALYSIS: Scale insects
Several different types of scale insects attack orchids. Some types can infest many different plants. Scales hatch from eggs. The young, called *crawlers*, are small (about 1/10 inch), soft-bodied, and move about on the plant and onto other plants. After moving about for a short time, they insert their mouthparts into the plant, feeding on the sap. The legs disappear, and the scales remain in the same place for the rest of their lives. Some develop a soft covering, others a hard covering. Some species of scales are unable to digest fully all the sugar in the plant sap and excrete the excess in a fluid called honeydew, which may cover the leaves or drip onto surfaces below. For additional information on spraying houseplants, see page 921.

SOLUTION: Spray infested plants outdoors with ORTHO Orthene Systemic Insect Control. Spraying is more effective against the crawlers than against the adults. Repeated applications may be necessary.

Mealybugs (twice life size).

PROBLEM: Oval, white insects up to ¼ inch long cluster in white, cottony masses on leaves, stems, and in the crotches where the leaves are attached. A sticky material may coat the leaves. Leaves may be spotted or deformed. When the condition is severe, leaves and plants may wither and die.

ANALYSIS: Mealybugs
Several species of this common insect feed on orchids. Mealybugs damage plants by sucking sap, causing leaf distortion and death. The adult female mealybug may produce live young, or may lay eggs in a white fluffy mass of wax. The immature mealybugs, called *nymphs*, crawl all over the plant and onto nearby plants. Soon after they begin to feed, they produce white waxy filaments that cover their bodies, giving them a cottony appearance. As they mature, they become less mobile. Mealybugs cannot digest all the sugar in the sap and excrete the excess in a fluid called honeydew, which coats the leaves and may drop onto furniture below the plant.

SOLUTION: Spray infested plants with ORTHO Orthene Systemic Insect Control. For rare or unusual varieties, test the spray on a few leaves before spraying the entire plant. (For instructions on spraying houseplants, see page 921.) Where practical, wipe mealybugs off the plant with a damp cloth or with cotton swabs dipped in alcohol. Inspect the pot, including the bottom, for mealybug egg masses. Wipe these off. Avoid bringing mealybugs into the house by carefully inspecting new plants. For additional information on mealybugs, see page 181.

PALMS

LIGHT: Most palms will grow better in full light, but many are adaptable to somewhat reduced light. Grow in an east-facing or curtained south or west-facing window, or in a room with light from a number of windows.

SOIL: Any of the standard houseplant soil mixes. For information on soil mixes, see page 920.

FERTILIZER: Fertilize once a month during early spring and summer when the plant is growing actively. Fertilizing is not necessary during the winter. Use ORTHO Fish Emulsion Fertilizer, ORTHO House Plant Food, or ORTHO Ortho-Gro Liquid Plant Food.

WATER:
How much: Add enough water so that some drains through the pot. Empty the saucer after draining is through.
How often: Water when the top soil is barely moist. For additional information on watering, see page 919.

TEMPERATURE: Most palms will grow better when warm, but will tolerate a wide range of temperatures. They will not do well when grown below 60°F.

Spider mites (half life size), webs, and damage.

PROBLEM: Fronds or leaflets are stippled, yellow, and dirty; they may dry out and drop. There may be webbing between leaflets or on the lower surfaces of the leaflets. To determine if a plant is infested with mites, hold a sheet of white paper underneath an affected plant and tap the frond sharply. Minute green, red, or yellow specks the size of pepper grains will drop to the paper and begin to crawl around. The pests are easily seen against the white background.

ANALYSIS: Spider mites
These mites, related to spiders, are major pests of many houseplants, including palms. They cause damage by sucking sap from the undersides of the leaflets. As a result of this feeding, the green pigment (chlorophyll) disappears, causing the stippled appearance. Under warm, dry conditions mites can build up to tremendous numbers. For more information about spider mites, see page 887.

SOLUTION: Spray infested plants with ORTHO Whitefly & Mealybug Killer, ORTHO House Plant Insect Killer, or ORTHO House Plant Insect Control. (For instructions on spraying houseplants, see page 921.) Plants need to be sprayed weekly for several weeks to kill the mites as they hatch. To avoid introducing mites, inspect new plants carefully.

PALMS

Salt damage.

PROBLEM: Margins of the older leaves die and turn brown, beginning at the base of the fronds and progressing outward. In severe cases, all fronds may have dead margins. Tissues adjacent to the dead margins of older fronds may turn yellow.

ANALYSIS: Salt damage
Palms are sensitive to excess salts. Soluble salts are picked up by the roots and accumulate in the leaf margins, where concentrations may become high enough to kill the tissues. Salts can accumulate from water or the use of fertilizers; or they may be present in the soil used in potting. Salts accumulate more rapidly and do more harm if the plant is not watered thoroughly.

SOLUTION: Leach excess salts from the soil by flushing with water. Water the plant at least three times, letting the water drain each time. This is done most easily in a bathtub or laundry sink or outside. Always water palms from the top of the pot. Enough water should be added at each watering so that some drains through the pot. Empty the saucer after the pot has finished draining. If the plant is too large to handle easily, use a turkey baster to remove the drainage water. (For additional watering instructions, see page 923.) Do not overfertilize. If practical, trim the damaged leaf tips to a point with a pair of scissors.

Mealybugs (half life size).

PROBLEM: Oval, white insects up to ¼ inch long cluster in white, cottony masses on fronds, leaflets, or stems, and in the crotches where fronds are attached. A sticky material may coat the leaflets. Leaflets may be spotted or deformed. When the condition is severe, leaves and plants may wither and die.

ANALYSIS: Mealybugs
Several species of this common insect feed on palms. Mealybugs damage plants by sucking sap, causing leaf distortion and death. The adult female mealybug may produce live young, or may lay eggs in a white fluffy mass of wax. The immature mealybugs, called *nymphs*, crawl all over the plant and onto nearby plants. Soon after they begin to feed, they produce white waxy filaments that cover their bodies, giving them a cottony appearance. As they mature, they become less mobile. Mealybugs cannot digest all the sugar in the sap and excrete the excess in a fluid called honeydew, which coats the leaflets and may drop onto furniture below the plant. For additional information on mealybugs, see page 181.

SOLUTION: Spray infested plants with ORTHO Whitefly & Mealybug Killer, ORTHO House Plant Insect Killer, or ORTHO House Plant Insect Control. (For instructions on spraying houseplants, see page 921.) Where practical, wipe mealybugs off the plant with a damp cloth or with cotton swabs dipped in alcohol. Inspect the pot, including the bottom, for mealybug egg masses. Wipe these off. Avoid bringing mealybugs into the house by carefully inspecting new plants.

Scale (life size).

PROBLEM: Stems and fronds are covered with white, cottony, cushionlike masses or brown crusty bumps. The bumps can be scraped or picked off easily. Fronds turn yellow and may drop. A shiny or sticky material may cover fronds and stems.

ANALYSIS: Scale insects
Several different types of scale insects attack palms. Some types can infest many different plants. Scales hatch from eggs. The young, called *crawlers*, are small (about ⅒ inch), soft-bodied, and move about on the plant and onto other plants. After moving about for a short time, they insert their mouthparts into the plant, feeding on the sap. The legs disappear, and the scales remain in the same place for the rest of their lives. Some develop a soft covering, others a hard covering. Some species of scales are unable to digest fully all the sugar in the plant sap and excrete the excess in a fluid called honeydew, which may cover the fronds or drip onto surfaces below. For more information about scales, see page 876.

SOLUTION: Spray infested plants with ORTHO Whitefly & Mealybug Killer, ORTHO House Plant Insect Killer, or ORTHO House Plant Insect Control. Spraying is more effective against the crawlers than against the adults. Repeated applications may be necessary. For additional information on spraying houseplants, see page 921.

Gliocladium rot.

PROBLEM: Brown spots appear on leaf stems. Leaflets turn yellowish brown on one side of the leaf stalk. The fronds die starting at the bottom, leaving only several alive at the top of the plant. When the condition is severe, the whole plant dies. A pinkish brown mold appears on the leaf bases. Sometimes the central bud area will rot, and the inner portions will be covered with a pinkish brown mass of fungal growth.

ANALYSIS: Gliocladium rot
This disease is caused by a fungus (*Gliocladium vermoeseni*) that infects parlor palm (*Chamaedorea*) and some other palms. The fungus produces large numbers of pink spores on infected leaf bases and in infected bud area. These spores are carried by air currents, and will infect other palms if the leaves are wet. The fungus kills the leaves, and may invade the central bud and kill it too. Gliocladium rot is favored by low temperatures.

SOLUTION: Remove any leaves that have symptoms. Avoid getting water on the fronds. Keep plants in warm rooms, and give them adequate light, water, and fertilizer. Plant sprays containing the fungicide *benomyl* may help. For information on spraying houseplants, see page 921.

PELARGONIUM (GERANIUM)

FLOWERING TIME: Summer, but will flower all year if given enough light.

LIGHT: Flowering plants need more light than foliage plants. Give geraniums as much light as possible. Grow in south-facing windows. Geraniums grown for foliage do not need as much light as flowering types.

SOIL: Any of the standard mixes for houseplants. For information on soil mixes, see page 920.

FERTILIZER: Fertilize once a month during spring and summer with ORTHO House Plant Food or ORTHO Ortho-Gro Liquid Plant Food.

WATER:
How much: Add enough water so that some drains out of the bottom of the pot.
How often: Water when the surface soil is dry. Avoid keeping the soil too wet or too dry because these conditions favor oedema. For more information on watering houseplants, see page 919.

TEMPERATURE: Average house temperatures are adequate for geraniums.

Spindly growth.

PROBLEM: Lower leaves turn yellow and may drop. New leaves are pale green. Plants fail to produce flower buds. Stems become elongated and lean toward the light.

ANALYSIS: Insufficient light
Plants use light as a source of energy, and grow slowly in light that is too dim for their needs. If most of the available light comes from one direction, the stems and leaves bend in that direction. If the light is much too dim, the plant has little energy and grows poorly. Plants grown for their flowers, such as geranium and pelargonium, have a relatively high need for light.

SOLUTION: Move the plant to a brighter location. Geranium and pelargonium need direct sun. But if they are allowed to become dry while in direct sunlight, they will sunburn. (For more information on sunburn, see page 178.) If a brighter location is not available, provide supplemental lighting as described on page 920. If you wish to grow a houseplant in a dim location, select a plant that is tolerant of dim light from the list on page 1001. Geranium and pelargonium can be grown outside in full sun. When moving them from inside to outside, put them in a semishady area for several days before moving them to direct sunlight. This will prevent them from sunburning.

PELARGONIUM (GERANIUM)

Oedema.

PROBLEM: Small spots appear on the undersides of the leaves. These spots are raised, corky, and water-soaked. Spots appear more frequently on older leaves, and rarely on new leaves. In old tissues, spots may become tan. When the condition is severe, leaves may yellow and drop. Corky streaks may appear on stems.

ANALYSIS: Oedema
Oedema is a disease found on many plants. It is not caused by infection, but results from environmental factors. It is believed to be caused by excessive watering during periods of high humidity, but it sometimes occurs on geraniums that have been kept dry and grown under low humidity. For more information about oedema, see page 860.

SOLUTION: Give geraniums bright light and enough water, and fertilize regularly. Avoid growing plants too close together. Do not keep the soil too wet during periods of damp, cloudy weather.

Whiteflies (life size).

PROBLEM: Tiny, winged insects 1/12 inch long feed on the undersides of the leaves. The insects are covered with white waxy powder. When the plant is touched, insects flutter rapidly around it. Leaves may be mottled and yellowing.

ANALYSIS: Greenhouse whitefly
(*Trialeurodes vaporariorum*)
This insect is a common pest of geranium. The four-winged adult lays eggs on the undersides of leaves. The larvae are the size of a pinhead, flat, oval, immobile, and semitransparent, with radiating white waxy filaments. In about a month, they change to the winged adult form. The larvae are more damaging because they suck more sap from the plants than do the adults. They cannot digest all the sugar in the sap they remove, and excrete the excess in a sugary material called honeydew, which coats the leaves and may drop from the plant onto furniture below.

SOLUTION: Spray with ORTHO House Plant Insect Control, ORTHO Whitefly & Mealybug Killer, ORTHO House Plant Insect Killer, or ORTHO Isotox Insect Killer. For instructions on spraying houseplants, see page 921. Spray weekly as long as the problem continues. Remove heavily infested leaves.

Bacterial leaf and stem blight.

PROBLEM: Small dark spots appear on the undersides of geranium or ivy geranium leaves. These spots enlarge, and are soon visible on both surfaces of the leaves. Spots turn brown or black, and usually have a water-soaked area around them. Large areas of the leaf may die in angular patterns surrounded by the veins. Affected leaves turn yellow and may drop. The stems and leaf stems turn black and shrivel. Roots may also turn black. Plants may die.

ANALYSIS: Bacterial leaf and stem blight
This disease is caused by a bacterium (*Xanthomonas pelargonii*) that infects leaves through wounds and natural openings. Once inside, it kills the tissues rapidly. The bacteria spread down the leaf stems into the main stem, killing tissue as they move. They may even spread into the roots. Martha Washington geranium (pelargonium) is not affected.

SOLUTION: Destroy infected plants. Avoid getting water on the foliage of geraniums. Do not touch the foliage of diseased plants and then the foliage of healthy plants. Make cuttings only from uninfected plants. Discard soil from diseased plants. Any tools used for trimming plants should be cleaned with rubbing alcohol before using on geraniums and pelargoniums.

PEPEROMIA

Root and stem rot.

PROBLEM: Lower leaves turn yellow or red and may drop from the plant. Plants are stunted. A black discoloration appears in the stem at the soil line and progresses upward. Upper leaves may wilt. The whole plant may die and be easily lifted from the soil. The rootball has many dead roots, which are brown, soft, and without white tips. For instructions on examining the rootball, see page 921.

ANALYSIS: Root and stem rot
This disease is caused by any of several soil-dwelling fungi, also known as *water molds* (see page 849 for more information about water molds). The fungi move rapidly through the root system and up the stem, killing the roots. Infected plants are unable to obtain water and nutrients, resulting in stunting and wilting.

SOLUTION: If the plant is only mildly affected, let the soil dry out between waterings. For more information on this technique, see page 849. If the soil mix is heavy, or the container does not drain well, transplant the plant into a container that drains freely. Use a well-drained soil mix. For information on soil mixes, see page 920. If stem or root rot occurs but the top of the plant is still vigorous, cut it off above the diseased area and root it according to the instructions on page 921. Discard severely infected plants and the soil in which they grew. Wash the pots thoroughly, and soak them in a mixture of 1 part household bleach to 9 parts water for 30 minutes. Rinse with plain water and dry thoroughly before reuse. Or, pasteurize the pots according to the directions on page 920.

Root and stem rot.

PROBLEM: Plants fail to grow, and are stunted. Roots are brown and soft, without white tips. (For information on examining roots, see page 921.) The stem may have brown, sunken areas at or below the soil line. Leaves may die and turn black. Plants may wilt and die.

ANALYSIS: Root and stem rot
Root rot is caused by any of several fungi, also known as *water molds* (see page 849 for more information about water molds). These soil-dwelling fungi (*Pythium* species, *Phytophthora parasitica*, or *Rhizoctonia solani*) infect the roots of many plants. They invade the small roots and spread through the root system, killing it. The fungi are favored by wet soil. Also, peperomia plants are weakened by wet soil, and become more susceptible to root rot. *Phytophthora* and *Rhizoctonia* can also infect the crown and lower stem, causing the tissues to collapse.

SOLUTION: If the plant is only mildly affected, let the soil dry out between waterings. For more information on this technique, see page 849. If the soil mix is heavy, or the container does not drain well, transplant the plant into a container that drains freely. Use a well-drained soil mix. For information on soil mixes, see page 920. If stem or root rot occurs but the top of the plant is still vigorous, cut it off above the diseased area and root it according to the instructions on page 921. Discard severely infected plants and the soil in which they grew. Wash the pots thoroughly, and soak them in a mixture of 1 part household bleach to 9 parts water for 30 minutes. Rinse with plain water and dry thoroughly before reuse. Or, pasteurize the pots according to the directions on page 920.

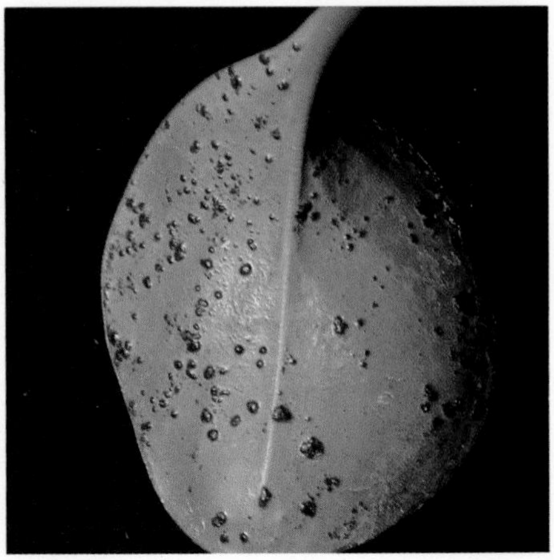
Oedema.

PROBLEM: Small corky spots appear on the undersides of the leaves. When first formed these spots are clear or water-soaked, but later become brown or black. If leaves are severely affected, they may turn yellow.

ANALYSIS: Oedema
Oedema is a disease found on many plants. It is not caused by infection, but results from unfavorable environmental conditions. It is believed to be caused by excessive watering during periods of high humidity, but it also develops occasionally on plants that are kept dry and in low humidity. For more information about oedema, see page 860.

SOLUTION: Grow peperomia under as favorable conditions as possible. Give adequate light, water, and fertilizer. Avoid keeping the soil too wet.

Peperomia cultural information
Light: Needs medium light
Water: When the soil just below the surface is dry

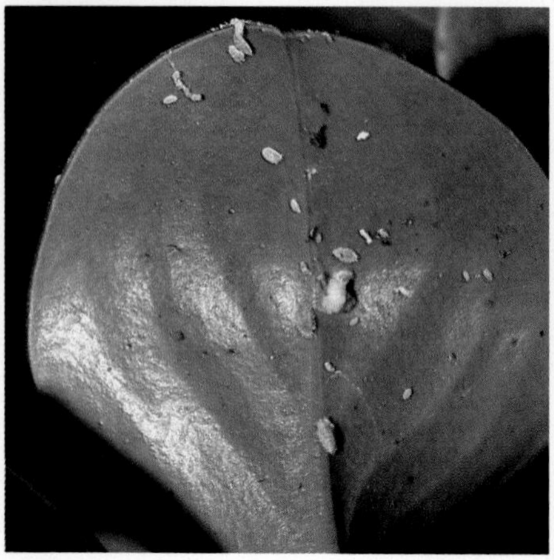

Mealybugs (life size).

PROBLEM: Oval, white insects up to ¼ inch long cluster in white, cottony masses on leaves, stems, and in the crotches where the leaves are attached. A sticky material may coat the leaves. Leaves may be spotted or deformed. When the condition is severe, leaves and plants may wither and die.

ANALYSIS: Mealybugs
Several species of this common insect feed on peperomia. Mealybugs damage plants by sucking sap, causing leaf distortion and death. The adult female mealybug may produce live young, or may lay eggs in a white fluffy mass of wax. The immature mealybugs, called *nymphs*, crawl all over the plant and onto nearby plants. Soon after they begin to feed, they produce white waxy filaments that cover their bodies, giving them a cottony appearance. As they mature, they become less mobile. Mealybugs cannot digest all the sugar in the sap and excrete the excess in a fluid called honeydew, which coats the leaves and may drop onto furniture below the plant. For additional information on mealybugs, see page 181.

SOLUTION: Spray infested plants with ORTHO Whitefly & Mealybug Killer, ORTHO House Plant Insect Killer, or ORTHO House Plant Insect Control. (For instructions on spraying houseplants, see page 921.) Where practical, wipe mealybugs off the plant with a damp cloth or with cotton swabs dipped in alcohol. Inspect the pot, including the bottom, for mealybug egg masses. Wipe these off. Avoid bringing mealybugs into the house by carefully inspecting new plants.

PHILODENDRON

LIGHT: Most philodendrons will tolerate a variety of light conditions, from filtered sunlight to that coming through a north window.

SOIL: Any standard houseplant soil mix. For information on soil mixes, see page 924.

FERTILIZER: Fertilize monthly with ORTHO Fish Emulsion Fertilizer, ORTHO House Plant Food, or ORTHO Ortho-Gro Liquid Plant Food.

WATER:
How much: Add enough water so that some drains through the pot. Discard any water that drains through the pot.
How often: Water when the top soil is barely moist. For additional information on watering houseplants, see page 919.

TEMPERATURE: Average house temperatures are adequate.

SPECIAL CONDITIONS: Philodendrons may be climbers or nonclimbers. Climbers need support, and may eventually get so large they have to be cut back severely. Climbing types produce aerial roots, which need to be attached to the support or removed.

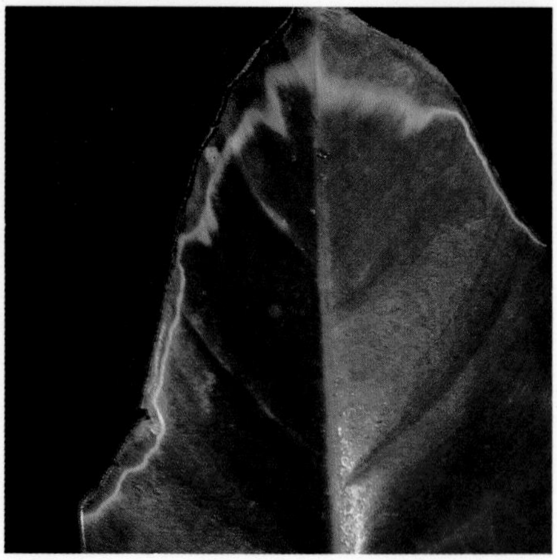

Salt damage.

PROBLEM: Margins of older leaves die and turn brown and brittle. In severe cases, all leaves may have dead margins. Tissues adjacent to the dead margins of older leaves may turn yellow.

ANALYSIS: Salt damage
Philodendron is sensitive to excess salts. Soluble salts are picked up by the roots and accumulate in the leaf margins, where concentrations may become high enough to kill the tissues. Salts can accumulate from water or the use of fertilizers; or they may be present in the soil used in potting. Salts accumulate more rapidly and do more harm if the plant is not watered thoroughly.

SOLUTION: Leach excess salts from the soil by flushing with water. Water the plants at least three times, letting the water drain each time. This is done most easily in a bathtub or laundry sink, or outside. Always water philodendron from the top of the pot. Enough water should be added at each watering so that some drains through the pot. Empty the saucer after the pot has finished draining. If the plant is too large to handle easily, use a turkey baster to remove the drainage water. (For additional watering instructions, see page 919.) Do not overfertilize.

Root rot.

PROBLEM: The lower leaves turn yellow. Leaves may drop from the plant. Plants may be stunted. Roots may be soft and dead, with no white tips. For information on examining roots, see page 921.

ANALYSIS: Root rot
This plant disease is caused by any of several fungi, also known as *water molds*, (for more information about water molds, see page 849). These fungi (*Pythium* and *Rhizoctonia* species) are favored by wet soil. The disease is usually an indication that the plant has been watered too frequently or that the soil mix is too heavy and does not drain well. The fungi are common in garden soils, but pasteurized soil or soilless potting mixes are free of them unless they are introduced on a plant, a dirty pot, or transferred from another pot on dirty fingers. Root rot spreads quickly through a root system if the soil remains wet.

SOLUTION: If the plant is only mildly affected, let the soil dry out between waterings. For more information on this technique, see page 849. If the soil mix is heavy, or the container does not drain well, transplant the plant into a container that drains freely. Use a well-drained soil mix. For information on soil mixes, see page 920. If stem or root rot occurs but the top of the plant is still vigorous, cut it off above the diseased area and root it according to the instructions on page 921. Discard severely infected plants and the soil in which they grew. Wash the pots thoroughly, and soak them in a mixture of 1 part household bleach to 9 parts water for 30 minutes. Rinse with plain water and dry thoroughly before reuse. Or, pasteurize the pots according to the directions on page 920.

Bacterial leaf spot.

PROBLEM: Small water-soaked spots appear on the leaves. These spots enlarge to irregular blotches, surrounded by yellow margins. The infected tissue turns brown or black. Severely infected leaves turn yellow, die, and drop from the plant.

ANALYSIS: Bacterial leaf spot
This disease is caused by bacteria that also attack dieffenbachia and other foliage plants. Under humid conditions, the bacteria gain entrance through wounds or natural openings in the leaves. Inside the leaf, the bacteria rot the tissue, causing the spots. Under very humid conditions large numbers of bacteria may be produced, and may ooze out of the tissues in a mass. If infection is severe, so much wilting results that the leaf dies.

SOLUTION: Once leaves are infected, no measures will control the spots already formed. To keep the disease from spreading to other plants, keep the leaves dry. Don't mist the plants. Keep plants in rooms where condensation does not form on the leaves. Remove and destroy infected leaves. Avoid touching diseased leaves and then touching uninfected leaves.

Spider mite damage.

PROBLEM: Leaves are stippled, yellow, and dirty; they may dry out and drop. There may be webbing between leaves or on the lower surfaces of the leaves. To determine if a plant is infested with mites, hold a sheet of white paper underneath an affected plant and tap the leaves sharply. Minute green, red, or yellow specks the size of pepper grains will drop to the paper and begin to crawl around. The pests are easily seen against the white background.

ANALYSIS: Spider mites
These mites, related to spiders, are major pests of many houseplants, including philodendron. They cause damage by sucking sap from the undersides of the leaves. As a result of this feeding, the green pigment (chlorophyll) disappears, causing the stippled appearance. Under warm, dry conditions, which favor mites, they can build up to tremendous numbers. For more information about spider mites, see page 887.

SOLUTION: Spray infested plants indoors with ORTHO Whitefly & Mealybug Killer, ORTHO House Plant Insect Killer, or ORTHO House Plant Insect Control; or take the plants outside and spray them with ORTHO Isotox Insect Killer. (For instructions on spraying houseplants, see page 921.) Plants need to be sprayed weekly for several weeks to kill the mites as they hatch. To avoid introducing mites, inspect new plants carefully.

PHILODENDRON

Mealybugs (half life size).

PROBLEM: Oval, white insects up to ¼ inch long cluster in white, cottony masses on leaves, stems, and in the crotches where branches or leaves are attached. A sticky material may coat the leaves. Leaves may be spotted or deformed. When the condition is severe, leaves and plants may wither and die.

ANALYSIS: Mealybugs
Several species of this common insect feed on philodendron. Mealybugs damage plants by sucking sap, causing leaf distortion and death. The adult female mealybug may produce live young, or may lay eggs in a white fluffy mass of wax. The immature mealybugs, called *nymphs*, crawl over the plant and onto nearby plants. Soon after they begin to feed, they produce white waxy filaments that cover their bodies, giving them a cottony appearance. As they mature, they become less mobile. Mealybugs cannot digest all the sugar in the sap and excrete the excess in a fluid called honeydew, which coats the leaves and may drop onto furniture below the plant. For additional information on mealybugs, see page 181.

SOLUTION: Spray infested plants indoors with ORTHO Whitefly & Mealybug Killer or ORTHO House Plant Insect Killer; or take the plants outside and spray them with ORTHO Orthene Systemic Insect Control or ORTHO Isotox Insect Killer. (For instructions on spraying houseplants, see page 921.) Where practical, wipe mealybugs off the plant with a damp cloth or with cotton swabs dipped in alcohol. Inspect the pot, including the bottom, for mealybug egg masses. Wipe these off. Avoid bringing mealybugs into the house by carefully inspecting new plants.

PILEA (ALUMINUM PLANT)

Mealybugs (half life size).

PROBLEM: Oval, white, insects up to ¼ inch long cluster in white, cottony masses on leaves, stems, and in the crotches where branches or leaves are attached. A sticky material may coat the leaves. Leaves may be spotted or deformed. If the condition is severe, leaves and plants may wither and die.

ANALYSIS: Mealybugs
Mealybugs damage plants by sucking sap, causing leaf distortion and death. The immature mealybugs, called *nymphs*, produce white, waxy filaments that give them a cottony appearance. As they mature, they become less mobile. Mealybugs cannot digest all the sap and excrete the excess as a fluid called honeydew. This coats the leaves and may drop onto furniture. For additional information on mealybugs, see page 181.

SOLUTION: Spray infested plants with ORTHO Whitefly & Mealybug Killer, ORTHO House Plant Insect Killer, or ORTHO House Plant Insect Control; or take the plant outdoors and spray with ORTHO Orthene Systemic Insect Control. (For instructions on spraying houseplants, see page 921.) If practical, wipe mealybugs off the plant with a damp cloth or with cotton swabs dipped in alcohol. Inspect the pot, including the bottom, for mealybug egg masses. Wipe these off. Carefully inspect new plants for mealybugs.

Pilea cultural information
Light: Needs medium light
Water: When the soil just below the surface is barely moist

PLECTRANTHUS (SWEDISH IVY)

Nitrogen deficiency.

PROBLEM: The oldest leaves—usually the lower leaves—turn yellow and may drop. Yellowing starts at the leaf margins and progresses inward without producing a distinct pattern. The yellowing may progress upward until only the newest leaves remain green. Growth is slow, new leaves are small, and the whole plant may be stunted.

ANALYSIS: Nitrogen deficiency
Nitrogen is a nutrient that is used by the plant in many ways, including the production of chlorophyll (the green pigment in leaves and stems). Nitrogen is used in large amounts by the plant. When there is not enough nitrogen for the entire plant, it is taken from the older leaves for use in new growth. Nitrogen is easily leached from the soil during regular watering. Of all the plant nutrients, it is the one most likely to be lacking in the soil.

SOLUTION: Take the plant outdoors and spray the leaves with Ra-Pid-Gro Plant Food for a quick response, or fertilize houseplants with ORTHO House Plant Food, ORTHO Fish Emulsion Fertilizer, or ORTHO Fern & Ivy Food. Add the fertilizer at regular intervals, as recommended on the label

Plectranthus cultural information
Light: Needs bright light
Water: When the soil surface is moist but not wet

Mealybugs (twice life size).

PROBLEM: Oval, white insects up to ¼ inch long cluster in white, cottony masses on the stems and leaves. They tend to congregate in the crotches where the leaves or branches are attached. Leaves may be spotted, deformed, and withered. Infested leaves may be shiny and sticky. Severely infested plants may die.

ANALYSIS: Mealybugs
Several species of this common insect feed on Swedish ivy. Mealybugs damage plants by sucking sap, causing leaf distortion and death. The adult female mealybug may produce live young, or may deposit her eggs in a white, fluffy mass of wax. The immature mealybugs, called *nymphs*, crawl all over the plant and onto nearby plants. Soon after they begin to feed, they produce filaments of white wax that cover their bodies, giving them a cottony appearance. As they mature, they become less mobile. Mealybugs cannot digest fully all the sugar in the sap and excrete the excess in a fluid called honeydew, which coats the leaves and may drop onto other leaves or furniture below the plant. For additional information on mealybugs, see page 181.

SOLUTION: Spray infested plants with ORTHO Whitefly & Mealybug Killer, ORTHO House Plant Insect Killer, or ORTHO House Plant Insect Control. Follow the directions on the label. Applications should be repeated every 7 to 10 days until the insects are controlled. Wash the mealybugs off the plant with a strong stream of water, or wipe them off with a cotton swab dipped in alcohol. For additional information on spraying houseplants, see page 921.

SAINTPAULIA (AFRICAN VIOLET)

LIGHT: African violets need abundant light to produce flowers. Grow them in bright light, but not in direct sunlight.

SOIL: Any standard houseplant mix. For information on potting mixes, see page 924.

FERTILIZER: Fertilize monthly with ORTHO House Plant Food or ORTHO Liquid African Violet Food.

WATER:
How much: Add enough water so that some drains out of the bottom of the pot.
How often: Water plants when the soil just under the surface is moist but not wet. For additional information on watering houseplants, see page 919.

TEMPERATURE: Average house temperatures are adequate, but do not leave African violets in rooms where the temperature falls below 60°F at night.

SPECIAL CONDITIONS: Avoid getting cold water on the leaves when watering, and don't let the plant sit in drainage water. Do not expose plants to cold drafts.

Failure to flower.

PROBLEM: Although the plant seems healthy, it does not bloom.

ANALYSIS: Insufficient light
Violets, like other flowering plants, won't bloom unless they are properly fed and watered. But if the plant is a good green color and is growing well but not blooming, it is probably not receiving enough light. Plants use light as a source of energy, and will not bloom unless they can afford the energy to do so. African violets will bloom at lower levels of light than will most other plants, but they do require a fairly bright location to bloom well.

SOLUTION: Move the plant to a brighter location. The ideal light level for African violets is as bright as possible without being direct sun. If the light is coming through a window that is exposed to the sun, the window should be curtained so that the sunlight coming through is not quite bright enough to make shadows. If the light is too bright, the leaves will lose their bright green color and become pale, with an orange or yellow cast. If the light is both bright and hot, the leaves will burn. If you don't have a location in your house bright enough, give the plants supplemental light as explained on page 920. Use fluorescent fixtures, and place them as close to the top of the plants as possible.

SAINTPAULIA (AFRICAN VIOLET)

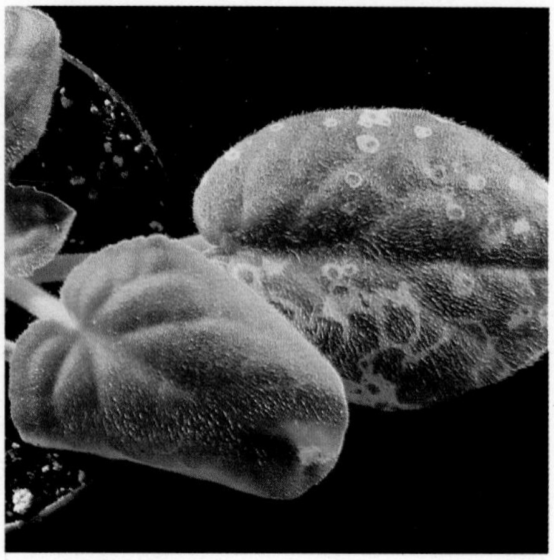

Water spots.

PROBLEM: White to light yellow blotches in various patterns, including circles, occur on the older leaves. Small islands of green may be separated by the discolored areas. Brown spots sometimes appear in the colored areas.

ANALYSIS: Water spots
Members of the African violet family are very sensitive to rapid temperature changes. Water spots occur most commonly when cold water is splashed on the leaves while the plant is being watered. If this happens in light, the chlorophyll (green pigment) is destroyed. In this plant family, all of the chlorophyll in the leaves is found in a single layer of cells near the upper surface. If the chlorophyll in that layer is broken down, the green color disappears, and the color of the underlying leaf tissue is exposed.

SOLUTION: Avoid getting cold water on African violet leaves when watering. Or use tepid water, which will not cause spotting if it touches the leaves. Spotted leaves will not recover. Pick them off if they are unsightly.

Cyclamen mite damage.

PROBLEM: Leaves in the center of the plant are severely stunted, and may be curled. These leaves may be bronze, gray, or tan. The hairs on these leaves are matted. Flower buds fail to open.

ANALYSIS: Cyclamen mite
(*Steneotarsonemus pallidus*)
Cyclamen mites infest a number of plants, including azaleas, begonias, cyclamen, gloxinia, ivy, kalanchoe, schefflera, and African violet. This very small mite (it can not be seen with the naked eye) feeds on the new growth, causing it to be stunted and curled. Buds fail to open. The female mite lays her eggs on the leaf surfaces. The young crawl about the same plant or other plants, where they feed and cause damage. These mites are favored by high humidity.

SOLUTION: Spray with *dicofol* (KELTHANE®). (For instructions on spraying houseplants, see page 921.) Isolate mildly infested plants from uninfested plants. Soak pots from which infested plants were removed for 30 minutes in a mixture of 1 part household bleach to 9 parts water. Wash the area where pots were sitting with the same dilution of household bleach.

Root and crown rot.

PROBLEM: Leaves appear dull. Those in the center of the plant turn dark green and then black. This darkening rapidly progresses outward until the whole top of the plant is dead. The roots are dead and rotted. For instructions on examining plant roots, see page 921.

ANALYSIS: Root and crown rot
This plant disease is caused by a soil-dwelling fungus (*Phytophthora parasitica*) that attacks the roots of African violet plants. The disease spreads rapidly through the root system and crown of the plant into the leaves, eventually killing the plant. The fungus is active over a wide range of soil moisture conditions. It is spread by using contaminated soil or pots, or it may be carried from one pot to another on the fingers when testing the soil for moisture. It may also be spread from pot to pot if pans are used to subirrigate plants.

SOLUTION: There is no available chemical for controlling this fungus. Discard diseased plants. Discard the soil in which diseased plants grew. Soak pots for 30 minutes in a mixture of 1 part household bleach to 9 parts water. After handling infected plants, wash your hands thoroughly before touching healthy plants.

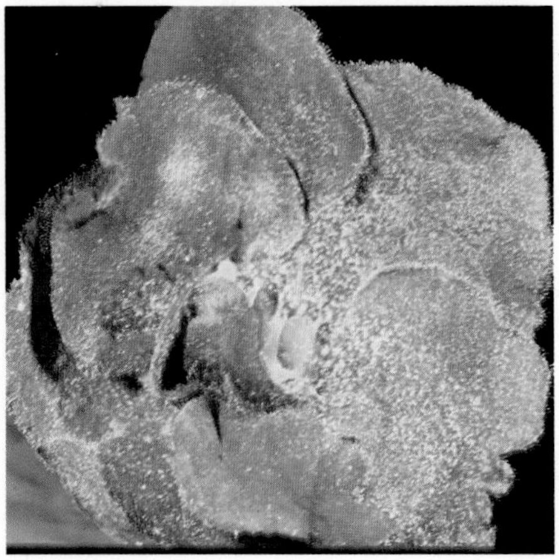

Powdery mildew.

PROBLEM: White or gray powdery patches appear on the leaves, stems, buds, and flowers. Leaves and flowers may be covered with the powdery growth. This material usually appears first on the upper surfaces of the older leaves. The affected plant parts may turn yellow or brown, and shrivel up and die.

ANALYSIS: Powdery mildew
Powdery mildew on African violet is caused by a fungus (*Oidium* species). The powdery patches consist of fungal strands and spores. The spores are carried by air currents to healthy leaves and flowers of the same plant and to other African violets. The fungus saps plant nutrients, causing yellowing or browning of the tissues. Dim light, warm days, and cool nights encourage the growth of powdery mildew.

SOLUTION: Spray with a fungicide containing *dinocap* or *benomyl* every 2 weeks until the disease is gone. (For information on spraying houseplants, see page 921.) Remove infected flowers and flower buds and badly infected leaves. Keep plants in bright, indirect light away from cold drafts.

Mealybugs (twice life size).

PROBLEM: Oval, white insects up to ¼ inch long cluster in white, cottony masses on leaves, stems, and in the crotches where the leaves are attached. A sticky material may coat the leaves. Leaves may be spotted or deformed. When the condition is severe, leaves and plants may wither and die.

ANALYSIS: Mealybugs
Several species of this common insect feed on African violet. Mealybugs damage plants by sucking sap, causing leaf distortion and death. The adult female mealybug may produce live young, or may lay eggs in a white fluffy mass of wax. The immature mealybugs, called *nymphs*, crawl all over the plant and onto nearby plants. Soon after they begin to feed, they produce white waxy filaments that cover their bodies, giving them a cottony appearance. As they mature, they become less mobile. Mealybugs cannot digest all the sugar in the sap and excrete the excess in a fluid called honeydew, which coats the leaves and may drop onto furniture below the plant. For additional information on mealybugs, see page 181.

SOLUTION: Spray infested plants with ORTHO Whitefly & Mealybug Killer or ORTHO House Plant Insect Killer. (For instructions on spraying houseplants, see page 921.) Where practical, wipe mealybugs off the plant with a damp cloth or with cotton swabs dipped in alcohol. Inspect the pot, including the bottom, for mealybug egg masses. Wipe these off. Avoid bringing mealybugs into the house by carefully inspecting new plants.

Elongated leaf stalks.

PROBLEM: Leaves turn a deep green. Plants stop flowering. Leaves and flowers are borne on elongated stems rather than on top of the fleshy root. Buds that are formed fail to open.

ANALYSIS: Insufficient light
Plants use light as a source of energy, and grow slowly in light that is too dim for their needs. They produce few flowers. If most of the available light is coming from one direction, the stems and leaves bend in that direction. If the light is much too dim the plant elongates, resulting in leaves and buds being produced in pairs along the stem rather than from a basal rosette. Plants grown for their flowers, such as gloxinia, need abundant light.

SOLUTION: Move the plant to a brighter location. Gloxinia will tolerate direct sun if it is kept well watered. But if it is allowed to become dry while in direct sunlight, it will sunburn. (For more information on sunburn, see page 178.) If a brighter location is not available, provide supplemental lighting as described on page 920. If you wish to grow a houseplant in a dim location, select a plant that is tolerant of dim light from the list on page 1001.

Sinningia cultural information
Light: Needs bright light
Water: When the soil just below the surface is barely moist

SINNINGIA (GLOXINIA)

Water spots.

PROBLEM: Pale green to light yellow rings or blotches appear on the upper surfaces of the leaves—usually the older leaves. These spots may be abundant and cover much of a leaf, or they may be small and scattered.

ANALYSIS: Water spots
Members of the African violet family—including gloxinia—are very sensitive to rapid temperature changes. Water spots occur most commonly when cold water is splashed on the leaves while the plant is being watered. If this happens in light, the chlorophyll (green pigment) is destroyed. In this plant family, all of the chlorophyll in the leaves is found in a single layer of cells near the upper surface. If the chlorophyll in that layer is broken down, the green disappears, and the color of the underlying leaf tissue is exposed.

SOLUTION: Avoid getting cold water on the foliage of gloxinia when watering. Or use tepid water, which will not cause spotting if it touches the leaves. Spotted leaves will not recover. Pick off unsightly leaves.

SPATHIPHYLLUM (SPATHE FLOWER)

Dead leaf tips.

PROBLEM: Tips of leaves turn brown or tan. The damaged area spreads slowly along the leaf. Older leaves are most severely affected.

ANALYSIS: Dead leaf tips
There are several reasons why spathe flower leaf tips die. Frequently the problem is a combination of causes.
1. *Salt damage:* Salts accumulate in the soil from irrigation water or fertilizer. Excess salts are carried to the leaves and deposited in the tips of pointed leaves like those of spathe flower plants. When enough salts accumulate there, the leaf tip dies.
2. *Too dry:* The leaf tip, being farthest from the roots, is the first part of the leaf to die when the plant is not getting enough water.
3. *Toxic salts:* Some chemicals, especially soluble salts, are damaging in very small amounts. They accumulate in leaf tips as other salts do, killing the tissue there. The most common of these chemicals are chloride and borate.

SOLUTION: Remove dead tips by trimming leaves to a point with scissors.
1. Flush the salts from the soil with several thorough waterings, discarding the drainage water each time.
2. Water the plant regularly, following the directions on page 919.
3. There isn't much you can do about traces of toxic chemicals in the water. Distilled or deionized water is always free of chemicals.

Spathiphyllum cultural information
Light: Tolerates dim light
Water: When the soil surface is moist but not wet

STREPTOCARPUS

Failure to flower.

PROBLEM: Plants fail to produce flowers; or, if they are flowering, they fail to produce new flower stems and buds. Lower leaves may become lighter green.

ANALYSIS: Insufficient light
Plants use light as a source of energy, and grow slowly in light that is too dim for their needs. If most of the available light is coming from one direction, the leaves bend in that direction. If the light is much too dim, the plant will stop producing flowers. Plants that are grown for their flowers, such as streptocarpus, need bright light.

SOLUTION: Move the plant to a brighter location. Streptocarpus will tolerate direct sun if it is kept well watered. But if it is allowed to become dry while in direct sunlight, it will sunburn. (For more information on sunburn, see page 178.) If a brighter location is not available, provide supplemental lighting as described on page 920. If you wish to grow a houseplant in a dim location, select a plant that is tolerant of dim light from the list on page 1001.

Streptocarpus cultural information
Light: Needs bright light
Water: When the soil just below the surface is barely moist

Water spots.

PROBLEM: Small, angular, white to light tan spots appear on the upper surfaces of the leaves—usually the older leaves.

ANALYSIS: Water spots
Members of the African violet family—including streptocarpus—are very sensitive to rapid temperature changes. Water spots occur most commonly when cold water is splashed on the leaves while the plant is being watered. If this happens in light, the chlorophyll (green pigment) is destroyed. In this plant family, all of the chlorophyll in the leaves is found in a single layer of cells near the upper surface of the leaf. If the chlorophyll in that layer is broken down, the green color disappears, and the color of the underlying tissue is exposed.

SOLUTION: Avoid getting cold water on the foliage of streptocarpus when watering. Or use tepid water, which will not cause spotting if it touches the leaves. Spots will not disappear. Pick off unsightly leaves.

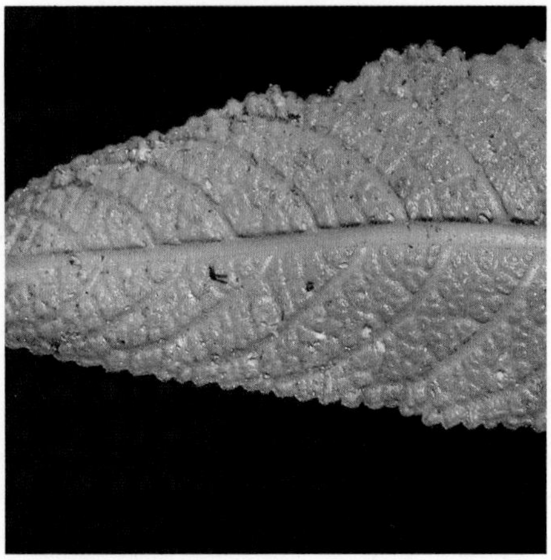

Mealybugs (half life size).

PROBLEM: Oval, white insects up to ¼ inch long cluster in white, cottony masses on leaves, stems, and in the crotches where the leaves are attached. A sticky material may coat the leaves. Leaves may be spotted or deformed. When the condition is severe, leaves and plants may wither and die.

ANALYSIS: Mealybugs
Several species of this common insect feed on streptocarpus. Mealybugs damage plants by sucking sap, causing leaf distortion and death. The adult female mealybug may produce live young, or may lay eggs in a white fluffy mass of wax. The immature mealybugs, called *nymphs*, crawl all over the plant and onto nearby plants. Soon after they begin to feed, they produce white waxy filaments that cover their bodies, giving them a cottony appearance. As they mature, they become less mobile. Mealybugs cannot digest all the sugar in the sap and excrete the excess in a fluid called honeydew, which coats the leaves and may drop onto furniture below the plant. For additional information on mealybugs, see page 181.

SOLUTION: Spray infested plants with an insecticide containing *diazinon*. (For instructions on spraying houseplants, see page 921.) Where practical, wipe mealybugs off the plant with a damp cloth or with cotton swabs dipped in alcohol. Inspect the pot, including the bottom, for mealybug egg masses. Wipe these off. Avoid bringing mealybugs into the house by carefully inspecting new plants.

Bacterial leaf spot.

PROBLEM: Irregular, oblong spots appear scattered on the leaves. New spots are very small but rapidly enlarge so that much of the leaf may be covered. Spots at first may be dark green, but eventually become dark brown or black as the tissue dies. Tissues around the dead areas look water-soaked, and have a yellow margin. Shiny drops may be found on the undersides of the spots. As these dry, they may become white or dark brown. Leaves may be killed.

ANALYSIS: Bacterial leaf spot
This disease is caused by either of two bacteria (*Erwinia chrysanthemi* or *Xanthomonas vitians*). The bacteria may be carried internally in the stems of syngonium, or may be on the leaf surfaces. High temperatures and high humidity favor infection and disease development. When conditions are favorable, the bacteria rapidly invade the leaf tissues, killing them as they progress.

SOLUTION: Break off and discard the infected leaves. Avoid getting water on the foliage. Space plants so that air can circulate around the leaves to keep them dry. Discard severely infected plants. Before using the pot again, wash it, and then soak it for 30 minutes in a solution of 1 part of household bleach to 9 parts of water.

Syngonium cultural information
Light: Tolerates dim light
Water: When the soil just below the surface is barely moist

SYNGONIUM (NEPHTHYTIS)

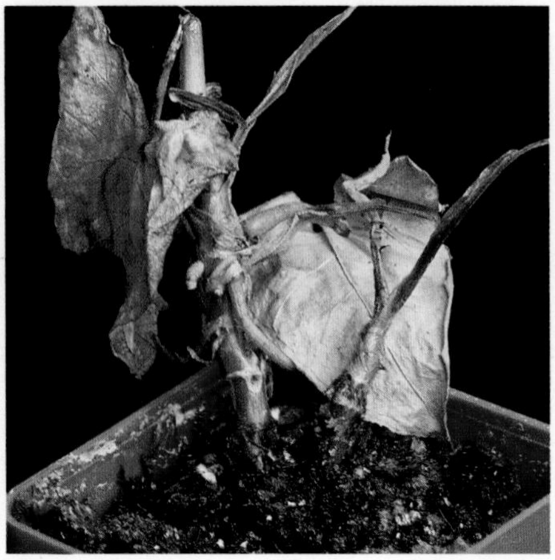

Root and stem rot.

PROBLEM: Older leaves turn yellow and wilt. All of the leaves may wilt. The stem at the soil line may be brown and sunken; this condition may girdle the stem. The plant may die. The roots are brown and soft, with no white tips. For information about examining roots, see page 921.

ANALYSIS: Root rot
Root rot of nephthytis is caused by either of two fungi (*Pythium splendens* or *Rhizoctonia solani*) that are favored by wet soil. The disease is usually an indication that the plant has been watered too frequently, or that the soil mix is too heavy and does not drain well. Stress from alternating periods of excessive dryness and wetness also will favor infection by the fungi. Root rot spreads quickly through the root system if the soil remains wet. *Rhizoctonia* can also rot the stem at or above the soil line.

SOLUTION: If most of the plant has wilted, or if there are no white tips remaining on the root system, the plant is probably too severely damaged to save. Discard it and the soil in which it grew. Wash the pot thoroughly before reusing it. Disinfect clay pots by soaking for half an hour in a solution of 1 part household bleach to 9 parts water. If only part of the plant is affected, or if white root tips are still visible on the root ball, dry the plant out as described on page 849. There are no fungicides presently available that adequately control this disease. Prevent recurrence by planting in a mix that drains well, and by letting the soil dry slightly between waterings. For more information on watering plants, see page 919.

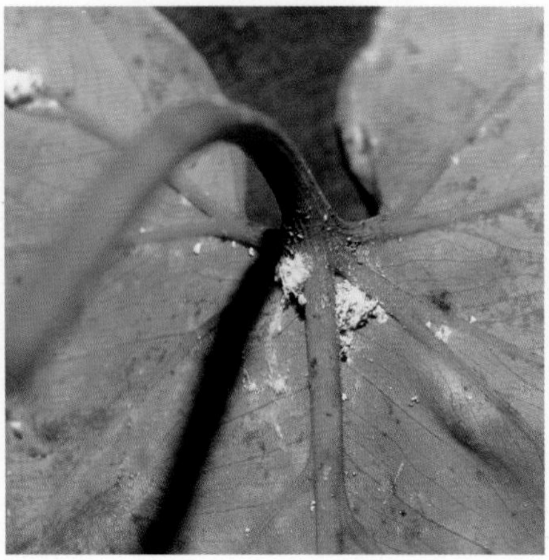

Mealybugs (life size).

PROBLEM: Oval, white insects up to ¼ inch long cluster in white, cottony masses on leaves, stems, and in the crotches where the leaves are attached. A sticky material may coat the leaves. Leaves may be spotted or deformed. When the condition is severe, leaves and plants may wither and die.

ANALYSIS: Mealybugs
Several species of this common insect feed on nephthytis. Mealybugs damage plants by sucking sap, causing leaf distortion and death. The adult female mealybug may produce live young, or may lay eggs in a white fluffy mass of wax. The immature mealybugs, called *nymphs*, crawl all over the plant and onto nearby plants. Soon after they begin to feed, they produce white waxy filaments that cover their bodies, giving them a cottony appearance. As they mature, they become less mobile. Mealybugs cannot digest all the sugar in the sap and excrete the excess in a fluid called honeydew, which coats the leaves and may drop onto furniture below the plant. For additional information on mealybugs, see page 181.

SOLUTION: Spray infested plants indoors with ORTHO Whitefly & Mealybug Killer, ORTHO House Plant Insect Killer, or ORTHO House Plant Insect Control; or take the plants outside and spray them with ORTHO Orthene Systemic Insect Control. (For instructions on spraying houseplants, see page 921.) Where practical, wipe mealybugs off the plant with a damp cloth or with cotton swabs dipped in alcohol. Inspect the pot, including the bottom, for mealybug egg masses. Wipe these off. Avoid bringing mealybugs into the house by carefully inspecting new plants.

TOLMIEA (PIGGYBACK PLANT)

Iron deficiency.

PROBLEM: The newest leaves turn yellow at the margins. The veins usually remain green. In severe cases, the entire leaf is yellow and small. The plant may be stunted.

ANALYSIS: Iron deficiency
This is a common problem with acid-loving plants like piggyback, which grow best in soil with a pH between 5.5 and 6.5. (For more information on soil acidity, see page 908.) The leaf yellowing is due to a deficiency of iron and other minor nutrients in the plant. Plants use iron in the formation of the green pigment (chlorophyll) in the leaves. The soil is seldom deficient in iron. However, iron is often found in an insoluble form that is not available to piggyback plants, especially when the soil pH is too high.

SOLUTION: To correct iron deficiency, spray the foliage with ORTHO Ortho-Gro Liquid Plant Food, and apply it to the soil in the pot. When potting or transplanting piggybacks, use an acid soil mix that contains about 50 percent peat moss. Use a minimum amount of lime or dolomite in the soil mix.

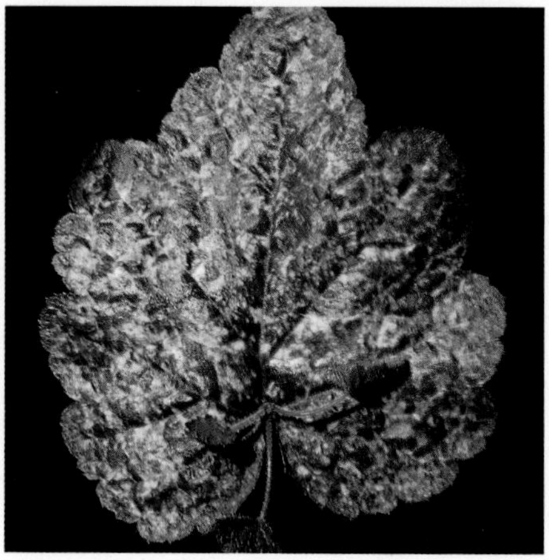
Virus.

PROBLEM: All leaves have blotches of various shades of yellow and green. Plants showing color blotches fail to grow as rapidly as green plants of the same type. Infected plants are of a variegated variety.

ANALYSIS: Virus
Several viruses have been found in variegated piggyback plants. The most common is cucumber mosaic virus. Viruses disrupt the normal functioning of the cells and, as a result, not as much chlorophyll is produced. This causes different shades of green and yellow to appear in the leaves. Aphids and other insects transmit the virus from one plant to another. Although viruses have been shown to be present in variegated piggyback plants, it has not been proven that viruses are the cause of the variegation. For more information about aphids, see page 180.

SOLUTION: Keep variegated piggyback plants isolated from other plants because aphids can transmit the virus to other susceptible plants. Control aphids as described on page 180.

Tolmiea cultural information
Light: Needs bright light
Water: When the soil surface is moist but not wet

Salt damage.

PROBLEM: Margins of older leaves die and turn brown and brittle. In severe cases, all leaves may have dead margins. Tissues adjacent to the dead margins of older leaves may turn yellow.

ANALYSIS: Salt damage
Piggyback is sensitive to excess salts. Soluble salts are picked up by the roots and accumulate in the leaf margins, where concentrations may become high enough to kill the tissues. Salts can accumulate from water or the use of fertilizers; or they may be present in the soil used in potting. Salts accumulate more rapidly and do more harm if the plant is not watered thoroughly.

SOLUTION: Leach excess salts from the soil by flushing with water. Water the plant at least three times, letting the water drain each time. This is done most easily in a bathtub or laundry sink or outside. Always water piggyback from the top of the pot. Enough water should be added at each watering so that some drains through the pot. Empty the saucer after the pot has finished draining. If the plant is too large to handle easily, use a turkey baster to remove the drainage water. (For additional watering instructions, see page 923.) Avoid overfertilizing.

Spider mite damage.

PROBLEM: Leaves are stippled, yellow, and dirty; they may dry out and drop. There may be webbing between leaves or on the lower surfaces of the leaves. To determine if a plant is infested with mites, hold a sheet of white paper underneath an affected plant and tap the leaves sharply. Minute green, red, or yellow specks the size of pepper grains will drop to the paper and begin to crawl around. The pests are easily seen against the white background.

ANALYSIS: Spider mites
These mites, related to spiders, are major pests of many houseplants, including piggyback plants. They cause damage by sucking sap from the undersides of the leaves. As a result of this feeding the green pigment (chlorophyll) disappears, causing the stippled appearance. Under warm, dry conditions, which favor mites, they can build up to tremendous numbers. For more information about spider mites, see page 887.

SOLUTION: Spray infested plants with ORTHO House Plant Insect Control, ORTHO House Plant Insect Killer, or ORTHO Whitefly & Mealybug Killer. (For instructions on spraying houseplants, see page 921.) Plants need to be sprayed weekly for several weeks to kill the mites as they hatch. To avoid introducing mites, inspect new plants carefully.

TOLMIEA (PIGGYBACK PLANT)

Powdery mildew.

PROBLEM: White powdery patches appear on the upper surfaces of the older leaves. The leaf tissue under the patches may show yellow or brown flecks. Whole leaves may die, become dry, and drop from the plant.

ANALYSIS: Powdery mildew
Powdery mildew on piggyback is caused by a fungus (*Sphaerotheca* species) that grows on the surfaces of the leaves. The powdery patches consist of fungal strands and spores. The spores are spread by air currents to uninfected plants. The fungus takes nutrients from the plant, causing yellowing or browning of tissues. When the condition is severe, the leaf may die. Powdery mildews are favored by reduced light, warm days, and cool nights.

SOLUTION: Spray with a fungicide containing *dinocap* or *cycloheximide*. (For information on spraying houseplants, see page 921.) Grow piggyback plants in bright light and in rooms where the temperature does not fluctuate much from day to night. Remove infected leaves as they appear.

Mealybugs (twice life size).

PROBLEM: Oval, white, insects up to ¼ inch long cluster in white, cottony masses on leaves, stems, and in the crotches where branches or leaves are attached. A sticky material may coat the leaves. Leaves may be spotted or deformed. If the condition is severe, leaves and plants may wither and die.

ANALYSIS: Mealybugs
Several species of this common insect feed on piggyback plant. Mealybugs damage plants by sucking sap, causing leaf distortion and death. The adult female mealybug may produce live young or may lay eggs in a white fluffy mass of wax. The immature mealybugs, called *nymphs*, crawl over the plant and to nearby plants. Soon after they begin to feed, they produce white, waxy filaments that give them a cottony appearance. As they mature, they become less mobile. Mealybugs cannot digest all the sugar in the sap and excrete the excess as a fluid called honeydew. This coats the leaves and may drop onto furniture below the plant. For additional information on mealybugs, see page 181.

SOLUTION: Spray infested plants with ORTHO Whitefly & Mealybug Killer, ORTHO House Plant Insect Killer, or ORTHO House Plant Insect Control. (For instructions on spraying houseplants, see page 921.) If practical, wipe mealybugs off the plant with a damp cloth or with cotton swabs dipped in alcohol. Inspect the pot, including the bottom, for mealybug egg masses. Wipe these off. Avoid bringing mealybugs into an area by carefully inspecting new plants.

Whiteflies (twice life size).

PROBLEM: Tiny, winged insects 1/12 inch long feed on the undersides of the leaves. The insects are covered with white waxy powder. When the plant is touched, insects flutter rapidly around it. Leaves may be mottled and yellowing.

ANALYSIS: Greenhouse whitefly
(Trialeurodes vaporariorum)
This insect is a common pest of piggyback plant. The four-winged adult lays eggs on the undersides of leaves. The larvae are the size of a pinhead, flat, oval, immobile, and semitransparent, with radiating white waxy filaments. In about a month, they change to the winged adult form. The larvae are more damaging because they suck more sap from the plants than do the adults. They cannot digest all the sugar in the sap on which they feed, and excrete the excess in a sugary material called honeydew; this coats the leaves and may drop from the plant onto furniture below.

SOLUTION: Spray with ORTHO House Plant Insect Control or ORTHO Whitefly & Mealybug Killer. Spray weekly as long as the problem continues. Remove heavily infested leaves.

TRADESCANTIA (WANDERING JEW)

Dieback.

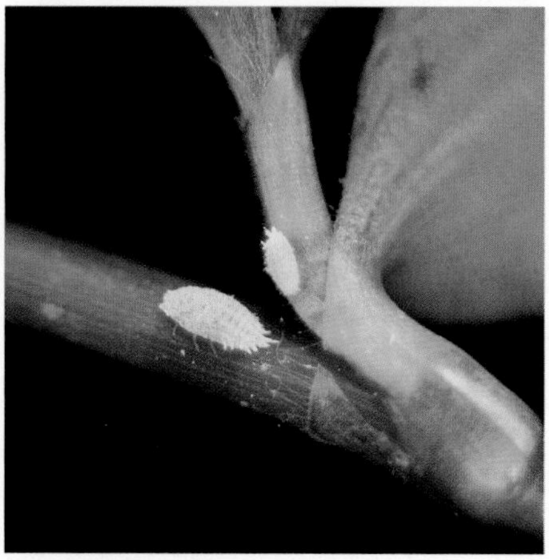

Mealybugs (twice life size).

PROBLEM: Tips of older leaves turn yellow, then die and turn brown. This condition occurs more frequently on long stems than on short stems. The longer the stem, the more tip burn is found.

ANALYSIS: Dieback
The cause of dieback is unknown. It looks like salt damage (see page 177), but often occurs on plants that have been leached regularly. As wandering Jew stems grow long, the plant does not support the old leaves, and they turn yellow and die starting at the tips.

SOLUTION: Remove dead leaves as they appear. Keep pinching the tips of the stems so they do not become too long. This will force new buds to grow farther back on the stems. New leaves will not show this problem. Plants may occasionally need to be cut back severely so that only several inches are left on each stem. After cutting back, reduce the amount of water and fertilizer given until the plant is actively growing again.

Tradescantia cultural information
Light: Needs medium light
Water: When the soil is just barely moist

PROBLEM: Oval, white,insects up to 1/4 inch long cluster in white, cottony masses on leaves, stems, and in the crotches where branches or leaves are attached. A sticky material may coat the leaves. Leaves may be spotted or deformed. If the condition is severe, leaves and plants may wither and die.

ANALYSIS: Mealybugs
Several species of this common insect feed on Wandering Jew. Mealybugs damage plants by sucking sap, causing leaf distortion and death. The adult female mealybug may produce live young or may lay eggs in a white fluffy mass of wax. The immature mealybugs, called *nymphs*, crawl over the plant and to nearby plants. Soon after they begin to feed, they produce white, waxy filaments that give them a cottony appearance. As they mature, they become less mobile. Mealybugs cannot digest all the sugar in the sap and excrete the excess as a fluid called honeydew. This coats the leaves and may drop onto furniture below the plant. For additional information on mealybugs, see page 181.

SOLUTION: Spray infested plants with ORTHO Whitefly & Mealybug Killer, ORTHO House Plant Insect Killer, or ORTHO House Plant Insect Control; or take the plant outdoors and spray with ORTHO Orthene Systemic Insect Control. (For instructions on spraying houseplants, see page 921.) If practical, wipe mealybugs off the plant with a damp cloth or with cotton swabs dipped in alcohol. Inspect the pot, including the bottom, for mealybug egg masses. Wipe these off. Avoid bringing mealybugs into an area by carefully inspecting new plants.

ZYGOCACTUS (CHRISTMAS CACTUS)

Stem rot.

PROBLEM: Stems wilt, and turn lighter green and dull. Plants stop flowering, are stunted, and may die. Large brown, circular, sunken areas may appear on the stem at or just below the soil line.

ANALYSIS: Root and stem rot
This plant disease is caused by any of several fungi, also known as *water molds*, (for more information about water molds, see page 849). These soil-inhabiting fungi (*Phythium* species or *Phytophthora* species) spread through the root system. Stems of plants weakened by these root-rotting fungi are susceptible to attack by the stem-rotting fungus *Fusarium oxysporum*. The fungus causes large brown, sunken areas on the main stems near the soil line. If it girdles the stem, the plant will die.

SOLUTION: If the plant is only mildly affected, let the soil dry out between waterings. If the soil mix is heavy, or the container does not drain well, transplant the plant into a container that contains a well-drained soil mix. For information on soil mixes, see page 920. If the top of the plant is still vigorous, cut it off above the diseased area and root it according to the instructions on page 921. Discard severely infected plants and the soil in which they grew. Wash the pots thoroughly, and soak them in a mixture of 1 part household bleach to 9 parts water for 30 minutes. Rinse with plain water and dry thoroughly before reuse. Or, pasteurize the pots according to the directions on page 920.

Zygocactus cultural information
Light: Needs bright light
Water: When the soil is just barely moist

On the next two pages, you will find some general guidelines for the care of lawns. Following that, lawn problems are grouped according to the general appearance of the problem. Find the description in the list below that most nearly describes your problem.

LAWNS

A lawn is made up of thousands of individual grass plants. Turfgrasses are adapted to growing in dense stands, and are fiercely competitive. If we give them conditions to their liking, they will grow so vigorously that few problems will be able to gain a toehold. You will find some basic guidelines for lawn care on the next two pages. If you follow these guidelines, most of the effort you expend on your lawn will be to keep it growing vigorously, rather than to fight weeds, diseases, and insects.

This is especially true of weeds. All weeds begin as seedlings in your lawn, and a vigorous turf will smother seedlings. Once weeds are established, however, they may be able to hold their own against the lawn. The two basic rules of lawn weed control are to keep the lawn growing vigorously, and to stop weeds before they gain a toe hold. If you follow these rules, the only weeding you will ever have to do will be to kill an occasional interloper before it goes to seed. For more information about weed control, see page 813.

All the diseases that attack lawns are caused by fungi. Fungi are simple plants that prefer moist conditions, and are usually controlled by keeping leaves or soil dry. But this cannot be done with lawns. Because of their shallow root system, they must be watered frequently, and because they are packed so closely together and are so close to the soil, the air around the grass blades is usually humid.

So the most frequently repeated disease preventative measure you will see in the next few pages is to regulate the amount of nitrogen the grass receives. Grass is greedy for nitrogen. If given large amounts when it can't grow fast enough to use it all, it hoards it in its tissues. This wealth of nutrients makes the grass an inviting target for fungi. But if the lawn is weakened from too *little* fertilizer, its defenses are lowered and it is unable to fight off diseases. So proper nitrogen fertilization is a key to preventing lawn diseases.

Lawn insects are often local problems, and their severity fluctuates from year to year. In some parts of the country, insects are minor lawn problems but in others, lawns may be destroyed by them. The key to solving insect problems is often to understand the life cycle of the insect, and to apply the proper measures at the right time.

You will find a little more information about lawn care on page 914, where methods for repairing the ravages of some disease and insect problems are described.

Above: Thatch. See page 262.
Left: A healthy, vigorous lawn eliminates many problems. See page 250.

CULTURAL GUIDELINES FOR LAWNS

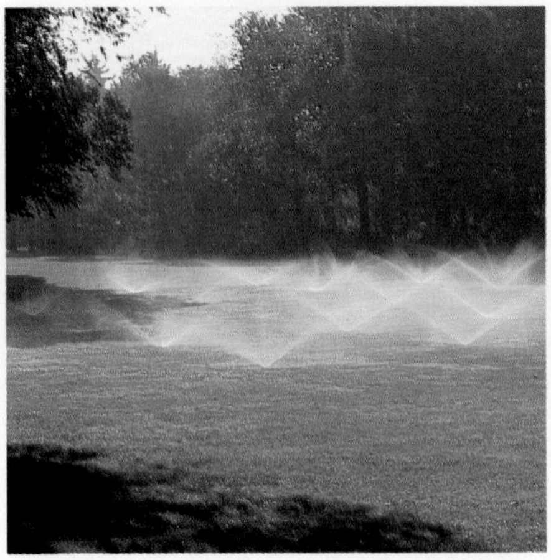

Sprinkler irrigation.

Mowing.

WATERING

Proper watering is essential in maintaining a healthy, vigorous lawn. Follow these guidelines for proper watering:

- Water deeply and infrequently. Apply 1 to 2 inches of water at each irrigation. Water every 3 days (in hot, dry areas) to 10 days if it does not rain. If the lawn wilts (see page 262), water immediately.
- Light and frequent watering promotes disease and encourages shallow roots. A lawn with shallow roots is more subject to drought damage than a lawn with deep roots.
- The lawn will use more water in hotter areas, or where there are tree roots near the surface.
- Water less often during cloudy and cool weather, and more often during hot and windy weather.
- Measure the amount of water you apply with several straight-sided cans scattered under the sprinkler.
- Check to see if you are applying enough water by digging a hole with a trowel a couple of hours after watering. The water should penetrate at least 8 inches.
- Apply the water slowly enough that it does not run off. If you cannot change sprinkler heads, turn off the sprinklers for 30 minutes whenever runoff occurs. Continue this cycle until you have applied enough water. Aerating (see page 262) will improve penetration.

MOWING

A well-groomed lawn—one that is mowed at the right height when it needs it—is better able to resist insects, diseases, and weeds. Follow these guidelines for proper mowing:

- Mow when the grass grows ⅓ to ½ times over the recommended height. For example, if the lawn's recommended mowing height is 2 inches, cut it when it is 3 inches high.
- Suggested mowing heights:

Bahiagrass	2 to 3 inches
Bentgrass	⅜ to ¾ inches
Bermudagrass	½ to 1½ inches
Bluegrass	2 to 3 inches
Carpetgrass	1 to 2 inches
Centipedegrass	1 to 2 inches
Fine fescue	1 to 2½ inches
Ryegrass	1 to 2½ inches
St. Augustine	1½ to 3 inches
Tall fescue	3 to 4 inches
Zoysia	½ to 1½ inches

- Sharpen mower blades frequently so they do not tear the grass blades. Torn blades give the lawn a whitish cast.
- Never cut off more than half of the grass blade at a mowing. Mowing too short exposes the shaded lower stems to sunlight, causing them to burn and turn brown. If the grass is much too high, reduce its height a little at a time.
- If the lawn is healthy, it is not necessary to remove grass clippings if the clippings are able to drop into the lawn out of sight. Clippings do not contribute to thatch. But if your lawn is maintained very short, or if the clippings sit on top of the grass, remove them to avoid smothering the grass.
- Mow the lawn when the grass is dry.

Uneven fertilization.

Dethatched lawn. The piles are thatch.

Seedlings emerging in new lawn.

FERTILIZING

Fertilizers supply the nutrients a lawn needs to grow well and remain healthy. Follow these guidelines for proper fertilizing:

- Use a fertilizer that supplies all 3 major nutrients: nitrogen, phosphate, and potash. For a discussion of plant nutrients, see page 859.
- Too much nitrogen fertilizer during periods of stress causes lawn diseases. Avoid heavy fertilization during stress periods. Warm season grasses are under stress during the cool part of the year; cool season grasses are under stress during hot weather.
- Spread the fertilizer evenly over the lawn with a drop spreader or a broadcast spreader.
- Apply fertilizer to moist soil, and water thoroughly immediately after application. This dilutes the dissolved fertilizer and prevents it from burning the lawn.
- Some general guidelines for feeding grasses: If you live in Zone A (see map on page 1002), feed in midspring, early fall, and late fall. If you live in Zone C, fertilize when the grass begins growing in the spring and repeat every 6 weeks until cool weather. If you live in Zone B and your lawn turns brown every winter, follow the directions for Zone C. If the lawn remains green during the winter, feed in early spring, late spring, early fall, and late fall.

THATCH

Thatch is an accumulation of partially decomposed grass stems and roots that accumulates between the live grass and the soil. Check the thickness of a thatch layer by cutting a triangular plug from the lawn with a knife. A thatch layer from ¼ to ½ inch thick is normal; when it exceeds ½ inch it becomes harmful to the lawn.

Thatch interferes with the flow of nutrients, water, and air to the roots. Insects and plant diseases live in a thick thatch layer. The thatch also interferes with the action of insecticides and fungicides, making control difficult.

Thatch accumulation gives the lawn a spongy texture. This causes the lawn mower to bounce, scalping the lawn in spots.

Thatch builds up when the lawn is overfertilized, overwatered, or when the soil is too acid. Grass clippings from mowing do not contribute to thatch.

Thatch accumulates over many years, and should not be removed all at once. Remove thatch with a dethatching machine, often called a verticutter (see page 262). These are available from rental agencies. Or, hire a contractor to do the job for you. Dethatch annually until the condition is corrected. The best time to dethatch is late spring for warm season grasses, or early fall for cool season grasses.

Test the pH of the thatch layer according to the instructions on page 909. If the pH is below 6.0, correct it with periodic applications of lime. Twice a year, spread 25 pounds of lime per 1000 square feet of lawn and water well.

NEW LAWNS

Avoid problems with new lawns by following these guidelines:

Getting ready

- The best time to plant a new lawn is just before a period of rapid growth for the type of grass you are planting.
- Kill old lawns or weeds with ORTHO Kleenup Systemic Weed & Grass Killer. You can plant 1 week after treatment.
- Improve the soil with organic amendments (page 907). Rototill, spade, or rake deeply to loosen the soil.
- Rake out any clods or rocks from the top 2 inches of soil. Level the ground, water it, roll with a garden roller to settle the soil, then level again. Repeat until the ground remains level after watering and rolling.

Seeding

- Spread seed with a drop spreader or a broadcast spreader. Rake lightly to mix the seed into the top ¼ inch of soil. Roll with a light roller to press the seed firmly into the soil. In dry weather, spread ⅛ to ¼ inch of mulch (sawdust or straw—don't use peat moss) to keep the seeds moist. Sprinkle lightly by hand whenever the mulch begins to dry out.

Laying sod

- Lay sod as soon as possible after it is cut. Fit the edges tightly together. Don't stretch the sod. Keep the sod moist until it is established—about 2 weeks. Test by tugging gently at a corner. When you feel resistance, it is established.

DEAD PATCHES

Dog urine spots.

PROBLEM: Circular spots, straw brown in color, 8 to 10 inches in diameter, appear in the lawn. A ring of deep green grass may surround each patch. There are no spots or webbing on the grass blades and the grass does not mat down. Dogs have been in the area.

ANALYSIS: Dog urine injury
Dog urine burns grass. The salts in the urine cause varying stages of damage, from slight discoloration to killing it outright. The nitrogen in the urine may encourage the immediately surrounding grass to grow rapidly, resulting in a dark green ring. Lawns suffer the most damage in hot, dry weather.

SOLUTION: Water the affected areas thoroughly to wash away the urine. This reduces but does not eradicate the brown discoloration. Surrounding grass eventually fills in the affected areas. For quick repair, spot sod as on page 914. If possible, keep dogs off the lawn.

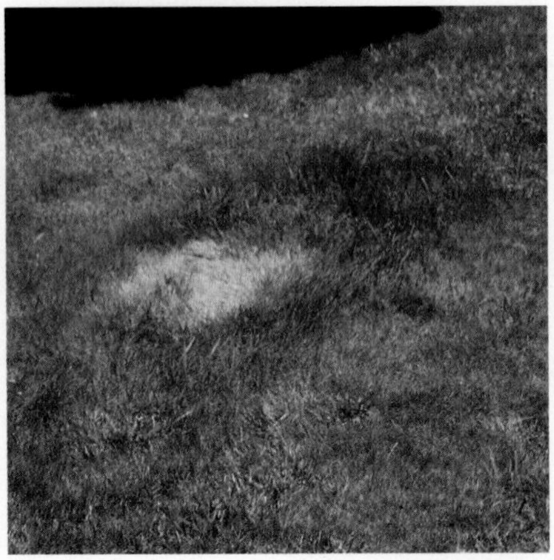

Burn caused by a fertilizer spill.

PROBLEM: Grass dies and turns yellow in irregular patches or definite regular stripes or curves. Grass bordering the areas is a healthy green color. Yellow areas do not spread or enlarge. They appear within 2 to 5 days after fertilizing or after a chemical is spilled on the lawn.

ANALYSIS: Chemical or fertilizer burn
Chemicals such as pesticides, fertilizers, gasoline, and hydrated lime may burn the grass if applied improperly or accidentally spilled. When excessive amounts of these materials contact grass plants, they cause the blades to dry out and die.

SOLUTION: Damage can be prevented or minimized by picking up the spilled material, then washing the chemical from the soil immediately. If the substance is water-soluble, water the area thoroughly—three to five times longer than usual. If the substance is not soluble in water, such as gasoline or weed oil, flood the area with a solution of dish soap diluted to about the same strength as used for washing dishes. Then water as indicated above. Some substances, such as pre-emergence herbicides, cannot be washed from the soil. Replace the top foot of soil in the spill area. Prevent further damage by filling gas tanks, spreaders, and sprayers on an unplanted surface, such as a driveway. Apply chemicals according to the label instructions. Apply fertilizers when the grass blades are dry and the soil is moist. Water thoroughly afterward to dilute the fertilizer and wash it into the soil. Keep drop spreaders closed when stopped or turning. Follow the directions on page 988.

Dead annual bluegrass.

PROBLEM: Areas of grass that were once lush and green die and turn straw brown. Irregular patches appear with the onset of hot summer weather in places where the grass had a whitish appearance in late spring.

ANALYSIS: Annual bluegrass
(*Poa annua*)
Annual bluegrass is one of the most troublesome but least noticed weeds in the lawn. This member of the bluegrass family is lighter green, more shallow-rooted, and less drought and heat tolerant than Kentucky bluegrass. Annual bluegrass, as its name suggests, lives for only 1 year, although some areas also have perennial strains. The seed germinates in cool weather from late summer to late fall. Annual bluegrass grows rapidly in the spring, especially if the lawn is fertilized then. Seed heads appear in mid- to late spring, the same height that the grass is cut. The seed heads give the lawn a whitish appearance. When hot, dry weather arrives, the plants die. The seeds fall to the soil and wait for cooler weather to germinate. Annual bluegrass is most serious where the soil is compacted.

SOLUTION: Weedkillers are only partially effective in controlling annual bluegrass. Prevent seeds from germinating by applying an herbicide containing *DCPA* (DACTHAL®) in early to mid-fall. Do not use *DCPA* if you plan to reseed the lawn in the fall. Replace the dead areas with sod. Do not cut the lawn too short. Lawns more than 2½ inches tall have very little annual bluegrass. Core the lawn in compacted areas (see page 262). For more information on annual bluegrass, see page 815.

Dead crabgrass.

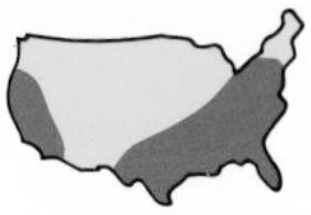

PROBLEM: Brown patches develop in the lawn with the first frost in the fall. Close examination of the dead spots reveals that it is not the lawn grass that has died, but a weed.

ANALYSIS: Crabgrass dying out

Crabgrass (*Digitaria* species) is an annual grassy weed in lawns. It forms large flat clumps, smothering the lawn grass as it spreads. Crabgrass dies with the first killing frost in the fall, or with the onset of cold weather, leaving dead patches in the lawn. Crabgrass sprouts from seeds in early spring. It is a prolific seed producer; a single plant can make thousands of seeds during the course of the summer.

SOLUTION: Treat with an herbicide containing *DCPA* (DACTHAL®) or *siduron* in the early spring 2 weeks before the last expected frost. These pre-emergence weed killers kill the seed as it germinates. Kill actively growing crabgrass with ORTHO Crab Grass Killer or ORTHO Crab Grass & Dandelion Killer. Maturing plants are harder to kill, so repeat the treatment two more times, 4 to 7 days apart, if necessary. Control crabgrass growing in cracks in sidewalks and driveways with ORTHO Kleenup Ready-To-Use Grass & Weed Killer. To keep your lawn healthy and vigorous, follow the guidelines on pages 250 and 251. A thick lawn has very little crabgrass. For more information on crabgrass, see page 270.

Anthracnose on bluegrass.

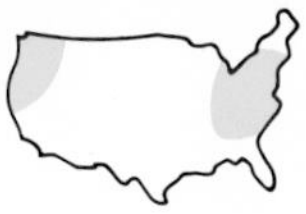

PROBLEM: In the summer and fall, irregular areas of reddish brown to light tan grass appear in the lawn. These areas may range from 2 inches to 10 to 20 feet in diameter. Small, oval, reddish purple spots occur on the blades. A fine webbing may cover the spots, or tiny black specks may be seen in the spots.

ANALYSIS: Anthracnose

This lawn disease is caused by a fungus (*Colletotrichum graminicola*) that attacks lawns under stress, especially those that are poorly fertilized or underwatered. The disease is active in warm (80° to 85°F), humid weather, and results in root decay and stem rot. When weather conditions are favorable for the disease, grass may be killed within 2 days.

SOLUTION: Treat the infected lawn with a fungicide containing *chlorothalonil* (DACONIL 2787®), *benomyl*, or *zineb*, at the first sign of the disease. Repeat the treatment three more times at intervals of 7 to 10 days. Reduce potential damage from anthracnose by fertilizing and watering as suggested on page 250.

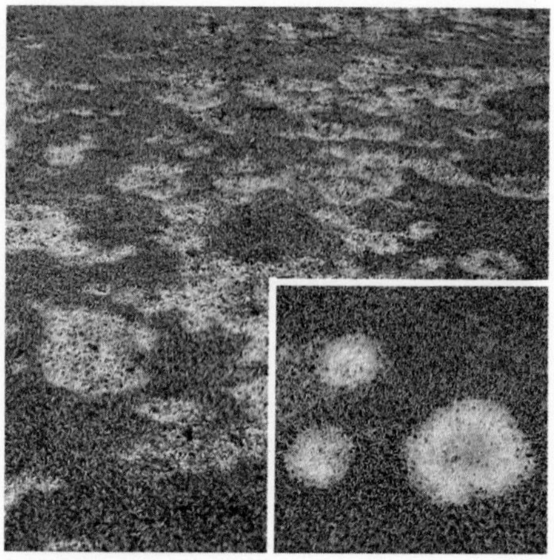

Fusarium patch. *Insert:* Closeup.

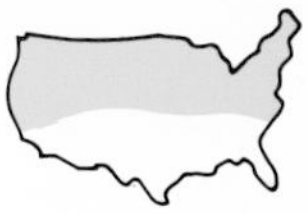

PROBLEM: Pale yellow areas, 2 inches to 1 foot in diameter and pink along the edges, occur in the lawn in the late winter and early spring. Blades are light tan and stick together. A white cottony growth may cover the blades.

ANALYSIS: Fusarium patch

This grass disease is caused by a fungus (*Fusarium nivale*) that may attack lawns in the fall, winter, or spring when the turf remains wet from snow, rain, or poor surface drainage. The disease, also called *pink snow mold*, is most severe on bentgrass, but also occurs on other grasses. It is most prevalent in cool (daytime temperatures below 65°F), humid weather, or when snow falls on unfrozen soil. The fungus often grows beneath the snow or as it melts. Usually, only the grass blades are affected, but when the snow mold is severe, the crowns also are attacked, killing the plants.

SOLUTION: Treat the lawn in early spring at the first sign of the disease with a fungicide containing *benomyl*, *iprodione*, or *methyl thiophanate*. Repeat the treatment in 10 to 14 days. Treat the lawn again in mid to late fall when the daytime temperatures remain below 60°F and the weather is wet. Make two applications, 10 to 14 days apart. To discourage snow mold, avoid applying fertilizers that are high in nitrogen late in the fall. To prevent matting, keep mowing the lawn until the grass stops growing in the fall. Reduce the thatch layer if necessary. For more information on lawn maintenance practices, see pages 250 and 251.

DEAD PATCHES

Fusarium blight.

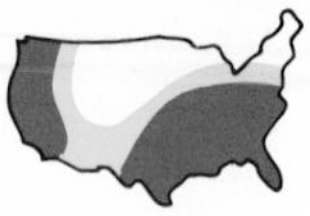

PROBLEM: Patches of grass turn light green, then straw-colored from June through August. "Hot spots" in the yard along driveways, sidewalks, and buildings usually discolor first. These circular, crescent-shaped, or streaked areas range from a few inches to several feet in size. Often the center patch remains green, resulting in a "frog-eye" pattern. Irregular tan lesions extend the full width of the blade. The basal portions of dead stems dry out and turn brown or black.

ANALYSIS: Fusarium blight
This lawn disease is caused by a fungus (*Fusarium roseum*) that is active during hot (75° to 100°F) summer weather, primarily attacking bentgrass and Kentucky bluegrass. Lawns under stress from lack of moisture, hot dry winds, low pH (pH 6.0 or less), thick thatch, and close mowing are most susceptible to the disease. Lush, dense growth from excessive nitrogen fertilization is readily attacked. In cool fall weather, new grass fills in the dead areas, but the disease may recur there the following year.

SOLUTION: Rake out the dead grass and follow the cultural practices outlined on pages 250 and 251. Reseed with resistant varieties. A mixture of 15 percent or more perennial ryegrass and 85 percent or less bluegrass greatly reduces the occurrence of fusarium blight. Next year, before the disease occurs, treat with a fungicide containing *benomyl* or *iprodione* in late May, followed by two applications 10 to 14 days apart. Water thoroughly the day before; water again afterwards. Complete control is difficult to achieve. For a list of resistant and susceptible varieties of bluegrass, see page 1002.

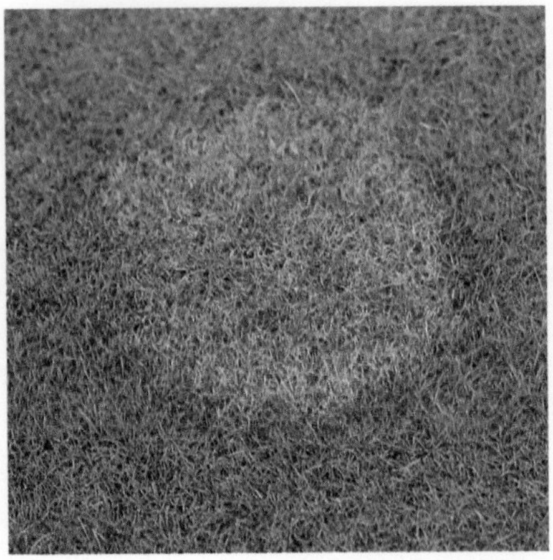
Brown patch.

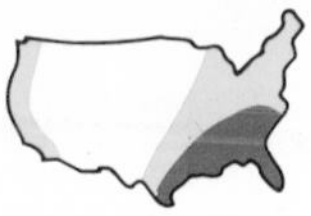

PROBLEM: Circular patches of dead grass a few inches to a few feet in diameter appear in the lawn during periods of high humidity and warm (75° to 85°F) temperatures. Brown areas are sometimes surrounded by dark, purplish smoky rings. Filmy white tufts cover blades in the early morning before the dew dries. Grass blades pull out easily from the base of the plant. After 2 to 3 weeks, the center brown grass may recover and turn green, giving brown areas a doughnut shape.

ANALYSIS: Brown patch
Brown patch is caused by a fungus (*Rhizoctonia solani*). It is one of the most prevalent diseases in warm, humid areas, attacking all turfgrasses. Lush, tender growth from excessive nitrogen fertilization is the most susceptible to attack. Sometimes only the blades are affected and the grass recovers in 2 to 3 weeks. When the infection is severe and warm weather continues, the disease attacks plant crowns and kills the grass.

SOLUTION: Control brown patch with ORTHO Liquid Lawn Disease Control. Spray when the disease is first noticed, and at least three more times at 7 to 10 day intervals. Continue to repeat the treatments as long as warm, humid weather continues. To reduce recurring infections, follow the cultural practices described on pages 250 and 251.

Resistant varieties of ryegrass: Birdie, Citation, Derby, Diplomat, Omega, Pennfine, Yorktown II.

Dollar spot damage. *Insert:* Close-up.

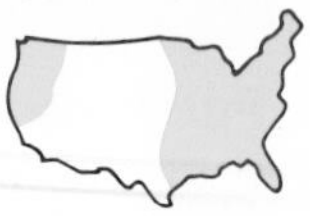

PROBLEM: The grass turns light brown to straw-colored in circular areas from the size of a silver dollar to 6 inches in diameter during the warm, wet weather of May to June and September to October. The small dead areas may merge to form large irregular patches. Small, light brown blotches with reddish brown borders appear on the leaf blades. These spots extend across the entire width of the blade. In the early morning before the dew dries, a white cobwebby growth may cover the infected blades.

ANALYSIS: Dollar spot
This lawn disease, also called *small brown patch*, is caused by a fungus (*Sclerotinia homoeocarpa*). It is most active during warm (60° to 85°F) moist days and cool nights. It attacks many kinds of lawn grasses, but is most severe on bentgrass, Bermudagrass, and Kentucky bluegrass. Lawns troubled by dollar spot are usually under stress from lack of moisture and nitrogen. An infection seldom causes permanent damage, although it takes the lawn several weeks or months to recover. The fungus is spread by shoes, hoses, mowers, and other equipment.

SOLUTION: Control dollar spot with ORTHO Liquid Lawn Disease Control. Make two applications, 7 to 10 days apart, beginning when the disease is first evident. The grass recovers quickly if treated promptly. Maintain the cultural practices outlined on page 250. For a list of resistant varieties, see page 1002.

Red thread. *Insert:* Infected blades.

PROBLEM: The grass turns light tan to pink in areas 2 inches to 3 feet in diameter. Pink webs bind the grass blades together. As the blades dry, pink threads, ¼ to ¾ inch long, protrude from the diseased leaf tips.

ANALYSIS: Red thread
This lawn disease is caused by a fungus (*Laetisaria fuciformis*). It is most serious on fine fescue lawns, but ryegrass, bentgrass, and bluegrass are also susceptible. Red thread is most active in mild (60° to 80°F), wet weather. Only the leaves and leaf sheaths are attacked. Lawns that are growing slowly because of a lack of nitrogen are the most severely affected. Red thread is seldom serious enough to kill the lawn.

SOLUTION: Mildy diseased lawns may improve if the nitrogen content of the soil is increased. For fertilization guidelines, see page 251. However, if weather conditions favorable for the disease continue and it becomes more severe, spray the lawn with ORTHO Liquid Lawn Disease Control. Repeat the treatment three more times at intervals of 7 to 10 days.

Ophiobolus patch.

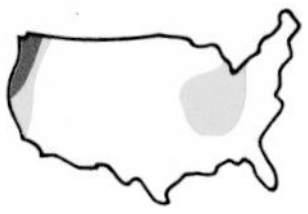

PROBLEM: In midsummer, primarily in the Pacific Northwest, the grass thins, turns light brown, and dies in doughnut-shaped rings or arcs. These areas, 2 to 36 inches in diameter, turn dull gray in winter. The centers are invaded by weeds and annual bluegrass. When the condition is severe the affected areas merge, forming large irregular patches.

ANALYSIS: Ophiobolus patch
This lawn disease is caused by a fungus (*Ophiobolus graminis*) that becomes active in cool, wet weather, but the symptoms develop in dry summer weather. The disease is especially common on bentgrass. Both roots and shoots are severely attacked. Affected areas do not recover for several months.

SOLUTION: Ophiobolus patch is difficult to control with fungicides. Spray with *wettable sulfur*, making two applications of 1¼ pounds per 1000 square feet, 1 month apart in early spring. Apply 7½ pounds of *ammonium sulfate* per 1000 square feet in March, May, June, and early September. Water thoroughly afterwards to prevent burning. Apply 7 pounds of 0–10–10 fertilizer per 1000 square feet in March and June. When the disease has disappeared, use a balanced lawn fertilizer for normal fertilization.

Spring dead spot.

PROBLEM: Circular dead spots develop in Bermudagrass lawns when the lawn begins growth in the spring. Spots vary from a few inches to several feet in diameter. The dead grass is straw-colored, and the stolons and roots are blackened and decayed. Weeds may invade the affected areas. Sometimes Bermudagrass slowly fills in by the end of summer, but the grass is shorter than the surrounding, healthy grass. Grass may grow back only in the center of the spot, creating a "frog-eye" or "island" pattern. In Bermudagrass lawns that have been overseeded with a cool-season grass, affected areas appear as light green spots.

ANALYSIS: Spring dead spot
This lawn disease affects Bermudagrass, causing a stolon and root rot. Spring dead spot is common in areas where temperatures drop low enough to promote winter dormancy of Bermudagrass. The organism that causes spring dead spot has not yet been determined, but current reasearch indicates that the disease is probably caused by a fungus or complex of several fungi. Spring dead spot is most likely to develop in lawns with excess thatch and in lawns that are overfertilized or fertilized late in the growing season.

SOLUTION: Avoid overfertilization and late season fertilization. Keep thatch to a thickness of no more than ¾ inch. Keep the lawn healthy and vigorous to encourage Bermudagrass regrowth into dead areas. Follow the guidelines for good lawn care on pages 250 and 251. Replace the sod and soil of badly diseased areas.

DEAD PATCHES

Damage. *Insert:* Sod webworm (twice life size).

PROBLEM: From mid-May to October the grass turns brown in patches the size of a saucer in the hottest and driest areas of the lawn. These areas may expand to form large irregular patches. Grass blades are chewed off at the soil level. Silky white tubes are found nestled in the root area. Inside are light brown or gray worms with black spots, from ¼ to ¾ inch long. White or gray moths fly in a zigzag pattern over the lawn in the evening. When it lands it folds its wings along the body, rather than letting them spread like most moths.

ANALYSIS: Sod webworms
Several different moths with similar habits are called sod webworms or *lawn moths.* These night-flying moths are the adults of this pest. The moths drop eggs into the grass as they fly. The eggs hatch into worms that feed on grass blades at night or on cloudy, rainy days. In the daytime the worm hides in white silky tubes in the soil. Sometimes an entire lawn is killed in a few days.

SOLUTION: Control sod webworms with ORTHO Lawn Insect Spray (liquid), ORTHO Chinch Bug & Sod Webworm Killer (liquid), or ORTHO Chinch Bug & Sod Webworm Control (granular) when large numbers of moths are noticed at dusk, or at the first sign of damage. First rake out all the dead grass and mow the lawn. Water thoroughly before spraying. For best results, apply the insecticide in the late afternoon or evening when the worms are most active. Do not cut or water the lawn for 1 to 3 days afterwards. To avoid recurring damage, treat the lawn again every 2 months beginning in late spring or early summer. Damaged lawns may recover rapidly if the insects are controlled early.

Damaged lawn. *Insert:* White grub (twice life size).

PROBLEM: In August and September the grass turns brown in large irregular patches. Brown areas of grass roll up easily like a carpet. Milky white grubs from ⅛ to 1 inch long, with brown heads and three pairs of legs, lie curled in the soil.

ANALYSIS: Grubs
Grubs are the larvae of different kinds of beetles, including May and June beetles (also called *white grubs*), Asiatic, Japanese, and masked chafer beetles. The grubs feed on turf roots and may kill the entire lawn. The adult beetles do not damage the lawn, but lay eggs in the soil. May and June beetles lay eggs in the spring and summer. The Asiatic, Japanese, and masked chafer beetles lay eggs in mid to late summer. The eggs hatch and the grubs feed on roots 1 to 3 inches deep in the soil. In late fall they move deep in the soil to overwinter, and resume feeding in the spring.

SOLUTION: The younger the grubs are, the easier they are to kill. Apply ORTHO Lawn Insect Spray (liquid), ORTHO Diazinon Insect Spray (liquid), or ORTHO Diazinon Soil & Turf Insect Control (granular) when you first notice damage and grubs. For preventive control, apply the insecticide just after eggs are laid. Contact your county agent (page 1029) for the correct time in your area. Water the lawn thoroughly within 1 hour after application to help carry the insecticide into the root zone where the grubs are feeding. Soil insecticides take time to be effective, so the grubs may be active for up to 35 days. Some grubs appear to be resistant to pesticides, so retreatments may be necessary. To save areas just beginning to fade, keep the soil moist but not wet.

Pythium blight on seedlings.

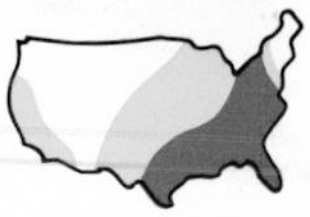

PROBLEM: In hot weather from April to October the grass wilts, shrivels, and turns light brown in irregular spots ½ to 4 inches in diameter. Spots enlarge rapidly, forming streaks a foot or more wide, or patches 1 to 10 feet in diameter. Infected blades mat together when walked on. Blades are often meshed together by white, cobwebby threads in the early morning before the dew dries. Grass sometimes dies within 24 hours.

ANALYSIS: Pythium blight
This lawn disease, also called *grease spot* and *cottony blight*, is caused by a fungus (*Pythium* species). It attacks lawns under stress from heat (85° to 95°F), poorly drained soil, and excessive moisture. Dense, lush grass is the most susceptible. All turfgrasses are affected, ryegrasses the most severely. The fungus spores spread easily in free-flowing water, on lawn mower wheels, and in footsteps. The disease is hard to control because it spreads so rapidly, killing large areas in hours. Pythium blight is common in the fall on topseeded ryegrass.

SOLUTION: Treat the lawn with a fungicide containing *chloroneb* or *ethazole* as soon as the disease is noticed. Repeat treatments every 5 to 10 days either until the disease stops, or until cooler weather resumes. Keep traffic off the diseased area to avoid spreading spores. To prevent recurring infections, follow the cultural practices outlined on pages 250 and 251. Severely infected areas often do not recover, so reseed or resod to reestablish the lawn. Treat next year during hot, humid weather.

Bare spots.

Poor seed germination.

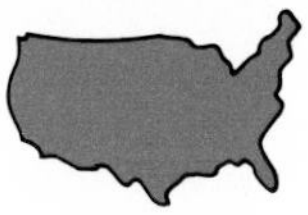

PROBLEM: Seeds in newly planted lawns sprout slowly or not at all. Or seedlings rot and fall over at the soil line.

ANALYSIS: Seeds fail to grow There are several reasons why lawn seeds may not grow.	**SOLUTION:** The numbered solutions below correspond to the numbers in the analysis.
1. *Lack of water:* Once the seed germinates and breaks its seed coat, the soil must stay evenly moist. If the soil around the seedling dries out, the seedling will die.	**1.** Sprinkle a newly planted lawn frequently enough that only the very surface is allowed to dry out. To help conserve moisture, mulch the seed bed lightly with a ¼ inch layer of straw or sawdust.
2. *Temperature:* Seeds planted at the wrong time of year take longer or fail to sprout. If planted at the proper time, seeds should sprout within 4 weeks. For seed germination times at optimum temperatures, see page 1002.	**2.** Plant warm season grasses (Bermudagrass, centipedegrass, and bahiagrass) in spring or early summer as the weather warms. Plant cool season grasses (rye, fescue, bentgrass, and bluegrass) in early to mid-fall or early spring.
3. *Old seeds:* Seeds left over from last year will sprout if they've been stored in a cool, dry place. Seeds older than 1 year, or that have not been stored properly, sprout poorly if at all.	**3.** Use seed produced for sale this year. Check the seed testing date on the box before purchasing.
4. *Seeds planted too deep:* Seeds planted deeper than ¼ inch to ½ inch usually don't sprout.	**4.** After sowing the seed, gently rake the soil to mix the seed into the top ¼ inch.
5. *Unprepared soil:* Seeds must be in direct contact with the soil to sprout. Seeds that sprout in thatch or directly on top of the soil are subject to drying out.	**5.** Till or rake the soil surface before planting. Don't throw seed on top of thatch or unprepared soil.
6. *Damping-off:* This fungus disease is caused by fungi (*Pythium* and *Rhizoctonia* species). Damping-off kills seedlings either before or after emergence if the soil is kept too wet and is rich in nitrogen. For more information on damping-off, see page 850.	**6.** When reseeding blank spots or the entire lawn, spray the seed bed with ORTHO Orthocide Garden Fungicide. Fill in any low spots where water may puddle. Water less often. Let the soil surface dry slightly between waterings until the seedlings are 1 inch high. Then reduce the frequency of watering to allow the top ¼ inch to dry between waterings. Don't add nitrogen fertilizer until the seedlings are 3 inches high.

Damage. *Insert:* Chinch bug (15 times life size).

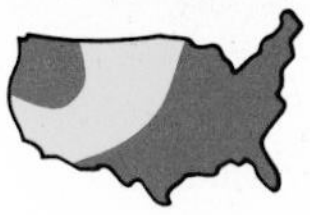

PROBLEM: The grass turns yellowish brown, dries out, and dies in sunny areas and and along sidewalks and driveways. To check for chinch bugs, select a sunny spot on the edge of an affected area where yellow grass borders healthy green grass. Cut out both ends of a tin can. Push one end of the can 2 to 3 inches into the soil. Keep it filled with water for 10 minutes. Black to brown insects with white wings, ⅛ to ¼ inch long, float to the surface in 5 to 10 minutes. Pink to brick red nymphs with a white stripe around the body may also be numerous.

ANALYSIS: Chinch bugs
(*Blissus* species)
These insects feed on many kinds of lawn grasses, but St. Augustine grass is a favorite. Both the adults and the nymphs suck the juices out of the blades. At the same time, they inject a poison that causes the blades to turn brown and die. Heavy infestations may completely kill the grass. These sun- and heat-loving insects seldom attack shady lawns. They can move across an entire lawn in several days.

SOLUTION: Control chinch bugs with ORTHO Lawn Insect Spray (liquid), ORTHO Chinch Bug & Sod Webworm Killer (liquid), or ORTHO Chinch Bug & Sod Webworm Control (granular) as soon as you see damage. Water the lawn before spraying, applying ½ to 1 inch of water to bring the insects to the surface. To prevent recurring damage from newly hatched nymphs, treat every 2 months until frost. In southern Florida, repeat the applications the year around.

DEAD PATCHES

Sod not rooted.

Dying patches of sod.

Scalped spot.

PROBLEM: Newly sodded areas turn yellow, then brown. Sod rolls up easily like a carpet. No roots are visible on the bottom of the sod.

ANALYSIS: Sod fails to establish	**SOLUTION:**
Sod should establish in 2 to 3 weeks. Test by gently tugging a corner. If it resists, then the roots have grown into the soil. Sod can fail to establish for a number of reasons:	The numbered solutions below correspond to the numbers in the analysis.
1. *Sod dried out:* Until the roots grow into the soil, sod is very susceptible to drying out.	**1.** Water frequently enough to keep the sod and the soil under it moist.
2. *Unprepared soil:* If the sod is laid directly on thatch it dries out quickly. If it is laid on hard soil, the roots have difficulty growing into the soil.	**2.** Before laying sod, the soil should be tilled or thoroughly raked. Remove all dead grass and debris, and level the grade.
3. *Old sod:* Old sod has many yellow blades among the green blades. It may be weak from water or heat stress, and will establish poorly or not at all. Sod may be damaged by remaining rolled up for only 2 days in hot weather. In cool weather it can remain rolled for over a week without damage.	**3.** Choose uniformly green sod that is not turning yellow or pale green. Lay the sod as soon as possible. Don't leave it rolled and stacked for more than a day in hot weather. However, it can be stored rolled for 2 to 3 days in a cool, shady area. Keep the soil on the outer pieces moist.
4. *Time of year:* Sod can be installed almost any time of the year, but it will establish slowly if it is laid when the grass is not actively growing.	**4.** Lay cool season grass sod (bluegrass or bentgrass) in late summer to early fall or early spring. Avoid midsummer. Lay warm season grass sod (Bermudagrass, St. Augustine grass, bahiagrass, or centipedegrass) in the late spring and early summer.

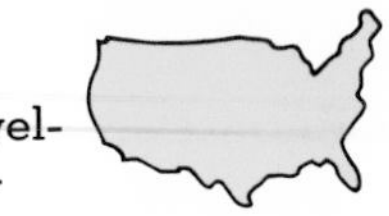

PROBLEM: Grass has yellow patches after mowing. A few days later, patches may turn brown and die.

ANALYSIS: Improper mowing
Too much grass was removed from the damaged places when the lawn was mowed. This can happen in two ways:
1. *Scalping*, or mowing near the soil level, occurs when the mower cuts too low in some areas. This can happen if the lawn is bumpy, in which case the high spots get scalped. Where the grass has been cut too short, the lower parts of the blades are exposed to sunlight, which burns them. If the base of the grass plant was damaged by the scalping, the grass may die. Otherwise, it will probably recover in a week or so.
2. *Grass has grown too tall* between mowings. If the mower is cutting at the proper height, but the grass has grown too long between mowings, the lower parts of the grass blades are exposed and burned. The grass is seldom killed from being mowed when it is too long, but it remains unsightly for a week or two.

SOLUTION: The damaged spots need no special care. To prevent further damage:
1. If the lawn surface is uneven, level the high spots with the procedure described on page 914. If the lawn is spongy from an accumulation of thatch, follow the procedure described on page 251. Raise the mower blade to the height suggested on page 250.
2. Mow frequently enough so that you don't remove more than half of the blade. If the grass is very tall when you mow, raise the blade to half the grass height, and lower it gradually over the next few mowings.

Dormant Bermudagrass.

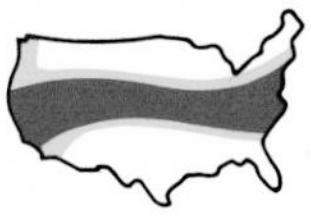

PROBLEM: Brown patches of irregular shape and size develop with the first frost in the fall. The leaf and stem structure of the dead grass look different from the living grass. There are no signs of insect or disease damage.

ANALYSIS: Warm weather grasses becoming dormant

Warm weather perennial grasses become dormant with the onset of cold weather. The tops die back, but the perennial roots live over the winter and resprout in the spring. Two of the most common invading warm weather grasses are zoysia and Bermudagrass. When these grasses invade cool weather (bluegrass) lawns, the warm weather grasses turn brown in the fall, while the cool weather grasses remain green through the winter. For more information on Bermudagrass, see page 269.

SOLUTION: It is very difficult to eradicate these grasses from the lawn. Once the grass turns brown, it is too late to treat. Next year, spot treat the undesirable grasses with ORTHO Kleenup Systemic Grass & Weed Killer or ORTHO Kleenup Ready-To-Use Grass & Weed Killer. Wait 1 week, and reseed. The grass will still be green, but the roots will die in 1 or 2 weeks and will not resprout. If new plants emerge in the spring, spot treat with the same herbicide or let the two kinds of grass grow together. If your lawn is in full sun, consider growing only warm season grass. As the warm season grass becomes dormant in the fall, camouflage the brown with a seeding of ryegrass or spray it with a green dye.

Billbug damage. *Insert:* Close-up.

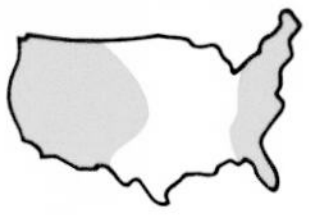

PROBLEM: The grass turns brown and dies in expanding patches from mid-June to late August. When pulled, the grass lifts easily. Lying in the soil are fat, humpbacked white grubs with brown heads, without legs, and from ¼ to ½ inch long. Black, slow-moving snouted weevils ¼ to ½ inch long occasionally walk on sidewalks and driveways in May and October.

ANALYSIS: Billbugs

(*Sphenophorus* species)

The larvae of this pest damage lawns by hollowing out the grass stems and chewing off the roots. They can destroy an entire lawn. In May, the adults lay eggs in holes they chew in grass stems. The newly hatched larvae feed inside the stems, hollowing out the stem and crown, leaving very fine sandlike excrement. Large larvae feed on roots. Once the larvae move down to the roots and inside the plant's crown, chemical control can't reach them.

SOLUTION: Control billbugs with ORTHO Diazinon Soil & Turf Insect Control (granular) or ORTHO Diazinon Insect Spray (liquid). Young larvae can be controlled if treated while still feeding on the grass blades. If the larvae have already moved down to the roots, then water and fertilize the lawn to stimulate new growth. Repeated treatments are not usually necessary unless the billbugs are migrating from your neighbors' yards. Small damaged areas usually recover if the larvae are killed. Reseed or resod large areas. Next year, treat in early May to kill the adults as they lay eggs.

Damaged lawn. *Insert:* Mole cricket (¾ life size).

PROBLEM: Small mounds of soil are scattered on the soil surface. The lawn feels spongy underfoot. Large areas of grass turn brown and die. To determine if the lawn is infested with mole crickets, make a solution of 1 ounce of liquid dishwashing detergent in 2 gallons of water. Drench the mixture into 4 square feet of turf. Mole crickets, greenish gray to brown insects, 1½ inches long, with short front legs and shovellike feet, will come to the surface within 3 minutes.

ANALYSIS: Mole crickets

(*Scapteriscus* species)

Several species of mole crickets attack lawns. They prefer bahia and Bermudagrass, but also feed on St. Augustine, zoysia, and centipedegrass. They damage lawns by tunneling through the top 1 to 2 inches of soil, loosening it and uprooting plants, causing them to dry out. They also feed on grass roots, weakening the plants. They feed at night, and may tunnel as much as 10 to 20 feet a night. In the daytime, they return to their underground burrows. Adults migrate from their burrows to new areas twice a year, in the spring from March to July, and again from November to December.

SOLUTION: In July, after the eggs hatch and before the young nymphs cause much damage, treat the lawn with ORTHO Mole Cricket Bait or ORTHO Diazinon Insect Spray. Mow grass and water before applying, since mole crickets are not active in dry soil. Do not water for 36 hours after application. If damage continues, treat again in late summer to early fall. Keep the lawn watered to encourage new root growth. For instructions on watering lawns, see page 250.

DEAD PATCHES

Dead patches caused by salt accumulation.

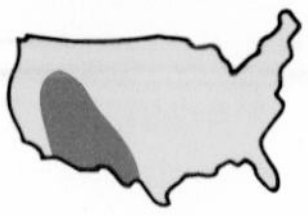

PROBLEM: Grass slowly dies, especially in the lowest areas of the lawn. A white or dark crust may be present on the soil.

ANALYSIS: Salt damage
Salt damage occurs when salt accumulates in the soil to damaging levels. This can happen in two ways: either the lawn is not receiving enough water from rainfall or irrigation to wash the salts from the soil, or the drainage is so poor that water does not pass through the soil. In either case, as water evaporates from the soil and grass blades, the salts that were dissolved in the water accumulate near the surface of the soil. In some cases, a white or dark brown crust of salts forms on the surface of the soil. Salts can originate in the soil, in the irrigation water, or in applied fertilizers.

SOLUTION: The only way to eliminate salt problems is to wash the salts through the soil with water. If the damage is only at a low spot in the lawn, fill in the spot to level the lawn. If the entire lawn drains poorly, improve drainage by aerating according to the directions on page 262; or improve the soil as described on page 907. If the soil drains well, increase the amount of water applied at each watering by 50 percent or more, so that excess water will leach salts below the root zone of the grass. Fertilize according to the instructions on page 251.

Leafhopper (6 times life size).

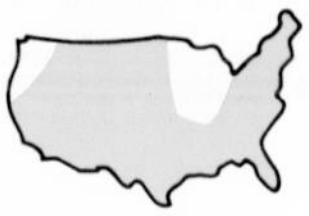

PROBLEM: The grass is bleached and dried, and has a stunted, thinned appearance. There are white to brown spots on individual blades of grass. Small wedge-shaped insects $\frac{1}{8}$ to $\frac{1}{4}$ inch long can be seen flying or hopping from blade to blade. The insects are light green to yellow to brownish gray. They may walk sideways or backwards on a blade of grass rather than forward.

ANALYSIS: Leafhoppers
These insects damage grasses and other plants by sucking the sap from the leaves and stems. The adult females lay eggs in or on the plant tissues. The immature leafhoppers that emerge from the eggs resemble the adults but are paler and wingless. Both immature and adult leafhoppers feed on plant sap. There may be only one generation a year in northern states, but as many as three or more in the warmer southern states. (See page 878 for more information on leafhoppers.)

SOLUTION: Treat the lawn with ORTHO Orthene Systemic Insect Control, ORTHO Diazinon Insect Spray, or ORTHO Diazinon Soil & Turf Insect Control. Mow the lawn and water well before the treatment. Treat after the grass blades have dried. Repeat the application in 1 month if reinfestation occurs.

Damage. *Insert:* Crane fly grub (half life size).

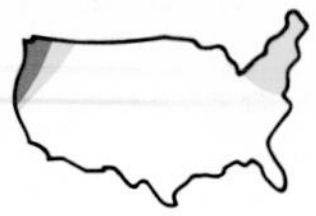

PROBLEM: Grass blades are eaten in patches, often beginning at the edges of the lawn. The patches may spread until most of the lawn is affected. A brownish paste covers the ground in heavily infested areas. Legless, brownish gray grubs, about an inch long, may be found just under the surface of the soil. Late last summer, many long-legged, mosquitolike insects were present around the house.

ANALYSIS: European crane fly
(*Tipula paludosa*)
The adult form of this insect looks like a large mosquito with very long legs that break off easily. They often swarm around houses in large numbers in late summer. Their numbers are alarming, but adult crane flies do not sting or do any other damage. They lay eggs in lawns, pastures, or fields in late summer. The grubs that hatch from the eggs feed on grass blades and clover during the fall, spend the winter buried in the soil, and resume feeding in the spring. The most severe damage is done in March and April. Feeding stops by mid-May. The adults emerge in late August and September. The grass is usually not killed in the damaged areas, and recovers after feeding stops.

SOLUTION: Treat the lawn with ORTHO Diazinon Insect Spray or ORTHO Diazinon Soil & Turf Insect Control when damage first appears. Treatment is most effective between April 1 and April 15.

Cutworm (half life size).

PROBLEM: Grass blades are chewed unevenly along the edges. In newly seeded lawns, young grass plants may be chewed or cut off near the ground. Gray, brown, or black worms, 1½ to 2 inches long, may be found in the thatch—the layer of dead grass stems and roots at the surface of the soil—by peeling back a section of grass.

ANALYSIS: Cutworms
Cutworms attack both newly seeded and established lawns. A single cutworm can sever the stems of many young grass plants in a single night. They also chew the edges of the blades. Cutworms spend the days hidden in debris or in the thatch layer of the lawn. They feed only at night, and are active throughout the growing season. In the adult stage, cutworms become dark, night-flying moths with bands or stripes on their forewings.

SOLUTION: Control cutworms in the lawn with ORTHO Diazinon Insect Spray or ORTHO Diazinon Soil & Turf Insect Control. Apply at the first sign of cutworms or damage. Since the cutworms are most active at night, treat in the evening. Repeat if damage continues.

Armyworm (life size).

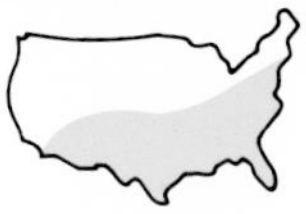

PROBLEM: Grass blades are chewed and circular bare areas appear in the lawn. Light tan to dark brown caterpillars with yellow, orange, or dark brown stripes, ¾ to 2 inches long, are found on the grass blades.

ANALYSIS: Armyworms *(Pseudaletia unipuncta)*
Armyworms attack a variety of plants including lawns, corn, and grains. The tan to gray adult moths lay eggs on blades of grass. The caterpillars that hatch from these eggs chew on the blades. They may completely strip a lawn in 2 to 3 days. Armyworms get their name from their feeding habit. After they have eaten everything in one area, they march in droves to another area in search of more food. After several weeks of feeding, the worms pupate in the soil, and later emerge as adult moths to repeat the cycle. There are several generations each year. The first begins in mid-May and causes the most damage. Armyworms are most numerous after cold, wet spring weather that slows the development of parasites and diseases that help keep the population in check. They do not overwinter in cold winter areas, but the moths migrate great distances in search of places to lay eggs.

SOLUTION: Treat infested lawns with ORTHO Lawn Insect Spray, ORTHO Diazinon Insect Spray, ORTHO Liquid Sevin, or ORTHO Diazinon Soil & Turf Insect Control at the first sign of damage. Repeat at weekly intervals if the lawn becomes reinfested.

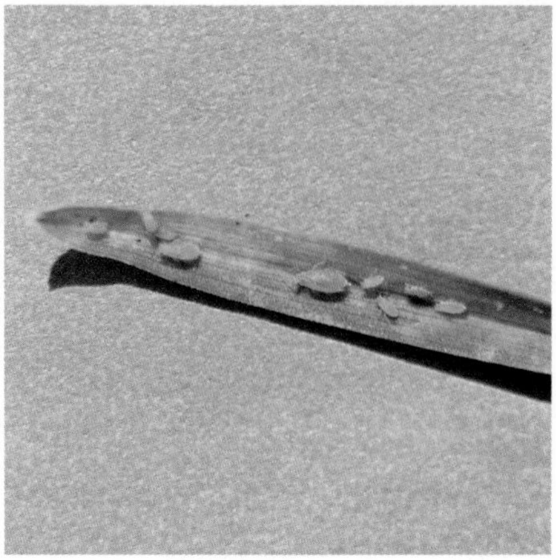
Greenbugs (3 times life size).

PROBLEM: Patches of grass under trees turn rust-colored, then brown, and die. Discolored areas then spread outward into sunny areas of the lawn. Yellow to rust-colored spots with dark centers occur on the blades.

ANALYSIS: Greenbug
(*Schizaphis graminum*)
The greenbug is a small aphid that feeds on grains such as wheat, corn, and sorghum. It has recently become a serious pest of Kentucky bluegrass lawns in some areas of the Midwest. The greenbug seldom attacks other kinds of turfgrass. Damage occurs as the greenbug pierces the leaf tissue, sucks the sap, and injects a toxin into the blades. This feeding weakens both the roots and aboveground plant parts. If uncontrolled, greenbugs can kill the turf. Greenbugs prefer well-maintained and managed lawns. However, underwatered lawns that are attacked also suffer severe damage. Overuse of fertilizers may predispose the lawn to attack. Greenbugs are most numerous after mild winters and cool springs.

SOLUTION: Spray the infested lawn with ORTHO Orthene Systemic Insect Control at the first sign of damage. Repeat if the damage and infestation continue. Prevent water stress by watering as suggested on page 250. Apply fertilizers as suggested on page 251.

GRASS THIN

Lawn damaged by drought.

PROBLEM: Footprints in the lawn make a long-lasting imprint instead of bouncing right back. The grass blades turn a bluish green or slate gray color and wilt. In the cool evening, the grass recovers until the sun and heat of the following day make it darken and wilt. Areas begin to thin out, and after a few days the lawn begins to look and feel like straw and dies.

ANALYSIS: Drought
A lawn suffers from drought damage when water evaporates from the lawn faster than it is absorbed. Drought damage occurs first in the hottest and driest areas of the lawn—along sidewalks, driveways, south or west-facing slopes, south sides of reflecting buildings, and areas with sandy soil. Grass blades don't wilt like broadleafed plants do. They don't droop, but roll or fold up lengthwise.

SOLUTION: Water the lawn immediately, following the guidelines on page 250. If the grass has turned yellow, it will take several weeks for the affected areas to recover. If you are not very conscientious about watering your lawn, consider planting a drought tolerant turfgrass.

Drought tolerant turfgrasses: Bahia, Bermudagrass, Red fescue, Tall fescue, Zoysia.

Thatch.

PROBLEM: Grass thins out in sunny or shady areas of the lawn. Weeds invade the sparse areas. Grass may suddenly die in large patches during summer heat and drought. Cut and lift several plugs of grass 2 to 3 inches deep. Look to see if the stringy, feltlike material between the grass and soil surface is thicker than ¼ inch.

ANALYSIS: Thatch
Thatch is a tightly intermingled layer of partially decomposed stems and roots of grass, which develops between the actively growing grass and the soil surface. Thatch slows grass growth by restricting the movement of water, air, and nutrients in the soil. Thatch is normal in a lawn, but when it is thicker than ½ inch, the lawn begins to suffer. As the layer accumulates, the grass roots grow in the thatch instead of down into the soil. Thatch is similar to peat moss—it dries out quickly and is very difficult to rewet. Thatch accumulation is encouraged by overly vigorous grass growth from excessive fertilization and frequent watering. Grass clippings do not contribute to thatch. For more information on thatch, see page 251.

SOLUTION: To reduce the thatch and increase the lawn's vigor, power rake or dethatch the lawn. Dethatch cool season grasses in the fall, and warm season grasses in the early spring before new growth begins. The machines for the job can be rented, or hire a contractor. Dethatchers have vertical rotating blades that slice through the turf, cutting out thatch. First, mow the lawn as short as possible. Go over the lawn one to three times with the the dethatcher. Take up the debris, fertilize, and water to hasten the lawn's recovery.

Lawn damaged by soil compaction.

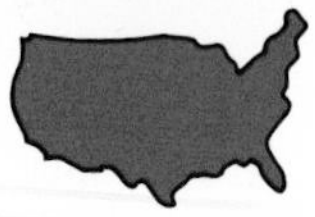

PROBLEM: In heavily traveled areas, the grass becomes thin and develops bare spots. Water runs off quickly.

ANALYSIS: Compacted soil
Soil is easily compacted, or pressed together, in areas where there is frequent foot or vehicular traffic. Clay soils are more likely to become compacted than loamy or sandy soils. Soil that has been compacted has few air spaces. Compaction prevents air, water, and nutrients from penetrating into the soil and reaching the grass roots. This results in a shallow root system, and frequent water and nutrient stress.

SOLUTION: Water daily during hot periods, and fertilize frequently to keep the grass alive until you can relieve the compacted soil. Aerate the compacted soil with a coring machine. These machines can be rented, or hire a contractor to do the job for you. Coring machines remove cores of soil, allowing water and nutrients to pass into the soil. Water the lawn a few days before aerating, so the soil is moist. Do not aerate dry or very wet soil. After aerating, allow the removed soil cores to dry a few days in the sun, then rake them up or break them by dragging a heavy flat board over them. In a few weeks the grass begins to fill in the holes in the lawn. Hand coring tools are available for aerating small areas. Aerate heavily trafficked areas annually. Reduce foot traffic in the area by installing a walk or patio, erecting a fence, or planting a hedge to divert traffic.

Surface roots.

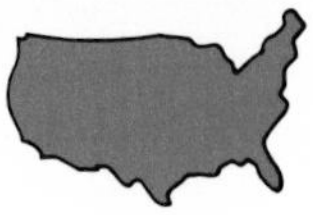

PROBLEM: Tree and shrub roots are exposed or are making bumps by growing just beneath it. Exposed roots may be lumpy and malformed.

ANALYSIS: Surface roots
Several factors can cause large surface roots to develop in lawns.
1. *Waterlogged soil:* Waterlogged soil has very little oxygen available for root growth. The only available oxygen is near the soil surface, so the roots develop there.
2. *Compacted or heavy soil:* Such soils contain very little oxygen, so root growth is restricted to near the surface.
3. *Light irrigation:* If plants growing in or near lawns are not deeply watered, they will often develop surface roots.
4. *Natural tendency:* Some trees and shrubs are more likely to develop surface roots than others.

SOLUTION: The numbered solutions below correspond to the numbers in the analysis.
1. If the soil is waterlogged, cut back on watering. (For information about watering, see pages 912 and 917.)
2. Loosen the soil around tree roots. Aerate the lawn area to improve soil compaction (see page 262). For more information about heavy soil, see page 904.
3. Water trees and shrubs deeply. Apply enough water to wet the soil to a depth of 6 inches to 3 feet, depending upon the species. Look up your plant in the section beginning on page 408 to determine the correct depth and frequency of irrigation.
4. For a list of plants likely to develop surface roots, see page 1010. If practical, replace them with plants adapted to growing in a lawn; see page 1009.

Lawn damaged by shade.

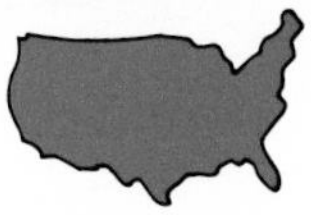

PROBLEM: Grass becomes thin under trees. Blades are thin and dark green. Moss and algae sometimes grow on the soil.

ANALYSIS: Shade
Planting and maintaining a good lawn under shade trees is difficult. Shallow-rooted trees like maples, pines, and beeches absorb much of the nutrients and water that are applied and intended for the grass. Trees that cast dense shade block out the sun that the grass needs to grow. It is especially difficult to grow grass under pines and other conifers. Some lawn diseases, such as powdery mildew, are more active in the shade, where they thrive in the higher humidity.

SOLUTION: Prune some of the branches from the trees to let more light to the grass. When seeding shady areas, select shade tolerant grasses: in the North, fescues and some bluegrasses such as Glade, Warrens A-34, and Nugget; in the South, St. Augustine grass. Seed in the fall so the seedlings have a chance to establish before the tree leafs out in the spring. Plant St. Augustine grass in the late spring. Rake up fallen leaves every 4 or 5 days in the fall so they do not suffocate the grass. Mow the grass in the shade higher than in the full sun. Water and fertilize more heavily under trees so there is enough for both the lawn and the tree. Or, replace the lawn with a shade-loving groundcover. For a list, see page 1003.

Lawn with leaf spot. *Insert:* Spotted blades.

PROBLEM: The grass turns brown and thins out in irregular patches 2 or more feet in diameter from spring until fall. Both the green and brown grass blades have small oval spots with straw-colored centers and dark maroon borders.

ANALYSIS: Helminthosporium leaf spot
This lawn disease, also called *melting out*, is caused by a fungus (*Helminthosporium* species). It is one of the most destructive lawn diseases, especially on Kentucky bluegrass. In cool spring and fall weather, *Helminthosporium* causes spots on grass blades, but does not kill them. In warm summer weather the fungus can kill the grass blades, spread to the base of the plant, and kill entire plants. Lawns that are excessively lush from high nitrogen fertilization or are under stress from short mowing, thick thatch, and light, frequent watering, are the most susceptible to attack.

SOLUTION: Spray the lawn with ORTHO Liquid Lawn Disease Control when leaf spotting is first noticed. Make at least three more applications, 7 to 10 days apart. Keep your lawn healthy and vigorous by following the guidelines for good lawn care on pages 250 and 251. Be particularly careful to use a balanced lawn fertilizer, reduce the thatch layer, and water thoroughly and infrequently. For a list of resistant and susceptible varieties of bluegrass, see page 1002.

GRASS THIN

Nematode damage.

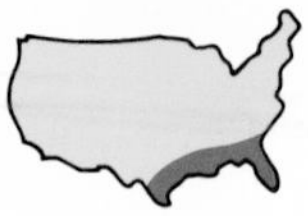

PROBLEM: The grass grows slowly, thins out, and turns pale green to yellow. In hot weather the blades may wilt. Main roots are short with few side roots, or many roots may grow from one point.

ANALYSIS: Nematodes
Nematodes are microscopic worms that live in the soil. They are not related to earthworms. Nematodes feed on grass roots, damaging and stunting them. The damaged roots can't supply sufficient water and nutrients to the leaf blades, and the grass is stunted or slowly dies. Nematodes are found throughout the country, but are most severe in the South. They prefer moist, sandy loam soils. They can move only a few inches each year on their own, but they may be carried long distances by soil, water, tools, or infested plants. Testing roots and soil is the only positive method for confirming the presence of nematodes. Contact your local Cooperative Extension Office (see page 1029) for sampling instructions and addresses of testing laboratories. Soil and root problems such as poor soil structure, drought stress, nutrient deficiency, and root rots can also produce symptoms of decline similar to those caused by nematodes. These problems should be eliminated as causes before sending soil and root samples for testing. For information on soil problems and root rots, see pages 907 and 849.

SOLUTION: There are no chemicals available to homeowners to kill nematodes in planted soil. However, they can be controlled before planting a new lawn by soil fumigation. For information on fumigating soil, see page 927.

LAWN PALE OR YELLOW

Unfertilized lawn with green clover.

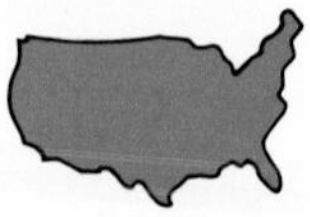

PROBLEM: Grass is pale green to yellow and grows more slowly than usual. If the condition persists, the grass will become sparse and weeds will invade the lawn.

ANALYSIS: Nitrogen deficiency
Nitrogen is a key element in maintaining a healthy lawn with few insect and disease problems. It is best to maintain a level of nitrogen in the soil that: (1) does not stimulate excessive leaf growth, which reduces mowing frequency; (2) doesn't encourage shoot growth at the expense of root growth; and (3) varies according to the cultural and environmental conditions present. Because heavy rains and watering leach nitrogen from the soil, periodic feedings are necessary throughout the growing season. Acid soil may cause nitrogen to be unavailable to the grass.

SOLUTION: Fertilize the lawn with a lawn fertilizer according to the instructions on the label. To prevent burning and to move the nutrients into the soil, water thoroughly after application. Grass begins using the nitrogen in the fertilizer within 15 to 24 hours. (For more information on fertilizing, see page 250.) If the soil is acid, below pH 5.5, liming is necessary for good nitrogen utilization. For more information on pH and liming, see pages 908 and 1019.

Grass blades damaged by a dull lawn mower.

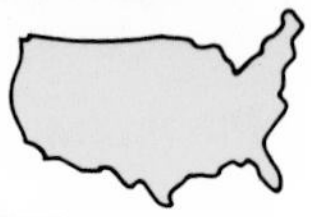

PROBLEM: When viewed from a distance, the lawn has a white or gray cast. The leaf ends are ragged and dead at the tip. White hairs may protrude from the cut tips.

ANALYSIS: Dull lawn mower
If a reel or rotary lawn mower is dull, it tears the tip off the grass blade rather than cutting it cleanly. Perennial ryegrass and tall fescues have fibers running the length of the blade that do not cut easily. If the blade tip is torn, these fibers usually remain protruding from the torn end. It is particularly important to keep the mower sharp when cutting these grasses.

SOLUTION: Reel mowers should be sharpened two or three times during the growing season. Rotary mowers should be sharpened after every few mowings. Reel mowers may be sharpened at a hardware store that offers this service. Rotary mower blades can be removed and sharpened with a file. For more information on mower care and sharpening, see the ORTHO book *How To Select, Use & Maintain Garden Equipment*.

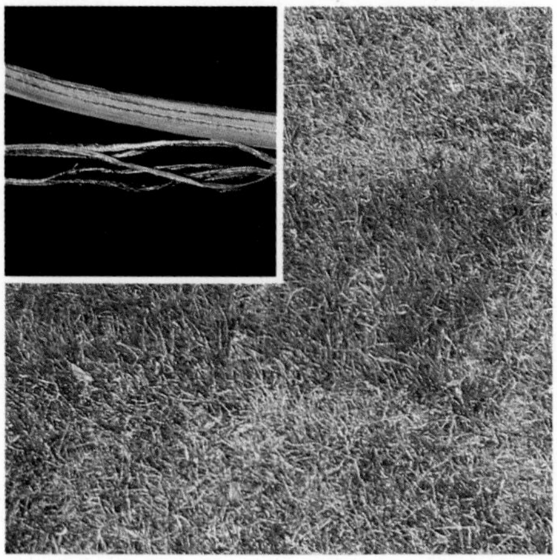

Stripe smut. *Insert:* Infected blades.

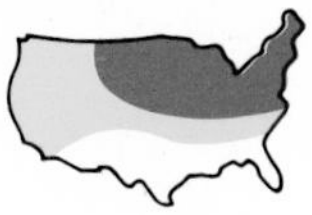

PROBLEM: Grass turns pale green to yellow in cool spring and fall weather. First, long yellowish streaks appear on the blades. These streaks turn gray to black. The blades then curl, wither, and shred in thin strips from the tip downward. Affected plants occur singly or in spots from a few inches to more than a foot in diameter. These areas grow more slowly and are shorter than surrounding healthy grass.

ANALYSIS: Stripe smut

This grass disease is caused by a fungus (*Ustilago striiformis*) that attacks many kinds of turfgrasses, but is most prevalent on Merion Kentucky bluegrass. The spores infect the plant's crown and adjoining underground stems. The fungus then grows throughout the plant's tissues. The disease is most active in cool (50° to 60°F) weather. The diseased plants then die during the next period of hot weather. Stripe smut is favored by high soil fertility and excessive watering.

SOLUTION: Stripe smut is difficult to eliminate completely, but its severity can be lessened. Treat the lawn with *benomyl* or *ethyl thiophanate* in October or early March with two applications 14 to 21 days apart. Water thoroughly afterwards to carry the fungicide to the roots so it can be absorbed into the plant. Follow the guidelines for good lawn care on pages 250 and 251. For a list of resistant varieties of bluegrass, see page 1002.

Bermudagrass mite damage.

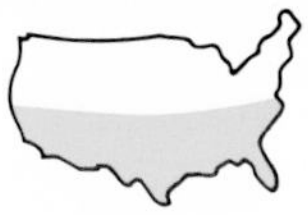

PROBLEM: Bermudagrass plants grow in a tight "knot" or rosette, turn yellow, then brown and die. To determine if the grass is infested with mites, shake one of these rosettes over a sheet of dark paper. Minute, creamy white specks the size of pepper grains will drop to the paper and begin to crawl around. These pests are easily seen against the dark background.

ANALYSIS: Bermudagrass mite

(*Aceria neocynodonis*)

These mites, related to spiders, are major pests of Bermudagrass, but do not attack other grasses. They damage the grass by sucking sap from the base of leaves, and from under leaf sheaths and stems. Their feeding causes the plant to form very short internodes (distance between leaves) so that the plants form tight rosettes or "knots." When the mite population is large, there is no new green growth. These pests are most numerous in warm (75°F and above) humid weather on well-fertilized lawns. They reproduce rapidly, and by midsummer build up to tremendous numbers.

SOLUTION: Treat the infested lawn with ORTHO Diazinon Insect Spray or ORTHO Diazinon Soil & Turf Insect Control when the grass turns green in the spring. Repeat whenever damage appears. Water and fertilize the lawn as discussed on pages 250 and 251 to keep it healthy and vigorous. Although fertilizer may increase the mite population, ultimately it hastens the lawn's recovery.

Septoria leaf spot.

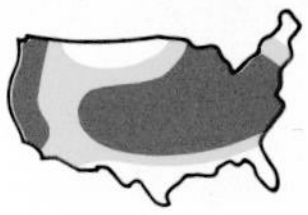

PROBLEM: In the spring and fall, the lawn has a gray cast. The tips of the blades are pale yellow to gray, with red or yellow margins. Pale areas may be ⅛ to 1 inch long. Tiny black dots are scattered in the diseased spots on the blades.

ANALYSIS: Septoria leaf spot

This lawn disease, also called *tip burn*, is caused by a fungus (*Septoria* species) that infects most northern grass species and Bermudagrass. It is most prevalent in the cool, wet weather of spring and fall. Unfertilized lawns are most susceptible. The disease usually attacks in the spring, declines during the hot summer months, and returns in the fall. Because the disease infects the leaf tips first, frequent mowing removes much of the diseased part of the blades.

SOLUTION: Treat the infected lawn with a fungicide containing *maneb*, *chlorothalonil* (DACONIL 2787®), or *iprodione* as soon as the discoloration appears. Repeat the treatment three more times, 7 to 10 days apart, or as long as weather favorable for the disease continues. Keep the lawn healthy and vigorous by following the guidelines for good lawn care on pages 250 and 251. Mow the lawn regularly. Since no variety is completely resistant, plant a blend of two or three disease-tolerant varieties.

Tolerant bluegrass varieties: A-20, A-34, Adelphi, Birka, Bonnieblue, Glade, Ruby, Sydsport, Touchdown, and Victa.

POWDERY MATERIAL ON GRASS

Rust.

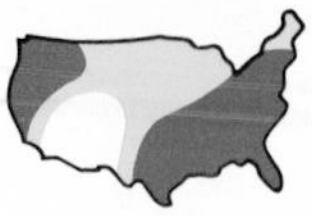

PROBLEM: Grass turns light green or yellow and begins to thin out. An orange powder coats the grass blades and rubs off on fingers, shoes, and clothing. Reddish brown lesions under the powder do not rub off.

ANALYSIS: Rust
This lawn disease is caused by a fungus (*Puccinia* species) that occurs most frequently on Merion Kentucky bluegrass, ryegrass, and zoysia. It is most active during moist, warm (70° to 75°F) weather, but can be active all winter in mild winter areas. Heavy dew favors its development. Grasses under stress from nitrogen deficiency, lack of moisture, and close mowing are most susceptible to attack. Rust is also more severe in the shade. The orange powder is composed of millions of microscopic spores which spread easily in the wind. Lawns attacked severely by rust are more likely to suffer winter damage.

SOLUTION: Rust develops slowly, often more slowly than the grass grows. Fertilize with a high-nitrogen fertilizer to maintain rapid growth. Mow frequently, removing the clippings. If the disease is severe, treat with ORTHO Liquid Lawn Disease Control. Repeat the application every 7 to 14 days until the lawn improves. For a list of rust-resistant varieties of bluegrass, see page 1002. A blend of two or more of these varieties is more resistant than a single variety.

Powdery mildew.

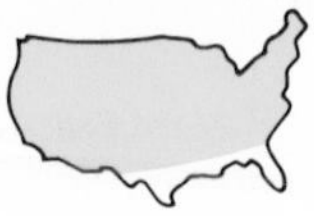

PROBLEM: Whitish gray mold develops on the upper surfaces of grass blades during cool rainy weather. The lawn looks as if it has been dusted with flour. The leaf tissue under the mold turns yellow and then tan or brown. Severely infected plants wither and die.

ANALYSIS: Powdery mildew
This lawn disease is caused by a fungus (*Erysiphe graminis*) that occurs when the nights are cool (65° to 70°F) and damp, and the days warm and humid. It is most severe on Merion Kentucky bluegrass, but also attacks other varieties of bluegrass, fescue, and Bermudagrass. Lawns growing in the shade are the most affected. Powdery mildew slows the growth of leaves, roots, and underground stems, causing gradual weakening of the grass and making it more susceptible to other problems. Lawns growing rapidly because of excessive nitrogen fertilization are very susceptible to attack from this fungus. The fine white mildew on the blades develops into powdery spores that spread easily in the wind. The spores can infect a grass plant in 2 to 4 hours.

SOLUTION: Treat the lawn with *benomyl* when the mildew is first seen. Repeat the application every 7 to 10 days until the mildew is no longer seen. Reduce the shade and improve air circulation by pruning surrounding trees and shrubs. Follow the guidelines on pages 250 and 251 for a healthy, vigorous lawn.

Mildew resistant varieties of Kentucky bluegrass: A-20, A-34, Aquila, Baron, Birka, Glade, Nugget, Rugby, Sydsport, Touchdown.

Slime mold.

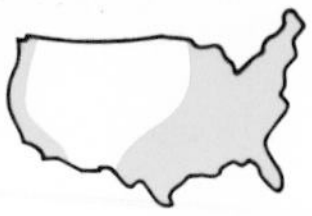

PROBLEM: Bluish gray, black, or yellow pinhead-size balls cover grass blades in the spring, summer, and fall following heavy rains or watering. Balls feel powdery when rubbed between the fingers. Affected areas range in size from a few inches to several feet.

ANALYSIS: Slime molds
These fungi feed on decaying organic matter in the soil. They do not feed on green plants. When the powdery covering is heavy, it may damage the grass by shading the blades from sunlight, causing them to turn yellow. Slime molds occur on dichondra, all turfgrasses, and some weeds. While slime molds are feeding on decaying organic matter in the soil, they are white, gray, or yellow slimy masses on the soil. When they are ready to reproduce, they extend up onto grass blades and form powdery balls containing spores. This phase of the life cycle is more noticeable than is the slimy mass phase.

SOLUTION: In most cases control is not necessary. Although slime molds are unsightly, they do not permanently damage the lawn. Remove the molds from the grass by hosing with a strong stream of water, or sweeping with a broom.

DARK GREEN AREAS

Fairy ring.

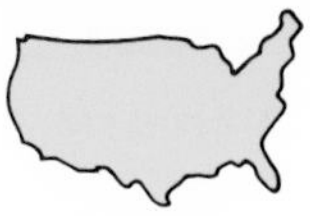

PROBLEM: Circles or arcs of dark green grass occur in the lawn. The circles may be as small as 1 foot or as large as hundreds of feet in diameter. The grass just inside the darker area may be lighter green than the rest of the lawn. Mushrooms may grow in the dark green area.

ANALYSIS: Fairy ring
This condition is caused by one of several fungi that grow on organic matter in the soil. These fungi do not harm the grass directly, but may inhibit water flow into the soil. The ring of darker green grass is caused by nutrients released as the fungus breaks down organic matter. If the lawn is low in nutrients, the darker area will be more pronounced in contrast to the paler grass around it. The fungus begins growth at a central point and grows outward at a rate of 1 or 2 feet a year, forming the circle. Mushrooms, which are the fruiting bodies of the fungus, appear when weather conditions are right for them.

SOLUTION: Fairy ring is not a turfgrass disease, and does not harm the lawn. It is very difficult to control, but its effects can be masked by fertilizing the lawn well so that all the grass will be dark green. If there is a region of pale green or yellow grass within the ring, aerate the lawn and water thoroughly so that water penetrates the soil surface. For information on aerating and watering, see pages 262 and 250.

DIGGING IN LAWN

Soil mounds from pocket gophers.

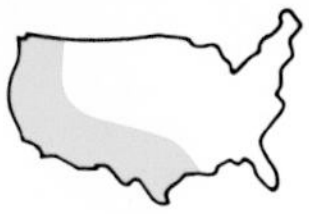

PROBLEM: Mounds of soil appear on the lawn. Usually crescent-shaped, these mounds open outward from a hole in the soil. There are no ridges on the surface of the lawn.

ANALYSIS: Pocket gophers
The pocket gopher lives and feeds almost entirely underground, coming to the surface only to bring up soil from its burrows, look for new territory, or feed close to its hole. Pocket gophers eat plant roots and occasionally whole plants. This rodent has fur-lined pouches on each side of its mouth. It has small eyes and ears, long sharp claws, a blunt head, and a tail sparsely covered with hair. Pocket gophers form their typical crescent-shaped mounds by pushing soil from their tunnels.

SOLUTION: Trapping is the quickest and surest way to eliminate pocket gophers from your yard. There are two types of traps—the wire trap and the box trap. Find the main runway by probing with a sharp rod about a foot deep a short distance on each side of a fresh mound. Dig a hole to intersect the run and insert two traps in the run, one facing in each direction. With cord or soft wire tie the traps together or to a stake above ground. To keep soil from falling on the traps, cover the hole with sod or a board, and sprinkle with soil to block out all light. Check and move the traps daily. For more information on pocket gophers, see page 896.

Ridges in lawn caused by mole tunnels.

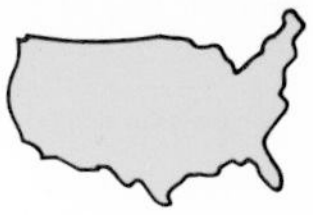

PROBLEM: Raised ridges, 3 to 5 inches wide, crisscross the lawn. These ridges sometimes turn brown.

ANALYSIS: Moles
Moles are small rodents that live underground. They feed on grubs, earthworms, and other insects. Moles are 4 to 6 inches long, with velvety fur and small hidden eyes. Their strong forelegs, with long, trowellike claws, are used to dig and push the soil as they move through the ground. As they mine their way through the soil, they sever the grass roots and raise the sod. These raised and loosened areas dry out quickly. Moles are also objectionable because their ridges give the lawn an uneven surface that can result in scalping when mowed. For more information about moles, see page 896.

SOLUTION: The best way to rid your lawn of moles is to control the insects they feed on. Their main diet is grubs. Treat the lawn with ORTHO Lawn Insect Spray (liquid), ORTHO Diazinon Insect Spray (liquid), or ORTHO Diazinon Soil & Turf Insect Control (granular). (For further information on grubs, see page 256.) Once their food supply is gone, moles will leave the area within a few weeks. If a few remain behind, traps are effective. Set the traps on active tunnels. To determine which tunnels are active, roll or tamp down the ridges in the early morning. Those that are raised by the afternoon are still active. Several kinds of mole traps are available in hardware and rental stores. Poison baits are not always effective, and should be used with caution around children and pets.

DIGGING IN LAWN

Bird damage.

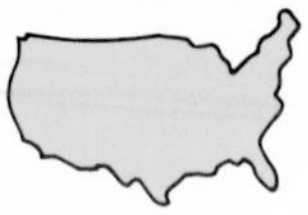

PROBLEM: Many birds are pecking in the lawn.

ANALYSIS: Birds tearing lawn
Birds pecking in the lawn indicate an insect problem in the lawn. Starlings, crows, sparrows, grackles, and robins are commonly found feeding on grubs, chinch bugs, and sod webworms. If left untended, the insects will probably do more damage than the birds, which disturb the lawn's root system only slightly by tearing and pulling the roots while searching for insects.

SOLUTION: The best way to keep birds from digging in your lawn is to rid it of insects. The following ORTHO products control the lawn insects that birds feed on. Select the most appropriate product and follow the label directions: ORTHO Lawn Insect Spray (liquid), ORTHO Diazinon Insect Spray (liquid), ORTHO Chinch Bug & Sod Webworm Killer (liquid), or ORTHO Chinch Bug & Sod Webworm Control (granular). Not all of the above products are sold in every region of the United States. For more information on controlling lawn insects, see page 256 for grubs and sod webworms, and page 257 for chinch bugs.

Earthworm (life size).

PROBLEM: Small mounds or clumps of granular soil appear scattered throughout the lawn. Earthworms may be seen at night or after a heavy rain.

ANALYSIS: Earthworms
Earthworms feed on dead roots and stems, and are usually an indication of fertile soil. They prefer moist, medium to fine-textured soil that is high in organic matter. They are seldom found in dry, sandy soil. Although the earthworm castings—small piles of soil—may mar the appearance of the lawn, and the earthworms may damage new seedlings, their activity improves the soil in several ways. Their movement from the surface to underlying soil helps mix the organic matter on the top with the soil below, and reduces thatch accumulation. Their channels in the soil improve air and water movement through the soil. The castings also help improve the soil structure.

SOLUTION: Earthworms are beneficial to the soil, so control measures are not required. Break up the mounds of soil with a rake.

Ant hill.

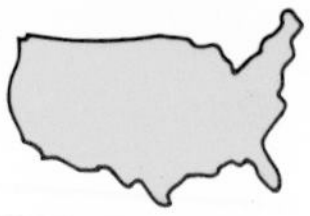

PROBLEM: Small mounds or hills of soil occur in the lawn. Each mound has a hole in the center. Black, brown, or red ants scurry about.

ANALYSIS: Ants
Ants live underground in hot, dry areas of the lawn. They do not feed on grass, but when numerous may damage the plants in several ways. The mounds of soil in their hills smother and kill grass plants. As the ants tunnel among grass roots the soil may dry out, killing the plants. Ants also feed on newly planted grass seeds and sometimes store the seeds in their nests. Some ants, especially fire ants and harvester ants, bite people and animals. Most ants become a nuisance when they travel from their mounds and invade homes. For more information about ants, see page 893.

SOLUTION: Treat ant hills with ORTHO Diazinon Granules, ORTHO Diazinon Soil & Turf Insect Control, or ORTHO Diazinon Insect Spray. Water lightly after the treatment. Repeat the application as new mounds appear and as long as the ants are active. Once the ants have disappeared, reseed any bare or dead spots.

GRASSLIKE WEEDS

Seed heads. *Insert:* Annual bluegrass plant.

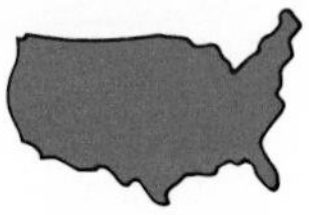

PROBLEM: In mid-spring, the grass has a whitish appearance. Pale green grassy weeds grow among desirable grasses.

ANALYSIS: Annual bluegrass
(*Poa annua*)
Annual bluegrass is one of the most troublesome but least noticed weeds in the lawn. This member of the bluegrass family is lighter green, more shallow-rooted, and less drought tolerant than Kentucky bluegrass. As its name suggests, annual bluegrass usually lives for only 1 year, although some strains are perennial strains. The seed germinates in cool weather from late summer to late fall. Annual bluegrass grows rapidly in the spring, especially if the lawn is fertilized then. Seed heads appear in mid- to late spring at the same height that the grass is cut. The seed heads give the lawn a whitish appearance. When hot, dry weather arrives, the plants die. The seeds fall to the soil and wait for cooler weather to germinate. Annual bluegrass is most serious where the soil is compacted. For more information on annual bluegrass, see page 815.

SOLUTION: Weedkillers are only partially effective in controlling annual bluegrass. Prevent seeds from germinating by applying an herbicide containing *DCPA* (DACTHAL®) or *bensulide* as a pre-emergence treatment in early to mid-fall. Do not use if you plan to reseed the lawn in the fall. Replace the dead areas in the summer with sod. Do not cut the lawn too short. Lawns more than 2½ inches tall have very little annual bluegrass. Aerate the lawn in compacted areas (see page 262).

Bentgrass invading a bluegrass lawn.

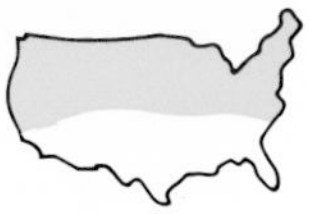

PROBLEM: Patches of soft, matted grass develop in the lawn. Sometimes the grass looks dead, with long straggly stems. In the spring, it greens up more slowly than the surrounding grass.

ANALYSIS: Bentgrass
(*Agrostis* species)
There are several kinds of bentgrass. It is most commonly grown on golf course putting greens, where the grass is cut very short, from ¼ inch to ½ inch. Bentgrass needs to be cut short to be attractive. The invasive nature of bentgrass makes it a weed in bluegrass and ryegrass lawns, which are cut 1½ to 2 inches tall. At this height, bentgrass becomes matted and straggly. Bentgrass is very invasive, and will crowd out other grasses. It is introduced into a lawn in several ways: seeds in the soil, lawn equipment, seed mixtures and sod, or from nearby unmowed areas.

SOLUTION: Kill bentgrass patches with ORTHO Kleenup Systemic Weed & Grass Killer while it is actively growing from early summer to early fall. Omit a regular mowing before treating to allow for enough leaf tissue to absorb the chemical. Spray enough to wet the foliage. Kleenup will also kill any desirable grasses it contacts. One week after spraying, mow the bentgrass close and reseed the area. The bentgrass will still be green when it is mowed, but the roots will die and not resprout.

Bermudagrass.

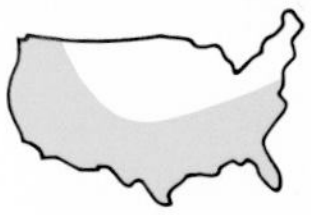

PROBLEM: In southern areas of the United States, patches of fine-textured grass grow in the lawn. The slightly hairy, gray-green stems creep along the soil, with erect shoots 6 to 18 inches tall. Leaf blades are ⅛ inch wide. This grass turns brown in the winter if subjected to temperatures below 50°F.

ANALYSIS: Bermudagrass
(*Cynodon dactylon*)
Bermudagrass is one of the most widely used lawn grasses in the South. It has a very deep root system and is drought and heat tolerant. The leaves are not cold tolerant, and turn brown when the temperature approaches freezing. Its vigorous, creeping growth habit makes it a weed that invades non-Bermudagrass lawns and flower beds.

SOLUTION: Spot treat the Bermudagrass with ORTHO Kleenup Grass & Weed Killer anytime the grass is actively growing, up to 2 to 4 weeks before the first killing frost. After 1 week, mow the treated grass as closely as possible, and reseed. The grass will still be green when it is mowed, but roots will die in 3 or 4 weeks and will not resprout. If regrowth occurs in the spring, spot treat with the same herbicide. To prevent Bermudagrass from invading your lawn from other lawns, mow higher than 1½ inches, spot treat as needed each summer, and water the lawn adequately during the summer. Fertilize more heavily in the fall than at any other time of year. In the South, Bermudagrass makes a nice lawn if mowed short (½ to 1 inch), grown in full sunlight, and given nitrogen throughout the growing season. For more information on Bermudagrass, see page 259.

GRASSLIKE WEEDS

Quackgrass.

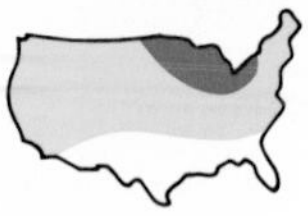

PROBLEM: A grassy weed with hollow stems grows in a newly seeded lawn. Wheatlike spikes grow at the tips of the stems. The narrow leaf blades are bluish green and rough on the upper surface. A pair of "claws" occurs at the junction of the blade and the stem. Rings of root hairs grow every ¾ to 1 inch along the underground stems.

ANALYSIS: Quackgrass
(*Agropyron repens*)
This cool season perennial, also called *couchgrass* or *witchgrass*, spreads extensively through the lawn by long white underground stems. It reproduces by seeds and these underground stems. Quackgrass is found most frequently in fertile, newly seeded lawns. It grows much more rapidly than grass seedlings, often crowding them out. For more information about quackgrass, see page 816.

SOLUTION: Kill clumps of actively growing quackgrass with ORTHO Kleenup Ready-To-Use Grass & Weed Killer.

Crabgrass.

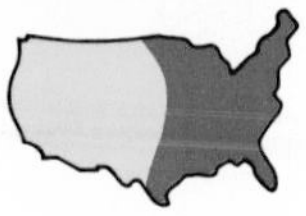

PROBLEM: A grassy weed forms broad, flat clumps in thin areas of the lawn. It grows rapidly through the summer, rooting easily at the stem joints. The pale green blades are 2 to 5 inches long and ⅓ inch wide. Seed heads 2 to 6 inches tall grow from the center of the plant.

ANALYSIS: Crabgrass
(*Digitaria* species)
Crabgrass sprouts from seeds in the early spring, growing rapidly and producing seeds all summer until the first killing frost in the fall. Then the plants turn brown and die. The seeds lie dormant over the winter and sprout in the spring. When a lawn begins to thin out from insects, disease, or poor maintenance, crabgrass is one of the first weeds to invade the area. For more information about crabgrass, see page 817.

SOLUTION: Kill actively growing crabgrass with ORTHO Crab Grass Killer or ORTHO Crab Grass & Dandelion Killer. Older plants are harder to kill; repeat the treatment two more times, at 4 to 7 day intervals. To kill crabgrass seeds as they germinate, apply the weedkiller *DCPA* (DACTHAL®) in the early spring, 2 weeks before the last expected frost, or about the time the forsythia bloom. Follow the guidelines on pages 250 and 251 for a healthy, vigorous lawn; crabgrass is usually not a serious problem in a thick, healthy lawn.

Goosegrass.

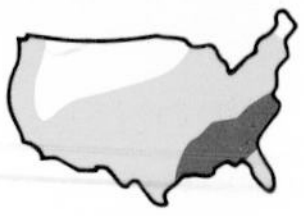

PROBLEM: A smooth, flat-stemmed, grassy weed forms a rosette in the lawn resembling the spokes of a wheel. Blades, ⅕ inch wide and 2 to 10 inches long, are slightly hairy near the base. Stems do not root at their joints. Seedstalks 2 to 6 inches tall grow from the tops of stems.

ANALYSIS: Goosegrass
(*Eleusine indica*)
This warm season annual weed, also known as *silver crabgrass*, resembles crabgrass, but is darker green, germinates later in the spring, and doesn't root at the stem joints. This weed reproduces by seeds and grows an extensive root system that is difficult to pull up. Goosegrass invades thin areas of the lawn where the soil is compacted and infertile. For more information about goosegrass, see page 818.

SOLUTION: Kill clumps of actively growing goosegrass with ORTHO Kleenup Ready-To-Use Grass & Weed Killer. After 7 days remove the weed. It will still be green, but the roots have been killed and will not resprout. Reduce the soil compaction, if necessary, as instructed on page 262. Then reseed or resod. To kill goosegrass seedlings as they germinate, apply a weed killer containing *DCPA* (DACTHAL®) in late spring or early summer. Maintain a healthy, dense lawn by following the guidelines on pages 250 and 251.

Dallisgrass.

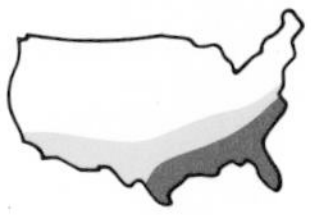

PROBLEM: A bunch-type, grassy weed with coarse-textured leaves grows in the lawn. The leaves are ½ inch wide and 4 to 10 inches long. Stems 2 to 6 inches long radiate from the center of the plant in a star pattern. Seed stalks with 3 to 5 fingerlike segments may grow from the top of the stems. The seeds are covered with fine, silken hairs.

ANALYSIS: Dallisgrass
(*Paspalum dilatatum*)
This warm season grassy weed is one of the most troublesome in the southern United States. It begins growth in very early spring and prefers warm, moist areas and high-cut lawns. However, once established in low-cut lawns it spreads rapidly. It is a deep-rooted perennial plant that reproduces by seeds and underground stems. For more information about dallisgrass, see page 817.

SOLUTION: Treat actively growing dallisgrass in early spring or summer with ORTHO Crab Grass Killer or ORTHO Kleenup Ready-To-Use Grass & Weed Killer. Repeat the treatment two more times at intervals of 7 days. Kleenup will also kill any desirable grasses it contacts. One week after spraying, mow the tall fescue and reseed the area. The tall fescue may still be green when it is removed, but the roots will die in 3 or 4 weeks and will not resprout.

Tall fescue.

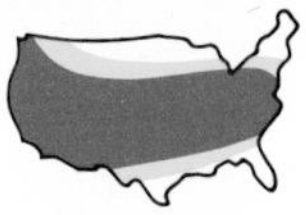

PROBLEM: Clumps of very coarse, tough grass invade thin areas of the lawn. The medium-dark green blades, ½ inch wide, are ribbed on the top surface, and smooth on the bottom. In the spring and fall, the lower parts of the stems turn reddish purple. The blades tend to shred when mowed.

ANALYSIS: Tall fescue
(*Festuca arundinacea*)
This cool season, perennial, bunch-type grass is very durable. It is commonly used on athletic fields because it holds up well under hard wear. Tall fescue makes an attractive turf when grown by itself. However, when it is seeded with, or invades, bluegrass, Bermudagrass, or ryegrass lawns, it is considered a weed. It becomes very clumpy and makes an uneven turf. When insects and diseases attack the desirable grasses in the lawn, the tall fescue is usually not affected. It resists diseases and grubs, and sod webworms attack it only if they've eaten everything else. It is also heat tolerant, and its deep roots help it survive periods of heavy moisture and drought.

SOLUTION: Kill clumps of tall fescue with ORTHO Kleenup Systemic Weed & Grass Killer while it is actively growing from early summer to early fall. Omit a regular mowing before treating to allow for enough leaf tissue to absorb the chemical. Kleenup will also kill any desirable grasses it contacts. One week after spraying, mow the tall fescue and reseed the area. The tall fescue may still be green when it is removed, but the roots will die in 3 or 4 weeks and will not resprout.

Barnyardgrass.

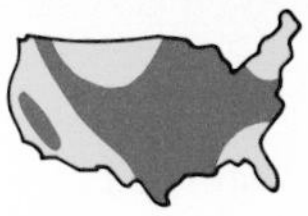

PROBLEM: In summer and fall, a low-growing grassy weed with reddish purple stems 1 to 3 feet long grows in the lawn. The smooth leaves are ¼ to ½ inch wide, with a prominent midrib.

ANALYSIS: Barnyardgrass
(*Echinochloa crus-galli*)
Barnyardgrass, also called *watergrass*, is a warm season annual weed that is usually found in poorly managed lawns of low fertility. It reproduces by seeds, and develops into a plant with a shallow root system. Although the natural growth habit of barnyardgrass is upright, when mowed regularly it forms ground-hugging mats. For more information about barnyardgrass, see page 819.

SOLUTION: Kill mats of actively growing barnyardgrass with an herbicide containing *DSMA*. Repeat the treatment two more times, at intervals of 7 to 10 days, until the plants die. *DSMA* may discolor the turf for 2 to 3 weeks. Improve soil fertility and maintain a dense, healthy lawn by following the guidelines on pages 250 and 251. To kill barnyardgrass seedlings as they sprout, apply a weed killer containing *DCPA* (DACTHAL®) in the early spring 2 weeks before the last expected frost.

GRASSLIKE WEEDS

Nutsedge. *Insert:* Underground stems and tubers.

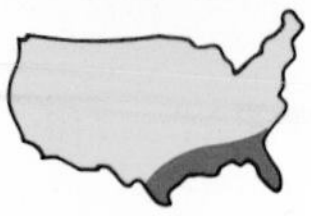

PROBLEM: In the summer, this weed grows more rapidly than the grass and stands above the turf. The erect, single, triangular stem has narrow, grasslike, yellow-green leaves arranged in threes from the base of the plant. Seed heads are yellow-brown.

ANALYSIS: Nutsedge
(*Cyperus* species)
Nutsedge, commonly called *nutgrass*, is a hard-to-kill perennial weed. It reproduces by underground stems, seeds, and tubers. The tubers, the size of popcorn kernels, sprout in late spring and early summer. The plant tops die back in the fall, leaving new tubers in the soil to repeat the cycle the following year. The tubers and underground stems are firmly anchored in the ground. When a plant is pulled up, some of the tubers and underground stems are left behind to resprout into new plants. For more information about nutsedge, see page 821.

SOLUTION: Nutsedge is difficult to control. Treat with ORTHO Crab Grass Killer or ORTHO Crab Grass & Dandelion Killer when the plants first become active in the spring. Repeat two or three more times, 10 to 14 days apart. If you miss a treatment, the weeds recover and take longer to control. Treat again the following spring to kill any persistent tubers. These herbicides may temporarily (2 to 4 weeks) discolor desirable grasses. On centipedegrass and St. Augustine grass lawns, use the weed killer *atrazine* in January, February, or March, before the weeds germinate.

Wild garlic. *Insert:* Aerial bulblets.

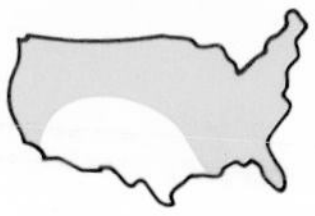

PROBLEM: An onion-like weed with a characteristic garlic odor grows in the lawn. The leaves are slender, hollow, and round. The leaves join together at the lower half of the main stem, just above where it emerges from the base of an underground bulb. Greenish purple flowers bloom at the same height as the leaves.

ANALYSIS: Wild garlic
(*Allium vineale*)
Wild garlic is also commonly called *wild onion*. This perennial weed reproduces mostly by bulbs and bulblets formed under and above ground. Both soft and hard bulblets are formed underground. The soft bulblets germinate in the fall. The hard bulblets remain dormant over the winter, germinating the following spring or later. Wild garlic also produces bulblets at the tips of some of its leaves. As they mature, they fall to the soil and sprout. Wild garlic spreads rapidly through the lawn and is very difficult to control.

SOLUTION: Treat the lawn with ORTHO Weed-B-Gon Lawn Weed Killer or ORTHO Weed-B-Gon Jet Weeder as the leaves emerge in the spring. Repeat the application in 2 weeks. Because the plants can regrow from the bulbs, and the bulbs sprout at different times of the year, repeat the treatments annually for the next 2 or 3 years. For more information about wild garlic, see page 821.

If wild garlic grows in pastures where milk cows feed, it makes the milk less appetizing by giving it a garlic flavor. Also, when this weed is harvested with wheat, the milled flour has a garlic odor.

BROADLEAF WEEDS

Prostrate knotweed.

PROBLEM: A very low-growing weed with oval, bluish green leaves grows in the thin and trampled areas of the lawn. The smooth leaves are 1 inch long and ¼ inch wide, and attach to the wiry stems at prominent "knots" or joints. This weed forms mats up to 2 feet in diameter. Very tiny greenish white flowers bloom at the leaf and stem joints from June to November.

ANALYSIS: Prostrate knotweed
(*Polygonum aviculare*)
Prostrate knotweed, sometimes called *wiregrass*, is an annual plant that reproduces from its numerous seeds, which germinate in the spring as the soil warms. Prostrate knotweed in a lawn is an indication of low fertility and compacted soil. It frequently grows in the compacted soils along driveways, and in paths cut through lawns. Sometimes it is also found in newly established lawns. Knotweed cannot get started in a vigorous, dense turf. For more information about prostrate knotweed, see page 827.

SOLUTION: Treat the lawn with ORTHO Weed-B-Gon Lawn Weed Killer or ORTHO Weed-B-Gon Jet Weeder in early spring when the seedlings are still young. Repeated treatments may be needed. Divert the traffic trampling the grass and loosen compacted soil (see page 262). Follow the guidelines on pages 250 and 251 for a healthy, vigorous lawn.

Clover.

PROBLEM: A weed with leaves composed of three round leaflets at the top of a hairy leaf stalk 2 to 4 inches tall grows in the lawn. The leaf stalks sprout from the base of the plant. White or pink-tinged flowers, ½ inch in size, bloom from June to September. They often attract bees.

ANALYSIS: Clover
(*Trifolium* species)
Clover is a common perennial weed in lawns throughout the country. Although some people like it in a lawn, others consider it messy, or they don't like the bees that are attracted to the flowers. Clover reproduces by seeds and aboveground rooting stems. The seeds can live in the soil for 20 years or more. The plant, which has a creeping, prostrate habit, suffocates lawn grasses, resulting in large patches of clover. When buying a box of grass seed, be sure to read the label carefully. Clover seeds are sometimes contained in seed mixtures. Since clover produces its own nitrogen, it thrives in lawns that are low in this plant nutrient.

SOLUTION: Treat the lawn with ORTHO Chickweed & Clover Control or ORTHO Weed-B-Gon Weed Killer in the spring and early fall. Repeated treatments are often necessary.

Black medic.

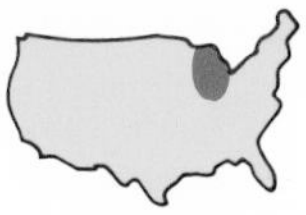

PROBLEM: A low-growing, trailing weed forms dense mats in the lawn. The stems are slightly hairy, and the three-leaflet cloverlike leaves are slightly toothed at the tips. Small, bright yellow flowers bloom in May and June, followed by black kidney-shaped pods.

ANALYSIS: Black medic
(*Medicago lupulina*)
This annual weed is also called *black clover* because of its cloverlike leaves and black seeds. It is common in lawns throughout the country in June, July, and August. Black medic reproduces by seed and has a shallow taproot. It usually invades lawns with poor, sterile soil where lawn grasses don't grow, or grow poorly. If not controlled, a single black medic plant enlarges into a thick mat that crowds out lawn grasses. For more information about black medic, see page 831.

SOLUTION: Treat the lawn with ORTHO Chickweed, Spurge & Oxalis Killer D, ORTHO Weed-B-Gon Lawn Weed Killer, or ORTHO Weed-B-Gon For Southern Grasses from late spring to early summer, or early to midfall, when the weeds are growing actively, and preferably before seeds form. Don't water for 24 hours after treating. Improve soil fertility by following the fertilizing guidelines on page 250.

Oxalis.

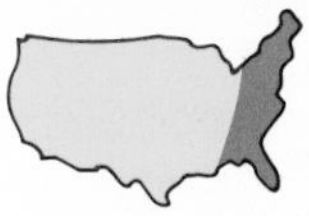

PROBLEM: A weed with pale green leaves divided into three heart-shaped leaflets invades thin areas of the lawn. The leaves are ¼ to ¾ inch wide, and are similar to clover. The stems root at the lower joints and are often thinly covered with fine hairs. Small, bright yellow flowers are ½ inch long with five petals. Cucumber-shaped light green seed pods develop from the fading flowers. Plants may be 4 to 12 inches high with a prostrate or erect growth habit.

ANALYSIS: Oxalis
(*Oxalis stricta*)
Oxalis, also called *yellow woodsorrel*, is a perennial plant that thrives in dry, open places. It invades lawns that are begining to thin from insect, disease, or maintenance problems. Oxalis reproduces from the seeds formed in the seed pods. When the pods dry, a light touch causes them to explode, shooting their seeds several feet in all directions. Oxalis leaves contain oxalic acid, which gives them a sour taste. For more information about oxalis, see page 830.

SOLUTION: Control oxalis with ORTHO Weed-B-Gon Lawn Weed Killer, ORTHO Weed-B-Gon Weed Killer, or ORTHO Weed-B-Gon For Southern Grasses. The most effective time to spray is when the weeds are actively growing in the spring or late summer to fall. Oxalis is not easy to kill; several treatments are usually needed. Check the soil pH level (see page 909), and follow the guidelines on pages 250 and 251 for a healthy, vigorous lawn. A healthy lawn helps smother the oxalis.

BROADLEAF WEEDS

Mouseear chickweed.

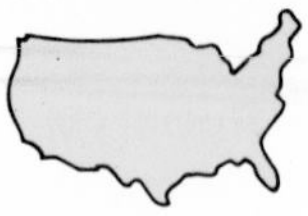

PROBLEM: A weed with extremely hairy, ½ inch-long lance-shaped leaves grows in sunny areas of the lawn. The leaves are attached directly to the stems without a leaf stalk. Starlike white flowers bloom from April to October. The stems root easily at their joints.

ANALYSIS: Mouseear chickweed
(*Cerastium vulgatum*)
Mouseear chickweed is a troublesome perennial weed found throughout the country. It grows in full sunlight on infertile and heavily watered soil. Mouseear chickweed invades lawns that thin out due to insects, disease, or mechanical damage. It reproduces by seeds and by the stems that root easily at their joints wherever they touch the soil. It has a low, prostrate growing habit, and forms a dense mat that crowds out the grass. For more information about mouseear chickweed, see page 829.

SOLUTION: Treat the lawn with ORTHO Chickweed & Clover Control, ORTHO Weed-B-Gon Weed Killer, or ORTHO Weed-B-Gon Lawn Weed Killer when the plant is growing actively in the early spring or late fall. Repeated applications may be needed. Don't water for 2 days after applying.

Spotted spurge.

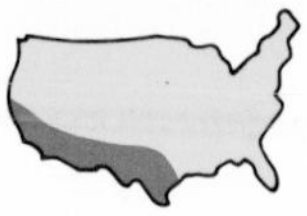

PROBLEM: A low-growing weed with oval pale to dark green leaves ¼ to ¾ inch long appears in the lawn. Each leaf may have a purple spot. Stems ooze milky white sap when broken. The leaves are slightly hairy on the underside and smooth on top. Tiny pinkish white flowers bloom in midsummer. The numerous pale green stems fan out on the soil surface and over the top of the grass, forming mats up to 2 feet in diameter.

ANALYSIS: Spotted spurge
(*Euphorbia maculata*)
Spotted spurge, also called *milk purslane*, invades thin areas of the lawn, smothering the grass. Spurge sprouts from seeds in the spring, and dies with the first frost. This weed commonly invades lawns that are dry and infertile, but it can also be found in well-maintained lawns. For more information about spotted spurge, see page 829.

SOLUTION: Treat the lawn with ORTHO Weed-B-Gon Lawn Weed Killer, ORTHO Weed-B-Gon Weed Killer, or ORTHO Weed-B-Gon For Southern Grasses or spot treat with ORTHO Weed-B-Gon Jet Weeder in the late spring or early summer. Keep the lawn well watered (see page 250) to discourage spurge from invading dry areas.

Common chickweed.

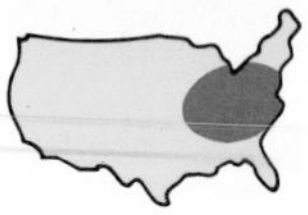

PROBLEM: A weed with small (½ inch long) heart-shaped leaves and starlike white flowers grows in thin spaces in the lawn. A row of hairs appears on the leaf stalk attaching the leaves to the stems. The stems root easily at their joints.

ANALYSIS: Common chickweed
(*Stellaria media*)
This weed grows from seeds that sprout in the fall and live for less than a year. It grows primarily in damp shady areas under trees and shrubs, and on the north side of buildings. Common chickweed invades home lawns when they begin to thin out from insects, disease, mechanical damage, or shade. It reproduces by seeds and by the creeping stems that root at their joints wherever they touch the soil. It has a low prostrate growing habit, forming a dense mat that crowds out the grass. For more information about common chickweed, see page 828.

SOLUTION: Treat the lawn with ORTHO Chickweed & Clover Control, ORTHO Weed-B-Gon Weed Killer, or ORTHO Weed-B-Gon Lawn Weed Killer when it is growing actively in the early spring or late fall. Repeated applications may be necessary. Do not water for 2 days after applying.

Henbit.

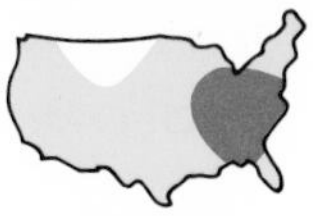

PROBLEM: A weed with rounded, toothed leaves, $\frac{3}{4}$ inch wide, grows in the lawn. The lower leaves are attached to the square (4-sided) upright stems by short leaf stalks; upper leaves attach directly to the stems. Stems root easily at lower joints. Lavender, $\frac{1}{2}$ inch flowers appear from April to June and again in September.

ANALYSIS: Henbit
(*Lamium amplexicaule*)
This weed, also known as *dead nettle* or *bee nettle*, is found in lawns and flower and vegetable gardens across the country. It is a winter annual that sprouts from seeds in September and grows rapidly in the fall and the following spring. Henbit also reproduces by stems that root easily wherever the stem joints touch the soil. Henbit most frequently invades thin areas in lawns with rich soil. For more information about henbit, see page 842.

SOLUTION: Treat the lawn with ORTHO Chickweed, Spurge & Oxalis Killer D or ORTHO Weed-B-Gon Weed Killer in early spring when henbit is growing most rapidly. Do not water for 24 hours after treating. A few small plants can be hand pulled.

English lawn daisy.

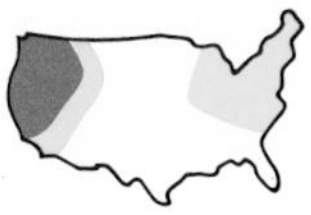

PROBLEM: A weed with slightly hairy, elongated oval leaves forms a tight rosette in the lawn. White to pink flowers with yellow centers, up to 2 inches across, appear from April to June and again from September to November.

ANALYSIS: English lawn daisy
(*Bellis perennis*)
As its name suggests, English lawn daisy came originally from Europe and was chiefly grown as an ornamental garden plant. Although it is a welcome member of the perennial garden, it often escapes cultivation and becomes a weed in the lawn. This perennial plant reproduces by seeds, and thrives in moist, cool soil. When growing in the lawn, English lawn daisy may indicate low soil fertility.

SOLUTION: Treat the lawn with ORTHO Weed-B-Gon Weed Killer before July 1. Repeat the treatment around September 15 to control any regrowth. Improve soil fertility by following the guidelines outlined on page 251.

Purslane.

PROBLEM: A low-growing weed with reddish brown, thick, succulent stems is found in thin areas or newly seeded lawns. The leaves are thick, fleshy, and wedge-shaped. Small yellow flowers sometimes bloom in the leaf and stem joints. Stems root where they touch the soil.

ANALYSIS: Purslane
(*Portulaca oleracea*)
Purslane, a summer annual weed that thrives in hot, dry weather, is seldom found in the spring when the lawn is being treated for other weeds. Purslane grows vigorously, forming a thick mat. The small yellow flowers open only in the full sunlight. Purslane primarily invades bare spots in lawns or thin lawns that have not been watered properly. Purslane stores water in its thick fleshy stems and leaves, and therefore survives longer than grass during dry weather. For more information about purslane, see page 829.

SOLUTION: Spray the lawn with ORTHO Weed-B-Gon Lawn Weed Killer, ORTHO Weed-B-Gon Weed Killer, or ORTHO Weed-B-Gon Jet Weeder when the weed is actively growing. If the lawn has just been reseeded, do not treat until the seedlings have been mowed three times. Wait 3 to 4 weeks before seeding bare areas. On St. Augustine grass, use ORTHO Weed-B-Gon For Southern Grasses.

BROADLEAF WEEDS

Ground ivy.

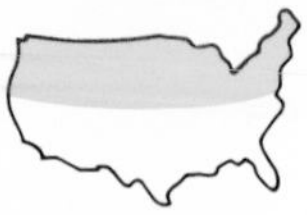

PROBLEM: A low-growing, creeping weed with rounded, scalloped leaves grows in shady areas of the lawn. The nickel- to quarter-size leaves grow at the end of a long leaf stalk. The stalks are paired opposite each other along the square stem. Light blue to purple flowers, ½ to ¾ inch long, bloom from April to July.

ANALYSIS: Ground ivy
(*Glechoma hederacea*)
Ground ivy, also called *creeping ivy*, is a perennial that was originally planted in some areas as a groundcover. It has now become a major weed in the North. Ground ivy reproduces by seeds and creeping stems that root wherever they touch the soil. This plant has shallow roots and forms a dense mat throughout the lawn, crowding out grasses. Although it is found primarily in shaded areas, ground ivy also survives in the sunlight. For more information about ground ivy, see page 831.

SOLUTION: Treat the lawn with ORTHO Weed-B-Gon Lawn Weed Killer or ORTHO Weed-B-Gon Jet Weeder in the spring or fall when the plants are growing actively. A spring treatment gives the best result by killing the plants before the leaves mature. Where the ground ivy has formed a dense mat, it may be necessary to apply the herbicide for several years in a row. Hand pulling is not a good way to control ground ivy since the roots will readily resprout into new plants. The ground ivy may indicate that the area is too shady to grow a lawn.

Creeping charlie.

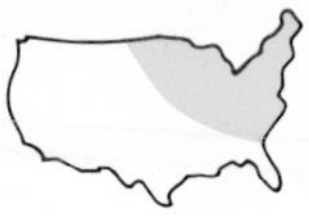

PROBLEM: A ground-hugging weed with creeping stems grows in moist, shady areas of the lawn. The leaves are oval to round and up to 1 inch long. Yellow flowers, ¾ inch in diameter, appear from May to September.

ANALYSIS: Creeping charlie
(*Lysimachia nummularia*)
Also called *moneywort* or *creeping jenny*, this weed invades areas of the lawn where grass won't grow because of shade and constantly moist soil. It is a perennial weed that reproduces by creeping stems that root easily at their joints wherever they touch the soil. It also reproduces by seeds. Creeping charlie is sometimes planted as a groundcover in shaded, moist rock gardens.

SOLUTION: Treat the weeds with ORTHO Kleenup Ready-to-Use Grass & Weed Killer or ORTHO Weed-B-Gon Weed Killer in early spring or fall. Kleenup may kill some surrounding grass. If so, reseed 7 to 10 days after treating. Improve the soil drainage as outlined on page 907.

Speedwell.

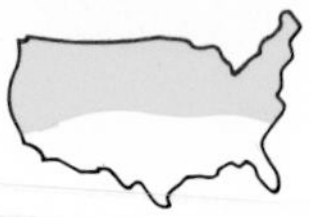

PROBLEM: A weed with roundish-oval bright green leaves grows in shady, moist areas of the lawn. The scallop-edged leaves are paired, growing opposite each other. Tiny white flowers with blue edges bloom on stalks taller than the leaves. On the stems below the flowers are characteristic heart-shaped seed pods.

ANALYSIS: Speedwell
(*Veronica filiformis*)
Speedwell, also called *creeping veronica,* was originally used as a rock garden plant. Over the years it has become a weed, invading lawns and flower beds. This perennial plant reproduces by creeping stems that root easily at their nodes wherever they touch the soil. The seeds in the heart-shaped seed pods seldom mature, so the plant does not reproduce from seeds. Speedwell thrives in moist, shady areas, but will grow in the sunlight if the soil remains moist. This ground-hugging plant spreads quickly. In a few years it can spread from a few patches to cover the entire lawn. However, it does not completely crowd out the desirable grass. Areas that are well fertilized, well drained, and get lots of sunlight are not invaded by speedwell. For more information about speedwell, see page 828.

SOLUTION: This weed is difficult to control. When the plant is flowering or actively growing, spray with ORTHO Weed-B-Gon Lawn Weed Killer. Several applications may be required.

Curly dock.

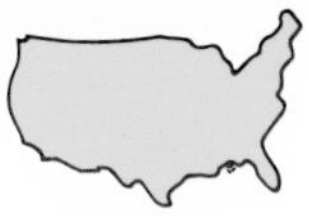

PROBLEM: A weed forming a rosette with large smooth leaves, 6 to 12 inches long, grows in thin areas of the lawn. The leaves are reddish green, with curly and wavy margins.

ANALYSIS: Curly dock
(*Rumex crispus*)
Curly dock is a persistent perennial weed that grows from a large, deep, brownish yellow taproot. It reproduces by seed and invades thin areas of the lawn. Because frequent mowing cuts off the flower stalk, curly dock seldom flowers when growing in the lawn. For more information about curly dock, see page 833.

SOLUTION: In mid to late spring, or early to late fall, treat curly dock with ORTHO Weed-B-Gon Lawn Weed Killer or ORTHO Weed-B-Gon Weed Killer. Treat again if plants resprout. Hand digging and removal is not only time consuming and tedious, but also impractical, since pieces of root that are left behind will sprout into new plants.

Dandelion.

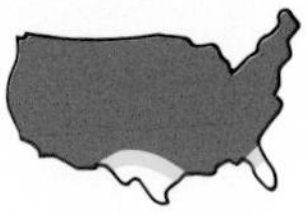

PROBLEM: From spring to fall, a weed with bright yellow flowers blooms in the lawn. Flower stems grow 2 to 10 inches above the plants. The medium green leaves, 3 to 10 inches long, are lobed along the sides. The plant has a deep, fleshy taproot.

ANALYSIS: Dandelion
(*Taraxacum officinale*)
This perennial is the most common and easily identified weed in the country. It reproduces by seeds and from shoots that grow from the fleshy taproot. This taproot grows 2 to 3 feet deep in the soil, surviving even the severest of winters. Dandelions grow in any soil, and are most numerous in full sunlight. In the early spring, new sprouts emerge from the taproot. As the yellow flowers mature and ripen, they form white "puff balls" containing seeds. The wind carries the seed for miles to other lawns. The tops die back in late fall and the taproot overwinters to start the cycle again in the spring. Dandelions prefer wet soil, and are often a sign of overwatering. For more information about dandelion, see page 836.

SOLUTION: Treat the lawn with ORTHO Weed-B-Gon Lawn Weed Killer, ORTHO Weed-B-Gon Weed Killer, or ORTHO Weed-B-Gon Jet Weeder for spot treatment. For best results make two applications, first in the early summer and again in the early fall. Do not water or mow for 2 days afterwards. Hand digging and removal is not only time consuming and tedious, but also impractical, since pieces of root that are broken off and left in the soil will sprout into new plants.

Sheep sorrel.

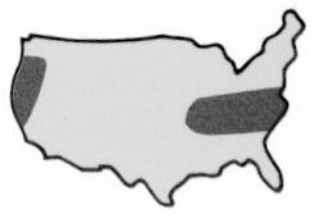

PROBLEM: Arrow-shaped leaves, 1 to 4 inches long, with two lobes at the base of each leaf, form a dense rosette. Erect, upright stems grow 4 to 14 inches tall. Two types of flowers appear in midspring; one is reddish green, the other yellowish green.

ANALYSIS: Sheep sorrel
(*Rumex acetosella*)
This cool-season perennial is also called *red sorrel* or *sour grass* because of its sour taste. It grows in dry, sterile, sandy or gravelly soil and is usually an indication of acid soil or low nitrogen fertility. Sheep sorrel reproduces by seeds and red underground rootstalks. The root system is shallow but extensive, and is not easily removed. For more information about sheep sorrel, see page 835.

SOLUTION: In spring or fall treat with ORTHO Weed-B-Gon Lawn Weed Killer, ORTHO Weed-B-Gon Weed Killer, or ORTHO Chickweed, Spurge & Oxalis Killer D. In the South, use ORTHO Weed-B-Gon For Southern Grasses. Don't mow for 5 days before treating, or for 2 days after. Sheep sorrel is difficult to control, so several treatments may be necessary. To discourage sheep sorrel, test the soil pH as outlined on page 909 and correct to between 6.0 and 7.0 if necessary. Improve the soil fertility by following the fertilization guidelines on page 250.

BROADLEAF WEEDS

Mallow.

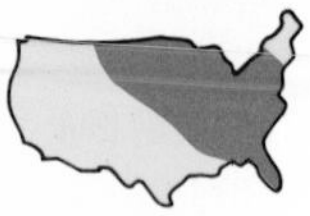

PROBLEM: A weed with hairy stems, 4 to 12 inches long, spreads over the lawn. The stem tips turn upward. Round, heart-shaped, hairy leaves, ½ to 3 inches wide and slightly lobed along the edges, are attached to the stems by a long leaf stalk. White to lilac flowers, 2½ inches in diameter with 5 petals, bloom singly or in clusters at the leaf and stem junction.

ANALYSIS: Mallow
(*Malva* species)
Mallow, also called *cheeseweed*, is found throughout the country in lawns, fields, and along roadways. It is an annual, or sometimes a biennial, and reproduces by seeds. It has a straight, nearly white taproot that is difficult to pull from the soil. Mallow is most commonly found in poorly managed lawns and in soils high in manure content. For more information about mallow, see page 832.

SOLUTION: Treat the lawn with ORTHO Weed-B-Gon Lawn Weed Killer or ORTHO Chickweed, Spurge & Oxalis Killer D from midspring to early summer. Don't water for 5 days before treating, or 2 days after. Maintain a thick, healthy lawn by following the guidelines on pages 250 and 251.

Buckhorn plantain. *Insert:* Broadleaf plantain.

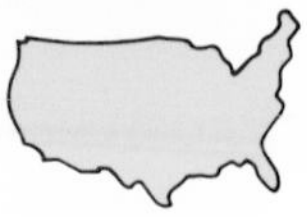

PROBLEM: A weed forming a rosette with lance-shaped leaves 4 to 12 inches long grows in the lawn. The leaves have 3 to 5 nearly parallel, prominent veins. Erect white flower spikes, 4 to 12 inches tall, appear from May to October. A similar weed has egg-shaped leaves attached to 1-inch leaf stalks, which are in turn attached to the center of a rosette. These leaves are 2 to 10 inches long, with 5 to 7 prominent veins. Erect greenish white flower spikes, 2 to 10 inches tall, bloom from May to September. The leaves of both plants lie flat on the soil.

ANALYSIS: Plantain
(*Plantago* species)
Both buckhorn plantain (*P. lanceolata*), with lance-shaped leaves, and broadleaf plantain (*P. major*), with egg-shaped leaves, are perennial weeds that resprout from their roots each year. They reproduce from seeds formed on the flower spikes, and from new shoots from the roots. As thin areas develop in the lawn from insect, disease, or maintenance problems, one or both of these weeds can move in. As the plants grow larger and lie flat on the soil, they suffocate the surrounding grass. For more information about plantain, see page 833.

SOLUTION: Spray the lawn with ORTHO Weed-B-Gon Lawn Weed Killer, ORTHO Weed-B-Gon Weed Killer, ORTHO Weed-B-Gon Jet Weeder or ORTHO Weed-B-Gon For Southern Grasses in the spring or fall when the plants are actively growing. Repeated applications are often necessary. An application in September gives the best results by reducing the infestation next year. Do not mow 5 days before or 2 days after spraying.

Morning glory.

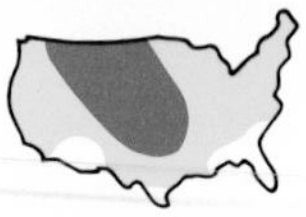

PROBLEM: A plant with long twining stems grows across the lawn. The leaves are arrowhead-shaped and up to 2 inches long. White to pink funnel-shaped flowers, about 1 inch across, appear from May to September.

ANALYSIS: Wild morning glory
(*Convolvulus arvensis*)
This deep-rooted perennial weed, also known as *field bindweed*, is found throughout most of the country in lawns, gardens, fields, and along roadways. It is one of the most troublesome and difficult weeds to eliminate because of its extensive root system. The roots may grow 15 to 20 feet deep. Roots or pieces of roots left behind from hand pulling or spading easily resprout. Morning glory reproduces by seeds and roots and twines and climbs over shrubs and fences, and up into trees. It prefers rich, sandy, or gravelly soil, but will grow in almost any garden soil. For more information about wild morning glory, see page 840.

SOLUTION: Treat plants from late spring through early summer, or early to late fall, with ORTHO Weed-B-Gon Lawn Weed Killer or ORTHO Chickweed, Spurge & Oxalis Killer D. In the South use ORTHO Weed-B-Gon For Southern Grasses. Because of the deep roots, another treatment may be necessary. Treat again whenever new growth appears. Or spot treat with ORTHO Kleenup Systemic Weed & Grass Killer and reseed.

MISCELLANEOUS

Mushrooms.

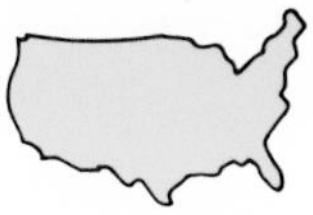

PROBLEM: Mushrooms sprout up in the lawn after wet weather. They may be growing in circles of dark green grass. When the weather gets colder or the soil dries out they disappear.

ANALYSIS: Mushrooms
Mushrooms, also called *toadstools* and *puffballs*, live on organic matter buried in the soil. The mushroom is the aboveground fruiting or reproductive structure of a fungus that lives on and helps to decay the organic matter. The organic matter may include buried logs, lumber, roots, or stumps. Most mushrooms do not damage the lawn, but are objectionable because they are unsightly. Mushrooms growing in circles of dark green grass, called fairy rings, may make the soil impervious to water and injure the grass. For more information on fairy rings, see page 267.

SOLUTION: There is no practical or permanent way to eliminate mushrooms. When the buried wood is completely decayed, the mushrooms will disappear. The easiest and most practical solution, although it is only temporary, is to break the mushrooms with a rake or lawn mower.

Algae.

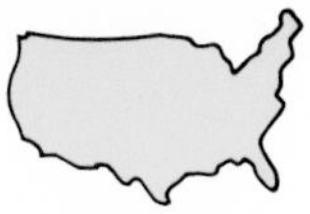

PROBLEM: A green to black slimy scum covers bare soil and crowns of grass plants. When dry, it becomes crusty, cracks, and peels easily.

ANALYSIS: Algae (*Symploca* species and *Oscillatoria* species)
Algae are fresh water plants that invade shady, wet areas of the lawn. They injure grass by smothering or shading it as they grow over the crowns of the plants. Invaded areas become slippery. Algae live in compacted soil and soil that is high in nitrogen and organic matter. They need constantly or frequently wet conditions to survive. Organic fertilizers encourage algae, especially in the cool seasons. Algae may be carried from place to place by animals, equipment, people, and birds. Water taken from ponds, lakes, and streams and used for irrigation usually contains algae. For more information about algae, see page 823.

SOLUTION: Patches of algae may be sprayed with *maneb, mancozeb,* or *wettable sulfur* two times, 1 month apart, in early spring. This is only a temporary solution. Algae will soon return if the conditions promoting them are not corrected. Reduce soil compaction as instructed on page 262. Improve drainage, as outlined on page 907, and prune nearby trees to reduce shading. Avoid high nitrogen fertilizers in late fall and winter. Maintain a healthy, vigorous lawn according to the lawn maintenance guidelines on pages 250 and 251.

Moss.

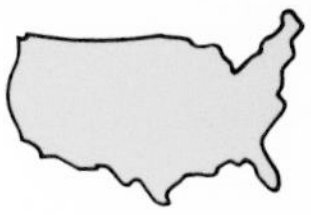

PROBLEM: Green, velvety, low-growing plants cover bare soil in shady areas of the lawn.

ANALYSIS: Moss
Moss invades thin or bare areas of the lawn. It does not grow in a vigorous lawn. Moss is encouraged by poor fertility, poor drainage, compacted soil, shade, and high acidity. Moss plants sprout from spores and fill in bare or thin areas. For more information about moss, see page 823.

SOLUTION: Remove moss by hand or by power raking. Reduce shade by pruning nearby trees. Correct soil compaction as outlined on page 262, and improve drainage as suggested on page 907. Test the soil pH as instructed on page 909, and correct if necessary. Follow the lawn maintenance guidelines on pages 250 and 251 for a healthy, vigorous lawn. Large patches of moss not easily removed by raking may be "burned" with *ammonium sulfate*. Apply to damp moss in early spring. Do not water after the application. Surrounding lawn grass may darken for about a week.

Some of the problems common to all groundcovers are described on the next 7 pages. If you don't find your problem there, look up your groundcover in the index on the next page. Only plants that are known primarily as groundcovers are listed here. If your groundcover is a dwarf form of a plant more commonly seen as a shrub, see page 405. If it is a perennial flower, see page 303.

PROBLEMS COMMON TO MANY GROUNDCOVERS	PAGE
Weeds in the groundcover	**282**
Groundcover is invading other areas	**283**
Bare spots in the groundcover	**283**
Discolored leaves	**285**
Insect or animal problems	**286**

GROUNDCOVERS

We often assume that the worst problem of groundcovers is weeds. Once weeds have invaded a groundcover, they are very difficult to control; the groundcover is too dense for a hoe, and it is often difficult or impossible to find an herbicide that will kill the weeds without killing the groundcover. So the weeds must be removed by hand pulling—the slowest and most tedious method of weeding.

Weeds are often only a symptom of some other problem. If a groundcover is dense and growing vigorously, it will smother any weed seedlings that germinate in it, and keep itself essentially weed-free. Weeds invade spots that are bare or getting thin from some other problem.

The most critical period in the life of a groundcover is the first couple of years after it is planted. If you can keep it free of weeds until it covers the ground completely, your groundcover will keep itself pretty much free of weeds from then on.

A related problem occurs when a groundcover itself becomes a weed, and invades adjacent areas. This happens when the groundcover chosen for the location is too vigorous.

Another common problem in groundcovers is that of traffic. Unlike most planting areas, groundcovers are neither clearly made for walking on nor clearly prohibit it. As a result, they are often trampled through, which breaks and crushes the plants and compacts the soil. Sometimes the solution is to erect barriers or put paths across the groundcover, but often the best thing to do is to select a different groundcover. Groundcovers that are knee-deep discourage traffic. Indeed, a deep groundcover can be used to divert traffic from other areas without cutting up the landscape with fences and hedges.

Above: Aphids on an ivy stem. See page 287.
Left: A healthy ajuga groundcover under a Japanese aralia. Ajuga looks best in the shade.

INDEX TO GROUNDCOVERS

PROBLEMS COMMON TO MANY GROUNDCOVERS

Weeds invading ivy planting.

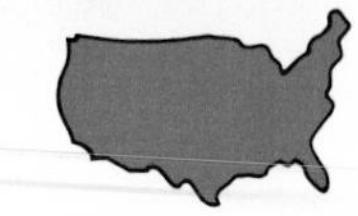

PROBLEM: Weeds are growing in the groundcover.

ANALYSIS: Weed invasion
A dense groundcover chokes out weeds and remains trouble-free. However, if the planting is new, or if bare spots are developing, weed control can be a difficult problem.

SOLUTION: If there are only a few weeds, pull them by hand. If the weeds are growing in bare spots in the groundcover, or if the weeds are projecting above the groundcover, spot treat them with ORTHO Kleenup Ready-To-Use Grass & Weed Killer or ORTHO Kleenup Systemic Weed & Grass Killer. To avoid dripping the solution on desirable plants, paint it on the weeds with a paint brush or roller. This will also prevent drift. To prevent reinfestation, apply ORTHO Casoron Granules around woody groundcovers, or ORTHO Garden Weed Preventer around nonwoody groundcovers. Apply according to label instructions. Replant bare areas immediately. Feed and water the groundcover well to keep it dense. To keep weeds out of new plantings, apply ORTHO Garden Weed Preventer after planting. If the groundcover is not one that spreads by rooting, apply a mulch of black plastic or an organic material from 3 to 5 inches deep between plants. As is true of weed control anywhere in the garden, it is best to remove weeds as soon as they are seen. Weeds are far more difficult to control once they are well established.

BARE SPOTS

African daisy groundcover invading landscaped area.

PROBLEM: Groundcover plants spread into surrounding lawns, shrubs, and flower beds.

ANALYSIS: Invading other areas
Some groundcovers are too vigorous for their location. In order to keep them from invading other garden areas, you must cut them back frequently. These plants are more suited to large areas where they receive little care. Some of these very vigorous groundcovers are Japanese honeysuckle, polygonum, African daisy, and crown vetch.

SOLUTION: Kill the existing planting with ORTHO Kleenup Systemic Weed & Grass Killer. After 1 week, cut off the old groundcover and replant. The plants may still be green when they are removed, but the roots will die in a couple of weeks and will not resprout. Kleenup is inactivated in the soil, so the new plants will not be affected. Consult your local nurseryman, County Extension Agent (see page 1029), or neighbors to learn which groundcovers grow well in your area and in the space you have selected. A plastic or metal strip or edging installed around the border helps restrict the plants. For more information on the many kinds of groundcovers and their care, see the ORTHO book *All About Groundcovers*.

Irish moss in a dark location.

PROBLEM: The planting is thin, with bare spots. Plants are spindly and leggy, with leaves that are darker green than usual. Leaves may drop, beginning with the lowest leaves and progressing upward.

ANALYSIS: Insufficient light
Plants use light to manufacture the food they need to survive. Without enough light they become weak, stunted, and susceptible to attack from insects and disease. The plants that suffer most in low light areas are those that require full sun. Shade-loving plants will tolerate varying degrees of shade.

SOLUTION: If a tree is shading the planting, consider pruning some of the branches to let more light pass through to the groundcover. If there is a group of trees, consider removing one or more of them. Or plant a groundcover that tolerates shade. For a list, see page 1003.

Compacted area in vinca.

PROBLEM: Leaves turn yellow and do not grow as large as usual. Plants are stunted and die in some areas, leaving bare spots. There are no signs of insect or disease damage. The soil is compacted.

ANALYSIS: Compacted soil
Soil compacts easily in areas where foot or vehicular traffic is heavy. This is especially a problem where a groundcover has been planted in an area that used to be a lawn or path. Compaction prevents air and water from penetrating into the soil and to the roots. Air in the soil is necessary for healthy root growth. Plants growing in compacted soil are more subject to disease, primarily root and crown rots, because the soil doesn't drain properly. Water often puddles on compacted soil.

SOLUTION: If the soil is dry, use a soil penetrant to increase the wetting capacity of the soil. Poke holes around the plants with a lawn aerator to allow air and water to penetrate the soil. The holes must be at least 3 inches deep, and no more than 3 inches apart. Cultivate the bare spots, add organic matter as outlined on page 926, and replant. Consider stepping stones or paths to keep traffic off the groundcover.

PROBLEMS COMMON TO MANY GROUNDCOVERS — BARE SPOTS

Polygonum dying from lack of water.

PROBLEM: Bare spots appear in the groundcover. Plants are pale green or yellow and grow slowly. The edges of the leaves turn brown and crisp. The soil is frequently dry.

ANALYSIS: Drought
The plants are not receiving enough water. This may be due to one of several problems.
1. Not enough water is applied at each watering. This frequently happens with hand watering. Although the ground is moist, or even muddy after watering, the water may not have penetrated to the plant roots.
2. Water is applied too infrequently. If rainfall is not supplemented by irrigation during drought periods, or if irrigation is too infrequent, the plants use up all the water in the soil and suffer stress before more water is applied.
3. Water is running off on the surface instead of entering the soil. This occurs when the soil is dense or compacted, or when water is applied faster than the soil can absorb it.

SOLUTION: Follow these guidelines to prevent drought damage.
1. Apply at least an inch of water at each watering. Set tin cans under the sprinkler, and water until an inch of water has accumulated in each can.
2. Water whenever the soil an inch or so deep feels just barely moist.
3. If water is running off the groundcover, irrigate with a sprinkler head that applies water more slowly. Or water until runoff begins, stop for half an hour to let the soil absorb the water, then continue until 1 inch has been applied. If the soil is compacted, improve water penetration by aerating the soil with a lawn aerator. See page 262 for instructions.

Bare spots from excess water.

PROBLEM: Leaves turn yellow, starting with the older, lower leaves and progressing to the younger leaves. Plants grow very little. The roots are shallow, and may be rotted. The soil is very moist.

ANALYSIS: Excess water
Excess moisture in the soil can result from watering too frequently or from too much rainfall. Roots need oxygen to grow and develop. Waterlogged soil has very little oxygen available for root growth because the soil pores are filled with water. The only available oxygen is near the soil surface, so roots grow only in the upper layer of soil. These shallow-rooted plants are smaller than usual and more susceptible to drought. Many root and crown rotting fungi thrive in wet soil, killing plants. Groundcovers growing in wet soil seldom spread out to fill in the planted area.

SOLUTION: Allow the soil to partially dry out between waterings. The soil an inch or so beneath the surface should be just barely moist before you water again. Of course, there is nothing you can do about the weather; but if you replant the area, improve drainage according to the instructions on page 907 before replanting. If the soil drains quickly, excess water seldom damages plants.

Spindly growth.

PROBLEM: Plants are spindly and leggy, with leaves that are darker green than usual. Leaves may drop, beginning with the lowest leaves and progressing upward.

ANALYSIS: Insufficient light
Plants use light to manufacture the food they need to survive. Without enough light they become spindly, stunted, and susceptible to attack from insects and diseases. The plants that suffer most in low-light areas are those that require full sun. Shade-loving plants will tolerate varying degrees of shade.

SOLUTION: If a tree is shading the planting, consider pruning some of the branches to let more light pass through to the groundcover. If there is a group of trees, consider removing one or more of them. Or plant a groundcover that tolerates shade, such as ajuga, English ivy, epimedium, hosta, pachysandra, or vinca.

DISCOLORED LEAVES

Underfertilized ajuga.

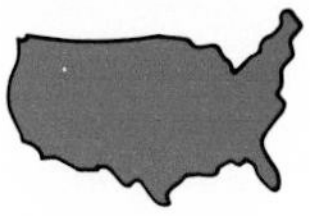

PROBLEM: Leaves are smaller than usual and turn pale green to yellow. Plants grow very little.

ANALYSIS: Lack of nutrients
Fertilizer supplies the nutrients plants need to stay vigorous and healthy; adequate fertilizing may result in fewer insect and disease problems. The three essential nutrients that plants require in the largest amounts are nitrogen (N), phosphorus (P), and potassium (K). *Nitrogen* gives the leaves their green color and encourages rapid growth. Without nitrogen, plants turn pale green to yellow. *Phosphorus* encourages flowering and fruiting, and helps build a strong root system. *Potassium* increases the plant's resistance to disease and aids in overall growth. Most garden fertilizers contain all three nutrients. On the bag are three numbers, called the N–P–K ratio or fertilizer grade, which state the nutrient content. For example, a fertilizer bag reading 5–10–10 has, by weight, 5 percent nitrogen, 10 percent phosphate (phosphorus), and 10 percent potash (potassium). Many fertilizers also supply trace, or minor, nutrients that plants need in minute amounts, which may be lacking in the soil.

SOLUTION: Fertilize your groundcover at regular intervals. Use a fertilizer that contains the three major nutrients unless you live in an arid region. In arid regions, the soil probably contains sufficient phosphate and potassium, so you only need to add nitrogen. Follow label instructions for amounts and timing of fertilizing. Water well after fertilizing to dilute the fertilizer and wash it into the soil.

Iron deficiency in pachysandra.

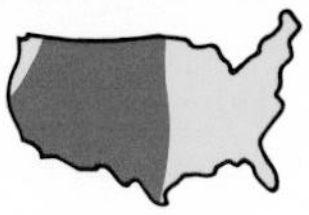

PROBLEM: Leaves turn pale green or yellow. The newest leaves (those at the tips of the stems) are most severely affected. Except in extreme cases, the veins of affected leaves remain green. In extreme cases, the newest leaves are small and all-white or yellow. Older leaves may remain green.

ANALYSIS: Iron deficiency
Plants frequently suffer from deficiencies of iron and other minor nutrients such as manganese and zinc, elements essential to normal plant growth and development. Deficiencies can occur when one more of these elements are depleted in the soil. Often, minor nutrients are present in the soil, but alkaline (pH 7.5 and higher) or wet soil conditions cause them to form compounds that cannot be used by the plant. An alkaline condition can result from overliming, or from lime leached from cement or brick. Regions where soil is derived from limestone, and those with low rainfall, usually have alkaline soils.

SOLUTION: Spray the foliage with ORTHO Greenol Liquid Iron, and apply it to the soil around the plants to correct the deficiency of minor nutrients. Check the soil pH (see the instructions on page 909). Correct the pH of the soil by treating it with *ferrous sulfate* or ORTHO Aluminum Sulfate and watering it in well. Maintain an acid pH by fertilizing with ORTHO Azalea, Camellia & Rhododendron Food.

Leaf yellowing on vinca caused by acid soil.

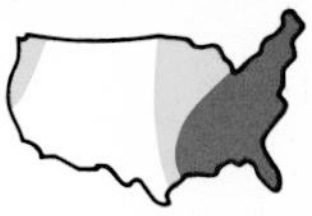

PROBLEM: Plants grow slowly and the leaves turn pale green to yellow. Plants don't improve very much when fertilized. A soil test shows a pH below 6.0.

ANALYSIS: Acid soil
Soils with a pH of less than 6.0 are common in areas of heavy rainfall. Heavy rains leach lime from the soil, making it more acid. The amounts and types of nutrients available to plants are limited in acid soils. Below a pH of 5.5, the availability of nitrogen, phosphorus, potassium, calcium, and other nutrients decreases. These nutrients are essential for healthy plants. Plants vary in their tolerance for acid soils. Most plants grow best with a soil pH between 6.0 and 7.5. For more information about soil pH, see page 908.

SOLUTION: Test your soil pH with an inexpensive test kit available in garden centers. Many County Extension Offices (see page 1029 for a list) also test soil pH. To make a soil less acid, apply lime. See page 1019 for instructions, or follow the directions given with the soil testing kit. Soil acidity corrections are only temporary. Add lime to your soil every year or two if you live in an acid-soil area.

Acid tolerant groundcovers: Epimedium, ferns, creeping gardenia, gaultheria, heaths and heathers, pachysandra, hosta, sarcococca, vancouveria, tiarella.

Scorched ivy leaves.

PROBLEM: Tips and edges of the leaves are brown and dead. Leaves may fall.

ANALYSIS: Scorch
Leaf scorch may be caused by any of a number of conditions.
1. *Heat scorch:* In hot weather, water evaporates rapidly from the leaves. If the roots can't absorb and convey water fast enough to replenish this loss, the leaves turn brown and wither. This condition is often seen when shade-loving plants receive too much sun.
2. *Winter injury* occurs on plants growing in full sun. On a clear winter day, the sun heats the leaf surface, increasing the need for water. If the ground is frozen, or if it has been a dry fall and winter, the roots can't absorb enough water.
3. *Salt injury* results from excess salts in the soil. These salts can come from irrigation water, de-icing salts, or fertilizers. This condition is worse in poorly drained soils, where salts can't be easily leached.

SOLUTION: Follow these guidelines to prevent scorching.
1. Keep groundcovers well watered during hot weather. For a list of sun and shade tolerant groundcovers, see page 909.
2. To prevent winter scorch, be sure that the soil is moist before the ground freezes. Provide shade during clear, cold weather.
3. Leach the salts from the soil with very heavy waterings. If your irrigation water is salty, leach regularly to keep salt from accumulating in the soil. When you fertilize, apply only the amounts recommended on the label, and water thoroughly afterward. For more information about salty soils, see page 909.

Powdery mildew on euonymus.

PROBLEM: Leaves and stems are partially or entirely covered with grayish white powdery patches. Leaves die and may drop off. The patches occur primarily on the upper surfaces of the leaves.

ANALYSIS: Powdery mildew
This common plant disease is caused by several fungi that thrive in both humid and dry weather. The powdery patches consist of fungal strands and spores. The spores are spread by the wind to healthy plants. The fungus saps plant nutrients, causing yellowing and sometimes death of the leaf. A severe infection may kill the plant. Since powdery mildews attack many different kinds of plants, the fungus from a diseased plant may infect other types of plants in the garden. See page 1006 for a list of powdery mildews and the plants they attack. Under favorable conditions, powdery mildew can spread through a groundcover in a matter of days or weeks.

SOLUTION: Spray with a fungicide containing *benomyl*, *triforine* (FUNGINEX®), or *folpet* (PHALTAN®). Make sure that your plant is listed on the product label. These fungicides do not kill the fungus on leaves that are already diseased. They do, however, protect healthy leaves by killing the mildew spores as they germinate on the leaf. Follow label directions regarding frequency of application. Clean infected leaves and debris from the garden.

Spider mite (50 times life size).

PROBLEM: Leaves are stippled, yellowing, and dirty. Leaves may dry out and drop. There may be webbing over flower buds, between leaves, or on the lower surfaces of the leaves. To determine if the plant is infested with mites, hold a sheet of white paper underneath an affected branch and tap the branch sharply. Minute green, red, or yellow specks the size of pepper grains will drop to the paper and begin to crawl around. The pests are easily seen against the white background.

ANALYSIS: Spider mites
Mites, related to spiders, are major pests of many garden and greenhouse plants. They cause damage by sucking sap from the underside of the leaves. As a result of feeding, the green leaf pigment disappears, producing the stippled appearance. Some mites are active throughout the growing season, but are favored by hot, dry weather (70°F and up). By midsummer, they build up to tremendous numbers. Other mites are most prolific in cooler weather. They feed and reproduce primarily during spring and, in some cases, fall. At the onset of hot weather (70°F and up), the mites have caused their maximum damage. For more information about spider mites, see page 887.

SOLUTION: Treat infested plants with ORTHO Isotox Insect Killer or ORTHO Diazinon Insect Spray when the mites first appear. Make sure that your plant is listed on the product label. Repeat the treatment two more times 7 to 10 days apart. Continue the treatments if the mites reappear.

Greenhouse whiteflies (10 times life size).

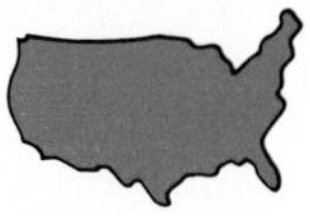

PROBLEM: Tiny, winged insects 1/12 inch long are found mainly on the undersides of the leaves. The insects are covered with white, waxy powder. When the plant is touched, insects flutter rapidly around it. Leaves may be mottled and yellowing. In warm winter areas, black mold may cover the leaves.

ANALYSIS: Greenhouse whitefly
(*Trialeurodes vaporariorum*)
Greenhouse whitefly is a common insect pest of many garden and greenhouse plants. The adult lays eggs on the undersides of leaves. The larvae are the size of a pinhead, and look quite different from the adult. The larvae are flat, oval-shaped, and semitransparent, with white waxy filaments radiating from the body. They feed for about a month before changing into adults. Both the larval and adult forms suck sap from the leaves. The larvae are more damaging because they feed more heavily. Adults and larvae cannot fully digest all the sugar in the plant sap and excrete the excess in a fluid called honeydew. Sooty mold, a black moldy fungus, grows on the honeydew. In warm winter areas, the insect can be active year-round with eggs, larvae, and adults present. The whitefly is unable to live through freezing winters. Spring reinfestations in freezing winter areas come from migrating whiteflies and infested plants placed in the garden.

SOLUTION: Control whiteflies by spraying with an insecticide containing either *diazinon*, *malathion*, or *acephate* (ORTHENE®). Make sure that your plant is listed on the product label. Treat every 7 to 10 days as necessary. Spray the foliage thoroughly, covering both the upper and lower surfaces of the leaves.

Aphids on ivy (twice life size).

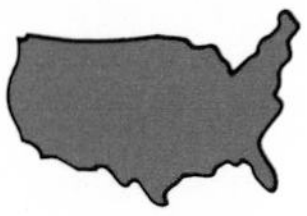

PROBLEM: The leaves are curled, distorted, and yellow. A shiny, sticky substance may coat the leaves. Tiny (1/8 inch) pale green to black soft-bodied insects cluster under leaves and stems. Ants may be present. If the infestation continues, plants may become stunted.

ANALYSIS: Aphids
Aphids do little damage in small numbers. However, they are extremely prolific and populations can rapidly build up to damaging numbers during the growing season. Damage occurs when the aphid sucks the juices from the leaves of the groundcover. The aphid is unable to digest fully all the sugar in the plant sap and excretes the excess in a fluid called honeydew. Ants feed on honeydew and are often present where there is an aphid infestation. For more information about aphids, see page 875.

SOLUTION: Spray with ORTHO Orthene Systemic Insect Control or ORTHO Isotox Insect Killer as soon as the insects appear. Repeat the spray if the plant becomes reinfested. Make sure that your plant is listed on the product label.

Snail and slug damage to ivy.

PROBLEM: Stems and leaves may be sheared off and eaten. Silvery trails wind around on the plants and soil nearby. Snails or slugs may be seen moving around or feeding on the plants, especially at night. Inspect the garden for them at night by flashlight.

ANALYSIS: Snails and slugs
These pests are mollusks, and are related to clams, oysters, and other shellfish. They feed on a wide variety of garden plants. Like other mollusks, snails and slugs need to be moist all the time. For this reason, they avoid direct sun and dry spots, and hide during the day in damp places, such as under flower pots or in thick groundcover. They emerge at night or on cloudy days to feed. Snails and slugs are similar, except that the snail has a hard shell into which it withdraws when disturbed. Slugs lay masses of white eggs encased in a slimy mass in protected places. Snails bury their eggs in the soil, also in a slimy mass. The young look like miniature versions of their parents.

SOLUTION: Scatter ORTHO Slug-Geta Snail & Slug Bait Granules or ORTHO Bug-Geta Snail & Slug Pellets in bands around the areas you wish to protect. Also scatter the bait in areas where snails or slugs might be hiding, such as in dense groundcover, weedy areas, compost piles, or pot storage areas. Before spreading the bait, wet down the areas to be treated to encourage snail and slug activity that night. Repeat the application every 2 weeks as long as snails and slugs are active.

PROBLEMS OF INDIVIDUAL GROUNDCOVERS

This section is arranged alphabetically by the botanical name of each plant. If you are not familiar with the botanical name of your plant, check the index on page 282.

AJUGA

Crown rot.

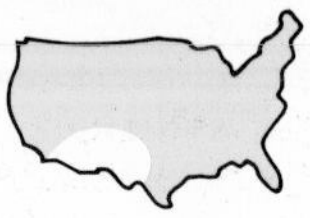

PROBLEM: Lower leaves turn yellow. White cobwebby strands may cover stems and spread over the soil. Large patches suddenly wilt and die during the first few warm, humid days of spring. Plants pull up easily, with most of the roots and crown rotted away. Tiny, hard, yellow-brown and white pellets are found in the soil.

ANALYSIS: Crown rot
This disease is caused by a fungus (*Sclerotium* species) that occurs mostly in wet, poorly drained soil. The fungus attacks many kinds of plants, and causes the only serious disease of ajuga. The fungus enters the plant through the roots and crown and spreads into the stem, rotting it and causing the plant to wilt and die. In mild infections, new growth sometimes sprouts from buds that have not been killed. The tiny fungal pellets found in the soil survive winters and other unfavorable conditions to infect other plants. The fungus most frequently enters the garden originally in infested soil or plants, and lives for years in the soil.

SOLUTION: Remove and destroy all infected plants. Do not replant in the area until the infected soil has either been removed, or drenched with a fungicide containing *PCNB*. To prevent crown rot, plant ajuga in well-drained soil. For instructions on improving soil drainage, see page 907.

Ajuga cultural information
Light: Light shade
Water: Do not allow to dry out
Soil: Rich, loamy, well drained
Fertilizer: Medium

Scorch.

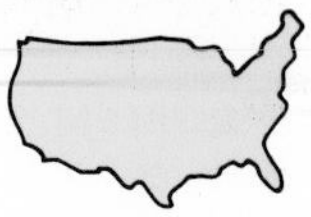

PROBLEM: Leaves turn light brown along the edges and then toward the center. Leaves feel crisp and then shrivel, sometimes falling off. Plants grow in full sun and are not watered regularly.

ANALYSIS: Scorch
Leaf scorch is caused by excessive evaporation of moisture from the leaves. In hot weather, water evaporates rapidly from the leaves. If the roots can't absorb and convey water fast enough to replenish this loss, the leaves turn brown and wither. Browning usually occurs first along the leaf edges and the top of the plant—those areas farthest from the roots and the water source. Unless it receives water, the plant dies. With small plants like ajuga, this process can happen within a few days. Leaf scorch can also occur in moist soil, if the weather is exceptionally hot and dry.

SOLUTION: Ajuga grows best in shade, but will tolerate the sun if the weather is not too hot. If you have a tendency to water irregularly or to neglect your landscape, plant ajuga in the shade. This low-maintenance groundcover requires well-drained soil that is not allowed to dry out.

DICHONDRA

Cutworms (life size).

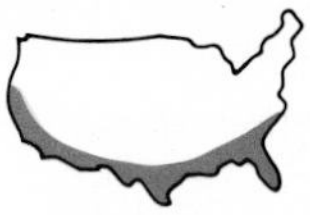

PROBLEM: Leaves are chewed along the edges. Young plants may be chewed or cut off near the ground. By using a flashlight at night, gray, brown, or black worms, 1½ to 2 inches long, may be seen feeding on the dichondra. The worms coil when disturbed.

ANALYSIS: Cutworms
Several species of cutworms attack plants in the garden. The most likely pests of dichondra plantings are the surface-feeding cutworms. For information on the climbing cutworms that may attack other plants in the garden, see page 871. Cutworms hide in the soil during the day, and feed only at night. Adult cutworms are dark, night-flying moths with bands or stripes on their forewings.

SOLUTION: Control cutworms in dichondra with ORTHO Diazinon Soil & Turf Insect Control, ORTHO Diazinon Insect Spray, or ORTHO Lawn Insect Spray. Apply at the first sign of cutworms or damage. Since cutworms are most active at night, treat in the evening. Repeat if damage continues.

Dichondra cultural information
Light: Sun or light shade
Water: While soil is still moist
Soil: Heavy or light
Fertilizer: Medium to heavy

Flea beetle damage. *Insert:* Flea beetle (life size).

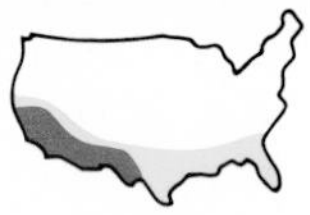

PROBLEM: From May to October, dichondra leaves turn brown, first along the edges of the lawn, then progressing toward the center. Small round holes like shotholes are chewed in the upper surfaces of the leaves. To determine if this is an insect problem, spread a white handkerchief on the border between a damaged area and a healthy area. Black insects, about $\frac{1}{25}$ inch long, will hop onto the white cloth, where they are easily seen.

ANALYSIS: Flea beetles
The adult flea beetle is the most damaging pest of dichondra. Although it hops like a flea, it is a true beetle. The adult spends the winter in garden trash and weeds, emerging with the warm spring weather to begin feeding and laying eggs. Damage is spotty at first because the beetles are so small. In a short time, however, they can destroy a lawn. The discoloration of the leaves is often mistaken for drought damage or fertilizer burn.

SOLUTION: Spray the infested dichondra with ORTHO Diazinon Insect Spray or ORTHO Lawn Insect Spray at the first sign of damage. Water the area first, then apply the insecticide according to the label directions. Repeat once a month throughout the growing season. A healthy planting of dichondra is more resistant to attack from flea beetles than an unhealthy one, and recovers more quickly if it does become infested. Fertilize once a month from March to September.

Slug on dichondra (life size).

PROBLEM: Holes are chewed in the leaves. Leaves may be sheared off entirely. Silvery trails wind around on the plants and nearby soil. If you inspect the lawn with a flashlight after dark, you will discover snails—slimy creatures with shells—or slugs—slimy creatures without shells—feeding on the dichondra.

ANALYSIS: Snails and slugs
Snails and slugs are not insects, but are related to mollusks—clams, oysters, and other shellfish. They feed on a wide variety of plants, including vegetables, flowers, and groundcovers. Snails feed mostly at night, but may also be active on cloudy, wet days. When not feeding, both snails and slugs hide in cool, dark places, such as in groundcovers, and under rocks, logs, and garbage cans.

SOLUTION: Control snails and slugs in dichondra with ORTHO Slug-Geta Snail and Slug Bait or ORTHO Bug-Geta Snail & Slug Pellets. First water the areas to be treated. Sprinkle lightly afterwards to wash the pellets off the leaves and onto the soil. Repeat every 2 weeks if further damage is seen.

DICHONDRA

Annual bluegrass.

PROBLEM: Clumps of pale green grass with whitish seed heads grow in the dichondra.

ANALYSIS: Annual bluegrass
(*Poa annua*)
Annual bluegrass is one of the most troublesome and difficult weeds to control in dichondra. This member of the bluegrass family is lighter green, more shallow-rooted, and less drought tolerant than the bluegrass used for lawns. As its name suggests, annual bluegrass lives only one year. The seeds germinate in cool weather from late summer to late fall. Annual bluegrass grows rapidly in the spring, especially if the dichondra is fertilized then. In mid to late spring, seed heads appear that give the grass a whitish appearance. When hot weather arrives, the annual bluegrass dies. For more information about annual bluegrass, see page 815.

SOLUTION: Weed killers are only partially effective in controlling annual bluegrass. Prevent seeds from germinating by applying weed killer containing *bensulide* in late summer. Water 10 to 15 minutes after application to wash the weed killer off the leaves and into the soil. Keep children and pets off the lawn until the weed killer has been washed into the soil and the leaves have dried. Keep your dichondra lawn healthy to help it resist invasion by annual bluegrass.

Bermudagrass.

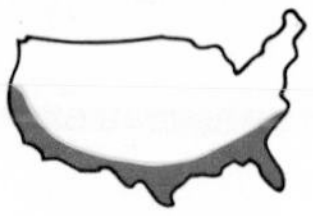

PROBLEM: Patches of a fine-textured grass grow in dichondra lawns. The slightly hairy, gray-green stems creep along the soil. The erect shoots are 6 to 8 inches tall, and the leaf blades are ⅛ inch wide. This grass turns brown in the winter if temperatures drop below 50°F.

ANALYSIS: Bermudagrass
(*Cynodon dactylon*)
Bermudagrass, also called *devilgrass* and *wiregrass*, is widely used as a lawn grass in the southern and western United States. Its deep root system makes it very drought tolerant, but its vigorous creeping habit makes it a weed in dichondra lawns, gardens, and other planted areas. This grass reproduces from seeds, roots, and stem segments. For more information about Bermudagrass, see page 816.

SOLUTION: Control Bermudagrass in dichondra lawns with a weed killer containing *dalapon* in late spring and summer. If the dichondra has not been recently fertilized, fertilize 5 to 7 days before treating with the weed killer. Water thoroughly 1 to 2 days before the weed killer treatment. Use the weed killer according to the directions, or the dichondra will turn yellow and the leaf edges will burn. Do not water after applying the weed killer until the dichondra shows signs of drought stress. Control of Bermudagrass is slow; retreatment will probably be necessary. Keep dichondra lawns thick and healthy by fertilizing once a month from March to September. If only a few patches exist, spot-treat with ORTHO Kleenup Systemic Weed & Grass Killer or ORTHO Kleenup Ready-To-Use Grass & Weed Killer, and replant after 7 days.

Crabgrass.

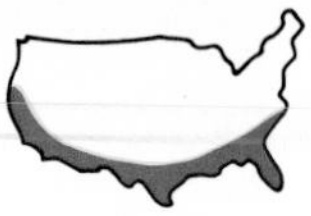

PROBLEM: A narrow-leaf weed forming broad, flat clumps invades thin areas of a dichondra lawn. The weed grows rapidly throughout the summer, rooting at the stem joints. The pale green blades are 2 to 5 inches long and ½ inch wide. Spikes 2 to 6 inches tall grow from the center of the plant.

ANALYSIS: Crabgrass
(*Digitaria* species)
Crabgrass, one of the most common annual weeds, completes its life cycle in 1 year. It sprouts in the early spring and produces seeds all summer, until the first killing frost in the fall when the plants turn brown and die. The seeds sprout the following spring. When dichondra begins to thin out from insect damage, disease, or poor maintenance, crabgrass is one of the first weeds to invade the area. For more information about crabgrass, see page 817.

SOLUTION: Apply a pre-emergence weed killer containing *bensulide* from mid-January to the end of February. Water after application for 10 to 15 minutes to wash the herbicide off the leaves and into the soil. If crabgrass is already in the planting, apply ORTHO Crab Grass Killer. Repeated applications may be required. Keep your dichondra lawn healthy to help it resist invasion by crabgrass.

Oxalis.

PROBLEM: A weed with pale green leaves divided into three heart-shaped leaflets invades thin areas of dichondra. The ¼- to ¾-inch wide leaves are similar to clover. The stems root at the lower joints and are often thinly covered with fine hairs. The small, bright yellow flowers are ½ inch long, with five petals. Plants grow prostrate to erect, 4 to 12 inches high.

ANALYSIS: Oxalis
(*Oxalis* species)
Oxalis, commonly called *yellow wood-sorrel*, is a perennial plant that thrives in dry, open places. When an area begins to thin from insect damage, disease, or drought, oxalis quickly moves in. Oxalis reproduces from seeds formed in cucumber-shaped seed pods. When the pods dry, a light touch causes them to explode, shooting their seeds several feet in all directions. Oxalis leaves contain oxalic acid, which gives them a distinctive sour taste. For more information about oxalis, see page 830.

SOLUTION: Apply a pre-emergent weed killer containing *monuron* in the spring before the oxalis germinates. Follow the directions carefully; over-application will injure the dichondra. Water immediately to prevent chemical leaf burn. Keep your dichondra lawn healthy and able to resist invasion by oxalis by following the cultural instructions on page 289.

DUCHESNEA

Rust.

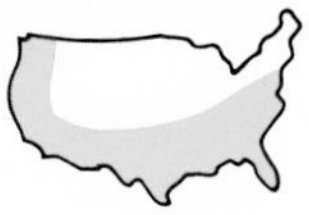

PROBLEM: Bright orange spots appear on the undersides of the leaves. Only the older leaves are affected; younger leaves show no spotting. Leaves yellow, and if severely infected, dry and drop. Severely infected plants may die.

ANALYSIS: Rust
This plant disease is caused by a fungus (*Frommea obtusa*) that causes extensive damage on duchesnea. Infection starts in the early spring, attacking only the older leaves. Rust spores are spread from plant to plant by the wind. The plant must be wet for 6 to 8 hours before the fungus infects the leaf. Rust fungi survive only on living plant tissue and as spores on seeds. They do not remain active on dead plant parts or in the soil. The fungus is most active in moist conditions, with cool nights and warm days. Temperatures of 90°F and higher kill the spores.

SOLUTION: No control measures for this rust fungus have been discovered. Since the fungus requires moisture on the leaves in order to infect them, avoid overhead watering. Instead, use a soaker hose that waters the plants along the soil surface. Water in the morning to allow the soil to dry as much as possible by nightfall. Pick off any infected leaves as soon as you notice them.

Duchesnea cultural information
Light: Light shade
Water: While soil is still moist
Soil: Sandy, well drained
Fertilizer: Medium

FRAGARIA (WILD STRAWBERRY)

Leaf spot.

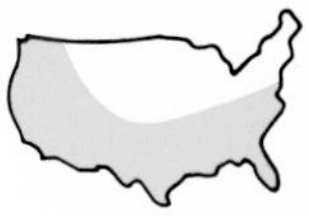

PROBLEM: Spots and blotches appear on the leaves. The spots may be yellow, red, tan, gray, or brown, ranging in size from barely visible to ¼ inch in diameter. Several spots may join to form blotches. Leaves often turn yellow, die, and fall off. Leaf spotting is most severe in warm, humid weather. In damp conditions, a fine gray mold sometimes covers the infected leaf tissue.

ANALYSIS: Leaf spot
Several different fungi cause leaf spots on wild strawberry. Some of these fungi eventually kill the plant. Others merely spot the leaves, and are unsightly but not harmful. The fungi are spread from plant to plant by splashing water, wind, and contaminated tools. They survive the winter on diseased plant debris not cleaned out of the garden. Most of the leaf spot fungi do their greatest damage in humid conditions and mild weather (temperatures between 50° and 85°F).

SOLUTION: Spray the infected planting with a fungicide containing *maneb*, *zineb*, or *mancozeb* every 3 to 10 days. Because leaf spot fungi are most active during warm, humid weather, spray more frequently during those weather conditions. These fungicides protect the new healthy foliage, but do not kill the fungus on leaves that are already infected.

Fragaria cultural information
Light: Full sun
Water: While soil is still moist
Soil: Sandy, well drained
Fertilizer: Medium

FRAGARIA (WILD STRAWBERRY)

Root rot.

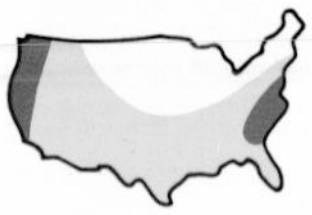

PROBLEM: Leaves turn yellow, starting with the older lower ones and moving up the stem to the younger ones. Plants grow very little. When they are pulled up, the roots are found to be black, soft, and rotted. The soil is very moist.

PROBLEM: Root rot
This disease is caused by a number of different fungi that persist indefinitely in the soil. They thrive in waterlogged, heavy soils. Waterlogged soil may result from overwatering or from poor soil drainage. Infection causes the roots to decay, resulting in wilting, yellowing leaves, and the death of the plant. These fungi are generally spread by infected soil and transplants, contaminated equipment, and moving water. For more information on root rot, see page 849.

SOLUTION: Allow the soil around the plant to dry out. (For more information on this technique, see page 849.) Remove and discard severely infected plants. Avoid future root rot problems by planting in well-drained soil. For information on improving soil drainage, see page 907.

Spider mite webbing.

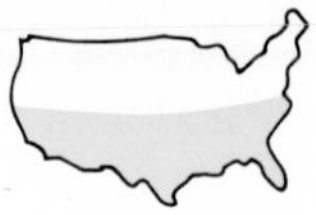

PROBLEM: Leaves are speckled or spotted, yellow, and dirty. Leaves may dry out and fall. Often there is webbing over flower buds, between leaves, or on the lower surfaces of the leaves. Discoloration is most severe during hot, dry weather. To check for an infestation of mites, hold a sheet of white paper underneath a few stippled leaves and tap the leaves sharply. Minute green, red, or yellow specks the size of pepper grains will drop to the paper and begin to crawl around. The mites are easily seen against the white background.

ANALYSIS: Spider mites
Spider mites, related to spiders, are major pests of many garden plants. They cause damage by sucking sap from the undersides of leaves. As a result of feeding, the green leaf pigment disappears, producing the stippled appearance. Mites are active throughout the growing season but are favored by hot, dry weather (70°F and up). By midsummer they build up to tremendous numbers.

SOLUTION: Spray with a miticide containing *dicofol* (KELTHANE®) when damage is first noticed. Cover all the leaves thoroughly and direct sprays to the undersides of the leaves. Repeat applications three more times at intervals of 7 days. Hose down plants frequently to knock off webs and mites.

GAZANIA

Crown rot.

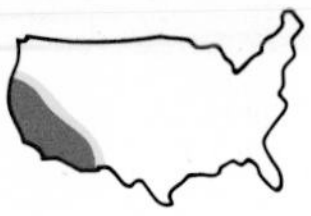

PROBLEM: Lower leaves turn yellow. Tan cobwebby strands may cover stems and spread over the soil. Large patches suddenly wilt and die during the first warm days of spring. Plants pull up easily with most of the roots and crown rotted away.

ANALYSIS: Crown rot
This fungus (*Rhizoctonia solani*) occurs mostly in heavy, poorly drained soil. Although this fungus attacks many kinds of plants, it is the cause of the only serious disease of gazania. The fungus rots the roots and crown, causing the plant to wilt and die. In mild infections, new growth sometimes sprouts from buds that have not been completely killed. The fungus lives indefinitely in the soil and is spread from plant to plant on contaminated tools and by splashing water.

SOLUTION: Remove and destroy all infected plants immediately. Do not replant in the same area until the infected soil has either been carefully removed, or drenched with a fungicide containing *PCNB*. Let the soil dry out between waterings (see page 849). Before replanting the area, improve the drainage. For instructions on improving drainage, see page 907.

Gazania cultural information
Light: Full sun
Water: Allow to dry between waterings
Soil: Loamy, well drained
Fertilizer: Light

HEDERA (IVY)

Heat scorch.

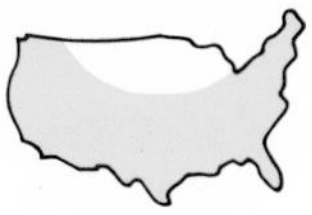

PROBLEM: Dead brown spots appear on the leaves. The spots are always on the part of the leaf that is exposed most directly to the sun. Plants grow in direct sun.

ANALYSIS: Scorch
Ivy can suffer from two kinds of scorch: heat and winter burn. Leaf scorch is caused by excessive evaporation from the leaves. In hot weather, water evaporates rapidly from the leaves. If the roots can't absorb and convey water fast enough to replenish this loss, then leaf tissue is killed. Ivy growing on a sunny wall is particularly affected by scorch because the wall radiates the sun's heat onto the plants. Winter injury occurs on plants growing in the full sun of a southern or western exposure. On a very sunny, clear winter day, the sun heats the leaf surface, increasing the plant's water requirement. If the ground is frozen, or if it has been a dry fall and winter, the ivy roots can't absorb the needed water. The leaf then turns brown and dries out.

SOLUTION: Keep ivy amply watered during hot weather. Pick off scorched leaves to improve the appearance of the planting. Fertilize heavily to encourage quick regrowth. In areas with hot summers, ivy does best in shady locations. To reduce the chance of winter scorch, be sure the soil is moist before the ground freezes.

Hedera cultural information
Light: Light shade to heavy shade
Water: While soil is still moist
Soil: Most soils
Fertilizer: Light to medium

Fungal leaf spot.

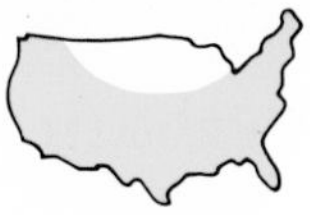

PROBLEM: Large tan to brown spots appear on the leaves. These oval or circular areas occur on both the upper and the lower surfaces of the leaves. Spots often enlarge to cover most of the leaf surface. Small black specks may be seen scattered over the surface of the spots. The leaves may turn brownish red, die, and fall.

ANALYSIS: Leaf spot
A number of different fungi cause leaf spotting on ivy. Some of these fungi may kill tender stems. Others merely spot the leaves and are unsightly. The fungi are spread from plant to plant by wind, splashing water, insects, and contaminated tools. They spend the winter on diseased plant debris left in the garden. Leaf spots affect a wide variety of plants including flowers, vegetables, and groundcovers. Most of the leaf spot fungi do their greatest damage in temperatures between 50° and 85°F.

SOLUTION: Spray the infected planting every 3 to 10 days with a fungicide containing *maneb* or *folpet* (PHALTAN®). Because leaf spots are most active during warm, humid weather, be sure to spray more frequently during those weather conditions. *Maneb* and *folpet* (PHALTAN®) protect the new healthy foliage, but do not remove the spots on leaves that are already infected. Leaves that are spotted over more than half their surface should be removed and thrown away to reduce the spread of the infection to less severely affected plants. Don't work in the diseased plants when the leaves are wet, or you will help spread the fungi.

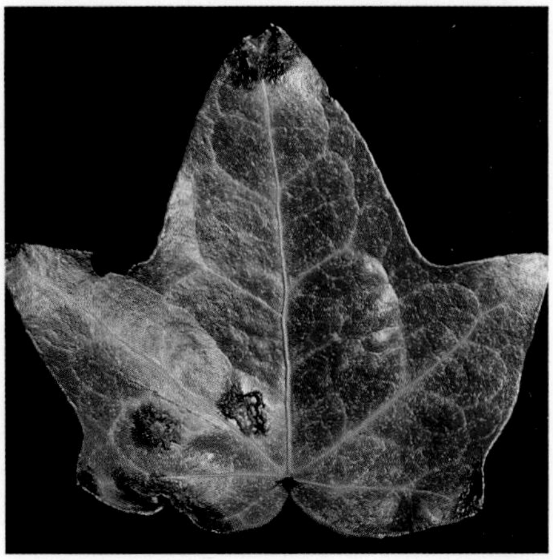

Bacterial leaf spot.

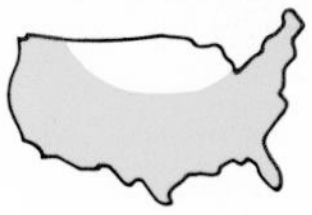

PROBLEM: Pale green angular areas spot the leaves. As the spots enlarge, they turn brown and black with red margins. They eventually dry out and crack. Leaf stems turn black and shrivel. A black decay begins on the stems and spreads to the older wood. Brown-black lesions form on the stems. During warm, humid weather, an ooze flows from the infected stems.

ANALYSIS: Bacterial leaf spot and stem canker
This disease, caused by a bacterium (*Xanthomonas hederae*), occurs frequently on English ivy growing in humid areas. Leaves kept constantly moist are particularly susceptible to invasion by these bacteria. It spreads from plant to plant in splashing rain, on insects such as ants, bees, and flies, and on contaminated equipment. People also spread the bacteria when they work around wet, infected plants. Other organisms often enter the dying tissue and stem lesions, causing further decay.

SOLUTION: When the foliage is dry, pick and remove infected leaves and plants. Spray the entire planting once a week with a fungicide containing *basic copper sulfate*, as long as the disease is present. Avoid planting English ivy in hot, humid areas. Water early in the day to allow the foliage to dry quickly.

HEDERA (IVY)

Stem rot.

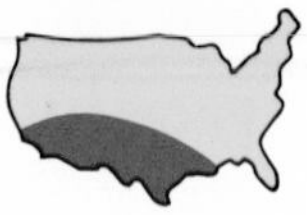

PROBLEM: Leaves turn dark green, wilt and then turn dark brown and cling to the stems. The stems become soft, sunken, and reddish brown. When the dying plants are dug up, many of the roots are found to be soft and rotting. There many be fine brown strands on the roots, and mats, 2 to 12 inches in diameter, of white powdery spores on the soil.

ANALYSIS: Root and stem rots
Root and stem rots on ivy are caused by several fungi that attack the roots, stems, and lower leaves, killing the plants rapidly. *Rhizoctonia solani* and *Phytophthora palmivora* cause wilting and root decay. *Phymatotrichum omnivorum*, a severe problem in the Southwest, causes a disease known as *cotton* or *Texas root rot*. It wilts the plant and also forms brown strands on the roots and powdery mats on the soil. These fungi live in the soil and on living roots, and are easily spread by contaminated tools, splashing water, and fungal strands in the soil. Plants growing in heavy alkaline soils are the most susceptible to attack.

SOLUTION: Once the plants wilt, nothing can be done. To reduce the spread of *Rhizoctonia* and *Phytophthora*, let the soil dry out between waterings according to the directions on page 849. Cotton root rot is more virulent in alkaline soil. Increase the acidity of the soil by spreading ORTHO Aluminum Sulfate and watering it in well according to the directions on page 908. When planting new beds, improve the drainage with the methods described on page 907.

Brown soft scale (twice life size).

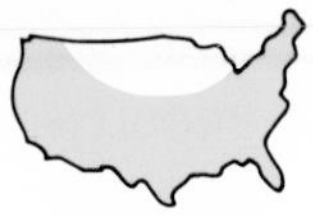

PROBLEM: The stems or the undersides of leaves are covered with raised tan to reddish black crusty or waxy bumps. The bumps can be picked off; the undersides are usually soft. Leaves may turn yellow and fall. In some cases, a sticky substance coats the leaves. A black sooty mold often grows on the sticky material. Ants may be present.

ANALYSIS: Scales
Scales are insects that spend the winter on the trunk and twigs of the plants. They lay eggs in spring and in early summer (late spring in the South); the young scales, called *crawlers*, settle on leaves and twigs. The small (1/10 inch), soft-bodied young feed by inserting their mouthparts and sucking sap from the plant. The legs usually atrophy and a hard crusty or waxy shell develops over the body. The mature female scales lay their eggs underneath the shell. Some species of scales that infest English ivy are unable to digest all the sugar in the plant sap and excrete the excess in a fluid called honeydew. A black sooty mold fungus may develop on the honeydew. Ants feed on the sticky substance and are often present where scales cluster. An uncontrolled infestation of scales may kill the vines after one or two seasons. For more information about scales, see page 876.

SOLUTION: Spray with an insecticide containing *malathion* or *carbaryl* (SEVIN®) in early summer (late spring in the South), when the young are active. The following early spring, before new growth begins, spray the vines with a *dormant oil spray* to control overwintering insects.

Sooty mold.

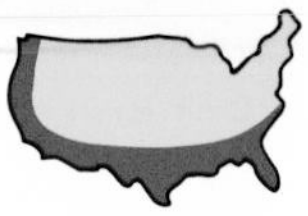

PROBLEM: A black sooty mold is growing on leaves and stems. It can be wiped off the leaves easily.

ANALYSIS: Sooty mold
This common black mold is a fungus, or one of several species of fungi. These fungi grow on the sugary material left on plants by aphids, scales, mealybugs, whiteflies, and other insects that suck sap from the plant. The insects are unable to digest all the sugar in the sap and excrete the excess in a fluid called honeydew, which coats the leaves. The honeydew may also drip from infested overhanging trees and shrubs onto ivy growing beneath them. Sooty mold is unsightly, but it is fairly harmless because it does not infect the leaf tissue. Extremely heavy infestations prevent light from reaching the leaf and may cause the leaf to turn yellow. The presence of sooty mold indicates that the ivy or another plant above it is infested with insects.

SOLUTION: Sooty mold will eventually be washed off by rain. Plants also can be rinsed off with a solution of soapy water, using a mild soap. If only a few leaves are infested, it may be practical to wipe off the mold with a wet rag. Prevent more sooty mold by controlling the insect that is producing the honeydew. Inspect the leaves and stems of the ivy and plants growing in the area to determine what type of insect is present. For control instructions for aphids, scales, mealybugs, and whiteflies, see pages 875 to 877.

HYPERCIUM (ST. JOHN'S WORT)

Leaf spot.

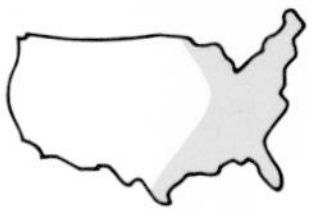

PROBLEM: Spots and blotches appear on the leaves. The spots may be yellow, red, tan, gray or brown. They range in size from barely visible to ¼ inch in diameter. Several spots may join to form blotches. Leaves often turn yellow, die, and fall. Leaf spotting is most severe in warm, humid weather. In damp conditions, a fine gray mold sometimes covers the infected leaf tissue.

ANALYSIS: Leaf spot
A number of different fungi cause leaf spotting on plants. Those that occur on hypericum spot the leaves and are unsightly, but not harmful. The fungi are spread from plant to plant by wind, splashing water, insects, and contaminated tools. They survive the winter on diseased plant debris left in the garden. Most of the leaf spot fungi do their greatest damage in temperatures between 50° and 85°F.

SOLUTION: Leaf spots on hypericum are not critical and won't kill the plant. If you don't like the unsightly leaves, a fungicide containing *maneb* or *folpet* (PHALTAN®) can be sprayed every 3 to 10 days. Because leaf spots are most active during warm, humid weather, spray more frequently during those weather conditions. *Maneb* and *folpet* (PHALTAN®) protect new healthy foliage, but do not kill the fungus on leaves that are already infected.

Hypericum cultural information
Light: Sun or partial shade
Water: While soil is still moist
Soil: Sandy or loamy
Fertilizer: Light to medium

Rust.

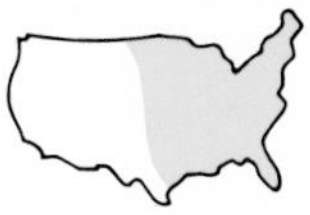

PROBLEM: Very small orange spots appear on the undersides of the leaves. On the upper surfaces, these areas are light yellow. Infected leaves may drop. Long orange areas appear on the stems.

ANALYSIS: Rust
This disease is caused by a fungus (*Mesospora hypericorum*) that attacks several plants beside hypericum. Infection starts in the early spring, at the same time that new plant growth begins. Rust spores are spread from plant to plant by wind and splashing water. The plant must be wet for 6 to 8 hours before the fungus infects the leaf. Rust survives only on living plant tissue and as spores on seeds. It does not remain active on dead plant parts or in the soil. The disease is most active in moist conditions, with cool nights and warm days. Temperatures of 90°F and higher kill the spores.

SOLUTION: Spray infected plants with a fungicide containing *zineb* once a week throughout the growing season. It is important to thoroughly spray both the upper and lower surfaces of the leaves. For even spray coverage, use a spreader-sticker according to the directions on page 922. *Zineb* protects the new, healthy foliage; it does not kill the fungus on leaves that are already diseased. Water in the morning rather than the late afternoon or evening to allow foliage time to dry. Remove and destroy all infected plants in the fall to reduce the chance of new infection next year.

Klamathweed beetles (life size).

PROBLEM: Leaf edges are chewed, giving the leaves a ragged appearance. There may be oval, metallic blue, green, purple, or bronze beetles ¼ inch long feeding on the leaves. Small, irregular, black specks may be seen on the leaves and unopened flowers. Complete defoliation may occur.

ANALYSIS: Klamathweed beetle
(*Chrysolina quadrigemina*)
This insect was introduced from Australia in 1946 to control klamathweed, a weed poisonous to livestock. Klamathweed beetles also feed on ornamental hypericum, which is related to klamathweed. During most years, klamathweed beetles do not cause significant damage, but occasionally they are significant enough to cause extensive defoliation. The beetles emerge in April and feed most heavily in May and June. They spend the summer beneath nearby rocks or other objects or in cracks in the ground. They lay eggs on hypericum in fall when the rains begin. The larvae feed on the plant during winter and form pupae in the soil debris under the plant in late winter.

SOLUTION: Spray plants with an insecticide containing *carbaryl* (SEVIN®). Water and fertilize the hypericum to stimulate regrowth.

MESEMBRYANTHEMUM (ICE PLANT)

Root rot. *Insert:* Closeup.

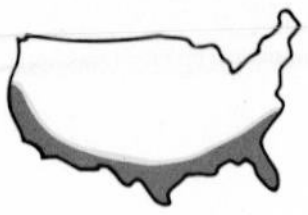

PROBLEM: Leaves turn yellow, starting with the older, lower leaves and progressing to the younger ones. Plants grow very little. When they are pulled up, the roots are black, soft, and rotted. The soil is very moist.

ANALYSIS: Root rot
This disease is caused by a number of different fungi that are present in moist soils. These fungi normally do little damage, but can cause root rot in waterlogged soils. Waterlogged soil may result from overwatering or poor soil drainage. Infection causes the roots to decay, resulting in wilting, yellowing leaves, and the death of the plant. For more information on root rots, see page 849.

SOLUTION: Ice plant is a drought tolerant plant that needs very little watering. Allow the soil around the plants to dry out between waterings. For more information on this technique, see page 849. Remove and discard severely infected plants. Avoid future root rot problems by planting in well-drained soil. For information on improving soil drainage, see page 907.

Mesembryanthemum cultural information
Light: Full sun
Water: Allow to dry between waterings
Soil: Well drained, sandy
Fertilizer: Light

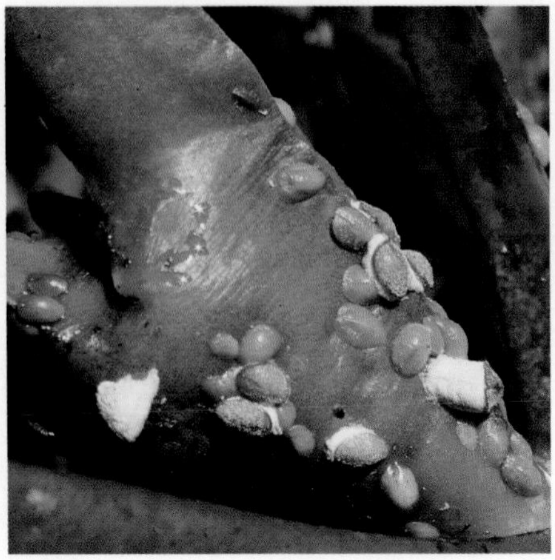

Mesembryanthemum scales (twice life size).

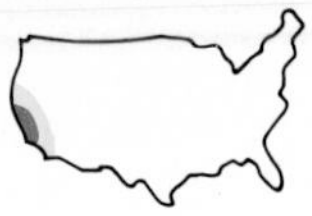

PROBLEM: White sacs appear on the new growth, stems, and undersides of the leaves in early spring and late summer to midfall. Lime green and yellow flecks, almost the same color as the plant, are on the stems and leaves. Plants may turn reddish purple.

ANALYSIS: Scales (*Pulvinaria delottoi, Pulvinariella mesembryanthemi*)
The two insects that attack ice plant are a serious problem in home gardens and in highway plantings along the California coast. They damage and kill plants by sucking the sap from the leaves and stems. Both scales feed actively yearround, but cause much less damage in the winter. The females mature and lay their eggs in white sacs from February to May and August to October. The eggs are spread from plant to plant by the wind. The fall generation causes the most damage because the plants are already under stress from the summer heat and dryness. For more information about scales, see page 876.

SOLUTION: These pests are very difficult to control. Once the plants have turned reddish purple, it is too late to spray. Discard them and plant new ones. For mildly infested plants, treat with *malathion* or *acephate* (ORTHENE®), mixed with a summer oil spray. Do not spray when the white sacs are first present, because the eggs are protected. Spray shortly afterward, when the young crawlers have hatched and begin feeding. For best control, spray both the upper and lower surfaces of the plants. Extensive studies are under way on the natural predators of these pests. Beetles and wasps have been very successful in keeping the scales under control on highway plantings.

PACHYSANDRA (JAPANESE SPURGE)

Scorch.

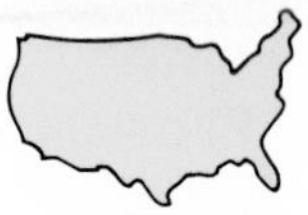

PROBLEM: Irregular blotches, light to dark brown, spot the leaves. Leaves are crisp, shrivel up, and sometimes fall off. Plants may be growing in the full sun.

ANALYSIS: Scorch
Pachysandra can suffer from two kinds of scorch: heat and winter burn. Leaf scorch is caused by excessive evaporation of moisture from the leaves. In hot weather, water evaporates rapidly from the leaves. If the roots can't absorb and convey water fast enough to replenish this loss, then the leaves turn brown and wither. In very hot weather, scorch may occur even though the soil is moist. Winter injury occurs on plants growing in the full sun of a southern or western exposure. Although the pachysandra may be in the shade during the spring and summer, in the winter after a sheltering tree has dropped its leaves, it is in the full sun. On a clear winter day, the sun heats the leaf surface, increasing the plant's water requirement. If the ground is frozen, or if it has been a dry fall and winter, the pachysandra roots can't absorb the needed water.

SOLUTION: Keep the soil moist. If scorch persists, consider growing a groundcover that is more resistant to drought in that area. To prevent winter scorch, keep the soil moist until the ground is frozen.

Pachysandra cultural information
Light: Shade
Water: While soil is still moist
Soil: Rich, loamy
Fertilizer: Medium

Leaf and stem blight.

PROBLEM: Irregular brown and black blotches appear on the leaves and spread to cover almost the entire leaf. Leaves are soft and water soaked. Areas on the stem turn black, soft, and sunken. In wet weather, pinkish spore masses appear along the stem.

ANALYSIS: Leaf and stem blight
This disease is caused by a fungus (*Volutella pachysandrae*). Plants are more susceptible to attack from this fungus if they are weak from spider mites or winter injury; if they are too crowded; if planted in the full sun; or if the area stays too moist from tree leaves falling into the bed. The fungus is most active in rainy, cool spring weather, and spreads from plant to plant on splashing water and contaminated tools. The spores survive the winter on infected stems and leaves that are left in the garden. If not controlled, this blight can kill an entire planting of pachysandra in one or two seasons.

SOLUTION: Pull out and discard all diseased plants. Although this may seem like an endless job, you will get much better control of this difficult-to-control disease. Then spray the cleaned bed with a fungicide containing *chlorothalonil* (DACONIL 2787®) or *captan* (ORTHOCIDE®) three times, at intervals of 1 week, beginning when the disease is discovered or when new growth starts in the spring. Thin and shear the beds periodically to improve air circulation. Rake out fallen leaves in the fall to reduce the chance of the disease occurring in the spring. Keep pachysandra healthy by controlling scale and reducing winter scorch.

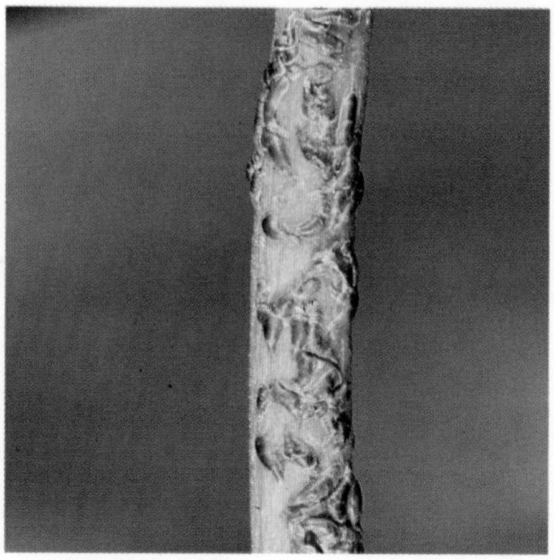

Oystershell scale (life size).

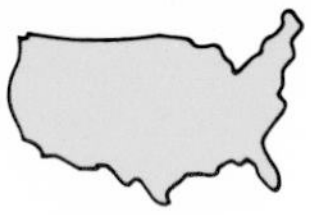

PROBLEM: The stems and the undersides of leaves are covered with gray, reddish brown, yellow, or white flecks or bumps. These bumps or flecks are round, pear-shaped, or narrow, and rub off easily. Leaves turn yellow and often fall. Plants seldom grow new leaves, and eventually die.

ANALYSIS: Scales
Scales are insects that spend the winter on the trunk and twigs of the plants. They lay eggs in spring and in early summer (late spring in the South); the young scales, called *crawlers,* settle on leaves and twigs. These small (1/10 inch), soft-bodied young feed by inserting their mouthparts and sucking sap from the plant. The legs usually atrophy and a hard crusty or waxy shell develops over the body. The mature female scales lay their eggs underneath the shell. Some species of scales that infest pachysandra are unable to digest all the sugar in the plant sap and excrete the excess in a fluid called honeydew. A black sooty mold fungus may develop on the honeydew. Ants feed on the sticky substance, and are often present where scales cluster. An uncontrolled infestation of scales may kill the vines after two or three seasons. For more information about scales, see page 876.

SOLUTION: Spray with an insecticide containing *malathion* or *carbaryl* (SEVIN®) in early summer (late spring in the South), when the young are active. The following early spring, before new growth begins, spray the vines with a *dormant oil spray* to control overwintering insects.

Spider mites (life size).

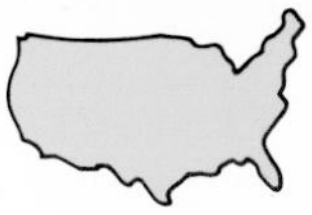

PROBLEM: Leaves are speckled or spotted, yellow, and dirty. Leaves may dry out and fall off. Often there is a fine webbing over the leaves or on the lower surfaces of the leaves. Plants lose vigor. Discoloration is most severe during hot, dry weather. To determine if the plant is infested with mites, hold a sheet of white paper underneath an affected leaf and tap the leaf sharply. Minute green, red, or yellow specks the size of pepper grains will drop to the paper. The mites are easily seen against the white background.

ANALYSIS: Two-spotted spider mite
(*Tetranychus urticae*)
Spider mites, related to spiders, are major pests of many garden plants. They cause damage by sucking sap from buds and the undersides of leaves. As a result of feeding, the green leaf pigment disappears, producing the stippled appearance. Mites are active during the growing season, but are favored by hot, dry weather (70°F and up).

SOLUTION: Spray with *dicofol* (KELTHANE®) or *malathion* when damage is first noticed. Cover all the leaves thoroughly and direct sprays to the undersides of the leaves. Repeat applications three more times at intervals of 7 days. Hose down plants frequently to knock off webs and mites.

Pachysandra cultural information
Light: Partial to full shade
Water: Water while soil is still moist
Soil: Loamy, acidic
Fertilizer: Light to medium

POTENTILLA (CINQUEFOIL)

Leaf spot.

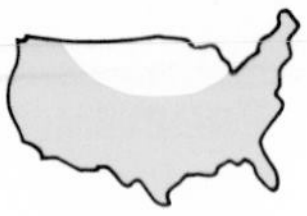

PROBLEM: Small reddish purple and brown spots with darker margins appear on the leaves. These oval to round spots occur on both the top and bottom surfaces of the leaves. Spots often enlarge to cover most of the leaf surface. Small black specks may be seen scattered over the surface of the spots. The leaves often turn yellow, die, and fall.

ANALYSIS: Leaf spot
A number of different fungi cause leaf spotting on potentilla. Some of these fungi may kill the plant. Others merely spot the leaves and are unsightly, but not too harmful. The fungi are spread from plant to plant by wind, splashing water, insects, and contaminated tools. They survive the winter on diseased plant debris left in the garden. Most of the leaf spot fungi do their greatest damage in temperatures between 50° and 85°F.

SOLUTION: Spray the infected planting every 3 to 10 days with a fungicide containing *zineb* or *mancozeb*. Because leaf spot fungi are most active during warm, humid weather, spray more frequently during those weather conditions. These fungicides protect the new healthy foliage, but do not kill the fungus on leaves that are already infected. Leaves that are spotted over more than half their surface should be removed and destroyed to reduce the spread of the fungus to less severely affected plants. Don't touch the diseased plants when the leaves are wet, or you will help spread the fungus.

Rust.

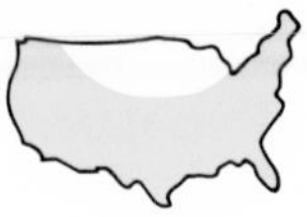

PROBLEM: Very small orange spots appear on the undersides of the leaves. On the upper surfaces, these areas are light yellow. Long orange areas appear on the stems. Plants wilt and drop their infected leaves.

ANALYSIS: Rust
A number of fungi (*Phragmidium* species) attack members of the rose family, including potentilla. Rust spores are spread from plant to plant by wind and splashing water. The plant must be wet for at least 4 hours before the fungus infects the leaf. Rust survives only on living plant tissue and as spores on seeds. It does not remain active on dead plant parts or in the soil. The disease is most severe in moist conditions, with cool nights and warm days.

SOLUTION: Spray infected plants with a fungicide containing *zineb* or *maneb* once a week throughout the growing season. It is important to wet both the lower and upper surfaces of the leaves. For even spray coverage, use a spreader-sticker according to the directions on page 922. *Zineb* and *maneb* protect the new, healthy foliage by killing the rust spores as they germinate on the leaf; they do not kill the fungus on diseased leaves. Water in the morning rather than the late afternoon or evening, to allow wet leaves time to dry. Remove and destroy all infected plants in the fall to reduce chances of infections next year.

Potentilla cultural information
Light: Full sun to partial shade
Water: While soil is still moist
Soil: Well drained, loamy
Fertilizer: Medium

TRACHELOSPERMUM (STAR JASMINE)

Iron deficiency.

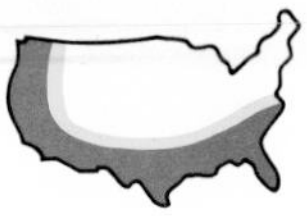

PROBLEM: Yellowing starts along the edges of the leaves and progresses inward. Eventually the areas between the veins are yellow, with the veins remaining bright green. The plant grows slowly, forming leaves that are smaller than usual.

ANALYSIS: Iron deficiency
Leaf yellowing in star jasmine is due to a deficiency of iron in the plant. The soil is seldom deficient in iron. However, the iron is often in an insoluble form and not available to the plant, especially in alkaline soils where the pH is above 7.0. (For more information about soil pH, see page 908.) Overliming the soil or lime leached from cement or brick will raise the soil pH. In addition, regions with low rainfall generally have high-pH soils. Iron is necessary for the formation of the green pigment in the leaf. Without it, the leaves yellow.

SOLUTION: Spray the leaves and the soil around the plants with ORTHO Greenol Liquid Iron. If the soil has a pH of over 7.0, treat it with *ferrous sulfate* or ORTHO Aluminum Sulfate. (For instructions, see page 908.) Do not lime soils with a pH of over 7.0.

Trachelospermum cultural information
Light: Sun or shade
Water: While soil is still moist
Soil: Loam
Fertilizer: Medium

VINCA (PERIWINKLE)

Root and stem rot.

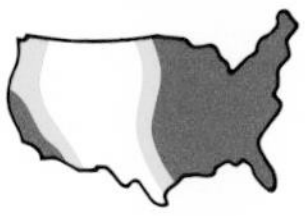

PROBLEM: Shoot tips wilt and die. There are no black specks on the affected stems. Plants pull up easily, with most of the roots and lower stem soft and rotted away. Individual plants are affected first, and within several weeks entire clumps wilt and die.

ANALYSIS: Root and stem rot
This plant disease is caused by a fungus (*Pellicularia filamentosa*). It is the most serious disease affecting periwinkle. It occurs mostly in heavy, poorly drained soil, and during periods of wet weather. It can be found throughout the growing season in most periwinkle plantings. The fungus enters the plant through the roots and crown and rots the cells, causing the plant to wilt and die. The fungus persists indefinitely in the soil, and spreads from plant to plant on contaminated tools and splashing water.

SOLUTION: Remove and destroy badly infected plants. Allow the soil to dry between waterings according to the method described on page 849 until the spread of the disease is halted. If the area is replanted, improve the drainage by one of the methods described on page 907. To prevent recurrence of the disease, allow the soil to dry between waterings until it is barely moist.

Vinca cultural information
Light: Light shade
Water: While soil is still moist
Soil: Well drained
Fertilizer: Medium

Gray mold.

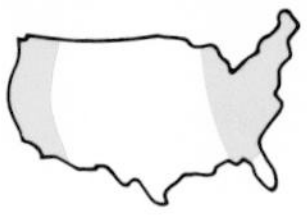

PROBLEM: Brown or black spots appear on the edges of the leaves and spread inward, sometimes covering the entire leaf. Flowers may be discolored or spotted. As the disease progresses, a fuzzy brown or grayish mold forms on the infected tissue during cool, wet weather.

ANALYSIS: Gray mold
This widespread plant disease is caused by a fungus (*Botrytis cinerea*) that is found on most dead plant tissue. The fungus initially attacks foliage and flowers that are weak or dead, causing spotting and mold. The fuzzy mold that develops is composed of fungus strands and millions of microscopic spores. Once gray mold has become established on plant debris and weak or dying leaves and flowers, it can invade healthy plant tissue. The fungus is spread by splashing water, or by infected pieces of plant tissue contacting healthy tissue. Cool temperatures and high humidity favor gray mold growth. Rain and overhead watering enhance the spread of the fungus. Infection is more of a problem in spring and fall, when temperatures are lower. In mild-winter areas where freezing is rare, gray mold can be a year-round problem.

SOLUTION: Remove and discard all fading flowers and diseased leaves. Treat plants with a fungicide containing *benomyl*, *captan* (ORTHOCIDE®), or *zineb*. For best control, add a spreader-sticker to the spray. For instructions on using a spreader-sticker, see page 922.

Dieback.

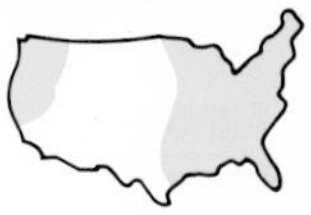

PROBLEM: Shoot tips wilt, turn brown, and die. The infection progresses down the stem to the soil surface, killing the plant. Affected stems turn black. Tiny black specks are often seen on the diseased stems. Dark brown spots sometimes develop on leaves, which then die and fall. Individual plants are affected first, and within several weeks entire clumps wilt and die.

ANALYSIS: Canker and dieback
This disease is caused by two fungi (*Phomopsis livella* and *Phoma exigua*) that attack periwinkle in the spring soon after the new growth begins. This disease is most prevalent during very rainy seasons. The fungal spores spread from plant to plant on splashing water and contaminated tools. This disease can be devastating, killing an entire planting in a few weeks.

SOLUTION: Thoroughly soak stems and soil with a fungicide containing *benomyl*. Apply two or three times, at intervals of 1 month, beginning in early spring. Prune and remove plants that are more than half affected. This helps reduce the chance of the fungus spreading. Drench soil and stems with *benomyl* when planting a new bed of periwinkle. Once the plants are established, these treatments may be reduced or eliminated unless the disease returns. To reduce the chances of new infections, water early in the day, rather than late afternoon or evening, so the leaves have time to dry out before nightfall.

VINCA (PERIWINKLE)

Scorch.

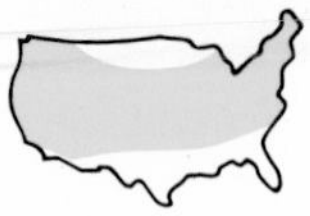

PROBLEM: Yellow or brown blotches appear on the leaves directly exposed to the sun. Severely affected leaves may die and fall off.

ANALYSIS: Scorch
Periwinkle can suffer from two kinds of scorch: heat scorch and winter burn. Scorch is caused by excessive evaporation from the leaves. In hot weather, water evaporates rapidly from the leaves. If the roots can't absorb and convey water fast enough to replenish this loss, leaf tissue is killed. Winter injury occurs on plants growing in the full sun of a southern or western exposure. On a very sunny, clear winter day, the sun heats the leaf surface, increasing the plant's water requirement. If the ground is frozen or dry, the periwinkle roots can't absorb the needed water. The leaves then turn yellow or brown and dry out.

SOLUTION: Keep periwinkle amply watered during hot weather. Fertilize the plants with a nitrogen-rich fertilizer to encourage quick regrowth. In areas with hot summers, periwinkle does best in shady locations. To reduce the chance of winter scorch, be sure the soil is moist before the ground freezes. Mulch plants or cover them with tree boughs during unusually cold sunny weather.

Leaf spot.

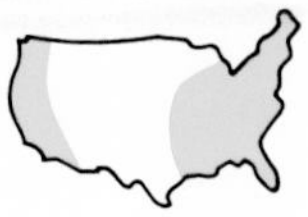

PROBLEM: Spots and blotches appear on the leaves. The spots may be yellow, red, tan, gray, or brown. They range in size from barely visible to ¼ inch in diameter. Several spots may join to form blotches. Leaves may yellow and die. Leaf spotting is most severe in warm, humid weather. In damp conditions, a fine gray mold may cover the infected leaf tissue.

ANALYSIS: Leaf spot
A number of different fungi cause leaf spots. Some of these fungi may eventually kill the plant, or weaken it so that it becomes susceptible to attack by other organisms. Others merely cause spotting that is unsightly but not harmful. These fungi are spread by splashing water, wind, insects, and tools. They generally survive the winter in diseased plant debris. Most of these fungi do their greatest damage in mild weather (50° to 85°F).

SOLUTION: Spray the infected planting every 3 to 10 days with a fungicide containing *basic copper sulfate*. Rake out infected fallen leaves.

Some of the problems common to many flowers and perennial ornamentals are discussed in the next 17 pages. If you don't find your problem here, look up your plant in the index to flowers on the next page.

PROBLEMS COMMON TO MANY FLOWERS	PAGE
Poor flowering	305
Slow growth	307
Discolored or spotted leaves	309
Wilting plants	313
Insects	315
Leaves and flowers chewed	317
Seedlings die	319

ANNUALS, PERENNIALS, AND BULBS

Annuals, perennials, and bulbs (including the soft-stemmed ornamentals) are the princesses of the garden. They are usually raised for their beauty alone, and serve no other function, such as diverting traffic or giving shade. So the measure of how well they perform their function is in their beauty.

Annuals are grown anew each year from seeds or transplants. They grow rapidly to the flowering stage, then bloom abundantly for the rest of the growing season. But ideal growing conditions are needed to keep them vigorous. They are most successful if treated like vegetables. Their bed should be cultivated and fertilized before planting, fertilizer should be added at regular intervals throughout their growing season, and they should be watered regularly.

Because annuals only last for a single season, one solution to their problems is to throw the plants away and begin with new ones instead of treating specific problems. Because annuals usually accumulate problems as they age, there is often a point toward the end of the season when the gardener decides that the annual bed is no longer attractive and cleans it out.

Perennials, on the other hand, are long-term investments. Because they are meant to last for many years, it is important that they be adapted to their environment. This means selecting the right types for your climate, and finding the right place in your yard for each plant. It is sometimes necessary to move a plant several times before finding just the right combination of shade, soil type, and protection from the elements. But finding that location is often the key to having trouble-free perennials.

Bulbs can be treated either as annuals or perennials. All bulbs are perennials, but those not adapted to your climate will not naturalize, multiplying their numbers each year. Tulips, for instance, make smaller and fewer blooms each year, and are usually most satisfactory if new bulbs are purchased each fall. But other bulbs, such as daffodils, are adapted to much of the United States, and will increase in number each year with a minimum of effort. If you wish to keep bulbs as perennials, feed and water the foliage after the blooming period is past, because it is during this period that energy is being stored in the bulb for next year's flower.

Above: Damage caused by gladiolus thrips. See page 359.
Left: A healthy perennial border, with lilies blooming in front of snake plant.

INDEX TO ANNUALS, PERENNIALS, AND BULBS

PROBLEMS COMMON TO MANY FLOWERS

Lobelia without flowers.

Flowerless geranium.

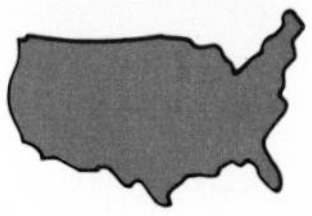

PROBLEM: The plant produces no flowers. The foliage is healthy, and there are no signs of insects or disease.

ANALYSIS: No flowers on a healthy plant Healthy plants may fail to bloom for several reasons.	SOLUTION: The numbered solutions below correspond to the numbers in the analysis.
1. *Wrong season:* Most plants bloom only during a specific season. Often, plants have particular seasonal light and temperature requirements that must be met before they will flower.	**1.** Find out the flowering season of your plants. For a list of common flowers and their blooming seasons, see page 1004.
2. *Unseasonable cool spell:* If the weather is unseasonably cool or cloudy, many plants adapted to hot, sunny weather stop flowering.	**2.** Plants will start to flower again when the weather warms up.
3. *Insufficient light:* Plants differ in the amount of light they require to flower properly. Generally, flowers that thrive in sunny conditions bloom poorly or fail to bloom in shaded locations.	**3.** Look up your specific plant in the alphabetical section beginning on page 320 to determine its light requirement. If your plant is not receiving enough light, transplant it to a sunnier location.
4. *Too much nitrogen:* All plants need nitrogen and several other nutrients to grow and flower properly. However, if they receive an excessive amount of nitrogen, some plants will grow lush, succulent foliage at the expense of flower production.	**4.** Fertilize your flowers with ORTHO Fruit & Bloom Builder according to label directions.
5. *Immature plants:* Biennials (plants that live for 2 years) and perennials (plants that live for many years) usually do not bloom during their first year of growth, even during their normal flowering season. They need to attain a minimum size or age before they will flower.	**5.** Check to see if your plant is either a biennial or a perennial (see page 1004). If it is, you can expect it to flower next year.
6. *Undersize bulbs:* Plants grown from bulbs or corms (such as daffodils, tulips, and gladioli) will not produce flowers if they are planted from undersize bulbs or corms.	**6.** Purchase only large, healthy bulbs and corms. After a year or two, plants grown from undersize bulbs and corms will eventually flower as the bulbs and corms increase in size.

PROBLEMS COMMON TO MANY FLOWERS — POOR FLOWERING

Transplant shock on cineraria.

PROBLEM: Recently transplanted flowers drop their flower buds before they open. Often, blossoms and leaves also drop prematurely. The plant may wilt during the hot part of the day even if the soil is moist.

ANALYSIS: Transplant shock
Even under ideal conditions, many plants drop some of their buds, flowers, and leaves when they are transplanted. Bud and leaf drop result from root damage that occurs during transplanting. Tiny hairlike rootlets that grow at the periphery of the root system absorb most of the water the plant uses. When these rootlets are damaged during transplanting, the amount of water that can be supplied to the foliage and flowers is decreased. Flower buds, flowers, and leaves fall off, and the plant wilts. The more the roots are damaged during transplanting, the greater will be the leaf and bud drop. Also, because plants lose water rapidly during hot, dry, windy periods, transplanting then will cause plants to undergo greater shock. They will not recover as quickly. As the root system regrows, new flower buds will form.

SOLUTION: Transplant when the weather is cool, in the early morning, late afternoon, and on cloudy days. When transplanting, disturb the soil around the roots as little as possible. Preserve as much of the root system as possible. If the roots have been disturbed, or if the plant is large or old, pinch off about a third of the growth, to reduce the amount of foliage needing water. Water immediately after transplanting with ORTHO Vitamin B–1 Plant Starter. For more information about transplanting, see page 924.

Poor flowering on gazanias.

Small petunia blossoms.

PROBLEM: There are few blooms, and the flowers may be small.

ANALYSIS: Poor flowering
Lack of flowers can result from any of several causes.

SOLUTION: The numbered solutions below correspond to the numbers in the analysis.

Analysis	Solution
1. *Insufficient light:* Many plants require full or part day sun to flower properly. Even plants that flower well in filtered light will not produce many blossoms when planted in deep shade. Plants receiving inadequate light are often leggy or spindly.	**1.** Check the light requirements of your plants by looking in the alphabetical section beginning on page 320. If plants are not receiving enough light, move them to a sunnier location.
2. *Diseased plants:* Frequently, plants that have been attacked by disease or insect pests do not flower well. Mottled, discolored, or dying foliage or chewed leaves usually indicate the presence of a disease organism or plant pest.	**2.** Look up your plant in the alphabetical section beginning on page 320 to find what diseases may affect it. Treat accordingly.
3. *Old flowers left on plant:* Many plants slow down their flower production when the older blossoms are allowed to fade and form seeds. The plant diverts its energy into producing seeds rather than flowers.	**3.** Remove flowers as they start to fade.
4. *Overcrowding:* Plants that are overcrowded must compete for light, nutrients, and water. When supplies of nutrients are inadequate, overall plant growth, including flowering, decreases.	**4.** Thin out overcrowded plantings.
5. *Too much nitrogen:* Plants require a balanced diet of nutrients (nitrogen, phosphorous, potassium) to grow and bloom properly. Excessive nitrogen from high-nitrogen fertilizers throws off the balance of nutrients and encourages lush, green leaf growth at the expense of flower production.	**5.** Fertilize your plants with ORTHO Fruit & Bloom Builder. The phosphorous and potassium in the fertilizer will promote flowering.

Thrips damage to gladiolus.

PROBLEM: Flower buds turn brown and die before they open. There are often silvery white streaks on the leaves. Flowers that have opened are often streaked and distorted. If the flower buds are peeled open, tiny (1/20 inch) insects resembling brown or straw-colored wood slivers can be seen moving around at the base of the petals.

ANALYSIS: Thrips
Several species of this common insect pest attack garden flowers. Thrips are found in protected parts of the plant, such as the insides of flower buds, where they feed by rasping the soft plant tissue, then suck the released plant sap. The injured tissue dies and turns white or brown, causing the characteristic streaking of the leaves and flowers. Because thrips migrate long distances on wind currents, they can quickly infest widespread areas. In cold climates, thrips feed and reproduce from spring until fall. With the onset of freezing weather, they find sheltered areas such as grass clumps and hibernate through the winter. In warm weather climates, thrips feed and reproduce all year. These pests reach their population peak in late spring to midsummer. They are especially troublesome during prolonged dry spells.

SOLUTION: Thrips cannot be eliminated completely, but they can be kept under control. Spray infested plants with ORTHO Orthene Systemic Insect Control or ORTHO Isotox Insect Killer. Spray 2 or 3 times at intervals of 10 days as soon as damage is noticed. Make sure your plant is listed on the product label. Repeat the spray if reinfestation occurs. Pick off and destroy old, infested flowers.

Mums that weren't disbudded.

PROBLEM: The plant produces many small flowers rather than a few large, showy flowers. The leaves are healthy.

ANALYSIS: Many small flowers
Large, showy flowers will not be produced on certain plants, such as chrysanthemums and carnations, unless most of the flower buds are removed. Generally, these plants produce long stems with a terminal flower bud at the end and secondary flower buds at the base of each leaf on the flower stem. The plant has only a limited amount of nutrients with which to nourish each bud. If there are many buds, each bud will receive only a small amount of nutrients, and will develop into a small flower.

SOLUTION: Pinch off the side flower buds as soon as they are large enough to be handled. The earlier they are removed, the larger the terminal flower will be.

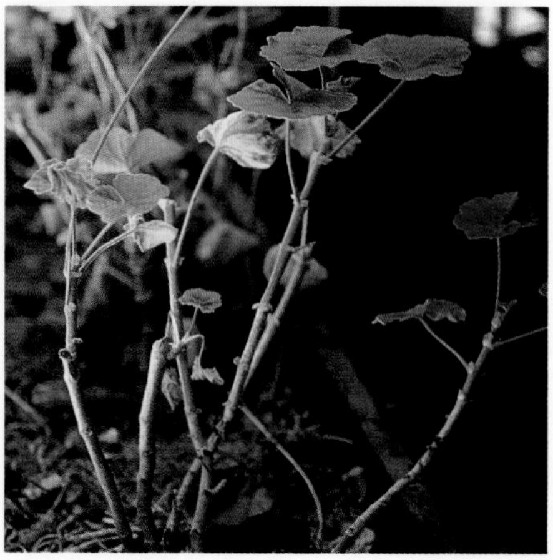

Geraniums in low light.

PROBLEM: The plant grows slowly or not at all, and is located in a shaded area. Growth is weak and leggy, and flowering is poor. The leaves may be dark green and larger than normal. The oldest leaves may drop off. There are no signs of disease or insect pests.

ANALYSIS: Insufficient light
Plants contain a green pigment, chlorophyll, which uses sunlight to produce energy. This energy is used to make food for plant growth and development. Plants differ in the amount of light they need to grow properly. Some plants need many hours of direct sunlight daily, while others thrive in shaded locations. Any plant that receives less light than it requires cannot produce as much food as it needs. It grows slowly and is weak and leggy.

SOLUTION: Look in the alphabetical section that begins on page 320 to determine the light requirement of your flower. If your plant is not receiving enough light, transplant it to a sunnier location.

PROBLEMS COMMON TO MANY FLOWERS — SLOW GROWTH

Zinnias planted too late.

Phosphorus-deficient columbine.

Slow-growing zinnias.

PROBLEM: The plant fails to grow, or grows very slowly. There are no signs of insects or diseases.

ANALYSIS: Poor growth
There are many reasons why a plant might grow slowly.

SOLUTION: The numbered solutions below correspond to the numbers in the analysis.

1. *Improper planting time:* Many plants require warm temperatures and long hours of sunlight to grow well. If transplants that need warm weather are set out too early in the spring, or too late in the fall when temperatures are cool, they will not grow.

1. Check page 1004 for a list of common flowers and their growing seasons. As the weather warms up, the plants will start to grow.

2. *Unseasonable cool spell:* If the weather is unseasonably cool or cloudy, most plants will slow down their growth rate, even those adapted to cool temperatures.

2. Plants will start to grow again when unseasonable cool spells have passed. If the weather is especially cloudy and moist, check for signs of disease. Fungal and bacterial infections are especially troublesome during periods of moist weather. For information about plant diseases, see the section beginning on page 848.

3. *Natural dormancy:* Many perennials and all bulbs undergo a period of no growth, which usually occurs soon after they have flowered. Although it may seem that the plant is inactive during this period, it is actually developing roots, bulbs, or rhizomes for next year's growth. The foliage of many perennials and bulbs eventually dies back completely, and the plant becomes entirely dormant.

3. Check the list of common flowers on page 1004 to see if your plant is a bulb or perennial with a natural dormancy period.

4. *Phosphorus deficiency:* Phosphorus is a plant nutrient essential to normal plant growth and development. Many garden soils are deficient in phosphorus. When plants do not receive enough phosphorus they usually grow very slowly, or stop growing altogether. Sometimes their foliage also turns dark green, or may redden slightly.

4. For a quick response, spray the leaves with Ra-Pid-Gro Plant Food. Fertilize plants with ORTHO Superphosphate according to label directions.

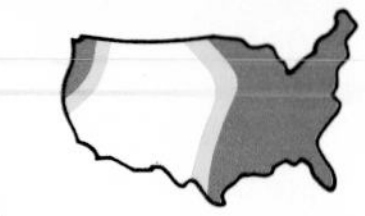

PROBLEM: Plants grow slowly, are stunted, and the leaves often turn pale green to yellow. Plants don't improve when fertilized. The pH of the soil is below 5.5.

ANALYSIS: Acid soil
Soils that have a pH of 5.5 or lower are too acid for most plants. Acid soils are commonly found in the Pacific Northwest and along the East Coast. The heavy rains in these areas leach the salts from the soils, leaving them acidic. The amounts and types of nutrients available to plants are limited in acid soils. Below a pH of 5.5, the amount of available nitrogen, phosphorus, potassium, calcium, magnesium, and other nutrients decreases. These nutrients are essential for healthy plants. Most plants grow best with a pH of 6.0 to 8.0. For more information about pH, see page 908.

SOLUTION: To make a soil less acidic, apply dolomitic limestone. This type of ground limestone contains calcium and magnesium, nutrients in which acid soils are usually deficient. The amount of lime you need to apply depends on the soil texture, how acid the soil is, and how much organic matter it contains. (For a chart of liming requirements, see page 1019.) Soil acidity corrections are only temporary because heavy rains leach the lime from the soil. Test your soil every 2 to 3 years, and correct accordingly.

DISCOLORED OR SPOTTED LEAVES

Discolored iris leaves caused by lack of water.

Dried-out crocus.

PROBLEM: Leaves turn pale green to yellow. The plant may be stunted. In many cases, leaf edges turn brown and crisp, and some of the leaves shrivel and die. There are no signs of disease or pests. Unlike nitrogen deficiency, the leaves do not discolor from the base of the plant upward. For information on nitrogen deficiency, see page 310.

ANALYSIS: Leaves discolored
There are several reasons why leaves discolor.

1. *Frequent stress:* Plants require at least a minimal supply of water to remain healthy and grow properly. When they are allowed to dry out once or twice, they usually survive. However, plants that suffer from frequent drought stress undergo changes in their metabolism that result in leaf discoloration, stunting, and lack of growth. If the soil is allowed to dry out completely, the plant will die.

2. *Salt buildup in the soil:* Leaf discoloration and browning occur when excess salts dissolved in the soil water are taken up into the plant and accumulate in the leaf tissue. Soil salts build up to damaging levels in soils that are not occasionally flushed. Salt buildup commonly occurs in arid regions of the country.

3. *Sunburn:* Shade-loving plants placed in a sunny location will develop discolored leaves. Sunburned leaves often develop a whitish or yellow bleached appearance. Leaves that are not directly exposed to the sun usually remain green and uninjured.

SOLUTION: The numbered solutions below correspond to the numbers in the analysis.

1. Do not let your plants wilt between waterings. Consult the alphabetical section beginning on page 320 for the moisture needs of your plant. Provide plants with adequate water. For more information about proper watering, see page 912.

2. Flush out soil salts periodically by watering deeply and thoroughly.

3. Check to see whether your plant is adapted to sun or to shade. Consult the alphabetical section beginning on page 320 for the light needs of your plant. Transplant shade-loving plants to a shaded location.

Overwatering damage on primrose.

PROBLEM: Leaves turn light green or yellow. Leaf edges may turn brown, and some of the leaves may die. In many cases the plant is stunted. Flowering is poor. If the plant is pulled out of the ground, the roots are found to be soft and rotted. The soil is frequently or constantly wet.

ANALYSIS: Overwatering
Overwatering is a serious and common problem that often results in the decay and death of the plant roots. Roots require oxygen to function normally. Oxygen is contained in tiny air spaces (pores) in the soil. When water is applied to the soil, the air is pushed out of the soil pores and replaced with water. If this water cannot drain properly, or is constantly reapplied, the soil pores will remain filled with water. The roots cannot absorb the oxygen they need in such saturated conditions, and they begin to decay. As the roots continue to rot, they are less able to supply the plant with nutrients and water, resulting in the decline and eventual death of the plant.

SOLUTION: Allow the soil to dry out slightly between waterings. For more information on watering see page 912. If your soil is poorly drained, improve the soil drainage. For information about improving soil drainage, see page 907. Use plants that will grow in wet soil (see page 1010).

PROBLEMS COMMON TO MANY FLOWERS — DISCOLORED OR SPOTTED LEAVES

Nitrogen-deficient impatiens.

PROBLEM: Leaves turn pale green, then yellow, beginning with the older leaves. Growth is slowed. Older leaves may drop. New leaves are small. Severely affected plants may die.

ANALYSIS: Lack of nitrogen
Garden soils are frequently deficient in nitrogen, the most important nutrient for plant growth. Nitrogen is essential in the formation of plant protein, chlorophyll (green leaf pigment), and many other compounds. When a plant becomes deficient in nitrogen, it breaks down proteins and chlorophyll in the oldest leaves to recover nitrogen to be recycled for new growth. This loss of chlorophyll causes the older leaves to turn yellow. A continuing shortage of nitrogen results in overall yellowing. Because nitrogen is leached from the soil more readily than are other plant nutrients, and because it is needed in larger quantities than are other nutrients, it must be added to almost all garden soils, and for all flowers. Nitrogen leaches from sandy soil more readily than from clay soil, and it leaches more quickly when rainfall or irrigation is heavy.

SOLUTION: Spray the leaves with Ra-Pid-Gro Plant Food for a quick response. Fertilize with ORTHO Ortho-Gro Liquid Plant Food or ORTHO General Purpose Plant Food. Repeat applications according to directions. Fertilize more frequently in sandy soils or where rainfall is heavy. For more information about fertilizers, see page 910.

Fungal leaf spot on impatiens.

Leaf spot.

PROBLEM: Spots and blotches appear on the leaves and flowers.

ANALYSIS: Leaf and flower spots
Several disease and environmental factors contribute to spotting and blotching of leaves and flowers.

SOLUTION: The numbered solutions below correspond to the numbers in the analysis.

1. *Fungal leaf spots:* Spots caused by fungi are usually small, circular, and may be found on all of the leaves. The spots range in size from barely visible to ¼ inch in diameter. They may be yellow, red, tan, gray, brown, or black. Often the leaves are yellow and dying. Infection is usually most severe during moist, mild weather (50° to 85°F).

1. Generally, picking off the diseased leaves gives adequate control. Clean up plant debris. Spray plants with *chlorothalonil* (DACONIL 2787®), *mancozeb*, or *zineb* if plants are severely infected. Make sure your plant is listed on the fungicide label before spraying.

2. *Bacterial leaf spots:* Spots caused by bacteria are usually tiny and angular in shape. They are usually dark-colored and are sometimes accompanied by rotting and oozing from infected areas. Bacterial spots may be found on all parts of the plant, and are most often favored by warm, moist conditions.

2. If practical, pick off and destroy spotted leaves. If the plant is severely infected, discard it. Clean up plant debris. Avoid overhead watering. Dip contaminated tools in rubbing alcohol.

3. *Sunburn:* Shade-loving plants placed in a sunny location will develop spots and blotches. Sun-loving plants may also develop sunburn symptoms if they are allowed to dry out. Initially, sunburned leaves develop a whitish or yellowish bleached appearance. Large, dark, angular blotches form on the damaged tissue. Leaves that are not directly exposed to the sun remain green and uninjured.

3. Pick off the injured leaves and plant parts. Check to see whether your plant is adapted to sun or shade. Transplant shade-loving plants to a shaded location, or provide shade. Provide plants with adequate water, especially during hot, sunny, or windy days. For a discussion of proper watering, see page 912.

4. *Spray damage:* Spotting of foliage and flowers may also be caused by insecticide, fungicide, and herbicide spray damage. Spots are usually irregular in shape, and vary in the patterns they form on the leaf. Spray injury includes distortion, browning, and death of flowers and young leaves. Sprays may drift in from other areas.

4. Once damage has occurred, there is nothing you can do. Read and follow directions carefully when spraying. Avoid spraying on windy days when the spray can drift onto the wrong plants. If spray drifts onto the wrong plant, rinse off the leaves immediately. Pick off dead or badly injured plant parts.

Iron-deficient pelargonium.

PROBLEM: Leaves turn pale green or yellow. The newest leaves—those at the tips of the stem—are most severely affected. Except in extreme cases, the veins of affected leaves remain green. In extreme cases, the newest leaves are small and all-white or yellow. Older leaves may remain green.

ANALYSIS: Iron deficiency
Plants frequently suffer from deficiencies of iron and other minor nutrients such as manganese and zinc, elements essential to normal plant growth and development. Deficiencies can occur when one or more of these elements are depleted in the soil. Often these minor nutrients are present in the soil, but alkaline (pH 7.5 or higher) or wet soil conditions cause them to form compounds that cannot be used by the plant. An alkaline condition can result from overliming, or from lime leached from cement or brick. Regions where soil is derived from limestone, and those with low rainfall, usually have alkaline soils. For more information about alkaline soils, see page 908.

SOLUTION: Spray the foliage with ORTHO Greenol Liquid Iron, and apply it to the soil around the plants to correct the deficiency of minor nutrients. Check the soil pH according to the instructions on page 909. Correct the pH of the soil using ORTHO Aluminum Sulfate according to the instructions on page 908. Maintain an acid pH by fertilizing with ORTHO Azalea, Camellia & Rhododendron Food .

Powdery mildew.

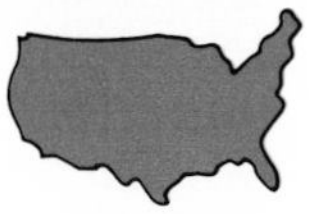

PROBLEM: Leaves and stems are covered with grayish white powdery spots and patches. In many cases, these patches occur on the upper surfaces of the leaves. The infected leaves eventually turn yellow.

ANALYSIS: Powdery mildew
This common plant disease is caused by a number of closely related fungi that thrive in both humid and dry weather. The powdery patches consist of fungal strands and spores. The spores are spread by the wind to healthy plants. The fungus saps the plant nutrients, causing the leaves to turn yellow and sometimes to die. A severe infection may kill the plant. Since some powdery mildews attack many different kinds of plants, the fungus from a diseased plant may infect other types of plants. (For a list of powdery mildews and the plants they attack, see page 1006.) Under favorable conditions, powdery mildew can spread through a closely spaced planting in a matter of days. In the late summer and fall, the fungus forms small, black, spore-producing bodies, which are dormant during the winter, but which can infect more plants the following spring. Powdery mildew is generally most severe in the late summer.

SOLUTION: There are a number of different fungicides that may be used to treat powdery mildew. Look up your specific plant in the alphabetical listing beginning on page 320 to determine which fungicide should be used. Spray at regular intervals of 10 to 12 days, or as often as necessary to protect new growth. Remove and destroy severely infected plants. Where practical, pick off diseased leaves. Clean up and destroy plant debris.

Rust on geranium.

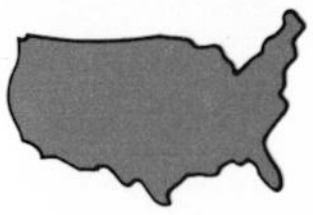

PROBLEM: Yellow or orange spots appear on the upper surfaces of the leaves. Yellowish orange, rust, or chocolate-colored pustules of spores develop on the undersides of the leaves. Infected leaves usually wilt and either hang down along the stem or drop prematurely. The plant may be stunted.

ANALYSIS: Rust
This plant disease is caused by any of a number of related fungi. Most rust fungi spend the winter as spores on living plant tissue and, in some cases, in plant debris. Some rust fungi also infect various weeds and woody trees and shrubs during part of their life cycle. Flower infection usually starts in the early spring as soon as conditions are favorable for plant growth. The spores are spread to healthy plants by splashing water and wind. Some rust fungi cannot infect the flower host unless the foliage is wet for 6 to 8 hours. Rust is favored by moist weather, cool nights, and warm days.

SOLUTION: Several different fungicides are used to control rust. Look up your specific plant in the alphabetical listing beginning on page 320 to determine which fungicide to use. Spray infected plants thoroughly, covering both the upper and lower surfaces of the leaves. Some plants are so susceptible to rust that you may need to spray at weekly intervals throughout the summer. Water in the morning rather than the late afternoon or evening. This will allow wet foliage to dry out more quickly. Remove and destroy all infected plants in the fall to prevent them from infecting new plantings. Plant rust-resistant varieties, if available. For a list of resistant flower varieties, see page 1004.

PROBLEMS COMMON TO MANY FLOWERS — DISCOLORED OR SPOTTED LEAVES

Nasturtiums damaged by ozone.

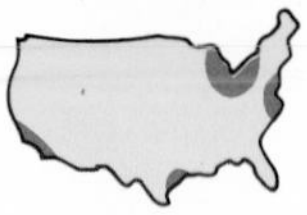

PROBLEM: The upper surfaces of the leaves may be bleached, with white flecks or reddish brown spots. Sometimes the leaves are distorted. Older leaves are more affected than younger ones.

ANALYSIS: Air pollution
Some gases released into the atmosphere from cars and factories damage plants. The most common type of pollution is *smog*. Air pollution damage is most commonly a problem in urban areas, but also occurs in rural areas where gardens are located downwind from factories. Some plants are severely affected, and may even die. Flower production is reduced on pollution damaged plants. For information on the three most common pollutants, *ozone*, *PAN*, and *sulfur dioxide*, see page 855. Many different environmental factors affect a plant's susceptibility to air pollution, including temperature, air movement, light intensity, and soil and air moisture.

SOLUTION: Air pollution injury is usually a localized problem. Check with your neighbors to see if the same kinds of plants in their gardens have been affected the same way. Because injury from air pollutants is similar in appearance to injury from nutrient deficiencies, insects, diseases, and mites, these problems should be eliminated as causes before attributing the damage to air pollution. Nothing can be done about air pollutants. If you live in a smoggy area, select plants that are smog resistant from the list on page 1008.

Leafminer damage to dahlia.

PROBLEM: Light-colored irregular trails wind through the leaves. Blotches may eventually appear on infested leaves. Some of the trails and blotches are filled with black matter. Severely infested leaves may dry up and die.

ANALYSIS: Leafminers
Most of the insects that cause this type of damage belong to the family of leaf-mining flies. The tiny adult flies lay their eggs on the undersides of the leaves. The maggots that hatch from these eggs penetrate the leaf and live between the upper and lower surfaces. They feed on the inner leaf tissue, creating winding trails and blotches. Their dark excrement may dot or partially fill sections of the trails. Generally, the larvae emerge from the leaves to pupate. Leafminers are continually present from the spring until the fall. The last generation of maggots pupates in the soil or plant debris through the winter, to emerge as adult flies the following spring. For more information about leafminers, see page 885.

SOLUTION: Spray infested plants with ORTHO Orthene Systemic Insect Control. Make sure that your plant is listed on the product label. Pick off and destroy infested leaves. Remove and destroy all plant remains in the fall.

Virus-damaged gladiolus.

PROBLEM: Leaves may be mottled yellow-green, or may be uniformly yellowing. In some cases, the foliage develops yellow rings, or the veins may turn yellow. Flowers and leaves may be smaller than normal, and distorted. The plant is usually stunted, and flowering is generally poor.

ANALYSIS: Viruses
Several different viruses infect flowering plants. These viruses include *mosaics*, *yellows*, and *ring-spots*. The severity of virus infections depends on the plant and on the strain of virus. In some cases, symptoms of infection may not show up unless several viruses are present in the plant at the same time. Virus infections do not generally kill the plant, but may greatly reduce its overall vigor and beauty. Many viruses are spread by aphids, which feed on diseased plants and transfer the virus to healthy plants. If diseased plants are touched or pruned, some viruses can be transferred to healthy plants on hands and equipment contaminated by plant sap. Viruses usually persist in the plant indefinitely. Cuttings or divisions made from diseased plants will also be infected.

SOLUTION: There are no chemicals that control or eliminate virus diseases. Remove weak, infected, and stunted plants. Wash your hands thoroughly and dip pruning shears in rubbing alcohol after working on infected plants. Purchase only healthy plants. (For more information on selecting healthy plants, see page 924.) Keep the aphid population under control. For more information about disease-carrying aphids and their control, see page 879.

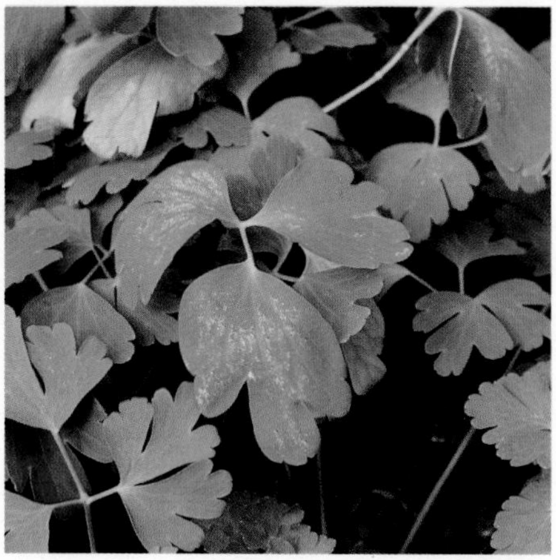
Mite damage to columbine.

PROBLEM: Leaves are stippled, yellowish, bronze, or reddish, and are often dirty. There may be webbing over flower buds, between leaves, or on the lower surfaces of the leaves. To determine if the plant is infested with mites, hold a sheet of white paper underneath an affected plant and tap the plant sharply. Minute green, red, or yellow specks the size of pepper grains will drop to the paper and begin to crawl around. These pests are easily seen against the white background.

ANALYSIS: Spider mites
These common pests of many garden and greenhouse plants are related to spiders. They cause damage by sucking sap from the undersides of the leaves. As a result of feeding, the green leaf pigment disappears, producing the stippled, discolored appearance. Mites are active throughout the growing season, but are favored by hot, dry weather (70°F and up). By midsummer, they build up to tremendous numbers. During cold weather, spider mites hibernate in the soil, on weeds and plants retaining foliage, and on tree bark. For more information about spider mites, see page 887.

SOLUTION: Spray infested plants with a pesticide containing *dicofol* (KELTHANE®). Make sure that your plant is listed on the product label. Spray plants thoroughly, being sure to cover both the upper and lower surfaces of the leaves. Repeat the spray at least two more times at intervals of 5 to 7 days.

Wilting snapdragons.

Wilting pincushion flowers.

PROBLEM: The plant is wilting. The leaves are discolored yellow or brown, and may be dying. The soil may be moist or dry.

ANALYSIS: Root problems
These symptoms are caused by one of several root problems:

SOLUTION: The numbered solutions below correspond to the numbers in the analysis.

1. *Stem and root rot diseases:* Many fungi and bacteria decay plant roots and stems. In addition to leaf wilting and discoloration, there are frequently spots and lesions on the leaves and stems. The infected tissue may be soft and rotted, and the plant pulls out of the ground easily to reveal rotted roots. Most of these disease-causing organisms thrive in wet soil.

1. Look up your plant in the alphabetical section beginning on page 320 to determine which root and stem rot diseases may affect it. Treat accordingly. See page 849 for more information about root rot.

2. *Fertilizer burn:* Excessive amounts of fertilizer cause plants to wilt. The leaves wilt and become dull and brown. Later they become dark brown or black and dry up. When too much fertilizer is applied and not watered in well, a concentrated solution of fertilizer salts is formed in the soil. This concentrated solution makes it difficult for plants to absorb the water they need and may even draw water out of the plant.

2. Dilute the fertilizer in the soil and leach it below the root zone by watering the plant heavily. Soak the affected area thoroughly with plain water, let it drain, then soak again. Repeat three to four times. Cut off dead plant parts. Follow directions carefully when fertilizing.

3. *Nematodes:* These microscopic worms (which are not related to earthworms) live in the soil and feed on plant roots. While feeding, they inject a toxin into the roots. The damaged roots can't supply adequate water and nutrients to the aboveground plant parts, so the plant slowly dies. Infested plants are weak, slow-growing, often turn bronze or yellowish, and wilt on hot, dry days, even when the soil is wet. If the plant is pulled up, the roots are seen to be stunted and often dark and stubby. There may be nodules on the roots.

3. If you have a chronic problem with wilting, yellowing plants that slowly die, and you've eliminated all other possibilities, test for nematodes. Testing roots and soil is the only positive method for confirming their presence. Contact your local Cooperative Extension Office (see page 1029 for a list of offices) for sampling instructions, addresses of testing laboratories, and control procedures for your area. For instructions for controlling nematodes, see page 854.

PROBLEMS COMMON TO MANY FLOWERS — WILTING PLANTS

Wilting hosta.

PROBLEM: The plant wilts frequently, and the soil is frequently or always dry. The leaves turn brown, shrivel, and may be crisp.

ANALYSIS: Lack of water
The most common cause of plant wilting is dry soil. Water in the soil is taken up by the plant roots. It moves up into the stems and leaves, and evaporates into the air through microscopic breathing pores in the surface of the leaf. Water pressure in the plant cells keeps the cell walls rigid and prevents the plant from collapsing. When the soil is dry, the roots are unable to furnish the leaves and stems with water, the water pressure in the cells drops, and the plant wilts. Most plants will recover if they have not wilted severely. However, frequent or severe wilting will curb a plant's growth and eventually kill it.

SOLUTION: Water the plant thoroughly, applying enough water to wet the soil to the bottom of the root zone. If the soil is crusted or compacted, cultivate the soil around the plant before watering. To help conserve soil moisture, apply a mulch around the plant. (For more information about proper watering, see page 912.) Do not allow the plant to wilt between waterings. Look up your plant in the alphabetical section to determine its moisture requirement.

Transplant shock—begonias.

Poor drainage—petunias.

PROBLEM: The plant is wilting, but the foliage looks healthy. There are no signs of disease or insects. The soil is moist.

ANALYSIS: Heat or acute root damage
If a plant wilts in moist soil, but the leaves look healthy, the problem has probably occurred recently:

1. *Intense heat or wind:* During hot, windy periods, plants may wilt even though the soil is wet. Wind and heat cause water to evaporate very quickly from the leaves. The roots can't take in water as fast as it is lost.

2. *Transplant shock:* Plants frequently wilt soon after being transplanted. Although called transplant "shock," this is not the same condition as shock in a human being, but refers to wilt resulting from injured roots. Roots are usually broken or injured to some degree during transplanting. Damaged roots are unable to supply the plant with enough water, even when the soil is wet. As the root system restores itself, its water-absorbing capacity increases. Unless they are severely injured, the plants will soon recover.

3. *Rodents:* The roots, underground stems, and bulbs of many plants are often disturbed or fed upon by various rodents, including pocket gophers and field mice. Root, bulb, and stem damage result in rapid wilting and sometimes death of the plant.

4. *Mechanical injury:* Cultivating, digging, hoeing, thinning, weeding, and any other kind of activity that damages plant roots can cause wilting and sometimes death.

SOLUTION: The numbered solutions below correspond to the numbers in the analysis.

1. As long as the soil is kept moist during periods of intense heat and wind, the plants will probably recover without harm when the temperature drops or the wind dies down. Recovery may be hastened by shading the plants and by sprinkling them with water to cool off the foliage and reduce the rate of water evaporation from the leaves.

2. Preserve the root system as much as possible when transplanting. Keep as much of the soil around the roots as possible. Transplant when the weather is cool, in the early morning, late afternoon, or on cloudy days. If the roots have been disturbed, or if the plant is large and old, prune off about a third of the growth. Water immediately after transplanting with ORTHO Vitamin B-1 Plant Starter. If possible, transplant when the plant is dormant. For more information about transplanting, see page 924.

3. Rodents may be trapped or baited. For details about rodent control, see page 896.

4. Prevent mechanical injury to plants by working very carefully around them.

INSECTS

Cucumber beetle feeding on zinnia (half life size).

PROBLEM: Insects are chewing holes in leaves and flowers. Their hard wing covers are folded across their backs, meeting in a straight line down the center of the back. They are frequently shiny and brightly colored.

ANALYSIS: Beetles
Many different species of beetles infest flowers. In the spring or summer, beetles fly to garden plants and feed on flowers, buds, and leaves. Punctured flower buds usually fail to open, and fully open flowers are often eaten. Because many beetles feed at night, only their damage may be noticed, not the insects. Female beetles lay their eggs in the soil or in the flowers in late summer or fall. The emerging larvae crawl down into the soil to spend the winter, or they mature and pass the winter in plant debris. The larvae of some beetles feed on plant roots before maturing in the fall or spring. For more information about beetles, see page 865.

SOLUTION: Spray infested plants with an insecticide containing *carbaryl* (SEVIN®), *diazinon, acephate* (ORTHENE®), or *malathion*. Make sure your plant is listed on the product label.

Damaged zinnias. *Insert:* Japanese beetle (life size).

PROBLEM: The leaf tissue has been eaten between the veins, making the leaves lacy. Flowers are eaten. Metallic green and bronze, winged beetles, ½ inch long, are feeding in clusters on the flowers and foliage.

ANALYSIS: Japanese beetles
(*Popillia japonica*)
As their name suggests, these beetles are native to Japan. They were first seen in New Jersey in 1916 and have since become a major pest in the eastern United States. They feed on hundreds of different species of plants. The adult beetles are present from June to October. They feed only in the daytime, and are most active on warm, sunny days. The female beetles live for 30 to 45 days. Just before they die, they lay their eggs just under the soil surface in lawns. The grayish white grubs that hatch from these eggs feed on grass roots. As the weather turns cold in the late fall, the grubs burrow 8 to 10 inches into the soil, where they hibernate. When the soil warms up in the spring, the grubs migrate back to the surface and resume feeding. They pupate and re-emerge as adult beetles in late May or June. For more information about Japanese beetles, see page 866.

SOLUTION: Spray infested plants with an insecticide containing *acephate* (ORTHENE®), *carbaryl* (SEVIN®), or *malathion*. Make sure that your plant is listed on the product label.

Caterpillar (life size).

PROBLEM: Holes appear in the leaves and buds. Leaves, buds, and flowers may be entirely sheared off. Caterpillars are feeding on the plants.

ANALYSIS: Caterpillars
Many species of these moth or butterfly larvae feed on garden plants. Usually the adult moths or butterflies begin laying eggs on garden plants with the onset of warm spring weather. The larvae that emerge from these eggs feed on the leaves, flowers, and buds for 2 to 6 weeks, depending on the weather conditions and the species. Mature caterpillars pupate in cocoons either buried in the soil or attached to leaves, tree bark, or buildings. Some caterpillar species have only one generation a year. With these species, all the caterpillars hatch, grow, and pupate at the same time. Other species have numerous generations, so caterpillars of various sizes may be present throughout the growing season. The last generation of caterpillars in the fall survives the winter as pupae. The adult moths and butterflies emerge the following spring. For more information about caterpillars, see page 870.

SOLUTION: Spray infested plants with an insecticide containing *acephate* (ORTHENE®), *carbaryl* (SEVIN®), or *diazinon*. Make sure that your plant is listed on the product label. Small numbers of caterpillars may be removed by hand.

PROBLEMS COMMON TO MANY FLOWERS — INSECTS

Ants on euphorbia (half life size).

PROBLEM: Ants are crawling on the plants and soil. In many cases, these plants are infested with aphids, scales, mealybugs, or whiteflies.

ANALYSIS: Ants

These insects, familiar to gardeners throughout the country, do not directly damage plants. Ants may be present for any of several reasons. Many ants feed on honeydew, a sweet, sticky substance excreted by several species of insects, including aphids, scales, mealybugs, and whiteflies. Ants are attracted to plants infested with these pests. In order to insure an ample supply of honeydew, ants may actually carry aphids to healthy plants. Aphid infestations are frequently spread in this manner. Ants may also feed on flower seeds and nectar. Although they do not feed on healthy plants, ants may eat decayed or rotted plant tissue. Ants generally live in underground colonies or nests. Certain species may form colonies in trees or in building foundations. For more information about ants, see page 893.

SOLUTION: Destroy ant nests by treating anthills with ORTHO Diazinon Granules or spraying the nest and surrounding soil with ORTHO Diazinon Insect Spray. Control aphids, scales, mealybugs, and whiteflies by spraying the plants with *malathion*, *carbaryl* (SEVIN®), or *diazinon*. Make sure that your plant is listed on the product label.

Aphids on ornamental pepper (half life size).

PROBLEM: Leaves are curled, distorted, and yellowing. Often the flowers are malformed. Tiny (⅛ inch) yellow, green, or dark-colored soft-bodied insects are clustered on the leaves, stems, and flowers. A shiny, sticky substance may coat the leaves. Ants are sometimes present.

ANALYSIS: Aphids

These common insects do little damage in small numbers. However, they are extremely prolific and populations can rapidly build up to damaging numbers during the growing season. Damage occurs when the aphid sucks the juices from the leaves and buds. The aphid is unable to digest fully all the sugar in the sap and excretes the excess in a fluid called honeydew, which often drops onto the leaves below. A sooty mold fungus may develop on the honeydew, causing the leaves to appear black and dirty. Ants feed on this sticky substance, and are often present where there is an aphid infestation. In warm areas, aphids are active year-round. In cooler climates, where winter temperatures drop below freezing, the adults cannot survive. However, the eggs they lay in the fall on tree bark, old leaves, and plant debris can survive the winter to cause reinfestation in the spring. Aphids transmit plant diseases such as mosaics and viral yellows.

SOLUTION: Spray with an insecticide containing *acephate* (ORTHENE®), *diazinon*, or *malathion*. Make sure that your plant is listed on the product label. Clean up plant debris in the fall. For more information about disease-carrying insects, see page 879.

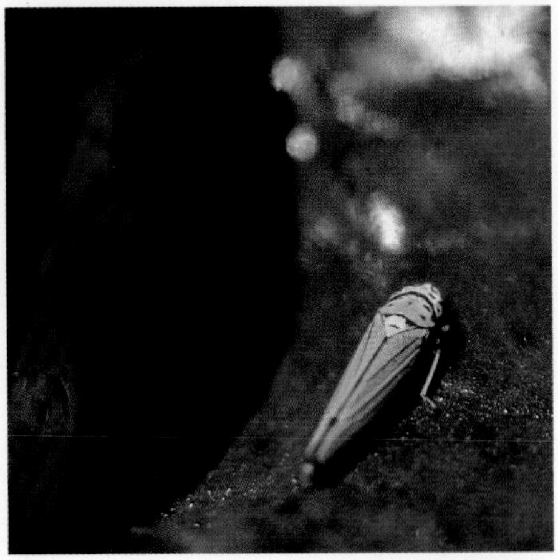

Aster leafhopper (4 times life size).

PROBLEM: Spotted, pale green insects up to ⅛ inch long hop or fly away quickly when the plant is touched. The leaves are stippled and may be yellowing.

ANALYSIS: Aster leafhopper
(*Macrosteles fascifrons*)

This insect, also known as the *six-spotted leafhopper*, feeds on many vegetable and ornamental plants. It generally feeds on the undersides of leaves, sucking the sap, which causes stippling. This leafhopper transmits *aster yellows*, a plant disease that can be quite damaging. (For more information, see page 854.) Leafhoppers at all stages of maturity are active during the growing season. They hatch in the spring from eggs laid on perennial weeds and ornamental plants. Even areas where the winters are so cold that the eggs cannot survive are not free from infestation because leafhoppers migrate in the spring from warmer regions.

SOLUTION: Spray plants with an insecticide containing acephate (ORTHENE®), *diazinon*, *carbaryl* (SEVIN®), or *malathion*. Check to make sure that your plant is listed on the product label. Eradicate nearby weeds that may harbor leafhopper eggs and aster yellows, especially thistles, plantains, and dandelions. For more information about controlling disease-carrying insects, see page 879.

Whiteflies on fuchsia (twice life size).

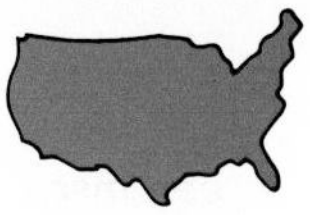

PROBLEM: Tiny, winged insects 1/12 inch long feed on the undersides of the leaves. The insects are covered with white waxy powder. When the plant is touched, insects flutter rapidly around it. Leaves may be mottled and yellowing. In warm winter areas, black mold may cover the leaves.

ANALYSIS: Greenhouse whitefly
(*Trialeurodes vaporariorum*)
This insect is a common pest of many garden and greenhouse plants. The four-winged adult lays eggs on the undersides of leaves. The larvae are the size of a pinhead, flat, oval-shaped, and semitransparent, with white waxy filaments radiating from the body. They feed for about a month before changing to the adult form. Both the larval and adult forms suck sap from the leaves. The larvae are more damaging because they feed more heavily. Adults and larvae cannot fully digest all the sugar in the plant sap and excrete the excess in a fluid called honeydew, which often drops onto the leaves below. A sooty mold fungus may develop on the honeydew. In warm winter areas these insects can be active year-round, with eggs, larvae, and adults present at the same time. Whiteflies are unable to live through freezing winters. Spring reinfestations in freezing winter areas come from migrating whiteflies and from infested greenhouse-grown plants placed in the garden.

SOLUTION: Spray infested plants with an insecticide containing *acephate* (ORTHENE®), *diazinon*, or *malathion*. Make sure that your plant is listed on the product label. When spraying, be sure to cover both the upper and lower surfaces of the leaves.

Spittlebug froth.

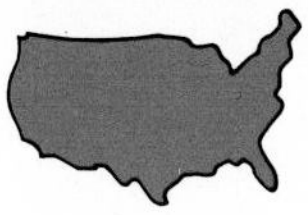

PROBLEM: Masses of white, frothy foam are clustered between the leaves and stems. If the froth is removed, small, green, soft-bodied insects can be seen feeding on the plant tissue. The plant may be stunted.

ANALYSIS: Spittlebugs
These insects, also known as *froghoppers*, appear in the spring. Spittlebug eggs, laid in the fall, survive the winter to hatch when the weather warms in the spring. The young spittlebugs, called *nymphs*, produce a foamy froth that protects them from sun and predators. This froth envelops the nymphs completely while they suck sap from the tender stems and leaves. The adult spittlebugs are not as damaging as the nymphs. The adults are 1/4 inch long, pale yellow to dark brown, and winged. They hop or fly away quickly when disturbed. Spittlebugs seldom harm plants, but if the infestation is very heavy, the plant may be stunted. Their presence is usually objectionable only for cosmetic reasons.

SOLUTION: Wash spittlebugs from plants with a garden hose. If plants are heavily infested, spray with an insecticide containing *malathion*, *acephate* (ORTHENE®), or *methoxychlor*. Make sure that the plant is listed on the product label. Repeated treatments are not usually necessary.

Cineraria damaged by nocturnal insects.

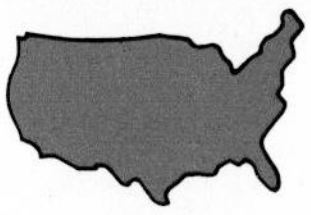

PROBLEM: Holes appear in the leaves and flowers. Some of the leaves, stems, and flowers may be sheared off. There are no insects to be seen feeding on the plants during the day. When the affected plants are inspected at night with a flashlight, insects may be seen feeding on the foliage and flowers.

ANALYSIS: Nocturnal insects
Several kinds of insects feed on plants only at night, including some beetles, weevils, and caterpillars, and all earwigs and cutworms. Beetles are hard-bodied insects with tough, leathery wing covers. The wing covers meet in the middle of the back, forming a straight line. Weevils look like beetles, except that they have elongated snouts. Earwigs are reddish brown, flat, elongated insects up to 1 inch long with pincers projecting from the rear of the body. Caterpillars and cutworms are smooth or hairy soft-bodied worms. These insects usually hide in the soil, in debris, or in other protected locations during the day.

SOLUTION: Control these insects by spraying with insecticides. For more information about controlling nocturnal insects, look up beetles on page 865; weevils on page 866; earwigs on page 893; caterpillars on page 870; and cutworms on page 871.

PROBLEMS COMMON TO MANY FLOWERS — SEEDLINGS DIE

Snails feeding on hosta (¼ life size).

Damping-off on petunia.

Damping-off on snapdragon.

PROBLEM: Holes are chewed in the leaves, or entire leaves may be sheared from the stems. Flowers are partially eaten. Silvery trails wind around on the plants and soil nearby. Snails or slugs may be seen moving around or feeding on the plants, especially at night. Check for them by inspecting the garden at night by flashlight.

ANALYSIS: Snails and slugs
These pests are mollusks, and are related to clams, oysters, and other shellfish. They feed on a wide variety of garden plants. Like other mollusks, snails and slugs need to be moist all the time. For this reason, they avoid direct sun and dry places, and hide during the day in damp places, such as under flower pots or in thick groundcover. They emerge at night or on cloudy days to feed. Snails and slugs are similar in appearance, except that the snail has a hard shell, into which it withdraws when disturbed. Slugs lay masses of white eggs encased in a slimy mass in protected places. Snails bury their eggs in the soil, also in a slimy mass. The young look like miniature versions of their parents.

SOLUTION: Scatter ORTHO Slug-Geta Snail & Slug Bait or ORTHO Bug-Geta Snail & Slug Pellets in bands around the areas you wish to protect. Also scatter the bait in areas where snails or slugs might be hiding, such as in dense groundcovers, weedy areas, compost piles, or pot storage areas. Before spreading the bait, wet down the treated areas to encourage snail and slug activity that night. Repeat the application every 2 weeks as long as snails and slugs are active.

PROBLEM: Seedlings fail to emerge.

ANALYSIS: Germination problems
Seeds may fail to emerge for several reasons:

1. *Dehydration:* Once the seeds have started to grow, even before they have emerged from the soil, they will die easily if allowed to dry out.

2. *Damping-off:* Germinating seedlings are very susceptible to damping-off, a plant disease caused by fungi. These fungi inhabit most soils, decaying the young seedlings as they emerge from the seed. Damping-off is favored by wet, rich soil.

3. *Slow germination:* Seeds of different kinds of plants vary considerably in the amount of time they require to germinate.

4. *Poor seed viability:* Seeds that are old, diseased, or of inferior quality may fail to germinate.

5. *Wrong planting depth:* Seeds of different kinds of flowers vary in their planting depth requirements. If planted too deeply or shallowly, the seeds may fail to germinate.

6. *Seeds washed away:* If a seedbed is flooded or watered with a forceful spray, the seeds may wash away. Heavy rains can also wash seeds away.

7. *Cold weather:* Cold weather may delay seed germination considerably, or prevent germination entirely.

SOLUTION: The numbered solutions below correspond to the numbers in the analysis.

1. Do not allow the soil to dry out completely. Check the seedbed and seed flats at least once a day. Water when the soil surface starts to dry slightly.

2. Allow the soil surface to dry slightly between waterings. Do not start seeds in soil that is high in nitrogen. Add nitrogen fertilizers after the seedlings have produced their first true leaves. For more information on starting seeds, see page 925.

3. Check the list of flower germination periods on page 1004 to see if your seeds germinate slowly.

4. Purchase seeds from a reputable nursery or seed company. Plant seeds packed for the current year.

5. Plant seeds at the proper depth. For a list of seed planting depths, see page 1004.

6. Water seedbeds gently. Do not allow the water to puddle and run off. Use a watering can or hose nozzle that delivers a gentle spray.

7. Even though germination may be delayed, many of the seeds will probably sprout when the weather warms up. Next year, plant seeds later in the season, after the soil has warmed up. For a list of common flowers and their ideal germination temperatures and planting times, see page 1004.

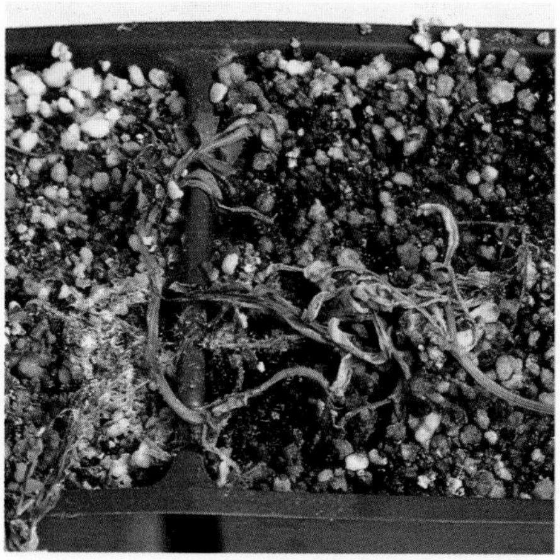
Damping-off of marigold seedlings.

PROBLEM: Seedlings die soon after emerging from the soil, and are found lying on the ground.

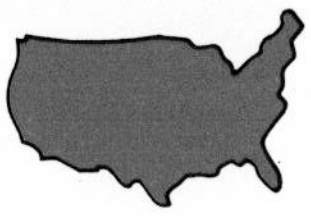

ANALYSIS: Wilted seedlings
Seedlings may wilt and die from lack of water or from disease:
1. *Dehydration:* Seedlings are succulent, and have shallow roots. If the soil dries out even an inch or so below the surface, they may die.
2. *Damping-off:* Young seedlings are very susceptible to damping-off, a plant disease caused by fungi. Damping-off is favored by wet soil with a high nitrogen level. Damping-off can be a problem when the weather remains cold, or cloudy and wet while seeds are germinating, or if seedlings are too heavily shaded.

SOLUTION: The numbered solutions below correspond to the numbers in the analysis.
1. Do not allow the soil to dry out completely. Water when the soil surface starts to dry slightly. During warm or windy weather, you may need to water several times a day.
2. Allow the soil surface to dry slightly between waterings. Do not start seeds in soil that is rich in nitrogen. Add nitrogen fertilizers after the seedlings have produced their first true leaves. Protect seeds during germination by coating them with a fungicide containing *captan* (ORTHOCIDE®), *thiram*, or *chloroneb*. Add a pinch of fungicide to a packet of seeds (or ½ teaspoon per pound), and shake well to coat the seeds with the fungicide. For more information about damping-off, see page 858. For more information about starting seeds, see page 917.

Seedlings sheared off by snails.

PROBLEM: Seedlings are sheared off and eaten, with only the stems emerging from the ground. Silvery trails wind around on the plants and soil nearby. Snails or slugs may be seen moving around or feeding on the plants, especially at night. Check for them by inspecting the garden after dark with a flashlight.

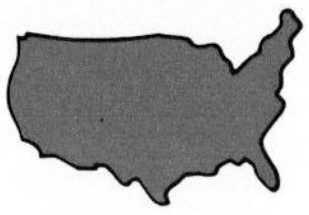

ANALYSIS: Snails and slugs
These pests are mollusks, and are related to clams, oysters, and other shellfish. They feed on a wide variety of garden plants. Like other mollusks, snails and slugs need to be moist all the time. For this reason, they avoid direct sun and dry places, and hide during the day in damp places, such as under flower pots or in thick groundcover. They emerge at night or on cloudy days to feed. Snails and slugs are similar in appearance, except that the snail has a hard shell into which it withdraws when disturbed. Slugs lay masses of white eggs encased in a slimy mass in protected places. Snails bury their eggs in the soil, also in a slimy mass. The young look like miniature versions of their parents.

SOLUTION: Scatter ORTHO Slug-Geta Snail & Slug Bait or ORTHO Bug-Geta Snail & Slug Pellets in bands around the areas you wish to protect. Also scatter the bait in areas where snails or slugs might be hiding, such as in dense groundcovers, weedy areas, compost piles, or pot storage areas. Before spreading the bait, wet down the treated areas to encourage snail and slug activity that night. Repeat the application every 2 weeks as long as snails and slugs are active.

Cutworm damage to petunia seedlings.

PROBLEM: Seedlings are chewed or cut off near the ground. Gray, brown, or black worms, 1½ to 2 inches long, may be found about 2 inches deep in the soil near the base of the damaged plants. The worms coil when disturbed.

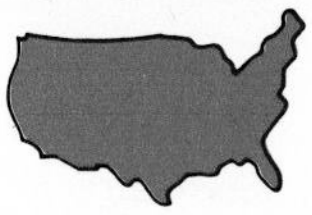

ANALYSIS: Cutworms
Several species of cutworms attack plants in the vegetable garden. The most likely pests of seedlings planted early in the season are the surface-feeding cutworms. A single surface-feeding cutworm can sever the stems of many young plants in one night. Cutworms hide in the soil during the day, and feed only at night. Adult cutworms are dark, night-flying moths with bands or stripes on their forewings. In the South, cutworms may also attack fall-planted seedlings. For more information about cutworms, see page 871.

SOLUTION: Apply ORTHO Soil & Turf Insect Control or ORTHO Vegetable Guard Soil Insect Killer around the base of undamaged plants when stem cutting is observed. Since cutworms are difficult to control, it may be necessary to repeat applications at weekly intervals. Before transplanting in the same area, apply a preventive treatment of one of the above products and work it into the soil. Cultivate the soil thoroughly in late summer and fall to expose and destroy eggs, larvae, and pupae. Further reduce damage with "cutworm collars" around the stem of each plant. These collars can be made of stiff paper, aluminum foil, tin cans, or milk cartons. They should be at least 2 inches high and pressed firmly into the soil.

PROBLEMS OF INDIVIDUAL ANNUALS, PERRENIALS, AND BULBS

This section is arranged alphabetically by the botanical name of each plant. If you are not familiar with the botanical name of your plant, check the index on page 304.

SEEDLINGS DIE

Rabbit.

PROBLEM: Plants and seedlings may be partially or entirely eaten. Mounds of soil, ridges, or tunnels may be clustered in the yard. There may be tiny holes in the soil and small, dry, rectangular brown pellets on the ground near the damaged plants. Various birds and animals may be seen feeding in the garden, or their tracks may be noticed around the damaged plants.

ANALYSIS: Animal pests
There are a number of different animals that feed on flowers. Pocket gophers (found primarily in the West), field mice, rabbits, and deer cause major damage by eating seedlings or mature plants. Certain species of birds feed on seedlings. Moles, squirrels, woodchucks, and raccoons are generally less damaging but may also feed on flower roots, bulbs, and seeds. Even if these animals are not directly observed, their presence is usually evidenced by their tunnels, burrows, droppings, and tracks.

SOLUTION: Fences, cages or screens, traps, repellents, or baits may be used to protect most garden plants from animal damage, or at least to greatly reduce the damage. For more information on specific animal pests and their control, see page 899.

ACHILLEA (YARROW)

Powdery mildew.

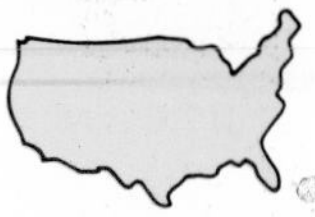

PROBLEM: Leaves and stems are partially or entirely covered with grayish white powdery patches. The patches occur primarily on the upper surfaces of the leaves. The leaves may turn yellow and die.

ANALYSIS: Powdery mildew
This common plant disease is caused by a fungus (*Erysiphe cichoracearum*) that thrives in both humid and dry weather. The powdery patches consist of fungal strands and spores. The spores are spread by the wind to healthy plants. The fungus saps plant nutrients, causing yellowing and sometimes death of the leaf. Under favorable conditions, powdery mildew can spread through a closely spaced planting in a matter of days or weeks.

SOLUTION: Spray with a fungicide containing *dinocap* to stop the spread of the disease. *Dinocap* protects the new healthy foliage, but will not eradicate the fungus on leaves that are already infected. Spray at regular intervals of 10 to 12 days, or as often as necessary to protect new growth. Use a spreader-sticker when spraying. (For information on spreader-stickers, see page 915.) Space plants far enough apart to allow good air circulation. Avoid watering in the late afternoon or evening. Clean up infected leaves and debris.

Achillea cultural information
Light: Full sun
Water: Allow to dry between waterings
Soil: Any kind
Fertilizer: Medium

AGERATUM (FLOSS FLOWER)

Gray mold.

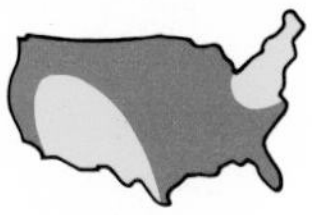

PROBLEM: Brown spots and blotches appear on the leaves and possibly on the stems. As the disease progresses, a fuzzy brown or grayish mold forms on the infected tissue. Gray mold and spots may appear on the flower, especially during periods of cool, wet weather. The leaves and stems may be soft and rotted.

ANALYSIS: Gray mold
This widespread plant disease is caused by a fungus (*Botrytis* species). The fungus initially attacks foliage and flowers that are weak or dead, causing spotting and mold. The fuzzy mold that develops is composed of millions of microscopic spores. Once gray mold has become established on plant debris and weak or dying leaves and flowers, it can invade healthy plant tissue. Splashing water spreads the fungus, as can bits of infected plant debris that land on the leaves. Crowded plantings, rain, and overhead watering enhance the spread of the disease. Cool temperatures and high humidity favor gray mold growth. In warm areas where freezing is rare, gray mold can be a year-round problem.

SOLUTION: Spray infected plants once every 10 to 14 days with a fungicide containing *maneb* or *mancozeb*. Continue spraying as long as mold is visible. Clean up plant debris, and remove old flowers and dying or infected leaves and stems. Avoid wetting the foliage.

Ageratum cultural information
Light: Sun
Water: While the soil is still moist
Soil: Rich, well drained
Fertilizer: Medium to heavy

Root and stem rot.

PROBLEM: Wilting may start on the lower leaves and progress up the plant until all the leaves are wilted; or it may occur very rapidly. Lower leaves and stems often rot. When the plant is pulled out of the ground, the roots are found to be very dark and sometimes badly rotted.

ANALYSIS: Root and stem rot
This disease is caused by fungi (*Rhizoctonia solani* and *Pythium mamillatum*) that are present in most soils. *Rhizoctonia* is a problem all over the country; *Pythium* is more common in the West. These fungi can live for several years on organic matter in the soil. They thrive in moist, fertile conditions. *Pythium* prefers heavy, poorly aerated soils, while *Rhizoctonia* favors aerated, well-drained soils. The fungi initially attack the main stem at the soil line or the root system, stunting the plant and causing it to wilt. They then move into the stems and lower leaves, causing rot and eventual death. They also attack seedlings and cause damping-off. For information about damping-off, see page 850.

SOLUTION: If all the foliage is wilted, it is best to replace the plants. Try to save plants not so severely affected by letting the soil dry out between waterings. (For further information on this technique, see page 849.) This drying out process also helps prevent further spread of the disease to healthy plants. Plant in well-drained soil. For information about improving soil drainage, see page 907.

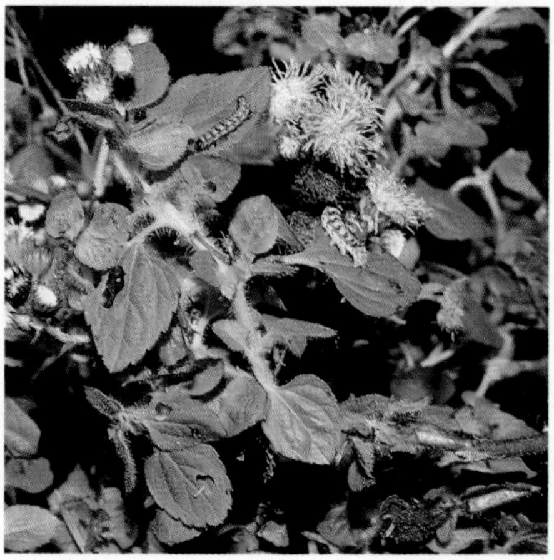

Corn earworms (⅛ life size).

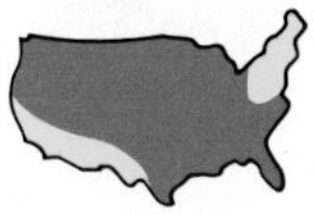

PROBLEM: Striped green, brown, or yellow caterpillars are chewing holes in leaves and buds. The caterpillars range in size from ¼ inch to 2 inches.

ANALYSIS: Tobacco budworm and corn earworm (*Heliothis* species)
These closely related caterpillars are the larval stages of night-flying moths. In addition to feeding on many different ornamental plants, the caterpillars of both moths are major agricultural pests. The corn earworm especially is considered one of the most destructive pests of corn in the country. The moths survive the winter as pupae in the soil, emerging in the spring to lay their light yellow eggs singly on the undersides of leaves. The caterpillars hatch in 2 to 8 days and feed for several weeks on leaves and buds, then crawl into the soil and pupate. One to three weeks later the new adults emerge to begin the cycle again, laying eggs in the evenings and on warm, overcast days. In cooler areas of the country, the caterpillars are present from early spring to the first frost. In warmer areas, the feeding caterpillars are present year-round.

SOLUTION: Control corn earworms and tobacco budworms with ORTHO Orthene Systemic Insect Control or ORTHO Liquid Sevin, applied when the caterpillars first appear. Repeat every 10 to 14 days as needed. Deep cultivating in the fall and winter will help destroy some of the overwintering pupae.

AGERATUM (FLOSS FLOWER)

Whiteflies (half life size).

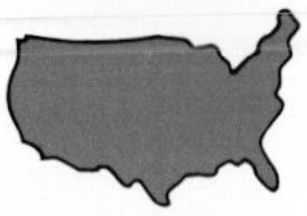

PROBLEM: Tiny, winged insects 1/12 inch long are found mainly on the lower surfaces of leaves. The insects are covered with white, waxy powder. When the plant is touched, insects flutter rapidly around it. Leaves may be mottled and yellowing.

ANALYSIS: Greenhouse whitefly
(*Trialeurodes vaporariorum*)
Greenhouse whitefly is a common insect pest of many garden and greenhouse plants. The four-winged adult lays eggs on the undersides of leaves. The larvae are the size of a pinhead and look quite different from the adult. The larvae are flat, oval-shaped, and semitransparent, with white waxy filaments radiating from the body. They remain attached to the underside of a leaf for about a month before changing to the adult form. Both the larval and adult forms suck sap from the leaves. The larvae are more damaging because they feed more heavily. In warm winter areas, the insect can be active year-round, with eggs, larvae, and adults present at the same time. The whitefly is unable to live through freezing winters. Spring reinfestations in freezing winter areas come from migrating whiteflies and infested greenhouse-grown plants placed in the garden.

SOLUTION: Control whiteflies by spraying with ORTHO Orthene Systemic Insect Control or ORTHO Isotox Insect Killer every 7 to 10 days as necessary, being careful to cover both the upper and lower surfaces of the leaves.

ALCEA (HOLLYHOCK)

Rust.

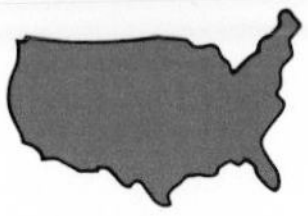

PROBLEM: Yellow or orange spots appear on the upper surfaces of the leaves in the early spring. Reddish brown pustules develop on the undersides of the leaves and possibly on the stems. These pustules may turn brown as the growing season progresses. Severely infected leaves shrivel, turn gray or tan, and hang down.

ANALYSIS: Rust
This fungus (*Puccinia malvacearum*) causes the most serious and widespread disease of hollyhock. The fungus spends the winter as spores on living plant tissue and plant debris. Infection starts in the early spring as soon as conditions are favorable for plant growth. The spores are spread to healthy plants by splashing water and air currents. A number of weeds known as cheeseweeds or mallows (*Malva* species) are frequently infected with rust, and are a source of spores. Rust is also favored by wet conditions.

SOLUTION: Spray with a fungicide containing *chlorothalonil* (DACONIL 2787®) in the spring as soon as the first signs of infection are noticed. Spray the foliage thoroughly, being sure to cover both the upper and lower surfaces of the leaves. These fungicides protect the new, healthy foliage, but do not eradicate the fungus on diseased leaves. Spray once every 7 to 10 days, or as often as necessary to protect new growth until the end of the growing season. Remove and destroy all infected foliage in the fall when the plant has stopped growing, and again in early spring just as the new foliage starts to grow. Pick off and destroy infected plant parts during the growing season. Remove and destroy any nearby cheeseweed plants that may harbor rust.

Spider mites and webbing.

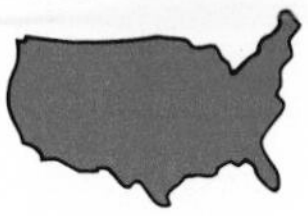

PROBLEM: Leaves are stippled, yellowing, and dirty. Leaves may dry out and drop. There may be webbing over flower buds, between leaves, or on the lower surfaces of the leaves. To determine if the plant is infested with mites, hold a sheet of white paper underneath an affected leaf and tap the leaf sharply. Minute green, red, or yellow specks the size of pepper grains will drop to the paper and begin to crawl around. These pest are easily seen against the white background.

ANALYSIS: Two-spotted spider mite
(*Tetranychus urticae*)
These mites, related to spiders, are major pests of many garden and greenhouse plants. They cause damage by sucking sap from the underside of the leaves. As a result the green leaf pigment disappears, producing the stippled appearance. Mites are active throughout the growing season, but are favored by hot, dry weather (70°F and up). By midsummer, they build up to tremendous numbers. For more information about spider mites, see page 887.

SOLUTION: Spray with a pesticide containing *dicofol* (KELTHANE®) when damage is first noticed. Spray the foliage thoroughly, covering both the upper and lower surfaces of the leaves. Repeat the spraying 3 more times at 7 day intervals. Remove severely infested leaves.

Alcea cultural information
Light: Full sun
Water: Do not allow to dry out
Soil: Rich, loamy
Fertilizer: Heavy

ALLIUM (ORNAMENTAL ONION)

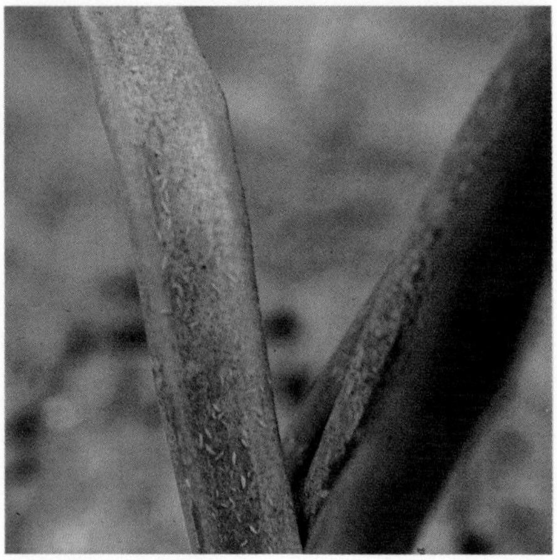

Onion thrips (life size).

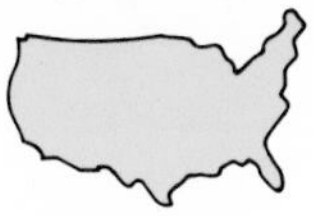

PROBLEM: Silvery white streaks appear on the leaves, and the leaf tips may be brown and distorted. The leaves may eventually wither and die. If the affected leaves are peeled away from the stem, tiny (1/25 inch) insects resembling brown or straw-colored wood slivers can be seen moving around.

ANALYSIS: Thrips
Several species of this common insect pest attack alliums, including the onion thrips (*Thrips tabaci*). Thrips are usually found in the protected area between the base of the leaves and the stem, where they feed by rasping the soft plant tissue, then sucking the released sap. In cold climates, thrips feed and reproduce from spring until fall. With the onset of freezing weather, they find sheltered areas such as grass clumps and hibernate through the winter. In warm winter climates, thrips feed and reproduce all year. These pests reach their population peak in late spring to midsummer. They are especially troublesome during prolonged dry spells.

SOLUTION: Thrips can be kept under control, although not eliminated entirely. Spray plants with an insecticide containing *acephate* (ORTHENE®) or *carbaryl* (SEVIN®) 2 or 3 times at weekly intervals. Repeat the spray if reinfestation occurs. Pick off and destroy old infested leaves and flowers.

Allium cultural information
Light: Sun
Water: While soil is still moist
Soil: Well drained
Fertilizer: Light

Onion white rot.

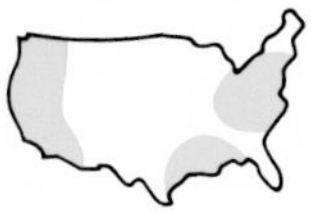

PROBLEM: Flower stalks fail to develop. Leaves decay at the base, yellow, wilt, and collapse, and the plant finally dies. Infected bulbs, roots, and stems are covered with white fluffy masses of fungal stands that eventually develop small black pellets the size of pinheads. Diseased bulbs may develop a soft, watery rot. Bulbs and roots are partially or entirely rotted.

ANALYSIS: Onion white rot
This soil-borne disease is caused by a fungus (*Sclerotium cepivorum*) that attacks the onion family. White rot initially attacks plant stems at the soil level, then moves down into the bulb and roots, causing rot and plant death. White rot is spread by diseased bulbs and transplants, moving water, wind, infested soils, and contaminated tools. The fungus remains viable indefinitely in the soil. White rot is favored by moist conditions and soil temperatures of 50° to 70°F.

SOLUTION: Chemical controls are not effective on diseased plants. White rot is best combatted by using preventive cultural controls. Plant only disease-free bulbs and transplants. Remove and destroy all infected plants and debris. Do not recycle them into compost; the fungal pellets will persist and reinfect new plants. Do not plant alliums in an area where white rot has occurred in previous years.

ANEMONE (WINDFLOWER)

Tuber rot.

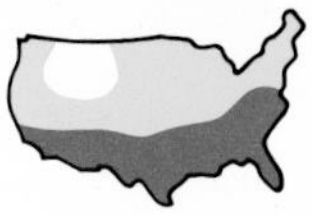

PROBLEM: Flowers fail to develop. Leaves decay at the base, yellow, wilt, and collapse, and the plant dies. The base of the plant and the lower stems are covered with white matted strands that eventually develop small brown pellets the size of pinheads. The tubers and roots are partially or entirely rotted. The diseased tubers may develop a soft rot. Tubers may fail to produce foliage at all in the spring.

ANALYSIS: Tuber rot
This disease, also known as *southern blight*, is caused by a fungus (*Sclerotium rolfsii*) that lives in the soil. It is widespread and attacks many different plants. Tuber rot may infect and decay tubers in the ground that have not yet produced foliage. It generally attacks plant stems at the soil level and then moves down into the tuber and roots, causing rot and plant death. The fungus can grow over the soil to attack adjacent plants. Tuber rot is spread by diseased tubers and transplants, seeds, moving water, infested soil, and contaminated tools. This fungus can persist in the soil for many years. It is favored by warm (70°F and up), moist conditions.

SOLUTION: Chemical controls are not effective on diseased plants. Remove and destroy all infected plants and surrounding soil for 6 inches beyond the diseased area. Drench the area where the infected plants were growing with a fungicide containing *PCNB*. To help prevent infection next year, spread a *PCNB* fungicide onto uninfested soil and dig it in to a depth of 6 inches before planting healthy tubers.

Leaf spot.

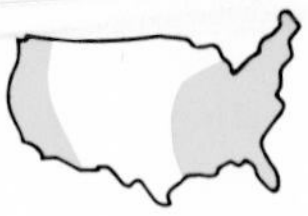

PROBLEM: Spots and blotches appear on the leaves. The spots may be yellow, red, tan, gray, or brown. They range in size from barely visible to ¼ inch in diameter. Several spots may join to form blotches. Leaves may be yellow and dying. Leaf spotting is most severe in warm, humid weather. In some cases, a fine gray mold covers the infected leaf tissue in damp conditions.

ANALYSIS: Leaf spot
Several different fungi cause leaf spots. Some of these fungi may eventually kill the plant, or weaken it so that it becomes susceptible to attack by other organisms. Others merely cause spotting that is unsightly but not harmful. These fungi are spread by splashing water, wind, insects, and tools. They generally survive the winter in diseased plant debris. Some of the leaf spot organisms affect a large number of plants. Most of these fungi do their greatest damage during mild weather (50° to 85°F).

SOLUTION: Spray with a fungicide containing *basic copper sulfate* at intervals of 3 to 10 days. Because leaf spots are favored by warm, humid conditions, it is important to spray frequently during these periods. *Basic copper sulfate* protects the new healthy foliage but will not eradicate the fungus on leaves that are already infected. Pick off infected leaves, and clean up plant debris.

Anemone cultural information
Light: Sun to partial shade
Water: Do not allow to dry out
Soil: Rich, well drained
Fertilizer: Medium

Aphids (life size).

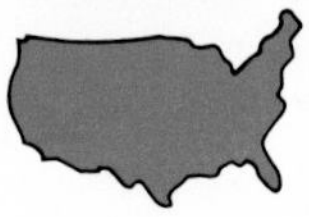

PROBLEM: Flowers are streaked and malformed. Young leaves are curled and distorted. A shiny, sticky substance may coat the leaves. Tiny (⅛ inch) green, soft-bodied insects cluster on the buds, leaves, and stems. Ants may be present.

ANALYSIS: Aphids
Aphids do little damage in small numbers. However, they are extremely prolific and populations can rapidly build up to damaging numbers during the growing season. Damage occurs when the aphid sucks the juices from the anemone leaves and flower buds. The aphid is unable to digest fully all the sugar in the plant sap, and excretes the excess in a fluid called honeydew, which often drops onto the leaves below. Ants feed on this sticky substance, and are often present where there is an aphid infestation. For more information about aphids, see page 875.

SOLUTION: Spray with ORTHO Liquid Sevin as soon as the insects appear. Repeat the spray if the plant becomes reinfested.

ANTIRRHINUM (SNAPDRAGON)

ADAPTATION: Throughout the United States.

FLOWERING TIME: Fall through late spring in zones 9 and 10. Spring through midsummer in colder areas. To determine your zone, see the map on page 1020.

LIGHT: Full sun.

PLANTING TIME: Plant in the fall in zones 9 and 10. In colder areas, plant in the spring when all danger of frost is past.

SOIL: Any good garden soil. pH 6.0 to 7.5

FERTILIZER: Fertilize with ORTHO Rose & Flower Food or ORTHO General Purpose Plant Food according to label directions.

WATER:
How much: Apply enough water to wet the soil to 12 inches deep.
Containers: Apply enough water so that 10 percent of the water drains from the bottom of the container.
How often: Water when the soil 1 inch below the surface is just barely moist.

HANDLING: For bushy plants, pinch off growing tips when the plants have 4 to 6 sets of leaves. Cut back the fading flower spikes to stimulate continued bloom.

Rust.

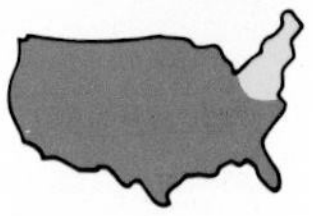

PROBLEM: Pale yellow spots appear on the upper surfaces of the leaves. Reddish brown pustules of spores develop on the undersides of the leaves. Often these pustules form concentric circles. There may be spores on the stems. Severely infected leaves dry up. The plant is stunted and may die prematurely.

ANALYSIS: Rust
This common disease of snapdragons is caused by a fungus (*Puccinia antirrhini*). Fungal spores are spread by wind and splashing water. Rust can survive only on living plant tissue and as spores on seed. It does not persist on dead plant parts. Plants must be wet for 6 to 8 hours before the fungus can infect the leaf surface. The disease is favored by moist conditions, cool nights (50° to 55°F), and warm days (70° to 75°F). Temperatures in the 90°F range and higher kill the spores.

SOLUTION: Spray infected plants with a fungicide containing *maneb* or *zineb* at intervals of 5 to 18 days. Avoid wetting the foliage. Water in the morning rather than the late afternoon or evening to give foliage a chance to dry out. Pick off and destroy infected plant parts during the growing season. Remove all snapdragon plants at the end of the growing season to prevent infected plants from reinfecting new plantings. Space plants far enough apart to allow good air circulation.

Root and stem rot.

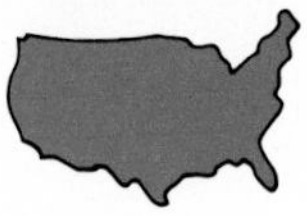

PROBLEM: The plant may suddenly wilt and die, or it may die slowly from the top down. The leaves turn yellow, and overall growth is stunted. There may be lesions on the stems. The roots are decayed.

ANALYSIS: Root and stem rot
This disease is caused by a number of different fungi that live in the soil. They thrive in waterlogged, heavy soils. The fungi can attack the plant stems and roots directly or enter them through wounds. Infection causes the stems and roots to decay, resulting in wilting, yellowing leaves, and plant death. These fungi are generally spread by infested soil and transplants, contaminated equipment, and moving water. Many of these organisms also cause *damping-off* of seedlings (see page 850).

SOLUTION: Let the soil dry out between irrigations. (For more information on this technique, see page 849.) Improve soil drainage. For more information about soil drainage, see page 907. Before planting next year, apply *PCNB* to the soil and work it in to a depth of 6 inches.

Spider mites and their damage.

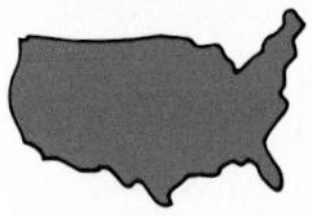

PROBLEM: Leaves are stippled, yellowing, and dirty. Leaves may dry out and drop. There may be webbing over flower buds, between leaves, or on the lower surfaces of leaves. To determine if the plant is infested with mites, hold a sheet of white paper underneath an affected plant and tap the stalk sharply. Minute green, red, or yellow specks the size of pepper grains will drop to the paper and begin to crawl around. These pests are easily seen against the white background.

ANALYSIS: Spider mites
(*Tetranychus urticae*)
These mites, related to spiders, are major pests of many garden and greenhouse plants. They cause damage by sucking sap from the underside of the leaves. As a result, the green leaf pigment disappears, producing the stippled appearance. Mites are active throughout the growing season, but are favored by hot, dry weather (70°F and up). By midsummer, they can build up to tremendous numbers. For more information about spider mites, see page 887.

SOLUTION: Spray with ORTHO Isotox Insect Killer when damage is first noticed. Spray the foliage thoroughly, covering both the upper and lower surfaces of the leaves.

ANTIRRHINUM (SNAPDRAGON) — AQUILEGIA (COLUMBINE)

Gray mold.

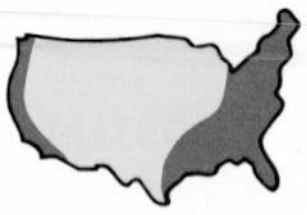

PROBLEM: Brown spots and blotches appear on leaves and possibly on stems. As the disease progresses, a fuzzy brown or grayish mold forms on the infected tissue. Gray mold and spots often appear on the flowers, especially during periods of cool, wet weather. The leaves and stems may be soft and rotted.

ANALYSIS: Gray mold
This widespread plant disease is caused by a fungus (*Botrytis cinerea*) that is found on most dead plant tissue. The fungus initially attacks foliage and flowers that are weak or dead, causing spotting and mold. The fuzzy mold that develops is composed of fungal strands and millions of microscopic spores. Once gray mold has become established on plant debris and weak or dying leaves and flowers, it can invade healthy plant tissue. The fungus is spread by splashing water, wind, or by infected pieces of plant tissue contacting healthy tissue. Cool temperatures and high humidity favor gray mold growth. Crowded plantings, rain, and overhead watering also enhance the spread of the disease. Infection is more of a problem in spring and fall, when temperatures are lower. In warm winter areas where freezing is rare, gray mold can be a year-round problem.

SOLUTION: Spray infected plants once every 10 to 14 days with a fungicide containing *benomyl*. Continue spraying as long as the mold is visible. Clean up plant debris, and remove dying or infected leaves, stems, and flowers. Provide enough space between plants to allow good air circulation. Try to avoid wetting the foliage and flowers when watering.

Leafminer damage.

PROBLEM: White or light green winding trails and blotches appear in the leaves. Some of the trails are filled with black matter. The infested leaves may turn white and die.

ANALYSIS: Columbine leafminer
(*Phytomyza* species)
This insect belongs to the family of leafmining flies. The pale brown adult fly lays its eggs on the undersides of leaves. The eggs hatch and the larvae that emerge penetrate the leaf and live between the upper and lower surfaces of the leaf. They feed on the inner leaf tissue, creating winding trails. Their dark excrement may dot or partially fill sections of the trails. The larvae may be continually present from spring until fall.

SOLUTION: Spray with an insecticide containing *malathion* and a spreader-sticker. (For information on spreader-stickers, see page 922.) Respray at the first sign of further infestation. Pick off and destroy infected leaves. Remove and destroy all plant remains in the fall.

Aquilegia cultural information
Light: Shade, filtered sun
Water: While the soil is still moist
Soil: Well drained
Fertilizer: Medium

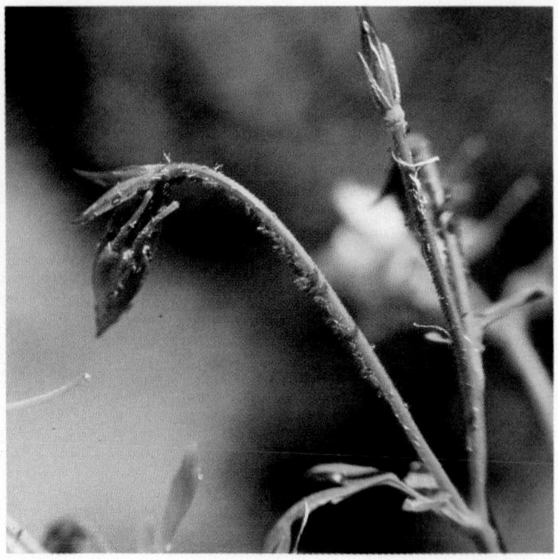

Aphids.

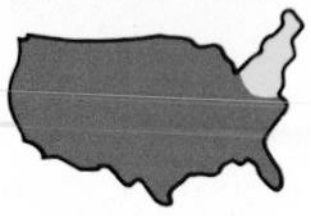

PROBLEM: Tiny (1/8 inch) green, cream-colored, or brown soft-bodied insects cluster on the buds, leaves, and stems. Young leaves are curled and distorted. There may be a shiny, sticky substance coating the leaves. Ants may be present.

ANALYSIS: Aphids
Aphids do little damage in small numbers. However, they are extremely prolific and populations can rapidly build up to damaging numbers during the growing season. Damage occurs when the aphid sucks the juices from the columbine leaves and flower buds. The aphid is unable to digest fully all the sugar in the plant sap and excretes the excess in a fluid called honeydew. The honeydew often drops onto the leaves below. Ants feed on this sticky material and are often present where there is an aphid infestation. For more information about aphids, see page 875.

SOLUTION: Spray with ORTHO Liquid Sevin or an insecticide containing *malathion* as soon as the insects appear. Repeat the spray if the plant is reinfested. Use a spreader-sticker when spraying. (For information on spreader-stickers, see page 922.)

Powdery mildew.

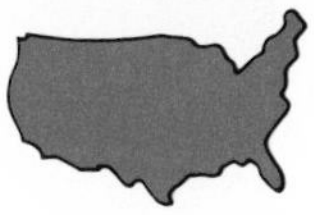

PROBLEM: Leaves and stems are partially or entirely covered with grayish-white, powdery patches. The patches occur primarily on the upper surfaces of the leaves. The leaves may be yellowing and dying.

ANALYSIS: Powdery mildew
This common plant disease is caused by a fungus (*Erysiphe polygoni*) that thrives in both humid and dry weather. The powdery patches consist of fungal strands and spores. The spores are spread by the wind to healthy plants. The fungus saps plant nutrients, causing yellowing and sometimes death of the leaf. Since this mildew attacks many different kinds of plants, the fungus from a diseased plant may infect other types of plants in the garden. (See page 1006 for a list of susceptible plants.) Under favorable conditions, powdery mildew can spread through a closely spaced planting in a matter of days or weeks.

SOLUTION: Spray with ORTHO Orthorix Spray to stop the spread of the fungus. Spray at regular intervals of 10 to 12 days, or as often as necessary to protect new growth. This fungicide protects the new healthy foliage, but will not eradicate the fungus on leaves that are already infected. Space plants far enough apart to allow good air circulation. Clean up infected leaves and debris.

Crown rot.

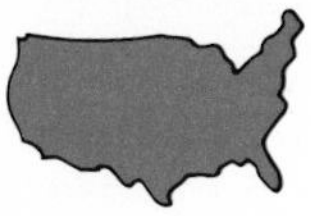

PROBLEM: Leaves and stems are wilting. The diseased branches slowly dry out and finally die. White fungal strands may grow on the stems of severely infected plants. When sliced open, an infected stem may be filled with white fungal threads and small black fungal pellets. The soil around the plant may be filled with white fungal strands and brown spherical pellets the size of a pinhead.

ANALYSIS: Crown rot or wilt
This disease is caused by a fungus (*Sclerotinia sclerotiorum*) that lives in the soil. The fungus survives the winter as fungal strands and dormant pellets in plant debris, or in the soil. It is favored by high humidity and moist soils, and attacks plant roots. *Sclerotinia* produces wind-blown spores in the spring and summer that may also infect the foliage. As the fungus spreads in the plant, wilting and eventual death occur. *Sclerotinia* can persist in the soil for 3 years or more, and is spread by infested soil and transplants.

SOLUTION: Let the soil dry out between waterings. (For more information on this technique, see page 849.) Cultivate the soil around the crown of the plant to help it dry out more quickly. Remove and destroy diseased plants and the soil immediately around them. Before planting columbine in an area that is known to be infested, broadcast a fungicide containing *PCNB* onto the soil and dig it in to a depth of 6 inches.

Leaf spot.

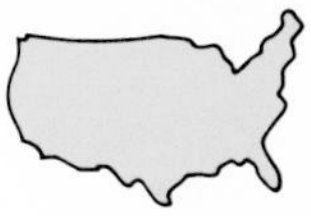

PROBLEM: Spots and blotches appear on the leaves. The spots may be yellow, red, tan, gray, brown, or black. They range in size from barely visible to ¼ inch in diameter. Several spots may join to form blotches. Leaves may be yellowing and dying. Leaf spotting is most severe in warm, humid weather.

ANALYSIS: Leaf spot
Asters are susceptible to several fungi that cause leaf spots. Some of these fungi may eventually kill the plant, or weaken it so that it becomes susceptible to attack by other organisms. Others merely cause spotting that is unsightly but not harmful. These fungi are spread by splashing water, wind, insects, tools, and infected seed. They generally survive the winter in diseased plant debris. Most of these fungi do their greatest damage during mild weather (50° to 85°F). Infection is favored by moist conditions.

SOLUTION: Spray at 7 to 10 day intervals with a fungicide containing *zineb* or *mancozeb*. Because leaf spots are favored by warm, humid conditions, it is important to spray frequently during these periods. These fungicides protect the new healthy foliage but will not eradicate the fungus on leaves that are already infected. Clean up infected leaves and debris.

Aster cultural information
Light: Sun
Water: When the soil is just barely moist
Soil: Well drained
Fertilizer: Medium

ASTER

Powdery mildew.

PROBLEM: Leaves and stems are partially or entirely covered with grayish white powdery patches. The patches occur primarily on the upper surfaces of leaves. The leaves may be yellowing and dying.

ANALYSIS: Powdery mildew
This common plant disease is caused by a fungus (*Erysiphe cichoracearum*) that thrives in both humid and dry weather. The powdery patches consist of fungal strands and spores. The spores are spread by the wind to healthy plants. The fungus saps the plant nutrients, causing yellowing and sometimes death of the leaf. Since this mildew attacks many different kinds of plants, the fungus from a diseased plant may infect other types of plants in the garden. (See page 1006 for a list of susceptible plants.) Under favorable conditions, powdery mildew can spread through a closely spaced planting in a matter of days or weeks.

SOLUTION: Spray with a fungicide containing *phaltan* or *triforine* (FUNGINEX®) to stop the spread of the disease. This fungicide protects the new healthy foliage, but will not remove the spots on leaves that are already infected. Spray at regular intervals of 10 to 12 days, or as often as necessary to protect new growth. Space plants far enough apart to allow good air circulation. Clean up infected leaves and debris.

ASTILBE

Aphid (10 times life size).

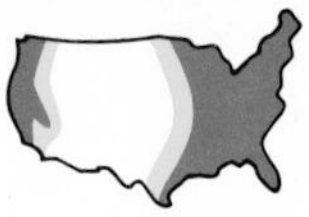

PROBLEM: Young leaves are curled, distorted, and yellowing. The flowers may be malformed. There may be a sticky or shiny substance coating the leaves. Tiny (1/8 inch), pale green to black, soft-bodied insects are clustered on the leaves and stems. Ants may be present.

ANALYSIS: Aphids
Aphids do little damage in small numbers. However, they are extremely prolific and populations can rapidly build up to damaging numbers during the growing season. Damage occurs when the aphid sucks the juices from the leaves and flower buds. The aphid is unable to digest fully all the sugar in the plant sap and excretes the excess in a fluid called honeydew. The honeydew often drops onto the leaves below. Ants feed on this sticky substance, and are often present where there is an aphid infestation. For more information about aphids, see page 875.

SOLUTION: Spray with ORTHO Liquid Sevin as soon as the insects appear. Repeat the spray if the plant is reinfested.

Astilbe cultural information
Light: Shade, filtered sun
Water: While the soil is still moist
Soil: Rich, well drained
Fertilizer: Medium

BEGONIA

BEGONIA

ADAPTATION: Throughout the United States.

FLOWERING TIME:
Tuberous: Early to late summer.
Fibrous: Spring to late fall.

LIGHT:
Tuberous: Filtered light to full shade.
Fibrous: Full shade to half-day sun. Dark-colored plants can tolerate full-day sun.

PLANTING TIME:
Tuberous: Start indoors in the spring in zones 1 through 9. To determine your zone, see the map on page 1020. You may start them outdoors in zone 10.
Fibrous: Start all year round in zones 9 and 10. Start in spring through summer in zones 2 through 8.

SOIL: Well drained, rich in organic matter. pH 6.0 to 7.0

FERTILIZER:
Tuberous: Fertilize with ORTHO Rose & Flower Food every 2 weeks at half the recommended rate. Stop fertilizing about 6 weeks before the first fall frost.
Fibrous: Fertilize with ORTHO Rose & Flower Food or ORTHO General Purpose Plant Food.

WATER:
How much: Apply enough water to wet the soil 6 to 8 inches deep.
Containers: Apply enough water so that 10 percent of the water drains from the bottom of the container.
How often: Water when the soil 1 inch below the surface is moist but not wet.

Gray mold.

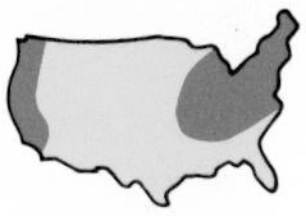

PROBLEM: Brown spots and blotches appear on the leaves and possibly on the stems. As the disease progresses, a fuzzy brown or grayish mold forms on the infected tissue. Gray mold and spots often appear on the flowers, especially during periods of cool, wet weather. The leaves and stems may be soft and rotted.

ANALYSIS: Gray mold
This widespread plant disease is caused by a fungus (*Botrytis cinerea*) that is found on most dead plant tissue. The fungus initially attacks foliage and flowers that are weak or dead, causing spotting and mold. The fuzzy mold that develops is composed of millions of microscopic dark spores. Once gray mold has become established on plant debris and weak or dying leaves and flowers, it can invade healthy plant tissue. Splashing water spreads the fungus, as can bits of infected plant debris that land on the leaves. Cool temperatures and high humidity favor the growth of gray mold. Crowded plantings, rain, and overhead watering also enhance the spread of the disease. Infection is a greater problem in spring and fall when temperatures are lower. In warm winter areas where freezing is rare, gray mold can be a year-round problem.

SOLUTION: Control gray mold with a fungicide containing *benomyl*. Spray every 1 to 2 weeks as long as the mold is visible. Clean up plant debris, and remove dying or infected leaves, stems, and flowers. Provide enough space between plants to allow good air circulation. Try to avoid wetting the foliage when watering.

Leaf spot.

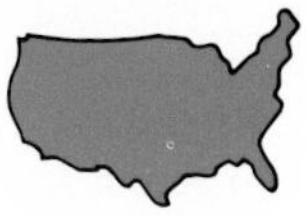

PROBLEM: Spots and blotches appear on the leaves. The spots may be yellow, red, tan, gray, or brown. They range in size from barely visible to ¼ inch in diameter. Several spots may join together to form blotches. Leaves may be yellowing and dying. Leaf spotting is most severe in warm, humid weather.

ANALYSIS: Fungal leaf spot
Begonias are susceptible to several fungi that cause leaf spots. Some of these fungi may eventually kill the plant, or weaken it so that it becomes susceptible to attack by other organisms. Others merely cause spotting that is unsightly but not harmful. These fungi are spread by splashing water, wind, insects, tools, and infected transplants and seed. They survive the winter in diseased plant debris. Some of the leaf spot organisms affect a large number of plants. Most of these fungi do their greatest damage during mild weather (50° to 85°F). Infection is favored by moist conditions.

SOLUTION: Spray with a fungicide containing *zineb* or *benomyl* at intervals of 7 to 10 days. Because leaf spots are favored by warm, humid conditions, it is important to spray frequently during these periods. These fungicides protect the new healthy foliage. In addition, *benomyl* will eradicate the fungus on leaves that are already infected. Clean up infected leaves and debris.

Bacterial leaf spot.

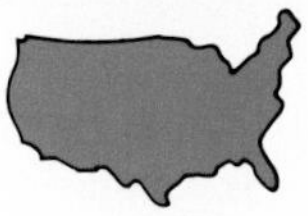

PROBLEM: Small, blister-like spots appear on the leaves. The spots are translucent and turn brown with yellow, translucent margins. The spots enlarge and run together, giving the leaf a blotched appearance. Sometimes a slimy substance oozes from the infected areas, turning light brown as it dries. Infected leaves often die prematurely. If the stems become infected, the entire plant may collapse.

ANALYSIS: Bacterial leaf spot
This disease is caused by bacteria (*Xanthomonas begoniae*) that infect tuberous and fibrous begonias. The slimy substance that oozes from infected lesions is composed of bacterial cells, which can live for 3 months or more. The bacteria are spread by splashing water, contaminated equipment, and infected transplants. Infection is favored by high humidity. Localized leaf infection causes early leaf drop. If the plant's water-conducting tissue is infected, the whole plant will soften and collapse.

SOLUTION: Spray with *basic copper sulfate* or *streptomycin* at intervals of 7 to 10 days to prevent the spread of the disease. Infected tissue will not recover, but new growth and healthy leaves will be protected. Cut off and discard infected plant parts. After working with diseased plants, disinfect tools by dipping them in rubbing alcohol. Remove and destroy severely infected plants and the soil immediately surrounding them. Avoid wetting or splashing the leaves. Space plants far enough apart to allow good air circulation.

BEGONIA

Powdery mildew.

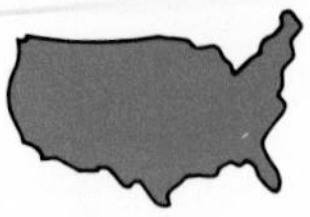

PROBLEM: The leaves and stems are covered with grayish white powdery spots and patches that occur primarily on the upper surfaces of the leaves. Older spots and patches often turn brown. The leaves may be yellow and dying.

ANALYSIS: Powdery mildew
This common plant disease is caused by either of two fungi (*Erysiphe cichoracearum* or *Oidium begoniae*) that thrive in both humid and dry weather. The powdery patches consist of fungal strands and spores. The spores are spread by the wind to healthy plants. The fungi sap plant nutrients, causing yellowing and sometimes death of the leaf. A severe infection may kill the plant. Since these powdery mildews attack many different kinds of plants, the fungus from a diseased plant may infect other types of plants in the garden. (See page 1006 for a list of powdery mildews and the plants they attack.) Under favorable conditions, powdery mildew can spread through a closely spaced planting in a matter of days or weeks.

SOLUTION: Spray ORTHO Orthocide Garden Fungicide or a fungicide containing *triforine* (FUNGINEX®), which protect the new, healthy leaves by preventing powdery mildew spores from entering them. Space plants far enough apart to allow good air circulation. Clean up infected leaves and debris.

Root and stem rot on tuberous begonia.

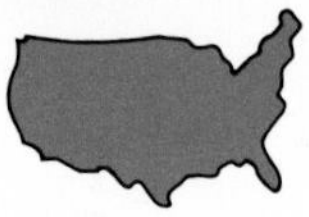

PROBLEM: Growth slows or stops. The roots are dark and rotted. The plant may wilt, topple over, and die. There may be discolored, water-soaked spots on the stems at the soil level. Leaves may be yellow, and the lower leaves and stems may rot. Cobwebby strands may appear on lower portions of the stems in wet weather.

ANALYSIS: Root and stem rot
This disease is caused by a number of different fungi, also known as *water molds,* that persist indefinitely in the soil. They thrive in waterlogged, heavy soils. Some of these fungi attack the plant stems at the soil level, while others attack the roots. Infection causes the roots and stems to decay, resulting in wilting, yellowing leaves, and the death of the plant. These fungi are generally spread by infested soil and transplants, contaminated equipment, and moving water. Many of these organisms also cause damping-off of seedlings. For more information about damping-off, see page 850.

SOLUTION: Allow the soil around the plants to dry out. For more information on this technique, see page 849. Remove and discard severely infected plants. Avoid future root rot problems by planting in well-drained soil. For information on improving soil drainage, see page 907.

Leaf nematode damage.

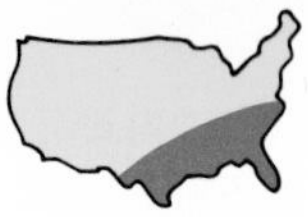

PROBLEM: Angular brown leaf blotches develop on the lower leaves first, then on the upper leaves. The blotches enlarge and eventually the leaves curl up, wither, and drop off. The plant is stunted, and new leaf buds may not develop.

ANALYSIS: Leaf nematode
(*Aphelenchoides olesistus*)
This plant condition is caused by nematodes—microscopic worms that live and feed inside the leaf tissue. Infestation occurs when the foliage is wet. Nematodes migrate in the thin film of water on the outside of the leaf to infect healthy tissue, and are spread from plant to plant by splashing water. They are most severe in warm, humid areas. Leaf nematodes can survive for 3 or more years in plant debris and in the soil.

SOLUTION: Remove and destroy severely infested plants. Pick off and destroy all the infested leaves and the next two leaves directly above them. As much as possible, avoid wetting the foliage. Inspect new plants carefully to be sure they are not diseased, and do not plant in infested soil. Spray weekly with an insecticide containing *malathion* or *dimethoate* using a spreader-sticker, until the symptoms stop spreading. For information on spreader-stickers, see page 915.

Mealybugs (half life size).

PROBLEM: Oval, white insects up to ¼ inch long cluster in white cottony masses on stems and leaves. Leaves may be deformed and withered. The infested leaves are often shiny and sticky.

ANALYSIS: Mealybugs
Several species of this common insect feed on begonias. Mealybugs damage plants by sucking sap, causing leaf distortion and death. The adult female mealybug may produce live young, or may deposit her eggs in white, fluffy masses of wax. The immature mealybugs, called *nymphs*, are very active and crawl all over the plant. Soon after the nymphs begin to feed, they exude filaments of white wax that cover their bodies, giving them a cottony appearance. As they mature, their mobility decreases. Mealybugs cannot fully digest all the sugar in the sap and excrete the excess in a fluid called honeydew. Mealybugs can be spread when they are brushed onto uninfested plants, or when young, active nymphs crawl to nearby plants. They may also be spread by the wind, which can blow egg masses and nymphs from plant to plant. Mealybug eggs and some adults can survive through the winter in warm climates. Spring reinfestations in colder areas come from infested new plants placed in the garden.

SOLUTION: Spray infested plants with ORTHO Orthene Systemic Insect Control. Spray at intervals of 7 to 10 days until the mealybugs are gone. Gently hose down plants to wash off honeydew. Remove and destroy severely infested leaves and plants.

Whitefly damage.

PROBLEM: Tiny, winged insects 1/12 inch long are feeding on the undersides of the leaves. The insects are covered with white, waxy powder. When the plant is touched, insects flutter rapidly around it. Leaves may be mottled and yellowing. In warm winter areas, black mold may cover the leaves.

ANALYSIS: Greenhouse whitefly
(*Trialeurodes vaporariorum*)
This insect is a common pest of many garden and greenhouse plants. The four-winged adult lays eggs on the undersides of leaves. The larvae are the size of a pinhead, flat, oval-shaped, and semitransparent, with white waxy filaments radiating from the body. Both the larval and adult forms suck sap from the leaves. Adults and larvae cannot fully digest all the sugar in the plant sap and excrete the excess in a fluid called honeydew. In warm winter areas the insect can be active year-round. The whitefly is unable to live through freezing winters. Spring reinfestations in freezing winter areas come from migrating whiteflies and from infested greenhouse-grown plants placed in the garden.

SOLUTION: Control whiteflies by spraying with an insecticide containing *malathion* every 7 to 10 days as necessary. Spray the foliage thoroughly, being sure to cover both the upper and lower surfaces of the leaves.

Browallia cultural information
Light: Shade, filtered sun
Water: While the soil is still moist
Soil: Rich, well drained
Fertilizer: Medium

CALENDULA

ADAPTATION: Throughout the United States.

FLOWERING TIME: Fall through late spring in zones 9 and 10. Spring through midsummer in colder areas. To determine your zone, see the map on page 1020.

LIGHT: Full sun.

PLANTING TIME: In zones 3 through 8, plant in the spring when all danger of frost is past. Calendulas can also be planted in the fall in zones 9 and 10.

SOIL: Any good well-drained garden soil. pH 6.0 to 7.5

FERTILIZER: Fertilize with ORTHO Rose & Flower Food or ORTHO General Purpose Plant Food according to label directions.

WATER:
How much: Apply enough water to plants in the ground to wet the soil 6 to 8 inches deep.
Containers: Apply enough water so that 10 percent of the water drains from the bottom of the container.
How often: Water when the soil 1 inch below the surface is just barely moist.

HANDLING: Pinch off fading flowers to encourage continued bloom. Calendulas reseed themselves readily.

CALENDULA

Powdery mildew.

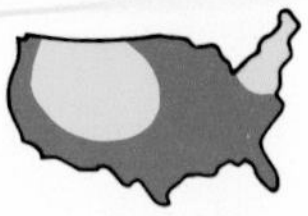

PROBLEM: Stems and the upper surface of leaves are covered with grayish white powdery spots and patches. Older spots and patches may turn brown. Severely infected plants wither and die.

ANALYSIS: Powdery mildew
This common plant disease is caused by a fungus (*Erysiphe cichoracearum*) that thrives in both humid and dry weather. The powdery patches consist of fungal strands and spores. The spores are spread by the wind to healthy plants. The fungus saps plant nutrients, causing yellowing and sometimes death of the leaf. A severe infection may kill the plant. Since some powdery mildews attack many different kinds of plants, the fungus from a diseased plant may infect other types of plants in the garden. (For a list of susceptible plants, see page 1006.) Under favorable conditions, powdery mildew can spread through a closely spaced planting in a matter of days or weeks.

SOLUTION: Spray with ORTHO Funginex Rose Disease Control as soon as the disease is noticed and at intervals of 7 to 10 days thereafter. Pick off yellowed, withered leaves. Space plants far enough apart to allow good air circulation. Clean up infected leaves and debris.

Leaf spot.

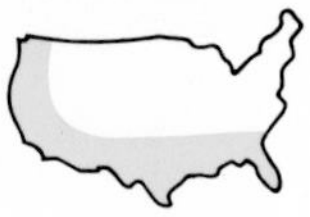

PROBLEM: Small reddish or yellowish spots on the leaves may run together to form blotches. The infected leaf tissue turns ashy gray and has a dry, papery texture. Leaves may die and fall off. Leaf spotting is most severe in warm, humid weather. Fine gray mold may cover infected leaf tissue in damp conditions.

ANALYSIS: Leaf spot
This disease of calendula is primarily caused by the fungus *Cercospora calendulae*, although several other leaf spotting fungi occasionally attack calendula. Some of these fungi may eventually kill the plant, or weaken it so that it becomes susceptible to attack by other organisms. Others merely cause spotting that is unsightly but not harmful. These fungi are spread by splashing water, wind, insects, and tools. Leaf spot organisms are favored by moist conditions and high temperatures. They are most common during the summer months and in warm climates. The fungus survives the winter in or on seeds and in plant debris.

SOLUTION: Spray with a fungicide containing *maneb* at intervals of 7 to 10 days. Because leaf spots are favored by warm, humid conditions, it is important to spray frequently during these periods. *Maneb* protects the new, healthy foliage but will not remove the spots on leaves that are already infected. Remove and destroy plant debris in the fall to help prevent reinfection next spring.

Cabbage loopers (⅓ life size).

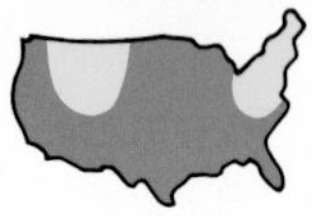

PROBLEM: Foliage and flower buds are chewed. Leaves have ragged edges and irregular or round holes. Green caterpillars up to 1½ inches long with white stripes feed on the leaves.

ANALYSIS: Cabbage looper
(*Trichoplusia ni*)
These destructive caterpillars feed on many garden ornamentals and vegetables. With the warm weather of spring, the brownish adult moth lays its tiny, pale green eggs at night on the upper surfaces of leaves. The eggs hatch into active green larvae, which feed extensively on buds and foliage for 2 to 4 weeks. Looper damage can occur from early spring through late fall. The caterpillars spend the winter as pupae attached to plant leaves.

SOLUTION: Spray with ORTHO Isotox Insect Killer or ORTHO Orthene Systemic Insect Control when the caterpillars first appear. Repeat 10 to 14 days later if reinfestation occurs. In the fall, remove plant debris and weeds that may harbor pupae. *Bacillus thuringiensis*, a biological control, is effective when sprayed on young loopers.

CALLISTEPHUS (CHINA ASTER)

ADAPTATION: Throughout the United States.

FLOWERING TIME: Summer to fall.

LIGHT: Full sun.

PLANTING TIME: Spring, after all danger of frost is past.

SOIL: Any good well-drained garden soil.

FERTILIZER: Fertilize with ORTHO Rose & Flower Food or ORTHO General Purpose Plant Food according to label directions.

WATER:

How much: Apply enough water to wet the soil 8 to 10 inches deep.

Containers: Apply enough water so that 10 percent of the water drains from the bottom of the container.

How often: Water when the soil 1 inch below the surface is just barely moist.

Rust.

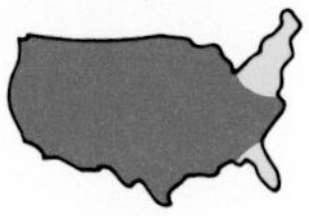

PROBLEM: Orange-red pustules appear on the undersides of the leaves. Severely infected leaves turn yellow and wither.

ANALYSIS: Rust

This plant disease is caused by a fungus (*Coleosporium solidaginis*) that infects china asters and several flowers in the daisy family. The fungus, which may spend part of its life cycle on pine trees, infects asters in the spring. Rust spores are spread from plant to plant by wind and splashing water. The foliage must be wet for at least 6 hours before the fungus can infect the leaf surfaces. Rust can survive only on living plant tissue or as spores on seed. It does not remain infectious on dead plant parts or in the soil. The disease is favored by moist conditions, cool nights, and warm days.

SOLUTION: Spray infected plants thoroughly with ORTHO Funginex Rose Disease Control or ORTHO Orthenex Insect & Disease Control. Pick off severely infected and dying leaves. Water in the morning rather than the late afternoon or evening to allow wet foliage to dry out more quickly. Remove and destroy all infected plants in the fall to prevent them from surviving the winter and reinfecting new plantings.

Fusarium wilt.

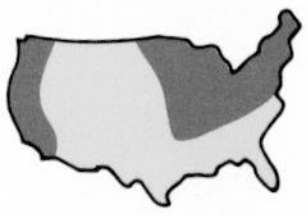

PROBLEM: The lower leaves turn yellow, then wilt and die; or all of the foliage may turn yellow and then wither. Older plants may be stunted. Yellowing and wilting often affect only one side of the plant. The flower heads droop. Dark brown areas may appear on the infected stem. When the stem is sliced open near the base of the plant, dark streaks and discolorations are seen on the inner stem tissue. The root system may be partially or entirely decayed. There may be a pink spore mass on the main stem at or below the soil line.

ANALYSIS: Wilt disease

This disease affects many ornamental plants. In *Callistephus* it is caused by either of two soil-inhabiting fungi (*Verticillium albo-atrum* and *Fusarium oxysporum f. callistephi*) that live on plant debris or in the soil. The disease is spread by contaminated seeds, plants, soil, and equipment. The fungus enters the plant through the roots and spreads up into the stems through the water-conducting vessels. The vessels become discolored and plugged. This plugging cuts off the flow of water to the leaves, which results in leaf yellowing, wilting, and death. For more information about wilt disease, see page 850.

SOLUTION: No chemical control is available. It is best to destroy infected plants. The fungi can be removed from the soil only by fumigation techniques. (For more information about soil fumigation, see page 927.) However, the best solution is usually to use plants that are resistant to wilt diseases. For a list of wilt-resistant plants, see pages 994 and 995.

Aster yellows.

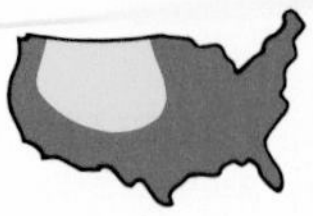

PROBLEM: The leaf veins pale and may lose all their color. Part or all of the foliage yellows. The flowers are distorted and may turn green. The plant may grow many thin stems bearing pale, spindly leaves. The plant is usually dwarfed.

ANALYSIS: Aster yellows

This plant disease is caused by mycoplasmas, microscopic organisms similar to bacteria. The mycoplasmas are transmitted from plant to plant by leafhoppers. (For further information about leafhoppers, see page 878.) The symptoms of aster yellows are more severe and appear more quickly in warm weather. Although the disease may be present in the plant, aster yellows may not manifest its symptoms in temperatures of 55°F or less. The disease also infects many ornamental plants, vegetables, and weeds. For a list of plants susceptible to aster yellows, see page 1005.

SOLUTION: Aster yellows cannot be eliminated entirely, but can be kept under control. Remove and destroy infected China asters. To remove sources of infection, eradicate nearby weeds that may harbor aster yellows and leafhopper eggs. Spray leafhopper-infested plants with ORTHO Orthene Systemic Insect Control. Repeat the spray whenever leafhoppers are seen.

CAMPANULA (BELLFLOWER)

ADAPTATION: Throughout the United States.

FLOWERING TIME: Spring through fall, depending upon the species.

LIGHT: Filtered sun to shade.

PLANTING TIME: Spring, when all danger of frost is past. Campanula can also be planted in fall in zones 9 and 10. To determine your zone, see the map on page 1004.

SOIL: Any good garden soil. pH 5.5 to 7.5

FERTILIZER: Fertilize with ORTHO Rose & Flower Food or ORTHO General Purpose Plant Food according to label directions.

WATER:

How much: Apply enough water to wet the soil 6 to 8 inches deep.

Containers: Apply enough water so that 10 percent of the water drains from the bottom of the container.

How often: Water when the soil 1 inch below the surface is moist but not wet.

Leaf spot.

PROBLEM: Spots and blotches appear on the leaves. The spots may be yellow, red, tan, gray, or brown. They range in size from barely visible to ¼ inch in diameter. Several spots may join to form blotches. Leaves may be yellow and dying. Leaf spotting is most severe in warm, humid weather. In damp conditions, a fine gray mold sometimes covers the infected leaf tissue.

ANALYSIS: Leaf spot

Several different fungi cause leaf spots. These fungi usually just cause spotting, which is unsightly but not harmful. They are spread by splashing water, wind, insects, and tools. They generally survive the winter in diseased plant debris. Most of the leaf spot organisms do their greatest damage in mild weather (50° to 85°F).

SOLUTION: Spray the diseased plants with a *basic copper sulfate* fungicide at intervals of 5 to 10 days. Pick off severely infected leaves. Because leaf spots are favored by warm, humid conditions, it is important to spray frequently during these periods. *Basic copper sulfate* protects the new healthy foliage but will not eradicate the fungus on leaves that are already infected.

CANNA

Crown rot.

PROBLEM: The leaves and stems turn yellow, wilt, and decay. The base of the plant and lower stems are covered with white matted fungal strands, which may develop small brown or black pellets the size of pinheads or black, irregular structures about ¼ inch in diameter. The decaying stems may be filled with thin, elongated black pellets. The plant pulls easily out of the ground to reveal decayed roots.

ANALYSIS: Crown rot
This disease is caused by two fungi (*Sclerotium rolfsii*, also known as *southern blight*, and *Sclerotinia sclerotiorum*), that live in the soil. These fungi usually attack the plant stems at or just below the soil level. Both of these fungi thrive in high humidity and moist soils. The southern blight fungus, in particular, is favored by warm temperatures (80° to 90°F), and is very damaging in this temperature range. Both fungi survive the winter as fungal strands and pellets in plant debris and as fungal pellets in the soil. They are spread by infested soil, seeds and transplants, moving water, and contaminated equipment. *Sclerotium* can also grow through the soil to attack adjacent plants.

SOLUTION: Let the soil dry out between waterings and improve soil drainage. (For further details on these techniques, see pages 849 and 907.) Remove and destroy all infected plants and surrounding soil for 6 inches beyond the diseased plant. Drench the area where the infected plants were growing with a fungicide containing *PCNB*. To help prevent infection next year, broadcast a *PCNB* fungicide onto uninfested soil and dig it in to a depth of 6 inches before replanting.

Bud rot.

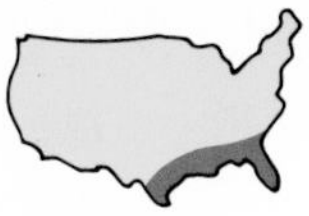

PROBLEM: The newly opened young leaves may be partially or entirely blackened, or they may be covered with tiny white spots. The older leaves may be distorted. Often they are covered with yellow or brown spots and streaks. In many cases, the flower buds turn black and die before they open. Entire stalks are often decayed. A sticky substance may coat infected leaf tissue.

ANALYSIS: Bud rot
This plant disease is caused by bacteria (*Xanthomonas* species) that usually attack the young canna leaves and flowers while they are still curled in the buds. The bacteria can spread from the leaves and flowers into the stems, causing plant death. Some of the infected tissue may exude a sticky ooze filled with bacteria. The bacteria are spread by splashing water and rain, and by direct contact with equipment, hands, and insects. Wet conditions enhance the spread of the disease. Bud rot survives through the winter in diseased rhizomes, contaminated soil, and infected plant debris to reinfect young plants the following spring.

SOLUTION: There are no effective chemical controls for this disease. In order to control bud rot, it is important to reduce excess moisture around the plants. Water in the morning so the foliage will dry out during the day. Try to avoid wetting the foliage. Space plants far enough apart to allow good air circulation. Pick off infected leaves and flowers. Remove severely diseased plants and the soil immediately surrounding them. Clean up plant debris. Plant only healthy plants and rhizomes. For information on choosing healthy plants, see page 924.

Corn earworms (⅓ life size).

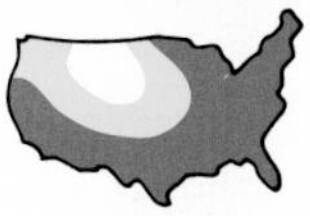

PROBLEM: The leaves are filled with holes and are often ragged. The flowers may not appear, or may be distorted. Striped green, brown, or yellow caterpillars are chewing on the leaves and inside the rolled leaf buds. The caterpillars range in size from ¼ inch to 2 inches.

ANALYSIS: Corn earworm
(*Heliothis zea*)
This caterpillar is the larva of a night-flying moth. In addition to feeding on many different ornamental plants, the corn earworm is one of the most destructive pests of corn in the country. The moths lay their light yellow eggs singly on the undersides of leaves. The caterpillars hatch in 2 to 8 days and feed for several weeks on leaves and buds, then crawl into the soil and pupate. 1 to 3 weeks later the new adults emerge to begin the cycle again, laying eggs in the evenings and on warm, overcast days. In cooler areas of the country, the caterpillars are present from early spring to the first frost. In warmer areas, the feeding caterpillars are present year-round.

SOLUTION: Control corn earworms with ORTHO Liquid Sevin, applied when the caterpillars first appear. Repeat every 10 to 14 days as needed. Deep cultivation in the fall and winter will help destroy some of the overwintering pupae.

Canna cultural information
Light: Sun
Water: While the soil is still moist
Soil: Rich
Fertilizer: Medium

CAPSICUM (ORNAMENTAL PEPPER) — CELOSIA (COCKSCOMB)

Verticillium wilt.

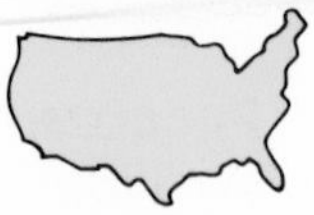

PROBLEM: The leaves and tender stems wilt, turn yellow, then brown, and finally die. The plant may be stunted and often drops many of its leaves. Some of the leaves may curl inward. When an infected stem is sliced open, dark streaks can be seen in the inner stem tissue. Flowering and fruiting are poor.

ANALYSIS: Verticillium wilt
This wilt disease affects many ornamental plants. It is caused by a soil-inhabiting fungus (*Verticillium dahliae*) that lives on plant debris or in the soil. The disease is spread by contaminated seeds, plants, soil, and equipment. The fungus enters the plant through the roots and spreads up into the stems and leaves through the water-conducting vessels in the stems. The vessels become discolored and plugged. This plugging cuts off the flow of water to the leaves, causing leaf yellowing and wilting. For more information about verticillium wilt, see page 850.

SOLUTION: No chemical control is available. It is best to destroy infected plants. Verticillium can be removed from the soil only by fumigation techniques. (For more information about soil fumigation, see page 927.) However, the best solution is usually to use plants that are resistant to verticillium. For a list of wilt-resistant plants, see page 1006.

Capsicum cultural information
Light: Sun
Water: When soil is just barely moist
Soil: Well drained
Fertilizer: Medium

Leaf spot.

PROBLEM: Yellow or brown spots appear on the leaves. The spots may run together to form blotches. The leaves may be yellowing and dying. Leaf spotting is most severe in humid weather.

ANALYSIS: Leaf spot
Several different fungi cause leaf spots on cockscomb. Some of these fungi may eventually kill the plant, or weaken it so that it becomes susceptible to attack by other organisms. Others merely cause spotting that is unsightly but not harmful. These fungi are spread by splashing water, wind, insects, and tools. They survive the winter in diseased plant debris. Some leaf spot organisms can affect a large number of plants. Most of these fungi do their greatest damage during mild weather (50° to 85°F).

SOLUTION: Spray with a fungicide containing *zineb* at intervals of 3 to 10 days. Because leaf spots are favored by humid conditions, it is important to spray frequently during these periods. *Zineb* protects the new healthy foliage but will not eradicate the fungus on leaves that are already infected. Clean up infected leaves and debris.

Spider mite webbing.

PROBLEM: Leaves are stippled, yellowing, and dirty. Leaves may dry out and drop. There may be webbing over flower buds, between leaves, or on the lower surfaces of leaves. To determine if the plant is infested with mites, hold a sheet of white paper underneath an affected plant and tap the stalk sharply. Minute green, red, or yellow specks the size of pepper grains will drop to the paper and begin to crawl around. These pests are easily seen against the white background.

ANALYSIS: Spider mites
(*Tetranychus urticae*)
These mites, related to spiders, are major pests of many garden and greenhouse plants. They cause damage by sucking sap from the underside of the leaves. As a result of feeding, the green leaf pigment disappears, producing the stippled appearance. Mites are active throughout the growing season, but are favored by hot, dry weather (70°F and up). By midsummer, they build up to tremendous numbers. For more information about spider mites, see page 887.

SOLUTION: Spray with a pesticide containing *dicofol* (KELTHANE®) when damage is first noticed. Spray the foliage thoroughly, making sure to cover both the upper and lower surfaces of the leaves. Repeat the spray three more times at intervals of 7 days.

Celosia cultural information
Light: Sun
Water: Do not allow to dry out
Soil: Rich
Fertilizer: Medium

CENTAUREA (BACHELOR BUTTONS, DUSTY MILLER)

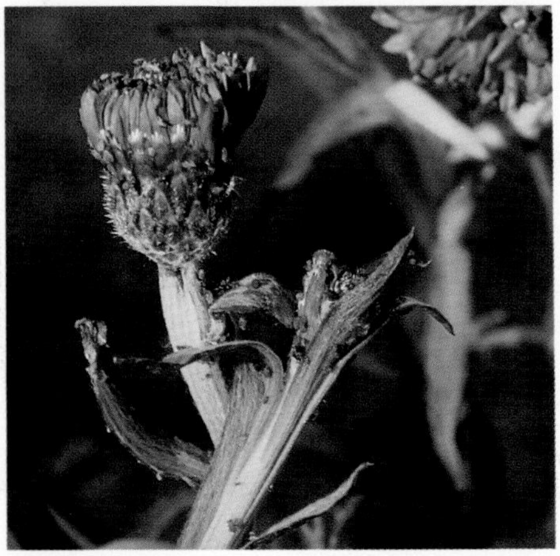
Aphids on bachelor buttons (life size).

PROBLEM: Tiny (1/8 inch) pale green to black soft-bodied insects are clustered on the leaves. Leaves may be curled, distorted, and yellowing. Flowers may be malformed. Overall growth is often stunted. A shiny, sticky substance may coat the leaves. Ants are often present.

ANALYSIS: Aphids
Several different species of aphids infest centaurea plants. Aphids do little damage in small numbers. However, they are extremely prolific and populations can rapidly build up to damaging numbers during the growing season. Damage occurs when the aphid sucks the juices from the leaves and flower buds. The aphid is unable to digest fully all the sugar in the plant sap and excretes the excess in a fluid called honeydew, which often drops onto the leaves below. Ants feed on this sticky substance, and are often present where there is an aphid infestation. For more information about aphids, see page 875.

SOLUTION: Spray the infested plants with an insecticide containing *malathion.* Repeat the spray if the plant becomes reinfested.

Centaurea cultural information
Light: Full sun
Water: Allow the soil to dry between waterings
Soil: Light, well drained
Fertilizer: Average

Root and stem rot on dusty miller.

PROBLEM: Leaves turn yellow, wilt, and eventually die. The roots and lower stems may be soft and rotten. There may be white fungal strands on infected stems and around the base of the plant.

ANALYSIS: Root and stem rot
This disease is caused by any of a number of different fungi, also known as *water molds,* that persist indefinitely in the soil . They thrive in waterlogged, heavy soil. Some of these fungi attack the plant stems at the soil level, while others attack the roots. Infection causes the roots and stems to decay. This results in wilting, then yellowing leaves, and eventually the death of the plant. These fungi are generally spread by infested soil and transplants, contaminated equipment, and splashing or running water. Many of these organisms also cause damping-off of seedlings. For more information, about damping-off, see page 850.

SOLUTION: Allow the soil around the plant to dry out. (For more information on this technique, see page 849.) Remove and discard severely infected plants. Avoid future root rot problems by planting in well-drained soil. For information on improving soil drainage, see page 907.

CHRYSANTHEMUM

CHRYSANTHEMUM (SHASTA DAISY, MARGUERITE, MUM)

ADAPTATION: Throughout the United States.

FLOWERING TIME:
Chrysanthemums: Late summer to late fall.
Shasta daisies: Late spring to late summer.
Marguerites: Spring to fall.

LIGHT: Full sun.

SOIL: Any good garden soil. pH 6.0 to 7.5

FERTILIZER: Fertilize with ORTHO Rose & Flower Food or ORTHO General Purpose Plant Food according to label directions.

WATER:
How much: Apply enough water to plants in the ground to wet the soil 8 to 12 inches deep.
How often: Water when the soil 1 inch below the surface is just barely moist.

HANDLING:
Chrysanthemums: Pinch plants frequently during the spring to encourage bushy growth. For more information, see page 338.
Shasta daisies: Divide clumps every 2 or 3 years. Pinch off old flowers to encourage continued bloom.
Marguerites: Replace plants every 3 years. Do not cut them back; they will not resprout.

CHRYSANTHEMUM (SHASTA DAISY, MARGUERITE, MUM)

Weak, leggy growth.

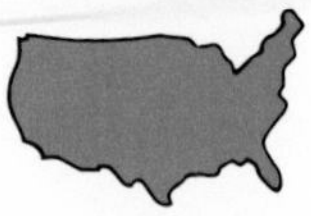

PROBLEM: Mums are leggy, and many of the stems are thin and spindly. Some plants topple and may need to be tied.

ANALYSIS: Leggy growth
Legginess in mums can be caused by two things:
1. *Natural growth pattern:* Most mum varieties grow tall and leggy naturally.
2. *Too much shade:* Mums are sun-loving plants. Chrysanthemums planted in a shaded area produce thin, leggy growth even when pinched back. Under shaded conditions, the plants may not flower well.

SOLUTION: To prevent leggy growth, follow these guidelines:
1. Plants that are leggy may be pinched back to encourage bushier growth as long as they have not yet formed flower buds. Next year, when your new plants are 6 to 8 inches tall, carefully pinch or nip off the young growing tips just above a leaf. The tiny side bud that is located between this leaf and the stem will grow into a new branch. Every 2 weeks, pinch back all the new growing points that have formed as a result of the previous weeks' pinching. Stop pinching the plant by August. For more information about pinching, see page 927. Purchase short-growing mum varieties.
2. Move or transplant your chrysanthemums to a location that receives at least 4 or 5 hours of direct sun daily. For more information about transplanting, see page 928.

Powdery mildew.

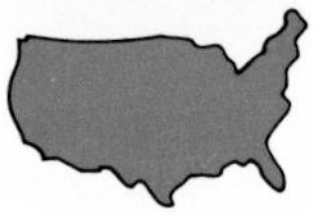

PROBLEM: The leaves and stems are covered with grayish white powdery spots and patches that occur primarily on the upper surfaces of the leaves. The leaves eventually yellow and wither.

ANALYSIS: Powdery mildew
This common plant disease is caused by a fungus (*Erysiphe cichoracearum*) that thrives in both humid and dry weather. The powdery patches consist of fungal strands and spores. The spores are spread by the wind to healthy plants. The fungus saps plant nutrients causing leaf yellowing and sometimes death of the leaf. Since this powdery mildew attacks many different kinds of plants, the fungus from a diseased plant may infect other types of plants in the garden. (See page 1006 for a list of susceptible plants.) Under favorable conditions, powdery mildew can spread through a closely spaced planting in a matter of days or weeks.

SOLUTION: Spray infected plants with ORTHO Phaltan Rose & Garden Fungicide to stop the spread of the disease. Spray at regular intervals of 7 to 10 days, or as often as necessary to protect new growth. Space plants far enough apart to allow good air circulation. Clean up infected leaves and debris.

Rust.

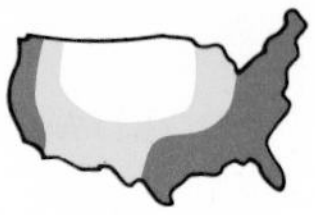

PROBLEM: Pale spots appear on the upper surfaces of the leaves. Chocolate brown pustules of spores form on the undersides of the leaves and on the stems. Infected leaves may wither and fall prematurely. The plant is stunted and may die.

ANALYSIS: Rust
This common disease of chrysanthemums is caused by a fungus (*Puccinia chrysanthemi*). The fungal spores are spread by wind and splashing water. Rust can survive only on living plant tissue and as spores on seed; it does not persist on dead plant parts. Plants must remain wet for 6 to 8 hours before the fungus can infect the leaf surface. The disease is favored by moist conditions, cool nights, and warm days. Temperatures of 90°F and higher will kill the spores. Rust can survive the winter on old infected plants.

SOLUTION: Spray infected plants with a fungicide containing *zineb* or *mancozeb* at weekly intervals as soon as the disease is noticed; continue spraying throughout the growing season. Water in the morning rather than the late afternoon or evening, to allow wet foliage to dry out more quickly. Pick off and destroy infected plant parts during the growing season. Space plants far enough apart to allow good air circulation. Remove and destroy all infected plants in the fall to keep them from reinfecting new plantings. Next year, grow only rust-resistant varieties. For a list of rust-resistant chrysanthemums, see page 1004.

Leaf spot.

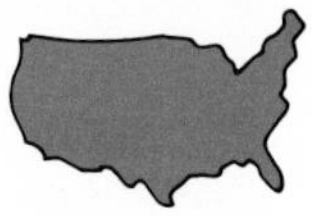

PROBLEM: Spots and blotches appear on the leaves. The spots may be yellow, tan, brown, or black. They range in size from barely visible to more than 1 inch in diameter. Several spots may join to form blotches. Leaves may turn yellow and drop, or wither and hang down along the stem.

ANALYSIS: Leaf spot
Several different fungi cause leaf spots on chrysanthemums. Some of these fungi may eventually kill the plant, or weaken it so that it becomes susceptible to attack by other organisms. Others merely cause spotting that is unsightly but not harmful. These fungi are spread by splashing water or by the wind. They generally survive the winter in diseased plant debris. Most of these fungi do their greatest damage in moist, mild (50° to 85°F) weather.

SOLUTION: Where practical, pick off infected leaves. Spray the plants with ORTHO Phaltan Rose & Garden Fungicide, or with a fungicide containing *maneb*, *folpet* (PHALTAN®), or *benomyl*. Spray weekly throughout the growing season.

Foliar nematode damage.

PROBLEM: Fan-shaped or angular yellow-brown to gray leaf blotches develop progressively upward from the lower leaves. The blotches join together and the leaf turns brown or black. The leaf then withers, dies, and hangs down along the stem. The plant is stunted and new leaf buds do not develop. In the spring, young, succulent, leafy growth becomes thickened, distorted, and brittle.

ANALYSIS: Leaf nematode
(*Aphelenchoides ritzema-bosi*)
The cause of this damage is a microscopic worm (*nematode*) that lives and feeds inside the leaf tissue. The nematode is restricted in its movement by larger leaf veins. This confined feeding range creates the angular shape of the blotch. When the foliage is wet, the nematode migrates in the thin film of water on the outside of the leaf to infect healthy tissue. This pest is spread from plant to plant by splashing water. It penetrates the plant tissue by entering through small breathing pores on the underside of the leaf. Leaf nematodes are most damaging in the wet-summer, warmer regions of the country. They can survive for 3 years or more in plant debris and in the soil.

SOLUTION: Remove and destroy severely infested plants. Pick off and destroy all of the infested leaves and the next 2 leaves directly above them. Avoid wetting the foliage as much as possible. Check new plants carefully to be sure they are not diseased, and do not replant them in infected soil. Spray with an insecticide containing *malathion*, using a spreader-sticker (see page 922). Spray weekly until the symptoms stop spreading.

Thrips damage.

PROBLEM: Silvery white streaks and flecks appear on the leaves and flowers. The leaves and flowers may be distorted and brown. If the flower buds are peeled open, tiny ($\frac{1}{20}$ to $\frac{1}{16}$ inch) insects resembling brown or straw-colored wood slivers can be seen moving around at the base of the petals.

ANALYSIS: Thrips
Several species of this common insect attack chrysanthemums, daisies, and many other garden plants. Thrips are generally found in protected locations such as the insides of the leaf and flower buds, where they feed by rasping the soft plant tissue, then sucking the released plant sap. The injured tissue dies and turns white, causing the characteristic streaking of the leaves and flowers. Because thrips migrate long distances on wind currents, they can quickly infest widespread areas. In cold climates, thrips feed and reproduce from spring until fall. With the onset of freezing weather, they find sheltered areas such as grass clumps and hibernate through the winter. In warm winter climates, thrips feed and reproduce all year. These pests reach their population peak in late spring to midsummer. They are especially troublesome during prolonged dry spells.

SOLUTION: Thrips can be kept under control, although not eliminated entirely. Spray plants before they bloom with ORTHO Orthene Systemic Insect Control, ORTHO Liquid Sevin or ORTHO Malathion 50 Insect Spray two to three times at regular intervals of 1 week. Repeat the spray if reinfestation occurs. Pick off and destroy old infested leaves and flowers.

CHRYSANTHEMUM (SHASTA DAISY, MARGUERITE, MUM)

Verticillium wilt.

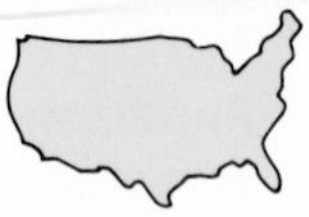

PROBLEM: Leaves yellow, wilt, and die, starting with the lower leaves and progressing up the plant. Older plants may be stunted. Leaf wilting and death often affect only one side of the plant. Flowering is poor. There may be dark brown areas on the infected stems. When the stem is sliced open near the base of the plant, dark streaks and discolorations of the inner stem tissue are revealed.

ANALYSIS: Verticillium wilt
This wilt disease affects many ornamental plants. It is caused by a soil-inhabiting fungus (*Verticillium* species) that persists indefinitely on plant debris or in the soil. The disease is spread by contaminated seeds, plants, soil, equipment, and ground water. The fungus enters the plant through the roots and spreads up into the stems and leaves through the water-conducting vessels in the stems. These vessels become discolored and plugged. This plugging cuts off the flow of water to the leaves, causing leaf yellowing and wilting. For more information about verticillium wilt, see page 850.

SOLUTION: No chemical control is available. It is best to destroy infected plants. Verticillium can be removed from the soil only by fumigation techniques. (For more information about soil fumigation, see page 927.) However, the best solution is usually to plant flowers that are resistant to verticillium. For a list of verticillium-resistant plants, see page 1006.

Nematode damage on chrysanthemum.

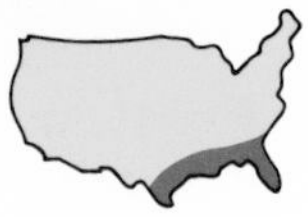

PROBLEM: Leaves turn bronze to yellow. On hot, dry days they may wilt, then recover at night. Plants are weak and grow slowly. Roots are stunted, often bushy and dark, and may have round nodules attached to them.

ANALYSIS: Nematodes
Nematodes are microscopic worms that live in the soil. They are not related to earthworms. Nematodes feed on plant roots, damaging and stunting them. The damaged roots can't supply sufficient water and nutrients to the aboveground plant parts, and the plant is stunted or slowly dies. Nematodes are found throughout the United States, but are most severe in the South. They prefer moist, sandy loam soils. Nematodes can move only a few inches each year on their own, but they may be carried long distances by soil, water, tools, or infested plants. Testing roots and soil is the only positive method for confirming the presence of nematodes. Contact your local Cooperative Extension Office (see page 1029) for sampling instructions and addresses of testing laboratories. Soil and root problems such as poor soil structure, drought stress, nutrient deficiency, and root rots can also produce symptoms of decline similar to those caused by nematodes. These problems should be eliminated as causes before sending soil and root samples for testing. For information on soil problems and root rots, see pages 907 and 849.

SOLUTION: There are no chemicals available to homeowners to kill nematodes in planted soil. However, they can be controlled before planting by soil fumigation. For information on fumigating soil, see page 927.

Two-spotted spider mite damage.

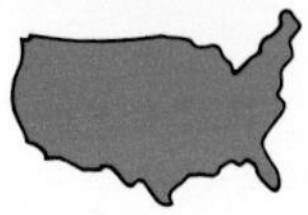

PROBLEM: Leaves are stippled, yellowing, and dirty. Leaves may dry out and drop. There may be webbing over flower buds, between leaves, or on the lower surfaces of leaves. To determine if the plant is infested with mites, hold a sheet of white paper underneath an affected leaf and tap the leaf sharply. Minute green, red, or yellow specks the size of pepper grains will drop to the paper and begin to crawl around. These pests are easily seen against the white background.

ANALYSIS: Spider mites
(*Tetranychus urticae*)
These mites, related to spiders, are major pests of many garden and greenhouse plants. They cause damage by sucking sap from the underside of the leaves. As a result of feeding, the green leaf pigment disappears, producing the stippled appearance. Mites are active throughout the growing season, but are favored by hot, dry weather (70°F and up). By midsummer, they build up to tremendous numbers. For more information about spider mites, see page 887.

SOLUTION: Spray with ORTHO Malathion 50 Insect Spray or a pesticide containing *dicofol* (KELTHANE®) when damage is first noticed. Spray the foliage thoroughly, making sure to cover both the upper and lower surfaces of the leaves. Repeat the spray three more times at intervals of 7 days.

Bacterial blight.

PROBLEM: Gray lesions with a water-soaked appearance occur on the stems. Stem portions above these lesions decay, turn brown or black, and fall over. Decay may progress downward to the base of the stems.

ANALYSIS: Bacterial blight
This disease, which is caused by a bacterium (*Erwinia chrysanthemi*), occurs most frequently in warm (80° to 90°F), humid areas. The bacteria enter the plant through stem wounds or through the root system. The infected stem is unable to transport water to the top of the plant, which wilts and dies. The rotted tissue contains millions of bacteria, which are spread to other plants through handling, and by contaminated tools and soil. The bacteria can live for several months in the soil and plant debris.

SOLUTION: There is no chemical control for this disease. Remove and destroy all infected plants. Clean up plant debris. After handling diseased plants, wash your hands before handling healthy plants. Disinfect tools by dipping them in rubbing alcohol. To avoid reinfection from contaminated soil, do not replant chrysanthemums in the same area for at least 6 months.

Mosaic.

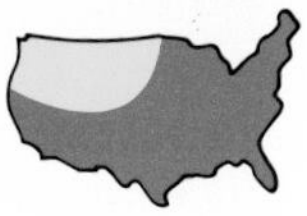

PROBLEM: Leaves are mottled, and the leaf veins may turn pale. Plants may be dwarfed and bushy. Flowers are small and may have brown streaks. Leaves, stems, and flowers may be deformed.

ANALYSIS: Mosaic
This plant disease is caused by several different viruses. Mosaic is primarily transmitted from plant to plant by aphids. The symptoms of mosaic virus can vary considerably in their severity depending on the type of virus, plant species, and variety. Viruses can be transmitted to chrysanthemums from many weeds and ornamental plants. Some plants may be infected with mosaic virus without showing the typical symptoms.

SOLUTION: Infected plants cannot be cured. They should be removed and destroyed. Spray aphid-infested plants in the area with ORTHO Diazinon Insect Spray or ORTHO Malathion 50 Insect Spray. Repeat the spray at intervals of 7 days as often as necessary to keep the aphids under control. For spot treatment of a few plants use ORTHO Rose & Flower Insect Killer according to label directions. To reduce the numbers of plants that may harbor viruses, keep your garden free of weeds. For more information about controlling disease-carrying insects, see page 879.

Aster yellows.

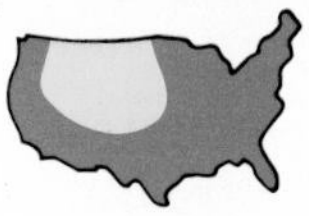

PROBLEM: The leaf veins pale and may lose all their color. Part or all of the foliage turns yellow. Leaf edges may turn brown. The flowers are dwarfed, distorted, and may turn green. The plant may grow many thin stems bearing pale, spindly leaves. The plant is generally stunted.

ANALYSIS: Aster yellows
This plant disease is caused by mycoplasmas, microscopic organisms similar to bacteria. The mycoplasmas are transmitted from plant to plant primarily by leafhoppers. (For more information about leafhoppers, see page 878.) The symptoms of aster yellows are more severe and appear more quickly in warm weather. Although the disease may be present in the plant, aster yellows may not manifest its symptoms in temperatures of 55°F or less. The disease also infects many ornamental plants, vegetables, and weeds. For a list of plants susceptible to aster yellows, see page 1005.

SOLUTION: Aster yellows cannot be eliminated entirely, but can be kept under control. Remove and destroy infected plants. To remove sources of infection, eradicate nearby weeds that may harbor aster yellows and leafhopper eggs. Spray leafhopper-infested plants with an insecticide containing *diazinon* or *malathion*. Repeat the spray whenever leafhoppers are seen. For more information about controlling disease-carrying insects, see page 879.

CHRYSANTHEMUM (SHASTA DAISY, MARGUERITE, MUM)

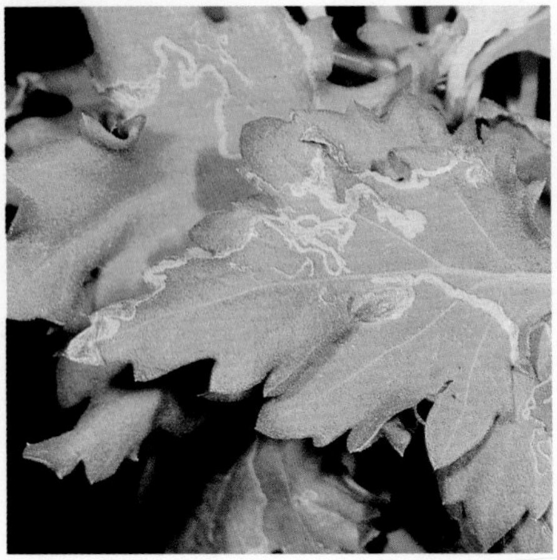

Leafminer trails in chrysanthemum leaf.

PROBLEM: Light-colored, irregular, winding trails or tunnels appear in the leaves. Some of the trails are filled with black matter. Severely infested leaves dry up and hang down along the stems.

ANALYSIS: Chrysanthemum leafminer (*Phytomyza syngenesiae*)
This insect belongs to the family of leaf-mining flies. The minute adult fly lays its eggs on the undersides of leaves. The eggs hatch and the larvae that emerge penetrate the leaf and live between the upper and lower surfaces of the leaves. They feed on the inner leaf tissue, creating winding trails. Their dark excrement may dot or partially fill sections of the trails. The larvae are continually present from the spring until the fall.

SOLUTION: Spray with ORTHO Orthene Systemic Insect Control. Respray at the first sign of further infestation. Pick off and destroy infected leaves. Remove and destroy all plant remains in the fall.

Aphids (life size).

PROBLEM: Young leaves are curled, stunted, and yellowing. The flowers may be malformed. There may be a sticky or shiny substance coating the leaves. Tiny (⅛ inch), soft-bodied insects that may range in color from pale green to dark brown or black are clustered on the leaves and stems. Ants may be present.

ANALYSIS: Aphids
Aphids do little damage in small numbers. However, they are extremely prolific and populations can rapidly build up to damaging numbers during the growing season. Damage occurs when the aphid sucks the juices from the chrysanthemum leaves and flower buds. The aphid is unable to digest fully all the sugar in the plant sap and excretes the excess in a fluid called honeydew. The honeydew often drops onto the leaves below. Ants feed on this sticky substance, and are often present where there is an aphid infestation. For more information about aphids, see page 875.

SOLUTION: Spray with ORTHO Orthene Systemic Insect Control, ORTHO Diazinon Insect Spray or ORTHO Malathion 50 Insect Spray as soon as the insects appear. Repeat the spray if the plant is reinfested. For spot treatment of a few plants use ORTHO Rose & Flower Insect Killer according to label directions.

CINERARIA

Chrysanthemum leafminer damage.

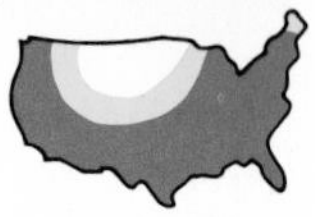

PROBLEM: Light-colored, irregular, winding trails or tunnels appear in the leaves. Some of the trails are filled with black matter. Severely infested leaves dry up and hang down along the stems.

ANALYSIS: Chrysanthemum leafminer (*Phytomyza syngenesiae*)
This insect, which is a serious pest of chrysanthemum as well as cineraria, belongs to the family of leaf-mining flies. The minute adult fly lays its eggs on the undersides of leaves. The eggs hatch and the larvae that emerge penetrate the leaves and live between the upper and lower surfaces of the leaves. They feed on the inner leaf tissue, creating winding trails. Their dark excrement can dot or partially fill sections of the trails. The larvae are continually present from the spring until the fall.

SOLUTION: Spray with ORTHO Diazinon Insect Spray. Respray at the first sign of further infestation. Pick off and destroy infested leaves. Remove and destroy all plant remains in the fall.

Cineraria cultural information
Light: Shade
Water: While the soil is still moist
Soil: Loamy, well drained
Fertilizer: Medium

Powdery mildew.

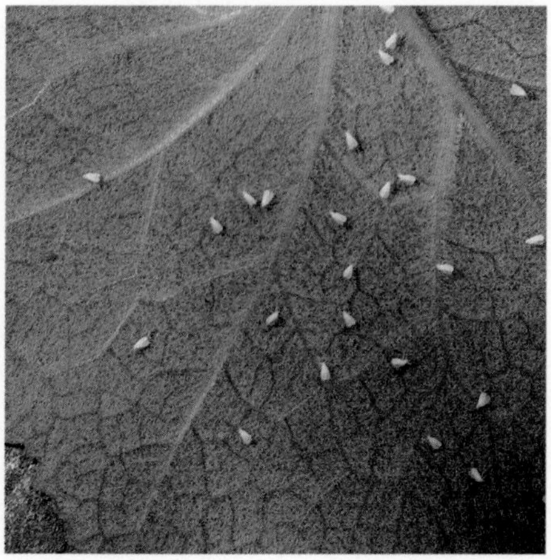
Whiteflies (life size).

Sunburn.

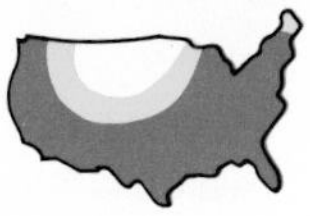

PROBLEM: Grayish white, powdery spots and patches cover the upper surfaces of the leaves, the stems, and possibly the flower buds. The infected plant parts are dwarfed and stunted. The leaves may eventually turn yellow and wither.

ANALYSIS: Powdery mildew
This common plant disease is caused by a fungus (*Erysiphe cichoracearum*) that thrives in both humid and dry weather. The powdery patches consist of fungal strands and spores. The spores are spread by the wind to healthy plants. The fungus saps plant nutrients, causing leaf yellowing and sometimes death of the leaf. A severe infection may kill the plant. Since this powdery mildew attacks many different kinds of plants, the fungus from a diseased plant may infect other types of plants in the garden. (See page 1006 for a list of susceptible plants.) Under favorable conditions, powdery mildew can spread through a closely spaced planting in a matter of days or weeks. The disease is generally most severe late in the growing season.

SOLUTION: Spray infected plants with a fungicide containing *benomyl* to stop the spread of the disease. *Benomyl* protects the new, healthy foliage by killing the powdery mildew spores as they germinate on the leaf. It will also eradicate the fungus on leaves that are already infected. Spray at regular intervals of 7 to 10 days, or as often as necessary to protect new growth. Space plants far enough apart to allow good air circulation. Clean up infected leaves and debris.

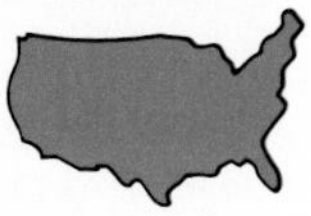

PROBLEM: Tiny, winged insects 1/12 inch long are feeding on the undersides of the leaves. The insects are covered with white waxy powder. When the plant is touched, insects flutter rapidly around it. Leaves may be mottled and yellowing. In warm winter areas, black mold may cover the leaves.

ANALYSIS: Greenhouse whitefly
(Trialeurodes vaporariorum)
This insect is a common pest of many garden and greenhouse plants. The four-winged adult lays eggs on the undersides of leaves. The larvae are the size of a pinhead, flat, oval-shaped, and semitransparent, with white waxy filaments radiating from the body. They feed for about a month before changing to the adult form. Both the larval and adult forms suck sap from the leaves. The larvae are more damaging because they feed more heavily. Adults and larvae cannot fully digest all the sugar in the plant sap and excrete the excess in a fluid called honeydew. A black, sooty mold fungus may develop on the honeydew, causing the cineraria leaves to appear black and dirty. In warm winter areas these insects can be active year-round, with eggs, larvae, and adults present at the same time. Whiteflies are unable to live through freezing winters. Spring reinfestations in freezing winter areas come from migrating whiteflies and from infested greenhouse-grown plants placed in the garden.

SOLUTION: Control whiteflies by spraying with an insecticide containing *resmethrin*. Repeat the spray at least two more times at intervals of 5 to 7 days. Spray the foliage thoroughly, being sure to cover both the upper and lower surfaces of the leaves.

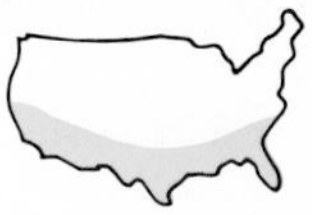

PROBLEM: Leaves are pale green to yellowish white in color; they may turn brown and brittle. There is very little new growth. Plants are exposed to at least several hours of direct sun during the day. Only the leaves exposed to the sun are affected. There are no signs of plant pests or diseases.

ANALYSIS: Sunburn
Clivias are adapted to shady conditions, and will not tolerate more than a few hours of direct sun, especially hot afternoon sunlight. Even if they receive only 1 or 2 hours of direct sunlight, they may discolor slightly, turning yellow-green. The bright light and intense heat break down the chlorophyll (green plant pigment), and eventually the plant tissue dies.

SOLUTION: Transplant your clivias to a shaded or partially shaded location. Do not place them in a western or southwestern exposure. Replace them with plants that are adapted to a sunny location.

Clivia cultural information
Light: Shade
Water: When the soil is just barely moist
Soil: Tolerates a wide variety
Fertilizer: Medium

COLEUS

Spider mites.

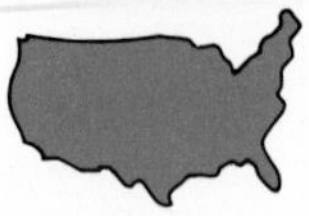

PROBLEM: Leaves are stippled, yellowing, and dirty. Leaves may dry out and die. There may be webbing over flower buds, between leaves and stems, or on the lower surfaces of leaves. To determine if the plant is infested with mites, hold a sheet of white paper underneath an affected leaf and tap the leaf sharply. Minute green, red, or yellow specks the size of pepper grains will drop to the paper and begin to crawl around. These pests are easily seen against the white background.

ANALYSIS: Mites
Mites, related to spiders, are major pests of many garden and greenhouse plants. They cause damage by sucking sap from the undersides of the leaves. As a result of feeding, the green leaf pigment disappears, producing the stippled appearance. Mites are active throughout the growing season, but are favored by hot, dry weather (70°F and up). By midsummer, they build up to tremendous numbers. For more information about mites, see page 887.

SOLUTION: Spray with a pesticide containing *dicofol* (KELTHANE®) when damage is first noticed. Spray the foliage thoroughly, making sure to cover both the upper and lower surfaces of the leaves. Repeat the spray three more times at intervals of 7 days.

Coleus cultural information
Light: Shade
Water: While the soil is still moist
Soil: Loamy, well drained
Fertilizer: Medium

Greenhouse whiteflies (life size).

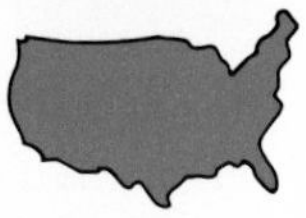

PROBLEM: Tiny, winged insects 1/12 inch long are found mainly on the undersides of the leaves. The insects are covered with white, waxy powder. When the plant is touched, insects flutter rapidly around it. Leaves may be mottled and yellowing. In warm winter areas, black mold may cover the leaves.

ANALYSIS: Greenhouse whitefly
(*Trialeurodes vaporariorum*)
Greenhouse whitefly is a common insect pest of many garden and greenhouse plants. The four-winged adult lays eggs on the undersides of leaves. The larvae are the size of a pinhead and look quite different from the adult. The larvae are flat, oval-shaped, and semitransparent, with white waxy filaments radiating from the body. They remain attached to the underside of a leaf for about a month before changing to the adult form. Both the larval and adult forms suck sap from the leaves. The larvae are more damaging because they feed more heavily. Whiteflies cannot fully digest all the sugar in the sap, and excrete the excess in a fluid called honeydew, which coats the leaves. A sooty mold fungus may develop on the honeydew, causing the coleus leaves to appear black and dirty. In warm winter areas, the insect can be active year-round with eggs, larvae, and adults present at the same time. The whitefly is unable to live through freezing winters. Spring reinfestations in freezing winter areas come from migrating whiteflies and infested greenhouse-grown plants.

SOLUTION: Control whiteflies by spraying with an insecticide containing *malathion* every 7 to 10 days as necessary. Spray both the upper and lower surfaces of the leaves.

Mealybugs (twice life size).

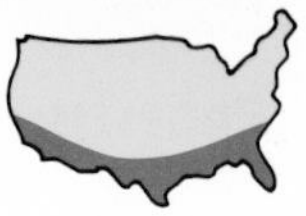

PROBLEM: Oval, white insects up to 1/4 inch long cluster in white, cottony masses on the stems and leaves. Leaves may be deformed and withered. The infested leaves are often shiny and sticky. Ants may be present.

ANALYSIS: Mealybugs
Several species of this common insect feed on coleus. Mealybugs damage plants by sucking sap, causing leaf distortion and death. The adult female mealybug may produce live young, or may deposit her eggs in white, fluffy masses of wax. The immature mealybugs, called *nymphs*, are very active and crawl all over the plant. Soon after the nymphs begin to feed, they exude filaments of white wax that cover their bodies, giving them a cottony appearance. As they mature, their mobility decreases. Mealybugs cannot fully digest all the sugar in the sap, and excrete the excess in a fluid called honeydew, which coats the leaves. Ants may feed on the honeydew. Mealybugs are spread by the wind, which may blow egg masses and nymphs from plant to plant. Ants may also move them, or young, active nymphs can crawl to nearby plants. Mealybug eggs and some adults can survive through the winter in warm climates. Spring reinfestations in colder areas come from infested new plants placed in the garden.

SOLUTION: Spray infested plants with an insecticide containing *malathion* and a spreader-sticker (see page 922). Spray at intervals of 7 to 10 days until the mealybugs are gone. Gently hose down plants to knock off mealybugs and wash off honeydew. Remove and destroy severely infested leaves and plants.

Sunburn.

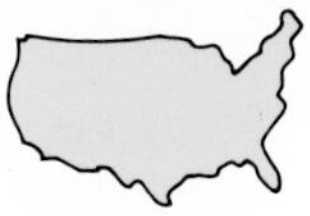

PROBLEM: The leaves are bleached and faded, and often turn pale green to yellowish white. Some of the leaves may turn brown and brittle. There is very little new growth. The plants have been recently purchased and planted, and they are exposed to at least several hours of direct sun during the day. There are no signs of plant pests or diseases.

ANALYSIS: Sunburn
Coleus plants that have been nursery or greenhouse grown are adapted to shady conditions, and will not tolerate more than a few hours of direct sun, especially intense afternoon sun. Even if they receive only 1 or 2 hours of direct sunlight, they may discolor slightly, turning yellow-green. The bright light and intense heat break down the chlorophyll (green plant pigment), and eventually the plant tissue dies.

SOLUTION: Transplant your coleus to a shaded or partially shaded location. Do not place them in a western or southwestern exposure. Replace them with plants that are adapted to a sunny location.

Root and stem rot.

PROBLEM: Leaves turn yellow, die, and drop off. The base of the stem may be soft and mushy, and the plant pulls out of the ground easily. The root system is small and rotted.

ANALYSIS: Root and stem rot
This disease is caused by a number of different fungi that live in the soil. They thrive in waterlogged, heavy soils. Some of these fungi attack the plant stems at the soil level, while others attack the roots. Infection causes the roots and stems to decay. This results in wilting, then yellowing, leaves and eventually the death of the plant. The fungi are generally spread by infested soil and transplants, contaminated equipment, and splashing or running water. Many of these organisms also cause damping-off of seedlings. For more information about damping-off, see page 850.

SOLUTION: Allow the soil around the plants to dry out. (For more information on this technique, see page 849.) Remove and discard severely infected plants. Avoid future root rot problems by planting in well-drained soil. For information on improving soil drainage, see page 907. For more information on root and stem rots, see page 813.

Spotted cucumber beetles.

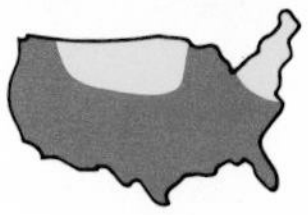

PROBLEM: Yellow-green, winged beetles ¼ inch long, with black spots, are chewing small holes in the leaves and flower petals.

ANALYSIS: Spotted cucumber beetle
(*Diabrotica* species)
Several closely related spotted cucumber beetles (one of which is also known as the *southern corn rootworm*) feed on many different vegetable and ornamental plants. The adult beetle hibernates in weeds and perennials. When temperatures reach 70°F in the spring, the adult resumes feeding on leaves and flowers. The female beetle lays eggs in or on the soil around the base of the plants. The wormlike yellowish white larvae feed on the plant roots and are very damaging to many vegetable crops such as corn, cucumbers, melons, and squash. The larvae pupate in midsummer and emerge as adult beetles, which feed exclusively on foliage and flowers. They are especially attracted to light-colored, late summer flowers like coreopsis.

SOLUTION: Spray plants with an insecticide containing *carbaryl* (SEVIN®) or *diazinon*. Repeat the spray when plants are reinfested, allowing at least 7 days between applications. To kill the larvae, thoroughly cultivate the soil as soon as temperatures reach 70°F in the spring. Reduce the number of hibernating beetles by cleaning up weeds in the fall.

Coreopsis cultural information
Light: Sun
Water: When almost dry
Soil: Well drained
Fertilizer: Medium

COREOPSIS

Aster leafhopper damage.

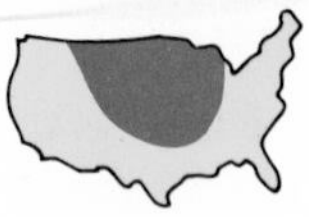

PROBLEM: Pale green, winged insects up to ⅛ inch long, usually feed on the undersides of the leaves. They hop away quickly when the plant is touched. The leaves may be stippled.

ANALYSIS: Aster leafhopper
(*Macrosteles fascifrons*)
This insect, also known as the *six-spotted leafhopper*, feeds on many different ornamental and vegetable plants. It generally feeds on the undersides of the leaves, sucking the plant sap, which causes the stippling. This leafhopper can infect plants with the disease *aster yellows* (see page 854). Leafhoppers at all stages of maturity are active throughout the growing season. Adult leafhoppers cannot overwinter where the temperatures approach freezing. However, the eggs they lay in the fall survive on perennial weeds and ornamental plants. The eggs hatch and the emerging insects reinfest plants when the weather warms up in the spring. Even areas that have winters so cold that the eggs cannot survive are not free from infestation, because leafhoppers can migrate in the spring from warmer regions.

SOLUTION: It is important to keep leafhoppers under control because, in addition to the damage their feeding causes, they can infect plants with aster yellows. Spray plants with an insecticide containing *diazinon* or *carbaryl* (SEVIN®), making sure to cover the lower surfaces of the leaves. Repeat the spray as necessary to keep the insects under control, allowing at least 10 days to pass between applications. Eradicate nearby weeds that may harbor leafhopper eggs and aster yellows. (For more information about controlling disease-carrying insects see page 879.)

COSMOS

Powdery mildew.

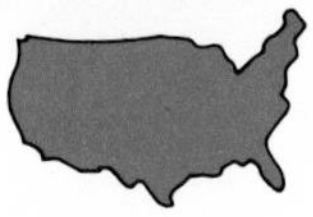

PROBLEM: The leaves and stems are covered with grayish white powdery spots and patches that occur primarily on the upper leaf surfaces. The leaves eventually turn yellow.

ANALYSIS: Powdery mildew
This common plant disease is caused by a fungus (*Erysiphe cichoracearum*) that thrives in both humid and dry weather. The powdery patches consist of fungal strands and spores. The spores are spread by the wind. The fungus saps plant nutrients, causing yellowing and sometimes death of the leaf. Since this powdery mildew attacks many different kinds of plants, the fungus from a diseased plant may infect other types of plants in the garden. (See page 1006 for a list of susceptible plants.) Under favorable conditions, powdery mildew can spread through a closely spaced planting in a matter of days or weeks. Generally it is most severe in late summer and early fall.

SOLUTION: Spray infected plants with a fungicide containing either *folpet* (PHALTAN®) or *benomyl* to stop the spread of the disease. These fungicides protect the new healthy foliage, but will not eradicate the fungus on leaves that are already infected. These may be picked off. Spray at regular intervals of 10 to 12 days, or as necessary to protect new growth. Space plants far enough apart to allow good air circulation.

Cosmos cultural information
Light: Sun
Water: When the soil is almost dry
Soil: Any good garden soil
Fertilizer: Medium

Root and stem rot.

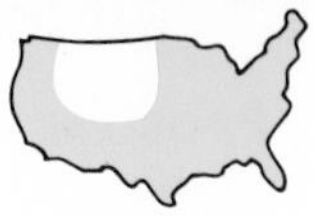

PROBLEM: The plant suddenly wilts and dies; or it may die slowly from the top down. The leaves may yellow, and overall growth may be stunted. Small black fungal pellets may appear on the lower stems and roots. The stem may be soft and mushy at the soil level. The roots may be decayed.

ANALYSIS: Root and stem rot
This disease is caused by a number of different fungi, also known as *water molds*, that persist indefinitely in the soil. They thrive in waterlogged, heavy soils. Some of these fungi primarily attack the plant stems at the soil level, while others attack the roots. Infection causes the roots, stems, or both to decay, resulting in wilting, yellowing leaves and plant death. These fungi are generally spread by infested soil and transplants, contaminated equipment, and moving water. Many of these organisms also cause damping-off of seedlings. For more information about damping off, see page 850.

SOLUTION: Allow the soil around the plants to dry out. For more information on this technique, see page 849. Remove and discard severely infected plants. Avoid future root rot problems by planting in well-drained soil. For information on improving soil drainage, see page 907.

Spider mite damage.

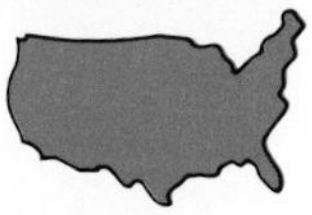

PROBLEM: Leaves are stippled, yellowing, and dirty. Leaves may dry out and drop. There may be webbing over flower buds, between leaves and stems, or on the lower surfaces of the leaves. To determine if the plant is infested with mites, hold a sheet of white paper underneath an affected leaf and tap the leaf sharply. Minute green, red, or yellow specks the size of pepper grains will drop to the paper and begin to crawl around. These pests are easily seen against the white background.

ANALYSIS: Spotted spider mites
(*Tetranychus urticae*)
These mites, related to spiders, are major pests of many garden and greenhouse plants. They cause damage by sucking sap from the underside of the leaves. As a result of feeding, the green leaf pigment disappears, producing the stippled appearance. Mites are active throughout the growing season, but are favored by hot, dry weather (70°F and up). By midsummer, they build up to tremendous numbers. For more information about spider mites, see page 887.

SOLUTION: Spray with ORTHO Isotox Insect Killer when damage is first noticed. Spray the foliage thoroughly, making sure to cover both the upper and lower surfaces of the leaves.

Aphids (life size).

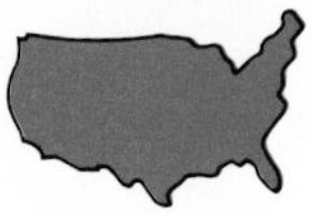

PROBLEM: Leaves may be curled, distorted, and yellowing. The flowers may be malformed. Tiny (⅛ inch) pale green to black, soft-bodied insects are clustered on the leaves and stems. A sticky, shiny substance may coat the leaves. Ants may be present.

ANALYSIS: Aphids
Aphids do little damage in small numbers. However, they are extremely prolific and populations can rapidly build up to damaging numbers during the growing season. Damage occurs when the aphid sucks the juices from the cosmos leaves and flower buds. The aphid is unable to fully digest all the sugar in the plant sap and excretes the excess in a fluid called honeydew. The honeydew often drops onto the leaves below. Ants feed on this sticky substance, and are often present where there is an aphid infestation. For more information about aphids, see page 875.

SOLUTION: Spray with ORTHO Isotox Insect Killer or ORTHO Liquid Sevin as soon as the insects appear. Repeat the spray if the plant is reinfested.

Aphids (life size).

PROBLEM: Leaves may be curled, distorted, and yellowing. The flowers may be malformed. Tiny (⅛ inch) yellow-green to black, soft-bodied insects are clustered on the undersides of the leaves and the base of the plant. A sticky, shiny substance may coat the leaves.

ANALYSIS: Aphids
Aphids do little damage in small numbers. However, they are extremely prolific and populations can rapidly build up to damaging numbers during the growing season. Damage occurs when the aphid sucks the juices from the crocus leaves and flower buds. The aphid is unable to digest fully all the sugar in the plant sap and excretes the excess in a fluid called honeydew. The honeydew often drops onto the leaves below. For more information about aphids, see page 875.

SOLUTION: Spray with ORTHO Liquid Sevin as soon as the insects appear. Repeat the spray if the plant becomes reinfested.

Crocus cultural information
Light: Sun
Water: When the soil is just barely moist
Soil: Any good garden soil
Fertilizer: Medium

Mosaic.

PROBLEM: Leaves are mottled or streaked. Pale rings may develop on the foliage. As the leaves grow older, black or brown stripes develop along the leaf veins, and irregular, sunken blotches may form. The flowers may be marred with dark green or light-colored rings or streaks.

ANALYSIS: Mosaic
This plant disease is caused by a number of closely related viruses. The symptoms of mosaic infections vary in their severity depending on the strain of virus and the cymbidium variety. Virus infections generally do not kill the plant, but may greatly reduce its overall vigor and beauty. Mosaic persists in the plant indefinitely. Cuttings or divisions made from the diseased plant will also be infected. If diseased plants are touched or pruned, the virus can be transferred to healthy plants on contaminated hands, knives, and other pruning equipment. Aphids and other insects may also transmit these viruses.

SOLUTION: There are no chemicals that control or eliminate virus diseases. Discard weak or severely infected plants. Wash your hands and dip pruning shears into rubbing alcohol after working on infected plants. Purchase only healthy plants. For information on selecting healthy plants, see page 924. Keep aphids under control. For more information about disease-carrying aphids and their control, see page 879.

Gray mold.

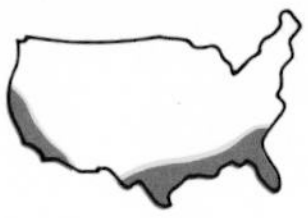

PROBLEM: Tiny brown spots appear on the blossoms. Spotting increases as the flower ages. If wet conditions continue, gray mold develops on the infected flower parts when the flower starts to die back naturally.

ANALYSIS: Gray mold
This widespread plant disease is caused by a fungus (*Botrytis cinerea*) that is found on most dead plant tissue. The fungus attacks the flowers, causing spotting and sometimes mold. The fuzzy gray mold that may develop is composed of millions of microscopic spores. The fungus is spread by the wind, splashing water, or by infected pieces of plant tissue contacting healthy tissue. Cool temperatures and high humidity favor gray mold growth. Infection is more of a problem in spring and fall, when temperatures are lower. In warm winter areas, where freezing is rare, gray mold can be a year-round problem.

SOLUTION: No chemicals are currently available that will control gray mold on cymbidium. Adequate sanitation controls this fungus satisfactorily. Clean up plant debris, and remove dying or moldy flowers. Provide enough space between plants to allow good air circulation. Try to avoid wetting the foliage and flowers when watering.

DAHLIA

ADAPTATION: Throughout the United States.

FLOWERING TIME: Summer to mid fall.

LIGHT: Full sun.

PLANTING TIME: In the spring when all danger of frost is past.

SOIL: High in organic matter. pH 6.0 to 7.5

FERTILIZER: Fertilize with ORTHO Rose & Flower Food or ORTHO General Purpose Plant Food according to label directions.

WATER:
How much: Apply enough water to plants in the ground to wet the soil to 1 to 1½ feet. For plants in containers, apply enough water so that 10 percent of the water drains from the bottom of the container.
How often: Water when the soil is moist but not wet. Dahlias cannot tolerate drying out. Mulch plants to help maintain soil moisture.

HANDLING: Dig up and divide tuberous roots in the fall. Store them in a perforated plastic bag packed in vermiculite or peat moss. Keep them in a dark, cool (35° to 45°F) location.

Tuber rot.

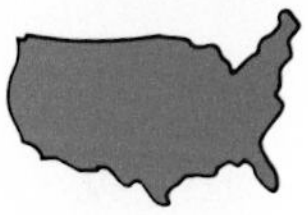

PROBLEM: Tuberous roots in storage develop dark brown, sunken areas that are usually dry and firm, but are sometimes soft and mushy. Tufts of pink and yellow mold may cover part or all of the roots. Tubers that have been planted may not produce any foliage. If they do, the foliage turns yellow and wilts. When dug up, the tubers and roots are rotted and moldy.

ANALYSIS: Tuber rot

This disease is caused primarily by two common soil-inhabiting fungi (*Fusarium* species and *Botrytis* species). The fungi generally don't infect the tubers unless they are wounded. If the roots are damaged when they are dug out of the ground, the fungi will penetrate the wounds and rot the tissue. The tubers rot rapidly when they are stored in warm, humid conditions. If tubers suffer frost damage while they are in storage, they will also be susceptible to fungal invasion. Sometimes tuberous roots in storage are contaminated but the fungal decay has not progressed far enough to be noticed. When they are planted the following spring, they may not produce foliage. If they do produce foliage, the fungus causes wilting, yellowing, and eventually death of the plant. For more information about fusarium wilt, see page 858.

SOLUTION: Infected roots cannot be saved. To prevent tuber rot next year, dig up the roots carefully after they have matured fully. Discard any roots that show decay. Handle them carefully to prevent injuries. Store the roots in peat moss in a cool, dark place that is safe from frost. For more information about storing bulbs and roots, see page 925.

Stem and root rot.

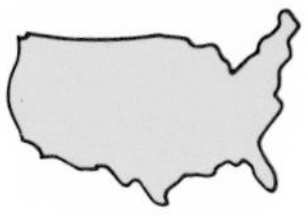

PROBLEM: Leaves and stems are wilted and dying. White fungal strands may be growing on the main stem at the base of the plant. When sliced open, infected stems may be found to be filled with small black fungal bodies. In many cases, the roots are black and rotted.

ANALYSIS: Root and stem rot

This disease is caused by a number of different fungi (including *Sclerotinia*, *Pythium*, and *Pellicularia* species) that persist indefinitely in the soil. They thrive in waterlogged, heavy soil. The fungi infect the plant roots and stems, causing them to decay. This results in wilting, then yellowing leaves, and eventually the death of the plant. These fungi are generally spread by infested soil and transplants, contaminated equipment, and splashing or running water. Many of these organisms also cause damping-off of seedlings. For more information about damping-off, see page 850.

SOLUTION: Allow the soil around the plants to dry out. (For more information on this technique, see page 849.) Remove and discard severely infected plants. Avoid future root rot problems by planting in well-drained soil. For information on improving soil drainage, see page 907. For more information on stem rots, see page 849.

Wilt disease.

PROBLEM: The lower leaves turn yellow, wilt and die; or all of the foliage may turn yellow and then wither. Older plants may be stunted. Yellowing and wilting often affect only one side of the plant. The flower heads droop. There may be dark brown areas on the infected stem. When the stem is sliced open near the base of the plant, dark streaks and discolorations are seen on the inner stem tissue. The root system may be partially or entirely decayed.

ANALYSIS: Wilt disease

Wilt disease affects many ornamental plants. It is caused by either of two soil-inhabiting fungi (*Verticillium dahliae* and *Fusarium* species) that persist indefinitely on plant debris or in the soil. The disease is spread by contaminated seeds, plants, soil, and equipment. The fungus enters the plant through the roots and spreads up into the stems through the water-conducting vessels. The vessels become discolored and plugged. This plugging cuts off the flow of water to the leaves, causing leaf yellowing and wilting. For more information about wilt disease, see page 850.

SOLUTION: No chemical control is available. It is best to destroy infected plants. Verticillium and fusarium can be removed from the soil only by fumigation techniques. (For more information about soil fumigation, see page 927.) However, the best solution is usually to use plants that are resistant to verticillium and fusarium. For a list of wilt-resistant plants, see pages 1005 and 1006.

DAHLIA

Powdery mildew.

PROBLEM: The leaves and stems are covered with grayish white powdery spots and patches that occur primarily on the upper surfaces of the leaves. The leaves eventually yellow and wither.

ANALYSIS: Powdery mildew
This common plant disease is caused by a fungus (*Erysiphe cichoracearum*) that thrives in both humid and dry weather. The powdery patches consist of fungal strands and spores. The spores are spread by the wind to healthy plants. The fungus saps the plant nutrients, causing yellowing and sometimes death of the leaf. Since this powdery mildew attacks many different kinds of plants, the fungus from a diseased plant may infect other types of plants in the garden. (See page 1006 for a list of susceptible plants.) Under favorable conditions, powdery mildew can spread through a closely spaced planting in a matter of days or weeks. It is generally most severe in the late summer.

SOLUTION: Spray infected plants with ORTHO Funginex Rose Disease Control or ORTHO Orthenex Insect & Disease Control to stop the spread of the disease. These fungicides protect the new, healthy foliage, but will not remove the fungus spots on leaves that are already infected. These leaves may be picked off. Spray every 10 to 12 days, or as often as necessary to protect new growth. Space plants far enough apart to allow good air circulation. Remove and destroy severely infected plants. Clean up plant debris.

Mosaic.

PROBLEM: The leaf veins and leaf tissue next to the veins turn pale green, or the leaves may be mildly to severely mottled. The leaves are often distorted or yellowing. The plant may be stunted and bushy.

ANALYSIS: Mosaic
This plant disease is caused by a virus that is transmitted from plant to plant by aphids. The symptoms of mosaic virus vary considerably in their severity, depending on the plant variety. Severely affected plants will not die from mosaic, but their overall vigor and beauty are greatly reduced. In contrast, some plants infected with mosaic don't show any symptoms at all. The virus survives the winter in the roots of perennial ornamental plants and weeds.

SOLUTION: Control mosaic virus by eliminating the virus-carrying aphids. Spray aphid-infested plants with ORTHO Isotox Insect Killer. Repeat the spray as often as necessary to keep the aphids under control, allowing 7 days to pass between sprays. For spot treatment of a few plants use ORTHO Rose & Flower Insect Killer according to label directions. Remove and destroy infected plants and nearby weeds that may harbor the virus.

DELPHINIUM

DELPHINIUM

ADAPTATION: Throughout the United States.

FLOWERING TIME: Late spring to fall.

LIGHT: Full sun.

PLANTING TIME: Plant in the fall for bloom next spring to summer, or plant in the spring for bloom in late summer and spring of the following year.

SOIL: Well drained, high in organic matter. pH 6.0 to 7.5

FERTILIZER: When planting, add a small handful of ORTHO Bone Meal or ORTHO Superphosphate to the bottom of the planting hole. During the growing season, fertilize with ORTHO Rose & Flower Food or ORTHO General Purpose Plant Food according to label directions.

WATER:
How much: Apply enough water to wet the soil to 1½ feet deep.
How often: Water when the soil 1 inch below the surface is just barely moist.

HANDLING: When planting, do not bury the crown of the plant. Cut back old flower stalks to promote further bloom. When new shoots are 6 to 8 inches high, cut back old stems to ground. Stake tall varieties.

Snail and slug damage.

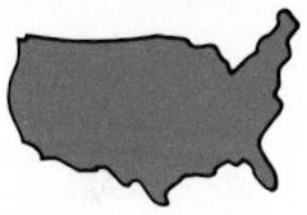

PROBLEM: Holes are chewed in the leaves, or entire leaves may be sheared from the stems. Silvery trails wind around on the plants and soil nearby. Snails or slugs may be seen moving around or feeding on the plants, especially at night. Check for them by inspecting the garden at night by flashlight.

ANALYSIS: Snails and slugs
These pests are mollusks, and are related to clams, oysters, and other shellfish. They feed on a wide variety of garden plants. Like other mollusks, snails and slugs need to be moist all the time. For this reason, they avoid direct sun and dry places, and hide during the day in damp places, such as under flower pots or in thick groundcover. They emerge at night or on cloudy days to feed. Snails and slugs are similar in appearance, except that the snail has a hard shell, into which it withdraws when disturbed. Slugs lay masses of white eggs encased in a slimy mass in protected places. Snails bury their eggs in the soil, also in a slimy mass. The young look like miniature versions of their parents.

SOLUTION: Scatter ORTHO Slug-Geta Snail & Slug Bait in bands around the areas you wish to protect. Also scatter the bait in areas where snails or slugs might be hiding, such as in dense groundcovers, weedy areas, compost piles, or pot storage areas. Before spreading the bait, wet down the treated areas to encourage snail and slug activity that night. Repeat the application every 2 weeks as long as snails and slugs are active.

Leaf spot.

PROBLEM: Spots and blotches appear on the leaves. The spots may be yellow, red, tan, gray, or brown. They range in size from barely visible to ¼ inch in diameter. Several spots may join to form blotches. Leaves may be yellow and dying. Leaf spotting is most severe in warm, humid weather. In damp conditions, a fine gray mold sometimes covers the infected leaf tissue.

ANALYSIS: Leaf spot
Several different fungi cause leaf spots. Some of these fungi may eventually kill the plant, or weaken it so that it becomes susceptible to attack by other organisms. Others merely cause spotting that is unsightly but not harmful. These fungi are spread by splashing water, wind, insects, and tools. They generally survive the winter in diseased plant debris. Most of the leaf spot organisms do their greatest damage in mild weather (50° to 85°F).

SOLUTION: Spray with a fungicide containing *chlorothalonil* (DACONIL 2787®), *maneb*, or *mancozeb* at intervals of 3 to 10 days. Because leaf spots are favored by warm, humid conditions, it is important to spray frequently during these periods. These fungicides protect the new healthy foliage but will not eradicate the fungus on leaves that are already infected. These leaves may be picked off. Clean up plant debris during the growing season and in the fall.

Powdery mildew.

PROBLEM: Leaves and stems are covered with grayish white powdery spots and patches, which occur primarily on the upper surfaces of the leaves. Severely infected young leaves become curled and distorted. The infected foliage eventually turns yellow and withers.

ANALYSIS: Powdery mildew
This common plant disease is caused by a fungus that thrives in both humid and dry weather. The powdery patches consist of fungal strands and spores. The spores are spread by the wind to healthy plants. The fungus saps the plant nutrients, causing leaf yellowing and often death of the leaf. A severe infection may kill the plant. Since some powdery mildews attack many different kinds of plants, the fungus from a diseased plant may infect other types of plants in the garden. (See page 1006 for a list of powdery mildews and the plants they attack.) Under favorable conditions, powdery mildew can spread through a closely spaced planting in a matter of days or weeks. It is generally most severe in the late summer.

SOLUTION: Spray infected plants with a fungicide containing *benomyl* or *triforine* (FUNGINEX ®) to stop the spread of the disease. *Benomyl* protects the new, healthy foliage by killing the powdery mildew spores as they germinate on the leaf. It will not remove the fungus spots on diseased leaves. These leaves may be picked off. Spray at regular intervals of 10 to 12 days or as often as necessary to protect new growth. Space plants far enough apart to allow good air circulation. Remove and destroy severely infected plants. Clean up plant debris.

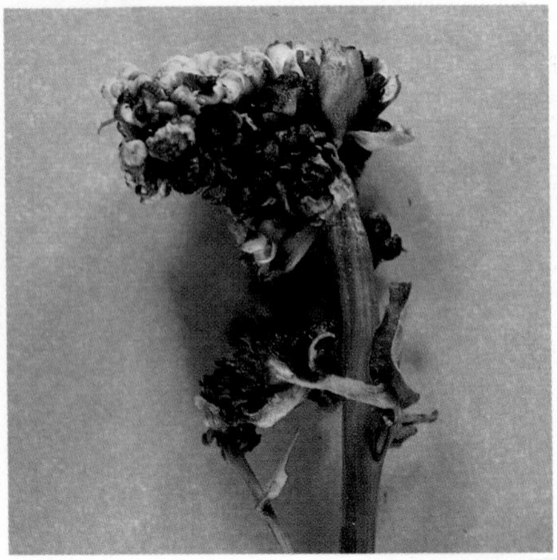

Cyclamen mite damage.

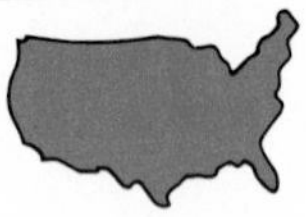

PROBLEM: Flower buds are deformed and blackened. The leaves are curled, distorted, thickened, and brittle. Dark brown or black streaks and blotches form on the leaves and stems. The plant may be stunted to only a quarter of its normal size.

ANALYSIS: Cyclamen mite
(*Steneotarsonemus pallidus*)
This microscopic plant pest is a member of the spider family. Cyclamen mites are 1/100 of an inch long and can be seen only with a powerful magnifying glass. Although the mites are not visible to the naked eye, their damage is very distinctive, and is often called *the blacks.* Mites generally live and feed in leaf and flower buds, and rarely venture out onto exposed plant surfaces. These pests spread by crawling from one overlapping leaf to another. They are also spread on contaminated tools, clothing, and hands. Cyclamen mites are not very active during the hot summer months, and are most injurious from the early spring until June and again in late summer. The adults live through the winter in the base of the delphinium plant, where the roots and stalks join, about ½ inch deep in the soil.

SOLUTION: Spray the infested plants with a pesticide containing *dicofol* (KELTHANE®); respray 3 more times at intervals of 7 to 10 days. Spray the foliage thoroughly, covering both the upper and lower surfaces of the leaves. Space plants far enough apart so that their foliage doesn't overlap. This prevents the mites from spreading. Wash your hands and tools after working on an infested plant to prevent spreading mites to healthy plants.

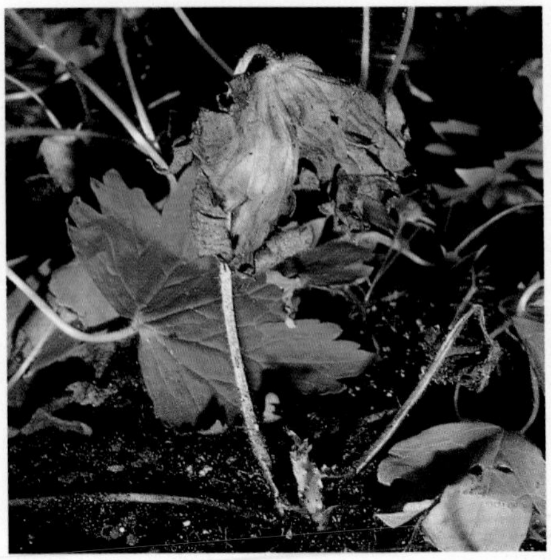

Crown and root rot.

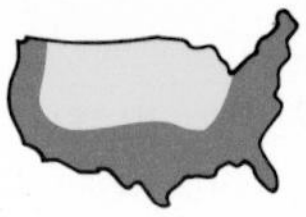

PROBLEM: The lower leaves turn yellow and the plant wilts and dies, sometimes in just a few days. The plant pulls up easily to reveal rotted dark-brown or black roots and lower stems. There may be white fungal strands on infected stems and around the base of the plant. Small tan to reddish brown pellets the size of pinheads or larger form on the infected plant tissue and on the soil surrounding the plant.

ANALYSIS: Crown and root rot
This plant disease is caused by either of 2 closely related fungi (*Sclerotium delphinii* and *Sclerotium rolfsii*), which infect many kinds of vegetable and ornamental plants. These fungi initially attack the root system and then move upward into the base of the plant. They decay the roots and clog the water-conducting tissue in the lower stems and base of the plant, causing wilting and death of the plant. Crown and root rots are most severe in poorly drained soil and during periods of warm, moist weather. Fungal pellets form which survive in dry soil and extremes of temperature to reinfect plants when conditions are suitable for plant growth. These pellets can persist in the soil or plant debris indefinitely. Both fungal strands and pellets are spread by moving water and contaminated soil and equipment.

SOLUTION: Remove and destroy infected plants and the soil immediately around them. Improve soil drainage and let the soil dry out between waterings. (For further information about these techniques see pages 849 and 907.) Do not put susceptible plants in areas that have been contaminated with these fungi. For a list of plants susceptible to sclerotium, see page 1007.

DIANTHUS (CARNATION, PINK, SWEET WILLIAM)

ADAPTATION: Throughout the United States. Carnations may be grown as annuals in zones 3 to 8, but may need winter protection to be grown as perennials in these areas. They do not need protection in zones 9 and 10. To determine your climate zone, see the map on page 1020.

FLOWERING TIME: Late spring and summer.

LIGHT: Full sun.

PLANTING TIME: Spring, after all danger of frost is past.

SOIL: Well drained, pH 6.5 to 7.5

FERTILIZER: Fertilize with ORTHO Rose & Flower Food or ORTHO General Purpose Plant Food according to label directions.

WATER:
How much: Apply enough water to wet the soil to the bottom of the root zone. For pinks and sweet william, wet the soil 4 to 6 inches deep. For carnations, wet the soil 8 to 10 inches deep.
Containers: Apply enough water to container plants so that about 10 percent of the water drains from the bottom of the container.
How often: Water when the soil is just barely moist.

Fusarium wilt.

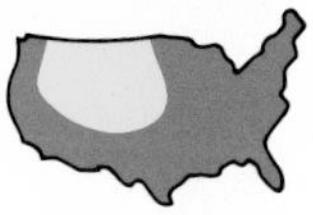

PROBLEM: Leaves and stems turn gray-green, then pale yellow, and wilt. Yellowing and wilting often affect only side side of the plant. Plant shoots may be curled and distorted. The stems are soft and can be easily crushed. When a stem is split open, dark streaks and discolorations of the inner stem tissue are revealed. The roots are generally healthy.

ANALYSIS: Fusarium wilt
This wilt disease affects many ornamental plants. It is caused by a soil-inhabiting fungus (*Fusarium oxysporum* var. *dianthi*) that persists indefinitely on plant debris or in the soil. The disease is spread by contaminated seeds, plants, soil, and equipment. The fungus enters the plant through the roots and spreads up into the stems and leaves through the water-conducting vessels in the stems. The vessels become discolored and plugged. This plugging cuts off the flow of water to the leaves, causing leaf yellowing and wilting. For more information about fusarium wilt, see page 850.

SOLUTION: No chemical control is available. It is best to destroy infected plants. Fusarium can be removed from the soil only by fumigation techniques. (For more information about soil fumigation, see page 927.) However, the best solution is usually to use plants that are resistant to fusarium.

Gray mold.

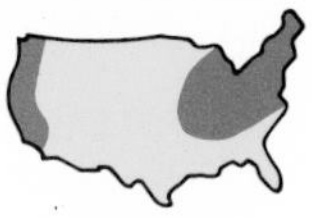

PROBLEM: Brown spots and blotches appear on leaves and possibly on stems. As the disease progresses, a fuzzy brown or grayish mold forms on the infected tissue. Gray mold and spots often appear on the flowers, especially during periods of cool, wet weather. The leaves and stems may be soft and rotted.

ANALYSIS: Gray mold
This widespread plant disease is caused by a fungus (*Botrytis cinerea*) that is found on most dead plant tissue. The fungus initially attacks foliage and flowers that are weak or dead, causing spotting and mold. The fuzzy mold that develops is composed of millions of microscopic spores. Once gray mold has become established on plant debris and weak or dying leaves and flowers, it can invade healthy plant tissue. The fungus is spread by wind and splashing water, or by infected pieces of plant tissue contacting healthy tissue. Cool temperatures and high humidity favor gray mold growth. Crowded plantings, rain, and overhead watering also enhance the spread of the disease. Infection is more of a problem in spring and fall, when temperatures are lower. In warm winter areas where freezing is rare, gray mold can a year-round problem.

SOLUTION: Spray infected plants once every 10 to 14 days with a fungicide containing *chlorothalonil* (DACONIL 2787®), *benomyl*, or *folpet* (PHALTAN®). Continue spraying as long as the mold is visible. Clean up plant debris, and remove dying or infected leaves, stems, and flowers. Provide enough space between plants to allow good air circulation. Try to avoid wetting the foliage when watering.

Bacterial wilt.

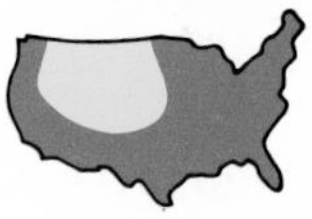

PROBLEM: Stems wilt or the entire plant may wilt. The leaves dry, turn yellow, and die. The roots are often rotted. Cracks may appear around the base of the stem, with yellow streaks extending up the length of the stem. When the stems are sliced open, yellowish to brownish discolorations of the stem tissue are revealed. The infected interior portions of the stem are sticky.

ANALYSIS: Bacterial wilt
This disease of carnations and pinks is caused by a bacterium (*Pseudomonas caryophylli*) that lives in the soil. The bacteria penetrate the plant stems through wounds or cuts in the roots or the base of the stem. Once inside, the wilt organisms multiply and clog the water-conducting stem tissue, causing the plant to wilt and die. The bacteria can also move down into the root system, causing decay. A sticky fluid, which coats infected stems and roots, contains millions of bacteria. The bacteria are spread to other plants by water, handling, contaminated soil, plant debris, and contaminated equipment. Bacterial wilt damage increases as the temperature grows warmer.

SOLUTION: Once a plant is infected, it cannot be cured. It is best to remove and destroy all infected plants. Clean up plant debris. If you've been handling infected plants, wash your hands thoroughly with soap and hot water and dip any contaminated tools in rubbing alcohol before working on healthy plants. Do not replant healthy carnations or pinks in contaminated soil. Avoid damage to plants when cultivating.

DIANTHUS (CARNATION, PINK, SWEET WILLIAM)

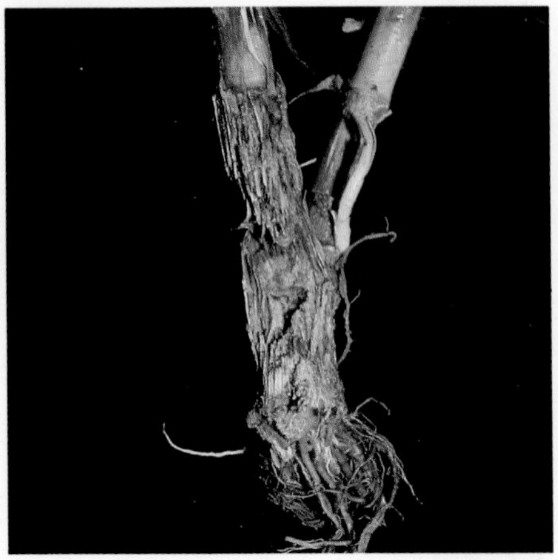

Rhizoctonia stem rot on carnation.

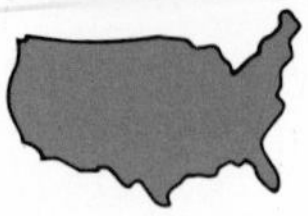

PROBLEM: The leaves turn pale and wilt, sometimes very suddenly. The lower leaves are rotted. The stem is slimy and decayed, and minute black pellets may be just barely visible around the base of the plant.

ANALYSIS: Stem rot
This plant disease is caused by a fungus (*Rhizoctonia solani*) that is found in almost all soils. It penetrates the plant at or just below the soil level, rotting through the outer stem bark into the inner stem tissue. Unlike the soft, outer stem rot, the inner stem tissue becomes dry and corky when it is infected. As the rot progresses up the stem, the lower leaves rot, the foliage pales and withers, and the plant may die. *Rhizoctonia* thrives in warm, moist conditions.

SOLUTION: If all the foliage is wilted, it is best to replace the plants. Plants not so severely affected can be saved. An effective cultural method to help control the disease is to let the soil dry out between waterings. (For further information on this technique, see page 849.) Next year before planting, spray or dust the soil with a fungicide containing *PCNB*.

Spider mite damage.

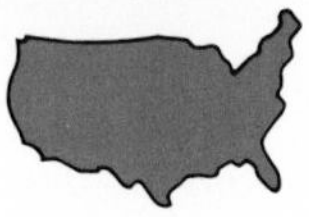

PROBLEM: Leaves are stippled, yellowing, and dirty. Leaves may dry out and drop. There may be webbing over flower buds, between leaves, or on the lower surfaces of the leaves. To determine if the plant is infested with mites, hold a sheet of white paper underneath an affected leaf and tap the leaf sharply. Minute green, red, or yellow specks the size of pepper grains will drop to the paper and begin to crawl around. The pests are easily seen against the white background.

ANALYSIS: Two-spotted spider mite
(*Tetranychus urticae*)
These mites, related to spiders, are major pests of many garden and greenhouse plants. They cause damage by sucking sap from the underside of the leaves. As a result of feeding, the green leaf pigment disappears, producing the stippled appearance. Mites are active throughout the growing season, but are favored by hot, dry weather (70°F and up). By midsummer, they build up to tremendous numbers.

SOLUTION: Spray with *dicofol* (KELTHANE®) when damage is first noticed. Spray the foliage thoroughly, covering the upper and lower surfaces of the leaves. Repeat the spray three more times at intervals of 7 days.

Virus.

PROBLEM: The leaves are mottled or have yellow to reddish spots, rings, or streaks parallel to the leaf veins. The lower leaves may turn yellow. Sometimes there are blotches on the leaves. The flowers may be streaked or blotched with light or dark colors, or coloring may be uneven.

ANALYSIS: Virus
Several different viruses infect carnations. Generally, virus infections are not very harmful to the plant. In fact, symptoms of infection may not show up unless several viruses are present in the plant at the same time. However, in severe infections, viruses can cause the lower leaves to turn yellow by suppressing the development of the green pigment (chlorophyll) in the leaf tissue. As a result, the leaves produce less food, causing the plant to be weakened. Certain viruses are spread by aphids, which feed on diseased plants and transfer the virus to healthy plants. Other viruses can be spread when the plants are pruned or handled. If diseased plants are touched or pruned, the virus can be transferred to healthy plants on contaminated hands or equipment.

SOLUTION: Once the plant is infected, there is no chemical that will control the virus. Remove weak and stunted plants. Wash your hands thoroughly and dip pruning shears into rubbing alcohol after working on infected plants. Keep the aphid population low by spraying infested plants with an insecticide containing *malathion*. For spot treatment of a few plants use ORTHO Rose & Flower Insect Killer according to label directions. Purchase only healthy plants. For further information on selecting healthy plants, see page 924.

Alternaria leaf spot.

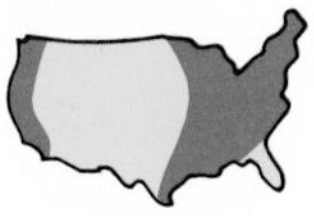

PROBLEM: Dark purple spots surrounded by yellow-green margins appear on the leaves and stems. Sunken, grayish-brown dead areas develop in the center of the spots. Individual spots enlarge and merge to form blotches. Infected leaves turn yellow, blacken, then die. Lesions develop on stems, especially at the bases. Flowers may be spotted. The leaves at the tips of infected stems may become mottled, turn yellow, and wilt. The entire plant may eventually wilt and die.

ANALYSIS: Alternaria leaf spot
This plant disease is caused by a fungus (*Alternaria dianthi*) that infects carnations, pinks, and sweet William. Infection is most severe in wet, humid conditions. Spores are spread by wind and splashing water. Infection occurs when spores germinate on wet leaves, stems, or petals. The fungus survives as spores on plant debris.

SOLUTION: Pick off and destroy infected plant parts and clean up plant debris. Spray with ORTHO Orthocide Garden Fungicide or a fungicide containing *chlorothalonil* (DACONIL 2787®) according to label directions. Water in the morning so the foliage will have a chance to dry out. Try to avoid wetting the foliage when watering.

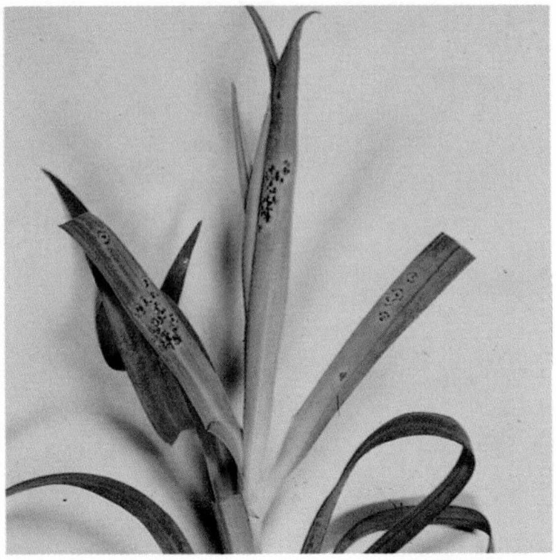

Rust.

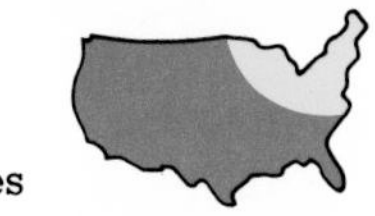

PROBLEM: Chocolate brown pustules of spores appear on the leaves, stems, and flower buds. Infected plants are often stunted and their leaves curl up. Severely infected leaves may wither and drop prematurely.

ANALYSIS: Rust
This fungus (*Uromyces dianthi*) causes a common and easily recognizable disease of carnations and pinks. Infection starts in the early spring as soon as conditions are favorable for plant growth. Rust spores are spread from plant to plant by wind and splashing water. The plant must be wet for 6 to 8 hours before the fungus can infect it. Rust survives only on living plant tissue and as spores on seed. It does not remain infectious on dead plant parts or in the soil. The disease is favored by moist conditions, cool nights, and warm days. Temperatures above 90°F kill the spores.

SOLUTION: Spray infected plants with ORHTO Funginex Rose Disease Control or ORTHO Orthenex Insect and Disease Control at intervals of 7 to 10 days throughout the growing season. Spray thoroughly, making sure to cover both the upper and lower surfaces of the leaves. Funginex protects the new, healthy foliage by killing the rust spores as they germinate on the leaf. It will not eradicate the fungus on diseased leaves. These leaves may be picked off. Water in the morning rather than the late afternoon or evening, to allow foliage a chance to dry out. Space plants far enough apart to allow good air circulation. Remove and destroy all infected plants in the fall to prevent them from surviving the winter and reinfecting new plantings.

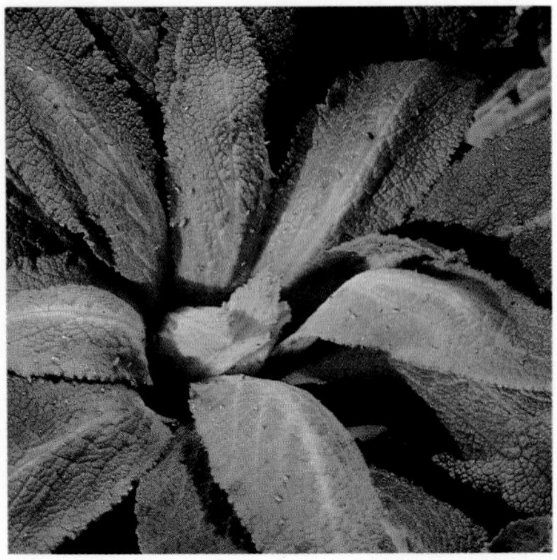

Aphid damage.

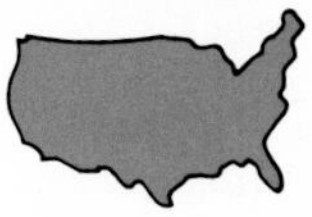

PROBLEM: Tiny (1/8 inch) pale green to black, soft-bodied insects cluster on the leaves and stems. The leaves may be curled, distorted, spotted, and yellowing. The flowers may be malformed. A sticky, shiny substance may coat the leaves. Ants are often present.

ANALYSIS: Aphids
Aphids do little damage in small numbers. However, they are extremely prolific and populations can rapidly build up to damaging numbers during the growing season. Damage occurs when the aphid sucks the juices from the foxglove leaves and flower buds. The aphid is unable to digest fully all the sugar in the plant sap and excretes it in a fluid called honeydew. The honeydew often drops onto the leaves below. Ants feed on this sticky substance, and are often present where there is an aphid infestation. For more information about aphids, see page 875.

SOLUTION: Spray with an insecticide containing *malathion* as soon as the insects appear. Repeat the spray if the plant becomes reinfested.

Digitalis cultural information
Light: Sun
Water: When the soil is just barely moist
Soil: Any good garden soil
Fertilizer: Medium

DIGITALIS (FOXGLOVE)

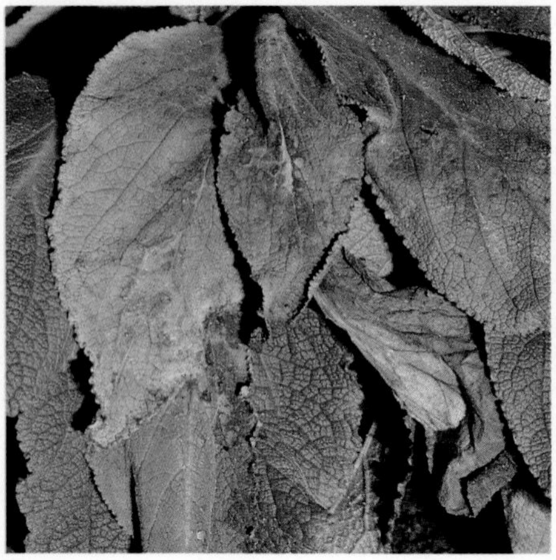

Foxglove anthracnose.

PROBLEM: Light or purplish brown spots up to ⅛ inch in diameter appear on the leaves. The spots are circular or angular, and have purplish margins. Often, black, rough areas develop in the centers of the leaf spots. There may be sunken lesions on the leaf veins and stems, and severely infected leaves turn yellow, wither, and drop off. Often the plants are stunted and die, especially during periods of warm, moist weather. Seedlings may wilt and die.

ANALYSIS: Foxglove anthracnose
This plant disease is caused by a fungus (*Colletotrichum fuscum*) that infects only foxgloves. The fungal spores are spread from plant to plant by splashing water or rain, insects, animals, and contaminated tools. If the leaves are wet, the spores germinate and infect the leaf tissue, creating spots and lesions. Anthracnose is favored by warm temperatures and moist conditions. The fungus survives the winter in diseased plant debris and infected seed. This fungus also causes damping-off of foxglove seedlings. For further information on damping-off, see page 850.

SOLUTION: Spray diseased plants with a fungicide containing *ferbam* or *ziram*. Repeat the spray throughout the growing season at intervals of 7 to 10 days. Remove and destroy plant debris in the fall. If practical, infected leaves may be picked off. Water in the morning so the foliage will have a chance to dry out. Try to avoid wetting the foliage when watering.

DIMORPHOTHECA (AFRICAN DAISY)

Wilt.

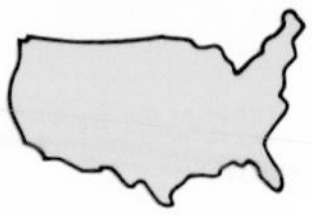

PROBLEM: The lower leaves turn yellow, then wilt and die; or all of the foliage may turn yellow and then wither. The flower heads may droop. Often, the plant is affected only on one side. When the stem is sliced open near the base of the plant, dark streaks and discolorations of the inner stem tissue are revealed. The root system may be partially or entirely rotted.

ANALYSIS: Wilt disease
Wilt disease affects many ornamental plants. It is caused by either of two soil-inhabiting fungi (*Verticillium albo-atrum* or *Fusarium* species) that persist indefinitely on plant debris or in the soil. The disease is spread by contaminated seeds, plants, soil, and equipment. The fungus enters the plant through the roots and spreads up into the stems and leaves through the water-conducting vessels in the stems. The vessels become discolored and plugged. This plugging cuts off the flow of water to the leaves, causing leaf yellowing and wilting.

SOLUTION: No chemical control is available. It is best to destroy infected plants. Verticillium and fusarium can be removed from the soil only by fumigation techniques. (For more information about soil fumigation, see page 927.)

Dimorphotheca cultural information
Light: Sun
Water: Allow to dry between waterings
Soil: Any good garden soil
Fertilizer: Medium

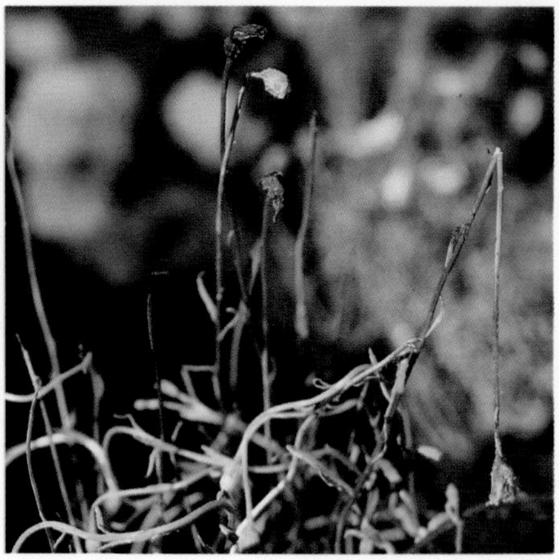

Gray mold.

PROBLEM: Brown spots and blotches appear on the leaves and possibly on the stems. As the disease progresses, a fuzzy brown or grayish mold forms on the infected tissue. Gray mold and spots often appear on the flowers, especially during periods of cool, wet weather. The leaves and stems may be soft and rotted.

ANALYSIS: Gray mold
This widespread plant disease is caused by a fungus (*Botrytis cinerea*) that is found on most dead plant tissue. The fungus initially attacks foliage and flowers that are weak or dead, causing spotting and mold. The fuzzy mold that develops is composed of millions of microscopic spores. Once gray mold has been established on plant debris and weak or dying leaves and flowers, it can invade healthy plant tissue. Crowded plantings, rain, and overhead watering enhance the spread of the disease. Cool temperatures and high humidity favor gray mold growth. Infection is more of a problem in spring and fall when temperatures are lower. In warm winter areas where freezing is rare, gray mold can be a year-round problem.

SOLUTION: Spray infected plants once every 10 to 14 days with a fungicide containing *captan* (ORTHOCIDE®) or *zineb*. Continue spraying as long as the mold is visible. Clean up plant debris, and remove dying or infected leaves, stems, and flowers. Provide enough space between plants to allow good air circulation. Try to avoid wetting the foliage when watering.

EUPHORBIA (POINSETTIA)

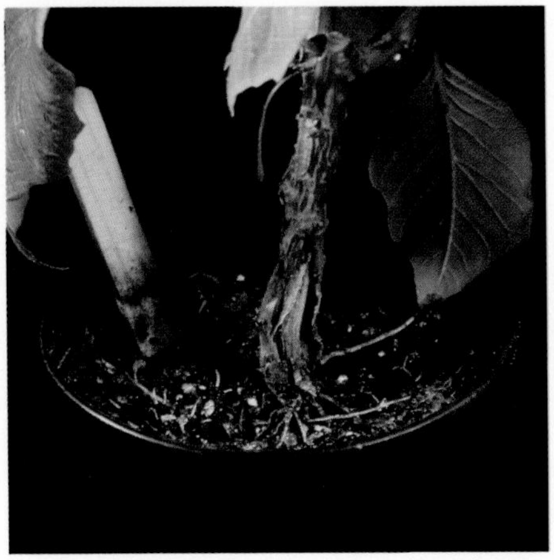

Root and stem rot.

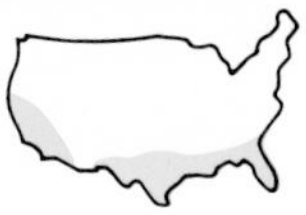

PROBLEM: Leaves turn yellow, wilt and die. Stems may be soft and rotted, and the plant may be easily pulled out of the ground. The roots are dark and rotted.

ANALYSIS: Root and stem rot
This disease is caused by any of several different fungi and bacteria that live in the soil. They thrive in waterlogged, heavy soil. Some of these fungi and bacteria attack the plant stems at the soil level, while others attack the roots. Infection causes the roots and stems to decay. This results in wilting, then yellowing leaves, and eventually the death of the plant. These fungi and bacteria are generally spread by infested soil and transplants, contaminated equipment, and splashing or running water.

SOLUTION: Allow the soil around the plants to dry out. (For more information on this technique, see page 849.) Remove and discard severely infected plants. Avoid future root rot problems by planting in well-drained soil. For information on improving soil drainage, see page 907. For more information on root and stem rots, see page 849.

Euphorbia cultural information
Light: Full sun
Water: When the soil is just barely moist
Soil: Any good, well-drained garden soil
Fertilizer: Medium

FREESIA

Aphids (life size).

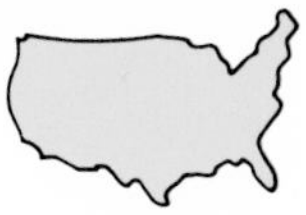

PROBLEM: Tiny (⅛ inch) pale green to black, soft-bodied insects are clustered on the leaves. The leaves may be curled, distorted, and yellowing. The flowers may be malformed. A shiny, sticky substance coats the leaves. Ants are often present.

ANALYSIS: Aphids
Aphids do little damage in small numbers. However, they are extremely prolific and populations can rapidly build up to damaging numbers during the growing season. Damage occurs when the aphid sucks the juices from the freesia leaves and flower buds. The aphid is unable to digest fully all the sugar in the plant sap and excretes the excess in a fluid called honeydew. The honeydew often drops onto the leaves below. Ants feed on this sticky substance and are often present where there is an aphid infestation. For more information about aphids, see page 875.

SOLUTION: Spray with an insecticide containing *malathion* as soon as the insects appear. Repeat the spray if the plant becomes reinfested.

Freesia cultural information
Light: Sun
Water: When soil is just barely moist
Soil: Any good garden soil
Fertilizer: Medium

GERBERA (TRANSVAAL DAISY)

Foot rot.

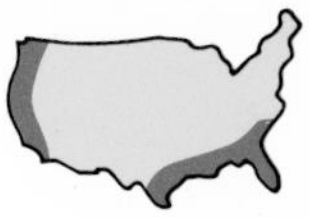

PROBLEM: Leaves wilt, turn reddish, and eventually die. The *crown* (where the leaves meet the roots) and roots are soft, water-soaked, and blackish brown.

ANALYSIS: Foot rot
This plant disease is caused by a soil-dwelling fungus (*Phytophthora* species) that penetrates the crown of the plant, then moves down into the roots. Infection causes the crown and roots to decay, resulting in wilting, reddened leaves, and eventually the death of the plant. Foot rot is most severe in heavy, poorly drained soil and generally moist conditions. The fungus is spread by contaminated soil, transplants, tools, and running water. For more information on root and stem rots, see the section beginning on page 849.

SOLUTION: Destroy all severely infected plants; they usually will not recover. Allow the soil around the plants to dry out. (For more information on this technique, see page 849.) Do not replant gerberas in infested soil for several years. Avoid future foot rot problems by planting in well-drained soil. For information on improving soil drainage, see page 907.

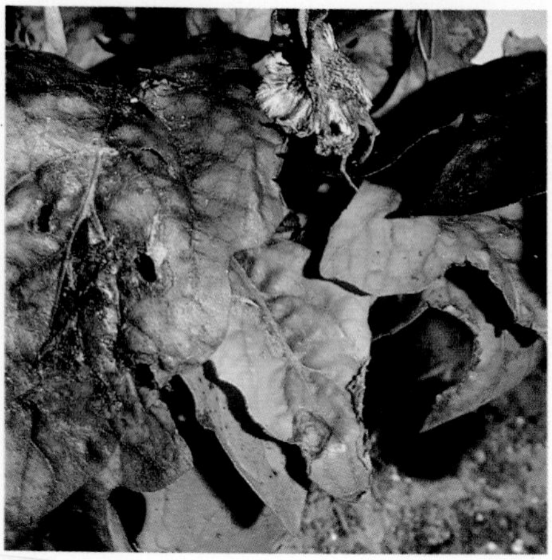

Gray mold.

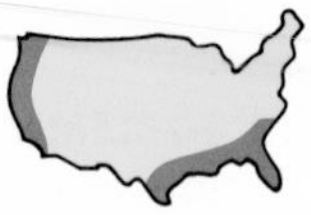

PROBLEM: Brown spots and blotches appear on the leaves and possibly on the stems. As the disease progresses, a fuzzy brown or grayish mold forms on the infected tissue. Gray mold and spots often appear on the flowers, especially during periods of cool, wet weather. The leaves and stems may be soft and rotted.

ANALYSIS: Gray mold
This widespread plant disease is caused by a fungus (*Botrytis cinerea*) that is found on most dead plant tissue. The fungus initially attacks foliage and flowers that are weak or dead, causing spotting and mold. The fuzzy mold that develops is composed of millions of microscopic spores. Once gray mold has become established on plant debris and weak or dying leaves and flowers, it can invade healthy plant tissue. The fungus is spread by splashing water, or by infected pieces of plant tissue contacting healthy tissue. Cool temperatures and high humidity favor gray mold growth. Crowded plantings, rain, and overhead watering also enhance the spread of the disease. Infection is more of a problem in spring and fall, when temperatures are lower. In warm winter areas where freezing is rare, gray mold can be a year-round problem.

SOLUTION: Spray infected plants once every 10 to 14 days with a fungicide containing *maneb* or *mancozeb*. Continue spraying as long as the mold is visible. Clean up plant debris, and remove dying or infected leaves, stems, and flowers. Provide enough space between plants to allow good air circulation. Try to avoid wetting the foliage when watering.

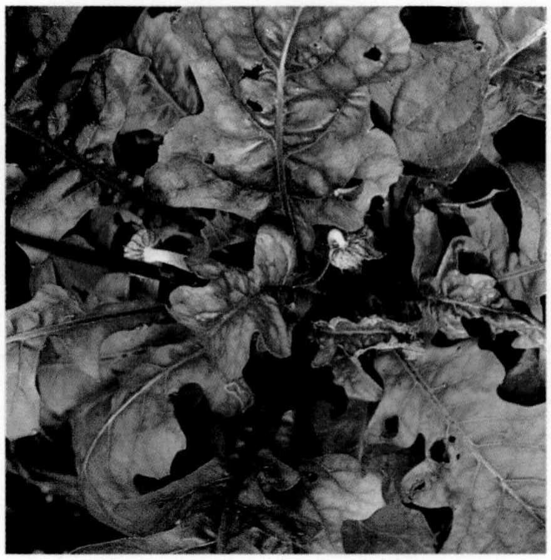

Aphid damage.

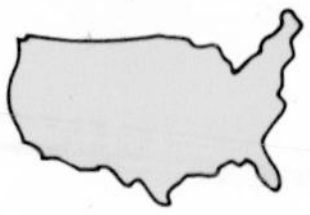

PROBLEM: The leaves may be curled, distorted, and yellowing. Often, the flowers are malformed. Tiny (1/8 inch) yellow to pale green soft-bodied insects cluster on the leaves, stems, and flowers. A shiny, sticky substance may coat the leaves. Ants are sometimes present.

ANALYSIS: Aphids
Aphids do little damage in small numbers. However, they are extremely prolific and populations can rapidly build up to damaging numbers during the growing season. Damage occurs when the aphid sucks the juices from the gerbera leaves and flower buds. The aphid is unable to digest fully all the sugar in the plant sap and excretes the excess in a fluid called honeydew. The honeydew often drops onto the leaves below. Ants feed on this sticky substance and are often present where there is an aphid infestation. For more information about aphids, see page 875.

SOLUTION: Spray with ORTHO Liquid Sevin or an insecticide containing *malathion* as soon as the insects appear. Repeat the spray if the plant becomes reinfested.

Gerbera cultural information
Light: Sun
Water: When the soil is just barely moist
Soil: Well drained
Fertilizer: Medium

GLADIOLUS

ADAPTATION: Throughout the United States.

FLOWERING TIME: Summer to fall.

LIGHT: Full sun.

PLANTING TIME: From late winter or spring, when all danger of frost is past, to midsummer.

SOIL: Any good garden soil. pH 5.5 to 7.5

FERTILIZER: Fertilize with ORTHO Rose & Flower Food or ORTHO General Purpose Plant Food according to label directions.

WATER:
How much: Apply enough water to wet the soil 6 to 8 inches deep.
How often: Water when the soil 1 inch below the surface is just barely moist.

HANDLING: For continuous summer bloom, make successive plantings at 2 week intervals from mid-April to mid-July. For cut flowers, harvest when the bottom flower is open. When cutting flowers, allow at least four leaves to remain on the plant.

Gladiolus thrips damage.

PROBLEM: Silvery white streaks appear on flowers and foliage. The leaves turn brown and die. Flowers may be deformed and discolored. In the early morning, late afternoon, or on overcast days, blackish brown, slender, winged insects 1/16 inch long can be seen on the foliage and flower petals. On warm, sunny days these insects hide between leaves and in flower buds. They can be detected only by pulling apart a flower bud or two overlapping leaves.

ANALYSIS: Gladiolus thrips
(*Thrips simplex*)
This insect, one of the most common pests of gladiolus plants, also feeds on many other garden ornamentals. Both the immature and adult thrips feed on plant sap by rasping the plant tissue. The injured tissue turns white, causing the characteristic streaking and silvering of the leaves and flowers. The adult female thrips inserts her eggs into growing plant tissue; the emerging young mature within 2 to 4 weeks. Thrips actively feed and reproduce from spring until the first frost of fall. They cannot survive freezing temperatures. In warm winter climates, the adult thrips hibernate in the soil until spring. In cold winter climates, they overwinter by hibernating on gladiolus corms in storage. Corms infested by thrips turn brown and corky and may fail to grow, or produce only stunted, poor quality flowers and foliage.

SOLUTION: Spray infested plants with ORTHO Isotox Insect Killer or ORTHO Diazinon Insect Spray. Repeat the spray at intervals of no less than 10 days if reinfestation occurs. Dust corms with an insecticide containing *malathion* before storing. Discard brown corms.

Streaking of gladiolus flowers caused by virus.

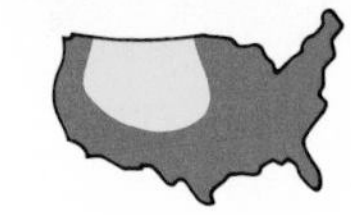

PROBLEM: Leaves and flowers are streaked, spotted, or mottled. The leaves may also be yellowing, stiff, or thickened. Often the plant blooms prematurely, and the flowers only partially open and then fade rapidly. The entire plant may be dwarfed, although sometimes only the flower spike is stunted.

ANALYSIS: Virus
There are a number of different viruses that infect gladiolus plants. Depending on weather conditions and plant variety, the symptoms of infection can vary from barely noticeable to quite severe. Viral infections rarely cause a plant to die, but can weaken it seriously. The virus increases in the corms (the "bulbs" of the gladiolus plant) year after year. Successive plantings from diseased corms provide flowers of poor quality. Viruses are spread by aphids. These insects feed on diseased plants and transfer the virus to healthy plants at subsequent feedings.

SOLUTION: Once the plant is infected, there is no chemical that will control the virus. To prevent the spread of the disease to healthy plants, remove and destroy infected plants. Keep the aphid population under control by spraying infested plants with ORTHO Diazinon Insect Spray. Because two of the viruses that infect gladioli are very common on vegetables in the bean and cucumber families, where practical, avoid planting gladioli near beans, clover, cucumbers, squash, melons, or tomatoes. For more information about controlling disease-carrying insects, see page 879.

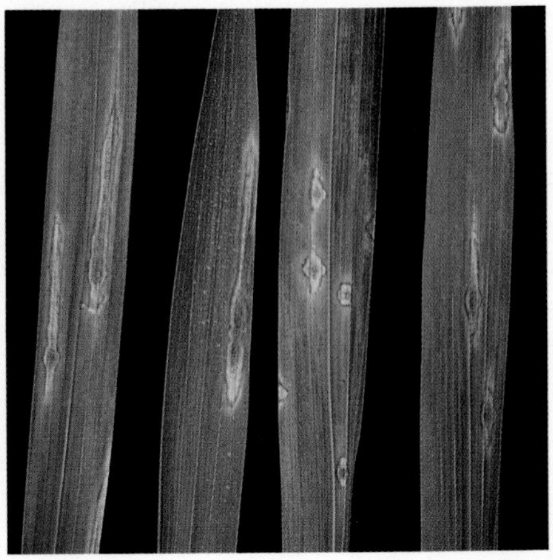

Leaf spot.

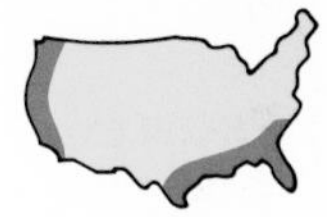

PROBLEM: Spots appear on the leaves. The spots may be yellow, brown, or black. Several spots may join to form blotches. The leaves may be yellowing and dying. Leaf spotting is most severe in humid weather.

ANALYSIS: Leaf spot
Several different fungi cause leaf spots on gladiolus. Some of these fungi may eventually kill the plant, or weaken it so that it becomes susceptible to attack by other organisms. Others merely cause spotting that is unsightly but not harmful. These fungi are spread by splashing water, wind, insects, and tools. They survive the winter in diseased plant debris. Most of these fungi do their greatest damage during wet, mild weather (50° to 85°F).

SOLUTION: Spray with a fungicide containing *chlorothalonil* (DACONIL - 2787®), *zineb, maneb,* or *mancozeb* at intervals of 7 to 10 days. Because leaf spots are favored by humid conditions, it is important to spray frequently during such periods. These fungicides protect the new healthy foliage but will not eradicate the fungus on leaves that are already infected. Clean up infected leaves and debris.

GLADIOLUS

Aster yellows.

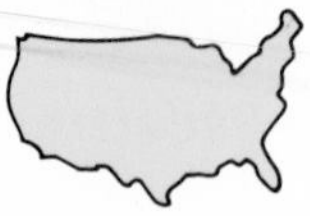

PROBLEM: There are many thin, weak leaves, which may turn yellowish green. The flower spikes are twisted and distorted. The flowers often remain green. The plant is generally small and spindly, and frequently the top of the plant is killed.

ANALYSIS: Aster yellows
This plant disease is caused by mycoplasmas, microscopic organisms similar to bacteria. The mycoplasmas are transmitted from plant to plant primarily by leafhoppers. (For more information about leafhoppers, see page 878.) The symptoms of aster yellows are more severe and appear more quickly in warm weather. Even when the disease is present in the plant, aster yellows may not manifest its symptoms in temperatures of 55°F or less. The disease also infects many ornamental plants, vegetables, and weeds. For a list of plants susceptible to aster yellows, see page 1005.

SOLUTION: Aster yellows cannot be eliminated entirely, but can be kept under control. Remove and destroy infected plants. To remove sources of infection, eradicate nearby weeds that may harbor aster yellows and leafhopper eggs. Spray leafhopper-infested plants with ORTHO Orthene Systemic Insect Control. Repeat the spray whenever leafhoppers are seen. For more information about controlling disease-carrying insects, see page 879.

Fusarium yellows.

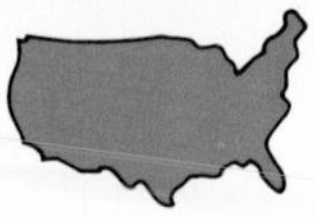

PROBLEM: Foliage and flower spikes are stunted, and flowers may be small and faded-looking. Yellowing starts on the leaf tips and spreads through the entire plant, which finally dies. When the dying plant is pulled out of the ground, the roots are found to be rotted and the corm (the "bulb" of the gladiolus plant) spotted with circular, firm, brown or black lesions. In some cases, the corm appears normal. However, when it is sliced open, brown, discolored inner tissue is revealed.

ANALYSIS: Fusarium yellows
This very common and widespread disease of gladiolus plants and corms is caused by a soil-inhabiting fungus (*Fusarium oxysporum* f. *gladioli*). The fungus may penetrate and rot the corms in storage or in the ground. Wet soils and warm temperatures (70°F and higher) favor the rapid development of this disease. Sometimes corms in storage are contaminated, but the fungal decay may not have progressed far enough to be noticed. When these corms are planted the following spring, they may not produce foliage, if severely infected. If they do produce feeble growth, it soon turns yellow and dies. The fungus survives in diseased corms and soil for many years. Corms that have been removed from the soil prematurely are especially susceptible to infection.

SOLUTION: Destroy all plants and corms that show signs of infection. Dig them up only when they have fully matured. Do not replant healthy corms in soil in which diseased plants have grown. Soak corms in a fungicide containing *benomyl* for 15 minutes before storing, and again before planting. Store them in a dry, cool (40° to 50°F) place.

Scab.

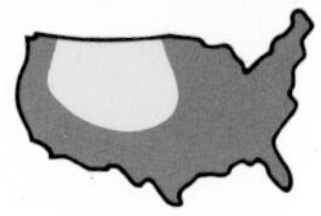

PROBLEM: Sunken black lesions on the corm (the "bulb" of the gladiolus plant) are covered with a shiny, varnish-like material and are encircled by raised, brittle rims. Later in the season, after the corms have been planted, many tiny, raised, reddish brown specks develop on the bases of the emerging leaves. These specks become soft, elongated dead spots, which may be covered with and surrounded by a shiny, oozing material in wet weather. The leaves usually fall over.

ANALYSIS: Scab
This disease, caused by bacteria (*Pseudomonas marginata*), earns its name from the scablike lesions it produces on the gladiolus corms. The bacteria penetrate the corm tissue and then move up into the stem base, producing a soft, watery rot. This decay causes the leaves to fall over. The shiny, varnish-like spots that form on the leaves and corms contain millions of bacteria. Wet, heavy soil and warm temperatures favor the rapid development of this disease. The bacteria can live for several years in infected corms and plant debris. The bacteria are spread by splashing water, and by contaminated corms, soil, tools, and insects. Severely infected plants may die.

SOLUTION: There is no chemical control for this disease. Destroy infected corms. Remove and destroy infected plants. Plant healthy corms in well-drained soil where diseased gladioli have not grown.

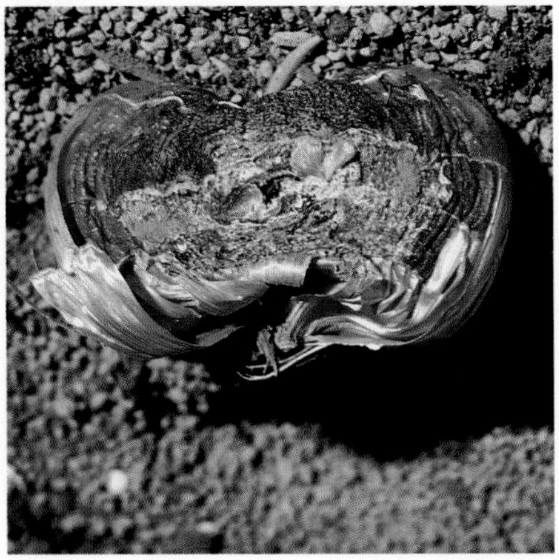

Penicillium corm rot.

PROBLEM: Corky, reddish brown, sunken lesions ½ inch or larger in diameter appear on the corm (the "bulb" of the gladiolus plant). In cool, moist conditions, the rotted areas of the corm become covered with a blue-green mold. Infected corms that have been planted may not produce any foliage. Foliage that is produced turns yellow and wilts. The corms are rotted and moldy.

ANALYSIS: Penicillium corm rot
This disease is caused by a common fungus (*Penicillium gladioli*) that is most often noticed on corms in storage. The fungi infect the corm through wounds or abrasions that usually occur when the corm is dug out of the ground to be put into storage. After the initial infection, the rot spreads throughout the corm and up into the stem tissue. The corms rot rapidly when they are stored in warm, humid conditions. The fungus forms masses of blue-green spores and tiny brown fungal pellets that can survive through dry conditions and extremes of temperatures to invade healthy corms. If mildly infected corms are planted, they may or may not produce foliage, depending upon how severely their infection has progressed. Eventually, any foliage produced will turn yellow and die.

SOLUTION: Destroy all corms showing decay. Store corms in a dry, cool (40° to 45°F) location. Dig them up carefully only when the gladiolus leaves have turned entirely yellow in the fall. Handle the corms carefully to prevent injuries. Dip them in a solution of ORTHO Phaltan Rose & Garden Fungicide before storing, and again before planting them.

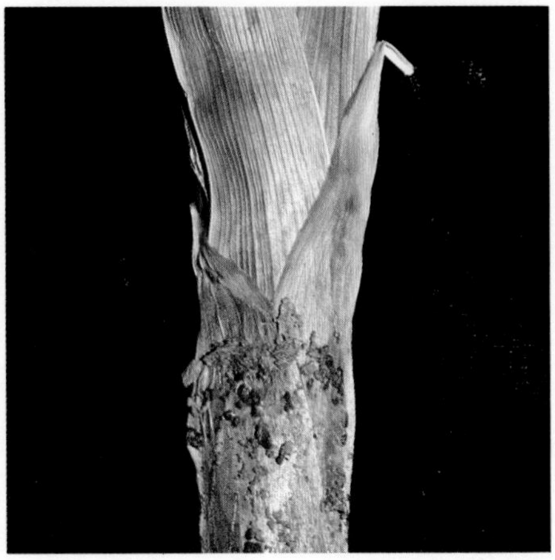

Dry rot.

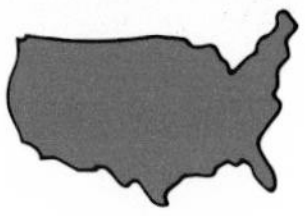

PROBLEM: Foliage turns yellow and dies prematurely. Leaf bases are rotted and may be shredded. Black fungal pellets the size of pepper grains may cover the decayed leaf bases and husks of the corms (the "bulbs" of the gladiolus plant). There are dark brown to black sunken lesions on the corms. These lesions are dry and corky. They may enlarge and join together, destroying the entire corm.

ANALYSIS: Dry rot
This plant disease is caused by a fungus (*Stromatinia gladioli*) that attacks corms either in storage or in the soil. After the initial infection, the decay spreads up into the leaf bases, killing the leaves prematurely. Corms that are planted in cold, wet soil or stored in moist conditions are most susceptible to dry rot. The fungus is spread by contaminated soil and corms. The tiny black fungal pellets that form on infected tissue can survive for 10 years or more in the soil.

SOLUTION: Discard infected corms and plants. Plant in well-drained soil. Dig corms before the onset of cold, wet weather and store them in a dry place. If you wish to replant in areas where infected corms have been growing, fumigate the soil. For information about soil fumigation, see page 927.

Leaf spot.

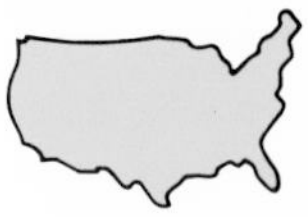

PROBLEM: Spots and blotches appear on the leaves, ranging in size from barely visible to ¼ inch in diameter. Several spots may join to form blotches. Leaves may be yellow and dying. Leaf spotting is most severe in warm, humid weather.

ANALYSIS: Leaf spot
Several different fungi cause leaf spots. Some of these fungi may cause leaf yellowing and death, while others merely cause spotting, which is unsightly but not harmful. These fungi are spread by splashing water, wind, insects, and tools. They survive the winter in diseased plant debris. Most of these leaf spot organisms do their greatest damage in mild weather (50° to 85°F).

SOLUTION: Spray at weekly intervals with a fungicide containing *basic copper sulfate*, *mancozeb*, or *ferbam*. Because leaf spots are favored by warm, humid conditions, it is important to spray conscientiously during these periods. These fungicides protect the new healthy foliage but will not eradicate the fungus on leaves that are already infected. Pick off severely infected leaves.

Helianthemum cultural information
Light: Sun
Water: Allow to dry between waterings
Soil: Well drained
Fertilizer: Light

HELIANTHUS (SUNFLOWER)

Verticillium wilt.

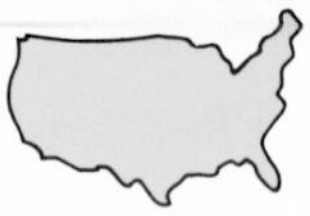

PROBLEM: Mottling, yellowing, and wilting start on the lower leaves and progress slowly upward. Diseased leaves soon wither. Dark brown areas may appear on the infected stems. When a stem is sliced open near the base of the plant, dark streaks and discolorations of the inner stem tissue are revealed. Sunflowers generally do not show symptoms until they flower.

ANALYSIS: Verticillium wilt
This wilt disease affects many ornamental plants. It is caused by a a soil-inhabiting fungus (*Verticillium albo-atrum*). The disease is spread by contaminated seeds, plants, soil, and equipment. The fungus enters the plant through the roots and spreads up into the stems and leaves through the water-conducting vessels in the stems. The vessels become discolored and plugged. This plugging cuts off the flow of water to the leaves, causing leaf yellowing and wilting. For more information about verticillium wilt, see page 850.

SOLUTION: No chemical control is available. It is best to destroy infected plants. Verticillium can be removed from the soil only by fumigation techniques. (For more information about soil fumigation, see page 927.) However, the best solution is usually to use plants that are resistant to verticillium. See page 1006 for a list of wilt-resistant plants.

Helianthus cultural information
Light: Sun
Water: When soil is just barely moist
Soil: Any good garden soil
Fertilizer: Medium to heavy

Powdery mildew.

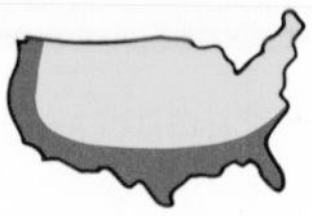

PROBLEM: Leaves and stems are partially or entirely covered with grayish-white powdery patches. The patches occur primarily on the upper surfaces of leaves. The leaves may be yellowing and dying.

ANALYSIS: Powdery mildew
This common plant disease is caused by a fungus *(Erysiphe cichoracearum)* that thrives in both humid and dry weather. The powdery patches consist of fungal strands and spores. The spores are spread by the wind to healthy plants. The fungus saps plant nutrients, causing yellowing and sometimes death of the leaf. Since this mildew attacks many different kinds of plants, the fungus from a diseased plant may infect other types of plants in the garden. (See page 1006 for a list of susceptible plants.) Under favorable conditions, powdery mildew can spread through a closely spaced planting in a matter of days or weeks.

SOLUTION: Treat infected plants with a fungicide containing *benomyl* or a *wettable sulfur.* Repeat every 7 to 10 days, or as often as necessary to protect new growth. Space plants far enough apart to allow good air circulation. Clean up infected leaves and debris.

HELLEBORUS

Crown rot.

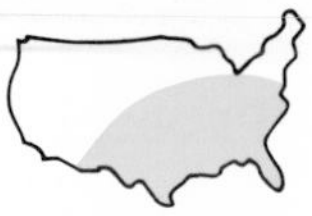

PROBLEM: The leaves turn yellow, wilt, and collapse and the plant finally dies. The base of the plant and the lower stems and leaves are covered with white matted strands. Reddish brown to black pellets the size of pinheads or larger form on the infected plant tissue and soil surrounding the plant.

ANALYSIS: Crown rot
This disease is caused by a soil-inhabiting fungus (*Sclerotium delphinii*). It is widespread and attacks many kinds of plants. The fungus penetrates the stems at or just below the soil level, causing decay and death of the root and stem tissue. The fungus can grow through the soil to attack adjacent plants. The crown rot fungus is spread by moving water, diseased transplants, infested soil, air currents, and contaminated tools. The fungal pellets that form can survive in plant debris and dry soil to reinfect healthy plants when conditions are suitable. Crown rot is most severe in moist soil during warm (70°F and up), moist weather.

SOLUTION: Remove and destroy all infected plants and surrounding soil to 6 inches beyond the diseased area. Drench the area where the infected plants were growing with a fungicide containing *PCNB.* To help prevent infection next year, broadcast a *PCNB* fungicide onto uninfested soil and dig it in to a depth of 6 inches before planting.

Helleborus cultural information
Light: Part to full shade
Water: While soil is still moist
Soil: Well drained
Fertilizer: Medium

HEMEROCALLIS (DAYLILY)

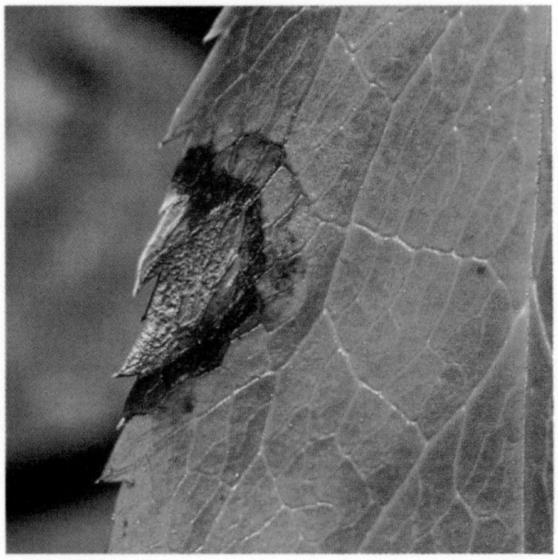

Black spot.

PROBLEM: Large, round or elliptical black spots develop on both sides of the leaves. Spots also form on the stems, flower stalks, and sometimes petals. Concentric rings may form within the spots. Infected stems shrivel and topple, and flower buds and leaves growing on infected stems wilt and die. Foliage yellows and dies prematurely, and overall growth is weak and sparse.

ANALYSIS: Black spot
This plant disease is caused by a fungus (*Coniothyrium hellebori*) that infects only helleborus. The fungal spores are spread from plant to plant by wind and splashing water. If the foliage is wet, the spores germinate and infect leaf, stem, and petal tissue. Black spot is favored by moist conditions. In continuously wet, humid weather, black spot can spread through an entire planting in several days. The fungus survives the winter in infected plant debris.

SOLUTION: Remove dying plants and plant debris. Cut off and destroy all diseased plant parts. Spray with a fungicide containing *captan* (ORTHOCIDE®) at intervals of 10 to 14 days until the spotting no longer occurs. Resume spraying during wet weather.

Leaf spot.

PROBLEM: Spots and blotches appear on the leaves, ranging in size from barely visible to 1/4 inch in diameter. Several spots may join to form blotches. Leaves may be yellow and dying. Leaf spotting is most severe in warm, humid weather.

ANALYSIS: Leaf spot
Several different fungi cause leaf spots. Some of these fungi may eventually kill the plant, or weaken it so that it becomes susceptible to attack by other organisms. Others merely cause spotting that is unsightly but not harmful. These fungi are spread by splashing water, wind, insects, and contaminated tools. They generally survive the winter in diseased plant debris. Most of these fungi do their greatest damage in mild weather (50° to 85°F).

SOLUTION: Spray at weekly intervals with a fungicide containing *basic copper sulfate* or *maneb*. Because leaf spots are favored by warm, humid conditions, it is important to spray conscientiously during these periods. These fungicides protect the new, healthy foliage but will not eradicate the fungus on leaves that are already infected. Pick off severely infected leaves.

Hemerocallis cultural information
Light: Sun or partial shade
Water: While soil is still moist
Soil: Any good garden soil
Fertilizer: Medium

Aphids (1/4 life size).

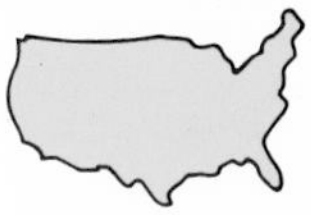

PROBLEM: Tiny (1/8 inch) pale green to brown soft-bodied insects are clustered on the leaves. Leaves may be curled, distorted, and yellowing. Flowers may be malformed. A sticky, shiny substance may coat the leaves. Ants are often present.

ANALYSIS: Aphids
Aphids do little damage in small numbers. However, they are extremely prolific and populations can rapidly build up to damaging numbers during the growing season. Damage occurs when the aphid sucks the juices from the daylily leaves. The aphid is unable to digest fully all the sugar in the plant sap and excretes the excess in a fluid called honeydew, which often drops onto the leaves below. Ants feed on this sticky substance, and are often present where there is an aphid infestation. For more information about aphids, see page 875.

SOLUTION: Spray the infested plants with an insecticide containing *malathion*. Repeat the spray if the plant becomes reinfested.

HEUCHERA (CORAL BELLS)

Leaf spots.

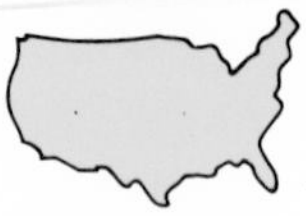

PROBLEM: Spots and blotches appear on the leaves. The spots may be yellow or brown. They range in size from barely visible to 1/4 inch in diameter. Several spots may join to form blotches. Leaves may be yellow and dying. Leaf spotting is most severe in warm, humid weather. In damp conditions, a fine gray mold sometimes covers the infected leaf tissue.

ANALYSIS: Leaf spot
Several different fungi cause leaf spots. Some of these fungi may eventually kill the plant, or weaken it so that it becomes susceptible to attack by other organisms. Others merely cause spotting that is unsightly but not harmful. These fungi are spread by splashing water, wind, insects, and contaminated tools. They generally survive the winter in diseased plant debris. Most of the leaf spot organisms do their greatest damage in mild weather (50° to 85°F).

SOLUTION: Where practical, pick off the diseased leaves. Spray with a fungicide containing *basic copper sulfate* or *maneb* every 7 to 10 days, or frequently enough to protect the new foliage as it grows. These fungicides protect the new healthy foliage but will not eradicate the fungus on leaves that are already infected. Because leaf spots are favored by humid conditions, it is important to spray frequently during these periods.

Heuchera cultural information
Light: Shade or partial shade
Water: Do not allow to dry out
Soil: Any good garden soil
Fertilizer: Medium

HOSTA (PLANTAIN LILY)

Snail damage.

PROBLEM: Irregularly shaped holes with smooth edges are chewed in the leaves. Leaves and stems may be chewed off entirely. Silvery trails wind around on the plants and nearby soil. Snails and slugs may be seen moving around or feeding on the plants, especially at night. Check for them in the garden at night by flashlight.

ANALYSIS: Snails and slugs
These pests are mollusks, and are related to clams, oysters, and other shellfish. They feed on a wide variety of garden plants. Like other mollusks, snails and slugs need to be moist all the time. For this reason, they avoid direct sun and dry places, and hide during the day in damp places, such as under flower pots or in thick groundcover. They emerge at night or on cloudy days to feed. The young look like miniature versions of their parents.

SOLUTION: Scatter ORTHO Bug-Geta Snail & Slug Pellets or ORTHO Slug-Geta Snail & Slug Bait granules around the areas you wish to protect. Also scatter the bait in areas where snails or slugs might be hiding, such as in dense groundcover, weedy areas, compost piles, or pot storage areas. Before spreading the bait, wet down the treated areas to encourage snail and slug activity that night. Repeat the application every 2 weeks as long as snails and slugs are active.

Hosta cultural information
Light: Partial to full shade
Water: Do not allow to dry out
Soil: Well drained
Fertilizer: Medium

HYACINTHUS (HYACINTH)

HYACINTHUS (HYACINTH)

ADAPTATION: Zones 4 through 8. Hyacinths may be grown in zones 9 and 10 if they are precooled (see below). To determine your zone, see the map on page 1020.

FLOWERING TIME: Spring.

LIGHT: Full sun to half-day sun.

PLANTING TIME: Fall.

SOIL: Well drained. pH 6.0 to 7.5

FERTILIZER: When planting, mix 1 teaspoon of ORTHO Bone Meal or ORTHO Superphosphate into the soil at the bottom of the planting hole. During the growing season, fertilize with ORTHO General Purpose Plant Food according to label directions.

WATER:
How much: Apply enough water to wet the soil 1 to 1½ feet deep.
How often: Water when the soil an inch below the surface is just barely moist. Stop watering the bulbs when the foliage turns yellow.

HANDLING: Continue to water and fertilize plants regularly until the foliage turns yellow. Remove foliage after it has turned yellow. In zones 9 and 10, precool bulbs for 6 weeks before planting by storing them in paper bags in the refrigerator crisper.

Short stems.

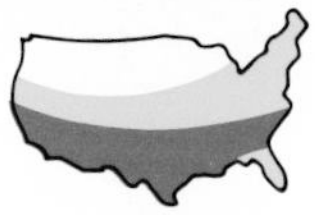

PROBLEM: Flower stems are very short, and the flowers may be smaller than normal. Sometimes only the tip of the flower stalk emerges and blooms at ground level. There are no signs of insects or disease, and the foliage appears healthy.

ANALYSIS: Short stems
This condition is the result of warm spring temperatures, lack of adequate chilling, or a combination of both. Hyacinth bulbs contain embryonic flowers and stems. A minimum of 6 weeks exposure to cool temperatures (45° to 50°F) during the winter stimulates the stem cells to elongate, causing the immature hyacinth to emerge from the ground. During cool spring weather (50° to 55°F) the stems continue to elongate to their full length, at which point the flowers mature and open. In warm winter areas, the hyacinth stems often fail to elongate properly due to inadequate chilling. Also, during unseasonal spring hot spells (when air temperature reaches 70°F or higher) the hyacinth flowers are stimulated by the heat to mature and open before the stems have entirely emerged from the ground.

SOLUTION: There is nothing you can do to increase the length of the hyacinth stem once the flower has matured. If warm spring temperatures are common in your area, plant hyacinths in locations where they will receive either filtered light, or direct sun only in the morning or late afternoon. The lower air and soil temperatures in such areas will help to increase stem lengths. If you live in a warm winter area, place hyacinth bulbs in paper bags in the fall, and chill them in the crisper section of the refrigerator for 6 weeks before planting.

Diseased bulb on left.

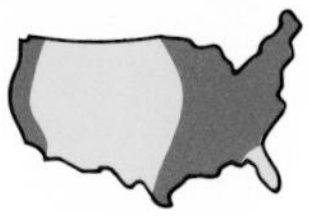

PROBLEM: Bulbs that have been planted may not produce any foliage; or if foliage is produced the flower stalk may not form. Sometimes the flower stalk develops, but the flowers open irregularly and rot off. The entire stalk may rot at the base and fall over. If pulled gently, the leaves and flower stalk may lift entirely off the bulb, which is soft, rotted, and filled with a white, thick, foul-smelling ooze.

ANALYSIS: Bacterial soft rot
This plant disease is caused by bacteria (*Erwinia carotovora*) that infect hyacinth bulbs both in storage and when planted in the ground. The bacteria initially penetrate and decay the upper portion of the bulb. The disease then progresses upward into the leaves and flower stalks, and down through the bulb and roots. The thick ooze that accompanies the decay is filled with millions of bacteria. Bulbs that are infected before they are planted will produce little, if any, growth. Even well-established, healthy plants may decay quite rapidly after they are infected, sometimes within three to five days. The bacteria survive in infected plant debris and bulbs, and are spread by contaminated insects and tools, and diseased bulbs and plants. Soft rot is favored by moist conditions. If bulbs freeze while they are in storage, they are especially susceptible to infection.

SOLUTION: There is no cure for this disease. Remove and destroy all bulbs and plants showing signs of decay. Store bulbs in a dry, cool (40° to 45°F) location. Plant only healthy bulbs in well-drained soil. Do not overwater. For instructions on proper watering, see page 912.

Rodent damage.

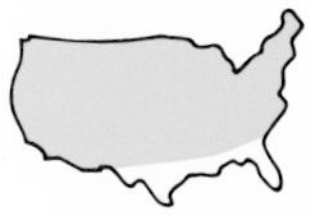

PROBLEM: Hyacinths do not emerge in the spring. When dug up, bulbs are found to have been partially eaten. Hyacinth stems and leaves may be chewed off. The entire plant sometimes disappears. When digging bulbs for storage, the ripened foliage may pull up unattached to the bulb, which is often found to be partly devoured. There may be crescent-shaped mounds of soil clustered in the yard, or tiny holes in the soil and small, dry, rectangular brown pellets on the ground.

ANALYSIS: Rodents
Pocket gophers and field mice are two types of rodents that feed on hyacinth bulbs. Pocket gophers, found in the West, are tan, furry, 6-inch-long rodents that live almost entirely underground. The clustered mounds of dirt they form are indicative of their presence. Field mice live both above ground in protective vegetation and below ground in shallow tunnels and burrows. Signs of field mice include clusters of tiny droppings and small holes in the soil that are entrances to the underground tunnels. Both of these animals feed on bulbs throughout the year.

SOLUTION: Prevent gopher damage by lining the inside of the planting bed with ½ inch mesh chicken wire along the bottom and up the sides. To prevent mouse damage, lay hardware cloth on the top of the planted area, burying the edges. Remove the hardware cloth before shoots emerge in the spring. For more information about rodents and their control, see pages 900 and 896.

IBERIS (CANDYTUFT)

Powdery mildew.

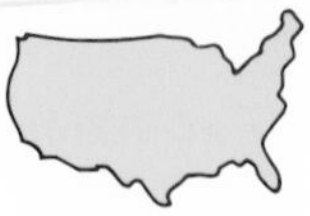

PROBLEM: The leaves and stems are covered with grayish white powdery spots and patches that occur primarily on the surfaces of the leaves. Leaves eventually turn yellow.

ANALYSIS: Powdery mildew
This common plant disease is caused by a fungus (*Erysiphe polygoni*) that thrives in both humid and dry weather. The powdery patches consist of fungal strands and spores. The spores are spread by the wind to healthy plants. A severe infection may kill the plant. Since this powdery mildew attacks several different kinds of plants, the fungus from a diseased plant may infect other types of plants in the garden. For a list of susceptible plants, see page 1006. Under favorable conditions, powdery mildew can spread through a closely spaced planting in a matter of days or weeks.

SOLUTION: Spray infected plants with a fungicide containing *folpet* (PHALTAN®) or *cycloheximide* to stop the spread of the disease. These fungicides protect the new, healthy foliage by killing the powdery mildew spores as they germinate on the leaves. They will not eradicate the fungus on leaves that are already infected. Severely infected plants should be removed. Spray at regular intervals of 7 to 10 days, or as often as necessary to protect new growth. Space plants far enough apart to allow good air circulation. Clean up plant debris.

Iberis cultural information
Light: Sun
Water: When the soil is just barely moist
Soil: Any good garden soil
Fertilizer: Medium

Damping-off.

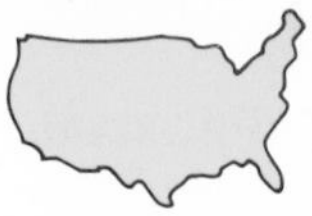

PROBLEM: Seeds don't sprout, or seedlings fall over soon after they emerge. Areas on the stem at the soil line are water-soaked and discolored. The base is soft and thin.

ANALYSIS: Damping-off
The fungi that cause damping-off are favored by wet soil with a high nitrogen level. Under these conditions, the fungi are more active, and the seedlings are more succulent and susceptible to attack. Damping-off often affects flowers that are planted too early in the spring, before the soil has had a chance to dry and warm sufficiently for quick seed germination. Damping-off can also be a problem when the weather remains cloudy and wet while seeds are germinating, or if seedlings are too heavily shaded.

SOLUTION: To prevent damping-off, take these precautions:
1. Allow the surface of the soil to dry slightly between waterings.
2. Do not start seeds in soil that has a high nitrogen level. Add nitrogen fertilizers after the seedlings have produced their first true leaves.
3. Plant seeds after the soil has reached the temperature needed for quick germination. For ideal germination temperatures, see page 1004.
4. Protect seeds during germination by coating them with fungicides containing *captan* (ORTHOCIDE®) or *PCNB*. Add a pinch of fungicide to a packet of seeds (or ½ teaspoon per pound), and shake well to coat the seeds with the fungicide. For more information on starting seeds, see page 925.

IMPATIENS (BALSAM)

ADAPTATION: Throughout the United States.

FLOWERING TIME: Spring to fall.

LIGHT: Filtered sun to deep shade. Impatiens may be planted in direct sun if they are not allowed to dry out.

PLANTING TIME: Spring, after all danger of frost is past.

SOIL: Any good garden soil that is rich in organic matter. pH 6.0 to 7.5

FERTILIZER: Fertilize with ORTHO Rose & Flower Food or ORTHO General Purpose Plant Food according to label directions.

WATER:
How much: Apply enough water to plants in the ground to wet the soil 8 to 10 inches deep.
Containers: Apply enough water so that 10 percent of the water drains from the bottom of the container.
How often: Water when the soil 1 inch below the surface is moist but not wet.

Sunburn.

PROBLEM: Leaves are light and faded, often turning pale green to yellowish white. Some of the leaves may turn brown and brittle, and drop. There is very little new growth. The plants are exposed to at least several hours of direct sun during the day. There are no signs of plant pests or diseases.

ANALYSIS: Sunburn

Impatiens are adapted to shady conditions, and will not tolerate more than a few hours of direct sun, especially intense afternoon sun. Even if they receive only 1 or 2 hours of direct sunlight, they may drop leaves and discolor slightly, turning yellow-green. The excess light breaks down the plant tissue, causing the chlorophyll (green plant pigment) to disappear. Impatiens are most sensitive to sunburn when they are allowed to dry out.

SOLUTION: Transplant your impatiens to a shaded or partially shaded location, or to a location where they will receive morning sun. Avoid placing them in an area where they are exposed to afternoon sun. Replace them with plants that are adapted to a sunny location.

Leaf spot.

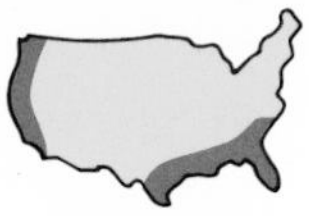

PROBLEM: The leaves are spotted or blotched with brown spots that may range in size from barely visible to ¼ inch in diameter. Several spots may join to form blotches. The leaves may turn yellow and die. Leaf spotting is most severe in wet weather.

ANALYSIS: Leaf spot

There are a number of different fungi that cause leaf spots. Some of these fungi will eventually kill the plant, while others merely cause spotting that is unsightly but not harmful. These fungi are spread by splashing water, wind, insects, and contaminated tools. Fungal strands or spores survive the winter in plant debris. Most of the leaf spot organisms do their greatest damage in humid conditions and temperatures of 50° to 85°F.

SOLUTION: Spray infected plants with a fungicide containing *captan* (ORTHOCIDE®), *benomyl*, or *folpet* (PHALTAN®) at intervals of 7 to 10 days. Make sure your plant is listed on the product label. Because leaf spots are favored by warm, wet conditions, it is important to spray conscientiously during these periods. Pick off spotted, diseased leaves and clean up plant debris.

Spider mite damage.

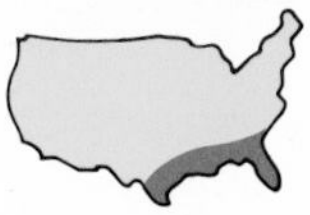

PROBLEM: Leaves are stippled, yellowing, and dirty. Leaves may dry out and drop. There may be webbing over flower buds, between leaves, or on the lower surfaces of the leaves. To determine if the plant is infested with mites, hold a sheet of white paper underneath an affected plant and tap the plant sharply. Minute green, red, or yellow specks the size of pepper grains will drop to the paper and begin to crawl around. These pests are easily seen against the white background.

ANALYSIS: Spider mites
(*Tetranychus urticae*)

These mites, related to spiders, are major pests of many garden and greenhouse plants. They cause damage by sucking sap from the undersides of the leaves. As a result of feeding, the green leaf pigment disappears, producing the stippled appearance. Mites are active throughout the growing season, but are favored by hot, dry weather (70°F and up). By midsummer, they build up to tremendous numbers. For more information about spider mites, see page 887.

SOLUTION: Spray the infested plants with ORTHO Isotox Insect Killer. Repeat the spray two more times at regular intervals 7 to 10 days.

IRIS

ADAPTATION:
Rhizomatous: Zones 5 through 10.
Bulbous: Zones 7 through 10.
Irises may be grown in colder areas if heavily mulched. To determine your zone, see the map on page 1020.

FLOWERING TIME:
Rhizomatous: Early summer.
Bulbous: Late spring through early summer.

LIGHT: Full sun.

PLANTING TIME:
Rhizomatous: Summer.
Bulbous: Fall.

SOIL: Well drained. pH 6.0 to 7.5

FERTILIZER: Fertilize with ORTHO Rose & Flower Food or ORTHO General Purpose Plant Food according to label directions.

WATER:
How much: Apply enough water to wet the soil to 1½ feet deep.
How often: Water when the soil 1 inch below the surface is just barely moist.

HANDLING: Mulch irises after the first hard fall frost. Divide rhizomatous iris clumps every 3 to 5 years.

Didymellina leaf spot.

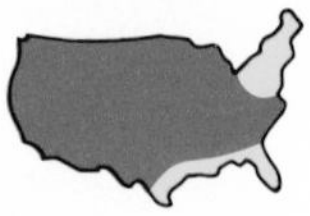

PROBLEM: Tiny brown spots from ⅛ to ¼ inch in diameter appear on the leaves. The spots have distinct reddish borders and may be surrounded by water-soaked margins that later turn yellow. After the plant has flowered, the spots enlarge rapidly and may join together to form blotches. Spotting is most severe in wet weather. The leaves die prematurely.

ANALYSIS: Leaf spots
This disease is caused by a fungus (*Didymellina macrospora*) that infects only irises and a few other closely related plants. This fungus attacks the leaves, and occasionally the flower stalks and buds. It will not affect iris roots, bulbs, or rhizomes. Although the fungus does not directly kill the plant, several years of repeated infection results in premature leaf death each summer, greatly reducing rhizome and bulb vigor. Some varieties of iris suffer leaf dieback even when they are only lightly spotted, while other varieties can be covered with spots before they start to die. When the leaves are wet, or during periods of high humidity, the fungal spots produce spores that are spread to other plants by wind or splashing water. The fungus spends the winters in old infected leaves and debris.

SOLUTION: Spray plants with ORTHO Vegetable Disease Control. Repeat the spray every 7 to 10 days until the foliage starts to die back. Clean up plant debris and clip off diseased foliage in the fall. Spray again when new growth appears, and repeat the spray four to six more times at intervals of 7 to 10 days. Use a spreader-sticker when spraying (see page 922).

Mosaic on Dutch iris.

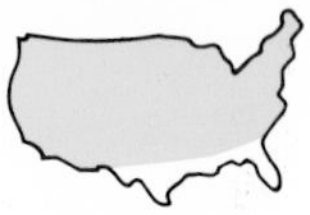

PROBLEM: Leaves are mottled light and dark green. Foliage may be streaked or stippled yellow. Young leaves are most severely affected. The plant may be stunted, and often the flowers are smaller than normal. There may be dark teardrop or feathery markings on the flowers.

ANALYSIS: Mosaic
This plant disease is caused by a virus. Depending upon the species or variety of iris, symptoms of infection can vary from barely noticeable to quite severe. Iris grown from bulbs (such as Dutch iris) are most severely affected by this virus. Mosaic rarely causes a plant to die, but can weaken or disfigure it extensively. The virus increases in the bulbs and rhizomes year after year. Successive plantings of diseased bulbs and rhizomes provide only poor quality flowers and foliage. Mosaic is spread by aphids. These insects feed on diseased plants and transfer the virus to healthy plants at later feedings.

SOLUTION: Once the plant is infected, there are no chemicals that will control the virus. Remove and destroy severely infected, weakened plants. Keep the aphid population under control by spraying infested plants with an insecticide containing *malathion*. Repeat the spray if reinfestation occurs. For more information about controlling disease-carrying insects, see page 879.

Rust.

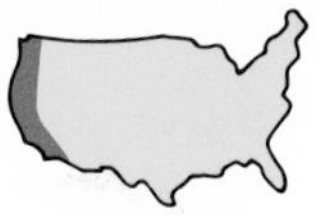

PROBLEM: Rust-colored, powdery pustules appear on both sides of the leaves. Later in the season, these pustules turn dark brown. Severely infected leaves may die prematurely.

ANALYSIS: Rust

This plant disease is caused by a number of closely related fungi (*Puccinia* species). The rust-colored pustules are composed of millions of microscopic spores. Some of the spores spend the winter on iris leaves that have not died back entirely, while others overwinter on other kinds of plants. Infection usually starts in the spring as soon as conditions are favorable for plant growth. The spores are spread to healthy plants by splashing water and wind. Because iris varieties vary greatly in their susceptibility to rust, some may be killed prematurely, while others may not be affected. Rust is greatly favored by wet weather.

SOLUTION: Spray infected plants with a fungicide containing *mancozeb*, *ferbam*, or *zineb*. Repeat the spray two or three more times at intervals of 7 to 10 days. Remove and destroy old and dying iris leaves in the fall. Water in the morning to allow the foliage a chance to dry out before nightfall. Plant rust-resistant varieties, if available.

Rust-resistant Dutch iris: Early Blue, Gold and Silver, Golden West, Imperator, Lemon Queen, and Texas Gold.

Iris borer damage.

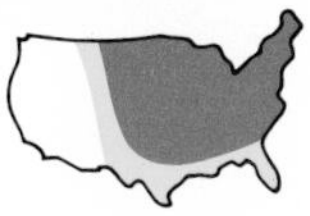

PROBLEM: Dark streaks, water-soaked spots, and possibly slits develop in new leaves in the spring to early summer. The leaf edges may be chewed and ragged. By midsummer, the foliage is wilting and discolored. The leaf bases are loose and rotted. The rhizomes are often filled with holes and may be soft and rotted. Pink caterpillars, from 1 to 2 inches long, are feeding inside the rhizomes.

ANALYSIS: Iris borer
(*Macronoctua onusta*)

The larva of this night-flying moth is the most destructive insect pest of iris. In the fall, the adult moth lays eggs in old leaf and flower stalks. The eggs hatch in late April or early May. The emerging larvae initially feed on the leaf surface, producing ragged leaf edges and watery feeding scars. They then bore into the inner leaf tissue, and gradually mine their way down into the rhizome, on which they feed throughout the summer. The damaged rhizome is very susceptible to bacterial soft rot. The larvae leave the rhizome, pupate in the soil, and emerge as adult moths in the fall.

SOLUTION: Clean up plant debris by April to eliminate overwintering borer eggs. Apply an insecticide dust containing *carbaryl* (SEVIN®), *dimethoate*, or *malathion* weekly from the time first growth starts until the beginning of June. In May and June, squeeze the leaves in the vicinity of feeding damage to kill feeding borers inside. Destroy heavily infested plants and rhizomes. To kill the borers in lightly infested rhizomes, poke a wire into borer holes.

Crown rot.

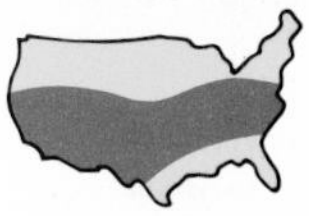

PROBLEM: The leaves of irises grown from rhizomes (such as bearded iris) die, starting with the leaftips and progressing downward. The leaf bases and possibly the rhizomes are dry, brown, and rotted. The leaves of irises grown from bulbs (such as Dutch iris) are stunted, turn yellow, and die prematurely. The leaves and stems at the soil level are rotted and the bulbs are soft and crumbly. White, matted, fungal strands cover the crowns and soil surrounding both rhizomatous and bulbous irises. Small, tan to reddish brown pellets the size of mustard seeds form on the infected plant tissue and soil.

ANALYSIS: Crown rot

This disease is caused by a widespread fungus (*Sclerotium rolfsii*) that initially penetrates the stems at the soil level. It decays and kills the leaf and stem bases, bulbs, and often part or all of the rhizomes. Crown rot is spread by moving water, diseased transplants, infested soil, and contaminated tools. The fungal pellets can survive for many years in dry soil and extremes of temperature to reinfect healthy plants when conditions are suitable. Crown rot is most severe in overcrowded plantings, warm temperatures (70°F and up), and moist conditions.

SOLUTION: Remove and destroy infected plants, bulbs, rhizomes, and the soil immediately surrounding them to 6 inches beyond the diseased area. Drench the area with a fungicide containing *PCNB*. Next year, repeat the soil drench at planting time and again when new growth is showing. Plant in well-drained soil, and thin out overcrowded plantings.

IRIS

Bacterial soft rot.

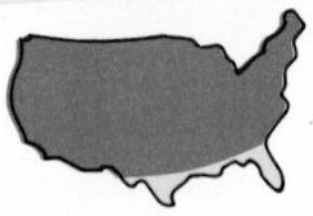

PROBLEM: Leaves turn yellow, wilt, and eventually die. Dieback often starts at the leaf tips and progresses downward. The entire leaf cluster (fan) may be found lying on the ground. If pulled gently, the leaf fan sometimes lifts off the rhizome (the elongated, jointed, underground stem). Leaf bases and rhizomes are often rotted and foul-smelling.

ANALYSIS: Bacterial soft rot
This plant disease is caused by a bacterium (*Erwinia carotovora*). It is a serious and common disease of bearded and other rhizomatous irises. The bacteria enter the plant through wounds in the leaves and rhizomes, which are frequently made by iris borers. As the infection develops, the plant tissue decays into a soft, foul-smelling mass. Finally, the plant dies and the inner rhizome tissue disintegrates. Infection and rapid decay are favored by moist, dark conditions. These bacteria live in the soil and in plant debris. They are spread by contaminated plants and rhizomes, soil, insects, and tools.

SOLUTION: Remove and destroy all diseased plants; they cannot be cured. Discard diseased rhizomes before planting. If only a small portion of the rhizome is infected, it may possibly be saved by cutting off the diseased portion. Avoid wounding the rhizomes when digging them up. After dividing rhizomes, let the wounds heal for a few days before replanting. Plant irises in a sunny, well-drained location. Plant the rhizome shallowly, so the upper portion is exposed. Clean up plant debris in the fall. Control iris borers.

LANTANA

Greenhouse whiteflies (twice life size).

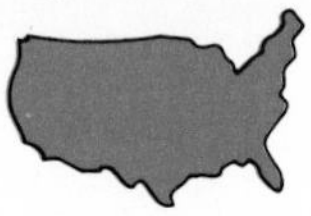

PROBLEM: Tiny, winged insects 1/12 inch long are found on the leaves. The insects are covered with white, waxy powder. When the plant is touched, insects flutter rapidly around it. The leaves may be mottled and yellowing.

ANALYSIS: Greenhouse whitefly
(*Trialeurodes vaporariorum*)
This insect is a common pest of many garden ornamentals and greenhouse plants. The four-winged adult lays eggs on the undersides of leaves. The larvae are the size of a pinhead, flat, oval-shaped, and semitransparent, with white, waxy filaments radiating from the body. They feed for about a month before changing to the adult form. Both the larval and adult forms suck sap from the leaves. The larvae are more damaging because they feed more heavily. In warm winter areas, the insect can be active year-round. The whitefly is unable to live through freezing winters. Spring reinfestations in such areas come from migrating whiteflies and from infested greenhouse-grown plants placed in the garden.

SOLUTION: Control whiteflies by spraying with ORTHO Orthene Systemic Insect Control, allowing at least 7 days to pass between applications.

Lantana cultural information
Light: Sun
Water: Let the soil dry out between waterings
Soil: Any good garden soil
Fertilizer: Light

LATHYRUS (SWEET PEA)

Powdery mildew. *Insert:* Closeup.

PROBLEM: The leaves and stems are covered with grayish white powdery spots and patches that occur primarily on the upper surfaces of the older leaves. Leaves eventually turn yellow and wither.

ANALYSIS: Powdery mildew
This common plant disease is caused by a fungus (*Erysiphe polygoni*) that can be severe on sweet peas. Powdery mildew thrives in both humid and dry weather. The powdery patches consist of fungal strands and spores. The spores are spread by the wind to healthy plants. The fungus saps plant nutrients, causing yellowing and sometimes death of the leaves, especially the older ones. A severe infection may occasionally kill the plant. Since this powdery mildew attacks many different kinds of plants, the fungus from a diseased plant may infect other types of plants in the garden. For a list of susceptible plants, see page 1006. Under favorable conditions, powdery mildew can spread through a closely spaced planting in a matter of days or weeks.

SOLUTION: Spray infected plants with a fungicide containing *benomyl*, or dust them with *sulfur*. These fungicides protect the new, healthy foliage by killing the powdery mildew spores as they germinate on the leaves. They will not eradicate the fungus on leaves that are already infected. If practical, these may be picked off. Severely infected plants should be removed. Spray or dust at regular intervals of 7 to 10 days, or as often as necessary to protect new growth. Clean up plant debris.

Wilt.

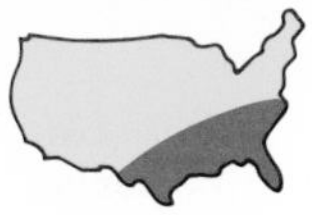

PROBLEM: Lower leaves turn yellow, then wilt and die; or all of the foliage may turn yellow and then wither. Flower heads may droop. When the stem is sliced open near the base of the plant, dark streaks and discolorations of the inner stem tissue are revealed.

ANALYSIS: Wilt disease

This widespread plant disease is caused by either of two fungi (*Verticillium* species or *Fusarium* species). These fungi live indefinitely on plant debris and in the soil. The disease is spread by contaminated seeds, plants, soil, and equipment. The fungus enters the plant through the roots and spreads up into the stems and leaves through the water-conducting vessels in the stems. The vessels become discolored and plugged. This plugging cuts off the flow of water to the leaves, causing leaf yellowing and wilting. For more information about wilt disease, see page 850.

SOLUTION: No chemical control is available. It is best to destroy infected plants. These fungi can be removed from the soil only by fumigation techniques. (For more information about soil fumigation, see page 927.) However, the best solution is usually to use plants that are resistant to verticillium and fusarium.

Lathyrus cultural information

Light: Sun
Water: Keep the soil moist
Soil: Any good garden soil
Fertilizer: Medium to heavy

Spider mite damage.

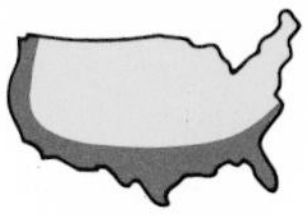

PROBLEM: Leaves are stippled, yellowing, and mealy. Leaves may dry out and drop. There may be webbing over flower buds, between leaves, or on the lower surfaces of the leaves. To determine if the plant is infested with mites, hold a sheet of white paper underneath an affected leaf and tap the leaf sharply. Minute green, red, or yellow specks the size of pepper grains will drop to the paper and begin to crawl around. The pests are easily seen against the white background.

ANALYSIS: Spider mites
(*Tetranychus urticae*)

These mites, related to spiders, are major pests of sweet peas and many other garden and greenhouse plants. Mites cause damage by sucking sap from the undersides of the leaves. As a result of feeding, the green leaf pigment disappears, producing the stippled appearance. Mites are active throughout the growing season, but are favored by hot, dry weather (70°F and up). By midsummer, they build up to tremendous numbers. For more information about spider mites, see page 887.

SOLUTION: Spray the infested plants with a pesticide containing *dicofol* (KELTHANE®). Repeat the spray two more times at regular intervals of 5 to 7 days.

LILIUM (LILY)

ADAPTATION: Throughout the United States.

FLOWERING TIME: Depending upon the species, late spring to late summer.

LIGHT: Full sun to part shade, depending on the variety.

PLANTING TIME: When bulbs are available (fall through spring).

SOIL: Well drained, high in organic matter. pH 6.0 to 7.5

FERTILIZER: When planting, mix 1 teaspoon of ORTHO Bone Meal into the soil at the bottom of the planting hole. During the growing season, fertilize with ORTHO Rose & Flower Food or ORTHO General Purpose Plant Food according to label directions.

WATER:

How much: Apply enough water to wet the soil 8 to 12 inches deep.

Containers: Apply enough water so that 10 percent of the water drains from the bottom of the container.

How often: Water when the soil 1 inch below the surface is just barely moist.

HANDLING: After the plants have bloomed, allow them to die back, then cut them off at ground level.

LILIUM (LILY)

Root and bulb rot. Diseased plant on right.

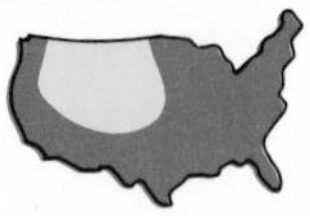

PROBLEM: Plants are stunted and wilting, and the lower leaves turn yellow. The tips of the lower leaves may be dying, and brown, dead patches may appear along the leaf edges. The flower buds may wither and fail to open. The bulbs and roots are rotted.

ANALYSIS: Root and bulb rots
Rot problems are common with lilies. These plant diseases are caused by various fungi (*Rhizoctonia,Phytophthora, Pythium, Fusarium, Cylindrocarpon*). These fungi attack and decay the bulbs and roots, causing stunting, wilting, and eventually the death of the foliage and flowers. These bulb and root rot organisms live in the soil and stored bulbs, and are favored by wet soil. Sometimes bulbs in storage are lightly infected but the fungal decay hasn't progressed far enough to be easily noticed. When planted, these bulbs may rot so quickly that they do not produce any foliage.

SOLUTION: Remove and destroy infected plants. Check all bulbs carefully and discard any that are moldy, rotted, or dry and crumbly. Before planting, dip clean, healthy bulbs in a fungicide solution containing *truban* or *benomyl.* Plant in well-drained soil. Store bulbs in a cool (40° to 45°F), dry location.

Aphids (life size).

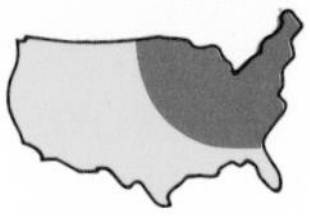

PROBLEM: Leaves may be curled, distorted, and yellowing. Flowers are sometimes malformed. Tiny ($1/8$ inch) pale green to black soft-bodied insects are clustered on the leaves and stems. A sticky, shiny substance may coat the leaves. Ants are often present.

ANALYSIS: Aphids
There are a number of different species of this common insect that feed on lilies. Aphids cause their damage by sucking plant sap; this feeding produces leaf curling, yellowing, and distortion. In the process of feeding, certain aphids can infect lilies with mosaic virus disease. The aphid is unable to digest fully all the sugar in the plant sap and excretes the excess in a fluid called honeydew. The honeydew often drops onto the leaves below. Ants feed on this sticky substance, and are often present where there is an aphid infestation. For more information about aphids, see page 875.

SOLUTION: Spray infested plants with an insecticide containing *malathion.* Repeat the spray if reinfestation occurs, allowing at least a week to pass between applications. In the fall, clean up plant debris that might harbor aphid eggs.

Virus.

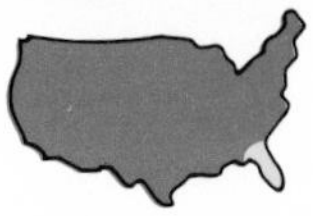

PROBLEM: The leaves are mottled and streaked light and dark green, and the plant may be stunted and dying. The leaves may be spotted with tiny yellow, brown, or gray flecks. These flecks are elongated and run parallel to the leaf veins. Plants with these flecks are often stunted and have small, streaked flowers that do not open fully. Their leaves may be twisted or curled, and frequently die prematurely, starting from the bottom of the plant.

ANALYSIS: Virus
There are several virus diseases of lilies that cause mottling or flecking of the foliage. *Mosaic viruses* produce leaf mottling and discoloration. Depending on the species or variety, the symptoms of infection can be mild or severe. *Fleck* is produced if a plant is simultaneously infected by the *symptomless lily virus* and the *cucumber mosaic virus* (which may or may not produce mottling by itself). Leaf flecking is usually accompanied by stunting and poor quality flowers and foliage. The plant is generally disfigured. Viruses remain in infected bulbs year after year, so successive plantings of diseased bulbs will produce only poor quality flowers and foliage. All of these viruses are spread by aphids, which pick up the virus while feeding on diseased plants and then transmit it to healthy plants at later feedings.

SOLUTION: There is no chemical control for viruses. Remove and destroy infected plants. Control aphids by spraying infested plants with an insecticide containing *malathion.* Respray if reinfestation occurs. Plant mosaic-resistant or immune lilies, a list of which can be found on page 1004.

LOBULARIA (SWEET ALLYSUM)

Leaf scorch.

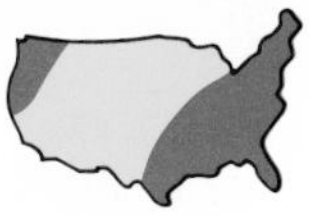

PROBLEM: Brown, semicircular or crescent-shaped areas develop along leaf margins. Leaf tips may be brown. Usually the lower leaves are affected first. When the soil pH is tested, it is found to be acidic.

ANALYSIS: Leaf scorch
Leaf scorch is a condition that may develop in lilies when they are growing in acid soil (lower than pH 6.5). Toxic amounts of aluminum and manganese salts become available and are absorbed by plant roots in acid soils. Leaf scorch is most likely to occur when the plant is not receiving adequate or balanced supplies of nutrients, such as nitrogen and calcium.

SOLUTION: Add ground dolomitic limestone to the soil to decrease its acidity. See pages 908 and 1019 for more information about decreasing soil acidity. Fertilize all plants with a balanced fertilizer such as ORTHO Rose & Flower Food.

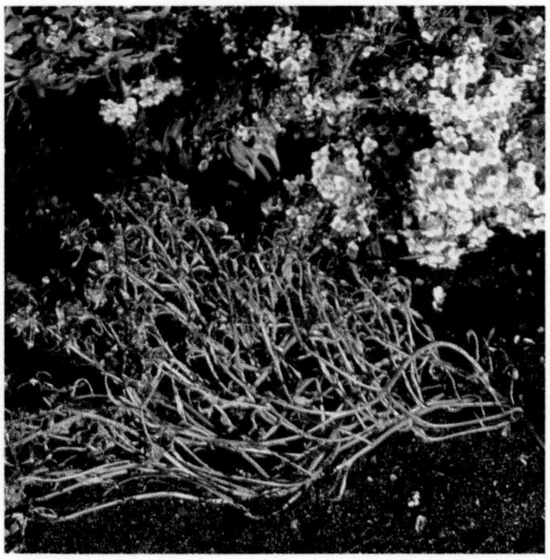

Root and stem rot.

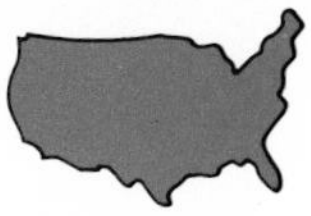

PROBLEM: Leaves and stems turn yellow, wilt, and die. The lower leaves and stems may be soft and rotted. White fungal strands may grow around the base of the plants.

ANALYSIS: Root and stem rot
This disease is caused by any of a number of different fungi, also known as *water molds*, that persist indefinitely in the soil. They thrive in waterlogged, heavy soil. Some of these fungi attack the plant stems at the soil level, while others attack the roots. Infection causes the roots and stems to decay. This results in wilting, then yellowing leaves, and eventually the death of the plant. These fungi are generally spread by infested soil and transplants, contaminated equipment, and splashing or running water. Many of these organisms also cause damping-off of seedlings. For more information about damping-off, see page 850.

SOLUTION: Allow the soil around the plants to dry out. (For more information on this technique, see page 849.) Remove and discard severely infected plants. Avoid future root rot problems by planting in well-drained soil. For information on improving soil drainage, see page 907.

Lobularia cultural information
Light: Part to full sun
Water: When the soil is almost dry
Soil: Well drained
Fertilizer: Light

Downy mildew.

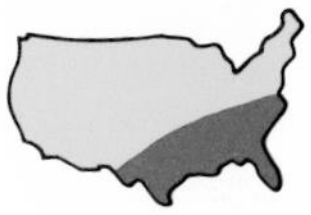

PROBLEM: Pale green to yellow spots develop on the leaves. A white, downy growth may be present on the upper and especially on the lower surfaces of the leaves. Infected leaves turn yellow, and the plant eventually dies.

ANALYSIS: Downy mildew
This plant disease is caused by a fungus (*Peronospora parasitica*) that infects flowers and vegetables in the cabbage family. The characteristic downy mold that develops on infected plants is composed of many microscopic spores. These spores may be blown or splashed to healthy plants, and germinate on wet stems and leaves. Downy mildew is favored by cool days and nights, and moist or humid weather conditions. The fungus survives the winter in plant debris or in perennial plants or roots.

SOLUTION: This fungus is difficult to eliminate entirely during cool, moist weather. However, you can control it by spraying infected plants with a fungicide containing *chlorothalonil* (DACONIL 2787®). Repeat at intervals of 7 to 10 days. Water early in the day to allow the plants to dry out before nightfall. Remove and destroy plant debris.

MATTHIOLA

ADAPTATION: Throughout the United States.

FLOWERING TIME: Spring through early summer. In zones 9 and 10, late winter through early summer. To determine your zone, see the map on page 1020.

LIGHT: Full sun.

PLANTING TIME: Spring, after all danger of frost is past. In zones 9 and 10, plant in early fall.

SOIL: Any good well-drained garden soil.

FERTILIZER: Fertilize with ORTHO Rose & Flower Food or ORTHO General Purpose Plant Food according to label directions.

WATER:
How much: Apply enough water to plants in the ground to wet the soil 6 to 8 inches deep.
Containers: Apply enough water so that about 10 percent of the water drains from the bottom of the container.
How often: Water when the soil 1 inch below the surface is just barely moist.

Verticillium wilt.

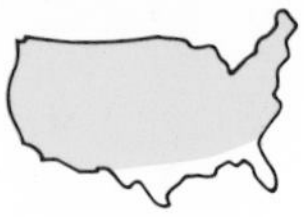

PROBLEM: Leaves turn yellow and die, starting at the base of the plant. The plant is stunted. When the stem near the base of the plant is sliced open, dark streaks and discolorations are seen in the inner stem tissue.

ANALYSIS: Fungal wilt
This widespread plant disease is caused by either of two fungi (*Verticillium* or *Fusarium*) that persist indefinitely on plant debris or in the soil. The disease is spread by contaminated seeds, plants, soil, and equipment. The fungus enters the plant through the roots and spreads up into the stems and leaves through the water-conducting vessels in the stems. The vessels become discolored and plugged. This plugging cuts off the flow of water to the leaves, causing leaf yellowing and wilting. For more information about fungal wilt, see page 850.

SOLUTION: No chemical controls are available. It is best to destroy infected plants. Verticillium and fusarium can be removed from the soil only by fumigation techniques. (For more information about soil fumigation, see page 927.) However, the best solution is usually to use plants that are resistant to verticillium and fusarium.

Bacterial wilt.

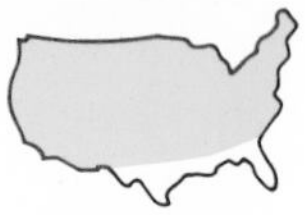

PROBLEM: Young plants (2 to 4 inches tall) wilt and collapse. The main stems are soft and yellowish, and have a water-soaked appearance. There may be dark green or brown lines along the stems. The lower leaves of older plants turn yellow and die. The scars on the stems where the leaves have fallen off have a water-soaked appearance and are darkened. When the stem is sliced open, a thick yellow fluid oozes out.

ANALYSIS: Bacterial wilt
This plant disease is caused by a bacterium (*Xanthomonas incanae*) that infects both young and mature plants. Because the bacteria are sometimes carried in the seed, infection may begin at germination. These bacteria usually penetrate older plants through leaf scars on the stems, or through wounds on the stems and roots. Once inside, they multiply and break down the inner stem tissue. This results in plant wilting, stunting, poor growth, and eventually death. The sticky yellowish fluid inside the stems is filled with millions of bacteria. These wilt organisms are spread to other plants by moving water, contaminated soil, plant debris, and tools. They can live in plant debris and the soil for up to 2 years, and are favored by cool, wet weather.

SOLUTION: Infected plants cannot be cured. It is best to remove and destroy them. Clean up plant debris. Wash your hands thoroughly with soap and hot water after handling infected plants. Dip contaminated tools in rubbing alcohol before working on healthy plants. Don't replant healthy stocks in contaminated soil for 3 years.

Powdery mildew.

PROBLEM: Leaves and stems are covered with grayish white powdery spots and patches. In many cases, these patches occur primarily on the upper surfaces of the leaves. The infected leaves eventually turn yellow and wither.

ANALYSIS: Powdery mildew
This common plant disease is caused by a fungus (*Erysiphe cichoracearum*) that thrives in both humid and dry weather. The powdery patches consist of fungal strands and spores. The spores are spread by the wind to healthy plants. The fungus saps the plant nutrients, causing yellowing and sometimes death of the leaves. A severe infection may kill the plant. Since powdery mildew attacks many different kinds of plants, the fungus from a diseased plant may infect other types of plants in the garden. (For a list of susceptible plants see page 1006). Under favorable conditions, powdery mildew can spread through a planting in a matter of days or weeks.

SOLUTION: Spray infected plants with a fungicide containing *folpet* (PHALTAN®), *dinocap*, or *cycloheximide*. Spray at regular intervals of 10 to 12 days, or as often as necessary to protect new growth. Remove and destroy severely infected plants. Where practical, pick off diseased leaves. Clean up and destroy plant debris.

Myosotis cultural information
Light: Part to full sun
Water: When the soil is just barely moist
Soil: Any good garden soil
Fertilizer: Medium

NARCISSUS (DAFFODIL, JONQUIL)

ADAPTATION: Throughout the United States.

FLOWERING TIME: Spring.

LIGHT: Full sun is best. Daffodils will tolerate light shade, but may stop blooming after several years.

PLANTING TIME: Fall.

SOIL: Any good well-drained garden soil. pH 6.0 to 7.5

FERTILIZER: When planting, mix 1 teaspoon of ORTHO Bone Meal or ORTHO Superphosphate into the soil at the bottom of the planting hole. During the growing season, fertilize with ORTHO Rose & Flower Food or ORTHO General Purpose Plant Food according to label directions.

WATER:
How much: Apply enough water to wet the soil $1\frac{1}{2}$ feet deep.
How often: Water when the soil 1 inch below the surface is just barely moist. Stop watering the bulbs after the foliage has turned yellow.

HANDLING: Continue to water and fertilize plants regularly until the foliage turns yellow, then remove the dead leaves.

Flower thrips (8 times life size).

PROBLEM: Silvery white streaks and flecks appear on the leaves and especially on the flowers. The leaves may turn brown. If the flowers or overlapping leaves are peeled open, slender, dark brown to straw-colored insects ranging in size from $\frac{1}{20}$ to $\frac{1}{16}$ inch can be seen moving around.

ANALYSIS: Thrips
This common insect pest attacks daffodils and many other garden plants. Thrips are found in protected parts of the plant like the insides of flower buds, where they feed by rasping the soft plant tissue, then sucking the released plant sap. The injured tissue turns white, causing the characteristic streaking of the leaves and flowers. Because thrips migrate long distances on wind currents, they can quickly infest widespread areas. In cold climates, thrips feed and reproduce from spring until fall. With the onset of freezing weather, they find sheltered areas such as grass clumps and hibernate through the winter. In warm weather climates, thrips feed and reproduce all year. These pests reach their population peak in late spring to midsummer. They are especially troublesome during prolonged dry spells.

SOLUTION: Thrips cannot be eliminated completely, but they can be kept under control. Spray with an insecticide containing *diazinon* as soon as damage is noticed. Repeat the spray if reinfestation occurs, allowing at least 10 days to pass between applications. Pick off and destroy infested flowers.

NARCISSUS (DAFFODIL, JONQUIL)

Failure to bloom.

No flowers due to weak growth.

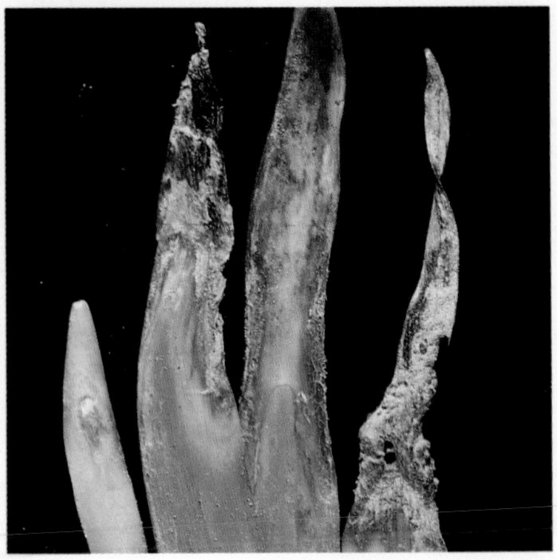

Smoulder.

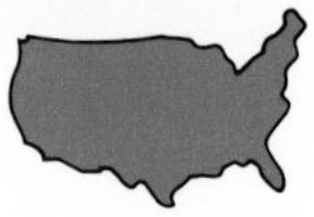

PROBLEM: Foliage is healthy, but may be sparse. Few or no flowers are produced. Flowers that are produced may be smaller than normal.

ANALYSIS: Failure to bloom
There are several cultural reasons why daffodils fail to flower:

SOLUTION: The numbered solutions below correspond to the numbers in the analysis.

1. *Overcrowding:* The bulbs multiply each year, producing larger clumps the following spring. If the bulbs are not divided and transplanted every few years, they become overcrowded.

1. Bulbs should be divided when flower production drops off. As a general rule, divide bulbs every three to four years.

2. *Too much shade:* Daffodils planted in a shaded spot will usually bloom well the first year. However, they require a sunny location for continued flowering over a long period of time. The leaves use light to manufacture food, which is stored in the bulbs for next year's growth and flowering. Inadequate light reduces the amount of stored food in the bulbs, resulting in few or no flowers.

2. Grow daffodils in a location where they will receive four or more hours of full sun. Plants in the shade can be transplanted to a sunny location any time after the flowering period. Try to keep the soil and roots immediately surrounding the bulb intact when transplanting.

3. *Overheating:* If bulbs are stored at high temperatures (80°F and up), the flower embryo inside the bulb is killed. Leaves will grow in the spring, but flowers will not be produced.

3. Store bulbs at a cool temperature (55° to 60°F) and in a well-ventilated location.

4. *Undersized bulbs:* If flower bulbs are much smaller than normal, they may produce only foliage for the first one or two years. Undersized bulbs don't store enough food to produce both leaves and blossoms. But the bulbs will grow larger, until finally they produce flowers.

4. Purchase only large, healthy bulbs.

5. *Foliage removed too soon:* After a daffodil flowers, the remaining foliage continues to use the sun's rays to manufacture food for new bulbs and next year's flowers. If the foliage is removed before it has a chance to die back naturally, the new bulbs may not have enough food stored to produce a flower.

5. Let the foliage turn yellow before removing it.

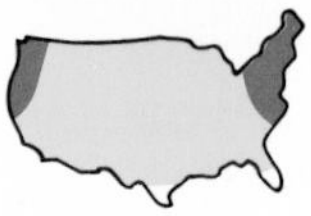

PROBLEM: Stored bulbs are yellow brown and rotted. Black crusty fungal mats may grow on the infected bulbs. When infected bulbs are planted, leaves that emerge from the soil are distorted and crumpled. They may be stuck together. Brown streaks develop on the leaf tips or edges. Black crusty fungal pellets appear on the streaked foliage. During cold, wet weather, a gray-brown fuzzy mold may appear on the infected tissues. Flowers may be spotted.

ANALYSIS: Smoulder
This plant disease is caused by a fungus (*Sclerotinia narcissicola*) that infects bulbs both in storage and in the ground, causing bulb rot and flower and foliage decay. When infected bulbs start to grow, the fungus spreads up into the foliage, causing leaf distortion and streaking. Smoulder is favored by wet, poorly drained soil. The fungus forms black pellets on the bulbs and leaves. These pellets can survive through dry conditions and extremes of temperature to invade healthy bulbs. The disease is spread by contaminated soil and bulbs.

SOLUTION: Remove and destroy infected plants and bulbs. During wet weather, spray plants weekly with a fungicide containing *basic copper sulfate*. Plant bulbs in well-drained soil. Avoid planting bulbs in soil where infected plants have grown previously.

Fusarium bulb rot.

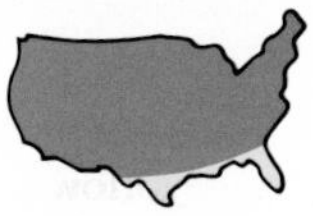

PROBLEM: Leaves turn yellow, and the plant is stunted and dies prematurely. If the bulb is unearthed, there may be few or no roots. Bulbs in storage develop a chocolate or purple-brown, spongy decay that is especially noticeable when the outer fleshy bulb scales are pulled away. There may be white fungal strands growing on the bulbs.

ANALYSIS: Fusarium bulb rot
This disease is caused by a fungus (*Fusarium oxysporum* var. *narcissi*) that attacks both growing plants and bulbs in storage. Growing plants are infected through their roots, while stored bulbs may be infected through wounds or abrasions in the bulb tissue. Infected bulbs that are planted continue to decay in the ground and produce few or no roots and stunted, yellowing foliage. The fungus persists in the soil indefinitely, and is spread by contaminated bulbs, soil, and tools. Generally, bulb rot is most destructive when soil temperatures reach 60° to 75°F. The disease is most common in warm climates where temperatures rarely drop below freezing, and in daffodils that are forced for indoor winter use.

SOLUTION: Discard all diseased plants and bulbs and the surrounding soil for 6 inches around the bulb. Dig bulbs up carefully to prevent wounds. Store them in a cool (55° to 60°F), well-ventilated place. Soak clean, healthy bulbs in a warm (80° to 85°F) bath of a fungicide containing *benomyl* (2 tablespoons per gallon) for 15 to 30 minutes. Do not replant healthy bulbs in an area where diseased plants have previously grown.

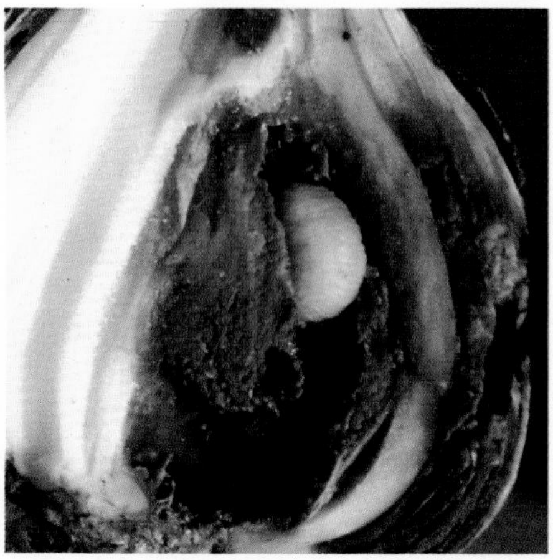

Narcissus bulb fly larva (life size).

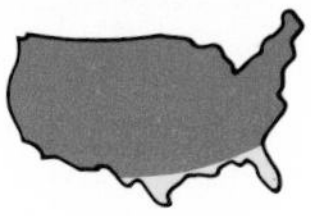

PROBLEM: Narcissus and daffodil bulbs feel soft and spongy, and produce little or no growth after they are planted. Foliage that does emerge is yellow, stunted, and looks grassy. No flowers are produced. In the spring, when the daffodils start to bloom, flying insects that resemble small bumblebees (½ to ¾ inch long), can be seen hovering around the plants. These black, hairy insects have bands of yellow, buff, or orange around their bodies.

ANALYSIS: Narcissus bulb fly
(*Merodon equestris*)
This insect, a member of the fly family, is a common pest of many ornamental bulb plants. In the spring, the adult fly lays its eggs on the leaf bases and soil immediately surrounding the plant. The emerging larvae tunnel through the soil to the bulb, and feed on the bulb tissue throughout the summer, making it soft and pulpy. The larvae spend the winter in the bulb as wrinkled, plump, grayish white to yellow maggots ½ to ¾ inches long. In the spring, they either remain in the bulb or move out into the surrounding soil to pupate. After 1 to 2½ months, the adult bulb fly emerges and starts the egg-laying cycle again.

SOLUTION: Check all bulbs carefully before planting. If they are soft or spongy, discard them. Dust the remaining bulbs with an insecticide containing *trichlorfon* before planting them, and again after they've been planted but before they're covered with soil. In May, drench the foliage and surrounding soil with a solution containing *trichlorfon* to kill the adults and emerging larvae. Make sure that daffodils are listed on the pesticide label.

Cutworm (¾ life size).

PROBLEM: Young plants are chewed or cut off near the ground. Gray, brown, or black worms, 1½ to 2 inches long, may be found about 2 inches deep in the soil near the base of the damaged plants. The worms coil when disturbed.

ANALYSIS: Cutworms
Several species of cutworms attack plants in the flower garden. The most likely pests of young nicotiana plants are the surface-feeding cutworms. A single surface-feeding cutworm can sever the stems of many young plants in one night. Cutworms hide in the soil during the day, and feed only at night. Adult cutworms are dark, night-flying moths with bands or stripes on their forewings. Cutworm damage is most severe on young plants in the spring.

SOLUTION: Apply an insecticide dust containing either *carbaryl* (SEVIN®) or *diazinon* around the bases of plants when damage is first noticed. Since cutworms are difficult to control, it may be necessary to repeat dusting at weekly intervals. Cultivate thoroughly in late summer and fall to expose and destroy eggs, pupae, and larvae. Further reduce damage with "cutworm collars" around the stem of each plant. These collars can be made of stiff paper or aluminum foil. They should be at least 2 inches high, and pressed firmly into the soil.

Nicotiana cultural information
Light: Sun
Water: When the soil is almost dry
Soil: Any good garden soil
Fertilizer: Medium

PAEONIA (PEONY)

ADAPTATION:
Herbaceous peonies: Zones 3 through 7.
Tree peonies: Zones 3 through 9. To determine your zone, see the map on page 1020.

FLOWERING TIME: Spring.

LIGHT: Full sun, or half-day sun in hot, dry areas.

PLANTING METHOD: Plant peonies in the fall, placing the eyes of the tubers 2 inches below the soil surface.

SOIL: Well drained, high in organic matter. pH 6.0 to 7.5

FERTILIZER: When planting, mix a half cup of ORTHO Superphosphate into the soil for each plant. During the growing season, fertilize with ORTHO Rose & Flower Food or ORTHO General Purpose Plant Food according to label directions.

WATER:
How much: Apply enough water to wet the soil 1½ to 2 feet deep.
How often: Water when the soil 1 inch below the surface is just barely moist.

HANDLING: Divide herbaceous peony clumps every 6 to 10 years. When cutting flowers, leave three or four leaves on the stems. To insure good bloom next year, pick only a third of this year's blooms for cut flowers.

Failure to bloom.

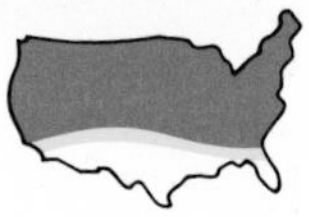

PROBLEM: Peonies fail to produce flower buds, or produce buds that fail to develop into flowers.

ANALYSIS: Failure to bloom
There are several reasons that peonies may fail to bloom:
1. *Roots buried at wrong depth:* Peonies that are planted too deeply or shallowly often fail to bloom.
2. *Immature transplants:* Peony roots that have been divided and transplanted usually fail to flower for at least 2 years. If the divisions were extremely small, the plants may not flower for as long as 5 years.
3. *Crowded plantings:* Old, established peony clumps eventually become overcrowded and stop producing flowers.
4. *Too much shade:* Peonies stop blooming when they are heavily shaded by trees, tall shrubs, or buildings.
5. *Lack of fertilization:* Peonies that are not being fed enough will fail to bloom. Sometimes they will form buds, but the buds will not develop.

SOLUTION: The numbers below correspond to the numbered sections in the analysis.
1. Carefully dig up and reset the roots so that the eyes are 1½ to 2 inches below the soil surface.
2. With time, the young plants will mature and start flowering.
3. Peonies usually need to be divided after 6 to 10 years, or any time after that when flower production starts to drop off. Dig up and divide old clumps into divisions containing 3 to 5 eyes. These divisions may be replanted.
4. Transplant peonies to a sunny location.
5. Apply a handful of ORTHO General Purpose Plant Food in early spring and work it in lightly around each plant.

Gray mold.

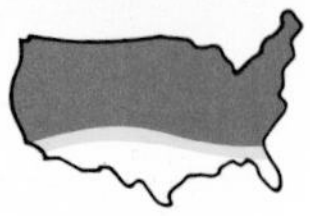

PROBLEM: New shoots wilt and die. The bases of the wilted stems are brownish black and rotted. Young flower buds turn black and wither. Older buds and open flowers turn soft and brown, and develop a gray or brown fuzzy covering in wet weather. This fuzzy growth, which may develop on all infected plant parts, is very distinctive. Its presence can be used to help distinguish this disease from *Phythophthora* (see the next column), with which it is often confused. Irregular brown lesions or patches form on the leaves. In severe cases, the plant base and roots may decay.

ANALYSIS: Gray mold
This common disease of peonies is caused by a fungus (*Botrytis paeoniae* or *B. cinerea*). Gray mold is most serious in the wet, cool conditions of early spring. Fungal growth on the stems, leaves, and flowers causes spotting, blackening, and decay. The fuzzy growth that forms on infected tissue is composed of millions of tiny spores. This fungus is spread by wind, splashing rain or water, or contaminated plants, soil, and tools. The fungus forms small black pellets that survive in plant debris and in the soil for many years.

SOLUTION: Remove and destroy all decayed or wilting plant parts. Clean up plant debris during the growing season and again in the fall. In the spring, spray emerging shoots with a fungicide containing *mancozeb*, *zineb*, or *benomyl*. Repeat the spray two more times at intervals of 5 to 10 days. Respray if the infection recurs. If available, *mancozeb* or *zineb* is preferable because they also control *Phytophthora*.

Peonies infected with phytophthora blight.

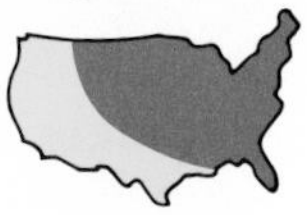

PROBLEM: New shoots wilt and turn black. Flowers, buds, leaves, and stems shrivel and turn dark brown and leathery. Black lesions several inches long often appear on the lower sections of the stem. The plant pulls up easily. Roots are black and rotted. The fuzzy mold that is characteristic of gray mold (see previous column) does not occur in this disease.

ANALYSIS: Phytophthora blight
This disease of peonies and many other plants is caused by a fungus (*Phytophthora cactorum*) that is common in most soils. Like gray mold, this fungus is favored by the cool, wet conditions of early spring. It can survive in the soil and in plant debris for many years in the form of tiny fungal pellets. Initially the fungus attacks either the roots or the developing shoots at the soil level, causing shoot wilting and a dark decay of the stem tissue. Wherever the fungus is splashed onto the plant, it may cause lesions, spots, and a typical brown, leathery decay. This disease is spread by splashing rain or water, and by contaminated plants, soil, and tools. It is most serious in heavy, poorly drained soils.

SOLUTION: Remove and destroy plants with decayed roots. Pick off and destroy infected plant parts. Clean up plant debris. Spray the foliage and drench the base of the plant with a fungicide containing *zineb*, *mancozeb*, or *maneb*. Spray three times at intervals of 5 to 10 days. Reapply the spray if infection recurs. Thin out overcrowded plants. Plant peonies in well-drained soil.

PAPAVER (POPPY)

Verticillium wilt.

PROBLEM: Leaves turn yellow, wilt, and die, starting with the lower leaves and progressing up the plant. Older plants may be stunted. Leaf wilting and death may affect only one side of the plant. Flowering is poor. There may be dark brown areas on the infected leaf stems.

ANALYSIS: Verticillium wilt
This wilt disease affects many ornamental plants. It is caused by a fungus (*Verticillium* species) that persists indefinitely on plant debris or in the soil. The disease is spread by contaminated seeds, plants, soil, and equipment. The fungus enters the plant through the roots and spreads up into the stems and leaves through the water-conducting vessels in the stems. These vessels become discolored and plugged. This plugging cuts off the flow of water to the leaves, causing leaf yellowing and wilting.

SOLUTION: No chemical control is available. It is best to destroy infected plants. Verticillium can be removed from the soil only by fumigation techniques. (For more information about soil fumigation, see page 927.) However, the best solution is usually to use plants that are resistant to verticillium. For a list of verticillium resistant plants, see page 1006.

Papaver cultural information
Light: Full sun
Water: Let the soil dry between waterings
Soil: Any good garden soil
Fertilizer: Medium

PELARGONIUM (GERANIUM)

ADAPTATION: Throughout the United States.

FLOWERING TIME: Spring and summer. In zones 9 and 10, some pelargoniums bloom throughout the year. To determine your zone, see the map on page 1020.

LIGHT: Full sun or light shade.

PLANTING TIME: Spring, when all danger of frost is past; or any time of year in zones 9 and 10.

SOIL: Well drained. pH 6.0 to 8.0

FERTILIZER: Fertilize with ORTHO Rose & Flower Food or ORTHO General Purpose Plant Food according to label directions.

WATER:
How much: Apply enough water to plants in the ground to wet the soil 8 to 10 inches deep.
Containers: Apply enough water so that 10 percent of the water drains from the bottom of the container.
How often: Water when the soil 1 inch below the surface is just barely moist.

HANDLING: Remove old flower clusters to encourage continuing bloom.

PELARGONIUM (GERANIUM)

Gray mold.

PROBLEM: Brown spots and blotches form on the leaves and possibly on the stems. As the disease progresses, a fuzzy brown or grayish mold forms on the infected tissue. Gray mold and spots often appear on the flowers, especially during periods of cool, wet weather. The leaves and stems may be soft and rotted.

ANALYSIS: Gray mold
This widespread plant disease is caused by a fungus (*Botrytis cinerea*) that is found on most dead plant tissue. The fungus initially attacks foliage and flowers that are weak or dead, causing spotting and mold. The fuzzy mold that develops is composed of millions of microscopic spores. Once gray mold has become established on plant debris and weak or dying leaves and flowers, it can invade healthy plant tissue. The fungus is spread by water, or by bits of infected plant debris that land on the leaves. Cool temperatures and high humidity favor gray mold growth. Crowded plantings, rain, and overhead watering enhance the spread of the disease. Infection is more of a problem in spring and fall when temperatures are lower. In warm winter areas where freezing is rare, gray mold can be a year-round problem.

SOLUTION: Clean up plant debris, and remove dying or infected leaves, stems, and flowers. Spray infected plants once every 10 to 14 days with ORTHO Vegetable Disease Control. Continue spraying as long as the mold is visible. Provide enough space between plants to allow good air circulation. Try to avoid wetting the foliage when watering.

Oedema on ivy geranium.

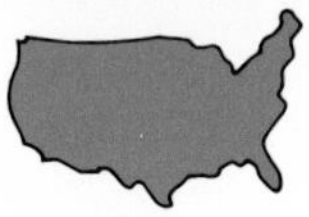

PROBLEM: Water-soaked spots appear on the leaves. Eventually, these spots turn brown and corky. Affected leaves may turn yellow and drop off. Corky ridges may form on the stems and leaf stalks. In most cases, the soil is moist and the air is cool and humid.

ANALYSIS: Oedema
Oedema is not caused by a pest, but results from an accumulation of water in the plant. Oedema often develops when the soil is moist or wet, and the atmosphere is humid and cool. Under these conditions, water is absorbed rapidly from the soil and lost slowly from the leaves, resulting in an excess amount of water in the plant. This excess water causes cells to burst. The ruptured cells eventually form spots and ridges. Oedema occurs most frequently in late winter and early spring during cloudy weather.

SOLUTION: Plant geraniums in soil that drains well, and avoid overwatering them. For information on proper watering, see page 912.

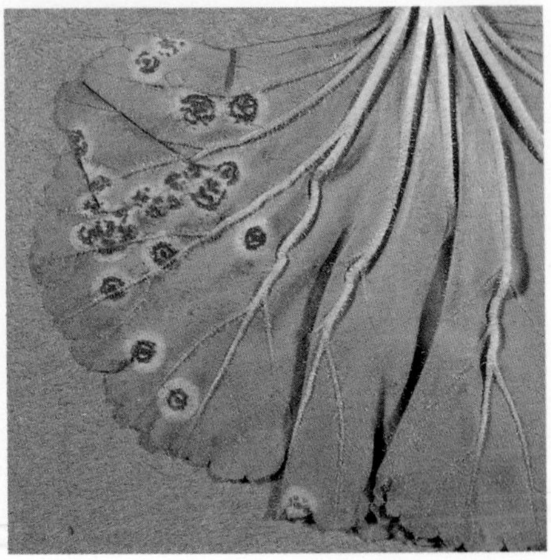

Rust.

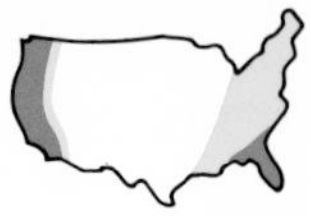

PROBLEM: Yellow spots up to ¼ inch in diameter appear on the leaves and stems. Reddish brown spore pustules develop on the undersides of the leaves. These pustules may be arranged in concentric circles. Severely infected leaves may turn yellow and drop prematurely.

ANALYSIS: Rust
This plant disease is caused by a fungus (*Puccinia pelargonii-zonalis*). Rust spores are spread by the wind and splashing water to healthy plants. After the leaf has been wet for 5 hours the spores germinate, forming a spot, and later a pustule. Rust generally does not kill the plant, but heavily infected plants may drop some leaves. The fungus survives only on living plant tissue. Wet conditions favor the development and spread of this disease.

SOLUTION: Spray with a fungicide containing *chlorothalonil* (DACONIL 2787®) at intervals of 10 days. Spray the foliage thoroughly, making sure to cover both the upper and lower surfaces of the leaves. These fungicides will protect the new, healthy foliage from infection, but they will not eradicate the fungus on diseased leaves, which should be picked off. If possible, avoid wetting the foliage. Water early in the day to allow foliage to dry out quickly.

Alternaria leaf spot.

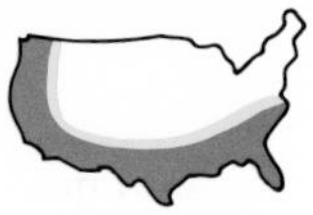

PROBLEM: Dark brown, irregularly shaped spots appear on the leaves. The spots range in size from barely visible to ⅓ inch in diameter. They are frequently surrounded by dark or yellow concentric circles. Spotting occurs mostly on the older leaves, although new growth may also be affected. Severely infected leaves shrivel, turn black, and fall off.

ANALYSIS: Alternaria leaf spot
This disease of geraniums is caused by a fungus (*Alternaria tenuis*) that is favored by prolonged cool, moist conditions. Infection rarely kills the plant, but can weaken and disfigure it. The fungus forms spores on the diseased leaves; these spores are readily blown or splashed to healthy leaves. Wherever the spores land, fungal strands grow, decay, and spot the plant tissue. The fungus survives on plant debris, and is spread by the wind and splashing water.

SOLUTION: Pick off and destroy infected leaves and clean up debris. If infection is severe and persistent, spray the plants with a fungicide containing *chlorothalonil* (DACONIL 2787®), *zineb,* or *basic copper sulfate.* Spray every 7 to 10 days until the spotting has diminished.

Bacterial leaf spot.

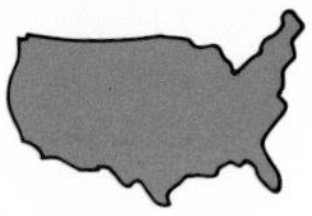

PROBLEM: Dark, circular, sunken spots up to ¼ inch in diameter, or larger, angular dead areas appear on the leaves. The leaves wilt and die. They either fall off the plant immediately, or hang down along the stem for several weeks. Many or all of the stems shrivel and turn brown or black. The roots are black but not rotted. When an infected stem is sliced open, a thick yellow fluid may ooze from the cut surface. Older diseased plants may retain only a few tufts of leaves at the stem tips.

ANALYSIS: Bacterial stem rot and leaf spot
This very common and widespread disease of geraniums is caused by bacteria (*Xanthomonas pelargonii* or *Pseudomonas* species). The disease develops most rapidly when the plants are growing vigorously and during periods of warm, moist weather. The bacteria decay the leaf tissue, causing the small spots and lesions, then may penetrate throughout the entire plant, causing wilting and rotting. The thick fluid that oozes from cut stems is filled with millions of bacteria. Infection is spread to healthy plants when bacteria are splashed onto the leaves, or when they make contact with contaminated tools. The bacteria can live in plant debris and in the soil for 3 months or more. Not all plants are killed by this disease. They often remain weak, stunted, and disfigured.

SOLUTION: Remove and destroy infected plants. Clean up plant debris. Avoid overhead watering. Sterilize contaminated tools by dipping them in rubbing alcohol. Wash your hands thoroughly after handling infected plants. Purchase only healthy plants. For information on plant selection, see page 924.

Root and stem rot.

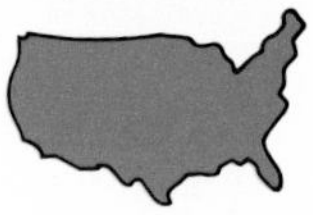

PROBLEM: Leaves turn yellow, wilt, and die. Stems may be soft and rotted, and the plant may be pulled out of the ground easily. The roots are dark and rotted.

ANALYSIS: Root and stem rot
This disease is caused by any of several different fungi, also known as *water molds,* that live in the soil. They thrive in waterlogged, heavy soil. Some of these fungi attack the plant stems at the soil level, while others attack the roots. Infection causes the roots and stems to decay. This results in wilting, then leaf yellowing, and eventually the death of the plant. These fungi are generally spread by infested soil and transplants, contaminated equipment, and splashing or running water.

SOLUTION: Allow the soil around the plants to dry out. (For more information on this technique, see page 849). Remove and discard severely infected plants. Avoid future root rot problems by planting in well-drained soil. For information on improving soil drainage, see page 907. For more information on root rot and stem rots, see page 849.

PELARGONIUM (GERANIUM)

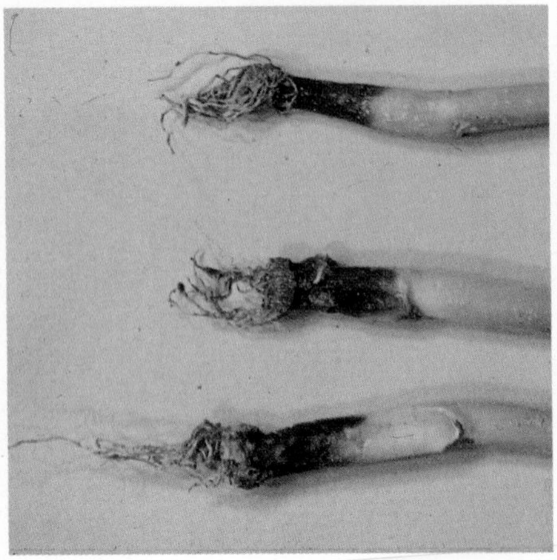

Blackleg.

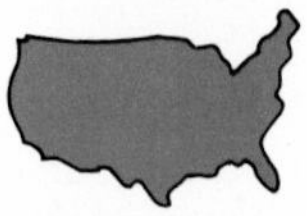

PROBLEM: Dark lesions form at the bases of the stems. These lesions enlarge and turn black and shiny. The blackening progresses up the stem. The leaves wilt and drop, and the plant may eventually die.

ANALYSIS: Blackleg
This common disease of geraniums is caused by a fungus (*Pythium* species) that lives in the soil. Blackleg is favored by wet, poorly drained soil. The fungus attacks the stems at the soil level, then spreads upward. The stems decay and the foliage wilts, shrivels, and eventually dies. Blackleg is spread by contaminated soil, transplants, and tools.

SOLUTION: Remove and destroy infected plants. If they have been growing in containers, throw out the soil in which they grew. Wash contaminated tools and pots, then dip them in a solution of 1 part chlorine bleach to 9 parts warm water for 1 minute or more. Plant healthy geraniums in well-drained soil and let them dry out between waterings. For further information on this technique, see page 849.

Greenhouse whiteflies (life size).

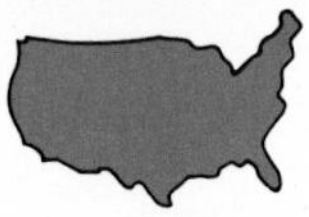

PROBLEM: Tiny, winged insects $\frac{1}{12}$ inch long are found mainly on the undersides of the leaves. The insects are covered with white, waxy powder. When the plant is touched, insects flutter rapidly around it. Leaves may be mottled and yellowing. In warm winter areas, black mold may cover the leaves.

ANALYSIS: Greenhouse whitefly
(*Trialeurodes vaporariorum*)
Greenhouse whitefly is a common insect pest of many garden and greenhouse plants. The four-winged adult lays eggs on the undersides of leaves. The larvae are the size of a pinhead, flat, oval-shaped, and semitransparent, with white waxy filaments radiating from the body. They feed for about a month before changing to the adult form. Both the larval and adult forms suck sap from the leaves. The larvae are more damaging because they feed more heavily. Adults and larvae cannot fully digest all the sugar in the sap, and excrete the excess in a fluid called honeydew, which often drops onto the leaves below. A sooty mold fungus may develop on the honeydew, causing the geranium leaves to appear black and dirty. In warm winter areas, the insect can be active year-round, with eggs, larvae, and adults present at the same time. The whitefly is unable to live through freezing winters. Spring reinfestations in freezing winter areas come from migrating whiteflies and from infested greenhouse-grown plants placed in the garden.

SOLUTION: Control whiteflies by spraying with ORTHO Isotox Insect Killer or ORTHO Orthene Systemic Insect Control. Be sure to cover both the upper and lower surfaces of the leaves.

Geranium budworm (twice life size).

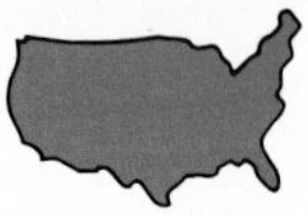

PROBLEM: Irregular or round holes appear in the leaves and buds. Leaves, buds, and flowers may be entirely chewed off. Worms or caterpillars are feeding on the plants.

ANALYSIS: Caterpillars
Many species of these moth or butterfly larvae feed on geraniums and other garden plants. Some common caterpillars include budworms, hornworms, and loopers. Usually, the adult moths or butterflies begin to lay their eggs on garden plants with the onset of warm spring weather. The larvae that emerge from these eggs feed on the leaves, flowers, and buds for two to six weeks, depending on weather conditions and species. Mature caterpillars pupate in cocoons attached to leaves or buildings, or buried in the soil. There may be one to several overlapping generations during the growing season. The last generation of caterpillars in the fall survives the winter as pupae. The adult moths and butterflies emerge the following spring.

SOLUTION: Spray infested plants with ORTHO Isotox Insect Killer or ORTHO Orthene Systemic Insect Control. Repeat the spray if reinfestation occurs, allowing at least seven to ten days to pass between applications. The bacterial insecticide *Bacillus thuringiensis* may also be used.

PETUNIA

ADAPTATION: Throughout the United States.

FLOWERING TIME: Summer and fall.

LIGHT: Full sun.

PLANTING TIME: Spring, when all danger of frost is past.

SOIL: Well drained.

FERTILIZER: Fertilize with ORTHO Rose & Flower Food or ORTHO General Purpose Plant Food according to label directions.

WATER:
How much: Apply enough water to plants in the ground to wet the soil 6 to 8 inches deep.
Containers: Apply enough water so that about 10 percent of the water drains from the bottom of the container.
How often: Water when the soil 1 inch below the surface is just barely moist.

HANDLING: If plants become rangy, pinch back about half of the growth to force additional bushy growth.

Gray mold.

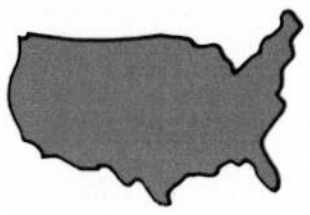

PROBLEM: Gray or brown spots appear on the flowers, especially during periods of wet weather. Brown spots and blotches may appear on the leaves and stems. As the disease progresses, a fuzzy brown or grayish mold may form on the infected tissue.

ANALYSIS: Gray mold
This widespread plant disease is caused by a fungus (*Botrytis* species) that is found on most dead plant tissue. The fungus initially attacks foliage and flowers that are weak or dead, causing spotting and sometimes mold. The fuzzy mold that may develop is composed of millions of microscopic spores. Once gray mold has become established on plant debris and weak or dying leaves and flowers, it can invade healthy plant tissue. The fungus is spread by the wind, splashing water, or infected pieces of plant tissue contacting healthy tissue. Cool temperatures and high humidity favor gray mold growth. Crowded plantings, rain, and overhead watering also enhance the spread of the disease. Infection is more of a problem in the spring and fall when temperatures are lower. In warm winter areas, where freezing is rare, gray mold can be a year-round problem.

SOLUTION: Spray infected plants once every ten to fourteen days with a fungicide containing *maneb* or *mancozeb*. Continue spraying as long as the mold is visible. Remove infected flowers and leaves, and clean up plant debris. Try to avoid wetting the flowers when watering.

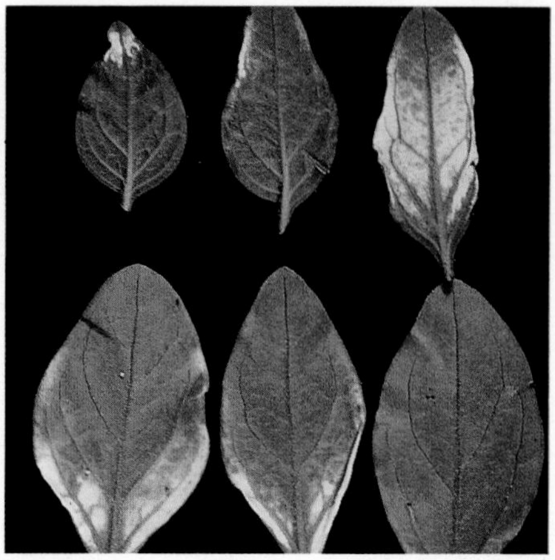

Smog damage.

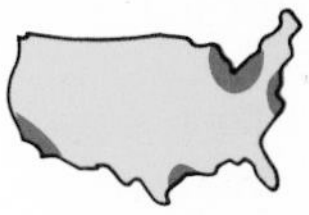

PROBLEM: Bands of bleached, dead tissue appear on the upper and lower surfaces of the leaves. Usually, the youngest leaves are the most severely affected, but in severe cases all of the leaves may be damaged. The leaf edges are pinched or twisted where damage has occurred. The plants are located in or near an urban area.

ANALYSIS: Smog damage
Petunias, especially white or light-colored varieties, are very sensitive to smog. PAN (peroxyacetyl nitrate) and ozone are two major components of smog that damage petunias and many other plants. PAN and ozone form as the result of chemical reactions between sunlight and products of petroleum combustion such as automobile exhaust. These compounds enter the plant through tiny breathing pores on the undersides of the leaves. Once inside the plant, PAN and ozone kill the leaf cells. Generally, injury first develops at the tips of young leaves and becomes more widespread as the leaves mature. The leaf edges become pinched or twisted where damage has occurred because the dead tissue is unable to expand with the rest of the growing leaf. Warm temperatures, high humidity, high light intensity, and moist soil stimulate leaf pores to open. When these conditions prevail, smog compounds can easily enter and damage the leaves.

SOLUTION: There is nothing you can do once damage has occurred. Pinch off severely damaged leaves. Do not plant white or light-colored petunias in smoggy areas. Shade plants on hot, smoggy days. Plant PAN and ozone tolerant flowers. For a list, see page 1008.

PETUNIA

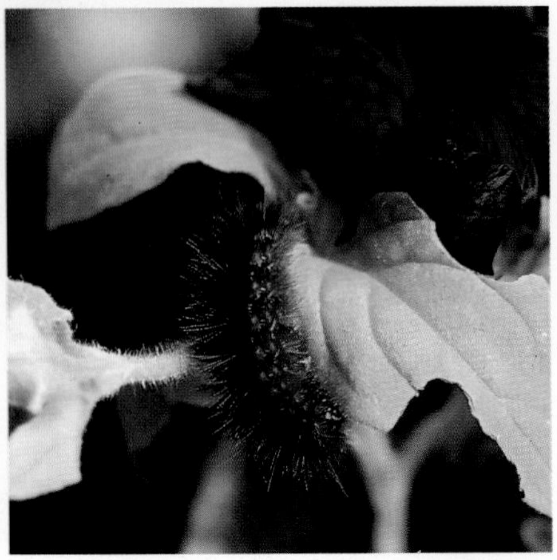

Caterpillar (life size).

PROBLEM: Irregular or round holes appear in the leaves and buds. Leaves, buds, and flowers may be entirely chewed off. Smooth or hairy caterpillars, up to 4 inches in length, are feeding on the plants.

ANALYSIS: Caterpillars
Numerous species of these moth or butterfly larvae feed on petunias and many other garden plants. Some common caterpillars include budworms, armyworms, hornworms, and loopers. As a rule, the adult moths or butterflies start to lay eggs on garden plants with the onset of warm weather in spring. The larvae that emerge feed on the leaves, flowers, and buds for two-to six weeks, depending on weather conditions and species. Mature caterpillars pupate in cocoons attached to leaves and structures, or in the soil. There may be one to several overlapping generations during the growing season. The last generation of caterpillars in the fall survives the winter as pupae. The adult moths and butterflies emerge the following spring.

SOLUTION: Spray infested plants with ORTHO Isotox Insect Killer or ORTHO Orthene Systemic Insect Control. Repeat the spray if reinfestation occurs, allowing at least seven to ten days to pass between applications.

Cutworm damage.

PROBLEM: Young plants are chewed or cut off near the ground. Many leaves may be sheared from the stems. Gray, brown, or black worms, 1½ to 2 inches long, may be found about 2 inches deep in the soil near the base of the damaged plants. The worms coil when disturbed.

ANALYSIS: Cutworms
Several species of cutworms attack petunias and many other flowers and vegetable plants. The most likely pests of young petunia plants set out early in the season are the surface-feeding cutworms and climbing cutworms. A single surface-feeding cutworm can sever the stems of many young plants in one night. Climbing cutworms shear the leaves off of older plants. Cutworms hide in the soil during the day, and feed only at night. Adult cutworms are dark, night-flying moths with bands or stripes on their forewings.

SOLUTION: Apply ORTHO Diazinon Soil & Turf Insect Control or ORTHO Diazinon Soil & Foliage Dust around the base of undamaged plants when stem cutting is observed. Since cutworms are difficult to control, it may be necessary to repeat the dusting at weekly intervals. Before transplanting into the area, apply a preventive treatment of ORTHO Diazinon Soil & Turf Insect Control and work it into the soil. Cultivate the soil thoroughly in late summer and fall to expose and destroy eggs, larvae, and pupae. Further reduce damage with "cutworm collars" around the stem of each plant. These collars can be made of stiff paper or aluminum foil. They should be at least 2 inches high, and pressed firmly into the soil.

Crown and root rot.

PROBLEM: There is a dark discoloration and dry rot of the lower stems and the base of the plant. Part or all of the foliage turns pale, wilts, and dies. The root system is small and the plant pulls up easily.

ANALYSIS: Crown and root rot
This disease is caused by a fungus (*Phytophthora* species) that lives in the soil. The fungus initially attacks the roots or stem at or just below the soil level. The dark, dry decay of the lower stem tissue and the roots eventually reduces the water flow to the leaves and flowers, causing the plant to wilt and finally die. Crown and root rot is most severe in heavy, poorly drained soils and wet conditions. The fungus is spread by contaminated soil, transplants, and tools.

SOLUTION: Remove and destroy the infected plants and the soil within 6 inches of their roots. If possible, improve the soil drainage (see page 907 for instructions). Replant with healthy plants. (For information on selecting healthy plants, see page 924.) Drench the entire bed with a solution containing *captan* (ORTHOCIDE®) in a concentration of 2 tablespoons per gallon of water. Repeat the drench at monthly intervals during the growing season. Let the soil dry out between waterings, as described on page 849.

PHLOX

ADAPTATION: Throughout the United States.

FLOWERING TIME: Early summer to fall.

LIGHT: Full sun.

PLANTING TIME: Spring or fall in zones 8 through 10. To determine your zone, see the map on page 1020. In colder areas, plant in spring, when all danger of frost is past.

SOIL: Any good garden soil.

FERTILIZER: Fertilize with ORTHO Rose & Flower Food or ORTHO General Purpose Plant Food according to label directions.

WATER:

How much: Apply enough water to plants in the ground to wet the soil 6 inches deep.

Containers: Apply enough water so that about 10 percent of the water drains from the bottom of the container.

How often: Water when the soil 1 inch below the surface is just barely moist.

Leaf spot.

PROBLEM: Spots and blotches appear on the leaves. The spots may be yellow, red, tan, gray, or brown. They range in size from barely visible to ¼ inch in diameter. Several spots may join to form blotches. The leaves may be yellow and dying. Leaf spotting is most severe in warm, humid weather. In some cases the infected leaf tissue turns ash gray and has a dry, papery texture.

ANALYSIS: Leaf spots
Several different fungi that cause leaf spots. Some of these fungi may eventually kill the plant, or weaken it so that it becomes susceptible to attack by other organisms. Others merely cause spotting that is unsightly but not harmful. These fungi are spread by splashing water or wind. They generally survive the winter in diseased plant debris. Most of the leaf spot fungi do their greatest damage in mild weather (50° to 85°F).

SOLUTION: Spray with a fungicide containing *maneb* or *benomyl* (or a combination) at intervals of 7 to 10 days. Because leaf spots are favored by humid conditions, it is important to spray frequently during these periods. Pick off severely infected leaves, and clean up plant debris.

Powdery mildew.

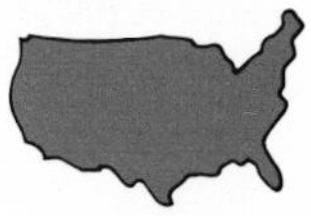

PROBLEM: Leaves and stems are covered with grayish white powdery spots and patches. The patches occur primarily on the upper surfaces of the older leaves. The leaves eventually turn yellow and wither.

ANALYSIS: Powdery mildew
This common plant disease can be caused by either of two closely related fungi (*Erysiphe cichoracearum* and *Sphaerotheca humuli*) that thrive in both humid and dry weather. The powdery patches consist of fungal strands and spores. The spores are spread by the wind to healthy plants. The fungus saps plant nutrients, causing yellowing and sometimes death of the leaves. A severe infection may kill the plant. Since these powdery mildews attack many different kinds of plants, the fungus from a diseased plant may infect other types of plants in the garden. (For a list of susceptible plants, see page 1006.) Under favorable conditions, powdery mildew can spread through a planting in a matter of days or weeks.

SOLUTION: Spray infected plants with ORTHO Funginex Rose Disease Control, ORTHO Orthenex Insect & Disease Control, or ORTHO Phaltan Rose & Garden Fungicide. These fungicides protect new, healthy foliage. Damaged leaves may be picked off. Severely infected plants should be removed. Spray at regular intervals of 7 to 10 days or as often as necessary to protect new growth. Space plants far enough apart to allow good air circulation. Clean up plant debris.

PRIMULA (PRIMROSE)

PRIMULA (PRIMROSE)

ADAPTATION: Throughout the United States.

FLOWERING TIME: In zones 9 and 10, winter through spring. In colder areas, most primroses bloom in early spring. To determine your zone, see the map on page 1020.

LIGHT: Deep shade or filtered sun.

PLANTING TIME: Fall in zones 9 and 10. In colder areas, spring, when all danger of frost is past.

SOIL: Any good garden soil that is rich in organic matter. pH 5.5 to 7.5

FERTILIZER: Fertilize with ORTHO Rose & Flower Food or ORTHO General Purpose Plant Food according to label directions.

WATER:

How much: Apply enough water to plants in the ground to wet the soil 6 inches deep.

Containers: Apply enough water so that 10 percent of the water drains from the bottom of the container.

How often: Water when the soil 1 inch below the surface is moist but not wet.

HANDLING: Divide every 3 or 4 years just after the plants have finished blooming.

Leaf spots.

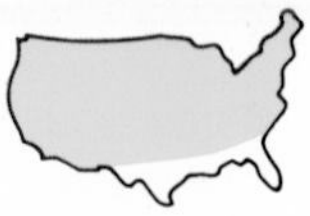

PROBLEM: Spots and blotches appear on the leaves. The spots range in size from ⅛ to ¼ inch, and are especially numerous on the lower leaves. The spots may be circular or irregular in shape, and are often brown with hazy yellow borders. They may also be yellow with ash-colored centers. Often, several spots join to form blotches. Severely infected leaves usually turn yellow and die.

ANALYSIS: Leaf spots

Primroses may be spotted by any of several different fungi (including *Ramularia primulae* and *Phyllosticta primulicola*). The spotting is unsightly but not harmful to the plant. However, the infected leaf tissue becomes susceptible to further attack by bacteria (*Pseudomonas primulae*), which cause dark brown spots with yellow borders. If bacterial infection becomes severe, many of the infected leaves will die. Both bacteria and fungi survive the winter in infected plant debris. They are spread by splashing water, contaminated tools, and transplants. In addition, some of the fungi form spores, which may be spread by the wind. Most of the leaf spot organisms do their greatest damage in mild weather (temperatures of 50° to 85°F).

SOLUTION: Remove and discard badly spotted leaves and all plant debris. Try to avoid splashing water on the foliage when watering. If spotting and blotching are persistent and severe, spray plants with a fungicide containing *benomyl*, *mancozeb*, or *basic copper sulfate* every ten to fourteen days.

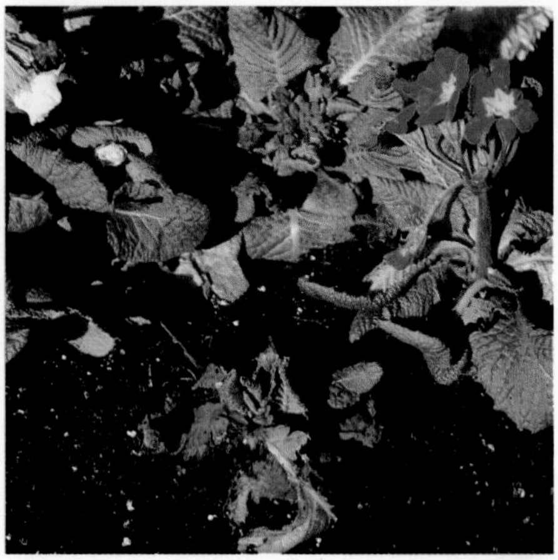

Root and stem rot.

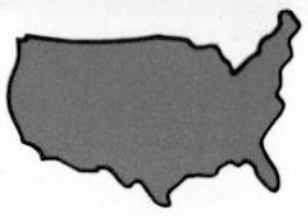

PROBLEM: Older leaves turn yellow, wilt, and die. The leaf bases may be soft and rotted, and the plant may pull out of the ground easily. The roots are dark and rotted.

ANALYSIS: Root and stem rot

This disease is caused by any of a number of different fungi (including *Pythium* and *Rhizoctonia* species) that persist indefinitely in the soil. They thrive in waterlogged, heavy soil. Some of these fungi attack the plant stems at the soil level, while others attack the roots. Infection causes the roots and stems to decay. This results in wilting, then yellowing leaves, and eventually the death of the plant. These fungi are generally spread by infested soil and transplants, contaminated equipment, and splashing or running water. Many of these organisms also cause damping-off of seedlings. For more information about damping-off, see page 850. For more information on root and stem rots, see the section beginning on page 849.

SOLUTION: Allow the soil around the plants to dry out. (For more information on this technique, see page 849.) Remove and discard severely infected plants. Avoid future root rot problems by planting in well-drained soil. For information on improving soil drainage, see page 907.

Slug (⅓ life size).

PROBLEM: Irregular holes with smooth edges are chewed in the leaves. Leaves may be sheared off entirely. Silvery trails wind around on the plants and soil nearby. Snails or slugs may be seen moving around or feeding on the plants, especially at night. Check for them by inspecting the garden at night by flashlight.

ANALYSIS: Snails and slugs
These pests are mollusks, and are related to clams, oysters, and other shellfish. They feed on a wide variety of garden plants. Like other mollusks, snails and slugs need to be moist all the time. For this reason, they avoid direct sun and dry places, and hide during the day in damp places, such as under flower pots or in thick groundcover. They emerge at night or on cloudy days to feed. Snails and slugs are similar in appearance, except that the snail has a hard shell, into which it withdraws when disturbed. Slugs lay masses of white eggs encased in a slimy mass in protected places. Snails bury their eggs in the soil, also in a slimy mass. The young look like miniature versions of their parents.

SOLUTION: Scatter ORTHO Bug-Geta Snail & Slug Pellets or ORTHO Slug-Geta Snail & Slug Bait Granules around the areas you wish to protect. Also scatter the bait in areas where snails or slugs might be hiding, such as in dense groundcovers, weedy areas, compost piles, or pot storage areas. Before spreading the bait, wet down the treated areas to encourage snail and slug activity that night. Repeat the application every 2 weeks as long as snails and slugs are active.

Iron deficiency.

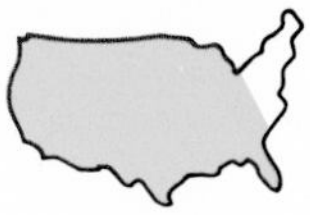

PROBLEM: Leaves turn pale green or yellow. The newest leaves (those at the tips of the stem) are most severely affected. Except in extreme cases, the veins of affected leaves remain green. In extreme cases, the newest leaves are small and all-white or yellow. Older leaves may remain green.

ANALYSIS: Iron deficiency
Plants frequently suffer from deficiencies of iron and other minor nutrients, such as manganese and zinc, elements essential to normal plant growth and development. Deficiencies can occur when one or more of these elements are depleted in the soil. Often, minor nutrients are present in the soil, but alkaline (pH 7.5 and higher) or wet soil conditions cause them to form compounds that cannot be used by primroses. An alkaline condition can result from overliming, or from lime leached from cement or brick. Regions where soil is derived from limestone, and those with low rainfall, usually have alkaline soils. For more information about alkaline soils, see page 908.

SOLUTION: To correct the deficiency of minor nutrients spray the foliage with ORTHO Greenol Liquid Iron , and apply it to the soil around the plants. Correct the pH of the soil by treating it with ORTHO Aluminum Sulfate or *ferrous sulfate* and watering it in well. Maintain an acid pH by fertilizing with ORTHO Azalea, Camellia & Rhododendron Food. If wet soil is a problem, improve the soil drainage. For information on improving soil drainage, see page 907.

RANUNCULUS

ADAPTATION: Throughout the United States. Ranunculus will overwinter in zones 8 through 10. To determine your zone, see the map on page 1020.

FLOWERING TIME: Summer.

LIGHT: Full sun.

PLANTING TIME: Plant tuberous roots in the fall in zones 8 through 10. In colder areas, start tuberous roots indoors in the fall or late winter, or plant them outside in the spring when all danger of frost is past.

SOIL: Well drained. pH 6.0 to 7.5

FERTILIZER: Fertilize with ORTHO Rose & Flower Food or ORTHO General Purpose Plant Food according to label directions.

WATER:
How much: Apply enough water to plants in the ground to wet the soil 6 to 8 inches deep.
Containers: Apply enough water so that 10 percent of the water drains from the bottom of the container.
How often: Water when the soil 1 inch below the surface is just barely moist.

HANDLING: Plant tuberous roots with the "toes" down. After the foliage dies in the late summer, dig up the tuberous roots and store them in a dry location.

RANUNCULUS

Bird damage.

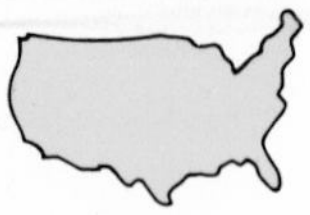

PROBLEM: Tender young leaves are torn. Seedlings may be entirely eaten. Birds may be seen feeding in the garden, or their tracks may be noticed around the damaged plants.

ANALYSIS: Bird damage
Birds are fond of ranunculus and frequently eat the tender parts of the plants. Individual birds may develop the habit of feeding on ranunculus, and visit the plants every day.

SOLUTION: Protect emerging shoots and young transplants with cages or coverings made of 1-inch-mesh chicken wire. Cages about 10″x10″x24″ are self-supporting. Larger cages may need to be reinforced with heavy wire. Cheesecloth cages supported with stakes, wire, or string may also be used. For more information about birds, see page 899.

Root rot.

PROBLEM: The plant is wilting. The leaves and stems are dark brown, limp, and have a water-soaked appearance. Roots and tubers are dark and rotted.

ANALYSIS: Root rot
This disease is caused by several fungi that persist indefinitely in the soil. They thrive in waterlogged, heavy soils. Some of these fungi attack the plant stems at the soil level, while others attack the roots. Infection causes the roots, tubers, and stems to decay. This results in wilting, then yellowing leaves, and eventually the death of the plant. These fungi are generally spread by infested soil and contaminated transplants, equipment, and splashing or running water.

SOLUTION: Remove and discard infected plants and the soil immediately surrounding them. Let the soil dry out between waterings. (For more information on this technique, see page 849.) Plant ranunculus in well-drained soil. For information on soil drainage, see page 907.

Ranunculus mosaic.

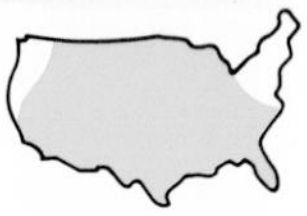

PROBLEM: Leaves are mottled yellow-green. Plants may be stunted, and flowers may be smaller than normal. In some cases, the petals are streaked.

ANALYSIS: Ranunculus mosaic
This virus disease infects ranunculus plants and tubers. The severity of infection varies from plant to plant. Mosaic does not kill ranunculus, but greatly reduces their overall vigor and beauty. The virus is spread by aphids that feed on diseased plants, then transmit the virus to healthy plants when they feed again. Mosaic persists in the plant indefinitely. Tubers obtained from diseased plants are also infected.

SOLUTION: There are no chemicals that control virus diseases. Discard infected plants. Prevent the spread of the virus by keeping the aphid population under control. For more information about disease-carrying aphids and their control, see page 880.

RUDBECKIA (GLORIOSA DAISY)

Verticillium wilt.

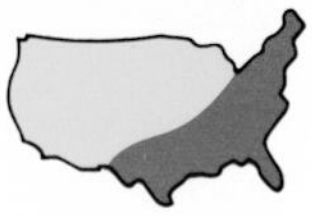

PROBLEM: Leaves yellow, wilt, and die, beginning with the lower leaves and progressing up the plant. Older plants may be stunted. Yellowing and wilting often affect only one of the plant. Flowering is poor. There may be dark brown areas on the infected stems. When the stem is sliced open near the base of the plant, dark streaks and discolorations of the inner tissue are seen.

ANALYSIS: Verticillium wilt
This wilt disease affects many ornamental plants. It is caused by a soil-inhabiting fungus (*Verticillium* species) that persists indefinitely on plant debris or in the soil. The disease is spread by contaminated seeds, plants, soil, and equipment. The fungus enters the plant through the roots and spreads up into the stems and leaves through the water-conducting vessels in the stems. The vessels become discolored and plugged. This plugging cuts off the flow of water to the leaves, causing leaf yellowing and wilting. For more information about verticillium wilt, see page 850.

SOLUTION: No chemical control is available. It is best to destroy infected plants. Verticillium can be removed from the soil only by fumigation techniques. (For more information about soil fumigation, see page 927.) However, the best solution is usually to use plants that are resistant to verticillium. For a list of verticillium-resistant plants, see page 1006.

Rudbeckia cultural information
Light: Sun
Water: When the soil is just barely moist
Soil: Well drained
Fertilizer: Medium

SALVIA (SAGE)

Gray mold.

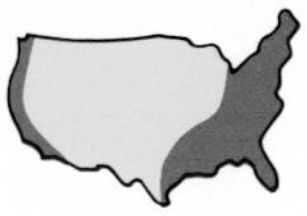

PROBLEM: Brown spots and blotches appear on the leaves and possibly on the stems. As the disease progresses, a fuzzy brown or grayish mold forms on the infected tissue. Gray mold and spots often appear on the flowers, especially during periods of cool, wet weather. The leaves and stems may be soft and rotted.

ANALYSIS: Gray mold
This widespread plant disease is caused by a fungus (*Botrytis* species) that is found on most dead plant tissue. The fungus initially attacks foliage and flowers that are weak or dead, causing spotting and mold. The fuzzy mold that develops is composed of millions of microscopic spores. Once gray mold has become established on plant debris and weak or dying leaves and flowers, it can invade healthy plant tissue. The fungus is spread by splashing water, or by bits of infected plant debris that land on the leaves. Cool temperatures and high humidity favor gray mold growth. Crowded plantings, rain, and overhead watering enhance the spread of the disease. Infection is more of a problem in spring and fall, when temperatures are lower. In warm winter areas where freezing is rare, gray mold can be a year-round problem.

SOLUTION: Spray infected plants every 10 to 14 days with a fungicide containing *chlorothalonil* (DACONIL 2787®) or *benomyl.* Continue spraying as long as the mold is visible. Clean up plant debris, and remove dying or infected leaves, stems, and flowers. Provide enough space between plants to allow good air circulation. Try to avoid wetting the foliage when watering.

Verticillium wilt. Diseased plant on right.

PROBLEM: Leaves yellow, wilt, and die, starting with the lower leaves and progressing up the plant. Older plants may be stunted. Yellowing and wilting often affect only one side of the plant. Flowering is poor. There may be dark brown areas on the infected stems. When the stem is sliced open near the base of the plant, dark streaks and discolorations of the inner stem tissue are seen.

ANALYSIS: Verticillium wilt
This wilt disease is caused by a soil-inhabiting fungus (*Verticillium* species) that persists indefinitely on plant debris or in the soil. The disease is spread by contaminated seeds, plants, soil, and equipment. The fungus enters the plant through the roots and spreads up into the stems and leaves through the water-conducting vessels in the stems. The vessels become discolored and plugged. This plugging cuts off the flow of water to the leaves, causing leaf yellowing and wilting. For more information about verticillium wilt, see page 850.

SOLUTION: No chemical control is available. It is best to destroy infected plants. Verticillium can be removed from the soil only by fumigation techniques. (For more information about soil fumigation, see page 927.) However, the best solution is usually to use plants that are resistant to verticillium. For a list of verticillium-resistant plants, see page 1006.

Salvia cultural information
Light: Sun
Water: When soil is just barely moist
Soil: Well drained
Fertilizer: Light

SEDUM

Stem and root rot.

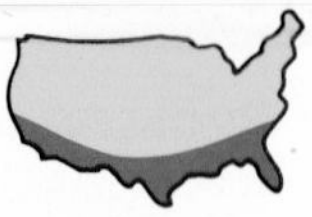

PROBLEM: The leaves and stems may be dark, soft, and rotted, or they may turn dull gray, then yellow. Finally, they shrivel and drop off. Sometimes the base of the plant and the lower stems are covered with white matted strands. These strands eventually develop small black or brown pellets the size of a pinhead.

ANALYSIS: Stem and root rot
This disease is caused by several different fungi (including *Sclerotium rolfsii*). These fungi may persist indefinitely in the soil. They thrive in waterlogged, heavy soil. Some of these fungi attack the roots directly, while others penetrate either the roots or stems. Infection causes the roots and stems to decay, resulting in wilting, rotting leaves, and finally the death of the plant. These fungi are generally spread by infested soil and contaminated transplants, equipment, and moving water. Some of these fungi may survive the winter in the form of fungal pellets and strands in the soil and plant debris.

SOLUTION: Let the soil dry out between waterings. (For information on this technique, see page 849.) Remove and destroy all infected plants and debris. Improve soil drainage by adding organic matter. For information on correcting soil drainage, see page 907.

Sedum cultural information
Light: Sun to shade
Water: Let soil dry between waterings
Soil: Any good garden soil
Fertilizer: Light

Snail (half life size).

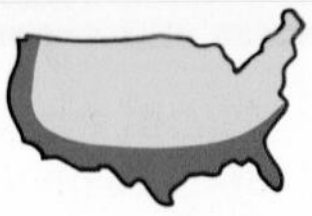

PROBLEM: Stems and leaves may be sheared off and eaten. Silvery trails wind around on the plants and soil nearby. Snails or slugs may be seen moving around or feeding on the plants, especially at night. Check for them by inspecting the garden at night by flashlight.

ANALYSIS: Snails and slugs
These pests are mollusks, and are related to clams, oysters, and other shellfish. They feed on a wide variety of garden plants. Like other mollusks, snails and slugs need to be moist all the time. For this reason, they avoid direct sun and dry places, and hide during the day in damp places, such as under flower pots or in thick groundcovers. They emerge at night or on cloudy days to feed. Snails and slugs are similar in appearance, except that the snail has a hard shell, into which it withdraws when disturbed. Slugs lay masses of white eggs encased in a slimy mass in protected places. Snails bury their eggs in the soil, also in a slimy mass. The young look like miniature versions of their parents.

SOLUTION: Scatter ORTHO Bug-Geta Snail & Slug Pellets or ORTHO Slug-Geta Snail & Slug Bait granules around the areas you wish to protect. Also scatter the bait in areas where snails or slugs might be hiding, such as in dense groundcovers, weedy areas, compost piles, or pot storage areas. Before spreading the bait, wet down the treated areas to encourage snail and slug activity that night. Repeat the application every two weeks as long as snails and slugs are active.

SOLANUM

Greenhouse whiteflies (¾ life size).

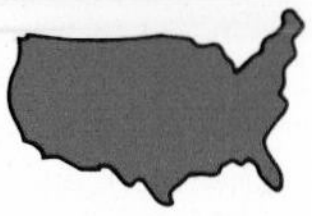

PROBLEM: Tiny, winged insects 1/12 inch long are found mainly on the undersides of the leaves. The insects are covered with white waxy powder. When the plant is touched, insects flutter rapidly around it. Leaves may be mottled and yellowing. Black mold may cover the leaves.

ANALYSIS: Greenhouse whitefly
(*Trialeurodes vaporariorum*)
Greenhouse whitefly is a common insect pest of many garden and greenhouse plants. The four-winged adult lays eggs on the undersides of leaves. The larvae are the size of a pinhead, flat, oval-shaped, and semitransparent, with white waxy filaments radiating from the body. They feed for about a month before changing to the adult form. Both the larval and adult forms suck sap from the leaves. The larvae are more damaging because they feed more heavily. Adults and larvae cannot fully digest all the sugar in the plant sap, and excrete the excess in a fluid called honeydew, which often coats the leaves. In warm winter areas the insect can be active all year, with eggs, larvae, and adults present at the same time. The whitefly is unable to live through freezing winters. Spring reinfestations in freezing winter areas come from migrating whiteflies and from infested greenhouse-grown plants placed in the garden.

SOLUTION: Control whiteflies by spraying infested plants with an insecticide containing *diazinon* or *malathion*. Spray at least three times at intervals of 7 to 10 days. Spray the foliage thoroughly, being sure to cover both the upper and lower surfaces of the leaves. For best results, use a spreader-sticker (see page 922.)

TAGETES (MARIGOLD)

ADAPTATION: Throughout the United States.

FLOWERING TIME: Summer to fall.

LIGHT: Full sun.

PLANTING TIME: Spring, after all danger of frost is past.

SOIL: Any good garden soil.

FERTILIZER: Fertilize with ORTHO Rose & Flower Food or ORTHO General Purpose Plant Food according to label directions.

WATER:

How much: Apply enough water to plants in the ground to wet the soil 10 to 12 inches deep.

Containers: Apply enough water so that 10 percent of the water drains from the bottom of the container.

How often: Water when the soil 1 inch below the surface is just barely moist.

HANDLING: Pinch off fading blooms to promote continuous flowering.

Leaf spot.

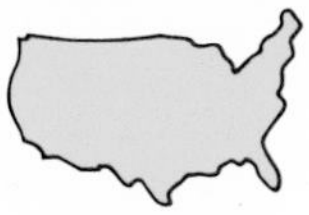

PROBLEM: Spots and blotches appear on the leaves. The spots may be yellow, reddish, brown, gray, or black. They range in size from barely visible to ¼ inch in diameter. Several spots may join to form blotches. Leaves and leaflets may be twisted or yellowing and dying. Leaf spotting is most severe in warm, humid weather.

ANALYSIS: Leaf spot

There are several different fungi that cause leaf spots. Some of these fungi may eventually kill the plant. Most of them merely cause spotting, which is unsightly but not harmful to the plant. These fungi are spread by splashing water or wind. They generally survive the winter in diseased plant debris. Most of these fungi do their greatest damage in mild weather (50° to 85°F).

SOLUTION: Remove and destroy badly spotted leaves and all plants. Try to avoid splashing water on the foliage when watering. Spray plants every 10 to 14 days with a fungicide containing *benomyl* or *basic copper sulfate.*

Mite damage.

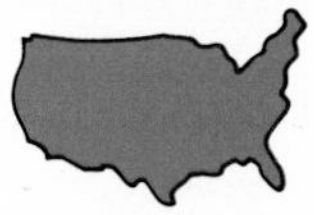

PROBLEM: Leaves are stippled, yellowing, and dirty. Leaves may dry out and drop. There may be webbing over flower buds, between leaves and stems, or on the lower surfaces of the leaves. To determine if the plant is infested with mites, hold a sheet of white paper underneath an affected leaf and tap the plant sharply. Minute green, red, or yellow specks the size of pepper grains will drop to the paper and begin to crawl around. These pests are easily seen against the white background.

ANALYSIS: Mites

These major pests of many garden and greenhouse plants are related to spiders. They cause damage by sucking sap from the underside of the leaves. As a result of feeding, the green leaf pigment disappears, producing the stippled appearance. Mites are active throughout the growing season, but are favored by hot, dry weather (70°F and up). By midsummer, they can build up to tremendous numbers. For more information about mites, see page 887.

SOLUTION: Spray with ORTHO Isotox Insect Killer according to label directions when damage is first noticed. Spray the foliage thoroughly, being sure to cover both the upper and lower surfaces of the leaves.

TAGETES (MARIGOLD)

Leafminer damage.

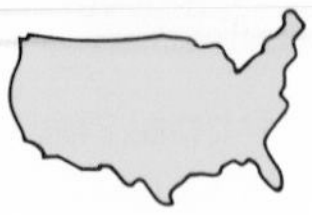

PROBLEM: Light-colored winding trails appear in the leaves. Blotches may eventually develop. Severely infested leaves may dry up and die.

ANALYSIS: Leafminers
Several species of leaf-mining flies cause this type of damage to marigolds and many other flowers. The minute adult flies lay their eggs on the undersides of the leaves. The larvae that emerge from these eggs penetrate the leaf and live between the upper and lower surfaces. They feed on the inner leaf tissue, creating winding trails and blotches. Their dark excrement dots or partially fills sections of the trails. The larvae usually emerge from the leaves to pupate. Leafminers are continually present from spring until fall. The last generation of larvae pupates in the soil or plant debris through the winter and emerges as adult flies the following spring. For more information about leafminers, see page 885.

SOLUTION: Spray infested plants with ORTHO Isotox Insect Killer or ORTHO Orthene Systemic Insect Control according to label directions. Pick off and destroy infested leaves. Remove and destroy all plant remains in the fall.

Wilt and stem rot.

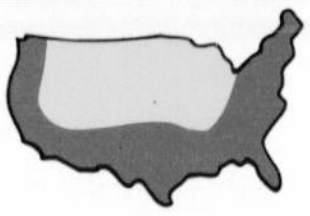

PROBLEM: Leaves wilt and die. The lower stems have a dark, water-soaked appearance. They eventually shrivel and turn brown near the soil line. The plant pulls up easily to reveal rotted roots. The plant usually dies within 1 to 3 weeks.

ANALYSIS: Wilt and stem rot
This disease is caused by a widespread fungus (*Phytophthora cryptogea*) that persists indefinitely in the soil. The fungus attacks the roots, then spreads up into the stems. As the roots and stems decay, the leaves wilt and turn yellow, and the plant dies. The fungus thrives in cool, waterlogged soils. This disease is spread by contaminated soil, transplants, equipment, and moving water. African marigolds (*Tagetes erecta*) are quite susceptible, but French marigolds (*T. patula*) and other dwarf varieties are resistant to this fungus.

SOLUTION: Remove and discard infected plants and the soil immediately surrounding them. Let the soil dry out between waterings. (For information on this technique, see page 849.) Plant marigolds in well-drained soil. (For information on improving soil drainage, see page 907.) A fungicidal drench of *captan* (ORTHOCIDE®) or *etridiazol* will help reduce the severity of the disease. Drench the flower bed in which diseased plants have been growing to help prevent the spread of the disease. Plant resistant French and dwarf marigolds.

Cutworm (¼ life size).

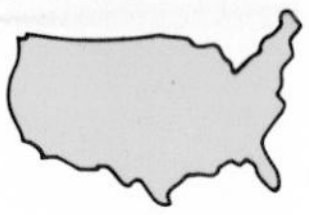

PROBLEM: Young plants are chewed or cut off near the ground. Many leaves may be sheared from their stems. Gray, brown, or black worms, 1½ to 2 inches long, may be found in the top 2 inches of soil near the base of the damaged plants. The worms coil when disturbed.

ANALYSIS: Cutworms
Several species of cutworms attack marigolds and many other flower and vegetable plants. The most likely pests of young marigold plants early in the season are surface-feeding and climbing cutworms. A single surface-feeding cutworm can sever the stems of many young plants in one night. Climbing cutworms may shear the leaves off older plants. Cutworms hide in the soil during the day, and feed only at night. The adult forms of cutworms are dark, night-flying moths with bands or stripes on their forewings.

SOLUTION: Apply an insecticidal dust or spray containing *diazinon* around the base of undamaged plants when stem cutting is observed. Since cutworms are difficult to control, it may be necessary to repeat the treatment at weekly intervals. Before transplanting into the area, apply a preventive treatment of insecticide and work it into the soil. Cultivate the soil thoroughly in late summer and fall to expose and destroy eggs, larvae, and pupae. Further reduce damage with cutworm "collars" around the stem of each plant. These collars can be made of stiff paper or aluminum foil. They should be at least 2 inches high, and pressed firmly into the soil.

TROPAEOLUM (NASTURTIUM)

Gray mold.

PROBLEM: Gray mold and spots often appear on the flowers, especially during periods of cool, wet weather. The petals may turn black. Brown spots and blotches appear on leaves and possibly on stems. Mold may appear on the infected leaf and stem tissues. The leaves and stems may be soft and rotted.

ANALYSIS: Gray mold
This widespread plant disease is caused by a fungus (*Botrytis cinerea*) that is found on most dead plant tissue. The fungus initially attacks foliage and flowers that are weak or dead, causing spotting and mold. The fuzzy mold that develops is composed of millions of microscopic spores. Once gray mold has become established on plant debris and weak or dying leaves and flowers, it can invade healthy plant tissue. The fungus is spread by wind, splashing water, or by infected pieces of plant tissue contacting healthy tissue. Cool temperatures and high humidity favor gray mold growth. Crowded plantings, rain, and overhead watering also enhance the spread of the disease. Infection is more of a problem in spring and fall, when temperatures are lower. In warm winter areas where freezing is rare, gray mold can be a year-round problem.

SOLUTION: Spray infected plants once every 10 to 14 days with a fungicide containing *mancozeb* or *maneb*. Continue spraying as long as the mold is visible. Clean up plant debris, and remove dying or infected leaves, stems, and flowers. Provide enough space between plants to allow good air circulation. Try to avoid wetting the foliage and flowers when watering.

Leaf spots.

PROBLEM: Spots and blotches appear on the leaves. The spots may be yellow, red, tan, gray, or black. They range in size from barely visible to $\frac{1}{4}$ inch in diameter. Several spots may join together to form blotches. Some of the leaves may be yellow and dying. Leaf spotting is most severe in warm, humid weather.

ANALYSIS: Leaf spot
Nasturtiums are susceptible to several fungi that cause leaf spots. Some of these fungi may eventually kill the plant or weaken it so that it becomes susceptible to attack by other organisms. Others merely cause spotting that is unsightly but not harmful. These fungi are spread by splashing water, wind, insects, tools, and infected transplants and seed. They survive the winter in diseased plant debris. Most of these fungi do their greatest damage during mild weather (50° to 85°F). Infection is favored by moist conditions.

SOLUTION: Picking off the diseased leaves generally gives adequate control. If infection is severe, spray with a copper-containing fungicide, such as *basic copper sulfate*. Clean up debris.

Aphids (twice life size).

PROBLEM: Tiny ($\frac{1}{8}$ inch) pale green to dark green or black soft-bodied insects are clustered on the leaves. Leaves may be curled, distorted, and yellowing. Flowers may be malformed. A shiny, sticky substance may coat the leaves. Ants are often present.

ANALYSIS: Aphids
Several species of aphids infest nasturtiums, including the *bean aphid* (*Aphis fabae*). Aphids do little damage in small numbers. However, they are extremely prolific and populations can rapidly build up to damaging numbers during the growing season. Damage occurs when the aphid sucks the juices from the nasturtium leaves. The aphid is unable to digest fully all the sugar in the plant sap and excretes the excess in a fluid called honeydew, which often coats the leaves. Ants feed on this sticky substance, and are often present where there is an aphid infestation. For more information about aphids, see page 875.

SOLUTION: Spray the plant with an insecticide containing *malathion*, *diazinon*, or *dimethoate*. Repeat the spray if the plant becomes reinfested. Hose off the foliage to remove the honeydew.

TROPAEOLUM (NASTURTIUM)

Caterpillars (half life size).

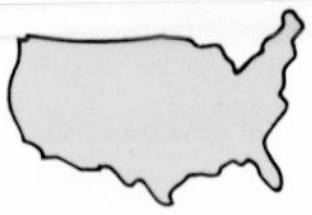

PROBLEM: Holes appear in the leaves and buds. Leaves, buds, and flowers may be entirely chewed off. Worms or caterpillars are feeding on the plants.

ANALYSIS: Caterpillars
Many species of these moth or butterfly larvae feed on nasturtiums and other garden plants. The adult moths or butterflies of most species start to lay their eggs on garden plants with the onset of warm spring weather. The larvae that emerge from these eggs feed on the leaves, flowers, and buds for 2 to 6 weeks, then pupate in cocoons either attached to leaves or structures or buried in the soil. The adult moths and butterflies emerge the following spring.

SOLUTION: Spray infested plants with an insecticide containing *malathion*. Repeat the spray if reinfestation occurs, allowing at least 7 to 10 days to pass between applications. You may also control caterpillars with a spray containing *Bacillus thuringiensis*. This bacterial insecticide is most effective while the caterpillars are small.

Tropaeolum cultural information
Light: Sun to partial shade
Water: When the soil is just barely moist
Soil: Any good garden soil
Fertilizer: Light

Bacterial wilt.

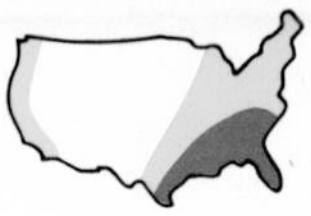

PROBLEM: The leaves wilt, turn yellow, and die. The stems have a water-soaked appearance and are soft and rotten. When sliced open, the stems are found to be discolored, and a thick gray fluid oozes out. The roots may be black and decayed.

ANALYSIS: Bacterial wilt
This disease is caused by a bacterium (*Pseudomonas solanacearum*) that is common in warm, humid climates. It attacks many different ornamentals and vegetables in the tomato family. The bacteria enter the plant through wounds or cuts in the roots. Once inside the roots, they move up into the stem and cause clogging and decay of the water-conducting stem tissue, resulting in wilting and death. The thick gray fluid that oozes from decayed or wounded tissue contains millions of bacteria. The bacteria are spread to other plants by water, contaminated soil, debris, and equipment. They can live for 6 years or more in the soil. Bacterial wilt is most damaging in warm areas (75° to 95°F) and moist conditions.

SOLUTION: There are no chemical controls for this disease. Remove and destroy all diseased plants. To avoid reinfection from contaminated soil, do not replant nasturtiums in the same area. When cultivating the soil, avoid damaging the stems, roots, and tubers. If bacterial wilt is prevalent in your garden, do not plant nasturtiums near vegetables like tomatoes, eggplants, peppers, and potatoes, which are also susceptible to this disease.

TULIPA (TULIP)

TULIPA (TULIP)

ADAPTATION: Throughout the United States. In zones 9 and 10, bulbs must be prechilled (see below for details).

FLOWERING TIME: Spring.

LIGHT: Full sun to filtered light.

PLANTING TIME: Fall.

SOIL: Well-drained soil, pH 6.0 to 7.5

FERTILIZER: When planting, add 1 teaspoon of ORTHO Bone Meal or ORTHO Superphosphate to the bottom of the planting hole and mix it into the soil. During the growing season, fertilize with ORTHO Rose & Flower Food or ORTHO General Purpose Plant Food according to label directions.

WATER:
How much: Apply enough water to wet the soil 1 to 1½ feet deep.
How often: Water when the soil an inch below the surface is just barely moist.

HANDLING: In zones 9 and 10, precool bulbs for 6 to 8 weeks before planting. Store bulbs in paper bags in the refrigerator crisper. Tulips usually do not flower as well the second or third year after planting. Either replace them, or dig, separate, precool if necessary and replant.

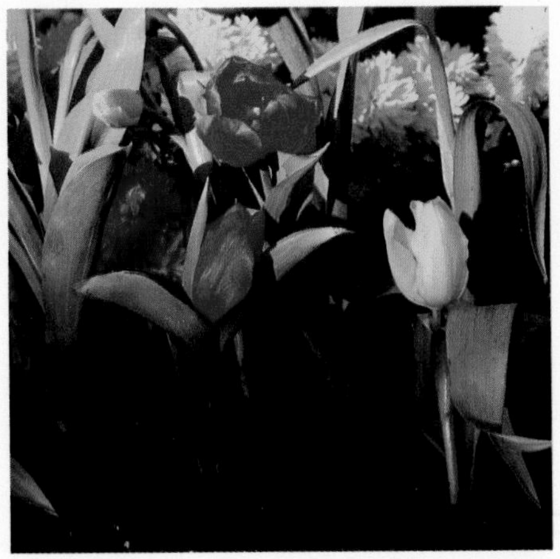

Short stems.

Old planting.

Undersized bulbs.

PROBLEM: Flower stems are very short, and the flowers may be smaller than normal. Sometimes the flowers bloom at ground level. The foliage appears healthy.

ANALYSIS: Short stems
This condition is the result of warm spring temperatures, a lack of adequate winter cooling, or a combination of both. Tulip bulbs contain embryonic flowers and stems. A minimum of six weeks exposure to cool temperatures (40° to 50°F) stimulates the stem cells to elongate, causing the immature tulip to emerge from the ground. During cool spring weather (40° to 50°F), the stems continue to elongate to their full length and then the flowers mature and open. In warm winter areas, stems often fail to elongate properly. Also, during unseasonable spring hot spells (when air temperatures reach 60°F and higher), the tulip flower is stimulated by the heat to mature and open before the stems have grown to their full potential.

SOLUTION: There is nothing you can do to increase the length of the tulip stem once the flower has matured. If warm spring temperatures are common in your area, plant tulips where they will receive either filtered light, or direct sun only in the early morning. Plant single-flowered, long-stemmed tulips such as the Darwin, Darwin hybrids, cottage, and lily-flowered tulips. If you live in a warm winter area, place tulip bulbs in paper bags in the fall, and chill them in the crisper section of the refrigerator for six weeks before planting; or buy precooled bulbs. In zones 9 and 10, delay planting tulips until mid-December.

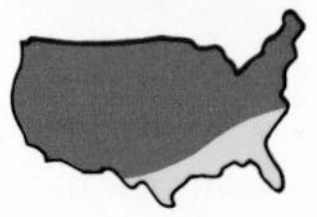

PROBLEM: Tulip bulbs produce healthy foliage, but fail to bloom.

ANALYSIS: Failure to bloom
Healthy tulips may fail to bloom for several reasons:

SOLUTION: The numbered solutions below correspond to the numbers in the analysis.

1. *Lack of cooling:* Tulip bulbs require a minimum exposure of 6 weeks to cool temperatures (40° to 50°F) in the fall in order to flower properly. Cooling stimulates the embryonic flower stem within the bulb to elongate and emerge from the ground.

1. In warm winter areas (zones 9 and 10), precool bulbs before planting, or buy precooled bulbs. For details on cooling bulbs, see page 394. Postpone planting until mid-December.

2. *Foliage removed too soon:* After a tulip flowers, the remaining foliage continues to to manufacture food for new bulbs and next year's flowers.

2. Let foliage turn yellow before removing it.

3. *Lack of fertilization:* When tulips are grown in infertile soil for more than one season, they form small, poor quality bulbs. Such bulbs produce only sparse foliage and few, if any, flowers.

3. Fertilize bulbs when planting, after the new leaves emerge in the spring, and after they bloom. For details on fertilizing, see page 394.

4. *Undersized bulbs:* Bulbs smaller than 2½ inches in circumference may not contain an embryonic flower. They will produce only foliage for 1 or 2 years, until they are large enough to produce a flower.

4. Purchase only large, healthy bulbs from a reputable nursery or mail order company.

5. *Old plantings:* Tulip flowers are largest and most prolific the first spring after newly purchased bulbs have been planted. After flowering, the original bulb usually disintegrates and several small "daughter bulbs" form. Often these daughter bulbs are too small to provide many flowers. Depending on the variety, a planting of tulips generally continues to flower for only 2 to 4 years, each year producing fewer flowers. Tulips are especially short-lived in warm winter areas (zones 9 and 10; see page 1020 for zone map).

5. Replace old tulips with fresh bulbs. You may also dig up, separate, and replant old bulbs. However, it will often be at least one year before they will flower again. Unless your soil and climate conditions are ideal for growing tulips, the bulbs and flowers will never be as large and prolific as they were the first year. You can prolong the flowering life of a tulip planting by planting the bulbs deeper than usual. Place them 12 inches deep in the soil rather than the usual 6 inches. The soil must be well drained to prevent rot.

TULIPA (TULIP)

Rodent damage.

Poor growth.

Diseased plants.

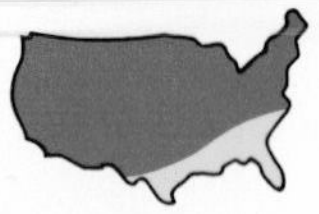

PROBLEM: Tulips do not emerge in the spring. Bulbs have been partially or completely eaten. Tulip stems may be chewed off. The entire plant sometimes disappears. There may be crescent-shaped mounds of soil clustered in the yard. There may also be tiny holes in the soil and small, dry, rectangular, brown pellets on the ground.

ANALYSIS: Rodents

Pocket gophers and field mice are rodents that feed extensively on tulip bulbs. *Pocket gophers*, found primarily in the West, are tan, furry, rodents, 6 inches long, that live almost entirely underground. They form crescent-shaped mounds of dirt. *Field mice* live both above ground in protective vegetation and below ground in shallow tunnels and burrows. Signs of field mice include clusters of tiny droppings, and small holes in the soil, which are entrances to their underground tunnels. Both of these animals feed on bulbs throughout the year.

SOLUTION: Prevent gopher damage by lining the inside of the planting bed with ½ inch mesh chicken wire along the bottom and up the sides. To prevent mouse damage, lay ¼ inch mesh hardware cloth on the top of the planted area, burying the edges several inches under the soil surface. Remove the hardware cloth before shoots emerge in the spring. For more information about rodents and their control, see pages 900 and 896.

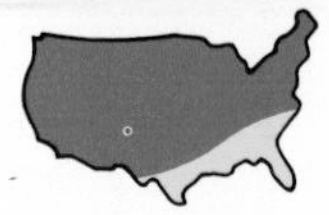

PROBLEM: Tulip bulbs do not produce any growth in the spring.

ANALYSIS: Failure to grow

Improper cultural techniques, diseases, animal pests, and natural decline can all contribute to lack of growth in tulips.

1. *Lack of cooling:* Tulip bulbs require a period of cooling to develop properly. They need to spend at least 6 weeks below 50°F in order to perform ideally. If newly purchased bulbs are not precooled, or soil temperatures remain at 55°F or above during the winter, root formation, flower emergence, and the production of new daughter bulbs for future flowering will be inhibited.

2. *Foliage removed too soon:* After a tulip flowers, the remaining foliage continues to use the sun's rays to manufacture food for the developing new bulbs and next year's flowers. If the foliage is removed before it has a chance to turn yellow naturally, the new bulbs will either be very small or will not form at all.

3. *Lack of fertilization:* After the first year, tulips will not continue to perform well when planted in infertile soil. They form only weak, small bulbs and flowers. After several years, they will stop producing growth.

4. *Root rot:* Infected tulip bulbs planted in heavy, poorly drained soil frequently decay.

5. *Rodents:* Mice, pocket gophers, and other rodents may feed on tulip bulbs. Dig in the area where the bulbs were planted and check for underground tunnels and half-eaten bulbs, both of which indicate rodent damage.

SOLUTION: The numbered solutions below correspond to the numbers in the analysis.

1. In warm winter areas (zones 9 and 10; see page 1020 for zone map), refrigerate newly purchased bulbs for 6 weeks. For details, see page 394.

2. Allow foliage to turn yellow before removing it.

3. Add ORTHO Bone Meal when planting bulbs. Fertilize emerging tulips in the spring with ORTHO Rose & Flower Food and refertilize once a month after the plants have flowered until the foliage dies back.

4. Before planting, discard discolored, spongy, or moldy bulbs. Plant in well-drained soil. For information on improving soil drainage, see page 907.

5. The most effective method of protecting tulips is to plant them in baskets made of ¼ inch wire mesh. Traps or baits may also be used. For further information on rodent control, see the information to the far left.

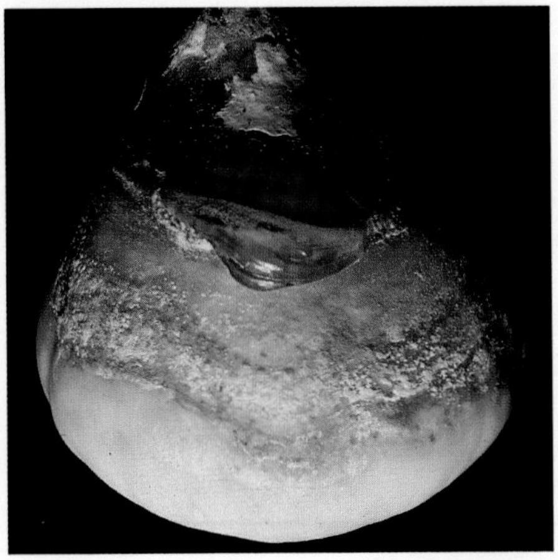

Bulb rot.

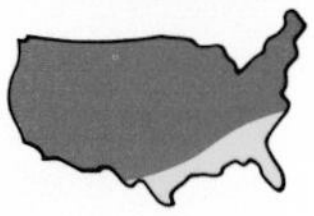

PROBLEM: Foliage is sparse and stunted. Often the leaves turn red, wilt, and die. When the plant is dug up, rotted bulbs are revealed. The bulbs may be either mushy or firm and chalky. Usually they are covered with a white, pink, or gray mold. There may be reddish brown to black pinhead-sized pellets on the bulb husks, leaf bases, and in the soil immediately surrounding the plant.

ANALYSIS: Root and bulb rot

This disease of tulips is caused by several different soil-inhabiting fungi that attack and decay the bulbs and roots. The fungi form tiny pellets on the bulbs and in the soil. These pellets survive through dry conditions and extremes of temperature. Bulbs and root rots are favored by wet, poorly drained soils. Bulbs injured during digging or storing are especially susceptible to infection. Sometimes bulbs in storage are lightly infected, but the fungal decay hasn't progressed far enough to be easily noticed. When planted, these bulbs may rot so quickly that they don't produce any foliage.

SOLUTION: Remove and destroy infected plants and the soil immediately surrounding them. Check and discard infected bulbs before planting. Avoid wounding bulbs when cultivating around them or handling them. Dip clean, healthy bulbs in a warm (80° to 85°F) solution of *benomyl* before storing, and again before planting them. Plant in a well-drained location. Do not replant tulips in infested soil for at least 3 years.

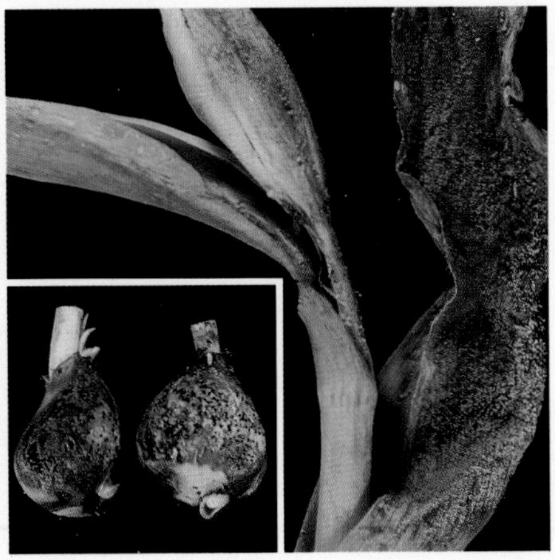

Botrytis blight. *Insert:* Infected bulbs.

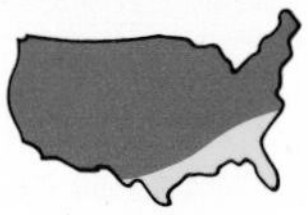

PROBLEM: Light to dark-colored spots appear on the leaves and flowers. The spots enlarge to form extensive gray blotches, which may cover the entire leaf and flower. During periods of cool, moist weather, a fuzzy brown or grayish mold forms on the infected tissue. Many of the leaves and stems are distorted, and often rot off at the base. There are dark, circular, sunken lesions on infected bulbs. Dark brown pinhead-sized pellets form on the bulb husks.

ANALYSIS: Botrytis blight

This common disease of tulips is caused by a fungus (*Botrytis tulipae*). The fungus persists through the winter and hot, dry periods as tiny fungal pellets in the soil, plant debris, and bulbs. In the spring, these pellets produce spores that attack foliage and flowers, causing spotting, decay, and mold. Wounded, weak, and dead plant tissues are especially susceptible to infection. The fungus is spread by splashing water. Botrytis blight is most serious during periods of cool, moist weather. Tulip bulbs that are injured when they are dug up to be stored are especially vulnerable to infection.

SOLUTION: Remove and destroy diseased plants, leaves, flowers, and debris. Before planting tulip bulbs, check them for signs of infection, and discard diseased bulbs. Start spraying emerging plants when they are 4 inches tall with a fungicide containing *zineb*, *mancozeb*, or *benomyl*. Use a spreader-sticker when spraying (see page 922). Spray plants every 5 to 7 days until the flowers bloom. Remove tulip flowers just as they start to fade, and cut off the foliage at ground level when it turns yellow. Rotate plants to a new location next year.

Aphids (half life size).

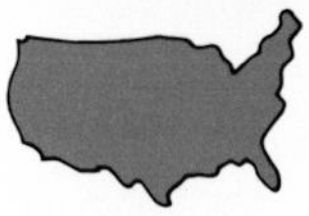

PROBLEM: Leaves are curled, distorted, and yellowing. Flowers may be malformed. Tiny (1/8 inch) yellow-green to gray soft-bodied insects are clustered on the leaves. A sticky, shiny substance may coat the leaves. Ants may be present.

ANALYSIS: Aphids

Aphids do little damage in small numbers. However, they are extremely prolific and populations can rapidly build up to damaging numbers during the growing season. Damage occurs when the aphid sucks the juices from the tulip leaves and flower buds. The aphid is unable to digest fully all the sugar in the plant sap and excretes the excess in a fluid called honeydew, which coats the leaves. Ants feed on the honeydew, and are often present where there is an aphid infestation. Aphids can also transmit virus diseases to tulips while feeding. For more information about aphids, see page 875.

SOLUTION: Spray infested plants with ORTHO Orthene Systemic Insect Control. Repeat the spray if the plant is reinfested.

TULIPA (TULIP)

Virus.

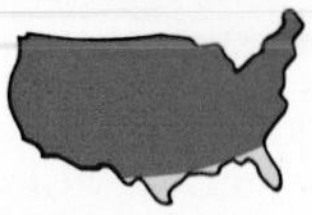

PROBLEM: Flowers are streaked, spotted, or mottled in an irregular pattern. The leaves may also be streaked or mottled with light green or white. The plant may be stunted and low in vigor.

ANALYSIS: Virus

Several viruses commonly infect tulips, causing a characteristic streaking or mottling of the flowers and foliage. Infection may be accompanied by stunted growth. Viral infections rarely cause the plant to die, but can weaken it seriously. The viruses increase in the bulbs year after year. Successive plantings from diseased bulbs yield infected flowers and foliage of poor quality. Some viruses are spread by aphids. These insects feed on diseased plants and transfer viruses to healthy plants at subsequent feedings. Sometimes tulips are intentionally infected to produce showy flowers.

SOLUTION: Once the plant is infected, no chemical will control the virus. To prevent the spread of the virus to healthy tulips, remove and destroy infected plants. Keep the aphid population under control by spraying with ORTHO Orthene Systemic Insect Control. Because these viruses may also infect lilies, avoid planting tulips near lilies. For more information about controlling disease-carrying insects, see page 879. The showy streaked patterns of Rembrandt tulips are caused by virus infections; they are a source of infection for solid colored tulips. Parrot tulips may also exhibit showy streaked patterns, but the streaking is genetic in origin and cannot be transferred to other tulips and lilies.

VERBENA

Powdery mildew.

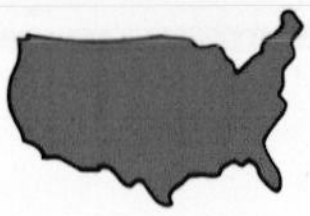

PROBLEM: Leaves and stems are covered with grayish white powdery spots and patches. These patches occur on the upper surfaces of the leaves. The infected leaves eventually turn yellow and wither.

ANALYSIS: Powdery mildew

This common plant disease is caused by a fungus (*Erysiphe cichoracearum*) that thrives in both humid and dry weather. The powdery patches consist of fungal strands and spores. The spores are spread by the wind to healthy plants. The fungus saps plant nutrients, causing yellowing and sometimes death of the leaves. A severe infection may kill whole plants. Since this powdery mildew attacks many different kinds of plants, the fungus from a diseased plant may infect other types of plants in the garden. (For a list of susceptible plants, see page 1006.) Under favorable conditions, powdery mildew can spread through a planting in a matter of days.

SOLUTION: Spray infected plants with a fungicide containing *folpet* (PHALTAN®), *dinocap*, or *cycloheximide*. Spray at regular intervals of 10 to 12 days or as often as necessary to protect new growth. Remove and destroy severely infected plants. Where practical, pick off diseased leaves. Clean up and destroy plant debris.

Verbena cultural information
Light: Sun
Water: When the soil is just barely moist
Soil: Well drained
Fertilizer: Medium

Gray mold.

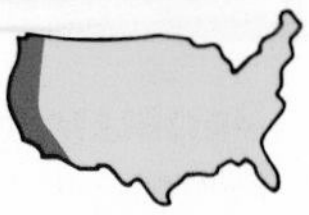

PROBLEM: Brown spots and blotches appear on the leaves and possibly on the stems. As the disease progresses, a fuzzy brown or grayish mold forms on the infected tissue. Gray mold and spots often appear on the flowers, especially during periods of cool, wet weather. The leaves and stems may be soft and rotted.

ANALYSIS: Gray mold

This widespread plant disease is caused by a fungus (*Botrytis* species) that is found on most dead plant tissue. The fungus initially attacks foliage and flowers that are weak or dead, causing spotting and mold. The fuzzy mold that develops is composed of millions of microscopic spores. Once gray mold has become established on plant debris and weak or dying leaves and flowers, it can invade healthy plant tissue. The fungus is spread by splashing water or by bits of infected plant tissue contacting healthy tissue. Cool temperatures and high humidity favor gray mold growth. Crowded plantings, rain, and overhead watering also encourage the spread of the disease. Infection is more of a problem in spring and fall when temperatures are lower. In warm winter areas where freezing is rare, gray mold can be a year-round problem.

SOLUTION: Spray infected plants every ten to fourteen days with a fungicide containing *maneb* or *mancozeb*. Continue spraying as long as the mold is visible. Clean up plant debris, and remove dying or infected leaves, stems, and flowers. Provide enough space between plants to allow good air circulation. Try to avoid wetting the foliage when watering.

Bacterial wilt.

PROBLEM: The plant wilts, turns yellow, and dies. When sliced open, the stem is found to be streaked and discolored. The lower stems near the soil may be soft and rotten.

ANALYSIS: Bacterial wilt
This disease is caused by a bacterium (*Pseudomonas solanacearum*) that is especially common in warm, humid climates. It attacks many different ornamental and vegetable plants. The bacteria enter the plant through wounds or cuts in the roots. Once inside the roots, they move up into the stem and cause clogging and decay of the water-conducting stem tissue, resulting in plant wilting and death. The infected tissue contains millions of bacteria, which are spread to other plants by water, contaminated soil, debris, and equipment. The bacteria may live for 6 years or more in the soil. They thrive and are most damaging in warm areas (75° to 95°F) and moist conditions.

SOLUTION: There are no chemical controls for this disease. Remove and destroy all wilted plants. To avoid reinfection from contaminated soils, do not replant verbenas in the same area next year. When cultivating the soil, avoid damaging the stems and roots. Plant in well-drained soil.

Mite damage.

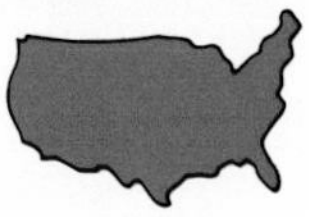

PROBLEM: Leaves are stippled, yellowing, and dirty. Leaves may dry out and drop. There may be webbing between the leaves or on the lower surfaces of the leaves. To determine if the plant is infested with mites, hold a sheet of white paper underneath an affected leaf and tap the leaf sharply. Minute green, red, or yellow specks the size of pepper grains will drop to the paper and begin to crawl around. These pests are easily seen against the white background.

ANALYSIS: Spider mites
(*Tetranychus urticae*)
These mites, related to spiders, are major pests of many garden and greenhouse plants. They cause damage by sucking sap from the undersides of the leaves. As a result of feeding, the green leaf pigment disappears, producing the stippled appearance. Mites are active throughout the growing season, but are favored by hot, dry weather (70°F and up). By midsummer, they build up to tremendous numbers. For more information about spider mites, see page 887.

SOLUTION: Spray the infested plants with a pesticide containing *dicofol* (KELTHANE®). Repeat the spray two more times at regular intervals of 5 to 7 days.

Greenhouse whiteflies (life size).

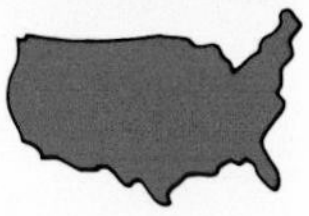

PROBLEM: Tiny, winged insects 1/12 inch long are found mainly on the undersides of the leaves. The insects are covered with white waxy powder. When the plant is touched, insects flutter rapidly around it. Leaves may be mottled and yellowing. Black mold may cover the leaves.

ANALYSIS: Greenhouse whitefly
(*Trialeurodes vaporariorum*)
This insect is a common pest of many garden and greenhouse plants. The four-winged adult lays eggs on the undersides of leaves. The larvae are the size of a pinhead, flat, oval-shaped, and semitransparent, with white waxy filaments radiating from the body. They feed for about a month before changing to the adult form. Both the larval and adult forms suck sap from the leaves. The larvae are more damaging because they feed more heavily. Adults and larvae cannot fully digest all the sugar in the plant sap, and excrete the excess in a fluid called honeydew, which often drops onto the leaves below. A sooty black mold fungus may develop on the honeydew, causing the verbena leaves to appear black and dirty. In warm winter areas the insect can be active year-round, with eggs, larvae, and adults present at the same time. The whitefly is unable to live through freezing winters. Spring reinfestations in freezing areas come from migrating whiteflies and from infested greenhouse-grown plants placed in the garden.

SOLUTION: Control whiteflies by spraying infested plants every 7 to 10 days with an insecticide containing *malathion*. Spray the foliage thoroughly, being sure to cover both the upper and lower surfaces of the leaves.

VIOLA (PANSY, VIOLET)

ADAPTATION: Throughout the United States.

FLOWERING TIME:
Violets: Spring and summer.
Pansies and violas: Fall, winter, and spring in zones 8 through 10. Spring and summer in colder areas. To determine your zone, see the map on page 1020.

LIGHT:
Violets: Half-day sun to full shade.
Pansies and violas: Full sun or filtered light.

PLANTING TIME: In zones 3 through 7, plant in spring when all danger of frost is past. In zones 8 through 10, plant fall through spring.

SOIL: Well drained and high in organic matter.

FERTILIZER: Fertilize with ORTHO Rose & Flower Food or ORTHO General Purpose Plant Food according to label directions.

WATER:
How much: Add enough water to plants in the ground to wet the soil 6 inches deep.
Containers: Add enough water so that about 10 percent of the water drains from the bottom of the container.
How often: Water when the soil 1 inch below the surface is moist but not wet.

HANDLING: Pinch off fading flowers to encourage continuous bloom. Pinch back weak, rangy growth.

Spindly growth and poor flowering.

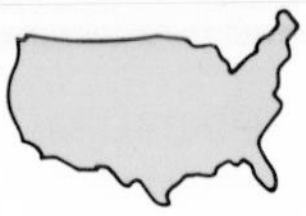

PROBLEM: Leaves are small and thin, and stems are long and spindly. Flowering is poor, and flowers are small.

ANALYSIS: Spindly growth and poor flowering
There are several cultural problems that may contribute to spindly growth.
1. *Failure to remove old flowers:* If the fading flowers remain on the plant, only a few small new flowers will be produced. When the old flowers are allowed to remain, the plant uses its energy in seed development instead of producing new flowers.
2. *Inadequate light:* Pansies and violas grow lanky and flower poorly when planted in deep shade. They require at least strong filtered light to grow compactly, and will flower most profusely in full sun during mild weather.
3. *Old age:* Pansies and violas are perennials, and theoretically will last from year to year. In cold winter climates, they are killed by freezing temperatures. In warm winter areas, they will often last for a year or more, but usually start to produce lanky, unattractive growth after the first growing season.

SOLUTION: The numbers below correspond to the numbers in analysis.
1. Pinch off flowers when they start to fade. For a discussion of pinching, see page 927.
2. Grow plants in full sun, part day sun, or strong filtered light.
3. Treat pansies and violas as annuals. Plant them in the spring (or fall in zones 9 and 10) and replace them when they start to decline in the summer. Rangy plants may be rejuvenated if one third of the spindly stems are pinched back to ⅓ of their height.

Leaf spot on viola.

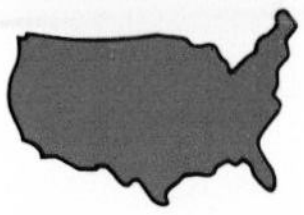

PROBLEM: Leaves and stems are spotted or blotched. The spots may be grayish white, yellow, tan, or brown, ranging in size from barely visible to ¼ inch in diameter. Sometimes these spots are bordered with black margins. Often, they join together to form blotches. The petals may be distorted and disfigured with brown lesions. The leaves may turn yellow and die. Sometimes elongated, sunken lesions also develop on the stems and flower stalks. Severely infected plants may die.

ANALYSIS: Leaf spot
Several different fungi cause leaf spots on pansies, violas, and violets. Some of these fungi will eventually kill the plant, while others merely cause spotting that is unsightly but not harmful. These fungi are spread by splashing water and wind. Fungal strands or spores survive the winter in plant debris and sometimes in infected seed. Most of the leaf spot organisms do their greatest damage in humid conditions and mild weather (50° to 85°F).

SOLUTION: Remove dying plants. Where practical, pick off infected leaves and clean up plant debris. Spray plants with a fungicide containing *zineb*, *maneb*, or *mancozeb* at weekly intervals. When spraying, use a spreader-sticker. For information about spreader-stickers, see page 922.

Root and stem rot.

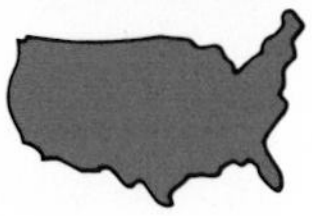

PROBLEM: Leaves turn yellow, wilt, and die. The roots and lower stems are soft and rotten. There may be white fungal strands on infected stems and around the base of the plant.

ANALYSIS: Root and stem rot
This disease is caused by a number of different fungi that persist indefinitely in the soil. They thrive in waterlogged, heavy soils. Infection causes the stem and roots to decay, resulting in wilting, yellowing leaves, and the death of the plant. These fungi are generally spread by infested soil and transplants, contaminated equipment, and splashing or running water.

SOLUTION: Remove dead and dying plants. It is important to allow the soil to dry between irrigations; root and stem rots are encouraged by waterlogged conditions. (For more information on this technique, see page 849.) Improve soil drainage. For more information about soil drainage, see page 907.

Slug damage.

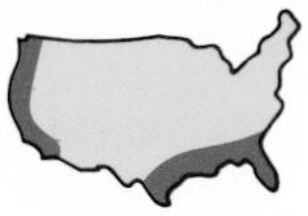

PROBLEM: Irregular holes with smooth edges are chewed in the leaves. Leaves, stems, and flowers may be chewed off entirely. Silvery trails wind around on the plants and soil nearby. Snails and slugs may be seen moving around or feeding on the plants, especially at night. Check for them by inspecting the garden at night by flashlight.

ANALYSIS: Snails and slugs
These pests are mollusks, and are related to clams, oysters, and other shellfish. They feed on a wide variety of garden plants. Like other mollusks, snails and slugs need to be moist all the time. For this reason, they avoid direct sun and dry places, and hide during the day in damp places, such as under flower pots or in thick groundcover. They emerge at night or on cloudy days to feed. Snails and slugs are similar in appearance, except that the snail has a hard shell, into which it withdraws when disturbed. Slugs lay masses of white eggs encased in a slimy mass in protected places. Snails bury their eggs in the soil, also in a slimy mass. The young look like miniature versions of their parents.

SOLUTION: Scatter ORTHO Bug-Geta Snail & Slug Pellets or ORTHO Slug-Geta Snail & Slug Bait granules around the areas you wish to protect. Also scatter the bait in areas where snails or slugs might be hiding such as in dense groundcovers, weedy areas, compost piles, or pot storage areas. Before spreading the bait, wet down the treated areas to encourage snail and slug activity that night. Repeat the application every two weeks as long as snails and slugs are active.

Soft rot.

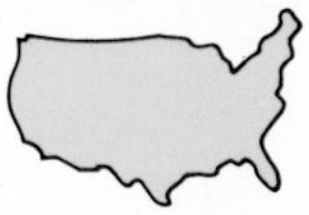

PROBLEM: Leaf bases and rhizomes (elongated underground stems) are soft and slimy. The edges of the leaves may appear as if they are soaked with water or oil, and are soft and slimy. In some cases, the leaves wilt, turn yellow, and die. Foliage and flower stalks rot off at the soil surface. The entire plant may wilt suddenly and die.

ANALYSIS: Soft rot
This plant disease is caused by a bacterium (*Erwinia carotovora*). The bacteria penetrate calla rhizomes and leaf bases through wounds. Leaf bases and rhizomes decay, turning soft and slimy. Sometimes the infection spreads up into the leaf tissue and down into the roots. Soft rot is favored by moist conditions and wet soils. The bacteria live in the soil and plant debris. They are spread by infected rhizomes, transplants, and contaminated soil and tools.

SOLUTION: Discard all diseased plants and the soil immediately surrounding them. Inspect all rhizomes before planting them, and discard those that are severely rotted. If only a small portion is decayed, cut out the diseased portion, then wash and dry the rhizome before planting. Plant in well-drained soil. Do not bury rhizomes deeper than 2 inches when planting.

Zantedeschia cultural information
Light: Half-day sun to shade
Water: When the soil is moist but not wet
Soil: Any good garden soil
Fertilizer: Medium

ZINNIA

ADAPTATION: Throughout the United States.

FLOWERING TIME: Summer and fall.

LIGHT: Full sun.

PLANTING TIME: Spring, after all danger of frost is past.

SOIL: Any good garden soil.

FERTILIZER: Fertilize with ORTHO Rose & Flower Food or ORTHO General Purpose Plant Food according to label directions.

WATER:
How much: Apply enough water to plants in the ground to wet the soil 8 to 10 inches deep.
Containers: Apply enough water so that 10 percent of the water drains from the bottom of the container.
How often: Water when the soil 1 inch below the surface is just barely moist.

HANDLING: Zinnias thrive in hot weather. They will grow more quickly and will be less susceptible to disease if they are planted out after the days and nights have warmed up in the spring or early summer.

Powdery mildew.

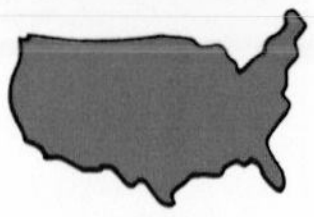

PROBLEM: Leaves and stems are covered with grayish white powdery spots and patches. These patches occur primarily on the upper surfaces of the leaves. The leaves eventually turn yellow and wither.

ANALYSIS: Powdery mildew
This common plant disease is caused by a fungus (*Erysiphe cichoracearum*) that thrives in both humid and dry weather. The powdery patches consist of fungal strands and spores. The spores are spread by the wind to healthy plants. The fungus saps plant nutrients, causing yellowing and sometimes death of the leaf. A severe infection may kill the plant. Since this powdery mildew attacks many different kinds of plants, the fungus from a diseased plant may infect other types of plants in the garden. (For a list of susceptible plants, see page 1006). Under favorable conditions, powdery mildew can spread through a closely spaced planting in a matter of days or weeks.

SOLUTION: Spray infected plants with ORTHO Funginex Rose Disease Control or ORTHO Orthenex Insect & Disease Control at regular intervals of 7 to 10 days, or as often as necessary to protect the new growth. The fungicide protects the new, healthy foliage, but does not remove the fungus spots on leaves that are already infected. Pick off severely infected leaves. Space plants far enough apart to allow good air circulation. Clean up plant debris.

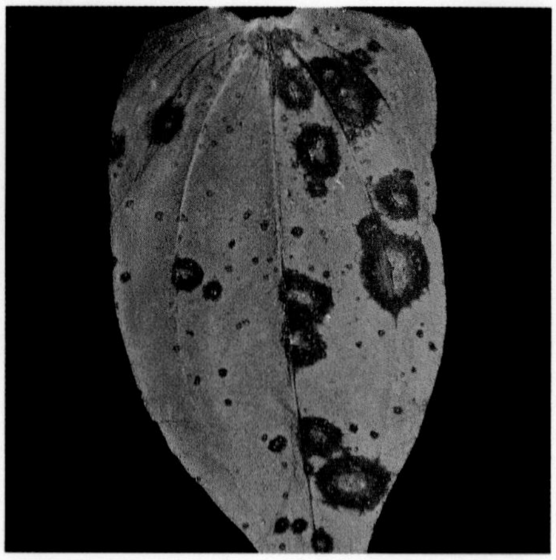

Alternaria blight.

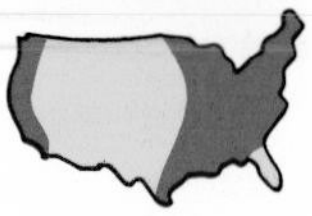

PROBLEM: Reddish brown circular or irregular spots up to ½ inch in diameter appear on the leaves. The centers of the spots may turn grayish white. The blossoms are also often spotted. Severely infected leaves, stems, and flowers turn brown and die. There may be dark, sunken lesions at the base of the stems. The entire plant frequently wilts and dies.

ANALYSIS: Alternaria blight
This common and widespread disease of zinnias is caused by a fungus (*Alternaria zinniae*). The disease is favored by moist conditions. The fungal spores are spread from plant to plant by wind and splashing water. The fungus survives on infected debris in the soil and in contaminated seed. This fungus also causes damping-off of seedlings. For more information about damping-off, see page 850.

SOLUTION: Remove dying plants. Spray infected plants with ORTHO Phaltan Rose & Garden Fungicide. Pick off infected leaves and flowers. Clean up plant debris. Avoid overhead watering.

Gray mold.

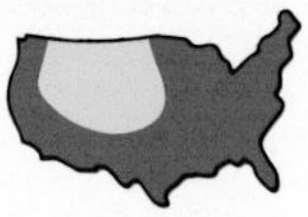

PROBLEM: Brown spots and blotches appear on the leaves and possibly on the stems. As the disease progresses, a fuzzy brown or grayish mold forms on the infected tissue. Gray mold and spots often appear on the flowers, especially during periods of cool, wet weather. The leaves and stems may be soft and rotted.

ANALYSIS: Gray mold
This widespread plant disease is caused by a fungus (*Botrytis cinerea*) that is found on most dead plant tissue. The fungus initially attacks foliage and flowers that are weak or dead, causing spotting and mold. The fuzzy mold that develops is composed of millions of microscopic spores. Once gray mold has become established on plant debris and weak or dying leaves and flowers, it can invade healthy plant tissue. The fungus is spread by splashing water, or by infected pieces of plant tissue contacting healthy tissue. Cool temperatures and high humidity favor gray mold growth. Crowded plantings, rain, and overhead watering also enhance the spread of the disease. Infection is more of a problem in spring and fall, when temperatures are lower. In warm winter areas, where freezing is rare, gray mold can be a year-round problem. For more information about gray mold, see page 849.

SOLUTION: Spray infected plants with a fungicide containing *chlorothalonil* (DACONIL 2787®), *maneb*, or *mancozeb* every 10 to 14 days. Continue spraying as long as the mold is visible. Clean up plant debris, and remove dying or infected leaves, stems, and flowers. Provide enough space between plants to allow good air circulation. Try to avoid wetting the foliage when watering.

Some of the problems common to all woody ornamentals are listed on the next 36 pages. If you don't find your problem here, locate your tree, shrub, or vine in the index on the next page.

TREES, SHRUBS, AND VINES

Trees, shrubs, and vines—the woody ornamentals—usually represent the greatest investment of all the plants in the garden. Not in dollars, perhaps, but in the years of care and waiting for them to reach maturity, and in their contribution to the landscape.

Shade trees are particularly valuable. The death of a single shade tree can drastically alter the nature of a garden, as well as lower the value of a home. As a result, this group of plants is probably better studied than other ornamental groups, and its problems are better understood.

But in spite of being more thoroughly studied than other groups of plants, the problems of woody ornamentals—and particularly of shade trees—are not easy to solve. The size of the plants is a major factor in their treatment. Many homeowners will decide to tolerate a leaf spot disease rather than spend hundreds of dollars a year to have their tree sprayed.

Also, because of the size of plants in this group, problems develop slowly and may be firmly entrenched before they are noticed. Root damage to a tree made during the installation of a new driveway may not cause any symptoms for a year or two, but may cause the death of the tree in 8 or 10 years.

Because of their permanence, woody ornamentals should be adapted to the spot in which they will grow. It is worth the time it takes to find out what species thrive in your area before buying. If a plant is adapted to the area and is properly fed, watered, and pruned, it is able to fight off many of the diseases and insects that might otherwise plague it.

One of the most serious problems of trees is internal decay, or heart rot. This disease occurs everywhere, and is one of the most common causes of tree death. It can be caused by many different fungi, all of which enter through breaks in the bark. A vigorous tree can wall off the diseased wood, stopping the spread of the rot. But as a tree grows older, or if it is weakened by some other condition, it loses its ability to wall off the fungus, and its wood slowly rots, often causing it to become hollow. Rotten or hollow trees are not only likely to die, they are also dangerous. When limbs break or entire trees fall, the cause is usually heart rot. For more information, see page 440.

Above: Powdery mildew on a rose. See page 567.
Left: Leaf spots on maple. See page 447.

INDEX TO TREES, SHRUBS AND VINES

PROBLEMS COMMON TO MANY TREES, SHRUBS, AND VINES

Flowerless dogwood in dark location.

Flower buds pruned off crapemyrtle.

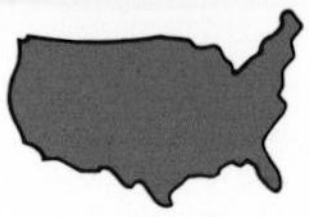

PROBLEM: Plants fail to bloom, or bloom only sparsely and sporadically.

ANALYSIS: Few or no flowers
Plants produce few or no buds or flowers for any of several reasons.

1. *Juvenility:* Plants, like people, must reach a certain age or size before they are able to reproduce. They will not develop flowers or fruit until this time.

2. *Inadequate winter cooling:* In order to produce flowers, many plants must undergo a period of cooling during the winter. The plant must be exposed for a certain number of hours to temperatures between 30° and 45°F. The number of hours needed is different for different plant species. If the cooling requirement is not satisfied, flowering will be delayed and reduced, and flower buds may drop off. This is a common problem when plants adapted to cold climates are grown in warmer, southern climates.

3. *Improper pruning:* If a plant is pruned improperly or too severely, flower and fruit production can be reduced or, in some cases, prevented. Drastic pruning, especially on young plants, stimulates a flush of green growth, which inhibits flowering. Flowering will also be reduced if flower buds are pruned off.

4. *Nutrient imbalance:* Plants overfertilized with nitrogen tend to produce a flush of green growth. Some plants will not make flowers while they are growing vigorously.

5. *Shade:* Flowering plants require a certain amount of light to produce flowers. If these plants are grown in inadequate light, they produce few or no flowers.

SOLUTION: The numbered solutions below correspond to the numbers in the analysis.

1. Plants will eventually begin to flower if they are otherwise healthy and adapted to the area. The juvenile stage in some trees and vines may last 15 years.

2. Plant trees and shrubs that are adapted to your area. Consult your local garden center, Cooperative Extension Office (for a list, see page 1029), or a book on plant selection, such as ORTHO's book *How to Select & Care for Shrubs & Hedges* or *The World of Trees*.

3. For instructions on proper pruning techniques, see ORTHO's book *All About Pruning*.

4. Do not overfertilize plants or make a heavy application of nitrogen before flowering. For more information about fertilizers, see page 910.

5. Thin out shading trees, or move plants to a sunnier area. For more information about transplanting, see page 924. For a list of shade loving plants, see page 1008.

Drought.

Bud drop caused by cold injury.

PROBLEM: Many or all of the buds or flowers die or drop off.

ANALYSIS: Buds die or drop
Buds may die or drop for any of several reasons.

SOLUTION: The numbered solutions below correspond to the numbers in the analysis.

1. *Transplant shock:* Whenever a tree or shrub is transplanted, it goes through a period of shock. Dormant plants usually recover more quickly and are injured less than growing plants. However, even when transplanted properly, dormant plants may still lose some of their buds. Plants that have begun growth or are in bloom often drop many of their flower buds or flowers shortly after transplanting. Some buds may remain on the plant but not open.

1. Whenever possible, transplant trees and shrubs during the dormant season. (For more information about transplanting, see page 924.) Avoid wounding the roots when planting, and do not let the plant dry out. (For more information about watering, see page 912.)

2. *Cold or frost injury:* Flower buds or flowers may be killed by cold or freezing temperatures. Many or all of them either fail to open or drop off. Cold injury occurs during the winter when temperatures drop below the lowest point that can be tolerated by buds of that particular plant species. Frost injury is caused by an unseasonal cold snap, in either fall or spring, which damages buds, developing flowers, and tender shoots of growing plants.

2. Plant trees and shrubs adapted to your area. Consult your local garden center, Cooperative Extension Office (see page 1029), or a book on plant selection, such as ORTHO's books *How to Select & Care for Shrubs & Hedges* or *All About Trees.* Protect shrubs and small trees from early or late cold snaps by covering them with burlap or a plastic tent. Placing a light underneath the covering will offer additional protection.

3. *Drought:* Flowers or flower buds dry and drop off when there is a temporary lack of moisture in the plant. This may be due to dry soil, minor root injuries, or anything else that disrupts water movement to the top of the plant.

3. Water trees and shrubs regularly. (For more information about watering, see page 912.) Most plants will recover from minor root injuries. Frequent shallow waterings and light fertilization (see page 910) may speed the recovery process. Avoid wounding plants.

4. *Insects:* Certain insects, such as thrips and mites, feed on flower buds. When infestations are heavy, their feeding kills flower buds, causing them to dry and drop off. Some infested buds may open, but are distorted.

4. Insects can be controlled with various chemicals. For more information about thrips and mites and their controls, look under your specific plant or on page 431.

Boxelder seeds will create messy litter.

PROBLEM: Trees and shrubs drop flowers, seedpods, or fruit, creating unwanted messy litter.

ANALYSIS: Excess flowers and fruits
All trees and shrubs produce flowers or flower structures that develop into seedpods or fruit. Some plants, such as juniper and boxwood, produce inconspicuous flowers and fruits. Others, such as ornamental crabapple, olive, sweet gum, horsechestnut, and glossy privet, produce many conspicuous flowers, seedpods, or fruits. The dropping flowers and fruits of such plants create litter that may detract from the beauty of the landscape and increase time spent in garden upkeep.

SOLUTION: Prevent flower and fruit production by spraying with a compound containing the growth regulator *NAA* (*napthalene acetic acid*), *ethephon*, or *dikegulac-sodium* when the flower buds are forming. Contact your local Cooperative Extension Office (see page 1029) to determine this period for your particular plant. Make sure your plant is listed on the product label and follow directions carefully. If plants are small enough to be moved, transplant them to a location where their flower and fruit drop will not be a nuisance. If spraying is impractical, replace messy trees and shrubs with plants that do not produce litter.

PROBLEMS COMMON TO MANY TREES, SHRUBS, AND VINES — INSECTS

Long-horned beetle (twice life size).

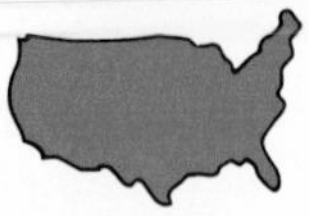

PROBLEM: Shiny or dull, hard-bodied insects with tough, leathery wing covers appear on the plant. The wing covers meet in the middle of the back, forming a straight line down the insect's body. Leaf tissue is chewed, notched, or eaten between the veins, giving the leaves a lacy appearance. The bark may be chewed, or flowers may be eaten. Holes may be found in branches or in the trunk.

ANALYSIS: Beetles
Many different types of beetles feed on ornamental trees and shrubs. In most cases, both larvae (grubs) and adults feed on the plants, so damage is often severe. The insects spend the winter as grubs inside the plant or in the soil, or as adults in bark crevices or in hiding places on the ground. Adult beetles lay eggs on the plant during the growing season. Depending on the species, the grubs may feed on foliage, mine inside the leaves, bore into stems or branches, or feed on roots. Beetle damage to leaves rarely kills the plant. Grubs feeding inside the wood or underground are much more damaging, and often kill branches or the whole plant. For more information about beetles, see page 865.

SOLUTION: Grubs feeding in the soil or inside the plant are difficult to detect and control. Control measures are often aimed at the adults. Several different insecticides, including ones containing *carbaryl* (SEVIN®), may be used to control these pests. Make sure your plant is listed on the label. Certain beetles are covered in this book. Look under your specific plant in the alphabetical section beginning on page 442.

Gypsy moth larvae (life size).

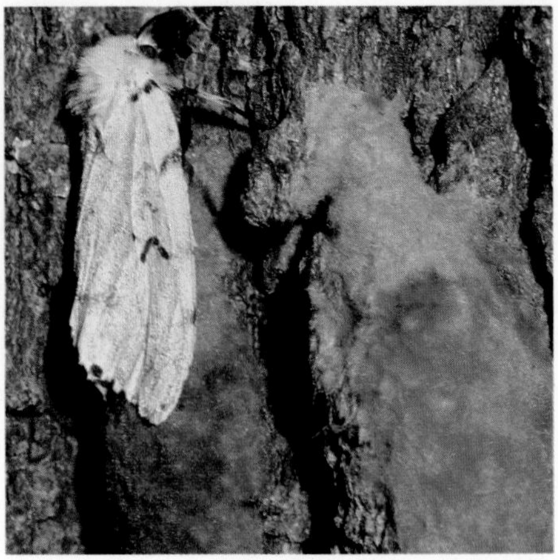

Gypsy moth and egg masses (life size).

PROBLEM: Leaves are chewed; the entire tree is often defoliated by early summer. Large (up to 2½ inches long), hairy, blackish caterpillars with rows of red and blue spots on their backs are feeding on the leaves, hiding under leaves or bark, or crawling on buildings, cars, or other objects outdoors. Insect droppings accumulate underneath the infested tree. Trees defoliated for several consecutive years may be killed, especially weak trees.

ANALYSIS: Gypsy moth (*Lymantria dispar*)
The gypsy moth is a general feeder, devouring over 450 species of plants. Gypsy moth populations fluctuate from year to year. When the moths' numbers are low, oaks are the preferred host. When their numbers increase, entire forests may be defoliated and the moths spread to other trees and shrubs. Repeated, severe defoliation weakens trees and reduces plant growth. Defoliated trees are rarely killed unless already in a weakened condition. However, they are more susceptible to attack by other insects and diseases, which may kill them. Gypsy moths are also an extreme nuisance in urban areas and in parks and campgrounds. The overwintering masses of eggs, covered with yellow hairs, are attached to almost any object outdoors. The eggs hatch from April to May. The tiny larvae crawl to trees where they feed, or drop on silken threads to be carried by the wind to other plants. As the caterpillars mature, they feed at night and rest during the day. The larvae may completely cover sides of houses or other objects during these resting periods. When population levels are high, the insects feed continually on the tree and large amounts of excrement accumulate beneath it. The larval hairs may cause allergies. The larvae pupate in sheltered places, and dark brown male or white female moths emerge in July.

SOLUTION: If the insects are bothersome or trees are weak or unhealthy either from last year's gypsy moth feeding or from drought, mechanical damage, or other insects and diseases, treatment with insecticides is required. Insecticides should be applied before larvae are 1 inch long, and the tree must be covered thoroughly. It is best to contact a professional arborist for large trees. Spray smaller trees with ORTHO Gypsy Moth & Japanese Beetle Killer, ORTHO Isotox Insect Killer, ORTHO Orthene Systemic Insect Control, or ORTHO Liquid Sevin when tiny larvae are first noticed. Repeat the sprays at weekly intervals if damage continues. Homeowners can reduce infestations by destroying egg masses during the winter months. During the spring when larvae are feeding, place burlap bands on trees, leaving the bottom edge unattached. Larvae will crawl under these flaps to hide during the day. Collect and destroy them. Keep trees healthy. Fertilize regularly and water during periods of drought. (For information about fertilizing and watering see pages 910 and 912.) When planting trees in the yard, choose species that are less favored by the gypsy moth. (For a list of these plants, and of plants favored by the gypsy moth, see page 1014.) Trees less favored by the insects are damaged only slightly by larval feeding. In addition, they may reduce damage to more favored hosts when interplanted by preventing a large buildup of insects in the area. Do not transport items that may have eggs or larvae attached to them.

Japanese beetle (life size).

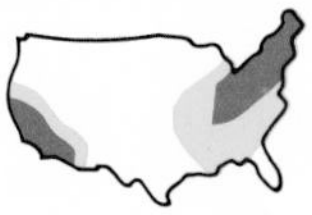

PROBLEM: The leaf tissue is chewed between the veins, giving the leaves a lacy appearance. If the plant is flowering, the flowers are also eaten. The entire plant may be defoliated. Metallic green and bronze winged beetles, ½ inch long, are feeding in clusters on the plant.

ANALYSIS: Japanese beetles
(*Popillia japonica*)
As their name suggests, these beetles are native to Japan. They were first seen in New Jersey in 1916 and have since become a major pest in the eastern United States. They feed on hundreds of different species of plants. The adult beetles are present from June to October. They feed only in the daytime, and are most active on warm, sunny days. The female beetles live for thirty to forty days. Just before they die, they lay their eggs just under the soil surface in lawns. Grayish white grubs soon hatch and feed on grass roots. As the weather turns cold in the late fall, the grubs move 8 to 10 inches down into the soil, where they remain dormant for the winter. When the soil warms up in the spring, the grubs move back up near the soil surface and resume feeding on roots. They soon pupate and reemerge as adult beetles in late May or June.

SOLUTION: Control the adults with ORTHO Isotox Insect Killer, ORTHO Gypsy Moth & Japanese Beetle Killer, ORTHO Liquid Sevin, or ORTHO Malathion 50 Insect Spray in late May or June. Make sure your plant is listed on the product label. Repeat the spray ten days later if damage continues. For a list of plants rarely fed upon by adult beetles, see page 1009.

Looper (twice life size).

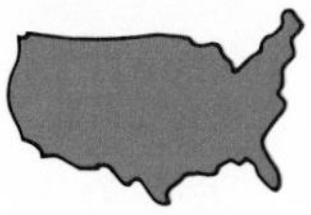

PROBLEM: Caterpillars are clustered or feeding singly on the leaves. The surface of the leaf is eaten, giving the remaining tissue a lacy appearance; or the whole leaf is chewed. Sometimes the leaves are webbed. The tree may be completely defoliated. Damage appears any time between spring and fall. Repeated heavy infestations may weaken or kill plants.

ANALYSIS: Leaf-feeding caterpillars
Many different species of caterpillars feed on the leaves of trees and shrubs. Depending on the species, the moths lay their eggs from early spring to midsummer. The larvae that hatch from these eggs feed singly or in groups on buds, on one leaf surface (skeletonizers), or on the entire leaf. Certain caterpillars web leaves together as they feed. In some years, damage is minimal due to unfavorable environmental conditions or control by predators and parasites. However, when conditions are favorable, entire plants may be defoliated by late summer. Defoliation weakens them because there are no leaves left to produce food. When heavy infestations occur several years in a row, branches or entire plants may be killed.

SOLUTION: Spray with ORTHO Isotox Insect Killer, ORTHO Orthene Systemic Insect Control, or ORTHO Liquid Sevin when damage is first noticed. Spray the leaves thoroughly. Repeat the spray if the plant becomes reinfested. Make sure your plant is listed on the product label.

Western tent caterpillars (¼ life size).

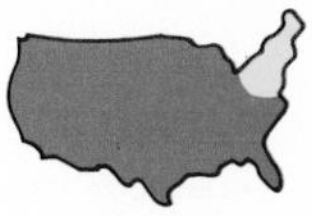

PROBLEM: In the spring or summer, silk nests appear in the branch crotches or on the ends of branches. Leaves are chewed; branches or the entire tree may be defoliated. Groups of caterpillars are feeding in or around the nests.

ANALYSIS: Tent caterpillars and fall webworm (*Malacosoma* species and *Hyphantria cunea*). These insects feed on many ornamental trees. In the summer, *tent caterpillars* lay masses of eggs in a cementing substance around twigs. They hatch in early spring as the leaves unfold, and the young caterpillars construct their nests. On warm, sunny days, they emerge from the nests to devour the surrounding foliage. In mid to late summer, brownish or reddish moths appear. The *fall webworm* lays many eggs on the undersides of leaves in the spring. In early summer, the young caterpillars make nests over the ends of branches, inside which they feed. As the leaves are devoured, the caterpillars extend the nests over more foliage. Eventually the entire branch may be enclosed with this unsightly webbing. The caterpillars drop to the soil to pupate. Up to four generations occur between June and September. Damage is most severe in the late summer.

SOLUTION: Spray with ORTHO Isotox Insect Killer, ORTHO Orthene Systemic Insect Control, ORTHO Liquid Sevin, or the bacterial insecticide *Bacillus thuringiensis*. Make sure your plant is listed on the product label. The bacterial insecticide is most effective against small caterpillars. Remove egg masses found in winter.

Bagworm case on honey locust (life size).

PROBLEM: Leaves are chewed; branches or the entire tree may be defoliated. Carrot-shaped cases or "bags," from 1 to 3 inches long, hang from the branches. The bags are constructed from interwoven bits of dead foliage, twigs, and silk. When a bag is cut open, a tan or blackish caterpillar or a yellowish grublike insect may be found inside. A heavy attack by bagworms may stunt deciduous trees or kill evergreens.

ANALYSIS: Bagworm
(*Thyridopteryx ephemeraeformis*)
Bagworms eat the leaves of many trees and shrubs. The larvae hatch in late May or early June and immediately begin feeding. Each larva constructs a bag that covers its entire body, and to which it adds as it develops. The worm partially emerges from its bag to feed. When all the leaves are eaten off the branch, the bagworm moves to the next branch, dragging its bag along. By late August the larva spins silken bands around a twig, attaches a bag permanently, and pupates. In the fall, the winged male moth emerges from his case, flies to a bag containing a female, mates, and dies. The female bagworm spends her entire life inside her bag. After mating, she lays 500 to 1000 eggs and dies. The eggs spend the winter in the mother's bag.

SOLUTION: Spray with ORTHO Bagworm Killer, ORTHO Orthene Systemic Insect Control, ORTHO Isotox Insect Killer, or ORTHO Liquid Sevin between late May and mid-July. Older bagworms are more difficult to control. Repeat the spray after 10 days if leaf damage is still occurring. Handpick and destroy bags in winter to reduce the number of eggs.

Aphids on hawthorn (life size).

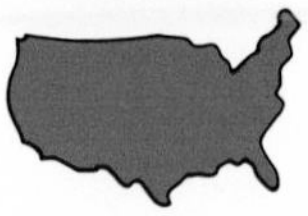

PROBLEM: Tiny (⅛ inch) green, yellow, black, brownish, or gray soft-bodied insects cluster on the bark, leaves, or buds. Some species are covered with white, fluffy wax. The insects may have wings. Leaves are discolored, and may be curled and distorted. They sometimes drop off. A shiny or sticky substance may coat the leaves. A black sooty mold often grows on the sticky substance. Plants may lack vigor, and branches sometimes die. Ants may be present.

ANALYSIS: Aphids
Many different aphids infest ornamental trees and shrubs. They do little damage in small numbers. However, they are extremely prolific, and populations can rapidly build up to damaging numbers during the growing season. Damage occurs when the aphid sucks the juices from the plant. Sap removal often results in scorched, discolored, or curled leaves and reduced plant growth. A severe infestation of bark aphids may cause branches to die. Aphids are unable to digest fully all the sugar in the plant sap, and excrete the excess in a fluid called honeydew, which contaminates anything beneath the tree or shrub. A sooty mold fungus may develop on the honeydew, causing the leaves to appear black and dirty. Ants feed on this sticky substance, and are often present where there is an aphid infestation. For more information about aphids, see page 875.

SOLUTION: Spray with ORTHO Isotox Insect Killer, ORTHO Orthene Systemic Insect Control, or ORTHO Malathion 50 Insect Spray when damage is first noticed. Make sure your plant is listed on the product label. Repeat the spray if the plant becomes reinfested.

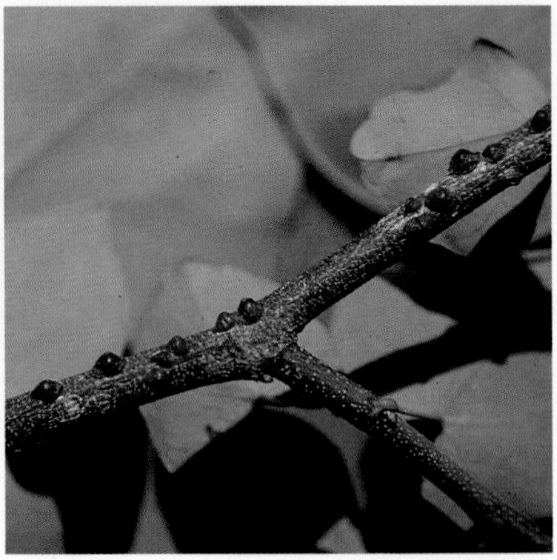
Lecanium scale on redbud (life size).

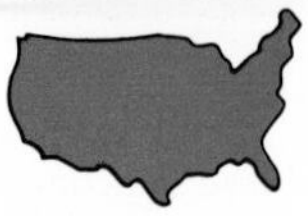

PROBLEM: Leaves, stems, branches, or trunk are covered with crusty or waxy bumps, or clusters of somewhat flattened scaly bumps. The bumps can be scraped or picked off; the undersides are usually soft. Leaves turn yellow and may drop. In some cases, a shiny or sticky substance coats the leaves. A black sooty mold often grows on the sticky substance.

ANALYSIS: Scales
Many types of scales infest trees and shrubs. They lay their eggs on leaves or bark, and in spring to midsummer the young scales, called *crawlers*, settle on leaves, branches, or the trunk. The small (1/10 inch), soft-bodied young feed by sucking sap from the plant. The legs usually atrophy, and a hard crusty or waxy shell develops over the body. The female scales lay their eggs underneath their shell. Some species of scales are unable to digest fully all the sugar in the plant sap, and excrete the excess in a fluid called honeydew. A sooty mold fungus may develop on the honeydew, causing the leaves to appear black and dirty. An uncontrolled infestation of scales may kill a plant after two or three seasons. For more information on scales, see page 876.

SOLUTION: Spray with ORTHO Isotox Insect Killer or ORTHO Orthene Systemic Insect Control when the young are active. Contact your local Cooperative Extension Office (see page 1029) to determine the best time to spray for scales in your area. The following early spring, before new growth begins, spray the trunk and branches with a *dormant oil spray* to control overwintering insects. Make sure your plant is listed on the product label.

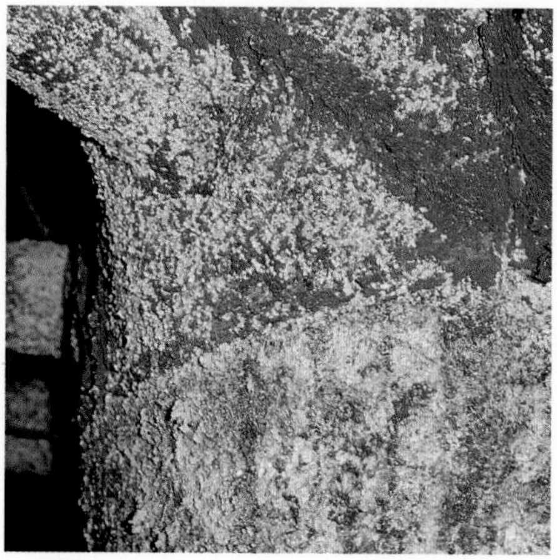

Pine bark aphid on white pine (1/4 life size).

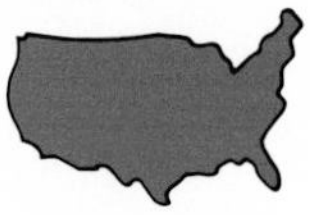

PROBLEM: The undersides of the leaves and stems, branch crotches, or trunk are covered with white, cottony masses. Leaves may be curled, distorted, and yellowing. Knotlike galls may form on the stems or trunk. Sometimes a shiny or sticky substance coats the leaves. A black sooty mold may be growing on the sticky substance. Twigs and branches may die.

ANALYSIS: Cottony scales, mealybugs, and woolly aphids
Cottony scales, mealybugs, and woolly aphids all produce white, waxy secretions that cover their bodies. This visual similarity makes separate identification difficult for the home gardener. Young insects are usually inconspicuous on the host plant. Their bodies range in color from yellowish green to brown, blending in with the leaves or bark. As the insects mature, they exude filaments of white wax, giving them a cottony appearance. Mealybugs and scales generally deposit their eggs in the white, fluffy masses. Damage is caused by the withdrawal of plant sap from the leaves, branches, or trunk. Because the insects are unable to digest fully all the sugar in the plant sap, they excrete the excess in a fluid called honeydew, which often drops onto the leaves or plants below. A sooty mold fungus may develop on the honeydew, causing the leaves and twigs to appear black and dirty.

SOLUTION: Spray with ORTHO Isotox Insect Killer or ORTHO Orthene Systemic Insect Control. Make sure your plant is listed on the product label.

Powdery mildew on London plane tree.

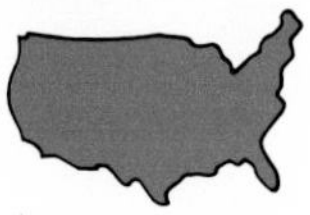

PROBLEM: Leaves, flowers, and young stems are covered with a thin layer or irregular patches of a grayish white powdery material. Infected leaves may turn yellowish or reddish and drop. Some leaves or branches may be distorted. In late fall, tiny black dots (spore-producing bodies) are scattered over the white patches like ground pepper.

ANALYSIS: Powdery mildew
This common plant disease is caused by any of several fungi that thrive in both humid and dry weather. Plants growing in shady areas are often severely infected. The powdery patches consist of fungal strands and spores. The spores are spread by the wind to healthy plants. The fungus saps the plant nutrients, causing discoloring and sometimes the death of the leaf. Certain powdery mildews also cause leaf or branch distortion. Since these powdery mildews often attack many different kinds of plants, the fungus from a diseased plant may infect other plants in the garden. For a list of powdery mildews and the plants they attack, see page 1006.

SOLUTION: Several different fungicides, including those containing *triforine* (FUNGINEX®), *chlorothalonil* (DACONIL 2787®), *benomyl*, *dinocap*, and *cycloheximide*, are used to control powdery mildew. For control suggestions, look under your specific plant in the alphabetical section beginning on page 442.

Rust on Oregon grape.

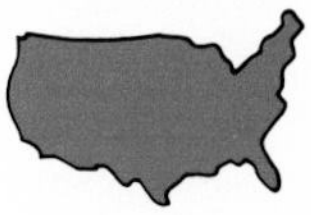

PROBLEM: Yellow, orange, red, or black powdery pustules appear on the upper or lower surfaces of the leaves, or occasionally on the bark. The powdery material can be scraped or rubbed off. Leaves are discolored or mottled yellow to brown. Leaves may become twisted, distorted, and dry, and drop off. Infected stems may be swollen, blistered, or develop oblong or hornlike galls, up to 2 inches long.

ANALYSIS: Leaf and stem rusts
Many different species of rust fungi infect trees and shrubs. Some rusts produce spore pustules on leaves or stems, and others produce galls or hornlike structures on various parts of the plant. Most rusts attack only one species or a few related species of plants. However, some rusts require two different plant species to complete their life cycles. Part of the life cycle is spent on the tree or shrub and part is spent on various other plants. In most cases, the symptoms produced on the two hosts are very different. Rust spores are spread to healthy plants by wind and splashing water. When conditions are favorable (moisture and moderate temperatures, 54° to 74°F), the spores germinate and infect the tissue.

SOLUTION: Several fungicides, including *triforine* (FUNGINEX®), *chlorothalonil* (DACONIL 2787®), *ferbam*, *mancozeb*, and *cycloheximide*, may be used to control rust. Look under the entry for your plant in the alphabetical section of the book beginning on page 442 to determine which fungicide is appropriate. Some rust fungi are fairly harmless to the plant and do not require control measures. Rake up and destroy leaves in the fall.

PROBLEMS COMMON TO MANY TREES, SHRUBS, AND VINES — SPOTS ON LEAVES

Sooty mold on yew.

PROBLEM: A black sooty mold is growing on the leaves and twigs. It can be completely wiped off the surfaces. Cool, moist weather hastens the growth of the mold.

ANALYSIS: Sooty mold
These common black molds are found on a wide variety of plants in the garden. They are caused by any of several fungi that grow on the sugary material left on plants by aphids, scales, mealybugs, whiteflies, and other insects that suck sap from the plant. The insects are unable to digest all the sugar in the sap, and excrete the excess in a fluid called honeydew, which drops onto the leaves below. The honeydew may also drop out of infested trees and shrubs onto plants growing beneath them. The sooty mold fungi develop on the honeydew, causing the leaves to appear black and dirty. Sooty molds are unsightly, but are fairly harmless because they do not attack the leaf directly. Extremely heavy infestations prevent light from reaching the leaf, so that the leaf produces fewer nutrients and may turn yellow. The presence of sooty molds indicates that the plant or a nearby plant is infested with insects.

SOLUTION: Sooty molds can be wiped from the leaves with a wet rag, or they will eventually be washed off by rain. Prevent more sooty mold by controlling the insect that is producing the honeydew. Inspect the leaves and twigs above the sooty mold to find what type of insect is present. See the following pages for control instructions: for aphids, page 875; for scales and mealybugs, page 876; for whiteflies, page 877.

Leaf spots on catalpa.

Leaf spots on liquidambar.

PROBLEM: Spots and blotches appear on the leaves and flowers.

ANALYSIS: Spots on leaves
Several diseases, insects, and environmental factors cause spots and blotches on leaves and flowers.

SOLUTION: The numbered solutions below correspond to the numbers in the analysis.

1. *Fungal leaf spot:* Spots caused by fungi are often small and circular, and may be found on all the leaves. Sometimes only the older or younger leaves are affected. The spots range in size from barely visible to ¾ inch in diameter. They may be yellow, red, tan, gray, brown, or black, and often have a definite margin. Spots sometimes join together to form blotches. Often the leaves turn yellow and die. Infection is usually most severe during moist, mild weather (50° to 85°F).

1. Spray plants with a fungicide containing *benomyl, chlorothalonil* (DACONIL 2787®), *maneb, mancozeb,* or *zineb* when new growth begins. Repeat at intervals of 2 weeks for as long as the weather remains favorable for infection. Make sure your plant is listed on the product label. Raking and destroying leaves in the fall may help control the fungus.

2. *Insects:* Several different types of insects, including lacebugs, leafhoppers, mites, plantbugs, and thrips, cause spotting of leaves. Leaves may be spotted brownish, yellow, or white, or they may be completely discolored. Sometimes the insects are visible, feeding on the lower or upper surfaces of the leaves. For more information about these insects, look in the insect section starting on page 865.

2. These insects can be controlled with various types of insecticides. For effective chemicals, look under the entry for your plant in the alphabetical section beginning on page 442.

3. *Sunburn:* Shade-loving plants placed in a sunny location will develop spots and blotches on the leaves most directly exposed to the sun. Sun-loving plants will also develop sunburn symptoms if they are allowed to dry out. Initially, sunburned leaves develop a whitish or yellowish bleached appearance between the veins. Large, dark blotches form on the damaged tissue. Leaves not directly exposed to the sun remain green and uninjured.

3. Where practical, pick off the injured leaves and plant parts. Check to see whether your plant is adapted to sun or shade by looking it up in the alphabetical section beginning on page 442. Provide shade, or transplant shade loving plants. (For a list of common shade plants, see page 1008.) Water plants regularly, especially on hot, sunny, or windy days. (For watering instructions, see page 912.)

GALLS OR GROWTHS

Gall rust on pine.

Leaf galls on willow.

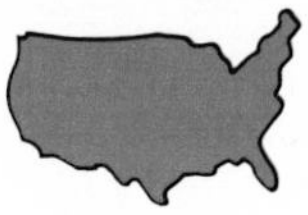

PROBLEM: Swellings, thickenings, and growths develop on the leaves, shoots, branches, or trunk. Plants with numerous galls on branches or the trunk may be weak, and leaves may be yellowing. Branches may die.

ANALYSIS: Galls or growths on leaves, branches, or trunk
These growths can be caused by three factors.

SOLUTION: The numbered solutions below correspond to the numbers in the analysis.

1. *Fungal leaf or stem gall:* Several different fungi, including rust fungi, cause enlargement and thickening of leaves and shoots. Affected plant parts are usually many times larger than normal, and are often discolored and succulent. Some leaf or stem galls turn brown and hard with age. The galls are unsightly but rarely harmful to the plant. Fungal galls are most severe when spring weather is wet.

1. Pick off and destroy affected parts as soon as they appear. If galls are a problem this year, spray next spring with a fungicide containing *ferbam*, *zineb*, *mancozeb*, or *maneb* just before the buds open. Add a spreader-sticker to the spray. (For more information about spreader-stickers, see page 922.) Repeat the spray 2 weeks later.

2. *Bacterial crown gall:* This plant disease is caused by a soil-inhabiting bacterium (*Agrobacterium tumefaciens*) that infects many ornamentals, fruits, and nuts in the garden. The bacteria enter the plant through wounds in the roots or the base of the trunk (the crown). The galls disrupt the flow of water and nutrients up the roots, stems, and trunk, weakening and stunting the top growth. Galls do not usually kill the plant. For more information on crown gall, see page 853.

2. Infected plants cannot be cured. However, they often survive for many years. To improve the appearance of shrubs with stem galls, prune out and destroy affected stems below the galled area. Sterilize pruning shears with rubbing alcohol after each cut. Destroy severely infected shrubs. Consult a professional horticulturist to remove galls from valued trees. The bacteria will remain in the soil for at least 2 to 3 years. For a list of plants resistant to crown gall, see page 1013.

3. *Insect galls:* Many different types of insects cause galls by feeding on plant tissue or by injecting a toxin into the tissue during feeding. As a result of this irritation, blisters or growths of various shapes form on leaves, swellings develop on roots or stems, and buds and flowers grow abnormally. Most gall-forming insects cause minor damage to the plant, but the galls may be unsightly.

3. Many gall-forming insects require no controls. However, if you feel the galls are unsightly or if the galls are causing dieback, control measures may be necessary. For recommended control measures, look under the entry for your plant in the alphabetical section beginning on page 442.

A conk on the trunk of a bigleaf maple.

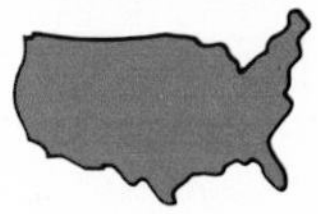

PROBLEM: Mushrooms appear around the base of the tree. Or white, yellow, gray, or brownish growths that are usually hard and woody protrude from the trunk. The plant may appear unhealthy.

ANALYSIS: Mushrooms and conks
Mushrooms and conks are the reproductive bodies of fungi. Most mushroom fungi live on decaying matter. When conditions are favorable, the fungi produce mushrooms and conks (hard, woody growths that protrude from tree trunks) containing spores, which are spread by the wind. A number of different mushroom fungi decay live trees. Most of these grow only in older wood, which they enter through wounds. Mushrooms or conks usually appear annually in the dead portions of the trees. Some conks may remain attached to the wood for years. *Armillaria mellea*, a fungus that causes a disease called *mushroom root rot*, *oak root fungus*, or *shoestring root rot*, invades healthy roots. In the fall or winter, mushrooms appear around the base of the plant, growing on the infected roots.

SOLUTION: By the time conks or mushrooms appear on the trunk, it is too late to do anything about the wood rot. Inspect the tree to determine the extent of decay (contact a professional arborist if necessary). Trees or branches with extensive decay should be removed. Keep plants vigorous by fertilizing and watering regularly. (For more information about fertilizers and watering, see pages 910 and 912.) The spread of armillaria root rot may be inhibited if it is found in only part of the roots. For more information about this root rot, see page 440.

PROBLEMS COMMON TO MANY TREES, SHRUBS, AND VINES — GALLS OR GROWTHS

Lichen.

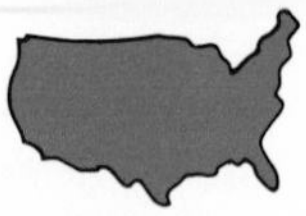

PROBLEM: Brown, gray, green, or yellow crusty, soft, or leaflike growths develop on trees in moist forested areas. The growths are usually found on the lower or shaded part of trunks and branches.

ANALYSIS: Algae, lichens, and mosses
Algae, lichens, and mosses are sometimes mistaken for diseases, especially if the tree they are attached to appears unhealthy. However, they do not harm the plant. Most algae grow where moisture is abundant, on the lower, shady side of the trunk. They appear only as a green color that is not very noticeable on the bark. Lichens are a combination of green algae and fungi. They range in color from brown to green and appear crusty or leaf-like. They are sensitive to air pollution, and are found only in areas where the air is clean. True mosses are small green plants with tiny leaves and stems growing in a mat. They are abundant in moist areas, and are much more apparent than algae. Spanish moss is a flowering plant (in the pineapple family) that is very noticeable hanging from branches of Southern trees.

SOLUTION: Algae, lichen, and mosses do not harm the plant, but may be unsightly. Control them by pruning away surrounding vegetation to increase the amount of light and air flow, which will reduce the soil and air moisture around the plants.

Leafy mistletoe.

PROBLEM: Leafy olive-green plants up to 4 feet across are attached to the branches. The tufts are most noticeable during the winter on trees without their leaves. Affected branches are often swollen. Some may break from the weight of the plants. Branches beyond the growth occasionally die.

ANALYSIS: Leafy mistletoe
(*Phoradendron* species)
Leafy mistletoes are semiparasitic plants that manufacture their own food but depend on their host plant for water and minerals. The plant produces sticky seeds that are spread by birds from one tree to another, or by falling from higher to lower branches. The seeds germinate almost anywhere, but penetrate only young, thin bark. The rootlike attachment organs of the plant penetrate the tree's water-conducting vessels, which they tap for mineral nutrients and water. At the point of attachment, the branch or trunk swells, sometimes to 2 or 3 times its normal size. Growth of mistletoe is slow at first, but after 6 or 8 years, plants may be 3 feet across. Trees heavily infested with mistletoe may be weakened, and sometimes die.

SOLUTION: Prune off limbs 18 inches below the point of mistletoe attachment. The rootlike attachment organs may spread through host tissue up to 1½ feet from the swollen area. They must be removed or the mistletoe will resprout. To prevent the spread of seeds, remove tufts before seeds form in the spring. If it is impractical to prune the tree limbs, remove the mistletoe and wrap the infected areas with black plastic to kill the re-sprouting mistletoe.

Dwarf mistletoe. *Insert:* Seeds.

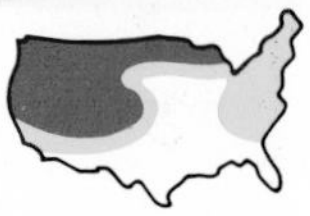

PROBLEM: Twigs and small branches of conifers are swollen and cankered. Witch's brooms (many small tufts of branches) usually form on infested branches. As swellings or witch's brooms increase in size, the tree loses vigor. Foliage becomes sparse and yellowish, and dieback develops in the upper part of the tree. Short, succulent, leafless, yellow, brown, or olive-green shoots develop in the bark of affected branches. Over a period of years the tree may die.

ANALYSIS: Dwarf mistletoe
This parasitic plant infests many conifers. Dwarf mistletoe lacks a normal root system and true leaves. It relies on its host plant to supply most of the nutrients it requires. In this respect it is different from leafy mistletoe (see this page), which depends on its host plant only for water and minerals. In midsummer, dwarf mistletoe spreads by sticky seeds that are explosively discharged for distances up to 50 feet. Seeds land on needles and then slide down to the bark when the needles are moistened. When seeds germinate, usually the following spring, rootlike structures penetrate the bark. The structures form a network in the branches, causing swellings and the formation of cankers. Dwarf mistletoe weakens the tree as it saps nutrients and water, and distorts the growth of branches. Within 1 to 3 years after infection, aerial shoots are produced that are from ½ to 4 inches long, depending on the species.

SOLUTION: Remove dying trees. Prune off branches of less severely infested trees, making the cuts at the trunk. Remove new infestations as they appear.

DISTORTED GROWTH

Witch's broom on hackberry.

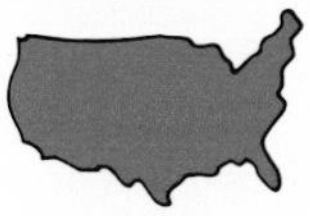

PROBLEM: A dense tuft of small, weak twigs develops on a branch. Leaves on the tuft may be smaller than normal and off-color. The branches are weak and unhealthy.

ANALYSIS: Witch's broom
A witch's broom is a dense proliferation of twig growth, usually caused by an insect, plant disease, or mistletoe (see page 416). The witch's broom looks messy, but is not harmful to the plant. The insect or disease that caused it, however, may be.

SOLUTION: If the witch's broom affects the appearance of the plant, prune it off. It may be difficult for the home gardener to identify the cause of brooming. If witch's brooms continue to develop, contact a professional arborist or your local Cooperative Extension Office. For a list of Cooperative Extension Offices, see page 1029.

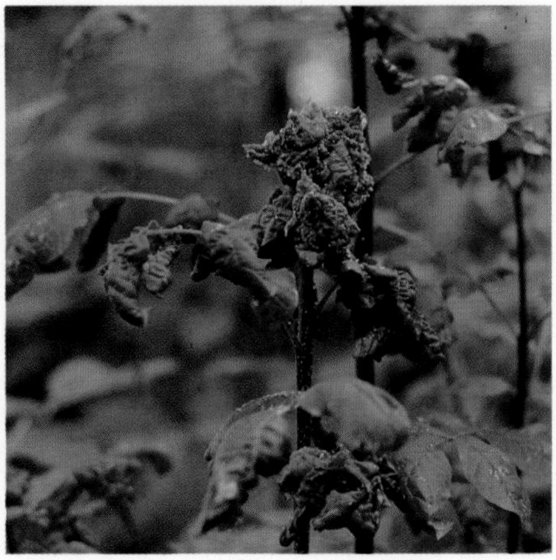
Leaf distortion on ash caused by aphids.

Herbicide damage on forsythia.

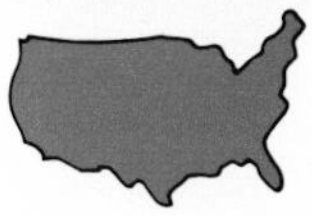

PROBLEM: Leaves are distorted or curled; new growth may also be deformed. Insects are sometimes found on distorted leaves, and affected leaves are often discolored.

ANALYSIS: Leaves distorted or curled
Leaves may be distorted by herbicides, insects, or cold:

SOLUTION: The numbered solutions below correspond to the numbers in the analysis.

1. *Herbicide damage:* Phenoxy herbicides, such as *2,4-D*, cause new growth on trees or shrubs to be deformed. Leaves and stem tips may be distorted and gnarled. Leaves are often discolored, but may remain green. Distorted new growth often continues to appear throughout the growing season. In severe cases, the plant is killed. Herbicide damage may be caused by misapplication of weedkillers, spray drift from neighbors, and spray equipment used for other purposes not cleaned after an herbicide application.

1. Damaged plants usually survive. Prune off injured parts and water the plant thoroughly. If a granular herbicide was applied, flush the soil with water several times. To avoid future damage, do not spray on windy days. Wash herbicides from sprayers thoroughly before spraying desirable plants, or keep a second sprayer for herbicides.

2. *Insects:* Many types of insects cause leaf distortion and curling. Thrips, certain caterpillars, and sucking insects, including aphids, scales, mealybugs, leafhoppers, mites, and whiteflies may cause leaf distortion or curling as a result of their feeding on plant tissue. These insects are usually found on the lower surfaces of the leaves or inside curled leaves during spring or summer. Leaves are often discolored, and plant growth is slowed.

2. Various insecticides are used to control these insects. For more information about the insects and their controls, check under your specific plant in the alphabetical section of the book beginning on page 442.

3. *Frost injury:* Leaves become distorted, crinkled, and discolored, and shoot tips on evergreens curl downward when they are exposed to cold temperatures. The injury is caused by low temperatures after growth starts in the spring, or by sudden cold periods, which damage young, tender tissue before plants are dormant in the fall. Buds and flowers may die, and bark may crack.

3. Where practical, remove injured parts. If cold temperatures are expected in spring or fall when plants are growing, cover them with burlap. Do not apply fertilizer late in the growing season. This encourages tender new growth, which may be damaged. Plant trees and shrubs adapted to your area.

Leafroller on linden.

PROBLEM: Leaves are rolled, usually lengthwise, and tied together with webbing. The rolled leaves are chewed. When a rolled leaf is opened a green caterpillar, ½ to ¾ inch long, may be found feeding inside. Flower buds may also be chewed.

ANALYSIS: Leafrollers
Several different leafrollers feed on the leaves and buds of woody ornamentals. Some species feed on only one plant. Others feed on many plants in the garden. Leafrollers are the larvae of small (up to ¾ inch) brownish moths. The insects spend the winter as eggs or larvae on the plant. In the spring the larvae feed on the young foliage, sometimes tunneling into and mining the leaf first. They roll one or more leaves around themselves, tying the leaves together with a silken webbing, then feed within the rolled leaves. This provides protection from weather, parasites, and chemical sprays. Some leafrollers mature in summer and have several generations each year. Other leafrollers have only one generation. In the fall, the larvae either mature into moths and lay the overwintering eggs, or they spend the winter inside the rolled leaf.

SOLUTION: Spray with ORTHO Isotox Insect Killer, ORTHO Orthene Systemic Insect Control, or ORTHO Liquid Sevin in the spring when leaf damage is first noticed. Make sure your plant is listed on the product label. For the insecticides to be most effective, they should be applied before the larvae are protected inside the rolled leaves. Check the plant periodically in the spring for the first sign of an infestation.

Leafminer damage to holly.

PROBLEM: Green or whitish translucent winding trails, blisters, or blotches develop on the leaves. The trails, blisters, or blotches later turn brown. If an infested leaf is torn open, one to several small green, yellowish, or whitish insects may be found between the upper and lower surfaces of the leaves.

ANALYSIS: Leafminers
Leafminers are the larvae of flies, moths, beetles, or sawflies. The larvae feed between the upper and lower surfaces of the leaves. The adult female moths lay their eggs on or inside the leaves, usually in early to late spring. The emerging larvae feed between the leaf surfaces, producing blisters, blotches, or trails. The infested tissue stands out prominently against the normal green foliage as it turns whitish or light green to brown. The insects pupate inside the leaves or in the soil and emerge as adults. Some adults also feed on the leaves, chewing holes or notches in them. For more information about leafminers, see page 885.

SOLUTION: Control of leafminers is difficult because they spend most of their lives protected inside the leaves. Insecticides are usually aimed at the adults. Once leafminers are noticed in the leaves, inspect the foliage periodically; or check with your local Cooperative Extension Office (see page 1029) to determine when the adults emerge. Then spray with ORTHO Orthene Systemic Insect Control, ORTHO Isotox Insect Killer, ORTHO Liquid Sevin, or ORTHO Diazinon Insect Spray. Make sure your plant is listed on the product label.

Root weevil notches in rhododendron leaves.

PROBLEM: Holes or notches appear in leaves and flowers. Some of the leaves, stems, and flowers may be sheared off. Severely infested plants may be stripped of foliage. No insects are visible on the plants during the day. When the affected plants are inspected at night with a flashlight, insects may be seen feeding on the foliage and flowers.

ANALYSIS: Nocturnal insects
Several types of insects feed on plants only at night, including beetles, weevils, and caterpillars. Beetles are hard-bodied insects with tough, leathery wing covers. The wing covers meet in the middle of the back, forming a straight line. Weevils look like beetles with elongated snouts. Caterpillars are smooth or hairy, soft-bodied worms. Nocturnal insects usually hide in the soil, debris, or other protected places during the day.

SOLUTION: Control these insects with insecticides. For more information about nocturnal insects and the specific insecticides that control them, look up beetles on page 865; weevils on page 866; and caterpillars on page 870.

WILTING

Snail damage to aucuba.

Leaf drop on dogwood due to borer infestation.

Wilting rhododendron.

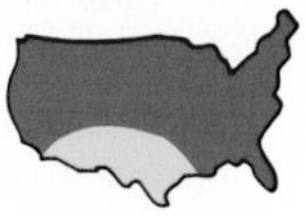

PROBLEM: Irregular holes with smooth edges are chewed in the leaves. Leaves may be sheared off entirely. Silvery trails wind around the plants and soil nearby. Snails and slugs may be seen moving around or feeding on the leaves, especially at night. Check for them by inspecting the garden at night by flashlight.

ANALYSIS: Snails and slugs
These pests are mollusks, and are related to clams, oysters, and other shellfish. They feed on a wide variety of plants, including ornamentals and vegetables. Like other mollusks, snails and slugs need to be moist all the time. For this reason, they avoid direct sun and dry places, and hide during the day in damp places, such as under flower pots or in thick groundcover. They emerge at night or on rainy days to feed. Snails and slugs are similar, except that the snail has a hard shell, into which it withdraws when disturbed. Slugs lay masses of white eggs encased in a slimy mass in protected places. Snails bury their eggs in the soil, also in a slimy mass. The young look like miniature versions of their parents.

SOLUTION: Scatter ORTHO Bug-Geta Snail & Slug Pellets, or ORTHO Slug-Geta Snail & Slug Bait granules around the trees and shrubs you wish to protect. Also scatter the bait in areas where snails or slugs might be hiding, such as in dense groundcovers, weedy areas, compost piles, or pot storage areas. Before spreading the bait, wet down the treated areas to encourage snail and slug activity that night. Repeat the application every 2 weeks as long as snails and slugs are active.

PROBLEM: All or part of the plant is wilting, and the leaves may turn yellow, then brown, and die. There are wounds or sunken lesions on the plant; or there are holes in the branches or trunk, surrounded by sap or sawdust.

ANALYSIS: Damaged trunk or stem
Damage to the wood or bark disrupts water and nutrient movement through the plant, causing wilting.

SOLUTION: The numbered solutions below correspond to the numbers in the analysis.

1. *Wounds:* Any kind of mechanical injury that breaks roots, stems, or bark causes the plant to wilt. Plants may be accidentally wounded by motor vehicles, animals, or foot traffic; or their roots may be damaged by cultivation, construction injuries, or other soil disturbance. In severe cases, the plants die.

1. Thin out some of the branches and keep the plant well watered. During hot weather, provide shade to reduce evaporation from the leaves. Prevent mechanical injuries to plants by being careful when working around the roots and stems. If necessary, place barriers around plants to prevent damage from vehicles, animals, and foot traffic.

2. *Cankers:* Cankers are sunken, dark-colored lesions that develop as a result of infection by fungi or bacteria. Cankers on small or young plants often cause the portion of the plant above the canker to wilt. Branches or the entire plant may eventually die.

2. Prune off dying branches. Avoid wounding plants. For more information about cankers and their controls, see page 424.

3. *Borers:* Most borers are the larvae of beetles or moths. Many kinds of borers infest stems, branches, or trunks. The larvae feed by tunneling through the bark, sapwood, and heartwood, stopping the flow of nutrients and water in that area. Large trees and shrubs usually turn yellow and brown rather than wilting.

3. Prune out stems with borers. Keep the plant well watered and fertilized. For more information about borers and their controls, see page 424.

PROBLEMS COMMON TO MANY TREES, SHRUBS, AND VINES — WILTING

Wilting philadelphus.

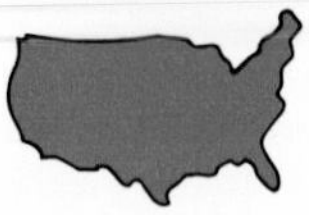

PROBLEM: The plant wilts often, and the soil is frequently or always dry. The leaves or leaf edges may turn brown and shrivel.

ANALYSIS: Lack of water
Water in the soil is taken up by the plant roots. It moves up into the stems and leaves, and evaporates into the air through tiny breathing pores in the surfaces of the leaves. Water pressure within plant cells keeps the cell walls rigid, and prevents the leaves and stems from collapsing. When the soil is dry, the roots are unable to furnish the leaves and stems with water, the water pressure in the cells drops, and the plant wilts. Most plants will recover if they have not wilted severely. However, frequent or severe wilting will curb a plant's growth and may eventually kill it.

SOLUTION: Water the plant immediately. To prevent future wilting, follow the cultural instructions for your plant in the alphabetical section beginning on page 442. For more information about watering, see page 912.

Wilting dogwood.

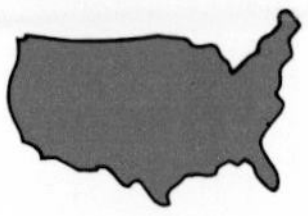

PROBLEM: The plant is wilting, but the foliage usually looks healthy. There are no signs of insects or disease, and the soil is moist. Wilting is most common on shrubs or plants with limited root systems.

ANALYSIS: Extreme heat or wind
During hot, windy periods small or young plants may wilt, even though the soil is wet. Wind and heat cause water to evaporate very quickly from the leaves. If the roots can't absorb and convey water fast enough to replenish this loss, the leaves wilt. For information about scorched leaves due to extreme heat and wind, see page 429.

SOLUTION: Keep the plant well watered during hot spells, and sprinkle it with water to cool off the foliage. The plant will usually recover when the temperature drops or the wind dies down. Provide shade during hot weather, and temporary windbreaks for protection from wind. Plant shrubs adapted to your area.

Arborvitae planted too shallow.

PROBLEM: A recently planted tree or shrub wilts frequently. Roots or the rootball may be exposed.

ANALYSIS: Planted too shallow
Newly planted trees and shrubs may wilt frequently if they are planted too shallow. Plants that have been set in the ground at a higher level than they were originally growing wilt because the exposed soil ball dries out quickly. This may kill the surface roots, especially if the soil washes away, exposing them.

SOLUTION: Remove the plant, along with its soil ball, and replant it more deeply. The plant should be set at the same level as when it was growing in the pot or the ground. Water the plant thoroughly so the entire soil ball is moistened. Keep the plant well watered until it becomes established. For more information about planting, see page 924.

Dry rootball.

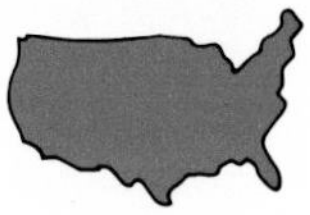

PROBLEM: The entire plant is wilting. The soil surrounding the plant is moist, but the rootball is dry.

ANALYSIS: Dry rootball
Plants that are sold in the nursery balled and burlapped are grown in fields. When the plants reach a size suitable for selling, they are dug up with a ball of soil around their roots. Sometimes the soil in which they are grown is extremely heavy. When the heavy soil is balled and burlapped, it sometimes shrinks as it dries or is compacted, and the ball becomes impermeable to water. After planting, water runs off the outside of the ball rather than moistening the soil, causing the roots to dry out. Rootballs of balled and burlapped plants or of container plants may also dry out if the soil in which the plant is set is much lighter or heavier than the soil in the rootball. The water runs into the lighter soil instead of moistening the soil around the roots; or the surrounding heavy clay soil draws out the water from the light soil in the rootball, causing the rootball to dry out.

SOLUTION: To wet the rootball, build a basin around the plant the diameter of the rootball. Keep water in the basin for 3 hours. Add a wetting agent (which can be purchased at your local nursery) to the water initially. Continue watering in the basin for 6 weeks. Water whenever the rootball (not the surrounding soil) is moist but not wet 1 inch below the surface. Water or soak the rootball before planting. If the soil texture in the rootball is very different from that of the surrounding soil, provide a transition zone, using a mix of rootball and native soil. Build a basin and water as above for 6 weeks.

Leaf drop on linden due to transplant shock.

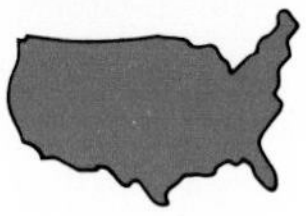

PROBLEM: The plant is wilting, but the foliage usually looks healthy. There are no signs of insects or disease, and the soil is moist. The plant was recently transplanted.

ANALYSIS: Transplant shock
Plants frequently wilt or stop growing for a while after being transplanted. Transplant "shock" is not related to shock in humans, but is the result of roots being cut or injured during transplanting. Wilting occurs when the roots are unable to supply the plant with enough water, even when the soil is wet.

SOLUTION: To reduce the water requirement of the plant, prune off one fourth to one third of the branches. Water the plant well until it becomes established. (For more information about watering, see page 912.) If necessary, provide shade during hot weather. In the future, transplant when the tree or shrub is dormant if possible, and when the weather is cool, in early morning, late afternoon, or on a cloudy day. For more information about transplanting, see page 924.

Slime flux on poplar.

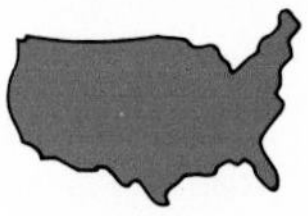

PROBLEM: Sour-smelling sap oozes from wounds, cracks, and branch crotches, mainly during the growing season. The sap drips down the bark and dries, causing unsightly gray streaks. There may be some wilting on affected branches. Insects are attracted to the sour-smelling ooze.

ANALYSIS: Slime flux
Slime flux, also called *wetwood*, is caused by a bacterium (*Erwinia nimipressuralis*). The bacteria infect the heartwood, producing abnormally high sap pressure. This pressure is caused by bacterial fermentation, and forces the fermented sap, or flux, out of wounds, cracks, or crotches in the tree. Flux is especially copious when the tree is growing rapidly. Large areas of the bark may be coated with the smelly, bacteria-laden sap, which dries to a grayish-white color. Also, wounds do not heal and the bark is unsightly. A tree with this problem is often under water stress, which may cause drought damage (wilting and scorched leaves) to the branches. The problem may persist for years.

SOLUTION: There are no chemical controls for this condition. Bore a slightly slanted drainage hole through the wood below each oozing wound. Insert a ½-inch-diameter plastic tube just until it stays firmly in place. If the tube penetrates the water-soaked wood inside the tree, it will interfere with drainage. The tube will carry the dripping sap away from the trunk. Disinfect tools with rubbing alcohol after pruning infected trees.

PROBLEMS COMMON TO MANY TREES, SHRUBS, AND VINES — FLUID ON BARK OR LEAVES

Oozing sap on cherry.

Oozing sap on Coulter pine.

Honeydew on maple.

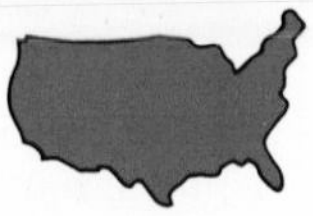

PROBLEM: Beads of amber-colored or whitish, sticky sap appear on healthy bark. Or sap oozes from patches of bark, cankers, wounds, or pruning cuts.

ANALYSIS: Oozing sap
Oozing sap, also called *gummosis,* occurs in all trees and shrubs to a greater or lesser degree. It is caused by one or a combination of the following factors.

SOLUTION: The numbered solutions below correspond to the numbers in the analysis.

1. *Natural tendency:* Certain species of plants have a tendency to ooze sap. Frequently, small beads of sap form on healthy bark of these plants.

1. As long as the bark appears healthy, there is nothing to worry about.

2. *Environmental stress:* Plants that are stressed because they are growing in wet soil may produce large quantities of sap, even though they are not diseased. Also, many plants respond to changes in weather conditions or soil moisture by oozing profusely.

2. If your plant is growing in wet, poorly drained soil, allow the soil to dry out between waterings. Provide for drainage away from trunks and roots. If oozing sap occurs as a result of rapid changes in weather and soil moisture, reduce the effects of stress on the plant by keeping it healthy. Maintain health and vigor of the plant by fertilizing and watering regularly. For more information about fertilizers and watering, see pages 910 and 912.

3. *Mechanical injury:* Almost all plants ooze sap when the bark is wounded. This is especially noticeable on maple and birch. If these trees are injured during the fall, they will ooze a large amount of sap the following spring.

3. Avoid mechanical injuries to the plant. Stake, tie, and prune properly. See page 917 for more information about pruning and treating wounds.

4. *Disease:* Plants respond to certain fungal and bacterial infections by forming cankers, dark, sunken areas that gum profusely. Gummosis or oozing sap is often one of the initial signs of infection.

4. Remove badly infected branches and cut out cankers. For details about canker removal and treatment, see page 917. Keep the plant in a vigorous growing condition by fertilizing and watering regularly.

5. *Borer damage:* Many different insects bore holes into bark. Sap oozes from these holes. The tunnels these insects bore in the wood often become infected by decay organisms.

5. Borers are difficult to control once they have burrowed into the wood. For more information about borers and their controls, see page 424.

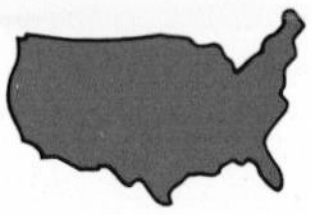

PROBLEM: A shiny or sticky substance coats the leaves and sometimes the twigs. Insects may be found on the leaves directly above, and ants, flies, or bees may be present. A black sooty mold is often growing on the sticky substance.

ANALYSIS: Honeydew
Honeydew is a sweet, sticky substance that is secreted by aphids, mealybugs, psyllids, whiteflies, and certain scales. These sucking insects cannot fully digest all the sugar in the plant sap, and excrete the excess in a fluid called honeydew, which drops onto the leaves directly below and adheres to anything beneath the tree or shrub. Lawn furniture or cars under infested plants may be stained. Ants and certain flies and bees feed on honeydew, and may be found around the plant. A sooty mold fungus often develops on the sticky substance, causing the leaves and twigs to appear black and dirty. The fungus does not infect the leaf, but grows superficially on the honeydew. Extremely heavy fungus infestations may prevent light from reaching the leaf, reducing food production.

SOLUTION: Honeydew can be wiped off the leaves with a wet rag, or it will eventually be washed off by rain. Prevent more honeydew by controlling the insect that is producing it. Inspect the leaves and twigs above the honeydew to find what type of insect is present. See the following pages for control instructions: for aphids, page 875; for scales and mealybugs, page 876; for whiteflies, page 877.

HOLES OR CRACKS IN BARK

Sapsucker holes.

PROBLEM: Rows of parallel holes, ¼ inch in diameter, appear on trunks. Sap often oozes from the holes, and portions of the surrounding bark may fall off. When damage is severe, part or all of the tree is killed. Yellow-bellied or red-breasted birds may be seen pecking on the tree.

ANALYSIS: Sapsuckers
Two different species of sapsuckers, members of the woodpecker family, feed on tree bark and sap. The red-breasted sapsucker is found in the Pacific Northwest. The yellow-bellied sapsucker is common throughout much of the United States. Sapsuckers peck into many trees before finding a suitable one that has sap with a high sugar content. Once the birds find a favorite tree, they visit it many times a day and feed on it year after year. Portions of the bark often fall off after sapsuckers have pecked many holes. If the trunk is girdled, the tree above the damaged area dies. Sometimes disease organisms enter the holes and damage or kill the tree.

SOLUTION: It is difficult to prevent sapsucker damage to trees. Wrapping the damaged trunk with burlap or smearing a sticky material, such as the latex used for ant control, above and below the holes may inhibit new pecking damage. For a list of trees most commonly attacked by sapsuckers, see page 1012.

Rodent damage to crabapple.

Porcupine damage to elm.

PROBLEM: Bark has been chewed or gnawed from the trunk and lower branches. In some cases, the trunk is entirely girdled. Deer, rabbits, mice, or squirrels may have been seen in the yard, or their tracks may be evident on the ground or snow. Damage is usually most severe during the winter, when other food sources are scarce.

ANALYSIS: Bark-feeding animals
Several animals chew on tree bark.
1. Deer feed on leaves, shoots, buds, and bark. They feed by pulling and twisting the bark or twig tissue, leaving ragged or twisted twig ends or patches of bark. Generally they feed on the lower branches and upper trunk. The males may also damage plants by rubbing their antlers on the trunk and branches.
2. Rabbits chew on the bark at the base of the trunk. They chew bark and twigs off cleanly, leaving a sharp break. The damaged trunk is often scarred with paired gouges left by the rabbit's front teeth. Rabbits generally feed no more than 2 feet above the ground or snow level. They damage small or young plants more severely.
3. Field mice, or *voles*, damage plants by chewing off the bark at the base of the trunk just at or slightly above or below ground or snow level. They may girdle the trunk, often killing the plant. Mice leave tiny scratches in the exposed wood. Some species of mice feed on plant roots, causing the slow decline and death of the plant.
4. Squirrels damage trees and shrubs by wounding the bark. Red squirrels feed on maple sap in the spring. The resulting bark wounds are V-shaped. Canker disease fungi sometimes invade the wounds, weakening or killing the tree. Some squirrels feed on bark when food is scarce in the winter. Other species of squirrels use bark and twigs for building nests.

SOLUTION: There are various methods that may be used to exclude or control deer, rabbits, mice and voles, and squirrels in the garden. These methods usually involve protecting the plants with fencing and tree guards, or controlling the animals with traps. For more information about the animals and their controls, see page 897 for deer, page 900 for rabbits and ground squirrels, and page 899 for tree squirrels.

PROBLEMS COMMON TO MANY TREES, SHRUBS, AND VINES — HOLES OR CRACKS IN BARK

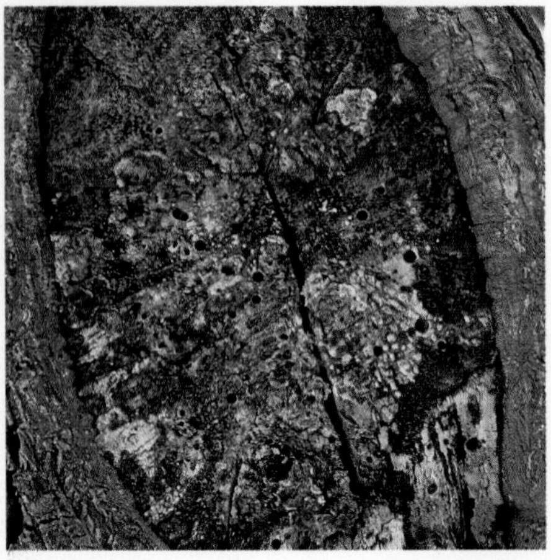

Borer emergence holes.

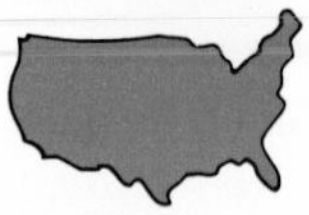

PROBLEM: Foliage on a branch or at the top of the tree is sparse; eventually the twigs and branches die. Holes or tunnels are apparent in the trunk or branches. Sap or sawdust usually surrounds the holes. The bark may die over the tunnels and slough off, or there may be knotlike swellings on the trunk and limbs. Weakened branches break during wind or snow storms. Weak, young, or newly transplanted trees may be killed.

ANALYSIS: Borers
Borers are the larvae of beetles or moths. Many kinds of borers attack trees and shrubs. Females lay their eggs in bark crevices throughout the summer. The larvae feed by tunneling through the bark, sapwood, and heartwood. This stops the flow of nutrients and water in that area by cutting the conducting vessels; branch and twig dieback result. Sap flow acts as a defense against borers if the plant is healthy. When the insect burrows into the wood, tree sap fills the hole and drowns the insect. Factors that weaken the tree, such as mechanical injuries, transplanting, damage by leaf-feeding insects, and poor growing conditions make it more attractive to egg-laying females.

SOLUTION: Cut out and destroy all dead and dying branches. Severely infested young plants should be removed. Spray or paint the trunk and branches with an insecticide containing *lindane.* Contact your local Cooperative Extension Office (see page 1029) for the best time to spray in your area. Repeat 3 more times at intervals of two weeks. Maintain plant health and vigor by watering and fertilizing regularly.

Canker on ceanothus.

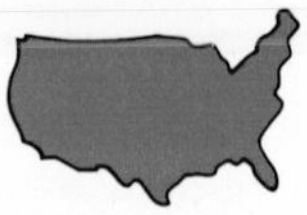

PROBLEM: Sunken, oval, or elongated dark-colored lesions (cankers) develop on the trunk or branches. The bark at the edge of the canker may thicken and roll inward. In some cases, sticky, amber-colored sap oozes from the canker. Foliage on infected plants may be stunted and yellowing. Some of the leaves may turn brown and drop off. Twigs and branches may gradually die, and the plant may eventually be killed.

ANALYSIS: Cankers
Many different species of fungi and bacteria cause cankers and dieback. Infection usually occurs through injured or wounded tissue. Bark that has been damaged by sunscald, cold, pruning wounds, or mechanical injury is especially susceptible. Some decay organisms infect the leaves first, then spread down into healthy twigs. Cankers form as the decay progresses. Some plants produce a sticky sap that oozes from the cankers. The portion of the branch or stem above the canker may die from the clogging of the water and nutrient-conducting vessels in the branch. Cankers that form on the trunk are the most serious, and may kill the tree. The plant may halt the development of a canker by producing callus tissue, a growth of bark-like cells, to wall off the decay.

SOLUTION: Remove badly infected branches and cut out cankers. For details about canker removal and treatment, see page 917. Avoid wounding the plant. Keep the plant vigorous by fertilizing and watering regularly. For instructions, see pages 910 and 912.

Bark shedding on madrone.

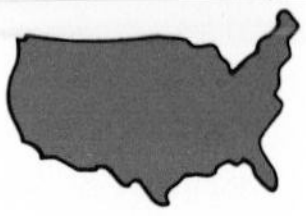

PROBLEM: Bark is cracking or peeling, usually on the older branches and trunk.

ANALYSIS: Bark shedding
The shedding or cracking of bark is often noticeable and may be of concern to people not familiar with this natural process. The outer bark changes over the lifetime of a tree. The bark of young trees is live tissue, usually smooth and relatively soft. As the trees mature, the bark dies and hardens, sometimes becoming rough. Trunks and branches increase in diameter with age. The increase in girth causes the outer bark of many plants to crack in a variety of patterns. With some tree species, such as white birch, cracking develops to such an extent that the bark peels and falls off. Newly exposed bark is often smooth and lighter in color than the bark that was shed. Some trees, such as sycamore and shagbark hickory, characteristically have loose outer bark. The bark is constantly in the process of peeling and shedding.

SOLUTION: This process is normal. No controls are necessary.

Lightning-damaged tree.

Sunscald.

Sunscald on dogwood.

PROBLEM: Part or all of the tree suddenly turns brown and dies. There may be no external signs of damage, or a strip of bark may be burned or stripped from the entire length of the trunk. In less severe cases, trees survive for several years or recover completely. Sometimes tops of trees or branches explode, leaving a jagged stub. There has been a lightning storm recently.

ANALYSIS: Lightning damage
Tall trees, trees growing in open locations, and trees growing in moist soil or along river banks are susceptible to damage by lightning. Lightning damage is variable. Some trees die suddenly from internal damage or burned roots without any external sign that lightning has struck. Other trees burst into flames or explode when struck. Sometimes only a strip of bark is burned or stripped from the trunk and the tree recovers. Some species of trees are more resistant to lightning bolts than others. (For a list of trees resistant and susceptible to lightning injury, see page 1012.) Some scientists believe that trees high in starch, deep-rooted species, and decaying trees are more susceptible to damage than trees high in oils, shallow-rooted species, or healthy trees.

SOLUTION: Remove all loose and injured bark. To reduce or prevent damage, water trees during dry spells. Remove severely damaged trees. Valuable old trees can be protected with lightning conductors. Contact a professional arborist.

PROBLEM: Patches of bark die, crack, and later develop into cankers. The dead bark eventually sloughs off, exposing undamaged wood. The affected bark area is always on the southwest side of the tree. Trees with dark bark may be more severely affected. The cracks and cankers develop in either summer or winter.

ANALYSIS: Sunscald
When a tree growing in a deeply shaded location is suddenly exposed to intense sunlight, or when a tree is heavily pruned, the southwest side of newly exposed bark is injured by the rapid change in temperature. This may develop when a forested area is excessively thinned, or when a tree is moved from a shaded nursery to an open area, such as a lawn.

1. *Summer sunscald:* With intense summer heat, exposed bark is killed and a canker develops, usually revealing the undamaged wood beneath the bark. Within several seasons, the tree may break at the cankered area and topple. Summer sunscald is most severe when the soil is dry.

2. *Winter sunscald:* Bark injury develops when there are rapid changes in bark temperature between cold nights and sunny winter days. Exposed bark, usually on the southwest side of the tree, becomes much warmer than the air during the day, but cools rapidly after sunset. This rapid temperature change often results in bark cracking and, later, cankering. Trees with thin, dark bark are most severely affected.

SOLUTION: Once the bark is injured, there is nothing you can do. Wrap the trunks of recently exposed or newly transplanted trees with tree-wrapping paper, available in nurseries. White interior latex or whitewash is also effective. The wrap or paint should be left on for at least 2 years. Reapply the paint the second season if it has washed off. Trees will eventually adapt to increased exposure by producing thicker bark. Give trees adequate water in the summer and, if necessary, in the fall, especially recently transplanted trees. Water transplants when the top 2 inches of the rootball are dry. For more information about watering, see page 912.

PROBLEMS COMMON TO MANY TREES, SHRUBS, AND VINES — TWIGS OR BRANCHES BREAK

Frost cracks.

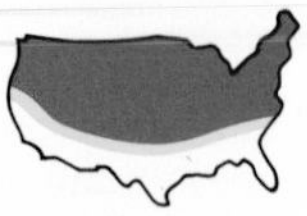

PROBLEM: Longitudinal cracks develop on the trunk, usually on the south and west sides. The cracks generally close during the growing season.

ANALYSIS: Frost cracks
Frost cracks develop from the expansion and shrinkage of bark and wood during periods of wide temperature fluctuations. This causes internal mechanical stress which causes already weakened or decayed areas of the bark and outer wood to split open. The sudden break is often accompanied by a loud noise. Cracks usually heal over during the growing season, but they may remain partially open after the weather warms, or reopen during the next winter.

SOLUTION: If a large crack fails to heal, a rod or bolt may be installed to hold it together. Consult a professional arborist. Plant trees adapted to your climate. Protect young susceptible trees by wrapping the trunks with tree-wrapping paper in late fall, or by painting the trunk with whitewash.

Trees that are most susceptible to frost cracks:

Botanical name	Common name
Acer	Maple
Aesculus	Horse chestnut
Liriodendron tulipifera	Tuliptree
Malus	Crabapple
Platanus acerifolia	London plane tree
Prunus	Flowering peach and cherry
Quercus	Oak
Salix	Willow
Tilia	Linden
Ulmus	Elm

Limb breakage caused by weak fork.

Limb breakage caused by snow load.

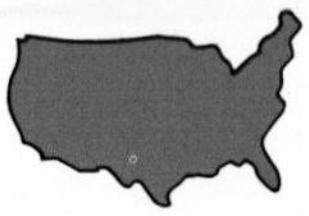

PROBLEM: Sound branches break and fall, usually during storms or high winds. Some may drop in the middle of the day during a hot spell.

ANALYSIS: Limb breakage
Several different environmental factors cause limb breakage.

Weak fork: The angle between a branch and the trunk, called the *fork*, is normally greater than 45°. If the angle is much less than this, bark is sometimes trapped between the branch and the trunk, preventing the wood from growing together at that point. This weakens the branch. As the branch and trunk increase in length, the additional weight causes the fork to split at the weak junction. A large portion of the tree may fall. Some trees that develop weak forks break more readily than others because of their growth habits and brittle wood.

Wind: Branches may fall during high winds, especially in areas where there are tornadoes, hurricanes, and other forms of extreme winds. Moderate winds often hasten the dropping of limbs weakened by injury, insects, or disease.

Sudden limb drop: Large limbs sometimes drop during the middle of the day for no apparent reason. This usually occurs on hot, calm days. The cause is not known.

Snow and ice: Plants heavily coated with snow or ice may lose large limbs due to the additional weight. Evergreen trees, or deciduous trees with leaves still attached, are most susceptible because of the greater surface to which the snow or ice can adhere.

SOLUTION: If the break is a split, or if a third of the bark at the break is intact, it can be bolted back in place. (For more information about bracing and cabling, see page 920.) If less than a third of the bark is intact, or if the branch has fallen off the tree, prune off the remaining branch stub. (For more information about pruning off broken branches, see page 916.) To prevent further damage, brace or cable trees, and knock off snow and ice constantly to prevent buildup. In areas with high winds, prune back some of the branches to reduce the wind load. In the future, do not plant trees with brittle wood that breaks easily. For a list of trees with weak forks and brittle wood, see page 1012.

Tree squirrel.

PROBLEM: Many small twigs with healthy leaves attached are lying under the tree or shrub. Squirrels may be seen in the area.

ANALYSIS: Tree squirrels
Tree squirrels may damage trees by shearing off small twigs, which they use for building nests. Twigs appear to have been cut off with a dull knife or shears. The squirrels gather the twigs up and carry them to their nests, but they usually leave many behind. They normally clip two or three times more twigs than they need. Trees heavily pruned by squirrels may be bushier than normal.

SOLUTION: Squirrels usually do not harm the tree by clipping twigs. However, if they are altering the shape of the tree, protect it with tree guards wrapped around the trunk, or control the squirrels by using live traps. For more information about tree squirrels, see page 899.

Twig girdler (twice life size).

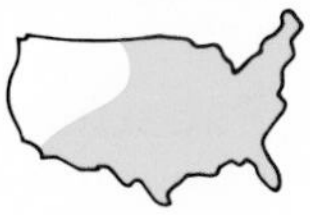

PROBLEM: Small, cleanly cut twigs, ¼ inch to 2 inches in diameter, are lying under the tree in the fall. The tree is often abnormally bushy. Small (up to 1 inch), whitish larvae may be found inside the fallen twigs.

ANALYSIS: Twig pruners and twig girdlers
Several species of wood-boring beetles cause unsightly damage to trees by altering their natural form. In midsummer to fall, the wood-boring beetles lay their eggs in the wood of small twigs. The *twig pruner* larvae tunnel toward the base of the twigs, eating all but the outer bark. In the fall, they back into the hollowed-out twigs. High winds cause the nearly severed twigs containing the larvae to break and drop to the ground. Adult *twig girdlers* lay eggs in twigs, then chew a circle arond the outside of the twigs. The girdled twigs die and break off. The eggs in the fallen twig are able to develop without being hindered by the flow of sap through the twig. Both twig pruner and twig girdler larvae mature in the twigs on the ground. The damage to the tree is the result of excessive pruning on the branch tips. Several new side shoots develop where the twigs break off, causing abnormal bushiness and an unnatural shape.

SOLUTION: Spray with an insecticide containing *lindane* after the first leaves are fully expanded in spring. Make a second application 30 days later. Gather and destroy all severed twigs in the late fall, when the insects are inside them.

Heart rot.

PROBLEM: Branches break and fall, usually during storms. The wood in the area of breakage is discolored and often spongy. Soft or woody mushroom-like growths may be found on the wood.

ANALYSIS: Heart rot
Heart rot is caused mainly by fungi. Decay organisms rot dead wood (such as fallen trees) as part of nature's recycling process. A number of them may also invade live trees through wounds. Healthy, vigorous trees may stop the spread of decay by producing cells that wall off the invaded area. Old trees with many wounds often have little resistance to microorganisms, and decay spreads through the wood. The decay does not usually kill the living tissue of the tree, so branches and leaves are kept alive. But internal decay reduces the strength of affected limbs. During a storm, weakened branches fall. Some of the decay organisms develop yellowish to brown, mushroomlike growths, called *conks*, on the outside wood in areas where decay is present. For more information about mushrooms and conks, see page 415.

SOLUTION: Cut off the remaining branch stub flush against the larger branch or tree trunk (see page 916). Inspect the rest of the tree to determine the extent of decay (it may be necessary to contact a professional arborist). Branches or the entire plant should be removed if decay is extensive. As much as possible, avoid wounding plants. Keep them in a vigorous growing condition by fertilizing and watering regularly. For more information about fertilizers and watering, see pages 910 and 912.

Roots plugging sewer.

Roots cracking pavement.

Surface roots in a lawn.

PROBLEM: Sewer drains are backed up. Trees or large shrubs are growing on the property.

ANALYSIS: Roots plugging sewer
The roots of trees and large shrubs plug up sewer lines. Roots cannot invade pipes by puncturing them. Unsealed pipe joints and cracks are common entrance points. Once inside, the invading root has a constant source of nutrients and moisture and grows rapidly. As the root expands it forces the crack open. Inside, the root branches and grows until it plugs the pipe, causing the drains to back up.

SOLUTION: Plugged drains must be cleared by a plumber. To prevent further plugging, pour 1 pound of *copper sulfate crystals* into the lowest entry point to the sewer line (a toilet or basement drain) before bedtime, when drains and sewer lines are not in use. Flush the toilet or wash the crystals into the pipes with a bucket of water. The copper sulfate crystals collect in the mass of roots and kill them. Copper sulfate is not absorbed by roots, so the rest of the plant is not harmed. The dead roots rot in a few weeks. Repeat the treatment every six months.

PROBLEM: Roots are exposed on the surface of the soil, or are making bumps by growing just beneath it. Or roots are cracking and raising the pavement. Exposed roots may be lumpy and galled.

ANALYSIS: Surface roots Several factors can cause roots near the surface to expand:	**SOLUTION:** The numbered solutions below correspond to the numbers in the analysis.
1. *Surface roots in lawns:* If plants receive only light irrigations on the soil surface, roots in this upper zone will expand, pushing above the surface. Plants growing in lawns that receive light irrigations often have shallow roots.	**1.** In addition to lawn watering, deep-water trees in lawns every two weeks, to a depth of 3 to 4 feet. Cover the roots by slowly raising the level of the lawn (1 inch per year) with soil topdressing.
2. *Waterlogged soil:* Roots need oxygen to grow and develop. Waterlogged soil has very little oxygen available for root growth because the soil pores are filled with water. The only available oxygen is near the soil surface, so the surface roots develop most.	**2.** If the soil is waterlogged from overwatering, cut back on watering. (For information about watering, see pages 912 and 917.) If necessary, improve drainage around the plant (see page 907). Cover the exposed roots with 2 to 4 inches of soil. Before planting new trees and shrubs, make sure drainage is adequate.
3. *Natural tendency:* Some plant species are more likely than others to develop surface roots.	**3.** For a list of plants likely to develop surface roots, see page 1010.
4. *Compacted soil:* Trees and shrubs growing in compacted soil develop surface roots.	**4.** Loosen compacted soil with a crowbar. Before planting in compacted soil, loosen the soil (see page 930).
5. *Confined roots:* Plants growing in areas with limited root space, such as in containers, often have roots growing on the soil surface.	**5.** Plant shrubs or small trees that are adapted to growing in confined root areas (see page 1009).
6. *Planting strips:* Trees growing in planting strips adjacent to lawns frequently crack the sidewalks that separate them from the lawns. All of the available water and food is beyond the walk, in the lawns. The roots that extend under the walk into the lawn expand rapidly, cracking the walk.	**6.** Sever small roots that are pushing up pavement. If possible, avoid cutting large roots. In the future, plant large trees on the lawn side of the sidewalk, and use shrubs in planting strips.

DISCOLORED LEAVES

Salt burn on philadelphus.

Leaf scorch on maple.

Leaf scorch on birch.

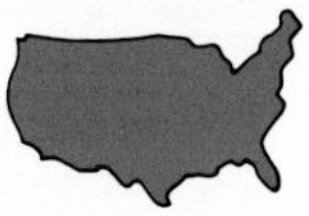

PROBLEM: Edges of older leaves turn brown or black, and die. The rest of the leaf may be lighter green than normal. The browning or blackening develops in dry or wet soil, but it is more severe in dry soil. In the worst cases, leaves drop from the plant.

ANALYSIS: Salt burn
This problem is common in areas of low rainfall. It also occurs in soils with poor drainage, in areas where salt has been used to melt snow and ice, and where too much fertilizer has been applied. Excess salts dissolved in the soil water accumulate in the leaf edges, where they kill the tissue. These salts also interfere with water uptake by the plant. This problem is rare in areas of high rainfall, where the soluble salts are leached from most soils. Poorly drained soils also accumulate salts because they do not leach well; much of the applied water runs off instead of washing through the soil. Fertilizers, which are soluble salts, also cause salt burn if too much is applied or if it is not diluted with a thorough watering after application. For more information about salt burn, see page 857.

SOLUTION: In areas with low rainfall, leach accumulated salts from the soil with an occasional heavy watering (about once a month). If possible, improve the drainage around the plants. (For instructions on improving drainage, see page 907.) If plants are severely damaged, replace them with healthy plants. Follow package directions when using fertilizers; several light applications are better than one application. Water thoroughly afterward. Avoid the use of bagged steer manure, which contains large amounts of salt.

PROBLEM: Leaf edges and the tissues between the veins turn tan or brown. Leaves are scorched and have a dry appearance. Brown areas often increase in size until little green is left except around the center vein. Dead leaves may remain attached to the plant, or they may drop. Leaf scorch is most severe in the upper branches, and when the soil is dry.

ANALYSIS: Leaf scorch
Scorch is caused by a lack of water in the leaves. This lack can result from any of several causes.

SOLUTION: The numbered solutions below correspond to the numbers in the analysis.

1. *Extreme heat and wind:* Leaf scorch is caused by excessive evaporation of moisture from the leaves. In hot or windy weather, water evaporates rapidly from the leaves. If the roots can't absorb and convey water fast enough to replenish this loss, the leaves turn brown and wither. This usually occurs in dry soil, but leaves can also scorch when the soil is moist and temperatures are near 100°F for extended periods. Young plants with limited root systems are most susceptible.

1. To prevent further scorch, deep-water plants during periods of hot weather to wet down the entire root space. Because of their limited root systems, recently transplanted trees and shrubs should be watered more often than established plants. Water them when the root ball is dry 2 inches below the surface. If the leaves scorched when the soil was moist, provide shade during periods of hot weather and screens for protection from wind; or transplant to a protected area.

2. *Winter burn:* Winter burn is similar to scorch from intense heat or wind except that it occurs during warm, windy days in late winter. In colder climates, water cannot be replaced by the roots because the soil is frozen, resulting in leaf desiccation. Conifers are most susceptible, especially those planted in exposed areas. The symptoms may not appear until spring.

2. Provide windbreaks and shelter for plants growing in cold, windy regions. Covering smaller plants with burlap helps prevent leaf drying. If necessary, water in late fall or winter to insure adequate soil moisture. Mulch plants after they are dormant to reduce the depth of frost penetration into the soil.

3. *Damaged roots:* Trees and shrubs may develop scorched and yellow leaves, early fall color, and dieback after the roots have been injured.

3. For more information about damaged roots, see pages 435 and 437.

4. *Underwatering:* Many plants that are regularly underwatered will survive. They do not function normally, however, and the leaves frequently burn and wilt over the entire plant.

4. Do not let the soil dry out to the point where leaves scorch. Check the moisture needs of your plant under its cultural information.

PROBLEMS COMMON TO MANY TREES, SHRUBS, AND VINES — DISCOLORED LEAVES

Cedar-apple rust on hawthorn.

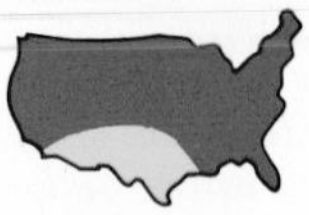

PROBLEM: Leaves are discolored or mottled yellow to brown. Yellow, orange, red, or blackish powdery pustules appear on the leaves. The powdery material can be scraped off. Leaves may become twisted, distorted, and dry, and drop off. Twigs may also be infected. Plants are often stunted.

ANALYSIS: Leaf rusts
Many different species of leaf rust fungi infect trees and shrubs. Some rusts require two different plant species to complete their life cycles. Part of the life cycle is spent on the tree or shrub and part is spent on various weeds, flowers, or other woody trees or shrubs. Rust fungi survive the winter as spores on or in living plant tissue or in plant debris. The spores are spread to healthy plants by wind and splashing water. When conditions are favorable (moisture on the leaf in the form of rain, dew, or fog, and moderate temperatures, 54° to 74°F), the spores germinate and infect the tissue. Leaf discoloration and mottling develop as the fungus saps the plant nutrients. Some rust fungi produce spores in spots or patches, while others develop into hornlike structures.

SOLUTION: Several fungicides, including those containing *triforine* (FUNGINEX®), *chlorothalonil* (DACONIL 2787®), *ferbam*, *maneb*, *zineb*, and *cycloheximide*, may be used to control rust. Look under the entry for your plant in the alphabetical section of the book beginning on page 442 to determine which fungicide is appropriate. Some rust fungi are fairly harmless to the plant and do not require control measures. Where practical, remove and destroy infected leaves as they appear. Rake up and destroy leaves in the fall.

Spirea aphids (4 times life size).

PROBLEM: The newest leaves are discolored. Leaves and twigs may be curled and distorted. Many leaves may drop from the plant, and branches sometimes die. A shiny or sticky substance often coats the leaves. A black sooty mold may grow on the sticky substance. Tiny ($\frac{1}{8}$ inch) green, yellow, black, brownish, or gray soft-bodied insects cluster on the leaves, stem tips, bark, or buds. The insects may have wings. Ants are sometimes present.

ANALYSIS: Aphids
Many different aphids infest ornamental trees and shrubs. They do little damage in small numbers. However, they are extremely prolific, and populations can rapidly build up to damaging numbers during the growing season. Damage occurs when the aphid sucks the juices from the leaves. Sap removal often results in scorched, discolored, or curled leaves and reduced plant growth. A severe infestation of bark aphids may cause branches to die. The aphid is unable to digest fully all the sugar in the plant sap, and excretes the excess in a fluid called honeydew, which drops onto the leaves and contaminates anything beneath the tree or shrub. A sooty mold fungus may develop on the honeydew, causing the leaves to appear black and dirty. Ants feed on the sticky substance, and are often present where there is an aphid infestation. For more information about aphids,see page 875.

SOLUTION: Spray with ORTHO Isotox Insect Killer, ORTHO Orthene Systemic Insect Control, or ORTHO Malathion 50 Insect Spray when damage is first noticed. Make sure your plant is listed on the product label. Repeat the spray if the plant becomes reinfested.

Leafhopper damage to dogwood.

PROBLEM: Leaves are stippled white, yellow, or light green, and leaves and stems may be distorted. Sometimes the plant has a burned appearance. Infested leaves may drop prematurely. When infestations are severe, twigs and small branches sometimes die. Whitish or green wedge-shaped insects, up to $\frac{1}{2}$ inch long, hop and fly away quickly when the plant is touched.

ANALYSIS: Leafhoppers
Many species of leafhoppers infest ornamental trees and shrubs. Some leafhoppers cause only minor damage to the leaves, while other species severely retard plant growth. Leafhoppers usually spend the winter as eggs in bark slits made by the females, although some may overwinter in the South and migrate north in the spring. Injury to the bark from egg laying may kill twigs. When the weather warms in the spring, the young leafhoppers emerge and settle on the undersides of the leaves, where they suck out the plant sap, causing the stippling and distortion. Severely infested leaves often drop in midsummer. Some leafhoppers cause a condition known as "hopperburn." Insect feeding causes distortion, and gives the leaves a burned appearance. There may be several generations of leafhoppers each year. For more information about leafhoppers, see page 878.

SOLUTION: Spray with ORTHO Isotox Insect Killer, ORTHO Orthene Insect Spray, or ORTHO Diazinon Insect Spray when damage is first noticed. Cover the lower surfaces of the leaves thoroughly. Make sure your plant is listed on the product label.

Spider mite damage to holly.

PROBLEM: Leaves are stippled yellow, white, or bronze and dirty. Sometimes there is a silken webbing on the leaves or stems. New growth may be distorted, and the plant may be weak and stunted. To determine if the plant is infested with mites, hold a sheet of white paper underneath an affected leaf or branch and tap it sharply. Minute green, red, or yellow specks the size of pepper grains will drop to the paper and begin to crawl around.

ANALYSIS: Spider mites
Spider mites, related to spiders, are major pests of many plants. They cause damage by sucking sap from the undersides of the leaves and buds. As a result of feeding, the green leaf pigment disappears, producing the stippled appearance. Many mites produce a fine webbing over the foliage as they feed, which collects dust and dirt. Some mites are active throughout the growing season, and are especially favored by hot, dry weather (70°F and up). Other mites, especially those infesting conifers, are most prolific in cooler weather. They are most active in the spring and sometimes fall, and during warm periods in winter in mild climates. At the onset of hot weather, these mites have usually caused their maximum damage. For more information about spider mites, see page 887.

SOLUTION: Spray with ORTHO Isotox Insect Killer, ORTHO Orthenex Insect & Disease Control, or ORTHO Orthene Systemic Insect Control when damage is first noticed. Repeat the spray two more times at intervals of seven to ten days. Make sure your plant is listed on the product label.

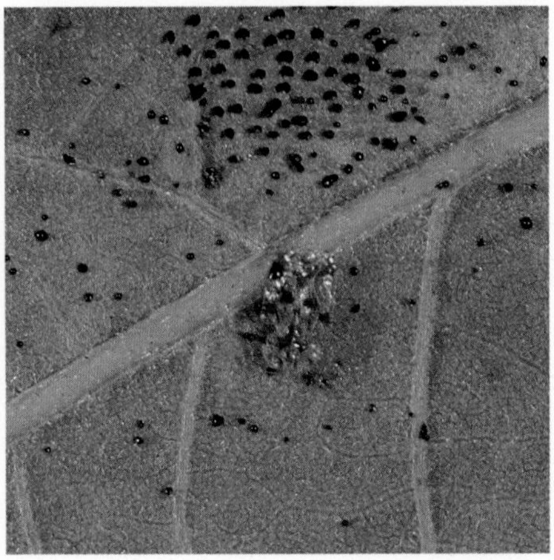
Lacebug and droppings (4 times life size).

PROBLEM: The upper surfaces of the leaves are mottled or speckled yellow, gray, or white and green. The mottling is distinguished from other insect damage—such as that caused by mites or leafhoppers—by the shiny, hard, black droplets found on the undersides of damaged leaves. Small (1/8 inch), light or dark, spiny, wingless insects or brownish insects with clear lacy wings may be visible around the droplets. The plant is usually stunted. Damage occurs in spring and summer.

ANALYSIS: Lacebugs
Many species of lacebugs feed on trees and shrubs. Each species usually infests only one type of plant. Depending on species, lacebugs spend the winter as adults in protected areas on the plant, or as eggs in leaf veins, or cemented in the black droplets on the lower surfaces of the leaf. Both the spiny, wingless, immature insects and the lacewing adults suck sap from the undersides of the leaves. The green leaf pigment disappears, resulting in the characteristic speckling or mottling. As the lacebugs feed, droplets of brown excrement accumulate around them. Damage is unsightly and food production by the leaf is reduced, resulting in loss of plant vigor.

SOLUTION: Spray with ORTHO Isotox Insect Killer or ORTHO Orthene Systemic Insect Control when damage first appears in the spring. Make sure your plant is listed on the product label. Cover the undersides of the leaves thoroughly. Repeat the spray seven to ten days later. A third application may be necessary if the plant becomes reinfested in midsummer.

Greenhouse thrips damage to coffee.

PROBLEM: Young leaves are severely curled and distorted. Parts of the leaf may die and turn black, or the entire leaf may drop from the plant. Or leaves are flecked and appear bleached or silvery, often becoming papery and wilted. Shiny black spots may cover the surfaces. Flowers and buds may also be affected. They either fail to open properly or are brown and distorted. Minute (1/25 inch), white or yellow, spindle-shaped insects and black or brown winged insects are barely visible either inside the distorted leaves and flowers or on the undersides of the leaves. Heavily infested plants may be stunted.

ANALYSIS: Thrips
Thrips are a common pest of many garden and greenhouse plants. Some species cause leaf or flower distortion; others cause a flecking of the leaves, producing a bleached appearance. Thrips feed by rasping the soft plant tissue, then sucking the released plant sap. Some leaf thrips leave unsightly, black, varnishlike spots of excrement around the areas where they feed. The black or brown adults have wings. They can spread rapidly by flying to new plants; or they may be blown long distances by the wind. They lay their eggs either on the plant or in surrounding weeds. The young are yellow or white and spindle-shaped.

SOLUTION: Spray the leaves or buds and flowers with ORTHO Isotox Insect Killer, ORTHO Orthene Systemic Insect Control, or ORTHO Malathion 50 Insect Spray. Make sure your plant is listed on the product label. Remove and destroy infested buds and flowers.

Air pollution damage.

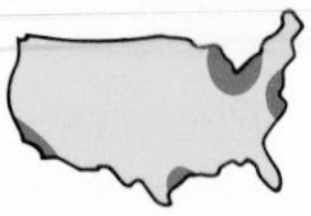

PROBLEM: Upper surfaces of leaves are stippled or flecked black, purple, or white. Dark spots soon fade to tan or brown. Or the tissue between the veins turns gray-green to light brown and bleaches to a light tan after several days. Leaves may curl, and many may drop off the plant. Growth is often slowed, and the plant is weak.

ANALYSIS: Air pollution
The breakdown products of some gases released into the atmosphere by cars and factories damage plants. The most common types of pollution affecting trees and shrubs are ozone and sulfur dioxide. (For more information, see page 855.) Air pollution damage is most commonly a problem in urban areas, but also can occur in rural areas where plants are located downwind from factories. Many different environmental and genetic factors affect a plant's susceptibility to air pollution, causing trees and shrubs to react differently. One plant may show leaf stippling and curling, while an identical plant growing next to it shows no symptoms.

SOLUTION: Air pollution damage cannot be cured or prevented. Because injury from air pollutants is similar in appearance to injury from nutrient deficiencies, insects, diseases, and mites, these problems should be eliminated as causes before attributing the damage to air pollution. Air pollution injury is usually a localized problem. Check with your neighbors to see if the same kinds of plants in their gardens have been affected the same way. If you live in a polluted area, select plants that are tolerant from the list on page 996.

Overwatering damage to viburnums.

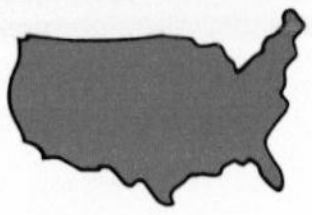

PROBLEM: Leaves turn light green to yellow and may drop. The edges of the leaves may be brown. In many cases, the plant grows very little. It may pull out of the ground easily, because the roots are soft and rotted. The soil is frequently or constantly wet.

ANALYSIS: Overwatering or poor drainage
Overwatering and poor drainage are serious common problems that often kill plants. Roots require air to function normally. Air is contained in tiny pores in the soil. When the soil is watered, air is forced out of the soil pores and replaced with water. If water cannot drain out of the soil, or if it is constantly reapplied, the soil pores remain filled with water. The roots cannot absorb the oxygen they need in such saturated conditions, and they die. As the roots rot, the root system is less able to supply the plant with nutrients and water, resulting in starvation and eventually the death of the plant.

SOLUTION: Do not apply water so frequently that the soil is constantly wet. Depending on the particular requirements of your tree or shrub (see cultural information for your specific plant in the alphabetical section beginning on page 442), allow the soil to dry partially or completely between waterings. If your soil drains poorly, improve drainage as described on page 907.

Nitrogen-deficient fuchsia.

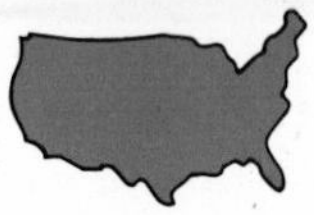

PROBLEM: Leaves turn yellow and may drop, beginning with the older leaves. New leaves are small, and growth is slow.

ANALYSIS: Lack of nitrogen
Nitrogen, one of the most important nutrients for plant growth, is deficient in most soils. Nitrogen is essential in the formation of green leaf pigment, and in many other compounds necessary for plant growth. When they are short on nitrogen, plants take nitrogen from their older leaves for new growth. Poorly drained, over-watered, compacted, and cold soils are often infertile. Plants growing in these soils often show symptoms of nitrogen deficiency. Various soil problems and other nutrient deficiencies also cause leaf discoloration. Study the symptoms carefully.

SOLUTION: For a quick response, spray the leaves and the soil beneath the plant with Ra-Pid-Gro Plant Food. Fertilize plants regularly with ORTHO Evergreen Tree & Shrub Food, ORTHO General Purpose Plant Food, or a fertilizer for a specific type of plant, such as ORTHO Rose Food. (For more information about fertilizers, see page 911.) ORTHO Blood Meal, which contains nitrogen in a long-lasting, slow-release form, can be used to supplement regular feeding. Add organic amendments to compacted soils and those low in organic matter, and improve drainage in poorly drained soils. (For more information about organic matter and drainage, see pages 930 and 907.) Do not keep the soil constantly wet. (For more information about watering, see page 912.)

Seasonal leaf drop on holly.

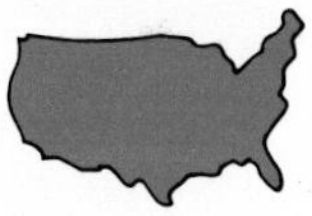

PROBLEM: Older needles or the leaves nearest the trunk or main stem turn yellow, reddish, or brown and drop. Or all the leaves drop off the plant. This condition may develop over a few days or several weeks.

ANALYSIS: Seasonal leaf drop

1. *Evergreen plants:*

This is a natural process similar to the dropping of leaves by deciduous plants. Evergreen leaves normally have a life span of 2 to 4 years. Leaf drop may occur every year, or only every second or third year. When growing conditions have been favorable the previous season, leaf shedding occurs over several weeks and is less noticeable. However, if the plant has been exposed to unfavorable conditions during the growing season, such as drying, or a spider mite or insect infestation, leaf drop develops within a few days. Some plants, such as arborvitae, drop their foliage in the fall. Holly leaf drop occurs in late winter. Many western trees drop old leaves in the spring, as new leaves are formed. Pines drop their needles at various times of the year, depending on the species. Leaf drop is also caused by new growth shading older, interior growth.

2. *Deciduous plants:*

In autumn, many trees and shrubs drop all their leaves as they become dormant before winter arrives. The leaves often turn beautiful colors before falling. If the plant is weak from poor growing conditions, diseases, or pests, leaf fall may develop prematurely, often in midsummer. A few plants, such as California buckeye, normally drop their leaves in midsummer.

SOLUTION: No control measures are necessary.

Iron-deficient azalea.

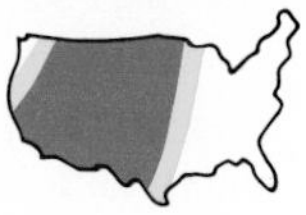

PROBLEM: Leaves turn pale green or yellow. The newest leaves (those at the tips of the stems) are most severely affected. Except in extreme cases, the veins of affected leaves remain green. Older leaves may remain green. The plant may be stunted.

ANALYSIS: Iron deficiency

Plants frequently suffer from deficiencies of iron and other minor nutrients, such as manganese and zinc, elements essential to normal plant growth and development. Deficiencies can occur when one or more of these elements are depleted in the soil. Often these minor nutrients are present in the soil, but alkaline (pH 7.5 or higher) or wet soil conditions cause them to form compounds that cannot be used by the plant. An alkaline condition can result from overliming, or from lime leached from cement or brick. Regions where soil is derived from limestone, and those with low rainfall, usually have alkaline soils.

SOLUTION: To correct the nutrient deficiency, spray the foliage with ORTHO Greenol Liquid Iron, and apply it to the soil around the plants. Apply ORTHO Aluminum Sulfate or ORTHO Orthorix Spray to correct the pH. (For more information about pH, see page 908.) Treating the soil with *ferrous sulfate* may also correct the pH of the soil. Place it in holes (6 inches deep for shrubs and 2 feet deep for trees) around the tree under the branches, and water it in well. Maintain an acid pH by fertilizing with ORTHO Azalea, Camellia & Rhododendron Food. When planting in an area with alkaline soil, add a handful of *soil sulfur*; or add at least 50 percent peat moss to the soil and mix it in well.

Lawn mower blight on oak.

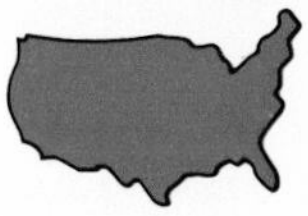

PROBLEM: Leaves are small and discolored, and often drop prematurely. Twigs may die. The plant is stunted and in a general state of decline. Bark at the base of the trunk is wounded. The tree is planted in a lawn.

ANALYSIS: Lawn mower blight

Trees growing in lawns may be severely injured by slight but repeated injuries to the bark from lawn mowers. Lawn mower blades may also slice through the bark into the wood. Nutrients and water cannot pass through the damaged part of the trunk to reach the top of the tree. In severe cases, young trees are killed. Lawn mower wounds are often entry points for diseases, which may also kill the tree. For more information about bark wounds, see page 435.

SOLUTION: Prune off dying twigs and branches, and fertilize with ORTHO Evergreen, Tree & Shrub Food or ORTHO General Purpose Plant Food. To prevent additional damage to the trunk, kill all grass from around the base of the tree by applying ORTHO Liquid Fence & Grass Edger as directed on the label. Or, install a tree guard to eliminate the need for edging and trimming grass around the trunk.

PROBLEMS COMMON TO MANY TREES, SHRUBS, AND VINES — WEAK OR DYING PLANT

Pines growing in shallow soil.

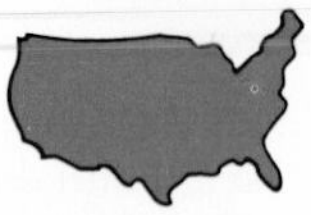

PROBLEM: Leaves are small and discolored, and often drop prematurely. Eventually twigs and then larger branches die. The plant is stunted and in a general state of decline. The tree is planted in soil that is less than 2 feet deep and underlaid with rock or rock-like soil.

ANALYSIS: Shallow soil or hardpan
Large plants growing in shallow soil with rock or hardpan (a rocklike layer of soil) beneath them are stunted and show symptoms of decline. Shallow soils usually do not provide adequate root space for large plants. As plants increase in size, they run out of food and water frequently. These soils usually do not drain during wet weather, so trees planted in them suffer from lack of air in the soil. Because the root system is shallow, the tree is liable to blow over in a storm.

SOLUTION: If possible, move the plant to an area with deeper soil and replace it with shallow-rooted plants. If the plant can't be moved, increase plant vigor by fertilizing and watering regularly. (For more information about fertilizers and watering, see pages 910 and 912.) Prune off any dead and dying branches. Avoid overwatering plants growing over an impervious soil layer. Guy or stake the tree to secure it in storms. If you wish to plant more trees in shallow soil, take one of these precautions. If the underlayment is hardpan, break holes in it as described on page 906. If it is bedrock, add at least 2 feet of soil and plant a tree or shrub that does not grow large. For a list of small trees for areas with restricted root space, see page 1009.

Stunted ash growing in compacted soil.

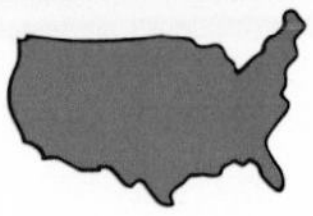

PROBLEM: Leaves are small and discolored, and often drop prematurely. Eventually twigs and then larger branches die. The plant is stunted and in a general state of decline. The soil under the tree is hard and dense, probably from heavy traffic.

ANALYSIS: Compacted soil
Constant vehicle or foot traffic in an area compacts soil. Compacted soil is too dense to admit air. Plant roots, which need air, stop growing or die. Water also enters the soil very slowly, so the tree or shrub suffers frequently from drought. Soil compaction is most common along roads or paths where traffic is heavy. Compacted soil is hard and difficult to probe when digging with a hand trowel or shovel.

SOLUTION: Divert traffic away from plants. If necessary, erect barriers to keep traffic out, using fences, walls, or dense or thorny shrubbery. Remove severely affected plants. Relieve the compaction to a depth of 4 to 6 inches with a soil aerator. Prevent further compaction by planting deep groundcovers, or by covering the compacted area with 2 to 4 inches of stone, crushed rock, or bark mulch. For more information about compaction, see page 906.

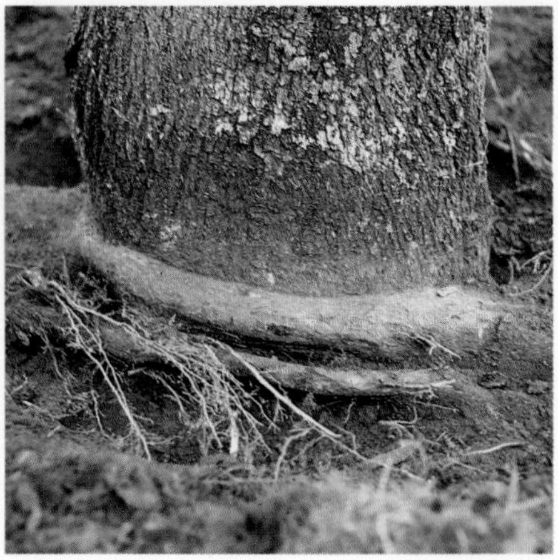

Girdling roots.

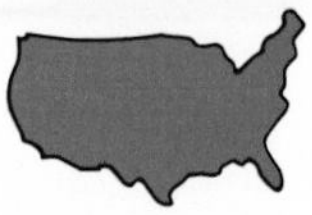

PROBLEM: Tree leaves are small and discolored, and often drop prematurely. Eventually twigs and then larger branches die. The plant is stunted and in a general state of decline. A root is wrapped around the trunk, at or just below the surface of the soil. It completely encircles the trunk, and is imbedded in it.

ANALYSIS: Girdling roots
A girdling root is a root that wraps itself around the main root system or the trunk. As the trunk enlarges, it is strangled by its own root, slowly reducing the flow of nutrients and water to the top of the tree. The girdling root may be visible above ground, or it may develop underground and remain undetected until the tree is in a severe state of decline. Trees with girdling roots often do not have a normal flare where the trunk enters the soil, but plunge directly into the soil like a telephone pole. The trunk may even be slightly constricted. Girdling roots usually develop when a containerized tree is planted or transplanted. If the roots that normally circle the inside of a container are not trimmed, they may eventually girdle the tree. Girdling roots occasionally develop spontaneously in field-grown or wild trees also. The trunk is weakened if it is severely constricted, and may break in a high wind.

SOLUTION: Remove the part of the root that is girdling the trunk. If the girdling root is large (more than a quarter of the diameter of the trunk), prune the tree to compensate for the roots that were lost. If the trunk is severely constricted, guy or stake the tree for a few years to prevent breakage at the narrow point.

Ash trunk injured by wire.

PROBLEM: Leaves are small and discolored, and often drop prematurely. Eventually twigs and then larger branches die. The plant is stunted and in a general state of decline. A large patch of bark is damaged, or a wire circles the trunk and is deeply imbedded in it.

ANALYSIS: Injury to trunk
Anything that slows the flow of water and nutrients through the trunk harms the tree. Since the nutrient and water circulation system of the tree is immediately under the bark, damage to the bark usually interrupts circulation between the tree and its roots. Damage most commonly occurs from a large wound on the trunk. If the wound covers over half the circumference of the trunk, it is major damage and threatens the life of the tree. Wires or cables wrapped around the trunk grow tighter as the trunk expands, cutting into the wood and slowly reducing circulation.

SOLUTION: Remove loose discolored bark splinters and wood from the wound according to the directions given on page 917. Remove any girdling wires and dead or dying branches. Fertilize and water well according to the directions on pages 910 and 912. Do not wrap wires around trees. Use rubber or plastic ties made for the purpose.

Bark beetle damage.

PROBLEM: Leaves are small and discolored, and often drop prematurely. Eventually twigs and larger branches die. The plant is stunted and in a general state of decline. There are many small holes in the bark. Sap, pitch, or sawdust may be coming out of the holes.

ANALYSIS: Bark beetles
Bark beetles may seriously damage older, mature trees growing in the home garden. They usually infest only weakened trees, but trees under stress from drought and healthy trees growing near stressed trees may also be attacked. In the spring, adults fly in search of weak or susceptible trees. When suitable trees are located, the beetles tunnel through the bark, making egg-laying galleries between the bark and the wood. They produce a chemical substance (pheromone) that attracts more beetles; the beetles mate and lay eggs in the galleries. The whitish larvae form tunnels that radiate from the egg gallery and cut off the flow of nutrients and water through the trunk. The larvae mature and may emerge that season to produce a new generation of beetles. Some beetles also transmit diseases.

SOLUTION: Cut down dead trees and those trees in which 50 percent of the foliage is yellowing. Do not leave infested wood in the area. Burn the wood immediately, or strip off and burn the bark before storing the stripped wood. Spray less severely infested trees with ORTHO Lindane Borer & Leaf Miner Spray. Make sure your tree is listed on the product label. Repeat the spray one month later. Water trees during periods of drought and fertilize weakened trees with ORTHO Evergreen, Tree & Shrub Food .

Dieback caused by injury to roots.

PROBLEM: Leaves turn yellow and then brown. Branches die. The tree declines, usually over a period of several years, and may die. Trenching or construction has occurred under the tree within the past two years.

ANALYSIS: Mechanical injuries to roots
Roots may be severed during excavation for building, trenching for cables and pipes, when soil is tilled, or when there is any other type of activity around a tree that disturbs its roots. Root injuries may be difficult to detect or diagnose. Check the area for overturned soil, patched lawn, or fresh patches of asphalt. If the tree is growing very near a recent construction site and is showing decline symptoms, it is likely that its roots were damaged and then covered with soil. Excavate the soil around the declining tree with a hand trowel to determine if the roots are injured, and the extent of the injury.

SOLUTION: Remove the tree if it is in a severe state of decline. If it is only mildly affected, thin out the branches so the top of the tree is in proportion to the remaining roots. (If 20 percent of the roots are damaged, prune off 20 percent of the branches.) If the roots are uncovered, refill the hole as soon as possible. Water during dry periods. In the future, avoid excavating or trenching around plants. If it is unavoidable, cut as few roots as possible. Dig as far away from the trunk as possible. If the trench must pass near the tree, fewer roots will be damaged if you tunnel under the tree rather than trench next to it.

PROBLEMS COMMON TO MANY TREES, SHRUBS, AND VINES — WEAK OR DYING PLANT

Root nematode damage.

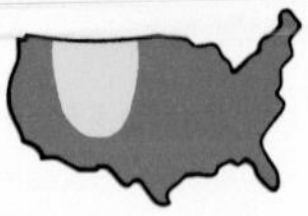

PROBLEM: Leaves are small and discolored, and often drop prematurely. Eventually twigs and then larger branches die. The plant is stunted and in a general state of decline.

ANALYSIS: Root nematodes
Root nematodes are microscopic worms that live in the soil. They feed on plant roots, damaging and stunting them, or causing them to become enlarged. The damaged roots can't supply sufficient water and nutrients to the aboveground plant parts, and the plant is stunted or slowly dies. Nematodes are found throughout the United States, especially in areas with moist, sandy loam soils. They can move only a few inches each year on their own, but they may be carried long distances by soil, water, tools, or infested plants. Laboratory testing of roots and soil is the only positive method for confirming the presence of nematodes. Contact your local Cooperative Extension Office (see page 1029) for sampling instructions and addresses of testing laboratories. Soil and root problems such as poor soil structure, drought stress, overwatering, nutrient deficiency, and root rots can also produce symptoms of decline similar to those caused by nematodes. These problems should be eliminated as causes before sending soil and root samples for testing.

SOLUTION: There are no chemicals available to homeowners to kill nematodes in planted soil. However, they can be controlled before planting by soil fumigation. For information on fumigating soil, see page 927.

Paving over roots.

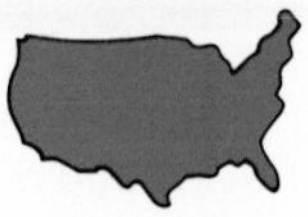

PROBLEM: Leaves turn yellow and then brown. Branches die back. The tree declines, usually over a period of several years, and may die. A large part of the soil under the tree has been recently paved.

ANALYSIS: Paving over roots
Impervious soil coverings, such as cement and asphalt, placed over the roots of an established tree may kill the tree. The greater the coverage of roots, the more likely it is that the tree will die. The supply of water and air to the roots is blocked, stopping their growth and eventually killing them. Some species of trees are more resistant than others, and young trees are more resistant than established trees. In areas where the water table is high, some trees may survive. Soil sterilants, often used by paving companies to kill weeds, will increase the probability of the tree dying.

SOLUTION: Remove the tree if it is in a severe state of decline. If the tree shows only mild symptoms and it is a valuable specimen, it may be saved by removing the pavement. Before laying pavement in the future, protect trees by installing a system of tile pipes in gravel under the paving, which allows for the passage of water and air. If it is necessary to kill weeds, use a weed killer rather than a soil sterilant.

Some trees that can tolerate paving over their roots are: *Ailanthus altissima* (tree of heaven), *Ficus retusa* (laurel fig), *Fraxinus* species (ash), *Morus* species (mulberry), and *Ulmus parvifolia* (Chinese elm).

Balled roots.

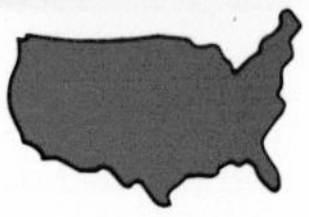

PROBLEM: Leaves are small and discolored, and often drop prematurely. Eventually twigs and then larger branches die. The plant is stunted and in a general state of decline. The plant is not firmly rooted, but may be rocked back and forth in the soil or pulled out easily.

ANALYSIS: Balled roots
Balled roots develop when the roots remain in the original soil ball instead of growing into the surrounding soil. This occurs when the planting hole is improperly prepared or when pot-bound plants are set in the ground without having their roots trimmed. Container plants are usually grown in a light soil mix. If they are placed in soil that is heavy, poorly aerated, or soggy, the roots may not grow into it. Instead, the roots twine around the original soil until they form a hard, tangled mass and can no longer supply adequate moisture. Container plants that sit in a nursery for a long time before they are sold become pot-bound. If roots are not trimmed, they will continue to grow in the original soil ball rather than growing out into the soil of the planting site. A plant with balled roots will become stunted and decline. It may blow over in a storm.

SOLUTION: If the planting hole was improperly prepared, remove the plant and add soil amendments to lighten the surrounding soil. (For more information about preparing a planting hole, see page 924.) Before replanting, untangle and prune the balled roots so they will grow into the surrounding soil. When planting container plants, trim roots to encourage new growth out of the soil ball. Keep the plant well watered until it becomes established.

Spruce killed by gas leak.

PROBLEM: The plant slowly or suddenly turns brown and dies. Lawn and flowers surrounding the plant usually die, and nearby trees and shrubs may turn yellow or slowly die. Soil removed from around the roots of the dying plant is very dark and smells like rotten eggs. An underground gas line runs within 100 feet of the plant.

ANALYSIS: Gas leak
Major leaks from underground natural gas pipes can cause severe injury or sudden death to nearby plants. Natural gas is not toxic to plants, but it forces the air out of the soil. Oxygen in the soil is necessary for plant growth. Methane-consuming bacteria use up any remaining oxygen. When oxygen is unavailable, roots die and the tree starves. In addition, other toxic compounds may be formed. A rotten egg smell may be noticed in the area, caused by bacteria that release sulfur compounds. Plants near the leak often die quickly, and plants further away decline slowly. Gas injury can also occur where plantings are made over or within several hundred feet of a landfill in which organic materials have been buried. The organic materials produce gas as they decompose. Sometimes utility companies will send manufactured gas (produced from coal or coke) through lines during peak loads when there is not enough natural gas. If there is a leak, manufactured gas will kill plants quickly.

SOLUTION: If you suspect a gas leak, contact your local utility company. Remove dead plants. The soil beneath the plant should be aerated to flush out the gas. Contact a professional arborist to aerate the soil.

Tree death caused by grade change.

Tree decline due to construction and grade change.

PROBLEM: Leaves turn yellow and may drop. Branches die. The tree declines, usually over a period of several years, and may die. The soil level under the tree was recently changed, either raised or lowered.

ANALYSIS: Grade change
Raising or lowering the level of the soil (the grade) around trees can be very damaging. If the grade has been raised, the tree emerges from the soil in a straight line (no flare at the base of the trunk). If the grade has been lowered, roots are exposed.

1. *Grade raised:* A large quantity of soil dumped around a tree usually suffocates the roots by cutting off their supply of air and water. The extent of damage depends on the kind of tree, its age and condition, the type and depth of fill, and how much of the root system is covered. Young, healthy trees are much more tolerant than old trees, and soil containing gravel or sand causes less severe injury than heavy clay soil. If only a portion of the root system is covered, or if the fill is relatively shallow (less than 3 inches of porous soil or less than 1 to 2 inches of clay soil), the tree will be weakened, but it does not usually die. Severe decline symptoms (progressive dieback from the top down) often do not occur for several years. Insects or diseases may kill the weakened plant sooner than it would have been killed otherwise.

2. *Grade lowered:* Many roots may be severed when soil is removed from around a tree, and exposed roots will dry out. The number and size of the roots severed determines the extent of damage. Cutting large roots close to the trunk is more likely to kill the tree than cutting the ends of roots. The plant is often unstable, and may blow down in a strong wind.

SOLUTION: Once the decline symptoms develop, considerable damage has already occurred.

1. By the time symptoms caused by raising the grade are noticed, it is usually too late to do anything. If possible, remove the fill if there are no symptoms and it has been around the tree for less than one growing season. If the tree is in a severe state of decline, remove it. If decline symptoms are not severe and fill is less than 12 inches deep, therapeutic treatments may save the tree. Remove all dead and dying branches and remove the soil from around the base of the trunk. Dig holes to the original soil level every few feet over the entire root area (under the branches) and place 6-inch bell tiles in the holes. In the future, valuable trees to be filled over should be protected by installing tile pipes in a thick bed of gravel covered with a minimum amount of fill. For a list of trees that are severely, moderately, or rarely damaged by fill, see page 1011.

2. Remove the tree if it is in a severe state of decline caused by lowering the grade. Unstable trees should be cabled to a stable object or removed. For trees with symptoms, prune off damaged roots and torn bark. Cut back the top growth so it is in balance with the remaining roots (if 20 percent of the roots are damaged, cut off 20 percent of the branches). Water trees during dry periods.

PROBLEMS COMMON TO MANY TREES, SHRUBS, AND VINES — WEAK OR DYING PLANT

Tree decline caused by poor drainage.

PROBLEM: Leaves are small, and discolored, and often drop prematurely. Eventually twigs and then larger branches die. The plant is stunted and in a general state of decline. The soil is constantly wet, either from frequent watering or because the soil drains slowly.

ANALYSIS: Overwatering
Many trees and shrubs do not grow well in soil that is constantly wet. This condition is most common around lawns, especially when the soil drains slowly. Lawns need much more water than do most trees and shrubs. When the soil is constantly wet, the roots cannot absorb the oxygen they need to function normally, they begin to decay, and the plant slowly declines. This problem is very common in areas of low rainfall when lawns are planted around established plants or native trees that cannot tolerate the increased soil moisture.

SOLUTION: Do not continually apply water so that the soil is constantly wet. Depending on the requirements of your tree or shrub (see cultural information for your specific plant), allow the soil to dry partially or fully between waterings. If possible, move the tree or shrub to a new location with better drainage. (For more information about transplanting, see page 924.) Replace it with a plant that tolerates poor drainage (for a list, see page 1010), or improve the drainage (see page 907). If the plant cannot be moved, water it less frequently. Cover the area under the tree with a mulch, or with a groundcover that requires little water.

Stunted ginkgo growing in a lawn.

PROBLEM: The tree or shrub is growing very slowly. Leaves may turn yellow, and twigs may die. The plant is growing in a lawn.

ANALYSIS: Lawn competition
The growth of plants can be retarded by grass growing over their roots. A lawn requires large amounts of fertilizer. Lawns will deplete the soil of nutrients that are necessary for vigorous growth of a tree or large shrub planted in it.

SOLUTION: If lawn is growing around a recently planted tree, remove an area of lawn at least 30 inches in diameter from around the trunk (18 to 24 inches is adequate for shrubs). Fertilize with ORTHO Evergreen, Tree & Shrub Food or ORTHO General Purpose Plant Food. This area can be mulched, or planted with flowers. As the plant grows, enlarge the cleared area. If you wish to keep a lawn under the tree or shrub, fertilize the plant as growth starts each spring with ORTHO Evergreen, Tree & Shrub Food, placed in holes 4 feet apart under the drip line (tips of outer branches). Make holes 2 feet deep with a crowbar or soil auger and pour in the fertilizer, using a total of 2 cups for each 1 inch diameter of tree trunk. For young trees—1 to 2 inches in diameter—use 1 cup of fertilizer; use ½ cup for trees under 1 inch in diameter. For shrubs, apply ½ cup of plant food for each 3 feet of height. Water the plant well after fertilizing. Plant trees adapted to growing in a lawn; for a list, see page 1009.

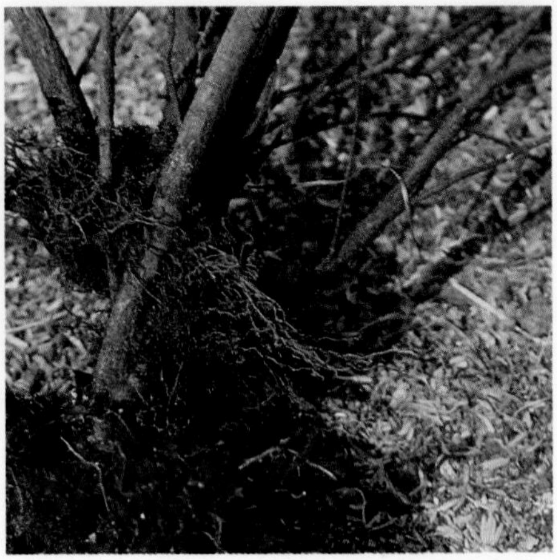

Root weevil damage to azalea.

PROBLEM: Leaves are small and discolored, and often drop prematurely. Eventually twigs and then larger branches die. The plant is stunted and in a general state of decline. If soil is removed from around the base of the plant, exposing some roots, small rootlets or bark on the roots are seen to be chewed. White grubs may be found in the soil around the roots.

ANALYSIS: Root weevil larvae
Root weevil larvae, called *grubs*, infest the roots of many ornamental plants. The damage caused by the white, legless grubs is often so gradual that the insects are well established before injury is apparent. If the grubs remain undetected, the plant may die abruptly with the onset of hot, dry weather. Female weevils lay eggs at the soil line near the stem during the summer months. The emerging grubs burrow into the soil. They feed on the roots in the fall, and then spend the winter in the soil. Most root weevils cause their major damage in the spring. Their feeding girdles the roots and stems, disrupting the flow of nutrients and water through the plant and causing the roots and the top of the plant to die.

SOLUTION: Discard dying plants. To prevent the next generation of weevils from causing damage, eliminate the adults. Spray the foliage and the ground under the plant with ORTHO Orthene Systemic Insect Control or ORTHO Isotox Insect Killer. Contact your Cooperative Extension Office (see page 1029) for the time of weevil emergence in your area. Before spraying, make sure that your plant is listed on the product label. Repeat the spray two more times three weeks apart.

BRANCHES DIE

Fireblight on crabapple.

Dog urine damage to boxwood.

Canker on sycamore.

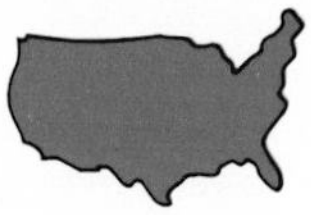

PROBLEM: Blossoms and leaves of some twigs suddenly wilt and turn black as if scorched by fire. Leaves curl and hang downward. The bark at the base of the blighted twig becomes water-soaked, then dark, sunken, and dry; cracks may develop at the edge of the sunken area. In warm, moist spring weather drops of brown ooze appear on the sunken bark.

ANALYSIS: Fireblight
This disease is caused by a bacterium (*Erwinia amylovora*) that is very destructive to many trees and shrubs. (For a list of susceptible plants, see page 1016.) The bacteria spend the winter in the sunken areas (cankers) on the branches. In the spring, the bacteria ooze out of the cankers and are carried by insects to the plant blossoms. Flies and other insects are attracted to the sweet, sticky ooze and become smeared with it. When the insects visit a flower for nectar, they infect it with the bacteria. The bacteria spread rapidly through the plant tissue in warm (65°F or higher), humid weather. Bees visiting these infected blossoms carry bacteria-laden nectar to healthy blossoms. Rain, wind, and tools may also spread the bacteria.

SOLUTION: During spring and summer, prune out infected branches about 12 inches beyond any visible discoloration and destroy. Sterilize the pruning tools with rubbing alcohol after each cut. A protective spray of a pesticide containing *basic copper sulfate* or *streptomycin* applied before bud break in the spring helps prevent infection. Repeat at intervals of 5 to 7 days until the end of bloom. In summer or fall, after the disease stops spreading, prune out infected branches.

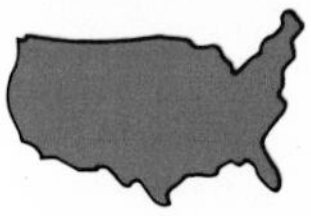

PROBLEM: Branches are dying. The leaves usually turn brown and may drop off. In some cases there may be wounds or sunken, dark-colored lesions on the dead branches, or there may be holes in the branches surrounded by sawdust or sap. Dogs may be seen in the area.

ANALYSIS: Twig or branch dieback Dieback can result from any of several causes:	**SOLUTION:** The numbered solutions below correspond to the numbers in the analysis.
1. *Mechanical injury:* Any type of injury that causes a wound may kill branches. Branches on shrubs or trees may be wounded by motor vehicles, animals, wires, nails, or tools. If the wound girdles the branch, nutrients and water can't reach the leaves and the branch dies. Wounds are also entrance points for many diseases and pests.	**1.** Dying limbs with large wounds that almost girdle the branch should be removed. Repair small wounds by removing ragged edges and dead bark. (For more information about bark wounds, see page 917.) Avoid wounding plants. Do not use bare wire on branches, and do not nail anything to trees. If necessary, place protective barriers around plants to prevent damage. Do not plant trees and shrubs in areas where they are likely to be hit by vehicles or trampled.
2. *Cankers:* Cankers are sunken dark-colored lesions that are caused by fungi and bacteria. They kill the living tissue underneath the bark, inhibiting the movement of nutrients and water through the tree. If a canker covers as much as half the circumference of a branch, the branch often dies.	**2.** For more information about cankers and their controls, see page 424.
3. *Borers:* Borers are the larvae of beetles or moths. The larvae feed by tunneling through bark, sapwood, and heartwood. This cuts the flow of nutrients and water in that area, killing the branch beyond the tunneling.	**3.** For more information about borers and their controls, see page 424.
4. *Dog urine:* The leaves on branches near the ground turn brown and die when dogs urinate on them. The salts in the urine burn the leaves. Dogs repeat their visits to certain shrubs or hedges, eventually killing branches.	**4.** If a dog has recently urinated on a plant, wash the urine off the leaves and soak the ground around the plant to dilute the salts in the urine. Twigs and branches already damaged may recover. Prune off any dead wood. Protect plants from new damage with ORTHO Scram Dog & Cat Repellent; or erect barriers around the plants.

PROBLEMS COMMON TO MANY TREES, SHRUBS, AND VINES—BRANCHES DIE ■ TREE FALLS OVER

Root rot of juniper.

Crown rot of madrone.

Internal decay.

PROBLEM: The normal leaf color dulls, and the plant loses vigor. Leaves may wilt or turn yellow or light brown. Major branches or the entire plant may die. The roots and lower stems are brownish, and the roots are often decayed. Fine woolly brown strands may form on the roots, and white powdery spores form on the soil surface. Or fan-shaped plaques of white strands may appear between the bark and wood of the roots and lower stems.

ANALYSIS: Root and crown rots
Root and crown rots are caused by any of several different fungi that live in the soil and on roots.

SOLUTION: The numbered solutions below correspond to the numbers in the analysis.

1. *Phytophthora* species: These fungi cause browning and decaying on the roots and browning of the lower stems. The plant usually dies slowly; however, young plants may wilt and die rapidly. The disease is most prevalent in heavy, waterlogged soils. For more information about *Phytophthora*, see page 849.

1. Remove dead and dying plants. When replanting, use plants that are resistant to *Phytophthora.* (For a list of resistant trees and shrubs, see page 1016.) Improve soil drainage (see page 907). Avoid overwatering plants.

2. *Phymatotrichum omnivorum:* This fungus causes the disease commonly known as *cotton root rot* or *Texas root rot.* It is a serious problem on many plants in the Southwest. The plant may suddenly wilt and die. Brown strands form on the roots, and white powdery spores form on the soil. The disease is most severe in heavy, alkaline soils. For more information about *Phymatotrichum*, see page 851.

2. Remove dead and dying plants. When replanting, buy only resistant plants. (For a list of resistant trees and shrubs, see page 1016.) Before planting, increase the soil acidity by adding 1 pound of *ammonium sulfate* for every 10 square feet of soil. Make a circular ridge around the planting area and fill the basin with 4 inches of water. Repeat the treatment in 5 to 10 days.

3. *Armillaria mellea:* This fungus causes a disease that is commonly known as *shoestring root rot*, *mushroom root rot*, or *oak root fungus. Armillaria* is identified by the presence of fan-shaped plaques of white fungal strands between the bark and the wood of the roots and lower stems. This fungus grows rapidly under wet conditions. Honey-colored mushrooms appear at the base of the plant in the fall. For more information about *Armillaria*, see page 851.

3. Remove dead and dying plants. The life of a newly infected plant may be prolonged if the disease has not reached the lower stems. Expose the base of the plant to air for several months by removing 3 to 4 inches of soil. Prune off diseased roots. Use a fertilizer to stimulate growth. (For more information about fertilizing trees and shrubs, see page 910.) When replanting, use only resistant plants. (For a list of plants resistant to *Armillaria*, see page 1016.) Avoid overwatering plants (see page 849).

PROBLEM: The plant bends over or the trunk breaks at or above the soil line.

ANALYSIS: Internal decay
This condition is caused by fungi that enter the tree through wounds. Healthy and vigorous trees may stop the spread of decay by walling off the invaded area. Old trees with many wounds often have little resistance against microorganisms, and decay spreads through the wood. There is usually enough healthy tissue left to keep the branches and leaves alive. But when a storm occurs, or sometimes on a calm day, the entire tree may crack in the decayed area and fall over. This condition can also develop on single branches.

SOLUTION: If only part of the plant has fallen, inspect the rest of it to determine the extent of decay. It may be necessary to contact a professional arborist. The entire plant should be removed if decay is extensive. Avoid wounding plants, and keep them in a vigorous growing condition by fertilizing and watering regularly. (For more information about fertilizers and watering, see pages 910 and 912.)

Broken trunk.

Shallow roots.

Tree blown over by wind.

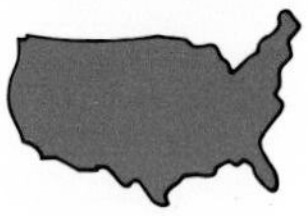

PROBLEM: The plant bends over and the trunk breaks. Breaks usually occur at or below discolored sunken lesions (cankers) on the trunk.

ANALYSIS: Cankers and canker rots

Cankers are localized dead areas on the bark and wood that begin at a wound. They are caused by disease, mechanical injury, or sunscald, or develop where branches have been cut off. (For more information about cankers, see page 424.) Microorganisms inhibit the normal healing process, preventing wounds from closing. The tissue appears sunken, and is often surrounded by callus tissue, a barklike growth of cells. These cankered areas lose the normal flexibility of wood. When a strong wind occurs, the plant cracks at the canker and falls. *Canker rots* develop when microorganisms attack healthy wood adjacent to and beneath a canker. Tree trunks or branches with this condition are more likely to fall because both the canker and wood decay are weakening the tree.

SOLUTION: Once the plant has fallen, there is nothing that can be done. In the future, avoid wounding plants. If you notice a large canker on the trunk, check to see if it is surrounded by callus tissue. If it is, the wound is healing properly and is less likely to become a canker rot. If little or no callus tissue surrounds the canker, and the canker appears sunken, decay may be starting. Consult a professional arborist to determine the possibility of the plant falling. To encourage wound healing, fertilize and water the plant regularly.

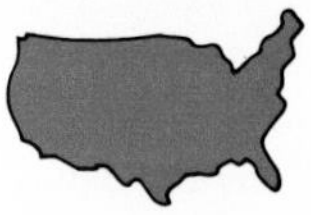

PROBLEM: The entire plant falls over with part or all of the roots attached.

ANALYSIS: Tree falls over

Anything that drastically affects the size or strength of the roots may decrease the stability of the tree.

SOLUTION: If the plant is only leaning slightly, saturate the soil and force the plant upright. Stake or wire it in place.

1. *Root rot:* A number of different soil fungi and bacteria cause the roots to rot. When the roots decay, they lose their ability to support the plant. The plant may fall when the foliage still appears healthy, or it may turn brown first. Only a few of the roots may be attached when the plant falls.

1. Once the plant has fallen, nothing can be done. In the future, avoid wounding roots, a common entrance point for root rot organisms. Do not overwater plants (see page 912), and keep them in a vigorous growing condition. For more information about root rots, see page 849.

2. *Severed roots:* Roots may be severed during construction where trenching and earthmoving equipment is used. The number and size of the roots severed determines the probability of the plant falling.

2. Avoid severing roots during construction activities, especially large supporting roots. If damaging many of the roots is unavoidable, either remove the plant or brace it. For more information about bracing, see page 916.

3. *Wet soil:* Plants growing in excessively wet soil may fall, especially after a long period of rain, when the soil no longer gives good support. A leaning tree, or one pushed by the wind, can pull loose. Plants with shallow root systems are most susceptible.

3. Do not keep the soil constantly wet. If you live in an area that receives heavy rains, cable or brace the plant (see page 916), or provide additional drainage. For more information about improving soil drainage, see page 907.

4. *Shallow roots:* Plants with a shallow root system may fall during strong winds. Those growing in compacted, shallow, or soggy soil, or where surface watering has been practiced, generally have shallow root systems.

4. For ways to encourage deeper root systems, see page 428.

5. *Undeveloped root system:* Young plants, or plants with girdled or balled roots, have root systems that may not support the rest of the plant. During a storm with high winds, the plant may blow over. The attached roots appear bunched or twisted.

5. Stake young trees (see page 917). Prevent girdled and balled roots by using proper planting techniques (see page 924). For more information about girdled and balled roots and their remedies, see page 434.

PROBLEMS OF INDIVIDUAL TREES, SHRUBS, AND VINES

This section is arranged alphabetically by the botanical name of each plant. If you are not familiar with the botanical name of your plant, check the index on page 406.

ABIES (FIR)

ADAPTATION: Zones 4 through 7. (To determine your zone, see the map on page 1020.) Not adapted to hot, dry areas.

LIGHT: Full sun.

SOIL: Grows best in well-drained, non-alkaline (below pH 7.0) soils.

FERTILIZER: Fertilize with ORTHO Evergreen, Tree & Shrub Food according to label directions.

WATER:

How much: Apply enough water to wet the soil 3 to 4 feet deep. To determine the proper amount of water for your soil type, see page 912.

How often: Firs grow best in moist soils. Water when the soil is moist but not wet 4 inches below the surface. For more information about watering, see page 912.

PRUNING: Plant firs in open areas where they have room to spread. Do not prune off branches unless necessary. New side growth can be sheared to develop a dense, bushy tree. New growth will not usually develop on the lower trunk if a limb is removed. To avoid altering the pyramidal growth of the tree, do not prune off the top.

Spruce budworm (twice life size).

PROBLEM: Needles on the ends of branches are chewed and webbed together. In mid-July the branch ends often turn reddish brown. Branches or the entire tree may die after 3 to 5 years of defoliation. Reddish brown caterpillars, $1\frac{1}{4}$ inches long, with yellow or white raised spots, are feeding on the needles.

ANALYSIS: Spruce budworms
(*Choristoneura* species)
Spruce budworms are very destructive to ornamental spruce, fir, and Douglas fir, and may infest pine, larch, and hemlock. The budworm is cyclical. It comes and goes in epidemics 10 or more years apart. The moths are small ($\frac{1}{2}$ inch long) and grayish, with bands and spots of brown. The females lay pale green eggs in clusters on the needles in late July and August. The larvae that hatch from these eggs crawl to hiding places in the bark or in lichen mats; or they are blown by the wind to other trees, where they hide. The tiny larvae spin a silken case and hibernate until spring. In May, when the weather warms, the caterpillars tunnel into needles. As they grow, they feed on opening buds; later they chew off needles and web them together. The larvae feed for about 5 weeks, pupate on twigs, and emerge as adults.

SOLUTION: Spray with an insecticide containing ORTHO Isotox Insect Killer when the buds begin to grow in late May.

Balsam twig aphid damage.

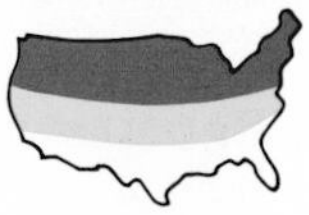

PROBLEM: The youngest needles are curled and twisted, with their lighter underside turned upward. Some needles are killed. Young twigs are twisted and bark is roughened. Shoots may become saturated with a shiny, sticky secretion called honeydew so that needles adhere to one another. A black sooty mold may grow on the honeydew. Tiny (1/8 inch) waxy bluish gray adult or pale green immature, soft-bodied insects cluster on the shoots.

ANALYSIS: Balsam twig aphid
(*Mindarus abietinus*)
The twig aphid does little damage in small numbers. However, aphids are extremely prolific and populations can rapidly build up to damaging numbers during the growing season. Damage occurs when the aphid sucks the juices from the fir shoots. The aphid is unable to digest fully all the sugar in the sap and excretes the excess in a fluid called honeydew. The honeydew often drops onto the shoots or other plants below. A sooty mold fungus may develop on the honeydew, causing the fir leaves to appear black and dirty. Late in the summer, females lay several large (1/10 inch) eggs, covered with tiny rods of white wax, in bark crevices. The eggs are conspicuous and are a useful index of the amount of injury that may occur during the next year.

SOLUTION: Control with ORTHO Orthene Systemic Insect Control or ORTHO Malathion 50 Insect Spray in late April or early May to kill aphids when they first appear. Repeat spray in mid-May if the tree becomes reinfested.

Tussock moth damage. *Insert:* Larva (life size).

PROBLEM: Much of the foliage is eaten, starting at the top of the tree and progressing downward. The entire tree may be defoliated in one season. Trees that lose most of their needles a second year are usually killed. Inch-long, hairy, gray or light brown caterpillars with tufts of orange hairs on their backs may be feeding on the needles.

ANALYSIS: Douglas fir tussock moth (*Orgyia pseudotsugata*)
Douglas fir tussock moth populations are cyclical. Every 7 to 10 years, forest populations build up to epidemic proportions. When this occurs, true firs, Douglas fir, spruce, pine, and larch may be completely defoliated. In cities, damaging numbers may be found every year. In mid to late summer the hairy, wingless female moths lay their eggs in a frothy substance covered with a layer of hairlike scales. When the eggs hatch the following spring, the caterpillars begin feeding on the new needles at the top of the tree. As the younger foliage is devoured the caterpillars move downward, feeding on older needles. Large numbers of tan excrement pellets accumulate around the base of the tree. Since conifers do not replace their old needles, defoliated trees are often killed after two seasons. Less severely damaged trees may be killed later by bark beetles. In August, the caterpillars pupate to emerge as adults.

SOLUTION: Spray with an insecticide containing ORTHO Orthene Systemic Insect Control when caterpillars or damage are first noticed in May or early June. Repeat the spray 2 weeks later if damage continues.

Balsam woolly aphid damage.

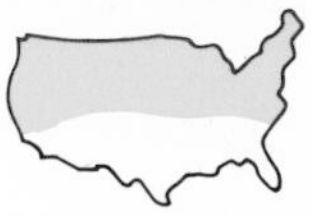

PROBLEM: The ends of twigs swell, forming knobs. The trunk, limbs, and needles may be covered by white, woolly masses or a dirty white crust. Young needles gradually turn yellow from the tip down and drop off. No new growth is evident. More susceptible species, such as balsam fir or subalpine fir, may be killed before swelling on terminal growth occurs.

ANALYSIS: Balsam woolly aphid
(*Adelges piceae*)
This small, soft-bodied insect is a pest only of true firs. The adult is covered by dense, white, woolly material. When this substance is removed, the minute wingless insect appears purplish to black. The adult lays eggs on the bark of fir trees in early spring. These eggs hatch into tiny spiderlike "crawlers" that are blown long distances by the wind. Once the aphid has found a suitable tree it sucks the juices from the needles. A growth-promoting substance is injected into the tree at the same time, causing the swelling of the branch tips. The wood becomes reddish and brittle. As the insect matures it becomes immobile, the legs atrophy, and it secretes white filaments of wax that eventually cover its body.

SOLUTION: Spray with ORTHO Orthene Systemic Insect Control or ORTHO Malathion 50 Insect Spray when woolly tufts first appear in early spring. The insects will be killed but the woolly material will remain on the tree. Thorough coverage is necessary to achieve adequate control. To penetrate the waxy filaments, high-pressure equipment should be used. A fall spray may help control overwintering insects on the tree.

ABIES (FIR)

Spider mite damage.

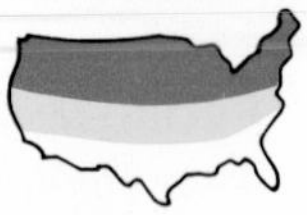

PROBLEM: The needles are stippled yellow and dirty. Sometimes there is a silken webbing on the shoots. Needles may turn brown and fall off. Hot, dry weather favors this problem. To determine if the tree is infested with mites, hold a sheet of white paper underneath some stippled needles and tap the foliage sharply. Tiny dark green or black specks about the size of a pepper grain will drop to the paper and begin to crawl around. The pests are easily seen against the white background.

ANALYSIS: Spruce spider mite
(*Oligonychus ununguis*)
The spruce spider mite is one of the most important pests of firs and many other conifers. It sucks sap from the underside of the needles, causing the stippled appearance. This symptom can be confused with certain types of air pollution damage (see page 855). Spider mites first appear in April or May, hatching from eggs laid at the base of fir needles the previous October. A complete generation may be produced in only seventeen days, so mites can rapidly build up to tremendous numbers during the growing season. Young fir trees may die the first season. If mites are left uncontrolled over a period of years, older trees die progressively from the lower branches upward.

SOLUTION: Control with ORTHO Orthene Insect Spray, ORTHO Isotox Insect Killer, or ORTHO Malathion 50 Insect Spray in early spring to kill young mites of the first generation. Spraying must be repeated three more times, seven to ten days apart, to kill young mites as they hatch from eggs. Additional sprays may be needed in early fall if the tree becomes reinfested.

ACACIA

Thornbugs (half life size).

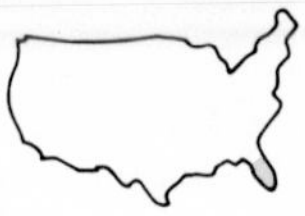

PROBLEM: Groups of ½-inch greenish sucking insects with red or brown markings and sharp spines on their backs are feeding on the tree. Small twigs and branches turn yellow and die.

ANALYSIS: Thornbug
(*Umbonia crassicornis*)
Thornbugs feed by sucking sap from the branches of several types of trees and shrubs, but seem to prefer earleaf acacia (*Acacia auriculiformis*). Large numbers of thornbugs of all sizes may often be found feeding together. Adults are strong fliers, and can travel long distances to find host plants. When large numbers of thornbugs are present, many small branches may be killed. Several generations of thornbugs are produced in a year. The greatest numbers occur during the winter and spring.

SOLUTION: Spray infested trees with an insecticide containing *diazinon* as soon as thornbugs are discovered. Repeat the treatment if the tree becomes reinfested.

Acacia cultural information
Light: Full sun
Water: Drought tolerant once established
Soil: Tolerates many types of soil
Fertilizer: Medium

Mushroom root rot.

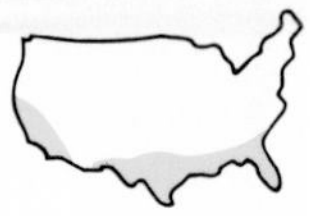

PROBLEM: Leaves turn light green, then yellow, and finally brown, and then fall off. Sometimes only one portion of the tree may be affected, but gradually the entire tree dies. Tan mushrooms may be seen at the base of infected trees. When the tree bark is cut open near the soil line, a white layer of fungal growth can be seen beneath the outer bark on the surface of the wood.

ANALYSIS: Mushroom root rot
Mushroom root rot affects certain species of Acacia, including the earleaf acacia (*acacia auriculiformis*) and the Sydney acacia (*A. floribunda*). This disease is caused by either of two closely related soil-dwelling fungi (*Clitocybe tabescens* and *Armillaria mellea*). *Armillaria* occurs throughout the United States, but is most severe in the West. *Clitocybe* occurs mainly in the Southeast. The fungi invade the root system, and slowly spread through the tree roots. When they enter the main stem, they girdle the stem and kill the tree. Death can occur in a few weeks in small trees, or may take months in large trees.

SOLUTION: There is no practical cure for this disease. By the time symptoms appear, the fungus is too far advanced to stop. In areas where diseased trees have been growing, use only plants that are resistant to mushroom root rot. (For a list of plants resistant to *armillaria*, see page 1016.) The fungi can be eradicated from the soil by fumigation techniques. For information, see page 927.

Some acacias resistant to *armillaria* are *Acacia longifolia*, *A. mearnsii*, and *A. verticillata*.

ACER (MAPLE, BOX ELDER)

ADAPTATION: Throughout the United States.

LIGHT: Full sun to part shade.

SOIL AND PLANTING: Any good, deep, well-drained garden soil. When choosing a planting site, pick an area that will handle the ultimate spread and height of the tree.

FERTILIZER: Fertilize with ORTHO Evergreen, Tree & Shrub Food according to label directions.

WATER:

How much: Apply enough water to wet the soil 3 to 4 feet deep. To determine the proper amount of water for your soil type, see page 912.

How often: Maples prefer moist soil. Water when the soil is moist but no longer wet 4 inches below the surface. For more information about watering, see page 912.

Boxelder bugs (3 times life size).

PROBLEM: New leaves are discolored and distorted. Flowers, seeds, and tender new shoots may also be affected. Small (½ inch) bright red bugs with dark heads may be found on the leaves throughout the summer. Black bugs with reddish lines on their backs may be seen in large numbers around buildings or in homes.

ANALYSIS: Boxelder bugs
(*Leptocoris* species)
Two species of plant bugs feed on boxelder trees, especially the female (seed-bearing) trees. They may also feed on other trees and plants around the home. The red, immature boxelder bugs suck sap from leaves and other plant parts, but they are rarely harmful to the tree. Boxelder bugs are mainly a problem because the black adults are a nuisance around homes. (For more information on boxelder bugs as household pests, see page 791.) Large numbers of adults hibernate inside homes or in the walls of buildings. In the spring, they fly to boxelder trees and lay their eggs in crevices in the bark. The larvae that hatch from these eggs feed until fall, mature, and then migrate back to buildings to spend the winter. In warmer areas of the country there may be two generations of bugs a year.

SOLUTION: Spray infested trees with ORTHO Malathion 50 Insect Spray or ORTHO Diazinon Insect Spray during the summer when insects are first noticed. Wet the tree thoroughly. This will reduce the number of migrating bugs in the fall, although it may not completely eliminate bugs around the home since they can migrate from plants not in the immediate area. Repeat the spray if the tree becomes reinfested.

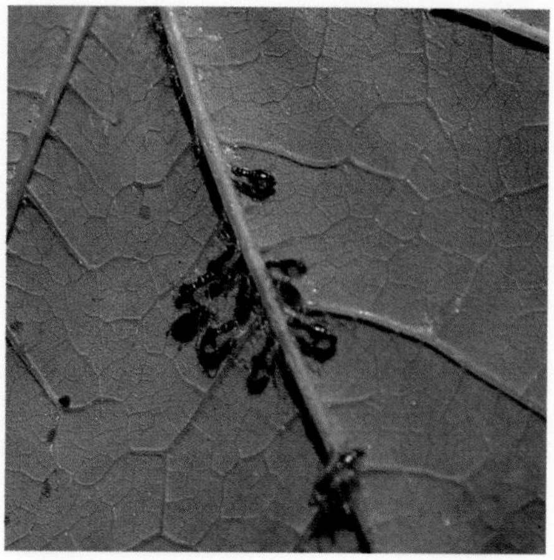

Aphids on maple leaves.

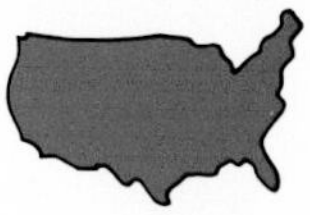

PROBLEM: The newest leaves are wrinkled, discolored, and reduced in size. Leaves may drop off. Silver and Norway maples may be nearly defoliated. A shiny, sticky substance may coat the leaves. A black sooty mold often grows on the sticky substance. Tiny (⅛ inch) green and black, or reddish, soft-bodied insects cluster on the undersides of leaves. Ants may be present.

ANALYSIS: Aphids
(*Periphyllus* and *Drepanaphis* species)
Aphids do little damage in small numbers. However, they are extremely prolific and populations can rapidly build up to damaging numbers during the growing season. Damage occurs when the aphid sucks the juices from the maple leaves. The aphid is unable to fully digest all the sugar in the plant sap and excretes the excess in a fluid called honeydew, which often drops onto the leaves below. Plants or objects beneath the tree may also be coated with honeydew. A sooty mold fungus may develop on the honeydew, causing the maple leaves to appear black and dirty; or rain may wash the honeydew off before the fungus has a chance to grow. Ants feed on this sticky substance, and are often present where there is an aphid infestation.

SOLUTION: Control with ORTHO Orthene Systemic Insect Control or ORTHO Diazinon Insect Spray or ORTHO Isotox Insect Spray when aphids first appear. Direct the spray to the undersides of the leaves. Repeat the spray if the tree becomes reinfested.

ACER (MAPLE, BOX ELDER)

Borer droppings.

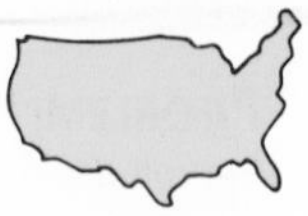

PROBLEM: The foliage is sparse on a branch or at the top of the tree; eventually the twigs and branches die back. Holes or tunnels are apparent in the trunk or branches. The bark may die over the tunnels and slough off, revealing trails. Sap or sawdust sometimes surrounds the holes. Weakened branches may break during wind or snow storms. Weak, young, or newly transplanted trees are most susceptible to injury, and may be killed.

ANALYSIS: Borers

Borers are the larvae of beetles or moths. Many kinds of borers attack maples. Throughout the summer, females lay eggs in bark crevices. The larvae feed by burrowing into the tree and tunneling through the bark, sapwood, or heartwood. This stops the flow of nutrients and water in that area by cutting the conducting vessels; branch and twig dieback result. Sap flow acts as a defense against borers. When the borer burrows into the wood, tree sap fills the hole and drowns the insect. Young or weakened trees are attractive to borers and may not produce enough sap to drown all the borers that invade them.

SOLUTION: Borers are difficult to control once they have burrowed into the wood. Cut out and destroy all dead and dying branches. Young trees that are severely infested should be removed. In spring, spray or paint the trunk and branches with ORTHO Lindane Borer & Leaf Miner Spray to kill young larvae before they burrow into the wood. Repeat two more times at intervals of 2 weeks. Maintain plant health and vigor by watering and fertilizing regularly.

Cottony maple scale (¼ life size).

PROBLEM: The undersides of leaves, stems, or branch crotches are covered with white, cottony, cushionlike masses. Leaves turn yellow and may drop prematurely. Sometimes there is a shiny or sticky substance coating the leaves. A black sooty mold often grows on the sticky substance. Numerous side shoots sometimes grow out of an infested crotch area. Twigs and branches may die back.

ANALYSIS: Cottony scales and mealybugs

Cottony scales and mealybugs are common on maples throughout the United States. The similarities in appearance of these insects make separate identification difficult. They are very conspicuous in late spring and summer because the females are covered with a white, cottony egg sac, containing up to 2500 eggs. The young insects that hatch from these eggs are yellowish brown to green. They feed throughout the summer on the stems and undersides of the leaves. Damage is caused by the withdrawal of plant sap from leaves and branches. The insects are unable to digest fully all the sugar in the sap and they excrete the excess in a fluid called honeydew. The honeydew often drops onto leaves or plants below. A sooty mold fungus may develop in the honeydew, causing the maple leaves and other plants to appear black and dirty. If the insects are not controlled, heavily infested branches may die after several seasons.

SOLUTION: Apply ORTHO Diazinon Insect Spray in midsummer when the young are active. The following spring, when trees are dormant, spray with *lime sulfur* to control insects on the bark.

Galls caused by bladder gall mites.

PROBLEM: In early spring, maple leaf tissue develops irregular, spherical, or bladderlike growths, known as galls, on the upper surfaces of the leaves. Leaves next to the trunk and on large branches are most affected. The galls are yellowish green at first but later turn pinkish to red and finally black. If the galls are numerous, leaves become deformed, and some turn yellow and drop prematurely.

ANALYSIS: Bladder gall mite and spindle gall mite

(*Vasates quadripedes* and *Vasates aceris-crumena*)

Bladder and spindle gall are caused by tiny mites, too small to be seen with the naked eye. Each gall contains one mite. The mites congregate on buds just before they open in the spring. As the buds open, each mite punctures and enters a leaf on the underside, injecting a growth-promoting substance that causes abnormal tissue formation. A gall encloses the mite, with an opening remaining on the underside. The mites feed and females lay eggs inside their galls. The eggs hatch, and as they mature, the young mites crawl out through the opening and infest new leaves. In July, mite activity stops and they migrate to the bark to spend the winter.

SOLUTION: Control measures are not necessary because galls generally cause no serious injury. However, if you wish to prevent unsightly leaves next year, spray buds, branches, and trunk with a *dormant oil spray* or an insecticide containing *dicofol* (KELTHANE®) before the buds start to open in spring.

Phyllosticta leaf spot.

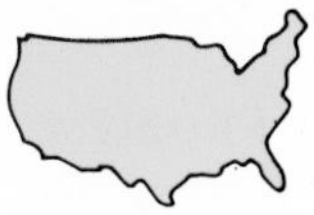

PROBLEM: Spots and blotches appear on the leaves. The spots may be yellow, red, gray, brown, or black. They range in size from being barely visible to ¾ inch in diameter. Several spots may join to form blotches. Leaves may be yellow and dying. Some leaves may drop. Leaf spotting is most severe in humid weather.

ANALYSIS: Fungal leaf spot
There are many different fungi that cause leaf spots; some of the common leaf spot diseases are *tar spot* and *phyllosticta spot.* Leaf spots are unsightly but rarely harmful to the tree. The fungi are spread by wind and splashing water. Spots develop where the fungi enter the tissue. If wet or humid weather persists, the infection spreads through the tissue and blotches form. The fungi survive the winter on twigs and fallen leaves. Most leaf spot organisms do their greatest damage in mild weather (between 50° and 85°F).

SOLUTION: Fungal leaf spots on maples are usually not harmful and do not require control measures. To protect valued specimens, spray with a fungicide containing *zineb*, *mancozeb*, or *basic copper sulfate.* Repeat 3 more times at intervals of 2 weeks. To thoroughly cover leaves on tall branches, use high-pressure equipment. To reduce recurrence next year, rake up and destroy the leaves in the fall.

Leaf scorch.

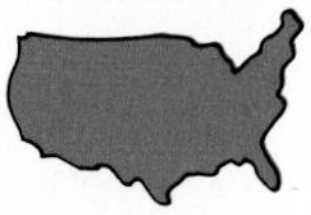

PROBLEM: During hot weather, usually in July or August, leaves turn brown on the edges between the veins. Sometimes the whole leaf dies. Many leaves may drop during late summer. This problem is most severe on the youngest branches. Trees do not generally die.

ANALYSIS: Summer leaf scorch
Leaf scorch is caused by excessive loss of moisture from the leaves due to evaporation. In hot weather, water evaporates rapidly from the leaves. If the roots can't absorb and convey water fast enough to replenish this loss, then the leaves turn brown and wither. This usually occurs in dry soil, but leaves can also scorch when the soil is moist. Drying winds, severed roots, limited soil area, or low temperatures can also cause scorch. For more information about scorch, see page 857.

SOLUTION: To prevent further scorch, deep-water trees during periods of hot weather to wet down the entire root space. (For more information about watering trees, see page 912.) Newly transplanted trees should be watered whenever the rootball is dry 1 inch below the surface. There are no controls for scorch occurring on trees in moist soil. Plant trees adapted to your climate.

Anthracnose on Norway maple.

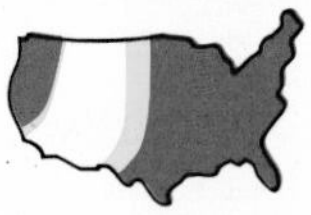

PROBLEM: Irregular, light brown spots of dead tissue appear on the leaf from late May to August. They develop during or just following wet, humid weather. Many spots occur along the veins. They may enlarge and run together, causing the death of the entire leaf. Leaves partially killed appear as if sunscorched. This disease is distinguished from sunscorch by the presence of dark dots (spore-producing structures) barely visible on the underside of the leaf. The spore-producing structures develop while the leaves are still on the tree. Sunken reddish oval areas often develop on the infected twigs.

ANALYSIS: Maple anthracnose
This plant disease is caused by a fungus (*Gloeosporium apocryptum*) that spends the winter on fallen leaves or in sunken cankers on twigs in the tree. During rainy weather, spores are blown and splashed onto young leaves. Dead spots develop on the leaf where the fungus enters the tissue. The spots expand and the fungus can kill the leaf in rainy seasons, causing defoliation. The tree will grow new leaves if defoliation takes place in spring or early summer. When the tree is severely affected for successive years, the fungus will enter and kill branches.

SOLUTION: Trees affected by this disease for a single year do not require a chemical control. Rake and burn old leaves and prune out dead twigs below the canker on the bark. This reduces the amount of disease next year. If the following spring is wet and humid, spray valuable specimens with a fungicide containing *zineb* or *maneb* when the leaves uncurl. Repeat the treatment two more times at two week intervals.

ACER (MAPLE, BOX ELDER)

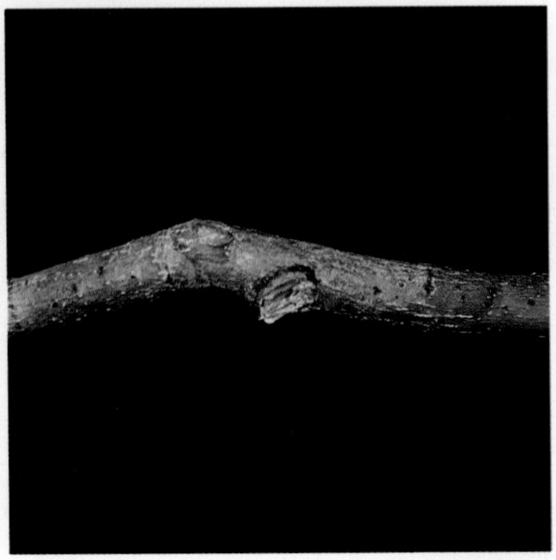

Cankers.

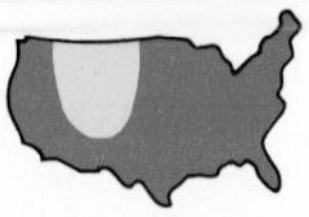

PROBLEM: Sunken, oval or elongated dark lesions (cankers) develop on the trunk or branches. Cankers also may develop at the base of the trunk, near the soil line; or, when the soil is removed from around the base of the tree, cracks in the trunk or roots may be revealed. Sometimes a brown or reddish liquid exudes from the canker or the fissures in the canker. The foliage on infected branches may be stunted and yellowing; some of the leaves may turn brown and drop off. Twigs and branches may die back, and the tree may eventually die.

ANALYSIS: Canker and dieback
A number of different fungi cause canker and dieback on maple. The fungi usually enter the tree at a wound, killing the surrounding healthy tissue. A sunken canker develops; tree sap containing the fungus may ooze from the wound. The canker cuts off the flow of nutrients and water to the branch or branches growing beyond it, causing the leaves to turn yellow. Leaf drop and twig dieback follow if infection continues. Cankers that form on the trunk are the most serious, and may kill the tree. The tree may halt the development of a canker by producing callous tissue—a growth of barklike cells—to wall off the infection.

SOLUTION: Remove badly infected branches and cut out cankers. For details about canker removal and treatment, see page 917. Avoid wounding the tree. Maintain the tree in good health to reduce the chances of future infection. For cultural information, see page 445.

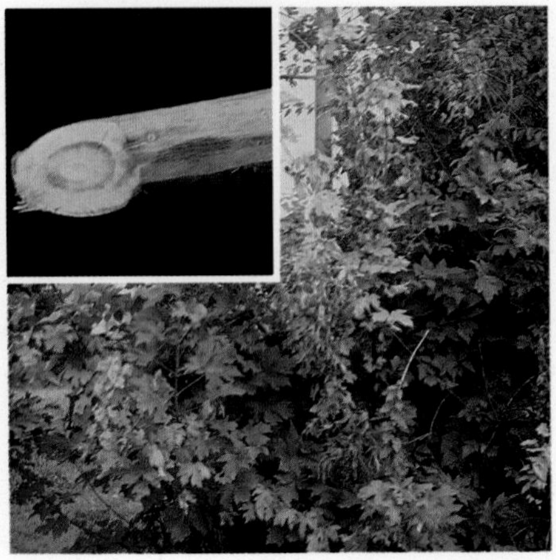

Verticillium wilt. *Insert:* Infected stem.

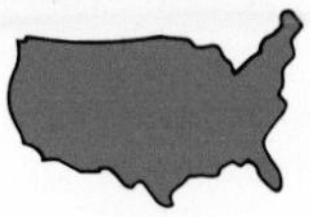

PROBLEM: The leaves on a branch turn yellow at the margins, then brown and dry. During hot weather, the leaves may wilt. New leaves may be stunted and yellowish. The infected tree may die slowly, branch by branch, over several seasons. Or the whole tree may wilt and die within a few months. Some trees may recover. The tissue under the bark on the dying side shows dark streaks which may be very apparent or barely visible when exposed. To examine for streaks, peel back the bark at the bottom of the dying branch.

ANALYSIS: Verticillium wilt
This wilt disease affects many ornamental trees and shrubs. It is caused by a soil-inhabiting fungus (*Verticillium* species) that persists indefinitely on plant debris or in the soil. The disease is spread by contaminated seeds, plants, soil, equipment, and ground water. The fungus enters the tree through the roots and spreads up into the branches through the water-conducting vessels in the trunk. The vessels become discolored and plugged. This plugging cuts off the flow of water and nutrients to the branches, causing the leaf discoloration and wilting. For more information about verticillium wilt, see page 850.

SOLUTION: No chemical control is available. Fertilize and water the affected tree to stimulate vigorous growth. Remove all dead wood. Do not remove branches on which leaves have recently wilted. These branches may produce new leaves in 3 to 4 weeks or next spring. Remove dead trees. If replanting in the same area, plant trees and shrubs that are resistant to verticillium. For a list of resistant trees and shrubs, see page 1006.

AESCULUS (HORSE CHESTNUT, BUCKEYE)

Leaf blotch.

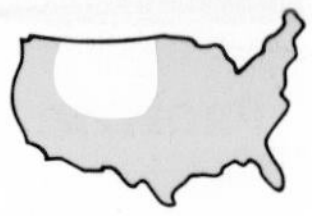

PROBLEM: Reddish brown blotches with bright yellow margins appear on the leaf. Spots may be as small as ¼ inch, or may nearly cover the leaf. When the whole leaf is infected, it becomes dry and brittle; many leaves may drop from the tree. The first infection occurs in spring, but blotches may not appear until July. Blotching is most severe in very wet springs. This problem is sometimes confused with leaf scorch caused by hot summer weather. It can be distinguished from scorch by the black specks in the center of the blotch.

ANALYSIS: Leaf blotch
This plant disease is caused by a fungus (*Guignardia aesculi*). In the spring, spores that develop on dead leaves on the ground are blown and splashed by rain onto young leaves. Water-soaked blotches appear in early summer, but are not usually noticed until they turn brown. In midsummer, numerous pinpoint black spore-producing structures develop in the blotches.

SOLUTION: Leaf blotch cannot be controlled once infection has occurred. Rake up and destroy leaves in the fall. When the first leaves appear the following spring, if the season is wet and there is danger of infection, spray with a fungicide containing *chlorothalonil* (DACONIL 2787®). Repeat two more times at intervals of 10 days.

Aesculus cultural information
Light: Full sun
Water: While soil is still moist
Soil: Tolerates many types of soil
Fertilizer: Light

Summer leaf scorch.

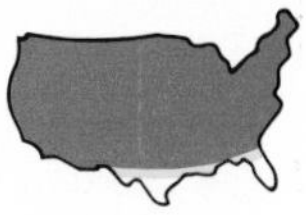

PROBLEM: During hot weather, usually in July or August, leaves turn brown around the edges and between the veins. Sometimes the whole leaf dies. Many leaves may drop during late summer. This problem is most severe on the youngest branches. Trees do not generally die.

ANALYSIS: Summer leaf scorch
In hot weather, water evaporates rapidly from the leaves. If the roots can't absorb and convey water fast enough to replenish this loss, the leaves turn brown and wither. This usually occurs in dry soil, but leaves can also scorch when the soil is moist. Chestnut trees vary in their susceptibility; one may be very susceptible while the tree next to it may show no sign of scorch. Drying winds, severed roots, limited soil area, or low temperatures can also cause scorch. For more information about scorch, see page 857.

SOLUTION: To prevent further scorch, deep-water trees during periods of hot weather to wet down the entire root space. (For more information about watering trees, see page 912.) Newly transplanted trees should be watered whenever the rootball is dry 1 inch below the surface. There are no controls for scorch on trees in moist soil. Plant trees adapted to your climate.

The California buckeye (*Aesculus californica*) is summer-deciduous. Every spring, about May or June, its leaves begin to show scorch symptoms that progress until all the leaves have dropped off. This is normal and cannot be prevented.

AILANTHUS (TREE-OF-HEAVEN)

Verticillium wilt.

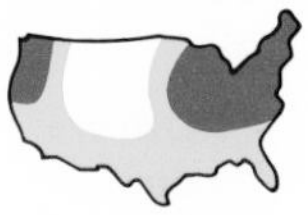

PROBLEM: The leaves on a branch turn yellow at the margins, then brown and dry. During hot weather, the leaves may wilt. New leaves may be stunted and yellowish. The infected tree may die slowly, branch by branch, over several seasons. Or the whole tree may wilt and die within a few months. Some trees may recover. The tissue under the bark on the dying side shows dark streaks when cut. To examine for streaks, peel back the bark at the bottom of the dying branch. The dark discoloration may be very apparent or barely visible in the area just underneath the bark.

ANALYSIS: Verticillium wilt
This wilt disease affects many ornamental trees and shrubs. It is caused by a soil-inhabiting fungus (*Verticillium* species) that persists indefinitely on plant debris or in the soil. The disease is spread by contaminated seeds, plants, soil, equipment, and ground water. The fungus enters the tree through the roots and spreads up into the branches through the water-conducting vessels in the trunk. The vessels become discolored and plugged. This plugging cuts off the flow of water and nutrients to the branches, causing the leaf discoloration and wilting. For more information about verticillium, see page 850.

SOLUTION: No chemical control is available. Fertilize and water the affected tree to stimulate vigorous growth. Prune off all dead wood. Remove dead trees. If replanting in the same area, plant trees or shrubs that are resistant to verticillium. For a list of resistant trees and shrubs, see page 1006.

ALBIZIA (MIMOSA, SILK TREE)

Mimosa webworm damage.

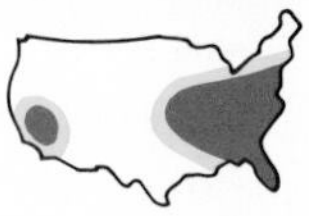

PROBLEM: Small clumps of leaves tied together with silk threads are scattered over the tree. The upper surfaces of the leaves are skeletonized. Leaves turn brown and die, causing the trees to appear as if scorched by fire. Small (up to 1 inch), pale gray or brown caterpillars with five white stripes feed inside the silken nests. Damage appears from June to September. Small trees may be completely defoliated in late summer. Trees are not killed, but repeated defoliations can seriously weaken them.

ANALYSIS: Mimosa webworm
(*Homadaula anisocentra*)
The mimosa webworm is the larval stage of a small moth that feeds only on mimosa and honey locust trees. The webworm passes the winter as a pupa in a white silken cocoon. The moth emerges in spring and lays eggs on leaf stems or on old silk from previous infestations. The eggs hatch and the larvae feed on the leaflets for several weeks, webbing the leaflets together for protection against predators and weather. In August a second generation of webworms appears. The larvae of this second generation are the most damaging because they are usually so numerous. In cooler areas of the country two generations occur each year between June and August. In warmer areas there is a third generation in September.

SOLUTION: Spray with ORTHO Isotox Insect Killer or ORTHO Orthene Systemic Insect Control when webbing first appears in early June. Repeat in August. Use high-pressure equipment to penetrate the webs and thoroughly cover the tree. In the fall, rake and destroy debris under infested trees, or turn over the soil and bury the leaves.

ALBIZIA (MIMOSA, SILK TREE)

Crown dieback. *Insert:* Discoloration under bark.

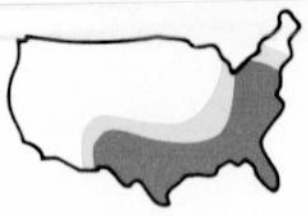

PROBLEM: The leaves wilt, usually in the upper portion of the crown. The wilted leaves turn yellow, then brown, and finally die, although they may remain green or yellowish for weeks. Eventually the leaves drop, often leaving the leaf stalk attached, and the branch dies. The tree may die very rapidly, in only a few months after the first symptoms appear, or it may live for a year or two. The tissue under the bark on the wilting branch shows brownish streaks when cut. To examine for discoloration, peel back the bark at the bottom of the dying branch. The streaks are visible in the area just underneath the bark.

ANALYSIS: Mimosa wilt
Mimosa wilt is a highly destructive disease that attacks only the mimosa tree. It is caused by a soil-inhabiting fungus (*Fusarium oxysporum f. perniciosum*). The fungus enters the tree through wounded roots, then spreads up into the branches through the water-conducting vessels in the trunk. These vessels become discolored and plugged, cutting off water to the branches. This causes the leaves and branches to wilt and eventually die.

SOLUTION: No controls are available. Cut down and destroy dead and dying trees to prevent spreading of the fungus. Do not plant another mimosa where a tree has died of wilt disease.

Albizia cultural information
Light: Full sun
Water: Water while soil is still moist
Soil: Well drained, tolerates alkaline soil
Fertilizer: Light

ALNUS (ALDER)

Aphids (twice life size).

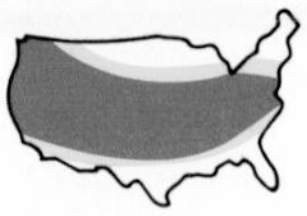

PROBLEM: Leaves may be discolored and reduced in size. A shiny or sticky substance usually coats the leaves. A black sooty mold may grow on the sticky substance. Tiny (1/8 inch), green, soft-bodied insects or gray insects coated with white, woolly, or waxy strands cluster on the undersides of the leaves or on the twigs.

ANALYSIS: Aphids
Several different types of aphids infest alder. Some are called *woolly aphids* because the waxy covering over their bodies looks like wool; others are green and have no woolly covering. Aphids do little damage in small numbers. However, they are extremely prolific and populations can rapidly build up to damaging numbers during the growing season. Damage occurs when the aphid sucks the juices from the alder leaves and twigs. The aphid is unable to digest fully all the sugar in the sap and excretes the excess in a fluid called honeydew, which often drops onto the leaves below. Plants or objects beneath the tree may also be coated with honeydew. A sooty mold fungus may develop on the sticky substance, causing the alder leaves to appear black and dirty.

SOLUTION: Spray with ORTHO Orthene Systemic Insect Control when aphids are noticed. Direct the spray to the branches and the undersides of the leaves. Repeat the spray if the tree becomes reinfested.

Alder flea beetles (life size).

PROBLEM: The leaf tissue is eaten between the veins. When infestations are severe, the tree may be completely defoliated. Small (1/5 inch) shiny blue to greenish blue beetles, with many fine punctures on their backs, may be seen on the tree or on the ground; or small (1/4 inch) dark brown larvae with black heads may be found on the leaves.

ANALYSIS: Alder flea beetle
(*Altica ambiens*)
Alder flea beetles are not normally found in large numbers. However, they periodically build up to epidemic proportions and devour alder leaves. The shiny blue or greenish beetles spend the winter in protected places, such as in litter on the ground and under wood. In the spring, the females lay orange eggs on the leaves. The brown larvae that hatch from these eggs eat the leaves between the veins throughout July and August. When mature, the larvae drop to the ground and pupate. In warm climates, there may be a second generation of beetles.

SOLUTION: Spray the leaves with an insecticide containing *carbaryl* (SEVIN®) when damage is first noticed in the spring. Repeat the spray at intervals of 7 to 10 days if the tree becomes reinfested.

Alnus cultural information
Light: Full sun
Water: Grows best in moist soil
Soil: Tolerates many types
Fertilizer: Medium

ARAUCARIA (NORFOLK ISLAND PINE)

Needle blight.

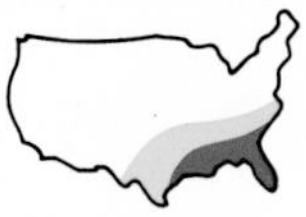

PROBLEM: Needles at branch tips turn yellowish, then reddish brown, and die. Branch tips may also die, and the condition usually begins on the branch tips and progresses back toward the main trunk. The problem can occur at any level on the tree, but is more severe on the middle and lower portions.

ANALYSIS: Needle blight
This plant disease is caused by any of several fungi that invade needles and twigs. Trees are infected by airborne spores from nearby plants. Infection is favored by warm, moist conditions. Large areas of severely infected trees may be killed, and small trees may be completely killed by needle blight.

SOLUTION: Spray infected trees with a fungicide containing *manzate* or *benomyl*. Repeat treatments as needed according to label directions. Keep tree foliage as dry as possible to reduce the chance of infection.

Araucaria cultural information
Light: Full sun
Water: Drought-tolerant once established
Soil: Tolerates many types
Fertilizer: Light to medium

Spider mite damage.

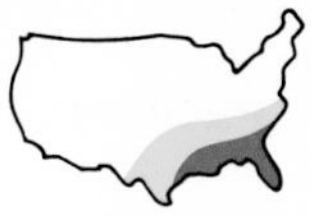

PROBLEM: Needles turn light green, then yellow, and finally brown. Damage almost always appears on the inside of the tree next to the trunk and then spreads upward and outward along the branches. Lower portions of the tree are usually affected first, and damage is most severe during periods of hot, dry weather. To check for pests, hold a piece of white paper beneath a dying area and tap the needles sharply. Minute red or yellow specks the size of a pepper grain will drop to the paper and begin to crawl around. They are easily seen against the white background.

ANALYSIS: Spider mites
(*Oligonychus* species)
This spider relative damages plants by sucking the juices from the leaves and stems. This feeding results in the discoloration and sometimes death of the needles. Damage is often severe enough to kill small trees. Mite levels increase rapidly in hot, dry weather (70°F and higher). Mites are most active during late spring and early summer, but some mite activity occurs throughout the year in warm regions. For more information about spider mites, see page 887.

SOLUTION: Apply ORTHO Isotox Insect Killer or ORTHO Malathion 50 Insect Spray when browning needles are first noticed. Repeat sprays at intervals of seven to ten days according to label directions until the mites are controlled. Mites in missed areas continue to reproduce and rapidly reinfest treated areas.

ARBUTUS (MADRONE)

Twig dieback on madrone. *Insert:* Canker.

PROBLEM: Leaves on infected trees are stunted and lighter green than normal. Some leaves turn brown and drop. Twigs may die back. There are sunken, brownish, water-soaked areas on branches or near the base of the trunk. The sunken areas have a definite margin. Sometimes a black liquid substance is exuded from the canker. The tree may be killed.

ANALYSIS: Canker and dieback
Several different fungi cause canker and dieback on madrone. The fungi are spread by wind, rain, soil, tools, and equipment. They enter the tree at a wound, killing the surrounding healthy tissue. A sunken canker develops and expands through the wood in all directions. Tree sap containing the fungus may ooze from the wound. The canker cuts off the flow of nutrients and water to the branch. The tree may stop the spreading disease by producing callus tissue, a rapid growth of barklike cells, to wall off the fungus. If the expanding canker is stopped before it covers half the diameter of the trunk, the tree usually survives. However, the fungus may grow faster than the callus, or the tree may not produce a callus, resulting in the death of the branch or the tree.

SOLUTION: Prune off dead twigs and small cankered branches, cutting at least 4 inches below the canker. Cankers on larger branches can be excised with a knife and chisel. Remove all discolored bark and wood, and a 1-inch border of apparently healthy bark around the wound. After each cut, sterilize the knife and chisel with rubbing alcohol. Clean the wound with the alcohol. To prevent the development of new cankers, avoid wounding trees.

ARCTOSTAPHYLOS (MANZANITA)

Leaf gall.

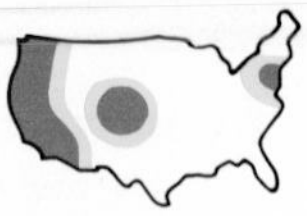

PROBLEM: Green or reddish galls appear at the edges or tips of the newest leaves. The leaves are twisted and distorted. When the gall is torn open, a small (1/8 inch), dark green to black insect or insect excrement is seen. On kinnikinnick (*Arctostaphylos uva-ursi*), the entire leaf may be thickened and reddish. Leaf galls appear in early summer.

ANALYSIS: Leaf gall aphid
(*Tamalia coweni*)
This leaf gall aphid is only a pest of *Arctostaphylos* species. Damage occurs when the aphid sucks the juices from the leaf and rolls a third of the leaf around itself. A growth-promoting substance is injected into the leaf at the same time, causing the thickening of the leaf. The aphid begins feeding in spring but the gall does not form until early summer. On most species of *Arctostaphylos*, the galls are more disfiguring than damaging. However, on kinnikinnick, all new leaves may be disfigured, preventing growth and spread of the groundcover.

SOLUTION: Once the gall has formed around the aphid, this insect is difficult to control. Pick off and destroy disfigured leaves. The following spring, spray with a systemic insecticide to protect new foliage.

Arctostaphylos cultural information
Light: Full sun to partial shade
Water: Allow the soil to dry between waterings
Soil: Well drained, loose
Fertilizer: Light

AUCUBA

Sunburn.

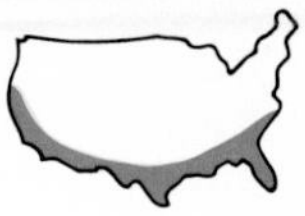

PROBLEM: Dark brown or black patches develop on leaves exposed to direct sunlight. The entire leaf or shoot may turn black.

ANALYSIS: Sunburn
Aucuba plants are shade-loving; they cannot tolerate direct sun, especially intense afternoon sun. The sunlight burns the leaves, causing them to turn brown or black. Sunburn is most severe when the soil is dry. Some pests and diseases may cause symptoms similar to those of sunburn. For more information, see page 857.

SOLUTION: There is nothing you can do once the foliage has been damaged. Prune off dead leaves and shoots. Prevent further sunburn by transplanting plants to a shady location, or providing shade around the plants. Keep plants well watered.

Aucuba cultural information
Light: Part shade to full shade
Water: Moist or dry conditions
Soil: Tolerates many types
Fertilizer: Light

BAMBOO

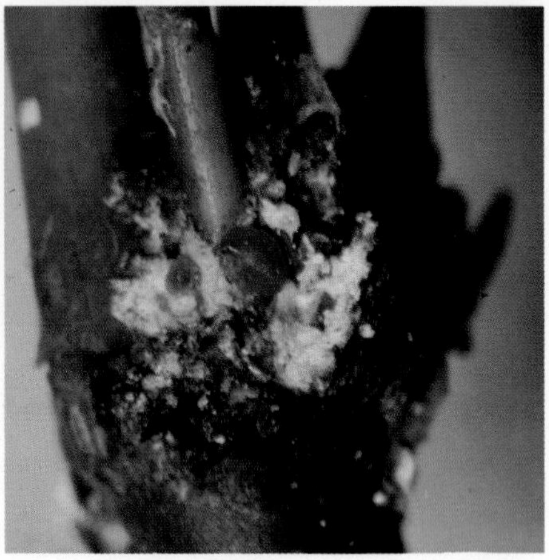
Aphids (twice life size).

PROBLEM: Young leaves are curled and yellowing. There may be a shiny or sticky substance coating the leaves. A black sooty mold often grows on the sticky substance. Tiny (1/8 inch), pale yellow, soft-bodied insects with black markings cluster on the undersides of leaves. Ants may be present. The plant is often weak and stunted.

ANALYSIS: Bamboo aphids
(*Takecallis* species)
Aphids do little damage in small numbers. However, they are extremely prolific and populations can rapidly build up to damaging numbers during the growing season. Damage occurs when the aphid sucks the juices from the bamboo leaves. The aphid is unable to digest fully all the sugar in the sap and excretes the excess in a fluid called honeydew. The honeydew often drops onto the leaves below. A sooty mold fungus may develop on the honeydew causing the bamboo leaves to appear black and dirty; or rain may wash the honeydew off before the fungus has a chance to grow. Ants feed on honeydew and are often present where there is an aphid infestation.

SOLUTION: Spray with ORTHO Malathion 50 Insect Spray when aphids first appear. Direct the spray to the undersides of the leaves. Repeat the spray in summer if the plant becomes reinfested.

Bamboo cultural information
Light: Full sun
Water: Drought tolerant once established
Soil: Tolerates many types
Fertilizer: Light to medium

BAUHINIA (ORCHID TREE)

Bamboo scale (life size). *Insert:* Close-up.

PROBLEM: Stems or leaves are covered with brownish crusty bumps or thick, white, waxy bumps, or clusters of somewhat flattened yellowish scaly bumps. The bumps can be scraped or picked off; the undersides are usually soft. Leaves turn yellow and may drop. In some cases, a shiny or sticky substance coats the leaves. A black sooty mold often grows on the sticky substance.

ANALYSIS: Scales

Several different types of scales infest bamboo. In spring to midsummer the young scales, called *crawlers*, settle on leaves and stems. The small (1/10 inch), soft-bodied young feed by inserting their mouthparts and sucking sap from the plant. The legs usually atrophy and a hard crusty or waxy shell develops over the body. The mature female scales lay their eggs underneath their shell. Some species of scales that infest bamboo are unable to digest fully all the sugar in the plant sap, and excrete the excess in a fluid called honeydew, which often drops onto the leaves below. A sooty mold fungus may develop on the honeydew, causing the bamboo leaves and stems to appear black and dirty. An uncontrolled infestation of scales may kill the plant after two or three seasons. For more information about scales, see page 876.

SOLUTION: Spray with ORTHO Liquid Sevin in late spring when the young are active. Contact your local Cooperative Extension Office (see page 1029) to determine the best time to spray for scales in your area. Or spray with a *summer oil* to kill the adults, and hose down the plants the next day.

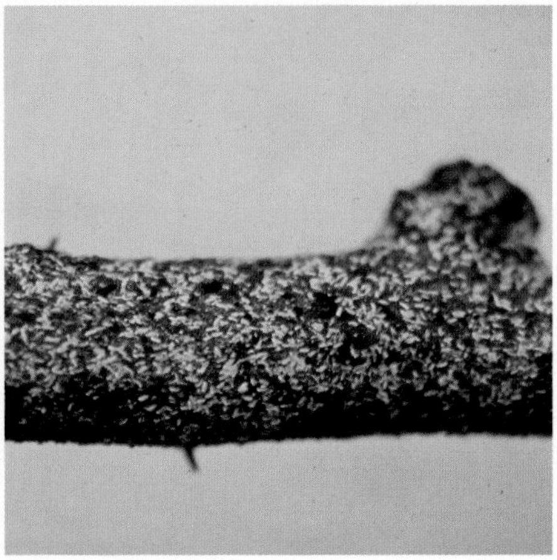

Snow scale (life size).

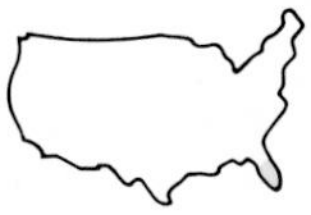

PROBLEM: Branches are infested with minute (1/32 to 1/16 inch) insects with white shells. Twigs and limbs that are heavily infested usually die, and small trees may be killed. Infested limbs have few, if any, leaves.

ANALYSIS: Snow scale

(*Unaspis citri*)

Snow scale gets its name from the color and appearance of the male scales. Female snow scales are brown to blackish, and are hard to see against the tree bark. Scales feed by sucking the plant sap. Often they are unable to digest fully all the sugar in the sap, and excrete the excess as a sugary fluid called honeydew. A sooty mold fungus may develop on the honeydew, causing the bauhinia leaves to appear black and dirty. Ants also feed on the honeydew, and are often present where scales are feeding. Scale infestations are most serious between spring and late fall.

SOLUTION: Spray infested trees with ORTHO Liquid Sevin. Repeat sprayings as needed according to label directions. Prune out dead branches on severely infested trees, and apply frequent, light applications of fertilizer to speed up recovery.

Bauhinia cultural information

Light: Full sun to part shade
Water: Keep the soil moist
Soil: Tolerates many types
Fertilizer: Medium

Iron deficiency.

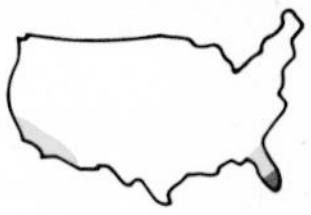

PROBLEM: Some leaves turn pale green to yellow. The newest leaves (those at the tips of the branches) may be completely yellow, with only the veins remaining green. Only the leaf edges of older leaves may be yellowing. The plant may be stunted.

ANALYSIS: Iron deficiency

This is a common problem in acid-loving trees like bauhinia. Bauhinia grows best in soil with a pH between 5.5 and 6.5. (For more information on soil acidity, see page 908.) The yellowing is due to a deficiency of iron and other minor nutrients in the tree. The soil is seldom deficient in iron. However, iron is often found in an insoluble form that is not available to the plant, especially in soil with a pH of 7.0 or higher. An alkaline soil can result from overliming, or from lime leached from cement or brick. Regions where soil is derived from limestone also have high-pH soils. Plants use iron in the formation of the green pigment in the leaves. When iron is lacking, new leaves are yellow.

SOLUTION: Spray the foliage with ORTHO Greenol Liquid Iron and apply it to the soil around the tree to correct the deficiency of minor nutrients. Correct the pH of the soil by treating it with *ferrous sulfate* or ORTHO Aluminum Sulfate. Maintain an acid pH by fertilizing with ORTHO Azalea, Camellia & Rhododendron Food. When planting orchid trees, add peat moss, acid topsoil, or other materials to help acidify the planting soil.

BETULA (BIRCH)

ADAPTATION: Zones 1 through 9. (To determine your zone, see the map on page 1020.) Most birches are not adapted to desert areas.

LIGHT: Full sun. Partial shade in warm areas.

SOIL: Birches tolerate a wide variety of soil types.

FERTILIZER: Fertilize with ORTHO Evergreen, Tree & Shrub Food according to label directions.

WATER:

How much: Apply enough water to wet the soil 3 to 4 feet deep. To determine the proper amount of water for your soil type, see page 912.

How often: Birches grow best in moist soil. Water when the soil is moist but not wet 4 inches below the surface. For more information about watering, see page 912.

PRUNING: Birches usually bleed heavily when pruned in winter or spring, so it is best to prune at other times of the year. Prune to maintain shape.

Aphids (half life size).

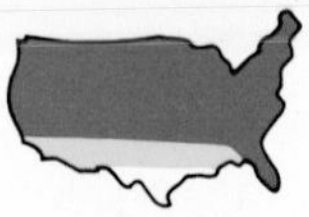

PROBLEM: Young leaves are puckered, twisted, and yellowing. There may be a shiny or sticky substance dripping from the trees and coating the leaves. Sometimes twigs or branches die back. Tiny ($1/8$ inch) yellow, green, or blackish soft-bodied insects cluster on the undersides of leaves or on the stems.

ANALYSIS: Aphids

Aphids do little damage in small numbers. However, they are extremely prolific and populations can rapidly build up to damaging numbers during the growing season. Damage occurs when the aphid sucks the juices from birch leaves or stems. Some aphid species attacking birch are unable to digest fully all the sugar in the sap and they excrete the excess in a fluid called honeydew. The honeydew often drops onto the leaves below. Plants or objects beneath the tree may also be coated with honeydew. Ants feed on honeydew and are often present where there is an aphid infestation.

SOLUTION: Control with ORTHO Orthene Systemic Insect Control or ORTHO Isotox Insect Killer when aphids first appear. Direct the spray to the undersides of the leaves or at the bark, depending on where the aphids are feeding. Repeat the spray in summer if the tree becomes reinfested.

Leafminer damage.

PROBLEM: Brown blisters appear in the new leaves. Eventually the blisters run together, forming a large blotch. The top of the tree is generally most severely affected, but in some areas the entire tree is infested and brown. A small (up to $1/4$ inch), whitish larva may be found inside the blister.

ANALYSIS: Birch leafminer

(*Fenusa pusilla*)

This sawfly is a common pest of gray birch (*Betula populifolia*), paper birch (*B. papyrifera*), white birch (*B. alba*), and cut leaf birch. It rarely attacks black (*B. lenta*), yellow (*B. alleghieniensis*), European white (*B. pendula*), or river birch (*B. nigra*). When the first birch leaves are half grown in spring, the fly hovers around the trees and lays eggs on the leaves. When the eggs hatch, the larvae feed between the upper and lower surfaces of the leaves, causing blisters. The mature larva chews its way out of the leaf and drops to the ground to pupate. The adult fly emerges and the cycle repeats itself two or more times during the growing season. The adult lays eggs only on young leaves, so later in the season only terminal growth and sprout growth are affected.

SOLUTION: Larvae are difficult to control once they are inside the leaf. If blotches are noticed in spring, spray with ORTHO Orthene Systemic Insect Control, ORTHO Isotox Insect Killer, or ORTHO Lindane Borer & Leaf Miner Spray in early July to control young larvae of the second generation. Repeat in mid-July. The following spring, spray as the leaves are unfolding (early May) to prevent leafminer damage. Repeat two more times, 10 days apart. Or apply ORTHO Systemic Rose & Flower Care to the soil.

Dieback. *Insert:* Adult borer (half life size).

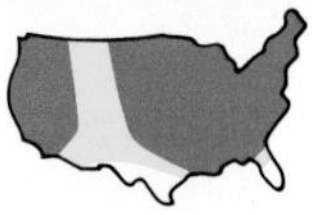

PROBLEM: Leaves are yellowing and the foliage is sparse at the top of the tree. There is increased side growth on the lower branches. Twigs and branches may die. The leaves on these branches turn brown but don't drop. There are D-shaped holes and ridges on the trunk and branches. Swollen ridges are packed with sawdust. Weak, young, or newly transplanted trees may be killed.

ANALYSIS: Bronze birch borer
(*Agrilus anxius*)
The birch borer is the larva of an olive-brown beetle about ½ inch long. For about six weeks in summer, adult beetles lay eggs in bark crevices, usually around a wound. They also feed on the leaves during egg laying. The larvae that hatch from these eggs are white and have flat heads. They bore into the wood just beneath the bark. The feeding and tunneling of the larvae stop the flow of nutrients and water in that area by cutting the conducting vessels; branch and twig dieback result. If the tree is healthy, sap flow acts as a defense against borers; when the insect burrows into the wood, tree sap fills the hole and drowns the insect. Factors that weaken the tree such as poor growing conditions, transplanting, and mechanical injuries make it more attractive to female beetles.

SOLUTION: Cut out and destroy all dead and dying branches. Severely infested young trees should be removed. In spring, spray or paint the trunk and branches with an insecticide containing *lindane* to kill young larvae before they burrow into the wood. Repeat three more times at intervals of two weeks. Maintain tree vigor by watering and fertilizing regularly.

Dieback.

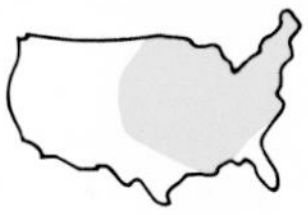

PROBLEM: Leaves on the ends of branches turn yellow and drop. The upper branches die from the tips back. The tree is weak and stunted.

ANALYSIS: Dieback
Dieback on birch is caused by any of several different species of fungi (*Melanconis* species) that attack trees weakened by drought. The fungus enters a branch and, if the tree is weak, produces a dark discoloration in the wood. Healthy trees can resist the attack of this weak fungus and show few symptoms. Upper branches progressively die as the fungus grows through the wood. Several other fungi that produce cankers on the branches or trunk of birches may also cause dieback. The bronze birch borer (see page 455) may cause similar dieback symptoms, and often invades trees weakened by dieback. In addition, birch trees under drought stress may show some twig dieback.

SOLUTION: No chemicals are known to control this fungus. Prune off affected branches well below the diseased area. Fertilize and water the tree regularly to promote vigorous growth. For more information about fertilizers and watering, see pages 910 and 912.

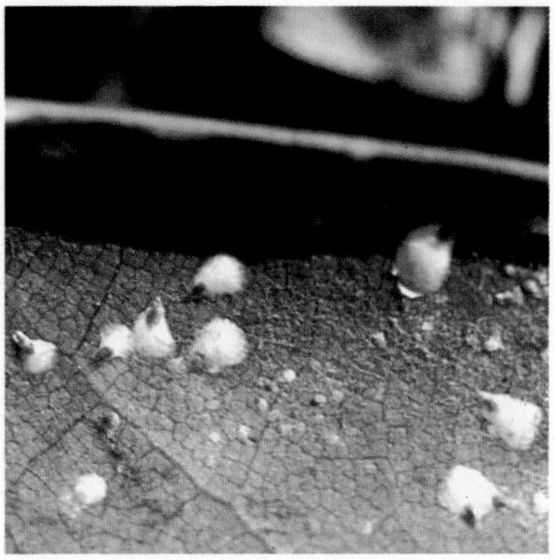

False oleander scale (twice life size).

PROBLEM: Yellow to greenish yellow spots develop on the leaves. Tiny, white to light brown raised bumps are often seen in the discolored areas. The bumps can be scraped or picked off; the undersides are usually soft. Leaves turn yellow and may drop. Sometimes a shiny or sticky substance coats the leaves.

ANALYSIS: False oleander scale
(*Pseudaulacaspis cockerelli*)
This insect feeds on many garden plants, and is capable of rapid reproduction. The female scale deposits large masses of eggs under her wax shell. After hatching, the young scales, called *crawlers*, move about the host plant until they locate a feeding site. They begin to feed and then develop the protective scale cover. Several generations of scales are produced each year. Scales feed by sucking the plant juices from tender leaves and stems. Some scales are unable to digest fully all the sugar in the plant sap, and excrete the excess in a fluid called honeydew, which often drops onto the leaves below. A sooty mold may develop on the honeydew, causing the leaves to appear dirty.

SOLUTION: Apply ORTHO Isotox Insect Killer thoroughly to infested trees. Repeat sprays at intervals of seven to ten days until scales are controlled. Dead scales remain on the plant but are dry and contain no fluids when scraped off and examined.

Bischofia cultural information
Light: Full sun
Water: Drought tolerant once established
Soil: Tolerates many types
Fertilizer: Medium

BOUGAINVILLEA

Bougainvillea caterpillar (life size).

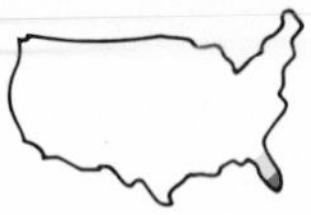

PROBLEM: Leaves have holes chewed in them, or they may be missing completely. New leaves are most severely affected, and the problem occurs most during warm weather from spring to fall. Green caterpillars 3/4 inch long may be present on the damaged leaves.

ANALYSIS: Bougainvillea caterpillars
(*Macalla thrysisalis*)
These caterpillars are the larval stage of a tiny moth that lays its eggs on bougainvillea leaves. After hatching, the caterpillars feed on the leaves and complete their development into the adult stage in 4 to 5 weeks. Several generations are produced during the year, with the greatest infestations occurring in the late spring.

SOLUTION: Apply ORTHO Liquid Sevin according to label directions. Repeat the sprayings at weekly intervals as long as caterpillars are present.

Bougainvillea cultural information
Light: Full sun to part shade
Water: Infrequent, deep watering
Soil: Loose, well drained
Fertilizer: Light to medium

BRASSAIA (SCHEFFLERA)

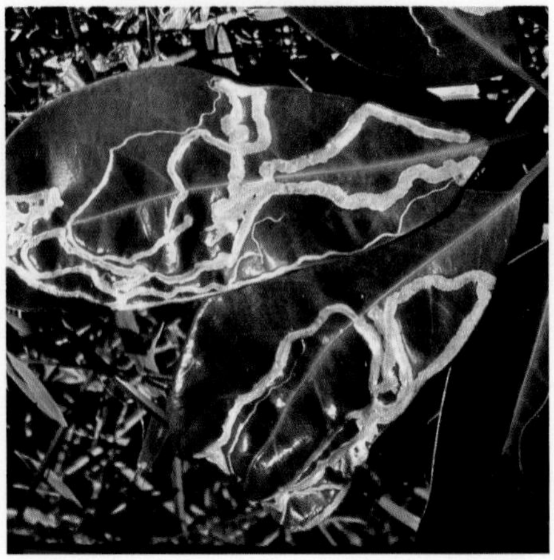

Leafminer trails.

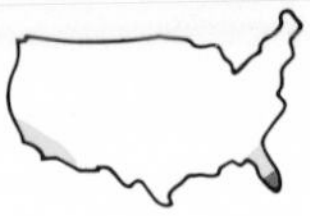

PROBLEM: Light-colored, irregular, winding trails appear in the leaves. Some of the trails are filled with black matter. Severely infested leaves may die or drop prematurely. Infested leaves are usually discolored.

ANALYSIS: Leafminer
Most of the insects that cause this type of damage belong to the family of leaf-mining flies. The minute adult flies lay their eggs on the undersides of the leaves. The larvae (maggots) that emerge from these eggs penetrate the leaf, and live between the upper and lower surfaces. They feed on the inner leaf tissue, creating winding trails. Their dark excrement can dot or partially fill sections of the trails. The larvae generally emerge from the leaves to pupate. Leafminers cause damage continually from spring until fall. The last generation of maggots pupates in the soil or plant debris throughout the winter to emerge as adult flies the following spring.

SOLUTION: Apply ORTHO Isotox Insect Killer or ORTHO Orthene Systemic Insect Control to infested plants according to label directions. Repeat sprayings as needed according to label directions. Remove and discard unsightly infested leaves.

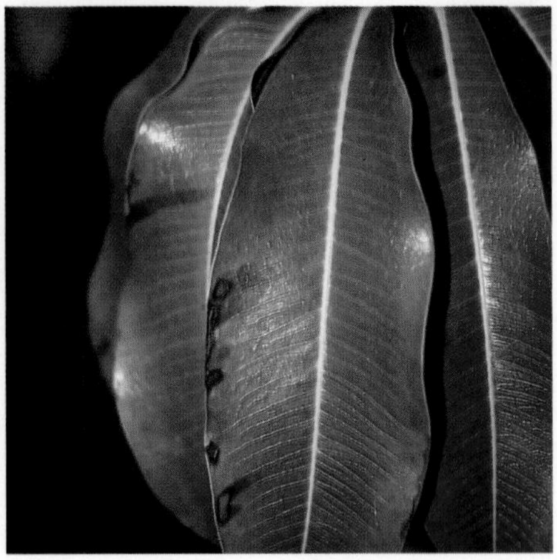

Alternaria leaf spot.

PROBLEM: Leaves have dark brown to black, water-soaked spots, often with a yellow halo. Spots range in size from a pinpoint to 2 inches or more, and may be found on branches and leaf stems as well as on leaves. Leaves drop off. Severely infected plants may lose many leaves.

ANALYSIS: Alternaria leaf spot
This leaf spot disease, caused by a fungus (*Alternaria* species), can be severe when plants are kept too moist. Alternaria fungus is found throughout the year, but is most prevalent during wet, warm weather. Once infected, plants rapidly develop symptoms. Spores from developing lesions are carried by the wind or splashing water to other parts of the plant or to nearby plants.

SOLUTION: Spray with a fungicide containing *manzate*. Repeat sprays at the intervals recommended on the label until no new spots are seen. Keep the leaves as dry as possible to reduce the danger of infection.

Brassaia cultural information
Light: Full sun to part shade
Water: When the soil is almost dry
Soil: Tolerates many types
Fertilizer: Medium

Blister mite damage.

PROBLEM: Leaves are deformed and have brown bumps of varying sizes. Severely infested leaves may drop. The problem is most severe in the spring and summer.

ANALYSIS: Blister mite
(*Eriophyes buceras*)
This tiny, pale white spider relative sucks fluids from the leaves to cause the brown blisterlike areas that may resemble leaf spots. Mite development is very rapid. They take only 5 to 7 days to reach the adult stage under ideal conditions, and many generations are produced each year. Mite activity is greatest during the spring and summer. These mites are difficult to see without magnification, and their damage is often blamed on other pests.

SOLUTION: Spray the tree with a pesticide containing *dicofol* (KELTHANE®). Repeat the spray every 1 to 2 weeks until mites are controlled. Be sure that the spray reaches all parts of the tree; otherwise, mites in missed areas quickly reinfest treated ones.

Bucida cultural information
Light: Full sun
Water: Drought tolerant once established
Soil: Tolerates many types
Fertilizer: Low to medium

Red leaves.

PROBLEM: Many leaves of all ages and sizes suddenly turn red or orange and fall off. No insects or diseases are observed on the fallen leaves. The problem may occur at any time, but is most severe during the winter and early spring. Trees usually replace the fallen leaves within a few weeks.

ANALYSIS: Leaf drop
Leaf drop on black olive may be sudden and dramatic. It is usually caused by abrupt changes in temperature or in soil moisture. Winter leaf drop is often caused by cold wind or by drought. Individual trees vary in the ease with which they drop leaves.

SOLUTION: No treatment is necessary once the leaves have fallen. Future leaf drop can be made less severe by keeping the tree in good condition. Apply ORTHO General Purpose Plant Food every 6 to 8 weeks during the growing season. Do not let the soil dry out.

BUXUS (BOXWOOD)

ADAPTATION: Zones 5 through 10. (To determine your zone, see the map on page 1020.) Protect from drying winds.

LIGHT: Full sun or partial shade, especially in hot climates.

SOIL: Well drained, rich in organic matter.

FERTILIZER: Fertilize with ORTHO Evergreen, Tree & Shrub Food or ORTHO General Purpose Plant Food according to label directions.

WATER:
How much: Apply enough water to wet the soil 1 to 2 feet deep. To determine the proper amount of water for your soil type, see page 912.
How often: Boxwood will not tolerate drought. Water when the soil is moist but not wet 2 inches below the surface. For more information about watering, see page 912.

BUXUS (BOXWOOD)

Boxwood psyllid damage.

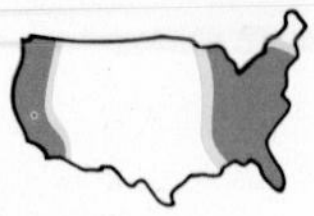

PROBLEM: Terminal leaves are cupped and yellowing. Buds inside the cupped leaves are often dead. There is no new growth on branch tips with damaged leaves. When the cupped leaves are peeled open, a tiny (1/16 inch), grayish green, immature insect is found inside. It is usually covered with a white, waxy material. Damage begins in early spring when buds first open. Small (1/8 inch) flies with transparent wings are sometimes seen jumping on leaves or flying around the plant in late May.

ANALYSIS: Boxwood psyllid
(*Psylla buxi*)
The boxwood psyllid is prevalent in temperate regions of the country where boxwood is grown. American boxwood is more severely attacked than English boxwood. The immature psyllid feeds by sucking the juices from growing leaves, resulting in the yellowing and cupping. As it feeds it secretes a white, waxy material that protects it from parasites and chemical sprays. The insect matures in early summer, and the female fly lays her eggs in the base of buds, where they remain until the following spring.

SOLUTION: Control with ORTHO Orthene Systemic Insect Control when damage is first noticed in early spring; repeat 2 weeks later. Spray the plant thoroughly to penetrate the waxy secretions and leaf buds.

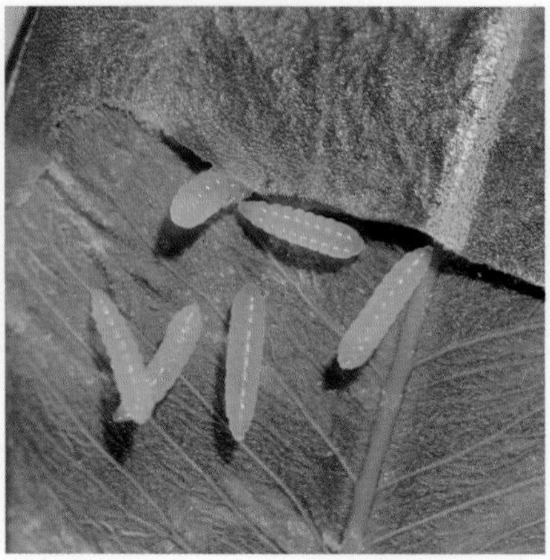

Boxwood leafminer larvae (twice life size).

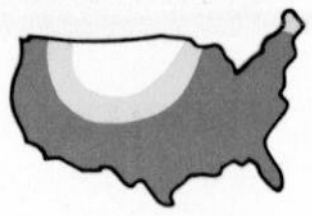

PROBLEM: The leaves are puckered or blistered. The lower surface of the leaf is spotted yellow; the upper surface is green at first and then flecked brown and yellow. Leaves may drop prematurely. Growth is poor and the plant is rangy. Twigs may die back if the plant is infested more than 1 year. When the leaf is torn open, two or more small (1/8 inch), yellowish maggots or brownish pupae may be found between the upper and lower surfaces of the leaf.

ANALYSIS: Boxwood leafminer
(*Monarthropalpus buxi*)
The boxwood leafminer is one of the most serious pests of boxwood. The larvae spend the winter in the leaf. When the weather warms in spring, they feed on the tissue between the leaf surfaces. In late April or May a tiny (1/10 inch), gnatlike, orange fly emerges from the pupal case inside the leaf. The emerging flies swarm around the plant in early morning, mating and laying eggs in the leaves. New blisters develop in midsummer from feeding by this next generation of larvae. When the weather turns cold, the larvae become inactive until the following spring.

SOLUTION: Leafminer control is most effective when insecticides are applied just before eggs are laid in late spring. Spray with ORTHO Orthene Systemic Insect Control in late April or early May. If eggs are laid before a control is applied, an insecticide containing *dimethoate* applied in late June may kill young miners.

Winter injury on Japanese boxwood.

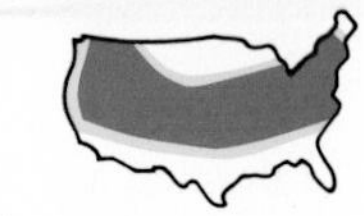

PROBLEM: Leaves are rusty brown to red, and dry. Twigs and branches may die back. The shrub is growing in an area where cold, dry, windy days are common or where plants may be exposed to late fall or early spring freezes.

ANALYSIS: Winter injury
Boxwood is severely damaged by cold, drying winter winds, especially if temperatures are below freezing and the weather is clear. The leaves lose their moisture more rapidly than it can be replaced by the root system. Cells in the leaf dry out and die. This condition is most pronounced when water is unavailable because the soil is frozen. Leaves, along with twigs and branches, also die during early fall or late spring freezes, when the plant is growing. Young succulent growth cannot withstand the cold temperatures.

SOLUTION: No cure is available once plants have been injured. Pick off damaged leaves where practical, and prune out dead twigs and branches. Provide shelter and windbreaks for plants growing in cold regions. Covering boxwoods with burlap bags helps prevent leaf drying. To avoid succulent growth in the fall, do not fertilize or prune late in the season. Water in late fall or winter, if necessary, to insure adequate soil moisture. Mulch plants after they become dormant to reduce the depth of frost penetration into the soil.

Volutella leaf and stem blight.

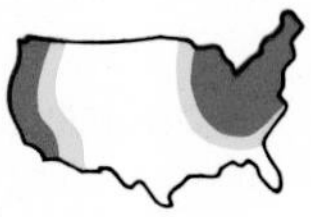

PROBLEM: In the spring before new growth appears, leaves on the tips of affected branches turn pale green, then red, tan, and finally yellow. The bark loosens and peels off at the base of infected stems and branches, revealing areas of darkened, discolored wood; the entire twig or stem eventually dies. Cream-pink pustules appear on the undersides of infected leaves that have survived the winter. Later in the season, new growth may turn yellow and develop pustules, especially if the weather is wet.

ANALYSIS: Volutella canker and blight

This plant disease is caused by a fungus (*Volutella buxi*) that attacks both American and English boxwood. Plants are more susceptible to the disease if they have been weakened by winter injury, poor growing conditions, or insect infestation. The fungus survives the winter on infected stems, leaves, and plant debris. Wind and splashing water spread the spores to healthy leaves and twigs. In the early spring, cankers form in twigs and branches, resulting in dieback. The fungus can continue to blight new growth throughout the growing season as long as conditions remain moist.

SOLUTION: Remove shrubs that are dying. Prune out and destroy infected twigs and branches. Clean up accumulated plant debris. Spray with a fungicide containig *benomyl*, *basic copper sulfate*, or *ferbam*, just before growth begins in the spring, or whenever the disease is first noticed. Repeat the spray three more times at intervals of 10 days. Maintain plants in good health. For cultural information, see page 457.

Dieback caused by phytophthora root rot.

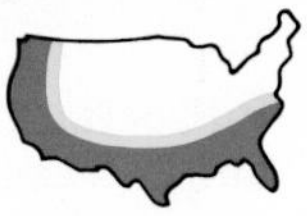

PROBLEM: The young leaves are yellowish or "off-color" and wilting. Eventually part or all of the plant wilts and dies, even though the soil is sufficiently moist. Dead leaves remain attached to the plant. Heavy, poorly drained soil favors disease development. When cut, the tissue under the bark close to ground level shows a dark discoloration. To look for discoloration, peel back the bark at the bottom of the plant. There is a distinct margin between white healthy wood and dark diseased wood. If the plant is pulled up, examination of young roots reveals browning, decaying, and an absence of white rootlets. Healthy roots are firm and white.

ANALYSIS: Root rot

This plant disease is caused by a soil-inhabiting fungus (*Phytophthora cinnamomi*) that attacks more than 100 kinds of ornamental plants. The fungus is carried in infected plants, infested soil, or soil water. It enters the roots and works its way up the plant, blocking the upward flow of water and nutrients. Plants in overwatered or poorly drained soils are more susceptible to attack.

SOLUTION: No chemical control is available. Once the fungus becomes established in the soil, it will remain indefinitely. Remove diseased plants; do not replant the same area with susceptible plants. For a list of resistant trees and shrubs, see page 1013. However, if replanting is necessary because the shrub is part of a hedge, replacing the soil in that area will reduce the chance of root rot. Remove as much soil as possible in the area where the old roots have penetrated and replace with uninfected soil. Avoid overwatering.

Spider mite damage.

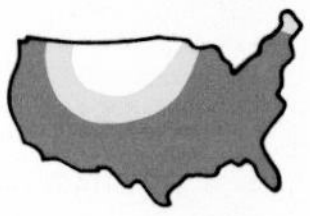

PROBLEM: Leaves are stippled yellow or whitish and dirty. There may be a silken webbing on the lower surfaces of the leaves. New leaves may be distorted. To determine if the plant is infested with mites, hold a sheet of white paper underneath a branch that has stippled leaves and tap the branch sharply. Minute reddish or green specks the size of a pepper grain will drop to the paper and crawl around. These pests are easily seen against the white background.

ANALYSIS: Spider mites

Spider mites, related to spiders, are major pests of many garden plants. They cause damage by sucking sap from the undersides of leaves. As a result of feeding, green leaf pigment disappears producing the stippled appearance. Mites infesting boxwood are most prolific in cooler weather. They are most active in the spring and occasionally, in the fall. At the onset of hot weather (70°F and up), the mites have caused their maximum damage. For more information about spider mites, see page 887.

SOLUTION: Control with ORTHO Diazinon Insect Spray or ORTHO Malathion 50 Insect Spray when stippling is first noticed in spring. Wet the undersides of the leaves thoroughly. Repeat three more times at 7 to 10 day intervals to kill young mites as they hatch from eggs. To prevent unsightly injury to foliage, it is important to apply control measures early in the season when damage first appears. Injured leaves remain on the plant for more than one growing season. Hose down plants frequently to knock off webs and mites.

BUXUS (BOXWOOD)

Nematode damage.

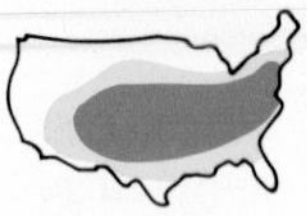

PROBLEM: The leaves are bronze to yellow. They may wilt on hot, dry days but recover at night. The plant lacks vigor. After several years, plants are noticeably stunted and branches may die back. The roots are stunted and often bushy and dark. There may be knots on the roots.

ANALYSIS: Nematodes
Nematodes are microscopic worms that live in the soil. They feed on plant roots, damaging and stunting them. The damaged roots can't supply sufficient water and nutrients to the aboveground plant parts, and the plant is stunted or slowly dies. Nematodes prefer moist, sandy loam soils. They can move only a few inches each year on their own, but they may be carried long distances by soil, water, tools, or infested plants. Testing roots and soil is the only positive method for confirming the presence of nematodes. Contact your local Cooperative Extension Office (see page 1029) for sampling instructions and addresses of testing laboratories. Soil and root problems such as poor soil structure, drought stress, nutrient deficiency, and root rots can also produce symptoms similar to those caused by nematodes. These problems should be eliminated as causes before sending soil and root samples for testing. For information on soil problems and root rots, see pages 907 and 849.

SOLUTION: There are no chemicals available to homeowners to kill nematodes in planted soil. However, they can be controlled before planting by soil fumigation. For information on fumigating soil, see page 927.

CACTUS

Root rot.

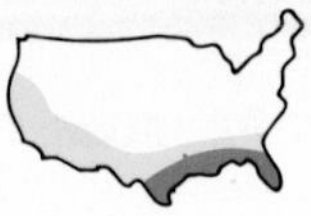

PROBLEM: The plant turns slightly yellow or gray. Soft, mushy areas may develop on the stems and around the base of the plant. The plant may topple, or easily break off at the base. The soil is frequently or constantly moist or wet.

ANALYSIS: Root rot
Cacti thrive in well-drained, sandy soil. They are very susceptible to root rot, a plant disease caused by any of several soil-dwelling fungi, also known as *water molds* (see page 849 for more information about water molds). These fungi thrive in waterlogged, heavy soil. Some of these fungi attack the plant stems at the soil level, while others attack the roots. Infection causes the roots and stems to decay, and eventually causes the plant to die.

SOLUTION: Allow the soil around the plants to dry out. (For more information on this technique, see page 849). Remove and discard severely infected plants. Plant cacti in well-drained soil and avoid overwatering. For information on improving soil drainage, see page 907.

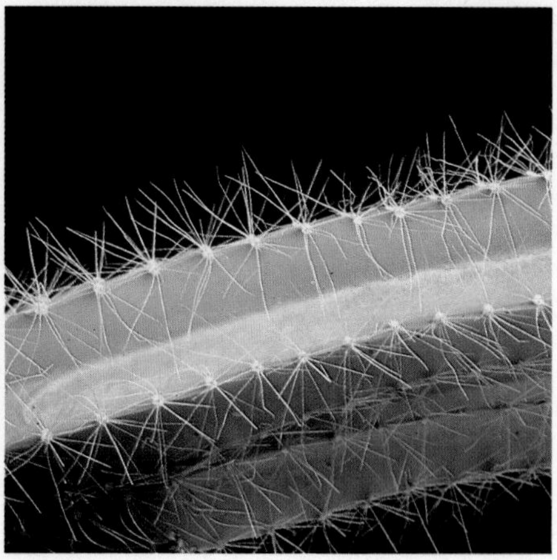

Sunburn.

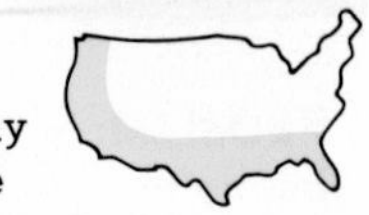

PROBLEM: During sunny weather, a section of the plant facing the sun turns yellow. Severely affected areas may turn brown later. The plant has been moved recently, from shade or low light to full sun.

ANALYSIS: Sunburn
Cacti are sun-loving plants. When growing in full sun, they produce thick cell walls that can withstand high light intensity and heat. However, plants may be burned by the sun if they are suddenly moved from a protected area (such as indoors) to an area that receives full sun. The cell walls cannot withstand high levels of ultraviolet light, and are damaged or killed.

SOLUTION: When moving plants out of the house or from areas of winter protection where light intensity has been low, place them in partial shade first (early morning, late afternoon, or filtered light) so they can adjust to the higher light intensity. In 1 to 2 weeks, cactus species that are adapted to full sun can be moved from partial shade into direct sunlight.

Cactus cultural information
Light: Full sun
Water: Allow to dry between waterings; reduce watering in fall
Soil: Sandy, loose, well drained
Fertilizer: Medium

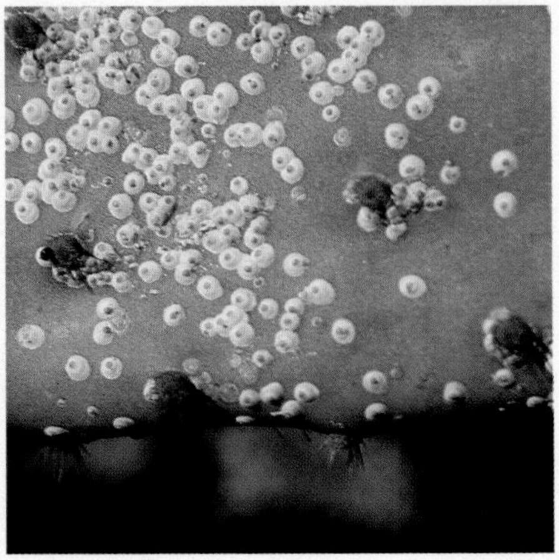

Cactus scale (twice life size).

PROBLEM: The plant is covered with clusters of somewhat flattened, circular, gray bumps, or with slender, white, scaly bumps. The bumps can be scraped or picked off; the undersides are soft. The plant may be yellowed.

ANALYSIS: Cactus scale
(*Diaspis echinocacti*)
This scale is common on cactus both outdoors and indoors. The infestation may be so heavy that the entire surface appears gray and crusty. The scale lays eggs in the spring. In late spring the young scales, called *crawlers*, settle on other parts of the plant. The tiny (1/30 inch), soft-bodied young feed by inserting their mouthparts and sucking sap from the plant. The legs atrophy and a hard, crusty, gray shell develops over the bodies of the females. The males are white and remain soft. The mature female scales lay their eggs underneath their shell. An uncontrolled infestation may kill the cactus after 2 or 3 seasons. Several other species of scales may also infest cactus.

SOLUTION: Spray with an insecticide containing *malathion* or *carbaryl* (SEVIN®) in late spring when the young are active. Some cacti are sensitive to *malathion* and may be injured. Test spray a small section of the plant and wait 24 hours to see if a burned area develops. Use a stiff brush to remove adult scales.

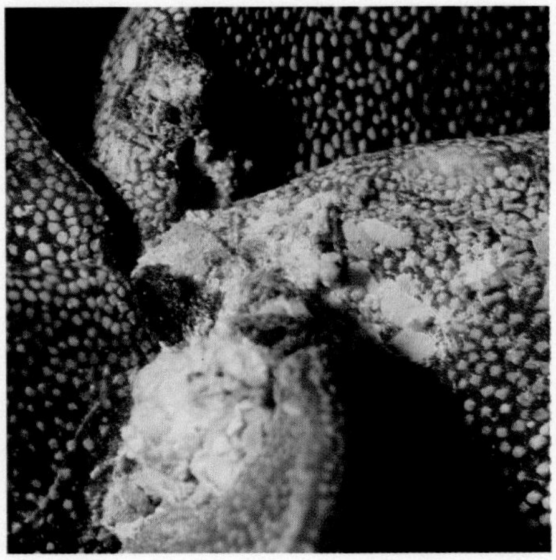

Mealybugs (twice life size).

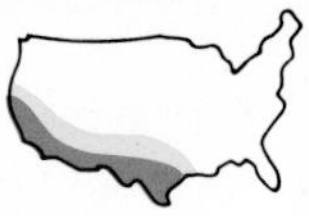

PROBLEM: The plant is covered with white, cottony, cushionlike masses. The plant may be yellowing, and a shiny sticky substance may coat the stems. When the masses are crushed, a red fluid may exude. A sticky or black substance may coat the plant.

ANALYSIS: Cottony scales and mealybugs
Cottony scales, including the cochineal scale (*Dactylopius* species), are common on cactus. The visual similarities between these insects make separate identification difficult. They are very conspicuous in late spring and summer because the females are covered with a white, cottony egg sac, containing up to 2500 eggs. Females lay their egg masses on leaves or branches. The young insects that hatch from these eggs are yellowish brown to green and inconspicuous. They feed throughout the summer on the stems and leaves. Damage is caused by the withdrawal of plant sap from the plant. Some species of scales and mealybugs that infest cacti are unable to digest fully all the sugar in the plant sap and excrete the excess in a fluid called honeydew. A sooty mold fungus may develop on the substance, causing the plant to appear black and dirty.

SOLUTION: Spray infested plants with an insecticide containing *malathion*. Spray at intervals of 7 to 10 days until mealybugs are gone. Some cacti are sensitive to *malathion*, and may be injured. Test spray a small section of the plant and wait 24 hours to see if a burned area develops.

CAMELLIA

ADAPTATION: Zones 7 through 10. Not adapted to desert areas.

FLOWERING TIME:
Common camellia (*C. japonica*): October to April.
Sasanqua camellia (*C. sasanqua*): September to December.

LIGHT: Protect from hot sun.

SOIL: Well drained, rich in organic matter, acid (pH 5.5 to 6.5). Mulch the soil to prevent drying.

FERTILIZER: Fertilize with ORTHO Azalea, Camellia & Rhododendron Food according to label directions.

WATER:
How much: Apply enough water to wet the soil 2 to 3 feet deep. To determine the proper amount of water for your soil type, see page 912.
How often: Camellias prefer moist soil. Water when the soil is moist but not wet under the mulch.

PRUNING: Prune just after flowering. Remove dead or weak wood and thin out overly dense growth. To encourage bushiness, cut back top growth, leaving 1 inch of new growth.

CAMELLIA

Leaf gall.

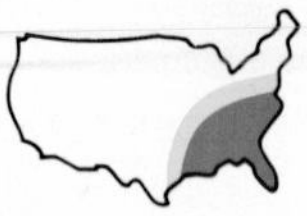

PROBLEM: Developing leaves and new shoots are thickened, fleshy, and enlarged. Diseased leaves can be up to ten times thicker than normal leaves. The upper surface of the leaf is green, but the underside is white and peeling. There are usually no more than a few diseased shoots on a plant. This problem is most common in periods of warm, moist weather.

ANALYSIS: Camellia leaf gall
This plant disease is caused by a fungus (*Exobasidium camelliae*); it is found on camellias only in the Southeast. The disease is more common on sasanqua varieties than on japonica. As the buds open in spring, fungal spores blown by wind to the plant or overwintering on the bark enter the tissue. The spores need moisture to germinate. Plants grown in areas of poor air movement, or in deep shade where moisture levels are high, are more likely to be infected.

SOLUTION: Sprays to control leaf gall must be applied before infection occurs. Once the galls develop, the best control is to remove them when they are first noticed. Search carefully to remove all galls. If they are not removed and destroyed, the disease will be more severe the following year. To prevent new infection next spring, spray with a fungicide containing *zineb* before new leaves open. Repeat at intervals of two weeks until new leaves are fully grown. If practical, move the plant to an area with better air circulation and avoid planting shrubs in areas of deep shade.

Camellia flower blight.

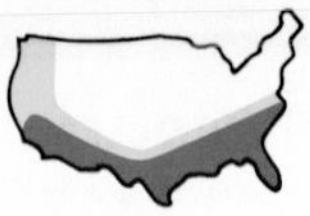

PROBLEM: Tan or brown spots or blotches spread across the flower. Infection takes place any time after the camellia buds begin to show color. The whole flower may turn brown. This disease is distinguished from frost, sunscald, or wind damage by a pattern of darkened veins, which give a netted effect in the spots. Dark brown to black resting structures an inch or more in diameter form in the base of the flower.

ANALYSIS: Camellia flower blight
This serious and widespread plant disease is caused by a fungus (*Sclerotinia camelliae*) that attacks only the flowers of camellias. In late winter to early spring, black fungal resting structures in the soil produce spores that are carried by the wind to new flowers. If moisture is present, the spores germinate and cause infection. The flowers may turn completely brown within 48 hours. The fungus continues to grow in the flower, eventually producing black resting structures that drop from the shrub with the flower. These resting structures can persist in the soil for at least five years.

SOLUTION: Remove and destroy infected flowers to eliminate the source of new infections the following spring. Many spores are produced in one infected flower. Rake up and destroy old leaves, flowers, and plant debris. A soil spray with a fungicide containing *PCNB* will inhibit spore production. Begin spray in December and repeat every three to four weeks throughout the blooming season. If this disease is a problem in your area, protect the flowers with a spray containing benomyl as soon as they begin to show color. Repeat every three days to protect new flowers.

Virus.

PROBLEM: Irregular yellow splotches of various sizes and shapes appear on the leaves. Some leaves may be entirely yellow. The uninfected portions remain dark green. Colored flowers may have irregular white blotches. White flowers show no symptoms. Some camellia varieties with extensive leaf yellowing may be weak and stunted.

ANALYSIS: Camellia yellow mottle leaf virus
The virus is transmitted by propagating from an infected plant or by grafting from an infected plant to a healthy one. This generally occurs in the nursery where the plant was grown. Sometimes the virus disease is intentionally transmitted to get variegated flowers. The disease is usually fairly harmless unless there is extensive leaf yellowing. Yellowing results from the suppression of green pigment (chlorophyll) development by the virus. The leaves produce less food, causing the plant to be weakened.

SOLUTION: Once the plant is infected there is no chemical that will control the virus. Remove excessively weak camellias. Buy only healthy plants. For further information on selecting healthy plants, see page 924.

Sunburn.

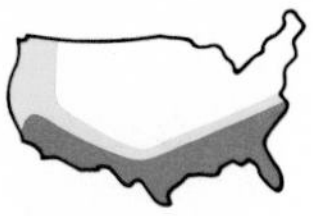

PROBLEM: During warm sunny weather, the center portion of the leaf turns yellowish or bronze,and severely affected areas turn brown and die. Flowers may be bleached or brown. The shrub is planted in direct sun or against a south- or west-facing wall.

ANALYSIS: Sunscald

Camellias are shade-loving plants. Their leaves and flowers are sensitive to the heat of direct sun, which kills the plant tissue. Scalding occurs when the shrub is planted in full sun or against a south- or west-facing wall. It takes only one hot summer day for damage to appear. The injury is unsightly but is not damaging to the plant. However, weakened leaves are more susceptible to invasion by fungi and bacteria. Plants deficient in water are more susceptible to sunscald.

SOLUTION: Once leaves and flowers are scalded, they will not recover. Remove affected leaves where practical. Move injured plants to a shaded location or provide some shade where they are now planted. For more information about transplanting, see page 924.

Aphids (half life size).

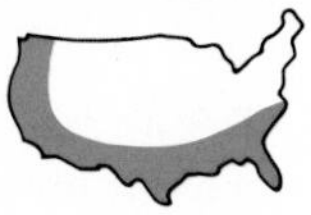

PROBLEM: Young leaves are cupped, twisted, and may be yellowing. Flower buds are malformed. A shiny, sticky substance may coat the leaves. A black sooty mold often grows on the sticky substance. Tiny ($\frac{1}{16}$ to $\frac{1}{8}$ inch) black, yellow, or green soft-bodied insects cluster on the buds, stems, and undersides of leaves. Ants may be present.

ANALYSIS: Aphids

The most common aphid infesting camellias is the black citrus aphid (*Toxoptera aurantii*), which causes leaf cupping and malformed buds. Several other aphids may also attack camellias. Aphids do little damage in small numbers. However, they are extremely prolific and populations can rapidly build up to damaging numbers during the growing season. Damage occurs when the aphid sucks the juices from the camellia leaves and stems. Some aphid species attacking camellias are unable to digest fully all the sugar in the plant sap and excrete the excess in a fluid called honeydew. The black citrus aphid produces large quantities of honeydew, which often drops onto the leaves below. Plants beneath the shrub may also be coated with honeydew. A black sooty mold fungus may develop on the honeydew, or rain may wash it off before the fungus has a chance to grow. Ants feed on the sticky substance, and are often present where there is an aphid infestation.

SOLUTION: Control with ORTHO Isotox Insect Killer or ORTHO Malathion 50 Insect Spray when aphids first appear. Direct the spray to the undersides of the leaves. Repeat the spray in midsummer if the plant becomes reinfested.

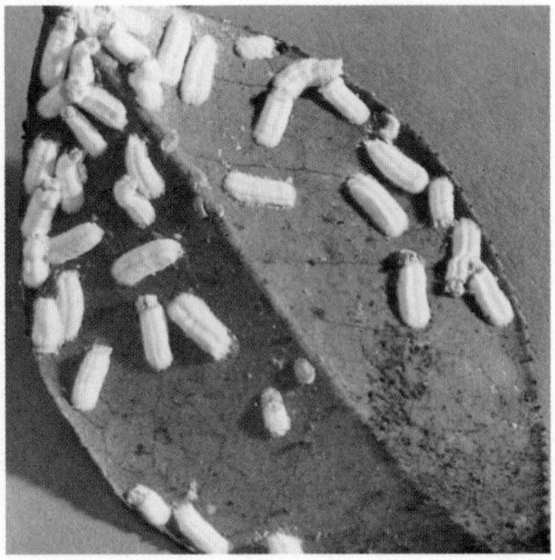

Cottony scales (life size).

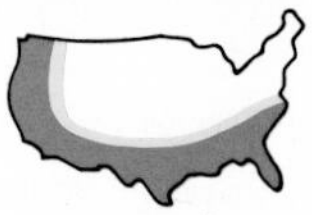

PROBLEM: Buds, young branches, or the undersides of leaves are covered with white, cottony masses. The leaves are yellowing and the plant may be weak and stunted. A shiny, sticky substance may coat the leaves. A black sooty mold often grows on this sticky substance. Ants may be present.

ANALYSIS: Cottony scales and mealybugs

Cottony scales and mealybugs are common on camellias. The visual similarities between these insects make separate identification difficult. They are very conspicuous in late spring and summer because the females are covered with a white, cottony egg sac, containing up to 2500 eggs. Females lay their egg masses on leaves or branches. The young insects are yellowish brown to green and inconspicuous. They feed throughout the summer on the stems and leaves. Damage is caused by the withdrawal of plant sap from the leaves and young branches. Some species of scales and mealybugs that infest camellias are unable to digest fully all the sugar in the plant sap and excrete the excess in a fluid called honeydew. A sooty mold fungus may develop on the sticky substance, causing the camellia leaves to appear black and dirty. Plants infested for more than a year are weakened and may be stunted.

SOLUTION: Control with ORTHO Orthene Systemic Insect Control, ORTHO Malathion 50 Insect Spray, or ORTHO Isotox Insect Killer in midsummer when the young are active. Repeat if plants become reinfested. To control scales early or late in the season, spray with ORTHO Volck Oil Spray in spring after blooming or in fall prior to blooming.

CAMELLIA

Camellia scales (twice life size).

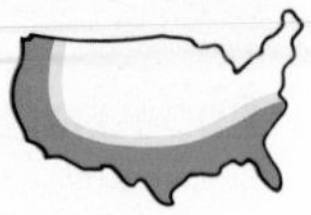

PROBLEM: Nodes, stems, buds, and leaves are covered with brown or black crusty bumps or thick, white, waxy bumps. The bumps can be scraped or picked off; the undersides are usually soft. Leaves may turn yellow and drop off, and twigs may die back. In some cases, a shiny, sticky substance coats the leaves. A black sooty mold often grows on the sticky substance. Ants are sometimes present.

ANALYSIS: Scales

Many species of scales infest camellias. They lay their eggs on leaves or bark, and in spring to midsummer the young scales, called *crawlers*, settle on the various parts of the shrub. These small (1/10 inch), soft-bodied young feed by sucking sap from the plant. The legs usually atrophy and a hard crusty or waxy shell develops over the body. The mature female scales lay their eggs underneath the shell. Some species of scales that infest camellias are unable to digest all the sugar in the plant sap, and excrete the excess in a fluid called honeydew. A sooty mold fungus may develop on the honeydew. An uncontrolled infestation of scales may kill the plant after two or three seasons. For more information about scales, see page 876.

SOLUTION: Control with ORTHO Isotox Insect Killer or ORTHO Orthene Systemic Insect Control when the young are active. Contact your local Cooperative Extension Office (see page 1011) to determine the best time to spray for scales in your area. To control scales early or late in the season, spray with ORTHO Volck Oil Spray in the spring after blooming, or in the fall prior to blooming.

Sooty mold.

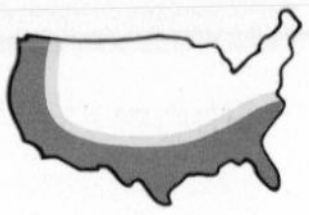

PROBLEM: A black sooty mold is growing on leaves and twigs. It can be completely wiped off the surfaces.

ANALYSIS: Sooty mold

This common black mold is caused by several species of fungi that grow on the sugary material left on plants by aphids, scales, mealybugs, whiteflies, and other insects that suck sap from the plant. The insects are unable to digest all the sugar in the sap and excrete the excess in a fluid called honeydew, which drops onto the leaves below. The honeydew may also drop out of infested trees and shrubs onto camellias growing beneath them. Sooty mold is unsightly, but it is fairly harmless because it does not attack the leaf directly. Extremely heavy infestations prevent light from reaching the leaf, so that the leaf produces fewer nutrients and may turn yellow. The presence of sooty mold indicates that the camellia or another plant near it is infested with insects.

SOLUTION: Sooty mold can be wiped from the leaves with a wet rag, or it will eventually be washed off by rain. Prevent more sooty mold by controlling the insect that is producing the honeydew. Inspect the leaves and twigs above the sooty mold to find what type of insect is present. For control instructions, see the following pages: for aphids, scales, and mealybugs, page 463; for whiteflies, page 877.

Iron deficiency.

PROBLEM: Some of the leaves are pale green to yellow. The newest leaves may be completely yellow with only the veins remaining green. On older leaves, only the leaf edges may be yellowing. The plant may be stunted.

ANALYSIS: Iron deficiency

This is a common problem in acid-loving plants like camellia. The plant prefers soil with a pH between 5.5 and 6.5. (For more information on soil acidity, see page 908.) The yellowing is due to a deficiency of iron and other minor nutrients in the plant. The soil is seldom deficient in iron. However, iron is often found in an insoluble form that is not available to the plant, especially in soil with a pH of 7.0 or higher. A high soil pH can result from overliming, or from lime leached from cement or brick. Regions where soil is derived from limestone, and those with low rainfall, also have high-pH soils. Plants use iron in the formation of the green pigment in the leaves. When it is lacking, new leaves are yellow.

SOLUTION: Spray the foliage with ORTHO Greenol Liquid Iron, and apply it to the soil around the plants to correct the iron deficiency. Correct the pH of the soil by treating it with ORTHO Aluminum Sulfate and watering it in well. Maintain an acid pH by fertilizing with ORTHO Azalea, Camellia & Rhododendron Food. When planting camellia, add at least 50 percent peat moss to the soil if you live in an area where the soil is alkaline or has poor drainage. Never lime the soil around camellia.

Algal spot.

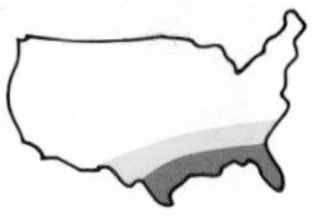

PROBLEM: Leaves and twigs are covered with reddish brown, velvety patches or greenish brown spots. Twigs may be stunted or die back.

ANALYSIS: Algal spot
Algal spot, also called *green scurf*, is caused by algae (*Cephaleuros virescens*) that are common on camellias and other ornamentals in the South. During moist weather, cells of the algae enter the leaves or twigs and spread rapidly. The invaded twig tissue may swell and crack. If the crack encircles the twig, the twig dies. The infected camellia leaves turn greenish brown at first. If the algae develop spore-producing bodies (tiny, round heads on fine, dense, reddish hairs) the patches appear reddish brown and velvety or cushiony. The algae spread rapidly when rains are frequent and heavy. Camellia plants weakened by poor growing conditions are most susceptible to algal spot.

SOLUTION: Control measures are not usually necessary. If trees are weak, improve growing conditions by watering and fertilizing regularly. Prune dead twigs. Improve air circulation around camellia plants by thinning out nearby dense vegetation. If algal spot is severe, spray with a fungicide containing *basic copper sulfate*, plus an oil or spreader-sticker, in December and January and at the start of the rainy season. Repeat 1 month later. For more information about spreader-stickers, see page 922.

CARISSA (NATAL PLUM)

Root rot.

PROBLEM: Small twigs and branches or entire plants turn brown and die. The leaves on affected branches may turn yellow before turning brown. No pests are seen on the dying plants, and plants of any age may be affected.

ANALYSIS: Root rot
This plant disease is caused by any of a number of different fungi, also known as *water molds,* that live in the soil. These fungi thrive in waterlogged, heavy soil. Some of these fungi attack the plant stems at the soil level, while others attack the roots. Infection causes the roots and stems to decay. This results in wilting, then yellowing leaves, and eventually the death of the plant. These fungi are generally spread by infested soil, contaminated equipment, and splashing or running water.

SOLUTION: Allow the soil around the plants to dry out. (For more information on this technique, see page 849.) Remove and discard severely infected plants. Avoid future root rot problems by planting in well-drained soil. For information on improving soil drainage, see page 907.

Carissa cultural information
Light: Full sun to part shade
Water: When the soil is almost dry
Soil: Loose, well drained
Fertilizer: Medium

CARPINUS (HORNBEAM)

Canker.

PROBLEM: Leaves on affected branches are stunted and lighter green than normal. Some leaves turn brown and drop. Twigs may die back. There are sunken, brownish, water-soaked areas on the branches. A liquid may exude from the canker. The tree may be killed.

ANALYSIS: Canker and dieback
A number of different fungi cause canker and dieback on hornbeam. They enter the tree at a wound, killing the surrounding healthy tissue. A sunken canker develops; tree sap containing the fungus may ooze from the wound. The canker cuts off the flow of nutrients and water through the vessels, causing the leaves to turn yellow. The tree may stop the spreading disease by producing callus tissue, a rapid growth of barklike cells that walls off the fungus. If the expanding canker is stopped before it covers half the branch, the branch usually survives. However, the fungus may grow faster than the callus.

SOLUTION: Prune off dead twigs and small cankered branches. Cankers on larger branches can be excised with a knife or chisel. Remove all discolored wood, and a 1-inch border of apparently healthy bark around the wound. After each cut, sterilize the knife or chisel with rubbing alcohol. To prevent the development of new cankers, avoid wounding trees. Do not overwater.

Carpinus cultural information
Light: Full sun
Water: Moist or dry conditions
Soil: Tolerates many types
Fertilizer: Light

CASTANEA (CHESTNUT)

Chestnut blight canker.

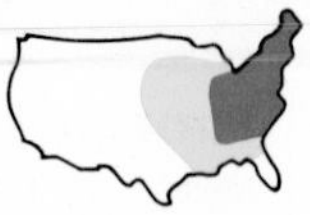

PROBLEM: Leaves on one or more branches are yellow or brown and dry.
Dead leaves hang on diseased branches long after normal leaf fall. On young wood, there are swollen, yellow-brown areas. On older wood, the areas are reddish and often split longitudinally. Trees usually die within four years.

ANALYSIS: Chestnut blight
This plant disease is caused by a fungus (*Endothia parasitica*). It is one of the most destructive plant diseases in North America. It was first discovered in New York in 1904, and within thirty years every stand of chestnut trees in the eastern half of the United States had been infected or killed. Almost all of the native chestnut trees are gone. The blight does not kill the roots, but leaves old sprouting stumps to harbor the fungus. New sprouts may grow for several years before they are killed. Trees planted on the West Coast or in the Midwest may grow to maturity. The spores enter the tree at a wound; a swollen canker develops and expands through the wood. The canker cuts off the flow of nutrients and water through the vessels, causing dieback of the parts beyond the affected area. Cankers develop throughout the tree, eventually killing it.

SOLUTION: There is no effective control for chestnut blight. Remove diseased trees, including the stump. Asiatic chestnuts are resistant to the disease.

Castanea cultural information
Light: Full sun
Water: Occasional deep watering
Soil: Well drained, nonalkaline
Fertilizer: Light

CATALPA

Catalpa sphinx caterpillars (half life size).

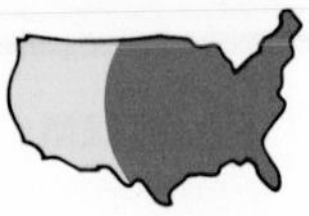

PROBLEM: Small holes are chewed in the upper surfaces of the leaves.
Large yellow and black striped caterpillars with a sharp "horn" at the tail end feed in groups on young leaves. As the caterpillars develop (to a length of 1 to 3 inches), they spread throughout the tree and feed singly on leaf edges. The tree may be completely defoliated. Damage occurs from May to August.

ANALYSIS: Catalpa sphinx
(*Ceratomia catalpae*)
The caterpillar is the larval stage of a large night-flying moth that is seldom seen. The moth passes the winter as a pupa in the ground. In spring, the moth emerges and the female lays her eggs on young catalpa leaves. The eggs hatch and the larvae feed for several weeks. If the larvae are left uncontrolled they develop into moths, producing a second generation of caterpillars that may completely defoliate the tree by mid to late summer.

SOLUTION: Control with ORTHO Orthene Systemic Insect Control or ORTHO Isotox Insect Killer when damage is first noticed in spring. Repeat in midsummer if the tree becomes reinfested. In fall, clean up debris beneath the tree to reduce the number of overwintering pupae.

The catalpa sphinx caterpillar is good fishing bait. Control the insects by handpicking them off the tree and then go fishing.

Leaf spot.

PROBLEM: Spots and blotches appear on the leaves. The spots may be yellow, brown, or black. They range in size from barely visible to ¼ inch in diameter. Several spots may join to form blotches. Spots may drop out of the leaf, leaving holes. Infected leaves may drop and, if spotting is severe, the tree may defoliate prematurely. Leaf spotting is most severe in moist, humid weather.

ANALYSIS: Leaf spot
Several different fungi cause leaf spots on catalpa. These spots are unsightly but rarely harmful to the plant. The fungi are spread by wind and splashing water. Spots develop where the fungi enter the tissue. The fungi survive the winter on twigs and in plant debris. Most leaf-spotting fungi do their greatest damage in mild (between 50° and 85°F), moist weather.

SOLUTION: Once leaves have become spotted, they will remain so. Reduce chances of spotting next year by cleaning up and destroying plant debris in the fall. To protect specimen plants, spray them with a fungicide containing *basic copper sulfate* or *ferbam* in the spring when the leaves emerge. Respray when the leaves are half-grown, and again when they are fully grown.

Scorched leaves.

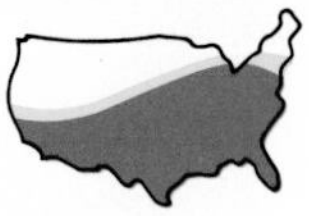

PROBLEM: During hot weather, usually in July or August, leaves turn brown around the edges and between the veins. Sometimes the whole leaf dies. Many leaves may drop during late summer. This problem is most severe on the youngest branches. Trees do not generally die. Browning and withering can develop whether the soil around the roots is moist or dry.

ANALYSIS: Summer leaf scorch
Leaf scorch is caused by excessive evaporation of moisture from the leaves. In hot weather, water evaporates rapidly from the leaves. If the roots can't absorb and convey water fast enough to replenish this loss, then the leaves turn brown and wither. This usually occurs in dry soil, but leaves also can scorch when the soil is moist. Drying winds, severed roots, limited soil area or low temperatures can also cause scorch. For more information about leaf scorch, see page 857.

SOLUTION: To prevent further scorch, deep-water trees during periods of hot weather to wet down the entire root space (see page 912 for more information about watering trees). Newly transplanted trees should be watered whenever the rootball is dry 2 inches below the surface. There are no controls for scorch on trees in moist soil. Plant trees adapted to your climate.

Catalpa cultural information
Light: Full sun
Water: Occasional deep watering
Soil: Tolerates many types
Fertilizer: Light

Verticillium wilt.

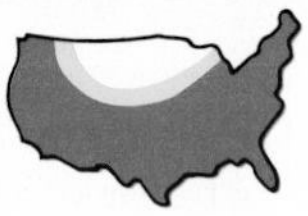

PROBLEM: The leaves on a branch turn yellow at the margins, then brown and dry. During hot weather, the leaves may wilt. New leaves are stunted and yellow. The leaves on uninfected portions remain green. The infected tree may die slowly, branch by branch, over several seasons. Or the whole tree may wilt and die within a few months. Some trees may recover. The tissue under the bark on the dying side shows brownish streaks when cut. To examine for streaks, peel back the bark at the bottom of the dying branch. The brown discoloration may be very apparent or barely visible in the cut.

ANALYSIS: Verticillium wilt
This wilt disease affects many ornamental trees and shrubs. It is caused by a soil-inhabiting fungus (*Verticillium* species). The disease is spread by contaminated seeds, plants, soil, equipment, and ground water. The fungus enters the tree through the roots and spreads up into the branches through the water-conducting vessels in the trunk. The vessels become discolored and plugged. The plugging cuts off the flow of water and nutrients to the branches, causing the leaf discoloration and branch wilting. For more information about verticillium wilt, see page 850.

SOLUTION: No chemical control is available. Fertilize and water the affected tree to stimulate vigorous growth. Remove all dead wood. Do not remove branches on which leaves have recently wilted. These branches may produce new leaves in 3 to 4 weeks or next spring. Remove dead trees. If replanting in the same area, plant trees and shrubs that are resistant to verticillium (see page 1006).

Leaf spot.

PROBLEM: Spots and blotches appear on the leaves. The spots may be yellow, red, tan, gray, or brown. They range in size from barely visible to ¼ inch in diameter. Several spots may join to form blotches. Leaves may yellow and die. Some leaves may drop. Leaf spotting is most severe in moist, humid weather.

ANALYSIS: Leaf spot
Several different fungi cause leaf spots on ceanothus. These spots are unsightly but rarely harmful to the plant. Plants weakened by low temperatures and wind exposure are most susceptible to invasion by leaf spot fungi. The fungi are spread by wind and splashing water. If wet or humid weather persists,the fungi spread through the tissue and blotches form. They survive the winter on the leaves and twigs. Most leaf organisms do their greatest damage in mild weather (between 50° and 85°F).

SOLUTION: Once leaves become spotted they will remain so. Where practical, remove infected leaves from the plant. Collect and destroy any fallen leaves. To reduce unsightly damage, spray with a fungicide containing *zineb* when new growth begins in spring. Repeat two more times at intervals of 2 weeks, or for as long as the weather remains favorable for infection. Add a spreader-sticker to the spray. For more information on spreader-stickers, see page 922.

Ceanothus cultural information
Light: Full sun
Water: Grows best in dry soil
Soil: Tolerates many types
Fertilizer: Light

CEANOTHUS (WILD LILAC)

Canker on ceanothus.

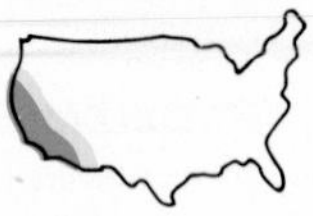

PROBLEM: The young leaves are yellowish or off-color. Many of the leaves wilt and fall off, and overall plant growth is sparse. Eventually the whole plant dies. The roots are dark and rotted. There may be a dark, sunken canker on the stem near the soil line.

ANALYSIS: Root and crown rot
This disease is caused by any of a number of different fungi, also known as *water molds,* that thrive in waterlogged, heavy soils. Some of these fungi attack the plant stems at the soil level, while others attack the roots. Infection causes the roots and stems to decay, resulting in wilting, then yellowing leaves, and eventually the death of the plant. These fungi are spread by infested soil and transplants.

SOLUTION: Remove dead and dying plants. Allow the soil around the plants to dry out. (For more information on this technique, see page 849.) Avoid future root rot problems by planting in well-drained soil. For information on improving soil drainage, see page 907.

CELASTRUS (BITTERSWEET)

Euonymus scale (4 times life size).

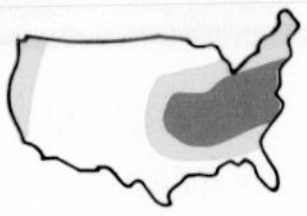

PROBLEM: Yellow or whitish spots appear on the upper surfaces of the leaves. Leaves may drop, and the plant may become bare by midsummer. In severe cases, stems die back. The stems and the undersides of the leaves are covered with dark brown, oystershell-shaped, crusty bumps or soft, white, elongated scales. The bumps and scales can be scraped off.

ANALYSIS: Euonymus scale
(*Unaspis euonymi*)
This scale, a serious pest of bittersweet and other ornamental shrubs, is found throughout the country. The scales spend the winter on the twigs and branches of bittersweet, laying their eggs in spring. In late spring to early summer the young scales, called *crawlers*, settle on leaves or stems. The small (1⁄10 inch), soft-bodied young feed by inserting their mouthparts and sucking sap. The legs atrophy and a crusty or waxy shell develops over the body. The males are white and very noticeable on the leaves and stems. The mature female scales are brown and shaped like an oystershell. They lay their eggs underneath the shell. The cycle may be repeated up to three times during the growing season. An uncontrolled infestation may kill the plant after 2 or 3 years. Other species of scale also infest bittersweet. For more information about scales, see page 876.

SOLUTION: Spray with ORTHO Isotox Insect Killer or ORTHO Orthene Systemic Insect Control in early summer (late spring in the South), when the young are active. The following spring, before new growth begins, spray the trunk and branches with a *dormant oil spray* to control overwintering insects.

CELTUS (HACKBERRY)

Witch's broom.

PROBLEM: There are broomlike growths of twigs throughout the tree. The clusters of twigs are most noticeable after leaf fall. Affected branches are weakened and break easily during windstorms.

ANALYSIS: Witch's broom
Witch's broom is most severe on common or American hackberry (*Celtis occidentalis*). The cause of this problem is not definitely known. However, a powdery mildew fungus (*Sphaerotheca phytophila*) and a gall mite (*Eriophyes* species) are usually associated with witch's broom. Gall mites cause proliferation of tissue in many plants. In spring, affected buds are larger and more open than normal. Microscopic mites and black spore-producing bodies from the fungus may be found inside. Branches from the affected buds become dwarfed and clustered, giving the witch's broom effect. Although the damage is unsightly, trees with this problem are not seriously harmed.

SOLUTION: There is no effective chemical control for this problem. If the brooms are unsightly, prune them off. For more information about pruning, see ORTHO's book *All About Pruning.*

Celtis cultural information
Light: Full sun
Water: Drought tolerant once established
Soil: Tolerates many types
Fertilizer: Light

CERCIS (REDBUD)

Galls caused by leaf gall psyllids.

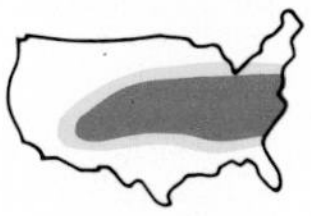

PROBLEM: The lower surfaces of the leaves are covered with cylindrical nipple- or crater-shaped or blisterlike growths. The upper surface of the leaf is spotted and yellowing. If the growth is broken open during the summer, a tiny (1/10 inch) yellowish orange insect is found inside. In late August or September, houses are invaded and windows and screens are covered with dark-colored flying insects, 1/8 inch long.

ANALYSIS: Hackberry leaf gall psyllids (*Pachypsylla* species)
The hackberry psyllid adults are considered more a nuisance than a destructive tree pest. The growth and vigor of the tree are not noticeably affected by the insects. Adult psyllids spend the winter in protected places such as buildings, trash, and bark crevices. In spring, just as the hackberry buds swell, the adults emerge from hibernation and fly or crawl around the ends of twigs. Eggs are deposited on the undersides of unfolded leaves; when they hatch, the immature insects feed by sucking the sap. This feeding stimulates abnormal leaf growth, producing the galls that enclose the insects and protect them from predators. The adults emerge in early fall, invading homes and buildings around hackberry trees.

SOLUTION: Once the protective galls have formed around the insects, there is no way to kill them. Spray trees with ORTHO Orthene Systemic Insect Control as leaves are unfolding in the spring to control overwintering adults and newly hatched immature psyllids before galls are formed. If adult psyllids invade the home, reduce the infestation by vacuuming them up. Destroy the sweeper bag contents.

Canker.

PROBLEM: The leaves on a branch wilt and turn brown. Eventually they drop. Twigs or branches are often dead or dying. There are sunken oval areas, with black centers and cracks along the edges, at the base of the affected twigs or branches.

ANALYSIS: Canker
This plant disease, caused by a fungus (*Botryosphaeria ribis*), is the most destructive disease of redbud. It also affects more than fifty woody plants in the eastern half of the country. (For a list of susceptible plants, see page 1018.) Spores, produced in the sunken areas during wet periods in spring and summer, are spread to healthy branches by splashing rain and wind. The fungus enters the tree through wounds or dead and dying twigs, and a sunken canker develops. The fungus slowly spreads through the wood in all directions, cutting off the flow of nutrients and water to the affected branch. The leaves wilt and die, and branches above the cankered area are usually killed.

SOLUTION: There is no effective chemical control available. Prune out and destroy dead twigs and branches, cutting at least 3 inches below the cankered area. Sterilize pruning shears after each cut with rubbing alcohol. Paint the cuts with ORTHO Pruning Seal. Remove dying trees. To help prevent infection, avoid wounding trees.

Cercis cultural information
Light: Full sun to shade
Water: Generally grows best in moist soil
Soil: Tolerates many types
Fertilizer: Light

Verticillium wilt.

PROBLEM: The leaves on a branch turn yellow at the margins, then brown and dry. During hot weather, the leaves may wilt. New leaves may be stunted and yellowish. The infected tree may die slowly, branch by branch, over several seasons. Or the whole tree may wilt and die within a few months. Some trees may recover. The tissue under the bark on the dying side shows dark streaks when cut. To examine for streaks, peel back the bark at the bottom of the dying branch. The dark discoloration may be very apparent or barely visible in the area just underneath the bark.

ANALYSIS: Verticillium wilt
This wilt disease attacks many ornamental trees and shrubs. It is caused by a soil-inhabiting fungus (*Verticillium* species). The disease is spread by contaminated seeds, plants, soil, equipment, and ground water. The fungus enters the tree through the roots and spreads up into the branches through the water-conducting vessels in the trunk. The vessels become discolored and plugged. The plugging cuts off the flow of water and nutrients to the branches, causing leaf discoloration and wilting. For more information about verticillium wilt, see page 850.

SOLUTION: No chemical control is available. Fertilize and water the affected tree to stimulate vigorous growth. Remove all dead wood. Do not remove branches on which leaves have recently wilted. These branches may produce new leaves in three to four weeks or next spring. Remove dead trees. If replanting in the same area, plant trees that are resistant to verticillium (see page 1006).

CHAENOMELES (FLOWERING QUINCE)

Rust.

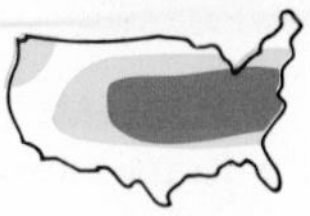

PROBLEM: Yellow or orange spots appear on young leaves and twigs. Heavy infection causes spotted leaves to fall prematurely. The plant may be weak and stunted.

ANALYSIS: Rust
This disease is caused by two species of fungi (*Gymnosporangium clavipes* and *G. libocedri*). These fungi require both quince and certain junipers or incense cedar to complete their life cycles. Rust spores on quince cannot infect another quince, but must alternate between quince and one of the evergreens. Wind-borne spores from the evergreen plant infect quince in spring. With warm, wet weather, the spores germinate and infect the leaves and twigs, causing the spotting. In August, spores are released during dry weather and carried by wind back to the evergreen plant. Rust (*G. clavipes*) on junipers causes swellings and possibly dieback on twigs. The main trunk has rough black patches or rings around the bark. Swellings and witch's broom (a dense bushy growth on the branches) develop from rust infection on incense cedars.

SOLUTION: To prevent infection from incense cedar and junipers, spray with a fungicide containing *chlorothalonil* (DACONIL 2787®), *ferbam, zineb*, or *mancozeb* as soon as new leaves appear. Repeat the spray 2 more times at weekly intervals. Do not plant flowering quince within several hundred yards of incense cedars and junipers. For a list of plants susceptible to quince rust, see page 1015.

CHOISYA

Spider mite damage.

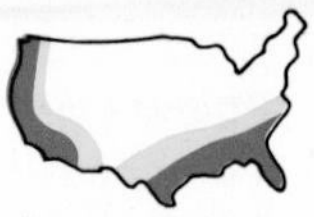

PROBLEM: Leaves are stippled yellow and dirty. Sometimes there is a silken webbing on the lower surfaces of the leaves. New leaves may be distorted. To determine if the plant is infested with mites, hold a sheet of white paper underneath an affected leaf and tap the leaf sharply. Minute green, red, or yellow specks the size of pepper grains will drop to the paper and begin to crawl around. The pests are easily seen against the white background.

ANALYSIS: Spider mites
Spider mites, related to spiders, are major pests of many garden plants. They cause damage by sucking sap from the undersides of leaves. As a result of feeding, the green leaf pigment disappears, producing the stippled appearance. Mites are active throughout the growing season, but most are favored by hot, dry weather (70°F and up). By midsummer, they build up to tremendous numbers. For more information about spider mites, see page 887.

SOLUTION: Spray with a pesticide containing *dicofol* (KELTHANE®) to control mites. Repeat spray three more times, five to seven days apart.

Choisya cultural information
Light: Full sun to part shade
Water: Occasional deep watering
Soil: Loose, well drained, nonalkaline
Fertilizer: Medium

CINNAMOMUM (CAMPHOR TREE)

Verticillium wilt.

PROBLEM: The leaves on a branch turn yellow at the margins, then brown and dry. During hot weather, the leaves may wilt. New leaves may be stunted and yellowish. The infected tree may die slowly, branch by branch, over several seasons. Or the whole tree may wilt and die within a few months. The tissue under the bark on the dying side shows dark streaks when cut. To examine for streaks, peel back the bark at the bottom of the dying branch.

ANALYSIS: Verticillium wilt
This wilt disease is caused by a fungus (*Verticillium dahliae*) that lives in the soil. The fungus enters the tree through the roots and spreads up into the branches through the water-conducting vessels in the trunk. The vessels become discolored and plugged. The plugging cuts off the flow of water and nutrients to the branches, causing the leaf discoloration and wilting. For more information about verticillium, see page 850.

SOLUTION: No chemical control is available. Fertilize and water the affected tree to stimulate vigorous growth. Remove all dead wood. If replanting in the same area, plant trees and shrubs that are resistant to verticillium. For a list of resistant trees and shrubs, see page 1006.

Cinnamomum cultural information
Light: Full sun
Water: Occasional deep watering
Soil: Loose, well drained, nonalkaline
Fertilizer: Light

CORNUS (DOGWOOD)

ADAPTATION: Throughout the United States except in desert areas.

FLOWERING TIME: February to July. Colors range from white to red. Clusters of reddish berries develop in fall that often persist after the leaves have fallen.

LIGHT: Partial shade to full sun.

SOIL: Well drained, rich in organic matter, acid (pH 5.5 to 6.5).

FERTILIZER: Fertilize with ORTHO Azalea, Camellia & Rhododendron Food according to label directions.

WATER:
How much: Apply enough water to wet the soil 2 to 3 feet deep. To determine the proper amount of water for your soil type, see page 912.
How often: Most dogwoods prefer moist soil. Water when the soil is moist but not wet 4 inches below the soil surface. For more information about watering, see page 912.

PRUNING: Shrubs grown for their colorful bark should be given a vigorous pruning in the spring every few years to force new, colorful growth. Shrubs grown as dense screens should be cut back at the base every spring.

Spot anthracnose.

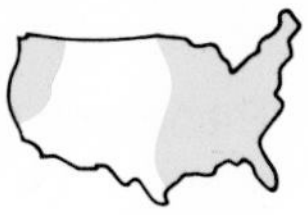

PROBLEM: Small (up to ⅛ inch) circular or elongated reddish purple spots appear on the flower petals (bracts). If spotting is severe, the flowers are malformed. The centers of the spots eventually dry and may drop out, leaving a small round hole. The leaves are infected after blooming, showing dark purple, circular spots or blotches. Young shoots and berries are also infected. Severely infected shoots die. The disease is worst in wet weather.

ANALYSIS: Spot anthracnose
This plant disease is caused by a fungus (*Elsinoë corni*). The fungus survives the winter on infected plant tissue. During wet weather in early spring, the fungus is splashed onto the dogwood blooms. Spots develop where the fungus enters the tissue. If wet weather continues, it spreads to the leaves and twigs.

SOLUTION: If spots are noticed on dogwood blooms in spring, spray with a fungicide containing *chlorothalonil* (DACONIL 2787®), *captan* (ORTHOCIDE®), or *mancozeb* at petal fall. Repeat 4 weeks later and again in September after flower buds form. The following spring, begin spraying when flower buds start to open. Prune out and destroy infected twigs. Rake up and destroy leaves in the fall.

Flower and leaf blight.

PROBLEM: In rainy seasons, irregular, brown, wrinkled patches appear on the flower petals (bracts) at the end of their bloom period. If the weather remains wet or humid, gray mold develops on the patches. When the bracts fall, young leaves they touch often become infected and shrivel. The infected leaves usually drop.

ANALYSIS: Flower and leaf blight
This plant disease is caused by a fungus (*Botrytis cinerea*) that infects many flowers, fruits, and vegetables in the garden. The fungus is spread to aging flowers by wind and splashing rain. Brown patches develop where the fungus enters the tissue. If the weather turns dry, the fungus stops spreading, and symptoms disappear when the flowers fall. However, if wet or humid weather continues throughout the spring, a grayish mold consisting of fungal strands and spores develops on the diseased flowers. As the bracts fall on young leaves, the fungal strands penetrate the leaf tissue and the leaves become blighted.

SOLUTION: Once the flowers and leaves are infected, it is too late to spray. Pick off all fading flowers and blighted leaves. Sprays must be applied early in the flowering period. If the weather is extremely wet or humid during early bloom the following spring, spray with a fungicide containing *chlorothalonil* (DACONIL 2787®), *benomyl*, *maneb*, or *mancozeb* at midbloom.

CORNUS (DOGWOOD)

Leaf spot.

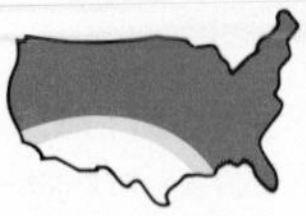

PROBLEM: Spots and blotches appear on the leaves. The spots may be yellow, red, tan, purple, gray, or black. They range in size from barely visible to ½ inch in diameter. Several spots may merge to form blotches. Leaves may be yellow and dying, and some leaves may drop. Leaf spotting is most severe in moist, humid weather.

ANALYSIS: Leaf spot
Many different fungi cause leaf spots on dogwood. These spots are unsightly but rarely harmful to the plant. The fungi are spread by wind and splashing water. Spots develop where the fungi enter the tissue. If wet or humid weather persists, the fungi spread through the tissue and blotches form. The fungi survive the winter on twigs and in plant debris. Most leaf spot organisms do their greatest damage in mild weather (between 50° and 85°F).

SOLUTION: Where practical, remove infected leaves from the plant. Clean up and destroy fallen leaves. To protect valuable trees, spray them in the spring with a fungicide containing *chlorothalonil* (DACONIL 2787®) or *benomyl,* beginning in April or when the new leaves emerge. Respray when the leaves are half-grown and again when they are fully grown. If the weather remains wet, spray at intervals of 2 to 3 weeks until late summer.

Summer leaf scorch.

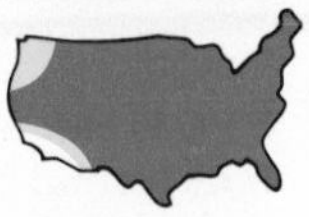

PROBLEM: During hot weather, usually in July or August, leaves turn brown at the edges and between the veins. Sometimes the whole leaf dies. Many leaves may drop during late summer. This problem is most severe on the youngest branches. Trees do not generally die. Browning and withering can develop whether the soil around the roots is moist or dry.

ANALYSIS: Summer leaf scorch
Leaf scorch is caused by excessive evaporation of moisture from the leaves. In hot weather, water evaporates rapidly from the leaves. If the roots can't absorb and convey water fast enough to replenish this loss, the leaves turn brown and wither. For optimum growth, dogwoods require moist soil. Leaf scorch is most severe when water is unavailable because the soil is dry. However, scorch may also develop when the soil is moist if the weather is extremely hot. Drying winds, severed roots, and limited soil area can also cause scorch. For more information about scorch, see page 857.

SOLUTION: To prevent further scorch, deep-water trees during periods of hot weather to wet down the entire root space. (For more information about watering trees, see page 912.) Newly transplanted trees should be watered whenever the rootball is dry 2 inches below the surface. There are no controls for scorch on trees in moist soil. Plant trees adapted to your climate. In hot summer areas, plant dogwoods in partial shade.

Dogwood borer. *Insert:* Adult (life size).

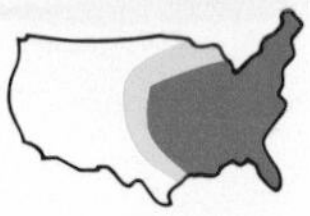

PROBLEM: In midsummer, the leaves turn red and drop prematurely; eventually twigs or branches die back. Bark sloughs off around holes in a swollen area on the trunk or at the base of branches. Late in the summer, a fine sawdust may drop from the holes. Young trees are usually killed.

ANALYSIS: Dogwood borer
(*Synanthedon scitula*)
The dogwood borer, also known as the *pecan borer,* is the larva of a brownish, clear-wing moth, ½-inch long. The borer infects flowering dogwood, pecan, and many other ornamental and fruit trees. The moths are active from May until September. They may be seen flying around trees during the summer. The moth lays its eggs on the bark, usually near a wound or old borer injury. After the eggs hatch, the ½-inch-long white larvae with brown heads find an opening in the bark. They feed in the wood just under the bark, girdling the branches and causing the dieback. The larvae spend the winter inside the tree. Several other borers also infest dogwood. For more information about borers, see page 865.

SOLUTION: Spray or paint the trunk and branches with ORTHO Lindane Borer & Leaf Miner Spray, beginning in April or May. Repeat 4 more times at monthly intervals. Water and fertilize the tree regularly to maintain vigor. (For a guide to watering and fertilizers for trees and shrubs, see pages 912 and 910.) To prevent borer entrance, avoid pruning during the summer months when the moths are present, and avoid wounding the trunks and branches. You can also reduce damage by inserting a fine wire up the entry hole to kill the larva.

Crown canker.

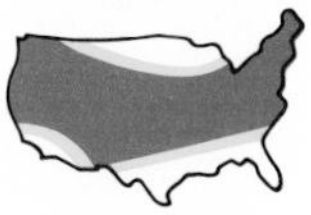

PROBLEM: The leaves on one or more branches at the top of the tree are small and pale green. They turn prematurely red in mid or late summer. Twigs and branches die back and sometimes the whole tree dies. The symptoms usually develop over several years. At the base of the tree dark-colored sap may ooze from one point. As the disease progresses, a sunken area develops around the oozing sap and the bark crumbles, leaving wood exposed. The exposed wood in the sunken area is dark and discolored.

ANALYSIS: Crown canker
This plant disease, also known as *collar-rot*, is caused by a soil-inhabiting fungus (*Phytophthora cactorum*). The fungus is carried in affected plants or in infested soil or soil water. It is often a problem following periods when flooding has resulted in standing water around the base of trees. It enters the root crown through wounds and slowly kills the tissue, causing a sunken canker. The above-ground symptoms are caused by the blockage of water and nutrients through the trunk. When the canker encircles the trunk, the tree dies.

SOLUTION: Small cankers can be removed surgically with some success if all discolored bark and wood, including a 1-inch border area of apparently healthy bark and wood, is removed. Remove an elliptical piece of wood from the tree with a sharp knife, sterilizing the knife with rubbing alcohol after each cut. Clean the wound with alcohol and cover with ORTHO Pruning Seal. If the tree dies, do not plant another dogwood in the same area for 3 to 5 years. Avoid wounding and watering the base of the tree.

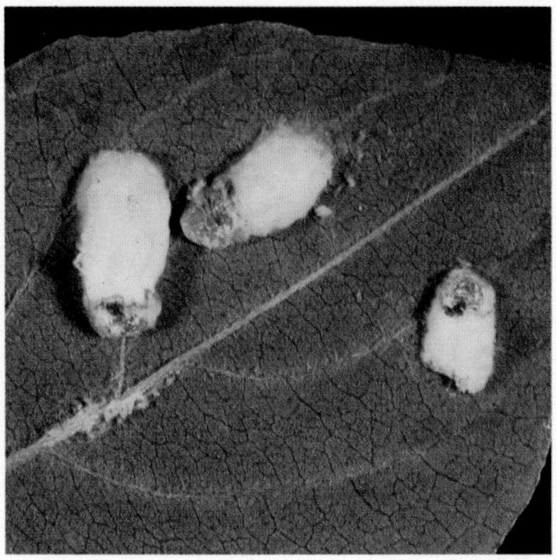

Cottony scale (3 times life size).

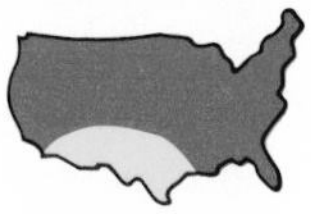

PROBLEM: The leaves, stems, and branches are covered with brownish crusty bumps or clusters of somewhat flattened brownish, yellow, or white scaly bumps. The bumps can be scraped or picked off; the undersides are usually soft. Leaves turn yellow and may drop. In some cases, twigs and branches die back. The plant may be killed.

ANALYSIS: Scales
Many different species of scales infest dogwood. Scales spend the winter on the trunk and twigs of dogwood. Most scales lay eggs in the spring. (Oystershell scales lay their eggs in the fall; the eggs hatch the following spring.) In late spring to early summer the young scales, called *crawlers*, settle on leaves and twigs. The small (1/10 inch), soft-bodied young feed by inserting their mouthparts and sucking sap from the plant. The legs usually atrophy and a hard crusty shell develops over the body. The mature female scale lays her eggs underneath the shell. An uncontrolled infestation may kill branches and possibly the entire tree after several seasons.

SOLUTION: Control with ORTHO Liquid Sevin in early or midsummer when the young are active. Repeat at intervals of 2 weeks if the plant becomes reinfested. To control scales early or late in the season, spray with ORTHO Volck Oil Spray in early spring before flowering or in late fall after leaves have dropped. For more information about scales, see page 412.

Verticillium wilt.

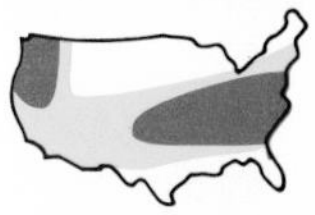

PROBLEM: The leaves on a branch turn reddish purple at the margins, then brown, and curl inward. During hot weather, the leaves may wilt. Generally, the leaves drop prematurely. The infected plant may die slowly, branch by branch, over several seasons. Or the whole plant may wilt and die within a few months. Some shrubs may recover. The tissue under the bark on the dying side shows brownish streaks when cut. To examine for streaks, peel back the bark at the bottom of the dying branch. The brown discoloration may be very apparent or barely visible in the area just underneath the bark.

ANALYSIS: Verticillium wilt
This wilt disease attacks many ornamental trees and shrubs. It is caused by a soil-inhabiting fungus (*Verticillium* species) that persists indefinitely on plant debris or in the soil. The disease is spread by contaminated seeds, plants, soil, equipment, and ground water. The fungus enters the tree through the roots and spreads up into the branches through the water-conducting vessels in the trunk. The vessels become discolored and plugged. This causes leaf discoloration and wilting. For more information about verticillium, see page 850.

SOLUTION: No chemical control is available. Fertilize and water the affected tree to stimulate vigorous growth. Remove all dead wood. Do not remove branches on which leaves have recently wilted. These branches may produce new leaves in 3 to 4 weeks or next spring. Remove dead shrubs. If replanting in the same area, plant trees and shrubs that are resistant to verticillium. For a list of resistant trees and shrubs, see page 1006.

COTONEASTER

Cotoneaster webworm damage.

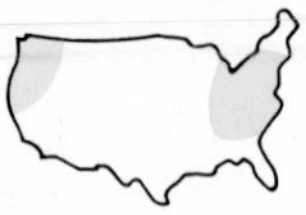

PROBLEM: Clumps of leaves tied together with silk threads are scattered all over the bush. The leaves are skeletonized and brown. Small (up to ½ inch) yellow to dark brown caterpillars are feeding inside the dense silken webbing. Small plants may die.

ANALYSIS: Cotoneaster webworm
(*Rhynchopacha triatomaea*)
This webworn is the larval stage of a grayish black night-flying moth that is seldom seen. The webworm spends the winter in a large silken nest in a branch junction. It pupates in the spring, and the emerging moth lays eggs on the leaf stems. The larvae that hatch from these eggs feed throughout the summer on the leaflets, webbing them together for protection against predators and weather.

SOLUTION: Spray with ORTHO Orthene Systemic Insect Control when webbing first appears. Repeat the spray in 2 weeks if damage continues.

Cotoneaster cultural information
Light: Full sun
Water: Drought tolerant once established
Soil: Tolerates many types
Fertilizer: Light

Fireblight.

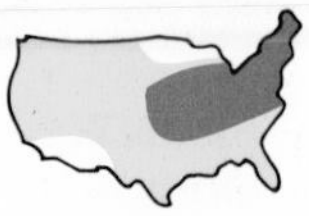

PROBLEM: New shoots suddenly wilt in spring and turn black as if scorched by fire. The bark at the base of the blighted shoots becomes water soaked, then dark, sunken, and dry; cracks may develop at the edge of the sunken area. In warm, moist spring weather, drops of brown ooze appear on the sunken bark. Young plants may die.

ANALYSIS: Fireblight
This plant disease is caused by a bacterium (*Erwinia amylovora*) that is very destructive to many trees and shrubs. For a list of susceptible plants, see page 1016. The bacteria spend the winter in sunken cankers on the branches. In spring, the bacteria ooze out of the cankers. Bees, flies, and other insects are attracted to the sweet, sticky ooze and become smeared with it. When the insects visit a cotoneaster flower for nectar, they infect it with the bacteria. The bacteria spread rapidly through the plant tissue in warm (65°F or higher), humid weather. Insects visiting these infected blossoms later carry bacteria-laden nectar to healthy blossoms. Rain, wind, and tools may also spread the bacteria. Tender or damaged leaves may be infected in midsummer.

SOLUTION: During spring and summer, prune out infected branches 12 to 15 inches beyond any visible discoloration and destroy them. A protective spray of a pesticide containing *basic copper sulfate* or *streptomycin*, applied before bud break in spring, will help prevent infection. Repeat at intervals of 5 to 7 days until the end of bloom. In the fall, prune out infected branches. Sterilize pruning shears with rubbing alcohol after each cut.

Damaged leaves. *Insert:* Lacebugs (⅓ life size).

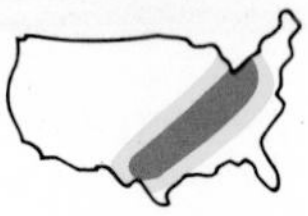

PROBLEM: The upper surfaces of the leaves are mottled yellow and green. The mottling may be confused with mite or leafhopper damage, but can be distinguished from other insect damage by the hard, black, shiny droplets found on the undersides of damaged leaves. Small (⅛ inch), light or dark spiny wingless insects or brownish insects with clear lace wings may be visible around the droplets and next to the midrib. The plant may be stunted. Damage occurs in spring and summer.

ANALYSIS: Hawthorn lacebug
(*Corythucha cydoniae*)
The hawthorn lacebug is found throughout the country on cotoneaster, hawthorn, pyracantha, and fruiting quince. It overwinters as an adult on the plant in bark crevices, branch crotches, or other protected areas on the shrub. Both the spiny, wingless, immature insects and the lacewinged adults suck sap from the undersides of leaves throughout the growing season. As a result of feeding, the green leaf pigment disappears, causing the characteristic yellowing. Droplets of black excrement accumulate around the insects while they feed. Damage is unsightly and food production by the leaf is reduced, resulting in a loss of plant vigor.

SOLUTION: Spray with ORTHO Isotox Insect Killer or ORTHO Orthene Systemic Insect Control when damage first appears in spring. Thoroughly cover the undersurfaces of the leaves where insects feed. Repeat 7 to 10 days later. A third application may be necessary if the plant becomes reinfested in the summer.

Blister mite damage.

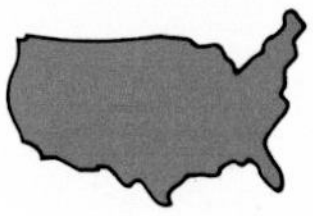

PROBLEM: Reddish or brownish blisters, ⅛ inch across, develop on the undersides of the leaves. The blisters may be massed together to almost cover the leaf. The upper surface of the leaf is mottled brown or blackish. Berries may be deformed.

ANALYSIS: Pear leaf blister mite
(*Phytoptus pyri*)
This microscopic pinkish or white mite is found wherever cotoneaster is grown. It also infests pear, apple, mountain ash, and service berry. Adults spend the winter in bud scales, often hundreds in a single bud. As the buds swell in spring, the mites lay their eggs; the young feed and burrow into the undersides of unfolding leaves. New generations of mites are produced inside the blisters throughout the summer. As cold weather approaches, the mites migrate back to the bud scales to overwinter.

SOLUTION: Once the mite has entered the underside of the leaf it is difficult to control. Spray the undersides of the leaves with a miticide containing *dicofol* (KELTHANE®) when damage is first noticed. Repeat 10 days later. The following early spring, just before growth starts, spray with ORTHO Volck Oil Spray or with ORTHO Orthorix Spray. As the leaves emerge, spray with a miticide containing *dicofol* (KELTHANE®). Repeat 10 days later.

CRATAEGUS (HAWTHORN)

ADAPTATION: Primarily zones 4 through 9. (To determine your climate zone, see the map on page 1020.) Not adapted to low desert areas.

FLOWERING TIME: Late spring.

LIGHT: Full sun.

SOIL: Hawthorns will thrive in almost any type of garden soil. However, most prefer a soil pH below 7.8.

FERTILIZER: Fertilize with ORTHO Evergreen, Tree & Shrub Food according to label directions.

WATER:
How much: Apply enough water to wet the soil 2 to 3 feet deep. To determine the proper amount of water for your soil type, see page 912.
How often: Keep plants on the dry side. Water when the soil is dry 4 inches below the surface. For more information about watering, see page 912.

PRUNING: Cut off any blighted or dead branches. Some shrubs may be sheared to form a dense hedge.

Fireblight.

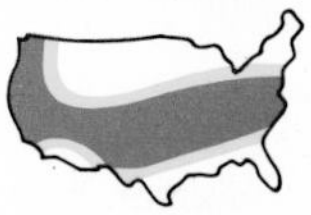

PROBLEM: Blossoms and leaves of infected twigs suddenly wilt and turn black as if scorched by fire. Brown or blackened leaves cling to the branches. The bark at the base of the blighted twig becomes water-soaked, then dark, sunken, and dry; cracks may develop at the edge of the sunken area. In warm, moist spring weather, drops of brown ooze appear on the sunken bark. Young trees may die.

ANALYSIS: Fireblight
This disease is caused by a bacterium (*Erwinia amylovora*) that is very destructive to hawthorn and many other related plants. (For a list of susceptible plants, see page 1001.) The bacteria spend the winter in the sunken cankers on the branches. In spring, the bacteria ooze out of the cankers and attract bees and other insects. When the insects visit a hawthorn flower for nectar, they infect it with the bacteria. The bacteria spread rapidly through the plant tissue in warm (65°F or higher), humid weather. Insects visiting these infected blossoms later carry bacteria-laden nectar to healthy blossoms. Rain, wind, and tools may also spread the bacteria.

SOLUTION: During spring and summer, prune out infected branches 12 to 15 inches beyond any visible discoloration and destroy them. A protective spray of a pesticide containing *basic copper sulfate* or *streptomycin*, applied before bud break in spring, will help prevent infection. Repeat at intervals of 5 to 7 days until the end of bloom. In the fall, prune out infected branches. Sterilize pruning shears with rubbing alcohol after each cut. When planting new trees, use resistant varieties. For a list of plants resistant to fireblight, see page 1016.

CRATAEGUS (HAWTHORN)

Hawthorn rust.

PROBLEM: In the summer, orange, red, gray, or brown spots develop on the upper surfaces of the leaves. Leaves are often distorted, and many may drop. Infected twigs and fruit are also deformed. Tiny whitish tubes may develop on the fruit and twigs, or brownish, horn-shaped bodies may develop in the fruit and on the undersides of leaves.

ANALYSIS: Hawthorn rust
This plant disease is caused by any of several species of fungi (*Gymnosporangium* species) that infect both hawthorns and red cedars or other species of junipers. The fungi cannot spread from hawthorn to hawthorn, but must alternate between junipers and hawthorns. In the spring, orange spores from junipers are carried by the wind to hawthorns. With warm, wet weather, the spores germinate and infect the leaves, twigs, and fruit. Depending on the species of rust, leaves become spotted, or the leaves, twigs, and fruit become deformed. Fruiting bodies develop on infected parts, which produce spores that are blown back to junipers. Some species of rust cause very little damage, while others may cause severe defoliation.

SOLUTION: If practical, eliminate junipers within a mile of hawthorns. If rust is a problem on your hawthorns, spray trees with a fungicide containing *chlorothalonil* (DACONIL 2787®) beginning just as the flower buds open. Repeat the spray two or three more times at intervals of 7 to 10 days.

Leaf spot.

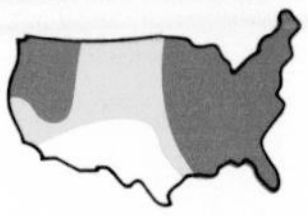

PROBLEM: Spots and blotches appear on the leaves. The spots may be red, purple, yellow, brown, or black. They range in size from barely visible to ¼ inch in diameter. Several spots may join to form blotches. Infected leaves may die and drop and, if spotting is severe, the tree may defoliate prematurely. Leaf spotting is most severe in moist, humid weather.

ANALYSIS: Leaf spot
Several different fungi, including *Fabraea theumenii*, cause leaf spots on hawthorn. These spots are unsightly but rarely harmful to the plant. However, severe, recurrent infections can cause repeated defoliations of the tree, which may weaken it and reduce its flowering potential. The fungi are spread by wind and splashing water. Spots develop where the fungi enter the leaf tissue. The fungi survive the winter on twigs and in fallen leaves and plant debris. Most leaf-spotting fungi do their greatest damage in mild (between 50° and 85°F), moist weather.

SOLUTION: Once the leaves have become spotted, they will remain so. To help prevent spotting next year, clean up and destroy fallen leaves and plant debris. In the spring, spray trees with a fungicide containing *chlorothalonil* (DACONIL 2787®) or *captan* (ORTHOCIDE®) when the leaves emerge. Respray when the leaves are half-grown, and again when they are fully grown. Continue spraying at intervals of 10 to 14 days as long as wet weather continues.

Lacebug damage.

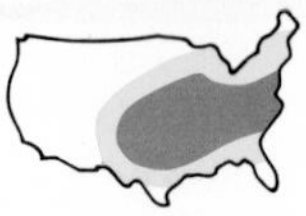

PROBLEM: The upper surfaces of the leaves are mottled yellow and green. The mottling may be confused with mite or leafhopper damage, but can be distinguished from other insect damage by the hard, black, shiny droplets found on the undersides of damaged leaves. Small (⅛ inch) light or dark spiny wingless insects or brownish insects with clear lace wings may be visible around the droplets and next to the midrib. The plant may be stunted. Damage occurs in spring and summer.

ANALYSIS: Hawthorn lacebug
(*Corythucha cydoniae*)
The hawthorn lacebug is found throughout the country on hawthorn, pyracantha, cotoneaster, and fruiting quince. It survives the winter as an adult on the plant in bark crevices, branch crotches, or other protected areas on the tree. Both the spiny, wingless, immature insects and the lace-wing adults suck sap from the undersides of leaves throughout the growing season. As a result of feeding, the green leaf pigment disappears, causing the characteristic yellowing. Droplets of black excrement accumulate around the insects while they feed. Damage is unsightly and food production by the leaf is reduced, resulting in a loss of plant vigor.

SOLUTION: Spray with ORTHO Orthene Systemic Insect Control or ORTHO Isotox Insect Killer when damage first appears in spring. Thoroughly cover the undersides of the leaves where insects feed. Repeat 7 to 10 days later. A third application may be necessary if the plant becomes reinfested in the summer.

Aphids (half life size).

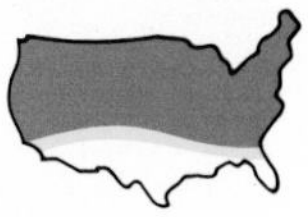

PROBLEM: Young leaves are tightly curled, stunted, and yellowing. New growth may stop completely. A shiny, sticky substance may coat the leaves and drip onto plants and other objects, such as cars parked beneath the tree. A black sooty mold often grows on the sticky substance. Tiny (1/8 inch) green, pinkish, yellow, or black soft-bodied insects cluster on branch tips and the undersides of leaves. Ants may be present.

ANALYSIS: Aphids
Aphids do little damage in small numbers. However, they are extremely prolific and populations can rapidly build up to damaging numbers during the growing season. Damage occurs when the aphid sucks the juices from hawthorn leaves and stems. Some aphid species that attack hawthorn are unable to digest fully all the sugar in the sap and excrete the excess in a fluid called honeydew. The honeydew often drops onto the leaves or plants below. A sooty mold fungus may develop on the honeydew, causing the hawthorn leaves to appear black and dirty. Ants feed on this sticky substance, and are often present where there is an aphid infestation. For more information about aphids, see page 875.

SOLUTION: Control aphids with ORTHO Isotox Insect Killer or ORTHO Orthene Systemic Insect Control when insects or damage are first noticed in late spring. Repeat at intervals of 2 weeks if damage continues.

Woolly aphids (half life size).

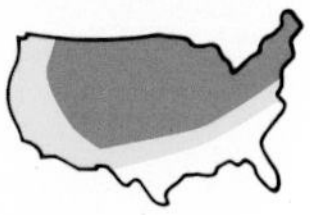

PROBLEM: The twigs, branches, and sometimes the trunk are covered with white, cottony masses. The leaves and twigs are yellowing and the tree may be stunted. A sticky substance may coat the leaves, stems, and trunk. A black sooty mold may be present.

ANALYSIS: Woolly aphids
(*Eriosoma* species)
Several species of woolly aphids attack hawthorn. They do little damage in small numbers. However, they are extremely prolific and populations can rapidly build up to damaging numbers during the growing season. Damage occurs when the woolly aphid sucks the juices from the hawthorn twigs, branches, or trunk. It is unable to digest fully all the sugar in the plant sap and excretes the excess in a fluid called honeydew. The honeydew often drops onto leaves or plants below. A sooty mold fungus may develop on the sticky substance, causing the hawthorn leaves to appear black and dirty. The woolly apple aphid (*Eriosoma lanigerum*) may also cause damage by burrowing down into the soil and feeding on the roots. The feeding causes marblelike knots to form and results in stunted roots and a weak tree.

SOLUTION: Control with ORTHO Isotox Insect Killer or ORTHO Orthene Systemic Insect Control when damage is first noticed. Repeat at intervals of two weeks if the plant becomes reinfested. If you suspect a root infestation, carefully dig away the soil from around some roots and check for aphids or galls. If aphids or galls are present, apply ORTHO Systemic Rose & Flower Care to the soil around the tree and water it in thoroughly.

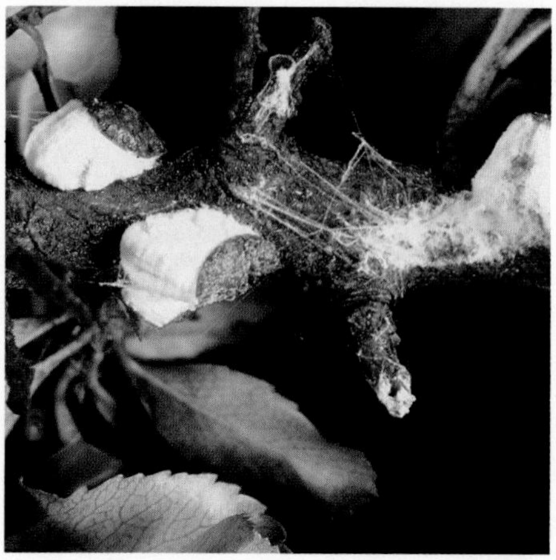

Cottony cushion scales (twice life size).

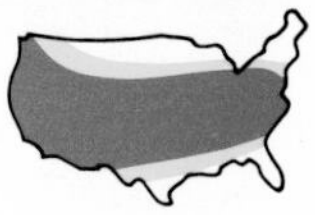

PROBLEM: The leaves or bark are covered with white, cottony masses; brown or whitish crusty bumps; or clusters of somewhat flattened brown or white scaly bumps. The bumps can be scraped off. Leaves turn yellow and may drop. Sometimes a sticky substance coats the leaves. A black sooty mold often grows on the substance. Branches are killed by heavy infestations.

ANALYSIS: Scales
Many species of scales infest hawthorn. They lay their eggs on leaves or bark and in spring to midsummer the young scales, called *crawlers*, settle around them. The small (1/10 inch), soft-bodied young feed by sucking sap from the plant. The legs usually atrophy and, with some types, a shell develops over the body. The types of scales that do not develop shells are very conspicuous. The females are covered with a white, cottony egg sac, containing up to 2500 eggs. Scales covered with a shell are less noticeable. The shell often blends in with the plant, and the eggs are inconspicuous beneath the covering. Some species of scales are unable to digest fully all the sugar in the plant sap, and excrete the excess in a fluid called honeydew. A sooty mold fungus may develop on the honeydew, causing the hawthorn leaves to appear black and dirty. For more information about scales, see page 876.

SOLUTION: Control with ORTHO Isotox Insect Killer or ORTHO Orthene Systemic Insect Control when the young are active. Contact your local Cooperative Extension Office (see page 1029) to determine the best time to spray for scales in your area. To control scales during the dormant season, spray with ORTHO Volck Oil Spray.

Borer hole.

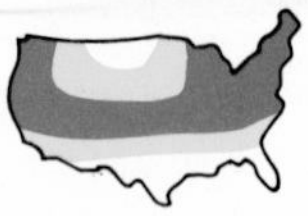

PROBLEM: Foliage is sparse on a branch or at the top of the tree; eventually the twigs and branch die. Holes or tunnels are apparent in the trunk or branches. The bark may die over the tunnels and slough off, revealing trails. Sap or sawdust usually surrounds the holes. Weakened branches break during wind or snow storms. Weak, young, or newly transplanted trees are most susceptible to injury, and may be killed.

ANALYSIS: Borers
The borers that attack hawthorn are the larvae of several different types of beetles that also infest a wide variety of other trees and shrubs. Throughout the summer, females lay eggs in bark crevices. The larvae feed by tunneling through the bark, sapwood, or heartwood. This stops the flow of nutrients and water in that area by cutting the conducting vessels; branch and twig dieback result. Sap flow acts as a defense against borers if the tree is healthy. When the borer burrows into the wood, tree sap fills the hole and drowns the insect. Factors that weaken the tree, such as mechanical injuries, damage by leaf-feeding insects, poor growing conditions, and transplanting make it more attractive to female beetles.

SOLUTION: Cut out and destroy all dead and dying branches. Reduce the amount of borer damage by inserting a fine wire into the entry hole and pushing it up the feeding channel to kill the larva. Insecticides containing *lindane* may help if damage is not too severe. Spray the trunk and branches at monthly intervals from May through July. Maintain plant health and vigor by watering and fertilizing regularly.

CYPRESS FAMILY (ARBORVITAE, CHAMAECYPARIS, INCENSE CEDAR)

ADAPTATION:
Chamaecyparis species: Zones 4 through 9. Plants should be protected from hot, dry winds.
Cupressocyparis and *Cupressus* species: Zones 5 through 10.
Thuja species: Zones 2 through 9. (To determine your climate zone, see the map on page 1020.)

LIGHT: Full sun.

SOIL:
Chamaecyparis species: Needs good drainage.
Cupressocyparis and *Cupressus* species: Tolerate a wide variety of soils.
Thuja species: Any good garden soil.

FERTILIZER: Fertilize with ORTHO Evergreen, Tree & Shrub Food according to label directions.

WATER:
How much: Apply enough water to wet the soil 3 to 4 feet deep. To determine the proper amount of water for your soil type, see page 912.
How often:
Chamaecyparis species: Grows best in moist soil, but will tolerate some drought. Water when the soil is moist but no longer wet 4 inches below the surface.
Cupressocyparis species: Water when the soil is barely moist 4 inches below the surface.
Cupressus species: Grows best if kept on the dry side. Water when the soil is dry 4 inches below the surface.
Thuja species: Will tolerate wet soil, but does best in moist soil. Water when the soil is moist but not wet 4 inches below the surface. For more information about watering, see page 912.

Twig and needle blight damage on western red cedar.

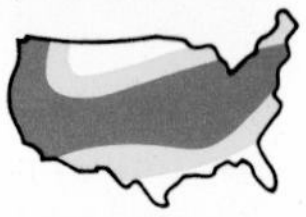

PROBLEM: Needles, twigs, and branches turn brown. In some cases, the upper branches die from the tips back; in other cases, the lower two thirds of the plant dies. The needles often drop in late summer, starting at the tips and leaving the infected branches bare. Sometimes minute black dots appear on the dead needles and stems. This disease is most serious in wet weather or in shady locations. Plants may be killed.

ANALYSIS: Twig and needle blight
A number of different fungi cause twig and needle blight on plants in the cypress family. During wet weather, spores germinate on twigs and spread into the needles and twigs above and below the point of entrance, killing them. Reinfection may continue until the whole plant dies, or the plant may persist for many years in an unsightly condition. With some fungi, black spore-producing bodies develop and spend the winter on dead needles.

SOLUTION: Prune out and destroy infected branches below the line between diseased and healthy tissue, making the cut into live tissue. Valuable specimens can be sprayed with a fungicide containing *basic copper sulfate* at weekly intervals throughout the growing season. Plant trees in areas with good air circulation and full sun.

Leaf browning on cedar.

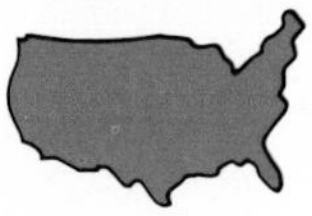

PROBLEM: The older leaves, on the inside of the tree nearest the trunk, turn brown and drop. This condition may develop in a few days or over several weeks, in either spring or fall.

ANALYSIS: Leaf browning and shedding

Leaf browning and shedding is a natural process similar to the dropping of leaves of deciduous trees. It is usually more pronounced on arborvitae (*Thuja*) than on other plants in the cypress family. Sometimes it takes place every year; in other cases, it occurs every second or third year. When growing conditions have been favorable the previous season, leaf shedding occurs over several weeks and is less noticeable. However, if the plant has been exposed to unfavorable conditions such as drying, or a spider mite or insect infestation, during the growing season, leaf drop develops within a few days. Leaf drop is also caused by new growth shading older interior growth.

SOLUTION: No chemical controls are necessary. Fertilize and water plants regularly. Provide full sun. Check plants for insects and mites during the growing season.

Leafminer damage to arborvitae.

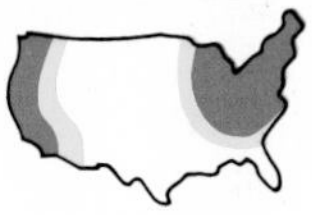

PROBLEM: Leaf tips turn yellow, then brown and dry, contrasting sharply with the healthy green foliage. Damage is most severe in plants growing in shady areas. When a yellow leaf is torn open, a small (⅕ inch long) greenish caterpillar with a dark head may be found inside. Gray or brownish moths with a ⅓-inch wingspread may be seen flying around the plant in April, May, or June.

ANALYSIS: Leafminers and tip moths

(*Argyresthia* species)

Several species of insects, known as leafminers in the eastern United States and tip moths on the West Coast, infest arborvitae, cypress, and juniper. Damage is unsightly, but plants may lose over half of their foliage and still survive. The larvae spend the winter inside the leaf tips. When the weather warms in late spring, adult moths emerge and lay eggs on the leaves. The eggs hatch and the larvae tunnel into the leaf tips, devouring the green tissue. The tips above the point of entry yellow and die. The larvae feed until late fall, or through the winter until early spring.

SOLUTION: Spray with an insecticide containing ORTHO Orthene Systsemic Insect Control or ORTHO Orthene Isotox Insect Killer when eggs are hatching in June or July (mid-August in the far northeastern states). Trim and destroy infested leaves in fall and spring.

Winter injury to arborvitae.

PROBLEM: Leaves turn yellow at first, then rusty brown and dry. Twigs and branches may die back. The tree is growing in a climate where cold, dry, windy days are common or where plants may be exposed to late fall or early spring freezes. The soil may be frozen.

ANALYSIS: Winter injury

Arborvitae are damaged by cold, drying winter winds, especially if temperatures are below freezing. These trees are commonly planted as windbreaks and in exposed areas where growing conditions may be unfavorable. Moisture is lost from the leaves more rapidly than it can be replaced by the root system. Cells in the leaves dry out and die. This condition is most pronounced when water is unavailable because the soil is dry or frozen. Leaves, along with twigs and branches, also die during early fall or late spring freezes when the plant is growing. Young succulent growth cannot withstand freezing temperatures.

SOLUTION: Prune out dead twigs and branches. Provide shelter for plants growing in extremely cold areas. To avoid succulent growth in fall, do not fertilize late in the season. During a dry fall, irrigate plants thoroughly to reduce winter injury.

CYPRESS FAMILY (ARBORVITAE, CHAMAECYPARIS, INCENSE CEDAR)

Aphid damage to cypress.

PROBLEM: Needles turn brown on twigs and branches; branches may die back. The plant is often weak and stunted. A white cottony material or a sticky substance may coat the needles. Small (⅙ inch) green or brown soft-bodied insects cluster on twigs and branches. Ants may be present.

ANALYSIS: Aphids
Aphids do little damage in small numbers. However, they are extremely prolific and populations can rapidly build up to damaging numbers during the growing season. Damage occurs when the aphid sucks the juices from the twigs and branches. The brown arborvitae aphid (*Cinara tujafilina*) excretes a white, cottony material as it feeds. Other aphids that attack plants in the cypress family are unable to digest all the sugar in the plant sap and excrete the excess in a fluid called honeydew. The honeydew often drops onto the leaves below. Ants feed on this sticky substance, and are often present where there is an aphid infestation.

SOLUTION: Spray with ORTHO Isotox Insect Killer or ORTHO Malathion 50 Insect Spray when insects or damage are first noticed. Repeat at intervals of two weeks if damage continues.

Spider mite webs on Italian cypress.

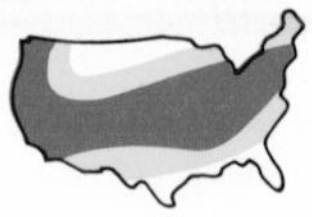

PROBLEM: The needles are stippled, yellowing, and dirty. Sometimes there is a silken webbing on the needles and stems. Needles may turn brown and fall off. To determine if the tree is infested with mites, hold a sheet of white paper underneath some stippled needles and tap the foliage sharply. Minute dark green, black, or red specks about the size of pepper grains will drop to the paper and begin to crawl around. The pests are easily seen against the white background.

ANALYSIS: Spider mites
Spider mites, especially the spruce spider mite (*Oligonychus ununguis*), are among the most destructive pests of evergreen trees. In the cypress family, they attack mainly arborvitae (*Thuja* species) and *Chamaecyparis*. They cause damage by sucking sap from the underside of the needles. As a result of feeding, the green leaf pigment disappears, producing the stippled appearance. This symptom can be confused with certain types of air pollution damage. Mites are active throughout the growing season but are favored by hot, dry weather (70°F and up). By midsummer, they build up to tremendous numbers. Young plants may die the first season. If mites are left uncontrolled over a period of years, older trees die progressively from the lower branches upward. For more information about spider mites, see page 887.

SOLUTION: Control with ORTHO Isotox Insect Killer or ORTHO Orthene Insect Spray in mid to late May to kill young mites of the first generation. Repeat the spray two more times, at intervals of seven to ten days. Additional spraying may be needed later in the season if the plant becomes reinfested.

Root rot on Port Orford cedar.

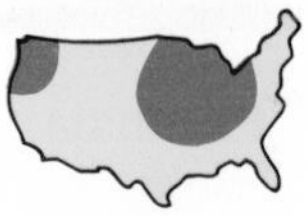

PROBLEM: Foliage turns off-color, starting from the bottom branches and progressing upward. Trees with green foliage fade to tan or light brown. Varieties of plants with blue foliage turn greenish at first, then fade to tan or light brown. The brownish foliage is crisp and dry, and eventually drops. By the time the trees turn brownish, they are dead. If bark is removed on the lower trunk, a sharp line is usually seen between healthy white tissue and infected red-brown tissue.

ANALYSIS: Root rot
This plant disease is caused by soil-inhabiting fungi (*Phytophthora* species) that infect many different plants. (For a list of susceptible plants, see page 1013.) The fungi are carried in plants, soil, or soil water. They invade and kill the roots and then spread into the main trunk, cutting off the flow of nutrients and water through the tree. The foliage turns brown, and the tree dies.

SOLUTION: There are no effective chemical controls. Once the fungus becomes established in the soil, it will remain indefinitely. Replace the trees with resistant plants. For a list of resistant plants, see page 1016.

DAPHNE

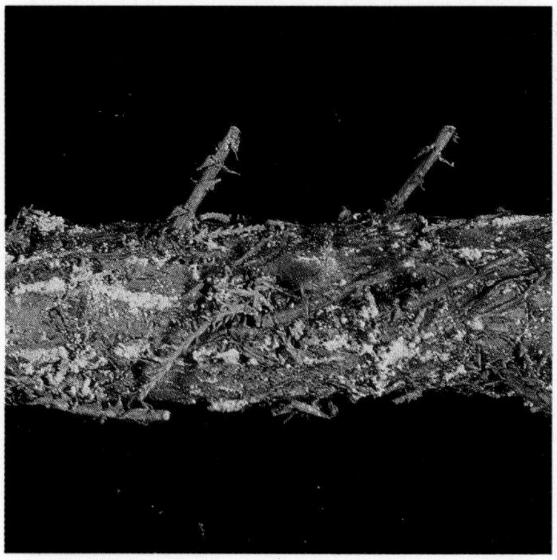

Cypress bark scale (half life size).

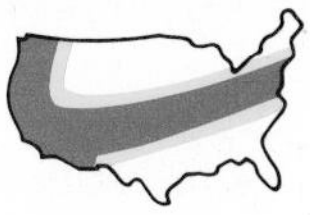

PROBLEM: Needles and stems are covered with white, cottony masses or brownish, crusty bumps. The bumps can be scraped or picked off. Needles turn yellow and new growth slows. In severe cases, branches die back. A shiny, sticky substance may coat the leaves. A black sooty mold often grows on the sticky substance.

ANALYSIS: Scales
Several species of scales infest plants in the cypress family. They lay their eggs on the needles or bark and in spring to midsummer the young scales, called *crawlers*, settle on needles and twigs. The small (1/10 inch), soft-bodied young feed by sucking sap from the plant. The legs usually atrophy and, with some types, a shell develops over the body. The types of scales that do not develop shells are very conspicuous. The females are covered with a white, cottony egg sac, containing up to 2500 eggs. Scales covered with a shell are less noticeable. The shell often blends in with the plant and the eggs are inconspicuous beneath the covering. Some species of scales are unable to digest fully all the sugar in the plant sap, and excrete the excess in a fluid called honeydew. A sooty mold fungus may develop on the honeydew, causing the leaves to appear black and dirty. For more information about scales, see page 876.

SOLUTION: Control with ORTHO Isotox Insect Killer or ORTHO Orthene Systemic Insect Control when the young are active. Contact your local Cooperative Extension Office (see page 1029) to determine the best time to spray for scales in your area. Repeat if the plant becomes reinfested. During the winter, spray with ORTHO Volck Oil Spray.

Crown rot.

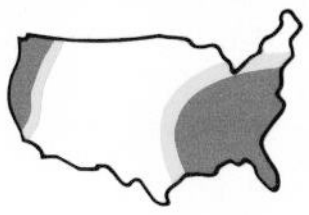

PROBLEM: Leaves turn yellow and wither. Diseased branches slowly dry out and die. White fungal strands, or brown irregular-shaped or round pellets may be found at the base of the plant or on the ground nearby. If the plant is pulled up, the roots appear black and decayed.

ANALYSIS: Crown rot
This disease is caused by fungi (*Sclerotium* species) that live in the soil and attack many different shrubs and flowers in the garden. The fungi penetrate the stems at or below the soil level. They move down into the roots and up into the base of the plant, causing death of the root system and stem tissue. Crown rot is spread by moving water, infested soil, and contaminated tools. The fungus can also grow over the soil to attack adjacent plants. The brown fungal pellets that form can survive in dry soil and extremes of temperatures to reinfect healthy plants when conditions are suitable. These pellets can live in the soil or in plant debris for many years. Crown rot is most severe during periods of warm (70°F and up), moist soil and weather conditions.

SOLUTION: Once the plant is infected, there is no chemical that will control the fungus. Remove and destroy the infected plant and the surrounding soil to six inches beyond the area of the plant. Removing the soil will help eliminate the fungus. Drench the remaining soil in the region of the diseased plant with a fungicide containing *PCNB* prior to planting more daphne. Plant in well-drained soil.

Aphids (half life size).

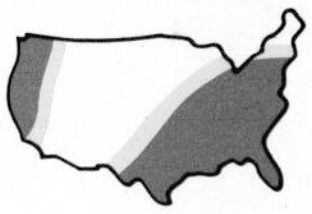

PROBLEM: Young leaves are curled, stunted, and yellowing. Buds and shoots are distorted and there may be little new growth. A shiny, sticky substance may coat the leaves. A black sooty mold may grow on the sticky substance. Tiny (1/8 inch) greenish soft-bodied insects cluster on the undersides of leaves or on the stems. Ants may be present.

ANALYSIS: Aphids
Aphids do little damage in small numbers. However, they are extremely prolific and populations can rapidly build up to damaging numbers during the growing season. Damage occurs when the aphid sucks the juices from the daphne leaves or stems. The aphid is unable to digest fully all the sugar in the sap and excretes the excess in a fluid called honeydew. The honeydew often drops onto the leaves below. A sooty mold fungus may develop on the honeydew, causing the daphne leaves to appear black and dirty. Ants feed on this sticky substance, and are often present where there is an aphid infestation. For more information about aphids, see page 875.

SOLUTION: Control with an insecticide containing *malathion* when damage or insects are first noticed in late spring. Repeat at intervals of 2 weeks if damage continues.

Daphne cultural information
Light: Full sun or part shade
Water: Keep the soil moist
Soil: Very well drained, neutral
Fertilizer: Medium

ELEAGNUS (RUSSIAN OLIVE, SILVERBERRY)

Verticillium wilt.

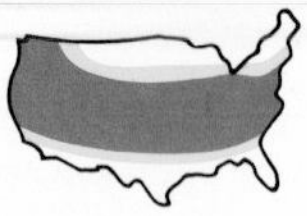

PROBLEM: The leaves on a branch turn yellow at the margins, then brown and dry. During hot weather, the leaves may wilt. New leaves may be stunted and yellowish. The infected tree may die slowly, branch by branch, over several seasons. Or the whole tree may wilt and die within a few months. Some plants may recover. The tissue under the bark on the dying side may show dark streaks when cut. To examine for streaks, peel back the bark at the bottom of the dying branch. The dark discoloration may be very apparent or barely visible in the area just underneath the bark.

ANALYSIS: Verticillium wilt
This wilt disease attacks many ornamental trees and shrubs. It is caused by a soil-inhabiting fungus (*Verticillium* species) that persists indefinitely on plant debris or in the soil. The fungal strands and spores are spread by contaminated seeds, plants, soil, equipment, and ground water. The fungus enters the tree through the roots and spreads up into the branches through the water-conducting vessels in the trunk. The vessels become discolored and plugged. The plugging cuts off water to the branches, causing the leaf discoloration and wilting. For more information about verticillium wilt, see page 850.

SOLUTION: No chemical control is available. Fertilize and water the affected tree to stimulate vigorous growth. Remove all dead wood. Do not remove branches on which leaves have recently wilted. These branches may produce new leaves in 3 to 4 weeks or next spring. Remove dead plants. If replanting in the same area, plant trees and shrubs that are resistant to verticillium (see page 1006).

Stem canker.

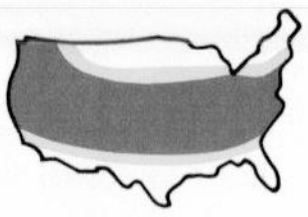

PROBLEM: The leaves on a branch, or the entire tree, wilt and turn brown. Eventually they drop. Twigs and branches are often dead and dying. Sunken or swollen brownish or reddish areas appear on the branches or trunk.

ANALYSIS: Canker and dieback
A number of different fungi cause canker and dieback on Russian olive. The fungi are spread by wind, rain, soil, tools, and equipment. They usually enter the tree at a wound, killing the surrounding healthy tissue. A sunken or swollen canker develops and expands through the wood in all directions. Tree sap containing the fungus may ooze from the wound. As a result of the canker, the flow of nutrients and water through the vessels is cut off, causing the leaves to wilt and die. The tree may stop the spread of the fungus by producing callus tissue. If the expanding canker is stopped before it covers half the diameter of the branch or trunk, the branch or tree usually survives. However, the fungus may grow faster than the callus, or the tree may not produce it, resulting in the death of the branch or the entire tree (if the canker is on the main trunk).

SOLUTION: No chemical control is available. Avoid wounding and overwatering trees. Prune out and destroy dead branches below the cankered area. Sterilize pruning shears with rubbing alcohol after each cut. Remove dying trees.

Eleagnus cultural information
Light: Full sun to part shade
Water: Drought tolerant
Soil: Tolerates many types
Fertilizer: Light

ERICA (HEATH, HEATHER)

Root rot.

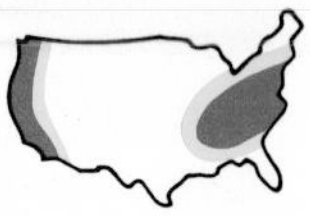

PROBLEM: One or more branches fade, turn yellow, and die. The plant is stunted. Eventually the whole plant wilts and dies, even though the soil may be sufficiently moist. The problem is more common where the soil is heavy and poorly drained. The tissue under the bark close to ground level shows a dark discoloration when cut. To look for discoloration, peel back the bark at the bottom of the plant. There is a distinct margin between white healthy wood and dark infected wood. If the plant is pulled up, young roots are brown and decaying.

ANALYSIS: Root rot
This plant disease is caused by a soil inhabiting fungus (*Phytophthora cinnamomi*) that is carried in affected plants or in infested soil or soil water. It enters the roots and works its way up into the plant. Water and nutrient uptake are blocked, causing the aboveground symptoms. Plants in overwatered or poorly drained soils, or those weakened from recent transplanting, are more susceptible to attack.

SOLUTION: Once the fungus becomes established in the soil, it will remain indefinitely. Remove diseased plants. Do not replant susceptible plants in the same area. (For a list of resistant trees and shrubs, see page 1016.) Buy only healthy plants, and plant them in well-drained soil or raised beds.

Erica cultural information
Light: Full sun
Water: Grows best in moist soil
Soil: Light, very well drained, acid
Fertilizer: Light

ERIOBOTRYA (LOQUAT)

Fireblight.

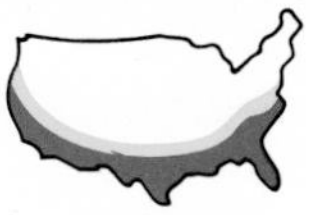

PROBLEM: Blossoms and leaves of infected twigs suddenly wilt and turn black as if scorched by fire. Leaves curl and hang downward. The bark at the base of the blighted twigs becomes water-soaked, then dark, sunken, and dry; cracks may develop at the edge of the sunken area. In warm, wet fall weather, drops of brown ooze appear on the sunken bark. Young plants may die.

ANALYSIS: Fireblight
This plant disease is caused by a bacterium (*Erwinia amylovora*) that is very destructive to loquat and many other closely related plant species. Blackened, dying branches are very noticeable in the fall and winter, and greatly detract from the beauty of the tree. The bacteria live in sunken cankers on the branches. In the fall, the bacteria ooze out of the cankers. Bees, flies, and other insects are attracted to the sticky ooze and become smeared with it. When the insects visit a flower for nectar, they infect it with the bacteria. The disease spreads rapidly through the plant tissue in warm (70° to 85°F), humid weather. Insects visiting these infected blossoms carry bacteria-laden nectar to healthy blossoms. Rain and wind may also spread the bacteria, infecting tender or damaged leaves in the winter.

SOLUTION: Prune out and destroy infected branches 12 to 15 inches beyond any visible discoloration. Sterilize pruning shears with rubbing alcohol after each cut. A protective spray of a pesticide containing *basic copper sulfate* or *streptomycin* applied before bud break in the fall will help prevent infection. Repeat at intervals of five to seven days until the end of bloom.

EUONYMUS

Powdery mildew.

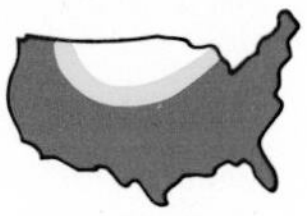

PROBLEM: The surfaces of the leaves are covered with a thin layer or irregular patches of a grayish white powdery mildew. Infected leaves are yellow and may drop prematurely. In late summer, tiny black dots (spore-producing bodies) are scattered over the white patches like ground pepper.

ANALYSIS: Powdery mildew
This plant disease is caused by two species of fungi (*Oidium euonymi japonici* and *Microsphaera alni*) that thrive in both humid and dry weather. The powdery patches or thin powdery layer consist of fungal strands and spores. The spores are spread by wind to healthy plants. The fungus saps plant nutrients, causing leaf yellowing and sometimes death of the leaf. In late summer and fall, the fungus forms small black spore-producing bodies that are dormant during the winter, but produce spores to reinfect new plants the following spring. The fungus is especially devastating in low-light situations, and is generally most severe in late summer and fall. Since *Microsphaera alni* attacks many different kinds of plants, the fungus from a diseased plant may infect other types of plants in the garden. For a list of powdery mildews and the plants they attack, see page 1006.

SOLUTION: Spray with ORTHO Funginex Rose Disease Control or ORTHO Orthenex Insect & Disease Control when mildew is first noticed. Clean up plant debris in late summer.

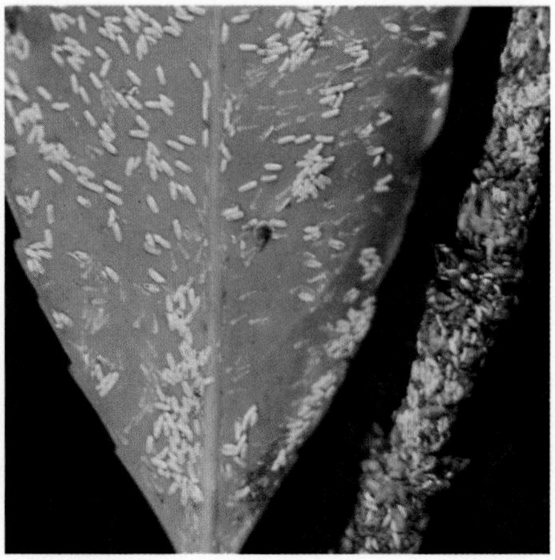

Euonymus scale (twice life size).

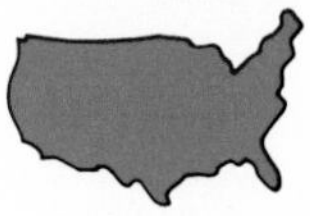

PROBLEM: Yellow or whitish spots appear on the leaves. Almost all the leaves may drop by midsummer. Branches often die, and heavy infestations may kill the plant. Stems and lower surfaces of the leaves are covered with somewhat flattened, white, scaly bumps and dark brown oystershell-shaped bumps. In severe cases, the whole plant appears white.

ANALYSIS: Euonymus scale
(*Unaspis euonymi*)
Many species of scales infest euonymus, but the most common and destructive is euonymus scale. It is especially damaging to evergreen euonymus. The dark brown females spend the winter on the plant and lay their eggs in the spring. In late spring to early summer the young scales, called *crawlers*, settle on the leaves and twigs, or are blown by the wind to other susceptible plants. The small ($\frac{1}{10}$ inch), soft-bodied young suck sap from the plant. The legs atrophy and a shell develops, brown over the females and white over the males. The females lay their eggs underneath their shell. For more information on scales, see page 876.

SOLUTION: Euonymus scale may be hard to detect until after it has caused serious damage. Check the plant periodically for yellow spotting and scales. Spray with ORTHO Isotox Insect Killer, ORTHO Orthene Systemic Insect Control, or ORTHO Volck Oil Spray in early June and mid-July. In the South, a third application may be necessary in early September. To control scales during the dormant season, spray with ORTHO Volck Oil Spray. For very heavy infestations, cut plants to the ground and spray new growth in June.

EUONYMUS

Leaf scorch.

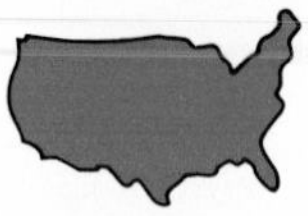

PROBLEM: During hot weather, usually in July or August, leaves turn brown on the edges and between the veins. Sometimes the whole leaf dies. Many leaves may drop during late summer. This problem is most severe on the youngest branches. Plants do not usually die.

ANALYSIS: Summer leaf scorch
Leaf scorch is caused by excessive evaporation of moisture from the leaves. In hot weather, water evaporates rapidly from the leaves. If the roots can't absorb and convey water fast enough to replenish this loss, the leaves turn brown and wither. This usually occurs in dry soil, but leaves can also scorch when the soil is moist. Drying winds, severed roots, or limited soil area can also cause scorch. For more information about scorch, see page 857.

SOLUTION: To prevent further scorch, deep-water plants during periods of hot weather to moisten the entire root space. Recently transplanted shrubs should be watered more often than established plants because of their limited root systems. Water them when the soil in the rootball is still moist, but no longer wet. If possible, shade the shrub during very hot weather. Hosing down the leaves may help cool the shrub and slow evaporation. Plant shrubs adapted to your climate.

Euonymus cultural information
Light: Full sun to part shade
Water: Moist or dry soils
Soil: Tolerates many types
Fertilizer: Light

Crown gall.

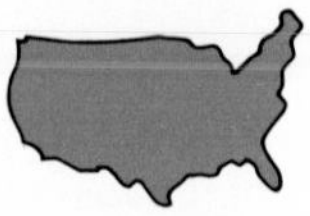

PROBLEM: Large, corky galls up to several inches in diameter appear at the base of the plant and on the stems and roots. The galls are rounded, with a rough, irregular surface. Plants with numerous galls are weak; growth is slowed and leaves turn yellow. Branches may die back.

ANALYSIS: Crown gall
This plant disease is caused by soil-inhabiting bacteria (*Agrobacterium tumefaciens*) that infect many ornamentals, fruits, and vegetables in the garden. The bacteria are often brought to a garden initially on the roots of an infected plant, and are spread with the soil and by contaminated pruning tools. The bacteria enter the shrub through wounds in the roots or at the base of the stem (the crown). They produce a substance that stimulates rapid cell growth in the plant, causing gall formation on the roots, crown, and sometimes branches. The galls disrupt the flow of water and nutrients up the roots and stems, weakening and stunting the top of the plant. Galls do not usually cause the shrub to die.

SOLUTION: Crown gall cannot be eliminated from the shrub. However, infected plants may survive many years. To improve the appearance of the plant, prune out and destroy affected stems below the galled area. Sterilize pruning shears after each cut with rubbing alcohol. Destroy severely infected shrubs. The bacteria will remain in the soil for 2 to 3 years. If you wish to replace the shrub soon, plant only resistant species. For a list of plants resistant to crown gall, see page 1013. For more information about crown gall, see page 853.

FAGUS (BEECH)

Aphids.

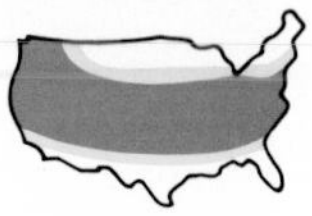

PROBLEM: Young leaves are curled, stunted, and yellowing. New growth may stop completely. A shiny, sticky substance may coat the leaves and drip onto plants and other objects, such as cars parked beneath the tree. A black sooty mold often grows on the sticky substance. Tiny (⅛ inch) green, whitish, or black soft-bodied insects cluster on the undersides of leaves and on stems. Ants are sometimes present.

ANALYSIS: Aphids
Aphids do little damage in small numbers. However, they are extremely prolific and populations can rapidly build up to damaging numbers during the growing season. Damage occurs when the aphid sucks the juices from beech leaves and stems. Some aphid species that attack beech are unable to digest fully all the sugar in the plant sap and excrete the excess in a fluid called honeydew. The honeydew often drops onto the leaves or other plants and objects below. A sooty mold fungus may develop on the honeydew, causing the beech leaves to appear black and dirty. Ants feed on this sticky substance, and are often present where there is an aphid infestation. Certain aphids that infest beech, called *woolly aphids*, excrete a white, cottony material while they feed. During heavy infestations, stems and the undersides of leaves may be covered with this secretion. For more information about aphids, see page 875.

SOLUTION: Spray with ORTHO Liquid Sevin or with an insecticide containing *malathion* when insects or damage are first noticed. Repeat at weekly intervals if the plant becomes reinfested.

Beech scale (1/4 life size)

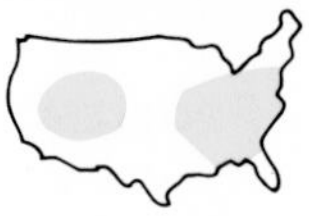

PROBLEM: Cottony, white masses cover portions of the trunk and branches. In severe cases, the entire woody portion of the tree may be covered. Leaves may turn yellow and drop, and branches may die. Cracks may appear in the bark, and sunken lesions (cankers) may develop. Sometimes, sap oozes from the cracks and cankers. In severe cases, the tree may die.

ANALYSIS: Beech scale
(Cryptococcus fagisuga)
These scales are very conspicuous because of the white waxy cottonlike material that they secrete over their bodies. Beech scales lay their eggs in early to mid-summer. The young scales, called *crawlers,* move around the bark, then settle down to feed in bark crevices. These tiny (1/50 inch), soft-bodied young feed by inserting their mouthparts into the bark and sucking plant sap. The legs atrophy so the scales are no longer mobile. Beech scale infestations spread when the crawlers are blown to nearby trees. The scales will not kill beech trees, but their feeding alters the bark and makes it susceptible to invasion by a seriously damaging fungus. This fungus causes canker formation, and eventual branch and tree death. (For more information about this fungus, see the canker and dieback discussion on this page.)

SOLUTION: Apply an insecticide containing *malathion* in early August and September when the crawlers are active. Next spring, when the trees are still dormant, spray with *lime sulfur* to control insects on the bark.

Canker.

PROBLEM: Leaves on affected branches are stunted and lighter green than normal. Some leaves turn brown and drop. Twigs and branches may die back. There are sunken, brownish, water-soaked areas on branches or base of the trunk. The sunken areas have a definite margin. Sometimes a brown or reddish liquid is exuded from the canker. A white waxy material may cover the tree, and the tree may die.

ANALYSIS: Canker and dieback
Several different fungi cause canker and dieback on beech. The fungi enter the tree at a wound, or where the bark has been damaged by insects. As the fungi spread through the bark, they kill the surrounding healthy tissue. A sunken canker develops; tree sap containing the fungus may ooze from the wound. The leaves turn yellow. Leaf drop and twig dieback follow. The tree may wall off the spreading fungus, and if the expanding canker is stopped before it covers half the diameter of the trunk or branch, the tree or branch usually survives. However, the fungus may grow faster than the callus, or the tree may not produce a callus, resulting in the death of the branch or the whole tree.

SOLUTION: Prune off dead twigs and small cankered branches, cutting at least 4 inches below the canker. Cankers on larger branches can be excised with a knife and chisel. Remove all discolored bark and wood, and a 1-inch border of apparently healthy bark around the wound. After each cut, sterilize the tools with rubbing alcohol, and clean the wound with alcohol. To prevent the development of new cankers, avoid wounding trees.

Aphids (1/8 life size).

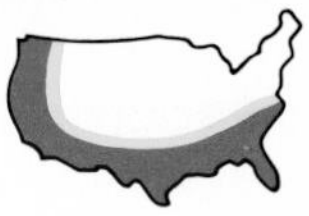

PROBLEM: Young leaves are curled, distorted, and yellowing. New growth may stop completely. A shiny or sticky substance may coat the leaves. A black sooty mold often grows on the sticky substance. Tiny (1/8 inch) greenish or black soft-bodied insects cluster on the leaves. Ants may be present.

ANALYSIS: Aphids
Aphids do little damage in small numbers. However, they are extremely prolific and populations can rapidly build up to damaging numbers during the growing season. Damage occurs when the aphid sucks the juices from fatshedera leaves and stems. Some aphid species attacking fatshedera are unable to digest fully all the sugar in the plant sap and excrete the excess in a fluid called honeydew. The honeydew often drops onto the leaves below. A sooty mold fungus may develop on the honeydew, causing the fatshedera leaves to appear black and dirty. Ants feed on this sticky substance, and are often present where there is an aphid infestation. For more information about aphids, see page 875.

SOLUTION: Spray with ORTHO Liquid Sevin when insects or damage are first noticed. Repeat at weekly intervals if damage continues.

Fatshedera cultural information
Light: Part shade to shade
Water: Keep the soil moist
Soil: Loose, well drained
Fertilizer: Medium

FATSIA (ARALIA)

Spider mite webbing.

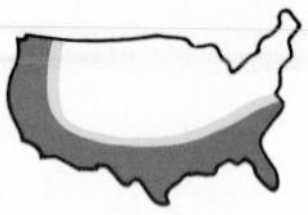

PROBLEM: Leaves are stippled, yellowing, and dirty. Sometimes there is a silken webbing on the lower surfaces of the leaves. New leaves may be distorted. To determine if the plant is infested with mites, hold a sheet of white paper underneath an affected leaf and tap the leaf sharply. Minute green, red, or yellow specks the size of pepper grains will drop to the paper and begin to crawl around. These pests are easily seen against the white background.

ANALYSIS: Spider mites
These mites, related to spiders, are major pest of many garden and greenhouse plants. They cause damage by sucking sap from buds and the undersides of leaves. As a result of feeding, the green leaf pigment disappears, producing the stippled appearance. Mites are active during the growing season, but are favored by hot, dry weather (70°F and up). By midsummer, they build up to tremendous numbers. For more information about spider mites, see page 887.

SOLUTION: Spray with ORTHO Isotox Insect Killer when damage is first noticed. Wet the undersides of the leaves thoroughly. Repeat the application if the plant becomes reinfested. Hose down plants frequently to knock off webs and mites.

Fatsia cultural information
Light: Part shade to shade
Water: Grows best in moist soil
Soil: Tolerates many types
Fertilizer: Heavy

FERNS

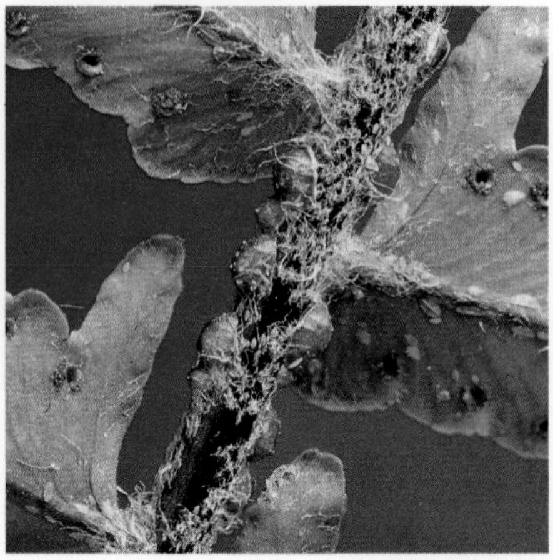

Brown scale (twice life size).

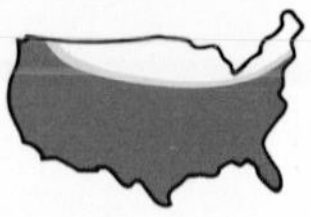

PROBLEM: The fronds are covered with brown crusty bumps or thick, white, waxy bumps or clusters of somewhat flattened yellow or whitish scaly bumps. The bumps can be scraped or picked off. Fronds may turn yellow and leaflets may drop. In some cases, a shiny, sticky substance coats the fronds. Scales are sometimes mistaken for reproductive spores produced by the fern. The round, flat, sometimes hairy spores are found only on the undersides of fronds, spaced at regular intervals. They are difficult to pick or scrape off.

ANALYSIS: Scales
Many different types of scales infest ferns. They lay their eggs on the fronds, and in spring to midsummer the young scales, called *crawlers*, settle down to feed. These small (1/10 inch), soft-bodied young feed by sucking sap from the plant. The legs usually atrophy and a hard crusty or waxy shell develops over the body. The mature female scales lay their eggs underneath the shell. Some species of scale are unable to digest fully all the sugar in the sap, and excrete the excess in a fluid called honeydew, which coats the fronds.

SOLUTION: Spray with an insecticide containing *malathion* when the young are active. Contact your local Cooperative Extension Office (see page 1029) to determine the best time to spray for scales in your area. Some ferns may be damaged by this chemical. Test the spray on a frond before spraying the entire plant. Wait a few days to see if the area turns brown. Cut off infested fronds on plants that are sensitive to sprays. Discard severely infested plants. To treat 1 or 2 small plants, use ORTHO Whitefly & Mealybug Killer.

Mealybugs (1/3 life size).

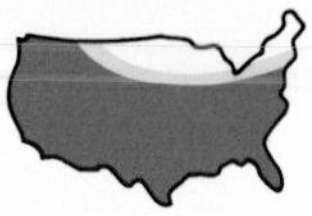

PROBLEM: Leaflets or stems are covered with white, cottony, cushion-like masses. Leaflets turn yellow and may drop; fronds may die.

ANALYSIS: Cottony scales and mealybugs
Cottony scales and mealybugs infest many plants in the garden. Mealybugs are usually found outdoors only in the warmer climates. The visual similarities between these insects make separate identification difficult. They are very conspicuous in late spring and summer because the females are covered with a white, cottony egg sac, containing up to 2500 eggs. Females lay their egg masses on leaves and stems. The young insects that hatch from these eggs are yellowish brown to green. They feed throughout the summer, causing damage by withdrawing plant sap from the ferns. Some species of scales and mealybugs are unable to digest fully all the sugar in the plant sap and excrete the excess in a fluid called honeydew.

SOLUTION: Spray with an insecticide containing *malathion* when insects are first noticed. Some ferns may be damaged by this chemical. Test the spray on a small portion of the plant before using. Wait a few days to see if the area turns brown. Cut off infested stems on plants that are sensitive to sprays. Discard severely infested plants. To treat 1 or 2 small plants, use ORTHO Whitefly & Mealybug Killer.

Fern cultural information
Light: Part shade to shade
Water: Keep the soil moist
Soil: Loose, rich, well drained
Fertilizer: Medium

Scorch.

PROBLEM: The tips and edges of fronds turn brown or black and die. Entire fronds may wilt, turn yellow or brown, and die. The problem usually occurs first on the youngest fronds. This condition usually develops when the soil is dry but may also occur when the soil is moist.

ANALYSIS: Scorch
Scorch is caused by excessive evaporation of moisture from the fronds. In hot weather, water evaporates rapidly from the fronds. Water loss is especially heavy when the weather is also dry and windy. If the roots can't absorb and convey water fast enough to replenish this loss, the fronds turn brown or black and wither. Scorch usually occurs when the soil is allowed to dry out, but ferns can also suffer from scorch when the soil is moist if the weather is exceptionally hot and dry. Winds, severed roots, limited soil area, and low temperatures can also cause scorch. For more information about scorch, see page 857.

SOLUTION: To prevent further scorch, water plants thoroughly. Ferns need to be kept moist. They must be watered frequently and deeply enough so that the soil doesn't dry out. During periods of exceptionally hot, dry weather, keep ferns wet by gently hosing down or sprinkling the fronds several times a day to reduce scorch damage. Grow ferns in shady areas that are protected from strong winds.

FICUS (ORNAMENTAL FIGS)

Cuban laurel thrips damage.

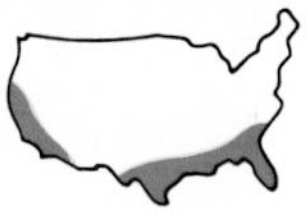

PROBLEM: Young, expanding leaves are curled and distorted, with purplish red spots on the undersides. The leaves soon turn yellow and drop. Minute ($\frac{1}{25}$ inch) black insects are feeding and laying tiny white eggs on the inside of the rolled leaves.

ANALYSIS: Cuban laurel thrips
(*Gynaikothrips ficorum*)
Ficus retusa (Cuban laurel), especially the variety *nitida*, may be severely infested with this thrips in California, Florida, and Texas. Other species of *Ficus* are attacked only if there are not enough Cuban laurel leaves to feed on when the insects are abundant. Thrips feed on plant sap by shredding and rasping the plant tissue, resulting in distortion and spotting. Damage is unsightly, but the feeding does not cause permanent injury to the plant. On hot days the adults fly around the plant and infest new leaves. Breeding is almost continuous, but populations are highest between October and December.

SOLUTION: Spray with ORTHO Isotox Insect Killer or ORTHO Orthene Systemic Insect Control when damage is first noticed. Repeat 3 more times at intervals of seven to ten days.

Ficus cultural information
Light: Full sun to part shade
Water: Grows best in moist soil
Soil: Loose, well drained
Fertilizer: Medium

FORSYTHIA

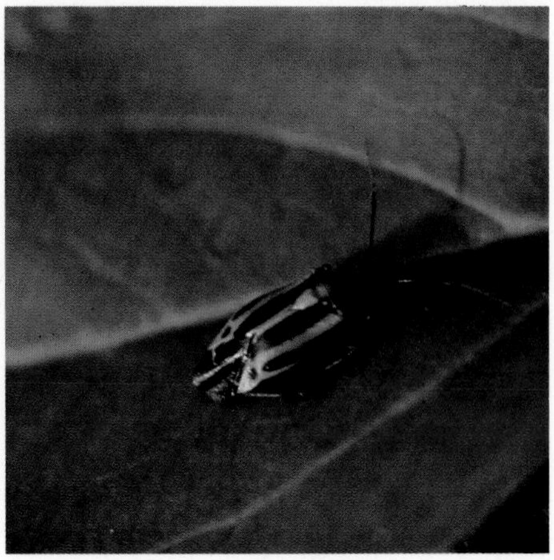

Fourlined plant bug (3 times life size).

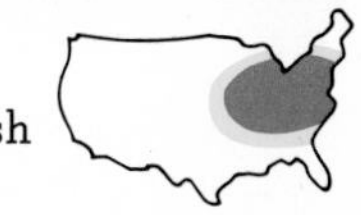

PROBLEM: Tan to reddish brown spots, $\frac{1}{16}$ inch in diameter, develop on young forsythia leaves. Spots may join together to form a blotch; leaves may be distorted. Yellowish green bugs, $\frac{1}{4}$ inch long, with four black stripes, may be found feeding on the leaves. Damage occurs during May and June.

ANALYSIS: Fourlined plant bug
(*Poecilocapsus lineatus*)
This plant bug is a pest on forsythia and many other ornamental and vegetable plants in the northern United States. A small number of bugs can cause many unsightly leaves. Eggs are laid inside the stems in slits cut by the adult females in early summer. The eggs spend the winter there, hatching in spring when the forsythia leaves unfold. The plant bugs feed for about 6 weeks. Their sharp mouthparts pierce the leaf tissue, injecting a toxic secretion at the same time. As a result of feeding, the green pigment disappears. Spots develop where the tissue is killed.

SOLUTION: Spray with ORTHO Malathion 50 Insect Spray or with an insecticide containing *carbaryl* (SEVIN®) when damage is first noticed in spring. Repeat the spray at intervals of 7 to 10 days if damage continues.

Forsythia cultural information
Light: Full sun
Water: When the soil is almost dry
Soil: Tolerates many types
Fertilizer: Medium

FRAXINUS (ASH)

FRAXINUS (ASH)

ADAPTATION: Throughout the United States. Some species are not adapted to windy areas, or develop winter injury due to temperature fluctuations.

FLOWERING TIME: Several species of ash (especially the flowering ash *F. ornus*) produce conspicuous fragrant white flowers in late spring.

LIGHT: Full sun.

SOIL: Ashes are adapted to a wide variety of soils, and some will tolerate soil that is soggy and poorly drained. Many are deep-rooted, making them good lawn trees.

FERTILIZER: Fertilize with ORTHO Evergreen, Tree & Shrub Food according to label directions.

WATER:
How much: Apply enough water to wet the soil 3 to 4 feet deep. To determine the proper amount of water for your soil type, see page 912.
How often: Some species of ashes are drought tolerant; others prefer periodic deep waterings.

PRUNING: Some species of ash, such as Modesto ash, develop narrow crotch angles (angles at which the branches attach to the tree). If a narrow-angled, small branch is removed, a dormant bud below it will grow, producing a branch with a wider angle.

Ash anthracnose.

PROBLEM: During wet or humid weather, irregular light brown spots of dead tissue appear on the leaves from late May to August. Sunken reddish areas develop and run together, killing the leaf. Partially killed leaves look as if they have been sunscorched. Anthracnose is distinguished from sunscorch by brown dots (spore-producing bodies) that are barely visible on the undersides of the leaves. There may be severe defoliation and twig dieback.

ANALYSIS: Ash anthracnose
This plant disease is caused by a fungus (*Gloeosporium aridum*). It may be very serious on Modesto ash (*Fraxinus velutina*) in California and the northeastern states. The fungus spends the winter on infected leaves and twigs. During rainy weather, spots develop where spores are blown and splashed onto young leaves. The spots expand and can kill the leaf in rainy seasons, causing defoliation. If defoliation takes place in the spring or early summer, the tree will grow new leaves. If the tree is severely affected for 2 or 3 successive years, the fungus may enter and kill entire branches.

SOLUTION: Trees affected by this disease for a single year do not require chemical control. Rake and destroy old leaves and, where practical, prune out dead twigs below the sunken reddish canker on the bark. Fertilize early in the growing season to stimulate vigorous growth. If the following spring is wet, spray with a fungicide containing *chlorothalonil* (DACONIL 2787®), *benlate*, or *captan* (ORTHOCIDE®) when the leaves uncurl. Repeat the treatment 2 more times at intervals of 14 days.

Leaf scorch.

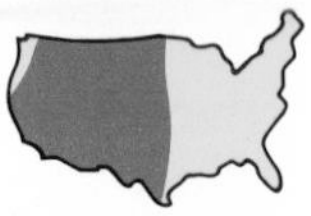

PROBLEM: During hot weather, usually in July or August, leaves turn brown around the edges and between the veins. Sometimes the whole leaf dies. Many leaves may drop during late summer. This problem is most severe on the youngest branches. Trees do not generally die.

ANALYSIS: Summer leaf scorch
Leaf scorch is caused by excessive evaporation from the leaves. In hot weather, water evaporates rapidly from the leaves. If the roots can't absorb and convey water fast enough to replenish this loss, then the leaves turn brown and wither. This usually occurs in dry soil, but leaves also can scorch when the soil is moist. Drying winds, severe roots, and limited soil area can also cause scorch. For more information about leaf scorch, see page 857.

SOLUTION: To minimize further scorch, deep-water trees during periods of hot weather to wet down the entire root space (see page 912 for more information about watering trees). Newly transplanted trees should be watered whenever the rootball is dry 2 inches below the surface. There are no controls for scorch on trees in moist soil. Plant trees adapted to your climate.

Aphid damage.

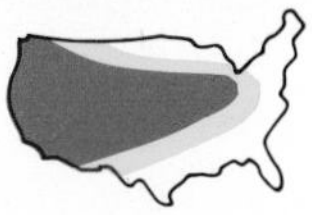

PROBLEM: Young leaves are curled and yellowing. Sometimes they are tightly folded into a mass. In other cases the undersides are covered with white cottony masses. A shiny, sticky substance usually coats the leaves. A black sooty mold may develop on the sticky substance. Inside the folded leaf or underneath the cottony masses are tiny (1/8 inch) green or purplish soft-bodied insects. Ants may be present.

ANALYSIS: Aphids
(*Prociphilus* species)
Several closely related species of aphids attack ash. Woolly aphids produce a white cottony mass over their bodies, which makes them very conspicuous. Leaf curl aphids cause the ash leaves to curl and fold tightly around themselves. Leaf curl aphids are mainly a problem on white, green, red, and Modesto ash. Neither of these aphids does much harm to the tree. However, when many leaves are tightly curled or covered with the woolly masses, they make the tree unsightly. Damage occurs when the aphids suck the juices from the ash leaves, causing them to curl and yellow. The aphids are unable to digest fully all the sugar in the plant sap and excrete the excess in a fluid called honeydew, which often drops onto the leaves or plants below. A sooty mold fungus may develop on the honeydew, causing the ash leaves to appear black and dirty. Ants feed on this sticky substance, and are often present where there is an aphid infestation.

SOLUTION: Spray with ORTHO Orthene Systemic Insect Control or ORTHO Isotox Insect Killer when aphids or damage are first noticed. Spray trees infested with woolly aphids thoroughly to penetrate the wool.

Ash flower galls.

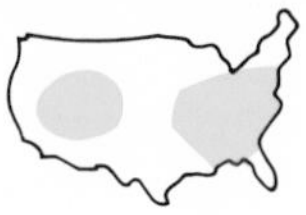

PROBLEM: Irregular galls, from 1/4 to 3/4 inch in diameter, form on flowers. The clusters of galls dry out and remain on the tree. They are very conspicuous throughout the winter.

ANALYSIS: Ash flower gall mite
(*Aceria fraxinivorus*)
Ash flower galls are caused by tiny mites, too small to be seen with the naked eye. The mites attack the male flowers of white ash (*Fraxinus americana*) and green ash (*F. pennsylvanica lanceolata*). As the buds open in the spring, the mites puncture the tissue, injecting a growth-promoting substance into it. The flowers develop abnormally and form clusters of galls. The galls are unsightly, but are rarely harmful to the tree.

SOLUTION: Once the galls form there is nothing you can do. Next spring, spray valuable specimens with a pesticide containing *dicofol* (KELTHANE®) after buds swell and before new growth emerges.

Borer damage.

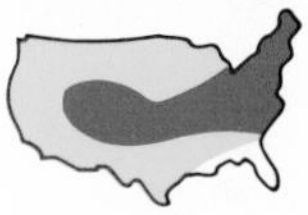

PROBLEM: Foliage is sparse on a branch or at the top of the tree; eventually the twigs and branches die back. Holes or tunnels are apparent in the trunk or branches. Sap or sawdust usually surrounds the holes. The bark may die over the tunnels and slough off, or there may be knotlike swellings on the trunk and limbs. Weakened branches break during wind or snow storms. Weak, young, or newly transplanted trees may be killed.

ANALYSIS: Borers
Borers are the larvae of beetles or moths. Many kinds of borers attack ash trees. Throughout the summer, females lay eggs in bark crevices. The borer larvae feed by tunneling through the bark, sapwood, or heartwood. This stops the flow of nutrients and water in that area by cutting the conducting vessels; branch and twig dieback result. If the tree is healthy, sap flow acts as a defense against borers. When the insect burrows into the wood, tree sap fills the hole and drowns the insect. Factors that weaken the tree, such as mechanical injuries, transplanting, damage by leaf-feeding insects, and poor growing conditions make it more attractive to egg-laying females.

SOLUTION: Cut out and destroy all dead and dying branches. Severely infested young trees should be removed. In the spring, spray or paint the trunk with ORTHO Lindane Borer & Leaf Miner Spray to kill young larvae before they burrow into the wood. Repeat three more times at intervals of 2 weeks. Maintain plant health and vigor by watering and fertilizing regularly.

FRAXINUS (ASH)

Canker.

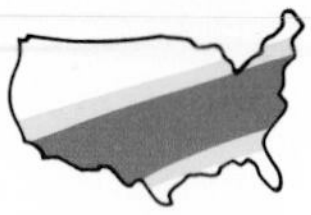

PROBLEM: Leaves of affected trees are stunted and lighter green than normal. Some leaves turn brown and drop. Twigs may die back. There are brownish, water-soaked, or cracked areas on branches or near the base of the trunk. The sunken areas have a distinct margin. A black liquid may ooze from the canker. The tree may be killed.

ANALYSIS: Canker and dieback
A number of different fungi cause canker and dieback on ash. The fungi are spread by wind, rain, soil, and equipment. They enter the tree at a wound, killing the surrounding healthy tissue. A canker develops; tree sap containing the fungus may ooze from the wound. The canker cuts off the flow of nutrients and water to the branch, causing the leaves to turn yellow. Leaf drop and twig dieback follow if infection continues. The tree may wall off the spreading fungus by producing callus tissue, a rapid growth of barklike cells. If the expanding canker is stopped before it covers half the diameter of the trunk or branch, the tree or branch usually survives. However, the fungus may grow faster than the callus, or the tree may not produce a callus, resulting in the death of the branch or the whole tree.

SOLUTION: Prune off dead twigs and small cankered branches, cutting at least 4 inches below the canker. Cankers on larger branches can be excised with a knife and chisel. Remove all discolored bark and wood, and a 1-inch border of apparently healthy bark around the wound. After each cut, sterilize the knife and chisel with rubbing alcohol, and clean the wound with alcohol. To prevent the development of new cankers, avoid wounding trees.

Oystershell scale (half life size).

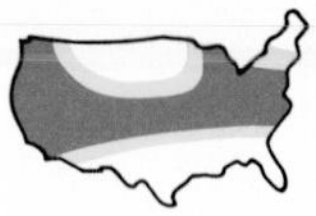

PROBLEM: Leaves on one or more branches turn yellow, and eventually drop. Affected branches often die. Large portions of the tree may be killed. The twigs, branches, or trunk are covered with small (1/8 inch by 1/16 inch), gray, crusty bumps that look like tiny oystershells.

ANALYSIS: Oystershell scale
(*Lepidosaphes ulmi*)
Oystershell scale is a common pest of many deciduous trees and shrubs. The scales lay their eggs in late summer, and the eggs hatch the following spring around late May or early June. The young scales, called *crawlers*, move around the bark, and then settle on twigs or branches. These small (1/10 inch) soft-bodied young feed by sucking sap from the plant. The legs atrophy and a crusty shell develops over the body. The mature female scales lay their eggs underneath their shell. Many other types of scales may infest ash.

SOLUTION: Remove dead and heavily encrusted, dying branches. Spray with ORTHO Isotox Insect Killer or ORTHO Orthene Systemic Insect Control in late May or early June when the young are active. The following early spring, before new growth begins, spray the trunk and branches with ORTHO Volck Oil Spray to control overwintering insects. For more information about scales, see page 876.

FUCHSIA

FUCHSIA

ADAPTATION: Zones 9 and 10. (To determine your zone, see the map on page 1020.) Protect in dry, windy areas. Roots are hardy with mulching in zone 8, but tops die back with hard frosts.

FLOWERING TIME: Summer until first frost. To promote continuous blooming, remove old flowers before berries form.

LIGHT: Partial shade. Full sun in foggy summer areas.

SOIL: Fast-draining soil high in organic matter. Mulch the base of the plant.

FERTILIZER: Fertilize with ORTHO Rose & Flower Food or ORTHO Ortho-Gro Liquid Plant Food.

WATER:
How much: Apply enough water to wet the soil 1 to 1½ feet deep. To determine the proper amount of water for your soil type, see page 912.
Containers: Apply enough water so that 10 percent of the water drains from the bottom of the container.
How often: Water when the soil is moist but not wet 2 inches below the surface.

PRUNING: Pinch the growing tips frequently in the spring. In frost-free areas, prune in the early spring by removing the same amount of wood as was formed the previous season. In cold winter areas, prune off twiggy growth in the fall. In the spring, cut back into live wood, leaving at least two healthy buds.

Whiteflies (twice life size).

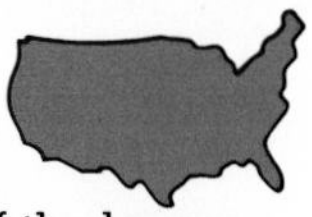

PROBLEM: Tiny, winged insects, 1/12 inch long, are found on the undersides of the leaves. The insects are covered with white waxy powder. When the plant is touched, the insects flutter rapidly around it. Leaves turn yellow and dry, and may be distorted. A black sooty mold may cover the foliage.

ANALYSIS: Greenhouse whitefly
(*Trialeurodes vaporariorum*)
This insect is one of the most serious pests of greenhouse-grown fuchsias and fuchsias growing in warm winter areas. The four-winged adult lays eggs on the undersides of leaves. The larvae are the size of a pinhead, flat, oval, and semitransparent, with white waxy filaments radiating from the body. They feed for about a month before changing to the adult form. Both the larval and adult forms suck sap from the leaves. Adults and larvae cannot fully digest all the sugar in the plant sap and excrete the excess in a fluid called honeydew. A black sooty mold fungus may develop on the honeydew. In warm winter areas the insects can be active year-round, with eggs, larvae, and adults present at the same time. Whiteflies are unable to live through freezing winters. Spring reinfestations in freezing winter areas come from migrating whiteflies and from infested greenhouse-grown plants placed in the garden.

SOLUTION: Spray with ORTHO Isotox Insect Killer. Or, treat small individual plants with ORTHO Whitefly & Mealybug Killer. Spray the foliage thoroughly, being sure to cover both the upper and lower surfaces of the leaves.

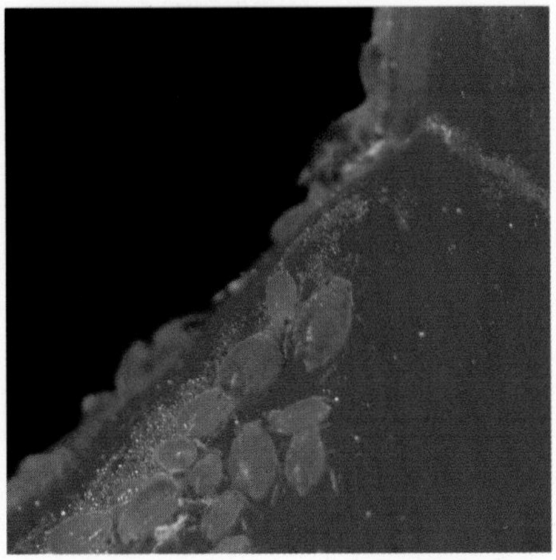

Aphids (3 times life size).

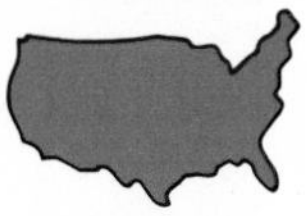

PROBLEM: Young leaves are curled, wrinkled, and yellowing. A shiny or sticky substance may coat the leaves. Tiny (1/8 inch) green, yellow, or pinkish soft-bodied insects cluster on the undersides of leaves or on the stems. Ants may be present.

ANALYSIS: Aphids
Aphids do little damage in small numbers. However, they are extremely prolific and populations can rapidly build up to damaging numbers during the growing season. Damage occurs when the aphid sucks the juices from fuchsia leaves. Some aphids that attack fuchsia are unable to digest fully all the sugar in the plant sap and excrete the excess in a fluid called honeydew. The honeydew often drops onto the leaves below. Ants feed on this sticky substance, and are often present where there is an aphid infestation.

SOLUTION: Control with ORTHO Isotox Insect Killer, ORTHO House Plant Insect Control, or ORTHO Whitefly & Mealybug Killer when insects or damage are first noticed. Repeat the spray if the plant becomes reinfested.

Fuchsia mite damage.

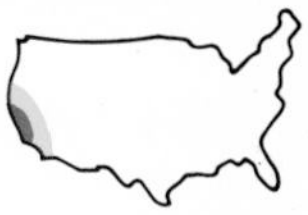

PROBLEM: New growth is severely curled, gnarled, and thickened, and flowers and flower buds are distorted. The plant is growing poorly, and may be weak.

ANALYSIS: Fuchsia mite
(*Aculops fuchsiae*)
The fuchsia mite is a microscopic wormlike mite that infests only fuchsia. It is a recent arrival in California, probably arriving from Brazil, where it is native. Unlike spider mites, fuchsia mites do not cause leaf stippling. Instead, they damage the plant by causing distortion and thickening that may be due to hormonelike materials secreted into the plant as they feed. Fuchsia mites are probably present all year long. They are spread from plant to plant by the wind, and probably by hummingbirds and bees as they visit plants.

SOLUTION: Pick off and destroy distorted growth. Spray with ORTHO Isotox Insect Killer, ORTHO Liquid Sevin, or ORTHO Systemic Rose & Floral Spray at intervals of 7 to 10 days.

FUCHSIA

Rust.

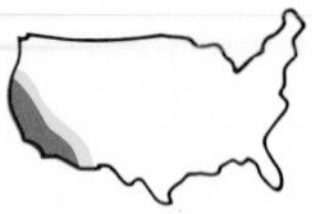

PROBLEM: Red spots and concentric rings of spots appear on the upper surfaces of the leaves. Reddish yellow pustules of spores develop on the undersides of leaves. Severely infected leaves turn brown, dry up, and die.

ANALYSIS: Rust
This plant disease is caused by a fungus (*Pucciniastrum epilobii*) that infects fuchsias. The fungus spends part of its life cycle on firs (*Abies*) and fireweed (*Epilobium*). Fuchsias are susceptible to infection throughout the growing season. Rust spores are spread from plant to plant by wind and splashing water. The disease is most severe when foliage is wet and humidity is high.

SOLUTION: No fungicides are currently registered for control of fuchsia rust. Pick off and destroy infected leaves. Remove leaves and plant debris lying on the ground and destroy fireweed plants. Wash your hands thoroughly after handling infected plants before touching healthy plants. Water in the morning rather than the late afternoon or evening to give wet foliage a chance to dry out. Avoid wetting the foliage when watering the plants. Space plants far enough apart to allow good air circulation.

GARDENIA

Yellow leaves.

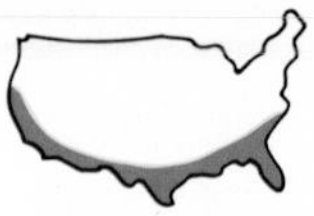

PROBLEM: Many older leaves turn yellow and fall off. No insects or diseases are observed on the fallen leaves, and the remaining leaves are a healthy green color. The problem may occur at any time, but is most often noticed during the winter and spring.

ANALYSIS: Leaf drop
Abrupt changes in soil moisture levels or air temperatures account for most yellowing leaves. A normal loss of foliage occurs in early spring just as bloom buds begin to appear and, in the Southeast, at the end of the rainy season. Yellowing and dropping of leaves at other times are almost always related to changes in weather or soil moisture levels. Gardenia varieties differ in the severity of leaf loss, but healthier plants generally have less leaf drop.

SOLUTION: Apply ORTHO Azalea, Camellia & Rhododendron Food or ORTHO Evergreen & Azalea Food every 4 to 6 weeks to keep plants in good health. Avoid letting plants dry out excessively between waterings.

Iron deficiency.

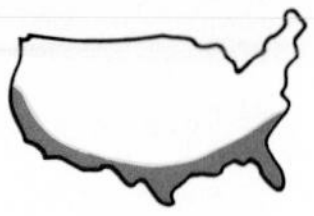

PROBLEM: Some of the leaves turn pale green to yellow. The newest leaves may be completely yellow, with only the veins and the tissue near the veins remaining green. On older leaves, only the leaf edges may be yellowing. The plant may be stunted.

ANALYSIS: Iron deficiency
This is a common problem with acid-loving plants like gardenias. These plants prefer soil with a pH between 5.0 and 6.0. (For more information on soil acidity, see page 908.) The yellowing is due to a deficiency of iron and other minor nutrients in the plant. The soil is seldom deficient in iron. However, iron is often found in an insoluble form that is not available to the plant, especially in soil with a pH of 7.0 or higher. A high soil pH can result from overliming, or from lime leached from cement or brick. Regions where soil is derived from limestone, and those with low rainfall, also have high-pH soils. Plants use iron in the formation of the green pigment in the leaves. When it is lacking, new leaves are yellow.

SOLUTION: Spray the foliage with ORTHO Greenol Liquid Iron, and apply it to the soil around the plants to correct the iron deficiency. Correct the pH of the soil by treating it with *ferrous sulfate* and watering it in well. Maintain an acid pH by fertilizing with ORTHO Azalea, Camellia & Rhododendron Food. If you live in an area where the soil is alkaline or has poor drainage, add at least 50 percent peat moss to the soil when planting gardenias. Never lime the soil around gardenias.

Spider mite damage.

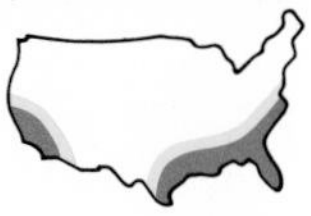

PROBLEM: Leaves are stippled, yellowing, and dirty. Sometimes a silken webbing appears on the lower surfaces of the leaves. New leaves may be distorted. To determine if the plant is infested with mites, hold a sheet of white paper underneath an affected leaf and tap the leaf sharply. Minute green, red, or yellow specks the size of pepper grains will drop to the paper and begin to crawl around. The pests are easily seen against the white background.

ANALYSIS: Spider mites

These mites, which are related to spiders, are major pests of many garden and greenhouse plants. They cause damage by sucking sap from buds and the undersides of the leaves. As a result of feeding, the green leaf pigment disappears, producing the stippled appearance. Mites are active throughout the growing season, but are favored by hot, dry weather (70°F and up). By midsummer, they increase to tremendous numbers. For more information about spider mites, see page 887.

SOLUTION: Spray with ORTHO Orthenex Insect & Disease Control or ORTHO Isotox Insect Killer when damage is first noticed. Wet the undersides of the leaves thoroughly. Repeat the application two more times at intervals of 7 to 10 days. Hose down plants frequently to knock off webs and mites.

Whiteflies (life size).

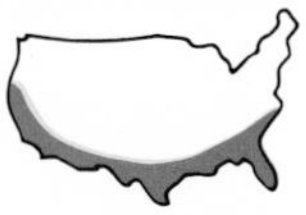

PROBLEM: Tiny, winged insects, 1/12 inch long, feed on the undersides of the leaves. The insects are covered with white waxy powder. When the plant is touched, insects flutter rapidly around it. Leaves may be yellow and dry. A black sooty mold may cover the leaves.

ANALYSIS: Greenhouse whitefly
(*Trialeurodes vaporariorum*)

This insect is a common pest of many garden and greenhouse plants. The four-winged adult lays eggs on the undersides of leaves. The larvae are the size of a pinhead, flat, oval-shaped, and semi-transparent, with white waxy filaments radiating from the body. They feed for about a month before changing to the adult form. Both the larval and adult forms suck sap from the leaves. The larvae are more damaging because they feed more heavily. Adults and larvae cannot fully digest all the sugar in the plant sap, and excrete the excess in a fluid called honeydew, which often drops onto the leaves below. A sooty mold fungus may develop on the honeydew, causing the gardenia leaves to appear black and dirty. In warm winter areas the insect can be active year-round, with eggs, larvae, and adults present at the same time.

SOLUTION: Spray with ORTHO Isotox Insect Killer or ORTHO Orthene Systemic Insect Control when the insects are first noticed, being sure to cover both the upper and lower surfaces of the leaves. Repeat three more times at intervals of 5 to 7 days.

Aphids (twice life size).

PROBLEM: Young leaves are curled, wrinkled, and yellowing. Buds may be distorted. Often, a sticky substance coats the leaves. A black sooty mold may grow on the sticky substance. Tiny (1/8 inch) yellowish green soft-bodied insects cluster on the undersides of the leaves, stems, or buds. Ants may be present.

ANALYSIS: Aphids

Aphids do little damage in small numbers. However, they are extremely prolific and populations can rapidly build up to damaging numbers during the growing season. Damage occurs when the aphid sucks the juices from the gardenia leaves. Some aphids that attack gardenia are unable to digest fully all the sugar in the plant sap and excrete the excess in a fluid called honeydew. The honeydew often drops onto the leaves below. A sooty mold fungus may develop on the honeydew, causing the gardenia leaves to appear black and dirty. Ants feed on the honeydew, and are often present where there is an aphid infestation.

SOLUTION: Spray with ORTHO Isotox Insect Killer or with ORTHO Liquid Sevin when insects or damage are first noticed. Repeat the spray if the plant becomes reinfested. Or spray with a combination of ORTHO Malathion 50 Insect Spray and ORTHO Volck Oil Spray, which will control the aphids and help to remove sooty mold.

Gardenia cultural information

Light: Full sun to part shade
Water: Keep the soil moist
Soil: Loose, rich, well drained, nonalkaline
Fertilizer: Heavy

Sooty mold.

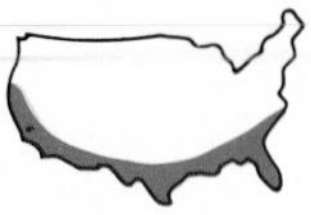

PROBLEM: A black sooty mold grows on the leaves and twigs. It can be completely wiped off the surfaces. Cool, moist weather hastens the growth of this substance.

ANALYSIS: Sooty mold
This common black mold is found on a wide variety of plants in the garden. It is caused by several species of fungi that grow on the sugary material left on plants by aphids, scales, mealybugs, whiteflies, and other insects that suck sap from the plant. The insects are unable to digest all the sugar in the plant sap and excrete the excess in a fluid called honeydew, which drops onto the leaves below. The honeydew may also drop out of infested trees and shrubs onto gardenias growing beneath them. The sooty mold fungus develops on the honeydew, causing the gardenia leaves to appear black and dirty. Sooty mold is unsightly, but it is fairly harmless because it does not attack the leaf directly. Extremely heavy infestations prevent light from reaching the leaf, so that the leaf produces fewer nutrients and may turn yellow. The presence of sooty mold indicates that the gardenia or another plant near it is infested with insects.

SOLUTION: Sooty mold can be wiped from the leaves with a wet rag, or it will eventually be washed off by rain. Prevent more sooty mold by controlling the insect that is producing the honeydew. Inspect the leaves and twigs above the sooty mold to find what type of insect is present. See the following pages for control instructions: for aphids and whiteflies, see page 493; for scales and mealybugs, see page 876.

Nematode-damaged roots.

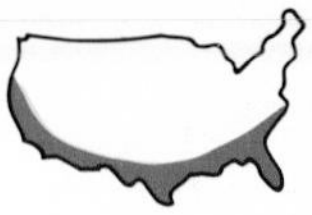

PROBLEM: Leaves are mottled yellow. They may wilt on hot, dry days but recover at night. The plant lacks vigor. After several years, plants are noticeably stunted and branches may die back. The roots are stunted, and often bushy and dark. Sometimes tiny galls are found on the roots.

ANALYSIS: Nematodes
Nematodes are microscopic worms that live in the soil. They feed on plant roots, damaging and stunting them. The damaged roots can't supply sufficient water and nutrients to the above-ground plant parts, and the plant is stunted or slowly dies. Nematodes prefer moist, sandy loam soils. They can move only a few inches each year on their own, but they may be carried long distances by soil, water, tools, or infested plants. Testing roots and soil is the only positive method for confirming the presence of nematodes. Contact your local Cooperative Extension Office (see page 1029) for sampling instructions and addresses of testing laboratories. Soil and root problems such as poor soil structure, drought stress, nutrient deficiency, and root rots can also produce symptoms similar to those caused by nematodes. These problems should be eliminated as causes before sending soil and root samples for testing. For information on soil problems and root rots, see pages 907 and 849.

SOLUTION: There are no chemicals available to homeowners to kill nematodes in planted soil. However, they can be controlled before planting by soil fumigation. For information on fumigating soil, see page 927.

GLEDITSIA (HONEYLOCUST)

ADAPTATION: Zones 4 through 10. (To determine your zone, see the map on page 1020.) Adapted to cold, hot, windy, or polluted areas.

LIGHT: Full sun.

SOIL: Tolerates a wide variety of soils.

FERTILIZER: Fertilize with ORTHO Evergreen, Tree & Shrub Food according to label directions.

WATER:
How much: Apply enough water to wet the soil 3 to 4 feet deep. To determine the proper amount of water for your soil type, see page 912.
How often: Honeylocust will tolerate some drought, but grows best when given periodic deep waterings. Water when the soil is barely moist 4 inches below the surface.

PRUNING: Prune off excessively long, weepy new growth in midsummer. Cut off about half of the new growth. Old trees in low vigor should be pruned severely every 2 to 4 years during the dormant season.

Mimosa webworm damage on honeylocust.

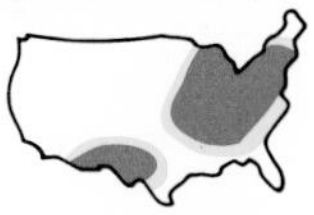

PROBLEM: Small clumps of leaves tied together with silk threads are scattered over the tree. The upper surfaces of the leaves are skeletonized. The leaves turn brown and die, causing infested trees to look as if they have been scorched by fire. Small (up to 1 inch), pale gray or brown caterpillars with 5 white stripes are feeding inside the silken nests. Small trees or the Sunburst variety of thornless honeylocust may be completely defoliated by late summer. Trees are not killed, but repeated defoliations can seriously weaken them.

ANALYSIS: Mimosa webworm
(*Homadaula anisocentra*)
The mimosa webworm is the larval stage of a small moth. It feeds only on honeylocust and mimosa trees. The webworm passes the winter as a pupa in a white silken cocoon. The cocoon is found in sheltered places such as crevices in the bark of the infested tree, or in soil and plant refuse beneath the tree. The moth emerges in the spring and lays her eggs. When the eggs hatch the larvae feed on the leaflets for several weeks. A second generation of webworms hatches in August. The larvae of this second generation are the most damaging because they are usually so numerous. In warmer areas, a third generation hatches in September.

SOLUTION: Spray with ORTHO Isotox Insect Killer or ORTHO Orthene Systemic Insect Control when webbing first appears. Repeat in August. Use high pressures to penetrate the webs and cover the tree thoroughly. In the fall, rake up and burn debris under infested trees, or turn over the soil and bury the leaves.

Plantbug-leafhopper damage.

PROBLEM: In early spring, the new expanding leaves become deformed, curled, and mottled yellow. Leaves drop and twigs die back in severe cases. When the leaves are disturbed, small (¼ inch) green or brownish wedge-shaped or shield-shaped insects hop or fly around the plant.

ANALYSIS: Plantbug-leafhopper complex
Several plantbugs and a leafhopper may be found on the same tree, feeding on the leaflets. The damage they cause is similar, making it difficult to distinguish the injury caused by each type of insect. Eggs, laid the previous summer near the buds and on small twigs, hatch as the leaves unfold. The young insects suck the sap from the leaves and may inject toxins, causing the mottling and distortion. Plantbugs and leafhoppers feed until the middle of summer. When infestations are heavy, twigs die back.

SOLUTION: Spray with ORTHO Isotox Insect Killer or ORTHO Orthene Systemic Insect Control when damage is first noticed in spring. Spray the foliage thoroughly, making sure to cover both the upper and lower surfaces of the leaves. To prevent damage next year, spray before the buds open in the spring.

Spider mite damage on honeylocust.

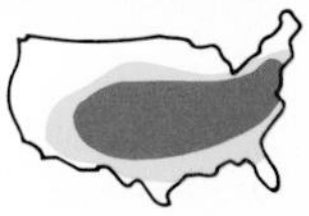

PROBLEM: The leaves are stippled yellow or whitish and dirty. By midsummer, all of the foliage may turn yellow or brownish and drop. Sometimes there is a silken webbing on the lower surfaces of the leaves. The tree may be weak and stunted. To determine if the plant is infested with mites, hold a sheet of white paper underneath a branch that has stippled leaves and tap the branch sharply. Minute reddish or green specks the size of pepper grains will drop to the paper and begin to crawl around.

ANALYSIS: Honeylocust spider mite
(*Platytetranychus multidigituli*)
These mites infest only honeylocust trees. They are a serious pest in the eastern half of the United States. The mites cause damage by sucking sap from the undersides of leaves. As as result of feeding, the green leaf pigment disappears, producing the stippled appearance. Hot, dry weather (70°F and up) favors rapid development of these mites, so by midsummer they may build up to tremendous numbers. If the injury is severe enough, the leaflets turn yellow or brown and drop in midsummer, and most of the mites die due to lack of food. The trees usually leaf out again in late summer, with conspicuous green leaves appearing on the branch tips. Trees infested for more than one year are weakened and may be stunted.

SOLUTION: Spray the undersides of the leaves with ORTHO Orthenex Insect & Disease Control or ORTHO Isotox Insect Killer. Repeat two more times at intervals of 7 to 10 days to kill mites as they hatch from eggs. Apply control measures early in the season to prevent unsightly injury to foliage.

GLEDITSIA (HONEYLOCUST)

Pod gall midge damage.

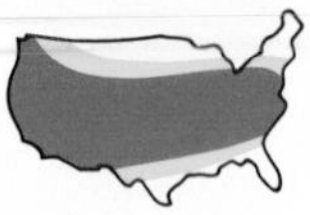

PROBLEM: Green, globular, podlike galls, 1/8 inch in diameter, develop on new leaflets in spring and early summer. The galls turn reddish, then brown, and many of the infested leaflets drop. Twigs or branches sometimes die back after several years of infestation. One to several whitish larvae, 1/4 inch long, are feeding inside the gall.

ANALYSIS: Honeylocust pod gall midge (*Dasineura gleditschiae*)
The larva of this tiny black fly causes unsightly galls on honeylocust trees, especially the thornless varieties. The adult female midge begins laying eggs on new leaflets in the spring. When the eggs hatch the larvae feed on the tissue, causing the leaflet to fold over them and form a pod gall. As the larvae develop inside, the galls turn brown. The flies emerge to lay more eggs. Honeylocust produces new leaves over a long period, so the cycle may repeat itself up to 7 times annually. The galls are not usually damaging to the tree. However, the ornamental value of the tree is reduced when the galled leaflets dry up and drop prematurely. Twigs sometimes die back after repeated attack, but new shoots normally form at the base of the dead twigs.

SOLUTION: Prune off dead twigs. Spray with an insecticide containing *malathion* or *carbaryl* (SEVIN®) in late May and again in late July.

Honeylocust borer damage.

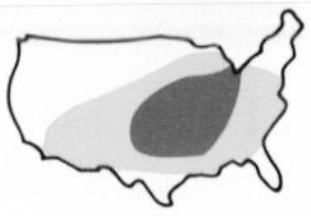

PROBLEM: Large quantities of wet, gummy sap ooze from holes in the trunk and branches. The sap dries to a varnishlike material. The leaves on a branch with oozing sap are often yellowing, and the branch may die back. Weakened branches break during wind or snow storms. Weak, young, or newly transplanted trees are most susceptible to injury, and may be killed.

ANALYSIS: Honeylocust borer (*Agrilus difficilis*)
This white, flat-headed borer is the larva of a metallic black beetle, 1/2 inch long. The adult lays eggs on the bark in June. The eggs hatch and the larvae feed by tunneling in the sapwood beneath the bark. This stops the flow of nutrients and water in that area by cutting the conducting vessels; twig and branch dieback may result. Feeding also weakens the tree structurally, causing limbs to break during storms. Sap flow through the tree acts as a defense against the borers. When the insect burrows into the wood, the tree sap fills the hole and drowns the insect. Young trees or those weakened by other factors are attractive to borers. Factors that weaken the trees, such as transplanting, storm injuries, defoliation by leaf-eating insects, and especially drought, predispose them to attack by borers.

SOLUTION: Cut out and destroy all dead and dying branches. Severely infested young trees should be removed. In the spring, spray or paint the trunk and branches with an insecticide containing *lindane*. Spray to kill young larvae before they burrow into the wood. Repeat three more times at intervals of 2 weeks. Maintain tree health and vigor by watering and fertilizing regularly.

Cankers.

PROBLEM: Leaves on an infected branch or throughout the tree are discolored and wilting. Eventually the leaves drop, and the branch or the entire tree dies. Small (up to 1/2 inch), slightly depressed, tan to black cankers on the affected area may grow together and enlarge to girdle the trunk or branch. The wood under the bark surrounding the canker is streaked reddish brown. Gummy sap may ooze from the canker.

ANALYSIS: Canker wilt
Canker wilt of honeylocust is caused by a fungus (*Thyronectria austro-americana*) that is spread by wind and splashing rain. The fungus enters the wood through wounds, killing the surrounding healthy tissue. A canker forms that ranges in size from a pinhead to 1/2 inch in diameter. The cankers often enlarge and grow together, cutting off the flow of nutrients and water through the branch or trunk. The leaves wilt, and the area above the canker dies. If cankers develop on the trunk, the entire tree may die. Several other fungi also cause cankers on honeylocust.

SOLUTION: There are no effective chemical controls. Prune off dying branches well below the cankered areas. Fertilize and water the tree regularly to promote vigorous growth. (For more information about fertilizing and watering, see pages 910 and 912.) Avoid wounding the tree. A fungicide containing *benomyl* applied as a paste to wounds may help prevent or slow down infection.

HAMAMELIS (WITCH HAZEL) ■ HIBISCUS (ROSE-OF-SHARON)

Galls caused by witch-hazel leaf gall aphid.

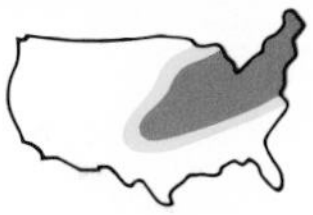

PROBLEM: The upper surfaces of the leaves are covered with $\frac{1}{2}$ inch long green cone-shaped galls with red tips. The galls develop in the spring but remain on the leaves throughout the summer. Underneath each gall on the lower surface of the leaf is a small opening. If the gall is broken open before late May, one or more tiny ($\frac{1}{12}$ inch), whitish insects are found inside.

ANALYSIS: Witch-hazel leaf gall aphid (*Hormaphis hamamelidis*)
Galls on witch hazel are unsightly but not damaging to the plant. The aphid is more injurious to birch (*Betula*), where it feeds on the leaves during the summer. No galls are produced on birch leaves. Gall aphids spend the winter as eggs on the twigs of witch hazel. In early spring, as the leaves unfold, the eggs hatch and the young crawl to the leaves. Each aphid initiates the formation of one gall by feeding on the leaf. The feeding activity stimulates abnormal leaf growth, producing galls that enclose the insects. The female aphid produces many young that fill the interior of the gall. When the aphids mature in late spring or early summer they develop wings, emerge through the opening in the lower surface of the leaf, and fly to birch leaves. Several generations are produced on birch. In the fall, the aphids fly back to witch hazel and lay eggs on the twigs.

SOLUTION: If the infested birch tree is in the area, spray it in summer with ORTHO Orthene Systemic Insect Control or ORTHO Isotox Insect Killer. This will prevent migration of the aphids back to witch hazel in the fall and prevent further damage to the birch tree. To control aphids on witch hazel, spray with a *dormant oil* before the buds open in spring.

Yellow leaves.

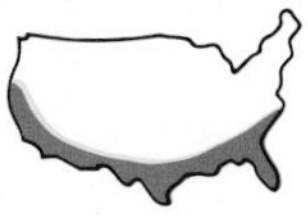

PROBLEM: Many older leaves turn yellow and fall off. No insects or diseases are observed on the fallen leaves, and the remaining leaves are a healthy green color. The problem may occur at any time but is most often noticed during the early fall and spring.

ANALYSIS: Leaf drop
Abrupt changes in soil moisture levels or air temperatures account for most yellowing leaves. A normal loss of older foliage occurs in early spring and at the end of the summer rainy seasons. Yellowing and dropping of leaves at other times is almost always related to changes in weather or soil moisture levels. Hibiscus varieties differ in the severity of leaf loss, but healthier plants generally have less leaf drop.

SOLUTION: Apply ORTHO Azalea, Camellia & Rhododendron Food every 4 to 6 weeks to keep plants in good health. Avoid letting plants dry out excessively between waterings.

Hibiscus cultural information
Light: Full sun to part shade
Water: Frequent, deep watering (deciduous shrubs take some drought)
Soil: Loose, very well drained
Fertilizer: Heavy (medium for deciduous)

Greenhouse whiteflies (twice life size).

PROBLEM: Tiny, winged insects, $\frac{1}{12}$ inch long, are found mainly on the lower surfaces of the leaves. The insects are covered with white waxy powder. When the plant is touched, insects flutter rapidly around it. The leaves may be mottled and yellowing. In warm winter areas, a black sooty mold may cover the foliage.

ANALYSIS: Greenhouse whitefly (*Trialeurodes vaporariorum*)
This insect is a common pest of many garden and greenhouse plants. The four-winged adult lays eggs on the undersides of leaves. The larvae are the size of a pinhead, flat, oval-shaped, and semitransparent, with white waxy filaments radiating from the body. They feed for about a month before changing to the adult form. Both the larval and adult forms suck sap from the leaves. The larvae are more damaging because they feed more heavily. Adults and larvae digest all the sugar in the plant sap and excrete the excess in a fluid called honeydew, which often drops onto the leaves below. A sooty mold fungus may develop on the honeydew causing the hibiscus leaves to appear black and dirty. In warm winter areas the insects can be active year-round, with eggs, larvae, and adults present at the same time. Whiteflies are unable to live through freezing winters. Spring reinfestations in freezing winter areas come from migrating whiteflies and from infested greenhouse-grown plants placed in the garden.

SOLUTION: Control with ORTHO Orthene Systemic Insect Control when whiteflies are first noticed. Repeat the spray three more times at intervals of 2 weeks to control the young as they hatch.

Aphids (half life size).

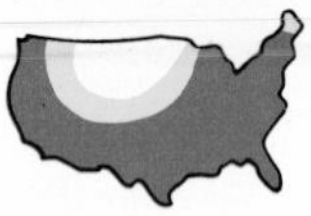

PROBLEM: Flowers and the newest leaves are wrinkled, distorted, and yellowing. On hot days the leaves may wilt, and eventually drop off. A shiny, sticky substance often coats the leaves. A black sooty mold sometimes grows on the sticky substance. Tiny (1/8 inch) yellowish green or black soft-bodied insects cluster on the branch tips and the leaves. Ants may be present.

ANALYSIS: Cotton aphid and cowpea aphid
(*Aphis gossypii* and *A. craccivora*)
Both of these aphids feed on many ornamentals in the garden. They do little damage in small numbers. However, they are extremely prolific and populations can rapidly build up to damaging numbers during the growing season. Damage occurs when the aphid sucks the juices from the hibiscus leaves. The aphid is unable to digest fully all the sugar in the plant sap and excretes the excess in a fluid called honeydew. The honeydew often drops onto the leaves below. A sooty mold fungus may develop on the honeydew, causing the hibiscus leaves to appear black and dirty. Ants feed on honeydew, and are often present where there is an aphid infestation.

SOLUTION: Spray with ORTHO Orthene Sytemic Insect Control when aphids are first noticed. Repeat the spray if the plant becomes reinfested.

HYDRANGEA

ADAPTATION: Zones 6 through 10. To determine your zone, see the map on page 1020.

FLOWERING TIME: Late spring to fall.

LIGHT: Partial shade (full sun in cool coastal areas).

SOIL: Rich, well drained, high in organic matter. Soil acidity affects the uptake of aluminum in the plant, which determines whether the flowers will be pink or blue. Blue flowers result from an acid soil pH and pink flowers occur in soils with an alkaline pH. (For more information about pH, see page 908.) White hydrangeas are not affected by soil acidity.

FERTILIZER: Fertilize with ORTHO Azalea, Camellia & Rhododendron Food or ORTHO General Purpose Plant Food according to label directions. For blue flowers, apply ORTHO Aluminum Sulfate to the soil to increase soil acidity and provide aluminum; for pink flowers, apply lime to decrease the soil acidity. Apply aluminum or lime in the spring to change the color of next spring's flowers.

WATER:
How much: Apply enough water to wet the soil 1½ to 2 feet deep. To determine the proper amount of water for your soil type, see page 912.
How often: Hydrangeas prefer moist soil. Water when the soil is moist but not wet 4 inches below the surface. For more information about watering, see page 912.

Flowerless plant.

PROBLEM: Hydrangeas fail to produce blooms in the spring.

ANALYSIS: Failure to bloom
Hydrangeas may fail to bloom for several reasons:
1. *Cold injury:* Extreme winter temperatures or late spring cold snaps will kill hydrangea flower buds, which form during the late summer or fall.
2. *Improper pruning:* Because some hydrangea species produce flower buds in the late summer or fall, pruning in the winter or spring will remove these potential flowers.
3. *Too much shade:* Hydrangeas growing in deep shade may fail to form flower buds.

SOLUTION: The numbers below correspond to the numbered sections in the analysis.
1. Plant hydrangeas in a protected spot in the garden. Protect them by placing a wire cylinder around each plant and then filling it with loosely-packed straw, or cover the cylinder with burlap. Protect hydrangeas grown in containers by moving them to a cool basement during the winter.
2. Prune hydrangeas after they have finished blooming by cutting back the longer branches.
3. Expose the plants to brighter light by pruning away some of the surrounding vegetation, or transplant hydrangeas to a location that receives filtered or half-day sun, or full sun in cool-winter areas.

Sunburn.

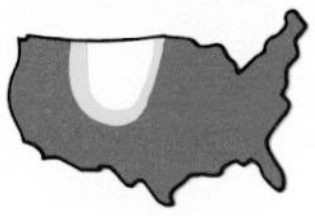

PROBLEM: During warm, sunny weather, leaves on the outside of the plant turn yellowish or brown in the center of the leaf tissue. Some leaves may drop.

ANALYSIS: Sunburn
Hydrangeas are shade plants; their leaves are sensitive to the heat of the sun. The outside leaves facing the light turn yellow or brown when the shrub is planted in full sun. The injury is unsightly, but is not damaging to the plant. Plants are more susceptible to sunburn when the soil in which they are planted is dry. Hydrangea leaves may also scorch (die and turn brown at the edges) during hot weather. For more information about sunburn, see page 429.

SOLUTION: Move the injured plant to a shaded location or provide some shade where it is now growing. (For more information about transplanting, see page 924.) Keep plants adequately watered. For more information about watering, see page 912.

Iron deficiency.

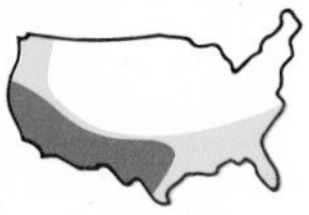

PROBLEM: Some of the leaves turn pale green to yellow. The newest leaves may be completely yellow, with only the veins remaining green. On older leaves, only the leaf edges may be yellowing. The plant may be stunted.

ANALYSIS: Iron deficiency
This is a common problem with acid-loving plants like hydrangea. The plant prefers soil with a pH between 5.5 and 6.5. (For more information on soil acidity, see page 908.) The yellowing is due to a deficiency of iron and other minor nutrients in the plant. The soil is seldom deficient in iron. However, iron is often found in an insoluble form that is not available to the plant, especially in soil with a pH of 7.0 or higher. A high soil pH can result from overliming, or from lime leached from cement or brick. Regions where soil is derived from limestone, and those with low rainfall, also have high-pH soils. Plants use iron in the formation of the green pigment in the leaves. When it is lacking, new leaves are yellow.

SOLUTION: Spray the foliage with ORTHO Greenol Liquid Iron, and apply it to the soil around the plants to correct the iron deficiency. Correct the pH of the soil by treating it with ORTHO Aluminum Sulfate and watering it in well. Maintain an acid pH by fertilizing with ORTHO Azalea, Camellia & Rhododendron Food. When planting hydrangea, add at least 50 percent peat moss to the soil. This is especially important if you live in an area where the soil is alkaline or has poor drainage.

Powdery mildew.

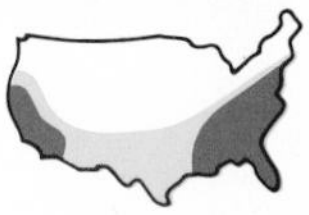

PROBLEM: Leaves, branch tips, buds, and flower stalks are covered with a thin layer or irregular patches of a grayish white powdery material. Infected leaves may turn purplish brown, and they usually drop prematurely. The buds and the blooms may be deformed or die.

ANALYSIS: Powdery mildew
This common plant disease is caused by a fungus (*Erysiphe polygoni*) that thrives in both humid and dry weather. The powdery patches consist of fungal strands and spores. The spores are spread by the wind to healthy plants. The fungus saps the plant nutrients, causing leaf browning, bud deformation, and occasionally the death of the leaf. Since this mildew attacks many different kinds of plants, the fungus from a diseased plant may infect other types of plants in the garden. For a list of susceptible plants, see page 1006.

SOLUTION: Spray the upper and lower surfaces of the leaves with a fungicide containing *benomyl* or *dinocap* when the plants show the first signs of mildew.

ILEX (HOLLY)

ADAPTATION: Zones 3 through 10. (To determine your climate zone, see the map on page 1020.)

BERRIES: Many species of holly are grown for their berries, which are showy in fall and winter. Most holly plants are either male or female, and both must be present in your neighborhood for female plants to develop berries. Male plants do not produce berries.

LIGHT: Full sun to shade. Berry production is greatest in full sun.

SOIL: Well drained and slightly acid (pH around 6.5).

FERTILIZER: Fertilize with ORTHO Azalea, Camellia & Rhododendron Food according to label directions.

WATER:

How much: Apply enough water to wet the soil 2 to 3 feet deep. To determine the amount of water for your soil type, see page 912.

How often: Holly grows best with ample water. Water when the soil is moist but no longer wet 4 inches below the surface.

PRUNING: Some varieties may be sheared for hedges.

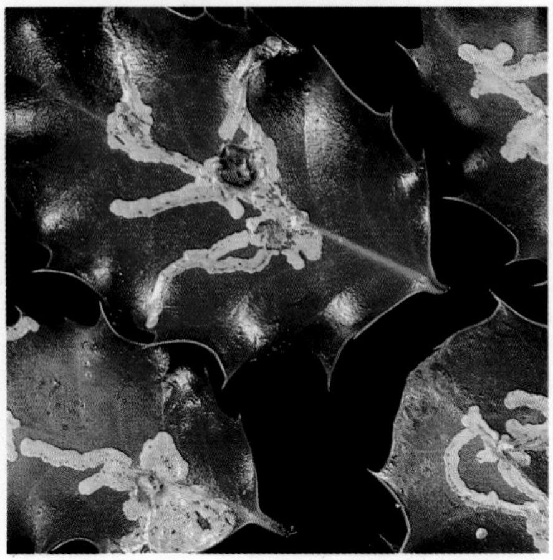

Leafminer damage on holly.

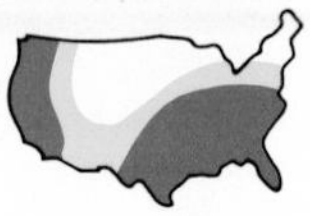

PROBLEM: Yellowish or brown winding trails or blotches appear in the leaves. The leaves may also be distorted and flecked with tiny brown dots. In severe cases, all the leaves are affected and most of them may drop from the plant. When the blotch is torn open, a small ($1/6$ inch), yellowish white maggot is found between the upper and lower surfaces of the leaf.

ANALYSIS: Holly leafminers
(*Phytomyza* species)
The damage caused by these leafminers is unsightly and ruins the value of those types of holly used as winter holiday decorations. Both the larva and adult cause damage. The insect spends the winter as a larva or pupa inside a fallen leaf or a leaf still attached to the plant. When new growth begins in spring, a tiny black fly emerges. The female deposits eggs inside the leaf by making a slit in the lower surfaces of the leaf. The flies (only the females in some species) feed on the sap by stabbing through the leaf surface. This feeding causes the brown flecking and distortion. The eggs deposited inside the leaves hatch into maggots that feed on the inner leaf tissue, producing the mines or trails. In a heavy infestation, the plant may drop almost all its leaves and will remain bare until the following spring.

SOLUTION: Control with ORTHO Isotox Insect Killer or ORTHO Orthene Systemic Insect Control as new leaves emerge in spring. Repeat the spray in 2 or 3 weeks. Rake up and destroy fallen leaves.

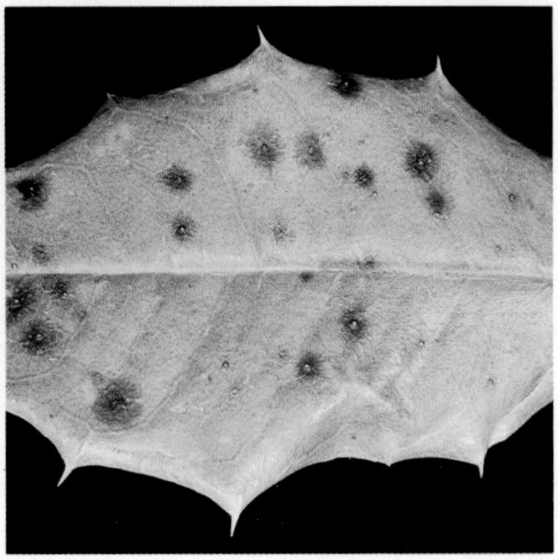

Leaf spots.

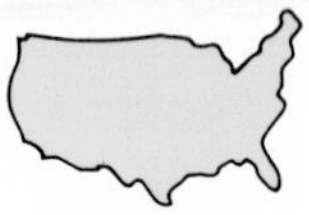

PROBLEM: Spots and blotches appear on the leaves. The spots may be yellow, red, tan, gray, or brown. They range in size from barely visible to $1/2$ inch in diameter. Several spots may join to form blotches. Leaves may turn yellow and die. Some leaves may drop. Leaf spotting is most severe in warm, humid weather.

ANALYSIS: Leaf spot
Several different fungi cause leaf spots on holly. These spots are unsightly but rarely harmful to the plant. The fungi are spread by splashing water and wind. Spots develop where the fungi enter the tissue. If wet or humid weather persists, the fungi spread through the tissue and blotches form. They survive the winter on the leaves and twigs. Most leaf spot organisms do their greatest damage in mild weather (between 50° and 85°F). Egg depositing sites of holly leafminers also cause leaf spotting. For more information, see page 500.

SOLUTION: Where practical, remove infected leaves from the plant. On valuable specimens, spray with a fungicide containing *chlorothalonil* (DACONIL 2787®), *ferbam*, or *maneb* when new growth begins in the spring. Repeat at intervals of 2 weeks for as long as the weather remains favorable for infection.

Small, pinhead-size gray spots with purple halos may be confused with fungal leaf spots. These spots, known as *spine spots*, are caused by the spines of adjacent leaves puncturing the tissue. Examination with a magnifying glass will reveal tiny holes in the center of the spot.

Iron deficiency.

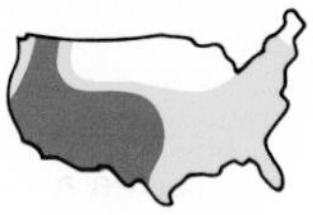

PROBLEM: Some of the leaves turn pale green to yellow. The newest leaves may be completely yellow with only the veins remaining green. On older leaves, only the leaf edges may be yellowing. The plant may be stunted.

ANALYSIS: Iron deficiency
This is a common problem with acid-loving plants like holly. The plant prefers soil with a pH between 6.0 and 6.5. (For more information on soil acidity, see page 908.) The yellowing is due to a deficiency of iron and other minor nutrients in the plant. The soil is seldom deficient in iron. However, iron is often found in an insoluble form that is not available to the plant, especially in soil with a pH of 7.0 or higher. A high soil pH can result from overliming, or from lime leached from cement or brick. Regions where soil is derived from limestone, and those with low rainfall, also have high-pH soils. Plants use iron in the formation of the green pigment in the leaves. When it is lacking, new leaves are yellow.

SOLUTION: Spray the foliage with ORTHO Greenol Liquid Iron, and apply it to the soil around the plants to correct the iron deficiency. Correct the pH of the soil by treating it with *ferrous sulfate* or ORTHO Aluminum Sulfate and watering it in well. Maintain an acid pH by fertilizing with ORTHO Azalea, Camellia & Rhododendron Food. When planting holly, add at least 50 percent peat moss to the soil if you live in an area where the soil is alkaline or has poor drainage. Never lime the soil around holly.

Southern red mite damage on Japanese holly.

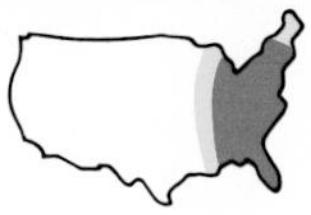

PROBLEM: Leaves are stippled yellow or grayish green and dirty, and are often smaller than normal. There may be a silken webbing on the lower surfaces of the leaves. To determine if the plant is infested with mites, hold a sheet of white paper underneath a branch that has stippled leaves and tap the branch sharply. Minute reddish specks the size of pepper grains will drop to the paper and begin to crawl around. The pests are easily seen against the white background.

ANALYSIS: Southern red mite
(*Oligonychus ilicis*)
The southern red mite, also known as *red spider*, is a major pest of many evergreen plants in the eastern half of the country. The mites cause damage by sucking sap from both the top and undersides of leaves. As a result of feeding, the green leaf pigment disappears, producing the stippled appearance. These mites are most prolific in cooler weather. They feed and reproduce primarily during spring and, in some cases, fall. At the onset of hot weather (70°F and up), the mites have caused their maximum damage.

SOLUTION: Control with ORTHO Isotox Insect Killer when stippling is first noticed in spring. Cover the leaves thoroughly. Repeat the spray 3 more times at intervals of 7 to 10 days to kill young mites as they hatch from eggs. It is important to apply control measures early in the season when damage first appears to prevent unsightly injury to foliage. Injured leaves remain on the plant for more than one growing season. Hose down plants frequently to knock off webs and mites.

Chinese wax scale (⅓ life size).

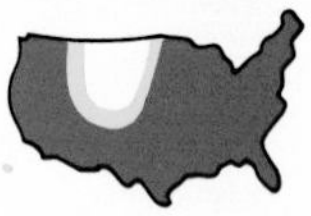

PROBLEM: The leaves, stems, or berries are covered with brown or black crusty bumps; or thick, white, waxy bumps; or clusters of somewhat flattened scaly bumps. The bumps can be scraped or picked off; the undersides are usually soft. Leaves may turn yellow and drop, and branches may die. In some cases, a shiny, sticky substance coats the leaves. A black sooty mold often grows on the sticky substance.

ANALYSIS: Scales
Many different species of scales infest holly. They lay their eggs on the leaves or bark in the spring, and in midsummer the young scales, called *crawlers*, settle on the various parts of the tree or shrub. The small (1/10 inch) soft-bodied young feed by sucking sap from the plant. The legs usually atrophy and a hard crusty or waxy shell develops over the body. The mature female scales lay their eggs underneath their shell. Some species of scales infesting holly are unable to digest fully all the sugar in the plant sap, and excrete the excess in a fluid called honeydew. A black sooty mold fungus may develop on the honeydew. An uncontrolled infestation of scales may kill the plant after two or three seasons. For more information about scales, see page 876.

SOLUTION: Spray with ORTHO Isotox Insect Killer or ORTHO Orthene Systemic Insect Control when the young are active. Contact your local Cooperative Extension Office (see page 1029) to determine the best time to spray for scales in your area. The following spring, before new growth begins, spray the trunk and branches with a *dormant oil spray*.

ILEX (HOLLY)

Yaupon psyllid damage.

PROBLEM: New leaves are deformed. A small, rough gall forms on the entire leaf or a portion of the leaf in the spring and summer. The galls gradually turn from green to dark red as the season progresses. There may be a white fluffy material and several tiny, yellow, wingless insects inside the galls.

ANALYSIS: Yaupon psyllid
(Metaphalaria ilicis)
This insect feeds exclusively on yaupon. It secretes a substance that stimulates abnormal leaf growth, producing galls that enclose the insects. Immature psyllids feed during the spring and summer, sucking the juices from the succulent tissues within the gall. In the fall they develop into winged adults. The female adults lay eggs in the late fall; the eggs hatch the following spring. Psyllid infestations do not kill yaupon but can greatly slow its growth. Severe, repeated infestations over several years give the plant a bushy, pruned appearance. See page 878 for more information about psyllids.

SOLUTION: Spray plants thoroughly with ORTHO Orthene Systemic Insect Control or ORTHO Isotox Insect Killer in the spring before extensive galling occurs. Repeat the spray in 2 weeks. The insecticide will not kill insects already in large galls. If galling has already occured, cut out deformed plant parts and compost or dispose of them, or wait until the following spring and spray to control the next generation.

IXORA

Cold damage.

PROBLEM: Many of the leaves have brown edges and tips. More than half of the leaf may be affected. Newer leaves show more symptoms than older ones. Shoot tips may be discolored or dead, and smaller branches may be killed. The problem occurs from December to March, following cold weather.

ANALYSIS: Cold damage
Ixora is a tropical plant, and is frequently injured by freezing temperatures in some growing areas. Mild damage results in leaf injury and discoloration. Severe injury can cause leaf and twig death or even kill plants back to the soil line.

SOLUTION: Delay pruning until spring, or until all danger of additional damage has passed. Fertilize injured plants lightly but frequently to speed recovery. Keep plants healthy to minimize damage. Cover and protect exposed plants on nights when freezing temperatures are expected. If possible, plant only in protected locations away from chilling winds. To reduce damage, water plants thoroughly the day before freezing temperatures are expected.

Ixora cultural information
Light: Full sun
Water: Occasional deep watering
Soil: Acid, well drained
Fertilizer: Medium to heavy

Iron deficiency.

PROBLEM: Some leaves turn pale green to yellow. The newest leaves (those at the tips of the branches) may be completely yellow, with only the veins remaining green. Only the leaf edges of older leaves may be yellowing. The plant may be stunted.

ANALYSIS: Iron deficiency
This is a common problem in acid-loving plants like ixora. Ixora grows best in soil with a pH between 5.5 and 6.5. (For more information on soil acidity, see page 908.) The yellowing is due to a deficiency of iron and other minor nutrients in the plant. The soil is seldom deficient in iron. However, iron is often found in an insoluble form that is not available to the plant, especially in soil with a pH of 7.0 or higher. An alkaline soil can result from overliming, or from lime leached from cement or brick. Regions where soil is derived from limestone also have high-pH soils. Plants use iron in the formation of the green pigment in the leaves. When iron is lacking, new leaves are yellow.

SOLUTION: Spray the foliage with ORTHO Greenol Liquid Iron, and apply it to the soil around the plants to correct the deficiency of minor nutrients. Correct the pH of the soil by treating it with *ferrous sulfate* or ORTHO Aluminum Sulfate and watering it in well. Maintain an acid pH by fertilizing with ORTHO Azalea, Camellia & Rhododendron Food. When planting ixora, add peat moss, acid soil, or other materials to help acidify the planting soil.

JASMINUM (JASMINE)

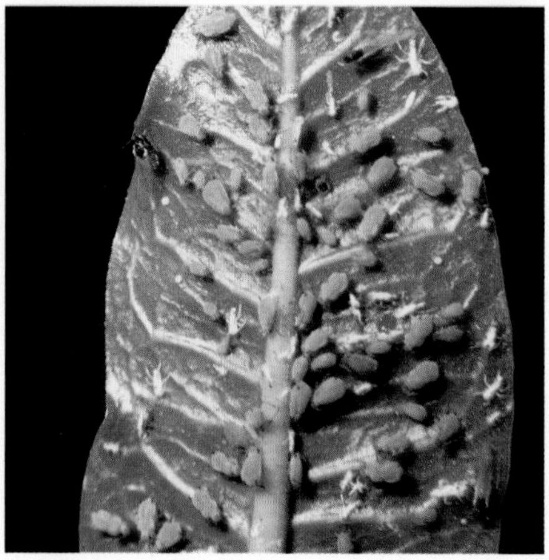

Aphids (twice life size).

PROBLEM: Leaves are yellow, curled, and often distorted. Soft-bodied insects, about $\frac{1}{8}$ inch long, cluster on the undersides of the leaves and on new growth. They may be green, black, or orange. A shiny or sticky substance may coat some of the leaves.

ANALYSIS: Aphids
Aphids do little damage in small numbers. However, they are extremely prolific and populations can rapidly build up to damaging numbers during the growing season. Damage occurs when the aphid sucks the juices from the ixora leaves. The aphid is unable to digest fully all the sugar in the plant sap and excretes the excess in a sugary fluid called honeydew, which often drops onto the leaves below. A sooty mold fungus may develop on the honeydew, causing the ixora leaves to appear black and dirty. Ants feed on the honeydew, and are often present where there is an aphid infestation. For more information about aphids, see page 875.

SOLUTION: Apply an insecticide containing *malathion* according to label directions. Repeat sprayings as needed. Make sure that ixora is listed on the product label.

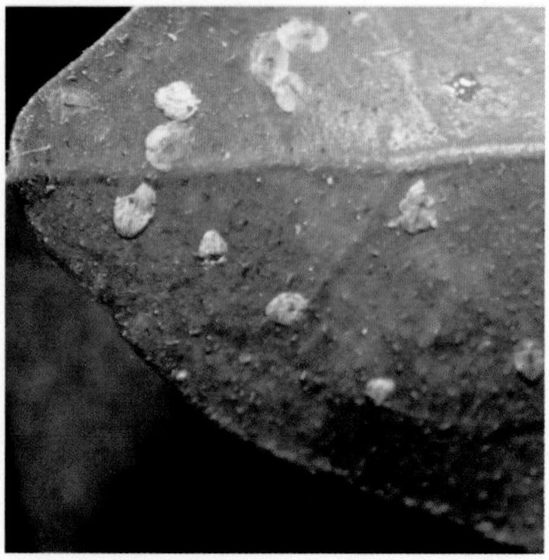

Soft scale (twice life size).

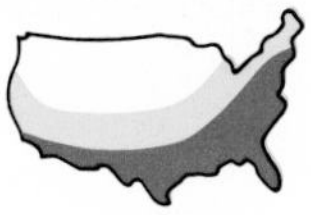

PROBLEM: The undersides of the leaves are covered with brownish or black crusty bumps or thick, white, waxy bumps or clusters of tan, yellowish, brown, or reddish scaly bumps. The bumps can be scraped or picked off; the undersides are usually soft. Leaves turn yellow and may drop; small branches may die back. In some cases, a sticky substance coats the leaves. A black sooty mold often grows on the sticky substance.

ANALYSIS: Scales
Many types of scales infest jasmine shrubs and vines. They lay their eggs on the leaves or bark, and in spring to midsummer the young scales, called *crawlers*, settle on leaves and twigs. The small ($\frac{1}{10}$ inch), soft-bodied young feed by sucking sap from the plant. The legs usually atrophy and a hard crusty or waxy shell develops over the body. The mature female scales lay their eggs underneath the shell. Some species of scales that infest jasmine are unable to digest fully all the sugar in the plant sap, and excrete the excess in a fluid called honeydew. A sooty mold fungus may develop on the honeydew, causing the jasmine leaves to appear black and dirty. For more information about scales, see page 876.

SOLUTION: Spray with an insecticide containing *malathion* or *carbaryl* (SEVIN®) when the young are active. Contact your local Cooperative Extension Office (see page 1029) to determine the best time to spray for scales in your area. The following early spring before new growth begins, spray the plant with a *dormant oil spray* to control overwintering insects.

Whiteflies (3 times life size).

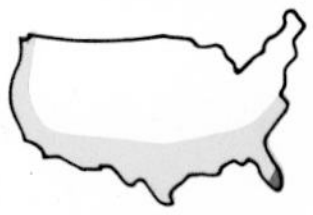

PROBLEM: Tiny, winged insects $\frac{1}{12}$ inch long feed on the undersides of the leaves. The insects are covered with a white waxy powder. When the plant is touched, insects flutter rapidly around it. Leaves may be mottled and yellowing.

ANALYSIS: Whitefly
This insect is a common pest of many garden and greenhouse plants. The four-winged adult lays eggs on the undersides of leaves. The larvae are flat, oval-shaped, and semitransparent. They feed for about a month before changing to the adult form. Both the larval and adult forms suck sap from the leaves. The larvae are more damaging because they feed more heavily. Adults and larvae cannot fully digest all the sugar in the plant sap, and excrete the excess in a fluid called honeydew, which often drops onto the leaves below. A sooty mold fungus may develop on the honeydew. In warm winter areas these insects can be active year-round.

SOLUTION: Spray with an insecticide containing *acephate* (ORTHENE®). Make sure your plant is listed on the product label.

Jasminum cultural information
Light: Full sun to part shade
Water: Drought-tolerant once established
Soil: Tolerates many types
Fertilizer: Medium

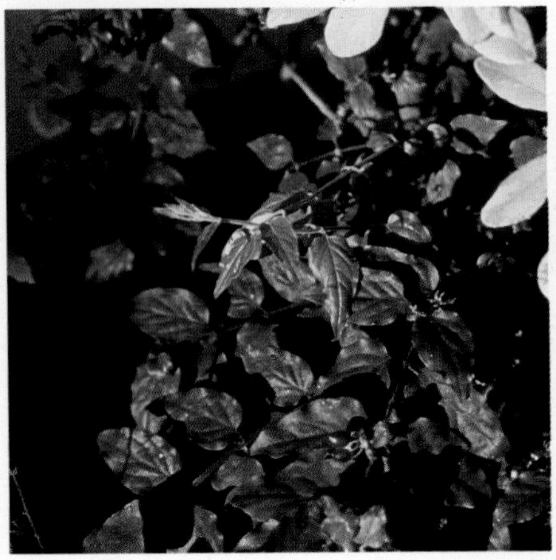

Sooty mold.

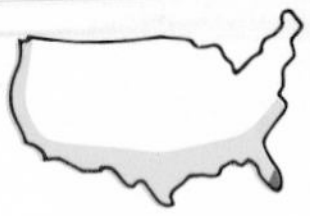

PROBLEM: A black sooty mold is growing on the leaves and twigs. It can be completely wiped off the surfaces. Cool, moist weather hastens the growth of this substance.

ANALYSIS: Sooty mold
This common black mold is found on a wide variety of plants in the garden. It is caused by any of several species of fungi that grow on the sugary material left on plants by aphids, scales, mealybugs, whiteflies, and other insects that suck sap from the plant. The insects cannot fully digest all the sugar in the sap and excrete the excess in a fluid called honeydew, which drops onto the leaves below. The sooty mold fungus develops on the honeydew, causing the jasmine leaves to appear black and dirty. Sooty mold is unsightly, but it is fairly harmless because it does not attack the leaf directly. Extremely heavy infestations prevent light from reaching the leaf, so that the leaf produces fewer nutrients and may turn yellow. The presence of sooty mold indicates that the jasmine is infested with insects.

SOLUTION: Sooty mold can be wiped from the leaves with a wet rag; or it will eventually be washed off by rain. Inspect the leaves and twigs above the sooty mold to find what type of insect is present. For information on controlling the insect, see the following pages: for aphids, page 875; for scales and mealybugs, page 876; for whiteflies, page 877.

JUNIPERUS (JUNIPER)

ADAPTATION: Throughout the United States.

LIGHT: Full sun (or partial shade in hot climates).

SOIL: Junipers prefer sandy, well-drained soil but they will thrive in almost any type of garden soil.

FERTILIZER: Fertilize with ORTHO Evergreen, Tree & Shrub Food or ORTHO General Purpose Plant Food according to label directions.

WATER:
How much: Apply enough water to wet the soil 1 to 3 feet deep, depending on the size of the juniper. To determine the proper amount of water for your soil type, see page 912.
How often: Young junipers should be watered when the soil 4 inches below the surface is just barely moist. Established plants are drought resistant and require summer watering only in the hottest climates. Water when the soil 4 inches below the surface is dry. Do not plant junipers where they will receive water meant for a lawn.

PRUNING: Some junipers grow tall (to 90 feet) or spread up to 15 feet. It is best to use a variety that will fit the area to be planted rather than depending on pruning. Older junipers will not sprout new growth from older wood, so never remove all the foliage from a branch. If a shrub is to be sheared, begin when the plant is young, and shear lightly and regularly.

Dieback. *Insert:* Girdler tunnels.

PROBLEM: One or more branches turn yellow. Eventually they turn brown and dry. Plants do not usually die. If the bark is peeled back at the base of the affected branch, holes or tunnels are found in the wood. There may be a small (1/4 inch long) cream-colored larva with a brown head feeding inside the tunnel.

ANALYSIS: Juniper twig girdler
(*Periploca nigra*)
The juniper twig girdler is found in the eastern half of the United States and in California, but it is damaging to junipers only in California. All species of junipers are attacked. The low-growing, thin-stemmed varieties are the most seriously damaged. The twig girdler is the larva of a tiny black moth. In Southern California, the female lays eggs on woody stems from March to May. In Northern California, the moth lays eggs from May to July. When the eggs hatch, the larvae tunnel into the stems beneath the bark. The plant may be infested for 2 or 3 years before damage becomes noticeable. Feeding by the larvae cuts off the flow of nutrients and water through the stems, so that the branches turn yellow and may die. If the stem is not entirely eaten or girdled, the branch may survive for several years.

SOLUTION: Control of this insect depends on applying insecticides before the larvae have tunneled into the stem. Spray with ORTHO Lindane Borer & Leaf Miner Spray in April and again in May in Southern California. In Northern California, spray in early June and again in late June or early July. Drench the woody stems thoroughly. Prune out and destroy dead branches.

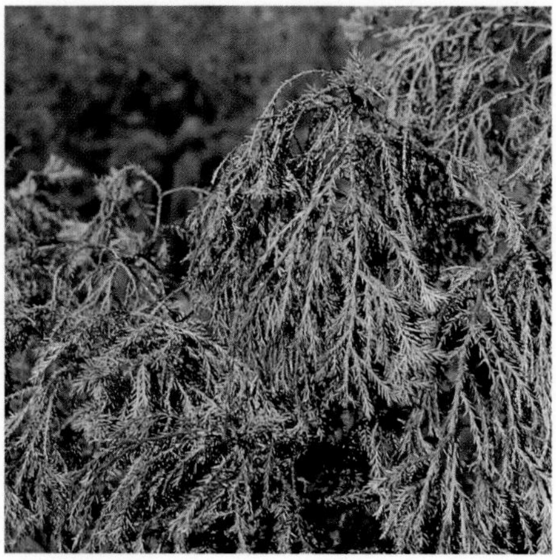
Drought damage.

Root rot damage.

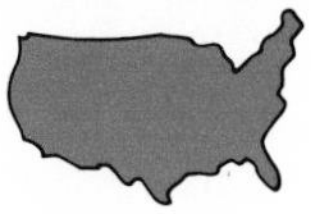

PROBLEM: Needles turn yellow and then brown and dry, either on the outer, lower branches; on the inside of the plant nearest the trunk; from the top of the plant down; or from the tips back. Sometimes only a branch or one side of the plant is affected. In other cases, the whole plant turns brown.

ANALYSIS: Needle browning
A number of different conditions may cause the needles to turn brown on junipers.

SOLUTION: The numbered solutions below correspond to the numbers in the analysis.

1. *Dog urine:* When dogs urinate on it, the foliage on the outer, lower branches turns yellow, then brown, as if scorched. The salts in the urine burn the foliage.

1. Wash the foliage and thoroughly soak the ground around the plant to dilute the salts in the urine if it is suspected that a dog has recently urinated on it.

2. *Natural leaf browning and shedding:* The older needles, on the inside of the plant nearest the trunk, turn brown and drop off in spring or fall. This is a natural process similar to the dropping of leaves of deciduous plants.

2. No controls are necessary.

3. *Drought or winter injury:* When the plant is damaged by drought or winter injury, needles gradually turn yellow, then brown or reddish from the top of the plant down and from the tips of the branches back. This may happen when the soil is dry and the plant is not getting enough water, or when the soil is frozen in the winter.

3. Prune out dead twigs and branches. Provide adequate water during periods of extended drought and shelter plants growing in windy locations. Water in late fall or early winter, if necessary, to insure adequate soil moisture during the winter. Mulch plants after they are dormant to reduce the depth of frost penetration into the soil. Do not plant junipers in areas where they are not adapted.

4. *Salt burn:* Needles turn brown from the tips back. This condition may develop on one side of the plant only, or on the whole plant. Salt burn is common in alkaline soils, when water has a high salt content, in soils with poor drainage, in overfertilized soils, or along roadsides where winter runoff contains road salts. The salts in the soil inhibit water and nutrient uptake, causing the needles to turn brown. Similar symptoms can occur in ocean-front plantings from wind-borne salt mist.

4. Prune off badly damaged areas. Avoid new injury by giving plants a heavy irrigation once during the growing season. If you suspect that your water contains salts, have it analyzed through your Cooperative Extension Office (see page 1029) or local water department. Do not overfertilize plants; follow package directions. Avoid planting in areas where road or sea salt may be a problem. Occasionally hose down ocean-front plantings to remove salt accumulations on the foliage.

Twig blight.

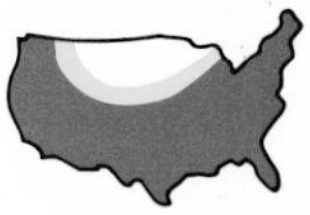

PROBLEM: Needles, twigs, and smaller branches turn light brown to reddish brown, then gray, gradually dying from the tips back. Plants less than 5 years old are often killed. Minute black dots may appear on the needles and stems when the needles have dried and turned grayish. The disease is most serious during wet weather or in shady, moist locations. This problem sometimes resembles drought damage. However, the border between healthy tissue and dead tissue is sharp with this disease but gradual with drought. In addition, the disease is found only on isolated branches rather than uniformly throughout the plant, as with drought.

ANALYSIS: Twig blight
This plant disease is caused by a fungus (*Phomopsis juniperovora*). It is highly destructive to junipers, cryptomeria, chamaecyparis, and arborvitae throughout most of the country. The spores are spread by splashing rain, overhead watering, insects, and tools. The fungus enters through wounds or healthy tissue, killing the stem and needles above and below the point of entrance. Black spore-producing structures develop and overwinter on dead needles.

SOLUTION: Spray with *benomyl* when symptoms first appear around May. Repeat three or four more times at weekly intervals. Prune out and destroy infected branches below the line between diseased and healthy tissue, making the cut into live tissue. Plant trees in areas with good air circulation and full sun. Plant resistant varieties (see page 1015).

JUNIPERUS (JUNIPER)

Dieback caused by phytophthora root rot.

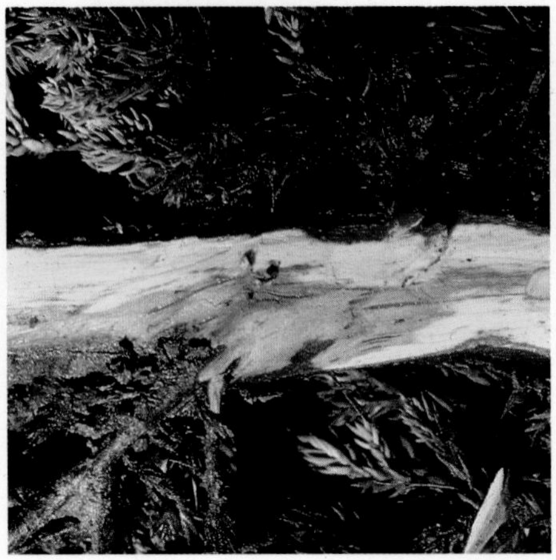

Stem browning.

Cypress tip moth and cocoon (life size).

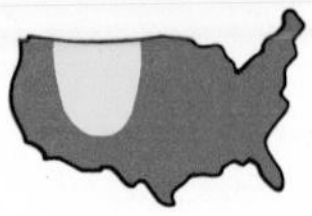

PROBLEM: The normal foliage color dulls, and the plant loses vigor. The foliage may wilt, or it may turn yellow or light brown. Major branches or the entire plant may die. The plant sometimes lives for many months in a weakened condition, or it may die quickly. The roots and lower stems are brownish and the roots are often decayed. There may be fine woolly brown strands on the roots and white powdery spores on the soil surface; or there may be fan-shaped plaques of white strands between the bark and wood of the roots and lower stems. Mushrooms may appear at the base of the plant in the fall.

ANALYSIS: Root and crown rots
Root and crown rots on junipers are caused by several different fungi. The fungi live in the soil and on living roots.

SOLUTION: The numbered solutions below correspond to the numbers in the analysis.

1. *Phytophthora* species: These fungi cause browning and decay on the roots, and browning of the lower stems. The plants usually dies slowly, but young plants may wilt and die rapidly. The disease is most prevalent in heavy, waterlogged soils. For more information about *Phytophthora*, see page 849.

1. Remove dead and dying plants. When replanting, use plants that are resistant to *Phytophthora*. (For a list of resistant trees and shrubs, see page 1016.) Improve soil drainage (see page 907). Avoid overwatering junipers.

2. *Phymatotrichum omnivorum:* This fungus, also known as *cotton root rot* or *Texas root rot*, is a severe problem on many plants in the Southwest. The plant often wilts and dies suddenly. Older plants may die more slowly, showing general decline and dieback symptoms. Brown strands form on the roots and white powdery spores form on the soil. The disease is most severe in heavy, alkaline soils. For more information about *Phymatotrichum*, see page 851.

2. Remove dead and dying plants. When replanting, buy only resistant varieties. (For a list of resistant trees and shrubs, see page 1013.) Before planting, increase the soil acidity by adding 1 pound of *ammonium sulfate* for every 10 square feet of soil. Make a circular ridge around the planting area and fill the basin with 4 inches of water. Repeat the treatment in 5 to 10 days. Improve drainage. For more information about soil drainage, see page 907.

3. *Armillaria mellea:* This disease, also known as *shoestring root rot*, *mushroom root rot*, or *oak root fungus*, is identified by the presence of fan-shaped plaques of white fungal strands between the bark and the wood of the roots and lower stems. This fungus grows rapidly under wet conditions. Honey-colored mushrooms appear at the base of the plant in the fall. For more information about *Armillaria*, see page 851.

3. Remove dead plants. The life of a newly infected plant may be prolonged if the disease has not reached the lower stems. Expose the base of the plant to air for several months by removing several inches of soil. Prune off diseased roots. When replanting, use only resistant varieties. (For a list of plants resistant to *Armillaria*, see page 1016.)

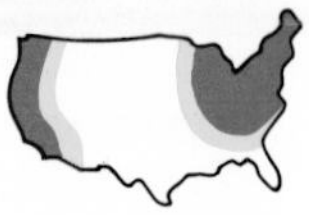

PROBLEM: Leaf tips turn yellow at first, then brown and dry. They contrast sharply with the healthy green foliage. Damage is most severe in plants growing in shady areas. When the yellow leaf is torn open, a small ($\frac{1}{5}$ inch long), greenish caterpillar with a dark head may be found inside. Gray or brownish moths with a $\frac{1}{3}$ inch wingspread may be seen flying around the plant in April, May, or June.

ANALYSIS: Leafminers and tip moths
(*Argyresthia* species)
Several species of insects, known as *leafminers* in the eastern United States and *tip moths* on the West Coast, infest junipers, arborvitae, and cypress. Damage is unsightly, but plants may lose over half their foliage and still survive. The larvae spend the winter inside the leaf tips. When the weather warms in late spring, the larvae pupate, then emerge as adult moths to lay eggs on the leaves. The larvae that hatch from these eggs tunnel into the leaf tips, devouring the green tissue. The tips above the point of entry yellow and die. The larvae feed until late fall or through the winter until early spring.

SOLUTION: Spray with ORTHO Isotox Insect Killer when eggs are hatching in June or July (mid-August in the far northeastern states). Trim and destroy infested leaves in fall and spring.

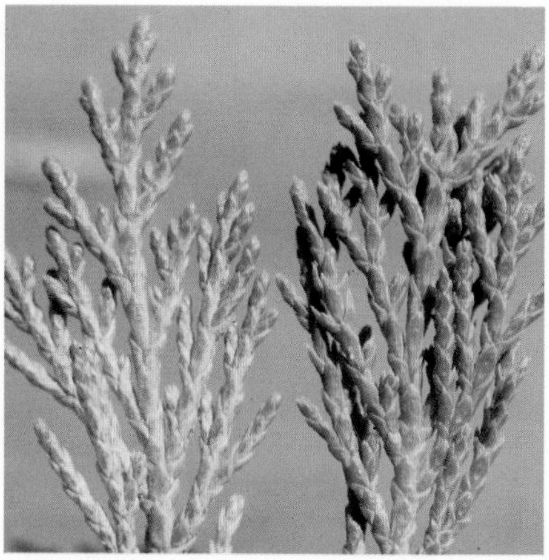

Spider mite damage (on left).

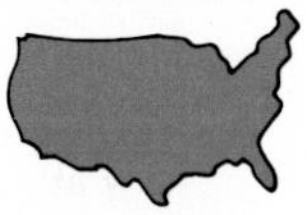

PROBLEM: The needles are stippled yellow or grayish and dirty. There may be a silken webbing on the twigs. Needles may turn brown and fall off. To determine if the plant is infested with mites, hold a sheet of white paper underneath some stippled needles and tap the foliage sharply. Minute green, red, yellow, or black specks the size of pepper grains will drop to the paper and begin to crawl around. The pests are easily seen against the white background.

ANALYSIS: Spruce spider mite (*Oligonychus ununguis*) **and two-spotted mite** (*Tetranychus urticae*)
Spider mites, related to spiders, are among the most important pests of junipers and other evergreen trees and shrubs. They cause damage by sucking sap from the needles. As a result of feeding, the green leaf pigment disappears, producing the stippled appearance. *Spruce spider mites* are more prolific in cooler weather. They feed and reproduce primarily during spring and, in some cases, fall. At the onset of hot weather (70°F and up), the mites have caused their maximum damage. *Two-spotted mites* develop rapidly in hot, dry weather (70°F and up), so by midsummer they build up to tremendous numbers.

SOLUTION: Spray with ORTHO Isotox Insect Killer or ORTHO Orthene Insect Spray when damage is first noticed. Repeat the application three more times at intervals of 7 days. Hose down plants frequently to knock off webs and mites.

Aphids (4 times life size).

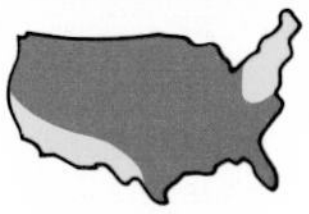

PROBLEM: Needles turn brown and eventually drop from the plant. When infestations are heavy, branches die back and the plant is stunted. A shiny, sticky substance may coat the needles and stems. A black sooty mold often grows on the sticky substance. Tiny (1/8 inch) black or brown soft-bodied insects cluster on the twigs and stems. Ants may be present.

ANALYSIS: Aphids
Aphids do little damage in small numbers. However, they are extremely prolific and populations can rapidly build up to damaging numbers during the growing season. Damage occurs when the aphid sucks the juices from the juniper bark, causing needle browning and branch dieback. The aphid is unable to digest fully all the sugar in the plant sap and excretes the excess in a fluid called honeydew. The honeydew often drops onto needles and plants below. A black sooty mold fungus may develop on the honeydew, or rain may wash it off before the fungus has a chance to grow. Ants feed on this sticky substance, and are often present where there is an aphid infestation. For more information about aphids, see page 875.

SOLUTION: Control with ORTHO Isotox Insect Killer or ORTHO Malathion 50 Insect Spray when aphids are first noticed. Cover the twigs and stems thoroughly. Repeat the spray if the plant becomes reinfested.

Juniper scale (4 times life size).

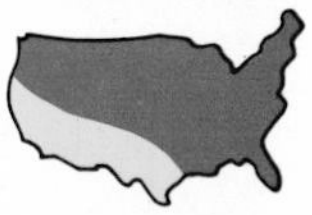

PROBLEM: The tree or shrub looks gray and off-color and there is no new growth. Eventually the needles turn yellow. Branches and possibly the whole plant may die back. The foliage is covered with clusters of tiny (1/8 inch), somewhat flattened yellow and white scaly bumps. A shiny, sticky substance may coat the needles. A black sooty mold often grows on the sticky substance.

ANALYSIS: Juniper scale (*Carulaspis juniperi*)
This scale is found throughout the country on many types of junipers and also on cypress (*Cupressus* species only) and incense cedar. The female scales spend the winter on the plant. They lay their eggs in spring, and in midsummer (late spring in the South) the new generation, called *crawlers*, settles on the needles. These small (1/10 inch), soft-bodied young feed by sucking sap from the plant. The legs atrophy and a crusty shell develops over the body. The mature female scales lay their eggs underneath the shell. Juniper scales are unable to digest fully all the sugar in the plant sap and excrete the excess in a fluid called honeydew. A sooty mold fungus may develop on the honeydew. An uncontrolled infestation of scales may kill the plant in two or three seasons. For more information about scales, see page 876.

SOLUTION: Spray with ORTHO Isotox Insect Killer or ORTHO Liquid Sevin in midsummer (late spring in the South) when the young are active. The following early spring, before new growth begins, spray the trunk and branches with a *dormant oil spray* to control overwintering insects.

JUNIPERUS (JUNIPER)

Damaged plant. *Insert:* Juniper webworm (life size).

PROBLEM: The needles on a branch or throughout the entire plant turn brown. Branches with extensive browning are usually heavily and tightly webbed. Brownish striped caterpillars, up to ½ inch long, are feeding on needles inside the webbing.

ANALYSIS: Juniper webworm (*Dichomeris marginella*)
This webworm feeds only on junipers. The damage caused by the caterpillars often goes unnoticed until the plant is heavily infested. The young larvae usually inhabit the inner parts of the plant first, which, on the bushier junipers, are well concealed. The small brown and gray female moths lay their eggs in May or June in the crotches of the needles. When the eggs hatch, the larvae burrow into the needles. As the larvae grow, they feed on other foliage but use their initial hollowed-out needles as "retreat cells." In late summer, the caterpillars web the foliage together as they feed and then spend the winter inside it. As the weather warms in spring, the caterpillars become active again and continue to produce large amounts of webbing until they pupate and mature into moths.

SOLUTION: Spray with an insecticide containing *diazinon* or *carbaryl* (SEVIN®) when damage is first noticed to kill young larvae. If the foliage is heavily webbed, use high pressure spray equipment for penetration and thorough coverage. A fall or early spring spray is effective against inactive caterpillars.

Bagworm case (half life size).

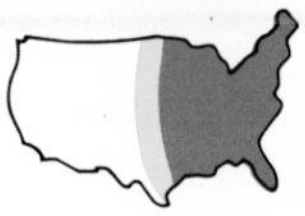

PROBLEM: The needles are chewed and individual branches or the entire tree or shrub may be defoliated. Carrot-shaped cases or "bags," from 1 to 3 inches long, hang from the branches. The bags are constructed from interwoven bits of dead foliage, twigs, and silk. When a bag is cut open, a tan or blackish caterpillar or a yellowish grublike insect may be found inside, or the bag may be empty. A heavy attack by this insect may retard or stunt tree growth.

ANALYSIS: Bagworm *(Thyridopteryx ephemeraeformis)*
The larval stage of the bagworm devours the foliage of junipers and many other tree species when populations of the insect are high. The larvae hatch in late May or early June and begin feeding on the juniper needles. The larva constructs a bag that covers its entire body. The worm partially emerges from its bag to feed. When the leaves are completely eaten off a branch, the bagworm moves to the next branch. By late August, the full-grown larva spins silken bands around a twig and attaches the bag permanently. In fall, the adult winged male emerges from his case, flies to a bag containing a female, mates, and dies. The black hairy male moths are sometimes seen at night around lights. The female lays 500 to 1000 eggs and dies.

SOLUTION: Spray with ORTHO Bagworm Killer, ORTHO Isotox Insect Killer, or ORTHO Orthene Systemic Insect Control between late May and mid-July. Older bagworms are more difficult to control. Spray again 10 days later if new leaf damage occurs. Handpicking and destroying bags between October and May will reduce the number of overwintering eggs.

Cedar-apple rust.

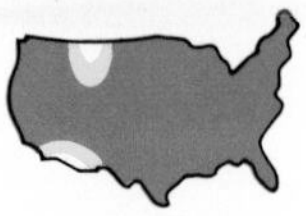

PROBLEM: In spring or early summer, brownish green swellings appear on the upper surface of the needles. The galls enlarge until, by fall, they range in size from 1 to 2 inches in diameter. The galls turn chocolate brown and are covered with small circular depressions. The following spring, during warm, rainy weather, the small depressions swell and produce orange, jellylike "horns" up to ¾ inch long. The galls eventually die, but remain attached to the tree for a year or more. Infected twigs usually die.

ANALYSIS: Cedar-apple rust
This disease is caused by a fungus (*Gymnosporangium juniperi-virginianae*) that infects both juniper and apple trees. It cannot spread from juniper to juniper or apple to apple, but alternates between the two. Wind-borne spores from apple leaves infect juniper needles in the summer. The fungus grows very little until the following spring, when the galls begin to form. The second spring spores from the orange "horns" are carried by the wind to infect apple trees. By midsummer, orange spots appear on the apples and upper surfaces of the leaves. (For more information about cedar-apple rust on apples, see page 609.) In August, spores are released and carried by the wind back to junipers. The entire cycle takes 18 to 20 months on juniper plus 4 to 6 months on apple. For a list of susceptible plants, see page 1015.

SOLUTION: Remove galls and destroy. When possible, do not plant junipers and apple trees within several hundred yards of one another. Spraying junipers with *ferbam* in August may help prevent new infections from apple trees.

KALMIA (MOUNTAIN LAUREL)

Fungal leaf spots.

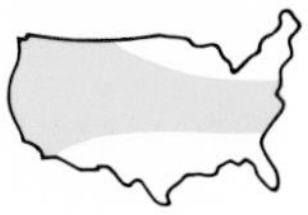

PROBLEM: Spots and blotches appear on the leaves. The spots may be yellow, red, tan, gray, or brown. They range in size from barely visible to ½ inch in diameter. Several spots may join to form blotches. Leaves may be yellow and dying. Some leaves may drop. Leaf spotting is most severe in moist, humid weather.

ANALYSIS: Fungal leaf spots
There are many different fungi that cause leaf spots on mountain laurel. These spots are unsightly but rarely harmful to the plant. Plants weakened by low temperatures and wind exposure may be more susceptible to invasion by leaf spot fungi. The fungi are spread by splashing water and wind. Spots develop where the fungi enter the tissue. If wet or humid weather persists, the fungi spread through the tissue and blotches form. They survive the winter on the leaves and twigs. Most leaf spot organisms do their greatest damage in mild weather (between 50° and 85°F).

SOLUTION: Where practical, remove infected leaves from the plant. Collect and destroy any fallen leaves. On valuable specimens, spray with fungicide containing *chlorothalonil* (DACONIL 2787®) when new growth begins in spring. Repeat two more times at intervals of 2 weeks for as long as the weather remains favorable for infection.

Kalmia cultural information
Light: Part shade
Water: When the soil is almost dry
Soil: Loose, rich, well drained, acid
Fertilizer: Medium

Iron deficiency.

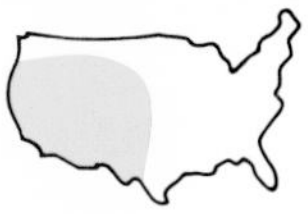

PROBLEM: Some of the leaves turn pale green to yellow. The newest leaves may be completely yellow with only the veins remaining green. On older leaves, only the leaf edges may be yellowing. The plant may be stunted.

ANALYSIS: Iron deficiency
This is a common problem with acid-loving plants like kalmia. The plant prefers soil with a pH between 5.5 and 6.5. (For more information on soil acidity, see page 908.) The yellowing is due to a deficiency of iron or other minor nutrients in the plant. The soil is seldom deficient in iron. However, iron is often found in an insoluble form that is not available to the plant, especially in soil with a pH of 7.0 or higher. A high soil pH can result from overliming, or from lime leached from cement or brick. Regions where soil is derived from limestone, and those with low rainfall, also have high-pH soils. Plants use iron in the formation of the green pigment in the leaves. When it is lacking, new leaves are yellow.

SOLUTION: Spray the foliage with ORTHO Greenol Liquid Iron, and apply it to the soil around the plants to correct the iron deficiency. Correct the pH of the soil by treating it with *ferrous sulfate* or ORTHO Aluminum Sulfate and watering it in well. Maintain an acid pH by fertilizing with ORTHO Azalea, Camellia & Rhododendron Food. When planting mountain laurel, add at least 50 percent peat moss to the soil. This is especially important if you live in an area where the soil is alkaline or has poor drainage. Never lime the soil around mountain laurel.

LABURNUM (GOLDENCHAIN TREE)

Aphids (half life size).

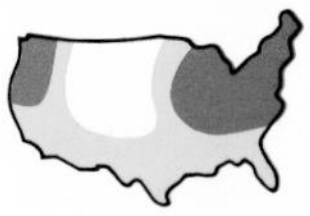

PROBLEM: The leaves may turn pale green or yellow. Sometimes they wilt and have a scorched appearance. A shiny, sticky substance coats the leaves. A black sooty mold may grow on this sticky substance. Tiny (⅛ inch) black or dark green soft-bodied insects cluster on the branch tips and leaf stalks. Ants may be present.

ANALYSIS: Cowpea aphid and bean aphid (*Aphis craccivora* and *A. fabae*)
Both of these aphids feed on many ornamental garden plants. They do little damage in small numbers. However, they are extremely prolific and populations can rapidly build up to damaging numbers during the growing season. The leaves often scorch and wilt because the aphids extract so much plant sap. The aphids are unable to digest fully all the sugar in the sap and excretes the excess in a fluid called honeydew. The honeydew often drops onto leaves below. Plants or objects beneath the tree may also be coated with honeydew. A black sooty mold fungus may develop on the honeydew, or rain may wash it off before the fungus has a chance to grow. Ants feed on this sticky substance, and are often present where there is an aphid infestation.

SOLUTION: Spray with an insecticide containing *carbaryl* (SEVIN®) or *malathion* when aphids are first noticed. Repeat the spray if the plant becomes reinfested.

Laburnum cultural information
Light: Full sun to part shade
Water: Grows best in moist soil
Soil: Well drained, nonalkaline
Fertilizer: Light

LAGERSTROEMIA (CRAPEMYRTLE)

Crapemyrtle aphids (life size).

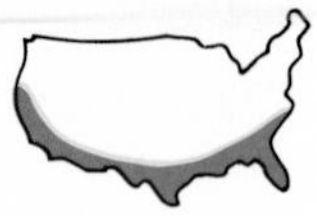

PROBLEM: Irregular yellow blotches appear on the leaves. Eventually the yellow areas turn brown. The leaves may drop prematurely. A shiny, sticky substance often coats the leaves. A black sooty mold may be growing on the sticky substance. Tiny (1/8 inch) soft-bodied insects are clustered on twigs and the upper and lower surfaces of the leaves.

ANALYSIS: Crapemyrtle aphid
(*Tinocallis kahawaluokalani*)
This aphid species attacks only crapemyrtle. It is usually abundant wherever the tree is grown. The aphids do little damage in small numbers. However, they are extremely prolific and populations can rapidly build up to damaging numbers during the growing season. Damage occurs when the aphid sucks the juices from the crapemyrtle leaves. The aphid is unable to digest fully all the sugar in the plant sap and excretes the excess in a fluid called honeydew. Plants or objects beneath the tree may also be coated with honeydew. A black sooty mold fungus may develop on this sticky substance. Ants feed on honeydew, and are often present where there is an aphid infestation.

SOLUTION: Control with ORTHO Isotox Insect Killer when aphids first appear. Spray the foliage thoroughly, being sure to cover the twigs and both the upper and lower surfaces of the leaves.

Lagerstroemia cultural information
Light: Full sun
Water: Infrequent, deep watering
Soil: Well drained, nonalkaline
Fertilizer: Light

Powdery mildew.

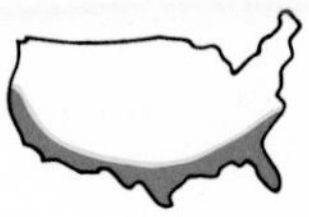

PROBLEM: Leaves, shoots, and flower buds are covered with a thin layer or irregular patches of a grayish white powdery material. The leaves and shoots are distorted and stunted, and the flower buds usually fail to open. Infected leaves may look reddish beneath the mildew; the leaves often drop prematurely.

ANALYSIS: Powdery mildew
This common plant disease is usually caused by a fungus (*Erysiphe lagerstroemiae*) that thrives in both humid and dry weather. The powdery patches consist of fungal strands and spores. The spores are spread by the wind to healthy plants. The fungus saps the plant nutrients, causing leaf and shoot distortion and bud failure. This particular powdery mildew infects only crapemyrtle. Several other species of powdery mildew that commonly infect other trees and shrubs occasionally infect this plant.

SOLUTION: Spray the upper and lower surfaces of the leaves with ORTHO Funginex Rose Disease Control or ORTHO Orthenex Insect & Disease Control when the plant shows the first signs of mildew. In the spring, before buds open, spray with a dormant *lime sulfur* spray.

LARIX (LARCH)

Woolly larch aphids (1/4 life size).

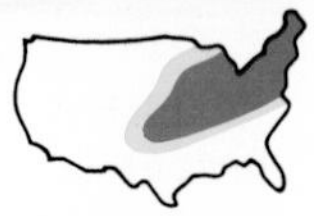

PROBLEM: Needles are covered with white, woolly masses. If the infestation is heavy, the tree appears to be covered with snow in midsummer. The needles may turn yellow, and the tree may be stunted.

ANALYSIS: Woolly larch aphids
(*Adelges laricis* and *A. lariciatus*)
Woolly larch aphids are small, soft-bodied insects. The adults infesting larch are always covered by a dense, white, woolly material. The larch aphids spend the winter on spruce trees. The females lay their eggs in the spring, and the newly hatched young feed at the base of the spruce buds, causing small pineapple-shaped galls to form. Within the galls are chambers, each containing several young larch aphids. The galls crack open in late spring, and the winged adults fly to larch trees, where the females lay their eggs. The next generation of aphids secretes white filaments of wax that eventually cover their bodies. The woolly material may completely cover the needles by midsummer. Generally, the tree is not injured unless it is infested for several consecutive seasons. In late summer, another generation of larch aphids with wings is produced that flies back to spruce to spend the winter.

SOLUTION: Next May when the aphids first appear, spray with an insecticide containing *malathion.*

Larix cultural information
Light: Full sun
Water: Moist or dry conditions
Soil: Tolerates many types
Fertilizer: Light

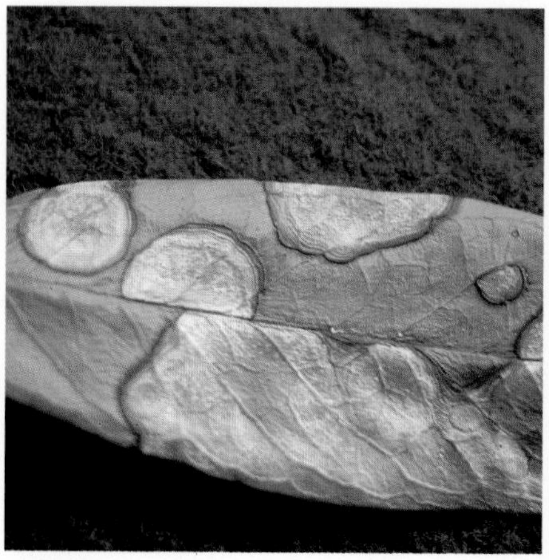

Leaf spots.

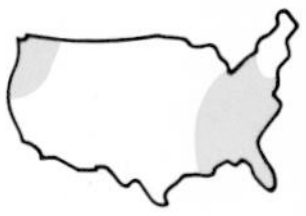

PROBLEM: Spots and blotches appear on the leaves. The spots may be yellow, red, tan, gray, or brown. They range in size from barely visible to ½ inch in diameter. Several spots may join together to form blotches. Leaves may turn yellow and die. Some leaves may drop. Leaf spotting is most severe in warm, humid weather.

ANALYSIS: Leaf spots
There are many different fungi that cause leaf spots. These spots are unsightly but rarely harmful to the plant. Plants weakened by low temperatures and wind exposure are more susceptible to invasion by leaf spot fungi. The fungi are spread by splashing water and wind. Spots develop where the fungi enter the tissue. If wet or humid weather persists, the fungi spread through the tissue and blotches form. They survive the winter on the leaves and twigs. Most leaf spot organisms do their greatest damage in mild weather (between 50° and 85°F).

SOLUTION: Once leaves become infected they will remain so. Where practical, remove infected leaves from the plant. In areas where spotting is severe every year, spray with a fungicide containing *ferbam* when the leaves appear in early spring. Repeat three more times at intervals of 2 weeks.

Leucothoe cultural information
Light: Part shade to shade
Water: Keep the soil moist
Soil: Loose, rich, well drained, acid
Fertilizer: Medium

LIGUSTRUM (PRIVET)

ADAPTATION: Throughout the United States.

FLOWERING TIME: Late spring to early summer.

LIGHT: Full sun to part shade.

SOIL: Must be well drained.

FERTILIZER: Fertilize with ORTHO Evergreen, Tree & Shrub Food or ORTHO General Purpose Plant Food according to label directions.

WATER:
How much: Apply enough water to wet the soil 2 to 3 feet deep. To determine the proper amount of water for your soil type, see page 912.
How often: Privets grow best when well watered, but they will tolerate drought. Water when the soil is barely moist 4 inches below the surface.

PRUNING: Prune to maintain shape or to hedge. If flowers are desired, prune after blooming. Otherwise, prune any time.

Privet rust mite damage.

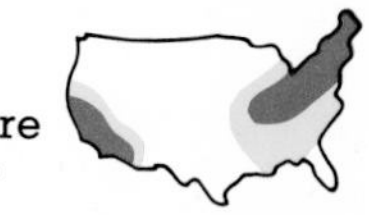

PROBLEM: The leaves are dull green and severely cupped. They may turn bronze, brown, or yellow and drop; or they may drop off the plant while still green. The plant is weak and often stunted.

ANALYSIS: Privet rust mite and privet mite (*Aculus ligustri* and *Brevipalpus obovatus*)
Both of these mites are extremely small, and generally cannot be seen without magnification. They cause damage by sucking sap from the leaf tissue. As a result of feeding, the leaf cups or curls under, and often drops from the plant. The privet rust mite may feed only on the cells in the surface of the leaf, causing a bronze russeting or browning. The green leaf pigment is unaffected. Or it may feed deeper in the tissue, resulting in leaf yellowing caused by the disappearance of the green pigment. Some types of privet drop their leaves before discoloration develops. The rust mite is most prolific during cool weather. It feeds and reproduces primarily during spring and fall. The privet mite is usually active throughout the growing season. By midsummer it may build up to tremendous numbers.

SOLUTION: Spray with a pesticide containing *dicofol* (KELTHANE®) or *diazinon* when damage is first noticed. Spray the foliage thoroughly, being sure to cover both the upper and lower surfaces of the leaves. Repeat the application three more times at intervals of 7 days.

LIGUSTRUM (PRIVET)

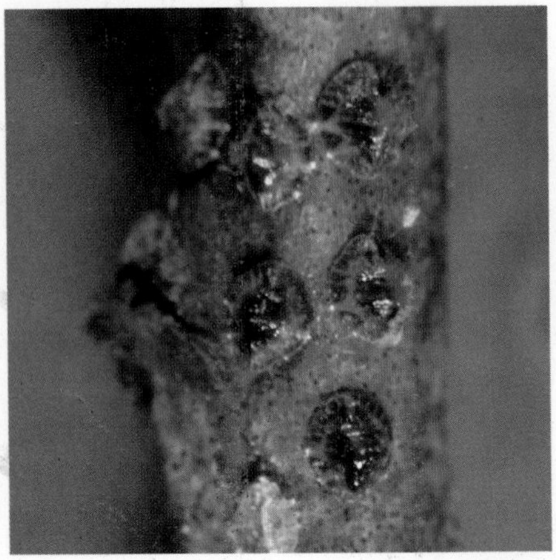

Scales (life size).

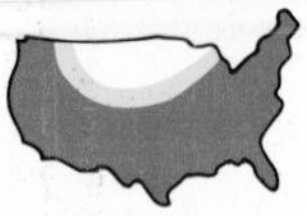

PROBLEM: The undersides of the leaves, trunk, or the branches are covered with brownish crusty bumps, or clusters of somewhat flattened yellowish, brown, reddish, gray, or white scaly bumps. The bumps can be scraped or picked off. Leaves turn yellow and may drop, and twigs or branches may die back. A shiny, sticky substance often coats the leaves. A black sooty mold may grow on the sticky substance.

ANALYSIS: Scales

Many different types of scales infest privet. They lay their eggs on the leaves or bark, and in spring to midsummer the young scales, called *crawlers*, settle on leaves, twigs, or the trunk. These small (1/10 inch), soft-bodied young feed by sucking sap from the plant. The legs usually atrophy and a hard crusty shell develops over the body. The mature female scales lay their eggs underneath the shell. Some species of scales that infest privet are unable to digest fully all the sugar in the plant sap, and excrete the excess in a fluid called honeydew. A sooty mold fungus may develop on the honeydew, causing the privet leaves to appear black and dirty. An uncontrolled infestation of scales may kill twigs or branches after two or three seasons. For more information about scales, see page 876.

SOLUTION: Spray with ORTHO Isotox Insect Killer or with ORTHO Liquid Sevin when the young are active. Contact your local Cooperative Extension Office (see page 1029) to determine the best time to spray for scales in your area. The following early spring, before new growth begins, spray the trunk and branches with ORTHO Volck Oil Spray to control overwintering insects.

Anthracnose.

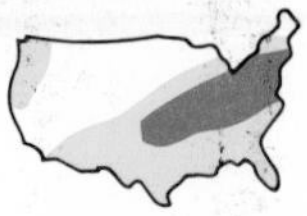

PROBLEM: Following warm, humid weather, leaves turn brown and dry and cling to the stem. Sunken oval areas, spotted with pink pustules, develop at the base of twigs and branches. The bark over the sunken areas turns brown and splits open. Twigs and branches may die back.

ANALYSIS: Anthracnose and twig blight

This plant disease is caused by a fungus (*Glomerella cingulata*) that infects many ornamentals and fruit trees in the garden. It is most severe in plants weakened by such factors as drought, nutrient deficiency, and low temperatures. The fungus spends the winter on infected twigs and stems on the plant. During warm, humid weather, spores are blown and splashed onto healthy stems. The spores enter the tissue, and the fungus grows through the wood in all directions. The cells collapse and a sunken area (canker) develops. The canker cuts off the flow of water and nutrients to the branch, causing the leaves to turn brown and dry. If the canker encircles the wood completely, the stem above it dies.

SOLUTION: Prune twigs and stems well below the infected area. Spray with a fungicide containing *zineb*, *ferbam*, or *chlorothalonil* (DACONIL 2787®) at weekly intervals as long as the weather remains favorable for infection.

Privets resistant to anthracnose and twig blight: Amur privet (*Ligustrum amurense*); California privet (*L. ovalifolium*); Ibota privet (*L. ibota*); and Regal privet (*L. obtusifolium* var. *regelianum*).

LIRIODENDRON (TULIPTREE)

Summer leaf yellowing.

PROBLEM: Starting in mid to late summer, the older leaves turn yellow and drop prematurely. Small brownish specks may appear between the veins before the leaves drop. Leaf drop develops during or just following hot, dry periods. It is most common in young or recently transplanted trees.

ANALYSIS: Summer leaf yellowing

Tuliptrees are sensitive to hot, dry summer weather, especially when the soil around the roots is allowed to dry out. The older leaves turn yellow and drop before the normal period of leaf drop in fall. Young or newly transplanted trees with limited root systems are particularly susceptible. Root injuries, soil level changes, and insects may also cause premature yellowing and leaf drop.

SOLUTION: Supply water during hot, dry periods. Newly transplanted trees require more water than established trees. Water when the top 2 inches of soil in the rootball are dry. (For more information about watering, see page 912.) Fertilize plants regularly to keep them vigorous and inspect them periodically for insects.

Sooty mold.

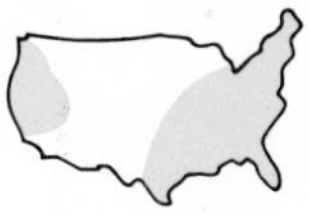

PROBLEM: A black sooty mold is growing on the leaves and twigs. It can be completely wiped off the surfaces. Cool, moist weather hastens the growth of this substance.

ANALYSIS: Sooty mold

This common black mold is found on a wide variety of plants in the garden. It is caused by any of several species of fungi that grow on the sugary material left on plants by aphids, scales, mealybugs, whiteflies, and other insects that suck sap from the plant. The insects are unable to digest all the sugar in the sap and excrete the excess in a fluid called honeydew, which drops onto the leaves below. The sooty mold fungus develops on the honeydew. Sooty mold is unsightly, but it is fairly harmless because it does not attack the leaf directly. The presence of sooty mold indicates that the plant or another plant near it is infested with insects.

SOLUTION: Sooty mold will eventually be washed off by rain. Prevent more sooty mold by controlling the insect that is producing the honeydew. Inspect the leaves and twigs above the sooty mold to find what type of insect is present. See the following pages for control instructions: for aphids, page 875; for scales, page 876; for whiteflies, page 877; for mealybugs, page 876.

Liriodendron cultural information

Light: Full sun
Water: Grows best in moist soil
Soil: Loose, rich, well drained, nonalkaline
Fertilizer: Light

Aphids (half life size).

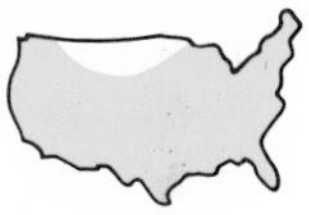

PROBLEM: The newest leaves turn yellow and may be small and distorted. A shiny, sticky substance coats the leaves and drips onto plants or objects below. A black sooty mold often grows on the sticky substance. Tiny ($\frac{1}{8}$ inch) greenish yellow soft-bodied insects cluster on the undersides of leaves. Ants may be present.

ANALYSIS: Tuliptree aphid
(*Macrosiphum liriodendri*)

This aphid infests the tuliptree wherever it is grown, and may be present from spring through fall. The aphids do not seriously harm the tree. However, they are extremely prolific and the population can rapidly build up and produce much unsightly damage. Damage occurs when the aphid sucks the juices from the tuliptree leaves. The aphid is unable to digest fully all the sugar in the plant sap and excretes copious quantities of the sugary material in a fluid called honeydew. The honeydew drops onto the leaves below. Plants or objects beneath the tree are also coated with it. A sooty mold fungus may develop on the honeydew, causing the tuliptree leaves and other coated plants to appear black and dirty. Ants feed on this sticky substance, and are often present where there is an aphid infestation.

SOLUTION: Spray with an insecticide containing *malathion* when aphids are first noticed. Direct the spray to the undersides of the leaves. Repeat the spray if the tree becomes reinfested.

Tuliptree scale ($\frac{3}{4}$ life size).

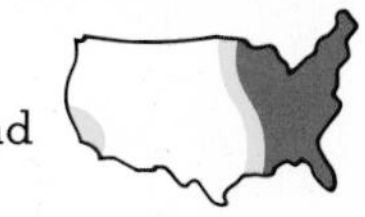

PROBLEM: The twigs and branches are covered with brown, turtle-shaped, crusty bumps, $\frac{1}{3}$ inch in diameter. Leaves turn yellow and may drop. A shiny, sticky substance coats the leaves. A black sooty mold often grows on the sticky substance. If the infestation is heavy, branches die back, starting at the bottom of the tree. The tree may be killed by severe infestations.

ANALYSIS: Tuliptree scale
(*Toumeyella liriodendri*)

The tuliptree scale is a serious pest of tuliptrees, magnolias, and lindens. The immature insect spends the winter on the twigs and branches of the tree. Starting in spring, it feeds by inserting its mouthparts and sucking the sap and nutrients from the bark tissue. The scale is unable to digest fully all the sugar in the plant sap, and excretes the excess in a fluid called honeydew, which drops onto leaves or other plants below. A sooty mold fungus may develop on the honeydew, causing the tuliptree leaves and other coated plants to appear black and dirty. The scale matures in August, and the female lays eggs underneath its brown shell. A single female lays up to 3000 eggs. In the fall the young scales, called *crawlers*, settle on the twigs to spend the winter. Repeated heavy infestations kill branches and possibly the whole tree. Several other types of scales also infest tuliptree. For more information about scales, see page 876.

SOLUTION: Spray with ORTHO Liquid Sevin or an insecticide containing *malathion* in mid-August when the young are active. The following early spring, before new growth begins, spray the trunk and branches with a *dormant oil spray* to control overwintering insects.

Witch's broom. *Insert:* Infested shoot.

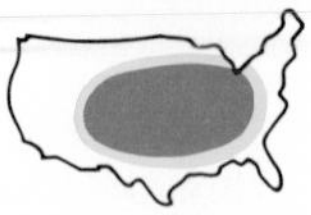

PROBLEM: Young leaves are curled and distorted, and growth is stunted. Affected leaves are curled upward. When these cupped leaves are peeled open, clusters of tiny, green-brown, soft-bodied insects may be found inside. As the growing season progresses the affected stems die, resulting in a tuft of dead twiggy branches (witch's broom). Witch's brooms are noticeable throughout the growing season, and are especially evident in early spring.

ANALYSIS: Honeysuckle aphid
(Hyadaphis tataricae)
These insects, also known as *Russian aphids,* commonly infest honeysuckle. Damage occurs on new growth when the aphid sucks the juice from the leaves. It is not known whether the characteristic witch's brooms are caused by the aphids' feeding or whether the aphids transmit a disease organism to the plant that causes the witch's brooms to develop. The adult aphids are present throughout the growing season. In the fall they lay eggs in the witch's brooms and around the base of the plant. These eggs hatch in the spring when the new leaves emerge.

SOLUTION: In winter, remove and destroy witch's brooms and other infested plant parts. In mid to late May, or whenever new infestations are noticed, spray with ORTHO Isotox Insect Killer or ORTHO Orthene Systemic Insect Control.

Powdery mildew.

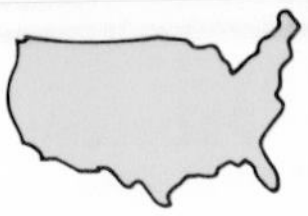

PROBLEM: The leaves, branch tips, and buds are covered with a thin layer or irregular patches of grayish white powdery material. Infected leaves may turn yellow and drop. The buds may be deformed or die. In fall, black dots (spore-producing bodies) are scattered over the powdery material like ground pepper.

ANALYSIS: Powdery mildew
This common plant disease is caused by two fungi (*Microsphaera alni* and *Erysiphe polygoni*) that thrive in both humid and dry weather. The powdery patches consist of fungal strands and spores. The spores are spread by the wind to healthy plants. The fungus saps the plant nutrients, causing leaf yellowing and bud deformation, and sometimes the death of the leaf and bud. Since these mildews attack many different kinds of plants, the fungus from a diseased plant may infect other types of plants in the garden. For a list of susceptible plants, see page 1006.

SOLUTION: Spray both the upper and lower surfaces of the leaves with a fungicide containing *benomyl, dinocap,* or *cycyloheximide* when the plants show the first sign of mildew. Repeat every 2 weeks as long as new mildew appears.

Lonicera cultural information
Light: Full sun to part shade
Water: When the soil is almost dry (some are drought tolerant)
Soil: Loose, well drained (some tolerate poor drainage)
Fertilizer: Medium

MAGNOLIA

ADAPTATION: Zones 5 through 9. To determine your zone, see the map on page 1020.

FLOWERING TIME: Late winter to fall, depending on the species.

LIGHT: Full sun (partial shade in desert areas).

SOIL: Well drained, rich in organic matter, neutral or slightly acid (pH 6.5 to 7.0). Magnolias will not tolerate salts in the soil or compacted soil. Avoid digging around their roots.

FERTILIZER: Fertilize with ORTHO Azalea, Camellia & Rhododendron Food according to label directions.

WATER:
How much: Apply enough water to wet the soil 3 to 4 feet deep. To determine the proper amount of water for your soil type, see page 912.
How often: Magnolias prefer moist growing conditions. Water when the soil is moist but not wet 4 inches below the surface. For more information about watering, see page 912.

PRUNING: Magnolias do not require pruning, except to remove dead wood. When planting, allow enough room for growth.

Leaf scorch.

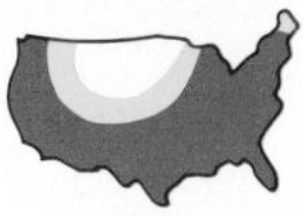

PROBLEM: During hot weather, usually in July or August, leaves turn brown around the edges and between the veins. Sometimes the whole leaf dies. Many leaves may drop during late summer. This problem is most severe on the youngest branches. Trees do not generally die.

ANALYSIS: Summer leaf scorch
Leaf scorch is caused by excessive evaporation from the leaves. In hot weather, water evaporates rapidly from the leaves. If the roots can't absorb and convey water fast enough to replenish this loss, the leaves turn brown and wither. For optimum growth, magnolias require moist soil. Leaf scorch is most severe when water is unavailable because the soil is dry. However, if the weather is extremely hot, scorch may also develop when the soil is moist. Drying winds, severed roots, limited soil area, or low temperatures can also cause scorch. For more information about scorch, see page 857.

SOLUTION: To prevent further scorch, deep-water trees during periods of hot weather to wet down the entire root space. (For more information about watering trees, see page 912.) Newly transplanted trees should be watered whenever the rootball is dry 2 inches below the surface. If possible, shade trees during very hot weather. Plant trees adapted to your climate.

Algal spot.

PROBLEM: Leaves and twigs are covered with reddish brown velvety patches or greenish brown spots. Twigs may be stunted or die back.

ANALYSIS: Algal spot
Algal spot, also called *green scurf*, is caused by algae (*Cephaleuros virescens*) that are common on magnolias and other ornamentals in the southern parts of the country. During moist weather, cells of the algae enter the leaves or the other tissue of twigs and spread rapidly. The invaded twig tissue may swell and crack. If the crack encircles the twig, the twig dies. The infected magnolia leaves turn greenish brown at first. If the algae develop spore-producing bodies (tiny round heads on fine, dense reddish hairs) the patches appear reddish brown and velvety or cushiony. The algae spread rapidly when rains are frequent and heavy. Trees weakened by drought or poor growing conditions are most susceptible to algal spot.

SOLUTION: Control measures are not usually necessary. If trees are weak, improve growing conditions by watering and fertilizing regularly. Prune dead twigs. If algal spot is severe, spray with a fungicide containing *basic copper sulfate*, plus an oil or a spreader-sticker, in December and January and at the start of the rainy season. Repeat 1 month later. For more information about spreader-stickers, see page 922.

Iron deficiency.

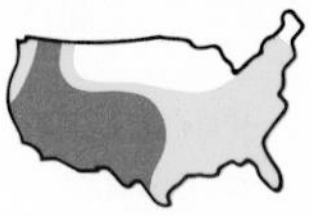

PROBLEM: Some of the leaves turn pale green to yellow. The newest leaves may be completely yellow with only the veins remaining green. On older leaves, only the leaf edges may be yellowing. The plant may be stunted.

ANALYSIS: Iron deficiency
This is a common problem with acid-loving plants like magnolia, which grow best in soil with a pH between 5.5 and 6.5. (For more information on soil acidity, see page 908.) The yellowing is due to a deficiency of iron and other minor nutrients in the plant. The soil is seldom deficient in iron. However, iron is often found in an insoluable form that is not available to the plant, especially in soil with a pH of 7.0 or higher. A high soil pH can result from overliming, or from lime leached from cement or brick. Regions where soil is derived from limestone, and those with low rainfall, also have high-pH soils. Plants use iron in the formation of the green pigment in the leaves. When it is lacking, new leaves are yellow.

SOLUTION: Spray the foliage with ORTHO Greenol Liquid Iron, and apply it to the soil around the plants to correct the iron deficiency. Correct the pH of the soil by treating it with *ferrous sulfate* and watering it in well. Maintain an acid pH by fertilizing with ORTHO Azalea, Camellia & Rhododendron.

MAGNOLIA

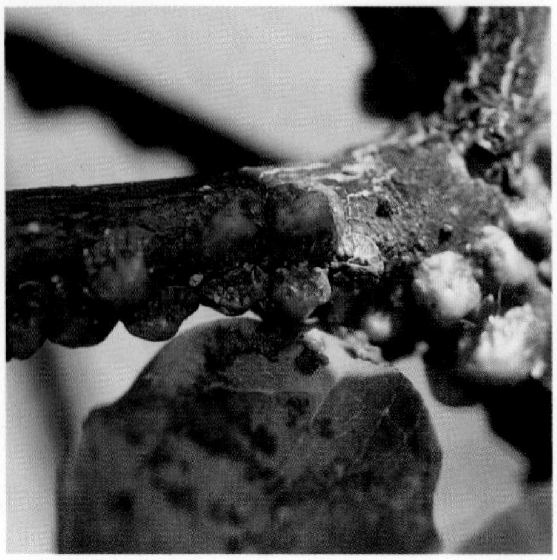

Magnolia scale (life size).

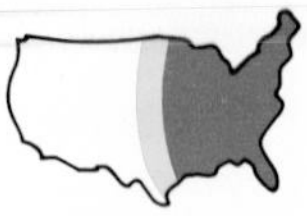

PROBLEM: Twigs and stems are covered with powdery white or shiny brown crusty bumps, ½ inch in diameter, or soft masses of purple insects. Stems that are normally light green may appear enlarged and purple or whitish. The crusty bumps can be scraped or picked off; the undersides are soft. Leaves may be yellowing and smaller than normal; trees may be weakened or killed. A shiny, sticky substance usually coats the leaves. A black sooty mold often grows on the sticky substance.

ANALYSIS: Magnolia scale
(*Neolecanium cornuparvum*)
This is the largest scale insect found in the United States. The immature purple insect spends the winter on the twigs and branches of the tree. Starting in spring, it feeds by inserting its mouthparts and sucking the sap and nutrients from the bark tissue. The scale is unable to digest fully all the sugar in the plant sap, and excretes the excess in a fluid called honeydew. A sooty mold fungus may develop on the honeydew. The scales mature in August and the female lays her eggs beneath her powdery white or shiny brown shell. In the fall the young scales, called *crawlers*, settle on the twigs to spend the winter. Repeated heavy infestations kill branches and possibly the whole tree. Several other types of scales also infest magnolia. For more information about scales, see page 876.

SOLUTION: Spray with ORTHO Orthene Systemic Insect Control or ORTHO Liquid Sevin in September when the young are active. The following early spring, before new growth begins, spray with a *dormant oil spray* to control overwintering insects.

MAHONIA (OREGON GRAPE)

Winter injury to Oregon grape.

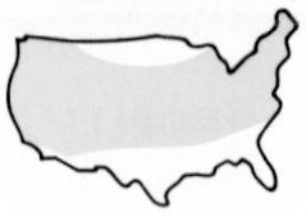

PROBLEM: The leaves are rusty brown to red, and dry. Twigs may die. The shrub is growing in a climate where cold, dry, windy days are common in winter or where plants may be exposed to late fall or early spring freezes. The soil may be frozen.

ANALYSIS: Winter injury
Oregon grape is damaged by cold, drying winter wind, especially if temperatures are below freezing and the weather is clear and sunny. The leaves lose their moisture more rapidly than it can be replaced by the root system. Cells in the leaves dry out and die. This condition is most pronounced when water is unavailable because the soil is frozen. Leaves and twigs may also die during early fall or late spring freezes when the plant is growing. Young, succulent growth cannot withstand the cold temperatures.

SOLUTION: No cure is available once plants have been injured. Where practical, pick off damaged leaves and prune out dead twigs. Provide shelter and windbreaks for plants growing in cold regions. Covering Oregon grape with burlap bags in winter helps prevent leaf drying. To avoid succulent growth in the fall, do not fertilize or prune late in the season. Water in late fall or winter, if necessary, to insure adequate soil moisture. Mulch plants after they are dormant to reduce the depth of frost penetration into the soil.

Rust.

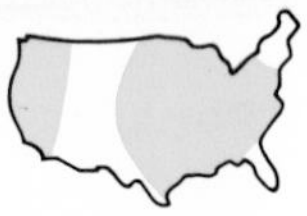

PROBLEM: Yellow spots appear on the upper surfaces of the leaves during the growing season. Corresponding to these spots, on the undersides of the leaves, are spots or pustules containing a powdery yellowish material. The powdery material can be rubbed or scraped off easily. Heavily infested plants usually lack vigor.

ANALYSIS: Rust
Rust on Oregon grape is caused by any of several different fungi. Some of these rust fungi spend their entire life on Oregon grape. Others must spend part of their life on another plant (weeds or wheat) before they can reinfect Oregon grape. The wind spreads spores to the leaves. With moisture (rain, dew, or fog) and moderate temperatures (55° to 75°F), the spores enter the tissue on the undersides of the leaves. Spots usually develop directly above on the upper surface of the leaf as the fungus saps the plant nutrients.

SOLUTION: Prune off and destroy heavily infested stems. In the early spring, just as new growth begins, spray with a fungicide containing *chlorothalonil* (DACONIL 2787®).

Mahonia cultural information
Light: Full sun to shade
Water: Keep the soil moist
Soil: Loose, rich, nonalkaline
Fertilizer: Medium

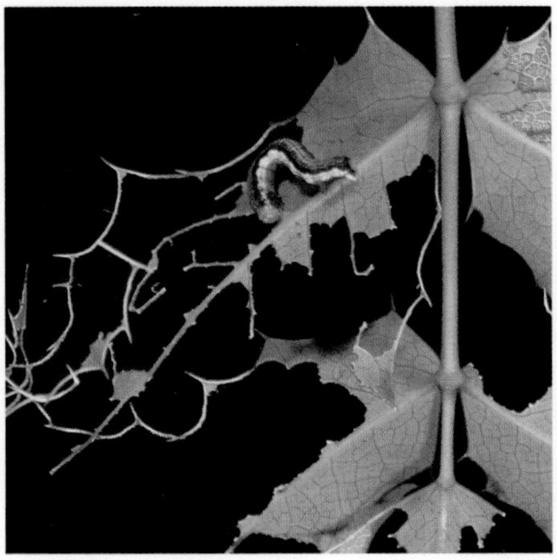

Barberry looper (half life size).

PROBLEM: Patches of tissue are eaten from one surface of the leaf; the corresponding upper or lower surface turns brown and appears lacy. Later, the entire leaf surface is eaten. By midsummer, the plant may be defoliated. Large (up to 1-inch long), brownish caterpillars with light and dark stripes may be found on the undersides of the leaves. The caterpillars crawl in a looping motion.

ANALYSIS: Barberry looper
(*Coryphista meadii*)
Barberry loopers, also called *mahonia loopers*, are the larvae of brownish gray moths with black bands across their wings. In the spring, the females lay their eggs on Oregon grape leaves. The emerging larvae feed as skeletonizers first, eating only one surface of the leaf. As the loopers mature, they feed on the entire leaf. When fully grown, the caterpillars drop to the ground and pupate in the soil. There may be as many as three generations of loopers during a growing season.

SOLUTION: Spray with an insecticide containing *carbaryl* (SEVIN®) or *acephate* (ORTHENE®) when insects are first noticed in the spring. Make sure your plant is listed on the product label. Repeat the spray if the plant becomes reinfested.

MALUS (CRABAPPLE)

ADAPTATION: Zones 2 to 10 (to determine your zone, see the map on page 1020). Most are not adapted to mild winter or desert areas.

FLOWERING TIME: Spring.

LIGHT: Full sun.

SOIL: Adapted to a wide variety of soils, but grows best in rich, well-drained garden soil.

FERTILIZER: Fertilize with ORTHO Evergreen, Tree & Shrub Food according to label directions.

WATER:
How much: Apply enough water to wet the soil 3 to 4 feet deep. To determine the proper amount of water for your soil type, see page 912.
How often: Water when the soil is barely moist 4 inches below the surface. For more information about watering, see page 912.

INSECTS AND DISEASES: Problems of crabapple are very similar to those of apple. For more information about plant problems on crabapple, see insects and diseases of apples in the section starting on page 605.

Fireblight.

PROBLEM: The blossoms and leaves of infected twigs suddenly wilt and turn black as if scorched by fire. The leaves curl and hang downward. The bark at the base of the blighted twig becomes water-soaked, then dark, sunken, and dry; cracks may develop at the edge of the sunken area. In warm, moist spring weather, drops of brown ooze appear on the sunken bark. Young trees may die.

ANALYSIS: Fireblight
This disease is caused by a bacterium (*Erwinia amylovora*) that is very destructive to many trees and shrubs. (For a list of susceptible plants, see page 1016.) The bacteria spend the winter in the sunken areas (cankers) on the branches. In the spring, the bacteria ooze out of the cankers. Insects that are attracted to this ooze become smeared with it, and when the insects visit a flower for nectar, they infect it with the bacteria. The bacteria spread rapidly through the plant tissue in warm (65°F or higher), humid weather. Insects visiting these infected blossoms later carry bacteria-laden nectar to healthy blossoms. Rain, wind, and tools may also spread the bacteria. Tender or damaged leaves may be infected in midsummer.

SOLUTION: Prune out infected branches 12 to 15 inches beyond any visible discoloration and destroy them. Sterilize pruning shears with rubbing alcohol after each cut. A protective spray of a pesticide containing *fixed copper* or *streptomycin*, applied before bud break in spring, will help prevent infection. Repeat at intervals of 5 to 7 days until the end of bloom. For a list of crabapples resistant to fireblight, see page 1017.

MALUS (CRABAPPLE)

Scab.

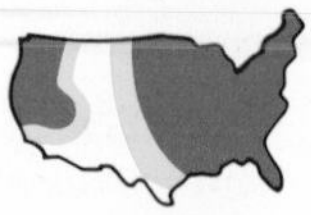

PROBLEM: Olive-colored, velvety spots, ¼ inch or more in diameter, appear on the leaves. The tissue around the spots may be puckered. The leaves often turn yellow and drop. In a wet year, the tree may lose all of its leaves by midsummer. The fruit and twigs develop circular, rough-surfaced, olive-green spots, which eventually turn corky and black. The fruit is usually deformed.

ANALYSIS: Apple scab
This plant disease is caused by a fungus (*Venturia inaequalis*). It is a serious problem on crabapples and apples in areas where spring weather is humid and mild (60° to 70°F). The fungus spends the winter in infected fallen leaves. In the spring, spore-producing structures in the dead leaves continuously discharge spores into the air. The spores are blown by the wind to new leaves and fruit buds. If there is water on the tissue surfaces, the fungus infects them and a spot develops. More spores are produced from these spots, and from twig infections from the previous year. The spores are splashed by the rain to infect new leaf and fruit surfaces. As temperatures increase during the summer, the fungus becomes less active.

SOLUTION: To obtain adequate control of scab, protective sprays must be applied starting as soon as bud growth begins in spring. Spray with a fungicide containing *chlorothalonil* (DACONIL 2787®). Repeat 5 to 8 times at intervals of 7 to 10 days. Rake up and destroy infected leaves and fruit in the fall. When planting new trees, use resistant varieties. For a list of crabapples resistant to scab, see page 1017.

Cedar-apple rust.

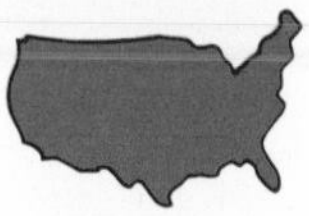

PROBLEM: Pale yellow spots appear on the leaves and fruit in mid to late spring. These spots gradually enlarge, turn orange, and develop minute black dots. Small (1/16 inch) cups with fringed edges form on the lower surfaces of the leaves. Infected leaves and fruit may drop prematurely; the fruit are often deformed.

ANALYSIS: Cedar-apple rust
This plant disease is caused by a fungus (*Gymnosporangium juniperi-virginianae*) that affects both crabapples and certain species of juniper and red cedar. This disease cannot spread from crabapple to crabapple, or from juniper to juniper, but must alternate between the two. In the spring, spores from brown and orange galls on juniper or cedar are blown up to 3 miles to crabapple trees. During mild, wet weather, the spores germinate and infect the leaves and fruit, causing spotting and premature leaf and fruit drop. During the summer, spores are produced in small cups on the undersides of the leaves. These spores are blown back to junipers and cedars, causing new infections. For more information about cedar-apple rust on junipers, see page 508.

SOLUTION: Cedar-apple rust cannot be controlled on this season's foliage and fruit. Next spring, spray trees with a fungicide containing *ferbam*, *maneb*, or *chlorothalonil* (DACONIL 2787®) when the flower buds turn pink, again when 75 percent of the petals have fallen from the blossoms, and once more 10 days later. If possible, do not plant crabapples within several hundred yards of junipers or red cedar.

Aphids (life size).

PROBLEM: The newest leaves are curled and discolored and twigs are often twisted. Leaves may drop off. A shiny or sticky substance may coat the leaves. A black sooty mold often is growing on the sticky substance. Tiny (1/8 inch), green, brown, or purplish soft-bodied insects cluster on the leaves and stems. Ants may be present.

ANALYSIS: Aphids
Several species of aphids infest crab-apple. The aphids do little damage in small numbers. However, they are extremely prolific and populations can rapidly build up to damaging numbers during the growing season. Damage occurs when the aphid sucks the juices from the crabapple leaves. The aphid is unable to fully digest all the sugar in the sap and excretes the sugary material in a fluid called honeydew. The honeydew often drops onto the leaves below. Plants or objects beneath the tree may also be coated with honeydew. A sooty mold fungus may develop on the honeydew, causing the leaves and other coated plants to appear black and dirty. Ants feed on the sticky substance and are often present where there is an aphid infestation.

SOLUTION: Spray with ORTHO Liquid Sevin or with an insecticide containing *malathion* when aphids first appear. Thoroughly cover the leaves and branch tips. Repeat the spray if the tree is reinfested.

Oystershell scale (twice life size).

PROBLEM: Stems or leaves are covered with brownish crusty bumps or thick, white, waxy bumps, or clusters of somewhat flattened yellowish scaly bumps. The bumps can be scraped or picked off; the undersides are usually soft. Leaves turn yellow and may drop. In some cases, a shiny or sticky substance coats the leaves. A black sooty mold often grows on the sticky substance.

ANALYSIS: Scales

Several different types of scales infest crabapples. They lay their eggs on leaves or bark, and in spring to midsummer the young scales, called *crawlers*, settle on leaves and twigs. The small (1/10 inch), soft-bodied young feed by inserting their mouthparts and sucking sap from the plant. The legs usually atrophy and a hard crusty or waxy shell develops over the body. The mature female scales lay their eggs underneath their shell. Some species of scales that infest crabapples are unable to digest fully all the sugar in the plant sap and excrete the excess in a fluid called honeydew, which often drops onto the leaves below. A sooty mold fungus may develop on the honeydew, causing the crabapple leaves to appear black and dirty. An uncontrolled infestation of scales may kill the plant after two or three seasons. For more information about scales, see page 876.

SOLUTION: Spray with ORTHO Liquid Sevin in late spring when the young are active. Contact your local Cooperative Extension Office (see page 1029) to determine the best time to spray for scales in your area. The following early spring, before new growth begins, spray the trunk and branches with a *dormant oil spray* to control overwintering insects.

Tent caterpillars (1/16 life size).

PROBLEM: In spring, silk nets appear in the crotches of trees or on the ends of branches. The leaves are chewed and the tree may be completely defoliated. Groups of bluish or black, hairy caterpillars with yellow or white stripes and blue or white spots are feeding in or around the nets.

ANALYSIS: Tent caterpillars (*Malacosoma* species)

Tent caterpillars feed on many ornamental and fruit trees in the garden. The insects are found in nearly all parts of the United States. In summer, tent caterpillars lay masses of 150 to 300 eggs in bands around twigs. The eggs hatch in early spring when leaves are beginning to unfold; the young caterpillars immediately begin to construct the nets. On warm, sunny days, they devour the surrounding foliage and may strip trees in just a few days. The caterpillars feed for 4 to 6 weeks and then pupate. In mid to late summer, brownish or reddish moths emerge and lay the overwintering eggs.

SOLUTION: Cut out and destroy large nets; or spray with ORTHO Liquid Sevin, an insecticide containing *malathion*, or a bacterial insecticide containing *Bacillus thuringiensis* when nets are first noticed. A bacterial insecticide is most effective against small caterpillars so it is best to spray before nets are large. Use high pressure spray equipment to penetrate the netting. To prevent damage next year, destroy the brown egg masses that encircle the twigs during the winter.

Slime flux.

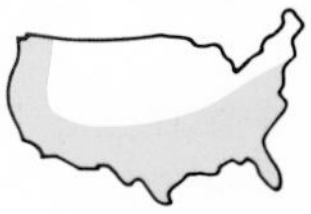

PROBLEM: Sour-smelling sap oozes from wounds, cracks, and branch crotches, mainly during the growing season. The sap drips down the bark and dries, causing unsightly gray or black streaks. Leaves may wilt on affected branches. Insects are attracted to the sour-smelling ooze.

ANALYSIS: Slime flux

Slime flux of mulberries, also called *wetwood*, is caused by bacteria (*Erwinia nimipressuralis*). The bacteria affect the heartwood, producing abnormally high sap pressure. This pressure is caused by bacterial fermentation, and forces the fermented sap, or flux, out of wounds, cracks, or crotches in the tree. Flux is especially copious when the tree is growing rapidly. Large areas of the bark may be coated with the smelly, bacteria-laden sap, which dries to a grayish white color. In addition, wounds do not heal and the bark is unsightly. A tree with this problem is often under water stress, which may cause drought damage (wilting and scorched leaves) to the branches. The problem may persist for years.

SOLUTION: There are no chemical controls for this condition. Bore a slightly slanted drainage hole through the wood below each oozing wound. Insert a ½-inch-diameter plastic tube just until it stays firmly in place. If the tube penetrates the water-soaked wood inside the tree, it will interfere with drainage. The tube will carry the dripping sap away from the trunk. Disinfect tools with rubbing alcohol after pruning infected trees.

Bacterial blight.

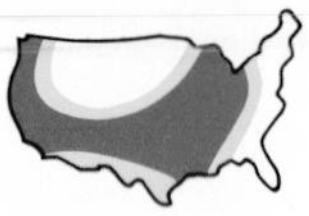

PROBLEM: Brown, water-soaked spots appear on the leaves and shoots. In wet weather, the spots enlarge rapidly, eventually becoming black and sunken. The leaves at the tips of the infected twigs are distorted; later they wilt and dry up. There are black streaks underneath the bark of infected twigs. The streaks extend downward from the blackened areas on the shoots. Infected shoots may exude an ooze in wet weather. Twigs often die, and the tree may be stunted.

ANALYSIS: Bacterial blight
This blight is caused by a bacterium (*Pseudomonas syringae mori*) that is common on both black and white mulberry. The bacteria spend the winter in the infected areas on the tree. During wet spring weather bacteria ooze out and are splashed by the rain to young leaves and twigs and nearby trees. Where the bacteria enter the tissue, a water-soaked spot develops. If rainy weather continues, the bacteria spread and twigs may die.

SOLUTION: In the fall, prune out infected branches well below the blighted area and destroy them. A protective spray used after pruning may help control the bacteria. Spray with a pesticide containing *basic copper sulfate* or *streptomycin.* Do not plant young mulberry trees near older infected trees.

Morus cultural information
Light: Full sun
Water: Occasional deep watering, tolerates some drought
Soil: Tolerates many types
Fertilizer: Light

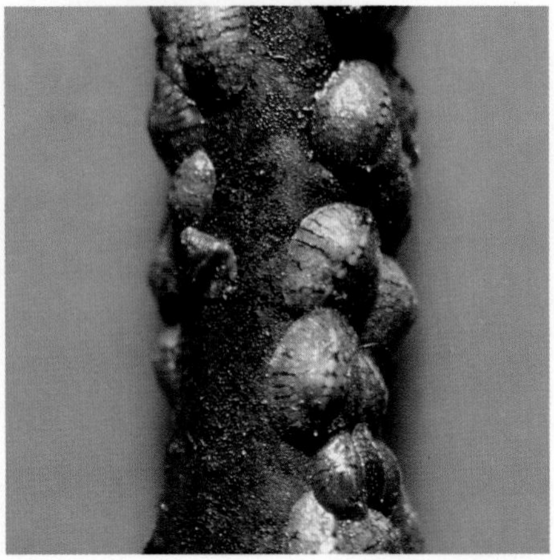

Scale (3 times life size).

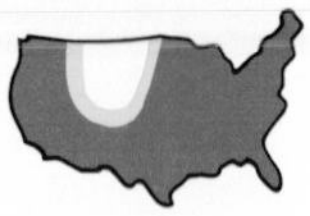

PROBLEM: The leaves, stems, or branches are covered with brownish purple crusty bumps or clusters of somewhat flattened brown, gray, or yellow scaly bumps. The bumps can be scraped or picked off; the undersides are usually soft. Leaves turn yellow and may drop. In some cases, a shiny, sticky substance coats the leaves. A black sooty mold often grows on the sticky substance.

ANALYSIS: Scales
Many different types of scales infest mulberry. They lay their eggs on leaves or bark, and in spring to midsummer the young scales, called *crawlers,* settle on leaves, twigs, and branches. These small ($\frac{1}{10}$ inch), soft-bodied young feed by sucking sap from the plant. The legs usually atrophy and a hard crusty shell develops over the body. The mature female scales lay their eggs underneath the shell. Some species of scales that infest mulberry are unable to digest fully all the sugar in the plant sap, and excrete the excess in a fluid called honeydew, which often drops onto the leaves or plants below. A sooty mold fungus may develop on the honeydew, causing the mulberry leaves or other plants to appear black and dirty. An uncontrolled infestation of scales may kill branches after 2 or 3 years. For more information about scales, see page 876.

SOLUTION: Spray with ORTHO Orthene Systemic Insect Control when the young are active. Contact your local Cooperative Extension Office (see page 1029) to determine the best time to spray for scales in your area. To control scales during the dormant season, spray the trunk and branches with ORTHO Volck Oil Spray.

Cottony scale (3 times life size).

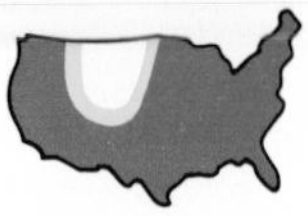

PROBLEM: The undersides of the leaves and the stems, branch crotches, or trunk are covered with white, cottony masses. Leaves may turn yellow and drop. A shiny, sticky substance may coat the leaves. A black sooty mold often grows on the sticky substance. Numerous side shoots sometimes grow out of an infested crotch area. Twigs and branches may die.

ANALYSIS: Cottony scales and mealybugs
Cottony scales and mealybugs are common on mulberry wherever it is grown. The visual similarities between these insects make separate identification difficult. They are very conspicuous in late spring and summer because the females are covered with a white, cottony egg sac, containing up to 2500 eggs. Females lay their egg masses on leaves or branches. The young insects that hatch from these eggs are yellowish brown to green. Damage is caused by the withdrawal of plant sap from the leaves and branches. The insects are unable to digest fully all the sugar in the plant sap and excrete the excess in a fluid called honeydew, which often drops onto the leaves or plants below. A sooty mold fungus may develop on the honeydew, causing the mulberry leaves and other plants to appear black and dirty. Leaf drop and twig dieback occur when the white masses completely cover the leaves and branches.

SOLUTION: Spray with ORTHO Orthene Systemic Insect Control in midsummer when the young are active. The following spring, when the tree is dormant, spray with *lime sulfur* to control overwintering insects on the bark.

NANDINA (HEAVENLY BAMBOO) ■ NERIUM (OLEANDER)

Iron deficiency.

PROBLEM: Some of the leaves are pale green (or pale red) to yellow. The newest leaves may be completely yellow, with only the veins remaining green. On older leaves, only the leaf edges may be yellowing. The plant may be stunted.

ANALYSIS: Iron deficiency
This is a common problem in plants, such as nandina, that do not tolerate alkaline soils. Nandina grows best in soil with a pH between 5.5 and 6.5. (For more information about soil acidity, see page 908.) The yellowing is due to a deficiency of iron and other minor nutrients in the plant. The soil is seldom deficient in iron. However, iron is often found in an insoluble form that is not available to the plant, especially in soil with a pH of 7.0 or higher. A high soil pH can result from overliming, or from lime leached from cement or brick. Regions where soil is derived from limestone, and those with low rainfall, also have high-pH soils.

SOLUTION: Spray the foliage with ORTHO Greenol Liquid Iron, and apply it to the soil around the plants to correct the iron deficiency. Correct the pH of the soil by treating it with *ferrous sulfate* or ORTHO Aluminum Sulfate and watering it in well. Maintain an acid pH by fertilizing with ORTHO Azalea, Camellia & Rhododendron Food.

Nandina cultural information
Light: Full sun to shade
Water: Grows best in moist soil
Soil: Loose, rich, well drained, nonalkaline
Fertilizer: Medium

Sooty mold.

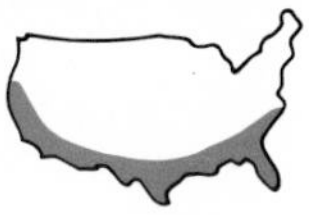

PROBLEM: A black sooty mold is growing on leaves and twigs. It can be completely wiped off the surfaces. Cool, moist weather hastens the growth of the mold.

ANALYSIS: Sooty mold
This common black mold is found on a wide variety of plants in the garden. It is caused by several species of fungi that grow on the sugary material left on plants by aphids, scales, mealybugs, whiteflies, and other insects that suck sap from the plant. The insects are unable to digest all the sugar in the sap and excrete the excess in a fluid called honeydew, which drops onto the leaves below. The honeydew may also drop out of infested trees and shrubs onto oleanders growing beneath them. The sooty mold fungus develops on the honeydew, causing the oleander leaves to appear black and dirty. Sooty mold is unsightly, but it is fairly harmless because it does not attack the leaf directly. Extremely heavy infestations prevent light from reaching the leaf, so that the leaf produces fewer nutrients and may turn yellow. The presence of sooty mold indicates that the oleander or another plant near it is infested with insects.

SOLUTION: Sooty mold can be wiped from the leaves with a wet rag; or it will eventually be washed off by rain. Prevent more sooty mold by controlling the insect that is producing the honeydew. Inspect the leaves and twigs above the sooty mold to find what type of insect is present. For control instructions, see the following pages: for aphids, page 875; for scales, page 876; for whiteflies, page 877; for mealybugs, page 876.

Oleander aphids (life size).

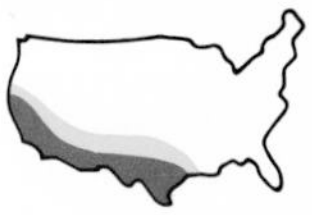

PROBLEM: Huge colonies of tiny ($\frac{1}{8}$ inch), soft-bodied insects cluster on the leaves, branch tips, and buds. The infested leaves may turn yellow, and new growth may be slowed and distorted.

ANALYSIS: Oleander aphid
(*Aphis nerii*)
This aphid heavily infests oleander in the southwestern states. The aphids appear in early spring. They are extremely prolific and populations rapidly build up to huge numbers during the early part of the growing season. The aphids suck the juices from the oleander leaves, but oleander is such a vigorous plant that the insect usually causes little damage. There may be some leaf yellowing and distortion on the ends of the branches. In early summer to midsummer, when temperatures increase and natural enemies, such as wasps and lady beetles, are abundant, the aphid population declines. Several other aphid species also infest oleander.

SOLUTION: If aphids are abundant and causing damage to the plant, spray the leaves and branch tips thoroughly with ORTHO Orthene Systemic Insect Control or ORTHO Isotox Insect Spray. Repeat the spray if the plant becomes reinfested.

NERIUM (OLEANDER)

Black scale (twice life size).

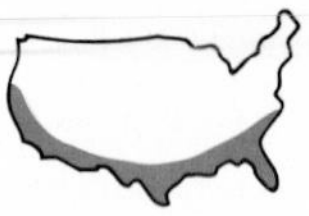

PROBLEM: The leaves, twigs, and branches are covered with brownish or black crusty bumps, $1/5$ inch in diameter. On the surface of the bumps, ridges form the letter H. Leaves turn brown in patches and may drop; twigs may die. A shiny sticky substance may coat the leaves. A black sooty mold often grows on the sticky substance.

ANALYSIS: Black scale
(*Saissetia oleae*)
Black scale is a serious pest of many trees and shrubs in the South. It may also infest greenhouse-grown plants in colder climates. The scales spend the winter on the trunk and twigs of oleander. They lay their eggs in the spring, and in late spring the young scales, called *crawlers*, settle on leaves, twigs, and branches. The small ($1/10$ inch), soft-bodied young feed by sucking sap from the plant. The legs atrophy and a hard shell develops over their body. The mature female scales lay their eggs underneath the shell. These scales are unable to digest fully all the sugar in the plant sap and excrete the excess in a fluid called honeydew. A sooty mold fungus may develop on the honeydew, causing the oleander leaves to appear black and dirty. An uncontrolled infestation of scales may kill branches or the entire plant after several seasons. Many other scales also infest oleander. For more information about scales, see page 876.

SOLUTION: Spray with ORTHO Isotox Insect Killer or ORTHO Orthene Systemic Insect Control in late spring when the young are active. The following early spring, spray the trunk and branches with a *dormant oil spray* to control overwintering insects.

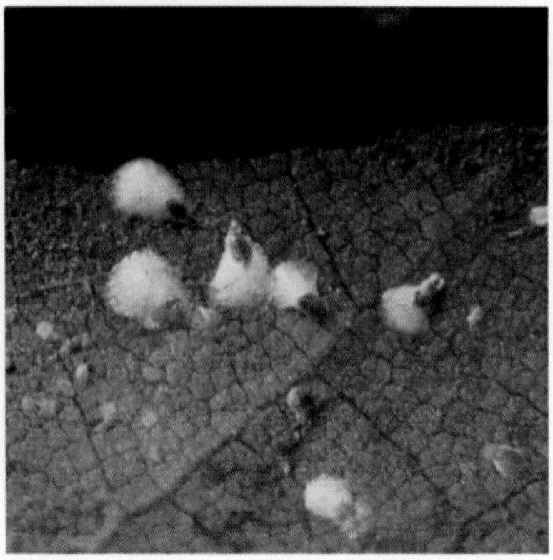

False oleander scale (twice life size).

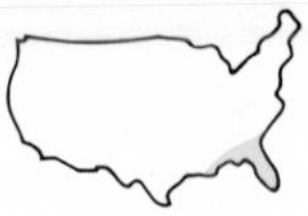

PROBLEM: Yellow to greenish yellow spots develop on the leaves. Tiny white to light brown raised bumps are often seen in the discolored areas. The bumps can be scraped or picked off; the undersides are usually soft. Stems may also be infested. Leaves turn yellow and drop. Small branches may be killed when infestations are heavy.

ANALYSIS: False oleander scale
(*Pseudaulacaspis cockerelli*)
This insect feeds on many garden plants, and is capable of rapid reproduction. The female scale deposits large masses of eggs under her wax shell. After hatching, the young scales, called *crawlers*, move about the host plant until they locate a feeding site. They then begin to feed and develop the protective scale cover. Several generations of scales are produced each year. Scales feed by sucking the plant juices from tender leaves and stems. Some scales are unable to digest fully all the sugar in the plant sap, and excrete the excess in a fluid called honeydew, which often drops onto the leaves below. A sooty mold may develop on the honeydew, causing the oleander leaves to appear black and dirty.

SOLUTION: Apply ORTHO Isotox Insect Killer or ORTHO Orthene Systemic Insect Control thoroughly to infested plants. Repeat sprays at intervals of 7 to 10 days until scales are controlled. Dead scales remain on the plant but are dry and contain no fluids when scraped off and examined.

Oleander caterpillar (half life size).

PROBLEM: Leaves are badly chewed or missing. Orange caterpillars up to 2 inches long with many short black hairs may be feeding on the damaged plants.

ANALYSIS: Oleander caterpillar
(*Syntomedia epilais juncundissima*)
This chewing pest is the larval stage of a colorful, purple, 2-inch moth with white markings on greenish black wings. The caterpillars hatch from eggs laid on the leaves. Development is rapid; the adult stage is reached in about a month. This rapid maturation enables several generations of caterpillars to be produced during the year. They cause their greatest damage from early spring until fall.

SOLUTION: Apply ORTHO Orthene Systemic Insect Control or ORTHO Liquid Sevin. Repeat treatments as needed according to label directions. Severely infested plants that have lost most of their leaves usually grow new leaves within a few weeks after caterpillars are controlled. Applying a light amount of a complete fertilizer will also help plants recover more quickly.

Bacterial gall.

PROBLEM: There are wartlike spongy growths on older branches, and longitudinal swellings on young green shoots. Leaves are distorted and yellowing, and may develop swellings. Ooze may drip from the leaf veins.

ANALYSIS: Bacterial gall
This plant disease is caused by a bacterium (*Pseudomonas syringae tonelliana*) that infects all of the aboveground parts of oleander. The bacteria enter the plant through wounds, possibly those caused by sucking insects such as scales and mealybugs. On younger shoots, cankers develop; on older woody stems, the bacteria initiate the development of wartlike galls. Growth above these galls is often scraggly. Large quantities of ooze that contains bacteria may be exuded from leaf veins.

SOLUTION: Prune out and destroy infected stems well below the galls. Sterilize pruning shears with rubbing alcohol after each cut.

All parts of the oleander plant are highly toxic, and contact with leaves can produce dermatitis. Smoke from burning plant parts can cause severe skin and respiratory irritations.

Witch's broom.

PROBLEM: Abnormal clusters of new shoots appear just below the branch tips. These shoots grow only a few inches, and then turn brown and die. On heavily infected plants, large areas may be killed.

ANALYSIS: Witch's broom
These abnormal growths on oleander are caused by a fungus (*Sphaeropsis tumefaciens*) that infects branch tips during the fall and winter. Witch's broom symptoms do not usually appear until spring, after additional growth has taken place and the infected tissue is several inches below the growing tip. Multiple shoots grow from the infected area, producing the witch's broom effect. Wind and insects spread the disease. Most oleanders are easily infected.

SOLUTION: No practical controls are available at present. Prune out affected areas as soon as symptoms are noticed, making cuts at least 6 inches below the witch's broom. Sterilize pruning tools in rubbing alcohol after pruning.

Nerium cultural information
Light: Full sun
Water: Drought tolerant once established
Soil: Tolerates many types
Fertilizer: Light

Cottony maple leaf scale (twice life size).

PROBLEM: The undersides of the leaves are covered with white, cottony, cushionlike masses. Leaves may turn yellow and drop. Sometimes a shiny, sticky substance coats the leaves. A black sooty mold often grows on the sticky substance. Twigs and branches may die back.

ANALYSIS: Cottony maple leaf scale (*Pulvinaria acericola*)
The cottony maple leaf scale is a pest of sour gum in the eastern part of the country. The immature scales spend the winter on the twigs and branches. Damage is caused when the insects suck plant sap from the leaves and branches. The scales feed in the spring, mate, and then the females migrate to the leaves to lay their eggs. The females are very conspicuous because they are covered with a white, cottony egg sac, containing up to 2500 eggs. The young scales that hatch from these eggs move to new leaves to feed, settling along the larger veins. The pale green insects are inconspicuous against the green leaves. In fall, the immature scales migrate back to the bark. The insects are unable to digest fully all the sugar in the plant sap, and excrete the excess in a fluid called honeydew, which often drops onto the leaves or plants below. A sooty mold fungus may develop on the honeydew, causing the black gum leaves and other plants to appear black and dirty. With repeated heavy infestations, twigs and branches die after several years.

SOLUTION: Spray with ORTHO Liquid Sevin in midsummer when the young are active. The following spring, while the tree is still dormant, spray with *lime sulfur* to control overwintering insects on the bark.

OLEA (OLIVE)

Olive knot.

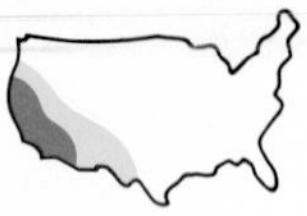

PROBLEM: Twigs, branches, leaves, and sometimes the fruit develop knotty swellings, up to several inches across. As the swellings enlarge the surfaces become rough, and irregular fissures form. Growth above these swellings slows, and shoots or the entire tree may die.

ANALYSIS: Olive knot
Olive knot is caused by a bacterium (*Pseudomonas syringae sevastanoi*) that lives and multiplies inside the knots. During rainy weather, between October and May, the bacteria ooze out of the knots and are washed and blown by rain and wind to the twigs, branches, and leaves. When new growth begins in spring, small swellings develop. The swellings enlarge, eventually becoming knotty and hard; growth above these knots is slowed. Trees grown for their fruit may produce few olives.

SOLUTION: Where practical, prune off the knots from the tree during the summer, sterilizing pruning shears after each cut with rubbing alcohol. Painting the knots with the bactericide Gallex® may help control the spread of the bacteria. Keep the tree in a vigorous growing condition by fertilizing and watering regularly to prevent large losses of leaves. Avoid wounding the tree. If branches require pruning, do so during the dry season to avoid new infections.

Olea cultural information
Light: Full sun
Water: Moist or dry soil
Soil: Rich, well drained, but tolerates many types
Fertilizer: Light

Scales (life size).

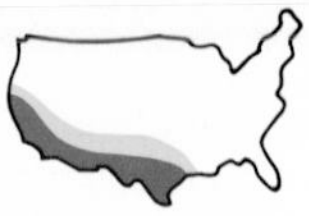

PROBLEM: The leaves, stems, or branches are covered with black or brownish crusty bumps or clusters of somewhat flattened yellowish or brown scaly bumps. The bumps can be scraped or picked off; the undersides are usually soft. Leaves turn yellow and may drop. In some cases, a shiny, sticky substance coats the leaves. A black sooty mold often grows on the sticky substance. Branches may die.

ANALYSIS: Scales
Several different types of scales infest olive. They lay their eggs on the leaves or bark, and in spring to midsummer the young scales, called *crawlers,* settle on leaves and twigs. The small (1/10 inch), soft-bodied young feed by sucking sap from the plant. The legs usually atrophy and a hard crusty shell develops over the body. The mature female scales lay their eggs underneath the shell. Some species of scales that infest olive are unable to digest fully all the sugar in the plant sap and excrete the excess in a fluid called honeydew. A sooty mold fungus may develop on the honeydew, causing the olive leaves to appear black and dirty. An uncontrolled infestation of scales may kill branches after two or three seasons.

SOLUTION: Spray with an insecticide containing *carbaryl* (SEVIN®) or *diazinon* when the young are active. Contact your local Cooperative Extension Office (see page 1029) to determine the best time to spray for scales in your area. For more information about scales, see page 876.

PALMS

Lethal yellowing.

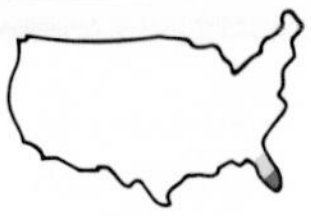

PROBLEM: Many palm fronds turn yellow and die, beginning with the lower fronds and progressing upward. On coconut palm (*Cocos nucifera*), fronds yellow, and all the nuts usually drop. The nuts are black where they were attached to the flower stalk. New flower stalks are blackened, and do not set any fruit. Dead fronds tend to cling to the tree instead of falling off, and after 3 to 6 months, all the fronds and the bud have been killed. Shortly thereafter the entire palm top falls off, leaving only the bare trunk. No insects can be recognized on the dying fronds.

ANALYSIS: Lethal yellowing
This serious palm disease is caused by bacterialike organisms called *mycoplasmas*, which are carried from palm to palm by leafhoppers, tiny sucking insects. Leafhoppers feed on fronds, especially the newly emerging ones, and are difficult to detect and control. For more information about leafhoppers, see page 878.

SOLUTION: There is no cure for lethal yellowing. To suppress the disease and prolong the life of palms showing lethal yellowing symptoms, inject them every 4 months with the antibiotic *oxytetracycline.* Avoid planting susceptible palms. (For a list, see page 1014.) Remove infected palms to avoid spreading the disease.

Bud rot. *Insert:* Close-up.

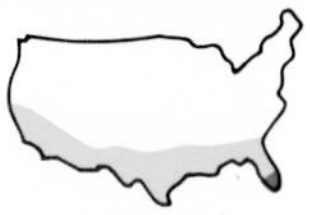

PROBLEM: The palm stops producing new fronds and the last new frond to appear turns yellow, then brown, and dies. The entire bud can be pulled out; it appears rotten, and may have a foul odor. One by one the fronds next to the bud turn yellow, then brown, and die. Eventually the entire top of the palm falls away, leaving the bare trunk standing. Palms of all ages and sizes are affected, and most damage follows periods of cold weather and high rainfall.

ANALYSIS: Bud rot
This often fatal palm disease is caused by a fungus (*Phytophthora palmivora*) that enters the palm through wounds or other openings. The spores can also be washed down into the palm bud by heavy rains. Once infected, palms may die within a short time. Most severe bud rot occurs from spring to fall.

SOLUTION: Spray the entire top of the palm with a fungicide containing *basic copper sulfate*. Be sure the bud area is thoroughly covered with the fungicide. Use a spreader-sticker with the fungicide to enable it to coat plant parts more effectively. (For more information on spreader-stickers, see page 922.) Repeat treatments as needed, following the label directions. Give a light application of fertilizer to speed the palm's recovery. Remove palms that die from bud rot as soon as possible to prevent infection of nearby healthy palms.

Palm leaf skeletonizer damage.

PROBLEM: Palm fronds become ragged and develop brown splotched areas covered with unsightly masses of webbing and excrement. Yellowish white caterpillars ⅝ inch long with several reddish brown stripes running the length of their bodies are feeding on the fronds. Fronds are rarely completely eaten.

ANALYSIS: Palm leaf skeletonizer
(*Homaledra sabalella*)
This caterpillar is the larva of a small brownish moth that lays eggs in clusters on the underside of the husk that surrounds new leaflets. Caterpillars feed on the fronds for 25 to 30 days after hatching, and then pupate in the webbing on the frond. Several generations of caterpillars are produced each year, primarily during the spring and summer.

SOLUTION: Apply an insecticide containing *carbaryl* (SEVIN®) according to label directions. Repeat sprays are often required. For a list of palms most frequently attacked, see page 1012.

Palm cultural information
Light: Full sun to partial shade
Water: When the soil is almost dry
Soil: Tolerates many types
Fertilizer: Medium

Frizzle top.

PROBLEM: Newly emerging fronds fail to grow to their normal length. Often they are light yellow to brown, and have a frizzled look. In severe cases, fronds turn dark brown to black, and the palm bud may die, resulting in the death of the tree.

ANALYSIS: Frizzle top
This problem in certain palms results from a lack of manganese, a minor nutrient. It occurs only where palms have been planted in infertile soil or soil that is subject to serious leaching of nutrient materials. A lack of regular fertilizing in home landscapes often greatly contributes to frizzle top.

SOLUTION: Apply *manganese sulfate* or a special palm fertilizer containing *manganese sulfate* according to label instructions. Severely affected palms may take 6 months or more to recover completely. Repeat fertilizer treatments at recommended intervals to prevent frizzle top from reappearing.

Palms most susceptible to frizzle top: Date palm (*Phoenix*), royal palm (*Roystonea*), and queen palm (*Arecastrum*).

PALMS

Lightning damage.

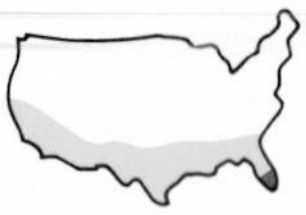

PROBLEM: Palm fronds suddenly begin to droop around the trunk, beginning with the lower ones. Frond color may be green at first, but changes rapidly to yellow and then to brown. After about 2 weeks most of the fronds have drooped down or fallen off, and the central bud area wilts and bends over. Sometimes a reddish fluid bleeds along the trunk. No pests or signs of diseases are seen on dying fronds, and the problem occurs shortly after a severe electrical storm.

ANALYSIS: Lightning damage
Severe electrical shock often kills palms very quickly, and each year hundreds are lost to lightning strikes in areas that have frequent thunderstorms.

SOLUTION: Usually nothing can save a palm that has suffered a severe lightning strike; however, some palms may recover. Regular applications of fertilizer to trees not killed outright will help them to recover. Dead palms should be removed so that they do not become a safety hazard. Do not plant tall-growing palms in open, exposed areas.

PARTHENOCISSUS (BOSTON IVY)

Leafhopper damage.

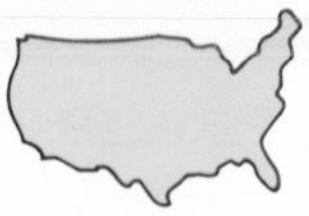

PROBLEM: Leaves are stippled with white specks. When the infestation is heavy, many leaves turn brown and drop from the plant. Small (⅛ inch), wedge-shaped yellow insects with red, yellow, or black markings are found on the undersides of the leaves. When the plant is touched, the insects run, hop, or fly away.

ANALYSIS: Leafhoppers
(*Erythroneura* species)
Many different species of leafhoppers feed on Parthenocissus. This group also feeds on several types of fruit trees and small fruits. The leafhoppers spend the winter as adults in protected areas, usually under fallen leaves or in weeds. When the weather warms in the spring, they fly to plants and feed on the undersides of the developing leaves. The leafhoppers suck the fluids from the plant cells, causing the stippled appearance. The adult females insert their eggs into the leaf tissue. The eggs hatch in 2 weeks and the wingless young leafhoppers feed and develop on the lower surfaces of the leaves. They mature in three to 5 weeks. There may be as many as three generations a year.

SOLUTION: Spray with ORTHO Isotox Insect Killer or with an insecticide containing *malathion* when the damage is first noticed. Direct the spray to the undersides of the leaves.

Parthenocissus cultural information
Light: Full sun
Water: Grows best in moist soil
Soil: Loose, well drained
Fertilizer: Medium

PHILADELPHUS (MOCK ORANGE)

Black bean aphids (life size).

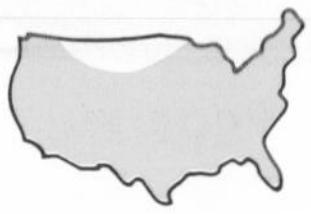

PROBLEM: The newest leaves are wrinkled and yellowing. Leaves may drop off and new growth may be slowed. A shiny, sticky substance may coat the leaves. A black sooty mold often grows on this sticky substance. Tiny (⅛ inch) greenish yellow or dark green soft-bodied insects cluster on the underside of leaves and on the branch tips. Ants may be present.

ANALYSIS: Aphids
Aphids do little damage in small numbers. However, they are extremely prolific and populations can rapidly build up to damaging numbers during the growing season. Damage occurs when the aphid sucks the juices from the mock orange leaves. The aphid is unable to digest fully all the sugar in the sap and excretes the excess in a fluid called honeydew, which often drops onto the leaves below. A sooty mold fungus may develop on the honeydew, causing the mock orange leaves to appear black and dirty. Ants feed on honeydew and are often present where there is an aphid infestation. For more information about aphids, see page 875.

SOLUTION: Control with ORTHO Orthene Systemic Insect Control when aphids first appear. Direct the spray to the undersides of the leaves. Repeat the spray if the plant becomes reinfested.

Philadelphus cultural information
Light: Full sun
Water: Allow the soil to dry between waterings
Soil: Loose, well drained
Fertilizer: Medium

Iron deficiency.

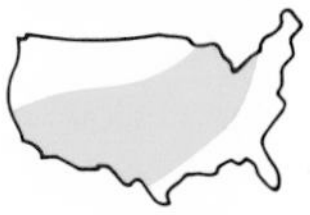

PROBLEM: Some of the leaves turn pale green to yellow. The newest leaves may be completely yellow, with only the veins remaining green. On older leaves, only the edges may be yellowing. The plant may be stunted.

ANALYSIS: Iron deficiency
This is a common problem in plants such as mock orange that do not tolerate highly alkaline soils. The plant grows best in soil with a pH between 6.0 and 6.5. (For more information about soil acidity, see page 908.) The yellowing is due to a deficiency of iron and other minor nutrients in the plant. The soil is seldom deficient in iron. However, iron is often found in an insoluble form that is not available to the plant, especially in soil with a pH of 7.5 or higher. A high soil pH can result from overliming, or from lime leached from cement or brick. Regions where soil is derived from limestone, and those with low rainfall, also have high-pH soils. Plants use iron in the formation of the green pigment in the leaves. When it is lacking, new leaves are yellow.

SOLUTION: Spray the foliage with ORTHO Greenol Liquid Iron, and apply it to the soil around the plants to correct the iron deficiency. Correct the pH of the soil by treating it with *ferrous sulfate* or ORTHO Aluminum Sulfate and watering it in well. Maintain an acid pH by fertilizing with ORTHO Azalea, Camellia & Rhododendron Food. Never lime the soil around mock orange.

Fungal leaf spots.

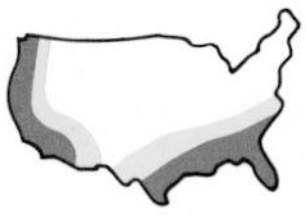

PROBLEM: Spots or blotches appear on the leaves. The spots are purple at first, then gray to brown with purple margins. They range in size from barely visible to ¾ inch in diameter. Several spots may join to form blotches. Leaves may be yellow and may fall to the ground. Leaf spotting is most severe in moist humid weather.

ANALYSIS: Fungal leaf spots
Several different fungi cause leaf spots on photinia. These unsightly spots rarely kill the plant. The fungi are spread by splashing water and wind. Spots develop where the fungi enter the tissue. If wet conditions persist, the fungi spreads and forms blotches. Most leaf spot organisms do their greatest damage in mild weather (between 50° and 85°F).

SOLUTION: Once leaves become spotted they will remain so. Where practical, remove infected leaves from the plant. Collect and destroy any fallen leaves. On valuable specimens, spray with a fungicide containing *chlorothalonil* (DACONIL 2787®), *ferbam,* or *benomyl,* when new growth begins in spring. Repeat at intervals of 2 weeks, or for as long as the weather remains favorable for infection. Add a spreader-sticker to the spray. (For more information about spreader-stickers, see page 922.) To reduce plant susceptibility, provide windbreaks and protection from low temperatures.

Photinia cultural information
Light: Full sun
Water: Moist or dry conditions
Soil: Any good garden soil
Fertilizer: Medium

PICEA (SPRUCE)

ADAPTATION: Zones 2 to 8 (to determine your zone, see the map on page 1020). Not adapted to desert areas.

LIGHT: Full sun to partial shade.

SOIL: Tolerates a wide variety of soils.

FERTILIZER: Fertilize with ORTHO Evergreen, Tree & Shrub Food or ORTHO Azalea, Camellia & Rhododendron Food according to label directions.

WATER:
How much: Apply enough water to wet the soil 3 to 4 feet deep. To determine the proper amount of water for your soil type, see page 912.
How often: Water when the soil is just barely moist 4 inches below the surface. For more information about watering, see page 912.

PRUNING: Prune to maintain shape. If two leaders (tops) develop, remove one. For dense, bushy growth, remove a third of each year's new growth. When planting, allow enough room for spread and height—some spruce grow to 150 feet.

PICEA (SPRUCE)

Spruce budworm larva (twice life size).

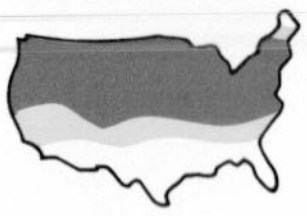

PROBLEM: Needles on the ends of branches are chewed and webbed together. In mid-July the branch ends often turn reddish brown. Branches or the entire tree may die after 3 to 5 years of defoliation. Reddish brown caterpillars, 1¼ inches long, with yellow or white raised spots, are feeding on the needles.

ANALYSIS: Spruce budworm
(*Choristoneura* species)
Spruce budworms are very destructive to ornamental spruce, fir, and Douglas fir, and may infest pine, larch, and hemlock. The budworm is cyclical. It comes and goes in epidemics 10 or more years apart. The moths are small (½ inch long) and grayish, with bands and spots of brown. The females lay pale green eggs in clusters on the needles in late July and August. The larvae that hatch from these eggs crawl to hiding places in the bark or in lichen mats; or they are blown by the wind to other trees, where they hide. The tiny larvae spin a silken case and hibernate there until spring. In May, when the weather warms, the caterpillars tunnel into needles. As they grow, they feed on opening buds; later they chew off needles and web them together. The larvae feed for about 5 weeks, pupate on twigs, and emerge as adults.

SOLUTION: Spray with ORTHO Orthene Systemic Insect Control when the buds begin to grow in late May.

Galls.

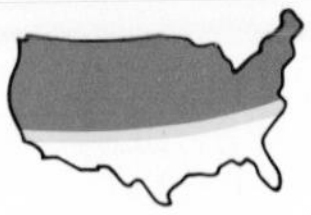

PROBLEM: The ends of branches develop green, pineapple-shaped galls in the spring; in late summer, they turn brown and dry. Growth continues beyond the galls, but the branch may be severely stunted. Galled stems are weak and may break during storms. When large numbers of galls are formed, the tree may be less vigorous.

ANALYSIS: Eastern spruce gall aphid
(*Adelges abietis*)
This gall aphid is most damaging to Norway spruce, but may occasionally infest white, black, and red spruce. The insect spends the winter at the base of a terminal bud. When buds begin to grow in the spring, the aphids lay clusters of several hundred eggs that are covered with white, waxy threads. The young that hatch from these eggs feed on developing needles. They suck the juices from the needles, inducing the formation of galls that enclose them. The aphids live and feed in chambers inside the galls. In mid to late summer, the galls turn brown and crack open. Aphids that emerge lay eggs near the tip of the needles. The young that hatch from these eggs spend the winter at the base of the buds.

SOLUTION: Spray with an insecticide containing *malathion* or *diazinon* in the spring just before growth begins, and again in the fall after the galls turn brown and crack open, around late September.

Stem gall.

PROBLEM: Green or purplish sausage-shaped galls, 2½ inches long, appear on the ends of side branches. The branches may be severely stunted. The galls turn brown and are very noticeable in late summer.

ANALYSIS: Cooley spruce gall aphid
(*Adelges cooleyi*)
The cooley spruce gall aphid requires 2 years to complete its life cycle, and may spend part of its life on both spruce and Douglas fir. In late spring the insect feeds, matures, and lays several hundred eggs at the base of needles near the branch tips. When the eggs hatch, the young insects move to growing needles. They suck the juices from the needles, inducing the formation of galls that enclose them. The aphids live and feed in chambers inside the galls. In July, the insects mature and emerge through openings in the dried galls. These aphids develop wings and migrate to Douglas fir or another spruce. The aphids on Douglas fir lay eggs, producing a generation of woolly aphids. (For more information about the spruce gall aphid on Douglas fir, see page 547.) Some of these aphids develop wings and migrate back to spruce. Others are wingless and remain on Douglas fir. Aphids that do not migrate to Douglas fir lay eggs on spruce after emerging from the galls.

SOLUTION: Where practical, remove galls before they open in midsummer. Spray with *lime sulfur* or with an insecticide containing *malathion* or *diazinon* just before buds break in the spring (early April). If using *malathion* or *diazinon*, repeat the spray after the galls open in late summer.

Damaged tree. *Insert:* Cocoons (1/3 life size).

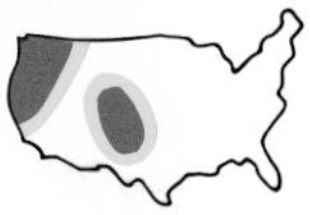

PROBLEM: Much of the foliage is eaten, starting at the top of the tree and progressing downward. The entire tree may be defoliated in one season. Inch-long, hairy, gray or light brown caterpillars, with tufts of orange hairs on their backs, may be found feeding on the needles. When populations are high, many tan-colored pellets drop from the tree and litter the ground.

ANALYSIS: Douglas fir tussock moth
(*Orgyia pseudotsugata*)
Douglas fir tussock moth populations are cyclical. Every 7 to 10 years, moth populations in forested areas build up to epidemic proportions. When this occurs, spruce, Douglas firs, true firs, pine, and larch may be completely defoliated. In cities, damaging numbers may be found every year. In mid to late summer, hairy, wingless female moths lay their eggs in a frothy substance covered with a layer of hairlike scales. When the eggs hatch the following spring, the caterpillars begin feeding at the top of the tree. As the younger foliage is devoured the caterpillars move downward, feeding on older needles. Large quantities of tan excrement pellets accumulate around the base of the tree. Since conifers do not replace their old needles, defoliated trees are often killed after two seasons. In August the caterpillars pupate, to emerge later as adults.

SOLUTION: Spray with an insecticide containing *acephate* (ORTHENE®), *carbaryl* (SEVIN®), or the bacteria *Bacillus thuringiensis* when caterpillars or damage are first noticed in May or early June. Repeat the spray 2 weeks later if damage continues.

Damaged needles. *Insert:* Larva (life size).

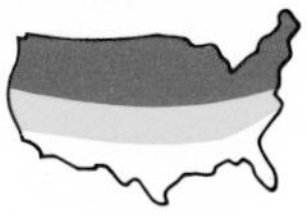

PROBLEM: Groups of brown needles are webbed together, usually near the inside of the lower branches. There is a sawdustlike material around the webbing. The entire tree may be severely infested, giving it an unsightly appearance. If a partially brown needle is broken open, a small (up to 1/4 inch), greenish brown larva may be seen feeding inside.

ANALYSIS: Spruce needle miner
(*Taniva albolineana*)
The spruce needle miner is the larva of a small (1/2 inch) dark brown moth. The moth lays eggs in late spring to early summer on the undersides of old needles. The larvae that hatch from these eggs bore into the base of the needles, feeding on the interior. When the interior is consumed, the caterpillars cut off the needles at their base and web them together, forming a nest. The needle miners feed until the first frost and then enter a hollow needle, where they spend the winter. When the weather warms in spring, the larvae continue feeding until April or May. They pupate inside the webbed nest of needles and emerge as adults to lay more eggs. Several other types of needle miners may cause similar damage to spruce trees.

SOLUTION: Wash out infested needles with a strong stream of water and destroy them. Spray with ORTHO Orthene Systemic Insect Control in late June. Repeat the treatment in 7 to 10 days.

Spruce aphid damage to blue spruce.

PROBLEM: Many of the older needles turn brown and drop. Only the newest needles remain green. The tree looks bare and sickly. Tiny (1/8 inch) green soft-bodied insects may be seen feeding on the needles.

ANALYSIS: Spruce aphid and green spruce aphid (*Elatobium abietinum* and *Cinara fornacula*)
These aphids may be very destructive to spruce in the North. The aphids appear in early spring, around February. They are extremely prolific and populations can rapidly build up to damaging numbers during March and April. Damage occurs when the aphids suck the juices from the spruce needles. They usually remain on a single needle until it is almost ready to drop. By the time the needles turn brown and the damage is noticeable, the insect population has declined. It may take a heavily damaged tree several years to recover and replace its lost foliage.

SOLUTION: By the time the damage is noticed, it is usually too late to treat the tree this year. Spray with ORTHO Isotox Insect Killer or ORTHO Diazinon Insect Spray the following February or March. Repeat the spray 10 days later.

PICEA (SPRUCE)

Pine needle scale (4 times life size).

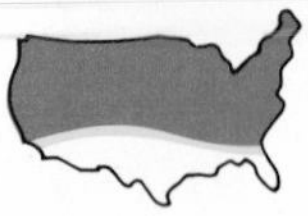

PROBLEM: Needles are covered with clusters of somewhat flattened, white, scaly bumps. When heavily infested, the foliage may appear completely white. The bumps can be scraped or picked off; the undersides are usually soft. Needles turn brown and eventually drop. Repeated severe infestations may kill young trees or weaken older trees.

ANALYSIS: Pine needle scale
(*Chionaspis pinifoliae*)
These scale insects may seriously damage spruce and pine trees and may infest fir, hemlock, and cedar. The scales survive the winter on the spruce needles as eggs beneath the dead mother scales. The eggs hatch in late spring and the young scales, called *crawlers*, move to new green needles. The small ($\frac{1}{10}$ inch) soft-bodied young feed by inserting their mouthparts and sucking sap from the plant. The legs atrophy and a crusty white shell develops over the body. The mature female scales lay their eggs underneath their shell in June or July. This next generation feeds throughout late summer and matures in fall. Females of this generation lay the overwintering eggs.

SOLUTION: Spray young trees with ORTHO Isotox Insect Killer or ORTHO Diazinon Insect Spray in late spring when the young are active. The following early spring, before new growth begins and when the danger of frost is past, spray with a pesticide containing *lime sulfur* to kill the overwintering eggs. Inspect ornamental spruce twice a year for evidence of infestation. Older trees seldom require controls.

Spruce spider mite damage.

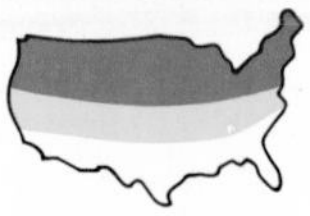

PROBLEM: Needles are stippled yellow and dirty. There may be a silken webbing on the twigs and needles. Needles usually turn brown and fall off. To determine if the tree is infested with mites, hold a sheet of white paper underneath some stippled needles and tap the foliage sharply. Minute dark green to black specks about the size of pepper grains will drop to the paper and begin to crawl around. The pests are easily seen against the white background.

ANALYSIS: Spruce spider mite
(*Oligonychus ununguis*)
The spruce spider mite is one of the most damaging pests of spruces and many other conifers. These mites suck sap from the undersides of the needles. As a result of feeding the green pigment disappears, causing the stippled appearance. This symptom may be mistaken for certain types of air pollution damage (see page 855). Spider mites first appear between April and June. In subtropical areas, mites may be active during warm periods in winter. A complete generation may be produced in only seventeen days, so mites can rapidly build up to tremendous numbers during the growing season. Young spruce trees may die the first season. If left uncontrolled for several years, older trees may die, with symptoms progressing from the lower branches upward. Several other kinds of mites may infest spruce trees.

SOLUTION: Control with ORTHO Orthene Insect Spray or ORTHO Isotox Insect Killer. Repeat the spray two more times, seven to ten days apart. Additional sprays may be needed in early fall or spring if the tree becomes reinfested.

Dieback. *Insert:* White pitch on bark.

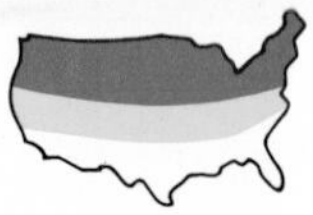

PROBLEM: The needles on the branches nearest the ground turn brown and dry. Occasionally this condition develops first in the upper branches. The needles may drop immediately, or they may remain attached for a year. Eventually the entire branch dies back. Amber-colored pitch usually oozes from the infected area, becoming white as it dries. The infection may spread to the higher branches. To determine if the tree is infected, slice off the bark on a dead branch in the area where the diseased tissue and healthy tissue meet. Small black spore-producing bodies are found beneath the bark.

ANALYSIS: Canker and dieback
This plant disease is caused by fungus (*Cytospora kunzei*) that is very destructive to Norway and Colorado blue spruce. The fungus enters the tree at a wound, killing the surrounding healthy tissue. A canker develops and expands through the wood in all directions. When the canker encircles a branch, the branch dies and the needles turn brown. Sap oozes from the dying branch. Eventually small black spore-producing bodies develop in the bark. Older (over fifteen years), weak, or injured trees are most susceptible to the disease.

SOLUTION: Prune off and destroy dead or dying branches well below the infected area, or where the branch meets the trunk. After each cut, sterilize the pruning shears with rubbing alcohol. Do not prune during wet weather. Avoid wounding trees with lawnmowers, tools, and other equipment. Keep trees vigorous by watering during dry spells and fertilizing every few years.

PIERIS (ANDROMEDA)

Lacebug damage.

PROBLEM: The upper sides of the leaves are mottled or speckled yellow or gray and green. The mottling may be confused with mite or leafhopper damage, but it can be distinguished from damage caused by other insects by the hard, black, shiny droplets found on the undersides of damaged leaves. Small (1/8 inch) light or dark spiny, wingless insects or brownish insects with clear lacy wings may be visible around the droplets. The plant may be stunted. Damage occurs in spring and summer.

ANALYSIS: Andromeda lacebug
(*Stephanitis takeyai*)
The andromeda lacebug is found throughout the Northeast on *Pieris japonica* and leucothoe. The lacebugs spend the winter as eggs in the leaf vein or cemented in the black droplets on the lower surface of the leaves. The eggs hatch in May. The spiny, wingless, immature insects and later the brown lacy-winged adults suck sap from the undersides of the leaves. The green leaf pigment disappears, resulting in the characteristic yellow or gray mottling. As the lacebugs feed, droplets of black excrement accumulate around them. Damage is unsightly and food production by the leaf is reduced, resulting in loss of plant vigor.

SOLUTION: Spray with ORTHO Isotox Insect Killer or with an insecticide containing *carbaryl* (SEVIN®) when damage first appears in spring. Cover the undersides of the leaves thoroughly. Repeat 7 to 10 days later. A third application may be necessary if the plant becomes reinfested in the summer. It is important to spray early, preventing as much damage as possible. Damaged leaves will be unsightly for more than a year.

Spider mites (half life size).

PROBLEM: Leaves are stippled yellow or bronze, and dirty. There may be a silken webbing on the lower surfaces of the leaves. New leaves may be distorted. To determine if the plant is infested with mites, hold a sheet of white paper underneath a branch that has stippled leaves and tap the branch sharply. Minute green, red, or yellow specks the size of pepper grains will drop to the paper and begin to crawl around. The pests are easily seen against the white background.

ANALYSIS: Spider mites
Spider mites, related to spiders, are major pests of many garden plants. They cause damage by sucking sap from the undersides of leaves. As a result of feeding, the green leaf pigment disappears, producing the stippled appearance. Mites are active during the growing season but are favored by hot, dry weather (70°F and up). By midsummer they can build up to tremendous numbers.

SOLUTION: Spray with ORTHO Isotox Insect Killer or with a pesticide containing *dicofol* (KELTHANE®) when damage is first noticed. Direct the spray to the undersides of the leaves. Repeat the application two more times at intervals of 7 days. Hose down plants frequently to knock off webs and mites.

Pieris cultural information
Light: Partial to full shade
Water: Grows best in moist soil
Soil: Loamy, well-drained
Fertilizer: Medium

PINUS (PINE)

PINUS (PINE)

ADAPTATION: Throughout the United States.

LIGHT: Full sun.

SOIL: Tolerates a wide variety of soils, but the soil should be well drained.

FERTILIZER: To avoid rank growth, do not fertilize pines heavily. When fertilizing, use ORTHO Evergreen, Tree & Shrub Food or ORTHO Azalea, Camellia & Rhododendron Food according to label directions.

WATER: Once established, pines require very little supplemental watering. Water young plants and potted plants when the soil is barely moist 2 inches below the surface. Established plants may require additional water during periods of extended drought, especially when growing in areas that normally receive water. For more information about watering, see page 912.

PRUNING: Prune to maintain shape. To slow growth or increase bushiness, cut back the candles (new growth before needles begin to emerge) at least halfway. When planting, allow large species enough room for growth. Pines often drop many needles annually. This is a natural process of growth, not a cause for concern.

PINUS (PINE) — BRANCHES DISCOLOR AND DIE

Blighted pine. *Insert:* Close-up of needles.

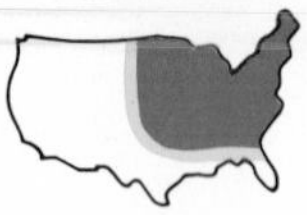

PROBLEM: New growth is stunted and brown. Dead buds and needles remain on the tree for several years, glued in place by resin (sap). With repeated infections, limbs die back and tree growth is stunted. The lowest branches are affected first. This disease may be mistaken for damage caused by insects or other diseases. Insect damage is recognized by the presence of larvae or tunnels and sawdustlike material in the shoot. No other disease causes resin production and the retention of needles.

ANALYSIS: Diplodia tip blight
This plant disease is causd by a fungus (*Diplodia pinea*) that may severely damage or kill Austrian pine. Several other types of pines may also be infected. (For a list, see page 1014.) Trees 20 to 30 years old are most susceptible. The fungus is commonly found on the decaying tissue of almost all pine trees that have died from other problems. The fungus from these and other infected trees spreads to living tissue when growing conditions are poor and trees are weakened. During moist weather in spring, spores ooze from black spore-producing bodies on dead tissue. The spores are carried by wind and rain to young needles and buds. The fungus enters and kills the tissue. Within a year, the fungus produces more spores.

SOLUTION: Spray the entire tree top with a fungicide containing *benlate* or *fixed copper* just before the buds begin to grow. Repeat 2 more times at intervals of 10 days. When the weather is dry, prune off dead branch tips. Keep trees vigorous by watering during dry periods and fertilizing every 3 to 5 years. For watering and fertilizing instructions, see pages 912 and 910.

Needle cast. *Insert:* Fruiting structures.

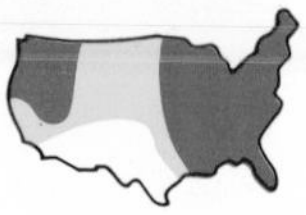

PROBLEM: The tips of the needles on last year's growth turn brown in winter. By spring, the infected needles are completely discolored, giving the tree a scorched appearance. Many needles may drop from the tree, leaving only the new green growth. Tiny, black, elongated structures develop on the midrib of dead needles. The black structures may be swollen, with cracks down the middle. In severe cases, branch tips die back. Shaded parts of the tree are more frequently infected.

ANALYSIS: Needle cast
This plant disease is caused by either of two species of fungi (*Hypoderma lethale* and *Lophodermium pinastri*). It is most severe on young pine trees, but older trees may be infected on the lower branches. In the summer, spores are released during wet weather from the elongated black fruiting structures on infected needles. Splashing rain and wind may carry the spores several hundred feet. The fungus enters the tissue but the symptoms do not appear until early the following spring. Brown spots with yellow margins develop on the needles in March or April. The fungus grows through the tissue, and by late April or May the needles are completely brown. The needles drop, and the spores from these infections continue the cycle.

SOLUTION: If needle cast was serious in the spring, spray valuable specimens with a fungicide containing *chlorothalonil* (DACONIL 2787®) starting in late July. Repeat the spray at intervals of 10 to 14 days through September. If trees are shaded, remove any shade-producing structures or plants, where practical.

Monterey pines killed by ips engraver beetles.

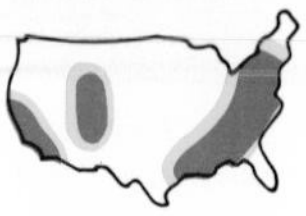

PROBLEM: The newest growth at the top of the tree turns yellow, then reddish brown. Within 4 to 6 weeks the whole tree may turn completely brown. There are numerous tiny (⅛ inch) holes in the main trunk. A sawdustlike material usually surrounds them. If the bark is peeled back around these holes, Y- or H-shaped engravings may be seen on the wood. Shiny black beetles, 3/16 inch long, with scooped-out rear ends, may be feeding in the wood.

ANALYSIS: Ips engraver beetles
(*Ips* species)
In some areas, ips beetles are serious pests of pines. Like other bark beetles, engraver beetles usually infest only weakened trees. However, trees under stress from drought, and healthy pines growing near stressed trees, are also susceptible to attack. In the spring, adults tunnel into the bark on either the upper or the lower part of the tree, depending on the species of ips beetle. A chemical substance is produced that attracts more beetles, which mate and lay their eggs in the tunnels. After the eggs hatch, the white grubs burrow under the bark, girdling the wood and cutting off the flow of nutrients and water through the trunk. The beetles also cause damage by introducing a blue stain fungus, which interrupts sap flow and hastens the death of the tree. A number of other bark beetles also infest pines (see page 435).

SOLUTION: Cut down dead trees and those trees where over 50 percent of the foliage is yellowed. Burn the wood, strip off the bark, or remove it from the area. Spray less severely infested trees with ORTHO Lindane Borer & Leaf Miner Spray. Water trees during droughts.

Sap oozing from damaged tree.

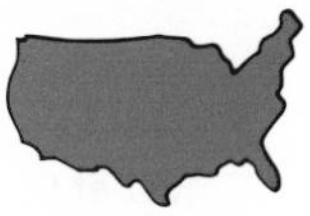

PROBLEM: Masses of pitch, often with a small tube or hole in the middle, appear on the lower part of the trunk. Pitch tubes may also appear on large exposed roots. Pitch may accumulate in piles around the base of the trunk. When the bark is cut away near a pitch mass, reddish to black beetles $\frac{1}{4}$ to $\frac{3}{8}$ inch long may be seen under the bark.

ANALYSIS: Turpentine beetles
(*Dendroctonus* species)
Turpentine beetles feed primarily on pine, and occasionally on spruce and larch; injured, weak, and dying trees are most susceptible to attack. The beetles burrow under the bark of the lower portion of tree trunks, freshly-cut logs, and stumps, where they lay their eggs. The larvae that emerge feed by tunnelling through the bark. They form pupae in their tunnels and emerge as adult beetles. A few beetles in a tree will not kill it; however, many pitch tubes indicate that enough beetles are present to kill the tree or seriously weaken it. Healthy trees can withstand numerous attacks.

SOLUTION: Knock off the pitch tubes and spray the lower 6 to 8 feet of the trunk with ORTHO Lindane Borer & Leaf Miner Spray. Keep the tree in good health by watering it thoroughly every 4 to 6 weeks during dry months. Fertilize weakened trees with ORTHO Evergreen, Tree & Shrub Food. Avoid injuring tree roots and trunk. Do not pile freshly cut pine wood or trimmings near trees because these may attract beetles to the tree.

Nematode damage to Japanese black pine.

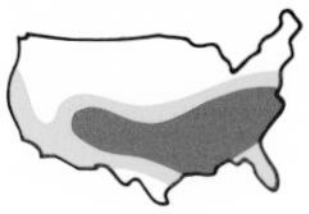

PROBLEM: The tree is yellowing and growing poorly. Branches die, or the entire tree turns brown and dies.

ANALYSIS: Root nematodes
Many different types of root nematodes infect pines. Nematodes are microscopic worms that live in the soil. They are not related to earthworms. Root nematodes feed on plant roots, damaging and stunting them. The damaged roots can't supply sufficient water and nutrients to the aboveground parts, and the plant is stunted or slowly dies. Root nematodes prefer moist, sandy loam soils. They can move only a few inches each year on their own, but they may be carried long distances by soil, water, tools, or infested plants. Testing roots and soil is the only positive method for confirming the presence of nematodes. Contact your local Cooperative Extension Office (see page 1029) for sampling instructions and addresses of testing laboratories. Soil and root problems such as poor soil structure, drought stress, nutrient deficiency, and root rots can also produce symptoms of decline similar to those caused by nematodes. These problems should be eliminated as causes before sending soil and root samples for testing. (For information on soil problems and root rots, see pages 907 and 849.) Another type of nematode that lives inside the conducting vessels causes similar aboveground symptoms.

SOLUTION: There are no chemicals available to homeowners to kill nematodes in planted soil. However, they can be controlled before planting by soil fumigation. For more information on fumigating soil, see page 927.

Pine wilt nematode damage. *Insert:* Dying shoot.

PROBLEM: Needles wilt and turn yellow, then brown. The dead needles remain on the branches. Some of the branches die, and in severe cases, the entire tree may die. Reddish brown beetles mottled with white may be seen on the bark. These beetles are 1 inch long with antennae longer than their bodies.

ANALYSIS: Pine wilt
Pine wilt is caused by microscopic nematodes *(Bursaphelenchus xylophilus)*. These nematodes usually damage only certain species of pine, but may also infest firs, spruces, and other conifers. Pine wilt is endemic to American forests, although it has been recognized as a problem only fairly recently. Pine wilt nematodes are spread by certain species of long-horned beetles, including the sawyer beetle *(Monochamus titillator)*. The beetles usually attack weak and dying trees, and transfer the nematodes from tree to tree while feeding. The nematodes damage the water-conducting vessels in the trunk and branches; this reduces or cuts off the flow of water through the tree. A diagnostic test is necessary to confirm the presence of pine wilt nematodes.

SOLUTION: If you suspect pine wilt, contact your local Cooperative Extension Office (see page 1029). They will monitor the problem and will direct you to a laboratory that can test for these nematodes. Remove and destroy all parts of infested trees. Clean up tree branches and other debris. Maintain trees in good health to reduce the chances of beetle infestation. Protect valuable specimens by spraying in late spring with an insecticide containing *lindane*. When planting, choose species resistant to pine wilt. For a list, see page 1015.

PINUS (PINE) — BRANCHES DISCOLOR AND DIE — INSECTS OR POWDERY MATERIAL ON TREE

Monterey pine damaged by spruce spider mite.

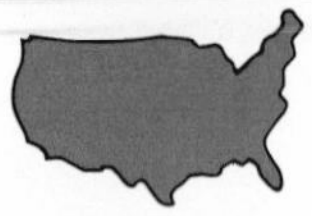

PROBLEM: Needles are stippled yellow, and dirty. Sometimes there is a silken webbing on the twigs and needles. To determine if the tree is infested with mites, hold a sheet of white paper underneath some stippled needles and tap the foliage sharply. Minute dark green or black specks the size of pepper grains will drop to the paper and begin to crawl around. The pests are easily seen against the white background.

ANALYSIS: Spruce spider mite
(*Oligonychus ununguis*)
The spruce spider mite is oneof the most damaging pests of evergreen trees. These mites suck sap from the undersides of the needles. As a result of feeding, the green leaf pigment disappears, producing the stippled appearance. This symptom may be mistaken for certain types of air pollution damage (see page 855). Spider mites first appear between April and June, hatching from eggs laid at the base of pine needles the previous October. Mites can rapidly build up to tremendous numbers during the growing season. Young pine trees may die the first season. If left uncontrolled for several years, older trees sometimes die, with symptoms progressing from the lower branches upward. Several other species of *Oligonychus* infest pines on the West Coast. Some of these mites are most numerous in the spring, while others are found throughout the summer and fall.

SOLUTION: Spray with ORTHO Isotox Insect Killer. Repeat the application two more times at intervals of 7 to 10 days. Additional sprays may be needed later in the season or in spring if the tree becomes reinfested.

Air pollution damage to white pine needles.

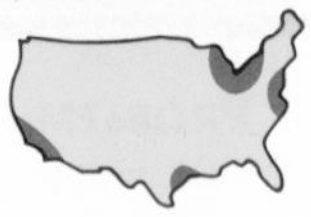

PROBLEM: The newest needles are flecked yellow, and the tips of the branches may turn red and die. The previous year's needles are deep yellow and dwarfed; many needles may drop from the branches. Repeated injury may cause the death of the tree. This problem is most noticeable in October. Air pollution damage is difficult to diagnose correctly. Damage due to fungi, insects, root injuries, and salts should be eliminated first as causes of these symptoms.

ANALYSIS: Air pollution injury
Air pollution injury, also called *white pine blight* because it was first noticed on Eastern white pine (*Pinus strobus*), is caused by ozone, a component of automobile exhaust, and sulfur dioxide, from the combustion of fossil fuels. (For more information about ozone and sulfur dioxide pollution, see page 855.) The optimum conditions of temperature, humidity, wind direction, and cloud cover, as well as of plant tissue development, are necessary for injury to occur. Therefore, air pollution damage may be more severe in certain years than in others. Injury develops as a flecking or reddening on young needles, then a yellowing and dropping of 1- or 2-year-old needles. Healthy pines also lose their older needles, but generally not until the third year.

SOLUTION: There are no controls for air pollution injury. Remove dead trees. Trees in a vigorous condition are less susceptible to severe damage. Water the trees during dry spells and fertilize regularly. For more information about watering and fertilizing trees, see pages 912 and 910.

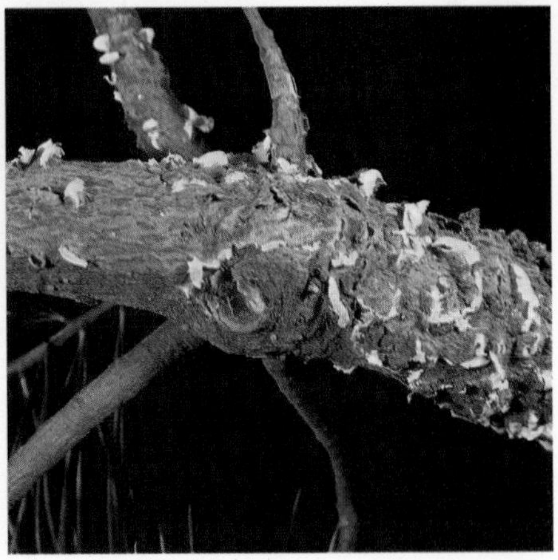

White pine blister rust.

PROBLEM: Branches or the main stem develop rough, elongated, slightly swollen areas. The infected areas are usually yellowish orange. Pitch may flow from the swollen areas. Branches or the entire tree often die. Dead foliage appears reddish brown, and may be very apparent if surrounded by green trees.

ANALYSIS: White pine blister rust
This plant disease is caused by a fungus (*Cronartium ribicola*) that alternately infects pines and either currants or gooseberries (*Ribes* species). Wind-blown spores from *Ribes* leaves infect pine needles in later summer. From there, the fungus grows into nearby branches. Small yellow to brownish spots develop. In 1 or 2 seasons, the bark develops swollen yellowish orange cankers. The canker grows, and the following season white blisters containing orange-yellow spores push through the bark. The spores are carried by the wind back to currants or gooseberies. (For more information about rust on *Ribes*, see page 721.) The pine bark in the cankered area dries out and cracks, resulting in the death of the underlying wood. The branches and foliage above this area die and turn reddish brown.

SOLUTION: Remove all gooseberry and currant bushes, including the root systems—which are capable of resprouting—for at least 1,000 feet from white pines. Cut off and destroy infected pine branches. Cankers on the trunk can be removed surgically with some success if all discolored bark and wood is destroyed, including a border of apparently healthy bark and wood. Use a sharp knife sterilized with rubbing alcohol after each cut. Spray the wound with a fungicide containing *cycloheximide*.

Woolly aphids on Austrian pine (life size).

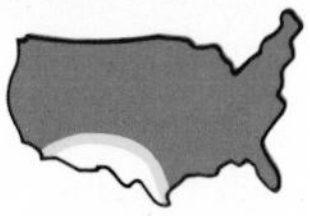

PROBLEM: The needles or trunk are covered with white, woolly masses. If the infestation is heavy, the tree appears to be covered with snow. Infested shoots may droop; the needles turn yellow and may die. Trees heavily infested for several years are usually stunted.

ANALYSIS: Woolly aphids
(*Pinus* species)
These small (1/8 inch), soft-bodied insects are not true aphids, but they are closely related. The adults are always covered with dense white filaments of wax. When this substance is removed, the insects appear purplish or green. Some species of these woolly "aphids" spend part of their life on other types of evergreens, usually spruce, often producing galls on the branches. In early summer, the insects migrate to pines and suck sap from the needles. Other species spend their entire life on pines, feeding and reproducing on the trunks. Those species that spend the winter on other plants produce a generation in the fall that flies to the winter host.

SOLUTION: Control with ORTHO Isotox Insect Killer or ORTHO Malathion 50 Insect Spray. Spray pines with infested trunks in late April; spray pines with infested needles in late June. Cover the tree thoroughly. Repeat the spray if the plant becomes reinfested.

Pine needle scale (life size).

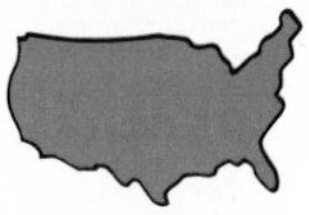

PROBLEM: Needles are covered with clusters of somewhat flattened, white scaly bumps. When heavily infested, the foliage may appear completely white. The bumps can be scraped or picked off; the undersides are usually soft. Needles turn brown and eventually drop. Repeated severe infestations may kill young trees or weaken older trees.

ANALYSIS: Pine needle scale
(*Chionaspis pinifoliae*)
These scale insects may seriously damage pine and spruce trees and may infest fir, hemlock, and cedar. The scales survive the winter on the pine needles as eggs beneath the dead mother scales. The eggs hatch in late spring and the young scales, called *crawlers*, move to new green needles. The small (1/10 inch) soft-bodied young feed by inserting their mouthparts and sucking sap from the plant. The legs atrophy and a crusty white shell develops over the body. The mature female scales lay their eggs underneath their shell in July. This next generation feeds throughout late summer and matures in fall. Females of this generation lay the overwintering eggs.

SOLUTION: Spray young trees with ORTHO Isotox Insect Killer or ORTHO Orthene Systemic Insect Control in late spring when the young are active. The following early spring, before new growth begins and when the danger of frost is past, spray with a pesticide containing *lime sulfur* to kill the overwintering eggs. Inspect ornamental pines twice a year for evidence of infestation. Older trees seldom require controls.

Irregular pine scale (3 times life size).

PROBLEM: Cream-colored, rough, scaly bumps with a black dot at one end appear on the branches. A shiny or sticky substance coats the needles. A black, sooty mold may be growing on the sticky substance. In heavy infestations, needles may be yellow or brown and shorter than normal. Young Monterey pine trees may be killed.

ANALYSIS: Irregular pine scale
(*Toumeyella pinicola*)
Where it occurs, this is the most serious scale insect of pine. Monterey pine (*Pinus radiata*) is particularly susceptible, but the scale attacks many other pines as well. The female scales lay their eggs on the needles or bark. In late winter or early spring, the young scales, called *crawlers*, settle on various parts of the trees. These small (1/10 inch), soft-bodied young feed by sucking sap from the plant. The legs usually atrophy and a hard crusty or waxy shell develops over the body. The scales are unable to digest all the sugar in the plant sap, and excrete the excess in a fluid called honeydew. A sooty mold fungus may develop on the honeydew. Irregular pine scale produces one generation a year.

SOLUTION: Spray in the early spring when the young are active. Use ORTHO Orthene Systemic Insect Control, ORTHO Isotox Insect Killer, ORTHO Malathion 50 Insect Spray, or ORTHO Sevin Garden Spray. Cover the needles thoroughly with spray. Make two applications: 2 to 3 weeks after crawlers first begin emerging in the early spring and 2 to 3 weeks later. Sprays at other times of the year do not provide effective control.

PINUS (PINE) — INSECTS OR POWDERY MATERIAL ON TREE

Needle rust.

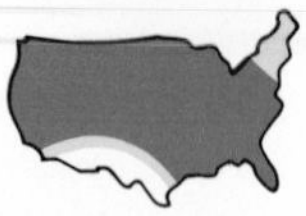

PROBLEM: Cream-colored, baglike pustules, 1/16 to 1/8 inch long, develop on the needles in the spring. The pustules rupture, releasing bright orange spores. Trees with heavy infestations often drop many needles. Young trees may be stunted.

ANALYSIS: Needle rust
This plant disease is caused by any of several different fungi (*Coleosporium* species) that infect pine trees, goldenrods, and asters. The fungi cannot spread from pine tree to pine tree, but must alternate between pines and goldenrods or asters. Wind-borne spores from goldenrods or asters infect pine needles in summer and fall. The following spring, cream-colored pustules (blisters) develop, and needles may drop. The pustules rupture, and orange spores are blown to goldenrods and asters, where bright orange-yellow pustules develop on the undersides of the leaves.

SOLUTION: Spray young or valuable pine trees with a fungicide containing *ferbam* or *zineb*. Where practical, remove goldenrods and asters around pines.

Aphids on white pine (life size).

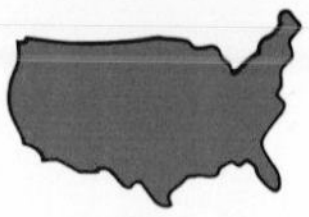

PROBLEM: Needles are discolored and may be deformed; many may drop from the tree. New growth is often slowed, and twigs may die. A shiny, sticky substance often coats the needles and branches. A black sooty mold may grow on the sticky substance. Small (up to 1/6 inch), green, brown, or black soft-bodied insects cluster on the needles, twigs, or main stems of small trees. An uncontrolled infestation may kill young trees.

ANALYSIS: Aphids
(*Cinara* species and *Eulachnus* species)
Several different aphids infest the needles or bark of pines. Aphids do little damage in small numbers. However, they are extremely prolific and populations can rapidly build up to damaging numbers during the growing season. Damage occurs when the aphid sucks the juices from the pine needles, growing tips, or bark. The aphid is unable to digest fully all the sugar in the sap and excretes the excess in a fluid called honeydew, which often drops onto the needles and bark below. Plants or objects beneath the tree may also be coated with honeydew. A sooty mold fungus may develop on the honeydew, causing the pine needles, bark, or other coated plants to appear black and dirty. Ants feed on this sticky substance, and are often present where there is an aphid infestation. For more information about aphids, see page 875.

SOLUTION: Control with ORTHO Isotox Insect Killer or ORTHO Malathion 50 Insect Spray when aphids first appear. Repeat the spray if the tree becomes reinfested in mid or late summer.

Pine spittlebug (3 times life size).

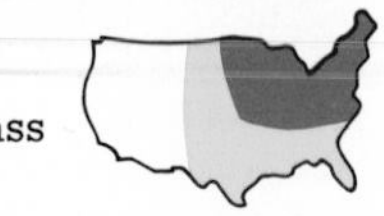

PROBLEM: A frothy mass of bubbles appears on the twigs at the base of the needles. A small (1/4 inch) tan or green wingless insect may be found inside the mass. Needles may turn yellow and drop off; black sooty mold may grow on surrounding branches. Continuous heavy infestations of insects kill branches or cause the death of young or weak trees.

ANALYSIS: Pine and Saratoga spittlebugs
(*Aphrophora parellela* and *A. saratogensis*)
The pine spittlebug may cause serious injury to Scotch and white pines. The Saratoga spittlebug kills branches of jack and red pines. The pine spittlebug adults are grayish brown, wedge-shaped insects, 1/2 inch long. The females lay their eggs at the base of buds in late summer. The eggs hatch the following May, and the young insects suck the sap from twigs and the main trunk. Drops of undigested sap mixed with air are excreted by the bug, producing the frothy "spittle" that surrounds its body. Some of the excreted sap drops onto lower branches, which may be colonized by a black sooty mold fungus. The life cycle of the Saratoga spittlebug is similar, but the tan females lay their eggs on plants beneath the tree. The adults migrate to trees in late June, feed until late fall, and then return to the low-growing plants to lay their eggs.

SOLUTION: Spray with ORTHO Isotox Insect Killer when insects are first noticed—in late May and again in July for the pine spittlebug, and in late June or early July for the Saratoga spittlebug. Use high pressures.

Pine webworm.

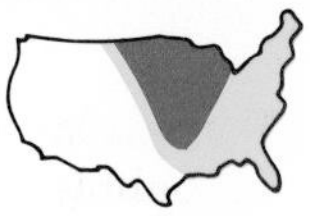

PROBLEM: Brown, globular nests made of silk, brown needles, and a sawdustlike material appear on the ends of branches in early or midsummer. The branches are often stripped of most of their foliage, and tree growth is slowed. Light brown caterpillars, up to ¾ inch long, may be feeding inside the nests.

ANALYSIS: Pine webworm
(*Tetralopha robustella*)
This webworm is found throughout the eastern United States on many different pines. The nests are unsightly only; rarely are trees seriously injured. The gray moths lay their eggs on pine needles between May and September. When the eggs hatch, the larvae feed within the needles until they are too large. Then they construct nests made of silk, dead needles, and brown excrement, which they wrap around twigs. Each nest may contain from 1 to 75 or more worms. When mature, the insects drop to the ground and pupate below the soil surface. In the South, moths may emerge to repeat the cycle one more time. The webworms spend the winter in the soil.

SOLUTION: Cut out and destroy the nests. Or spray with an insecticide containing *carbaryl* (SEVIN®), or the bacterial insecticide *Bacillus thuringiensis* when the larvae are small and before the needles are webbed in mid-June. Repeat the spray in early August if the tree becomes reinfested.

Sawfly larvae (life size).

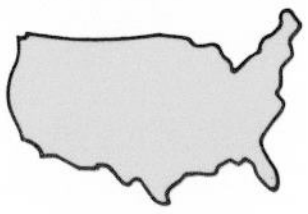

PROBLEM: The needles are partially chewed, or the entire branch may be defoliated. In some cases, only the younger needles are eaten. Usually, however, the older needles are preferred. Gray-green, tan, or black caterpillarlike larvae, up to an inch long, are clustered on the needles. The larvae have many legs (prolegs) on their abdomens.

ANALYSIS: Sawflies
(*Neodiprion* species and *Diprion* species)
Many species of sawflies infest pines. The dark, clear-winged adults are nonstinging wasps. The females insert rows of eggs in the needles with sawlike egg-laying organs. The larvae that hatch from these eggs feed in groups on the outer part of the needles. As the larvae grow, they feed on a larger portion of the foliage; eventually, entire needles are devoured. Small trees may be completely defoliated. The larvae then move to adjacent trees to feed. Some species of sawflies feed only in the spring or summer. Others are present throughout the growing season, producing five or six generations a year. When the larvae mature, they drop to the ground and spin cocoons. Most sawflies spend the winter in the soil, although several species overwinter as eggs on the needles.

SOLUTION: Spray the needles with ORTHO Orthene Systemic Insect Control or ORTHO Isotox Insect Killer when damage or the insects are first noticed. Inspect the trees periodically during the growing season to detect infestations before severe defoliation occurs.

European pine shoot moth damage.

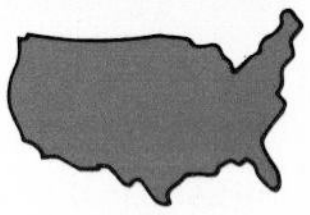

PROBLEM: Branch tips turn yellow, then brown and dry. The dead branches contrast sharply with healthy green foliage. In the summer, pitch accumulates around the dead needles. Trees may appear bushier than normal, or they may be crooked and distorted. At the base of needles or inside a brown, resin-coated tip, cream-colored to reddish brown worms, up to ¾ inch long, may be found feeding on the tissue. Young trees may die.

ANALYSIS: Pine tip or shoot moths
(*Rhyacionia* species)
Seven species of tip moths infest various pines in different parts of the country. The adult is a reddish brown and gray moth, up to an inch long. The moths fly at night, but they may be seen during the day if a branch is disturbed. The moths lay their eggs in mid to late spring at the ends of branches. The larvae that hatch from these eggs bore into needles and buds where they feed and mature. Depending on the species, pupation occurs in the mined out area or in the soil around the base of the tree. Most species of tip moths produce one generation a year. The Nantucket pine tip moth, *Ryacionia frustrana*, has as many as four or five generations yearly in warm climates.

SOLUTION: If practical, prune out and destroy infested twigs in May or early June. Spray with ORTHO Orthene Systemic Insect Control or ORTHO Isotox Insect Killer in mid-April or early May. Repeat the spray in mid-May. If reinfestation occurs the same year, the Nantucket pine tip moth is probably involved. Repeat sprays every 4 weeks from early May to August may be necessary.

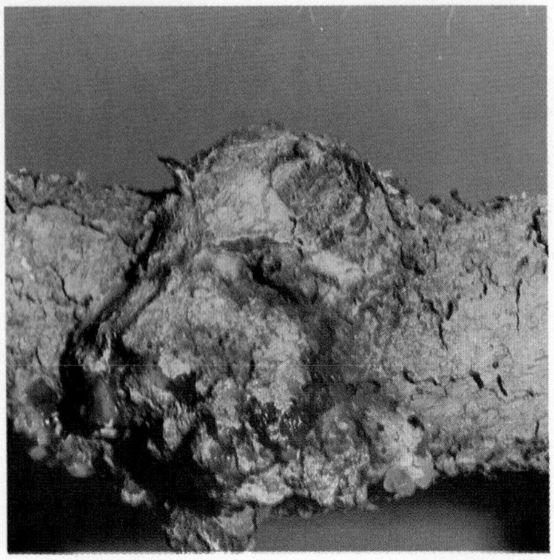

Pitch moth damage.

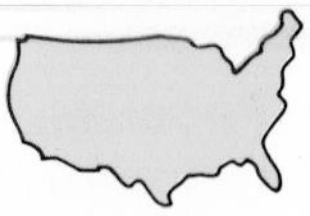

PROBLEM: One or more masses of sticky cream, yellow, or pinkish pitch appear on the trunk. These masses may be 2 or 3 inches wide and protrude 1 to 2 inches from the side of the trunk. The pitch masses are usually found in wounds or in branch crotches. When the pitch mass is scraped away, a larva up to 1 inch long may be found underneath.

ANALYSIS: Pitch moths
(*Vespamima* species)
Pitch moths attack pine, spruce, and Douglas fir. The adults are clear-winged moths that resemble yellowjackets. They lay eggs during the spring and summer in the trunks and larger limbs, particularly at sites of recent trunk injury or where old pitch masses exist. Usually there is one larva per pitch mass. It feeds on the inner bark for 1 to 2 years, pupates, and finally emerges as the adult moth during the summer. Although pitch masses are unsightly, pitch moths do not usually threaten the life of a tree. However, tree limbs may be weakened enough to break under the weight of snow.

SOLUTION: Scrape away fresh pitch masses and kill the larva. The larva can be found in the bark under the pitch mass or in the pitch mass itself. Avoid mechanical injury to trees. Confine pruning of larger limbs to fall and early winter months.

White pine weevil damage.

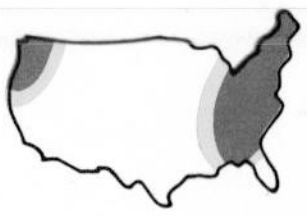

PROBLEM: The main shoot at the top of the tree stops growing and turns yellow in midsummer. The shoot tip usually droops, producing a "shepherd's crook." Several new shoots may develop from below the dying shoot so that the top of the tree is forked. In fall and winter the drooping shoot appears brown and dry. There is a white resin on the bark, and small holes in the dead shoot.

ANALYSIS: White pine weevil
(*Pissodes strobi*)
The white pine weevil attacks the leaders of both pines and spruce. This small (1/5 inch), brown, snouted beetle with white patches spends the winter in dead plant material at the base of the tree. In the spring, just before new growth begins, it moves to the top of the tree to feed on the inner bark tissue. Eggs are then laid in small punctures in the bark. Resin droplets ooze from the punctures, which later dry and turn white. The 1/4-inch larvae that hatch from these eggs bore into the wood. The feeding cuts off the flow of water and nutrients through the stem, causing the shoot to droop and die. Several new shoots often develop from below the dead shoot, destroying the natural shape of the tree. In late summer, the larvae mature and return to the ground to spend the winter.

SOLUTION: Control the adults with ORTHO Lindane Borer & Leaf Miner Spray in late April when the buds begin to swell. Spray the top of the tree thoroughly. It is usually impractical to spray large trees. Prune out and destroy infested twigs in early June before the beetles emerge. Train one side branch to replace the dead leader by pruning off all but one of the new shoots.

Western gall rust on Monterey pine.

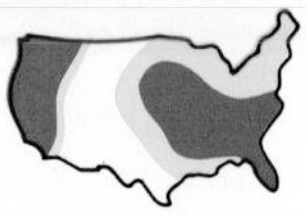

PROBLEM: Rough, spherical swellings develop on branches or on the main trunk. In the spring, the swellings appear orange or yellow. Growth beyond the galls is often stunted, distorted, and off-color.

ANALYSIS: Western gall rust and eastern gall rust
These plant diseases are caused by two species of fungi (*Cronartium harknessii* and *C. quercuum*). Western gall rust requires only one host to complete its life cycle; spores from one pine can infect another. Eastern gall rust requires both pine and oak to complete its life cycle. In early spring, orange or yellow spores are produced over the ruptured surfaces of the swellings (galls). The spores are blown and carried by wind and insects to susceptible trees. When moisture and temperatures are optimum, western gall rust spores infect pine tissue, causing an increase in the number and size of plant cells. Within 6 months to a year, swellings develop. The galls enlarge and produce spores after 1 to 2 years. Eastern gall rust spores infect only oak. Spores produced on the oak trees reinfect pines. The galls caused by both fungi interrupt the sap movement in the tree. They also stimulate witch's brooms, dense stunted growth beyond the galls. If many of these develop the tree becomes unsightly and weak, and limbs break during storms.

SOLUTION: Where practical, prune off galled branches before the galls produce spores in early spring.

PISTACIA (PISTACHE)

Verticillium wilt. *Insert:* Infected stem.

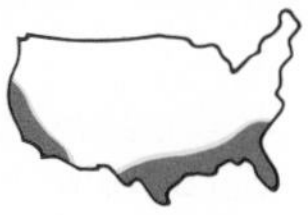

PROBLEM: The leaves on a branch turn yellow at the margins, then brown and dry. During hot weather, the leaves may wilt. New leaves may be stunted and yellowish. The infected tree may die slowly, branch by branch, over several seasons. Some trees may recover. The tissue under the bark on the dying side shows dark streaks when cut. To examine for streaks, peel back the bark at the bottom of the dying branch.

ANALYSIS: Verticillium wilt
This wilt disease affects many ornamental trees and shrubs. It is caused by a soil-inhabiting fungus (*Verticillium* species). The disease is spread by contaminated seeds, plants, soil, equipment, and ground water. The fungus enters the tree through the roots and spreads up into the branches through the water-conducting vessels in the stems. The vessels become discolored and plugged. This plugging cuts off the flow of water and nutrients to the branches, causing the leaf discoloration and wilting. For more information about verticillium, see page 850.

SOLUTION: No chemical control is available. Fertilize and water the affected plant to stimulate vigorous growth. Prune off all dead wood. Remove dead plants. If replanting in the same area, plant trees or shrubs that are resistant to verticillium.

Pistacia cultural information
Light: Full sun
Water: Moist or dry soil
Soil: Well drained
Fertilizer: Light

PITTOSPORUM

Aphid damage.

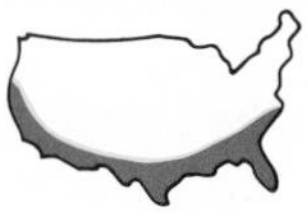

PROBLEM: The newest leaves are wrinkled and yellowing. Leaves may drop off, and new growth may be slowed. A shiny, sticky substance often coats the leaves. A black sooty mold may grow on the sticky substance. Tiny (1/8 inch) greenish yellow soft-bodied insects cluster on the underside of leaves and on branch tips. Ants may be present.

ANALYSIS: Aphids
Aphids do little damage in small numbers. However, they are extremely prolific and populations can rapidly build up to damaging numbers during the growing season. Damage occurs when the aphid sucks the juices from the pittosporum leaves. The aphid is unable to digest fully all the sugar in the plant sap and excretes the excess in a fluid called honeydew, which often drops onto the leaves below. A sooty mold fungus may develop on the honeydew, causing the pittosporum leaves to appear black and dirty. Ants feed on this sticky substance, and are often present where there is an aphid infestation. For more information about aphids, see page 875.

SOLUTION: Control with ORTHO Orthene Insect Spray or ORTHO Isotox Insect Killer when aphids first appear. Direct the spray to the undersides of the leaves. Repeat the spray if the plant becomes reinfested.

Pittosporum cultural information
Light: Full sun to part shade
Water: Allow the soil to dry between waterings
Soil: Loose, well drained
Fertilizer: Medium

Cottony cushion scale (twice life size).

PROBLEM: The undersides of the leaves, stems, branch crotches, and trunk are covered with white, cottony, cushionlike masses. Leaves may turn yellow and drop. A shiny, sticky substance may coat the leaves. A black sooty mold often grows on the sticky substance. Numerous side shoots may grow out of an infested crotch area. Twigs and branches may die back.

ANALYSIS: Cottony scales and mealybugs
Cottony scales and mealybugs are common on pittosporum wherever it is grown. The similarity in appearance between these insects makes separate identification difficult. They are very conspicuous in late spring and summer because the females are covered with a white, cottony egg sac, containing up to 2500 eggs. Females lay their egg masses on leaves or branches. The young insects that hatch from these eggs are yellowish brown to green. They feed throughout the summer on the trunk, stems, and leaves. Damage is caused by the withdrawal of plant sap from the leaves and branches. The insects are unable to digest fully all the sugar in the plant sap and excrete the excess in a fluid called honeydew, which often drops onto the leaves below. A sooty mold fungus may develop on the honeydew, causing the pittosporum leaves to appear black and dirty. Leaf drop and twig dieback occur when the white masses completely cover the leaves and branches.

SOLUTION: Spray with ORTHO Isotox Insect Killer in midsummer when the young are active. The following spring, when the tree is dormant, spray with ORTHO Volck Oil Spray to control overwintering insects on the bark.

PLATANUS

ADAPTATION: Zones 4 through 9. (To determine your zone, see the map on page 1020.) Adapted to harsh city conditions.

LIGHT: Full sun.

SOIL: Tolerates a wide variety of soils. pH 5.5 to 7.5

FERTILIZER: Fertilize with ORTHO Evergreen, Tree & Shrub Food according to label directions.

WATER: Once established, plane trees require very little supplemental watering. Water newly transplanted and young trees when the soil is barely moist 2 inches below the surface. For more information about watering, see page 912.

PRUNING: Prune to maintain shape. Plane trees can also be pollarded (branches cut back to the same spot every year), producing a dense, ball-shaped growth habit. When planting, allow enough room for the height and large trunk of these trees.

Powdery mildew.

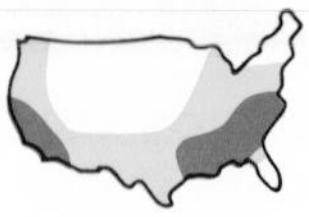

PROBLEM: Young leaves and twigs are covered with a thin layer or irregular patches of grayish white powdery material. Infected leaves are distorted, and many may turn yellow and drop off. New growth is often stunted. In late summer, tiny black dots (spore-producing bodies) are scattered over the white patches like ground pepper. The problem is often more serious on heavily pruned trees.

ANALYSIS: Powdery mildew
This common plant disease is caused by a fungus (*Microsphaera alni*) that thrives in both humid and dry weather. The powdery patches consist of fungal strands and spores. The spores are spread by the wind to healthy plants. The fungus saps the plant nutrients, causing distortion, yellowing, and sometimes death of the leaf. Since this mildew attacks many different kinds of trees, the fungus from a diseased tree may infect other trees in the garden. For a list of susceptible plants, see page 1006.

SOLUTION: Spray young trees with a fungicide containing *benlate* or *karathane* when the trees show the first sign of mildew. It is seldom practical to spray large trees. When planting new trees, plant the resistant variety Yarwood if it is adapted to your climate.

Sycamore lacebug damage.

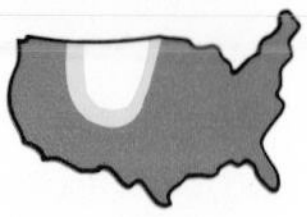

PROBLEM: The upper surfaces of the leaves are mottled or speckled white and green. The mottling may be confused with mite or leafhopper damage. However, it can be distinguished from damage caused by other insects by the shiny, hard, brown droplets found on the undersides of damaged leaves. Small (1/8 inch), light or dark, spiny, wingless insects, or brownish insects with clear lacy wings, may be visible around the droplets. Foliage on severely infested trees may be completely white, then turn brown by mid-August.

ANALYSIS: Sycamore lacebug
(*Corythucha* species)
Two species of lacebugs infest sycamores and London plane trees. They survive the winter as adults in bark crevices or in other protected areas on the tree. When the buds begin to open in the spring, the adults attach their eggs to the undersides of the leaves with a brown, sticky substance. The eggs hatch and the spiny, wingless, immature insects, and later the brown lacy-winged adults, suck sap from the undersides of the leaves. The green leaf pigment disappears, resulting in the characteristic white and green mottling. As the lacebugs feed, droplets of brown excrement accumulate around them.

SOLUTION: Spray young trees with ORTHO Isotox Insect Killer or ORTHO Orthene Systemic Insect Control when damage first appears in spring. Cover the undersurfaces of the leaves thoroughly. Repeat 7 to 10 days later. It is important to spray early, preventing as much damage as possible. It is usually impractical to spray large trees.

Anthracnose. *Insert:* Spore-producing bodies.

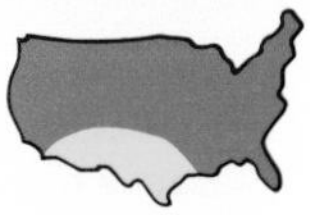

PROBLEM: In the spring, buds or expanding shoots turn brown and die. Dead areas appear along the veins of young leaves. As the leaves mature, the spots may expand and cover them entirely. Most infected leaves drop from the tree. Later in the season, twigs and older leaves may be infected. Infected twigs hang on the tree or drop to the ground with the leaves. Larger limbs may die. Dark brown spore-producing bodies appear on the bark and dead leaves. The tree is often stunted and bushy.

ANALYSIS: Sycamore anthracnose
This plant disease is caused by a fungus (*Gnomonia platani*) that is the most serious problem of sycamore and causes minor damage to the London plane tree. The fungus survives the winter on fallen leaves and twigs, and in swollen cankers in the tree. During cool (below 55°F), wet weather, spores are blown and splashed onto buds, expanding shoots, and young leaves. The fungus enters the tissue and kills it, causing the buds and shoots to die back. The fungus moves down onto the twigs, and spores develop. The spores may infect mature leaves or any new growth on the tree, causing a sun-scorched appearance. Swollen, cracked cankers develop on infected twigs and branches. When the cankers encircle the wood, the limbs die.

SOLUTION: Prune off and destroy infected twigs and dead branches. In areas where spring is cool and moist, spray trees with a fungicide containing *chlorothalonil* (DACONIL 2787®) when buds begin to grow in the spring. Repeat when leaves reach full size, and again 2 weeks later.

Summer leaf scorch.

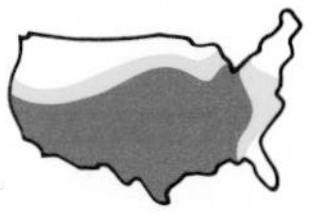

PROBLEM: During hot weather, usually in July or August, leaves turn brown around the edges and between the veins. Sometimes the whole leaf dies. Many leaves may drop during late summer. This problem is most severe on the youngest branches. Trees do not usually die. This problem may be mistaken for damage caused by anthracnose or lacebugs. However, the brown areas caused by anthracnose cross over the veins and often cover the entire leaf. Lacebugs leave brown droplets of excrement on the lower surfaces of the leaves.

ANALYSIS: Summer leaf scorch
Leaf scorch is caused by excessive evaporation of moisture from the leaves. In hot weather, water evaporates rapidly from the leaves. If the roots can't absorb and convey water fast enough to replenish this loss, the leaves turn brown and wither. This usually occurs in dry soil, but leaves can also scorch when the soil is moist. Drying winds, severed roots, limited soil area or salts in the soil also cause scorch. For more information about scorch, see page 857.

SOLUTION: To prevent further scorch, deep-water trees during periods of hot weather to wet the entire root space. (For more information about watering trees, see page 912.) Newly transplanted trees should be watered whenever the rootball is dry 2 inches below the surface. There are no controls for scorch occurring on trees in moist soil. Plant trees adapted to your climate.

Cankers.

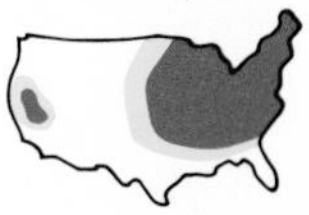

PROBLEM: The leaves are small and yellow on part or all of the tree, and the foliage is sparse. Dark, elongated, sunken areas appear on the trunk or larger branches. If an affected branch is cut off, bluish black or reddish discoloration is seen running toward the center of the wood.

ANALYSIS: Canker stain disease
This plant disease, caused by a fungus (*Ceratocystis fimbriata* f. *platani*), is very destructive to the London plane tree (*Platanus acerifolia*). Other sycamores may also be affected. The fungus is very contagious. It enters the tree through a wound, or may be spread by pruning tools, ladders, contaminated wound dressings, or sap-feeding beetles. The surrounding healthy tissue is killed and a sunken canker develops. The vessels become discolored and plugged as the fungus spreads through the wood. This plugging cuts off the flow of water and nutrients, causing leaf yellowing and the death of the branch or tree.

SOLUTION: Avoid all unnecessary cutting, and avoid injuring trees. Prune trees in winter when the fungus is less active. Disinfect tools after each use with rubbing alcohol. Remove and destroy infected trees.

Giant bark aphids (life size).

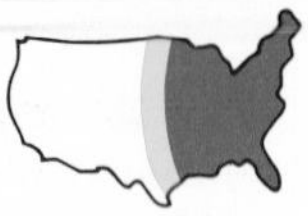

PROBLEM: Small (¼ inch) black and beige soft-bodied insects with long black legs cluster on twigs and the undersides of limbs. Twigs may be completely covered with a mat of black eggs. When populations are large, twigs and branches die back. A shiny, sticky substance may coat the limbs. A black sooty mold often grows on the sticky substance. Ants may be present.

ANALYSIS: Giant bark aphid
(*Longistigma caryae*)
The giant bark aphid is the largest species of aphid known. Because of its long legs, it appears much larger than its actual size of ¼ inch. The aphids do little damage in small numbers. However, they are extremely prolific and populations can rapidly build up to damaging numbers during the late summer. When populations are large, black eggs are matted all over the bark of infested limbs. Damage occurs when the aphid sucks the juices from the twigs and branches. The aphid is unable to digest fully all the sugar in the sap, and excretes the excess in large quantities in a fluid called honeydew, which often coats plants or objects beneath the tree. A sooty mold fungus may develop on the honeydew, causing the bark to appear black and dirty. Ants feed on the sticky substance, and are often present where there is an aphid infestation. Several other species of aphids may infest sycamore leaves and twigs.

SOLUTION: Spray with ORTHO Isotox Insect Killer or ORTHO Liquid Sevin when aphids first appear. Spray the bark thoroughly. Repeat the spray if the tree becomes reinfested.

Aphids (twice life size).

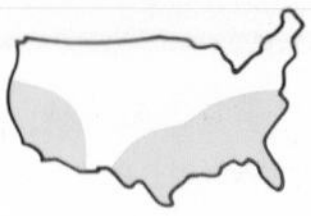

PROBLEM: Leaves near branch tips may be curled and are sometimes covered with a shiny or sticky substance. Gray-blue, ⅛-inch, soft-bodied insects cluster on the stems and undersides of the leaves, especially on new growth.

ANALYSIS: Aphids
Aphids do little damage in small numbers. However, they are extremely prolific and populations can rapidly build up to damaging numbers during the growing season. Damage occurs when the aphid sucks the juices from the podocarpus leaves. The aphid is unable to digest fully all the sugar in the plant sap and excretes the excess in a sugary material called honeydew, which often drops onto the leaves below. A sooty mold fungus may develop on the honeydew, causing the podocarpus leaves to appear black and dirty. Ants feed on the honeydew, and are often present where there is an aphid infestation. For more information about aphids, see page 875.

SOLUTION: Apply ORTHO Isotox Insect Killer at recommended rates. Repeat sprayings as needed according to label directions to keep aphids from reinfesting the plant.

Podocarpus cultural information
Light: Full sun to part shade
Water: When the soil is almost dry
Soil: Loose, well drained
Fertilizer: Light to medium

Wax scale (life size).

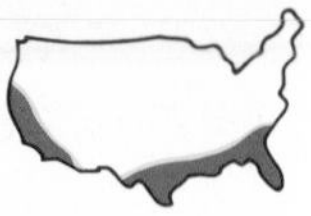

PROBLEM: The stems or the undersides of the leaves are covered with somewhat flattened yellowish, brown, or white scaly bumps. The bumps can be scraped or picked off; the undersides are usually soft. Leaves turn yellow and may drop, and twigs and branches may die.

ANALYSIS: Scales
Several different types of scales infest podocarpus. They lay their eggs on the trunk and twigs, and in spring to early summer the young scales, called *crawlers*, settle on leaves and twigs. The small (1/10 inch), soft-bodied young feed by inserting their mouthparts and sucking sap from the plant. The legs usually atrophy and a crusty shell develops over the body. The mature female scales lay their eggs underneath their shell. An uncontrolled infestation of scales may kill the plant after two or three seasons. For more information about scales, see page 876.

SOLUTION: Spray with ORTHO Isotox Insect Killer, ORTHO Orthene Systemic Insect Control, or ORTHO Liquid Sevin when the young are active. Contact your local Cooperative Extension Office (see page 1029) to determine the best time to spray for scales in your area. The following winter or spring, spray the trunk and branches with a *dormant oil spray* to control overwintering insects.

POPULUS (POPLAR, ASPEN, COTTONWOOD)

POPULUS

ADAPTATION: Throughout the United States.

LIGHT: Full sun.

SOIL: Tolerates a wide variety of soils. Roots are invasive.

FERTILIZER: Fertilize with ORTHO Evergreen, Tree & Shrub Food according to label directions.

WATER:
How much: Apply enough water to wet the soil 3 to 4 feet deep. To determine the proper amount of water for your soil type, see page 912.
How often: Some poplars are drought tolerant once established. However, most poplars prefer moist soils, and some even tolerate soils that are soggy or flooded.

PRUNING: Prune off suckers and broken branches, and prune to maintain shape.

Slime flux.

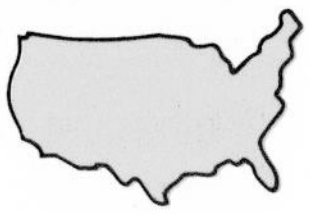

PROBLEM: Sour-smelling sap oozes from wounds, cracks, and branch crotches, mainly during the growing season. The sap drips down the bark and dries, causing unsightly gray streaks. There may be some wilting on affected branches. Insects are attracted to the sour-smelling ooze.

ANALYSIS: Slime flux
Slime flux of poplars, also called *wetwood*, is caused by a bacterium (*Erwinia nimipressuralis*). The bacteria affect the heartwood, producing abnormally high sap pressure. The pressure is caused by bacterial fermentation, and forces the fermented sap, or flux, out of the wounds, cracks, or crotches in the tree. Flux is especially copious when the tree is growing rapidly. Large areas of the bark may be coated with the smelly, bacteria-laden sap, which dries to a grayish white color. In addition, wounds do not heal and the bark is unsightly. A tree with this problem is often under water stress, which may cause drought damage (wilting and scorched leaves) to the branches. The problem may persist for many years.

SOLUTION: There are no chemical controls for this condition. Bore a slightly slanted drainage hole through the wood below each oozing wound. Insert a ½-inch-diameter plastic tube, just until it holds firmly in place. If the tube penetrates the water-soaked wood inside the tree, it will interfere with drainage. The tube will carry the dripping sap away from the trunk. Disinfect tools with rubbing alcohol after pruning infected trees.

Satin moth caterpillars (life size).

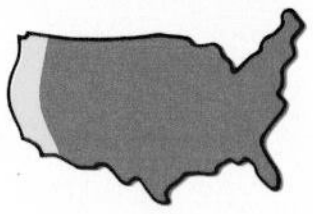

PROBLEM: The surface of the leaf is eaten, giving the remaining tissue a lacy appearance, or the whole leaf is chewed. Sometimes leaves or branches are webbed. The tree may be completely defoliated. Damage appears any time between spring and fall. Caterpillars are feeding on the leaves. Repeated heavy infestations may weaken or kill trees.

ANALYSIS: Leaf-feeding caterpillars
Many different species of caterpillars feed on poplar leaves wherever the trees are grown. Depending on the species, the moths lay their eggs from early spring to midsummer. The larvae that hatch from these eggs feed singly or in groups on buds, on one leaf surface (skeletonizers), or on the entire leaf. Certain caterpillars web leaves together, or web a branch as they feed. In some years, damage is minimal due to unfavorable environmental conditions or control by predators and parasites. However, when conditions are favorable, entire trees may be defoliated by late summer. Defoliation weakens trees because there are no leaves left to produce food. When heavy infestations occur several years in a row, branches or entire trees may be killed.

SOLUTION: Spray with ORTHO Isotox Insect Killer, ORTHO Liquid Sevin, or with the bacterial insecticide *Bacillus thuringiensis* when damage is first noticed. Cover the leaves thoroughly. Repeat the spray if the tree becomes reinfested.

POPULUS (POPLAR, ASPEN, COTTONWOOD)

Damaged leaves. *Insert:* Leaf beetles (half life size).

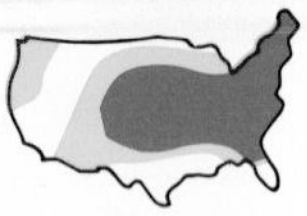

PROBLEM: The leaf tissue is eaten between the veins, giving the leaves a lacy appearance. Sometimes only the major veins remain. The bark of young trees may be chewed. Small blackish larvae or ¼-inch-long yellow beetles with round or oblong black spots are feeding on the leaves. Clusters of yellow eggs may be found on the lower sufaces of the leaves. With repeated infestations, young trees may die.

ANALYSIS: Leaf beetles
(*Chrysomela* species)
Several species of leaf beetles may seriously damage poplars, especially in urban plantings. They spend the winter as adults under the bark in plant debris on the ground, or in homes. When new growth begins in the spring, the beetles fly to trees to feed on the leaves and twigs. The females lay groups of yellow eggs on the undersides of the leaves. The clusters of larvae that hatch from these eggs feed on the leaf tissue between the veins, skeletonizing the leaf. There are four or more generations of leaf beetles each year, so larvae and adults may be present throughout the growing season.

SOLUTION: Spray with ORTHO Isotox Insect Killer when damage is first noticed in spring. If necessary, repeat the spray in mid-July.

Oystershell scales (¼ life size).

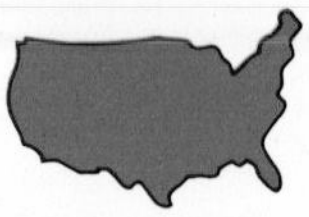

PROBLEM: The trunk, stems, or the undersides of the leaves are covered with brown, black, or red-orange crusty bumps or somewhat flattened brownish, white, or grayish scaly bumps. The bumps can be scraped or picked off; the undersides are usually soft. Leaves turn yellow and may drop. In some cases, a shiny, sticky substance coats the leaves. A black sooty mold often grows on the sticky substance. Large portions of the tree may be killed if infestations are heavy.

ANALYSIS: Scales
Many different types of scales infest poplar. They lay their eggs on leaves or bark, and in spring to midsummer the young scales, called *crawlers*, settle on leaves, twigs, and the trunk. The small (⅒ inch), soft-bodied young feed by sucking sap from the plant. The legs usually atrophy and a hard crusty shell develops over the body. The mature female scales lay their eggs underneath the shell. Some species of scales that infest poplar are unable to digest fully all the sugar in the plant sap, and excrete the excess in a fluid called honeydew. A sooty mold fungus may develop on the honeydew, causing the poplar leaves to appear black and dirty. An uncontrolled infestation of scales may kill the tree after two or three seasons. For more information about scales, see page 876.

SOLUTION: Spray with ORTHO Isotox Insect Killer or ORTHO Liquid Sevin when the young are active. Contact your local Cooperative Extension Office (see page 1029) to determine the best time to spray for scales in your area. To control overwintering insects, spray with ORTHO Volck Oil Spray before growth begins in the spring.

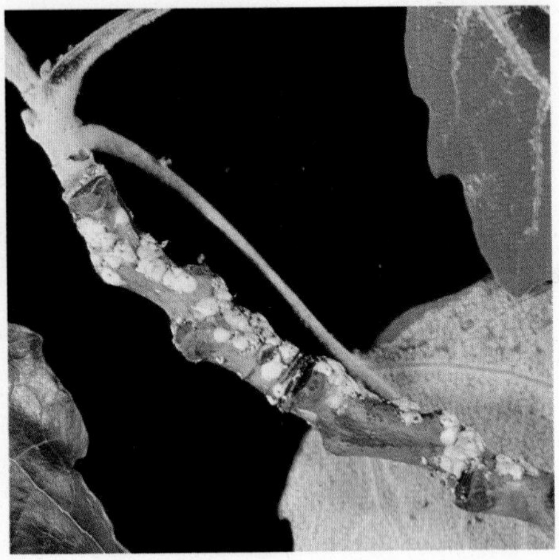

Poplar scales (life size).

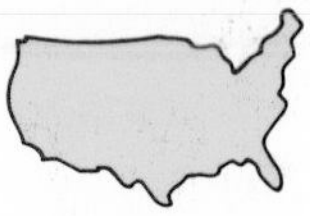

PROBLEM: The undersides of the leaves, and the stems, branch crotches, or trunk are covered with white, cottony masses. Leaves may turn yellow and drop. A shiny, sticky substance may coat the leaves. A black sooty mold often grows on the sticky substance. Numerous side shoots sometimes grow out of an infested crotch area. Twigs and branches may die back.

ANALYSIS: Cottony scales and mealybugs
Cottony scales and mealybugs are common on poplar wherever it is grown. The visual similarity between these insects makes separate identification difficult. They are very conspicuous in late spring and summer because the females are covered with a white, cottony egg sac, containing up to 2500 eggs. Females lay their egg masses on leaves or branches. The young insects that hatch from these eggs are yellowish brown to green. They feed throughout the summer on leaves, stems, and trunk. Damage is caused by the withdrawal of plant sap from the leaves and branches. The insects are unable to digest fully all the sugar in the plant sap and excrete the excess in a fluid called honeydew, which often drops onto the leaves or plants below. A sooty mold fungus may develop on the honeydew, causing the poplar leaves and other plants to appear black and dirty. Leaf drop and twig dieback occur when the white masses completely cover the leaves and branches.

SOLUTION: Spray with ORTHO Isotox Insect Killer in midsummer when the young are active. The following spring, when the tree is dormant, spray with a dormant oil to control overwintering insects on the bark.

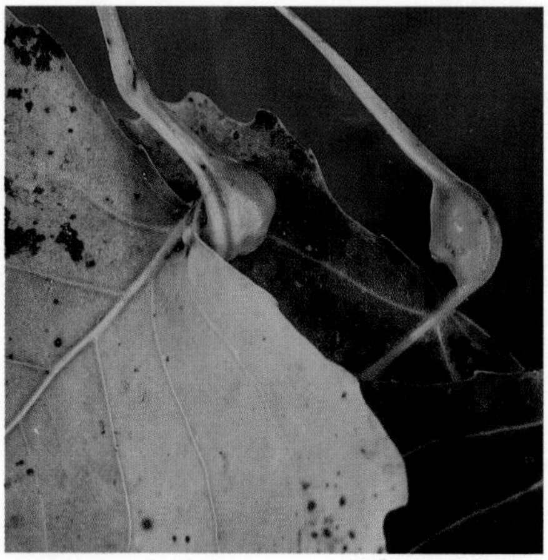

Petiolegalls (life size).

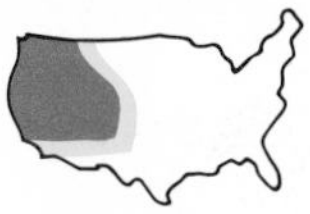

PROBLEM: Galls appear on the leaf stalks. Inside the gall a white or gray fluffy material covers a colony of small (⅛ inch) greenish-yellow, soft-bodied insects. Galls also may occur on the leaves.

ANALYSIS: Poplar petiolegall aphid
(*Pemphigus populitransversus*)
These aphids cause galls to form on poplar leaves. The galls are unsightly but not seriously harmful to the tree. The aphids hatch from eggs in the spring and begin feeding on the leaves. A substance that they inject during feeding causes galls to form. They multiply within the galls for several generations. In summer they produce winged aphids which fly to vegetables such as lettuce, beets, and turnips, and many weeds. The aphids feed on the roots of these plants throughout the summer. In fall the aphids fly back to poplar trees where a final generation of aphids lays eggs on the bark.

SOLUTION: Spray poplar trees in the winter with ORTHO Volck Oil Spray to control overwintering aphid eggs. Once the galls are formed in the spring, the aphids are protected from insecticides.

Poplar willow borer (half life size).

PROBLEM: Swollen areas with holes in their centers develop on twigs, branches, or the trunk. Many side shoots may grow from below the swellings, destroying the tree's natural form. The leaves on infested twigs and branches turn yellow and may be chewed on the edges. There is usually a sawdustlike material and many broken twigs beneath the tree.

ANALYSIS: Poplar borers
(*Saperda* species)
At least five species of beetles feed on poplars, causing galls to form. The inch-long, striped and spotted, brownish or gray beetles with long antennae appear in late spring or early summer. The females lay eggs in small holes gnawed in the bark of twigs and branches that are more than ½ inch in diameter. As the legless, whitish grubs hatch from these eggs, they tunnel into the wood. Excess tissue grows around the wound, resulting in a swollen area or gall. When infestations are severe, nearly all twigs and branches more than ½ inch in diameter have one or more galls. The galls weaken the twigs and branches, causing them to break and litter the ground during stormy weather. The grubs remain in the wood for 1 or 2 years.

SOLUTION: Remove and destroy severely damaged trees. Spray the bark of less severely damaged trees with ORTHO Lindane Borer & Leaf Miner Spray in late May or early June. Repeat the treatment 2 weeks later.

Damaged tree. *Insert:* Adult borer (half life size).

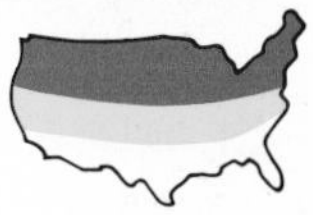

PROBLEM: The leaves turn yellow and there are holes in the twigs. Large quantities of sawdustlike material cling to the bark just below the holes. Sap often oozes from the holes. Young trees may be killed and older trees may lose their natural form due to the production of numerous side shoots. Small (⅜ inch) black or dark brown weevils, with pale yellow spots and long snouts, may be seen around the tree from midsummer until fall.

ANALYSIS: Poplar and willow borer
(*Cryptorhynchus lapathi*)
Most species of poplar and all willow trees may be attacked by this weevil. The adult weevils cause minor injury by chewing holes in the bark of twigs. The major damage is caused by the white, C-shaped larvae. During mid to late summer, the larvae hatch from eggs laid in holes chewed by the female weevils. The larvae burrow into and feed on the inner bark. In the spring, large quantities of frass (sawdust and excrement) are expelled from the holes as the larvae tunnel into the center of the twigs to pupate. The feeding and tunneling cause branches to break easily and disrupt nutrient and water movement through the tree. The leaves yellow and the tree often becomes bushy from the growth of numerous side shoots. The larvae pupate in June, and emerge as adults in midsummer. Several other types of borers may also infest the trunk and branches of poplars.

SOLUTION: Remove and destroy severely infested trees or branches before early summer. Spray the bark of trees with ORTHO Lindane Borer & Leaf Miner Spray in late July or early August.

POPULUS

Dieback. *Insert:* Canker.

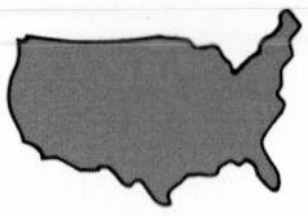

PROBLEM: Dark sunken areas appear on the twigs, branches, or trunk. Leaves on infected branches may be spotted, or they may be stunted and lighter green than normal. Twigs and branches are often killed. Young or weakened trees are most susceptible.

ANALYSIS: Canker and dieback
Several different fungi cause canker and dieback on poplars. Lombardy poplars are especially vulnerable. The fungi enter the tree through a wound or, in some cases, through the leaves, killing the surrounding healthy tissue. A dark sunken canker develops in the wood and expands through it in all directions. If the fungus infects the leaves first, it grows down through the leaf stems and forms cankers on the twigs. The canker cuts off the flow of nutrients and water to the twigs or branch, causing the leaves to turn yellow. Twig or branch dieback follow if the canker girdles the wood. The tree may wall off the spreading fungus by producing callus tissue, a rapid growth of barklike cells. If the expanding canker is stopped before it covers half the diameter of the trunk, the tree usually survives. However, the fungus may grow faster than the callus, or the tree may not produce a callus, resulting in the death of the branch or the whole tree.

SOLUTION: Prune off dead twigs and small cankered branches, cutting well below the canker. Remove and destroy severely infected trees. To prevent the development of new cankers, avoid wounding trees. Keep trees vigorous by fertilizing and watering. For information on fertilizers and watering, see pages 910 and 912.

PRUNUS (FLOWERING FORMS)

PRUNUS (FLOWERING FORMS)

ADAPTATION: Zones 3 to 9 (to determine your zone, see the map on page 1020).

FLOWERING TIME: Spring.

LIGHT: Full sun.

SOIL: Any good, fast-draining garden soil.

FERTILIZER: Fertilize with ORTHO Evergreen, Tree & Shrub Food according to label directions.

WATER:
How much: Apply enough water to wet the soil 3 to 4 feet deep. To determine the proper amount of water for your soil type, see page 912.
How often: Water when the soil is barely moist 4 inches below the surface. For more information about watering, see page 912.

PRUNING: Most species require only maintenance pruning. Remove dead or broken branches. The flowering peaches and nectarines produce a better show of flowers if cut back severely every year immediately after flowering.

INSECTS AND DISEASES: Problems of flowering fruit trees are very similar to those of trees that produce fruit. For more information about plant problems on flowering fruit trees, see page 604 for almond; page 616 for cherry; page 633 for peach; and page 648 for plum.

Citrus whitefly (5 times life size).

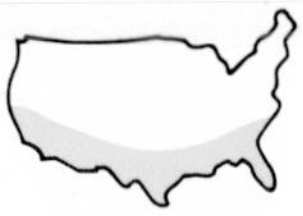

PROBLEM: Tiny, winged insects, 1/12 inch long, feed on the leaf surfaces. The insects are covered with white waxy powder. When the plant is touched, insects flutter rapidly around it. Leaves may be mottled and yellowing. In warm winter areas, a black sooty mold may cover the leaves.

ANALYSIS: Citrus whitefly
(*Dialeurodes citri*)
This insect is a common pest of many garden plants. The adult lays her eggs on the undersides of leaves. The larvae are the size of a pinhead, flat, oval-shaped, and semitransparent, with white waxy filaments radiating from the body. They feed for about a month before changing to the adult form. Both the larval and adult forms suck sap from the leaves. The larvae are more damaging because they feed more heavily. Adults and larvae cannot fully digest all the sugar in the plant sap, and excrete the excess in a fluid called honeydew, which often drops onto the leaves below. A sooty mold fungus may develop on the honeydew, causing the laurel leaves to appear black and dirty. In warm winter areas the insects can be active year-round, with eggs, larvae, and adults present at the same time. Whiteflies are unable to live through freezing winters. Spring reinfestations in freezing winter areas come from migrating whiteflies.

SOLUTION: Control with ORTHO Isotox Insect Killer if the whiteflies are noticebly damaging the leaves. Repeat the spray at least two more times at intervals of 2 weeks to control the young as they hatch.

PRUNUS (EVERGREEN FORMS)

PRUNUS (EVERGREEN FORMS)

ADAPTATION: Zones 7 through 10. To determine your zone, see the map on page 1020.

FLOWERING TIME: Spring or summer.

LIGHT: Full sun (some species prefer partial shade in hot summer areas).

SOIL: Any good, well-drained garden soil.

FERTILIZER: Fertilize with ORTHO Azalea, Camellia & Rhododendron Food or ORTHO Evergreen, Tree & Shrub Food according to label directions.

WATER:

How much: Apply enough water to wet the soil 2 to 3 feet deep. To determine the proper amount of water for your soil type, see page 912.

How often: Most cherry laurels are drought tolerant once established, but they grow best with periodic deep watering. Water when the soil is dry 4 inches below the surface. For more information about watering, see page 912.

PRUNING:

Tree forms: Prune to a single trunk.

Shrubs: Prune to maintain shape. Cut back overly long growth. Some species can be pruned to form a hedge.

Leaf spot.

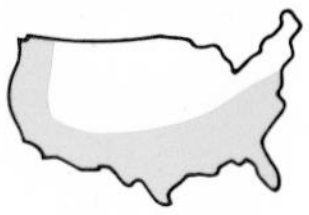

PROBLEM: Spots and blotches appear on the leaves. The spots may be yellow, purple, red, tan, gray, or brown. They range in size from barely visible to ¾ inch in diameter. Several spots may join to form blotches. The infected tissue sometimes dries up and falls out, causing a shothole appearance. Leaves may turn yellow and drop off. Leaf spotting is most severe in warm, humid weather.

ANALYSIS: Leaf spot

Several different fungi and bacteria cause leaf spot. These spots are unsightly but rarely harmful to the plant. Plants weakened by low temperatures and wind exposure may be more susceptible to invasion by leaf spotting organisms. The fungi and bacteria are spread by splashing water and wind. Spots develop where the organisms enter the tissue. If wet or humid weather persists, the disease spreads through the tissue and blotches form. Most leaf spot organisms do their greatest damage in mild weather (between 50° and 85°F).

SOLUTION: Once leaves become spotted they will remain so. Where practical, remove infected leaves from the plant. Collect and destroy any fallen leaves. To reduce plant susceptibility, provide windbreaks and protection from low temperatures.

PSEUDOTSUGA (DOUGLAS FIR)

Cooley spruce gall aphid (3 times life size).

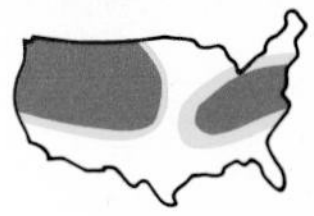

PROBLEM: White, cottony tufts appear on the undersides of needles in midsummer. Small (⅛ inch) blackish insects may be found underneath the cottony material. The needles are spotted yellow and distorted; many may drop from the tree prematurely.

ANALYSIS: Cooley spruce gall aphid

(*Adelges cooleyi*)

The cooley spruce gall aphid requires both Douglas fir and spruce to complete its two-year life cycle. The aphids spend the winter on spruce. The following spring, the females lay their eggs around the new needles. The young feed there, inducing the formation of galls that enclose them (see page 528). In midsummer, the galls open and the mature aphids migrate to Douglas fir, where the females lay their eggs on the needles. The young aphids cover themselves with a white cottony or woolly material. They suck sap from the needles, causing yellowing and distortion. When infestations are heavy, many needles drop off. The next spring, winged aphids develop; some fly back to spruce, while others may remain on Douglas fir.

SOLUTION: Spray with an insecticide containing *acephate* (ORTHENE®), *diazinon*, or *lindane* when new growth is expanding to control the young insects as they hatch.

Pseudotsuga cultural information

Light: Full sun to light shade
Water: Allow the soil to dry between waterings
Soil: Well-drained
Fertilizer: Light

Douglas fir tussock moth larvae (twice life size).

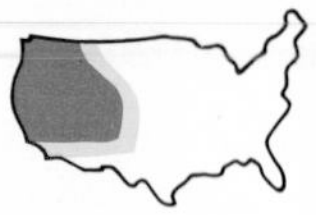

PROBLEM: Starting at the top of the tree and progressing downward, much of the foliage is eaten. The entire tree may be defoliated in one season. Trees that lose most of their needles the second year are usually killed. Inch-long, hairy, gray or light brown caterpillars, with tufts of orange hairs on their backs may be found feeding on the needles. Tan-colored pellets may drop from the tree and litter the ground.

ANALYSIS: Douglas fir tussock moth
(*Orgyia pseudotsugata*)
Douglas fir tussock moth populations are cyclical. Every 7 to 10 years, forest populations build up to epidemic proportions. When this occurs, Douglas firs, true firs, spruce, pine, and larch may be completely defoliated. In cities, damaging numbers may be found every year. In mid- to late summer, hairy, wingless female moths lay eggs in a frothy substance covered with a layer of hairlike scales from the cocoon from which they emerged. The eggs hatch the following spring, and the caterpillars begin feeding on the new needles at the top of the tree. As the younger foliage is devoured, the caterpillars move downward, feeding on older needles. Defoliated trees are often killed after two seasons. Less severely damaged trees may be killed later by bark beetles. In August, the caterpillars pupate, and later emerge as adults.

SOLUTION: Spray with an insecticide containing *acephate* (ORTHENE®), sevin, or the bacteria *Bacillus thuringiensis* when caterpillars or damage are first noticed, usually in May or early June. Repeat the spray 2 weeks later if damage continues.

PYRACANTHA

ADAPTATION: Zones 5 through 10. To determine your zone, see the map on page 1020.

FLOWERING TIME: Small white flowers, usually in the spring. Yellow, orange, or red berries in the fall, sometimes lasting through the winter.

LIGHT: Full sun to partial shade.

SOIL: Any good, well-drained, slightly acid (pH 5.5 to 6.5) garden soil.

FERTILIZER: Fertilize with ORTHO Azalea, Camellia & Rhododendron Food according to label directions.

WATER:
How much: Apply enough water to wet the soil 1 to 2 feet deep. To determine the proper amount of water for your soil type, see page 912.
How often: Do not keep the soil constantly wet or plant pyracantha near sprinkler systems. Water when the soil is dry 4 inches below the surface. For more information about watering, see page 912.

PRUNING: Give pyracantha plenty of room to spread. To maintain shape, pinch off young growth or prune back long branches just before growth starts. Pyracantha is often used as an espalier (a plant trained to grow flat against a wall or fence). For more information about this technique, see ORTHO's book *All About Pruning*.

Fireblight.

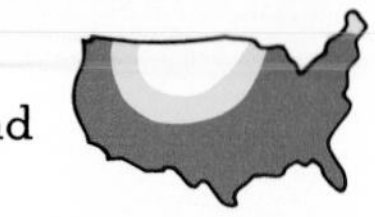

PROBLEM: Blossoms and leaves of infected twigs suddenly wilt and turn black as if scorched by fire. The leaves curl and hang downward. The bark at the base of the blighted twigs becomes water-soaked, then dark, sunken, and dry; cracks may develop at the edge of the sunken area. In warm, moist spring weather, drops of brown ooze appear on the sunken bark. Young plants may die.

ANALYSIS: Fireblight
This disease is caused by a bacterium (*Erwinia amylovora*) that is very destructive to many trees and shrubs. (For a list of susceptible plants, see page 1016.) The bacteria spend the winter in the sunken areas (cankers) on the branches. In the spring, the bacteria ooze out of the canker. Bees, flies, and other insects are attracted to the sweet, sticky ooze and become smeared with it. When the insects visit a flower for nectar, they infect it with the bacteria. The bacteria spread rapidly through the plant tissue in warm (65°F or higher), humid weather. Insects visiting these infected blossoms later carry bacteria-laden nectar to healthy blossoms. Tender or damaged leaves may be infected in midsummer.

SOLUTION: During spring and mid to late summer, prune out infected branches 12 to 15 inches beyond any visible discoloration and destroy. A protective spray of a bactericide containing *basic copper sulfate* or *streptomycin*, applied before bud break in spring, will help prevent infection. Repeat at intervals of 5 to 7 days until the end of bloom. In the fall, prune out infected branches. Sterilize pruning shears after each cut with rubbing alcohol. For a list of pyracantha varieties resistant to fireblight, see page 1016.

Scab.

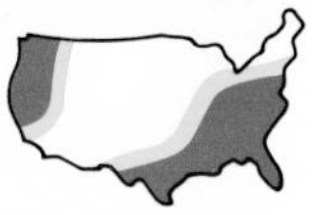

PROBLEM: Dark blotches, with fringed edges, 1/4 inch or more in diameter, appear on the leaves. The leaves turn yellow, then brown, and drop from the plant. Berries and twigs develop circular, rough-surfaced, olive-green spots that eventually turn corky and black. The infected berries die.

ANALYSIS: Scab
This plant disease is caused by a fungus (*Fusicladium pyracanthae*) that produces scabby lesions on pyracantha leaves and berries similar to those caused by scab fungi on apple and other fruit trees. Scab may be a serious problem in areas where winter or spring weather is humid and mild (60° to 70°F). In the spring, spores are blown by the wind to new leaves and flower buds. If the leaves and buds are wet, the fungus infects them and a spot develops. More spores are produced from these spots. These spores are splashed by rain to infect new leaf, twig, and berry surfaces. The spots on the berries and twigs turn corky and black and the berries become deformed during development. As the temperature increases in summer, the fungus becomes less active.

SOLUTION: To obtain adequate control of scab, protective sprays must be started as soon as bud growth begins in spring. Spray with a fungicide containing *chlorothalonil* (DACONIL 2787®). Repeat 3 more times at intervals of 10 days. Plant scab-resistant varieties (see page 1015).

Damage. *Insert:* Hawthorn lacebugs (half life size).

PROBLEM: The upper surfaces of the leaves are mottled or speckled gray and green. The mottling may be confused with mite or leafhopper damage. It can be distinguished from other insect damage by the black, shiny, hard droplets found on the undersides of damaged leaves. Small (1/8 inch), light or dark, spiny, wingless insects or brownish insects with clear, lacy wings may be visible around the droplets and next to the midrib. The plant is usually stunted. Damage occurs in spring and summer.

ANALYSIS: Hawthorn lacebug
(*Corythucha cydoniae*)
The hawthorn lacebug is found throughout the United States on pyracantha, hawthorn, cotoneaster, and fruiting quince. It spends the winter as an adult on the plant in bark crevices, branch crotches, or other protected areas on the host. When growth begins in spring, the adults attach their eggs to the undersides of the leaves with a brown, sticky substance. The eggs hatch and the spiny, wingless, immature insects, and later the brown lacy-winged adults, suck sap from the undersides of the leaves. The green leaf pigment disappears, resulting in the characteristic gray and green mottling. As the lacebugs feed, droplets of brown excrement accumulate around them. Damage is unsightly and food production by the leaf is reduced, resulting in a loss of plant vigor.

SOLUTION: Spray with ORTHO Isotox Insect Killer or ORTHO Orthene Systemic Insect Control when damage first appears in spring. Thoroughly cover the undersides of the leaves where insects feed. Repeat 7 to 10 days later. A third application may be necessary if the plant becomes reinfested in the summer.

Kuno scales (twice life size) and honeydew drops.

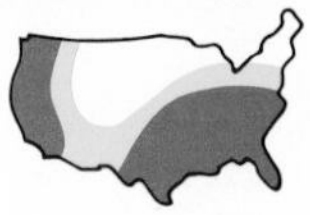

PROBLEM: The stems or the undersides of the leaves are covered with white and brown crusty bumps or thick, white, waxy bumps or clusters of somewhat flattened scaly bumps. The bumps can be scraped or picked off; the undersides are usually soft. Leaves turn yellow and may drop, and the plant may be stunted. A sticky substance may coat the leaves. A black sooty mold often grows on the sticky substance.

ANALYSIS: Scales
Many different types of scales infest pyracantha. In spring to midsummer the young scales, called *crawlers*, settle on leaves and twigs. The small (1/10 inch), soft-bodied young feed by sucking sap from the plant. The legs usually atrophy and a hard crusty or waxy shell develops over the body. The mature female scales lay their eggs underneath the shell. Some species of scales that infest pyracantha are unable to digest fully all the sugar in the plant sap, and excrete the excess in a fluid called honeydew. A sooty mold fungus may develop on the honeydew, causing the pyracantha leaves to appear black and dirty. An uncontrolled infestation of scales may kill the plant after two or three seasons. For more information about scales, see page 876.

SOLUTION: Spray with ORTHO Isotox Insect Killer or ORTHO Orthene Systemic Insect Control when the young are active. Contact your local Cooperative Extension Office (see page 1029) to determine the best time to spray for scales in your area. To control overwintering insects, spray the trunk and branches with ORTHO Volck Oil Spray in spring.

PYRACANTHA

Woolly apple aphids (twice life size).

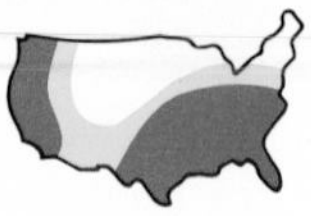

PROBLEM: Woody growths and a white, woolly material form on the twigs and branches in summer. The plant has an unthrifty appearance, with yellowing leaves and possibly some twig dieback. A shiny, sticky substance often coats the leaves. A black sooty mold may grow on the sticky substance.

ANALYSIS: Woolly apple aphid
(*Eriosoma lanigerum*)
The woolly apple aphid causes woody growths or galls to form on the twigs, branches, and roots of pyracantha, apple trees, and flowering fruit trees. The aphids spend the winter on elm trees or, in the West, on pyracantha or fruit trees. In the summer, they migrate to the plant and cluster on the stems, twigs, and around old pruning wounds. They also crawl down to the roots. Damage occurs when the aphids suck the juices from the wood. Their feeding induces galls to form, weakening the plant. A white, woolly material covers the aphids as they feed, making them very conspicuous on the shrub. The aphids are unable to digest fully all the sugar in the plant sap and excrete the excess in a fluid called honeydew, which often drops onto the leaves below. A sooty mold fungus may develop on the honeydew, causing the pyracantha leaves to appear black and dirty. The woolly hawthorn aphid and several leaf-feeding aphids may also infest pyracantha.

SOLUTION: Spray the plant with ORTHO Orthene Systemic Insect Control or ORTHO Isotox Insect Killer in summer when aphids or their damage are first noticed.

Sooty mold.

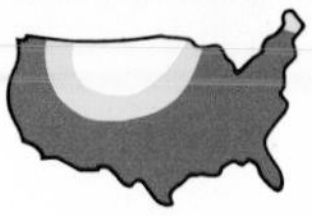

PROBLEM: A black sooty mold is growing on the leaves and twigs. It can be completely wiped off the surfaces. Cool, moist weather hastens the growth of this substance.

ANALYSIS: Sooty mold
This common black mold is found on a wide variety of plants in the garden. It is caused by any of several species of fungi that grow on the sugary material left on plants by aphids, scales, mealybugs, whiteflies, and other insects that suck sap from the plant. The insects are unable to digest all the sugar in the sap and excrete the excess in a fluid called honeydew, which drops onto the leaves below. The honeydew may also drop out of infested trees and shrubs onto pyracantha growing beneath them. The sooty mold fungus develops on the honeydew, causing the pyracantha leaves to appear black and dirty. Sooty mold is unsightly, but it is fairly harmless because it does not attack the leaf directly. Extremely heavy infestations prevent light from reaching the leaf, so that the leaf produces less food and may turn yellow. The presence of sooty mold indicates that the pyracantha or another plant near it is infested with insects.

SOLUTION: Sooty mold can be wiped from the leaves with a wet rag, or it will eventually be washed off by rain. Prevent more sooty mold by controlling the insect that is producing the honeydew. Inspect the leaves and twigs above the sooty mold to find what type of insect is present. See the following pages for control instructions: for aphids, see the column to the left; for scales, see page 549; for whiteflies, see page 877; for mealybugs, see page 876.

PYRUS (ORNAMENTAL PEAR)

PYRUS (ORNAMENTAL PEAR)

ADAPTATION: Zones 4 to 10 (to determine your zone, see the map on page 1020). Tolerant of harsh city conditions.

FLOWERING TIME: Late winter to early spring.

LIGHT: Full sun.

SOIL: Tolerates a wide variety of soils.

FERTILIZER: Fertilize with ORTHO Evergreen, Tree & Shrub Food according to label directions.

WATER: Drought-resistant once established, but will also tolerate moist soil. Water during periods of extended drought.

PRUNING: Heavily pruned trees seldom flower. Prune only to maintain shape. Evergreen pears need to be pruned to a single trunk to obtain a tree form.

INSECTS AND DISEASES: Problems of flowering pear are very similar to those found on pears that produce fruit. For information about plant problems on flowering pear, see the section starting on page 639.

QUERCUS (OAK)

ADAPTATION: Throughout the United States. There are oaks for all climates and conditions, including salt air, heat, wind, and moist areas.

LIGHT: Full sun.

SOIL: Any good, deep, well-drained garden soil. Some oaks do not tolerate alkaline soils (pH 7.0 and above).

FERTILIZER: Some oaks benefit from periodic feedings under the outer branches. Fertilize with ORTHO Evergreen, Tree & Shrub Food according to label directions.

WATER: Some oaks grow best with ample water and will thrive in lawns. Others, such as the western native oaks, prefer drier conditions. They will decline and eventually die if overwatered. For a list of oaks and their water requirements, see page 1010.

How much: Apply enough water to wet the soil 4 to 5 feet deep. To determine the proper amount of water for your soil type, see page 912.

How often: Water young trees when the soil is barely moist 4 inches below the surface. *Oaks requiring ample water:* established trees should be watered when the soil is barely moist 4 inches below the surface. *Oaks preferring dry conditions:* never water around the trunk. Most of these oaks need no supplemental water once established.

PRUNING: Prune to maintain shape and to remove dead wood. When planting, allow room for growth.

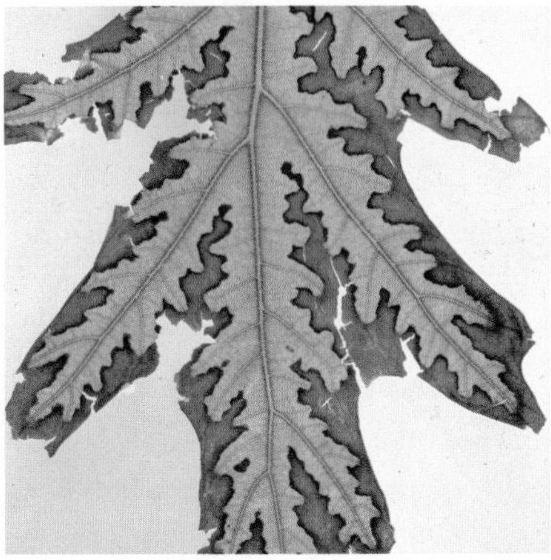

Summer leaf scorch.

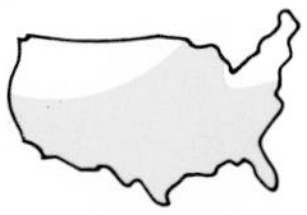

PROBLEM: During hot weather, usually in July or August, leaves turn brown around the edges and between the veins. Sometimes the whole leaf dies. Many leaves may drop during late summer. This problem is most severe on the youngest branches. Trees do not generally die.

ANALYSIS: Summer leaf scorch
Leaf scorch is caused by excessive evaporation of moisture from the leaves. In hot weather, water evaporates rapidly from the leaves. If the roots can't absorb and convey water fast enough to replenish this loss, the leaves turn brown and wither. This usually occurs in dry soil, but leaves can also scorch when the soil is moist. Drying winds, severed roots, limited soil area, or soil with a high salt concentration contribute to scorch. For more information about scorch, see page 857.

SOLUTION: To prevent further scorch, deep-water trees during periods of hot weather to wet down the entire root space. For more information about watering trees, see page 912. Newly transplanted trees should be watered whenever the rootball is dry 1 inch below the surface. There are no controls for scorch on trees in moist soil. Plant trees adapted to your climate.

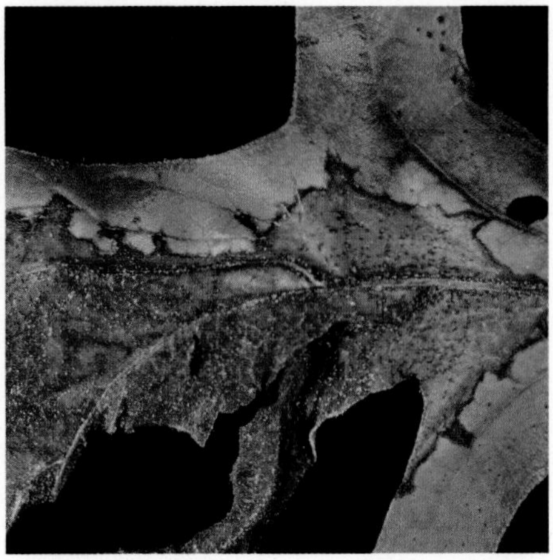

Oak anthracnose.

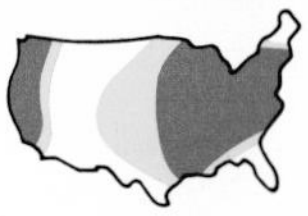

PROBLEM: Brown, dead spots appear along the veins in the spring, and expand outward to the leaf edges. Leaves become curled, puckered, and twisted. In wet seasons, many leaves may fall. Leaves on the lower branches are generally more severely infected. Small sunken areas may form on twigs; the twigs may die.

ANALYSIS: Oak anthracnose
This plant disease is caused by fungi (*Gnomonia* species) that infect the leaves of white oaks and, in California, several other oaks. The fungi spend the winter on fallen leaves or in sunken cankers on twigs in the tree. During rainy weather, spores are blown and splashed onto young leaves. Dead spots develop where the fungi enter the tissue. The spots enlarge and the leaves become puckered and twisted. When moist weather continues into summer, the fungi may kill the leaves, causing severe defoliation. The fungi may also enter twigs, causing canker and twig dieback.

SOLUTION: There is nothing you can do to control anthracnose this year. If next spring is wet, spray young trees and valuable specimens with a fungicide containing *chlorothalonil* (DACONIL 2787®) when the buds are opening.

QUERCUS (OAK) — LEAVES DISCOLORED

Oak leafminer damage.

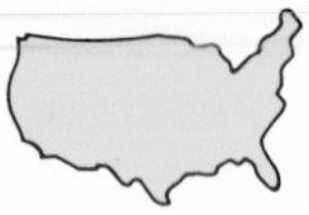

PROBLEM: Brown patches or trails appear on the leaves, starting in the spring. By August, the leaves may be completely brown and drop from the tree. When a brown spot is torn open, one to several small green or whitish caterpillars may be found inside.

ANALYSIS: Oak leafminers
The larvae of several species of moths mine the leaves of oak. The insects spend the winter as pupae inside dried, fallen leaves. In the spring, the moths emerge and lay their eggs on the newly developed green leaves. The larvae that hatch from these eggs burrow into the leaf and feed on the tissue between the upper and lower surfaces of the leaves. The outer tissue turns brown, producing patches or trails. The larvae mature, pupate, and emerge as moths to repeat the cycle up to five times during the growing season. When infestations are heavy, the trails run together, covering the entire leaf surface, and nearly all the leaves are affected. When this occurs the leaves drop prematurely, reducing the ornamental value of the tree.

SOLUTION: Spray young trees or heavily infested valuable specimens with ORTHO Orthene Systemic Insect Control when damage is first noticed in late spring or early summer. Spray the leaves thoroughly. Repeat the spray if new mines are noticed in July. Rake up and destroy the fallen leaves in autumn.

Oak mite damage.

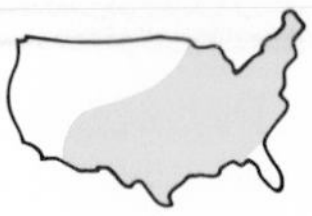

PROBLEM: Leaves are stippled yellow or bronze and dirty. Sometimes there is a silken webbing on the leaf surfaces. New leaves may be slightly distorted. To determine if the plant is infested with mites, hold a sheet of white paper underneath a stippled leaf and tap the leaf sharply. Minute yellow, brown, or red specks the size of pepper grains will drop to the paper and begin to crawl around. The pests are easily seen against the white background.

ANALYSIS: Oak mite
(*Oligonychus bicolor*)
Mites, related to spiders, are major pests of many garden plants. The oak mite causes damage by sucking sap from the upper surfaces of the leaves. As a result of feeding, the green pigment disappears, producing the stippled appearance. Mites infesting oak are most prolific in warm weather, and are most active in midsummer. Mite damage is usually not noticeable until much of the foliage is stippled. This damage seldom seriously injures oak trees, but it is unsightly.

SOLUTION: Control with ORTHO Isotox Insect Killer when damage is first noticed in the summer. Wet the upper surfaces of the leaves thoroughly. Repeat the spray 2 weeks later. A *dormant oil* or *lime sulfur* spray may be applied before growth starts in early spring to control the overwintering mites.

Oak leaf blister.

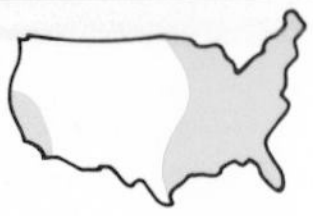

PROBLEM: Puckered, circular areas, up to ½ inch in diameter, appear on the leaves in the spring. The blisterlike spots are yellowish green at first, and later die and turn brown. The leaves usually remain attached to the tree.

ANALYSIS: Oak leaf blister
Leaf blister is caused by a fungus (*Taphrina caerulescens*) that is unsightly but rarely harmful to the tree. It is a problem on various species of oaks, particularly red, black, scarlet, and live oaks. The fungus spends the winter in the bud scales on the tree. During cool, wet springs, it enters the developing leaves. Green blisters form where the fungus enters the tissue. The infected tissue eventually dies and turns brown. In the fall, the fungus produces the overwintering spores. If the following spring is cool and wet, the cycle begins again.

SOLUTION: If leaf blister was a problem the previous year and the weather this spring is cool and wet, spray the tree with a fungicide containing *chlorothalonil* (DACONIL 2787®) 1 or 2 weeks before the leaves appear. Wet the entire tree thoroughly.

INSECTS

Powdery mildew on bur oak.

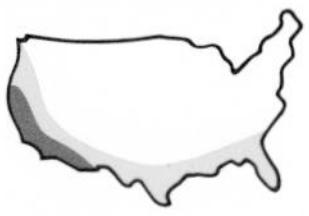

PROBLEM: The leaf surfaces and the new shoots are covered with a dense layer of grayish white powdery material, which later becomes tan, then brown. Affected new shoots are usually swollen, fleshy, and shortened. The leaves on these shoots may be small and yellow; eventually they turn brown and shrivel. Many side shoots may develop from the infected branch, producing a "witch's broom."

ANALYSIS: Powdery mildew
This common plant disease is caused by a fungus (*Sphaerotheca lanestris*) that thrives in both humid and dry weather. It is sometimes called *brown mildew* because the fungus changes in color from grayish white to brown with age. It is most destructive to coast live oak (*Quercus agrifolia*) in California, but is also found on white, southern red, holly, bur, and post oaks in the southern and western states. The powdery layer consists of fungal strands and spores. The spores are spread by the wind to healthy plants. The fungus saps the plant nutrients, causing stunted, yellow leaves and swollen, distorted branches, which often develop into a witch's broom. Several other common powdery mildews that do not cause witch's brooms also infect oaks.

SOLUTION: Where practical, remove the witch's brooms during the winter to reduce the amount of fungus. Succulent summer growth is most susceptible. Avoid causing new growth by excessive pruning, fertilization, and irrigation during this period.

Lacebugs (three times life size).

PROBLEM: The upper surfaces of the leaves are mottled or speckled white and green. The mottling may be mistaken for damage caused by mites or leafhoppers. However, it can be distinguished from other insect damage by the shiny, hard, brown droplets found on the undersides of damaged leaves. Small (⅛ inch), light or dark, spiny, wingless insects, or brownish insects with clear lacy wings, may be visible around the droplets. Foliage on severely infested trees may curl, turn brown, and drop prematurely.

ANALYSIS: Oak lacebug
(*Corythucha arcuata*)
The oak lacebug may be found feeding in great numbers on the undersides of oak leaves. The lacebugs spend the winter as adults in bark crevices or in other protected areas on the tree. When the buds begin to open in spring, the adults attach their eggs to the undersides of the leaves with a brown, sticky substance. When the eggs hatch, the spiny, wingless immature insects, and later the brown lacy-winged adults, suck sap from the leaves. The green leaf pigment disappears, resulting in the characteristic white and green mottling. As the lacebugs feed, droplets of brown excrement accumulate around them. The damage is unsightly, and food production by the leaf is reduced, resulting in a loss of plant vigor.

SOLUTION: Spray with ORTHO Orthene Systemic Insect Control or ORTHO Isotox Insect Killer when damage first appears in the spring. Cover the undersides of the leaves thoroughly. It is important to spray early, to prevent as much damage as possible.

Borer hole.

PROBLEM: Foliage on a branch or at the top of the tree is sparse; eventually the twigs and branches die. Holes or tunnels are apparent in the trunk or branches. The bark may die over the tunnels and slough off, revealing trails. Sap or a sawdustlike material sometimes surrounds the holes. Weakened branches may break during wind or snow storms. Weak, young, or newly transplanted trees are more susceptible to injury, and may be killed.

ANALYSIS: Borers
Borers are the larvae of beetles or moths. Several kinds of borers attack oaks. Throughout the summer, females lay their eggs in bark crevices. The larvae feed on the bark, sapwood, and heartwood. This stops the flow of nutrients and water in that area by cutting the conducting vessels; branch and twig dieback results. Sap flow acts as a defense against borers if the tree is healthy; when the borer burrows into the wood, tree sap fills the hole and kills the insect. Factors that weaken the tree, such as mechanical injuries, transplanting, damage by leaf-feeding insects, and poor growing conditions make it more attractive to egg-laying females.

SOLUTION: Borers are difficult to control once they have burrowed into the wood. Cut out and destroy all dead and dying branches. Severely infected young trees should be removed. Spray the trunk and branches with an insecticide containing *lindane* in May. Repeat the spray 2 weeks later, and again in July and August. Maintain plant vigor by watering during periods of drought and fertilizing regularly. (For more information about fertilizing and watering see page 910 and 912.)

QUERCUS (OAK) — INSECTS

Oak twig girdler damage.

PROBLEM: Patches of dead leaves appear throughout the tree, contrasting sharply with healthy green foliage. To determine if the tree is infested with this insect, prune off an affected twig with dead leaves. Peel back the bark between the healthy green and brown foliage. A winding trail filled with a brown sawdustlike material and possibly a 3/4-inch flattened, legless, white larva may be seen just underneath the bark.

ANALYSIS: Oak twig girdler
(*Agrilus angelicus*)
The twig girdler is the larva of a 1/4-inch brownish bronze beetle. The adults feed on leaves, then lay their eggs on twigs in early summer. When the eggs hatch, the larvae burrow into the wood. They tunnel through the twig, just underneath the bark, in the direction of the trunk. As the larvae tunnel, they fill their trails with brown frass—excrement mixed with sawdust. The tunneling cuts off the flow of nutrients and water in that area, causing the leaves on the ends of the twigs to turn brown and die. More leaves die as the larvae continue to tunnel. After 2 years of feeding, the insect burrows back into the dead twig, pupates, and emerges as an adult.

SOLUTION: When practical, prune out and destroy infested twigs in midsummer. Keep oaks vigorous by giving them optimum growing conditions (see cultural information on page 551).

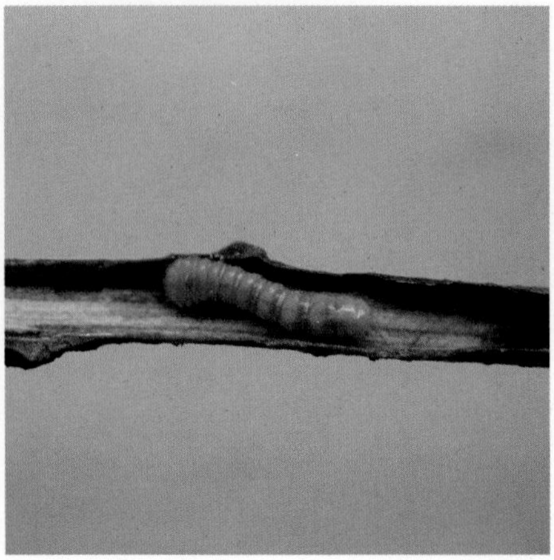

Oak twig pruner (life size).

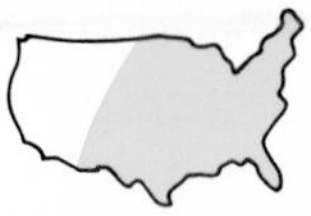

PROBLEM: Small, cleanly cut twigs, 1/4 inch to 2 inches in diameter, are lying under the tree in the fall. The tree is often abnormally bushy. There may be small (up to 1 inch) whitish larvae inside the fallen twigs.

ANALYSIS: Twig pruners and twig girdlers
Several species of wood-boring beetles cause unsightly damage to oaks by altering the natural form of the tree. In midsummer to fall, these wood-boring beetles lay their eggs in the wood of small twigs. The twig pruner larvae tunnel toward the base of the twigs, eating all but the outer bark. In the fall, they back into the hollowed-out twig. High winds cause the nearly severed twigs containing the larvae to break and drop to the ground. With twig girdlers, it is the adults that cause the damage to the twigs. After laying their eggs, the adults chew a circle around the outside of the twigs. Girdled twigs die and break off. The eggs in the fallen twig are then able to develop without being hindered by the flow of tree sap through the twig. Both twig pruner and twig girdler larvae mature in the twigs on the ground. The damage to the tree is the result of excessive pruning on the branch tips. Several new side shoots develop where the twigs break off, causing abnormal bushiness and an unnatural shape.

SOLUTION: Gather and destroy all severed twigs in late fall when the insects are inside.

Gypsy moth caterpillars (half life size).

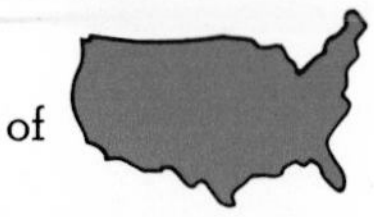

PROBLEM: The surface of the leaf is eaten, giving the remaining tissue a lacy appearance, or the whole leaf is chewed. Sometimes the leaves are webbed together. The tree may be completely defoliated. Damage appears any time between spring and fall. Caterpillars are feeding on the leaves. Repeated heavy infestations may weaken or kill trees.

ANALYSIS: Leaf-feeding caterpillars
Many different species of caterpillars feed on oak leaves wherever the trees are grown. Depending on the species, the moths lay their eggs from early spring to midsummer. The larvae that hatch from these eggs feed singly or in groups on buds, on one leaf surface (skeletonizers), or on the entire leaf. Certain caterpillars web the leaves together as they feed. In some years, damage is minimal due to unfavorable environmental conditions or control by predators and parasites. However, when conditions are favorable, entire trees may be defoliated by late summer. Defoliation weakens trees because there are no leaves left to produce food. When heavy infestations occur several years in a row, branches or entire trees may be killed.

SOLUTION: Spray with ORTHO Isotox Insect Killer, ORTHO Orthene Systemic Insect Control, or ORTHO Gypsy Moth & Japanese Beetle Killer when damage is first noticed. Spray the leaves thoroughly. Repeat the spray if the tree becomes reinfested.

Oak moth larva (twice life size).

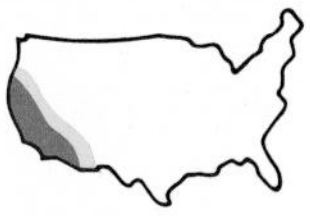

PROBLEM: Dead brown patches appear on the leaves in the spring. One of the leaf surfaces inside these patches has been eaten. Later, the whole leaf is chewed and the tree may be completely defoliated. Large (up to 1 1/4 inches) olive-green caterpillars with black and yellow stripes and a brownish head are feeding on the leaves.

ANALYSIS: Oak moth
(*Phryganidia californica*)
This insect, also called the *California oakworm*, may completely defoliate oaks in California. Defoliated trees are not usually killed, but it may take them years to recover. Defoliation 2 years in a row can kill the tree. In addition, falling excrement and young larvae hanging from silken threads may be a nuisance around homes. The oak moth spends the winter as an egg or young larva on the leaves of evergreen oaks. When temperatures warm in the spring, the caterpillars begin feeding on one surface of the leaf. The leaf surface opposite this chewed area turns brown. When the caterpillars are half grown, they feed on the entire leaf. In May or June, the mature larvae pupate, emerge as pale brown moths, mate, and lay eggs. The larvae that hatch from these eggs feed on leaves until fall. Deciduous oaks are attacked only by this second generation.

SOLUTION: Spray evergreen oaks with ORTHO Orthene Systemic Insect Control when insects are first noticed, or with the bacteria *Bacillus thuringiensis* in the spring as soon as the larvae begin eating through the entire leaf. In the summer, spray deciduous oaks or reinfested evergreen oaks when damage is first noticed.

Giant bark aphids (twice life size).

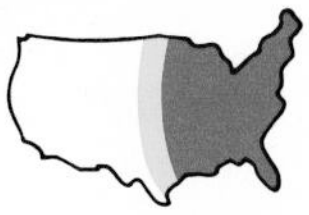

PROBLEM: Small (1/4 inch) black and beige soft-bodied insects with long black legs cluster on twigs and the undersides of limbs. Twigs may be completely covered with a mat of black eggs. When populations are large, twigs and branches die. A shiny, sticky substance may coat the limbs. A black sooty mold often grows on the sticky substance. Ants may be present.

ANALYSIS: Giant bark aphid
(*Longistigma caryae*)
The giant bark aphid is the largest species of aphid known. Because of its long legs, it appears much larger than its 1/4-inch size. The aphids do little damage in small numbers. However, they are extremely prolific and populations can rapidly build up to damaging numbers during the late summer. When populations are large, black eggs are matted all over the bark of infested limbs. Damage occurs when the aphid sucks the juices from the twigs and branches. The aphid is unable to digest fully all the sugar in the sap, and excretes large quantities in a fluid called honeydew, which may coat plants or objects beneath the tree. A sooty mold fungus may develop on the honeydew, causing the bark to appear black and dirty. Ants feed on the sticky substance, and are often present where there is an aphid infestation. Several other species of aphids may also infest oak leaves.

SOLUTION: Spray with ORTHO Isotox Insect Killer or ORTHO Orthene Systemic Insect Control when aphids first appear. Wet the bark thoroughly. Repeat the spray if the tree becomes reinfested.

Oak pit scales (3 times life size).

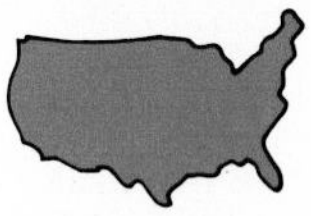

PROBLEM: During the summer or early fall, leaves turn brown and twigs or branches die back. Dead leaves usually remain attached to the branches throughout the winter. In the spring, new leaves may appear 3 weeks late on infested deciduous oaks. Repeated heavy infestations often kill young trees. Small (1/12 inch), somewhat flattened, green, golden, or brown scaly bumps cluster on the twigs and branches. The bark is pitted where these insects cluster.

ANALYSIS: Pit scales
(*Asterolecanium* species)
Several species of pit scales may seriously damage oaks. The scales lay their eggs in spring and summer. The young scales, called *crawlers*, that hatch from these eggs settle on new growth and last year's branches, not far from the parent. The small (1/16 inch), soft-bodied young feed by inserting their mouthparts and sucking sap from the plant. Pits develop where the scales feed. The legs atrophy and a hard, crusty shell develops over the body. The mature female scales lay eggs underneath their shells. Several other types of scales also infest oak. For more information about scales, see page 876.

SOLUTION: Spray with ORTHO Isotox Insect Killer or ORTHO Orthene Systemic Insect Control in mid-May to June when the young are active. To control overwintering insects, spray with ORTHO Volck Oil Spray in winter or spring. Cover the tree thoroughly.

QUERCUS (OAK) — GROWTHS ON TREE

Gall caused by gall wasps.

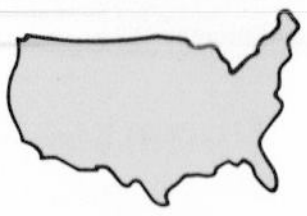

PROBLEM: Round balls grow on twigs, or abnormal growths in a wide variety of shapes, sizes, and colors develop on the leaves, twigs, or branches. Infected leaves may be discolored or distorted and drop prematurely. In some cases, infected twigs and branches die.

ANALYSIS: Oak galls

Tiny insects, called *gall wasps* or *gallflies*, cause hundreds of different types of growths (galls) to develop on oak trees. The galls may be round, spiny, star-shaped, flattened, or elongated. Each species of insect (either a fly or a nonstinging wasp) causes its own specific gall to form. The galls are thought to be caused by a chemical that the insect injects into the plant tissue. The mature female lays her eggs on the various parts of the plant. The eggs hatch into legless grubs around which the gall forms. The insects feed and develop inside the galls, mature, and either spend the winter inside them or emerge to produce another generation. Most galls do not harm the tree. However, some leaf galls inhibit food production, and several types of twig galls disrupt water and nutrient movement through the wood, causing twig dieback.

SOLUTION: If galled branches are distorted and unsightly, cut them off and destroy them before the adults emerge from the galls in spring.

Leafy mistletoe.

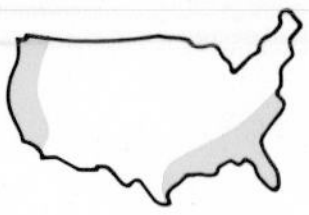

PROBLEM: Leafy, olive-green tufts of plants up to 3 feet across are attached to the branches. The plants may be covered with white, pink, or red berries. The tufts are most noticeable during the winter when there are no leaves on the tree. In severe cases, twigs may die or affected branches may be swollen where the tufts are attached.

ANALYSIS: Leafy mistletoe

(*Phoradendron* species)

Mistletoes are semi-parasitic plants that manufacture their own food but depend on their host plant for water and minerals. Those infecting oak are unsightly, but are rarely harmful to the tree. The plant produces sticky seeds that are spread by birds from one tree to another. The seeds germinate almost anywhere, but penetrate only young, thin bark. The attachment organs of the plant penetrate the tree's water-conducting vessels, from which they obtain their water and minerals. Growth of the mistletoe is slow at first, but in 6 to 8 years plants may be 3 feet across.

SOLUTION: If control is desired, prune off limbs 12 to 18 inches below the point of mistletoe attachment. The rootlike attachment organs may spread through the host tissue up to a foot from the place of original infection. They must be removed from the wood or the mistletoe will resprout. To prevent the spread of seeds, remove tufts before seeds form in spring. If it is not practical to prune a branch, cut off the mistletoe flush with the bark and wrap the area with several layers of black plastic, taped firmly to the tree. Since the mistletoe needs light to grow, the new sprouts will be killed by the darkness under the plastic.

TREE DYING

Oak wilt.

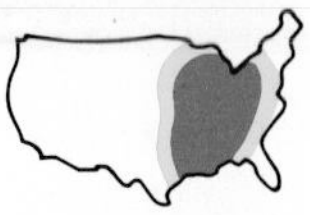

PROBLEM: The leaves on one or more branches wilt, turn bronze, and then fall prematurely. Infected trees of the red oak group may die within a few weeks. Infected trees of the white oak group may die within a few weeks or may die slowly over a period of 2 to 3 years. If an affected branch is cut off, a brown discoloration or ring is seen in the wood just beneath the bark. In the spring, the bark around the infected area may rupture, exposing mats of fungus.

ANALYSIS: Oak wilt

This plant disease is caused by a fungus (*Ceratocystis fagacearum*) that is spread from tree to tree by insects, grafted (intertwined) roots, and tools. Sap-feeding beetles and other insects become coated with the sticky spores that are formed under ruptured bark, and carry them to healthy trees. The fungus spreads through the water-conducting vessels in the wood, causing the discoloration and plugging. The leaves wilt, and the branches—or the entire tree—die. Bark-feeding beetles, which feed on dying trees, may spread the disease long distances. Closely planted trees (50 feet or less between trees) of the same species may pass the fungus through grafted roots.

SOLUTION: Remove infected trees. If the wood is saved, peel off the bark and split the wood immediately. To prevent the spread of the disease through root grafts of closely planted infected and healthy trees, cut a trench midway between the trees, 2 feet deep and extending beyond the spread of the branches. Prune trees in November when the fungus is less active, sterilizing tools after each cut with rubbing alcohol.

Cankers.

Fungal mats.

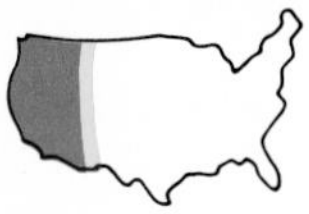

PROBLEM: Leaves are stunted and yellow, and the foliage throughout the tree may be sparse. Branches eventually die. Weakened trees are most severely infected. Occasionally, trees die suddenly without showing symptoms; but in most cases trees die slowly over a period of several years. Honey-colored mushrooms, 2 to 5 inches in diameter, may grow singly or in clusters during the fall or winter on the lower trunk or on the ground near infected roots. If the soil is removed from around the base of the tree black rootlike strands, about the diameter of pencil lead, are seen attached to the larger roots. A white fan-shaped growth occurs between the bark and wood of these larger roots and on the trunk just below the soil surface. The infected tissue has a mushroom odor.

ANALYSIS: Armillaria root rot
This plant disease, also called *oak root fungus* or *shoestring root rot*, is caused by a fungus (*Armillaria mellea*) that rots the roots of many woody and nonwoody plants. Oaks are often lightly infected with this fungus for years with no damage. However, when the trees are under stress from drought, overwatering, physical injuries, insects, or diseases, they often succumb to *Armillaria*. The fungus is spread short distances (under a foot) through the soil by the rootlike fungal strands. When they contact susceptible plant roots, the strands penetrate the host if conditions are favorable. Once the fungus enters the bark tissue it produces a white fan-shaped mat of fungal strands that invade and decay the tissue of the roots and lower trunk. The fungus spreads rapidly if the oak tree is in a weakened state. Water and nutrient uptake by the roots is inhibited, causing the foliage and branches to die. In the fall, mushrooms—the reproductive bodies of the fungus—often appear around infected trees. A closely related fungus (*Clitocybe tabescens*) found in the Southeast produces symptoms on oak very similar to armillaria root rot.

SOLUTION: Remove and destroy infected trees, including the stump and the root system. The fungus can live on the stumps and roots for many years, infecting susceptible plants nearby. Healthy-appearing plants growing adjacent to diseased trees may already be infected. Check around the roots and lower stems for signs of the fungus. The life of a tree may be prolonged if it is not severely infected. Remove the soil from around the rotted parts of the roots and trunk. Cut out the diseased tissue down to healthy wood and allow them to air dry through the summer. Do not water the tree. Cover the exposed parts before temperatures drop below freezing. When replacing trees that have been infected with *Armillaria*, use resistant plants. (For a list, see page 1016.) Avoid planting susceptible species in recently cleared forest lands where armillaria root rot is common. To inhibit disease development in an established oak tree, provide optimum growing conditions, avoid injuring the tree, and control pests and diseases.

Polyporos rot.

PROBLEM: The leaves are yellowing and the foliage is sparse on a branch or on one section of the tree; the tree slowly dies. Large branches may break off. The tree is planted in a lawn or in an area that receives summer watering; or the soil has been raised around the base of the trunk.

ANALYSIS: Crown rot and decline
This plant disease is a common and serious problem of oaks, especially native oaks growing in urban parts of California. It is the result of too much moisture around the base of the tree in summer. Many oaks prefer dry soil. Planting in a lawn or in an area that receives summer watering weakens the tree. These conditions are favorable to the development of soil fungi (especially *Phytophthora* species) that enter weakened roots and slowly destroy them. The flow of nutrients and water is cut off to the top of the tree, causing the foliage to yellow and drop. The fungi may also move up into the trunk and destroy the wood. Entire branches eventually die. The diseased branches can no longer support their weight and they crack and fall. A raised soil level also weakens a tree by keeping the base of the tree too moist, leaving it susceptible to attack by soil fungi.

SOLUTION: Stop all watering of the soil beneath the tree. Remove all plants and lawn that require summer watering from around the trunk. Prune off dead or dying branches. Do not raise the soil around the trunk. If the base of the trunk is covered, remove the soil down to its original level. For more information about raised soil level under trees, see page 437.

RHODODENDRON (AZALEA) — FLOWERS DYING

RHODODENDRON (AZALEA)

ADAPTATION: Zones 4 through 10 except in desert areas. (To determine your zone, see the map on page 1020.) Azaleas are more tolerant of warm, dry climates than rhododendrons.

FLOWERING TIME: Late winter to early summer.

LIGHT: Partial shade (full sun in cool summer areas). Plants don't bloom well in deep shade.

SOIL: Rich, well-drained, acid (pH 4.5 to 6.0) soil, high in organic matter and low in salts. (For more information about pH, see page 908.) When planting, add at least 50 percent peat moss to the soil, and keep 2 inches of mulch around the base of the plant.

FERTILIZER: Fertilize with ORTHO Azalea, Camellia & Rhododendron Food according to label directions.

WATER:
How much: Apply enough water to wet the soil 1 to 2½ feet deep. To determine the proper amount of water for your soil type, see page 912.
How often: Water when the soil is moist but not wet under the mulch. For more information, see page 912.

PRUNING: Prune just after flowering.
Azaleas: For a bushier plant, pinch off growing tips.
Rhododendrons: Remove dead flower trusses. Be careful not to break the new buds. To renew old, lanky plants, reduce the height of the plant by a third for 3 successive years.

Azalea petal blight.

PROBLEM: Circular spots the size of pinheads form on the flower petals. The spots are pale or whitish on colored flowers, and rust-colored on white flowers. Spots quickly enlarge to form irregular blotches until the entire flower collapses. The petals feel slimy when rubbed between the fingers. Diseased flowers dry up and cling to the plant. Leaves and stems are not injured.

ANALYSIS: Azalea petal blight
Petal blight is very destructive to azaleas and rhododendrons in humid coastal regions. It is caused by a fungus (*Ovulinia azaleae*). In early spring, the fungus infects early-flowering azaleas. With favorable weather conditions, the disease spreads rapidly, turning the flowers to mush within a day. Spores from early-flowering azaleas infect later-flowering varieties. Small hard black "resting structures," composed of fungal strands, form on dead flowers if the weather stays wet. Many of these resting structures drop to the ground and remain in the litter. The following season, they produce spores that cause the initial infection on the early-flowering varieties.

SOLUTION: Spray the flowers with a fungicide containing *chlorothalonil* (DACONIL 2787®), *triforine* (FUNGINEX®), or *benomyl* when the disease is first noticed. Test the fungicides on a few flowers before spraying the entire plant; some varieties may discolor. Repeat every 3 to 4 days until flowering ends. To prevent infection the following year, begin spraying as the first color begins to show. Clean up litter around the base of the plants and pick off diseased flowers. Spray the ground under the shrub before flowering begins with a fungicide containing *PCNB*.

Spider mite damage on azalea.

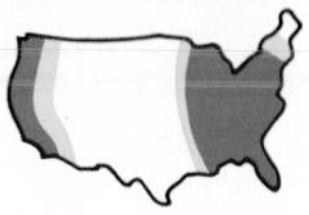

PROBLEM: Leaves are stippled yellow or bronze and dirty. There may be a silken webbing on the lower surfaces of the leaves. New leaves may be distorted. To determine if the plant is infested with mites, hold a sheet of white paper underneath an affected leaf or branch and tap sharply. Minute green, red, or yellow specks the size of pepper grains will drop to the paper and begin to crawl around. The pests are easily seen against the white background.

ANALYSIS: Spider mites
Spider mites, related to spiders, are major pests of many garden plants. They cause damage by sucking sap from buds and the undersides of leaves. As a result of feeding, the green leaf pigment disappears, producing the stippled appearance. The southern red mite (*Oligonychus ilicis*), found in the Northeast, Southeast, and Great Lakes states, is most prolific in cooler weather. It feeds and reproduces primarily during spring and fall. Other spider mites found on rhododendrons develop rapidly in hot, dry weather (70°F and up); by midsummer they build up to tremendous numbers. For more information about spider mites, see page 887.

SOLUTION: Spray with ORTHO Isotox Insect Killer or ORTHO Diazinon Insect Spray when damage first appears. Direct sprays to the undersides of the leaves. Repeat application if plant becomes reinfested. To prevent unsightly injury to foliage, it is important to apply control measures early in the season when damage first appears. Injured leaves remain on the plant for more than one growing season. Hose down plants frequently to knock off webs and mites.

GROWTH ON LEAVES

Leaf gall on azalea.

PROBLEM: Developing leaves and flowers are thickened, fleshy, and distorted. Initially the thickenings are whitish or light green. As the thickenings enlarge they become white or pink, with a powdery appearance. Later in the growing season, the distorted leaves turn dark and hard. This problem is most severe in spring, during cool moist weather, and where plants are growing in areas of poor air circulation or in full shade.

ANALYSIS: Leaf gall
This plant disease is caused by a fungus (*Exobasidium vaccinii*). It is most common on azaleas but sometimes occurs on rhododendrons. As the buds open in spring, fungal spores blown by wind to the plant or washed by rain from the bark enter the tissue. The spores need moisture to germinate. Plants grown in areas of poor air movement or in deep shade, where moisture levels are high, will usually have more galls than will other plants. After infection takes place, a growth-promoting substance is triggered in the plant, causing the thickening and distortion. By midsummer the white powdery fungal spores cover the distorted leaves.

SOLUTION: Sprays must be applied before infection occurs. Once the galls develop, the best control is to remove them when they are first noticed. If the galls are not removed and destroyed, the disease will be more severe the following year. To reduce new infection next spring, spray with a fungicide containing *tribasic copper sulfate* or *zineb* before buds open. Repeat at intervals of 2 weeks until new leaves are fully grown. Provide air circulation and avoid planting shrubs in areas of deep shade.

DISCOLORED OR SPOTTED LEAVES

Lacebug damage on rhododendron.

PROBLEM: The upper sides of the leaves are mottled or speckled yellow and green. The mottling may be confused with mite or leafhopper damage. It can be distinguished from other insect damage by hard, black, shiny droplets that are found on the undersides of damaged leaves. Small (1/8 inch) spiny wingless insects or brownish insects with clear lacy wings may be seen around the droplets. The plant is usually stunted. Damage occurs in spring and summer.

ANALYSIS: Lacebugs
(*Stephanitis* species)
Populations of lacebugs are highest when rhododendrons and azaleas are grown in sunny rather than shady locations. The wingless, immature insects and the lacy-winged adults suck sap from the undersides of leaves. As they feed, droplets of black excrement accumulate around them. Damage is unsightly and food production by the leaf is reduced, making the plant less vigorous.

SOLUTION: Spray with ORTHO Orthene Systemic Insect Control or ORTHO Isotox Insect Killer when damage first appears. Cover the undersurfaces of the leaves thoroughly. Repeat 7 to 10 days later. A third application may be necessary if plants become reinfested in summer. It is important to spray early to prevent as much damage as possible.

Rust on rhododendron.

PROBLEM: Yellow spots, up to 1/4 inch in diameter, may appear on the upper surfaces of the leaves during the growing season. Directly under the spots, on the undersides of the leaves, are spots or blisters containing a yellow to orange-red powdery material. The powdery material can be rubbed or scraped off easily. Infected leaves may drop off the plant prematurely. Heavily infected plants usually lack vigor.

ANALYSIS: Rust
Several different fungi cause rust on rhododendrons and azaleas. The yellow to orange-red spores are spread by the wind to the leaves. With moisture (rain, dew, or fog) and moderate temperatures (55° to 75°F), the spores enter the tissue on the undersides of the leaves. Spots usually develop directly above—on the upper surfaces—as the fungus saps the plant nutrients.

SOLUTION: No chemicals are available to control rust on rhododendrons and azaleas. Where practical, pick off infected leaves.

RHODODENDRON (AZALEA) — DISCOLORED OR SPOTTED LEAVES

Iron deficiency on rhododendron.

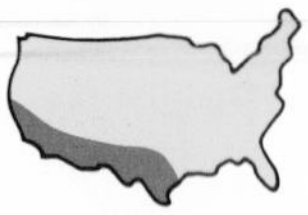

PROBLEM: The leaves are pale green to yellow. The newest leaves may be completely yellow with only the veins, and the tissue right next to the veins, remaining green. With progressively older leaves, only the leaf edges may be yellowing. The plant may be stunted.

ANALYSIS: Iron deficiency

This is a common problem in acid-loving plants like azaleas and rhododendrons. These plants prefer soil with a pH between 5.0 and 6.0. (For more information on soil acidity, see page 908.) The yellowing is due to a deficiency of iron in the plant. The soil is seldom deficient in iron. However, iron is often found in an insoluble form that is not available to the plant, especially in soil with a pH of 7.0 or higher. A high soil pH can result from overliming, or from lime leached from cement or brick. Regions where soil is derived from limestone and those with low rainfall also have high pH soils. Plants use iron in the formation of the green pigment in the leaves. When it is lacking, new leaves are yellow.

SOLUTION: Spray the foliage with ORTHO Greenol Liquid Iron, and apply it to the soil around the plants to correct the iron deficiency. Correct the pH of the soil by treating it with ORTHO Aluminum Sulfate and watering it in well. Maintain an acid pH by fertilizing with ORTHO Azalea, Camellia & Rhododendron Food. When planting azaleas or rhododendrons, add at least 50 percent peat moss to the soil. This is especially important if you live in an area where the soil is alkaline or has poor drainage. Never lime the soil around azaleas or rhododendrons.

Leaf spots on azalea.

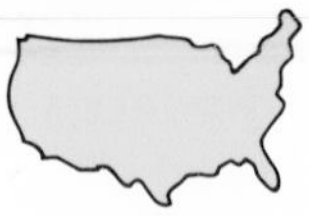

PROBLEM: Spots and blotches appear on the leaves. The spots may be yellow, red, tan, gray, or brown. They range in size from barely visible to ¾ inch in diameter. Several spots may join to form blotches. Leaves may be yellow and dying. Some leaves may drop. Leaf spotting is most severe in warm, humid weather.

ANALYSIS: Fungal leaf spot

There are a number of different fungi that cause leaf spots. These spots are unsightly but rarely harmful to the plant. Plants weakened by low temperatures and wind exposure are most susceptible to invasion by leaf spot fungi. The fungi are spread by splashing water and wind. Spots develop where the fungi enter the tissue. If wet or humid weather persists, the fungi spread through the tissue and blotches form. They survive the winter on the leaves and twigs. Most leaf spot organisms do their greatest damage in mild weather (between 50° and 85°F).

SOLUTION: Once leaves become spotted they will remain so. Where practical, remove infected leaves from the plant. Collect and destroy any fallen leaves. Spray with a fungicide containing *chlorothalonil* (DACONIL 2787®), *mancozeb*, *benlate*, or *zineb* when new growth begins in the spring. Repeat two more times at intervals of 2 weeks, or for as long as the weather remains favorable for infection. Add a spreader-sticker to the spray. (For more information about spreader-stickers, see page 922.) To reduce plant susceptibility, provide windbreaks and protection from low temperatures.

LEAVES OR BRANCHES DIE

Rhododendron borer damage.

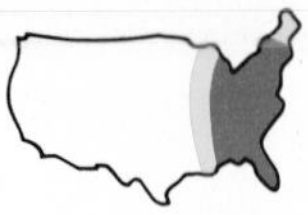

PROBLEM: Crisp, round spots, the size of a dime or nickel, are scattered like polka dots on the leaves. Leaves and shoots on the outer edge of the plant may wilt. The bark on the main stem and lower branches flakes off easily. Underneath this area shallow tunnels, ridges, and holes are seen.

ANALYSIS: Rhododendron borer
(*Synanthedon rhododendri*)

The larva of this clear-winged moth is a serious pest of rhododendrons in the Atlantic coast states. The small (up to ½ inch), yellowish white caterpillar with brown legs and head causes severe wounds by tunneling into the bark and wood of the trunk and branches. The borer is seldom seen because the larva develops inside the wood. In early summer, it emerges as an adult moth, lays its eggs on the bark, and dies. The eggs hatch in June and the larvae burrow into the wood to feed.

SOLUTION: The rhododendron borer is difficult to control once it has burrowed into the wood. In fall, winter, or early spring (before May), cut out and destroy all dead and dying branches. Severely bored sections should be sacrificed. In early May, spray or paint the trunk and branches with ORTHO Lindane Borer & Leaf Miner Spray to kill young larvae before they burrow. Repeat three more times at intervals of 2 weeks. Maintain plant health and vigor by watering and fertilizing regularly.

Salt burn.

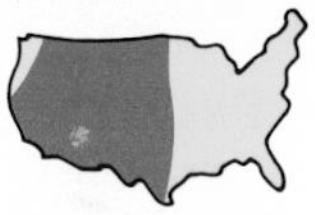

PROBLEM: Leaf edges are brown and dead. Browning usually occurs on older leaves first. This distinguishes the problem from wind burn, which develops on young, exposed leaves first. Leaves may be lighter green than normal. In a severe case, leaves drop off.

ANALYSIS: Salt burn
This problem is most common in areas of low rainfall. It also occurs in soils with poor drainage, and where too much fertilizer has been applied. Excess salts dissolved in the soil water accumulate in the leaf edges, where they kill the tissue. These salts also interfere with water uptake by the plant. This problem is rare in areas of high rainfall, where the soluble salts are leached from most soils. Poorly drained soils do not leach well; much of the applied water runs off the surface instead of washing through the soil. Fertilizers, which are soluble salts, also cause salt burn if too much is applied or if they are not diluted with a thorough watering after application.

SOLUTION: Salt burn damage does not disappear from the leaves, but injury can be avoided in the future. In areas of low rainfall, leach accumulated salts from the soil with an occasional heavy irrigation (about once a month). If possible, improve the drainage around the plants by removing them and adding soil amendments. For instructions on improving drainage, see page 907. If plants are severely damaged, replace them with healthy plants. Follow package directions when using commercial fertilizers; water thoroughly after application. Avoid the use of bagged steer manure, which contains large amounts of salt, on azaleas and rhododendrons.

Sunburn on azalea.

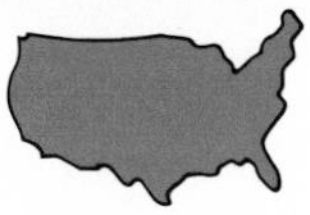

PROBLEM: During warm, sunny weather, the center portion of the leaf bleaches to a tan or off-white color. Once the initial damage has occurred, the spot does not usually increase in size. Injury is generally more severe on plants with light-colored flowers.

ANALYSIS: Sunburn
Rhododendrons and azaleas are generally classified as shade plants. Their leaves are sensitive to the heat of direct sun, which kills the leaf tissue. Scalding occurs when the shrub is planted in full sun. The intense reflection from a light-colored, south-facing wall can also scald leaves. It takes only one hot summer day for damage to appear. The injury is unsightly but is not damaging to the plant. However, weakened leaves are more susceptible to invasion by fungi and bacteria. Plants that do not receive enough water are more susceptible to sunscald.

SOLUTION: Move the injured plant to a shaded location, or provide some shade where it is now planted. (For more information about transplanting, see page 924.) Once leaves are scalded, they will not recover. Where practical, remove affected leaves. Don't let plants dry out during hot weather.

Winter injury on rhododendron.

PROBLEM: Young and exposed leaves are brown and dry, especially around the leaf margins and near the tips. The shrub is planted in a windy location, or is growing in a cold climate where cold, dry, windy days are common. The soil may be frozen or dry.

ANALYSIS: Windburn and winter injury
Windburn and winter injury on rhododendron and azalea leaves are common on plants growing in wind-swept locations. In cold climates, where temperatures commonly fall below freezing, strong winds cause leaves to lose their moisture more rapidly than it can be replaced by the root system. The leaf edges dry out and die. This is most pronounced when water is unavailable because the soil is frozen. Leaf burning also occurs on exceptionally windy, dry days in summer.

SOLUTION: Once the leaf edges have been damaged, the injury remains. Where practical, pick off damaged leaves. To prevent winter injury and windburn, plant shrubs in locations protected from wind; or provide windbreaks. Plants should be watered and fertilized regularly to maintain health and vigor. Water in late fall or winter, if necessary, to ensure adequate soil moisture. Mulch plants after they are dormant to reduce the depth of frost penetration into the soil.

Dieback on rhododendron.

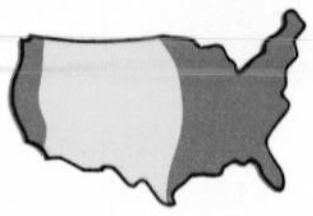

PROBLEM: The leaves and terminal portion of a branch are permanently wilted, and dying. Leaves may turn reddish brown and remain attached to the plant. Or the leaves may be rolled and have spots that look water-soaked. There are often sunken, brownish, dead areas at the base of the wilted branch. Generally it is the older branches that are affected. In hot weather, the entire plant may die.

ANALYSIS: Dieback
Dieback is caused by several different fungi. The fungi are spread by splashing water, rain, and infected soil and tools. They enter the plant through wounds, through dead and dying twigs, and through the leaves. A sunken dead area or canker usually develops on the twigs or branches, cutting off the flow of nutrients and water on that side of the plant. The leaves and stems above the canker wilt and die. With some fungi, no canker develops. Instead, the fungus is carried through the water-conducting tissue, producing toxins and plugging the tissue, which causes the leaves and branch tips to wilt and die back. Plants under stress from hot weather die more rapidly.

SOLUTION: Once the branch is wilted and dying, there is no chemical that will control the disease. Prune out and destroy all wilted or cankered branches by cutting into healthy tissue a few inches below the canker. Those plants in which infection started at the leaves with water-soaked spots can be protected with a spray the following year. Spray with a *basic copper* fungicide after blooming. Repeat two more times at intervals of 14 days.

Phytophthora root rot.

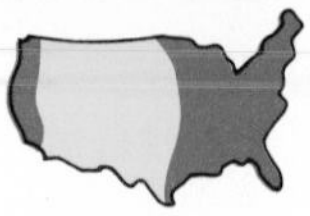

PROBLEM: The young leaves are yellowish and wilting. Eventually the whole plant wilts and dies, even though the soil is moist. Dead leaves remain attached to the plant and are rolled along the midrib. The symptoms may develop over a few weeks, or may take many months. Heavy, poorly drained soil favors disease development. The tissue under the bark close to ground level shows a dark discoloration when cut. To check for discoloration, peel back the bark at the bottom of the plant. There is a distinct margin between white healthy wood and dark diseased wood.

ANALYSIS: Wilt and root rot
This plant disease is caused by several different soil-inhabiting fungi, also known as *water molds*. These fungi (*Phytophthora* and *Pythium* species) attack a wide variety of ornamental plants. The fungi destroy the roots, and may work their way up the stem. If they girdle the stem, the plant wilts and dies. Very wet conditions favor the fungi, which are most common in heavy, poorly drained soils. Although azaleas and rhododendrons need constant moisture, they must also have good drainage.

SOLUTION: No chemical control is available. Dry the plant out, following the technique on page 849. Improve the drainage of the soil before replanting azaleas or rhododendrons in the same location. For methods of improving soil drainage, see page 907. If drainage cannot be improved, plant in beds raised a foot or more above grade. Or plant shrubs that are resistant to wilt and root rot. See page 1016 for a list.

Damaged azalea. *Insert:* Grub (twice life size).

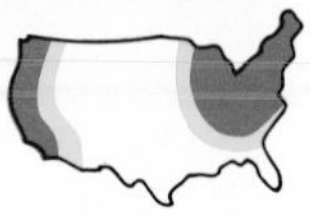

PROBLEM: The leaves on a branch or the entire plant may be yellowing and stunted, or the leaves may droop and curl, especially with the onset of hot weather. The leaf margins may be notched. To determine if the plant is infested with these insects, wash the soil away to expose the base of the stem and a few inches of the main roots. Inspect the bark for signs of chewing. Look for small (¼ to ½ inch), legless grubs in the soil.

ANALYSIS: Root weevil larvae
Several species of root weevils infest rhododendrons and azaleas. The larval stage of the insect (the grub) causes the most damage by feeding on roots and the base of the stem. If the grubs remain undetected, the plant may die abruptly with the onset of hot weather. Female weevils lay eggs at the soil line near the stem during the summer months. The emerging grubs burrow into the soil. They feed on the roots in fall, and then spend the winter in the soil. Most root weevils cause their major damage when they resume feeding in spring. Their feeding girdles the roots and stems, disrupting the flow of nutrients and water through the plant and causing the roots and the top of the plant to die. Minor damage may be caused by the night-feeding adults notching the foliage.

SOLUTION: Discard severely wilted plants. To prevent the next generation of weevils from causing damage, eliminate the adults. Spray the foliage and the ground under the plant with ORTHO Isotox Insect Killer or ORTHO Orthene Systemic Insect Control when notching first appears in May or June. Repeat the spray 2 more times at intervals of 3 weeks.

INSECTS

Notching caused by root weevils.

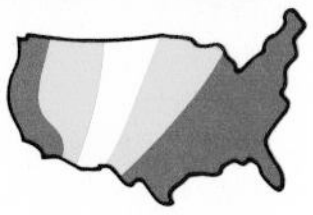

PROBLEM: The leaf margins are scalloped or notched. The leaves may be green and healthy, or they may be yellowing and curled. To determine if the plant is infested with this insect, inspect the foliage after dark, using a flashlight. Black or grayish insects, 1/5 to 2/5 inches long, with elephantlike snouts and with rows of tiny round depressions on their backs, are feeding on the leaf edges. These insects are present from May or June to as late as September.

ANALYSIS: Root weevil adults
Root weevils are common pests of many garden plants. The adult weevils feed at night, notching leaf margins. This feeding detracts from the appearance of the plant, but usually does not cause serious injury. Severe damage and death of the plant may result from larvae feeding on roots, if the weevils are left uncontrolled. The grubs feed unseen on the roots in spring, and from mid or late summer into fall.

SOLUTION: To control adults, spray with ORTHO Orthene Systemic Insect Control or ORTHO Isotox Insect Killer when notching first appears in May or June. Thoroughly cover the foliage and the soil beneath the plant. Repeat two more times at intervals of 3 weeks.

Check for the presence of these weevils with a pitfall trap. Sink a tin can in the soil so the rim is flush with the surface. Pour a few inches of soapy water in the bottom. Inspect the trap daily and replenish the water as necessary. When adults are trapped, begin spraying.

Azalea bark scale (life size).

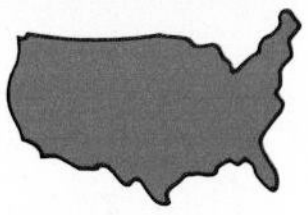

PROBLEM: The undersides of the leaves, the young branches, or the branch crotches, are covered with clusters of somewhat flattened white, yellowish, brown, reddish, or gray scaly bumps. The bumps can be scraped or picked off; the undersides are usually soft. Leaves may turn yellow and drop off, and branches may die back. The plant is killed when infestations are heavy.

ANALYSIS: Scales
Many species of scales infest rhododendrons and azaleas throughout the country. Scales spend the winter on the trunk and twigs of the plant. They lay eggs in spring and in midsummer; the young scales, called *crawlers*, settle on the various parts of the shrub. The small (1/10 inch), soft-bodied young feed by inserting their mouthparts and sucking sap from the plant. The legs usually atrophy and a scaly or crusty shell develops over the body. The mature female scales lay their eggs underneath the shell. Leaf drop and twig dieback occur when scales completely cover the leaves and branches. An uncontrolled infestation may kill a plant after two or three seasons. For more information about scales, see page 876.

SOLUTION: Spray with ORTHO Isotox Insect Killer or ORTHO Orthene Systemic Insect Control in midsummer (late spring in the South), when the young are active. The following early spring, before new growth begins, spray the branches and trunk with a *dormant oil spray* to control overwintering insects.

Aphids (1/4 life size).

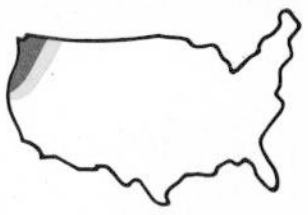

PROBLEM: Tiny (1/8 inch) green or pink soft-bodied insects cluster on the leaves and developing buds. The flower buds may be deformed, and the leaves often have curled edges. A shiny or sticky substance usually coats the leaves. A black sooty mold may grow on the sticky substance. Ants may be present.

ANALYSIS: Rhododendron aphid
(*Macrosiphum rhododendri*)
Rhododendron aphids do little damage in small numbers, and plants can tolerate large numbers without much effect. However, aphids are extremely prolific and populations can rapidly build up to damaging numbers during the growing season. Damage occurs when the aphid sucks the juices from the rhododendron leaves and buds. The aphid is unable to digest fully all the sugar in the plant sap and excretes the excess in a fluid called honeydew. The honeydew often drops onto the leaves below. A sooty mold fungus may develop on the honeydew, causing the rhododendron leaves to appear black and dirty. Ants feed on the sticky substance, and are often present where there is an aphid infestation.

SOLUTION: Spray with ORTHO Isotox Insect Killer or ORTHO Orthene Systemic Insect Control when aphids are noticed. Spray the plant thoroughly. Repeat the spray if the plant becomes reinfested.

RHODODENDRON — INSECTS

Whiteflies on rhododendron (life size).

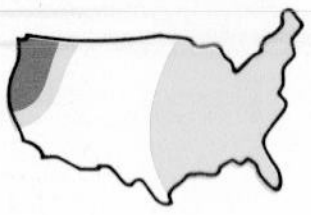

PROBLEM: Tiny, white, winged insects 1/12 inch long are found mainly on the undersides of the leaves. When the plant is touched, the insects flutter rapidly around it. The upper surfaces of new leaves may be mottled and yellow; sometimes the leaf edges curl. A shiny or sticky substance usually coats the leaves. A black sooty mold may grow on the sticky substance.

ANALYSIS: Rhododendron whitefly
(*Dialeurodes chittendeni*)
This whitefly attacks only rhododendrons. The four-winged adult lays eggs on the undersides of leaves. The larvae are the size of a pinhead, flat, greenish, oval, and semitransparent. They feed for about a month before changing to the adult form. Both the larvae and adults suck sap from the leaves. The larvae are more damaging because they feed more heavily. Adults and larvae cannot fully digest all the sugar in the plant sap, and excrete the excess in a fluid called honeydew, which drops onto leaves below. A sooty mold fungus may develop on the honeydew, causing the rhododendron leaves to appear black and dirty. Only rhododendrons that have leaves with smooth undersurfaces are infested. A similar whitefly, called the *azalea whitefly* (*Pealius azaleae*), infests the hairy-leaved, evergreen snow azalea (*Rhododendron mucronatum*).

SOLUTION: Spray with ORTHO Isotox Insect Killer or ORTHO Orthene Systemic Insect Control when insects are first noticed. Repeat the spray 2 more times at intervals of 7 to 10 days. Thoroughly spray both the upper and lower surfaces of the leaves.

RHUS (SUMAC)

Verticillium wilt.

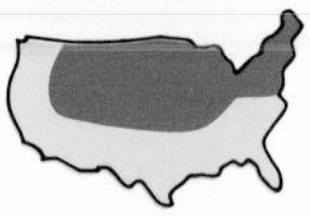

PROBLEM: The leaves on a branch turn yellow at first, and then redden prematurely. During hot weather, the leaves may wilt. New leaves may be stunted and yellow. The infected plant may die slowly, branch by branch, over several seasons. Or the whole plant may wilt and die within a few months. Some plants may recover. The tissue under the bark on the dying side shows dark streaks when cut. To examine for streaks, peel back the bark at the bottom of the dying branch. The dark discoloration may be very apparent or barely visible in the area just underneath the bark.

ANALYSIS: Wilt
This disease affects many ornamental plants. It is caused by either of two soil-inhabiting fungi (*Verticillium albo-atrum* or *Fusarium oxysporum* f. *rhois*) that live on plant debris or in the soil. The disease is spread by contaminated seeds, plants, soil, equipment, and groundwater. The fungus enters the plant through the roots and spreads up into the branches through the water-conducting vessels in the main stem. The vessels become discolored and plugged. This plugging cuts off the flow of water and nutrients to the branches, causing the leaf discoloration and wilting. For more information about wilt, see page 850.

SOLUTION: No chemical control is available. Fertilize and water the affected plant to stimulate vigorous growth. Prune off all dead wood. Do not remove branches on which leaves have recently wilted. These branches may produce new leaves in 3 to 4 weeks or next spring. Remove dead plants.

ROBINIA (LOCUST)

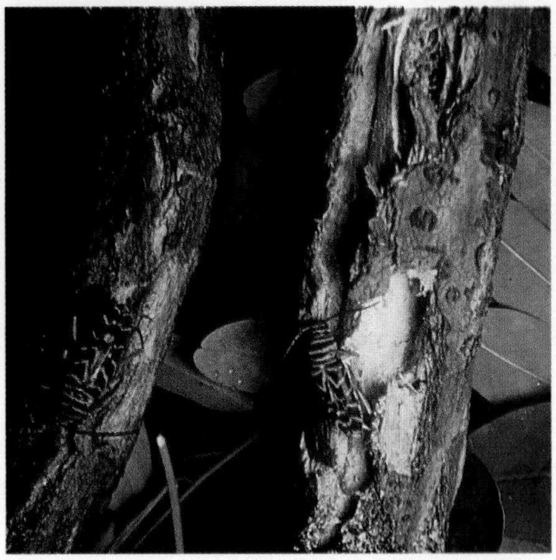

Locust borers (life size).

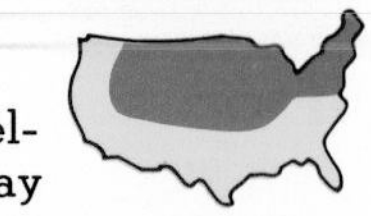

PROBLEM: Foliage is yellow and stunted, and may be sparse. Swellings form on the branches and trunk. The bark cracks, and scars develop at the cracks. Sawdust is often found around the scars. Branches may break off.

ANALYSIS: Locust borer
(*Megacyllene robiniae*)
The locust borer is found wherever black locust is grown, but its damage is more severe in the eastern half of the country. Trees more than 4 years old are most heavily damaged. The female beetles lay their eggs from August to October in bark crevices and around wounds. The white, legless larvae that hatch from these eggs bore through to the inner bark and spend the winter there. In spring, the larvae tunnel into the sapwood and, eventually, the heartwood. The tunneling stops the flow of nutrients and water in that area by cutting the conducting vessels. The leaves yellow, branches and the trunk are weakened and scarred, and they often break. In late summer, the larvae pupate in the tunnel and emerge as adults to lay eggs. Several other borers may also infest black locust.

SOLUTION: Spray the trunk and larger branches with ORTHO Lindane Borer & Leaf Miner Spray in the middle of August. Repeat the spray during the first week of September.

Robinia cultural information
Light: Full sun
Water: Drought tolerant once established
Soil: Tolerates many types
Fertilizer: Light

Locust leafminers (half life size).

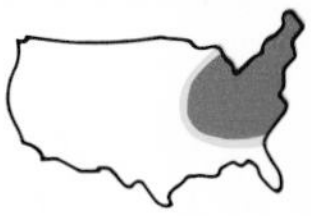

PROBLEM: Yellow to brown patches or trails appear on the leaves in late spring. Some of the leaves may also be chewed. The patches or trails enlarge to form blotches. If a blotch is torn open, whitish larvae with black heads may be found inside. During midsummer, the upper surfaces of the leaves are eaten, giving the leaves a lacy appearance. Small (¼ inch) orange-yellow beetles with a broad black stripe may be seen on the leaves. Many or all of the leaves may turn brown and drop off.

ANALYSIS: Locust leafminer
(*Odontota dorsalis*)
The locust leafminer is destructive in both the larval and adult stages. In the spring, adult beetles feed on the developing locust leaves. After a short time, the females deposit eggs in brown fecal matter on the undersides of the leaves. The emerging larvae burrow into the leaf tissue and feed, making a single trail between the upper and lower surfaces of the leaf. As they increase in size, the larvae feed in separate mines. They pupate, and the beetles emerge from the leaf in midsummer. The beetles skeletonize the leaves by feeding on their lower surfaces. The leaves turn brown, and many or all of them drop off the tree. If the tree grows another set of leaves, a second generation of leafminers often destroys all of them. Infested trees are unsightly, and with repeated infestations they may die.

SOLUTION: Spray with ORTHO Lindane Borer & Leaf Miner Spray as the leaves are developing and again in early July. If you notice damage late in the season, begin spraying the following spring.

ROSA (ROSE)

ADAPTATION: Throughout the United States.

FLOWERING TIME: Spring and summer (through fall in the south).

LIGHT: Full sun. Plant in areas with good air circulation.

SOIL: Any good, well-drained garden soil.

FERTILIZER: Fertilize with ORTHO Rose Food according to label directions.

WATER:
How much: Apply enough water to wet the soil 1½ to 2 feet deep. To determine the proper amount of water for your soil type, see page 912.
How often: Roses need plenty of water. Water when the soil is moist but not wet 4 inches deep. For more information about watering, see page 912.

PRUNING: Remove dead or unhealthy wood. Remove branches that cross through the center of the plant. Prune off at least a third to half of last year's growth. For more information about pruning and care of roses, see ORTHO's book *All About Roses.*

Flower thrips damage.

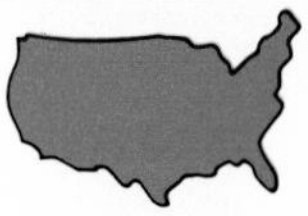

PROBLEM: Young leaves are distorted and foliage may be flecked with yellow. Flower buds are deformed, and usually fail to open. The petals of open blossoms, especially those of white or light-colored varieties, are often covered with brown streaks and spots. If a deformed or streaked flower is pulled apart and shaken over white paper, tiny yellow or brown insects fall out and are easily seen against the white background.

ANALYSIS: Flower thrips
(*Frankliniella tritici*)
Flower thrips are the most abundant and widely distributed thrips in the country. They live inside the buds and flowers of many garden plants. Both the immature and the adult thrips feed on plant sap by rasping the tissue. The injured petal tissue turns brown and the young expanding leaves become deformed. Injured flower buds usually fail to open. Thrips initially breed on grasses and weeds. When these plants begin to dry up or are harvested, the insects migrate to succulent green ornamental plants. The adults lay their eggs by inserting them into the plant tissue. A complete life cycle may occur in 2 weeks, so populations can build up rapidly. Most damage to roses occurs in early summer.

SOLUTION: Thrips are difficult to control because they continuously migrate to roses from other plants. Immediately remove and destroy infested buds and blooms. Spray with ORTHO Orthene Systemic Insect Control, ORTHO Isotox Insect Killer, or ORTHO Orthenex Insect & Disease Control, three times at intervals of 7 to 10 days.

ROSA (ROSE) — FEW OR NO BLOOMS

Failure to bloom.

Poor flowering caused by lack of pruning.

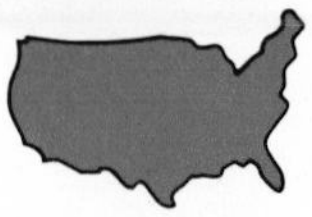

PROBLEM: Plants fail to bloom, or bloom only sparsely.

ANALYSIS: Few or no blooms
Roses produce few or no buds or flowers for any of several reasons.

SOLUTION: The numbered solutions below correspond to the numbers in the analysis.

1. *Too much shade:* Roses grow and bloom best in full sun. They need at least 4 to 5 hours of direct sunlight for normal blooming.

1. Thin out shading trees and shrubs or transplant roses to a sunnier location. Replace them with shade-loving plants. For a list, see page 1008.

2. *Improper dormant pruning:* Most rose varieties are grafted onto a rootstock. Tree roses and some climbing roses are grafted onto an intermediate trunkstock. If the hybrid canes are pruned off below the bud union, the rootstock or trunkstock will produce suckers that are flowerless or that produce flowers very different from the desired variety. Some climbing roses and many old-fashioned roses bloom from flower buds formed the previous season. Heavy pruning of such plants will remove all of these buds.

2. Do not prune roses below the bud union. Take special care when pruning climbing roses and standard tree roses since the bud union between the trunkstock and the grafted variety may be several feet from the ground. Prune old-fashioned roses lightly during the dormant season. If heavy pruning is needed, wait until after the plants have bloomed in spring. For more information about pruning high roses, see ORTHO'S book *All About Roses.*

3. *Excessive or improper pruning during the growing season:* If roses are excessively trimmed and pruned during the growing season, many or all of the developing flower buds may be inadvertently removed.

3. During the growing season, prune roses only to shape them, or to remove suckers and dead or dying growth. When cutting flowers or removing faded flowers, leave at least two five-leaflet leaves on the cane to ensure continued flower production.

4. *Old flowers left on plant:* Roses do not produce as many new flowers when the old blooms are allowed to fade and form seeds.

4. Remove flowers as they begin to fade.

5. *Flushes of bloom:* Many roses bloom in flushes. The first flush usually occurs in late spring, and the second flush occurs in late summer or early fall.

5. There is nothing you can do; this is a natural plant cycle.

6. *Diseased or infested plants:* Roses that have been attacked by diseases or insects do not flower well.

6. Look up the symptoms beginning on page 565 to determine what the cause is. Treat accordingly.

LEAVES DISCOLORED OR SPOTTED

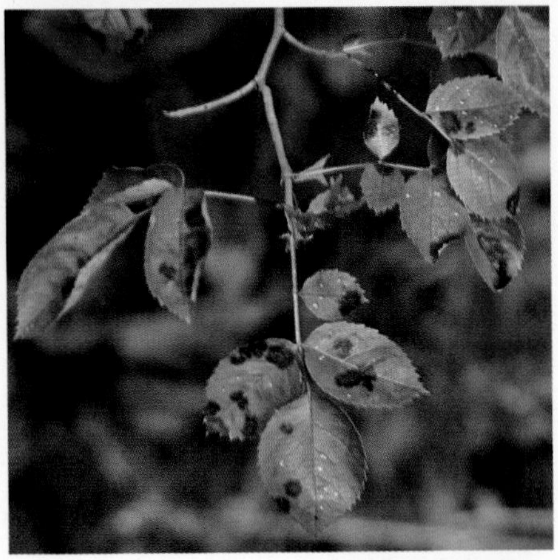

Black spot.

PROBLEM: Circular black spots with fringed margins appear on the upper surfaces of the leaves in the spring. The tissue around the spots or the entire leaf may turn yellow, and the infected leaves may drop prematurely. Severely infected plants may lose all of their leaves by midsummer. Flower production is often reduced and quality is poor.

ANALYSIS: Black spot
Black spot is caused by a fungus (*Diplocarpon rosae*) that is a severe problem in areas where high humidity or rain is common in spring and summer. The fungus spends the winter on infected leaves and canes. The spores are spread from plant to plant by splashing water and rain. The fungus enters the tissue, forming spots the size of a pinhead. The black spots enlarge, up to ¾ inch in diameter, as the fungus spreads; spots may join to form blotches. Twigs may also be infected. Plants are often killed by repeated infections.

SOLUTION: Spray or dust with ORTHO Funginex Rose Disease Control, ORTHO Orthenex Insect & Disease Control, ORTHO Phaltan Rose & Garden Fungicide, or ORTHO Rose & Floral Dust. Repeat the treatment at intervals of 7 to 10 days for as long as the weather remains wet. Sprays may be omitted during hot, dry spells in summer. Prune off infected canes. Avoid overhead watering. In the fall, rake up and destroy the fallen leaves. After pruning plants during the dormant season, spray with ORTHO Orthorix Spray. The following spring, when new growth starts, begin the spray program again. For a list of tolerant and susceptible varieties, see page 1005.

Powdery mildew.

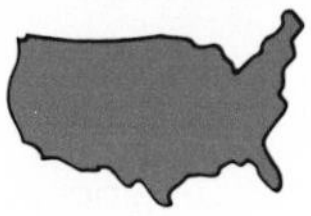

PROBLEM: The young leaves, young twigs, and flower buds are covered with a thin layer of grayish white powdery material. Infected leaves may be distorted and curled and many may turn yellow or purplish and drop off. New growth is often stunted, and young canes may be killed. Badly infected flower buds do not open properly. In late summer, tiny black dots (spore-producing bodies) may be scattered over the powdery covering like ground pepper.

ANALYSIS: Powdery mildew
This common plant disease is caused by a fungus (*Sphaerotheca pannosa* var. *rosae*). It is oneof the most widespread and serious diseases of rose. The powdery covering consists of fungal strands and spores. The spores are spread by the wind to healthy plants. The fungus saps the plant nutrients, causing distortion, discoloring, and often death of the leaves and canes. Powdery mildew may occur on roses any time during the growing season when rainfall is low or absent, temperatures are between 70° and 80°F, nighttime relative humidity is high, and daytime relative humidity is low. In areas where there is high rainfall in spring and summer, control may not be needed until the drier months of late summer. Rose varieties differ in their susceptibility to powdery mildew.

SOLUTION: Apply ORTHO Funginex Rose Disease Control or ORTHO Orthenex Insect & Disease Control at the first sign of mildew. Repeat the spray at intervals of 7 to 10 days if mildew reappears. Rake up and destroy leaves in the fall. For a list of roses tolerant of and susceptible to powdery mildew, see page 1005.

Rust.

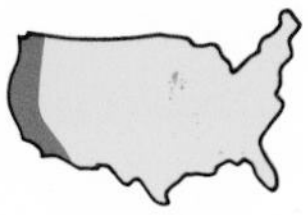

PROBLEM: Yellow to brown spots, up to ¼ inch in diameter, appear on the upper surfaces of the leaves, starting in the spring or late fall. The lower leaves are affected first. On the undersides of the leaves are spots or blotches containing a red, orange, or black powdery material that can be scraped off. Infected leaves may become twisted and dry, and drop off the plant, or they may remain attached. Twigs may also be infected. Severely infected plants lack vigor.

ANALYSIS: Rust
Rose rust is caused by any of several species of fungi (*Phragmidium* species) that infest only rose plants. The orange fungal spores are spread by wind to rose leaves. With moisture (rain, dew, or fog) and moderate temperatures (55° to 75°F), the spores enter the tissue on the undersides of the leaves. Spots develop directly above, on the upper surfaces. Rose varieties differ in their susceptiblity to rust. In the fall, black spores develop in the spots. These spores can survive the winter on dead leaves. In spring, the fungus produces the spores that cause new infections. Rust may also infect and damage young twigs.

SOLUTION: At the first sign of rust, spray with ORTHO Funginex Rose Disease Control or ORTHO Orthenex Insect & Disease Control. Repeat at intervals of 7 to 14 days for as long as conditions remain favorable for infection. Rake up and destroy infected leaves in the fall. Prune off infected twigs. Apply ORTHO Orthorix Spray as a dormant application. Plant resistant varieties (for a list, see page 1005).

Spider mite damage.

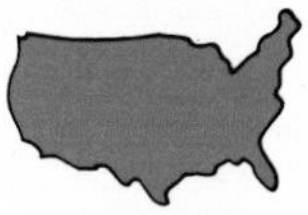

PROBLEM: Leaves are stippled, bronzed, and dirty. There may be a silken webbing on the lower surfaces of the leaves or on the new growth. Infested leaves often turn brown, curl, and drop off. New leaves may be distorted. Plants are usually weak and appear unthrifty. To determine if the plant is infested with mites, hold a sheet of white paper underneath an affected leaf and tap the leaf sharply. Minute green, red, or yellow specks the size of pepper grains will drop to the paper and begin to crawl around. The pests are easily seen against the white background.

ANALYSIS: Spider mites
These mites, related to spiders, are major pests of many garden and greenhouse plants. They cause damage by sucking sap from the undersides of the leaves. As a result of feeding, the green leaf pigment disappears, producing the stippled appearance. Many leaves may drop off. Severely infested plants produce few flowers. Mites are active throughout the growing season, but are favored by hot, dry weather (70°F and up). By midsummer, they build up to tremendous numbers. For more information about spider mites, see page 887.

SOLUTION: Spray with ORTHO Orthenex Insect & Disease Control or ORTHO Isotox Insect Killer when damage is first noticed. Cover the undersides of the leaves thoroughly. Repeat the application two more times at intervals of 7 to 10 days.

ROSA (ROSE) — LEAVES MOTTLED

Damaged leaf. *Insert:* Leafhopper (twice life size).

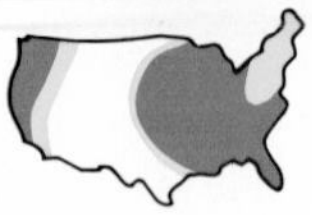

PROBLEM: Whitish insects, up to ½ inch long, hop and fly away quickly when the plant is touched. The leaves are stippled white. Severely infested plants may be killed.

ANALYSIS: Rose leafhopper
(*Edwardsiana rosae*)
The rose leafhopper is a serious pest of roses and apples, and infests a number of ornamental trees as well. It spends the winter as an egg, usually in pimplelike spots on rose canes or on apple bark. When the weather warms in the spring, the young leafhoppers emerge and settle on the undersides of the leaves. They feed by sucking out the plant sap, which causes the stippling of the leaves. The insects mature, and the females produce a second generation of leafhoppers. Eggs may be deposited in the leaf veins or leaf stems of the rose; or the leafhopper may fly to another woody plant to lay her eggs. This second generation of leafhoppers feeds until fall. The damage caused by their feeding on the leaves, and by egg-laying in the rose canes, may kill the plant.

SOLUTION: Spray with ORTHO Isotox Insect Killer, ORTHO Orthenex Insect & Disease Control, or ORTHO Rose & Flower Insect Killer when damage is first noticed. Cover the lower surfaces of the leaves thoroughly. Repeat the spray if the plant becomes reinfested.

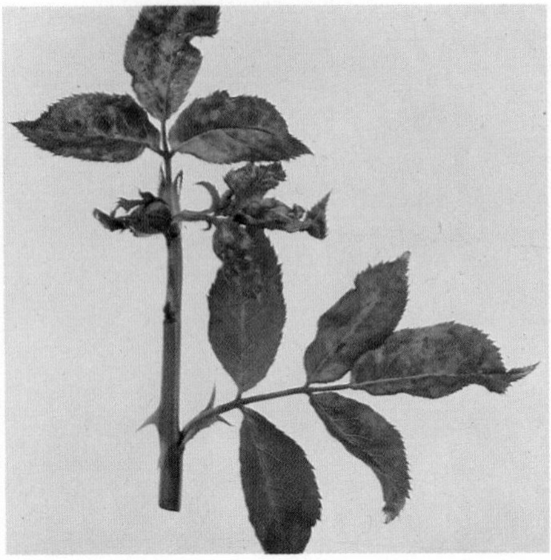

Rose midge damage.

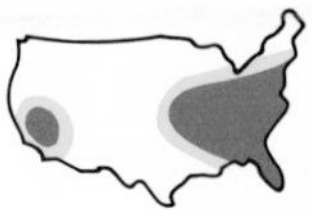

PROBLEM: The buds are deformed, or black and crisp, and the stem tips are dead. Tiny whitish maggots may be seen feeding at the base of buds or on the stem tips.

ANALYSIS: Rose midge
(*Dasineura rhodophaga*)
The rose midge is the larva of a tiny (1/20 inch) yellowish fly that appears in mid or late summer. The females lay their eggs in the growing tips, flower buds, and unfolding leaves, often 20 or 30 eggs to a bud. The eggs hatch in about 2 days and the maggots feed, causing the tissue and buds to become distorted and blackened. When mature, the larvae drop to the ground to pupate. New adults appear in 5 to 7 days to lay more eggs. When infestations are severe, most or all of the buds and new shoots in an entire rose garden are killed.

SOLUTION: Cut out and destroy infested stem tips and buds, and spray with ORTHO Orthene Systemic Insect Control. Repeat the spray if the plant becomes reinfested.

Virus disease.

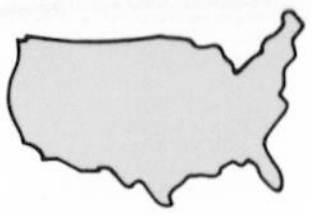

PROBLEM: Yellow or brown rings, or yellow splotches of various sizes, appear on the leaves. The uninfected portions remain dark green. New leaves may be puckered and curling; flower buds may be malformed. Sometimes there are brown rings on the canes. The plants are usually stunted.

ANALYSIS: Mosaic and streak viruses
A number of viruses infect roses. The viruses are transmitted when an infected plant is grafted or budded to a healthy one. This generally occurs in the nursery where the plant was grown. Some plants may show symptoms in only a few leaves. However, the virus is throughout the plant, and further symptoms may appear later. Most rose viruses are fairly harmless unless there is extensive yellowing or browning. The virus suppresses the development of the green pigment (chlorophyll), causing the splotches or rings. Food production is reduced, which may result in stunted plant growth.

SOLUTION: No cure is available for virus-infected plants. There is little natural spread of rose viruses; therefore only weak plants need to be removed. When purchasing rose bushes, buy only healthy plants from a reputable dealer. For further information on selecting healthy plants, see page 924.

INSECTS

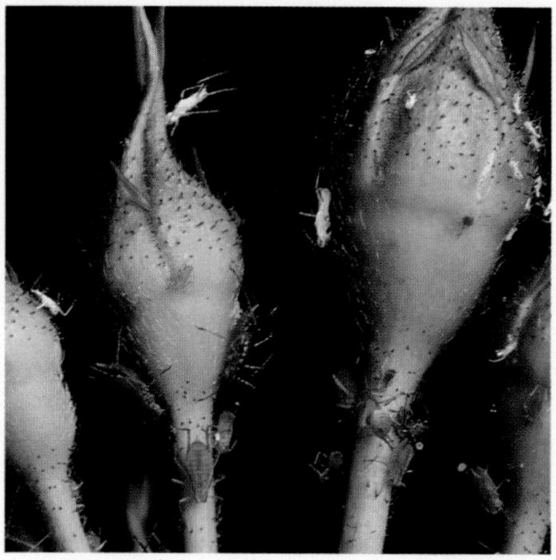

Rose aphids (life size).

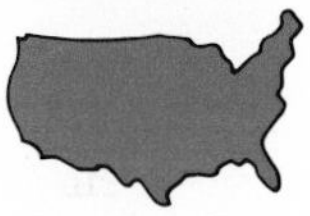

PROBLEM: Tiny (1/8 inch) green or pink soft-bodied insects cluster on leaves, stems, and developing buds. When insects are numerous, flower buds are usually deformed and may fail to open properly. A shiny, sticky substance often coats the leaves. A black sooty mold may grow on the sticky substance. Ants may be present.

ANALYSIS: Rose aphid
(*Macrosiphum rosae*)
Rose aphids do little damage in small numbers. Plants can tolerate fairly high populations without much effect. However, the aphids are extremely prolific, and populations can rapidly build up to damaging numbers during the growing season. Damage occurs when the aphid sucks the juices from the rose stems and buds. The aphid is unable to digest fully all the sugar in the plant sap and excretes the excess in a fluid called honeydew, which often drops onto the leaves below. A sooty mold fungus may develop on the honeydew, causing the rose plants to appear black and dirty. Ants feed on the sticky substance, and are often present where there is an aphid infestation. When aphid populations are high, flower quality and quantity are reduced.

SOLUTION: Spray with ORTHO Isotox Insect Killer, ORTHO Orthenex Insect & Disease Control, or ORTHO Rose & Flower Insect Killer or dust with ORTHO Rose & Floral Dust when clusters of aphids are noticed. Repeat the treatment if the plant becomes reinfested.

Rolled leaves.

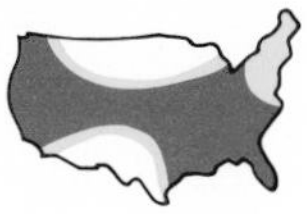

PROBLEM: Leaves are rolled, usually lengthwise, and tied together with webbing. The rolled leaves are chewed and the plant may be defoliated. When a rolled leaf is opened, a green caterpillar, 1/2 to 3/4 inch long may be found inside, surrounded by silky webbing. Flower buds also may be chewed.

ANALYSIS: Leafrollers
Several different leafrollers feed on rose leaves and buds. They may also feed on many other plants in the garden. Leafrollers are the larvae of small (up to 3/4 inch) brownish moths. The larvae feed on the young foliage in the spring, sometimes tunneling into and mining the leaf first. They roll one to several leaves around themselves, tying the leaves together with silken webbing. The leafrollers feed very little once the leaves are rolled. The rolled leaves provide protection from weather, parasites, and chemical sprays. Some leafrollers mature in summer and have several generations during the growing season. Other leafrollers have only one generation a year.

SOLUTION: Spray with ORTHO Isotox Insect Killer or ORTHO Orthene Systemic Insect Control in the spring when leaf damage is first noticed. For the insecticide to be most effective, it should be applied before the larvae are protected inside the rolled leaves. Check the plant periodically in spring for the first sign of an infestation.

Leafcutter bee damage.

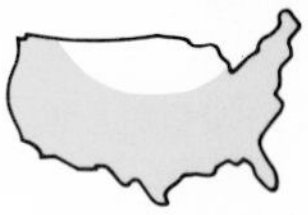

PROBLEM: Small, precise ovals or circles are cut from the leaves. Rose twigs with broken or cut ends may die back for several inches. Hairy, black or metallic blue, green, or purple bees are sometimes seen flying around the plant.

ANALYSIS: Leafcutter bees
(*Megachile* species)
The leafcutter bees are important pollinators of plants such as alfalfa, clover, and forage crops. The females cut circular pieces of leaf tissue from rose plants to line their nests and plug their egg cells. They usually make their nests in dead rose twigs or other plant twigs tht accumulate in the garden. Sometimes they nest in the ends of dying or dead rose stems still attached to the plant. Damage to rose plants is minor.

SOLUTION: Cut out dead and dying stems. Remove dead twigs and plant debris. Since leafcutter bees are pollinators, no chemical controls should be used.

ROSA (ROSE) — INSECTS

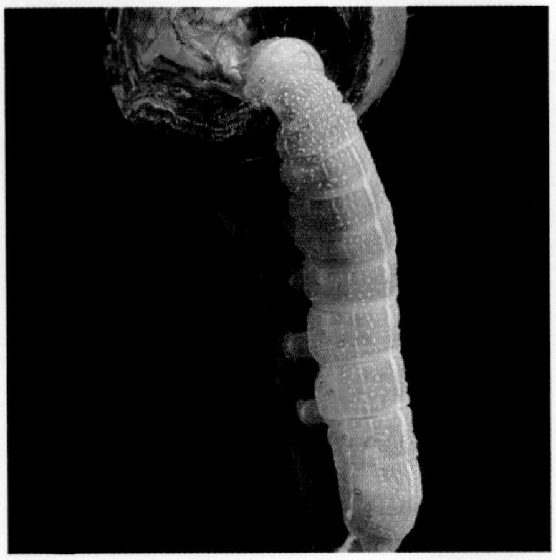

Caterpillar (life size).

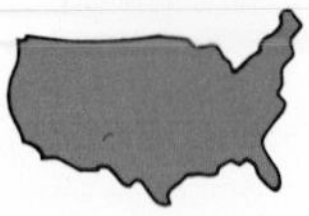

PROBLEM: Holes appear in the leaves and buds. Leaves, buds, and flowers may be entirely chewed off. Worms or caterpillars are feeding on the plants.

ANALYSIS: Caterpillars
Many species of these moth or butterfly larvae feed on roses and other garden plants. The adult moths or butterflies of most species start to lay their eggs on garden plants with the onset of warm spring weather. The larvae that emerge from these eggs feed on the leaves, flowers, and buds for 2 to 6 weeks, then pupate in cocoons attached to leaves or structures, or buried in the soil. The adult moths and butterflies emerge the following spring.

SOLUTION: Spray infested plants with ORTHO Household Insect Control, ORTHO Orthene Systemic Insect Control, or ORTHO Liquid Sevin according to label directions. You may also control caterpillars with a spray containing *Bacillus thuringiensis*. This bacterial insecticide is most effective while the caterpillars are small.

Io caterpillar (life size).

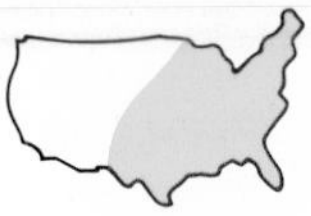

PROBLEM: Round or irregular holes appear in the leaves and buds. Leaves, buds, and flowers may be entirely chewed off. Two-inch, greenish caterpillars covered with short green spines and with a red and white stripe running the length of the body are found on the plants. Caterpillars are most active at night, and can occur in large numbers.

ANALYSIS: Io caterpillar
(*Automeris io*)
This caterpillar is the larva of a 3-inch, yellowish brown moth that lays its eggs on the rose leaves. After hatching, caterpillars eat leaves and flowers, and develop into adults within a few weeks. Several generations of caterpillars are produced each year, primarily between early spring and late fall. Their spines give a painful sting.

SOLUTION: Spray infested plants with ORTHO Isotox Insect Killer or the bacterial insecticide *Bacillus thuringiensis*. If additional caterpillars are found, allow at least 7 days to pass between spray applications.

Roseslug (life size).

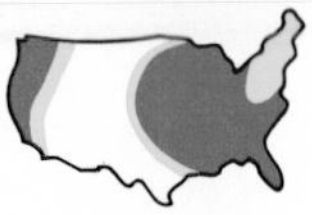

PROBLEM: The upper or lower surfaces of the leaves are eaten between the veins, leaving a lacy, translucent layer of tissue that turns brown. Later, large holes or the entire leaf, except the main vein, may be chewed. Pale green to metallic green sluglike worms, up to ¾ inch long, with large brown heads, may be found feeding on the leaves. Some have hairs covering their bodies, and others appear wet and slimy.

ANALYSIS: Roseslugs
Roseslugs are the larvae of black and yellow wasps called *sawflies*. The adult flies appear in spring. They lay their eggs between the upper and lower surfaces of the leaves along the leaf edges, with a sawlike egg-laying organ. Depending on the species of roseslug, some of the larvae that emerge exude a slimy substance, giving them a sluglike appearance. Others are hairy. The roseslugs begin feeding on one surface of the leaf tissue, skeletonizing it. Later, several species of these slugs chew holes in the leaf or devour it entirely. When they are mature, the larvae drop to the ground, burrow into the soil, and construct cells in which to pass the winter. Some roseslugs pupate, emerge, and repeat the cycle 2 to 6 times during the growing season. Severely infested roses may be greatly weakened, and produce fewer blooms.

SOLUTION: Dust with ORTHO Rose & Floral Dust or spray with ORTHO Liquid Sevin when damage is first noticed.

BUMPS ON STEM

Japanese beetle (life size).

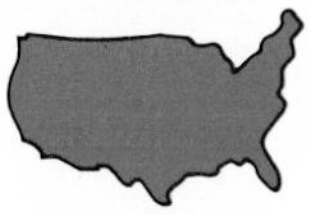

PROBLEM: Holes appear in the flowers and flower buds; open flowers may be entirely eaten. Affected buds often fail to open, or they open deformed. The stem tips may be chewed, or the leaves may be notched or riddled with holes. Red, green spotted, brownish, or metallic green beetles up to ½ inch long are sometimes seen on the flowers or foliage.

ANALYSIS: Beetles
A number of different beetles infest roses. They may destroy the ornamental value of the plant by seriously damaging the flowers and foliage. The insects usually spend the winter as larvae in the soil or as adults in plant debris on the ground. In late spring or summer, mature beetles fly to roses and feed on the flowers, buds, and sometimes the leaves. Punctured flower buds usually fail to open, and open flowers are often devoured. Many beetles feed at night, so their damage may be all that is noticed. The female beetles lay their eggs in the soil or in the flowers in late summer or fall. The emerging larvae crawl down into the soil to spend the winter, or mature and pass the winter as adults. The larvae of some beetles feed on plant roots before maturing in fall or spring.

SOLUTION: Spray with ORTHO Gypsy Moth & Japanese Beetle Killer, ORTHO Isotox Insect Killer or ORTHO Liquid Sevin, or dust with the combination insecticide-fungicide ORTHO Rose & Floral Dust.

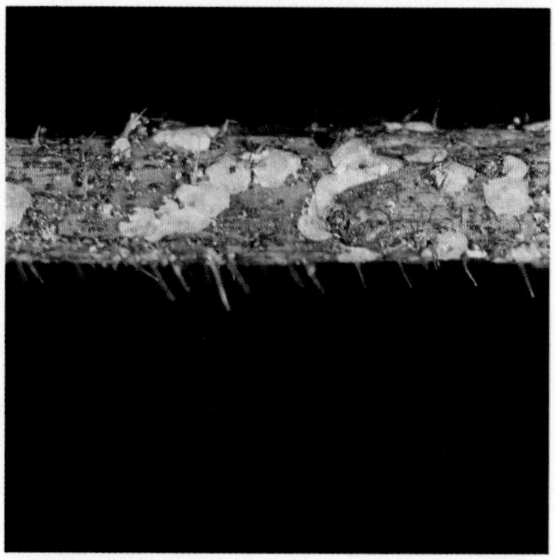

Rose scale (life size).

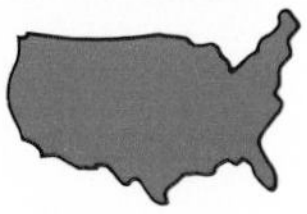

PROBLEM: Stems and leaves are covered with white, cottony masses, or brown or black crusty bumps, or clusters or somewhat flattened white, yellowish, or brown scaly bumps. The bumps can be scraped or picked off. Leaves turn yellow and may drop. In some cases, a shiny, sticky substance coats the leaves. A black sooty mold often grows on the sticky substance. Stems are killed by heavy infestations.

ANALYSIS: Scales
Many different types of scale insects infest roses. They lay their eggs on the leaves or canes, and in spring to midsummer the young scales, called *crawlers*, settle on the leaves and twigs. These small (1/10 inch), soft-bodied young feed by sucking sap from the plant. The legs usually atrophy and with some types, a shell develops over the body. The types of scale that do not develop shells are very conspicuous. The females of the cottony cushion scale are covered with a white, cottony egg sac, containing up to 2500 eggs. Scales covered with a shell are less noticeable. The shell often blends in with the plant, and the eggs are inconspicuous beneath their covering. Some species of scales are unable to digest fully all the sugar in the plant sap, and excrete the excess in a fluid called honeydew. For more information about scales, see page 876.

SOLUTION: Control with ORTHO Isotox Insect Killer or ORTHO Orthene Systemic Insect Control when the young are active. Contact your local Cooperative Extension Office (see page 1029) to determine the best time to spray in your area. To control overwintering insects, spray with ORTHO Volck Oil in spring.

Crown gall.

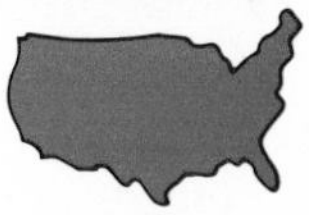

PROBLEM: Large, corky galls, up to several inches in diameter, appear at the base of the plant and on the stems and roots. The galls are rounded, with rough, irregular surfaces, and may be dark and cracked. Plants with numerous galls are weak; growth is slowed and leaves turn yellow. Branches or the entire plant may die back.

ANALYSIS: Crown gall
This plant disease is caused by a soil-inhabiting bacterium (*Agrobacterium tumefaciens*) that infects many ornamentals and fruits in the garden. The bacteria are spread with the soil and contaminated pruning tools, and are often brought to a garden initially on the roots of an infected plant. The bacteria enter the shrub through wounds in the roots or the base of the stem. They produce a compound that stimulates rapid cell growth in the plant, causing gall formation on the roots, crown, and sometimes the branches. The galls disrupt the flow of water and nutrients up the roots and stems, weakening and stunting the top of the plant. Galls do not usually cause the death of the shrub. For more information about crown gall, see page 853.

SOLUTION: Crown gall cannot be eliminated from the shrub. However, infected plants may survive for many years. To improve the appearance of the plant, prune out and destroy galled stems. Sterilize pruning shears after each cut with rubbing alcohol. Destroy severely infected shrubs. The bacteria will remain in the soil for 2 to 3 years. If you wish to replace the shrub soon, plant resistant species. For a list of plants resistant to crown gall, see page 1013.

ROSA (ROSE) — BRANCH DIES

Dieback.

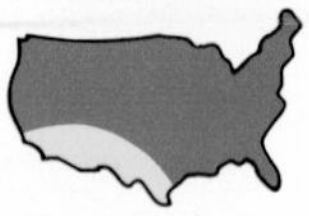

PROBLEM: Yellowish, reddish, or brown sunken areas develop on the canes. The sunken areas may have a purple margin, or they may be cracked. The leaves on affected canes are sometimes spotted, yellow, or wilting. Stems may die back.

ANALYSIS: Stem cankers and dieback
A number of different fungi cause stem cankers on roses. During wet or humid weather the fungi enter the plant at a wound caused by the thorns, or at a cut stem. A sunken canker develops and expands through the tissue in all directions. The fungus may cut off the flow of nutrients and water through the stem, causing the leaves to wilt or yellow, and twigs to die back. Rose plants that are infected with black spot (see page 566) or in a weakened condition are more susceptible to invasion by stem canker fungi.

SOLUTION: Cut out and destroy cankered canes at least 5 inches below the infected area. Sterilize pruning tools after each cut with rubbing alcohol. After pruning, spray the canes with a fungicide containing *lime sulfur*. Sprays aimed at controlling black spot will help control canker. Or spray with a fungicide containing *chlorothalonil* (DACONIL 2787®), *mancozeb*, *benlate*, or *folpet* (PHALTAN®) starting in the spring. Repeat every 10 to 14 days for as long as the weather is wet or humid.

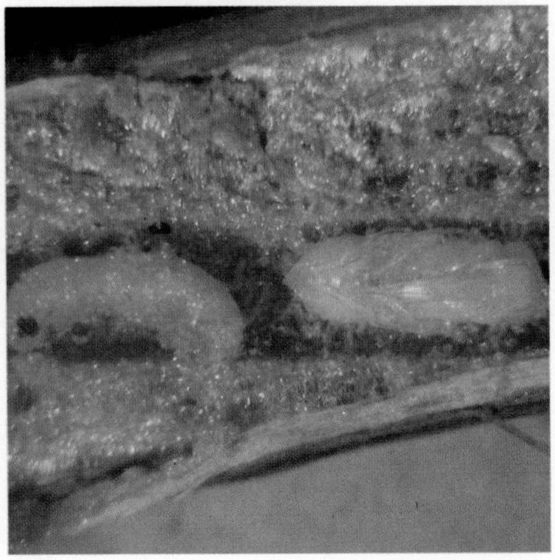

Carpenter bee larvae (3 times life size).

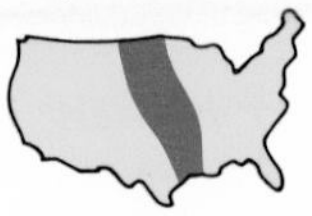

PROBLEM: Several or all of the larger canes and stems wilt and die. If the bark is peeled back, or dying stems are sliced open, white to yellowish worms or legless grubs up to 3/4 inch long may be revealed. Affected stems may be swollen at the base.

ANALYSIS: Borers
There are many kinds of insects which bore into rose stems. They include certain sawflies, beetles, horntail wasps, and solitary bees. Some of these attack old, weakened plants or plants that are under stress from recent transplant or improper care; such borers often attack at the base of the plant. Other borers attack healthy rose plants, either traveling in a spiral pattern just under the bark, or burrowing down through the center of the rose stems. Most rose borers produce one generation a year.

SOLUTION: Prune out and destroy infested rose stems. Make the cut several inches below the point where the stem is wilted or swollen. If there is a hole through the center of the stem where an insect has tunneled, keep cutting the stem lower to the ground until you find and destroy the insect or see the end of the tunnel. If this is a problem year after year, seal rose canes immediately after pruning with ORTHO Pruning Seal to prevent borers from penetrating the soft tissue in the center of the stem. Keep rose plants in good health (see page 565 for information on rose care.)

Verticillium wilt.

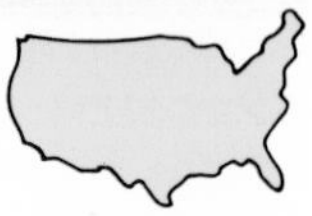

PROBLEM: The leaves on a branch turn yellow at the margins, then brown and dry. During hot weather, the leaves may wilt. New leaves may be stunted and yellowish. The infected plant may die slowly, branch by branch, over several seasons. Or the whole plant may wilt and die within a few months. Some plants may recover. Infected rose canes frequently turn purple at the base. The tissue under the bark on dying canes shows dark streaks when cut. To examine for streaks, peel back the bark at the bottom of the dying branch.

ANALYSIS: Verticillium wilt
This wilt disease affects many ornamental trees and shrubs. It is caused by a soil-inhabiting fungus (*Verticillium* species) that persists indefinitely on plant debris or in the soil. The fungus is spread by contaminated seeds, plants, soil, equipment, and ground water. The fungus enters the rose plant through the roots and spreads up into the branches through the water-conducting vessels in the main stem. The vessels become discolored and plugged. This plugging cuts off the flow of water and nutrients to the branches, causing the leaf discoloration and wilting. For more information about verticillium, see page 850.

SOLUTION: No chemical control is available. Fertilize and water the affected plant to stimulate vigorous growth. Prune off all dead wood. Do not remove branches on which leaves have recently wilted. These branches may produce new leaves in 3 to 4 weeks. Remove dead shrubs. If replanting in the same area, plant trees and shrubs that are resistant to verticillium (see page 1006).

SALIX (WILLOW)

ADAPTATION: Throughout the United States.

LIGHT: Full sun.

SOIL: Tolerates a wide variety of soils, including those that are wet. Roots are shallow, invasive, and fiercely competitive.

FERTILIZER: Fertilize with ORTHO Evergreen, Tree & Shrub Food according to label directions.

WATER:
How much: Apply enough water to wet the soil 3 to 4 feet deep. To determine the proper amount of water for your soil type, see page 912.
How often: Willows require ample water. Water when the soil is moist but not wet 4 inches below the surface. For more information about watering, see page 912.

PRUNING: Willows are fast-growing, short-lived trees with brittle wood. Prune to maintain the shape and to remove dead or broken branches. If you wish to be able to walk under weeping willows, prune so that the lowest branches are at least 10 feet above the ground.

Willow hornworm (half life size).

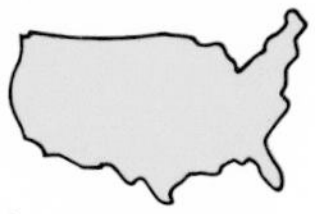

PROBLEM: The surface of the leaf is eaten, giving the remaining tissue a lacy appearance, or the whole leaf is chewed. Sometimes the leaves are webbed together. The tree may be completely defoliated. Damage appears any time between spring and fall. Caterpillars are clustered or feeding singly on the leaves. Repeated heavy infestations may weaken or kill trees.

ANALYSIS: Leaf-feeding caterpillars
Many different species of caterpillars feed on willow leaves wherever the trees are grown. Depending on the species, the moths lay their eggs any time between early spring and midsummer. The larvae that hatch from these eggs feed on buds, on one surface of the leaf (skeletonizers), or on the entire leaf. Certain caterpillars web the leaves together as they feed. In some years, damage is miminal due to unfavorable environmental conditions or control by predators and parasites. However, when conditions are favorable, entire trees may be defoliated by late summer. Defoliation weakens trees because there are no leaves left to produce food. When heavy infestations occur several years in a row, branches or entire trees may be killed.

SOLUTION: Spray with ORTHO Orthene Systemic Insect Control when damage is first noticed. Spray the leaves thoroughly. Repeat the spray if the tree becomes reinfested.

Leaf beetle larva (8 times life size).

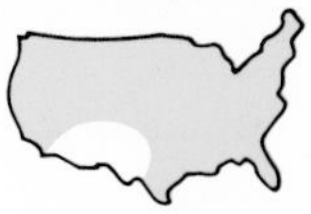

PROBLEM: Leaf tissue is eaten between the veins, giving the leaves a lacy appearance; or circular holes are chewed out of the leaves. The foliage may turn brown and dry. Twigs may die. With severe infestations, the tree may lose most of its leaves. Small blackish or white larvae, or brown, yellowish, or metallic green or blue beetles may be found feeding on the leaves.

ANALYSIS: Leaf beetles
A number of different beetles feed on willow leaves. In late spring or summer, the beetles fly to willow trees. Some feed on the willow leaves for a number of weeks, while others lay eggs soon after arriving. The females lay groups of eggs on the undersides of the leaves. The emerging larvae feed on the leaf tissue between the veins, or on one surface of the leaf.

SOLUTION: Spray valuable specimens with ORTHO Isotox Insect Killer or ORTHO Orthene Systemic Insect Control when damage is first noticed in spring. Repeat the spray if the tree becomes reinfested.

SALIX (WILLOW)

Giant bark aphids (twice life size).

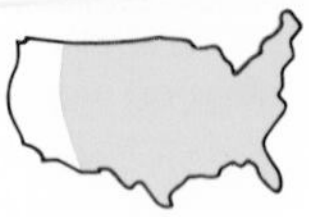

PROBLEM: Small (¼ inch) black and beige soft-bodied insects with long black legs cluster on twigs and the undersides of limbs. They usually persist after leaf fall until freezing weather. Twigs may be completely covered with a mat of black eggs. When populations are large, twigs and branches die. A shiny, sticky substance may coat the limbs. A black sooty mold often grows on the sticky substance. Ants may be present.

ANALYSIS: Giant bark aphid
(*Longistigma caryae*)
The giant bark aphid is the largest species of aphid known. Because of its long legs, it appears much larger than its ¼ inch size. The aphids do little damage in small numbers. However, they are extremely prolific and populations can rapidly build up to damaging numbers during the late summer. When populations are large, black eggs are matted all over the bark of infested limbs. Damage occurs when the aphid sucks the juices from the twigs and branches. The aphid is unable to digest fully all the sugar in the sap, and excretes large quantities in a fluid called honeydew, which may coat plants and objects beneath the tree. A sooty mold fungus may develop on the honeydew, causing the bark to appear black and dirty. Ants feed on the sticky substances, and are often present where there is an aphid infestation. Several other species of aphids may also infest willow leaves and twigs.

SOLUTION: Spray with ORTHO Isotox Insect Killer or ORTHO Orthene Systemic Insect Control when aphids first appear. Spray the bark thoroughly. Repeat the spray if the tree becomes reinfested.

Scurfy scale (life size).

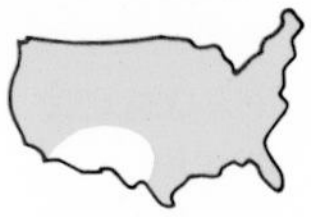

PROBLEM: Stems and leaves are covered with white, cottony masses or brownish, crusty bumps or clusters of somewhat flattened yellow, brown, gray, or white scaly bumps. The bumps can be scraped or picked off. Leaves turn yellow and may drop. In some cases a shiny, sticky substance coats the leaves. A black sooty mold often grows on the sticky substance. Branches are killed by heavy infestations.

ANALYSIS: Scales
Many different types of scale insects infest willow. They lay their eggs on leaves or bark. In spring to midsummer the young scales, called *crawlers*, settle on leaves and twigs. The small (1/10 inch), soft-bodied young feed by sucking sap from the plant. The legs usually atrophy and, with some types, a shell develops over the body. The types of scales that do not develop shells are very conspicuous. The females are covered with a white, cottony egg sac, containing up to 2500 eggs. Scales covered with a shell are less noticeable. The shell often blends in with the plant, and the eggs are inconspicuous beneath their covering. Some species of scales are unable to digest fully all the sugar in the plant sap, and excrete the excess in a fluid called honeydew. A sooty mold fungus may develop on the sticky substance, causing the willow leaves to appear black and dirty. For more information about scales, see page 876.

SOLUTION: Spray with ORTHO Isotox Insect Killer or ORTHO Orthene Systemic Insect Control when the young are active. Contact your local Cooperative Extension Office (see page 1029) to determine the best time to spray for scales in your area.

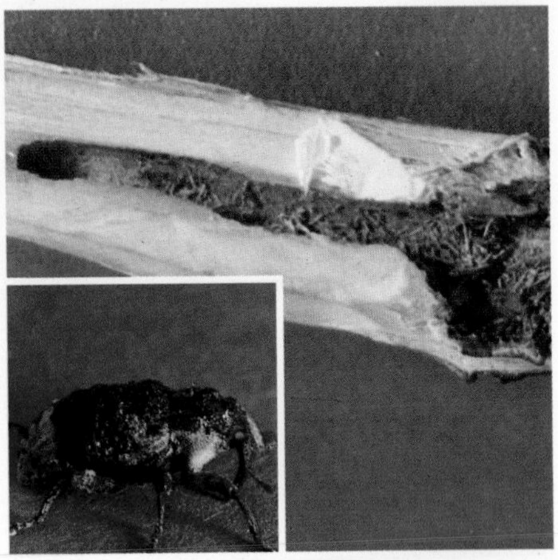

Damaged stem. *Insert:* Adult (3 times life size).

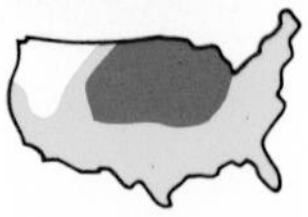

PROBLEM: Swollen areas with holes in their centers develop on twigs, branches, or the trunk. Many side shoots may grow from below the swellings, destroying the tree's natural form. The leaves on infested twigs and branches turn yellow and may be chewed on the edges. Sawdust and many broken twigs are often found beneath the tree.

ANALYSIS: Willow borers
(*Saperda* species)
At least five species of this beetle feed on willows, causing galls, or swollen areas, to form. The 1-inch, striped and spotted, brownish or gray beetles with long antennae appear in late spring or early summer. The females lay their eggs in small holes that they gnaw in the bark of twigs and branches that are more than ½ inch in diameter. The emerging legless, whitish grubs tunnel into the wood. Excess tissue accumulates around the wound, resulting in a gall. When infestations are severe, nearly all twigs and branches more than ½ inch in diameter have one or more galls. The galls weaken the twigs, causing them to break and litter the ground during stormy weather. The grubs remain in the wood 1 to 2 years before maturing into adults.

SOLUTION: Remove and destroy severely damaged trees. Spray the bark of less severely damaged trees with ORTHO Lindane Borer & Leaf Miner Spray in late May or early June. Repeat the spray 2 weeks later.

Mottled willow borer (life size).

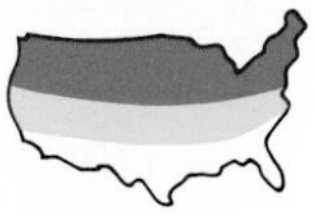

PROBLEM: Leaves turn yellow and holes appear in the twigs. Large quantities of sawdust cling to the bark just below the holes. Sap often oozes from the holes. Young trees may be killed, and older trees may lose their natural form due to the production of numerous side shoots. Small (3/8 inch) black or dark brown weevils with pale yellow spots and long snouts may be seen around the tree from midsummer until fall.

ANALYSIS: Mottled willow borer
(*Cryptorhynchus lapathi*)
All willows and most species of poplars may be attacked by this weevil, also called the *poplar and willow borer*. The adult weevils cause minor injury by chewing holes in the bark of twigs. The major damage is caused by the C-shaped larvae, which are white with brown heads. During mid to late summer, the larvae hatch from eggs laid in holes chewed by the female weevils. The larvae burrow into and feed on the inner bark. In the spring, large quantities of frass (sawdust and excrement) are expelled from the holes as the larvae tunnel into the center of the twigs to pupate. The feeding and tunneling cause branches to break easily and disrupt nutrient and water movement through the tree. The leaves turn yellow, and the tree often becomes bushy from the growth of numerous side shoots. The larvae pupate in June and emerge as adults in midsummer. Several other borers may also infest the trunk and branches of willows.

SOLUTION: Remove and destroy severely infested trees or branches before early summer. Spray the bark of trees with ORTHO Lindane Borer & Leaf Miner Spray in late July or early August.

Blighted twigs.

PROBLEM: Soon after leaves develop in the spring, many turn blackish, wither, and drop from the tree. The tree may look as if it has been scorched by fire. Brown sunken areas develop on the young twigs; the twigs may die. After wet weather, green, feltlike masses form on the large veins on the undersides of the leaves.

ANALYSIS: Willow scab
This plant disease is caused by a fungus (*Fusicladium saliciperdum*). Willow scab survives the winter on fallen leaves and infected twigs. Soon after the leaves appear in the spring, spores are blown and splashed onto leaf tissue. Spots develop, the leaves wither, and then drop from the tree. The fungus moves down into the twigs, forming sunken cankers and causing dieback. Dark green spore masses develop on the veins on the lower surfaces of infected leaves. Repeated infections by willow scab may kill the tree after several seasons.

SOLUTION: When practical, prune out infected twigs below the canker. Spray valuable specimens with a fungicide containing *mancozeb, maneb, zineb,* or *dodine* when growth begins in the spring. Repeat the spraying 2 or 3 more times at intervals of 7 to 10 days. Weeping, bay-leaved, and osier willows are resistant to willow scab.

Dieback.

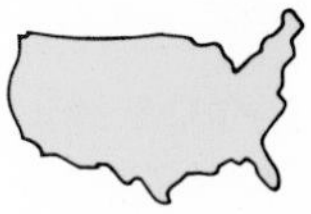

PROBLEM: Dark sunken areas appear on the twigs, branches, or trunk. Leaves on infected branches may be spotted, or they may be stunted and lighter green than normal. Twigs and branches are often killed. Young or less vigorous trees are most susceptible.

ANALYSIS: Canker and dieback
Several different fungi cause canker and dieback on willows. The fungi enter the tree through a wound or, in some cases, the leaves, killing the surrounding healthy tissue. A dark sunken canker develops in the wood. If the fungus infects the leaves first, it grows down through the leaf stems and forms cankers on twigs. The canker cuts off the flow of nutrients and water to the twigs or branch, causing the leaves to turn yellowish. Twig or branch dieback follows if the canker girdles the wood. The tree may stop the spreading canker by producing callus tissue, a rapid growth of barklike cells, to wall off the fungus. If the expanding canker is stopped before it covers half the diameter of the branch or trunk, the tree usually survives.

SOLUTION: Prune off twigs and small cankered branches, cutting at least 4 inches below the canker. Cankers on larger branches can be excised with a knife and chisel. Remove all discolored bark and wood, and a 1-inch border of apparently healthy bark around the wound. After each cut, sterilize the tools with rubbing alcohol. Remove and destroy severely infected trees. To prevent the development of new cankers, avoid wounding trees. Keep trees vigorous by fertilizing and watering (see pages 910 and 912).

SALIX (WILLOW)

Slime flux.

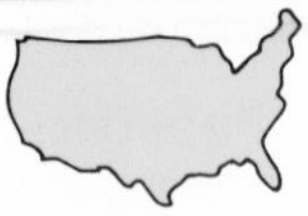

PROBLEM: Sour-smelling sap oozes from wounds, cracks, and branch crotches, mainly during the growing season. The sap drips down the bark and dries, causing unsightly gray streaks. There may be some wilting on affected branches. Insects are attracted to the sour-smelling ooze.

ANALYSIS: Slime flux
Slime flux, also called *wetwood*, is caused by a bacterium (*Erwinia nimpressuralis*). The bacteria infect the heartwood, producing abnormally high sap pressure. This pressure is caused by bacterial fermentation, and forces the fermented sap, or flux, out of wounds, cracks, or crotches in the tree. Flux is especially copious when the tree is growing rapidly. Large areas of the bark may be coated with the smelly, bacteria-laden sap, which dries to a grayish-white color. In addition, wounds do not heal and the bark is unsightly. A tree with this problem is often under water stress, which may cause drought damage (wilting and scorched leaves) to the branches. The problem may persist for years.

SOLUTION: There are no chemical controls for this condition. Bore a slightly slanted drainage hole through the wood below each oozing wound. Insert a ½-inch-diameter plastic tube just until it stays firmly in place. If the tube penetrates the water-soaked wood inside the tree, it will interfere with drainage. The tube will carry the dripping sap away from the trunk. Disinfect tools with rubbing alcohol after pruning infected trees.

SARCOCOCCA

Sunburned foliage.

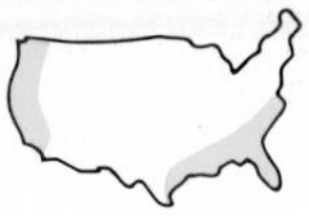

PROBLEM: During warm, sunny weather the leaves turn yellowish; or the center portions of the leaves bleach out to a tan color. Once the initial damage has occurred, the yellowing does not usually increase in size.

ANALYSIS: Sunburn
Sarcococca is a shade plant. It can't tolerate the heat of direct sunlight. Burning occurs on hot days if the shrub is exposed to direct sunlight or to sunlight reflected from a light-colored, south-facing wall. It takes only one hot day for damage to appear. The injury is unsightly but does not seriously injure the plant. However, weakened leaves are more susceptible to invasion by fungi and bacteria. Plants in dry soil are much more susceptible to sunscald.

SOLUTION: Move the injured plant to a shaded location; or provide shade where it is now planted. (For more information about transplanting, see page 924.) Once leaves are scalded they will not recover. Where practical, remove affected leaves.

Sarcococca cultural information
Light: Part shade to deep shade; sun in cool summer areas
Water: Keep the soil moist
Soil: Loose, rich, well drained, nonalkaline
Fertilizer: Medium

SASSAFRAS

Sassafras weevil damage.

PROBLEM: Holes appear in the leaves in spring; buds may also be eaten. Brown blotches develop at or near the leaf tips in early summer. Small (1/12 inch) black weevils with long snouts may be found feeding on the foliage in spring and midsummer.

ANALYSIS: Sassafras weevil
(*Odontopus calceatus*)
Both the larva and adult of the sassafras weevil, also called the *yellow poplar weevil* or *magnolia leafminer*, feed on sassafras leaves. The adults survive the winter in leaf litter beneath the plant. When the weather warms in early spring, the beetles fly to the trees and feed on the buds and developing leaves. In late spring, the females lay their eggs on the undersides of the leaves. The emerging white, legless larvae burrow into the leaf tips, between the upper and lower surfaces of the leaves, causing brown blotches to form. The larvae pupate inside the leaves and emerge as adults. The beetles feed, usually until July, and then drop to the ground to spend the winter. Japanese beetles may also seriously damage sassafras. For information on Japanese beetles, see page 866.

SOLUTION: Spray with an insecticide containing *carbaryl* (SEVIN®) when damage is first noticed in the spring.

Sassafras cultural information
Light: Full sun to part shade
Water: Keep the soil moist
Soil: Sandy, well drained
Fertilizer: Light

SORBUS (MOUNTAIN ASH)

ADAPTATION: Zones 2 through 8. To determine your zone, see the map on page 1020.

FLOWERING TIME: White flowers in late spring. Bright orange-red berries develop in midsummer and usually last until the following spring.

LIGHT: Full sun to partial shade.

SOIL: Any good, well-drained garden soil.

FERTILIZER: Fertilize with ORTHO Evergreen, Tree & Shrub Food according to label directions.

WATER:

How much: Apply enough water to wet the soil 2 to 3 feet deep. To determine the proper amount of water for your soil type, see page 912.

How often: Water when the soil is just barely moist 4 inches below the surface. For more information about watering, see page 912.

Fireblight.

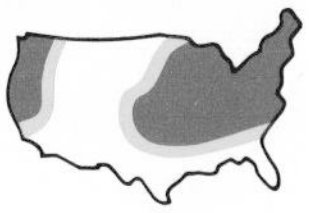

PROBLEM: The blossoms and leaves of infected twigs suddenly wilt and turn black as if scorched by fire. The leaves curl and hang downward. The bark at the base of the blighted twig becomes water-soaked, then dark, sunken, and dry; cracks may develop at the edge of the sunken area. In warm, moist spring weather drops of brown ooze appear on the sunken bark. Young trees may die.

ANALYSIS: Fireblight

This plant disease is caused by a bacterium (*Erwinia amylovora*) that is very destructive to many trees and shrubs. (For a list of susceptible plants, see page 1016.) The bacteria spend the winter in the sunken cankers on the branches. In the spring, the bacteria ooze out of the cankers. Bees, flies, and other insects are attracted to the sticky ooze and become smeared with it. When the insects visit a mountain ash flower for nectar, they infect it with the bacteria. The bacteria spread rapidly through the plant tissue in warm (65°F or higher), humid weather. Insects visiting these infected blossoms later carry bacteria-laden nectar to healthy blossoms. Rain, wind, and tools may also spread the bacteria. Tender or damaged leaves may be infected in mid-summer.

SOLUTION: Prune out infected branches 12 to 15 inches beyond any visible discoloration and destroy them. Sterilize pruning shears with rubbing alcohol after each cut. A protective spray of a pesticide containing *basic copper sulfate* or *streptomycin*, applied before bud break in the spring, will help prevent infection. Repeat at intervals of 5 to 7 days until the end of bloom.

Rust.

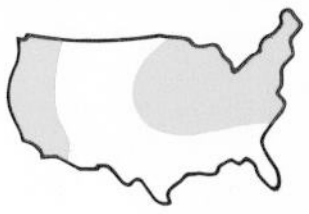

PROBLEM: Light yellow, thickened, circular spots appear on the leaves in summer. Later in the season, orange cups develop on the lower surfaces of the leaves, directly below the thickened spots. Spotted leaves may drop.

ANALYSIS: Rust

This plant disease is caused by any of a number of different fungi (*Gymnosporangium* species). These fungi require both mountain ash and certain junipers or incense cedar to complete their life cycles. Rust spores on mountain ash cannot infect another mountain ash, but can infect only one of the evergreens. Windborne spores from the evergreen plant infect mountain ash in the spring. The spores germinate during warm, wet weather and infect the leaves, causing spotting. In late summer, spores are released during dry weather and carried by the wind back to the evergreen plant. Rust on junipers and incense cedar causes swellings, dieback, and excessive branching.

SOLUTION: Protect valuable specimens with a fungicide containing *ferbam* at the first sign of spotting. The spray will not eradicate the fungus on leaves that are already infected, but will protect uninfected leaves. Repeat the spray at weekly intervals throughout the spring. If possible, do not plant junipers or incense cedars within several hundred yards of mountain ash.

SORBUS (MOUNTAIN ASH)

Pearleaf blister mite damage.

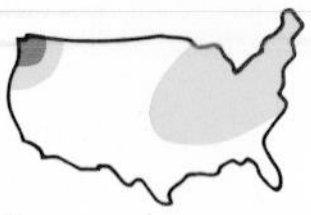

PROBLEM: Reddish or brownish blisters, 1/8 inch across, appear on the undersides of the leaves. The blisters may be massed together to nearly cover the leaf. The upper surface is mottled brown or blackish. Affected leaves may drop off, and berries may be deformed.

ANALYSIS: Pearleaf blister mite
(*Phytoptus pyri*)
This microscopic, elongated, pinkish or white mite is generally found throughout the country wherever mountain ash is grown. It also infests pear, apple, cotoneaster, and serviceberry. The adults spend the winter in bud scales, often hundreds in a single bud. As the buds swell in the spring, the mites lay their eggs. The young burrow into the undersides of unfolding leaves, forming blisters. New generations of mites are produced inside the blisters throughout the summer. As cold weather approaches, the mites migrate back to the buds to spend the winter.

SOLUTION: Once the mites have entered the undersides of the leaves, they are difficult to control. Spray the undersides of the leaves with *lime sulfur* or a *dormant oil spray* in late fall or early spring.

Woolly apple aphid (1/4 life size).

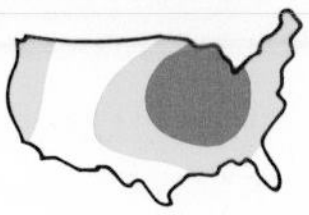

PROBLEM: Twigs, branches, and possibly the trunk are covered with white, cottony masses. Underneath the white masses are clusters of small (1/8 inch), purplish brown, soft-bodied insects. Leaves and twigs are yellowing, and the tree may be stunted. A sticky substance may coat the leaves, stems, and trunk. A black sooty mold may develop on the sticky substance.

ANALYSIS: Woolly aphids
(*Eriosoma* species)
Several species of woolly aphids attack mountain ash. They do little damage in small numbers. However, they are extremely prolific and populations can rapidly build up to damaging numbers during the growing season. Damage occurs when the woolly aphid sucks the juices from twigs, branches, or the trunk. It is unable to digest fully all the sugar in the plant sap and excretes the excess in a fluid called honeydew, which often drops onto the leaves below. A sooty mold fungus may develop on the sticky substance, causing the mountain ash leaves to appear black and dirty. The woolly apple aphid (*Eriosoma lanigerum*) may also cause damage by burrowing down into the soil and feeding on roots. This feeding causes marblelike knots to form, and results in stunted roots. The tree is weakened and growth is poor.

SOLUTION: Control with an insecticide containing *malathion* or *diazinon* when damage is first noticed. Aphids protected with the white, woolly material are more difficult to control. Spray the tree thoroughly. Repeat the spray if the tree becomes reinfested.

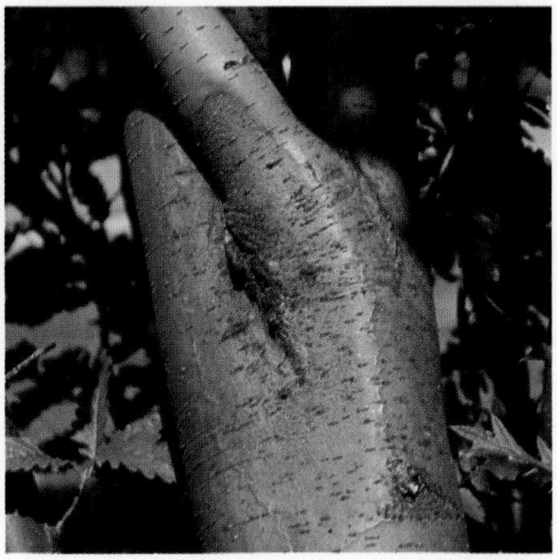
Canker.

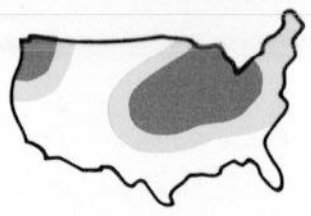

PROBLEM: Vertical cracks or sunken areas appear on the branches or trunk. The bark is discolored, and a liquid may ooze from the sunken areas. The leaves and twigs above these areas turn brown and die. Young trees, wounded trees, or trees of low vigor are most susceptible, and are usually killed.

ANALYSIS: Canker and dieback
Several different fungi cause canker and dieback on mountain ash. The fungi are spread by rain, wind, soil, tools, and equipment. They enter the tree through a wound, killing the surrounding healthy tissue. A sunken canker or crack develops as the fungi grow through the wood. Tree sap containing the fungus may ooze from the wound. The canker cuts off the flow of nutrients and water to the branch, causing the leaves to turn brown and the branch to die. This process may take several years. After one or more branches begin to turn brown, the tree usually dies within a year.

SOLUTION: The tree usually will not survive once the branches start dying, so it is best to remove and destroy the tree. Prevention is the only control. Avoid wounding trees. Do not use a lawn mower near the base of the tree. Keep the tree in optimum health by watering and fertilizing regularly (see pages 912 and 910), and by controlling insects, especially borers (see page 865).

Spirea aphids (twice life size).

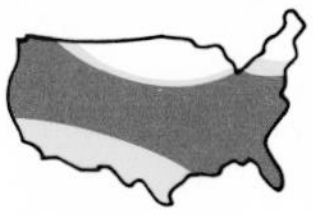

PROBLEM: Tiny (⅛ inch), dark green, soft-bodied insects cluster on the flowers, undersides of the leaves, and young shoots. Leaves are curled, yellowing, and stunted, and growth of the plant is slowed. A shiny or sticky substance may coat the leaves. A black sooty mold often grows on the sticky substance.

ANALYSIS: Spirea aphid
(*Aphis spiraecola*)
These aphids do little damage in small numbers. However, they are extremely prolific in the early summer, and populations can rapidly build up to damaging numbers by late June. Damage occurs when the aphid sucks the juices from the spirea leaves. The aphid is unable to digest fully all the sugar in the plant sap and excretes the excess in a fluid called honeydew, which often drops onto the leaves below. A sooty mold fungus may develop on the honeydew, causing the spirea leaves to appear black and dirty.

SOLUTION: Control with ORTHO Isotox Insect Killer or ORTHO Orthene Systemic Insect Control when damage is first noticed. Spray the plant thoroughly. Repeat the spray if the plant becomes reinfested.

Spiraea cultural information
Light: Full sun to part shade
Water: Keep the soil moist
Soil: Tolerates many types
Fertilizer: Light

SYRINGA (LILAC)

ADAPTATION: Zones 3 through 7. (To determine your zone, see the map on page 1020.) Generally not adapted to warm climates, but some species grow in zones 8 and 9.

FLOWERING TIME: May or June.

LIGHT: Full sun.

SOIL: Any good garden soil high in organic matter with a neutral pH (approximately 6.5 to 7.5). For more information about pH, see page 908.

FERTILIZER: Fertilize with ORTHO General Purpose Plant Food according to label directions. Add lime to acid soils (pH 4.5 to 5.5). For more information about adding lime to the soil, see page 1019.

WATER:
How much: Apply enough water to wet the soil 2 to 3 feet deep. To determine the proper amount of water for your soil type, see page 912.
How often: Water when the soil is barely moist 4 inches below the surface. For more information about watering, see page 912.

PRUNING: To shape young plants, pinch off growing tips. Remove dead flowers immediately after blooming and prune out dead and weak wood. To renew old plants, cut a few of the oldest stems to the ground each year after flowering; or cut the entire plant almost to the ground.

Powdery mildew.

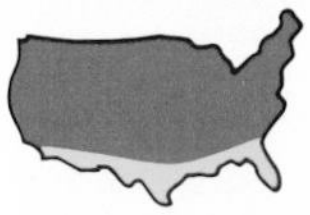

PROBLEM: The leaves are covered with a thin layer or irregular patches of a grayish white powdery material. Infected leaves may turn yellow and drop off. New growth is often stunted. In late summer, tiny black dots (spore-producing bodies) are scattered over the white patches like ground pepper.

ANALYSIS: Powdery mildew
This common plant disease is caused by a fungus (*Microsphaera alni*) that thrives in both humid and dry weather. The powdery patches consist of fungal strands and spores. The fungus saps plant nutrients, causing yellowing and sometimes the death of the leaf. Since this mildew attacks many different kinds of trees and shrubs, the fungus from a diseased plant may infect other plants in the garden. For a list of susceptible species, see page 1006.

SOLUTION: Spray plants with ORTHO Funginex Rose Disease Control or ORTHO Orthenex Insect & Disease Control when the plant shows the first sign of mildew. Cover the upper and lower surfaces of the leaves thoroughly. Repeat the treatment at intervals of 7 to 10 days until mildew disappears.

SYRINGA (LILAC)

Bacterial blight.

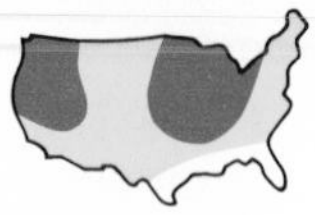

PROBLEM: Brown spots, surrounded by large areas of yellow, appear on the leaves in early spring. On older leaves, spots slowly increase in size during rainy periods. The leaves are usually distorted. Immature leaves turn black and die. Infected young stems bend over at the lesion, wither and die. Mature stems develop spots that enlarge along the length of the stem. The leaves die within the infected area. Flowers often become limp, turn dark brown, and die.

ANALYSIS: Bacterial blight

This plant disease is caused by a bacterium (*Pseudomonas syringae*) that may seriously damage lilacs during cool, wet weather. The bacteria overwinter in lilac buds, infected twigs and plant debris, and on other hosts. (For a list, see page 1013.) They are spread by wind, rain, and splashing water. The bacteria cause spots on leaves that are olive-green at first, later turning brown, surrounded by yellow. If wet weather persists, the bacteria spread through the tissue, forming blotches. Young plant parts are more severely affected. Leaves and young shoots blacken rapidly and die. Leaves die on older stems within the infected area. Flowers often become limp and blighted. White-flowered lilacs are most susceptible to bacterial blight.

SOLUTION: Prune out and destroy blighted shoots immediately, cutting well below the infected tissue. Sterilize pruning tools after each cut with rubbing alcohol. If the disease has been serious, spray with a fungicide containing *basic copper sulfate* early the following spring. Repeat the spray at intervals of 7 to 10 days for as long as the weather remains wet.

Lilac leafminer damage.

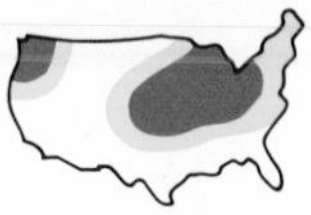

PROBLEM: Light green blotches appear on the leaves in early summer; the blotches turn brown and are often wrinkled. Later, the leaf tips are curled and tied together with silken webbing. The upper surfaces of the rolled leaves appear eaten. If a blotch is torn open, a tiny green worm may be found inside. The rolled leaf tips may contain a thin white cocoon or a pale yellow worm, up to 1/3 inch long. With heavy infestations, nearly every leaf turns brown, giving the plant a burned appearance.

ANALYSIS: Lilac leafminer
(*Caloptilia syringella*)

The lilac leafminer is the larva of a small brown moth that infests both lilac and privet. In late spring, moths emerge and deposit their eggs on the lower surfaces of the leaves. The emerging larvae enter the leaves and mine within the tissue between the upper and lower surfaces. Blotches, or mines, develop as the larvae increase in size. About the time the mines turn brown, the worms crawl to the leaf tips and curl the leaves around themselves. They feed for several weeks inside the leaves and then drop to the ground to pupate. The adults that emerge in late summer lay the eggs of a second generation, which survives the winter as pupae in plant litter.

SOLUTION: If the infestation is heavy, spray with ORTHO Isotox Insect Killer, ORTHO Orthenex Insect & Disease Control, or ORTHO Orthene Systemic Insect Control when green mines are first noticed (before the leaves are rolled), or when adults are laying eggs in June and August. If the infestation is light, pick off and destroy both mined and curled leaves before the larvae drop to the ground to pupate.

Scales (1/4 life size).

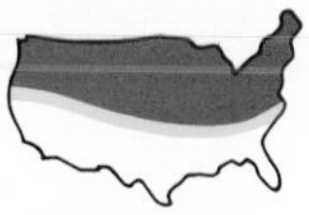

PROBLEM: The trunk and branches are covered with clusters of somewhat flattened grayish, brownish, or white scaly bumps that can be scraped or picked off; the undersides of the bumps are usually soft. Leaves are dwarfed and yellow, and may drop; plant growth is poor. Twigs and branches may die.

ANALYSIS: Scales

Several species of scales infest lilacs. They lay their eggs on the bark, and in early to late spring the young scales, called *crawlers*, settle on the trunk, branches, and twigs. The small (1/10 inch), soft-bodied young feed by sucking sap from the plant. The legs usually atrophy and a hard, crusty shell develops over the body. The mature female scales lay their eggs underneath their shell. In warmer climates, there may be several generations a year. An uncontrolled infestation of scales may kill the plant after two or three seasons. For more information about scales, see page 876.

SOLUTION: Spray with ORTHO Isotox Insect Killer or ORTHO Orthene Systemic Insect Control in early to late spring when the young are active. Spray the trunk and the branches thoroughly. Repeat the spray if the plant becomes reinfested. Early the following spring, spray the trunk and branches with ORTHO Volck Oil Spray to control the overwintering insects.

Borer damage.

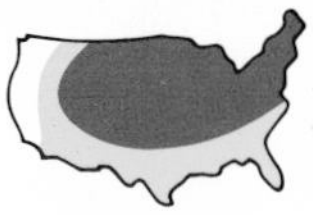

PROBLEM: Branch tips wilt in late summer, especially during warm, dry periods. Affected branches may die or break off. The stems near the ground are swollen and cracked. Sawdust is often found around holes in the stems and on the ground below infested stems.

ANALYSIS: Lilac borer
(*Podosesia syringae*)
The lilac borer is the larva of a brownish, clear-winged moth that resembles a wasp. Moths may be seen flying around the plant in late spring. The moths lay their eggs in cracks or bark wounds at the base of the stems. The cream-colored larvae bore into the wood and feed on the sapwood and heartwood. The stems become swollen and may break where the larvae are feeding. Their feeding also cuts off the flow of nutrients and water through the stems, causing the shoots to wilt and die. The larvae spend the winter in the stems. In the spring, they feed for a few weeks before maturing into moths. Several other borers may infest lilac.

SOLUTION: Before the moths emerge in the spring (April to May), cut out infested stems to ground level and destroy them. In late April, spray or paint the trunks and stems with ORTHO Lindane Borer & Leaf Miner Spray. Repeat the treatment two more times at intervals of 7 to 10 days. Borers can also be destroyed by injecting liquid insecticides into the holes with an oil can. Holes should then be plugged with putty or a caulking compound. Or kill borers by inserting a flexible wire into the borer hole in early summer. Avoid pruning during the spring months are moths are present.

TAXUS (YEW)

ADAPTATION: Zones 4 through 8.

LIGHT: Sun or shade. Plant in shade in hot, dry climates and protect from wind.

SOIL: Any good, very well-drained garden soil. Plants will be stunted and sickly in heavy, wet soil.

FERTILIZER: Fertilize with ORTHO Evergreen, Tree & Shrub Food according to label directions.

WATER:
How much: Apply enough water to wet the soil 2 to 3 feet deep. To determine the proper amount of water for your soil type, see page 912.
How often: Yews are drought tolerant once established, but they grow best in moist soil as long as it is well drained. Water when the soil is barely moist 3 to 6 inches below the surface. Hose the foliage frequently during the driest periods. For more information about watering, see page 912.

Yew in poorly drained soil.

PROBLEM: Young leaves turn yellow. Eventually the entire plant may turn yellow, wilt, and die. The plant is growing in heavy, poorly drained, acid, or alkaline soil.

ANALYSIS: Poor soil
Yews are particularly sensitive to improper growing conditions. When they are planted in soil that is heavy, poorly drained, very acid (between pH 4.5 and 5.5) or very alkaline (above pH 7.5), the plants do not usually survive. The bark on the roots decays and sloughs off, and the roots die. The roots can no longer supply sufficient amounts of nutrients and water to the leaves, resulting in leaf yellowing and wilting. The plant usually dies within several months.

SOLUTION: Improve the soil drainage (see page 907) or, if the plant is small, move it to an area with better drainage. Check the acidity of your soil (see page 909). If the pH is below 6.0, add ground limestone around the base of the plant. Add ORTHO Aluminum Sulfate to the soil if the pH is above 7.0. The optimum pH for yews is between 6.0 and 6.5. Do not water yews heavily.

Root rot.

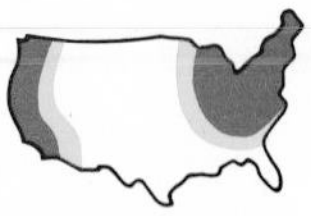

PROBLEM: The young leaves are yellowish or off-color and wilting. Eventually the whole plant wilts and dies, even though the soil is sufficiently moist. Dead, brown leaves remain attached to the plant. The symptoms may develop over a few weeks, or may take many months. Heavy, poorly drained soil favors disease development. When cut, the tissue under the bark close to ground level shows a dark discoloration. To look for discoloration, peel back the bark at the bottom of the plant. There is usually a distinct margin between white, healthy wood and dark, diseased wood. If the plant is pulled up, examination of young roots reveals browning, decay, and an absence of white rootlets. Healthy roots are firm and white.

ANALYSIS: Root rot
This plant disease is caused by a soil-inhabiting fungus (*Phytophthora cinnamomi*) that attacks more than 100 kinds of ornamental plants. The fungus is carried in plants, soil, or soil water. It enters the roots and works its way up the plant, blocking the upward flow of water and nutrients. Plants in overwatered or poorly drained soils are more susceptible to attack.

SOLUTION: No chemical control is available. Once the fungus becomes established in the soil, it will remain indefinitely. Remove diseased plants. Do not replant the same area with susceptible plants. (For a list of resistant trees and shrubs, see page 1016.) However, if replacement is necessary because the shrub is part of a hedge, remove as much soil as possible in the area where the old roots have penetrated and replace with light, clean soil before planting. Avoid overwatering.

Needles notched by taxus weevils.

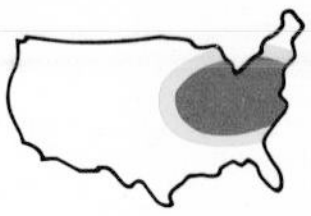

PROBLEM: Needles turn yellow and often wilt in hot weather. The edges of some needles may be notched. The plant is growing poorly, and branches or the entire plant may die. To determine if the plant is infested with this insect, in mid to late June inspect the foliage after dark, using a flashlight. Black weevils, ⅜ inch long, with elephantlike snouts and rows of tiny round depressions on their backs, are feeding on the needle edges, especially near the trunk.

ANALYSIS: Taxus weevil
(*Otiorhynchus sulcatus*)
This root weevil, also known as the *black vine weevil*, is a serious pest of yews and many other plants in the garden. The weevil spends the winter either as an adult, in trash and weeds, or as a larva, on the roots of plants. The adult emerges from its hiding place in June. It feeds on the needle edges during the night, and hides during the day. Its feeding does not usually cause serious injury, but many notched needles usually indicates a high larval population on the roots. During the summer, the weevil lays eggs for a month or more. The white larvae feed on roots from midsummer until fall, and again in spring. When infestations are heavy, the plant no longer receives enough nutrients and water, and dies.

SOLUTION: Inspect the center of the plant every year for insects and recently notched needles (notched needles from a previous year may still be on the plant). To control the adults, spray the foliage and soil beneath the plant with ORTHO Isotox Insect Killer or ORTHO Orthene Systemic Insect Control, starting in mid-June. Repeat the spray three more times at intervals of 3 weeks.

TILIA (LINDEN)

ADAPTATION: Zones 4 through 10. (To determine your zone, see the map on page 1020.) Good street or lawn tree.

FLOWERING TIME: Summer.

LIGHT: Full sun.

SOIL: Tolerates a wide variety of soils, but grows best in deep, rich soils.

FERTILIZER: Fertilize with ORTHO Evergreen, Tree & Shrub Food according to label directions.

WATER:
How much: Apply enough water to wet the soil 3 to 4 feet deep. To determine the proper amount of water for your soil type, see page 912.
How often: Lindens are somewhat drought tolerant, but they grow best in moist soils. Water when the soil is barely moist 4 inches below the surface. For more information about watering, see page 912.

Gypsy moth caterpillars (half life size).

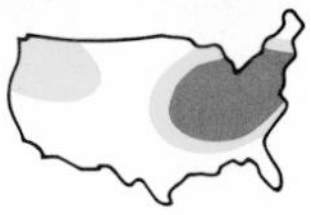

PROBLEM: The surface of the leaf is eaten, giving the remaining tissue a lacy appearance; or the whole leaf is chewed. Sometimes the leaves and branches are webbed. The tree may be completely defoliated. Damage appears any time between spring and fall. Caterpillars are clustered or feeding singly on the leaves. Repeated heavy infestations may weaken or kill trees.

ANALYSIS: Leaf-feeding caterpillars
Many different species of caterpillars feed on linden leaves wherever the trees are grown. Depending on the species, the moths lay their eggs in early spring to midsummer. The larvae that hatch from these eggs feed singly or in groups on buds, on one leaf surface (skeletonizers), or on the entire leaf. Certain caterpillars web the branches or leaves as they feed. In some years, damage is minimal due to unfavorable environmental conditions or control by predators and parasites. However, when conditions are favorable, entire trees may be defoliated by late summer. Defoliation weakens trees because there are no leaves left to produce food. When heavy infestations occur several years in a row, branches or entire trees may be killed.

SOLUTION: Spray with ORTHO Gypsy Moth & Japanese Beetle Killer or ORTHO Isotox Insect Killer when damage is first noticed. Spray the leaves thoroughly. Repeat the spray if the tree becomes reinfested.

Aphids (twice life size).

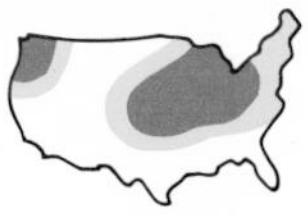

PROBLEM: Leaves are curling, discolored, and reduced in size. A shiny or sticky substance may coat the leaves. A black sooty mold often grows on the sticky substance. Tiny (⅛ inch), winged, green, soft-bodied insects with black stripes cluster on the leaves. Ants may be present.

ANALYSIS: Linden aphid
(*Myzocallis tiliae*)
Aphids do little damage in small numbers. However, they are extremely prolific and populations can rapidly build up to damaging numbers during the growing season. Damage occurs when the aphid sucks the juices from the linden leaves. The aphid is unable to digest fully all the sugar in the plant sap and excretes the excess in a fluid called honeydew, which often drops onto the leaves below. Plants or objects beneath the tree may also be coated with honeydew. A sooty mold fungus may develop on the sticky substance, causing the linden leaves to appear black and dirty. Ants feed on honeydew, and are often present where there is an aphid infestation.

SOLUTION: Spray with ORTHO Isotox Insect Killer when aphids appear. Direct the spray to the undersides of the leaves. Repeat the spray if the plant becomes reinfested.

Sunscorch and drought injury.

PROBLEM: During hot weather (95°F and over), usually in July or August, the ends of the branches die. The top of the tree appears brown and scorched. Browning can develop whether the soil around the roots is moist or dry. During prolonged periods of drought, the tree may die.

ANALYSIS: Scorch
Hemlocks are very sensitive to hot weather, which scorches the needles. In hot weather, water evaporates rapidly from the needles. If the roots can't absorb and convey water fast enough to replenish this loss, the needles turn brown and the branch tips die. This usually occurs in dry soil, but needles can also scorch when the soil is moist and temperatures are near 100°F for extended periods. Hemlocks growing in shallow, rocky soil or on sites with southern exposure are especially susceptible to scorch, and sometimes the entire tree turns brown and dies.

SOLUTION: To prevent further scorch, water trees deeply during periods of hot weather and prolonged drought. Wet the entire root space. (For more information about watering trees, see page 912.) Newly transplanted trees should be watered whenever the rootball is dry 2 inches below the surface. There are no controls for scorch on trees in moist soil. Plant trees adapted to your climate.

Fiorinia hemlock scale (life size).

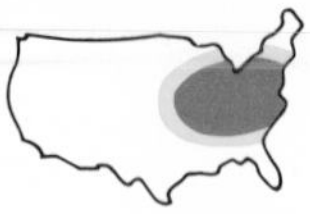

PROBLEM: The stems and undersides of the needles are covered with thick, white, waxy bumps or clusters of somewhat flattened grayish, white, or brown scaly bumps. The bumps can be scraped or picked off; the undersides are usually soft. Needles turn yellow and may drop.

ANALYSIS: Scales
Several species of scales infest hemlock. They lay their eggs on the leaves or bark, and in spring to midsummer the young scales, called *crawlers*, settle on the needles and twigs. These small (1/10 inch), soft-bodied young feed by sucking sap from the plant. The legs usually atrophy and a hard crusty or waxy shell develops over the body. The mature female scales lay their eggs underneath their shell. An uncontrolled infestation of scales may kill branches after two or three seasons. For more information about scales, see page 876.

SOLUTION: Spray with ORTHO Isotox Insect Killer, ORTHO Orthene Systemic Insect Control, ORTHO Volck Oil Spray, or ORTHO Liquid Sevin when the young are active. Contact your local Cooperative Extension Office (see page 1029) to determine the best time to spray for scales in your area. The following spring, before new growth begins, spray the trunk and branches with a *dormant oil spray* to control the overwintering insects.

Tsuga cultural information
Light: Full sun to part shade
Water: Keep the soil moist
Soil: Loose, rich, deep, acid
Fertilizer: Light

Spruce spider mite damage.

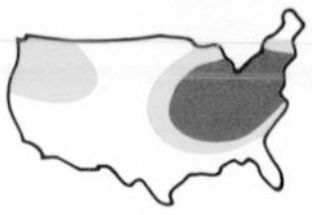

PROBLEM: Needles are stippled, gray, and dirty. When the infestation is heavy, the tree may appear totally gray. There is usually a silken webbing between the needles. Young trees may die the first season; older trees die progressively from the lower branches upward, over a period of years. To determine if the plant is infested with mites, hold a sheet of white paper underneath an affected branch and tap the branch sharply. Minute dark green to black specks the size of pepper grains will drop to the paper and begin to crawl around. The pests are easily seen against the white background.

ANALYSIS: Spruce spider mite
(*Oligonychus ununguis*)
This mite is a major pest of conifers throughout the country. It attacks hemlocks, spruce, junipers, and several other trees. The mites cause damage by sucking sap from the needles. As a result of feeding, the green pigment disappears, producing the stippled appearance. The spruce spider mite is most prolific in cooler weather. It is active in the spring and fall. At the onset of hot weather (70°F and up), the mite goes dormant and usually has caused its maximum damage. Several other mites infest hemlock. The microscopic hemlock rust mite (*Nalepella tsugifoliae*) causes needles to turn bluish, then to yellow and drop off.

SOLUTION: Spray the needles thoroughly with ORTHO Orthene Insect Spray or ORTHO Malathion 50 Insect Spray when damage is first noticed. Repeat two more times at intervals of 7 to 10 days to kill young mites as they hatch. To control insects during the dormant season, apply ORTHO Volck Oil Spray.

ULMUS (ELM)

ADAPTATION: Zones 3 to 10 (to determine your zone, see the map on page 1020). Not adapted to desert areas.

LIGHT: Full sun.

SOIL: Tolerates a wide variety of soils.

FERTILIZER: Fertilize with ORTHO Evergreen, Tree & Shrub Food according to label directions.

WATER: Water during periods of extended drought. (For more information about watering, see page 912.)

PRUNING: Prune off dead wood and destroy or strip off the bark to eliminate breeding sites for elm beetles (see page 587), which transmit Dutch elm disease.

Dutch elm disease.

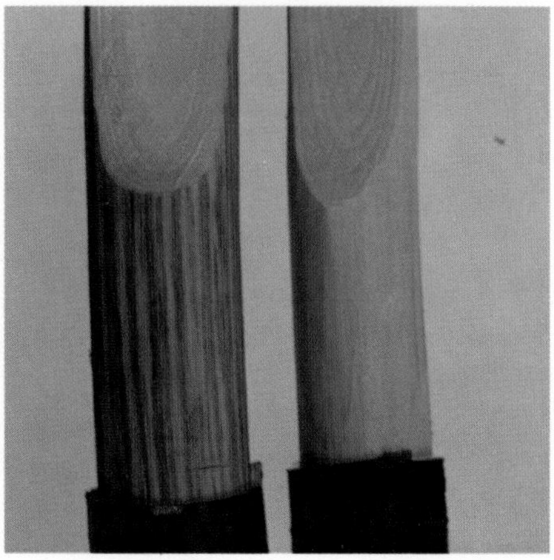
Diseased stem on left.

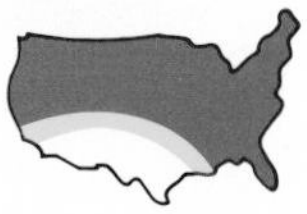

PROBLEM: Leaves wilt, curl, and turn yellow on one or more branches in the top of the tree; many leaves drop off. Trees may die slowly over a period of a year or longer. Or trees wilt and die within a few weeks, often in the spring soon after they have leafed out. Cross sections of infected branches may show a ring of brown dots in the wood, just underneath the bark. Small holes may be found in the bark of infected branches.

ANALYSIS: Dutch elm disease
Dutch elm disease is caused by a fungus (*Ceratocystis ulmi*) that invades and plugs the water-conducting vessels in the tree. The fungus enters the wood through feeding wounds made by elm bark beetles (see page 587). In the spring, the adult beetles emerge from holes in the bark of elm trees where they have spent the winter. If the trees are infected with the Dutch elm fungus, the beetles have sticky spores of the fungus on and inside their bodies. The beetles disperse to healthy elm trees, where they feed in crotches of small twigs, usually high in the tree, and deposit the fungus spores in the wounds. The fungus then spreads through the tree. The infected elm usually develops the disease that summer. The fungus produces a toxin that interferes with the water-conducting vessels in the wood, reducing the amount of water available to the leaves. The foliage on the infected branch wilts, turns yellow, and drops. Surrounding branches, and eventually the entire tree, become infected and the tree dies. When elms are closely planted (50 feet or less between trees), the fungus may spread through natural root grafts between trees. Trees infected through the roots generally wilt and die rapidly, often when growth begins in spring. These trees do not show browning in the wood when the branches are cut.

SOLUTION: Curing a tree of Dutch elm disease is usually not possible. Disease development may be delayed on lightly infected trees (less than 5 percent of the crown is infected) that were initially infected by bark beetles rather than by root grafts. Removal of early infections by tree surgery may save a tree for a number of years. Remove yellowing branches at least 10 feet below the point where brown streaks are visible in the wood. Sterilize pruning tools with rubbing alcohol after each cut. Spray the wound with an insecticide containing *methoxychlor*. Systemic fungicides (fungicides that are carried throughout the tree) injected into the tree by a trained arborist may increase the life span of a lightly infected tree. Contact an arborist when yellowing is first noticed. Prevention involves three different measures that should be carried out on a communitywide basis. (1) A good sanitation program will slow the spread of the fungus. Since bark beetles carrying the fungus breed in dead or dying elm wood, all dead or dying trees, damaged limbs, and prunings should be removed and burned or buried. The bark of all stumps should be peeled to just below ground level. (2) Controlling bark beetles with insecticides is practical only on valuable specimens, when used in conjunction with a sanitation program. Spray with an insecticide containing *methoxychlor* in early spring before leaves come out. Use high-pressure spray equipment, and cover the entire tree thoroughly. (3) To prevent transmission of the fungus through the roots of closely planted trees, grafted roots should be severed either by mechanical trenching or by soil injection of a chemical. This is especially important if there is a diseased tree nearby. Contact a professional arborist.

Phloem necrosis. *Insert:* Diseased stem.

PROBLEM: Leaves on the entire tree droop, curl, and turn bright yellow; eventually they turn brown and fall. Trees infected during spring or early summer may live over the winter, produce a thin crop of leaves, and die the next summer. Trees infected in midsummer may wilt and die within 3 to 4 weeks. If the bark on the roots or lower trunk is peeled back, the inner layers will be found to be a butterscotch color and will have a faint odor of wintergreen.

ANALYSIS: Phloem necrosis
This destructive plant disease of American elms is caused by mycoplasmas, microscopic organisms similar to bacteria. They are transmitted from tree to tree by leafhoppers. The organisms are introduced into plant sap as the leafhoppers feed on the undersides of the leaves. The nutrient-conducting vessels (phloem) are destroyed, first in the roots, then in the lower portions of the tree. The bark loosens and falls away, and the tree wilts. American elms may be attacked at any age.

SOLUTION: There is no cure for this disease. Infected trees should be removed and burned. To prevent phloem necrosis, control leafhoppers with ORTHO Isotox Insect Killer in late May or early June. A second application may be necessary if a flush of new growth occurs during July or August. For more information about controlling disease-carrying insects, see page 879.

ULMUS (ELM)

Whitebanded elm leafhopper damage.

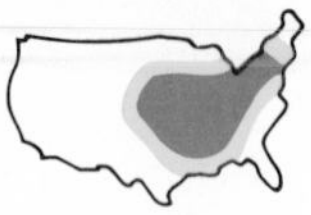

PROBLEM: Leaves are stippled white, and small twigs may be killed. Grayish-brown insects up to ½ inch long hop and fly away quickly when the leaves are touched.

ANALYSIS: Whitebanded elm leafhopper (*Scaphoideus luteolus*)
Elm leafhoppers by themselves cause only minor damage to elms. However, they carry mycoplasmas (microscopic organisms similar to bacteria) within their bodies that cause the very serious disease *phloem necrosis*. The leafhoppers spend the winter as eggs in the bark of twigs. Slits made by the egg-laying organ of the female leafhopper may injure or kill twigs. When the weather warms in spring, the young leafhoppers emerge and settle on the undersides of the leaves. They suck the plant sap, causing stippling. The leafhoppers that are carrying phloem necrosis transmit it as they feed. Infected trees often die. Several other leafhoppers that infest elms may also transmit phloem necrosis.

SOLUTION: Control leafhoppers with ORTHO Isotox Insect Killer in late May or early June. A second application may be necessary if a flush of new growth occurs during July or August. Insects carrying the phloem necrosis organism are difficult to control because it takes only one to infect the tree. For more information about controlling disease-carrying insects, see page 879.

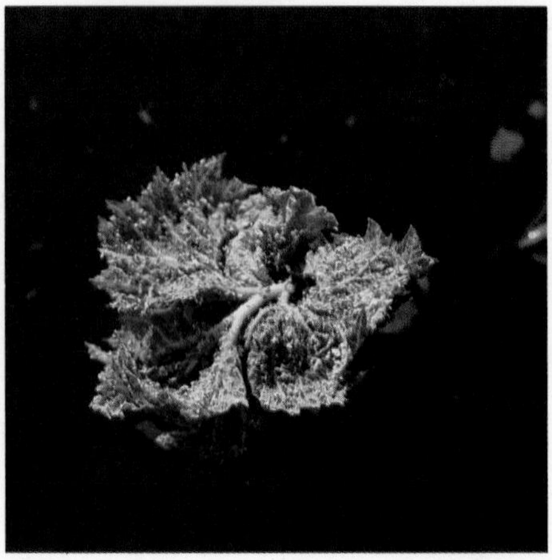

Woolly aphids (¼ life size).

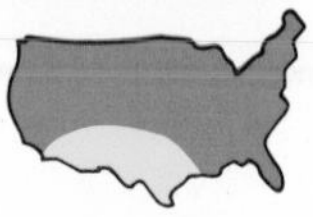

PROBLEM: Leaves are covered with white, cottony masses. Underneath the white masses are clusters of small (⅛ inch), purplish brown, soft-bodied insects. The leaves are curled, distorted, and yellowing, and the tree is often weak and growing poorly.

ANALYSIS: Woolly aphids (*Eriosoma* species)
Several species of woolly aphids attack elm throughout the country. When present in large numbers, they are both unsightly and severely damaging to the leaves. The aphids overwinter as eggs in bark crevices. The eggs hatch in spring as the elm leaves unfold. The aphids crawl to the undersides of the leaves to feed on plant sap. They cover themselves with a white, cottony mass as they feed. At the end of June, a generation of winged aphids may develop. They often leave the elm tree and fly to one of their summer hosts, such as apple, serviceberry, pyracantha, hawthorn, or mountain ash. In the fall, these aphids return to elms and lay the overwintering eggs.

SOLUTION: Spray with ORTHO Isotox Insect Killer when insects are first noticed in the spring. Cover the undersides of the leaves thoroughly. Repeat the spray 7 to 10 days later if damage continues.

Larva and Beetle (*insert*) (3 times life size).

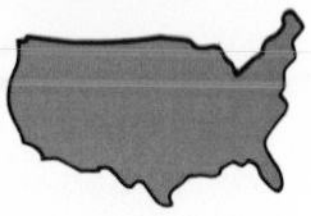

PROBLEM: The lower surface of the leaf is eaten between the veins, giving the leaves a lacy appearance. There may also be small holes in the leaves. Severely infested leaves turn brown; the entire tree may appear scorched. Many leaves drop off by midsummer. Small (½ inch) yellow and black insects, or ¼-inch yellowish green and black striped beetles, may be found on the undersides of the leaves.

ANALYSIS: Elm leaf beetle (*Pyrrhalta luteola*)
All species of elm are attacked by the leaf beetle, but the beetles may have local preferences. The beetles spend the winter as adults in buildings or in protected places outside. In the fall, when the beetles are looking for shelter, they often become a nuisance inside homes. The adults fly back to elm trees in the spring. They eat small holes in the developing leaves, mate, and lay their eggs. The emerging black larvae feed on the lower surface of the leaf between the veins. As the larvae mature, they turn a dull yellow with black stripes. After feeding for several weeks, the larvae pupate. Bright yellow pupae may be seen around the base of the tree in late June or early July. Adults emerge, and there may be one or two more generations. Trees that lose many of their leaves early in the season may grow new ones, which also may be eaten.

SOLUTION: Spray with ORTHO Isotox Insect Killer, ORTHO Orthene Systemic Insect Control, or ORTHO Liquid Sevin when damage is first noticed. To prevent severe leaf damage, sprays should be applied just as the leaves grow to full size. Repeat the spray if the tree becomes reinfested.

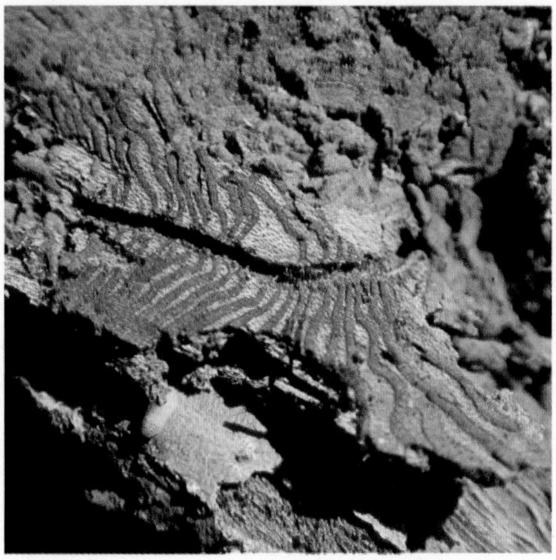

Galleries of elm bark beetles (1/4 life size).

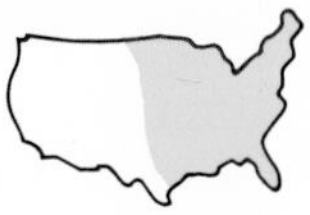

PROBLEM: Small (1/8 inch), shiny, dark reddish brown beetles or dull brown beetles with a rough body surface may be found feeding in the crotches of twigs around the middle of May. The bark is chewed and appears rough. Small holes may be found in the bark of weak or dying trees.

ANALYSIS: Elm bark beetles
These bark beetles by themselves cause very little injury to elm trees. However, they can be extremely damaging because they often carry the destructive Dutch elm fungus (see page 585). The fungus is carried on the bodies of the beetles as they move from infected breeding sites. The shiny reddish brown European bark beetle is generally a more important carrier than the dull brown native species because it usually outnumbers the native beetles. Spore-bearing beetles infect a healthy tree with the fungus as they feed on small twigs. The beetles then seek breeding sites under the bark of weakened, dead, or recently cut elm trees up to several miles away. The female beetles tunnel galleries in the wood under the bark, where they lay their eggs. The white larvae mine the wood at right angles to the gallery, producing many radiating tunnels. If these dead or dying trees are infected with the Dutch elm fungus, the larvae become covered with fungal spores. They emerge as adults in the spring and fly to healthy trees. These trees then become infected with Dutch elm fungus, which spreads through the whole tree.

SOLUTION: For information about controlling bark beetles and preventive and control measures for Dutch elm disease, see page 585.

Elm bark scale (life size).

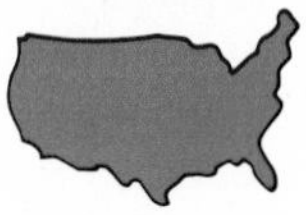

PROBLEM: The leaves, branches, or trunk are covered with white, cottony, cushionlike masses, or brownish or whitish crusty bumps. The bumps can be scraped or picked off. Leaves turn yellow and may drop. In some cases, a shiny or sticky substance coats the leaves. A black sooty mold often grows on the sticky substance. Branches are killed by heavy infestations.

ANALYSIS: Scales
Many different types of scales infest elm. They lay their eggs on leaves and bark, and in spring to midsummer the young scales, called *crawlers*, settle on leaves, twigs, and branches. These small (1/10 inch), soft-bodied young feed by sucking sap from the plant. The legs usually atrophy and, with some types, a shell develops over the body. The types of scale that do not develop shells are very conspicuous. The females are covered with a white, cottony egg sac, containing up to 2500 eggs. Scales covered with a shell often blend in with the plant, and the eggs are inconspicuous beneath their covering. Some species of scales are unable to digest fully all the sugar in the plant sap, and excrete the excess in a fluid called honeydew. A sooty mold fungus may develop on the honeydew, causing the elm leaves to appear black and dirty. For more information about scales, see page 876.

SOLUTION: Spray with ORTHO Orthene Systemic Insect Control, ORTHO Volck Oil Spray, or ORTHO Liquid Sevin when the young are active. Contact your local Cooperative Extension Office (see page 1029) for the best time to spray for scales in your area. Control scales during the dormant season with ORTHO Volck Oil Spray.

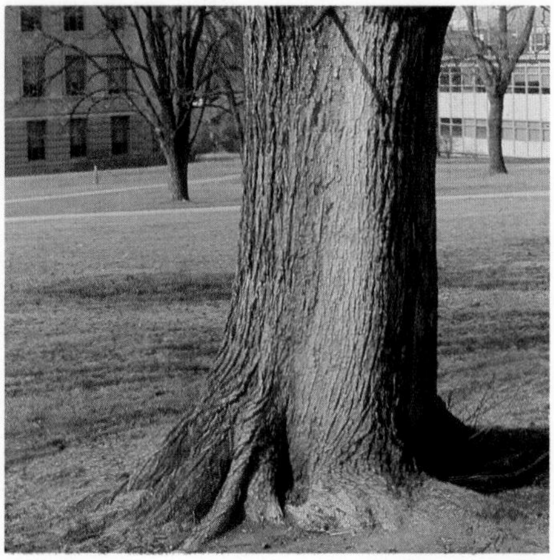

Slime flux.

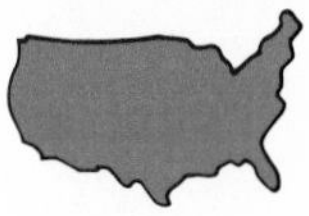

PROBLEM: Sour-smelling sap oozes from wounds, cracks, and branch crotches, mainly during the growing season. The sap drips down the bark and dries, causing unsightly gray streaks. There may be some wilting on affected branches. Insects are attracted to the sour-smelling ooze.

ANALYSIS: Slime flux
Slime flux of elms, also called *wetwood*, is caused by a bacterium (*Erwinia nimipressuralis*). The bacteria infect the heartwood, producing abnormally high sap pressure. This pressure is caused by bacterial fermentation, and forces the fermented sap, or flux, out of wounds, cracks, or crotches in the tree. Flux is especially copious when the tree is growing rapidly. Large areas of the bark may be coated with the smelly, bacteria-laden sap, which dries to a grayish-white color. In addition, wounds do not heal and the bark is unsightly. A tree with this problem is often under water stress, which may cause drought damage (wilting and scorched leaves) to the branches. The problem may persist for years.

SOLUTION: There are no chemical controls for this condition. Bore a slightly slanted drainage hole through the wood below each oozing wound. Insert a 1/2-inch-diameter plastic tube just until it stays firmly in place. If the tube penetrates the water-soaked wood inside the tree, it will interfere with drainage. The tube will carry the dripping sap away from the trunk. Disinfect tools with rubbing alcohol after pruning infected trees.

VIBURNUM

Aphids (life size).

PROBLEM: Tiny (⅛ inch), ash-gray, reddish brown, or dark green soft-bodied insects cluster on the leaves and stem tips. Leaves are discolored, and may be extremely curled and distorted. Leaves sometimes drop off. A shiny or sticky substance may coat the leaves. A black sooty mold often grows on the sticky substance.

ANALYSIS: Aphids
Several different kinds of aphids infest viburnum. They do little damage in small numbers. However, they are extremely prolific and populations can rapidly build up to damaging numbers during the growing season. Damage occurs when the aphid sucks the juices from the viburnum leaves. The aphid is unable to digest fully all the sugar in the plant sap and excretes the excess in a fluid called honeydew, which often drops onto the leaves below. A sooty mold fungus may develop on the honeydew, causing the viburnum leaves to appear black and dirty. The ash-gray snowball aphid (*Neoceruraphis viburnicola*) causes severe curling and distortion of the leaves and leaf stems of the snowball viburnum (*Viburnum opulus*). Other species of viburnum are usually immune. The other species of aphids that infest viburnum do not cause leaf curling.

SOLUTION: Spray with ORTHO Isotox Insect Killer or ORTHO Orthene Systemic Insect Control when aphids first appear. Direct the spray to the undersides of the leaves. Repeat the spray if the plant becomes reinfested.

Powdery mildew.

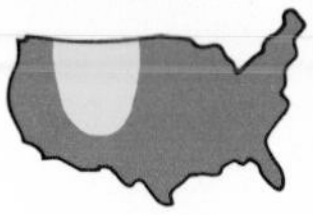

PROBLEM: Leaves are covered with a thin layer or irregular patches of a grayish white powdery material. Infected leaves may turn yellow and drop. In late fall, tiny black dots (spore-producing bodies) are scattered over the white patches like ground pepper.

ANALYSIS: Powdery mildew
This common plant disease is caused by a fungus (*Microsphaera alni*) that thrives in both humid and dry weather. Plants growing in shady areas are often severely infected in the fall. The powdery patches consist of fungal strands and spores. The spores are spread by the wind to healthy plants. The fungus saps the plant nutrients, causing yellowing and sometimes death of the leaf. Since this powdery mildew attacks many different kinds of woody plants, the fungus from a diseased plant may infect other woody plants in the garden. (For a list of susceptible plants, see page 1006.)

SOLUTION: Spray the surfaces of the leaves with a fungicide containing *chlorothalonil* (DACONIL 2787®) when the plants show the first sign of mildew. Repeat the spray at intervals of 7 to 10 days until mildew disappears.

Viburnum cultural information
Light: Full sun or part shade
Water: When soil is moist but not wet
Soil: Heavy loam
Fertilizer: Heavy

WISTERIA

ADAPTATION: Throughout the United States (protect in zones below zone 5). To determine your zone, see page 1020.

FLOWERING TIME: April and May.

LIGHT: Full sun to partial shade (Japanese wisteria blooms best in full sun).

SOIL: Any good, well-drained garden soil.

FERTILIZER: Fertilize with ORTHO General Purpose Plant Food according to label directions.

WATER:
How much: Apply enough water to wet the soil 2 to 3 feet deep. To determine the proper amount of water for your soil type, see page 912.
How often: Young wisteria needs ample water. Water when the soil is moist but not wet 4 inches below the surface. Established plants flower best with less water. Water established plants when the soil is barely moist 4 inches below the surface. For more information about watering, see page 912.

PRUNING: Establish a framework on young wisterias. Pinch off long streamers and buds that develop on the trunk. Prune older plants during the dormant season. Thin out or cut back side shoots. Shorten the flower-producing spurs (short shoots containing flower buds that grow from the side shoots) to 2 or 3 buds. In the summer, cut back some streamers.

Failure to bloom.

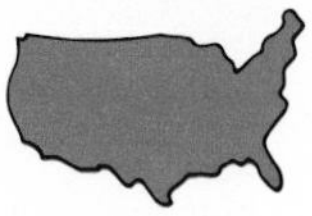

PROBLEM: No flowers appear in the spring, but the vine is healthy and vigorous.

ANALYSIS: Not blooming
Most wisterias purchased from nurseries bloom well after 2 or 3 years. These plants are usually asexually propagated (plants started from cuttings or by some method other than from seed). Vines started from seed often do not bloom for 10 to 15 years or longer. Wisterias also may fail to bloom because of improper growing conditions, poor pruning practices, or freeze damage. Young plants should be well fed and watered. Plants old enough to bloom flower best with less food and water. Too much nitrogen fertilizer during the growing season causes lush, overly vigorous, green growth and poor flower bud production (flower buds for next season's bloom are produced in early summer). Heavy pruning also may produce lush, overly vigorous growth, or flower buds may be mistakenly removed.

SOLUTION: Do not grow wisteria from seed. Buy nursery-grown vines. If your old wisteria did not bloom in spring and is lush and growing vigorously, do not use nitrogen fertilizer for an entire season. Fertilize in early summer with ORTHO Fruit & Bloom Builder to promote flower bud formation for next season. Prune back vigorous shoots in summer. In winter, cut back or thin out side shoots from the main stems. Spurs (short fat stems bearing flower buds) develop on these side shoots. Cut back spurs to 2 to 3 buds. Do not drastically prune the side shoots. Drastic pruning will eliminate all the spurs so no flowers are produced.

Bird injury.

PROBLEM: Flower buds disappear from the clusters. This becomes most noticeable when the remaining buds open; long, bare stalks protrude from the plant, with blossoms only at the base. Birds may be seen around the plant.

ANALYSIS: Birds
Birds are pests of many berries and soft, sweet fruits in the garden. Some birds also feed on blossoms, especially when other food is limited. In early spring, when wisteria flowers are developing, birds may devour many of the buds, leaving long bare stalks. The damage does not harm the plant, but flowering may be drastically reduced.

SOLUTION: Once most of the buds have disappeared, there is nothing you can do. If you notice birds around the plant before many buds have been eaten, protect the vines with netting. For more information about bird control, see page 899.

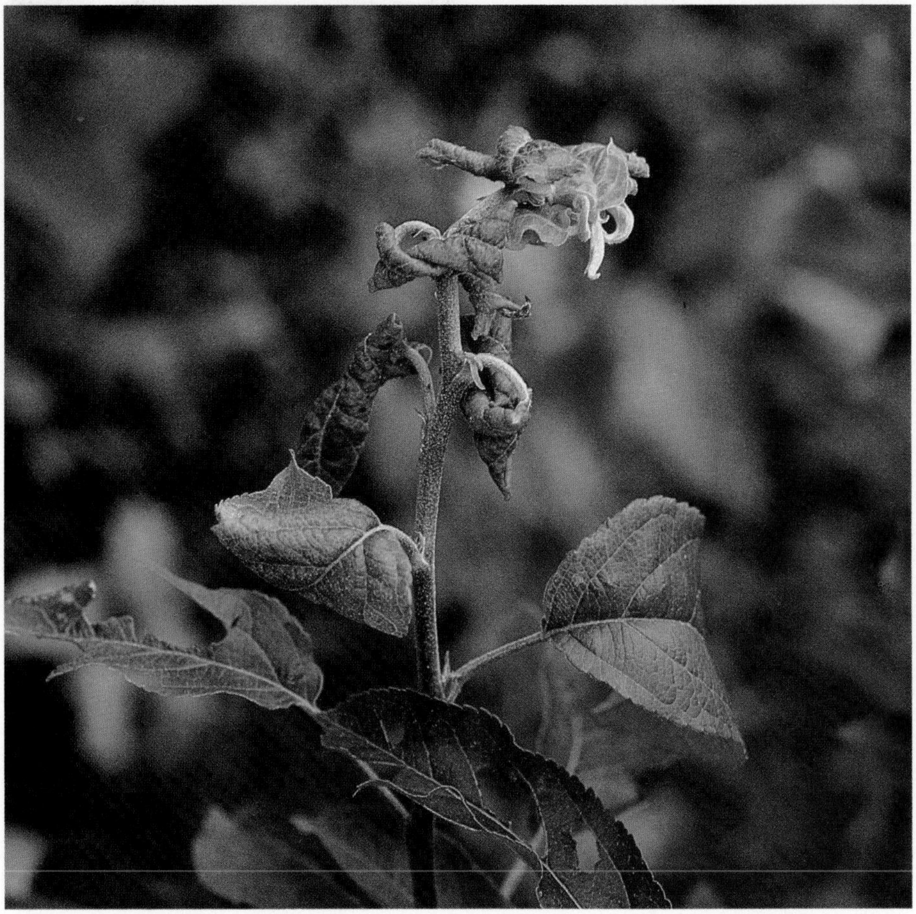

Some of the problems common to all fruit and nut trees are listed on the next 12 pages. If you don't find your problem there, look up your specific fruit or nut tree in the index on the next page. Several problems that occur in all trees may also be found in the section discussing problems common to trees, shrubs, and vines, on page 408.

PROBLEMS COMMON TO MANY FRUIT AND NUT TREES:	PAGE
Poor fruiting	593
Animal damage	594
Bark or wood problems	595
Insects	597
Powdery material on leaves	599
Leaves discolored or mottled	600
Tree stunted or declining	602

FRUIT AND NUT TREES

Although fruit and nut trees are increasingly valued for the ornamental contribution to the landscape, they are primarily raised for food. The measure of success with these trees lies in the quality and quantity of their fruit. And, since the production of fruit and nuts takes energy over and above the energy needed for simple growth, fruit and nut trees are seldom satisfactory if they just barely survive.

The production of large crops of tasty fruit or nuts requires more time and skill than does the successful raising of ornamentals, or even vegetables. In addition to the soil preparation, regular feeding, and watering that most garden plants require to flourish, fruit and nut trees need proper pruning and pest control.

All fruit trees need some pruning, at least while they are young. Some, such as citrus, need very little when mature. But others, such as peach, need fairly heavy, skillful pruning to remain fruitful and problem-free. Proper pruning requires an understanding of the growth and bearing habits of each type of fruit or nut tree. It is an easy skill to learn, but some study must be given to master it. If you don't have a skilled friend to teach you, you can learn from a book, such as Ortho's book, *All About Growing Fruits and Berries*.

In the course of evolution, the trees that we raise for their fruit and nuts developed a large seed (in the case of nuts) or seed package (in the case of fruit) in order to be attractive to animals and birds. The animals and birds then dispersed their seeds over a far larger area than could be accomplished by gravity or the wind. But in developing fruit that was attractive to animals and birds, they also developed fruit that was attractive to insects and diseases.

Most fruit trees need regular spraying to produce a large crop that is free of holes and blemishes. Commercial orchardists spray many times each season to produce the superior fruit we have become accustomed to in supermarkets. Most home gardeners will tolerate a few more wormy apples than supermarket buyers, but usually find it necessary to follow some sort of spray schedule.

Because these schedules are different in different parts of the country, depending on local problems and climate, we are unable to offer spray schedules in this book. But spray schedules are available from local Cooperative Extension offices. See page 1029.

Fruit and nut trees may be more trouble than ornamentals, but the rewards are also greater. Fresh, sweet fruit right off the tree is a reward worth a great deal of effort.

Above: Aphid-damaged apple leaves. See page 607.
Left: A bountiful harvest is the reward for solving fruit tree problems.

INDEX TO FRUIT AND NUT TREES

PROBLEMS COMMON TO MANY FRUIT AND NUT TREES

Premature drop of cherries.

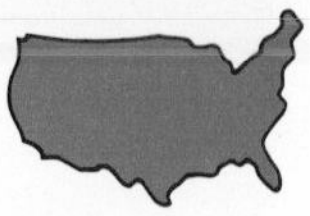

PROBLEM: Fruit drops prematurely. The tree appears to be healthy; there are no signs of insect pests or diseases.

ANALYSIS: Premature fruit drop
Premature fruit drop has several causes:
1. *Natural thinning:* Most fruit trees initially produce more fruit than they can mature. Premature fruit drop is a natural means of thinning out the excess fruit. Such fruit may be as small as a fraction of an inch in diameter.
2. *Stress:* Large quantities of fruit may drop when the tree is under stress. Stress may be caused by conditions such as excessive heat, drought, cold, or overwatering, and by rapid changes in soil moisture and air temperature.
3. *Freeze damage:* Unseasonal spring frosts often freeze and kill developing young fruits, causing them to drop off.
4. *Lack of pollination:* If the flowers are not pollinated, they may develop into pea-sized fruits, then fall off.

SOLUTION: The numbers below correspond to the numbers in the analysis.
1. As long as your tree appears healthy, there is nothing to worry about.
2. Help reduce stress to the tree by watering and fertilizing it properly. For cultural information, look up your tree in the alphabetical section beginning on page 604.
3. Once fruits are damaged by frost, there is nothing you can do. For information on how to protect your trees from frost damage, see page 919. Plant trees that are hardy in your area. For a list of common fruit and nut trees and their hardiness, see page 1021.
4. Check the lists on page 1021 to determine if your tree requires a pollinator.

Poor fruiting on almond.

Failure to fruit on peach.

PROBLEM: Trees produce few or no fruits. The tree appears healthy, and is growing vigorously. There are no signs of insect pests or diseases.

ANALYSIS: Few or no fruits
Fruit trees may fail to bear fruit for any of several reasons.

1. *Lack of pollination:* In order to produce fruit, many varieties of fruit trees must be cross-pollinated (pollinated with pollen from a different variety). If a cross-pollinating variety is not present in the garden or nearby neighborhood, the tree may bloom profusely, but produce few or no fruits.

2. *Lack of pollinators:* Most fruit trees are pollinated by bees. If, due to rain or cold weather, bees are not present when the tree is flowering, or if they are killed by tree-spraying, pollination and fruit set will not occur.

3. *Cold damage:* Flowers may be killed when temperatures drop below freezing. Some fruit tree flowers can tolerate temperatures in the 20°F range, but flower hardiness varies considerably with the species and variety.

4. *Biennial bearing:* Certain types of fruit trees, especially apples, pears, and some citrus varieties, tend to bear a heavy crop of fruit one year, and few or no fruits the following year. The production of large quantities of fruit inhibits the formation of next year's flowers. Then the lack of fruit stimulates the production of many flowers for the following year.

5. *Improper pruning:* If the fruit-bearing wood is pruned off during the dormant season, the tree will fail to flower and fruit.

SOLUTION: The numbered solutions below correspond to the numbers in the analysis.

1. Check the list of common fruit tree varieties on page 1005 to determine whether your tree requires a pollinator.

2. There is nothing you can do about lack of bee activity due to rain or cold weather. If your trees bloom early in the season when inclement weather is more likely, plant late-blooming varieties.

3. Once flowers have been killed or damaged by an unseasonal cold spell, there is nothing you can do. If you expect temperatures to drop during the night, you can protect your trees in several ways (see page 919). Plant late-blooming varieties to avoid cold damage.

4. To help even out fruit production from year to year, thin fruits about 4 to 6 weeks after the trees have bloomed. For information about thinning fruits, look up your tree in the alphabetical section beginning on page 604.

5. Avoid pruning off large amounts of fruit-bearing wood. To determine where the fruit is produced, look up your fruit tree in the alphabetical section.

Small cherries.

PROBLEM: The tree is healthy, and produces many small fruits. There are no signs of pests or diseases.

ANALYSIS: Fruit too small
Certain fruit trees, including peaches, nectarines, Japanese plums, and apples, tend to produce large quantities of small fruit when the trees are not pruned or thinned adequately. If the fruit-bearing wood is not pruned during the dormant season, the tree will set many more fruits than can grow to full size. Even when properly pruned, certain fruit trees have a tendency to overbear. A tree has only a limited amount of nutrients that can be supplied to the fruits. When a tree overbears, it distributes smaller quantities of nutrients to each maturing fruit, resulting in large numbers of small fruits.

SOLUTION: Prune your tree properly during the dormant season, and thin the young fruits when they are thumbnail size (4 to 8 weeks after bloom). For pruning and thinning details, look up your fruit tree in the alphabetical section beginning on page 604.

Poor-quality pear.

Poor-quality apples.

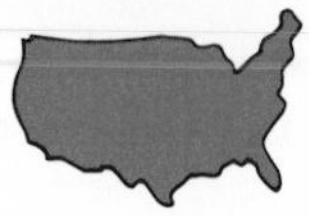

PROBLEM: Fruits and nuts are not flavorful. Fruits may be dry, watery, pulpy, or grainy, and may taste sour or tart.

ANALYSIS: Poor-tasting fruit and nuts
Fruits and nuts may be poor in flavor for a number of reasons.

SOLUTION: The numbered solutions below correspond to the numbers in the analysis.

1. *Lack of nutrients:* Trees planted in infertile soil grow poorly and often produce small crops of inferior-tasting fruits and nuts.

1. Fertilize trees regularly according to label directions with ORTHO Evergreen, Tree & Shrub Food.

2. *Environmental stress:* Trees may be stressed by too much or too little soil moisture, excessively high or low temperatures, or rapid, unseasonable weather changes. Under environmental stress, many types of trees may fail to ripen fruits or nuts properly, producing dry, pulpy, or otherwise poor-tasting fruits and nuts.

2. To reduce stress caused by too much or too little soil moisture, avoid overwatering or underwatering your tree. (For details on proper watering, see page 912.) Minimize tree stress resulting from weather and temperature fluctuations by maintaining the tree in good health. For specific cultural information, look up your tree in the alphabetical section starting on page 604.

3. *Disease or insect damage:* Diseases and pests often slow root, shoot, and leaf growth, and prevent fruits and nuts from ripening properly. Fruits and nuts themselves may also be infected or infested, resulting in poor flavor.

3. To help ensure high-quality fruit and nut crops, keep your trees as free of insect pests and diseases as possible. To determine what is infecting or infesting your tree, look up your tree in the alphabetical section.

4. *Untimely harvest:* When fruits are prematurely harvested, they may taste tart, flavorless, dry, or starchy. But pears taste gritty or mealy if they are allowed to ripen on the tree. For more information about harvesting pears, see page 641.

4. As a general rule, fruits are ripe when they are fully colored, slightly soft, and easy to separate from the branch when gently lifted. For details on harvesting, look up your specific tree.

5. *Fruit naturally unflavorful:* Tree varieties vary considerably in the quality of their fruits and nuts. No matter how healthy and vigorous your tree is, the variety may just naturally produce a flavorless crop. Seedling trees often produce insipid fruit.

5. If your tree appears to be healthy, but has continued to produce poor-quality fruits over several years, plant a variety that bears more flavorful fruits. Check with your local Cooperative Extension Office (see page 1029) for a list of flavorful fruit and nut trees that are adapted to your area.

Ground squirrel damage to almond trees.

PROBLEM: Leaves and buds or shoots are chewed from the trees. Bark may be chewed or gnawed from the trunk or lower branches. In some cases, the trunk is entirely girdled. Deer, rabbits, or mice may be seen in the yard, or their tracks may be seen on the ground or snow. Damage is usually most severe during the winter months.

ANALYSIS: Bark-feeding animals
Several animals chew on tree bark.
1. Deer damage trees by feeding on leaves, shoots, buds, and bark. They feed by pulling or twisting the bark or twigs, leaving ragged or twisted twig ends or patches of bark. The males may also damage trees by rubbing their antlers on the trunk and branches.
2. Rabbits damage fruit trees by chewing on the bark at the base of the trunk, and clipping off tender shoots. They chew bark and twigs off cleanly, leaving a sharp break. The damaged trunk is often marked with paired gouges where the rabbits have fed. They generally feed no more than 2 feet above the ground or snow level. Rabbits damage young or dwarf trees most severely.
3. Field or meadow mice damage fruit trees by chewing off the bark at the base of the trunk, just at or slightly above or below ground or snow level. They may girdle the trunk, killing the tree. Mice leave tiny scratches in the exposed wood.

SOLUTION: Various methods may be used to control deer, rabbits, and mice. For more information, see page 897 for deer control; page 900 for rabbit control; and page 896 for mouse control.

Bird-damaged apple.

Squirrel eating green cherry.

PROBLEM: Ripened fruits and nuts have holes in them and may be partially eaten. Fruits and nuts may disappear from the tree, or may have been knocked to the ground. Birds, tree squirrels, or raccoons may be seen feeding in the trees.

ANALYSIS: Animals eating fruit and nuts
Some birds and animals, especially tree squirrels and raccoons, feed on tree fruits and nuts.

SOLUTION: The numbered solutions below correspond to the numbers in the analysis.

1. Birds are notorious pests of many tree fruits, especially cherries, figs, persimmons, and other soft, sweet fruits. They peck at the ripening fruit, leaving holes in the flesh. The wounded fruits may decay, becoming inedible. Some birds also feed on the fruit blossoms and tiny developing fruits, greatly reducing the overall fruit yield.

1. The most effective way of controlling birds is to throw nets over the trees, securing the nets tightly around the trunk. Birds are most likely to damage ripening fruits. Check the trees every morning, and harvest fruits and nuts that have ripened. Bright, shiny objects hung in trees frighten birds, and will repel them for a while.

2. Tree squirrels feed on a large variety of foods, including bark, leaves, insects, and eggs. However, they prefer maturing nuts and fruits. They can strip entire trees of nuts, many of which they store for later use. They often leave partially eaten nuts on the ground around the tree. Tree squirrels are especially fond of filberts.

2. Prevent tree squirrels from climbing fruit and nut trees by wrapping 2-foot-wide bands of metal (made from materials like aluminum roof flashing) snugly around tree trunks at least 6 feet above the ground level. Prune trees so that all their branches are at least 6 feet above the ground and 6 feet away from other trees and structures. If necessary, dwarf trees or shrubs can be completely enclosed in a chicken-wire cage. If permissible in your area, you can also trap tree squirrels. For more information about trapping, see page 897.

3. Raccoons are usually found in wooded areas near a source of water. They feed on a wide variety of foods, including ripening fruits and nuts. Raccoons may strip off fruits and nuts and carry them away, or feed on them in the tree. In the process of feeding, they often knock many fruits and nuts to the ground.

3. Raccoons are intelligent, inquisitive animals that can be very difficult to control. To discourage raccoons from climbing between trees, or from a building to a tree, keep the limbs pruned so that they do not touch each other, and do not make contact with the roof. Wrap metal guards at least 18 inches wide around tree trunks at least 3 feet above the ground. For more information about controlling raccoons, see page 900.

Fruit overload on apple branch.

PROBLEM: Branches laden with large quantities of ripening fruit break off.

ANALYSIS: Limb breakage
Trees that produce large fruit, such as peaches, nectarines, apples, and pears, have problems with limbs breaking as the fruit reaches full size. Branches that have not been pruned or thinned properly are most likely to break. Trees that produce fruit on thin, year-old wood, like peaches and nectarines, are most susceptible to limb breakage.

SOLUTION: Prune off stubs where branches have broken. (For information about pruning stubs, see page 916.) Prop up any branches that are bent or appear ready to break. Cut a notch at one end of a board and place the board about a third of the way inward from the tip of the sagging branch. Set the branch into the notch, and then push the board into the ground. If the soil is not soft, you may need to dig a hole in the ground first. The board should be pushed in at a slight angle (20°), leaning toward the center of the tree. During the dormant season prune the tree properly, and thin young fruit. For pruning and thinning details, look up your fruit tree in the alphabetical section beginning on page 604.

PROBLEMS COMMON TO MANY FRUIT AND NUT TREES — BARK OR WOOD PROBLEMS

Gummosis on peach.

Gummosis on apricot.

Cytospora canker on peach.

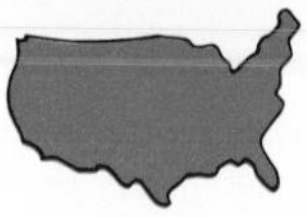

PROBLEM: Beads of sticky, amber-colored sap appear on healthy bark, cankers (sunken lesions), wounds, or pruning cuts.

ANALYSIS: Gummosis	**SOLUTION:**
Oozing sap (gummosis), which occurs in all trees to a greater or lesser extent, is caused by one or several of the following factors.	The numbered solutions below correspond to the numbers in the analysis.
1. *Natural tendency:* Certain species of fruit trees, especially cherries, apricots, peaches, and plums, have a natural tendency to ooze sap. Small beads of sap often form on the bark of these trees.	**1.** As long as the bark appears healthy, there is nothing to worry about.
2. *Environmental stress:* Trees that are under stress because they are growing in wet, poorly drained, or very dry soil may produce large quantities of sap, even though they are not diseased. Also, many fruit trees respond to rapid changes in weather conditions or soil moisture by gumming profusely.	**2.** If your tree is growing in wet, poorly drained soil, allow the soil to dry out between waterings. Provide for drainage of water away from tree trunks and roots. To help prevent crown rot, carefully remove enough soil around the base of the trunk to expose the first major roots.
3. *Mechanical injury:* Almost all trees ooze sap when the bark or wood is wounded. Wounding results from limb breakage; lawnmower injury; pruning; improper staking, tying, or guying techniques; and other practices that damage the bark and wood.	**3.** Avoid unnecessary mechanical injuries to the tree. Stake, tie, and prune properly. For more information, see ORTHO's book *All About Pruning.* For instructions on staking and tying, see page 917.
4. *Disease:* Fruit trees respond to certain fungal and bacterial infections by forming cankers that gum profusely. Gummosis is often one of the initial signs of infection.	**4.** Remove badly infected branches and cut out cankers. For details about canker removal and treatment, see page 917. Keep the tree healthy. For cultural information, look up your tree in the alphabetical section beginning on page 604.
5. *Insect damage:* Several species of insects bore into tree bark, causing sap to ooze from the damaged areas. The larvae of certain beetles and moths are the most damaging types of boring insects. The tunnels they form in the wood often become infected with decay organisms.	**5.** Borers are difficult to control once they have burrowed into the wood. For instructions on borer control, see page 597.

PROBLEM: Sunken, oval, or elongated dark lesions (cankers) develop on the trunk or branches. The bark at the edge of the canker may thicken and roll inward. Sticky, amber-colored sap may ooze from the canker. The foliage on infected branches may be stunted and yellowing; some of the leaves may turn brown and drop off. Twigs and branches may die back, and the tree may eventually die.

ANALYSIS: Cankers
Several different species of fungi and bacteria cause cankers on fruit and nut trees. These organisms may be spread by wind, splashing water, or contaminated tools. Infection usually occurs through injured or wounded tissue. Bark that has been damaged by sunscald, cold, pruning wounds, or mechanical injury is especially susceptible. The decay organisms sometimes infect the leaves directly, then spread down into healthy twigs. Cankers form as the decay progresses. Many fruit trees produce a sticky sap that oozes from the cankers. The portion of the branch or stem above the canker may die from decay or from clogging of the water and nutrient-conducting vessels in the branch. Cankers that form on the trunk are the most serious, and may kill the tree. The tree may halt the development of a canker by producing callus tissue, a growth of bark-like cells, to wall off the infection.

SOLUTION: Remove badly infected branches and cut out cankers. For details about canker removal and treatment, see page 917. Avoid wounding the tree, and keep it healthy. For cultural information, see the alphabetical section beginning on page 604.

INSECTS

Sunscald.

PROBLEM: Patches of bark on the trunk or branches darken and die. Often, these patches appear on the southwest side of the tree. Cracks and sunken lesions (cankers) may eventually develop in the dead bark. Damaged trees have been recently transplanted or heavily pruned.

ANALYSIS: Sunscald
When a tree is shaded by other trees or structures, or is covered with dense foliage, the bark on the trunk and branches remains relatively thin. If the tree is suddenly exposed to intense sunlight, the newly exposed bark and the wood just beneath the bark may be injured by the sun's heat. This frequently happens when young trees are moved from a shaded nursery to an open area, and when trees are heavily pruned during periods of intense sunlight. The problem also occurs on cold, clear days in winter, as cold bark is quickly warmed by the sun. The damaged bark usually splits open, forming long cracks or cankers. Decay fungi may invade the exposed wood. Sunscald is most severe when the soil is dry. Young trees may die from sunscald.

SOLUTION: Unless the tree is very young, or extremely damaged, it will usually recover with proper care. Water and fertilize the tree to stimulate new growth. To prevent further damage, wrap the trunks and main branches of recently pruned or newly transplanted trees with tree-wrapping paper. Or paint the exposed bark with a white interior latex or whitewash. The tree will eventually adapt to increased exposure by growing more foliage and producing thicker bark.

Borer holes.

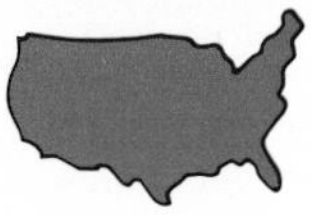

PROBLEM: Foliage on a branch or at the top of the tree is sparse; eventually the twigs and branches die. Holes or tunnels are apparent in the trunk or branches. Sap or sawdust may be present near the holes. The bark over the tunnels may die or slough off, or there may be knotlike swellings on the trunk and limbs. Weakened branches break during wind or snow storms. Weak, young, or newly transplanted trees may be killed.

ANALYSIS: Borers
Borers are the larvae of beetles or moths. Many kinds of borers attack fruit and nut trees. Females lay their eggs in bark crevices throughout the summer. The larvae feed by tunneling through the bark or wood. Borer tunnels stop the flow of nutrients and water through the area by damaging the conducting vessels; branch and twig dieback result. Sap flow may act as a defense against borers if the tree is healthy. When the borer burrows into the wood, tree sap fills the hole and drowns the insect. Trees that are weakened by mechanical injuries, disease, poor growing conditions, or insect infestation are more susceptible to borer attack.

SOLUTION: Cut out and destroy all dead and dying branches. Severely infested young trees should be removed. Spray or paint the trunk and branches with an insecticide containing *lindane* to kill young larvae before they burrow into the wood. Contact your local Cooperative Extension Office (see page 1029) to determine the appropriate time to apply the insecticide in your area. Make sure that your tree is listed on the product label. Maintain tree health and vigor by watering and fertilizing regularly.

Cherry scale. *Insert:* Leucanium scale (life size).

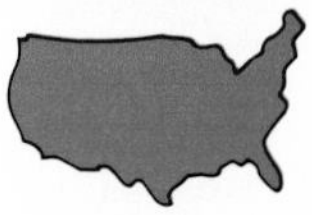

PROBLEM: The stems or undersides of the leaves are covered with crusty bumps or thick, white, waxy bumps or clusters of somewhat flattened scaly bumps. The bumps can be scraped or picked off; the undersides are usually soft. Leaves turn yellow and may drop. In some cases, a shiny or sticky substance coats the leaves.

ANALYSIS: Scales
Several different types of scales infest fruit trees. They lay their eggs on leaves or bark, and in spring to midsummer the young scales, called *crawlers*, settle on leaves and twigs. The small ($\frac{1}{10}$ inch), soft-bodied young feed by sucking sap from the plant. The legs usually atrophy and a hard crusty or waxy shell develops over the body. The mature female scales lay their eggs underneath their shell. Some species of scales are unable to digest fully all the sugar in the plant sap, and excrete the excess in a fluid called honeydew. An uncontrolled infestation of scales may kill the plant after 2 or 3 seasons. For more information about scales, see page 876.

SOLUTION: Spray with an insecticide containing *malathion* when the young are active. Make sure that your fruit tree is listed on the product label. Contact your local Cooperative Extension Office (see page 1029) to determine the best time to spray for scales in your area. Early the following spring, before new growth begins, spray the trunk and branches with a *dormant oil spray* to control overwintering insects.

PROBLEMS COMMON TO MANY FRUIT AND NUT TREES — INSECTS

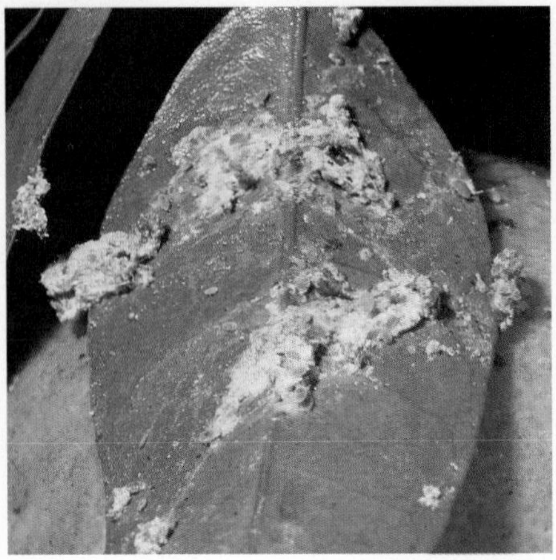

Citrus mealybugs.

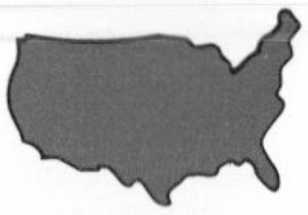

PROBLEM: The undersides of the leaves, stems, branch crotches, or trunk are covered with white, cottony masses. Leaves may be curled, distorted, and yellowing, and knotlike galls may form on the stems or trunk. Sometimes a shiny or sticky substance coats the leaves. Twigs and branches may die.

ANALYSIS: Cottony scales, mealybugs, and woolly aphids
Cottony scales, mealybugs, and woolly aphids produce white, waxy secretions that cover their bodies. Their similarity makes separate identification difficult. When the insects are young, they are usually inconspicuous on the host plant. Their bodies range in color from yellowish green to brown, blending in with the leaves or bark. As the insects mature, they exude filaments of white wax, giving them a cottony appearance. Mealybugs and scales generally deposit their eggs in white, fluffy masses. Damage is caused by the withdrawal of plant sap from the leaves, branches, or trunk. The insects are unable to digest fully all the sugar in the plant sap and excrete the excess in a fluid called honeydew, which often drops onto the leaves or plants below.

SOLUTION: Spray the branches, trunk, and foliage with ORTHO Fruit & Vegetable Insect Control or ORTHO Malathion 50 Insect Spray. Make sure that your fruit tree is listed on the product label. During the dormant season, spray the trunk and branches with ORTHO Volck Oil Spray.

Aphids (life size).

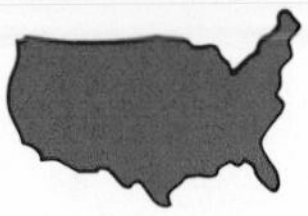

PROBLEM: The youngest leaves are curled, twisted, discolored, and stunted. Leaves may drop, and in severe cases the tree may defoliate. The developing fruits may be small and misshapen. A shiny or sticky substance may coat the leaves. A black sooty mold often grows on the sticky substance. Tiny (⅛ inch) yellow, green, purplish, or black soft-bodied insects cluster on the young shoots and undersides of the leaves.

ANALYSIS: Aphids
Many species of these insects infest fruit trees. Aphids do little damage in small numbers. However, they are extremely prolific and populations can rapidly build up during the growing season. Damage occurs when the aphid sucks the juices from the leaves and immature fruit. The aphid is unable to digest fully all the sugar in the sap and excretes the excess in a fluid called honeydew, which often drops onto the leaves below. A sooty mold fungus may develop on the honeydew, causing the leaves to appear black and dirty. At harvest time, the fruit may be small, misshapen, and pitted due to aphid damage earlier in the season. For more information about aphids, see page 875.

SOLUTION: Spray with ORTHO Fruit and Vegetable Insect Control or ORTHO Home Orchard Spray. Make sure that your fruit is listed on the product label. Repeat the spray if the tree becomes reinfested.

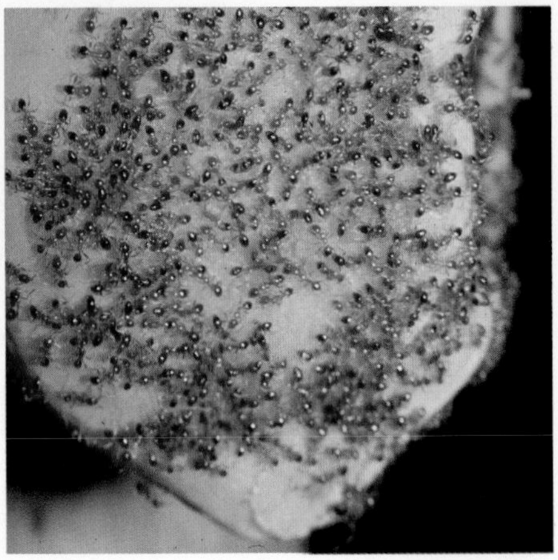

Ants feeding on papaya (half life size).

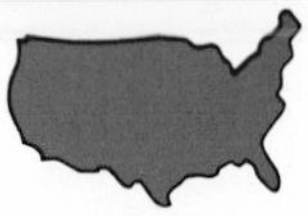

PROBLEM: Ants are crawling on the trunk, branches, and fruit. In many cases, the trees are also infested with aphids, scales, and leafhoppers.

ANALYSIS: Ants
Most ants do not directly damage plants. They may be present for any of several reasons. Many ants feed on honeydew, a sweet, sticky substance excreted by several species of insects, including aphids, scales, mealybugs, whiteflies, and leafhoppers. Ants are attracted to plants infested with these pests. In order to supply them with food, ants may carry aphids to an uninfested tree. Ants may also feed on flower nectar, fruit, or tree exudate, or on fruit that has had its skin broken or is rotting. Ants usually live in underground nests. Some species make colonies in trees and building foundations. For more information about ants, see page 893.

SOLUTION: Destroy ant nests by treating anthills with ORTHO Diazinon Granules, or by spraying the nest and surrounding soil with ORTHO Diazinon Insect Spray. Control aphids, scales, mealybugs, and whiteflies by spraying the infested plants with an insecticide containing *carbaryl* (SEVIN®), *malathion*, or *diazinon*. Make sure that your fruit tree is listed on the product label. To prevent ants from crawling up the trunk, apply a ring of sticky latex ant deterrent to the trunk.

POWDERY MATERIAL ON LEAVES

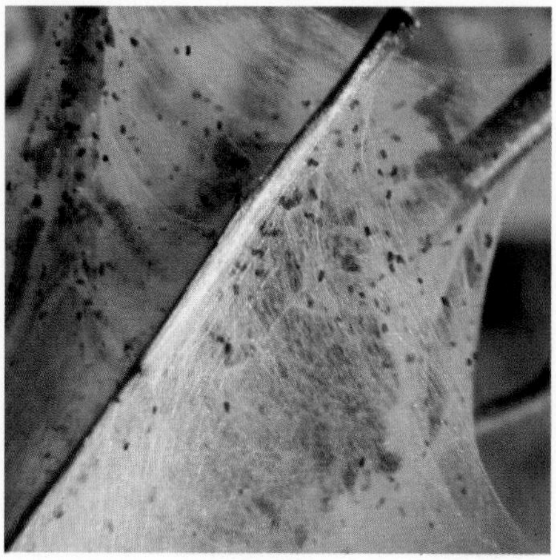

Tent caterpillar nest (life size).

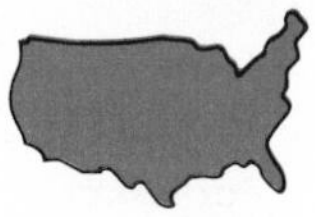

PROBLEM: In the spring or summer, silk nests appear in the branch crotches or on the ends of branches. The leaves are chewed; branches or the entire tree may be defoliated. Groups of bluish, black, tan, or greenish hairy caterpillars, with spots or stripes, are feeding in or around the nests.

ANALYSIS: Tent caterpillars and fall webworm (*Malacosoma* species and *Hyphantria cunea*)
These insects feed on many fruit and ornamental trees. The fall webworm and several species of tent caterpillars are distributed throughout the country. In the summer, adult tent caterpillar moths lay masses of eggs in a cementing substance around twigs. The eggs hatch in early spring as the leaves unfold, and the young caterpillars immediately begin to construct their nests. On warm, sunny days, they devour the surrounding foliage. In mid to late summer, brownish or reddish adult moths appear. The fall webworm moth lays many eggs on the undersides of leaves in the spring. In early summer, the young caterpillars begin feeding and surrounding themselves with silk nests. The caterpillars drop to the soil to pupate. Up to 4 generations occur between June and September.

SOLUTION: Spray with ORTHO Fruit & Vegetable Insect Control, ORTHO Home Orchard Spray, or with the bacterial insecticide *Bacillus thuringiensis.* Make sure your plant is listed on the product label. For best results, use *Bacillus thuringiensis* while the caterpillars are small. Remove egg masses found in the winter.

Yellowjacket feeding on honeydew.

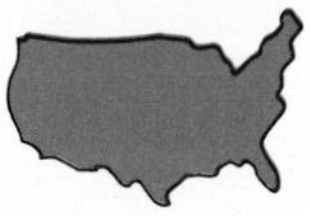

PROBLEM: A shiny or sticky substance coats the leaves, fruit, and sometimes twigs. A black sooty mold often grows on the sticky substance. Insects may be found on the leaves, and ants, flies, or bees may be present.

ANALYSIS: Honeydew
Honeydew is a sweet, sticky substance that is secreted by aphids, mealybugs, whiteflies, and some scales. These sucking insects cannot digest all the sugar in the plant sap, and excrete the excess in this sticky fluid. The honeydew drops onto the leaves directly below and onto anything beneath the tree. Ants, flies, and bees feed on honeydew, and may be found around the plant. A sooty mold fungus often develops on the sticky substance, causing the leaves, fruit, and twigs to appear black and dirty. The fungus does not infect the leaf but grows on the honeydew. Extremely heavy infestations may prevent light from reaching the leaf, reducing food production.

SOLUTION: Honeydew will eventually be washed off by rain, or may be hosed off. Prevent more honeydew by controlling the insect that is producing it. Inspect the foliage to determine what type of insect is present. See the following pages for control instructions: for aphids, page 875; for scales, page 876; for whiteflies, page 877; for mealybugs, page 876.

Powdery mildew.

PROBLEM: Gray-white powdery patches appear on the leaves. New growth is often stunted, curled, and distorted. Infected buds may be shriveled and open later than usual, and infected leaves often turn brittle and die. The fruit is sometimes small and misshapen, and may be russet-colored or covered with white powdery patches.

ANALYSIS: Powdery mildew
This common plant disease is caused by a fungus that thrives in both humid and dry weather. The fungus spends the winter in leaf and flower buds. In the spring, spores are blown to the new leaves, which are very susceptible to infection. The fungus saps the plant nutrients, causing distortion and often death of the tender foliage. Fruit yield may be greatly reduced. Powdery mildew is favored by warm days and cool nights.

SOLUTION: Spray infected trees with a fungicide containing *benomyl, dinocap,* or *sulfur.* (Do not use *sulfur* on apricots.) Make sure that your fruit tree is listed on the spray label. Most fruit trees should be sprayed at regular intervals of 10 to 14 days until 3 to 4 weeks after the petals have fallen from the blossoms. Resume spraying whenever the mildew recurs. For more details about spraying, check your specific fruit tree in the alphabetical section beginning on page 604.

PROBLEMS COMMON TO MANY FRUIT AND NUT TREES — LEAVES DISCOLORED OR MOTTLED

Sooty mold on citrus.

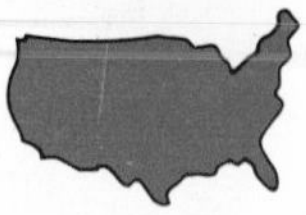

PROBLEM: A black sooty mold is growing on the leaves, fruit, and twigs. It can be completely wiped off the surfaces of the leaves. Cool, moist weather hastens the growth of this substance.

ANALYSIS: Sooty mold
This common black mold is found on a wide variety of plants in the garden. It is caused by any of several species of fungi that grow on the sugary material left on plants by aphids, scales, mealybugs, whiteflies, and other insects that suck sap from the plant. The insects are unable to digest fully all the sugar in the sap, and excrete the excess in a fluid called honeydew, which drops onto the leaves and fruit below. The sooty mold fungus develops on the honeydew, causing the leaves to appear black and dirty. Sooty mold is unsightly, but it is fairly harmless because it does not attack the leaf directly. Extremely heavy infestations prevent light from reaching the leaf, so that the leaf produces fewer nutrients and may turn yellow. The presence of sooty mold indicates that the tree is infested with insects.

SOLUTION: Sooty mold will eventually be washed off by rain. Prevent more sooty mold by controlling the insect that is producing the honeydew. Inspect the foliage to determine what type of insect is present. See the following pages for control instructions: for aphids, page 875; for scales, page 876; for whiteflies, page 877; for mealybugs, page 876.

Leaf scorch on hickory.

PROBLEM: During hot weather, usually in July or August, leaves turn brown around the edges and between the veins. Sometimes the whole leaf dies. Many leaves may drop during late summer. This problem is most severe on the youngest branches. Trees do not generally die.

ANALYSIS: Leaf scorch
Leaf scorch is caused when water evaporates from the leaves faster than it can be supplied. In hot weather, water evaporates rapidly from the leaves. If the roots can't absorb and convey water fast enough to replenish this loss, the leaves turn brown and wither. This usually occurs in dry soil, but leaves can also scorch when the soil is moist and temperatures are very high for extended periods. Drying winds, severed roots, limited soil area, salt buildup, or low temperatures can also cause scorch. For more information about leaf scorch, see page 857.

SOLUTION: To prevent further scorch, deep-water trees during periods of hot weather to wet down the entire root space. (For more information about watering trees, see page 912.) Newly transplanted trees should be watered whenever the rootball is dry 2 inches below the surface. There are no controls for scorch on trees in moist soil. Plant trees adapted to your climate.

Iron-deficient apple leaves.

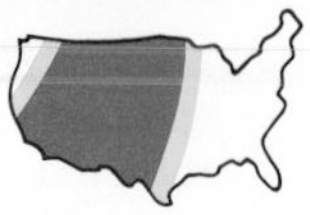

PROBLEM: Leaves turn pale green or yellow. The newest leaves (those at the tips of the branches) are most severely affected. Except in extreme cases, the veins of affected leaves remain green. Older leaves may remain green. Fruit production may be reduced, and fruit flavor may be poor.

ANALYSIS: Iron deficiency
Plants frequently suffer from deficiencies of iron and other minor nutrients, such as manganese and zinc, elements essential to normal tree growth and development. Deficiencies can occur when one or more of these elements are depleted in the soil. Often, these minor nutrients are present in the soil but alkaline (pH 7.5 or higher) or wet soil conditions cause them to form compounds that cannot be used by the tree. An alkaline condition can result from overliming, or from lime leached from cement or brick. Regions where soil is derived from limestone, and those with low rainfall, usually have alkaline soils.

SOLUTION: To correct the deficiency of nutrients, apply ORTHO ORTHO-GRO Liquid Plant Food to the soil around the plants. Check the soil pH. (For information on pH, see page 908.) Correct the pH of the soil by treating it with *ferrous sulfate* and watering it in well.

Nitrogen-deficient peach.

Nitrogen-deficient citrus.

PROBLEM: The older leaves turn yellow. Eventually, the rest of the leaves turn yellow-green, and then yellow. Yellow leaves usually die and drop off. New leaves are small, and growth is slow. Fruit production is poor.

ANALYSIS: Nitrogen deficiency
Nitrogen, the most important nutrient for plant growth and development, is deficient or unavailable in almost all soils. Nitrogen is essential in the formation of plant tissue, green leaf pigment, and many other compounds necessary for plant growth. When the tree cannot obtain enough nitrogen from the soil, it utilizes nitrogen from its older leaves for new growth. The older leaves become deficient in nitrogen, and turn yellow. A continuing shortage of nitrogen causes overall yellowing, stunting, and death of the older leaves, and a reduced fruit yield. Fast-growing, young fruit trees usually require large amounts of nitrogen. If it is not supplied, the foliage turns yellow and grows poorly. Nitrogen naturally present in the soil is made available to trees as organic matter decomposes. Soils that are low in organic matter, such as sandy and readily leached soils, are often infertile. Also, nitrogen is leached from the soil more quickly when rainfall or irrigation is heavy. Poorly drained, overwatered, and compacted soils lack oxygen that is necessary for the utilization of nitrogen. Trees growing in these soils often exhibit symptoms of nitrogen deficiency. In addition, trees growing in cold (50°F and below), hot (90°F and up), acid (pH 5.5 and lower), or alkaline (pH 7.8 and higher) soils are often low in nitrogen.

SOLUTION: Fertilize trees regularly with ORTHO Evergreen, Tree & Shrub Food or ORTHO General Purpose Plant Food. (For more information about fertilizers, see page 910.) ORTHO Blood Meal, which contains nitrogen in a long-lasting, slow-release form, can be used to supplement a regular feeding program. Add organic matter to compacted soils and those low in organic substances. Improve soil drainage in poorly drained soils. (For more information about improving soil drainage, see page 907.) Do not keep the soil constantly wet. (For more information about watering, see page 912.) Raise or lower soil pH in soils that are acid or alkaline. For more information about pH, see page 908.

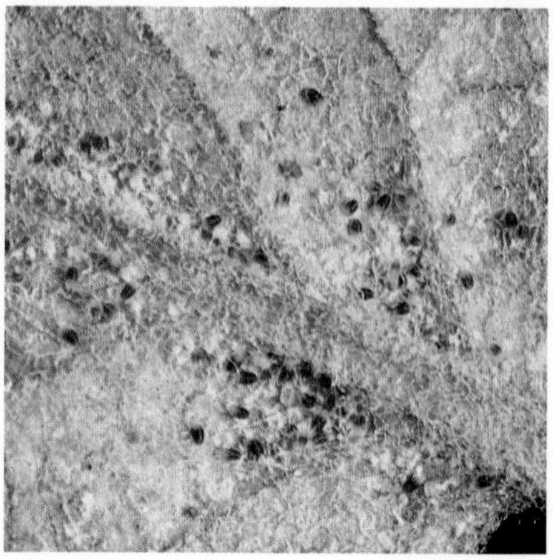
Spider mites (6 times life size).

PROBLEM: Leaves are stippled, yellowing, silvered, or bronzed. There may be webbing over flower buds, between leaves, or on the lower surfaces of the leaves. The fruit may be roughened or russet-colored. To check for certain species of mites, hold a sheet of white paper underneath an affected leaf and tap the leaf sharply. Minute green, red, or yellow specks the size of pepper grains will drop to the paper and begin to crawl around.

ANALYSIS: Mites
These pests, related to spiders, commonly attack fruit trees and other garden plants. Certain mites, like the two-spotted spider mite, are large enough to be detected as described above. Smaller mites, like the plum and pear rust mites, are microscopic, and cannot be seen without the aid of a strong hand lens or microscope. Mites cause damage by sucking sap from the fruit surface and the undersides of the leaves. As a result of feeding, the green leaf pigment disappears, producing the stippled or silvered appearance. Mites are active throughout the growing season, but are favored by hot, dry weather (70°F and up). By midsummer, they build up to tremendous numbers. For more information about mites, see page 887.

SOLUTION: Spray infested trees with ORTHO Fruit & Vegetable Insect Control, or with a pesticide containing *dicofol* (KELTHANE®). Repeat the spray at least two more times at intervals of 7 to 10 days. Make sure that your tree is listed on the spray label. If you are not sure whether your tree is infested with microscopic mites, bring an infested shoot or twig to your local County Extension Office (see page 1029) for confirmation.

PROBLEMS COMMON TO MANY FRUIT AND NUT TREES — TREE STUNTED OR DECLINING

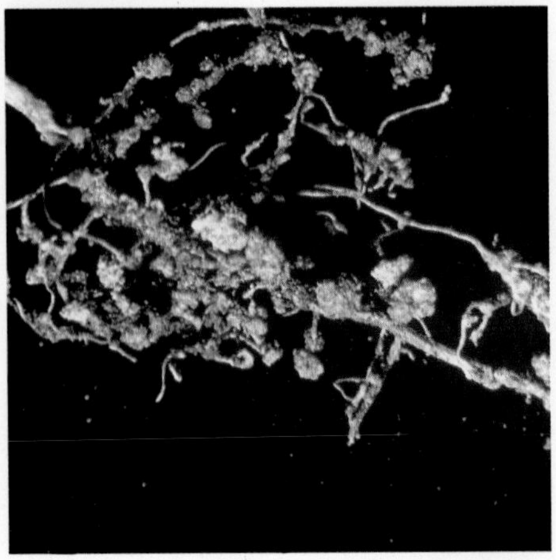
Root knot nematode damage.

Crown rot on cherry.

Phytophthora rot on apple.

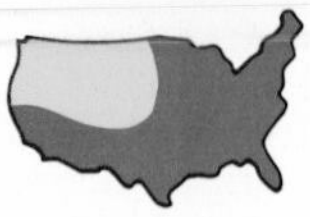

PROBLEM: Leaves are bronzed and yellowing. They may wilt on hot, dry days, but recover at night. The tree is generally weak. After several years, the tree is noticeably stunted, and branches may die.

ANALYSIS: Nematodes
Nematodes are microscopic worms that live in the soil. They are not related to earthworms. Nematodes feed on tree roots, damaging and stunting them. The damaged roots can't supply sufficient water and nutrients to the branches and leaves, and the tree is stunted or slowly dies. Nematodes are found throughout the United States, but are most severe in the South. They prefer moist, sandy loam soils. Nematodes can move only a few inches each year on their own, but they may be carried long distances by soil, water, tools, or infested plants. Testing roots and soil is the only positive method for confirming the presence of nematodes. Contact your local Cooperative Extension Office (see page 1029) for sampling instructions and addresses of testing laboratories. Soil and root problems such as poor soil structure, drought stress, nutrient deficiency, and root rots can also produce symptoms of decline similar to those caused by nematodes. These problems should be eliminated as causes before sending soil and root samples for testing. For information on soil problems and root rots, see pages 907 and 849.

SOLUTION: There are no chemicals available to kill nematodes in planted soil. However, they can be controlled before planting by soil fumigation. For information on fumigating soil, see page 927.

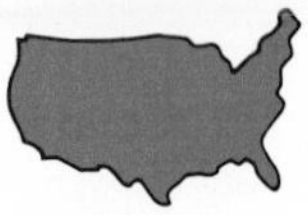

PROBLEM: The normal leaf color dulls, and the plant loses vigor. Leaves may wilt, or turn yellow or light brown. Major branches or the entire tree may die. The tree sometimes lives for many months in a weakened condition, or it may die quickly. The roots and lower trunk are brownish, and the roots may be decayed. Fine woolly brown strands may form on the roots, and white powdery spores form on the soil surface. Or fan-shaped plaques of white strands may appear between the bark and wood of the roots and lower stems. Mushrooms may appear at the base of the plant in the fall.

ANALYSIS: Root and crown rots
Root and crown rots are caused by any of several different fungi that live in the soil and on roots. They are spread by water, soil, and transplants.

SOLUTION: The numbered solutions below correspond to the numbers in the analysis.

1. *Phytophthora* species. These fungi cause browning and decay of the roots and browning of the lower trunk. The tree usually dies slowly, but young trees may wilt and die rapidly. The disease is most prevalent in heavy, waterlogged soils. For more information about phytophthora, see page 849.

1. Remove dead and dying trees. When replanting, use plants that are resistant to phytophthora. (For a list, see page 851.) Improve soil drainage. (For more information, see page 907.) Avoid overwatering plants, as discussed on page 849.

2. *Phymatotrichum omnivorum.* This fungus, commonly known as *cotton root rot* or *Texas root rot*, is a serious problem on many plants in the Southwest. Young trees may suddenly wilt and die. Brown strands form on the roots, and white powdery spores form on the soil. The disease is most severe in heavy, alkaline soils. For more information about phymatotrichum, see page 851.

2. Remove dead and dying trees. When replanting, use only resistant varieties. (For a list, see page 1016.) Before planting, increase the soil acidity by adding 1 pound of *ammonium sulfate* for every 10 square feet of soil. Make a circular ridge around the planting area, and fill the basin with 4 inches of water. Repeat the treatment in 5 to 10 days. Improve soil drainage. For more information, see page 907.

3. *Armillaria mellea.* This disease is commonly known as *shoestring root rot*, *mushroom root rot*, or *oak root fungus.* It is identified by the presence of fan-shaped plaques of white fungal strands between the bark and the wood of the roots and lower trunk. Honey-colored mushrooms appear at the base of the plant in the fall. For more information about armillaria, see page 851.

3. Remove dead trees. The life of a newly infected plant may be prolonged if the disease has not reached the lower trunk. Expose the base of the plant to air for several months by removing 3 to 4 inches of soil. Prune off diseased roots. Use a fertilizer to stimulate growth. (For more information, see page 910.) When replanting, use only resistant plants. (For a list, see page 1016.) Avoid overwatering plants, as discussed on page 849.

PROBLEMS OF INDIVIDUAL FRUIT AND NUT TREES

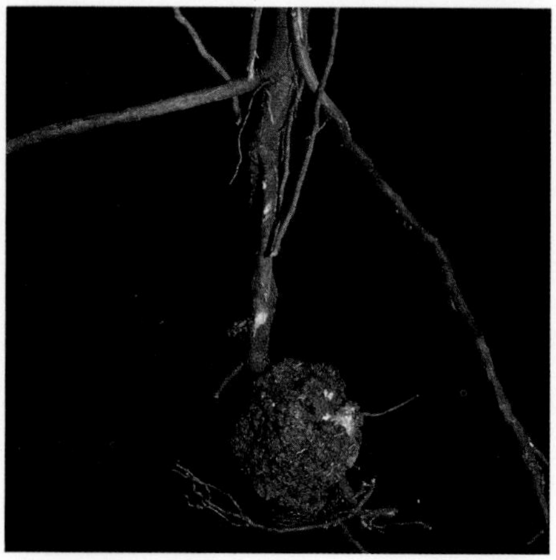

Crown gall on cherry.

PROBLEM: Large corky galls, up to several inches in diameter, appear at the base of the tree and on the roots. The galls are rounded, with a rough, irregular surface. Trees with numerous galls are weak; growth may be slowed, and the foliage may turn yellow.

ANALYSIS: Crown gall
This plant disease is caused by a soil-inhabiting bacterium (*Agrobacterium tumefaciens*) that infects many ornamentals, fruits, and vegetables in the garden. The bacteria are spread in the soil, and are often brought to a garden initially on the roots of an infected plant. The bacteria enter the tree through wounds in the roots or the base of the trunk (the crown). They produce a substance that stimulates rapid cell growth in the plant, causing gall formation. The galls disrupt the flow of water and nutrients up the roots and trunk, weakening and stunting the top growth. They do not usually cause the tree to die. For more information about crown gall, see page 853.

SOLUTION: Infected trees cannot be cured. However, they often survive for many years. Although the disease cannot be eliminated from the tree, individual galls can be removed by professionals. If you wish to remove galls from valued trees, consult a professional horticulturist or landscape contractor. The bacteria will remain in the soil for as long as 3 years after an infected tree has been removed. Replant with one of the resistant trees from the list on page 1013.

Neglected fruit tree.

PROBLEM: Overall growth is slow. Foliage may be sparse, discolored, or stunted. Branches are dense and intertwined. Twigs and branches may be dying or dead, and fruit is small and of poor quality. The tree may be diseased or infested with insects.

ANALYSIS: Tree neglect
Most fruit trees will decline in vigor and fruitfulness if they are neglected for several years. Fruit trees are susceptible to a number of fungal and bacterial diseases that can affect the roots, crown, branches, foliage, and fruits. Many insect pests also weaken fruit trees by feeding, boring into, or otherwise damaging them. Most fruit trees need to be pruned annually in order to stimulate the production of new fruiting wood, or eliminate excess or old fruiting wood. In addition, proper watering and fertilizing is important in maintaining tree health and fruitfulness.

SOLUTION: Control pests and diseases. To determine what types of insects and diseases are affecting your tree and how to control them, look up your tree in the alphabetical section beginning on this page. Thin out weak, diseased, intertwined, and dying twigs and branches. If the tree needs to be heavily pruned, or restructured, gradually prune it into proper shape over a period of 3 years. Remove all invasive growth (grass, groundcover) from around the base of the tree. Water and fertilize the tree properly. For specific details on pruning, watering, and fertilizing, look up your tree in the alphabetical section. For general information on pruning, see ORTHO's book *All About Pruning*. For more information on fertilizers and watering, see pages 910 and 912.

ALMOND

ADAPTATION: Zones 8 through 10.

POLLINATION: Cross-pollinate with another variety.

SOIL: Any good, deep, well-drained soil. pH 5.5 to 8.0

FERTILIZER: Fertilize with ORTHO Evergreen, Tree & Shrub Food according to label directions.

WATER:
How much: Apply enough water to wet the soil 3 to 4 feet deep. To determine the proper amount of water for your soil type, see page 912.
How often: Water when the soil 6 inches below the surface is just barely moist.

PRUNING: Almonds bear on short fruiting branches (spurs) on 2 to 5-year-old wood. Thin out weak, crossing, or dead twigs and branches. The maturing almonds themselves do not need to be thinned.

HARVEST: Harvest almonds when most of the hulls have split open. Pick them off, or knock them off of the tree by striking the branches with a rubber mallet or cloth-covered stick. After removing the hulls, pile the almonds 1 to 2 inches deep in the sun to dry them. Drying usually takes several days to a week.

Peach twig borer (life size).

PROBLEM: New growth at the tips of the twigs wilts and dies. When new shoots or maturing nuts are cut open, reddish brown caterpillars, about ½ inch long, may be visible inside. There may be silken cocoons in the crotches of the branches.

ANALYSIS: Peach twig borer
(*Anarsia lineatella*)
This borer, the larva of a gray night-flying moth, infests peaches, apricots, nectarines, and plums, as well as almonds. The young larvae hibernate during the winter in silk-lined cavities under loose bark or in the crotches of the branches. In the spring they emerge and bore into new twigs and buds, usually killing them. When fully grown, they pupate in silken cocoons on the branches. About 2 weeks later they emerge as moths and lay eggs on twigs and nuts. This second generation burrows into and feeds almost entirely on the nuts.

SOLUTION: Once the borers have infested the nuts, they cannot be killed. Next spring, spray with an insecticide containing *diazinon* just before the flower buds open. Repeat when 90 percent of the petals have dropped from the blossoms, and spray a third time when the late portions of the blossoms split from the small developing almond fruit. Don't spray during full bloom, or you will kill the bees that are pollinating the almond flowers.

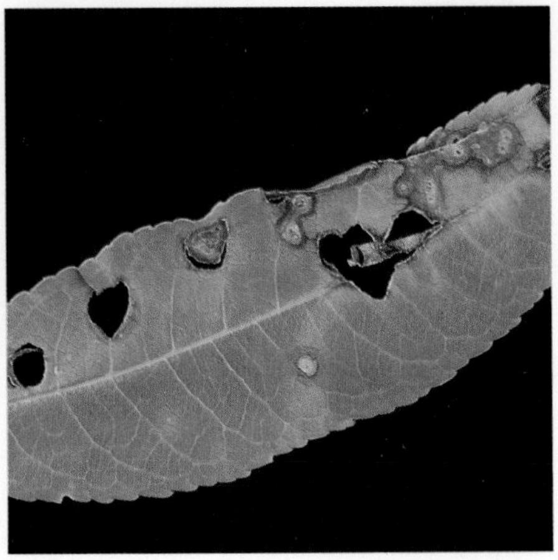

Shothole fungus.

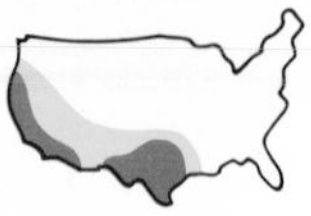

PROBLEM: Small purplish spots appear on the leaves in early spring. The spots turn brown and enlarge to ¼ inch in diameter. The centers of the spots die and drop out, leaving a small round hole. The blossoms may turn brown and have a gummy exudate at the base. The almond yield may be reduced, and corky spots may appear on the hulls. In severe cases, the tree may drop all its leaves.

ANALYSIS: Shothole fungus
This disease is also called *coryneum blight* and *peach blight.* It is caused by a fungus (*Coryneum beijerinckii*) that attacks almonds and stone fruits. The fungus spends the winter in lesions on the twigs and buds. The spores are spread by spring rains and infect the new leaves. Infection causes the leaf tissue to produce a layer of cells that wall off the damaged area. The center of the spot then drops out. Severe infection may defoliate the tree, produce smaller almonds, and cause some almonds to drop. The disease is favored by wet spring weather.

SOLUTION: There is no adequate control during the growing season. Next spring, spray the tree with ORTHO Dormant Disease Control, ORTHO ORTHORIX spray or *chlorothalonil* (DACONIL 2787®) fungicide when the petals have emerged from the bud, but before they are fully opened. Spray again when the petals have fallen from the flowers.

APPLE

ADAPTATION AND POLLINATION: See variety chart on page 1021.

SOIL: Any good, deep, well-drained soil. pH 5.5 to 7.5

FERTILIZER: Fertilize with ORTHO Evergreen, Tree & Shrub Food according to label directions.

WATER:
How much: Apply enough water to wet the soil 3 to 4 feet deep. To determine the proper amount of water for your soil type, see page 912.
How often: Water when the soil 6 inches below the surface is just barely moist.

PRUNING: Apples are borne on short fruiting branches (spurs) that grow on year-old wood. The spurs continue to fruit for about 10 years. Prune lightly, since the removal of many spurs will reduce the apple yield. Thin out weak, crossing, or dead twigs and branches. When apples are thumbnail size, thin them to 6 inches apart, with one fruit per spur.

HARVEST: Apples are ripe when their seeds turn dark brown to black, the flesh turns creamy white, and the apple stem separates easily from the spur when the fruit is gently lifted. Harvest earlier if you prefer tart apples.

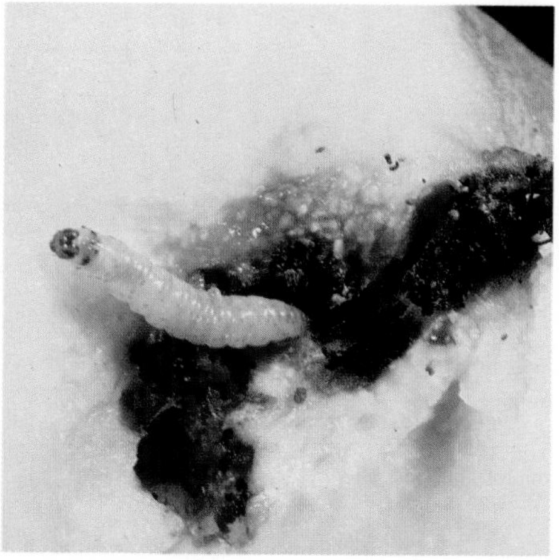

Codling moth larva (life size).

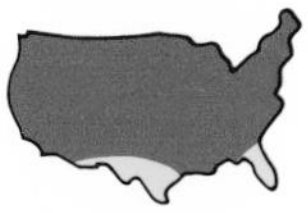

PROBLEM: The fruit is blemished by small holes surrounded by dead tissue. A brown, crumbly material resembling sawdust may surround the holes. Brown-headed, pinkish white worms up to 1 inch long may be found in the fruit. The interior of the fruit is often dark and rotted. Many apples drop prematurely.

ANALYSIS: Codling moth
(*Laspeyresia pomonella*)
This worm, the larva of a small gray-brown moth, is one of the most serious apple pests in the United States. This insect attacks pears, quinces, and several other fruit and nut trees in addition to apples. The moths appear in the spring when the apple trees are blooming. They lay their eggs on the leaves, twigs, and developing fruit. When the eggs hatch, the larvae tunnel into the fruit. They feed for several weeks, then emerge from the fruit, often leaving a mass of dark excrement on the skin and inside the fruit. After pupating in sheltered locations on or around the tree, another generation of moths emerge in midsummer. Apples may be damaged by worms continuously throughout the summer. In the fall, mature larvae spin cocoons in protected places, such as under loose bark or in tree crevices. They spend the winter in these cocoons, emerging as moths in the spring.

SOLUTION: Once the worms have penetrated the apples, it is impossible to kill them. To protect uninfested apples, spray with ORTHO Home Orchard Spray or ORTHO Fruit & Vegetable Insect Control at intervals of 10 days, as directed on the label. Remove and destroy all fallen apples, and clean up debris. Next spring, spray according to label direction when the new growth appears.

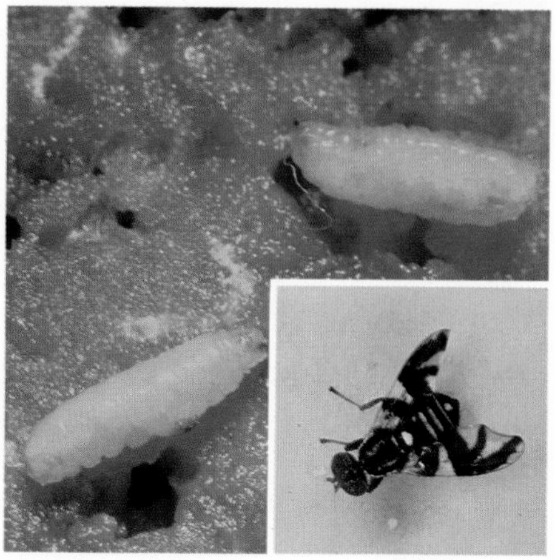

Apple maggot (4 times life size). *Insert:* Adult.

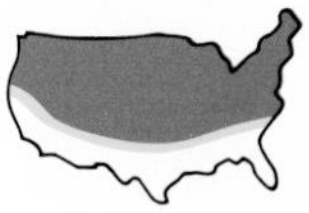

PROBLEM: The fruit may be dimpled and pitted, with brown trails winding through the flesh. White, tapered, legless maggots about ⅜ inch long may be present in the fruit. Severely infested apples are brown and pulpy inside. Frequently, many apples drop prematurely.

ANALYSIS: Apple maggot
(*Rhagoletis pomonella*)
These worms, also known as *railroad worms* and *apple fruit flies*, are the larvae of flies that resemble the common housefly. Apple maggots infest plums, cherries, and pears in addition to apples. The adult flies emerge from pupae between late June and the beginning of September. They lay eggs in the fruit through holes they puncture in the skin. The maggots that emerge from the eggs make brown trails through the flesh as they feed. Infested apples usually drop to the ground. The mature maggots emerge from the apple and burrow in the soil to pupate. They remain in the soil throughout the winter, and emerge as adult flies the following June.

SOLUTION: There is no way to kill the maggots after apples are infested. Protect healthy apples from the adult flies by spraying at intervals of 7 to 10 days from the end of June until the beginning of September with ORTHO Fruit & Vegetable Insect Control, ORTHO Liquid Sevin or ORTHO Home Orchard Spray. Pick up and destroy fallen apples every week throughout the summer.

APPLE

Damage. *Insert:* Plum curculio (3 times life size).

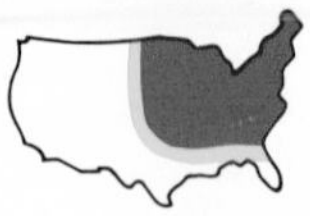

PROBLEM: The ripening fruit is misshapen, rotten, and often drops prematurely. Holes about ⅛ inch in diameter and deep, crescent-shaped scars appear on the fruit. When cut open, such fruits may be found to contain crescent-shaped, yellow-gray grubs with brown heads.

ANALYSIS: Plum curculio
(*Contrachelus nenuphar*)
These insects, found east of the Rocky Mountains, attack stone fruits and pears, as well as apples. The adult insects are brown beetles with long, curved snouts. They hibernate in debris and other protected places during the winter. The beetles emerge in the spring when new growth starts and begin feeding on young leaves, blossoms, and developing fruit. After 5 to 6 weeks, the female beetles start to lay eggs in the young fruit. The grubs that hatch from the eggs feed for several weeks in the fruit. The infested apples usually drop to the ground. The grubs eventually leave the apples and bore into the soil, where they pupate. The emerging beetles feed on fruit for a few weeks, then go into hibernation. Or, in the South, they lay eggs, producing a second generation of grubs in the late summer.

SOLUTION: Once the fruit is infested, there is no way to kill the grubs inside the fruit. Spray with ORTHO Home Orchard Spray or ORTHO Malathion 50 Insect Spray to kill beetles that may be feeding on fruit, or laying eggs. Pick up and destroy all fallen fruit. Next spring, spray the trees when the petals are falling from the blossoms; repeat applications according to the directions on the label.

Bitter rot.

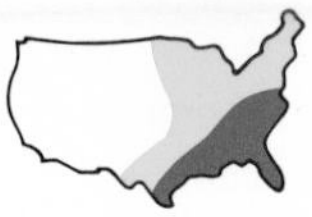

PROBLEM: Sunken, light brown, circular spots appear on the half-grown fruit. These spots gradually enlarge to 1 inch in diameter. Concentric rings and sticky pink masses of spores may appear on the spotted areas during moist weather. The rotted apple flesh tastes bitter. Sunken lesions may form on the branches.

ANALYSIS: Bitter rot
This plant disease, which also affects pears, is caused by a fungus (*Glomerella cingulata*). The fungus spends the winter in rotted apples left on the tree and on the ground, and in sunken lesions on the branches. Spores are spread by splashing rain to healthy apples in the spring. Infection can occur throughout the fruiting season. In areas where hot, humid conditions last for long periods of time, bitter rot can quickly destroy an entire apple crop. This disease primarily attacks the fruit, and does not severely damage the health of the tree.

SOLUTION: Spray infested trees with ORTHO Home Orchard Spray or ORTHO Orthocide Garden Fungicide, according to label directions. To prevent recurrence next year, prune out branches with lesions, and remove and destroy rotted apples from the tree. Next spring, spray the trees with ORTHO Home Orchard Spray or ORTHO Orthocide Garden Fungicide just before the blossoms start to open. Continue spraying according to label directions. Plant resistant varieties (see page 1021).

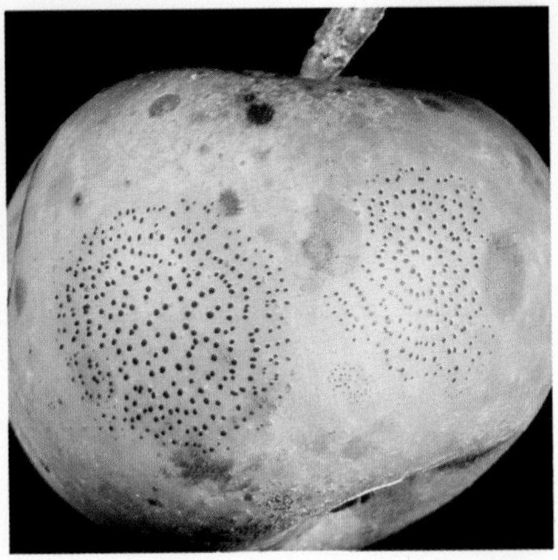

Sooty blotch and fly speck.

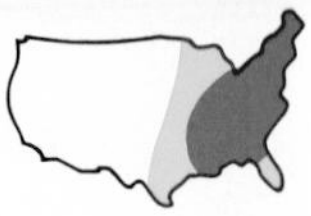

PROBLEM: Clusters of 10 to 30 or more raised, shiny, black specks appear on the apple skins. There are indefinite dark brown to olive-green smudges on the surface of the fruit.

ANALYSIS: Sooty blotch and fly speck
Although these two plant diseases are not caused by the same fungus, they are so commonly found in association that they are usually described together. Sooty blotch is caused by the fungus *Gloeodoes pomigena*, and fly speck is caused by the fungus *Microthyriella rubi*. These fungi spend the winter on the twigs of apples and many other woody plants. During mild, wet weather in spring, the fungi produce spores that are blown to and infect the developing apples. About a month after the initial infection, specks and blotches appear on the maturing fruit. Although these diseases are unsightly, they are external and do not generally affect the taste of the apples. Spores are not produced when temperatures rise above 85°F, so infection generally occurs during the spring and late summer or fall, but rarely in midsummer.

SOLUTION: To prevent the possible infection of healthy fruit, spray with ORTHO Home Orchard Spray. Infected apples are edible; rub them vigorously to remove the specks and blotches. Next spring, spray with ORTHO Home Orchard Spray according to label directions when the new growth appears.

Aphid damage.

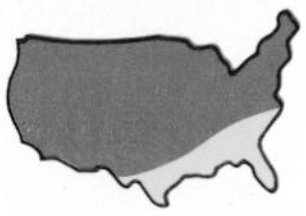

PROBLEM: The newest leaves are curled, twisted, discolored, and stunted. Leaves may drop off, and in severe cases the tree may defoliate. The developing apples are often small and misshapen. A shiny, sticky substance may coat the leaves. A black sooty mold often grows on this sticky substance. Tiny (⅛ inch) green, red, purplish, or rosy brown soft-bodied insects cluster on the young shoots and undersides of the leaves. Ants may be present.

ANALYSIS: Aphids

Aphids do little damage in small numbers. However, they are extremely prolific and populations can rapidly build up to damaging numbers during the growing season. Damage occurs when the aphid sucks the juices from the leaves and immature fruit. The aphid is unable to digest fully all the sugar in the sap and excretes the excess in a fluid called honeydew. The honeydew often drops onto the leaves below. Plants or objects beneath the tree may also be coated with honeydew. A sooty mold fungus may develop on the honeydew, causing the leaves to appear black and dirty. Ants feed on this sticky substance, and are often present where there is an aphid infestation. At harvest time, apples may be small, misshapen, and pitted due to aphid damage earlier in the season. For more information about aphids, see page 875.

SOLUTION: Control with ORTHO Home Orchard Spray, ORTHO Malathion 50 Insect Spray, or ORTHO Fruit & Vegetable Insect Control as soon as the insects appear. Repeat according to label directions if the tree becomes reinfested.

Woolly apple aphids (twice life size).

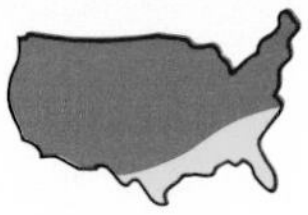

PROBLEM: Twigs, branches, leaves, and possibly the trunk of the tree are covered with white, cottony masses. There may be galls on the infested limbs. Beneath the white masses are clusters of small (⅛ inch), purplish brown, soft-bodied insects. The leaves are yellowing. Young trees are often stunted, and may die.

ANALYSIS: Woolly apple aphid

(*Erisosoma lanigerum*)

These insects may be found wherever apples are grown. Woolly apple aphids usually suck sap from the twigs and branches, but cause their most serious damage when some of the aphids burrow into the soil and feed on the roots. This feeding causes root galls to form, inhibiting the flow of water and nutrients up into the tree. In addition to forming galls and nodules, the roots also become fibrous and stunted. Young trees often die from root infestations.

SOLUTION: Spray the tree trunk, branches, and foliage with ORTHO Fruit & Vegetable Insect Control or ORTHO Diazinon Insect Spray as soon as the pests are noticed. Repeat the spray as directed on the label. If you suspect root infestation, carefully dig away the soil from around the crown and check the roots for aphids and galls. Although it is not possible to rid the roots of aphids, you can usually control them by keeping the trunk, branches, and foliage free of aphids. In addition to spraying, hose off clusters of aphids on the tree between sprays. Remove dying trees.

San Jose scale (half life size).

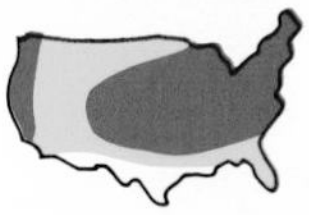

PROBLEM: Some of the leaves are pale green to yellow and may drop prematurely from weakened limbs. The bark is encrusted with small (1/16 inch) hard, circular, slightly raised bumps with dull yellow centers. If the hard cover is scraped off, the insect underneath is yellow or olive-colored. There may be severe limb dieback, and entire branches may be killed. Red spots with white centers mar the apple skins.

ANALYSIS: San Jose scale

(*Quadraspidiotus perniciosus*)

These insects infest the bark, leaves, and fruit of many fruit trees. The scales bear live young in the spring. In late spring to midsummer the young scales, called *crawlers*, settle on leaves and twigs. The soft-bodied young feed by inserting their mouthparts and sucking sap from the plant. The legs atrophy and a hard, crusty shell develops over the body. An uncontrolled infestation of San Jose scales may kill large branches after 2 or 3 seasons. For further information about scales, see page 876

SOLUTION: During the dormant season, spray the trunk and branches with ORTHO Volck Oil Spray. Spray with ORTHO Fruit & Vegetable Insect Control or ORTHO Malathion 50 Insect Spray to kill the crawlers. For further information about scales, see page 876.

APPLE

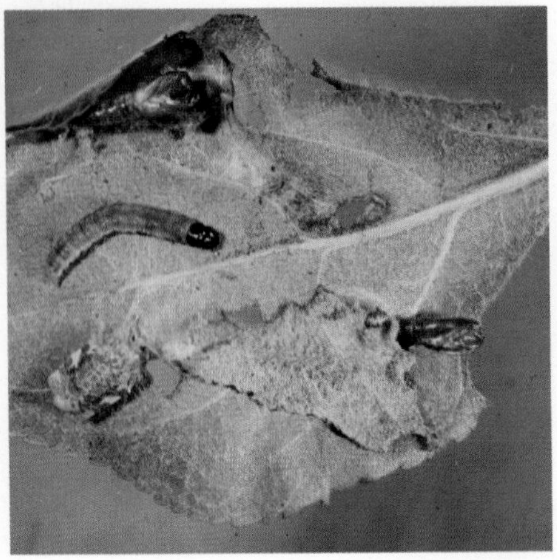

Fruit tree leafrollers (life size).

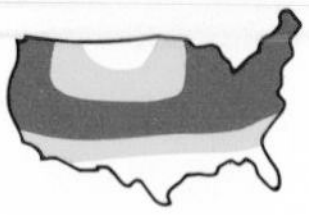

PROBLEM: Irregular holes appear in the leaves and fruit. Some of the leaves are rolled and held together with a web. Inside these rolled leaves are pale green worms with brown heads, up to ¾ inch long. The maturing apples are scarred and misshapen.

ANALYSIS: Fruit tree leafroller
(*Archips argyrospilus*)
These worms, the larvae of brown moths, are common pests of many fruit and ornamental trees. The moths lay their eggs on branches or twigs in June or July. The eggs hatch the following spring, and the emerging larvae feed on the blossoms and developing fruit and foliage. Leafrollers often wrap leaves around ripening fruit, then feed on the fruit inside. After about a month, the mature larvae pupate within rolled leaves, to emerge as moths in June or July.

SOLUTION: If practical, pick off and destroy rolled leaves to reduce the numbers of moths that will emerge later in the season. Next spring, spray the tree with ORTHO Home Orchard Spray or ORTHO Fruit & Vegetable Insect Control when 75 percent of the petals have fallen from the blossoms. Repeat the spray according to the directions on the label.

Scab.

PROBLEM: Olive-brown velvety spots, ¼ inch or more in diameter, appear on the leaves and young fruit. As the infected apples mature, the spots develop into light to dark brown corky lesions. The fruit is often cracked and malformed, and may drop prematurely. Severely infected trees may completely defoliate.

ANALYSIS: Scab
This plant disease is caused by a fungus (*Venturia inaequalis*). It is one of the most serious diseases of apples in areas where spring weather is mild (60° to 70°F) and wet. The fungus spends the winter in infected leaf debris. In the spring, spores are produced and blown by the wind. If there is adequate moisture on the foliage and fruit, the fungus infects them, and spots develop. The infected tissues produce more spores, which infect other leaf and fruit surfaces, where further spotting and decay occur. As the temperature increases, the fungus becomes less active. However, late summer rains initiate additional spore production, and apples that are infected when they are almost ready to be harvested will develop scab lesions after.

SOLUTION: Unless severely infected, the apples are edible. To prevent recurrence of the disease next year, remove and destroy leaf debris and infected fruit in the fall. Next spring, spray with ORTHO Home Orchard Spray, ORTHO Orthocide Garden Fungicide, or a fungicide containing *triforine* (FUNGINEX ®) according to label directions.

Apple varieties resistant to scab: Prima, Priscilla, Sir Prize.

Black rot.

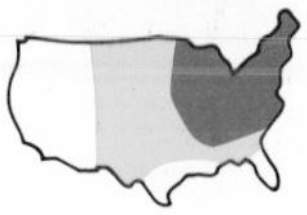

PROBLEM: A firm spot composed of concentric light and dark brown rings appears on the apple. This spot gradually turns dark brown or black and enlarges, rotting part or all of the fruit. Spots on the leaves are also formed of light and dark concentric rings. There are often reddish brown, slightly sunken lesions up to several feet in length on the branches or trunk of the tree.

ANALYSIS: Black rot
This plant disease, also known as *frog-eye leaf spot*, is caused by a fungus (*Physalospora* species) that also attacks pears. The fungus spends the winter in rotted apples and in cankers. When temperatures reach 60°F and higher in the spring, spores are produced on infected tissues and splashed by water to the foliage and fruit. Branches and trunks may be infected with black rot, especially when the bark has been weakened by sun scald, cold, or heavy shading. Pruning cuts also encourage fungal infection. As the fungus decays the wood, cankers form, weakening the branches and reducing the overall vigor of the tree. Fruit infection is generally more severe in warm, moist areas, and canker formation is more prevalent in cooler climates.

SOLUTION: Spray with ORTHO Home Orchard Spray according to label directions as soon as infestation is noticed. The next spring, repeat the spray when the new growth appears. Remove all rotted apples from the tree and ground and destroy them. Prune out infected branches at least 12 inches below visible cankers. Densely-branched trees should be thinned to provide adequate light and air circulation.

Powdery mildew.

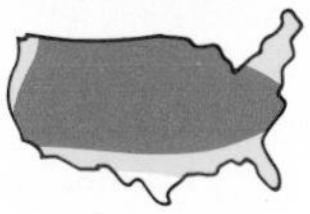

PROBLEM: Gray-white powdery patches appear on the leaves. The new growth is often stunted, curled, and distorted. Infected buds may be shriveled and open later than usual, and infected leaves often turn brittle and die. The fruit may turn russet colored and be dwarfed.

ANALYSIS: Powdery mildew
This plant disease is caused by a fungus (*Podosphaera leucotricha*) that thrives in both humid and dry weather. The fungus spends the winter in leaf and flower buds. In the spring, spores are blown to the emerging young leaves, which are very susceptible to infection. The fungus saps plant nutrients, causing distortion and often death of the tender foliage. The fruit yield may be greatly reduced, since the infected blossoms do not set fruit. Young, developing apples that are attacked become dwarfed and turn russet colored. However, the fruit can be eaten if peeled. Powdery mildew is favored by warm spring days and cool nights.

SOLUTION: Spray infected trees with a fungicide containing *benomyl* and continue spraying at intervals of 10 to 14 days until 3 to 4 weeks after the petals have fallen from the blossoms. Resume spraying whenever the mildew recurs.

Apple varieties particularly susceptible to mildew: Cortland, Gravenstein, Idared, Jonathan, Rome Beauty.

Cedar-apple rust.

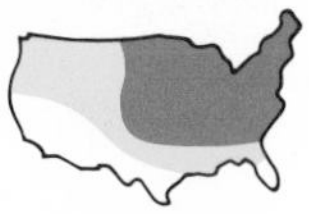

PROBLEM: Pale yellow spots appear on the leaves and fruit in mid to late spring. These spots gradually enlarge, turn orange, and develop minute black dots. Small (1/6 inch) cups with fringed edges form on the lower surfaces of the leaves. Infected leaves and fruit may drop prematurely; the fruit is often small and deformed.

ANALYSIS: Cedar-apple rust
This plant disease is caused by a fungus (*Gymnosporangium juniperi-virginianae*) that affects both apples and certain species of juniper and red cedar. This disease cannot spread from apple to apple, or juniper to juniper, but must alternate between the two. In the spring, spores from brown and orange galls on juniper or cedar are blown up to 3 miles to apple trees. During mild, wet weather, the spores germinate and infect the leaves and fruit, causing spotting, and eventually premature leaf and apple drop. During the summer, spores are produced in the small cups on the underside of the leaves. These spores are blown back to junipers and cedars, causing new infections and starting the cycle over again. For more information about cedar-apple rust on junipers, see page 508.

SOLUTION: Cedar-apple rust cannot be controlled on this season's apples and leaves. Next spring, spray apple trees with a fungicide containing *zineb* or *ferbam* when the flower buds turn pink, again when 75 percent of the petals have fallen from the blossoms, and once more 10 days later. When practical, do not plant apples within several hundred yards of junipers or red cedar.

Twig dieback. *Insert:* Bacterial ooze.

PROBLEM: Blossoms turn brown and die. Young, leafy twigs wilt from the tips down, turn brown, and die. A bend often develops at the tips of the twigs. On the branches, and at the base of the blighted twigs, the bark becomes water-soaked in appearance, then dark, sunken, and dry. In warm, moist spring weather, drops of brown ooze appear on the surface of these lesions. During the summer, shoots or branches may wilt and turn dark brown.

ANALYSIS: Fireblight
This plant disease is caused by a bacterium (*Erwinia amylovora*) that commonly affects apples, pears, and several ornamental plants. (For a list of susceptible plants, see page 1016.) The bacteria spend the winter in sunken lesions (cankers) on the branches and twigs. In the spring the bacteria ooze out of the canker and are carried by insects to the apple blossoms. Splashing rain, honeybees, and other insects continue to spread the bacteria to healthy blossoms. Bacterial decay causes cankers to develop on the twigs and branches, often resulting in conspicuous branch and twig dieback. Wounded leaves, twigs, and suckers are also susceptible to infection. For more information about fireblight, see page 640.

SOLUTION: Prune and destroy infected twigs and branches at least 12 inches beyond visible decay. Sterilize pruning shears with rubbing alcohol after each cut. A protective spray of *basic copper sulfate* or *streptomycin* applied before the blossoms open next spring will help prevent infection. Repeat at intervals of 5 to 7 days until the end of the blooming period. For a list of resistant apple varieties, see page 1021.

APPLE ■ **APRICOT**

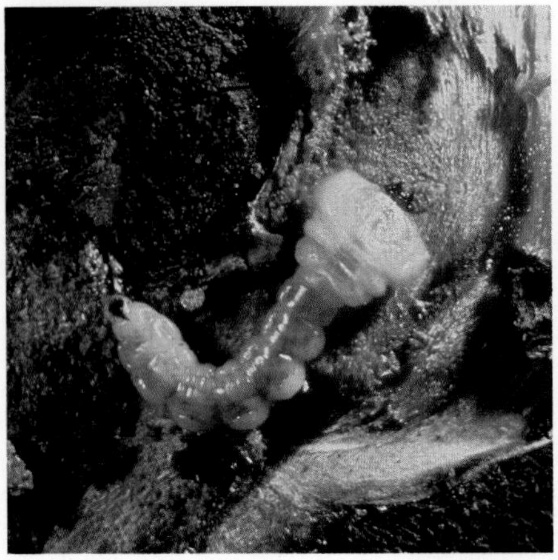

Pacific flatheaded borer (twice life size).

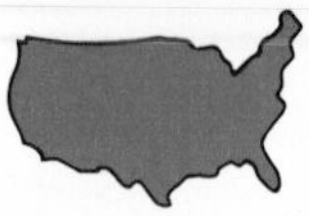

PROBLEM: Leaves wilt and turn brown. Patches of bark on the trunk are sunken, discolored, and may be soaked with sap. There may be holes about $\frac{3}{8}$ inch in diameter in the affected bark. Sawdust-filled tunnels in the wood may contain yellowish white, flat-headed grubs about $\frac{3}{4}$ inch long. In late spring to midsummer, bronze or copper-colored beetles $\frac{1}{2}$ to $\frac{3}{4}$ inch long may be seen feeding on the foliage. Newly planted or weak trees are most severely affected.

ANALYSIS: Flatheaded borers
(*Chrysobothris* species)
In addition to damaging apples, these insects attack many other trees and shrubs. In late spring to midsummer, the females begin to lay eggs in crevices in the bark. The emerging larvae bore through the bark into the outer layer of wood, creating winding tunnels. These tunnels damage the nutrient and water-conducting vessels in the tree, causing twig and branch dieback and sometimes killing the tree. The mature larvae bore deep into the heartwood to pupate; adult beetles emerge the following spring. Newly transplanted, weakened, and diseased trees are most susceptible to borer infestation.

SOLUTION: Apply ORTHO Lindane Borer & Leaf Miner Spray according to label directions. Keep your tree healthy and vigorous by watering, fertilizing, and pruning it properly. For more cultural information, see page 605. Discourage borer infestation by wrapping the trunk soon after bloom with tree wrapping paper or burlap. Prune out and destroy infested branches.

APRICOT

ADAPTATION AND POLLINATION:
See variety chart on page 1021.

SOIL: Any good, deep, well-drained garden soil. pH 5.5 to 8.0

FERTILIZER: Fertilize with ORTHO Evergreen, Tree & Shrub Food according to label directions.

WATER:
How much: Apply enough water to wet the soil 3 to 4 feet deep. To determine the proper amount of water for your soil type, see page 912.
How often: Water when the soil 6 inches below the surface is just barely moist.

PRUNING: Apricots are borne on short fruiting branches (spurs), which grow on 2-year-old wood. The spurs continue to fruit for 2 to 4 years. Prune back last year's growth to half its length, and thin out spurred branches that have stopped fruiting (4 years or older). Thin out weak, crossing, or dead twigs and branches. For large apricots, thin fruits when they are large enough to handle to 3 to 5 inches apart, with no more than 2 fruits per spur.

HARVEST: Harvest when the fruits are fully colored and slightly soft. When they are ripe, the apricot stem separates easily from the spur when the fruit is gently lifted.

Plum curculio (5 times life size).

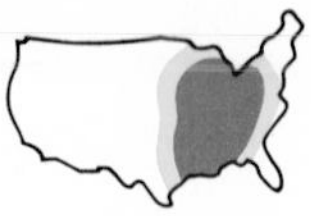

PROBLEM: The ripening fruit is misshapen, rotten, and often drops prematurely. There are holes about $\frac{1}{8}$ inch in diameter and deep, crescent-shaped scars on the fruit. When cut open, the damaged fruit may contain crescent-shaped yellow-gray grubs with brown heads.

ANALYSIS: Plum curculio
(*Conotrachelus nenuphar*)
These insects, found east of the Rockies, attack other stone fruits, apples, and pears, as well as apricots. The adult insects are brown beetles with long curved snouts. They hibernate in debris and other protected places during the winter. The beetles emerge in the spring when new growth starts and begin feeding on young leaves, blossoms, and developing fruit. After 5 to 6 weeks, the female beetles start to lay eggs in the young fruit. The grubs that hatch from the eggs feed for several weeks in the fruit. Usually the infested apricots drop to the ground. The grubs eventually leave the fruit and bore into the soil, where they pupate. The emerging beetles feed on fruit for a few weeks, then go into hibernation. Or, in the South, they will lay eggs, producing a second generation of grubs in the late summer.

SOLUTION: Once the fruit is infested, there is no way to kill the grubs inside the fruit. Spray with ORTHO Home Orchard Spray or ORTHO Malathion 50 Insect Spray to kill beetles that may be feeding on fruit, or laying eggs. Pick up and destroy all fallen fruit. Next spring, spray the trees when the petals are falling from the blossoms; repeat applications according to directions on the label.

Twig blight.

Fruit rot.

PROBLEM: The blossoms and young leaves decay, wilt, and turn brown during the first 2 weeks of the bloom period. Often the decayed blossoms fail to drop and hang on the tree throughout the growing season. In humid conditions, masses of gray spores may appear on the infected flower parts. There is often extensive twig dieback. Sunken lesions (cankers) may develop on the twigs and branches as the season progresses; a thick gummy material often oozes from these cankers.

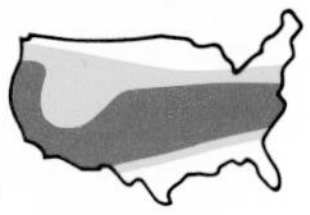

PROBLEM: Small circular brown spots appear on the young apricots. Later in the season, as the apricots start to mature, these spots may enlarge to rot part or all of the fruit. During moist weather, the rotted apricots are covered with tufts of gray spores. When the infected fruit is sliced open, the flesh inside is seen to be brown, firm, and fairly dry. Infected apricots either drop prematurely or dry out, turn dark brown, and remain on the tree past the normal harvest period. Many twigs die. There are sunken lesions (cankers) on some of these twigs. A thick, gummy material often oozes from these cankers.

ANALYSIS: Brown rot
This plant disease, caused by either of two closely related fungi (*Monolinia laxa* or *M. fructicola*), is very destructive to apricots and to all of the stone fruits. The fungi spend the winter in twig cankers or in rotted apricots (mummies) in the tree or on the ground. In the spring, spores are blown or splashed from cankers or mummies to the healthy flower buds. After penetrating and decaying the flowers, the fungus grows down into the twigs, producing brown, sunken cankers. During moist weather a thick, gummy sap oozes from the lesions, and tufts of gray spores may form on the infected areas. Spores from cankers and infected blossoms or mummies are splashed and blown to the maturing fruit. Young apricots are fairly resistant to infection, but maturing apricots are vulnerable. Brown rot develops most rapidly in mild, moist conditions.

SOLUTION: If there are still uninfected blossoms left on your tree, spray with ORTHO Home Orchard Spray or a fungicide containing *triforine* (FUNGINEX®) to protect them from further infection. Spray twice at 10-day intervals. Next spring, spray trees at early bloom and continue to spray according to label directions. To protect maturing apricots from infection, spray them with ORTHO Home Orchard Spray or a fungicide containing *triforine* (FUNGINEX®) about 3 weeks before they are to be harvested. Remove and destroy all infected apricots and mummies. Prune out cankers and blighted twigs. Clean up and destroy all debris around the tree. Plant resistant varieties.

Apricot resistance to brown rot:
Most susceptible: Blenheim, Derby Royal, Royal
Fairly resistant: Tilton

Bacterial leaf spot.

PROBLEM: Water-soaked spots on the undersides of the leaves turn brown or black; often the centers of the spots fall out. The tips of the leaves may die, and eventually the leaves will drop. When the fruit sets, the surface may be dotted with spots that later turn into deep sunken brown pits, often surrounded by yellow rings. Sunken lesions can often be seen at the joints of the twigs.

ANALYSIS: Bacterial leaf spot
This disease is caused by a bacterium (*Xanthomonas pruni*) that also attacks peach, nectarine, and plum. The disease is common east of the Rocky Mountains, and is one of the more destructive stone fruit diseases. The bacteria spend the winter in the lesions on the twigs, oozing out in the spring to be carried by splashing raindrops to the young leaves and shoots, which they infect and decay. Periods of frequent rainfall favor the infection.

SOLUTION: There is no adequate control for this disease. Spraying with *basic copper sulfate* when the buds open may help suppress the disease, but will not eliminate it.

APRICOT

Scab.

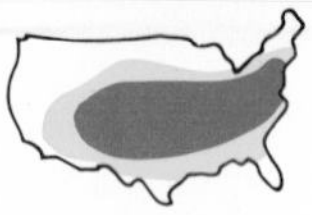

PROBLEM: Small, olive-green spots appear on the half-grown fruit. These spots are usually centered around the stem end of the apricot. The spots eventually turn brown and velvety. The fruit is often dwarfed, deformed, or cracked. There may be small brown spots and holes in the leaves, and many twigs die back.

ANALYSIS: Scab
This plant disease is caused by a fungus (*Cladosporium carpophilum*), that attacks peaches, nectarines, cherries, and plums as well as apricots. The fungus spends the winter on twig lesions. In the spring, spores are splashed and blown to the developing foliage and fruit. The young fruit do not show scab lesions for at least a month after they are initially infected. Spores produced on the infected leaves, twigs, and fruit will continue to infect healthy apricots throughout the growing season.

SOLUTION: It's too late to do anything about the spots on this year's fruit, but they are edible if peeled. Next year, spray a fungicide containing *chlorothalonil* (DACONIL 2787®) or *captan* (ORTHOCIDE®) on the tree when the petals have fallen from the blossoms. If scab is serious in your area, continue to spray at intervals of 10 to 14 days about a month before the apricots are harvested.

Shothole fungus.

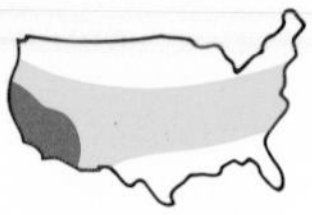

PROBLEM: Small purplish spots appear on the leaves and developing fruit in early spring. There may be small round holes in the infected leaves. Infected leaf buds and leaves often die. The spots on the maturing apricots turn scablike, drop off, and leave rough, corky lesions.

ANALYSIS: Shothole fungus
This plant disease, also called *coryneum blight* and *peach blight*, is caused by a fungus (*Coryneum beijerinckii*) that attacks almonds and some of the stone fruits. The fungus spends the winter in lesions on the twigs and buds. In the spring, the spores are splashed by rain to the developing blossoms, leaves, and fruit, causing spotting and tissue death. Infection causes the leaf tissue to produce a layer of cells that walls off the damaged area. The center of the spot then drops out. Severe infection may defoliate the tree and reduce the apricot yield. The disease is favored by wet spring weather.

SOLUTION: There is no adequate control during the growing season. To prevent twig and leaf bud infection, spray the tree this fall with a fungicide containing *chlorothalonil* (DACONIL 2787®) or *captan* (ORTHOCIDE®) soon after the leaves have fallen. Spray again in the spring when the petals have fallen from the flowers.

Cytospora canker.

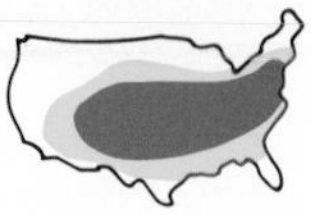

PROBLEM: Oval or oblong sunken lesions on the bark enlarge gradually. A sticky gum may ooze from the lesion, sometimes followed by the emergence of curly orange threads. Later, small black freckles appear on the bark along the edge of the lesions. Leaves on the affected branches may turn brown and die, or the entire branch may die.

ANALYSIS: Cytospora canker
This plant disease, also known as *perennial canker*, is caused by 2 related fungi (*Cytospora cincta* and *C. leucostoma*) that also attack peach, plum, and cherry. The fungi spend the winter in sunken lesions (cankers) or on dead wood. In the spring, black fungal bodies develop in the bark, and curly orange fungal chains form. These chains release spores that are spread by wind and splashing rain to healthy trees. Infection usually occurs through injured tissues. Bark that is damaged by sunscald, cold, pruning wounds, or mechanical injury is especially susceptible. Fungal decay causes the formation of depressed lesions (cankers). A sticky gum may ooze from the cankers. The branch or stem above the canker may die due to decay or clogging of the water-conducting tissue in the branch. Mild, wet weather (70° to 85°F) enhances the development of this disease.

SOLUTION: No fully adequate control is available; a combination of procedures must be used. Remove badly infected branches and cut out cankers. For more information about canker removal and treatment, see page 917. Avoid mechanical injuries to the tree and paint the trunk with white latex paint to protect against cold injury and sunburn.

Peachtree borer (twice life size).

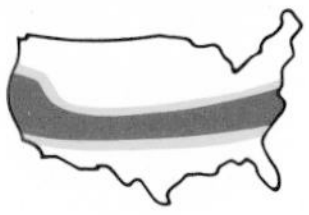

PROBLEM: Holes appear in the lower part of the trunk or in the upper trunk and lower crotches. A thick gummy substance may ooze from these holes. There may be sawdust around the holes or base of the tree. In mid to late summer, empty pupa skins may protrude from these holes. During the spring and summer, some of the leaves and branches may wilt. Severely affected trees may die.

ANALYSIS: Peachtree borers
(*Synanthedon* species)
These moth larvae are most damaging to peaches, but also attack other stone fruits and some ornamental trees. The clear-winged moths (which resemble wasps) lay their eggs in mid to late summer. The larvae that emerge bore into the bark. Their tunnels interfere with the circulation of water and nutrients, causing twig and branch wilting and dieback. The borers feed throughout the winter and into the spring. A gummy sap often oozes from the borer tunnels. This sap is often mixed with sawdustlike particles, the product of larval feeding. The borers pupate in early to midsummer. Their cocoons are located at the base of the tree or just inside their tunnels. The moths emerge several weeks later.

SOLUTION: Apply a spray containing *lindane* to the trunk and lower branches. Do not spray the fruit or foliage. Next year, in late May or early June, kill the egg-laying moths by spraying the trunk and crotches with an insecticide containing *malathion*. Continue spraying at intervals of 3 weeks until early August. Individual borers may be killed by inserting a wire into the borer holes.

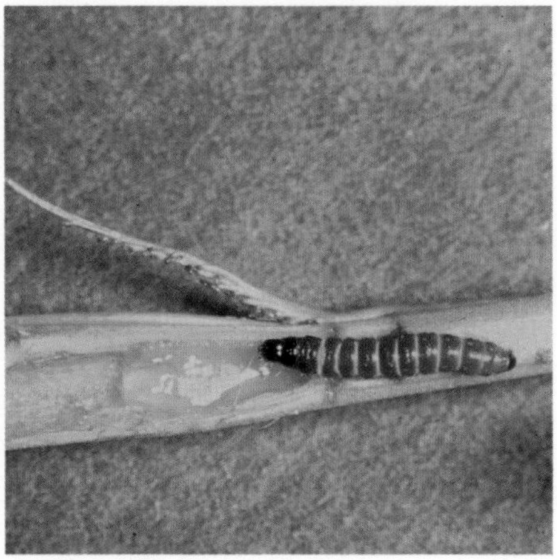

Peach twig borer (twice life size).

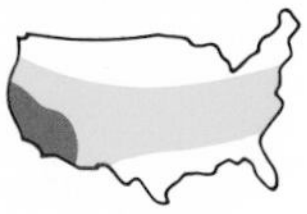

PROBLEM: New growth at the tips of the twigs wilts and dies. When the affected twigs are sliced open lengthwise, worms about ½ inch long are found inside. The reddish brown color of these worm distinguishes them from Oriental fruit moth worms, which cause similar damage. Later in the season, some of the maturing fruit when cut open are also found to contain these worms. During the summer, there may be cocoons attached to the branches or tree crotches.

ANALYSIS: Peach twig borer
(*Anarsia lineatella*)
This borer attacks all of the stone fruits, and is particularly damaging along the Pacific Coast. The young larvae hibernate during the winter in burrows under loose bark or in other protected places on the tree. When the tree blooms in the spring, the larvae emerge and bore into the young buds, shoots, and tender twigs, causing twig and leaf death. When mature, they leave the twigs and pupate in cocoons attached to branches. After several weeks, gray moths emerge and lay eggs on the twigs, leaves, and fruit. Egg laying and larval damage can occur all through the growing season. Later in the summer, larvae feed almost exclusively on the maturing fruit. In addition to ruining the fruit, these pests may cause abnormal branching patterns on young trees.

SOLUTION: Worms in the twigs and fruit cannot be killed with pesticides. To prevent future worm damage, kill the moths by spraying infested trees with ORTHO Home Orchard Spray according to label directions. Next spring, spray again just before the blossoms open. Repeat the treatment 2 more times at intervals of 10 to 14 days.

Oriental fruit moth larva (twice life size).

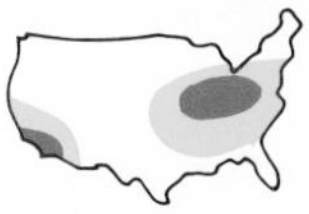

PROBLEM: New growth at the tips of the twigs wilts and dies. When the affected twigs are sliced open lengthwise, worms about ½ inch long are found inside. The pinkish white color of these worms distinguishes them from peach twig borers, which cause similar damage. Later in the season, some of the maturing fruit when cut open are also found to contain these worms. Often there are holes filled with a sticky gum in the apricots.

ANALYSIS: Oriental fruit moth
(*Grapholitha molesta*)
The larvae of these night-flying moths damage stone fruits, apples, and pears. In the spring brown adult moths lay eggs on the young apricot twigs and leaves. The larvae emerge and bore into the young buds, shoots, and tender twigs, causing twig and leaf death. Egg laying and larval damage can occur all through the growing season. Late in the summer, larvae feed almost exclusively on the maturing fruit. They leave gum-filled holes in the apricots when they exit to pupate. In addition to ruining fruit, these pests may cause abnormal branching patterns on young trees when large numbers of twigs are infested.

SOLUTION: Worms in the twigs and fruit cannot be killed with pesticides. To prevent future worm damage, kill the moths by spraying infested trees with ORTHO Fruit & Vegetable Insect Control according to label directions. Next spring, spray again when the petals start to fall from the blossoms. Repeat the treatment 2 more times at intervals of 10 to 14 days.

APRICOT

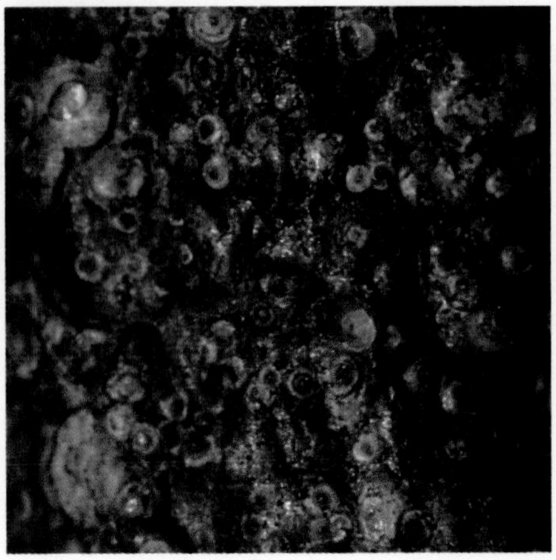

San Jose scale (1/4 life size).

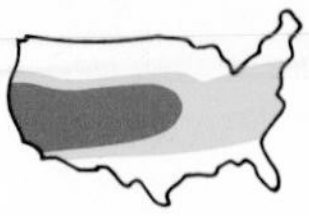

PROBLEM: The leaves are pale green to yellow, and may drop prematurely from weakened limbs. The bark is encrusted with small (1/10 inch or smaller) hard, circular, slightly raised bumps with dull yellow centers. If the hard cover is scraped off, the insect underneath is found to be yellow or olive. There may be severe limb dieback, and entire branches may be killed. Fruit may be marred by red-purple specks.

ANALYSIS: San Jose scale
(*Quadraspidiotus perniciosus*)
These insects infest the bark, leaves, and fruit of many fruit trees. The scales bear live young in the spring. In late spring to midsummer the young scales, called *crawlers*, settle on leaves and twigs. The small (1/16 inch), soft-bodied young feed by inserting their mouthparts and sucking sap from the plant. The legs usually atrophy and a hard, crusty shell develops over the body. An uncontrolled infestation of San Jose scale may kill large branches after 2 or 3 seasons. For further information about scales, see page 876.

SOLUTION: During the dormant season, spray the trunk and branches with ORTHO Volck Oil Spray. The crawlers may be killed with ORTHO Malathion 50 Insect Spray or ORTHO Fruit & Vegetable Insect Control, applied in the late spring.

AVOCADO

ADAPTATION: See the variety chart on page 1016.

SOIL: Any good, deep, very well-drained soil. pH 6.0 to 8.0

FERTILIZER: Fertilize with ORTHO Citrus & Avocado Food according to label directions.

WATER:
How much: Apply enough water to wet the soil 3 to 4 feet deep. To determine the proper amount of water for your soil type, see page 912.
How often: Water when the soil 6 inches below the surface is just barely moist.

PRUNING: During the summer, prune lightly to shape the tree. Remove weak, diseased, or dead twigs and branches. Thin the fruits only if there is danger of branch breakage from excessive weight.

HARVEST: Avocados do not soften on the tree, so it is difficult to tell when the fruit is ripe. Purple or dark varieties are usually mature when the fruit starts to darken. When fruits of green varieties begin to mature, the bright green color diminishes, a yellow tinge appears on the skin and stem, the fruit becomes smoother, and small corky areas may appear on the skin. The seed coat will turn brown and papery. When picking, cut the stem as close to the fruit as possible without injury.

Omnivorous looper (twice life size).

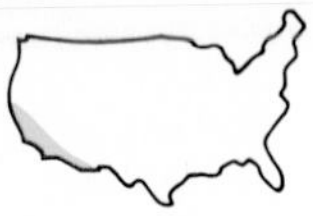

PROBLEM: The upper surfaces of the leaves may be stripped away, leaving a thin brown membrane; or the leaves may be entirely chewed between the veins. The fruit may be distorted or scarred. Striped yellow to pale green worms up to 2½ inches long are eating the leaves. These worms may be seen on the leaf edges, or in between two leaves that are webbed together. Severely infested trees may be partially defoliated.

ANALYSIS: Omnivorous looper
(*Sabulodes caberata*)
This worm, the larva of a brown night-flying moth, attacks avocados and other trees and shrubs. The moths lay eggs on the undersides of the leaves. The larvae that hatch from these eggs feed on the foliage and developing fruit for about 6 weeks. Then they pupate inside leaves that they web together. Larval damage occurs all year, but is most severe during the spring and summer.

SOLUTION: There are several natural predators that keep this pest under control, including tiny wasps (*Trichogramma* species), flies, viruses, and fungi. If infestation is severe, spray with *Bacillus thuringiensis*, a bacterial insecticide. *Bacillus thuringiensis* is most effective when the loopers are small.

Fruit scab.

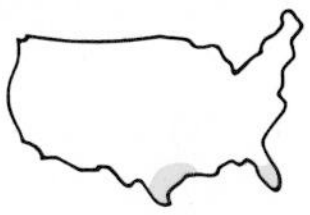

PROBLEM: Fruit develop raised, dark brown to purplish brown, scablike areas. Spots may be scattered, or they may grow together to form large scabby areas that cover the entire surface of the fruit. Heavily infected fruit may be deformed or dwarfed. Fruit of all sizes can be affected. The disease does not affect the eating quality of the mature fruit. However, other decay organisms may gain entrance into the fruit through scab lesions.

ANALYSIS: Fruit scab
This disfiguring disease is caused by a fungus (*Sphaceloma perseae*) that is carried over from one season to the next on stem and leaf lesions. Young fruit are usually infected just after the petals fall from the flowers. As fruit ages, it becomes more resistant to infection, but does not acquire immunity until it is more than half grown.

SOLUTION: Spray the entire tree with a fungicide containing *basic copper sulfate*. Use a spreader-sticker with the fungicide for better coverage. (For more information on spreader-stickers, see page 922.) Apply sprays at the following times:
1. Late January to mid-February, when flower buds swell.
2. Mid-February to mid-March, at fruit set.
3. Three to four weeks after second spray.
4. May 1 to May 15 (all varieties).
5. June 1 to June 15 (midseason and late varieties).
6. July 15 (late varieties only).

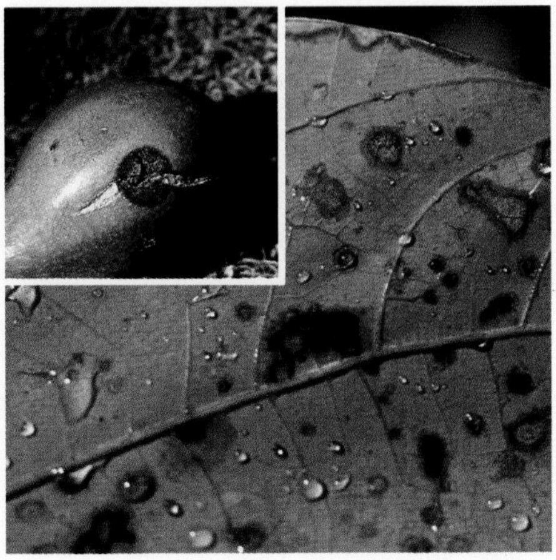

Cercospora leaf spot. *Insert:* Infected fruit.

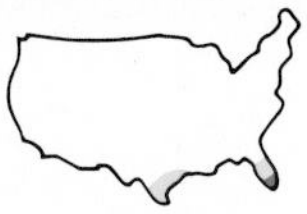

PROBLEM: Leaves are covered with angular brown spots, about $1/16$ inch in diameter, that often penetrate completely through the leaf. Individual spots may grow together to form large spots. During moist periods throughout the year, spores are produced in grayish tufts on either surface of the spot. Severely infected leaves often drop.

ANALYSIS: Cercospora leaf spot
This plant disease is caused by a fungus (*Cercospora purpurea*) that infects avocado leaves and fruit. Old leaf infections are the usual source of spores. In some years, much leaf loss can occur, weakening the tree and slowing fruit development. When the fungus attacks the fruit, the spots often provide convenient entryways for other fungi that rot the fruit.

SOLUTION: Spray the tree with a fungicide containing *basic copper sulfate*. Use a spreader-sticker for better coverage. (For more information on spreader-stickers, see page 922.) Apply sprays at the following times:
1. Late January to mid-February, when flower buds begin to swell.
2. Mid-February to mid-March, at fruit set.
3. Three to four weeks after second spray.
4. May 1 to May 15 (all varieties).
5. June 1 to June 15 (midseason and late varieties).
6. July 15 (late varieties only).

Animal damage.

PROBLEM: Fruit has large holes chewed in it. In some cases, the entire fruit except for the seed may be eaten. Fruit loss is heaviest during the ripening season, but some losses may occur earlier. No insects or similar pests can be found doing the damage.

ANALYSIS: Animal damage
Birds, squirrels, and rats are fond of avocados, and can destroy large quantities of fruit. Birds attack immature fruit; rats and squirrels tend to attack mature or nearly mature fruit.

SOLUTION: When the problem becomes too severe on mature fruit, pick all remaining fruit. Traps may be used to catch squirrels and rats, but birds cannot usually be discouraged easily. Netting may have to be placed over fruit to protect them. Scare devices are sometimes effective in controlling most animal pests. Physical barriers are also effective. For more information, see page 595.

Phytophthora root rot.

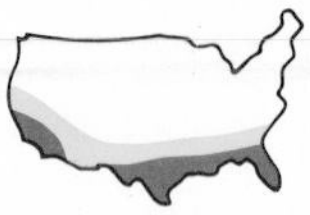

PROBLEM: Leaves are smaller than normal, yellowish, and may wilt and drop. The foliage is sparse, and there is little new growth. Entire branches may die, and the fruit is often small. Eventually the entire tree may wilt and die, even though the soil is sufficiently moist. The bark on part or all of the trunk just above or below the soil line may be darkened. When the diseased bark is scraped away, the underlying sapwood is discolored tan to black.

ANALYSIS: Phytophthora root rot
This plant disease is caused by a soil-inhabiting fungus (*Phytophthora cinnamomi*) that infects many fruit, nut, and ornamental trees and shrubs. It penetrates the roots and crown of the tree. As the fungus decays the sapwood, the flow of water and nutrients is blocked, eventually resulting in the death of the tree. The fungus is spread by infected plants, and by infested soil and soil water. Phytophthora root rot is greatly favored by wet or poorly drained soil. Trees planted in lawns, flower beds, or other moist or poorly drained areas are highly susceptible to this disease.

SOLUTION: No chemical control is available. Once the fungus becomes established in the soil, it will remain indefinitely. The lives of mildly infected trees may be prolonged. Remove the soil from around the crown of the tree, exposing the major roots. Always keep this area dry by providing drainage away from the tree. Avoid overwatering. Remove severely diseased and dying trees. Do not replant susceptible plants in the same area. For a list of resistant trees and shrubs, see page 1013.

CHERRY

ADAPTATION AND POLLINATION: See the variety chart on page 1023.

SOIL: Any good, deep, well-drained garden soil. pH 5.5 to 8.0

FERTILIZER: Fertilize with ORTHO Evergreen, Tree & Shrub Food according to label directions.

WATER:
How much: Apply enough water to wet the soil 3 to 4 feet deep. To determine the proper amount of water for your soil type, see page 912.
How often: Water when the soil 6 inches below the surface is just barely moist.

PRUNING: Cherries are borne on short fruiting branches (spurs) that grow on 2-year-old wood. The spurs are very long-lived and often continue to bear for 10 years or more. Prune lightly, thinning out weak, crossing, or dead twigs and branches.

HARVEST: Harvest when the cherries are fully colored. With ripe cherries, the stem will easily separate from the spur when the fruit is gently lifted or pulled. When picking cherries, avoid damaging the spurs.

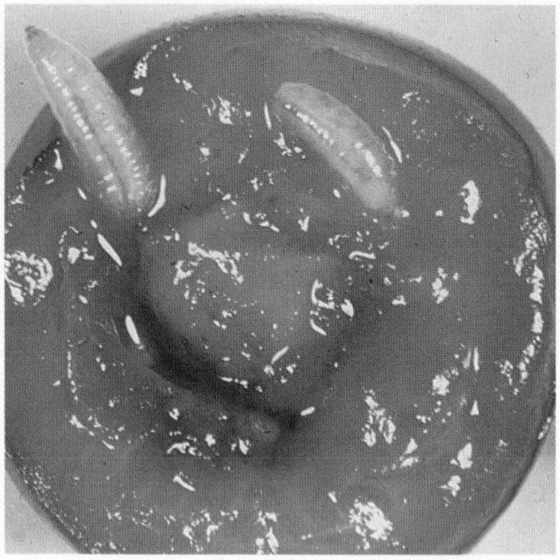
Cherry fruit fly maggots (3 times life size).

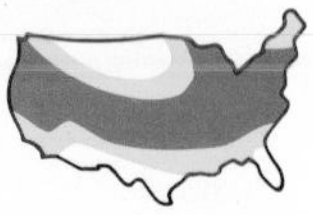

PROBLEM: The fruit is malformed, shrunken, or shriveled. Often the cherries are rotten and pulpy; there may be holes in the fruit. Tapered, yellow-white, legless worms up to ¼ inch long may be found in the cherries. Many cherries drop prematurely.

ANALYSIS: Cherry fruit flies
(*Rhagoletis* species)
These worms are the larvae of several closely related flies. The adult flies, about half the size of the common house fly, appear in the late spring for a period of about a month. They lay eggs in the cherries through holes they puncture in the skin. After several days the eggs hatch into maggots that tunnel through the cherry flesh. Infested cherries usually drop to the ground, and the mature maggots burrow into the soil to pupate. They remain in the soil throughout the winter, and emerge as adults next spring.

SOLUTION: You cannot control the worms in this year's fruit, but you can probably prevent the recurrence of the problem next year. Look for the adult flies in late spring as the fruit is forming. As soon as fruit flies appear, spray with ORTHO Fruit & Vegetable Insect Control. Repeat the application 2 more times at intervals of 14 days.

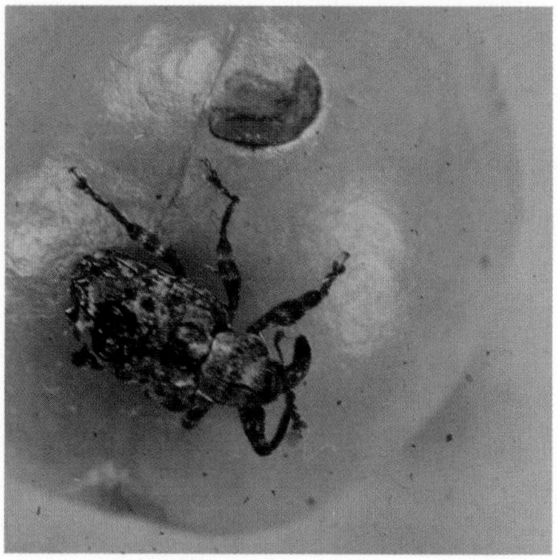

Plum curculio (4 times life size).

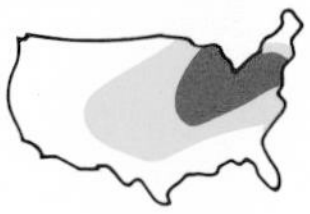

PROBLEM: The fruit is shriveled, blackened, and soft, and often drops prematurely. There are holes about 1/8 inch in diameter and deep, crescent-shaped scars on the fruit. When damaged fruit is cut open, crescent-shaped yellow-gray grubs with brown heads may be found.

ANALYSIS: Plum curculio
(*Conotrachelus nenuphar*)
These insects, found east of the Rocky Mountains, attack other stone fruits, apples, and pears as well as cherries. The adult insects are brown beetles with long curved snouts. They hibernate in debris and other protected places during the winter. The beetles emerge in the spring when new growth starts and feed on young leaves, blossoms, and developing fruit. After 5 to 6 weeks, the female beetles lay eggs in the young cherries. During this process, they cut distinctive crescent-shaped slits into the fruit. The young grubs that hatch from the eggs feed for several weeks in the fruit. Usually the infested cherries drop to the ground. The grubs eventually leave the fruit and bore into the soil, where they pupate. The emerging beetles feed on fruit for a few weeks, then go into hibernation. Or, in the South, they lay eggs, producing a second generation of grubs in the late summer.

SOLUTION: Once the fruit is infested, there is no way to kill the grubs inside the fruit. Spray with ORTHO Home Orchard Spray or ORTHO Malathion 50 Insect Spray to kill beetles that may be feeding on fruit, or laying eggs. Pick up and destroy all fallen cherries. Next spring, spray all trees when the petals are falling from the blossoms; repeat applications according to label directions.

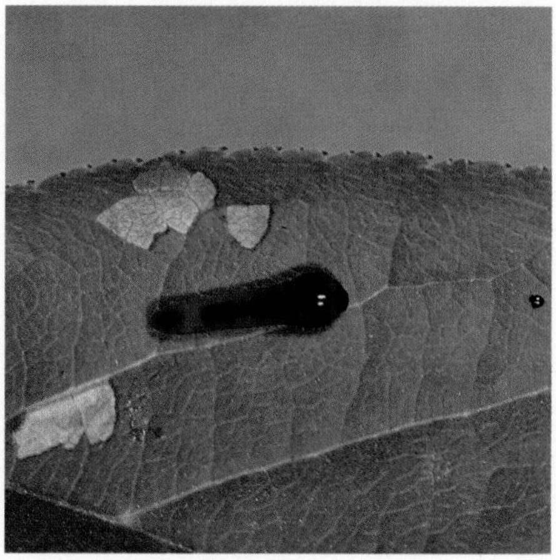

Pearslug larva (twice life size).

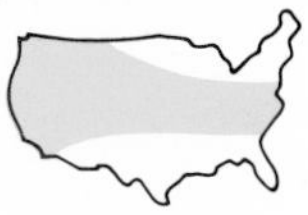

PROBLEM: The upper surfaces of the leaves are chewed between the veins, leaving a lacy, translucent layer of tissue that turns brown. Dark green to orange, wet, sluglike worms up to 1/2 inch long may be feeding on the leaves. Severely infested trees may be defoliated.

ANALYSIS: Pearslug
(*Caliroa cerasi*)
Although pearslugs closely resemble slugs, they are actually the larvae of black and yellow flies that infest pears, plums, and some ornamental trees in addition to cherries. The adult flies, which appear in the late spring, lay their eggs in the leaves. The young larvae that hatch from these eggs exude a slimy, olive-green substance, giving them a sluglike appearance. They feed on the foliage for about a month, then drop to the ground, burrow into the soil, and pupate. Young trees that are severely infested by pearslugs may be greatly weakened and will produce fewer, poor quality cherries.

SOLUTION: Spray the infested tree with ORTHO Home Orchard Spray. Repeat the spray if infestation recurs.

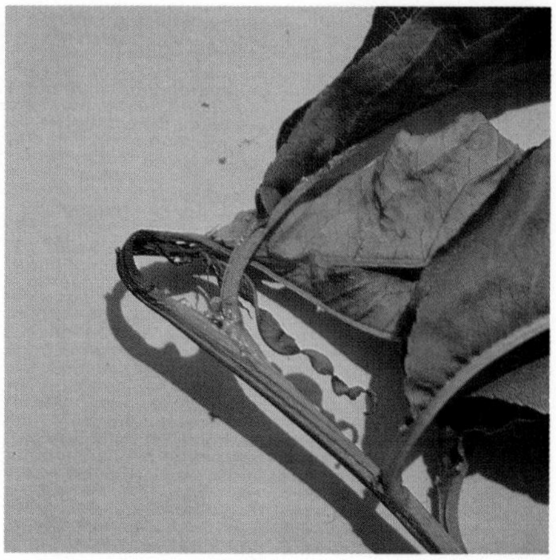

Oriental fruit moth damage.

PROBLEM: New growth at the tips of the twigs wilts and dies. When the affected twigs are sliced open lengthwise, pinkish white worms up to 1/2 inch long are found inside. Later in the season, some of the maturing fruit when cut open may also be found to contain these worms.

ANALYSIS: Oriental fruit moth
(*Grapholitha molesta*)
The larvae of these night-flying moths damage stone fruits, apples, and pears. The larvae hibernate in cocoons on the tree bark, or in branch crotches. In the spring they pupate, emerge as brown adult moths, and lay eggs on the young cherry twigs and leaves. The larvae bore into the young buds, shoots, and tender twigs, causing twig and leaf death. When mature they leave the twigs, spin cocoons, and pupate in the tree or in debris on the ground. After several weeks, moths emerge to lay their eggs. Egg laying and larval damage can occur all through the growing season. Later in the summer, larvae feed almost exclusively on the maturing cherries. They leave gum-filled holes in the cherries when they exit to pupate. In addition to ruining the fruit, these pests may cause abnormal branching patterns on young trees when large numbers of twigs are infested.

SOLUTION: Worms in the twigs and fruit cannot be killed with pesticides. To prevent future worm damage, kill the moths by spraying infested trees with ORTHO Fruit & Vegetable Insect Control or ORTHO Liquid Sevin. Apply as directed on the label.

CHERRY

Shothole borer beetle.

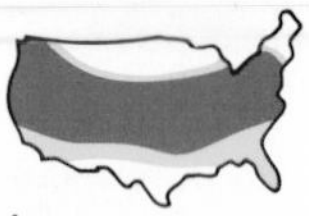

PROBLEM: Many small holes (1/16 to 1/8 inch in diameter) are bored in the twigs, branches, and sometimes trunk of the tree. A sticky gum often oozes from the holes. The holes may be plugged with the bodies of dead insects. When sliced open, the branches reveal sawdust-filled tunnels in the wood. Pinkish white, slightly curved grubs may be found in the tunnels. Brownish black beetles 1/10 inch long are often present on the bark. The foliage on damaged branches sometimes wilts and turns brown. Twigs and buds may be killed, and entire branches may die.

ANALYSIS: Shothole borer
(*Scolytus rugulosus*)
This beetle, sometimes known as the *fruit tree bark beetle*, also attacks other stone fruits and many ornamental trees. The adult beetles that emerge in the late spring or early summer feed at the base of buds and small twigs, often killing them. The female beetles bore into the wood, creating tunnels in which they lay their eggs. The grubs that hatch from the eggs bore into the inner wood, creating sawdust-filled burrows 2 to 4 inches long. The grubs pupate just under the bark, then emerge as adult beetles. The last generation of grubs spends the winter in the tunnels, emerging the following spring. Weakened, diseased, and dying trees and branches are most susceptible to borer infestation.

SOLUTION: Apply a spray containing *lindane* to the lower part of the trunk, wetting the bark thoroughly. Avoid spraying the fruit and foliage. During the dormant season, remove and destroy infested branches. Keep the tree healthy by watering and fertilizing it properly. For cultural information, see page 616.

Sap oozing from borer hole.

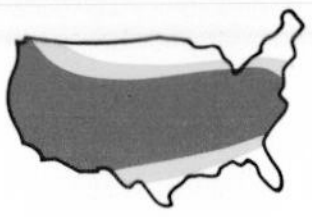

PROBLEM: Holes appear in the lower part of the trunk or in the upper trunk and lower crotches. A thick, gummy substance may ooze from these holes. There may be sawdust around the holes or the base of the tree. In mid to late summer, empty pupa skins may protrude from these holes. During the spring and summer, some of the leaves and branches may wilt. Severely affected trees may die.

ANALYSIS: Peachtree borers
(*Synanthedon species*)
The larvae of these moths are damaging to stone fruits and some ornamental trees. The clear-winged moths (which resemble wasps) lay their eggs in mid to late summer. The larvae bore into the bark either just above or just below the ground level, or in the upper trunk and main crotches. Their tunnels interfere with the circulation of water and nutrients, causing twig and branch wilting and dieback. The borers feed throughout the winter and into the spring in their tunnels. A gummy sap may ooze from the borer tunnels. This sap is often mixed with sawdustlike particles, the product of larval feeding. The borers pupate in early to midsummer; their cocoons are located at the base of the tree or just inside their tunnels. The moths emerge several weeks later.

SOLUTION: Apply a spray containing *lindane* to the trunk and lower branches. Do not spray the fruit or foliage. Next year, in late May or June, kill the egg-laying moths by spraying the trunk and crotches with a pesticide containing *malathion*. Continue spraying at intervals of 3 weeks until early August. Individual borers may be killed by inserting a wire into the borer holes.

Bacterial canker.

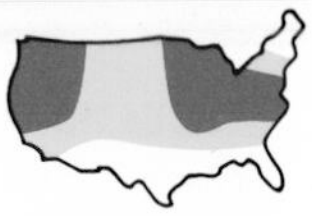

PROBLEM: Sunken, elliptical lesions appear on the trunk or branches. Throughout the fall, winter, and spring, thick, amber, sour-smelling gum oozes from these lesions. In the spring, especially when the weather is very wet and cold, blossoms may turn brown and wither. Individual branches may fail to produce foliage, or, as the season progresses, entire branches may die back. There may be angular holes in the leaves. Sometimes dark, sunken lesions appear in the fruit.

ANALYSIS: Bacterial canker
This plant disease, also known as *bacterial gummosis* or *bacterial blast*, attacks various fruit and nut trees, but is most severe on cherries. This disease is caused by bacteria (*Pseudomonas syringae*). During the fall, winter, and early spring, large quantities of bacteria-containing gum ooze from the cankers. Splashing rain spreads the bacteria to dormant buds, twigs, and branches. Infection occurs through wounds in the twigs and branches, and bacterial decay causes cankers to form. Bacterial activity decreases in summer. However, slowly developing cankers may encircle a branch, and by midsummer, the affected branches and limbs start to die back. With the onset of cool, wet, fall weather, bacterial activity increases again. This disease is most serious on young trees.

SOLUTION: Bacterial canker is difficult to control. Prune out diseased branches. After each cut, sterilize pruning shears with rubbing alcohol. In the fall, spray with a fungicide containing *basic copper sulfate*. Keep the tree healthy. For care of cherries, see page 616. For a list of resistant cherries, see page 1023.

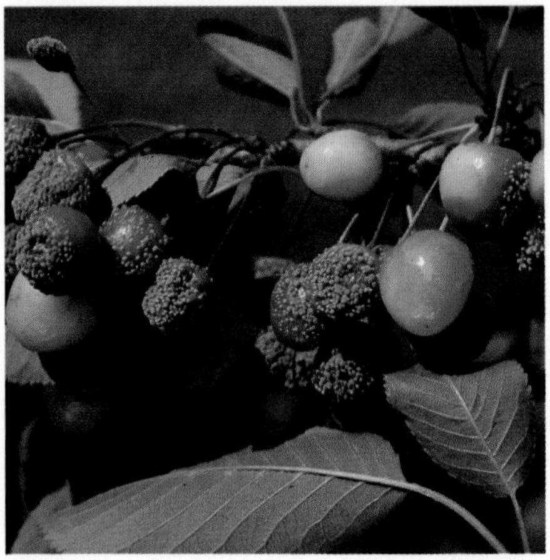

Fruit rot.

PROBLEM: Blossoms and young leaves decay, wilt, and turn brown during the first 2 weeks of the bloom period. The decayed blossoms may fail to drop and hang on the tree through the growing season. In humid conditions, masses of gray spores may appear on the infected flower parts. There is often extensive twig dieback. Sunken lesions sometimes develop on the twigs and branches as the season progresses. These lesions may exude a sticky ooze.

Blighted shoots.

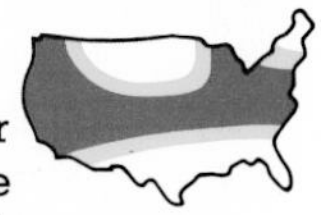

PROBLEM: Small, circular brown spots appear on the young cherries. Later in the season, as the fruit begins to mature, these spots may enlarge to rot part or all of the cherries. During moist weather, the rotten fruit is covered with tufts of gray spores. Infected cherries either drop prematurely or dry out, turn dark brown, and remain on the tree past the normal harvest period. Many twigs die. There are sunken lesions (cankers) on some of these twigs. A thick, gummy material often oozes from these cankers.

ANALYSIS: Brown rot

This plant disease, caused by either of two closely related fungi (*Monilinia laxa* or *M. fructicola*), is very destructive to all of the stone fruits. The fungi spend the winter in twig cankers or in rotted cherries (mummies) in the tree or on the ground. In the spring, spores are blown or splashed from cankers or mummies to the healthy flower buds. After penetrating and decaying the flowers, the fungus grows down into the twigs, producing brown, sunken cankers. During moist weather a thick, gummy sap oozes from the lesions, and tufts of gray spores may form on the infected areas. Spores from cankers and infected blossoms or mummies are splashed and blown to the maturing cherries. Young cherries are fairly resistant to infection, but maturing cherries are vulnerable. Brown rot develops most rapidly in mild, moist conditions.

SOLUTION: If there are still uninfected blossoms left on the tree, spray with ORTHO Home Orchard Spray or ORTHO Orthocide Garden Fungicide to protect them from further infection. Spray twice at intervals of 10 days. To protect maturing cherries from infection, spray again about 3 weeks before they are to be harvested. Remove and destroy all infected fruits and mummies. Prune out cankers and blighted twigs. Clean up and destroy all debris around the tree. Next spring, spray trees at early and full bloom with ORTHO Home Orchard Spray or ORTHO Orthocide Garden Fungicide.

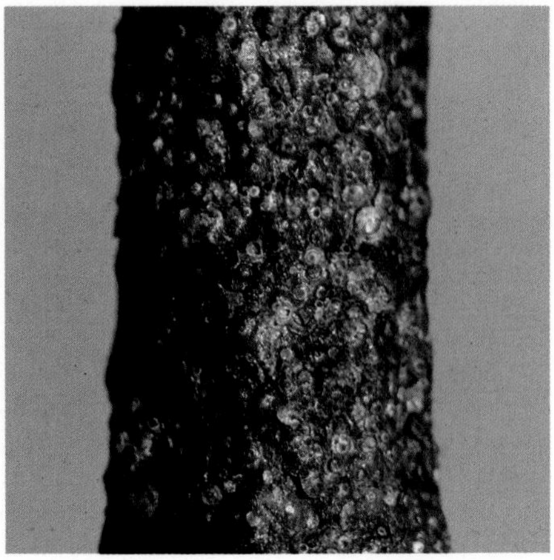

San Jose scales.

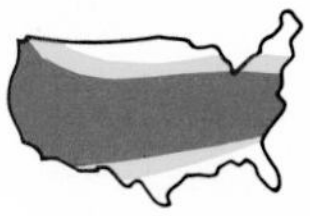

PROBLEM: Some of the leaves are pale green to yellow and may drop prematurely from weakened limbs. Or they may turn brown and wither, and remain attached to the tree into the winter. The bark is encrusted with small (1/10 inch) hard, circular, slightly raised bumps with dull yellow centers. If the hard cover is scraped off, the insect underneath is yellow or olive. There may be severe limb dieback and entire branches may be killed. The fruit may be marred by specks.

ANALYSIS: San Jose scale
(*Quadraspidiotus perniciosus*)

These insects infest the bark, leaves, and fruit of many fruit trees. The scales bear live young in the spring. In late spring to midsummer the young scales, called *crawlers*, settle on leaves and twigs. The small (1/16 inch), soft-bodied young feed by inserting their mouthparts and sucking sap from the plant. The legs atrophy and a hard, crusty shell develops over the body. An uncontrolled infestation of San Jose scale may kill large branches after 2 or 3 seasons. For further information about scale, see page 876.

SOLUTION: During the dormant season, spray the trunk and branches with ORTHO Volck Oil Spray. The crawlers may be killed with ORTHO Malathion 50 Insect Spray or ORTHO Fruit & Vegetable Insect Control, applied in the late spring.

CHERRY

Powdery mildew.

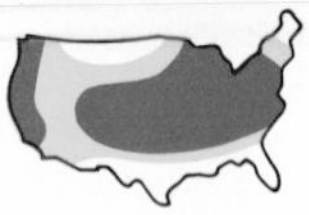

PROBLEM: Gray-white powdery patches appear on the leaves. New growth is often stunted, curled, and distorted. Infected buds may be shriveled and open later than usual. Infected leaves often die. The fruit may be covered with white, powdery patches, and is sometimes small and misshapen.

ANALYSIS: Powdery mildew
This common plant disease is caused by a fungus (*Podosphaera oxycanthae*) that thrives in both humid and dry weather. The fungus spends the winter in leaf and flower buds. In the spring, spores are blown to the emerging young leaves, which are very susceptible to infection. The fungus saps plant nutrients, causing distortion and often death of the tender foliage. The fruit yield may be greatly reduced, since the mildewed cherries are often not edible. Powdery mildew is favored by warm days and cool nights. For a list of plants that are susceptible to this fungus, see page 1006.

SOLUTION: Spray with a fungicide containing *sulfur* when mildew appears, and continue spraying at regular intervals for 10 days until 3 weeks after the petals have fallen from the flowers. Respray during periods of wet weather, or if reinfection occurs.

Cherry leafspot.

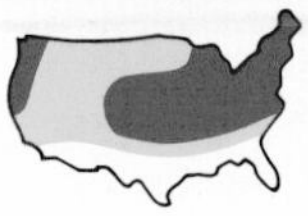

PROBLEM: Purple spots appear on the upper surfaces of the leaves. The centers of the spots may fall out, leaving holes in the leaves. Many of the spotted leaves are yellow and dying. The undersides of the leaves may be dotted with cream-colored masses of spores. In severe cases, the fruit is also spotted. The tree defoliates prematurely, and the cherry yield is reduced and of poor quality. The fruit is often soft and watery.

ANALYSIS: Cherry leafspot
This plant disease, also known as *yellow leafspot*, is caused by a fungus (*Coccomyces hiemalis*). The fungus spends the winter in fallen leaves. About the time the cherry trees are finished blooming, large numbers of spores are splashed and blown from the ground to the emerging leaves. The infection and premature death of the leaves greatly reduces the amount of food the tree can make and store. This results in weakened trees and reduced, poor quality fruit yields. Such trees are much more susceptible to cold injury during the following winter. Cherry leafspot is most severe during mild (60° to 70°F), wet weather.

SOLUTION: Spray with ORTHO ORTHOCIDE Garden Fungicide or ORTHO Home Orchard Spray according to label directions. In the fall, remove and destroy all leaf debris around the trees. Next spring, spray when the petals fall from the tree; repeat the spray at least 2 more times at intervals of 10 to 14 days. If the problem is severe, continue spraying until 7 days before harvest. Meteor and Northstar cherries are resistant to cherry leafspot.

CITRUS

ADAPTATION: See the variety chart on page 1021.

SOIL: Any good, well-drained soil. pH 5.5 to 8.0

FERTILIZER: Fertilize with ORTHO Citrus & Avocado Food according to label directions.

WATER:
How much: Apply enough water to wet the soil 3 to 4 feet deep. To determine the proper amount of water for your soil type, see page 912. To avoid wetting the trunk and crown of the plant, water into a basin that keeps the water at least 12 inches out from the trunk.
How often: Water when the soil 6 to 12 inches below the surface is just barely moist.

PRUNING: Prune only to shape the tree, and to remove suckers and dead twigs and branches. Lightly thin the inside of the tree if the growth is dense.

HARVEST: When the fruits are fully colored, taste one to determine if it is ripe. If the flavor is not yet sweet enough for the variety, allow the fruits to ripen for another few weeks, then try again. To harvest, clip fruits off with pruning shears rather than pulling them off.

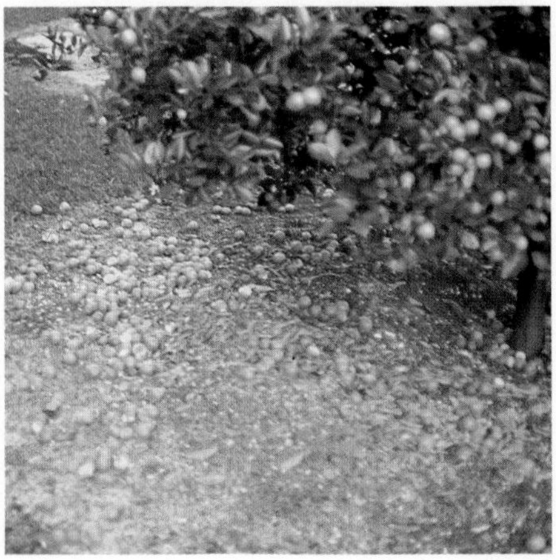

Fruit drop.

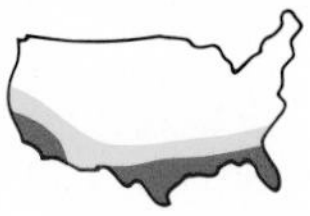

PROBLEM: Large amounts of young, newly formed fruit drop from the tree. Fruit drop continues until the fruit has grown to about ½ inch in diameter. The tree appears healthy otherwise.

ANALYSIS: Fruit drop
Some fruit normally drops every year. This is a natural thinning process, and does not mean the tree is diseased or injured. If more fruit seems to be dropping than usual, the tree is being watered too little or too often. Or the supply of nitrogen may be inadequate. For more information about excessive fruit drop, see page 592.

SOLUTION: The only control you have over the amount of fruit that is lost this way is to see that the tree is maintained in healthy condition. There will still be natural thinning, but it will not be excessive. Be sure the tree has the amounts of water and fertilizer it needs while it is setting fruit. If the weather has been warmer or more windy than usual, water deeply and more frequently.

Split grapefruit.

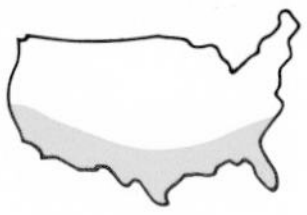

PROBLEM: The rind splits as the fruit ripens. The split may be short and shallow, or it may be deep and wide, exposing the fruit segments.

ANALYSIS: Fruit splitting
Fruit splitting usually results from fluctuations in temperature, humidity, soil moisture, and possibly fertilizer levels. This condition may be a result of several of these factors rather than any one cause. The amount of split fruit varies from year to year. Usually, only a small portion of fruit on each tree is affected. Fruit splitting is most serious on thin-skinned citrus varieties.

SOLUTION: There is no chemical control. Avoid extreme fluctuations in soil moisture and fertilization levels. For more information about citrus culture, see page 620.

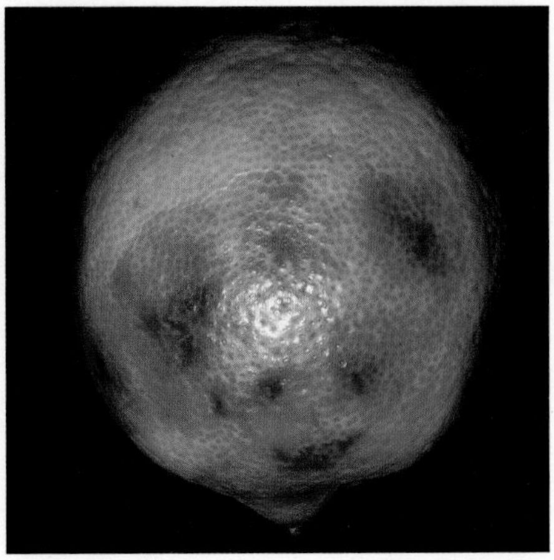

Brown rot on lemon.

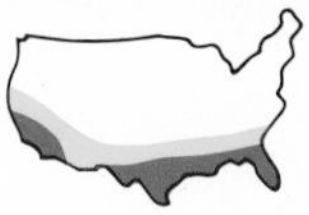

PROBLEM: Firm light-brown spots appear on the rind. These spots may cover a large part or all of the fruit. During periods of high humidity, a white mold often appears on the infected rind. Diseased fruit usually drops. Sometimes leaves and twigs die. Dark lesions that exude a sticky ooze may appear on the trunk near the base of the tree.

ANALYSIS: Brown rot
This plant disease is caused by any of several closely related soil-inhabiting fungi (*Phytophthora* species), some of which may also cause a debilitating canker and gummosis disease of citrus. (For more information about *brown rot gummosis*, see page 627.) These fungi thrive in heavy wet soil, and are most damaging during periods of wet weather. Spores are spread by splashing rain or irrigation water to the maturing fruit, blossoms, and tender shoots on the lower portion of the tree. The fungi that attack and decay the fruit produce spores that are splashed to additional fruit higher in the tree. During periods of rainy weather, an entire crop may be infected.

SOLUTION: Spray the ground and the bottom 3 to 4 feet of the foliage with ORTHO ORTHOCIDE Garden Fungicide. To prevent recurrence of the disease, spray again just before seasonal rains begin. Remove and destroy infected fruit and blighted twigs. Prune off branches that touch the ground.

CITRUS

Citrus scab.

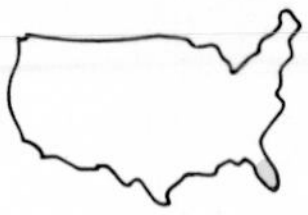

PROBLEM: Fruit has raised, corky areas. Leaves may be deformed and twisted, with brown scablike lesions. Heavily infected fruit fail to develop normally, and infected leaves may fall prematurely.

ANALYSIS: Citrus scab

This plant disease is caused by a fungus (*Elsinoë fawcetti*) that attacks the new leaves, fruit, and stems of many types of citrus, especially sour orange, lemons, Temple and Murcott honey orange, grapefruit, and Satsumas. Leaves and fruit are infected in early spring from spores released from old scab lesions. Once infection has taken place, scablike, corky, brown areas develop on leaves and fruit. Scab is more severe following a rainy spring or overwatering.

SOLUTION: Spray trees at least twice with ORTHO Phaltan Rose & Garden Fungicide. Apply the first spray in late winter prior to spring growth, and the second spray just after the petals have fallen from the blossoms, before the new fruits are larger than a large pea. To discourage infection, keep foliage as dry as possible during the spring growth period.

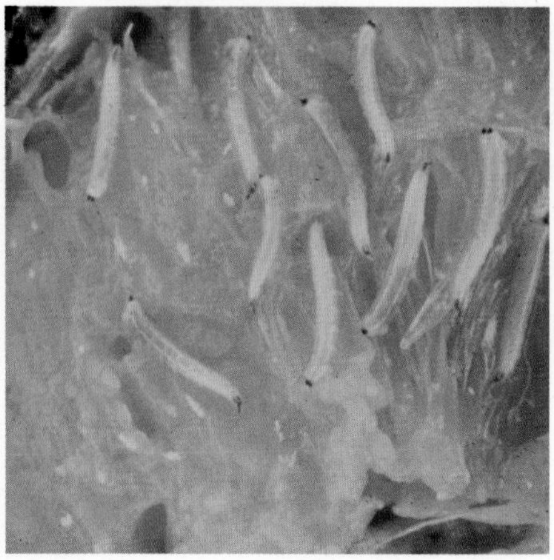

Caribbean fruit fly larvae (3 times life size).

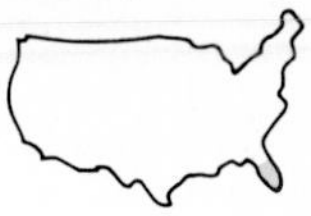

PROBLEM: Many ripe fruit fall from trees. Each fallen fruit has a small rotten spot and a tiny hole in the skin. Small white maggots are found in the flesh just beneath the rotten areas.

ANALYSIS: Caribbean fruit fly

(*Anastrepha suspensa*)

Female flies deposit their eggs in ripe fruit just beneath the skin, where they hatch in 2 to 3 days into tiny maggots. The larvae feed inside the fruit for 7 to 10 days; during this period the fruit usually drops to the ground. The larvae enter the soil to pupate, emerging 14 to 18 days later as adult flies. The adults, which are seldom seen, are brown with brown markings on their wings and are about ½ inch long.

SOLUTION: No chemical is available for controlling flies on home citrus trees. Because adult flies are attracted to mature and overripe fruit, pick fruit as soon as it matures. Pick up any fallen fruit and dispose of it so that fly larvae do not have a chance to mature.

Citrus thrips damage.

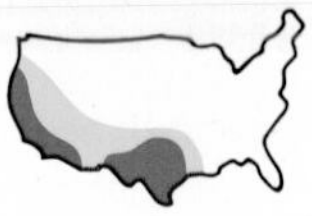

PROBLEM: Leaf buds shrivel and turn brown. Some of the leaves are silvery gray, leathery, curled, and distorted. The fruit may be silvery, scabbed, streaked, and deformed. To determine if the plant is infested with these insects, hold a sheet of white paper underneath an affected shoot and tap the stem sharply. Minute yellow-brown insects, resembling wood slivers, will drop to the paper and begin to crawl around.

ANALYSIS: Citrus thrips

(*Scirtothrips citri*)

These insects are pests of citrus and various ornamental trees. Thrips cause their damage by rasping the tissue of young leaves and immature fruits. They feed on the plant sap that exudes from the injured tissue. Adult thrips lay their eggs in leaves and stems in the fall. The following spring, the young thrips that emerge from these eggs begin feeding on the new growth. These pests are often found in protected areas like the insides of leaf buds. Thrip damage occurs throughout the growing season, and is especially severe during hot, dry weather.

SOLUTION: Spray infested plants with ORTHO Fruit & Vegetable Insect Control or ORTHO Malathion 50 Insect Spray. Follow directions carefully, and repeat at regular intervals of 7 to 10 days as long as new damage is seen.

Damage. *Insert:* Citrus whiteflies (3 times life size).

PROBLEM: Tiny, winged insects $1/12$ inch long feed mainly on the undersides of the leaves. The insects are covered with a white waxy powder. When the plant is touched, insects flutter rapidly around it. A black film or mold may cover the leaves and stems.

ANALYSIS: Citrus whitefly (*Dialeurodes citri*)
This tiny sucking insect lays eggs on the undersides of leaves, where they hatch into flat, oval-shaped semitransparent larvae. The larvae feed by sucking the plant juices from the leaves. Citrus whiteflies cannot fully digest all the sugar in the plant sap, and the excess is excreted in a fluid called honeydew, which often drops onto the leaves below. A sooty mold fungus may develop on the honeydew, causing the leaves to appear black and dirty. There are several generations of citrus whiteflies each year, with peaks of activity in March-April, June-July, and September-October.

SOLUTION: Apply ORTHO Malathion 50 Insect Spray or ORTHO Citrus Insect Spray as directed on the label for the specific type of citrus involved. Thorough coverage of both the upper and lower surfaces of the leaves is very important to get adequate control. Complete control of adult whiteflies is difficult, but spraying will usually control the immature stages and lessen the problem of sooty mold.

Aphids (life size).

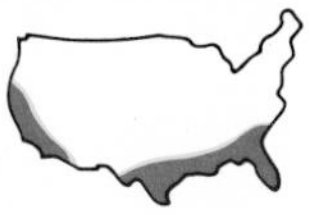

PROBLEM: The newest leaves are curled, cupped, and thickened. Leaves and fruit directly under the curled leaves may be coated with a shiny, sticky substance. A black sooty mold may grow on this sticky substance. Tiny ($1/8$ inch) green or black, soft-bodied insects cluster on the stems and leaves. Blossoms may be deformed. Ants may be present.

ANALYSIS: Aphids
Aphids do little damage in small numbers. However, they are extremely prolific and populations can rapidly build up to damaging numbers during the growing season. Damage occurs when the aphid sucks the juices from the citrus leaves. The aphid is unable to digest fully all the sugar in the sap and excretes the excess in a fluid called honeydew. The honeydew often drops onto the leaves and fruit below. Plants or objects beneath the tree may also be coated with honeydew. A sooty mold fungus may develop on the honeydew, causing the leaves and fruit to appear black and dirty. Ants feed on this sticky substance and are often present where there is an aphid infestation. Repeated aphid attacks may greatly slow the growth and development of young citrus trees. For more information about aphids, see page 875.

SOLUTION: Apply ORTHO Citrus Insect Spray, ORTHO Malathion 50 Insect Spray, or ORTHO Fruit & Vegetable Insect Control as soon as the insects appear.

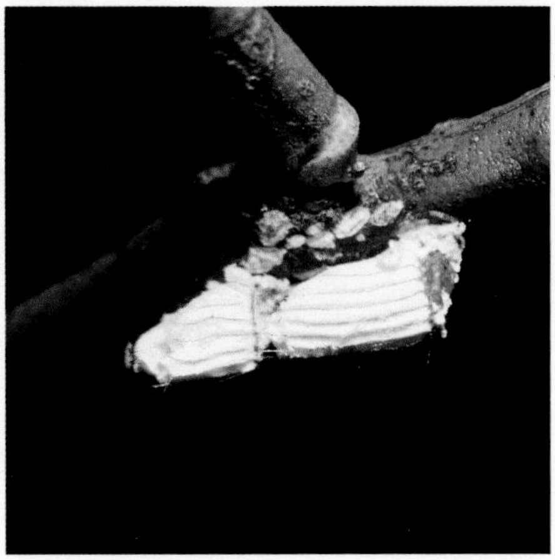

Cottonycushion scale (twice life size).

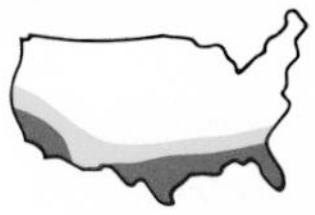

PROBLEM: White, cottony masses cluster on the leaves, stems, branches, and possibly the trunk. Some of the foliage may wither and turn yellow; leaves and fruit may drop. A shiny or sticky substance often coats the leaves. A black, sooty mold may grow on the sticky substance.

ANALYSIS: Mealybugs (*Planococcus citri*) **and cottonycushion scale** (*Icerya purchasi*)
These insects, frequently found together on citrus plants, look so much alike that separate identification is difficult. In late spring and summer, the females are covered with white, cottony masses containing up to 2500 eggs. Females lay their conspicuous egg masses on leaves, twigs, and branches. The inconspicuous young insects that hatch from these eggs are yellowish brown to green. They feed by sucking sap from the plant tissues. They are unable to digest fully all the sugar in the plant sap, and excrete the excess in a fluid called honeydew. A sooty mold fungus may develop on the honeydew, causing the citrus leaves to appear black and dirty. Mealybugs and scales can be spread in any of several ways. The wind can blow egg masses and insects from plant to plant. Ants can carry them to new locations on the plant. Or the active young insects can crawl to new locations by themselves.

SOLUTION: Spray infested trees with an insecticide containing *malathion* or *diazinon*, covering both surfaces of the leaves. Repeat the spray 5 to 7 days later. Use a spreader-sticker when spraying. For more information about spreader-stickers, see page 922. Do not spray when the plant is in full bloom. Do not apply within 7 days of harvest.

CITRUS

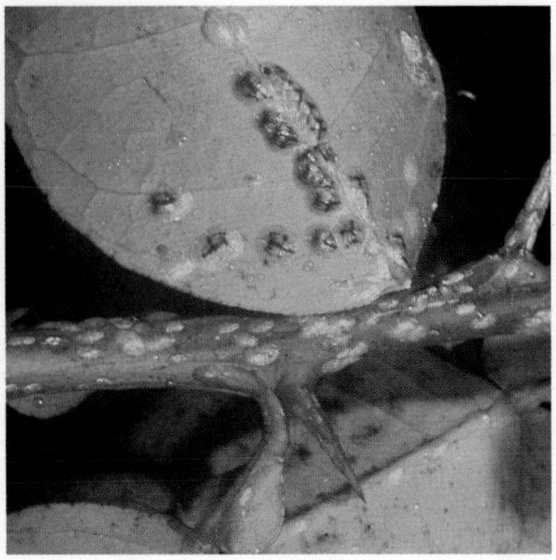

Brown soft scale (twice life size).

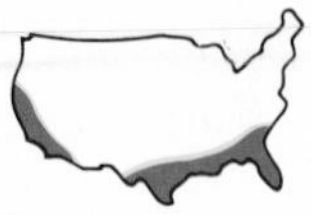

PROBLEM: Crusty, waxy, or smooth bumps, up to ¼ inch in diameter, are found on the trunk, stems, foliage, and sometimes fruit. Often the leaves turn yellow and drop. Fruit may also drop. In some cases, a shiny or sticky substance coats the leaves.

ANALYSIS: Scales

Many species of these insects attack citrus. Some of the most damaging are *California red scale, Florida red scale, brown soft scale, black scale,* and *citrus snow scale.* Scales spend the winter on the trunk and twigs of the tree. They lay eggs or bear live young in late spring to midsummer. The young scales, called *crawlers*, settle on the leaves, twigs, and sometimes on the developing fruit. The tiny (1/10 inch), soft-bodied young resemble small aphids. They feed by sucking sap from the plant. As they mature, the legs usually atrophy, and a hard crusty or waxy shell develops over the body. Some species of scale are unable to digest fully all the sugar in the plant sap and excrete the excess in a fluid called honeydew. An uncontrolled infestation of scales may seriously damage or even kill limbs after 2 or 3 seasons. For more information about scales, see page 875.

SOLUTION: Spray with ORTHO Citrus Insect Spray, ORTHO Fruit & Vegetable Insect Control, or ORTHO Malathion 50 Insect Spray according to label directions in the spring after the bloom period. In late summer or fall, spray with ORTHO Volck Oil Spray. Do not apply products containing petroleum oil during hot (90°F) or freezing weather.

Orangedog caterpillar larva (half life size).

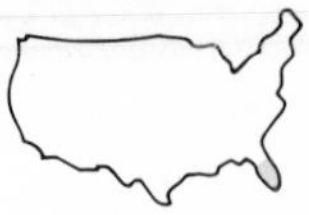

PROBLEM: Leaves are chewed or entirely eaten. Large, brown 1½ to 2-inch caterpillars with yellow or white patches are found on damaged leaves. When disturbed, the caterpillars push out two red, hornlike projections from skin folds just behind the head; the projections give off a strong, disagreeable odor.

ANALYSIS: Orangedog caterpillar

(*Papilio cresphontes*)

This caterpillar is the immature stage of a beautiful black and yellow butterfly. The butterfly lays tiny orange eggs on the new citrus leaves. The caterpillars that hatch from these eggs resemble bird droppings and have few natural enemies, so they feed almost unmolested. Most damage occurs during the spring and summer. Young trees can be defoliated in only a few days, but they usually grow new leaves within a short time, and no permanent damage results.

SOLUTION: When practical, pick off and destroy caterpillars. Spraying is not needed unless large numbers of trees are involved, or trees are so large that it is too difficult to reach caterpillars. If necessary, spray with an insecticide containing *malathion.*

Snail (half life size).

PROBLEM: Holes are chewed in the leaves, and the fruit may be pitted or scarred. Silvery trails wind around on the trunk, branches, and nearby soil. Snails or slugs may be seen moving around or feeding on the tree. They often cluster on the trunk or under leaf debris that accumulates around the tree. Check for them by lifting up the lower branches and removing the leaf debris, or by inspecting the damaged tree at night by flashlight.

ANALYSIS: Snails and slugs

These pests are related to mollusks such as clams and oysters, and are widespread and very troublesome to many garden plants. They hide or feed in shaded, cool locations during the day, venturing out to feed in exposed locations at night, or during cloudy, wet days. They prefer cool, dark, moist conditions, and may frequently be found under rocks, leaves, in groundcovers, and under logs or garbage cans. Because citrus trees are often surrounded by leaf debris and have low-hanging branches, they provide a protected environment ideal for snails and slugs.

SOLUTION: Clean up leaf debris under citrus trees, and remove low-hanging branches to eliminate snail and slug hiding places. Scatter ORTHO Bug-Geta Snail & Slug Pellets in bands around the infested trees and around other daytime hiding places. Wet down the treated areas to encourage snail and slug activity that night; they will be more likely to feed on fresh pellets. Snails and slugs that are visible on the tree can be removed by hand.

Damaged leaves. *Insert:* Mite (12 times life size).

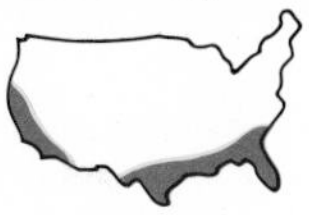

PROBLEM: Leaves are stippled, yellowing, or scratched in appearance. There may be webbing over flower buds, between leaves, or on the lower surfaces of the leaves. The fruit is often brown or russet colored, leathery, or silvery, and may drop prematurely. To determine if the plant is infested with mites, hold a sheet of white paper underneath an affected branch and tap the branch sharply. Minute green, red, or yellow specks will drop to the paper and begin to crawl around. In some cases, you will need to inspect the leaves with a 10-power magnifying glass.

ANALYSIS: Mites

These pests, related to spiders, are very damaging to all types of citrus. There are several species of mites that attack citrus, including *citrus red mites, citrus bud mites, purple mites,* and *citrus rust mites.* Mites cause damage by sucking sap from the leaves and young fruit. As a result of feeding, the green leaf pigment disappears, producing a yellowed, stippled appearance. Feeding damage also causes tissue death, resulting in the browning and silvering of the fruit and foliage. Mites are active throughout the growing season, but are favored by hot, dry weather (70°F and up). By midsummer, they build up to tremendous numbers. A severe mite infestation weakens the plant, and can seriously reduce the size and quality of the fruit. For more information about mites, see page 887.

SOLUTION: Spray infested trees with ORTHO Citrus Insect Spray, or a pesticide containing *dicofol* (KELTHANE®). Be sure to cover both the upper and lower surfaces of the leaves. Repeat the spray at least 2 more times at intervals of 7 days.

Nitrogen-deficient citrus leaves.

PROBLEM: Foliage turns pale green, and the older leaves gradually turn yellow and often fall off. Overall growth is stunted. The tree may flower profusely, but usually fails to set much fruit.

ANALYSIS: Lack of nitrogen

Nitrogen, the most important nutrient for plant growth and development, is deficient in almost all soils. Nitrogen is essential in the formation of plant protein, fiber, enzymes, chlorophyll (green leaf pigment), and many other compounds. When a plant becomes deficient in nitrogen, it breaks down chlorophyll and other compounds in its older leaves to recover nitrogen, which it reuses for new growth. This loss of chlorophyll causes the older leaves to turn yellow. Soils that are low in organic matter, and sandy, readily leached soils are frequently deficient in nitrogen. These kinds of soils, in particular, need to be supplemented with fertilizers. Poor drainage, cold (50°F and below), and acidity or alkalinity can also cause soil nitrogen to become less available for plant use.

SOLUTION: Spray the foliage with Ra-Pid-Gro Plant Food for a quick response. Fertilize plants with ORTHO Citrus & Avocado Food as directed on the label. For more information about fertilizers, see page 910.

Iron deficiency on orange leaves.

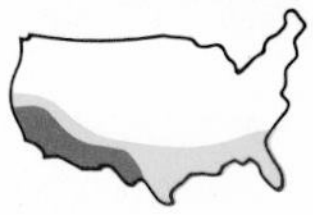

PROBLEM: Some of the leaves turn pale green or yellow. The newest leaves (those at the tips of the branches) are most severely affected. Except in extreme cases, the veins of affected leaves remain green. In extreme cases, the newest leaves are small and all-white or yellow. Older leaves may remain green.

ANALYSIS: Iron deficiency

Citrus trees frequently suffer from deficiences of iron and other minor nutrients such as manganese and zinc, elements essential to normal plant growth and development. Deficiencies can occur when one or more of these elements are depleted in the soil. Often these minor nutrients are present in the soil but alkaline (pH 7.5 and higher) or wet soil conditions cause them to form compounds that cannot be used by the tree. An alkaline condition can result from overliming, or from lime leached from cement or brick. Regions where soil is derived from limestone, and those with low rainfall, usually have alkaline soils. Some citrus trees turn yellow naturally in cold weather. However, if iron is available the foliage will turn green again when the weather warms.

SOLUTION: Apply ORTHO Citrus & Avocado Food to the soil around the plants to correct the deficiency of minor nutrients. Improve soil drainage (see page 907).

CITRUS

Greasy spot.

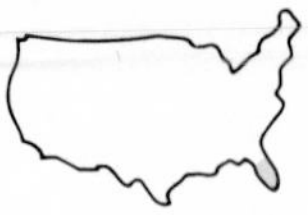

PROBLEM: Yellowish blistered spots develop on the undersides of leaves. These spots become orange and finally a greasy black or brown. Heavily infected leaves fall from the tree prematurely, especially in the fall and winter. On fruit, tiny pitted areas may develop between the oil glands in the peel, causing an unsightly blemish, but fruit quality is not affected.

ANALYSIS: Greasy spot
This disease is caused by a fungus (*Cercospora citri-grisea*) that attacks many types of citrus. Fungi that have spent the winter in fallen, infected leaves begin releasing spores in the spring. The spores infect the lower surface of the leaves; infection peaks in June and July. Fungus spores also invade fruit skin, causing pitting between the oil glands.

SOLUTION: Pick up and remove fallen leaves to reduce sources of new spores. Apply a fungicide containing *basic copper sulfate* or *benomyl* in June or July. A second spray may have to be applied in August or September to protect late summer growth. To slow down infection, keep trees as dry as possible, especially in early summer.

Tristeza.

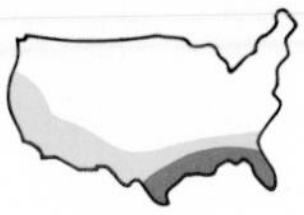

PROBLEM: Leaves are ash-colored, bronze, or yellowing, and often curl upward around the midrib. New growth is sparse. Growth has been slow, and some twigs and branches die. Or the tree may suddenly die within several weeks or months, leaving the foliage attached. The upper portion of the bud union often bulges over the lower rootstock portion. When small patches of bark along the rootstock area of the bud union are removed, tiny pinholes can frequently be seen with the aid of a hand lens dotting the inner surface of the patches.

ANALYSIS: Tristeza
This plant disease, also known as *quick decline*, is caused by a virus that affects the rootstocks of citrus plants. Aphids spread the virus to trees grafted onto susceptible rootstocks. Orange and grapefruit trees grafted onto *sour orange* rootstocks are especially susceptible to this disease. The virus attacks the food-conducting vessels in the rootstock bark, impeding the flow of nutrients, causing the starvation and death of the root system. Trees often live for several years after they have been infected, although continuing to decline in vigor and fruit yield. Sometimes trees die rapidly after infection, especially during periods of drought.

SOLUTION: There is no cure for this disease. Remove severely infected trees. Purchase plants with rootstocks tolerant to tristeza.

Rootstock varieties tolerant to tristeza: Mandarin Orange, Rangpur Lime, Sweet Orange, and Trifoliate Orange.

Psorosis.

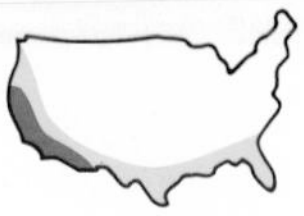

PROBLEM: Rough flaky or scaly lesions develop on the trunk or main branches of mature trees. Gummy deposits may form on the bark as the disease progresses. Greenish yellow or clear flecks or streaks usually appear on the young leaves. Severely infected fruit and foliage may have pale blotches or sunken, circular spots or rings.

ANALYSIS: Psorosis
This plant disease, which is caused by a virus, is also known in California as *scaly bark*, a name that, in Florida, is used for a different disease. Psorosis is a serious problem on orange, grapefruit, and tangerine, and can affect all citrus trees. This virus is spread by grafting infected citrus plant tissue (budwood) to healthy plants. As the disease develops the tree weakens, and twigs and limbs may die.

SOLUTION: No cure is known. Prune out diseased branches. If the lesions on the trunk are still small (not more than 3 to 4 inches across), scrape deeply enough to remove all diseased bark and wood layers. Also scrape clean an area of outer bark to about 5 inches out from the lesion. Wipe the treated area with rubbing alcohol, and seal with ORTHO Pruning Sealer. Disinfect tools with rubbing alcohol. If you are planting new trees, ask for stock registered as being free of the disease.

Brown rot gummosis.

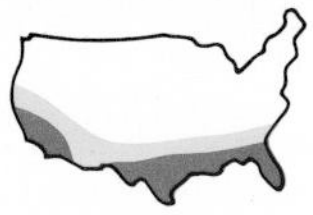

PROBLEM: Firm brownish patches of bark appear at the base of the trunk. Often a thick amber gum oozes from the infected area. The bark eventually dries, cracks, and weathers away, leaving a dark sunken canker. Some of the maturing fruit may be brown and decaying. The foliage may turn yellow and die.

ANALYSIS: Brown rot gummosis
This plant disease, also known as *foot rot* or *collar rot*, is caused by a soil-inhabiting fungus (*Phytophthora* species). The fungus thrives in heavy, wet soils. Infection occurs when spores are splashed to the trunk, penetrating the bark directly or through wounds. As the canker develops, the branches above the infected trunk may start to die. Fruit infection can occur when spores are splashed to the developing fruit. (For information about *brown rot*, see page 621.) Sometimes cankers heal over by themselves, but often they continue to spread, causing a loss in vigor and fruit production, and eventually killing the tree.

SOLUTION: Do not let water settle around the base of the tree. Gently remove the soil from around the trunk until the main lateral roots are just barely covered. Small trunk lesions may be removed by cutting away the diseased bark plus an additional surrounding ½ inch of the healthy bark. Spray around the base of the trunk with a fungicide containing *basic copper sulfate*. When planting new trees, purchase plants that are grafted onto phytophthora-resistant rootstocks such as *Trifoliate orange* and *Troyer citrange*.

Cold-damaged Valencia oranges.

Cold damage.

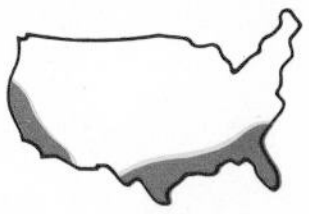

PROBLEM: The tree has been exposed to freezing temperatures. Tender shoots may blacken and die; older foliage often turns yellowish brown, leathery, and eventually withers and falls. The fruit rind may be scarred with brown or green sunken lesions. Or, even though the fruit rind appears normal, when the fruit is cut open, the flesh is dry. Severely damaged trees suffer twig and branch dieback. The bark along the branches or trunk may split open.

ANALYSIS: Cold damage
Citrus plants are frost-tender, and are easily damaged by temperatures below 32°F. Although many citrus plants can recover from a light frost, they cannot tolerate long periods of freezing weather. Damage to fruit occurs when the juice-filled cells freeze and rupture. The released fluid evaporates through the rind, leaving the flesh dry and pulpy. In addition to causing leaf and twig dieback, temperatures of 20°F and lower promote bark splitting, which may not become apparent for several weeks or months.

SOLUTION: Don't prune back damaged branches immediately. If there is still danger of frost, drive four stakes into the ground around the tree, and cover the tree with fabric, cardboard, or plastic. Remove this cover when the weather warms up. The trunks and main limbs of young trees may be protected by wrapping them with corn stalks, palm fronds, or fiberglass building insulation. Do not shade the foliage. Keep the soil moist during a freeze but be careful not to overwater. Limit fertilizer to a minimum. Damaged fruit can be removed immediately following the freeze. Always wait for new growth to appear before pruning. As soon as the danger of frost is past, you can prune blackened shoots and withered foliage. If the tree has suffered serious injury, it may take as long as 6 months before you will be able to determine the extent of the damage to the trunk and main limbs. You can then prune out the dead wood. For more information on pruning, see ORTHO's book *All About Pruning*.

FIG

ADAPTATION: See the variety chart on page 1003.

SOIL: Any good, deep, well-drained soil. pH 5.5 to 8.0

FERTILIZER: Fertilize with ORTHO Evergreen, Tree & Shrub Food according to label directions.

WATER:
How much: Apply enough water to wet the soil 3 to 4 feet deep. To determine the proper amount of water for your soil type, see page 912.
How often: Water when the soil 6 inches below the surface is just barely moist.

PRUNING: Lightly thin out branches, and head back long shoots to maintain tree vigor and shape during the dormant season. Remove weak, diseased, dead, or crossing twigs and branches.

HARVEST: Harvest figs when they have fully ripened. They are ripe when the fruits bend over at the neck, and the flesh is soft. Remove the fruit with the stem still attached. If you find the milky sap irritating, wear gloves and protective clothing when picking figs.

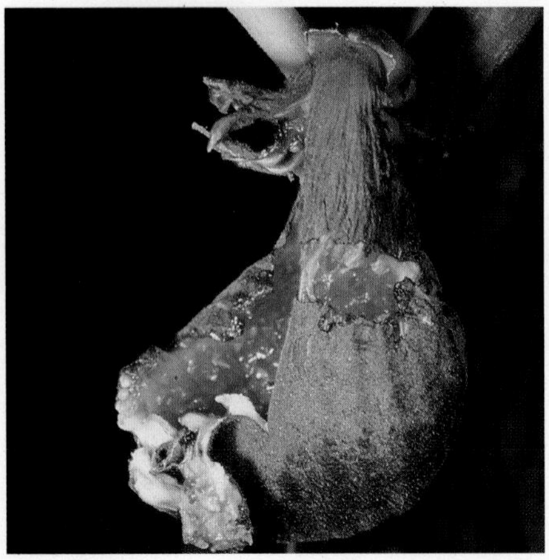

Bird damage to mission fig.

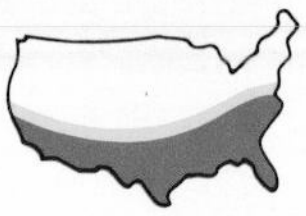

PROBLEM: Ripened figs have holes in them and may be partially eaten. They may have been knocked to the ground. Birds may be seen feeding on ripening figs.

ANALYSIS: Bird damage
Some birds feed heavily on ripening figs. When the fruit is fully ripe, birds peck at the soft flesh, leaving holes in the fruit. The wounded figs may decay, becoming inedible.

SOLUTION: You can save many of your figs by harvesting daily. Check the tree every morning, and harvest those figs that have ripened. Nets thrown over the tree are also effective in reducing bird damage. Nets may be purchased at your local nursery or hardware store. For more information about birds, see page 899.

Souring.

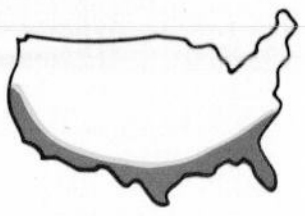

PROBLEM: A pink, sticky fluid may drip from the tiny hole ("eye") at the end of the ripening fig. The fruit is soft and mushy. When cut open, an infected fig has a strong fermented or alcoholic odor.

ANALYSIS: Souring
This plant disease is caused by various types of yeast. The yeasts that cause souring are spread by insects (including the dried fruit beetle and the vinegar fly). The insects enter the fig through the eye. If the fig is infected, the insects become contaminated with yeast cells while crawling around inside the fig. They can then infect healthy figs. The dark, moist conditions inside the ripening fig provide an ideal environment for the rapid decay and fermentation of the fruit.

SOLUTION: There is no chemical control for this disease. Pick off and destroy infected figs. Plant closed-eye fig varieties.

Fig varieties with small or closed eyes: Brown Turkey, Celeste, Green Ischia, and Mission.

Rust.

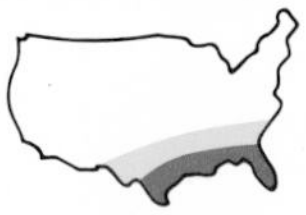

PROBLEM: Rust-colored, raised spots appear on the undersides of the leaves. Opposite these spots, on the upper surfaces of the leaves, are dark brown, smooth spots. Infected leaves turn yellow and die prematurely. Fruit yields may be reduced.

ANALYSIS: Rust

This plant disease is caused by a fungus (*Cerotelium fici*) that infects figs and several other closely related plants. The fungi spend the winter as spores on the bark or in plant debris. Infection starts in the spring as soon as the tree begins growing. The spores are spread to healthy leaves by wind and splashing water. They germinate on wet foliage, causing spotting and eventually premature leaf drop. Although rust infects the leaves rather than the fruit, premature leaf drop may weaken the tree after several years, causing a reduction in fruit yields.

SOLUTION: Spray the tree with a fungicide containing *basic copper sulfate.* Repeat the spray every 3 to 4 weeks throughout the growing season. Spray thoroughly, covering both the upper and lower surfaces of the leaves.

Fig mosaic.

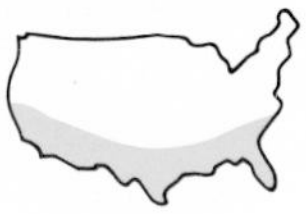

PROBLEM: Leaves are mottled yellow, and may have translucent areas. Often, the fruit is spotted yellow. The leaves may be stunted, and the foliage and fruit may drop prematurely.

ANALYSIS: Fig mosaic

This plant disease is caused by a virus. Mosaic rarely causes a plant to die, but can weaken it extensively, greatly reducing the fruit yield. The virus may be spread by microscopic fig mites (*Eriophyes fici*), which feed on diseased figs and transfer the virus to healthy trees at later feedings. The virus is also spread by infected cuttings.

SOLUTION: The virus cannot be chemically controlled. Reduce the numbers of fig mites by applying ORTHO Volck Oil Spray in the winter. If you are planting new trees, select healthy stock from a reliable nursery. For information on selecting healthy nursery plants, see page 924.

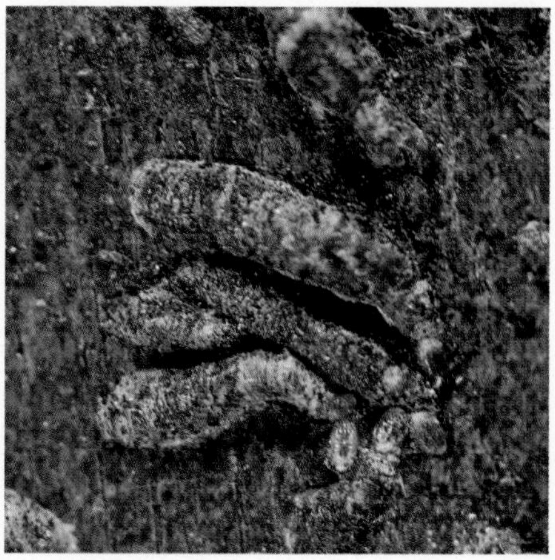

Fig scale (twice life size).

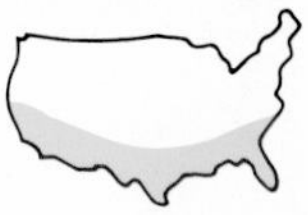

PROBLEM: The stems or undersides of the leaves are covered with brownish crusty bumps or thick, white, waxy bumps, or clusters of somewhat flattened yellowish, gray, or brownish scaly bumps. The bumps can be scraped or picked off; the undersides are usually soft. Leaves turn yellow and may drop. In some cases, a shiny or sticky substance coats the leaves. A black sooty mold often grows on the sticky substance.

ANALYSIS: Scales

Several different types of scale insects infest figs. They lay their eggs on leaves or bark, and in spring to midsummer the young scales, called *crawlers*, settle on leaves and twigs. These small (1/10 inch), soft-bodied young feed by sucking sap from the plant. The legs usually atrophy, and a hard, crusty or waxy shell develops over the body. The mature female scales lay their eggs underneath their shell. Some species of scales infesting figs are unable to digest fully all the sugar in the plant sap and excrete the excess in a fluid called honeydew, which often drops onto the leaves below. A sooty mold fungus may develop on the honeydew, causing the fig leaves to appear black and dirty. For more information about scales, see page 876.

SOLUTION: Spray with an insecticide containing *malathion* in early to midsummer when the young crawlers are active. The following late winter or early spring, before new growth begins, spray the trunk and branches with ORTHO Volck Oil Spray to control overwintering insects.

FILBERT (HAZELNUT)

ADAPTATION AND POLLINATION: Filberts grow well in the Pacific Northwest, the East, and the Southeast. Plant at least two different cultivars to ensure good nut production.

SOIL: Any good, deep, well-drained soil. pH 5.5 to 7.5

FERTILIZER: Fertilize with ORTHO Evergreen, Tree & Shrub Food according to label directions.

WATER:

How much: Apply enough water to wet the soil 3 to 4 feet deep. To determine the proper amount of water for your soil type, see page 912.

How often: Water when the soil 6 inches below the surface is just barely moist.

PRUNING: Filberts form on the current season's growth. Prune lightly, removing weak, diseased, or dead twigs and branches. To encourage heavy nut production, prune off half of the new growth every second or third year.

HARVEST: In the fall, the husks will open up, and the nuts will fall to the ground. Remove nuts from the ground as soon as possible, or squirrels and other animals will remove them first.

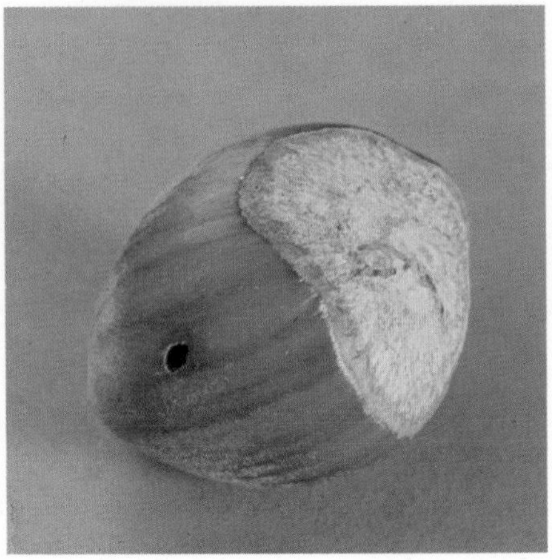

Filbertworm hole.

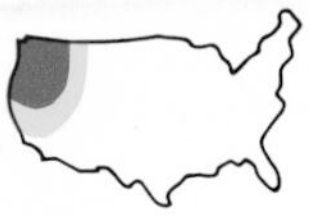

PROBLEM: The kernel of the nut is blackened and destroyed. There may be a hole in the shell, and winding trails at the flattened base of the nut. Or amber-headed white worms, up to ½ inch long, may be feeding in the nuts.

ANALYSIS: Filbertworm
(*Melissopus latiferreanus*)
The larvae of these reddish brown moths infest many different types of nut trees, including chestnuts, beechnuts, and almonds, but they are most damaging to filberts. The adult moths lay their eggs on or near the developing nuts during the spring and summer. The larvae that hatch from these eggs crawl down between the shell and the husk, then tunnel into the husk until they reach the base of the nut. They then bore up into the developing kernel, where they feed for several weeks. After maturing, the larvae exit through holes they make in the shells. They drop to the ground, spin cocoons, and pupate. Adult moths may either emerge later in the summer or remain in the cocoons until the following spring or summer.

SOLUTION: Spray the trees with an insecticide containing *carbaryl* (SEVIN®) when the moths emerge in the spring. Repeat the spray 2 weeks later. Contact your County Extension Office to find out the dates of moth emergence in your area. (For a list of Extension Offices, see page 1029.) In the fall, clean up debris around the trees to reduce the number of overwintering cocoons.

Filbert leafroller larvae (twice life size).

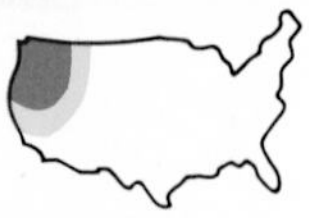

PROBLEM: Irregular holes appear in the leaves and buds. Some of the leaves are rolled and held together with a web. Young buds and nuts are often enclosed within the rolled leaves. When these rolled leaves are peeled open, pale green worms up to ¾ inch long with brown heads are found inside. Some of the maturing nuts may be damaged.

ANALYSIS: Filbert leafroller
(*Archips rosanys*)
These worms, also known as *European leafrollers*, are the larvae of brown moths. They infest many different ornamental trees. The moths lay their eggs on branches or twigs in June or July. The eggs hatch the following spring, and the emerging larvae feed on the buds and developing foliage. Leafrollers often wrap leaves around ripening nuts and tender buds, then feed inside. After about a month, the mature larvae pupate within rolled leaves to emerge later as moths that lay the eggs for a second generation of leafrollers that summer. Heavy leafroller infestations may cause tree stunting and sometimes defoliation.

SOLUTION: If practical, pick off and destroy rolled leaves to reduce the numbers of moths that will emerge later in the season. Next spring, kill the young larvae by spraying with ORTHO Fruit & Vegetable Insect Control or *carbaryl* (SEVIN®) when the filbert leaves are about ¾ to 1 inch long.

Bacterial blight.

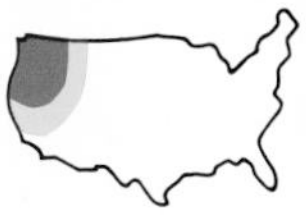

PROBLEM: Small angular or irregular spots develop on the leaves. Initially these spots are yellow-green, and appear water-soaked. They later turn reddish brown. Dark green lesions on the stems eventually turn reddish brown. Stems and twigs may die back. Often the leaves wither, die, and cling to the dead stems. There may be sunken lesions (cankers) on the branches and trunk. Young trees (up to 4 years old) may die.

ANALYSIS: Bacterial blight
This plant disease is caused by a bacterium (*Xanthomonas corylina*) that is common on filberts in the Northwest. The bacteria are spread by splashing rain and contaminated pruning tools. They may attack leaves and buds directly, or penetrate twigs and stems through wounds. As the infection progresses down into the branches and trunk, cankers may form that encircle and kill the branches and trunks of young trees. Trees weakened by sunburn, winter injury, and poor growing conditions are most susceptible to infection. Bacterial blight is most severe after heavy fall rains.

SOLUTION: Spray trees with *tribasic copper sulfate* in the fall before rains begin. In late winter, prune out infected twigs and branches, sterilizing pruning tools with rubbing alcohol between cuts.

HICKORY

ADAPTATION AND POLLINATION: Hickories grow throughout the eastern half of the United States. Plant several varieties to assure nut production.

SOIL: Any good, deep, well-drained soil. pH 5.5 to 8.0

FERTILIZER: Fertilize with ORTHO Evergreen, Tree & Shrub Food according to label directions.

WATER:
How much: Apply enough water to wet the soil 5 to 6 feet deep. To determine the proper amount of water for your soil type, see page 912.
How often: Water when the soil 6 inches below the surface is just barely moist.

PRUNING: Nuts form on the current season's growth. Prune hickories lightly, removing weak, diseased, or dead twigs and branches.

HARVEST: Harvest the nuts in the fall by gently knocking the tree with a rubber mallet or cloth-covered pole.

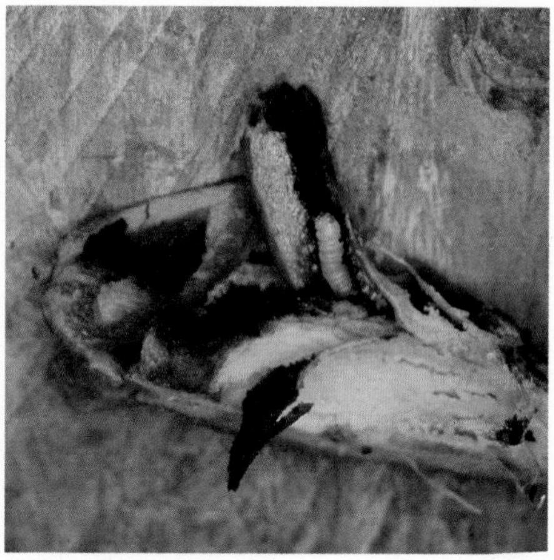

Hickory shuckworm (life size).

PROBLEM: Cream-colored worms up to 3/8 inch long are feeding in the immature nuts, many of which fall to the ground prematurely. Later in the season, after the shells have hardened, the worms may be found in the green shucks.

ANALYSIS: Hickory shuckworm
(*Laspeyresia caryana*)
These worms, the larvae of small brown moths, are also known as *pecan shuckworms*. They are pests of hickory and pecan trees wherever they are grown. The larvae spend the winter in shucks on the ground or in the tree. The shuckworms pupate and emerge as adult moths in the spring to lay their eggs on hickory leaves and nuts. The larvae that hatch from these eggs tunnel into the soft green hickory nut shells and feed on the developing kernels. Infested nuts usually drop. Later in the season, after the nut shells have hardened, the larvae tunnel into the shucks. Their feeding damage interferes with the proper development of the kernels. Shuckworm damage may occur throughout the spring and summer.

SOLUTION: Chemical controls are not practical for the home gardener. Clean up and destroy all dropped nuts and shucks to eliminate many of the overwintering larvae. If infestations are severe, contact a professional tree spraying company.

Bark beetles and larvae (twice life size).

PROBLEM: Leaves turn brown and wilt, and some of the twigs and branches may die. Severely infested trees sometimes defoliate prematurely. Dark brown beetles $\frac{1}{8}$ to $\frac{1}{4}$ inch long may be seen on the buds, leaf stalks, and bark. When sliced open, an infested branch reveals tunnels running through the sapwood. There may be slightly curved, white grubs, up to $\frac{1}{4}$ inch long, in the tunnels. There are usually small perforations in the bark of the branches and trunk.

ANALYSIS: Hickory bark beetle
(*Scolytus quadrispinosus*)
These beetles are pests of all the hickory species, including pecans. The adult beetles that appear in early summer feed at the bases of tender buds, leaf stalks, and sometimes the developing nuts. The female beetles bore down through the twigs into the branches, forming tunnels in which they lay their eggs. The grubs that hatch from these eggs tunnel into the inner wood. These tunnels interfere with the flow of water and nutrients through the tree, and may result in branch or tree death. The grubs pupate in their tunnels, then exit through the bark as adult beetles either later in the summer or the following spring. Weakened, diseased, and dying trees and branches are most susceptible to beetle infestation.

SOLUTION: Spray infested trees with an insecticide containing *carbaryl* (SEVIN®) or *methoxychlor* to kill the exposed beetles. During the dormant season, remove and destroy infested branches. Keep the tree healthy by watering and fertilizing it properly.

MANGO

ADAPTATION: Zone 10. To determine your climate zone, see the map on page 1020.

SOIL: Any good, deep, well-drained soil. pH 5.5 to 7.5

FERTILIZER: Fertilize with ORTHO Evergreen, Tree & Shrub Food according to label directions.

WATER:
How much: Apply enough water to wet the soil 2 to 3 feet deep. To determine the proper amount of water for your soil, see page 912.
How often: Water when the soil 6 inches below the surface is just barely moist.

PRUNING: Mangoes grow on shoots that form on last year's wood. Prune trees lightly, removing weak, diseased, or dead twigs and branches.

HARVEST: Harvest when the fruits have turned yellow or reddish, and the flesh yields slightly when squeezed. Pick the fruit by twisting it sideways or upward sharply to snap the stem, or clip the fruit off with pruning shears, leaving a small piece of stem attached to the fruit. The milky mango stem sap can cause dermatitis in some people.

Scab.

PROBLEM: Fruits have grayish to grayish brown spots that become covered with cracked, fissured, corky tissue as the spots and fruit enlarge. Velvety, grayish brown spore masses are present on fruit lesions during moist periods. Small ($\frac{1}{16}$ inch), brown to black angular spots may be present on the leaves, causing crinkling and distortion on new leaves and shotholes on mature leaves.

ANALYSIS: Scab
This plant disease is caused by a fungus (*Elsinoë mangiferae*) that infects young fruit, twigs, leaves, and blossom spikes. During the bloom period and throughout the warmer months, infection takes place from spores on previously infected areas. Spores may be produced on fruit until it reaches maturity.

SOLUTION: Spray the tree with a fungicide containing *basic copper sulfate.* Use a spreader-sticker with the fungicide to enable it to coat plant parts more effectively. (For more information on spreader-stickers, see page 922.) Apply sprays at the following times:
1. Weekly from the first appearance of flower spikes until all fruit have set.
2. Monthly from the time fruit sets until mid-May for early varieties and mid-June for late varieties.

Anthracnose. *Insert:* Infected fruit.

PROBLEM: Minute black or brown angular or irregular spots appear on the leaves, flowers, and fruit. As the spots enlarge, dead areas are formed on leaves, flowers may be killed, and fruit may have large infected areas with surface cracks extending into the flesh. Affected areas decay rapidly. The most serious problems occur in the late winter to summer on leaves, late winter to spring on flowers, and near or at the time of maturity on fruit.

ANALYSIS: Anthracnose
This plant disease is caused by a fungus (*Colletotrichum gloeosporioides*) that attacks mango leaves, flowers, and fruit. Spores from infections on older leaves infect flowers, new leaves, and fruit. Periods of wet, rainy weather favor disease development. On fruit, the highest fungus activity occurs when the fruit begins to soften near maturity.

SOLUTION: Spray the tree with a fungicide containing *basic copper sulfate*. Use a spreader-sticker with the fungicide to enable it to coat plant parts more effectively. (For more information on spreader-stickers, see page 922.) Apply sprays at the following times:
1. Weekly from the first appearance of flower spikes until all fruit have set.
2. Monthly from the time fruit sets until mid-May for early varieties and mid-June for late varieties.

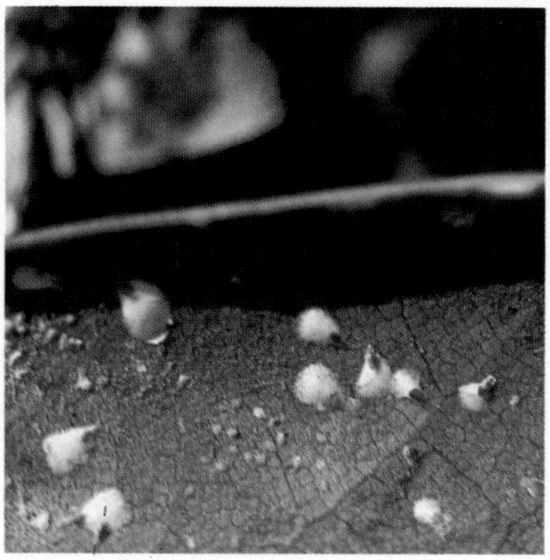

False oleander scale (life size).

PROBLEM: Stems and leaves are covered with brownish crusty bumps or clusters of somewhat flattened reddish, white, or brownish scaly bumps. The bumps can be scraped or picked off; the undersides are usually soft. Leaves turn yellow and may drop. A shiny or sticky substance may coat the leaves. A black sooty mold often grows on the sticky substance. Ants may be present. Branches are killed by heavy infestations.

ANALYSIS: Scales
Members of this diverse group of insects are damaging to many trees. Scales lay their eggs in spring to midsummer. The young scales, called *crawlers*, settle on leaves and twigs. The small ($\frac{1}{10}$ inch), soft-bodied young feed by sucking sap from the plant. The legs usually atrophy and a shell develops over the body. Some species of scales are unable to digest fully all the sugar in the plant sap, and excrete the excess in a fluid called honeydew. A sooty mold fungus may develop on the honeydew, causing the mango leaves to appear black and dirty. Ants feed on this sticky substance, and are often present where scales cluster. For more information about scales, see page 876.

SOLUTION: Spray trees with a combination of ORTHO Volck Oil Spray and ORTHO Malathion 50 Insect Spray at the rate of 1 tablespoon of each per gallon of water. Repeat sprays as needed up to 2 days before harvest.

PEACH AND NECTARINE

ADAPTATION AND POLLINATION: See the variety chart on page 1022.

SOIL: Any good, deep, well-drained soil. pH 5.5 to 7.5

FERTILIZER: Fertilize with ORTHO Evergreen, Tree & Shrub Food according to label directions.

WATER:
How much: Apply enough water to wet the soil 3 to 4 feet deep. To determine the proper amount of water for your soil type, see page 912.
How often: Water when the soil 6 inches below the surface is just barely moist.

PRUNING: Peaches and nectarines bear on 1-year-old wood. Prune half of last year's growth annually. Thin out weak, crossing, or dead twigs and branches. Thin fruits to 6 inches apart when they are thumbnail size.

HARVEST: Harvest when the fruits are fully colored and slightly soft. With a ripe peach or nectarine, the stem will easily separate from the branch when the fruit is gently lifted.

PEACH AND NECTARINE

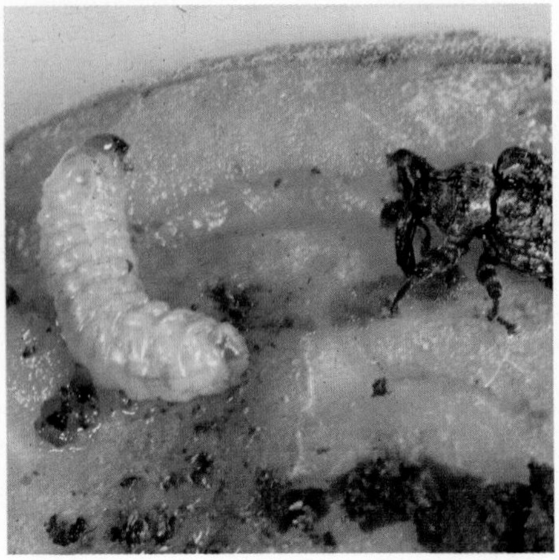

Plum curculio and larva (4 times life size).

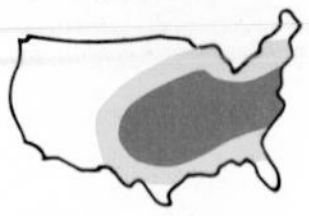

PROBLEM: The ripening fruit is misshapen and rotten, and often drops prematurely. Holes about ⅛ inch in diameter and deep, crescent-shaped scars appear on the fruit. When cut open, damaged fruits may be found to contain crescent-shaped yellow-gray grubs with brown heads.

ANALYSIS: Plum curculio
(*Conotrachelus nenuphar*)
These insects, found east of the Rocky Mountains, attack stone fruits, apples, and pears. The adults are brown beetles with long, curved snouts. They hibernate in debris and other protected places during the winter. The beetles emerge in the spring when new growth starts, and begin feeding on young leaves, blossoms, and developing fruit. After 5 to 6 weeks, the female beetles start to lay their eggs in the young fruit, cutting distinctive, crescent-shaped slits into the peaches and nectarines. The grubs that hatch from the eggs feed for several weeks in the fruit. The infested fruits usually drop to the ground. The grubs eventually leave the fruit and bore into the soil, where they pupate. The emerging beetles feed on fruit for a few weeks, and then go into hibernation. In the South, they lay eggs, producing a second generation of grubs in late summer.

SOLUTION: There is nothing you can do to kill the grubs inside the fruit. Spray with ORTHO Home Orchard Spray or ORTHO Malathion 50 Insect Spray to kill beetles that are feeding on fruit or laying eggs. Pick up and destroy all fallen fruit. Next spring, spray the trees when the petals are falling from the blossoms. Repeat applications according to directions on the label.

Scab.

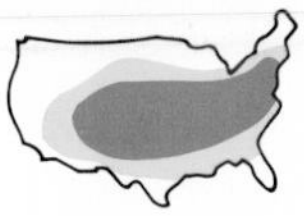

PROBLEM: Small, olive-green spots appear on the half-grown fruit. These spots are generally centered around the stem end of the peach or nectarine. The spots eventually turn brown and velvety. The fruit is often dwarfed, deformed, or cracked. There are usually small brown spots and holes in the leaves, and many twigs die.

ANALYSIS: Scab
This plant disease is caused by a fungus (*Cladosporium carpophilum*) that attacks all the stone fruits. In the spring, spores are splashed and blown from lesions on the twigs to the developing foliage and fruit. The young fruit do not show scab lesions for at least a month after they are initially infected. Spores that are produced on the infected leaves, twigs, and fruit will continue to infect healthy peaches and nectarines throughout the growing season.

SOLUTION: It's too late to do anything about the spots on this year's fruit, but they are edible if peeled. Next year, spray with ORTHO Orthocide Garden Fungicide or ORTHO Home Orchard Spray when the petals have fallen from the blossoms. If scab is a serious problem in your area, continue to spray at intervals of 10 to 14 days until about a month before the fruits are harvested.

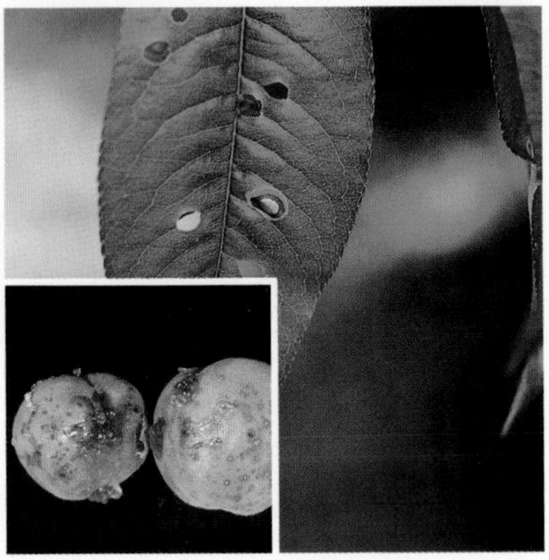

Shothole fungus. *Insert:* Infected fruit.

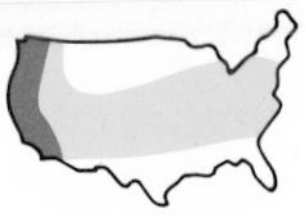

PROBLEM: Small purplish spots appear on the young twigs, leaves, and developing fruit in early spring, and eventually turn brown. These leaf spots often drop out, leaving shotholes in the leaf. Infected buds, shoots, and leaves may die. The spots on the maturing peaches turn scablike, drop off, and leave rough, corky lesions.

ANALYSIS: Shothole fungus
This plant disease, also called *coryneum blight* and *peach blight*, is caused by a fungus (*Coryneum carpophilum*) that attacks peaches, nectarines, apricots, and almonds. The fungus spends the winter in lesions on the twigs and buds. In the spring, the spores are splashed by rain to the developing buds, leaves, and fruit, causing spotting and tissue death. Infection causes the leaf tissue to produce a layer of cells, which walls off the damaged area. The center of the spot then drops out. Severe infection may cause extensive twig and bud blighting, and possibly premature defoliation, reducing the peach and nectarine yield. The disease is favored by wet spring weather.

SOLUTION: To prevent twig and leaf bud infection, spray the tree with ORTHO Orthorix Spray, ORTHO Dormant Disease Control, or *chlorothalonil* (DACONIL 2787®) in the fall immediately after the leaves have dropped. To reduce or prevent fruit infection, apply a fungicide containing *chlorothalonil* (DACONIL 2787®) 1 to 2 weeks after petal fall.

Bacterial leaf spot.

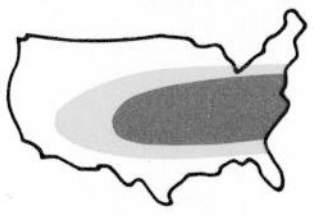

PROBLEM: Brown or black angular spots appear on leaves. The centers of the spots often fall out. The tips of the leaves may die, and eventually the leaves turn yellow and drop. The surface of the fruit may be dotted with brown to black spots, and become pitted and cracked. Sunken lesions may form on the twigs. Severely infected trees may drop all their leaves.

ANALYSIS: Bacterial leaf spot
This plant disease is caused by a bacterium (*Xanthomonas pruni*) that also attacks apricots and plums. This is one of the more destructive diseases of stone fruit east of the Rocky Mountains. In the spring, bacteria ooze from lesions on the twigs, to be carried by splashing rain to the young leaves, shoots, and developing fruits. Frequent rainfall favors the infection. Trees that defoliate early in the summer are weakened, and produce small crops of peaches and nectarines of poor quality.

SOLUTION: There is no adequate control for this disease. Spraying with *basic copper sulfate* when the flower buds open in the spring may help suppress the disease, but will not eliminate it. When planting new trees, use resistant varieties.

Peach variety resistance to bacterial leaf spot:
Susceptible: Blake, Elberta, and Rio-Oso-Gem.
Fairly resistant: Lizzie, Redhaven, Redskin, and Sunhaven.
Resistant: Belle of Georgia, Early-Free-Red, and Hiley.

Leaf curl on peach.

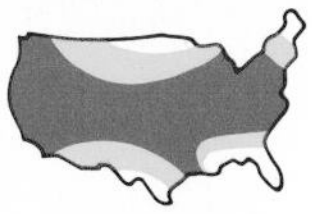

PROBLEM: Leaves are puckered, thickened, and curled from the time they first appear in the spring. Emerging shoots are swollen and stunted. Initially the infected foliage is red or orange, but it later turns pale green to yellow. As the season progresses, a grayish white powdery material develops on the leaves. Eventually these leaves shrivel and drop. Fruiting is poor, and the fruit that is present may be covered with raised, wrinkled, irregular lesions.

ANALYSIS: Leaf curl
This plant disease is caused by a fungus (*Taphrina deformans*) that attacks peaches and nectarines wherever they are grown. Infection occurs as soon as the buds begin to open in the spring. Fungal spores are splashed from the bark to the buds by spring rains. Later in the season, the infected leaves develop a grayish white covering of spores that are blown onto the bark. Infected trees are greatly weakened by the premature loss of foliage in early summer. Leaf curl is most severe when spring weather is cool and wet.

SOLUTION: Infected leaves cannot be cured. To prevent the recurrence of the disease next year, spray the trees with ORTHO ORTHORIX Spray, ORTHO Dormant Disease Control, or *chlorothalonil* (DACONIL 2787®) in the fall immediately after the leaves have dropped or in the spring before the buds begin to swell, but before they open. If the disease has been severe, spray in both fall and spring.

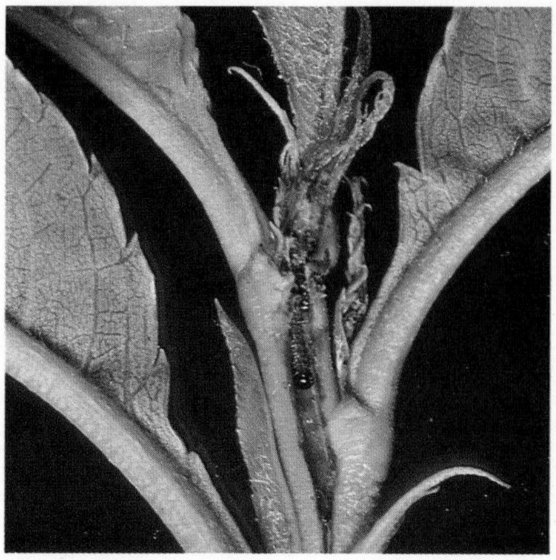

Peach twig borer (life size).

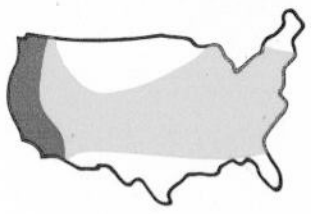

PROBLEM: New growth at the tips of the twigs wilts and dies. When affected twigs are sliced open lengthwise, worms about ½ inch long are discovered inside. The reddish brown color of these worms distinguishes them from oriental fruit moth worms, which cause similar damage. Later in the season, some of the maturing fruits also contain these worms. During the summer, cocoons may be attached to the branches or tree crotches.

ANALYSIS: Peach twig borer
(*Anarsia lineatella*)
This borer attacks all of the stone fruits, and is particularly damaging on the Pacific Coast. The young larvae hibernate during the winter in silk-lined burrows under loose bark or in other protected places on the tree. When the tree starts to bloom in the spring, the larvae bore into young buds and shoots. They feed on the tender twigs, killing twigs and leaves. When mature, they leave the twigs and pupate in cocoons attached to branches. After several weeks, gray moths emerge and lay their eggs on the twigs, leaves, and fruit. Egg laying and larval damage can occur all through the growing season. Later in the summer, larvae feed almost exclusively on the maturing fruit. In addition to ruining the fruit, peach twig borers may cause abnormal branching patterns on young trees when large numbers of twigs are infested.

SOLUTION: Worms in the twigs and fruit cannot be killed with pesticides. To prevent future worm damage, kill the moths by spraying infested trees with ORTHO Home Orchard Spray. Next spring, spray again just before the blossoms open. Repeat the treatment 2 more times at intervals of 10 to 14 days.

PEACH AND NECTARINE

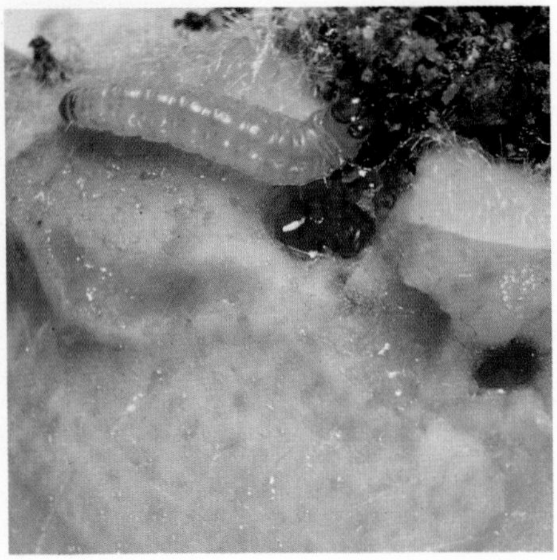

Oriental fruit moth larva (twice life size).

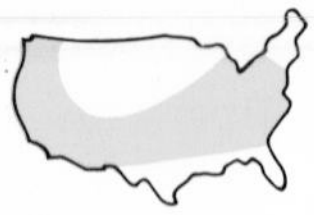

PROBLEM: New growth at the tips of the twigs wilts and dies. When affected twigs are sliced open lengthwise, worms about ½ inch long are found inside. The pinkish white color of these worms distinguishes them from peach twig borers, which cause similar damage. Later in the season, some of the maturing fruit also contain these worms. Often the peaches and nectarines have holes filled with a sticky gum.

ANALYSIS: Oriental fruit moth
(*Grapholitha molesta*)
The larvae of these night-flying moths damage stone fruits, apples, and pears. The larvae hibernate in cocoons on the tree bark or buried in crotches. In the spring they pupate, emerge as brown adult moths, and lay eggs on the young twigs, leaves, and fruit. The larvae bore into the young buds and shoots, killing twigs and leaves. When mature, they leave the twigs, spin cocoons, and pupate in the tree or in debris on the ground. After several weeks, moths emerge and lay eggs. Larval damage can occur all through the growing season. Later in the summer, the larvae feed almost exclusively on the maturing fruit. They leave gum-filled holes in the peaches and nectarines when they exit to pupate.

SOLUTION: Worms in the twigs and fruit cannot be killed with pesticides. To prevent future worm damage, kill the moths by spraying infested trees with ORTHO Home Orchard Spray or ORTHO Liquid Sevin. Next spring, spray again when the petals start to fall from the blossoms. Repeat the treatment 2 more times at intervals of 10 to 14 days.

Blighted shoots.

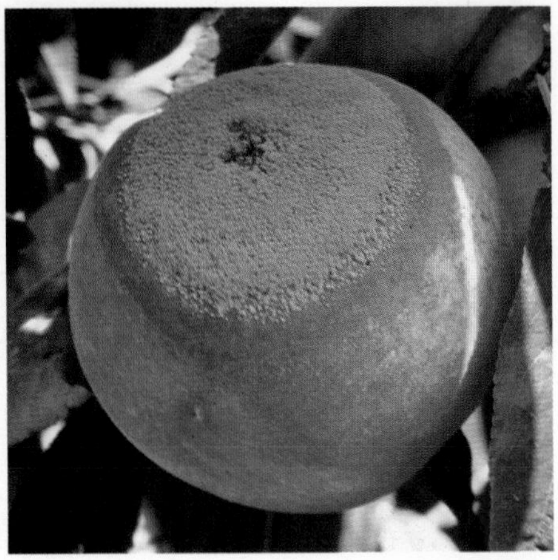

Fruit rot.

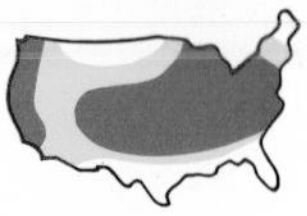

PROBLEM: Blossoms and young leaves decay, wilt, and turn brown during the first 2 weeks of the bloom period. The decayed blossoms may fail to drop, and hang on the tree throughout the growing season. In humid conditions, masses of gray spores may appear on the infected flower parts. There is often extensive twig dieback. Sunken lesions develop on the twigs and branches as the season progresses. These lesions usually exude a sticky ooze.

PROBLEM: Small circular brown spots appear on the young fruits. Later in the season, as the peaches or nectarines start to mature, these spots may enlarge to rot part or all of the fruit. During moist weather, the rotted fruits are covered with tufts of gray spores. When the infected peaches or nectarines are sliced open the flesh inside is found to be brown, firm, and fairly dry. Infected fruits either drop prematurely or dry out, turn dark brown, and remain on the tree past the normal harvest period. Healthy fruits may rot when they contact infected fruits in storage.

ANALYSIS: Brown rot
This plant disease, caused by either of two closely related fungi (*Monilinia laxa* or *M. fructicola*), is very destructive to all of the stone fruits. The fungi spend the winter in twig cankers or in rotted fruits (mummies) in the tree or on the ground. In the spring, spores are blown or splashed from cankers or mummies to the healthy flower buds. After penetrating and decaying the flowers, the fungus grows down into the twigs, producing brown, sunken cankers. During moist weather, a thick, gummy sap oozes from the lesions, and tufts of gray spores may form on the infected areas. Spores from cankers and infected blossoms or mummies are splashed and blown to the maturing fruit. Young peaches and nectarines are fairly resistant to infection, but maturing fruits are vulnerable. Brown rot develops most rapidly in mild, moist conditions.

SOLUTION: If there are still uninfected blossoms left on your tree, spray with ORTHO Home Orchard Spray, ORTHO Orthocide Garden Fungicide, or a fungicide containing *chlorothalonil* (DACONIL 2787®) or *triforine* (FUNGINEX®) to protect them from further infection. Repeat the spray 10 days later. To protect maturing peaches and nectarines from infection, spray them with ORTHO Home Orchard Spray or ORTHO Orthocide Garden Fungicide about 3 weeks before they are to be harvested. Remove and destroy all infected fruits and mummies. Prune out cankers and blighted twigs. Clean up and destroy all debris around the tree. Next spring, spray trees as the first flowers begin to open, and continue to spray according to label directions.

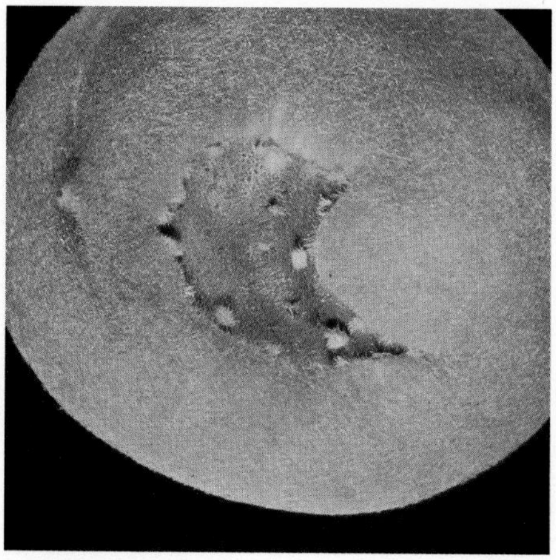

Catfacing on peach.

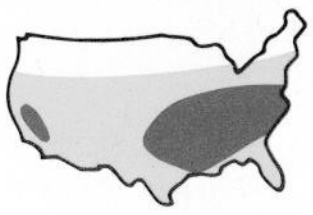

PROBLEM: Sunken, corky areas mar the fruit surface. Blossoms may drop without setting fruit. Many of the young fruits drop prematurely. Some of the developing leaves and twigs are deformed. Brown, green, or rust-colored bugs ¼ to ½ inch long may be seen feeding on the buds and fruit.

ANALYSIS: Catfacing
The sunken, corky "catface" disfigurations that appear on the fruit are usually caused by the tarnished plant bug (*Lygus lineolaris*) and various species of stinkbugs. The insects hibernate in vetch or other broadleafed weeds during the winter. When the trees start to bloom in the spring, these bugs feed on the young buds, blooms, and fruits, causing bud and fruit drop, twig malformation, and catfacing. Most of the damage occurs early in the season, although the bugs may occasionally feed on the fruits up until harvest. Hail or cold weather may also damage the tender blooms and fruit surfaces, causing catface injuries.

SOLUTION: To control plant bugs, spray with ORTHO Home Orchard Spray or ORTHO Malathion 50 Insect Spray when the buds turn pink. Repeat the spray when the petals have dropped from most of the blossoms and whenever bugs are seen in the trees. Next fall, clean up weeds and plant debris to eliminate hibernating locations for the overwintering bugs.

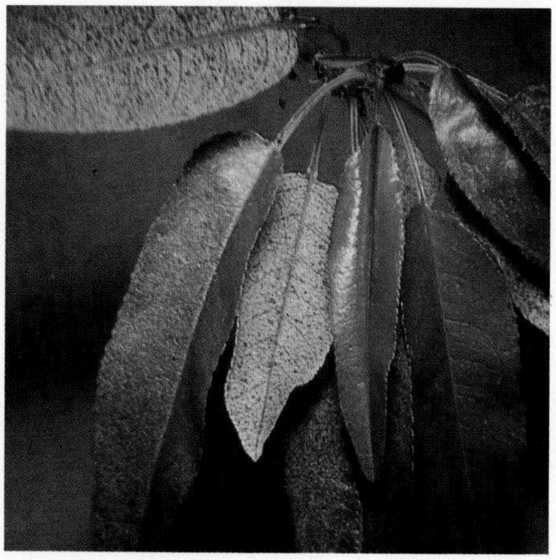

Spider mite damage.

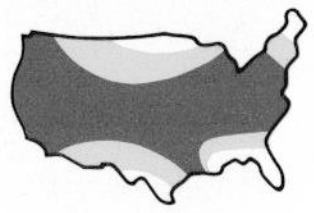

PROBLEM: Leaves are stippled, yellowing, and dirty. Leaves may dry out and drop. There may be webbing between leaves or on the lower surfaces of the leaves. To determine if the plant is infested with mites, hold a sheet of white paper underneath an affected leaf and tap the leaf sharply. Minute green, red, or yellow specks the size of pepper grains will drop to the paper and begin to crawl around. The pests are easily seen against the white background.

ANALYSIS: Mites
These pests, related to spiders, attack many garden and greenhouse plants. They cause damage by sucking sap from the undersides of the leaves. As a result of feeding, the green leaf pigment disappears, producing the stippled appearance. Mites are active throughout the growing season, but are favored by hot, dry weather (70°F and up). By midsummer, they build up to tremendous numbers. Severely infested trees may produce small, poor-quality fruits. For more information about mites, see page 887.

SOLUTION: Spray infested trees with ORTHO Home Orchard Spray or ORTHO Fruit & Vegetable Insect Control. Repeat the spray 2 more times at intervals of 7 to 10 days. Do not apply pesticides within 3 weeks of harvest.

Aphid damage.

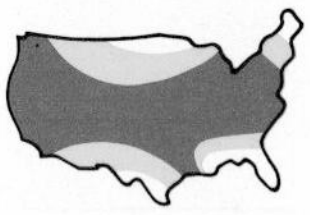

PROBLEM: New leaves are curled and twisted. Leaves may turn yellow and drop. The developing fruits may be small and misshapen. A shiny or sticky substance may coat the leaves. A black sooty mold often grows on the sticky substance. Tiny (⅛ inch) yellow, light green, or black soft-bodied insects cluster on the young shoots and undersides of the leaves. Ants may be present.

ANALYSIS: Aphids
Several species of aphids infest peaches and nectarines, including the green peach aphid (*Myzus persicae*). Aphids do little damage in small numbers. However, they are extremely prolific and populations can rapidly build up to damaging numbers during the growing season. Damage occurs when the aphid sucks the juices from the young peach and nectarine leaves. The aphid is unable to digest fully all the sugar in the sap, and excretes the excess in a fluid called honeydew, which often drops onto the leaves below. A sooty mold fungus may develop on the honeydew, causing the leaves to appear black and dirty. Ants feed on this sticky substance, and are often present where there is an aphid infestation.

SOLUTION: Spray with ORTHO Home Orchard Spray, ORTHO Malathion 50 Insect Spray, or ORTHO Fruit & Vegetable Insect Control as soon as the insects appear. Repeat the spray according to label directions if the tree becomes reinfested.

PEACH AND NECTARINE

Terrapin scale (4 times life size).

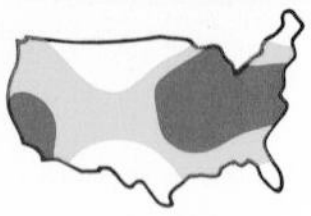

PROBLEM: Some of the leaves are pale green to yellow and may drop prematurely. The bark is encrusted with small (1/16 inch), hard, raised bumps that are often light gray to white, or dark brown with raised yellow centers. There may be severe limb dieback. The fruit may be mottled or spotted.

ANALYSIS: Scales

Although peaches and nectarines are attacked by many different species of scale insects, the two most common are *San Jose scale* (*Quadraspidiotus perniciosus*) and *white peach scale* (*Pseudaulacaspis pentagona*). The scales lay their eggs or bear live young in the spring. In late spring to midsummer the young scales, called *crawlers*, settle on leaves and twigs. These small (1/16 inch), soft-bodied young feed by sucking sap from the plant. Their legs usually atrophy, and a hard, crusty shell develops over the body. An uncontrolled infestation of scales may kill large branches after two or three seasons. For further information about scales, see page 876.

SOLUTION: During the dormant season, spray the trunk and branches with ORTHO Volck Oil Spray. The crawlers may be killed with ORTHO Malathion 50 Insect Spray or ORTHO Fruit & Vegetable Insect Control applied in the late spring.

Bacterial canker on peach.

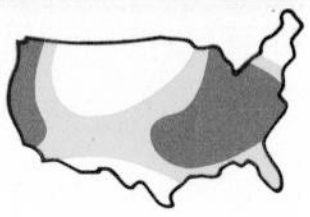

PROBLEM: Sunken elliptical lesions appear on the trunk or branches. Throughout the fall, winter, and spring a thick, sour-smelling, amber gum oozes from these lesions. In the spring, especially when the weather is excessively wet and cold, blossoms may turn brown and wither, and some of the leaf and flower buds die and become covered with gum. Individual branches may fail to produce foliage, or, as the season progresses, entire branches may die back. There may be angular holes in the leaves. Often, many shoots sprout from the rootstock.

ANALYSIS: Bacterial canker

This plant disease, also known as *bacterial gummosis* or *bacterial blast*, is caused by a bacterium (*Pseudomonas syringae*). During the fall, winter, and early spring, large quantities of bacteria-containing gum ooze from the cankers. Splashing rain spreads the bacteria to dormant buds, twigs, and branches. Infection occurs through wounds in the twigs and branches, and bacterial decay causes cankers to form. Slowly developing cankers may encircle a branch, and by midsummer the affected branches and limbs die back. With the onset of cool fall weather, bacterial activity increases. This disease is most serious on young trees.

SOLUTION: Prune out diseased branches. After each cut, sterilize the pruning shears by dipping them in rubbing alcohol. In the fall, spray with a fungicide containing *basic copper sulfate* to obtain partial control. Keep the tree healthy by fertilizing and watering properly. For cultural information, see page 633.

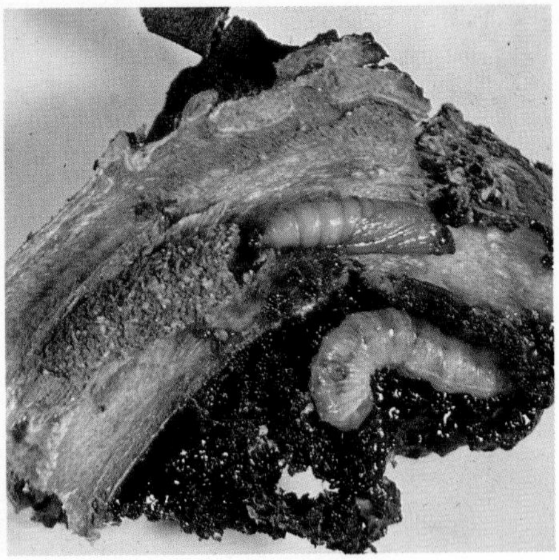

Peachtree borer larva and pupa (life size).

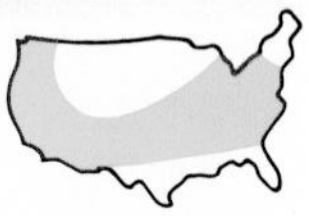

PROBLEM: Holes appear in the lower part of the trunk or in the upper trunk and lower crotches. A thick, gummy substance often oozes from these holes. Sawdust may surround the holes or collect at the base of the tree. In mid to late summer, empty pupa skins may protrude from the holes. During the spring and summer, some of the leaves and branches may wilt. Severely affected trees may die.

ANALYSIS: Peachtree borers

(*Synanthedon* species)

These moth larvae are very damaging to peaches and nectarines. The clear-winged moths, which resemble wasps, lay their eggs in mid to late summer. The larvae that emerge bore into the bark. Their tunnels interfere with the circulation of water and nutrients, causing twigs and branches to wilt and die. These borers feed throughout the winter and into the spring. A gummy sap—often mixed with sawdustlike particles—may ooze from the tunnels. The borers pupate in early to midsummer in cocoons located at the base of the tree or just inside their tunnels. The moths emerge several weeks later.

SOLUTION: Spray the trunk and lower branches with ORTHO Lindane Borer & Leaf Miner Spray. Next year, in late May or early June, kill the egg-laying moths by spraying the trunk and crotches with ORTHO Liquid Sevin. Spray at intervals of 3 weeks until early August. Contact your local Cooperative Extension Office (see page 1029) for peachtree borer emergence dates in your area. Individual borers may be killed by inserting a wire into their holes.

Phony peach.

PROBLEM: Leaves are abnormally dark green and flattened. Branching is profuse at the sides of the tree while upward growth is stunted. The tree has a compact, rounded appearance with few or no branches above the dense mass of leaves. Fruit ripens early and is usually more highly colored than normal.

ANALYSIS: Phony peach

This disease is caused by *rickettsias*, microscopic organisms similar to bacteria. Leafhoppers inject the rickettsias while they feed on the tree's leaves and twigs. The rickettsias travel downward and infect the root system of the tree. Visual symptoms of the disease appear after the root system has been severely affected, usually within 18 months. Plum trees, which are also attacked by the disease, do not show any visual symptoms. However, leafhoppers can transmit the disease from plum to nearby peach trees. Trees may live many years, but the wood becomes brittle, twigs and branches die, and the tree eventually looks ragged.

SOLUTION: No cure is available for diseased trees. Once the visual symptoms appear, the tree cannot be saved. Since sprouts from a cut tree can still carry the disease, an infected tree must be pulled out. For more information on tree removal, see page 918. The spread of the disease may be slowed by a yearly spray program to control leafhoppers. Contact your local Cooperative Extension Office (see page 1029) to determine the best time to spray for leafhoppers in your area. Spray with ORTHO Diazinon Insect Spray, ORTHO Fruit & Vegetable Insect Control, or ORTHO Home Orchard Spray. Repeat according to label directions.

PEAR

ADAPTATION AND POLLINATION: See the variety chart on page 1022.

SOIL: Any good, deep, well-drained soil. pH 5.5 to 8.0

FERTILIZER: Fertilize with ORTHO Evergreen, Tree & Shrub Food according to label directions.

WATER:

How much: Apply enough water to wet the soil 3 to 4 feet deep. To determine the proper amount of water for your soil type, see page 912.

How often: Water when the soil 6 inches below the surface is barely moist.

PRUNING: Pears are borne on short fruiting branches (spurs) that grow on 1-year-old wood. The spurs continue to fruit for 5 to 8 years. Prune lightly, because removal of many spurs will reduce the pear yield. Thin out weak, crossing, or dead twigs and branches.

HARVEST: Unlike most other fruit, pears should not be allowed to ripen on the tree. Pick them when they have reached their mature size and are starting to lose their green color. Don't let them soften or turn entirely yellow before harvesting. Most pears may be safely harvested during September. Contact your local Cooperative Extension Office (see page 1029) for specific harvest dates for your location. After harvesting, place the pears in a plastic bag, and refrigerate them for at least 2 weeks. To ripen them, remove them from the refrigerator and keep at room temperature. After 5 to 10 days, they should be fully ripe.

Scab.

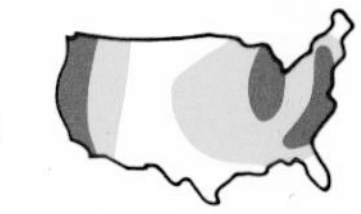

PROBLEM: Olive-brown velvety spots, 1/4 inch or more in diameter, appear on the leaves and young fruit. As the infected pears mature, the spots develop into light to dark brown corky lesions. The fruit is often cracked and malformed, and may drop prematurely. There are small, blisterlike pustules on many of the twigs.

ANALYSIS: Scab

This plant disease is caused by a fungus (*Venturia pyrina*) that commonly infects pears. The fungus spends the winter in infected plant debris and twig lesions. In the spring, spores are produced and discharged into the air. They are blown to the developing leaves, flowers, twigs, and young pears. If the leaves and fruit are wet the fungus infects them, and spots develop. The infected tissues produce more spores, which further spread the disease. As temperatures increase in the summer, the fungus becomes less active.

SOLUTION: Unless they are severely infected, the pears are edible if the scabby areas are removed. To prevent recurrence of the disease next year, remove and destroy leaf debris and infected fruit in the fall. Next spring, spray with ORTHO Home Orchard Spray or ORTHO Orthocide Garden Fungicide according to label directions.

PEAR

Infected blossoms.

Blighted twig.

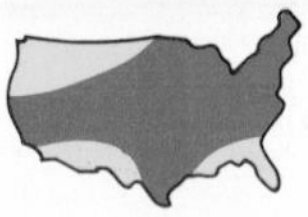

PROBLEM: Blossoms turn black and die. Young leafy twigs wilt from the tips down, turn black, and die. A bend often develops at the tips of the infected twigs. On the branches, and at the base of the blighted twigs, the bark becomes water-soaked in appearance, then dark, sunken, and dry. Cracks may develop at the edge of the sunken area. In warm, moist spring weather, drops of brown ooze appear on the surface of these lesions. During the summer, shoots or branches may wilt and turn dark brown to black. Infected fruit shrivels, turns black, and remains on the tree.

ANALYSIS: Fireblight
This plant disease is caused by a bacterium (*Erwinia amylovora*) that is very severe on pears, and also affects apples and several ornamental plants in the rose family. (For a list of susceptible plants, see page 1016.) The bacteria spend the winter in sunken lesions (cankers) on the branches and twigs. In the spring, the bacteria ooze out of the cankers and are carried by insects to the pear blossoms. Once a few of the blossoms have been contaminated, splashing rain, honeybees, and other insects continue to spread the bacteria to healthy blossoms. The bacteria spread down through the flowers into the twigs and branches, where cankers develop. Often, developing cankers will encircle a shoot or branch by midsummer, causing conspicuous branch and twig dieback. Although fireblight is spread primarily through flower infection, leaves and twigs damaged by hail or wounded in some other manner are also susceptible to infection. Tender, succulent shoots and sprouts are also vulnerable to infection. Although severely diseased trees may be killed, more commonly only the fruiting stems (spurs) are killed, resulting in greatly reduced fruit yields. Fireblight is most severe during warm (65° to 85°F), wet weather.

SOLUTION: After the infection has stopped spreading in the summer or fall, prune out and destroy infected twigs and branches at least 12 inches beyond visible decay. Sterilize pruning shears after each cut with rubbing alcohol. A protective spray of *basic copper sulfate* or *streptomycin* applied before the blossoms open next spring will help prevent infection. Repeat at intervals of 5 to 7 days until the end of the blooming period. Avoid fertilizing with high-nitrogen fertilizers to prevent excess growth of shoots and suckers. Plant varieties that are less susceptible to fireblight.

Pear varieties resistant and susceptible to fireblight:
Susceptible: Barlett, Bosc, and Clapp.
Fairly Resistant: Baldwin, Dutchess, Garber, Moonglow, Orient, Seckel, and Starking Delicious.

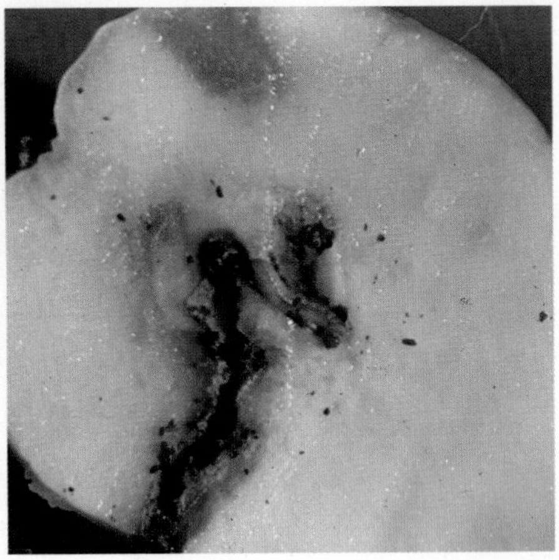
Codling moth larva (¾ life size).

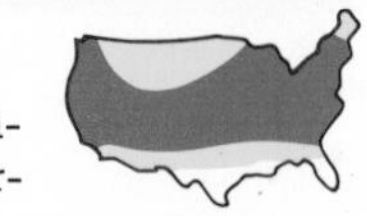

PROBLEM: Fruit is blemished by small holes surrounded by dead tissue. A brown, crumbly material that resembles sawdust may surround the holes. Brown-headed, pinkish white worms up to 1 inch long may be found in the fruit. The interior of the fruit may be dark and rotted. Many pears drop prematurely.

ANALYSIS: Codling moth
(*Laspeyresia pomonella*)
This worm, the larva of a small gray-brown moth, attacks apples, quinces, and several other fruit and nut trees in addition to pears. The moths appear in the spring, and lay their eggs on the leaves, twigs, and developing fruit. The eggs soon hatch, and the larvae that emerge tunnel into the fruit. They feed for several weeks, then emerge from the pears, often leaving a mass of dark excrement on the skin and inside the fruit. After pupating in sheltered locations on or around the tree, another generation of moths emerges in midsummer. Pears may be damaged by worms continuously throughout the summer. In the fall the mature larvae spin cocoons in protected places, such as under loose bark or in tree crevices. They spend the winter in these cocoons and, with the warming temperatures of spring, pupate and emerge as moths.

SOLUTION: Once the worms have penetrated the pears, it is impossible to kill them. To protect uninfested pears, spray with ORTHO Home Orchard Spray or ORTHO Fruit & Vegetable Insect Control at intervals of 10 to 14 days as directed on the label. Remove and destroy all fallen pears, and clean up debris around the trees. Next spring, spray 10 to 14 days after petals have fallen, according to label directions.

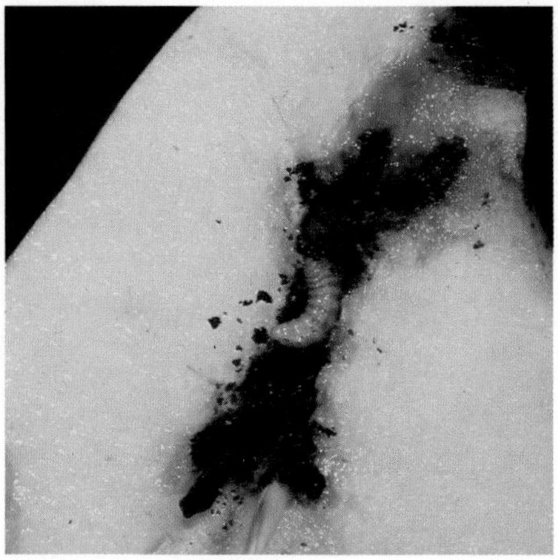

Plum curculio larva (life size).

PROBLEM: The ripening fruit is misshapen, rotten, and often drops prematurely. Holes about ⅛ inch in diameter and deep, crescent-shaped scars appear on the fruit. When cut open, such fruit may be found to contain crescent-shaped yellow-gray grubs with brown heads.

ANALYSIS: Plum curculio
(*Conotrachelus nenuphar*)
These insects, found east of the Rocky Mountains, commonly attack stone fruits, apples, and pears. The adult insects are brown beetles with long curved snouts. They hibernate in debris and other protected places during the winter. The beetles emerge in the spring when new growth starts and begin feeding on young leaves, blossoms, and developing fruit. After 5 to 6 weeks, the female beetles start to lay eggs in the young fruit. During this process they cut distinctive crescent-shaped slits into the pears. The grubs that hatch from the eggs feed for several weeks in the fruit. Usually the infested pears drop to the ground. The grubs eventually leave the fruit and bore into the soil, where they pupate. The emerging beetles feed on fruit for a few weeks, then hibernate. Or, in the South, they lay eggs, producing a second generation of grubs in the late summer.

SOLUTION: There is no way to kill the grubs inside the fruit. Spray with ORTHO Malathion 50 Insect Spray, ORTHO Liquid Sevin, or an insecticide containing *methoxychlor* to kill beetles that may be feeding on fruit or laying eggs. Pick up and destroy all fallen fruit. Next spring, spray the trees when the petals are falling from the blossoms; repeat applications according to the directions on the label.

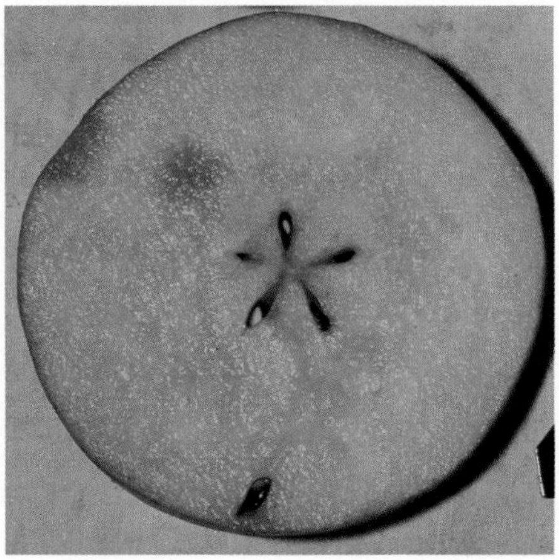

Overripe pear.

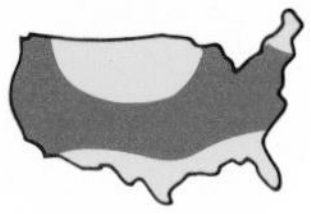

PROBLEM: The fruit tastes mealy, mushy, or gritty. The flavor is poor, and the inner flesh may be soft and discolored. The fruit was picked when it had softened or turned yellow on the tree.

ANALYSIS: Fruit harvested too late
Unlike most other fruits, pears must be harvested before they are fully ripe. When left to ripen on the tree, they turn mealy, develop clusters of hard cells (stone cells), and lose their flavor and succulence.

SOLUTION: Most pear varieties should be picked when they have reached their mature size and are starting to lose their green color. Do not allow them to soften or turn entirely yellow before harvesting. As a general rule, most pears may be safely picked during September. Contact your local Cooperative Extension Office (see page 1029) for specific harvest dates for your location and pear varieties. After harvesting, place the pears in a closed plastic bag and refrigerate them for at least 2 weeks. To soften them, remove them from the bag, and keep them at room temperature. After 5 to 10 days, they should be fully ripe.

Spider mite damage.

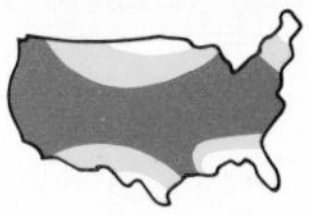

PROBLEM: Leaves are stippled, yellowing, or bronzed. There may be webbing over flower buds, between leaves, or on the lower surfaces of the leaves. Fruit may be russeted. To determine if the tree is infested with certain species of mites, hold a sheet of white paper underneath an affected leaf and tap the leaf sharply. Minute green, red, or yellow specks the size of pepper grains will drop to the paper and begin to crawl around.

ANALYSIS: Mites
Several species of mites, including the two-spotted spider mite (*Tetranychus urticae*) and the pear rust mite (*Epitrimerus pyri*) attack pears. Two-spotted spider mites, which cause leaf stippling and webbing, may be detected as described above. Pear rust mites, which cause fruit russeting and leaf stippling and bronzing, cannot be seen without the aid of a microscope or strong hand lens. These pests, related to spiders, cause damage by sucking plant sap. As a result of feeding, the green leaf pigment disappears, producing the stippled or bronzed appearance. Mites are active throughout the growing season, but are favored by hot, dry weather (70°F and up).

SOLUTION: Spray infested trees with ORTHO Fruit & Vegetable Insect Control or ORTHO Malathion 50 Insect Spray. Repeat the spray 2 more times at intervals of 7 to 10 days. After the leaves have dropped next fall, spray the tree with a *lime sulfur* solution and a *dormant oil*. If you are not sure whether your trees are infested with pear rust mites, bring an infested fruit spur to your local County Extension Office (see page 1029) for confirmation.

PEAR

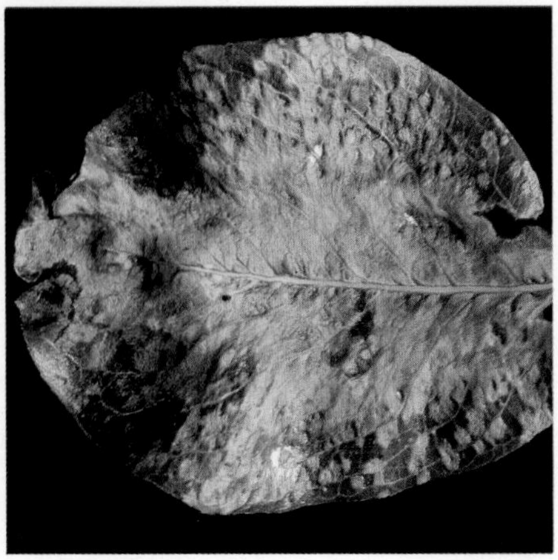

Pearleaf blister mite damage.

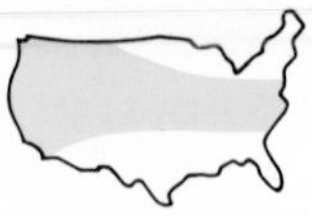

PROBLEM: Yellow to green blisters about 1/8 inch across appear on the undersides of the leaves. These blisters turn red, then black. Buds are deformed and may not set fruit, so the fruit yield is often reduced. Many of the pears that do mature are russet-colored and deformed. They may crack open. If one of the leaf blisters is opened and inspected with a strong hand lens, tiny pinkish white mites may be seen.

ANALYSIS: Pearleaf blister mite
(*Phytoptus pyri*)
These microscopic mites are related to spiders. They attack pears, apples, and several other ornamental trees and shrubs. The mites spend the winter under leaf and flower bud scales. They lay eggs in the spring when the buds begin to swell. The young mites that hatch from these eggs burrow into the emerging leaves, causing blisters to form. Blister mite damage may continue throughout the growing season. With the onset of cold weather, the adult mites move back under the bud scales.

SOLUTION: There is no control for damage on the fruit this year. To help prevent blister mite damage next year, spray the infested tree with ORTHO Orthorix Spray or ORTHO Dormant Disease Control in the fall and again the following spring as directed on the label. Early next spring, before the buds open, spray with a *dormant oil spray.*

Damaged leaf. *Insert:* Pear psylla (4 times life size).

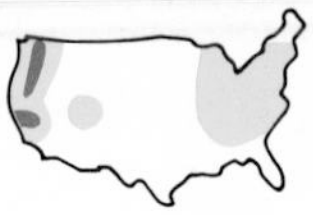

PROBLEM: Leaves and fruit are covered with a shiny or sticky substance called honeydew. A black mold usually grows on the honeydew. Tiny (1/10 inch) reddish brown winged insects may be seen feeding on the foliage. Some of the leaves may turn yellow and drop. Severely infested trees may defoliate prematurely.

ANALYSIS: Pear psylla
(*Psylla pyricola*)
These insects are related to aphids. The adults overwinter in crevices in the tree trunks, in groundcover, or in other protected places. In the late winter or early spring the females lay eggs on the bark, and later on the emerging foliage. The young psyllas feed on the leaves and developing pears, causing damage by sucking the plant sap. The psyllas are unable to digest fully all the sugar in the plant sap, and excrete the excess in a fluid called honeydew, which drops onto the leaves and fruit. A sooty mold fungus may develop on the honeydew, causing the pear leaves and fruit to appear black and dirty. Psylla damage may occur throughout the growing season.

SOLUTION: These pests are often very hard to kill during the growing season. Spray trees thoroughly with ORTHO Fruit & Vegetable Insect Control or ORTHO Home Orchard Spray at the first sign of damage. To control them next year, kill the overwintering adults and eggs by spraying the tree with ORTHO Volck Oil Spray in the early spring.

Fabraea leaf spot.

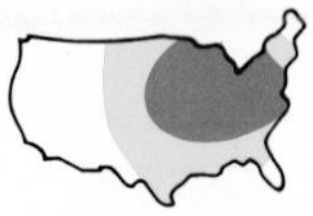

PROBLEM: Tiny purplish black spots appear on the leaves and shoots. These spots enlarge up to 1/4 inch in diameter and turn dark brown. Spots on shoots may join together, forming twig cankers. Infected leaves turn yellow and drop. Small red spots develop on the fruit, eventually turning into dark, sunken lesions. Diseased pears may be cracked and misshapen, with rough skins. Severely infected trees may defoliate prematurely.

ANALYSIS: Fabraea leaf spot
This plant disease, also known as *pearleaf blight*, is caused by a fungus (*Fabraea maculata*) that attacks pears and quinces. The fungus spends the winter in twig cankers and leaf debris. In the spring, spores are splashed to the leaves, shoots, and young fruit. Spots develop where the fungus penetrates the plant tissue. Infection may continue throughout the growing season. The premature death of the infected foliage greatly reduces the amount of food the tree can make and store. This results in weakened trees and lower yields of poor quality fruit.

SOLUTION: To protect leaves and fruit that have not yet been infected, spray with a fungicide containing *captan* (ORTHOCIDE®) or *ferbam.* Remove and destroy all leaf debris around the trees. Next spring, spray just before the trees bloom, and again after the petals fall from the tree.

Fruit tree leafroller (twice life size).

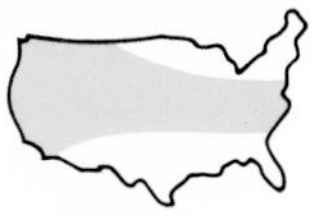

PROBLEM: Irregular holes appear in the leaves and fruit. Some of the leaves are rolled and held together with a web. One or several young fruit may be enclosed within the rolled leaves. When these rolled leaves are peeled open, pale green worms up to ¾ inch long with brown heads are found inside. The maturing pears are scarred and misshapen.

ANALYSIS: Fruit tree leafroller
(*Archips argyrospilus*)
These worms, the larvae of brown moths, are common pests of many fruit and ornamental trees. In June or July, the moths lay eggs on twigs and branches. When the eggs hatch the following spring, the larvae feed on the blossoms and developing fruit and foliage. Leafrollers often wrap leaves around ripening fruit, then feed on the fruit inside, causing much damage to the pears. After about a month, the mature larvae pupate inside rolled leaves.

SOLUTION: If practical, pick off and destroy rolled leaves to reduce the number of moths that will emerge later in the season. Next spring, spray the tree with ORTHO Home Orchard Spray, ORTHO Liquid Sevin, or ORTHO Fruit & Vegetable Insect Control when 75 percent of the petals have fallen from the blossoms. Repeat the spray according to the directions on the label.

Pearslug (twice life size).

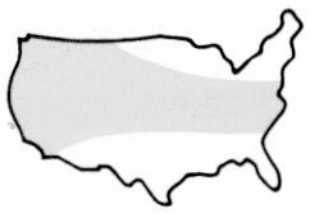

PROBLEM: The upper surfaces of the leaves are chewed between the veins, leaving a lacy, translucent layer of tissue that turns brown. Dark green to orange, wet, sluglike worms up to ½ inch long may be feeding on the leaves. Severely infested trees may be defoliated.

ANALYSIS: Pearslug
(*Caliroa cerasi*)
Although pearslugs resemble slugs, they are actually the larvae of black and yellow flies that infest pears, cherries, plums, and some ornamental trees. The adult flies appear in the late spring and lay their eggs in the leaves. The larvae that hatch from these eggs exude a slimy, olive-green substance, giving them a sluglike appearance. They feed on the foliage for about a month, then drop to the ground, burrow into the soil, and pupate. The second generation of larvae spends the winter in cocoons buried in the soil. Young trees that are severely infested with pearslugs may be greatly weakened, producing pears of poor quality.

SOLUTION: Spray the infested tree with an ORTHO Home Orchard Spray. Repeat the spray if reinfestation occurs.

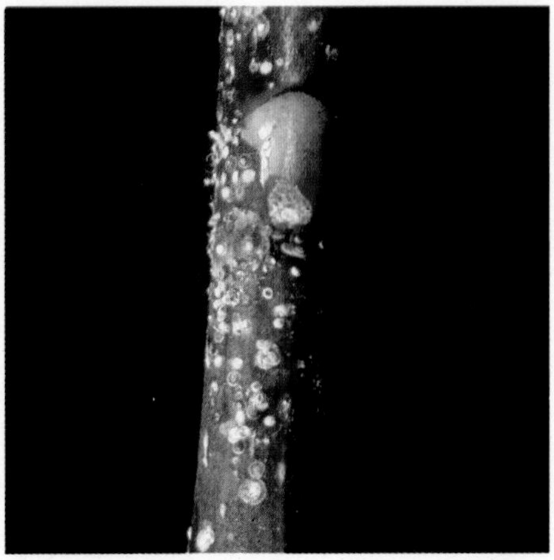
San Jose scales (life size).

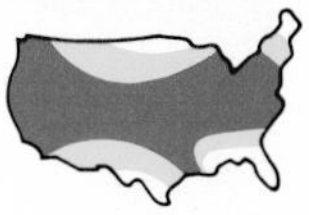

PROBLEM: Some of the leaves are pale green to yellow, and may drop prematurely on weakened limbs. The bark is encrusted with small (1/16 inch), hard, circular, slightly raised bumps with dull yellow centers. If the hard cover is scraped off, the insect underneath is yellow or olive. Entire branches may be killed. Red-purple spots mar some of the infested fruits and shoots.

ANALYSIS: San Jose scale
(*Quadraspidiotus perniciosus*)
These insects infest the bark, leaves, and fruit of many fruit trees. The scales bear live young in the spring. In late spring to midsummer the young scales, called *crawlers*, settle on leaves, twigs, and fruit. The small (1/16 inch), soft-bodied young feed by inserting their mouthparts and sucking sap from the plant. The legs usually atrophy and a hard, crusty shell develops over the body. An uncontrolled infestation of San Jose scales may kill large branches after 2 or 3 seasons. For further information about scales, see page 876.

SOLUTION: During the dormant season, spray the trunk and branches with ORTHO Volck Oil Spray. The crawlers may be killed with ORTHO Malathion 50 Insect Control or ORTHO Fruit & Vegetable Insect Control applied in the late spring.

PECAN

PECAN

ADAPTATION AND POLLINATION: See the variety chart on page 1017.

SOIL: Any good, deep, well-drained soil. pH 5.5 to 8.0

FERTILIZER: Fertilize with ORTHO Evergreen, Tree & Shrub Food according to label directions.

WATER:
How much: Apply enough water to wet the soil 3 to 4 feet deep. To determine the proper amount of water for your soil type, see page 912.
How often: Water when the soil 6 inches below the surface is just barely moist.

PRUNING: Nuts form on the current season's growth. Prune pecans lightly, removing weak, diseased, or dead twigs and branches.

HARVEST: Harvest the nuts in the fall by gently knocking the tree with a rubber mallet or cloth-covered pole when the shucks have split and the nuts are exposed.

Pecan weevil (twice life size).

PROBLEM: Immature pecans that drop to the ground during August are marked with dark patches and tobacco-like stains. Later in the season, there are 1/8-inch holes in some of the ripe nuts. When cut open, the kernels are found to be destroyed, and may contain creamy-white curved grubs up to 1/2 inch long. Reddish brown to gray long-beaked beetles, 1/2 inch long, may be seen in the tree. If the limbs are shaken, these beetles will drop to the ground.

ANALYSIS: Pecan weevil
(*Curculio caryae*)
This insect is very damaging to pecans and hickories in both its immature and adult stages. The adult weevils appear in late summer and feed on the immature pecans. The injured nuts drop from the tree. As soon as the kernels harden, the female weevils drill holes through the shucks and shells, and lay their eggs in the kernels. The grubs that hatch from these eggs feed on the kernels for several weeks, then leave the nut, drop to the ground, and burrow into the soil. They will emerge after 2 to 3 years as adult weevils.

SOLUTION: Spray severely infested trees with an insecticide containing *carbaryl* (SEVIN®). Spray at intervals of 10 to 14 days until the shucks split from the shells. Weevils may also be partially controlled by shaking them from lightly infested trees. Place sheets under the tree, then lightly jar the limbs. Collect and kill the dislodged weevils that fall onto the sheet. Repeat every 2 weeks until the weevils are no longer present.

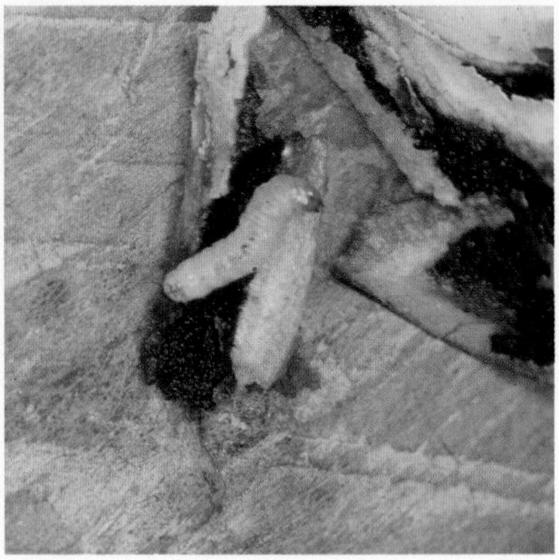

Hickory shuckworm (twice life size).

PROBLEM: Cream-colored worms up to 3/8 inch long, are feeding in the immature nuts, many of which fall to the ground prematurely. Later in the season, after the shells have hardened, the worms may be found in the green shucks.

ANALYSIS: Hickory shuckworm
(*Laspeyresia caryana*)
These worms, the larvae of small brown moths, are also known as *pecan shuckworms.* They are pests of pecan and hickory trees wherever they are grown. The larvae spend the winter in shucks on the ground or in the tree. The shuckworms pupate and emerge as adult moths in the spring to lay their eggs on pecan leaves and nuts. The young larvae that hatch from these eggs tunnel into the soft green pecan shells and feed on the developing kernels. Infested nuts usually drop. Later in the season, after the nut shells have hardened, the larvae tunnel into the shucks. Their feeding damage interferes with the development of the kernels. Shuckworm damage may occur throughout the spring and summer.

SOLUTION: Chemical controls are not practical for the home gardener. Clean up and destroy all dropped nuts and shucks to eliminate many of the overwintering larvae.

Pecan phylloxeras (life size).

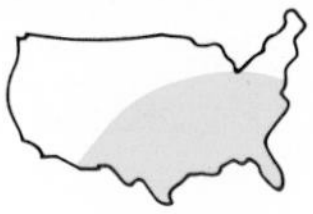

PROBLEM: Green to yellow-green swellings (galls) appear on the leaves, shoots, and nuts. These galls, which range in size from 1/8 to 1 inch in diameter, split open in the late spring. Shoots with galls on them may be weak and dying. When the galls are cut open, tiny soft-bodied insects resembling aphids may be seen inside.

ANALYSIS: Pecan phylloxera
(*Phylloxera* species)
These insects, closely related to aphids, are common pests of pecan and hickory trees. Phylloxera eggs, laid in the fall, survive the winter on branches and twigs. The eggs hatch when the leaf buds open in the spring. The emerging insects feed on the new spring growth by sucking the plant sap. They inject a substance into the plant while feeding that causes the plant tissue to swell, forming galls. Eventually the galls envelop the feeding insects. After the phylloxeras mature, they lay their eggs and die. When this second generation of winged insects matures, the galls split open, releasing them. Although these pests are present throughout the summer, they are most damaging to the new spring growth.

SOLUTION: Once the galls have formed, the insects cannot be killed. During the dormant season, spray the tree with a *dormant oil spray* to kill the overwintering eggs. Next spring when the buds start to open, spray with an insecticide containing either *malathion* or *lindane*.

Pecan nut casebearer damage.

PROBLEM: Olive-green worms up to ½ inch long with yellow-brown heads are feeding on the twigs, foliage, and developing nuts. Some of the young shoots are wilting. Nut clusters may be webbed together. There are holes in some of the nuts, and many of the kernels have been destroyed. Many nuts drop prematurely. Some of the nuts may contain worms or pupae, either in the kernel or in the shuck.

ANALYSIS: Pecan nut casebearer
(*Acrobasis nuxvorella*)
These worms, the larvae of small, dark gray moths, are very damaging to pecans. The larvae come out of hibernation when the buds open in the spring. They feed on the developing buds for a short time, then tunnel into the new shoots to pupate. The adult moths emerge just as the nuts start to form, and lay their eggs on the young pecans. This second generation of worms webs clusters of nuts together, then bores into and feeds on them. This generation of casebearers usually damages many pecans because each worm eats 3 or 4 of the immature nuts during its larval stage. After reaching their mature size, the larvae pupate inside the nuts and become moths. Larval damage continues throughout the summer, but lessens in severity as the nuts enlarge.

SOLUTION: Spray with ORTHO Fruit & Vegetable Insect Control. Next spring, contact your local County Extension Office (see page 1029) to determine when moths are laying eggs in your area. Spray during this period and again 6 weeks later. Destroy all infested nuts that fall to the ground.

Spittlebugs.

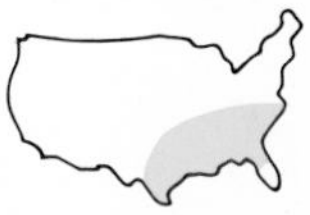

PROBLEM: Masses of white, frothy foam cluster on the twigs, buds, and nuts. If the froth is washed off, small, green, soft-bodied insects can be seen feeding on the plant tissue. Young, tender shoots sometimes die, and the nut yield may be reduced.

ANALYSIS: Spittlebugs
(*Clastoptera achatina* and *C. obtusa*)
These insects, also known as *froghoppers*, appear in the spring and again in the midsummer. Spittlebug eggs are laid in the fall and survive the winter in cracks in the bark. The young spittlebugs—called *nymphs*—emerge soon after the pecan nuts have set. The foamy froth they produce completely envelops them while they suck the sap from the tender buds, twigs, and nuts. The adult spittlebugs are not as damaging as the nymphs. The adults are ¼ inch long, yellow to reddish brown, and winged. They hop or fly away quickly when disturbed. Large numbers of spittlebugs can kill many young shoots, resulting in a reduced nut yield.

SOLUTION: Spray infested trees with an insecticide containing *malathion*. Repeat the spray if reinfestation occurs.

Scab.

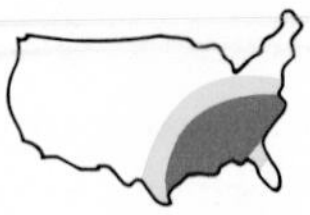

PROBLEM: Olive-colored spots up to $\frac{1}{4}$ inch across appear on the twigs and the undersides of the leaves. Large areas of the leaves may turn black. The tree may defoliate prematurely. Tiny black dots that develop on the shucks usually enlarge to form black sunken lesions. Infected nuts drop prematurely.

ANALYSIS: Scab

This plant disease is caused by a fungus (*Fusicladium effusum*). It is the most serious disease of pecans. The fungus spends the winter on twigs and old leaves and shucks on the tree and ground. In the spring, fungal spores are splashed and blown to new growth. If there is adequate moisture, the spores infect the plant tissue, causing spotting and blighting. The infected tissue produces more spores, which spread to the young nuts. As the pecan leaves mature they become resistant to scab infection. However, the shucks are susceptible to fungal attack as long as they continue to grow and develop.

SOLUTION: If there are some healthy nuts left on the tree, spray with a fungicide containing *benomyl*. Remove and destroy old shucks and plant debris. Next spring, spray again when the buds open, and spray 3 more times at intervals of 2 to 3 weeks. Do not spray after the shucks begin to split open.

Pecan resistance to scab:

Susceptible: Burkett, Mahan, Schley, Success, and Western.

Fairly resistant: Curtis, Dependable, Elliot, Gloria Grande, and Shawnee.

Resistant: Cheyenne, Desirable, Kiowa, and Mohawk.

Damage. *Insert:* Pecan aphid (life size).

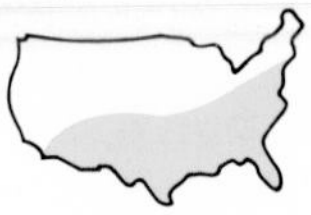

PROBLEM: Small ($\frac{1}{16}$ to $\frac{1}{8}$ inch) yellow, light to dark green, or black soft-bodied insects are feeding on the foliage. Rectangular yellow areas about $\frac{1}{4}$ inch long may appear on the leaves. These yellow areas turn brown, and the affected leaves drop. In some cases, the youngest leaves are curled, twisted, and dying. A shiny or sticky substance may coat the leaves. A black sooty mold may grow on this sticky substance. The pecan yield is often reduced. Severely infested trees may defoliate prematurely.

ANALYSIS: Aphids

Several species of aphids infest pecans, including the black pecan aphid (*Tinocallis caryaefoliae*) and yellow aphid (*Monellia* species). Aphids do little damage in small numbers. However, they are extremely prolific and populations can rapidly build up to damaging numbers during the growing season. Damage occurs when the aphid sucks the juices from the pecan leaves. The aphid is unable to digest fully all the sugar in the plant sap and excretes the excess in a fluid called honeydew, which often drops onto the leaves below. A sooty mold fungus may develop on the honeydew, causing the pecan leaves to appear black and dirty. Black pecan aphids are especially damaging to pecans. They are responsible for the yellow-spotted, dying leaves of many pecans in the Southeast. For more information about aphids, see page 875.

SOLUTION: Spray infested trees with ORTHO Fruit & Vegetable Insect Control. If reinfestation occurs, repeat the spray as directed on the label.

Cotton root rot.

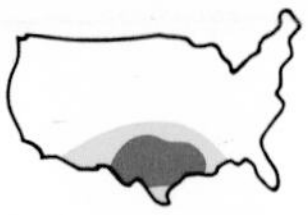

PROBLEM: During the summer, the foliage turns yellow, wilts, and dies. The dead leaves may remain attached to the tree. Cottony white or powdery tan mats of spores 2 to 12 inches in diameter may appear on the soil near the affected tree. If the soil around the base of the tree is loosened and removed to expose some of the roots, the bark of the roots is usually found to be brownish, rotted, and soft. There may be light to dark brown spherical fungal pellets the size of pinheads on the infected roots.

ANALYSIS: Cotton root rot

This plant disease, also known as *Texas root rot*, is caused by a fungus (*Phymatotrichum omnivorum*). Cotton root rot, a serious problem in the Southwest, infects many kinds of flowers, trees, and shrubs. The fungus becomes active as the soil warms in the spring. Fungal strands grow through the soil to penetrate and decay the roots, eventually killing the tree. The fungal strands may spread up to 30 feet in 1 year. Cotton root rot is often brought into a garden initially in infected transplants or contaminated soil and tools. The fungus thrives in heavy, moist, alkaline soils. It may persist in the soil for 5 years or more.

SOLUTION: There is no practical chemical control. Mildly affected trees may be saved by fertilizing with *ammonium sulfate*. For more information about this technique, see page 851. It is best to replace dying trees with plants that are resistant to cotton root rot. For a list of resistant plants, see page 1007.

PERSIMMON

ADAPTATION: Oriental persimmons can be grown in zones 7 through 10. Native persimmons can be grown in zones 4 through 10. To determine your climate zone, see the map on page 1020.

SOIL: Any good, deep, well-drained soil. pH 5.5 to 8.0

FERTILIZER: Fertilize with ORTHO Evergreen, Tree & Shrub Food according to label directions.

WATER:
How much: Apply enough water to wet the soil 3 to 4 feet deep. To determine the proper amount of water for your soil type, see page 912.
How often: Water when the soil 6 inches below the surface is just barely moist.

PRUNING: Prune lightly. Remove weak or lank growth and crossed, diseased, and broken limbs.

HARVEST: Allow astringent persimmons to become soft and fully colored before harvesting. Nonastringent varieties may be harvested and eaten before they have softened. Clip fruit off rather than pulling them off.

Fruit drop.

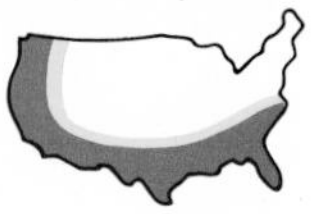

PROBLEM: Fruit drops prematurely. The tree appears to be healthy; there are no signs of insects, pests, or diseases.

ANALYSIS: Fruit drop
Persimmons have a natural tendency to drop their fruit prematurely. Large quantities of fruit may drop when the tree is under stress. Stress may be caused by conditions such as excessive heat, drought, cold, or overwatering. Excessive fruit drop may also occur on trees that are growing vigorously due to heavy nitrogen fertilization.

SOLUTION: Although fruit drop cannot be eliminated, it can be reduced. Avoid overfertilizing and overwatering or underwatering the tree. For more information about the proper culture of persimmons, see the column to the left.

Sunburn.

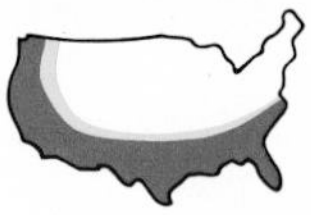

PROBLEM: During hot weather, usually in August or September, dark brown or black patches appear on the developing fruit. Leaves may turn brown around the edges and between the veins.

ANALYSIS: Sunburn
Sunburn is caused by excessive evaporation of moisture from the leaves and fruit. In hot weather, water evaporates rapidly from the fruit and foliage. If the roots can't absorb and convey water fast enough to replenish this loss, the fruit surfaces exposed to the sun overheat and burn; in severe cases, the leaves turn brown and wither. This usually occurs in dry soil, but fruit and leaves can also burn when the soil is moist and temperatures are around 100°F. Drying winds, severed roots, and limited soil area can also cause sunburn. For more information about leaf scorch, see page 857.

SOLUTION: There is nothing you can do once the fruit has been damaged, but it is still edible. To help prevent further sunburn, deep-water plants during periods of hot weather to wet down the entire root space. (For more information about watering, see page 916.) Newly transplanted trees should be watered whenever the rootball is dry 2 inches below the surface.

PLUM

PLUM

ADAPTATION AND POLLINATION: See the variety chart on page 1022.

SOIL: Any good, deep, well-drained soil. pH 5.5 to 8.0

FERTILIZER: Fertilize with ORTHO Evergreen, Tree & Shrub Food according to label directions.

WATER:
How much: Apply enough water to wet the soil 3 to 4 feet deep. To determine the proper amount of water for your soil type, see page 912.
How often: Water when the soil 6 inches below the surface is just barely moist.

PRUNING: European and American plums are borne on short fruiting branches (spurs) that continue to fruit for many years. Prune lightly, because removal of many spurs will reduce the plum yield. Thin out weak, crossing, and dead twigs and branches. Japanese plums are borne on 1-year-old wood and on spurs that grow on 2-year-old wood. The spurs continue to fruit for 2 to 4 years. Prune back last year's growth to half its length, and thin out spurred branches that have stopped fruiting. Thin out weak, crossing, or dead twigs and branches. For large plums, thin fruit to 4 to 6 inches apart.

HARVEST: Harvest when the fruit are fully colored and slightly soft. When they are ripe, the plum stem will easily separate from the spur or branch when the fruit is gently lifted.

Plum curculio damage.

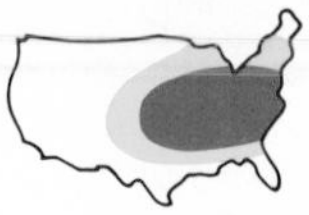

PROBLEM: Ripening fruit is misshapen, rotten, and often drops prematurely. Holes about ⅛ inch in diameter and deep, crescent-shaped scars appear on the fruit. When cut open, such fruit may be found to contain crescent-shaped, yellow-gray grubs with brown heads.

ANALYSIS: Plum curculio
(*Conotrachelus nenuphar*)
These insects, found east of the Rocky Mountains, commonly attack other stone fruits, apples, and pears, as well as plums. The adult insects are brown beetles with long curved snouts. They hibernate in debris and other protected places during the winter. The beetles emerge in the spring when new growth starts and begin feeding on young leaves, blossoms, and developing fruit. After 5 to 6 weeks, the female beetles start to lay eggs in the young fruit. During this process they cut distinctive crescent-shaped slits into the plums. The grubs that hatch from the eggs feed for several weeks in the fruit. The infested plums usually drop to the ground. The grubs eventually leave the fruit and bore into the soil, where they pupate. The emerging beetles feed on fruit for a few weeks, then go into hibernation. Or, in the South, they lay eggs, producing a second generation of grubs in the late summer.

SOLUTION: Once the fruit is infested, there is no way to kill the grubs inside the fruit. Spray with ORTHO Home Orchard Spray, ORTHO Malathion 50 Insect Spray, or ORTHO Liquid Sevin to kill beetles that may be feeding on fruit or laying eggs. Pick up and destroy all fallen fruit. Next spring, spray the trees when the petals are falling from the blossoms; repeat applications according to the directions on the label.

Bacterial leaf spot on Stanley prunes.

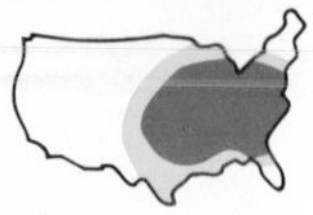

PROBLEM: Brown or black angular spots develop on the leaves. The centers of the spots often fall out. The tips of the leaves may die, and severely infected leaves turn yellow and drop. When the fruit sets, the surface may be dotted with brown to black spots. The surface of the fruit becomes pitted and cracked. Sunken lesions may form on the twigs. Severely infected trees may defoliate.

ANALYSIS: Bacterial leaf spot
This plant disease, caused by bacteria (*Xanthomonas pruni*), also attacks apricots and peaches. The disease is common east of the Rocky Mountains. The bacteria spend the winter in lesions on the twigs, oozing out in the spring to be carried by splashing rain to young leaves, shoots, and developing fruit. Periods of frequent rainfall favor the infection. Trees that defoliate early in the summer become weakened, and produce few plums of poor quality.

SOLUTION: There is no adequate control for this disease. Spraying when the flower buds open in the spring with *basic copper sulfate* may help suppress the disease, but will not eliminate it.

Fruit rot.

Blossom blight.

PROBLEM: Blossoms and young leaves decay, wilt, and turn brown during the first 2 weeks of the bloom period. Often the decayed blossoms fail to drop, and hang on the tree through the growing season. In humid conditions, masses of gray spores may appear on the infected flower parts. There is often extensive twig dieback. Sunken lesions sometimes develop on the twigs and branches as the season progresses. These lesions usually exude a sticky ooze.

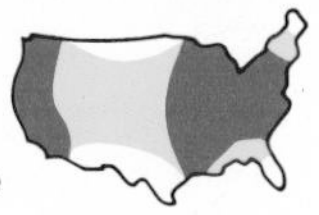

PROBLEM: Small circular brown spots appear on the young fruits. Later in the season, as the plums start to mature, these spots may enlarge to rot part or all of the fruit. During moist weather the rotted fruits are covered with tufts of gray spores. When the infected plums are sliced open, the flesh inside is brown, usually firm, and fairly dry. Infected fruits either drop prematurely or dry out, turn dark brown, and remain on the tree past the normal harvest period. Many twigs die. There are sunken lesions (cankers) on some of these twigs. A thick, gummy material often oozes from these cankers.

ANALYSIS: Brown rot
This plant disease, caused by either of two closely related fungi (*Monilinia laxa* or *M. fructicola*), is very destructive to all the stone fruits. The fungi spend the winter in twig cankers or in rotted fruits (mummies) in the tree or on the ground. In the spring, spores are blown or splashed from cankers or mummies to the healthy flower buds. After penetrating and decaying the flowers, the fungus grows down into the twigs, producing brown, sunken cankers. During moist weather a thick, gummy sap oozes from the lesions, and tufts of gray spores may form on the infected areas. Spores from cankers and infected blossoms or mummies are splashed and blown to the maturing fruit. Young fruits are fairly resistant to infection, but maturing fruits are vulnerable. Brown rot develops most rapidly in mild, moist conditions.

SOLUTION: If there are still uninfected blossoms left on the tree, spray with ORTHO Home Orchard Spray, or with a fungicide containing *captan* (ORTHOCIDE®), *triforine* (FUNGINEX®), *chlorothalonil* (DACONIL 2787®), or *benomyl* to protect them from further infection. Spray twice at intervals of 10 days. To protect maturing plums and nectarines from infection, spray them with ORTHO Home Orchard Spray or with a fungicide containing *captan* (ORTHOCIDE®) or *benomyl* about 3 weeks before they are to be harvested. Remove and destroy all infected fruits and mummies. Prune out cankers and blighted twigs. Clean up and destroy all debris around the tree. Next spring, spray trees at early bloom. Continue to spray according to label directions.

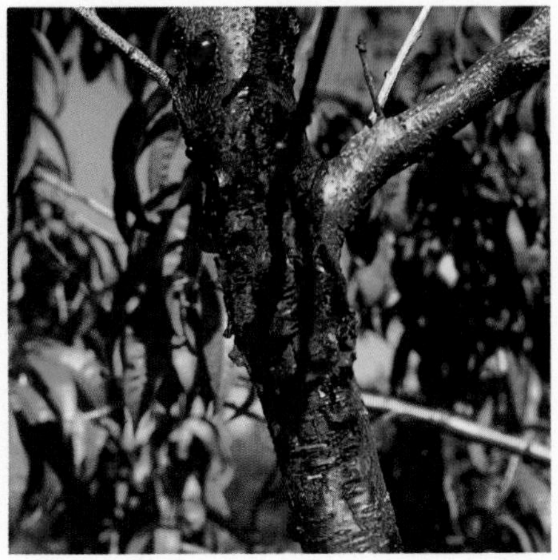
Cytospora canker.

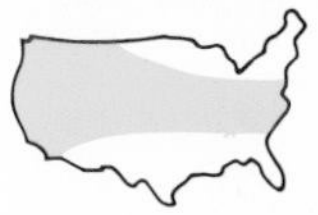

PROBLEM: Oval or oblong sunken lesions develop in the bark and enlarge gradually. The bark at the edges of the lesions may thicken and roll inward. Often a sticky gum oozes from the lesion; this is often followed by the emergence of curly orange threads. Later, small black freckles appear on the bark along the edges of the lesions. Leaves on the affected branches may turn brown and die, or the entire branch may die.

ANALYSIS: Cytospora canker
This plant disease, also known as *perennial canker*, is caused by several related fungi (*Cytospora species*). The fungi spend the winter in sunken lesions (cankers) or on dead wood. In the spring, black fungal bodies develop in the bark, and curly orange fungal chains form. These chains release spores that are blown and splashed to healthy trees. Infection usually occurs through injured or wounded tissue. Bark that has been damaged by sunburn, cold injury, pruning wounds, or mechanical injury is especially susceptible. Fungal decay causes the formation of cankers from which a sticky gum may ooze. The portion of the branch or stem above the canker may die due to the decay of the water-conducting tissue in the branch. Wet, mild weather (70° to 85° F) enhances the development of this disease.

SOLUTION: There is no fully adequate control for this plant disease; a combination of procedures must be used. Remove badly infected branches and cut out cankers. For details about canker removal and treatment, see page 917. Avoid mechanical injuries to the tree, and paint the trunk and exposed main limbs with white interior latex paint to protect against cold injury and sunscald.

PLUM

Spider mite damage.

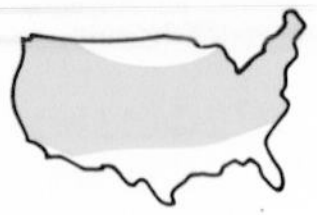

PROBLEM: Leaves are stippled, yellowing, or silvery and curling. There may be webbing over flower buds, between leaves, or on the lower surfaces of the leaves. Fruit may be roughened or russeted. To determine if the tree is infested with certain species of mites, hold a sheet of white paper underneath an affected leaf and tap the leaf sharply. Minute green, red, or yellow specks the size of pepper grains will drop to the paper and crawl around.

ANALYSIS: Mites

Several species of mites attack plums, including the two-spotted spider mite (*Tetranychus urticae*) and the plum rust mite (*Aculus fockeui*). Two-spotted spider mites, which cause leaf stippling and webbing, may be detected as described above. Plum rust mites, which cause leaf silvering and curling and fruit russeting, are microscopic, and cannot be seen without the aid of a microscope or strong hand lens. These pests, related to spiders, cause damage by sucking sap from the fruit surface and the undersides of the leaves. As a result of feeding, the green leaf pigment disappears, producing the stippled or silvered appearance. Mites are active throughout the growing season, but are favored by hot, dry weather (70°F and up). By midsummer, they build up to tremendous numbers.

SOLUTION: Spray infested trees with ORTHO Home Orchard Spray or ORTHO Fruit and Vegetable Insect Control. Repeat the spray 2 more times at intervals of 7 to 10 days. If you are not sure whether your tree is infested with plum rust mites, bring an infested fruit spur to your local Cooperative Extension Office (see page 1029) for confirmation.

Aphids (twice life size).

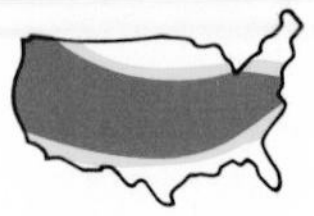

PROBLEM: The youngest leaves are curled, twisted, discolored, and stunted. Leaves may drop off; in severe cases, the tree may defoliate. The developing plums may be small and misshapen. A shiny or sticky substance may coat the leaves. A black sooty mold often grows on the sticky substance. Tiny (1/8 inch) green, yellow, purplish, or black soft-bodied insects cluster on the young shoots and undersides of the leaves.

ANALYSIS: Aphids

Several species of these insects infest plums. Aphids do little damage in small numbers. However, they are extremely prolific and populations can rapidly build up to damaging numbers during the growing season. Damage occurs when the aphid sucks the juices from the plum leaves. The aphid is unable to digest fully all the sugar in the plant sap and excretes the excess in a fluid called honeydew, which often drops onto the leaves and fruit below. A sooty mold fungus may develop on the honeydew, causing the plum leaves to appear black and dirty. For more information about aphids, see page 875.

SOLUTION: Spray with ORTHO Home Orchard Spray or ORTHO Fruit & Vegetable Insect Control as soon as the insects appear. Repeat according to label directions if the tree becomes reinfested. To kill overwintering insects or eggs, spray with ORTHO Volck Oil Spray in the spring while the tree is still dormant.

Peach twig borer (4 times life size).

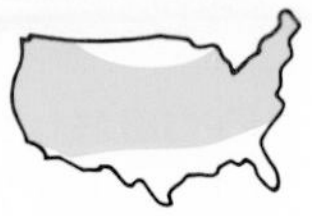

PROBLEM: New growth at the tips of the twigs wilts and dies. When the affected twigs are sliced open lengthwise, worms about 1/2 inch long are found inside. The reddish brown color of these worms distinguishes them from *oriental fruit moth worms*, which cause similar damage. Later in the season, some of the maturing fruit also contain these worms.

ANALYSIS: Peach twig borer
(*Anarsia lineatella*)

This borer attacks all of the stone fruits, and is particularly damaging on the Pacific Coast. The young larvae hibernate during the winter in silk-lined burrows under loose bark or in other protected places on the tree. When the tree blooms in the spring, the larvae emerge and bore into young buds and shoots, causing twig and leaf death. When mature, they leave the twigs and pupate in cocoons attached to branches. After several weeks, gray moths emerge and lay eggs on the twigs, leaves, and fruit. Egg laying and larval damage can occur throughout the growing season. Later in the summer, larvae feed almost exclusively on the maturing fruit. These pests may cause abnormal branching on young trees.

SOLUTION: Worms in the twigs and fruit cannot be killed with pesticides. To prevent future worm damage, kill the moths by spraying infested trees with ORTHO Home Orchard Spray according to label directions. Next spring, spray again just after the petals fall from the blossoms. Repeat the treatment 2 more times at intervals of 10 to 14 days.

Oriental fruit moth damage.

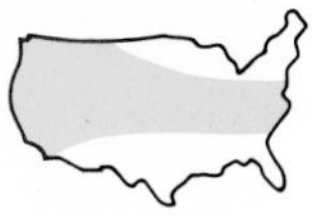

PROBLEM: New growth at the tips of the twigs wilts and dies. When the affected twigs are sliced open lengthwise, worms about ½ inch long are found inside. The pinkish white color of these worms distinguishes them from *peach twig borers*, which cause similar damage. Later in the season, some of the maturing fruits also contain these worms. Often there are holes filled with a sticky gum in the plums.

ANALYSIS: Oriental fruit moth
(*Grapholitha molesta*)
The larvae of these night-flying moths damage stone fruits, apples, and pears. The larvae hibernate in cocoons on the tree bark or buried in crotches. In the spring they pupate, emerge as brown adult moths, and lay eggs on the young plum twigs and leaves. The larvae bore into the young buds, shoots, and tender twigs, causing twig and leaf death. When mature they leave the twigs, spin cocoons, and pupate in the tree or in debris on the ground. After several weeks, moths emerge to lay eggs. Egg laying and larval damage continues throughout the growing season. Later in the summer, the larvae feed mainly on the maturing fruit. They leave gum-filled holes in the plums when they exit to pupate. In addition to ruining the fruit, these pests may cause abnormal branching on young trees.

SOLUTION: Worms in the twigs and fruit cannot be killed with pesticides. To prevent future worm damage, kill the moths by spraying infested trees with ORTHO Home Orchard Spray according to label directions. Next spring, spray again when the petals start to fall from the blossoms. Repeat the treatment 2 more times at intervals of 10 to 14 days.

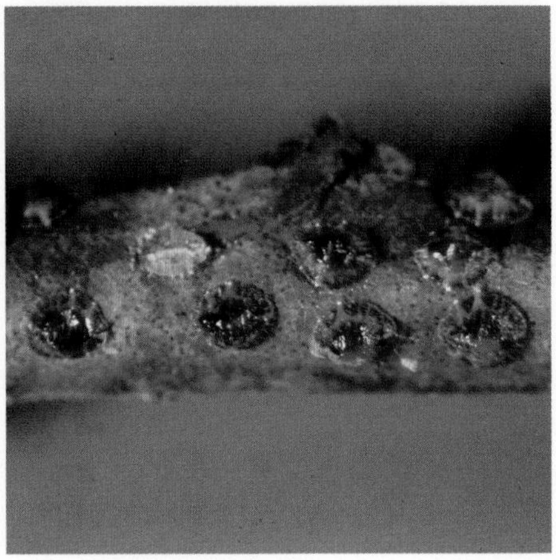
Terrapin scale (twice life size).

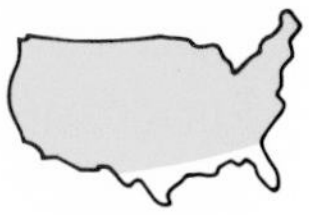

PROBLEM: Stems, small branches, or the undersides of the leaves are covered with brownish crusty bumps or thick, white, waxy bumps, or clusters of flattened yellowish, gray, or brownish scaly bumps. The bumps can be scraped or picked off; the undersides are usually soft. Leaves turn yellow and may drop. In some cases, a shiny or sticky substance coats the leaves. A black sooty mold often grows on the substance.

ANALYSIS: Scales
Several different types of scales infest plum trees. They lay their eggs on leaves or bark, and in spring to midsummer the young scales, called *crawlers*, settle on leaves and twigs. The small (¹⁄₁₀ inch), soft-bodied young feed by inserting their mouthparts and sucking sap from the plant. The legs usually atrophy and a hard crusty or waxy shell develops over the body. The mature female scales bear live young or lay their eggs underneath their shell. Some species of scales are unable to digest fully all the sugar in the plant sap, and excrete the excess in a fluid called honeydew, which often drops onto the leaves below. A sooty mold fungus may develop on the honeydew, causing the plum leaves to appear black and dirty. For more information about scales, see page 876.

SOLUTION: Spray with ORTHO Fruit & Vegetable Insect Control in midsummer when the crawlers are active. The following early spring, while the tree is still dormant, spray the trunk and branches with ORTHO Volck Oil Spray to control overwintering insects.

Peachtree borer (twice life size).

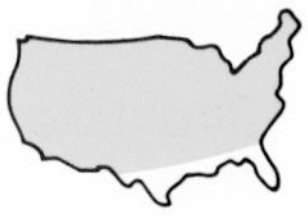

PROBLEM: Holes appear in the lower part of the trunk or in the upper trunk and lower crotches. A thick, gummy substance may ooze from these holes. There may be sawdust around the holes or base of the tree. In mid to late summer, empty pupa skins may protrude from these holes. During the spring and summer, some of the leaves and branches may wilt. Severely affected trees may die.

ANALYSIS: Peachtree borers
(*Synanthedon* species)
The larvae of these moths are most damaging to stone fruits, but also attack other ornamental trees. The clear-winged moths (which resemble wasps) lay their eggs in mid to late summer. The larvae that emerge bore into the bark. Their tunnels interfere with the circulation of water and nutrients, causing twigs and branches to wilt and die. These borers feed throughout the winter and into the spring. A gummy sap may ooze from the borer tunnels. This sap is often mixed with sawdustlike particles, the product of larval feeding. The borers pupate in early to midsummer. Their cocoons are located at the base of the tree or just inside their tunnels. The moths emerge several weeks later.

SOLUTION: Apply a spray containing *lindane* to the trunk and lower branches. Do not spray the fruit or foliage. Next year, in late May or early June, kill the egg-laying moths by spraying the trunk and crotches with ORTHO Home Orchard Spray. Continue spraying at intervals of 3 weeks until early August. Individual borers may be killed by inserting a wire into the borer holes.

Black knot.

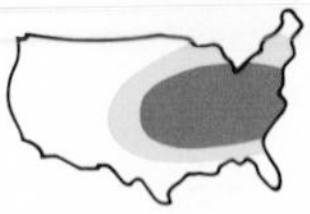

PROBLEM: Soft greenish knots or elongated swellings form on twigs and branches. These knots develop into black, corky, cylindrical galls that may range from ½ to 1½ inches in diameter and be more than 12 inches in length. Twigs and branches beyond the galls are usually stunted, and eventually die.

ANALYSIS: Black knot
This plant disease is caused by a fungus (*Dibotryon morbosum*) that is severe on plums, and occasionally attacks cherries. Fungal spores form during wet weather in the spring. Galls appear 6 months to a year after infection. The galls slowly enlarge and elongate. They eventually cut off the flow of water and nutrients to the branches, causing stunting, wilting, and dieback. Black knot spreads most rapidly during warm (55° to 75°F), wet spring weather.

SOLUTION: Prune out and destroy infected twigs and branches during the fall and winter. When pruning, cut at least 4 inches below visible signs of infection. Cut out knots on the trunk or large limbs down to the wood, and at least ½ inch outward past the diseased tissue. Next spring, spray the tree with a fungicide containing *captan* (ORTHOCIDE®) or *benomyl* just before the buds open. Repeat the spray 2 more times at intervals of 7 to 10 days. Plant resistant varieties.

Plum resistance to black knot:
Very susceptible: Bluefre, Damson, Shropshire, and Stanley.
Moderately resistant: Bradshaw, Early Italian, Fellenberg, Formosa, Methley, Milton, Santa Rosa, and Shiro.
Resistant: President.

Bacterial canker on Santa Rosa plum.

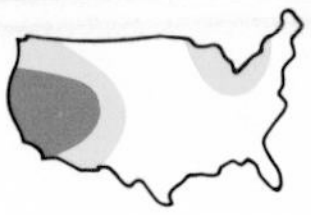

PROBLEM: Sunken, elliptical lesions (cankers) appear on the trunk or branches. Throughout the fall, winter, and spring a thick, amber, sour-smelling gum may ooze from these cankers. In the spring, especially during wet, cold weather, blossoms may turn brown and wither. Some of the leaf and flower buds die and become covered with gum. Entire branches may die. There may be angular holes in the leaves, and sometimes there are dark, sunken lesions in the fruit.

ANALYSIS: Bacterial canker
This plant disease is also known as *bacterial gummosis* or *bacterial blast*, and is caused by a bacterium (*Pseudomonas syringae*). During the fall, winter, and early spring, bacteria-containing gum that oozes from the cankers is spread by splashing rain to dormant buds, twigs, and branches. Infection occurs through wounds in the twigs and branches, and bacterial decay causes cankers to form. Bacterial activity decreases as the weather warms up. However, slowly developing cankers may encircle a branch, and by midsummer the affected branches and limbs start to die. With the onset of cool, wet, fall weather, bacterial activity increases. This disease is most severe on young trees.

SOLUTION: Although this disease cannot be entirely controlled, partial control may be obtained by spraying with a fungicide containing *basic copper sulfate* in the fall just after the leaves have dropped. Prune out diseased branches. After each pruning cut, sterilize pruning shears by dipping in rubbing alcohol. Keep the tree healthy by fertilizing and watering properly. For cultural information, see page 648.

QUINCE

ADAPTATION: Zones 4 through 10. To determine your climate zone, see the map on page 1020.

SOIL: Any good garden soil. pH 5.5 to 7.5

FERTILIZER: Fertilize with ORTHO Evergreen, Tree & Shrub Food according to label directions.

WATER:
How much: Apply enough water to wet the soil 3 to 4 feet deep. To determine the proper amount of water for your soil type, see page 912.
How often: Water when the soil 4 inches below the surface is just barely moist.

PRUNING: The fruit is borne on the branch tips of the current year's growth. Prune to shape the plant as a tree rather than as a shrub. Remove diseased, dead, or crossing twigs and branches, and suckers and twigs along the trunk.

HARVEST: Harvest fruits in the fall when they are fully colored.

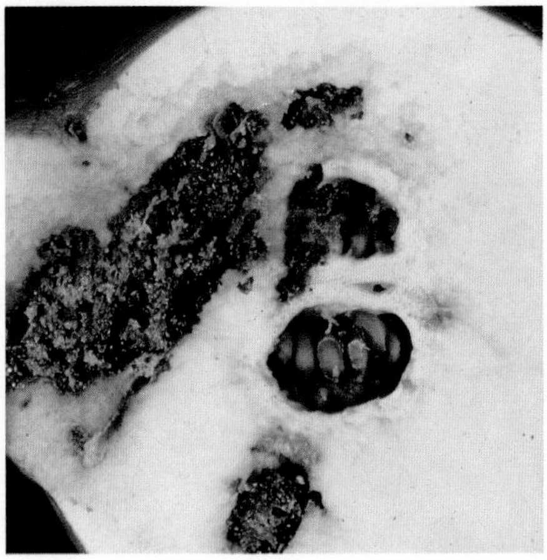

Codling moth damage.

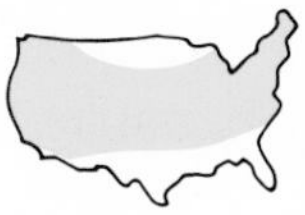

PROBLEM: The fruit is blemished with small holes surrounded by dead tissue. Brown, crumbly material resembling sawdust may surround the holes. Brown-headed, pinkish white worms up to 1 inch long may be found in the fruit. The interior of the fruit is often dark and rotted. Many quinces drop prematurely.

ANALYSIS: Codling moth
(*Laspeyresia pomonella*)
This worm, a serious pest of apples, attacks several other fruit and nut trees in addition to quinces. The gray-brown moths appear in the spring when the quince trees are blooming. They lay their eggs on the leaves, twigs, and developing fruit. The larvae feed for several weeks, then emerge from the fruit, often leaving a mass of dark excrement on the skin and inside the fruit. After pupating in sheltered locations on or around the tree, another generation of moths emerges in midsummer. Quinces may be damaged by worms continuously throughout the summer. In the fall, the mature larvae spin cocoons in protected places, such as under loose bark or in tree crevices. They spend the winter in these cocoons, emerging as moths in the spring.

SOLUTION: Once the worms have penetrated the quinces, it is impossible to kill them. To protect uninfested quinces, spray with an insecticide containing *carbaryl* (SEVIN ®) at intervals of 3 weeks. Remove and destroy all fallen quinces, and clean up debris around the trees. To control infestation next spring, spray quinces with *carbaryl* (SEVIN®) 2 weeks after the petals fall from the blossoms, then spray again 3 weeks later.

WALNUT

ADAPTATION AND POLLINATION: Zones 4 through 8. To determine your climate zone, see the map on page 1020.

SOIL: Any good, deep, well-drained soil. pH 5.5 to 8.0

FERTILIZER: Fertilize with ORTHO Evergreen, Tree & Shrub Food according to label directions.

WATER:
How much: Apply enough water to wet the soil 5 to 6 feet deep. To determine the proper amount of water for your soil, see page 912. Avoid wetting the trunk and crown of the tree by watering into a basin that keeps the water at least 4 feet away from the trunk.
How often: Water when the soil 6 inches below the surface is just barely moist.

PRUNING: Walnuts form on the current season's growth. Prune trees lightly, removing weak, diseased, or dead twigs and branches. Thin the inside of the tree if the growth is dense.

HARVEST: In the fall, the nuts drop to the ground. You may hasten nut drop by striking the branches with a rubber mallet or cloth-covered stick. After removing the husks, spread the nuts one layer deep in a shaded, well-ventilated location to dry.

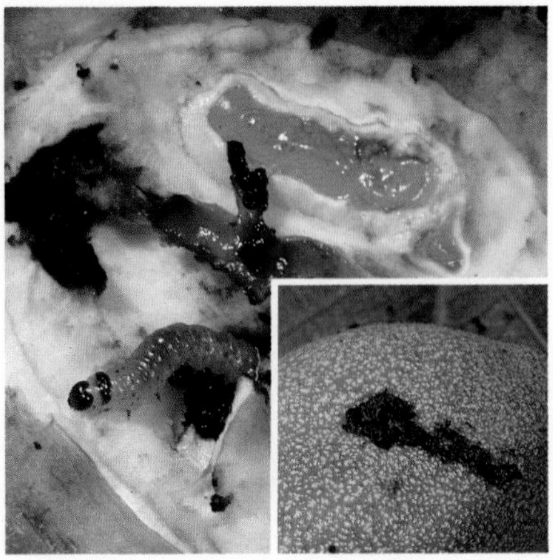

Larvae (¾ life size). *Insert:* Frass on husk.

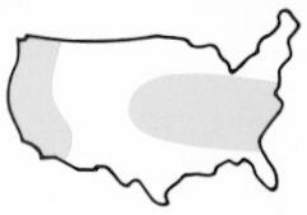

PROBLEM: Nut shells are stained, and there may be holes at the base of the nuts. A brown, crumbly material that resembles sawdust (frass) may surround the holes. Brown-headed, pinkish white worms up to 1 inch long may be found in the nuts. Infested nuts usually drop prematurely.

ANALYSIS: Codling moth
(*Laspeyresia pomonella*)
The larva of this small gray brown moth is a very serious pest of apples and pears, in addition to attacking walnuts and several other fruit and nut trees. The moths appear in the spring when the young nuts are forming. They lay their eggs on the leaves, twigs, and developing walnuts. The larvae that emerge from these eggs tunnel into the nuts. They feed for several weeks, then leave the nut, often leaving a mass of dark excrement on the husks and inside the nuts. After pupating in sheltered locations on or around the tree, another generation of moths emerges in midsummer. Walnuts may be damaged by worms throughout the summer. The larvae spend the winter in cocoons in protected places, such as under loose bark or in tree crevices. Early blooming walnut varieties are most susceptible to codling moth damage.

SOLUTION: Once the worms have penetrated the nuts, it is impossible to kill them. Next spring, spray trees with ORTHO Fruit & Vegetable Insect Control when the developing nuts are ⅜ to ½ inch in diameter. Repeat the spray 6 to 8 weeks later. Remove and destroy all fallen nuts, and clean up debris around the trees. Plant late-blooming varieties such as Hartley and Vina.

WALNUT

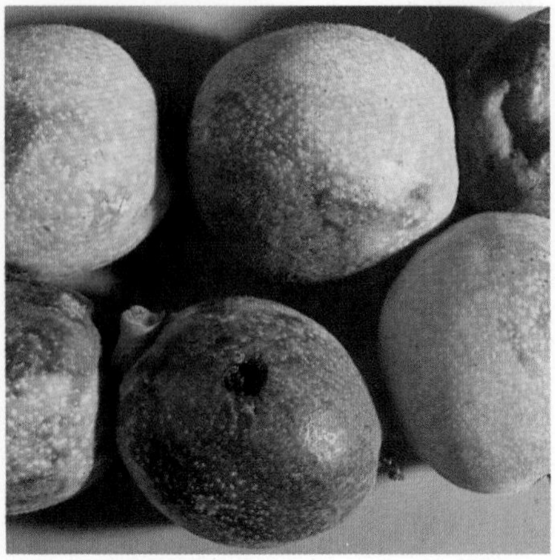

Walnut husk fly damage.

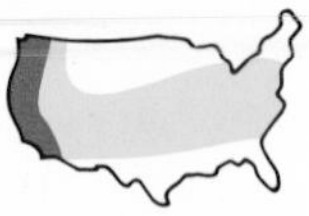

PROBLEM: Soft, blackened, decayed areas cover part or all of the walnut husk. Cream to yellow-colored maggots up to 3/8 inch long are feeding inside the husk. The walnut shells are stained dirty black; sometimes the husks stick to the shells. The kernels are often stained, and may be shriveled.

ANALYSIS: Walnut husk fly
(*Rhagoletis* species)
These maggots are the larvae of several closely related flies. The adult flies, slightly smaller than a housefly, are yellow-brown with banded wings. The flies begin laying their eggs in the developing walnut husks in late July and early August. The maggots that hatch from these eggs feed in the husks for about a month, then drop to the ground and pupate in the soil until the following summer. As a result of maggot feeding, the husks become black and decayed, and the shells and kernels are stained. The maggots never feed on the kernels, and although the walnut meats may be shriveled or discolored, they usually taste normal.

SOLUTION: Walnut husk flies are very difficult to control. Partial control may be obtained by killing the adult flies before they lay their eggs. Spray with an insecticide containing *malathion*, covering all of the foliage thoroughly. Respray 2 weeks later. Contact your local County Extension Office (see page 1029) for information regarding husk fly emergence dates in your area.

Walnut blight.

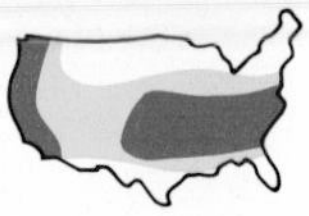

PROBLEM: Buds turn dark brown to black, and die. There are brown spots on the leaves and dead, sunken lesions on the shoots. Some of the leaves may be deformed. Black, sunken, hard areas develop on the nuts. A shiny black fluid may exude from these lesions. Infected nuts have stained shells or shriveled kernels. Nut yield may be reduced.

ANALYSIS: Walnut blight
This plant disease is caused by a bacterium (*Xanthomonas juglandis*) that is common on walnuts. The bacteria spend the winter in diseased buds, twig lesions, and old infected nuts attached to the tree. A thick, shiny fluid containing millions of bacteria exudes from the infected plant parts in the spring. Spring rains splash the bacteria to the buds, shoots, flowers, and developing nuts, starting new infections. Bacterial infection reduces nut set and can continue to spread to healthy nuts and foliage throughout the summer during periods of wet weather. If the nuts are infected before their shells harden (when the nuts are 3/4 grown), the bacteria may spread into and decay the kernels. Because the wet, rainy conditions of spring favor the rapid spread of walnut blight, early-blooming walnut varieties are most susceptible to this disease.

SOLUTION: Next spring, spray with a pesticide containing *basic copper sulfate* when catkins start to shed pollen, then spray again when the small nutlets start to appear. If the weather remains wet, spray once more after 2 weeks. Plant late-blooming varieties such as Vina and Hartley.

Walnut aphid (12 times life size).

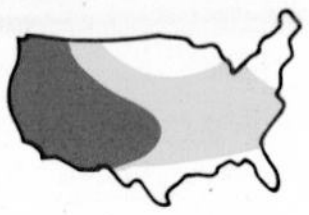

PROBLEM: Tiny (1/16 inch) soft-bodied yellow insects are clustered on the leaves and stems. The youngest leaves may be curled, thickened, and discolored. A shiny or sticky substance coats the leaves. A black sooty mold may grow on the sticky substance. Ants are sometimes present. Severely infested trees may suffer a reduction in nut yield.

ANALYSIS: Aphids
Several species of aphids infest walnuts, including the walnut aphid (*Chromaphis juglandicola*) and the European dusky-veined walnut aphid (*Panaphis juglandis*). These insects do little damage in small numbers. However, they are extremely prolific and populations can rapidly build up to damaging numbers during the growing season. Damage occurs when the aphid sucks the juices from the walnut leaves. The aphid is unable to digest fully all the sugar in the plant sap and excretes the excess in a fluid called honeydew, which often drops onto the leaves below. A sooty mold may develop on the honeydew, causing the walnut leaves to appear black and dirty. Ants feed on the honeydew, and are often present where there is an aphid infestation. For more information about aphids, see page 875.

SOLUTION: Moderate numbers of aphids do little harm. If there are more than 15 or 20 aphids per leaflet, spray with ORTHO Fruit & Vegetable Insect Control. Repeat as directed on the label.

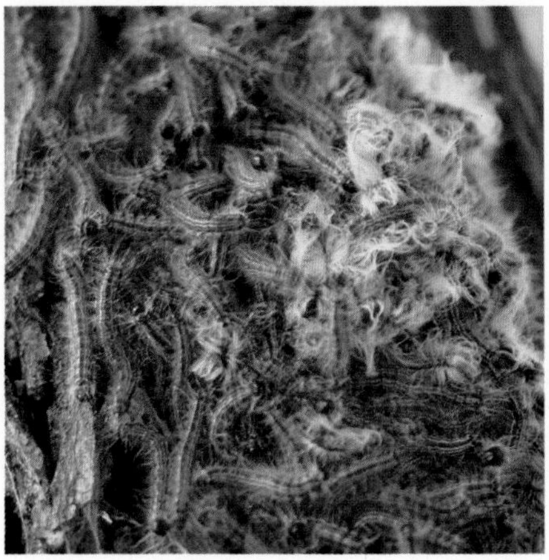

Walnut caterpillars (half life size).

PROBLEM: Reddish brown to black hairy caterpillars with pale yellow to gray stripes running lengthwise along their bodies are feeding on walnut leaves. These caterpillars, which range in size up to 2 inches, feed in clusters. The leaves are chewed, and severely infested trees may be completely defoliated.

ANALYSIS: Walnut caterpillar
(*Datana integerrima*)
These caterpillars, the larvae of brown moths, are common pests of walnut, pecan, and several other nut trees. The adult moths emerge in the spring to lay their eggs on the young leaves. The larvae that hatch from these eggs feed on the foliage, often clustered together. Caterpillars group together on the trunk and molt (shed their skins) several times during their life cycle. When mature, they drop to the ground and pupate in the soil, emerging as adult moths either later in the season or the following spring. Caterpillar damage may occur throughout the growing season. These pests can be very destructive. Severely infested trees may be defoliated within 24 hours.

SOLUTION: Spray infested trees with ORTHO Fruit & Vegetable Insect Control. Repeat as directed on the label. Pick off and kill caterpillars when they are clustered on the trunk while molting.

Oystershell scales (life size).

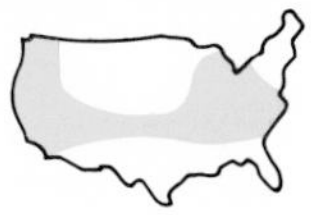

PROBLEM: The undersides of the leaves, stems, or small branches are covered with brownish crusty bumps or thick, white, waxy bumps, or clusters of flattened yellowish, gray, or brownish scaly bumps. The bumps can be scraped or picked off; the undersides are usually soft. Leaves turn yellow and may drop. In some cases, a shiny or sticky substance coats the leaves. A black sooty mold often grows on the substance.

ANALYSIS: Scales
Several different types of scale insects infest walnut trees. They lay their eggs on leaves or bark, and in spring to midsummer the young scales, called *crawlers*, settle on leaves and twigs. The small ($\frac{1}{10}$ inch), soft-bodied young feed by sucking sap from the plant. The legs usually atrophy and a hard crusty or waxy shell develops over the body. The mature female scales lay their eggs underneath their shell. Some species of scales that infest walnuts are unable to digest fully all the sugar in the plant sap, and excrete the excess in a fluid called honeydew, which often drops onto the leaves below. A black sooty mold fungus may grow on the honeydew. For more information about scales, see page 876.

SOLUTION: Spray with ORTHO Fruit & Vegetable Insect Control in midsummer when the crawlers are active. Contact your local Cooperative Extension Office (see page 1029) to determine the best time to spray for scales in your area. The following early spring, before new growth begins, spray the trunk and branches with an insecticide containing *methidathion* or dormant oil to control overwintering insects.

Walnut blister mite damage.

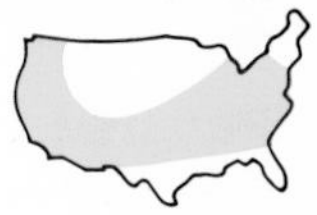

PROBLEM: Leaves are stippled, yellowing, or bronzed; they may dry out and drop. There may be webbing between the leaves or on the lower surfaces of the leaves. Severely infested trees may drop all their leaves. To determine if the tree is infested with mites, hold a sheet of white paper underneath an affected leaf and tap the leaf sharply. Minute green, red, or yellow specks the size of pepper grains will drop to the paper and begin to crawl around. These pests are easily seen against the white background.

ANALYSIS: Spider mites
These mites, related to spiders, are major pests of many trees, shrubs, and flowers. They cause damage by sucking sap from the undersides of the leaves. As a result of feeding, the green leaf pigment disappears, producing the stippled, bronzed appearance. Mites are active throughout the growing season, but are favored by hot, dry weather (70°F and up). By midsummer, they build up to tremendous numbers. For more information about spider mites, see page 887.

SOLUTION: Spray the infested tree with ORTHO Fruit & Vegetable Insect Control or a pesticide containing *dicofol* (KELTHANE®). To kill overwintering mites on the branches, spray the tree with ORTHO Volck Oil Spray early next spring just before the buds open.

WALNUT

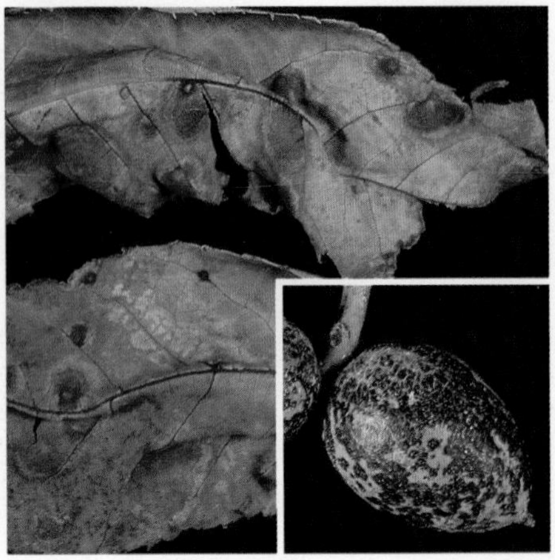

Anthracnose. *Insert:* Infected nut.

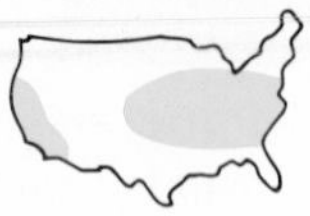

PROBLEM: Circular reddish to grayish brown spots up to ¾ inch in diameter appear on the leaves from May to the end of the summer. Oval or irregular brown sunken lesions may develop on the green shoots. Tiny, dark, sunken spots may appear on the walnut husks. Infected nuts often drop prematurely. The kernels of harvested nuts may be dark and shriveled. Infected leaves usually drop, and the tree may defoliate by midsummer.

ANALYSIS: Walnut anthracnose
This plant disease is caused by a fungus (*Gnomonia leptostyla*) that attacks walnuts and butternuts. The fungus spends the winter in twig lesions and on plant debris on the ground. In the spring, spores are discharged during rainy weather and blown to the new growth. If the surfaces of the leaves are wet, the spores can infect the leaves and shoots. The fungus can continue to infect healthy leaf, nut, and shoot tissue throughout the growing season, especially during periods of wet and humid weather. Trees that defoliate prematurely become weakened, and frequently suffer a large reduction in nut yield and size.

SOLUTION: If you notice the problem early in the summer, spray the infected tree with a fungicide containing *benomyl, maneb,* or *zineb.* Repeat the spray 2 more times at intervals of 2 weeks. Remove and destroy all plant debris. Next spring, spray the tree when the leaves are half their mature size. Spray again 2 more times at intervals of 2 weeks.

Crown rot.

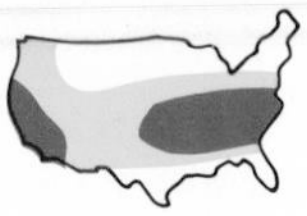

PROBLEM: The bark on part or all of the trunk just above or below the soil line is darkened. Sap may ooze from the affected bark. When the diseased bark is scraped away, the underlying sapwood is found to be discolored tan to black. Foliage may be sparse and yellowing. There is little new growth, and the tree may be stunted.

ANALYSIS: Crown rot
This plant disease is caused by soil-inhabiting fungi (*Phytophthora* species) that infect many trees and shrubs. The fungi penetrate the bark of the lower trunk or upper roots, forming lesions. As the fungi progress inward, they decay the nutrient-conducting tissue under the bark, interfering with the flow of nutrients to the roots. If left unchecked, the fungi will encircle and decay the entire trunk, eventually causing the death of the tree. Crown rot is greatly favored by wet soil. Trees planted in lawns, flower beds, or other moist areas are highly susceptible.

SOLUTION: If the rot has not completely encircled the tree, it can probably be saved. To let the crown dry out, remove the soil within 4 feet of the base of the tree, exposing the major roots. Keep this area dry. During the rainy season, slope the remaining soil away from the hole to keep it from filling with water. After the tree shows signs of recovering (look for healthy new growth), replace the soil around the base of the tree. Or, if possible, fill the hole with stones instead of soil to help keep the roots dry. Avoid planting flowers, shrubs, or other vegetation immediately around the tree.

Blackline. *Insert:* Closeup.

PROBLEM: Growth is weak and sparse, and many of the leaves are drooping and yellow. Foliage may drop prematurely. Many of the shoots die. Eventually the upper part of the tree dies. Numerous shoots sprout from the root stock. Small holes and cracks may be seen on the graft union between the rootstock and the upper part of the tree. When patches of bark along the graft union are removed, a dark brown or black line of corky tissue up to ¼ inch wide is exposed.

ANALYSIS: Blackline
This plant disease is caused by a virus that infects English walnuts grafted onto black walnut rootstock. Blackline usually affects trees 5 years of age or older. The virus is spread in the pollen of English walnuts to healthy trees. Infected trees develop a layer of black, corky cells at the graft union. This layer initially forms in small portions of the union. As it increases in size and encircles the entire graft union, the flow of water and nutrients between the rootstock and the top is reduced and finally cut off entirely, killing the upper part of the tree.

SOLUTION: Infected trees cannot be cured. They will need to be replaced eventually. If desired, the black walnut rootstock may be saved. To do so, remove the dead top growth, then prune out most of the sprouts, leaving a few of the most vigorous ones to develop into a new top.

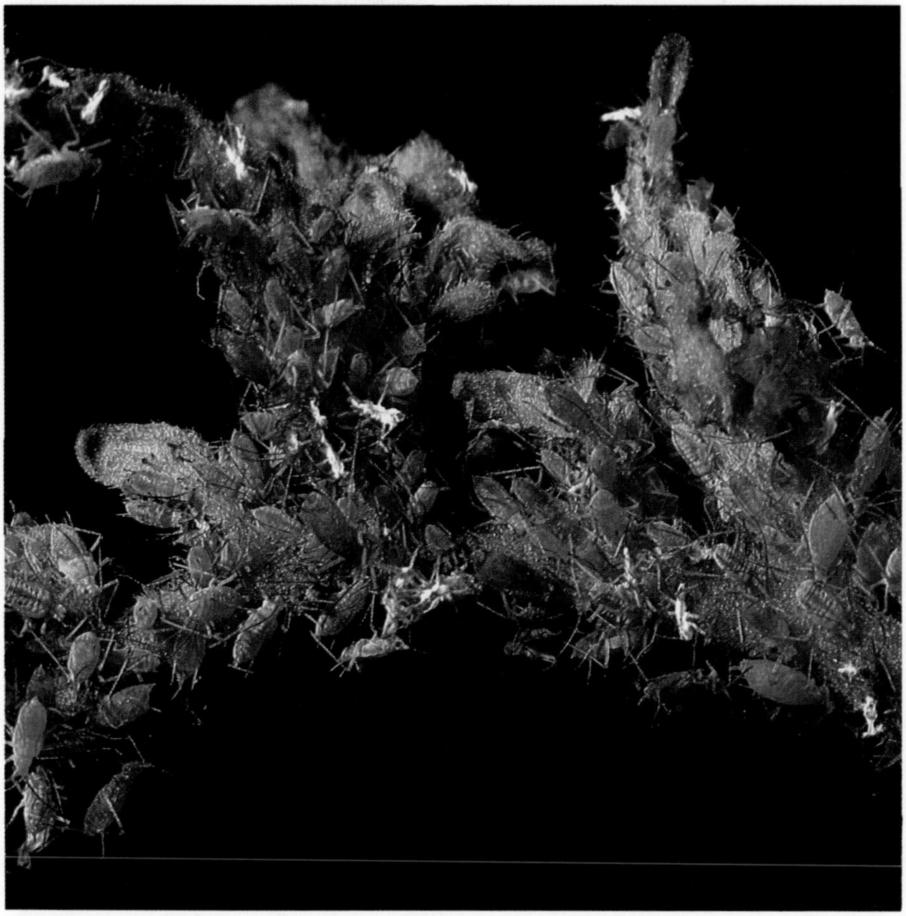

Some of the problems common to many vegetables, berries, and grapes are described on the next 17 pages. If you don't find your problem here, look up your plant in the index on the next page.

VEGETABLES, BERRIES, & GRAPES

The secret to growing food crops that are both delicious and prolific is to grow them quickly. If growth continues at its maximum rate from the time the seedling emerges until harvest, the plant not only grows bigger and makes more fruit*, but it has less time to store the chemicals that give strong or bitter flavors.

The way to grow plants quickly is to give them ideal growing conditions. In the vegetable garden, this usually means selecting the right location, preparing the soil properly, feeding and watering as the plants need it, and keeping the garden free of weeds and pests.

But rich soil and ideal growing conditions are ideal for weeds, too. Weeds slow the growth of vegetables by competing with them for light, water, and food. And, studies are revealing that many weeds also inhibit the growth of plants with which they share garden space.

It's easy to think of our garden problems as mostly dealing with weeds, insects, or disease. But often problems are encouraged by our habitual garden practices. We can seldom eliminate a disease or insect problem by changing our garden practices, but by adopting garden practices that minimize our problems, we can often turn a catastrophe into a mere nuisance.

The most effective solution for disease and insect problems on vegetables is usually to select plant varieties that are resistant to a particular pest or disease. For many years, plant breeders have been concentrating on breeding vegetables that are resistant to the major problems that plague that plant. Some of their successes have been astonishing, and have done a great deal to help vegetable gardeners.

Above: Aphids on a tomato plant. See page 777.
Left: Healthy vegetables can be decorative as well as delicious.

*Throughout this section, we use the word "fruit" in the botanical sense, to mean the part of the plant associated with the seeds. In the kitchen, a "tomato" is a vegetable, but in the garden, a "tomato" is a tomato plant; the part we eat is the tomato fruit.

INDEX TO VEGETABLES, BERRIES, AND GRAPES

PROBLEMS COMMON TO MANY VEGETABLES, BERRIES, AND GRAPES

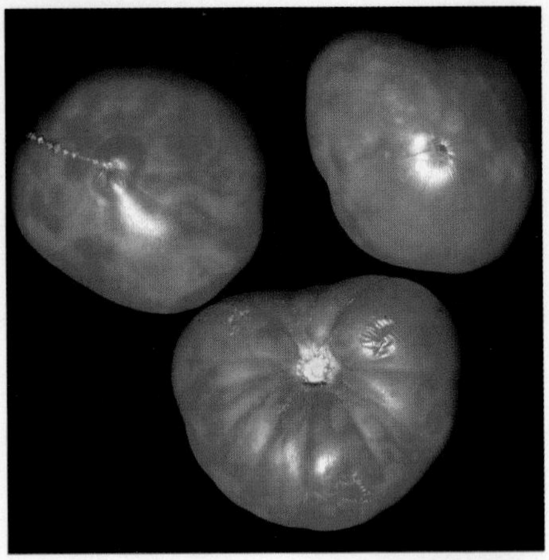

Poor-quality tomatoes.

PROBLEM: Fruit have poor or strong flavor and are smaller than normal. Fruit yield is low.

ANALYSIS: Poor-quality produce

Vegetables and berries may yield poor-quality produce for many reasons.

1. *Hot weather* affects the flavor of some fruit, especially cool season crops such as lettuce and members of the cabbage family. Their taste becomes strong and bitter.

2. *Fluctuations in soil moisture* affect the flavor of many fruits, especially cucumbers. Sweet and white potato tubers crack and appear unappetizing. Alternating wet and dry soil results in erratic growth with poor-quality fruit and reduced yields.

3. *Poor soil fertility* causes plants to grow poorly and yield few if any fruit. Those fruits produced are frequently off-flavor and may not develop fully.

4. *Overmature fruit* deteriorate rapidly and lose their flavor. Allowing fruit to overripen on the plant reduces future yields by using energy the plant could have used to produce more fruit.

SOLUTION: Follow these guidelines for better-quality produce. (For more information on each of these recommendations, see the entry for your plant in the alphabetical section beginning on page 676.)

1. Plant vegetables and small fruits at the times of year suggested on page 1025.

2. Follow the irrigation guidelines for your vegetable.

3. Fertilize your plants as instructed.

4. Pick fruit as they mature, so more fruit will be produced. Follow the harvesting guidelines specific to your plant.

Slow growth caused by insufficient light.

Phosphorus deficiency on corn.

Slow growth from too acid soil.

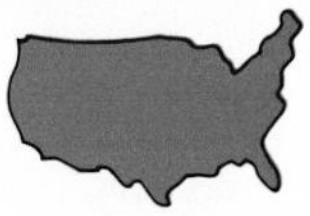

PROBLEM: Plants grow slowly or not at all. Leaves are light green, and few or no flowers or fruit are produced. Plants are shaded for much of the day. Lower leaves may turn yellow and drop.

ANALYSIS: Insufficient light
Plants need sunlight to manufacture food and produce fruit. Without adequate sunlight they grow slowly. Vegetable and berry plants that yield fruit, such as tomatoes, brambles, strawberries, beans, and peppers, require at least 6 hours of sunlight a day. Some leafy and root vegetables, however, will tolerate light shade. These vegetables include beets, cabbage, carrots, chives, kale, leeks, lettuce, mustard, green onions, parsley, radishes, Swiss chard, and turnips.

SOLUTION: Prune any surrounding trees to allow more sunlight. Plant vegetables that require less sunlight in somewhat shady areas of the garden. If possible, move your garden site, or grow vegetables in containers on a sunny patio or porch.

PROBLEM: Plants grow slowly. Leaves are pale green to yellow, or darker than normal, and dull. Few flowers and fruit are produced. Fruit that are produced mature slowly. Plants pulled from the soil may have small, black, and rotted root systems. Plants may die.

ANALYSIS: Poor soil or cool weather
Vegetables and small fruits may grow slowly and produce few fruit for any of several reasons.

1. *Excess water:* If the soil is constantly wet, either from frequent watering or poor drainage, roots become shallow, stunting the plant. Wet soil also encourages root rotting fungi, which destroy the root system and kill the plant.

2. *Phosphorus deficiency:* Phosphorus is a major nutrient needed by plants for root formation, flower and fruit production, and overall cell growth. Phosphorus-deficient plants grow slowly, and have dark leaves that may be tinted with purple or have purple veins. This nutrient may be lacking either because it is not present in the soil, or because it is in a form that is unavailable to plants.

3. *Incorrect pH:* The soil pH limits the amounts and kinds of nutrients available to plants. Vegetables grow best with a pH of 6.0 to 8.0. Required nutrients are usually available in adequate amounts at this range. For more information on pH, see page 908.

4. *Cool weather:* Warm-season vegetables such as tomatoes, beans, and okra require temperatures over 70°F for best growth and fruit production. If they are planted too early in the season, the cool weather slows their growth. Affected plants may take several months to recover from this setback, and still may not produce abundantly.

SOLUTION: The numbered solutions below correspond to the numbers under analysis.

1. Allow the soil around plants to dry out. (For more information on this technique, see page 857.) Remove and discard any plants with rotting roots. Avoid future root rot problems by planting in well-drained soil. For information on improving soil drainage, see page 901.

2. Spray the leaves with Ra-Pid-Gro Plant Food for a quick response. Fertilize with a balanced fertilizer such as ORTHO Vegetable Food or ORTHO General Purpose Plant Food. Follow the rates on the package, or those given for each vegetable on the following pages.

3. Test the soil pH and correct to 6.0 to 8.0 according to the instructions on page 909.

4. Plant vegetables at the correct time of year. For planting times for your area, see page 1009. Discard warm-season vegetable plants that have been set back by cool temperatures. Replant with healthy transplants.

PROBLEMS COMMON TO MANY VEGETABLES, BERRIES, AND GRAPES — SEEDLING PROBLEMS

Dehydration.

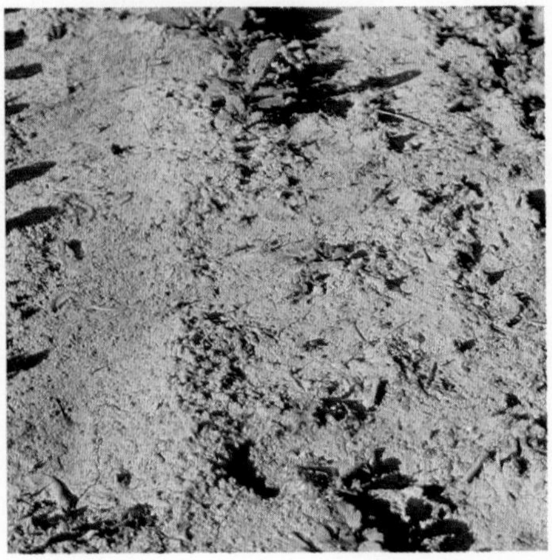

Crusted soil.

Wilted broccoli.

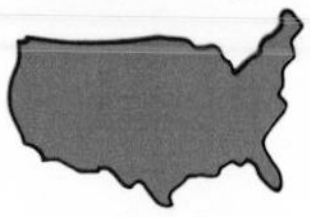

PROBLEM: Few or no seedlings emerge through the soil.

ANALYSIS: Seedlings don't emerge Seedlings may fail to sprout for any of several reasons.	**SOLUTION:** The numbered solutions correspond to the numbers under analysis.
1. *Lack of water:* Seeds need water to soften and break the seed coat. Seeds planted in dry soil will not germinate.	**1.** Keep the soil moist, letting the surface dry slightly between waterings.
2. *Seeds washed away:* Heavy rains or watering may wash seeds from the planting site or deeper into the soil than they were planted.	**2.** Water carefully with a spray or mist or cover the seed row with burlap or cheesecloth to keep the soil and seeds from washing away.
3. *Slow germination:* Some seeds require a longer time to germinate than others.	**3.** Read the seed packet for information on special germinating conditions.
4. *Soil temperature:* Warm-season vegetables (tomatoes, beans, peppers) germinate best at soil temperatures between 60° and 85°F. If temperatures fall below this range, the inside of the seed is damaged. Cool-season vegetables (cabbage, peas, lettuce) germinate best at soil temperatures below 75°F, and become dormant at higher temperatures.	**4.** Plant seeds at the correct time of year. For planting times for your area, see page 1009. If starting seeds indoors, improve the germination rate by providing bottom heat with soil heating cables or placing the seeded containers in a warm place, such as the top of a refrigerator.
5. *Incorrect planting depth:* Seeds need oxygen for good germination. If planted too deep, they suffocate. If planted too shallow, they dry out.	**5.** Plant seeds according to the depth stated on the packet.
6. *Crusted soil:* Seedlings are unable to push their way up through crusted soil.	**6.** Plant seeds in loose, crumbly soil, or cover the seed row with vermiculite, sand, or burlap to keep the soil from crusting. For more information on starting seeds, see page 925.
7. *Damping-off:* This disease is caused by soil-inhabiting fungi, which attack seeds as they germinate, killing them before they emerge. For more information on damping-off, see page 850.	**7.** Protect seeds during germination by coating them with a fungicide containing *captan* (ORTHOCIDE®), *thiram*, or *chloroneb*. Add a pinch of fungicide to a packet of seeds (or ½ teaspoon per pound), and shake well to coat the seeds with the fungicide.

PROBLEM: Seedlings wilt and die. The soil is dry.

ANALYSIS: Dehydration
Seedlings need a continuous supply of water. Seedlings growing in sandy soil are especially susceptible to drying out, because sandy soil does not hold much water. Seedling roots may penetrate only the top inch of soil. If that top inch dries out, the seedling has no moisture on which to draw. The young roots are tender and very susceptible to drying. Seedlings are so small that if they wilt, they seldom recover as do older plants. If they do recover, it may take some time for them to resume their normal growth.

SOLUTION: Water seedlings whenever the surface of the soil dries. In hot weather, you may have to water more than once a day. To reduce their need for water, shade seedlings with a layer of cheesecloth during hot weather. By the time the young plants have formed their first true leaves (the leaves that look like those on a mature plant), their root systems are a few inches deep, and they are no longer as susceptible to drying out.

Damping-off of radish seedlings.

Peas eaten by rabbits.

Bean seedlings eaten by slugs.

PROBLEM: Seedlings fall over soon after they emerge. Areas on the stem at the soil line are water-soaked and discolored. The base of the stem is soft and thin.

ANALYSIS: Damping-off
Damping-off is a common problem in wet soil with a high nitrogen level. Wet, rich soil promotes damping-off in two ways: the fungi that cause it are more active under these conditions, and the seedlings are more susceptible to attack. Damping-off is often a problem when the weather remains cloudy and wet, and when seedlings are heavily shaded or crowded. Seedlings started indoors in a wet, unsterilized medium are also susceptible.

SOLUTION: To prevent fungi from attacking your seedlings, take these precautions:
1. Allow the surface of the soil to dry slightly between waterings.
2. Do not start seeds in soil that has a high nitrogen level. Add nitrogen fertilizers after the seedlings have produced their first true leaves.
3. Protect the seeds during germination with a fungicide containing *captan* (ORTHOCIDE®) or *thiram*. Add a pinch of fungicide to a packet of seeds (or ½ teaspoon per pound) and shake well to coat the seeds.
4. Use a sterilized medium for starting seeds indoors, such as a sterilized potting soil or a mixture of peat moss, perlite, and vermiculite.
5. Thin seedlings to allow good air circulation through the planting.

PROBLEM: Seedling leaves are chewed ragged. Seedlings may completely disappear, or short stubs of the stems may remain.

ANALYSIS: Seedlings eaten Several animal and insect pests feed on seedlings.	**SOLUTION:** The numbered solutions below correspond to the numbers in the analysis.
1. Many kinds of *birds*, especially grackles, blackbirds, and crows eat entire seedlings. The plants are most susceptible to bird attack when they have just emerged.	**1.** Cover seedlings with a tent made of cheesecloth or netting stretched over a wooden frame. Scarecrows and dangling aluminum pie plates may help to deter birds. For more about birds, see page 899.
2. *Snails and slugs* feed at night and on cloudy days, chewing holes in leaves or devouring entire seedlings. Silvery winding trails are evidence of their presence. During the day they hide in damp places under rocks, flower pots, or debris.	**2.** Control snails and slugs with ORTHO Bug-Geta Snail & Slug Pellets. Sprinkle lightly after application to activate the pellets. The moisture will also attract snails and slugs. Treat along the seeded rows, and in hiding places such as rocks, boards, flower pots, or compost piles. For more information on snails and slugs, see page 670.
3. *Earwigs* are dark brown insects with pinchers on their tail end. They feed at night, and chew holes in leaves and stems.	**3.** To control earwigs, treat with an insecticide containing *carbaryl* (SEVIN®) along the seeded rows and in hiding places under stones, rocks, and debris. For more information on earwigs, see page 673.
4. *Rabbits* may eat an entire seedling, or leave only a short stub of the stem standing in the soil.	**4.** Keep rabbits out of the garden by erecting a 1-foot-high fence of small-gauge fencing wire around the garden. Anchor the bottom of the fence with boards 1 to 2 inches deep in the soil to prevent the rabbits from digging underneath. For more information on rabbits, see page 900.
5. *Grasshoppers* are present throughout the growing season, and migrate from area to area as their food source is depleted. They eat entire seedlings. Grasshoppers are prevalent in hot, dry weather.	**5.** Control grasshoppers and protect uneaten seedlings with an insecticide containing *carbaryl* (SEVIN®), *diazinon*, or *malathion*. Repeat at weekly intervals as long as grasshoppers are present. For more information on grasshoppers, see page 672.

PROBLEMS COMMON TO MANY VEGETABLES, BERRIES, AND GRAPES

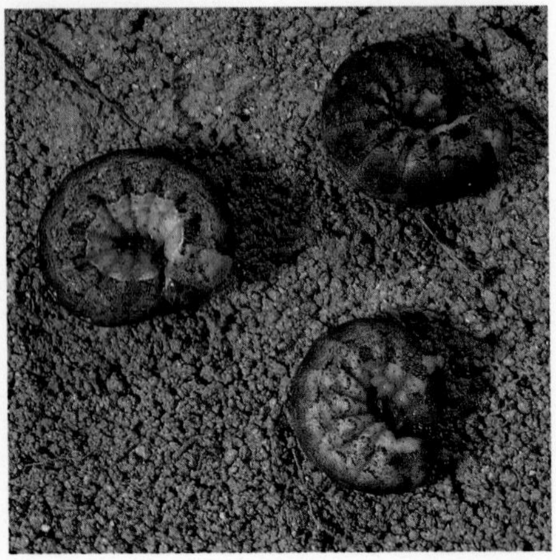
Variegated cutworms (life size).

Cutworms on celery (life size).

PROBLEM: Stems of young plants are chewed or cut off near the ground. Gray, brown, or black worms, up to 2 inches long, may be found in the top 2 inches of the soil near the base of the damaged plants. The worms coil when disturbed.

ANALYSIS: Cutworms
Several species of cutworms attack plants in the vegetable garden. Surface-feeding cutworms are common pests of young vegetables planted early in the season. A single surface-feeding cutworm can sever the stems of many young plants in one night. They eat through the stems just above ground level. Tomatoes, peppers, peas, beans, and members of the cabbage family are particularly susceptible. Some cutworms can climb up the stem or trunk of grapes, blueberries, tomatoes, and other garden crops to feed on young leaves, buds, and fruit. Cutworms hide in the soil during the day and feed only at night. Adult cutworms are dark, night-flying moths with bands or stripes on their forewings.

SOLUTION: Apply ORTHO Vegetable Guard Soil Insect Killer, ORTHO Diazinon Soil & Turf Insect Control, or ORTHO Diazinon Soil & Foliage Dust around the base of undamaged plants where cutworm damage has been observed. Make sure your plant is listed on the product label. Since cutworms are difficult to control, it may be necessary to repeat the dusting at weekly intervals. Before transplanting new plants into the area, apply a preventive treatment of ORTHO Vegetable Guard Soil Insect Killer, or ORTHO Diazinon Soil & Turf Insect Control and work it into the soil. Cultivate the soil thoroughly in late summer and fall to expose and destroy eggs, larvae, and pupae. Further reduce damage with a "cutworm collar" around the stem of each plant. These collars can be made of any stiff material, such as a cottage cheese carton with the bottom removed. They should be at least 2 inches high, and pressed firmly into the soil. For more information on cutworms, see page 871.

WILTING

Wilting French sorrel.

PROBLEM: Plants wilt. Soil is dry. Plants may recover when watered.

ANALYSIS: Dehydration
Plants need water for both root and leaf growth. Plants growing in sandy soil are very susceptible to drying out because the soil does not retain much water. Plants usually recover in a short time after being watered. Repeated wilting will stunt plants, reducing their yield and the quality of their produce. Ripening fruit on repeatedly wilted plants do not mature fully, sometimes crack, and are frequently flavorless. Some members of the cabbage family wilt on hot days even though the soil is moist. This is normal and does not harm the plant.

SOLUTION: Water immediately and thoroughly. Follow the watering guidelines for your plant found in the alphabetical section beginning on page 676. To reduce the need for watering, use mulches as discussed on page 926.

Root rot on broccoli.

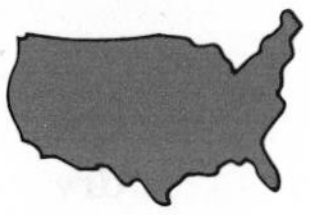

PROBLEM: Leaves wilt and turn yellow. Lower leaves are affected first, then the upper ones. Few or no fruit are produced. Plants do not recover when watered, and usually die.

ANALYSIS: Root and stem rot
This disease is caused by any of a number of different fungi, also known as *water molds*. These fungi live in the soil. They thrive in waterlogged, heavy soils. The fungi attack the plant roots or the stems at the soil level. Infection causes the roots and stems to decay, resulting in wilting, then yellowing leaves, and eventually the death of the plant. Many of these fungi also cause *damping-off* of seedlings. For more information about damping-off, see page 663.

SOLUTION: Allow the soil around the plants to dry out. (For more information on this technique, see page 857.) Remove and discard severely infected plants. Avoid future root rot problems by planting in well-drained soil. (For information on improving soil drainage, see page 901.) Avoid overwatering by following the watering guidelines for your plant found in the alphabetical section beginning on page 676.

Fusarium wilt on tomato.

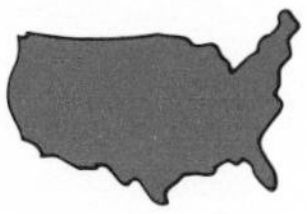

PROBLEM: Leaves wilt, turn yellow, and may turn brown. Few or no fruit are produced. Growth slows and plants may be stunted. When the stem is sliced open lengthwise, the tissue just under the bark may be brown.

ANALYSIS: Wilt diseases
Wilt diseases infect many vegetables and berries. They may be caused by any of several fungi that live in the soil. The fungi are spread by contaminated plants, soil, and equipment. They enter the plant through the roots and spread through the water-conducting vessels in the stems. The vessels become discolored and plugged. This plugging cuts off the flow of water and nutrients to the leaves, resulting in leaf yellowing and wilting. The plugging also results in a reduced yield and poor quality fruit. Severely infected plants die. For more information about wilt diseases, see page 850.

SOLUTION: No chemical controls are available. Wilt fungi can be removed from the soil only by fumigation techniques. (For more information about soil fumigation, see page 919.) However, the best solution is usually to avoid plants that are susceptible to wilt diseases. For a list of vegetables and berries that are susceptible to wilt diseases, see page 1009.

Nematode damage on beans.

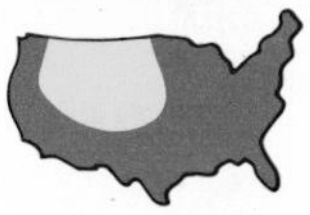

PROBLEM: Plants wilt in hot, dry weather and recover at night. They are stunted and yellow. Round and elongated nodules may occur on the roots. Plants may die.

ANALYSIS: Nematodes
Nematodes are microscopic worms that live in the soil. They are not related to earthworms. Nematodes feed on plant roots, damaging and stunting them. The damaged roots can't supply sufficient water and nutrients to the aboveground plant parts, and the plant is stunted or slowly dies. Nematodes are found throughout the United States, but are most severe in the South. They prefer moist, sandy loam soils. Nematodes can move only a few inches each year on their own, but they may be carried long distances by soil, water, tools, or infested plants. Testing roots and soil is the only positive method for confirming the presence of nematodes. Contact your local Cooperative Extension Office (see page 1029) for sampling instructions and addresses of testing laboratories. Soil and root problems such as poor soil structure, drought stress, nutrient deficiency, and root rots can also produce symptoms of decline similar to those caused by nematodes. These problems should be eliminated as causes before sending soil and root samples for testing. For information on soil problems and root rots, see pages 907 and 665.

SOLUTION: No chemicals are available to homeowners to kill nematodes in planted soil. However, they can be controlled before planting by soil fumigation. For information on fumigating soil, see page 927. Plant resistant varieties (see page 1026).

PROBLEMS COMMON TO MANY VEGETABLES, BERRIES, AND GRAPES — LEAVES DISCOLORED OR MOTTLED

Nitrogen-deficient tomato.

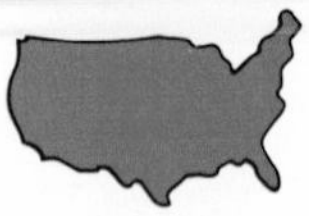

PROBLEM: The bottom leaves turn light green to pale yellow, and may die or drop. Growth slows, and new leaves are small. Flowers turn yellow and drop. Fruit are small, and may be distorted and discolored.

ANALYSIS: Nitrogen deficiency
Plants need nitrogen for making chlorophyll, the green pigment in their leaves, and for overall healthy growth and high-quality fruit production. When plants lack nitrogen, growth slows, blossoms drop, and fruit yield is reduced. Nitrogen may either be lacking in the soil, or be present in a form that is not available to the plant. In cool, rainy, early spring weather, little or no nitrogen is available. Later in the season, as vegetables are growing rapidly and maturing, the plants may deplete the supply of nitrogen in the soil. During a drought, nitrogen is carried to the soil surface as the water it is dissolved in evaporates. Once the nitrogen is above the plant's root zone, the roots are unable to absorb it. Rain or irrigation water carries the nitrogen back to the root zone where it is available to the plant.

SOLUTION: For a quick response, spray the foliage with ORTHO ORTHO-GRO Liquid Plant Food or Ra-Pid-Gro Plant Food. Water the plant with the same solution. Remove any fruit from severely affected plants to allow them time to resume normal growth. Fertilize according to the recommendations for your plant in the alphabetical section beginning on page 676. For more information about nitrogen deficiency, see page 859.

Root rot on bush beans.

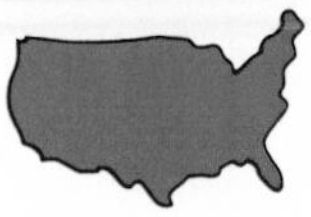

PROBLEM: Leaves turn yellow, starting with the older, lower leaves and progressing to the younger ones. Plants grow very little. Flowers yellow and drop. Fruit shrivel and do not ripen. When the plant is pulled up, the roots are black, soft, and rotted. The soil has frequently been very moist.

ANALYSIS: Root rot
This plant disease is caused by any of a number of different fungi that are present in most soil. These fungi normally do little damage, but can cause root rot in wet or waterlogged soils. Waterlogged soil may result from overwatering or poor soil drainage. Infection causes the roots to decay, resulting in wilting, yellowing leaves, flower and fruit drop, reduced fruit yield, and eventually the death of the plant.

SOLUTION: To avoid root rot problems, do not overwater. Follow the watering guidelines under the entry for your plant in the alphabetical section beginning on page 676. Remove and discard severely infected plants. Avoid future root rot problems by planting in well-drained soil. For information on improving soil drainage, see page 901. For more information on root rots, see the section beginning on page 856.

Iron-deficient beans.

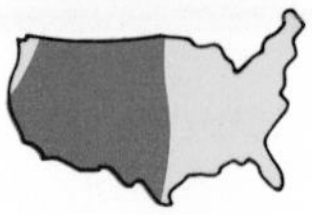

PROBLEM: Leaves turn pale green or yellow. The newest leaves (those at the tips of the stems) are most severely affected. Except in extreme cases, the veins of affected leaves remain green. In extreme cases, the newest leaves are small and all-white or yellow. Older leaves may remain green.

ANALYSIS: Iron deficiency
Plants frequently suffer from deficiencies of iron and other minor nutrients, such as manganese and zinc, elements essential to normal plant growth and development. Deficiencies can occur when one or more of these elements are depleted in the soil. Often, these minor nutrients are present in the soil, but alkaline (pH 7.5 and higher) or wet soil conditions cause them to form compounds that cannot be used by the plant. An alkaline condition can result from overliming, or from lime leached from cement or brick. Regions where soil is derived from limestone, and those with low rainfall, usually have alkaline soils.

SOLUTION: Feed the plants with a fertilizer containing *chelated iron.* Check the soil pH. Correct to the recommended level for your plant as given in the alphabetical section beginning on page 676. Make alkaline soil more acid with *ferrous sulfate.*

Spider mite damage on string beans.

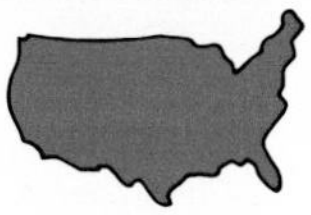

PROBLEM: Leaves are stippled, yellowing, and dirty. Leaves may dry out and drop. There may be webbing over flower buds between leaves, or on the lower surfaces of the leaves. To determine if the plant is infested with mites, hold a sheet of white paper underneath an affected leaf or stem and tap the leaf or stem sharply. Minute green, red, or yellow specks the size of pepper grains will drop to the paper and begin to crawl around. The pests are easily seen against the white background.

ANALYSIS: Mites
Mites, related to spiders, are major pests of many garden and greenhouse plants. They cause damage by sucking sap from the undersides of the leaves. As a result of feeding, the green leaf pigment disappears, producing the stippled appearance. Although mites do not attack the fruit directly, they do cause leaf drop, which weakens the plant and reduces fruit yield. If the plants are severely infected, flowers do not form or do not bloom, resulting in no fruit. Mites are active throughout the growing season, but are favored by hot, dry weather (70°F and up). By midsummer, they may build up to tremendous numbers.

SOLUTION: Treat infested plants with *dicofol* (KELTHANE®) at the first sign of damage. Repeat at weekly intervals until no further damage occurs. Make sure that your vegetable or small berry is listed on the label. Hose plants frequently with a strong stream of water to wash off mites and webs.

Salt damage on radishes.

PROBLEM: Leaf edges and areas between the veins turn dark brown and die. Burned leaves may drop. Growth slows or stops. A white or dark crust may be on the soil.

ANALYSIS: Salt damage
Salt damage occurs when salt accumulates in the soil to damaging levels. This can happen in either of two ways: the garden is not receiving enough water from rainfall or irrigation to wash the salts from the soil, or the drainage is so poor that water does not pass through the soil. In either case, as water evaporates from the soil and plant leaves, the salts that were dissolved in the water accumulate near the soil surface. In some cases, a white or dark brown crust of salts forms on the surface. Salts can originate in the soil, in the irrigation water, or in applied fertilizers.

SOLUTION: The only way to eliminate salt problems is to wash the salts through the soil with water. If the damage is only at a low spot in the garden, fill in the spot to level the area. If the entire garden drains poorly, improve the drainage according to the directions on page 907. If the soil drains well, increase the amount of water applied at each watering by 50 percent or more, so that excess water will leach salts below the root zone of the plants. Fertilize according to instructions for your plant in the alphabetical section beginning on page 676.

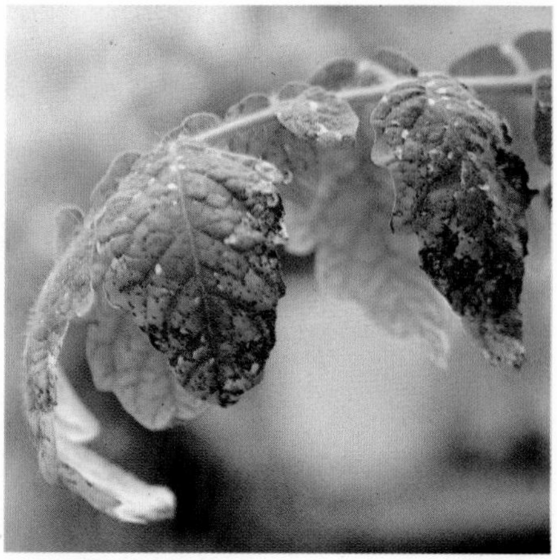

Potassium-deficient tomato.

PROBLEM: Plants grow slowly. Small brown spots appear along the leaf margins. Leaf edges turn yellow, then bronze and finally brown, curl downward, and die. The discoloration may then spread from the leaf edges to areas between the veins. Few fruit are produced, and those that are produced ripen poorly and may be distorted.

ANALYSIS: Potassium deficiency
Potassium is a major nutrient that plants need for overall growth and to help move food manufactured in the leaves to stems, roots, and other parts. Without this movement of food, plants are unable to produce new growth. Plants require larger amounts of potassium as their fruit matures. Fruit yields are reduced in plants deficient in potassium, and such plants are more susceptible to attack from some diseases. Sandy soils, and soils in regions of high rainfall, are often deficient in potassium.

SOLUTION: Spray the foliage with Ra-Pid-Gro Plant Food or ORTHO Ortho-Gro Liquid Plant Food. Water the plant with the same solution. Fertilize with ORTHO Vegetable Food, or follow the fertilization guidelines for your plant in the alphabetical section beginning on page 676.

PROBLEMS COMMON TO MANY VEGETABLES, BERRIES, AND GRAPES — LEAVES DISCOLORED OR MOTTLED

Grapes with spray injury.

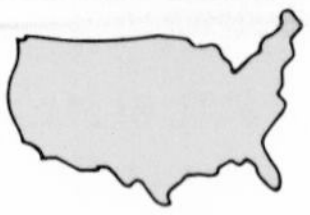

PROBLEM: Irregular spots occur on leaves. Young leaves and blossoms may be distorted and brown. Plants may have been recently sprayed with pesticides.

ANALYSIS: Pesticide burn
Insecticides, fungicides, and herbicides damage plants when used improperly. Damage usually occurs within 24 hours of the time the plants were sprayed. Pesticides may drift from other areas on windy days and damage plants. Pesticides may burn plants when the temperature is above 90°F at the time of spraying, or if it rises above 90°F within a few hours of spraying. Pesticides not mixed and applied according to the label directions also burn plants. Pesticides used in tanks that were once used for herbicides may be contaminated, since traces of herbicides are difficult to remove from sprayers.

SOLUTION: Once plants are damaged, there is nothing to do. Keep the plants healthy with regular watering and fertilizing. In the future, do not spray when temperatures are above 90°F. Avoid spraying on windy days, when sprays may drift. Mix according to the label directions. Do not increase the dosage. When mixing two or more chemicals, be sure they are compatible. Always keep the solution well mixed by shaking the tank periodically while spraying. This is especially important when using wettable powder formulations. Purchase fresh pesticides each year. Wash herbicides thoroughly from sprayers before filling with other pesticides or fertilizer. Or keep a separate sprayer for herbicides.

Air pollution damage to bean.

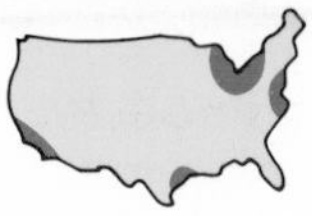

PROBLEM: The upper surfaces of the younger leaves are stippled yellow, tan, or bronze. The entire leaf may be stippled, giving the leaf a yellowish or pale green appearance.

ANALYSIS: Air pollution
Some gases released into the atmosphere from cars and factories damage plants. The most common type of pollution is *smog*. Air pollution damage is most commonly a problem in urban areas, but also occurs in rural areas where gardens are located downwind from factories or large urban centers. Some plants are severely affected, and may even die. Fruit and vegetable production is reduced on pollution-damaged plants. For information on the three most common pollutants, *ozone*, *PAN*, and *sulfur dioxide*, see page 855. Many different environmental factors affect a plant's susceptibility to air pollution including temperature, air movement, light intensity, and soil and air moisture.

SOLUTION: Air pollution injury is usually a localized problem. Check with your neighbors to see if the same kinds of plants in their gardens have been affected the same way. Because injury from air pollutants is similar in appearance to injury from nutrient deficiencies, insects, diseases, and mites, these problems should be eliminated as causes before attributing the damage to air pollution. Nothing can be done about air pollution damage. If you live in a smoggy area, select plants that are smog resistant from the list on page 1008.

Leaf spot on strawberry.

PROBLEM: Spots and blotches appear on the leaves. The spots may be yellow, red, tan, gray, or brown. They range in size from barely visible to ¼ inch in diameter. Several spots may join to form blotches. Leaves may be yellow and dying. Leaf spotting is most severe in warm, humid weather. Fruit may be spotted like the leaves, or be discolored brown or yellow. A fine gray or white mold sometimes covers the infected leaf or fruit tissue in damp conditions.

ANALYSIS: Leaf spot
Several different fungi cause leaf spots. Some of these fungi may eventually kill the plant, or weaken it so that it becomes susceptible to attack by other organisms. Others merely cause spotting that is unsightly but not harmful. Infected fruit are less appetizing, some are inedible, and the yield is reduced. Fruit infected only slightly are still edible if the discolored tissue is cut away. Leaf spotting fungi are spread by splashing water or wind. They generally survive the winter in diseased plant debris. Most of the fungi do their greatest damage in mild weather (50° to 85°F).

SOLUTION: Treat infected plants with a fungicide containing *chlorothalonil* (DACONIL 2787®) or *captan* (ORTHOCIDE®) at the first sign of the disease. Repeat the treatment at intervals of 7 to 10 days until weather conditions favorable to the spread of the disease no longer occur. Make sure that your plant is listed on the product label. Remove all plant debris from the garden after harvest to reduce the amount of overwintering spores.

Powdery mildew on a cucumber.

PROBLEM: The upper surfaces of the leaves are covered with a white powdery growth. Areas of the leaves turn brown and dry. Older leaves are affected first, progressing to younger leaves. Fruit may also be covered with the white powdery growth.

ANALYSIS: Powdery mildew
This common plant disease is caused by fungi that thrive in both humid and dry weather. The powdery patches consist of fungal strands and spores. The spores are spread by the wind to healthy plants. The fungus saps the plant nutrients, causing yellowing and sometimes death of the leaf. Fruit yield may also be reduced. A severe infection may kill the plant. Since powdery mildews attack many different kinds of plants, the fungus from a diseased plant may infect other types of plants in the garden. For a list of powdery mildews and the plants they attack, see page 995. Under favorable conditions, powdery mildew can spread through a closely spaced planting in a matter of days or weeks.

SOLUTION: Control powdery mildew on vegetable and berry plants with ORTHO Vegetable Disease Control at the first sign of the disease. Continue at intervals of 7 days as long as the disease is a problem. Make sure that your plant is listed on the fungicide label. Remove all plant debris from the garden after harvest. When available, grow varieties of vegetables and small fruits that are resistant to powdery mildews.

Leafminer trails on tomato.

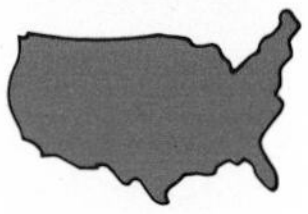

PROBLEM: Light-colored, irregular blotches, blisters, or tunnels appear on the leaves. The tan areas peel apart easily like facial tissue. Tiny black specks are found inside the tunnels.

ANALYSIS: Leafminers
These insect pests belong to a family of leaf-mining flies. The tiny black or yellow adult fly lays its white eggs on the undersides of leaves, or in the leaves. The maggots that hatch from these eggs tunnel between the upper and lower surfaces of the leaves, feeding on the inner tissue. The tunnels and blotches are called *mines*. The black specks inside are the maggots' droppings. Damaged portions of leaves are no longer edible. The yield is usually not affected on fruit-producing vegetables and berries unless many of the leaves are damaged. Several overlapping generations occur during the growing season, so larvae are present continually from spring until fall.

SOLUTION: Control leafminers with ORTHO Fruit & Vegetable Insect Control when the egg clusters are first seen under the leaves. Repeat two more times at weekly intervals to control succeeding generations. Once the leafminers enter the leaves, the sprays are ineffective. Spraying after the mines first appear will control only those leafminers that attack after the application. Make sure that your plant is listed on the insecticide label. Clean all plant debris from the garden after harvest to reduce overwintering spots for the pupae.

Hail damage to tomato.

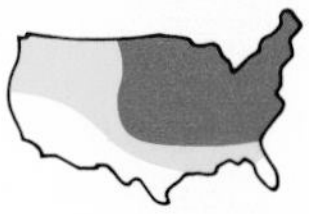

PROBLEM: Leaves are shredded or entirely stripped from the plant during a hail storm. Wounds or deep gouges appear on the fruit and stems; scars form several days after the storm. Young, tender plants may be knocked to the ground.

ANALYSIS: Hail damage
Hail storms often occur from July through September in the midwestern and northeastern United States. Beans, tomatoes, eggplants, peppers, and other maturing vegetables may be stripped of their leaves. The developing fruits are often wounded; usually the wounds heal and the fruit is still edible. However, the wounds may form unsightly scars, and fruit growth may be distorted. Hail-damaged fruit is sometimes mistakenly thought to be diseased or infested.

SOLUTION: Prune off dead and dying shoots and decaying fruit. Fertilize plants with ORTHO Vegetable Food, ORTHO General Purpose Plant Food, or ORTHO Tomato & Vegetable Food to stimulate new growth. Plants will produce new leaves and fruit if the damage has occurred early enough in the growing season. When hail storms are expected, protect plants by covering them with burlap or plastic tarp suspended over stakes.

PROBLEMS COMMON TO MANY VEGETABLES, BERRIES, AND GRAPES — INSECTS ON THE PLANT

Cabbage plants damaged by nocturnal pests.

PROBLEM: Young plants are chewed or cut off near the ground. Some of the leaves, stems, flowers, and fruit are chewed. When the affected plants are inspected at night with a flashlight, insects may be seen feeding on the plants.

ANALYSIS: Nocturnal pests
Several kinds of insects feed on plants only at night, including some beetles, weevils, caterpillars, and all earwigs and cutworms. Beetles are hard-bodied insects with tough, leathery wing covers. Weevils look like beetles, except that they have elongated snouts. Earwigs are reddish brown, flat, elongated insects up to 1 inch long with pincers projecting from the rear of the body. Caterpillars and cutworms are smooth or hairy, soft-bodied worms. All of these nocturnal pests usually hide in the soil, in debris, or in other protected locations during the day.

SOLUTION: Control nocturnal pests by treating with insecticides. For more information about these pests and control measures, see beetles on page 865, weevils on page 866, earwigs on page 893, caterpillars on page 870, and cutworms on page 664.

Slug damage.

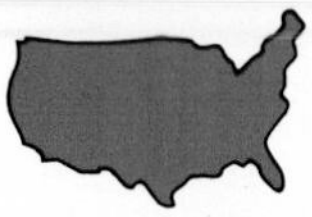

PROBLEM: Irregular holes with smooth edges are chewed in the leaves. Some leaves may be sheared off entirely. Silvery trails wind around the plants and soil nearby. At night, check with a flashlight for slimy creatures with or without hard brown shells feeding on the leaves.

ANALYSIS: Snails and slugs
These pests are mollusks, and are related to clams, oysters, and other shellfish. They feed on the leaves of a wide variety of garden plants, and may completely devour a young seedling. Ripe and unripe fruit lying on the ground may be attacked by snails and slugs. This is especially true when the fruit are shaded by the foliage, as with strawberries and unstaked tomatoes. Like other mollusks, snails and slugs need to be moist all the time. For this reason, they avoid direct sun and dry places, and hide during the day in damp places, such as under flower pots or in thick groundcovers. They emerge at night or on cloudy days to feed. Slugs lay masses of white eggs encased in a slimy mass in protected places. Snails bury their eggs in the soil, also in a slimy mass. The young look like miniature versions of their parents.

SOLUTION: Scatter ORTHO Bug-Geta Snail & Slug Pellets in bands around the areas you wish to protect. Also scatter the pellets in areas where snails and slugs might be hiding, such as in dense groundcovers, weedy areas, compost piles, or pot storage areas. Wet down the treated areas to encourage snail and slug activity that night. Repeat every 2 weeks as needed.

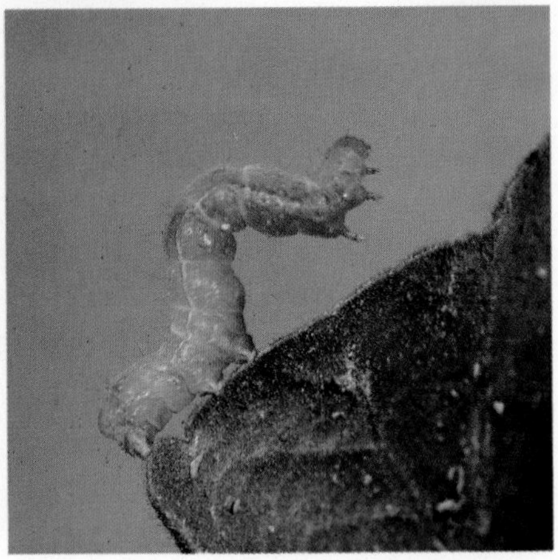

Cabbage looper (twice life size).

PROBLEM: Irregular or round holes appear in the leaves and buds. Leaves, buds, and flowers may be entirely chewed off. Worms or caterpillars are feeding on the plants.

ANALYSIS: Caterpillars
Several species of these moth or butterfly larvae feed on many vegetable and berry plants. Some common caterpillars are budworms, hornworms, and loopers. Most moths or butterflies start to lay their eggs on garden plants with the onset of warm weather in the spring. The larvae that emerge from these eggs feed on the leaves, flowers, and buds for 2 to 6 weeks, depending on weather conditions and species. Mature caterpillars pupate in cocoons attached to leaves or structures, or buried in the soil. There may be one generation a year, or overlapping generations during the growing season. The last generation of caterpillars in the fall survives the winter as pupae. Moths and butterflies emerge from the pupae the following spring.

SOLUTION: Spray infested plants with an insecticide containing *carbaryl* (SEVIN®), *diazinon*, or *methoxychlor*, or ORTHO Tomato & Vegetable Insect Killer. The bacterium *Bacillus thuringiensis* is effective against the early stages of some caterpillars. Make sure that your plant is listed on the product label. Repeat the treatment if reinfestation occurs, allowing at least 7 days to pass between applications.

Japanese beetles on grape (1/3 life size).

PROBLEM: The leaf tissue has been chewed between the veins, giving the leaf a lacy appearance. Metallic green and bronze, winged beetles, ½ inch long, are feeding in clusters on the foliage, especially on the tender new leaves.

ANALYSIS: Japanese beetles
(*Popillia japonica*)
As their name suggests, these beetles are native to Japan. They were first seen in New Jersey in 1916 and have since become a major pest in the eastern United States. They feed on hundreds of different plant species. The adult beetles are present from June to October. They feed only in the daytime, rapidly defoliating plants. Leaves exposed to direct sun are the most severely attacked. Badly damaged leaves drop. Any reduction in leaf tissue ultimately affects the overall vigor and production of fruit. Japanese beetles can fly up to 5 miles, and travel from yard to yard. Consequently, repeated sprays are necessary to control them. (For a list of plants rarely attacked by the adult beetle, see page 997.) The larva of the Japanese beetle, a white grub, feeds on grass roots, frequently killing entire lawns.

SOLUTION: Treat infested plants with ORTHO Malathion 50 Insect Spray, ORTHO Tomato Vegetable Dust, or ORTHO Home Orchard Spray. Make sure that your plants are listed on the product label. Treat for grubs in the lawn as outlined on page 256.

Spotted cucumber beetle (half life size).

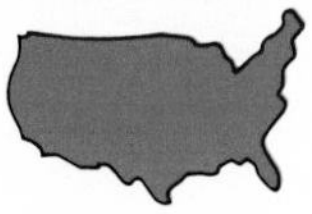

PROBLEM: Holes are chewed in the leaves, leaf stalks, and stems by yellow-green beetles with black spots or stripes.

ANALYSIS: Cucumber beetles
Both *striped cucumber beetles* (*Acalymma* species) and *spotted cucumber beetles* (*Diabrotica* species) are common pests of vegetable plants. It is important to control these beetles because they may infect plants with two serious diseases that damage and may kill cucurbits (squash, melons, and cucumbers): *squash mosaic* (page 720) and *bacterial wilt* (page 718). Adult beetles survive the winter in plant debris and weeds. As soon as vegetable plants are set in the garden in the spring, the beetles attack the leaves and stems, and may totally destroy the plants. Adults lay their yellow-orange eggs in the soil at the base of the plants. The grubs that hatch from these eggs eat the roots and the stems below the soil line, causing the plants to be stunted or to die prematurely. Severely infested plants produce few fruit. The slender white grubs feed for several weeks, pupate in the soil, and emerge as adults to repeat the cycle. There is one generation a year in the North and two or more in the South.

SOLUTION: Treat the plants with ORTHO Fruit & Vegetable Insect Control, ORTHO Tomato & Vegetable Insect Killer, or ORTHO Tomato Vegetable Dust at the first sign of the beetles. Make sure that your plant is listed on the product label.

Flea beetle on turnip leaf (twice life size).

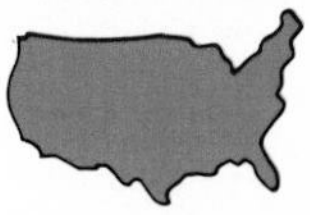

PROBLEM: Leaves are riddled with shotholes about ⅛ inch in diameter. Tiny (1/16 inch) black beetles jump like fleas when disturbed. Leaves of seedlings and eventually whole plants may wilt and die.

ANALYSIS: Flea beetles
These beetles jump like fleas, but are not related to them. Both adult and immature flea beetles feed on a wide variety of garden vegetables and berries. The immature beetle, a legless gray grub, injures plants by feeding on the roots and the lower surfaces of leaves. Adults chew holes in leaves. Flea beetles are most damaging to seedlings and young plants. Leaves of seedlings riddled with holes dry out quickly and die. Adult beetles survive the winter in soil and garden debris. They emerge in early spring to feed on weeds until vegetables sprout or plants are set in the garden. Grubs hatch from eggs laid in the soil and feed for 2 to 3 weeks. After pupating in the soil, they emerge as adults to repeat the cycle. There are 1 to 4 generations a year. Adults may feed for up to 2 months.

SOLUTION: Control flea beetles on vegetable and small fruit plants with ORTHO Diazinon Insect Spray, ORTHO Tomato Vegetable Dust, or ORTHO Tomato & Vegetable Insect Killer when the leaves first show damage. Watch new growth for evidence of further damage, and repeat the treatment at weekly intervals as needed. Make sure that your plant is listed on the insecticide label. Remove all plant debris from the garden after harvest to reduce the number of overwintering spots for adult beetles.

PROBLEMS COMMON TO MANY VEGETABLES, BERRIES, AND GRAPES — INSECTS ON THE PLANT

Grasshopper on blueberry (half life size).

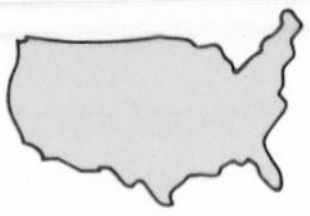

PROBLEM: Large holes are chewed in the margins of the leaves. Greenish yellow to brown jumping insects, $\frac{1}{2}$ to $1\frac{1}{2}$ inches long, with long hind legs are eating the plants. Some fruit and corn ears may be chewed.

ANALYSIS: Grasshoppers
Grasshoppers attack a wide variety of plants. They eat leaves and occasionally fruit, migrating as they deplete their food sources. They are most numerous in the rows near weedy areas. In late summer, adult grasshoppers lay their eggs in pods in the soil. The adults continue feeding until cold weather kills them. The eggs hatch the following spring. Grasshopper problems are most severe during hot, dry weather. Grasshoppers migrate into green gardens and yards as surrounding areas dry up in the summer heat. Periods of cool, wet weather help keep their numbers under control.

SOLUTION: Treat the plants with ORTHO Fruit & Vegetable Insect Control as soon as grasshoppers appear. Repeat at weekly intervals if the plants become reinfested. Make sure that your plant is listed on the product label.

Leafhopper (3 times life size).

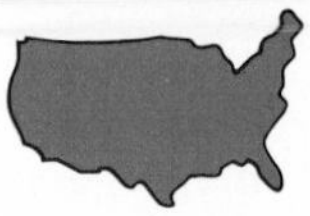

PROBLEM: Spotted, pale green insects up to $\frac{1}{8}$ inch long hop, move sideways, or fly away quickly when a plant is touched. The leaves are stippled.

ANALYSIS: Leafhoppers
Leafhoppers feed on many vegetables and small fruits. They generally feed on the undersides of leaves, sucking the sap, which causes stippling. Severely infested vegetable and small fruit plants may become weak and produce few edible fruit. One leafhopper, the *aster leafhopper* (*Macrosteles fascifrons*), transmits *aster yellows*, a plant disease that can be quite damaging. For further details see page 854. Leafhoppers at all stages of maturity are active during the growing season. They hatch in the spring from eggs laid on perennial weeds and ornamental plants. Even areas where the winters are so cold that the eggs cannot survive are not free from infestation because leafhoppers migrate in the spring from warmer regions.

SOLUTION: Spray infested plants with ORTHO Diazinon Insect Spray, ORTHO Tomato Vegetable Dust, or ORTHO Tomato & Vegetable Insect Killer. Be sure to cover the lower surfaces of the leaves. Repeat the spray as often as necessary to keep the insects under control. Allow at least 10 days between applications. Make sure that your plants are listed on the product label. Eradicate nearby weeds, especially thistles, plantains, and dandelions, which may harbor leafhopper eggs. For more information about controlling disease-carrying insects, see page 879.

Whiteflies (life size).

PROBLEM: Tiny, winged insects $\frac{1}{12}$ inch long feed on the undersides of the leaves. The insects are covered with white waxy powder. When the plant is touched, insects flutter rapidly around it. Leaves may be mottled and yellowing. Black mold may cover the leaves.

ANALYSIS: Whitefly
This insect is a common pest of many garden and greenhouse plants. The 4-winged adult lays eggs on the undersides of leaves. The larvae are the size of a pinhead with white waxy filaments radiating from the body. They feed for about a month before changing to the adult form. The larval and adult forms suck sap from the leaves. The larvae are more damaging because they feed more heavily. Whiteflies cannot fully digest all the sugar in the plant sap, and excrete the excess in a fluid called honeydew, which often drops onto the lower leaves. A sooty mold fungus may develop on the honeydew, causing the leaves to appear black and dirty. In warm winter areas these insects can be active year-round, with eggs, larvae, and adults present at the same time. Whiteflies are unable to live through freezing winters. Spring reinfestations in freezing winter areas come from migrating whiteflies and infested greenhouse-grown plants placed in the garden.

SOLUTION: Control whiteflies by treating with ORTHO Tomato & Vegetable Insect Killer, ORTHO Fruit & Vegetable Insect Control, ORTHO Malathion 50 Insect Spray, or ORTHO Diazinon Insect Spray every 7 to 10 days as necessary. Spray the foliage thoroughly, being sure to cover both the upper and lower surfaces of the leaves. Make sure your plant is listed on the product label.

INSECTS IN THE SOIL

Aphids on spinach (half life size).

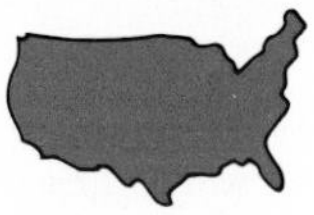

PROBLEM: Pale green, yellow, purple, or black soft-bodied insects cluster on the undersides of the leaves. Leaves turn yellow, and may be curled, distorted, and puckered. Plants may be stunted and produce few fruit.

ANALYSIS: Aphids
Aphids are one of the most common pests in the garden. They do little damage in small numbers, but are extremely prolific and populations can rapidly build up to damaging numbers during the growing season. Damage occurs when the aphids suck the juices from vegetable or small fruit leaves and flower buds. Aphids usually prefer young tender leaves. Severely infested plants may be stunted and weak, producing few fruit. Fruit yield is also reduced when the aphids spread plant virus diseases. Aphids feed on nearly every plant in the garden, and are spread from plant to plant by the wind, water, and people. Aphids are unable to digest fully all the sugar in the plant sap and excrete the excess in a fluid called honeydew, which often drops onto lower leaves. Ants feed on this sticky substance, and are often present where there is an aphid infestation. For more information about aphids, see page 875.

SOLUTION: Control aphids on vegetables and berries with ORTHO Malathion 50 Insect Spray, ORTHO Tomato & Vegetable Insect Killer, or ORTHO Fruit & Vegetable Insect Control as soon as the insects appear. Repeat the spray if the plants become reinfested. Make sure that your plant is listed on the product label. For more information on controlling disease-carrying insects, see page 880.

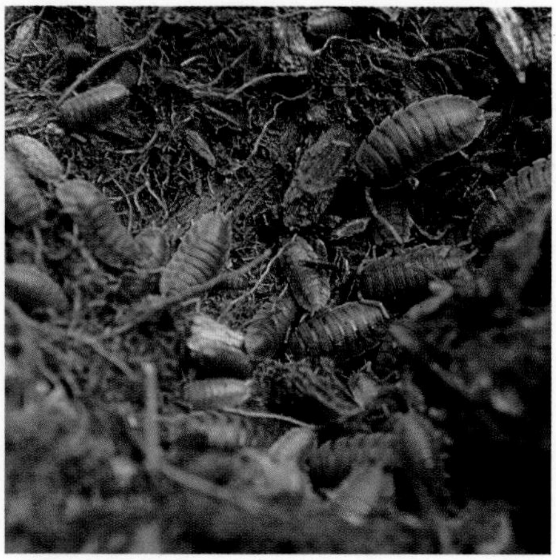

Sowbugs (life size).

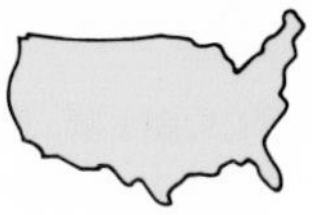

PROBLEM: Flat, oval, brown or gray creatures up to ½ inch long are found on and in the soil. These crusty pests have 7 pairs of legs, and may roll up into a ball when disturbed.

ANALYSIS: Sowbugs and pillbugs
These soil-inhabiting pests are not insects, but are related to crabs. They live in damp protected places and feed on decaying plant parts. They are frequently found in manure, and may be brought into the garden in a fresh load. Although found in many gardens, sowbugs and pillbugs are a minor pest of vegetables unless populations are high. They may feed on seedling roots and underground stems, and occasionally may feed on tender new growth. They may eat lettuce leaves and heads, tomatoes, and other soft fruit and leaves that are in contact with the soil.

SOLUTION: Since sowbugs and pillbugs are more of a nuisance than a destructive pest, insecticide treatments are seldom needed in the home vegetable garden. However, if they are numerous and troublesome, treat the soil and hiding places with an insecticide containing *carbaryl* (SEVIN®), *diazinon*, *malathion*, or *methoxychlor*. Make sure that your plants are listed on the product label.

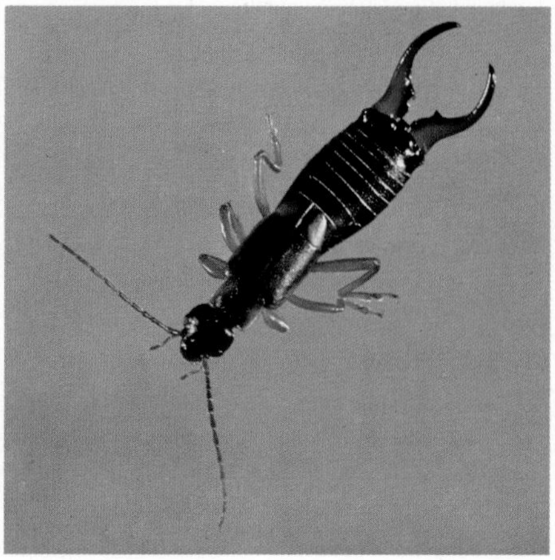

Earwig (twice life size).

PROBLEM: Dark, reddish brown insects up to ¾ inch long, with pincers projecting from the rear of the body, are found under objects in the garden. They scurry for cover when disturbed. Holes may be chewed in leaves and blossoms.

ANALYSIS: Earwigs
Although seen in most gardens, earwigs are only minor pests of vegetables and berries, unless populations are high, when they can become major pests. They feed predominantly on decaying plant material and other insects. Earwigs feed at night and in the daytime hide under stones, debris, and bark . They have wings but seldom fly, preferring to run instead. Adult earwigs lay eggs in the soil in late winter to early spring. The young that hatch from these eggs may feed on green shoots and eat holes in leaves. As the earwigs mature, they feed occasionally on blossoms and ripening fruit. Earwigs are beneficial when they feed on other insect larvae and on snails. They sometimes invade homes.

SOLUTION: Because earwigs typically cause only minor damage, insecticide sprays are seldom needed in the vegetable garden. However, if they are numerous and troublesome, treat the soil with an insecticide containing ORTHO Diazinon Soil & Turf Insect Control. Since earwigs are most active at night, treat in the late afternoon or evening. Make sure that your plant is listed on the product label. Pick fruit as it ripens. For information on controlling earwigs indoors, see page 789.

PROBLEMS COMMON TO MANY VEGETABLES, BERRIES, AND GRAPES

Symphylans (3 times life size).

PROBLEM: Slender white pests about ¼ inch long with 6 to 12 pairs of legs and long antennae are present in the soil. Plants may be stunted.

ANALYSIS: Garden symphylans
(*Scutigerella immaculata*)
These soil-inhabiting pests, also called *garden centipedes*, are a problem in both outdoor plantings and greenhouses. They thrive in damp soil that is high in organic matter, and avoid sunlight. Symphylans damage plants by feeding on the fine roots and root hairs, which reduces the amount of water the plant absorbs. They also tunnel through underground stems, stunting and sometimes killing plants. These weakened plants produce few fruit, if any at all. Symphylans are most active in the spring, but egg-laying occurs from spring through summer. They lay their white eggs in clusters 1 foot deep in the soil. The young have short antennae and 6 pairs of legs, but these develop to long antennae and 12 pairs as they mature into adults. Symphylans may live 4 to 5 years, so symphylans of all ages are found in the soil at one time.

SOLUTION: Treat the soil around vegetable plants with an insecticide containing *diazinon* at the first sign of symphylans. Repeat the treatment as needed to control these pests. Make sure that your plant is listed on the insecticide label.

Millipedes (half life size).

PROBLEM: Hard-shelled, cylindrical worms up to an inch long are found in the soil, frequently coiled like a watch spring. They are brown to pinkish brown, with two pairs of legs on each body segment.

ANALYSIS: Millipedes
Millipedes may have from 30 to 400 legs, but not as many as 1000, as their name suggests. They prefer soils high in organic matter. These scavengers feed on decaying vegetable matter and manure. They may also feed on seedlings or small roots, and sometimes eat bean, pea, or corn seeds. They frequently tunnel into root crops such as carrots, potatoes, parsnips, beets, and turnips, and into ripening fruit that is in contact with damp soil.

SOLUTION: Treat infested soil with an insecticide containing *carbaryl* (SEVIN®) or ORTHO Diazinon Soil & Turf Insect Control. Repeat the treatment as needed. Make sure that your plant is listed on the insecticide label. Place straw or newspapers under ripening fruit. Pick fruit as it ripens.

ANIMAL PESTS

Mole.

PROBLEM: Raised ridges, 3 to 5 inches wide, crisscross the garden. Plants may be disturbed. Mounds of soil with no holes appear in the garden.

ANALYSIS: Moles
Moles are small animals that live underground and feed on earthworms and insects. They are 4 to 6 inches long, with velvety fur and tiny, hidden eyes. They use their strong forelegs with broad, trowellike claws to dig and push the soil as they move through the ground. Although they seldom eat plants, they often loosen the soil around plant roots as they search for earthworms and grubs. This loosened soil dries out quickly, causing the plants to wilt.

SOLUTION: Tamp down the soil around wilted plants, water them thoroughly, and shade them until they recover. Because moles seldom eat the roots, the damage is usually not permanent. In the East, trap moles by setting spear-type traps over active surface runs. Locate active runs by tamping down the ridges in a few spots. Spots that are raised again the next day are active runs. Western moles are not easily caught in surface traps. Locate a main run, usually 6 to 10 inches deep, by probing around a fresh pile of soil. Dig down to the run and set a scissors-type trap according to package directions. Poison baits are not very effective with moles. Poison gas is dangerous and difficult to use properly. For more information about moles, see page 896.

Raccoon.

Snapbeans eaten by rabbits.

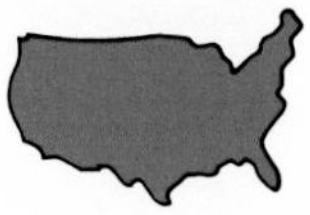

PROBLEM: Plants are chewed or completely eaten. Ripening fruit, pods, and ears are partially or completely eaten. Deer, raccoons, squirrels, rabbits, woodchucks, or mice may be seen in the garden.

ANALYSIS: Wildlife Various forms of wildlife feed in the garden.	**SOLUTION:** There are several ways to exclude or repel wildlife from your garden.
1. *Deer* feed on leaves and fruit. They are most active at dawn and dusk.	**1.** The only sure way to exclude deer is with a woven wire fence 8 feet tall. Cotton drawstring bags filled with bloodmeal fertilizer or human hair and suspended on stakes in the garden sometimes repel them. For more information on deer, see page 901.
2. *Raccoons* knock over cornstalks to feed on maturing ears. They may also feed on other ripening fruit. Raccoons feed at night.	**2.** Exclude raccoons with a 6-foot-tall fence. Electric fencing above the fence may also be needed. Protect corn by interplanting with members of the cucurbit family. Raccoons will not walk on the prickly vines. Sprinkle ripening corn with cayenne pepper. For more information on raccoons, see page 900.
3. *Squirrels* feed on ripening fruit and climb cornstalks to feed on maturing ears.	**3.** Protect ears of corn from squirrels by sprinkling corn silks with cayenne pepper. For more information on squirrels, see page 899.
4. *Rabbits* feed on young bean, pea, lettuce, and cabbage plants, eating the young leaves and frequently leaving short stubs of the stems standing in the soil.	**4.** To exclude rabbits, erect a fence 18 inches tall and anchor it by burying the edges 5 to 6 inches deep in the soil. For more information on rabbits, see page 900.
5. *Woodchucks*, also called *groundhogs*, feed in the afternoons and avoid tomatoes, eggplants, red and green peppers, chives, and onions.	**5.** Deter woodchucks with a wire fence that is buried 1 foot deep and extended horizontally underground 10 to 12 inches. For more information on woodchucks, see page 901.
6. *Mice* may bite into ripening tomatoes, cucumbers, and beans that are close to the ground to eat the seeds inside. Mice frequently travel underground in mole tunnels.	**6.** Stake, trellis, or cage plants to keep fruit off the ground, and away from mice. For more information on mice, see page 896.

Pocket gopher mound.

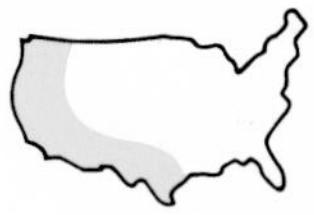

PROBLEM: Plants wilt suddenly or disappear. Mounds of soil are clustered in the garden. These mounds are usually crescent shaped, and open outward from a hole in the soil. There are no ridges on the soil surface.

ANALYSIS: Pocket gophers
Pocket gophers live and feed almost entirely underground. They come to the surface only to bring up soil from their burrows, to look for new territory, or to feed within a few inches of their holes. Gophers feed on plant roots. This rodent has fur-lined pouches on each side of its mouth. It has small eyes and ears, a sparsely haired tail, long sharp claws, and a blunt head. Gophers are solitary, and only one inhabits a burrow at a time. The mounds of soil are formed as gophers push soil out of their holes to enlarge their burrow system. Gophers may be present without mounding soil.

SOLUTION: Trapping is the quickest and surest way to eliminate pocket gophers from your yard. Find the main runway (which runs in both directions) by probing with a sharp rod about a foot deep near a fresh mound or an eaten plant. Dig a hole to intersect the run and insert two traps, one facing in each direction. Tie the traps to a stake above ground. Keep animals and children away from the traps by covering the hole with sod or a board. Sprinkle the board with soil to block out all light. Check and move the traps daily. Although only one gopher occupies a burrow at a time, migrating gophers will move into an abandoned burrow. Level all the mounds and watch for signs that the burrow has been reoccupied.

PROBLEMS OF INDIVIDUAL VEGETABLES, BERRIES, AND GRAPES

GLOBE ARTICHOKE

ADAPTATION: Frost-free areas with cool, humid summers.

PLANTING TIME: Early to midspring.

PLANTING METHOD: Set crown or root pieces 6 to 8 inches deep, and 4 to 6 feet apart. Set containerized plants so that the top of their rootball is even with the garden soil. Space 4 to 6 feet apart. Or, start seeds indoors 4 to 6 weeks before planting outdoors. Store seeds in the refrigerator in moist peat moss for 2 weeks before planting.

SOIL: Any good garden soil that is rich in organic matter. pH 6.0 to 6.5

FERTILIZER: Feed twice a year, in the spring and fall, with ½ pound of ORTHO General Purpose Plant Food per plant.

WATER:
How much: Apply enough water at each irrigation to wet the soil 1 to 1½ feet deep.
How often: Water when the soil 1 inch deep is dry.

HARVEST: Cut artichokes with 1 inch of stem, while the buds are still tight. Overmature artichokes have loose scales that point outward with purple flowers in between. The bud scales of the Creole variety, commonly grown in southern Louisiana, naturally point outward. Smaller artichokes will be produced along the stalk after the first one is cut. Remove the entire stalk after it stops producing.

Cold damage.

PROBLEM: White blisters or dark streaks and patches appear on artichoke leaves (bud scales). Discoloration appears soon after temperatures have dropped to freezing.

ANALYSIS: Cold damage
Artichokes are tender perennials; they are easily injured by freezing temperatures. Damage is most likely to occur in the late summer or early fall after a frosty night. The damage may not be noticed in the early morning following the frost, but as the temperature warms throughout the day the discoloration appears.

SOLUTION: Discolored artichokes are still edible; in most cases damage is only cosmetic. Discard artichokes so badly damaged that they are entirely shriveled and brown. If you anticipate freezing temperatures, protect plants by covering them with newspaper or burlap.

Slug damage.

PROBLEM: Artichoke buds (heads), stems, and leaves are disfigured with white or tan scars. Silvery trails wind around on the plants and soil nearby. Snails or slugs may be seen moving around or feeding on the plants, especially at night. Inspect the garden for them at night by flashlight.

ANALYSIS: Snails and slugs
These pests are mollusks, and are related to clams, oysters, and other shellfish. They feed on a wide variety of garden plants. Like other mollusks, snails and slugs need to be moist all the time. For this reason, they avoid direct sun and dry places, and hide during the day in damp places, such as under flower pots or in thick groundcover. They emerge at night or on cloudy days to feed. Snails and slugs are similar except that the snail has a hard shell, into which it withdraws when disturbed. Slugs lay masses of white eggs encased in a slimy mass in protected places. Snails bury their eggs in the soil, also in a slimy mass. The young look like miniature versions of their parents.

SOLUTION: Scatter a snail and slug bait containing *metaldehyde* on the ground around the artichoke plants. Also scatter the bait in areas where snails or slugs might be hiding, such as in dense groundcovers, weedy areas, compost piles, or pot storage areas. Before spreading the bait, wet down the areas to be treated to encourage snail and slug activity that night. Repeat the application every 2 weeks as long as snails and slugs are active. Do not apply bait to the plant itself.

Damaged artichoke. *Insert:* Larva (half life size).

PROBLEM: Irregular holes appear in the artichoke bud scales (the "leaves" of the artichoke bud), in the stem, and in the new foliage. Small worms may be seen feeding on new foliage and beneath the bud scales. Brown moths with plumed wings, about 1 inch across, fly near the plant in the evening.

ANALYSIS: Artichoke plume moth
(*Platyptilia carduidactyla*)
The larvae of this moth feed on the tender parts of the artichoke plant. The adult moth lays eggs on the underside of the foliage or on the stem below the bud. The larvae bore into the artichoke, blemishing the bud scales and tunneling the heart. Insect damage may occur all year around, but is particularly severe in the spring. This insect also lives on thistles (*Cirsium* species).

SOLUTION: Apply an insecticide containing *carbaryl* (SEVIN®) to the foliage, buds, and stems, when the worms first appear or when the plant shows damage. Repeat the dusting weekly as long as new damage appears. Pick and destroy all wormy artichoke buds and foliage. In the fall, remove or bury all plant debris. Also remove all nearby thistles that may harbor the insect.

Curly dwart.

PROBLEM: The plant is stunted. The foliage may be curled, and the artichokes are misshapen and small. The plant eventually dies.

ANALYSIS: Curly dwarf
This plant disease is caused by a virus transmitted by sucking insects such as aphids and leafhoppers. The most common—and often the only—symptom of virus infection is stunting. Curly dwarf virus is transmitted from infected artichokes or, on the Pacific Coast, from milk thistle (*Silybum marianum*), a common weed.

SOLUTION: There are no chemical controls for virus diseases in plants. Remove and destroy the infected plants. To prevent reintroducing the virus, use a virus-free root stock. Also protect your artichokes by removing milk thistle and other weeds from the area. For more information about controlling disease-carrying insects, see page 880.

ASPARAGUS

ASPARAGUS

ADAPTATION: Throughout the United States, except in the Southeast.

PLANTING TIME: See page 1009.

PLANTING METHOD: Set crowns, buds upward, in a trench 6 to 8 inches deep, and 12 inches apart. As the plants grow, gradually fill in the trench with soil until even with the surrounding soil. Or, sow seeds 1 inch deep and 3 inches apart.

SOIL: Any good garden soil. pH 6.5 to 8.0

FERTILIZER: At planting time, use 4 pounds of ORTHO Vegetable Food per 100 square feet. Side-dress in late July to early August with 1½ pounds per 100-foot row. After the first year, fertilize twice a year, once in the spring before the shoots emerge, and again just after harvest.

WATER:
How much: Apply enough water at each irrigation to wet the soil 1 to 1½ feet deep.
How often: Water when the soil is just barely moist.

HARVEST: Plants must grow for 2 years before harvesting to build strong roots to insure crops for at least 10 years. In the spring of the third year, pick when the spears are 7 to 10 inches tall with tight heads. To avoid wounding the crown, snap the spears, do not tear or cut them. Harvest for 2 weeks. The fourth year, pick for 4 weeks, and the fifth and following years for 8 weeks. In California, harvest for 4, 8, and 12 weeks respectively.

Small spears.

PROBLEM: Spears are small and skinny.

ANALYSIS: Small spears
Asparagus spears may be small for any of several reasons:
1. *Poor fertility:* Underfertilized plants cannot produce adequate fern growth and food for next year's crop.
2. *Immature plants:* Asparagus crowns produce small spears for the first 2 or 3 years following planting.
3. *Poor drainage:* Asparagus plants do not produce well in poorly drained soil.
4. *Overharvested plants:* When harvest continues late in the season, the plants are unable to produce enough foliage and do not store enough food for next year's crop.

SOLUTION: Follow the growing and harvesting guidelines on this page. Improve the soil drainage and aeration as outlined on page 907.

Crooked spears.

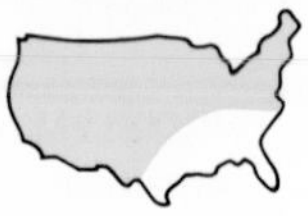

PROBLEM: Spears are crooked or misshapen.

ANALYSIS: Crooked spears
Asparagus spears grow crooked when the growing shoot is damaged by insects (especially the asparagus beetle—see page 679), cultivation wounds on the crown, or windblown sand that pelts the tender shoots. The injured areas grow more slowly than the uninjured side, causing the stem to curve. Although the spears are misshapen, they are still edible.

SOLUTION: Control asparagus beetles. To avoid wounding the crown, do not cultivate closer or deeper than 2 inches. Tall plants or fencing can be used as windbreaks to prevent sandblasting.

For gourmet white asparagus spears, blanch the emerging shoots in the spring. Mound 10 or 12 inches of soil over the plants as the first shoots appear. Harvest when the spear tips emerge through the hill of soil. Carefully dig down about 8 inches and cut the spear with a sharp knife. Use the spears fresh or cooked.

Damaged spear.

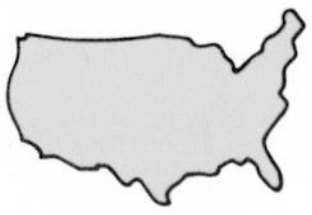

PROBLEM: Spears turn brown and may be soft, or they may dry and wither.

ANALYSIS: Freeze injury
Asparagus is the earliest vegetable in the spring garden and is sometimes damaged by spring frosts. The damage may not be noticed in the early morning following the frost, but as the temperature warms through the day the tissue discolors and softens. Damaged spears then dry rapidly as temperatures rise and humidity drops. A slight freeze injury may result in a crooked spear or slightly damaged tip of the spear. For information on other causes of crooked spears, see page 678.

SOLUTION: Harvest and discard frost-damaged spears. When night temperatures below 32° F are predicted, protect the spears with a mulch of straw, newspaper, or leaves. Remove the mulch in the morning.

Fusarium wilt.

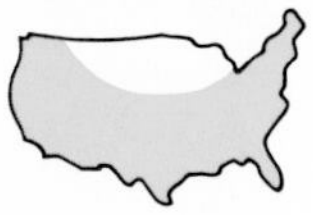

PROBLEM: The growing shoot turns yellow to dingy brown and wilts. During wet weather, white or pink cottonlike strands often appear under the leaf scales. Wilting is most severe among full-grown plants during the months of July and August. When the infected plant is dug up, all or part of the root system is seen to be a reddish color. The plant eventually dies.

ANALYSIS: Fusarium wilt
This wilt disease is caused by a fungus (*Fusarium* species). Asparagus plants under stress from poor growing conditions (drought, poor drainage, insect or disease injury, etc.) are more severely affected. The fungus lives on organic matter in the soil. The disease is spread by contaminated seeds, plants, soil, and equipment; it often enters a garden on the roots of a transplant. The fungus enters the plant through the roots and spreads up into the stems and leaves through the water-conducting vessels in the stems. The vessels become discolored and plugged, cutting off the flow of water to the leaves. Because fusarium is favored by wet weather and warm temperatures (70° to 85°F), the fungi build up in warm soils. For more information about fusarium wilt, see page 858.

SOLUTION: No chemical control is available. It is best to destroy infected plants. Next year, plant healthy crowns where asparagus has not been planted for 2 to 4 years. If you plant in infected soil, fumigate the soil about 3 weeks before planting. For more information about soil fumigation, see page 919.

Larvae. *Insert:* Adults (twice life size).

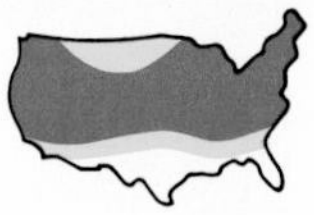

PROBLEM: The tips of young asparagus spears are chewed and scarred. Later, when the spears develop into asparagus ferns, they are also chewed. Small (¼ inch) metallic blue or black beetles with yellow markings and a narrow red head may feed on the tips of the spears, and later on the ferns and stems. Reddish orange beetles with black spots may be present. Shiny black specks are found on the spear tips. Humpbacked orange or slate-gray grubs may also be seen.

ANALYSIS: Asparagus beetle (*Crioceris asparagi*) **and spotted asparagus beetle** (*Crioceris duodecimpunctata*)
These two beetles injure asparagus plants throughout the growing season. The blue-black *asparagus beetle* is found throughout the United States. The orange and black *spotted asparagus beetle* is found east of the Mississippi River. The beetles are particularly a problem when young asparagus shoots emerge in the spring. Both adults and grubs injure the plants by feeding on shoots, ferns, and stems. This feeding robs the root system of food manufactured in the foliage and necessary for healthy growth next year.

SOLUTION: Apply ORTHO Tomato & Vegetable Insect Killer or ORTHO Rotenone Dust or Spray when the beetles are first noticed. Repeat the applications as long as the beetles or grubs are feeding. Also treat the fern growth in late summer or early fall to prevent adults from overwintering on the ferns and reinfesting next year's crop.

Rust.

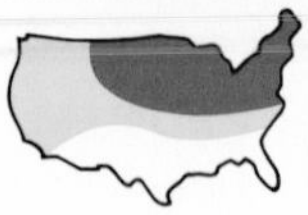

PROBLEM: Tops turn yellow, then brown, and die back in early to midsummer. Reddish brown, orange, or black blisters appear on the ferns and stems. Spears mature earlier than usual.

ANALYSIS: Rust

This plant disease is caused by a fungus (*Puccinia asparagi*). This year's rust weakens the plant by reducing the amount of food manufactured in the leaves to be stored in the roots. Since this stored food supplies the energy for next year's crop, fewer shoots are produced the following year. Damage is most severe when the tops are attacked several years in a row. In severe cases, the plants die. Warm temperatures and high humidity from fog, heavy dew, or overhead watering favor rust infection. Rust spores from diseased tops that have been left in the garden infect new shoots as they emerge in the spring. The wind spreads the spores from plant to plant.

SOLUTION: After the harvest, spray the ferns and stems with a fungicide containing *maneb* or *zineb*. Repeat the treatment at intervals of 10 days when weather conditions favor rust infection. Do not spray while spears are still being harvested. Cut the tops down close to the ground after they die in the fall, and destroy them. Don't add them to the compost pile or leave them lying around the garden. If you plant more asparagus, select rust-resistant varieties.

Rust-resistant asparagus varieties: California 500, Martha Washington, Mary Washington, and Waltham Washington.

BEANS

ADAPTATION: Throughout the United States.

PLANTING TIME: See page 1009.

PLANTING METHOD: Sow seeds 1 to 1½ inches deep and 1 to 2 inches apart. Thin to 2 to 4 inches apart when the seedlings have their first set of leaves.

SOIL: Any good garden soil, somewhat friable for easy seedling emergence. pH 6.0 to 8.0

FERTILIZER: At planting time, use 3 pounds of ORTHO Vegetable Food per 100 square feet, or 1 pound per 25-foot row. Side-dress every 3 to 4 weeks with 1 pound per 25-foot row.

WATER:
How much: Apply enough water to wet the soil 8 to 10 inches deep.
How often: Water when the soil is just barely moist.

HARVEST: Break the beans from the vines, being careful not to jerk or tear the vine. Pick beans when they are ready. If over-mature beans remain on the vines, production is greatly reduced. Cool beans in the refrigerator until use.
Harvesting times:
Snap (green) beans: When the seed in the pod begins to swell.
Lima Beans: When the pods are well-filled, but still bright green.

Mexican bean beetle (twice life size).

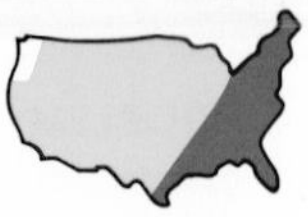

PROBLEM: The tissue between the leaf veins is eaten, giving the leaves a lacelike appearance. Copper-colored beetles about ¼ inch long feed on the undersides of the skeletonized leaves. The beetles have 16 black spots on their backs. Orange to yellow soft-bodied grubs about ⅓ inch long with black-tipped spines on their backs may also be present. Leaves dry up, and the plant may die.

ANALYSIS: Mexican bean beetle
(*Epilachna varivestis*)

This beetle is found throughout the United States. It prefers lima beans, but also feeds on pole and bush beans and cowpeas. Feeding damage by both adults and larvae can reduce pod production. The adult beetles spend the winter in plant debris in the garden and emerge in late spring and early summer. They lay yellow eggs on the undersides of the leaves. Larvae that hatch from these eggs, in early to midsummer, are green at first, gradually turning yellow. There are 1 to 4 generations per year. Frequently, all stages of beetles appear at the same time throughout the season. Hot, dry summers and cold winters reduce the beetle population.

SOLUTION: Apply ORTHO Sevin Garden Dust, ORTHO Diazinon Insect Spray, or ORTHO Fruit & Vegetable Insect Control when the adults first appear. Be sure to spray the undersides of the leaves where the insects feed. Early treatments to control the adults may save extra applications later to control the larvae, which are more damaging and harder to control. Remove and destroy all plant debris after the harvest to reduce overwintering spots for adults.

Bean leaf beetle (5 times life size).

PROBLEM: Holes are chewed in the leaves. Yellow to red beetles with black spots and a black band around the outer edge of the body are feeding on the undersides of the leaves. The plant may later turn yellow and wilt. If you pull the plant up you may see slender white grubs up to ⅓ inch long feeding on the roots and stem.

ANALYSIS: Bean leaf beetle
(*Cerotoma trifurcata*)
This widely distributed insect attacks all beans, as well as peas. Adult beetles feed on the undersides of leaves, blossoms, and pods throughout the growing season. Grubs feed on the roots and stems below the soil line. Females lay clusters of orange eggs on the soil at the base of plants. The grubs that hatch from these eggs attack the plant below the soil, feeding on the roots and sometimes girdling the stem at the soil level. This feeding can kill the plant. Both adults and grubs cause serious damage to young plants. There are 1 to 3 generations per year.

SOLUTION: Apply ORTHO Sevin Garden Dust or ORTHO Diazinon Insect Spray at the first sign of damage. Be sure to spray the undersides of the leaves where the beetles feed. Repeat at intervals of 7 to 10 days whenever damage occurs. Clean all debris from the garden at the end of the season to eliminate overwintering spots for adults.

Bean aphids (half life size).

PROBLEM: Young leaves are curled, distorted, and yellow. Tiny (⅛ inch) pale green to black, soft-bodied insects cluster on leaves and stems. There may be a shiny, sticky substance coating the leaves. Ants may be present.

ANALYSIS: Aphids
Aphids do little damage in small numbers. However, they are extremely prolific and populations can rapidly build up to tremendous numbers during the growing season. Damage occurs when the aphid sucks the juices from the bean leaves. The aphid is unable to digest fully all the sugar in the plant sap and excretes the excess in a fluid called honeydew. The honeydew often drops onto the leaves below. Ants feed on the sticky substance and are often present where there is an aphid infestation. For more information about aphids, see page 875.

SOLUTION: Treat with ORTHO Fruit & Vegetable Insect Control, ORTHO Malathion 50 Insect Spray, ORTHO Tomato & Vegetable Insect Killer, ORTHO Diazinon Insect Spray, or ORTHO Diazinon Soil & Foliage Dust as soon as the insects appear. Repeat as directed on the label if the plant is reinfested.

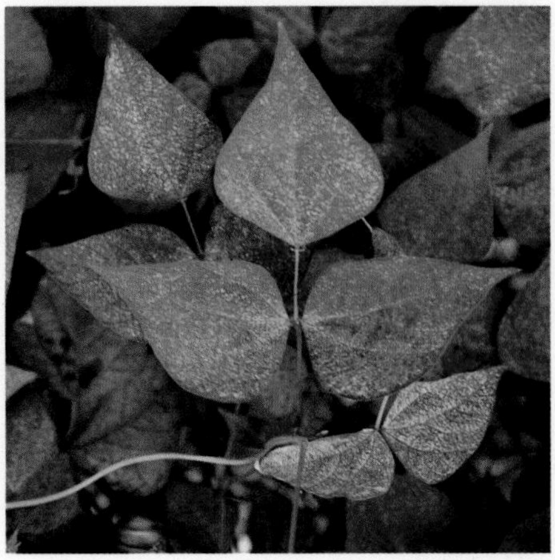

Two-spotted spider mite damage.

PROBLEM: Leaves are stippled, yellowing, and dirty. Leaves may dry out and drop. There may be webbing between leaves or on the lower surfaces of the leaves. To determine if the plant is infested with mites, hold a sheet of white paper underneath an affected leaf and tap the leaf sharply. Minute green, red, or yellow specks the size of pepper grains will drop to the paper and begin to crawl around. The pests are easily seen against the white background.

ANALYSIS: Two-spotted spider mite
(*Tetranychus urticae*)
These mites, related to spiders, are major pests of many garden and greenhouse plants. They cause damage by sucking sap from the undersides of the leaves. As a result of feeding, the green leaf pigment disappears, producing the stippled appearance. Mites are active throughout the growing season, but are favored by hot, dry weather (70°F and up). By midsummer, they build up to tremendous numbers. For more information about spider mites, see page 887.

SOLUTION: Apply ORTHO Malathion 50 Insect Spray, ORTHO Fruit & Vegetable Insect Control, ORTHO Diazinon Insect Spray, or a pesticide containing *dicofol* (KELTHANE®) when the damage is first seen. Spray thoroughly, being sure to cover both the upper and lower surfaces of the leaves. Mites are difficult to control because they reproduce so rapidly. Repeated applications are necessary, especially during hot, dry weather, at intervals of 7 to 10 days. Hose down plants every few days to knock off webs and mites.

BEANS

Failure to set pods.

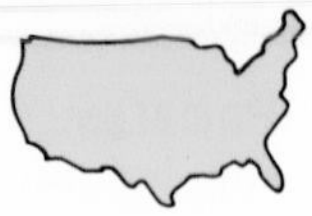

PROBLEM: The plants look healthy but there are only a few fully formed pods.

ANALYSIS: Failure to set pods
Failure to set pods may result from any of several factors.
1. *High temperatures:* Maturing bean plants prefer temperatures between 70° and 80°F. If the maximum temperature is consistently over 85°F, as it often is in the summer, flowers often drop off without setting pods—a condition known as *blossom drop.* Heat can also cause the blossoms to deteriorate on the plant without actually dropping off. This condition is known as *blossom blast.* Hot, dry winds also contribute to both blossom drop and blast.
2. *Extremes in soil moisture:* Plants growing in soil that is either too wet or too dry are stressed by a lack of oxygen and water. Irregular watering contributes to this problem. Weakened plants produce few pods.
3. *Overmature pods:* Leaving mature pods on the vine forces the plant to put its energy into seed formation in the pod, rather than to forming new pods.

SOLUTION: The numbers below correspond to the numbers in the analysis.
1. In areas where very hot summers or hot, dry winds are common, plant beans for late spring harvest and again for fall harvest.
2. Water regularly, allowing the soil surface to dry out between waterings. To conserve moisture during hot, dry weather, use a 3 to 4 inch mulch of straw or chopped leaves.
3. Pick the pods regularly when they are young and tender and before large seeds develop inside. Do not allow any pods to mature.

Anthracnose spots.

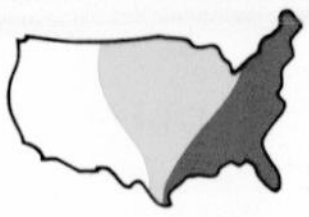

PROBLEM: Small brown specks on pods enlarge to black, circular, sunken spots. In wet weather, a salmon-colored ooze appears in the infected spots. Elongated dark reddish brown spots appear on the stems and veins on the underside of the leaves. If seedlings are attached, the stems may rot, or the first young leaves may be spotted. In either case, the seedlings die.

ANALYSIS: Bean anthracnose
This bean disease is caused by a fungus (*Colletotrichum lindemuthianum*) that affects all kinds of beans, but is most destructive on lima beans. It occurs in the eastern and central states, rarely west of the Rocky Mountains. The fungus thrives in cool, wet weather. The salmon-colored ooze that often appears in the infected spots during wet weather consists of slime spores. The spores are carried by splashing water, animals, people, or tools to healthy plants. The fungus lives on diseased bean seeds and on plant debris that has been left in the garden.

SOLUTION: Apply a fungicide containing *chlorothalonil* (DACONIL 2787®) at flowering and repeat 3 more times at intervals of 7 to 10 days. Continue treatments whenever wet weather occurs. Remove and destroy any diseased plants. The disease spreads rapidly on moist foliage, so do not work in the garden when the plants are wet. To avoid reintroducing this fungus into your garden, purchase seeds from a reputable seed company. Do not plant beans in the infected area for 2 or 3 years. Rotate your bean planting site every year.

Halo blight.

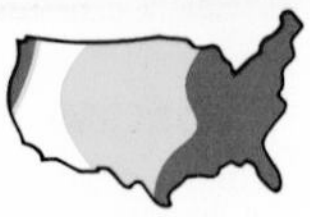

PROBLEM: Small, water-soaked spots appear on the leaves. These spots enlarge, turn brown, and may kill the leaf. In cool weather, narrow greenish yellow halos may border the infected spots. The leaves either turn yellow and die slowly or turn brown rapidly and drop off. Long reddish lesions may girdle the stem. In moist conditions, a tan or yellow ooze is produced in spots on pods.

ANALYSIS: Bacterial blights
Two widespread bacterial blights on beans are *common blight* (caused by *Xanthomonas phaseoli*) and *halo blight* (caused by *Pseudomonas phaseolicola*). These bacteria attack all kinds of beans. Common blight is more severe in warm, moist weather; halo blight is favored by cool temperatures. The bacteria are usually introduced into a garden on infected seed, and can live on infected plant debris in the soil for as long as 2 years. They are spread by rain, splashing water, and contaminated tools. The bacteria multiply rapidly in humid weather. If the water-conducting tissue is invaded, bacteria and dead cells eventually clog the veins, causing leaf discoloration. Often bacteria ooze from infected spots in a yellow or cream-colored mass.

SOLUTION: There are no chemical controls for bacterial blights. Avoid overhead watering. Do not work with the beans when the plants are wet. Do not plant beans in the same area more often than every third year. Purchase new seed each year from a reputable company.

Rust.

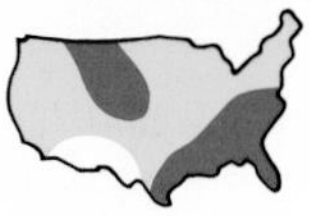

PROBLEM: Rust-colored spots form, mostly on the undersides of the leaves. Severely infected leaves turn yellow, wilt, dry up, and fall off. Stems and pods may also have spots.

ANALYSIS: Bean rust
This plant disease is caused by a fungus (*Uromyces phaseoli*) that affects only bean plants. It is most common on mature plants, and most damaging to pole beans and lima beans. Scarlet runner beans are sometimes mildly affected. Each rust spot develops thousands of spores that are spread by wind and splashing water. The disease develops rapidly during periods of cool nights and warm days. High humidity from rain, dew, or watering also encourages rust. Heavy vine growth, which shades the ground and prevents air circulation, produces ideal conditions for the disease. At the end of the summer when the nights are longer, the fungus produces another type of spore. This thick-walled black spore spends the winter on infected bean plant debris.

SOLUTION: Apply ORTHO Vegetable Disease Control to snap beans at the first sign of the disease. Weekly applications may be necessary if conditions favorable to the disease continue. Avoid overhead irrigation. Water in the morning rather than evening to allow wet foliage to dry quickly. Thin seedlings and space plants far enough apart to allow air to circulate freely. In the fall, remove and destroy all infected plants to prevent the fungus from surviving and reinfecting in the spring. Do not plant beans in the same area more often than every third year. Plant resistant varieties (see page 1027).

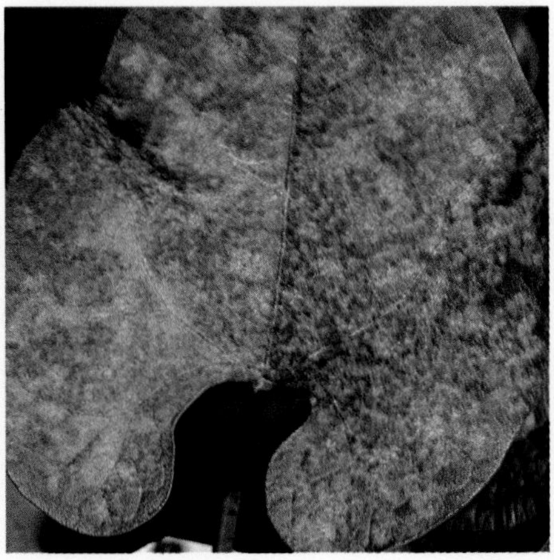

Powdery mildew.

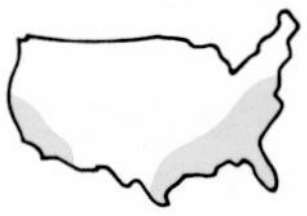

PROBLEM: Leaves are covered with a white, powdery growth. Later they turn yellow and may drop from the plant. Pods are small and are also covered with white powder.

ANALYSIS: Powdery mildew
This common bean disease may be caused by either of two fungi (*Erysiphe polygoni* or *Microsphaera*) that thrive in both humid and dry weather. The powdery patches consist of fungal strands and spores. The spores are spread by the wind to healthy plants. The fungi sap the plant nutrients, causing yellowing and sometimes death of the leaf. A severe infection may kill the plant. Infected pods are inedible. Since powdery mildew attacks several different kinds of plants, the fungus from a diseased plant may infect other types of plants in the garden. (For a list of susceptible plants, see page 1006.) Under favorable conditions, powdery mildew can spread through a closely spaced planting in a matter of days or weeks.

SOLUTION: Treat infected plants with ORTHO Flotox Garden Sulfur at the first sign of the disease. The fungicide protects healthy leaves from infection. Repeat the treatment at intervals of 7 to 10 days until the disease is no longer present.

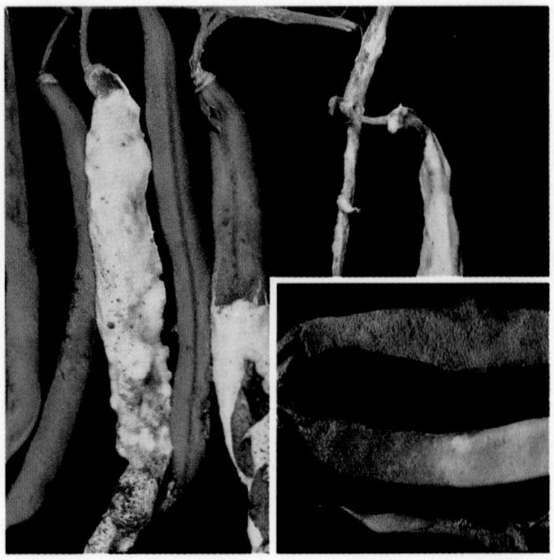

White mold. *Insert:* Gray mold.

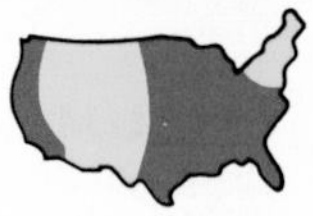

PROBLEM: Soft, watery spots appear on the stems, leaves, or pods. Under moist conditions, these spots enlarge rapidly. A fuzzy gray, gray-brown, or white mold forms on the infected tissue. There may be small, hard, black, seedlike structures embedded in the white mold. Bean plants may yellow, wilt, and die. Rotted pods are soft and mushy.

ANALYSIS: Mold
Mold on beans is caused by two related fungi. One fungus, *Sclerotinia sclerotiorum*, is responsible for *white mold*, also known as *watery soft rot*. The white mold fungus forms dark, seedlike structures that can drop to the soil and survive through adverse conditions to infect bean crops for the next few years. The fungus *Botrytis cinerea* is responsible for *gray mold*. This fungus produces tan to gray-brown fungal strands. Both fungi often attack plant parts that are weak or dead, such as old blossoms. Once established on a plant, the diseases can be spread to healthy plants by wind, splashing water, or when infected plant parts touch healthy ones. Mold spreads quickly in cool, wet weather.

SOLUTION: Remove all diseased plants as soon as symptoms appear. Water healthy plants early in the day. Avoid wetting plant foliage. Do not plant beans in the affected area for 3 to 4 years. Until then, plant other nonsusceptible vegetables such as corn, beets, Swiss chard, or spinach. Always plant beans in well-drained soil, and avoid overcrowding to improve air flow between plants. Spray the foliage with a fungicide containing *benomyl* when approximately 25 percent of the buds are open, and again about 7 to 10 days later.

BEANS

Hopperburn. *Insert:* Leafhopper (3 times life size).

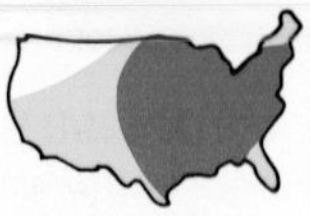

PROBLEM: Leaves are stippled. Some are scorched, with a green midrib and brown edges curled under. Spotted, pale green, winged insects up to ⅛ inch long hop, run, or fly away quickly when the plant is touched.

ANALYSIS: Hopperburn
Hopperburn is caused by the potato leafhopper (*Empoasca fabae*), which injects a toxin into the leaves as it feeds. Bean yields may be drastically reduced from hopperburn. Leafhoppers are active throughout the growing season. They hatch in the spring from eggs laid on perennial weeds and ornamental plants. Even areas that have winters so cold that the eggs cannot survive are not free from infestation, because leafhoppers migrate in the spring from warmer regions.

SOLUTION: Treat infested plants with ORTHO Malathion 50 Insect Spray, ORTHO Fruit & Vegetable Insect Control, ORTHO Tomato & Vegetable Insect Killer, or ORTHO Sevin Garden Dust at the first sign of damage. Be sure to cover the lower surfaces of the leaves, where the leafhoppers feed. Repeat the spray as often as necessary to keep the insects under control. Allow at least 10 days between applications.

Snakehead.

Baldhead.

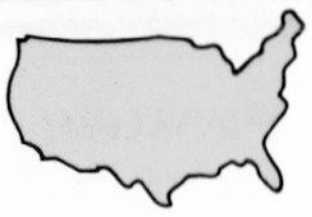

PROBLEM: Seedlings have no leaves or only one leaf. The young plants may sprout late and are often stunted. A normal seedling pushes its way through the soil with a curved stem. The stem then straightens and unfolds two seed leaves.

ANALYSIS: Snakehead and baldhead
Snakeheads are seedlings whose seed leaves have been broken or injured. *Baldheads* are seedlings with no true leaves or stem tip above the seed leaves. They may be caused by:

SOLUTION: Pull out damaged seedlings;they rarely grow into normal plants.

1. *Seed damage:* In the seed, the tiny plant is connected to the seed leaves by slender threads. Despite careful handling by seed companies, seeds can be damaged during harvesting or handling.

1. Buy seed from a reputable garden company. Handle carefully before and during planting.

2. *Soil texture and planting depth:* Bean sprouts push their large seed up and out of the soil. During that struggle the seeds may be damaged, particularly in clay soils, when the soil surface is crusted.

2. Plant new seeds in loose soil 1 to 1½ inches deep. Cover with a layer of sand, vermiculite, or some other loose material to prevent the soil from crusting. Do not use peat moss—it dries out quickly.

3. *Snails, slugs, birds, or insects:* The succulent young leaves may be eaten by animal or insect pests before or after emergence. The seedcorn maggot (see page 686) is sometimes responsible.

3. For protection from birds, cover the seedbed with cheesecloth. Remove once the seedlings emerge through the soil. Discourage soil-inhabiting pests with ORTHO Diazinon Soil & Foliage Dust at planting; for slugs and snails use ORTHO Bug-Geta Snail & Slug Pellets.

Fusarium root rot.

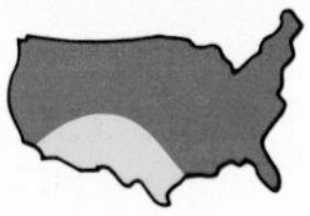

PROBLEM: Leaves turn yellow. Overall growth is slow, and the plant may be dwarfed. In hot, dry weather the plant suddenly wilts and sometimes dies. Few pods are produced. Red spots or streaks may be seen on stems and roots. Underground stems may be streaked dark brown or black.

ANALYSIS: Root rot
This plant disease is caused by several soil-inhabiting fungi (*Fusarium* species, *Pythium* species, and *Rhizoctonia solani*) that attack beans and many other vegetables. The fungi live in the soil, invading the plant through the roots and underground stem. As the disease progresses, the roots decay and shrivel. The leaves turn yellow, and growth slows. The plant becomes dwarfed, wilts, and sometimes dies. Under favorable growing conditions, the bean plants may grow new side roots to replace the rotted ones. These plants will survive, but the yield will be reduced. Root rots develop most rapidly at soil temperatures between 60° and 85°F.

SOLUTION: There is no completely effective chemical control for this problem. Pull out and discard wilted plants. Rotate your bean planting site yearly. If this is not practical, sprinkle with a fungicide containing *captan* (ORTHOCIDE®) or *PCNB* in the row at planting time (1 teaspoon per 20 foot row). Plant in well-drained soil and let the soil surface dry out between waterings.

Bean yellow mosaic.

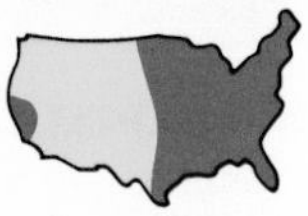

PROBLEM: Leaves are mottled yellow and green, and may be longer and narrower than usual, and puckered. Raised dark areas develop along the central vein, and the leaf margins curl downward. The whole plant is stunted. Pods on the affected plants may be faded, rough, and few in number. The seeds inside are shriveled and small. The damage is most noticeable when the temperature is between 60° and 75°F.

ANALYSIS: Bean mosaic
Bean common mosaic and bean yellow mosaic are widespread virus diseases. Common mosaic virus affects only French and snap beans; yellow mosaic virus affects lima beans, peas, summer squash, clover, gladiolus, and other perennial flowers. Both diseases are spread by aphids, which transmit the virus as they feed. (For more information on aphids, see page 673.) In warmer parts of the country with large aphid populations, the disease spreads rapidly. Common bean mosaic is also spread in infected seed. If the infection occurs early in the season when the plants are young, the plants may not bear pods. Infection later in the season does not affect pod production as severely. For more information on virus diseases, see page 853.

SOLUTION: There are no chemical controls for plant viruses. To reduce the aphid population and the spread of disease, apply ORTHO Malathion 50 Insect Spray or ORTHO Fruit & Vegetable Insect Control as soon as the first insects appear. Remove all infected plants and all clover plants in the vicinity of the garden. Plant virus resistant varieties of beans listed on page 1010.

Curly top.

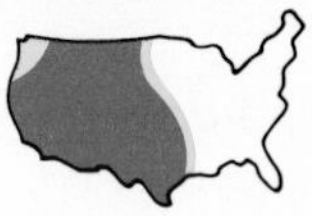

PROBLEM: Leaves are pale green, puckered, and curl downward, and are thick and brittle. The plant is dwarfed and bushy, stops growing, and may die. Bean pods are stunted.

ANALYSIS: Curly top
This virus disease affects many vegetables, including beans, beets, tomatoes, squash, and melons. The virus is transmitted from plant to plant by the beet leafhopper (*Circulifer tenellus*), so the disease is common only in the West, where this insect lives. The pale greenish yellow leafhopper feeds from early May through June. It sucks the sap and virus from the infected leaves, and then injects the virus into healthy plants at its next feeding stop. Curly top symptoms vary in their severity, depending on the variety and age of the plant. Young infected plants usually die. Older plants may turn yellow and die.

SOLUTION: There are no chemical controls for this virus. Remove and destroy all infected plants. To reduce the chances of infection in your garden, control the beet leafhopper with ORTHO Sevin Garden Dust, ORTHO Fruit & Vegetable Insect Control, ORTHO Tomato & Vegetable Insect Killer, or ORTHO Tomato Vegetable Dust. For more information about controlling disease-carrying insects, see page 879. Begin when the insect swarms first appear in early May. Beans planted after the insect stops feeding in June are not infected.

Weak seedlings. *Insert:* Seedcorn maggot (life size).

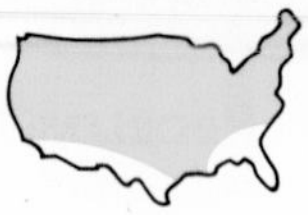

PROBLEM: Seeds may not sprout. If they do, the weak plants wilt and collapse shortly after emerging. Cream-colored, legless maggots about ¼ inch long are feeding on the seeds.

ANALYSIS: Seedcorn maggot
(*Hylemya platura*)
The seedcorn maggot feeds on many vegetables including beets, beans, peas, onions, cucumbers, and cabbage. It damages seeds and germinating seedlings by tunneling into them and feeding on the tissue. If the seed is only partially destroyed, the plants that sprout are weak, sickly, and soon die. These pests can be responsible for snakeheads (see page 684). The seedcorn maggot is favored by cold, wet soil with a high manure content. It spends the winter as a larva or a pupa in soil, plant debris, or manure, and becomes active in the early spring. Small adult flies emerge from May to July, and lay eggs in the rich soil or on seeds or seedlings. The overwintering maggots cause the most damage. Those of later generations are of less importance. There are 3 to 5 generations a year.

SOLUTION: Remove any damaged seeds and sickly plants. Replant with insecticide-treated seeds. To treat the seed yourself, mix one packet of seed with ¼ teaspoon of an insecticide powder that contains *diazinon.* Shake carefully in a jar until the seeds are thoroughly coated. Or work the *diazinon* into the soil at planting time, or spray over the row. Plant seeds when the soil has warmed above 55°F in the spring so they germinate quickly. Shallow-planted seeds germinate more quickly. Use only moderate amounts of manure and till it in thoroughly.

BEETS

ADAPTATION: Throughout the United States.

PLANTING TIME: See page 1009.

PLANTING METHOD: Sow seeds ½ to 1 inch deep. Thin seedlings to stand 2 to 4 inches apart when they have 2 to 3 leaves. Thinnings can be eaten in salads.

SOIL: Any good garden soil. pH 6.0 to 7.0

FERTILIZER: At planting time, use 3 to 4 pounds of ORTHO Vegetable Food per 100 square feet, or 1 pound per 25-foot row. Side-dress every 3 to 4 weeks with 1 pound per 25-foot row.
Containers: Water thoroughly every 2 to 3 weeks with a solution of ORTHO Tomato & Vegetable Food.

WATER:
How much: Apply enough water at each watering to wet the soil 8 to 10 inches deep.
How often: Water when the soil 1 inch deep is just slightly moist.

HARVEST: Beets are edible at different stages of maturity, but smaller ones are more colorful and less tough and stringy than larger ones. Pull beets from the ground when they reach the size listed on the seed packet. Leave 1 to 2 inches of the leaf stalk attached to the beet. Beet greens are also edible, and should be harvested when 4 to 6 inches tall.

Flea beetle (5 times life size).

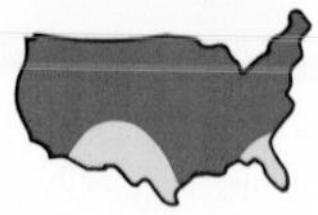

PROBLEM: Leaves are riddled with shotholes about ⅛ inch in diameter. Tiny (1/16 inch) black beetles jump like fleas when disturbed. Leaves of seedlings and eventually whole plants may wilt and die.

ANALYSIS: Flea beetles
These beetles jump like fleas, but are not related to them. Both adult and immature flea beetles feed on a wide variety of garden vegetables. The immature beetle, a legless gray grub, injures plants by feeding on the roots and the lower surface of leaves. Adults chew holes in leaves. Flea beetles are most damaging to seedlings and young plants. Leaves of seedlings riddled with holes dry out quickly and die. Adult beetles spend the winter in soil and garden debris. They emerge in early spring to feed on weeds until vegetables sprout or plants are set in the garden. Grubs hatch from eggs laid in the soil and feed for 2 to 3 weeks. After pupating in the soil, they emerge as adults to repeat the cycle. There are one to four generations a year. Adults may feed for up to 2 months.

SOLUTION: Control flea beetles with an insecticide containing *carbaryl* (SEVIN®) or *methoxychlor* when the leaves first show damage. Watch new growth for further evidence of feeding, and repeat treatments at weekly intervals as needed. Remove all plant debris from the garden after the harvest to eliminate overwintering areas for the adult beetle.

Leafminer damage.

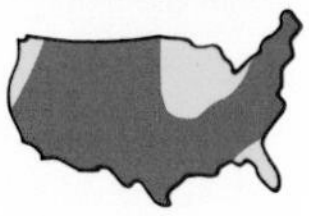

PROBLEM: Light colored, irregular blotches, blisters, or tunnels appear in the leaves. Brown areas peel apart easily like facial tissue. Tiny black specks are found inside the tunnels.

ANALYSIS: Beet leafminer
(*Pegomya hyoscyami*)
This insect pest belongs to a family of leaf-mining flies. The tiny black or yellow adult fly lays its white eggs on the underside of leaves. When the eggs hatch, the cream-colored maggots bore into the leaf. They tunnel between the upper and lower surfaces of the leaf, feeding on the inner tissue. The tunnels and blotches are called *mines*. The black specks inside are the maggot's droppings. The beet leaves are no longer edible, but the root is. Several overlapping generations occur during the growing season, so larvae are present continually from spring until fall.

SOLUTION: Spray with an insecticide containing *malathion* or *diazinon* when the white egg clusters are first seen under the leaves. Repeat two more times at weekly intervals to control succeeding generations. Once the miners enter the leaves, the sprays are ineffective. Spraying after the mines first appear will control only those leafminers that attack after the application. Leafminers are not active in the fall and winter, so if beets will grow in your area at this time of year, you can avoid most of the damage from this pest.

Cercospora leaf spot.

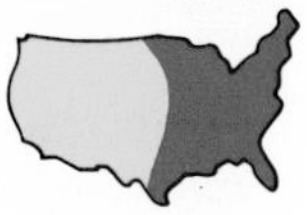

PROBLEM: The leaves have small, circular, distinct spots with dark borders. These spots may run together to form blotches or dead areas. The leaves often turn yellow and die. Leaf spotting is most severe in warm, humid weather, when a fine gray mold may cover the infected tissue. Older leaves are more severely affected than younger ones.

ANALYSIS: Leaf spot
This common, destructive fungus (*Cercospora beticola*) attacks beets, spinach, and Swiss chard. The fungus invades the leaves but not the beet root. However, severe infection damages many leaves and hinders the development of the root. The spotting makes the leaves unappetizing. The fungus is spread by wind, contaminated tools, and splashing water, and is favored by moist conditions and high temperatures. Leaf spot is most common during the summer months and in warm areas. This fungus survives the winter on plant debris not cleaned out of the garden.

SOLUTION: Picking off and destroying the first spotted leaves retards the spread of leaf spot. Leaf spots on beets seldom cause enough damage to warrant fungicide sprays. If your planting is large or the disease becomes very severe, you may spray with a fungicide containing *zineb* at weekly intervals. Do not work among wet plants. If possible, avoid overhead watering; use drip or furrow irrigation instead. Use a mulch to reduce the need for watering. Clean all plant debris from the garden after the harvest to reduce the number of overwintering spores.

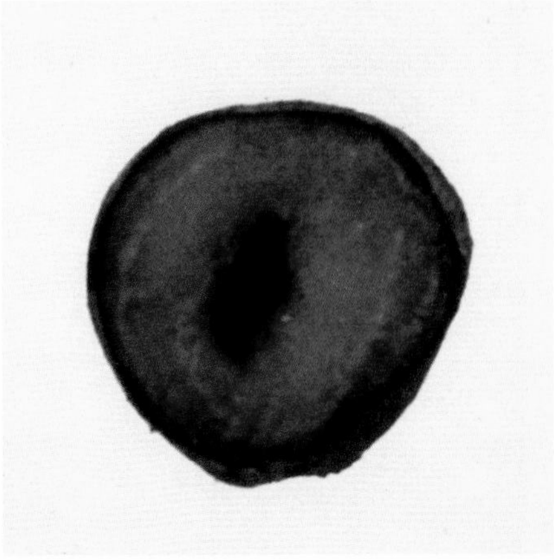

Boron-deficient beet.

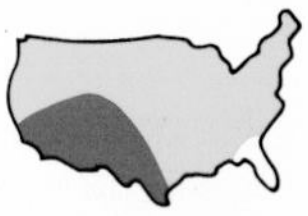

PROBLEM: Black areas occur on the outer skin and inside the beet root. The root may be wrinkled and cracked. Plants are stunted and the leaves brown along the edges. The lower surfaces of the leaves turn reddish purple. Bottom leaves die.

ANALYSIS: Boron deficiency
Boron is a plant nutrient that is present in most soils. All vegetables require boron, but some require a greater amount than others. Boron is used by the plant to manufacture food and to move the food from one part of the plant to another. Plants suffer from a boron deficiency when boron is either lacking in the soil, or is in a form the plants can't use. Boron deficiency is most common during dry weather and in alkaline soil. Boron may be lacking in any type of soil, but most frequently in sandy soil. Beets are affected when they are more than 1 inch in diameter. The roots are still edible if the discolored areas are cut away. Root rotting fungi and bacteria may invade cracked roots.

SOLUTION: Treat plants as soon as damage is noticed with a solution of 1 tablespoon of household borax dissolved in 12 quarts of water. Apply this solution to a 100-foot row. Next year, treat the soil soon after planting. Repeat the treatment in 2 to 3 weeks. Test the soil pH as instructed on page 903, and correct if necessary to maintain a pH between 6.0 and 7.0. Add organic matter to sandy soil as outlined on page 930. Maintain even soil moisture, so that the soil never dries out.

BEETS

Curly top.

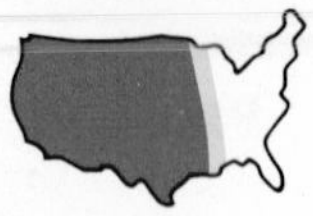

PROBLEM: The leaf margins roll upward and feel brittle. The undersides of the leaves are rough, with puckering along the veins. The leaves and roots are stunted; the plant may die.

ANALYSIS: Curly top
This virus disease affects many vegetables, including beets, beans, tomatoes, squash, and melons. The virus is transmitted from plant to plant by the beet leafhopper (*Circulifer tenellus*), and is common only in the West, where this insect lives. The beet leafhopper is a pale greenish yellow insect about ⅛ inch long that feeds from early May through June. It sucks the sap and virus from the infested leaves, and then injects the virus into healthy plants at its next feeding stop. (For more information about leafhoppers, see page 880.) Curly top symptoms vary in their severity, depending on the variety and the age of the plant. Young infected plants usually die. Older plants may turn yellow and die.

SOLUTION: There is no direct control for curly top. To reduce the chance of infection, control the beet leafhopper with an insecticide containing *malathion*, beginning when the insect swarms first appear. For information about controlling disease-carrying insects, see page 880. Destroy infected plants. A light screening of cheesecloth over the plants keeps leafhoppers from landing on the plants.

Damping-off.

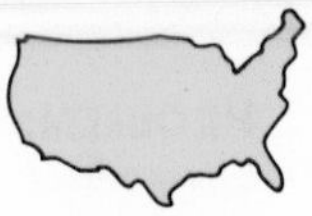

PROBLEM: Seeds don't sprout, or seedlings fall over soon after they emerge. Areas on the stem at the soil line are water-soaked and discolored. The base of the stem is soft and thin.

ANALYSIS: Damping-off
Damping-off is a common problem in wet soil with a high nitrogen level. Wet, rich soil promotes damping-off in two ways: the fungi are more active under these conditions, and the seedlings are more succulent and susceptible to attack. Damping-off is often a problem with crops that are planted too early in the spring, before the soil has had a chance to dry and warm sufficiently for quick seed germination. Damping-off can also be a problem when the weather remains cloudy and wet while seeds are germinating, or if seedlings are too heavily shaded.

SOLUTION: To prevent damping-off, take these precautions:
1. Allow the surface of the soil to dry slightly between waterings.
2. Do not start seeds in soil that has a high nitrogen level. Add nitrogen fertilizers after the seedlings have produced their first true leaves.
3. Plant seeds after the soil has reached the temperature needed for quick germination, at least 60°F.
4. Protect seeds during germination by coating them with a fungicide containing *captan* (ORTHOCIDE®) or *thiram*. Add a pinch of fungicide to a packet of seeds (or ½ teaspoon per pound), and shake well to coat the seeds with the fungicide. For more information on starting seeds, see page 917.

Misshapen roots.

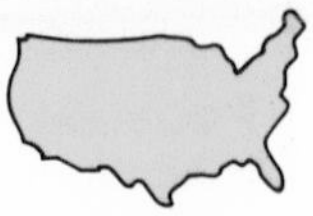

PROBLEM: Beet roots are distorted, elongated, knobby, and crooked. They are not smooth and round.

ANALYSIS: Misshapen roots
Beet roots may be misshapen for any of several reasons.
1. *Overcrowding:* The beet "seed" is actually a dried fruit containing two or more seeds. As the "seed" germinates, seedlings emerge through the soil in clusters instead of individually as do beans and corn. When the seedlings are too crowded, the root does not have room to develop properly.
2. *Lumpy soil:* Beet roots may be distorted because rocks, clods of soil, or clumps of manure do not allow even expansion of the root.
3. *Variety:* Some beet varieties do not produce smooth, round roots. Some are roughly cylindrical, and others long and smooth.

SOLUTION: Follow these suggestions for round, smooth beets.
1. Plant beet seeds ½ inch deep and 1 inch apart. When the young seedlings have their first set of leaves, thin them to stand 2 to 3 inches apart. If you wait until the plants are 3 inches tall, you can cook the greens like spinach.
2. Rake out and discard rocks ½ inch in diameter and larger. Break up clods of soil and manure.
3. Plant varieties that grow smooth, round roots (see page 1027).

BLUEBERRIES

ADAPTATION: Throughout the United States. For varietal adaptations, see page 1003.

PLANTING TIME:
Cold winter areas: Spring.
Mild winter areas: Fall or spring.

PLANTING METHOD: For best fruit set, plant at least three different varieties. Select dormant 2 to 3-year-old plants that are 12 to 36 inches tall. Prune back to 3 or 4 strong shoots. Set plants so the top of their rootball is 1 to 2 inches deeper than the surrounding garden soil. Mulch with a 4 to 6-inch layer of sawdust, pine bark, or leaf mold.

SOIL: Light, acid soil that is high in organic matter. pH 4.0 to 5.2

FERTILIZER: As soon as the bushes begin to grow after planting, feed with ORTHO General Purpose Plant Food, 1½ ounces per plant. For the next 2 years, feed with 3 ounces per plant just as the buds break in the spring. Thereafter, feed with 3 to 8 ounces of *ammonium sulfate* per plant. *Ammonium sulfate* also helps maintain an acid soil.

WATER:
How much: Apply enough water to wet the soil 1 foot deep at each irrigation.
How often: Water when the soil under the mulch is just barely moist.

HARVEST: Pick blueberries when they are solid blue with a light whitish bloom. Pull them gently from the cluster.

Cranberry fruitworms (¾ life size).

PROBLEM: Clusters of berries are webbed together with silk. Berries may be shriveled and full of sawdustlike material. Inside the berries are smooth pink-red or pale yellow-green caterpillars about ⅜ to 1 inch long.

ANALYSIS: Cherry fruitworm (*Grapholitha packardii*) **or cranberry fruitworm** (*Acrobasis vaccinii*)
These 2 fruitworms are serious pests of blueberries and cranberries. They also attack cherries and apples. Each caterpillar destroys 2 to 6 berries. They do not damage the leaves. In midspring, adult moths lay eggs on developing berries and leaves. The caterpillars that hatch from these eggs bore into the berries at the junction of the stem and berry. When they are about half grown, the fruitworms move to another berry, usually one touching the infested berry. This way the fruitworm can move to a new food source without exposing itself. About mid-June, when the caterpillar is full grown, it crawls to the soil, garden debris, or a pruning stub, where it remains through the remainder of the growing season and the winter. Adult moths emerge in midspring to start the cycle again.

SOLUTION: Once the fruit is infested there is no way to kill the worms inside. Handpick and destroy all infested fruit. If your planting is large, or if the fruitworm infestation this year was severe, spray the plants immediately after bloom, before the berries are ¼ inch in diameter, with ORTHO Fruit & Vegetable Insect Control. Repeat once 10 days later.

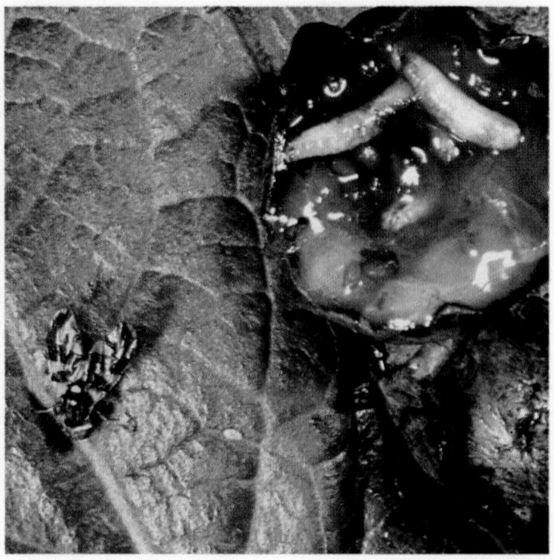

Blueberry maggots and adult (twice life size).

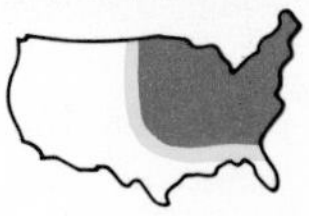

PROBLEM: Ripening blueberries leak juice and are soft and mushy. White, tapered maggots about ⅜ inch long are feeding inside the berries.

ANALYSIS: Blueberry maggot
(*Rhagoletis mendax*)
This insect, also called the *blueberry fruitfly*, is the most important pest of blueberries in the Midwest and on the East Coast. Maggots attack both green and ripe fruit, and often ruin an entire crop. They are most severe after unusually cold winters and when the weather is very wet at harvest time, and frequent pickings are not possible. The maggots spend the winter as pupae in the soil. From late June through August, the adult flies lay eggs just under the skin of the fruit. The maggots that hatch from the eggs feed in the berry for about 20 days, then drop to the soil where they pupate for 1 to 2 years. There is only one generation a year.

SOLUTION: Harvest frequently, destroying any infested berries. Next year, beginning in early July, treat the plants with ORTHO Fruit & Vegetable Insect Control. Repeat the treatment at intervals of 10 days through the harvest. Treatments the following year may be necessary to control any pupae that mature after 2 years.

BLUEBERRIES

Plum curculio (twice life size).

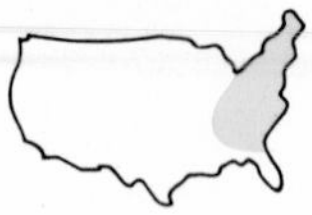

PROBLEM: Fruit ripens earlier than usual. Shriveled, hollow berries lie on the soil beneath the plants. Berries still on the plants have small circular indentations in them. Inside are smooth, legless, yellowish white grubs with brown heads.

ANALYSIS: Plum curculio
(*Conotrachelus nenaphar*)
This insect prefers plums and peaches, but also damages blueberries, apples, and cherries. The adult weevil is ¼ inch long, with an elongated snout and brown warty body with gray or white patches. In midspring, it lays 1 egg in a small circular indentation in each berry. Each female weevil lays about 150 eggs. When the eggs hatch, the grubs bore into the center of the fruit, where they feed for several weeks. The infested berries stop growing and fall to the ground. When the grubs are fully grown, the berries are completely hollow. The larvae burrow into the soil to pupate. Several weeks later the adult emerges. If green berries are still on the bushes, the adult lays eggs, starting the cycle again.

SOLUTION: Once the fruit is infested there is no way to kill the grubs inside. Pick and destroy the infested fruit. Next spring, spray the plants with an insecticide containing *carbaryl* (SEVIN®) or *malathion* immediately after bloom, before the fruits are ¼ inch in diameter. Repeat 2 more times, 7 to 10 days apart.

Mummy berry.

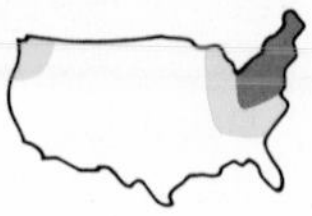

PROBLEM: As the berries ripen, they become reddish buff or tan in color. Many fall off before they ripen. Mature berries are gray, shriveled, and hard. Blossoms turn brown and wither. The centers of new leaves are black. Eventually the entire leaf and/or shoot tips wilt and die.

ANALYSIS: Mummy berry
This plant disease is caused by a fungus (*Monilinia vaccinii-corymbosi*) that occurs irregularly, and may be severe some years and nonexistent other years. This is due primarily to the spring weather. Cold, wet weather favors the fungus. The disease spores spend the winter on infected fruit mummies on the ground and on twigs. The spores infect leaves, shoots, and flowers shortly after they begin growing in the spring. The spores infect young fruit through the flower. In order for the disease to develop, spores must land on very young tissue before a natural waxy layer covers the plant surfaces.

SOLUTION: This disease is very difficult to control. Once the berries have mummied, it is too late to do anything this year. Discard all mummies on the twigs and the ground. Next spring, apply the fungicide *triforine* (FUNGINEX®) 3 times, 7 to 10 days apart, beginning at bud break. Cultivate around the plants in early spring to bury any remaining mummies. Add 2 inches of sawdust mulch to keep the spores from reaching the new growth.

Botrytis blossom blight.

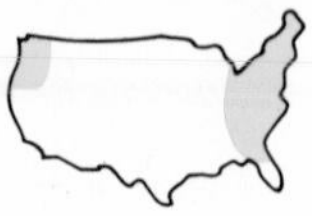

PROBLEM: Brown spots and blotches appear on the flowers and stems. As the disease progresses, a fuzzy brown or grayish mold forms on the infected tissue. Gray mold often appears on the flowers, especially during periods of cool, wet weather. The leaves and stems may be soft and rotted.

ANALYSIS: Stem and blossom blight
This plant disease is caused by a fungus (*Botrytis cinerea*) that is found on most dead plant tissue. The fungus initially attacks flowers that are weak or dead, causing spotting and mold. The fuzzy mold that develops is composed of fungus strands and millions of microscopic spores. Once gray mold has become established on plant debris and weak or dying flowers, it can invade healthy plant tissue. The fungus is spread by splashing water, or by infected pieces of tissue contacting healthy tissue. Cool temperatures and high humidity favor gray mold growth. Crowded plantings, rain, and overhead watering also enhance the spread of the fungus. Infection is more of a problem in spring and fall, when temperatures are lower. In mild winter areas, where freezing is rare, gray mold can be a year-round problem.

SOLUTION: Spray plants with a fungicide containing *captan* (ORTHOCIDE®) or *benomyl* at the first sign of the disease. Continue spraying at intervals of 10 to 14 days as long as wet weather continues. Clean up plant debris and infected parts. Provide enough space between plants to allow good air circulation. Try to avoid wetting the foliage when watering.

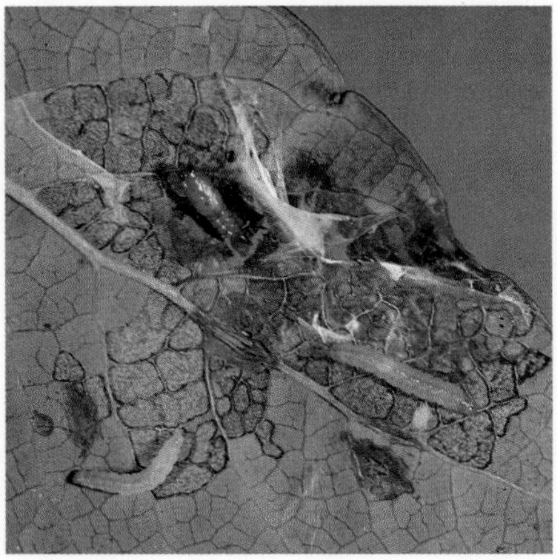

Red banded leafroller larva and pupa (life size).

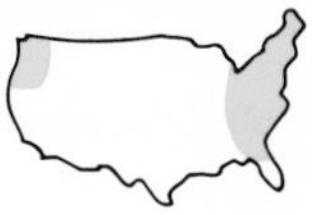

PROBLEM: Leaves are rolled or tied together. Inside the rolled leaves is a tubelike shelter made of black sawdust and silk threads. A yellowish white or purple-brown caterpillar may be found in the tube. The caterpillar may have red stripes.

ANALYSIS: Leafrollers and leaftiers

Leafrollers are caterpillars that roll up leaves and feed inside. Leaftiers tie leaves together with silk threads and feed inside. Several kinds of leafrollers and tiers attack blueberries. Although they may slightly weaken the plant, they do not significantly reduce berry production. Adult moths lay eggs in early spring. From April to September the larvae feed on leaves near the stem tips. They roll the leaves together, and feed on the upper leaf tissue within the tied leaves. This area becomes somewhat discolored on the outside of the leaf. They may also feed on the tips of the tied leaves. After feeding, they move to another set of leaves, roll or tie them, and feed again.

SOLUTION: Spray the plants with ORTHO Fruit & Vegetable Insect Control as soon as the problem is discovered or immediately after bloom. Repeat at intervals of 7 to 10 days as the rolling continues. If only a few stem tips are affected, pick them off and squash the caterpillar inside.

Blueberry scale (life size).

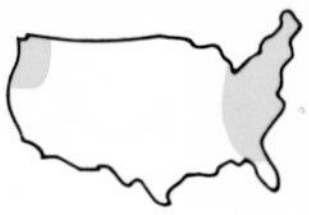

PROBLEM: Nodes, stems, and leaves are covered with white, cottony, cushionlike masses or brownish, crusty bumps or clusters of somewhat flattened reddish, gray, or brownish scaly bumps. The bumps can be picked off. Leaves turn yellow and may drop. Branches are killed by heavy infestations.

ANALYSIS: Scales

These insects are damaging to many plants in the garden. They damage blueberries by reducing berry production and weakening the plant. The scales lay their eggs on leaves or bark, and in spring to midsummer the young scales, called *crawlers*, settle on leaves and twigs. The small (1/10 inch), soft-bodied young feed by inserting their mouthparts and sucking sap from the plant. The legs usually atrophy and, with some types, a shell develops over the body. The types of scale that do not develop shells are very conspicuous. The females are covered with a white, cottony egg sac containing up to 2500 eggs. Scales covered with a shell are less noticeable. The shell often blends in with the plant and the eggs are inconspicuous beneath the covering. For more information about scales, see page 876.

SOLUTION: Control scales with ORTHO Fruit & Vegetable Insect Control when the young are active. Contact your local Cooperative Extension Office (see page 1029) to determine the best time to spray for scales in your area. Repeat if the plants become reinfested. Next spring, just before the new leaves emerge, spray the plants with a *dormant oil*.

BRAMBLES (BLACKBERRIES, RASPBERRIES)

ADAPTATION: Throughout the United States. For varietal adaptions, see page 1023.

PLANTING TIME: Late fall or early spring.

PLANTING METHOD: Select 1-year-old dormant plants that are 12 to 24 inches tall. Set plants 3 to 6 feet apart, and deep enough so that the top of their rootball is 1 inch deeper than the surrounding garden soil. Prune canes back to 6 to 12-inch stubs.

SOIL: Any good garden soil that is high in organic matter. pH 5.5 to 6.8

FERTILIZER: At planting time, use 1 pound of ORTHO General Purpose Plant Food per 20-foot row. Thereafter, apply 2 pounds per 20-foot row once a year in early spring before new growth begins.

WATER:

How much: Apply enough water at each irrigation to wet the soil 1 to 2 feet deep.

How often: Water when the soil 2 inches deep is barely moist.

HARVEST: Berries are ripe when they are a deep, rich color and slightly soft. Ripe fruit are easily removed when pulled gently. When picked, only raspberries pull free of their central core. All other bramble fruits have a central core. Pick every 2 to 3 days. Protect ripening fruit from birds with netting available in your garden center or through mail-order garden supply companies. Store berries in the refrigerator until use.

BRAMBLES (BLACKBERRIES, RASPBERRIES)

Torn leaf.

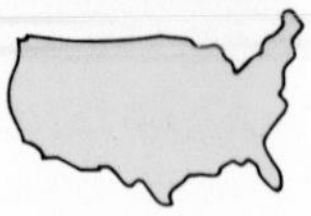

PROBLEM: Leaves are torn or shredded. There are no signs of insects or diseases.

ANALYSIS: Leaves torn
Bramble leaves are torn during gusty winds by the thorns on their canes. This damage does not harm the plants or reduce fruit production. Plants set too close together are damaged most seriously. Plants whose cane movement is restricted by staking or trellising are the least affected.

SOLUTION: If you live in a very windy area, construct a windbreak out of burlap and wood to protect the plants. Tie plants to a trellis or staking system.

To keep berry rows manageable, remove most of the suckers as they appear in the spring. Leave only a few of the strongest to replace this year's fruiting canes. When the new canes are long enough, tie them to a trellis.

Raspberry fruitworm (twice life size).

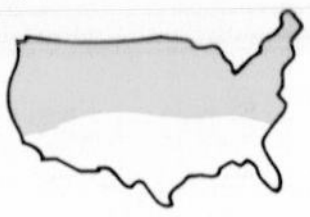

PROBLEM: Berries drop or decay before they are fully ripe. Inside the fruit are light yellow worms, ¼ inch long, with brown markings. Holes are chewed in the leaves.

ANALYSIS: Raspberry fruitworm
(*Byturus* species)
Raspberries and loganberries in the northern part of the country are attacked by these pests. Early red raspberries are the most severely damaged. Both the adults and larvae feed on buds, blossoms, leaves, and fruit. Feeding damage to the blossoms and developing fruit reduces fruit set and yield. When infestations are large, many leaves are eaten. Light brown adult beetles ⅛ inch long emerge from the soil in early spring as the new leaves are unfolding. They feed on these leaves and buds, and the females lay their white eggs in the blossoms and fruit. The larvae that hatch then feed in the fruit. After feeding, they drop to the soil, where they pupate, and emerge the following spring as adults. There is only one generation a year.

SOLUTION: Once the fruit is infested, sprays are ineffective. Remove and destroy all infested berries. Next year, treat the plants with ORTHO Fruit & Vegetable Insect Control. Spray first when the blossom buds first appear, and again just before the blossoms open.

Fruit rot on blackberries.

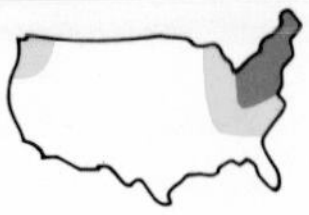

PROBLEM: Ripening berries are covered with tufts of gray, green, white, or black cottony growths. A smelly, watery liquid may ooze from berries.

ANALYSIS: Fruit rot
Several different fungi (*Botrytis cinerea*, *Monilinia fructicola*, and *Rhizopus nigricans*) cause fruit rot on raspberries and blackberries. These diseases are widespread and develop fastest on overripe and bruised raspberries. Warm, wet weather, especially during harvest, favors these fungi. They can infect the fruit before or after harvest.

SOLUTION: Fungicide sprays help reduce fruit rot, but good harvest practices are a must. Pick ripening berries frequently to avoid an accumulation of overripe fruit. Harvest in the cool early morning, and handle the fruit carefully to avoid bruising. Cool the picked berries in the refrigerator immediately. To reduce fruit rot, spray the plants with a fungicide containing *captan* (ORTHOCIDE®). Repeat at intervals of 7 to 10 days during the harvest.

Verticillium wilt of raspberry.

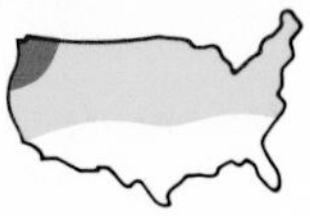

PROBLEM: In mid to late summer the leaves turn yellow, wilt, dry, and fall off. Yellowing starts on the lower leaves and moves up the stems. Canes may turn bluish black from the soil line upward. Fruit withers, or is small and tasteless. Plants may die the following year.

ANALYSIS: Verticillium wilt
This wilt disease affects many garden plants. It is caused by a soil-inhabiting fungus (*Verticillium albo-atrum*) that persists indefinitely on plant debris or in the soil. The disease is spread by contaminated seeds, plants, soil, and equipment. The fungus enters the plant through the roots and spreads into the canes and leaves through the water-conducting vessels in the stems. The vessels become discolored and plugged. This plugging cuts off the flow of water and nutrients to the leaves, causing leaf yellowing and wilting. Plants under stress from hot, dry midsummer weather are most susceptible. For more information about verticillium wilt, see page 850.

SOLUTION: No chemical control is available. It is best to destroy infected plants. Verticillium can be removed from the soil by fumigation techniques. For more information about soil fumigation, see page 919. However, the best solution is usually to use varieties that are resistant to verticillium wilt.

Blackberry varieties resistant to verticillium wilt: Evergreen and Himalaya. Ollalieberry and loganberry are also resistant.

Raspberry crown borer (life size).

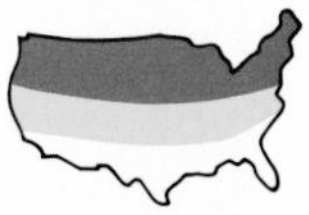

PROBLEM: In early summer, canes wilt and begin dying. Some canes are spindly, lack vigor, and grow very little. Canes often break off easily at ground level. There may be white grubs, ¼ to 1¼ inches long inside some of the canes.

ANALYSIS: Raspberry crown borer
(*Pennitsetia marginata*)
This insect pest, also called the *raspberry root borer*, attacks brambles in the northern United States. The borer damages plants by feeding on the roots and crown (base) of the plant. Root feeding weakens all cane fruits, but often kills raspberries. The crown borer has a 2-year life cycle. In late summer, the adult moth lays a total of about 100 eggs on the undersides of several leaves. The eggs hatch in early fall, and the larvae move to the soil near the plant crown, where they spend the winter. As the weather warms in the spring, the larvae enter the plant and begin hollowing out the crown. This feeding causes the canes to swell and eventually die. The larvae continue feeding throughout the year, spend the winter in the canes, and feed again the spring. They mature and emerge from the canes as adults in late summer. One and two year old larvae may be present at the same time.

SOLUTION: In early spring, drench the crown and lower 2 feet of the canes with an insecticide containing *diazinon*. Repeat controls annually for at least 2 years because of this insect's 2-year life cycle. Cut out and destroy canes when pruning.

Borer damage.

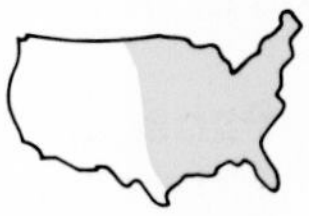

PROBLEM: Shoot tips wilt. Some canes die. Two rows of small holes, 1 inch apart, may encircle the cane below the wilted tips. Cigar-shaped swellings, ¼ to 3 inches long, may occur on the cane. The cane breaks off easily at the swelling. Some leaves may be chewed and ragged.

ANALYSIS: Raspberry cane borer and red-necked cane borer
(*Oberea maculata* and *Agrilus ruficollis*)
These two cane borers attack blackberries, raspberries, and dewberries. The adult beetles are black with copper or yellow just behind the head, and are ½ inch long. On sunny summer days, the adult red-necked cane borers may be seen feeding on the leaves. The females lay their eggs in the bark of new, tender growth. The white grublike larvae then tunnel around and inside the cane, feeding on the inner tissue. This feeding often causes cane swellings; it also interferes with the flow of water and nutrients through the cane, resulting in shoot wilting and cane death. The borers spend the winter in tunnels in the canes.

SOLUTION: Cut off infested canes 6 inches below the swelling or wilted tip, and destroy them. The following year, apply an insecticide containing *rotenone* or *malathion* immediately before bloom and again 2 weeks later.

BRAMBLES (BLACKBERRIES, RASPBERRIES)

Cane blight on raspberry.

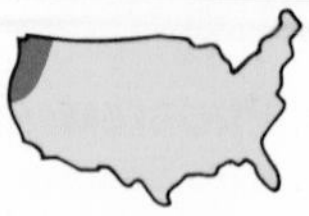

PROBLEM: Branches wilt and die in midsummer. Brownish purple areas occur on pruned ends or wounded areas of canes and extend downward, sometimes encircling the stem. Infected canes turn gray in late summer.

ANALYSIS: Cane blight
This plant disease is caused by a fungus (*Leptosphaeria coniothyrium*). It is more prevalent on black raspberries than on red and purple raspberries and blackberries. The fungus spends the winter on diseased canes. The spores are spread from plant to plant by the wind. In wet weather in late spring and early summer, the spores enter canes through cracks in the bark, broken fruit stems, and wounds from pruning and insects. The spores don't infect young tissue directly. Canes weakened from cane blight are more subject to winter injury.

SOLUTION: Apply ORTHO Dormant Disease Control in late fall and early spring. Follow with two applications of a fungicide containing *ferbam* or *folpet* (PHALTAN®): one just before bloom, when the new canes are 1½ to 2 feet tall; and the other just after harvest. Remove infected canes before growth starts in the spring. Prune just above a bud in dry weather at least 3 days before rain, so the wounds have time to dry up.

Spider mite damage.

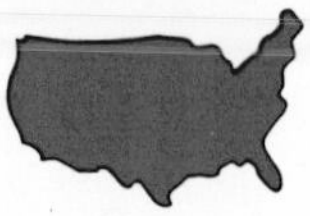

PROBLEM: Leaves are stippled, yellowing, and dirty. Leaves may dry out and drop. There may be webbing between leaves, or on the young stems and lower surfaces of the leaves. To determine if the plant is infested with mites, hold a sheet of white paper underneath an affected leaf and tap the leaf sharply. Minute green, red, or yellow specks the size of pepper grains will drop to the paper and begin to crawl around. These pests are easily seen against the white background.

ANALYSIS: Spider mites
These mites, related to spiders, are major pests of many garden plants, including brambles. They cause damage by sucking sap from the underside of the leaves. As a result of feeding, the green leaf pigment disappears, producing the stippled appearance. Mites are active throughout the growing season, but are favored by hot, dry weather (70°F and up). By midsummer, they build up to tremendous numbers. For more information about spider mites, see page 887.

SOLUTION: Spray with ORTHO Fruit & Vegetable Insect Control when damage is first noticed. Spray the leaves thoroughly, being sure to cover the undersides of the leaves. Repeat the treatment three more times at intervals of 7 days. Hose down the plants frequently to knock off webs and mites. Next spring, spray the plants with *lime sulfur* when the leaves are just beginning to emerge.

Crown gall on blackberry.

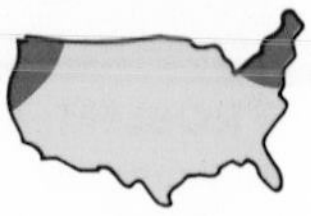

PROBLEM: Plants are stunted, break and fall over easily, and produce dry, seedy berries. Irregular, wartlike growths (galls) may appear on canes. The canes may dry out and crack. Galls also occur just below the soil level on roots and crown. They range from pinhead-sized to several inches in diameter, and are white or grayish brown.

ANALYSIS: Cane and crown gall
These diseases are caused by bacteria (*Agrobacterium rubi* and *A. tumefaciens*) that occur on blackberries, raspberries, boysenberries, loganberries, and youngberries throughout the United States. The plants become weak and produce fewer berries. The bacteria are often brought to a garden initially on the roots of an infected plant, and are spread with the soil and by contaminated pruning tools. The bacteria enter the plant through wounds in the roots or the base of the stem (the crown). They produce a substance that stimulates rapid cell growth in the plant, causing gall formation on the roots, crown, and canes. The galls disrupt the flow of water and nutrients up the roots and stems, weakening and stunting the top of the plant. Galls do not usually cause the plant to die.

SOLUTION: Crown gall cannot be eliminated from the plant. Although infected plants may survive for many years, they will produce few berries. Dig up and discard diseased plants and the soil within 6 inches of a gall. Wait at least 3 years before replanting brambles in areas where the disease has occurred. Plant gall-free plants in clean soil. Prune and cultivate carefully to avoid wounding plants. For more information on crown gall, see page 853.

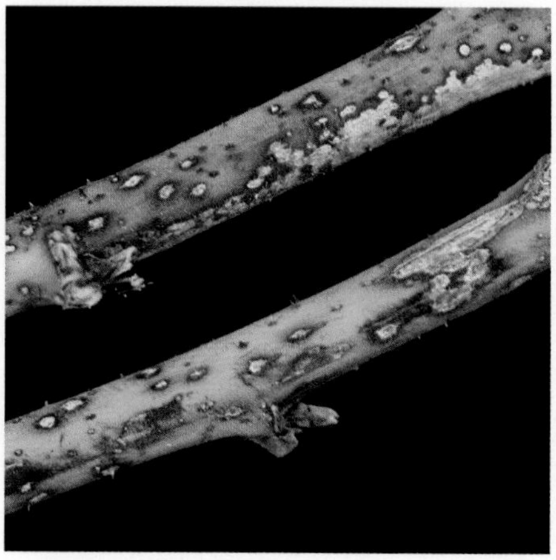

Anthracnose spots on raspberry.

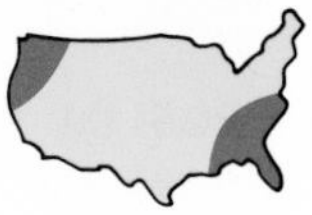

PROBLEM: Stem tips die. Oval spots with purple edges and light gray centers appear on the canes. Spots enlarge, sometimes circling the entire stem. Canes may dry and crack. Most of the spots occur on the inside of the canes toward the center of the plant, and from 6 to 30 inches up from the ground. The leaves may have small yellow spots with purple margins. The centers of the spots often drop out, leaving a hole.

ANALYSIS: Anthracnose
This disease, caused by a fungus (*Elsinoe veneta*), is one of the most important diseases of black and purple raspberries. Although the disease is common on red raspberries, they are not seriously affected by it. Overgrown, unpruned bushes are very susceptible to anthracnose. The disease is most serious when heavy rains continue late in the spring and into the summer. The fungus survives the winter in infected canes, and infects new growth in the early spring. Canes weakened by anthracnose are more susceptible to winter injury.

SOLUTION: Apply a fungicide containing *lime sulfur* in early spring when the leaf buds swell and expose from ½ to ¾ inch of the new leaves. This is the most important and effective time to spray. Follow with three applications of a fungicide containing *ferbam* or *captan* (ORTHOCIDE®): (1) when the new canes are 6 to 8 inches tall; (2) when they are 12 to 15 inches tall; and (3) just before bloom. After harvest, prune out old infected canes.

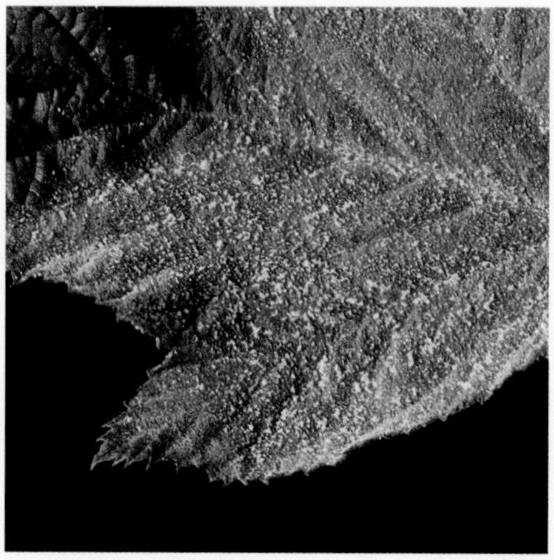

Powdery mildew on raspberry.

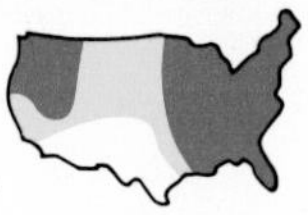

PROBLEM: A whitish gray powder covers the leaves, fruit, and young growing tips of the canes. Canes may be dwarfed or distorted. Fruit may wither and die.

ANALYSIS: Powdery mildew
This common plant disease seriously affects red raspberries and occasionally attacks purple and black raspberries and blackberries. It is caused by a fungus (*Sphaerotheca humuli*) that thrives in both humid and dry weather. The powdery patches consist of fungal strands and spores. The spores are spread by the wind to healthy plants. The fungus saps plant nutrients, causing yellowing and sometimes the death of the leaf. A severe infection may kill the plant. Since this powdery mildew attacks many different kinds of plants, the fungus from a diseased plant may infect other types of plants in the garden. (For a list of susceptible plants, see page 1006.) Under favorable conditions, powdery mildew can spread through a row of berries in a matter of days or weeks.

SOLUTION: Spray the plants with a fungicide containing *benomyl* when the blossoms first open. Repeat at weekly intervals if the plants become reinfected. Next fall, and again in the spring as the buds begin to swell, spray the plants with ORTHO Orthorix Spray. Space the plants far enough apart to allow good air circulation so they can dry rapidly after rain or watering.

Red raspberry varieties resistant to powdery mildew: Meeker, Sumner, and Willamette.

Orange rust on blackberry.

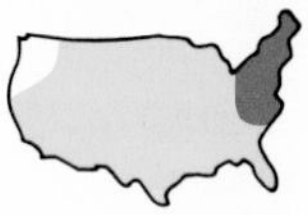

PROBLEM: Leaves are dwarfed, misshapen, and yellowish. Blisterlike pustules and bright orange dust cover the undersides of the leaves.

ANALYSIS: Orange rust
This plant disease is caused by a fungus (*Gymnoconia peckiana*). It is severe on wild and cultivated blackberries and dewberries. It sometimes attacks black raspberries, but doesn't affect red and purple raspberries. The disease spreads throughout the entire plant. Infected plants never recover and never bloom. Spores are produced on the plant each year after it is infected. The fungus spreads from plant to plant on the wind. In the spring, orange spores land on leaves. After infecting them, the fungus spreads throughout the plant into the canes, crown, and roots. The disease spreads into new shoots as the plant grows.

SOLUTION: Fungicide sprays and pruning are not effective. Remove and destroy infected plants as soon as they are noticed. Remove any wild blackberries growing nearby. Thin the plants for good air circulation. Pull out all weeds. Grow rust-resistant varieties.

Blackberry varieties resistant to rust: Boysenberry, Ebony King, Eldorado, Lawton, Orange Evergreen, and Youngberry. Leucretia is a rust-resistant dewberry.

CABBAGE FAMILY

PROBLEMS WITH THE HEAD

CABBAGE FAMILY (BROCCOLI, BRUSSELS SPROUTS, CABBAGE, CHINESE CABBAGE, CAULIFLOWER, COLLARDS, KALE, KOHLRABI)

ADAPTATION: Throughout the United States.

PLANTING TIME: See page 1025.

PLANTING METHOD: Set transplants so the top of their rootball is even with the garden soil.

Spacing: Cabbage, cauliflower, and broccoli—15 to 24 inches apart; Brussels sprouts—30 to 36 inches apart; kohlrabi—4 to 6 inches apart; kale and collards—8 to 12 inches apart. Or, sow seeds ½ to 1 inch deep and 1 inch apart. Thin according to the spacings listed above when the seedlings have 2 or 3 leaves.

SOIL: Any good garden soil. pH 6.0 to 7.0

FERTILIZER: At planting time use 2 to 4 pounds of ORTHO Vegetable Food per 100 square feet, or 1 pound per 25-foot row. Side-dress every 3 to 4 weeks with 1 pound per 25-foot row, or 1 to 2 tablespoons per plant.

Containers: Water thoroughly every 2 to 3 weeks with a solution of ORTHO Tomato & Vegetable Food.

WATER:

How much: Apply enough water at each irrigation to wet the soil 8 to 10 inches deep.

How often: Water when the soil 1 inch deep is barely moist.

HARVEST:

Broccoli: When the buds are still tight, before they open into yellow flowers. Smaller heads will grow along the stem after the first head is harvested.

Brussels sprouts: Pick sprouts from the bottom up when they are about 1 inch in diameter and still tight. Remove the leaves as you pick.

Cabbage: Cut just below the head when firm and before it cracks.

Chinese cabbage: Cut the entire head when it is 12 to 16 inches tall.

Cauliflower: Cut when the heads are 6 to 8 inches in diameter with tight curds. For information on blanching, see page 697.

Collards and kale: Pick the leaves when the plant is 1 foot tall. Or the entire plant may be harvested. Kale flavor improves after a freeze.

Kohlrabi: Harvest when the bulb is 2 to 3 inches in diameter.

Growth cracks.

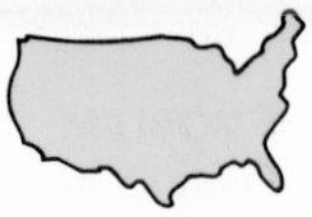

PROBLEM: The head of the cabbage plant cracks open soon after it reaches picking size.

ANALYSIS: Growth cracks

A cabbage head may crack if not harvested soon after it matures. Splitting results from the pressure of water taken up into the head after it is solid and mature. Tomatoes, carrots, potatoes, and sweet potatoes are also susceptible to growth cracking. Cracked vegetables are still edible.

SOLUTION: Harvest cabbage heads as soon as they feel firm. Stagger planting times so that all the heads don't mature at the same time. Or select several varieties that will ripen at different times. There are 3 ways to delay harvest by reducing the water supply to mature heads: (1) When the heads are firm, give the plants less water at each watering; (2) Break off some of the roots by lifting and twisting the cabbage plant; (3) Cut the roots on 2 sides of the plant by pushing a spade into the soil 6 to 8 inches deep. Surplus cabbage heads can be stored in the crisper section of your refrigerator.

Bolting broccoli.

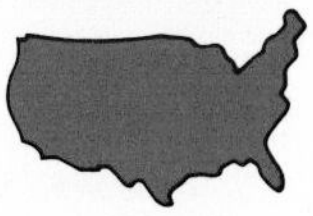

PROBLEM: In hot weather, an elongated stalk with flowers grows from the main stem of broccoli, cauliflower, and Brussels sprouts plants. On cabbage, the head splits open, and the stalk emerges from within.

ANALYSIS: Bolting
Bolting, or seed stalk formation, results from exposure of the plants to cold temperatures early in their lives. Once a plant has matured to the point where its leaves are about 2 inches wide, exposure to cold (40° to 50°F) temperatures for several days in a row causes flower buds to form within the growing point. These buds remain dormant until hot weather arrives. With the arrival of hot weather, the buds develop into tall flower stalks. As the plant bolts, its flavor deteriorates and bitterness develops.

SOLUTION: Discard plants that have bolted. Avoid setting out plants too early in the winter or spring. If cabbage plants are set out in the fall or winter, harvest them before hot weather causes them to bolt. Cutting the flower stalk will not prevent poor flavor from developing.

Small broccoli head.

PROBLEM: Broccoli plants form small heads or none at all. Plant may be slightly wilted, yellow, or flowering.

ANALYSIS: Poor heading
Broccoli plants may develop small or no heads for any of several reasons. Small heads are of low quality, with either a bitter taste or little flavor.
1. *Planted too close:* Roots compete with each other for water and nutrients.
2. *Dry soil:* Broccoli needs constant moisture throughout the growing season.
3. *Root maggots:* These pests feed on roots and weaken the plants.
4. *Nematodes:* These soil-inhabiting microscopic worms also weaken plants.
5. *Clubroot:* This fungal root disease weakens and kills plants.
6. *Bolting:* Plants go to seed in hot weather.
7. *Poor soil fertility:* Broccoli plants are heavy feeders, and need additional nutrients throughout the season.

SOLUTION: Follow these steps to produce large broccoli heads.
1. Set plants 15 to 24 inches apart in rows 24 to 36 inches apart.
2. For watering instructions, see page 696.
3. To control root maggots, see the recommendations on page 699.
4. For information on nematodes, see page 665.
5. For information on clubroot, see page 701.
6. To prevent bolting, see the recommendations on this page.
7. Follow the fertilizing instructions on page 696.
If possible, rotate your cabbage family planting site every year.

Discolored cauliflower head.

PROBLEM: Yellow, green, or purple discolorations mar cauliflower heads. The leaves are healthy and green.

ANALYSIS: Discolored head
Developing cauliflower heads need to be protected from the sunlight to remain white. Exposure to light causes yellow, green, or purple pigment to form. The resulting discoloration not only affects the appearance, but also causes a stronger flavor. Brown or black spots, up to 1 inch in diameter, on the head may be caused by the disease *downy mildew*, as described on page 700.

SOLUTION: Prevent further discoloration by tying the lower leaves up over the developing heads. To avoid possible head rotting, wait until the head is 2½ inches in diameter. Be sure the heads are dry, then tie the leaves loosely, giving the head room to grow. Secure the leaves with soft twine or a wide elastic band. This "blanching" or whitening process takes 1 to 2 weeks, depending on the weather and the variety of cauliflower. Check under the protective canopy occasionally for hiding pests. The head is ready for harvest when it is firm and shows no signs of splitting.

To avoid the need for blanching, plant the variety "Self Blanch," which does what its name implies—its leaves naturally curl over the head without assistance. The "Purple Head" variety doesn't need blanching either. Its head is a purple color that turns green when cooked.

CABBAGE FAMILY — INSECTS

Imported cabbageworm. *Insert:* Adult (life size).

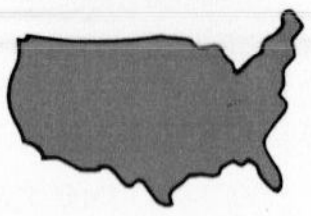

PROBLEM: Round or irregular holes appear in leaves. Green worms with light stripes down their backs, up to 1½ inches long, feed on the leaves or heads. Masses of green or brown pellets may be found between the leaves. Cabbage and cauliflower heads may be tunnelled.

ANALYSIS: Cabbage worms
These destructive worms are either the *cabbage looper* (*Trichoplusia ni*) or the *imported cabbageworm* (*Pieris rapae*). Both worms attack all members of the cabbage family, as well as lettuce. Adults lay eggs throughout the growing season. Adults of the imported cabbageworm attach yellow, bullet-shaped eggs to the undersides of leaves. These white butterflies are frequently seen around cabbage plants in the daytime. The brownish cabbage looper moth lays pale green eggs on the upper surfaces of leaves in the evening. Worms may be present from early spring until late fall. In the South, they may be present all year. Worms spend the winter as pupae attached to a plant or nearby object.

SOLUTION: Control cabbage worms with ORTHO Sevin Garden Dust, ORTHO Diazinon Insect Spray, ORTHO Fruit & Vegetable Insect Control, ORTHO Tomato & Vegetable Insect Killer, or ORTHO Rotenone Dust or Spray as soon as damage is seen. Cabbage worms can also be killed with *Bacillus thuringiensis*, a biological control, while they are small. Repeat treatments weekly as long as worms are found, but stop 3 days before harvest. Remove plant debris after harvest to destroy the pupae.

Diamondback moth larvae (life size).

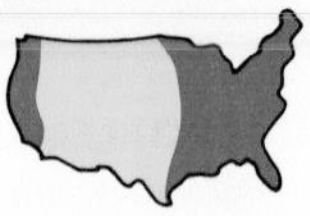

PROBLEM: Small holes and transparent holes appear in the leaves. Small (¼ inch) green worms feed on the undersides of the leaves. When disturbed, the worms wriggle rapidly and often drop from the plant on a silk thread.

ANALYSIS: Diamondback moth
(*Plutella xylostella*)
These worms are the larvae of gray or brown moths that fly in the evening. The adults don't damage plants. The larvae feed on the undersides of leaves of members of the cabbage family, chewing holes and eating the lower surfaces of the leaves. After feeding for about 2 weeks, the larvae pupate in transparent silken cocoons attached to the undersides of leaves. Adult moths spend the winter hidden under plant debris. There are 2 to 7 generations a year that damage both spring and fall plantings.

SOLUTION: Apply ORTHO Tomato & Vegetable Insect Killer, ORTHO Diazinon Soil & Foliage Dust, or ORTHO Diazinon Insect Spray to the foliage when the young worms first appear, or when the leaves show feeding damage. The insecticide must reach the undersides of the leaves in order to be most effective. Repeat the treatment each week as long as the caterpillars are found. Clean up plant debris in the fall and cultivate the soil thoroughly to expose and destroy overwintering moths.

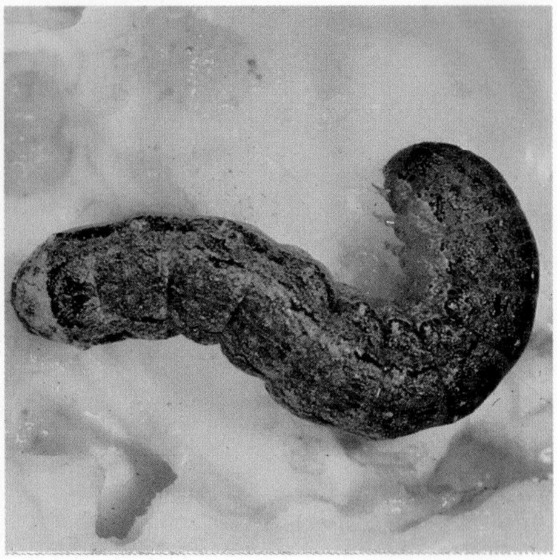

Cutworm (twice life size).

PROBLEM: Seedlings and young transplants are chewed or cut off near the ground. If you dig near the freshly damaged plant you may find dull gray, brown, or black worms about 2 inches deep. They have spots or stripes on their smooth bodies, are about 1½ to 2 inches long, and coil when they are disturbed.

ANALYSIS: Cutworms
Several species of these moth larvae are pests in the vegetable garden. The most likely pests of young cabbage plants set out early in the season are the surface-feeding cutworms. Cutworms spend the days hidden in the soil, and feed only at night. A cutworm can sever the stems of several young plants in a single night. All adult cutworms are dark, night-flying moths with stripes on their forewings. In the South, cutworms may also attack fall-planted cabbage.

SOLUTION: Apply ORTHO Vegetable Guard Soil Insect Killer, ORTHO Diazinon Soil & Turf Insect Control, or ORTHO Diazinon Soil & Foliage Dust around the base of the plants when stem cutting is observed. Since cutworms are difficult to control, it may be necessay to repeat dusting at weekly intervals. Before transplanting in the same area of planting in an area previously full of weeds, apply a preventive treatment of ORTHO Diazinon Soil & Turf Insect Control or ORTHO Vegetable Guard Soil Insect Killer and work it into the soil. Further reduce damage with "cutworm collars" around the stem of each plant. These collars can be made of stiff paper or aluminum foil. They should be at least 2 inches high and be pressed firmly into the soil. Cultivate the soil in late summer and fall to expose and destroy eggs, pupae, and larvae.

Cabbage root maggot (life size).

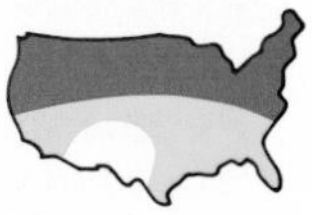

PROBLEM: Young plants wilt in the heat of the day. They may later turn yellow and die. Soft-bodied, white maggots about ⅓ inch long, are feeding in the roots. The roots are honeycombed with slimy channels and scarred by brown grooves. Damage is particularly severe during cool, moist weather in spring, early summer, and fall.

ANALYSIS: Cabbage maggot
(*Hylemya brassicae*)
The cabbage maggot is an important pest in the northern United States. Early maggots attack the roots and stems of cabbage, cauliflower, broccoli, radishes, and turnips in the spring and early summer. Later insects injure late cabbage, turnips, and radishes in the fall. The adult is a gray fly, somewhat smaller than a housefly, with black stripes and bristles down its back. It lays eggs on stems and nearby soil. The maggots hatch in 2 to 3 days and tunnel into the stems and roots of plants, sometimes to a depth of 6 inches. Not only does the cabbage maggot cause feeding damage, but it spreads black rot bacteria (see page 701).

SOLUTION: Once the growing plant wilts and turns yellow, nothing can be done. To control maggots in the next planting, mix ORTHO Diazinon Soil & Turf Insect Control (granules), ORTHO Vegetable Guard Soil Insect Killer, or ORTHO Diazinon Soil & Foliage Dust 4 to 6 inches into the soil before seeding or transplanting. Control lasts about 1 month. Since control depends on the maggots coming into direct contact with the insecticide, correct timing and thorough mixing are important. To prevent egg laying, screen flies from the seedbed with a cheesecloth cover.

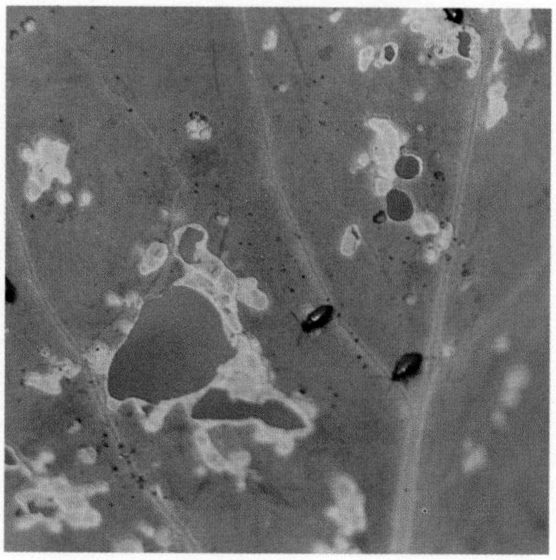
Flea beetles (twice life size).

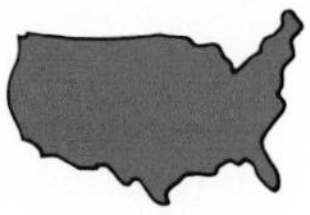

PROBLEM: Leaves are riddled with shotholes, about ⅛ inch in diameter. Tiny (1/16 inch) black beetles jump like fleas when disturbed. Leaves of seedlings and eventually whole plants may wilt and die.

ANALYSIS: Flea beetles
These beetles jump like fleas, but are not related to them. Both adult and immature flea beetles feed on a wide variety of garden vegetables. The immature beetle, a legless grey grub, injures plants by feeding on the roots and the lower surface of leaves. Adults chew holes in leaves. Flea beetles are most damaging to seedlings and young plants. Leaves of seedlings riddled with holes dry out quickly and die. Adult beetles spend the winter in soil and garden debris. They emerge in early spring to feed on weeds until vegetables sprout or plants are set in the garden. Grubs hatch from eggs laid in the soil and feed for 2 to 3 weeks. After pupating in the soil, they emerge as adults to repeat the cycle. There are 1 to 4 generations a year. Adults may feed up to 2 months.

SOLUTION: Control flea beetles with ORTHO Sevin Garden Dust, ORTHO Fruit & Vegetable Insect Control, ORTHO Tomato & Vegetable Insect Killer, or ORTHO Rotenone Dust or Spray when the leaves first show damage. Watch new growth for evidence of further damage, and repeat the treatment at weekly intervals as needed. Clean all debris from the garden after harvest to eliminate overwintering spots for adult beetles.

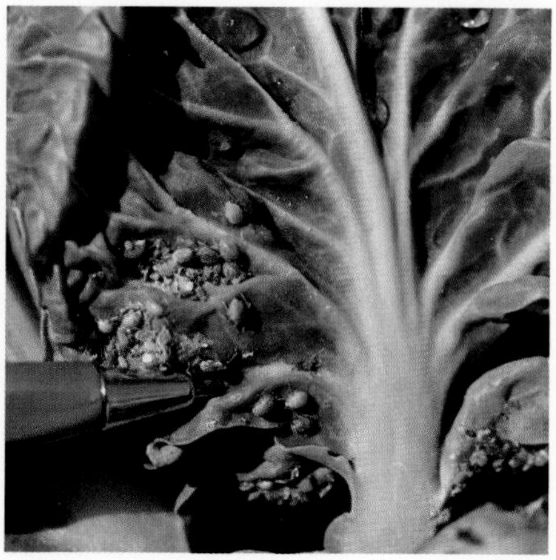
Aphids on cabbage (twice life size).

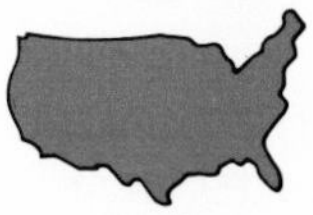

PROBLEM: Some leaves are yellowed and cupped downward. Tiny (⅛ inch) pale green or gray soft-bodied insects cluster under leaves, on stems, and on heads. There may be a shiny, sticky substance coating the leaves. Ants may be present.

ANALYSIS: Aphids
Aphids do little damage in small numbers. However, they are extremely prolific and populations can rapidly build up to damaging numbers during the growing season. Damage occurs when the aphid sucks the juices from the plant. The aphid is unable to digest fully all the sugar in the plant sap and excretes the excess in a fluid called honeydew. The honeydew often drops onto the leaves below. Ants feed on the sticky substance, and are often present where there is an aphid infestation. The most common aphid attacking the cabbage family is the *cabbage aphid* (*Brevicoryne brassicae*). The cabbage aphid spends the winter as eggs on plant debris in the garden. In the South, they are active year-round. For more information about aphids, see page 875.

SOLUTION: Treat with ORTHO Malathion 50 Insect Spray, ORTHO Tomato & Vegetable Insect Killer, or ORTHO Diazinon Soil & Foliage Dust as soon as the insects appear. Repeat at intervals of 1 week if the plant is reinfected. Clean all plant debris from the garden after harvest to reduce the number of overwintering eggs.

CABBAGE FAMILY — DISCOLORED LEAVES

Downy mildew on broccoli.

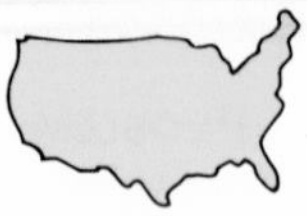

PROBLEM: Small irregular tannish purple to dark brown spots appear on the lowest leaves. Later, these spots enlarge, turn yellow, dry, and the leaves drop off. In moist weather a downy white mold appears on the undersides of the leaves opposite the leaf spot. There may be sunken black spots up to 1 inch in diameter on cabbage heads, and a similar blackening on cauliflower curds and broccoli. Seedlings turn yellow and die in a few days.

ANALYSIS: Downy mildew
This plant disease is caused by a fungus (*Peronospora parasitica*) that affects all members of the cabbage family at any stage in their growth. It is most devastating to seedlings, which can die in only a few days. Moisture and temperature are important to the spread, growth, and development of the fungus. The downy growth consists of fungus spores that are spread by splashing water and wind to other leaves or plants. The disease develops most rapidly when night temperatures range from 45° to 60°F for four nights in a row, and day temperatures do not go above 75°F. Affected heads and leaves are edible but unappetizing.

SOLUTION: Apply ORTHO Vegetable Disease Control when the young plants are first set out. Repeat at weekly intervals as long as cool, moist conditions prevail. To discourage furthur infection, take steps to reduce the excess moisture in the garden. Allow enough space between maturing plants for air to circulate freely. Avoid overhead watering.

Alternaria leaf spot on Chinese cabbage.

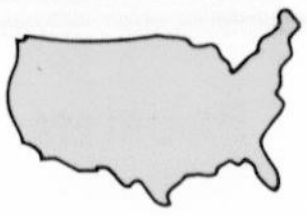

PROBLEM: Small, circular, yellow spots appear on the older leaves. As the spots enlarge to 2 to 3 inches in diameter, they develop brown concentric rings. The spots may be covered with a black growth. Seedlings may be stunted and have dark spots on the stems. Cauliflower and broccoli heads turn brown along the margins.

ANALYSIS: Alternaria leaf spot
This plant disease is caused by fungi (*Alternaria* species) that attack members of the cabbage family that are low in vigor, poorly fertilized or under environmental stress. When spotting is severe, the size and flavor of the yield may be reduced. The fungi are most active in hot (75° to 85°F), wet weather, when rain or dew keeps the leaves wet for more than 9 hours. These fungi are spread by splashing water or wind. They generally survive the winter in plant debris, and may be introduced into the garden on contaminated seeds or plants.

SOLUTION: Treat infected plants at the first sign of the disease with ORTHO Vegetable Disease Control. Repeat the treatment at intervals of 7 to 10 days until the weather is no longer favorable to the spread of the disease. To reduce the amount of overwintering spores, remove all plant debris from the garden after harvest. Rotate the cabbage family planting site every year. Keep plants healthy by following the cultural guidelines on page 696.

Black rot.

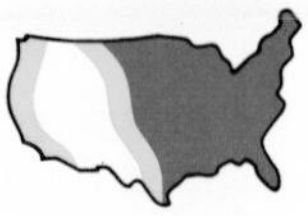

PROBLEM: Young plants turn yellow, then brown, and die. On older plants, yellow areas develop along the leaf margins, then progress into the leaf in a V-shape; these areas later turn brown and die. Lower (older) leaves wilt and drop off. The veins running from the infected leaf margins to the center stem are black. When the stem is cut across, a black ring and sometimes yellow ooze are seen in the cross-section.

ANALYSIS: Black rot
This plant disease is caused by a bacterium (*Xanthomonas campestris*) that affects all members of the cabbage family at any stage in their growth. The bacteria live in or on seed or in infected plant debris for as long as 2 years. Insects, splashing water, and garden tools carry bacteria to other leaves and plants. They enter the plant through natural openings or wounds and spread in the water- and nutrient-conducting vessels of the plant. The infected tissue may form pockets where dead cells and bacteria accumulate as a yellow ooze. Warm, humid weather favors the spread and development of the bacteria. Black rot can kill seedlings rapidly. The diseased heads are edible but unappetizing.

SOLUTION: There are no chemical controls for black rot. Discard infected plants. To avoid further infection, plant only disease-free seed and healthy plants. Place plants far enough apart to allow good air circulation. Avoid overhead irrigation. Plant in soil that has not grown cabbage for at least 2 years.

Watery soft rot.

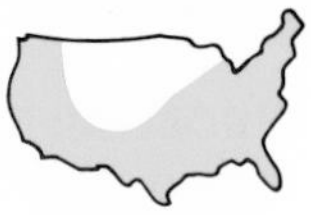

PROBLEM: A water-soaked area develops on the stem near the soil line. As it extends upward leaves die, wither, and droop to the ground. The head becomes wet and slimy. In moist weather, a thick, white, cottony mold covers the head. White to black pellets about the size of a pea are found in the mold and between dead leaves.

ANALYSIS: Watery soft rot
This plant disease is caused by a fungus (*Sclerotinia sclerotiorum*) that attacks cabbage and Chinese cabbage. All parts of the plant may become infected. The infection starts on the stem and spreads downward, rotting the roots. As it spreads upward, the leaves die and the head rots. The fungus is most active in moderate (55° to 75°F), wet weather. Water on the leaves from rain, fog, dew, and irrigation provide the moisture necessary for infection. The fungus survives the winter inside the pellets in the soil and on infected plant debris.

SOLUTION: There are no chemical controls for this disease. Remove and destroy all infected plants when symptoms are first observed. Avoid overhead watering by using drip or furrow irrigation. Clean all plant debris from the garden after harvest to reduce the amount of overwintering spores. Rotate the cabbage planting site every year.

Black leg on cabbage.

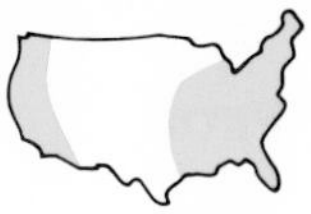

PROBLEM: Brown spots with gray centers appear on the lower stems and leaves. Tiny black specks appear in the spots. Stems turn black. Plants become stunted, yellow, wilt, and may die. Wilted leaves remain attached to the stem.

ANALYSIS: Black leg
This plant disease is caused by a fungus (*Phoma lingam*) that is prevalent in wet weather, especially in early summer. All parts of the plant may be infected. Infections on the stem spread downward, rotting the roots. Plants usually die, but when the soil is moist they may grow new roots. The fungal spores live in the soil and on plant debris for up to 3 years, and may be introduced into the garden on infected seeds or plants. The spores spread to healthy plants in splashing water. The leaves must be wet from rain, dew, or irrigation for infection to occur.

SOLUTION: There are no chemical controls for this disease. Remove and destroy all infected plants. Do not work among wet plants. Avoid overhead watering by using drip or furrow irrigation. Remove all plant debris from the garden after harvest to reduce the number of overwintering spores. Rotate the cabbage family planting site every year. Purchase treated seeds and healthy plants from a reputable nursery. Before planting, seeds may be immersed in hot (122°F) water for 25 minutes to kill any spores that may be on them.

Clubroot on kohlrabi.

PROBLEM: The plant wilts on hot, sunny days and recovers at night. The older (outer) leaves turn yellow and drop. The roots are swollen and misshapen. The largest swellings are just below the soil surface. Growth slows, and the plant eventually dies.

ANALYSIS: Clubroot
This plant disease is caused by a soil-inhabiting fungus (*Plasmodiophora brassicae*) that persists in the soil for many years. Warm, moist weather conditions, together with an acid soil favor the infection. The fungus causes cells to grow and divide within the root tissue. This causes swelling and a general weakening of the plant, allowing other fungi and bacteria to invade the roots and cause root rot. As the roots decompose, they liberate millions of spores into the soil, where they are spread by shoes, tools, or in drainage water. Most members of the cabbage family are susceptible to clubroot. Most rutabaga varieties and many turnip varieties are resistant. Weeds in this family, such as mustard, pennycress, and shepherds purse, can also harbor the disease.

SOLUTION: Once a plant is infected, it cannot be cured. To reduce the severity of the disease next year, do not grow susceptible plants where any members of the cabbage family have grown for the past 7 years. If you must plant in infected soil, pour ¾ cup of a solution of 3 tablespoons of *PCNB 75 WP* fungicide per gallon of water in the soil around the roots of each transplant. To discourage infection, lime the soil to a pH of 7.2. For liming instructions, see page 1019.

CARROTS

ADAPTATION: Throughout the United States.

PLANTING TIME: See page 1025.

PLANTING METHOD: Sow carrot seeds ¼ inch deep. When they have 2 or 3 leaves, thin them to stand 1 to 3 inches apart. Thinning is very important for good shape.

SOIL: Light, friable, and free from rocks and clods. For heavy soil, see page 702. pH 6.0 to 7.5

FERTILIZER: At planting time, use 2 pounds of ORTHO Vegetable Food per 100 square feet, or ¾ pound per 25-foot row. Side-dress every 3 to 4 weeks with ¾ pound per 25-foot row.

WATER:
How much: Apply enough water at each irrigation to wet the soil 12 to 15 inches deep.
How often: Water when the soil 1 inch deep is barely moist. Do not let the soil dry out.

HARVEST: Pull carrots any time from finger-size until they reach the size stated on the seed packet. When pulling carrots, select the largest first, so that those remaining have room to enlarge. Carrots can be left in the ground and harvested over the winter.

Green root top.

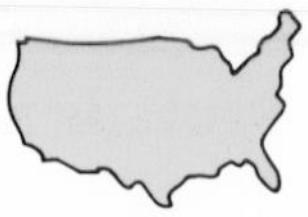

PROBLEM: Carrot root tops are green and have a strong flavor. Leaves are healthy.

ANALYSIS: Green root tops
Tops of carrot roots turn green when exposed to sunlight. The root tops may become exposed when heavy rains or irrigation water wash away the soil. Soil may also be moved away during cultivation. The green portions of the root have a strong flavor. The orange part of the root is edible.

SOLUTION: Cut away the green portion of the carrot before eating. Protect the carrot root tops in the ground by covering with a 1 to 2-inch layer of soil whenever exposed. Or mulch the plants with a 4 to 6-inch layer of straw or several sheets of newspaper to prevent water from washing away the soil. Do not cultivate closer than 6 to 8 inches to the plants.

Carrots stunted from growing in heavy soil.

PROBLEM: Roots are forked, twisted, or abnormally shaped.

ANALYSIS: Misshapen roots
Carrot roots may be misshapen for any of several reasons.
1. *Overcrowding:* Crowded seedlings do not have room to develop properly.
2. *Soil debris:* Stones or clods of soil prevent even expansion of the root.
3. *Fresh manure:* Fresh, undecomposed manure stimulates root branching.
4. *Heavy soil:* Carrot roots have difficulty expanding in heavy, tight soil. Soil-inhabiting rot fungi that may cause forking are also prevalent in these wet soils.
5. *Nematodes:* These microscopic worms live in the soil and feed on plant roots.

SOLUTION: Follow these suggestions for smooth, elongated carrots.
1. Plant carrot seeds ¼ to ½ inch deep and ½ inch apart. When the seedlings are 1 inch tall, thin them to stand ½ to 2 inches apart, depending on the variety planted.
2. Before planting, rake out and discard stones ½ inch and larger in diameter. Break up soil clods.
3. If you add manure, use only decomposed manure. Or fertilize with a balanced fertilizer such as ORTHO Vegetable Food or ORTHO Tomato Food.
4. Incorporate organic matter such as peat moss or humus into heavy soil. Short, blunt varieties of carrots that do well in heavy soil include Short 'n Sweet, Oxhart, and the Nantes and Chantenay types.
5. For information on nematodes, see page 703.

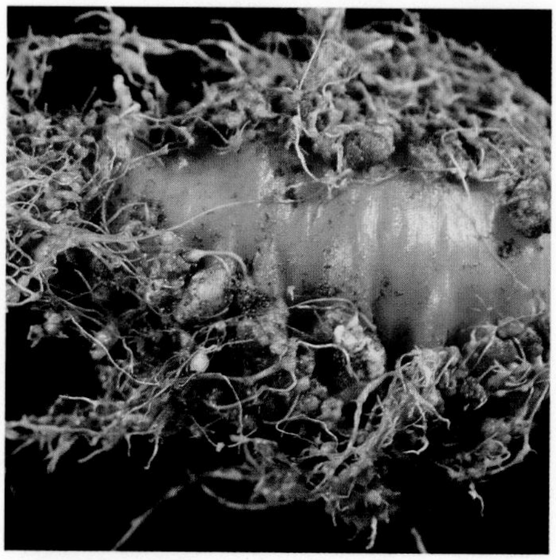

Misshapen carrots.

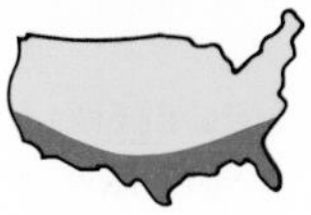

PROBLEM: Plants are stunted and yellow. The main root may be forked, and numerous side roots are produced, or tiny beads or knots are attached to the roots.

ANALYSIS: Nematodes
Nematodes are microscopic worms that live in the soil. They are not related to earthworms. Nematodes feed on plant roots, damaging and stunting them. The damaged roots can't supply sufficient water and nutrients to the above-ground plant parts, and the plant is stunted or slowly dies. Nematodes are found throughout the country, but are most severe in the South. They prefer moist, sandy loam soils. Nematodes can move only a few inches each year on their own, but they may be carried long distances by soil, water, tools, or infested plants. Testing roots and soil is the only positive method for confirming the presence of nematodes. Contact your local Cooperative Extension Office (see page 1029) for sampling instructions and addresses of testing laboratories. Soil and root problems such as poor soil structure, drought stress, nutrient deficiency, and root rots can also produce symptoms of decline similar to those caused by nematodes. These problems should be eliminated as causes before sending soil and root samples for testing. For information on soil problems and root rots, see pages 907 and 849.

SOLUTION: There are no chemicals available to homeowners to kill nematodes in planted soil. However, they can be controlled before planting by soil fumigation. For information on fumigating soil, see page 927.

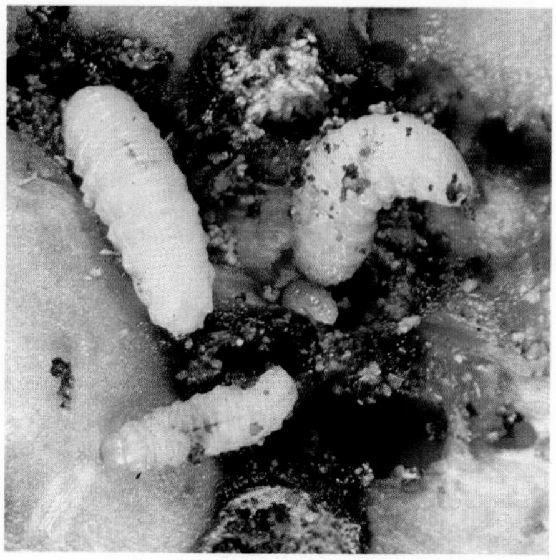

Carrot weevil larvae damage (3 times life size).

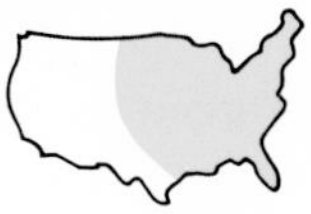

PROBLEM: The upper part of the root is scarred with zigzag tunnels. White, curved, legless grubs, about ⅓ inch long, may be found in the root and soil.

ANALYSIS: Carrot weevil
(*Listronotus oregonensis*)
This insect feeds on carrots, dill, celery, parsley, and parsnips. The adult is a dark brown beetle that lays eggs in the carrot tops. In May and June the eggs hatch into white grubs, which travel down to the developing root. Here the grub tunnels into and feeds on the upper tissue, scarring the root. After a short resting period in the soil, the pest emerges as an adult and lays eggs that hatch into a second generation in August. The adults of this second generation spend the winter in debris in and around the garden. The following spring, the cycle repeats itself.

SOLUTION: There are no insecticides currently registered for use on this insect pest. Some control may be obtained when spraying for leafhoppers (see page 878). Clean up garden debris in the fall to eliminate overwintering spots for the adults. Do not add infested debris to the compost pile.

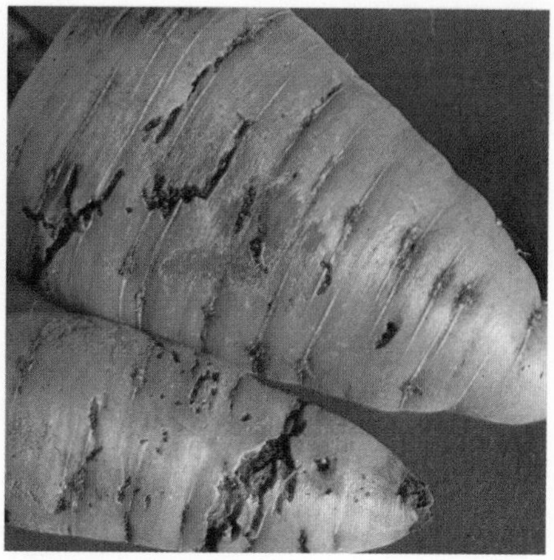

Carrot rust fly damage.

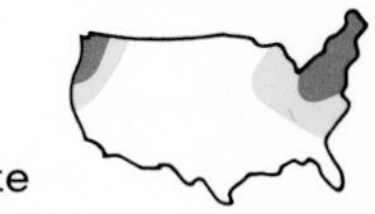

PROBLEM: Burrows with rust-red sawdustlike material inside wind through the carrot root. Scars also mar the surface. Plant tops may look healthy, or they may be stunted, turn yellow, and die.

ANALYSIS: Carrot rust fly
(*Psila rosae*)
This insect pest attacks carrots, celery, parsnips, and parsley. It damages the plants by eating small roots and tunneling into larger roots. The rust-red excrement in the tunnels gives the insect its name. The adult fly, which causes no damage, lays eggs on the soil surface in late spring and early summer. The eggs hatch into yellowish white maggots, ⅓ inch long. The maggots feed on and in the roots until they pupate and emerge as adults in late summer. These adults lay eggs that hatch into a second generation of maggots in August and September. It is this second generation that does the most damage. The maggots may also feed in stored carrots. Disease-causing organisms often enter carrot roots through wounds made by the rust fly maggot. These diseases cause the roots to rot before they are ready to be harvested, and also in storage. Roots with only a few tunnels are still edible; cut out the damaged part.

SOLUTION: Destroy badly damaged plants to reduce the source of next year's population. Next year at planting time, work ORTHO Diazinon Soil & Turf Insect or ORTHO Vegetable Guard Soil Insect Killer Control into the top 4 inches of soil.

CARROTS

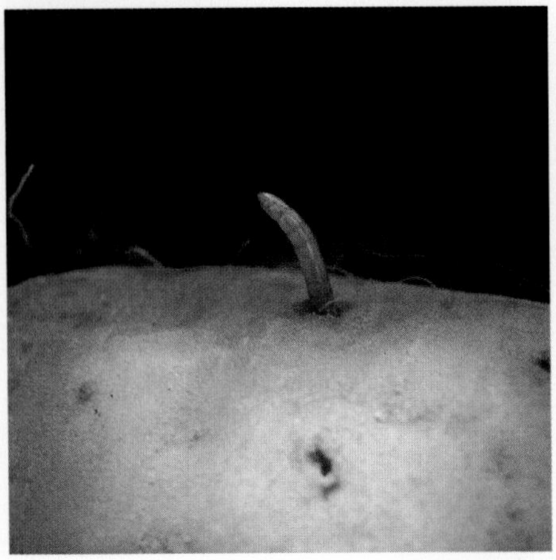

Wireworm (twice life size).

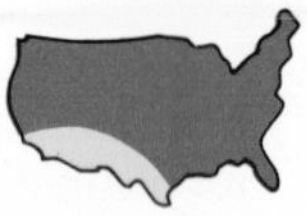

PROBLEM: Plants are stunted and grow slowly. Roots are poorly formed. Tunnels wind through the roots. Shiny, hard, jointed, creamy yellow, dark brown, or gray worms up ⅝ inch long are found in the roots and soil.

ANALYSIS: Wireworms

Wireworms attack carrots, corn, potatoes, beets, peas, beans, lettuce and many other plants. They feed only on underground plant parts, devouring seeds, underground stems, tubers, and roots. Infestations are most extensive in soil where lawn grass was previously grown. The adult is known as a *click beetle* because it makes a clicking sound when turning from its back to its feet. The adult lays eggs in the spring. After the eggs hatch, the wireworms feed for 2 to 6 years before maturing into adult beetles. All sizes and ages of wireworms may be found in soil at the same time.

SOLUTION: Treat with ORTHO Diazinon Soil & Foliage Dust, ORTHO Vegetable Guard Soil Insect Killer, or ORTHO Diazinon Soil & Turf Insect Control just before planting, working the insecticide into the top 6 to 8 inches of soil.

Cercospora leaf blight.

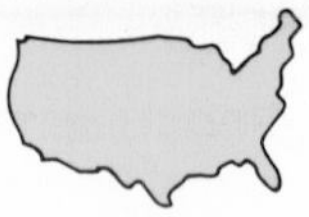

PROBLEM: Tan, gray-brown, or black spots with pale centers appear on the leaves. The spots enlarge, forming blotches that may eventually kill the leaves. Similar spots also occur on the leaf stems. Infected leaf stems shrivel and die. Severely infected plants look as if they've been burned by fire.

ANALYSIS: Leaf blights

Leaf blights on carrots are caused by two different fungi (*Alternaria dauci* and *Cercospora carotae*) that produce similar symptoms. They also attack parsley. The diseases spread rapidly in humid weather with frequent rains and heavy dews. The leaves and stems must remain wet for several hours for the spores to infect them. The spores are spread from plant to plant by wind and splashing water. Plants under stress from poor nutrition are most susceptible. Although these fungi don't attack the carrot root directly, if enough leaves die to reduce the amount of food manufactured, root size and flavor may be reduced.

SOLUTION: Pick off infected leaves. Treat the plants with ORTHO Vegetable Disease Control at the first sign of the disease. Continue the treatments at intervals of 10 to 14 days until the leaf blights are no longer present. Water the garden by midafternoon so the foliage is dry at night. Do not work among wet plants. Clean all plant debris from the garden after the harvest to reduce next year's infection. Plant blight-resistant carrot varieties.

Carrot varieties resistant to leaf blight: Ace, Denver 126, Imperator 58, Imperator 408, and Spartan Bonus.

Aster yellows. *Insert:* Infected root.

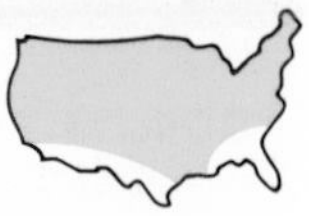

PROBLEM: Inner leaves are yellow, stunted, and grow in tight bunches. Outer leaves turn rusty red to reddish purple. The roots are stunted, deformed, and have a bitter taste. Tiny hairlike roots grow in great protusion out of the main root. Numerous tiny leaves grow from the top of the root.

ANALYSIS: Aster yellows

This plant disease is caused by mycoplasmas, microscopic organisms similar to bacteria. The mycoplasmas are transmitted from plant to plant primarily by leafhoppers. (For information about leafhoppers, see page 878.) The symptoms of aster yellows are more severe and appear more quickly in warm weather. Even when the disease is present in the plant, aster yellows may not manifest its symptoms in temperatures of 55°F or less. The disease also infects many other vegetables, ornamental plants, and weeds. For a list of plants susceptible to aster yellows, see page 1005.

SOLUTION: Aster yellows cannot be eliminated entirely, but can be kept under control. Move and destroy infected plants. To remove sources of infection, eradicate nearby weeds that may harbor aster yellows and leafhopper eggs. Treat leafhopper-infested plants with ORTHO Sevin Garden Dust or ORTHO Malathion 50 Insect Spray. Repeat the treatment whenever leafhoppers are seen. For more information about controlling disease-carrying insects, see page 879.

CELERY

ADAPTATION: Zones 4 through 10. To determine your zone, see the map on page 1020.

PLANTING TIME: See page 1025.

PLANTING METHOD: Set transplants so that the top of their rootball is even with the garden soil. Space 6 to 10 inches apart. Or, sow seeds indoors 8 to 10 weeks before planting outside. Soak the seeds in warm water overnight, and plant 1/8 inch deep. Thin to stand 1½ to 2½ inches apart when the seedlings have 2 or 3 leaves. At the recommended time, set outdoors as stated above.

SOIL: Any good garden soil that is high in organic matter. pH 6.0 to 8.0

FERTILIZER: At planting time, apply 5 pounds of ORTHO Vegetable Food per 100 square feet, or 2 pounds per 25-foot row. Side-dress every 3 to 4 weeks with 2 pounds per 25-foot row.

WATER:

How much: Apply enough water at each irrigation to wet the soil 8 to 10 inches deep.

How often: Keep the soil evenly moist, never allowing it to dry out.

HARVEST: Cut the plants at the base of the stalks with a sharp knife when they are 10 to 12 inches tall, and before they become tough and stringy. Outside stalks may also be harvested as needed. For white celery, blanch the stalks when they are 6 to 8 inches tall by wrapping with paper or shading with boards. Store in the refrigerator.

Overmature plant.

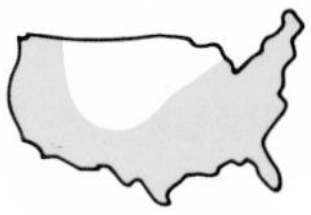

PROBLEM: Celery stalks are tough, stringy, and off-flavor. There are no signs of insects or disease. A tall stalk may emerge from the plant.

ANALYSIS: Tough, stringy, and bitter stalks

Celery stalks become tough, stringy, and off-flavor for any of several different reasons.

1. *High temperatures when maturing:* Celery is a cool season crop that grows poorly in temperatures over 70°F.

2. *Lack of water:* Celery requires a constant and abundant supply of moisture. Without this moisture, the stalks are not tender. Celery plants have shallow roots and are very subject to drought damage.

3. *Low fertility:* Celery plants are heavy feeders and must be adequately fertilized at planting time and throughout the season.

4. *Overmaturity:* The tenderness and flavor of celery deteriorate rapidly when it becomes overmature.

5. *Seedstalk formation:* Celery plants form seedstalks prematurely when exposed to cool temperatures when young. Temperatures between 40° and 50°F for 2 weeks, or between 50° and 60°F for 1 to 2 months initiate seedstalk formation. When plant growth is later stimulated by fertilizing, the stalk elongates.

SOLUTION: Celery grows best when the night temperatures are around 50°F and daytime temperatures range between 60° and 70°F. It requires a long growing season of 120 to 140 days. To help reduce tough, stringy, and bitter stalks, follow the feeding, watering, and harvesting instructions on page 705.

Leaf webbed together by celery leaftier.

PROBLEM: Leaves are webbed together with white silken threads. Inside the webs are pale green to yellow caterpillars, ½ to ¾ inch long, with a white and green stripe down the back. They wriggle when disturbed.

ANALYSIS: Celery leaftier

(*Udea rubigalis*)

This moth larva attacks many garden and greenhouse plants, especially celery, aster, beets, dahlias, sweetpeas, and spinach. The brown moth lays its eggs on the underside of the celery leaf. The pale green caterpillars that hatch from these eggs feed on celery foliage and leaf stalks, mining into the soft stems and hearts of the plants and webbing the foliage together. As they mature, the caterpillars turn yellow, pupate in the webs, then emerge as adult moths to continue the cycle. There are several generations each year, and leaftiers may be active all year in warm areas of the country.

SOLUTION: Spray with an insecticide containing *malathion* as soon as webbing appears. Clean up garden debris to reduce overwintering spots.

CELERY

Late blight.

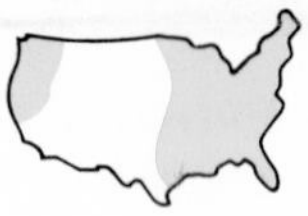

PROBLEM: Small yellow spots appear on older leaves in cool, moist weather in the fall, winter, and spring. Spots turn dark brownish gray and are speckled with tiny black dots. Seriously affected leaves die. Stalks may also be affected.

ANALYSIS: Late blight
This plant disease is caused by a destructive fungus (*Septoria apiicola*) that is prevalent in cool, rainy weather. It attacks celery in the fall, winter, and early spring. Only wet leaves are infected. The tiny black dots in the leaf spots contain spores that live in infected celery debris and are spread by splashing raindrops, people, animals, and tools. The spores may also survive on the seeds for many months. Severely infected leaves die, and if weather conditions that are favorable for the disease continue, eventually the whole plant may die.

SOLUTION: Spray the plants with ORTHO Vegetable Disease Control as soon as the disease appears. Repeat at intervals of 7 to 10 days. Remove and destroy plant debris after harvest. In the future, use treated seed, or soak seed in hot water (118°F) for 30 minutes, then dry at room temperature. Grow late blight tolerant varieties.

Celery variety tolerant to late blight: Emerson Pascal.

Early blight.

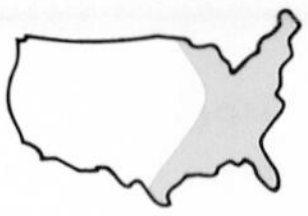

PROBLEM: In summer and early fall small yellow spots appear on both sides of the leaves. These spots enlarge, turning ash gray in color. Elongated tan spots appear on stalks just before harvest. During warm, humid weather, a velvety growth covers the affected spots.

ANALYSIS: Early blight
This plant disease is caused by a fungus (*Cercospora apii*) that usually attacks celery in the summer and early fall. It is most prevalent when days are warm and night temperatures are in the 60s. Only wet leaves are infected. Heavy dews and light rains provide enough moisture for infection. The fungus attacks the entire plant and, when severe, all the foliage may be killed. The spores survive from one crop to the next in celery debris left in the garden.

SOLUTION: Spray the plants with ORTHO Vegetable Disease Control as soon as the disease appears. Repeat at intervals of 7 to 10 days. Remove and destroy plant debris after harvest. Next spring, purchase treated or resistant seeds, or soak the seeds in hot water (118°F) for 30 minutes, then dry at room temperature.

Celery varieties that are tolerant to early blight: Early Belle, Emerson Pascal, and June Belle.

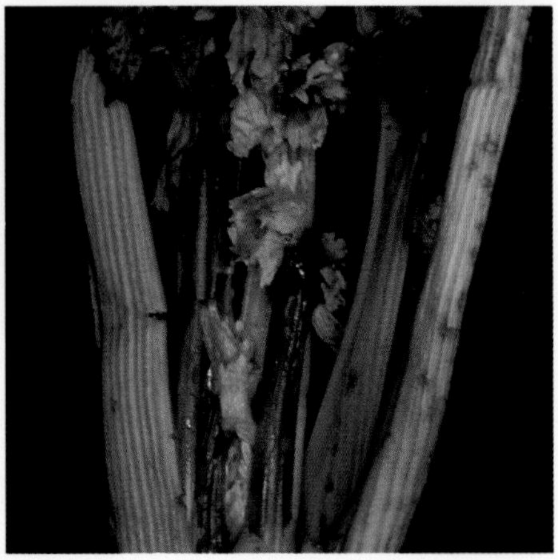

Black heart.

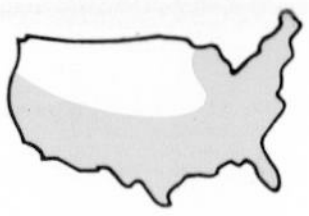

PROBLEM: Early maturing leaves turn pale yellow and the heart of the plant turns black and dies. A slimy decay may follow.

ANALYSIS: Black heart
This disorder is caused by a calcium deficiency in the growing tip. It occurs most frequently in crops where the soil moisture fluctuates from very dry to very wet, rather than remaining constant. Heavy watering after a long dry period frequently induces black heart. High temperatures, excess soil salts, and rapid growth from excess nitrogen may also promote the condition. A bacterial soft rot often enters the dying heart, resulting in slimy, watery, rotting tissue.

SOLUTION: Discard affected plants. Keep the soil constantly moist, and use a complete fertilizer such as ORTHO Vegetable Food. Avoid fertilizers that are extremely high in nitrogen. Test your soil pH as outlined on page 909 and correct if necessary. Celery grows best at a pH of 6.5 to 8.0.

Aster yellows.

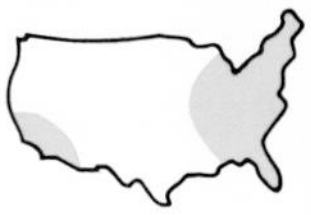

PROBLEM: Plants are stunted and light yellow. Stems become curled, twisted, and brittle. Leaves thicken and become brittle.

ANALYSIS: Aster yellows

This plant disease is caused by mycoplasmas, microscopic organisms similar to bacteria. The mycoplasmas are transmitted from plant to plant primarily by leafhoppers. (For more information on leafhoppers, see page 878.) Green celeries and some self-blanching varieties are resistant to aster yellows. The symptoms of aster yellows are more severe and appear more quickly in warm weather. Even when the disease is present in the plant, aster yellows may not manifest its symptoms in temperatures of 55°F or less. The disease also infects many other vegetable plants, ornamentals, and weeds. For a list of plants susceptible to aster yellows, see page 1005.

SOLUTION: Aster yellows cannot be eliminated entirely, but can be kept under control. Remove and destroy infected plants. To remove sources of infection, eradicate nearby weeds that may harbor aster yellows and leafhopper eggs. Spray leafhopper-infested plants with an insecticide containing *malathion*. Repeat the spray whenever leafhoppers are seen. For more information on controlling disease-carrying insects, see page 879. Grow resistant varieties.

Self-blanching varieties resistant to aster yellows: Florida Golden, Forbes Golden Plume, and Michigan Golden.

CORN

ADAPTATION: Throughout the United States.

PLANTING TIME: See page 1025.

PLANTING METHOD: Sow seeds 1 to 2 inches deep and 12 to 16 inches apart. Or, set transplants so that the top of their rootball is even with the garden soil. Space 12 to 16 inches apart.

SOIL: Any good garden soil that is high in organic matter. pH 6.0 to 7.5

FERTILIZER: At planting time, use 3 pounds of ORTHO Vegetable Food per 100-foot row. Side-dress with the same amount when the plants are 8 inches tall, and again when they are 18 inches tall.

WATER:

How much: Apply enough water at each irrigation to wet the soil 8 to 10 inches deep.

How often: Keep the soil moist, never allowing it to dry out. Corn needs constant moisture all season, especially from tasseling to picking time.

HARVEST: Corn is generally ready to be picked 3 weeks after the silks appear. When ready, the silks become dark brown and dry. Test ripeness by pressing a kernel with your finger. If it spurts milky juice, it is ready. To pick, grab the ear at its base, bend it downward, and twist. Do not damage the main stalk. Pick corn just before cooking, as its flavor deteriorates rapidly when stored.

Corn earworm (¾ life size).

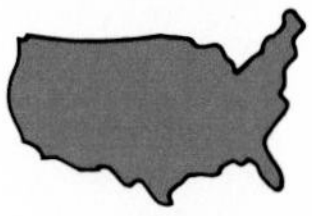

PROBLEM: Striped yellow, brown, or green worms are feeding on the tip of the ear inside the husk. The worms range in size from ¼ to 2 inches long. Leaves may be chewed and ragged.

ANALYSIS: Corn earworm
(*Heliothis zea*)

This is the most serious pest of corn. It also attacks many other garden vegetables and flowers, and is also known as the *tomato fruitworm* and the *cotton bollworm*. The worm is the larva of a light gray-brown moth with dark lines on its wings. In the spring, the moth lays yellow eggs singly on corn silks and the undersides of leaves. The worms that hatch from these eggs feed on the new leaves in the whorls. This feeding doesn't reduce the corn yield, but the leaves that develop are ragged and the plant may be stunted. More serious damage is caused when the worms feed on the silks, causing poor pollination, and when they feed on the developing kernels. Worms enter the ear at the silk end, or they may bore through the husk. There are several generations a year. In the South, where these pests survive the winter, early and late plantings suffer the most damage. Adult moths migrate into northern areas, where late plantings are severely damaged. Uneaten parts of infested ears are still edible.

SOLUTION: Once the worms are in the ears, insecticides are ineffective. In the future, dust plants with ORTHO Sevin Garden Dust when 10 percent of the ears show silk. Repeat the treatment 3 to 4 times at intervals of 3 days. If the infestation continues, repeat as necessary until harvest.

CORN — PROBLEMS WITH THE EAR

Armyworm (¼ life size).

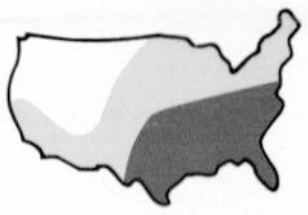

PROBLEM: Leaf edges are chewed and some leaves may be completely eaten. Light tan to dark brown caterpillars 1½ to 2 inches long, with yellow, orange, or dark brown stripes, are feeding on the leaves and may be boring into the ears.

ANALYSIS: Armyworm
Armyworms attack corn, grains, grasses, and other garden crops. These pests do not overwinter in cold winter areas, but the moths migrate great distances in the spring in search of places to lay their eggs. The tan to gray adult moths lay eggs on the blades of grasses and grains. The caterpillars that hatch from these eggs feed on corn leaves, ears, and ear stalks. They get their name from their feeding habits. After they have eaten everything in one area, they crawl in droves to another area in search of more food. After several weeks of feeding they pupate in the soil, then emerge as adult moths to repeat the cycle. There are several generations each year, beginning in mid-May. These pests are most numerous after cold, wet spring weather that slows the development of the natural parasites and diseases that help keep the population in check.

SOLUTION: When the worms are first seen, spray with ORTHO Fruit & Vegetable Insect Control, or dust with ORTHO Sevin Garden Dust. It may be 4 or 5 days before results are seen. Repeat at weekly intervals if the plants become reinfested. To control worms that bore into the ears, spray when 10 percent of the ears show silk, and repeat three or four more times at intervals of 3 days.

Poor pollination.

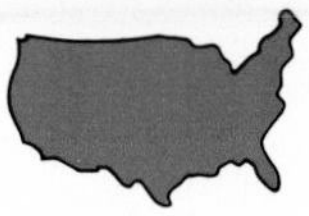

PROBLEM: Corn ears are not completely filled with kernels. Plants are healthy.

ANALYSIS: Poor pollination
Poorly filled ears result from ineffective or incomplete pollination. Pollen grains produced on the tassels must fall on the sticky silks for complete pollination. Each strand of silk is attached to a kernel, so for each silk that is pollinated, one kernel will develop on the ear. Corn pollen is spread by the wind; if the wind is blowing across a single row of corn, the pollen on the tassels will be carried away from the silks, resulting in poorly filled ears. Poor pollination can also result from dry soil during pollination and from hot, dry winds. Prolonged periods of rain reduce the amount of pollen shed from the tassels. Damage to the silks from corn earworms, (see page 707), rootworm adults (see page 711), armyworms (see page 708), and grasshoppers (see page 711) may also result in incomplete ears.

SOLUTION: To help ensure pollination, grow corn in blocks of at least 3 or 4 short rows rather than in 1 long row. Plant seeds 12 to 16 inches apart in rows 30 to 36 inches apart. Keep the soil moist, letting the surface dry slightly between waterings. Control corn insect pests. Corn can be hand-pollinated by shaking the tassels onto the silks.

Bird damage.

PROBLEM: Holes are pecked in the ears through the husk. Some kernels are missing from the ears. Birds are active in the corn.

ANALYSIS: Birds
Birds are attracted to certain grains, including corn. Blackbirds, grackles, cowbirds, starlings, and crows frequently feed on corn seed and developing ears. The developing ears are particularly inviting to birds from the milk stage to harvest. Blackbirds and grackles pierce the husk and puncture the soft kernels. Cowbirds feed on ears where the husk has been removed by other birds.

SOLUTION: To protect developing ears, put a paper bag over each ear after it has been pollinated—when the silk begins to turn brown. Bird netting placed over the rows also protects the ears. These nets are available at garden centers and through mail order garden supply companies. For more information on birds in the garden, see page 899.

Corn smut.

PROBLEM: Puffballs or galls appear on the stalk, leaves, ears, or tassels. Galls are white and may be smooth, or they may be covered with a black greasy or powdery material. They range from peasize to 5 inches in diameter.

ANALYSIS: Corn smut
This plant disease is caused by a fungus (*Ustilago maydis*) that attacks any aboveground part of corn. Germinating seedlings are not affected. Galls are full of black powdery spores that survive the winter on or in soil, corn debris, and manure. They are spread from plant to plant by wind, water, and manure. A gall forms only where a spore lands. The disease does not spread throughout the plant. Younger plants are more susceptible; most plants are infected when they are from 1 to 3 feet tall. Corn is less susceptible after the ears have formed. Corn smut is most prevalent in warm (80° to 95°F) temperatures, and when dry weather early in the season is followed by moderate rainfall as the corn matures. Stem and leaf smut doesn't reduce the corn yield directly, but rather saps the plant's energy, reducing ear development.

SOLUTION: There are no chemical controls for this disease. Cut off smuts before they break open and release the black powdery spores. Grow varieties tolerant to corn smut (see page 1027). Clean all plant debris from the garden after harvest. Avoid using manure in the soil if corn smut is a problem in your garden.

Fusarium ear rot.

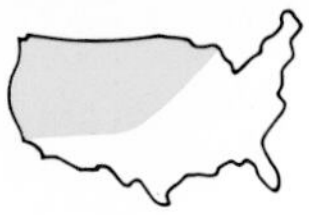

PROBLEM: Dark brown lesions spot the corn stalks near their joints. The stalks are rotted inside, are often pink, and break easily. Kernels are moldy, and pink to reddish brown. Plants die.

ANALYSIS: Root, stalk, and ear rot
This plant disease is caused by a soil-inhabiting fungus (*Fusarium moniliforme*) that attacks roots, stalks, and ears. It is prevalent during warm, dry weather, and can attack corn plants any time during their life. The fungi are prevalent in nutrient-deficient soils. The rot often originates in the roots and crown of the plant, and spreads upward into the stalk. Stalks injured by insects, disease, or hail are very susceptible. The fungal spores survive the winter on or in seeds and dead stalks left in the garden. Infected seeds don't sprout, or the seedlings die soon after emerging. The spores are spread from plant to plant by the wind, splashing water, insects, and infected tools. Spores that land on the stalks are washed into the leaf sheaths where they germinate and infect the stalk, resulting in lesions at the stalk joints.

SOLUTION: There is no chemical control for this disease. Destroy infected plants and ears. Maintain balanced nutrition by fertilizing with ORTHO Vegetable Food. Clean all plant debris from the garden after harvest.

Small yellow plants.

PROBLEM: Corn plants are short and produce few or no ears. Leaves may be pale green to yellow.

ANALYSIS: Poor yield
Sweet corn is exacting in its growth requirements and, if these requirements are not met, can be a disappointment in the garden. Corn plants may be small, yellow, and yield poorly for any of several reasons.

1. *Planted too close:* Corn plants have extensive root systems and are very competitive.
2. *Nutrient deficiency:* Plants are heavy feeders and require abundant supplies of nutrients, especially nitrogen, throughout the season.
3. *Poor irrigation:* Corn needs abundant water throughout the season, but especially from tasseling to picking time.
4. *Poorly drained soil:* Shallow, weak roots develop in poorly drained soil. Corn plants are vigorous and need deep healthy roots.
5. *Nematodes:* These soil-inhabiting, microscopic worms damage corn roots, reducing the plant's vigor. For more information on nematodes, see page 665.

SOLUTION: Follow the cultural guidelines on page 707 for healthy and productive sweet corn. Plant seeds 12 to 16 inches apart, in rows 30 to 36 inches apart. Improve soil drainage as described on page 907.

CORN — DISCOLORED LEAVES

Bacterial wilt.

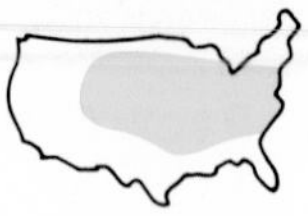

PROBLEM: Long irregular streaks up to 1 inch wide appear on leaves. The streaks turn brown and dry. Plants may be stunted and produce few ears, or wilt rapidly and die. Seedlings rapidly wilt and die. Brown cavities occur inside the stalks near the soil line.

ANALYSIS: Bacterial wilt
This plant disease, also called *Stewart's wilt*, is caused by a bacterium (*Erwinia stewartii*). The bacteria spend the winter in the bodies of corn flea beetles and then infect healthy plants as the flea beetles feed on the corn leaves. (For more information on the corn flea beetle, see page 691.) The bacteria then move through and infect the entire plant. The severity of the wilt disease depends on the number of flea beetles that survive the winter. Bacterial wilt is most severe after mild winters when numerous beetles survive. Plants growing in rich soil are the most susceptible to attack, as are early yellow varieties. Spotted cucumber beetles (see page 671) also spread the bacteria during the growing season.

SOLUTION: There are no chemical controls for this disease. Remove and destroy all infected plants. Control flea beetles and cucumber beetles with ORTHO Fruit & Vegetable Insect Control. Plant varieties tolerant of this disease (see page 1027).

Northern corn leaf blight.

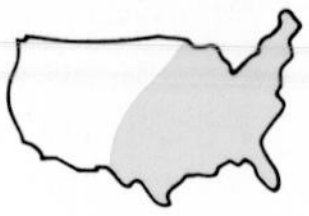

PROBLEM: Greenish yellow to grayish tan elliptical spots appear on the lower leaves first and on the upper leaves later. The spots may be surrounded by a reddish brown or yellow margin, and range in size from very small to 1 to 5 inches long and 1 inch wide. In humid weather, the spots may be covered with tiny black specks on a velvety growth.

ANALYSIS: Leaf blights
Northern and southern leaf blights are caused by fungi (*Helminthosporium* species) that usually attack corn plants when they are about 15 inches tall. The fungi thrive in warm (70° to 85°F), wet weather. The spores can infect leaves only when the leaves remain wet for 6 to 18 hours. Leaf blights are seldom a problem in hot, dry weather. The spores spend the winter on diseased plant parts left in the garden, and are spread to new crops in the early summer by the wind. Leaf blights seldom kill the corn plants, but may weaken them and make them more susceptible to root and stalk rots.

SOLUTION: Spray the plants with ORTHO Vegetable Disease Control when spotting first appears. Continue spraying every 4 to 7 days until dry weather resumes. Grow corn varieties that are tolerant of leaf blight (see page 1027). Clean all corn debris from the garden after harvest.

Maize dwarf mosaic.

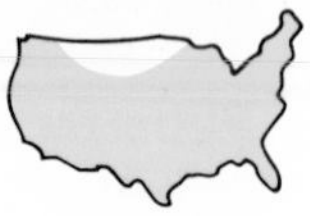

PROBLEM: The upper part of the plant is dwarfed, causing the plant to look like a feather duster. Leaves are striped with yellow and green in a mosaic pattern. As the plant matures the mosaic disappears, and late in the season the leaves turn yellow-green with red blotches or streaks.

ANALYSIS: Maize dwarf mosaic
This plant disease is caused by a virus that is transmitted primarily by aphids, and occasionally by equipment and man. It also infects wild and cultivated grasses, especially Johnsongrass, in which it survives the winter. The symptoms are most obvious in plants that are infected before silking. If infected after silking or later, the symptoms may not show, and the plants appear to be healthy.

SOLUTION: There are no chemical controls for virus diseases. Destroy all infected plants. Do not touch a healthy plant after touching an infected one. Prevent the spread of the disease by controlling aphids when they appear with ORTHO Fruit & Vegetable Insect Control. (For information on aphids, see page 875.) Grow varieties of corn tolerant of maize dwarf mosaic (see page 1027). Kill Johnsongrass outside the garden with ORTHO Kleenup Systemic Weed & Grass Killer. For more information on virus diseases, see page 853.

INSECTS

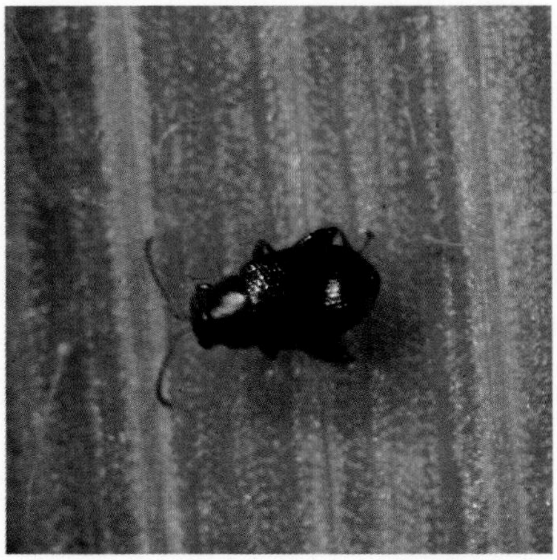

Flea beetle (12 times life size).

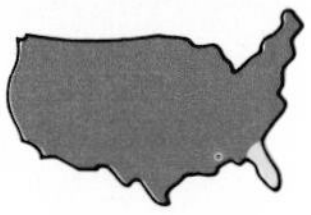

PROBLEM: Leaves are riddled with shotholes about 1/8 inch in diameter. Tiny (1/16 inch) black beetles jump like fleas when disturbed. Leaves of seedlings and eventually whole plants may wilt and die.

ANALYSIS: Flea beetles
These beetles jump like fleas, but are not related to them. Both adult and immature flea beetles feed on a wide variety of garden vegetables. Some flea beetles are responsible for spreading the bacterial wilt that kills corn plants. For more information on these wilts, see page 710. The immature beetle, a legless gray grub, injures plants by feeding on the roots and the lower surfaces of leaves. Adults chew holes in leaves. Flea beetles are most damaging to seedlings and young plants. Leaves of seedlings riddled with holes dry out quickly and die. Adult beetles survive the winter in soil and garden debris. They emerge in early spring to feed on weeds until vegetables sprout or plants are set in the garden. Grubs hatch from eggs laid in the soil and feed for 2 to 3 weeks. After pupating in the soil, they emerge as adults to repeat the cycle. There are one to four generations a year. Adults may feed for up to 2 months.

SOLUTION: Control flea beetles on corn with ORTHO Fruit & Vegetable Insect Control, ORTHO Sevin Garden Dust, or ORTHO Tomato & Vegetable Insect Spray when the leaves first show damage. Watch new growth for evidence of further damage, and repeat the treatment at weekly intervals as needed. Remove all plant debris from the garden after harvest to eliminate overwintering spots for adult beetles.

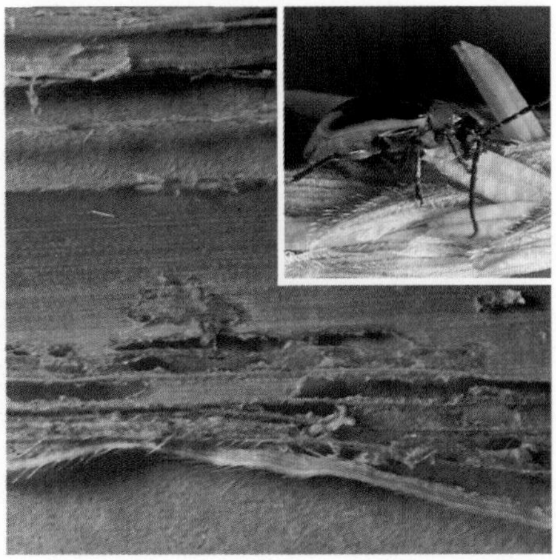

Damage. *Insert:* Adult (3 times life size).

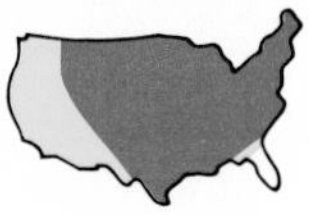

PROBLEM: Yellow, pale green, or brownish red beetles with very long antennae crawl on the plants. Some may have black spots or stripes. The ears are malformed, with undeveloped or partially developed kernels; leaves may be chewed.

ANALYSIS: Corn rootworm
(*Diabrotica* species)
Both adult beetles and young worms of this pest attack corn. For information on the larva, see page 713. The adult beetles feed on the pollen, silks, and tassels, resulting in malformed ears and undeveloped kernels from improper or incomplete pollination. Some beetles may also feed on the leaves. The adults lay yellow-orange eggs in the soil at the base of the corn plants. The young worms that hatch from these eggs feed on the corn roots for several weeks, then pupate in the soil to emerge as beetles in late July and August. These pests are most common where corn has grown consecutively for 2 or more years. Late-planted corn and corn under drought stress are the most susceptible.

SOLUTION: Dust the plants with ORTHO Sevin Garden Dust when the beetles first appear on the plants. Repeat at weekly intervals if the plants become reinfested. Control the rootworm larvae as suggested on page 713.

Grasshoppers (half life size).

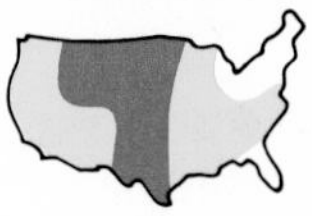

PROBLEM: Large holes are chewed in the margins of the leaves. Greenish yellow to brown jumping insects, 1/2 to 1 1/2 inches long, with long hind legs infest corn plants. Kernels on ears may be chewed or undeveloped.

ANALYSIS: Grasshoppers
Grasshoppers attack a wide variety of plants including corn, grains, and grasses. They eat corn leaves and silk, migrating as they mature and as they deplete their food sources. They are most numerous in the rows adjacent to weedy areas. In the late summer, adult grasshoppers lay eggs in pods in the soil. The adults continue feeding until cold weather kills them. The eggs hatch the following spring. Grasshopper populations are most severe during hot, dry weather. They migrate into green gardens and yards as surrounding areas dry up in the summer heat. Periods of cool, wet weather help keep their numbers under control. The loss of a small amount of leaf tissue by a small population of grasshoppers doesn't reduce the corn yield significantly.

SOLUTION: Treat the plants with ORTHO Fruit & Vegetable Insect Control as soon as grasshoppers appear. Repeat at weekly intervals if the plants become reinfested. Clean up weedy areas near the garden and remove all plant debris from the garden after harvest.

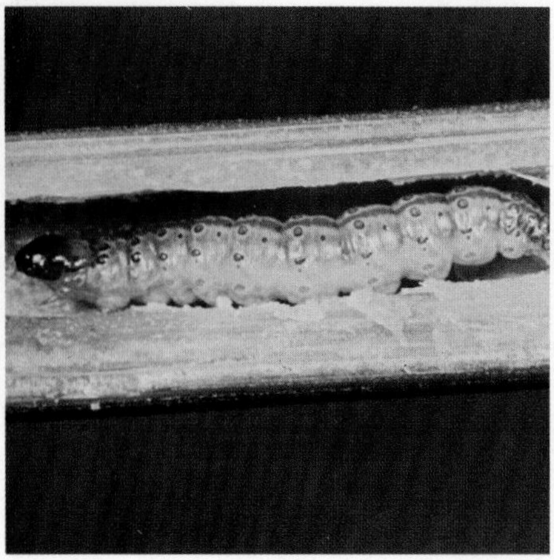

European corn borer (twice life size).

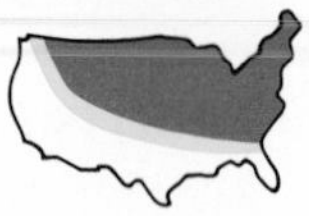

PROBLEM: Leaves are riddled with tiny shotholes. Tassels may be broken and ear stalks bent. Holes filled with sawdust are bored into the main stalks. Pinkish caterpillars with dark brown heads and two rows of brown dots are found inside the stalks.

ANALYSIS: European corn borer
(*Ostrinia nubilalis*)
The European corn borer is one of the most destructive pests of corn. It also feeds on tomatoes, potatoes, and peppers. Early plantings are the most severely affected. The borer survives the winter in corn plants, pupates in the spring, and emerges as an adult moth in early summer. The moth, which is tan with dark wavy lines on the wings, lays clusters of about 20 white eggs on the undersides of the lower corn leaves. The borers that hatch from these eggs feed first in the whorl of leaves, riddling the leaves with shotholes. Later they bore into stalks and the bases of ears. This feeding results in broken stalks and tassels, poor ear development, and dropped ears. The borers continue feeding for a month, pupate, and emerge as moths to repeat the cycle. Cool, rainy weather in the early summer inhibits egg laying and washes the hatching larvae from the plants, reducing borer populations. Very dry summers and cold winters also reduce borer populations.

SOLUTION: Treat ear shoots and centers of leaf whorls at the first sign of borers or when 10 percent of the ears show silk with ORTHO Sevin Garden Dust or ORTHO Rotenone Dust or Spray. Repeat at weekly intervals until borers are no longer seen. Destroy the plants at the end of the season. Avoid early planting.

Stalk borer damage. *Insert:* Larva (life size).

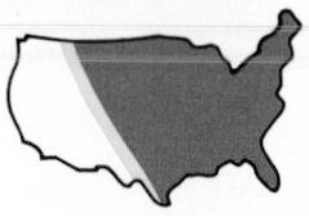

PROBLEM: Leaves are chewed and ragged. Stalks don't produce ears and may be distorted and curled. Dark brown to purple caterpillars, 1 inch long, with white stripes and bands may be found inside the stalks.

ANALYSIS: Common stalk borer
(*Papaipema nebris*)
The common stalk borer is a serious pest of corn east of the Rocky Mountains. These borers feed on a variety of plants, but prefer corn. They spend the winter as eggs on grasses and weeds, especially giant ragweed. After hatching in the early spring, the worms feed in the leaf whorls and then bore into the side of the stalks and burrow upward. After pupating in the soil, the adult moths emerge in late summer and early fall. These grayish brown moths lay eggs on grasses for next year's generation. There is only one generation per year.

SOLUTION: Once the damage is noticed, it is too late for any controls. Destroy all infested plants. Clean all plant debris from the garden after harvest. Eliminate nearby grasses and weeds, especially giant ragweed. If stalk borers were serious this year, next year treat the plants with an insecticide containing *diazinon* or *carbaryl* (SEVIN®) in early to midspring.

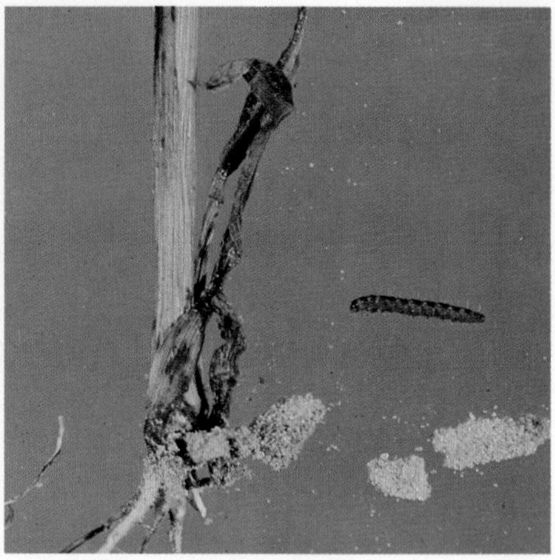

Lesser corn stalk borer (half life size).

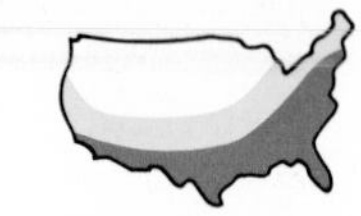

PROBLEM: Leaves are chewed and ragged. Stalks are distorted and curled, with few or no ears. A hole appears in the corn stalk about 2 inches above the soil surface. A ¾ inch bluish-green caterpillar with brown stripes may be found in the soil near the plants.

ANALYSIS: Lesser corn stalk borer
(*Elasmopalpus lignosellus*)
These worms damage plants by boring and tunneling into the stalks. One larva may injure or kill several plants. In the spring a brownish yellow moth with black spots lays eggs on corn leaves and stalks. The borers that hatch from these eggs feed on the leaves and burrow into the lower 2 inches of the stalk, causing curled and distorted plants. After feeding for about 3 weeks the borers pupate in the soil and emerge as adults to repeat the cycle. There are two or more generations a year. The lesser corn stalk borer feeds on a variety of plants, and is often found on Johnsongrass.

SOLUTION: Once the damage is noticed, it is too late for any controls. Destroy all infested plants, and clean all plant debris from the garden after harvest. Pull out surrounding weeds and grasses, especially Johnsongrass, where the borers may breed and spend the winter. Next year at planting time, apply an insecticide containing *diazinon* granules to the soil.

SOIL INSECTS

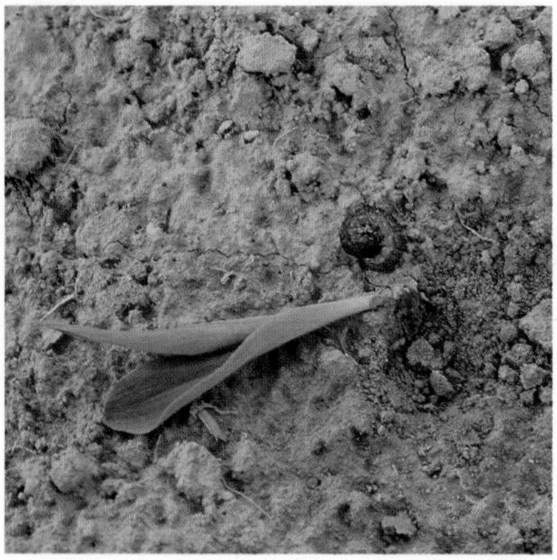

Black cutworm (⅓ life size).

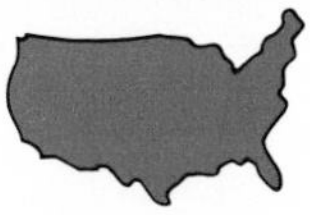

PROBLEM: Young plants are chewed or cut off near the ground. Gray, brown, or black worms, 1½ to 2 inches long, may be found about 2 inches deep in the soil near the base of the damaged plants. The worms coil when disturbed.

ANALYSIS: Cutworms
Several species of cutworms attack plants in the vegetable garden. The most likely pests of corn seedlings are the surface-feeding cutworms. The two most common on corn are the black cutworm (*Agrotis ipsilon*) and the dingy cutworm (*Feltia ducens*). For information on the climbing cutworms, see page 670. A single surface-feeding cutworm can sever the stems of many young plants in one night. Cutworms hide in the soil during the day, and feed only at night. All adult cutworms are dark night-flying moths with bands or stripes on their forewings.

SOLUTION: Apply ORTHO Vegetable Guard Soil Insect Killer, ORTHO Diazinon Soil & Turf Insect Control, or ORTHO Diazinon Soil & Foliage Dust around the base of undamaged plants when stem cutting is observed. Since cutworms are difficult to control, it may be necessary to repeat dusting at weekly intervals. Before planting more corn in the same area, apply a preventive treatment of ORTHO Vegetable Guard Soil Insect Killer and work it into the soil. Cultivate the soil thoroughly in late summer and fall to expose and destroy eggs, larvae, and pupae. Further reduce damage with "cutworm collars" around the stem of each plant or group of plants. These collars can be made of stiff paper or aluminum foil. They should be at least 2 inches high, and pressed firmly into the soil.

Corn rootworm larva (life size).

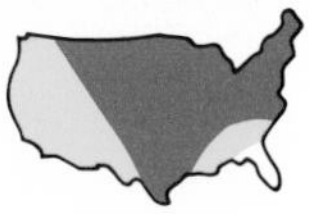

PROBLEM: Corn plants are dwarfed, yellow, and fall over easily. The base of the stalks may have a crook-necked shape. White worms, from ½ to ¾ inch long, with brown heads are eating the roots.

ANALYSIS: Corn rootworm larvae
(*Diabrotica* species)
Several species of this pest attack corn. The beetle larva, or worm, feeds on corn roots, completely devouring small ones and tunneling into larger ones. The worms hatch from eggs in early summer to midsummer and migrate through the soil, feeding on corn roots. This feeding damage can be so serious to young plants that some gardens may need to be replanted. When populations are large, all the roots may be destroyed. The worms pupate in the soil and emerge as greenish yellow or light brown beetles, some with black spots or stripes, to repeat the cycle. There are one to three generations per year. Adult beetles feed on larvae and silks. For information on adult corn rootworms, see page 711. Corn plants are affected most severely when they are growing in dry soil, where root regrowth is minimal. Rot diseases may enter the damaged roots, injuring them further. Several parasitic insects and diseases help keep beetle populations under control most years.

SOLUTION: Discard damaged plants and clean up weedy areas where the insects lay eggs and spend the winter. Apply ORTHO Diazinon Soil & Turf Insect Control or ORTHO Vegetable Guard Soil Insect Killer to the soil at planting time. Don't grow corn in the same soil for more than 2 consecutive years.

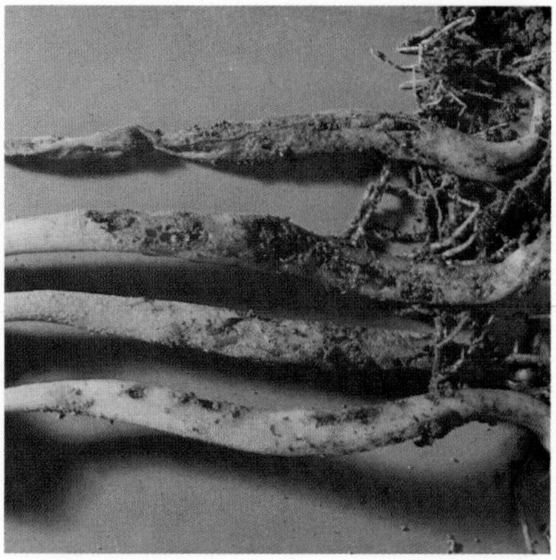

Seedcorn maggot damage.

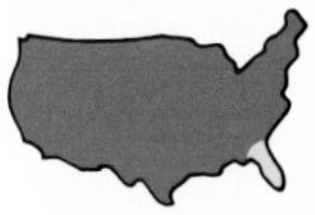

PROBLEM: Seeds don't sprout, or the seedlings are weak and don't develop leaves. Pearly white worms, ¼ inch long, are feeding in the seeds. The seeds are hollow.

ANALYSIS: Seedcorn maggot
(*Hylemya platura*)
Seedcorn maggots feed on seeds and seedlings. They are attracted to large-seeded vegetables such as peas, beans, and corn. The maggots are most numerous in cool periods in the spring and fall, and in cold soil that is high in organic matter. The black, hairy adult flies are attracted to the organic matter, and lay eggs in the soil. The maggots that hatch from these eggs burrow into the seeds and eat the inner tissue, leaving a hollow shell. Rot fungi may enter a damaged seed and further destroy it. After 1 to 2 weeks, the maggots burrow deep into the soil and pupate. The adult flies that emerge feed on nectar and plant juices before laying more eggs. There are several generations a year. In warm winter areas, these pests are active all year. In cold winter areas, they survive the winter as pupae, emerging as adults in the early spring.

SOLUTION: Treat seed with an insecticide powder that contains *diazinon*. Mix ¼ teaspoon of insecticide with each packet of seed. Shake off the excess, and plant the seeds 1 to 2 inches deep. Since adult flies are attracted to organic matter, don't add manure to the soil in the spring when planting beans, peas, or corn.

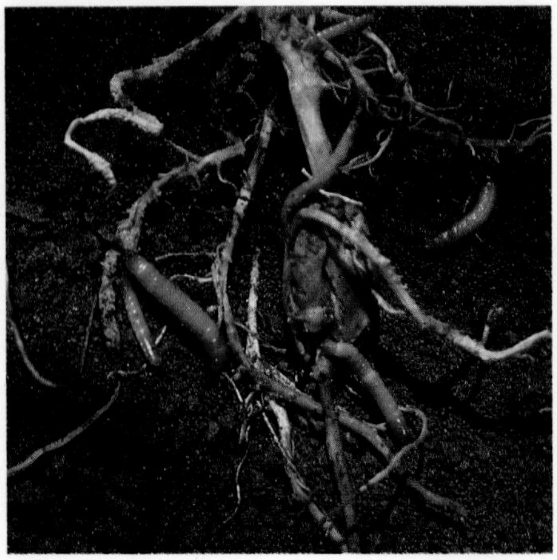

Wireworms (life size).

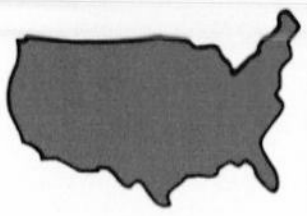

PROBLEM: Plants are stunted and grow slowly. Holes are drilled into the base of the plants. Shiny, hard, jointed, cream to yellow worms up to ⅝ inch long are found in the soil or on plant roots. Seeds don't sprout. Unsprouted seeds are hollow.

ANALYSIS: Wireworms
Wireworms are found throughout the United States. They feed on corn, carrots, potatoes, beets, peas, and many other plants. Wireworms feed entirely on underground plant parts, devouring seeds, underground stems, tubers, and roots. Infestations are most extensive in soil where lawn grass was previously grown, in poorly drained soil, and in soil that is high in organic matter. The adult form is known as the *click beetle* because it makes a clicking sound when turning from its back to its feet. Click beetles lay eggs in the spring. The eggs hatch into wireworms, which feed for 2 to 6 years before maturing into adult beetles. All sizes and ages of wireworms may be in the soil at the same time. Infestations may be scattered throughout a planting. Sometimes damaged plants resprout from the base, resulting in a bushy, stunted plant.

SOLUTION: Destroy damaged plants, since they won't produce ears. Replant unsprouted rows. At planting time, incorporate ORTHO Diazinon Soil & Turf Insect Control, ORTHO Vegetable Guard Soil Insect Killer, or ORTHO Diazinon Soil & Foliage Dust into the top 4 to 6 inches of soil.

CUCURBITS (CUCUMBERS, GOURDS, MUSKMELONS, PUMPKINS, SUMMER SQUASH, WATERMELON, AND WINTER SQUASH)

ADAPTATION: Throughout the United States.

PLANTING TIME: See page 1025.

PLANTING METHOD: Start seeds indoors or directly in the garden. Plant cucumber, muskmelon, and watermelon seeds 1 to 2 inches deep. Plant squash and pumpkins 2 to 3 inches deep. Set transplants in the garden so that the top of their rootball is even with the surrounding garden soil. Space transplants or thin seedlings as follows: Cucumbers and muskmelons—12 inches apart, or 24 to 36 inches apart if planted in hills. Pumpkins and vining squash—36 to 40 inches apart. Bush squash and watermelon—24 to 36 inches apart.

SOIL: Any good garden soil high in organic matter. pH 5.5 to 8.0.

FERTILIZER: At planting time, use 2 pounds of ORTHO Vegetable Food per 50-foot row, or 1 to 2 tablespoons per plant. Side-dress when the runners are 12 to 18 inches long and again when the first fruit have set.

WATER:
How much: Apply enough water at each irrigation to wet the soil 1 to 1½ feet deep.
How often: Water when the soil 2 inches deep is barely moist.

HARVEST:
Cucumbers: Slicing: 8 to 10 inches long. Pickles: 2 to 4 inches. Dill and larger pickles: 6 to 8 inches.
Muskmelons: When netting becomes pronounced and skin color turns yellow-tan; stem should separate or slip easily from the fruit.
Pumpkins and gourds: After the vines die in the fall but before a hard frost.
Summer squash: Continuous picking insures a steady supply. Zucchini and crook-neck: 1½ to 2 inches in diameter. Bush scallop: 3 to 4 inches.
Watermelon: When the spot where the melon touches the ground turns from white to creamy yellow. Green skin is dull, not shiny; the melon makes a dull thud when hit with the palm of the hand.
Winter squash: After the vines die in the fall, but before a hard frost; when your fingernail doesn't scratch the hardened skin.

STORING: Most cucurbits are used soon after harvesting. Cool in refrigerator until use. Winter squash and pumpkins can be stored over the winter. Pick only mature fruit, and cure them at temperatures between 80° and 85°F for 10 days. Then move the squash or pumpkins to a well-ventilated place with temperatures between 50° and 60°F. Store in a single layer; they rot easily if stored in piles.

PROBLEMS WITH THE FRUIT

Healthy plants with no fruit.

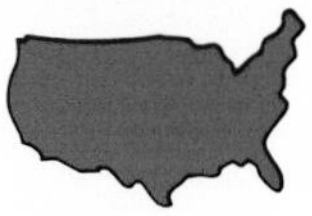

PROBLEM: Few or no fruit are produced on melon, squash, or cucumber plants. Plants are healthy, with no signs of insect or disease problems.

ANALYSIS: Few fruit
Few or no fruit are produced on cucurbit plants because of poor pollination. Members of this family produce two kinds of flowers, male and female. For fruit production, pollen produced on male flowers must be carried by insects, especially honeybees, to the female flowers. The male flower, on the end of a long stalk, is the first to bloom. The female flowers bloom shortly thereafter. The female flower is not on a stalk, but is attached to a swelling resembling a miniature fruit. Once pollination is complete, the small swelling at the base of the female flower grows into a full-size edible fruit. Anything that interferes with pollination reduces fruit set and yield. Cold, rainy weather reduces bee activity. Improper use of insecticides may kill bees. Sometimes male and female flowers do not bloom at the same time.

SOLUTION: Male and female flowers are produced all season, so be patient. To aid pollination, hand pollinate by transferring pollen from the male flowers to the female flowers with a small paintbrush. Spray insecticides in the late afternoon when bees are not flying.

Misshapen and tough cucumbers.

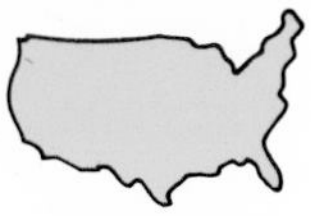

PROBLEM: Fruit are misshapen or tough with large seeds inside. Plants may be wilted or growing slowly.

ANALYSIS: Misshapen and tough fruit
Cucumbers are misshapen when the flowers are improperly pollinated. This can result from reduced honeybee activity or from hot temperatures that kill the pollen. For more information on cucurbit pollination, see page 715. Squash and cucumber plants growing in dry soil with low fertility frequently produce misshapen fruit. Overmature fruit are tough with large seeds inside. They lack a sweet flavor.

SOLUTION: Discard all misshapen fruit. To keep your plants healthy and productive, follow the cultural and harvesting guidelines on page 714.

For a tasty treat, dip fading squash flowers in batter and pan fry in butter, or deep fry in vegetable oil. Serve hot.

Bitter cucumbers.

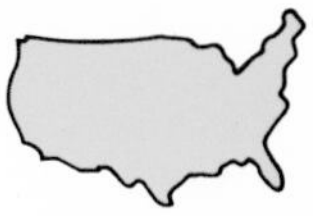

PROBLEM: Cucumbers taste bitter.

ANALYSIS: Bitterness
Bitter cucumbers are usually produced on unhealthy plants late in the season. A bitter taste results from adverse growing conditions that stress the plant. These conditions include hot temperatures, dry soil, and low fertility. Plants with diseased foliage may also produce bitter fruit. Usually only the stem end is affected, but sometimes the entire fruit is bitter. Some older varieties produce fruit that is more bitter than newer varieties. Bitter fruit does not result from cross pollination between cucumbers and squash or melons. These plants do not cross pollinate. Different varieties of cucumbers will cross pollinate with each other, but they will not cross pollinate with melons or squash.

SOLUTION: As long as hot weather continues or the plant is stressed, it will continue to produce bitter fruit. This is especially true late in the season. For healthy, productive plants, follow the cultural guidelines on page 714.

CUCURBITS — PROBLEMS WITH THE FRUIT

Blossom-end rot on melon.

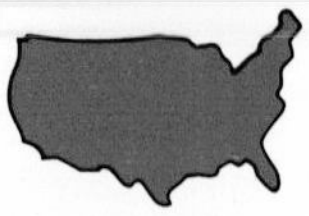

PROBLEM: A water-soaked, sunken spot develops on the blossom end (opposite the stem end) of squash and watermelons. The spot enlarges and turns brown to black. Mold may grow on the spot.

ANALYSIS: Blossom-end rot
This disorder of squash, watermelons, tomatoes, and peppers is caused by a lack of calcium in the developing fruit. This lack of calcium is the result of slowed growth and damaged roots caused by any of the following factors:
1. Extreme fluctuations in soil moisture, either very wet or very dry.
2. Rapid plant growth early in the season followed by extended dry weather.
3. Excessive rains that smother root hairs.
4. Excess soil salts.
The first fruit are the most severely affected. As the name implies, the disorder always starts at the blossom end, and may enlarge to affect half of the fruit. Moldy growths on the rotted area are caused by fungi or bacteria that frequently invade the damaged tissue. The rotted area is unsightly, but the rest of the ripened fruit is edible.

SOLUTION: The numbers below correspond to numbers in the analysis.
1. Maintain uniform soil moisture by mulching (see page 926), and by following the watering guidelines on page 714.
2. Avoid high-nitrogen fertilizers and large quantities of fresh manure.
3. Plant in well-drained soil, as outlined on page 907.
4. If your soil or water is salty, provide more water at each watering to help leach salts through the soil.

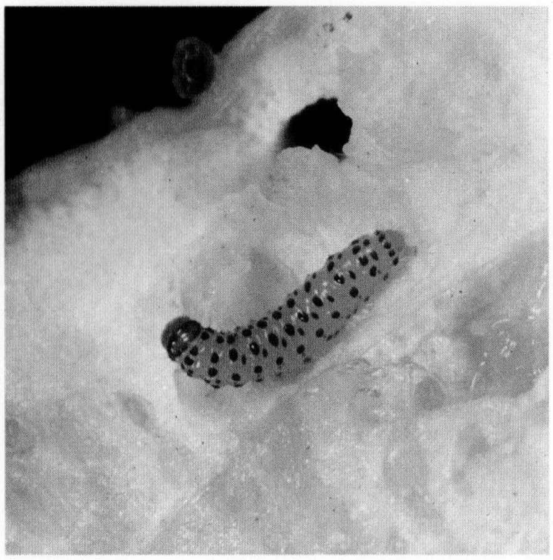

Pickleworm (twice life size).

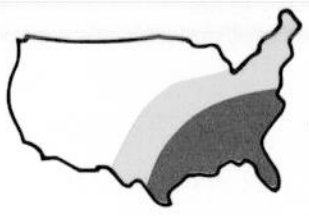

PROBLEM: Light green worms about 5/8 inch long, with black dots and dark brown heads, feed on blossoms and vines and tunnel into the fruit.

ANALYSIS: Pickleworm
(*Diaphania nitidalis*)
This moth larva favors summer squash, but also attacks cucumbers and muskmelons. Pickleworms can be a serious problem in some areas of the South. They damage plants by feeding on the vines, and reduce the fruit yield by feeding on the blossoms. Their tunneling into the fruit makes it unappetizing and often inedible. The adult moth lays clusters of eggs on the plant in late spring. The worms that hatch from these eggs feed on blossoms, buds, vines, and fruit for 2 to 3 weeks, then pupate in silken tubes on the leaves. In several days, adults emerge to repeat the cycle. The worms are active throughout the growing season. In southern Florida they are active all year.

SOLUTION: Apply ORTHO Tomato Vegetable Dust, ORTHO Sevin Garden Dust, or ORTHO Liquid Sevin at the first sign of worms in buds or blossoms. Repeat at weekly intervals as long as the pickleworms are present. Clean up plant debris and pupae to reduce the infestation.

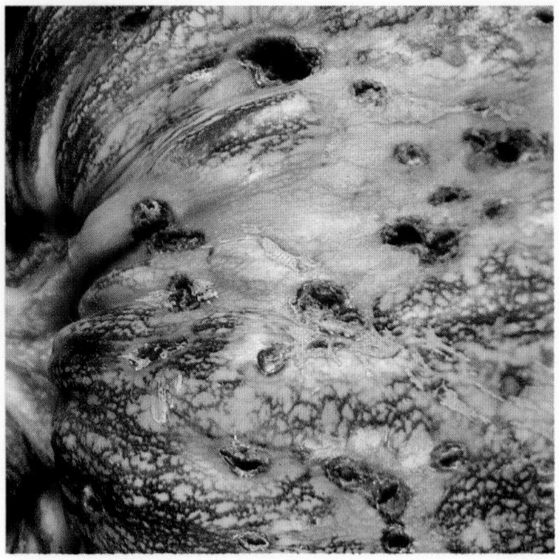

Scab on pumpkin.

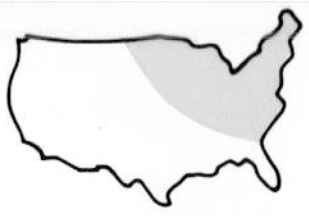

PROBLEM: Dry corky spots up to ½ inch in diameter appear on the fruit. A sticky substance may ooze from the spots. In moist weather, a dark green velvety growth covers the spots. Fruit may be cracked and decay. White or gray spots appear on leaves. The dead tissue falls out of these spots, leaving ragged holes.

ANALYSIS: Scab
This plant disease is caused by a fungus (*Cladosporium cucumerinum*) that attacks cucumbers, squash, and muskmelons. All aboveground parts are affected. Fruit is attacked at all stages of growth, but young fruit are the most susceptible. The disease is most prevalent in foggy, cool (60° to 65°F) weather, and when night temperatures fall below 60°F for several nights in a row. The fungal spores spend the winter in diseased plant debris left in the garden and on seeds.

SOLUTION: Treat the plants with ORTHO Vegetable Disease Control at the first sign of the disease. Repeat at weekly intervals until harvest. Next year, begin spraying when the runners are 6 inches long. Clean all plant debris from the garden after harvest. Rotate your cucurbit planting site every year. Grow resistant varieties (see page 1028).

Beet leafhopper damage to zucchini.

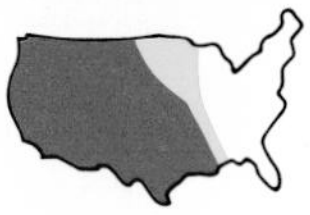

PROBLEM: Spotted, pale green, winged insects up to 1/8 inch long hop and fly away quickly when a plant is touched. The leaves are stippled, and may be curled, puckered, and brittle.

ANALYSIS: Beet leafhopper
(*Circulifer tenellus*)
The beet leafhopper is a western insect that is found only as far east as Missouri and Illinois. It attacks all members of the cucurbit family and frequently infects them with the virus that causes curly top. Plants infected with curly top are stunted, brittle, and sometimes die. (For more information on curly top, see page 853.) The beet leafhopper feeds from early May through June. It sucks the sap and virus from the infected leaves, and then injects the virus into healthy plants at its next feeding stop.

SOLUTION: Treat infested plants with ORTHO Fruit & Vegetable Insect Control, ORTHO Sevin Garden Dust, or ORTHO Tomato Vegetable Dust. Be sure to cover the lower surfaces of the leaves. Repeat the treatment at intervals of 7 to 10 days if the plants become reinfested. For more information on controlling disease-carrying insects, see page 879.

Striped cucumber beetle (4 times life size).

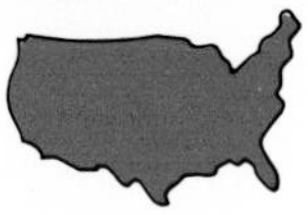

PROBLEM: Holes are chewed in the leaves, leaf stalks, and stems by yellow-green beetles with black stripes or spots. Plants may wilt and die.

ANALYSIS: Cucumber beetles
Cucumber beetles, both *striped* (*Acalymma* species) and *spotted* (*Diabrotica* species), are common pests of cucumbers, melons, squash, and pumpkins. It is important to control these beetles because they carry two serious diseases that damage and may kill cucurbits: mosaic (page 720) and bacterial wilt (page 718). The adults survive the winter in plant debris and weeds. They emerge in the early spring and feed on a variety of plants. As soon as cucurbits are planted in the garden, the beetles attack the leaves and stems, and may totally destroy the plant. They lay their yellow-orange eggs in the soil at the base of the plants. The grubs that hatch from these eggs eat the roots and the stems below the soil line, causing the plant to be stunted or to wilt. The slender white grubs feed for several weeks, pupate in the soil, and emerge as adults to repeat the cycle. There is one generation a year in the North and two or more in the South. The adults and larvae of the spotted cucumber beetle also attack corn, as described on pages 711 and 713.

SOLUTION: Treat the plants with ORTHO Fruit & Vegetable Insect Spray, ORTHO Sevin Garden Dust, or ORTHO Tomato & Vegetable Insect Spray at the first sign of the beetles. Repeat at weekly intervals as the plants become reinfested. Control early in the season helps prevent susceptible young seedlings and plants from becoming infected with bacterial wilt.

Squash bugs (1/3 life size).

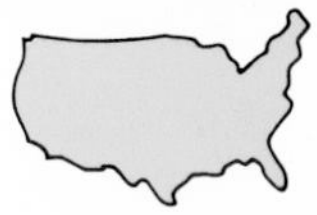

PROBLEM: Squash and pumpkin leaves wilt and may become black and crisp. Bright green to dark gray or brown flat-backed bugs, about 1/2 inch long, cluster on the plants.

ANALYSIS: Squash bug
(*Anasa tristis*)
Both the young (nymphs) and adult squash bugs attack cucurbits, but they are most serious on squash and pumpkins. They injure and kill the plants by sucking the sap from the leaves and stems. The dark brown adults, which are sometimes incorrectly called stink bugs, emit a disagreeable odor when crushed. They lay brick-red egg clusters on the leaves in the spring. Although there is only one generation each year, all stages are found throughout the summer.

SOLUTION: Squash bugs are elusive and difficult to control. Treat the plants and the soil around the plants with ORTHO Sevin Garden Dust or ORTHO Tomato Vegetable Dust when the bugs first appear. Repeat the treatment every 7 days until the bugs are controlled. Plant varieties that are resistant to attack by squash bugs.

Squash varieties resistant to squash bugs: Butternut, Royal Acorn, and Sweet Cheese.

CUCURBITS — INSECTS

Spider mite damage on cucumber.

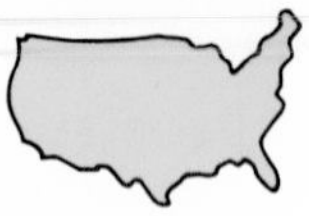

PROBLEM: Leaves are stippled, yellowing, and dirty. Leaves may dry out and drop. There may be webbing over flower buds, between leaves, or on the lower surfaces of the leaves. To determine if the plant is infested with mites, hold a sheet of white paper underneath an affected leaf and tap the leaf sharply. Minute green, red, or yellow specks the size of pepper grains will drop to the paper and begin to crawl around. The pests are easily seen against the white background.

ANALYSIS: Spider mites
(*Tetranychus urticae*)
These mites, related to spiders, are major pests of many garden and greenhouse plants. They cause damage by sucking sap from the underside of the leaves. As a result of feeding, the green leaf pigment disappears, producing the stippled appearance. Mites are active throughout the growing season, but are favored by hot, dry weather (70°F and up). By midsummer, they build up to tremendous numbers. In mild winter areas, mites can be a problem throughout the winter. For more information about spider mites, see page 887.

SOLUTION: Spray infested plants with ORTHO Fruit & Vegetable Insect Control when damage is first noticed. Spray the foliage thoroughly, being sure to cover both the upper and lower surfaces of the leaves. Repeat applications three more times at intervals of 7 days. Hose plants frequently to knock off webs and mites.

Borer damage. *Insert:* Borer in stem (¾ life size).

PROBLEM: Squash vines suddenly wilt. Holes in the stems are filled with a tan sawdustlike material. Fat white worms up to 1 inch long are found in the affected vines when the stems are slit open lengthwise with a knife.

ANALYSIS: Squash vine borer
(*Melittia satyriniformis*)
This insect pest primarily attacks squash and gourds, and only rarely attacks cucumbers and melons. Hubbard squash is especially susceptible. The larvae damage and kill the plants by tunneling in the stems, preventing the rest of the vine from receiving the water and nutrients it needs. The metallic green adult moth lays eggs on the vines in early summer. Egg laying occurs in April and May in the South, and June and July in the North. When the eggs hatch, the white larvae bore into the stems and feed for 4 to 5 weeks. They then crawl out of the stem and into the soil to pupate.

SOLUTION: Insecticides applied after the borer is inside the stem are not effective. Instead, slit the affected stems with a knife and destroy the borer. If the plant has not died, cover the damaged portion of the stem with soil. Keep the soil moist to encourage new roots to grow. The vine may recover. Next year, dust the plant with ORTHO Tomato Vegetable Dust during the egg-laying period.

DISCOLORED OR SPOTTED LEAVES

Bacterial wilt. *Insert:* Bacterial ooze.

PROBLEM: A few leaves wilt and dry and may be chewed. Wilted leaves often recover at night, but wilt again on sunny days and finally die. Fruit shrivels. To test for bacteria, cut a wilted stem near the base of the plant and squeeze out the sap, looking for a milky white substance. Touch a knife to the sap and withdraw it slowly. Look for a white ooze that strings out in a fine thread as you withdraw the knife.

ANALYSIS: Bacterial wilt
This plant disease is caused by a bacterium (*Erwinia tracheiphila*) and is more prevalent on cucumbers and muskmelons than on pumpkins and squash. Watermelons are not affected. The bacteria spend the winter in striped or spotted cucumber beetles, and are spread to plants when the beetles feed. (For more information on cucumber beetles, see page 717.) An entire plant may become infected within 15 days. The disease is most prevalent in cool weather in areas with moderate rainfall.

SOLUTION: There are no chemical controls for bacterial wilt. Remove and discard all infected plants promptly. Control cucumber beetles with ORTHO Fruit & Vegetable Insect Control, ORTHO Sevin Garden Dust, or ORTHO Diazinon Insect Spray. Repeat the treatments every 7 days if the plants become reinfected. For more information about controlling disease-carrying insects, see page 879. Grow varieties resistant to this disease.

Cucumber variety resistant to bacterial wilt: Saladin. There are no resistant muskmelon varieties.

Alternaria leaf spot on muskmelon.

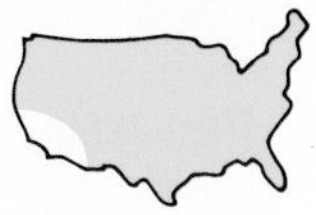

PROBLEM: Circular water-soaked spots up to ½ inch in diameter appear on the leaves. Dark concentric circles appear in the spots. Spots eventually enlarge into dry blotches and the leaves drop. Center or older leaves are affected first, progressing to those at the tips of the vines.

ANALYSIS: Alternaria leaf spot
This plant disease, which is caused by a fungus (*Alternaria cucumerina*), is severe on muskmelons, and also occurs on cucumbers and other cucurbits. The fungus defoliates the vines, reducing fruit yields. Weak plants, especially those bearing heavily, and those suffering from poor fertility, are most susceptible to attack. Vigorous, healthy vines are rarely attacked. The fungal spores survive the winter in plant debris left in the garden, and in and on seeds. They infect plants at temperatures between 60° and 90°F, causing the most damage from 80° to 90°F.

SOLUTION: Treat plants at the first sign of the disease with a fungicide containing *maneb*, *chlorothalonil* (DACONIL 2787®), or *anilazine*. Repeat every 7 to 10 days. Keep the plants healthy with adequate water and fertilizer and the correct soil pH (6.0 to 7.0). For more information on soil pH, see page 908.

Anthracnose on melon.

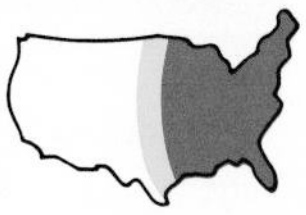

PROBLEM: Yellow, water-soaked areas spot melon and cucumber leaves, enlarge rapidly, and turn brown and dry. These spots then shatter, leaving a ragged hole in the spot. On watermelon leaves, the spots turn black. Elongated dark spots with light centers may appear on the stems. Whole leaves and vines die. Large fruit are spotted with sunken, dark brown, circular spots. Pinkish ooze may emerge from the spots. Young fruit darkens, shrivels, and dies.

ANALYSIS: Anthracnose
This plant disease is caused by a fungus (*Colletotrichum lagenarium*) and is the most destructive disease of melons and cucumbers in the East. It rarely attacks squash and pumpkin. The disease affects all aboveground parts of the plant, and is most prevalent in warm (70° to 80°F), humid weather with frequent rains. The spores overwinter in seeds and plant debris not removed from the garden. They are spread by splashing water, cucumber beetles, and tools.

SOLUTION: Treat plants with ORTHO Vegetable Disease Control at the first appearance of the disease. Repeat every 7 days, or more frequently if warm, humid weather occurs. Grow varieties resistant to this disease (see page 1028).

Angular leaf spot.

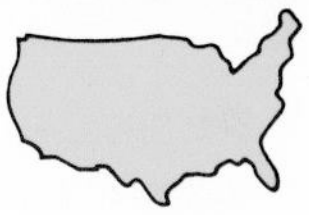

PROBLEM: Water-soaked, angular spots appear on the leaves. Tearlike droplets may ooze from the spots and dry into a white residue. Spots turn gray or tan, then drop out, leaving ragged holes. Fruit may be covered with cracked white spots.

ANALYSIS: Angular leaf spot
This plant disease is caused by a bacterium (*Pseudomonas lachrymans*) that attacks the leaves, stems, and fruits of cucurbits. The bacteria survive the winter on seed and plant debris not removed from the garden. The bacteria are spread from the soil to the plants by splashing rain, cucumber beetles, and hands and clothing, and infect the leaves and stems when they are wet with dew, rain, or irrigation water. The disease is most active between 75° and 80°F.

SOLUTION: Treat the plants with a pesticide containing *basic copper sulfate* at the first sign of the disease. Repeat every 7 to 10 days as long as the disease is a problem. To reduce the spread of the bacteria, don't work among wet plants. Avoid overhead watering by using drop or furrow irrigation. Clean all plant debris from the garden after harvest to reduce the amount of overwintering bacteria. Purchase seeds and plants from a reputable company. Grow varieties resistant to this disease (see page 1028).

CUCURBITS — DISCOLORED OR SPOTTED LEAVES

Mosaic on squash. *Insert:* Mosaic on cucumbers.

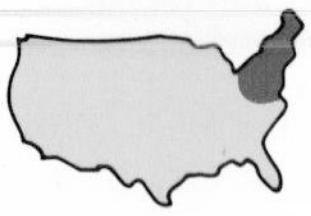

PROBLEM: Leaves are mottled yellow and green, and are distorted, stunted, and curled. Cucumber fruits are mottled with dark green and pale green to white blotches and covered with warts. Sometimes the skin is smooth and completely white. Summer squash fruit may be also covered with warts.

ANALYSIS: Mosaic virus
This plant disease is caused by several viruses that attack cucumbers, muskmelons, and summer squash. The viruses overwinter in perennial plants, and weeds, including catnip, pokeweed, wild cucumber, motherwort, and milkweed. The viruses are spread from plant to plant by aphids and cucumber beetles, and can infect plants at any time from the seedling stage to maturity. Infection early in the season is more damaging. Affected fruits taste bitter. Fruits that are more than half grown at the time of infection are immune to attack. Roots are not affected.

SOLUTION: There are no chemical controls for virus diseases. Remove and destroy all infected plants immediately. Control aphids and cucumber beetles with ORTHO Fruit & Vegetable Insect Control. Repeat at intervals of 7 to 10 days if the plants become reinfested. For more information on controlling disease-carrying insects, see page 879. Remove weeds in and near the garden. Grow resistant cucumber varieties. For a list of these varieties, see page 1028. There are not yet any resistant varieties of summer squash or muskmelon.

Powdery mildew on cucumber.

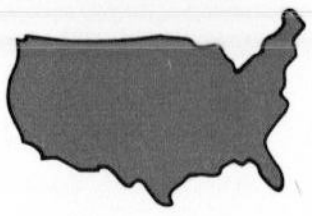

PROBLEM: The upper surfaces of the leaves are covered with a white powdery growth. Areas of the leaves and stems turn brown, wither, and dry. Fruit may be covered with the white powdery growth.

ANALYSIS: Powdery mildew
This common plant disease is caused by either of two fungi (*Erysiphe cichoracearum* and *Sphaerotheca fuliginea*) that thrive in both humid and dry weather. The powdery patches consist of fungal strands and spores. The spores are spread by the wind to healthy plants. The fungus saps the plant nutrients, causing yellowing and sometimes death of the leaf. A severe infection may kill the plant. Since these powdery mildews attack several different kinds of plants, the fungus from a diseased plant may infect other types of plants in the garden. For a list of powdery mildews and the plants which they attack, see page 1006. Under favorable conditions, powdery mildew can spread through a closely spaced planting in a matter of days or weeks.

SOLUTION: Treat the plants with ORTHO Vegetable Disease Control at the first sign of the disease. Continue treatments at intervals of 7 days as long as the disease is a problem. Grow varieties resistant to powdery mildew (see page 1028).

Downy mildew.

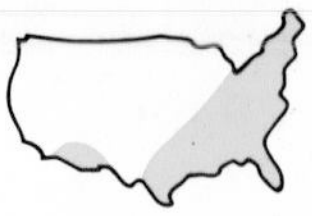

PROBLEM: Areas between the leaf veins turn yellow and then brown. In humid weather, the lower surfaces of the leaves are covered with a white, purple, or black hairy growth. Leaves die quickly. The older leaves are attacked first, progressing outward until the entire vine dies. Fruit is small and has a poor taste.

ANALYSIS: Downy mildew
This plant disease is caused by a fungus (*Pseudoperonospora cubensis*). The disease is severe on cucumbers and muskmelons, and less severe on pumpkins and squash. Watermelons are rarely attacked. The downy growth on the undersides of the leaves consists of fungus spores that break off and are spread by splashing water, tools, and clothing to other plants and leaves. The disease develops most rapidly in warm (60° to 85°F), wet weather.

SOLUTION: Treat the plants with ORTHO Vegetable Disease Control at the first sign of the disease. Repeat at intervals of 7 days as long as the disease continues. Those leaves already infected will not be cured. However, the sprays will protect healthy leaves from becoming infected. Clean all plant debris from the garden after harvest. Grow varieties resistant to this disease (see page 1028).

CURRANTS AND GOOSEBERRIES

ADAPTATION: Northern United States.

PLANTING TIME: Early spring and fall.

PLANTING METHOD: Select 1 to 2-year-old plants that are 12 to 24 inches tall. Set the plants 3 to 4 feet apart, and deep enough so that the top of their rootball is 1 inch deeper than the surrounding garden soil.

SOIL: Any good garden soil that is high in organic matter. pH 5.5 to 7.5

FERTILIZER: At planting time, incorporate a 1 to 2-inch layer of partially decomposed manure. In early spring before new growth begins, add 1 pound of ORTHO General Purpose Plant Food per 100 square feet, or 1 tablespoon per plant. Side-dress with the same amount in midspring and midsummer.

WATER:
How much: Apply enough water at each irrigation to wet the soil 1½ to 2 feet deep.
How often: Water when the soil 2 inches deep is dry.

HARVEST: Gently pull fruit from the stem when evenly colored, plump, and slightly soft. Use currants right after picking. Nearly ripe currants can be left on the bush for a week or more before picking. Immature gooseberries make tasty pies.

Powdery mildew on gooseberries.

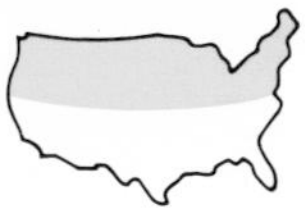

PROBLEM: White powdery material covers leaves and stems. Fruit is covered with a white or brown powdery growth.

ANALYSIS: Powdery mildew
This common plant disease is caused by a fungus (*Sphaerotheca mors-uvae*) that thrives in both humid and dry weather. The powdery patches consist of fungal strands and spores. The spores are spread by the wind to healthy plants. The fungus saps plant nutrients, causing yellowing and sometimes death of the leaf. A severe infection may kill the plant. The white or brown growth on the fruit makes them unpalatable. Under favorable conditions, powdery mildew can spread through a closely spaced planting or a dense bush in a matter of days or weeks.

SOLUTION: Treat the plants with a *lime sulfur* fungicide when the tips of the new leaves show green through the bud. Use a *wettable sulfur* for the following additional three sprays: as the blossoms open, at full bloom, and 2 weeks later. Prune the bushes for good air circulation.

White pine blister rust on currant.

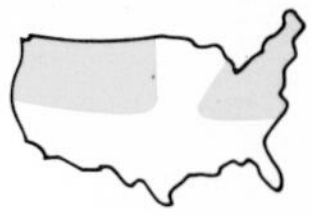

PROBLEM: In midsummer, orange-brown blisters appear on the undersides of older leaves. A yellow material may ooze from the blisters. Leaves turn yellow.

ANALYSIS: White pine blister rust
This plant disease is caused by a fungus (*Cronartium ribicola*) that requires both white pines and currants or gooseberries (*Ribes* species) to complete its life cycle. If either one is not present, the disease does not occur. Wild gooseberries, and black, skunk, stink, and red-flowering currants are all highly susceptible. Cultivated red currants are somewhat resistant. Currants and gooseberries are not severely affected by this disease. However, white pine trees are often killed. Federal and state quarantine laws prohibit planting currants or gooseberries closer than 300 to 900 feet to white pine plantings. In midsummer, yellow spores are produced in blisters on currant or gooseberry leaves, and then blown to pine trees. White blisters form on pine bark and rupture to release another type of spore. These orange-yellow spores are then blown back to currants or gooseberries, where the cycle begins again. For information on this disease on white pine, see page 534.

SOLUTION: Quarantine regulations require elimination of all black currant bushes within 1 mile of white pine plantings. Remove red currant and gooseberry bushes closer than 300 feet to pines.

Red currant varieties resistant to blister rust: Viking and Red Dutch.

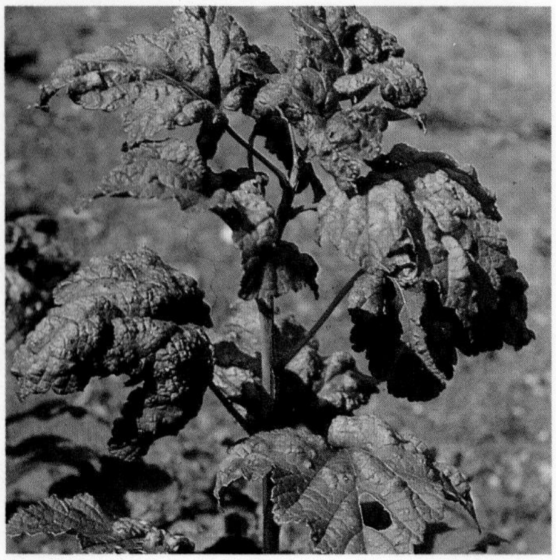
Aphid damage on currant.

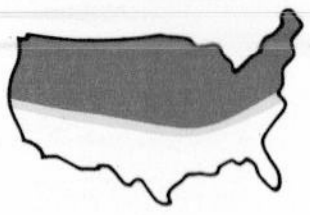

PROBLEM: Leaves are cupped and distorted, and may turn red. Small yellow soft-bodied insects cluster on the undersides of the leaves. A shiny, sticky substance often covers the leaves and fruit.

ANALYSIS: Aphids
Aphids do little damage in small numbers. However, they are extremely prolific and populations can rapidly build up to damaging numbers during the growing season. Damage occurs when the aphid sucks the juices from the currant or gooseberry leaves and flower buds. The aphid is unable to digest fully all the sugar in the plant sap and excretes the excess in a fluid called honeydew. The honeydew is unsightly and makes the fruit undesirable. Ants feed on this sticky substance and are often present where there is an aphid infestation. For more information about aphids, see page 875.

SOLUTION: Spray the plants with an insecticide containing *malathion* as soon as the insects appear. Repeat the spray at intervals of 10 days if the plant becomes reinfested.

Currant borer (4 times life size).

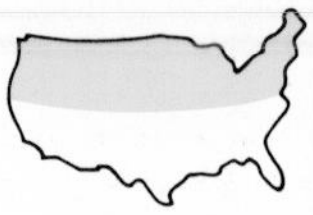

PROBLEM: Leaves turn yellow and wilt in the summer and fall. Canes produce fewer fruits and eventually die. Pale yellow caterpillars, ½ inch long, are found inside the canes.

ANALYSIS: Currant borer
(*Synanthedon tipuliformis*)
This insect pest attacks currants and gooseberries, but red currants are the most susceptible. The borer feeds on the inner cane tissue and weakens the canes, thereby reducing the fruit yield. Weakened canes eventually die. The immature borer hibernates for the winter in the canes and pupates in the spring. In June and July, the adult black and yellow moth emerges and lays eggs on the bark of the canes. The larvae that hatch from these eggs bore into the canes. They feed in the canes all summer and hibernate there for the winter. There is one generation each year.

SOLUTION: The chemical used to control this pest is not available to home gardeners. Contact a pest control operator. Prune out and destroy all infested canes as soon as the borers are noticed. Keep the plants healthy with regular maintenance as outlined on page 721.

EGGPLANT

ADAPTATION: Throughout the United States.

PLANTING TIME: See page 1025.

PLANTING METHOD: Sow eggplant seeds ¼ to ½ inch deep. Thin seedlings or plant transplants to stand 18 to 24 inches apart.

SOIL: Any good garden soil high in organic matter. pH 5.5 to 7.5

FERTILIZER: At planting time, use 3 to 4 pounds of ORTHO Vegetable Food per 100 square feet, or 1 pound per 25-foot row. Side dress every 3 to 4 weeks with 1 pound per 25-foot row, or 1 to 2 tablespoons per plant.
Containers: Water thoroughly every 2 to 4 weeks with a solution of ORTHO Tomato & Vegetable Food.

WATER:
How much: Apply enough water at each irrigation to wet the soil 10 to 12 inches deep.
How often: Water when the soil 2 inches deep is barely moist.

HARVEST: Fruit is usually mature 80 to 90 days after transplanting. Pick it while the skin is glossy, before it turns dull. When you press the skin with your thumb, a slight indentation should remain. Seeds inside should not be brown or hardened. Cut the stem with sharp knife, leaving ½ to 1 inch attached to the fruit. Store in the refrigerator until use.

Flea beetle (twice life size).

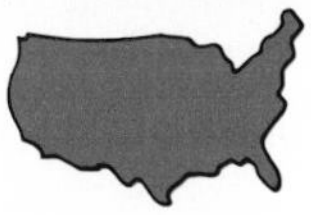

PROBLEM: Leaves are riddled with shotholes about 1/8 inch in diameter. Tiny (1/16 inch) black beetles jump like fleas when disturbed. Leaves of seedlings and eventually whole plants may wilt and die.

ANALYSIS: Flea beetles
These beetles jump like fleas, but are not related to them. Both adult and immature flea beetles feed on a wide variety of garden vegetables, including eggplants. The immature beetle, a legless gray grub, injures plants by feeding on the roots and the lower surface of leaves. Adults chew holes in leaves. Flea beetles are most damaging to seedlings and young plants. Leaves of seedlings riddled with holes dry out quickly and die. Adult beetles survive the winter in soil and garden debris. They emerge in early spring to feed on weeds until vegetable seeds sprout or plants are set in the garden. Grubs hatch from eggs laid in the soil and feed for 2 to 3 weeks. After pupating in the soil, they emerge as adults to repeat the cycle. There are one to four generations a year. Adults may feed for up to 2 months.

SOLUTION: Control flea beetles on eggplants with ORTHO Sevin Garden Dust, ORTHO Tomato & Vegetable Insect Killer, or ORTHO Tomato Vegetable Dust when the leaves first show damage. Watch new growth for evidence of further damage, and repeat the treatment at weekly intervals as needed. Clean all plant debris from the garden after harvest to eliminate overwintering spots for adult beetles.

Colorado potato beetle (life size).

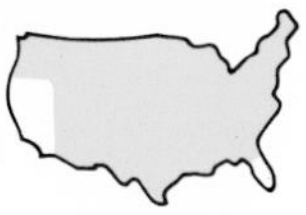

PROBLEM: Yellow beetles 3/8 inch long with black stripes are chewing holes in the leaves. Fat, red, humpbacked grubs with two rows of black dots also feed on the leaves.

ANALYSIS: Colorado potato beetle
(*Leptinotarsa decemlineata*)
This insect pest, also known as the *potato bug*, often devastates eggplant, potato, tomato, and pepper plantings. Both the adults and the larvae damage plants by eating leaves and stems. Small plants are most severely affected. The beetle was originally native to the Rocky Mountains, and spread eastward in the late 1800s as potato plantings increased. Now they are found in all states except California, Nevada, and parts of Florida. In some areas of the country the beetle population may reach epidemic proportions. Adult beetles overwinter in the soil and emerge in the spring as eggplants are set in the garden. They lay orange-yellow eggs on the undersides of the leaves. The larvae that hatch from the eggs are dark red. They feed for 2 to 3 weeks, pupate in the soil, and emerge 1 to 2 weeks later as adults. One generation is completed in a month. There are 1 to 3 generations a year, depending on the part of the country.

SOLUTION: Control Colorado potato beetles with ORTHO Sevin Garden Dust, ORTHO Tomato & Vegetable Insect Killer or ORTHO Tomato Vegetable Dust. Treat when the insects are first noticed, and repeat every 7 days as long as the infestation continues.

Blister beetles (life size).

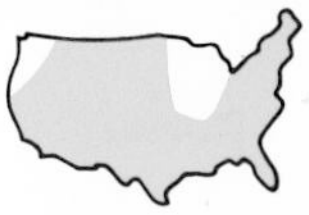

PROBLEM: Leaves are chewed. Black, gray, brown, or yellow beetles cluster on the leaves. These slender beetles range from 1/2 to 3/4 inch long, and are sometimes striped.

ANALYSIS: Blister beetle
(*Epicauta* species)
These insect pests feed on a wide variety of vegetables and flowers. The adult beetles damage plants by chewing the leaves, often defoliating an entire plant. The larvae, however, feed on grasshopper egg masses, and help to reduce the grasshopper population. Adult beetles emerge from hibernation in swarms in June and July. They feed voraciously, and after stripping one plant they move on to another. They lay yellow egg clusters in the soil. The grubs that hatch from these eggs migrate through the soil, feeding on grasshopper eggs. There is only one generation each year. Be careful when handling these beetles; the juices from crushed beetles cause blisters.

SOLUTION: Treat the plants with ORTHO Tomato Vegetable Dust or ORTHO Tomato & Vegetable Insect Spray as soon as the beetles appear in June or July. Repeat the treatments if the plants become reinfested.

EGGPLANT

Tomato hornworm (⅓ life size).

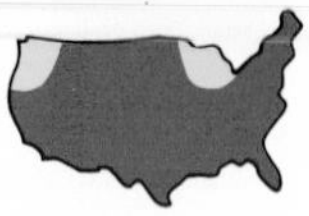

PROBLEM: Fat green or brown worms, up to 5 inches long, with white diagonal side stripes, chew on the leaves. A red or black "horn" projects from the rear end. Black droppings soil the leaves.

ANALYSIS: Tomato hornworm (*Manduca quinquemaculata*) **and tobacco hornworm** (*M. sexta*)
Hornworms feed on the fruit and foliage of eggplants, peppers, and tomatoes. Although there may be only a few worms present, each worm consumes large quantities of foliage and causes extensive damage. The large gray or brown adult moth with yellow and white markings emerges from hibernation in late spring, and drinks nectar from petunias and other garden flowers. The worms hatch from eggs laid on the undersides of the leaves, and feed for 3 to 4 weeks. Then they crawl into the soil, pupate, and later emerge as adults to repeat the cycle. There is one generation a year in the North and two to four in the South. Some worms may have white sacs that look like puffed rice on their bodies. These sacs are the cocoons of parasitic wasps that feed on and eventually kill the hornworm.

SOLUTION: Treat the plants with ORTHO Sevin Garden Dust or ORTHO Tomato & Vegetable Insect Spray. Don't destroy worms covered with white sacs. Let the wasps inside the worms mature, emerge, and infest other hornworms. If practical, handpick unaffected worms.

Whiteflies (half life size).

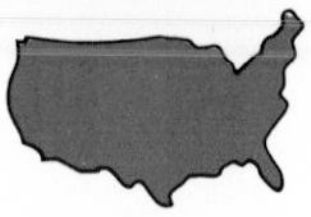

PROBLEM: Tiny, winged insects 1/12 inch long feed on the undersides of the leaves. The insects are covered with white waxy powder. When the plant is touched, insects flutter rapidly around it. Leaves may be mottled and yellowing. In warm winter areas, black mold may cover the leaves.

ANALYSIS: Greenhouse whitefly (*Trialeurodes vaporariorum*)
This insect is a common pest of many garden and greenhouse plants. The four-winged adult lays eggs on the undersides of leaves. The larvae are the size of a pinhead, flat, oval-shaped, and semitransparent, with white waxy filaments radiating from the body. They feed for about a month before changing to the adult form. Both the larval and adult forms suck sap from the leaves. The larvae are more damaging because they feed more heavily. Adults and larvae cannot fully digest all the sugar in the plant sap, and excrete the excess in a fluid called honeydew, which often drops onto the leaves below. A sooty mold fungus may develop on the honeydew, causing the eggplant leaves to appear black and dirty. In warm winter areas the insect can be active year-round, with eggs, larvae, and adults present at the same time. The whitefly is unable to live through freezing winters. Spring reinfestations in freezing winter areas come from migrating whiteflies and from infested greenhouse-grown plants placed in the garden.

SOLUTION: Control whiteflies by spraying with ORTHO Tomato & Vegetable Insect Killer every 7 to 10 days as necessary. Spray the foliage thoroughly, being sure to cover both the upper and lower surfaces of the leaves.

Aphids (life size).

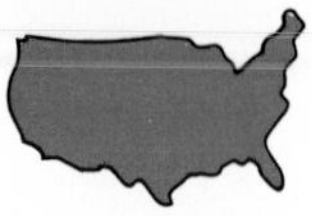

PROBLEM: Leaves are yellow, curled, and often distorted. Soft-bodied insects cluster on the undersides of the leaves and new growth. They are about 1/8 inch long, and may be green, black, or purple. A shiny, sticky substance may coat some of the leaves and fruit.

ANALYSIS: Aphids
Aphids do little damage in small numbers. However, they are extremely prolific and populations can rapidly build up to damaging numbers during the growing season. Damage occurs when the aphid sucks the juices from the eggplant leaves, flower buds, and fruit. The aphid is unable to digest fully all the sugar in the plant sap and excretes the excess in a fluid called honeydew. The honeydew often drops onto the leaves below. Ants feed on this sticky substance, and are often present where there is an aphid infestation. For more information about aphids, see page 875.

SOLUTION: Spray with ORTHO Tomato Vegetable Dust, ORTHO Tomato & Vegetable Insect Spray, or ORTHO Tomato & Vegetable Insect Killer as soon as the aphids appear. Repeat the treatment if the plants become reinfested. Occasionally hose down the plants with a strong stream of water to wash the aphids off.

Blossom about to drop.

PROBLEM: Few or no fruits develop. Those that do develop may have rough skin or be misshapen.

ANALYSIS: Blossom drop
Eggplant, tomato, and pepper blossoms are sensitive to temperature fluctuations during pollination. Normal pollination and fruit set don't occur on eggplant when night temperatures fall below 58°F. At this low temperature the blossoms fall off, often before pollination. However, if pollination has occurred and the fruit has begun to set but isn't completely fertilized, rough and misshapen fruit result.

SOLUTION: Blossom drop only delays fruit production. When the temperatures becomes less extreme a full crop of fruit will set, and the plants will be productive for the rest of the season. Discard rough or misshapen fruit, as they never develop fully. Planting through a black plastic mulch helps provide the heat eggplants require.

Verticillium wilt.

PROBLEM: Plants are stunted. The lower leaves turn yellow. Finally the entire plant wilts and dies. The inside of the stem, near the surface, is discolored brown.

ANALYSIS: Verticillium wilt
This wilt disease affects many ornamental plants. It is caused by a soil-inhabiting fungus (*Verticillium albo-atrum*) that persists indefinitely on plant debris or in the soil. The disease is spread by contaminated seeds, plants, soil, and equipment. The fungus enters the plant through the roots and spreads up into the stems and leaves through the water-conducting vessels in the stems. The vessels become discolored and plugged. This plugging cuts off the flow of water and nutrients to the leaves, causing leaf yellowing and wilting. For more information about verticillium wilt, see page 850.

SOLUTION: No chemical control is available. It is best to destroy infected plants. Verticillium can be removed from the soil only by fumigation techniques. (For more information about soil fumigation, see page 927.) There are no eggplant varieties resistant to this wilt disease. Do not plant members of the tomato family (tomato, pepper, eggplant, potato) or okra in the same area of the garden more frequently than once every 3 years.

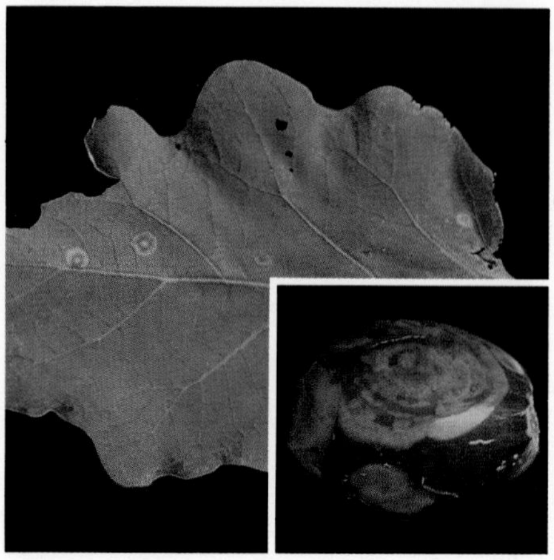

Phomopsis leaf spot. *Insert:* Infected fruit.

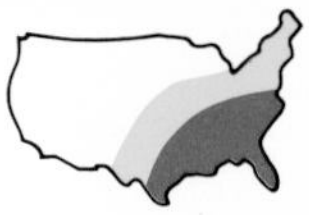

PROBLEM: Circular gray to brown spots with light centers appear on the lower leaves. The spots may be covered with tiny black specks and affected leaves may turn yellow and die. The base of the stem darkens, and the plant falls over easily. Fruit is speckled with pale sunken spots that often spread to include the whole fruit. Fruit then rots and shrivels.

ANALYSIS: Leaf spot and fruit rot
This plant disease is caused by a fungus (*Phomopsis vexans*) that attacks every aboveground part of the plant, and can infect the plant at any stage in its life. It causes the death of seedlings, lesions on the main stem, leaf blight, and fruit rot. The disease is most prevalent in very warm (70° to 90°F), wet weather. The fungal spores spend the winter in and on diseased seeds, plant debris, and soil. They are spread from plant to plant by splashing rain, tools, and insects.

SOLUTION: Treat the plants with ORTHO Tomato Vegetable Dust at the first sign of the disease. Repeat the treatment every 10 to 14 days until harvest. Discard affected fruit and plants immediately. Clean the garden at the end of the season. If the disease develops in your garden, wait 3 years before planting eggplant in that area again.

Eggplant varieties resistant to leaf spot and fruit rot: Florida Beauty, Florida High Bush, and Florida Market.

EGGPLANT

Spider mite damage.

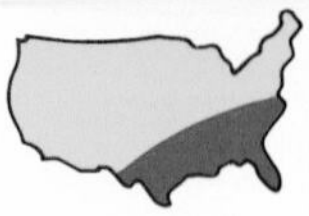

PROBLEM: Leaves are stippled, yellowing, and dirty. Leaves may dry out and drop. There may be webbing over flower buds, between leaves, or on the lower surfaces of the leaves. To determine if the plant is infested with mites, hold a sheet of white paper underneath an affected leaf and tap the leaf sharply. Minute green red or yellow specks the size of pepper grains will drop to the paper and begin to crawl around. The pests are easily seen against the white background.

ANALYSIS: Two-spotted spider mite
(*Tetranychus urticae*)
These mites, related to spiders, are major pests of many garden and greenhouse plants. They cause damage by sucking sap from the underside of the leaves. As a result of feeding, the green leaf pigment disappears, producing the stippled appearance. Mites are active throughout the growing season, but are favored by hot, dry weather (70°F and up). By midsummer, they build up to tremendous numbers. For more information about spider mites, see page 887.

SOLUTION: Treat the infested plants with ORTHO Fruit & Vegetable Insect Control, or an insecticide containing *malathion*, as soon as the damage appears. Repeat the treatment three more times at intervals of 7 to 10 days.

GRAPES

GRAPES

ADAPTATION: Throughout the United States; for regional recommendations, see page 1024.

PLANTING TIME: Spring.

PLANTING METHOD: Purchase 1-year-old rooted vines, either bare-root or in containers. Plant them 6 to 10 feet apart and so that the top of their rootball is even with the surrounding soil. Cut the tops back, leaving only 2 or 3 buds.

SOIL: Any good garden soil that is high in organic matter. pH 6.0 to 8.0

FERTILIZER: At planting time, use 1 pound of ORTHO General Purpose Plant Food per 100 square feet, or 1 tablespoon per plant. For the first year, side-dress with the same amount in midspring and midsummer. In subsequent years, fertilize each spring before new growth begins with ½ to 1 pound of fertilizer per plant.

WATER:
How much: Apply enough water at each irrigation to wet the soil 1½ to 3 feet deep.
How often: Water when the soil 6 to 12 inches deep is almost dry.

HARVEST: Table grapes should taste sweet and be plump with even color. Wine grapes may be slightly tart, but plump and slightly soft with even color.

PROBLEMS WITH THE FRUIT

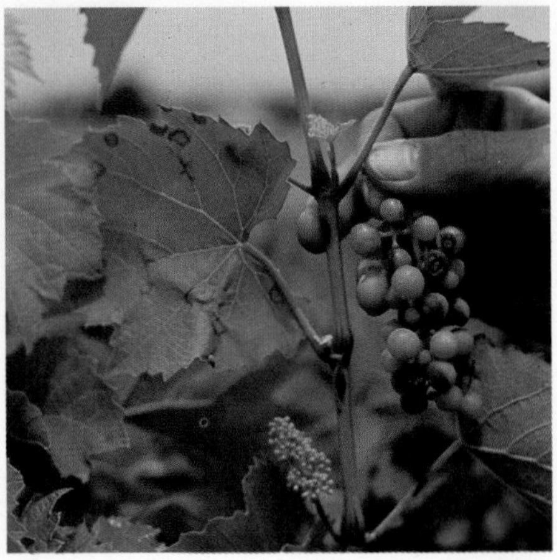

Black rot.

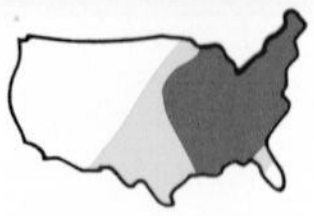

PROBLEM: Light brown spots surrounded by a dark brown line appear on the grapes. The grapes turn black, shrivel, and dry up like raisins. They remain attached to the stems. Reddish brown circular spots appear on the leaves. Sunken purple to black elongated lesions spot the canes, leaf stems, and tendrils.

ANALYSIS: Black rot
This plant disease is caused by a fungus (*Guignardia bidwelli*). It is the most destructive disease that attacks grapes, often destroying all the fruit. The fungus spends the winter in infected dormant canes, tendrils on the support wires, and mummified fruit. In warm, moist spring weather, spores infect new shoots, leaves, tendrils, and eventually the developing fruit. The fruit is affected in all stages of development, but most severely when it is half to two-thirds grown. Spores for future infections are produced on infected leaves, canes, and fruit. The severity of the disease depends on the amount of diseased material that survives the winter, and on the spring and early summer weather.

SOLUTION: Discard all infected fruit and prune out infected canes and tendrils. Once the fruit has begun to shrivel, fungicide sprays are ineffective. Next year, spray the plants with ORTHO Home Orchard Spray. Spray early in the season to keep the spread of the disease to a minimum. Treat when new shoots are 6 to 10 inches long; just before and immediately after bloom; and continue at intervals of 10 to 14 days until the grapes are full size. Treat more frequently if leaf symptoms develop, or if the season is wet. For a list of grapes resistant to this disease, see page 1024.

INSECTS

Grapes damaged by grape berry moth larvae.

PROBLEM: Grapes are webbed together and to leaves. Dark green to purple worms, up to ⅜ inch long, with dark brown heads are inside the grapes. White cocoons cling to the leaves between flaps of leaf tissue.

ANALYSIS: Grape berry moth
(*Endopiza viteana*)
The grape berry moth is the most serious insect pest of grapes in the East. The worms damage both green and ripening fruit by feeding on the inner pulp and seeds. They web the grapes together and to leaves with silken threads as they feed and move from cluster to cluster of grapes. One worm can injure several berries. The worms spend the winters as pupae on leaves and on the ground. The brown moths emerge in early June, and lay eggs on blossom stems and small fruit. The larvae that hatch from these eggs feed on the buds, blossoms, and fruit. After 3 to 4 weeks of feeding, they cut a small bit of leaf, fold it over, and make a cocoon inside, where they pupate. Within a few weeks, adult moths emerge to repeat the cycle, this time laying eggs on ripening fruit. This second generation feeds for 3 to 4 weeks, then pupates for the winter.

SOLUTION: Discard infested grapes. At the end of the season, clean up all fallen grape leaves to reduce the number of overwintering pupae. Next year, treat the plants immediately after bloom with ORTHO Fruit & Vegetable Insect Control or ORTHO Home Orchard Spray. Repeat the application 7 to 10 days later. To control the second generation, spray again in late July to early August.

Leafroller damage.

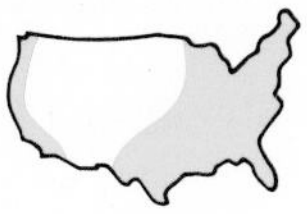

PROBLEM: Leaves are rolled up in a curl. A white webbing covers grape clusters and leaves. Inside the webbing are pale green to yellow caterpillars, up to ¾ inch long, with brown heads. Holes are chewed in leaves and fruit.

ANALYSIS: Redbanded leafroller
(*Argyrotaenia velutinana*)
and omnivorous leafroller
(*Platynota stultana*)
These caterpillars feed on buds, fruit, and leaves in the protection of rolled and webbed leaves and fruit. They feed on the surface of the berry, not inside. They also chew into the cluster stem, so the grape clusters dangle from the plants by a slender thread, causing the fruit to shrivel and drop. Leafrollers spend the winter as larvae and pupae on vines and fruit clusters lying on the ground. As the weather warms in the spring, they emerge and begin feeding on the young foliage. They later pupate and emerge as brown adult moths to lay light green eggs on bark, leaves, and fruit. There are two to three generations a year, so damage may continue from April until October or November.

SOLUTION: Sprays are ineffective once the caterpillars are rolled in the leaves. Pinch rolled leaves or webbing around grapes and leaves to kill the leafrollers inside. Destroy all mummified fruit. Control future generations with ORTHO Home Orchard Spray or ORTHO Malathion 50 Insect Spray. Next year, treat when the shoots are 6 to 8 inches long; when they are 18 inches long; at petal fall; when the fruit is ⅛ inch in diameter; and when the fruit just touch each other in the cluster.

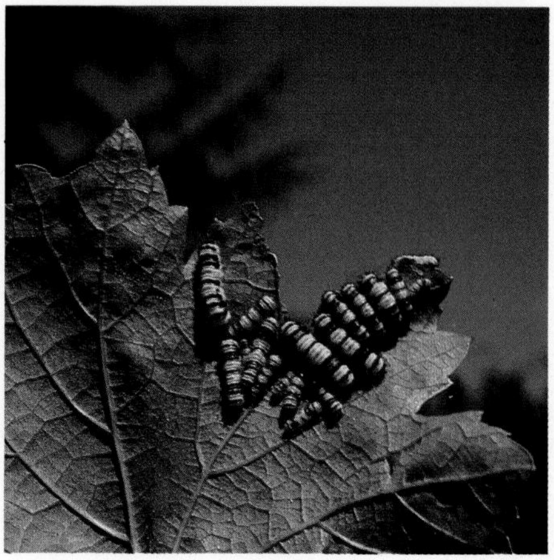
Grape leaf skeletonizers (life size).

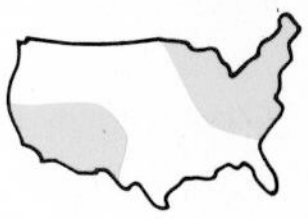

PROBLEM: Yellow caterpillars with purple or black stripes feed in rows on the leaves. The caterpillars may be covered with black spines. They chew on the upper and lower surfaces of the leaves, eating everything but the leaf veins.

ANALYSIS: Grape leaf skeletonizer
(*Harrisina* species)
These pests frequently attack grapes in home gardens and abandoned vineyards. The young caterpillars characteristically feed side by side in a row on the leaves. They feed heartily, and may defoliate a vine in several days. The loss of leaf tissue slows the growth of the vine and fruit, and reduces production. These pests survive the winter as pupae in cocoons on leaves and in debris on the ground. In late spring the metallic green or smoky black adult moths emerge, and lay their eggs on the lower surfaces of the leaves. The yellow caterpillars that hatch from those eggs feed on the leaves, usually chewing on the upper or lower surfaces; but sometimes as they mature, they eat all the tissue between the veins. There are two to three generations each year, so damage continues from mid-May to August. The black spines on the western grape skeletonizer may cause welts on your fingers if you touch them.

SOLUTION: Treat the infested plants with an insecticide containing *carbaryl* (SEVIN®) as soon as the caterpillars appear. Spray both the upper and lower surfaces of the leaves. Repeat the treatment if the plants become reinfested.

GRAPES — INSECTS

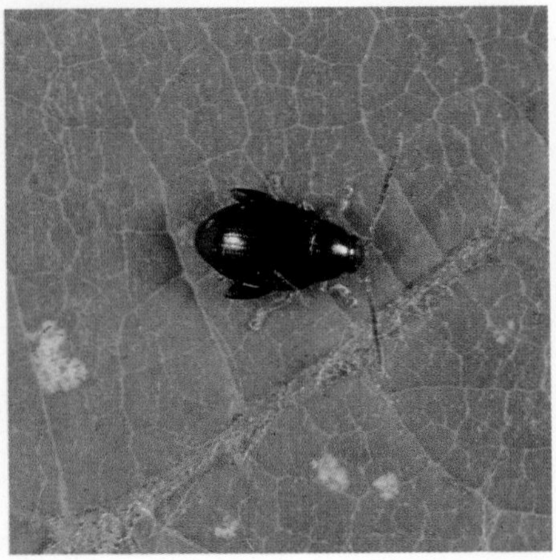
Grape flea beetle (3 times life size).

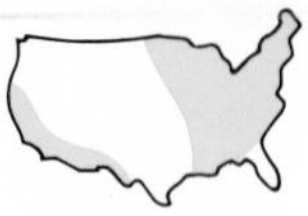

PROBLEM: Metallic, blue-green beetles, 1/5 inch long, feed on buds and unfolding leaves. Brown grubs with black spots damage the foliage by feeding on the upper surfaces of the leaves, causing the lower surfaces to turn brown.

ANALYSIS: Grape flea beetle
(*Altica chalybea*)
Both the adults and larvae of the grape flea beetle damage grape plants. In the early spring, as the leaf buds swell, the adult beetles migrate to the plants from wild grapes and abandoned plantings. They feed on the tender buds, chewing out the centers and destroying future canes. One adult beetle damages several buds; if the beetles are numerous, crop yield and cane growth may be reduced. The adults lay yellow eggs on the buds, bark, and leaves. From June to mid-July the eggs hatch and the larvae feed for 3 to 4 weeks on the leaves. They then pupate in the soil for 1 to 2 weeks, and emerge as adults. The adults feed on new growth through the summer and hibernate for the winter under leaves and other garden debris. There is only one generation each year. Grape flea beetles are most prevalent on neglected plants.

SOLUTION: Treat infested plants with ORTHO Diazinon Insect Spray or ORTHO Home Orchard Spray as soon as these pests appear. Repeat applications 10 to 14 days apart if the beetles reappear.

Aphids (life size).

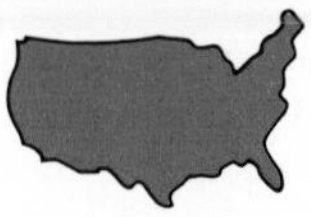

PROBLEM: Leaves are curled, puckered, and distorted. Soft-bodied purple, brown, or green insects cluster under the leaves and on stems and new growth. They may disappear after a heavy rain. Some grapes may drop from the clusters. A shiny, sticky substance may coat the leaves and discolor the fruit. A black sooty fungus may cover affected leaves and fruit.

ANALYSIS: Aphids
Aphids do little damage in small numbers. However, they are extremely prolific and populations can rapidly build up to damaging numbers during the growing season. Damage occurs when the aphid sucks the juices from the grape leaves. The aphid is unable to digest fully all the sugar in the plant sap and excretes the excess in a fluid called honeydew, which often drops onto the leaves below. Ants feed on this sticky substance and are often present where there is an aphid infestation. For more information about aphids, see page 875.

SOLUTION: Treat the infested plants with ORTHO Home Orchard Spray, ORTHO Malathion 50 Insect Spray, ORTHO Diazinon Insect Spray or ORTHO Fruit & Vegetable Insect Control as soon as the aphids appear. Repeat at intervals of 10 to 14 days if the plants become reinfested.

DISCOLORED LEAVES

Grape leafhopper (15 times life size).

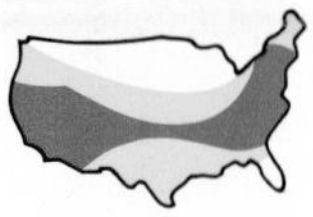

PROBLEM: Areas on the leaves are stippled and turn pale yellow, white, then brown. Some of the leaves may fall. On the undersides of the leaves are found pale yellow or white, 1/8 inch, flying or jumping insects, with red or yellow body markings.

ANALYSIS: Grape leafhoppers
(*Erthroneura* species)
Both the young and adult grape leafhoppers suck the juices from grape leaves, causing white spots that later turn brown. This damage reduces normal vine growth, resulting in delayed maturity of fruit and poor vine growth the following year. Their black droppings may also mar the fruit, making it unappetizing. Leafhoppers survive the winter as adults in protected places. When new growth begins in the spring, these adults emerge and begin feeding. The adults lay their eggs in the leaves, causing blisterlike swellings. There are two or three overlapping generations each season, so leafhoppers of all stages of maturity can be found feeding from the time of new growth in the spring until the leaves drop in the fall.

SOLUTION: Treat infested grape vines with ORTHO Fruit & Vegetable Insect Control, ORTHO Home Orchard Spray, or ORTHO Malathion 50 Insect Spray as soon as leafhoppers are noticed. Spray both the upper and lower surfaces of the leaves. Repeat the treatment at intervals of 10 to 14 days if the plants become reinfested. Clean all plant debris from the planting after harvest to reduce the number of overwintering leafhoppers.

Spider mite damage.

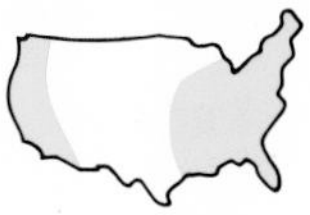

PROBLEM: Leaves are stippled, yellowing, and dirty. Leaves may dry out and drop. There may be webbing between leaves or on the lower surfaces of the leaves. To determine if the plant is infested with mites, hold a sheet of white paper underneath an affected leaf and tap the leaf sharply. Minute green, red, or yellow specks the size of pepper grains will drop to the paper and begin to crawl around. The pests are easily seen against the white background.

ANALYSIS: Spider mites
These mites, related to spiders, are major pests of many garden and greenhouse plants. They cause damage by sucking sap from the undersides of the grape leaves. As a result of feeding, leaf pigment disappears, producing the stippled appearance. Mites are active throughout the growing season, but are favored by hot, dry weather (70°F and up). By midsummer, they build up to tremendous numbers. For more information about spider mites, see page 887.

SOLUTION: Treat the infested grape vines with ORTHO Home Orchard Spray, ORTHO Malathion 50 Insect Spray, or ORTHO Fruit & Vegetable Insect Control as soon as damage appears. Repeat three more times at intervals of 7 to 10 days.

Eutypa dieback.

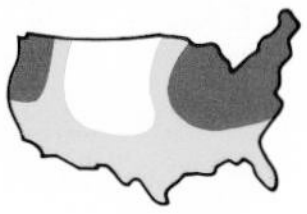

PROBLEM: Dark, irregular spots develop on the young leaves. These spots may drop out, leaving holes in the leaves. Elongated, sunken spots develop on the current season's canes. Shoot growth may be weak and stunted, and the leaves are small, yellowish, and cupped, with crinkled margins. Later in the season, the leaves may become scorched and tattered. Sunken lesions (cankers) may develop on the woody canes and trunk. Entire branches may die.

ANALYSIS: Eutypa dieback
This plant disease is caused by a fungus (*Eutypa armeniacae*). The fungus survives the winter in trunk and branch cankers. Fungal spores that form in the cankers are carried by splashing water to pruning wounds, where they infect the plant. Infection causes the formation of cankers that reduce the flow of water and nutrients through the trunk and branches. The portion of the plant above the canker will weaken and may eventually die.

SOLUTION: Prune out and destroy infected branches and canes. Make the pruning cut at least 6 inches below the canker and any discolored wood. If cankers are present on the trunk, remove and destroy the entire plant, cutting the trunk below the lowest canker but above the bud union. Maintain 2 to 4 suckers on the trunk. The plant will not produce grapes this year but will yield a normal crop next year. Treat fresh pruning wounds with a fungicide containing *benomyl*.

Anthracnose.

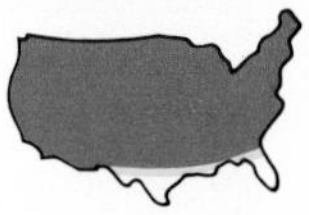

PROBLEM: Circular, sunken spots with light gray centers and dark borders appear on shoots, fruit, tendrils, and leaf stalks. The fruit remains firm. The leaves may curl downward, and the brown areas drop out.

ANALYSIS: Anthracnose
This plant disease is caused by a fungus (*Elsinoe ampelina*) that may do considerable damage a few years in a row, and then disappear. It is often called *birds-eye rot* because of the similarity of the spots on the fruit to a bird's eye. It is seldom severe on Concord or muscadine grape vines. The disease first attacks the new growth. The spots on the stems often merge, girdling the stem and killing the vine tips. Anthracnose is prevalent during wet periods in the spring and in poorly maintained vineyards. The fungus survives the winter on old lesions on the canes. Although this disease doesn't kill the grape vines, the infected fruit are often misshapen and unappetizing. Several years of attack from anthracnose sufficiently weakens the vines to make them more susceptible to other problems.

SOLUTION: Discard infected fruit, and prune out diseased canes. Sprays applied after spotting occurs are ineffective. Next spring, before the buds open, spray the vines with a fungicide containing *lime sulfur*. Treat the plants with a fungicide containing *ferbam* when the shoots are 1 to 2 inches long, when they are 6 to 10 inches long, just before bloom, just after the blossoms fall, and 2 to 3 more times at intervals of 2 weeks. Spray all canes and leaves thoroughly.

GRAPES — DISCOLORED LEAVES

Armillaria root rot.

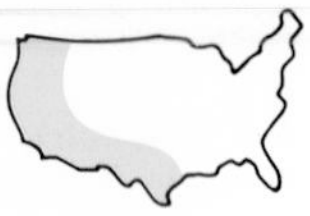

PROBLEM: Leaves are reddened or yellow. Shoot growth is stunted. Few grapes are produced. Plants decline, produce no new growth, and die. In the fall and winter, honey-colored mushrooms 2 to 5 inches in diameter may develop singly or in clusters on the lower trunks or on the soil. Black rootlike strands somewhat smaller than the diameter of a pencil lead grow in the soil out of larger roots. A white, fan-shaped growth occurs between the bark and the wood of large roots and on the main stem just below the soil line.

ANALYSIS: Armillaria root rot

This plant disease, also called *oak root fungus* and *shoestring root rot*, is caused by a fungus (*Armillaria mellea*) that attacks the roots of many woody and nonwoody plants. Plants under stress from severe drought, overwatering, physical injury, insects, or disease are the most susceptible to attack. Once the fungus enters the plant, it produces the white fungal strands under the bark that invade and decay the roots and lower trunk. Water and nutrient uptake are inhibited, causing the foliage and branches to die. In the fall and winter, mushrooms appear at the base of the plant. For more information on this disease, see page 851.

SOLUTION: No chemical controls are available that are suitable for the home gardener. Remove and destroy infected plants, including the stump and root. Check the roots and stems of surrounding plants, and remove if infected. Avoid planting grapes in recently cleared forest land, especially where old oak trees existed.

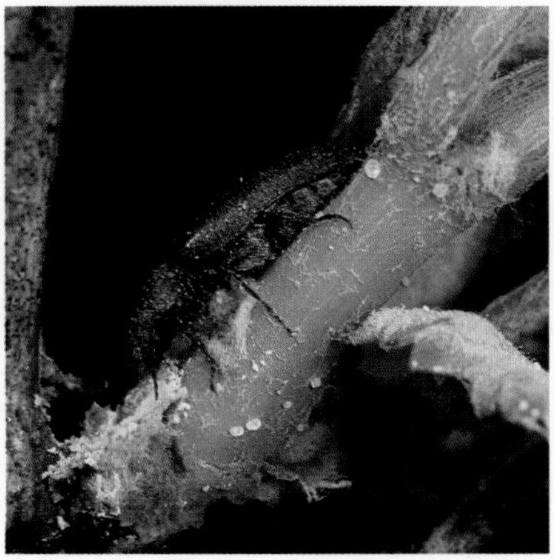

Twig and branch borer (3 times life size).

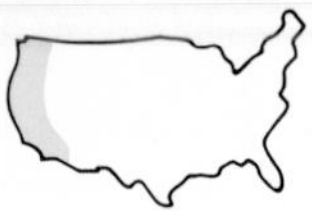

PROBLEM: Grape shoots wilt and die. Holes about 1/8 inch in diameter appear in the year-old wood below the shoots. A white flaky material is exuded from the hole. Inside the shoots are 1/2-inch white grubs.

ANALYSIS: Twig and branch borer
(*Polycaon confertus*)

This insect pest is common in grape plantings neighboring brushy or wooded areas, or in plantings adjacent to piles of year-old prunings or dead vines. The borers damage grape vines by boring into the base of succulent new shoots. Infested shoots are weak and frequently break during wind storms. Sap flows freely from damaged branches. A few broken or dead shoots will not severely damage grape plants, but when borers are numerous many of the leaves may drop, weakening the vine. The brownish black adult beetles emerge from hibernation in mid to late spring, chew holes about 1/8 inch in diameter in the base of the tender shoots, and lay their eggs. The larvae that hatch from these eggs feed inside the branch, mining downward through the pith. The borers pupate and spend the winter in the dormant canes. There is only one generation a year.

SOLUTION: No chemical controls are available. Prune out and destroy any shoots infested with the borers. Remove and destroy all dead vines. Destroy all pruned brush from adjacent orchards, vineyards, and shade trees before the grape vines start growth each spring. Keep the plants healthy with regular maintenance as outlined on page 726.

Powdery mildew.

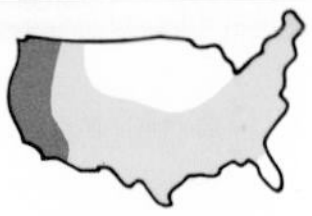

PROBLEM: The upper surfaces of the leaves, the fruit, and cluster stems are covered with a white powdery growth. Leaves turn brown and fall. Fruit may be rusty or scaly.

ANALYSIS: Powdery mildew

This common plant disease is caused by a fungus (*Uncinula necator*) that thrives in both humid and dry weather. It is encouraged by warm days and cool nights. The powdery patches consist of fungal strands and spores. The spores are spread by the wind to healthy leaves. The fungus saps the plant nutrients, causing yellowing and sometimes the death of the leaf. Seriously affected leaves retard fruit ripening. The vine's overall vigor may be reduced, resulting in poor wood maturity and increased susceptibility to winter damage. Fruit may also be attacked. Powdery mildew is a major problem in the West. Under favorable conditions, powdery mildew can spread through a closely spaced planting in a matter of days or weeks.

SOLUTION: Treat infected grape plants with ORTHO Flotox Garden Sulfur or a spray containing *folpet* (PHALTAN®) at the first sign of the disease. Clean up and discard any debris around the plants at the end of the season. Next year, begin spraying the plants when the shoot growth is 4 to 6 inches long, and repeat at intervals of 2 weeks for four to six applications. Sulfur sprays may burn leaves when temperatures are above 85°F.

BIRDS

Bird damage.

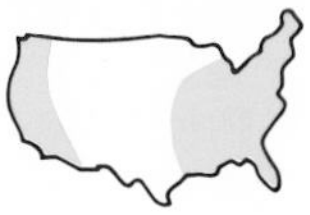

PROBLEM: Ripening grapes disappear. Some may be broken, with holes pecked in them. Birds are active in the grape planting.

ANALYSIS: Birds
Starlings, robins, finches, grackles, and blackbirds like the sweetness of ripe grapes. Entire bunches of grapes may disappear within a few hours. Birds are hearty eaters, and if not discouraged from the vineyard, may devour all the grapes in a planting. The sugar level in grapes increases during the ripening process. As the grapes approach maturity, birds keep a watchful eye on their progress. Birds seem to be more attracted to the wine or vinifera type grapes than to the American bunch types. Early-ripening varieties and those with red or black fruit are most often attacked. However, when they are hungry, birds are not choosy.

SOLUTION: To protect ripening grapes, put a brown paper bag or cheesecloth over each cluster as it begins to ripen. Do not use plastic bags, because moisture will build up inside. Pick grapes promptly as they ripen. Bird netting placed over the plants and secured at the base with rocks or logs also protects the bunches. Nets are available at garden centers. For more information on birds in the garden, see page 899.

GROWTHS ON LEAVES

Grapevine tomato gall.

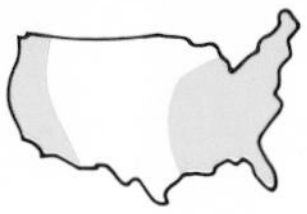

PROBLEM: Green to deep red round or slender swellings appear on grape leaves, canes, or tendrils. Greenish yellow to red grubs may be found inside.

ANALYSIS: Galls
Tiny insects, called gall wasps or gall midges cause different types of galls to develop on grapes. The growths may be round, slender, or pear-shaped. Each species of insect (midge, nonstinging wasp, or weevil) causes its own type of gall to form. The galls are caused by a chemical that the insect injects into the plant tissue. The mature female lays her eggs on various parts of the plant. The eggs hatch into legless grubs that cause galls to form around themselves. The insects feed and develop inside the galls, mature, and either spend the winter there or emerge to produce another generation. Young, tender growth is the most susceptible to attack. Most galls do not harm the vines. However, one gall maker, the grape phylloxera, attacks the roots and leaves and interrupts the flow of nutrients in the vines, killing the plants.

SOLUTION: Chemical controls are not necessary for galls. Prune out and destroy severely infested leaves and canes before the grubs inside emerge.

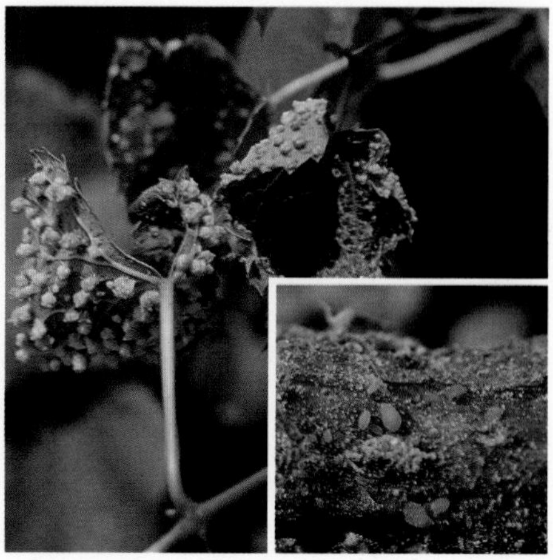

Galls. *Insert:* Grape phylloxeras (3 times life size).

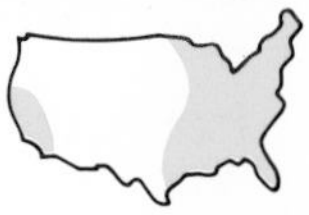

PROBLEM: Vines grow slowly and produce few clusters of grapes. Very often plants die. Tubers or swellings are found on the roots. Pea-shaped galls that are open on the underside may appear on the leaves.

ANALYSIS: Grape phylloxera
(*Phylloxera vitifoliae*)
The grape phylloxera is a serious pest of grape vines in California and Europe. In the late 1800s it killed almost a third of the vineyards in France before it was discovered that American-type grapes were resistant, and that European varieties could be grafted onto these rootstocks and then be planted in phylloxera-infested soil. This orange to yellow aphidlike pest is native to the eastern United States, where cultivated grapes have become resistant to its attack, and only wild grapes are affected. There are two forms of this pest. One form, found only in the East, attacks the leaves and roots. The other form, found only in California, attacks only the roots. The grape phylloxera sucks the juices from the roots, causing galls to form. These galls interrupt the nutrient flow in the roots, and the vines become stunted and unproductive, and often die. American-type varieties that are commonly grown in the East are resistant to this pest, but the European types or vinifera varieties grown in California are very susceptible. French hybrid types are only mildly affected.

SOLUTION: There are no chemical controls for the grape phylloxera for home gardeners. Select resistant American grape varieties, or plant European varieties with phylloxera-resistant rootstocks.

GRAPES

Downy mildew.

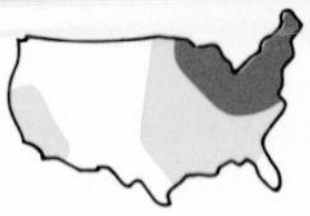

PROBLEM: Small yellow spots appear on the upper surfaces of the leaves. The surfaces are covered with a white cottony growth. Older leaves are affected first. Leaves, shoots, and tendrils turn brown and brittle, and are often distorted. Grapes may be covered with the white growth, or they may be shriveled and brown, yellow, or red.

ANALYSIS: Downy mildew
This plant disease is caused by a fungus (*Plasmopara viticola*) that attacks grape foliage and fruit from before bloom to the end of harvest. Downy mildew causes leaf defoliation and prevents proper ripening. When the disease is severe, entire grape clusters may be killed. Reduced vine vigor results in poor growth the following season. This disease is more prevalent in cool, moist weather, and is always more serious in rainy growing seasons. The most damage occurs during August and September. The fungus survives the winter in diseased leaves on the ground.

SOLUTION: Discard severely infected leaves and fruit. At the first sign of the disease, spray the vines with a fungicide containing *captan* (ORTHOCIDE®) or *folpet* (PHALTAN®). Repeat every 10 days until 7 days before harvest. Remove all plant debris from the vineyard at the end of the season to reduce the number of overwintering spores. Next year, spray just before bloom, just after bloom fall, when the grapes are about the size of peas, and every 10 days thereafter until 7 days before harvest.

Concord grape is resistant, but not immune, to downy mildew.

HERBS

ADAPTATION: Throughout the United States.

PLANTING TIME: See page 1025.

PLANTING METHOD: Transplants or seeds.

SOIL: Any good garden soil. pH 6.0 to 7.5.

FERTILIZER: At planting time, use 1 to 2 pounds of ORTHO Vegetable Food per 100 square feet, or ½ pound per 25-foot row. Side dress every 6 to 8 weeks with ½ pound per 25-foot row, or ½ teaspoon per plant.
Containers: Water thoroughly every 4 to 6 weeks with a solution of ORTHO Tomato & Vegetable Food.

WATER:
How much: Apply enough water at each irrigation to wet the soil 10 to 12 inches deep.
How often: Water when the soil 1 inch deep is dry.

HARVEST: Pick young leaves for use any time. Flavor is best just before blooming. After the dew dries in the morning, snip leaves or sprigs with sharp scissors. Wash and use or hang to dry. After herbs are thoroughly dry, store in an airtight container. Never harvest more than a third of the plant at a time.

Caterpillars feeding on dill (life size).

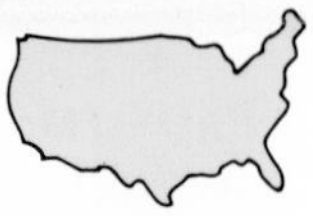

PROBLEM: Holes appear in the leaves and buds. Leaves, buds, and flowers may be entirely chewed off. Worms or caterpillars are feeding on the plants.

ANALYSIS: Caterpillars
Many species of these moth or butterfly larvae feed on herbs and many other garden plants. Some common caterpillars include budworms, hornworms, and loopers. As a rule, the adult moths or butterflies begin to lay their eggs on garden plants with the onset of warm weather in the spring. The larvae that emerge from these eggs feed on the leaves, flowers, and buds for 2 to 6 weeks, depending on weather conditions and species. Mature caterpillars pupate in cocoons attached to leaves or structures, or buried in the soil. There may be one to several overlapping generations during the growing season. The last generation of caterpillars in the fall survives the winter as pupae. The adult moths and butterflies emerge the following spring.

SOLUTION: If practical, handpick caterpillars as they appear. Or spray with the bacterial insecticide *Bacillus thuringiensis*.

LETTUCE

ADAPTATION: Throughout the United States.

PLANTING TIME: See page 1025.

PLANTING METHOD: Sow seeds ¼ inch deep. Thin seedlings or set transplants 4 to 6 inches apart. For a continuous harvest, plant some seeds or plants every 2 weeks.

SOIL: Any good garden soil. pH 6.0 to 7.0

FERTILIZER: At planting time, use 3 to 4 pounds of ORTHO Vegetable Food per 100 square feet, or 1 pound per 25-foot row. Side-dress every 3 to 4 weeks with 1 pound per 25-foot row, or 1 to 2 tablespoons per plant; or fertilize with a solution of ORTHO Tomato & Vegetable Food.

WATER:

How much: Apply enough water at each irrigation to wet the soil 8 to 10 inches deep.

How often: Water when the soil 1 inch deep is barely moist. Do not allow the soil to dry out.

HARVEST: Cut plants with a sharp knife in the early morning.

Head types: Head should be full and firm. Cut just above the soil line.

Looseleaf types: The entire plant may be cut when it is the size of your hand; or pick the outer leaves as you need them, leaving a few center leaves for future picking.

Bibb lettuce bolting.

PROBLEM: A seed stalk emerges from the center of the lettuce plant. The lettuce tastes bitter.

ANALYSIS: Bolting

Lettuce is a cool-weather crop, and grows best between 55° and 60°F. When temperatures rise above 60°F for several days in a row, the plants will form a flower stock if they are mature enough. As the stalk grows, sugars and nutrients are withdrawn from the leaves for the growth of the stalk, making the leaves bitter and tough. The formation of a flower stalk in vegetables that are grown for their leaves is known as "bolting." Once bolting begins, it cannot be stopped; cutting off the stalk does not help.

SOLUTION: If it is harvested as soon as bolting begins, the lettuce may still be edible, but quality deteriorates rapidly as the stalk forms. In the future, plant lettuce so that it matures during cool weather, or grow varieties that are slow to bolt.

Lettuce varieties that are resistant to bolting:

Head—Great Lakes 659.

Loose Leaf—Oak Leaf, Royal Oak Leaf, Salad Bowl, and Slo-Bolt.

Butterhead—Augusta, Buttercrunch, Butter King, Green Lake, and Hot Weather.

Potato aphid (5 times life size).

PROBLEM: Leaves turn yellow and may be distorted, curled, and puckered. Pale green, yellow, or purple insects, some with 3 dark lines on the back, cluster on the undersides of the leaves.

ANALYSIS: Aphids

Aphids do little damage in small numbers. However, they are extremely prolific and populations can rapidly build up to damaging numbers during the growing season. Damage occurs when the aphid sucks the juices from the lettuce leaves. The green peach aphid (*Myzus persicae*) may also spread lettuce mosaic virus, which dwarfs lettuce plants, rendering them unproductive. (For more information on lettuce mosaic virus, see page 736.) The green peach aphid is pale green with 3 dark lines on the back. Its shiny black eggs spend the winter on the bark of fruit trees. About the time peach trees bloom, the eggs hatch and the aphids begin feeding, first on the tree, then migrating to vegetable and flower plants.

SOLUTION: Control aphids on lettuce with ORTHO Fruit & Vegetable Insect Control, ORTHO, Tomato & Vegetable Insect Killer or ORTHO Malathion 50 Insect Spray as soon as the aphids appear. Repeat the spray if the plant becomes reinfested.

To rid lettuce of aphids at harvest time, swish the head or leaves in a solution of ½ cup salt in a bucket of water. The aphids and other insects will drop off the lettuce. Rinse the lettuce thoroughly afterwards.

LETTUCE

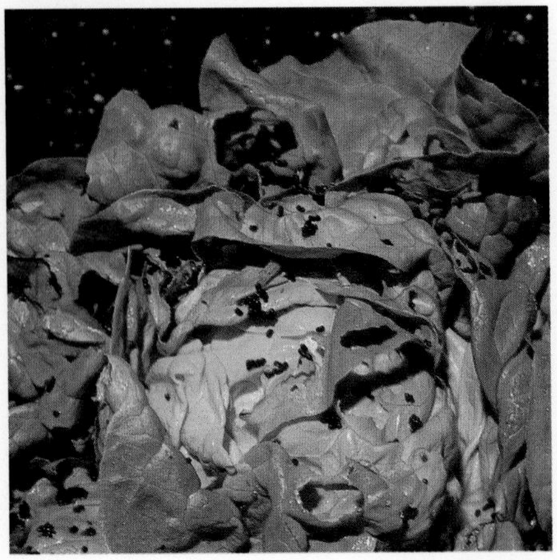
Cabbage looper damage and droppings.

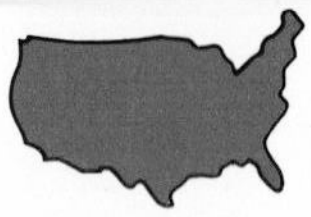

PROBLEM: Leaves have round or irregular holes. Green worms up to 1½ inches long, with light stripes down their backs, feed on the leaves or heads. Masses of green or brown pellets may be found between the leaves.

ANALYSIS: Cabbage looper
(*Trichoplusia ni*)
Several worms attack lettuce, the most damaging of which is the cabbage looper. The looper attacks all varieties of lettuce, as well as members of the cabbage family. Adults lay eggs throughout the growing season. The brownish cabbage looper moth lays pale green eggs on the upper sides of the leaves in the evening. The worms eat lettuce leaves and heads. Their greenish brown excrement makes the plants unappetizing. Worms may be present from early spring until late fall. In the South, they may be present all year. Worms spend the winter as pupae attached to a plant or nearby object.

SOLUTION: Control cabbage loopers with ORTHO Fruit & Vegetable Insect Control, ORTHO Tomato & Vegetable Insect Killer, ORTHO Sevin Garden Dust, or with the bacterial spray *Bacillus thuringiensis. Bacillus thuringiensis* is effective only while the caterpillars are small. Repeat treatments at weekly intervals if the plants become reinfested. Clean all plant debris from the garden to reduce the number of overwintering pupae.

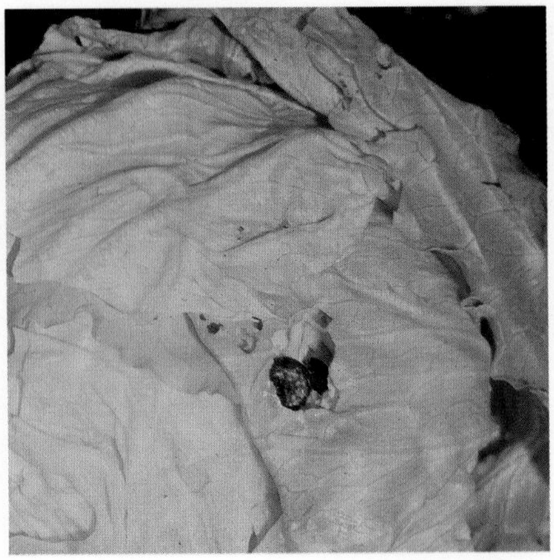
Cutworm (⅓ life size).

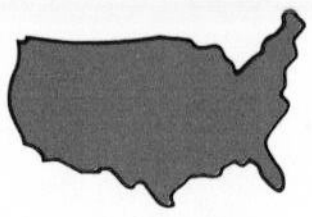

PROBLEM: Young plants are chewed or cut off near the ground. Gray, brown, or black worms, 1½ to 2 inches long, may be found about 2 inches deep in the soil near the base of the damaged plants. The worms coil when disturbed.

ANALYSIS: Cutworms
Several species of cutworms attack plants in the vegetable garden. The most likely pests of lettuce plants in the spring are the surface-feeding cutworms. A single surface-feeding cutworm can sever the stems of many young plants in one night. Cutworms hide in the soil during the day, and feed only at night. Adult cutworms are dark, night-flying moths with bands or stripes on their forewings. In the South, cutworms may also attack fall-planted lettuce.

SOLUTION: Apply ORTHO Diazinon Soil & Turf Insect Control,ORTHO Vegetable Guard Soil Insect Killer, or ORTHO Diazinon Soil & Foliage Dust around the base of undamaged plants when stem cutting is observed. Since cutworms are difficult to control, it may be necessary to repeat the dusting at weekly intervals. Before transplanting into the area, apply a preventive treatment of ORTHO Vegetable Guard Soil Insect Killer or ORTHO Diazinon Soil & Turf Insect Control and work it into the soil. Cultivate the soil thoroughly in late summer and fall to expose and destroy eggs, larvae, and pupae. Further reduce damage with "cutworm collars" around the stem of each plant. These collars can be made of stiff paper or aluminum foil. They should be at least 2 inches high, and pressed firmly into the soil.

Leafhopper (8 times life size).

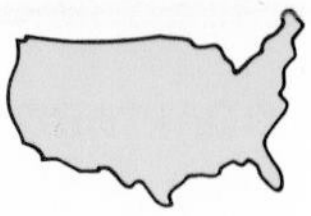

PROBLEM: Spotted, pale green insects up to ⅛ inch long hop or fly away quickly when a plant is touched. The leaves are stippled and may turn brown.

ANALYSIS: Aster leafhopper
(*Macrosteles fascifrons*)
This insect, also known as the *six-spotted leafhopper*, feeds on many vegetable and ornamental plants. It generally feeds on the undersides of leaves, sucking the sap, which causes stippling. This leafhopper transmits *aster yellows*, a plant disease that can be quite damaging. (For further details, see page 736.) Leafhoppers at all stages of maturity are active during the growing season. They hatch in the spring from eggs laid on perennial weeds and ornamental plants. Even areas where the winters are so cold that the eggs cannot survive are not free from infestation because leafhoppers migrate in the spring from warmer regions.

SOLUTION: It is important to keep leafhoppers under control because, in addition to their feeding damage, they can infect plants with aster yellows. Spray infested plants with ORTHO Fruit & Vegetable Insect Control, ORTHO Malathion 50 Insect Spray, ORTHO Tomato & Vegetable Insect Killer, or ORTHO Sevin Garden Dust at the first sign of infestation, being sure to cover the lower surfaces of the leaves. Repeat the spray as often as necessary to keep the insects under control, leaving at least 10 days between applications. Eradicate nearby weeds, especially thistles, plantains, and dandelions, which may harbor leafhopper eggs and aster yellows. For more information about disease-carrying insects, see page 879.

Tip burn.

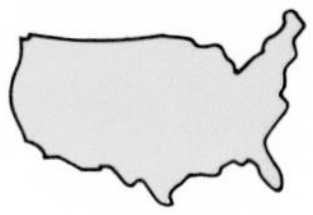

PROBLEM: Small, dark brown spots appear ¼ inch from the margins of outer and inner leaves. Spots enlarge and the entire margins die and turn brown. Leaves may become slimy and black.

ANALYSIS: Tip burn
This problem on lettuce is caused by a lack of calcium in the leaves. There is probably enough calcium in the soil, but it is not being transported to the leaf tips. Tip burn is most severe when lettuce is grown under conditions of fluctuating soil moisture. The disease frequently occurs when bright, warm days follow damp or foggy weather. Overmature heads and rapidly growing succulent plants are particularly susceptible to injury. Leaf lettuce varieties are seldom affected. Head varieties are affected after the plants have begun to develop solid heads. Soft rot organisms often invade the dead tissue and turn the plants slimy and black.

SOLUTION: Clip off the brown tissue and use the rest of the head. Keep the soil evenly moist, letting the surface dry out slightly between waterings. Pick the heads when they are mature. Grow loose-leaf types or resistant head varieties (see page 1027).

Bottom rot.

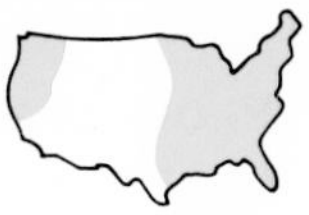

PROBLEM: Rust-colored sunken spots appear on the lower leaf stems and midribs, especially on leaves touching the ground. The entire leaf then turns brown and slimy. The infection spreads to adjacent leaves until the entire head is infected. The head may dry and shrivel into a mummylike form.

ANALYSIS: Bottom rot
This plant disease is caused by a fungus (*Rhizoctonia solani*) that is widespread on lettuce grown in soil high in organic matter, or after a period of excessive rainfall. Head lettuce is more commonly affected than loose-leaf types. The fungus lives in the soil and on diseased plant debris. The spores infect the head whenever the plant is large enough to retain dampness between itself and the moist soil. This is usually after the head has developed and is approaching maturity. The lower leaves or those touching the soil are the first infected.

SOLUTION: There are no chemical controls for this disease. Harvest infected heads immediately, discarding the infected leaves. Store the healthy portion in the refrigerator. Pick healthy heads as soon as possible so they don't become infected. Harvest every other head to improve air circulation and reduce the chances of infection. Plant lettuce in well-drained soil or raised beds, spacing the plants 5 to 8 inches apart in rows 12 to 14 inches apart. Or grow lettuce in containers. Plant lettuce in the same area only once every 4 years. Other years plant nonsusceptible crops such as sweet corn and onions. Tomatoes, celery, and cabbage are also susceptible to bottom rot.

Watery soft rot. *Insert:* Close-up.

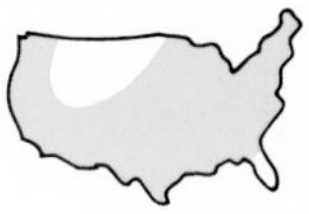

PROBLEM: A water-soaked area develops on the stem near the soil line. As it extends upward the outer leaves die, wither, and droop to the ground. The head becomes wet and slimy. In moist weather a thick white cottony mold covers the head. White, gray, or black pellets about the size of a pea are found in the mold and between dead leaves.

ANALYSIS: Watery soft rot
This plant disease, also called *white mold*, is caused by a fungus (*Sclerotinia sclerotiorum*) that attacks many vegetables in the garden, including lettuce. All parts of the plant may be infected. The infection starts on the stem and spreads downward, rotting the roots. As it spreads upward, the outer leaves die and the head rots. This fungus is most active in moderate (55° to 75°F), wet weather. Moisture on the leaves from rain, fog, dew, or irrigation provides the water necessary for infection. The spores survive the winter inside pellets in the soil and plant debris. They are generally spread by diseased plant parts and the wind.

SOLUTION: There are no chemical controls for this disease. Remove and destroy all infected plants at the first sign of the disease. Avoid overhead watering by using drip or furrow irrigation. Clean all plant debris from the garden after harvest to reduce the amount of overwintering spores. Rotate your lettuce planting site every year into an area where the disease has not yet occurred.

Mosaic virus.

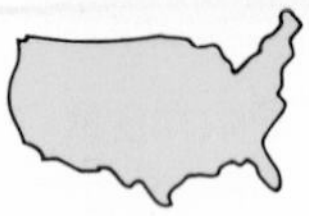

PROBLEM: Leaves turn yellow or are mottled light green and yellow. The veins are pale, and the leaf edges may curl inward or be ruffled. The plants are stunted, and heading varieties don't produce heads.

ANALYSIS: Mosaic virus
This plant disease is caused by at least two viruses that attack all varieties of lettuce. It is most evident in cool, cloudy weather, usually disappearing in midsummer. The viruses usually enter the garden in infected seed, but they may also live in weeds, including wild lettuce, pokeweed, wild cucumber, and groundsel. Once the infection is present in the garden, aphids, primarily the green peach aphid, spread the viruses from plant to plant. The viruses can also be transmitted mechanically as diseased and healthy plants rub together. Symptoms appear 8 to 14 days after infection. Occasionally a plant will show symptoms and then recover and grow to normal size.

SOLUTION: Once the symptoms occur, there are no practical controls. Discard severely infected plants; they will produce very little. If the plants are infected just before harvest, they are still edible. There are no resistant varieties. Buy lettuce seed from a reputable company. Do not save seed from infected plants. Control aphids with ORTHO Fruit & Vegetable Insect Control, ORTHO Tomato & Vegetable Insect Killer, or ORTHO Malathion 50 Insect Spray, repeating at intervals of 7 to 10 days if the plants become reinfested. For information on controlling disease-carrying insects, see page 879. For information about aphids, see page 733.

Aster yellows.

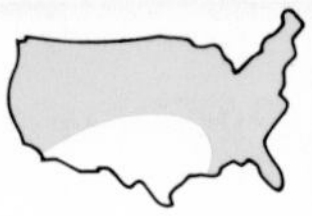

PROBLEM: Heart leaves turn pale yellow to white. They may be short, thick stubs. Pink to tan latex deposits occur on leaf midribs and deep in the heart of mature plants. Plants are stunted and fail to head.

ANALYSIS: Aster yellows
This plant disease is caused by mycoplasmas, microscopic organisms similar to bacteria. The mycoplasmas are transmitted from plant to plant primarily by leafhoppers. (For information about leafhoppers, see page 734.) The symptoms of aster yellows are more severe and appear more quickly in warm weather. Even when the disease is present in the plant, aster yellows may not manifest its symptoms in temperatures of 55°F or less. Infected lettuce heads are often bitter. The disease also infects celery, onion, potato, and several ornamentals and weeds. For a list of plants susceptible to aster yellows, see page 1005.

SOLUTION: Aster yellows cannot be eliminated entirely, but can be kept under control. Remove and destroy infected plants. To remove sources of infection, eradicate nearby weeds that may harbor aster yellows and leafhopper eggs. Spray leafhopper-infested plants with ORTHO Fruit & Vegetable Insect Control, ORTHO Tomato & Vegetable Insect Killer, or ORTHO Malathion 50 Insect Spray. Repeat the spray whenever leafhoppers are seen. For more information about disease-carrying insects,see page 879.

OKRA

ADAPTATION: Throughout the warmer areas of the United States.

PLANTING TIME: See page 1025.

PLANTING METHOD: Soak seeds overnight in warm water for better germination. Plant them ½ to 1 inch deep. When they have 2 or 3 leaves, thin to stand 1 to 2 feet apart.

SOIL: Any good garden soil high in organic matter. pH 6.0 to 7.5.

FERTILIZER: At planting time, use 1 to 1½ pounds of ORTHO Vegetable Food per 25-foot row. Side-dress every 4 to 6 weeks with ½ to 1 pound per 25-foot row.

WATER:
How much: Apply enough water at each irrigation to wet the soil 12 to 14 inches deep.
Containers: 10 percent of the water should drain from the bottom of the container.
How often: Water when the soil 1 inch deep is dry.

HARVEST: Cut pods close to the stem with a sharp knife or shears when they are about 4 inches long, and before they become fibrous. A knife should pass easily through a mature, edible pod. Harvest every 2 or 3 days so the plants will continue to produce. Handle pods carefully to avoid bruising them. Store in the refrigerator.

Corn earworm (life size).

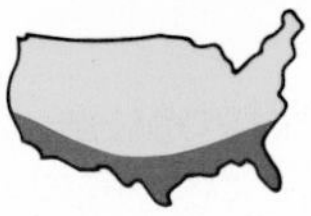

PROBLEM: Holes are chewed into the okra pods. Inside the pods are striped yellow, green, or brown worms ¼ to 2 inches long. These worms may also be feeding on the leaves.

ANALYSIS: Corn earworm
(*Heliothis zea*)
The corn earworm, also known as the *tomato fruitworm* or *cotton bollworm*, attacks many vegetables and flowers. The worms feed on the foliage, and also chew holes in the fruit, making them worthless. The worm is the larva of a light gray-brown moth with dark lines on its wings. In the spring, the moth lays yellow eggs on leaves and stems. The worms that hatch from these eggs feed on the new leaves. When they are about ½ inch long, the worms move to the pods and bore inside. After feeding for 2 to 4 weeks, they drop to the ground, pupate, and emerge in several weeks as adults. There are several generations a year. In the South, where these pests survive the winter, early and late plantings suffer the most damage.

SOLUTION: Once the worms are inside the pods, sprays are ineffective. Handpick and destroy infested pods.
Clean all plant debris from the garden after harvest to reduce the number of overwintering adults. Next year treat your plants with ORTHO Sevin Garden Dust when the worms are feeding on the foliage, or when the pods are about ½ to 1 inch long. Repeat in 2 to 4 weeks if the plants become reinfested.

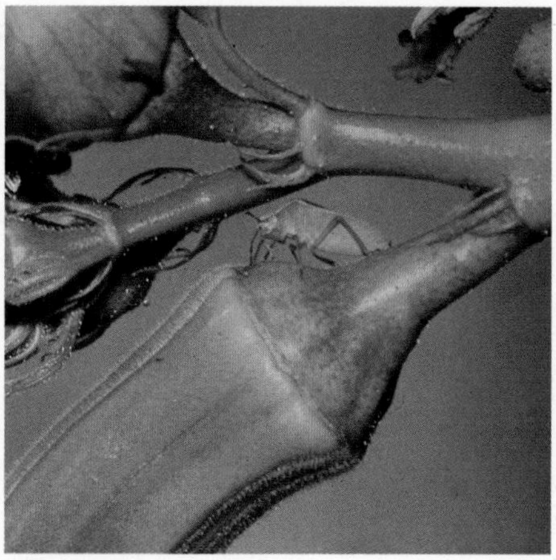

Stink bug (twice life size).

PROBLEM: Fruit is distorted and spotted with hard calluses. Some fruit may drop. Green, blue, or red insects, ⅝ inch long and shaped like a shield, are found on the plants.

ANALYSIS: Stink bugs
Stink bugs attack a wide variety of vegetables including okra, squash, beans, peas, and tomatoes. They get their name because they emit a strong odor when crushed. Both the adults and nymphs damage okra plants by sucking the sap from buds, blossoms, and fruit. This feeding causes the fruit to become distorted and dimpled. Hard calluses form around the spot where the stink bug inserted its mouthparts to feed. Young tender growth is the most susceptible to attack. In the spring, stink bugs lay clusters of eggs on the undersides of the leaves. Young stink bugs look like smaller versions of the adult. There are several generations each year, so damage occurs throughout the growing season.

SOLUTION: Treat infested okra plants with ORTHO Sevin Garden Dust as soon as stink bugs or their damage are noticed. Repeat at intervals of 5 to 7 days if the plants become reinfested.

Nematode damage.

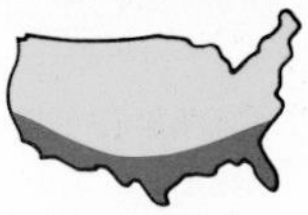

PROBLEM: Plants are stunted and yellow, and wilt in hot, dry weather. Few pods are produced. Round or elongated nodules occur on the roots.

ANALYSIS: Nematodes
Nematodes are microscopic worms that live in the soil. They are not related to earthworms. Nematodes feed on plant roots, damaging and stunting them. The damaged roots can't supply sufficient water and nutrients to the aboveground plant parts, and the plant is stunted or slowly dies. Nematodes are found throughout the United States, but are most severe in the South. They prefer moist, sandy loam soils. Nematodes can move only a few inches each year on their own, but they may be carried long distances by soil, water, tools, or infested plants. Testing roots and soil is the only positive method for confirming the presence of nematodes. Contact your local Cooperative Extension Office (see page 1029) for sampling instructions and addresses of testing laboratories. Soil and root problems such as poor soil structure, drought stress, nutrient deficiency, and root rots can also produce symptoms of decline similar to those caused by nematodes. These problems should be eliminated as causes before sending soil and root samples for testing. For information on soil problems and root rots, see pages 907 and 849.

SOLUTION: There are no chemicals available to homeowners to kill nematodes in planted soil. However, they can be controlled before planting by soil fumigation. For information on fumigating soil, see page 927.

ONION FAMILY (ONIONS, GARLIC, SHALLOTS, CHIVES, AND LEEKS)

ADAPTATION: Throughout the United States.

PLANTING TIME: See page 1025.

PLANTING METHOD:
Onions: Sow onion seeds ½ inch deep and thin to stand ¼ to 3 inches apart. Plant sets 1 to 2 inches deep, side by side or up to 3 inches apart. Set transplants 2 to 3 inches deep and 3 to 5 inches apart. When growing for green onions, plant bulbs closer than when growing for dry onions. For a continuous harvest, plant every couple of weeks.
Garlic: Plant individual cloves 1 to 2 inches deep and 5 to 6 inches apart.
Shallots: Plant individual sections 1 to 1½ inches apart and 3 to 5 inches apart.
Chives: Sow seeds ½ inch deep. Thin seedlings or set transplants to grow 8 inches apart. Plant transplants so that the top of their rootball is even with the surrounding garden soil.
Leeks: Plant as for onion transplants or seeds.

SOIL: Loose, crumbly soil that is rich in organic matter. pH 6.0 to 7.0

FERTILIZER: At planting time, use 2 pounds of ORTHO General Purpose Plant Food per 100 square feet, or 1½ pounds per 50-foot row. Side-dress every 3 to 4 weeks with 1 pound per 25-foot row.

WATER:
How much: Apply enough water at each watering to wet the soil 8 to 10 inches deep.
How often: Water when the soil 2 inches deep is barely moist.

HARVEST:
Green onions: Pull the largest as needed, when about pencil size.
Dry onions: Harvest when half or more of the tops have turned yellow and fallen over. Dry in a warm, airy spot for 4 to 5 days. Shake off loose soil and skins. Place bulbs in a slatted crate or mesh bag, and continue drying in a well-ventilated, dry area for 2 to 4 weeks. After drying, store in a dry area between 35° and 40°F.
Garlic: Harvest when the tops dry; cure as for dry onions.
Shallots: Treat like dry onions.
Chives: Snip with sharp shears any time there are young, fresh leaves. Use fresh, or dry or freeze for later use.
Leeks: For white stems, gradually hill soil around the plants through the growing season. Pick when the stems are ¾ to 1 inch in diameter. Store in a root cellar or in the refrigerator until used.

Onion seedstalk.

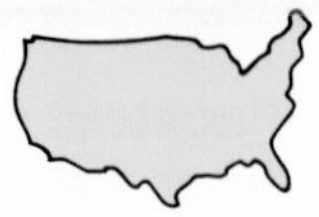

PROBLEM: A tall seedstalk emerges from the onion bulb. Purple or white flowers bloom on top.

ANALYSIS: Seedstalk formation
Onions prefer cool temperatures in their early growth, and warm temperatures near maturity. When temperatures fluctuate between cool and warm, the plants may become dormant. Dormancy then initiates seedstalk formation. Plants from larger bulbs or sets form seedstalks more readily than do those from smaller bulbs. As the seedstalk grows, sugars and nutrients are withdrawn from the bulb for the growth of the stalk, inhibiting future bulb enlargement. Once the seedstalk begins growing, it cannot be stopped; cutting off the stalk does not help.

SOLUTION: Onion bulbs with seedstalks are still edible, but should not be stored. Harvest and use bulbs as soon as possible. In the future, plant onions recommended for your area at the proper time. See page 1025 for a list of regional onion recommendations and planting times.

Onion maggot damage.

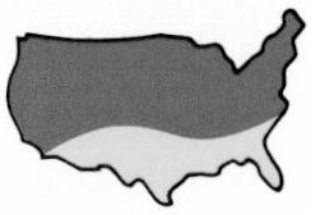

PROBLEM: Plants grow slowly, turn yellow, wilt, and die. Bulbs may rot in storage. White legless maggots, up to ⅓ inch long, burrow inside the bulb.

ANALYSIS: Onion maggot
(*Hylemya antiqua*)
This fly larva is the most serious pest of onions. The larvae burrow into the onion bulb, causing the plant to wilt and die. Once the bulb is damaged by the mag-got's feeding, it is susceptible to attack by bacterial soft rot. Early plantings are the most severely injured. When the on-ions are young and growing close to-gether, the maggots move easily from one bulb to another, destroying several plants. Cool, wet weather favors serious infestations. Maggots spend the winter as pupae in plant debris or in the soil. The brownish gray adult fly emerges in the spring to lay clusters of white eggs at the base of plants. The maggots that hatch from these eggs burrow into the soil and bulbs. After feeding, they pu-pate in the soil and emerge as adults to repeat the cycle. There are two or three generations a year, the last one attacking onions shortly before they are harvested. When maggot-infested bulbs are placed in storage, the maggots continue to feed and damage the bulbs.

SOLUTION: Discard and destroy mag-got-infested onions. Clean all debris from the garden at the end of the season to reduce the number of overwintering pupae. At planting time, treat the soil in the row with ORTHO Diazinon Soil & Fo-liage Dust, ORTHO Vegetable Guard Soil Insect Killer, or ORTHO Diazinon Soil & Turf Insect Control. Repeat the treatment 7 to 10 days after plants emerge through the soil.

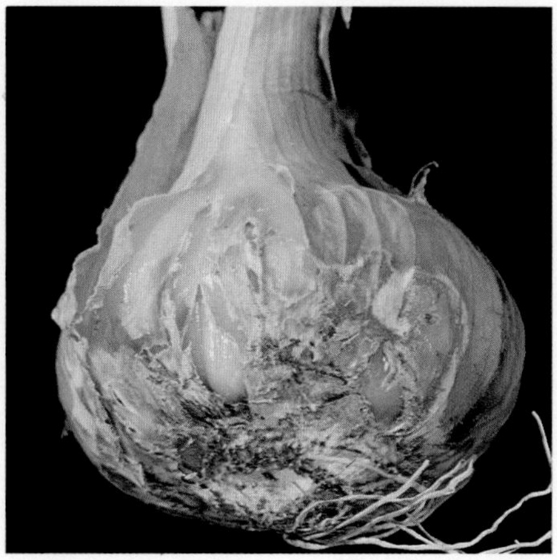

Fusarium basal rot.

PROBLEM: Leaf tips wilt and die back. The neck of the bulb is soft. A white fungal growth may appear on the base of the bulb. The bulb is soft and brown inside. Bulbs may also be affect-ed in storage.

ANALYSIS: Fusarium basal rot
This plant disease is caused by a soil-in-habiting fungus (*Fusarium* species) that attacks onions, shallots, garlic, and chives. It persists indefinitely in the soil. The disease is spread by contaminated bulbs, soil, and equipment. The fungus enters the bulb through wounds from maggots and old root scars, and spreads up into the leaves, resulting in leaf yel-lowing and dieback. Bulbs approaching maturity are the most susceptible to at-tack. If infection occurs during or after harvest, the rot may not show until the bulbs are in storage. Fusarium basal rot is most serious when bulbs are stored in a moist area at temperatures above 70°F.

SOLUTION: No chemical controls are available. Destroy infected plants and bulbs. Harvest healthy bulbs promptly at maturity. Dry according to the instruc-tions on page 738. Fusarium can be re-moved from the soil only by fumigation techniques. For information on soil fumi-gation, see page 927. Control onion maggots to reduce chances of infection. Store bulbs in a cool (35° to 40°F), dry area. Rotate the planting site if possible.

Pink root.

PROBLEM: Plants grow slowly and their tops may be stunted. Roots turn light pink, shrivel, then a darker pink, and die. Leaves may turn yellow or white and die.

ANALYSIS: Pink root
This plant disease is caused by a fungus (*Pyrenochaeta terrestris*) that attacks on-ions, garlic, shallots, leeks, and chives. It persists indefinitely in the soil, and in-fects plants at all stages of growth. Mature and weakened bulbs are the most susceptible to attack. Plants infect-ed early in their life seldom produce large bulbs. Pink root is favored by warm (60° to 85°F) weather.

SOLUTION: No chemical control is available. Discard all infected plants. Pink root fungus can be removed from the soil only by fumigation techniques. (For information on soil fumigation, see page 927.) Weak plants are the most sus-ceptible to attack, so keep the plants healthy with adequate water and nutri-tion, as discussed on page 738. Grow varieties that are resistant to pink root (see page 1027).

ONION FAMILY

Neck rot.

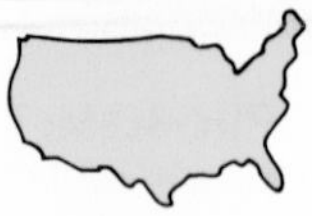

PROBLEM: Just before harvest, or in storage, sunken dry areas develop on the bulb. Gray mold grows between the inside tissues of the bulb. A crusty layer of hard black tissue develops around the neck.

ANALYSIS: Neck rot
This plant disease is caused by a fungus (*Botrytis allii*). It is seldom evident on onions, shallots, and garlic while they are growing on the ground but appears after harvest and during storage. Neck rot develops only on bulbs that are injured or diseased. Infection most commmonly occurs on bulbs that have not been properly harvested. The fungus penetrates the bulb through the trimmed tops if they have not dried completely and are still succulent at harvest. The fungus may also attack elsewhere on the bulbs through man-made, insect, and disease injuries. Neck rot often rots the inside of the bulb before the injury shows on the outside. Infected bulbs are susceptible to a soft rot and are foul-smelling. The neck rot fungus overwinters in infected bulbs and plant debris left in the garden. The spores are spread to susceptible plant tissue by wind and water. Infections may occur in moist conditions between 50°and 75°F.

SOLUTION: There are no recommended fungicides to control this disease. Harvest bulbs only when plant tops turn yellow and fall over naturally. Put the bulbs in a slatted crate or mesh bag, and continue drying in a well-ventilated, dry area for 2 to 4 weeks, then store in a dry area between 35° and 40°F. If roots appear, the area is too moist; if tops sprout, the temperature is too high.

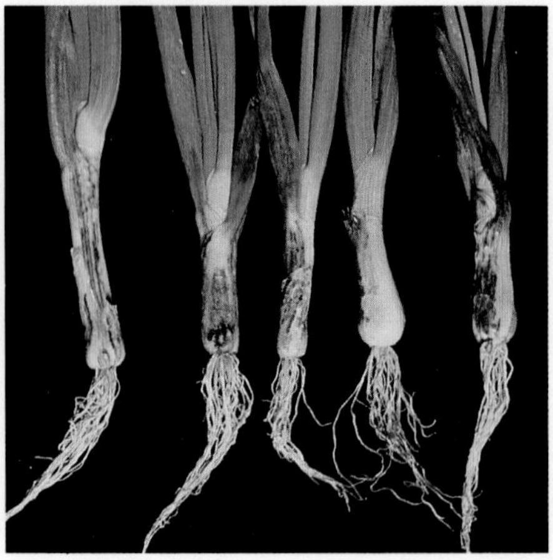

Smut on green onions.

PROBLEM: Black elongated streaks or blisters appear on seedling leaves, break open, and emit a black powdery substance. Seedlings may die.

ANALYSIS: Smut
This plant disease is caused by a fungus (*Urocystis cepulae*) that attacks onions, leeks, and shallots. Garlic is not affected. The disease persists in the soil for several years, attacking only seedlings. The seedlings are susceptible to attack only from the second day of seed germination until the seedling has one leaf—a period of approximately 10 to 15 days. Many seedlings may die from smut, requiring replacement. If the seedling does survive, the bulb is often distorted, with dark streaks and lesions. Smut is prevalent in cool summer areas with soil temperatures between 60° and 75°F. The black fungal spores live in the soil. They often enter a garden initially on diseased sets or plants.

SOLUTION: Sprays are not effective on infected seedlings. Discard all diseased plants. Since only seedlings are attacked, grow onions from sets or transplants, rather than from seeds. Select clean sets and transplants free of black streaking or stripes. If using seeds, dust the soil at planting time with a fungicide containing *thiram*, *chlorothalonil* (DACONIL 2787®), or *captan* (ORTHOCIDE®).

Purple blotch.

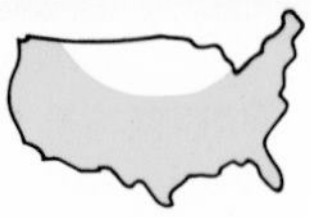

PROBLEM: Pale yellow, slightly sunken spots with purple centers and yellow margins appear on the leaves. The spots enlarge rapidly, covering the entire leaf. In moist weather, the spots may be covered with a brown to black powdery growth. Bulbs in storage may be rotted around the neck, and yellow to wine-red inside.

ANALYSIS: Purple blotch
This plant disease is caused by a fungus (*Alternaria porri*) that attacks onions, garlic, and shallots. Infection often occurs following injury from other fungi or insects. Plants are seldom killed, but bulbs infected in storage are inedible. The fungal spores pass the winter in infected bulbs and plant debris left in the garden. Infection occurs and spreads rapidly in warm (75° to 80°F), rainy weather or heavy dew.

SOLUTION: Spray infected plants with a fungicide containing *maneb*, *zineb*, or *chlorothalonil* (DACONIL 2787®) as soon as blotches appear on the leaves. Repeat at weekly intervals until dry weather resumes. Discard infected bulbs in storage. To prevent infection in storage, dry harvested bulbs properly as outlined on page 738. Clean all debris from the garden at the end of the season.

Downy mildew.

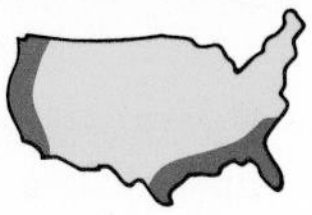

PROBLEM: Pale green to yellow spots appear on the outer, older leaves. In humid weather, a fuzzy purple growth may cover these spots. The entire leaf eventually yellows, drops over, and dies. Young leaves may be twisted and distorted. The bulb is soft and small.

ANALYSIS: Downy mildew
This plant disease is caused by a fungus (*Peronospora destructor*) that attacks onions and shallots primarily, although garlic, leeks, and chives are also susceptible. The occurrence of downy mildew may be sporadic—appearing 1 year and disappearing the next—or it may continue for several consecutive years. It is most prevalent during cool, moist nights and warm, cloudy days. Most infections occur when the temperature is between 50° and 65°F. Downy mildew is especially troublesome, and many plants are killed, during periods of heavy dew or high humidity. If dry weather resumes before the plant dies, new growth may emerge. The spores are spread from plant to plant by the wind, and die rapidly when exposed to the sun and low humidity.

SOLUTION: Treat infected plants with a fungicide containing *zineb* or *maneb* at the first sign of the disease. Repeat at intervals of 7 to 10 days as long as weather conditions continue that are favorable for the spread of the disease. For best results, add a spreader-sticker to the spray. (For instructions on using spreader-stickers, see page 922.) The recommended fungicides will not cure infected leaves, but will protect healthy ones from infection. Avoid overhead watering by using drip irrigation.

Onion thrips damage (life size).

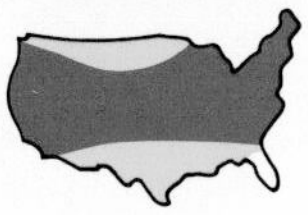

PROBLEM: White streaks or blotches appear on onion leaves. Tips may be distorted. Plants may wilt, wither, turn brown, and die. Bulbs may be distorted and small.

ANALYSIS: Onion thrips
(*Thrips tabaci*)
Onion thrips attack many vegetables, including onions, peas, and cabbages. Thrips are barely visible insects, less than 1/25 inch long, dark brown to black. They reduce the quality and yield of onion bulbs by rasping holes in the leaves and sucking out the plant sap. This rasping causes the white streaks. Plants often die when thrips populations are high. Damage is most severe in the leaf sheath at the base of the plant. Thrips favor this protected area where the elements and pesticides have difficulty reaching them. Onion thrips survive the winter in grass stems, plant debris, and bulbs in storage. Thrips are active throughout the growing season; in warm climates they are active all year.

SOLUTION: Treat infested onion plants with ORTHO Fruit & Vegetable Insect Control, ORTHO Vegetable Guard Soil Insect Killer, or ORTHO Diazinon Soil & Foliage Dust at the first sign of thrips damage. Repeat at weekly intervals until the new growth is no longer damaged.

PARSLEY

ADAPTATION: Throughout the United States.

PLANTING TIME: See page 1025.

PLANTING METHOD: For best germination, soak seeds in warm water overnight. Then plant 1/4 to 1/2 inch deep. Thin seedlings or set transplants to grow 3 to 6 inches apart. Plant transplants so the top of their rootball is even with the surrounding garden soil.

SOIL: Any good garden soil that is rich in organic matter. pH 5.5 to 7.5

FERTILIZER: At planting time, use 2 tablespoons of ORTHO Vegetable Food for each plant, or 1 pound per 25-foot row. Side-dress every 3 to 4 weeks with 1 to 2 tablespoons per plant, or 1 pound per 25-foot row.

WATER:
How much: Apply enough water at each irrigation to wet the soil 8 to 10 inches deep.
How often: Water when the soil 2 inches deep is moist but not wet.

HARVEST: Snip or pinch parsley stems after the plants are at least 6 inches tall. Store in the refrigerator until use. Parsley can also be frozen or dried. To dry, place sprigs on a screen in a shady, well-ventilated area. To freeze, wash and dry parsley sprigs and immediately freeze in plastic bags or containers.

PARSLEY

Parsleyworm (life size).

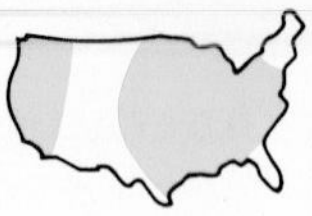

PROBLEM: Parsley leaves are eaten. Green worms, 2 inches long, with a black band on each body segment, feed on the leaves. When disturbed, these worms emit a sickly sweet odor, and two orange horns project behind the head.

ANALYSIS: Parsleyworm
(*Papilio polyxenes asterius*)
This insect pest is the larva of the *black swallowtail butterfly*. It is also called the *celeryworm*. As its names suggest, it feeds on parsley and celery, as well as on dill and parsnips. Although seldom a serious pest, these worms may strip plants of foliage. In the North, they spend the winter in tan cocoons hanging from host plants. The adult butterfly overwinters in the South. The butterfly has black wings spotted with yellow, orange, and blue dots, and a wingspan of 3 to 4 inches. The worms that hatch from eggs laid on the leaves feed on the foliage for several weeks, pupate in suspended cocoons, and emerge as adults to repeat the cycle. There are two to four generations a year.

SOLUTION: Handpick as the worms appear. They are seldom serious enough to warrant sprays. However, if they are numerous, treat with an insecticidal spray containing *malathion* or the bacteria *Bacillus thuringiensis. Bacillus thuringiensis* is effective only while the caterpillars are small.

PARSNIPS

PARSNIPS

ADAPTATION: Throughout the United States.

PLANTING TIME: See page 1025.

PLANTING METHOD: Sow seeds ½ inch deep directly in the garden. Thin to stand 3 to 4 inches apart. Parsnip seeds germinate slowly (up to 30 days) and poorly, so plant twice as many seeds as the number of plants you need.

SOIL: Light, crumbly, and free from rocks and clods. pH 6.0 to 7.0

FERTILIZER: At planting time, use 2 pounds of ORTHO Vegetable Food per 100 square feet, or ¾ pound per 25-foot row. Side dress every 3 to 4 weeks with ¾ pound per 25-foot row.

WATER:
How much: Apply enough water at each irrigation to wet the soil 15 to 18 inches deep.
How often: Water when the soil 1 inch deep is barely moist. Do not let the soil dry out.

HARVEST: For best flavor, parsnips should be exposed to a frost or continuous cold weather. They can remain in the garden through the winter, or be stored in moist sand in a cool garage or root cellar. Dig carefully, being careful not to damage the foot-long root.

Poor germination.

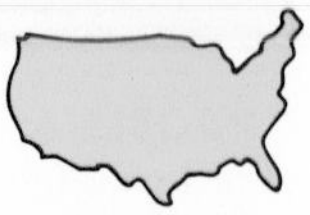

PROBLEM: Seeds germinate slowly, or not at all.

ANALYSIS: Poor germination
Parsnip seeds take longer to germinate than most other vegetables, requiring 21 to 25 days to sprout. Be sure the soil is well drained and loose, or the seedlings may have difficulty pushing up through the heavy soil. Loose soil also gives the root room to expand and makes harvesting easier. Parsnip seeds are seldom attacked by insects or diseases.

SOLUTION: The percentage of seeds that germinate is usually low, so increase your chances of success by soaking the seeds in warm water for 24 hours before planting. Sow the seed heavily. Plant seeds ½ inch deep in rows 15 to 18 inches apart. Thin the seedlings to stand 3 to 4 inches apart when they are 1 inch tall. Radish seeds planted along with parsnip seeds will break the soil and loosen any crust before parsnip seedlings emerge. Or keep the soil from crusting by covering the seed row with burlap strips, sand, or vermiculite. Parsnip seeds are short-lived, so buy fresh seed every year.

PEAS

ADAPTATION: Throughout the United States.

PLANTING TIME: See page 1025.

PLANTING METHOD: Plant peas 1 to 2 inches deep and 1 to 4 inches apart directly in the soil outdoors. Do not thin.

SOIL: Any good garden soil. pH 5.5 to 7.5

FERTILIZER: At planting time, use 3 pounds of ORTHO Vegetable Food per 100 square feet, or 1 pound per 25-foot row. Side-dress every 3 to 4 weeks with 1 pound per 25-foot row.

WATER:
How much: Apply enough water to wet the soil 8 to 10 inches deep.
How often: Water when the soil 1 inch deep is barely moist.

HARVEST:
Garden peas: Pick as soon as the peas fill the pods. Pods should be tender and bright green. Faded pods are overmature, and peas inside will be tough and starchy.
Edible podded peas: Harvest pods when peas inside just begin to form and pods are tender and bright green.
Southern or blackeye peas: Pick when the pods change from deep green to light yellow, silver, red, or purple, depending on the variety. Seeds inside should be fully developed but not hard.

Hot weather damage.

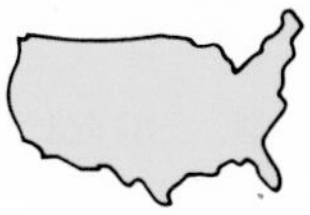

PROBLEM: Pea plants stop producing pods. Leaves turn yellow, then brown, wither, and die.

ANALYSIS: Hot weather
The garden pea is a cool season vegetable. It grows best with daytime temperatures below 80°F and nighttime temperatures below 65°F. When temperatures are hotter than this, the plants stop producing and gradually die. In the South, garden peas grow best in the fall, winter, and spring. In the North, grow them as a spring and fall crop.

SOLUTION: Plant peas early enough in the season so they mature in cool weather. Follow the cultural guidelines on page 743 so the plants grow quickly with high yields. Grow varieties that are tolerant of hot weather.

Pea varieties that are heat tolerant: Freezer 692, Sugar Snap, and Wando.

Powdery mildew.

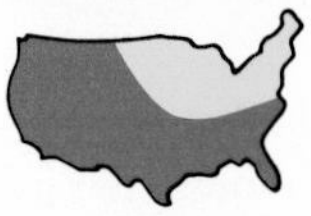

PROBLEM: A white powdery coating develops first on the upper surfaces of the lower leaves. Stems, pods, and other leaves may then become infected. Leaves may turn yellow and be malformed. Pods may be distorted, with dark streaks or spots.

ANALYSIS: Powdery mildew
This common plant disease is caused by a fungus (*Erysiphe polygoni*) that thrives in both humid and dry weather. The powdery coating consists of fungal strands and spores. The spores are spread by the wind to healthy plants. The fungus saps plant nutrients, causing yellowing and sometimes death of the leaf. A severe infection reduces pea yield considerably, and may kill the plant. Fall crops are most susceptible to serious damage; spring crops are attacked late in the season. Since this powdery mildew attacks many vegetables, the fungus from a diseased plant may infect other plants in the garden. (For a list of susceptible plants, see page 1006.) Under favorable conditions, powdery mildew can spread through a planting in a matter of days or weeks.

SOLUTION: Treat plants with ORTHO Flotox Garden Sulfur. Repeat at intervals of 7 to 10 days as needed. This fungicide does not cure infected leaves, but does protect healthy ones from infection.

PEAS

Ascochyta blight.

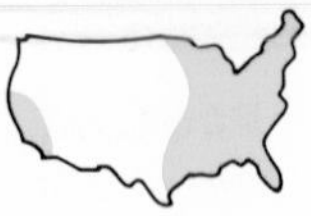

PROBLEM: Small, light brown to purple spots appear on leaves, stems, and pods. Spots enlarge, turning brown to black, and may have gray centers and purple margins. Concentric rings may appear in the spots. Lower leaves shrivel and drop off. The stem may darken at the soil line, and the plant may die.

ANALYSIS: Ascochyta blight
This plant disease is caused by several fungi that attack both garden peas and sweet peas. All parts of the plant are affected. Ascochyta blight is favored by warm (65° to 80°F), wet weather. The fungal spores overwinter in plant debris left in the garden, and are spread to susceptible plants by splashing water and moist winds. The disease is also spread through infected seeds. When infected seeds are planted, they either don't sprout or sprout into weak seedlings that soon die. Although slightly blemished pods and peas are unattractive, they are still edible.

SOLUTION: No chemical controls are available. Discard infected plants and clean the garden thoroughly at the end of the season. Buy pea seeds from a reputable dealer, and plant in well-drained soil.

Pea aphids (twice life size).

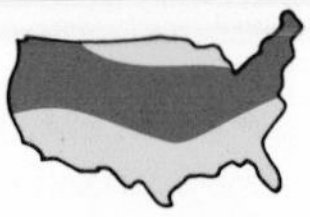

PROBLEM: Plants turn yellow and wilt. Pods may not be completely filled with peas. Clustered on the leaves, especially the young, tender ones, are tiny, soft-bodied, light to deep green insects with red eyes. Leaves may be covered with a sticky material or black powder.

ANALYSIS: Pea aphid
(*Acyrthosiphon pisum*)
Several species of aphids attack peas, but the most common and damaging is the pea aphid. Aphids generally do little damage in small numbers. However, they are extremely prolific and populations can build up to damaging numbers during the growing season. Damage occurs when the aphid sucks the juices from the pea leaves, stems, blossoms, and pods. This feeding results in stunted plants and fewer and smaller pods that may be only partially filled with peas. The aphid is unable to digest fully all the sugar in the plant sap and excretes the excess in a fluid called honeydew. The honeydew often drops onto the leaves below. Ants feed on this sticky substance, and are often present where there is an aphid infestation. Some aphids also transmit viruses, plant diseases which can be quite damaging. Infected pea plants and pods are distorted, and plants sometimes die. For more information on viruses, see page 861.

SOLUTION: Spray infested plants with ORTHO Fruit & Vegetable Insect Control or ORTHO Malathion 50 Insect Spray as soon as the aphids appear. Repeat the spray if the plants become reinfested.

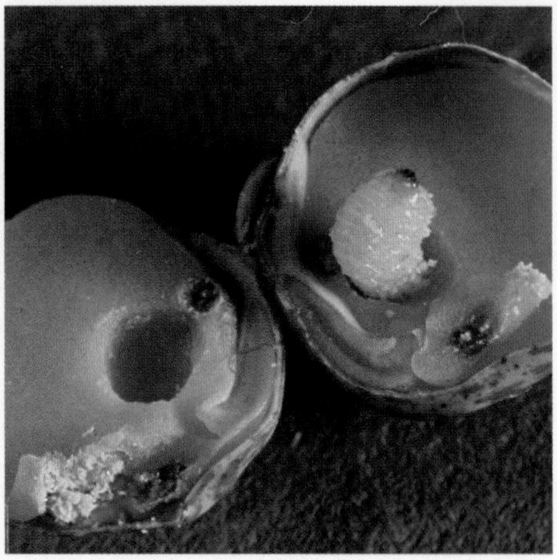

Pea weevil (5 times life size).

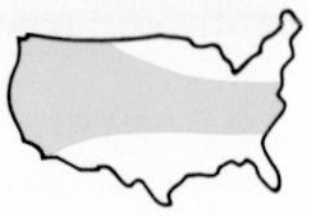

PROBLEM: Peas have small round holes. The peas are partially or completely hollow, and fat white grubs with brown heads may be found inside. When the pea plants are blooming, ⅕-inch-long dark brown beetles with light markings may be seen crawling or flying about the plants.

ANALYSIS: Pea weevil
(*Bruchus pisorum*)
This insect pest attacks all varieties of edible peas. Weevils emerge from hibernation as peas are beginning to bloom. The adults feed on pea nectar and pollen. This feeding does not harm the plant. Adults can migrate up to 3 miles in search of food. They lay orange to white eggs on the developing pods. The white grubs that hatch from these eggs eat through the pod and into the pea. They continue feeding for 6 to 8 weeks, then pupate inside the hollow pea. The adult weevil emerges in 1 to 3 weeks, and hibernates to repeat the cycle the following year. There is only one generation each year. Infested peas are inedible.

SOLUTION: Insecticides must be applied to kill the adults before they lay eggs. Once the eggs are laid on the pods it is too late to prevent injury. Treat the plants with ORTHO Rotenone Dust or Spray soon after the first blooms appear, and before pods start to form. Additional sprays may be needed to control migrating weevils.

PEANUTS

ADAPTATION: Southeast and Southwest.

PLANTING TIME: See page 1025.

PLANTING METHOD: Plant peanuts 1 to 2 inches deep. For Spanish types, allow 4 to 6 inches between plants; between Virginia types, allow 6 to 8 inches.

SOIL: Loose and crumbly soil. pH 5.5 to 6.5

FERTILIZER: At planting time, use 2 to 3 pounds of ORTHO Vegetable Food per 100 square feet, or 2 pounds per 100-foot row. Peanuts need adequate calcium. To avoid empty pods, dust the plants with gypsum (calcium sulfate) when flowering. Use 2½ pounds per 100-foot row.

WATER:

How much: Apply enough water at each irrigation to wet the soil 10 to 12 inches deep.

How often: Water when the soil 1 inch deep is barely moist. Stop watering before harvest, as the leaves just begin to yellow.

HARVEST: When the leaves have turned yellow and veins in the pods have darkened, dig the plants and shake off soil. Hang upside down in a warm airy place for 2 to 3 weeks. Then strip the peanuts and use. Discard any rotted or moldy pods.

To roast: Preheat the oven to 500°F. Put nuts in a wire basket or colander. Place them in the oven and turn it off. When the peanuts are cool enough to touch, they are finished roasting.

Spider mite damage.

PROBLEM: Leaves are stippled, yellowing, and dirty. Leaves may dry out and drop. There may be webbing over flower buds, between leaves, or on the lower surfaces of the leaves. To determine if the plant is infested with mites, hold a sheet of white paper underneath an affected leaf and tap the leaf sharply. Minute green, red, or yellow specks the size of pepper grains will drop to the paper and begin to crawl around. The mites are easily seen against the white background.

ANALYSIS: Spider mites
(*Tetranychus urticae*)
These mites, related to spiders, are major pests of many garden and greenhouse plants. They cause damage by sucking sap from the underside of the peanut leaves. As a result of feeding, the green leaf pigment disappears, producing the stippled appearance. Mites are active throughout the growing season, but are favored by hot, dry weather (70°F and up). By midsummer, they build up to tremendous numbers. For more information about spider mites, see page 887.

SOLUTION: There are no chemical controls for use by homeowners to control spider mites. Hose plants frequently to knock off webbing and spider mites.

Leaf spot.

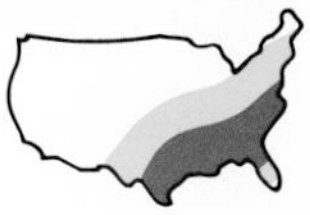

PROBLEM: Pale green to brownish black spots occur on the lower leaves first, then spread to the upper leaves. A pale green to yellow "halo" may surround the spots. The spots range in size from barely visible to ¼ inch in diameter. Several spots may join to form blotches. Leaf spotting is most severe in warm, humid weather. Infected leaves drop off.

ANALYSIS: Leaf spot
There are a number of different fungi that cause leaf spot on peanuts. Some of these fungi may eventually kill the plant, or weaken it so that it is susceptible to other organisms. Although peanut leaves are susceptible to attack by leaf spot throughout the growing season, the problem is most severe in hot (75° to 95°F), humid weather. Plants affected by leaf spot have low yields of poor quality peanuts. Leaf spot spores survive the winter in plant debris in the garden.

SOLUTION: Treat infected plants with a *copper sulfur* fungicide or one containing *chlorothalonil* (DACONIL 2787®). Repeat every 7 to 10 days while warm, humid weather persists. Discard severely infected and fallen leaves. Thoroughly clean the garden at the end of the season to reduce the number of overwintering spores.

Stem rot.

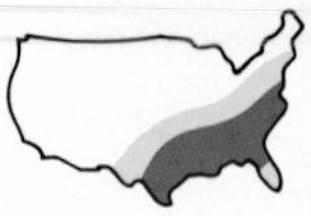

PROBLEM: Plants suddenly wilt. Leaves turn pale green, then brown and dry. A brown rot occurs at the base of the stems. During humid weather a white, cottony growth covers the soil and infected plant. White to dark brown pellets may form a crust on the soil around the infected plant.

ANALYSIS: Stem rot
This plant disease, also called *Southern blight* or *Southern stem rot*, is caused by a fungus (*Sclerotium rolfsii*). It attacks and kills a wide variety of vegetables and flowers. Peanut roots, stems, pegs, and pods are attacked. The fungus invades the plant through the stems at the soil line, then progresses into the pegs, pods, and roots. Affected pegs are weakened, so pods break off easily during harvest. Infection occurs in hot (85° to 95°F), dry weather. The fungus persists from one crop to the next in plant debris.

SOLUTION: Remove and destroy plants at the first sign of infection. Clean all debris from the garden at the end of the season. Rotate peanuts with a nonsusceptible crop every year. For a list of resistant plants, see page 1007. Before planting peanuts or any crop in an area where stem rot has been a problem, incorporate a fungicide containing *PCNB* into the top 6 inches of soil.

PEPPERS

ADAPTATION: Throughout the United States.

PLANTING TIME: See page 1025.

PLANTING METHOD: Sow seeds ¼ inch deep. Thin seedlings or set transplants to grow 18 to 24 inches apart. Plant transplants so the top of their rootball is even with the surrounding garden soil.

SOIL: Any good garden soil that is rich in organic matter. pH 5.5 to 7.5

FERTILIZER: At planting time, use 3 to 4 pounds of ORTHO Vegetable Food per 100 square feet, or 1 pound per 25-foot row. Side-dress every 3 to 4 weeks with 1 pound per 25-foot row, or 1 to 2 tablespoons per plant.

WATER:
How much: Apply enough water at each irrigation to wet the soil 10 to 12 inches deep.
Containers: 10 percent of the applied water should drain out the bottom.
How often: Water when the soil 2 inches deep is barely moist.

HARVEST:
Green or yellow peppers: Pick when of usable size with a rich color. Fruit should be slightly soft.
Red peppers: Red peppers are green peppers that have remained on the plants and matured. Pick when they have a rich red color. Cut peppers from the plant with pruning shears or a sharp knife, leaving ½ to 1 inch of the stem attached. Cool in the refrigerator.

Blossom drop.

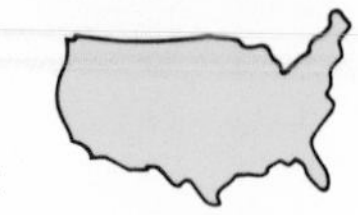

PROBLEM: Few or no fruit develop. Those that do develop may have rough skin or be misshapen. Plants remain vigorous, with lush foliage.

ANALYSIS: Blossom drop
Pepper blossoms are sensitive to temperature fluctuations during pollination. Normal pollination and fruit set don't occur when night temperatures fall below 58°F and daytime temperatures rise above 85°F. Under these temperature conditions, the blossoms fall off, often before pollination. If pollination has occurred and the fruit has begun to set, but isn't completely fertilized at the time the blossoms drop, rough and misshapen fruit result.

SOLUTION: Blossom drop only causes a delay in fruit production. When the temperatures are less extreme, a full crop of fruit will set, and the plants will be productive the rest of the season. Discard rough or misshapen fruit; they will never develop fully. Irrigation for cooling during hot periods can help to reduce losses.

Sunscald.

PROBLEM: An area on the pepper fruit becomes soft, wrinkled, and light in color. Later, this area dries and becomes slightly sunken, with a white, paperlike appearance. An entire side of the fruit may be affected. Black mold may grow in the affected areas.

ANALYSIS: Sunscald
Pepper fruit exposed directly to sunlight may be burned by the heat of the sun. The fruit may be exposed to the sun as a result of leaf diseases that cause leaf drop. Early fruits on small plants without enough protective foliage may be burned. Also, some varieties do not produce enough foliage to shade the fruit. Rot organisms sometimes enter the fruit through the damaged area, making the fruit unappetizing or inedible. Sunscalded fruit without these molds is still edible if the discolored tissue is removed.

SOLUTION: Control leaf diseases that may defoliate the plants. (See pages 748 and 749.) Fertilize according to the guidelines on the previous page to keep plants healthy with lush foliage. Select pepper varieties that form a protective canopy of leaves.

Blossom-end rot.

PROBLEM: A round, sunken, water-soaked spot develops on the bottom of the fruit. The spot enlarges, turns brown to black, and feels leathery. Mold may grow on the rotted surface.

ANALYSIS: Blossom-end rot
Blossom-end rot occurs on peppers, tomatoes, squash, and watermelons from a lack of calcium in the developing fruit. This lack results from slowed growth and damaged roots caused by the following factors:
1. Extreme fluctuations in soil moisture, either very wet or very dry.
2. Rapid plant growth early in the season, followed by extended dry periods.
3. Excessive rains that smother root hairs.
4. Excess soil salts.
5. Cultivating too close to the plant.
The first fruit are the most severely affected. The disorder always starts at the blossom end, the end farthest from the stem, and may enlarge to affect up to half of the fruit. Moldy growths on the rotted area are from fungi or bacteria that frequently invade the damaged tissue. This rotted area is unsightly, but the rest of the fruit is edible.

SOLUTION: Blossom-end rot is difficult to eliminate, but it can be controlled by following these guidelines.
1. Maintain uniform soil moisture by mulching and proper watering.
2. Avoid overuse of high nitrogen fertilizers and large quantities of fresh manure.
3. Plant in well-drained soil.
4. If your soil or water is salty, provide more water at each watering to help leach salts through the soil.
5. Do not cultivate deeper than 1 inch within 1 foot of the plant.

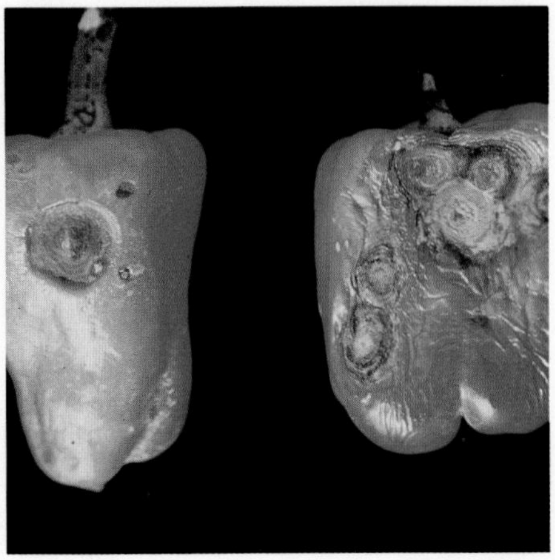

Anthracnose.

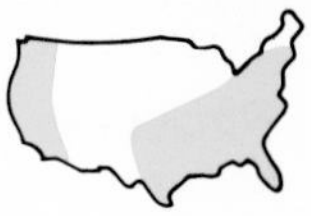

PROBLEM: Dark brown to black sunken spots appear on both green and ripe fruit. The centers of the spots are darker, with concentric rings. The spots may enlarge, covering a large part of the fruit. Small dark spots may appear on leaves and stems.

ANALYSIS: Anthracnose
This plant disease is caused by a fungus (*Gloesoporium piperatum*) that is a common rot of peppers. Both green and ripe fruit are attacked, and become worthless. Occasionally spots may occur on leaves and stems. The fungus is most active in warm (70° to 80°F), wet weather. When it is severe, many fruits become infected in a short period. Heavy dew, overhead watering, fog, and drizzling rain provide the water necessary for infection. The fungal spores are carried on and in seed. Young plants can become infected through the diseased seed, although the disease is not evident until the fruits form. Spores are spread to healthy plants by splashing water, people, and tools.

SOLUTION: Remove and discard infected fruit. Treat plants with ORTHO Tomato Vegetable Dust at the first sign of the disease. Repeat the treatment at intervals of 1 to 2 weeks as long as weather continues that is favorable to the spread of the disease. Avoid overhead watering by using drip or furrow irrigation. Do not work among wet plants. Clean all plant debris from the garden after harvest. Purchase seeds or transplants from a reputable garden company.

PEPPERS

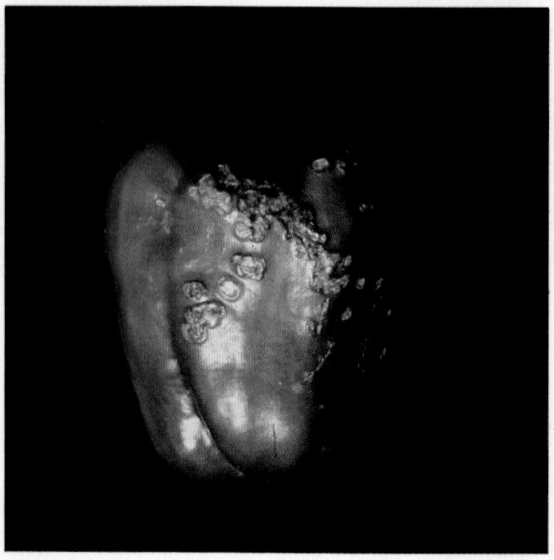

Bacterial spot.

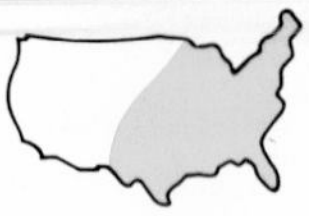

PROBLEM: Tan to dark brown spots, ⅛ to ¼ inch in diameter, occur on the lower leaves. Spotted leaves turn yellow and drop. Brown, corky, wartlike, raised spots appear on the fruit.

ANALYSIS: Bacterial spot
This plant disease is caused by a bacterium (*Xanthomonas vesicatoria*) that also attacks tomatoes. It affects all aboveground parts of the plant at any stage of growth. When the disease is serious, many blossoms may drop, reducing the fruit yield. The bacteria are most prevalent after heavy rains and in very warm (75° to 85°F) weather. In damp weather, with frequent splashing rains, they spread very rapidly, often resulting in complete leaf drop. Fruit are unsightly, but edible if the blemishes are removed. Molds and decay organisms may enter the fruit through the corky spots and rot the fruit. The bacteria are carried on seed, and persist from one crop to the next in the soil and on diseased plant parts left in the garden.

SOLUTION: Clean all infected plant debris from the garden. Spray the plants with *basic copper sulfate* when the fruit first forms or at the first sign of the disease. Continue the sprays every 10 to 14 days as long as weather conditions are favorable for the spread of the disease. Fertilize plants (see page 746) to help them to replace any leaves lost to bacterial spot. Plant pepper and tomato plants in the same area only once every 3 or 4 years. Purchase healthy transplants. Avoid overhead watering by using drip or furrow irrigation.

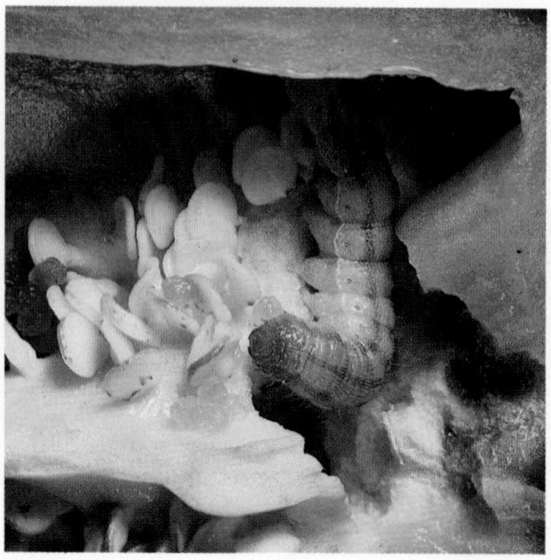

Corn earworm larva (life size).

PROBLEM: Holes are chewed in the fruit. Inside the fruit are striped yellow, green, or brown worms from ½ to 2 inches long. These worms may also be feeding on the leaves.

ANALYSIS: Corn earworm
(*Heliothis zea*)
The corn earworm attacks many vegetables and flowers. It is also known as the *tomato fruitworm* and *cotton bollworm*. The worms feed on the foliage, and also chew holes in the fruit, making them worthless. The worm is the larva of a light gray-brown moth with dark lines on its wings. In the spring, the moth lays yellow eggs on the leaves and stems. The worms that hatch from these eggs feed on the new leaves. When they are about ½ inch long, the worms move to the fruit and bore inside. After feeding for 2 to 4 weeks, they drop to the ground and pupate 2 to 6 inches deep in the soil. After several weeks they emerge as adults to repeat the cycle. There are several generations a year. In the South, where earworms survive the winter, early and late plantings suffer the most damage. Adult moths migrate into northern areas, where they do not survive the winter.

SOLUTION: Once the worms are inside the fruit, sprays are ineffective. Pick and destroy infested fruit. Clean all plant debris from the garden after harvest to reduce the number of overwintering adults. Next year, treat the plants with ORTHO Sevin Garden Dust or ORTHO Sevin Garden Spray when the worms are feeding on the foliage, or when the fruit are about 1 to 2 inches in diameter. Repeat the treatment at intervals of 10 to 14 days if the plants become reinfested.

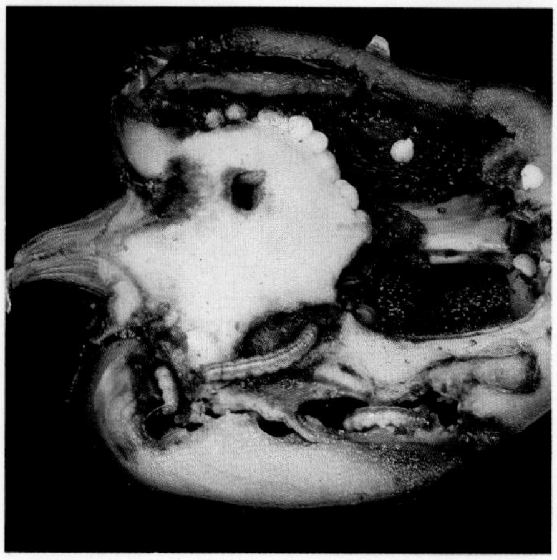

European corn borers (half life size).

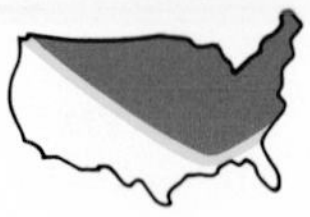

PROBLEM: Pink or tan worms, up to 1 inch long, with dark brown heads and two rows of brown dots, are feeding inside the pepper. The fruit is decayed inside.

ANALYSIS: European corn borer
(*Ostrinia nubilalis*)
This moth larva is a destructive pest of peppers, corn, tomatoes, beans, and eggplant. The worms feed and promote decay inside the fruit. The borers spend the winter in plant debris, pupate in the spring, and emerge as adults in early summer. The adults are tan moths with dark wavy lines on their wings. The moths lay clusters of 15 to 30 white eggs on the undersides of the leaves. In midsummer, the eggs hatch and young borers enter the fruit where it attaches to the cap. After feeding for 1 month inside the fruit, they pupate and later emerge as adults to repeat the cycle. There are two to three generations a year. Cool, rainy weather in early summer inhibits egg laying and washes the hatching larvae from the plants, reducing borer populations. Very dry summers and cold winters also reduce borer populations. Peppers are edible if the damaged part is cut away.

SOLUTION: Remove infested fruit. Treat the plants with ORTHO Liquid Sevin or ORTHO Sevin Garden Dust when the fruits are 1 to 1½ inches in diameter. Repeat the treatment 2 more times, 7 days apart. Clean all debris from the garden after harvest to reduce overwintering sites for the larvae.

Tomato hornworm (⅓ life size).

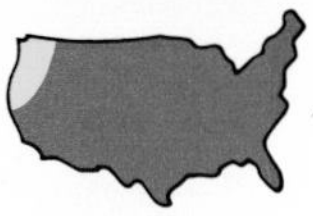

PROBLEM: Fat green or brown worms, up to 5 inches long, with white diagonal side stripes, chew on the leaves. A red or black "horn" projects from the rear end. Black droppings soil the leaves.

ANALYSIS: Tomato hornworm (*Manduca quinquemaculata*) **or tobacco hornworm** (*M. sexta*)
Hornworms feed on the fruit and foliage of peppers, eggplants, and tomatoes. Although there may be only a few worms present, each worm consumes large quantities of foliage and causes extensive damage. The large gray or brown adult moth with yellow and white markings emerges from hibernation in late spring, and drinks nectar from petunias and other garden flowers. The worms hatch from eggs laid on the undersides of the leaves, and feed for 3 to 4 weeks. Then they crawl into the soil, pupate, and later emerge as adults to repeat the cycle. There is one generation a year in the North, and two to four in the South. Some worms may have white sacs that look like puffed rice on their bodies. These sacs are the cocoons of parasitic wasps that feed on and eventually kill the hornworm.

SOLUTION: Treat the plants with ORTHO Sevin Garden Dust or ORTHO Tomato & Vegetable Insect Spray. Don't destroy worms covered with white sacs. Let the wasps inside the worms mature, emerge, and infest other hornworms. If practical, handpick unaffected worms.

Cutworm (⅓ life size).

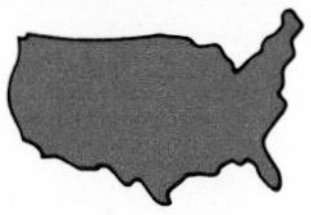

PROBLEM: Young plants are chewed or cut off near the ground. Gray, brown, or black worms, 1½ to 2 inches long, may be found about 2 inches deep in the soil near the base of the damaged plants. The worms coil when disturbed.

ANALYSIS: Cutworms
Several species of cutworms attack plants in the vegetable garden. The most likely pests of young pepper plants are the surface-feeding cutworms. For information on the climbing cutworms, see page 670. A single surface-feeding cutworm can sever the stems of many young plants in one night. Cutworms hide in the soil during the day and feed only at night. Adult cutworms are dark, night-flying moths with bands of stripes on their forewings.

SOLUTION: Apply ORTHO Diazinon Soil & Turf Insect Control, ORTHO Vegetable Guard Soil Insect Killer, or ORTHO Diazinon Soil & Foliage Dust around the base of undamaged plants when stem cutting is observed. Since cutworms are difficult to control, it may be necessary to repeat the dusting at weekly intervals. Destroy any cutworms found hiding in the soil. Before transplanting into the area, apply a preventive treatment of ORTHO Diazinon Soil & Turf Insect Control or ORTHO Vegetable Guard Soil Insect Killer and work it into the soil. Cultivate the soil thoroughly in late summer and fall to expose and destroy eggs, larvae, and pupae. Further reduce damage with "cutworm collars" around the stem of each plant. These collars can be made of stiff paper or aluminum foil. They should be at least 2 inches high, and pressed firmly into the soil.

Cercospora leaf spot.

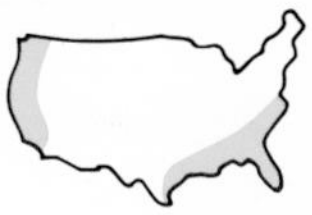

PROBLEM: Circular or oblong spots, up to ½ inch in diameter, develop on the leaves and stems. The spots have light gray centers and dark margins. Leaves may yellow and drop.

ANALYSIS: Cercospora leaf spot
This plant disease is caused by a fungus (*Cercospora capsici*). It is also known as *frog-eye leaf spot* because of the resemblance of the spots to frog's eyes. The disease is most prevalent during hot (75° to 85°F), wet weather. Under these conditions, complete leaf defoliation may occur within 2 to 3 weeks. This leaf drop not only reduces fruit yield, but also exposes the fruit to sunscald. For information on sunscald, see page 747. The fungal spores persist from crop to crop in plant debris, and also survive in the soil for at least 1 year. Spores are spread by the wind, and may also be carried in the seed.

SOLUTION: Treat the plants with ORTHO Tomato Vegetable Dust at the first sign of the disease. Repeat the treatment at intervals of 7 to 10 days until no new infections occur. Destroy severely infected plants. Discard all plant debris at the end of the season. Purchase disease-free seeds or plants from a reputable company.

Mosaic.

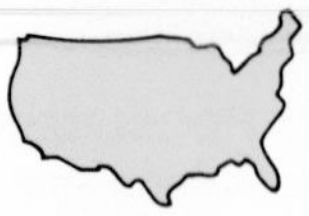

PROBLEM: Leaves are curled and mottled yellow and green. Fruit is misshapen, with rough skin and brown streaks, rings, or yellow, green, and red mottling. Plants are stunted.

ANALYSIS: Mosaic
This plant disease may be caused by any of several different viruses. One common virus that infects peppers is *tobacco mosaic virus* (*TMV*). Young plants infected with viruses seldom produce fruit. Plants infected at maturity are less severely affected, and produce misshapen but edible fruit. Seed is one source of infection, but viruses more commonly are transmitted from weeds, including pokeweed, plantain, catnip, and motherwort. Aphids spread viruses from plant to plant while feeding. Viruses are also transmitted mechanically when diseased and healthy leaves rub together.

SOLUTION: Discard infected plants at the first sign of infection. Control aphids with ORTHO Fruit & Vegetable Insect Control, ORTHO Tomato & Vegetable Insect Spray, or ORTHO Tomato & Vegetable Insect Killer. Repeat the treatment at intervals of 7 to 10 days if the plants become reinfested. For more information on controlling disease-carrying insects, see page 879. Because some viruses are present in tobacco products, wash your hands thoroughly with soap and water after smoking and before working in the garden. Plant varieties resistant to mosaic (see page 1028).

POTATOES

ADAPTATION: Throughout the United States.

PLANTING TIME: See page 1025.

PLANTING METHOD: Plant 1½ to 2-ounce seed pieces (about the size of a medium egg) in trenches 3 to 4 inches deep. Allow 12 to 18 inches between pieces. Plant pieces whole or cut, with at least one eye on each piece. Certified potato seed pieces are certified by the State Department of Agriculture to be free of viruses. Purchase new seed pieces each year.

SOIL: Any good garden soil that is rich in organic matter. pH 4.8 to 6.8

FERTILIZER: At planting time, use 1 to 2 pounds of ORTHO Vegetable Food per 100 square feet, or ½ pound per 25-foot row. Side-dress when the plants are 4 to 6 inches tall.

WATER:
How much: Apply enough water at each irrigation to wet the soil 8 to 12 inches deep.
How often: Water when the soil 2 inches deep is barely moist.

HARVEST: Dig potatoes as needed about 2 to 3 weeks after flowering. Dig those to be stored after the tops naturally turn yellow and die. Carefully dig with a spade or pitchfork, being careful not to wound the tubers. Discard any diseased tubers.
To store: Cure in the dark for 1 week at 70°F and high humidity. Then store in a humid area at between 40° and 45°F until used. Check stored tubers periodically for storage rot.

Green potato tuber.

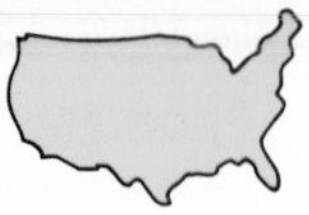

PROBLEM: Potato tubers turn green while in the ground or in storage.

ANALYSIS: Green tubers
Potato tubers turn green when exposed to light. Tubers are modified stems, and produce the green pigment chlorophyll when they receive light. Tubers may be exposed to light when the plants are not properly hilled, or when they are stored in a light place. Excessively green tubers are bitter and inedible. If only slightly green, the tubers are still edible if the green tissue is peeled off.

SOLUTION: Discard tubers, or peel them before eating. Protect tubers in the ground from sunlight by mounding loose soil around the plants when they are 5 to 6 inches tall to completely cover developing tubers. Replace the soil if it is washed away by rain or irrigation water. Store potatoes in a dark, humid place at temperatures between 35° and 45°F.

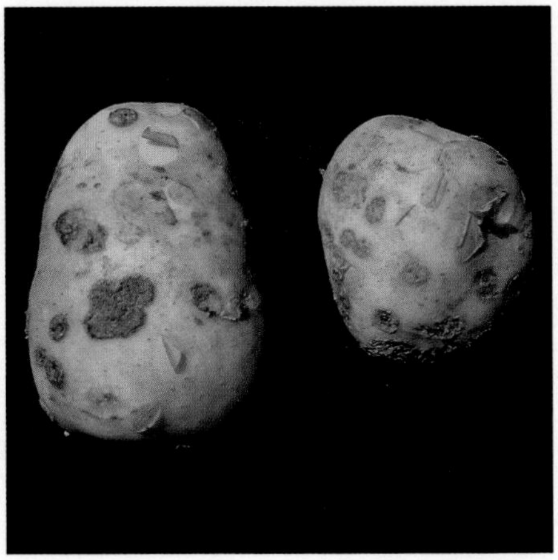

Scab.

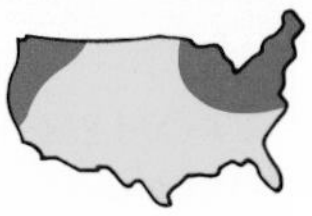

PROBLEM: Brown corky scabs or pits occur on potato tubers. Spots enlarge and merge together, sometimes covering most of the tuber. Leaves and stems are not affected.

ANALYSIS: Common scab
This plant disease is caused by a fungus (*Streptomyces scabies*) that persists in the soil for long periods of time. Besides potatoes, scab also infects beets, carrots, and parsnips. Scab affects only the tubers, not the leaves and stems. The fungus spends the winter in the soil and in infected tubers left in the garden. Infection occurs through wounds and through the breathing pores in the tuber skins when the tubers are young and growing rapidly. Scab is most severe in warm (75° to 85°F) dry soil with a pH of 5.7 to 8.0. The severity of scab often increases when the pH is raised with lime or wood ashes. Scab is not a problem in acid soils with a pH of 5.5 or less. Poorly fertilized soil also encourages scab. The fungal spores withstand temperature and moisture extremes. Because the spores pass intact through the digestive tracts of animals, manure can spread the disease. Tubers infected with scab are edible, but much may be wasted as the blemishes are removed.

SOLUTION: No chemical control is available. Test your soil pH, and if necessary correct it to 5.0 to 5.5 with *aluminum sulfate*. (For information on soil testing, see page 909.) Avoid alkaline materials such as wood ashes and lime. Do not use manure on potatoes. Plant potatoes in the same area only once every 3 to 4 years. Use certified seed pieces that are resistant to scab (see page 1027).

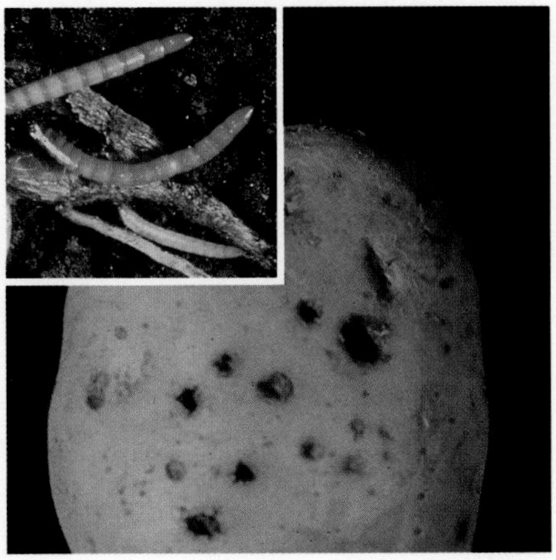

Damaged potato. *Insert:* Wireworms (twice life size).

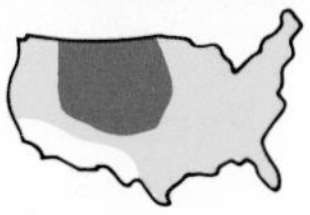

PROBLEM: Plants are stunted and grow slowly. Tunnels wind through stems, roots, and in and on the surface of tubers. Shiny, hard, jointed, cream to yellow worms up to $\frac{5}{8}$ inch long are found in the tuber and in the soil.

ANALYSIS: Wireworms
Wireworms feed on potatoes, corn, carrots, beets, peas, beans, lettuce, and many other plants. Wireworms feed entirely on underground plant parts, devouring seed potatoes, underground stems, tubers, and roots. Infestations are most extensive in soil where lawn grass was recently grown. Adults are known as "click" beetles because they make a clicking sound when turning from their back to their feet. Wireworm larvae feed for 2 to 6 years before maturing into adult beetles, so all sizes and ages of wireworms may be found in the soil at the same time. Undamaged portions of the tubers are edible.

SOLUTION: Control wireworms with ORTHO Diazinon Soil & Foliage Dust or ORTHO Vegetable Guard Soil Insect Killer at the first sign of damage. Incorporate into the top 6 to 8 inches of soil. Do not store damaged tubers. Repeat the soil treatment next year just before planting.

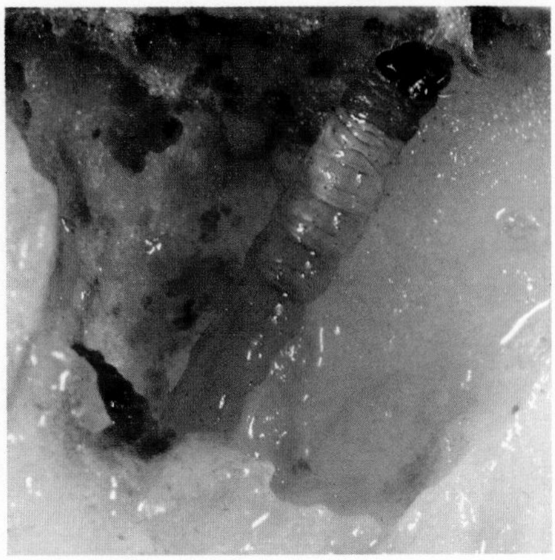

Potato tuberworm (3 times life size).

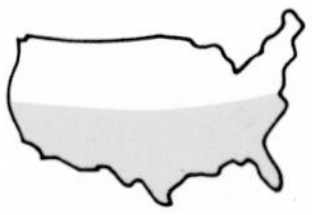

PROBLEM: Holes are bored into the tubers. The flesh surrounding the tuber may be decayed. When sliced open, damaged tubers are found to contain dirty, silk-lined tunnels. Worms up to $\frac{3}{4}$ inch long with dark heads and pinkish white or green bodies may be seen in the tunnels. There may also be tunnels in the stems and leaves.

ANALYSIS: Potato tuberworm
(*Phthorimaea operculella*)
Potato tuberworms are the larvae of small, brownish gray moths. The moths lay eggs in the spring on the underside of leaves or in the eyes of potato tubers. Moths emerging late in the season crawl down through cracks in the soil and lay eggs on potato tubers. The emerging larvae either mine leaves or burrow into stems and tubers to feed. When mature, they pupate in debris on the ground. The adult moths emerge from these pupae. There may be as many as six generations yearly, depending on the area of the country. The larvae may continue to develop in the tubers even after harvested, and later emerge from storage.

SOLUTION: Dust foliage with ORTHO Diazinon Soil & Foliage Dust while the plants are young to control both adults and the leafminer stage. Check all tubers carefully before planting; if they appear infested, discard them. Keep the developing tubers covered with at least 2 inches of soil. Water the plants on a regular basis to keep the soil moist and prevent soil cracking, or apply a mulch. Do not leave potato tubers exposed overnight in the field. Remove infested plants, tubers, and debris to eliminate larvae that may overwinter.

POTATOES — PROBLEMS WITH THE TUBER

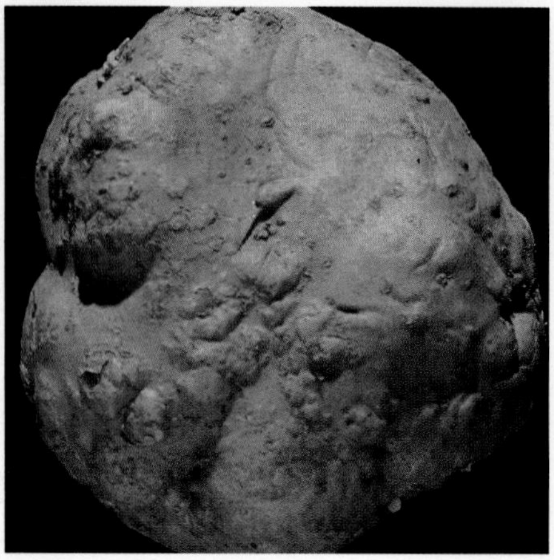

Root knot nematode damage.

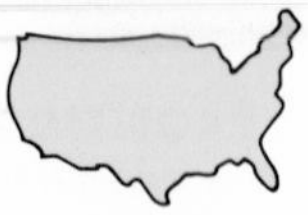

PROBLEM: The leaves turn bronze to yellow. They may wilt on hot, dry days, then recover at night. Plants are stunted. Tubers may have a roughened and pebbly skin.

ANALYSIS: Nematodes
Nematodes are microscopic worms that live in the soil. They are not related to earthworms. Nematodes feed on plant roots, damaging and stunting them. The damaged roots can't supply sufficient water and nutrients to the above-ground plant parts, and the plant is stunted or slowly dies. Infested tubers are unsightly, but edible if peeled. Nematodes are found throughout the United States, but are most severe in the South. They prefer moist, sandy loam soils. Nematodes can move only a few inches each year on their own, but they may be carried long distances by soil, water, tools, or infested plants. Testing roots and soil is the only positive method for confirming the presence of nematodes. Contact your local Cooperative Extension Office (see page 1029) for sampling instructions and addresses of testing laboratories. Soil and root problems such as poor soil structure, drought stress, nutrient deficiency, and root rots can also produce symptoms of decline similar to those caused by nematodes. These problems should be eliminated as causes before sending soil and root samples for testing. For information on soil problems and root rots, see pages 907 and 849.

SOLUTION: There are no chemicals available to homeowners to kill nematodes in planted soil. However, they can be controlled before planting by soil fumigation. For information on fumigating soil, see page 927.

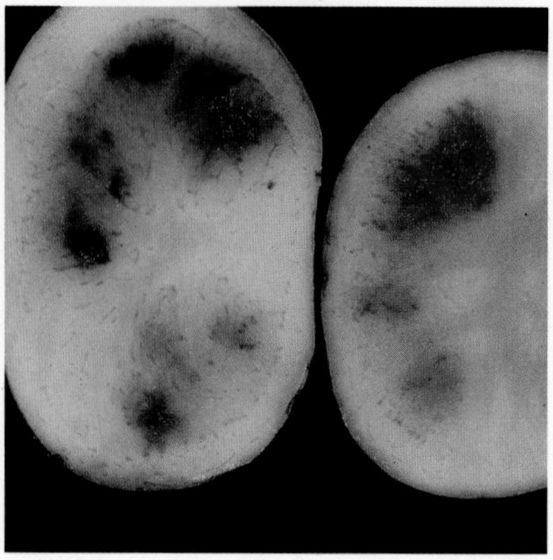

Internal discolorations.

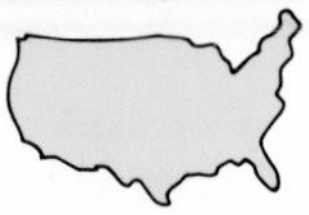

PROBLEM: The inside of a tuber is streaked or spotted with brown to black discolorations. The discolorations may extend throughout the tuber, or occur in just a few small spots.

ANALYSIS: Internal discoloration
Discoloration inside potato tubers results from unfavorable growing and harvesting conditions. It can be caused by an early frost, by alternating periods of very wet and very dry soil, or by drought conditions at harvest time. Plants infected with leaf roll or mosaic virus also produce discolored tubers. For information on these diseases, see page 756. Discolored tubers are inedible.

SOLUTION: Provide good growing conditions, as outlined on page 750. Control aphids, which spread virus diseases, with ORTHO Malathion 50 Insect Spray or ORTHO Fruit & Vegetable Insect Control. Plant only certified seed pieces.

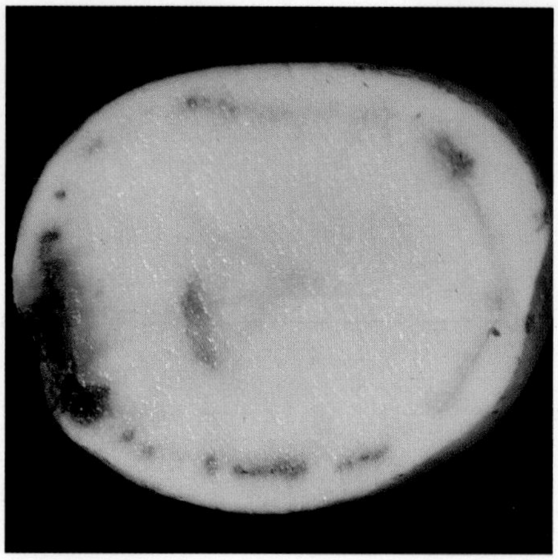

Bacterial ring rot.

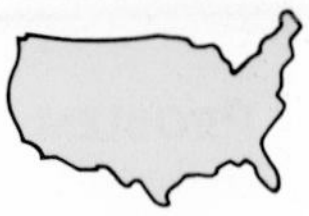

PROBLEM: Shoot tips are stunted, forming rosettes. Leaves turn yellow, then brown between the veins. Leaf margins curl upward, and stems may wilt. Stems cut at the ground level exude a creamy white ooze. Only a few stems on a plant may show symptoms. Tubers may be cracked and, when cut near the stem end, reveal a yellow to light brown ring of crumbly decay.

ANALYSIS: Ring rot
This disease is caused by a bacterium (*Corynebacterium sepedonicum*) that attacks both tubers and stems. Infected tubers are inedible. Tuber decay may be evident at harvest, or it may not develop until after several months in storage. Other rot organisms frequently invade and completely rot the tubers. Ring rot bacteria enter plants through wounds, especially those caused by cutting seed pieces before planting. They do not spread from plant to plant in the field. The bacteria survive between seasons in infected tubers and storage containers.

SOLUTION: Discard all infected tubers and plants at the first sign of the disease. Next year, use only certified potato seed pieces for plants. Plant whole; or if you cut them, disinfect the knife between cuts by dipping it in rubbing alcohol. Disinfect storage containers with a chlorine bleach. Wash storage bags in hot water.

INSECTS

Hollow heart.

PROBLEM: Tubers develop irregular white to brown cavities. Tubers are generally very large.

ANALYSIS: Hollow heart
Discolored cavities result when potato tubers develop too rapidly during the growing season. This rapid growth may be encouraged by excessive soil fertility and moisture. Plants spaced too far apart may also develop hollow heart. These cavities occur mainly on very large or oversized tubers. Tubers are still edible if the discolored cavities are cut away. The cavities do not decay unless bacterial or fungal rot organisms enter the tuber from the outside.

SOLUTION: Follow the planting and maintenance guidelines outlined on page 750.

If you're short of space, grow potatoes in bushel baskets, buckets, or large plastic garbage bags.

Adult (half life size). *Insert:* Larva (life size).

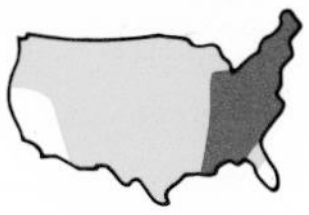

PROBLEM: Yellow-orange beetles with black stripes, about 3/8 inch long, are eating the leaves. Fat, red, humpbacked larvae with 2 rows of black dots may also be present.

ANALYSIS: Colorado potato beetle
(*Leptinotarsa decemlineata*)
This insect pest, also known as the *potato bug*, often devastates potato, tomato, and pepper plantings. Both the adults and the larvae damage plants by devouring leaves and stems. Small plants are most severely damaged. The beetle was originally native to the Rocky Mountains, and spread eastward in the late 1800s as potato plantings increased. In some areas of the country, the beetle population may reach epidemic proportions. The beetles lay their yellow-orange eggs on the undersides of the leaves as the first potatoes emerge from the ground in the spring. The larvae that hatch from these eggs feed for 2 to 3 weeks, pupate in the soil, and emerge 1 to 2 weeks later as adults, which lay more eggs. One generation is completed in a month. There are one to three generations a year, depending on the area of the country.

SOLUTION: Control Colorado potato beetles with ORTHO Fruit & Vegetable Insect Control, ORTHO Tomato & Vegetable Insect Killer, ORTHO Sevin Garden Dust, or ORTHO Tomato Vegetable Dust. Treat when the insects are first noticed, and repeat every 7 days as long as the infestation continues.

Blister beetle (twice life size).

PROBLEM: Black or gray slender beetles feed in clusters on the leaves. They are 1/2 to 3/4 inch long, and may be striped.

ANALYSIS: Blister beetle
(*Epicauta* species)
This insect pest feeds on a wide variety of vegetables and flowers. The adult beetles eat plant leaves, and can defoliate entire plants. The larvae, however, eat grasshopper eggs, and help to reduce the grasshopper population. Adult beetles emerge from hibernation in swarms in June and July. They feed voraciously, and after stripping one plant move on to another. They lay yellow egg clusters in the soil. The grubs that hatch from these eggs migrate through the soil, feeding on grasshopper eggs. There is only one generation each year. Be careful when handling these beetles; the juice from crushed beetles causes blisters.

SOLUTION: Treat the plants with ORTHO Tomato Vegetable Dust, ORTHO Tomato & Vegetable Insect Killer, or ORTHO Tomato & Vegetable Insect Spray as soon as the beetles appear in June or July. Repeat the treatments at intervals of 7 to 10 days if the plants become reinfested.

POTATOES — INSECTS ——— **LEAVES DISCOLORED OR DYING**

Flea beetle damage.

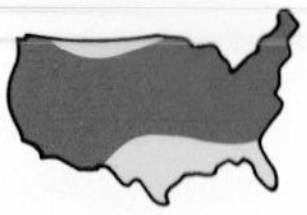

PROBLEM: Leaves are riddled with shotholes about 1/8 inch in diameter. Tiny (1/16 inch) black beetles jump like fleas when disturbed. Leaves of seedlings and eventually whole plants may wilt and die.

ANALYSIS: Flea beetles
These beetles jump like fleas, but are not related to them. Both adult and immature flea beetles feed on a wide variety of garden vegetables, including potatoes. The immature beetle, a legless gray grub, injures plants by feeding on the roots and the lower surfaces of leaves. Adults chew holes in leaves. Flea beetles are most damaging to young plants. Adult beetles survive the winter in soil and garden debris. They emerge in early spring to feed on weeds until potatoes sprout. Grubs hatch from eggs laid in the soil and feed for 2 to 3 weeks, damaging the tubers. After pupating in the soil, they emerge as adults to repeat the cycle. There are one to four generations a year. Adults may feed for up to 2 months.

SOLUTION: Control flea beetles on potatoes with ORTHO Fruit & Vegetable Insect Control, ORTHO Sevin Garden Dust, ORTHO Tomato & Vegetable Insect Killer, or ORTHO Tomato Vegetable Dust when the leaves first show damage. Spray or dust carefully at the base of stems. Watch new growth for evidence of further damage, and repeat the treatment at weekly intervals as needed. Clean all plant debris from the garden after harvesting to eliminate overwintering spots for adult beetles.

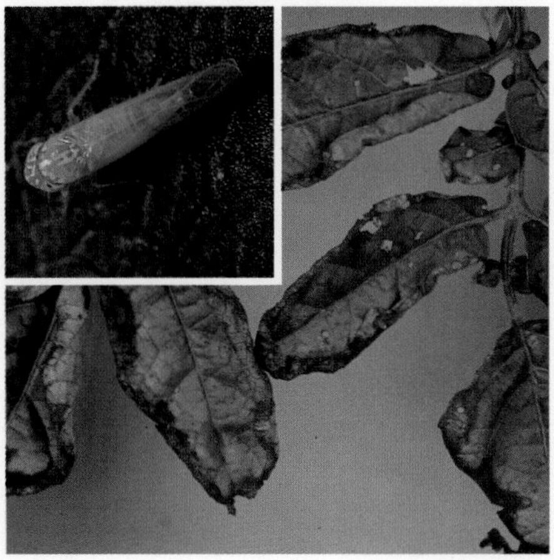

Damage. *Insert:* Potato leafhopper (4 times life size).

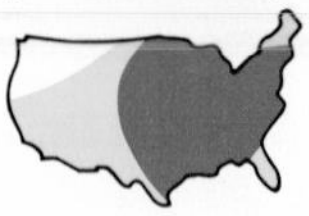

PROBLEM: Spotted, pale green insects up to 1/8 inch long hop, run sideways, or fly away quickly when a plant is touched. The leaves are stippled or appear scorched, with a green midrib and brown edges curled under.

ANALYSIS: Potato leafhopper
(*Empoasca fabae*)
This insect feeds on potatoes, and beans, and on some fruit and ornamental trees. It sucks plant sap from the undersides of the leaves, causing leaf stippling. This leafhopper is responsible for *hopperburn*, and the browning and curling of the edges of potato leaves. The leafhopper injects toxic saliva into the nutrient-conducting tissue, interrupting the flow of food within the plant. Potato yields may be reduced drastically by hopperburn. Leafhoppers at all stages of maturity are active during the growing season. Both early and late varieties of potatoes are infested. Leafhoppers live year-round in the Gulf States, and migrate northward on warm spring winds, so even areas that have winters so cold that the eggs cannot survive are not free from infestation.

SOLUTION: Spray infested plants with ORTHO Tomato & Vegetable Insect Spray, ORTHO Malathion 50 Insect Spray, ORTHO Tomato & Vegetable Insect Killer, or ORTHO Sevin Garden Dust. Be sure to cover the lower surfaces of the leaves. Repeat the spray as often as necessary to keep the insects under control. Allow at least 10 days between applications. Eradicate nearby weeds that may harbor leafhopper eggs.

Early blight.

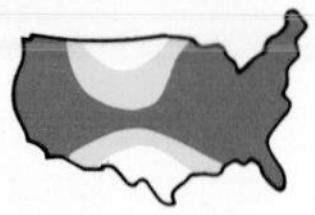

PROBLEM: Irregular dark brown to black spots, 1/8 to 1/2 inch in diameter, appear on the lower leaves. Concentric rings develop in the spots. Spots may enlarge, causing the leaf to die and fall off. Tubers may be infected with brown, corky, dry spots.

ANALYSIS: Early blight
This plant disease is caused by a fungus (*Alternaria solani*) that attacks both vines and tubers. It is most severe toward the end of the growing season when the vines approach maturity and after tubers are formed. Many leaves may be killed. The potato yield is reduced, but the plant seldom dies. Tubers are frequently infected through wounds inflicted during harvest. Early blight is favored by warm (75° to 85°F) weather and moisture. The fungal spores spend the winter in plant debris left in the garden. Infected tubers are inedible.

SOLUTION: Spray plants with ORTHO Vegetable Disease Control as soon as leaf spotting occurs. Repeat the treatment every 7 to 10 days until the leaves die back naturally. Clean all plant debris from the garden after harvest. Do not store infected tubers. Next year, begin spraying the plants when they are 6 inches tall, and continue at intervals of 7 to 10 days until the tops die back. Avoid overhead watering by using drip or furrow irrigation. Maintain adequate fertility as outlined on page 750. Use seed potatoes certified by State Departments of Agriculture to be free of diseases.

Late blight.

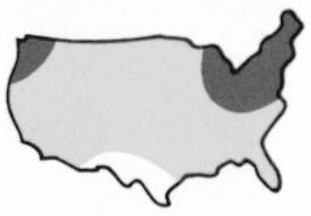

PROBLEM: Brownish water-soaked spots appear on the leaves. Spots enlarge rapidly, turn black and kill leaves, then leaf stems and stems. In moist weather, a gray mildew grows on the lower surfaces of the leaves. Tuber skins are infected in the ground or in storage with brownish purple spots that become a wet or dry rot.

ANALYSIS: Late blight

This plant disease is caused by a fungus (*Phytophthora infestans*) that seriously injures potatoes and tomatoes. This disease was responsible for the great famine in Ireland from 1845 to 1850. The fungus spreads very rapidly, killing an entire planting in a few days. Infected tubers are inedible. The tubers are infected when the spores wash off the leaves and into the soil. Tubers may also be attacked during harvest and rot in storage. A soft rot often invades the damaged tubers. (For information on soft rot, see page 755.) Late blight is prevalent in moist humid weather with cool nights and warm days. Foggy, misty weather and heavy dews provide enough moisture for infection. The spores survive the winter in infected tubers in the garden or compost pile.

SOLUTION: If late blight is an annual problem in your area, spray plants with ORTHO Vegetable Disease Control when the plants are 6 inches tall. Continue at intervals of 7 to 10 days until the plants naturally turn yellow and die. Avoid overhead watering; use drip or furrow irrigation. Wait at least a week after plants die naturally before digging the tubers. This allows time for the spores to die.

Black leg.

PROBLEM: Leaves roll, turn yellow, and wilt. The lower stem becomes black, slimy, and smelly from the soil line to 3 or 4 inches up the stem. Aerial tubers may form along the stems.

ANALYSIS: Black leg

This plant disease is caused by a bacterium (*Erwinia carotovora var. atroseptica*) that is spread in seed potatoes and sometimes persists in the soil. Bacteria in the soil may infect the plants through wounds in the stem or through the seed piece. If infected seed is planted, it rots after it sprouts. The rot spreads from the seed piece into the stem of the potato plant. As the tuber rots, toxic substances are released that cause the plant to wilt, collapse, and often die. The lower stem turns black and rots. If the plant does not die, it yields poorly, and the tubers may rot in storage. Plants growing in wet soil are very susceptible.

SOLUTION: No chemical controls are available. Avoid overwatering and damaging the plants in any way. Use certified seed potatoes that are resistant to black leg. Plant small whole tubers 2 to 3 inches deep in well-drained soil.

Potato varieties that are resistant to black leg: Atlantic, Katahdin, Kennebec, La Rouge, Red LaSoda, Red Norland, Red Pontiac, and Superior.

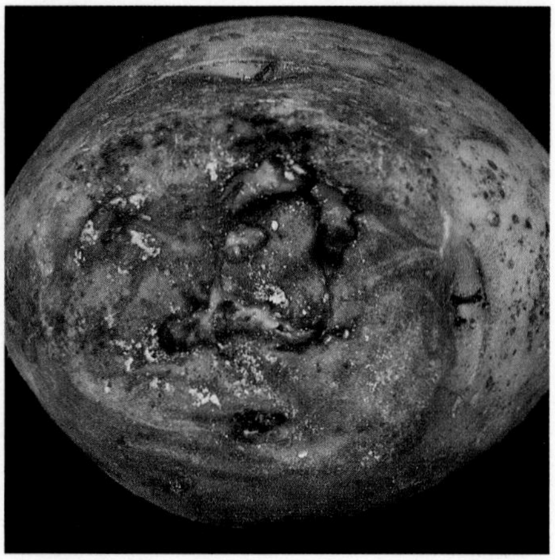

Bacterial soft rot.

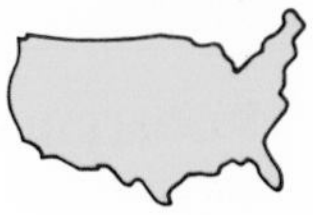

PROBLEM: A slimy, smelly decay infects potatoes either in the ground or in storage. Small, soft, circular discolored spots may occur on tubers.

ANALYSIS: Bacterial soft rot

This plant disease is caused by a bacterium (*Erwinia carotovora var. aroideae*) that attacks potatoes, tomatoes, peppers, parsnips, carrots, and many other vegetables. The bacteria rarely attack potato leaves, but severely infect the tubers, rendering them inedible. The tubers may be infected either in the ground or in storage. Bacteria can rot tubers completely in 3 to 10 days. Tubers bruised during harvest are likely to become infected and rot in storage. The bacteria that cause soft rot are almost always present in the soil, but they infect only potatoes that have been wounded, or are growing in wet soil.

SOLUTION: No chemical controls are available. Keep potato plants healthy and control insect and disease problems. Wait until vines turn yellow and die before digging potatoes. Dig carefully to avoid bruising them. If you want to store the tubers, cure them in the dark for one week at 70°F to heal any bruises and to condition them. Then store them in a humid area between 35° and 45°F. Do not store blemished tubers. Next year, plant in well-drained soil, and ridge or hill the plants to encourage excess water to flow away from them.

Virus.

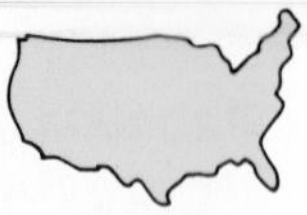

PROBLEM: Leaves are small, mottled light and dark green, and may be wrinkled or curled. Plants are stunted and may die prematurely. Tubers may be elongated, cracked, or discolored inside.

ANALYSIS: Viruses
Several viruses infect potatoes, causing distortion, slów growth, a reduction in the size, quality, and number of tubers, and sometimes death of the plant. Infected tubers are inedible. Viruses may be introduced into the garden in infected seed pieces; or they may live in weeds, including pokeweed, plantain, horsenettle, catnip, and motherwort. Once the infection is present in or near the garden, aphids spread the viruses from plant to plant while feeding.

SOLUTION: There are no chemical controls for viruses. Discard infected plants and tubers promptly. At the first sign of aphids, treat the potato plants with ORTHO Malathion 50 Insect Spray or ORTHO Fruit & Vegetable Insect Control. Repeat the treatment at intervals of 7 to 10 days if the plants become reinfested. (For more information about controlling disease-carrying insects, see page 879.) Plant only pieces certified by State Departments of Agriculture to be free of disease. Do not save your own tubers for replanting. Do not plant tubers from the grocery store.

Potato leaf roll.

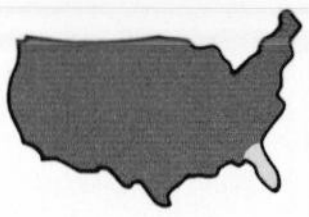

PROBLEM: Leaves roll upward, turn light green to yellow, and feel leathery. Lower leaves are affected first, then upper leaves. Plants may be stunted and produce few tubers. Tubers may be discolored inside. Pale green or yellow insects may cluster on the leaves and stems.

ANALYSIS: Leaf roll
This plant disease is caused by a virus that is carried in infected tubers and spread by aphids. As a result of the widespread distribution and severity of leaf roll virus by infected tubers, the seed potato certification program was started. Potato tubers are tested for the virus, and if clean, are certified by State Departments of Agriculture. Several species of aphids transmit this virus, the most common being the green peach aphid. This is a pale green aphid with three dark lines on its back. The aphid injects the virus into the plant while sucking the sap from the leaves and stems. Leaf roll virus affects potatoes in two ways: by reducing the yield, and by discoloring the tuber. Discolored tubers are inedible.

SOLUTION: No chemical control is available for leaf roll, although controlling aphids with ORTHO Fruit & Vegetable Insect Control or ORTHO Malathion 50 Insect Spray will help. Repeat at intervals of 7 to 10 days if the plants become reinfested. For more information on controlling disease-carrying insects, see page 879. Discard all infected plants and tubers. Plant only certified seed potatoes.

RADISHES

ADAPTATION: Throughout the United States.

PLANTING TIME: See page 1025.

PLANTING METHOD: Sow seeds ½ inch deep and thin to grow 1 inch apart. Do not transplant. For a continuous harvest, plant seeds every 2 weeks.

SOIL: Any good garden soil. pH 5.5 to 7.0

FERTILIZER: At planting time, add 3 to 4 pounds of ORTHO Vegetable Food per 100 square feet, or 1 pound per 25-foot row.
Containers: Water thoroughly 1 to 2 weeks after seeds sprout with a solution of ORTHO Tomato & Vegetable Food 6–18–6.

WATER:
How much: Apply enough water at each irrigation to wet the soil 6 to 8 inches deep.
Containers: 10 per cent of the applied water should drain out the bottom.
How often: Water when the soil 2 inches deep is barely moist.

HARVEST: Pull radishes and use as needed. They are usually ready for eating 25 to 30 days after sprouting. Large radishes may be tougher and more stringy than smaller ones. Dig winter radishes or daikon when the roots attain the length stated on the seed packet. Pull oneor two to check. Store radishes in the refrigerator.

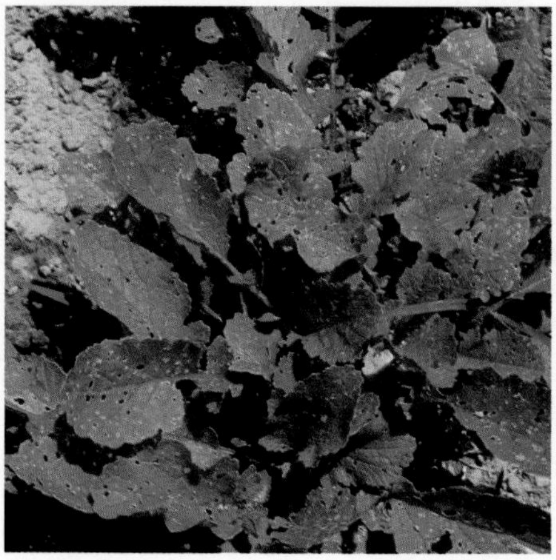
Flea beetle damage.

PROBLEM: Leaves are riddled with shotholes about 1/8 inch in diameter. Tiny (1/16 inch) black beetles jump like fleas when disturbed.

ANALYSIS: Flea beetles
These beetles jump like fleas, but are not related to them. Both adult and immature flea beetles feed on a wide variety of garden vegetables. The immature beetle, a legless gray grub, injures plants by feeding on the roots and the lower surfaces of leaves. Adults chew holes in leaves. Adult beetles survive the winter in soil and garden debris. They emerge in early spring to feed on weeds until vegetable seeds sprout. Grubs hatch from eggs laid in the soil and feed for 2 to 3 weeks. After pupating in the soil, they emerge as adults to repeat the cycle. There are one to four generations a year. Adults may feed for up to 2 months.

SOLUTION: Control flea beetles on radishes with ORTHO Tomato & Vegetable Insect Killer when the plants first emerge through the soil or at the first sign of damage. Watch new growth for evidence of further damage, and repeat the treatment at weekly intervals as needed. Clean all plant debris from the garden after harvest to eliminate overwintering spots for adult beetles.

Root maggot (life size).

PROBLEM: Young plants wilt in the heat of the day. They may later turn yellow and die. Soft-bodied, yellow-white maggots, about 1/4 inch long, are feeding in the roots. The roots are honeycombed with slimy channels and scarred by brown grooves.

ANALYSIS: Root maggots
(*Hylemya* species)
Root maggots are most numerous during cool, wet weather in spring, early summer, and fall. Early maggots attack the roots, stems, and seeds of radishes, cabbage, broccoli, and turnips in the spring and early summer. Later insects damage fall crops. The adult is a gray fly slightly smaller than a housefly, with black stripes and bristles down its back. It lays eggs on stems and nearby soil. The maggots hatch in 2 to 5 days and tunnel into radish roots, making them inedible.

SOLUTION: Once the growing plant wilts and turns yellow, nothing can be done. To control maggots in the next planting of radishes, mix ORTHO Vegetable Guard Soil Insect Killer or, ORTHO Diazinon Soil & Turf Insect Control 4 to 6 inches into the soil before seeding. Control lasts about 1 month. To prevent egg laying, screen adult flies from the seedbed with a cheesecloth cover.

Black root rot.

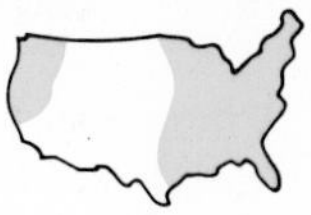

PROBLEM: Bluish black spots develop on the roots of white radishes. The spots enlarge, infecting the entire root. The infected tissue remains firm. A black discoloration extends into the root in radial streaks.

ANALYSIS: Black root rot
This plant disease is caused by a fungus (*Aphanomyces raphani*) that is especially severe on long-rooted white radish varieties. The variety White Icicle is the most susceptible. Colored and late-maturing varieties are also affected, but less severely. Plants may be infected at any time from the seedling stage to maturity. The fungus is most active in warm (68° to 80°F), wet soils, and the spores may live in the soil for several years. Abundant water is necessary for infection, and spores are spread by splashing and running water.

SOLUTION: Discard all infected roots. Clean all plant debris from the garden after harvest. Plant radishes in the same area only once every 3 or 4 years. Because this fungus requires abundant water for infection, grow radishes in well-drained soil and avoid overwatering. The soil should remain moist, but not soggy. Before planting, dust seeds with a fungicide containing *captan* (ORTHOCIDE®) or *thiram*.

The variety White Spike is less susceptible to black root rot than White Icicle. Red Prince is more resistant than other red globe varieties.

Poorly developed roots.

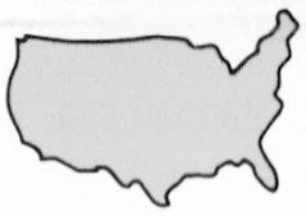

PROBLEM: Radish plants are all leaves with no plump roots. Any roots that do develop are thin.

ANALYSIS: Poor root development
Radishes fail to develop bulbous roots for any of several reasons.
1. Seedlings that are not thinned and that grow too close together compete with each other for water and nutrients, and never fully develop.
2. Plants may be growing at temperatures above 85°F. Radishes prefer the cooler temperatures of the spring and fall.
3. Plants may not be receiving enough sunlight to make the food they need to develop plump roots.
4. High-nitrogen fertilizers or soils high in organic material promote bushy top growth at the expense of root development.

SOLUTION: Follow these guidelines for good radish root development.
1. Plant seeds in rows 9 to 18 inches apart. When seedlings are 1 to 2 inches tall, thin to ½ to 1 inch apart.
2. In warmer areas of the country, plant radish seeds in the spring and fall so that they mature when temperatures are below 85°F.
3. Plant radishes in an area that receives at least 6 hours of sunlight a day.
4. Fertilize with a balanced fertilizer such as ORTHO Vegetable Food. Use moderate amounts of organic matter.

RHUBARB

ADAPTATION: Northern United States.

PLANTING TIME: See page 1025.

PLANTING METHOD: Plant root divisions or crowns so the buds are no deeper than 2 inches. Allow 2½ to 3 feet between plants.

SOIL: Any well-drained soil that is rich in organic matter. pH 5.0 to 7.0

FERTILIZER: At planting time, use 2 to 3 pounds of ORTHO General Purpose Plant Food per 100 square feet, or 1½ pounds per 50-foot row. Following years, fertilize with 1½ to 2 pounds of ORTHO General Purpose Plant Food each spring before the new leaves begin to grow. After harvest, side-dress with ORTHO Blood Meal using 1½ pounds per 50-foot row.

WATER:
How much: Apply enough water at each irrigation to wet the soil 15 to 18 inches deep.
How often: Water when the soil 2 inches deep is barely moist.

HARVEST: Do not pick stalks the first year after planting. The second year, pick for about 2 weeks. The third and following years, pick for about 6 to 8 weeks, or until the stalks become small. Pull only large stalks, leaving smaller ones to grow. Never pick more than two-thirds of the stalks present on the plant. To pick, hold the stalk near its base and pull toward one side until it breaks. Do not cut. Discard the leaf blade, which is not edible.

Crown rot.

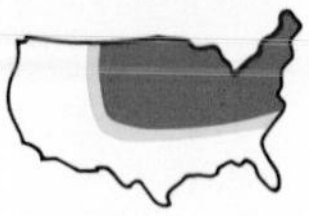

PROBLEM: Leaves wilt. Brown, sunken, water-soaked spots appear on the base of the leaf stalks. Leaves yellow and stalks collapse and die. The whole plant eventually dies.

ANALYSIS: Crown rot
This plant disease, also called *foot rot* or *root rot*, is caused by a fungus (*Phytophthora* species) that lives in the soil. It thrives in waterlogged, heavy soils, and attacks the crown and base of the stems. The stems and eventually the roots rot, resulting in wilting and finally the death of the plant. The fungus is most active in warm (60° to 75°F), moist soils in the late spring and early summer. The spores are spread to healthy plants in running or splashing water, or by contaminated soil or infected plants brought into the garden.

SOLUTION: Remove and destroy dying leaves and plants. Apply a drench of fungicide containing *captan* (ORTHOCIDE®) or *basic copper sulfate* to the crown or base of the plant and to the surrounding soil. When replanting, purchase disease-free plants from a reputable company, and plant in well-drained soil. (For information on improving soil drainage, see page 907.) Avoid overwatering.

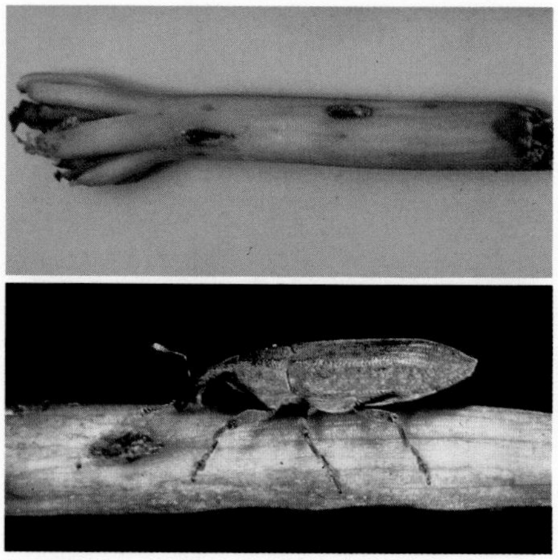
Damaged rhubarb and curculio (twice life size).

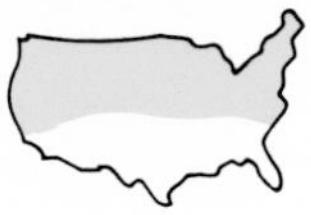

PROBLEM: Small black spots occur on the stalks. Slow-moving, ½ inch, black weevils covered with rusty-yellow powder are found on the stalks. They have long curved snouts.

ANALYSIS: Rhubarb curculio
(*Lixus concavus*)
The rhubarb curculio is one of the largest snout-nosed beetles in the United States. It does not feed on rhubarb at all, but injures the plants by boring into or puncturing the stalks, roots, and crown to lay eggs. This causes black spots on the stalks. After laying eggs, the adult curculio travels to nearby large-stemmed weeds, usually curly dock, and feeds on the foliage. (For information about curly dock, see page 833.) When the eggs in the rhubarb hatch, the larvae also leave the rhubarb plants to feed on curly dock roots. Rhubarb stalks marred with puncture holes are edible if the discolored area is cut away.

SOLUTION: There are no chemical controls currently available for curculio. Control grassy and large-stemmed weeds, especially curly dock, in the vicinity of your garden. Handpick adult beetles when you see them.

Small stalks.

PROBLEM: Rhubarb stalks are thin and small.

ANALYSIS: Small stalks
Rhubarb stalks may be small for any of several reasons.
1. *End of the harvest season:* Rhubarb stalks are produced from food stored in their roots. Toward the end of the harvest season, the food is used up and the stalks become smaller and smaller.
2. *Lack of fertilization*: Rhubarb plants are heavy feeders, requiring large amounts of fertilizer to encourage healthy growth so that an adequate food supply will be stored for the following year's harvest.
3. *Young plants:* Rhubarb stalks are small until the plants establish their roots and are able to store an adequate amount of food. This may take 2 years after planting.
4. *Overcrowding*: Rhubarb plants are vigorous growers with deep roots, and may compete with each other if not divided every 5 to 7 years.
5. *Crown rot*: This disease reduces plant vigor and kills the roots. For more information, see page 758.
6. *Poor soil drainage:* Rhubarb does not tolerate wet soil. The roots rot and the plants eventually die.

SOLUTION: To improve your harvest, follow the growing and harvesting guidelines on page 758. Control crown rot, and improve the soil drainage as outlined on page 907.

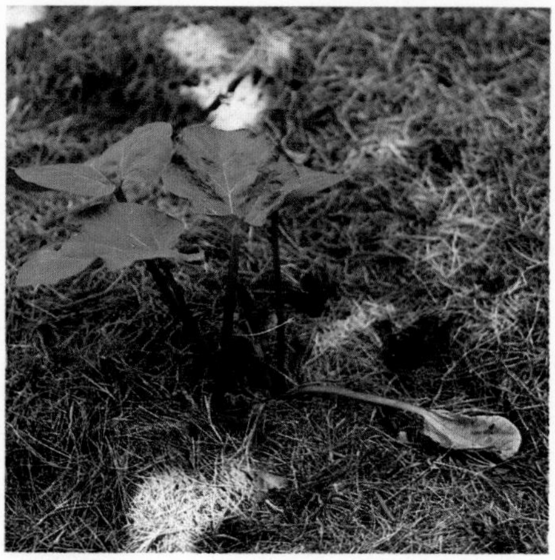
Seedstalks.

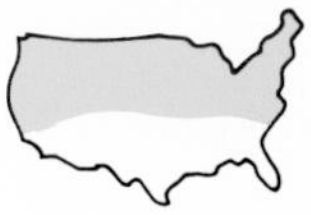

PROBLEM: Large yellow seedstalks grow from the center of rhubarb plants.

ANALYSIS: Seedstalk formation
Rhubarb forms seedstalks when the days become long and warm enough to trigger this response in the plant, usually about the time the harvest is ending. Sugars that are manufactured in the leaves are moved to the rapidly growing seedstalk at the expense of the roots. As a result, less sugar is stored in the roots to produce next year's crop, so the yield is reduced.

SOLUTION: Cut off the seedstalks as soon as they begin to grow.

Rhubarb leaves contain large amounts of oxalic acid, enough to make them poisonous. They should never be eaten or fed to animals.

SPINACH

ADAPTATION: Throughout the United States.

PLANTING TIME: See page 1025.

PLANTING METHOD: Sow seeds ½ inch deep and 1 inch apart. When the plants have 2 to 3 leaves, thin to stand 4 to 8 inches apart.

SOIL: Any good garden soil that is rich in organic matter. pH 6.0 to 8.0

FERTILIZER: At planting time, use 2 pounds of ORTHO General Purpose Plant Food per 100 square feet, or 1½ pounds per 50-foot row. Side-dress in 2 weeks with 1 to 2 pounds per 50-foot row.

Containers: Water thoroughly every 2 weeks with a solution of ORTHO Tomato & Vegetable Food.

WATER:

How much: Apply enough water at each irrigation to wet the soil 8 to 10 inches deep.

Containers: 10 per cent of the applied water should drain out the bottom.

How often: Water when the soil 2 inches deep is barely moist.

HARVEST: Pick individual leaves as needed. Just before seed stalks emerge, use a sharp knife to cut the entire plant just above the soil line.

Bolting spinach.

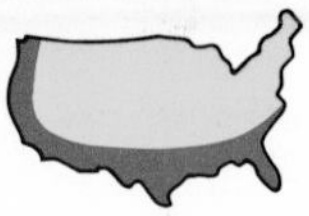

PROBLEM: Flower stalks grow from the center of spinach plants in late spring and summer.

ANALYSIS: Bolting

Spinach makes seed stalks (bolts) in late spring and summer as temperatures rise and the length of the day increases. Some varieties bolt more easily than others. Once the flower stalk forms, leaves may become bitter, and edible foliage is no longer produced. Fall-planted spinach seldom bolts.

SOLUTION: Plant spinach as soon as possible in the late winter or early spring. Plant approximately 4 to 6 weeks before the last spring frost, and no later than 6 to 8 weeks before the daytime temperatures remain over 75°F. Use bolt-resistant or long-standing varieties for spring planting. For a summer crop, plant New Zealand spinach, a spinach substitute that thrives in summer heat. Although it is not a true spinach, the taste is similar.

Bolt-resistant spinach varieties: America, Bloomsdale, Long Standing, and Melody.

Downy mildew.

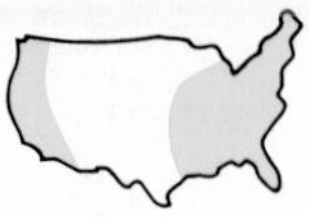

PROBLEM: During cool, humid weather, pale yellow spots appear on the upper surfaces of the lower leaves. These spots enlarge and spread to the upper leaves. A gray-purple mold grows on the undersides of the leaves. Leaves may turn black, and the whole plant may die.

ANALYSIS: Downy mildew

This plant disease, also called *blue mold,* is caused by a fungus (*Peronospora effusa*) that attacks only spinach. Bloomsdale variety is particularly susceptible. During prolonged cool (45° to 65°F), humid weather, the fungus spreads rapidly, often destroying the entire planting. The fungus can invade a healthy leaf only if the leaf remains wet for extended periods. Spores are produced on the undersides of the leaves.

SOLUTION: Fungicidal sprays for the control of this disease are seldom practical in home gardens. It is difficult to spray the lower surfaces of the spinach leaves. If downy mildew is severe, and your planting is large, you may treat with a fungicide containing *maneb* or *zineb.* Repeat the treatment at weekly intervals until the disease is no longer seen, or until the weather becomes less favorable for the disease. Remove all plant debris from the garden after harvest. Plant disease-resistant varieties (see page 1027). Water early in the day, so that the plants dry before nightfall.

White rust.

PROBLEM: White, blisterlike spots with a yellow border appear on the undersides of leaves. The upper surfaces of the leaves are pale green to yellow, and may also have blisterlike spots.

ANALYSIS: White rust
This plant disease is caused by a fungus (*Albugo occidentalis*) that attacks all varieties of spinach. Infected plants are weakened and collapse quickly. White rust is most active during prolonged periods of cool, humid nights and mild days, with temperatures between 55° and 80°F. The leaves must be wet for infection to take place. The fungal spores survive the winter in plant debris in the garden, and are spread to healthy plants by the wind, or by splashing or running water.

SOLUTION: Fungicidal sprays are seldom practical in home gardens for this disease. The spinach usually matures before enough applications can be made to control the disease. If white rust is severe in your area, or if your planting is large, treat the plants with a fungicide containing *maneb* or *zineb* when the first three to four leaves are three-quarters grown. Controls are effective only if started early. Repeat at weekly intervals until 10 days before harvest. To help reduce infections, water early in the day so the plants dry before nightfall. Remove all plant debris from the garden after harvest. Don't plant spinach in the same spot more often than once every 3 years.

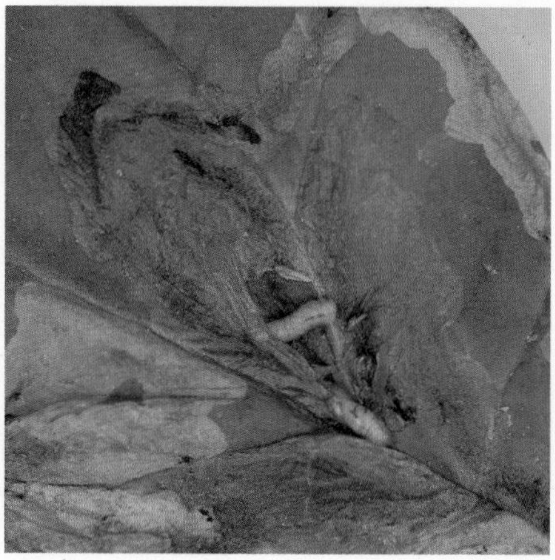
Leafminers (life size).

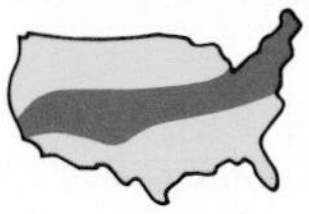

PROBLEM: Irregular tan blotches, blisters, or tunnels appear in the leaves. The tan areas peel apart like facial tissue. Tiny black specks and white or yellow maggots are found inside the tunnels.

ANALYSIS: Leafminers
These insect pests belong to a family of leaf-mining flies. The tiny black or yellow adult fly lays her white eggs on the undersides of leaves. The maggots that hatch from these eggs bore into the leaf and tunnel between the upper and lower surfaces, feeding on the inner tissue. The tunnels and blotches are called *mines*. The black specks inside are the maggots' droppings. Several overlapping generations occur during the growing season, so larvae are present continually from spring until fall. Infested leaves are not edible.

SOLUTION: Control leafminers on spinach with ORTHO Fruit & Vegetable Insect Control when the white egg clusters are first seen under the leaves. Repeat 2 more times at weekly intervals to control succeeding generations. Once the leafminers enter the leaves, the sprays are ineffective. Spraying after the mines first appear will control only those leafminers that attack after the application. Clean all plant debris from the garden after harvest to reduce overwintering spots for the pupae.

STRAWBERRIES

ADAPTATION: Throughout the United States.

PLANTING TIME: See page 1025.

PLANTING METHOD: Select dormant or growing plants. Pick off all but two or three of the healthiest leaves. Prune away a third of the roots. Set the plants 18 inches apart and so that the roots fan outward. The crown should be just above the soil level. As runners develop, maintain the rows no wider than 18 to 24 inches.

SOIL: Any good garden soil that is high in organic matter. pH 5.5 to 7.5

FERTILIZER: At planting time, add 2 pounds of ORTHO General Purpose Plant Food per 100 square feet, or ½ pound per 25-foot row. Side-dress after harvest each year with ½ to 1 pound of fertilizer per 25-foot row.
Containers: Water thoroughly every 3 to 4 weeks with a solution of ORTHO Tomato & Vegetable Food.

WATER:
How much: Apply enough water at each irrigation to wet the soil 8 to 10 inches deep.
How often: Water when the soil 1 inch deep is barely moist.

HARVEST: For maximum production the second year, remove blossoms and runners the first year. Pick berries, with the stem and cap attached, when they are completely red. Pinch the stem between your fingers, being careful not to uproot the plants. Store berries in the refrigerator until used.

STRAWBERRIES

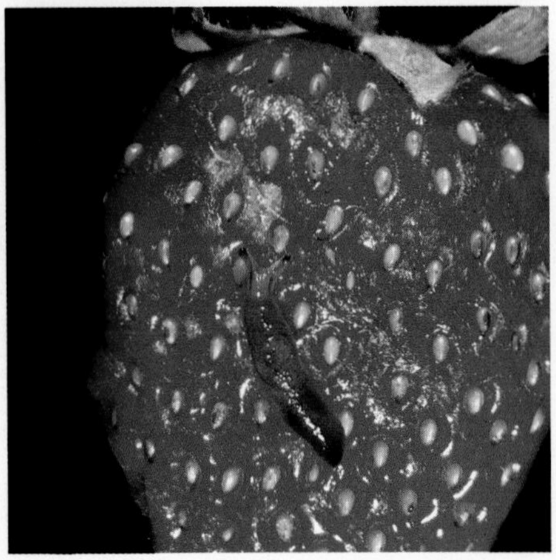

Slug (3 times life size).

PROBLEM: Stems and leaves may be sheared off and eaten. Silvery trails wind around on the plants and soil nearby. Snails or slugs may be seen moving around or feeding on the plants, especially at night. Inspect the garden for them at night by flashlight.

ANALYSIS: Snails and slugs

These pests are mollusks, and are related to clams, oysters, and other shellfish. They feed on a wide variety of garden plants. Like other mollusks, snails and slugs need to be moist all the time. For this reason, they avoid direct sun and dry places, and hide during the day in damp places, such as under flower pots or in thick groundcover. They emerge at night or on cloudy days to feed. Snails and slugs are similar except that the snail has a hard shell, into which it withdraws when disturbed. Slugs lay masses of white eggs encased in a slimy mass in protected places. Snails bury their eggs in the soil, also in a slimy mass. The young look like miniature versions of their parents.

SOLUTION: Scatter ORTHO Bug-Geta Snail & Slug Pellets around the areas you wish to protect. Also scatter the pellets in areas where snails or slugs might be hiding, such as in dense groundcover, weedy areas, compost piles, or pot storage areas. Before spreading the pellets, wet down the areas to be treated to encourage snail and slug activity that night. Repeat the application every 2 weeks as long as snails and slugs are active. Do not apply pellets to leaves.

Meadow spittlebug (half life size).

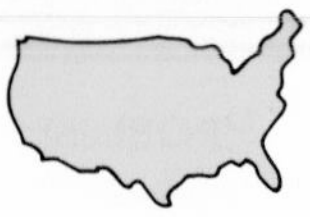

PROBLEM: White, frothy masses of bubbles, ½ inch long, appear on leaves, stems, and flowers. Hidden in this froth is a small, smooth, tan to green insect.

ANALYSIS: Meadow spittlebug

(*Philaenus spumarius*)

Spittlebugs are related to leafhoppers (see page 880). Both the adults and the nymphs damage plants by sucking the sap from the leaves and stems. When populations are high, this results in stunted plants that are low in vigor and produce few berries. Small numbers of spittlebugs do little damage to strawberry plants. Spittlebug eggs survive the winter in plant debris, and hatch in the early spring. The nymphs produce the frothy "spittle," which protects them from the sun and from other insects. The nymphs remain in the spittle until they emerge in early summer as hopping, tan to black adults. The adults feed until frost, laying eggs in August and September. Spittlebugs are most numerous in areas with high humidity. There is one generation a year.

SOLUTION: Once the nymphs are protected inside the froth, insecticides are ineffective. Hose off the frothy masses with a strong stream of water. If spittlebugs are numerous in your area and your plants are suffering, control the adults in the summer and fall with ORTHO Home Orchard Spray or ORTHO Malathion 50 Insect Spray. Clean all plant debris from the garden at the end of the season to reduce the number of overwintering eggs.

Gray mold.

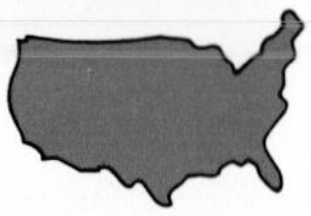

PROBLEM: A light tan spot appears on berries. Some berries are soft, mushy, and rotting. A fluffy gray mold may cover rotting berries.

ANALYSIS: Gray mold

Gray mold is caused by a fungus (*Botrytis cinerea*). It is the most damaging rot of strawberries, and greatly reduces the amount of edible fruit. Both flowers and berries are attacked. The flowers are infected when in bloom, and may not produce berries. Berries are attacked at all stages of development. They are infected directly when a healthy berry touches a decaying one, the ground, or a dead leaf. Infected berries are inedible. The fuzzy gray mold on the berries is composed of fungal strands and millions of microscopic spores. The fungus is most active in cool, humid weather, and is spread by splashing water, people, or infected fruit. Crowded plantings, rain, and overhead watering enhance the spread of the fungus.

SOLUTION: Discard infected fruit. To reduce the spread of the fungus to uncontaminated fruit, treat with ORTHO Home Orchard Spray, ORTHO Orthocide Garden Fungicide, or ORTHO Tomato Vegetable Dust at the first sign of the disease. Continue treating every 8 to 10 days. Pick berries as they ripen. Avoid overhead watering by using soaker or drip hoses. Mulch with straw, pine needles, or other material to keep fruit off the ground. To prevent infection next year, treat the plants when in bloom, and repeat every 8 to 10 days. When setting out new plants, provide enough space between plants to allow for good air circulation and rapid drying after rain and irrigation.

Strawberry leafroller (life size).

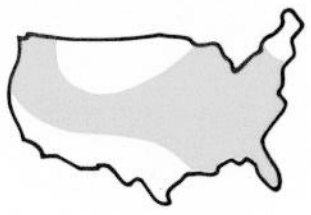

PROBLEM: Leaves are rolled, folded, or webbed together. Some leaves may turn brown and die. Inside the rolled leaves are ½-inch brown or green worms that wriggle when disturbed.

ANALYSIS: Strawberry leafroller
(*Ancylis comptana fragariae*)
This moth larva damages plants by feeding from inside the rolled leaves. This feeding weakens the plant, causing leaves to die and fruit to be deformed. Leafrollers hibernate for the winter as larvae and pupae in plant debris and folded leaves. In May, the adult moths, rusty red with brown and white markings, lay their eggs on the undersides of the leaves. The worms that hatch from these eggs roll the leaves and feed inside. After feeding for 4 to 7 weeks, the worms pupate in the rolled leaves, and emerge as adults to repeat the cycle. There are two or three generations a year.

SOLUTION: Treat with ORTHO Fruit & Vegetable Insect Control or ORTHO Diazinon Insect Spray as soon as the worms or rolled leaves are noticed. Repeat the treatments at intervals of 10 to 14 days if leaf rolling continues. If practical, pick the worms off by hand.

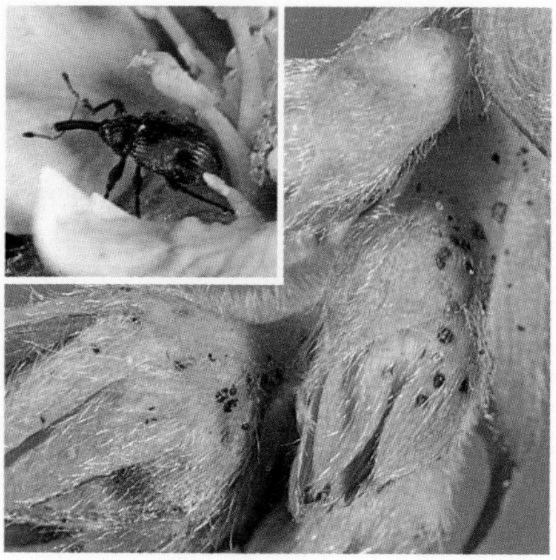

Damaged buds. *Insert:* Adult (5 times life size).

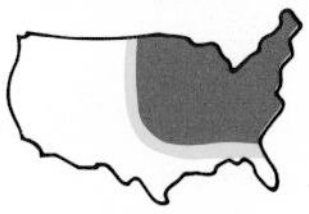

PROBLEM: Flower buds droop, turn brown and dry, and hang from the plant or fall to the ground. Small holes appear in the sides of the buds. Dark reddish brown, ⅛ inch weevils with curved snouts crawl on the plants.

ANALYSIS: Strawberry weevil
(*Anthonomous signatus*)
These insect pests of strawberries, dewberries, and wild blackberries are also known as *clippers* because they clip the flower bud stems, causing buds to droop and fall to the ground. By destroying the flower buds they reduce the berry crop. Adult weevils survive the winter in debris in and near the garden. In the spring, they puncture holes in the sides of unopened flower buds and lay an egg in each hole. Then the adult cuts a notch in the flower stem ⅛ to ¼ inch below the bud. The buds droop for a few days and then fall to the ground. Within a week the eggs hatch and fat, white grubs feed on the pollen inside the bud. After feeding for about 4 weeks, the grubs pupate and emerge as adults in early to midsummer. These adults feed on blackberry and dewberry pollen, hibernate for the winter, and emerge in the spring to repeat the cycle. There is only one generation a year.

SOLUTION: Treat plants with ORTHO Home Orchard Spray or ORTHO Sevin Garden Dust when cut buds first appear. Repeat through the closed bud stage as long as damage occurs. Clean all plant debris from the garden and adjacent areas at the end of the season to reduce overwintering locations for the adults.

Spider mite webbing.

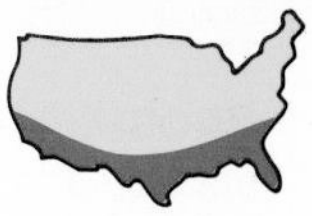

PROBLEM: Leaves are stippled, yellowing, and dirty. Leaves may dry out and drop. There may be webbing between leaves, or on the lower surfaces of the leaves. Few berries are produced. To determine if the plant is infested with mites, hold a sheet of white paper underneath an affected leaf and tap the leaf sharply. Minute green, red, or yellow specks the size of pepper grains will drop to the paper and begin to crawl around. These pests are easily seen against the white background.

ANALYSIS: Spider mites
Spider mites, related to spiders, are major pests of many garden and greenhouse plants. Spider mites are larger than cyclamen mites, which also attack strawberries. Spider mites attack the older leaves, while cyclamen mites attack the younger leaves. For more information on cyclamen mites, see page 764. Spider mites cause damage by sucking sap from the undersides of the leaves. As a result of feeding, the green leaf pigment disappears, producing the stippled appearance. Berry production is also reduced. Mites are active throughout the growing season, but are favored by hot, dry weather (70°F and up). By midsummer, they build up to tremendous numbers. For more information about spider mites, see page 887.

SOLUTION: Treat infested strawberry plants with ORTHO Fruit & Vegetable Insect Control or a miticide containing *dicofol* (KELTHANE®) when the damage first appears. Repeat the treatment at intervals of 7 to 10 days until harvest, or until damage no longer occurs. Be sure the pesticide contacts the lower surfaces of the leaves where the mites live.

STRAWBERRIES

Cyclamen mite damage.

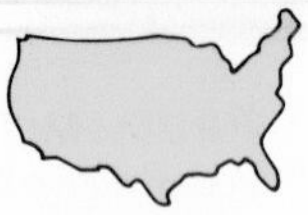

PROBLEM: Leaves are curled, distorted, and stunted. Leaves in the center of the plant grow in tight bunches. Flower buds fall prematurely. Berries are distorted and shriveled.

ANALYSIS: Cyclamen mites
(*Steneotarsonemus pallidus*)
These pests of strawberries, also called *strawberry crown mites*, attack many garden and greenhouse plants including delphiniums, dahlias, African violets, and snapdragons. They attack the young leaves and damage them by sucking sap from the midvein on the undersides of the folded leaves. This causes the leaves to remain curled and tight in the center of the plant. Berry production is also reduced. Cyclamen mites are very tiny (1/100 of an inch) and can be seen only with a microscope or high-power hand lens. The mites survive the winter in the crowns of the strawberry plants. They feed in cool weather, and are seldom found in hot weather.

SOLUTION: Treat infested plants and those nearby with ORTHO Diazinon Soil & Foliage Dust, or with a miticide containing *dicofol* (KELTHANE®). Be sure the pesticide contacts the lower surfaces of the leaves where the mites live. Repeat at intervals of 7 to 10 days until the new leaves grow normally and are no longer curled or distorted. Avoid touching healthy plants after handling infested ones.

Virus disease.

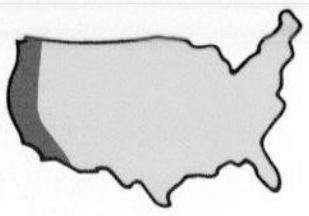

PROBLEM: Strawberry leaves are crinkled, yellowed, or distorted.
Plants may be stunted with cupped leaves, or may grow in a tight rosette. Small, dull fruits or no fruits are produced. Plants grow few runners.

ANALYSIS: Viruses
Two types of viruses attack strawberries: killer viruses and latent viruses. Killer viruses have obvious symptoms, and kill individual mother plants and daughter plants attached to the ends of runners. Latent viruses show few or no symptoms. A single latent virus may merely reduce the number of runners and fruit produced. However, plants infected with more than one kind of latent virus are so weakened that they are frequently attacked and killed by other diseases. Viruses are transmitted by aphids and through runners from mother to daughter plants. Aphids are most numerous in cool spring and fall weather.

SOLUTION: Remove and discard all infected plants. If aphids are present, control them with ORTHO Diazinon Insect Spray, ORTHO Home Orchard Spray, or ORTHO Malathion 50 Insect Spray. (For more information about controlling disease-carrying insects, see page 879.) When replanting, buy certified plants from a reputable company. Certified plants are grown in special isolated conditions, and are essentially virus-free. Or choose virus-tolerant varieties.

Strawberry varieties tolerant of viruses: Florida Belle, Florida 90, Klonmore, Shasta, Tennessee Beauty, and Tioga.

Fungal leaf spot.

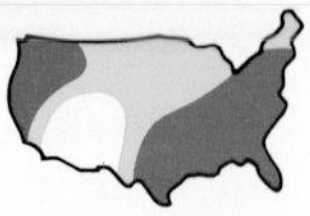

PROBLEM: Purple spots, 1/8 to 1/4 inch in diameter, with tan to white centers occur on young leaves, fruitstalks, runners, and berry caps. Black spots may appear on unripe berries.

ANALYSIS: Leaf spot
A number of fungi cause leaf spots on strawberries. One of the most prevalent (*Mycosphaerella fragariae*) may kill many leaves. The most serious injury, however, occurs from spotting on fruitstalks and caps. This spotting reduces the size of the fruit, or kills the entire cluster. Berries attacked before they ripen never fully ripen and are inedible. Infected caps are discolored and killed, making the fruit unappetizing. Plantlets growing at the end of infected runners are weak and produce poorly. Leaf spot is most prevalent in cool, damp, humid weather in spring and fall, but occurs through the summer as long as moist weather continues.

SOLUTION: Treat plants with a fungicidal spray containing *benomyl* or *basic copper sulfate* at the first sign of leaf spotting. Repeat at intervals of 7 to 10 days until 3 days before harvest. Be sure to spray both the upper and lower surfaces of the leaves. Treat the plants in the fall if spotting occurs. Repeat as long as weather favorable for the spread of the disease continues. Clean all plant debris from the garden at the end of the season. Grow resistant varieties.

Strawberry varieties resistant to leaf spot: Albritton, Apollo, Atlas, Daybreak, Earlibelle, Fairfax, Guardian, Headliner, Howard 17 (Premier), Klonmore, Midland, Surecrop, and Tennessee Beauty.

Leaf scorch.

PROBLEM: Purple to brown spots, up to ¼ inch in diameter, occur on the leaves, fruitstalks, and runners. The spots enlarge into blotches that may cover the entire leaf. Leaves become dry as if scorched. Berry caps may be black.

ANALYSIS: Leaf scorch

This plant disease is caused by a fungus (*Diplocarpon earliana*) that attacks strawberry leaves, fruitstalks, runners, and berry caps. Both older and younger leaves are attacked. When severe, the disease may destroy many leaves, weakening and killing plants. Spots on fruitstalks reduce berry size and cause flowers and young fruit to die. Infected berry caps turn black, making the fruit unattractive. Leaf scorch is most prevalent in cool, damp, humid weather in the spring and fall, but may occur throughout the summer as long as moist weather continues.

SOLUTION: Treat plants with a fungicidal spray containing *benomyl* or *basic copper sulfate* at the first sign of leaf spotting. Repeat at intervals of 7 to 10 days before harvest. Be sure to spray both the upper and lower surfaces of the leaves. Treat the plants in the fall if spotting occurs. Repeat as long as weather favorable to the spread of the disease continues. Clean all plant debris from the garden at the end of the season. Grow resistant varieties.

Strawberry varieties resistant to leaf scorch: Albritton, Apollo, Atlas, Catskill, Earlibelle, Fairfax, Fletcher, Hood, Howard 17 (Premier), Midland, Pocahontas, Rainier, Redstar, Southland, and Tennessee Beauty.

Salt damage.

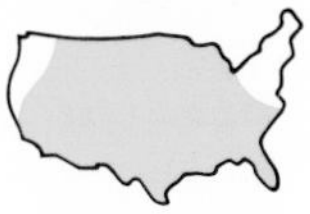

PROBLEM: Leaf edges and areas between the veins turn dark brown and die. Burned leaves may drop. Growth slows or stops. A white or dark brown crust may form on the soil.

ANALYSIS: Salt damage

Salt damage occurs when salt accumulates in the soil to damaging levels. This can happen in either of two ways: the strawberry patch is not receiving enough water from the rainfall or irrigation to wash the salts from the soil, or the drainage is so poor that water does not pass through the soil. In either case, as water evaporates from the soil and plant leaves, the salts that were dissolved in the water accumulate near the soil surface. In some cases, a white or dark brown crust of salts forms on the surface of the soil. Salts can originate in the soil, in the irrigation water, or in applied fertilizers.

SOLUTION: The only way to eliminate salt problems is to wash the salts through the soil with water. If the damage is only at a low spot in the planting, fill in the spot to level the area. If the entire planting drains poorly, improve the drainage according to the directions on page 907. If the soil drains well, increase the amount of water applied at each watering by 50 percent or more, so that excess water will leach salts below the root zone of the strawberry plants. Fertilize according to the instructions on page 761.

Verticillium wilt.

PROBLEM: Outer leaves wilt and turn dark brown along the margins and between the veins. Few new leaves are formed. Plants are flattened and few berries are produced. Brown spots or streaking may appear on leafstalks and runners and in crown tissue.

ANALYSIS: Verticillium wilt

This wilt disease affects many ornamental plants. It is caused by a soil-inhabiting fungus (*Verticillium dahliae*) that persists indefinitely on plant debris or in the soil. The disease is spread by contaminated seeds, plants, soil, and equipment. The fungus enters the plant through the roots and speads up into the crown and leaves through water-conducting vessels, which become discolored and plugged. This plugging cuts off the flow of water and nutrients to the leaves, causing leaf yellowing and wilting. Affected plants may or may not recover and yield fruit the following year. Sometimes the disease appears in mother plants, but not in rooted daughter plants. For more information about verticillium wilt, see page 850.

SOLUTION: No chemical control is available. It is best to destroy infected plants. Verticillium can be removed from the soil only by fumigation techniques. (For more information about soil fumigation, see page 927.) However, the best solution is usually to plant varieties that are tolerant of verticillium wilt.

Strawberry varieties tolerant of verticillium wilt: Catskill, Empire, Gala, Guardian, Hood, Rainier, Redchief, Robinson, Salinas, Shuksan, Sunrise, Surecrop, and Vermillion.

STRAWBERRIES

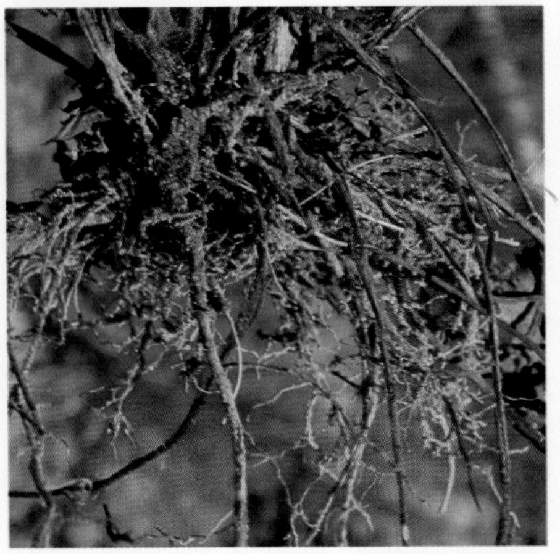

Black root rot.

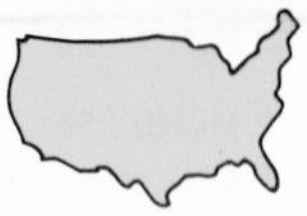

PROBLEM: Plants grow poorly, wilt, and produce very few berries. Leaves turn yellow, then red and finally brown, and die. Dark brown to black spots occur on roots. The outer tissue layer of the main roots blackens, while the center core remains a normal pale yellow.

ANALYSIS: Black root rot
Black root rot is caused by any of several soil-inhabiting fungi. These fungi thrive in waterlogged, heavy soils. The fungi attack the plant roots, causing them to decay. This results in wilting, then yellowing leaves, and eventually the death of the plant. Plants weakened by frost injury, drought stress, nematodes, buried crowns, or wet soil are more susceptible to these fungi.

SOLUTION: Remove and discard all infected plants. Avoid future black root rot problems by planting in well-drained soil. For information on improving soil drainage, see page 901. Buy healthy plants from a reputable company. Do not purchase any plants with black or darkened roots.

Damaged roots. *Insert:* Root weevil (4 times life size).

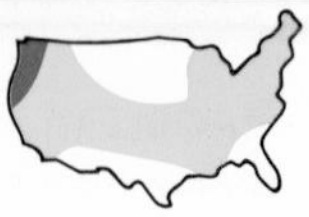

PROBLEM: Plants grow slowly and are stunted. Leaves turn reddish brown. Notches or scallops are chewed in the edges of the leaves. White, legless, C-shaped, grubs with brown heads, up to ⅜-inch long, are found in the soil feeding on plant roots.

ANALYSIS: Root weevils
Several weevils attack strawberries. The brown to black, hard shelled, ¼-inch-long adult beetles with long snouts feed on the leaves at night. They hide during the day under leaves and clods of soil. Their feeding causes little damage, but is a warning sign that grubs may be present. Adults are present from spring through summer, and lay their eggs in the crowns of plants in early summer. The grubs that hatch from these eggs burrow into the soil and feed on the roots until late fall, then resume feeding in the spring. Their feeding reduces berry production and sometimes kills the plant. There is only one generation a year. The adult weevils occasionally become a nuisance in the house. As they migrate in search of more food, they enter homes through open doors and windows and cracks in the foundation. Although they may feed on some houseplants, they do not eat food or clothing.

SOLUTION: There are no chemicals available to home gardeners to control root weevils on strawberries. Destroy infested plants and any grubs found in the soil. Do not plant in infested soil.

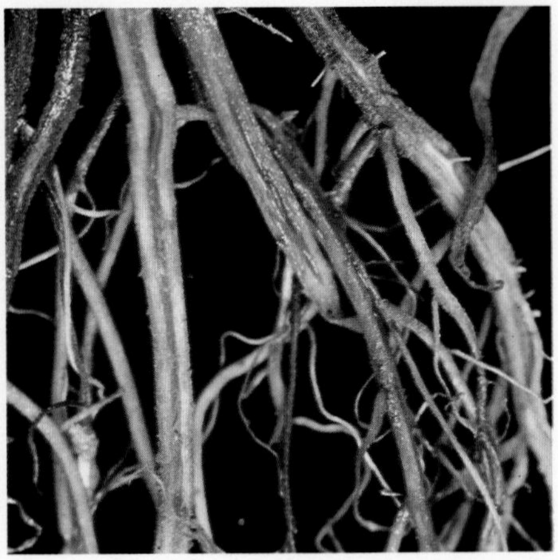

Red stele.

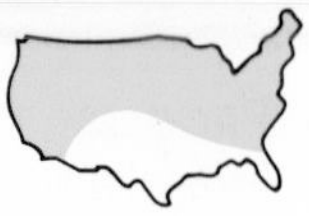

PROBLEM: Plants grow poorly, are stunted, and frequenty wilt. The young leaves turn bluish-green. Older leaves turn yellow and red. In the spring, the center of the root is discolored reddish brown instead of the normal pale yellow color. Black tips or patches may appear on feeder roots. Few berries are produced, and the plants eventually die.

ANALYSIS: Red stele
This root rot disease of strawberries is caused by a fungus (*Phytophthora fragariae*) that persists in the soil for many years. It is the most damaging disease that attacks strawberries. The small feeder roots are attacked first. Then the fungus invades the center core—the stele—of the roots. The reddish brown discoloration is most visible in the spring. In the summer the rotted roots are replaced by new healthy roots, so the symptoms often disappear. Red stele is most destructive in cool spring and fall weather in poorly drained, heavy soil or low spots in the garden. Plants growing in well-drained soil are less frequently attacked.

SOLUTION: There is no chemical control available for red stele on strawberry. The most practical method of control is to plant tolerant varieties in well-drained soil. For instructions on improving drainage, see page 763.

Strawberry varieties tolerant to red stele:
East Coast—Earliglow, Guardian, Midway, Redchief, Red Glow, Sparkle, Sunrise, and Surecrop.
West Coast—Columbia, Hood, Olympus, Rainier, Shuksan, and Totem.

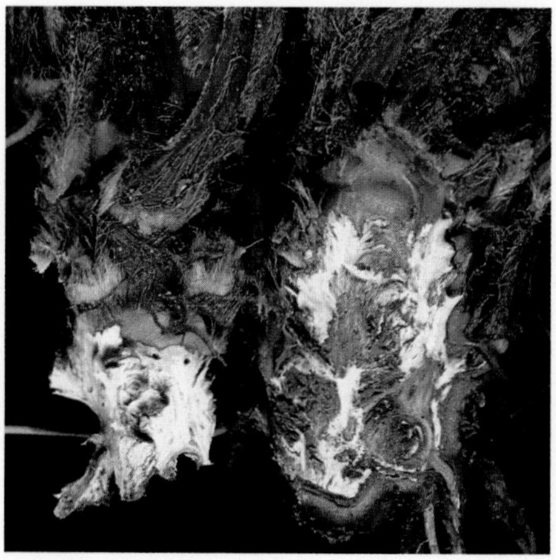

Armillaria root rot.

PROBLEM: Leaves are stunted and yellow. Few berries are produced. Plants decline, produce no new growth, and die. In the fall, honey-colored mushrooms, 2 to 5 inches in diameter, may develop singly or in clusters on the base of the plant or in the soil. Black, rootlike strands about the diameter of a pencil lead grow out of the roots into the soil.

ANALYSIS: Armillaria root rot
This plant disease, also called *oak root fungus* and *shoestring root rot*, is caused by a fungus (*Armillaria mellea*) that rots the roots of many woody and nonwoody plants. Plants under stress from severe drought, overwatering, physical injuries, insects, or diseases are the most susceptible to attack. The fungus is spread long distances by spores from the mushrooms, or short distances through the soil by the rootlike fungal strands. Once the fungus enters the plant, the roots decay, and water and nutrient uptake are inhibited, causing the plant to die. In the fall, mushrooms appear at the base of the plant.

SOLUTION: No chemical controls are available. Remove and destroy infected plants, including the roots. Check surrounding plants and remove if infected. Keep strawberry plants healthy with regular maintenance as outlined on page 761. Avoid planting strawberries in recently cleared forest lands or old orchards, where armillaria root rot is common.

Symphylan damaged plants.

PROBLEM: Slender, white pests about ¼ inch long with 6 to 12 pairs of legs and long antennae are present in the soil. Plants may be stunted.

ANALYSIS: Garden symphylans
(*Scutigerella immaculata*)
These soil-inhabiting pests, also called *garden centipedes*, are a problem in both outdoor plantings and greenhouses. They live in damp soil that is high in organic matter, and avoid sunlight. Symphylans feed on the fine roots and root hairs of many different plants, and tunnel through crowns, stunting and sometimes killing plants. They may also invade fruit close to the ground. Symphylans are most active in the spring, but egg laying occurs from spring through summer. They lay white eggs in clusters 1 foot deep in the soil. The young have 6 pairs of legs and short antennae, but these develop to 12 pairs and long antennae as they mature into adults. Symphylans may live 4 to 5 years, so symphylans of all ages are found in the soil at one time.

SOLUTION: Treat the soil around strawberry plants with an insecticide containing *diazinon* at the first sign of symphylans. Repeat the treatment as needed to control these pests. Mulch plants with straw or leaf mold to keep the fruit off the ground. For more information on these pests, see page 890.

SUNFLOWER

ADAPTATION: Throughout the United States.

PLANTING TIME: See page 1025.

PLANTING METHOD: Sow seeds 1 inch deep and 5 to 6 inches apart. When the seedlings have 2 or 3 leaves, thin to stand 16 to 24 inches apart.

SOIL: Any good garden soil. pH 6.0 to 7.5

FERTILIZER: At planting time, use 2 pounds of ORTHO Genreral Purpose Plant Food per 100 square feet, or 1 pound per 25-foot row. Side-dress every 3 to 4 weeks with 1 pound per 25-foot row, or 1 to 2 tablespoons per plant.

WATER:
How much: Apply enough water at each irrigation to wet the soil 12 to 15 inches deep.
How often: Water when the soil 1 inch deep is dry.

HARVEST: Sunflower seeds begin to mature when the seeds along the outside of the head fatten. When the back of the head becomes tough, leathery, and dries out, cut the entire head with a sharp knife and shake or scrape out the seeds, collecting them on newspaper or a sheet. Wash thoroughly, and dry at room temperature. Store in an air-tight container.

SUNFLOWERS

Powdery mildew.

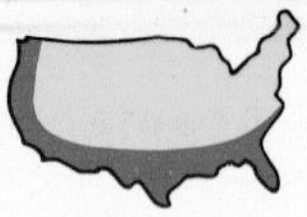

PROBLEM: A grayish white, powdery growth appears on the upper surfaces of the leaves. Infected leaves shrivel and die.

ANALYSIS: Powdery mildew
This common plant disease is caused by a fungus (*Erysiphe cichoracearum*) that thrives in both humid and dry weather. The powdery patches consist of fungal strands and spores. The spores are spread by the wind to healthy plants. The fungus saps the plant nutrients, causing yellowing and sometimes death of the leaf. A severe infection may kill the plant. Since this powdery mildew attacks many different kinds of plants, the fungus from a diseased plant may infect other types of plants in the garden. (For a list of susceptible plants, see page 995.) Under favorable conditions, powdery mildew can spread though a closely spaced planting in a matter of days or weeks.

SOLUTION: Treat infected plants with a fungicidal spray containing *benomyl* or *wettable sulfur* at the first sign of the disease. Repeat at weekly intervals as long as new growth is attacked. Do not use sulfur when temperatures are above 90°F. Clean all debris from the garden at the end of the season to eliminate overwintering spores.

Sunflower moth larva (life size).

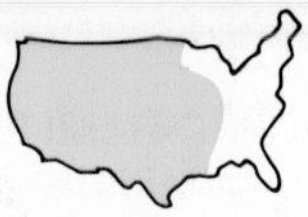

PROBLEM: Sunflower heads are covered with a silken webbing mixed with black flecks and plant debris. In the flower heads are light brown worms, ¾ inch long, with five brown stripes down their backs.

ANALYSIS: Sunflower moth
(*Homoeosoma electellum*)
This insect is one of the most destructive pests of sunflowers, as well as of cosmos, marigolds, and coreopsis. The larvae damage the plants by feeding on and destroying seeds in the flower heads. Sometimes the entire head is destroyed. The first sunflowers to bloom in an area are the most susceptible to attack. Adult moths, ⅜ inch long, with buff to grayish wings emerge in early to mid-July and lay eggs on the flower heads. The larvae that hatch from these eggs begin feeding on the florets and seeds. While feeding, they spin over the flower head a silken webbing intertwined with their black excrement and plant debris.

SOLUTION: Remove webbing on flower heads and destroy any worms inside. The following year, treat with an insecticidal spray containing *diazinon* when the flowers first appear. Repeat one or two more times, 5 to 7 days apart.

Rust.

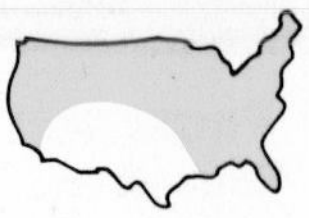

PROBLEM: Yellow-white specks spot the upper surfaces of the leaves. Rust-colored pustules form on the lower surfaces of the leaves and often on the stem. Infected leaves may wither and drop. Plants are stunted and sometimes die.

ANALYSIS: Rust
This plant disease is caused by a fungus (*Puccinia helianthi*) that attacks sunflower relatives, including Jerusalem artichokes and ornamental sunflowers. The spores are spread by splashing water and wind. The disease is favored by moist conditions with cool nights and warm days. Temperatures above 90°F kill the spores. Plants must remain wet for 6 to 8 hours before the fungus can infect the leaf. Rust spores spend the winter on infected plant debris that has been left in the garden. Rust seldom affects the flavor of the sunflower seeds.

SOLUTION: Rust is not easy to control. Pick off and destroy infected leaves. Apply a fungicide containing *zineb*, *maneb*, or *wettable sulfur* as soon as the disease is noticed. Since rust needs water on the leaves in order to infect them, water in the morning rather than the evening to allow wet foliage time to dry. Avoid overhead watering; if possible, use drip or furrow irrigation. Thin seedlings and space plants far enough apart to allow air to circulate freely. Remove all plant debris at the end of the season to reduce the number of overwintering spores.

SWEET POTATOES

ADAPTATION: Southern United States.

PLANTING TIME: See page 1025.

PLANTING METHOD: Plant slips or sprouts 2 to 3 inches deep and 12 to 16 inches apart. In poorly drained soil, plant in ridges or hills so the roots do not rot in the ground.

SOIL: Loose, crumbly soil high in organic matter. pH 5.0 to 6.5

FERTILIZER: At planting time, use 1½ to 2 pounds of ORTHO Vegetable Food per 50-foot row. Side-dress 3 to 4 weeks after planting with the same amount as at planting time.

WATER:
How much: Apply enough water at each irrigation to wet the soil 8 to 10 inches deep.
How often: Water when the soil 2 inches deep is dry. Sweet potatoes are drought-hardy, and grow well under dry conditions.

HARVEST: Sweet potatoes are usually ready for eating about 110 to 120 days after planting. With a shovel, dig around a few plants to check tuber size. When ready, dig carefully to avoid bruising, and use as needed.
To store: Brush off all soil and discard infected or damaged roots. Cure at 85°F with high humidity for 6 to 8 days. After curing, store the roots at 55° to 60°F with high humidity until use.

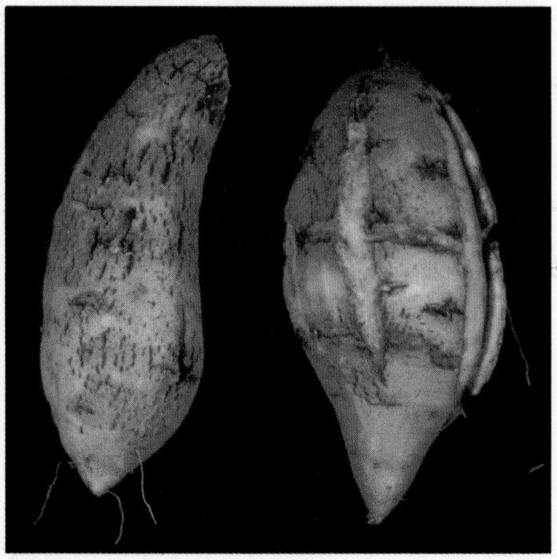

Growth cracks.

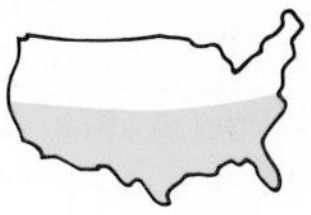

PROBLEM: Sweet potato roots are cracked when harvested. Some may also crack in storage.

ANALYSIS: Growth cracks
Cracking of sweet potato roots is a disorder that results from prolonged dry periods followed by excessive moisture. In some varieties, it seems to be an inherited characteristic. The cracks heal over by harvest time, with no loss in eating or storage quality. Roots may also crack in storage if the temperature and humidity fluctuate greatly.

SOLUTION: Avoid excessively wet or dry soil. For best yields, sweet potatoes require adequate water throughout the growing season, especially when they are older and growing vigorously in hot weather in sandy soil. Store roots in a cool (55° to 60°F) place with high humidity (85 percent).

Sweet potato varieties less susceptible to cracking: Jewel and Porto Rico 198.

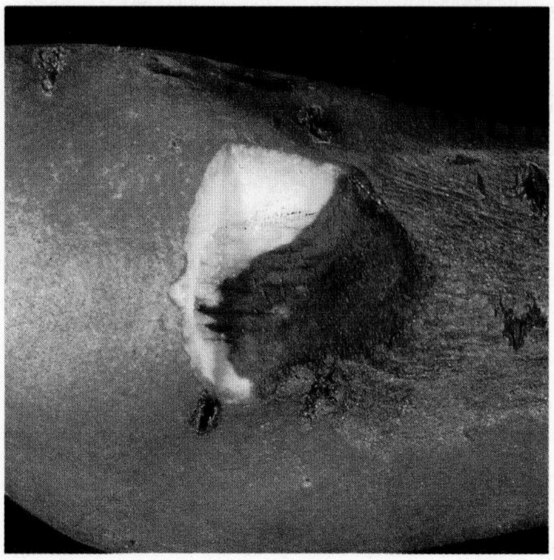

Black rot.

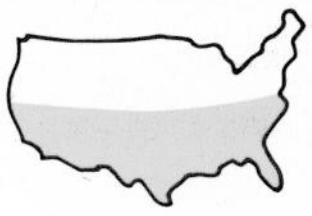

PROBLEM: Black spots occur on roots in the ground and in storage. Tiny black specks appear in the center of blackened areas. Black lesions occur on stems at the soil line. Leaves are yellow and dwarfed.

ANALYSIS: Black rot
This plant disease is caused by a fungus (*Ceratocystis fimbriata*) that attacks all underground parts of sweet potato plants. The fungi usually enter the plants through injuries, but healthy parts may also be attacked under favorable conditions. Infections occur between 75° and 85°F during periods of high humidity. Infected roots may not show symptoms when dug up, but once in storage they develop blackened areas. Both discolored tissue and the surrounding healthy tissue taste bitter. The fungus survives in sweet potato debris, manure, and weeds for at least 2 years. Spores are spread by wind, water, and insects, including the sweet potato weevil. For information on the sweet potato weevil, see page 770.

SOLUTION: There are no chemical controls for this disease. Remove and discard all infected plants and roots. Disinfect the storage area thoroughly with a solution of 1 part household bleach to 9 parts water. Purchase certified slips or seed potatoes. Do not plant sweet potatoes in the same soil 2 years in a row.

SWEET POTATOES

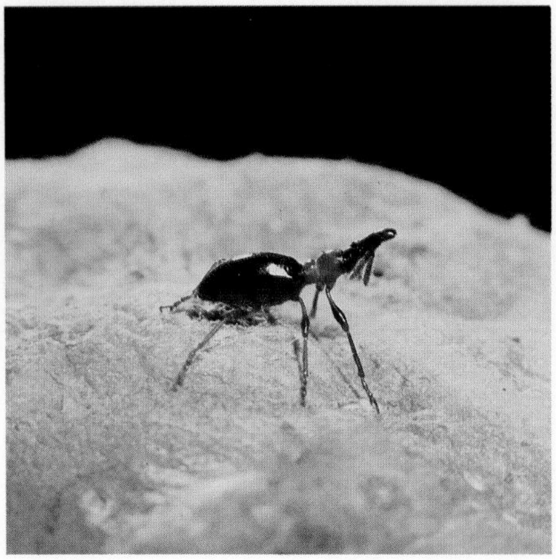

Sweet potato weevil (4 times life size).

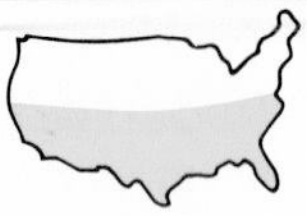

PROBLEM: Tunnels are bored into sweet potato vines and roots. Inside the tunnels are white, $\frac{3}{8}$ inch legless grubs with pale brown heads. Reddish antlike weevils with bluish black heads and long snouts may be seen feeding on leaves. Roots in storage may also be tunneled by grubs.

ANALYSIS: Sweet potato weevil
(*Cylas formicarius elegantulus*)
This weevil, also called the *sweet potato borer,* attacks roots both in the ground and in storage. Both adults and larvae damage the plants. Adult weevils feed on leaves, vines, and roots, and lay their eggs on the plant near the soil surface. The grubs that hatch from these eggs burrow into the vines and through the roots. This feeding kills the plants and makes the roots unappetizing. Roots are edible if the damaged parts are removed. The grubs pupate inside the roots and adults emerge in 1 week. There may be as many as eight generations a year. The sweet potato weevil does not hibernate for the winter, but feeds on weeds, especially wild morning glory, through the winter. The weevil also feeds and breeds in stored sweet potatoes.

SOLUTION: There are no chemical controls available for this pest. Carefully select and store only clean tubers. Purchase only certified, weevil-free sweet potato slips or seed potatoes. Mound the soil slightly around the stems to make it difficult for the grubs to reach the roots. Clean all plant debris and weeds, especially wild morning glory, from the garden to reduce the amount of food available to adults for the winter.

Scurf.

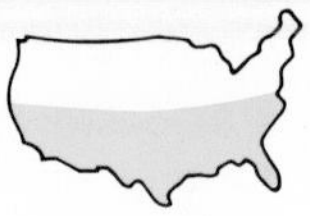

PROBLEM: Dark brown to black spots or irregular patches stain sweet potato skins. Discoloration affects only the skin, not the inside of the root.

ANALYSIS: Scurf
This disease, also called *soil stain,* is caused by a fungus (*Monilochaetes infuscans*) that attacks only the roots. Although their appearance is somewhat unappetizing, the flavor of the tubers is not affected and they are still edible. Scurf is most severe in wet, poorly drained soils and those high in organic matter. It is more prevalent in soils with a high pH and at temperatures between 70° and 80°F. It also appears more frequently when heavy rains occur just before harvest. The spots may enlarge in storage. Injury to the root surface allows rapid water loss, causing roots to shrivel. The fungus is introduced into the garden on infected roots and slips. The spores persist from one crop to the next in infected vines rotting in the garden, and in humus or partially decomposed organic matter.

SOLUTION: Use scurf-infected roots promptly, without storing them. Avoid planting in heavy soil. Improve soil drainage as instructed on page 763. If you add organic matter, till it into the soil a year before planting so it will decompose. Test the soil pH according to the directions on page 909 and make it more acid (see page 1019) if necessary. Purchase disease-free slips from a reputable company. If possible, rotate the sweet potato planting site every 3 or 4 years.

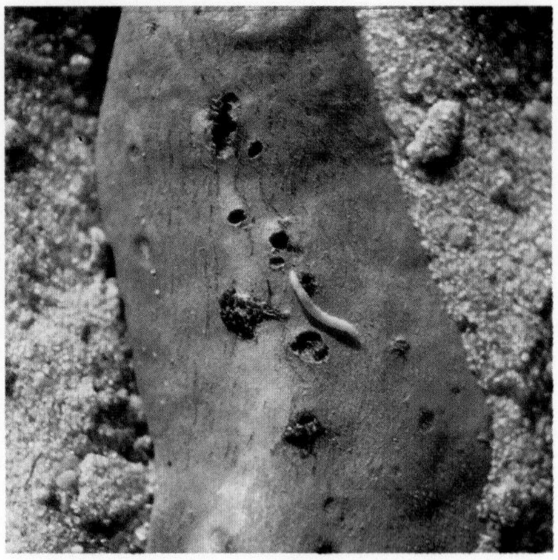

Flea beetle larva (half life size).

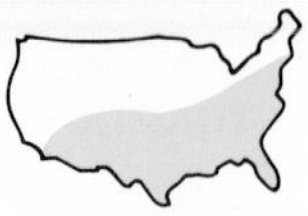

PROBLEM: Yellow irregular channels are chewed in the surface of the leaves. Tiny ($\frac{1}{16}$ inch) black beetles jump like fleas when disturbed. Shallow, dark tunnels scar the surface of the root.

ANALYSIS: Sweet potato flea beetle
(*Chaetocnema confinis*)
These beetles jump like fleas, but are not related to them. Both adults and immature flea beetles feed on sweet potatoes. The immature beetle, a legless white grub, feeds on the surface tissue of the roots, making them unattractive but still edible. Adults chew channels in leaves. Flea beetles are present nearly everywhere sweet potatoes are grown. They are most damaging to young plants. Adult beetles survive the winter in soil and garden debris. They emerge in early spring to feed on weeds until slips are set in the garden. Grubs hatch from eggs laid in the soil and feed for 2 to 3 weeks. After pupating in the soil, they emerge as adults to repeat the cycle. There are several generations a year.

SOLUTION: Control flea beetles on sweet potatoes with an insecticidal spray containing *methoxychlor* when the leaves first show damage. Watch new growth for evidence of further damage, and repeat the treatment at weekly intervals as needed. Clean all plant debris from the garden after harvest to eliminate overwintering spots for the adult beetles.

SWISS CHARD

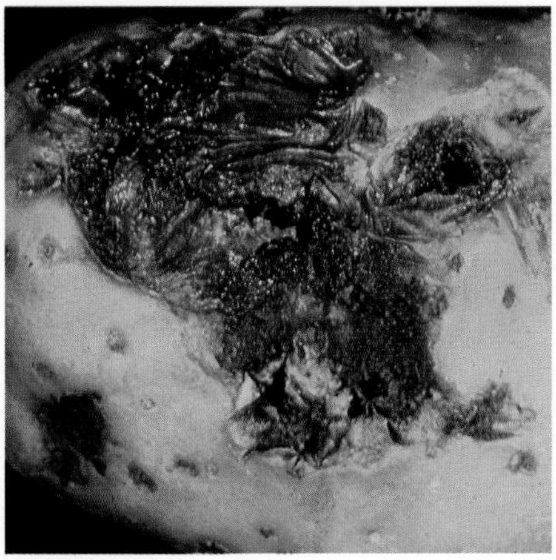

Nematode damage.

PROBLEM: Sweet potato plants turn yellow, are stunted, and wilt. Roots are cracked, and may be marred with surface blemishes and pitting. Black lesions occur on smaller roots.

ANALYSIS: Nematodes
Nematodes are microscopic worms that live in the soil. They are not related to earthworms. Nematodes feed on plant roots, damaging and stunting them. The damaged roots can't supply sufficient water and nutrients to the aboveground plant parts, and the plant is stunted or slowly dies. Nematodes are found throughout the United States, but are most severe in the South. They prefer moist, sandy loam. Testing roots and soil is the only positive method for confirming the presence of nematodes. Contact your local Cooperative Extension Office (see page 1029) for sampling instructions and addresses of testing laboratories. Soil and root problems such as poor soil structure, drought stress, nutrient deficiency, and root rot can also produce symptoms of decline similar to those caused by nematodes. These problems should be eliminated as causes before sending soil and root samples for testing. For information on soil problems and root rots, see pages 906 and 666.

SOLUTION: There are no chemicals available to homeowners to kill nematodes in planted soil. However, they can be controlled before planting by soil fumigation (see page 927). Choose varieties that are resistant to nematodes.

Nematode-resistant varieties: Heart, Jasper, Jewel, Kandee, Nemagold, and Nugget.

SWISS CHARD

ADAPTATION: Throughout the United States.

PLANTING TIME: See page 1025.

PLANTING METHOD: Sow seeds ½ inch deep and 1 to 2 inches apart. Thin seedlings when they have 2 to 3 leaves, and set transplants to grow 12 inches apart. Use the thinnings as greens. Plant transplants so the top of their rootball is even with the surrounding garden soil.

SOIL: Any good garden soil high in organic matter. pH 6.0 to 7.5

FERTILIZER: At planting time, use 2 pounds of ORTHO General Purpose Plant Food per 100 square feet, or 1½ pounds per 50-foot row. Side-dress every 3 to 4 weeks with 1 to 2 pounds per 50-foot row.
Containers: Water every 2 to 3 weeks with a solution of ORTHO Tomato & Vegetable Food.

WATER:
How much: Apply enough water at each irrigation to wet the soil 10 to 12 inches deep.
Containers: 10 per cent of the applied water should drain out the bottom.
How often: Water when the soil 2 inches deep is barely moist.

HARVEST: Harvest leaves about 50 to 60 days after planting. Using a sharp knife, cut the outer leaves about 1 inch above the soil level. Be careful not to damage young leaves and center buds. Store in the refrigerator.

Aphids (twice life size).

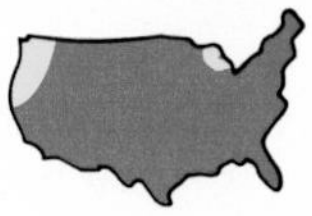

PROBLEM: Leaves turn yellow and may be curled, distorted, and puckered. Pale green, yellow, or purple soft-bodied insects cluster on the undersides of the leaves.

ANALYSIS: Aphids
Aphids do little damage in small numbers. However, they are extremely prolific and populations can rapidly build up to damaging numbers during the growing season. Damage occurs when the aphid sucks the juices from the Swiss chard leaves. Aphids feed on nearly every plant in the garden, and are spread from plant to plant by wind, water, and people. For more information about aphids, see page 875.

SOLUTION: Spray infested plants with an insecticide containing *diazinon* or *malathion* as soon as the insects appear. Repeat the spray if the plant becomes reinfested. If aphids are present during harvest, hose them off with a strong stream of water.

SWISS CHARD

Leafminer damage.

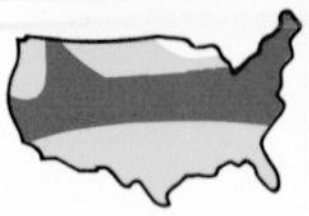

PROBLEM: Light-colored irregular blotches, blisters, or tunnels appear in the leaves. The tan areas peel apart like cleansing tissue. Tiny black specks are inside the tunnels.

ANALYSIS: Spinach leafminer
(*Pegomyahyoscyami*)
This insect belongs to a family of leafmining flies. The tiny, black adult fly lays its white eggs on the undersides of the leaves. The maggots that hatch from these eggs bore into the leaves. Once inside a leaf, the maggot tunnels between the upper and lower surfaces of the leaves, feeding on the inner tissue. The tunnels are called "mines." The black specks inside the mines are the maggots' droppings. Several overlapping generations occur during the growing season, so the white larvae are present continually from spring until fall. Leaves are edible if the damaged portions are cut away.

SOLUTION: Once the leafminers enter the leaves, sprays are ineffective. Squash the miners inside the leaves when you first notice the mines. Spraying after the mines first appear will control only those leafminers that attack after the application. To control succeeding generations of leafminers, treat with an insecticidal spray containing *malathion.* Repeat two more times at weekly intervals. Clean all plant debris from the garden after harvest to reduce the number of overwintering pupae.

TOMATOES

TOMATOES

ADAPTATION: Throughout the United States.

PLANTING TIME: See page 1025.

PLANTING METHOD: Sow seeds ½ inch deep. Thin seedlings when they have 2 or 3 leaves, or set transplants to grow 18 to 36 inches apart. Set transplants horizontally with only the top third of the plant above the soil.

SOIL: Any good garden soil that is high in organic matter. pH 5.5 to 7.5

FERTILIZER: At planting time, use 3 to 4 pounds of ORTHO Vegetable Food per 100 square feet, or 1 pound per 25-foot row. In hot summer areas, sidedress every 3 to 4 weeks with 1 pound per 25-foot row, or 1 to 2 tablespoons per plant. In cool summer areas, sidedressing may produce excess foliage and green fruit that don't ripen.
Containers: Water thoroughly every 2 to 4 weeks with a solution of ORTHO Tomato & Vegetable Food.

WATER:
How much: Apply enough water at each irrigation to wet the soil 18 to 20 inches deep.
How often: Water when the soil 2 inches deep is barely moist.

HARVEST: Harvest tomatoes when they have a deep, rich color. Store at room temperature until use. If your plants still have many green fruit at the first frost, the fruit can be ripened in either of two ways. Hang the plants upside down in the garage until the fruit ripen; or pick the green fruit and store in boxes at room temperature until they ripen.

PROBLEMS WITH THE FRUIT

Poor fruit set.

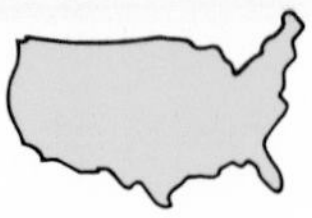

PROBLEM: Few or no fruit develop. The plants are healthy, and may even be extremely vigorous.

ANALYSIS: Poor fruit set
Poor fruit set occurs on tomatoes for any of several reasons:
1. *Extreme temperatures:* The blossoms drop off without setting fruit when night temperatures fall below 55°F or day temperatures rise above 90°F.
2. *Dry soil:* Blossoms dry and fall when the plants don't receive enough water.
3. *Shading:* Few blossoms are produced when the plants receive less than 6 hours of sunlight a day.
4. *Excessive nitrogen:* High levels of nitrogen in the soil promote leaf growth at the expense of blossom and fruit formation.

SOLUTION: Follow these guidelines to reduce the chances of poor fruit set.
1. Plant early, mid, and late-season varieties at the appropriate time of year. For a list of these varieties, see page 1026.
2. Water tomatoes regularly, never allowing the soil to dry out. Mulch with straw or black plastic, as discussed on page 926, to reduce the need for watering.
3. Plant tomatoes in an area that receives at least 6 hours of sunlight a day. If your yard is shady, grow tomatoes in containers on your porch or patio.
4. Correct the nitrogen imbalance with ORTHO Superphosphate or ORTHO Fruit & Bloom Builder. To prevent future problems, follow the fertilizing recommendations on this page.

Growth cracks.

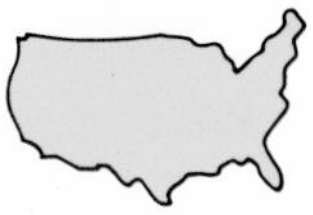

PROBLEM: Circular or radial cracks mar the stem end (top) of ripening fruit. Cracks may extend deep into the fruit, causing it to rot.

ANALYSIS: Growth cracks
Tomatoes crack when certain environmental conditions encourage rapid growth during ripening. The rapid growth is frequently promoted by heavy rains or watering following a drought period. Tomatoes are most susceptible to cracking after they have reached full size and begin to change color. Some varieties crack more easily than others. Cracking is more severe in hot weather. Some cracks may be deep, allowing decay organisms to enter the fruit and rot it. Shallow cracks frequently heal over, but may rupture if the fruit is roughly handled when picked. Cracked tomatoes are still edible.

SOLUTION: Maintain even soil moisture with regular watering according to the instructions on page 772. Grow crack-tolerant varieties.

Tomato varieties that are crack tolerant: Avalanche, Bragger, Early Girl, Glamor, Heinz 1350, Heinz 1439, Jet Star, Marglobe Supreme F, Red Glow, Roma, and Willamette.

Sunscald on tomatoes.

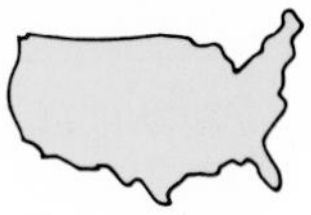

PROBLEM: On green and ripening fruit, a light patch develops on the side facing the sun. These areas blister, and finally become slightly sunken and grayish white, with a paperlike surface. A black mold may grow on the affected area, causing the fruit to rot.

ANALYSIS: Sunscald
Sunscald occurs on tomatoes when they are exposed to the direct rays of the sun during hot weather. It is most common on green fruit, but ripening fruit is also susceptible. It is most prevalent on staked plants that have lost their foliage due to leaf diseases such as early or late blight (see pages 780 and 779), septoria leaf spot (see page 780), fusarium and verticillium wilt (see pages 778 and 779), or leaf roll (see page 780). Fruit on plants that have been pruned to hasten ripening are also subject to sunscald. Tomatoes need warm temperatures—not direct sun—to ripen. Tomatoes are still edible if the sunscalded area is removed. Rot fungi frequently invade the damaged tissue, resulting in moldy and inedible fruit.

SOLUTION: Cover exposed fruit with straw or other light material to protect them from the sun's rays. Do not prune leaves to hasten ripening. Control leaf diseases. Grow verticillium and fusarium wilt-resistant plants. For a list of these varieties, see page 1026.

Blossom-end rot.

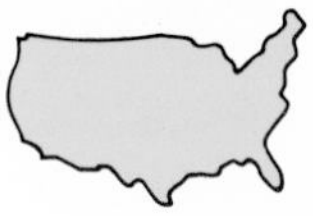

PROBLEM: A round, sunken, water-soaked spot develops on the bottom of the fruit. The spot enlarges, turns brown to black, and feels leathery. Mold may grow on the rotted surface.

ANALYSIS: Blossom-end rot
Blossom-end rot occurs on tomatoes, peppers, squash, and watermelons from a lack of calcium in the developing fruit. This results from slowed growth and damaged roots caused by any of several factors:
1. Extreme fluctuations in soil moisture, from very wet to very dry.
2. Rapid plant growth early in the season, followed by extended dry weather.
3. Excessive rains that smother root hairs.
4. Excess soil salts.
5. Cultivating too close to the plant.
The first fruit are the most severely affected. The disorder always starts at the blossom end, and may enlarge to affect up to half of the fruit. Moldy growths on the rotted area are from fungi or bacteria that invade the damaged tissue. The rotted area is unsightly but the rest of the fruit is edible.

SOLUTION: To prevent future blossom-end rot, follow these guidelines:
1. Maintain uniform soil moisture by mulching (see page 926), and by following the watering guidelines on page 772.
2. Avoid using high-nitrogen fertilizers or large quantities of fresh manure.
3. Plant in well-drained soil, as outlined on page 907.
4. If your soil or water is salty, provide more water at each watering to help leach salts through the soil.
5. Do not cultivate deeper than 1 inch within 1 foot of the plant.

TOMATOES — PROBLEMS WITH THE FRUIT

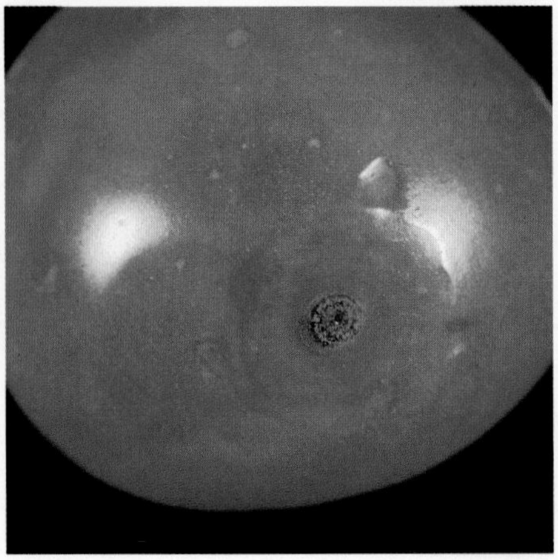

Anthracnose.

PROBLEM: Sunken spots up to 1/2 inch in diameter occur on ripe tomatoes. The centers of the spots darken and form concentric rings. Spots may merge, covering a large part of the tomato.

ANALYSIS: Anthracnose
This plant disease is caused by a fungus (*Colletotrichum coccodes*) that rots ripe tomatoes. Green tomato fruit are also attacked, but the spots don't appear until the fruit ripen. Infected fruit are inedible. Anthracnose is most common on overripe fruit and those close to the ground. Fruit on plants partially defoliated by leaf spot diseases are also prone to infection. The leaves may be infected, but are usually not severely damaged. The fungus is most active in warm (60° to 90°F), wet weather and when infection is severe many fruit are damaged in a short period of time. Infections frequently become epidemic in hot, rainy weather. Water from heavy dews, overhead watering, and frequent abundant rains provides the moisture necessary for infection.

SOLUTION: Spray tomato plants at the first sign of the disease with ORTHO Vegetable Disease Control. Repeat at intervals of 7 to 10 days until harvest. Discard all infected fruit. Pick tomatoes as they mature and use promptly. To reduce the spread of the disease, do not work among wet plants. Remove all plant debris from the garden after harvest.

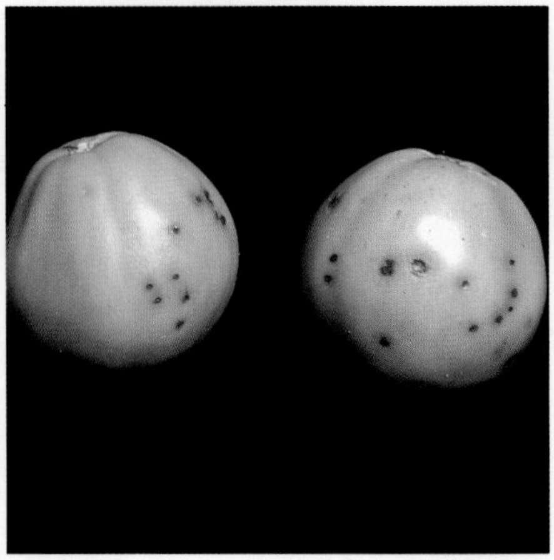

Bacterial spot.

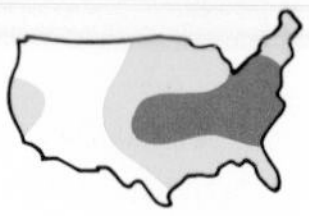

PROBLEM: Dark, raised, scablike spots, 1/8 to 1/4 inch in diameter, appear on green tomatoes. The centers of the spots are slightly sunken. Dark, greasy, 1/8 inch spots occur on the older leaves, causing them to drop.

ANALYSIS: Bacterial spot
This plant disease is caused by a bacterium (*Xanthomonas vesicatoria*) that attacks green but not red tomatoes. Peppers are also attacked. The bacteria infect all aboveground parts of the plant at any stage of growth. Infected blossoms drop, reducing the fruit yield. Fruit are infected through skin wounds caused by insects, blowing sand, and mechanical injuries. Infected fruit do not ripen properly, and are frequently invaded by rot organisms. The bacteria are most active after heavy rains and in very warm (75° to 85°F) weather. They spread rapidly in the rain, often resulting in severe defoliation, which weakens the plant and exposes the fruit to sunscald. The bacteria spend the winter in the soil, and are carried on tomato seeds.

SOLUTION: Pick and discard all infected green fruit. If the infection is severe, spray with a fungicide containing both *maneb* and *basic copper sulfate* at the first sign of the disease. Repeat at intervals of 7 to 10 days as long as weather conditions continue that are favorable to the spread of bacterial spot. To reduce the spread of the disease, do not work among wet plants. Avoid overhead watering by using drip or furrow irrigation. Purchase disease-free plants or seeds from a reputable dealer.

Bacterial speck.

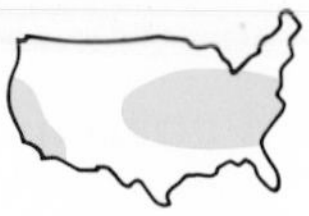

PROBLEM: Many tiny (1/16 inch), slightly raised, dark brown specks appear on the green fruit. A white border surrounds each speck. Dark brown to black spots 1/16 inch in diameter occur on the leaves. The surrounding tissue turns yellow.

ANALYSIS: Bacterial speck
This plant disease is caused by a bacterium (*Pseudomonas syringae*) that attacks young tomatoes. This disease is commonly confused with bacterial spot. Bacterial speck attacks tomatoes only; peppers are not infected. The specks on the fruit mar the skin but do not extend into the inner tissue. The fruit appear unappetizing, but are still edible when they ripen. The bacteria are most active in warm (65° to 75°F) weather following heavy rains when the bacteria are splashed from plant to plant. The bacteria spend the winter in the soil. They may also be carried on tomato seeds.

SOLUTION: If the infection is severe, spray the plants with a fungicide containing *maneb* or *basic copper sulfate* at the first sign of the disease. Repeat at intervals of 7 to 10 days as long as weather conditions continue that are favorable to the spread of bacterial speck. To reduce the chances of spreading the bacteria, do not work among wet plants. Avoid overhead watering by using drip or furrow irrigation. Do not save seeds from infected fruit.

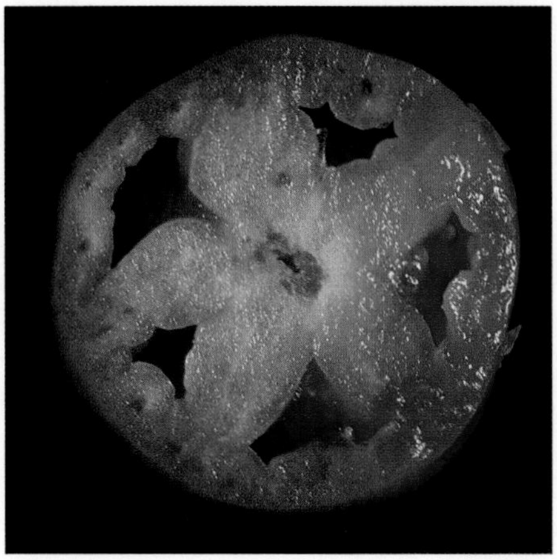

Blotchy ripening.

PROBLEM: Irregular grayish brown or yellow blotches appear on green tomatoes. When the tomato is cut open crosswise, the tissue just inside the skin may be brown, sometimes with pits and cavities. Fruits feel hard and are sometimes ridged.

ANALYSIS: Blotchy ripening and internal browning
Blotchy ripening results from any of a variety of environmental factors:
1. Tomatoes ripen poorly and irregularly at temperatures below 60°F.
2. Compacted soil and overly wet soil inhibit the root system, which restricts fruit ripening.
3. Low levels of potassium in the soil inhibit proper fruit growth and maturity.

Brown wall tissue, called *internal browning*, results when the plant is infected with tobacco mosaic virus (TMV) as the fruit begin to ripen. For information on TMV, see page 781. Usually only the first and sometimes the second pickings are affected by blotchy ripening and internal browning. Later fruit ripen normally.

SOLUTION: Plant tomatoes according to the planting chart on page 1025. Improve soil drainage as instructed on page 907. Water and fertilize according to the guidelines on page 772. Give your plants a boost of potassium with ORTHO Fruit & Bloom Builder. To prevent internal browning, see page 781 for ways to prevent tobacco mosaic virus.

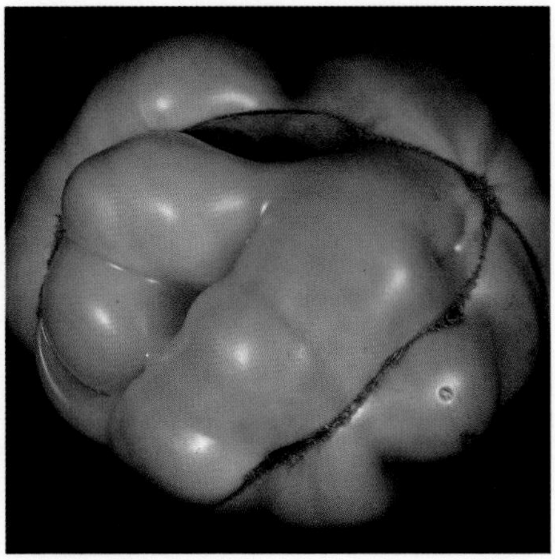

Catface.

PROBLEM: Green and red tomatoes are malformed, scarred, and puckered. Greenish tan streaks and bands of scar tissue mar the blossom end (bottom) of the fruit.

ANALYSIS: Catface
Certain conditions that occur during bloom disturb the normal growth of the tomato flower, resulting in catfaced fruit. These conditions include extreme heat (above 85°F) or cold (below 55°F), drought, and 2,4-D herbicide sprays. Usually only the first fruits to form are affected. These fruits are of poor quality and ripen unevenly. Although some varieties seem to be more susceptible to this disorder, many of the modern varieties are seldom affected.

SOLUTION: Water tomatoes regularly according to the instructions on page 772. Avoid exposing tomato plants to herbicides by washing sprayers thoroughly after herbicide use, or by keeping separate sprayers for herbicides and other sprays. Select varieties that seldom catface.

Tomato varieties that seldom catface: Avalanche, Bonus, Floramerica, and Floridol.

Tomato fruitworm damage.

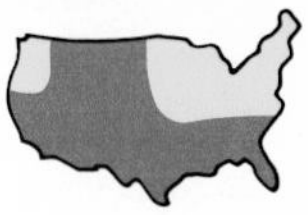

PROBLEM: Deep holes are chewed in the fruit. Striped yellow, green, or brown worms from $\frac{1}{4}$ to 2 inches long are feeding in them. Worms may also be feeding on the leaves.

ANALYSIS: Tomato fruitworm
(*Heliothis zea*)
Tomato fruitworms, also known as *corn earworms* and *cotton bollworms*, attack many plants, including tomatoes, corn, and cotton. The worms feed on the foliage, and also chew deep holes in the fruit and feed inside. Damaged fruit is inedible. The adult tomato fruitworm is a light grayish brown moth with dark lines on the wings. In the spring, the adults lay white eggs on the leaves and stems. The worms that hatch from these eggs feed on the leaves until they are about $\frac{1}{2}$ inch long. Then they move to the fruit and bore inside. After feeding for 2 to 4 weeks, they drop to the ground, burrow 2 to 6 inches deep, pupate, and emerge in several weeks as adults. There are several generations of worms a year, so damage can continue until fall.

SOLUTION: Once the fruitworms are inside the tomatoes, there is nothing you can do. Destroy infested fruit. Clean all plant debris from the garden after harvest to reduce the number of overwintering adults. If fruitworms were numerous this year, next year treat your plants with ORTHO Liquid Sevin, ORTHO Sevin Garden Dust, or ORTHO Tomato Vegetable Dust when the worms are feeding on the foliage, and fruit are about $\frac{1}{2}$ inch in diameter. Repeat in 2 and 4 weeks if the plants become reinfested.

TOMATOES — INSECTS

Tomato (top) and tobacco hornworms (life size).

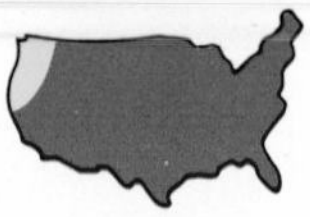

PROBLEM: Fat green or brown worms, up to 5 inches long, with white diagonal stripes chew on the leaves. A red or black "horn" projects from the rear end. Black droppings soil the leaves.

ANALYSIS: Tomato hornworm (*Manduca quinquemaculata*) **and tobacco hornworm** (*M. sexta*)
Hornworms feed on the fruit and foliage of tomatoes, peppers, and eggplants. Although only a few worms may be present, each worm consumes large quantities of foliage and causes extensive damage. The large gray or brown adult moth with yellow and white markings emerges from hibernation in late spring, and drinks nectar from petunias and other garden flowers. The worms that hatch from eggs laid on the undersides of the leaves feed for 3 to 4 weeks. Then they crawl into the soil, pupate, and later emerge as adults to repeat the cycle. There is one generation a year in the North and two to four in the South. Some worms may have white sacs that look like puffed rice on their bodies. These sacs are the cocoons of parasitic wasps that feed on and eventually kill the hornworm.

SOLUTION: Treat the plants with ORTHO Sevin Garden Dust or ORTHO Fruit & Vegetable Insect Control. But don't destroy worms covered with white sacs. Let the wasps inside the worms mature, emerge, and infest other hornworms. If practical, handpick and destroy unaffected worms.

Flea beetle damage.

PROBLEM: Leaves are riddled with shotholes about $\frac{1}{8}$ inch in diameter. Tiny $\frac{1}{16}$ inch black beetles jump like fleas when disturbed. Leaves of seedlings may wilt and die.

ANALYSIS: Flea beetles
These beetles jump like fleas, but are not related to them. Both adult and immature flea beetles feed on a wide variety of garden vegetables, including tomatoes. The immature beetle, a legless gray grub, injures plants by feeding on the roots and the lower surfaces of the leaves. Adults chew holes in leaves. Flea beetles are most damaging to seedlings and young plants. Leaves of seedlings riddled with holes dry out quickly and die. Adult beetles survive the winter in soil and garden debris. They emerge in early spring to feed on weeds until vegetables sprout or plants are set in the garden. Grubs hatch from eggs laid in the soil and feed for 2 to 3 weeks. After pupating in the soil, they emerge as adults to repeat the cycle. There are one to four generations a year. Adults may feed for up to 2 months.

SOLUTION: Control flea beetles on tomatoes with ORTHO Fruit & Vegetable Insect Control, ORTHO Sevin Garden Dust, ORTHO Tomato & Vegetable Insect Killer, or ORTHO Tomato Vegetable Dust. Treat when the leaves first show damage. Watch new growth for evidence of further damage, and repeat the treatment at weekly intervals as needed. Clean all plant debris from the garden after harvest to eliminate overwintering spots for adult beetles.

Stink bug (twice life size).

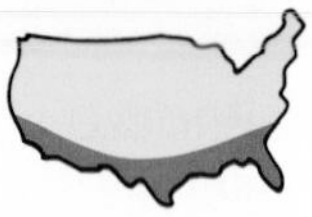

PROBLEM: Light yellow to white, cloudy spots occur on the tomato fruit. The tissue under these spots is pithy and corky. Young fruits are deformed and may drop. Bright green, gray, blue, or red insects, $\frac{5}{8}$ inch long and shaped like a shield are present on the plants.

ANALYSIS: Stink bugs
Stink bugs attack a wide variety of vegetables, including tomatoes, okra, squash, and beans. They emit a strong odor when crushed. Both the adults and nymphs damage tomato plants by sucking sap from buds, blossoms, and fruit. This feeding causes the fruit to become distorted and dimpled with corky inner tissue. Hard calluses form around the spots where the stink bugs feed. Damaged tomatoes are edible, but unappetizing. Young tender growth is the most susceptible to attack. Stink bugs spend the winter as adults in sheltered areas. In the spring, they lay clusters of eggs on the undersides of leaves. The young that hatch from these eggs mature into adults in 6 weeks. There are several generations each year, so damage occurs throughout the season.

SOLUTION: Treat infested tomato plants with ORTHO Tomato & Vegetable Insect Spray or ORTHO Sevin Garden Dust as soon as stink bugs and their damage are noticed. Repeat the treatment at intervals of 7 to 10 days if the plants become reinfested.

Potato aphids (life size).

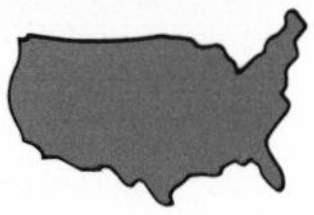

PROBLEM: Leaves turn yellow, and may be curled, distorted, and puckered. Pale green, yellow, or purple soft-bodied insects cluster on the stems and the undersides of the leaves.

ANALYSIS: Aphids

Aphids do little damage in small numbers. However, they are extremely prolific and populations can rapidly build up to damaging numbers during the growing season. Damage occurs when the aphid sucks the juices from the tomato leaves. Aphids feed on nearly every plant in the garden and are spread from plant to plant by wind, water, and people.

SOLUTION: Control aphids on tomatoes with ORTHO Fruit & Vegetable Insect Control, ORTHO Malathion 50 Insect Spray, ORTHO Tomato & Vegetable Insect Killer, or ORTHO Tomato Vegetable Dust. Treat at the first sign of infestation, and repeat at intervals of 7 to 10 days if the plants become reinfested.

Whiteflies (life size).

PROBLEM: Tiny, winged insects $\frac{1}{12}$ inch long feed on the undersides of the leaves. The insects are covered with white waxy powder. When the plant is touched, insects flutter rapidly around it. Leaves may be mottled and yellowing. A black mold may cover the leaves.

ANALYSIS: Greenhouse whitefly
(*Trialeurodes vaporariorum*)

This insect is a common pest of many garden and greenhouse plants. The four-winged adult lays eggs on the undersides of leaves. The larvae are the size of a pinhead, flat, oval-shaped, and semitransparent, with white waxy filaments radiating from the body. They feed for about a month before changing to the adult form. Both the larvae and adult forms suck sap from the leaves. The larvae are more damaging because they feed more heavily. Adults and larvae cannot fully digest all the sugar in the plant sap, and excrete the excess in a fluid called honeydew, which often drops onto the leaves or plants below. A sooty mold fungus may develop on the honeydew, causing the tomato leaves to appear black and dirty. In warm winter areas, these insects can be active yearround. Whiteflies are unable to live through freezing winters. Spring reinfestations in freezing winter areas come from migrating whiteflies and infested greenhouse-grown plants placed in the garden.

SOLUTION: Control whiteflies by spraying with ORTHO Malathion 50 Insect Spray, ORTHO Tomato & vegetable Insect Killer, or ORTHO Fruit & Vegetable Insect Control every 7 to 10 days as necessary. Spray thoroughly, being sure to cover both the upper and lower surfaces of the leaves.

Mite damage.

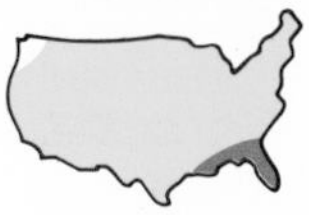

PROBLEM: Leaves may be stippled, yellowing, and dirty. There may be webbing over flower buds, between leaves, or on the lower surfaces of the leaves. Lower stems and leaves may be bronzed, with cracks in the main stem. Leaves dry out and drop. To determine if the plant is infested with mites, hold a sheet of white paper underneath an affected leaf and tap the leaf sharply. Minute green, red, or yellow specks the size of a pepper grain or smaller will drop to the paper and begin to crawl around. The pests are easily seen against the white background.

ANALYSIS: Spider mites (*Tetranychus urticae*) **and tomato russet mite**
(*Aculops lycopersici*)

These mites, related to spiders, are major pests of many garden and greenhouse plants. Tomato russet mites, which bronze the stems and leaves, are a problem mainly in the Southwest and California. Mites cause damage by sucking sap from the undersides of the leaves and stems. As a result of feeding, the green leaf pigment disappears, producing the stippled or bronze appearance. Fruit are seldom attacked. When populations are high and not controlled, many leaves may drop, weakening the plant and exposing the fruit to sunscald. Mites are active throughout the growing season, but are favored by hot, dry weather (70°F and up). By midsummer, they build up to tremendous numbers.

SOLUTION: Treat infested plants with ORTHO Malathion 50 Insect Spray or ORTHO Fruit & Vegetable Insect Killer when the first fruit begin to set or at the first sign of damage. Repeat at intervals of 7 to 10 days if plants become reinfested.

Wilting caused by nearby walnut tree.

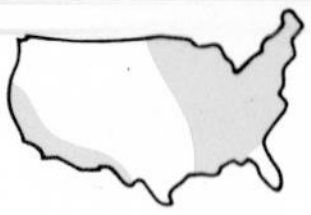

PROBLEM: Tomato plants suddenly wilt and die. Inner stem tissue is dark brown. A black walnut tree is growing nearby.

ANALYSIS: Walnut wilt
Some plants growing within 50 feet of black walnut trees are killed by a toxic substance called juglone that is released from the tree roots. Tomato plants are very sensitive to juglone, which is emitted from both living and dead tree roots. Juglone remains active in the soil and root debris for at least 3 years after a black walnut tree is removed. The substance kills the tomato roots, causing the inner tissue to darken and the plant to suddenly wilt and die.

SOLUTION: Plant tomato plants at least 50 feet from black walnut trees. Wait at least 3 years before planting tomatoes in an area where black walnut trees once grew.

Fusarium wilt.

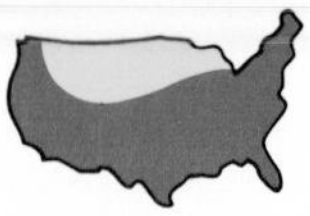

PROBLEM: Lower leaves turn yellow, wilt, and die. Then upper shoots wilt, and eventually the whole plant dies. Wilting usually occurs first on one side of the leaf or plant, then the other. When the stem is sliced lengthwise near the soil line, the tissue ⅛ inch under the bark is found to be dark brown.

ANALYSIS: Fusarium wilt
This wilt disease is caused by a soil-inhabiting fungus (*Fusarium oxysporum f. lycopersici*) that infects only tomatoes. The fungus persists indefinitely on plant debris or in the soil. Fusarium is more prevalent in warm-weather areas. The disease is spread by contaminated soil, seeds, plants, and equipment. The fungus enters the plant through the roots and spreads up into the stems and leaves through the water-conducting vessels in the stems. These vessels become discolored and plugged. This plugging cuts off the flow of water and nutrients to the leaves, causing leaf yellowing and wilting. Affected plants may or may not produce fruit. Fruit that is produced is usually deformed and tasteless. Many plants will die. For more information about fusarium wilt, see page 850.

SOLUTION: No chemical control is available. Destroy infected plants promptly. Fusarium can be removed from the soil only by fumigation techniques. (For more information on soil fumigation, see page 927.) However, the best solution is usually to use plants that are resistant to fusarium wilt. This is denoted by the letter "F" after the tomato variety name. For a list of wilt-resistant varieties, see page 1026.

Bacterial canker.

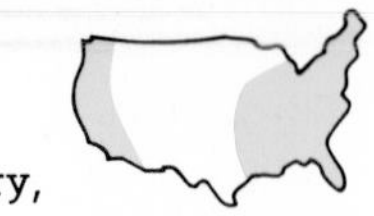

PROBLEM: Margins of the lower leaves wilt, dry, and then curl upward. one side of the plant may be affected first, then the other. Yellow-white streaks develop on the stem, break open, and may ooze. When the stem is split lengthwise, the center tissue appears pale yellow and mealy, and separates easily from the outer woody tissue. Plants may die. Raised tan spots with flattened white margins mar the fruit. Dark cavities may occur inside the fruit.

ANALYSIS: Bacterial canker
This destructive disease of tomatoes is caused by a bacterium (*Corynebacterium michiganense*) that also attacks peppers, potatoes, and eggplants. The bacteria are carried on seeds and are most frequently introduced into the garden on infected transplants. The bacteria can survive in the soil for 2 to 3 years. Plants may be infected at any stage of growth. Some infected plants die, but others survive weakly until harvest. If fruit is produced, it is deformed or spotted. The fruit is infected in either of two ways: the bacteria pass from the stem into the fruit, resulting in dark inner cavities; or the bacteria are washed by the rain onto the fruit skin, resulting in skin spotting.

SOLUTION: There are no chemical controls for this disease. Remove and destroy infected plants and fruit at the first sign of infection. Don't plant tomatoes in the same spot every year. Purchase healthy plants from a reputable company. Do not save seeds from infected fruit.

LEAVES DISCOLORED OR DISTORTED

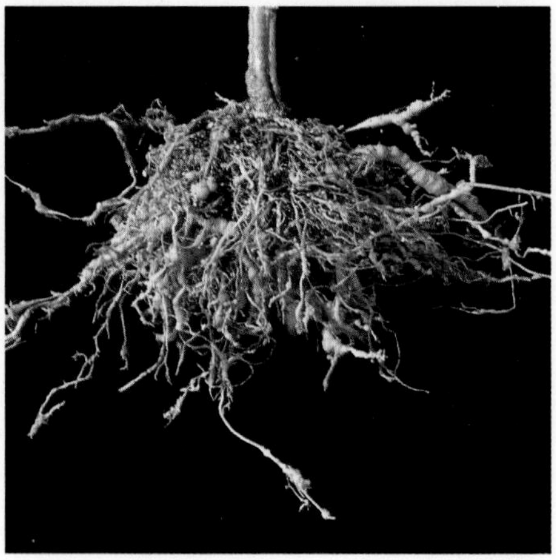

Nematode-infested roots.

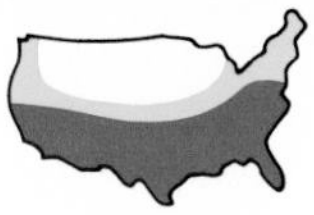

PROBLEM: Plants are stunted, yellow, and wilt in hot, dry weather. Round and elongated nodules occur on roots.

ANALYSIS: Nematodes
Nematodes are microscopic worms that live in the soil. They are not related to earthworms. Nematodes feed on plant roots, damaging and stunting them. The damaged roots can't supply sufficient water and nutrients to the aboveground plant parts, and the plant is stunted or slowly dies. Nematodes are found throughout the country, but are most severe in the South. They prefer moist, sandy loam soils. Nematodes can move only a few inches each year on their own, but they may be carried long distances by soil, water, tools, or infested plants. Testing roots and soil is the only positive method for confirming the presence of nematodes. Contact your local Cooperative Extension Office (see page 1029) for sampling instructions and addresses of testing laboratories. Soil and root problems such as poor soil structure, drought stress, nutrient deficiency, and root rots can also produce symptoms of decline similar to those caused by nematodes. These problems should be eliminated as causes before sending soil and root samples for testing. For information on soil problems and root rots, see pages 907 and 849.

SOLUTION: No chemicals are available to homeowners to kill nematodes in planted soil. However, they can be controlled before planting by soil fumigation (see page 927). Some varieties are resistant to nematodes. Resistance is indicated by an "N" after the variety name. For a list of resistant varieties, see page 1026.

Verticillium wilt.

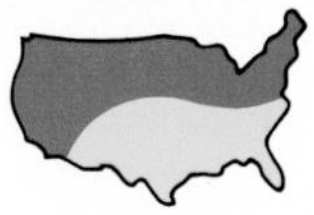

PROBLEM: Older lower leaves turn yellow, dry, and fall. Tip leaves curl upward at the margins, but remain green. When the stem is sliced lengthwise near the soil line, the tissue ⅛ inch below the bark is seen to be tan in color.

ANALYSIS: Verticillium wilt
This wilt disease affects many plants in the garden, including potatoes, eggplants, peppers, strawberries, and raspberries. It is caused by a soil-inhabiting fungus (*Verticillium albo-atrum*) that persists indefinitely on plant debris or in the soil. It is more prevalent in cool-weather areas. The disease is spread by contaminated seeds, soil, plants, and equipment. The fungus enters the plant through the roots and spreads into the stems and leaves through the water-conducting vessels in the stems. The vessels become discolored and plugged. This plugging cuts off the flow of water and nutrients to the leaves, causing leaf yellowing and death. Affected plants may or may not produce fruit. Fruit that is produced is usually small, deformed, and tasteless. The plant is not usually killed. For more information about verticillium wilt, see page 850.

SOLUTION: No chemical control is available. Destroy infected plants promptly. Verticillium can be removed from the soil only by fumigation techniques. (For more information about soil fumigation, see page 919.) However, the best solution is usually to use plants that are resistant to this wilt disease. This is denoted by the letter "V" after the tomato variety name. For a list of wilt-resistant tomato varieties, see page 1010.

Late blight. *Insert:* Close-up.

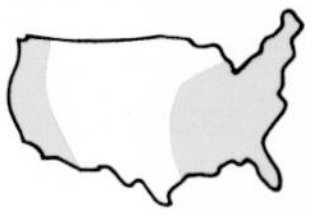

PROBLEM: Bluish gray water-soaked patches appear on the leaves. During humid weather, a white downy mold grows on the lower surfaces of the leaves. Leaves dry, shrivel, and turn brown. Water-soaked spots also occur on the stems. Grayish green water-soaked spots appear on the fruit. The spots turn dark brown, become wrinkled and corklike, and may enlarge to cover the entire fruit. Dying plants have an offensive odor.

ANALYSIS: Late blight
This plant disease is caused by a fungus (*Phytophthora infestans*) that attacks both tomatoes and potatoes. Late blight does not attack tomatoes every year, but is very destructive when it does occur. The fungus attacks leaves, stems, and fruit, causing severe defoliation and rotted fruit. Infected fruit is inedible. Plants can be infected at all stages of growth. Late blight frequently enters the garden on infected transplants or infected potato seed pieces. The fungus is most active in wet weather with cool (45° to 60°F) nights and warm (70° to 85°F) days. Spores spend the winter in infected potato tubers in the garden or compost pile.

SOLUTION: Treat infected plants promptly with ORTHO Vegetable Disease Control at the first sign of the disease. Repeat the treatments at intervals of 7 to 10 days as long as weather conditions continue that are favorable to the spread of the disease. Remove all potato and tomato debris from the garden after harvest. Do not compost infected tubers.

TOMATOES — LEAVES DISCOLORED OR DISTORTED

Early blight. *Insert:* Infected fruit.

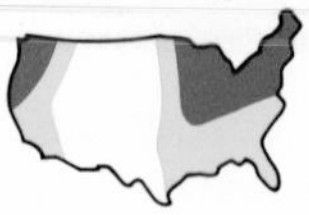

PROBLEM: Irregular brown spots, ¼ to ½ inch in diameter, with concentric rings in their centers appear on the lower leaves. A yellow margin may outline the spot. When many spots appear, the entire leaf turns yellow and drops. Dark spots with light centers and concentric rings may occur on the stems. Dark, leathery, sunken spots with concentric rings mar the fruit where it joins the stem. The discoloration extends into the fruit.

ANALYSIS: Early blight
This plant disease is caused by a fungus (*Alteraria solani*) that attacks tomatoes at any stage of growth. Some leaf spotting appears early in the season, but most occurs as the fruit matures. Plants heavily loaded with fruit and those that are poorly fertilized are the most susceptible to attack. Severe early blight causes partial to complete defoliation, which weakens the plant, reduces the size and quality of fruit, and exposes the fruit to sunscald. Infected fruit should not be canned, but can be eaten fresh if the diseased portion is removed. The spores survive in plant debris in the soil for at least a year. The fungus is most active in warm (75° to 85°F), humid weather.

SOLUTION: Treat infected plants with ORTHO Orthocide Garden Fungicide or ORTHO Vegetable Disease Control at the first sign of the disease. Repeat at intervals of 7 to 10 days as long as weather conditions continue that are favorable to the spread of the disease. Remove all plant debris from the garden after harvest to reduce the amount of overwintering spores. Fertilize according to the guidelines on page 772.

Septoria leaf spot.

PROBLEM: Numerous brown spots, ⅛ inch in diameter, with dark borders appear on the older lower leaves. A few tiny black specks appear in the center of the spots. Severely spotted leaves turn yellow, dry, and fall. In warm, wet weather, all the leaves may become spotted and drop except for a few at the top of the plant.

ANALYSIS: Septoria leaf spot
This tomato plant disease is caused by a fungus (*Septoria lycopersici*) that is most severe in warm (60° to 80°F) wet weather. Tomato plants are attacked at any stage of growth, but most commonly after the first fruit are set. Fruit are rarely infected. Severe infection causes extensive leaf yellowing and defoliation. This weakens the plant, reduces the size and quality of the fruit, and exposes the fruit to sunscald. Spores are formed in the tiny black specks in the leaf spots, and are spread by splashing rain and by people and animals brushing against wet foliage. Foggy, misty weather and heavy dews provide enough moisture for infection. The fungus survives on tomato plant debris for at least 3 years.

SOLUTION: Treat infected plants with ORTHO Orthocide Garden Fungicide or ORTHO Tomato Vegetable Dust at the first sign of the disease. Repeat treatment at intervals of 7 to 10 days as long as weather conditions continue that are favorable to the spread of the disease. To help prevent the spread of the disease, do not work among wet plants. Remove all plant debris from the garden after harvest to reduce the amount of overwintering spores. Avoid overhead watering by using drip or furrow irrigation.

Tomato leaf roll.

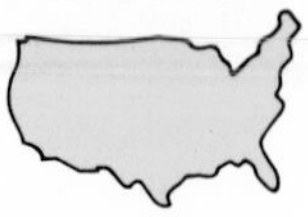

PROBLEM: Older lower leaves roll upward until the margins touch or overlap each other. Eventually most of the leaves may be rolled. Leaves feel leathery and remain green. No other symptoms develop.

ANALYSIS: Leaf roll
Leaf roll on tomatoes is a temporary disorder resulting from excessively wet soil, especially after heavy rains. It occurs most commonly during wet springs on staked tomatoes, although unstaked tomatoes may also be affected. Leaf roll does not slow the plant's growth, and a normal crop of fruit is produced. Within a few days, as the soil dries, the symptoms disappear and the plants return to normal. The varieties Big Boy, Floramerica, and Beefsteak are affected more often than are other varieties.

SOLUTION: Plant tomatoes in well-drained soil, where this problem is least likely to occur. Water regularly, following the guidelines on page 772, so that the soil is neither excessively wet nor dry.

Curly top.

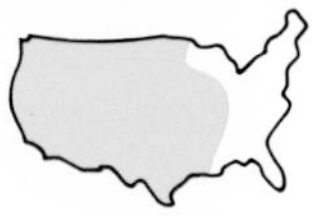

PROBLEM: Leaflets roll upward, twist, and feel tough and leathery. Veins turn purple, and the whole plant is dull yellow and stunted. Young plants die.

ANALYSIS: Curly top
This virus disease affects many vegetables including tomatoes, beets, peppers, beans, and squash. The virus is transmitted from plant to plant by the beet leafhopper (*Circulifer tenellus*), and is common only where this insect lives, west of the Mississippi River. The beet leafhopper is a pale greenish yellow insect about ⅛ inch long that feeds from early May through June. It sucks the sap and virus from the infected leaves, and then injects the virus into healthy plants at its next feeding stop. (For more information on leafhoppers, see page 878.) Curly top symptoms vary in their severity depending on the variety and age of the plant. Young infected plants usually die. Older plants may turn yellow and die. Little if any fruit is produced.

SOLUTION: There is no direct control for curly top. To reduce the chances of infection, control the beet leafhopper with an insecticidal spray containing *malathion*, beginning when insect swarms first appear. (For information about controlling disease-carrying insects, see page 879.) Destroy infected plants. Keep leafhoppers away from tomato plants with a screen of cheesecloth stretched on a frame. Where possible, plant tolerant varieties from the list on page 1026. But if the leafhopper population is large, even resistant varieties may become infected.

Mosaic.

PROBLEM: Leaves are mottled light and dark green, curled, and deformed. Plants are stunted. Fruit is mottled and deformed, with a rough texture and poor flavor.

ANALYSIS: Mosaic
Mosaic is caused by a plant virus. The two most common virus diseases that infect tomatoes are *tobacco mosaic virus* and *cucumber mosaic virus*. Viruses weaken the plants, reducing fruit quality and yield. Plants infected when young do not produce fruit. Viruses may be introduced into the garden on infected transplants, but most viruses live in weeds, including pokeweed, Jimson weed, catnip, plantain, horsenettle, and motherwort. Once the viruses are present in or near the garden, aphids spread them from plant to plant while feeding. Viruses are also transmitted when diseased and healthy leaves rub together, especially during weeding and transplanting. Tobacco mosaic virus is sometimes present in cigar, pipe, and cigarette tobacco, and smokers may carry the virus on their hands.

SOLUTION: There are no chemical controls for viruses. Discard infected plants promptly. Control aphids with ORTHO Fruit & Vegetable Insect Control or ORTHO Malathion 50 Insect Spray. Repeat the treatment at intervals of 7 to 10 days if the plants become reinfested. (For more information about controlling disease-carrying insects, see page 879.) Wash your hands thoroughly with soap and water after smoking and before working in the garden. Remove host weeds around the garden.

Cutworm (life size).

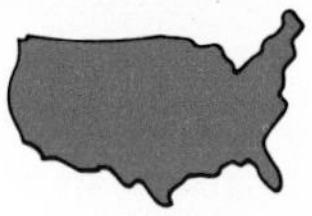

PROBLEM: Young plants are chewed or cut off near the ground. Gray, brown, or black worms, 1½ to 2 inches long, may be found about 2 inches deep in the soil near the base of the damaged plants. The worms coil when disturbed.

ANALYSIS: Cutworms
Several species of cutworms attack plants in the vegetable garden. The most likely pests of young tomato plants set out early in the season are the surface-feeding cutworms. For information on climbing cutworms, see page 670. A single surface-feeding cutworm can sever the stems of many young plants in one night. Cutworms hide in the soil during the day, and feed only at night. Adult cutworms are dark, night-flying moths with bands or stripes on their forewings.

SOLUTION: Apply ORTHO Diazinon Soil & Turf Insect Control, ORTHO Vegetable Guard Soil Insect Killer, or ORTHO Diazinon Soil & Foliage Dust around the base of undamaged plants when stem cutting is observed. Since cutworms are difficult to control, it may be necessary to repeat the dusting at weekly intervals. Before transplanting into the area, apply a preventive treatment of ORTHO Diazinon Soil & Turf Insect Control, ORTHO Vegetable Guard Soil Insect Killer, and work it into the soil. Cultivate the soil thoroughly in late summer and fall to expose and destroy eggs, larvae, and pupae. Further reduce damage with "cutworm collars" around the stem of each plant. These collars can be made of stiff paper or aluminum foil. They should be at least 2 inches high, and pressed firmly into the soil.

Damping-off.

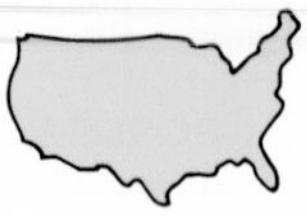

PROBLEM: Seeds don't sprout, or seedlings fall over soon after they emerge. The stem at the soil line is watersoaked and discolored. The base of the stem is soft and thin.

ANALYSIS: Damping-off
Damping-off is a common problem in wet soil with a high nitrogen level. Wet, rich soil promotes damping-off in two ways: the fungi are more active under these conditions, and the seedlings are more succulent and susceptible to attack. Damping-off is often a problem with crops that are planted too early in the spring, before the soil has had a chance to dry and warm sufficiently for quick seed germination. Damping-off can also be a problem when the weather remains cloudy and wet while seeds are germinating, or if seedlings are too heavily shaded.

SOLUTION: To prevent damping-off, take these precautions:
1. Allow the surface of the soil to dry slightly between waterings.
2. Do not start seeds in soil that has a high nitrogen level. Add nitrogen fertilizers after the seedlings have produced their first true leaves.
3. Plant seeds after the soil has reached at least 70°F or start seeds indoors in sterilized potting mix.
4. Protect seeds during germination by coating them with a fungicide containing *captan* (ORTHOCIDE®), *thiram*, or *chloroneb*. Add a pinch of fungicide to a packet of seeds and shake well to coat the seeds with the fungicide. For more information on starting seeds, see page 925.

TURNIPS

ADAPTATION: Throughout the United States.

PLANTING TIME: See page 1025.

PLANTING METHOD: Sow seeds ½ inch deep. When the seedlings have 2 or 3 leaves, thin to stand 2 to 6 inches apart.

SOIL: Any good garden soil. pH 5.5 to 7.0

FERTILIZER: At planting time, use 3 to 4 pounds of ORTHO Vegetable Food per 100 square feet, or 1 pound per 25-foot row. Side dress every 3 to 4 weeks with 1 pound per 25-foot row.
Containers: Water thoroughly every 2 to 3 weeks with a solution of ORTHO Tomato & Vegetable Food.

WATER:
How much: Apply enough water at each irrigation to wet the soil 8 to 10 inches deep.
Containers: 10 percent of the applied water should drain out the bottom.
How often: Water when the soil 2 inches deep is barely moist.

HARVEST: Pull turnips when the root is about 2 to 4 inches in diameter. Use both greens and roots.

Root maggots (half life size).

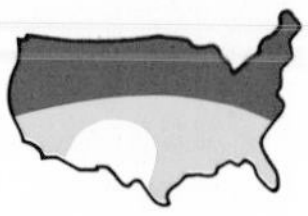

PROBLEM: Young plants wilt in the heat of the day. They may later turn yellow and die. Soft-bodied, yellow-white maggots, ¼ to ⅓ inch long, are feeding in the roots and on seeds. The roots are honeycombed with slimy channels and scarred by brown grooves.

ANALYSIS: Root maggots
(*Hylemya* species)
Root maggots are a damaging pest of turnips in the northern United States. They are most numerous during cool, wet weather in the spring, early summer, and fall. Early maggots attack the roots, stems, and seeds of turnips, cabbage, broccoli, and radishes in the spring and early summer. Later insects damage crops in the fall. The adult is a gray fly somewhat smaller than a housefly, with black stripes and bristles down its back. It lays eggs on stems and in nearby soil. The maggots hatch in 2 to 5 days to feed and tunnel into the roots, rendering them inedible.

SOLUTION: Once the maggots are in the roots, nothing can be done. To control maggots in the planting of turnips, mix ORTHO Vegetable Guard Soil Insect Killer or ORTHO Diazinon Soil & Turf Insect Control into the top 4 to 6 inches of soil before seeding. Control lasts about a month. To prevent egg laying, screen adult flies from the seedbed with a cheesecloth cover.

Wireworm (3 times life size).

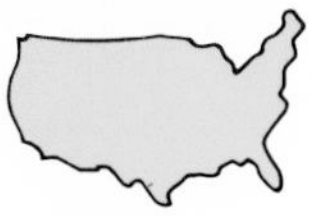

PROBLEM: Plants are stunted and grow slowly. Holes are drilled into the base of the plants. In the soil and throughout the roots are hard, jointed, shiny, cream-colored to yellow worms up to ⅝ inch long.

ANALYSIS: Wireworms
Wireworms feed on turnips, corn, carrots, beets, peas, and many other plants. They feed on the roots and seeds of turnips. Infestations are most extensive in soil where lawn grass was previously grown, in poorly drained soil, and in soil that is high in organic matter. The adult is known as the *click beetle* because it makes a clicking sounds when turning from its back to its feet. Adults lay their eggs in the spring. Wireworms feed for 2 to 6 years before maturing into adult beetles, so all sizes and ages of wireworms may be present in the soil at the same time. Infestations are often spotty.

SOLUTION: Control wireworms with an insecticide containing *diazinon*. Both granular and liquid forms are effective. Treat the soil 1 week before planting, working the insecticide into the top 6 inches of soil.

Cabbage looper (life size).

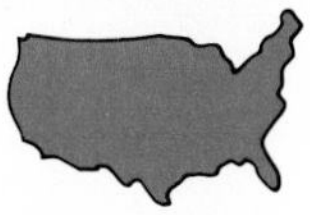

PROBLEM: Leaves have ragged, irregular, or round holes. Green caterpillars, up to 1½ inches long, are feeding on the leaves. Masses of greenish brown pellets may be found when the outer leaves are parted.

ANALYSIS: Cabbage caterpillars
These destructive caterpillars are either the *cabbage looper* (*Trichoplusia ni*), native to the United States, or the *imported cabbageworm* (*Pieris rapae*), introduced into North America from Europe around 1860. Both species attack all members of the cabbage family, including turnips. Adults lay their eggs singly on leaves in the spring. The white cabbage butterfly attaches its tiny, yellow, bullet-shaped eggs to the underside of leaves; the brownish cabbage looper moth lays its pale green eggs at night on the upper surfaces of leaves. The larvae that hatch from these eggs feed on leaves. The cabbageworm also causes damage by contaminating plants with its greenish brown excrement. There are as many as five generations in a season, so caterpillar damage can occur from early spring through late fall. The caterpillars spend the winter as pupae attached to a plant or nearby object.

SOLUTION: Treat the turnip leaves with ORTHO Fruit & Vegetable Insect Control or ORTHO Tomato & Vegetable Insect Killer when the caterpillars first appear. Or, if practical, handpick and destroy caterpillars on the leaves. Clean all plant debris from the garden to reduce the number of overwintering pupae.

Flea beetles (life size).

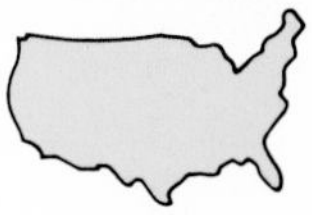

PROBLEM: Leaves are riddled with shotholes about ⅛ inch in diameter. Tiny (1/16 inch) black beetles jump like fleas when disturbed. Leaves of seedlings and eventually whole plants may wilt and die.

ANALYSIS: Flea beetles
These beetles jump like fleas, but are not related to them. Both adult and immature flea beetles feed on a wide variety of garden vegetables, including turnips. The immature beetle, a legless gray grub, injures plants by feeding on the roots and the lower surfaces of leaves. Adults chew holes in leaves. Flea beetles are most damaging to seedlings and young plants. Leaves of seedlings riddled with holes dry out quickly and die. Adult beetles survive the winter in soil and garden debris. They emerge in early spring to feed on weeds until vegetables sprout or plants are set in the garden. Grubs hatch from eggs laid in the soil and feed for 2 to 3 weeks. After pupating in the soil, they emerge as adults to repeat the cycle. There are one to four generations a year. Adults may feed for up to 2 months.

SOLUTION: Control flea beetles on turnips with ORTHO Fruit & Vegetable Insect Control or ORTHO Tomato & Vegetable Insect Killer when the leaves first show damage, or when the plants first emerge through the ground. Watch new growth for evidence of further damage, and repeat the treatment at weekly intervals as needed. Clean all plant debris from the garden after harvest to eliminate overwintering spots for adult beetles.

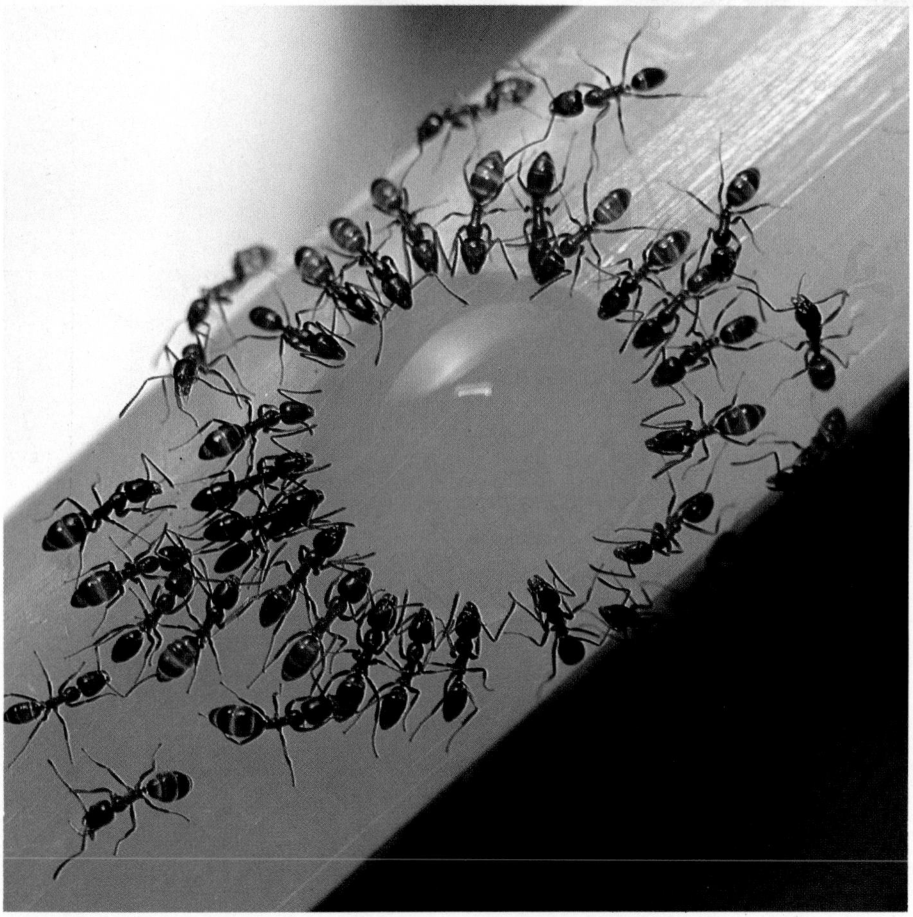

If you don't know the name of a household pest, look through the photographs in the next 25 pages, and read the descriptions of the pests and the damage they cause. This section is grouped into these categories:

HOUSEHOLD PESTS

Finding cockroaches, mice, or ants in the home can be a shocking experience—as if your privacy was being invaded. But it happens to everybody occasionally, and to some people frequently. Some of these pests are only nuisances, such as boxelder bugs or clover mites, which often invade our homes in the fall looking for a warm place to spend the winter. They do no direct harm, but their presence is distasteful. But other pests spoil our food, weaken our homes, or even feed on us!

The two most effective ways to control pests in the house are to remove their reason for invading the house, and to make the house so tight that they can't get in. Many of these pests enter our homes because they find food more easily there than outside. They way to avoid them is to keep food locked up tight. This means practicing careful sanitation in the kitchen, and keeping attractive foods in glass jars or other tight containers. It may also mean sealing woolen clothes in plastic bags, or washing a pet's bedding frequently.

We think of the walls of our houses as barriers but, to an insect, they may have open portals. Many insect problems can be solved by making a careful inspection of the house, then patching holes and caulking cracks.

Also included in this section are some of the biting and stinging pests that annoy or alarm us outside. Although it is usually not possible to erect barriers against outside pests, sanitation helps to limit their numbers. Some dangerous pests such as black widow spiders and scorpions can most easily be eliminated by ridding the yard of the places they like to hide. Honey bees will stay away from the yard if you don't plant their favorite flowers.

As with many of the garden pests, household pests are most easily controlled by avoiding the conditions that attract them.

Above: Ants around a drop of bait. See page 791.
Left: A pest-free patio makes outdoor living more pleasant.

INDEX TO HOUSEHOLD PESTS

Housefly (4 times life size).

PROBLEM: Flies are present in the home and other living areas.

ANALYSIS: Houseflies
(*Musca domestica*)
These insect pests are common throughout the world. In addition to their annoying presence, they can spread a number of serious human diseases and parasites such as diarrhea, dysentery, typhoid, cholera, intestinal worms, and *Salmonella* bacteria. Several other fly species may also infest the home, including face flies (*M. autumnalis*) and little houseflies (*Fannia canicularis*). Flies feed on and lay their eggs in decaying organic materials. The eggs hatch within several days, and even within 12 hours if conditions are ideal. The creamy-white maggots (about ⅓ inch long) burrow into and feed on the decaying material for several days, pupate, and then emerge as adult flies. Under warm conditions, the entire life cycle may be completed within 14 days. However, cooler conditions will greatly extend this period. The adults usually live for 15 to 25 days.

SOLUTION: To reduce the fly population, maintain sanitary conditions in the home and garden. Keep garbage tightly covered, and dispose of it regularly. Maintain door and window screens in good condition. Kill flies indoors with ORTHO Flying & Crawling Insect Killer, ORTHO Hi-Power Indoor Insect Fogger, or ORTHO Home Pest Insect Control. Kill flies outdoors with ORTHO Malathion 50 Insect Spray or ORTHO Outdoor Insect Fogger. Apply according to label directions.

Vinegar fly (10 times life size).

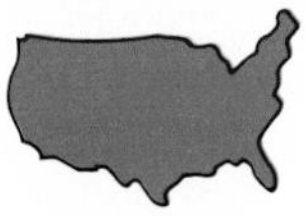

PROBLEM: Tiny (up to $\frac{1}{6}$ inch), yellowish brown, clear-winged insects fly around rotting fruits and vegetables, garbage cans, and other wet, fermenting, or rotting materials. These insects fly in a slow, hovering manner.

ANALYSIS: Vinegar flies
(*Drosophila* species)
These insects, also known as *fruit flies*, do not constitute a serious health menace, but can be annoying in locations where fruit, vegetables, or garbage are allowed to rot and ferment. The adult flies lay their eggs in the decaying fruits or vegetables. The eggs hatch in a few days, and the tiny maggots feed on yeasts growing in the decaying food. The maggots pupate and become adults; the entire life cycle takes only 10 to 12 days.

SOLUTION: To reduce the fly population, maintain sanitary conditions. Keep garbage tightly covered, and dispose of it regularly. Kill flies with ORTHO Flying & Crawling Insect Killer, ORTHO Hi-Power Indoor Insect Fogger, or ORTHO Home Pest Insect Control. Apply according to label directions.

Spider (half life size).

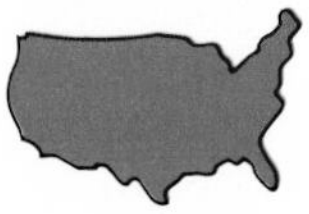

PROBLEM: Spider webs and spiders are in secluded, rarely-disturbed areas in and around the home.

ANALYSIS: Household spiders
Many kinds of spiders wander into the home. With only a few exceptions, these familiar creatures are harmless and often beneficial. Spiders feed on other spiders and insects, including such household pests as flies and moths. The more insects there are inside the home, the more likely spiders will live there. Most spiders spin silken webs. Some, such as tarantulas, are active hunting spiders that do not spin webs. When spiders bite humans, it is usually because they have been squeezed, lain on, or somehow provoked. Only a few spiders, particularly the black widow and brown recluse, are dangerous to people, but their bites are rarely fatal. (For more information about black widow and brown recluse spiders, see page 805).

SOLUTION: Knock down webs with brooms or dusters. Kill spiders and the insects they feed on by spraying infested areas with ORTHO Ant, Roach & Spider Killer, ORTHO Hi-Power Indoor Insect Fogger, or ORTHO Home Pest Insect Control. To reduce the numbers of spiders entering the home, seal cracks in the home, inspect and repair window screens, and clean up accumulations of debris outdoors that may harbor spiders or their prey. Spray around doors, windows, and foundations where spiders may enter with ORTHO Ant, Roach & Spider Killer or ORTHO Home Pest Insect Control.

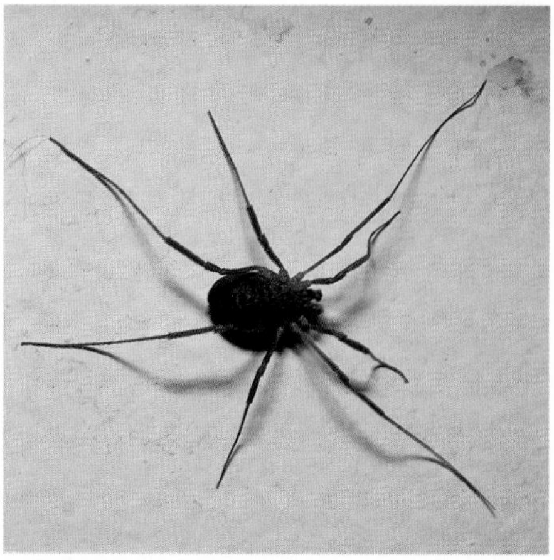

Daddy-long-legs (twice life size).

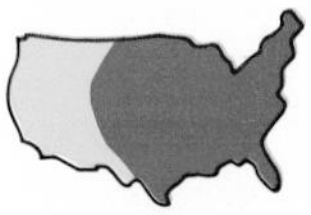

PROBLEM: Spiderlike creatures with a small body and long delicate legs are found in or around the home and garden. They are sometimes seen in large gatherings, standing with their legs interlaced.

ANALYSIS: Daddy-long-legs
Daddy-long-legs, also called *harvestmen,* are closely related to spiders, but are not true spiders. They are not capable of producing silken webbing. They are most common in areas near a source of water. In northern states, most daddy-long-legs die in autumn after the female lays eggs. In southern states, females usually spend the winter under ground litter and lay eggs in the spring. They lay eggs in the soil under stones, wood, and other debris. Daddy-long-legs feed mainly on small insects. They are most active at night, and do not bite humans. Occasionally they wander indoors, but do not cause any damage.

SOLUTION: Reduce the number of daddy-long-legs coming indoors by cleaning up wood, trash, and other debris outside the home that may harbor them. Trim plant growth away from the house. Seal cracks and crevices around windows and doors, and repair any broken screens.

PESTS AROUND THE HOME

House cricket (life size).

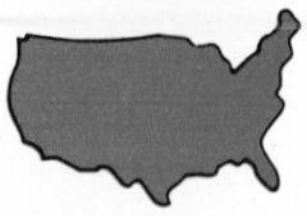

PROBLEM: Crickets are chirping in the home. These insects, which look like grasshoppers, are light to dark brown, ½ to ¾ inch long, and have long antennae that curve back along the sides of the body. Holes may be chewed in clothing, curtains, carpets, and upholstery in severely infested homes.

ANALYSIS: Crickets (*Gryllus assimilis* and *Acheta domesticus*)

The two types of crickets that may invade the home are *field crickets* and *house crickets.* Field crickets usually live outdoors, feeding on vegetation and plant debris. In the fall, when their natural food supply fails, or during periods of heavy rainfall, they may invade buildings in search of food. Field crickets cannot reproduce in the home, and usually die by winter. House crickets, however, can survive and reproduce indoors. During the day, both types of crickets hide in dark, warm locations such as behind baseboards, in closets, and in attics. Male crickets make a chirping sound by rubbing their legs together. Crickets may feed on fabrics and paper items, and large numbers of them may cause serious problems.

SOLUTION: To control crickets outdoors, dust along foundations with ORTHO Ortho-Klor Indoor & Outdoor Insect Killer or ORTHO Pest-B-Gon Roach Bait according to label directions. To control crickets indoors, spray with ORTHO Ant, Roach & Spider Killer or ORTHO Home Pest Insect Control according to label directions. Remove dense vegetation and debris around the building foundation where crickets may hide. Seal openings around doors and windows.

Moth on door screen.

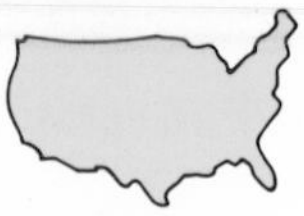

PROBLEM: Numerous insects are flying around indoor or outdoor lights at night. Their physical presence as well as their buzzing or droning is bothersome. Dead insects may accumulate below lights, attracting ants and other insects to the site.

ANALYSIS: Night-flying insects

Many night-flying insects use the moon and stars as points of orientation to help them discern direction. When they see a brighter source of light, such as a light bulb, they mistake it for one of these objects and orient to it, eventually colliding with the light. Lights attract a wide variety of night-flying insects, including most moths, and certain beetles, mosquitoes, flies, gnats, and leafhoppers. When many insects become adults during a short period, large numbers may be attracted to lights.

SOLUTION: Spray ORTHO Outdoor Insect Fogger or burn citronella candles to temporarily eliminate outdoor flying insects. Spray ORTHO Household Insect Killer to control flying insects indoors. Replace white light bulbs with yellow ones; yellow light is less visible to insects and therefore less attractive to them. Use light bulbs of lower wattage, and turn off lights when not needed. Locate outdoor lights behind shrubs or walls rather than where they are visible to insects from long distances. Install or repair screens to prevent insects from moving indoors. If entertaining outdoors, consider using candles for light. Their lower light intensity is less attractive to insects. For more information on insects and lighting, see the ORTHO book *How to Design & Install Outdoor Lighting.*

Giant water bug (twice life size).

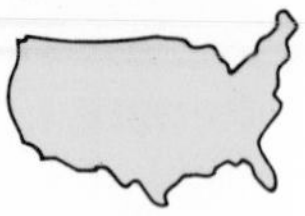

PROBLEM: Insects are in the swimming pool. The insects may be actively swimming in the pool, or may be floundering or dead. Even well-maintained pools can have this problem. Some of these insects may inflict painful bites.

ANALYSIS: Swimming pool pests

Many insects and related organisms become pests in swimming pools. They may either fall in the pool and drown or live in the pool. Sowbugs, millipedes, springtails, and other insects that are living in nearby vegetation may crawl into the pool and drown. They are particularly common if there is an abundance of organic matter under shrubbery near the pool. Bees and wasps may fall into the pool as they search for water. Insects that can live even in chlorinated and clean pools include some beetles and several bugs: backswimmers, giant water bugs, water boatmen, and water striders. Backswimmers and giant water bugs can inflict painful bites similar to bee stings. These insects, as well as many moths, are attracted to pool lights. If a swimming pool is not kept chlorinated and clean, mosquitoes and midges may breed in the water.

SOLUTION: Skim insects off the surface of the water with a dip net. Use lights sparingly near pools, and switch to yellow lights (which are less attractive to insects) if there is a continual problem. Or, place a very bright light source a couple hundred feet away to attract night fliers away from the pool. Keep the pool chlorinated and reasonably clean. Keep grass and shrubbery trimmed near the pool. Control insects in nearby shrubbery. (Look up the control for the insect in the Insect Gallery beginning on page 865.) Do not spray the pool directly.

Earwig (twice life size).

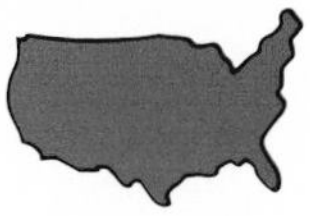

PROBLEM: Reddish brown, flat, elongated insects up to an inch long with straight or curved pincers projecting from the rear of the body are present in the home. They are often found in dark, secluded places such as in pantries, closets, and drawers, and even in bedding. They may be seen scurrying along baseboards, or moving from room to room.

ANALYSIS: Earwigs
Several species of these nocturnal insects may infest the home, including the European earwig (*Forficula auricularia*), the ringlegged earwig (*Euborellia annulipes*), and the striped earwig (*Labidura riparia*). Earwigs are usually found in the garden, where they feed on mosses, decaying organic matter, vegetation, and other insects. However, large numbers of earwigs may invade homes through cracks or openings in the foundation, doors, and window screens, especially during hot, dry spells. Although they do not damage household furnishings, their presence is annoying, and they may feed on stored food items, or hide in areas where food is kept. They may inflict painful pinches when provoked.

SOLUTION: Store food in sealed containers. Repair cracks or openings in window screens, doors, and the building foundation. Control earwigs indoors by baiting with ORTHO Earwig, Roach & Sowbug Bait or spraying with ORTHO Home Pest Insect Control or dusting with ORTHO Ortho-Klor Indoor & Outdoor Insect Killer. Use according to label directions. To prevent reinfestations, control earwigs outdoors. For more information about controlling earwigs outdoors, see page 893.

Smokybrown cockroach (3 times life size).

PROBLEM: Cockroaches are found outdoors in wood piles, groundcovers, leaf litter, and other protected areas. Occasionally they wander indoors.

ANALYSIS: Outdoor-originating cockroaches
Unlike many species of cockroaches, these cockroaches, often called *wood roaches*, live mainly outdoors; they occasionally wander inside but cannot reproduce there. The American cockroach (*Periplaneta americana*) and the smokybrown cockroach (*P. fuliginosa*) are two species that can live equally well indoors and outdoors in warm climates. The smokybrown cockroach, in particular, is a pest in many southern states. It moves indoors when weather conditions outside become adverse. Outdoor-living cockroaches are more likely to wander indoors if there are suitable places for them to live and breed next to the house. Favorite habitats include plantings of groundcovers, and piles of wood, compost, and other debris. These cockroaches are general scavengers, eating decaying plant and animal material.

SOLUTION: To eliminate cockroaches outdoors, move compost and wood piles away from the structure. Clean up litter and debris near the home. Apply ORTHO Diazinon Insect Spray in a 5 foot band around the foundation and in nearby groundcovers. Make sure your groundcover is listed on the product label. Repair window and door screens, and plug cracks and crevices in the walls and foundation. Inspect firewood before bringing it indoors and remove any cockroaches. Follow the indoor control measures in the adjacent section on "cockroaches" to eliminate cockroaches living indoors.

Silverfish (3 times life size).

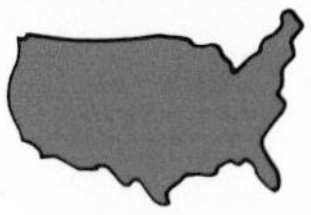

PROBLEM: Paper and fabric products, especially those made with glue, paste, or sizing, are stained yellow, chewed, or notched, and may be covered with excrement and silver or gray scales. When infested products are moved, flattened, slender, wingless insects up to ½ inch long may scurry away. These insects have long, thin antennae, and may be silvery and shiny, or dull and mottled gray.

ANALYSIS: Silverfish and firebrats
(*Lepisma* and *Thermobia* species)
These common household pests are similar in size, shape, and feeding habits except for their coloration and hiding places. Silverfish are silvery, and prefer damp, cool to warm (70° to 80°F) locations such as basements and wall voids. Firebrats are mottled gray, and prefer damp, hot (90° to 105°F) locations such as hot-water pipes and areas near the oven or furnace. These pests are active at night, and hide during the day. They feed on a wide range of foods, especially products high in starches, including human food, paper, paste, and linen and other fabrics. Silverfish damage books by feeding on the bindings. These pests crawl throughout the house along pipes and through holes or crevices in the walls or floor. The adult females lay eggs in cracks or openings behind baseboards and other protected areas.

SOLUTION: Treat with ORTHO Home Pest Insect Control, ORTHO Ant, Roach & Spider Killer, or ORTHO Ortho-Klor Indoor & Outdoor Insect Killer according to label directions. Where practical, seal all cracks and crevices in the infested areas. Store valued papers and clothes in tightly sealed plastic bags.

PESTS AROUND THE HOME

House centipede (life size).

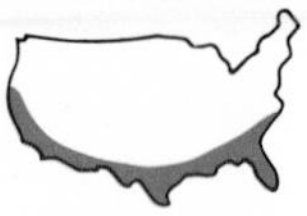

PROBLEM: A thin centipedelike creature with long legs is crawling on the floor or wall. It is up to $1\frac{1}{2}$ inches long, with very long antennae and legs in comparison to its body size. The antennae and rear set of legs can be more than twice the length of the body. The creature runs quickly, with sudden stops.

ANALYSIS: House centipede
(*Scutigera coleoptrata*)
House centipedes are found both indoors and outdoors in warm regions of the country, but only indoors where winters are colder. Unlike other centipedes, which wander indoors but cannot reproduce there, house centipedes live and reproduce indoors. House centipedes prey on other insects, and become most numerous where there is an abundance of insects to feed on. They prefer dampness, and thrive in typically moist areas such as cellars, closets, or bathrooms. Outdoors they are common in moist piles of compost and other debris. House centipedes are most active at night. They seldom bite humans, and when they do, the bite is no more severe than a bee sting.

SOLUTION: To control house centipedes and the insects they feed on, spray indoor areas with ORTHO Household Insect Killer or ORTHO Flying & Crawling Insect Killer, especially along baseboard cracks. Or, fog the premises with ORTHO Hi-Power Indoor Insect Fogger. Eliminate moist areas in and around the home. Air out damp places. Outdoors, remove piles of compost and other materials that provide hiding places near the house.

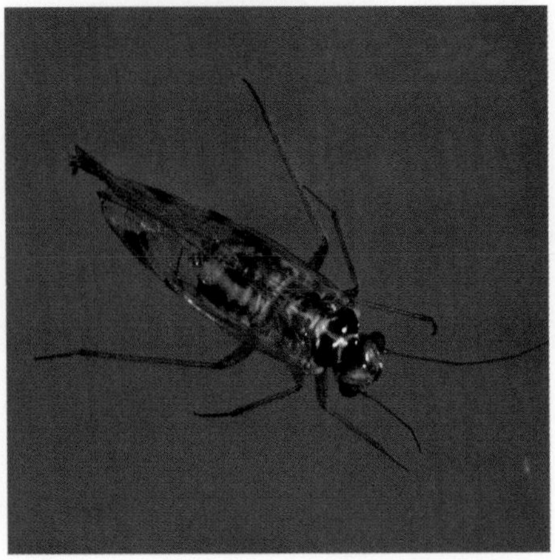
Winged psocid (12 times life size).

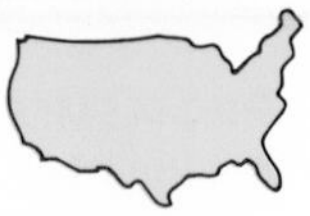

PROBLEM: Numerous tiny insects the size of a pinhead are crawling in stored food products or around books. These insects may emerge from behind walls for several months after construction of a building. They run along surfaces in a hesitating, jerky manner.

ANALYSIS: Booklice
These insects, also known as *psocids*, thrive in warm, damp, undisturbed places. They feed mainly on microscopic molds that may develop on certain kinds of adhesives used in book binding and wallpaper. Booklice sometimes infest damp Spanish moss, straw, or other vegetable matter used in making upholstered furniture. They feed directly on cereals and other starchy materials (particularly if these products are stored for a long period in damp conditions), and on dead insects. Although booklice contaminate stored food with their body parts, they do not cause other damage. Insect damage seen on books is caused by other insects such as silverfish (see page 789) or cockroaches (see page 807). Booklice do not bite or carry disease organisms.

SOLUTION: Dry out infested areas of the home. If booklice are in the food pantry, search for and throw out any infested food. Ventilation and artificial heat can aid in drying out cupboards. Booklice will disappear in new homes as the structure dries. Control infested furniture by thoroughly drying the item in sunlight for several days, having it fumigated by a pest control operator, or, if practical, discarding the infested stuffing. Infested areas also can be treated with an insecticide containing *pyrethrins*. Make sure the site you spray is listed on the product label.

Carpet beetles and larvae (3 times life size).

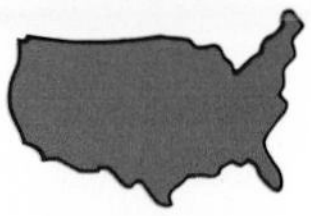

PROBLEM: Irregular holes are chewed in carpets, blankets, clothing, and other articles made of animal fur, hair, feathers, or hides. Light brown to black grubs up to $\frac{1}{4}$ inch long may be seen crawling on both damaged and undamaged items. The grubs are distinctly segmented, and covered with circular rows of stiff, dark hairs.

ANALYSIS: Carpet beetles
(*Attagenus megatoma* and *Anthrenus* species)
The larvae of these beetles damage carpets, clothes, upholstery, and other products of animal origin. Some species also feed on stored foods. The adult beetles are about $\frac{1}{8}$ inch long, and may be black or mottled gray, brown, and white. They usually live outdoors, feeding on pollen and nectar. The beetles fly into homes during the late spring or early summer and lay their eggs in cracks or crevices, or on clothes, carpets, or other materials. The emerging larvae seek out dark, undisturbed locations in which to feed. They shed their skins a number of times during their development. Most of the larvae hibernate during the winter, and pupate in the spring.

SOLUTION: Shake out, brush, and air infested clothes and blankets. To kill remaining grubs, dry clean infested items. Pack clean clothes with *paradichlorobenzene* crystals (mothballs) in airtight closets or containers. Vacuum or sweep infested rooms, and destroy the sweepings immediately. Kill remaining insects by treating rooms with ORTHO Hi-Power Indoor Insect Fogger, ORTHO Home Pest Insect Control, or ORTHO Ortho-Klor Indoor & Outdoor Insect Killer. Seek professional help to protect carpets and furs.

Black ants (twice life size).

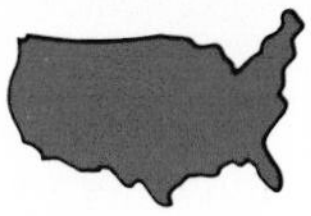

PROBLEM: Ants are present in the house. Trails of ants may be seen crawling on floors, walls, baseboards, counters, and in cupboards. They are generally most troublesome in the kitchen or pantry.

ANALYSIS: Ants
A number of closely related species of ants invade households. Most ants are strongly attracted to sweets, starches, fats, and grains, and invade households in order to carry these foods back to their nests. Adverse outdoor conditions, such as flooding or drought, may cause ants to move their nests or colonies into buildings. Ant colonies are often built underground in the garden, but may also be found in building foundations, under flooring, between wall partitions, in attics, and in other protected locations. The colonies may contain from several hundred to several thousand individuals. Ant colonies may be located by following the established ant trails to their source. For more information about ants, see page 893.

SOLUTION: Destroy ant colonies by dusting with ORTHO Ortho-Klor Indoor & Outdoor Insect Killer or spraying the nests and ant trails with ORTHO Home & Garden Insect Killer, ORTHO Home Pest Insect Control, or ORTHO Ant, Roach & Spider Killer, as directed on the label. Eliminate ant colonies from the garden by treating the anthills with ORTHO Diazinon Granules or spraying the nest and surrounding soil with ORTHO Diazinon Insect Spray. Store food in sealed containers, and keep kitchens and pantries free of exposed foods.

Clothes moths (life size).

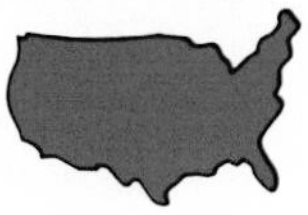

PROBLEM: Holes are chewed in clothing, blankets, carpets, pillows, upholstery, and other items. Infested articles may be covered with a webbing of silken tubes, cases, and strands. Shiny white worms up to ½ inch long may be seen crawling on damaged items.

ANALYSIS: Clothes moths (*Tineola bisselliella* and *T. pellionella*)
The larvae of these small, yellowish to tan moths damage clothes and other items made of fur, wool, feathers, and leather. The female moths attach their eggs to the fabric. Soon after the larvae emerge they spin silken tubes, mats, or cases. The larvae usually feed from within these protective casings, but may crawl out to feed unprotected. The larvae pupate in cocoons attached by silken threads to the infested item, and emerge as adult moths. New infestations occur when moths lay eggs on clothing, carpets, and other articles, and when moth, larva, and egg-ridden items are stored with uninfested articles.

SOLUTION: Shake out, brush, and air infested clothes and blankets in a sunny location. To kill remaining moths, dry clean infested items. Pack clean clothes with *paradichlorobenzene* crystals (mothballs) in airtight closets or containers. Vacuum or sweep infested rooms, and destroy the sweepings immediately. Seek professional help to protect carpets and furs.

Boxelder bug (4 times life size).

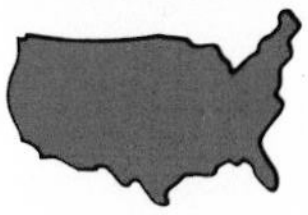

PROBLEM: During the fall, hordes of brownish black bugs ½ inch long with red stripes on their wings swarm into the home and outdoor living areas. They congregate on walls, walks, furniture, drapes, and other objects. When crushed, they emit a strong, unpleasant odor.

ANALYSIS: Boxelder bugs (*Leptocoris* species)
These insects are common in all parts of the country. They are most numerous in areas where boxelder trees (*Acer negundo*) grow. In the spring, the female bugs lay their eggs in the bark of boxelders, or sometimes of maples, ash, and fruit trees. The young feed on tender twigs, foliage, and seeds through the spring and summer. During the fall, especially on bright, sunny days, the bugs migrate in large numbers into tree trunks, homes, buildings, or other dry, protected locations to hibernate for the winter. Boxelder bugs do not feed on fabric or furniture, but may stain household items with their excrement. Occasionally, boxelder bugs will bite, and they may feed on houseplants.

SOLUTION: Vacuum boxelder bugs with a tank-type vacuum cleaner, and then destroy the bag. Or spray the bugs with an insecticide containing *malathion*, *diazinon*, or *pyrethrum*. Spray outdoor areas with ORTHO Malathion 50 Insect Spray or ORTHO Diazinon Insect Spray. Keep the doors and windows screened and the cracks around them well sealed.

PESTS AROUND THE HOME

Clover mite (30 times life size).

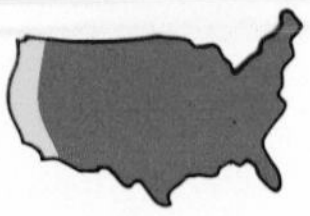

PROBLEM: Reddish brown mites smaller than a pinhead, with long front legs, are present in the home in the fall. They may be found on walls, window sills, floors, and furniture and even in bedding and clothes. When crushed, these mites leave a blood-red stain. They are often so numerous that they give infested surfaces a reddish appearance.

ANALYSIS: Clover mites (*Bryobia praetiosa*)

These pests, related to spiders, are found throughout the United States. Clover mites feed and reproduce on clover, grasses, and other plants. They are most active in the spring and fall, and on warm winter days. The mites lay eggs during the summer and fall. The young that hatch from these eggs feed on vegetation, and then migrate into homes and other protected areas during the early fall. Mites enter homes through cracks or openings in the foundation and around doors and windows. Mite activity usually decreases when temperatures rise above 85°F or fall below 40°F.

SOLUTION: Remove mites from household furnishings by vacuuming them from infested surfaces. Kill mites indoors by spraying them directly with ORTHO Home Pest Insect Control. Treat outdoor areas with ORTHO Home Pest Insect Control, ORTHO ORTHO-KLOR Indoor & Outdoor Insect Killer, or ORTHO Malathion 50 Insect Spray as directed on the label. Keep a strip of soil 18 to 24 inches wide around the foundation of the building free of vegetation and debris to reduce mite movement into homes.

Pigeon.

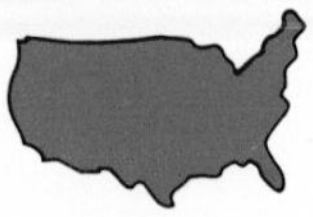

PROBLEM: Birds are roosting or nesting in wall voids, under eaves, and in other areas around the home.

ANALYSIS: Birds

Most birds are harmless and pleasant, but a few species, especially pigeons, starlings, and sparrows, may become a nuisance around the home. These birds are adapted to urban and suburban environments. They roost and build nests on chimneys, ledges, rafters, eaves, drainpipes, and similar locations, and often return to the same nesting site year after year. In addition to their messy droppings and irritating chirping, birds may transmit to humans such diseases as pigeon ornithosis, aspergillosis, encephalitis, and histoplasmosis.

SOLUTION: Where possible, exclude birds with screens. Apply a bird repellent adhesive or jelly to roosting and nesting areas. Clean up possible food or nest-building materials (such as dried weeds or vegetation) to discourage bird activity in the vicinity. Place flashings of wood, plastic, or metal at a 45 degree angle on nesting or roosting areas. Birds may also be trapped or poisoned. If you are considering poison, contact a licensed pest control operator or your county agricultural commissioner's office for regulations pertaining to your city.

Raccoon.

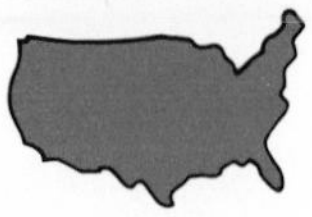

PROBLEM: Raccoons are present around the home. They overturn garbage cans at night, scattering and feeding on the contents and causing a great commotion. They occasionally invade attics, crawl spaces under buildings, and other secluded locations.

ANALYSIS: Raccoons (*Procyon lotor*)

Raccoons are a nuisance mainly in rural and suburban areas. They generally live near a source of natural water such as a stream, marsh, or pond. Raccoons are very dextrous and inquisitive animals. They frequently turn over garbage cans in their search for food. They sometimes take up residence in attics, basements, barns, or similar locations. Although these animals carry fleas and ticks, they are not a serious health threat. Raccoons can be dangerous if cornered.

SOLUTION: Keep garbage cans securely anchored in racks or immovable frames. Lids should be tightly secured to the can. Screen or seal openings into buildings. Consult your Department of Fish and Game regional office to find out about local raccoon control restrictions and regulations. Live traps baited with pieces of melon, prunes, honey-coated bread, or smoked fish are usually effective in controlling raccoons. Attach traps to a tree, stake, or fence post. If possible, push the trap back and forth in the ground until the soil covers the wire mesh on the bottom of the trap. Wait a few days before setting the trap; this allows the animal a chance to become accustomed to it. Transport the trapped animal to a wooded area at least several miles away.

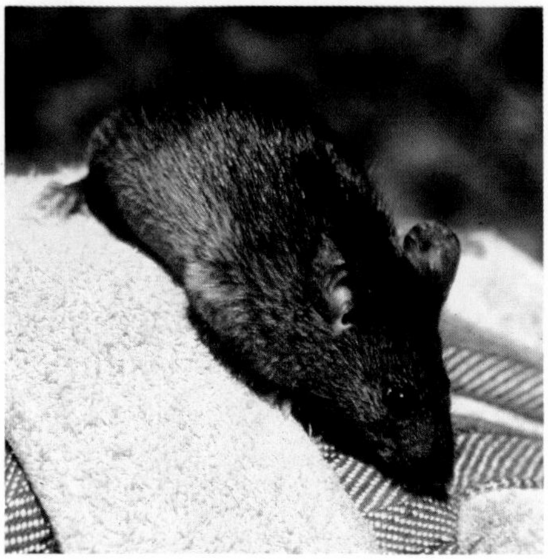
House mouse.

House mouse.

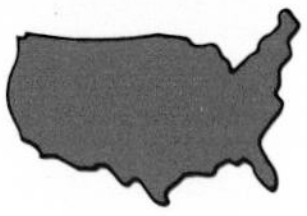

PROBLEM: Mice are seen in the garage or home. Or signs of mouse infestation are found, including droppings and tracks, or gnawed doors, baseboards, or kitchen cabinets. Books, fabrics, furniture, and other objects may be chewed or shredded, and packages of food may be gnawed open and the contents eaten.

ANALYSIS: House mice (*Mus musculus*)
These familiar pests often go unnoticed if only a few are present, but may cause significant damage when their numbers are large. In addition to gnawing on clothing, furniture, and other items, mice contaminate food with their urine and droppings, and may spread parasites and diseases. Mice are generally active at night. Under ideal conditions, the females produce up to 50 young in a year. Mice are very agile, and can jump to 12 inches off the ground, run up almost any rough vertical surface, swim, and squeeze through openings slightly larger than ¼ inch. House mice feed primarily on cereal grains, but will eat many other kinds of food including butter, fat, meat, sweets, and nuts.

SOLUTION: The best way to eliminate mice in the home is to trap them. Mice are more likely to seek bait in traps if their normal source of food is scarce. Remove food from areas where mice can get to it, and store grains in sealed metal, glass, or heavy plastic containers. Place traps where mouse droppings, gnawings, and damage indicate their presence such as behind refrigerators and other protective objects, in dark corners, along baseboards, and in cupboards. Bait the traps with pieces of bacon, nutmeats, raisins, or peanut butter. Tie the bait to the trigger so the mouse won't be able to remove the bait without springing the trap. Check the traps daily to dispose of trapped mice. Wear gloves when handling dead mice, or use tongs to pick them up to avoid bites from mouse parasites. Poisoned baits are also effective in controlling mice. If you are unable to eliminate all the mice, contact a professional pest control operator. After the mice have been eliminated, prevent them from returning by sealing holes or cracks larger than ¼ inch in the walls, floors, windows, doors, and foundation that open to the outside. For details on mouse-proofing your home, contact your local Cooperative Extension Office. For a list of extension offices, see page 1029.

Gray squirrel.

PROBLEM: Squirrels are seen or heard in the building. Or nuts or other food remnants, droppings, gnawed holes, and nesting materials in the attic, garage, wall voids, and other areas indicate their presence.

ANALYSIS: Tree squirrels
Several species of tree squirrels invade houses, including the fox squirrel (*Sciurus niger*), eastern gray squirrel (*S. carolinensis*), and flying squirrels (*Glaucomys* species). Squirrels enter buildings through vents, broken windows, construction gaps under eaves and gables, and occasionally chimneys and fireplaces. They may build nests or store food in attics, wall voids, garages, and similar locations, and damage items stored in attics or garages.

SOLUTION: Contact your State Department of Fish and Game regional office for regulations governing the control of tree squirrels in your area. Eliminate animals inside the building by placing traps in the areas they are inhabiting. Bait the traps with nutmeats, chunk-style peanut butter, sunflower seeds, or raisins. If tree squirrels are entering the building via trees or power lines, secure traps to tree limbs or the roof top to intercept them. For more information about traps, see page 897. Once squirrels have been eliminated from the building, seal entry routes into the home with sheet metal or hardware cloth. Prune off tree limbs at least 6 feet away from the roof or any other part of the building.

PESTS AROUND THE HOME

Roof rat.

Norway rat.

Skunk.

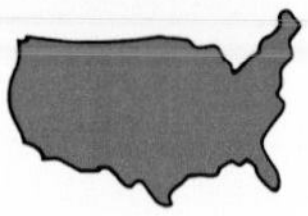

PROBLEM: Rats are seen or heard in the attic, garage, basement, wall voids, or other areas of the home. Or signs of rat infestation are found, including droppings, tracks, and loosely constructed nests made of rags, paper, and other scraps. Pipes, beams, and wiring may be gnawed. Books, fabrics, furniture, and other objects may be chewed or shredded, and packages of food may be gnawed open and the contents eaten.

ANALYSIS: Rats *(Rattus* species)
Rats are distributed world-wide, and infest well-maintained suburban residences as well as run-down urban houses and apartments. The species that most frequently infest houses are the Norway rat (also known as the brown, house, wharf, or sewer rat) and the roof rat. Rats enter buildings through any opening, including toilets, pipes, chimneys, and garbage chutes. Young rats can squeeze through openings as small as ½ inch wide. These animals make their nests and breed in wall voids, attics, crawl spaces, basements, and other secluded locations. They also breed in heavy vegetation near the home, such as ivy or juniper groundcovers. Their long front teeth grow constantly. To keep them worn down, rats gnaw on almost anything, including clothing, furniture, and electrical wires. They can also gnaw through gas lines, causing gas leaks. Rats are notorious for contaminating food with their urine, droppings, and hair, spreading parasites and diseases. They occasionally bite people, especially sleeping infants. The bites are dangerous, and should be treated by a doctor.

SOLUTION: Control rats in the home by trapping them. Rats are more likely to seek bait in traps if their normal source of food is scarce. Remove food from areas where rats can get to it easily. Store food in glass or tin containers with screw-on or otherwise tightly sealed lids. Place traps along rat runways, anchoring the trap securely to a nearby object so the animal won't drag it away. Bait traps with pieces of beef, bacon, fish, nutmeats, or carrots. Tie the bait to the trigger so the rat won't remove the bait without springing the trap. Check the traps daily to dispose of captured rats. Wear gloves when handling dead rats, or use tongs to pick them up to avoid bites from rat parasites such as fleas and mites. Poisoned baits may also be used. If you are unable to eliminate the rats, contact a professional pest control operator. Keep rats out by rat-proofing the building. Rat-proofing may involve much expense and work because it involves sealing all openings larger than ½ inch leading into the building from the outside. For details, contact your Cooperative Extension Office. For a list of extension offices, see page 1029.

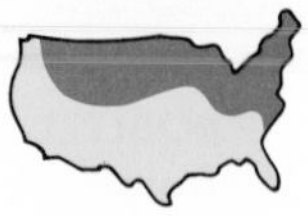

PROBLEM: Skunks are observed living beneath the building, or their tracks and strong scent are present around the home.

ANALYSIS: Skunks
Skunks become household pests when they take up residence under a house. They are most likely to make a den under a house when natural burrows or dens are not readily available. The strong scent they spray when threatened may cause nausea and even temporary blindness. Skunks can eject this potent fluid as far as 10 feet. Skunks carry a variety of diseases, including rabies. They may transmit rabies to humans and pets. Rabid skunks often show abnormal behavior such as listlessness, unprovoked aggressiveness, or a tendency to wander around during the day. Such animals will bite if handled.

SOLUTION: Contact your local Department of Fish and Game office for skunk control regulations. Eliminate skunks by placing moth balls or open pans of household ammonia under the building, or place several floodlights under the building to drive them out. Live-catch box-type traps may also be used. For more information about traps, see page 897. When handling skunks, wear old clothing and goggles. After the animals have been eliminated, screen off or seal openings into the building. Skunk bites should be treated immediately by a physician or veterinarian. Skunk scent may be neutralized with *neutroleum alpha*, a compound that may be obtained through a hospital supply outlet. For information about controlling skunks in the garden, see page 901.

PET AND BODY PESTS

Fleas.

Flea larvae (6 times life size).

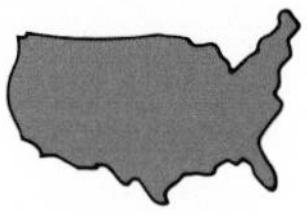

PROBLEM: Fleas infest pets, pet quarters, rooms, carpets, upholstered furniture, or the garden.

ANALYSIS: Fleas

These pests of humans, dogs, cats, and many other warm-blooded animals are found throughout the world. In addition to causing annoying bites, they can transmit several serious diseases such as bubonic plague, murine typhus, and tapeworms. The cat flea (*Ctenocephalides felis*), the dog flea (*C. canis*), and the human flea (*Pulex irritans*) are the most common species found around the home. These fleas have a wide host range, attacking humans, dogs and cats, and a number of other animals. The female fleas lay eggs shortly after feeding upon animal blood. The eggs are usually laid on the host's body, or the host's bedding. The eggs often fall off of the host's body into floor crevices, dog and cat boxes, carpets, and other areas where the infested animals spend time. Within 10 days, the eggs hatch into tiny, wormlike larvae that feed on dried blood, lint, excrement, and other organic debris. Pupation occurs after one week to several months. The adult fleas may emerge after only a week if conditions are favorable, or emergence may be delayed up to a year. The adults often remain in their pupal cocoons until a host is present. A flea's life cycle may vary from 2 weeks up to 2 years. Because fleas have the ability to survive for many months without a blood meal, they can remain in vacated residences for long periods of time, ready to bite returning pets and humans. Fleas are mainly spread by infested animals. Uninfested animals can easily pick up fleas when visiting flea-ridden premises. Fleas may also be spread by infested articles of clothing or furniture.

SOLUTION: Treat infested pets. Dust them with ORTHO Sevin Garden Dust, or spray them with ORTHO Flea-B-Gon Flea Killer. Spray infested animal quarters with ORTHO Flea-B-Gon Flea & Tick Killer, or dust with ORTHO Ortho-Klor Indoor & Outdoor Insect Killer. Read and follow label directions carefully. Flea-repellent collars may help to control fleas on animals. Destroy infested pet bedding, or wash it thoroughly in hot, soapy water. Vacuum carpeting, chairs, sofas, and other areas or objects that may contain eggs and larvae-ridden lint or debris, and then dispose of the vacuum bag. Kill remaining fleas with ORTHO Flea-B-Gon Flea & Tick Killer, ORTHO Hi-Power Indoor Insect Fogger used according to label directions. Kill fleas in the yard by spraying with ORTHO Malathion 50 Insect Spray or ORTHO Diazinon Insect Spray, used according to label directions. To prevent reinfestations, do not allow infested animals to enter the house and yard, and keep pets away from infested areas.

Chigger-infested field.

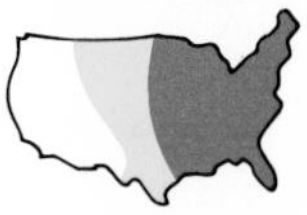

PROBLEM: Welts and hard, raised bumps (papules) appear on the skin, particularly on parts of the body where clothing is binding or where body parts come in contact, such as the belt line, the armpits, the backs of the knees, and under cuffs and collars. Itching is severe and may last as long as 2 weeks. Welts and itching often develop within several hours to a day after the affected person has been in a scrubby, thicket-covered, or otherwise heavily vegetated area.

ANALYSIS: Chiggers

(*Trombicula* species)

These parasites, also known as *red bugs*, are the larval forms of several closely related microscopic mites. Only the larvae are harmful. They hatch from eggs laid in the soil of uncultivated, scrubby woodland or marshy areas, and attach themselves to people and other hosts as they pass by. Chiggers insert their mouthparts into the skin and feed on blood for several days until they become engorged and drop off. Chiggers are sometimes a problem in lawns around new home developments.

SOLUTION: To remove chiggers from your skin, bathe thoroughly in hot, soapy water. Contact your druggist for compounds to relieve the itching. When walking through chigger-infested areas, wear protective clothing, and tightly button or tape sleeves, pant cuffs, and collars. Apply repellents such as *diethyl toluamide* or *ethyl hexanediol* to the skin and clothing, especially around the ankles, underarms, waist, sleeves, and cuffs. Treat infested areas around your home with ORTHO Diazinon Soil & Turf Insect Control or ORTHO Diazinon Insect Spray according to label directions.

PET AND BODY PESTS

Pajaroello tick (twice life size).

Pacific coast tick (4 times life size).

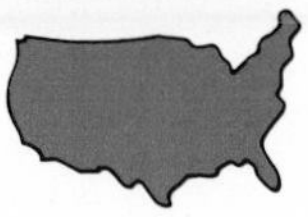

PROBLEM: Oval, leathery, reddish brown to dark brown ticks are attached to a person or pet. These pests, which range in size from 1/16 to 1/8 inch before feeding, are usually found on the pet's ears and neck, and between the toes. Engorged ticks are round, 1/2 inch in diameter, and blue to olive-gray.

ANALYSIS: Ticks

These blood-sucking pests, which are related to spiders, attack humans, dogs, cats, and other animals. Most ticks are found in grassy or brushy areas. In addition, the *brown dog tick* may drop off infested dogs in households, and establish itself in the home. Ticks attach themselves to passing people and pets, and sink their "heads" and mouthparts into the flesh. If left undisturbed, they may continue to suck blood for 5 to 50 days before dropping off. Tick-infested dogs become restless and often lose their vitality because of the irritating bites and loss of blood. Ticks can live for up to 18 months without food or water.

SOLUTION: When ticks are sharply pulled or brushed off the skin, their mouthparts usually break off, remaining embedded in the flesh. This may cause small ulcers or infections to develop in the wounded areas. There are no foolproof methods to make a tick withdraw its mouthparts, but the following techniques may be tried.

1. Touch the tick with the lit end of a cigarette, a hot needle, or a just extinguished match. The heat may cause it to remove its mouthparts.

2. Suffocate the tick by covering it with petroleum jelly, fingernail polish, or butter. After several minutes to half an hour, the tick will withdraw its mouthparts.

3. Slowly and steadily pull the tick from the skin.

If the wound becomes infected, or illness ensues, contact a doctor or veterinarian. Dust infested pets lightly with ORTHO Sevin Garden Dust according to label directions. If the animal is severely infested, contact a veterinarian. Spray grassy or brushy areas around the home with ORTHO Ant, Roach & Spider Killer or ORTHO Home Pest Insect Control according to label directions. Kill ticks in the home by fogging with ORTHO Hi-Power Indoor Insect Fogger or dusting with ORTHO Ortho-Klor Indoor & Outdoor Insect Killer. Destroy infested animal bedding, and spray animal quarters and other infested indoor areas with ORTHO Ant, Roach & Spider Killer according to label directions.

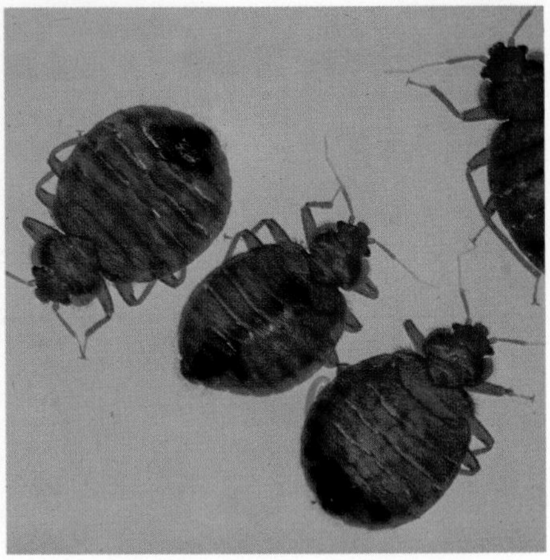

Bedbugs (6 times life size).

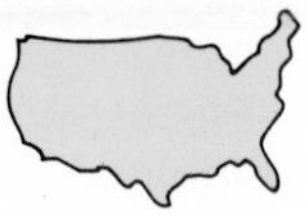

PROBLEM: Painful swellings develop on the body. Dark brown to black spotted stains appear on pillows, sheets, and other bedding. When the lights are turned on at night, reddish brown, oval-shaped bugs about 1/4 inch long may be seen crawling on the skin and bedding.

ANALYSIS: Bedbugs

(*Cimex lectularius*)

These distasteful bugs have become an infrequent problem in the United States. However, they still infest homes where living conditions are unsanitary, and may be transported to well-maintained residences on infested clothing and furniture. Bedbugs hide during the day behind baseboards, in mattresses and upholstered furniture, in cracks and crevices in the floor, bedframes, and similar locations. These pests are nocturnal, and become very active at night. They crawl onto a sleeping person, pierce their skin, and suck their blood for several minutes. Bedbugs usually deposit telltale masses of dark excrement on bedding after they feed. They are very active, and may crawl from room to room or even from house to house during the night.

SOLUTION: Spray baseboards, wall crevices, and floor cracks with a 2 percent solution of *malathion* or *ronnel*. Spray bed frames and springs with a 1 percent solution of *malathion* or *ronnel*. Mist mattresses with a 1 percent solution of *malathion*, but do not soak them. Be sure to spray mattress seams and tufts. Let mattresses dry completely before reusing. Do not spray infant cribs and bedding. If bedbugs reinfest the home, treat again after an interval of 2 weeks. Launder all bedding thoroughly. Keep the house clean.

Subterranean termites (twice life size).

Termite-damaged book.

Dampwood termites ($\frac{3}{4}$ life size).

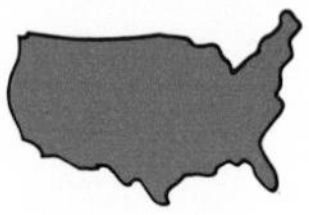

PROBLEM: On warm, sunny spring or fall days, brown to brownish black winged insects, about $\frac{3}{8}$ inch long, swarm in and around the building. These insects resemble flying ants, but have thick rather than constricted waists. Their discarded wings may be found around the building. Earthen tubes extend from the soil up along the building foundation and any other termite-proof surface to the infested wooden structures. These tubes are commonly found in basements and crawlspaces under the building. When broken off, they are rebuilt within several days. Dark or blistered areas may develop in the flooring.

ANALYSIS: Subterranean termites
These wood-feeding insects cause more structural damage to buildings than any other insect. Subterranean termites live in colonies as deep as 5 feet in the ground, and move up to infest wooden structures through tubes of soil they build over masonry or metal to bridge the gap from soil to wood. Except for the dark, winged swarmers, these termites are white, wingless, and very sensitive to moisture loss. They always remain within the nest, soil tubes, or infested wood, protected from desiccation and insect predators. Termites maintain a complicated caste system within their colony that includes sterile workers and soldiers, winged reproducers, and an egg-laying queen. Colonies are formed when a pair of winged reproducers leaves the parent colony and excavates a nest in a piece of wood that is on top of or buried in the ground. As the new colony develops, galleries are formed deep in the soil. Termite colonies develop slowly; 3 or 4 years usually pass before the reproductive swarmers develop, and structural damage may not be noticed for several more years. However, when buildings are erected over established termite colonies, serious damage may occur within a year. Termites hollow out the inside of a wooden structure, leaving only an outer shell. Damage is most severe when they infest main supporting wooden beams and girders. One species of subterranean termite, the *Formosan termite* (*Coptotermes formosanus*), is not native to the United States, but is present in areas of the Southeast and Southwest. This termite is more vigorous and aggressive than native North American species, and is more difficult to control.

SOLUTION: Termite infestations can be treated most effectively only after a thorough and accurate diagnosis of the damage is made. Accurate diagnosis is usually very difficult and requires the aid of a professional termite or pest control operator. Once the termite colony has been located, and the damage has been revealed, a physical or chemical barrier is placed between the soil and the building to prevent the termites from reaching the building. An insecticide containing *chlordane*, or *chlorpyrifos* (DURSBAN®) is applied to the soil around and underneath the building. If infestations are small and localized, you may control them by applying ORTHO Ortho-Klor Soil Insect & Termite Killer to the soil according to label directions. Discourage additional infestations by keeping the area under and around the house free of wood debris above and below the ground. If the soil around the foundation remains moist due to faulty plumbing or improper grade, repair the plumbing and alter the grade; termites prefer moist soil. For details on termite-resistant construction methods, contact a reliable building contractor or your local Cooperative Extension Office (see page 1029).

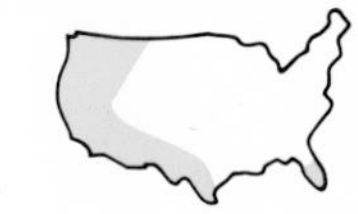

PROBLEM: Yellowish brown, winged insects 1 inch long swarm in or around buildings at dusk, and tend to fly toward lights. They usually appear in the late summer or early fall, but may be seen in small numbers throughout the year. These insects resemble large flying ants, but have thick rather than constricted waists. Their wings, which are shed after the reproductive stage, may be found around the building. Tiny, round or elongated, brown fecal pellets may be piled below cracks in infested wood.

ANALYSIS: Dampwood termites
These wood-feeding insects cause structural damage to buildings with moist or wet, poorly ventilated timbers—typically, beach houses or other buildings situated on wet soil, and buildings with leaky plumbing. Dampwood termites cannot tolerate desiccation, and can establish themselves only in moist wood. Except for the dark, winged swarmers, termites are white and wingless. Infestations start when a pair of winged reproductive termites leaves the main colony and burrows into a moist wood structure. As the colony grows, the wood is hollowed out. Infestations develop slowly, and are usually small. Damage is most severe when many colonies are present.

SOLUTION: If many swarmers emerge from the floorboards, or from the perimeter of the building, contact a professional pest control operator. If the soil around the foundation and the foundation itself remain moist due to faulty plumbing or improper grade, repair the plumbing or alter the grade. Prevent reinfestations by following the same procedures used to prevent subterranean termite infestations.

STRUCTURAL PESTS

Powderpost beetle and larva (3 times life size).

Emergence holes.

Drywood termites (twice life size).

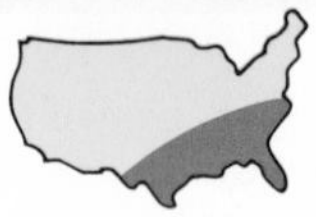

PROBLEM: Wood flooring, structural timbers, cabinets, furniture, and other items are riddled with round holes that range in size from 1/16 to 3/8 inch. Wood powder or tiny pellets may be piled around the holes or on the floor below. When the infested item is tapped, additional pellets or wood powder are expelled from the holes. Tiny red, brown, or black beetles ranging in size from 1/12 to 1/3 inch may be seen crawling around the infested wood, or flying around windows and electric lights in the evening. When the damaged wood is cut open, the inside is found to be riddled with sawdust-filled tunnels; or it may be pulverized into a mass of wood powder or pellets.

ANALYSIS: Powderpost beetles
These wood-feeding beetles, including the *powderpost, false powderpost,* and *deathwatch* beetles, damage wood houses and household furnishings throughout the country. Powderpost beetles feed only on dead wood. They are brought into the home in infested timber or furnishings; or they may fly from infested lumber or wood piles in the yard. The female beetles deposit their eggs in unfinished wood. The grubs that hatch from the eggs tunnel through the wood, leaving masses of wood powder or pellets behind them. They pupate just under the surface of the wood, and emerge as adult beetles through the round holes they chew in the wood. Beetle eggs or larvae present in wood before it has been coated with paint, varnish, shellac, or other finishings can chew through the finished surface when they have matured, leaving round emergence holes. However, they do not lay eggs in coated wood surfaces, and reinfestation cannot occur.

SOLUTION: If the infestation is localized, remove and destroy badly infested timbers. Replace them with kiln-dried or insecticide-treated wood. Or treat unfinished wood yourself by painting or spraying it with ORTHO Ortho-Klor Soil Insect & Termite Killer. Wherever possible, apply paint, shellac, varnish, paraffin wax, or other wood coatings to unfinished wood around the home to prevent further infestation. Inspect wood piles periodically for signs of powderpost beetle infestation. Infested wood may also be treated with ORTHO Ortho-Klor Soil Insect & Termite Killer. If the infestation is widespread, contact a professional pest control operator to fumigate the building. Individual pieces of furniture may also be fumigated to kill beetle eggs and larvae. Many pest control operators maintain fumigation chambers for movable items. Eggs and larvae in small wooden items may be killed by placing them in the freezer for 4 days.

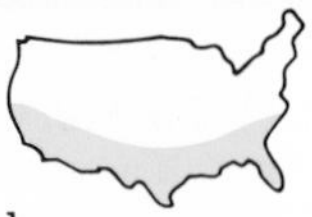

PROBLEM: On warm, sunny days, 1/2-inch winged insects with reddish brown heads may be seen flying in and around a building. These insects resemble flying ants, but have thick rather than constricted waists. Their discarded wings may be found around the building. Tiny elongated brown fecal pellets are piled below cracks or chinks in infested rafters, window frames and sills, door and window jambs, and other wooden structures.

ANALYSIS: Drywood termites
These wood-feeding insects cause structural damage to buildings in the warmer areas of the country. Drywood termites live in colonies within wooden structures, including furniture. Except for the dark, winged swarmers, drywood termites are white and wingless. They can withstand desiccation for long periods of time. Infestations start when a pair of winged reproductive termites leaves the main colony and burrows into a wood structure. As the colony grows, the wood is slowly hollowed out. Piles of termite pellets are pushed out through cracks in the weakened wood. Drywood termite infestations develop slowly and are usually small. These pests may be spread long distances in infested pieces of wood.

SOLUTION: Drywood termites are most effectively controlled by fumigation, which must be done by a professional pest control operator. Several preventive measures should be followed when building new structures to prevent future infestation. For details on termite-resistant construction methods, contact your local County Extension Office (see page 1029) or a reliable building contractor.

Old house borer damage.

Old house borer (twice life size).

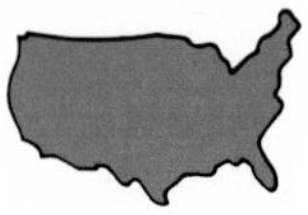

PROBLEM: Oval holes $\frac{1}{4}$ to $\frac{1}{3}$ inch wide appear in walls and flooring. Or holes appear in wallpaper, plaster, linoleum, and other types of wood coverings. Sawdustlike borings may be piled around the holes. In some cases, rasping or ticking sounds may be heard before the holes appear, and the wood may be blistered or rippled. Grayish brown to black beetles 1 inch long with antennae may be seen around the house.

ANALYSIS: Roundheaded borers
The larvae of these beetles, including the *new house borer* (*Arhopalus productus*) and the *old house borer* (*Hylotrupes bajulus*), cause damage to softwood (fir, pine) structural timbers. New house borers mainly infest fir subflooring. They do not cause structural damage; the holes they make in wood or covered wood surfaces are of cosmetic concern only. The adults lay their eggs in the bark of weak and dying forest trees. The yellow grubs tunnel into wood that is later incorporated into a building before the adult beetles emerge. New house borers continue to emerge through holes in wood and wood coverings for up to a year after construction. They cannot reinfest the building. Old house borer beetles do not emerge from timbers until 3 to 5 years after the building has been constructed. They continue to reinfest the damaged wood, and may cause serious structural damage. Sometimes the grubs make rasping or clicking noises while they feed. If they are tunneling close to the surface, wood blistering or rippling may result.

SOLUTION: New house borers are the problem if damage occurs within a year after construction. To repair new house borer damage, seal or fill emergence holes. Localized areas may be painted with ORTHO Ortho-Klor Soil Insect & Termite Killer following label directions. Because damage is only cosmetic and will stop within a year, this expensive procedure is seldom justified. Old house borers are the problem if damage occurs at least 3 years after construction. Buildings infested with old house borers must be fumigated. Contact a professional pest control operator to fumigate the building. To prevent future infestations of old house borers when building new structures, purchase pressure-treated wood.

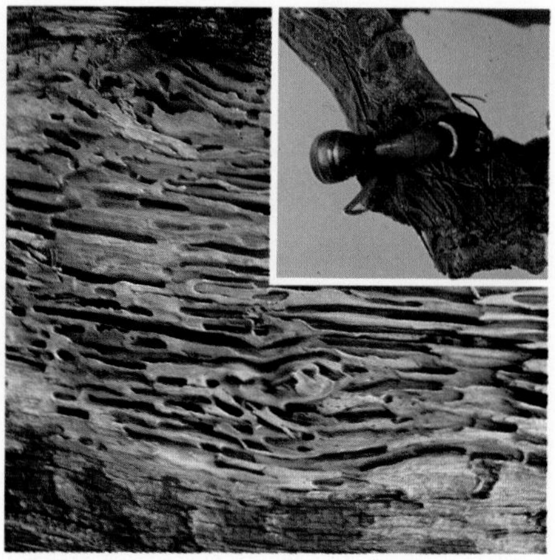
Carpenter ants (twice life size).

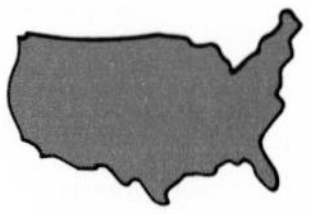

PROBLEM: Black or reddish black winged or wingless ants up to $\frac{1}{2}$ inch long are seen around the home. Piles of sawdust may be found in basements or attics, under porches, or near supporting girders or joists. Slitlike holes are often present in woodwork. On warm spring days, swarms of winged ants may cluster around windows. Unlike termites, these pests have constricted waists.

ANALYSIS: Carpenter ants
(*Camponotus* species)
Many closely related species of these wood-damaging ants are found throughout the country. Carpenter ants bore into moist, decaying wood, forming extensive galleries in which they make nests. They do not eat their sawdustlike wood borings, but feed on other insects, plant sap, pollen, and seeds. When ant colonies grow too large, part of the colony will migrate, often invading nearby homes through windows and other similar entry points. They will either colonize undisturbed hollow spaces such as walls or bore into structural timbers, ceilings, and floor areas. They prefer damp and rotted wood. In addition to weakening wood, carpenter ants may infest pantries, and inflict painful bites when disturbed.

SOLUTION: Spray baseboards, window sills, door frames, and other surfaces where ants crawl with ORTHO Ortho-Klor Soil Insect & Termite Killer. Spray into nests if possible. Remove nearby logs, stumps, and woodpiles. Seal openings in the foundation, windows, and other access areas into the home. Dust along the foundation with ORTHO Ortho-Klor Indoor & Outdoor Insect Killer.

STRUCTURAL PESTS

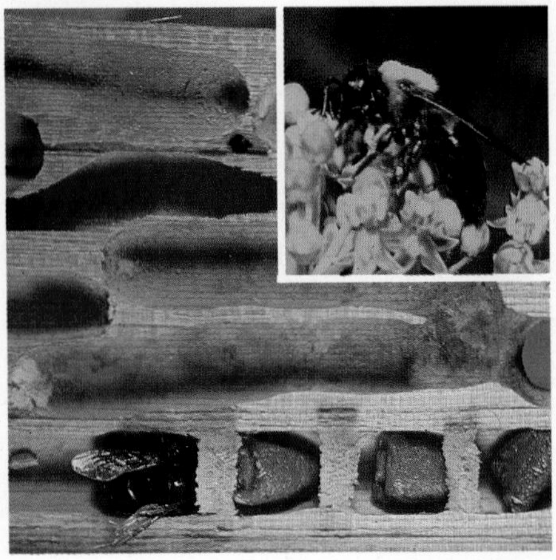

Galleries. *Insert:* Adult carpenter bee (life size).

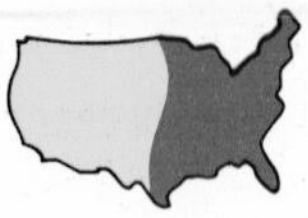

PROBLEM: Metallic blue or black buzzing bees fly around the home and yard. They may be seen entering and leaving holes about 1 inch wide in decks, posts, beams, rafters, and other wooden structures. When damaged wood is sliced open, partitioned galleries may be seen. The partitions may contain immature bees.

ANALYSIS: Carpenter bees
(*Xylocopa* species)
These insects do not usually cause serious damage; however, continued burrowing and gallery formation year after year will eventually weaken wooden structures. These insects burrow into wood to make their nests. The female bees partition the galleries into small cells in which the carpenter bee larvae mature. When bee nests are approached, the males hover around the head of the intruder. Although they are frightening because of their loud buzzing and large size, the male bees do not sting, and the females sting only when handled.

SOLUTION: Paint wood surfaces once a year to discourage bee tunneling. Flood galleries in exposed wood with ORTHO Ortho-Klor Soil Insect & Termite Killer. Close the holes with putty, caulking compound, dowel pins, or plastic wood to prevent bees from returning to the nest.

Woodwasp (life size).

PROBLEM: Round holes about ¼ inch in diameter appear in wood floors, walls, doors, and other surfaces. Or holes appear in wallpaper, linoleum, carpeting, and other types of covering over wood. Metallic blue, black, or multicolored wasplike insects may be seen flying around the home. These buzzing insects are 1 to 2 inches long, and may have hornlike "tails."

ANALYSIS: Woodwasps
These insects, also known as *horntails*, do not cause structural damage; the holes they make in wood or covered wood surfaces are of cosmetic concern only. Woodwasps lay their eggs in weak and dying forest trees. The adult insects emerge from the wood 2 to 5 years later, often long after the tree has been used for construction. However, most woodwasp holes occur within the first 2 years after the cut wood has been used. These insects lay their eggs only in forest trees; they do not reinfest buildings.

SOLUTION: Seal or fill emergence holes. There is nothing you can do to prevent the woodwasps from emerging. For future construction, purchase lumber that has been kiln-dried or vacuum fumigated. These processes kill woodwasp larvae embedded in the wood.

Dry rot.

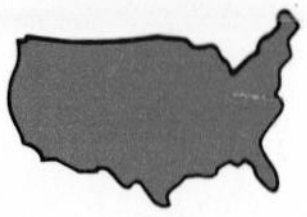

PROBLEM: Foundation timbers, paneling, flooring, and other wooden structures are damp and soft, or dry, cracked, brown, and crumbling. Often the wood is broken into small, cubical pieces. Thin mats of white fungal strands may be seen on the rotted wood. Thick white, brown, or black fungal cords up to 2 inches wide may extend across the rotted area. These cords often extend over impenetrable surfaces such as brick and concrete to reach wood surfaces beyond.

ANALYSIS: Dry rot
Dry rot is caused by fungi that live in the soil, and grow into wood that is in direct contact with damp soil. The white fungal strands penetrate and decay the wood fibers, causing a soft rot. In some cases, the fungus draws water from the soil up through the thick fungal cords that extend across the rotted area. The water is used to moisten dry wood, providing the damp condition in which the fungus thrives. After the fungus dies, badly rotted wood cracks and crumbles into chunks when handled.

SOLUTION: Remove any water-conducting fungal cords from the wood. Eliminate moist soil conditions around wood structures as much as possible by improving ventilation, changing soil grade and drainage, or fixing leaky plumbing. As soon as the soil and wood dry out, the fungus will die. Replace badly rotted wood with wood that has been pressure-treated with preservatives. Remove all wood scraps around the building foundation. When building new structures, use pressure-treated wood in all areas where wood and soil make contact.

Infested firewood.

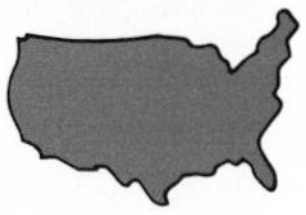

PROBLEM: Firewood is riddled with holes. Small piles of sawdust accumulate around the holes or on the ground around the firewood. If the wood has been stored indoors, insects may be crawling around the firewood pile or flying around lights or windows.

ANALYSIS: Firewood insects
Many insects develop in and emerge from cut firewood. If infested wood is stored either indoors or outdoors so that it rests against the house, there is a chance that insects will invade the wooden structure of the house. Insects that are capable of moving from firewood into the structure include carpenter ants (see page 799), termites (see pages 797 and 798), and powderpost beetles (see page 798). Some insects, such as bark beetles (see page 435), most flatheaded and roundheaded borers (see page 799), and woodwasps (see page 800) emerge from firewood but attack only living or recently killed trees; these insects will not damage structural wood or household articles.

SOLUTION: Spray infested firewood outdoors with ORTHO Ortho-Klor Soil Insect & Termite Killer, ORTHO Diazinon Insect Spray, or ORTHO Lawn Insect Spray. Sprayed firewood may be burned 2 weeks following treatment. Store all firewood outdoors unless you plan to burn it within a couple of days. Do not lean an outdoor wood pile against the home; stack it so that there is at least an inch between the wood and the structure. If practical, choose a location for the wood pile at least 10 feet away from the home.

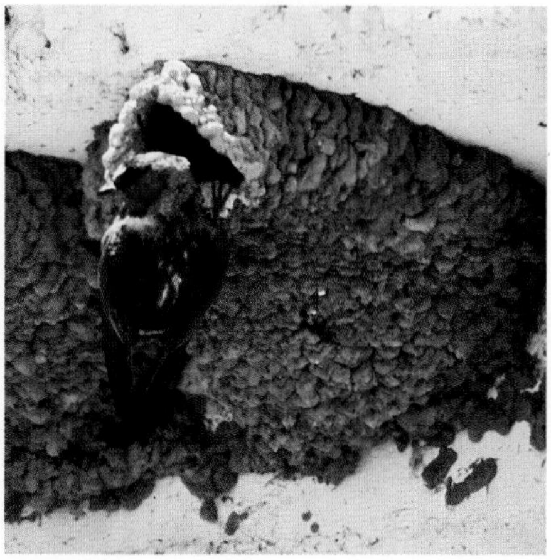

Cliff swallow.

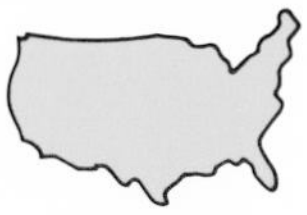

PROBLEM: Mud nests are found beneath eaves of the building. The nests are shaped like gourds, about 6 inches in diameter, with a necklike round entrance. Nests are usually grouped together. Bird droppings and mud are scattered beneath the nests. In spring, birds are seen flying in and out of the nests.

ANALYSIS: Cliff swallows
(Petrochelidon pyrrhonota)
These birds, also known as *mud swallows,* spend their winters in South America and annually migrate northward to the United States. From March through June they build their mud nests, usually against a vertical wall just beneath an overhang such as an eave. The same nesting sites are used year after year, and many of the birds will return to the same area they nested in the year before. The birds abandon the nests by the end of June.

SOLUTION: Wash down the nests with a strong stream of water. This must be done consistently over an extended period or the birds will rebuild their nests. Or, after washing the nests down, string a wire across the area where the birds are building their nests (usually that means stringing the wire along the junction of the wall and the roof overhang). Drape a 12 inch curtain of aluminum foil or polyethylene sheeting over the wire. This prevents cliff swallows from attaching their nests to the wall because the new surface is too smooth. If the problem continues, contact a licensed pest control operator.

Woodpecker.

PROBLEM: Loud tapping sounds are heard around the building. Holes are found in roof shakes, wood sidings, and other wooden parts of the building. Birds may be seen rapidly pecking on wood, glass, or metal.

ANALYSIS: Woodpeckers
Woodpeckers often rapidly peck at wood and glass, creating annoying tapping noises as well as causing cosmetic and sometimes structural damage to buildings and other structures. Woodpeckers drill into wood to make nesting sites or to make holes where they store acorns and other nuts. They may peck at wood in their search for insects. The males also drill on wood, glass, and other surfaces in a territorial activity called "drumming," which proclaims their territory to other male birds. Drumming is especially noticeable in the spring when woodpeckers begin nesting. Woodpeckers are most common in wooded areas. Usually only a few birds inhabit an area.

SOLUTION: Prevent damage by fastening sheet metal or ¼ to ½ inch hardware cloth over areas where birds are pecking. Woodpeckers are protected by federal and state laws. Contact your Department of Fish and Game to determine local regulations regarding woodpecker control.

BITING AND STINGING PESTS

Yellowjackets (twice life size).

Yellowjacket (twice life size).

Swarm (1/10 life size). *Insert:* Honey bee.

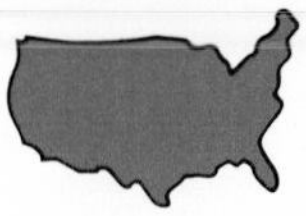

PROBLEM: Yellowjackets are present around the home. They hover around patios, picnic areas, garbage cans, and other areas where food or garbage is exposed. Yellowjackets may be seen flying into underground nests. Yellowjackets inflict painful stings when threatened or harmed, or when their nests are approached.

ANALYSIS: Yellowjackets (*Vespa* and *Vespula* species)
Unlike most other species of wasps, yellowjackets live in large colonies, often numbering in the thousands. Some species of yellowjackets feed on insects and spiders, while others scavenge scraps of meat from recreational areas or dumpsites. These pests may also feed on nectar, sap, and other sugary fluids, and may be seen hovering around soft drinks and cut fruit. Yellowjackets can inflict painful stings, and are capable of repeated stings. The venom injected along with the sting causes reddening, swelling, and itching of the affected area. Some people who are very sensitive to the stings experience extreme swelling, dizziness, difficulty in breathing, and even death. Yellowjackets are very protective of their nests, and large numbers may emerge to sting intruders. Some species of yellowjackets build their nests underground; the only evidence of the nest is a raised mound of dirt surrounding a depression several inches deep. Other species build football-shaped nests in trees or shrubs, or under eaves. Almost all yellowjackets die in the late fall, and new nests are started the following spring in a different location.

SOLUTION: Keep food and garbage covered, and empty garbage frequently. To kill yellowjackets before picnicking, spray with ORTHO Outdoor Insect Fogger according to label directions. To remove yellowjackets from the vicinity, you must eliminate the nests. After locating the nests, spray them at dusk or during the night with ORTHO Hornet & Wasp Killer. Stay 8 feet away from the nest, and spray directly into the entrance hole. If you need to illuminate the area, use a flashlight covered with red cellophane. Use it for only short periods of time. Stop spraying when the yellowjackets begin to emerge; leave the nest area quickly by walking, not running away. Repeat the spraying every evening until the insects fail to emerge, then quickly cover the hole with moistened soil. Contact a professional pest control operator to remove yellowjacket nests in difficult locations. If you are stung, apply a cold compress or ice pack to the affected area. If a severe reaction develops, call your doctor.

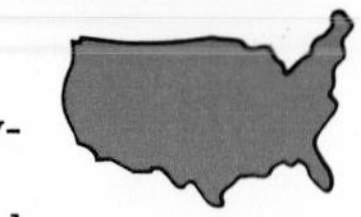

PROBLEM: Bees are hovering around flowering plants in the garden, and may inflict stings when threatened or harmed. Large numbers of bees may cluster on shrubs or trees. Hives may be located in attics, chimneys, and wall voids.

ANALYSIS: Honey bees
(*Apis mellifera*)
These familiar and often feared insects provide honey and wax, and are very important as pollinators. On warm, sunny days, bees forage for nectar among flowering garden plants, then return to their hives in the evening. When an established hive gets too crowded, thousands of bees leave in a swarm. Swarms fly for a mile or so before settling in a new location. En route, they often rest in a tight cluster on a tree branch or other object. Some people are allergic to bee stings, and experience extreme swelling, dizziness, difficulty in breathing, and possibly death. A bee does not sting more than once because the stinger and venom sac rip out of its body when it flies away. The injured bee soon dies.

SOLUTION: When stung, scrape the stinger off the skin with a knife or fingernail. Avoid squeezing it; this forces more venom into the wound. Apply cold compresses or ice packs to the swollen area. If a severe reaction develops, call a doctor immediately. Avoid using plants that are attractive to bees, especially around pools, patios, and other recreational areas. For a list of plants that are attractive to bees, see page 1007. Do not try to remove hives or swarms yourself. Contact a professional beekeeper or pest control operator if bees are nesting in your home or garden.

Paper wasps (life size).

PROBLEM: Single-layered paper nests are suspended from eaves, ceilings, or branches. These nests are composed of exposed, open cells, and have a honeycomb appearance. They are often umbrella-shaped. Black or brown wasps with yellow or red stripes may be seen hovering around or crawling on the nests.

ANALYSIS: Paper wasps
(*Polistes* species)
Paper wasps, also known as *umbrella wasps*, usually live in small colonies consisting of 20 to 30 wasps. They build paper nests in which they raise their young. Paper wasps feed on insects, nectar, and pollen. They are not as aggressive and protective of their nests as are yellowjackets. (For more information about yellowjackets, see page 802.) However, they will sting if threatened, causing swelling, itching, and more generalized symptoms in sensitive individuals.

SOLUTION: To remove paper wasps from the vicinity, you must eliminate their nests. Spray the nests at dusk or during the night with ORTHO Hornet & Wasp Killer or ORTHO Outdoor Insect Fogger. Spray the nest from a distance of 8 feet. Stop spraying when wasps begin to emerge; leave the nest area quickly by walking, not running away. Repeat the spraying every evening until the insects fail to emerge. Remove the nest and dispose of it. If you are stung, apply a cold compress or ice pack to the swollen area. If a severe reaction develops, call your doctor.

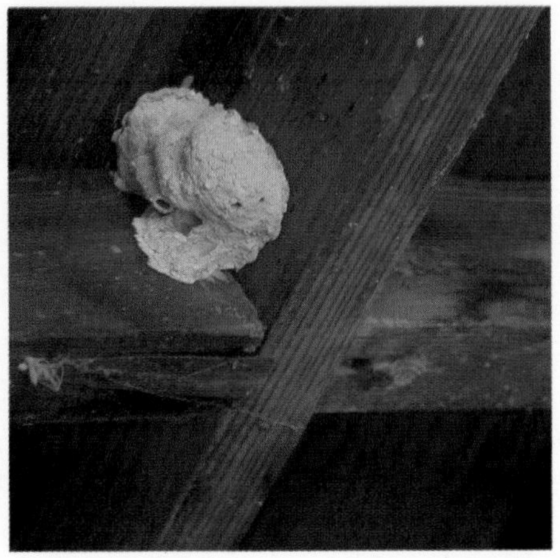

Mud dauber nest.

PROBLEM: Wasps are flying around the garden. Some of these insects are black with yellow, red, or white markings. Others are black, brown, blue, red, or yellow. Many wasps have very thin elongated waists. Their mud nests may be found under eaves and on plants or rocks.

ANALYSIS: Solitary wasps
Unlike the social yellowjackets, many species of wasps, including the potter and mason wasps, mud daubers, and spider wasps, live alone. Most of them build nests of mud and sand in which they raise their young. Many of these wasps feed on insects; a few feed on pollen and nectar. These wasps are not as aggressive and protective of their nests as are yellowjackets, and will not sting as readily. (For more information about yellowjackets, see page 802.) If highly provoked, however, they can sting, causing swelling, itching, and more generalized symptoms in sensitive individuals.

SOLUTION: Eliminate mud nests by hosing or knocking them down. Kill wasps by spraying them with ORTHO Hornet & Wasp Killer or ORTHO Outdoor Insect Fogger according to label directions. Even though many of the solitary wasps are docile, they may be confused with yellowjackets; it is best to avoid threatening or provoking them. If you are stung, apply a cold compress or ice pack to the swollen area. If a severe reaction develops, call your doctor.

Puss caterpillar (twice life size).

PROBLEM: An irritating rash forms where a hairy or spiny caterpillar touches the skin. Reactions vary depending on the caterpillar and the individual, and include mild itching, rash, swelling, local severe pain, local lesions, and fever.

ANALYSIS: Stinging caterpillars
There are about 25 species of stinging caterpillars. These insects have hollow hairs that contain a mild poison. The hairs release the irritating substance when people handle the caterpillars or accidently brush against them. Most of these caterpillars are capable of causing only a mild itching or skin rash. The caterpillar that causes one of the most severe reactions is the *puss caterpillar, Megalopyge opercularis*. It can cause intense itching, swelling, local numbness, nausea, and fever (especially in children). This caterpillar is widely distributed in the southeastern and south central states and feeds on a wide variety of deciduous trees and shrubs. During some years it increases to unusually large numbers. The *saddleback caterpillar* (*Sibine stimulea*), the *io moth caterpillar* (*Automeris io*), and the *flannel moth caterpillar* (*Norape ovina*) are other caterpillars known for their stinging hairs.

SOLUTION: Avoid handling the caterpillars. Spray shrubs and trees on which these caterpillars are found with an insecticide containing *carbaryl* (SEVIN®). Make sure your plant is listed on the product label. Contact a physician if a severe reaction begins to develop.

BITING AND STINGING PESTS

Horsefly (3 times life size).

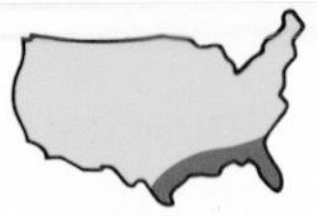

PROBLEM: Black, brown, or black and white biting flies about $\frac{1}{2}$ to 1 inch long are present around the home. They are especially bothersome in areas where horses and domestic animals are common.

ANALYSIS: Biting flies
These flies, including several species of *horseflies* and *deerflies*, attack humans and domestic animals in rural and suburban areas. The female flies deposit their eggs in still pools of water, in moist soil, or on vegetation. The larvae feed on other insects or decaying vegetation, and pupate in damp plant debris. The adult flies inflict painful bites that often continue to bleed after the fly has left. Some people bitten by horseflies may suffer from fever and general illness.

SOLUTION: Keep doors and windows tightly screened. Spray outdoor living areas with ORTHO Outdoor Insect Fogger or ORTHO Home & Garden Insect Killer. Kill biting flies indoors by spraying with ORTHO Household Insect Killer, ORTHO Home & Garden Insect Killer, or ORTHO Hi-Power Indoor Insect Fogger. Apply insect repellents to the skin. Such repellents may be purchased at drugstores. Remove fly breeding areas by cleaning up stagnant pools of water and wet, decaying vegetation around the yard.

Blackflies (3 times life size).

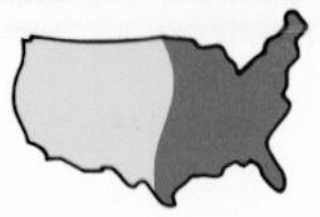

PROBLEM: During the late spring and summer, many black or gray humpbacked flies $\frac{1}{25}$ to $\frac{1}{5}$ inch long are present around the home. They inflict painful bites.

ANALYSIS: Black flies
These annoying flies, also known as *buffalo gnats* or *turkey gnats*, attack humans and domestic animals in rural and suburban areas throughout the United States. The female flies deposit their eggs in swiftly running water, including streams and irrigation ditches. The larvae develop in the water, and emerge as adult flies during the spring and summer. Black flies may be blown many miles from their breeding areas. They bite any exposed part of the body and may also bite under clothing, especially where clothes are binding, such as around belts and collars. These irritating bites often swell and itch for several days. The victim may suffer headaches, fever, and nausea.

SOLUTION: Keep windows and doors tightly screened. Spray outdoor living areas with ORTHO Outdoor Insect Fogger or ORTHO Home & Garden Insect Killer. Kill black flies indoors by spraying with ORTHO Household Insect Killer or ORTHO Home & Garden Insect Killer. Apply insect repellents to the skin. Repellents may be purchased at drugstores.

Biting midge (15 times life size).

PROBLEM: During the spring and summer, tiny black biting midges $\frac{1}{25}$ to $\frac{1}{8}$ inch long infest the yard. They are most common in coastal areas and near lakes, streams, marshlands, and swamps.

ANALYSIS: Biting midges
These annoying insects are also known as *no-see-ums*, *sand flies*, or *black gnats*. They feed on humans, many warm-blooded animals, and birds. Biting midges breed in wet sand or mud, damp, rotting vegetation, very shallow stagnant or brackish water, and similar locations. They rarely infest the home, but are bothersome outdoors, inflicting bites around the feet, legs, ears, and eyes, and under clothes, especially in cuff, collar, and belt areas where clothing binds. The bites are not usually painful, but produce tiny swellings or blisters that continue to itch for several days.

SOLUTION: Spray infested areas of the yard with ORTHO Outdoor Insect Fogger according to label directions. Apply insect repellents to the skin. Such repellents may be purchased at drugstores.

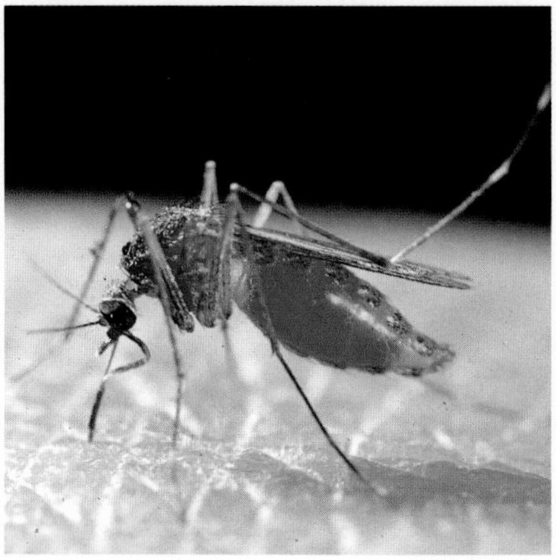

Mosquito (8 times life size).

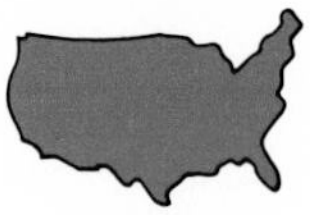

PROBLEM: Biting mosquitoes are present in the home and yard. They are most bothersome at dusk and during the night.

ANALYSIS: Mosquitoes
Many different species of this insect pest occur throughout the world. In addition to their annoying bites, they transmit encephalitis within the United States, and other serious diseases such as yellow fever and malaria in other parts of the world. Adults emerge from hibernation with warm spring weather. The males feed on nectar, honeydew, and plant sap; the females require a blood meal in order to produce their eggs. Larval development takes place exclusively in water. Typically, eggs are laid in shallow accumulations of fresh, stagnant, or salty water. The larvae may mature within 5 days, or may take months to mature.

SOLUTION: Maintain door and window screens in good repair. Kill mosquitoes indoors by fogging with ORTHO Hi-Power Indoor Insect Fogger or spraying with ORTHO Home & Garden Insect Killer. Kill mosquitoes outdoors by spraying with ORTHO Lawn Insect Spray or ORTHO Malathion 50 Insect Spray around the lawn and foundation of the house. Spray resting areas under eaves with ORTHO Home & Garden Insect Killer or ORTHO Outdoor Insect Fogger. Apply insect repellents to the skin. Drain unnecessary accumulations of water. Stock ornamental ponds with mosquitofish (*Gambusia affinis*), which eat mosquito larvae. Goldfish also eat mosquito larvae, but are not as effective as mosquitofish.

Black widow spider (life size).

PROBLEM: Black widow spiders are shiny, black, about the size of a quarter, and have a red hourglass marking on the underside of the abdomen. Outdoors, they live under rocks or clods of dirt, or in wood and rubbish piles. Indoors, they are found in garages, attics, cellars, and other dark secluded places such as under boards or cluttered debris, in old clothing, or in crevices. Black widow webs are coarse and irregular, about 1 foot wide.

ANALYSIS: Black widow spiders
(*Latrodectus* species)
Several species of these poisonous spiders are found throughout the United States. Black widows live in secluded locations and feed on insects trapped in their webs. If the spiders are accidentally touched, or their webs are disturbed, they will bite the intruder. The venom may cause serious illness and, in rare occasions, death. The females produce egg sacs that contain hundreds of eggs. The tiny spiderlings that emerge are also capable of inflicting poisonous bites. They may be carried long distances by the wind.

SOLUTION: Kill spiders by spraying webs and infested areas with ORTHO Ant, Roach & Spider Killer or ORTHO Home Pest Insect Control, or dust areas where spiders may hide with ORTHO ORTHO-KLOR Indoor & Outdoor Insect Killer. Remove loose wood, trash, and clutter from areas where spiders might hide. Wear gloves and protective clothing when cleaning up infested areas. Vacuum infested areas to remove eggs sacs, and destroy the contents of the vacuum cleaner bag. Put ice on spider bites, and call a doctor immediately.

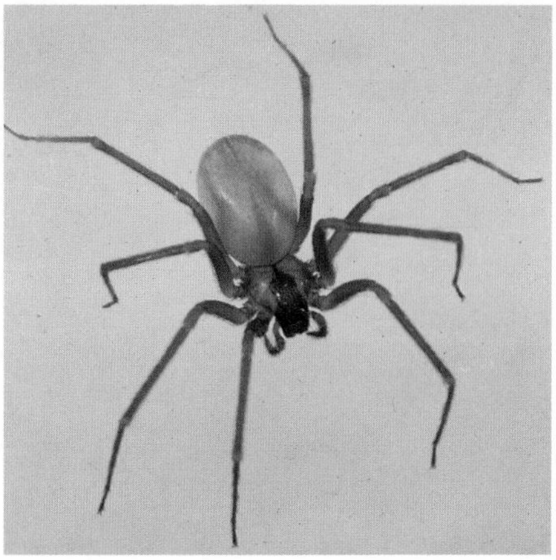

Brown recluse spider (twice life size).

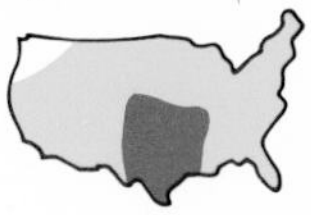

PROBLEM: Brown recluse spiders are light to dark brown, 1/3 to 1/2 inch in length, with a violin-shaped marking behind the head. Outdoors, they are found under rocks. Indoors, they are found in old boxes, among papers and old clothes, behind baseboards, underneath tables and chairs, and in other secluded places. Grayish, irregular, sticky webs and round white egg sacs 3/4 inch wide may be found in the infested areas.

ANALYSIS: Brown recluse spiders
(*Loxosceles reclusa*)
These poisonous spiders are found in the Midwest and Southeast. Other related but less poisonous spiders (*Loxosceles* species) are found throughout most of the United States. Brown recluse spiders live in secluded places and are very shy, moving away quickly when disturbed. If they are touched or trapped in shoes, clothing, or bedding, they may bite. Their venom is rarely fatal, but causes a severe sore that is slow to heal, and sometimes causes illness.

SOLUTION: Kill spiders by spraying webs and infested areas with ORTHO Ant, Roach & Spider Killer or ORTHO Home Pest Insect Control. Or, dust areas where spiders may hide with ORTHO ORTHO-KLOR Indoor & Outdoor Insect Killer. Remove loose wood, trash, or clutter from areas where spiders might hide. Wear gloves and protective clothing when cleaning up infested areas. Spray outdoor living areas, and clean up debris around the home that may harbor spiders. Vacuum infested areas to remove egg sacs, and destroy the contents of the vacuum bag. Put ice on spider bites and call a doctor immediately.

BITING AND STINGING PESTS

Mound. *Insert:* Fire ant (4 times life size).

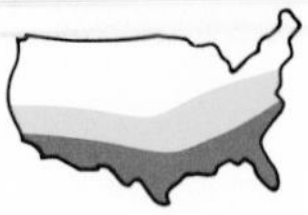

PROBLEM: Small (¼ inch) reddish to black ants crawl to and from large mounds of soil in the lawn and garden. These ants inflict painful stings to people or animals that disturb the mounds.

ANALYSIS: Fire ants
(*Solenopsis* species)
These ants are notorious for their large mounds and painful stings. The mounds, which are their nests, are usually found in lawns and gardens. Occasionally the ants move into or underneath homes during periods of rain or drought. They mainly feed on other insects, but will also feed on young succulent plants, seeds, fruits, household foods, and even small, weak animals such as newly hatched birds. Because fire ants feed on other insects, they are of some benefit in the yard. However, their presence can greatly limit use of the garden without the threat of painful stings. The sting results in a pustule that develops within 24 hours. The bite heals within several weeks.

SOLUTION: Control fire ants in the lawn by drenching the mounds with ORTHO Fire Ant Control, ORTHO Lawn Insect Spray, ORTHO Ortho-Klor Soil Insect & Termite Killer, or ORTHO Diazinon Insect Spray. Also treat the area surrounding the mounds out to a distance of 4 feet. Spray ants indoors with ORTHO Ant, Roach & Spider Killer. If a severe reaction to fire ant stings develops, call your doctor.

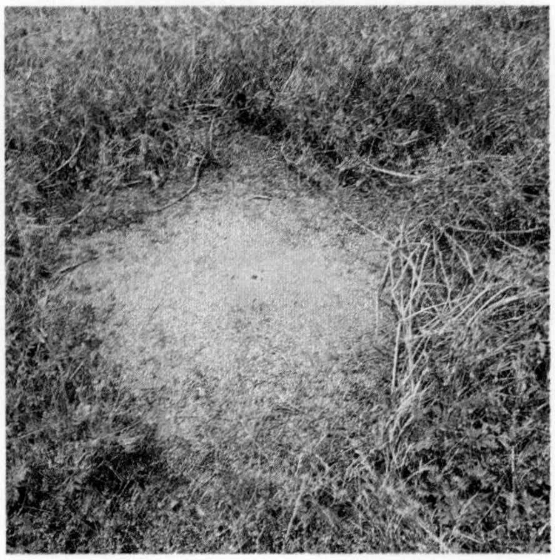

Harvester ant mound.

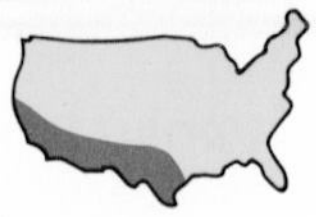

PROBLEM: Large ants up to ½ inch long, are crawling on cleared areas on the ground. Ants are seen entering holes or large craters in the ground. The holes are surrounded by a large cleared area of from 3 to 35 feet in diameter. The cleared area my be strewn with small pebbles and seed husks. Ant trails radiate out from the nest in all directions. If there is a mound, it is usually low. If disturbed, the ants will inflict a painful sting.

ANALYSIS: Harvester ants
(*Pogonomyrmex* species)
Harvester ants do not invade the home but may be a problem in lawns and gardens. These ants eat all tender vegetation surrounding their nests, resulting in a large cleared area where they dump small pebbles removed from their nest as well as husks and other inedible portions of seeds. They are primarily seed eaters. The holes in the center of the cleared areas lead to their underground nests. Harvester ants aggressively sting and bite anyone who disturbs their nests. They have been known to kill very small animals which accidentally wander over their nests.

SOLUTION: Treat the entrances to the ant nests and the cleared area around them with ORTHO Lawn Insect Spray, ORTHO Diazinon Granules, or ORTHO Diazinon Insect Spray. If you are stung, apply a cold compress or ice pack to the swollen area. If a severe reaction develops, call your doctor.

Scorpion (twice life size).

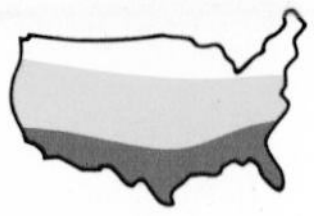

PROBLEM: Scorpions are usually found in the garden under rocks, boards, and protective debris. Indoors, they may inhabit attics or crawl spaces under the home. They may move down into living areas such as kitchens and bathrooms when attic temperatures rise above 100°F.

ANALYSIS: Scorpions
All scorpions are capable of inflicting stings; however, only a few species found in the Southwest are dangerous. Scorpions are nocturnal creatures, feeding at night on insects and small animals. During the day, they hide in dark, protected locations. They are shy, and sting only when touched, trapped, or otherwise provoked. Except for a few fatally poisonous scorpions (*Centruroides* species), most scorpions deliver stings that are no more serious than a bee sting. The venom varies in potency from season to season, however, and like many insect stings may cause severe illness in a sensitive individual. Although they live mostly in the garden, scorpions may crawl into the home through open or loose doors and windows.

SOLUTION: Remove loose boards, rocks, clutter, and other debris around the yard and in the home to eliminate scorpion hiding places. Wear gloves and protective clothing when cleaning up infested areas. Spray or dust locations where scorpions might hide in the yard and home with ORTHO Diazinon Insect Spray. Maintain window and door screens and weather stripping in good repair. Call a doctor if you are stung by a scorpion.

■ PANTRY PESTS

Tarantula (half life size).

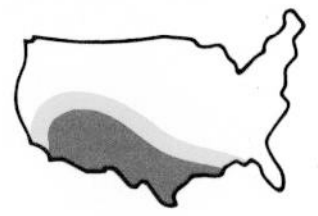

PROBLEM: A large, hairy spider, up to 5 inches across, is crawling around on the floor indoors or outside in the garden.

ANALYSIS: Tarantula

These spiders are often feared because of their large size and hairy bodies. Although a few South American species can give a very painful bite, all tarantulas occurring in this country inflict a bite that is like a bee sting. Their hairs, which easily rub off their bodies, can irritate the skin. When cornered, tarantulas may make a purring sound or rear up on their back legs. Tarantulas are sluggish, bite only rarely, and can be handled with ease. In recent years, tarantulas have become more acceptable as pets and are often sold in pet stores. Female tarantulas may live 20 years or more in captivity. Males are shorter-lived. Tarantulas are nocturnal, living in dark cavities or burrows during the day and hunting at night.

SOLUTION: Capture the spider in a large jar or box and release it in a secluded area. Chances of being bitten while catching it are minimal, but it is wise to wear protective clothing such as long rubber gloves, and to avoid sudden, quick movement. If a severe reaction develops to a tarantula bite, call your doctor. To control spiders, spray a 5 foot band around the home with ORTHO Diazinon Insect Spray.

German cockroaches (life size).

Oriental cockroach (twice life size).

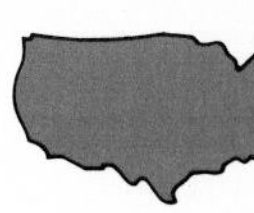

PROBLEM: Cockroaches infest the kitchen, bathroom, and other areas of the home. These flat, shiny insects range in size from ½ to 1¾ inches long. They may be light brown, golden tan, reddish brown, or black. In large numbers, they emit a fetid odor.

ANALYSIS: Cockroaches

These insect pests thrive in human habitations throughout the world. The most important household species in the United States are the *German cockroach* (*Blattella germanica*), the *brown-banded cockroach* (*Supella longipalpa*), the *Oriental cockroach* (*Blatta orientalis*), and the *American cockroach* (*Periplaneta americana*). In addition to their annoying presence, cockroaches spread diseases such as salmonella poisoning and parasitic toxoplasmosis by contaminating food with their infected droppings. These pests proliferate in areas where food and water are available. Cockroaches prefer starchy foods, but will feed on any human and pet food scraps, garbage, paper, or fabrics soiled with food. Unless infestations are heavy, or their hiding places are disturbed, they are rarely seen in exposed locations during the day. These nocturnal insects seek out dark, protected areas in which to live and breed. Usually they congregate in kitchens and bathrooms. They may be found behind or under sinks, refrigerators, and water heaters, within the walls of household appliances, behind baseboards and molding, in wall voids, around pipes, in garbage cans, and in piles of cluttered paper or grocery bags. They may be present in cracks or crevices in cupboards, cabinets, desks, dressers, and closets. They may infest basements, crawl spaces, and sewers. Cockroaches move from one room to another through wall voids or through cracks in walls, floors, and ceilings, and along pipes and conduits. If their living conditions become too crowded, they may migrate. Infestations usually begin when stray insects or egg cases are brought into the home with shipped items, second-hand furniture or appliances, grocery bags, or debris. They may also move into homes from sewers.

SOLUTION: Eliminate cockroach food sources by keeping the kitchen and other areas of the home free of food scraps. Clean up the kitchen after each meal and store food in tightly sealed metal, glass, or heavy plastic containers. Empty household garbage and pet litter regularly. Do not leave pet food out overnight. Fix leaking faucets and pipes. Clean up water puddles or moist areas around the kitchen, basement, and other infested areas. Plug cracks around baseboards, shelves, cupboards, sinks, and pipes with a filling material, such as putty or caulk. Remove food and utensils, then apply ORTHO Home Pest Insect Control, ORTHO Ortho-Klor Indoor & Outdoor Insect Killer, or ORTHO Ant, Roach & Spider Killer in cracks in cupboards, surfaces underneath sinks, along molding, behind appliances, and in other areas where insects are likely to congregate. Allow the spray to dry and then reline the shelves with fresh paper before replacing food and utensils. Bait with ORTHO Pest-B-Gon Roach Bait under sinks and refrigerators and in other hiding places according to label directions. Boric acid dust may also be used. Avoid inhaling or ingesting boric acid dust when applying. If infestations remain severe or persistent, contact a professional pest control operator.

PANTRY PESTS

Angoumois grain moth (6 times life size).

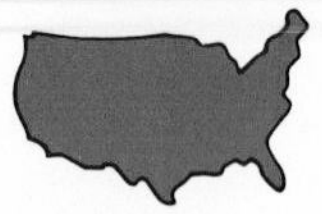

PROBLEM: Pinkish or greenish caterpillars up to $\frac{5}{8}$ inch long are feeding inside silken webbing in stored grain, flour, cereals, and other grain products. Beige, gray, and coppery-winged moths $\frac{1}{3}$ inch long may be seen flying around in the home.

ANALYSIS: Flour moths
The larvae of *Indian meal moths* (*Plodia interpunctella*) and *Mediterranean flour moths* (*Anagasta kuehniella*) damage ground or broken grain products, dried fruits, powdered milk, and other pantry items. The larvae of *angoumois grain moths* infest whole wheat and corn kernels. The adult moths lay eggs in stored grain products. The larvae that emerge spin silken webs, under which they feed. When mature, they usually leave the infested food to pupate in a corner or crack in the cupboard.

SOLUTION: Discard all infested food. Clean out cupboards thoroughly before restocking. If infestation is widespread, remove all food and utensils, and fog the infested area with ORTHO Hi-Power Indoor Insect Fogger; or dust cracks and crevices along shelves in the pantry with ORTHO Ortho-Klor Indoor & Outdoor Insect Killer. Wipe off excess dust on food bearing surfaces. Do not treat countertops or other food work areas. Reline shelves with paper and replace food after the spray has dried. If you suspect that food is infested, kill the eggs, larvae, and pupae by deep-freezing food for 4 days or heating it in a shallow pan at 150°F for half an hour. Keep foods in airtight glass, plastic, or metal containers. Keep the pantry clean, and avoid buying broken packages; they are more likely to be infested.

Mealworms (life size).

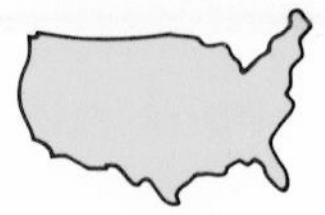

PROBLEM: Shiny, yellow to brown grubs up to $1\frac{1}{4}$ inches long are feeding in damp or moldy flour, grain, or cereal products. Flat, shiny, brown to black beetles $\frac{1}{4}$ to $\frac{3}{4}$ inch long may also be found.

ANALYSIS: Mealworms
(*Tenebrio* and *Alphitobius* species)
These insects prefer to feed on damp or moldy grain products stored in dark, rarely disturbed, dusty locations such as warehouses. However, if infested food items are brought into the pantry, the mealworms and beetles may migrate to infest and reproduce in poorly sealed bags of flour, bran, crackers, and other grain products.

SOLUTION: Chemical control is not necessary. Discard infested food items. Clean out cupboards thoroughly. Keep grain products in dry, tightly sealed glass, plastic, or metal containers.

Red flour beetle (6 times life size).

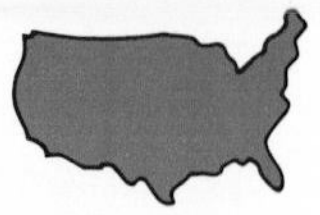

PROBLEM: Reddish to dark brown, elongated beetles $\frac{1}{10}$ to $\frac{1}{7}$ inch long, and yellowish white, wiry grubs $\frac{1}{8}$ inch long are feeding in flour, cereals, cake mix, macaroni, and other flour and grain products.

ANALYSIS: Flour beetles
(*Tribolium* and *Oryzaephilus* species)
Several species of beetles infest grain products in the pantry, grocery store, and packing plant, including the *saw-toothed grain beetle*, the *red flour beetle*, and the *confused flour beetle*. These pests feed on and reproduce in stored flour products. They can migrate to and infest nearby broken or poorly sealed containers, and can also chew through and infest flimsy paper and cellophane packages. Even when infested packages are removed, the beetles can live on flour and cereals that sift into cracks in the cupboard.

SOLUTION: Discard all infested food. Clean out cupboards thoroughly before restocking. If infestation is widespread, remove all food items and treat behind shelves and cracks in the pantry with ORTHO Ortho-Klor Indoor & Outdoor Insect Killer (wipe off excess dust on food bearing surfaces); or fog the infested area with ORTHO Hi-Power Indoor Insect Fogger. Let the spray dry before replacing food. Keep foods in air-tight glass, plastic, or metal containers. If you suspect food is contaminated, kill the beetles, grubs, and eggs by deep-freezing for 4 days; or heat the food in a shallow pan at 130°F for half an hour. Keep the pantry clean, and avoid buying broken packages; they are more likely to be infested.

Rice weevils (4 times life size).

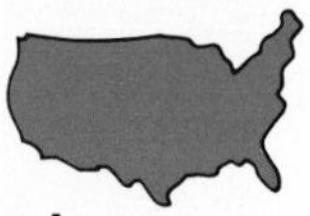

PROBLEM: Reddish brown to black beetles ⅛ to ⅙ inch long with elongated snouts are feeding in stored whole grain rice, corn, wheat, and beans. The beetles may be seen crawling around the pantry. Yellow-white grubs may be found inside infested kernels.

ANALYSIS: Grain weevils (*Sitophilus* species)
These pantry pests include the *granary weevil* and the *rice weevil*. They usually damage whole grains, but occasionally infest flour and other broken or processed grain products. The adult weevils lay eggs inside grain kernels. Larvae that hatch from the eggs mature inside the kernels, pupate, and emerge as adult weevils. The adults wander about, and are often seen far from the site of infestation.

SOLUTION: Discard all infested food. Clean out cupboards thoroughly before restocking. If the infestation is widespread, remove all food items and fog the kitchen with ORTHO Hi-Power Indoor Insect Fogger according to label directions; or spray shelves and cracks in pantry cupboards with an insecticide containing *malathion* or *propoxur* (BAYGON®). Do not spray countertops or other food preparation areas. Reline shelves with paper and replace food after the spray has dried. Keep foods in air-tight glass, plastic, or metal containers, and avoid buying broken packages; they are more likely to be infested.

Cigarette beetle, larva, and pupa (twice life size).

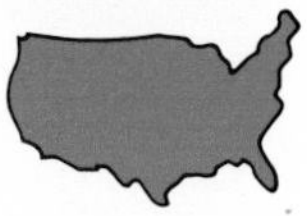

PROBLEM: Reddish or reddish brown, oval-shaped beetles, ⅛ inch long, or yellowish white, curved grubs are feeding in stored tobacco, cigars, or cigarettes. They may also be found in spices, such as red pepper and paprika, coffee beans, and other stored foods derived from plants.

ANALYSIS: Cigarette and drugstore beetles (*Lasioderma serricorne* and *Stegobium paniceum*)
These beetles are native to tropical parts of the world and can survive in the United States only in warm buildings (65°F and up). These pests feed on and reproduce in foods and spices. They may also feed on wool, leather, paper, drugs, and other household items. When infested products are brought into the home, the beetles can invade nearby uncontaminated foods that are kept in unsealed, broken, or flimsy containers. They may also chew through sealed paper containers.

SOLUTION: Remove and destroy all infested foods. Clean out cupboards thoroughly before restocking. If the infestation is widespread, remove all food items and spray shelves and cracks with an insecticide containing *malathion* or *rotenone*. Let the spray dry before replacing food. Keep foods and spices in air-tight glass, metal, or plastic containers. Refrigerate food kept in paper packages. Do not purchase items in broken or unsealed packages; they are more likely to be infested.

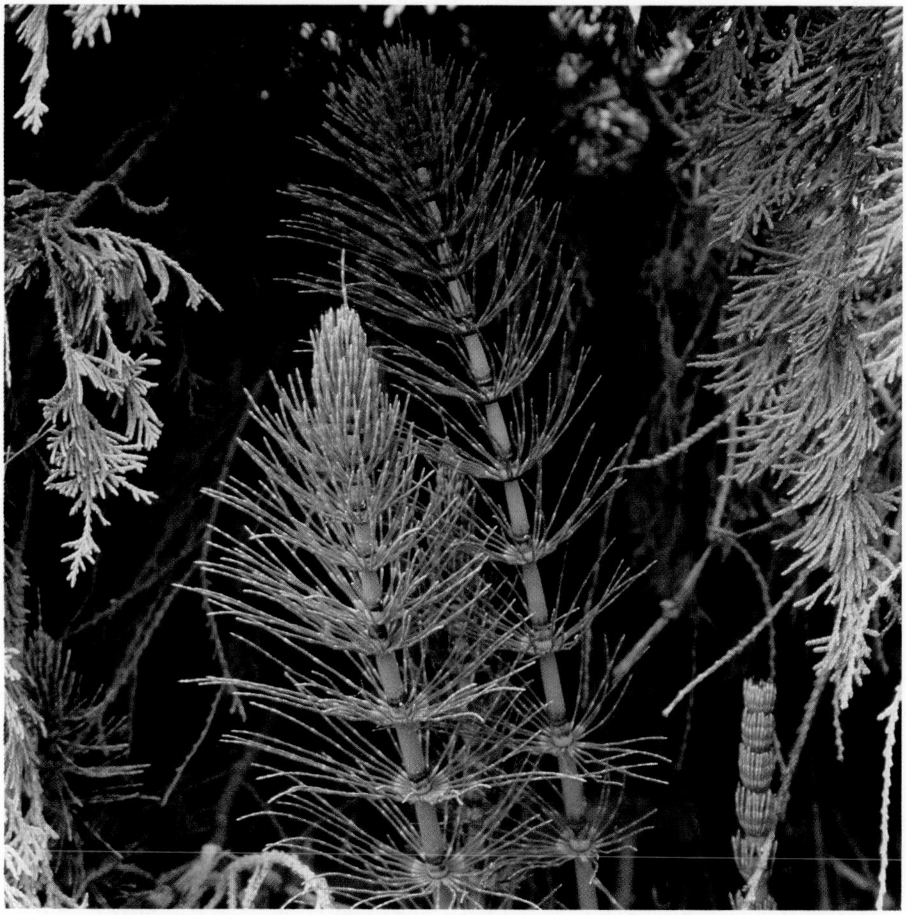

If you know the name of your weed, look for it in the index on the next page. If you don't know its name, scan through the pictures of weeds on the next 34 pages. This section is arranged with weeds that look alike located near one another, to make identification easier. If you have a problem with many different kinds of weeds in an area of your garden, see one of these area weed control articles:

A GALLERY OF WEEDS

Most gardeners would agree that weeds are the most time-consuming and persistent garden problem. Yet, for most gardeners, they don't need to be. Weed control can be reduced to a minimum by spending one or two growing seasons diligently removing every weed before it makes seeds. This year or two of extra effort will pay off with many years of reduced work in the garden.

Weeds can be divided into two categories. Some weeds produce a copious amount of seed, and begin producing it early in life. These weeds often are easy to kill, either with herbicides or with a hoe, but new ones keep appearing. Weeds in the second category are hard to kill, often because they have persistent underground parts that can sprout into new plants. And a few weeds, such as dandelions, have both of these characteristics.

The first category of weeds is most easily controlled by keeping its seeds from sprouting. Begin the battle in the spring, or whenever seeds germinate, by applying a pre-emergent herbicide—an herbicide that kills seeds as they germinate—or a mulch wherever the weed has been a problem. Then, once a week throughout the growing season, remove every weed that appears in your yard, either with a hoe, or by spot-treating with an herbicide.

The second category of weeds is best controlled with a translocated herbicide—one that is carried to every part of the plant. *Glyphosate*, the active ingredient in ORTHO Kleenup Systemic Weed & Grass Killer, has been a real help to gardeners (but it can't be used in the vegetable garden). It controls most of the difficult weeds, then breaks down in the soil, so it has no lasting effect on garden plants. Or cover the area with a black plastic mulch for a growing season. This treatment kills all plants under the mulch by excluding light.

Then, as with weeds in the first category, inspect the entire garden once a week and pull every weed seen. If this routine is followed carefully for a year, all the weeds in your garden will be eliminated, and only a few that blow in from outside will bother you in future years. Weed control will have been reduced to a routine chore.

Above: Horsetail. See page 822.
Left: Dandelions in a lawn. These common weeds are a nuisance in many lawns. See page 836.

INDEX TO WEEDS

WEED CONTROL

Effective weed control on right.

WEED CONTROL IN LAWNS

The best way to control weeds in a lawn is to keep the lawn thick and vigorous by following the guidelines beginning on page 250. A vigorous lawn is a strong competitor, and will crowd out most weeds.

Broadleaf weeds: Kill broadleaf weeds in lawns with ORTHO Weed-B-Gon Lawn Weed Killer or ORTHO Weed-B-Gon For Southern Grasses. Or, spot treat individual weeds with ORTHO Weed-B-Gon Weed Killer.

Weed grasses: Kill crabgrass and dallisgrass in lawns with ORTHO Crab Grass Killer. Other weed grasses can be spot treated with ORTHO Kleenup Systemic Weed & Grass Killer or ORTHO Kleenup Ready-To-Use Grass & Weed Killer. You can reseed or resod the dead spots 1 week after treatment. For instructions on lawn repair, see page 914.

Reestablishing the lawn: If the lawn is in disrepair, and is mostly weeds rather than turfgrass, the best solution might be to kill it all, then reseed or resod a new lawn. For instructions on establishing a new lawn, see page 251.

Preventive care: Pre-emergence herbicides kill seedlings as they germinate, but do not harm existing plants. ORTHO Garden Weed Preventer is a pre-emergence herbicide for lawns and gardens. One application in early spring will prevent most lawn weeds from emerging from the soil.

Weed-free annual bed.

WEED CONTROL IN ANNUAL BEDS

Annuals have a short life, growing quickly from seeds to bloom. Any weeds that compete with the annuals for water and nutrients slow their growth and bloom. Before tilling and planting an annual bed, kill the existing weeds or lawn grass. Annual weeds can be killed by an herbicide or by cultivation. If the area is being reclaimed from a lawn, or if perennial weeds are present, use ORTHO Kleenup Systemic Weed & Grass Killer. For small gardens or to spot treat individual weeds, use ORTHO Kleenup Ready-To-Use Grass & Weed Killer, the same product in a premixed formulation. Kleenup will not affect the roots of untreated annual flowers, since it is inactivated on contact with soil. Once the flower bed is weed-free, prevent weed seeds from germinating with a pre-emergence herbicide such as ORTHO Garden Weed Preventer. Established weeds and plants are not affected, so use only on weed-free soil. Don't use in an area where you have planted annual flower seeds. Pre-emergence herbicides form a barrier to emerging seedlings. If the barrier is disturbed by cultivating or hoeing, the herbicide's effectiveness is reduced, so don't disturb the soil until you reapply the herbicide. For more information on the products mentioned, see the gallery of ORTHO products beginning on page 920.

WEED CONTROL

Weeds growing in vegetable garden.

Weed-free perennial bed.

Poor weed control.

WEED CONTROL IN VEGETABLE GARDENS

It is important to remove weeds in the vegetable garden because they compete with vegetables, reducing their growth and yield. However, control measures are complicated by the fact that the vegetable garden offers an ideal environment for plant growth, with lots of water and fertilizer. Also, because vegetables are eaten, the use of herbicides around them must be limited. Remove existing weeds by cultivating with a sharp hoe. Cut off the weeds just below the soil line, rather than trying to dig them from the ground. Most vegetable garden weeds are killed by this treatment, and the roots of the vegetables are not disturbed. To remove small weeds close to seedlings, pinch them off, or cut them at the ground line with a pair of scissors. Prevent weeds from returning with ORTHO Garden Weed Preventer. This preemergence herbicide kills weed seedlings as they germinate, but does not harm existing plants. Or smother weeds with a mulch. Black plastic stops all weed growth, and 2 to 4 inches of sawdust, straw, or other loose material discourages most weeds. Be careful in choosing an organic mulch. It should be free of weed seeds, and must not have been treated with herbicides before being cut. A mulch of organic materials can be turned under in the fall to improve the tilth of the soil. To save yourself much weeding next year, be diligent about weeding this year. Only a few weed seeds blow in from outside the garden; most of this year's weeds are the progeny of last year's weeds.

WEED CONTROL IN PERENNIAL BEDS

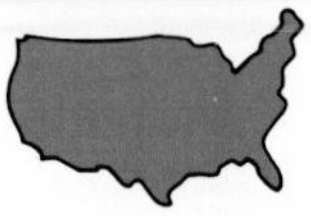

Weeds are usually more numerous, vigorous, and difficult to control in flower beds growing in full sun. Before establishing a perennial bed in an area that was once lawn or a neglected plot, kill all the present weeds or they will be a continuous maintenance problem. Kill the existing weeds with ORTHO Kleenup Systemic Weed & Grass Killer. These herbicides are also effective in cleaning up an established but neglected bed. In small flower beds or to spot treat individual weeds, use ORTHO Kleenup Ready-To-Use Grass & Weed Killer, a premixed formulation. Kleenup is inactivated on contact with the soil, so it won't harm the roots of established perennials. Once the flower bed is established, use a pre-emergence herbicide to keep the area weed-free. Pre-emergence herbicides such as ORTHO Garden Weed Preventer kill seedlings as they emerge. They don't affect established plants or weeds, so use only on weed-free soil. Pre-emergence herbicides form a barrier to emerging seedlings. If the barrier is disturbed by cultivating or hoeing, the herbicide's effectiveness is reduced, so don't disturb the soil until you are ready to reapply the herbicide. For more information on the products mentioned, see the gallery of ORTHO products beginning on page 928.

WEED CONTROL UNDER TREES AND SHRUBS

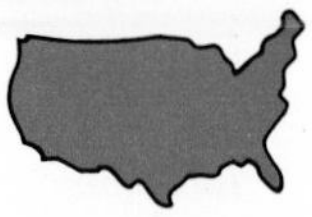

Weed control under trees and shrubs is usually simpler and easier than weed control in other areas because the trees and shrubs shade the bed, reducing the vigor of the weeds. If the area has been neglected for some time, and is full of perennial weeds, kill them with ORTHO Kleenup Systemic Weed & Grass Killer. If the area is small, or to spot treat individual weeds, use ORTHO Kleenup Ready-To-Use Grass & Weed Killer. It will probably not be necessary to remove the dead weeds, since small weeds dry up and disappear. Kleenup is inactivated on contact with soil so it won't harm the roots of nearby plants. To prevent weed seeds from germinating after you have cleared an area, apply ORTHO Casoron Granules or ORTHO Garden Weed Preventer. These pre-emergence herbicides kill young seedlings as the seeds germinate. They won't kill existing weeds, so apply them only to weed-free soil. The herbicide forms a barrier that kills emerging seedlings. If the barrier is disturbed by hoeing or cultivating, the protection is dispersed. Once the herbicide is applied and watered in, don't disturb the soil until you reapply the herbicide. (For more information on these products, see the gallery of ORTHO products beginning on page 928.) Light, shallow cultivation and mulching (see page 926) under trees are also effective in controlling weeds.

Weeds growing in patio.

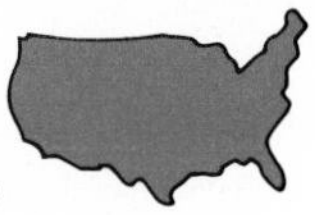

WEED CONTROL IN DRIVEWAYS, WALKWAYS, AND PATIOS

Weeds growing in the cracks and crevices of walkways, brick patios, and driveways are often difficult to hand-pull. Most perennial weeds have deep roots that become anchored underneath the permanent surface. To eliminate weeds in these situations, use an herbicide that won't harm surrounding lawn grasses, trees, and shrubs if it is washed from the treated area by rain or irrigation water. Treat existing weeds with an herbicide such as ORTHO Kleenup Ready-To-Use Grass & Weed Killer. For scattered or few weeds, treat with ORTHO Kleenup Spot Weed & Grass Killer. All of these herbicides are inactivated on contact with the soil, so they won't harm the roots of surrounding desirable plants. For longer-term control where desirable plants are not present nearby, kill existing weeds with ORTHO Triox Vegetation Killer. This residual herbicide prevents weed growth for up to a year. For more information on the products mentioned, see the gallery of ORTHO products beginning on page 928.

Weeds growing in unimproved area.

WEED CONTROL IN UNIMPROVED AREAS

One reason to keep weeds to a minimum in vacant lots and fields is that these weeds produce the seeds that germinate in your garden. If you prevent them from setting seeds, you can often nip your garden weed problems in the bud.

Mowing: One way to control weeds in unused places is to mow them regularly. While this method keeps the area neat, and keeps some of the weeds from setting seed, many weed varieties set seed in only a few days, and others have flower heads close to the ground, so that a mower misses them.

Killing weeds: If you wish to kill all the weeds in an empty lot, use a nonselective herbicide—an herbicide that kills just about any plant it touches. If you wish to replant the area soon, choose ORTHO Kleenup Systemic Weed & Grass Killer, which becomes inactive on contact with the soil. If most of the weeds are woody, such as shrubs or vines, use ORTHO Brush-B-Gon Brush Killer.

Keeping the weeds out: If you wish to keep the area clear of all vegetation, apply ORTHO Triox Vegetation Killer. Triox not only kills the weeds it contacts, but remains in the soil for up to a year to prevent further weed growth. For more information about these products, see the gallery of ORTHO products beginning on page 928.

Annual bluegrass.

ANNUAL BLUEGRASS
Poa annua

Annual bluegrass, also called *annual speargrass*, *dwarf speargrass*, or *walkgrass*, is a troublesome weed in all areas of the yard. In lawns it is not easily noticed because it resembles Kentucky bluegrass. Annual bluegrass prefers areas with moist, rich, or compacted soil. This pale green grass reproduces by seeds and lives for only 1 year, although in some areas there are perennial strains. Annual bluegrass grows most rapidly in cool spring weather. In mid to late spring, white seed heads appear on the plants. The seeds fall to the soil, and germinate in the cooler weather of late summer to midfall. Annual bluegrass is not heat or drought tolerant, and dies in the summer.

CONTROL: For information on controlling annual bluegrass in lawns, see page 269. Around trees and shrubs, and in flower and vegetable gardens, use ORTHO Garden Weed Preventer. Apply to the soil in late summer to midfall. While the weeds are actively growing around trees and shrubs, flower beds, and in nonplanted areas, use ORTHO Kleenup Ready-To-Use Grass & Weed Killer or ORTHO Kleenup Spot Weed & Grass Killer. Prevent annual bluegrass near trees and shrubs with ORTHO Casoron Granules. On compacted soil, correct as outlined on page 906. Reduce the chances of invasion by allowing the soil to become moderately dry between waterings when the seeds are germinating in the fall.

GRASSLIKE WEEDS

Quackgrass.

QUACKGRASS

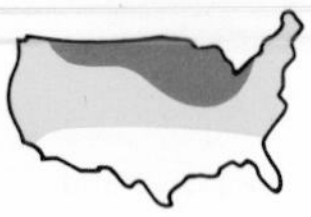

Agropyron repens

Quackgrass, also called *couchgrass* or *witchgrass,* is one of the most troublesome perennial grasses in the northern United States. Its extensive fibrous system consists of long, yellow-white roots that may grow 5 feet or more in one growing season. The narrow, bluish green blades grow on stalks 1 to 3 feet tall. Wheatlike spikes produce seeds from May to September. These seeds may survive in the soil for up to 4 years, but most germinate in the spring within 2 years. The underground creeping rootstocks also send up new shoots, increasing the infestation. Quackgrass tolerates any type of soil. Its roots are very competitive, and crowd out desirable plants.

CONTROL: Hand-digging is not a practical solution, since any rootstock pieces left behind will generate new plants. Kill existing weeds in lawns, around trees and shrubs, and in nonplanted areas with ORTHO Kleenup Systemic Weed & Grass Killer or ORTHO Kleenup Ready-To-Use Grass & Weed Killer. Use an herbicide containing *eptam* or *trifluralin* to prevent quackgrass seedlings from becoming established in flower beds and landscaped areas. Apply in early spring 2 weeks before the last expected frost, or about the time the forsythia bloom. Patches of quackgrass can be killed by covering with black plastic sheeting for 1 year.

Velvetgrass.

GERMAN VELVETGRASS

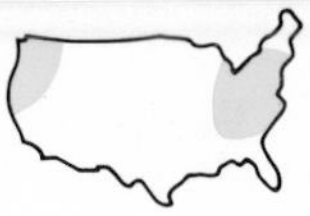

Holcus mollis

German velvetgrass is a perennial grassy weed. In unmowed areas, the stems grow 2 to 4 feet tall. In mowed areas, they grow flat, and root wherever their joints touch the soil. The 4 to 8-inch leaves are velvety and bright green. Seeds are produced from July to August on seedheads 2 to 4 inches long. They lie dormant in the soil over the winter, and germinate in the spring. Plants grow from vigorous, slender underground rootstocks. Velvetgrass thrives in damp areas with rich soil. Although mostly a problem in fields and along roadways and walkways, it can become established and unsightly in lawns.

CONTROL: Kill existing velvetgrass in walkways and lawns and around trees, shrubs, and flower beds with an herbicide containing *glyphosate* (KLEENUP®). Treat any time the plants are actively growing, but preferably before the seeds appear.

Bermudagrass.

BERMUDAGRASS

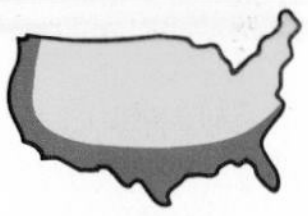

Cynodon dactylon

This perennial grass is also called *devilgrass, wiregrass,* or *dog's tooth grass.* It is adapted to areas where the ground does not freeze. Its vigorous creeping habit makes it a weed that invades lawns, flower and landscaped beds, and nonplanted areas where it crowds out desirable plants. The leaf blades are ⅛ inch wide and attached to slightly hairy, gray-green stems. The leaves are not cold tolerant, and turn brown when the temperature falls below 50°F. Seeds are formed on 3 to 7 short, fingerlike segments that are about 3 inches across and grow taller than the stems. The vigorous roots may grow several feet deep making the plants drought and heat tolerant, and also difficult to eliminate. Bermudagrass reproduces by seeds, stems, and underground stems. It prefers sandy soil, and will not grow in dense shade.

CONTROL: To control Bermudagrass in non-Bermudagrass lawns, see page 269. To control Bermudagrass around trees and shrubs, flower beds, and nonplanted areas, use ORTHO Kleenup Systemic Weed & Grass Killer, ORTHO Kleenup Spot Weed & Grass Killer, or ORTHO Kleenup Ready-To-Use Grass & Weed Killer. Apply any time the plants are actively growing. A treatment in the early fall about 2 to 3 weeks before the first killing frost is very effective. Treat again in the spring as soon as plants are noticed. Repeated treatments are usually necessary because of the tough, extensive rhizomes. Hand-digging is not effective; any pieces left behind will sprout into new plants.

Crabgrass.

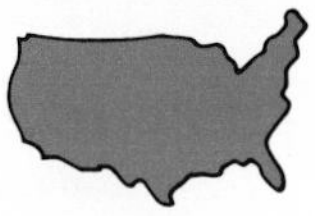

CRABGRASS
Digitaria species

Crabgrass is one of the most troublesome weeds in yards throughout the country. Although it is known to most gardeners as a lawn weed, it is frequently found in flower and vegetable gardens and growing in cracks in sidewalks and driveways. In some areas of the country crabgrass is called *fingergrass* or *crowfootgrass*. This annual grassy weed grows in most soils, but prefers light, sandy areas. Crabgrass is most troublesome in hot, dry weather. The pale, bluish green blades are 2 to 5 inches long and ⅓ inch wide. They may be slightly hairy. Stems root at the lower joints. Seed heads 4 to 5 inches across grow from the center of the plant from July to October. The seeds remain dormant over the winter, then sprout in the spring. The tops of the plants are killed by the first frost in the fall. Plants grow in broad, flat clumps that crowd out desirable plants.

CONTROL: To control crabgrass in lawns, see page 270. Around trees and shrubs, and in flower beds and nonplanted areas, kill existing weeds with ORTHO Kleenup Systemic Weed & Grass Killer or ORTHO Kleenup Spot Weed & Grass Killer. Prevent crabgrass from sprouting around trees and shrubs with ORTHO Casoron Granules. In flower and vegetable gardens and around trees and shrubs, prevent crabgrass with ORTHO Garden Weed Preventer. Apply the preventive measures in the early spring about 2 weeks before the last expected frost, or about the time the forsythia bloom. The many fibrous roots make this weed difficult to remove by digging.

Nimblewill.

NIMBLEWILL
Muhlenbergia schreberi

The leaves of this perennial grass are flat, smooth, bluish green, and ½ to 2 inches long. The wiry stems grow up to 10 inches tall, first outward, then upward from the central crown. The stems root at the lower nodes, increasing the size of the plant. Seeds are produced on inconspicuous spikes from August to October. The seeds lie dormant in the soil for the winter, and sprout in late spring. Plants develop a shallow root system. Plant tops turn whitish tan and become dormant with the first killing frost in the fall. They begin growth again late the following spring. This warm-season grass invades moist lawns, gardens, and nonplanted areas with rich, gravelly soil.

CONTROL: Eliminate nimblewill in lawns with an herbicide containing *DSMA*. Around trees and shrubs and in flower beds and nonplanted areas, kill existing weeds with ORTHO Kleenup Systemic Weed & Grass Killer or ORTHO Kleenup Ready-To-Use Grass & Weed Killer. Nimblewill is easiest to kill when it is a seedling, from late spring to early summer. In vegetable gardens, remove the weeds by hand-digging.

Dallisgrass.

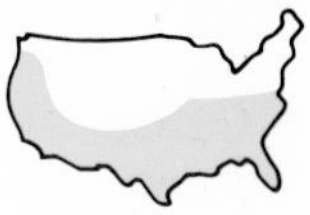

DALLISGRASS
Paspalum dilatatum

The coarse leaves of this perennial grass are ½ inch wide and 4 to 10 inches long. Stems 2 to 6 inches long radiate from the center of the plant in a star pattern. Plants grow in spreading clumps with deep roots. Seeds are produced on 3 to 5 fingerlike segments that grow from May to October from the top of the stems. Silken hairs cover the seeds, which lie dormant over the winter, and sprout very early in the spring. Dallisgrass also reproduces by underground stems. Dallisgrass grows across the southern states in lawns, gardens, and fields. It prefers moist soil, but will tolerate any type of soil. It grows most vigorously in warm summer weather.

CONTROL: Treat actively growing clumps of dallisgrass in lawns with ORTHO Crab Grass Killer in spring or summer. Repeated treatments are often necessary, since dallisgrass has deep roots. In landscaped beds and nonplanted areas, treat with ORTHO Kleenup Spot Weed & Grass Killer. Patches of dallisgrass can also be killed by covering with black plastic sheeting for 1 year.

GRASSLIKE WEEDS

Goosegrass.

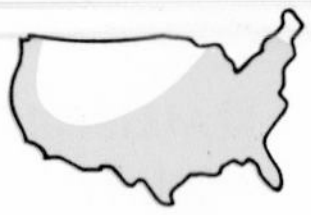

GOOSEGRASS
Eleusine indica

This annual grassy weed is also called *silver crabgrass* or *yardgrass.* Goosegrass is frequently confused with crabgrass, but it is darker green, does not root at the stem joints, and germinates later in the spring. (For more information on crabgrass, see page 817.) Goosegrass stems are smooth and flat, forming a rosette that resembles the spokes of a wheel. The leaf blades are ⅕ inch wide and 2 to 10 inches long. Seeds are produced on stalks 2 to 6 inches tall from July to October. The seeds fall to the soil, remain dormant over the winter, and sprout in the spring. The plants are killed in the fall by the first frost. Goosegrass has an extensive root system, and grows in lawns, gardens, and cracks in walkways where the soil is compacted and low in fertility.

CONTROL: Eliminate existing goosegrass in lawns by spot treating with ORTHO Kleenup Ready-To-Use Grass & Weed Killer. Around trees and shrubs and in nonplanted areas, kill existing weeds with ORTHO Kleenup Spot Weed & Grass Killer or ORTHO Kleenup Ready-To-Use Grass & Weed Killer. Prevent goosegrass in vegetable and flower gardens and lawns and around trees and shrubs with ORTHO Garden Weed Preventer. Apply to the soil before the plants sprout in early spring. Where appropriate, reduce the soil compaction as outlined on page 906. Improve soil fertility with regular fertilization.

Fall panicum.

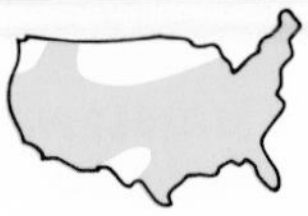

FALL PANICUM
Panicum dichotomiflorum

This grassy annual is also known as *spreading* or *smooth witchgrass.* The rough leaves, 4 to 8 inches long, have a prominent midrib. The stems grow 1 to 4 feet tall, and root wherever the nodes touch the soil. Seeds are produced from June to October on gray-brown panicles that grow 4 to 10 inches long on the tips of the stems. When mature, the panicles break off and tumble about, scattering the seeds. The seeds do not sprout until the following spring. Fall panicum thrives in moist soil in fields and waste places and along roadways and stream banks.

CONTROL: Kill existing weeds with an herbicide containing *glyphosate* (KLEENUP®). Prevent the seeds from germinating throughout the yard with ORTHO Garden Weed Preventer. Apply in early spring about 2 weeks before the last expected frost, or when the forsythia bloom. Fall panicum has shallow roots and can be hand-pulled or hoed.

Johnsongrass.

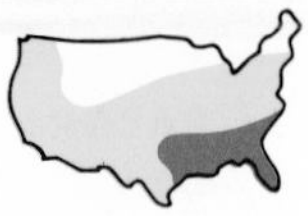

JOHNSONGRASS
Sorghum halepense

Also called *Egyptiangrass,* this persistent perennial plant is a serious problem in the South. The roots may penetrate 3 to 6 feet into loose, rich soil. The stems grow 1 to 6 feet tall, and frequently root at their lower nodes, forming dense clusters that crowd out desirable plants. The leaves grow 1 to 2 feet long and up to 1 inch wide, with a conspicuous greenish white midvein. Hairy purple seedheads, from 4 to 16 inches long, appear on the ends of the stems from June to October. The reddish brown seeds germinate in the spring. New plants also sprout from creeping rootstocks. Johnsongrass is commonly found in areas with rich, moist soil along roadways and in fields, lawns, landscaped beds, and nonplanted areas.

CONTROL: Johnsongrass is difficult to control because of its extensive rootstocks. To eliminate the weeds in landscaped beds and nonplanted areas and to spot treat in lawns, use ORTHO Kleenup Spot Weed & Grass Killer. Repeated treatments may be necessary if new growth appears. To prevent seeds from sprouting, use ORTHO Garden Weed Preventer. Apply to the soil in the spring about the time of the last frost, or 2 weeks after the forsythia bloom. Handpulling is not a practical solution, since new plants will sprout from any rootstocks left in the soil.

Barnyardgrass.

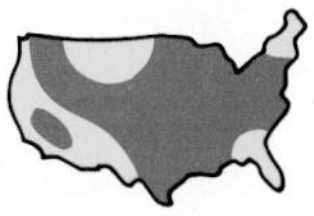

BARNYARDGRASS

Echinochloa crus-galli

Also called *cockspurgrass* or *watergrass*, this annual has upright, reddish purple stems that grow 1 to 4 feet tall. When mowed in lawns, the stems grow close to the ground. The large, smooth leaves are ¼ to ½ inch wide with a prominent midvein. Plants develop deep, fibrous root systems. Seeds are produced on 6 to 8 segments on the stems from July to September. One plant may produce as many as 40,000 seeds. The seeds fall to the soil, remain dormant over the winter, and sprout the following year in early summer. Barnyardgrass is a troublesome weed from midsummer to midfall. It thrives in lawns, gardens, and nonplanted areas with rich, moist soil.

CONTROL: To control barnyardgrass in lawns, see page 271. Kill existing weeds around trees and shrubs and in nonplanted areas with an herbicide containing *glyphosate* (KLEENUP®). Plants can also be hand-pulled. To prevent barnyardgrass from becoming established, treat the soil with ORTHO Garden Weed Preventer. Apply in early spring before the plants sprout.

Sandbur.

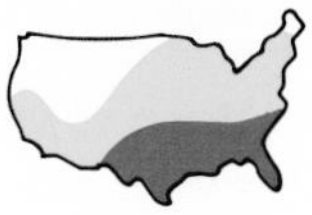

SANDBUR

Cenchrus species

Sandbur, also called burgrass or sandburgrass, is an annual grass that grows 6 inches to 2 feet tall. The narrow, yellow-green leaf blades are ¼ inch wide and 2 to 5 inches long. They may be rough on the upper surface. The blades are attached to flattened stems that may grow upright or spread along the soil. Plants have shallow, fibrous roots, and when growing in mowed lawns, they form low mats. From July to September, seeds are produced inside the spiny, ½-inch, straw-col-ored burs that are formed on the stems. Each bur contains only two seeds, but one plant may produce as many as 1000 seeds. Seeds are spread to new areas when the burs cling to clothing and animals. The seeds germinate in the spring. Sandbur is most troublesome in orchards, vineyards, fields, and lawns with light, sandy, well-drained soils.

CONTROL: In lawns, kill sandbur by spot treating with ORTHO Kleenup Systemic Weed & Grass Killer or ORTHO Kleenup Spot Weed & Grass Killer. Also use around trees and shrubs and in flower beds and nonplanted areas. For best results, treat in early to midsummer before burs and seeds are produced. Prevent sandbur from returning to these areas by applying a pre-emergence herbicide containing trifluralin or eptam in early spring. Plants can be removed by hand if handled carefully with gloves.

Foxtails.

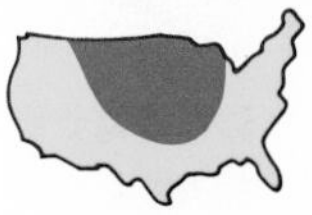

FOXTAILS

Setaria species

Foxtails, sometimes called bristlegrass or pigeongrass, are summer annual grasses that grow 1 to 2 feet tall. In a mowed lawn, they will form low mats. The leaves are flat, sometimes twisted, ¼ to ½ inch wide, and 2 to 6 inches long. Spikelets consisting of 5 to 20 bristles, 2 to 4 inches long, appear from July to September. The bristle resembles a fox's tail, hence the name. The bristles contain seeds that sprout from midspring to early summer. Foxtails grow in clumps and are often mistaken for crabgrass, but form smaller clumps than crabgrass. (For information on crabgrass, see page 817.) Foxtails are found in yards with rich soil bordering fields, roadways, and other unmaintained areas.

CONTROL: Spot treat existing weeds in lawns, around trees and shrubs, and in flower beds and nonplanted areas with ORTHO Kleenup Ready-To-Use Grass & Weed Killer. To prevent foxtails in lawns and flower and vegetable gardens and around trees and shrubs, apply ORTHO Garden Weed Preventer in early spring 2 weeks before the last expected frost, or about the time the forsythia bloom. Plants can also be successfully removed by hand.

GRASSLIKE WEEDS

Downy brome.

Wild oats.

Wild iris.

DOWNY BROME

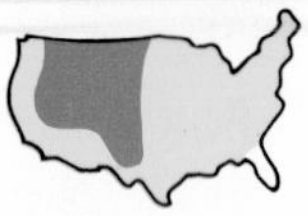

Bromus tectorum

This annual grass is also known as *bromegrass*, *cheatgrass*, or *military grass*. The smooth stems grow ½ to 2 feet tall with fibrous, shallow roots. The light green leaves are 2 to 6 inches long and covered with soft hairs. Drooping purple panicles appear from April to May. The seeds they produce mature in May and June, and germinate in the fall or early spring. They may remain viable in the soil for more than 2 years. The plants turn purplish tan when mature. When dry, they are a fire hazard, burning very rapidly and creating intense heat. Downy brome is most troublesome in areas with dry, sandy, or gravelly soil.

CONTROL: Kill existing weeds with ORTHO Kleenup Systemic Weed & Grass Killer. Apply any time the plants are actively growing, but preferably right after they sprout in the fall or early spring. To keep downy brome from returning, apply an herbicide containing *trifluralin*, *eptam*, or *DCPA* (DACTHAL®) to the soil before the seeds sprout. Downy brome can also be removed by hand-pulling.

WILD OATS

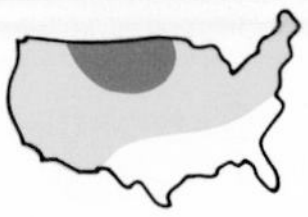

Avena fatua

Also called *wheat oats* or *oatgrass*, this annual grassy weed has smooth stems that grow 1 to 4 feet tall. The leaves are ¼ inch wide and 3 to 8 inches long, with hairs along the margins. The extensive, fibrous roots make the plants somewhat drought tolerant. Seeds are produced from June to October on 1-inch spikelets in 6 to 10-inch panicles. The seeds may lie dormant in the soil for several years before sprouting in the fall or spring. Plants are very conspicuous when they turn yellow in early or midsummer, while surrounding plants remain green. This weed tolerates many types of soil. It is found most frequently in fields and along roadsides, occasionally invading neighboring yards.

CONTROL: Kill existing plants around trees and shrubs and in flower beds and nonplanted areas with an herbicide containing *glyphosate* (KLEENUP®). Prevent seeds from germinating in lawns, flower beds, and around trees and shrubs with an herbicide containing *eptam* or *simazine*. Apply in the fall or early spring.

WILD IRIS

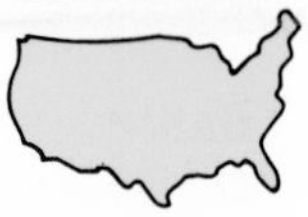

Iris species

Wild irises closely resemble the cultivated irises grown in home gardens. They grow slowly in clumps from underground, tightly gnarled rootstocks. The plants grow ½ to 1½ feet tall with swordlike bright green leaves. Yellow to purple flowers bloom from spring through summer. The petals are marked with very conspicuous veins. Wild irises are most notable for gracing meadows, hillsides, and woodlands with their delicate flowers. However, in some situations they may become noxious. Wild irises that grow along the edges of ponds and lakes may gradually creep into the water, reducing water flow and flora and fauna habitats. The dense clumps of wild iris may be a nuisance when an uncultivated area is being reclaimed for cultivated gardens or lawns.

CONTROL: Spot treat individual plants or clumps of wild iris with an herbicide containing *dalapon* or *2,4-D*. Apply when the plants just begin to bloom. Cover all the foliage thoroughly. Avoid contaminating any nearby bodies of water. Clumps of wild iris may be hand-dug, although new plants will sprout from any rootstocks left in the soil. Because the rootstocks grow in tight groups, the entire clump can be removed with some effort.

RUSHES

Wild onion.

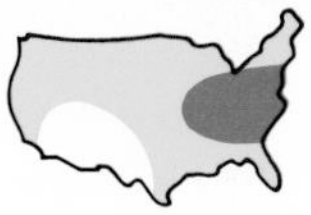

WILD GARLIC AND WILD ONION

Allium vineale and
A. canadense

These perennial weeds grow from underground bulbs. They are easily recognized by the garlic or onion odor of their crushed leaves. The slender, hollow leaves grow 10 to 15 inches tall. Greenish purple or white flowers bloom from May to July. Although they produce seeds in the spring that germinate in the fall, they reproduce mostly by bulbs and bulblets formed in the summer. In addition to the bulbs that are formed underground, tiny bulblets that look like leaves are formed at the tips of the flower stalks. Some of the new bulbs germinate in the fall; others can remain dormant in the soil for a year or two before germination. Wild garlic and onion thrive in heavy soil, and tolerate wet soil. They are hardy to both cold and drought. They spread rapidly and are difficult to control.

CONTROL: In the lawn, control these weeds with ORTHO Weed-B-Gon Lawn Weed Killer, ORTHO Weed-B-Gon Weed Killer, or ORTHO Chickweed, Spurge & Oxalis Killer D. Around trees and shrubs and in flower beds, spot treat with ORTHO Weed-B-Gon Jet Weeder. Treat as soon as the leaves emerge in the spring, or any time the plants are actively growing. Because dormant bulbs sprout at different times, it will probably be necessary to repeat the treatments for the next 2 or 3 years. Hand-digging is impractical, since any bulbs left behind will sprout into new plants.

Nutsedge.

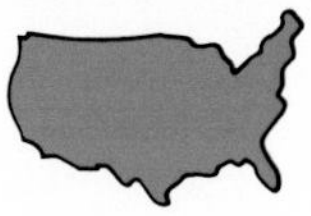

NUTSEDGES

Cyperus species

The two most common nutsedges troublesome as weeds are *yellow nutsedge* (*Cyperus esculentus*) and *purple nutsedge* (*C. rotundus*). Purple nutsedge is primarily a problem in the southeastern and in coastal California. Yellow nutsedge is found throughout the country. These perennials are also called *nutgrass*, *cocosedge*, or *cocograss*. There are also some annual nutsedges that are troublesome in the southeastern United States. Nutsedges prefer poorly drained, rich soil. They thrive in frequently watered garden areas. Nutsedges are particularly noticeable in lawns in the summer, when they grow more quickly than the mowed grass and stand above it. The grasslike, yellow-green leaves grow on erect triangular stems. Seed heads are purple or yellow, appearing from July to October. Nutsedges reproduce by seeds, underground stems, and nutlike tubers. The tubers store food and are drought tolerant.

CONTROL: To control nutsedges in lawns, see page 272. To control existing plants around trees and shrubs and in flower beds and nonplanted areas, use ORTHO Kleenup Ready-To-Use Grass & Weed Killer or ORTHO Kleenup Spot Weed & Grass Killer. Treat as soon as the plants are noticed, preferably before seed heads appear. Nutsedges are difficult to control, so repeated treatments may be necessary. To control nutsedge seeds as they germinate around trees and shrubs and in flower beds, use an herbicide containing *eptam* in the mid to late spring. Hand-pulling is not practical, since any tubers left behind will sprout into new plants.

Bulrush.

BULRUSH

Scirpus species

These perennials, also called *tule* or *meadow rush*, grow from thick tubers, underground rhizomes, or seeds. Olive green, round stems grow 3 to 9 feet tall. Clusters of reddish brown spikelets grow on the tips of the stems from June to October. Seeds produced on these spikelets germinate in the spring and rapidly grow into mature plants. There are several different kinds of bulrush, but all grow in moist, marshy ground in swamps and shallow water and along shores. They are troublesome in cranberry bogs, rice fields, and ornamental ponds. Many cultures use bulrush stems to build small boats and to weave mats.

CONTROL: Treat established plants with an herbicide containing *2,4-D* in the spring before the spikelets appear. Spot treat the stems of individual plants, being careful not to contaminate any surrounding water. Repeated treatments, 3 to 4 weeks apart, are necessary because of the thick rootstocks. Hand-dig young bulrushes before the fleshy tubers or rhizomes form. Or if possible, dry out the area and cultivate to expose and dry the tubers.

RUSHES

Invasive bamboo.

Cattails.

Horsetail.

BAMBOO

Many species of bamboo are aggressive weeds. Creeping types of bamboo in particular can become very invasive. Unlike the slower-spreading clumping bamboos, creeping bamboos form underground rootstocks that spread quickly. The rootstocks grow through the soil and send up shoots every couple of feet. The large types of creeping bamboo are especially vigorous, and are very difficult to control. Removal of the shoot is ineffective because the rootstocks will resprout.

CONTROL: Locate the rootstock where it leaves the original planting. It is usually 2 to 4 inches below the soil surface in a direct line between the invasive shoot and the parent planting. Cut the rootstock and pull it up, with all the shoots attached to it. Prevent reinvasion by surrounding the bamboo planting with an underground barrier. Sink lengths of an impregnable material such as copper or galvanized iron sheeting 12 to 18 inches deep into the soil. Or dig a trench to the same depth and fill it with concrete. Alternatively, spray two or more applications of *glyphosate* (KLEENUP ®) to actively growing bamboo. Do not prune bamboo before spraying.

COMMON CATTAIL
Typha latifolia

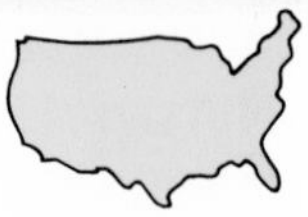

Cattails grow from perennial, creeping rootstocks in swamps, marshes, shallow water, and frequently wet areas. The flat swordlike leaves are pale to grayish green, and 1 inch wide. The plants grow 3 to 8 feet tall. Two types of flowers bloom from May to July. Female flowers are borne on the brown, 8-inch cattails for which the plants are known. Above these are produced the light yellow spikes of male flowers. The brown cattails are used in dried flower arrangements, and by the redwing blackbird in making its nest. Before using freshly picked cattails in flower arrangements, dry in a well-ventilated area to avoid odors.

CONTROL: Cattails are difficult to control because of their vigorous creeping roots. Hand-pulling is not practical because any pieces of root left behind will sprout into new plants. For top kill, use an herbicide containing *diquat*. Apply before the cattails are fully developed. Repeated treatments are necessary to kill the regrowth. For complete elimination of cattails, treat the plants with an herbicide containing *dalapon*, from after the cattails are formed until frost. Do not use around water used for drinking, swimming, irrigation, or washing, or if fish are present. Repeated treatments may be necessary if the plants are firmly established and re-growth occurs.

HORSETAIL
Equisetum species

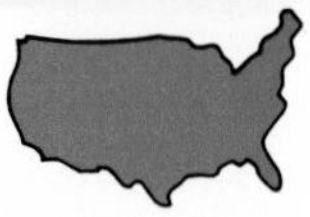

Horsetail is a perennial that grows in wooded areas, roadsides, and stream banks with wet, sandy, or gravelly soil. Two types of stalks—branched and unbranched—grow from the deep, thick rootstocks. The unbranched stalks, topped by cones, appear from April to May. The cones, 1 to 4 inches long, are filled with pale green to yellowish spores. Horsetail reproduces from these spores, as well as from the rootstocks. After the spores mature, these stalks die. From late spring until fall, jointed hollow stalks grow 1 to 3 feet tall. Branches 4 to 6 inches long grow in whorls at the joints on the stalks. These stems are killed by the first frost in the fall. Food is stored in the thick roots to enable the plant to survive under adverse growing conditions.

CONTROL: There are no chemicals that are effective against existing horsetail plants. Dig out the roots, being careful to get them all; any pieces of root or rootstock left in the ground will resprout. Or, if possible, cover the area with a sheet of black plastic for a full year. This will starve the horsetail by preventing light from reaching it. Prevent the spores from germinating in landscaped beds by applying ORTHO Casoron Granules in the late spring as the unbranched stalks die.

Bracken.

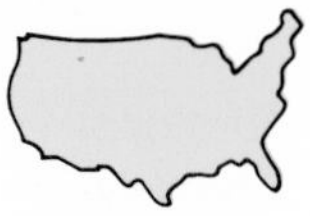

BRACKEN

Pteridium species

Bracken, also known as *brake fern*, is a nonbunching fern that grows from rootstocks that may extend up to 20 feet in the soil. The fronds grow 1 to 4 feet tall directly from the roots. Plants are usually found in clusters or colonies since new plants sprout from the creeping rootstocks. Light brown spores are produced along the margin on the undersides of the fronds. The spores mature in late summer, lie dormant over the winter, and sprout the following spring. Bracken prefers dry, sandy, acid soils in woodlands, pastures, and fields. It sometimes creeps into home gardens from these surrounding areas.

CONTROL: Kill existing bracken with an herbicide containing *glyphosate* (KLEENUP®) any time the plants are actively growing. Hand-pull young bracken. Be sure to get all the rootstocks, as any pieces left behind will sprout into new plants.

Liverworts.

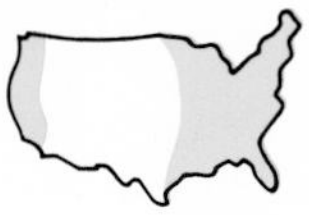

MOSSES, LIVERWORTS, AND ALGAE

Most mosses grow only ¼ of an inch to 2 inches tall. A mat of moss consists of thousands of tiny plants with stems and leaves. They attach themselves to the soil and absorb nutrients through threadlike *rhizoids*, or rootlike structures. Liverworts grow in thin, lobed sheets along the ground. Algae are simple, primitive, freshwater plants that thrive in constantly or frequently wet conditions. Algae may be found growing on wet, compacted soil that is high in nitrogen and organic matter. Both mosses and liverworts grow best in moist, shady areas with acid soil. In cultivated gardens and lawns, they are an indication of excess acidity, poor fertility, or poor drainage or aeration. Mosses, liverworts, and algae sometimes grow on pavement and structures.

CONTROL: Remove mosses and liverworts from lawns and gardens by hand-raking. Reduce shade by pruning nearby trees. Improve soil fertility with regular fertilization, and follow the guidelines on page 907 to improve soil drainage. Correct pH is necessary (see page 908). Large patches of moss also may be removed by "burning" with *ferrous ammonium sulfate*. Apply to damp moss in early spring. Surrounding lawn grass may darken for about a week. Patches of algae may be sprayed with *maneb, mancozeb,* or *wettable sulfur* two times, 1 month apart, in early spring. Prevent algae from returning by reducing soil compaction (see page 907) and pruning nearby vegetation to reduce shading. Remove mosses, liverworts, and algae from structures by treating with a soap or compound containing *potassium salts*.

Virginia peppergrass.

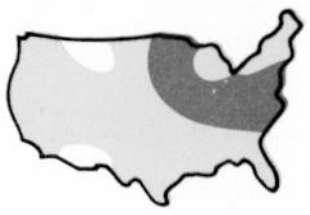

VIRGINIA PEPPERGRASS

Lepidium virginicum

This annual grass, also known as *bird's pepper* or *tonguegrass*, grows 1 to 2 feet tall with slightly hairy, branched stems. The blades are toothed and 1 to 3 inches long. Very small white flowers with greenish petals bloom from May to November. They produce seeds in ½-inch reddish yellow pods. Seedpods and flowers are usually present on the plant at the same time. Peppergrass is usually found along roadsides and in waste places and fields. It grows in most soils, but is more troublesome in dry areas. In home gardens, it frequently sprouts in landscaped beds, lawns, and cracks in walkways.

CONTROL: Eliminate peppergrass in lawns with ORTHO Chickweed, Spurge & Oxalis Killer D. Treat when the plants are actively growing in the spring or early summer, preferably before the flowers and seedpods appear. To prevent peppergrass seeds from germinating in landscaped beds, use a pre-emergence herbicide containing *diphenamid*. Apply to the soil in early spring about the time of the last expected frost, or when the forsythia bloom. In nonplanted areas, kill existing weeds with an herbicide containing *linuron*. Treat in the spring when the plants are actively growing. Peppergrass plants have shallow roots and can be hand-pulled.

BROADLEAF WEEDS

Klamath weed.

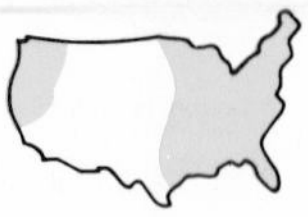

KLAMATH WEED
Hypericum perforatum

Klamath weed, also known as *St. Johnswort*, is a perennial that reproduces by seeds and short runners. These horizontal stems grow from the crown of the plant out along the soil or just below it. The roots grow deep in the soil. The main upright stems are branched, and grow 1 to 2 feet tall. The ½ to 1-inch-long, oblong leaves are marked with clear dots. From June to September, flowers ¾ inch in diameter bloom and produce seeds. The flowers are orange-yellow with black dots along the edges of the petals. Black fruit capsules are evident from late summer into the fall. Each contains several seeds that lie dormant over the winter, and sprout in the spring. The tops of the plants die back to the ground in cold weather. Klamath weed is poisonous to livestock that graze on it. It prefers dry, sandy, or gravelly soil in fields and pastures and along roadways. In home gardens, it may become established in landscaped beds and unmaintained areas.

CONTROL: Around trees and shrubs and in flower beds, nonplanted areas, and lawns, kill existing weeds with an herbicide containing *glyphosate* (KLEENUP®). Repeated applications are often necessary because of this plant's deep root system.

Wild mustard.

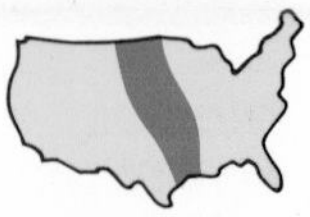

WILD MUSTARD
Brassica kaber

Wild mustard is an annual also known as *field mustard* or *charlock*. The erect stems grow 1 to 3 feet tall, and have bristly hairs at their base. The upper portion is branched. The lower leaves are irregularly lobed or toothed, and the upper leaves are oval. From May to August, yellow clusters of flowers bloom and produce seeds. Severely infested fields appear completely yellow. Seeds lie dormant in the soil for 1 or more years, germinating in the spring or fall. Although primarily troublesome in grain fields in the Midwest, wild mustard may also occur in home gardens throughout the country.

CONTROL: In lawns, kill existing weeds with ORTHO Chickweed & Clover Control or ORTHO Chickweed, Spurge & Oxalis Killer D. Treat any time the plants are actively growing, but preferably before they bloom and produce seeds. Around trees and shrubs, prevent the seeds from sprouting with ORTHO Casoron Granules. Apply in early fall or in early spring before the seeds germinate. Wild mustard has a shallow root system, and can be removed by hand-pulling or hoeing.

Russian thistle.

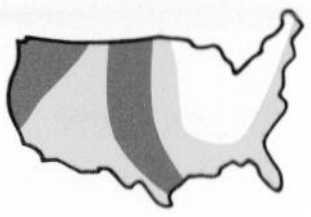

RUSSIAN THISTLE
Salsola kali var. tenuifolia

A native of eastern Europe, this annual is also known as *tumbleweed*. The plants grow ½ to 3 feet tall with reddish, spreading, or erect stems. The leaves on seedlings and younger plants are fleshy and cylindrical. As the leaves mature they drop, and stiff, narrow leaves ending in a spike appear. From July to October, greenish flowers bloom and produce seeds throughout the plant. Each plant produces thousands of seeds. When the plants mature in early fall, they break off at the soil line and tumble about, distributing the seeds. Russian thistle prefers areas with dry soil along roadways, fields, and unmaintained areas. It is a host to the beet leafhopper, which spreads *curly top*, a plant disease.

CONTROL: Eliminate Russian thistle in lawns with ORTHO Weed-B-Gon Lawn Weed Killer. To prevent seeds from germinating around trees and shrubs and in flower beds, use a pre-emergence weed killer containing *trifluralin*. Apply to the soil in the spring about the time of the last frost, or 2 weeks after the forsythia bloom.

Spanishneedles.

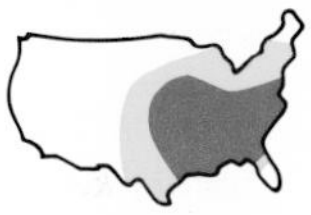

SPANISHNEEDLES
Bidens bipinnata

Spanishneedles, also known as *cuckold,* is a summer annual. The stems grow erect 1 to 5 feet tall, with the upper portion branched. Leaves are smooth, segmented, and 4 to 8 inches long. From July to October, flowers with yellow centers and white petals bloom on the ends of leafless branches. They produce ½-inch long, brown to black seeds with spines and bristles. These seeds lie dormant in the soil over the winter, sprouting in the spring. The plants are killed with the first frost in the fall. Spanishneedles grows in moist or wet places and in areas with sandy soil. Although native to fields and woodlots, it is occasionally found in yards and gardens.

CONTROL: Plants have somewhat shallow roots, and can be hand-pulled. Around trees and shrubs and in lawns, prevent Spanishneedles with a preemergence herbicide containing *simazine.* Apply to the soil 2 weeks before the last expected frost, or about the time the forsythia bloom.

Puncturevine.

PUNCTUREVINE
Tribulus terrestris

Puncturevine, also called *caltrop* or *ground burnut,* is an annual weed found in dry sandy areas. The prostrate stems branch from the crown of the plant, forming dense mats that crowd out desirable plants. The stems grow 6 to 8 feet long, and may twine up buildings and fences. Oblong leaves, 1 to 2 inches long, consist of 5 to 8 pairs of oval leaflets. Both the stems and the leaves are covered with silken hairs, giving the plants a silvery appearance. Small yellow flowers bloom in the leaf axils from June to September. They open only in the morning on clear days. They are followed by pods consisting of 5¼-inch spiny burs. When the burs mature, they separate and fall to the soil, where they may lie for several years before germinating. The burs are able to puncture shoe leather and bicycle and automobile tires. They not only injure animals by sticking in their feet, but also adhere to their fur, and are spread from place to place. The plant develops from a short taproot that branches into many fine rootlets, enabling it to survive periods of drought.

CONTROL: Treat puncturevine around trees, shrubs, and buildings and in nonplanted areas with ORTHO Kleenup Systemic Weed & Grass Killer. For best results, treat before burs are produced. To prevent seedlings from becoming established, apply a pre-emergence herbicide containing *trifluralin* or *dichlobenil* (CASORON®) to the soil before seedlings emerge.

Redstem filaree.

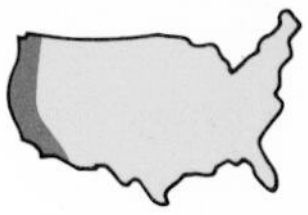

REDSTEM FILAREE
Erodium cicutarium

Redstem filaree is a low-growing spreading annual or biennial with stems 3 to 12 inches long and fernlike, dark green leaves, ½ to 4 inches long. Both the stems and leaves are hairy. Plants form a rosette, especially when young. Rose-purple clusters of flowers bloom and produce seeds from April to June. Because the seeds are inside capsules with one long pointed end, resembling a crane's beak, this plant is also known as *cranesbill* or *storksbill.* When mature, the capsules fall to the soil. In alternately moist and dry weather, the beaks coil and uncoil, gradually planting themselves. Seeds sprout in the fall, or remain dormant until spring. Redstem filaree thrives in dry soil. It is most commonly found in lawns, but also occurs in landscaped beds and cracks in walkways.

CONTROL: To kill existing weeds around trees and shrubs and in flower beds and nonplanted areas, use ORTHO Kleenup Systemic Weed & Grass Killer. In lawns, use an herbicide containing *2,4-D.* For best results, treat in the spring before the flowers appear and produce seeds. Prevent redstem filaree from returning by using a pre-emergence herbicide containing *trifluralin* or *DCPA* (DACTHAL®). Apply to the soil in early fall or spring before seeds sprout. Keep redstem filaree from returning to the lawn by increasing the lawn's fertility. Follow the fertilization guidelines on page 251. Redstem filaree can be hand-pulled or hoed when small.

BROADLEAF WEEDS

Wild carrot.

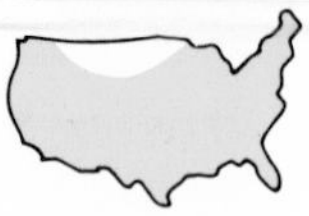

WILD CARROT

Daucus carota

Wild carrot, also called *Queen Anne's lace* or *bird's nest plant*, is a biennial that grows in a rosette the first year. The second year, hollow, branching stems grow 2 to 3 feet high. The fleshy, carrot-shaped root is not edible. The finely dissected leaves give the plant a lacy appearance. Flat-tipped clusters of white or pinkish flowers bloom and produce seeds from May to October. The seeds lie dormant in the soil over the winter, and sprout in early spring. At the end of the second year, the entire plant is killed by the first frost in the fall. Wild carrot prefers dry soil in fields and meadows and along roadways. It is occasionally found in landscaped beds and lawns.

CONTROL: Kill existing weeds in landscaped beds and in nonplanted and unmaintained areas with ORTHO Kleenup Ready-To-Use Grass & Weed Killer. Treat any time the plants are actively growing, but preferably before they bloom. In lawns, treat wild carrot with ORTHO Weed-B-Gon Lawn Weed Killer or ORTHO Weed-B-Gon Weed Killer in the spring and fall. Young plants can be hand-pulled or hoed.

Common yarrow.

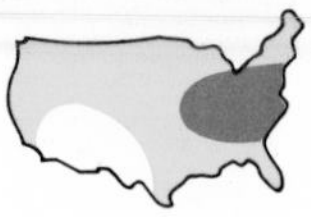

COMMON YARROW

Achillea millefolium

Common yarrow, also called *milfoil*, is a perennial that grows 1 to 3 feet tall. If it occurs in mowed lawns, it forms a rosette. The fernlike leaves are covered with fine gray hairs, and are aromatic when crushed. The flattened flower heads are white or yellow, and bloom and produce seeds from June to November. It reproduces by creeping underground rootstocks as well as by seeds. Yarrow flowers are sometimes dried and used in flower arrangements. Some other species of *Achillea* are valued as ornamental perennials. Yarrow is most common in gardens bordering roadways, fields, and vacant lots, and thrives in poor, dry soil where few plants can survive.

CONTROL: Eliminate yarrow in lawns with ORTHO Weed-B-Gon Lawn Weed Killer or ORTHO Chickweed, Spurge & Oxalis Killer D. Treat any time the plants are actively growing, from spring to fall. In flower beds and vegetable gardens and around trees and shrubs, dig the plants while still young before flowers bloom and seeds form.

Cudweed.

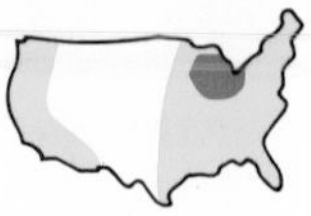

CUDWEED

Gnaphalium species

Cudweed, also called *fragrant everlasting* or *cotton batting plant*, is an annual or biennial. The stems branch at their base and grow ½ to 2 feet tall. They are woolly-white, and fragrant when rubbed. The lance-shaped leaves are also fragrant and woolly on the underside. The top is smooth and dark green. Tubular white, tan, or purple flowers bloom and produce seeds in August and September. They appear at the ends of the branches and in the axils of the upper leaves. Seeds lie dormant in the soil over the winter, sprouting in the cool, moist spring weather. They grow slowly in the summer heat, resuming normal growth in late summer until the first killing frost in the fall. Cudweed grows in moist or dry soil. It is most commonly found along roadways and in fields and wooded lots, but may appear in lawns and landscaped beds.

CONTROL: Use ORTHO Kleenup Ready-To-Use Grass & Weed Killer to control existing cudweed in lawns and around trees and shrubs in flower beds and nonplanted areas. For spot treating a few individual clumps in lawns, use ORTHO Weed-B-Gon Weed Killer. Treat any time the plants are actively growing, but preferably in the spring before they bloom and produce seeds. For overall lawn treatment, use ORTHO Weed-B-Gon For Southern Grasses or an herbicide containing *2,4-D* and *dicamba*. Treat in the spring when the plants are growing most rapidly.

Pineappleweed.

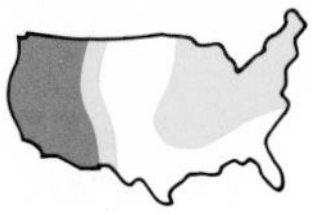

PINEAPPLEWEED
Matricaria matricarioides

The stems and leaves of this annual have a pleasant pineapple fragrance when crushed. Many stems, 6 to 18 inches tall, grow from the base of the plant. The finely dissected leaves grow 1 to 4 inches long. Greenish yellow, ¼-inch flowers bloom at the ends of the branches from May to September. The seeds they produce do not sprout until early the following spring. Pineappleweed grows along roadsides, in fields, waste places, and sometimes in landscaped beds. It tolerates many types of soil, and frequently grows where other plants do not survive.

CONTROL: To kill established plants around trees and shrubs, in flower beds and unplanted areas, and to spot treat in lawns, use an herbicide containing *glyphosate* (KLEENUP®). Use ORTHO Casoron Granules to prevent pineappleweed seeds from sprouting around trees and shrubs. Apply in the early spring about 2 weeks before the last expected frost, or when the forsythia bloom. Regular mowing will help control pineappleweed in lawns. The plants have shallow roots, and can be hand-pulled or hoed, especially when young and the soil is moist.

Mayweed.

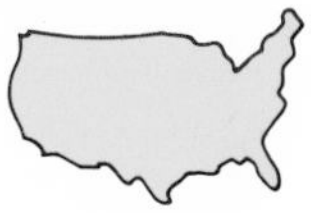

MAYWEED
Anthemis cotula

This annual weed is also called *dog fennel* or *stinkweed.* The erect stems grow ½ to 2 feet tall with a short, thick taproot. The 1 to 3-inch long, fernlike leaves have a pungent odor when crushed. Daisylike flowers, ¼ to ½ inch in diameter, have yellow centers with white petals. They bloom and produce seeds from May to October. The seeds lie dormant in the soil over the winter, and sprout in the spring. The plants die with the first killing frost in the fall. In warm weather areas, seeds germinate in both the spring and fall. Those which germinate in the fall grow through the winter and flower in the spring. Mayweed grows in fields and gardens with rich, gravelly soil.

CONTROL: Eliminate mayweed by spot treating around trees and shrubs in lawns, around trees and flower beds, and nonplanted areas with ORTHO Kleenup Systemic Weed & Grass Killer or ORTHO Kleenup Ready-To-Use Grass & Weed Killer. Treat any time the plants are actively growing, but preferably before they flower and produce seeds. Plants can be hoed or hand-pulled.

Prostrate knotweed.

PROSTRATE KNOTWEED
Polygonum aviculare

This annual weed is also called *knotgrass, doorweed,* and *matgrass.* It grows in areas with compacted, infertile soil, such as driveways, dirt walkways, and recreation areas where the soil and grass are heavily trampled. Oval, bluish green leaves, 1 inch long and ¼ inch wide, are attached to the stems at swollen joints. Very tiny greenish white flowers bloom and produce seeds at the leaf and stem joints from June to November. The seeds produced by these flowers remain dormant over the winter and germinate in the spring as the soil warms. Prostrate knotweed grows low to the ground, forming dense wiry mats up to 2 feet in diameter that crowd out desirable plants.

CONTROL: For overall treatment in lawns, use ORTHO Weed-B-Gon Lawn Weed Killer. Spot treat with ORTHO Weed-B-Gon Jet Weeder. To help prevent knotweed in the lawn, maintain a vigorous turf by following the guidelines beginning on page 250. Around trees and shrubs kill existing weeds with ORTHO Kleenup Systemic Weed & Grass Killer or ORTHO Kleenup Ready-To-Use Grass & Weed Killer. Or prevent the weeds in the early spring with ORTHO Casoron Granules. Cultivating is also helpful. In driveways, walkways, and other nonplanted areas, use ORTHO Kleenup Systemic Weed & Grass Killer. Prevent knotweed in flower and vegetable gardens with an herbicide containing *trifluralin,* applied in the spring before the weeds germinate. Knotweed may also be hand-pulled or hoed.

BROADLEAF WEEDS

Common chickweed.

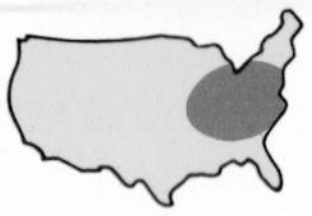

COMMON CHICKWEED
Stellaria media

This weed, also called *starwort, satin flower*, or *starweed*, prefers damp, shady areas with rich cultivated soil. Common chickweed is a winter annual that grows from seeds that sprout in the fall. It grows vigorously in cool wet weather, forming a dense mat that crowds out desirable plants. The ½ to 2-inch heart-shaped leaves are attached to the stems by a slightly hairy stalk. Fine white hairs grow in a single line on one side of the stem. The creeping stems root at their joints wherever they touch the soil. Small, white, starlike flowers bloom in clusters on the ends of the stems from March to December. In mild winter areas they bloom and produce seeds throughout the winter. Seeds are carried by birds and by the wind.

CONTROL: In lawns, control chickweed with ORTHO Weed-B-Gon Lawn Weed Killer, ORTHO Chickweed & Clover Control, or ORTHO Chickweed, Spurge & Oxalis Killer D. To help prevent chickweed in lawns, maintain a vigorous turf by following the guidelines beginning on page 250. Around trees and shrubs, and in nonplanted areas, kill existing weeds with ORTHO Kleenup Systemic Weed & Grass Killer. Apply these herbicides to actively growing plants in the early spring or late fall just after they have sprouted. Cultivating is also helpful. Prevent weeds from returning around trees and shrubs with ORTHO Casoron Granules. Prevent chickweed in vegetable gardens and flower gardens with ORTHO Garden Weed Preventer. Apply in the fall before the seeds sprout.

Creeping veronica.

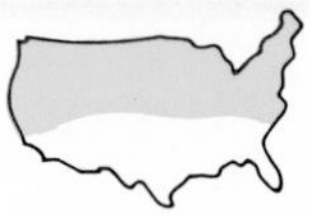

CREEPING VERONICA
Veronica filiformis

Creeping veronica, also called *speedwell*, is a perennial weed that prefers acid soil in moist, shady garden areas. It is found in sunny areas if the soil remains moist. Areas that are well fertilized, well drained, and get lots of sunlight are not invaded by this weed. Creeping veronica was originally used as a rock garden plant, but over the years has become a nuisance by invading lawns and flower beds. Oval bright green leaves with scalloped edges are paired opposite each other on low-growing creeping stems. Tiny white flowers with blue or lavender edges bloom from May to July. Seeds are produced in heart-shaped pods. The seeds seldom mature, so the plant does not reproduce from them. The creeping stems, however, root easily wherever the stem joints touch the soil. Pieces of stem cut and distributed by lawn mowers also root to start new plants. If uncontrolled, veronica can cover an entire lawn or flower bed within a few years. However, it does not completely crowd out other plants.

CONTROL: Creeping veronica is difficult to control. In lawns, treat with ORTHO Chickweed, Spurge & Oxalis Killer D or ORTHO Weed-B-Gon Lawn Weed Killer. In landscaped beds and flower beds, treat in the spring or early fall with an herbicide containing *DCPA* (DACTHAL®). Veronica dies slowly, so repeated applications may be necessary. Veronica can also be hand-pulled, removing all parts of the plant so new plants do not emerge.

Florida pusley.

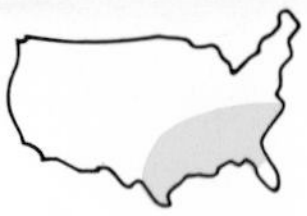

FLORIDA PUSLEY
Richardia scabra

This annual is also known as *Florida purslane* or *Mexican clover*. The hairy stems grow 4 to 12 inches tall, and are tinged with red. The leaves are oblong, 1 to 3 inches long, and are also hairy. Starlike white flowers bloom in the leaf axils at the ends of the branches from May to September. The seeds produced by these flowers do not germinate until the following spring. Florida pusley thrives in sandy soils in the warm southern states. This weed hugs the ground, forming dense patches that crowd out desirable plants, especially lawn grasses. It also grows in landscaped beds and cracks in walkways.

CONTROL: In lawns, eliminate Florida pusley with ORTHO Weed-B-Gon Lawn Weed Killer, ORTHO Weed-B-Gon Weed Killer, or ORTHO Weed-B-Gon For Southern Grasses. Use ORTHO Kleenup Systemic Weed & Grass Killer to kill existing weeds around trees and shrubs, in nonplanted areas, and to spot treat in lawns. Treat when the weeds are actively growing. For best results, apply before the plants flower and produce seeds for the following year. To prevent Florida pusley seeds from germinating throughout the yard, apply ORTHO Garden Weed Preventer to the soil in early spring, 2 weeks before the last expected frost, or when the forsythia bloom. Florida pusley has shallow roots and can be hand-pulled or hoed.

Purslane.

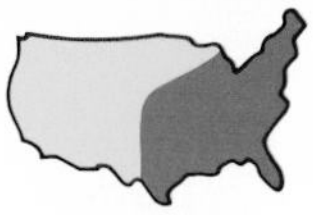

PURSLANE

Portulaca oleracea

Purslane, also called *wild portulaca* or *pusley*, is a particularly troublesome weed in vegetable and flower gardens. This summer annual thrives in hot, dry weather and is seldom found in the spring when gardeners are controlling other weeds. Leaves are ½ to 1½ inches long, rubbery, and wedge-shaped. Small yellow flowers open only in full sunlight from midsummer to frost. The seeds may remain viable in the soil for many years, and will sprout in warm weather when brought to the surface during plowing or cultivating. The thick reddish brown stems grow vigorously, forming a thick mat and rooting wherever they touch the soil. The stems and leaves store water that enables purslane to survive drought periods, and to grow in cracks in sidewalks and driveways. Plants pulled and allowed to lie on the soil will reroot. Plants are killed by the first frost in the fall.

CONTROL: In lawns, control purslane with ORTHO Weed-B-Gon Lawn Weed Killer, ORTHO Weed-B-Gon For Southern Grasses, or spot treat with ORTHO Weed-B-Gon Jet Weeder. To help prevent purslane in the lawn, maintain a vigorous turf by following the guidelines beginning on page 250. Kill existing weeds around trees and shrubs and in driveways and flower beds with ORTHO Kleenup Systemic Weed & Grass Killer. Keep weeds from returning around trees and shrubs with ORTHO Casoron Granules. Prevent weeds from sprouting in vegetable and flower gardens with ORTHO Garden Weed Preventer. Purslane may also be hand-pulled. Remove the plants from the garden.

Spotted spurge.

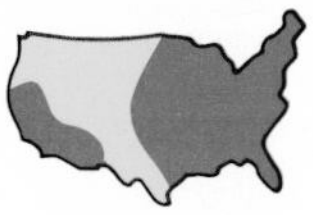

SPOTTED SPURGE

Euphorbia maculata

This annual weed, also called *milk purslane*, thrives in infertile soil and in sandy, poorly maintained areas. It is often found in lawns and shrub beds, and in cracks in walkways and driveways. Spurge is a low-growing plant that may form dense mats up to 2 feet in diameter. Leaves are oval, ¼ to ¾ inch long, and pale to dark green with a purple smudge. The slender reddish stems ooze a milky white sap when broken. The sap may irritate the skin. Pinkish white flowers bloom and produce seeds from May to October. Many of the seeds remain dormant over the winter and sprout the following spring. Some sprout immediately. Plants may complete one generation within 2 weeks. They die with the first frost in the fall.

CONTROL: For overall lawn treatment, use ORTHO Weed-B-Gon Lawn Weed Killer or ORTHO Chickweed, Spurge & Oxalis Killer D. To spot treat weeds in lawns, use ORTHO Weed-B-Gon Weed Killer. Kill existing weeds around trees and shrubs and in walkways and driveways with ORTHO Kleenup Systemic Weed & Grass Killer. Treat spurge any time the plants are actively growing in the spring and summer. Do not treat in the fall, since the plants will be killed anyway by the first frost. Prevent spurge seeds from germinating in lawns, flower beds, and landscaped beds with an herbicide containing *DCPA* (DACTHAL®). ORTHO Casoron Granules can also be used to prevent the seeds from sprouting around trees and shrubs. These shallow-rooted plants can also be hand-pulled or hoed. Because spotted spurge forms seeds when only 2 weeks old, it is especially important to follow a regular control program.

Mouseear chickweed.

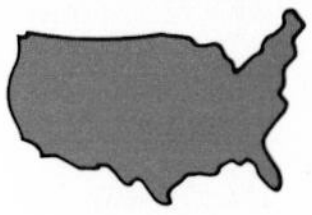

MOUSEEAR CHICKWEED

Cerastium vulgatum

This perennial weed is troublesome throughout the United States in lawns, vegetable and flower gardens, around trees and shrubs, and in nonplanted areas. It thrives in full sunlight on wet, infertile soil. The hairy leaves are ½ inch long and lance-shaped. Starlike white flowers bloom and produce seeds from April to October. These low-growing plants root easily wherever their stem joints touch the soil, starting new plants. Seeds germinate throughout the growing season, rapidly increasing the number of plants. Dense mats of mouseear chickweed crowd out desirable plants.

CONTROL: For overall lawn treatment use ORTHO Weed-B-Gon Lawn Weed Killer when plants are actively growing in the early spring and fall. Or spot treat with ORTHO Weed-B-Gon Weed Killer or ORTHO Weed-B-Gon Jet Weeder. Around trees and shrubs, and in flower beds, kill existing weeds with ORTHO Kleenup Systemic Weed & Grass Killer or ORTHO Kleenup Spot Weed & Grass Killer. To prevent mouseear chickweed seeds from germinating around trees and shrubs, use ORTHO Casoron Granules. Mouseear chickweed is difficult to control, so repeated treatments may be necessary. These shallow-rooted plants can also be hand-pulled or hoed, but be sure to remove all parts of the plants so they do not resprout.

Lippia.

LIPPIA

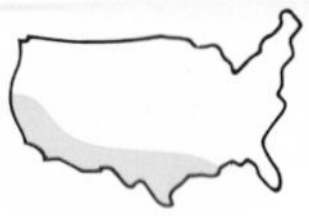

Phyla nodiflora

This perennial, also known as *matchweed* or *matgrass*, is used in hot, dry areas as a groundcover or lawn substitute. The creeping stems grow 1 to 3 feet long, and root wherever their nodes touch the soil, forming dense mats that crowd out desirable plants. Lippia has wedge-shaped, slightly hairy leaves up to 1¾ inches long. The edges are toothed. Bees are attracted to the white or pink flowers that bloom on oblong heads from late spring through early summer. In the sun, lippia grows 1 to 2 inches tall; in the shade, it grows up to 6 inches tall. Lippia grows vigorously, creeping from its planted areas into surrounding areas.

CONTROL: In lawns, eliminate lippia with ORTHO Weed-B-Gon Lawn Weed Killer. In landscaped beds and noncrop areas, treat with an herbicide containing *glyphosate* (KLEENUP®). Apply in the spring or fall. The plants have shallow roots, and can also be hand-pulled.

Dichondra.

DICHONDRA

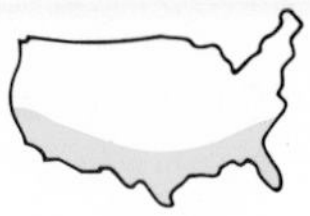

Dichondra repens

This popular grass substitute in the South and West sometimes becomes a weed when it creeps into nondichondra lawns and landscaped beds. Dichondra is a broadleafed perennial with heart-shaped, rounded leaves ¼ to ½ inch in diameter. The leaves are attached to the stems opposite each other. The creeping stems root wherever the nodes touch the soil. Inconspicuous flowers produce seeds that may remain in the soil for many years before sprouting. Dichondra will not grow where temperatures fall below 25°F. It grows in both sun and shade, but prefers fertile soil in areas that are watered frequently. Dichondra seldom grows in areas that are not maintained.

CONTROL: Eliminate dichondra in nondichondra lawns with ORTHO Weed-B-Gon Lawn Weed Killer or ORTHO Weed-B-Gon For Southern Grasses. Treat any time the plants are actively growing. Or use ORTHO Garden Weed Preventer containing *DCPA* (DACTHAL®). Several applications may be necessary. Dichondra has shallow roots, and can be removed by hand in landscaped beds and other areas.

Oxalis.

OXALIS

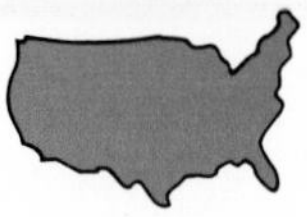

Oxalis species

Some oxalis are grown for ornamental purposes, but two, *Oxalis stricta* and *O. corniculata*, are common weeds throughout the yard and in greenhouses. Also called *yellow woodsorrel* or *sourgrass*, these perennials grow most commonly in well-maintained areas. The pale green or purple leaves are divided into three heart-shaped leaflets, like clover leaves. The leaflets usually close up at night. Small, bright yellow flowers, ½ inch long with 5 petals, bloom from May to September. Cucumber-shaped light green seed pods develop from the fading flowers. When the pods dry, a light touch causes them to explode, shooting their seeds several feet in all directions. The seeds germinate throughout the growing season. Plants grow 4 to 12 inches tall. Although the stems root wherever they touch the soil, new plants do not form at these spots. Oxalis leaves contain oxalic acid, which gives them a sour taste.

CONTROL: In lawns, treat oxalis with ORTHO Chickweed, Spurge & Oxalis Killer D or ORTHO Weed-B-Gon Lawn Weed Killer. Around trees and shrubs, flower beds, driveways, and other nonplanted areas, kill the weeds with ORTHO Kleenup Systemic Weed & Grass Killer or ORTHO Kleenup Spot Weed & Grass Killer. Treat weeds when they are actively growing in the spring or late summer to fall. The late summer to fall application is the most effective. Oxalis is not easy to kill, so several treatments may be necessary. Oxalis can also be hand-pulled or hoed if it is done before rooting occurs on stems.

Black medic.

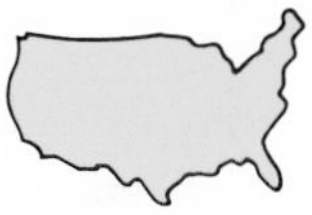

BLACK MEDIC
Medicago lupulina

Black medic, sometimes called *black clover* or *trefoil*, is frequently confused with clover. The low-growing, hairy, trailing stems of this summer or winter annual form dense mats that crowd out desirable plants. Cloverlike leaves grow in threes on the stems. Small bright yellow flowers bloom and produce seeds in black, kidney-shaped pods from May to September. In warm-weather areas, blooming may last until December. Seeds lie dormant in the soil, sprouting in the spring, and, in warm-weather areas, also in the fall. Black medic grows in lawns with low nitrogen fertility, in gardens, and in cracks in sidewalks and driveways.

CONTROL: Eliminate black medic in lawns with ORTHO Chickweed, Spurge & Oxalis Killer D, ORTHO Weed-B-Gon Lawn Weed Killer, or ORTHO Weed-B-Gon For Southern Grasses. Treat from late spring to early summer or midfall when the weeds are actively growing, and preferably before seeds form. In landscaped beds and nonplanted areas, kill existing weeds with ORTHO Kleenup Systemic Weed & Grass Killer. Prevent black medic from becoming established by mulching landscaped beds as discussed on page 926. Where appropriate, improve the nitrogen fertility with regular fertilization to reduce black medic invasion. Black medic can also be hand-pulled.

Wild violets.

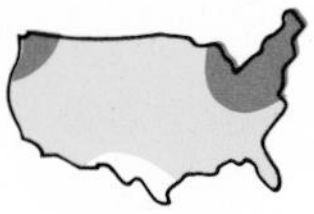

WILD VIOLET
Viola species

Wild violet, also called *violet, field pansy*, or *hearts-ease*, is an annual or short-lived perennial with dense, fibrous roots. The leaves emerge from the crown of the plant on long, angular leafstalks, forming a rosette from 6 to 24 inches tall. The leaves are dark green, heart-shaped, or almost round, and 1 to 2½ inches long with slightly saw-toothed edges. Small flowers resembling florist's violets are individually borne on slender flower stalks. The flowers may be pale yellow, purple, white, or a combination of these colors. The plants bloom from April to June and produce seed from May to July. Wild violets produce seeds that sprout in spring, or in fall and spring in mild-winter areas. The plants often produce small bulblets in the fall that resprout the following spring. Wild violets thrive in moist shaded or semi-shaded conditions. They are a persistent weed in partially-shaded lawns and planting beds.

CONTROL: Spot treat wild violets with an herbicide containing *glyphosate* (KLEENUP®). Violets are persistent, so retreatment probably will be necessary. Apply ORTHO Garden Weed Preventer in early spring to prevent seeds from sprouting. In warm winter areas, apply ORTHO Garden Weed Preventer in late fall and early spring.

Ground ivy.

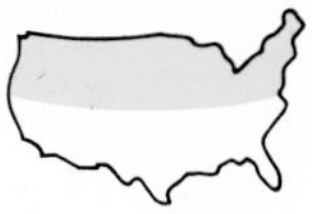

GROUND IVY
Glechoma hederacea

Ground ivy, a perennial, is also called *creeping ivy, creeping charlie*, and *gill-over-the-ground*. It was originally planted in many areas as a shade tolerant ground cover, but has since become a nuisance, invading lawns and landscaped areas. Rounded, scalloped leaves, about the size of a nickel or quarter, grow opposite each other on creeping stems. Light blue to purple flowers, ½ to ¾ inch long, bloom and produce seeds from April to July. These seeds germinate as soon as they ripen. Ground ivy also reproduces by the creeping stems that root wherever they touch the soil. It has shallow roots and forms a dense mat, crowding out desirable plants. Ground ivy prefers damp, shady areas with rich soil, but may also grow in the sun.

CONTROL: Control ground ivy in the lawn with ORTHO Weed-B-Gon Lawn Weed Killer or spot treat with ORTHO Weed-B-Gon Weed Killer or ORTHO Weed-B-Gon Jet Weeder. Around trees and shrubs and nonplanted areas, use an herbicide containing *glyphosate* (KLEENUP®). Treat any time the plants are actively growing, but preferably in the spring when the leaves are still tender. If ground ivy has grown into a dense mat, annual treatments may be necessary for the next 2 to 3 years. Although ground ivy has shallow roots, hand-pulling is not a practical solution. Any pieces of stem left behind in the soil will sprout into new plants.

BROADLEAF WEEDS

Lawn pennywort.

LAWN PENNYWORT

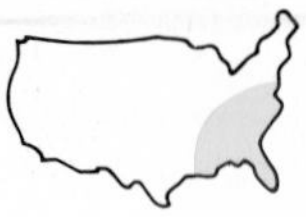

Hydrocotyle sibthorpioides

Lawn pennywort is a member of the parsley family. It is a perennial that has bright green, ½ inch, rounded leaves with wavy margins. Small white flowers bloom from July to August. The creeping stems root wherever their nodes touch the soil, increasing the number of plants. If not controlled, pennywort can form dense mats that crowd out desirable plants. Pennywort grows in moist, shady lawns, gardens, and nonplanted areas. It is frequently mistaken for ground ivy (previous column). Some gardeners prefer to allow pennywort to grow as a shade-toler-ant groundcover rather than try to eliminate it.

CONTROL: In lawns, control pennywort with ORTHO Weed-B-Gon Lawn Weed Killer or spot treat with ORTHO Weed-B-Gon Weed Killer or ORTHO Weed-B-Gon Jet Weeder. Around trees and shrubs and in flower beds and nonplanted areas, kill existing weeds with ORTHO Kleenup Systemic Weed & Grass Killer. Treat weeds any time they are actively growing, from late spring to fall. In vegetable gardens, remove weeds by hand-digging. Be careful to remove all the stem pieces so they do not resprout into new plants.

Mallow.

MALLOW

Malva species

These weeds, also called cheeseweed, cheeses, or musk plant, are found in lawns, fields, vacant lots, and landscaped beds throughout the country. They are annuals, or—in warmer climates—biennials. Although mallow tolerates all types of soil, it prefers infertile, poorly maintained areas. The hairy stems grow from several inches to a foot or more in length. They may grow from close to the soil to 3 to 6 feet tall. The taproot is straight and deep. The hairy, round, heart-shaped leaves are ½ to 5 inches wide. The edges are slightly lobed. From April to October, flowers with 5 white to lavender petals bloom at the leaf and stem joints. Mallow reproduces by seeds that remain dormant in the soil over the winter and germinate in the spring. The plants are killed by the first frost in the fall. In warmer climates, the plant survives the winter and grows and flowers a second year.

CONTROL: In lawns, eliminate mallow with ORTHO Weed-B-Gon Lawn Weed Killer or ORTHO Chickweed, Spurge & Oxalis Killer D. Around trees and shrubs and in flower beds and nonplanted areas, treat existing weeds with ORTHO Kleenup Systemic Weed & Grass Killer. Treat with these herbicides from midspring to early summer when the plants are still young, and before they produce flowers and seeds for next year's generation. Follow the lawn maintenance guidelines beginning on page 250 to help prevent mallow from becoming established in the lawn.

Prickly lettuce.

PRICKLY LETTUCE

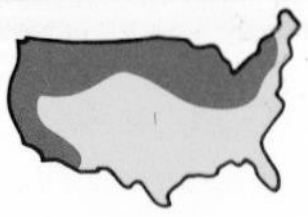

Lactuca serriola

Prickly lettuce, also known as wild lettuce, is an annual or biennial. Pale green or straw-colored stems grow 1½ to 6 feet tall. The lower part is covered with prickly spines. The lower leaves are 2 to 12 inches long and lobed, with prickly edges. The upper leaves are short, elongated, and lobed or prickly toothed. Both kinds of leaves are bluish green with prickles on the midrib. A milky sap oozes from the leaves and taproot when they are broken. Prickly lettuce reproduces by seeds that are formed on flowers that bloom from July to September. These yellow flowers are ⅓ inch in diameter and bloom at the ends of the lateral stems. When the seeds are mature, they fall to the soil and either sprout in the fall or, in colder areas, the following spring. Prickly lettuce prefers areas with dry or light soil, and is troublesome along roadways and in fields, walkways, and unmaintained areas.

CONTROL: Control this weed in lawns with ORTHO Chickweed, Spurge & Oxalis Killer D. Around trees and shrubs, in flower beds and nonplanted areas, and to spot treat in lawns, use ORTHO Kleenup Ready-To-Use Grass & Weed Killer. Apply either herbicide when the plants are actively growing, preferably before they bloom and produce seeds.

Curly dock.

Ladysthumb.

Broadleaf plantain.

CURLY DOCK
Rumex crispus

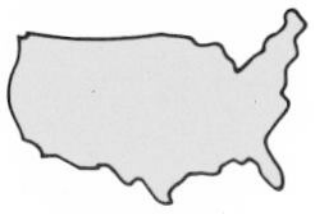

Curly dock, a persistent perennial, is also called *sour dock* or *yellow dock*. Plants may be found anywhere in the yard, except in the shade. Curly dock prefers wet, low areas with heavy soil. The curly leaves, which form a rosette, are 6 to 12 inches long and reddish green. A 2 to 3-foot stalk with green to brown flowers grows from June to September. The flowers turn dark brown and dry and cling to the stalk. Seeds produced by these flowers fall to the soil and remain dormant over the winter, sprouting in the spring and summer. The plant tops are killed in the fall by the first frost. The thick, yellow taproot is drought resistant and very difficult to dig from the soil. It remains dormant over the winter and resprouts in the spring. Once curly dock is established, it is very difficult to eliminate.

CONTROL: To control curly dock in the lawn, use ORTHO Weed-B-Gon Lawn Weed Killer. Or spot treat individual plants with ORTHO Kleenup Systemic Weed & Grass Killer. Around trees and shrubs and in flower gardens and nonplanted areas, kill existing weeds with ORTHO Kleenup Systemic Weed & Grass Killer. Hand-digging is not practical, since any root pieces left behind will resprout into new plants.

LADYSTHUMB
Polygonum persicaria

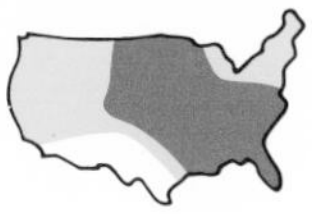

Ladysthumb, also known as *spotted smartweed*, prefers moist soil. It is usually found growing in waste places and fields, and along roadways. It may occur in lawns, as well as in landscaped beds and cracks in walkways. The smooth stems grow 6 inches to 3 feet tall. The narrow leaves are pointed at both ends, and have a peppery taste. They are marked in the middle with a triangular purple spot. Tiny pink flowers bloom on 1-inch spikes from July to October. The seeds they produce lie dormant in the soil over the winter, sprouting in the spring.

CONTROL: Eliminate ladysthumb in lawns with ORTHO Weed-B-Gon Lawn Weed Killer. Around trees and shrubs, in flower beds and nonplanted areas, and to spot treat in lawns, use ORTHO Kleenup Ready-To-Use Grass & Weed Killer. Treat any time the plants are actively growing, but preferably before they flower and produce seeds for next year. To prevent seeds from germinating around trees and shrubs, apply ORTHO Casoron Granules to the soil just after the last expected frost in the spring, or 2 weeks after the forsythia bloom. This weed has shallow roots, and can be hand-pulled or hoed.

PLANTAINS
Plantago species

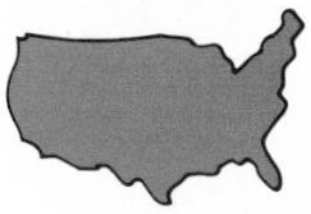

The two most common plantains that invade landscaped areas are *buckhorn plantain* (*P. lanceolata*) and *broadleaf plantain* (*P. major*). These are perennial weeds that grow in all kinds of soil, but prefer rich, moderately moist areas. The lance-shaped leaves of buckhorn plantain are 4 to 12 inches long, with 3 to 5 prominent veins in each leaf. White flower spikes 4 to 12 inches tall appear from May to October. Broadleaf plantain has oval leaves, 2 to 10 inches long, with 5 to 7 veins per leaf. Greenish white flower spikes, 2 to 10 inches tall, appear from May to September. The plantains reproduce from seeds formed on the flower spikes through the summer and fall. Seeds remain dormant over the winter and germinate the following spring. New plants also sprout from the perennial roots throughout the growing season. These ground-hugging, rosette-shaped plants suffocate desirable plants as they increase in size.

CONTROL: Control plantains in lawns with ORTHO Weed-B-Gon Lawn Weed Killer or ORTHO Weed-B-Gon For Southern Grasses. Spot treat lawns with ORTHO Weed-B-Gon Weed Killer or ORTHO Weed-B-Gon Jet Weeder. Around trees and shrubs and in flower beds, driveways, and nonplanted areas, use ORTHO Kleenup Systemic Weed & Grass Killer or ORTHO Kleenup Spot Weed & Grass Killer. Treat in the spring or fall when the plants are actively growing. Repeated applications are often necessary.

BROADLEAF WEEDS

Ragweed.

Canada thistle.

Yellow starthistle.

RAGWEED
Ambrosia species

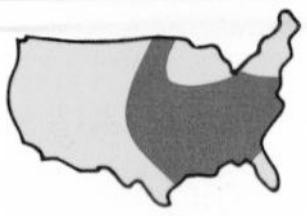

This group of both annual and perennial plants is responsible for the agony of hay fever sufferers in late summer and fall. Ragweeds may also be called *wild tansy* or *hogweed*. The hairy stems grow 1 to 6 feet tall with shallow roots. The fernlike smooth leaves are 2 to 4 inches long. Two kinds of flowers bloom from August to September. The greenish male flowers appear at the tips of the stems and produce vast quantities of pollen. The female flowers are less noticeable, since they bloom in the axils of the leaves. The seeds produced by the female flowers lie dormant for the winter, to sprout in the spring. Ragweed tolerates many types of soil, and is found most commonly in fields and vacant lots and along roadways.

CONTROL: Eliminate ragweed in lawns with ORTHO Weed-B-Gon Lawn Weed Killer, ORTHO Chickweed & Clover Control, or ORTHO Chickweed, Spurge & Oxalis Killer D. Around trees and shrubs and in flower beds and nonplanted areas, kill existing weeds with ORTHO Kleenup Systemic Weed & Grass Control. Treat ragweed any time it is actively growing. For best results, treat by midsummer, before the flowers open and produce seeds. Plants have shallow roots, and can be hand-pulled.

CANADA THISTLE
Cirsium arvense

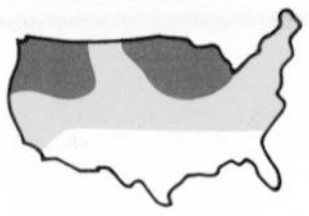

Also known as *creeping thistle*, this perennial is adapted only to cool climates. The slender, prickly stems grow 1 to 4 feet tall. The prickly leaves have smooth upper surfaces, with woolly undersides. They are lobed and 4 to 8 inches long. Small purple, rose, or white flowers bloom from June to October. The seeds they produce are attached to a tuft of hairs that makes them readily windborne. Seeds germinate throughout the growing season, usually within 2 weeks from the time they mature and fall from the flower. The tops of the plants are killed in the fall by the first frost. The rootstocks grow horizontally through the soil, often up to 15 feet from the plant. New plants that sprout from the rootstocks grow rapidly, blooming in 7 to 8 weeks. Food stored in the roots enables the plants to survive extended droughts and other adverse growing conditions for several years. Canada thistle tolerates many types of soil, but is most troublesome in moist areas with rich, heavy soil. It is very competitive in fields and pastures.

CONTROL: Treat Canada thistle in lawns with ORTHO Weed-B-Gon Lawn Weed Killer in the spring and fall. Around trees and shrubs, in flower beds and nonplanted areas, and for spot treating in lawns, use ORTHO Kleenup Systemic Weed & Grass Killer, ORTHO Kleenup Spot Weed & Grass Killer, or ORTHO Weed-B-Gon Weed Killer. For best results, treat in the spring when the food reserves in the roots are low. Repeated treatments are necessary. Repetitive mowing or weekly hand-pulling gradually weakens the roots, eventually killing the plant.

YELLOW STARTHISTLE
Centaurea solstitialis

Yellow starthistle, also known as *Barnaby's thistle*, is an annual, or sometimes a biennial. The stems grow 1 to 3 feet tall, and branch at the base. Both the stems and the leaves are covered with a white, cottony fleece. The deeply lobed basal leaves are 2 to 3 inches long, and form a rosette. The upper leaves are narrow and ½ to 1 inch long. Small yellow tubular flowers grow at the ends of the branches. They bloom and produce seeds from May to the first killing frost in the fall. The seeds germinate readily throughout the growing season, and are spread by the wind. The sharp, ¼ to 1-inch spines at the base of the flowers make this plant injurious to livestock and people. Yellow starthistle is found in fields and vacant lots and along roadways.

CONTROL: In lawns, treat young plants with ORTHO Weed-B-Gon Lawn Weed Killer before spines form. Prevent weeds from becoming established in landscaped beds with a pre-emergence herbicide containing *dichlobenil* (CASORON®). Apply to the soil before any seedlings emerge. Hand-pull or hoe the plants when small, before they develop a long taproot.

Common groundsel.

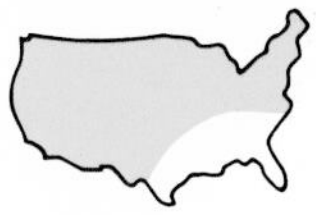

COMMON GROUNDSEL
Senecio vulgaris

This annual, also known as *grimsel*, grows ½ to 1½ feet tall with hollow stems that may root at the lower nodes. The toothed leaves are 4 inches long. The lower leaves are attached to the stems by a short leafstalk, and the upper ones cling directly to the stems. From April to October, yellow flowers up to 1 inch in diameter bloom on the ends of the branches. The seeds they produce germinate in cool, moist weather. Common groundsel is most troublesome in the fall and spring. It prefers areas with moist, rich soil, and is found in fields, along roadways, and throughout home gardens.

CONTROL: To control this weed around trees and shrubs, in flower beds and nonplanted areas, and to spot treat in lawns, use ORTHO Kleenup Systemic Weed & Grass Killer. Treat any time the plants are actively growing, but preferably soon after they germinate. To prevent the seeds from sprouting around trees and shrubs, apply ORTHO Casoron Granules to the soil in early fall and again in early spring. Hand-pull groundsel plants before they produce seeds.

Chicory.

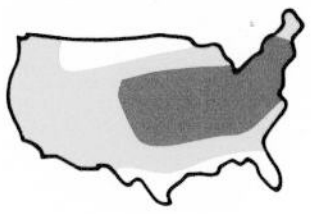

CHICORY
Cichorium intybus

Chicory, also called *succory* or *blue daisy*, is a perennial weed along roadways, in fields, and occasionally in lawns. Although it tolerates most types of soil, it is most troublesome in areas with neutral or alkaline soil. Chicory reproduces by seeds and by a deep, fleshy taproot. Hollow stems grow erect 1 to 3 feet tall. In lawns, the leaves grow in a tight rosette. Stems and roots ooze a white milky juice when broken. The 3 to 8-inch basal leaves spread outward into a rosette. The oval upper leaves have toothed or smooth edges. Flowers bloom and produce seeds on the ends of the branches or in the axils of the upper leaves. Flowers appear from March to August, and are usually sky blue, but sometimes white, or rarely, pink. They open in the early morning, and close by midday. Roasted chicory root is used as a coffee substitute. Young leaves may be eaten fresh in salads or cooked as greens if they haven't been sprayed.

CONTROL: In lawns, control chicory with ORTHO Chickweed, Spurge & Oxalis Killer D. Treat in the spring or early fall. Repeated treatments may be necessary because of the deep taproot.

Red sorrel.

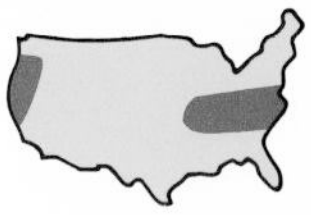

RED SORREL
Rumex acetosella

This perennial weed is also called *sheep sorrel, field sorrel,* and *sour grass.* It prefers cool, moist weather, but thrives in dry, sandy soil in lawns and landscaped beds. It is frequently an indication of low nitrogen fertility and acid soil, but will survive in neutral or slightly alkaline soil. (For more information on soil acidity, see page 908.) The stems on this rosette-shaped plant grow 4 to 14 inches tall. The leaves are 1 to 4 inches long and arrow-shaped, with 2 lobes at the base of each leaf. Flowers bloom from May to September. The yellow male flowers are on separate plants from the red female flowers. Plant tops are killed by the first frost in the fall. The rootstocks and seeds remain dormant until spring. Red sorrel has a shallow but extensive root system. The plants reproduce by seeds and red underground rootstalks.

CONTROL: In lawns, treat red sorrel with ORTHO Weed-B-Gon Lawn Weed Killer or ORTHO Weed-B-Gon Weed Killer in the spring or fall. To help prevent it in lawns, maintain a vigorous turf by following the guidelines beginning on page 250. There are no herbicides to kill existing weeds around trees, shrubs, and flower beds. To prevent seeds from sprouting in these areas, apply an herbicide containing *dichlobenil* (CASORON®) in early spring before the seeds sprout. Red sorrel can be removed by cultivating or hand-pulling. Remove all the rootstocks, since any left behind will resprout. Test the soil pH (see page 909), and correct if necessary.

BROADLEAF WEEDS

Dandelion.

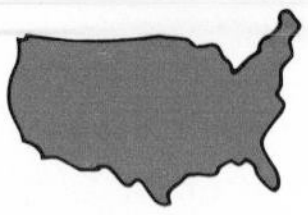

DANDELION
Taraxacum officinale

Dandelions are the most common and easily identified weed in the United States. They grow anywhere there is bare soil and full sunlight. They do, however, prefer wet soil, and may indicate overwatering or poor drainage. These rosette-shaped, perennial plants grow from thick fleshy taproots that may grow 2 to 3 feet deep in the soil. A white milky sap oozes from broken flower stems and leaves. The yellow flowers bloom from midspring until frost. In warm weather areas they bloom all year. As the flowers mature and ripen, they form white "puffballs" containing seeds. The wind carries the seeds for miles to other lawns and bare spots of soil. The seeds sprout the following spring. The tops of the plants are killed in the fall by the first frost, but the taproot survives even the severest winters to resprout in the spring.

CONTROL: In lawns, control dandelions with ORTHO Weed-B-Gon Lawn Weed Killer, or spot treat with ORTHO Weed-B-Gon Jet Weeder or ORTHO Weed-B-Gon Weed Killer. To help prevent dandelions in the lawn, maintain a vigorous turf by following the guidelines beginning on page 250. Around trees and shrubs and in flower beds and nonplanted areas, treat with ORTHO Kleenup Systemic Weed & Grass Killer or ORTHO Kleenup Ready-To-Use Grass & Weed Killer. Apply to actively growing plants, preferably before the seeds ripen. Hand-digging is impractical, since pieces of root that are broken off and left in the soil will sprout new plants.

Sowthistle.

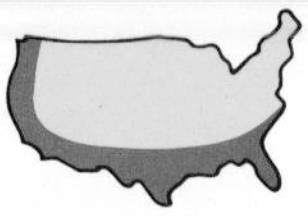

SOWTHISTLE
Sonchus species

These annual weeds are found throughout the United States, but are most common in the South and along the West Coast. The reddish stems arise from a short taproot and grow upright 1 to 6 feet. In mowed lawns they form tight rosettes. A milky sap oozes from the stems when broken. The upper branches may be covered with hairs. From July to September, yellow flowers, ½ to 1 inch in diameter, bloom on branches at the top of the plants. In Florida, Texas, and California, the plants may germinate or bloom year round. The seeds these flowers produce are contained in brownish seedheads. They germinate either that fall, or the following spring. Sowthistles prefer rich soil along roadways and in fields, lawns, and landscaped beds.

CONTROL: Treat lawns with ORTHO Weed-B-Gon Lawn Weed Killer. To spot treat, use ORTHO Weed-B-Gon Jet Weeder. Or frequently mow off the flower stalks before they produce seeds. The plants will then be killed in the fall by frost. Around trees and shrubs and in nonplanted areas, use ORTHO Kleenup Systemic Weed & Grass Killer or ORTHO Kleenup Ready-To-Use Grass & Weed Killer. Prevent sowthistle seedlings from becoming established in landscaped beds by applying a pre-emergence herbicide containing *dichlobenil* (CASORON®) to the soil in early fall or early spring. Sowthistle can be hand-pulled, but wear gloves. The fine hairs are irritating.

Horseweed.

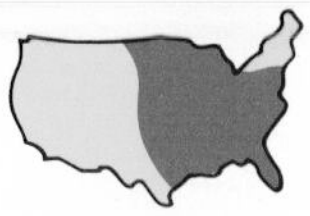

HORSEWEED
Conyza canadensis

Horseweed is an annual plant that grows in dry soil in fields, along roadways, in lawns and landscaped beds, and in nonplanted areas. It is also known as *fleabane*, *mare's tail*, and *bitterweed*. The erect, bristly stems grow 1 to 4 feet tall, branching in the upper portion. In lawns, the stems form a rosette. The narrow, dark green leaves are covered with white bristles. Clusters of small yellow to white flowers bloom on the upper stems from July to October. The seeds they produce may blow long distances in the wind, then lie dormant in the soil over the winter, germinating in the early spring. The plants are killed by the first frost in the fall. Horseweed grows from a short taproot that can be hand-pulled or hoed.

CONTROL: Eliminate horseweed in lawns with ORTHO Weed-B-Gon Lawn Weed Killer. Apply in the spring and early summer. For best results, treat before the plants bloom and produce seed for next year. Hand-pull or hoe any plants growing in landscaped beds.

Shepherds purse.

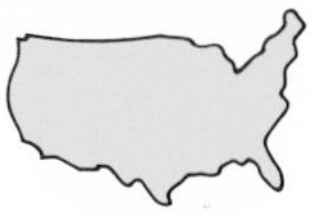

SHEPHERDS PURSE
Capsella bursa pastoris

Shepherds purse, also called *lady's purse* or *shepherds bag*, is a common summer or winter annual. It grows in lawns, landscaped beds, nonplanted areas, and fields throughout the United States. It tolerates most types of soil, but will not grow in the shade. Lobed or toothed leaves form a rosette at the base of the plant. Arrow-shaped leaves and tiny white flowers grow on stems 3 to 18 inches tall. Flowers bloom and produce seeds in triangular pods from March to December. The seeds fall to the soil and may remain dormant for several years before germinating in the spring. The plants are killed in the fall by the first frost. In warm winter areas, seeds may germinate in the fall. The plants then grow through the winter until the fall. The triangular seed pods resemble purses once carried by shepherds; hence the name shepherds purse.

CONTROL: Eliminate shepherds purse in lawns with ORTHO Weed-B-Gon Lawn Weed Killer or ORTHO Chickweed & Clover Control. Follow the lawn maintenance guidelines beginning on page 250. Treat when the weeds are actively growing. Around trees and shrubs, flower beds, and nonplanted areas, kill existing weeds with ORTHO Kleenup Ready-To-Use Grass & Weed Killer. Prevent this weed around trees and shrubs with ORTHO Casoron Granules. Apply in the early spring, or in warm winter areas in the early fall, before the weeds sprout. Shepherds purse can also be hand-pulled or hoed.

Tansy ragwort.

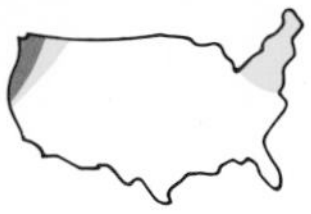

TANSY RAGWORT
Senecio jacobaea

Tansy ragwort is a prolific biennial or perennial that grows 1 to 4 feet tall and is most noticeable when the daisylike golden flowers bloom in late summer. The leaves are 5 to 9 inches long, and lobed with a full blade at the tip. Seeds produced by the flowers germinate in the fall into rosette-shaped plants. The first year, the plants remain rosettes. The second year, most plants blossom, produce seeds, and die. Sometimes the plants survive a third year, blossom again, and produce more seeds. Each plant may produce as many as 150,000 seeds, which remain viable in the soil for 3 or 4 years. Tansy ragwort survives most soil conditions. It is troublesome in fields and pastures and along roadways and unmaintained areas. It may be introduced into home gardens by windblown seeds or when straw contaminated by tansy ragwort is used for mulching. Several insects—including the cinnabar moth larvae—eat this weed, helping keep it under control.

CONTROL: Hand-pull tansy ragwort. If it is in bloom, cover with a plastic bag before you pull to keep the seeds from spreading. Or spray with ORTHO Kleenup Ready-To-Use Grass & Weed Killer. Treat in early spring or midfall when the plants are rosettes. Plants in bloom are much more difficult to control, and repeated treatments are often necessary.

Goldenrod.

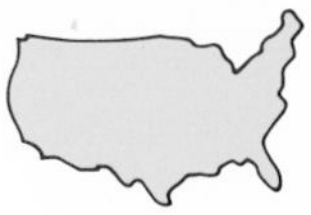

GOLDENROD
Solidago species

Goldenrod is widely known for the discomfort hayfever sufferers feel when it is in bloom in late summer and early fall. The yellow flower clusters, 2 to 8 inches long, give fields a yellowish cast. The seeds produced by these flowers lie dormant in the soil over the winter, sprouting into new plants in the spring. New plants also arise from the short, creeping rootstocks. Goldenrod thrives in rich soil in either dry or moist areas. It is most frequently seen on hillsides, in fields, and along roadways. The seeds may be windblown, so plants occasionally appear in home gardens. The stems grow ½ foot to 4 feet tall, and are covered with grayish hairs. The hairy leaves are 3 to 5 inches long, and lanceolate, with toothed edges. The upper leaves are the same shape, only smaller. The yellow flower heads are used to make a dye for coloring yarns and fabric.

CONTROL: Treat goldenrod growing in fields or along roadsides with an herbicide containing *dicamba*. Spray in spring when the new leaves have begun to grow but before they have developed fully. Repeat the application if necessary.

BROADLEAF WEEDS

Milkweed.

MILKWEED
Asclepias syriaca

This perennial is also known as *silkweed* or *cottonweed.* The hairy, erect stems grow 2 to 5 feet tall. A milky sap oozes from the stems when broken. The 4 to 8-inch elliptical leaves are smooth on the upper surface; the lower surface is covered with white hairs. Young milkweed shoots resemble asparagus shoots. Plants reproduce from their thick creeping rootstocks, as well as from seeds. Clusters of fragrant, pinkish white flowers bloom from June to August. The milkweed plant is best known for its gray pods, 2 to 4 inches long, covered with soft spines. Evident in late summer and fall, the pods contain brown seeds with white silken hairs attached. When mature, they split open, releasing the seeds. The seeds lie dormant over the winter, sprouting in the spring. Milkweed usually grows in patches in rich, sandy, or gravelly loam soils in fields and along roadways. Because the seeds are windborne, it is occasionally found in flower and vegetable gardens.

CONTROL: Spot treat milkweed plants with an herbicide containing *glyposate* (KLEENUP®). Or pull plants while young before they develop extensive rootstocks. Plants will resprout from pieces of rootstock left behind.

Pigweed.

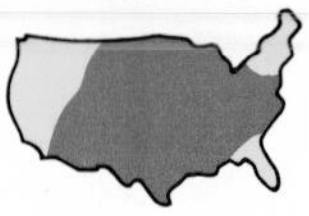

PIGWEEDS
Amaranthus species

Members of the pigweed group are annuals that grow upright, except in mowed lawns, where they form mats. Leaves are oval to egg-shaped, and may be hairy. Flower spikes bloom and produce seeds from July to October. In one season, each plant may produce thousands of seeds, which sprout in the spring. Pigweeds prefer hot, dry weather and dry soil. They are found in fields and vacant lots, along roadways, and in lawns and gardens.

CONTROL: Control pigweeds in lawns with ORTHO Weed-B-Gon Lawn Weed Killer any time they are actively growing. In other areas, use ORTHO Kleenup Ready-To-Use Grass & Weed Killer. For best results, and to reduce the number of plants the following year, treat before flowers and seeds are produced. Prevent pigweeds around trees and shrubs, in flower and vegetable gardens, and in lawns with ORTHO Garden Weed Preventer. Apply to the soil 2 weeks before the last expected frost, or about the time the forsythia bloom. Pigweeds have shallow roots and can be removed by hand.

Mugwort.

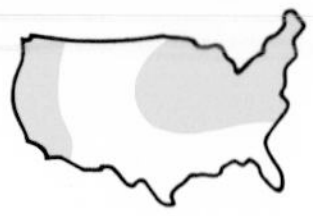

MUGWORT
Artemisia vulgaris

Mugwort, also called *chrysanthemum weed* or *wormwood,* is a perennial with underground creeping rootstocks and upright stems 3 to 6 feet high. The segmented leaves, green on the upper surface, and woolly-white on the lower surface, are 2 to 6 inches long and aromatic when crushed. From July to September, greenish yellow flower spikes bloom and produce seeds. Mugwort reproduces by these seeds, which germinate in the spring, and by the extensive rootstocks. It prefers limey soil and grows primarily in moist areas near streams, highways, and fields. In yards, mugwort often creeps from lawns into landscaped beds and sprouts in cracks in walkways.

CONTROL: Mugwort is difficult to control. Spot treat with an herbicide containing *glyphosate* (KLEENUP®). To prevent seeds from germinating around trees and shrubs and in flower beds, use a pre-emergence herbicide containing *eptam.* Apply to the soil in the spring, 2 weeks before the last expected frost, or about the time the forsythia bloom. Hand-pull-ing is not effective, since any rootstock pieces left behind will sprout into new plants.

Common lamb's-quarters.

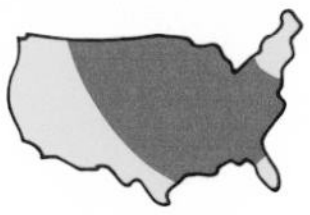

COMMON LAMB'S-QUARTERS
Chenopodium album

This annual is also known as *white pigweed* or *white goosefoot.* The ridged stems are frequently lined with red or light green stripes. They grow 1 to 4 feet tall from a short, branched taproot. The wedge-shaped leaves are 1 to 3 inches long with toothed edges. The undersides of the leaves are covered with a white, mealy coating. At the ends of the branches and in the leaf axils, small green flowers bloom and produce seeds from June to October. The pollen from these flowers irritates hay fever sufferers. The seeds remain dormant over the winter, and sprout in the spring. The entire plant is killed by the first frost in the fall. Common lamb's-quarters is a troublesome weed in cultivated fields and gardens. It is a major host for the beet leafhopper, which transmits *curly top*, a virus disease.

CONTROL: In lawns, eliminate lamb's-quarters with ORTHO Weed-B-Gon Lawn Weed Killer. Treat in the spring when the plants are young. Kill existing weeds around trees and shrubs and in flower beds and nonplanted areas with ORTHO Kleenup Systemic Weed & Grass Killer. Treat any time the plants are actively growing, but preferably before they bloom and produce seeds. Prevent the seeds from germinating in these areas as well as in vegetable gardens with ORTHO Garden Weed Preventer. Apply in the spring 2 weeks before the last expected frost, or about the time the forsythia bloom. Lamb's-quarters can also be hand-pulled or hoed.

Horsenettle.

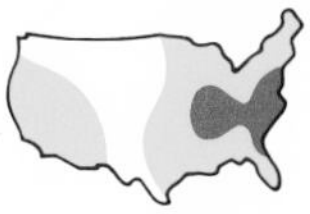

HORSENETTLE
Solanum carolinense

Also called *bull nettle* or *Carolina nettle*, this perennial grows 1 to 3 feet tall. The stems, petioles, midribs, and veins of the leaves are prickled with yellow spines. Oval, 2 to 6-inch leaves with lobed or wavy margins are covered with fine hairs. Clusters of white to purple flowers that look like tomato flowers bloom from the sides of the stems from May to October. They are followed by ½ inch yellow-orange berries that are first smooth and later become wrinkled. New plants sprout from the seeds contained in these berries, as well as from the rootstocks. The berries and leaves are poisonous to humans and animals. Horsenettle thrives in areas with sandy, well-drained soil. It spreads 5 or more feet across, crowding out desirable plants.

CONTROL: Horsenettle has deep roots and is difficult to control. To kill existing weeds around trees and shrubs, in flower beds and nonplanted areas, and to spot treat lawns, use an herbicide containing *glyphosate* (KLEENUP®). Regular mowing will also control horsenettle in lawns. Hand-pulling is not practical, as any root pieces left behind will sprout into new plants. Contact your doctor or veterinarian if horsenettle berries or leaves are eaten.

Stinging nettle.

STINGING NETTLE
Urtica dioica

Tiny hairs on stinging nettle cause welts or inflammations on the skin when touched. The 3 to 8-foot-tall stems and the leaves are covered with these stinging hairs. The irritation caused by contact with nettles usually heals in a day or so. The egg-shaped leaves are 5 inches long and 3 inches wide, with saw-toothed margins. Small greenish flowers bloom on clusters of spikes in the leaf axils from June to September. Stinging nettle grows in damp, rich soil. It is found along creeks, in waste places, on the edges of wooded lots, and occasionally in lawns, nonplanted areas, and landscaped beds. It reproduces by seeds and underground creeping rootstocks. A greenish yellow dye can be made from the upper part of the plant.

CONTROL: Spray nonplanted areas with an herbicide containing *glyphosate* (KLEENUP®). Repeated applications may be necessary to kill all the roots. Treat the plants any time they are growing actively, but preferably before they bloom. Prevent seeds from germinating in vegetable gardens with a pre-emergent herbicide containing *trifluralin.* Apply to the soil in the early spring, about 2 weeks before the last expected frost, or when the forsythia are in bloom.

BROADLEAF WEEDS

Field dodder.

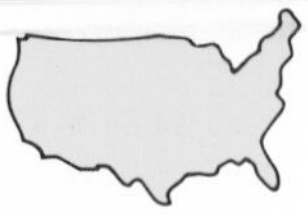

FIELD DODDER
Cuscuta campestris

This leafless, parasitic annual is also known as *strangleweed* or *devil's hair.* The threadlike, golden yellow stems twine and coil on other plants. Short suction-cup-like suckers then sprout along the undersides of the dodder stems, penetrating the stems of the host plant. Dodder obtains its nourishment through these suckers. The stems branch repeatedly, attacking additional host plants. White or creamy flowers, ¼ inch in diameter, bloom and produce seeds from April to October. The seeds may germinate that year, or lie dormant in the soil for many years before sprouting in the spring. The seeds germinate in the soil, but the roots die as soon as the dodder is attached to a host plant. Once attached, the dodder lives completely off its host plant. Dodder is killed in the fall by the first frost. It is found most commonly in pastures and fields where alfalfa has been grown. Occasionally it may be found living on herbaceous plants in the home garden.

CONTROL: Once dodder has attached itself to another plant, there is no way to remove it. Destroy infested host plants. Do not pull dodder off the plants, since any stem pieces left behind will continue to grow. Prevent the seeds from germinating with a pre-emergence herbicide containing *DCPA* (DACTHAL®). For best results, apply in early spring, about the time of the last expected frost, when the majority of dodder seeds sprout. Repeat the application in 6 to 8 weeks.

Morning glory.

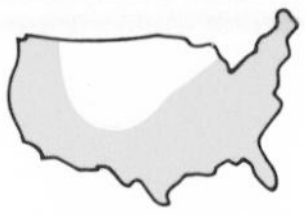

MORNING GLORY
Ipomoea species

These annual weeds have twining, hairy stems that grow 2 to 10 feet long. The heart-shaped, hairy leaves may be lobed and 2 to 6 inches long. Trumpet-shaped white, purple, or blue flowers bloom in the leaf axils from July to October. Seeds are formed within bristly, brown, egg-shaped pods that adhere to clothing or animal fur and are carried to other areas. The seeds lie dormant in the soil over the winter, and germinate in the spring. The plants are killed in the fall by the first frost. Morning glories are found in fields and along roadsides. They may sprout anywhere in the yard, and frequently creep into yards from neighboring areas. They tolerate any type of soil, but are most troublesome in areas with sandy soil.

CONTROL: In lawns, control morning glories with ORTHO Weed-B-Gon Lawn Weed Killer. Treat in the spring and early summer when the plants are growing most actively. Kill existing weeds around trees and shrubs and in noncrop areas with ORTHO Kleenup Systemic Weed & Grass Killer or ORTHO Kleenup Ready-To-Use Grass & Weed Killer. To prevent morning glory seeds from sprouting around trees and shrubs, use a pre-emergent herbicide containing *simazine* or *eptam.* Apply to the soil in the spring about the time of the last expected frost. Young plants can be hand-pulled or hoed.

Field bindweed.

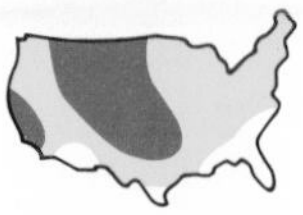

FIELD BINDWEED
Convolvulus arvensis

Field bindweed, a troublesome perennial, is also called *wild morning glory* or *cornbind.* It grows in lawns and flower and vegetable gardens, and around trees and shrubs. The creeping, twining stems frequently invade yards from nearby roadways, fields, and vacant lots. Field bindweed thrives in rich, heavy soil. The stems may be 3 to 9 feet long with arrow-shaped leaves 1 to 2 inches long. White to pink funnel-shaped flowers, the size of a nickel, bloom and produce seed from May to September. Field bindweed is difficult to control because the roots may grow 15 to 20 feet deep in the soil. The roots store food and water so the plant can survive under adverse growing conditions. It reproduces by seeds and pieces of the root. The seeds may remain dormant in the soil for many years before sprouting. Any root pieces left behind after hand-pulling will sprout into new plants.

CONTROL: In lawns, control field bindweed with ORTHO Weed-B-Gon Lawn Weed Killer. Apply from late spring through early summer, or early to late fall. Around trees and shrubs and in flower beds and nonplanted areas, kill existing weeds with ORTHO Kleenup Systemic Weed & Grass Killer or ORTHO Kleenup Ready-To-Use Grass & Weed Killer. Repeat the treatments as new growth emerges. In vegetable gardens, control this weed with an herbicide containing *trifluralin.* Apply in the spring before the plants emerge. Bindweed cannot be controlled by hand-pulling or hoeing.

Nightshade.

NIGHTSHADES
Solanum species

This group of annual and perennial weeds includes *bitter nightshade* (*S. dulcamara*), *black nightshade* (*S. nigrum*), and *hairy nightshade* (*S. sarachoides*). Nightshades belong to the same family as tomatoes, potatoes, and eggplant. They grow in rich, moist soil and frequently creep into home gardens from surrounding fields, hedgerows, and unmaintained areas. The stems may grow up to 9 feet long, creeping along the ground or twining on fences and plants. The stems frequently root where they touch the soil. Dark green to purple leaves, 1 to 4 inches long, have varying shapes. They may be mitten-shaped, heart-shaped, or lobed at the base. Blue, violet, or white flowers with yellow centers resemble tomato flowers. They bloom from May to November. The flowers are followed by green berries, which turn red or black when ripe. The berries are very attractive to children and small pets, and are poisonous ifaten in quantity. The leaves are also poisonous. Yellow seeds inside the berries are often spread by birds, and sprout into new plants in the spring.

CONTROL: Spot treat around trees and shrubs and in other noncrop areas with an herbicide containing *glyphosate* (KLEENUP®). Repeated treatments are often necessary because of the long, woody stems. Or hand-pull the vines, being careful not to drop any berries. Any pieces of stem left behind will sprout into new plants. If berries or leaves are eaten by children or pets, call your doctor or veterinarian promptly.

Florida betony.

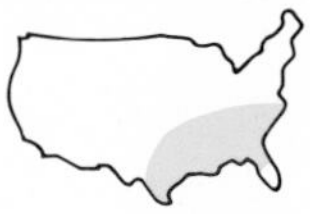

FLORIDA BETONY
Stachys floridana

Also known as *rattlesnakeweed*, this perennial sprouts from white tubers that resemble the rattles on a rattlesnake. The four-sided stems grow 6 to 20 inches tall. The elliptical leaves have saw-toothed edges. Trumpet-shaped white to lavender flowers bloom in the leaf axils from late spring to early summer. The seeds lie dormant through the summer, and sprout in the fall. New plants emerge from seeds and tubers in cool, moist fall weather. The plants grow and spread rapidly through the winter and spring until the heat of the summer, when the tops die. Florida betony is a nuisance in lawns and landscaped beds. If not controlled, it rapidly takes over large areas.

CONTROL: In lawns, use ORTHO Weed-B-Gon For Southern Grasses in the spring when the plants are rapidly growing. Kill existing weeds in landscaped beds and nonplanted areas with an herbicide containing *glyphosate* (KLEENUP®). To prevent Florida betony seedlings from becoming established, apply a pre-emergence herbicide containing *dichlobenil* (CASORON®) or *eptam* to the soil in September. Individual plants may be hand-dug before the tubers become large.

Carpetweed.

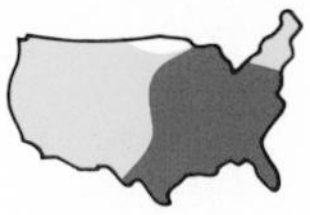

CARPETWEED
Mollugo verticillata

Also known as *Indian chickweed* or *whorled chickweed*, this annual weed's smooth, prostrate stems form circular mats up to 20 inches in diameter, crowding out desirable plants. Whorls of 5 to 6 leaves grow at each stem joint. Small white flowers bloom in the leaf axils from June to November. They produce orange-red, kidney-shaped seeds that lie dormant in the soil over the winter and sprout slowly in the spring. The plants develop a short taproot and grow rapidly in the summer heat. Carpetweed prefers fertile, dry sandy or gravelly soil in lawns and gardens and along walkways.

CONTROL: In lawns, treat with ORTHO Weed-B-Gon Lawn Weed Killer. Apply in early to midsummer when the plants are actively growing. Prevent seeds from germinating throughout the yard with ORTHO Garden Weed Preventer. Apply to the soil in midspring about the time of the last expected frost, or 2 weeks after the forsythia bloom. Carpetweed can be hand-pulled or hoed.

BROADLEAF WEEDS

Douglas fiddleneck.

DOUGLAS FIDDLENECK

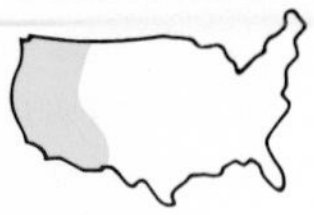

Amsinckia douglasiana

Douglas fiddleneck is also called *bur-weed* or *buckthorn.* The erect stems grow 1 to 4 feet tall and are covered with stiff white hairs. The lance-shaped leaves are also covered with white hairs. From May to July, 5 to 10-inch-long, orange to yellow flower spikes resembling a fiddle's neck bloom and produce seeds. The seeds germinate in the winter, and the plants mature in the summer. Douglas fiddleneck is common in fields and pastures and along roadways. It is occasionally found in yards bordering these areas.

CONTROL: Use ORTHO Kleenup Systemic Weed & Grass Killer to spot treat around trees and shrubs and in lawns, flower beds, and nonplanted areas. Apply any time the plants are actively growing. Plants have shallow roots and can be hand-pulled. Wear gloves so the spiny hairs don't prick the skin.

Henbit.

HENBIT

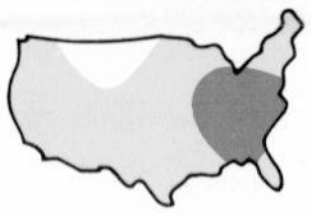

Lamium amplexicaule

This winter annual or biennial is also called *dead nettle* or *bee nettle.* It grows rapidly in early spring, fall, and winter in lawns and in landscaped beds with rich soil. Rounded, toothed leaves up to ¾ inch wide grow on creeping square stems. Lavender flowers, ½ inch in diameter, bloom and produce seeds from April to June and again in September. Seeds sprout in the fall. Henbit also reproduces by the creeping stems that root wherever they touch the soil.

CONTROL: In lawns, eliminate henbit with ORTHO Chickweed, Spurge & Oxalis Killer D. Or spot treat individual plants with ORTHO Weed-B-Gon Jet Weeder or ORTHO Weed-B-Gon Weed Killer. Treat in the spring when henbit is actively growing. Around trees and shrubs and in flower beds, kill existing weeds with ORTHO Kleenup Ready-To-Use Grass & Weed Killer, or ORTHO Kleenup Spot Weed & Grass Killer. Around trees and shrubs, prevent henbit with ORTHO Casoron Granules. Apply it in the fall before the plants sprout. Follow the lawn maintenance guidelines beginning on page 250 to help keep henbit out of your lawn.

MUSHROOMS

Mushrooms.

MUSHROOMS

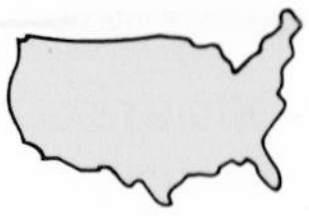

The folklore surrounding mushrooms has given them the additional name of *toadstool.* Some types are also known as *puffballs.* The mushroom is the aboveground fruiting or reproducing structure, the "flower," of a fungus that lives on and helps to decay organic matter in the soil. In wooded areas, some mushrooms live on the leaves that accumulate each year on the ground. Others may grow on the roots of trees and benefit both the trees and the mushrooms. Mushrooms thrive in warm, damp areas. They are seldom found in cool, dry spots. In cold winter areas, they disappear with the first frost, and return with wet spring weather. Spores are produced on the underside of the mushroom cap, and are spread by the wind. Some mushrooms are poisonous; identify them carefully before eating. Mushrooms growing in circles in lawns are called fairy rings. For more information on fairy rings, see page 267.

CONTROL: There is no practical way to eliminate mushrooms. When the buried organic matter is completely decayed, the mushrooms will disappear. For temporary control, break the mushrooms with a rake, or mow the lawn. For information on suppressing mushrooms in lawns, see page 279.

WOODY WEEDS

Japanese honeysuckle.

JAPANESE HONEYSUCKLE
Lonicera japonica

Japanese honeysuckle, a perennial woody vine, is best known for its fragrant flowers, which are used to scent soaps, perfumes, and bath oils. They are white, tinged with pink or yellow, and bloom in pairs in the upper leaf axils from April to November. The twining, climbing stems grow on valuable plants, strangling them. As the stems creep along the ground, they root wherever the nodes touch the soil. The oval leaves, 1 to 3 inches long, smooth on the upper surface and hairy below, frequently remain on the plant through the winter. Honeysuckle fruit, evident from September to November, are $\frac{1}{4}$-inch black berries that contain 2 or 3 seeds. The seeds sprout the following spring. New plants also sprout from underground rootstocks.

CONTROL: Control honeysuckle in lawns with an herbicide containing *2,4-D*, *dicamba*, and *mecoprop*. In landscaped beds and nonplanted areas, spot treat with an herbicide containing *glyphosate* (KLEENUP®). Apply in mid to late summer when the plants will readily absorb the herbicide. Hand-pulling is not a practical solution, since any underground rootstocks left behind will sprout into new plants.

Ivy invading juniper planting.

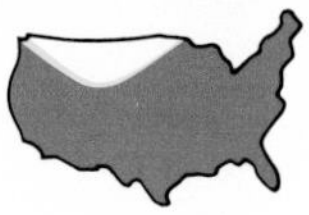

ENGLISH IVY
Hedera helix

English ivy is a popular evergreen woody vine that is often used as a ground cover. Some varieties of English ivy are bicolored with unusually shaped leaves, but most commonly the leaves are 1 to 4 inches long, dark green, and glossy. They usually have three to five lobes. The plant trails and roots as it spreads, creating a dense mat of foliage. Sometimes English ivy becomes invasive. The vines can climb onto and smother nearby shrubs, flowers, and lawns. The small rootlike projections (holdfasts) produced along the stems enable vigorous ivy plants to cling to walls, fences, tree trunks, and other vertical surfaces.

CONTROL: English ivy is a very persistent weed. Remove as much of it as possible by pruning off the runners and digging out major roots. Spot treat remaining ivy and any ivy that resprouts with an herbicide containing *glyphosate* (KLEENUP®); treatment is most effective in the spring or summer when ivy is actively growing. Retreat if necessary.

Kudzu. *Insert:* Kudzu flowers.

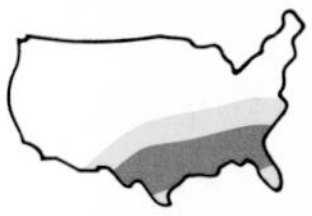

KUDZU VINE
Pueraria lobata

Kudzu vine is a woody perennial vine with heavy, brown, hairy stems. The leaves have three leaflets, 3 to 6 inches long, with margins that may be smooth or slightly lobed. Tiny, reddish purple, fragrant flowers produced in July and August are followed by small, long, hairy seed pods. In the past, kudzu vine was widely planted in the Southeast for erosion control and for use as a forage crop. In many areas, kudzu has become an aggressive weed. This twining vine spreads rapidly, growing up to 60 feet per year. It invades roadsides, vacant lots, fence lines, and neglected yards. Kudzu can twine over trees and shrubs, limbs and branches. Plants completely covered may be killed by the shade.

CONTROL: Treat kudzu vine with ORTHO Brush-B-Gon Brush Killer or *glyphosate* (KLEENUP®). Control is most effective during mid- to late summer when the weed is in full leaf and growing actively. Spot treat if resprouting occurs. If kudzu vine has climbed into or over trees and shrubs, cut off the runners and remove them before treatment.

WOODY WEEDS

Wild blackberry.

Poison ivy berries.

Poison ivy.

WILD BLACKBERRY

Rubus species

Wild blackberries are perennial shrubs with thorny, arching stems that grow 3 to 8 feet tall and live for only 2 years. The first year only leaves are produced. They have 3 to 5 leaflets that are hairy with toothed edges, green on the upper surface, and silver on the lower surface. Spines grow on the midrib on the underside of the leaflets. The second year, clusters of 12 to 30 white or pink flowers bloom in May and June. Red to black edible fruit then appear in July. New plants may sprout from underground runners or from seeds that are spread by birds that eat the fruit. Wild blackberry plants have deep roots, making them difficult to control. They prefer dry gravelly or sandy soil along roadways, fences, and unmaintained areas.

CONTROL: Treat existing plants with ORTHO Kleenup Systemic Weed & Grass Killer, ORTHO Kleenup Spot Weed & Grass Killer, or ORTHO Brush-B-Gon Brush Killer any time the plants are actively growing. Repeated treatments are often necessary to kill the deep roots. Hand-pulling is not effective against blackberries; any pieces of rootstock left behind will sprout into new plants. If feasible, control blackberries by allowing the soil to dry out in the summer.

POISON IVY

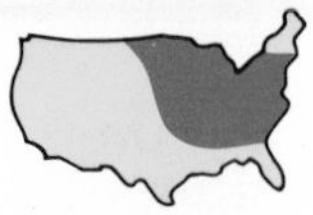

Rhus radicans

This woody perennial may grow as a small shrub in full sunlight. The stems often grow up to 8 feet long, and may be 5 inches in diameter. The leaves have 3 leaflets, 2 to 4 inches long, with margins that may be toothed, smooth, or lobed. All three forms may occur on the same plant. The terminal leaflet is attached by an elongated leafstalk. In the spring, the small new leaves are red, turning a glossy or dull green as they enlarge. In the fall, they turn bright red or reddish yellow. Poison ivy is sometimes confused with Virginia creeper (*Parthenisisus quinquefolia*), which has 5 leaflets and blue berries. Clusters of greenish white flowers bloom on poison ivy from late spring to early summer. They produce white, waxy, ¼-inch berries with seeds. The fruit first appear in the late summer, and remain on the plant through the winter. They are a way of identifying the plant in the winter, when there are no leaves. Some plants produce only male flowers, so fruit will not be present on all poison ivy plants. Poison ivy reproduces by seeds, which birds distribute, and by underground creeping stems and roots. It is frequently found climbing buildings, trees, fences, and along the ground. An oil present in all parts of poison ivy plants causes skin irritations. Poisoning can occur throughout the year, and from live or dead plants. These irritations develop after contact with the plant, or with contaminated clothing, tools, pet hair, or smoke from burning plants.

CONTROL: Hand-pulling and burning are not practical solutions. Any pieces of root left behind will sprout into new plants. The irritating oil in poison ivy vaporizes when burned, and the smoke causes lung, eye, and skin irritations. Control poison ivy around trees, on fences and buildings, and in noncrop areas with ORTHO Brush-B-Gon Brush Killer, ORTHO Poison Ivy & Poison Oak Killer, or ORTHO Kleenup Systemic Weed & Grass Killer. Treat any time the plants are actively growing, but at least 2 weeks before the first killing frost in the fall. Spray the leaves thoroughly. Plants turn white or brown in 10 days to 2 weeks. The vigorous roots are difficult to kill, so repeated treatments may be necessary if new growth appears. Handle dead plants with rubber gloves, since they may still be toxic. Dispose of plants and rubber gloves in tightly sealed garbage bags. If you come in contact with poison ivy, wash as soon as possible with a drying agent such as rubbing alcohol or a solution of baking soda and water.

Poison oak (in the fall).

Poison oak (in the summer).

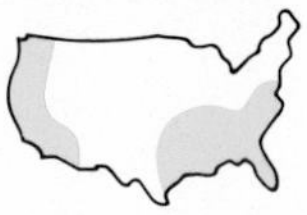

POISON OAK AND PACIFIC POISON OAK

Rhus toxicodendron and *R. diversiloba*

This perennial grows as an upright shrub as well as a twining vine. The leaves, 1½ to 4 inches long with 3 to 7 shallow lobes, are composed of 3 elliptical or oval leaflets. The terminal leaflet is attached with an elongated petiole. The lower surfaces of the leaves and the petiole are velvety; the upper surfaces are hairy. The leaflets resemble white oak leaves, except that oak leaves are smooth. Poison oak leaves turn a brilliant orange to red color in the fall. In May and June, clusters of greenish flowers bloom from the centers of the leaves. They are followed by round, green to tan fruit containing seeds. New plants sprout from these seeds, as well as from the creeping underground stems. Poison oak prefers dry areas with poor, sandy soil. It is frequently found in wooded lots, along roadways, and in yards and noncrop areas. It is well known for the irritating rash caused by the oily sap. The oil is found in all parts of the plant. The greatest irritations occur in the spring and summer when the sap is flowing freely. However, rashes can develop if the plant is contacted any time of year. Irritations develop after contact with the plant directly, or with contaminated clothing, tools, pet hair, or smoke from burning plants.

CONTROL: Do not hand-pull or burn poison oak plants. Any pieces of root left behind will sprout into new plants. The oil also remains potent on clothing for up to 2 years. When burned, the oil vaporizes and the smoke causes skin, eye, and lung irritations. Herbicides are the safest way to rid an area of this weed. Around homes, buildings, fences, noncrop areas, and trees, treat the plants with ORTHO Poison Ivy & Poison Oak Killer, ORTHO Brush-B-Gon Brush Killer, or ORTHO Kleenup Systemic Weed & Grass Killer. Treat any time the plants are actively growing, but at least 2 weeks before the first killing frost in the fall. Spray the leaves thoroughly. Plants begin to turn white or brown in 10 days to 2 weeks. The vigorous roots are difficult to kill, so repeated treatments may be necessary if new growth appears. Handle dead plants with rubber gloves, since they may still be toxic. Place dead plants in plastic bags and tie securely. Discard bags and rubber gloves. If you come in contact with poison oak, wash as soon as possible with a drying agent such as rubbing alcohol or a solution of baking soda and water.

This section was included for the person who wants to learn more about plant diseases than was presented in the first part of the book. It contains additional information about some of the most common plant diseases, especially those that attack a wide variety of plants. Locate the disease you are looking for in the index on the next page.

A GALLERY OF PLANT DISEASES

Most plant diseases are caused by either fungi or bacteria. A key to understanding plant diseases and their prevention lies in the fact that both fungi and bacteria need wet conditions.

Plant diseases can be divided into two broad categories: those that are spread by wind or splashing water, and those that live in the soil.

Most diseases in the first category are spread as spores by wind or splashing raindrops to plant leaves or flowers. The spores sprout—usually within a drop of water on the leaf surface—and enter the leaf. Infection from this type of disease can be prevented by protecting the leaf with a fungicide, and by keeping the leaf as dry as possible. Most fungicides provide a protective barrier on the leaf surface, preventing the spore from germinating or killing it before it can enter the leaf. To be effective, the protective barrier must be in place before the spore lands on the leaf, so timing is important with fungicidal sprays. The fungicide must also be renewed periodically as it wears off.

If you live in an area where summer rainfalls are frequent, there isn't much you can do to keep the leaves dry. But if you must irrigate during the summer, chose irrigation methods that don't wet the leaves. Or water in the morning, so the leaves will dry as rapidly as possible.

The second category of plant diseases includes those diseases that live in the soil. These diseases usually attack plants through their roots or the base of the stem or trunk. Some of these organisms—such as the water molds—are present in most soils, but are not a problem if the soil is allowed to dry out periodically. This can be done by improving the drainage so that water can escape from the soil, and by watering thoroughly but infrequently, so that the soil has a chance to dry out between waterings.

Other disease organisms are only present in some soils. They are usually transferred to a garden on the roots of infected plants. It's a good idea to buy plants only from reputable nurseries, most of which pasteurize their planting mixes or use soilless mixes. Or keep new plants in "quarantine" for a few weeks before planting them in your garden, to make sure they are healthy.

Above: Gray mold spots on a calceolaria blossom. See page 849.
Left: Disease-free impatiens and begonias brighten a garden corner.

INDEX TO PLANT DISEASES | **FUNGUS DISEASES**

INDEX TO PLANT DISEASES

Fungal leaf spot on rhubarb.

FUNGUS DISEASES

Fungi are plants that lack chlorophyll, the green pigment that enables plants to make their own food in the presence of light. Most fungi live on decaying organic matter, but about 8000 species infect live plants. In fact, most plant diseases are caused by fungi. Some of these fungi require a live host plant to survive. Others continue to live and grow in the soil or plant debris after their host plant has died. Although individual fungal filaments are microscopic, some species form dense mats of visible growth on the plant surface. Most fungi cannot grow without water or in temperatures colder than 25°F or hotter than 110°F. When their plant hosts die, or during periods of temperature extremes or drought, fungi produce resistant dormant strands or pellets that can survive for long periods until the environment is favorable for growth again. Fungi reproduce by means of spores, which are microscopic equivalents of seeds. In some cases, the fruiting bodies that produce spores are very noticeable. These are the familiar mushrooms and conks. Other fungi, such as gray mold, powdery mildew, and rust, produce spores on the surface of leaves they infect. Spores are usually spread to new host plants by wind or water. Most spores must be in a drop of water for 6 to 8 hours in order to germinate and infect the leaf. Powdery mildew is the exception to this rule.

CONTROL: Many fungus diseases may be controlled or prevented by applying fungicides, keeping plant leaves dry, and growing disease-resistant plants.

Rust on geranium.

RUSTS

These fungi are aptly named: most rusts produce rust-colored or brown powdery pustules on the leaves and stems of their host plants. Rusts infect all kinds of plants, but most rust fungi infect only 1 or 2 plant species, or only certain varieties of a species. Some rusts, such as cedar-apple rust (see page 609), must alternate between two specific host plants. Diseased plants are usually weak and stunted, and severely infected plants may die. Spores may be blown hundreds of miles to infect healthy plants. Some rust fungi cannot infect their host unless the foliage remains wet for at least 6 hours. Most rusts require a living host to survive the winter; others can survive on plant debris.

CONTROL: Many methods can be used to control or prevent rust infections. Spray infected plants with a fungicide containing *folpet* (PHALTAN®), *triforine* (FUNGINEX®), *chlorothalonil* (DACONIL 2787®), *mancozeb*, or *zineb*. Make sure your plant is listed on the product label. Pick off badly infected plant leaves as long as the practice doesn't damage the overall beauty of the plant. Keep the foliage as dry as possible. One way to do this is to water in the morning, which gives the plant a chance to dry out quickly, reducing the chance of infection. The best way to avoid rust infections is to plant resistant varieties of grasses, flowers, vegetables, and woody ornamentals, which may be found in local nurseries or through seed companies.

Botrytis blight on calceolaria.

Phytophthora rot of rhododendron.

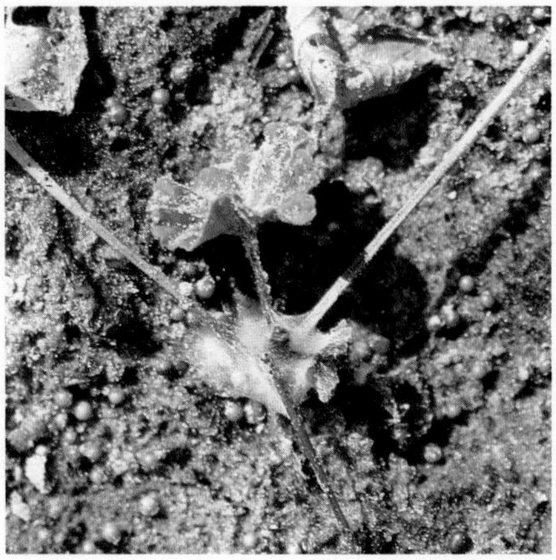
Pythium stem and root rot of geranium.

BOTRYTIS BLIGHT

This plant disease, also known as *gray mold*, *blossom blight*, and *bud and flower blight*, is caused by any of several closely related species of fungi (*Botrytis* species) that infect many vegetables, flowers, trees, and shrubs. The fungus usually begins to grow on plant debris or weak or inactive plant tissue, such as old leaves, flowers, and overripe fruit. After the fungus becomes established, it invades healthy, actively growing plant tissue. Botrytis causes spotting and decay of flowers and foliage, and of fruits and berries, both before and after harvest. In some plants, it causes cankers or rots stems, corms, and bulbs. Botrytis spores are present in most soils. The fungus thrives in cool, moist conditions. It is responsible for the fuzzy gray mold that grows on vegetables left too long in the refrigerator.

CONTROL: The key to avoiding problems is good sanitation. Keep dead leaves and flowers picked up so the fungus will not have a chance to produce the thousands of spores necessary to mount an assault on healthy plants. Keep the foliage as dry as possible. Water the plants at the soil level, instead of overhead, and space them far enough apart so that air can circulate between plants. Fungicides can also be helpful. Spray with *chlorothalonil* (DACONIL 2787®), *captan* (ORTHOCIDE ®), *maneb* or *mancozeb* every 10 to 14 days as long as the mold is visible. Check to make sure that your plant is listed on the product label.

WATER MOLDS

Water molds are fungi (*Pythium* species and *Phytophthora* species) that thrive in wet, poorly drained soils. They produce motile spores that swim through soil water to attack the roots of susceptible plants. Water molds are most active in warm (55° to 80°F) soils, but they survive as spores when the soil is cold or dry. Water molds are especially troublesome in frequently watered areas such as lawns or flower beds. They cause *damping-off* of seedlings and young plants (see page 850). Both fungi cause root rots of many plants. In addition, phytophthora causes crown rots and collar rots of many herbaceous and woody plants. The fungus attacks stems or trunks just at or below the soil surface. Reddish to brown lesions usually form on the infected tissue, and sunken, girdling cankers may develop. In some cases, phytophthora attacks the roots, and then spreads to the trunk. The foliage of infected plants dulls, and individual branches or the entire plant wilts, turns yellow, and eventually dies. Gardeners frequently mistake this wilting for drought stress and water more heavily, speeding the demise of the plant.

CONTROL: If the plant is so severely infected that most or all of the branches are dying, remove it. You may be able to save plants that are mildly infected by water molds by letting the soil dry out. If the plant is a tree or large shrub, remove the soil from around the rotted parts of the trunk and roots. Exposure to air will slow down or stop further decay.

The drying-out technique: This process involves careful observation in order to let the soil dry out as much as possible without placing plants under too much drought stress. Stop watering infected plants. To dry the soil as quickly as possible, place container plants in a well-ventilated, even breezy location. If they can tolerate direct sun, put them in a sunny spot. But if the roots are damaged badly enough that plants wilt or drop leaves, don't put them in the sun. Eventually the soil will dry out to the point where the plants would normally need another watering. Allow the soil to become drier yet to stop the fungi from continuing their decay. Take steps to minimize the water needs of the plants. Place container plants in a shaded location to reduce evaporation from the foliage. Provide shade for plants in the ground. Spray trees and shrubs that are growing in the shade with an antitranspirant, which reduces the amount of water that evaporates from the leaves. (Antitranspirants are available in many nurseries.) Further relieve drought stress by placing clear plastic tents over the plants. The tents maintain high humidity, reducing the plants' water loss. Use tents only in the shade; if used in the sun, they can heat up enough to kill plants. Begin watering again when the plant shows signs of drought stress, such as heavy wilting or yellowing and dropping of leaves.

Prevention: To help prevent future root rot problems, allow the soil to dry slightly between waterings, and provide good drainage. (For details about proper watering techniques and improving soil drainage, see pages 912 and 907.) Phytophthora-resistant plants may be used in wet areas that are hard to drain. For a list, see page 1013.

Leaf spot on tuliptree.

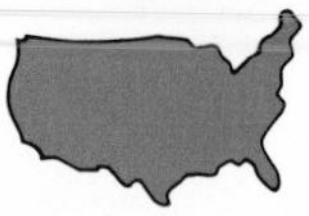

LEAF SPOTS

Most plants are occasionally blemished by leaf spots. There are thousands of leaf-spotting fungi and bacteria, most of which cause only cosmetic damage. Many of these organisms infect only one plant species. Spotting is sometimes accompanied by oozing, leaf yellowing, wilting, and decay. Fungal spores are blown or splashed to healthy leaves, and a spot forms wherever spores infect a leaf. Leaf-spotting bacteria are usually spread by splashing water or contaminated hands or tools. Leaf spots are most severe in mild, wet weather.

CONTROL: If your plant is only lightly spotted, pick off the infected leaves. If spotting is severe in your garden, try some additional control methods. Control fungal leaf spots by spraying infected plants with a fungicide containing *maneb*, *chlorothalonil* (DACONIL 2787®), *captan* (ORTHOCIDE ®), or *zineb*. Bacterial leaf-spot organisms cannot be as easily controlled. Fungicides containing *basic copper sulfate* or *zineb*, or antibiotics such as *streptomycin* will help control bacterial leaf spotting if used in combination with good sanitation practices. Badly infected plants should be discarded. After working with infected plants, wash your hands and sterilize your tools in rubbing alcohol. Keeping foliage as dry as possible will reduce spotting. Avoid overhead watering, and water in the morning to give the foliage a chance to dry quickly. When using fungicides, make sure your plant is listed on the product label.

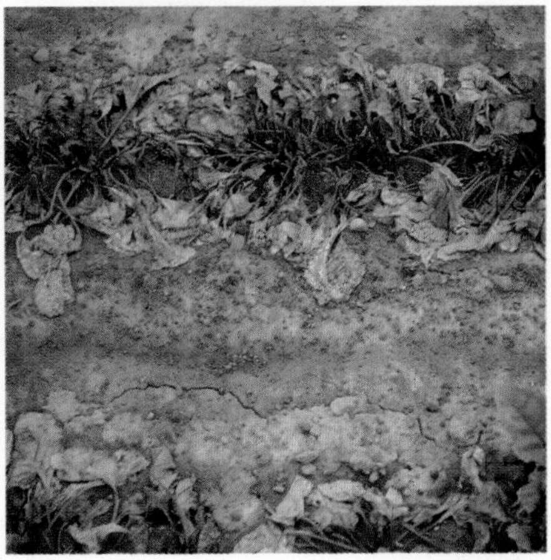

Damping-off of beet seedlings.

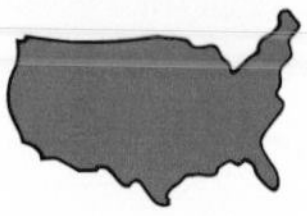

DAMPING-OFF

This plant disease is caused by any of several species of fungi (including *Pythium*, *Rhizoctonia*, *Fusarium*, *Phytophthora*, and *Sclerotium* species). These fungi, common in soils throughout the world, are one of the major causes of poor germination. They infect seeds and seedlings at several stages. Seeds are often attacked before they germinate. Or seeds germinate, but the growing tips are infected and killed before they emerge from the soil. Seedlings are susceptible even after they emerge. The fungi can attack the stems and roots just at or below the soil level, causing the seedlings to fall over. Although older seedlings are more resistant, damping-off fungi may still infect them, producing dark lesions on the lower stems and roots that stunt and weaken their growth. Damping-off is most severe in soil with lots of nitrogen and soil that is constantly wet. Seedlings growing in soils that are too warm or cold for rapid germination and growth are also more susceptible to infection.

CONTROL: Incorporate lots of sand or perlite into the soil mix to increase drainage. Don't add fertilizers that are high in nitrogen until your seedlings have produced at least one pair of true leaves. Encourage rapid growth by planting seeds in soils that are the proper temperature for rapid germination (see page 1025). Also, coating seeds with recommended fungicides will help discourage damping-off. For more information on starting seeds, see page 925.

Fusarium wilt of cabbage.

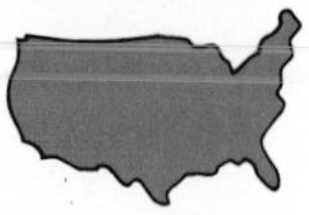

VERTICILLIUM OR FUSARIUM WILT

These fungi (*Verticillium* species and *Fusarium* species) cause wilting, stem and leaf discoloration, and the death of many plants. Both types of fungi live in the soil for years, even after the host plants have died. Fusarium thrives in warm soils, and is most severe in the southern states. Verticillium is more of a problem in the cooler soils of the northern states. They both infect annual vegetables, flowers, and herbaceous perennials. Verticillium also infects many woody shrubs, and ornamental, fruit, and nut trees. Infection begins when fungal strands penetrate the roots of a susceptible plant. The fungus spreads up into the water-conducting vessels in the stems and leaves and breaks down some of the plant cells, producing gels and gums. The accumulation of gels, gums, cell debris, and fungal strands and spores in the vessels reduces the water flow up into the leaves. The clogging results in wilting, leaf and stem discoloration, and eventually the death of the plant. The fungus also produces toxins that move up into uninfected leaves. These toxins interfere with photosynthesis and the production of chlorophyll, the green pigment necessary for plant health and growth.

CONTROL: Once these fungi have infected the plant, you cannot save it. Diseased flowers and vegetables often last through the season if they are cared for properly. Replace infected plants with varieties resistant to these wilt diseases (see pages 1007 and 1006). If you want to use susceptible plants, remove the fungus from the soil by fumigation. For information on soil fumigation, see page 927.

Armillaria root rot on sour cherry.

ARMILLARIA ROOT ROT

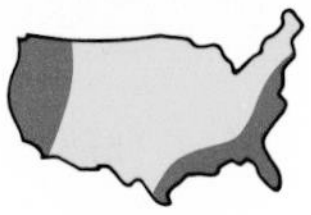

This plant disease, also known as *mushroom root rot, honey mushroom, oak root fungus*, and *shoestring fungus*, is caused by a soil-borne fungus (*Armillaria mellea*) that rots the roots of a wide range of plants. Many diseased ornamental and fruit trees die slowly over a period of years. However, these plants may die suddenly, especially if they are under stress. The fungus spreads short distances (under a foot) through the soil by thick fungal strands (rhizomorphs) that penetrate the roots of nearby susceptible plants. Infection is most severe in heavy, poorly drained soil. Once the fungus enters the plant, it produces a white, fan-shaped mat between the bark and the wood that decays the roots and lower trunk. As the roots die, the top of the plant slowly starves. If the crown is girdled by the fungus, the top wilts and dies quickly. In the fall, mushrooms—the spore-producing fruiting bodies of the fungus—often appear around the base of the infected plant. A different fungus (*Clitocybe tabescens*) also known as *mushroom root rot*, causes similar and often identical damage to woody trees and shrubs in the Southeast.

CONTROL: Remove badly infected trees, including the stumps and, if possible, the roots. You can usually save mildly infected plants, or at least prolong their lives. Remove the soil from around the rotted parts of the roots and trunk. Cut out the diseased tissue and allow the healthy wood to air through the summer. When temperatures drop toward freezing, cover the exposed roots with loose soil. Replace dying plants with armillaria-resistant plants. For a list, see page 1016.

Sclerotium rot of carrot.

SCLEROTIUM ROOT ROT

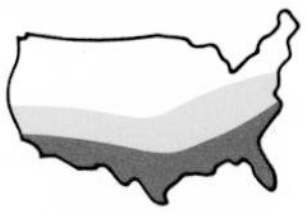

This plant disease, also known as *southern wilt, southern blight*, and *crown rot*, is caused by a soil-borne fungus (*Sclerotium rolfsii*) that occurs primarily in the southern states. The fungus infects many flowers and vegetables, and a few woody shrubs. *Sclerotium* causes root and crown rots, stem cankers, and bulb and tuber rots. It usually attacks plant stems at or just below the soil level. Infected plants wilt, turn yellow, and decay as the fungus spreads throughout the roots and stems. White fungal threads that surround or cover infected plants produce oxalic acid, which kills healthy plant cells, allowing the fungus to gain entrance. *Sclerotium* forms yellow or tan pellets that resemble mustard seeds. Under adverse conditions, these pellets and fungal strands survive in the soil and plant debris to reinfect healthy plants when conditions become favorable. This disease is most severe in warm (80°F and up), moist, sandy soils that are low in nitrogen.

CONTROL: Once plants become infected, there is no way to save them. It's best to pull out and destroy infected plants and remove the soil in the diseased area and 6 inches beyond. You can discourage rapid reinfection by making the soil unfavorable for fungal growth. Add a fertilizer, such as ORTHO General Purpose Plant Food, and liberal quantities of compost, leaf mold, or other organic matter. Clean up plant debris to eliminate fungal pellets.

Cotton root rot on pecan.

COTTON ROOT ROT

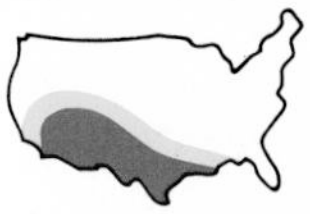

This plant disease, also known as *Texas root rot*, is caused by a fungus (*Phymatotrichum omnivorum*) that lives in soils throughout much of the Southwest. This fungus infects more than 1700 species of plants, eventually killing them by rotting their roots. Infected plants wilt and may die within a few days if they are suffering from drought or heat stress. When pulled out of the ground, the roots are covered with yellow or tan fungal growth. The fungus thrives in warm, poorly aerated, alkaline (pH 8.0 and up) soils that are low in organic matter. In many areas, the fungal strands and spores are concentrated 1 to 3 feet below the soil surface. Cotton root rot can survive in the soil for 5 years after plants have died. It is spread from plant to plant by brown fungal strands that grow through the soil, and by the movement of contaminated soil and transplants. Cotton root rot is most active from midsummer to frost.

CONTROL: Creating a soil environment unfavorable to its development can reduce the severity of cotton root rot. Improve soil aeration by digging or tilling your soil. To improve the drainage and increase the number of competing beneficial microorganisms, incorporate lots of mulch, compost, or other organic matter into the soil. Reducing the alkalinity of the soil also helps. Fumigating the soil will kill the fungus (see page 927). For a list of plants resistant to cotton root rot that may be used to replace infected plants, see page 1007.

BACTERIAL DISEASES

Bacterial crown rot on orchid.

Bacterial wilt on cucumber.

Bacterial soft rot of cabbage.

BACTERIAL DISEASES

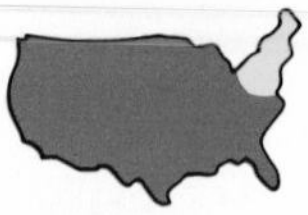

Bacteria are microscopic organisms that are neither plant nor animal; they do not have an organized, well-defined cell nucleus like plant and animal cells. Most bacteria live on decaying organic matter. About 200 species of bacteria cause plant diseases. Bacteria vary in their ability to survive in the soil without a host; some can live and multiply in the soil, while others die off. They damage plants by causing leaf spots, soft rots, blights, wilts, cankers, and galls. Bacteria often live within a protective ooze that they produce on infected plant parts. When conditions are warm and moist, this ooze, containing millions of bacteria, is exuded by infected plants. Infection spreads when the ooze is splashed to healthy plant parts or other plants, and when bacteria are transferred from diseased plants to healthy plants by contaminated hands, tools, and insects.

CONTROL: Bacterial diseases are more difficult to control than fungal diseases. The available chemicals, such as *streptomycin* or *basic copper sulfate*, are not very effective, but when used in combination with good sanitation, can usually keep infection to a minimum. When possible, use resistant plant varieties.

BACTERIAL WILTS

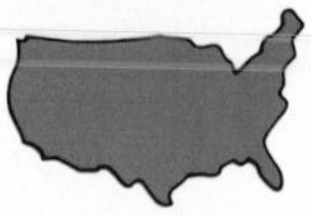

Several kinds of bacteria can cause bacterial wilt in vegetables, flowers, tropical plants, and other herbaceous plants. Infection begins when bacteria in the soil or on contaminated tools and hands penetrate wounds in the roots, leaves, or stems, or when infected seed is planted. In some cases, infection begins when insects transmit the bacteria to healthy plants. The bacteria enter the water-conducting vessels of the plant, where they break down plant cells, producing gums and gels. The bacteria also move out of these vessels to attack and dissolve the walls of adjacent cells. Sometimes bacterial ooze emerges from cracks in the leaf and stem tissue. The accumulation of gels, gums, cell debris, and bacteria in the vessels clogs the water flow throughout the plant. This clogging and the destruction of cell walls causes the plant to discolor, wilt, and finally die.

CONTROL: Once the bacteria infect the plant, there is no way to stop them. It's best to throw out the plants to avoid spreading the infection. Keep the garden clean; destroy plant debris. If you want to replant in infested soil, use resistant varieties. Because bacteria may remain in the seed, do not plant seed obtained from infected plants. If infection is widespread and severe, you can kill the bacteria in the soil by using fumigation techniques. For information on soil fumigation, see page 927.

BACTERIAL SOFT ROT

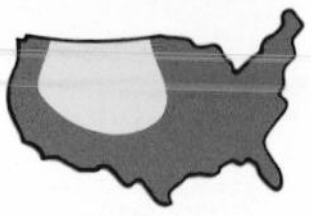

Bacterial soft rot occurs on succulent fruits, vegetables, bulbs, and tubers. Any diseased, weak, or overripe fruit, vegetables, or flowers are susceptible. However, a few kinds of bacteria can infect and decay actively growing plants. These bacteria penetrate the plant through wounds made by insect feeding or damage from tools or handling. The bacteria produce enzymes that break down plant cells, causing the infected tissue to turn soft, mushy, and watery. Masses of bacteria and cell debris may ooze through growth cracks in the plant tissue. This sticky ooze dries and turns tan, gray, or brown. Bacterial soft rot is most severe in warm (80° to 85°F), moist conditions. The bacteria survive from season to season in infected plant debris and soil. Infection is spread by diseased plants or plant parts, water, and contaminated tools, soil, and plant debris.

CONTROL: Chemicals aren't effective in controlling this disease; once your plants are infected, there is nothing you can do. The key to control is good sanitation. Help prevent bacterial soft rot by cleaning up plant debris around the garden. When working in the yard, be careful not to injure plants with hoes, cultivators, or other garden tools. You can further reduce infection by leaving enough space between plants so they get a chance to dry out after they are watered. Plant in well-drained soil. For more information about improving soil drainage, see page 907.

VIRUS DISEASES

Crown gall on euonymus.

Squash mosaic.

Virus infection of mint.

CROWN GALL

Crown gall is caused by soil-inhabiting bacteria (*Agrobacterium tumefaciens*) that infect the plant through wounds in the roots, crown, or stems. After infection, they produce a substance that stimulates plant cells to enlarge and divide rapidly and continuously, independent of the normal hormonal control of the host plant. This uncontrolled growth is similar in several respects to tumors in animals and humans. As the galls enlarge, they become woody and hard, and the outer layers die, turning brown and corky. Growing galls may exert pressure on the underlying normal plant tissues. The galls interfere with the plant's circulation, slowing the flow of water and nutrients through the galled area to the top of the plant. Infected plants are often weak, stunted, and more susceptible to other sources of plant stress, such as drought and winter injury. The bacteria are spread by infested soil, transplants, and contaminated tools, and through soil water.

CONTROL: Even though infected plants cannot be cured, they usually survive for many years. The plants look better if stems with galls are pruned off. It's much more difficult to properly remove galls on tree roots and trunks. Professional horticulturists or landscape contractors can remove large galls. When you replant in infested soil, choose plants that are resistant to crown gall. For a list, see page 1013.

VIRUS DISEASES

Viruses are complex, submicroscopic particles composed of proteins and nucleic acids. They are much smaller than fungi or bacteria, and are not made of cells. A few virus diseases of plants are serious or fatal. These are usually transmitted by insects or spread by hands or equipment. Most viruses only slightly impair the growth of the plant, and manifest symptoms only under certain conditions. They are usually transmitted when diseased stock is propagated by cuttings or grafting. Viruses may spread slowly from cell to cell, eventually infecting all of the plant tissue. Or they may spread quickly through the nutrient-conducting vessels to specific parts of the plant. Infection usually decreases the plant's ability to manufacture food. Less chlorophyll (green plant pigment) is produced, and the amounts of nitrogen and stored foods in the plant are reduced. Some of the common types of viruses, such as *mosaics, ring spots*, and *stunts*, produce specific symptoms. *Mosaic* viruses cause the foliage to become mottled or streaked. *Ring-spot* viruses cause pale rings to form on the leaves. *Stunts* viruses cause stunting of plant foliage. Often the symptoms overlap. In some hosts, these viruses cause leaf thickening, curling, and distortion; slow growth; and reduced yields of fruit, flowers, and vegetables. The severity of virus infections varies, depending on the host plant and strain of virus. Sometimes viruses infect certain host plants without showing symptoms of disease. In other cases, symptoms appear with changes in the environment, such as a rise or drop in temperature.

CONTROL: There are no chemical cures for virus infections. Aphids, leafhoppers, and certain other insects transmit viruses while feeding, so you can control infection by keeping the insect population down. For more information about controlling virus-carrying insects, see page 879. Pulling out infected plants will also help reduce the spread of virus diseases. Because seed, bulbs, corms, and cuttings taken from infected plants are likely to be infected, it's best to purchase healthy plants and seed from a reputable nursery and discard seeds and cuttings from diseased plants.

DISEASES

Aster yellows. Infected marigold bud on left.

ASTER YELLOWS

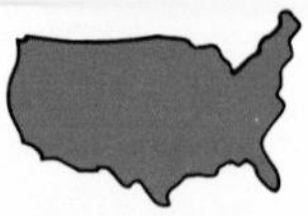

Aster yellows is a plant disease that is caused by *mycoplasmas*, microscopic organisms similar to bacteria. Many vegetables, ornamentals, and weeds are susceptible to this disease. Infected plants are usually stunted and yellowing. They produce many spindly stems and flower stalks. The flowers are often green, and don't produce seeds or fruit. Mycoplasmas are spread from plant to plant by leafhoppers. (For more information about leafhoppers, see page 878.) When a leafhopper feeds on a diseased plant, mycoplasmas are transferred into its body along with the plant sap. The mycoplasmas multiply in the insect's body. After an incubation period of 10 days, the leafhopper infects healthy plants when it feeds.

CONTROL: Once the plant is infected, there is no way to cure it. Keep aster yellows under control by destroying infected plants and keeping the garden free of weeds, especially those weeds that are likely to be infected. It's also a good idea to spray for leafhoppers early in the season to keep populations from soaring later. Spray leafhopper-infested plants with ORTHO Diazinon Insect Spray, or ORTHO Isotox Insect Killer according to label directions. Make sure your plant is listed on the product label.

Weeds commonly infected with aster yellows: Black-eyed Susan, dandelion, field daisy, thistle, wideleafed plantain, wild carrot, and wild chicory.

NEMATODES

Root knot nematode damage to snap bean.

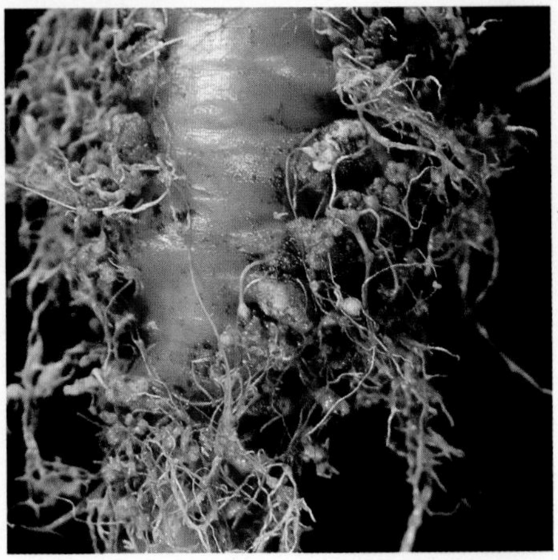

Root knot nematode damage to carrot.

NEMATODES

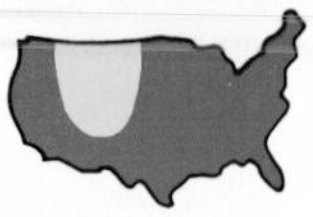

Nematodes are also known as *eelworms*, *nemas*, or *round worms*. They include some well-known parasites of humans, such as pinworms. Nematodes are found throughout the world in soil, fresh and salt water, and plants and animals. The several hundred species of nematodes that parasitize plants are microscopic. Most of them live in the soil and feed on plant roots; a few (foliar nematodes) feed on aboveground plant parts. Nematodes are found throughout the United States, but they are most severe in the Southeast. They prefer moist, sandy soils.

Root nematodes: Root-feeding nematodes are attracted to substances exuded by plant roots. Some of them remain on the outside of the root while feeding; others penetrate the root tissue, and live inside the root. Roots may be damaged from the punctures made during feeding, but the most significant damage occurs when nematodes inject "saliva" into the roots. This saliva contains a toxin that causes cells to collapse or disintegrate, resulting in dark lesions and dead areas along the roots. In some cases, the toxin stimulates rapid cell growth or enlargement, resulting in numerous dark, bushy roots, or galls or swellings on roots. Nematode damage limits the ability of the root system to supply the aboveground plant parts with water and nutrients, causing plant wilting, discoloration, stunting, and in severe cases death. Some nematodes indirectly injure plants by rendering them more susceptible to root-rot fungi. Although the nematodes do not directly transmit fungi, they can transmit certain virus diseases while feeding. Nematodes can move through the soil by themselves, but they move slowly, traveling at most 3 feet during a season. They are spread more rapidly by infested soil and transplants, contaminated equipment, and irrigation water.

Foliar nematodes: Foliar nematodes live and feed mainly inside plant stems and leaves. They spread through the plant by swimming through moisture on wet leaves. The foliage of infested plants is stunted and distorted, and brownish black blotches develop on the leaves.

CONTROL: Nematode damage is difficult to distinguish from other soil and root problems. Test the plants and a soil sample to confirm nematode damage. (For more information about soil testing, see page 909.) There are no chemicals that can be used to kill nematodes in planted soil. Remove and destroy infested plants, and fumigate the soil to control nematodes. (For more information on soil fumigation, see page 931.) Many varieties of plants are resistant to nematodes. If you have a serious problem with nematodes, plant resistant varieties. For a list of nematode-resistant plants adapted to your area, check with your local Cooperative Extension Office (see page 1029). Avoid moving infested soil and transplants to clean soil.

AIR POLLUTION

Ozone damage to bean.

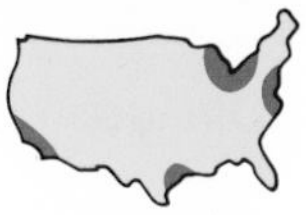

OZONE

Ozone forms when gases produced by combustion engines and other industrial processes interact in the presence of sunlight with materials given off by automobiles, solvents, and vegetation. Ozone is common throughout the United States, and is the primary air pollutant on the East Coast. All types of plants are affected. Ozone causes small white to tan flecks to appear on the upper surfaces of the leaves. On some plants the flecks are visible on both the upper and lower surfaces. Conifers display mottled needles, or the needle tips turn reddish brown to gray. Repeated exposure to ozone reduces growth, causes blossom, fruit, and needle drop, and may eventually kill the plant. Ozone injury usually occurs when the air is still; concentrations are highest in the early afternoon from mid to late summer. Ozone is absorbed through the leaf pores. Once inside the leaf, it disrupts the cell membranes. This causes the cells to collapse, resulting in the white flecks. Environmental factors influence the susceptibility of plants to injury. Plants growing in light, moist soil with optimum nutrient levels are more sensitive to injury, as are those growing in warm temperatures (80° to 90°F) and high light levels at the time of exposure.

CONTROL: Once plants are damaged, regular watering and fertilizing will speed recovery. In smoggy areas, select plants that are tolerant of ozone from the list on page 1008.

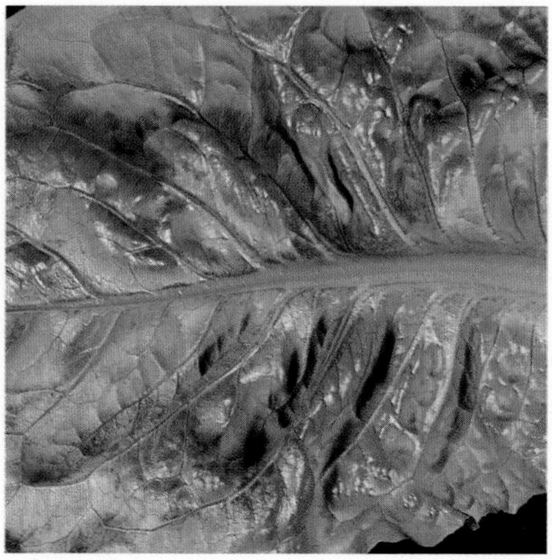

PAN damage to lettuce.

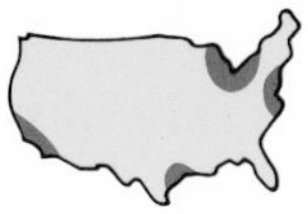

PAN

PAN (*peroxyacetyl nitrate*), an ingredient of smog, damages herbaceous plants mainly on the West Coast. Trees are seldom affected by this pollutant. PAN enters the leaves through microscopic breathing pores causing a characteristic silvering or glazing on the lower surfaces of the leaves. When damage is severe, the injured tissue dies and turns whitish tan. Young, rapidly growing leaves and plants are especially sensitive to PAN exposure. Injury may also occur in bands across the leaf, with each band corresponding to a different exposure. Healthy green tissue separates each band. Plants repeatedly exposed to PAN grow slowly and drop their leaves. Sunscald, frost injury, and damage by mites, thrips, and leafhoppers resemble PAN injury. The most severe injury occurs at midday on sunny days. Plants growing in moist soil in very warm weather (80° to 95°F) are highly sensitive.

CONTROL: Water and fertilize injured plants regularly to help speed recovery. In smoggy areas, select PAN-tolerant plants from the list on page 1008.

Sulfur dioxide damage to azalea.

SULFUR DIOXIDE AND NITROGEN DIOXIDE

Sulfur dioxide is an industrial pollutant resulting from burning sulfur-containing fuels such as coal and refining oil, and from smelting ores. Full grown and nearly grown leaves are the most susceptible to injury. All types of plants are affected. Injured areas first become water-soaked and then turn yellowish; or they dry up, turning ivory or brown. Injured areas may appear along the margins and between the veins on both surfaces of the leaves. On conifers, the young needles turn orange-red. Severely injured plants drop their leaves or needles and eventually die. Plants are most sensitive to sulfur dioxide from late spring to late summer. Sensitive plants are more likely to be injured at midday than in the early morning or evening. Plants are more sensitive at temperatures above 60°F, and when they are growing in moist soil. *Nitrogen dioxide* causes symptoms very similar to those caused by sulfur dioxide. It can be a problem in areas near factories that manufacture munitions or nitric acid, or that do electroplating, engraving, or welding. The greatest concentrations of this pollutant occur in midsummer. Nitrogen dioxide damage occurs mainly during the night. Plants growing in moist soil are especially sensitive to injury. Nitrogen dioxide frequently interacts with other pollutants, causing extensive injury.

CONTROL: Help injured plants to recover by watering and fertilizing them regularly. In industrial areas, select plants tolerant to sulfur dioxide and nitrogen dioxide from the list on page 1008.

Dwarf mistletoe.

Leafy mistletoe.

Drought.

DWARF MISTLETOE

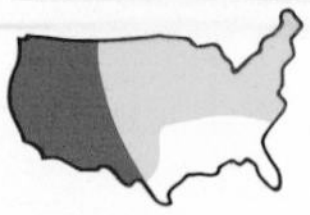

Dwarf mistletoes (*Arceuthobium* species) are parasitic plants that grow only on conifers. The grayish green to brownish green scaly shoots of this parasite rarely grow longer than 8 inches; they are usually 4 inches or shorter. Unlike leafy mistletoes, dwarf mistletoes are true parasites, obtaining all their food from the host plant. Their rootlike attachment organs (haustoria) penetrate the host's food-conducting vessels. As the haustoria continue to spread through a limb, they form buds that sprout tufts of dwarf mistletoe along the infected branch. This parasite disrupts the normal functioning and hormonal balance of infected branches, often starving the branch growth beyond the point of infection. Limbs usually swell around the infected area, and cankers and witch's brooms (many small tufted branches) may form. Infected trees are stunted, weakened, and sometimes killed by this parasite.

CONTROL: The only effective way to get rid of dwarf mistletoe is to prune off the limbs on which it is growing. The haustoria spread several feet inside the branch from the site of the mistletoe tufts, so cut the branch off at the trunk to make sure that you've eliminated all of the haustoria. Be on the lookout for additional resprouting of the mistletoe; prune it out as soon as you see it. If a tree is severely infected (more than half of the branches are parasitized), consider removing the entire tree. The tree is bound to decline in health if it hasn't already, and will be a source of infection for other trees.

LEAFY MISTLETOE

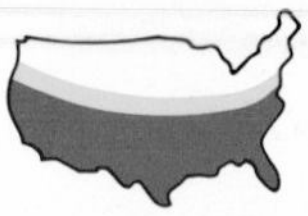

Leafy mistletoes (*Phoradendron* species) are plants that grow on broadleafed trees throughout the United States; they rarely attack conifers. Leafy mistletoes have chlorophyll (green plant pigment) and can manufacture their own food. To obtain water and minerals, their rootlike attachment organs (haustoria) penetrate the host plant's water-conducting vessels. These haustoria can grow through the branch, sending up more leafy tufts several feet from the original site of attachment. Branches usually swell around the infected area, and branch growth is sometimes sparse beyond the mistletoe site. Leafy mistletoes are spread to other areas of the tree when their sticky seeds drop to branches below. Also, the seeds may be eaten or accidentally carried by birds and other tree-dwelling animals and deposited on other trees. Trees infested with leafy mistletoe usually continue to survive for many years, but their overall growth and vigor may be reduced.

CONTROL: The most effective way to get rid of leafy mistletoe is to prune off the branch on which it is growing. To be sure that the haustoria have been removed, prune off the branch at least 3 feet below the point of mistletoe attachment. The haustoria are visible as green streaks or dots in the wood. For more information about controlling leafy mistletoe, see page 416.

DROUGHT

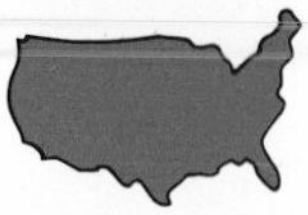

Plants suffer from drought stress any time they receive less water than they need. Water is essential to the normal maintenance and growth of all plants. It moves into plant roots from the soil and is transported up through the water-conducting vessels in the branches, stems, and foliage to all the plant cells. The pressure exerted by water in the cells keeps them turgid. Eventually it evaporates from the plant through tiny breathing pores in the leaves. When plants don't receive enough water, the water pressure in the cells drops, the cells lose their turgidity, and the plant wilts. If drought continues, normal metabolic functions are disrupted. Plants grown in mild drought conditions are usually stunted and slow growing. They are also hardier and better able to withstand stress. Plants grown in more severe drought conditions stop growing, discolor, drop their leaves and fruit, and eventually starve and die. Plants wilt permanently when deprived of water for long periods, or when grown in soil so dry that the roots cannot extract water at all.

CONTROL: Growth will be more rapid and luxuriant if you give plants enough water. For more information about proper watering techniques, see page 912. If drought is a common problem in your area because of low rainfall, plant drought tolerant plants. For a list, see page 1009.

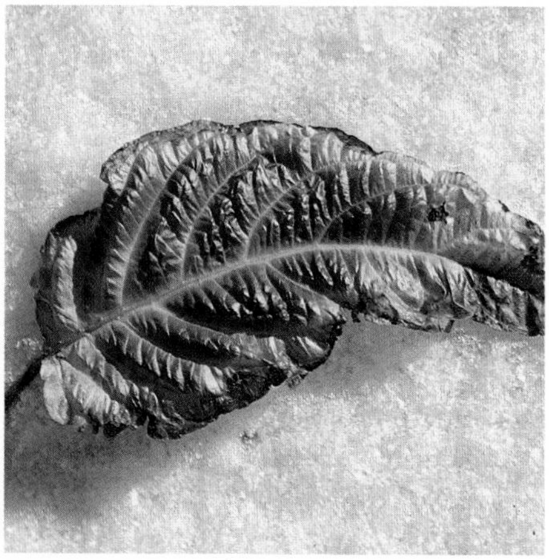

Salt damage.

Leaf burn on fuchsia.

Leaf scorch on poplar.

SALT DAMAGE

Salts in the soil come from natural minerals in the soil or dissolved in the irrigation water; from improperly applied manure, lime, or fertilizer; or from deicing salts. If the concentration of salts dissolved in the soil water is too high, plants can't get enough water for healthy growth. As a result, growth slows and the leaves turn yellow. Salt also enters the plant, where it is deposited in the leaf tips or edges as the water in which it was dissolved evaporates. When enough salt accumulates, the tissue at the edge of the leaf turns yellow, then dies. As water evaporates from the soil, the salts become more concentrated, and more damaging. Salt damage and drought damage often occur together, compounding the problem. Salt accumulation in the soil is often caused by poor drainage, which keeps the salts from being leached through the soil. For information on inexpensive laboratory tests for salts, see page 909.

CONTROL: Leach salts from the soil with periodic heavy irrigations. Enough water should be applied to wash the salts below the plant roots. If the soil does not drain well, improve drainage according to the instructions on page 907. Keep the soil moist enough so that the plants are never under stress. Follow label instructions when using fertilizer. Apply the fertilizer to moist soil, and water it in thoroughly. If you are applying lime to soil already high in salts, use ground limestone rather than agricultural lime or quicklime; it is less soluble, and less likely to cause problems. If you have salt problems, do not use bagged steer manure (feedlot manure), which contains high levels of salts.

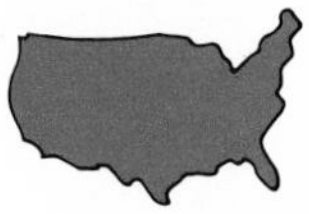

LEAF BURN AND LEAF SCORCH

Leaf burn and *leaf scorch* occur when leaf cells overheat. Although the two terms are often used interchangeably, leaf scorch usually refers to browning and tissue death around leaf margins and between veins, while leaf burn usually refers to dead patches in the middle of the leaf. Normally, leaves are cooled by the evaporation of water from their surfaces. When leaves dry out, the amount of water that evaporates is reduced and they overheat, then burn or scorch. Sometimes entire leaves or shoots are damaged. Several different conditions may cause leaf burn or leaf scorch. Many of these factors are interrelated; when they occur in combination, damage may be severe.

Lack of water: Leaf burn and leaf scorch often occur when plant roots can't get enough water. Many soil conditions may cause dehydration. Plants growing in dry, salty, frozen, or restricted soil areas may not get as much water as they need.

Too much water: Overwatered or heavy, poorly drained soils can cause burn or scorch. Roots require oxygen to function properly. Wet soils are often low in oxygen, causing root death. As the roots start to die, they absorb less water.

Wind and heat: Hot, windy conditions cause burn and scorch in some plants, even when the soil is moist. Wind and heat cause water to evaporate more quickly from the leaves than it can be replaced.

Freezing damage: Leaf burn or leaf scorch may result when foliage freezes. Frozen leaf cells rupture or dry out and die.

Other factors: Roots that are diseased or mechanically damaged often cannot supply as much water as the plant needs, resulting in leaf burn or leaf scorch. Burn and scorch can also be caused by an accumulation of salt in the leaf tissue. For more information, see page 857.

CONTROL: Leaves damaged by leaf scorch or leaf burn will not recover. Keep plants properly watered to help reduce further damage. For more information about proper watering, see page 916. If possible, shade plants during very hot weather, and hose down foliage a couple of times a day. (For more information about heat protection, see page 918.) Make sure the soil is moist when it freezes, and reduce chances of dehydration resulting from frozen soils by applying a mulch around the base of the plant. (For more information about mulching, see page 926.) Inspect damaged plants for root rot or mechanical damage. (For more information on root rots, see page 849.) Protect shade-loving plants by providing adequate shade.

WEATHER AND CULTURAL DISEASES ■ TEMPERATURE-RELATED DISEASES

Root rot of succulent caused by overwatering.

Upper flower buds killed by winter cold.

Frost cracks.

OVERWATERING

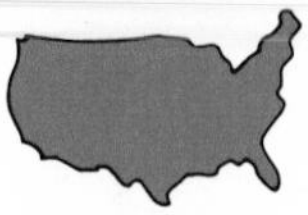

Overwatering is one of the most common plant problems, especially in areas where the soil is heavy and poorly drained. Plant roots require oxygen to function normally. They obtain oxygen from tiny air spaces (pores) in the soil. When the soil is irrigated, air is pushed out of the soil pores and replaced with water. Pores refill with air when water drains through the soil, as plant roots absorb water, and as water evaporates up through the soil surface. If water is constantly reapplied, the soil pores will remain filled with water. Roots growing in such soil die because they cannot absorb the oxygen they need. The dying roots decay and are unable to supply the plant with water and nutrients. This results in plant stunting, weakening, and eventually death. Sometimes plants respond to wet soil conditions by growing roots just under the soil surface where the soil dries out more rapidly and oxygen is more available. These plants are often stunted and slow growing. They may wilt and die quickly if the soil is allowed to dry out past their shallow root zone. Overwatering frequently causes root rot diseases. For more information about root rot, see page 849.

CONTROL: Allow the soil to dry out somewhat between waterings. (For information on watering, see page 912.) If your soil is heavy and poorly drained, improve the soil drainage. (For more information on improving drainage, see page 907.) Some plants can tolerate wet soil; for a list, see page 1010.

COLD DAMAGE

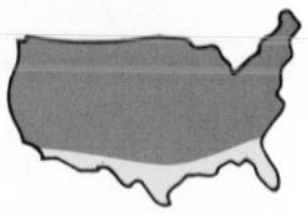

Low temperatures damage plants in several ways.

Freezing: Leaves, stems, and sometimes the entire plant may be killed by freezing. Foliage damaged by freezing temperatures looks water-soaked and wilts. In a few hours or days, it darkens and turns black.

Tender plants: Tender plants are most likely to suffer from freezing temperatures in the fall and spring. Seedlings or plants that have been raised in the house or greenhouse are very susceptible to freezing damage if they are planted outdoors too early in the spring or left out too late in the fall.

Early or late cold snaps: Plants that are hardened off (adjusted to outdoor conditions) and adapted to the area in which they are growing do not usually suffer from freezing damage unless the temperature drops much lower than normal. However, during mild fall weather hardening off is delayed, and unexpected cold snaps in early fall may freeze tender leaves and stems. When premature warm spells during the spring stimulate the production of new growth, cold snaps can be very damaging to this tender foliage.

Chilling injury: Cold-sensitive, tender plants growing in warm winter areas, and greenhouse-grown or house-raised plants, may be susceptible to chilling temperatures (50°F and lower). Chilling injury usually occurs when these plants are set outdoors when night temperatures drop below 50°F. Even though the leaf tissue doesn't freeze, these tender plants cannot tolerate cool conditions. Their foliage may discolor and die.

Winter sunscald and frost cracks: For information about cold damage to woody plants, see page 457.

CONTROL: There is not much you can do about unanticipated freezing or chilling temperatures during cold snaps. If you anticipate damagingly low temperatures, cover plants with burlap, cardboard, or heavy paper during the night. It's usually a good idea to wait until spring before pruning out dead twigs and branches. Often the full amount of dieback caused by cold damage isn't obvious until the tree or shrub begins to grow again in the spring. However, it's best to prune or pinch off frozen leaves, flowers, and stems of herbaceous flowers and vegetables as soon as damage is noticed. Use only plants adapted to your area, or be prepared to shelter or protect tender plants when temperatures drop below 50°F. Harden off house-raised plants before setting them outside by gradually exposing them to cool temperatures over a period of a week.

■ NUTRIENT DEFICIENCIES

Sunscald on maple.

SUNSCALD

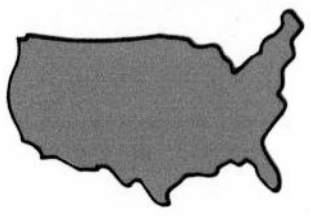

Sunscald occurs when bark is killed by overexposure to the sun. Trees that have been recently transplanted or pruned are most susceptible to sunscald. When a tree is shaded by other trees, buildings, or dense foliage, the bark on the trunk and branches remains thin and tender. If exposed to intense sunlight, the bark cells heat up rapidly. Because they are not adapted to such high temperatures, the cells are easily injured or killed. Dark brown or black barks are particularly susceptible to sunscald because they absorb more heat than lighter barks. Sunscald may also occur during cold, sunny winter days. The killed bark turns dark and splits open, forming long cracks or cankers, usually on the southwest side of the tree. Decay organisms may invade the damaged bark and wood. Sunscald is most severe when the tree is suffering from drought stress.

CONTROL: Unless the tree is very young or extremely damaged, it will usually recover with proper care. Water and fertilize the tree to stimulate new growth. As the tree adapts to its sunnier location, its bark will thicken; new growth will also shade the bark, protecting it from sunscald. To prevent damage, wrap the trunks and main branches of recently pruned or newly transplanted trees with burlap or tree-wrapping paper. Or paint the exposed bark with whitewash or white interior latex paint. If possible, transplant in overcast, cool weather, and water trees as soon as they've been transplanted. For more information about watering, see page 912.

Nitrogen-deficient Swedish ivy.

NITROGEN DEFICIENCY

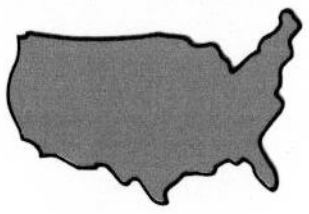

Nitrogen is the most commonly deficient plant nutrient. Nitrogen-starved plants grow slowly. New leaves are small and pale green. The older leaves turn yellow and fall off or die and remain hanging on the plant.

Nitrogen in the plant: Nitrogen is taken up by plant roots from the soil, and is used in the formation of many plant tissues and compounds such as proteins, chlorophyll (green plant pigment), enzymes, and nucleic acids. Because plants use nitrogen whenever they form new tissue this nutrient is used in large quantities whenever growth is rapid; plants that are dormant or growing slowly use less nitrogen.

Soil deficient in nitrogen: If the soil is deficient in nitrogen, plants break down the compounds in older leaves to recycle the nitrogen to new growth. This is why the older leaves of plants suffering from nitrogen deficiency turn yellow and die.

High nitrogen levels: High nitrogen levels stimulate leaf growth, often at the expense of root growth or flower production.

CONTROL: Most plants need to be fertilized regularly with nitrogen fertilizers. While nitrogen is needed all the time a plant is not dormant, it is needed in the greatest amounts when leaves are growing most rapidly. For most plants, this is from spring through early summer. Use fertilizers such as ORTHO General Purpose Plant Food, ORTHO Evergreen, Tree & Shrub Food, or ORTHO Blood Meal. For more information about fertilization, see page 910.

Phosphorus-deficient tomato seedling.

PHOSPHORUS DEFICIENCY

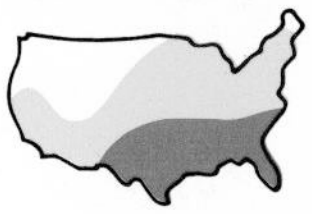

Plants that are starved for phosphorus are stunted, and darker than usual. The leaves are dull and gray-green, and may be tinged with magenta. Some plants develop magenta coloring under the leaves, especially on the veins or around the edge of the leaf. Flowering and fruiting are usually poor. Plants that are only slightly deficient in phosphorus grow more slowly than normal, and produce fewer flowers and fruit, but often have no specific symptoms.

Phosphorus in the plant: Phosphorus is used in the enzyme systems that produce new cells and supply energy to the plant tissues. It promotes healthy root growth and the production of flowers and fruit.

Seedlings: Seedlings and other plants with limited root systems need more phosphorus than plants with more developed root systems. Even in areas where phosphorus seldom needs to be applied to growing plants, seedlings may be deficient. If this is the case, their growth is slowed for a few weeks until the root system develops enough to supply the plant with phosphorus. Trees seldom need added phosphorus.

CONTROL: For a quick response, spray the leaves with Ra-Pid-Gro Plant Food. Add ORTHO Superphosphate to the soil, placing it within the root zone, either by cultivation or by dropping it into holes dug into the root zone. Water transplants with ORTHO Up-Start Plant Starter. In the future, use a fertilizer that contains at least 5 percent phosphate, such as ORTHO General Purpose Plant Food or ORTHO Rose & Flower Food.

Potassium-deficient walnut leaf.

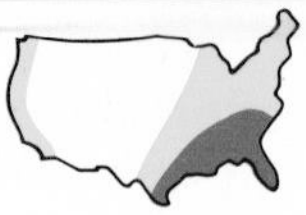

POTASSIUM DEFICIENCY

Plants that are deficient in potassium grow slowly. The older leaves are mottled with yellow or pale green smudges. The edges of the leaves scorch and die. The dead area may extend inward between the leaf veins. Badly scorched leaves usually drop. Slightly deficient plants grow more slowly than usual and have low yields of flowers and fruit. They are especially susceptible to disease.

Potassium in the plant: Potassium is essential to the normal functioning of many plant enzymes, and facilitates the production of chlorophyll (green plant pigment), proteins, carbohydrates, and other plant tissues. Potassium is used in the production of new cells, and is necessary for the proper opening and closing of the tiny breathing pores (stomata) in leaves. This nutrient is used most heavily in rapidly growing plant parts.

Lack of potassium: When potassium is in short supply, plants break down potassium-containing compounds in their older leaves, and recycle the potassium to the new growth. That is why the symptoms develop first on older leaves.

CONTROL: Spray the leaves with Ra-Pid-Gro Plant Food. Fertilize the plant with ORTHO Fruit & Bloom Builder. In the future, use a fertilizer that contains at least 5 percent potassium, such as ORTHO General Purpose Plant Food, ORTHO Evergreen, Tree & Shrub Food, or ORTHO Azalea, Camellia & Rhododendron Food.

Iron-deficient oak.

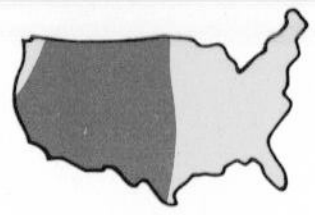

MINOR NUTRIENT DEFICIENCY

The leaves of plants deficient in minor nutrients are pale green or yellow between the veins; the veins remain bright green. In extreme cases, the entire leaf is bright yellow or almost white, and small, so that the new growth looks like a flower. Older leaves usually remain green.

Minor nutrients in the plant: Iron and several other elements (including manganese and zinc) are essential plant nutrients. They are called "minor" only because they are needed by the plant in small quantities. Minor nutrients are required for the production of chlorophyll (green plant pigment), and are essential to the proper functioning of many plant enzymes.

Minor nutrients in the soil: These nutrients are present in most soils. However, alkaline soil or wet soil often cause them to form compounds that cannot be used by the plant. Minor nutrients are not mobile throughout the plant. Once they have been incorporated into leaf tissue, the plant cannot reuse them for new growth. Therefore minor nutrient deficiencies show up in the newest growth first.

CONTROL: Spray the foliage with ORTHO Greenol Liquid Iron, and apply it to the soil around the plants to correct the deficiency of minor nutrients. Check the soil pH. (For information on pH, see page 908; for information on soil testing, see page 909.) If your soil is too alkaline, correct the pH by treating with ORTHO Aluminum Sulfate or ORTHO Orthorix Spray. Maintain an acid pH by fertilizing with ORTHO Azalea, Camellia & Rhododendron Food.

Oedema on cabbage.

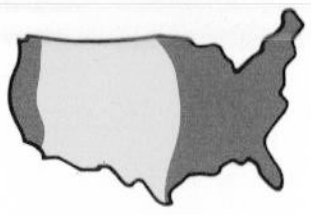

OEDEMA

Oedema, also known as *edema*, affects houseplants and some outdoor herbaceous plants. This condition is not caused by an insect or disease, but by a buildup of water in the plant. Oedema usually develops in plants that are overwatered and growing in a cool, humid atmosphere. Under these conditions, water is absorbed rapidly from the soil, and lost slowly through the leaves. The excess water that builds up in the plant causes cells to burst. Water-soaked spots or pale green blisters or bumps form on the leaves and stems. Eventually these bumps and spots develop into reddish brown corky ridges and spots. Some of the badly affected leaves may turn yellow and drop off.

CONTROL: Oedema is not a serious condition in itself, but often indicates an overwatering problem. Eliminate oedema by planting in well-drained soil and watering properly. For information on proper watering, see page 916. For information on improving soil drainage, see page 907.

Cankers on chestnut.

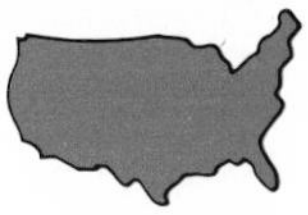

CANKERS

Most cankers are dark, sunken areas on trunks or branches. The bark over these areas cracks, then usually dies and falls off, revealing the wood beneath. Many trees produce a sticky sap that oozes from cankers. Cankers are caused by fungi and bacteria that infect the soft tissue just under the bark. Bark that has been damaged by sunscald, cold injury, pruning or insect wounds, or mechanical injury is especially susceptible. As the infection spreads, the infected bark and wood tissues darken and die. The water and nutrient-conducting vessels that pass through the cankered area are cut off. If the canker girdles a branch, the branch dies; if the trunk is girdled, the whole tree dies. Sometimes the plant walls off and stops canker growth by surrounding the canker with corky, barklike cells. Trees and shrubs are not usually killed by cankers, but are weakened and become more vulnerable to insects, diseases, and winter injury.

CONTROL: Remove badly infected branches, and cut out cankers. For details about canker removal and treatment, see page 917. Keep tree wounds to a minimum to cut down on canker formation. When pruning or working around plants, use the proper equipment and work carefully. Steer carefully around trunks when mowing the lawn. Infected trees will heal more quickly if they are watered and fertilized properly. For information about fertilizers, see page 910; for information about watering, see page 912.

Oak gall.

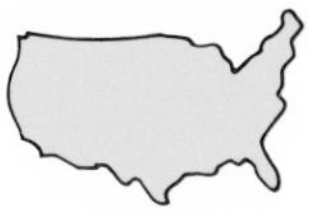

GALLS

Galls are growths on plants. They may be simple lumps, or they may have a complicated structure. Some galls are brightly colored. Galls form on leaves, twigs, and branches. In most cases they are unsightly but not damaging to the plant, although small plants may be stunted. The water and nutrient circulatory system of a small plant may be disrupted by the galls. Some galls form when insects (certain wasps, midges, and aphids) or mites feed on or lay eggs in leaves, stems, and twigs. While feeding or laying eggs, these insects inject a toxin that stimulates rapid and abnormal cell growth. Galls may also develop as a response to infection by any of several kinds of fungi, bacteria, and viruses. Galls caused by fungi and bacteria are usually most numerous in wet years. A soil-inhabiting bacterium (*Agrobacterium tumefaciens*) causes a common plant disease called *crown gall*. For more information about crown gall, see page 853.

CONTROL: Pruning off gall-infested growth usually takes care of the problem. If galls are especially unsightly and numerous, you can control the insects or diseases that are causing them. Look up your plant in the index to determine which pests may be causing the galls.

Witch's broom on hackberry.

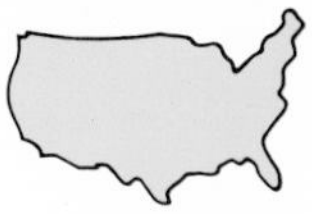

WITCH'S BROOM

Witch's brooms are dense tufts of weak, twiggy growth that develop on the branches of woody trees and shrubs. The foliage that grows on a witch's broom is usually smaller and paler than normal. Witch's brooms are not a disease in themselves; they grow when a hormonal imbalance develops in the plant, usually as the result of disease. Some mites or an infestation of dwarf mistletoe can also cause witch's brooms. (For more information about dwarf mistletoe, see page 856.) Sometimes environmental factors or chemicals (such as herbicides) stimulate the growth of witch's brooms. Certain kinds of plants are more likely to develop these growths. Although witch's brooms weaken the affected branch, they do not seriously damage the plant. However, the disease or mite that caused the witch's broom may kill the plant.

CONTROL: If a plant has many witch's brooms it is probably diseased or infested. You can improve the appearance of the tree or shrub by pruning off the witch's brooms, but unless you can control the disease or mite that is causing these growths, witch's brooms will continue to develop. Look up your plant in the index to determine what may be causing these growths. Contact a professional horticulturist or your local Cooperative Extension Office (see page 1029) for additional help.

Only a few of the thousands of insects are represented here, but these few are the insects that are mostly likely to be problems in the garden. Locate your insect in the index on the next page.

A GALLERY OF INSECTS

Insects and plants have evolved together. Insects exist in vast numbers; they will always be present in our gardens. Our goal should not be to eradicate all insects, or even the harmful ones, but to control their numbers so the damage they do is held in check.

Entomologists—scientists who study insects—place a great deal of importance on developing *life histories* of insects they study. A life history tells when the eggs hatch, what the larvae eat, how they survive the winter, and where they lay eggs, and other information about an insect's growth and development.

Life histories help us to locate weaknesses—times of year or stages of growth when the insect is most amenable to control measures. Scale insects, for instance, are covered with a waxy shell for most of their life. This shell protects them from predators and insecticides. But when they first hatch out they are soft-bodied and easily killed by insecticides. A well-timed spray or two can control a whole generation of scales.

Timing is particularly important with insects that have a single generation each year. All the eggs of single-generation insects hatch at once, and they go through the life stages at once. But other insects, such as aphids, have multiple generations a year. All life stages are apt to be present at once. Control of multiple-generation insects usually depends on a series of treatments over a period of time to kill new generations as they hatch from eggs.

Winter is a particularly vulnerable time for many insects. Being cold-blooded, they must spend the winter in an inactive state, often as eggs or pupae. Sanitation measures—such as removing dead plants from the garden, picking up trash, and tilling—remove, kill, or expose to the cold many insect pests. Dormant oil sprays suffocate eggs and insects on trees. Although we don't often think of insect control in the winter, this may be the best time to reduce next summer's insect population.

Also, many plants are now being bred that are resistant to their most damaging pests. Ask your Cooperative Extension agent about insect-resistant varieties for your area.

Above: Tent caterpillar. See page 870. Left: This tomato harnworm is feeding on a pepper plant. The "horn" is harmless.

INDEX TO INSECTS

BEETLE FAMILY

Elm leaf beetles (4 times life size).

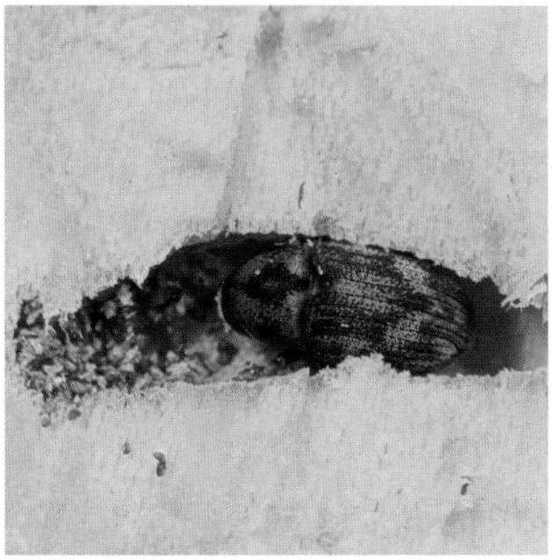
Eastern ash bark beetle (4 times life size).

Flatheaded borer (10 times life size).

BEETLES

Beetles are members of the order *Coleoptera*, which is the largest insect order, containing 40 percent of all insects. The shiny or dull insects are easily recognized by their tough, leathery wing covers, called *elytra*. The wing covers meet in the middle of the back, forming a straight line down the insect's body. Some beetles, distinguished by their long snouts, are also called *weevils* or *curculios*. When beetles are at rest, the elytra hide a pair of clear, membranous wings. Some beetles don't have wings, and can't fly. The larvae of beetles are sometimes called *grubs*. Those grubs that have legs usually have three pairs. The larvae of weevils and curculios are legless. Both the larvae and adults may be harmful to plants. They have chewing mouthparts, and feed on plant tissue, other insects, or as scavengers. Plant feeders may devour any part of the plant. Some beetles feed inside the leaf tissue as leafminers (page 885), borers (next column), or bark beetles (next column and page 435). Others feed outside the plant or on the roots.

CONTROL: There are many methods of controlling beetles, depending on the part of the plant they infest. Control measures are often aimed at the adults, because grubs may be hidden or protected from chemicals inside plants or in the ground. Several different insecticides, including *malathion*, *carbaryl* (SEVIN®), and *diazinon*, are used to control adult beetles. Look under the entry for your specific plant.

BARK BEETLES AND BORERS

Most borers are the larvae of beetles or moths that tunnel in wood or soft stems. Their presence is usually indicated by the sap or sawdust that surrounds holes in the tissue, and by wilting and dying foliage on the affected stems or branches. Hundreds of different kinds of borers infest trees, shrubs, and herbaceous plants. Borers that infest trees and shrubs usually favor weak, wounded, or recently set plants. However, borers commonly attack healthy flowers and vegetables as well. Vigorous trees and shrubs are often able to resist borer infestations. When the larvae try to burrow into such plants, they are overcome by oozing plant sap. Weak plants, such as those that have damaged roots or are suffering from drought, have reduced sap flow, making it easier for borers to enter them and develop inside. There are hundreds of different species of beetle borers that infest plants. They fall into two general catagories: bark beetles, and flat-headed or round-headed borers.

Bark beetles: These beetles mainly attack and kill weak trees, but are also capable of attacking and killing a healthy tree when present in large numbers. The larvae are white or cream and from $\frac{1}{16}$ to $\frac{1}{4}$ inch long. Adult bark beetles are $\frac{1}{16}$ to $\frac{1}{4}$ inch long and are usually black, brown, or dark red. The adults tunnel into and under the bark and lay eggs along the tunnels. The larvae hatch and generally bore away from the parent tunnel, creating characteristic tunnel designs which can be used by experts to identify the kind of bark beetle involved.

Round and flatheaded borers: These larger insects attack severely weakened trees or freshly killed trees. The larvae, usually white or cream colored, are approximately $\frac{3}{4}$ inch in length at maturity. Some have heads that are flattened and triangular; others have rounder heads. Adults are from $\frac{1}{4}$ to 1 $\frac{1}{2}$ inches long and are often metallic or brightly colored. The larvae leave tunnels that travel in a meandering, random path.

CONTROL: The best control for borers in many herbaceous plants is to cut out and destroy infested stems and remove dying plants. To control with chemicals, sprays must be applied before the insects burrow into the plant. The time varies with different species. For timing of sprays, look up your plant in the index, or contact your local Cooperative Extension Office (see page 1029). Many woody plants can be sprayed with ORTHO Lindane Borer & Leaf Miner Spray. Spray herbaceous plants with an insecticide containing *carbaryl* (SEVIN®). Make sure your plant is listed on the product label. Keep plants in vigorous growing condition by fertilizing and watering regularly, and by controlling diseases and other insects. Avoid wounding plants.

BEETLE FAMILY

Japanese beetle (life size).

Damaged rose. *Insert:* Rose curculio (life size).

Black vine weevil larvae (life size).

JAPANESE BEETLES

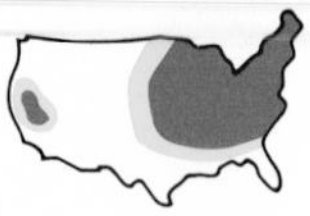

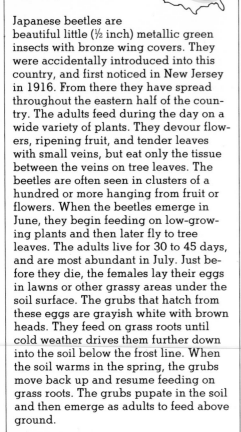

Japanese beetles are beautiful little (½ inch) metallic green insects with bronze wing covers. They were accidentally introduced into this country, and first noticed in New Jersey in 1916. From there they have spread throughout the eastern half of the country. The adults feed during the day on a wide variety of plants. They devour flowers, ripening fruit, and tender leaves with small veins, but eat only the tissue between the veins on tree leaves. The beetles are often seen in clusters of a hundred or more hanging from fruit or flowers. When the beetles emerge in June, they begin feeding on low-growing plants and then later fly to tree leaves. The adults live for 30 to 45 days, and are most abundant in July. Just before they die, the females lay their eggs in lawns or other grassy areas under the soil surface. The grubs that hatch from these eggs are grayish white with brown heads. They feed on grass roots until cold weather drives them further down into the soil below the frost line. When the soil warms in the spring, the grubs move back up and resume feeding on grass roots. The grubs pupate in the soil and then emerge as adults to feed above ground.

CONTROL: Adult beetles can be controlled on ornamentals with ORTHO Malathion 50 Insect Spray, ORTHO Liquid Sevin, ORTHO Gypsy Moth & Japanese Beetle Killer, or ORTHO Isotox Insect Killer. Spray food crops with ORTHO Malathion 50 Insect Spray or ORTHO Fruit & Vegetable Insect Control. To control grubs in the soil, follow the instructions on page 256. Before spraying, make sure your plant is listed on the product label.

WEEVILS

Weevils, also known as *snout beetles*, are beetles that have long snouts with chewing mouthparts at the end. Some weevils are called *curculios*. Curculios usually have snouts that are longer and more curved than those of weevils. Weevil adults are hard-bodied, usually dark-colored insects that play dead when disturbed. They feed on many different types of plants, often chewing holes in leaves, buds, and flowers. The larvae are white, fleshy, legless grubs that usually live inside plant tissue. Grubs may feed inside seeds, fruit, buds, leaves, or stems. Some weevil grubs live in the soil and feed on plant roots. These *root weevils* are very damaging to their host plants. For more information about root weevils, see page 866.

CONTROL: Control is most often aimed at the adults, since the larvae are usually protected inside plant tissue. To control weevils on fruit and nut trees, spray with ORTHO Home Orchard Spray. Several different insecticides, including *malathion*, *lindane*, and *carbaryl* (SEVIN®), are used to control weevils on vegetables and ornamentals. Look under the entry for your specific plant.

ROOT WEEVILS

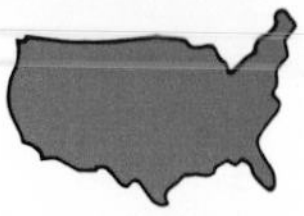

Root weevils are serious pests of berries, ornamentals, and grasses. Both adults and larvae cause damage. The adults are snout beetles, with chewing mouthparts at the end of their long snouts. They have light brown to black hard-shelled bodies, with rows of tiny round depressions on their backs. In most species the adults cannot fly because their elytra (wing covers) are fused down the middle of the back. The adult weevils feed at night, notching the edges of leaves. In the summer, each female lays hundreds of eggs on the soil at the base of plants. The emerging larvae are white, C-shaped, legless grubs with brown heads. The grubs sometimes feed on the base of plant stems before burrowing down into the soil to feed on roots. They spend the winter in the soil and resume feeding in the spring. Larval feeding is most severe in spring and often results in severe weakening or death of the plant.

CONTROL: Since the grubs are protected by soil, there are no effective controls for them. Control of root weevils must be aimed at the adults. The best time to spray is in May or June as the adults emerge from the soil. Check your plants periodically for notched leaves; or contact your local Cooperative Extension Office (see page 1029) for the time of weevil emergence. Spray the foliage and the ground under the plant thoroughly with ORTHO Orthene Systemic Insect Control or ORTHO Isotox Insect Killer on ornamentals. Make sure your plant is listed on the product label. Repeat the spray two more times at intervals of 3 weeks.

Soldier beetle (twice life size).

SOLDIER BEETLES

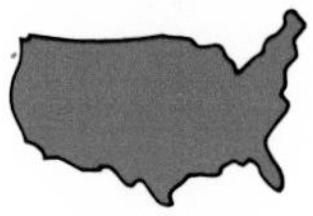

Soldier beetles, belonging to the beetle family *Cantharidae,* are commonly seen in the garden. They resemble fireflies, but lack light-producing organs. The adult beetles are up to ⅝ inch long. Their wing covers are overlaid with downy hair and may be dull gray or black or brightly colored with yellow, orange, or red. They rest on vegetation during the day; at night some are attracted to lights. The beetles eat flower pollen and nectar as well as small insects. The larvae of soldier beetles feed on other insects, and are found beneath bark or debris on the ground.

CONTROL: Controls are not necessary.

Darkling ground beetles (twice life size).

DARKLING BEETLES

Darkling beetles are a large group of slow-moving beetles that range from 1/16 inch to over 1 inch in length. They are mostly black or brown; a few have white or red markings. The head is broad and short. Some darkling beetles have a peculiar habit of raising their abdomen in the air at about 45 degrees from the ground, and running in this position. When disturbed, they emit a black, foul-smelling fluid. Darkling beetle adults and larvae both live under stones and leaf debris. They are commonly seen around dusk. Both adults and larvae of most species eat decaying plant material or fungi, and are harmless. The larvae of some, known as *false wireworms,* feed on the roots and young seedlings of grasses and other plants, but these are not common. A few species eat stored grain products; these are known as *mealworms* or *flour beetles* (see page 808). Darkling beetles occasionally wander indoors.

CONTROL: Collect and remove darkling beetles that wander indoors. To control mealworms and flour beetles, see page 808.

Predaceous ground beetle (3 times life size).

GROUND BEETLES

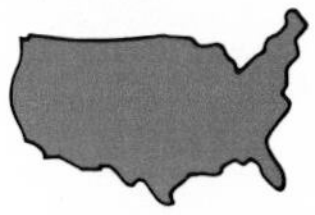

Ground beetles, also known as *predaceous ground beetles*, are a large group of common insects. They vary from ⅛ inch to over 1 inch in length. Many are a shiny black color; others are brown or an iridescent green, blue, or purple. A characteristic of these beetles is that their rather thin head is narrower than the thorax (the middle body segment). Almost all ground beetles and their larvae feed on other insects or slugs. They have strong jaws, some are even able to kill and eat very large caterpillars. Ground beetles rarely fly but are usually fast runners. They are active at night and hide during the day under stones, loose bark, or other debris. Most ground beetles are beneficial predators, though one in California, known as the *tule beetle* (*Agonum maculicolle*), can become a pest when it invades homes in large numbers at dusk following fall rains. These beetles also have an offensive odor. Tule beetles breed in the marshlands along rivers or in moist, weedy areas, and invade homes from the direction of their breeding grounds.

CONTROL: Most ground beetles are beneficial. If the tule beetle becomes a problem by invading homes in large numbers, collect and destroy beetles already indoors and spray outdoors along the foundation and beneath and around porches and doorsills with an insecticide containing *carbaryl* (SEVIN®). Also spray along the edge of the property from which the beetles invade. Seal cracks and crevices in the wall and foundation, and make sure screens fit tightly.

BEETLE FAMILY

Firefly (twice life size).

FIREFLIES

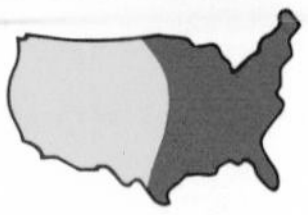

Fireflies, or *lightning bugs*, are actually beetles. These insects are well known for their ability to produce light by means of a luminescent organ near the abdomen. Both the male and female fireflies occurring east of the Rockies can fly and blink their light organs. In the West the adult female glows but cannot fly, and the male flies but does not produce light. Larvae of some fireflies also produce light and are called *glowworms.* Adult fireflies are soft-bodied beetles ¼ to ¾ inch in length. Their head is concealed from above by a hard covering. All larvae and some adults are beneficial, predaceous insects that feed at night on other insects and small slugs and snails. The larvae live in moist places among debris on the ground or on low-growing herbs and grasses. The adult fireflies use their flashing lights as signals in courting. They become active at dusk, with the number of flashes increasing as the night gets darker, and continuing well into the night.

CONTROL: Controls are not necessary.

BUTTERFLY FAMILY

Tiger swallowtail butterfly (life size).

Alfalfa looper moth (twice life size).

BUTTERFLIES AND MOTHS

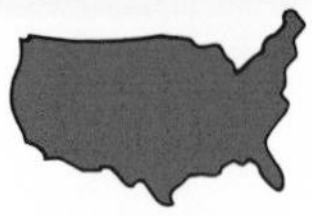

Insects in the butterfly and moth family (Lepidoptera) include some of the most beautiful insects in the world. The adults have two pairs of wings covered with tiny overlapping scales. The scales, which rub off easily, give the wings their striking colors. A few moths are wingless. *Female cankerworms* (page 872), female *bagworms* (page 873), and some *tussock moths* (page 443) are examples. Butterflies can be distinguished from moths by their slender bodies and slender antennae with small clubs on the ends. Moths have stout bodies and antennae without clubs. Moths usually fly at night and have wings with dull colors, while butterflies fly during the day and are usually brightly colored. Butterflies and moths are not harmful in the adult stage, and many are beneficial. They feed on flower nectar with a long, coiled tongue, and are a minor aid in pollinating some flowers. A few butterflies and moths lap up tree sap or juices from rotting fruit, carrion, or animal droppings.

Butterfly and moth development: The caterpillar, or immature stage, has chewing mouthparts. Some caterpillars are serious pests of plants, stored food, and fabrics. (See page 870 for more information on caterpillars and their control.) Butterflies and moths lay their tiny eggs singly or in groups, usually on the plant or other food that the caterpillar eats. The eggs usually hatch in just a few days, although some are laid in the fall and do not hatch until warm spring weather arrives. The caterpillars emerge and immediately begin to eat and grow. They reach maturity after several weeks to several months, depending on the species, the abundance of food, and the temperature. Development is fastest in warm temperatures.

Pupation: At maturity, the caterpillars look for a place to pupate. The moth pupa is either enclosed in a silken cocoon or formed in some protected place such as within the plant itself, in debris on the soil surface, or buried in soil. The butterfly pupa, also called a *chrysalis,* is attached to a stem or some other support and usually is much more exposed than a moth pupa. At this stage a dramatic transformation takes place. Many of the internal organs, muscles and nerves dissolve and the resulting fluids form new structures, producing a creature whose appearance and functions are entirely different. Some of the butterflies and moths emerge from their pupae in as little as 10 days; others spend the winter as pupae. The adult butterfly or moth emerges by splitting the pupal shell, spends several hours pumping fluid into its wings and hardening them, and then flies off. Male and female mate and the female then lays eggs. Butterflies and moths live a few days to several months. Some gardeners attract butterflies to their garden by providing the kinds of plants the caterpillars feed on, as well as plants that produce flowers that are particularly attractive to the adults. Good flowers to attract butterflies are butterfly bush (Buddleia), butterfly weed, lantana, thistles, tithonia, zinnia, and many herbs. Plants that are eaten by caterpillars of particularly pretty butterflies include milkweed, nettles, parsley, fennel, spicebush, and willow.

CONTROL: Most butterflies and moths are harmless and do not require control. If you are having a problem with caterpillars, look up your plant to determine what kind of caterpillars may be damaging it, and follow the control method described.

Gypsy moth larvae (half life size).

Gypsy moth adult and pupae (half life size).

Larva (half life size). *Insert:* Monarch butterfly.

GYPSY MOTH

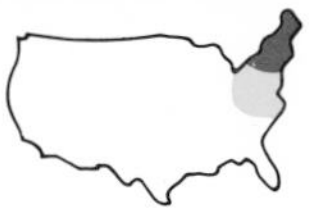

Gypsy moth (*Porthetria dispar*) larvae are large (up to 2½ inches), hairy, blackish caterpillars, with two rows of longitudinal red and blue spots on their backs. They are the most serious shade tree pest in this country. When their numbers are small, the caterpillars prefer to feed on oak leaves. As population levels increase, entire forests may be defoliated and then the insects spread to other types of trees and shrubs. The gypsy moth was introduced into this country in the mid-1800s from Europe, where it is a native pest. It was brought in by an entomologist searching for a hardy silk moth. Some of the larvae escaped and became established on plants. The East Coast has large forests of the insects' preferred food (oak) that can support huge populations of gypsy moths. This allowed the moths to increase in numbers rapidly. Besides defoliating and weakening plants, the insects are a nuisance. In mid to late summer, the female moths attach masses of eggs covered with yellow hairs to almost any outdoor object. The larvae that hatch from these eggs from April to June may completely cover the sides of houses or other objects during the day when they're not feeding. Some people are allergic to the hairs of the larvae, which blow about in the wind. Where insects are feeding, large amounts of excrement accumulate beneath the plant. There is only one generation of gypsy moths a year.

CONTROL: It may not be necessary to spray your tree if it is healthy and vigorous. Hardwood trees can generally withstand 2 to 5 successive years of defoliation before dying (although a single season's defoliation can stress a tree so badly that it may take many years to recover fully). Evergreen trees may die after one complete defoliation since they cannot totally replace their foliage. If the insects are bothersome, or if trees are weak or unhealthy either from last year's gypsy moth feeding or from drought, mechanical damage, or other insects and diseases, treatment with insecticides should be considered. Insecticides should be applied in the spring or early summer before the larvae are 1 inch long; the tree must be covered thoroughly. It is best to contact a professional arborist for spraying large trees. Spray smaller trees with ORTHO Gypsy Moth & Japanese Beetle Killer, ORTHO Liquid Sevin, ORTHO Orthene Systemic Insect Control, or ORTHO Isotox Insect Killer. Repeat the sprays at weekly intervals if damage continues. Homeowners can reduce infestations by destroying egg masses found on walls, wood piles, buildings, trees, and other objects when they are noticed during the winter months. During the spring when larvae are feeding, place burlap bands on trees, leaving the bottom edge unattached. Larvae will crawl under these flaps to hide during the daylight hours. Collect and destroy them. This is most effective when infestations are light to moderate. Keep trees in a healthy growing condition; avoid damaging the roots or injuring the tree. Fertilize and water trees during periods of drought. When planting trees in the yard, choose species that are less favored by the gypsy moth. (For a list of these plants, see page 1014.) Trees less favored by the insects are damaged only slightly by larval feeding. In addition, they may reduce the mortality of more favored hosts when interplanted, by preventing a large buildup of insects in the area.

MONARCH BUTTERFLY

The monarch is perhaps the best known butterfly. Its wings are orange with black veins and black margins. The margins are sprinkled with white and orange spots. This large butterfly has a wingspan of up to 4 inches. They are often seen flying from plant to plant, sipping nectar from a wide variety of flowers. Monarchs lay pale green eggs on the leaves of milkweed, a plant that has a white milky sap. The eggs hatch in about 4 days. The caterpillar is banded with white, black, and yellow stripes and has a pair of soft spines at both its front and rear end. It feeds on the leaves of milkweed for about 10 days, and when fully mature, reaches a length of about 2 inches. It then attaches itself to a leaf or stem and forms a cocoon (chrysalis). The chrysalis is a jade green color with gold trimmings. It slowly darkens. After about 12 days, the butterfly emerges from the chrysalis. There may be up to four generations a year. The monarch is the only butterfly species that migrates yearly both north and south. In the spring you can observe them migrating in a northerly direction, laying eggs and sipping nectar in the process. In the fall they migrate in a southerly direction. They are capable of flying up to 2,000 miles during a migration. Monarchs that emerge in late summer and fall in the East or Midwest spend the winter in fir forests in northern Mexico; monarchs in the West spend the winter on the coast of central and southern California in groups of pine, cypress, and eucalyptus. There are also certain stands of trees along the Atlantic and Gulf Coasts and the Great Lakes where they are seen yearly.

CONTROL: Controls are not necessary.

BUTTERFLY FAMILY

Mourning cloak butterfly. *Insert:* Larva.

Tent caterpillar (life size).

Redhumped caterpillars (¾ life size). *Insert:* Close-up.

MOURNING CLOAK BUTTERFLY

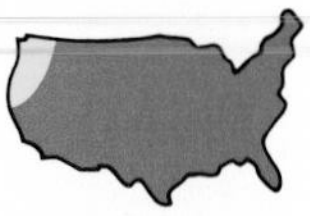

The mourning cloak butterfly (*Nymphalis antiopa*) is a beautiful and common butterfly. The wings are a dark purplish brown color with blue spots along the back edge next to a band of yellowish gold. The wingspread is about 3 inches. The mourning cloak caterpillar is sometimes called the *spiny elm caterpillar* because of the large spinelike projections on its body that are harmless to touch. The caterpillar is black with tiny white dots, red legs, and a row of red spots along its back. A fully grown caterpillar is about 2 inches long. It feeds on many hardwood trees, particularly elm, willow, and poplar. Caterpillars feed in groups, devouring the leaves one branch at a time. When mature each caterpillar suspends itself from a twig and hangs downward, then forms a brown and gray pupa (chrysalis). Within a week a mourning cloak butterfly emerges. The butterfly mates and the female lays eggs in masses of 300 to 450 on twigs. Butterflies emerging in the late summer spend the winter in protected spots. There is one generation yearly in northern states and two generations yearly in southern states.

CONTROL: Prune off the branches containing caterpillars or spray with an insecticide containing *carbaryl* (SEVIN®) when the caterpillars are first seen. Make sure your plant is listed on the label.

CATERPILLARS

Caterpillars, the larvae of moths and butterflies, are serious pests of garden plants. Moths and butterflies do not feed on tissue or harm plants, but drink nectar from flowers. They may also help to pollinate flowers. Caterpillars are smooth, hairy, or spiny wormlike creatures with 3 pairs of legs near their heads and several pairs of prolegs (false legs) in the middle and rear of the abdomen. Their mouthparts are adapted for chewing plant tissue. They generally confine themselves to tissue that is soft and succulent. After hatching, caterpillars go through as many as 11 stages of development (instars). At the end of each instar, caterpillars must molt (shed their skin) to make room for their larger body size. During the first instars, caterpillars may feed as leafminers between the upper and lower surfaces of leaves; or as skeletonizers, eating only one leaf surface. As the caterpillars increase in size in later stages, they require more food, devouring entire leaves. Caterpillar populations often fluctuate greatly from year to year due to unfavorable environmental conditions and to control by natural enemies such as birds, rodents, diseases, and other insects.

CONTROL: Inspect garden plants periodically for signs of caterpillar infestation. Control caterpillars on ornamentals with ORTHO Orthene Systemic Insect Control, ORTHO Isotox Insect Killer, or ORTHO Liquid Sevin. Spray food crops with ORTHO Fruit & Vegetable Insect Control, ORTHO Liquid Sevin, or ORTHO Malathion 50 Insect Spray. Make sure your plant is listed on the label.

REDHUMPED CATERPILLAR

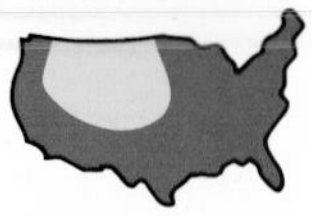

The redhumped caterpillar (*Schizura concinna*) is so named because of the characteristic brick-red hump on its back. This caterpillar also has a red head and red stripes along its body. It is a fairly large caterpillar, as much as 1½ inches long when fully grown, and has the unusual characteristic of resting with its hind end elevated. The redhumped caterpillar feeds on a wide variety of deciduous fruit, nut, and ornamental trees. Sweet gum, walnut, and plum are favorite hosts. The caterpillars feed in groups on the lower leaf surfaces when young. As they grow they tend to disperse and eat entirely through leaves, leaving only the largest leaf veins. Often, just one section of a tree will be defoliated, but occasionally a large population will defoliate the entire tree. This slows growth and may reduce fruit quality, but the tree will usually recover from the defoliation. When mature, the caterpillars form cocoons in plant litter on the ground. The emerging adults are grayish brown moths with a wingspan of 1 to 1⅜ inches. They lay eggs in groups on the undersides of leaves. There are as many as four or five generations a year.

CONTROL: Spray infested areas of trees with an insecticide containing *carbaryl* (SEVIN®). Make sure your plant is listed on the product label. The bacterial insecticide *Bacillus thuringiensis* can also be used. If caterpillars are no longer present, delay spraying until the next generation of caterpillars is seen. Branches containing caterpillars can also be cut off and destroyed while the caterpillars are young and grouped together.

Climbing cutworms (half life size).

Surface cutworm (twice life size).

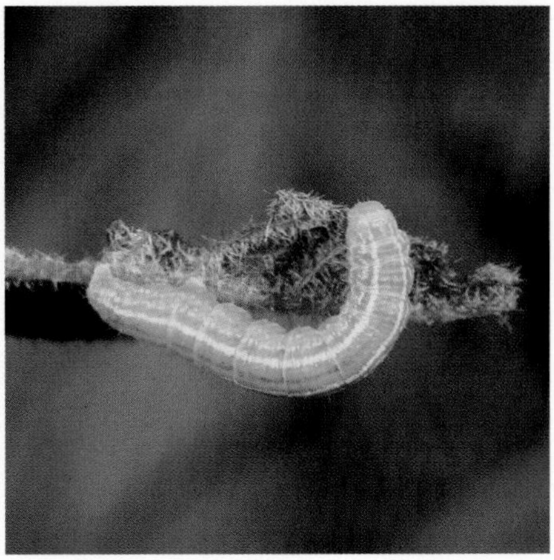
European winter moth larva (twice life size).

CUTWORMS

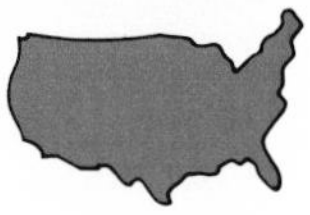

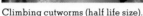

Cutworms are large (up to 2 inches), fleshy, hairless caterpillars that curl up when disturbed. They are serious pests of vegetables and flowers, and sometimes infest vines and trees. There are many species of cutworms in the United States. They are grouped according to their feeding habits.

Surface cutworms are pests of early season vegetables and flowers, feeding on the succulent tissue of newly transplanted or emerging plants. A single surface-feeding cutworm may destroy many plants in one night. They chew or cut off the plant at or below the soil surface, and then hide under dirt clods or in the soil during the day. They do not eat much of the plant, but take only a few bites from the stem, often causing the plant to topple over.

Climbing cutworms feed aboveground on any part of the plant. Their favorite foods are the tender young leaves, buds, and flowers of vegetables and herbaceous plants. Sometimes they infest vines or climb up into the tops of fruit trees to feed on leaves or buds. In one night, climbing cutworms may devour all but the stem of a young plant and then move to another plant to feed.

Subterranean cutworms spend their lives in the soil. They feed day and night on the roots and underground stems of vegetables, sod, and grains, causing plants to wilt and die. Many other insects and diseases cause similar symptoms. Dig in the soil around the dying plant for cutworms to confirm that they are the cause of the problem.

The adults of all cutworms are dark, night-flying moths with bands or stripes on their forewings and lighter-colored hindwings. They feed at dusk on the nectar from flowers, and may be seen fluttering around lights at night.

CONTROL: Since cutworms feed in the soil or hide there during the day, insecticides are most effective if they are applied around the base of plants. Use ORTHO Diazinon Soil & Foliage Dust, ORTHO Diazinon Soil & Turf Insect, or ORTHO Vegetable Guard Soil Insect Killer on vegetables and lawns when stem cutting or leaf chewing is observed. To control subterranean cutworms, water the soil lightly after applying the insecticide. Control cutworms on flowers with ORTHO Diazinon Insect Spray. Make sure your plant is listed on the product label. Since cutworms are difficult to control, it may be necessary to repeat the dusting or spraying at weekly intervals. Before transplanting in the area, apply a preventive treatment of ORTHO Diazinon Soil & Turf Insect Control or ORTHO Vegetable Guard Soil Insect Killer and work it into the soil. Cultivate the soil thoroughly in late summer and fall to expose and destroy larvae and pupae. Further reduce damage with "cutworm collars" around the stem of each plant or group of plants. These collars can be made of stiff paper, milk cartons, tin cans, or aluminum foil. They should be at least 2 inches high and pressed firmly into the soil. To reduce injury from climbing cutworms, inspect your plants at night with a flashlight and pick off and destroy any cutworms you find.

EUROPEAN WINTER MOTH

The European winter moth (*Operophtera brumata*) is best known for its larva, a green caterpillar with three pale yellow stripes along each side of the body. It crawls in a looping movement similar to cankerworms (see page 872) and is about 1 inch long when fully grown. These caterpillars can damage an estimated 200 different kinds of plants by feeding on their leaves and flowers. When abundant they can defoliate entire trees. The trees develop new leaves after defoliation, but growth may be slowed. Deciduous trees such as elm, oak, apple, plum, pear, and cherry are especially favored food plants. As they feed, the caterpillars hide inside leaves that they tie together with silken strands. They form pupae in the ground in June and July. Adult moths appear in late October. The males have light brown-gray wings and a wingspan of about 1 inch; the tiny female is wingless. The moths mate and lay eggs on tree trunks and larger branches. The eggs hatch in early spring and the young caterpillars crawl to the foliage to begin feeding or are carried to adjacent trees by wind currents. There is one generation each year.

CONTROL: Several insects that parasitize and kill the European winter moth have been introduced to this country to control it. Chemical controls have not yet been registered for control of this insect.

BUTTERFLY FAMILY

Cankerworm (3 times life size).

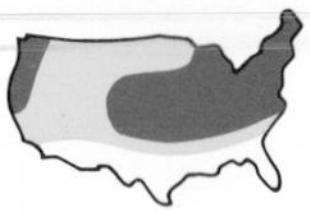

CANKERWORMS

The spring cankerworm (*Paleacrita vernata*) and fall cankerworm (*Alsophila pometaria*) belong to the group of insects known as inchworms or loopers. Cankerworms have legs only at the front and the rear of their body. They move by drawing the rear portion of their slender body up to the front, causing their body to form a wide loop, and then moving the front portion of their body forward. Spring cankerworms are about 1 inch long when mature. They spend the winter as pupae in the soil and emerge as adults in early spring. The adult male is an ash gray moth with a wingspread of about 1 inch. The female is entirely wingless. She lays eggs on the branches; they hatch when the foliage begins to appear in the spring. The young cankerworms eat the leaves for 3 to 5 weeks before dropping to the ground and forming pupae. Fall cankerworms lay their eggs in November and early December. The eggs hatch the following spring, and the emerging young feed, pupate, and emerge as adults in the fall. Trees defoliated 2 or 3 years in succession are weakened and may die. Favored host trees include elm, apple, oak, hickory, and maple.

CONTROL: Spray ORTHO Home Orchard Spray on fruit and nut trees, and ORTHO Orthene Systemic Insect Control or ORTHO Isotox Insect Killer on ornamentals. Apply the spray in late April or early May—soon after the caterpillars become active and after the leaves have expanded. A spray applied too early when the leaves are still rapidly expanding is not effective. The bacterial insecticide *Bacillus thuringiensis* can also be used.

Woollybear caterpillar (life size).

WOOLLYBEAR CATERPILLAR

These hairy caterpillars, sometimes called *saltmarsh caterpillars*, are commonly seen crawling across roads and pathways. Woollybears are large caterpillars that can grow to over 2 inches long. They are covered with dense, stiff, reddish brown to black hairs that give them a woolly or furry appearance. The hairs break off easily when the caterpillar is picked up. One of the common woollybears, the *banded woollybear*, (*Isia isabella*), has black hairs at each end and reddish brown hairs around its middle. In the fall, woollybears become very active and crawl about in search of a protected place to spend the winter, such as under loose bark or dry leaves. There they either form a cocoon and emerge as an adult moth in the spring, or simply curl up for the winter and continue feeding in the spring. The adult is a pretty moth with a wingspan up to 2½ inches. Depending on the species of woollybear, the wings may be white with black spots or have bold patterns of orange or yellow. The moths mate and lay eggs on low vegetation. The caterpillars eat the leaves of a wide variety of plants, including many weeds.

CONTROL: If caterpillars are feeding on garden plants, hand pick them or spray them with an insecticide containing *carbaryl* (SEVIN®). Make sure your plant is listed on the product label. A few caterpillars crawling about the garden can be safely ignored.

Uglynest caterpillars (¼ life size).

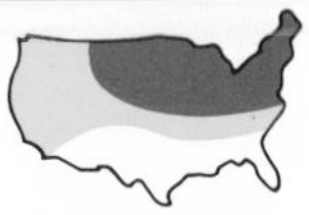

UGLYNEST CATERPILLAR

The uglynest caterpillar (*Archips cerasivoranus*) gets its name from the unsightly silken nests it forms on the ends of branches. The nests are built around several small stems and are filled with pieces of dead leaves and black droppings from the caterpillars. Inside the webbing are numerous yellowish green caterpillars with shiny black heads. Uglynest caterpillars feed on the foliage of a variety of trees and shrubs including cherry, hawthorn, and rose, but they are seldom abundant enough to cause any lasting damage to their hosts. Other caterpillars that form webs or tents and are sometimes confused with the uglynest caterpillar include fall webworms, which produce lighter, gauzier webs; tent caterpillars, which form silken tents at the branch crotches (see page 411); and mimosa webworms, which only attack mimosa and honeylocust (see page 449). The caterpillars feed from late spring through the summer, when they form pupae within their nests. The adult moths emerge from July to September. They are dull orange with a wingspread of just under 1 inch.

CONTROL: Prune out and destroy the webbed portions of branches, or spray with an insecticide containing *diazinon* or *carbaryl* (SEVIN®) when the webs are first seen. Use ORTHO Orthene Systemic Insect Control or ORTHO Isotox Insect Killer on the oak webworm. Make sure your plant is listed on the product label. Apply the spray at a high spray pressure to force it into the webs and improve control.

Bagworm cases (half life size).

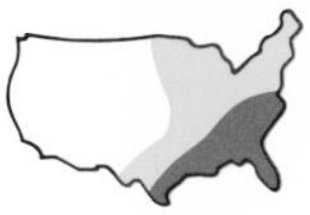

BAGWORMS

Bagworms are the larvae of moths. The characteristic brown bags are often seen attached to twigs. The bags are up to 2 inches long and composed of interwoven bits of dead foliage, twigs, and silk. During the summer, a dark brown to black caterpillar can be found in the bag. At first it drags the bag around as it feeds on leaves, enlarging the bag as it grows. By late August, the caterpillar finishes feeding and attaches the bag to a twig. Inside the bag it forms a pupa. Several days later an adult moth emerges from the pupa. The female is wingless and stays within her bag. The male flies to the bag containing the female and they mate while she is still inside. She then lays a mass of eggs within the bag and dies. The eggs hatch in May or June. Newly hatched caterpillars crawl out of the old bag and immediately begin feeding on leaves. In severe infestations, the entire plant is defoliated and there are bags hanging on many of the twigs. Such an infestation often kills evergreens such as arborvitae and cedar but may only slow the growth of a deciduous plant.

CONTROL: Spray with ORTHO Bagworm Killer, ORTHO Isotox Insect Killer, ORTHO Liquid Sevin, or the bacterial insecticide *Bacillus thuringiensis* between late May and mid-July. Make sure your plant is listed on the product label. Repeat the spray after 10 days if leaf damage is still occurring. Hand pick and destroy bags on small plants in the winter to reduce the number of eggs.

Leafroller feeding on hickory leaf.

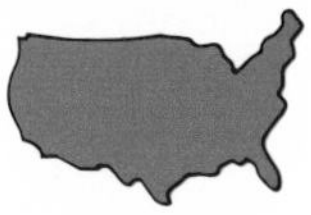

LEAFROLLERS AND LEAFTIERS

Leafrollers and leaftiers are small caterpillars that feed inside leaves, which they roll or tie together. They are similar in their habits, but leafrollers roll leaves around themselves, and leaftiers tie leaves together with silk threads. This feeding habit gives the insects some protection from unfavorable weather, predators, and chemical sprays. Leafrollers and leaftiers may be serious pests in the garden, feeding on many fruits, vegetables, and ornamentals. Their feeding habits vary, depending on their age. Only part of their life may be spent feeding inside the rolled or tied leaves. At other times they may feed inside buds, flowers, or fruit. The species of leafrollers and leaftiers that feed on flowers and fruits are usually much more damaging than the species that feed exclusively on the leaves.

CONTROL: Insecticides are most effective if they are applied before the larvae are protected inside the leaves. Check your plants periodically in the spring for the first sign of infestation. Spray ornamentals with ORTHO Isotox Insect Killer, ORTHO Orthene Systemic Insect Control, or ORTHO Liquid Sevin. Spray fruits with ORTHO Liquid Sevin or ORTHO Malathion 50 Insect Spray. Control insects on food crops with ORTHO Fruit & Vegetable Insect Control or with an insecticide containing *carbaryl* (SEVIN®) or *malathion*. Make sure your plant is listed on the product label.

Harlequin bugs (life size).

PLANT BUGS

Plant bugs are a large group of insects that infest many plants in the garden. This group includes many species of *plant bugs*, *leaf bugs*, *lygus bugs*, *predaceous bugs*, and *stinkbugs*. These insects are true bugs, of the order *Hemiptera*. They have long legs and antennae, large eyes, and the adults hold their wings flat over their bodies. Immature plant bugs have no wings. Both the immature and mature bugs feed on succulent plant tissue. They pierce the tissue and remove the cell contents, resulting in tan or bleached spots and distortion. Infested fruits and flowers often drop off the plant. The mature females may also damage plants by laying eggs inside the leaves or stems. Many plant bugs have two or more generations a year, so late-season populations can be very large and damaging.

CONTROL: It is important to control plant bugs before they build up to damaging numbers. Watch for signs of infestation during the growing season. If damage is noticed, spray or dust plants with ORTHO Malathion 50 Insect Spray, ORTHO Tomato & Vegetable Insect Killer, or ORTHO Sevin Garden Dust. Make sure your plant is listed on the product label. If migrating plant bugs reinfest the plant, repeat the spray.

BUG FAMILY

Stinkbug (twice life size).

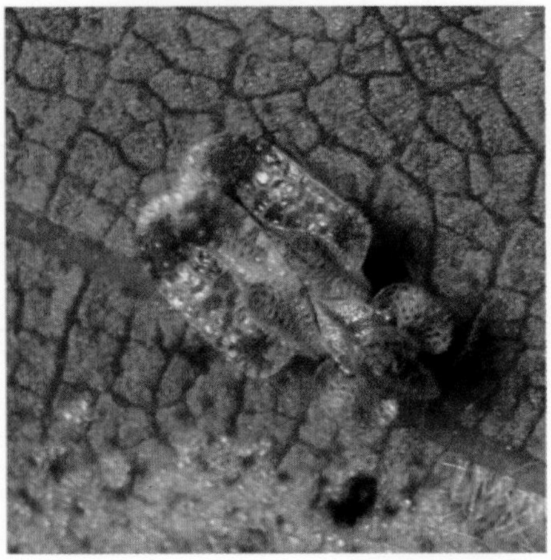

Lacebug (10 times life size).

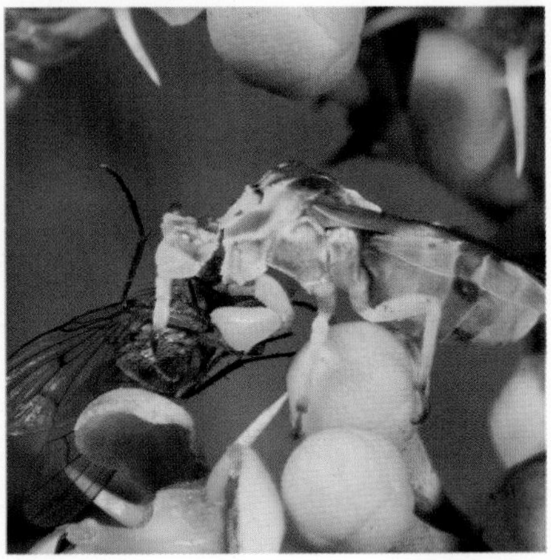

Ambush bug (3 times life size).

STINKBUGS

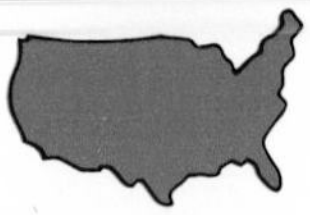

Stinkbugs are medium to large-sized bugs, usually ¼ to ¾ inches long. They are usually dull green, gray, or brown, but one common stink bug, the *harlequin bug,* is black with bright orange marks. Stinkbugs get their name from the foul smell they produce when disturbed. This smell comes from a fluid they discharge from special stink glands. The great majority of stinkbugs suck the juices from tender young foliage and fruit. They can be destructive pests when numerous. Infested fruit develops hard calluses around the feeding punctures, and the fruit may be deformed if punctured early in its development. Leaves that are heavily infested may become distorted and scorched. Stinkbugs lay barrel-shaped eggs in groups of 10 to 20 on leaves. The eggs are often brightly colored with stripes.

CONTROL: Treat infested plants with ORTHO Tomato & Vegetable Insect Spray or an insecticide containing *carbaryl* (SEVIN®). Repeat the treatment at intervals of 7 to 10 days if the plants become reinfested. Make sure your plant is listed on the product label. Hand pick egg masses when seen. Clean up weeds in orchards and gardens to eliminate stinkbug breeding places.

LACEBUGS

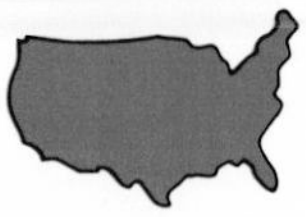

Lacebugs are small (⅛ inch) insects of the family *Tingidae,* which means "ornamented." The adults have delicate clear wings that they hold flat over their bodies. The wings have many veins, giving them a lacy appearance. Immature lacebugs are dark and wingless, with spines radiating from the edges of their bodies. Lacebugs are pests primarily of ornamental trees and shrubs, although several species infest a few vegetables. Most lacebugs feed on only one type of plant. They damage plants by sucking the sap and cell contents from the undersides of the leaves, producing a mottling or speckling on the upper surfaces. Lacebug damage often resembles leafhopper or spider mite damage. However, lacebugs excrete drops of shiny, varnishlike excrement, which accumulates around them as they feed. Several generations of lacebugs occur each year. Certain lacebugs may build up to such tremendous numbers on their host plant that very little green tissue remains to produce food for the plant.

CONTROL: Lacebugs should be controlled early, before they cause much damage. This is especially important on broadleaved evergreen plants because they retain the unproductive leaves for several years. Spray ornamentals with ORTHO Orthene Systemic Insect Control or ORTHO Isotox Insect Killer. Control lacebugs on food crops with ORTHO Fruit & Vegetable Insect Control. Make sure your plant is listed on the product label. Reinfestations may come from infested plants in nearby gardens. Check your plant periodically for insects. Repeat the spray if the plant becomes reinfested.

PREDACEOUS BUGS

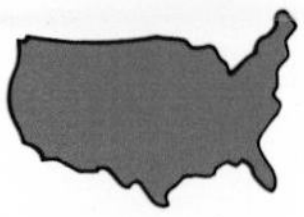

Many true bugs are beneficial because they prey on other insects. Some of these are difficult to distinguish from other bugs that feed on plants. Common predaceous bugs include *assassin bugs, minute pirate bugs, damsel bugs,* and *ambush bugs.* Predaceous bugs are general feeders, eating any insect eggs or small insects they can catch. They are never very abundant and seldom reduce pests to numbers below damaging levels. Some of these bugs will bite if they are handled. The bite of most predaceous bugs feels like a pin prick, but a few species of assassin bugs feed on blood and can cause severe pain that lasts several days. If a severe reaction develops, call your doctor.

CONTROL: Controls are not necessary.

APHID FAMILY

Aphids on ivy (life size).

APHIDS

Aphids, also called *plant lice* or *aphis*, are small (up to ¼ inch), soft-bodied insects that infest most garden plants. Some aphids spend their entire life on one type of plant; others infest several different plant species. Aphids have a complicated life history because they produce an additional form besides male and female aphids. Aphids that hatch from overwintering eggs are wingless females, called *stem mothers*. They give live birth without fertilization by a male. Many generations of females may be produced throughout the summer. Some of these aphids are born with wings so they can fly to less densely populated plants, or to another species of plant. In the fall, stem mothers give birth to males and females that mate and produce the fertilized eggs that survive the winter. In warm climates there may be continuous production of living young, with no development of sexual males and females. Large numbers of aphids may cause little damage to a plant; or just a few aphids on a plant may cause severe distortion and stunting. Certain aphids are also vectors of plant diseases (see page 879).

CONTROL: Aphids are usually easy to control if they are not protected by tightly curled leaves, galls, or cottony material. Use ORTHO Fruit & Vegetable Insect Control or ORTHO Malathion 50 Insect Spray to quickly knock out existing aphids on food crops. Use ORTHO Isotox Insect Killer or ORTHO Orthene Systemic Insect Control on ornamentals, to protect them for a couple of weeks from new infestations. Make sure your plant is listed on the product label. Aphids may continually reinfest the garden from other plants nearby. Inspect your plants regularly for aphids.

Green peach aphids on pyracantha (half life size).

GREEN PEACH APHID

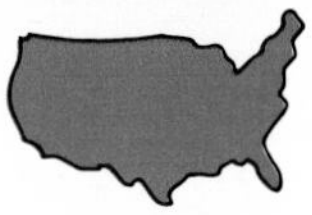

The green peach aphid (*Myzus persicae*) is one of the most common aphids in the country. It is present in every state and is often seen on vegetables, fruit, and ornamental plants. It is a yellowish green aphid with tiny red eyes. The green peach aphid lays black shiny eggs that survive the winter on peach, plum, cherry, and related trees. In spring, the eggs hatch and two or three generations of aphids develop on the trees. The aphids then migrate to other, usually herbaceous, plants such as weeds, flowers, and vegetables. In the vegetable garden, green peach aphids are especially attracted to spinach and potatoes, but they also feed on many other vegetables and flowers. They complete many generations on these plants during the summer. In the autumn, winged females fly back to fruit trees, complete one or more generations, mate and produce females, which lay the overwintering eggs. Green peach aphids rarely damage fruit trees, but at times they seriously injure vegetables and flowers because they remove plant sap and can transmit plant viruses. Many other insects feed on aphids, but do not always keep the population under control.

CONTROL: Apply control measure as for other aphids (see page 875). Apply ORTHO Volck Oil Spray to peach, plum, cherry, and related trees to kill overwintering eggs.

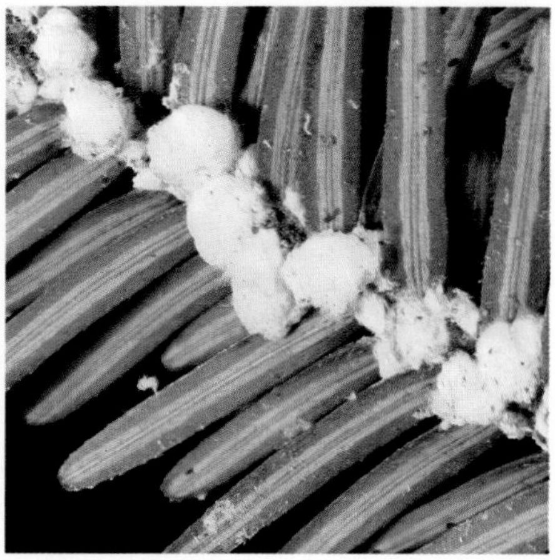

Woolly hemlock aphids (twice life size).

WOOLLY APHIDS

Aphids that cover themselves with white or gray waxy threads that look like wool or cotton are called woolly aphids. If the threads are removed, small (⅛ inch), dark, soft-bodied insects will be found clustered beneath. Woolly aphids infest only woody plants. Some species infest leaves, often causing them to curl inward. The damage is unsightly but rarely fatal to the plant. Other types of woolly aphids cover the trunk, branches, and roots. Galls may develop where they feed, and infested roots may be heavily branched. Young plants severely infested with woolly aphids are often stunted and may die. Older plants with galls on the roots may be weak and produce few fruits. Most of these aphids have a summer and a winter host. They spend the summer on one type of plant and then, in the fall, produce a generation that migrates to another plant species. Sometimes, especially in warmer climates, woolly aphids spend their entire life on the summer host.

CONTROL: Woolly aphids protected inside curled leaves are best controlled with a systemic insecticide such as ORTHO Isotox Insect Killer or ORTHO Orthene Systemic Insect Control. Use these sprays or ORTHO Malathion 50 Insect Spray on woolly aphids infesting branches or trunks, which are more exposed. Make sure your plant is listed on the product label. Repeat the spray if the plant becomes reinfested.

APHID FAMILY

Mealybugs on oleander (life size).

Cottony cushion scale (twice life size).

Japanese wax scale on holly (twice life size).

MEALYBUGS

Mealybugs are soft-bodied insects that are close relatives of scales. Their name derives from the white or gray threads of wax with which they cover themselves. Plant parts heavily infested with mealybugs often appear to be covered with cotton. Mealybugs may damage any part of the plant by sucking out the sap, which may cause leaf distortion, yellowing, stunting, galls, and the death of the plant. They also coat the plant with large quantities of undigested sap, called *honeydew*. Most species of mealybugs are garden pests only in the subtropical areas of the country, infesting house plants and greenhouse plants in the colder northern states. However, several species that infest woody plants can survive through the extreme cold of northern winters. Mealybugs are very active when young, crawling all over the plant until they find a suitable place to settle. As the young mealybugs mature, they become sluggish. Mature females move around very little, but males develop into winged insects that look like minute flies. Adult males do not feed, but die after mating.

CONTROL: Mealybugs are often difficult to control because they are protected by their waxy threads. Spray ornamentals thoroughly with ORTHO Isotox Insect Killer or ORTHO Malathion 50 Insect Spray. Spray food crops with ORTHO Fruit & Vegetable Insect Control or ORTHO Malathion 50 Insect Spray. Check to make sure your plant is listed on the product label. Repeat the spray if the plant becomes reinfested.

COTTONY SCALES

Cottony scales are a type of soft scale (see page 877). Like other soft scales, they have a crusty skeleton on the outside of their bodies. However, it is rarely seen because the mature female scales lay hundreds of eggs in white, waxy egg sacs that are attached to their bodies, giving them a cottony appearance. The females die and shrivel after they lay their eggs. The young scales, called *crawlers*, emerge from the egg sacs and migrate to leaves and young twigs. They insert their mouthparts into the plant and suck sap throughout the summer. Trees and shrubs infested with cottony scales may be coated with large quantities of a sticky substance called *honeydew*, undigested sap excreted by the insects. Male cottony scales are tiny winged insects, which mature before females. They mate with immature females and die. Many species of cottony scales remain mobile throughout their life. Before the leaves drop, scales migrate to bark to spend the winter.

CONTROL: Cottony scales may be difficult to control because they are protected by the waxy egg sacs. Control is often aimed at the crawler stage, whose time of appearance varies with the species. Spray crawlers on ornamentals with ORTHO Orthene Systemic Insect Control or ORTHO Isotox Insect Killer. Crawlers on fruit trees can be controlled with ORTHO Fruit & Vegetable Insect Control or ORTHO Diazinon Insect Spray. Contact your local Cooperative Extension Office (see page 1029) to determine the best time to spray for scales in your area. ORTHO Volck Oil Spray is very effective against the eggs and often against the crawlers.

WAX SCALES

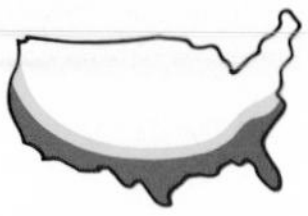

Wax scales are a type of soft scale (see page 877) that are serious pests of hundreds of ornamental plants in the warmer parts of the country. Their reddish or brown bodies are covered with a hard, thick, white wax, often tinged pink or gray. Females lay hundreds of eggs underneath their bodies, which shrink as the eggs accumulate. The young scales, called *crawlers*, leave the waxy covering and settle down to feed on leaves and stems. As the young scales mature, they begin excreting cones of wax on top of their bodies. The wax gives the scales a different appearance when they are in various stages of development (instars). When the immature insects have reached their second instar, they have a "cameo" appearance. The wax is secreted rapidly during the third instar, producing a cone—the "dunce-cap" stage. By the time the insects mature, the wax is very thick, and convex or globular.

CONTROL: Mature female wax scales are difficult to control because they are protected by the thick wax covering. Control is often aimed at the crawler stage, whose seasonal appearance varies with each species. Spray crawlers with ORTHO Orthene Systemic Insect Control or ORTHO Isotox Insect Killer. Contact your local Cooperative Extension Office (see page 1029) to determine the best time to spray for scales in your area. ORTHO Volck Oil Spray is very effective against the eggs and often against the crawlers.

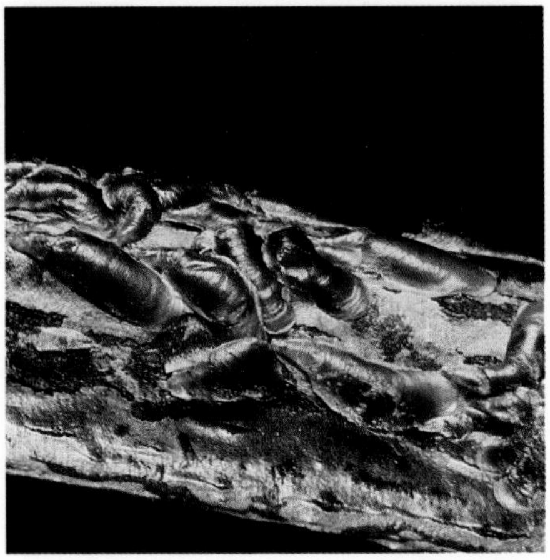

Oystershell scale (3 times life size).

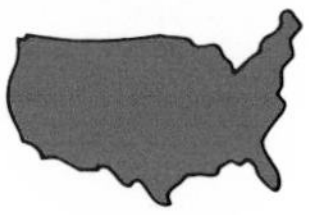

ARMORED SCALES

Armored scales appear as somewhat flattened bumps, either round or very elongated, and are often clustered together on leaves, stems, or bark. Small, immobile, soft-bodied insects live beneath these shells, which are made of wax and cast skins. The shells are not attached to the insect; if the shells are picked off, the insect remains attached to the plant. Females lay their eggs underneath the shells. The young scales, called *crawlers*, are active, usually moving from beneath their mothers' shells to find suitable feeding sites. The crawlers eventually settle down in one spot, where they remain for the rest of their lives, feeding on plant sap. Some armored scales produce a toxin that causes discolored or dead spots on leaves or fruit. Armored scales do not produce honeydew, as other scales do.

CONTROL: Mature scales are difficult to control because they are protected by their shell. Control is usually aimed at the crawlers, whose seasonal appearance varies with species. Spray crawlers with ORTHO Orthene Systemic Insect Control or ORTHO Isotox Insect Killer. Contact your local Cooperative Extension Office (see page 1029) to determine the best time to spray for scales in your area. ORTHO Volck Oil Spray may be used very effectively to smother scales during the dormant season and during the growing season. Before spraying, check to make sure your plant is listed on the product label.

Hemispherical scale (3 times life size).

SOFT SCALES

Soft scales are serious pests of hundreds of woody plants, appearing as crusty bumps on bark and leaves. This scale group contains some of the largest species of scales found in the United States. Soft scales (also see page 876) are related to both mealybugs (page 876) and armored scale (this page). Many soft scales look like mealybugs; they are covered with a white, powdery wax during part of their life. Like mealybugs, soft scales excrete large quantities of undigested sap, called *honeydew*, as they feed on plant tissue. Soft scales develop an external skeleton that looks like the armored scales' shell-like covering. This skeleton can't be removed without killing the insect. Depending on the species, female scales lay eggs or produce living young beneath their bodies. The egg-laying females die and shrivel, and the skeletons protect the eggs until they hatch. The young scales, called *crawlers*, move away from their protected sites to find a suitable spot to feed. This stage of the insect, when it is not protected by a skeleton, is most susceptible to insecticides.

CONTROL: Control is often aimed at the susceptible crawler stage, whose seasonal appearance varies with each species. Spray crawlers on ornamentals with ORTHO Orthene Systemic Insect Control or ORTHO Isotox Insect Killer. Contact your local Cooperative Extension Office (see page 1029) for the best time to spray for scales in your area. Control scales on fruit trees with ORTHO Fruit & Vegetable Insect Control or ORTHO Malathion 50 Insect Spray. ORTHO Volck Oil Spray is very effective against the eggs and often against the crawlers.

Whiteflies (life size).

WHITEFLIES

Whiteflies are tiny (1/12 inch), winged insects that are found mainly on the undersides of leaves. When the plant is touched, insects flutter rapidly around it. Whiteflies belong to a family of insects called *Aleyrodidae*, which means "flourlike." The wings of the adults are covered with a white, powdery substance. Whiteflies are mostly tropical insects that are able to survive outdoors only in the southern parts of the country. Their population may build up to tremendous numbers during the growing season. Whiteflies may also infest outdoor plants in colder climates. Infestations come from migrating whiteflies and infested greenhouse-grown plants placed in the garden.

CONTROL: Whiteflies have five stages of development, and each stage has a different tolerance to insecticides. The minute eggs are resistant to most insecticides. The crawlers that hatch from the eggs can be controlled by contact insecticides, such as ORTHO Malathion 50 Insect Spray or ORTHO Tomato & Vegetable Insect Killer. The crawlers settle to feed, inserting their mouthparts into plant tissue. They soon lose their legs and take on the appearance of a scale insect. The "scale" stage is resistant to contact insecticides, but can be controlled on ornamentals by insecticides—such as ORTHO Isotox Insect Killer or ORTHO Orthene Systemic Insect Control—that act systemically. On vegetables, the adults can be controlled with ORTHO Fruit & Vegetable Insect Control. All life stages may be present at the same time, but a single application of insecticide affects only susceptible stages, leaving other stages to survive and reproduce. Sprays must be applied at least 3 times at intervals of 4 to 6 days to achieve control.

APHID FAMILY

Blue sharpshooter leafhopper (10 times life size).

LEAFHOPPERS

Leafhoppers are small (under ½ inch), wedge-shaped insects that hop or fly away quickly when disturbed. Some can run backwards and sideways as rapidly as they move forward. The adults have wings that are held over their bodies in a rooflike position. Immature leafhoppers are wingless. All stages have large eyes on the sides of their heads and piercing-sucking mouthparts for feeding on plant sap. Leafhoppers feed on many garden plants, causing leaf stippling, stunting, and distortion of the leaves and stems. As they feed, most leafhoppers excrete large quantities of a sticky substance called *honeydew*, undigested sap that coats the plants. Many of these pests are also vectors of plant diseases that can damage plants severely. In addition, certain leafhoppers cause a condition called *hopperburn*. Infested leaves turn brown on the edges and curl upward. Leafhopper saliva kills leaf tissue as it is injected into the conducting vessels.

CONTROL: Leaves that are severely damaged by leafhoppers are unsightly and lose much of their ability to produce food. Insects should be controlled early before damage is serious. Spray ornamentals with ORTHO Isotox Insect Killer or ORTHO Diazinon Insect Spray. Spray food crops with ORTHO Fruit & Vegetable Insect Control, ORTHO Tomato & Vegetable Insect Killer, or ORTHO Malathion 50 Insect Spray. Cover the lower surfaces of the leaves thoroughly. Make sure your plant is listed on the product label.

Oak treehopper (4 times life size).

TREEHOPPERS

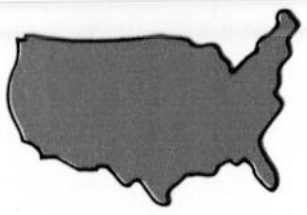

Treehoppers are small to medium-sized insects, ¼ to ⅝ inch long. They may be dull colored or brightly colored. These insects are distinctive for the hard covering that protrudes up and back from the head. The covering makes some appear humpbacked; on others it takes the form of a sharp point which makes the insect look like a thorn. Treehoppers suck plant juices, but this seldom causes significant injury. More severe damage is caused when they lay eggs. The female cuts slits in the stems of trees, shrubs, and herbaceous plants, and inserts her eggs underneath the bark at the wound. A canker forms at the injury site and the stem may die. Sometimes disease-causing fungi enter through the wounds. Most treehoppers never become abundant enough to be serious pests.

CONTROL: Treehoppers can be safely ignored unless abundant. When numerous, spray infested plants with an insecticide containing *malathion* or *carbaryl* (SEVIN®). Spray with ORTHO Volck Oil Spray to kill overwintering eggs.

Apple sucker psyllid (4 times life size).

PSYLLIDS

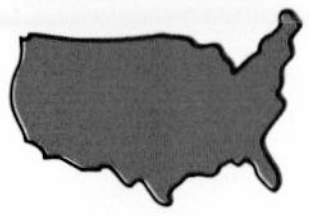

Psyllids are related to aphids, and are often called *jumping plant lice*. The winged adults are small (up to ⅙ inch) brownish or green insects that can spring from leaves into flight with their large hind legs. The wingless immature psyllids are often covered with white, waxy threads, or with drops of honeydew. Psyllids damage plants by sucking the plant sap. They feed on shoots and leaves, causing distortion, stunted growth, and sometimes tip dieback. They may also cover the plant with honeydew, undigested plant sap that is excreted as they feed. Some psyllids transmit plant diseases; others cause leaf galls to form. Infested leaves curl around one or more insects and enlarge to form a gall that completely surrounds them; or blisterlike galls develop in the center of leaves (for more information about galls, see page 861). The insects feed inside the galls, mature, and the galls split open to release the adult psyllids. When plants are heavily infested, thousands of adults may swarm around and invade homes.

CONTROL: Psyllids should be controlled early before they are protected inside curled leaves and galls. In mid-May, spray ornamentals with ORTHO Isotox Insect Killer or ORTHO Orthene Systemic Insect Control; spray fruits and vegetables with an insecticide containing *malathion*. Make sure your plant is listed on the product label. Repeat the spray in 10 to 14 days.

Grape leafhoppers (three times life size).

VECTORS OF PLANT DISEASES

Many different insects transmit plant diseases, but the most common and widespread carriers are aphids and leafhoppers. Aphids transmit most plant diseases, especially those caused by viruses. A single species of aphid may transmit up to 50 different viruses. Aphids and leafhoppers are small insects with sucking mouthparts. Their needlelike "mouths" pierce plant tissue and suck out the sap. Aphids and leafhoppers may acquire disease organisms as they feed on an infected plant. Disease organisms may also be transmitted to offspring through the eggs laid by the infective mother. When the infective insects feed on healthy, susceptible plants, they inject the disease organisms into the tissue, infecting the plant. Less common disease vectors are treehoppers, whiteflies, mealybugs, grasshoppers, beetles, earwigs, and mites.

CONTROL: Controlling insect vectors is especially difficult because it takes only one insect to infect a plant. If you are troubled by a vector-borne disease, you can reduce future damage by taking these precautions:

1. Begin a spray program before the insect is expected in the spring. To determine when the insect is expected, contact your local Cooperative Extension Office (see page 1029). Spray the plants you wish to protect and any nearby plants that the insect may feed on.

2. Destroy any diseased plants and any weeds that may harbor the disease.

3. If possible, construct a cage of cheesecloth around the plants you wish to protect to keep the insect vector from reaching them.

Spittlebugs on rosemary.

SPITTLEBUGS

Immature spittlebugs (nymphs) are small, green, soft-bodied insects that have an unusual and distinctive characteristic that distinguishes them from other insects. The nymphs, clustered in between leaves and stems, surround themselves with a frothy, white mass that looks like spittle, which protects them from sun and preying insects. Adult spittlebugs are small ($\frac{1}{4}$ inch), winged insects that hop or fly away quickly when disturbed. They feed on plant sap and lay their eggs inside stems or between the leaf blades and stems of many garden plants and forage crops. The greenish nymphs that hatch from the eggs suck sap from the plant. The insect excretes drops of undigested sap mixed with air. Its tail moves up and down as if working a bellows, forcing out bubbles of sap. The bug then reaches back and covers itself with the frothy spittle. Spittlebugs are most noticeable in the spring when the nymphs are feeding, but adults may be found on the plants throughout the summer.

CONTROL: A few spittlebugs on a plant do little harm. However, if the insects appear to be weakening the plant, control them on ornamentals with ORTHO Isotox Insect Killer or ORTHO Orthene Systemic Insect Control, and on food crops with an insecticide containing *malathion.* Make sure your plant is listed on the product label.

Cicada (twice life size).

CICADAS

Cicadas are large (up to $1\frac{1}{2}$ inches long), dark-bodied insects, with transparent wings held over their bodies in a rooflike position. The males have special vibratory organs that produce loud, strident sounds. Immature cicadas suck sap from roots (large numbers on the roots of fruit trees may severely reduce flowers and fruit), and adults may suck sap from young twigs. However, the main damage to plants is from egg-laying. Females use their sawlike egg-laying organ to cut the bark and sapwood of twigs. Rows of 24 to 48 eggs are deposited in the sapwood, up to 20 times per female, causing the leaves on damaged twigs to turn brown. Damaged twigs may eventually break and fall to the ground. The young insects that hatch from the eggs enter the soil, where they burrow down to the roots. There are many species of cicadas in the United States. The periodical cicada (*Magicicada septendecim*), found only in the eastern United States, is the longest-lived insect in North America. The southern race has a 13-year life cycle; the northern race, called the *17-year locust,* occurs every 17 years. The various broods (populations) are numbered, so their appearance can be accurately predicted. On the thirteenth or seventeenth spring, as many as 40,000 cicadas may appear from beneath a single tree.

CONTROL: Mature cicadas can be controlled by spraying with ORTHO Liquid Sevin when their singing is first heard and then repeating the spray after 6 or 7 days. Cut off and destroy injured twigs as soon as possible. Young trees can be protected with mosquito netting. Do not plant new trees in the spring when periodical cicada emergence is predicted.

BEE AND WASP FAMILY

Honey bee (3 times life size).

Bumble bee (twice life size).

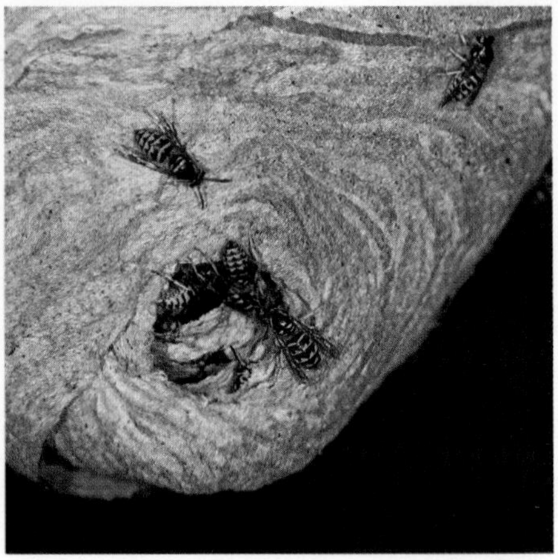

Yellowjackets (half life size).

HONEY BEES

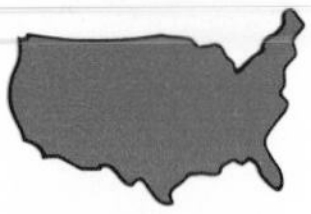

Honey bees are members of the insect order *Hymenoptera.* Other insects in this group include wasps, ants, and sawflies. Although some of these insects are plant and household pests, a great many prey on other insects or are important pollinators (well over 100 food crops depend on or benefit from insect pollination). Of all these insects, bees—and particularly honeybees—are by far the most important pollinators of flowers. They can be recognized by the furry body, two pairs of wings, and the bands of black or brown alternating with lighter brown or tan on the abdomen . The queen is ¾ inch long. Other bees are slightly shorter. One reason the honey bee is such an effective pollinator is that its body and legs are covered with special split hairs to which pollen clings. The bee is attracted to flowers for their sweet nectar, which it sucks up through its hollow tongue. Once the bee is on the flower, pollen rubs off onto the hairy body. Some of the pollen falls off when the bee visits other flowers, thus completing the pollination process. Honeybees also collect pollen as food for their young. It is collected on a special "pollen basket" on the hind legs. Honey bees usually visit flowers within ¼ mile of their colony, but have been known to forage as far away as 8½ miles. They use a "bee dance" to communicate the direction, distance, and quantity of pollen to other bees in the colony. (See page 802 for more information on honey bees.)

CONTROL: See page 802 for information on controlling honeybees.

BUMBLE BEES

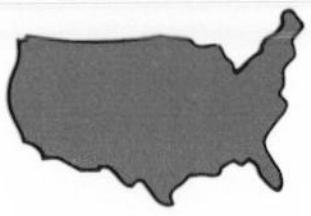

Bumble bees are recognized by their robust shape, hairy bodies, and large size (⅜ to 1 inch long). They are usually black with a yellow or orange patch on the abdomen. Bumble bees are closely related to honey bees and are excellent pollinators. Bumble bees nest in the ground, often in abandoned rodent nests, or among dry grass or other debris on the ground. The colonies are small, usually containing no more than several hundred adults. The individual cells that make up bumble bee nests are roundish and shaped like pots. The cells may contain honey, pollen, or immature bumble bees. Bumble bee colonies die out in the fall; only younger queens survive the winter. Queens start a new colony in the spring. The colony is small at first and attains its largest size in the late summer or early fall. Bumble bees visit many kinds of flowers. Because they have longer tongues than honey bees, they feed on the nectar of some flowers from which honeybees cannot feed. Bumble bees are not aggressive insects unless they are defending their nest. Most stings result when the nest is accidently stepped on.

CONTROL: Control of a bumble bee colony is seldom necessary unless there is a possibility that the nest will be disturbed by children or pets. Contact a professional pest control operator to spray the nest. If you are stung, apply a cold compress or ice pack to the swollen area. If a severe reaction develops, call a doctor.

SOCIAL WASPS

Social wasps are so named because they live in colonies. Some common social wasps include *yellowjackets, hornets,* and *umbrella* or *paper wasps.* These insects all live in paper nests they build either in abandoned rodent burrows or hanging from eaves or branches. The paper nest material is a combination of plant fibers and wasp saliva. A mature colony contains from 200 to as many as 15,000 individuals, depending on the kind of wasp. In fall, most of the wasps die and the colony is abandoned. Only recently-mated females (queens) live until the next year. They establish new colonies in the spring and by late summer the number of individuals in the colony is at a peak. It is at this time that social wasps become pests around picnic tables, ripe fruits, and garbage cans as they search for sweets and bits of meat. Normally, however, social wasps prey on other insects. They feed partially digested bits of the prey to their young. The adults also feed on sweet substances such as nectar and honeydew. Some social wasps aggressively defend their nests and may attack in mass if disturbed. Unlike honey bees, they can easily withdraw their stinger and escape or sting again.

CONTROL: Keep food and garbage covered to discourage wasps from becoming pests. For more information about controlling yellowjackets and wasps, see pages 802 and 803.

Digger wasp (1½ times life size).

Larvae (1½ times life size). *Insert:* Adult (life size).

Grasshopper (life size).

SOLITARY WASPS

Solitary wasps include *mud daubers, spider wasps, tarantula hawks*, and *cicada killers*. These wasps live alone. Some build mud nests under eaves, against walls, or under twigs or rocks; others dig tunnels in the ground and use these as nests. Although nests of several solitary wasps may be built close to each other, the wasps do not cooperate in building nests or feeding their young. Most solitary wasps resemble yellowjackets and other social wasps. Some, though, are a beautiful metallic blue or black. Many have a long, thin waist and are sometimes called thread-waisted wasps. Solitary wasps stock their nests with insects or spiders that they either kill or paralyze with their sting. The wasp larvae in the nests feed on the paralyzed prey, and later form a cocoon and emerge as adults. Solitary wasps rarely defend their nests and do not sting unless they are handled, stepped on, or highly provoked.

CONTROL: If mud nests are a problem, eliminate them by hosing or knocking them down. Kill wasps by spraying them with ORTHO Hornet & Wasp Killer or ORTHO Insect Fogger according to label directions. Control solitary wasps nesting in the ground (sometimes known as *digger wasps*) in lawns and other areas where they may be a nuisance by applying ORTHO Diazinon Soil & Turf Insect Control in and around the nest openings. Apply it at dusk when the wasps are not active. If you are stung, apply a cold compress or ice pack to the swollen area. If a severe reaction develops, call your doctor.

SAWFLIES

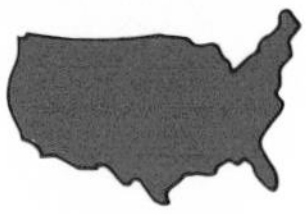

Sawflies are one of the few insects in the bee and wasp family that feed on plants. They are a diverse group of insects. The immature sawfly resembles either a slug, having a soft, glistening body and tiny legs, or a caterpillar, having three pairs of larger legs and seven pairs of smaller legs. When feeding, most sawflies eat almost the entire leaf, leaving only the larger leaf veins. Some sawflies eat just one leaf surface (upper or lower), leaving translucent tan spots ("windows") where they have fed. Others are leafminers that live and feed entirely between the upper and lower surfaces of the leaves. Adult sawflies are wasplike in general body shape but do not have the constricted threadlike waist characteristic of wasps. Some adults are colored like wasps, with yellow and black markings, others are entirely black. The adults do not eat and cannot sting. They lay eggs on or in leaves. The hatching larvae feed and spin a cocoon when fully grown. Most sawflies go through one generation a year; some go through two or three. If there are enough sawflies their feeding may weaken a plant, stunting its growth and causing fewer blooms and fruit. Sawflies feeding on conifers can kill the plant if they defoliate it for one to several years in a row.

CONTROL: Spray sawflies feeding on ornamental plants with ORTHO Orthene Systemic Insect Control or ORTHO Isotox Insect Killer. If it is a leafmining sawfly on an ornamental tree or shrub, spray with ORTHO Lindane Borer & Leaf Miner Spray. Spray sawflies on fruit trees with ORTHO Home Orchard Spray. Make sure your plant is listed on the product label. Repeat the spray if reinfestation occurs.

GRASSHOPPERS

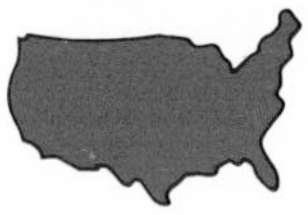

Grasshoppers, also called *locusts*, are large (up to 2½ inches), light and dark-mottled insects with hind legs enlarged for jumping. There are hundreds of different species throughout the country, but only a few of these are damaging to garden plants. Grasshoppers are not a serious pest every year. Seasonal conditions must be ideal for them to build up to large numbers. They are found primarily in areas that receive only 10 to 30 inches of rain annually. When winter temperatures are mild and other conditions are optimum, grasshopper populations increase to tremendous numbers and food becomes scarce. Under these conditions, many types of grasshoppers become nonselective in their food preference. Millions of migratory grasshoppers have been known to form swarms hundreds of miles across, devouring every green plant in their path. When infestations build up to such tremendous numbers, these grasshoppers pollute water, invade homes, destroy fabric, and become a hazard to motorists.

CONTROL: Handpicking eliminates small populations of grasshoppers. In order to minimize damage, controls should be applied while the grasshoppers are young. (Young grasshoppers are distinguished from the adults by their lack of fully developed wings.) As grasshoppers mature and increase in size, they require larger quantities of food. They will migrate, usually from mature and drying crops and weeds, to the garden to find food. Spray with ORTHO Fruit & Vegetable Insect Control or with an insecticide containing *carbaryl* (SEVIN®) or *malathion*. Repeat at weekly intervals if the plants become reinfested.

Walkingstick (half life size).

Cricket (life size).

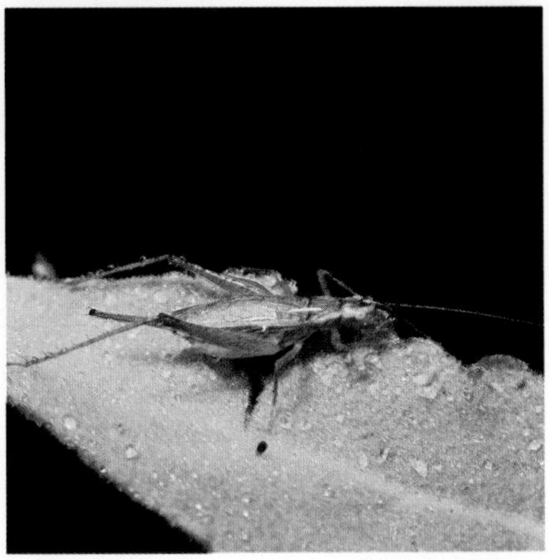

Tree cricket (twice life size).

WALKINGSTICKS

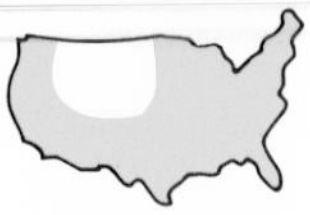

Walkingsticks are slow-moving insects that resemble twigs. They have long slender legs, a thin twig-like body, and long slender antennae. They are usually green when immature and turn brown as adults. Some walkingsticks may grow to a length of 5 or 6 inches. At night they feed on a wide variety of plants; oak is a favored food plant. Walkingsticks have been known to become numerous enough to defoliate trees, but such occurrences are rare. Females lay eggs while in trees. The eggs fall to the ground, lie among the leaf litter during the winter, and hatch in the spring. Only one generation is produced each year.

CONTROL: Walkingsticks seldom are numerous enough to cause plant damage, and are usually more of a curiosity than anything else. No insecticides are registered for their control; hand pick them if they are numerous and causing damage.

CRICKETS

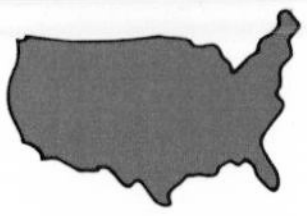

Crickets are black, brown, or green insects, up to 1½ inches long, that are closely related to grasshoppers (see page 881). Outdoors they feed on many plants; indoors they feed on clothes or other materials that have food or perspiration on them. Some crickets are beneficial, feeding on aphids and other small pests. Crickets fly or jump with their long legs, and have long antennae that reach down their backs. The males produce a loud chirping sound by rubbing together parts of their front wings. Females have long, spear-shaped ovipositors (egg-laying organs). Depending on the species, females insert eggs either in the soil or in plant tissue, which may kill the tissue. Crickets have chewing mouthparts and feed at night on foliage, flowers, seeds, and seedlings, or on other insects. They hide during the day in trash, around plants, along walkways, at the foot of walls or fences, or in the ground. The ground species are called *mole crickets.* (For more information about mole crickets, see page 259.) Crickets also invade homes, especially in the fall when their natural food supply disappears. For more information about crickets as household pests, see page 788.

CONTROL: If crickets become a problem in the garden, spray with ORTHO Diazinon Insect Spray or scatter ORTHO Diazinon Soil & Turf Insect Control, ORTHO PEST-B-GON Roach Bait or ORTHO Earwig, Roach & Sowbug Bait in a 2 to 4-foot band around ornamental plants or other areas where they congregate. Do not use around food crops.

TREE CRICKETS

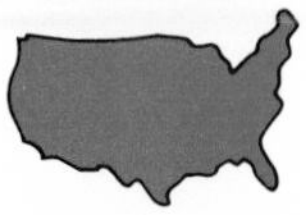

Tree crickets are slender, whitish to pale green or brown insects up to ¾ inch long, with long slender antennae. They live in trees and shrubs, where they feed on aphids and other insects, and to a lesser extent on fruit, flowers, and foliage. The main damage they cause occurs when the female makes a place to lay her eggs by cutting a row of deep punctures in berry canes or twigs of trees and shrubs. The twigs or canes may later break or die at the puncture sites. Tree crickets lay their eggs in the fall, and the young crickets emerge in the spring. There is only one generation a year. Tree crickets produce a high-pitched, sustained chirping or trilling sound. They emit the sound in unison; if one cricket stops, it restarts in time with the others. The *snowy tree cricket* (*Oecanthus fultoni*) is common throughout the country except in southeastern states. This famous species alters its rate of chirping in relation to the temperature; a good approximation of the temperature can be obtained by adding 40 to the number of chirps made in 15 seconds; the resulting number is the temperature in degrees Farenheit.

CONTROL: Prune out and destroy infested canes and twigs during the winter. There are no insecticides registered for control of tree crickets.

Jerusalem cricket (¾ life size).

JERUSALEM CRICKETS

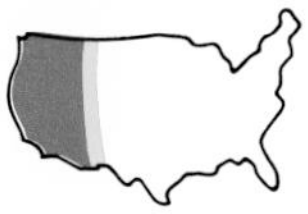

Jerusalem crickets (*Stenopelmatus fuscus*), also known as *potato bugs*, are large (up to 2 inches), brown insects. Their large head and legs, and long antennae give them a somewhat bizarre appearance. Jerusalem crickets are often found under rocks or other debris, or when spading up garden soil. Sometimes they accidentally wander into a home or garage where they may become trapped in a bowl or box. Jerusalem crickets are harmless, nonpoisonous insects. However, handle them with care; their powerful jaws can deliver a forceful pinch, and the spines on their legs can pierce skin. They are called potato bugs because they occasionally damage potatoes on newly cleared land. Although they feed on roots, their preferred diet is other small insects. They find their food by burrowing in the soil, and are most commonly found in freshly cultivated or light loamy or sandy soil.

CONTROL: Scoop the insect into a jar or box, or onto a newspaper, and throw it outdoors or dispose of it. There are no insecticides registered for control of this insect.

Katydid (life size).

KATYDIDS

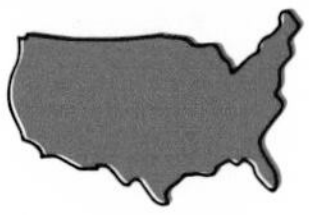

Katydids belong to the same order (*Orthoptera*) as grasshoppers, crickets, walkingsticks, praying mantids, cicadas, and cockroaches. The immature katydid, called a nymph, looks like the adult, except that its wings are shorter or not visible at all. Nymphs gradually develop into the adult form. Katydids are usually green, but are sometimes brown. The adults are from ¾ to over 2 inches long. Wings of many katydids look very similar to leaves; even the veins in the wings look like leaf veins. Katydids have large hind legs for jumping, and slender antennae which are usually longer than the body. The female has a flattened swordlike egg-laying device, called an ovipositor, which protrudes from the tail end of the body. She lays eggs in overlapping rows, usually on stems or leaves. The eggs are about the shape of pumpkin seeds, but a little smaller. There is only one generation a year. Katydids chew holes in the margins of leaves. They seldom occur in large enough numbers to do much damage, but occasionally they defoliate citrus trees or ornamental plants. Katydids are well known for their chirping sounds, which are an important part of courtship.

CONTROL: The presence of a few katydids is not enough to harm plants. If numerous, hand pick and destroy the insects, or spray with an insecticide containing *sodium aluminum flouride.* Make sure your plant is listed on the product label.

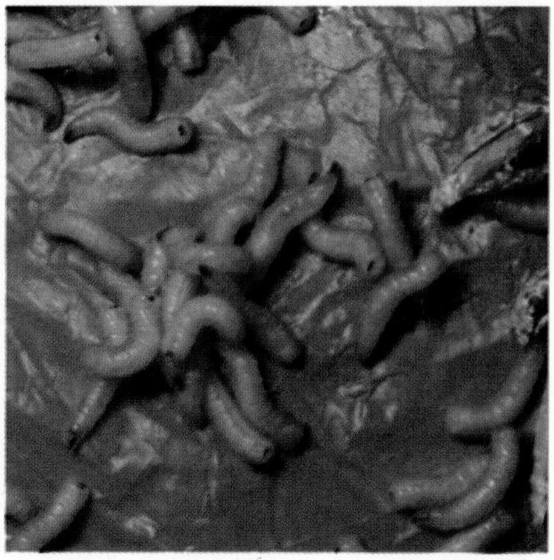

Housefly maggots (life size).

FLIES AND MAGGOTS

All flies are two-winged insects belonging to the insect order *Diptera.* Some familiar flies include *crane flies, fruit flies, blue bottle flies, house flies, hover flies, mosquitoes,* and *gnats.* Depending on the species, adult flies feed on other insects, blood, nectar, or liquids from decaying organic matter; some adult flies do not eat at all. Immature flies, called maggots, are legless creatures that lead a lifestyle quite different from the adults. Many live in and feed on moist decaying organic material such as compost, animal manure, and human garbage. Others are beneficial parasites or predators of other insects. Some feed on living plants. When the maggots have completed their development they change into brownish pupae and finally emerge as adults. Some flies complete their life cycle in days, while others may take a full year. Flies can transmit diseases to humans through their bites or as they crawl over food. Some flies are important pollinators, help to decompose decaying matter, help control other insects, and are used as food by other small animals.

CONTROL: Kill household flies indoors with ORTHO Flying and Crawling Insect Killer, ORTHO Hi-Power Indoor Insect Fogger, or ORTHO Home Pest Insect Control. Kill flies outdoors with ORTHO Malathion 50 Insect Spray or ORTHO Outdoor Insect Fogger. Apply according to label directions. For more information about controlling household flies and biting flies, see the section beginning on page 786. For information on flies infesting plants, look under the entry for your plant.

FLY FAMILY

Mediterranean fruit fly larvae (¾ life size).

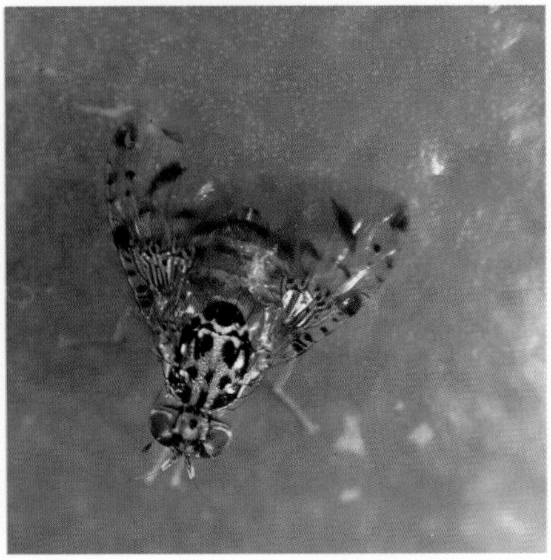

Mediterranean fruit fly (4 times life size).

Larva (5 times life size) *Insert:* Adult (life size).

MEDITERRANEAN FRUIT FLY

The Mediterranean fruit fly, commonly known as the *medfly*, is a tropical insect that infests over 250 species of plants, including many fruits, nuts, and vegetables. (For a list, see page 1018.) Because of its rapid development and wide host range, the medfly is one of the most serious agricultural problems in warm parts of the world. The adult is a little smaller than a housefly, with drooping wings that are banded with yellow, brown, and black.

The spread of the medfly: The medfly is a native of tropical West Africa. Since the mid-1800s it has been spreading to many of the warmer parts of the world, including Hawaii, Southern Europe, and Central and South America. It has been found in the United States off and on since 1929, when it was first discovered in central Florida. Since that time, outbreaks in Florida, Texas, and Southern California have been eradicated. The medfly is usually transported into the country as a larva in infested fruit. Most new infestations are the result of travelers bringing home infested fruit and vegetables.

The life cycle: Egg laying begins in the spring after the weather has remained warm (over 75°F) for a week. Male and female flies congregate on fruit, where they mate. The female then finds a fruit that is beginning to ripen. She drills a hole through the skin with her ovipositor (egg-laying organ) and inserts up to 10 white eggs in a cavity. One female can produce up to 1000 eggs during her lifetime. The larvae feed on the ripening fruit, which may rot on the inside. The fruit may appear normal, but fall off the plant prematurely. The mature larvae bore an exit hole and drop to the ground. They pupate in the soil or under objects on the ground. The adults feed on honeydew (see page 422) that is excreted by aphids, mealybugs, and scale insects. Medflies can fly over a mile, but usually remain near the plants in which they developed as larvae. There may be as many as 14 generations during the growing season.

CONTROL: The Mediterranean fruit fly is under quarantine laws and its spread is constantly monitored by detection traps operated by state and federal departments of agriculture. Fruit shipped from countries with medfly infestations must be fumigated or otherwise treated before it is accepted by countries in which the medfly is likely to survive. Despite these precautions, the insect sometimes gains entry and spreads. Summer and fall (May to October) are the most likely times to detect the fly. If you live in an infested area or an area where infestations have occurred, you should learn to identify the medfly, and notify your local Cooperative Extension Office (see page 1029) if you suspect an outbreak in your neighborhood.

CRANE FLIES

Crane flies resemble huge, overgrown mosquitoes. They range from ⅜ to 2½ inches long, with the wings spanning as much as 3 inches. They have long, slender legs that break off easily. Crane flies often find their way into homes and garages where they can cause alarm because of their large size. Fortunately they cannot bite and are completely harmless. The adult flies do not eat. Most crane fly larvae (or maggots) feed on decaying plant material in damp soil or shallow water. One, the *European crane fly,* is a lawn pest (see page 260 for more information). Crane fly larvae range from ½ to 1½ inches long when fully grown. There are one or two generations a year.

CONTROL: Usually only one or two crane flies are seen indoors. Spray them with ORTHO Household Insect Killer or capture them and release them outdoors.

THRIPS FAMILY

Leafminer trails.

LEAFMINERS

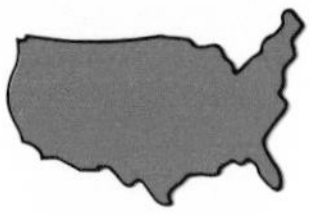

Leafminers are insect larvae that feed inside a leaf, between the upper and lower surfaces. They may be the larvae of flies, moths, sawflies, or beetles. Females lay their eggs on or in the leaves, and the larvae that hatch from these eggs burrow into the leaves. Leafminers must be able to survive in a small living space, so they are tiny and somewhat flattened. The thinner the leaf the flatter and smaller the leafminer. As the larvae mine the leaf tissue, there is more room for them to expand, but their heads always remain somewhat flattened. Leafminer feeding produces blisters, blotches, or tunnels in the leaf, which turns yellow or brown as the tissue dies. If more than one larva is mining the tissue, the tunnels often run together, forming large blotches that cover much of the leaf. Infested plants may have a scorched appearance.

CONTROL: Leafminers are protected inside leaves for most of their lives, which makes control difficult. If the spray used for control is not a systemic insecticide, then sprays must be applied when the adults emerge to lay their eggs. Most ornamentals can be sprayed with the systemic insecticides ORTHO Orthene Systemic Insect Control or ORTHO Isotox Insect Killer. Food crops can also be treated with ORTHO Diazinon Insect Spray or ORTHO Fruit & Vegetable Insect Control if the spray is carefully timed. Check with your local Cooperative Extension Office (see page 1029) for the best time to spray for the insect in your area. Make sure your plant is listed on the spray label.

Leaf thrips damage to viburnum.

THRIPS

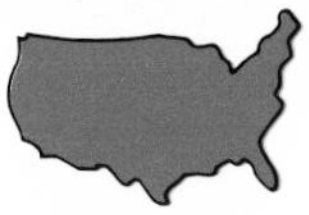

Thrips are tiny (less than 1/16 inch), slender insects of the order *Thysanoptera*, which means "bristle wings" or "fringe wings." Adults are tan to dark brown or black with two pairs of featherlike wings. The immature insects (nymphs) are wingless, and usually lighter in color. Thrips are serious pests of hundreds of plants in the garden. Nymphs and adults feed by scraping or rasping the plant tissue and then sucking the released plant sap. Blossoms, fruit, foliage, and shoots become flecked, streaked, or distorted. Females lay fertilized or unfertilized eggs in plant tissue. The unfertilized eggs develop only into males. Most species of thrips complete a life cycle in 2 to 3 weeks, so populations can rapidly build up to tremendous numbers. In warm winter areas, reproduction may continue throughout the year.

CONTROL: Exposed thrips (those that feed unprotected on foliage) are easier to control than flower thrips, which are protected from chemicals inside the flowers or growing points of the plant. Remove infested buds and blooms. Spray flowers with a systemic insecticide such as ORTHO Isotox Insect Killer or ORTHO Orthene Systemic Insect Control. Spray ornamentals for exposed thrips with ORTHO Isotox Insect Killer, ORTHO Malathion 50 Insect Spray, or ORTHO Liquid Sevin. Control thrips on food crops with ORTHO Fruit & Vegetable Insect Control or ORTHO Malathion 50 Insect Spray. Apply sprays 2 more times at intervals of 7 to 10 days to control thrips as they hatch. Because most types of thrips migrate long distances on wind currents, they can quickly reinfest plants. Check your plants periodically for new damage.

Flower thrips damage to pansy.

FLOWER THRIPS

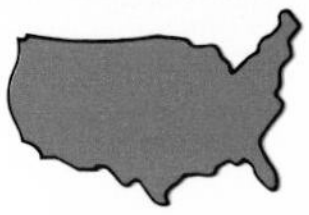

Flower thrips (*Frankliniella* species) are tiny (1/20 inch long) insects that infest the flowers, flower buds, and growing points of many plants. They are able to distinguish different colors of flowers, usually preferring those that are yellow or light-colored. The amber-colored adults and lemon-yellow nymphs (immature thrips) feed by rasping the plant tissue and then sucking the released plant sap. The injured tissue dies, producing dead spots, distorted blossoms and new leaves, and balled flowers (flower buds that turn brown and never open). Flower thrips are most abundant between late spring and midsummer. They reproduce mainly on the flowers of trees, grasses, and weeds, and then migrate to gardens nearby. In the western states, thrips are most damaging when uncultivated plants dry up in summer, forcing the insects to migrate to gardens where plants are still green.

CONTROL: Flower thrips are difficult to control because they are usually protected in plant tissue, and they constantly reinfest garden flowers from nearby plants. Spraying ornamentals with a systemic insecticide (one that moves through the plant) will protect flowers for up to 10 days. Use ORTHO Orthene Systemic Insect Control or ORTHO Isotox Insect Killer at the first sign of damage. Control thrips on food crops with ORTHO Malathion 50 Insect Spray or ORTHO Fruit & Vegetable Insect Control. Make sure your plant is listed on the label. Repeat the spray two more times at intervals of 7 to 10 days to control thrips as they hatch.

THRIPS FAMILY

Greenhouse thrips (twice life size).

GREENHOUSE THRIPS

Greenhouse thrips (*Heliothrips haemorrhoidalis*) are serious pests of many greenhouse plants, and also damage many garden ornamentals and fruits in the southern states. They feed openly in dense colonies on leaves and fruit. Greenhouse thrips do not survive well in hot, dry conditions, so they are usually found in shady areas, or on the inner parts or north side of a plant. As the thrips remove sap from the plant tissue, leaves become silvery or bleached. Damaged leaves wilt, become papery, and usually drop prematurely. The thrips also leave large quantities of black, varnishlike spots of excrement around the areas where they feed, giving the plant an unsightly appearance. Adult greenhouse thrips are black with silvery-black wings. They are not strong fliers like other types of thrips, so infestations spread slowly. Females insert their eggs inside leaves or fruit, producing blisters. The young thrips that hatch from these eggs are translucent white and wingless. They feed for several weeks and then develop into adults. There may be seven or more generations a year.

CONTROL: Greenhouse thrips are easier to control than other types of thrips that are protected in buds and flowers (see page 885). Spray infested plants with ORTHO Isotox Insect Killer, ORTHO Malathion 50 Insect Spray, or ORTHO Liquid Sevin. Cover the leaf surfaces thoroughly. Before spraying, make sure your plant is listed on the product label. Do not use Isotox on food crops.

TERMITES

Termites (3 times life size).

Termite soil tube.

TERMITES

Termites cause great economic damage in this country. These insects have special protozoa in their stomachs that help them digest wood. Termites may be winged or wingless. The winged forms emerge from the nests in the spring and fall, often on a warm day following a rain. After mating in the air, the winged termites drop their wings and search for a suitable place to start a new colony. Only a small percentage survive and are successful. Colonies consist of eggs, nymphs, workers, soldiers, one or more egg-laying queens, and winged termites that will one day leave the colony. There are three kinds of termites. *Subterranean termites* are the most common (see page 797). They maintain their colonies within the ground, and build their characteristic mud tubes over rocks and cement foundations to bridge the gap between soil and wood. Their galleries in wood always contain soil. *Drywood termites* (see page 798) do not require such contact with the ground, and do not build mud tubes. Their galleries are free of soil. *Dampwood termites* (see page 797) do not require contact with the ground, but do require wood or soil with a high moisture content. Their galleries are free of soil. Although termites are beneficial in nature because they help decompose the wood of fallen trees and shrubs, they sometimes weaken or kill living trees and shrubs. They usually enter the plant through wounds, dead branches, or roots. Drywood termites confine their feeding primarily to dried heartwood. They seldom kill the plant, but they weaken it structurally if they continue feeding over a long period. In warm climates subterranean termites sometimes eat the bark and living tissues underneath, killing the plant.

CONTROL: If termites are in the structure of a building, identify the kind of termite involved, determine the extent of damage, and apply the control measures given for that termite. Use Ortho-Klor Soil Insect & Termite Killer for localized areas. For more information, see page 797 for subterranean termites, page 798 for drywood termites, and page 797 for dampwood termites. Accurate diagnosis and effective control of termites usually requires the aid of a professional termite or pest control operator. Prevent termite occurrences in the garden by pruning out dead branches, burning or digging out stumps, removing wood debris, and painting or treating garden stakes and fence posts with a wood preservative. Remove debris from around termite-infested plants and prune out infested plant parts if possible. No insecticides are registered for control of termites in plants.

SPIDERS

Spider with egg sac (life size).

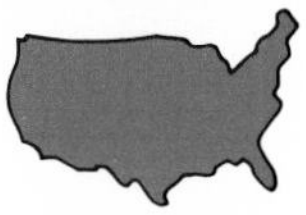

SPIDERS

Spiders are not insects but belong to the class Arachnida, along with mites, ticks, scorpions, and harvestmen. All Arachnida have four pairs of legs and two main body segments, unlike insects which have three pairs of legs and three main body segments. There are many different kinds of spiders. Many spin intricate webs to trap their prey; others do not spin webs. Spiders which do not build webs either actively hunt their prey or wait motionless and grab their victims as they approach. Most spiders in homes and gardens build neat, organized webs or sheets of webbing that lead into a funnel. The poisonous black widow and the brown recluse spiders (see page 805), both spin an irregular, tangled web in a dark, quiet location or among debris on the ground. Many nonpoisonous species also build tangled webs. Most spiders lay eggs in silken sacs. The young spiderlings resemble adults and are cannabalistic. Some spiderlings leave the egg sac by sending out a long silken thread that catches the wind and pulls the spider into the air. This process is called ballooning. In the fall the air is sometimes filled with masses of these threads, called gossamer. Spiders feed mostly on insects, but play only a minor role in controlling insect pests.

CONTROL: They usually do not need to be controlled unless they become a nuisance in or around the home. See page 787 for control of household spiders, and page 805 for control of specific poisonous spiders.

MITES

Mite damage on hollyhock.

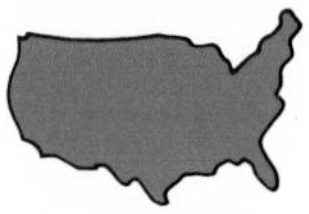

MITES

Mites are minute pests that infest many garden plants. There are many injurious species, some of which are commonly called *spider mites.* Some mites may injure humans or animals; others are beneficial predators of plant pests. Mites are not insects, but belong to the animal class Arachnida, along with spiders, ticks, and several other groups. They have four pairs of legs instead of three, and lack antennae and true jaws. Each mite has a pair of needlelike stylets that pierce plant tissue. The sap and cell contents are sucked out, resulting in leaf stippling. Most mites have many generations each year, often completing a life cycle in 7 to 10 days. Mites, cast skins, egg shells, and webbing may cover the surfaces of leaves or other plant parts. Heavy rains usually limit spider mite populations by washing them off the plant.

CONTROL: Mites can be difficult to control because the egg stage is resistant to most chemical sprays. Chemicals are effective against other stages, however. They must be applied at least 3 times at intervals of 7 to 10 days for effective control. Spray ornamentals with ORTHO Isotox Insect Killer. Control mites on fruits and vegetables with ORTHO Fruit & Vegetable Insect Control, ORTHO Diazinon Insect Spray, or ORTHO Malathion 50 Insect Spray.

SILVERFISH

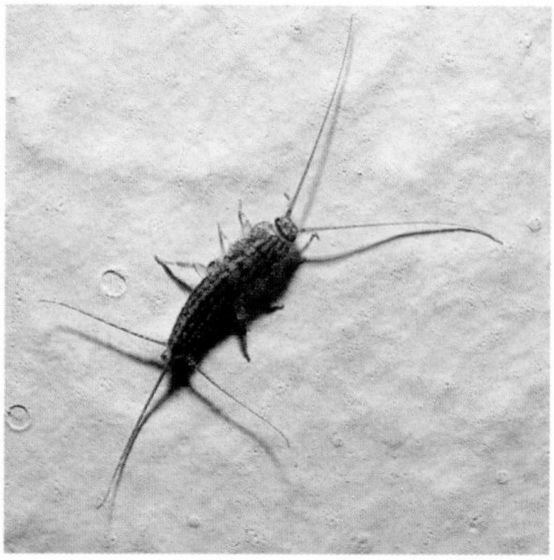

Silverfish (twice life size).

SILVERFISH

Silverfish belong to the order Thysanura, a name that refers to the three long antennaelike tails at the rear of the insect. They are sometimes called *bristletails.* These insects are less than ½ inch long and are covered with silvery scales that rub off easily. Immature silverfish resemble the adults except for their smaller size. After hatching, they periodically shed their skin (molt) as they grow. They may molt as many as 50 times during their lifetime. In very warm climates, silverfish take as little as 3 months to become adults; in cooler climates, they mature in about 2 years. Under optimum conditions silverfish can live for 3 or 4 years. Silverfish are commonly found indoors, where they feed on materials with a high starch content such as paper, wallpaper, book bindings, and starched clothing. The species that live outdoors, usually called bristletails, are found under stones, beneath bark, in leaf litter, and in other dark, protected spots. They mainly feed on lichens, molds, and dead insects. Silverfish and bristletails are most active at night. See page 789 for more information on silverfish occurring in homes.

CONTROL: Spray with ORTHO Ant, Roach and Spider Killer or ORTHO Home Pest Insect Control in areas such as cracks along baseboards and door and window frames, closets, behind drawers and shelves, and around bookcases. Store valued papers and clothes in tightly sealed plastic bags. Dispose of unwanted books, papers, and magazines. Seal holes in walls around pipes, and other cracks and crevices. Eliminate sources of excess moisture such as leaking plumbing.

DRAGONFLIES AND DAMSELFLIES ■ **MAYFLIES** ■ **ANTLIONS** ■

Dragonfly (¾ life size).

Mayfly (twice life size).

Antlion pit. *Insert:* Antlion (twice life size).

DRAGONFLIES AND DAMSELFLIES

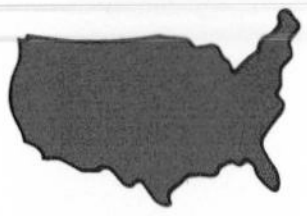

Dragonflies and damselflies are both in the order Odonata, a name referring to their toothed "jaws". They are common around lakes and streams. Dragonflies, which have wider bodies and stiffer wings than damselflies, are strong fliers, and may be seen well away from water. Dragonflies hold their wings perpendicular to their body when at rest, while damselfies hold their wings parallel to their body and behind them. Both may have clear wings or wings with black or colored bands. Colorful, sometimes iridescent, markings cover their bodies. The largest dragonflies in this country are over 4 inches long with a wingspan of nearly 6 inches. Dragonflies and damselflies deposit their eggs in water or boggy areas close to water. The immature insects, called naiads, live at the bottom of streams and ponds where they feed on insects, tadpoles, and small fish. Naiads are in turn eaten by larger fish. Naiads bear little resemblence to the adults; they are broad-bodied, wingless, and have 3 pairs of legs which are as long as or longer than their bodies. They range up to 2½ inches long. When naiads are fully grown they crawl out of the water on a plant stem, post, or other nearby object, shed their skin, and emerge as adults. Their outgrown skins may be seen along the water's edge.

CONTROL: Controls are not necessary.

MAYFLIES

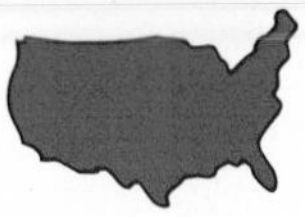

Mayflies, are in the order Ephemeroptera, a name referring to the extremely short life of the adults. Mayflies are soft-bodied, delicate creatures, from ⅛ to 1 inch long, with triangular wings that are held upright over their body when at rest. They have two or three long antennaelike filaments at their tail end. Mayfly adults cannot feed. They live only 1 to 3 days. Large numbers of them often emerge at the same time. On certain spring and summer nights swarms of mayflies may be seen flying around lights near lakes and streams. Their dead bodies may pile up in enormous numbers. The dried out bodies and skins of mayflies cause allergy problems in some people when large flights of adults occur. Mayflies swarm and mate at twilight, and lay eggs within an hour in nearby water. The immature mayflies, known as naiads, live at the bottoms of streams, ponds, and lakes, feeding on tiny aquatic plants and animals. Naiads are wingless and have three tail-end filaments which are shorter than the body and about as long as the antennae. Most naiads live from 1 to 4 years before emerging as adults. Both naiads and adult mayflies are important food sources for fish, frogs, and other creatures in and around water.

CONTROL: Controls are not necessary.

ANTLIONS

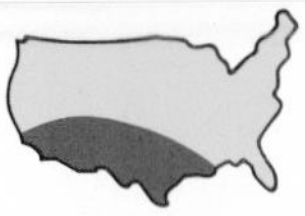

These peculiar insects are related to damselflies; the adult antlion closely resembles a damselfly except for its antennae, which have tiny clubs on the tips. The immature antlions, also known as *doodlebugs,* make cone-shaped pits in dry, sandy, or dusty soil. The pits are often located at the base of trees and near or beneath buildings. The largest pits are up to 2 inches in diameter. The antlion lies concealed at the bottom of the pit, ready to grab any ant or other small insect that tumbles in. The antlion has large sickle-shaped jaws which it uses to hold the prey as it sucks out the body fluids. It lives from 1 to 3 years and makes many pits during its lifetime. It makes a cocoon at the base of the pit and emerges as an adult antlion during the summer. Antlions are very weak fliers and are easily blown by the wind. They are sometimes attracted to lights. Although antlions are beneficial predators, their role in controlling garden pests is minor.

Ants (twice life size).

ANTS

Ants are social insects, relatives of bees and wasps, and live in colonies or nests. Each colony has large egg-laying queens, larvae, pupae, and wingless, sterile workers, which are all females. In the spring or early summer, the queen produces winged males and females that may leave the nest to start new colonies or enter established colonies. After mating, the males die, and the queens shed their wings and begin laying eggs. Many different types of ants are found throughout the United States. All ants have a constricted abdomen, and they range in color from yellow to black. Some ants invade homes looking for food (see page 791). Others find their food outside, where they feed on insects, seeds, vegetable roots, flower nectar, or honeydew, a sweet, sticky excretion from sucking insects, including aphids, soft scales, mealybugs, leafhoppers, and whiteflies. Certain ants caress aphids to increase their production of honeydew, or carry them to uninfested plants to supply them with ample food. Ant colonies or mounds located in the garden, lawn, or cultivated fields disturb plant roots and interfere with the use of equipment. The mounds are often more of a nuisance than the ants themselves.

CONTROL: Ant mounds in the garden can be treated with ORTHO Diazinon Granules or sprayed with ORTHO Diazinon Insect Spray. Control aphids (page 875), scales (page 877), mealybugs (page 876), leafhoppers (page 878) and whiteflies (page 877) to eliminate the production of honeydew, which attracts ants.

Fire ant mound.

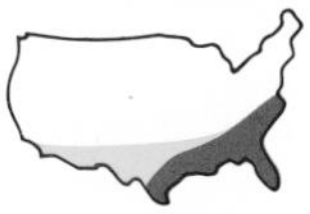

FIRE ANTS

Fire ants (*Solenopsis* species) are small (up to ¼ inch) red or black ants that build large, hard nests in the ground, 1 to 2 feet high. Mounds or nests are found in lawns and gardens, or in houses, when ants are driven inside by rain or drought. They are especially numerous in pasture lands, where there may be up to 60 mounds per acre. Damage from fire ants is due mainly to their mounds, which interfere with mowing or cultivating in the garden, and with harvest operations in commercial vegetable production. The large mounds ruin garden equipment and machinery. Fire ants may also damage plants. Some species feed on young succulent vegetables, bark, and insects, while others eat almost anything, including seeds, plants, insects, nesting birds, household foods, and clothes. The ants may attack and kill young animals and ground birds, such as quail; they also sting people, usually on the feet or legs, who accidentally disturb their nests. Depending on the degree of allergy, people react differently to the sting, which may be very painful and serious. The ant first bites the skin, raising it slightly, and then inserts its stinger, leaving it there for up to 25 seconds. It may repeat this procedure two or three more times, causing a cluster of stings. Within 24 hours, pustules develop that are up to ⅛ inch in diameter.

CONTROL: Fire ants can be controlled in the lawn by treating their mounds as they appear with ORTHO Fire Ant Control or ORTHO Ortho-Klor Soil Insect & Termite Killer. If you have a severe reaction to fire ant stings, call your doctor.

Earwig (twice life size).

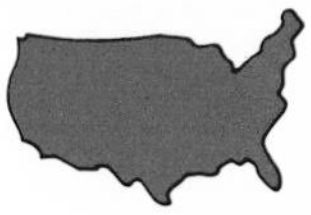

EARWIGS

Earwigs are hard, flattened, reddish brown insects, up to 1 inch long with forcepslike pincers that extend from the back end. The pincers on the females are almost straight, with a sharp inward curve on the end. On the males, the pincers are longer and have a wide curve. The pincers are used as offensive and defensive weapons, and sometimes to catch insects, on which they feed. However, their main source of food is from plants, ripe fruit, and decaying organic matter. Young earwigs eat ragged holes in the leaves of many vegetables and flowers in spring or early summer. Older earwigs feed on blossoms and corn silk, causing poor kernel development on the cobs. The insects may even climb into large fruit trees, such as apricot and peach trees, and feed on ripening fruit. Earwigs are nocturnal insects, feeding at night and hiding during the day. In daylight hours they hide in damp, dark places, such as in wood piles or plant refuse, under flower pots, or in homes, where they become household pests. For more information about earwigs as household pests, see page 789.

CONTROL: If you think earwigs are eating your plants, inspect the plants at night with a flashlight. Spray with ORTHO Diazinon Insect Spray, dust with ORTHO Ortho-Klor Indoor & Outdoor Insect Killer, or scatter ORTHO Earwig, Roach & Sowbug Bait lightly in a 2 to 4-foot band around plants, flower pots, house and porch foundations, woodpiles, or anywhere else you think earwigs may be hiding. Do not use on food crops. To keep earwigs out of fruit trees growing in lawn areas, sprinkle ORTHO Diazinon Soil & Turf Insect Control around the base of the trees about a month before the fruit ripens.

SOIL PESTS

Centipede (life size).

Millipede (4 times life size).

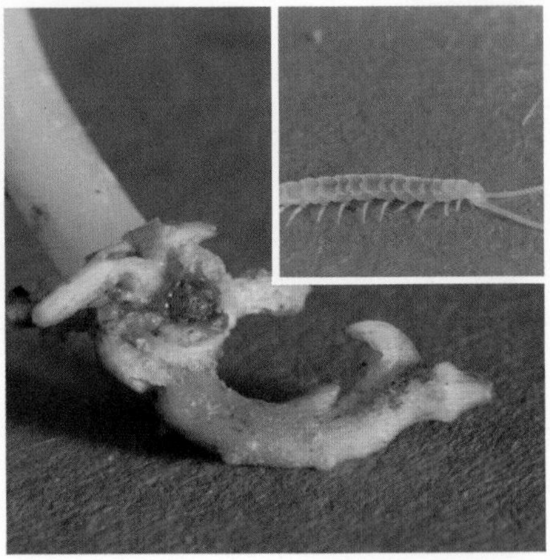

Damaged root. *Insert:* Symphylan (4 times life size).

CENTIPEDES

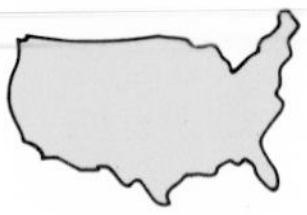

Centipedes, often called *hundred-legged worms*, are not true insects, but they are closely related. They have no wings; only two main body parts instead of three; and instead of three pairs of legs like true insects, they have one pair on each segment of their body. Most centipedes have at least 15 pairs of legs. Their bodies are long in relation to width and somewhat flattened, which make it possible for them to squeeze into cracks and crevices of foundations and around windows. Most centipedes are about 1 inch long, but some of the tropical species reach 18 inches in length. Centipedes look like millipedes (see page 890), but are more active. Centipedes scurry rapidly away when disturbed; millipedes usually curl into a tight spiral. Centipedes do not injure plants. They are beneficial, preying on snails, insects, and earthworms. Centipedes hide in damp areas under logs and stones, and in plant debris. They can move swiftly to catch their prey, which they paralyze by injecting poison from claws located behind the head. Some of the larger species of centipedes may inflict a painful bite if they are handled by humans.

CONTROL: It is usually unnecessary to control centipedes unless they start infesting your home. Sealing cracks in the foundation or holes in window frames will help prevent centipedes from entering the house. Clear wood, stones, and dead vegetation away from the base of the house. Scatter ORTHO Pest-B-Gon Roach Bait or ORTHO Earwig, Roach & Sowbug Bait around areas where centipedes hide. Do not use on food crops. Inside the home, use ORTHO Flying & Crawling Insect Killer.

MILLIPEDES

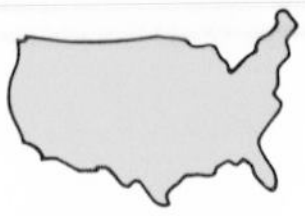

Millipedes, also called *thousand-legged worms*, are distant relatives of centipedes (see page 890). Millipedes are one to several inches long, hard-bodied, cylindrical, and wormlike, usually brown, pinkish brown, or grayish. They have two very short legs on each body segment, numbering from 30 to 400 legs. Young millipedes look like the adults, but initially have only 3 pairs of legs. Millipedes curl up in a coil when they are touched or picked up. They hide in damp, dark places, such as under stones or boards, or in plant debris. Large numbers of them may crawl into houses during heavy rains or during dry periods in summer and fall. Millipedes normally feed on decaying matter. But when they become numerous, they may feed on small roots, seedlings, or vegetable seeds. Root crops, decaying flower bulbs, and overripe fruit that touch damp ground, especially muskmelons, tomatoes, and strawberries, may attract millipedes.

CONTROL: If millipedes are a problem in your garden, dust with ORTHO Ortho-Klor Indoor & Outdoor Insect Killer, or scatter ORTHO Earwig, Roach & Sowbug Bait lightly in a 2 to 4-foot band around plants and other areas where millipedes hide. Do not use around food crops. Protect ripening fruits on the ground with straw or other mulch. To reduce the number of millipedes that enter your home, remove vegetation and plant debris from around your house foundation and spray around the foundation with ORTHO Diazinon Insect Spray. Millipedes move slowly, which makes them simple to remove from inside the house. Pick them up by hand or with a vacuum cleaner, or sweep them up with a broom.

SYMPHYLANS

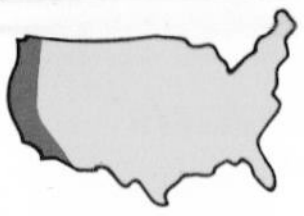

Symphylans are small (up to ¼ inch), pure white, soft-bodied animals with 12 pairs of legs. They are often called *garden centipedes* because of their similarity to centipedes (see page 890). The tiny animals are very active in damp soil, outside in warm climates or in greenhouses everywhere. They feed on many vegetables, fruits, and flowers, attacking germinating seeds, plant root systems, and aboveground parts in contact with the soil. Small plants may die or be severely stunted. Larger, more mature plants can usually withstand a symphylan infestation. When the weather warms in the spring, symphylans migrate up to the top 6 inches of soil where they usually remain feeding throughout the summer. In late fall, they move deeper in the soil to more protected sites. Symphylans are often found in large numbers in localized areas, marked by a group of stunted plants. Sifting through a shovelful of soil from the site will confirm their presence.

CONTROL: Drenching the soil with an insecticide containing *malathion* may reduce injury to plants. An insecticide containing *diazinon* granules mixed into the top 4 to 8 inches of soil before planting may allow vegetable plants to establish a good root system and become resistant to damage by symphylans. Seeds and plants must be set immediately after treatment. An insecticide containing *lindane* can be used for nonfood crops. Thorough discing or tilling of the soil before planting will scatter and destroy many symphylans, which gives plants time to grow before the symphylan population builds up again.

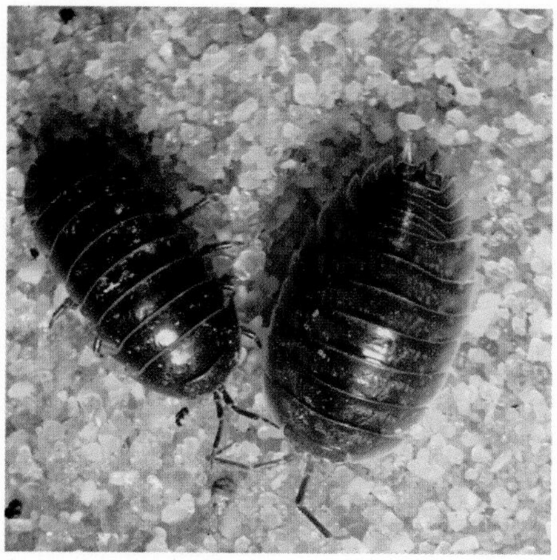

Sowbugs (6 times life size).

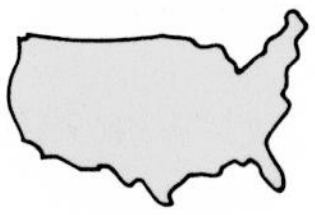

SOWBUGS AND PILLBUGS

Sowbugs and pillbugs are crustaceans, and are related to lobsters and shrimp. They are dark gray, with hard, flattened, segmented bodies, about ½ inch long, and have many legs. Pillbugs roll up into a ball when disturbed. Sowbugs and pillbugs are nocturnal insects. They feed at night on decaying vegetable matter, and are destructive to plants only when their populations build up to very large numbers. When this happens, they feed on the fine roots of seedlings in the garden or greenhouse. They also feed on fruit and leaves that are in contact with the ground. During the day, sowbugs and pillbugs hide in damp, dark places, such as under boards, rocks, or flower pots, or in plant debris. Sometimes they invade homes through cracks or windows, and hide in dark places like basements. They do no damage inside, but they can be a nuisance.

CONTROL: If you notice large numbers of sowbugs or pillbugs under your flower pots or in the garden, scatter ORTHO Slug-Geta Snail & Slug Bait, ORTHO Pest-B-Gon Roach Bait, or ORTHO Earwig, Roach & Sowbug Bait lightly in a 2 to 4-foot band around plants, flower pots, boards, plant debris, and other areas where sowbugs and pillbugs congregate. Do not use around food crops. Where possible, eliminate moist, dark breeding sites (rocks, boards, leaves). Spray around house foundations with ORTHO Diazinon Insect Spray, or dust with ORTHO Ortho-Klor Indoor & Outdoor Insect Killer.

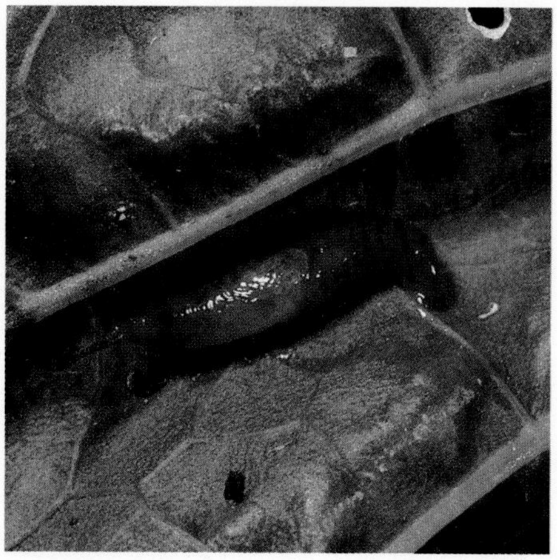

Slug (life size).

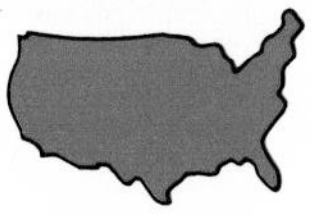

SNAILS AND SLUGS

Snails and slugs are mollusks, belonging to the same group as oysters and clams. Snails and slugs are quite similar to each other except that snails have an external shell. Both secrete mucus which helps them to glide along. The mucus dries to become the familiar shiny "slime trail," a good clue to their presence. These land mollusks require moisture to survive and therefore are most troublesome in wet areas. When conditions become dry they go dormant, becoming active again only when moisture is available. They lay their eggs in damp soil under rocks or plant debris. Snails and slugs take from 2 months to 2 years to become adults. Dense ground covers, such as ivy, are ideal hiding and breeding places for them. They feed on either living or decaying plant material, or both. Some species are more troublesome than others, and size alone is not a good indicator of how serious a pest it is.

CONTROL: Scatter ORTHO Slug-Geta Snail & Slug Bait granules or ORTHO Bug-Geta Snail & Slug Pellets in bands around the areas you wish to protect. Also scatter the bait in areas where snails or slugs might be hiding, such as in dense ground cover, weedy areas, compost piles, or pot storage areas. Before spreading the bait, wet down the areas to be treated to encourage snail and slug activity that night. Repeat the application every 2 weeks as long as snails and slugs are active. Hand picking and disposing of snails and slugs consistently over a long period will greatly reduce populations.

Lady beetle (twice life size).

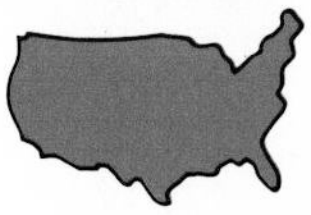

LADY BEETLES

Lady beetles, also called *ladybugs* and *ladybird beetles*, are beneficial insects that prey mostly on aphids, but also eat scales, mealybugs, and mites. They belong to the large insect family *Coccinellidae*, which means "scarlet red." People often think of lady beetles as red with black spots, but there are many different species that range in color from gray and black to bright orange. The larvae are flat, orange or gray, alligator-shaped insects, with legs on the front half of the body. Unlike the adults, they have no wings or wing covers. The cigar-shaped eggs are usually orange, and stand upright in clusters of a dozen or more. A single lady beetle may lay up to 1500 eggs during her life. The larvae that hatch from the eggs feed on aphids or other insects, devouring up to 25 aphids a day. Because lady beetles are such voracious eaters, they require high populations of aphids to maintain themselves. Adults may eat 50 or more aphids a day. If the prey population is reduced to such low numbers that there are not enough aphids on which to feed, the lady beetles will migrate or starve to death. The aphid population will gradually rebuild, possibly followed by a return of the lady beetle population. These population fluctuations are very common between predators and their prey. Lady beetles can be purchased at garden stores or through mail-order houses. These insects have been collected from huge masses in areas where they hibernate. When they are placed out in the garden, there is no guarantee they will stay. Even when there is food available, lady beetles often have an urge to migrate. Some may remain in the garden, but most will move to your neighbors' yards.

BENEFICIAL INSECTS

Praying mantid (¾ life size).

Larva (6 times life size). Adult (twice life size).

Hover fly. (twice life size).

PRAYING MANTIDS

Praying mantids are considered beneficial insects because they prey on many insect pests. However, they are just as likely to prey on a harmless insect or even another beneficial insect, such as a honey bee, as they are on a pest species. Their name comes from the position in which they wait for their prey—a position of prayer. They are large (up to 5 inches), slender, green or straw-colored insects with wings and long legs. The front legs are larger than the hind legs and have spines that are used to grasp and hold their prey. The immature mantids look just like the adults but are smaller and do not have wings. In the fall, the females lay 100 or more eggs in foamlike, straw-colored masses attached to any type of plant in the garden. After mating, the female often devours the male mantid. The following May or June the emerging young begin feeding on aphids or other small, slow-moving prey. They may also feed on one another. As they increase in size, they feed on larger insects. The mantids kill their prey by biting the back of the neck, which severs the main nerves and renders the animal helpless. Praying mantid eggs can be purchased or gathered from roadside borders, around fields, or from shrubs. Leave them attached to a section of the plant and place them in your garden off the ground where they won't be soaked by rain. Because they are not heavy feeders, mantids are relatively ineffective as insect controls. But they are interesting.

LACEWINGS

Lacewings are beneficial insects that belong to a group called *nerve-winged* insects. The adults are up to ¾ inch long, have long antennae, and transparent green or brown lacy wings held over the body in a rooflike position. The green species has iridescent red-gold eyes and, in its adult form, is one of the most beautiful insects. The larvae are small (up to ½ inch), flat, spindle-shaped insects resembling miniature alligators. They are yellow to gray with reddish brown markings and sickle-shaped jaws for capturing their prey. The larvae suck the body fluids from aphids, mealybugs, scales, and other small insects. Some species carry the remains of their victims on their backs. The larvae are such voracious eaters that they are commonly called *aphid lions*. The female lacewings lay their eggs singly on top of a delicate, hairlike stalk projecting from the surface of a leaf or twig. This prevents the hatching larvae from devouring other unhatched eggs. At night, the adult lacewings are attracted to bright lights, and may cling to screen doors. Lacewings can be purchased from insectaries, companies that raise insect predators and parasites. Because they don't survive the winter well, they should be reintroduced each spring.

HOVER FLIES

Hover flies, or flower flies, are flies that closely resemble bees and wasps. They are about the same size as these other insects (¼ to ¾ inch long) and have very similar color patterns—black with bands of yellow or orange. Some are fuzzy like bees and wasps. However, unlike bees and wasps they can fly stationary, or hover, in the air. A close inspection will reveal that they have one pair of wings rather than two, as bees and wasps do. They cannot sting. Hover flies sip nectar from flowers. Immature hover flies are maggots with feeding patterns that vary, depending on the species. One, the narcissus bulb fly (see page 377), feeds on bulbs. Others feed on decaying plant material. But, most hover fly larvae prey on plant-feeding insects, particularly aphids, young mealybugs, and scale insects. They grasp and puncture these insects with tiny hooks in their mouths, suck out the body fluids, and then toss the empty carcass to the side. Predaceous hover fly larvae are very common in gardens and are often seen feeding on aphids. They have voracious appetites and are highly beneficial. When abundant, they can completely control a colony of aphids within a few days.

Parasitic wasp pupae on hornworm (life size).

Parasite of pine tip moth (3 times life size).

PARASITIC WASPS

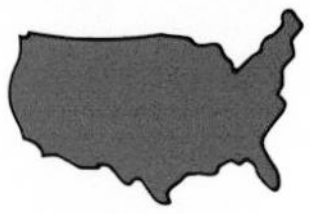

A number of wasps are insect parasites. They lay eggs in or on living insects, and the emerging immature wasp, which is white and grublike in appearance, feeds on tissues inside the host insect, eventually killing it. Many of these parasitic wasps are far more effective in controlling a certain pest than are predators such as lady beetles, praying mantids, and lacewings.

Aphid parasites: One parasitic wasp that attacks aphids (*Aphidius testaceipes*) is present throughout the country. It is responsible for creating the aphid "mummies" so commonly seen. The mummy is the brown shell of an aphid that has been killed by this tiny wasp parasite. The wasp larva develops in the aphid's body. After the larva pupates, it emerges as an adult wasp through a round hole it cuts in the mummy's back. This wasp reproduces throughout the warmer months of the year and effectively controls many aphid colonies.

Whitefly parasites: The whitefly parasite (*Encarsia formosa*) is a wasp that is particularly useful for control of whiteflies in greenhouses. The adult wasp lays eggs in whitefly pupae and larvae. As the immature wasp develops inside, the whitefly host turns black and dies. Several days later an adult wasp emerges. The entire life cycle takes as little as 20 days in warm weather. The whitefly parasite is only effective when temperatures average 75°F or warmer. In cooler temperatures the development of this parasite is delayed too much to effectively control the whitefly population.

Caterpillar parasites: Another common wasp parasite is *Trichogramma*. This minute wasp is so small it can lay its egg inside another insect egg. The adult is about 1/64 of an inch long. The host egg dies and turns black as the wasp larva develops. *Trichogramma* primarily attacks eggs of butterflies and moths. It is an important parasite of codling moth eggs. However, attempts to control codling moths by releasing large numbers of wasps have not been very successful. For maximum effectiveness, thousands of wasps must be released weekly during the time the pests are laying their eggs. The common wasp parasite of tomato and tobacco hornworms is *Apanteles congregatus*. This wasp lays eggs on the skin of the caterpillar. The wasp larvae hatch and burrow into the host. Many immature wasps feed and develop within the body of the caterpillar. They then move to the surface of the host and form small white cocoons which protrude from the back of the insect. Adult wasps emerge from the cocoons. The hornworm usually dies before the adult parasites emerge.

Locate the animals that are bothering your garden in this index:

A GALLERY OF ANIMAL PESTS

Animals in the garden can be the worst problem the gardener has. Their presence influences the way he gardens and often which plants he selects. Control of animals in the garden is difficult for a couple of reasons.

One reason is that animals are more intelligent than insects or plant diseases, and can overcome the obstacles we place in their path. The other reason is that we often can't kill them as we can insects or disease-causing organisms. The sight of a deer and her fawn browsing in our back yard in the morning may give us as much pleasure as the roses she is eating. Or the culprit may be our neighbor's cat—or even our own!

Over the centuries, gardeners have developed a multitude of ways to repel animals. Most of these methods work for some and not for others, or work 1 year and fail the next. Repellents are not very reliable because animals and birds learn from experience. A radio in the orchard may frighten off the deer 1 year, or for a few months, but eventually the deer learn that the radio is harmless and will browse next to it. Deer in populated areas even learn which dogs to fear and which are harmless nuisances.

Usually the most effective way to control animal pests is to fence them out. This may mean a fence around the garden, or a sheet of hardware cloth laid over the bulb bed to keep mice from digging up the bulbs.

When animal pests need to be removed, traps are usually more effective than poisons, although in some cases poison baits work well. Traps let you see that you have caught the animal, for one thing. And if the animal is one you don't want to kill, you can catch it in a live trap (see page 897) and release it in a nearby wilderness area. But there are local regulations governing this—ask your county agricultural commissioner about the rules in your area.

Above: Tree squirrel. See page 899.
Left: A doe browsing at the edge of a yard. See page 897.

ANIMAL PESTS

Damaged tree. *Insert:* Meadow mouse.

MICE

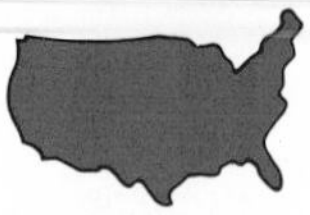

Several kinds of mice, or *voles,* invade gardens throughout the United States. Mice live in grassy or brushy areas, nesting underground in shallow burrows, or aboveground in densely vegetated, protected spots. They may also establish nests in thick hay or leaf mulches in the garden. Mice usually move along narrow runways from their nesting areas to their source of food. They are active throughout the year, digging up and feeding on seeds and nuts. They also feed on bulbs and tender vegetables and flowers, and may severely damage young trees by gnawing on the bark and roots. Mice are nocturnal, and do most of their damage at night.

CONTROL: You can keep mice out of the garden by putting up a fence. Surround the area you wish to protect with a woven wire fence (¼-inch mesh) at least 12 inches high. To prevent mice from tunneling underneath, extend the fence 12 inches below the soil surface. Or bend 12 inches of the wire mesh outward before burying it a few inches deep. Protect young tree trunks by placing hardware cloth cylinders 12 inches high around the tree, burying several inches of the cylinder in the soil. You may also protect the trunk by wrapping tree-wrapping plastic, available in nurseries, around the bottom of the trunk. Keep your garden free of grassy areas and hay or leaf mulches to reduce possible hiding and breeding areas for mice. Protect bulbs by covering the planted areas with hardware mesh, burying the edges in the ground. Traps or poisoned baits placed along mouse runways may be used. For more information about traps, see page 897. A few active cats will help reduce the mouse population.

Mole tunnels.

MOLES

Moles are small (up to 9 inches), gray to black mammals with fine velvety fur. They have slender hairless snouts and inconspicuous eyes and ears. Their eyesight is poor but they have superior senses of smell, touch, and hearing. The front feet are much larger than the hind feet and have long trowellike claws used for tunneling in the ground. Moles live in burrows made up of many interconnecting runways that are usually about 6 to 8 inches underground. Some species also dig many shallow feeding runways only a few inches below ground, which produces ridges on the soil surface. These ridges are especially noticeable in lawns. Moles dig lateral tunnels to the surface, where they deposit surplus soil in volcano shaped mounds. Occasionally they leave their tunnels to search for food or to move to new areas. Moles seldom feed on plants. They eat slugs, earthworms, grubs, and other small insects. Damage to plants is caused by their tunneling, which uproots plants or loosens the soil around roots so they dry out and die.

CONTROL: The best way to rid your lawn of moles is to control the insects that they feed on. (For more information, see page 267.) Traps are generally used for the rest of the garden, and can also be used in lawns. Before placing traps on shallow tunnels, you must determine which tunnels are still active. Roll or tamp down the ridges. Those that are raised the following day are still active. Trapping in main runways is usually more productive. To detect these deeper runways, probe between mounds with a rod. Poison baits, fumigants, and repellents are generally ineffective.

Gopher mound. *Insert:* Gopher.

POCKET GOPHERS

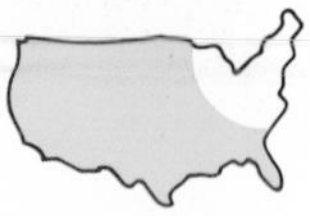

These burrowing rodents live and feed almost entirely underground. Pocket gophers eat roots and bulbs, and plants that they pull down into their burrows. They can kill shrubs by eating most of the roots and girdling the underground part of the trunk or stems. Damaged plants wilt, sometimes on only one side. Pocket gophers are solitary and fiercely territorial, so only one gopher inhabits a run system at a time. They are also quite active, and seem to be constantly digging new tunnels. The crescent-shaped mounds of soil they leave on the surface are excavated from new runs. Their tunnels sometimes drain irrigation ditches or basins, so the water does not soak into the soil.

CONTROL: Gophers are best controlled by trapping. Find the main runway by probing with a sharp rod about a foot deep near a fresh mound or an eaten plant. Dig a hole to intersect the run, and insert 2 wire or box traps in the run, one facing in each direction. Tie the traps together or to a stake above ground. To keep soil from falling on the traps, cover the hole with sod or a board, and sprinkle with soil to block out all light. Check and move the traps daily. Although only one gopher occupies a burrow system at a time, migrating gophers will move into an abandoned burrow. Level all the mounds, and watch for signs that the burrow has been reoccupied. Gophers can also be controlled by an active cat.

Deer.

Snap beans damaged by deer.

Live-catch traps.

DEER

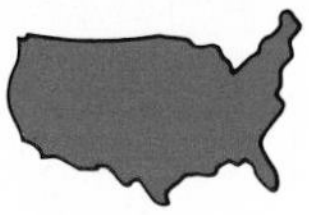

Deer can be very damaging to gardens in rural and suburban areas. They feed on many vegetables and flowers, stripping off new growth and often eating the entire plant. Deer may also browse on the tender bark, leaves, and twigs of shrubs and trees. Usually they feed on tree buds and bark during the winter or when other sources of food are scarce. The males may damage trees by rubbing their antlers on the trunks and branches. While feeding, they may trample on plants.

CONTROL: The best way to prevent deer damage is to fence them out. Deer are strong and agile jumpers; to be effective, a vertical fence must be at least 8 feet high. Enclose all areas of the garden that are accessible to deer. The fencing material should be a woven wire mesh. Stretch it between wooden or steel posts placed 10 to 12 feet apart. The wire mesh should fit tightly along the ground to prevent deer from forcing their way under the fence. A strand of barbed wire stretched along the ground will discourage deer from attempting to go under the fence. If the ground is uneven, secure the mesh to depressions in the ground, or fill in the depressions with soil, rocks, or other material.

Slanted fences: A slanted fence may also be used. Although deer are good high jumpers, they will not jump a barricade that is both high and wide. You can keep deer out with a fence that is only 4 feet high if it is also 4 feet wide. Anchor 6-foot steel posts in the ground 30 to 40 feet apart, burying the bottom third of the post. Attach a heavy guy wire along the top. Stretch 6-foot-wide wire mesh fencing at a 45° angle along the posts, securing the mesh with stakes at the bottom, and attaching it to the guy wires at the top. Build the fence so that the deer will approach it from the side where the posts are anchored. If you live in an area where snowfall is heavy, wire mesh is likely to be crushed by settling snow pack. Instead, use smooth wire stretched horizontally 4 inches apart.

Other methods: Electric fences are also effective. After deer have been shocked a few times, they will learn to avoid the fence. Individual trees or small areas can be protected with individual wire mesh cages (1 or 2-inch mesh). You can also spray repellents such as *tetramethylthiuram disulfide* or *zinc dithiocarbamate amine* on trees to prevent browsing damage. Deer may also be repelled by nylon stockings filled with human hair or small sacks of blood meal hung on trees you wish to protect. Kerosene or creosote-soaked rags, or perforated cans of mothballs hung from trees, may also repel deer. Sometimes all deer control measures fail, and killing certain problem deer may be the only solution. Because deer are protected by law, contact your agricultural commissioner or State Department of Fish and Game regional office for regulations.

ABOUT TRAPS

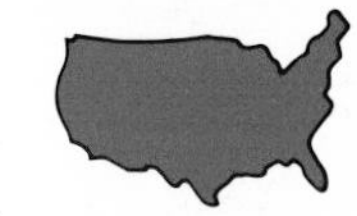

Traps are used to control many animal pests, either in combination with other methods or when other methods fail. The two most commonly used types are live-catch traps and snap traps. Before purchasing a trap, check with your agricultural commissioner or regional Department of Fish and Game to determine what regulations govern the type of animal you are trying to control. Some states prohibit trapping or killing certain animal species. Purchase the appropriate size trap for the animal you are trapping. Live-catch traps are the most humane. They are rectangular boxes with trap doors at both ends that shut when the animal touches a trigger in the box. The animal may be safely carried in the trap to your local humane society, or released in an acceptable area. Snap traps close on the leg or body of the animal when it touches the trigger. Some types, such as mousetraps, kill or severely injure the animal. Others, such as leg-hold traps, hold on to the animal until the trapper disposes of it. When using snap traps, fasten them to a stake or tree to prevent the animal from dragging the trap away. Snap traps should not be used in areas where pets can be trapped accidentally. If possible, tie the bait to the trigger with a piece of string or wire to prevent the animal from stealing the food. Most animals are fearful of new objects. If allowed to explore the unset trap and feed on the bait for a few days, they'll become accustomed to the trap, and will be easier to capture after you set it. Check traps daily.

ANIMAL PESTS

Dog digging in garden.

DOGS

Dogs can devastate a garden, especially when allowed to play or romp freely in a small yard. They cause damage by trampling or lying on plants, digging up the soil, and depositing droppings and urine around the yard.

CONTROL: Discourage dogs from digging around or urinating on plants by spraying the affected area with ORTHO Scram Dog & Cat Repellent according to label directions. Further dog-proof these spots by putting up a fence. The sturdiness of the fence will depend on the size, strength, and determination of your pet. A flimsy fence made of wire strung between stakes may be adequate for a small, well-behaved animal. Larger, more rambunctious dogs will require sturdier fences. Eventually the animal will adjust to the new boundaries, and will be less likely to damage planted areas when the fence is removed. Proper discipline and the provision of an alternate location in which the animal can play will reduce damage to garden plants.

Cat.

CATS

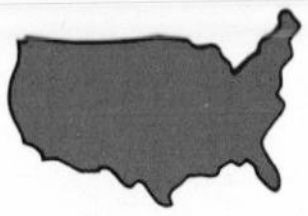

Cats are usually beneficial to a home garden; they help keep mice, rats, and other rodents under control, and frighten away nuisance birds. But cats can be damaging in newly planted areas. They dig up soft, loose soil where they bury their droppings and urine. They unearth seeds and transplants while digging, and may continue to damage these areas until the soil becomes compacted or plants fill in the area.

CONTROL: You can discourage cats from digging in newly planted areas by spraying the soil with ORTHO Scram Dog & Cat Repellent according to label directions. Protect seedbeds by laying chicken wire on the soil; remove the wire before the plants are too large to slip through the mesh. If plants are already present, set up cages made of 1-inch chicken wire over newly planted spots. You can take away protective devices after the soil packs down, or when vegetation covers bare areas.

Earthworm (life size).

EARTHWORMS

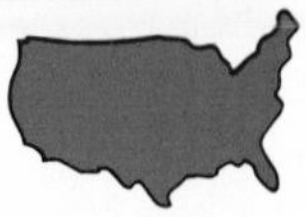

Earthworms are beneficial soil-dwelling animals. They surface in large numbers during a heavy rain or other times when the soil is saturated with water. As they tunnel through the ground earthworms ingest soil, digesting any organic matter in it. They may deposit the soil that passes through their bodies as crumbly mounds (castings) on the soil surface. A large population of earthworms can sometimes be a nuisance in a lawn when many castings accumulate. Earthworm tunnels help to aerate and loosen the soil, improving soil drainage and tilth and facilitating root growth. Although they are most numerous in the top 6 inches of soil, earthworms may tunnel 6 feet down into the ground, bringing up deep layers of soil to the surface. Sometimes earthworms enter the drainage holes of containers sitting on the soil, or sunken into the ground. As their castings accumulate in the container, the drainage becomes clogged.

CONTROL: For the most part, earthworm activity in the ground is beneficial, and should be encouraged. If you are having trouble with castings on your lawn, see page 268 for information on how to treat this problem. To prevent earthworms from getting into containers in or on the ground, place a piece of screen over the drainage hole. Or set the container on a layer of gravel or cinders; earthworms will not move through such a coarse layer.

Starling.

Sapsucker damage.

Tree squirrel.

BIRDS

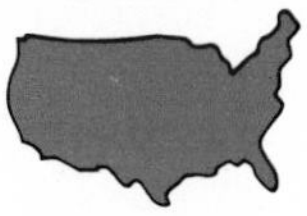

Many types of birds feed on seeds, seedlings, fruit, and berries in the garden. Birds scratch away at soft soil to unearth newly planted seeds. They peck at seedlings and young leaves. Birds are especially damaging to berries, grapes, and soft fruit.

CONTROL: Once birds develop the habit of feeding in your garden, you will probably have to exclude them with wire or fabric cages. Make wire cages out of 1-inch chicken wire. Cages that are about 10″x10″x24″ are self-supporting. Larger cages may need to be reinforced with heavy wire. You can also make cages or protective coverings with cheesecloth or plastic bird netting supported by stakes or a wooden frame. If birds have not yet developed the habit of feeding in your garden, you may be able to repel them without having to construct cages. Set up stakes around the plantings you wish to protect and tie criss-crossing strings between the stakes. Attach strips of aluminum foil to the strings. Birds will not readily fly through the crossing strings, and will avoid the shiny aluminum. Scarecrows are usually not effective for long. You can remove protective devices once plants have produced several sets of mature leaves, or in the case of berries, after you've harvested all of the fruit. To prevent birds from digging up seeds, lay hardware cloth (¼-inch mesh) over the seed bed. It must be removed before the plants are too large to slip through the mesh. For information on controlling bird damage on trees, see page 595 and 423.

SAPSUCKERS

Sapsuckers are members of the woodpecker family that feed on tree bark and sap. The red-breasted sapsucker (*Sphyrapicus varius ruber*) is found in the Pacific Northwest and British Columbia. The yellow-breasted sapsucker (*S. varius varius*) is common throughout much of the United States. Sapsuckers peck into many trees before finding a suitable one that has sap with a high sugar content. Once the birds find a favorite tree, they visit it many times a day and feed on it year after year. Sapsucker damage to the tree is very distinctive. They drill uniform round or rectangular holes in the bark, ¼ inch in diameter, arranged in horizontal rings around the trunk. Sap often oozes from the holes, and portions of the tree bark may fall off after sapsuckers have drilled many holes. The tree trunk may eventually be girdled by sapsucker drilling, causing the tree above the damaged area to die. Sometimes the birds' beaks are contaminated with fungus spores, or the spores are blown or splashed into the holes. Once inside the tree, the disease organisms may damage or kill the tree.

CONTROL: It is difficult to prevent sapsucker damage to trees. Wrapping the damaged trunk with burlap or smearing a sticky material (such as the latex used for ant control) above and below the holes may inhibit new pecking damage. For a list of trees most commonly attacked by sapsuckers, see page 1012.

TREE SQUIRRELS

Tree squirrels are mainly a problem in forested or lightly wooded rural or suburban areas. These animals establish nests in tree hollows, or build nests of leaves, twigs, and bark in trees. They are omnivorous, feeding on fruit, seeds, nuts, insects, and bark. Tree squirrels are agile climbers and jumpers; they can easily jump 6 feet from the ground to a branch or structure, or between branches. These animals damage gardens by digging up newly planted seeds and bulbs, and sometimes entire plants. They may strip the bark or leaves from trees and shrubs, and feed on fruits and nuts.

CONTROL: Keep tree squirrels out of newly planted seed and bulb beds by placing chicken wire over the planted area. Bury the edges of the mesh in the soil, or weight them down with bricks. Remove the wire before the plants are too large to fit through the mesh. Prevent tree squirrels from climbing up fruit and nut trees by snugly placing 2-foot-wide bands of metal (made from material such as aluminum roof flashing) around tree trunks at least 6 feet above the ground. Prune branches so that they are at least 6 feet above the ground, and 6 feet away from structures or the branches of other trees. If permissible in your area, you can also trap tree squirrels. Contact your Department of Fish and Game to determine local regulations. Place or tie traps near tree squirrel trails or nests. Bait the traps with nuts, sunflowers seeds, peanut butter, or raisins. For more information about trapping, see page 897.

Ground squirrel.

Rabbit damage to dwarf apples.

Raccoon.

GROUND SQUIRRELS

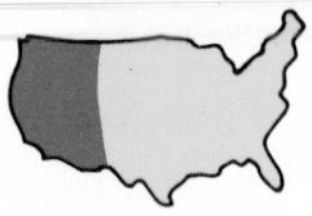

Several types of ground squirrels are found throughout the United States, but these animals are mainly a problem west of the Rocky Mountains. Ground squirrels live in underground burrows located in open, sunny areas. Many species are social, forming large underground colonies that may extend over an acre. Sometimes ground squirrels excavate burrows under buildings, causing stress cracking of the foundation. In certain areas, ground squirrels and some of their parasites may transmit serious diseases to humans. These animals can be very damaging to gardens. In the late winter and spring, they emerge from hibernation to invade gardens, feeding on tender green growth. Later in the season they feed on seeds, grains, vegetables, fruits, and nuts.

CONTROL: Ground squirrels are agile climbers; they can climb over most fences. If there are only a few ground squirrels causing damage, trap them. Set the traps near burrow entrances or along pathways used by the animals. Use baits such as peanut butter, nuts, raisins, or cereals. Because ground squirrels may carry diseases, always wear gloves and protective clothing when handling them. For more information about traps, see page 897. Contact the Humane Society for information on how to get rid of the trapped animals. If large colonies (more than a dozen ground squirrels) are present, contact a pest control operator, who will eliminate the colony using fumigants or poisoned baits.

RABBITS

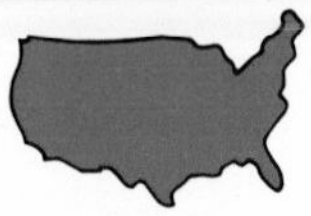

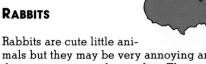

Rabbits are cute little animals but they may be very annoying and damaging pests in the garden. Their reproductive rate is high. They produce several litters a year, with four to seven babies in each litter. Rabbits are active all year long, mainly during the day. In the summer, they feed on any tender young plants, especially garden vegetables. During the winter, they gnaw on bark, twigs, and buds. They are especially destructive to young fruit trees in the winter. Much of the bark on small trees may be eaten, and young branches are often clipped off. Clipped twigs are removed cleanly, without ragged edges. Rabbits can also clip off twigs on older trees up to 2 feet above snow or ground level.

CONTROL: The best way to keep rabbits out of a vegetable garden or small orchard is to enclose it with a 1½-inch mesh chicken wire fence. The fence should be 2 feet high in areas with little snow, or 2 feet above the snow level in areas where snow accumulates. The bottom must be tight to the ground. Or build portable cages to place over small garden plots. Single trees can be protected by building a cylindrical chicken wire fence 2 feet high around the trunk. Several other methods of control may help prevent rabbit damage. Sprinkling dried blood meal near plants may repel rabbits, and it is also beneficial to the soil. It must be reapplied every few days during wet weather. Chemical repellents, cats, dogs, or live traps may also be used to protect the garden from rabbits.

RACCOONS

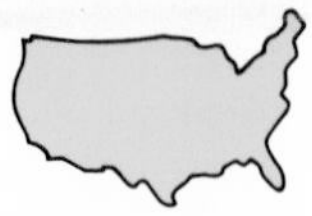

Raccoons are a nuisance mainly in wooded rural or lightly populated suburban areas. They usually establish their dens in hollow logs, trees, or other natural shelters near a source of water. Raccoons are omnivorous, feeding on insects, small mammals, fish, fruit, nuts, grains, and vegetables; they are especially fond of corn. Raccoons are nocturnal animals, foraging at night and returning to their dens during the day. They are agile climbers, and climb trees to feed on fruit or nuts, often knocking many to the ground. Sometimes they invade attics and basements.

CONTROL: Raccoons are intelligent, inquisitive animals that can be very difficult to exclude. You can discourage raccoons from invading your vegetable garden by erecting a 4-foot-high chicken wire fence, with its top extending 18 inches above the fence post. As the raccoon climbs up onto the unattached portion of the fence, his weight will pull him down to the ground. Low-voltage electric fences are also effective in excluding raccoons from the garden. To keep raccoons from climbing between trees or from a building to a tree, keep the limbs pruned so that they do not touch each other or make contact with the roof. Prevent raccoons from climbing up trees by wrapping metal guards at least 18 inches wide around the trunk. Place the guards at least 3 feet above the ground. For information about controlling raccoons as household pests, see page 792.

Skunk.

SKUNKS

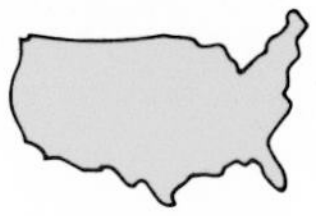

Skunks are mainly a problem in rural and outlying suburban areas. They are omnivorous, feeding on insects, small rodents, fruits, berries, corn and other garden vegetables, and garbage. They do not usually cause much damage in the garden, but are unacceptable to many people because of the strong scent they spray when threatened or provoked. In addition, skunks may carry rabies. Rabid skunks often show abnormal behavior such as listlessness, unprovoked aggressiveness, or a tendency to wander around during the day. Such animals will bite when handled.

CONTROL: The best way to keep skunks out of the garden is to fence them out. Enclose the area you want to protect with a 3-foot-high fence made of chicken wire. Extend 12 inches of the bottom outward below the soil surface to discourage animals from digging beneath it. You may also trap skunks, placing traps near their dens or trails. Bait traps with sardines or cat food. When handling skunks, wear protective goggles and old clothing in case you are sprayed. Before attempting to trap or kill skunks, contact your agricultural commissioner's office or local Department of Fish and Game to find out if these animals are protected in your area. For more information about trapping, see page 897. If you or your pets are sprayed, neutralize the scent with *neutroleum alpha*, a compound that is available through pest control operators or hospital supply outlets. Contact a doctor or veterinarian if you or a pet are bitten by a skunk.

Woodchuck.

WOODCHUCKS

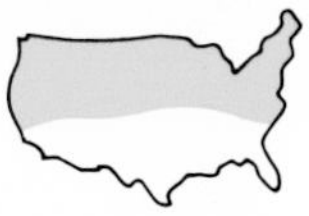

Woodchucks are also known as *groundhogs*. They are a problem in rural and suburban areas throughout most of the country. They live in underground burrows, from which they emerge in the early morning and late afternoon to feed. Woodchucks prefer tender vegetables, flowers, and other succulent greenery, but they may occasionally gnaw on tree bark. These animals seldom invade gardens in large numbers. They do not tunnel to their food source, but feed aboveground. Woodchucks occasionally contract diseases that they may transmit to humans.

CONTROL: The best way to eliminate damage is to fence the woodchucks out. Surround the area you wish to protect with a woven wire fence about 3 feet high. To prevent woodchucks from burrowing under the fence, bend the bottom 12 inches of the wire mesh outward before burying it a few inches deep in the soil. To prevent woodchucks from climbing over the top, leave the upper 18 inches of mesh unattached to the supporting stakes. Bend this upper portion outward. As the animal climbs the fence, the weight of its body will pull the upper portion down toward the ground. Traps may also be used. For more information about traps, see page 897. In some states, these animals are protected by law. Before attempting to trap or kill woodchucks, contact your agricultural commissioner's office or Department of Fish and Game for proper regulations in your area. Always wear gloves and protective clothing when handling woodchucks; they may be diseased.

Locate the problem or practice in which you are interested in the index on the next page. This section is arranged into these categories:

SOIL, CULTURAL, AND CLIMATE PROBLEMS

This section contains garden problems that aren't related to a particular plant, or even to a particular section of the garden. It also contains some cultural guidelines.

Most of the soil problems a gardener might experience are in this section. Some soils are more difficult to work with than others, but any garden soil that will grow weeds will grow garden plants, too. The difference between good garden soil and difficult garden soil is the amount of latitude the gardener has in his cultural practices. If your soil drains well, you don't have to worry about overwatering. If, in addition, it holds ample water, you are also less likely to underwater. But if you have a heavy clay or a droughty sand, proper watering takes skill and attention. These soils can still raise good garden plants, though; they just take more careful handling.

There are two basic approaches to both soil and climate problems. One—and by far the simplest one—is to grow plants that are adapted to the soil and climate of your garden. This requires no extra work on your part, and little skill or garden knowledge beyond that needed to select adapted plants.

The limitation of this system is that you may not like the plants available to you, or you may want plants not adapted to your area. For instance, lawns are not adapted to much of the arid West. In some areas, it takes almost heroic measures to keep a lawn healthy. But gardeners are so fond of lawns that the majority of homes in these areas have them.

The second method is to adapt your garden to the plants. This may involve installing irrigation systems, or building structures to shelter garden plants from the sun, wind, or cold.

You will also find some garden practices in this section. These are practices that are solutions to garden problems in general, but not to any one problem. For instance, you will find directions for patching a lawn, which may have been damaged by a fungus disease or an insect. After you have dealt with the fungus or insect, you can use these guidelines to clear up the secondary problem of dead patches in the lawn.

Above: Deep-watering of pumpkin seedlings. The slow flow from this punctured can allows water to penetrate deep into the soil.
Left: Turning organic amendments into the soil. These materials improve almost any soil. See page 926.

INDEX TO SOIL, CULTURAL, AND CLIMATE PROBLEMS

INDEX TO SOIL, CULTURAL, AND CLIMATE PROBLEMS

SOIL PROBLEMS

Heavy soil.

HEAVY SOIL

When used to describe soil, the word "heavy" does not mean weight, but the sensation of working the soil. Heavy soils can be difficult to work. Heaviness comes from a high proportion of clay in the soil. If the soil does not have a crumbly texture, the pores in clay soil are very small. It is these pores that let air and water into the soil.

Difficulties with heavy soil: Heavy soil may be sticky when wet and hard when dry, and may go rapidly from one to the other. Water passes through its small pores very slowly. If the soil is not managed properly, it is easy to overwater, keeping the soil pores full of water and excluding air.

Advantages of heavy soil: When heavy soil has a crumbly structure it drains well, yet still retains much water. Heavy soils also hold onto nutrients well, and are fertile. Because they need feeding and watering less often than other soils, they are easier to manage.

Managing heavy soil: Be careful not to overwater. Water slowly and deeply, but infrequently. The heavier your soil, the more important it is to work it when the water content is just right. There is a point between too wet and too dry when it works easily. Gypsum will sometimes improve the structure of clay soils. Work a cup of gypsum into the soil in a watering basin to see if drainage is improved. Organic matter, such as manure, compost, or ammoniated sawdust, always improves heavy soil. Spread from 1 to 4 inches of organic matter on the surface and turn it in every time you work the soil. In 2 or 3 years, the soil will be vastly improved.

Sandy soil.

Shallow soil.

Erosion.

SANDY SOIL

Sandy soil contains a high proportion of sand. It can be identified by the characteristic grittiness when the soil is rubbed between the thumb and fingers. Sandy soil has large pore spaces, so water and air enter it easily; however, the soil dries out rapidly and it does not retain nutrients well. Sandy soil cultivates easily either dry or wet. It seldom puddles or becomes muddy or sticky, and seldom has erosion problems because water enters it immediately, so there is none to run off on the surface.

Managing sandy soil: Sandy soil must have both water and fertilizer applied lightly and frequently. Because it retains very little water, plants wilt quickly. This type of soil is often called "droughty." A simple way to feed the garden is to use liquid fertilizers, such as ORTHO Ortho-Gro Liquid Plant Food or ORTHO Tomato & Vegetable Food. These can be added to the irrigation water with an ORTHO Lawn Sprayer or a siphoning fertilizer injector. Fertilize once a month during the growing season. Improve sandy soil by adding organic matter, such as peat moss, compost, or manure. Spread from 1 to 4 inches of organic material on the surface and turn it in every time you till the soil. The organic matter acts like a sponge, retaining water and nutrients. (For more information about organic amendments, see page 926.) Drip irrigation systems are especially effective and useful in sandy soils. Use plants that are adapted to sandy soil (see page 1011).

SHALLOW SOIL

Depth of soil is important for the growth of plants. Shallow soil does not provide enough root space and has less water storage capacity than deep soil. It dries out rapidly, but since, on flat land, the water has no place to drain, it is also easy to overwater. Soil depth can be determined by digging a hole. A lawn can be grown in 6 inches of soil, but trees need from 1½ feet to 4 feet. Sometimes the underlayment is not bedrock but a rocklike layer called *hardpan*, which can be penetrated. For more information about hardpan, see page 906.

Living with shallow soil: If your garden is already planted, watch the amount of water you apply. You may need to water more frequently than if the soil were deeper, but apply less at each watering. Guy trees to keep them from blowing over.

Improving shallow soil: In areas that are not yet planted, you have two options. One is to choose shallow-rooted plants, such as lawns and annuals. A second option is to deepen the soil in raised planting beds. But avoid planting large trees, even in raised beds. Resist the temptation to deepen the soil by digging into the underlayment. Drainage would be nonexistent in these holes, so maintenance would be very difficult.

EROSION

Erosion occurs on bare ground when soil is worn away by wind and water. Eroding winds can carry away dry soil, but water erosion is more common and more severe. When raindrops fall on bare soil, their impact loosens soil particles. On a slope, water starts to flow over the surface as soon as the ground stops absorbing it. The force of the moving water and the scouring action of the soil particles carried in the water erode the bare ground further down the slope. Erosion is most severe on long, steep slopes.

Stop erosion by covering the soil. If the slope is not too steep, cover it with a heavy mulch, such as gravel or fir bark. Cover steep slopes with burlap or coarse netting sold for this purpose. Plant a groundcover through holes in the fabric. By the time the fabric rots, the groundcover will be established. The most effective plantings for erosion control are low, dense groundcovers or turfgrasses. The roots help to hold soil particles in place, and the leaves and stems break the impact of water drops and reduce the momentum of runoff. If slopes are already deeply eroded, it may be necessary to construct retaining walls or check dams to prevent further erosion.

Rocky soil.

Compacted soil.

Turf over hardpan killed by drought.

ROCKY SOILS

Rocky soils do not usually affect plant growth. Water drainage is not impaired in rocky soil, and plant roots easily grow around rocks. The major problem with rocky soil is that planting and cultivating are difficult, especially in vegetable and flower beds where plants are replaced frequently and the soil is intensely cultivated. If your garden is not yet planted, hire a contractor with a stonepicker attachment on a tractor to clear it of surface rocks. If this is not practical, hand-pick rocks in vegetable gardens and other areas where cultivation is intense, or plant in raised beds. If rocks are so numerous throughout your garden that there is very little soil, add topsoil.

COMPACTION

Soil compaction is the result of foot or vehicle traffic. The pressure packs the soil tightly, squeezing the pores closed. Compacted soil contains little air, restricting root growth to the surface levels. Also, roots have difficulty in penetrating the dense soil. Water penetrates the soil slowly, making irrigation difficult. Some soils, especially clay soils and some loamy sands, are more susceptible to compaction than others, and dry soil has more resistance to compaction than wet soil. Soil compaction should be corrected before planting in the area. Different techniques are needed in planted and unplanted areas.

Before planting: Till the soil to loosen the compaction. Large areas that are badly compacted require the use of a rotary tiller. Organic matter should be mixed in as the soil is tilled. (For information about adding organic matter to the soil, see page 926.) If the compaction was caused by heavy construction equipment, it may be necessary to have the soil loosened to a depth of 2 feet with a chisel plow. Foot traffic compacts only a couple of inches of surface soil.

In planted areas: Relieve compaction in planted areas by aeration (see pages 262 and 434).

Preventing compaction: The most effective way to prevent compaction is to keep traffic off the soil. Make paths, or place fences or shrubs to act as barriers. If heavy equipment must be driven across the soil, make sure the soil is as dry as possible at the time. If foot traffic can't be kept off an area, mulch it with 4 inches of gravel or rocks.

HARDPAN

Hardpan is a cementlike layer of soil that impedes the downward flow of water and restricts root growth. Soil particles in the hardpan layer are cemented together by minerals, usually iron compounds, that have accumulated there. Hardpan is usually within a foot or so of the surface, and is only a few inches thick. Or it may be very close to the soil surface if erosion has washed away the topsoil. The hardpan has two effects on plants growing above it. Since roots cannot grow through hardpan, they are restricted to the shallow soil layer above it. Trees grow slowly, and may be blown over in a wind storm. Also, since water does not penetrate it, the hardpan impedes drainage. To determine if your soil has a hardpan layer, dig a hole 2 to 3 feet deep. The rocklike layer can, with persistence, be penetrated. It's not necessary to remove hardpan, but only to provide a hole or channel through it for water flow and root growth. Around established plants, break holes in the hardpan with a crowbar or jackhammer. Depending on the depth of the soil, the holes should be 4 to 6 feet apart. When establishing a new planting area, break up hardpan with a chisel plow or backhoe. Hardpan reforms very slowly, so any holes made in it will last for many years. Or install drain pipes on top of the hardpan to drain water away from the plant roots. Another possibility is to grow vegetables and flowers in raised beds.

DRAINAGE PROBLEMS

Drainage problems due to heavy soil.

Poor drainage due to layered soil.

Drain line.

SOIL TYPE

Certain types of soil naturally have drainage problems.

Soils that crust: Some types of soil form a thin (⅛ to ¼ inch) crust on the soil surface. The crust can be broken with the fingers, and flakes when handled. Even though the soil below the crust drains well, water does not penetrate quickly and tends to puddle or run off. Prevent crusting by cultivating organic matter into the soil, or by mulching. For more information about organic matter and mulching, see page 926.

Sodic soil: Sodic soils are high in certain forms of sodium. They are impermeable to water; puddling and runoff are common. Sodium hydroxide (caustic soda) in sodic soils dissolves organic matter, which becomes suspended in puddled water, turning it brown or black. For more information about sodic soils, see page 913.

Heavy soil: Heavy soils are those with a large proportion of clay. They crack and are very hard when dry, and are sticky and difficult to mix or turn over when wet. To determine if your soil is heavy, dig a hole 2 feet deep in a poorly drained area. Fill the hole with water. If the water level drops more slowly than 1⁄10 inch per hour, heavy soil is probably causing your problem. Runoff and puddling may be reduced on heavy soils (and other poorly drained soils) by applying water more slowly. Use sprinkler heads with a lower water output, or oscillating or impulse hose-end sprinklers. Or cycle sprinklers by pausing for half an hour when runoff begins. For more information about heavy soil, see page 904.

SOIL STRUCTURE

The soil structure may be altered by natural processes or by human activities, causing poor drainage.

Compacted soil: Compacted soils are hard, dense, and impermeable to water. Compacted areas are usually on the surface, and only 2 to 4 inches deep. Compaction is usually caused by foot traffic, but construction equipment can compact the soil 2 feet deep. Dig a hole through the compacted layer in the poorly drained area when the soil is moist but not wet. Fill the hole with water. Compaction is the problem if the water level drops faster than 1⁄10 inch per hour. For more information about compacted soil, see the adjacent page.

Layered soil: Layered soils are those in which soils of different textures are layered like a cake. If the layers are very different in texture, drainage problems may result. This kind of problem is most often caused when soil of a different texture than the native soil is added as fill material. Even a thin layer of added soil can slow drainage. Dig a hole to see if your soil has distinctly different layers. If this is what is causing your drainage problem, stir the layers together by tilling or, if the layers are deep, chisel-plowing. If the area is planted, dig holes or a trench through the layers. Fill the holes to the surface with gravel or wood chips. Water will drain quickly through these holes.

Hardpan: Hardpan is a cementlike layer of soil that forms a foot or two below the surface. Water does not drain through this layer. When struck with a shovel or pick, hardpan feels like rock. For more information about hardpan, see page 906.

GROUNDWATER

Poor drainage occurs in soils where the water table is high.

High water table: The water table is usually tens or hundreds of feet below the surface, but in some areas it is close enough to the surface to keep the soil wet. The water table rises and falls during the year, and is most likely to be high in the spring. If a hole, such as a well, is dug into the water table, it will spontaneously fill with water. The water level in the hole is the same as that in the water table. A high water table must be drained with underground drain lines or deep ditches. See a contractor.

Springs: Springs may surface in the garden, especially on a hillside. Even though free-flowing water is not produced, springs may produce soggy areas that never dry out. Drain away the excess water by installing an interception drain. To do this, dig a ditch several feet up the slope from the wet area, and parallel to it. The ditch should be dug straight down until it fills with water, intercepting the spring. Install a drain line in the ditch to carry away the water. Or, better yet, dig into the spring and use its water in the garden.

SOIL ACIDITY

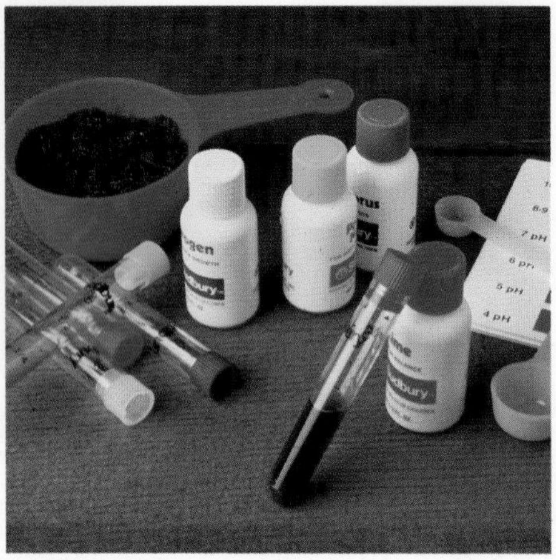

Soil pH test kit.

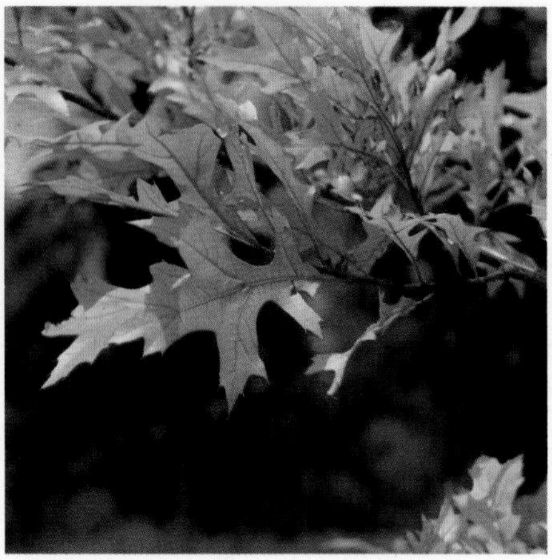

Pin oak in alkaline soil.

Magnesium deficiency caused by acid soil.

pH

pH is a measure of acidity and alkalinity, on a scale from 0 to 14. The lower the number, the more acid the soil. A pH of 7.0 is neutral, neither acid or alkaline. (For a list of common substances and their pH, see the chart below.) Many of the chemical reactions that occur in all soils depend on the pH. The soil pH often determines what nutrients are available for plant use. Soils are rarely more acidic than 4.0 or more alkaline than 9.0. Most plants will grow in soils with a pH of 5.5 to 7.5. Some plants need acid soil (4.0 to 5.5). Others will tolerate alkaline conditions (7.5 to 9.0). (For a list, see page 1019.) To determine your soil pH, have your soil tested. For more information about soil testing, see page 909.

The pH Scale

Some common substances	Acid	Soils
Grapefruit	3	Peat moss
Grapes	4	Best for rhododendrons, azaleas, and other acid-loving plants
Bread	5	
Milk	6	Average Eastern soils
Pure water Neutral	7	Average Western soils
Baking soda	8	
Soap	9	Alkali Soils
Milk of magnesia	10	
	11	
	Alkaline	

ALKALINE SOILS

Alkaline soils are those with a pH of more than 7.0, the neutral point. The soil is usually alkaline in regions that receive less than 20 inches of rain a year.

Effect on plants: Most plants grow well in slightly alkaline soil (pH 7.0 to 8.0). However, in soils that are more alkaline than 8.0 some plant nutrients, including iron and manganese, become insoluble and are not available to plants even though they are present in the soil. Plants growing in soil that is too alkaline for them develop yellow areas between the veins on their newest leaves. Older leaves usually remain green, unless the plant has been growing for some time in soil that is too alkaline.

Acid-loving plants: Plants that are adapted to acid soil, such as azaleas and rhododendrons, may show symptoms of iron deficiency even when the soil is slightly acid.

Over-limed soils: If soil that is naturally acid has so much lime added to it that the pH rises above about 7.2, plants may show iron deficiency symptoms.

Decreasing soil alkalinity: Make soils more acid by adding ORTHO Aluminum Sulfate, *ferrous sulfate*, or *soil sulfur.* Add 2 pounds per 100 square feet, wait 2 weeks, then test the soil pH. Reapply these acidifying amendments until the desired pH has been attained. Or, apply ORTHO Orthorix Spray to the soil according to label directions. Amounts will vary depending upon the soil type. Maintain acidity by using a fertilizer that has an acid reaction in the soil, such as ORTHO Azalea, Camellia & Rhododendron Food. Or select plants that are tolerant of alkaline soil from the list on page 1003.

ACID SOILS

Strictly speaking, any soil with a pH below 7.0—the neutral point—is acid. However, the term *acid soils* usually refers to soils that are too acid for good plant growth, those with a pH below about 5.5. As the pH decreases, the soil becomes increasingly acidic. Acidity develops naturally in soils that are heavily leached by rainfall. Most plants grow well in slightly acid soils (pH 6.0 to 7.0).

Effect on plant nutrients: As acidity increases, chemical changes occur in the soil that reduce the overall growth and health of most plants, except for acid-loving plants such as rhododendrons, azaleas, and blueberries. Many plant nutrients, especially phosphorous, calcium, and magnesium, become less available for plant use in acid soils. Other elements, such as aluminum and manganese, become available in quantities toxic to plants. The beneficial soil organisms that decompose organic matter are less active in acid soils, so the nitrogen obtained from the breakdown of organic matter is reduced.

Effect on plants: Plants growing in acid soils are often stunted and off-color. Their roots are sparse and small.

Decreasing soil acidity: To decrease soil acidity, add ground dolomitic limestone according to the chart on page 1019. In addition to raising the soil pH, dolomitic limestone supplies magnesium and calcium, nutrients in which acidic soils are usually deficient. Do not overlime acid soils, because when the soil pH is too high the availability of some nutrients may be decreased.

SOIL SALTS

Leaf scorch on oleander caused by salty soil.

Salt damage to white pine.

Soil sampling tube.

SALTY SOIL

Soil salts are soluble minerals. They include table salt (sodium chloride) as well as salts of calcium, magnesium, and potassium. Salty soil occurs mainly in arid regions where there is not enough rainfall to wash the salts from the soil. Soil salts originate from several sources. As soil minerals weather, they slowly break down into salts that dissolve in the soil water. Irrigation water that contains dissolved salts contributes to soil salinity, and so do fertilizers. As water evaporates from the surface it moves up through the soil, bringing dissolved salts up into the topsoil. Salts may accumulate in poorly drained soils because rainfall and irrigation water cannot drain through and leach the soil. Roadside soil may become very saline in areas where deicing salts are used in the winter. Salty soil may develop a white crust of salt deposits on the surface. Most garden plants will not tolerate much salt in the soil. For more information about plant reactions to salt, see page 857.

Removing salts: Leach salty soils periodically by watering them deeply. About 12 inches of water are needed to remove most of the salts in a foot of soil. If soil salinity is a result of poor drainage, improve the soil drainage. (For information on drainage, see page 907.) The use of mulches in arid regions helps reduce the evaporation of soil water and the subsequent salt accumulation in the topsoil. For a list of plants that are tolerant of salty soils, see page 1011.

Sodic soils: Soils with a high concentration of free sodium are called *sodic* or *alkali* soils. Sodium destroys the soil structure and causes clay particles to become lodged in soil pores, making the soil impermeable to water. Water puddles on sodic soils, and usually evaporates before it enters the soil. Some of the sodium forms caustic soda (sodium hydroxide), which dissolves organic matter. The organic substances in solution are dark brown or black. A black crust often forms on sodic soils. Sodic soils are often very alkaline, and usually do not support plant growth. To improve sodic soils, add gypsum at a rate of 5 pounds to every 100 square feet. Cultivate the gypsum into the soil, then water it well to leach the sodium from the soil. If drainage is only slightly improved, add more gypsum.

SOIL TESTING

Every few years, test the acidity of your soil. If you live in an area that gets less than 25 inches of rain a year, test also for soluble salts. In most states, the Cooperative Extension Offices will test your soil. (For a list of Cooperative Extension Offices, see page 1029.) Commercial soil laboratories, listed under *Soil* in the yellow pages, also test soil. Or test soil acidity yourself with a test kit, available in most garden centers. It is not practical for home gardeners to test for nutrient levels because the cost of the test is usually more than might be saved in fertilizers. Take a soil sample like this:

1. Use a clean bucket and trowel, as any traces of fertilizer or lime will offset the test.

2. Select the areas that you wish to test separately. Different soil types should be tested separately, as should areas you put to different uses.

3. Dig a hole 6 inches deep, or deeper when testing for soil around tree roots.

4. With a trowel, cut a thin slice from the side of the hole. Scrape the top ½ inch of soil from the slice.

5. Place the slice in a bucket. Take more samples from the same area.

6. Mix the soil in the bucket thoroughly. Measure out 2 cups for testing.

7. If someone other than yourself is testing the soil, be sure to note what type of plants are growing, or will be planted, in the area.

8. Repeat the sampling procedure for each area you wish to test. Rinse the trowel and bucket between areas.

FERTILIZING

Nitrogen-deficient euonymus.

Nitrogen-deficient tomato.

Phosphorus-deficient corn.

NITROGEN

Nitrogen is one of the three primary nutrients necessary for plant growth. It is used by plants to form proteins that are required for the development of new shoots and leaves, and to make chlorophyll, the green pigment in leaves. Most soils require additional nitrogen to produce healthy plants. (For information about nitrogen deficiency in plants, see page 859.) There are three major forms of nitrogen.

Ammoniacal nitrogen: Ammoniacal nitrogen includes ammonium, ammonia, and urea, all of which quickly become ammonium in the soil. Ammonium is not readily leached from the soil. It binds to the surfaces of the soil particles, which keeps it from washing away. Although many plants use ammonium, the availability of ammoniacal nitrogen is low to most plants, because it must be changed to nitrate by soil microorganisms before it can be washed to the plant roots. The activity of these microbes depends on soil moisture, aeration, and temperature. In warm, well-aerated soils, the nitrogen is changed to nitrate and is available to plants for a couple of weeks. The process is much slower in cold, wet soils, and will not take place at all when the soil temperature is below 30° to 40°F. If a plant growing in cold soil is in immediate need of nitrogen, a fertilizer should be applied that also contains *nitrate nitrogen* (see below). Ammoniacal nitrogen fertilizers have an acidifying effect on the soil. In areas of high rainfall, where soils are already acidic, it may be necessary to add lime.

Nitrate nitrogen: Fertilizers containing nitrate nitrogen are fast acting. They are very useful for plants in immediate need of nitrogen. The nitrogen is in a form that is readily available to plants. Microorganisms are not needed to break down the nitrogen, so the fertilizers are effective in cold or warm soils. Nitrate nitrogen does not become attached to soil particles, but floats freely in the soil water. With heavy rains or deep watering, the nitrogen may be washed below the root zone. Nitrate fertilizers are most effective if applied in frequent, light feedings, or in combination with a long-lasting ammoniacal or organic nitrogen.

Organic nitrogen: Organic nitrogen is in the form of protein or other insoluble compounds. It is found in plant and animal derivatives such as blood meal, manure, and sewage sludge. In uncomposted organic material, the nitrogen is not available to plants. The protein must be decomposed by soil microorganisms to ammonium, and then to nitrate, before the plant can use it. As with ammoniacal nitrogen, the rate of decomposition depends on soil temperature and moisture. Organic nitrogen usually lasts for a few months in the soil.

PHOSPHORUS

Phosphorus is one of the three primary plant nutrients. It is used in all phases of plant growth, and in all parts of the plant. In the soil, phosphorus is taken up by plants in the form of phosphate. Phosphate compounds have two qualities that govern phosphate use by the plant. One of these qualities is that only a tiny amount of phosphate dissolves at any time in the soil water. Because the part that does not dissolve cannot be washed from the soil, phosphorus lasts for a long time in the soil. One application lasts for months or years. This also means that plants must have an extensive root system to get enough phosphate from this dilute soil solution. The other quality of phosphate is that it is very active chemically, and quickly forms compounds with many chemicals. Because of this quality, phosphate does not move through the soil. Therefore phosphorus fertilizers should be placed in the root zone of the plant. Southern and eastern soils are often deficient in phosphorus.

Rock phosphate: Most phosphorus fertilizers begin as phosphate rock. This material is almost insoluble, and only slightly available to plants.

Superphosphate: Superphosphate is phosphate rock that has been treated with acid to make it soluble. In this form, the phosphate remains soluble for a few weeks or months in the soil.

Bone meal: This organic form of phosphate is made of ground bones. Chemically, it is similar to rock phosphate, and is almost insoluble.

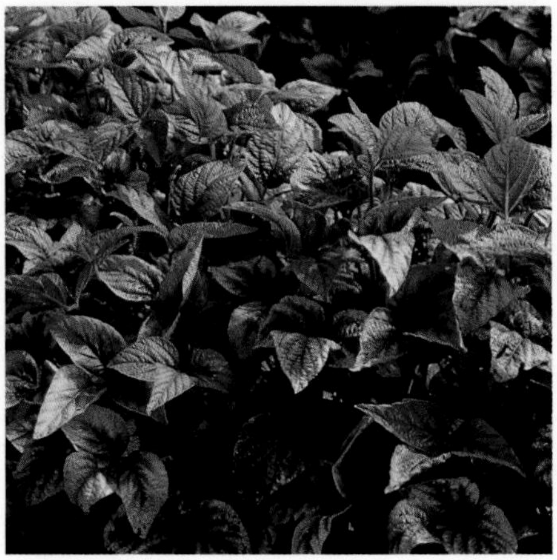

Potassium-deficient soybeans.

Iron-deficient piggyback.

GUARANTEED ANALYSIS

Total Nitrogen (N) 8%
  5.3% Ammoniacal Nitrogen
  2.7% Urea Nitrogen
Available Phosphoric Acid (P_2O_5) 8%
Soluble Potash (K_2O) 8%

Calcium (Ca) 1.5%
Magnesium ..... Water Soluble Mg 0.2% .... Total Mg 1.0%
Sulfur (S) as Combined 4.5%
Iron (Fe) 0.2%
Manganese (Mn) 0.08%
Zinc (Zn) 0.09%
  Primary Nutrients from Ammonium Sulfate, Urea, Ammonium Phosphates, Sulfate of Potash, and Muriate of Potash

  Secondary and Trace Nutrients from Dolomitic Limestone, Magnesium Oxide, Sulfate of Potash, Ammonium Sulfate, Iron Sulfate, Manganese Oxide and Zinc Oxide
Chlorine, not more than 6.5%
Potential Acidity 400 lbs. Calcium Carbonate Equivalent per ton

Fertilizer label.

POTASSIUM

Potassium is the third primary nutrient contained in complete fertilizers. Plants use potassium to maintain their salt balance, and in many other ways. (For information about potassium deficiency in plants, see page 860.) All potassium fertilizers are mined from the ground, either as potassium sulfate or as potassium chloride. They can be bought in these forms, but are most commonly purchased as part of a complete fertilizer. Potassium is soluble, and usually remains in solution in the soil water, but it adheres to clay particles and humus in the soil, so it is not as readily leached from the soil as nitrogen. Potassium is about midway between nitrogen and phosphorus in persistence in the soil. In soils that are rich in clay or humus, one application a year is often enough. But in sandy soils or in containers, potassium should be applied more frequently. Eastern and southern soils, which receive abundant rainfall, are usually deficient in potassium, and need regular applications. Western soils usually need added potassium only for heavily cropped areas, such as vegetable gardens or annual beds, and on lawns and container plants.

MINOR NUTRIENTS

Minor nutrients, also called *trace elements* or *micronutrients*, are nutrients that are needed in small amounts by plants. They include boron, iron, manganese, copper, zinc, molybdenum, and chlorine. Yearly applications of minor nutrients are not necessary; they need to be added only when deficiency symptoms appear in the plant. (For more information about deficiency symptoms, see page 860.)

Minor nutrient deficiencies in the soil: When deficiencies develop in soils, they are usually in localized areas. The most commonly deficient minor nutrient is iron, which is tied up in insoluble forms in alkaline or poorly aerated soils. Alkaline soils may also be deficient in manganese and zinc. (For more information about minor nutrient deficiencies in alkaline soil, see page 908.) Zinc deficiency is much more common than manganese deficiency, especially in citrus and other tree and vegetable crops.

Correcting minor nutrient deficiencies: Minor nutrient deficiencies in the plant are corrected by applying fertilizers to the soil or spraying the foliage. Minor nutrients may be contained in complete fertilizers, and are often contained in specialty fertilizers, such as Ortho-Gro Liquid Plant Food. For immediate results, minor nutrients can be applied in a foliar spray using Ra-Pid-Gro Evergreen & Azalea Food or ORTHO Greenol Liquid Iron.

HOW TO READ A FERTILIZER LABEL

The law requires that fertilizer labels inform the consumer of the minimum guaranteed contents of the product. Information on labels is fairly standardized. Manufacturers give the percentages of nitrogen, phosphate, and potash, and the sources of the nutrients. Some manufacturers also include secondary nutrients (calcium, magnesium, and sulfur) or minor nutrients in their fertilizers, which may or may not be listed. The brand name of the product is listed first, followed by the formula or analysis of the fertilizer. The analysis always gives the percentages of nitrogen, phosphate, and potash that the fertilizer contains, listed in that order. For example, a fertilizer with an analysis of 8–12–4 contains 8 percent nitrogen, 12 percent phosphate, and 4 percent potash. The guaranteed analysis is the manufacturer's warranty of the minimum nutrient content of the fertilizer. The analysis may also list some secondary nutrients or minor nutrients. The source of the primary nutrients—the chemicals from which they were derived—is stated next. The derivation determines their availability to plants. Some fertilizers have an acid reaction in the soil. If this potential exists, the label will indicate the number of pounds of lime it would take to neutralize the acidity of the fertilizer once it is in the soil. Other fertilizers have an alkaline reaction in the soil. If this potential exists, the label will indicate the degree to which the fertilizer will add to the alkalinity of the soil; this is stated in equivalent pounds of lime. On the labels of some specialty fertilizers, the words "chelating agent" appear. A chelating agent is a substance that is added to fertilizers containing nutrients derived from metals.

WATERING

Measuring sprinkler output.

Sprinkler irrigation.

Punctured can for deep-watering.

HOW MUCH WATER TO APPLY

Each time you water, apply enough water to wet the soil to the bottom of the root zone. Water is measured in inches. If a tin can is placed on a lawn when the sprinklers are turned on, the soil has received an inch of water when the water in the container is an inch deep. If a watering basin is 3 inches deep, 3 inches of water is applied to the soil when the basin is filled with water. Because sandy soils do not hold as much water as clay soils, it takes less water to wet them to the same depth. To wet one foot of a sandy loam that has dried out to the point where average plants need water (just barely moist), apply about 1 inch of water. To wet 1 foot of a loam or clay loam that is just barely moist, apply about 1½ inches of water. Soils vary greatly in their ability to hold water, so these figures are only guidelines. To see how much water your soil needs to wet it a foot deep, measure the amount of water you apply at an irrigation. The next day, after the wetting front has moved down as far as it will go (clay soils may take 2 or 3 days), dig a hole to see where the wetting front is. You will be able to calculate from this how much water you need to apply to wet the soil to the bottom of the root zone. Then, by measuring the time it takes your sprinkler system to apply an inch of water, you can calculate how long you need to leave the system on to apply enough water.

ABOUT WATERING

Plants suffer more from improper watering than from any other cause. Watering is more difficult to master than other gardening techniques because it depends on many variables. The amount of water a plant needs varies with the kind of plant, the soil, the location, and all of the continually changing components of the weather including temperature, humidity, and wind, so it is easy to overwater or underwater. Several methods are commonly used to irrigate plants.

Hand watering: This method involves watering the garden with a hand-held hose, usually with a spray head on the end. Hand watering is the simplest method of irrigation. It involves no previous soil preparation or equipment installation. But it is time-consuming, and leads to underwatering because most gardeners do not have the patience to water for many hours at a time.

Furrow irrigation: Furrow irrigation works best when you are watering rows of plants; it is often used in vegetable gardens. Furrows are dug beside plant rows and filled with water. The water is left in the furrows for several hours. Plant foliage stays dry when furrow irrigation is used; only the roots receive water.

Basin irrigation: Watering basins are used mainly around shrubs and trees. A ridge of soil is built to contain the water, then the basin formed by this ridge is filled with water, either from a hand-held hose or a bubbler head on a permanent sprinkler system. A few basins can be filled quickly with water, but if many plants are irrigated by hand in this manner, watering may be time-consuming. Plant foliage stays dry when water basins are used.

Sprinklers: Both hose-end sprinklers and underground installed sprinklers irrigate a large area at once. They are most effective when used to water heavily planted areas. Sprinklers are wasteful if they are used to irrigate sparsely planted areas. They are also hard to control in windy areas, and they get plant leaves wet, which may lead to disease problems. But they are effective for delivering water evenly over a large area, and require less time than most other systems.

Drip irrigation: Drip irrigation systems apply the water very slowly, allowing it to seep into the soil. They are left on for many hours at a time, often for 4 to 16 hours a day. Many types of delivery systems are available. If they are properly operated, drip systems do the best watering job because they keep the soil at a relatively constant state of moisture, without the wet-to-dry fluctuations of other methods. Drip systems work best in light soils, and are a perfect solution to watering plants on steep slopes. They do not wet the leaves.

Some methods, including hand watering and some sprinklers, make water puddle or run off long before the soil receives as much water as it needs. Many gardeners stop watering when the soil surface becomes soggy, or when water starts to puddle or run off. This practice wets only the top few inches of the soil. Because the rate of water absorption into the soil is slow, it may take several hours to several days to wet some types of soil 3 to 4 feet deep. To water deeply and prevent runoff, apply water at the same rate at which it enters the soil. If your irrigation system cannot be adjusted to apply water that slowly, use another system, or water until runoff begins, stop watering for an hour, then water again, until the soil has been wetted as deeply as necessary.

Irrigating vegetable seedlings.

Furrow irrigation.

Watering annual bed.

HOW WATER MOVES IN SOIL

Water enters soil by moving into the pores between the soil particles. As water fills the pores, the soil becomes saturated, and water can move farther down into deeper air-filled pores. This wetting front cannot move down in the soil unless the soil above it is saturated. The rate at which the wetting front moves through the soil varies, depending on the texture of the soil. Water moves quickly through soil with large pores, such as sandy soil, and much more slowly in soil with tiny pores, such as compacted or clay soil. It is important to remember that each layer of soil must get very wet before the wetting front moves deeper into the soil. After the wetting front stops moving downward, the soil below it remains dry. There is no such thing as "keeping the soil slightly moist." Some of the soil always gets very wet. The more water you put on, the deeper you are watering. At each rainfall or irrigation, the soil gets as wet as possible, then it dries slowly until the next wetting. Soil moisture is in a constant state of flux.

Soil drainage: If you place a sponge in water and lift it out, water runs freely from it, pulled by gravity. Soil drains in the same way. Eventually the sponge will stop dripping. Gravity has pulled out all the water it can; the rest of the water in the sponge is held by capillary forces, the forces that make water stick to some surfaces instead of beading. When soil has finished draining, it is holding all the water it can against the pull of gravity. The amount of water in the soil at this point varies greatly from one type of soil to another. As water drains from the soil, air is drawn into it, so the amount of air in the soil also depends on the soil type. Sandy soils hold the least water and the most air; clay soils hold the most water.

Plants and soil water: If you squeeze a sponge that has quit draining, more water will drip from it. As you squeeze the sponge, it requires more and more effort to get it to drip, until you can't squeeze out more water, no matter how hard you try. But the sponge is not yet dry. In the same way, a plant can get water easily from very moist soil, but as the soil dries out, the water moves less and less freely into the plant, until finally the plant can't extract any more water at all. But even at this point, the soil still contains some water. Healthy plant growth requires free movement of water into the plant. When the soil is so dry that the plant cannot get enough water for its needs, the plant is under drought stress. The best time to water is when the plant has used about half the water available to it, before the plant is under any stress.

WHEN TO WATER

There are two primary skills involved in watering plants: knowing how much water to apply at each irrigation (see page 912), and knowing when to water. There are many methods for knowing when to water, some of them very sophisticated. The method described here is one of the simplest and easiest to learn, and it always works. The first step is to dig a hole into the root zone of the plant, from 2 to 6 inches deep. In loose soil you can dig a hole with a finger. Otherwise use a trowel or a shovel. Then feel the soil in the hole. Dig a new hole each time you check. In this book, plants are divided into 3 watering categories: those that can't tolerate drought, average plants, and those that can't tolerate wet soil. When the soil reaches a certain level of dryness, it is time to water again.

Plants that can't tolerate drought: The soil in the root zone is moist but not wet. When you touch it, it makes your finger damp but not muddy. If you squeeze a ball of this soil, water will not run out.

Average plants: The soil in the root zone is just barely moist. When you touch it, it feels cool and moist, but does not dampen your finger. Most soils are crumbly at this stage, but not dusty.

Plants that can't tolerate wet soil: When it is time to water, the soil in the root zone feels completely dry. It is not cool to the touch, and it is probably dusty. It is important to water these plants as soon as the soil reaches this state. Although they can usually withstand long periods of drought, they grow much better if they are watered regularly.

REPAIRING THE LAWN

Lawn renovation.

Patching.

Drip emitter.

LAWN REPAIR

Lawn repair is necessary when dead or bare spots develop, or when a neglected lawn needs to be renovated.

Patching dead spots: With a sharp spade, outline a triangle or a rectangle around the dead spot. With the spade held horizontally, cut the sod free, removing about 1 inch of soil. If the patch is large, roll up the sod as you cut it. Using the removed piece as a pattern, cut a replacement piece of sod from an inconspicuous part of the lawn. Loosen the surface of the soil in the bare spot, and lay the new piece. Press it firmly into place, and water thoroughly. Keep the soil moist until the new piece mends. For more information about laying sod, see page 251.

Sod nursery: Establish your own sod nursery so that matching sod will always be available for patching dead spots. Plant the nursery in an out-of-the-way part of the yard, or use an edge of the lawn. Plant either seed or sod of the same kind as the lawn. Maintain the turf nursery as you do the rest of the lawn. Use as needed.

Spot seeding: Do not plant seeds on top of dead grass or crusted soil. Remove all debris and dead grass. Scratch the surface of the soil ¼ to ½ inch deep. Sow seeds, and top dress lightly with fine soil. Press the soil down firmly. If the weather is dry, mulch lightly (⅛ inch) with sawdust or leaf mold. Water thoroughly and keep the surface of the soil moist until the seedlings are established. For more information about sowing grass seeds, see page 251.

Edging: For a neat, straight edge of grass, use a board as a cutting guide. Trim the edge with a sharp spade or half-moon edging tool. Slice through the turf at an outward angle. Cutting inward will remove the roots of the grass plants growing along the edge. Throughout the season, trim any overhanging grass with grass shears or a trimmer.

Leveling: To level bumps, cut an "H" across the bump. Roll the two flaps of sod back like a carpet. Scrape off enough soil to level the bump. Roll back the cut turf, making sure it is level. Press into place and water thoroughly. Keep the sod moist until it mends. To raise depressions, follow the instructions above, but bring the exposed soil to level by filling and tamping. Or without cutting the sod, sift ¼ inch of soil into the depression at each mowing until the lawn is level. Use soil that is similar to the soil in the lawn.

Renovating the lawn: You can renovate a neglected lawn without beginning over. First kill any weeds. Carry out the renovation just before a period of rapid growth—early summer for southern grasses, spring or fall for northern grasses. (To determine which type you have, see page 1007.) Relieve any compaction as described on page 262. Remove thatch as described on page 262. Mow the lawn as short as possible. Loosen the soil surface with a rake in bare or thin spots. Reseed with matching grass seed. Top dress lightly with fine soil. Water thoroughly, and keep the surface moist until the seedlings are established.

TROUBLESHOOTING DRIP IRRIGATION SYSTEMS

The most common problems with drip irrigation systems are uneven watering, clogging, and breaking.

Uneven watering: In drip systems installed on slopes, the emitters at the base of the slope may apply more water than those at the top. Install pressure-compensating emitters on the circuit. Or split up the circuit into several circuits, so that the emitters on each circuit are on approximately the same level. This will require installation of a new valve and line for each circuit.

Clogged lines or emitters: Once a month, turn the system on and check each emitter. Remove clogged emitters from the line and blow through them, or insert a small wire through the orifice. Make sure that a filter is installed at the valve, and keep it clean.

Surface flooding caused by broken or separated lines: Remove the damaged piece of line or the broken fitting. Cut the line ends cleanly with a pocket knife, insert new line or fittings, and slip it together. Use digging tools with care around drip systems, since the polyethylene plastic is easily cut. If a particular fitting frequently pulls out of the line, check the pressure reducer to make sure the setting is correct (20 to 25 pounds per square inch for most drip systems). Attach the fitting to the line with metal screw clamps if necessary.

Malfunctioning sprinklers.

Electronic sprinkler system.

Shrub sprinkler.

TROUBLESHOOTING SPRINKLER SYSTEMS

Three types of problems are common with sprinkler systems: dry spots, flooding, and stuck electric valves.

Dry spots: First check the sprinkler heads (the parts that spray water). Clean them if they are clogged. Next check the sprinkler circuit (the group of heads that operate from the same valve). A complete sprinkler system often has many circuits. If the circuit is new and the heads clog repeatedly, flush the circuit by removing the heads. Unscrew the nozzles first, and turn on the valve for a moment to flush out the sprinkler heads. Then remove the sprinkler heads and flush out the entire circuit. Working from the valve outward, toward the end sprinklers, replace the heads one by one while the water is running. This will remove debris from the lines. If the circuit is over 10 years old, and the pipes are galvanized iron, consider replacing them with plastic lines, since they are probably clogged with pipe scale or corrosion. If the heads are covered by foliage, reset them at a greater height by substituting longer risers (the upright pipes that run from the buried lines to the heads above ground). Pruning the plants may also help. If you have done all this and you still have dry patches between the sprinkler heads or at the corners of the planted areas, you may need to replace the heads with others that cover a larger area. Another possible reason for dry spots is inadequate pressure for the number of heads on each circuit. Replace the existing heads with heads that will give full coverage of the area with the lower available pressure. Many manufacturers make low-pressure heads. If none of these steps solves the problem, you may have to rebuild the circuit. Sometimes several heads can be moved a few inches each to fill in gaps in coverage, or a head can be added to an existing circuit, if the water pressure will permit it. This is usually a matter for professional determination. The last possible step involes splitting a circuit that has too many heads into two or more circuits. Install a new valve for each new circuit, and new pipe from the valve to the sprinkler heads.

Flooding: When water is delivered more rapidly than the soil can absorb it, flooding results. This problem is most common on slopes. Improve the drainage of the soil by one of the methods described on page 907, or replace the heads with a type that delivers water more slowly. Or turn the circuit on until flooding begins, then turn it off until the water has been absorbed. Repeat this cycle until enough water has been applied, allowing the water to soak in each time. Flooding in one spot is probably caused by a break in the pipe or fittings, especially on PVC plastic or polyethylene systems. Dig up the line, cut out the damaged part cleanly, refit and glue in the new piece of pipe or fitting. Compression couplings can be useful in difficult places, eliminating the need for glue. Pipe breaks at the base of risers are common. Replace the broken fitting and replace the riser with a flexible type to prevent future breakage.

Stuck electric valves on automatic sprinkler systems: If the valve fails to shut off automatically, check the screws holding the valve together. If they are loose, they can allow a pressure leak and activate the valve. If the valve fails to turn on automatically, check the wiring at the clock and the valve. Look for loose or corroded electrical connections, and be sure that all outdoor connections are thoroughly waterproofed. If these steps do not solve your problem, you may need professional help to detect and repair defects in the clock or valve.

REPAIRING TREES

Broken apple branches.

Cabling.

Rod bracing.

BROKEN BRANCHES

Broken branches that are not removed or repaired properly are a potential threat to the life of the tree.

Removing broken branches: If the branch is broken beyond repair (the branch is split so that the bark is intact over less than a third of the circumference of the branch, or only a stub remains), remove it with a pruning saw. First, prune off the dangling part of the broken branch. Next, remove any attached stubs. If a stub is less than a foot long, remove it by making one cut almost flush against the trunk or branch where it is attached. To remove a larger stub, make three cuts in the wood to prevent the bark from tearing as the stub falls off. Make the first cut on the bottom of the branch 1 foot out from where the stub is attached and at least a third of the way through the wood. A second cut on top of the branch, an inch beyond the first cut, will sever the branch. Remove the remaining small stub as described above.

Repairing branches: If broken branches are still attached to the tree they can sometimes be repaired by splinting. Do not attempt to repair large branches, because they never regain their full strength, and may be hazardous. Lift it back into position, matching the wood as carefully as possible. Prune off loose bark and ragged edges, but do not remove any more bark than necessary. Spray a thin film of ORTHO Pruning Sealer on the bark edges. Support the branch by nailing a board to it to serve as a splint. If additional support is needed, prop it in place as described on page 595, or cable it as described on this page.

CABLING AND BRACING

Cables and braces are used to support weak tree branches or crotches, or to repair split crotches. Cables and braces are often used to support heavy branches overhanging homes and other buildings. Weak branches (with narrow, creased or wrinkled crotches), and branches or trunks that are partially hollowed-out or rotted may also require the support of cables and braces.

Rigid bracing (rods): Rods are used to repair or prevent a split crotch. If the crotch is already split, repairs should be made within 3 weeks. Rods are always used in horizontal pairs. If the wood is sound, threaded rods (obtained from an arboriculture supply house) can be used. Drill a hole slightly smaller than the rod, and screw the rod into the hole with a pipe wrench. Cut off the rod flush with the trunk and paint the end with ORTHO Pruning Seal. If the tree is hollow, drill a hole all the way through and insert a length of all-thread rod. Fasten the ends with large washers and nuts, countersinking the holes through the bark so the washers are pressing against the wood. To reinforce a sound crotch, insert one or two pairs of rods above the crotch. If the crotch has already split, close the split with a block and tackle, and insert the rods right through the split.

Cabling: Wire rope or cables are used to provide a flexible brace for tree branches. Cables must be galvanized, and are attached to screw hooks or lag-screw hooks that are screwed into the branches. The hooks should be in line with the cable for the greatest strength. The best place to attach a cable is ⅔ of the way from the crotch to the branch tip. For maximum strength, cable three branches together in a triangular pattern. Branches may also be cabled to buildings or other structures. To provide support, the cable must be taut. Tighten it with a turnbuckle, or attach the cable while the branches are pulled together slightly with a block and tackle.

Caution: Tree work is dangerous. If your tree is tall or very large, have the job done by a professional arborist.

Canker removal.

Bark wound caused by lawn mower.

Staked tree.

CANKER REMOVAL

Cankers are caused by any of a number of different fungi and bacteria. They usually appear as discolored, sunken areas on a branch or on the main trunk, and often have sap oozing from them. As the organisms spread through the tissue, the cankers increase in size. If the cankers girdle the wood, the portion of the tree above the canker dies. Remove cankered branches by pruning off the branch at the trunk, or at least 6 inches below the canker. When the canker appears on the main trunk or a large branch, the tree or branch can sometimes be saved by surgical removal of the canker. Using a chisel and a sharp knife, excise all discolored bark and wood from the wound. All tools should be sterilized with rubbing alcohol after each cut to prevent spreading the disease organisms to healthy tissue. Spray the wound lightly with ORTHO Pruning Sealer. To hasten the healing process and promote vigorous growth, fertilize and water the tree regularly. For more information about fertilizers and watering, see pages 910 and 916.

BARK WOUNDS

The bark is a protective layer that serves many of the same functions as our skin. When this layer is breached, disease organisms and insects may invade the plant through the break. Directly under the bark is the conductive tissue of the plant—the circulatory system that carries water and minerals to the leaves, and sugar and protein to the roots. If the break in the bark does not heal quickly, this tissue dries out and dies, stopping circulation through that part of the trunk or branch. Bark wounds that encircle more than a quarter of the circumference of a trunk or branch slow the growth of the plant past that point. Small breaks in a healthy tree—those less than ½ inch wide—usually heal within a couple of weeks during the growing season. Larger breaks heal more slowly, as the tree grows a layer of tissue across them. If the break remains open for too long, heart-rot fungi often invade the wound, rotting the wood and beginning the process that leads to hollow trees.

If the edges of a wound are ragged, trim the bark with a sharp knife to make a clean edge, but don't remove any more bark than is necessary. Smooth the underlying wood with a chisel. On wounds over ½ inch across, spray the exposed wood lightly with ORTHO Pruning Sealer. If the wound has begun to heal, a roll of new tissue can be seen at the edge of the wound. Do not cut into this tissue.

STAKING AND GUYING

Many newly transplanted trees require temporary support until the roots grow into the surrounding soil and the tree establishes itself. This is especially true of shade trees, which just after transplanting have much larger crowns (branch systems at the top of the tree) than root systems, making them top heavy. Most trees are able to support themselves after 1 to 2 years. To avoid girdling the tree, stakes and ties should be checked annually and either readjusted or removed. Staked trees that are held rigidly in place develop weaker trunks than unstaked trees, so support should allow some natural sway.

Trees with trunks less than 3 inches in diameter: Support the tree with two directly opposed stakes (8 feet long by 3 inches in diameter), driven at least 2 feet into the ground. The stakes should not interfere with the roots. Loop two strands of plastic tape or rubber ties (available in garden centers) around the tree trunk, and tie them around each stake. Leave enough slack in the tie to allow the trunk to sway slightly.

Trees with trunks greater than 3 inches in diameter: Space three stakes (3 feet by 2 inches by 4 inches), or 18-inch screw-type ground anchors, around the tree and drive them into the soil at an angle away from the tree. Place the stakes or anchors at a distance from the tree equal to ⅔ of the height of attachment to the tree. Loop three strands of thick tape or rubber ties around the tree trunk and over a branch or nail, and tie one to each of the stakes. Tighten the ties as in the method above. Flag the ties so that people don't trip over them.

REMOVING TREES

Stump grinder.

Tree stump.

TREE AND SHRUB REMOVAL

Small trees and shrubs can be dug out of the ground if their root systems are small and shallow. To remove large trees and shrubs, follow the guidelines below.

Cutting the plant to a stump: Saw larger, established plants to a stump. Contact a professional arborist to do this job if the tree or shrub is very large or in an area where the falling branches and trunk might damage nearby structures or property, injure people, or fall on power lines. Kill the remaining stump before removing it; stumps that are alive are much more difficult to remove. If you choose to keep the stump as a decorative element in your landscape, it may continue to resprout if you do not kill it.

Killing freshly-cut stumps: Remove any sprouts growing from the trunk, then paint or daub undiluted ORTHO Brush-B-Gon Brush Killer over the entire surface of the stump within 30 minutes after the tree or shrub has been cut. If there is a chance of runoff from rain affecting adjacent desirable plants, cover the stump with a plastic bag and secure it around the base of the stump.

Killing old, resprouting stumps: With a hatchet, make a continuous horizontal cut or an overlapping ring of notches around the base of the stump, angling downwards into the bark. Cut through but do not remove any of the bark. Pour as much ORTHO Brush-B-Gon Brush Killer into the cut as it will hold. Reapply the treatment if the stump resprouts. Cover the stump with plastic as mentioned above if runoff may be a problem.

Killing root-grafted stumps: Sometimes tree and shrub roots merge with the roots of nearby plants of the same or closely-related species, forming root grafts. If you suspect that the stump roots are grafted to nearby desirable plants, use the following method to avoid harming root-grafted plants when killing a stump. Bore holes in the soil around the stump in a ring pattern. The holes should be 1 inch in diameter, 15 inches deep, and 18 inches from the trunk. Fill each hole with a mixture of 1 part *vapam* to 3 parts water. Pour the *vapam* mixture into the holes to within 2 inches of the soil surface. Tamp each hole closed.

Removing the stump: You will know the stump is dead if it fails to resprout during the next growing season. Dig it out, or contact a professional landscape contractor or arborist who can quickly remove a living or dead stump with a stump grinder.

TEMPERATURE PROBLEMS

Protecting tomato transplant from the sun.

HEAT PROTECTION

Plants cool their leaves by evaporation. If the soil dries out during hot weather, leaf temperatures rise rapidly to killing levels. To prevent heat injury to plants, keep them well watered during hot weather, never letting the soil around them dry out. For small plants such as annuals and vegetables, and plants growing in containers, this may mean watering as often as twice a day during heat waves. The lawn grasses that are used in the northern states are especially susceptible to heat. Keep the soil moist during hot weather. The lawn—and most other plants in the garden—benefits by being wet down during the hottest part of the day. To further protect sensitive plants, erect temporary shade structures. Shade larger plants with burlap or cheesecloth stretched on a wooden frame. Shade small plants with shingles or pieces of cardboard, set at an angle in the soil beside the plant.

Fir branches used as protective mulch.

PROTECTING PLANTS FROM THE COLD

Low temperatures can cause severe damage in the home garden. Take these precautions against winter cold:

1. Protect tender plants from light frost with newspapers or sheets of fabric or plastic. When night temperatures below 32°F are predicted, cover the plants loosely. Remove the covers in the morning. In the South, protect tender or half-hardy plants during especially cold weather by covering them, or by providing heat sources throughout the garden. Many small heat sources are more effective than a few large ones. Use electric lights, piles of charcoal, cans of jellied alcohol, or other slow-burning material.

2. In the North, continue watering the garden until the ground freezes in the winter. Plants need water in the soil to replace any lost through their leaves to the winter winds.

3. After the ground freezes, mulch perennials and trees and shrubs with chopped leaves, wood chips, straw, evergreen boughs, or pine needles. A 4 to 6-inch layer will help maintain even soil temperatures and prevent alternate freezing and thawing, which can heave plants out of the soil, tearing their roots. If plants are heaved, replant them as soon as the soil can be worked. Meanwhile, mulch the disrupted roots. For more information on mulching, see page 926.

4. Wrap the trunks of newly planted trees with burlap or tree-wrap paper to prevent sunscald or cracks in the trunk caused by fluctuating day and night temperatures.

5. Shield evergreens from drying winds and sun with burlap stretched over wooden frames, or with snow fencing.

Ageratum seedlings damaged by cold.

CHILLING INJURY

Plants that have been grown in a house or greenhouse may be damaged if they are planted in the garden while night temperatures are still below 50°F. The growth of damaged plants may be temporarily halted, or parts of the leaves may die and turn black. To prevent this damage, accustom your plants to cool weather by hardening them off. A week or 2 before planting them outdoors, place them outside in a sunny spot for 1 to 3 hours. Each day, increase the time they are outside until they are being left outside for a full day by the end of the 1 to 2 week period. If frost is predicted, bring them indoors. Water wilted plants promptly. Plants can also be hardened off in a cold frame. Gradually open the sash more each day to expose the plants to cooler temperatures. Remove any shading gradually to allow in more sunlight. If it is impractical to take plants outside, they may be hardened off by gradually increasing the length of time between waterings. Repeated drought stress has the same effect as cold.

Watering containerized shrub.

WATERING CONTAINER PLANTS

Apply enough water to container plants so that some water drains from the bottom. Drainage water should flow freely away from the container so that water doesn't collect around the base. If the container is sitting in a saucer, wait for all of the water to drain through (10 to 15 minutes is adequate for most plants), then empty the water from the saucer. Sometimes the drainage hole becomes blocked and water accumulates inside the container rather than flowing out. Make sure the container drains after you've watered. If it doesn't, poke a stick up into the drainage hole to loosen compacted soil. Water again when the soil just below the surface is barely moist. In large containers (more than 10 inches wide and 10 inches high), water when the soil 1 to 2 inches below the surface is barely moist. Plants in containers without drainage holes are difficult to water properly. Water accumulates in the bottom of the container, causing root rot. If the soil in a container is allowed to become too dry, it may be difficult to rewet. Instead of penetrating the soil, the water runs down the inside edge of the container and immediately drains out the bottom. To wet the soil, soak the container in a tub or sink full of water for a few hours. The rim of the container should be submerged. Or add a soil penetrant (available in garden centers) to the irrigation water.

HOUSEPLANT PRACTICES

Potting.

Filling container with potting mix.

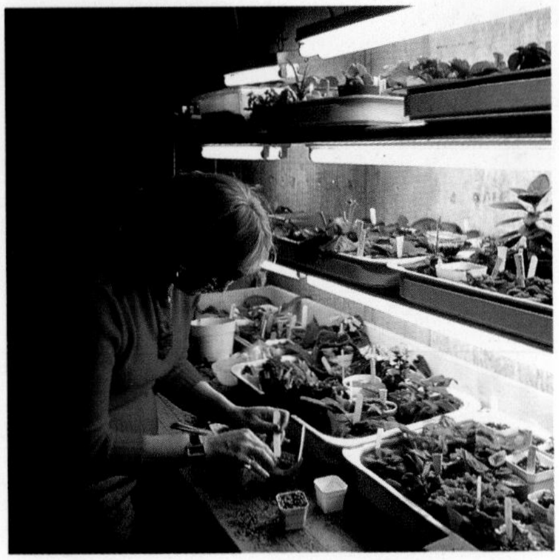

Supplemental light.

PLANTING IN CONTAINERS

Potting soils: Potting soils may be purchased or made. The best potting mixes provide good drainage, yet retain enough water so that the soil doesn't dry out too frequently. Any of the following recipes will provide 1 cubic foot of good potting mix, enough to fill ten to twelve 1-gallon containers.
Mix thoroughly and store in a closed container until use:

1. 4 gallons of medium or coarse sand
   4 gallons of moistened peat moss
   4 gallons of composted bark or sawdust
   ¼ cup dolomitic limestone
   3 tablespoons of ORTHO Superphosphate
   1 tablespoon ORTHO General Purpose Plant Food
2. 6 gallons of moistened peat moss
   6 gallons of perlite
   ¼ cup dolomitic limestone
   3 tablespoons of ORTHO Superphosphate
   1 tablespoon ORTHO General Purpose Plant Food
3. 4 gallons of pasteurized garden soil
   4 gallons of medium or coarse sand
   4 gallons of leaf mold
   3 tablespoons of ORTHO Superphosphate
   1 tablespoon of ORTHO General Purpose Plant Food

Pasteurizing soil: To pasteurize garden soil, moisten it and spread it about 2 inches deep on a cookie sheet. Place a thermometer so that the bulb is about in the center of the soil, but not touching the metal sheet. Put the pan of soil in the oven and turn it on. Heat the soil to 140°F, and keep it at that temperature for 30 minutes. If your oven thermostat can't be set as low as 140°F, heat the soil to that temperature, then turn off the oven and crack the door slightly. Do not heat the soil higher than 140°F or for longer than 30 minutes. This temperature is high enough to kill all disease producing organisms and insect pests, and will even kill some weed seeds. However, many of the beneficial soil organisms will survive. Clean clay pots can be pasteurized at the same time as the soil.

Planting in containers: When potting, do not put a layer of gravel in the bottom of the container. A gravel layer does not improve drainage, and it reduces the amount of soil that can be used by the roots. If necessary, keep soil from spilling out of the drain holes by placing a piece of screen or broken crockery over the hole before planting. Do not fill the container to the rim with soil. The space between the surface of the soil and the container rim is a watering reservoir. The reservoir should be deep enough after settling so that one filling provides enough water to wet the mix to the bottom.

SUPPLEMENTARY LIGHTING

In many homes, it is hard to find enough bright locations for all the plants. It is particularly important that plants grown for their flowers or colorful foliage have bright light.

Lengthening the day: Giving some extra light after nightfall is often enough to keep a plant vigorous. This is especially true in the winter, when the days are short. These extra hours of light can be achieved by placing the plant near a reading light in the evening, but not so near that the heat burns the leaves.

Making extra light: If the plant cannot be moved, bring more light to the plant by training a decorator spotlight on it in its present location. This light can be used to extend the day or, if the location is dim, it can be left on all day to brighten the location.

Growing under lights: You can make plants independent of natural light by supplying all their light needs with artificial lighting. Fluorescent fixtures with cool-white bulbs are most practical. Use a reflector to focus the light on the plants. About 15 to 20 watts are needed for each square foot you wish to illuminate. Fix the lights 1 to 2 feet above the tops of the plants, and leave them on for 12 hours a day for foliage plants, and 16 hours a day for flowering plants. Most houseplants can be grown under fluorescent fixtures, but a few that need full sun, such as miniature roses, may not get enough light to bloom.

Rooting a dieffenbachia cutting.

ROOTING CUTTINGS

Many houseplants root easily (for a list, see page 1001). If a houseplant has lost many of its lower leaves, or is suffering from root rot, the top can often be saved by following these guidelines:

Preparing the rooting mix: Fill flower pots with equal parts of perlite and peat moss. Add 1 teaspoon of lime per quart of mix, and blend it in thoroughly. Wet the mix thoroughly and let it drain.

Making the frame: Bend 1 or 2 wire coathangers or sturdy wire into a U shape and insert the ends of the wire into the rooting mix.

Preparing the cuttings: Cut off the top of the plant you wish to save. Take the part that will be the new plant, plus 2 to 4 inches of stem. Strip off all of the leaves on the extra stem portion. Dip the bottom of the stem in a rooting powder. Insert the stem into the rooting mix. Press the mix gently around the stem, then slip a clear plastic bag over the wire frame. Secure the bag around the pot with rubber bands. The bag acts as a miniature greenhouse by maintaining high moisture levels in the soil and air. Keep the cuttings in a warm place where they receive bright, indirect light, but not direct sunlight. Remove the plastic cover once a week to make sure the rooting mix has not dried out; water if necessary.

Checking for roots: Check for roots after 3 weeks by gently tugging the cutting. If the cutting is firmly bound to the mix by the new roots, it is ready to transplant into potting soil. If the cutting has not rooted adequately, check weekly until it is well rooted.

Examining plant roots.

EXAMINING PLANT ROOTS

Rootballs can be inspected without harming the plant. However, the plant must be established in the container—that is, roots must have grown all through the potting mix—or else much of the rootball will fall apart when the plant is removed from the pot. It is easier to remove the plant from the container when the soil is moist. If your plant is small enough to hold in one hand, put your hand on the soil surface, with the plant stems between your fingers. Invert the container and gently knock the rim on the edge of a table or other firm surface. The rootball will dislodge from the inside of the pot and fall into your hand. To inspect the rootball of a plant that is too large to hold, lay the container on its side, and place a piece of 2×4 or 4×4 lumber across the rim of the container as close to the stem of the plant as possible. Strike the board with a hammer to dislodge the rootball. Slide the plant gently out of the container. Roots will be visible on the outside of the rootball. Healthy roots have many white or tan threadlike tips. These tips are the part of the root system that most actively absorbs water and nutrients. Unhealthy roots have fewer white tips, and the larger roots may be dark and rotting. Dead roots have no white tips.

Spraying coleus plant.

SPRAYING HOUSEPLANTS

Some houseplant sprays, such as ORTHO House Plant Insect Control, ORTHO House Plant Insect Killer, and ORTHO Whitefly & Mealybug Killer, are designed to be used inside the house. But if the label does not say the product can be used indoors, take the plants outside to a shady spot to spray them. In cold weather, spray in a heated garage or basement. Don't spray in front of air intakes for heating units. Let the plants dry thoroughly before taking them back into the living quarters.

Applying the spray: Read the label and follow the directions exactly. Be sure the plant you wish to spray is listed on the label. The chemical may damage the leaves if it is applied in too high a concentration, or if the plants are sprayed more frequently than recommended. Leaves may also be burned if aerosol cans are held too close to them when spraying. Do not spray in the sun, or when the temperature is higher than 85°F.

Applying insecticides: Spray both sides of the leaves, all around the stems, the surface of the soil, and the outside of the pot. Unless a product is specially formulated for mealybugs, adding a few drops of a spreader-sticker—a wetting agent available in most garden centers—will help the insecticide penetrate this insect's waxy coating and increase its effectiveness. A spreader-sticker will also help to keep the spray from beading on waxy leaves. ORTHO products are formulated to wet foliage quickly, so additional spreader-stickers are usually not needed.

GARDENING PRACTICES

Mixing pesticides.

Using a hose-end sprayer.

Applying an insecticidal spray to plum.

MIXING AND STORING PESTICIDES

Proper mixing and storage of pesticides is necessary in order to use them safely and to their full benefit (for more information about specific pesticides, see page 1040 and pages 929 to 1000).

Mixing pesticides: Always read the label carefully before mixing pesticides. Mix pesticides according to the proportions and as directed by the label. Keep a special set of measuring spoons, cups, stirring rods, and other tools to be used only for mixing and measuring pesticides. Make sure mixing and spraying utensils are clean before using them. Mix only the amount needed for the job. Protect your skin from contact with pesticides by wearing clothing that covers your arms and legs. Wear goggles and a cap to protect your head and face if the label carries a *Warning* or *Danger* cautionary word. Wash your hands and face and any other area that may have come in contact with the pesticide with soap and water. Remove pesticide-contaminated clothes immediately. Wash them in a strong detergent before wearing them again.

Storing chemicals: Always keep pesticides in their original containers. Do not remove the labels, and keep the containers securely capped. Pesticide storage shelves should be strong, stable, and not too high to reach easily, though they should be out of the reach of children. Do not store pesticides near food. Pesticides are best stored in a locked, well-ventilated space, out of the sun and away from pilot lights and other open flames or sparks, since the fumes may be flammable.

APPLYING PESTICIDES

In order for pesticides to be most effective, they must be properly applied. Choose a calm day when the temperature is under 85°F and no rain is expected for 12 hours. Early morning is often the best time. Before spraying or dusting, remove toys, food, dishes, garden furniture, and other objects away from the area that you intend to treat. Keep children, pets, and anyone else involved well away from the areas where you apply pesticides. Wear clothing that covers your arms and legs. If the label carries a *Warning* or *Danger* cautionary word, wear goggles and a cap.

Spraying: It is important that the plant be thoroughly covered. If the label instructions say "wet thoroughly" or "to the drip point," apply as much spray as possible, until the plant begins to drip. To get thorough coverage, spray the plant from two or three directions, and from underneath as well as from above. If there is breeze, spray downwind to avoid having the mist drift back to you.

Dusting: Since dust is carried by air currents, it is especially important that dusting be done when the air is still. Apply a thin coat of dust, not a heavy layer. Work the duster vigorously, so that the air currents carry the dust onto the foliage and cover all the surfaces of the leaves. Dust from the bottom of the plant as well as from the top.

Spreader-stickers: These additives perform two functions: they break the surface tension of the spray droplets, preventing them from beading on waxy leaves and helping them to penetrate wax-covered insects, such as mealybugs and scales. They also make pesticides adhere better in rainy weather. ORTHO products are formulated to wet foliage quickly, so additional spreader-stickers are usually not needed.

INSECTICIDES

There are many different types of insecticides on the market today. Most of our common insecticides have *broad-spectrum* activity; they are effective against many different types of plant pests. A few insecticides are *selective;* control is aimed at only one type or group of insects. Insecticides use different methods to control insects. Most insecticides are either systemic or kill on contact. A *systemic* insecticide is a chemical that is absorbed by the roots, stems, or leaves and is carried with the sap throughout the plant. Any type of pest that feeds on sap from the treated plant is killed. Systemic insecticides usually remain active in the plant for at least 2 weeks, protecting the plant from reinfestations. They are applied either as granules to the soil or as sprays or drenches. *Nonsystemic* chemicals may control the insect by direct contact (the spray is absorbed through the body) or through ingestion, as the insect feeds on plant tissue. The *persistence* of an insecticide determines how quickly it breaks down in the environment. The persistance of most nonsystemic insecticides ranges from several days to months. The less persistent the insecticide, the shorter the time interval between applications.

Applying a fungicidal spray.

Weed control in juniper planting.

Thistle treated with herbicide.

FUNGICIDES

Fungicides are chemicals that kill or inhibit the growth and development of fungi found on or in plants or in the soil. Most fungicides, called *protectants,* work by protecting healthy plant parts from infection. They form a chemical barrier between the fungus and the plant tissues, killing the spores and fungal strands. Protective fungicides cannot cure fungal infections that are already established on or in plant tissues. A few fungicides, called *eradicants,* can kill fungi growing on and sometimes in infected plant parts.

Most fungicides are *nonsystemic;* they do not penetrate the leaves, stems, and roots, but protect only the surface of the plant. Protective, nonsystemic fungicides must be applied so that the plant is thoroughly and evenly covered. Areas that are missed and new growth that is not treated are susceptible to infection. The activity of fungicides diminishes as they are washed off by rain or irrigation water, or broken down by ultraviolet light from the sun. A *spreader-sticker* helps a fungicide spread over leaf, stem, and fruit surfaces, and stick to the foliage and resist degradation. Some fungicides are pre-mixed with a spreader-sticker; check the label. A few fungicides are *systemic.* They are absorbed into the plant roots, leaves, or stems, and are transferred throughout part or all of the plant, providing protection against invading fungi. Some fungicides (broad-spectrum) control many types of fungi, while others (narrow-spectrum) control only a few types of fungi. Fungi may develop resistance to fungicides, especially narrow-spectrum fungicides that are used exclusively.

HERBICIDES

Herbicides are chemicals that kill or inhibit the development of plants. They are mainly used to kill weeds or plants growing in areas where they are not wanted. A wide variety of herbicides are available, differing greatly in their characteristics.

Herbicides vary in the kinds of plants they will kill. *Non-selective* herbicides kill any kind of plant and are usually used to kill vegetation indiscriminately. *Selective* herbicides are more specific and kill only certain kinds of plants. For example, many of the herbicides used in grass lawns selectively kill broad-leaved plants and do not harm grasses when used properly. Herbicides can usually be classified as either *preemergent* or *postemergent. Preemergent* herbicides kill weeds before they come up as seedlings. *Postemergent* herbicides kill plants that have already produced above-ground growth. Postemergent herbicides are further classified as *contact* or *systemic. Contact* herbicides kill only the part of the plant with which they come in contact, usually the leaves, stems, and flowers. To ensure complete killing, it is essential to cover the weed thoroughly when using a contact herbicide. *Systemic* herbicides are absorbed into the plant roots, leaves, or stems, and are carried throughout the plant. Thorough coverage is not as important with systemic herbicides. As long as enough herbicide makes contact with some part of the plant, it will spread throughout the plant's system. Systemic herbicides are most effective if they are applied when the weed is actively growing.

APPLYING HERBICIDES

There are two categories of herbicides: *pre-emergence* herbicides, which are applied to the soil before weed seeds germinate, and *post-emergence* herbicides, which are applied to actively growing weeds.

Pre-emergence herbicides: These herbicides do not kill growing weeds. They should be applied to weed-free soil, either before weed seeds sprout in the spring, or after weeds have been removed. Pre-emergence herbicides attach to soil particles in the top inch of soil, where most seed germination takes place, and kill weed seeds as they germinate. If the soil is cultivated after application, the herbicide will be diluted and its effectiveness diminished.

Post-emergence herbicides: These herbicides control weeds that are actively growing. When spraying them, be careful not to allow the material to touch desirable plants. This can be most easily done by following these guidelines:

1. Spray on a windless day.
2. Use low pressures when spraying.
3. Keep the nozzle as close to the weeds as possible.
4. Use a shield of cardboard, plywood, or sheet metal to protect garden plants when working near them.

Clean sprayers carefully before using them for fungicides or insecticides. Some gardeners keep separate sprayers for herbicides.

GARDENING PRACTICES

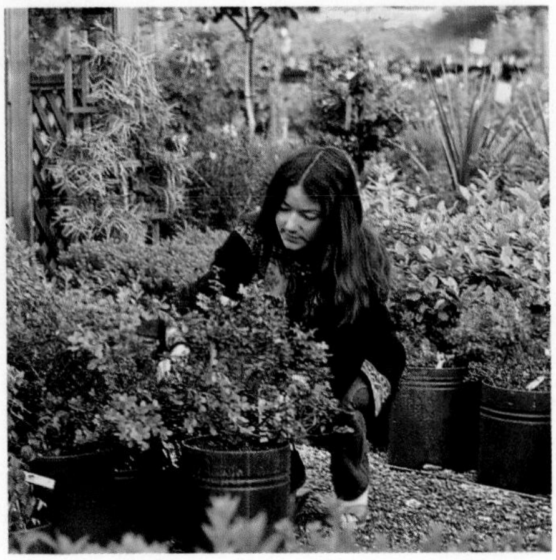
Choosing plants.

Planting a tomato.

Planting a balled and burlapped shrub.

CHOOSING PLANTS

Plants are available in several different forms. Inspect all plants for visible insects and diseases. Here are some standards for choosing plants.

Balled and burlapped (B&B): The leaves are large, of good color, and free from spots or dead areas. The stems do not show signs of recent heavy pruning. Stem diameter is in good proportion to the size of the plant. The roots do not encircle the base of the trunk, and the rootball inside the burlap is not broken or very dry.

Bare root: The trunk is a good diameter for the size of the plant. The stem is flexible and the bark is not broken or dried. The roots are symmetrical and flexible. The buds and roots are still dormant, with no new growth evident.

Containerized: The leaves are large, of good color, and free from spots or dead areas. The stems do not show signs of recent heavy pruning. The stem diameter is in proportion with the size of the plant. The roots do not encircle the base of the trunk, and the plant is firmly rooted. When the plant is removed from the container, many roots are visible on the outside of the rootball, but they are not thick or woody.

Flats or small pots: Plants are young and stocky, without dead or discolored leaves. No plants should be missing from the flat.

Sod: The grass is a good green color without yellow blades. The soil is about ¾ inch thick, and moist. The sod holds together when handled.

Bulbs: The bulbs are firm without wounds, or soft or deep blemishes. They are not moldy or dried, and the basal plate is firm and not cracked. The skins may be loose.

PLANTING AND TRANSPLANTING

Survival of a plant after transplanting often depends on how much care was taken during planting. This includes selection of the plant, site selection, preparation of the planting site, and the actual setting of the plant. To avoid problems after transplanting, all of these factors must be considered. Choose a plant that will survive in your climate. Do not transplant at a time when the plant will be damaged by unfavorable weather (extreme heat or cold).

Storing the plant: Before planting, protect the plant from heat, cold, or drying. It is best to plant soon after purchase. Bare root plants and balled and burlapped plants are extremely susceptible to drying. If planting is to be delayed more than a few days, cover the roots of a balled and burlapped plant with moist mulch or loose soil. To store a bare root plant, dig a trench in a shady location, place the plant in the trench, and cover the roots with mulch or soil.

The planting site: Select a planting site in an area where the plant will have room for spread and height, and receive the right light for its needs. Choose a site that has good drainage. If the area has poor drainage, improve it, following the directions on page 907. If planting in a lawn, keep the lawn away from the root area of the plant to avoid competition.

Planting: Prepare the planting hole by digging a hole approximately twice as wide as the root system and deep enough so that the plant will be at the same level as it was in the nursery. Leave the sides of the hole rough, so the roots can penetrate the soil. Use topsoil for backfill. Break up dirt clods and remove rocks. If the soil is very sandy or heavy clay, improve it by adding organic matter (see page 930). Carefully remove the container from potted plants. Make three vertical cuts down the sides of the rootball. This pruning prevents circling roots that may later constrict the trunk, and stimulates new root growth into the surrounding soil. Inspect bare root plants for broken or damaged roots, and prune off any that are damaged. Do not remove the burlap from balled and burlapped plants before setting them in the planting hole. Spread out the roots on bare root plants. Fill in the hole with soil until it is ¾ full, settling the soil around the roots to prevent large air pockets from forming. Cut the twine on balled and burlapped plants and fold back the burlap so it is below the soil surface. Fill the hole with water, then cover the rest of the roots with soil. Do not tamp the soil down.

Care of the plant: Proper care after transplanting is essential for the survival of the plant. Prune off broken branches, and if necessary prune to shape the plant. On bare root plants, prune off about a third of the branches to compensate for root loss. Newly transplanted trees with tops that are large in proportion to their roots should be staked (see page 917). To prevent sunscald, wrap trunks of trees (especially those with smooth, thin bark) with tree-wrap paper or burlap. Build a basin around the plant and water the plant by filling the basin whenever the rootball is barely moist. Water in the basin until the roots grow into the surrounding soil. For more information about watering, see page 912.

Starting seeds indoors.

Starting seeds outdoors.

Storing bulbs.

STARTING SEEDS INDOORS

Growing transplants requires bright light and moderate temperatures.
1. Wash containers (milk or egg cartons, cans, flower pots) to remove soil and debris. Disinfect in a solution of 1 part household bleach to 9 parts water.
2. Fill the containers to within ½ inch of the top with vermiculite, or a mix of 1 part peat moss and 10 parts perlite.
3. Wet and drain the mix.
4. Sprinkle the seeds over the surface.
5. Cover lightly with soil mix or peat moss.
6. Place the containers in clear plastic bags and seal, to provide humidity and prevent the soil from drying out. Place the container in a location in which the temperature is suitable for seed germination (see page 1025).
7. As soon as the seedlings emerge, remove the bag and move the containers to a warm area with bright light, either a windowsill or under fluorescent lights.
8. As soon as the seedlings are large enough to handle, transplant them into disinfected flats or peat pots containing a mix of equal parts peat moss and perlite, and ½ teaspoon limestone per quart of mix.
9. Place the flats in a warm area with bright light.
10. Feed the seedlings weekly with ORTHO Tomato & Vegetable Food mixed at half strength.
11. One week before planting outdoors, harden off the plants by placing them outdoors a few hours a day, until they are outside a full day by the end of the week. Transplant into the garden according to the spacing recommended on the seed packet.

STARTING SEEDS OUTDOORS

Some plants should be seeded directly in the garden.
1. Till the soil, incorporating a fertilizer that is high in phosphate such as ORTHO Up-Start® Plant Starter. Rake to level and remove stones and clods larger than ½ inch. Water well 1 or 2 days before planting.
2. If you have been troubled with damping-off fungi in the past, treat the seeds with a fungicide containing *captan* (ORTHOCIDE®) or *thiram*. Add a pinch to a packet of seeds, or ½ teaspoon per pound. For more information on damping-off, see page 850.
3. Using a board or a string stretched between two stakes as a guide, make a furrow as deep as the planting depth suggested on the seed packet, or four times as deep as the seed is wide.
4. Drop the seeds into the furrow, spacing them about twice as close together as you wish the mature plants to stand.
5. Fill the furrow with sand, compost, or light soil.
6. Press firmly to settle the seeds and soil.
7. Water gently, sprinkling the soil. Be careful not to wash away the newly planted seeds. Allow the soil surface to dry slightly between waterings.
8. In hot, dry weather, mulch the seed row lightly with straw, sawdust, or leaf mold. Or place a board or a strip of burlap on the row. Remove the latter promptly as soon as the seeds begin to germinate.
9. When the seedlings are large enough to handle, thin according to the recommended spacings on the seed packet. To avoid disturbing the roots of the remaining seedlings, pinch the thinnings off at the ground level, or cut them with a pair of scissors.

STORING BULBS

In areas where bulbs are not winter hardy, they must be dug up and stored for the winter.
1. After the foliage has yellowed or been killed by a frost in the fall, carefully dig up the bulbs with a spading fork.
2. Discard any wounded, diseased, or deformed bulbs.
3. Cut off the foliage close to the bulb, and shake off any loose soil. Dry the bulbs in a well-ventilated area out of direct sunlight for about a week.
4. Carefully brush off any soil. To protect the bulbs from storage rots, dust them with a fungicide containing *captan* (ORTHOCIDE®).
5. Bulbs are live plants, and continue to breathe. Store them in shallow trays or plastic buckets, covered with dry sand, peat moss, perlite, or vermiculite.
6. Store the bulbs at temperatures between 35° and 45°F. They must not be allowed to freeze.
7. Store until the proper planting time for your plant.

Precooling: In mild winter areas where the bulbs' chilling requirements are not satisfied, purchase precooled bulbs, or precool them yourself. To do this, place the uncovered bulbs in a shallow pan. Store in the refrigerator or any area where the temperature remains just above freezing for 6 weeks. Plant outdoors or in pots. Blooms will appear in 2 to 4 months, depending on the plant variety.

GARDENING PRACTICES

Measuring organic matter.

Compost bin.

Pine cone mulch.

ORGANIC MATTER

The organic matter that is added to soil is derived from plants or animals. Any soil will benefit from the addition of organic material, but heavy or sandy soils are especially helped.

How organic matter improves the soil: Organic matter incorporated into clay or compacted soils opens up the soil, giving it a crumbly structure. This reduces stickiness, improves drainage, and allows air to move more easily into the soil. In sandy soils, organic matter acts like a sponge, holding moisture and nutrients in the root zone. The quantity of organic matter added to the soil must be large enough to change the soil structure. Spread from 1 to 4 inches over the soil and then till or mix it in. As organic matter decomposes into humus, it continues to improve the soil. For best results, add organic matter whenever the soil is worked. Many different types of organic matter can be used as soil amendments. The amendments should be free of weed seeds, toxic materials, and disease organisms. When buying organic matter, especially in bulk, it is best to buy from a well-established, reputable dealer. The most commonly used types of organic matter are compost, peat moss, manure, ground bark, and sawdust, but other materials may be available locally.

Compost: Compost can be purchased or made at home. Besides improving soil structure, compost also provides some of the essential nutrients for plant growth, depending on what originally went into it.

Peat moss: Peat moss is one of the most commonly used soil conditioners. Since peat moss is acid (pH 3.5 to 4.5), it is especially good for acid-loving plants, and as much as 50 percent may be added to the soil before planting. If peat moss is allowed to dry out, it will shed water. It can be remoistened by loosening the peat moss, spreading it under a sprinkler, and then mixing it several times while it is absorbing water. If the peat moss is already mixed into the soil and it does not moisten, add a wetting agent, which can be purchased from your local nursery, to the water.

Manure: Manure is a very common and widely available soil amendment. It is a good conditioner, but has several drawbacks. Fresh manure may burn tender roots, so it should be partially decomposed before it is used. Some manure, especially bagged steer manure, has a high salt content, and should be used in moderation if you already have salt problems or alkaline soil. (For more information about salt damage, see page 857.)

Ground bark and sawdust: Ground bark and sawdust are byproducts of the lumber industry. Unless they have been fortified with nitrogen (if they are purchased in bags it will say so on the bag) or are well composted, the bacteria that decompose them will rob the soil of nitrogen. To prevent a nitrogen deficiency, add ½ pound of nitrogen to every cubic yard of bark or sawdust. For example, 10 pounds of ORTHO Tomato & Vegetable Food or 6¼ pounds of ORTHO General Purpose Plant Food should be added to a cubic yard of bark or sawdust during tillage.

MULCHING

A mulch is an insulating layer of material that is spread over the ground. The most important types of mulches are:

Organic material: A wide variety of organic materials are used for mulching. Some of the most common are straw, leaves, lawn clippings, wood chips, shredded bark, and ground corncobs. All organic mulches conserve soil moisture and modify the soil temperature near the surface. As these materials decompose, they improve the tilth of the soil. Choose a mulching material that is free of weed seeds, and that has not been recently sprayed with an herbicide. Apply organic mulches 3 to 6 inches thick. A thick mulch also controls weeds.

Inorganic material: These materials do not decompose, so they are more permanent than organic mulches. Inorganic mulches include rocks, gravel, and coarse sand. These materials are more expensive but longer lasting than organic mulches. There is also less danger of bringing weed seeds or diseases into your garden.

Impervious films: The most popular impervious film mulch is black polyethylene. Clear plastic and builder's paper are also used. Black plastic gives excellent control of weeds. It can even be placed over existing weeds to kill them. Films also control water loss and warm the soil slightly. Clear plastic does not control weeds, but warms the soil quickly, and can even be used to pasteurize the soil with heat (see page 927). Because plastic films reduce the amount of oxygen that penetrates the soil, do not use them over large areas around trees and shrubs.

Soil fumigation with methyl bromide.

Fumigation with *VPM* (VAPAM®).

Pinching.

SOIL FUMIGATION

Soil fumigants kill all living matter present in the soil, including plants, weed seeds, nematodes, insects, and disease organisms. Soil fumigation is used to kill organisms for which there are no other controls. For best results, treat when the soil temperature is between 60° and 85°F. Do not use around desirable plants where the roots growing into the treated soil may be killed. The only soil fumigant available to home gardeners is *VPM* (VAPAM®), a liquid. More potent fumigants are available to commercial pest control operators, the most common of which is *methyl bromide.*

Using VPM (VAPAM®):
1. Till the soil 6 inches deep. Remove all debris larger than 2 inches.
2. Water thoroughly and let the soil sit for 1 to 3 days.
3. Divide the area to be treated into sections 5 feet by 10 feet (50 square feet).
4. Add 1 pint (2 cups) of VPM (VAPAM®) to a watering can full of water.
5. Sprinkle the solution on the first 50 square foot section. Water immediately.
6. Repeat the same procedure for each section.
7. When the entire area is treated, water with a sprinkler, applying 1 or 2 inches of water.
8. Break up the soil crust with a rake in 7 to 10 days. Otherwise, do not disturb the area for 2 to 3 weeks following the treatment.
9. After this time, loosen the soil with a rake. To be sure the fumigant has completely dissipated, test by planting some radish seeds. If the seeds germinate, then the soil is ready for planting. If they don't germinate, wait a week and plant again. Repeat this procedure until the seeds sprout.

Pasteurizing the soil with clear plastic:
This method of soil pasteurization has only recently been developed, and is still being tested, but initial results look promising for controlling fungus diseases. Shallow tree roots may be killed by soil pasteurization.
1. This method uses the heat of the sun to sterilize the soil. It must be applied during the hottest part of the summer.
2. Till and water the soil as described in steps 1 and 2 above.
3. Cover the soil with clear polyethylene, sealing the edges and all seams with soil.
4. Leave the plastic in place for 6 weeks. During this period, the heat of the sun will warm the surface of the soil to 120°F or more, enough to kill many disease organisms.

PINCHING

The technique of pinching plants is used to produce dense, stocky plants and more (but smaller) blossoms. When the growing tip of the stem is removed, the plant's energy is channeled into the side branches and buds, forcing them to grow. Although annuals, perennials, and houseplants are the plants most commonly pinched, woody ornamentals—especially azaleas and rhododendrons—may also be pinched. With your thumbnail and finger, gently squeeze the stem just above a set of leaves until it breaks. Most annuals and perennials are pinched when they are 2 to 4 inches tall, with several sets of leaves. Usually only the growing tip with one set of leaves is removed, but for tall, spindly plants up to a third of the height of the plant may be pinched. Herbaceous plants are usually pinched when they are transplanted into the garden, and any time throughout the season if they become leggy. Pinch off old flowers to encourage more blossoms. Pinch houseplants whenever they become leggy. Pinching woody ornamentals periodically will help save on pruning later. Pinch out the growing tip of any erratically growing branches when the tip is still tender, before it becomes woody. Pinching is also an easy way to harvest sprigs of herbs.

To find out more about an ORTHO product, locate the product in the index on the next page. This section is arranged into these broad categories:

A GALLERY OF ORTHO PRODUCTS

Each ORTHO product in this section solves a garden or household problem. Some of them, such as ORTHO Mole Cricket Bait, solve a very specific problem; others, such as ORTHO General Purpose Plant Food, are solutions to a wide range of plant problems.

This section presents information about each of these products as an aid to the reader in selecting a solution to a garden problem. Most of the problems discussed in this book have a number of possible solutions. Where several products have been offered as solutions to a problem, any of them may be chosen, depending on availability in your region.

Aside from some of the obvious considerations, such as whether you already have a bottle of one of the recommended products in your garage, there are a few major product differences to take into account when making your selection.

One difference is the way a product is formulated. For instance, a dust can be used right from the package without mixing or measuring, and may be applied with a dust applicator. Liquids or wettable powders must be mixed with water so that they can be applied. The choice depends on your preference.

Another consideration in choosing a product is the size of the job it is meant to do. ORTHO Weed-B-Gon Jet Weeder, for instance, is quick and convenient for spot-treating a few weeds in a lawn, but is not suitable for killing many weeds in a large lawn area. ORTHO Weed-B-Gon Lawn Weed Killer can be applied over the entire lawn and is more suitable for large jobs.

Perhaps the most important consideration, though, is the plant or the part of the garden on which a product is to be used. A product intended for use on trees and shrubs may not be registered for use in the vegetable garden, and a product intended for the vegetable garden may not be effective on lawn problems.

You should always read a product label twice: once when you buy it, to decide if it is the right product for the job you need done, and a second time before you use it, to get specific instructions for applying it. Always use chemical products exactly as the label directions say; these directions have been carefully worked out by the manufacturer (and approved by the government) to give you the maximum satisfaction from the use of the product.

Above: A sample of ORTHO products.
Left: It's easy with ORTHO sprayers.

INDEX TO ORTHO HOME AND GARDEN PRODUCTS

INDEX TO ORTHO BOOKS

FERTILIZERS

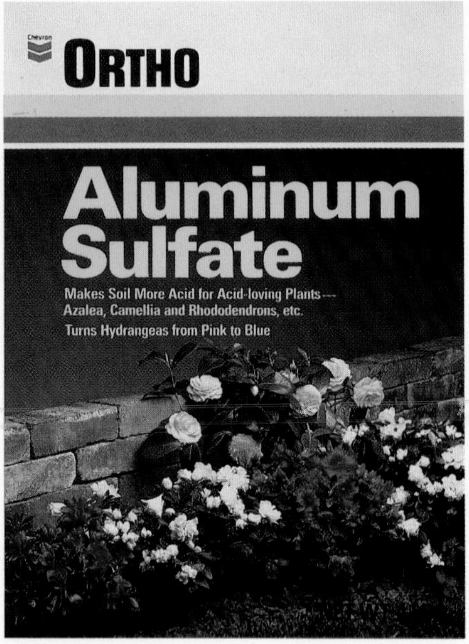

BENEFITS THESE PLANTS:
Azaleas
Camellias
Hydrangeas
Rhododendrons

FOR USE IN THESE AREAS:
Acid-loving plants

ALUMINUM SULFATE

GENERAL DESCRIPTION:
A granular soil amendment for making soils more acid. It is especially useful in changing the color of hydrangeas to a deep blue. It is beneficial to acid-loving plants (azaleas, camellias, gardenias, rhododendrons, hydrangeas, orchids, ixora, hibiscus, etc.) by helping to keep the soil acid.

AREAS SOLD:
National

GUARANTEED ANALYSIS:
100% Hydrated aluminum sulfate

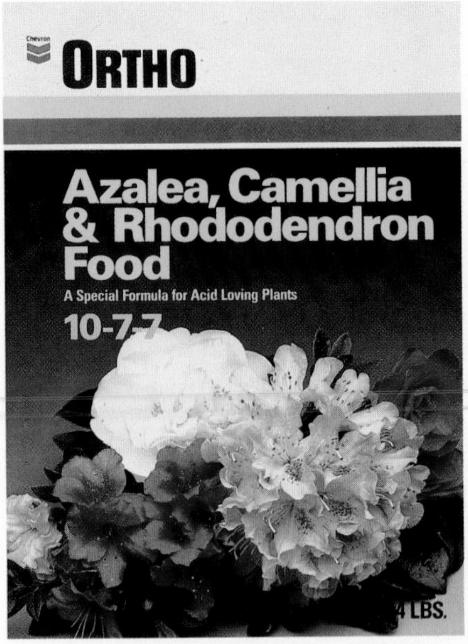

BENEFITS THESE PLANTS:
Aucuba
Azalea
Caladium
Calla Lilly
Camellia
Clevera
Columbine
Crape Myrtle
Croton
Cyclamen
Delphinium
Dogwood
Easter Lily
Fern
Fir
Gardenia
Heather
Hibiscus
Holly
Hydrangea
Ixora
Japanese Maple
Juniper
Laurel
Ligustrum
Magnolia
Mahonia
Pine
Pyracantha
Rhododendron
Spruce
Star Jasmine
Tuberous Begonia
Viburnum
White Cedar
Yew

FOR USE IN THESE AREAS:
Acid-loving plants

AZALEA, CAMELLIA & RHODODENDRON FOOD
(10–7–7)

GENERAL DESCRIPTION:
A granular fertilizer specially designed for acid-loving plants. It contains the 3 major plant nutrients—nitrogen, phosphate, and potash and sulfur—to provide a balanced food for acid-loving plants. The label lists over 35 acid-loving plants that respond well to this formula, along with rates of application for established plants and potted plants.

AREAS SOLD:
National

GUARANTEED ANALYSIS:
10% Nitrogen
7% Phosphate
7% Potash
3% Sulfur

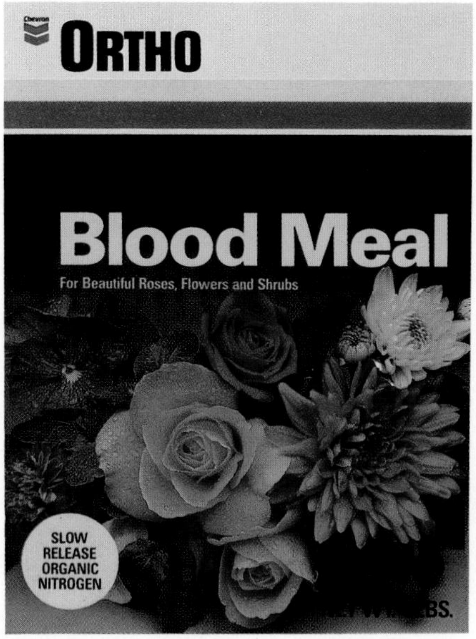

BENEFITS THESE PLANTS:
Bedding Plants
Flowers
Roses
Shrubs
Vegetables

FOR USE IN THESE AREAS:
Roses and flowers
Vegetables
Shrubs

BLOOD MEAL
(12–0–0)

GENERAL DESCRIPTION:
This granular fertilizer is a natural, organic source of long-lasting, slow-release nitrogen. Nitrogen is the most important element for vigorous plant growth and greenness. The fertilizer is easy to use as a supplement to a regular feeding program on flowers, vegetables, bedding plants, shrubs, and roses. For best results, scatter the recommended amount evenly on the soil surface, rake into the top 1 or 2 inches, and water thoroughly.

AREAS SOLD:
National

GUARANTEED ANALYSIS:
12% Nitrogen

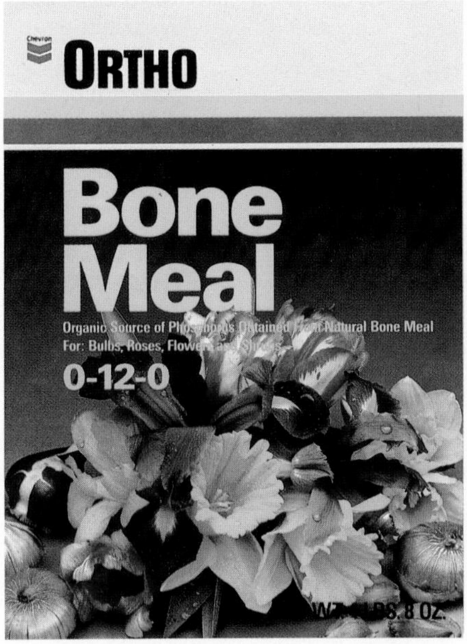

BENEFITS THESE PLANTS:
Bulbs
Container Plants
Flowers
Roses
Shrubs
Trees
Vegetables

FOR USE IN THESE AREAS:
Roses and flowers
Trees and shrubs
Bulbs and vegetables

BONE MEAL
(0–12–0)

GENERAL DESCRIPTION:
A granular phosphorus obtained from bone meal for use as a natural organic supplemental source of phosphorus, one of the important plant nutrients. Since phosphorus does not move much once placed in the soil, it is important to incorporate it into the soil to a depth of 6 to 8 inches. Bulbs respond especially well to bone meal placed in the bottom of the planting hole. Do not use ORTHO Bone Meal for acid-loving plants such as azaleas, rhododendrons, and blueberries.

AREAS SOLD:
National

GUARANTEED ANALYSIS:
12% Phosphate

CITRUS & AVOCADO FOOD
(14–7–10)

BENEFITS THESE PLANTS:
Avocados
Grapefruit
Lemons
Limes
Oranges
Other citrus trees
Tangerines

FOR USE IN THESE AREAS:
Citrus and avocados

GENERAL DESCRIPTION:
A granular fertilizer specially designed for citrus and avocados. It is clean and odorless, and contains the essential primary plant nutrients of nitrogen phosphate, and potash for good plant growth and fruit production. It also contains zinc, a trace element required by many soils for optimum plant growth.

AREAS SOLD:
South
West

GUARANTEED ANALYSIS:
14% Nitrogen
7% Phosphoric Acid
10% Potash
Traces of these nutrients:
Zinc

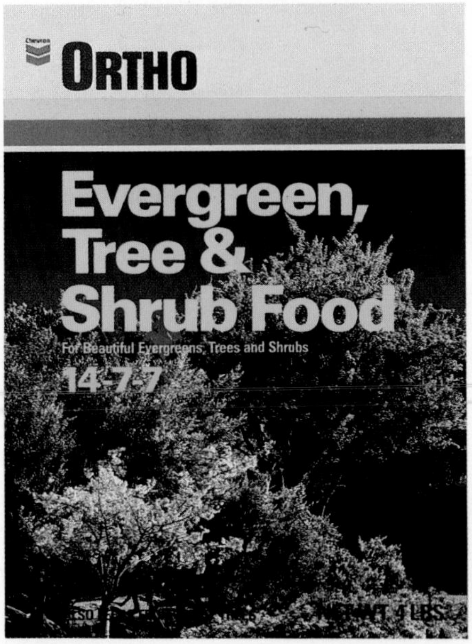

EVERGREEN, TREE & SHRUB FOOD
(14–7–7)

BENEFITS THESE PLANTS:
Arborvitae
Almond
Apple
Apricot
Ash
Beech
Birch
Cherry
Citrus
Elm
Euonymus
Fir
Hazelnut
Hickory
Juniper
Ligustrum
Maple
Mulberry
Oak
Palm
Peach
Pear
Pecan
Pine
Plum
Poplar
Spirea
Spruce
Sycamore
Walnut and many other trees and shrubs

FOR USE IN THESE AREAS:
Trees and shrubs

GENERAL DESCRIPTION:
A pelleted fertilizer made with a balance of nutrients to promote hardy, sturdy plants. It is formulated for use on evergreens, shrubs, shade trees, citrus, and fruit and nut trees. It supplies plants with the three major plant nutrients, nitrogen, phosphate, and potash. This fertilizer is clean, odorless, and easy to use on new plantings and established trees and shrubs. For best results, apply evenly beneath the outer ends of the branches and away from the trunk. Water thoroughly afterward to dissolve the pellets and carry the nutrients down into the root zone.

AREAS SOLD:
National

GUARANTEED ANALYSIS:
14% Nitrogen
7% Phosphoric acid
7% Potash

FERN & IVY FOOD 10-8-7

BENEFITS THESE PLANTS:
Ferns
Ivy

FOR USE IN THESE AREAS:
Fern and ivy houseplants

GENERAL DESCRIPTION:
A ready-to-use fertilizer solution specially formulated for ferns and ivy houseplants. It helps promote vigorous green growth and healthy root systems by supplying plants with the three major plant nutrients, nitrogen, phosphate, and potash, plus several minor elements. For easy, no-mess fertilization, simply add the recommended number of drops directly to the soil and then water in the usual way. Or dilute 1 capful in 1 quart of water and water plants with this solution.

AREAS SOLD:
National

GUARANTEED ANALYSIS:
10% Nitrogen
8% Phosphoric acid
7% Potash
Traces of these nutrients:
- Iron
- Manganese
- Zinc

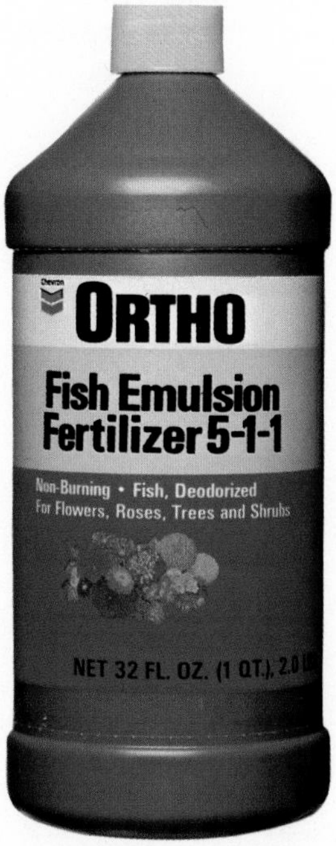

FISH EMULSION FERTILIZER (5-1-1)

BENEFITS THESE PLANTS:
African Violets
Azaleas
Beans
Berries
Cabbage
Camellias
Carrots
Ferns
Fuchsias
Lettuce
Orchids
Peas
Philodendrons
Rhododendrons
Roses
Tuberous Begonias
and many other plants

FOR USE IN THESE AREAS:
Fruits and vegetables
Roses and flowers
Trees and shrubs
Houseplants

GENERAL DESCRIPTION:
A liquid organic fertilizer made entirely of seagoing fish and designed for general indoor and outdoor use. It is absorbed by plants through their roots and leaves. When used as directed, it is nonburning. It promotes overall strong, healthy growth by supplying plants with the three major plant nutrients, nitrogen, phosphate, and potash. Because it does not burn, it is a very popular houseplant fertilizer. The label gives detailed dilution directions for use on various plants.

AREAS SOLD:
National

GUARANTEED ANALYSIS:
5% Nitrogen
1% Phosphoric acid
1% Potash

FERTILIZERS

BENEFITS THESE PLANTS:
Acid-loving Plants
Azaleas
Camellias
Flowers
Fruit Trees
Rhododendrons
Shade Trees
Shrubs
Vegetables

FOR USE IN THESE AREAS:
Trees and shrubs
Fruits and vegetables
Flowers
Container plants

FRUIT & BLOOM BUILDER (0-10-10)

GENERAL DESCRIPTION:
A liquid fertilizer specially formulated to increase the size, color, and quality of fruit, strengthen the branches of fruit and shade trees, and promote beautiful blossoms on annual and perennial flowers, flowering shrubs and trees, azaleas, camellias, rhododendrons, and other acid-loving plants, potted or container-grown flowering plants, and fruits and vegetables. It contains equal amounts of phosphate and potash and should be used before the plant's blooming period when a flush of foliar growth is not desired. It mixes readily with water to be applied with a sprinkling can or an ORTHO hose-end sprayer.

AREAS SOLD:
South
West

GUARANTEED ANALYSIS:
10% Phosphoric Acid
10% Potash

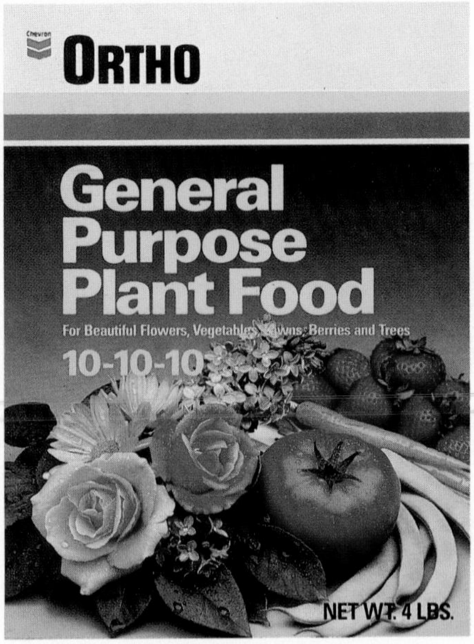

BENEFITS THESE PLANTS:
Bush Berries
Evergreens
Flowers
Lawns
Roses
Shrubs
Strawberries
Trees
Vegetables

FOR USE IN THESE AREAS:
Fruits and vegetables
Trees and shrubs
Roses and flowers
Lawns

GENERAL PURPOSE PLANT FOOD (10-10-10)

GENERAL DESCRIPTION:
A pelleted fertilizer designed for use on listed flowers, roses, shrubs, trees, and lawns. It is clean, odorless, and easy to use on new plantings as well as on established plants. It supplies equal amounts of the three major plant nutrients, nitrogen, phosphate, and potash. It helps promote strong healthy growth with abundant flowering and high fruit yields. For best results, water immediately after application to dissolve the pellets and carry the nutrients down into the root zone. Detailed instructions on fertilization timing and amount for each area of the garden are included on the box.

AREAS SOLD:
National

GUARANTEED ANALYSIS:
10% Nitrogen
10% Phosphoric acid
10% Potash

GREENOL® LIQUID IRON 6.13%

GENERAL DESCRIPTION:
A liquid concentrate containing the specific trace elements necessary to correct iron deficiency and to produce vigorous, green growth of lawns, flowers, and ornamentals. It is a supplemental fertilizer, and should be used in conjunction with a regular fertilization program. Dilute the concentrate according to the label directions and apply to either the soil or the foliage. Water thoroughly following soil treatments. To treat lawns, use an ORTHO Lawn Sprayer, diluting so that 32 ounces of concentrate treats 1,000 square feet of turf.

AREAS SOLD:
National

GUARANTEED ANALYSIS:
3.64% Sulfur
0.13% Copper
6.13% Iron
0.10% Zinc

BENEFITS THESE PLANTS:
Azalea
Camellia
Carnation
Chrysanthemum
Gardenia
Gladiolus
Golf Course Greens
Hibiscus
Holly
Ixora
Lawns
Ligustrum
Petunia
Rhododendron
Rose
Snapdragon
Turf and other annuals, perennials, and shrubs

FOR USE IN THESE AREAS:
Flowers and shrubs
Lawns
Ornamentals

HOUSE PLANT FOOD (5–10–5)

GENERAL DESCRIPTION:
A liquid fertilizer designed for all houseplants to promote overall strong, healthy growth. It provides plants with the three major plant nutrients, nitrogen, phosphate, and potash plus numerous minor elements. For quick, no-mess weekly fertilizing, just add the required number of drops directly to the soil. Then immediately water the plant in the usual way. Or dilute 1 capful in 1 quart of water and fertilize every 2 weeks. Water immediately afterward. Slow-growing plants need less frequent feeding.

AREAS SOLD:
National

GUARANTEED ANALYSIS:
5% Nitrogen
10% Phosphoric acid
5% Potash
Traces of these nutrients:
- Iron
- Manganese
- Zinc

BENEFITS THESE PLANTS:
All Houseplants

FOR USE IN THESE AREAS:
Houseplants

FERTILIZERS

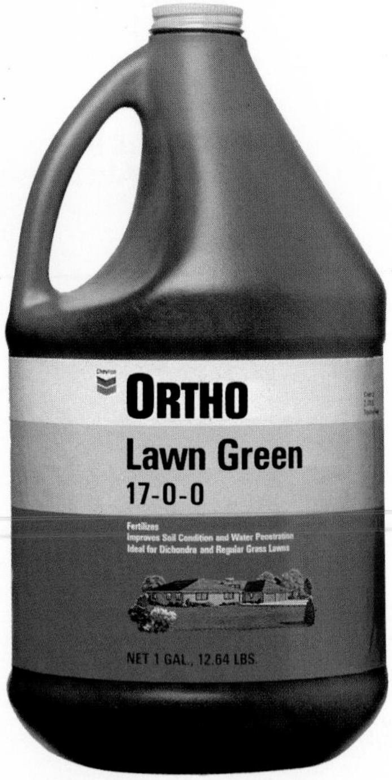

BENEFITS THESE PLANTS:
Dichondra Lawns
Grass Lawns

FOR USE IN THESE AREAS:
Lawns

LAWN GREEN 17–0–0

GENERAL DESCRIPTION:
A liquid lawn fertilizer designed for use on both grass and dichondra lawns. It fertilizes with two forms of nitrogen to promote greenness and rapid growth. It also contains soluble calcium for the improvement of soil tilth, increased water penetration, more efficient water utilization, and plant growth. One gallon of this fertilizer dilutes readily in water to cover 2,000 square feet of lawn. The label contains detailed instructions for applying with an ORTHO Lawn Sprayer or other applicator. For a quicker response, water heavily afterward to wash the spray off the grass and into the soil.

AREAS SOLD:
West

GUARANTEED ANALYSIS:
17% Nitrogen
Traces of this nutrient:
Calcium

POLISHES THESE PLANTS:
Anthuriums
Dieffenbachias
Gardenias
Ivy
Philodendrons
Pothos
Rubber Plants
Snake Plants
And all other houseplants with hard-surfaced leaves

FOR USE IN THESE AREAS:
Houseplants

LEAF POLISH (AEROSOL)

GENERAL DESCRIPTION:
An easy-to-use aerosol spray that forms a lasting dust-resistant natural glow on all houseplants with hard-surfaced leaves, including philodendrons, pothos, and dieffenbachias. Clean all leaves with a damp clean cloth before using this spray. When the leaves dry, hold the can 10 to 12 inches away from the plant and evenly spray the leaves. Protect furniture and floors from the spray with newspaper or cloth. The spray dries in 5 to 10 minutes. For a higher gloss, gently rub the leaves after the spray dries. Do not apply to succulents.

AREAS SOLD:
National

LEAF POLISH (PUMP)

GENERAL DESCRIPTION:
A liquid designed to give hard-surfaced leaves a lasting natural glow. When used as directed, it will not injure plants. The hand pump makes application quick and easy. Before using, wipe dusty leaves clean with a damp cloth, and dry. Direct the nozzle at the leaves and gently pump, covering the leaves evenly. Protect furniture and floors from the spray with newspaper or cloth. Do not use on succulents such as jade plants, or on plants with soft or hairy foliage. Do not apply more often than every 3 to 4 weeks.

AREAS SOLD:
National

POLISHES THESE PLANTS:
Dieffenbachias
Gardenias
Ivy
Philodendrons
Rubber Plants
Scheffleras
Wax Plants
And all other houseplants with hard-surfaced leaves

FOR USE IN THESE AREAS:
Houseplants

LIQUID AFRICAN VIOLET FOOD (6–9–5)

GENERAL DESCRIPTION:
A liquid fertilizer designed for growing African violets. It helps promote vigorous green growth and numerous full-size blossoms by supplying plants with the three major plant nutrients, nitrogen, phosphate, and potash, plus several minor elements. For easy, no-mess fertilization, simply add the recommended number of drops directly to the soil and then water in the usual way. Or dilute 1 capful in 1 quart of water and water plants with this solution.

AREAS SOLD:
National

GUARANTEED ANALYSIS:
6% Nitrogen
9% Phosphoric acid
5% Potash
Traces of these nutrients:
Manganese
Zinc

BENEFITS THESE PLANTS:
African Violets

FOR USE IN THESE AREAS:
African Violets

FERTILIZERS

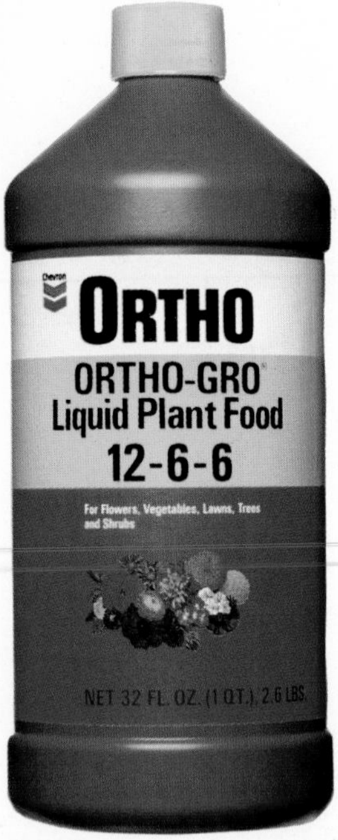

ORTHO-GRO® LIQUID PLANT FOOD (12–6–6)

GENERAL DESCRIPTION:
A liquid fertilizer formulated for general garden use. As a liquid, it is readily available to the roots and foliage. This fertilizer dilutes readily in water and is easy to use on established plants and also when transplanting. It promotes vigorous overall growth by supplying plants with the three major plant nutrients, nitrogen, phosphate, and potash, plus several minor elements. For fertilizing flowers, vegetables, and shrubs, dilute the concentrate in a bucket or sprinkling can and apply from 1 quart to 1 gallon of liquid to the foliage and soil, depending on the size of the plant. For fertilizing houseplants, apply the diluted material to the soil or in the trays when watering.

AREAS SOLD:
National

GUARANTEED ANALYSIS:
12% Nitrogen
6% Phosphoric acid
6% Potash
Traces of these nutrients:
Iron
Zinc

BENEFITS THESE PLANTS:
African Violets
Azaleas
Beans
Berries
Camellias
Carrots
Fuchsias
Lawns
Peas
Philodendrons
Primroses
Radishes
Roses
Tomatoes
Trees
Tuberous Begonias
Other flowers and vegetables
Other houseplants and potted plants

FOR USE IN THESE AREAS:
Houseplants
Lawns and flowers
Trees and shrubs
Vegetables and berries

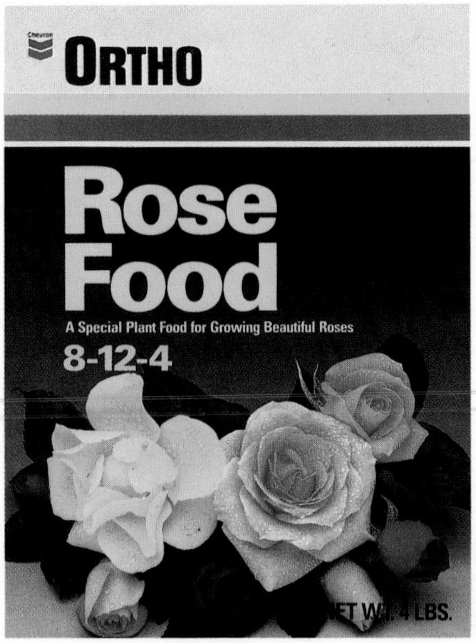

ROSE FOOD (8–12–4)

GENERAL DESCRIPTION:
A granular plant food specially formulated for roses. It is clean, odorless, and easy to apply. The formula provides nitrogen, phosphate, and potash. These plant nutrients help produce healthy, productive plants with beautiful blooms. The label contains complete directions for using this fertilizer on new plantings and on established plants.

AREAS SOLD:
National

GUARANTEED ANALYSIS:
8% Nitrogen
12% Phosphoric acid
4% Potash

BENEFITS THESE PLANTS:
Roses

FOR USE IN THESE AREAS:
Roses

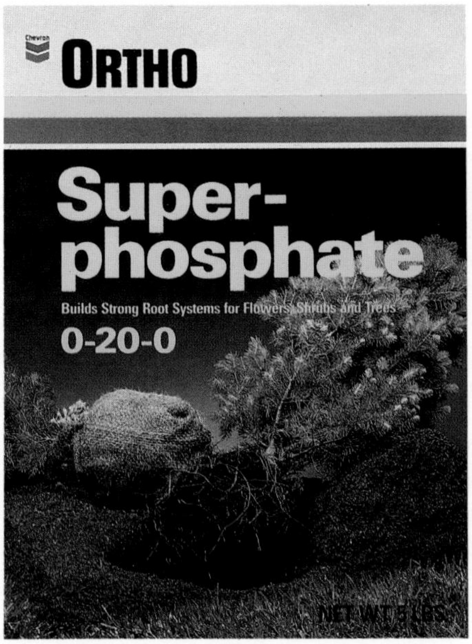

BENEFITS THESE PLANTS:
Bulbs
Flowers
Roses
Shrubs
Vegetables

FOR USE IN THESE AREAS:
Vegetables and flowers
Roses and shrubs
Compost piles

SUPERPHOSPHATE (0–20–0)

GENERAL DESCRIPTION:
This granular fertilizer is a rich source of phosphorus. Phosphorus is one of the three primary plant nutrients, and is used by plants to build sturdy root systems, to develop new tissues, and to aid in the formation of blooms and fruit. Since phosphorus moves very little in the soil, it is necessary to place it where the roots can obtain a good supply. Superphosphate is often used as a supplement to a regular fertilizer program where additional phosphorus is needed. In the home garden use Superphosphate when planting vegetables, shrubs, bulbs, roses, and other flowers. It can also be used around established roses and shrubs if carefully worked into the soil. Also add this material to compost piles to improve their phosphorus content.

AREAS SOLD:
National

GUARANTEED ANALYSIS:
20% Phosphoric acid

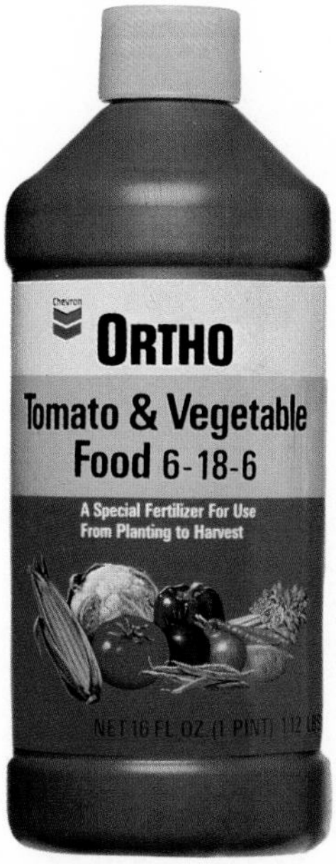

BENEFITS THESE PLANTS:
Asparagus
Beans
Beets
Broccoli
Brussels Sprouts
Cabbage
Carrots
Cauliflower
Celery
Corn
Cucumbers
Eggplant
Endive
Lettuce
Melons
Onions
Peas
Peppers
Potatoes
Pumpkins
Radishes
Spinach
Squash
Strawberries
Swiss Chard
Tomatoes
Turnips

FOR USE IN THESE AREAS:
Vegetables

TOMATO & VEGETABLE FOOD 6–18–6

GENERAL DESCRIPTION:
A liquid fertilizer specially formulated for use on tomatoes and other vegetables including carrots, eggplants, peas, and strawberries. It promotes healthy green growth, abundant flowering, and high yields by supplying the three major plant nutrients, nitrogen, phosphate, and potash. It mixes readily with water and is easy to use when transplanting and seeding, and to maintain healthy plants. It can also be used on container vegetable plants. The label lists dilution rates for foliar and soil feedings. For best results, apply this fertilizer with an ORTHO hose-end sprayer.

AREAS SOLD:
National

GUARANTEED ANALYSIS:
6% Nitrogen
18% Phosphoric acid
6% Potash

FERTILIZERS

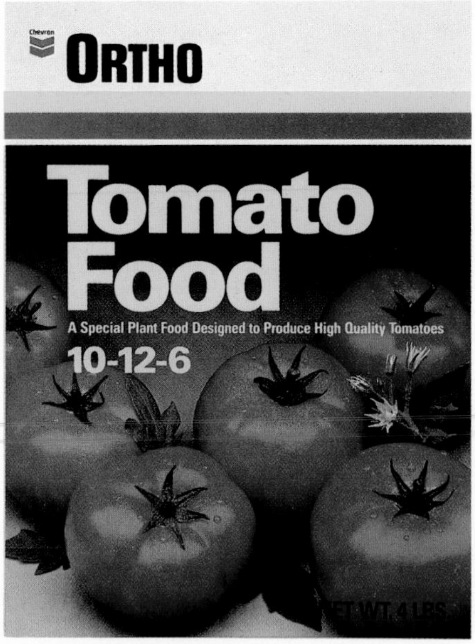

TOMATO FOOD
(10–12–6)

BENEFITS THESE PLANTS:
Beans
Beets
Broccoli
Cabbage
Carrots
Cauliflower
Collards
Corn
Cucumbers
Eggplant
Lettuce
Onions
Peas
Peppers
Radishes
Spinach
Squash
Tomatoes
Turnips and other vegetables

FOR USE IN THESE AREAS:
Tomatoes and other vegetables

GENERAL DESCRIPTION:
A granular fertilizer specially formulated for use on tomatoes. It is designed to produce sturdy plants with many top-quality tomatoes. This product can also be used on other vegetable crops. It supplies plants with the nutrients they need most, nitrogen, phosphate, and potash. It can be worked into the soil before planting, and also used later to side-dress plantings.

AREAS SOLD:
National

GUARANTEED ANALYSIS:
10% Nitrogen
12% Phosphoric acid
6% Potash

UP-START® PLANT STARTER
(5–15–5)

BENEFITS THESE PLANTS:
Bedding plants
Berries
Container plants
Fruit and nut trees
New lawn plantings
Roses
Shade trees
Shrubs
Vegetables

FOR USE IN THESE AREAS:
Fruits and vegetables
Lawns
Roses and flowers
Trees and shrubs

GENERAL DESCRIPTION:
This granular fertilizer is a clean, odorless, easy-to-use plant food especially formulated for use at planting to aid in early root formation and get plants off to a good start. This product can be used when planting vegetable and flower seeds or seedlings, when transplanting bedding plants, shrubs, or trees, or when planting in containers. It supplies plants with nitrogen, phosphate, and potash, essential nutrients for plant growth.

AREAS SOLD:
National

GUARANTEED ANALYSIS:
5% Nitrogen
15% Phosphoric Acid
5% Potash

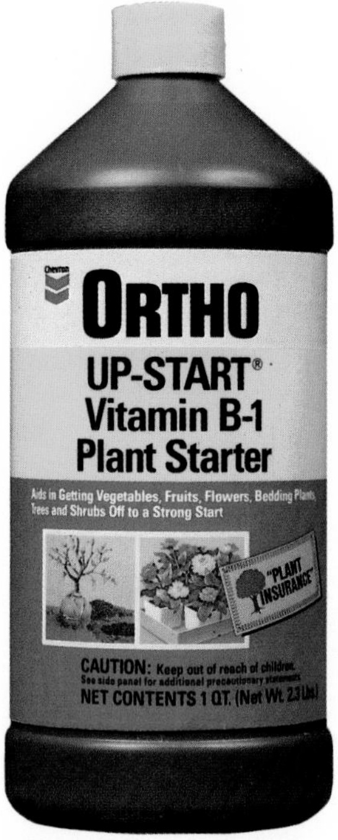

UP-START® VITAMIN B-1 PLANT STARTER

(3–10–3)

GENERAL DESCRIPTION:
This liquid starter solution is a combination of a fertilizer and a hormonelike root stimulator. When it is diluted with water, this solution stimulates early root formation and stronger root development. It also reduces transplant shock and promotes a greener, more vigorous plant. Simply pour the diluted solution into the planting hole and over the soil as the roots are being covered. It supplies plants with the three major nutrients, nitrogen, phosphate, and potash.

AREAS SOLD:
National

GUARANTEED ANALYSIS:
3% Nitrogen
10% Phosphoric acid
3% Potash
Vitamin B-1 (0.01%)

BENEFITS THESE PLANTS:
Azaleas
Bedding Plants
Camellias
Flowers
Fruit Trees
Gardenias
Hibiscus
Holly
Large Ornamentals
Roses
Shade Trees
Vegetables

FOR USE IN THESE AREAS:
Bedding Plants
Fruits and vegetables
Roses and flowers
Trees and shrubs

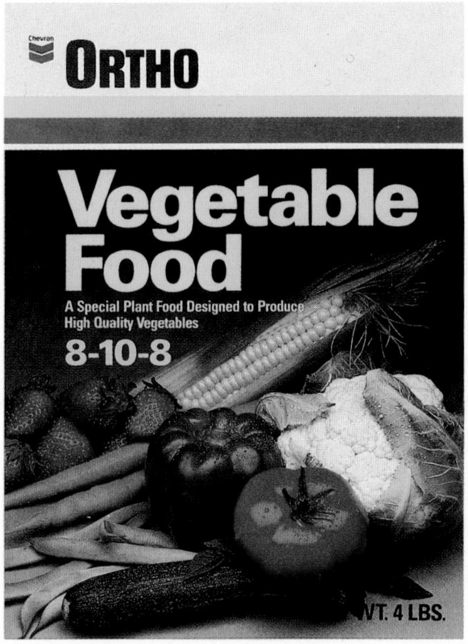

VEGETABLE FOOD

(8–10–8)

GENERAL DESCRIPTION:
A granular fertilizer specially formulated for vegetables and strawberries. It is designed to produce sturdy plants with vigorous root systems, healthy green leaves, abundant flowers, and high-quality produce. It is clean and easy to use. Work it into the soil at planting time and also use it later in the season to side-dress plantings. Around established plants, water thoroughly after applying to dissolve the pellets and wash the nutrients down into the root zone. This fertilizer provides vegetable plants with the three major plant nutrients, nitrogen, phosphate, and potash.

AREAS SOLD:
National

GUARANTEED ANALYSIS:
8% Nitrogen
10% Phosphoric acid
8% Potash

BENEFITS THESE PLANTS:
Asparagus
Beans
Beets
Broccoli
Brussels Sprouts
Cabbage
Carrots
Cauliflower
Celery
Corn
Cucumbers
Eggplant
Endive
Melons
Onions
Peas
Peppers
Potatoes
Pumpkins
Radishes
Spinach
Squash
Swiss Chard
Tomatoes
Turnips
Strawberries

FOR USE IN THESE AREAS:
Vegetables

FERTILIZERS

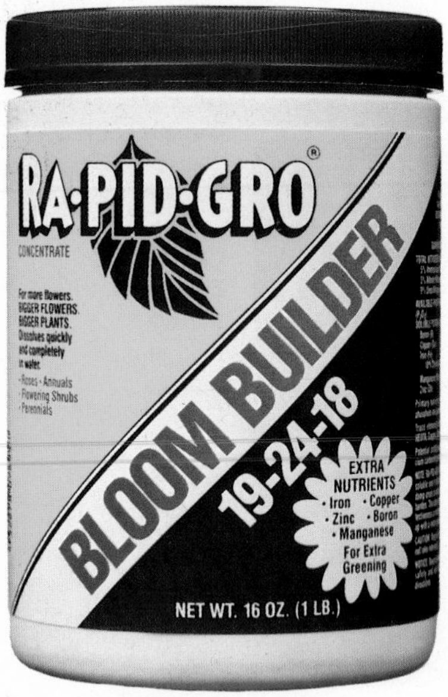

BENEFITS THESE PLANTS:

Bulbs
Container plants and hanging baskets
Flowers
Flowering evergreens and shrubs
Transplanting-Balled and Burlapped, Bare Root Bedding Plants, Container Stock

FOR USE IN THESE AREAS:

Flowers and shrubs
Transplanting and bulbs

RA-PID-GRO® BLOOM BUILDER (19–24–18)

GENERAL DESCRIPTION:
This water-soluble fertilizer is especially formulated to promote beautiful blossoms on flowering shrubs, annual and perennial flowers, roses and container grown flowering plants. It contains the three major plant nutrients, nitrogen, phosphate, and potash as well as the essential trace elements, iron, copper, zinc, boron, and manganese. Apply the fertilizer solution to small areas with a sprinkling can. Large areas can be fed quickly and easily with a hose-end sprayer. The label contains complete dilution and application directions.

AREAS SOLD:
Midwest

GUARANTEED ANALYSIS:
19% Nitrogen
5% Ammoniacal Nitrogen
5% Nitrate Nitrogen
9% Urea Nitrogen
24% Phosphoric Acid
18% Potash
.02% Boron
.05% Copper
.10% Iron
.05% Manganese
.05% Zinc

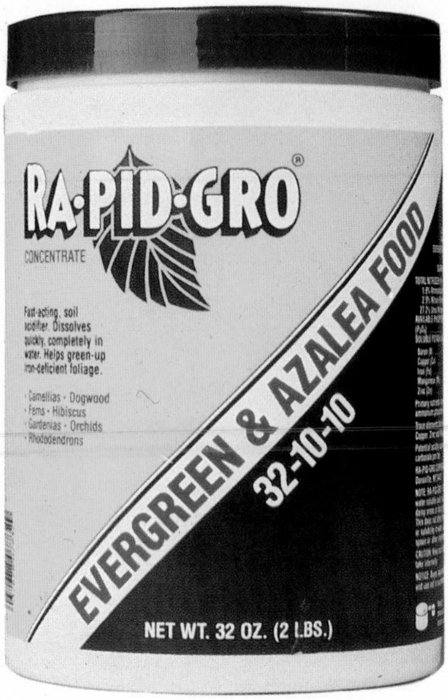

BENEFITS THESE PLANTS:

Arborvitae
Azalea
Camellia
Dogwood
Douglas Fir
Euonymus
Ferns
Gardenia
Hawthorn
Hemlock
Hibiscus
Holly
Hydrangea
Juniper
Larch
Laurel
Ligustrum
Magnolia
Mountain Ash
Oak
Orchid
Pine
Privet
Pyracantha
Rhododendron
Spirea
Spruce
Taxus
Other acid-loving trees and shrubs

FOR USE IN THESE AREAS:

Ferns
Flowers
Trees and shrubs

RA-PID-GRO® EVERGREEN AND AZALEA FOOD (32–10–10)

GENERAL DESCRIPTION:
This water-soluble fertilizer is formulated for use on evergreens, rhododendrons, azaleas, and other acid-loving plants. It acidifies the soil, provides the primary plant nutrients, nitrogen, phosphate, and potash, and contains the important micronutrients, iron, copper, zinc, manganese, and boron. This product dissolves quickly in water to form a solution that is readily absorbed by plants. The label contains directions for applying and diluting this fertilizer.

AREAS SOLD:
National

GUARANTEED ANALYSIS:
32% Nitrogen
1.9% Ammoniacal Nitrogen
2.9% Nitrate Nitrogen
27.2% Urea Nitrogen
10% Phosphoric Acid
10% Potash
.02% Boron
.05% Copper
.10% Iron
.05% Manganese
.05% Zinc

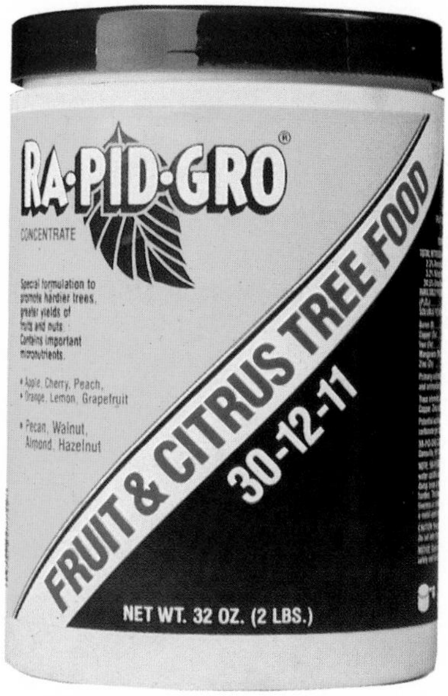

RA-PID-GRO®
FRUIT & CITRUS TREE FOOD
(30–12–11)

GENERAL DESCRIPTION:
This water-soluble fertilizer is specifically designed for fruit and nut trees, citrus, and berries. It contains nitrogen, phosphate, and potash as well as important micronutrients. It does not need to be worked into the soil like dry fertilizers; the water in the solution carries the nutrients down to the roots naturally. Not only roots, but also the leaves, stems, and buds of many plants can absorb the fertilizer solution. The label contains complete directions for application timing and dilutions rates.

AREAS SOLD:
South, West

GUARANTEED ANALYSIS:
30% Nitrogen
- 2.3% Ammoniacal Nitrogen
- 3.2% Nitrate Nitrogen
- 24.5% Urea Nitrogen

12% Phosphoric Acid
11% Potash
.02% Boron
.05% Copper
.10% Iron
.05% Manganese
.05% Zinc

BENEFITS THESE PLANTS:
Almond
Apple
Cherry
Grapefruit
Hazelnut
Lemon
Orange
Peach
Pecan
Walnut

FOR USE IN THESE AREAS:
Berries
Fruit and nut trees

RA-PID-GRO®
HOUSE PLANT FOOD
(23–19–17)

GENERAL DESCRIPTION:
This water-soluble fertilizer is designed for use on all houseplants, and may be used on patio plants, hanging baskets, roses, and flowers as well. Feed plants every 2 weeks or as often as plants require watering. This fertilizer dissolves quickly and completely in water and is readily absorbed by plant roots, leaves, stems, and buds. To fertilize, pour the solution around the base of the plant, or spray or mist the leaves of all but "fuzzy" leafed houseplants. The label contains complete directions for proper dilution rates.

AREAS SOLD:
National

GUARANTEED ANALYSIS:
23% Nitrogen
- 4% Ammoniacal Nitrogen
- 5% Nitrate Nitrogen
- 14% Urea Nitrogen

19% Phosphoric Acid
17% Potash

BENEFITS THESE PLANTS:
Flowers
Houseplants
Roses

FOR USE IN THESE AREAS:
Container plants and hanging baskets
Houseplants
Roses and flowers

FERTILIZERS | **PEST AND DISEASE CONTROL PRODUCTS**

BENEFITS THESE PLANTS:
Bedding Plants
Berries
Bulbs
Evergreens
Flowers
Fruit Trees
Houseplants
Lawns
Roses
Shade Trees
Shrubs
Tomatoes
Vegetables

FOR USE IN THESE AREAS:
Roses and flowers
Fruits and vegetables
Trees and shrubs
Lawns
Houseplants

RA-PID-GRO® PLANT FOOD (23–19–17)

GENERAL DESCRIPTION:
This water-soluble fertilizer is designed for use on a wide variety of plants including shrubs, vegetables, and flowers. The RA-PID-GRO® method of regular, continuing applications gives plants a steady, even supply of nutrients for uniform growth. Because it is soluble in water, it is readily available to the plant through the roots, leaves, stems, and buds. Fertilize small areas and individual plants with a sprinkling can. Large areas can be fed quickly and easily with a hose-end sprayer. Combine the fertilizer with insecticides and fungicides to help strengthen pest-damaged plants as you kill the pests. The label contains complete directions for diluting and applying this fertilizer.

AREAS SOLD:
National

GUARANTEED ANALYSIS:
23% Nitrogen
19% Phosphoric acid
17% Potash

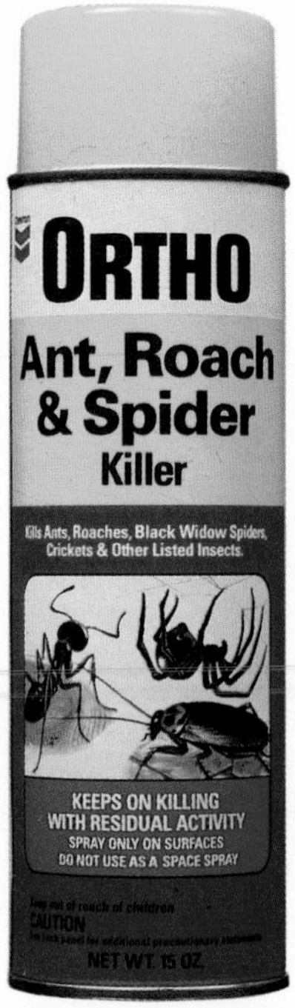

KILLS THESE INSECTS:
Ants
Brown Dog Ticks
Crickets
Earwigs
Roaches
Silverfish
Sowbugs
Spiders

FOR USE IN THESE AREAS:
Indoors
Outdoors
Not for use on plants

ANT, ROACH & SPIDER KILLER

GENERAL DESCRIPTION:
An aerosol that gives rapid contact kill of crawling pests as listed, including those resistant to certain chlorinated hydrocarbon and phosphate insecticides. In addition to rapid initial kill, it also provides residual insect killing power after the spray deposit has dried.

AREAS SOLD:
National

ACTIVE INGREDIENT:
1% Propoxur (BAYGON®) *2-(1-Methylethoxy)phenyl methylcarbamate*

HINTS FOR USE:
To enhance performance, use this spray in conjunction with an ORTHO Hi-Power Indoor Insect Fogger. The fogger flushes the insects out of hiding into the treated area.

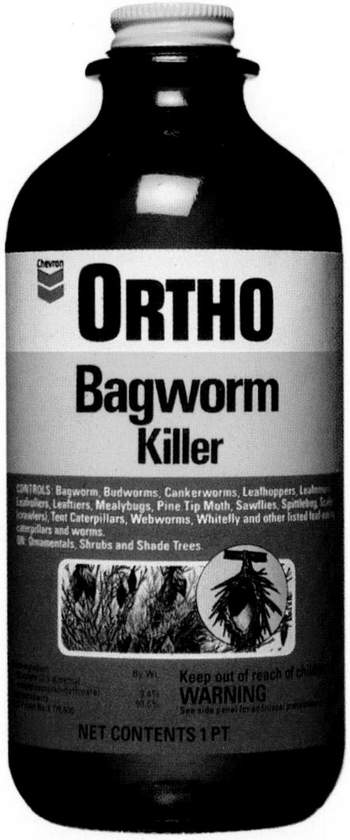

BAGWORM KILLER

GENERAL DESCRIPTION:
A liquid concentrate contains ORTHENE® insecticide and is designed to control bagworms, tent caterpillars, webworms, sawflies, and other listed leaf-eating insects that damage ornamentals, shrubs, and shade trees. It dilutes readily with water to be applied with an ORTHO SPRAY-ETTE®, hose-end sprayer, tank-type, or power sprayer. Spray when insects are present or feeding injury is first noticed.

AREAS SOLD:
Midwest
South

GUARANTEED ANALYSIS:
9.4% Acephate (ORTHENE®)
(0,5-dimtheyl acetylphosphoroamidothioate)

KILLS THESE INSECTS:
Bagworm
Budworms
Elm Leafbeetle
Fall Cankerworm
Fall Webworm
Hornworm
Lace Bugs
Leafhoppers
Leafminers
Obliquebanded Leafrollers
Omnivorous Leaftier
Maple Shoot Moth
Mealybugs
Mimosa Webworm
Nantucket Pine Tip Moth
Oak Webworm
Orange-striped Oakworm
Poplar Tentmaker
Sawflies
Scales
Spittlebug
Tent Caterpillars
Willow Leafbeetle
White-marked Tussock Moth
Whiteflies
Yellow-necked Caterpillar

FOR USE IN THESE AREAS:
Ornamentals, shrubs and shade trees

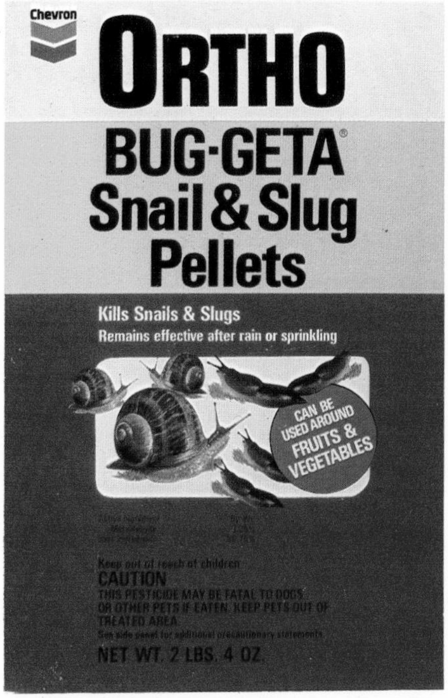

BUG-GETA® SNAIL & SLUG PELLETS

GENERAL DESCRIPTION:
A pellet bait specially formulated to attract and kill snails and slugs. The highly compressed pellets are easy to use, clean to handle, and economical. Two pounds of pellets will bait approximately 2,000 square feet. The presence of snails and slugs can be detected by their shiny mucouslike trail. They are night feeders and prefer damp, cool places. Do not apply the bait to the foliage or place in piles, but scatter the bait to the foliage or place in piles, but scatter pellets on the soil surface around plants. Repeated treatments every 2 weeks are usually sufficient to protect plants. This bait can be used around fruit and vegetable plantings.

AREAS SOLD:
National

ACTIVE INGREDIENT:
3.25% Metaldehyde

HINTS FOR USE:
To encourage snail and slug movement and feeding, sprinkle the soil lightly after application.

KILLS THESE PESTS:
Snails
Slugs

FOR USE ON THESE PLANTS:
Fruits:
Apples
Avocados
Blackberries
Cherries
Citrus
Grapes
Melons
Peaches
Plums
Strawberries

Vegetables:
Asparagus
Beans
Beets
Cabbage
Carrots
Corn
Cucumbers
Eggplant
Lettuce
Onions
Peas
Peppers
Potatoes
Radishes
Spinach
Squash
Tomatoes
Turnips

FOR USE IN THESE AREAS:
Fruits and vegetables
Greenhouse and lath Houses

PEST AND DISEASE CONTROL PRODUCTS

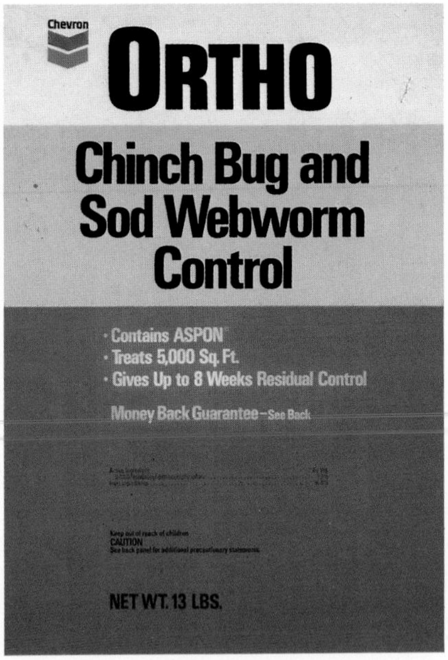

KILLS THESE INSECTS:
Chinch Bugs
Sod Webworms

FOR USE IN THESE AREAS:
Lawns

CHINCH BUG & SOD WEBWORM CONTROL

GENERAL DESCRIPTION:
This granular material controls chinch bugs and sod webworms for up to 8 weeks, and can be applied with a fertilizer drop spreader. St. Augustine and zoysia lawns in particular are often attacked by chinch bugs. As a preventive treatment, apply every 2 months starting in early summer. The entire lawn should be treated if either of these pests is found.

AREAS SOLD:
Midwest
Northeast
South

ACTIVE INGREDIENT:
3.2% *0,0,0,0-Tetrapropyl dithiopyrophosphate* (ASPON®)

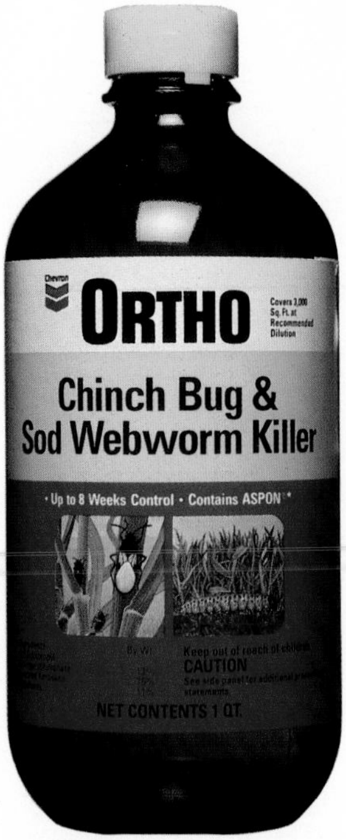

KILLS THESE INSECTS:
Chinch Bugs
Sod Webworms

FOR USE IN THESE AREAS:
Lawns

CHINCH BUG & SOD WEBWORM KILLER

GENERAL DESCRIPTION:
This liquid concentrate contains ASPON® insecticide and controls chinch bugs and sod webworms (lawn moth larvae) for up to 8 weeks. It mixes readily with water and may be applied with an ORTHO Lawn Sprayer, or tank-type sprayer. When diluted, one quart treats up to 3,000 spuare feet of lawn. St. Augustine and zoysia lawns in particular are often attacked by chinch bugs. The entire lawn should be treated if either of these insects is found.

AREAS SOLD:
National

GUARANTEED ANALYSIS:
13% *0,0,0,0-Tetrapropyl dithiopyrophosphate* (ASPON®)
76% Deodorized Kerosene

ASPON® is a registered trademark of Stauffer Chemical Co.

CITRUS INSECT SPRAY

KILLS THESE INSECTS:
Aphids
Black Scales
Chaff Scales
Citrus Red Mites
Citrus Rust Mites
Florida Red Scales
Glover Scales
Purple Scales
Snow Scales
Texas Citrus Mites
Yellow Scales
Whiteflies

FOR USE IN THESE AREAS:
Citrus

GENERAL DESCRIPTION:
A liquid concentrate containing *ethion*—a proven and widely recommended organic phosphate insecticide—and petroleum oil for excellent control of scales, mites, aphids, and whiteflies on oranges, grapefruit, tangerines, tangelos, lemons, and limes. This product helps protects citrus plantings with only one or two sprayings per season. Apply with an ORTHO SPRAY-ETTE® for good coverage of all foliage and branches wherever these insects are found. In addition to controlling insects and mites, this product improves the appearance of the plant by giving a bright, shiny finish to the leaves, and helps eliminate the sooty mold fungus that grows on the honeydew excreted by the insects listed above.

AREAS SOLD:
South

ACTIVE INGREDIENT:
10% Ethion *0,0,0′,0′-Tetraethyl S,S′-methylene bisphosphorodithioate*
75% Petrolium oil

DIAZINON GRANULES

KILLS THESE INSECTS:
Ants
Armyworms
Bermuda Mites
Billbugs
Brown Dog Ticks
Chinch bugs
Clover Mites
Crickets
Cutworms
Digger Wasps
Earwigs
Fleas
Leafhoppers
Millipedes
Sod Webworms (Lawn Moths)
Sowbugs
Springtails (Collembola)
Ticks
White Grubs

FOR USE IN THESE AREAS:
Lawns
Building foundations

GENERAL DESCRIPTION:
These granules kill home-invading pests including ticks, ants, crickets, fleas, and sowbugs. Apply the granules to individual nesting areas, or in a band around the house. The granules also control sod webworms, Bermuda mites, grubs, and other lawn pests in both grasses and dichondra lawns. They can be easily sprinkled directly from the canister without any additional equipment. One canister treats an area of up to 200 square feet.

AREAS SOLD:
National

ACTIVE INGREDIENT:
2% Diazinon *0,0-Diethyl 0-(2-isopropyl-6-methyl-4-pyrimidinyl) phosphorothioate*

HINTS FOR USE:
This product is an effective replacement for chlordane dust for ant control.

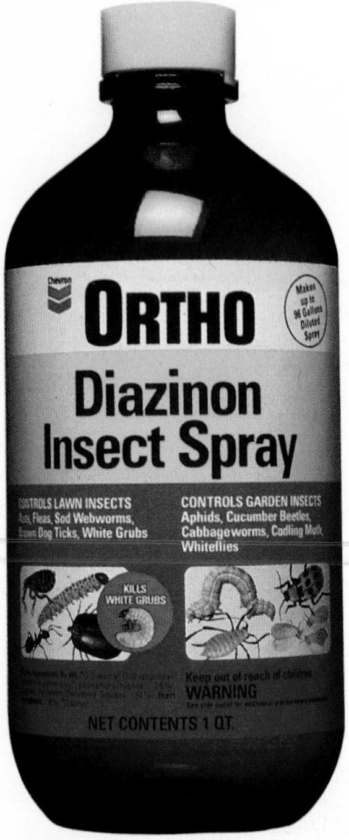

DIAZINON INSECT SPRAY

GENERAL DESCRIPTION:
This liquid concentrate kills many outdoor insects that can destroy lawns, roses, flowers, trees, and shrubs, or annoy people and pets. It controls white grubs, sod webworms, armyworms, and other listed pests in lawns for up to 8 weeks. When diluted, one quart treats up to 4,000 square feet of lawn. It also controls vegetable pests including aphids, whiteflies, and flea beetles. Use it on tomatoes to within one day of harvest. On ornamental trees and shrubs, control such pests as leafhoppers, leafminers, and mealybugs. Treat around patios, windows, and foundations to control home-invading pests. The label contains complete dilution directions and lists days to harvest for fruits and vegetables.

AREAS SOLD:
National

ACTIVE INGREDIENT:
25% Diazinon *0,0-Diethyl 0-(2-isopropyl-6-methyl-4-pyrimidinyl) phosphorothioate*

KILLS THESE INSECTS:
Ants
Aphids
Armyworms
Bagworms
Bean Beetles
Bermuda Mites
Box Elder Bugs
Brown Dog Ticks
Cabbageworms
Chiggers
Chinch Bugs
Clover Mites
Cockroaches
Codling Moths
Crickets
Cucumber Beetles
Cutworms
Dichondra Flea Beetles
Earwigs
European Craneflies
Fire Ants
Flea Beetles
Fleas
Flies
Holly Bud Moths
Lacebugs
Lawn Billbugs
Lawn Moths
Leafhoppers
Leafminers
Leafrollers
Mealybugs
Millipedes
Mites
Mole Crickets
Scale Crawlers
Scorpions
Sod Webworms
Sowbugs (Pillbugs)
Spiders
Thrips
Whiteflies
White Grubs

FOR USE IN THESE AREAS:
Lawns
Fruits and vegetables
Roses and flowers
Shrubs and Shade Trees

DIAZINON SOIL & FOLIAGE DUST

GENERAL DESCRIPTION:
This insecticide controls both soil-inhabiting and foliage-feeding pests. It dusts easily from the container onto the soil to control cutworms and wireworms; 2 pounds covers up to 900 square feet. When treating plants, use ORTHO WHIRLY® Duster or similar applicator to avoid over-application. It may be applied to tomatoes and melons up to 3 days before harvest.

AREAS SOLD:
National

ACTIVE INGREDIENT:
4% Diazinon *0,0-Diethyl 0-(2-isopropyl-6-methyl-4-pyrimidinyl) phosphorothioate*

HINTS FOR USE:
For cutworm and wireworm control, dust the soil before planting and work into the top 6 to 8 inches of soil.

KILLS THESE INSECTS:
Aphids
Cucumber Beetles
Cutworms
Diamondback Moth Larvae
Flea Beetles
Imported Cabbage Worms
Lacebugs
Leafhoppers
Leafminers
Mealybugs
Mites
Root Maggots
Scale Crawlers
Spittlebugs
Thrips
Whiteflies
Wireworms

FOR USE IN THESE AREAS:
Fruits and vegetables
Roses and flowers
Shrubs

DIAZINON SOIL & TURF INSECT CONTROL

GENERAL DESCRIPTION:

These granules are formulated to control ants, chinch bugs, grubs, and other listed insect pests on both grass and dichondra lawns. Apply the material with a fertilizer spreader according to the spreader settings listed on the bag. Also use the granules at planting time to control root maggots, cutworms, wireworms, and other listed pests on most vegetables including broccoli, melons, onions, and tomatoes. Foliage-feeding pests on sweet corn are also controlled. When applied in a band along foundations, it helps to control and prevent clover mites, earwigs, fleas, and other pests from entering homes.

AREAS SOLD:

National

ACTIVE INGREDIENT:

5% Diazinon *0,0-Diethyl 0-(2-isopropyl-6-methyl-4-pyrimidinyl) phosphorothioate*

KILLS THESE INSECTS:

Ants
Armyworms
Bermuda Mites
Billbugs
Brown Dog Ticks
Carrot Rust Flies
Chiggers
Chinch Bugs
Clover Mites
Corn Rootworms
Crickets
Cutworms
Digger Wasps
Earwigs
European Corn Borers
European Cranefly (larvae)
Fleas
Hyperodes Weevils
Lawn Moths (Sod Webworms)
Leafhoppers
Millipedes
Mole Crickets
Root Maggots
Southwestern Corn Borers
Sowbugs (Pillbugs)
Springtails (Collembola)
Vinegar Flies
White Grubs
Wireworms

FOR USE IN THESE AREAS:

Lawns
Vegetables
Building foundations

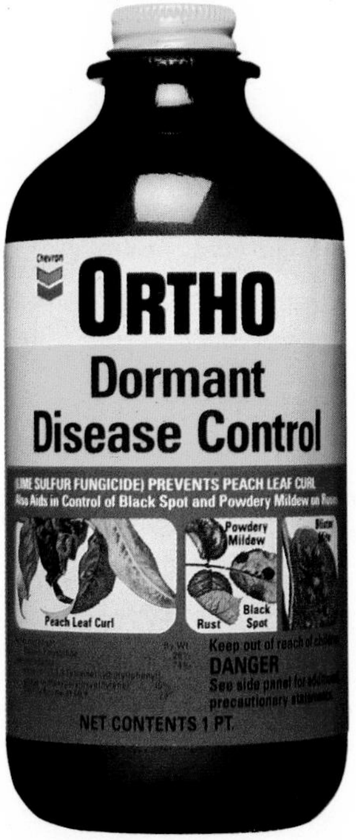

DORMANT DISEASE CONTROL

GENERAL DESCRIPTION:

A liquid spray designed for use on listed fruits, berries, and roses to prevent foliage diseases during the growing season. When applied in late fall, winter, and spring, it kills disease-causing spores that overwinter on buds, twigs, and bark. It also forms a protective coating over buds before they open in the spring, to give control of peach leaf curl. It mixes readily with water, and can be applied with an ORTHO SPRAY-ETTE®, or a tank-type or power sprayer.

AREAS SOLD:

West

ACTIVE INGREDIENT:

26% Lime sulfur *Calcium polysulfide*

HINTS FOR USE:

It is important that sprays be applied before the buds open. If the buds have begun to open, it is too late to obtain satisfactory control of peach leaf curl disease, since infection has already occurred.

CONTROLS THESE DISEASES AND PESTS:

Black Spot
Blister Mites
Cane Blight
Leafspot
Powdery Mildew
Peach Blight
Peach Leaf Curl
Powdery Mildew
Rust

FOR USE IN THESE AREAS:

Fruits
Roses

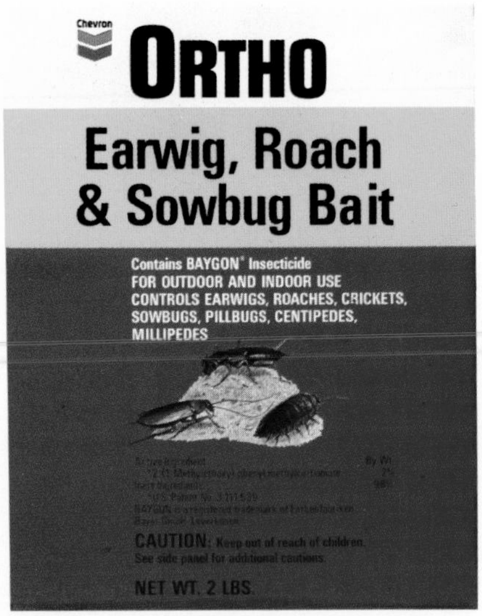

KILLS THESE INSECTS:
Centipedes
Cockroaches
Crickets
Earwigs
Pillbugs
Millipedes
Sowbugs

FOR USE IN THESE AREAS:
Indoors
Outdoors

EARWIG, ROACH & SOWBUG BAIT

GENERAL DESCRIPTION:
A granular, ready-to-use formulation for use indoors and outdoors to control the listed pests that feed upon it or come in contact with it. It rapidly kills both resistant and nonresistant cockroaches. Use the bait any time insects are noticed. Since most of the listed outdoors pests are night feeders, distribute the bait in late afternoon or early morning wherever pests congregate, and along foundations to prevent them from entering buildings. Indoors, sprinkle lightly under sinks and refrigerators and in areas where the pests hide, but which are inaccessible to children and pets. Do not place in piles or use on food crops.

AREAS SOLD:
West

ACTIVE INGREDIENT:
2% Propoxur *2-(1-Methylethoxy)phenyl methylcarbamate*

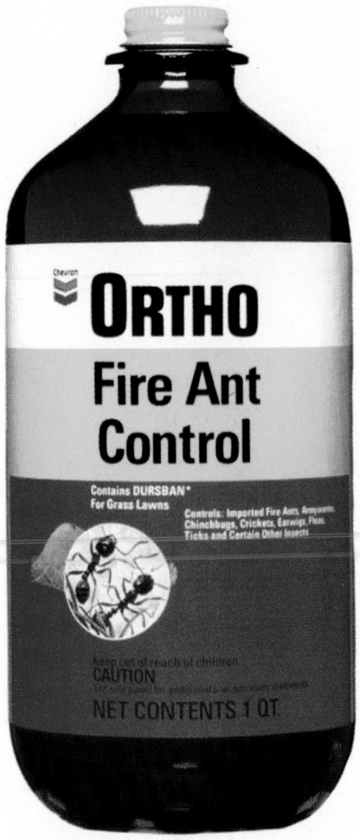

KILLS THESE INSECTS:
Ants
Armyworms
Brown Dog Ticks
Chiggers
Chinch Bugs
Clover Mites
Crickets
Earwigs
Fire Ants
Fleas
Grasshoppers
Lawn Moth Larvae (Sod Webworms)
Millipedes
Sowbugs (Pillbugs)

FOR USE IN THESE AREAS:
Lawns
Building foundations

FIRE ANT CONTROL

GENERAL DESCRIPTION:
This liquid concentrate controls fire ants, numerous lawn pests, and home-invading pests outside buildings. Treat the entire fire ant mound or lawn when the pests first appear. For best results, apply Fire Ant Control to the lawn 2 hours before dark, when lawn insects become active. Use a sprinkling can to treat fire ant mounds and surrounding areas, and an ORTHO Lawn Sprayer for treating lawns and building foundations for general pest control. Mosquitoes coming to rest on treated lawns and foundations will also be killed.

AREAS SOLD:
South

ACTIVE INGREDIENT:
5.3% Chloropyrifos *0,0-Diethyl 0-(3,5,6-trichloro-2-pyridyl) phosphorothioate*

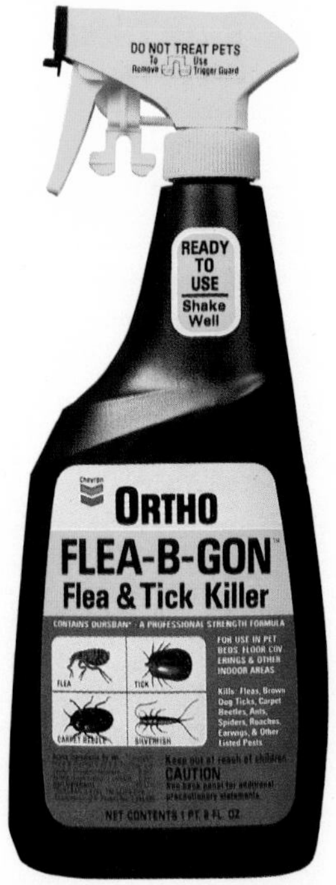

KILLS THESE INSECTS:
Ants
Brown dog ticks
Carpet beetles
Clover mites
Crickets
Firebrats
Fleas
Roaches
Silverfish
Spiders

FOR USE IN THESE AREAS:
Pet beds, floor coverings and other indoor areas

FLEA-B-GON®
FLEA & TICK KILLER

GENERAL DESCRIPTION:
A ready-to-use liquid insecticide that contains DURSBAN® and controls fleas, ticks, roaches, ants, and other listed insects. This product is meant to be used on carpets and other floor coverings, and is nonstaining, nonflammable, low-odor, and convenient to use. This professional strength formula kills insects on contact and its residual action keeps on killing for weeks. It's easy to use and comes in its own applicator container.

AREAS SOLD:
National

GUARANTEED ANALYSIS:
0.50% Chlorpyrifos *O,O-diethyl O-(3,5,6-Trichloro-2-pyridyl) phosphorothioate* (DURSBAN®)
0.33% Xylene range aromatic solvent
99.17% Inert ingredients

KILLS THESE INSECTS:
Ants
Centipedes
Earwigs
Fleas
Roaches
Sowbugs
Spiders

FOR USE IN THESE AREAS:
Pets
Indoors

FLEA-B-GON®
FLEA KILLER

GENERAL DESCRIPTION:
This aerosol controls fleas on dogs and cats, in their bedding, and inside doghouses. It can also be sprayed on carpets and in cracks and crevices where fleas hide. To ensure good coverage when treating pets, part the animal's fur so that the spray contacts the skin. This spray is also effective against cockroaches, spiders, and other listed indoor pests throughout the home.

AREAS SOLD:
National

ACTIVE INGREDIENT:
.250% Resmethrin *[5-(Phenylmethyl)-3-furanyl]methyl 2,2-dimethyl-3-(2-methyl-1-propenyl) cyclopropanecarboxylate*

HINTS FOR USE:
The aerosol's hissing sound and cool sensation may startle nervous pets, so hold them securely. They will soon become accustomed to the spray.

PEST AND DISEASE CONTROL PRODUCTS

KILLS THESE PESTS:
Aphids
Leafhoppers
Red Spider Mites
Russet Mites
Thrips

CONTROLS THESE DISEASES:
Black Spot
Brown Rot
Powdery Mildew
Scab

FOR USE IN THESE AREAS:
Fruits and vegetables
Roses and flowers
Shrubs and lawns

FLOTOX® GARDEN SULFUR

GENERAL DESCRIPTION:
A wettable powder designed for use as a dust or spray to control powdery mildew, brown rot, black spot, and certain other pests on listed fruits and ornamentals. It also controls russet and red spider mites on tomatoes. For lasting disease and mite protection, repeat the applications throughout the season. Use around acid-loving plants, including camellias, azaleas, rhododendrons, and heather, and in new lawn soil to make the soil more acidic. It may cause foliage injury if the temperature is over 90°F. When it is used as a spray, continue to agitate the solution during application to keep it dissolved.

AREAS SOLD:
National

ACTIVE INGREDIENT:
90% Sulfur

KILLS THESE INSECTS:
Ants
Centipedes
Earwigs
Fleas
Flies
Gnats
Mosquitoes
Roaches
Sowbugs
Spiders
Wasps

FOR USE IN THESE AREAS:
Indoors
Outdoors
Pets

FLYING & CRAWLING INSECT KILLER

GENERAL DESCRIPTION:
An aerosol contact insecticide that kills both flying and crawling insects. Used as a room spray, it controls flies, mosquitoes, and gnats. It also kills cockroaches, spiders, and other listed pests when sprayed on the pests and along baseboards, cabinets, and areas where these crawling insects are found. It controls fleas on dogs and in their bedding, and also kills wasps when sprayed into their nests.

AREAS SOLD:
National

ACTIVE INGREDIENT:
0.250% Resmethrin *[5-(Phenylmethyl)-3-furanyl] methyl 2,2-dimethyl-3-(2-methyl-1-propenyl) cyclopropane-carboxylate*

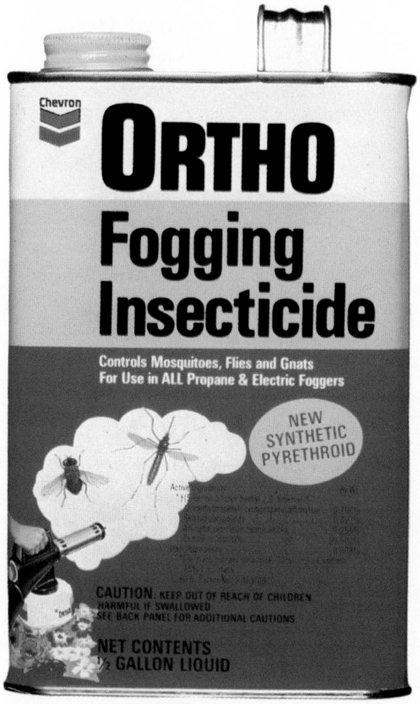

FOGGING INSECTICIDE

KILLS THESE INSECTS:
Flies
Gnats
Mosquitoes

FOR USE IN THESE AREAS:
Patios
Yards
Picnic Areas
Pools
Horse Stables
Drive-in Restaurants
Campsites

GENERAL DESCRIPTION:
Contains the synthetic pyrethroid *resmethrin,* which controls mosquitoes, flies, and gnats in listed *outdoor* areas. It is specially formulated to be used undiluted in portable electric, propane, or gas-powered thermo-foggers that produce spray particles in the aerosol size range. Use at dusk when the wind dies down and the ground and air temperatures are approximately the same. The fog will then linger longer in the treated area. Do not re-enter the treated area until after the fog dissipates.

AREAS SOLD:
National

ACTIVE INGREDIENT:
0.200% Resmethrin *(5-Benzyl-3-furyl) methyl 2,2-dimethyl-3-(2-methylpropenyl) cyclopropanecarboxylate*

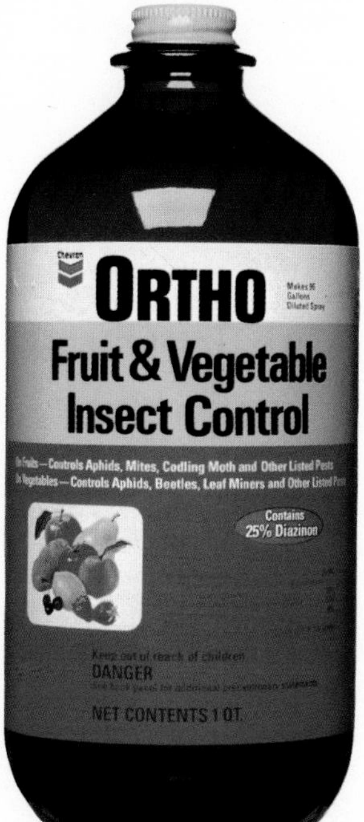

FRUIT & VEGETABLE INSECT CONTROL

GENERAL DESCRIPTION:
A liquid concentrate used to control codling moths, leafrollers, mites, beetles, and other listed pests on fruits, nuts, and vegetables. One quart mixes readily with water to make 96 gallons of diluted spray, and it may be used in all types of sprayers. It can be used on tomatoes and peas up to 1 day before harvest. For a combination spray on fruits, combine with ORTHO ORTHOCIDE® Garden Fungicide; for vegetables, combine with ORTHO Vegetable Disease Control.

AREAS SOLD:
National

ACTIVE INGREDIENT:
25% Diazinon *0,0-Diethyl 0-(2-isopropyl-6-methyl-4-pyrimidinyl) phosphorothioate*

KILLS THESE INSECTS:
Aphids
Apple Maggots
Armyworms
Blueberry Maggots
Cherry Fruit Flies
Cherry Fruitworms (Maggots)
Citrus Thrips
Codling Moths
Colorado Potato Beetles
Cranberry Fruitworms
Cucumber Beetles
Diamondback Moths (Larvae)
Dipterous Leafminers
Dried Fruit Beetles
Flea Beetles
Fruit Tree Leafrollers
Grape Berry Moths
Grape Leaf-folders
Grasshoppers
Imported Cabbage Worms
Leafhoppers
Mealybugs
Mexican Bean Beetles
Mites
Pecan Nut Casebearers
Pear Psyllas
Raspberry Sawflies
Raspberry Fruitworms
Scale Crawlers
Strawberry Leafrollers
Tentiform Leafminers
Thrips
Vinegar Flies
Walnut Caterpillars
Whiteflies

FOR USE IN THESE AREAS:
Fruits and nuts
Vegetables

PEST AND DISEASE CONTROL PRODUCTS

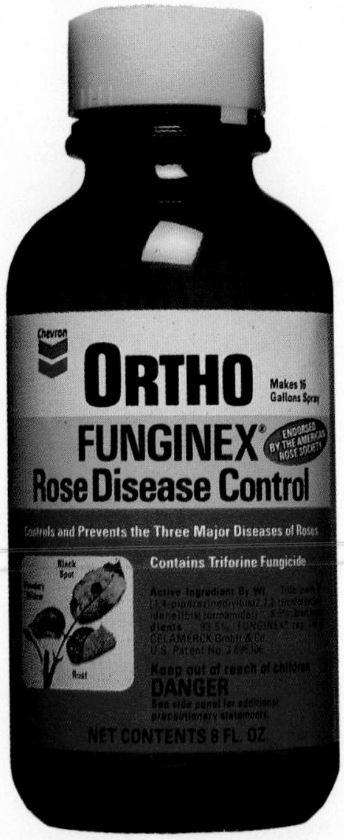

FUNGINEX® ROSE DISEASE CONTROL

CONTROLS THESE DISEASES:
Black Spot
Powdery Mildew
Rust

FOR USE ON THESE PLANTS:
Aster
Calendula
Carnation
Crapemyrtle
Dahlia
Euonymus
Jerusalem Thorn
Lilac
Phlox
Photinia
Poplar
Rose
Snapdragon
Zinnia

FOR USE IN THESE AREAS:
Roses and flowers

GENERAL DESCRIPTION:
A quick-wetting liquid spray, containing the systemic fungicide *triforine*, designed to control or prevent the three most important diseases of roses—black spot, powdery mildew, and rust. When used as directed, it gives uniform coverage and does not leave an unsightly residue on foliage or flowers. Spots on diseased leaves will not be removed, but unaffected leaves will be protected if a regular spray program is followed. One quart of concentrate makes up to 64 gallons of spray, which can be applied with any ORTHO hose-end SPRAY-ETTE® sprayers or pump-up sprayer.

AREAS SOLD:
National

ACTIVE INGREDIENT:
6.5% Triforine *N,N'(1,4-piperazinediyl-bis [2,2,2-trichloroethylidene])bis (formamide)*

HINTS FOR USE:
A systemic fungicide is absorbed into the plant roots, leaves, or stems and moves throughout the plant.

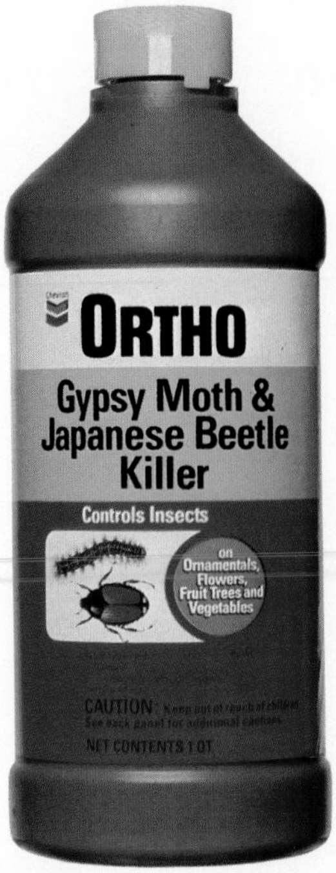

GYPSY MOTH & JAPANESE BEETLE KILLER

KILLS THESE INSECTS:
Aphids
Apple Maggots
Bagworms
Blister Beetles
Codling Moths
Corn Borers
Elm Leaf Beetles
Fall Armyworms
Fruitworms
Gypsy Moths
Hornworms
Japanese Beetles
Leafminers
Leafrollers
Melonworms
Oriental Fruit Moths
Peachtree Borers
Periodical Cicadas
Pickleworms
Plum Curculios
Rose Slugs
Scale Insects
Tent Caterpillars
Thrips

FOR USE IN THESE AREAS:
Trees and shrubs
Roses and flowers
Fruits and vegetables

GENERAL DESCRIPTION:
A liquid concentrate designed to control gypsy moth larvae, Japanese beetles, and a broad range of pests that damage vegetables, fruits, roses, flowers, and other ornamentals. It dilutes readily with water to be applied with all types of sprayers. It can be applied to tomatoes, peppers, and other listed vegetables up to the day of harvest.

AREAS SOLD:
Northeast
Midwest

ACTIVE INGREDIENT:
27% Carbaryl *1-Naphthyl N-methylcarbamate*

HINTS FOR USE:
Thoroughly spray both the upper and the lower surfaces of the leaves so that any Japanese beetles that may fly to your plants from surrounding areas will be controlled. For rapid control of gypsy moth larvae, spray when they are young, up to 1 inch long. Thoroughly spray the entire plant, including the trunk, where the larvae frequently congregate.

KILLS THESE INSECTS:

Ants
Crickets
Fleas
Gnats
Flies
Mosquitos
Roaches
Silverfish
Small flying insects
Spiders
Wasps

FOR USE IN THESE AREAS:

Indoors

HI-POWER INDOOR INSECT FOGGER

GENERAL DESCRIPTION:

This fogger rapidly knocks down flies, mosquitoes, fleas, silverfish, and many other flying and crawling household and pantry pests. When activated, the aerosol can automatically releases its entire contents, filling the room with a penetrating fog that flushes pests out of hiding. Keep the treated area closed for 2 hours or more, and then air out for 30 minutes before re-entering. This easy-to-use formulation treats up to 7,500 cubic feet.

AREAS SOLD:

National

ACTIVE INGREDIENT:

0.50% Pyrethrins
1.00% *Piperonyl Butoxide
1.67% ***N-octyl bicycloheptene dicarboximide*
11.83% Petroleum distillate

KILLS THESE INSECTS:

Ants
Aphids
Biting Flies
Centipedes
Earwigs
Fleas
Gnats
House Flies
Japanese Beetles
Leafhoppers
Mosquitoes
Noctuid Flying Moths
Plant Bugs
Pyralids
Roaches
Sowbugs
Spiders
Spittlebugs
Thrips
Wasps
Whiteflies

FOR USE ON THESE PLANTS:

African Violet
Ageratum
Azalea
Begonia
Camellia
Ceanothus
Chrysanthemum
Coleus
Cotoneaster
Daisy
Daphne
Dogwood
Euonymus
Fatshedera
Forsythia
Geranium
Iris
Ivy
Juniper
Marigold
Nasturtium
Ornamental Quince
Peony
Philodendron
Pyracantha
Rhododendron
Rose
Snapdragon
Spirea
Viburnum
Zinnia

FOR USE IN THESE AREAS:

Indoors
Outdoors
Flowers and shrubs
Houseplants
Pets

HOME & GARDEN INSECT KILLER

GENERAL DESCRIPTION:

An aerosol household and garden contact insecticide. Indoors, use it as a room and surface spray for flying and crawling pests including cockroaches, flies, and earwigs. It also controls whiteflies, aphids, and other pests on African violets, philodendrons, coleus, begonias, and geraniums. Outdoors, use it as an area spray against flying insects and as a plant spray to control the listed foliage-feeding pests.

AREAS SOLD:

National

ACTIVE INGREDIENT:

0.250% Resmethrin *[5-(Phenylmethyl)-3-furanyl] methyl 2,2-dimethyl-3-(2-methyl-1-propenyl) cyclopropanecarboxylate*

PEST AND DISEASE CONTROL PRODUCTS

KILLS THESE INSECTS:
Aphids
Apple Maggots
Cankerworms
Codling Moths
Curculios
Flea Beetles
Grape Berry Moths
Japanese Beetles
Leafhoppers
Leafrollers
Oriental Fruit Moths
Peachtree Borers
Peach Twig Borers
Pear Psylla
Pear Slugs
Plant Bugs
Red Spider Mites
Rose Chafers
Spittlebugs
Strawberry Leaf Beetles
Strawberry Weevils
Tent Caterpillars
Thrips

HOME ORCHARD SPRAY

GENERAL DESCRIPTION:
A multipurpose formulation designed to be used as a dust or spray. It is formulated to control a broad range of insects and diseases on many fruits including apples, cherries, peaches, grapes, and strawberries. The fungicide *captan* kills fungal infections as listed on the label. The insecticides *malathion* and *methoxychlor* kill both sucking and chewing insects. The label contains detailed application instructions and days to harvest for each fruit and berry.

CONTROLS THESE DISEASES:
Bitter Rot
Black Pox
Black Rot
Botryosphaeria
Botrytis Rot
Brooks Fruit Spot
Brown Rot
Dead Arm
Fly Speck
Scab

FOR USE IN THESE AREAS:
Fruits

AREAS SOLD:
National

ACTIVE INGREDIENTS:
14.2% Captan *N-([Trichloromethyl] thio)-4-cyclohexene-1,2-dicarboximide*
7.5% Malathion *0,0-Dimethyl dithiophosphate of diethyl mercaptosuccinate*
15% Methoxychlor *2,2-Bis (p-methoxyphenyl)-1,1,1-trichloroethane*

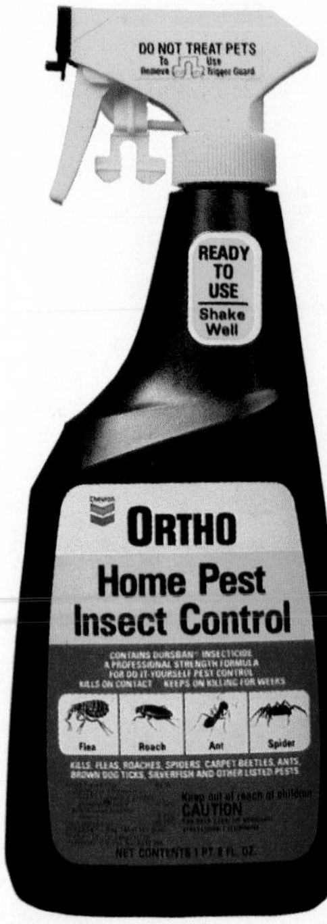

KILLS THESE INSECTS:
Ants
Brown dog ticks
Carpet beetles
Clover mites
Crickets
Firebrats
Fleas
Roaches
Silverfish
Spiders (including Black Widow spiders)

FOR USE IN THESE AREAS:
Homes
apartments
attics
garages
basements
storage areas.

HOME PEST INSECT CONTROL

GENERAL DESCRIPTION:
This ready-to-use liquid insecticide contains DURSBAN® for controlling cockroaches, fleas, and other hard-to-kill pests is suitable for indoor or outdoor use. It kills insects on contact and keeps on killing for weeks with residual action. It can be purchased in the 24-ounce applicator size, or in a one-gallon applicator size for bigger jobs. Both applicators are easy to carry, and can be adjusted to deliver spray patterns from a coarse stream to a fine mist. The active ingredient in this product is the proven insecticide DURSBAN®. This low-odor product has been formulated with a water base, so it is nonflammable and will not stain.

AREAS SOLD:
National

ACTIVE INGREDIENTS:
0.50% Chlorpyrifos *0.0-diethyl 0-(3,5,6-Trichloro-2-pyridyl) phosphorothioate* (DURSBAN®)
0.33% Xylene range aromatic solvent

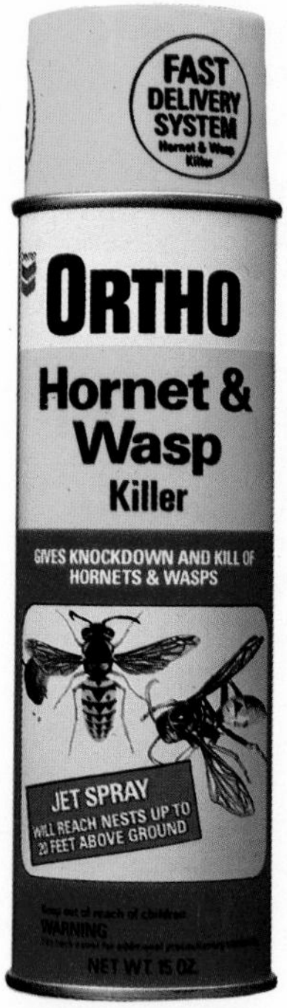

KILLS THESE INSECTS:
Ants
Brown Dog Ticks
Clover Mites
Crickets
Earwigs
Fleas
Hornets
Millipedes
Sowbugs
Spiders
Wasps

FOR USE IN THESE AREAS:
Outdoors
Not for use on plants

HORNET & WASP KILLER

GENERAL DESCRIPTION:
An aerosol that shoots a jet of spray up to 20 feet to eliminate hornets and wasps from a safe distance. For best results, treat the nest after dark when all the insects are inside. Soak the entire nest, inside and out. The spray also controls clover mites, fleas, crickets, earwigs, and other listed pests outdoors to prevent them from entering homes.

AREAS SOLD:
National

ACTIVE INGREDIENT:
0.50% Propoxur *2-(1-Methylethoxy)phenylmethylcarbamate*

KILLS THESE INSECTS:
Ants
Centipedes
Earwigs
Fleas
Flies
Gnats
Mosquitoes
Roaches
Sowbugs
Spiders
Wasps

FOR USE IN THESE AREAS:
Indoors
Outdoors
Pets

HOUSEHOLD INSECT KILLER

GENERAL DESCRIPTION:
An easy-to-use aerosol that kills both flying and crawling pests. Use it as a room spray to control flying pests, such as mosquitoes, flies, and gnats, and as a surface spray for crawling pests, including cockroaches, earwigs, and sowbugs. Keep the room closed for at least 15 minutes after treatment; air out thoroughly before re-entering. It also kills fleas on dogs, and reduces reinfestations when bedding and doghouses are sprayed. It effectively eliminates wasps when sprayed into their nests after dark.

AREAS SOLD:
National

ACTIVE INGREDIENT:
0.250% Resmethrin *[5-(Phenylmethyl) 3-furanyl] methyl 2,2-dimethyl-3-(2-methyl-1-propenyl) cyclopropanecarboxylate*

HOUSE PLANT INSECT CONTROL

GENERAL DESCRIPTION:
An aerosol designed for use in interior and exterior plantscapes. It kills chewing and sucking pests that attack houseplants, roses, flowers, and other ornamentals. It kills both on contact and by systemic action. Provides residual control of aphids for up to 3 weeks. This spray is particularly effective on hard-to-control pests such as mites, whiteflies, scale crawlers, and thrips. For best results, apply a light spray at the first sign of the pests, and repeat at intervals of 7 to 10 days.

AREAS SOLD:
National

ACTIVE INGREDIENTS:
.25% ORTHENE® (Acephate) *0,S-dimethyl acetylphosphoramidothioate*
.10% Resmethrin *5-(phenylmethyl)-3-furanyl methyl 2,2-dimethyl-3-(2-methyl-1-propenyl) cyclopropanecarboxylate*

KILLS THESE INSECTS:
Aphids
Armyworms
Bagworms
Catalpa Sphinx Moth (Larvae)
Cuban Laurel Thrips
Diabrotica Beetles
Eastern Tent Caterpillars
Fall Webworms
Flower Thrips
Lace Bugs
Leafbeetles
Leafhoppers
Leafminers
Maple Shoot Moths (Larvae)
Mealybugs
Oleander Caterpillars
Orange-striped Oakworms
Poplar Tentmakers
Psyllids
Rose Midges
Salt Marsh Caterpillars
Sawflies
Scale Crawlers
Southern Red Mites
Spittlebugs
Two-spotted Spider Mites

FOR USE IN THESE AREAS:
Roses and flowers
Houseplants
Trees and shrubs

HOUSE PLANT INSECT KILLER

GENERAL DESCRIPTION:
This ready-to-use liquid formula kills all the major house plant pests (aphids, mealybugs, whiteflies, scale crawlers, spider mites) on contact. The hand-pump nozzle makes it easy to treat both the upper and lower surfaces of the leaves. Plants may be treated either indoors or outdoors as soon as pests or their damage is noticed. The treatment may be repeated weekly if needed.

AREAS SOLD:
National

GUARANTEED ANALYSIS:
0.180% Petroleum oil
0.220% Plant spray oil
0.050% Resmethrin *5-(phenylmethyl)-3-furanyl methyl 2,2-dimethyl-3-(2-methyl-1-propenyl) cyclopropanecarboxylate*

KILLS THESE INSECTS:
Aphids
Mealybugs
Whiteflies
Scale Crawlers
Spider Mites

FOR USE ON THESE PLANTS:
African Violet
Aluminum Plant
Angelwing Begonia
Asparagus Fern
Bird's-nest Fern
Bird's-nest Sansevieria
Boston Fern
Coleus
Dieffenbachia
Dracaena
English Ivy
False Aralia
Fiddle Leaf Philodendron
Fuchsia
Geranium
Holly Fern
Ivy Geranium
Jade Plant
Japanese Aralia
Kalanchoe
Lace Fern
Marigold
Neanthe Bella Palm
Needle Point Ivy
Parlor Palm
Philodendron
Piggyback Plant
Polka Dot Plant
Pothos
Prayer Plant
Purple Passion
Ribbon Plant
Rubber Plant
Salvia
Schefflera
Shasta Daisy
Spider Plant
Sprengei Fern
Strawberry Begonia
Swedish Ivy
Table Fern
Variegated Spider Plant
Variegated Vanilla
Wandering Jew
Wax Plant
Weeping Fig
Zebra Plant

FOR USE IN THESE AREAS:
Houseplants

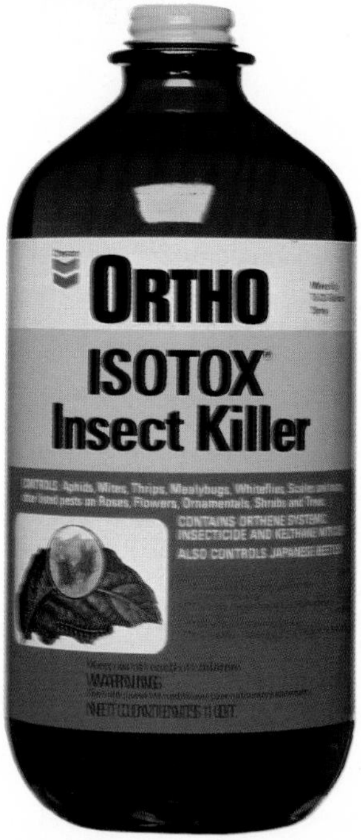

ISOTOX®
INSECT KILLER

GENERAL DESCRIPTION:
This liquid concentrate contains *acephate* (ORTHENE®), a systemic insecticide, and *dicofol* (KELTHANE®), a miticide. It controls chewing and sucking pests, including hard-to-control scales, flower thrips, whiteflies, and mites on the many ornamentals specified on the label. It gives both contact and residual control; Orthene's systemic killing action remains effective for up to 3 weeks. For best results, treat at the first sign of insects, before populations become large. Apply with any ORTHO hose-end sprayer or any tank-type or power sprayer. Not for use on food crops.

AREAS SOLD:
National

ACTIVE INGREDIENTS:
8.0% ORTHENE® (Acephate) *(0,S-Dimethyl-acetylphosphoramidothioate)*
3.0% Dicofol *1,1-Bis (p-chlorophenyl)-2,2,2-trichloroethanol*

KILLS THESE INSECTS:
Aphids
Ash Plant Bugs
Bagworms
Beet Armyworms
Birch Leafminers
Black Vine Weevils
Budworms
Cabbage Loopers
Catalpa Sphinx Moths (Larvae)
Cottonwood Leaf Beetle
Cuban Laurel Thrips
Elm Leaf Beetles
Fall Cankerworms
Fall Webworms
Grasshoppers
Gypsy Moths (Larvae)
Holly Leafminers
Japanese Beetles
Lacebugs
Leafhoppers
Leafrollers
Lilac Leafminers
Maple Shoot Moths (Larvae)
Mealybugs
Mimosa Webworms
Nantucket Pine Tip Moths (Larvae)
Oak Webworms
Obscure Root Weevils
Orange-striped Oakworms
Poplar Tentmakers
Psyllids
Saddled Prominent Caterpillars
Sawflies (Dusky Birch, Blackheaded Ash, Redheaded Pine, European Pine)
Scales (Crawlers)
Spittlebugs
Spruce Mites
Stinkbugs
Tent Caterpillars
Thrips
Two-spotted Spider Mites
Whiteflies
Willow Leaf Beetles

FOR USE IN THESE AREAS:
Roses and flowers
Trees and shrubs

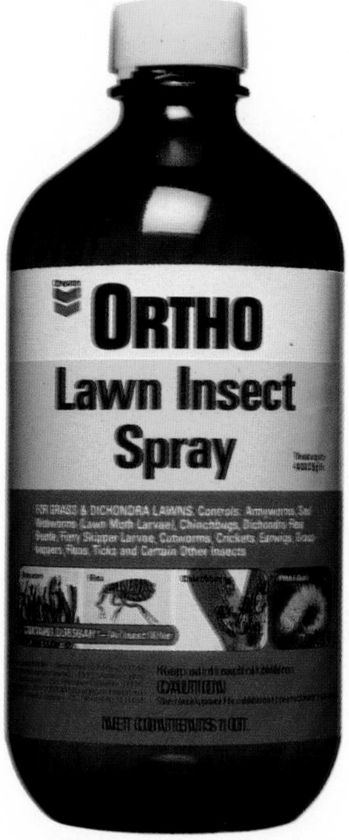

LAWN
INSECT SPRAY

GENERAL DESCRIPTION:
A liquid concentrate used to control common lawn pests, home-invading pests, and imported fire ants. It is effective on both grass and dichondra lawns, and also prevents ants, ticks, and other listed pests from invading buildings when applied around and on foundations. When diluted, one quart of concentrate treats up to 4,000 square feet. Apply with an ORTHO Lawn Sprayer. For best results, treat the entire lawn rather than spot spraying.

AREAS SOLD:
National

ACTIVE INGREDIENT:
5.3% Chlorpyrifos *[0,0-Diethyl 0-(3,5,6-trichloro-2-pyridyl) phosphorothioate]*

KILLS THESE INSECTS:
Ants
Armyworms
Brown Dog Ticks
Chiggers
Chinch Bugs
Clover Mites
Crickets
Cutworms
Dichondra Flea Beetles
Earwigs
European Cranefly (larvae)
Fiery Skipper Larvae (California and Hawaii only)
Fire Ants
Fleas
Grasshoppers
Lawn Moth Larvae (Sod Webworms)
Millipedes
Sowbugs (Pillbugs)
Tropical Grass Webworms (Hawaii only)
White Grubs

FOR USE IN THESE AREAS:
Lawns
Building foundations

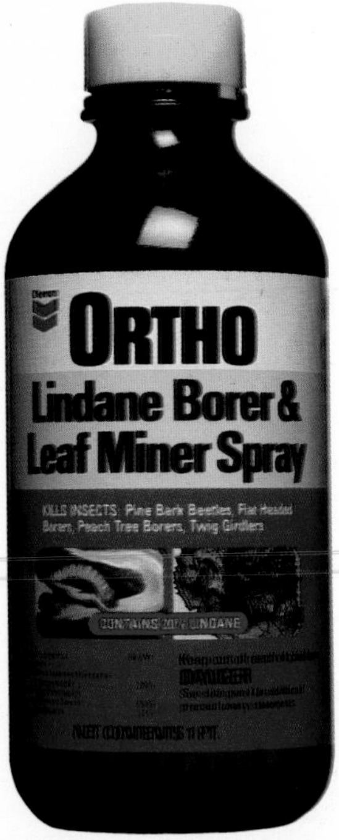

KILLS THESE INSECTS:
Bark Beetles
Dogwood Borers
Flat-headed Borers
Fruit Tree Bark Beetles
Iris Borers
Leafminers
Lilac Borers
Peach Tree Borers
Pine Bark Beetles
Rhododendron Borers
Round-headed Borers
Taxus Weevils
Twig Girdlers
White Pine Weevils
Wood-Boring Beetles

FOR USE IN THESE AREAS:
Flowers and fruits
Trees and shrubs

LINDANE BORER & LEAF MINER SPRAY

GENERAL DESCRIPTION:
A liquid that is applied as a foliage spray, trunk paint, and soil drench. It controls wood-boring beetles, weevils, and leafminers that are not easily contacted by insecticides. It kills borers inside trees as the vapor penetrates into their feeding tunnels. To prevent new infestations, drench tree trunks to form a protective coating. Invading borers ingest the chemical as they chew into the trunk.

AREAS SOLD:
National

ACTIVE INGREDIENT:
20% Lindane *Gamma isomer of benzene hexachloride*

HINTS FOR USE:
Some borers, including peachtree borers, pupate in the soil below infested trees. Soak the soil to give residual control of the adults as they emerge.

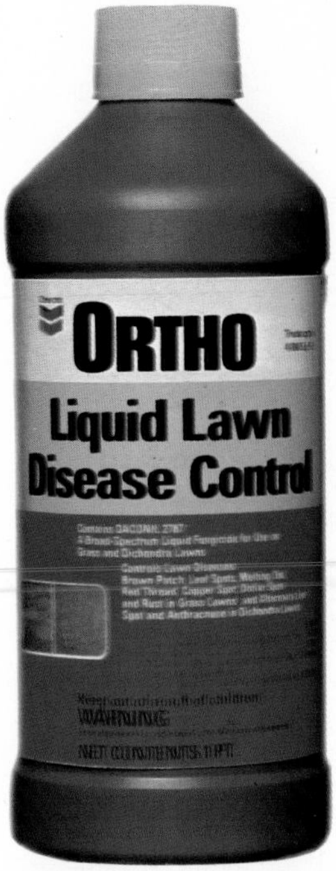

CONTROLS THESE DISEASES:
Alternaria Leaf Spot
Anthracnose
Copper Spot
Curvularia Leaf Spot
Dollar Spot
Gray Leaf Spot
Large Brown Patch
Leaf Spot (Melting Out)
Red Thread
Stem Rust of Bluegrass

FOR USE IN THESE AREAS:
Lawns

LIQUID LAWN DISEASE CONTROL

GENERAL DESCRIPTION:
A broad-spectrum, liquid fungicide for use on all grass and dichondra lawns. It controls brown patch, dollar spot, leaf spot, anthracnose, and other listed diseases. It contains the proven fungicide *chlorothalonil* (DACONIL 2787®) to kill existing infections, and also provides protection against additional infections. For best results, spray whenever weather conditions favor disease development, or before the problem becomes extensive. The label lists weather conditions that favor various diseases and the appropriate dilution rates for control. One quart of concentrate mixes readily with water to treat up to 4,000 square feet. Mow and water the lawn prior to use. Apply with an ORTHO SPRAY-ETTE® or a tank-type or power sprayer.

AREAS SOLD:
National

ACTIVE INGREDIENT:
29.6% Chlorothalonil *Tetrachloroisophthalonitrile*

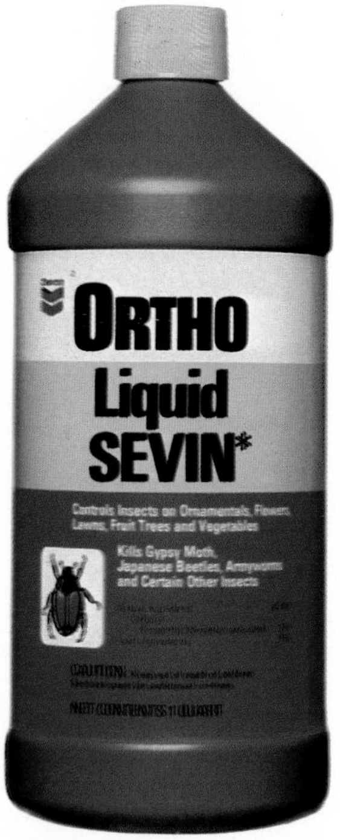

LIQUID SEVIN®

GENERAL DESCRIPTION:

A liquid concentrate designed to control a broad range of insects on contact and as they feed on roses, ornamentals, lawns, and food crops. It mixes readily with water to be used in all types of sprayers. For best results, apply when the insects first appear. Treat all exposed parts of plants, especially the upper and lower surfaces of the leaves. Liquid SEVIN® may be applied to specified vegetables up to the day of harvest. Combine with ORTHO FUNGINEX® Rose Disease Control for a combination spray on roses.

AREAS SOLD:

National

ACTIVE INGREDIENT:

27% Carbaryl *1-Naphthyl N-methylcarbamate*

KILLS THESE INSECTS:

Ants
Aphids
Apple Aphids
Apple Maggots
Bagworms
Blister Beetles
Codling Moths
Corn Borers
Earwigs
Elm Leaf Beetles
Fall Armyworms
Fleas
Fruitworms
Grasshoppers
Gypsy Moths
Hornworms
Japanese Beetles
Leafminers
Leafrollers
Melon Worms
Oriental Fruit Moths
Peachtree Borers
Periodical Cicadas
Pickleworms
Plum Curculios
Rose Slugs
Scale Insects
Sod Webworms
Tent Caterpillars
Thrips

FOR USE IN THESE AREAS:

Fruits and vegetables
Trees and shrubs
Roses and flowers
Lawns

SEVIN® is a registered trademark of Union Carbide Corporation. FUNGINEX® is a registered trademark of Celamerck GmbH & Co.

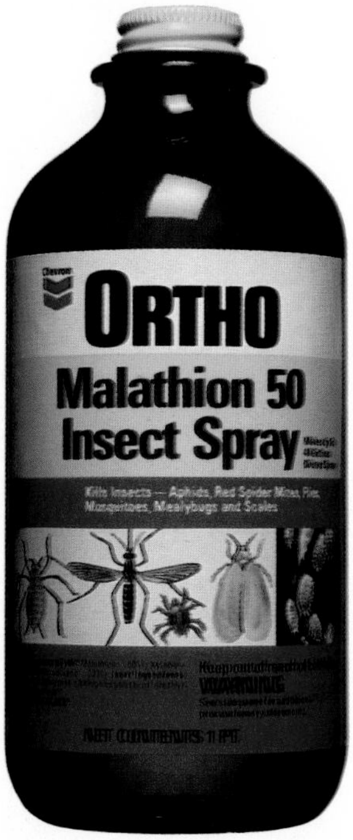

MALATHION 50 INSECT SPRAY

GENERAL DESCRIPTION:

A multipurpose liquid that kills on contact a broad range of chewing and sucking insects on lawns, ornamentals, and food crops. Thorough coverage of branches and the upper and lower surfaces of the leaves is necessary to control insects. *Malathion* may be applied to broccoli and peas within 3 days of harvest, and to citrus within 7 days of harvest. Use around building foundations to control fleas, clover mites, and mosquitoes. One quart of concentrate readily mixes with water to make 96 gallons of diluted spray. *Malathion* is one of the least toxic insecticides used in home gardens, and has been used successfully for many years.

AREAS SOLD:

National

ACTIVE INGREDIENT:

50% Malathion *0,0-Dimethyl dithiophosphate of diethyl mercaptosuccinate*

KILLS THESE INSECTS:

Aphids
Bagworms
Bean Leafhoppers
Box Elder Bugs
Bud Moths
Clover Mites
Codling Moths
Fleas
Florida Red Scales
Fourlined Leaf Bugs
Fruit Tree Leafroller
Grape Leafhoppers
Houseflies
Japanese Beetle Adults
Lacebugs
Mealybugs
Mosquitoes
Pear Psyllids
Plum Curculios
Potato Leafhoppers
Red Spider Mites
Purple Scales
Red-Banded Leafrollers
Rose Leafhoppers
Scales (black, oyster shell, soft brown)
Spittlebugs
Spruce Mites
Strawberry Leafroller
Tarnished Plant Bugs
Tent Caterpillars
Thrips
Whiteflies
Woolly Aphids
Yellow Scale

FOR USE IN THESE AREAS:

Trees and shrubs
Roses and flowers
Fruits and vegetables
Outdoors
Around dwellings
Lawns

PEST AND DISEASE CONTROL PRODUCTS

KILLS THESE INSECTS:
Cockroaches
Field Crickets
Mole Crickets

FOR USE IN THESE AREAS:
Indoors
Outdoors

MOLE CRICKET BAIT

GENERAL DESCRIPTION:
A ready-to-use granular bait containing BAYGON® insecticide for controlling mole crickets, field crickets, and cockroaches. It rapidly kills these insects, including cockroaches resistant to certain chlorinated hydrocarbon and phosphate insecticides. Three pounds of granules treats up to 6,000 square feet of lawn. For fast, easy application outdoors, use an ORTHO WHIRLYBIRD® Spreader. Indoors, lightly sprinkle in cracks and crevices and other areas where pests may hide, but which are inaccessible to children and pets. Do not place in piles or use on food crops.

AREAS SOLD:
South

ACTIVE INGREDIENT:
2% Propoxur (BAYGON®) *2-(1-Methylethoxy)phenylmethylcarbamate*

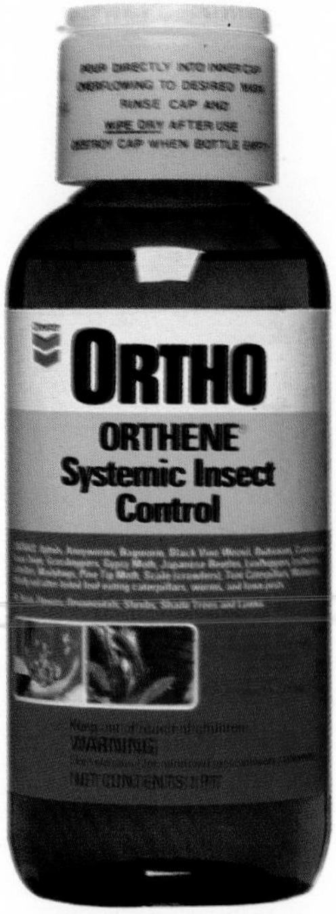

ORTHENE® SYSTEMIC INSECT CONTROL

GENERAL DESCRIPTION:
A liquid that effectively controls on contact and with residual systemic action many of the chewing and sucking pests that attack roses, flowers, ornamentals, and lawns. It is absorbed systemically by plants, so it controls present insects and future infestations for up to 3 weeks. It is particularly effective on hard-to-control insects such as scales, thrips, mealybugs, and black vine weevils. It controls imported fire ants and listed lawn pests, including fall armyworms and sod webworms. It may be applied with an ORTHO SPRAY-ETTE®, or a tank-type or power sprayer.

AREAS SOLD:
National

ACTIVE INGREDIENT:
9.4% Acephate (ORTHENE®) *0,S-Dimethyl acetylphosphoramidothioate*

KILLS THESE INSECTS:
Aphids
Armyworms
Bagworms
Black Vine Weevils
Budworms
Cabbage Loopers
Casebearers
Catalpa Sphinx Moths
Cherry Laurel Leaftiers
Cuban Laurel Thrips
Elm Leafbeetles
Fall Armyworms
Fall Cankerworms
Fall Webworms
Flower Thrips
Gladiolus Thrips
Grasshoppers
Greenbugs
Green Striped Mapleworms
Gypsy Moths
Hornworms
Imported Fire Ants
Japanese Beetles
Lacebugs
Leafhoppers
Leafminers
Maple Shoot Moths
Mealybugs
Mimosa Webworms
Nantucket Pine Tip Moths
Oak Webworm
Obscure Root Weevils (Adults)
Oleander Caterpillars
Orange-striped Oakworms
Poplar Tentmakers
Psyllids
Rose Midges
Sawflies
Scales (Crawlers)
Sod Webworms
Spittlebugs
Sunflower Moths
Tent Caterpillars
Whiteflies
White-marked Tussock Moths
Willow Leafbeetles
Yellow-necked Caterpillars

FOR USE IN THESE AREAS:
Roses and flowers
Trees and shrubs
Lawns

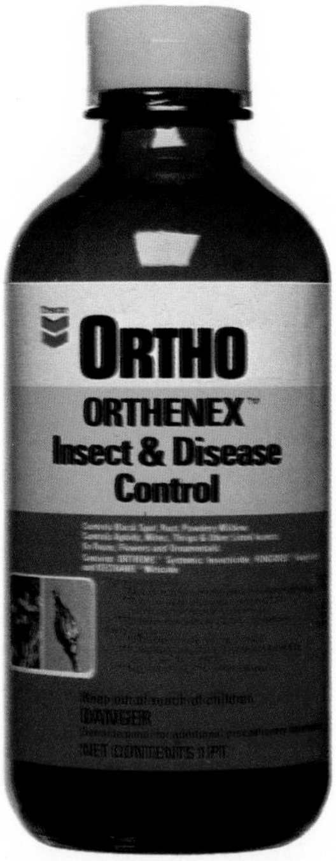

ORTHENEX® INSECT & DISEASE CONTROL

KILLS THESE INSECTS:
Aphids
Budworms
Flower Thrips
Lacebugs
Leafhoppers
Leafminers
Spittlebugs
Two-spotted Mites

CONTROLS THESE DISEASES:
Black Spot
Powdery Mildew
Rust

FOR USE IN THESE AREAS:
Roses and flowers
Trees and shrubs

GENERAL DESCRIPTION:
A liquid combination of three highly effective pesticides, *acephate* (ORTHENE®) for insects, *dicofol* (KELTHANE®) for mites, and *triforine* (FUNGINEX®)for disease control on roses, flowers, and ornamentals. The systemic action of the ingredients (ORTHENE®) and *triforine* enables them to be absorbed into plants through the leaves and stems, resulting in longer, more effective protection with no unsightly residue on the foliage. Insects and mites are killed on contact. For best results, use as a preventive spray, applying before or at the first sign of insects and diseases. One quart of concentrate dilutes easily with water to make 32 gallons of diluted spray. Apply with an ORTHO SPRAY-ETTE® or a tank-type or power sprayer.

AREAS SOLD:
National

ACTIVE INGREDIENTS:
4.00% Acephate (ORTHENE®) *O,S-Dimethyl acetylphosphoramidothioate*
3.25% Triforine (FUNGINEX®) *N,N'-(1,4-Piperazine-diylbis [2,2,2-trichloroethylidene])bis (formamide)*
3.00% Dicofol (KELTHANE®) *1,1-Bis(p-chlorophenyl)-2,2,2-trichloroethanol*

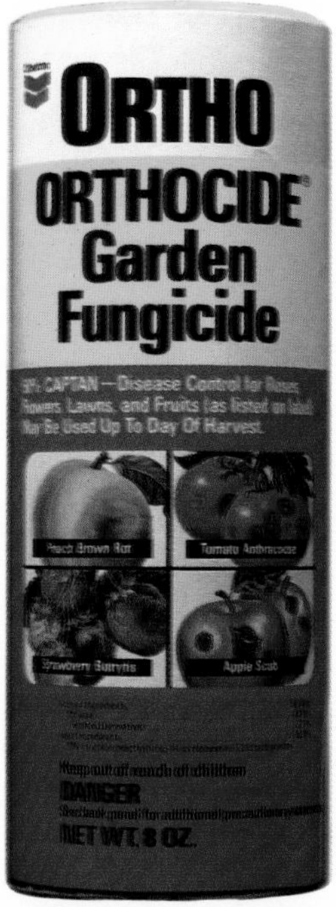

ORTHOCIDE® GARDEN FUNGICIDE

CONTROLS THESE DISEASES:
Alternaria (Leaf Spot)
Angular Leaf Spot
Anthracnose
Bitter Rot
Black Spot
Botrytis Flower Blight
Botrytis Rot
Brown Patch
Brown Rot
Cercospora Spot or Blotch
Cherry Leaf Spot
Damping-off
Downy Mildew
Early Blight
Fruit Spot
Gray Leaf Spot
Helminthosporium (Melting Out)
Late Blight
Leaf Spot
Peach Scab
Powdery Mildew
Root Rot
Rust
Scab
Seed Rot
Septoria Leaf Spot

FOR USE IN THESE AREAS:
Roses and flowers
Fruits and vegetables
Lawns

GENERAL DESCRIPTION:
A wettable powder used to control many garden plant diseases on roses, flowers, lawns, vegetables, and fruits as listed on the label. It contains the fungicide *captan* to kill existing fungal infections, and provides protection against additional infections for 1 to 2 weeks. It is also used on cuttings, bulbs, and seeds before planting to prevent damping-off. For best results, apply with an ORTHO SPRAY-ETTE® garden hose sprayer or power sprayer; continue to agitate during application to keep the powder dissolved. It is compatible with most commonly used insecticides and fungicides except for highly alkaline materials such as hydrated lime.

AREAS SOLD:
National

ACTIVE INGREDIENTS:
47.3% Captan *N-([Trichloromethyl] thio)-4-cyclohexene-1,2-dicarboximide*
2.7% Related derivatives

HINTS FOR USE:
An eradicant fungicide kills fungi that are present on, and sometimes in, infected plant parts. For best control, apply the fungicide at the first sign of the disease.

PEST AND DISEASE CONTROL PRODUCTS

ORTHO-KLOR® INDOOR & OUTDOOR INSECT KILLER

KILLS THESE INSECTS:
Ants
Brown Dog Ticks
Carpenter Ants
Clover Mites
Cockroaches
Confused Flour Beetles
Crickets
Firebrats
Earwigs
Fleas
Mediterranean Flour Moths
Millipedes
Sowbugs
Spiders (incl. Black Widow Spider)
Ticks

FOR USE IN THESE AREAS:
Indoors
Outdoors

GENERAL DESCRIPTION:
This ready-to-use insecticidal dust contains DURSBAN® and controls ants, spiders, fleas, ticks, and other household pests found in and around the home. Apply it along doors and windowsills, in cracks in cement walks and patios, around garbage containers, under porches, and as a spot treatment or in a continuous band. A one-pound container is enough to treat a continuous band 2 feet wide and 72 feet long.

AREAS SOLD:
National

ACTIVE INGREDIENT:
1% Chlorpyrifos */0,0-diethyl-0-(3,5,6-trichloro-2-pyridyl)phosphorothioate/* (DURSBAN®)
99% Inert Ingredients

HINTS FOR USE:
Effective *chlordane* replacement for ant control.

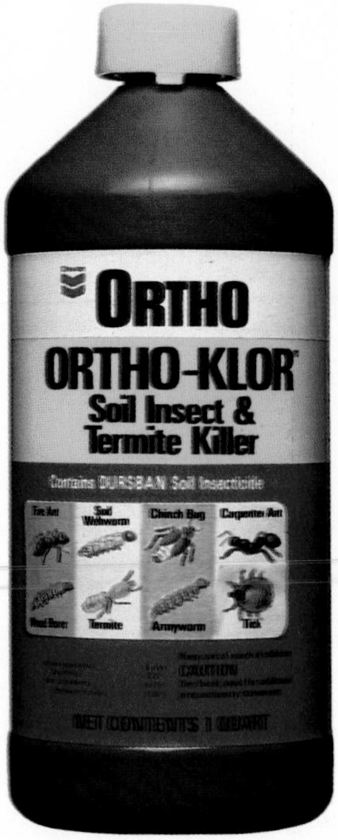

ORTHO-KLOR® SOIL INSECT & TERMITE KILLER

KILLS THESE INSECTS:
Ants
Armyworms
Carpenter Ants
Carpenter Bees
Chiggers
Chinch Bugs
Clover Mites
Crickets
Cutworms
Deathwatch Beetles
Dichondra Flea Beetles
Earwigs
European Crane Fly
Fiery Skipper Larvae (California and Hawaii only)
Fire Ants
Fleas
Furniture Beetles
Grasshoppers
Grubs
Lawn Moth Larvae
Millipedes
Mosquitoes
Powderpost Beetles
Round-headed House Borers
Sod Webworms
Sowbugs
Subterranean Termites
Ticks
Tropical Grass Webworms (Hawaii only)
Wood Borers

FOR USE IN THESE AREAS:
Around foundations
Lawns
Outdoor wood structures

GENERAL DESCRIPTION:
This liquid concentrate contains DURSBAN® insecticide, and controls a wide range of nuisance soil and home invading insects, including ants, subterranean termites, powderpost beetles, and wood borers. It is particularly useful as an effective replacement for chlordane for the prevention and control of listed wood-destroying insects, but also effectively controls many common pests in lawns and other outdoor areas around the home. Its residual activity provides nuisance pest control for months and termite control for years. Do not use on vegetables or food crops.

AREAS SOLD:
National

ACTIVE INGREDIENT:
12.6% Chlorpyrifos */0,0-diethyl 0-(3,5,6-Trichloro-2-pyridyl)phosphorothioate* (DURSBAN®)
87.4% Inert Ingredients

HINTS FOR USE:
Effective *chlordane* replacement for termite and ant control.

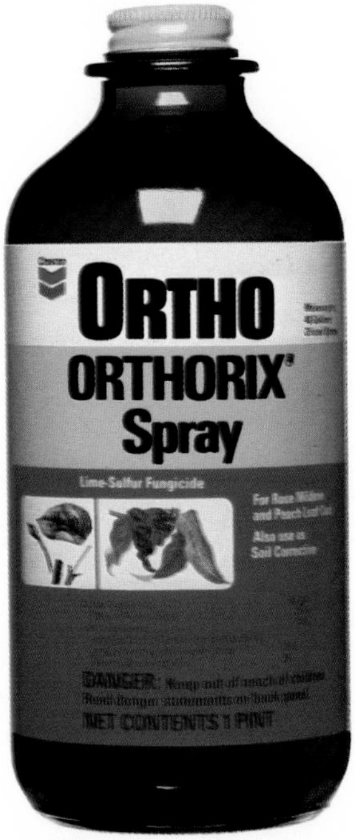

ORTHORIX® SPRAY

KILLS THESE INSECTS:
Blister mites
Red Spider Mites
Rust mites

CONTROLS THESE DISEASES:
Blackspot
Cane Blight
Leaf Spot
Peach Blight
Peach Leaf Curl
Powdery Mildew
Red Berry Trouble
Rust
Scab

FOR USE IN THESE AREAS:
Trees and shrubs
Roses and flowers
Fruits

GENERAL DESCRIPTION:
A liquid formulated for use in both dormant and growing seasons to kill overwintering fungal spores and existing infections on roses and listed ornamentals, fruits, and berries. It also controls rust mites on citrus, and can be used as a soil correction for acid-loving plants including rhododendrons, azaleas, and camellias. It can also be used as a lawn and soil treatment to condition soils and to improve water penetration and moisture retention in heavy soils. One pint of concentrate makes up to 48 gallons of diluted spray. Depending on use, apply the solution with an ORTHO SPRAY-ETTE®, ORTHO Lawn Sprayer or watering can. Combine it with ORTHO ISOTOX® Insect Killer for a combination spray on roses and many ornamentals. It can also be combined with ORTHO VOLCK® Oil Spray for a combination winter spray on dormant deciduous fruits, ornamentals and roses.

AREAS SOLD:
National

ACTIVE INGREDIENT:
26% Lime sulfur *Calcium polysulfides*

OUTDOOR INSECT FOGGER

KILLS THESE INSECTS:
Ants
Centipedes
Crickets
Flies
Flying Moths
Gnats
Hornets
Mosquitoes
Sowbugs
Spiders
Wasps

FOR USE IN THESE AREAS:
Outdoors

GENERAL DESCRIPTION:
This insecticide is specially formulated for use in backyards, patios, and picnic areas to control flying and crawling insects in a wide area, as far as 21 feet away. When sprayed, it blankets the area with a penetrating insect-killing fog that contains both an insecticide and a repellent. It is very effective against mosquitoes, gnats, flies, ants, spiders, and other outdoor pests. For best results, spray in the direction of a slight breeze that will carry the fog into the infested areas. Do not reenter the area until after the spray dissipates.

AREAS SOLD:
National

ACTIVE INGREDIENTS:
0.250% Resmethrin *(5-[Phenylmethyl]-3-furanyl)methyl 2,2-dimethyl-3-(2-methyl-1-propenyl) cyclopropane-carboxylate*
0.950% MGK Repellent 874 *2-Hydroxyethyl-n-octyl sulfide*

HINTS FOR USE:
For pest-free outdoor parties, spray into shrubs around the perimeter of gardens and lawns one hour before using outdoor patio areas.

PEST AND DISEASE CONTROL PRODUCTS

KILLS THESE INSECTS:
Centipedes
Cockroaches
Crickets
Earwigs
Millipedes
Pillbugs
Sowbugs

FOR USE IN THESE AREAS:
Indoors
Outdoors

PEST-B-GON® ROACH BAIT

GENERAL DESCRIPTION:
A ready-to-use granular bait for indoor and outdoor control of the listed pests that feed upon it or come in contact with it. It rapidly kills both resistant and non-resistant cockroaches. For best results outdoors, distribute the granules where pests congregate late afternoon or the early morning, when they are most active; also sprinkle around foundations to prevent pests from entering buildings. Indoors, treat in cracks and crevices and in other areas where pests hide. Do not apply directly to foliage of ornamentals—apply the bait to the soil around the plants.

AREAS SOLD:
National

ACTIVE INGREDIENT:
2% Propoxur *2-(1-Methylethoxy)phenyl methylcarbamate*

CONTROLS THESE DISEASES:
Anthracnose
Black Spot
Citrus Scab
Damping-off (Cylindrocladium)
Leaf Spot (Alternaria)
Leaf Spot (Didymellina)
Leaf Spot (Septoria)
Melanose
Powdery Mildew
Root Rot (Pythium)
Rust

FOR USE IN THESE AREAS:
Roses and flowers
Citrus

PHALTAN® ROSE & GARDEN FUNGICIDE

GENERAL DESCRIPTION:
A wettable powder used to control black spot, powdery mildew, leaf spot, and other listed diseases on roses, flowers, and citrus. When applied as a preventive spray at the intervals specified on the label, it provides lasting protection against future infections. It is also used as a dip solution prior to planting to prevent corm rot on gladiolus. Mix it with any rooting medium to prevent damping-off on azalea cuttings. It may be combined with most common insecticides and fungicides, except for strongly alkaline materials as hydrated lime.

AREAS SOLD:
National

ACTIVE INGREDIENT:
75% Phaltan (Folpet) *N-([Trichloromethyl]thio)phthalimide*

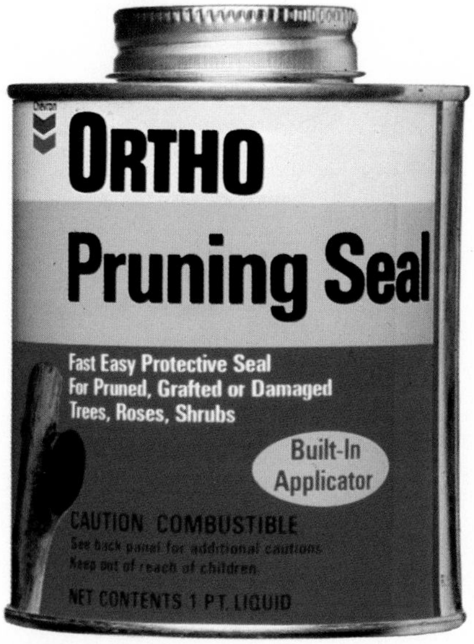

PRUNING SEAL

FOR USE IN THESE AREAS:
Roses and ornamental shrubs
Fruit and shade trees

GENERAL DESCRIPTION:
A ready-to-use liquid designed as a fast, effective dressing to aid in the healing of pruning cuts, grafts, abrasions, and wounds on woody plants, and fruit and shade trees. The material provides a protective coating that prevents the entry of moisture into the exposed cut and also prevents excessive sap flow. The built-in applicator makes the application fast and easy, and requires no additional equipment.

AREAS SOLD:
National

HINTS FOR USE:
Trim and clean tree wounds before applying ORTHO Pruning Seal. Using a sharp knife, trim away all splinters and dead wood, making a smooth wound. Then shape the wound into a vertical ellipse, pointed at the top and bottom. This shape hastens healing and callusing. Then apply the pruning seal evenly over the entire wound.

PRUNING SEALER

FOR USE IN THESE AREAS:
Roses and ornamentals
Fruit and shade trees

GENERAL DESCRIPTION:
An aerosol spray formulated as a fast, easy, effective dressing to aid in the healing of pruning cuts, grafts, abrasions, and wounds on woody plants and trees. It provides a protective coating against moisture, and helps prevent excessive sap flow. It can also be used to waterproof planting pots and wooden tubs. The ready-to-use aerosol makes application clean and easy.

AREAS SOLD:
National

PEST AND DISEASE CONTROL PRODUCTS

KILLS THESE INSECTS:
Aphids
Bagworms
Boxwood Leafminers
Japanese Beetles
Lacebugs
Leafrollers
Rose Chafers
Rose Leafhoppers
Rose Slugs
Scale Crawlers
Spider Mites

CONTROLS THESE DISEASES:
Black Spot
Leaf Spot
Powdery Mildew

FOR USE IN THESE AREAS:
Roses and flowers

ROSE & FLORAL DUST

GENERAL DESCRIPTION:
A dust specially formulated to control insects and major diseases on roses and other flowers. The insecticides kill both sucking and chewing pests that feed on leaves and blossoms. The fungicide protects the foliage from fungal infections. For best results, begin applying as new growth appears in the spring. Repeated applications are necessary through the growing season for good insect and disease control. The unique patented squeeze duster easily treats all parts of the plants, including the upper and lower surfaces of the leaves, without clumping or clogging. Apply in early morning or late evening when the temperature is low and the air is still.

AREAS SOLD:
National

ACTIVE INGREDIENTS:
3.0% Carbaryl (SEVIN®) *1-Naphthyl N-methylcarbamate*
4.0% Malathion 0,0-*Dimethyl dithiophosphate of diethyl mercaptosuccinate*
5.0% Phaltan (Folpet) *N-([Trichloromethyl]thio)phthalimide*
1.5% Dicofol (KELTHANE®) *1,1-Bis (p-chlorophenyl)-2,2,2-trichloroethanol*

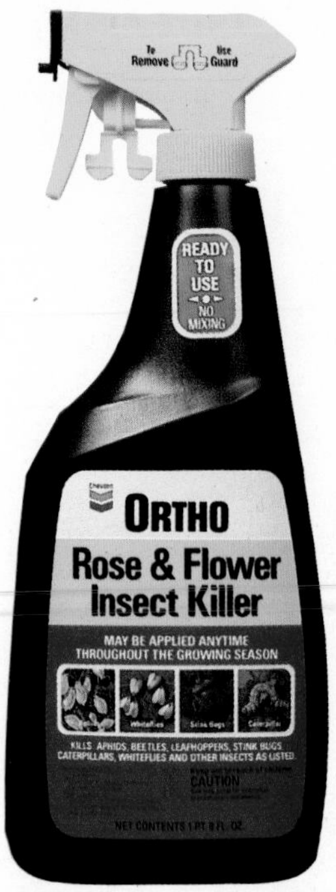

KILLS THESE INSECTS:
Aphids
Cabbage Looper
Caterpillars
Flea Beetles
Leafhoppers
Stink Bugs
Twelve-Spotted Cucumber Beetles
Whiteflies

FOR USE IN THESE AREAS:
Roses
Flowers

ROSE & FLOWER INSECT KILLER

GENERAL DESCRIPTION:
A ready-to-use liquid that kills aphids, whiteflies, and other insects that infest roses and other flowering plants. Ideal for spot-treatment, this product leaves no residue and comes in its own applicator container. ORTHO Rose & Flower Insect Killer can be applied any time during the growing season.

AREAS SOLD:
National

ACTIVE INGREDIENTS:
0.02% Pyrethrins
0.20% *Piperonyl Butoxide, Technical
0.08% Petroleum Distillate
*Equivalent to 0.16% (butylcarbityl)

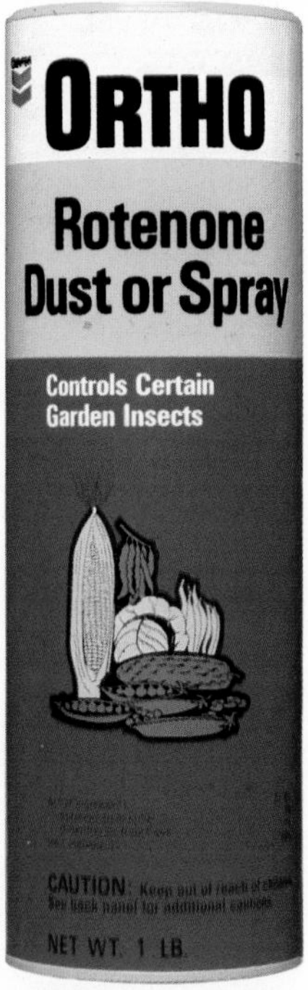

ROTENONE DUST OR SPRAY

KILLS THESE INSECTS:
Asparagus Beetles
Cabbage Worms
Cucumber Beetles
European Corn Borers
Flea Beetles
Pea Weevils
Thrips
Twelve-spotted Beetles

FOR USE IN THESE AREAS:
Vegetables

GENERAL DESCRIPTION:
A wettable powder insecticide designed to be used as either a dust or a spray to control certain garden pests on the vegetables listed on the label. *Rotenone*, the active ingredient, is a botanical insecticide derived from the roots of leguminous plants. One application provides protection for about a week. Repeated treatments are necessary for continuous insect control. When used as a dust, 1 pound will treat 1,000 square feet. It may be used on vegetables to within 1 day of harvest.

AREAS SOLD:
National

ACTIVE INGREDIENT:
1% Rotenone

HINTS FOR USE:
A contact insecticide kills insects by direct contact when absorbed through the insect's body. For best results, the plant must be thoroughly sprayed so that all insects are contacted.

SCRAM® DOG & CAT REPELLENT

FOR USE IN THESE AREAS:
Indoors
Outdoors

GENERAL DESCRIPTION:
An aerosol spray designed to repel dogs and cats from forbidden areas of the home such as furniture and rugs. Outdoors it prevents pets or stray animals from damaging garden areas, including ornamentals beds and lawns. However, do not apply the spray directly to the foliage of shrubs or to ornamental soft-bodied plants. When applied daily, this repellent is effective for 12 to 24 hours. The spray may stain or soften some fabrics or plastics, so test first by treating a small inconspicuous area. The label contains complete instructions for indoor and outdoor use.

AREAS SOLD:
National

ACTIVE INGREDIENT:
1.9% MGK 1770 Repellent *Methyl nonyl ketone*

HINTS FOR USE:
This product works best in conjunction with voice commands to pets. Read the label completely and follow directions for best results.

PEST AND DISEASE CONTROL PRODUCTS

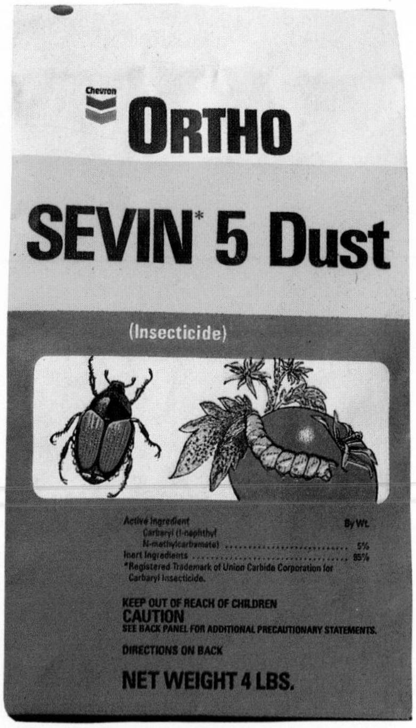

SEVIN® 5 DUST

GENERAL DESCRIPTION:
A 5 percent dust designed to control chewing and sucking insects including beetles, leafhoppers, and fruitworms on the vegetables listed on the label. It can be applied to beans, corn, carrots, cucumbers, melons, and squash up to the day of harvest. It also kills ticks and fleas on dogs and cats when lightly dusted on their fur. Treat poultry and in and around their houses to control lice, fleas, chicken mites, and northern fowl mites. Apply at the first sign of insects or damage, and repeat at intervals of 7 days unless the label specifies otherwise. For easy application in evenly covering both the upper and lower surfaces of the leaves, and in treating cracks and crevices in poultry houses and doghouses, apply with an ORTHO WHIRLY® Duster. *Note:* Do not use inside the home.

AREAS SOLD:
South

ACTIVE INGREDIENT:
5% Carbaryl (SEVIN®) *1-Naphthyl N-methylcarbamate*

KILLS THESE INSECTS:
Armyworms
Bean Leaf Beetles
Bedbugs
Cabbage Caterpillar
Chicken Mites
Colorado Potato Beetles
Corn Earworms
Corn Rootworm Adults
Cucumber Beetles
European Corn Borers
Fall Armyworms
Flea Beetles
Fleas
Harlequin Bugs
Imported Cabbageworms
Japanese Beetles
Lace Bugs
Leafhoppers
Lice
Lygus Bugs
Melonworms
Mexican Bean Beetles
Northern Fowl Mites
Pickleworms
Salt Marsh Caterpillars
Sap Beetles
Six-spotted Leafhoppers
Spittlebugs
Squash Bugs
Stink Bugs
Strawberry Leafrollers
Strawberry Weevils
Tarnished Plant Bugs
Ticks
Tomato Fruitworms
Tomato Hornworms
Velvetbean Caterpillars
Western Bean Cutworms
Young Cabbage Loopers

FOR USE IN THESE AREAS:
Vegetables and fruits
Pets and poultry

SEVIN® is a registered trademark of Union Carbide Corp.

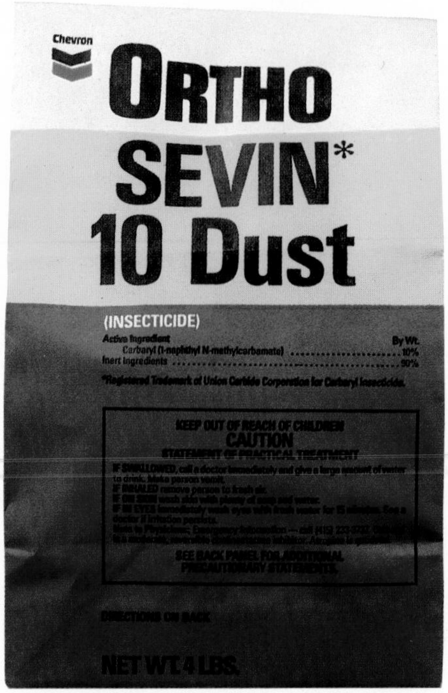

SEVIN® 10 DUST

GENERAL DESCRIPTION:
A 10 percent SEVIN® dust formulated to kill a wide range of vegetable and fruit insect pests on the listed crops. It can be applied to many fruits and vegetables up to harvest. The label gives detailed directions, with days to harvest for all listed fruits and vegetables. It also controls ticks and fleas on dogs and cats. Apply the dust at the first sign of insects or their damage. For best results, dust in early morning or late evening when the temperature is low and the air is still. Note: Do not use inside the home.

AREAS SOLD:
South

ACTIVE INGREDIENT:
10% Carbaryl (SEVIN®) *1-naphthyl N-methylcarbamate*

KILLS THESE INSECTS:
Armyworms
Bean Leaf Beetle
Blueberry Maggot
Cat-facing Insects
Cherry and Cranberry Fruitworms
Codling Moth
Colorado Potato Beetle
Corn Earworm
Corn Rootworm Adults
Cucumber Beetles
Eastern Tent Caterpillar
European Corn Borer
Fall Armyworm
Fleas
Flea Beetles
Fruit Tree Leafroller
Harlequin Bug
Imported Cabbageworm
Japanese Beetles
Leafhoppers
Lygus Bugs
Melonworm
Mexican Bean Beetle
Orange Tortrix
Oriental Fruit Moth
Peach Twig Borer
Periodical Cicada
Pickleworm
Plum Curculio
Red-Banded Leafroller
Sapbeetles
Six-spotted Leafhopper
Spittlebugs
Squash Bugs
Stink Bugs
Stink Bugs
Tarnished Plant Bug
Ticks
Tomato Fruitworm
Tomato Hornworm
Velvet Bean Caterpillar
Western Bean Cutworm
Western Tussock Moth
Young Cabbage Looper

FOR USE IN THESE AREAS:
Vegetables
Fruit and fruit trees
Dogs and cats

SEVIN®
GARDEN DUST

GENERAL DESCRIPTION:
A dust formulated to kill vegetable garden pests including hornworms, cutworms, beetles, and squash bugs on the listed vegetables. It can be applied to many vegetables up to harvest, including tomatoes, peppers, and beans. The label gives full instructions, with days to harvest for all listed vegetables. It also controls ticks and fleas on dogs and cats. Ruffle their fur while treating to ensure contact with the skin. For even application to plants and in and around doghouses and kennels, apply the dust with an ORTHO WHIRLY® Duster. Not for use inside the home.

AREAS SOLD:
National

ACTIVE INGREDIENT:
5% Carbaryl (SEVIN®) *1-Naphthyl N-methylcarbamate*

KILLS THESE INSECTS:
Armyworms
Bean Leaf Beetles
Cabbage Caterpillars
Colorado Potato Beetles
Corn Earworms
Corn Rootworm Adults
Cucumber Beetles
European Corn Borers
Fall Armyworms
Flea Beetles
Fleas
Harlequin Bugs
Japanese Beetles
Lace Bugs
Leafhoppers
Lygus Bugs
Melonworms
Mexican Bean Beetles
Pickleworms
Sap Beetles
Spittlebugs
Squash Bugs
Stink Bugs
Strawberry Leafrollers
Strawberry Weevils
Tarnished Plant Bugs
Ticks
Tomato Fruitworms
Tomato Hornworms
Velvetbean Caterpillars
Western Bean Cutworms

FOR USE IN THESE AREAS:
Fruits and vegetables
Pets

SEVIN® is a registered trademark of Union Carbide Corp.

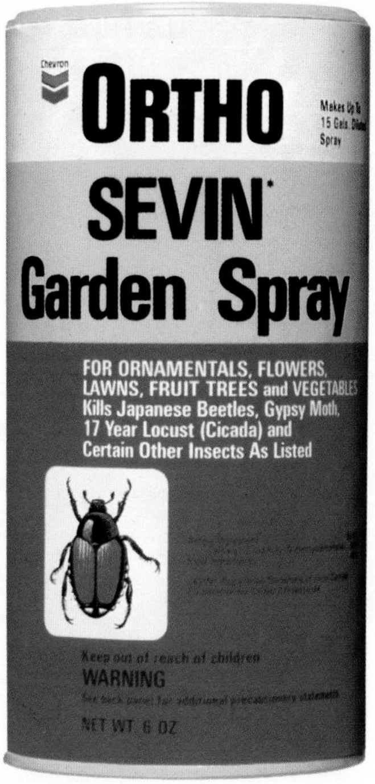

SEVIN®
GARDEN SPRAY

GENERAL DESCRIPTION:
A wettable powder containing *carbaryl* (SEVIN®), designed to control a wide range of chewing and sucking pests that damage and reduce yields of vegetables, fruits, flowers, ornamentals, and lawns. It is especially effective on hard-to-control apple maggots, gypsy moths, Japanese beetles, and cicadas. For best results and even coverage, apply the solution with an ORTHO SPRAY-ETTE® or ORTHO Lawn Sprayer at the first sign of insects or damage. Repeat the treatment weekly, or as noted on the label. SEVIN® Garden Spray may be used on the listed vegetables up to harvest. Six ounces of concentrate makes up to 15 gallons of diluted spray.

AREAS SOLD:
Midwest
Northeast
South

ACTIVE INGREDIENT:
50% Carbaryl (SEVIN®) *1-Naphthyl N-methylcarbamate*

HINTS FOR USE:
To dilute easily, mix the measured amount of powder with a little water to form a paste, then add the required amount of water.

KILLS THESE INSECTS:
Ants
Aphids
Apple Aphids
Apple Maggots
Bagworms
Blister Beetles
Codling Moths
Corn Borers
Earwigs
Elm Leaf Beetles
Fall Armyworms
Fleas
Fruitworms
Grasshoppers
Gypsy Moths
Hornworms
Japanese Beetles
Leafminers
Leafrollers
Melon Worms
Oriental Fruit Moths
Peachtree Borers
Periodical Cicadas (17-Year Locusts)
Plum Curculio
Pickleworms
Rose Slugs
Scale Insects
Sod Webworms
Tent Caterpillars
Thrips

FOR USE IN THESE AREAS:
Fruits and vegetables
Lawns
Roses and flowers
Trees and shrubs

PEST AND DISEASE CONTROL PRODUCTS

SLUG-GETA® SNAIL & SLUG BAIT

KILLS THESE INSECTS:
Crickets
Millipedes
Slugs
Snails
Sowbugs

FOR USE IN THESE AREAS:
Lawns and groundcovers
Ornamental gardens
Noncrop areas

GENERAL DESCRIPTION:
A granular, easy-to-use formulation of MESUROL® bait that effectively controls snails and slugs and other listed pests in ornamental gardens, dichondra and grass lawns, and turf. Simply scatter the granules directly from the canister, or apply them with an ORTHO WHIRLY-BIRD® Spreader. One pound of granules covers up to 1,000 square feet. Do not put granules in piles. Snails and slugs prefer damp, protected areas, so lightly sprinkle the area to be treated before application. This encourages movement and increases feeding on the bait. Do not use on or around food crops.

AREAS SOLD:
National

ACTIVE INGREDIENT:
2% Methiocarb *3.5-Dimethyl-4-(methlthio)phenyl methylcarbmate*

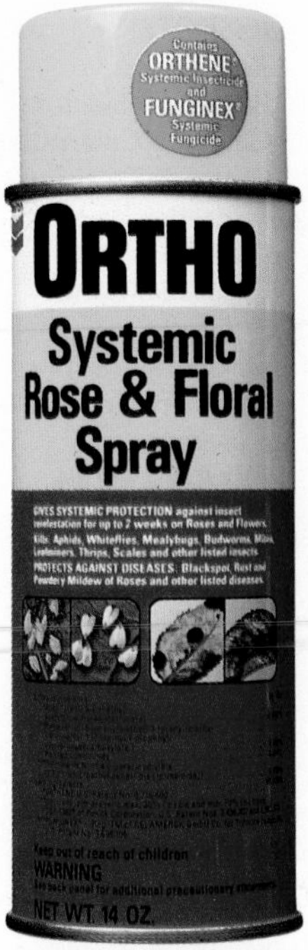

SYSTEMIC ROSE & FLORAL SPRAY

KILLS THESE INSECTS:
Aphids
Armyworms
Bagworms
Budworms
Cuban Laurel Thrips
Diabrotica Beetles
Flower Thrips
Lacebugs
Leafhoppers
Leafminers
Leaftiers
Mealybugs
Oleander Caterpillars
Rose Midges
Salt Marsh Caterpillars
Scales (Crawlers)
Southern Red Mites
Spittlebugs
Two-spotted Spider Mites
Whiteflies

CONTROLS THESE DISEASES:
Blackspot
Powdery Mildew
Rust

FOR USE IN THESE AREAS:
Roses and flowers
Trees and shrubs
Not for use on houseplants

GENERAL DESCRIPTION:
An aerosol containing the insecticide *acephate* (ORTHENE®) and *resmethrin* (SBP–1382®) and the systemic fungicide *triforine* (FUNGINEX®) to control a broad range of insects and diseases on plants listed on the label. The insecticides kill both on contact and by systemic action to provide protection of all plant parts against insect reinfestations for up to 2 weeks. The fungicide kills present fungal infections and systemically protects against additional infections for 1 to 2 weeks. Systemic action is internal, and cannot be washed off by rain or sprinkling. The 14-ounce size is especially convenient for gardeners with only a few plants to treat.

AREAS SOLD:
National

ACTIVE INGREDIENTS:
0.250% Acephate (ORTHENE®) *O,S-Dimethyl acetylphosphoramidothioate*
0.100% Resmethrin *(5-[Phenylmethyl]-3-furanyl)methyl 2,2-dimethyl-3-(2-methyl-1-propenyl) cyclopropane-carboxylate*
0.100% Triforine *N,N'-(1,4-Piperazine-diylbis [2,2,2-trichloroethylidene])bis (formamide)*

SYSTEMIC ROSE & FLOWER CARE 8-12-4

KILLS THESE INSECTS:
Aphids
Birch Leafminers
Holly Leafminers
Lacebugs
Leafhoppers
Mimosa Webworms
Pine Tip Moths
Spider Mites
Whiteflies

FOR USE IN THESE AREAS:
Roses and flowers
Shrubs
Potted plants

GENERAL DESCRIPTION:
This granular formulation is an effective systemic insecticide combined with a fertilizer containing the three essential plant food elements, nitrogen, phosphate, and potash. It provides the proper amount of plant food and systemic insecticide necessary for strong, vigorous plants free of damage from sucking and certain chewing insects. The insecticide is absorbed through the roots and moves to all parts of the plant. The protection is internal and cannot be washed off by rain or sprinkling. All parts of the plant, including new growth, are protected for up to 6 weeks. Do not use near food crops.

AREAS SOLD:
National

ACTIVE INGREDIENT:
1% Disulfoton *0,0-Diethyl S-(2-[ethylthio]ethyl) phosphorodithioate*

GUARANTEED ANALYSIS:
8% Nitrogen
12% Phosphoric Acid
4% Potash

3-WAY ROSE AND FLOWER CARE

KILLS THESE INSECTS:
Aphids
Birch Leafminers
Holly Leafminers
Lacebugs
Leafhoppers
Mimosa Webworms
Pine Tip Moths
Spider Mites
Whiteflies

KILLS THESE WEEDS:
Annual Bluegrass
Barnyardgrass
Bromegrass
Carelessweed
Carpetweed
Cheat
Chickweed
Crabgrass
Florida Pusley
Foxtail
Goosefoot
Goosegrass
Johnsongrass
Jungle Rice
Knotweed
Kochia
Lamb's Quarters
Pigweed (Spiny and Redfoot)
Puncturevine
Purslane
Russian Thistle
Sandbur
Sprangeletop
Stinging Nettle
Stinkgrass
Texas Panicum

FOR USE IN THESE AREAS:
Roses and flowers

GENERAL DESCRIPTION:
A granular formulation that kills sucking and chewing insects, prevents weeds, and feeds plants. It contains *disulfoton*, a systemic insecticide that is absorbed by the roots and then moves into the branches, leaves, and blossoms. The pre-emergence herbicide *trifluralin* kills annual grasses and broadleaf weeds as they germinate. The fertilizer supplies plants with nitrogen, phosphate, and potash, plus minor elements. Do not use near the roots of food crops.

AREAS SOLD:
Midwest, Northeast, West

ACTIVE INGREDIENT:
1.000% Disulfoton *0,0-Diethyl S-(2-[ethylthio]ethyl) phosphorodithioate*
0.174% Trifluralin *a,a,a-trifluoro-2,6-dinitro-N,N-dipropyl-p-toluidine*

GUARANTEED ANALYSIS:
8% Nitrogen
12% Phosphoric Acid
4% Potash
10% Calcium
1% Magnesium
9.5% Sulfur
Traces of these nutrients: Boron, Iron, Manganese, Molybdenum, Zinc

TOMATO & VEGETABLE INSECT KILLER

GENERAL DESCRIPTION:
A ready-to-use liquid with a convenient pump sprayer quickly kills whiteflies, aphids, beetles, caterpillars and other insects as listed on the label. Ideal for spot application on tomatoes and many other vegetable crops, and can be applied up to harvest. For best results, apply the spray to both the upper and lower surfaces of the leaves and fruits.

AREAS SOLD:
National

ACTIVE INGREDIENT:
0.02% Pyrethrins
0.20% *Piperonyl Butoxide, Technical
0.08% Petroleum Distillate
*Equivalent to 0.16% *(butylcarbityl)(6-propylpiperonyl)* ether and 0.04% related compound.

KILLS THESE INSECTS:
Aphids
Asparagus Beetles
Blister Beetles
Cabbage Looper
Colorado Potato Beetles
Cross Striped Cabbage Worms
Diamond-back Moth Larvae
Flea Beetles
Harlequin Bugs
Imported Cabbageworms
Leafhoppers
Leaftiers
Mexican Bean Beetles
Stink Bugs
Twelve-spotted Cucumber Beetles
Webworms
Whiteflies

FOR USE IN THESE AREAS:
Asparagus
Beans
Broccoli
Brussels Sprouts
Cabbage
Cauliflower
Celery
Collards
Eggplant
Kale
Lettuce
Mustard Greens
Peppers
Potatoes
Radishes
Spinach
Tomatoes
Turnips

FOR USE IN THESE AREAS:
Tomatoes
Vegetables

TOMATO & VEGETABLE INSECT SPRAY

GENERAL DESCRIPTION:
An aerosol spray designed for rapid control of flea beetles, hornworms, stinkbugs, and other listed insects on vegetables. This formulation contains two insecticides that are derived from plants and have quick contact-killing power. For best results, repeat the treatments to prevent a buildup of insect populations. The ready-to-use can makes treating both the upper and lower surfaces of the leaves an easy task. Food crops may be treated to within 1 day of harvest.

AREAS SOLD:
National

ACTIVE INGREDIENTS:
0.030% Pyrethrins
0.128% Rotenone

KILLS THESE INSECTS:
Aphids (Green Peach)
Blister Beetles
Colorado Potato Beetles
Flea Beetles
Hornworms
Japanese Beetles
Leafhoppers
Mexican Bean Beetles
Stinkbugs
Striped Cucumber Beetles
Twelve-spotted Cucumber Beetles
Whiteflies

FOR USE IN THESE AREAS:
Vegetables

TOMATO VEGETABLE DUST

GENERAL DESCRIPTION:
A multipurpose garden dust that contains the insecticides *methoxychlor* and *rotenone* and the fungicide *captan* for insect and disease control on listed vegetables and berries including tomatoes, melons, squash, potatoes, and strawberries. When applied according to the label directions, it kills fungal infections and protects the foliage from additional infections for up to 2 weeks. It kills insects both on contact and as they feed on the leaves. Repeated treatments are necessary for good insect and disease control. It can be used on most vegetables and berries up to 7 days before harvest.

AREAS SOLD:
National

ACTIVE INGREDIENTS:
4.7% Captan *N-([trichloromethyl]thio)-4-cyclohexene-1,2-dicarboximide*
5.00% Methoxychlor *2,2-bis (p-methoxyphenyl)-1,1,1-trichloroethane* and related compounds
0.75% Rotenone

KILLS THESE INSECTS:
Aphids
Blister Beetles
Colorado Potato Beetles
Cucumber Beetles
Flea Beetles
Fleahoppers
Japanese Beetles
Leafhoppers
Melonworms
Mexican Bean Beetles
Omnivorous Leaftiers
Pickleworms
Raspberry Fruitworms
Spittlebugs
Squash Bugs (Nymphs)
Squash Vine Borers
Thrips
Tomato Fruitworms

CONTROLS THESE DISEASES:
Alternaria
Anthracnose
Botrytis Rot
Cercospora
Downy Mildew
Early Blight
Fruit Rot
Late Blight
Phomopsis
Septoria Leaf Spot
Spur Blight

FOR USE IN THESE AREAS:
Vegetables

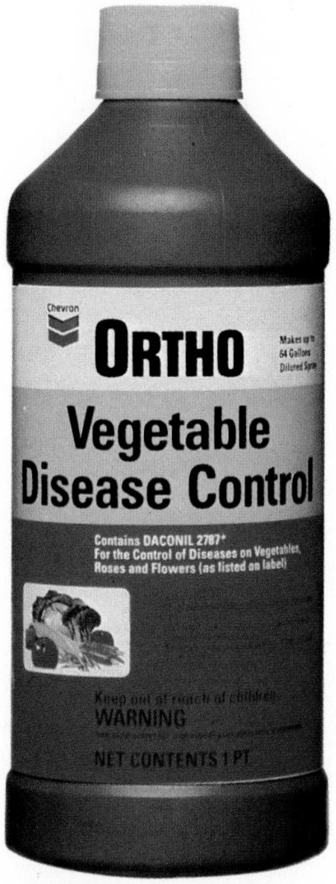

VEGETABLE DISEASE CONTROL

GENERAL DESCRIPTION:
A liquid spray used to control diseases on vegetables, roses, and flowers as listed on the label. When applied according to the label directions and repeated at specified intervals, it provides protection against fungal infections. One pint of concentrate makes up to 64 gallons of diluted spray. It dilutes easily in water to be applied with an ORTHO SPRAY-ETTE® or a tank-type or power sprayer. Use up to the day of harvest on tomatoes, cucumbers, broccoli, and carrots. The label lists days to harvest for other vegetables.

AREAS SOLD:
National

ACTIVE INGREDIENT:
29.6% Chlorothalonil (DACONIL 2787®) *Tetrachloroisophthalonitrile*

CONTROLS THESE DISEASES:
Alternaria Fruit Rot or Black Mold on Tomatoes
Alternaria Leaf Spot on Broccoli, Brussels Sprouts, Cabbage, and Cauliflower
Anthracnose on Cucumbers, Melons, Pumpkins, Squash, and Tomatoes
Basal Stalk Rot on Celery
Blackspot on Roses
Blossom Blight on Roses
Botrytis Blight on Geraniums and Iris
Botrytis Vine Rot on Potatoes
Cercospora Leaf Spot on Melons, Pumpkins, and Squash
Downy Mildew on Broccoli, Brussels Sprouts, Cabbage, and Cauliflower
Early Blight on Carrots, Celery, Potatoes, and Tomatoes
Fruit Rot (Rhizoctonia) on Cucumbers and Tomatoes
Gray Mold (Botrytis) on Tomatoes and Chrysanthemums
Gummy Stem Blight on Cucumbers, Melons, Pumpkins, Squash, and Tomatoes
Helminthosporium Leaf Blight on Sweet Corn
Late Blight on Carrots, Celery, Potatoes, and Tomatoes
Leaf Blight on Cucumbers, Melons, Pumpkins, Squash, and Tomatoes
Leaf Spot on Iris
Powdery Mildew (*Erysiphe*) on Cucumbers, Melons, and Zinnias
Ring Spot on Brussels Sprouts
Rust on Beans
Scab

FOR USE IN THESE AREAS:
Roses and flowers
Vegetables

PEST AND DISEASE CONTROL PRODUCTS

KILLS THESE INSECTS:
Cutworms
Mole Crickets
Wireworms
Root Maggots
Carrot Rust Flies
Onion Maggots
European Corn Borers
Fall Armyworms
Vinegar Flies

FOR USE IN THESE AREAS:
Vegetables

VEGETABLE GUARD SOIL INSECT KILLER

GENERAL DESCRIPTION:
This insecticide is formulated as ready-to-use granules that control cutworms, wireworms, and other soil-dwelling insects. Apply the granules when seeding or transplanting the listed vegetables. Then mix the granules into the soil to the specified depth. The granules can be easily sprinkled directly from the canister without additional equipment.

AREAS SOLD:
National

ACTIVE INGREDIENT:
5% Diazinon *(0,0-diethyl-0-[2-isopropyl-6-methyl-4-pyrimidinyl]phosphorothioate)*

KILLS THESE INSECTS:
Codling Moth Eggs
Lacebug Larvae
Mealybugs
Oak Moth Eggs
Red Spider Mites
Red Spider Mite Eggs
Scales
Whitefly Larvae

FOR USE IN THESE AREAS:
Trees and shrubs
Fruits
Greenhouses

VOLCK® OIL SPRAY

GENERAL DESCRIPTION:
A liquid dormant and growing season insect spray that controls scale insects, mealybugs, and red spider mites on ornamentals, citrus, fruits, and palms, and in greenhouses. It also acts as a leaf polish to brighten the leaves of hardy houseplants, and helps to suffocate listed insect eggs. It can be combined with ORTHO ORTHORIX® Spray for a winter spray on dormant deciduous fruits, roses, and ornamentals. Or combine it with ORTHO Malathion 50 Insect Spray for improved insect control on citrus, avocados, mangos, gardenias, and ixora. It is also effective in removing sooty mold fungus by controlling whitefly larvae.

AREAS SOLD:
Midwest
Northeast
South

ACTIVE INGREDIENT:
97% Petroleum Oil

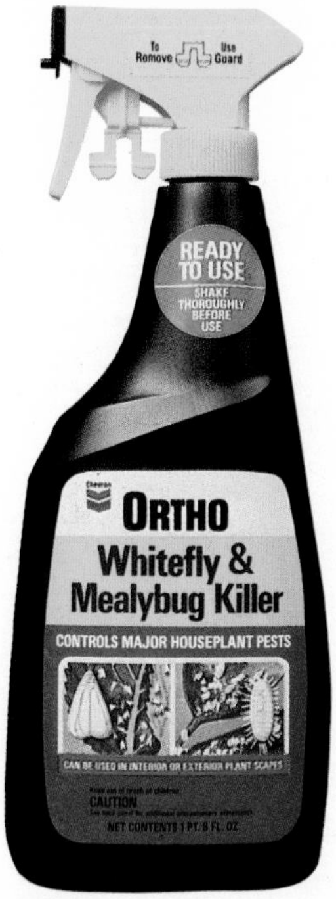

WHITEFLY & MEALYBUG KILLER

GENERAL DESCRIPTION:
A liquid designed to control all the major houseplant pests, including hard-to-kill mealybugs, whiteflies, and two-spotted spider mites. It kills on contact, so pests must be sprayed directly. This spray can be used on the listed plants indoors or out. The ready-to-use container with hand-pump nozzle makes treating both the upper and lower surfaces of the leaves a quick and easy task. Repeat the treatment if needed, but not more frequently than every 7 days.

AREAS SOLD:
National

ACTIVE INGREDIENT:
0.050% Resmethrin *(5-[Phenyl-methyl]-3-furanyl) methyl 2,2-dimethyl-3-(2-methyl-1-propenyl) cyclopropane-carboxylate*
0.180% Petroleum
0.220% Plant Spray Oil

KILLS THESE INSECTS:
Aphids
Mealybugs
Scales (Crawlers)
Two-spotted Spider Mites
Whiteflies

FOR USE ON THESE PLANTS:
Aluminum Plant
Asparagus Fern
African Violet
Angelwing Begonia
Bird's-nest Fern
Bird's-nest Sansevieria
Boston Fern
Coleus
Dieffenbachia
Dracaena
English Ivy
False Aralia
Fiddle Leaf Philodendron
Fluffy Ruffles
Fuchsia
Geranium
Holly Fern
Ivy Geranium
Jade Plant
Japanese Aralia
Marigold
Neanthe Bella Palm
Needle Point Ivy
Nephthytis
Parlor Palm
Philodendron
Piggyback Plant
Polka Dot Plant
Pothos
Prayer Plant
Purple Passion
Ribbon Plant
Rubber Plant
Salvia
Schefflera
Shasta Daisy
Silver Tree
Spider Plant
Sprengeri Fern
Strawberry Begonia
Swedish Ivy
Variegated Spider Plant
Wandering Jew
Wax Plant
Weeping Fig
Zebra Plant

FOR USE IN THESE AREAS:
Houseplants

BRUSH-B-GON® BRUSH KILLER

GENERAL DESCRIPTION:
This liquid concentrate effectively controls 36 listed undesirable brushy plants and a variety of weeds, including poison oak, poison ivy, blackberry, willow, and kudzu vine. The active ingredient is the systemic herbicide Garlon. A systemic, ORTHO BRUSH-B-GON®, translocates to all parts of the plant, including the root system. When diluted, one quart of concentrate will make up to 8 gallons of spray.

AREAS SOLD:
National

ACTIVE INGREDIENT:
8.0% *Triclopyr *(3,5,6-trichloro-2-pyridinyl-oxyacetic acid)*, as the triethylamine salt
*Equivalent to 5.7% acid

KILLS THESE WEEDS:
Arkansas Rose
Big Leaf Maple
Black Cottonwood
Black Willow
Box Elder
California Rose
Choke Cherry
Common Ragweed
Elderberry
Elm
Evergreen Blackberry
Giant Ragweed
Himalayan Blackberry
Honeysuckle
Kudzu
Mackenzie Willow
Mesquite
Mimosa
Maple
Narrow Leaved Willow
Oak
Persimmon
Poison Ivy
Poison Oak
Raspberry
Red Alder
Sassafras
Scouler Willow
Sweet Gum
Trailing Blackberry
Trumpet Creeper
Virginia Creeper
Wild Blackberry
Wild Grape
Wild Rose
Willow

FOR USE IN THESE AREAS:
Unwanted Woody Plants

WEED CONTROL PRODUCTS

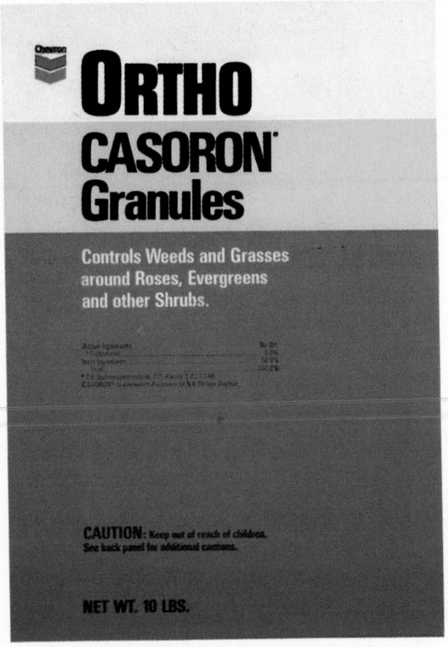

KILLS THESE WEEDS:
Annual Bluegrass
Carpetweed
Chickweed
Crabgrass
Foxtail
Groundsel
Henbit
Horsetail
Knotweed
Lamb's-quarters
Pigweed
Pineapple Weed
Purslane
Mustard
Shepherds Purse
Smartweed
Spurge

FOR USE IN THESE AREAS:
Trees and shrubs
Roses

CASORON® GRANULES

GENERAL DESCRIPTION:
A granular pre-emergence weed killer designed to control annual and perennial weeds and grasses around roses, evergreens, and other shrubs and trees. Before applying, existing weeds should be removed and the soil worked and smoothed. Sprinkle the granules uniformly over the soil and water in lightly. Do not disturb soil in a treated area as long as the weed control program is being maintained.

AREAS SOLD:
West (Oregon, Washington, and Idaho)

ACTIVE INGREDIENT:
2.0% Dichlobenil *2,6-Dichlorobenzonitrile*

CASORON® is a registed trademark of Thompson-Hayward Chemical Co.

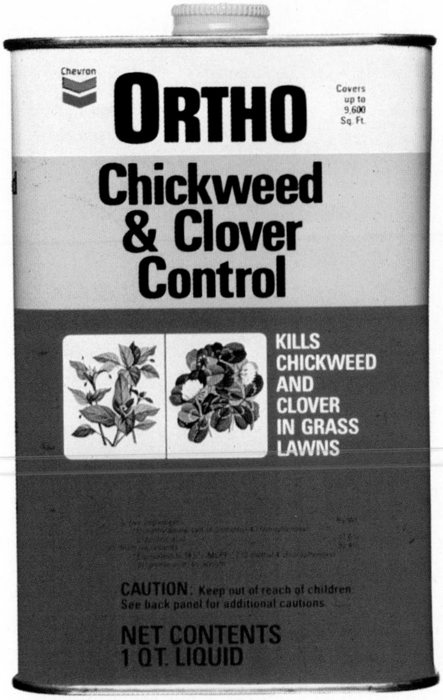

KILLS THESE WEEDS:
Clover
Common Chickweed
Dandelion
Dichondra
Ground Ivy
Knotweed
Lamb's-quarters
Mouseear Chickweed
Mustard
Pigweed
Plantain
Ragweed
Shepherds Purse

FOR USE IN THESE AREAS:
Lawns

CHICKWEED & CLOVER CONTROL

GENERAL DESCRIPTION:
A liquid broadleaf weed killer concentrate to be mixed with water and applied with any ORTHO hose end sprayer to control chickweed, clover, and a number of broadleaf weeds in grass lawns as listed. It can be used any time that weeds are actively growing; however, applications are most effective in the spring and fall when the weeds are small and temperatures are mild. For best results, apply when the air is calm in the morning (after the leaves are dry) on a sunny day when no rain is expected and the temperatures will not exceed 85°F for 24 hours. Water the lawn thoroughly 2 or 3 days before spraying, and do not water for 48 hours after application. When diluted, one quart of concentrate covers up to 9,600 square feet.

AREAS SOLD:
Midwest
Northeast
South

ACTIVE INGREDIENT:
17.6% MCPP *Dimethylamine salt of 2-(methyl-4-chlorophenoxy) propionic acid*

CHICKWEED, SPURGE & OXALIS KILLER D

GENERAL DESCRIPTION:
A liquid broadleaf weed killer concentrate that mixes with water; for best results, apply when weeds are small and tender. If weeds are older and harder to kill, use the higher rates listed on the label. This product is especially effective against the troublesome lawn weeds—spotted spurge, oxalis, chickweed, knotweed, sheep sorrel, and henbit. In addition to these, it kills virtually all broadleaf weeds. For best results, apply when the air is calm in the morning (after the leaves are dry) on a sunny day when no rain is expected for 24 hours. Water the lawn thoroughly 2 or 3 days before spraying. When diluted, one pint covers up to 6,400 square feet.

AREAS SOLD:
West

ACTIVE INGREDIENTS:
3.05% 2,4-D *Dimethylamine salt of 2,4-dichlorophenoxyacetic acid*
10.60% MCPP *Dimethylamine salt of 2-(2-methyl-4-chlorophenoxy) propionic acid*
1.30% Dicamba *Dimethylamine salt of Dicamba (3,6-dichloro-o-anisic acid)*

KILLS THESE WEEDS:
Bedstraw
Black Medic
Buckhorn
Bull Thistle
Burdock
Buttercup
Chicory
Chickweed
Clover
Cocklebur
Dandelion
Dock
Galinsoga
Ground Ivy
Hawkweed
Heal-all
Henbit
Knotweed
Lambsquarters
Lespedeza
Mallow
Morning Glory
Mustard
Oxalis
Peppergrass
Pigweed
Plantain
Poison Ivy
Poison Oak
Purslane
Ragweed
Sheep Sorrel
Shepherdspurse
Speedwell
Spurge
Tansy Mustard
Thistle
Velvet Leaf
Wild Carrot
Wild Garlic
Wild Lettuce
Wild Onion
Yarrow and many other broadleaf weeds

FOR USE IN THESE AREAS:
Lawns

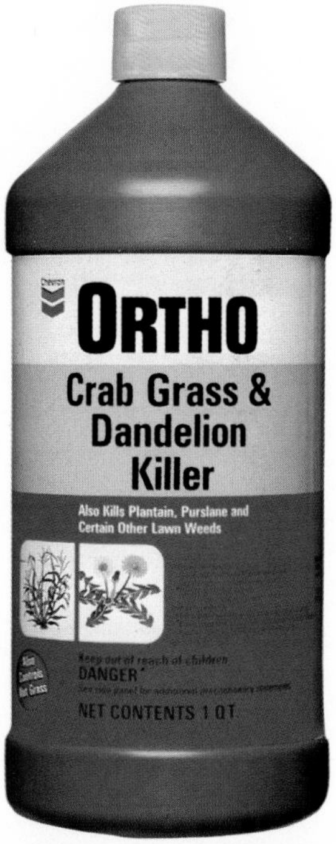

CRAB GRASS & DANDELION KILLER

GENERAL DESCRIPTION:
A liquid post-emergence herbicide that controls established crabgrass, dandelions, nutgrass, and other listed weeds in major turf grasses. It mixes readily with water as directed, to be applied as a coarse spray. For best results, apply when weeds are 1 to 2 inches tall and temperatures are below 90°F. Reseed bare spots 3 weeks after treatment. Do not apply to newly seeded lawns until after 3 mowings. Do not use on dichondra, St. Augustine, carpet, centipede, bahia, or bentgrass lawns. Avoid spray or drift onto nearby desirable plants.

AREAS SOLD:
Midwest
Northeast

ACTIVE INGREDIENTS:
8.0% *Dodecylammonium methanearsonate*
8.0% *Octylammonium methanearsonate*
7.67% 2,4-D *Octylammonium salt of 2,4-dichlorophenoxyacetic acid*

KILLS THESE WEEDS:
Crabgrass
Dandelion
Knotweed
Nutgrass
Pennywort
Plantain
Purslane

FOR USE IN THESE AREAS:
Lawns

WEED CONTROL PRODUCTS

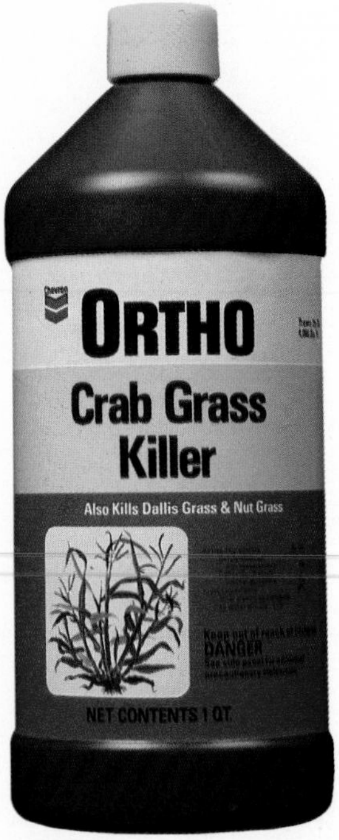

KILLS THESE WEEDS:
Crabgrass
Dallisgrass
Nutgrass

FOR USE IN THESE AREAS:
Lawns

CRAB GRASS KILLER

GENERAL DESCRIPTION:
A liquid, selective post-emergence weed killer used to control crabgrass, dallisgrass, and nutgrass on all major turf grasses including dichondra, bent, and fescue grasses. One quart of concentrate mixes readily with water to treat up to 4,000 square feet. For best results, treat when weeds are 1 to 2 inches tall. Control older weeds with repeated applications. This herbicide may be used on newly seeded lawns after two mowings. When the weeds are dead, remove and reseed bare spots. Do not use on St. Augustine, carpet, or centipedegrass lawns.

AREAS SOLD:
National

ACTIVE INGREDIENTS:
8% *Octylammonium methanearsonate*
8% *Dodecylammonium methanearsonate*

KILLS THESE WEEDS:
Annual and perennial weeds and grasses

FOR USE IN THESE AREAS:
Driveways
Along fences
Sidewalks
Walkways
Patios
Curbs
Gutters
Not for use in vegetable gardens

FENCE & GRASS EDGER FORMULA II

GENERAL DESCRIPTION:
This convenient, ready-to-use liquid comes with its own handy applicator. It gives complete kill of annual and perennial weeds and grasses, and will prevent germination of weeds and grasses for up to 3 months. Apply ORTHO Fence & Grass Edger Formula II where no vegetation is desired, such as driveways, along fences, sidewalks, walkways, patios, curbs, gutters, and even cracks in sidewalks. One gallon will cover a band 2 inches wide and 1200 feet long.

AREAS SOLD:
National

ACTIVE INGREDIENT:
0.25% *Isopropylamine salt of *glyphosate*
0.25% *Oxyfluorfen-2-chloro-1-(3-ethoxy-4-nitrophenoxy)-4-(trifluoromethyl) benzene*
**N-(phosphonomethyl) glycine*

GARDEN WEED PREVENTER

KILLS THESE WEEDS:
Annual Bluegrass
Barnyardgrass
Carpetweed
Common Chickweed
Crabgrass (Both Smooth and Large)
Florida Pusley
Goosegrass
Green and Yellow Foxtail
Johnsongrass (From Seed)
Lamb's-quarters
Lovegrass
Nodding Spurge
Pigweed
Purslane
Witchgrass

FOR USE IN THESE AREAS:
Lawns
Trees and shrubs
Vegetables and flowers

GENERAL DESCRIPTION:
A granular pre-emergence herbicide used to prevent annual grasses and broadleafed weeds weeds from becoming established in lawns and flower gardens and around trees, shrubs, and vegetables as listed on the label. Use this herbicide at seeding or transplanting time and around established plants as directed. When applied according to label directions, it keeps treated areas free of listed weeds for up to 4 months.

AREAS SOLD:
National

ACTIVE INGREDIENT:
5% DCPA (DACTHAL®)
Dimethyltetrachloroterephthalate

HINTS FOR USE:
Pre-emergence herbicides kill only germinating seedlings, not existing weeds. So for best results clean all weeds from the area to be treated, and cultivate. Then spread the herbicide immediately and rake it into the top 1 or 2 inches of soil, or water lightly. The herbicide forms a barrier on the soil that kills seedlings. Disturbing the soil after application reduces the herbicide's effectiveness.

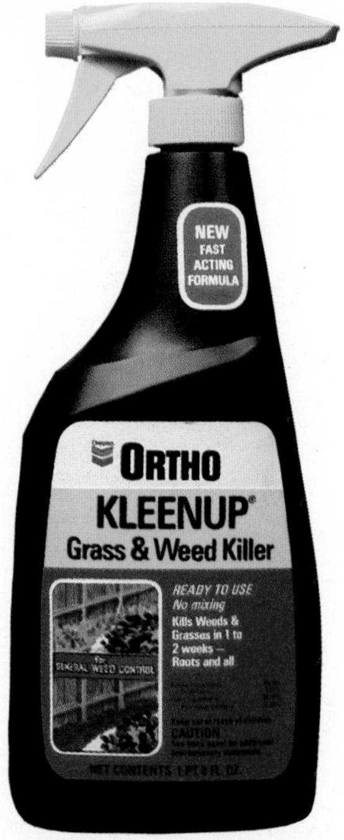

KLEENUP® GRASS & WEED KILLER

KILLS THESE WEEDS:
Annual Bluegrass
Bahiagrass
Bermudagrass
Bentgrass
Blackseed Plantain
Broadleaf Plantain
Canada Thistle
Chickweed
Clover
Common Fiddleneck
Common Mollein
Common Plantain
Common Ragweed
Creeping Charlie
Cudweed
Dandelion
Evening Primrose
False Dandelion
Field Bindweed (Wild Morning Glory)
Garden Spurge
Goosegrass
Green Foxtail
Hairy Crabgrass
Henbit
Hypericum
Johnsongrass
Kentucky Bluegrass
Lambsquarter
Large Crabgrass
Nutgrass (Nutsedge)
Orchardgrass
Oxalis
Poison Ivy
Poison Oak
Prostrate Knotweed
Prostrate Pigweed
Purslane
Puncture Vine
Quackgrass
Ragweed
Red Dead Nettle
Sandspur
Sheperdspurse
Smooth Crabgrass
Sowthistle
Spurge
St. Augustinegrass
Tall Fescue
Torpedograss
Virginia Creeper
Wild Blackberry
Wild Geranium
Yellow Oxalis
Zoysiagrass

FOR USE IN THESE AREAS:
Flower Beds
Around Trees and Shrubs
Lawns
Walks
Driveways

GENERAL DESCRIPTION:
This ready-to-use liquid glyphoste systemic weed killer formulation is formulated for spot application to individual annual and perennial weeks, including annual bluegrass, oxalis, dandelion and many others. Its systemic action moves throughout the plant's leaves, stems and roots. Visible effects usually occur within 1 week on most weeks with complete kill in 1 to 2 weeks. For best results, spray on a calm day when the air is still to avoid possible drift. Treated areas in lawns can be reseeded 7 days after application.

AREAS SOLD:
National

ACTIVE INGREDIENT:
0.50% *Isopropylamine salt of *glyphosate *[N-(phosphoromethyl)glycine]*
0.12% *Sodium salt of **acifluorfen **[sodium 5-2-chloro-4(triflouromethyl)-phenoxy-2-nitrobenzoate]*

WEED CONTROL PRODUCTS

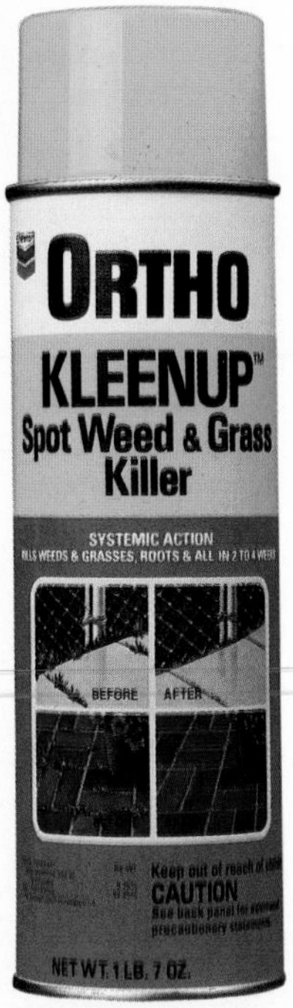

KLEENUP® SPOT WEED & GRASS KILLER

GENERAL DESCRIPTION:
An easy-to-use aerosol containing glyphosate systemic weed killer is formulated with a foam marker for spot application to individual weeds. Ideal for use in flower beds, around trees and shrubs, in walks and driveways, and for spot weed treatment in lawns. It kills tough annual and perennial grasses and broadleaf weeds with a systemic action that assures complete kill, roots and all, in 2 to 4 weeks.

AREAS SOLD:
National

ACTIVE INGREDIENT:
0.75% *Isopropylamine salt of *glyphosate *[N-(phosphoromethyl)glycine]*

KILLS THESE WEEDS:
Bahiagrass
Bentgrass
Bermudagrass
Bluegrass
Canada Thistle
Centipedegrass
Cheeseweed
Chickweed (common)
Clover
Common Lambquarters
Common Ragweed
Crabgrass
Creeping Charlie
Creeping Lantana
Curly Dock
Dallisgrass
Dandelion
Dog Fennel
Evening Primrose
Florida Pusley
Goosegrass
Hairy Crabgrass
Henbit
Ironweed
Johnsongrass
Knotweeds
Maiden Cane
Mouseear Chickweed
Nutgrass (Nutsedge)
Oxalis
Pigweeds
Plantains
Poison Ivy
Poison Oak
Prickly Lettuce
Purple Cudweed
Purslane
Quackgrass
Sandspur
Smartweeds
Sowthistle
Spurges
St. Augustinegrass
Tall Fescue
Torpedograss
Velvetweed
Virginia Creeper
Wild Blackberry
Wild Carrot
Wild Geranium
Wild Morning Glory
Yarrow
Yellow Oxalis

FOR USE IN THESE AREAS:
Driveways, Walks
Flower Gardens
Lawns
Mulches
Ornamentals

KLEENUP® SYSTEMIC WEED & GRASS KILLER

GENERAL DESCRIPTION:
A liquid, nonselective herbicide that controls annual and perennial grasses, weeds, and other unwanted vegetation. Also use it for spot treatment in lawns. It contains the proven herbicide *glyphosate,* which moves systemically through the plant, killing tops and roots. Its killing power is inactivated on contact with soil, so the roots of surrounding trees and shrubs are not harmed. Treated lawn areas can be tilled and seeded after 7 days. Treated plants generally begin to show symptoms within a week, with complete kill in 2 to 4 weeks.

AREAS SOLD:
National

ACTIVE INGREDIENT:
5.00% *Isopropylamine salt of *glyphosate *[N-(phosphoromethyl)glycine]*

KILLS THESE WEEDS:
Bahiagrass
Bentgrass
Bermudagrass
Bindweed (Wild Morning Glory)
Blackberries
Black Medic
Bluegrass
Broadleaf Plantain
Bromegrass
Burclover
Canada Thistle
Chickweed
Common Groundsel
Common Plantain
Crabgrasses
Creeping Bentgrass
Creeping Charlie
Curly Dock
Dandelion
Diffuse Lovegrass
Dog Fennel
Evening Primrose
False Dandelion
Fennel
Fescue
Fiddleneck
Filaree
Florida Pusley
Garden Spurge
Henbit
Johnsongrass
Knotweed
Lamb's-quarters
London Rocket
Mallow
Mayweed
Mouseear Chickweed
Oldenlandia
Orchardgrass
Oxalis
Pennsylvania Smartweed
Pennywort
Perennial Ryegrass
Poison Ivy
Poison Oak
Primrose
Prostrate Spurge
Puncture Vine
Quackgrass
Ragweed
Sandspur
Shepherds Purse
Smooth Cat's Ear
Sowthistle
Spotted Spurge
St. Augustinegrass
Tall Fescue
Torpedograss
White Clover
Whitetop
Wild Barley
Yellow Nutgrass
Zoysia

FOR USE IN THESE AREAS:
Trees and shrubs
Flower beds and lawns
Noncrop areas

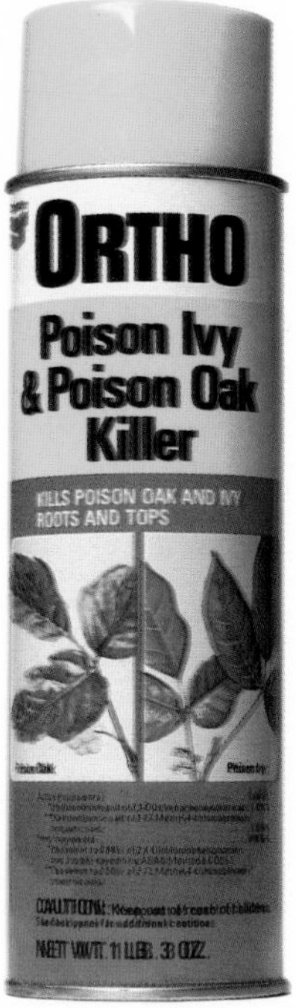

KILLS THESE PLANTS:
Poison Ivy
Poison Oak

FOR USE IN THESE AREAS:
Noncrop areas

POISON IVY & POISON OAK KILLER

GENERAL DESCRIPTION:
An easy-to-use aerosol for controlling poison ivy and poison oak around homes and buildings, along fence rows, in vacant lots, and on tree trunks. It contains two proven selective herbicides, 2,4-D and MCPP, that are translocated throughout the entire plant, killing roots and tops. An added foam marker helps ensure complete coverage of all leaves. In warm and sunny summer weather, the treated leaves turn brown in 10 days to 2 weeks after spraying. Discard dead plants in sealed plastic bags. Wear rubber gloves whenever handling poison ivy or poison oak, whether it is alive or dead. Discard the gloves after use, since irritating oils may remain potent for months.

AREAS SOLD:
South
West

ACTIVE INGREDIENT:
0.70% 2,4-D *Diethanolamine salt of 2,4-Dichlorophenoxyacetic acid*
0.75% MCPP *Diethanolamine salt of 2-(2-Methyl-4-chlorophenoxy) propionic acid*

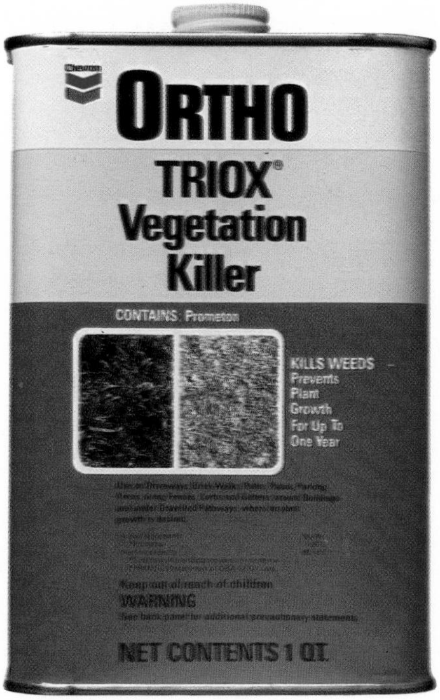

KILLS THESE PLANTS:
General weed conrol

FOR USE IN THESE AREAS:
Noncrop areas

TRIOX®
VEGETATION KILLER

GENERAL DESCRIPTION:
A liquid semi-soil-sterilant containing *prometon*, designed to kill existing vegetation and prevent plant growth for up to a year after treatment. Use it only in areas where plant growth is unwanted, such as driveways, brick walks, gravel pathways, patios, parking areas, along fences, curbs and gutters, and in cracks in sidewalks. Do not apply over root systems of desirable plants. Treat any time, but for best results apply to bare soil or just as new growth emerges in the spring. See label for detailed instructions.

AREAS SOLD:
National

ACTIVE INGREDIENT:
1.86% Prometon *2-Methoxy-4,6-bix(isopropylamino)-s-triazine*

HINTS FOR USE:
If the weeds are taller than 5 inches, cut them down and remove before application. If no rain has fallen after 2 to 3 days, water thoroughly to help move the herbicide into the soil. Do not apply to slopes or where desired vegetation is to be grown in the future.

WEED CONTROL PRODUCTS

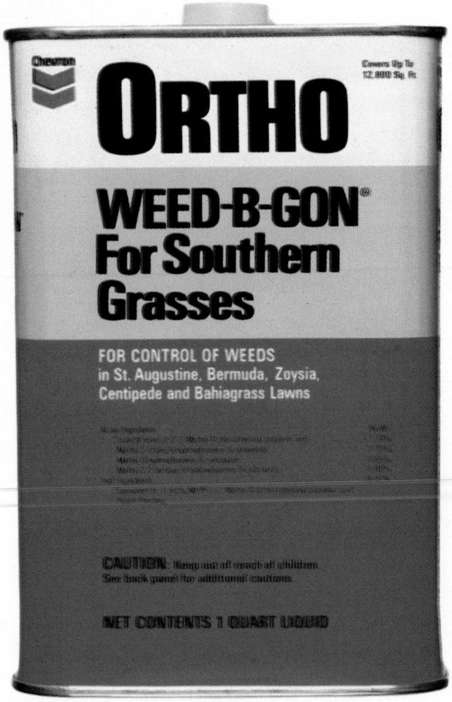

KILLS THESE WEEDS:
Black Medic
Bracted Plantain
Chickweed
Clover
Cudweed
Dichondra
Evening Primrose
Florida Betony
Florida Pusley
Oxalis
Pigweed
Purslane
Sensitive Mimosa
Shepherds Purse
Sow Thistle
Spurge
Toadflax
Wild Geranium

FOR USE IN THESE AREAS:
Lawns

WEED-B-GON® FOR SOUTHERN GRASSES

GENERAL DESCRIPTION:
A liquid herbicide containing MCPP and *chlorflurecol* and designed for control of broadleaf weeds in St. Augustine, Bermuda, zoysia, centipede, and bahiagrass lawns. When used as directed, it does not injure the lawn grass, and control a wide range of broadleaf weeds including hard-to-kill oxalis, spurge, and wild geranium. One quart of concentrate diluted as directed covers up to 12,800 square feet. For best results, apply with an ORTHO SPRAY-ETTE® or tank-type sprayer. Treated weeds may remain green for 2 to 3 weeks following the application. Complete kill may take 4 to 6 weeks. Do not use on dichondra, lippia, clover, bluegrass, or fescue lawns, or around desirable plants.

AREAS SOLD:
South

ACTIVE INGREDIENTS:
17.74% MCPP *Isooctyl ester of 2-(2-Methyl-4-chlorophenoxy) propionic acid*
2.71% *Methyl 2-chloro-9-hydroxyfluorene-9-carboxylate*
0.65% *Methyl 9-hydroxyfluorene-9-carboxylate*
0.49% *Methyl 2,7 dichloro-9-hydroxyfluorene-9-carboxylate*

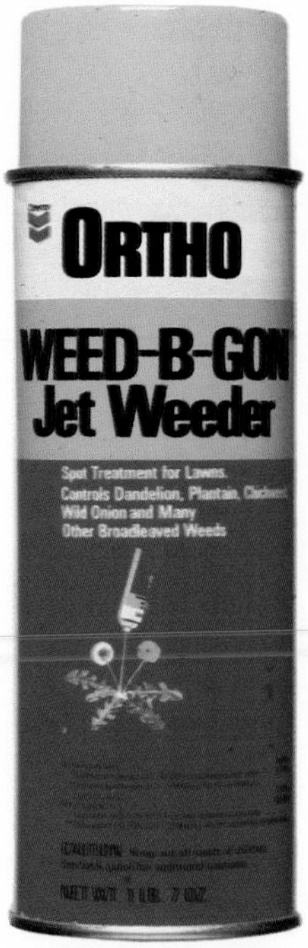

KILLS THESE WEEDS:
Annual Morning Glory
Chickweed
Cinquefoil
Clovers
Dandelions
Ground Ivy
Henbit
Knotweed
Pennywort
Plantain
Poison Ivy
Poison Oak
Purslane
Spotted Spurge
Thistles
Wild Onion

FOR USE IN THESE AREAS:
Lawns

WEED-B-GON® JET WEEDER

GENERAL DESCRIPTION:
A clean, easy-to-use aerosol for spot treating individual broadleaf weeds in most grass lawns. It produces a foamy white lather for direct weed contact and to avoid drift. The foam also serves as a marker to prevent repeated applications. This herbicide is effective on persistent broadleaf weeds including chickweed, thistles, annual morning glory, and dandelions. It contains 2,4-D and MCPP, hormonal weed killers that cause susceptible weeds to shrivel up and disappear. One application kills most weeds listed.

AREAS SOLD:
National

ACTIVE INGREDIENTS:
0.70% 2,,4-D *Diethanolamine salt of 2,4-Dichlorophenoxyacetic acid*
0.75% MCPP *Diethanolamine salt of 2-(2-Methyl-4-chlorophenoxy) propionic acid*

WEED-B-GON® LAWN WEED KILLER

GENERAL DESCRIPTION:
A liquid formulation containing 2,4-D and MCPP that effectively controls broadleaf weeds in most grass lawns. It singles out broadleaf weeds growing among grasses and, without injuring the grasses, kills the weeds from the tops right down to the roots. Susceptible weeds shrivel up and disappear completely. One quart of concentrate mixes readily with water to treat up to 9,600 square feet. Apply this herbicide with an ORTHO hose-end sprayer. It can be used on newly seeded lawns after three mowings. Reseed bare treated spots 3 to 4 weeks after the treatment. Do not apply to dichondra, lippia, St. Augustine, or clover lawns.

AREAS SOLD:
National

ACTIVE INGREDIENTS:
10.8% 2,4-D *Dimethylamine salt of 2,4-dichlorophenoxyacetic acid*
11.6% MCPP *Dimethylamine salt of 2-(2-methyl-4-chlorophenoxy) propionic acid*

KILLS THESE WEEDS:
Annuals:
Black Medic
Carpetweed
Clover
Common Chickweed
Creeping Beggarweed
Fennel
Fleabane
Florida Pusley
Hawkweed
Knotweed
Lamb's-quarters
Mallow
Mouseear Chickweed
Oxalis
Pigweed
Purslane
Ragweed
Shepherds Purse
Smartweed
Sow Thistle
Speedwell
Spurge
Wild Geranium

Biennials and Perennials:
Buckhorn Plantain
Canada Thistle
Common Burdock
Common Plantain
Curly Dock
Dandelion
Dichondra
Ground Ivy
Lawn Pennywort
Lippia
Morning Glory
Oxalis
Sheep Sorrel
Thistles
Wild Carrot
Wild Garlic
Wild Onion
Yarrow

FOR USE IN THESE AREAS:
Lawns

WEED-B-GON® WEED KILLER

GENERAL DESCRIPTION:
This ready-to-use liquid containing *2,4-D* and MCPP selective weed killers is ideal for spot treatment of dandelion, clover, chickweed, and many other listed broadleafed weeds in grass lawns. One application is sufficient for most; a repeat application may be needed for hard-to-kill weeds. Treatment is most effective when weeds are actively growing. The convenient applicator container can be easily refilled. For use on lawns only.

AREAS SOLD:
National

ACTIVE INGREDIENTS:
0.20% **Dimethylamine salt of 2,4-dichlorophenoxyacetic acid*
0.20% ***Dimethylamine salt of 2-(2-methyl-4-chlorophenoxy) propionic acid*
*Equivalent to 0.16% *2,4-dichlorophenoxyacetic acid. Isomer specific by* AOAC Method 6.275
**Equivalent to 0.17% MCPP *2-(2-methyl-4-chlorophenoxy) propionic acid*

KILLS THESE WEEDS:
Bur Clover
Carpetweeds
Chickweeds
Creeping Charlie
Cudweed
Curly Dock
Dandelion
English Daisy
False Dandelion
Filaree
Florida Pusley
Heart-leaf Drymary
Henbit
Oxalis
Pennywort
Plantains
Purslane
Red Sorrel
Sheep Sorrel
Spurges
Spurweed
Thistles
Toadflax
White Clover
Wild Carrot
Wild Geranium
Wild Onion

FOR USE IN THESE AREAS:
Lawns
Not for use in vegetable gardens, flower beds, or around ornamentals

BROADCAST SPREADER

The broadcast spreader distributes granular materials and grass seed in a wide arc in all directions across the lawn and garden. Designed for use on large areas, it covers a larger area more efficiently than does a drop spreader. It is useful on nonlevel surfaces for fertilizing landscaped beds, vegetable gardens, and other large areas. The broadcast spreader consists of a hopper, agitator, and spinning disc. The sturdy plastic hopper holds up to 55 pounds of fertilizer, and won't rust or corrode. The shape of the hopper allows the fertilizer bag to be tipped, package and all, into the hopper, preventing blowing, spilling, and extra handling of the material. As you begin walking with the spreader, the material moves down the hopper to the agitator, which ensures that the material flows evenly onto the spinning disc. The spinning disc broadcasts the material in a uniform pattern from 6 to 16 feet in diameter. Fertilizers are usually broadcast 10 to 12 feet. The micrometer setting for the disc is easily adjusted for dispensing almost any kind of fertilizer, pesticide, or seed. The on-off control is located on the T-bar handle. Occasionally lubricate the wheel bearings and rotor shaft lightly. The drive gear unit is self-lubricating and needs no servicing. The ORTHO Broadcast Spreader is covered by a limited 4-year parts guarantee.

Using a broadcast spreader:

1. Fill the spreader off the lawn, measuring the amount of fertilizer that is put into the hopper.
2. Spread that much fertilizer across the area listed on the bag. For example, if the bag says to apply 20 pounds of fertilizer per 1,000 square feet, and the hopper holds 10 pounds, measure off 500 square feet and spread the fertilizer evenly across it.
3. Overlap the patterns about a third of their width.
4. Open the hopper only when you are walking and the disc or plate is spinning.

DROP SPREADER

The drop spreader is designed to apply granular fertilizers, insecticides, and grass seed on small to medium-sized lawns and gardens. It distributes the material in a path as wide as the spreader itself. The sturdy plastic hopper holds up to 55 pounds of fertilizer. As you begin walking with the hopper open, the fertilizer or other material falls down the hopper onto the agitator bar. This bar ensures that the material flows evenly through the hopper opening onto the ground. The shutoff blade that opens and closes the hopper is made of nonrusting stainless steel; the on-off control for this blade is located on the T-bar handle. The hopper opening can be adjusted easily for dispensing many different kinds of fertilizers, pesticides, and grass seed. The plastic wheels provide good traction on both grass and dichondra lawns. Lubricate the wheel bearings and shutoff blade with light oil. The ORTHO Drop Spreader is covered by a limited 4-year parts guarantee.

Using a drop spreader:

1. Fill the spreader off the lawn.
2. Open the hopper only after you have begun walking.
3. Make two passes at each end of the lawn first, as a turnaround space, and then go back and forth the long way.
4. Close the hopper on the turns.
5. Overlap the wheel marks on each pass.
6. Calibrate the spreader occasionally to make sure it is dropping the correct amount of fertilizer. To calibrate, mark out a 100-square foot area (10′ X 10′) on the driveway or patio. Spread the fertilizer over the marked area with the spreader adjusted to the proper setting. Sweep up and weigh the fertilizer in the measured area. It should be within 10 percent of what the bag says should be spread per 100 square feet. If it is too much or too little, try another setting and test again.

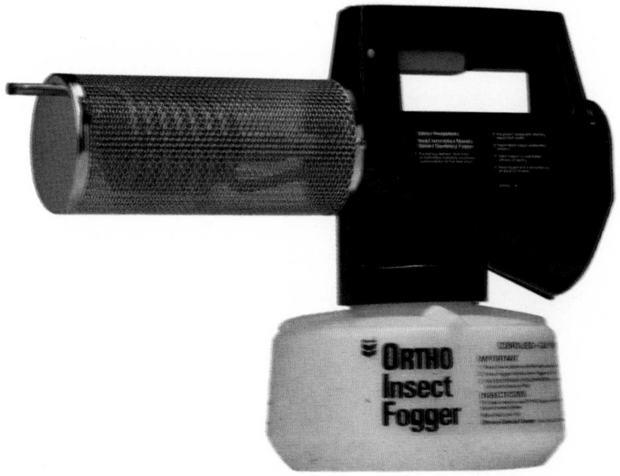

INSECT FOGGER

This device is designed to fog outdoor areas with insecticides to control flies, gnats, mosquitoes, and other pests. The main components of the fogger are an insecticide jar, pressurized propane cylinder, coil, and trigger. A recommended insecticide such as ORTHO Fogging Insecticide is poured into the jar, which is then attached to the bottom of the fogger. The propane cylinder attaches to the rear of the fogger and serves as the fuel source to vaporize the liquid insecticide into a fog. When the propane valve is opened, propane flows from the cylinder into the shroud where a burner unit heats the coil. The fogger is ignited by holding a lighted match under the tip of the coil. Pressure on the trigger activates the pump inside the insecticide jar, causing the material to flow up to and through the heated coil. The insecticide then emerges as a fog from the nozzle. For the most effective fog, pump the fogger once every 3 or 4 seconds. Safety features on this fogger include a safety button and an "on-off" fuel valve. The safety button engages the trigger lock to prevent accidental pumping of insecticide into the coil. The fuel valve controls the emission of propane from the cylinder.

Reading a pesticide label:
Federal law requires that the following information be stated on a pesticide label.

1. Product name
2. Kind of formulation
3. Active ingredients
4. A statement of hazard to people and wildlife
Caution—relatively safe
Warning—intermediately toxic
Danger—Poison, with skull and crossbones—highly toxic
5. Environmental Protection Agency registration number
6. The manufacturer or formulator
7. The type of pesticide (insecticide, fungicide, herbicide, etc.) or its purpose
8. Net contents
9. General information and directions for use

LAWN SPRAYER

This hose-end sprayer is designed to spray fungicides, insecticides, and herbicides on lawns, and to foliar-feed ornamentals and lawns. The garden hose provides the pressure to suction material from the jar through the siphon tube, into the mixing jets, and then through the nozzle and onto the plant. The sprayer is designed with a 60:1 dilution ratio to accurately dilute the product with the large volume of water necessary to carry liquid fertilizers down to the root zone, or to apply other garden chemicals that must be carried into the soil with sufficient water. It operates on all water pressures from 20 to 90 pounds. The wide-mouthed plastic jar is easy to fill, and has a spray capacity of 15 gallons. The thumb-controlled valve shuts off the water supply, and in the "on" position sprays a mixture of water and spray material. A swivel hose-nut connector with an antisiphoning device enables you to connect the hose to a filled jar without spilling any material or twisting the hose.

Cleaning a clogged sprayer:
Sprayers fail to work when they are clogged by undissolved pesticides, soil, or garden debris. To unclog the sprayer, insert a piece of copper wire or toothpick in the sprayer jet with a small amount of water running. Move the cleaner straight in and out a few times to scrape loose the material that has caked or dried in the spray jet hole. Finish cleaning with a final back flush. Poke out any material that may be clogging the breather hole on the sprayer lid. To prevent getting soil and garden debris in the sprayer, do not place the sprayer on the bare ground, and clean the end of the hose before each connection.

ORTHOMATIC® GARDEN SPRAY-ETTE

This hose-end sprayer is especially designed to produce a precise spray pattern, ideal for small or closely-planted gardens. It features a rotating nozzle that provides UP, DOWN, and JET spray patterns useful for treating the entire garden—lawns, trees, shrubs, flowers, and vegetables. It has a 6-gallon spray capacity, and operates on all water pressures from 20 to 90 pounds. Your garden hose provides the pressure that automatically mixes water with garden chemicals in a ratio of 24:1. The control valve incorporates an "INSTANT-ON" and "INSTANT-OFF" feature with a "THUMB-TOUCH®" valve that can be operated easily by a right-handed or left-handed person. The valve also features a "THUMB-SLIDE" that locks the sprayer in the "ON" position for sustained spraying. The hose nut rotates so that a full sprayer an be attached to the garden hose. This prevents spilling of garden chemicals or twisting of the garden hose. An anti-siphon device is included in the swivel hose nut to prevent chemicals from going back into the waterline.

Spraying instructions:

1. Select your spray mode by rotating the nozzle to the desired position for your application requirements.
2. When you are ready to start spraying, hold the sprayer (in either hand) and with the thumb depress the "INSTANT-ON-OFF" "THUMB-TOUCH®" valve. This valve also incorporates a slide mechanism to lock the sprayer in an "ON" position. Simply slide the "THUMB SLIDE" back white depressing until it locks. To disengage, simply slide it forward. The "THUMB-TOUCH®" valve can be used as either instant "ON-OFF" or locked "ON" for large areas.
3. You are now spraying properly diluted material.
4. All material can be emptied by tilting jar to allow material to flow to part of jar where siphon tube is located.
5. After spraying, clean according to instructions, never leave any unused product in this precision sprayer.

ORTHOMATIC® LAWN SPRAYER

This convenient hose-end sprayer is especially designed to produce a precise, fan-shaped spray pattern, ideal for applying soil insecticides or liquid fertilizers on lawns where the uniform spray pattern lets you know exactly where you have treated so you don't have any skips in coverage which could result in poor control. It has a 15-gallon spray capacity, and operates on all water pressures from 20 to 90 pounds. Your garden hose provides the pressure that automatically mixes water with garden chemicals in a ratio of 24:1. The control valve incorporates an "INSTANT-ON" and "INSTANT-OFF" feature with a "THUMB-TOUCH®" valve that can be operated easily by a right-handed or left-handed person. The valve also features a "THUMB-SLIDE" that locks the sprayer in the "ON" position for sustained spraying. The hose nut rotates so that a full sprayer an be attached to the garden hose. This prevents spilling of garden chemicals or twisting of the garden hose. An anti-siphon device is included in the swivel hose nut to prevent chemicals from going back into the waterline.

Spraying instructions:

1. When you are ready to start spraying, hold the sprayer (in either hand) and with the thumb depress the "INSTANT-ON-OFF" "THUMB-TOUCH®" valve. This valve also incorporates a slide mechanism to lock the sprayer in an "ON" position. Simply slide the "THUMB SLIDE" back white depressing until it locks. To disengage, simply slide it forward. The "THUMB-TOUCH®" valve can be used as either instant "ON-OFF" or locked "ON" for large areas.
2. You are now spraying properly diluted material.
3. All material can be emptied by tilting jar to allow material to flow to part of jar where siphon tube is located.
4. After spraying, clean according to instructions, never leave any unused product in this precision sprayer.

SPRAY-ETTE® 4

This hose-end sprayer applies up to 4 gallons of diluted spray to trees and shrubs, lawns, flowers, or vegetables. Your garden hose provides the pressure that develops the suction to force the spray material from the jar, to the mixing jets, and out the nozzle onto the plant. The sprayer mixes water with the spray material in a ratio of 24:1, and operates on all water pressures from 20 to 90 pounds. The thumb-controlled valve on the lid shuts off the water supply, and in the "on" position sprays a mixture of water and spray material. The deflector on the end of the nozzle can be pushed in or out of the spray stream for a fan-shaped or straight spray pattern. It can also be turned 360° to spray up, down, or sideways to treat all plant surfaces. The hose connector rotates so that a full sprayer can be attached to the hose without spilling any material or twisting the hose. The antisiphoning device in the connector prevents any spray material from being sucked back down the hose in case of a sudden drop in water pressure.

When to spray:
To control the army of insects and diseases that destroy your garden, spray thoroughly at the first signs of damage and repeat as necessary. For best results, spray when the insects are most active so that the insecticide will kill them more rapidly. Avoid spraying in the heat of the day during hot summer months because of the possibility of injury to the foliage. Irrigate plants the day before you spray during summer weather because thirsty plants will absorb spray material, which could burn the leaves and damage the plant.

TRACTOR PULL SPREADER

This broadcast spreader attaches easily to the back of any size riding lawn mower or tractor for easy application of granular material including fertilizers, insecticides, and grass seed to large lawns and gardens. The spreader consists of a hopper, agitator, and spinning disc. The plastic hopper holds up to 55 pounds of fertilizer, and is easy to fill with no spilling and no tipping. When the spreader is moving and the spinning disc is rotating, the material flows down the hopper to the agitator. The agitation ensures that the material flows evenly from the hopper onto the spinning disc. The spinning disc then throws the material in a 6 to 16-foot-wide arc in all directions across the lawn or garden. Fertilizers are usually broadcast 10 to 12 feet. The micrometer setting that regulates the disc movement adjusts easily for dispensing many different kinds of granular material and grass seed. Hose off the spreader after each use to keep it clean. Occasionally lubricate the wheel bearings and the rotor shaft lightly. The drive gear is self-lubricating and needs no servicing. The ORTHO Tractor Pull Spreader is covered by a limited 4-year guarantee.

Here is a way to determine the area of your lawn or garden with about 5 percent accuracy:

Measure a long axis of the area. At every 10 feet on the length line measure the width at right angles to the length line. Total all widths and multiply by 10.

$$A = (A_1A_2 + B_1B_2 + C_1C_2) \times 10$$
$$A = (40' + 60' + 32') \times 10$$
$$A = 132' \times 10'$$
$$A = 1{,}320 \text{ square feet}$$

EQUIPMENT

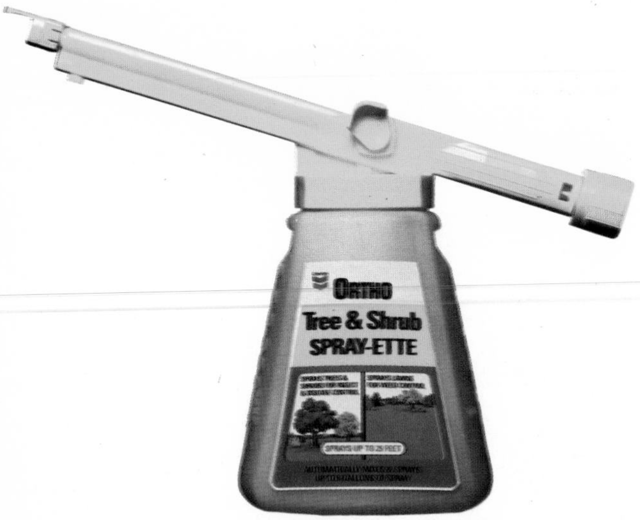

TREE & SHRUB SPRAY-ETTE®

This hose-end sprayer is especially designed with an elongated nozzle shaft for spraying the tops of trees and inside shrubs and hedges. It has a 8-gallon spray capacity, and operates on all water pressures from 25 to 90 pounds. The wide-mouth jar and sprayer lid are made of shatterproof plastic that won't corrode. With the pressure of the garden hose, the sprayer automatically mixes water with the material in a ratio of 24:1. The "on-off" valve that controls the water supply is easily controlled by thumb. The deflector on the nozzle tip is adjustable for a fan-shaped or straight spray. It also turns 360° to spray up, down, and sideways to cover all plant surfaces. The hose-nut connector with an antisiphoning device swivels so a full sprayer can be attached to the hose without spilling any material or twisting the hose. The antisiphoning device prevents any spray from being sucked back down the hose in case of a sudden drop in water pressure.

How to spray trees and shrubs:
Using as much pressure as possible, spray the plant until the excess spray begins to drip off. The spray that drips off isn't wasted, since it wets the leaves, grass, and soil under the plant where insects often live. It is important to get thorough coverage of the plant when you spray. The sucking insects that are not actually hit by the spray, and the chewing insects that feed on untreated areas of leaves, are still alive. Insects not killed can spread new infestations. Spray more than just the outside foliage. Spray the trunks, branches, and leaves. Get into the main trunk area of densely-leaved shrubs and hedges. Be sure to spray both sides of the leaves, because many insects are found on the undersides. Adjust the nozzle so the spray is directed upward.

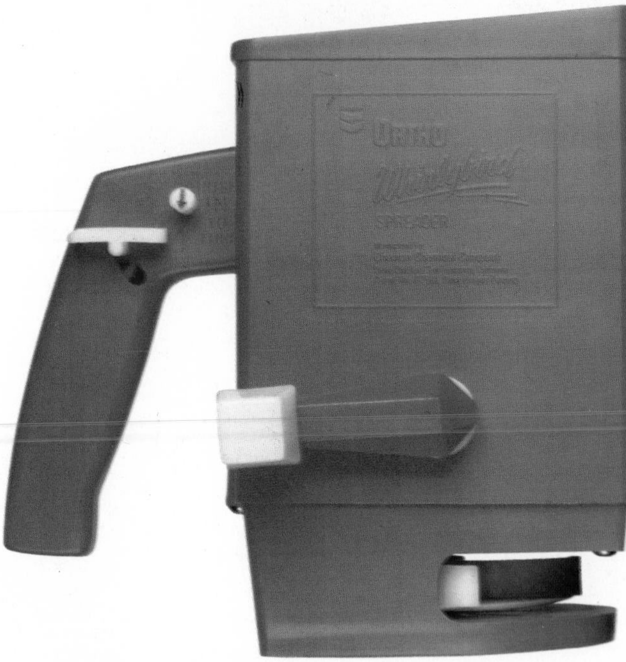

WHIRLYBIRD® SPREADER

This hand-held broadcast spreader is designed for fertilizing lawns, groundcovers, landscaped beds, and vegetable gardens, and for seeding lawns. It consists of a hopper, crank handle, and broadcast wheel. The polypropylene hopper won't rust or corrode. As you turn the crank handle, the material flows from the hopper down onto the broadcast wheel. This rotating wheel throws the material outward in an 8 to 12-foot arc. For uniform coverage, walk at a comfortable, even pace, turning the handle one complete turn for each step forward with your right foot. There are four adjustable settings on the pistol-grip handle for dispensing different kinds of fertilizers and grass seed. The trigger control that opens and closes the hopper is also located on the handle for quick, easy use. The bearings are self-lubricating, and require no additional servicing. Keep the spreader clean and in good working order by washing it with tap water after each use.

Here are some formulas for determining the area or square footage of your lawn or garden.

SQUARE OR RECTANGLE:
Area = LW
L = Length
W = Width
A = 90′ × 60′ = 5,400 square feet

TRIANGLE:
A = 0.5 BH
B = Base
H = Height
A = 0.5 × 60′ × 120′ = 3,600 square feet

CIRCLE:
A = πR^2
π = 3.14
R = Radius
A = 3.14 × 20′ × 20′ = 1,256 square feet

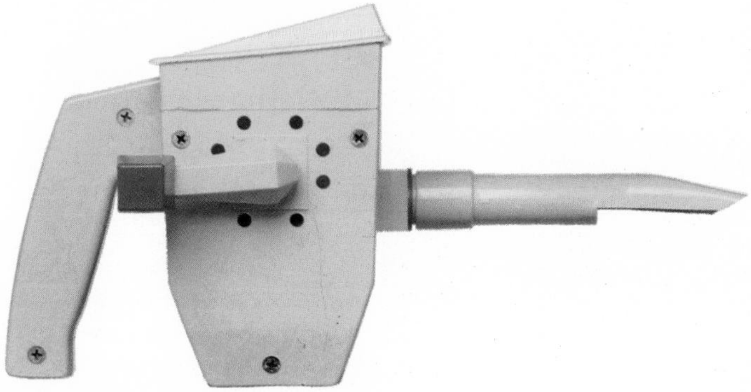

WHIRLY® DUSTER

This hand-held duster is designed for applying insecticide and fungicide dusts to vegetables, flowers, roses, shrubs, and small trees. It consists of a polypropylene hopper, crank handle, blower, and extension tubes. The nonrusting, noncorroding hopper holds up to 8 ounces of dust. The lid helps reduce contact with the material during use. As the crank handle is turned, the dust is propelled by the blower from the hopper down the elongated extension tubes and onto the plant. The deflector at the end of the tubes helps direct the material to avoid creating a cloud of dust. The tubes enable you to dust the undersides of the leaves and to reach inside and around shrubs. Dust is expelled only when the handle is turned. The pistol-grip handle ensures a firm, steady hold. The gears are nylon-fiberglass reinforced and require no special servicing. After dusting, wash the duster with tap water, turning the crank handle to clean the blower and the tubes.

Storing pesticides and equipment:
Store pesticides in their original containers. Do not put them in other containers, especially containers that are commonly used to store food or drink. Do not store any diluted solutions; make a new mixture for each use. Place the tightly sealed containers in a locked cabinet, room, or shed out of reach of children and pets. A dry, well-ventilated area where the temperature remains above freezing is best. Date the container when purchased, so outdated materials can be disposed of promptly. Store weedkillers containing *2,4-D* away from other pesticides, as the vapor may contaminate other materials. Thoroughly clean and dry all equipment at the end of the season. Lubricate any moving parts as specified in your instruction manual.

ORTHO BOOKS

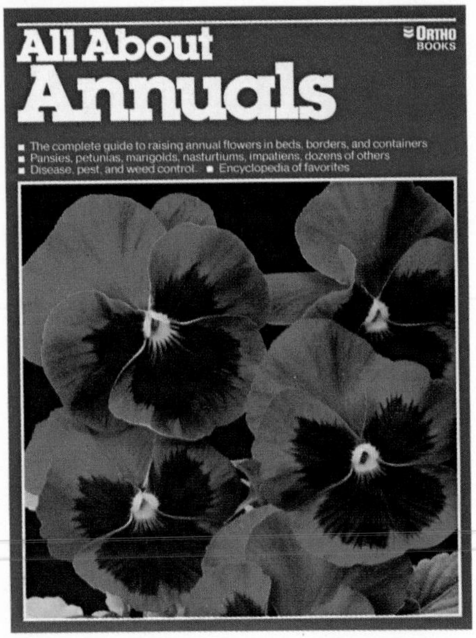

ORTHO's complete guide to raising favorite annuals in beds, borders, and containers. Disease, pest, and weed control. Encyclopedia of favorite annuals. Full color, 96 pages.

Learn how to design, plant, and care for a spectacular bulb garden that will please you every year. Complete encyclopedia of favorites. Full color, 96 pages.

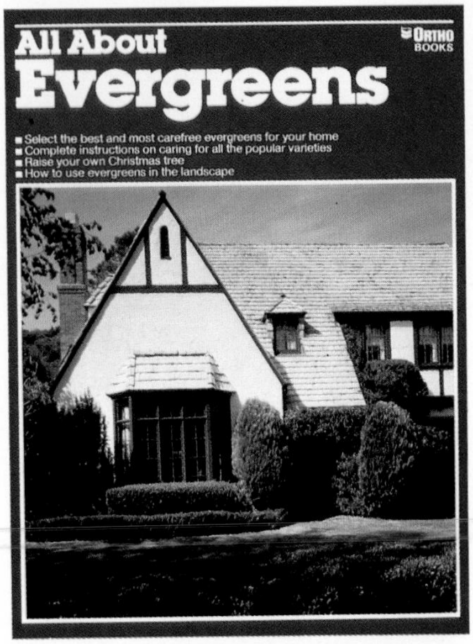

How to select, plant, and care for evergreen trees and shrubs in your landscape. Guide to over 200 evergreen species and varieties. Also contains ideas for landscape design with evergreens. Full color, 96 pages.

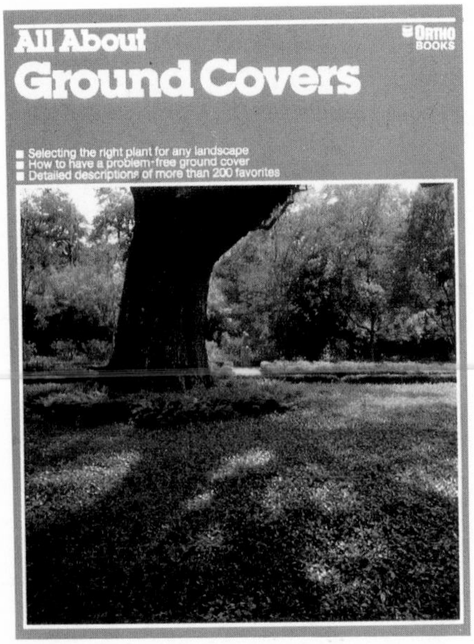

Revised. How to select and successfully grow plants that creep, mat, vine, or spread to cover the ground. Full color, 96 pages.

Revised. A guide to growing more than 25 different kinds of fruits and berries. Climate maps and pest and disease charts. Full color, 112 pages.

All about plants you can grow indoors. Detailed instructions and tips on designing with plants, cultivation, maintenance, and propagation. Many color photographs illustrating types of plants. Full color, 96 pages.

All About
Landscaping
ORTHO BOOKS
How to create a beautiful landscape that is uniquely your own
Professional guidance through all aspects of landscaping from design to construction
Special sections on design techniques and garden remodeling

The techniques, tools, and insights you need to create a landscape that is uniquely your own. Covers all aspects, from design through construction. Full color, 96 pages.

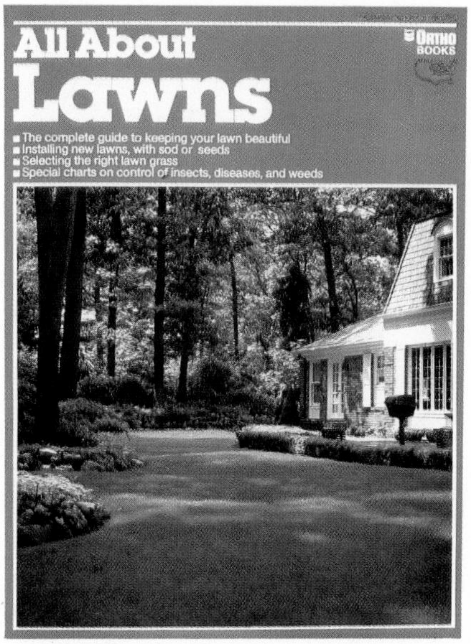
All About
Lawns
ORTHO BOOKS
The complete guide to keeping your lawn beautiful
Installing new lawns, with sod or seeds
Selecting the right lawn grass
Special charts on control of insects, diseases, and weeds

Clearly and completely shows the way to a beautiful lawn with a climatized guide to seeding, sodding, fertilizing, and watering. Full color, 96 pages.

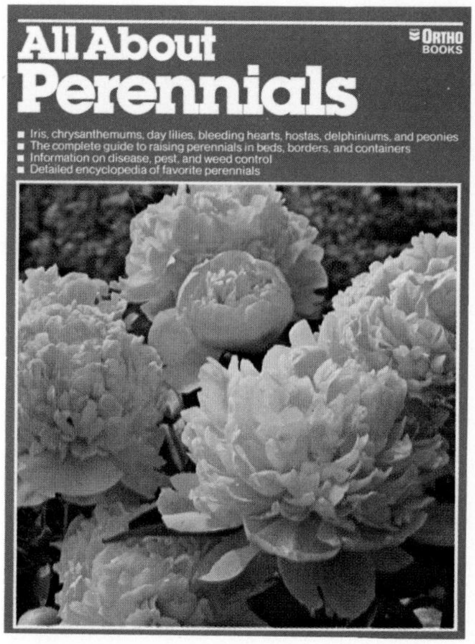
All About
Perennials
ORTHO BOOKS
Iris, chrysanthemums, day lilies, bleeding hearts, hostas, delphiniums, and peonies
The complete guide to raising perennials in beds, borders, and containers
Information on disease, pest, and weed control
Detailed encyclopedia of favorite perennials

How to select and grow perennials that are just right for you. Fresh ideas on how to mix and coordinate your flowers for every season. Encyclopedia of favorite perennials. Full color, 96 pages.

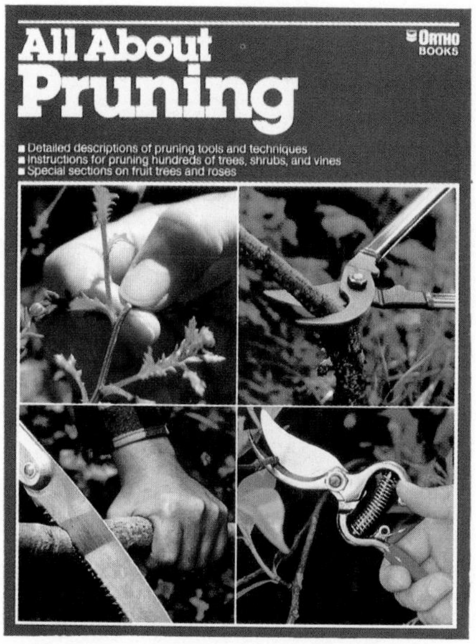
All About
Pruning
ORTHO BOOKS
Detailed descriptions of pruning tools and techniques
Instructions for pruning hundreds of trees, shrubs, and vines
Special sections on fruit trees and roses

When, why, and how to prune everything—from trees and shrubs to vines and perennials. Includes tools, techniques, and tricks of the trade. Full color, 96 pages.

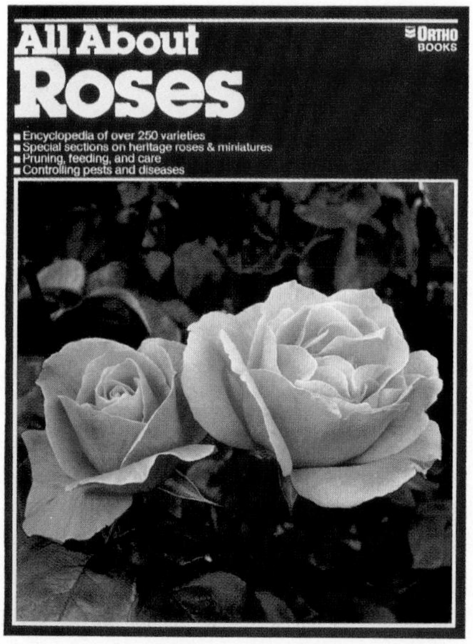
All About
Roses
ORTHO BOOKS
Encyclopedia of over 250 varieties
Special sections on heritage roses & miniatures
Pruning, feeding, and care
Controlling pests and diseases

Endorsed by the American Rose Society, this book tells you everything you need to know to raise beautiful roses, from choosing the right variety to pruning. This revision adds dozens of new varieties to a favorite Ortho book, as well as new sections on miniature roses and old varieties that are making a comeback today. Full color, 96 pages.

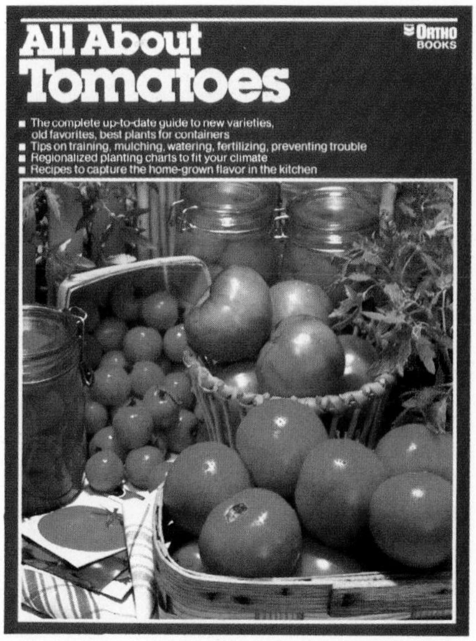
All About
Tomatoes
ORTHO BOOKS
The complete up-to-date guide to new varieties, old favorites, best plants for containers
Tips on training, mulching, watering, fertilizing, preventing trouble
Regionalized planting charts to fit your climate
Recipes to capture the home-grown flavor in the kitchen

Revised. How to select, plant, grow, and harvest tomatoes especially suited to your climate. Recipes that capture the home-grown flavor in the kitchen. Full color, 96 pages.

If any of these ORTHO gardening books are not available from your local dealer, or if you would like a complete catalog, write to: Chevron Chemical Company, Ortho Books, 575 Market Street, San Francisco, CA 94105

ORTHO BOOKS

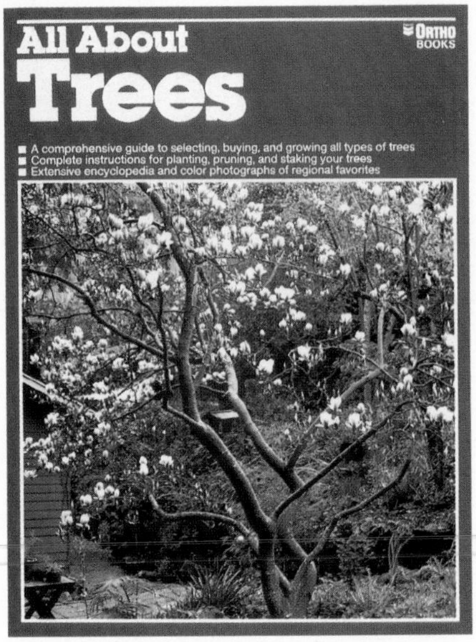

Revised. How to select and care for trees in any climate and situation. Extensive encyclopedia filled with photographs and information for over 100 popular trees. Full color, 112 pages.

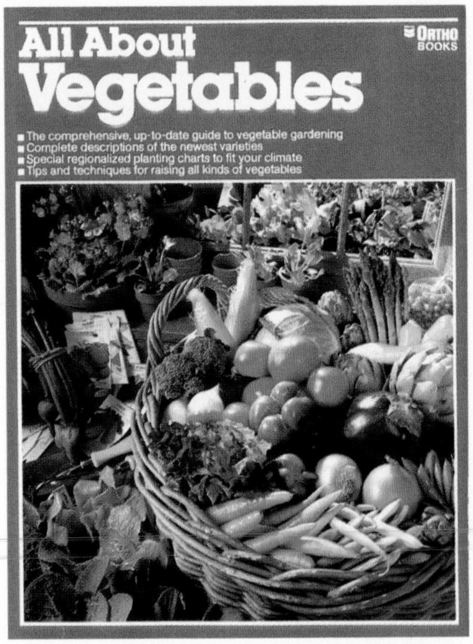

Revised, up-to-date edition of the most complete guide to planting, growing, and harvesting vegetables. Special regionalized planting charts. Latest recommendations on varieties. Full color, 112 pages.

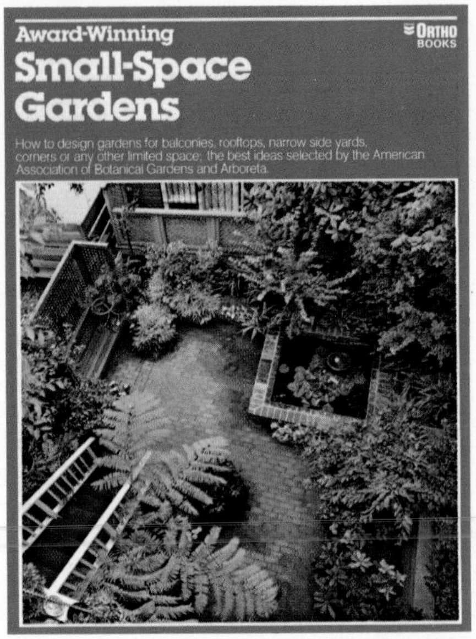

Learn to design both flower and food gardens for balconies, rooftops, narrow side yards, or any limited space. Full color, 112 pages.

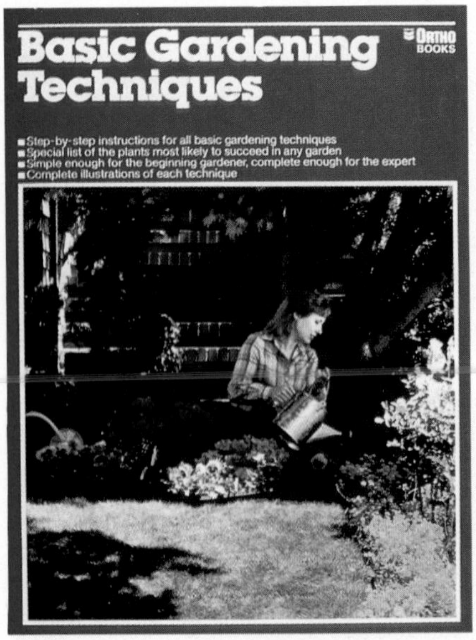

Clear color photos, illustrations, and instructions show the latest and best ways to prepare and manage every major garden task. An outstanding reference guide for beginning or experienced gardeners. Full color, 192 pages.

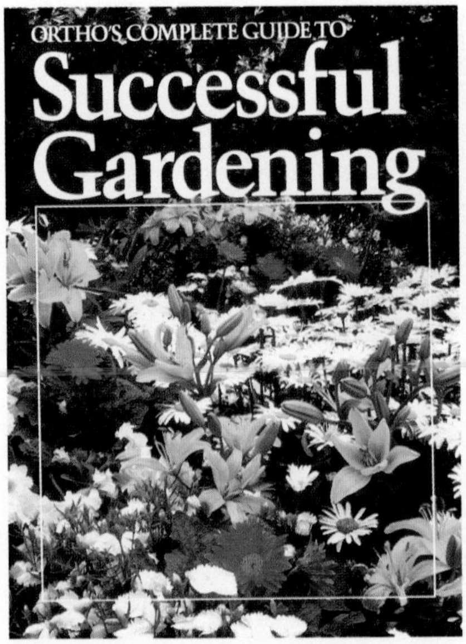

Filled with solid information on basic culture, *Successful Gardening* also covers special topics such as easy garden planning, blending flower colors and textures, timing bloom, and growing cut flowers. Encyclopedic charts list details on over 1000 individual plants. Hardbound, full color, 504 pages.

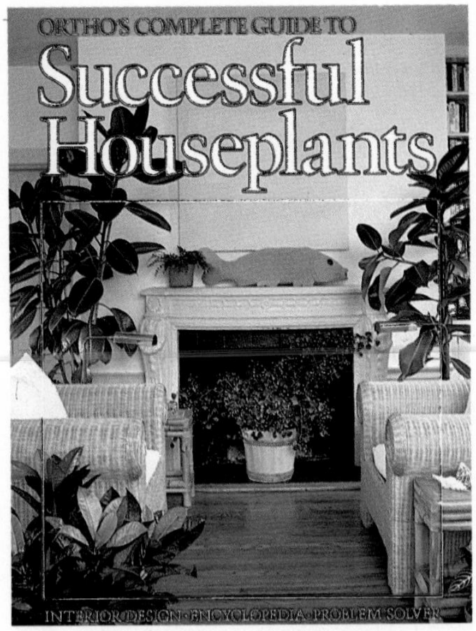

Successful Houseplants offers beautiful color photography, clear illustrations, and informative text to cover methods of propagating, watering, feeding, grooming, and problem-solving. A Gallery of Houseplants provides details on over 300 plants. Hardbound, full color, 320 pages.

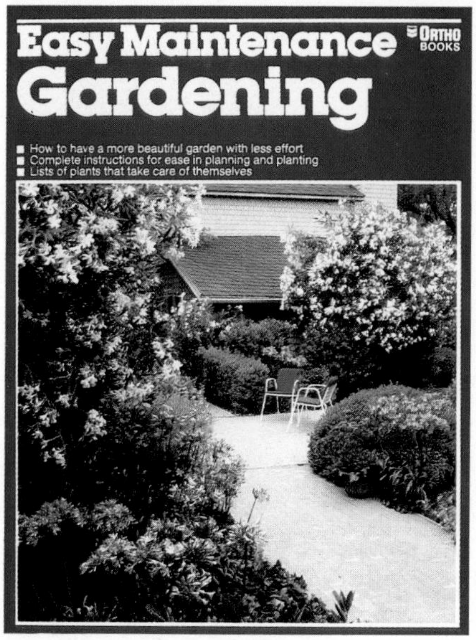

Instructions for planning and planting beautiful gardens and landscapes that require minimal care. A selection guide for choosing plants and tools that save time and labor. Full color, 96 pages.

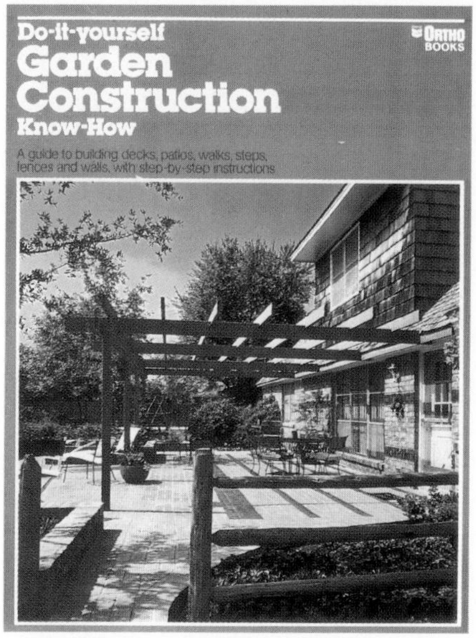

A do-it-yourself guide to building garden floors, decks, patios, walks, steps, fences, gazebos amd more. With step-by-step instructions; section on inexpensive materials. Full color, 96 pages.

Teaches principles of color combination in your garden, using nature's colors as your gardening palette. Full color, 96 pages.

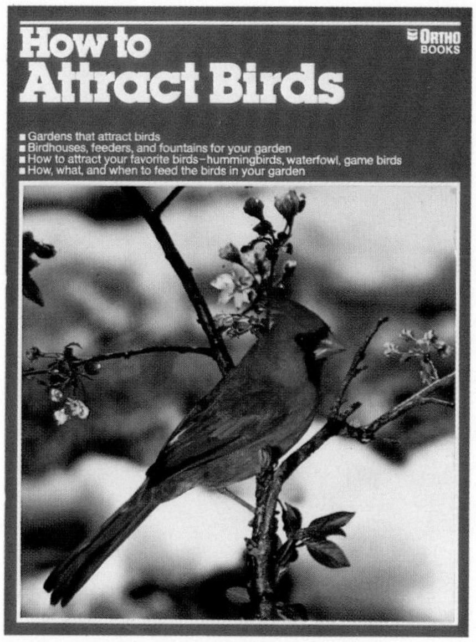

Learn to attract the birds you love—and keep the others away!—by filling their needs for food, water and shelter. Learn which foods and nesting sites attract your favorite birds. Photos and information about feeding and nesting habits of dozens of common backyard birds. Learn to make birdhouses, feeders, and birdbaths. Full color, 96 pages.

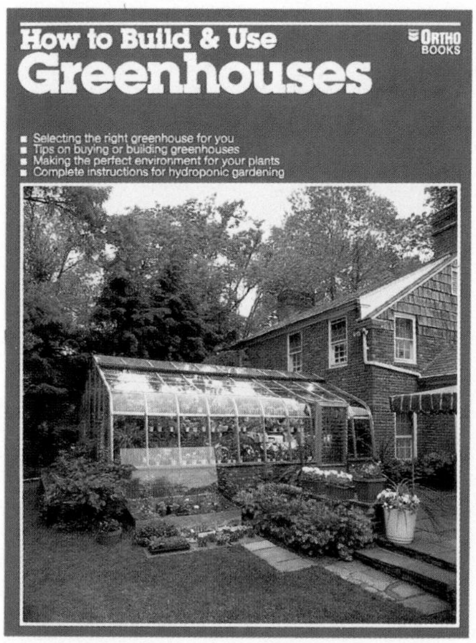

How to select, plan, buy or build, equip and use your greenhouse. Sections on solar heating, hydroponics, growing techniques, lighting control, and special projects. Full color, 96 pages.

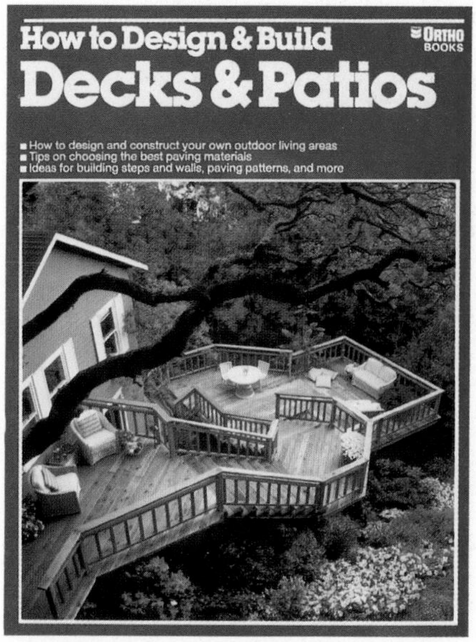

Learn how to create decks and patios to suit every type of situation. With detailed information on design and construction; special charts on building and paving materials. Full color, 112 pages.

ORTHO BOOKS

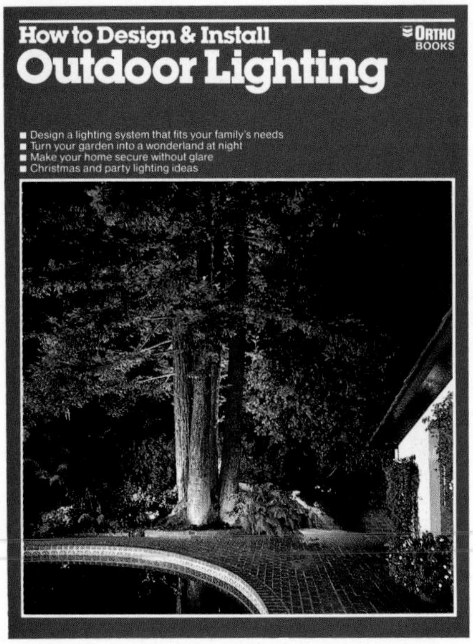

Basic design techniques, charts, and photographs illustrate the many ways to light plants, patios, pools, and other areas to make your yard a nighttime wonderland, and still provide safety and security lighting. Full color, 96 pages.

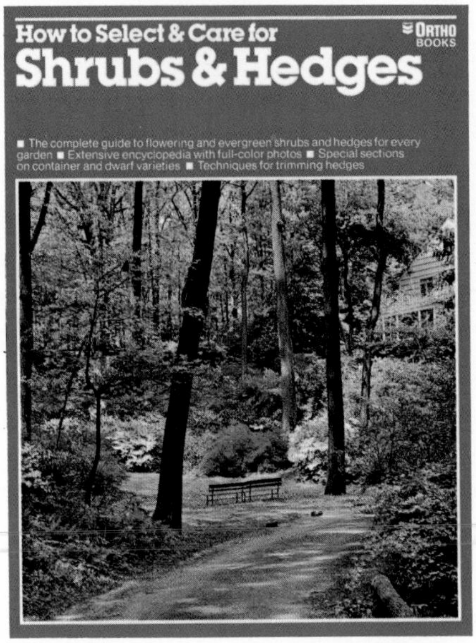

The complete guide to flowering and evergreen shrubs and hedges. Extensive encyclopedia of types. Special sections on container and dwarf varieties. Full color, 96 pages.

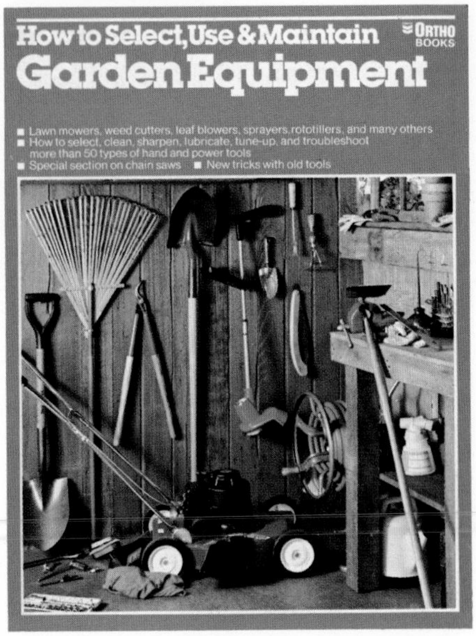

The authoritative guide to all types of garden equipment. Professional tips on how to select, use, clean, sharpen, and tune up more than 50 hand and power tools. Full color, 96 pages.

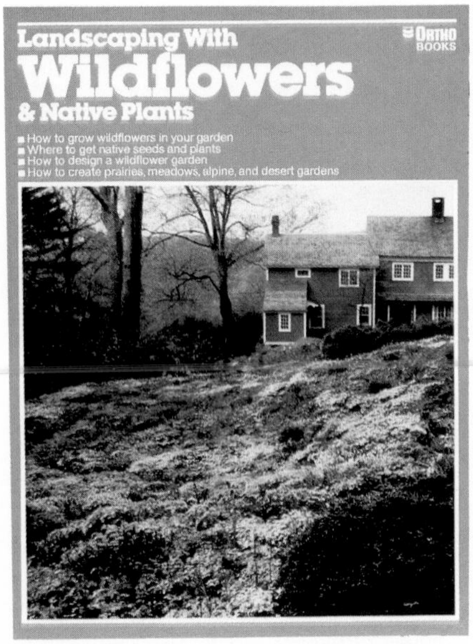

What plants are native to your area? This book answers that question and gives plenty of ideas for incorporating native plants into your garden or landscape. Also listings of native plant societies which are good sources of native plants. Full color, 96 pages.

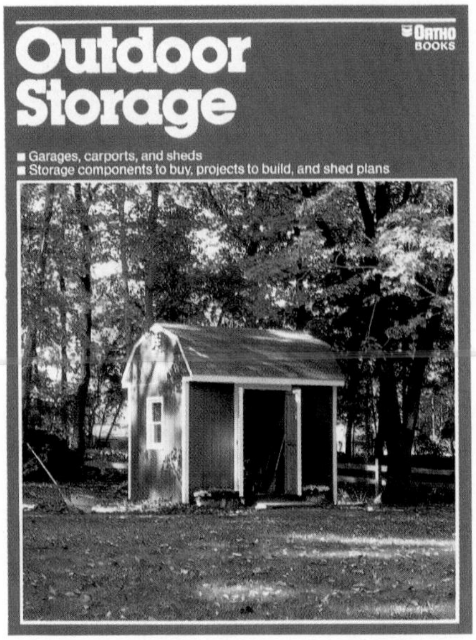

This idea-packed book illustrates simple steps for consolidating storage space in garages, carports, and sheds. Both ready-made storage components and build-it-yourself options are presented. Full color, 96 pages.

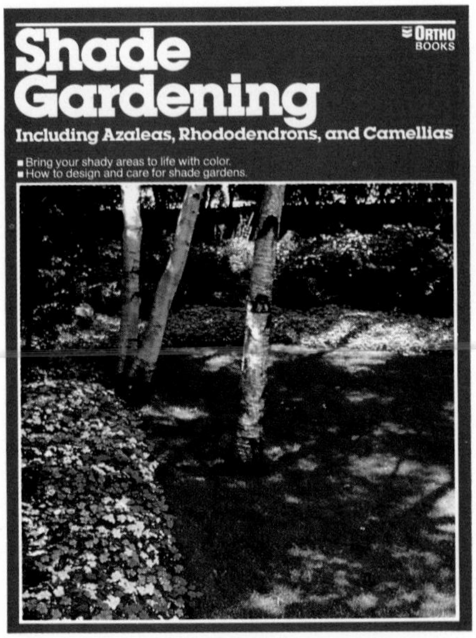

How to choose plants that thrive in the shade. Ideas for creating shade and landscapes in various climates. Emphasis on growing azaleas, rhododendrons, and camellias. Full color, 96 pages.

Detailed plans for 87 easy-to-build garden accesories made of wood—containers, trellises, benches, tables, duckboards and more. Clear, easy-to-follow, illustrated instructions. Full color, 96 pages.

Covers 240 herbs and spices, including how to select and grow them indoors or out. Ideas for landscaping, and creative recipes for foods, cosmetics, dyes, and crafts. Full color, 96 pages.

How to select and grow cacti and other succulents indoors and outdoors, with an explanation of botanical nomenclature. Full color, 96 pages.

APPENDIX

Some houseplants that tolerate low light:

Botanical name	Common name
Aglaonema	Chinese evergreen
Aspidistra elatior	Cast iron plant
Cissus rhombifolia	Grape ivy
Dieffenbachia	Dumbcane
Dracaena	
Palmae	
Neanthebella	Parlor palm
Kentia,	Kentia palm
Raphis	Lady palm
Philodendron	
Sansevieria trifasciata	Mother-in-law tongue
Scindapsus and *Epipremnum*	Pothos
Spathiphyllum	Spathe flower
Syngonium	Nephthytis

Plants that produce easily-rooted cuttings:

Botanical name	Common name
Aglaonema	Chinese evergreen
Begonia	
Chlorophytum	Spider plant
Chrysanthemum morifolium	Florist's chrysanthemum
Cissus rhombifolia	Grape ivy
Coleus hybridus	Coleus
Crassula argentea	Jade plant
Fittonia	Nerve plant
Gynura	Purple passion vine
Hedera helix	English ivy
Impatiens	
Maranta	Prayer plant
Pelargonium	Geranium
Philodendron	
Pilea cadierei	Aluminum plant
Plectranthus australis	Swedish ivy
Saintpaulia ionantha	African violet
Scindapsus	Pothos
Syngonium	Nephthytis
Tolmiea menziesii	Piggyback plant
Tradescantia	Wandering Jew

Some houseplants that are sensitive to salts in the soil:

Botanical name	Common name
Aphelandra	
Aspidistra	Cast iron plant
Asplenium	Bird's-nest fern
Avocado	
Calathea	Zebra plant
Chamaedorea	Parlor palm
Chlorophytum	Spider plant
Cissus	Grape ivy
Citrus	
Coffea	Coffee tree
Cordyline	Ti plant
Cycas	Sago palm
Dracaena	
Fatshedera	
Fatsia	Japanese aralia
Ferns	
Ficus	Ornamental fig, rubber plant
Haworthia	
Hedera	English ivy
Howea	Kentia palm
Maranta	Prayer plant
Monstera	Split-leaf philodendron
Pandanus	Screw pine
Philodendron	
Saxifraga	Strawberry geranium
Spathiphyllum	Spathe flower
Tolmiea	Piggyback plant

Some houseplants that tolerate full sun:

Botanical name	Common name
Aeschynanthus	Lipstick plant
Amaryllis	
Asparagus	Asparagus fern
Begonia semperflorens	Wax begonia
Cacti	
Caladium	
Capsicum	Ornamental pepper
Chrysanthemum	
Citrus	
Codiaeum	Croton
Coffea arabica	Coffee plant
Coleus hybridus	Coleus
Columnea	
Cycas	Sago palm
Dizygotheca	False aralia
Euphorbia pulcherrima	Poinsettia
Fatsia japonica	Japanese aralia
Ficus	Ornamental figs
Gynura	Purple passion vine
Hedera	Ivy
Hoya	Wax plant
Passiflora	Passion flower
Pelargonium	Geranium
Rosa	Miniature rose
Schefflera	
Senecio mikanioides	Parlor ivy
S. rowleyanus	String-of-pearls

Turfgrass climate zones:

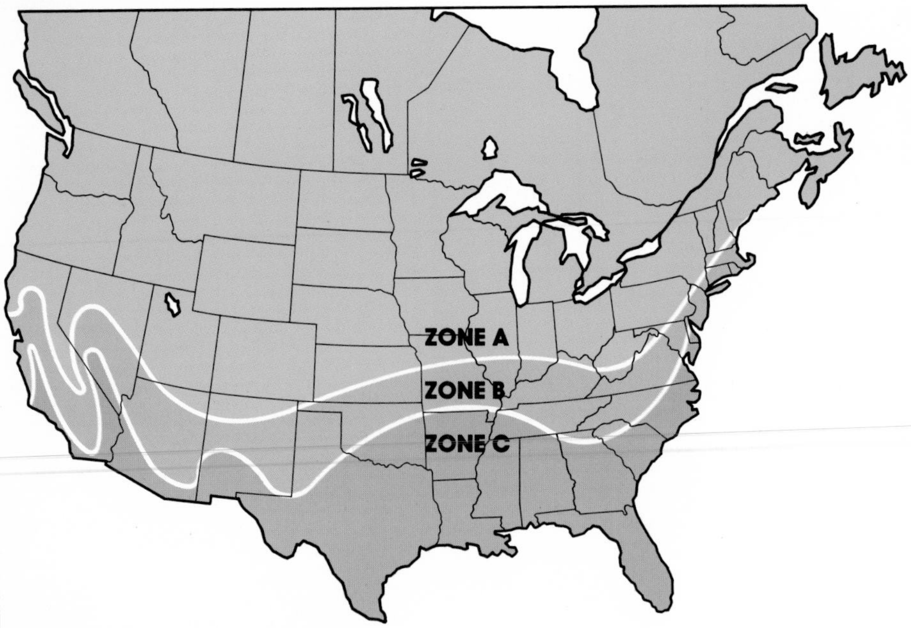

Zone A Cool-season grasses.

Zone C Warm-season grasses.

Zone B This is a transition zone, where the climate zones overlap. Both warm-season and cool-season grasses are grown here. Because warm-season grasses have long dormant periods in this zone, cool-season grasses are usually preferred. Tall fescue does particularly well in this zone.

From *Turf Managers Handbook*, W.H. Daniel and R.P. Freeborg.

Characteristics of some turfgrasses:

Grass	Zone	Drought Resistant	Shade Tolerant	Days to Germinate	Low* Maintenance
Bahiagrass	C			21-28	•
Bentgrass	A		•	5-12	
Bermudagrass, Common	C	•		14-20	•
Bermudagrass, Improved	C	•		Sprigs	•
Carpetgrass	C			21	•
Centipedegrass	C			14-20	•
Fescue, Red	A	•	•	5-12	•
Fescue, Tall	A	•	•	5-12	•
Kentucky Bluegrass	A			20-30	
St. Augustine grass	C		•	Sprigs	
Zoysiagrass	C	•	•	Sprigs	

*Low maintenance turfgrasses are those that tolerate irregular fertilizing, watering, and mowing.

Turfgrass varieties resistant to dollar spot:

BLUEGRASS
A-20
Adelphi
Bonnieblue
Columbia
Bristol
Majestic
Parade
Park
Touchdown
Vantage
Victa

FESCUE
Jamestown chewings
Pennlawn creeping

BENTGRASS
Arlington
Pennpar

Bluegrass resistance to fusarium blight:

RESISTANT
A-20
Adelphi
Bonnieblue
Columbia
Enmundi
Glade
Parade
Rugby
Sydsport
Trenton
Vantage
Windsor

MODERATELY RESISTANT
Majestic
Merit
Ram #2

SUSCEPTIBLE
Arboretum
Belturf
Brunswick
Campus
Cougar
Delft
Enita
Fylking
Geronimo
Merion
Modena
Newport
Nugget
Park
Pennstar
Pio-Cebaco
Plush
Ram #1
South Dakota Certified

Bluegrass varieties resistant to stripe smut:

A-20
A-34
Adelphi
Aquila
Birka
Bonnieblue
Brunswick
Enmundi
Glade
Newport
Plush
Ram #1
Sydsport
Touchdown
Vantage

Bluegrass resistance to helminthosporium leaf spot:

RESISTANT
A-20
Adelphi
Birka
Bonnieblue
Bristol
Brunswick
Majestic
Merion
Newport
Nugget
Parade
Pennstar
Rugby
Sydsport
Touchdown
Vantage
Victa

MODERATELY RESISTANT
Baron
Cheri
Enmundi
Glade

SUSCEPTIBLE
Delta
Geary
Kenblue
Newport
Park

Bluegrass varieties resistant to rust:

A-20
A-34
Bonnieblue
Fylking
Glade
Majestic
Park
Pennstar
Rugby

Bluegrass varieties resistant to red thread:

A-34
Adelphi
Birka
Bonnieblue
Touchdown

Bluegrass varieties resistant to fusarium patch:

Adelphi
Birka
Bonnieblue
Touchdown

Some drought-resistant groundcovers:

Botanical name	Common name
Aegopodium podograria	Goutweed
Arctostaphylos uva-ursi	Bearberry
Artemisia	Wormwood
Baccharis pilularis 'Twin Peaks'	Coyote bush
Carpobrotus, Lampranthus, Mesembryanthemum	Ice plant
Cistus	Rock rose
Coronilla varia	Crown vetch
Cotoneaster adpressus	Creeping cotoneaster
C. dammeri	Bearberry cotoneaster
C. horizontalis	Rock cotoneaster
Festuca ovina glauca	Blue fescue
Helianthemum nummularium	Sunrose
Hypericum	St. John's wort
Juniperus	Juniper
Phalaris arundinacea 'Picta'	Ribbon grass
Phyla nodiflora	Lippia
Rosmarinus officinalis 'Prostratus'	Dwarf rosemary
Santolina	Lavender cotton
Sedum	Stonecrop
Thymus	Thyme
Verbena peruviana	Peruvian verbena

Some groundcovers for shady areas:

Botanical name	Common name
Adiantum pedatum	Maidenhair fern
Ajuga	Carpet bugle
Asarum	Wild ginger
Asparagus densiflorous	Asparagus fern
Athyrium goeringianum	Japanese painted fern
Cyrtomium falcatum	Holly fern
Dryopteris	Wood fern
Duchesnea indica	Mock strawberry
Epimedium	Barrenwort
Euonymus fortunei	Winter creeper
Galium odoratum	Sweet woodruff
Hedera	Ivy
Hypericum	St. John's wort
Liriope	Lily turf
Ophiopogon japonicus	Mondo grass
Pachysandra terminalis	Japanese spurge
Sarcococca hookerana humilis	Small Himalayan sarcococca
Soleirolia soleirolii	Baby's tears
Vinca	Periwinkle
Viola odorata	Sweet violet

Some groundcovers for sunny areas:

Botanical name	Common name
Achillea tomentosa	Woolly yarrow
Arabis	Rock cress
Arctostaphylos uva-ursi	Bearberry
Artemisia schmidtiana	Satiny wormwood
Baccharis pilularis 'Twin Peaks'	Dwarf coyote bush
Carpobrotus, Lampranthus, Mesembryanthemum	Ice plant
Ceanothus	Wild lilac
Cerastium tomentosum	Snow-in-summer
Cotoneaster adpressus	Creeping cotoneaster
C. dammeri	Bearberry cotoneaster
C. horizontalis	Rock cotoneaster
Helianthemum nummularium	Sunrose
Hypericum	St. John's wort
Juniperus	Juniper
Lantana	
Myrica pensylvanica	Bayberry
Phlox subulata	Moss pink
Phyla nodiflora	Lippia
Pyracantha koidzumii 'Santa Cruz'	Santa Cruz firethorn
Rosmarinus officinalis 'Prostratus'	Dwarf rosemary
Santolina	Lavender cotton
Sedum	Stonecrop
Taxus media 'Chadwicki'	Chadwick yew
Thymus	Creeping thyme
Trachelospermum	Star jasmine
Vaccinium angustifolium	Lowbush blueberry

Planting and blooming of some common flowers:

Flower	Plant	Planting season	Blooming season	Ideal soil temperature for germination	Days to germination
Achillea	P	Sp	Su-F	70°F	5-15
Ageratum	A	Sp*	Sp-Su	60-65	10
Alcea	Bi	Sp-Su	Sp-Su	68	7-21
Allium	B	Sp or F	Sp-Su	**	**
Amaranthus	A	Sp	Sp-Su	60-70	12
Anemone	Tu	F or Sp	Sp	**	**
Antirrhinum	A	Sp*	Sp-Su	70	15
Aquilegia	P	F or Sp	Sp-Su	70-85	21-28
Aster	A, P	Sp	Sp-Su-F	70	12-14
Astilbe	P	Sp	Sp-Su	60-70	14-21
Begonia	Tp	Sp	Sp-Su	70-75	15-20
Calendula	A	Sp*	W-Sp	70-85	7-14
Campanula	P	Sp	Sp-F	68-86	10-14
Canna	Tu	Sp	Su-F	**	**
Capsicum	A	Sp	Su	70	15-20
Celosia	A	Sp	Su	70-85	7-14
Chrysanthemum	A, P	Sp	Su-F	70	7-10
Cineraria	A	Sp*	W-Sp	45-60	20
Cleome	A	Sp*	Su	55-85	10-14
Coleus	Tp	Sp	Sp-Su	70-85	15-20
Convallaria	P	F (from pips)	Sp	**	**
Coreopsis	A, P	F or Sp	Su-F	70	15-20
Cosmos	A	Sp	Su-F	70-85	10-15
Crocus	Corm	F	Sp	**	**
Dahlia	Tu	Sp	Su-F	70-85 (seed)	15-20
Delphinium	A, P	Sp*	Su	55-60	15-30
Dianthus	A, P	Sp*	Sp-Su	70	15-30
Digitalis	Bi, P	Su	Sp-Su	70-85	15-20
Dimorphotheca	A	Sp	Su	70-85	15-20
Freesia	Corm	Sp	Sp	**	**
Gaillardia	A, P	Sp*	Su-F	70	15-20
Gerbera	Tp	Sp	Su	70	15
Gladiolus	Corm	Sp	Su-F	**	**
Helianthemum	P	F or Sp	Su	70	15-20
Helianthus	A, P	Sp	Su	70-85	15-20
Hemerocallis	Tu	Sp*	Su	**	**
Heuchera	P	F or Sp	Sp-Su	70-85	5-20
Hosta	P	Sp	Su-F	70	15-20
Hyacinthus	Bu	F	Sp	**	**
Iberis	A, P	Sp*	Sp-Su	70-85	7-15
Impatiens	A, P	Tp	Su	70	15-20
Iris	Rh	F	Sp-Su	**	**
Lantana	Tp	Sp	Sp-F	70	40-50
Lathyrus	A	W-Sp	Sp	70	15
Lilium	Bu	Sp	Su	**	**
Lobelia	A	Sp*	Su-F	70-85	15-20
Lobularia	A, P	Sp	Sp-Su-F	70	7-15
Matthiola	A	Sp	Sp-Su	55-90	15
Pelargonium	P	Sp	Sp-Su-F	68-86	5-15
Phlox	A, P	Sp*	Su-F	55-65	8-20
Primula	A, P	Sp	Sp	55-65	20
Ranunculus	Tu	F	Su	**	**
Rudbeckia	A, P	Sp	Su-F	70-75	5-10
Salpiglossis	A	Sp	Su	70-75	15-20
Salvia	A, P	Sp	Su	70	12-15
Sedum	P	Sp	Su	70-80	15-30
Solanum	A, P	Sp	Su-F	70	15-30
Tagetes	A	Sp	Su-F	70-75	5-7

Florida gardeners may find differences in planting times and soil temperatures. Check with your local extension agent.

* Planted in the fall in zones 9 and 10. See page 1020 for USDA zone map.

** Not usually planted from seed.

KEY: A – Annual; Bu – Bulb; Bi – Biennial; P – Perennial; Rh – Rhizome; Tp – Tender perennial, grown as annual in all but zones 9 and 10; Tu – Tuber; Sp – Spring; Su – Summer; F – Fall; W – Winter.

Some lily species resistant and susceptible to lily mosaic:

RESISTANT TO MODERATELY RESISTANT

Lilium amabile
L. brownii
L. davidii
L. hansonii
L. henryi
L. martagon
L. monadelphum
L. paradalinum
L. pumilum
L. regale

SUSCEPTIBLE

L. auratum
L. canadense
L. concolor
L. formosanum
L. lancifolium
L. maculatum
L. pennsylvanicum
L. superbum
*L. tigrinum**

* Easily infected, but not apparently injured; can become a carrier to other susceptible species.

Some chrysanthemum cultivars that are resistant to chrysanthemum rust:

Achievement
Copper Bowl
Escapade
Helen Castle
Mandalay
Matador
Miss Atlanta
Orange Bowl
Powder Puff

Adapted from "Chrysanthemum Cultivars Resistant to Verticillium Wilt and Rust," University of California leaflet 21057.

Some flowers susceptible to various fusarium wilts:

Botanical name	Common name
Antirrhinum	Snapdragon
Astilbe	
Browallia	
Callistephus	China aster
Campanula	Bellflower
Centaurea	Bachelor's button
Chrysanthemum	
Cineraria	
Cosmos	
Cyclamen	
Dahlia	
Delphinium	
Dianthus	Carnation, Pink, Sweet William
Digitalis	Foxglove
Dimorphotheca	Cape marigold
Lantana	
Lilium	Lily
Matthiola	Stock
Narcissus	Daffodil
Paeonia	Peony
Salpiglossis	Painted tongue
Tagetes	Marigold
Tulipa	Tulip

Some plants susceptible to aster yellows:

FLOWERS

Botanical name	Common name
Anemone	
Antirrhinum	Snapdragon
Aster	
Calendula	Pot marigold
Callistephus	China aster
Celosia	Cockscomb
Centaurea	Bachelor's buttons
Chrysanthemum	
Coreopsis	
Cosmos	
Delphinium	
Dianthus	Sweet William, Carnation, Pinks
Dimorphotheca	Cape marigold
Gaillardia	Blanket flower
Gladiolus	
Helichrysum	Straw flower
Lobelia	
Petunia	
Phlox	
Scabiosa	Pincushion flower
Tagetes	Marigold

VEGETABLES

Broccoli
Cabbage
Carrot
Cauliflower
Celery
Endive
Lettuce
New Zealand spinach
Onion
Parsley
Parsnip
Potato
Pumpkin
Radish
Spinach
Squash
Tomato

WEEDS

Botanical name	Common name
Ambrosia	Ragweed
Cirsium	Thistle
Conyza	Horseweed
Daucus	Wild carrot
Erigeron	Fleabane
Plantago	Plantain
Taraxacum	Dandelion

Some rose varieties with resistance to black spot (BS), powdery mildew (PM), or rust (R):

HYBRID TEAS

Audie Murphy	R
Aztec	PM, R
Carousel	PM
Charlotte Armstrong	BS
Chrysler Imperial	BS
Command Performance	BS, R
Coronado	BS
Ernest H. Morse	BS
Fred Howard	R
Fortyniner	BS
Garden Party	BS, R
Golden Rapture	PM
Grand Opera	BS
Jamaica	PM
John F. Kennedy	BS, R
Lowell Thomas	PM
Lucy Cramphorn	BS
Matterhorn	PM
Miss All American Beauty	PM
Pascali	PM
Pink Favorite	R
Queen Charlotte	PM
Radiant	BS
Sante Fe	PM
Sierra Dawn	PM, R
Simon Bolivar	PM, R
Sphinx	BS
Sutter's Gold	BS, PM
Tiffany	BS
Trade Winds	R
Tropicana	BS
White Bouquet	R

CLIMBERS

Blaze	BS, PM
Bonfire	PM
Cecile Brunner	PM
Paul's Scarlet	BS, PM

FLORIBUNDAS

Alain	R
Burma	R
Donald Prior	R
Fashionette	R
Etiole De Hollande	R
Garden Party	R
Gold Cup	R
Red Gold	BS, R
Red Radiance	R
Sarabande	BS, PM, R
Simplicity	BS
Summer Snow	R
Tiara	BS
Wildfire	PM

Some plants that are resistant to verticillium wilt:

PLANT GROUPINGS

Ferns
Conifers (Cypress, fir, larch, juniper, pine, sequoia, spruce, and others.)
Monocots (Bamboo, bulbs, corn, gladiolus, grasses, iris, onion, orchids, palm, and others.)
Cacti

TREES AND SHRUBS

Botanical name	Common name
Arctostaphylos	Manzanita
Betula	Birch
Buxus	Boxwood
Carpinus	Hornbeam
Ceanothus	
Cornus	Dogwood
Crataegus	Hawthorn
Eucalyptus	
Fagus	Beech
Gleditsia	Locust
Ilex	Holly
Juglans	Walnut
Liquidambar	Sweet gum
Malus	Apple, crabapple
Morus	Mulberry
Nerium	Oleander
Platanus	Plane tree, sycamore
Pyracantha	Firethorn
Quercus	Oak
Salix	Willow
Tilia	Linden

FLOWERS

Botanical name	Common name
Ageratum	
Alcea	Hollyhock
Alyssum	
Anemone	
Aquilegia	Columbine
Begonia	
Calendula	Pot marigold
Dianthus	Carnation, pink, sweet William
Gaillardia	
Gypsophila	Baby's breath
Helianthemum	Sun rose
Helianthus	Sunflower
Helleborus	Christmas rose
Heuchera	Coral bells
Iberis	Candytuft
Impatiens	
Lantana	
Mimulus	Monkey flower
Nemesia	
Nemophila	Baby-blue-eyes
Penstemon	
Platycodon	Balloon flower
Portulaca	Moss rose
Potentilla	
Primula	Primrose
Ranunculus	
Scabiosa	
Tropaeolum	Nasturtium
Verbena	
Vinca	Periwinkle
Viola	Pansy, viola, violet
Zinnia	

VEGETABLES

Asparagus	Lettuce
Beans	Peas
Carrot	Sweet potato
Celery	

Adapted from *Plants Resistant or Susceptible to Verticillium Wilt*, University of California Cooperative Extension Leaflet 2703.

Powdery mildews and some of the plants they infect:

ERYSIPHE CICHORACEARUM:

Botanical name	Common name
Achillea	Yarrow
Ajuga	Carpet bugle
Alcea	Hollyhock
Antirrhinum	Snapdragon
Aster	
Baccharis	Coyote bush
Begonia	
Calendula	Pot marigold
Centaurea	Bachelor's button
Chrysanthemum	
Cineraria	
Citrullus	Watermelon
Cosmos	
Cotinus	Smoke tree
Dahlia	
Eucalyptus	
Gerbera	Transvaal daisy
Hebe	
Helianthus	Sunflower
Lactuca	Lettuce
Myosotis	Forget-me-not
Papaver	Poppy
Ranunculus	
Rhus	Sumac
Rudbeckia	Black-eyed Susan
Salpiglossis	Painted tongue
Salvia	
Spiraea	
Verbena	
Zinnia	

ERYSIPHE POLYGONI:

Botanical name	Common name
Amaranthus	Amaranth
Aquilegia	Columbine
Begonia	
Beta	Beet
Brassica	Cabbage family
Delphinium	
Eschscholzia	California poppy
Iberis	Candytuft
Lathyrus	Sweet pea
Lobularia	Sweet alyssum
Phaseolus	Beans
Pisum	Peas
Raphanus	Radish
Vinca	Periwinkle
Viola	Pansy, viola

MICROSPHAERA ALNI:

Botanical name	Common name
Alnus	Alder
Corylus	Hazelnut
Lonicera	Honeysuckle
Platanus	Plane tree
Quercus	Oak
Symphoricarpos	Snowberry
Syringa	Lilac

Adapted from, "A List of Powdery Mildews of California," California Cooperative Extension Service. Leaflet 217.

MICROSPHAERA SPECIES:

Botanical name	Common name
Acacia	
Catalpa	
Ceanothus	
Erica	Heath
Euonymus	
Hydrangea	
Juglans	Walnut
Lagerstroemia	Crapemyrtle
Ligustrum	Privet
Liriodendron	Tuliptree
Lonicera	Honeysuckle
Magnolia	
Passiflora	Passion flower
Platanus	Plane tree
Populus	Poplar
Raphiolepis	India hawthorn
Rhododendron	Rhododendron, azalea
Robinia	Locust
Vaccinium	Blueberry
Viburnum	

PHYLLACTINIA CORYLEA:

Botanical name	Common name
Aesculus	Horse chestnut
Cornus	Dogwood
Philadelphus	Mock orange
Quercus	Oak
Rubus	Brambles

PODOSPHAERA SPECIES:

Botanical name	Common name
Acer	Maple
Fraxinus	Ash
Malus	Apple, crabapple
Photinia	
Prunus	Peach, plum, etc.
Pyracantha	Firethorn
Pyrus	Pear
Spiraea	

SPHAEROTHECA FULIGINEA:

Cantaloupe
Cucumber
Winter squash

SPHAEROTHECA SPECIES:

Botanical name	Common name
Cotoneaster	
Crataegus	Hawthorn
Dianthus	Sweet William, carnation, pink
Erica	Heath
Fragaria	Strawberry
Gaillardia	Blanket flower
Heuchera	Coral bells
Kalanchoe	
Nicotiana	
Petunia	
Phlox	
Potentilla	Cinquefoil
Ribes	Currant, gooseberry
Rosa	Rose
Tolmiea	

Some plants resistant to cotton root rot (*Phymatotrichum*):

TREES AND SHRUBS

Botanical name	Common name
Celtis	Hackberry
Deutzia	
Morus alba 'Pendula'	Weeping mulberry
Palmae	Palm family
Polypodiaceae	Ferns
Punica	Pomegranate
Quercus	Oak

FLOWERS

Botanical name	Common name
Amaranthus	Amaranth
Antirrhinum	Snapdragon
Calceolaria	
Canna	
Cyclamen	
Digitalis	Foxglove
Eschscholzia	California poppy
Freesia	
Gypsophila	Baby's breath
Hyacinthus	
Iberis	Candytuft
Iris	
Lobularia	Sweet alyssum
Matthiola	Stock
Narcissus	Daffodil
Nasturtium	
Papaver	Poppy
Petunia	
Phlox	
Portulaca	Moss rose
Primula	Primrose
Zantedeschia	Calla
Zinnia	

VEGETABLES AND BERRIES

Asparagus
Cabbage family
Cantaloupe
Celery
Cranberry
Cucumber
Currant
Dewberry
Garlic
Grape
Leek
Onion
Pumpkin
Spinach
Squash
Strawberry
Watermelon

Some plants susceptible to southern blight (*Sclerotium rolfsii*):

SHRUBS

Botanical name	Common name
Daphne	
Hydrangea	
Pittosporum	
Rosa	Rose

FLOWERS

Botanical name	Common name
Anemone	
Alcea	Hollyhock
Calendula	Pot marigold
Callistephus	China aster
Campanula	Bell flower
Canna	
Chrysanthemum	Mum, daisy, marguerite
Cosmos	
Dahlia	
Delphinium	
Dianthus	Sweet William, carnation, pinks
Gladiolus	
Iris	
Lathyrus	Sweet pea
Lilium	Lily
Lupinus	Lupine
Narcissus	Daffodil, narcissus
Phlox	
Rudbeckia	Black-eyed Susan
Scabiosa	Pincushion flower
Sedum	
Tagetes	Marigold
Tulipa	Tulip
Viola	Pansy, viola
Zinnia	

VEGETABLES AND FRUITS

Apple
Artichoke
Avocado
Bean
Beet
Cabbage
Cantaloupe
Carrot
Cucumber
Eggplant
Lettuce
Okra
Onion
Pea
Peanut
Pepper
Potato
Rhubarb
Squash
Strawberry
Tomato
Turnip
Watermelon

*Southern blight has been reported on hundreds of plants. This is a partial list of plants that are frequently infected by this disease.

Some plants attractive to bees:

TREES AND SHRUBS

Botanical name	Common name
Abelia	
Acacia	
Arctostaphylos	Bearberry
Berberis	Barberry
Callistemon	Bottlebrush
Calluna	Heather
Ceanothus	Wild lilac
Cotoneaster	
Cytisus	Broom
Erica	Heath
Eriobotrya	Loquat
Escallonia	
Gleditsia	Honeylocust
Lantana	
Ligustrum	Privet
Lonicera	Honeysuckle
Myrtus	Myrtle
Nerium	Oleander
Pittosporum	Mock orange
Pyracantha	Firethorn
Raphiolepis	India hawthorn
Rosmarinus	Rosemary
Thymus	Thyme
Trachelospermum	Star jasmine
Wisteria	

FLOWERS

Botanical name	Common name
Achillea	Yarrow
Campanula	Bell flower
Helianthus	Sunflower
Lavandula	Lavender
Lobularia	Sweet alyssum
Myosotis	Forget-me-not
Nicotiana	Flowering tobacco
Salvia	

A few small trees for areas with restricted root space:

Botanical name	Common name
Acer campestre	Hedge maple
Acer ginnala	Amur maple
Acer palmatum	Japanese maple
Albizia julibrissin	Silk tree
Carpinus	Hornbeam
Cercis	Redbud
Cornus	Dogwood
Crataegus	Hawthorn
Elaeagnus angustifolia	Russian olive
Ilex	Holly
Koelreuteria	Golden-rain tree
Magnolia soulangiana	Saucer magnolia
Magnolia stellata	Star magnolia
Malus	Crabapple
Pistacia chinensis	Chinese pistache
Prunus	Flowering peach, plum, cherry
Styrax	Snowbell
Viburnum prunifolium	Black haw
Viburnum rufidulum	Southern black haw
Viburnum sieboldii	Siebold viburnum

Some plants tolerant of smog (ozone and PAN):

TREES AND SHRUBS

Botanical name	Common name
Abies balsamea	Balsam fir
A. concolor	White fir
Acer platanoides	Norway maple
A. saccharum	Sugar maple
Betula pendula	European white birch
Cornus racemosa	Gray dogwood
Euonymus alatus	Winged euonymus
Pinus resinosa	Red pine
Quercus robur	English oak
Rhododendron molle	Chinese azalea
Thuja occidentalis	American arborvitae

FLOWERS

Botanical name	Common name
Agapanthus	Lily-of-the-Nile
Antirrhinum majus	Snapdragon
Aquilegia	Columbine
Eschscholzia californica	California poppy
Heuchera sanguinea	Coral bells
Iris	
Lilium	Lily
Narcissus	Daffodil, narcissus

GROUNDCOVERS

Botanical name	Common name
Hedera helix	English ivy
Vinca minor	Periwinkle

FRUITS AND VEGETABLES

Strawberry
Sweet potato

Some plants tolerant of industrial pollution (SO2):

TREES AND SHRUBS

Botanical name	Common name
Acer campestre	Hedge maple
A. spicatum	Mountain maple
Carpinus betulus	European hornbeam
Citrus aurantifolia	Lime
C. limon	Lemon
C. paradisi	Grapefruit
C. sinensis	Sweet orange
Fraxinus pennsylvanica	Green ash
Gingko biloba	Gingko
Ilex aquifolium	English holly
I. opaca	American holly
Juniperus	Juniper
Ligustrum	Privet
Nyssa sylvatica	Sourgum
Oxydendron arboreum	Sourwood
Pinus mugo var. *mugo*	Dwarf mugho pine
Platanus occidentalis	Eastern sycamore
P. acerifolia	London plane tree
Populus deltoides	Cottonwood
Quercus robur	English oak
Q. rubra	Red oak
Robinia pseudoacacia	Black locust
Thuja occidentalis	Eastern arborvitae
T. plicata	Western red cedar
Tilia	Linden

FRUITS AND VEGETABLES

Cabbage
Celery
Corn
Muskmelon
Onion

Some trees and shrubs for shady areas:

Botanical name	Common name
Acer circinatum	Vine maple
Acer palmatum	Japanese maple
Amelanchier	Serviceberry
Aucuba	
Buxus	Boxwood
Calycanthus	Sweet shrub
Camellia	
Cercis	Redbud
Chamaecyparis	False cypress
Cornus	Dogwood
Daphne	
Halesia	Silver-bell
Hamamelis	Witch hazel
Hydrangea	
Ilex	Holly
Kalmia	Mountain laurel
Laurus nobilis	Laurel
Leucothoe	
Ligustrum	Privet
Mahonia	Oregon grape, holly grape
Nandina	Heavenly bamboo
Pieris	Andromeda
Pittosporum	
Podocarpus	
Rhododendron	Azalea, rhododendron
Sarcococca	
Taxus	Yew
Thuja	Arborvitae
Tsuga	Hemlock
Viburnum davidii	David viburnum
Viburnum tinus	Laurustinus

Plants rarely fed upon by adult Japanese beetles:

TREES AND SHRUBS

Botanical name	Common name
Abies	Fir
Acer negundo	Boxelder
Acer rubrum	Red maple
Acer saccharinum	Silver maple
Cercis	Redbud
Celastrus	Bittersweet
Clematis	
Cornus	Dogwood
Forsythia	
Fraxinus	Ash
Ginkgo	
Hydrangea	
Ilex	Holly
Juniperus	Juniper
Kalmia	Mountain laurel
Ligustrum	Privet
Liquidambar	Sweet gum
Lonicera	Honeysuckle
Magnolia	
Morus	Mulberry
Picea	Spruce
Pinus	Pine
Quercus alba	White oak
Q. coccinea	Scarlet oak
Q. rubra	Red oak
Q. stellata	Post oak
Q. velutina	Black oak
Rhododendron	Rhododendron, azalea
Robinia	Locust
Symphoricarpos	Snowberry
Syringa	Lilac
Thuja occidentalis	Arborvitae
Tsuga	Hemlock

FLOWERS

Botanical name	Common name
Aquilegia	Columbine
Aster	
Celosia	Cock's comb
Chrysanthemum	Mum, daisy
Dianthus	Sweet William, carnation, pink
Digitalis	Foxglove
Iberis	Candytuft
Iris	
Lathyrus	Sweet pea
Papaver	Poppy
Petunia	
Phlox	
Portulaca	
Viola	Pansy, viola

GROUNDCOVERS

Botanical name	Common name
Hedera	Ivy
Pachysandra	

VEGETABLES

Brussels sprout
Cabbage
Cantaloupe
Carrot
Cauliflower
Cucumber
Eggplant
Lettuce
Onion
Pea
Pumpkin
Radish
Spinach
Squash
Sweet potato
Turnip
Watermelon

FRUIT TREES

Pear

Adapted from "Japanese Beetle," Cooperative Extension Service, West Virginia University, Pest Information Series 68.

Some drought tolerant plants suitable for growing in areas with restricted root space:

Botanical name	Common name
Albizia julibrissin	Silk tree
Arbutus unedo	Strawberry tree
Carpinus	Hornbeam
Cercis	Redbud
Cercocarpus	Mountain mahogany
Cotoneaster	
Crataegus	Hawthorn
Elaeagnus	
Ginkgo	Maidenhair tree
Juniperus	Juniper
Koelreuteria	Golden-rain tree
Pinus edulis	Pinon pine
Pinus mugo mugo	Mugho pine
Potentilla fruticosa	Cinquefoil
Rosmarinus	Rosemary

A few trees that tolerate competition from lawn grasses:

Botanical name	Common name
Acer campestre	Hedge maple
Acer ginnala	Amur maple
Acer palmatum	Japanese maple
Albizia	Silk tree
Cornus	Dogwood
Cotinus	Smoke tree
Crataegus	Hawthorn
Fraxinus velutina glabra	Modesto ash
Koelreuteria	Golden-rain
Lagerstroemia	Crapemyrtle
Magnolia soulangiana	Saucer magnolia
Magnolia stellata	Star magnolia
Prunus	Flowering cherry, peach, plum

Some trees, shrubs, and perennials for wet soil:

TREES

Botanical name	Common name
Acer rubrum	Red maple
A. saccharinum	Silver maple
Alnus	Alder
Amelanchier arborea	Serviceberry
Betula nigra	River birch
Casuarina equisetifolia	Horsetail tree
Ilex cassine	Dahoon holly
I. opaca	American holly
Larix laricina	American larch
Liquidambar styraciflua	Sweet gum
Magnolia virginiana	Sweetbay magnolia
Nyssa sylvatica	Sour gum
Platanus	Sycamore
Populus	Poplar
Quercus bicolor	Swamp white oak
Q. palustris	Pin oak
Salix	Willow
Taxodium distichum	Bald cypress
Tristania laurina	Kanooka tristania

SHRUBS

Botanical name	Common name
Aronia arbutifolia	Red chokeberry
Bambusa disticha	Fernleaf bamboo
Betula occidentalis	Water birch
Calycanthus	Sweet shrub
Cephalanthus occidentalis	Buttonbush
Cornus sericea	Red-osier dogwood
Ilex glabra	Gallberry
I. verticillata	Winterberry
Lindera benzoin	Spicebush
Myrica pensylvanica	Bayberry
Rhododendron arborescens	Smooth azalea
R. vaseyi	Pink-shell azalea
Rosa palustris	Swamp rose
Salix	Willow
Thuja	Arborvitae
Viburnum trilobum	Cranberry bush

PERENNIALS

Botanical name	Common name
Aconitum	Monkshood
Acorus calamus	Sweet flag
Althaea officinalis	Marsh mallow
Aster novae-angliae	New England aster
Astilbe	
Caltha palustris	Marsh marigold
Cimicifuga racemosa	Black snakeroot
Colocasia esculenta	Elephant's ear
Cyperus	Sedge
Eupatorium maculatum	Joe-Pye weed
Ferns	
Hydrophyllum virginianum	Virginia waterleaf
Iris kaempferi	Japanese iris
I. sibirica	Siberian iris
Lilium canadense	Canada lily
Lobelia cardinalis	Cardinal flower
L. siphilitica	Great lobelia
Lysimachia nummularia	Moneywort
Mentha	Mint
Mimulus	Monkey flower
Myosotis scorpioides	Forget-me-not
Phalaris arundinacea 'Picta'	Ribbon grass
Primula japonica	Japanese primrose
Ranunculus	Persian buttercup
Sanguinaria canadensis	Bloodroot
Sisyrinchium californicum	Golden-eyed grass
Tolmiea menziesii	Piggyback plant
Trollius	Globeflower
Typha latifolia	Common cattail
Viola blanda	Sweet white violet
V. lanceolata	Lance-leaved violet
Zantedeschia	Calla

Some oaks that need no water after the first two seasons in the ground:

Botanical name	Common name
Quercus agrifolia	Coast live oak
Q. chrysolepis	Canyon live oak
Q. douglasii	Blue oak
Q. dumosa	California scrub oak
Q. engelmannii	Mesa oak
Q. garryana	Oregon white oak
Q. ilex	Holly oak
Q. kelloggii	California black oak
Q. lobata	Valley oak
Q. suber	Cork oak
Q. wislizenii	Interior live oak

Some oaks that need added water during periods of drought:

Botanical name	Common name
Quercus alba	White oak
*Q. bicolor**	Swamp white oak
Q. coccinea	Scarlet oak
Q. macrocarpa	Bur oak
*Q. palustris**	Pin oak
Q. phellos	Willow oak
Q. robur	English oak
Q. rubra	Red oak

*Will tolerate wet soil.

Some trees and shrubs with shallow root systems:

Botanical name	Common name
Acacia	
Acer saccharinum	Silver maple
Ailanthus altissima	Tree-of-heaven
Alnus	Alder
Cornus nuttallii	Pacific dogwood
Eucalyptus	
Ficus	Fig
Fraxinus uhdei	Evergreen ash
Gleditsia	Honeylocust
Morus	Mulberry
Platanus	Sycamore
Populus	Poplar
Rhus	Sumac
Robinia	Black locust
Salix	Willow
Ulmus	Elm

Trees, shrubs, vines, and groundcovers for sandy soil:

TREES

Botanical name	Common name
Crataegus phaenopyrum	Washington hawthorn
Elaeagnus angustifolia	Russian olive
Ilex opaca	American holly
Juniperus virginiana	Red cedar
Malus	Crabapple
Nyssa sylvatica	Sourgum
Parkinsonia aculeata	Jerusalem thorn
Picea glauca	White spruce
Pinus banksiana	Jack pine
P. clausa	Sand pine
P. echinata	Yellow pine
P. elliottii	Slash pine
P. resinosa	Red pine
P. rigida	Pitch pine
P. strobus	Eastern white pine
P. thunbergii	Japanese black pine
P. virginiana	Scrub pine
Platanus x acerifolia	London plane
Populus alba	White poplar
Quercus alba	White oak
Q. palustris	Pin oak
Q. stellata	Post oak
Sophora japonica	Japanese pagoda tree

SHRUBS

Botanical name	Common name
Aronia arbutifolia	Red chokeberry
Berberis thunbergii	Japanese barberry
Buddleia davidii	Orange-eye butterfly bush
Chaenomeles speciosa	Japanese quince
Juniperus chinensis 'Pfitzerana'	Pfitzer's juniper
Kalmia angustifolio	Sheep laurel
K. latifolio	Mountain laurel
Kerria japonica	Japanese rose
Lespedeza thunbergii	Bush clover
Ligustrum amurense	Amur privet
Lonicera tatarica	Tatarian honeysuckle
Myrica cerifera	Wax myrtle
M. pensylvanica	Bayberry
Philadelphus coronarius	Mock orange
Potentilla fruticosa	Shrubby cinquefoil
Prunus maritima	Beach plum
Pyracantha coccinea	Firethorn
Rhamnus cathartica	Common buckthorn
Rhus glabra	Smooth sumac
Rosa rugosa	Japanese rose
Spiraea japonica	Japanese spirea
Tamarix parviflora	Tamarisk
Vaccinium corymbosum	Highbush blueberry
Weigela florida	Weigela

VINES AND GROUNDCOVERS

Botanical name	Common name
Actinidia arguta	Bower actinidia
Arctostaphylos uva-ursi	Common bearberry
Campsis radicans	Trumpet creeper
Celastrus scandens	American bittersweet
Juniperus chinensis procumbens	Japanese garden juniper
J. conferta	Shore juniper
J. horizontalis	Creeping juniper
Lantana montevidensis	Trailing lantana
Liriope spicata	Lilyturf
Lonicera japonica 'Halliana'	Hall's Japanese honeysuckle
Parthenocissus quinquefolia	Virginia creeper
Phyla nodiflora	Lippia
Pteridium aquilinum	Bracken
Rhus aromatica	Fragrant sumac
Rosa wichuraiana	Memorial rose
Sedum acre	Golden-carpet
Thymus vulgaris	Common thyme
Vitis	Grape
Wedelia triloba	Wedelia

Some plants tolerant of saline soil:

Botanical name	Common name
Araucaria heterophylla	Norfolk Island pine
Arctotheca calendula	Arctotheca
Baccharis pilularis	Coyote bush
Bougainvillea	
Callistemon viminalis	Weeping bottlebrush
Carissa grandiflora	Natal plum
Chamaerops humilis	European fan palm
Coprosma repens	Mirror plant
Cordyline indivisa	Blue dracaena
Cortaderia selloana	Pampas grass
Delosperma 'Alba'	White ice plant
Drosanthemum	Rosea ice plant
Euonymus japonica	
Gazania	
Lampranthus	Trailing ice plant
Nerium oleander	Oleander
Phyla nodiflora	Lippia
Pinus halepensis	Alleppo pine
Pittosporum crassifolium	Evergreen pittosporum
Pyracantha	Firethorn
Rosmarinus lockwoodii	Rosemary
Syzygium paniculatum	Brush cherry

Susceptibility of some trees to injury from fill:

MOST SUSCEPTIBLE

Botanical name	Common name
Acer saccharum	Sugar maple
Cornus	Dogwood
Fagus	Beech
Liriodendron	Tuliptree
Picea	Spruce
Pinus	Pine
Quercus	Oak

MODERATELY SUSCEPTIBLE

Botanical name	Common name
Betula	Birch
Carya	Hickory
Tsuga	Hemlock

LEAST SUSCEPTIBLE

Botanical name	Common name
Platanus	Sycamore
Populus	Poplar
Quercus palustris	Pin oak
Robinia	Locust
Salix	Willow
Ulmus	Elm

Some trees with weak forks and brittle wood:

Botanical name	Common name
Acacia	
Acer saccharinum	Silver maple
Aesculus	Horse chestnut
Ailanthus	Tree-of-heaven
Callistemon citrinus	Bottlebrush
Casuarina stricta	She-oak
Eucalyptus	
Fraxinus velutina glabra	Modesto ash
Liriodendron	Tuliptree
Magnolia grandiflora	Southern magnolia
Melaleuca	
Melia azedarach	Chinaberry
Morus alba	White mulberry
Populus	Poplar
Quercus prinus	Chestnut oak
Robinia	Locust
Salix	Willow
Sassafras	
Sequoia sempervirens	Coast redwood
Ulmus pumila	Siberian elm

Low-growing trees suitable for planting under wires along streets:

Botanical name	Common name
Acer campestre	Hedge maple
Acer ginnala	Amur maple
Acer palmatum	Japanese maple
Acer spicatum	Mountain maple
Acer tataricum	Tatarian maple
Cercis	Redbud
Cotinus	Smoketree
Koelreuteria paniculata	Golden-rain tree
Lagerstroemia indica	Crapemyrtle
Malus	Crabapple
Prunus	Flowering cherry, peach, plum
Styrax japonicus	Snowbell

Some trees susceptible to lightning injury:

SUSCEPTIBLE

Botanical name	Common name
Fraxinus	Ash
Liriodendron	Tuliptree
Picea	Spruce
Pinus	Pine
Populus	Poplar
Quercus	Oak
Ulmus	Elm

LESS SUSCEPTIBLE*

Botanical name	Common name
Aesculus	Horse chestnut
Betula	Birch
Fagus	Beech

*No species is totally immune, and location and size of the tree are also factors influencing susceptibility.

From *Tree Maintenance*, P.P. Pirone. Copyright © 1978 Oxford University Press, Inc. Reprinted by permission.

Some trees that are commonly damaged by sapsuckers:

Botanical name	Common name
Abies	Fir
Acacia	
Acer rubrum	Red maple
Acer saccharum	Sugar maple
Betula	Birch
Casuarina	Beefwood
Eriobotrya	Loquat
Fagus	Beech
Grevillea	Silk oak
Larix	Larch
Magnolia	
Malus	Apple
Palmae	Palms
Picea rubens	Red spruce
Pinus	Pine
Populus tremuloides	Quaking aspen
Pseudotsuga menziesii	Douglas fir
Salix	Willow
Tsuga	Hemlock

Palms most frequently attacked by the palm leaf skeletonizer (*Homaledra sabalella*):

Botanical name	Common name
Acoelorrhaphe wrightii	Paurotis palm
Butia capitata	Pindo palm
Cocos nucifera	Coconut palm
Livistona chinensis	Chinese fan palm
Phoenix	Date palms
Sabal palmetto	Cabbage palm
Washingtonia	Washington palms

Trees and shrubs that are relatively free of insects and diseases:

Botanical name	Common name
Ailanthus	Tree-of-heaven
Brachychiton	Bottletree
Carpinus	Hornbeam
Cedrus	Cedar
Celtis australis	European hackberry
Ceratonia siliqua	Carob
Cercidiphyllum japonicum	Katsura tree
Clematis	
Cornus mas	Cornelian cherry
Cornus officinalis	Japanese cornelian cherry
Corylus colurna	Turkish filbert
Cotinus	Smoke tree
Cytisus	Broom
Eucommia ulmoides	Hardy rubber tree
Ficus	Fig
Franklinia	Franklin tree
Gingko	Maidenhair tree
Grevillea robusta	Silk oak
Gymnocladus dioica	Kentucky coffeetree
Kalopanax pictus	Castor-aralia
Kerria	Japanese rose
Koelreuteria paniculata	Varnish tree
Laburnum	Bean tree
Libocedrus decurrens	Incense cedar
Ligustrum lucidum	Glossy privet
Magnolia acuminata	
M. Kobus borealis	
M. salicifolia	Anise magnolia
M. stellata	Star magnolia
Metasequoia	Dawn redwood
Myrica	Bayberry
Myrtus	Myrtle
Nyssa	
Ostrya	Hop hornbeam
Parrotia persica	Persian parrotia
Phellodendron	Cork tree
Pistacia chinensis	Chinese pistache
Podocarpus	
Potentilla	Cinquefoil
Rhamnus	Buckthorn
Sciadopitys verticillata	Umbrella pine
Sophora japonica	Japanese pagoda tree
Stewartia	
Styrax	Snowbell
Tamarix	Tamarisk
Taxodium	Bald cypress
Viburnum sieboldii	Siebold viburnum
Xylosma congestum	Shiny xylosma

Some trees and shrubs that are resistant to crown gall:

Botanical name	Common name
Abelia	
Ailanthus	Tree-of-heaven
Albizia	Mimosa
Amelanchier	Serviceberry
Berberis	Barberry
Betula	Birch
Buxus	Boxwood
Calluna	Heather
Carpinus	Hornbeam
Catalpa	
Cedrus	Cedar
Cercis	Redbud
Cladrastis	Yellowwood
Cotinus	Smoke tree
Cryptomeria	
Deutzia	
Fagus	Beech
Ginkgo	Maidenhair tree
Gymnocladus	Coffee tree
Ilex	Holly
Kalmia	Mountain laurel
Koelreuteria	Golden-rain tree
Laburnum	Golden-chain tree
Larix	Larch
Leucothoe	
Liquidambar	Sweet gum
Liriodendron	Tuliptree
Magnolia	
Mahonia	Oregon grape
Nyssa	Black gum
Picea	Spruce
Pieris	Andromeda
Pyracantha	Firethorn
Rhus	Sumac
Sambucus	Elderberry
Sassafras	
Tsuga	Hemlock
Zelkova	

Adapted from *Crown Gall*, W.A. Sinclair and W.T. Johnson. Cornell Tree Pest Leaflet A-5.

Some plants susceptible and resistant to *Phytophthora cinnamoni* and *P. lateralis*:

SUSCEPTIBLE TREES AND SHRUBS

Botanical name	Common name
Abelia	
Abies	Fir
Acacia	
Arctostaphylos	Manzanita
Calluna	Heather
Camellia japonica	
Castanea	Chestnut
Casuarina	Beefwood
Ceanothus	
Cedrus	Cedar
Chamaecyparis	False cypress
Cinnamomum	Camphor tree
Cornus	Dogwood
Cupressus	Cypress
Daphne	
Erica	Heath
Eucalyptus	
Fatsia	Aralia
Hibiscus	
Hypericum	St. John's wort
Juglans	Walnut
Juniperus	Juniper
Larix	Larch
Laurus	Sweet bay
Libocedrus	Incense cedar
Myrtus	Myrtle
Olea	Olive
Picea	Spruce
Pieris	Andromeda
Pinus	Pine
Pittosporum	Mock orange
Platanus	Sycamore
Pseudotsuga	Douglas fir
Quercus	Oak
Rhododendron	Rhododendron, azalea
Salix	Willow
Sequoia sempervirens	Coast redwood
Taxodium	Bald cypress
Taxus	Yew
Thuja	Arborvitae
Viburnum	

SUSCEPTIBLE FRUITS AND BERRIES

Apricot
Avocado
Blueberry (highbush)
Cherry
Citrus
Peach
Pear

RESISTANT TREES AND SHRUBS

Botanical name	Common name
Camellia sasangua	
Chamaecyparis nootkatensis	Alaska cypress
Chamaecyparis pisifera var. *filifera*	Sawara
Chamaecyparis thyoides	White cedar
Daphne cneorum	Rock daphne
Juniperus chinensis 'Pfitzerana'	Pfitzer's juniper
Juniperus sabina	Savin juniper
Juniperus squamata 'Meyeri'	Meyer juniper
Pinus mugo var.*mugo*	Mugho pine
Rhododendron obtusum	Hiryu azalea
Thuja occidentalis	Arborvitae

RESISTANT BERRY

Blueberry (rabbiteye)

Some plants susceptible to bacterial blight (*Pseudomonas syringae*):

Almond	Citrus	Oleander
Apple	Lilac	Plum
Avocado	Pea	Rose
Bean	Peach	Stock
Cherry	Pear	

Susceptibility of palm species to lethal yellows disease in Florida:

HIGHLY SUSCEPTIBLE

Botanical name	Common name
Cocos nucifera L. 'Jamaica Tall'	Coconut palm
Pritchardia species	

MODERATELY SUSCEPTIBLE

Botanical name	Common name
Arenga engleri	Englers palm
Caryota mitis	Fishtail palm
Corypha elata	Buri palm
Dictyosperma album	Hurricane palm
Latania species	Latan palm
Phoenix canariensis	Canary Island date palm
Phoenix dactylifera	Date palm
Trachycarpus fortunei	Chinese windmill palm
Veitchia merrillii	Christmas (adonidia) palm

SLIGHTLY SUSCEPTIBLE

Botanical name	Common name
Arikuryroba schizophylla	Arikury palm
Borassus flabellifer	Palmyra palm
Chrysalidocarpus cabadae	Cadaba palm
Hyophorbe vershaffeltii	Spindle palm
Livistona chinensis	Chinese fan palm
Phoenix reclinata	Senegal date palm
Phoenix sylvestris	Wild date palm
Veitchia montgomeryana	Montgomery's palm

Pines susceptible to diplodia tip blight:*

Botanical name	Common name
Pinus mugo var. *mugo*	Mugho pine
Pinus nigra	Austrian pine
Pinus ponderosa	Ponderosa pine
Pinus resinosa	Red pine
Pinus strobus	White pine
Pinus sylvestris	Scotch pine
Pinus virginiana	Scrub pine

*Susceptibility may vary according to region.

Gypsy moth food plant preferences:

MOST PREFERRED

Botanical name	Common name
Amelanchier	Serviceberry
Betula alleghaniensis	Gray birch
Betula papyrifera	Paper birch
Crataegus species	Hawthorn
Hamamelis	Witch hazel
Malus	Apple, crabapple
Populus tremuloides	Quaking aspen
Quercus	Oak
Rosa	Rose
Salix	Willow
Sorbus	Mountain ash
Tamarix	Tamarisk
Tilia	Linden

INTERMEDIATE

Botanical name	Common name
Acer	Maple
Carya	Hickory
Celtis	Hackberry
Cercis	Redbud
Fagus	Beech
Liquidambar	Sweet gum
Magnolia	
Nyssa	Tupelo
Pinus	Pine
Populus deltoides	Cottonwood
Prunus avium	Cherry
Sassafras	
Tsuga	Hemlock
Ulmus	Elm

LEAST PREFERRED

Botanical name	Common name
Abies	Fir
Aesculus	Horse chestnut
Catalpa	
Cornus	Dogwood
Fraxinus	Ash
Ilex	Holly
Juglans nigra	Black walnut
Kalmia	Mountain laurel
Liriodendron	Tuliptree
Morus	Mulberry
Platanus	Sycamore, plane tree
Robinia	Locust

Juniper varieties resistant to twig blight:

Botanical name	Common name
Juniperus chinensis	Chinese juniper
var. *'Aureo-Pfitzerana'*	Golden pfitzer juniper
'Foemina'	
'Keteleeri	Keteleer juniper
'Sargenti'	Sargent juniper
'Sargenti glauca'	
J. communis	Common juniper
var. *'Aureospica'*	
'Depressa'	Prostrate juniper
'Repanda'	
'Suecica'	Swedish juniper
J. horizontalis	Creeping juniper
J. sabina	Savin juniper
var. *'Broadmoor'*	Broadmoor juniper
'Campbelli'	
'Fargesi'	
'Prostrata'	
'Pumila'	
'Skandia'	
'Tripartita'	Tripartite juniper

Some varieties of pyracantha resistant to scab:

Mohave
Orange glow
Rogersiana
Shawnee
Watereri

Some pines susceptible to and resistant to pine wilt:

SUSCEPTIBLE PINES

Botanical name	Common name
Pinus contorta latifolia	Lodgepole pine
P. densiflora	Japanese red pine
P. lambertiana	Sugar pine
P. monticola	Western white pine
P. mugo	Mugho pine
P. nigra	Austrian pine
P. pinaster	Cluster pine
P. radiata	Monterey pine
P. sylvestris	Scotch pine
P. taeda	Loblolly pine
P. thunbergii	Japanese black pine
P. virginiana	Scrub pine

RESISTANT PINES

Botanical name	Common name
Pinus banksiana	Jack pine
P. caribaea	Slash pine
P. echinata	Shortleaf pine
P. eliottii	Slash pine
P. jeffreyi	Jeffrey pine
P. palustris	Longleaf pine
P. pungens	Table mountain pine
P. rigida	Pitch pine
P. strobus	White pine

Some plants that are susceptible to quince rust (*Gymnosporangium clavipes* or *G. libocedri*):

Botanical name	Common name
Amelanchier	Serviceberry
Aronia	Chokeberry
Crataegus	Hawthorn
Juniperus communis and its varieties	Common juniper
Juniperus virginiana	Red cedar
Libocedrus decurrens	Incense cedar
Sorbus	Mountain ash

Some plants that are resistant and susceptible to cedar-apple rust (*Gymnosporanglum juniperi-virginianae*):

RESISTANT VARIETIES

Botanical name	Common name
Juniperus chinensis	Chinese juniper
var. *'Foemina'*	
'Keteleeri'	Keteleer juniper
'Sargenti'	Sargent juniper
J. communis	Common juniper
var. *'Aureospica'*	
'Depressa'	Prostrate juniper
'Saxatilis'	
'Suecica'	Swedish juniper
J. sabina	Savin juniper
var. *'Broadmoor'*	Broadmoor juniper
'Knap hill'	
'Skandia'	
J. squamata	Singleseed juniper
var. *'Fargesi'*	
J. virginiana	Eastern red cedar
var. *'Tripartita'*	Fountain red cedar

SUSCEPTIBLE VARIETIES

Botanical name	Common name
Juniperius scopulorum and its varieties	Rocky Mountain juniper
Juniperis virginiana	Red cedar
Malus	Apples

PARTICULARLY SUSCEPTIBLE APPLE VARIETIES

Jonathan
Rome
Wealthy
York Imperial
Bechtel crabapple
Parkman flowering crabapple

Some plants that are resistant to armillaria root rot:

TREES AND SHRUBS

Botanical name	Common name
Abies concolor	White fir
Acacia longifolia	Bush acacia
Acacia mearnsii	Black wattle
Acacia verticillata	Star acacia
Acer macrophyllum	Bigleaf maple
Acer palmatum	Japanese maple
Ailanthus altissima	Tree-of-heaven
Arbutus menziesii	Madrone
Berberis polyantha	Barberry
Betula pumila	Swamp birch
Buxus sempervirens	Boxwood
Calocedrus decurrens	Incense cedar
Catalpa bignonioides	Common catalpa
Celtis species	Hackberry
Ceratonia siliqua	Carob
Cercis occidentalis	California redbud
Cercis siliquastrum	Judas tree
Chaenomeles lagenaria	Japanese quince
Chamaecyparis lawsoniana 'Ellwoodii'	Elwood cypress
Cotinus coggygria	Smoke tree
Cryptomeria japonica	Japanese cedar
Cupaniopsis anacardioides	Carrotwood
Cupressocyparis leylandii	Leyland cypress
Cupressus arizonica var. *glabra*	Smooth Arizona cypress
Elaeagnus angustifolia	Russian olive
Erica arborea	Tree heath
Eucalyptus camaldulensis	Red gum
Eucalyptus cinerea	Silver-dollar tree
Eugenia species	Eugenia
Fraxinus uhdei	Evergreen ash
Fraxinus velutina var. *glabra* 'Modesto'	Modesto ash
Ginkgo biloba	Ginkgo
Gleditsia triacanthos 'Shademaster'	Shademaster locust
Hibiscus syriacus	Rose-of-Sharon
Hypericum patulum	St. John's wort
Ilex aquifolium	English holly
Jacaranda acutifolia	Jacaranda
Liquidambar orientalis	Oriental sweet gum
Liquidambar styraciflua	Sweet gum
Liriodendron tulipifera	Tuliptree
Lonicera nitida	Box honeysuckle
Magnolia grandiflora	Southern magnolia
Mahonia aquifolium	Oregon grape
Malus floribunda	Japanese flowering crab
Maytenus boaria	Mayten tree
Metasequoia glyptostroboides	Dawn redwood
Morus species	Mulberry
Myrica pensylvanica	Bayberry
Nandina domestica	Heavenly bamboo
Palms	
Pinus canariensis	Canary Island pine
Pinus nigra	Austrian pine
Pinus radiata	Monterey pine
Pinus sylvestris	Scotch pine
Pinus torreyana	Torrey pine
Pistacia chinensis	Chinese pistache
Pittosporum rhombifolium	Queensland pittosporum
Platanus species	Sycamore
Prunus caroliniana	Cherry laurel
Prunus ilicifolia	Holly-leaved cherry
Prunus lyonii	Catalina cherry
Quercus ilex	Holly oak
Quercus lobata	Valley oak
Raphiolepis umbellata	Yedda hawthorn
Rhus aromatica	Fragrant sumac
Sambucus canadensis	American elder
Sequoia sempervirens	Coast redwood
Sophora japonica	Japanese pagoda tree
Taxodium distichum	Bald cypress
Ternstroemia species	Ternstroemia
Ulmus parvifolia	Chinese elm
Vitex agnus-castus	Chaste tree
Wisteria sinensis	Chinese wisteria

FRUITS, NUTS, AND BERRIES

Botanical name	Common name
Carya illinoinensis	Pecan
Castanea dentata	American chestnut
Diospyros kaki	Japanese persimmon
Diospyros virginiana	Common persimmon
Ficus carica 'Kadota'	Kadota fig
Ficus carica 'Mission'	Mission fig
Juglans hindsii	Black walnut
Malus pumila	Common apple
Malus species	Crabapple
Persea americana	Avocado
Prunus cerasifera	Cherry plum
Prunus serotina salicifolia	Black cherry
Pyrus calleryana	Callery pear
Pyrus communis	Pear
Rubus ursinus loganobaccus	Loganberry
Rubus ursinus	Ollalie

Some plants that are susceptible to fireblight:

TREES AND SHRUBS

Botanical name	Common name
Amelanchier	Serviceberry
Chaemoneles	Flowering quince
Cotoneaster	
Crataegus	Hawthorn
Eriobotrya	Loquat
Malus	Apple, crabapple
Photinia	
Prunus	Flowering almond, plum, and cherry
Rosa	Rose
Sorbus	Mountain ash
Spireaea	

FRUIT TREES AND BERRIES

Apple
Pear
Quince
Raspberry

Varieties of pyracantha and hawthorn that are tolerant of fireblight.

PYRACANTHA

Botanical name	Common name
P. coccinea 'Lalandei'	Laland's firethorn
P. fortuneana	

HAWTHORN

Botanical name	Common name
Crataegus phaenopyrum	Washington hawthorn

These varieties are not immune to fireblight, but are not damaged by it as severely as are other varieties.

Some avocado varieties for California and Florida, from most hardy to least hardy:

For California	For Florida
Bacon	Brogdon
Zutano	Tonnage
Fuerte	Choquette
Hass	Pollock

Disease-resistant crabapples

Species or Cultivar	Disease Resistance	Description
Adams	S+, F+, P+	Flowers opening to pink; fruit vivid red, ¾″ across.
Malus baccata Jackii	S+, F-, P+	Flowers white, fragrant; fruit glossy red, ½″ across.
Beverly	S+, F-	Flowers opening to white; small red fruit, ½″ to ¾″ across.
Centurion	S	Flowers rose-red; fruit glossy, cherry-red, ⅝″ across.
Christmas Holly (P.A.F.)	S+	Flowers open to white; fruit bright red and lasting, ⅛″ across.
David	S+, F	Flowers opening to white; fruit scarlet, ½″ across.
Dolgo	S+, F+	Flowers white; fruit red, 1¼″ across.
Donald Wyman	S+, F-, P+	Flowers opening to white; fruit glossy red, ¾″ across.
M. Floribunda	S+, F, P+	Flowers opening to pink and white; fruit yellow and red, ⅜″ across.
Harvest Gold	S-	Flowers white; fruit gold and lasting, ⅜″ across.
Henningi	S+	Flowers white; fruit orange-red, ⅝″ across.
Jewelberry	S+, F+	Flowers pink and white; fruit glossy red, ½″ across. Dwarf, shrubby tree.
Liset	S+, F+, P	Flowers rose-red to light crimson; fruit glossy dark red, ⅝″ across.
Mary Potter	S, F, P	Flowers open to white; fruit red, ½″ across.
Ormiston Roy	S+, F+	Flowers pink; fruit yellow, ⅜″ across, persistent.
Red Baron	S, F+	Flowers very dark red; fruit glossy dark red, medium size. Columnar habit.
Red Jewel	S, F-, P+	Flowers white; fruit cherry red, ⅜″ across. Broad habit.
M. sargentii	S+, F	Flowers white, fragrant; fruit dark red, ¼″ across. Broad habit.
Selkirk	S, F+ P	Flowers purplish-pink; fruit glossy bright red.
Sentinel	S, F+	Flowers pale pink; fruit red, small.
Silver Moon	S, F-	Flowers white; fruit tiny, red, persistent.
Sugartyme (P.A.F.)	S+	Flowers white, fruit bright red, persistent, ¼″ across.
White Angel	S+, F	Flowers open to white; fruit red, ½″ across.
White Cascade	S+, F+, P+	Flowers open to white; fruit lime-yellow, weeping habit.

DISEASE KEY

F+ Strong resistance to fireblight
F Moderate resistance to fireblight
F- Slight resistance to fireblight

P+ Strong resistance to powdery mildew
P Moderate resistance to powdery mildew
P- Slight resistance to powdery mildew

S+ Strong resistance to scab
S Moderate resistance to scab
S- Slight resistance to scab

Some pecan varieties—regional adaptation, pollination requirements, and disease resistance:

Variety	Regional Adaptation	Pollination Requirements	Disease Resistance
Cape Fear	I, II	A	
Cheyenne	II	B	S
Colby	III	D	
Elliot	II	B	S+
Mahan	II	A	
Major	III	D	
Missouri Hardy	III	C	
Schley	I, II	A	
Stuart's Paper Shell	I, II	A	S+
Success	II	A	
Western Schley	II	B	

REGIONAL ADAPTATION

I Louisiana to Florida.
II Areas of Texas, Arizona, New Mexico, and California within USDA Plant Hardiness Zones 7 through 9. See page 1020.
III Oklahoma, Kansas, Missouri, Iowa, Illinois, Indiana, Kentucky, and Tennessee.

POLLINATION REQUIREMENTS

Pecans are self-fruitful, but crops will be improved by use of a pollinator.
A Use another A.
B Use another B.
C Plant two of this variety.
D Use another D.

DISEASE RESISTANCE

S+ Resistant to scab.
S Moderately resistant to scab.

Some fig varieties, with special regional adaptations:

Variety	South*	California interior valleys	California coastal areas	Northwest coastal areas
Brown Turkey		•	•	
Celeste	•			
Eastern Brown Turkey**	•			
Green Ischia	•			
Kadota		•		
King ('Desert King')				•
Latterula				•
Magnolia	•			
Mission		•	•	

* Southern areas suitable for growing figs are Florida, Georgia, South Carolina, North Carolina, Alabama, Mississippi, Louisiana, southern Arkansas, and Texas.

** Also called Lee's Perpetual, Brunswick, Ramsey, Harrison, and Everbearing.

Some plants that may be infested by the Mediterranean fruit fly:

Apple
Apricot
Avocado
Cantaloupe
Cherry
Citrus
Cucumber
Fig
Grape
Guava
Loquat
Olive
Peach
Pear
Pepper
Persimmon
Plum
Pumpkin
Pyracantha
Quince
Squash (Hubbard)
Strawberry
Tomato
Walnut

Adapted from "California Agriculture," March-April 1981.

Some plants susceptible to *Botryosphaeria ribis*:

TREES AND SHRUBS

Botanical name	Common name
Acer	Maple
Castanea	Chestnut
Cercis	Redbud
Cornus	Dogwood
Forsythia	
Ilex	Holly
Liquidambar	Sweet gum
Nyssa	Tupelo, sour gum
Populus	Poplar
Pyracantha	Firethorn
Rhododendron	Rhododendron, azalea
Rosa	Rose
Salix	Willow

FRUIT AND NUT TREES AND SMALL FRUITS

Apple
Avocado
Citrus
Currant
Fig
Hickory
Pear
Pecan

Regional adaptations of some blueberry varieties:

FOR THE SOUTH AND SOUTHERN CALIFORNIA:

Rabbiteye *(Vaccinium ashei)*

Bluebelle, Bluegem, Climax, Tifblue, Woodward

Highbush *(Vaccinium species)*

Avonblue, Flordablue, Sharpblue

FOR THE VERY COLDEST REGIONS:

Meader, Northland

WIDELY ADAPTED:

Berkeley, Bluecrop, Blueray, Bluetta, Collins, Jersey, Patriot

Cold hardiness of citrus, from most hardy to least hardy:

Kumquat
Meyer lemon
Mandarin orange
Orange
Grapefruit
Lemon
Lime

Home gardeners in Florida and California can plant a wide variety of citrus in the milder areas of their states. In the warmest areas, you will have success with the more tender citrus such as grapefruit, lemons, and limes. South Texas gardeners can plant Meyer lemon, Satsuma mandarin, and Marr's Early Orange.

The pH Scale

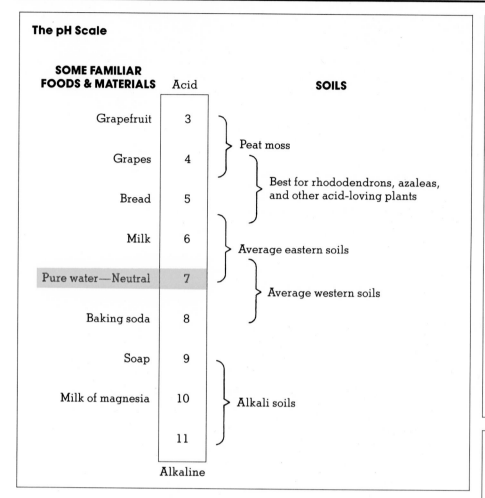

SOME FAMILIAR FOODS & MATERIALS	Acid	SOILS
Grapefruit	3	Peat moss (3–4)
Grapes	4	Best for rhododendrons, azaleas, and other acid-loving plants (4–5.5)
Bread	5	
Milk	6	Average eastern soils (5.5–7)
Pure water—Neutral	7	Average western soils (6.5–8)
Baking soda	8	
Soap	9	Alkali soils (9–11)
Milk of magnesia	10	
	11	
	Alkaline	

Apply limestone to raise pH

Pounds of ground limestone needed per 100 square feet to raise pH to 6.5:

Present pH of soil	Pounds needed to raise sandy loam to pH 6.5	Pounds needed to raise loam to pH 6.5	Pounds needed to raise clay loam to pH 6.5
4.0	11.5	16	23
4.5	9.5	13.5	19.5
5.0	8	10.5	15
5.5	6	8	10.5
6.0	3	4	5.5

Dolomitic limestone is recommended because it adds magnesium as well as calcium to the soil. The limestone should be cultivated into the soil.

Adapted from "Soil acidity needs of plants," New York Cooperative Extension Service, publication D-2-25.

Some plants that will grow in alkaline soil (pH 7.5 to 8.4):

TREES AND SHRUBS

Botanical name	Common name
Acer negundo	Box elder
Albizia	Silk tree
Berberis thunbergii	Japanese barberry
Casuarina	Beefwood
Celtis	Hackberry
Cercocarpus	Mountain mahogany
Deutzia	
Elaeagnus angustifolia	Russian olive
Forsythia	
Fraxinus velutina	Velvet ash
Hibiscus syriacus	Rose-of-Sharon
Kerria	
Lonicera fragrantissima	Fragrant honeysuckle
Malus sargentii	Sargent crabapple
Philadelphus	Mock orange
Phoenix dactylifera	Date palm
Populus fremontii	Fremont cottonwood
Potentilla fruticosa	Bush cinquefoil
Robinia	Black locust
Sophora japonica	Japanese pagoda
Spiraea vanhouttei	Vanhoutte spirea
Viburnum dentatum	Arrowwood
Viburnum dilatatum	Linden viburnum
Washingtonia	Washington palm
Ziziphus jujuba	Common Jujube

Some plants that will grow in acid soil (pH 4.5 to 5.5):

TREES AND SHRUBS

Botanical name	Common name
Amelanchier	Serviceberry
Arctostaphylos	Manzanita, kinnikinick
Calluna	Heather
Camellia	
Cytisus	Broom
Erica	Heath
Gardenia	
Hydrangea	
Ilex	Holly
Kalmia	Mountain laurel
Lagerstroemia indica	Crapemyrtle
Leucothoe	
Magnolia	
Picea	Spruce
Pieris	Andromeda
Pinus	Pine
Populus tremuloides	Quaking aspen
Quercus palustris	Pin oak
Rhododendron	Azalea, rhododendron
Salix babylonica	Weeping willow
Sorbus	Mountain ash
Tsuga	Hemlock

FLOWERS

Botanical name	Common name
Convallaria	Lily-of-the-valley
Coreopsis	
Gypsophila	Baby's-breath
Lupinus	Lupine

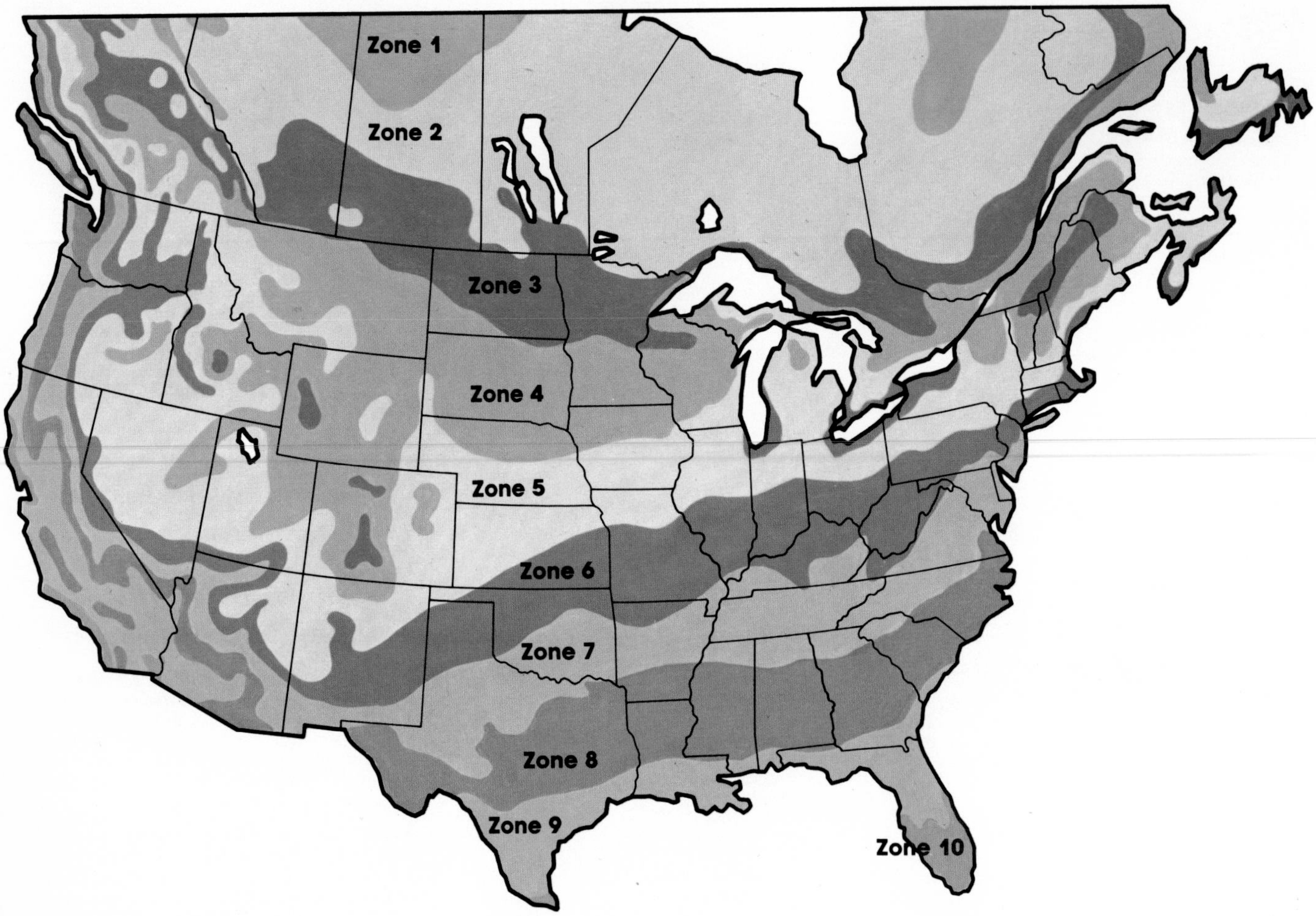

Plant Climate Zone Map

These zones are based on mean minimum temperatures, and represent only an *average* for areas within the zone. Your location might be a zone or two warmer than the map shows if you live near a large body of water, or a zone or two colder if you live at a high elevation or on a north-facing slope. Adapted from the USDA Plant Climate Zone Map.

Range of average minimum temperatures for each zone:

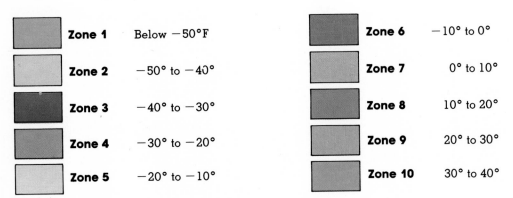

Zone 1	Below −50°F
Zone 2	−50° to −40°
Zone 3	−40° to −30°
Zone 4	−30° to −20°
Zone 5	−20° to −10°
Zone 6	−10° to 0°
Zone 7	0° to 10°
Zone 8	10° to 20°
Zone 9	20° to 30°
Zone 10	30° to 40°

Apples

Variety	Pollination	Disease Resistance	Zone Adaptation[1] 2	3	4	5	6	7	8	9	10[2]
Anna	D								•	•	•
Baldwin	A	FB	•	•	•	•					
Cortland	B	PM-		•	•	•	•				
Dorsett Golden	D							•	•	•	•
Ein Shemer	D								•	•	•
Empire	B	FB		•	•	•					
Golden Delicious	A					•	•	•	•		
Granny Smith	B								•	•	
Gravenstein	E	PM-					•	•	•	•	
Idared	E	FB-, PM-			•	•	•	•			
Jonathan	B	CAR-, FB-, PM-			•	•	•	•	•		
McIntosh	B			•	•	•	•				
Newton Pippin	B					•	•	•	•		
Northern Spy	B		•	•	•	•	•				
Prima	C	PM, S+, FB				•	•	•	•		
Priscilla	C	CAR+, S+, FB				•	•	•	•		
Red Delicious	B	BR, CAR-				•	•	•	•		
Red Rome Beauty	A	FB-, PM-				•	•	•	•		
Rhode Island Greening	E	FB-		•	•	•					
Sir Prize	C	S+, PM				•	•	•	•		
Stayman Winesap	E	BR, FB				•	•	•	•		
Winesap	E					•	•	•	•		
Winter Banana	B					•	•	•	•		
Yellow Transparent	B	FB-			•	•	•	•	•		

[1]Based on USDA Plant Hardiness Zone Map. See page 1020.
[2]Florida only.

POLLINATION KEY
- A Self-fruitful, but crop is improved with a pollinator.
- B Pollinate with any A or B.
- C Prima and Priscilla cross-pollinate well. Sir Prize needs either Prima or Priscilla for pollination, but will not pollinate them.
- D Pollinate with another D.
- E Not a pollinator. Pollinate with an A or a B.

DISEASE KEY
- BR Fairly resistant to bitter rot.
- CAR- Highly susceptible to cedar-apple rust.
- CAR+ Resistant to cedar-apple rust.
- FB Fairly resistant to fireblight.
- FB- Highly susceptible to fireblight.
- PM Fairly resistant to powdery mildew.
- PM- Highly susceptible to powdery mildew.
- S+ Resistant to scab.

Apricots

Variety	Pollination	Disease Resistance	Zone Adaptation[1] 2	3	4	5	6	7	8	9[2]	10
Blenheim	A	BR-					•	•	•	•	
Goldcot	A					•	•	•	•		
Perfection	B						•	•	•		
Royal	A	BR-					•	•	•		
Tilton	A	BR					•	•	•	•	
Stella	A					•	•	•	•		

[1]Based on USDA Plant Hardiness Map. See page 1020.
[2]California only.

POLLINATION KEY
- A Self-fruitful. Needs no pollinator.
- B Not self-fruitful. Pollinate with Blenheim or Royal.

DISEASE KEY
- BR Fairly resistant to brown rot.
- BR- Highly susceptible to brown rot.

Peaches

Variety	Pollination	Disease Resistance	Zone Adaptation[1] 2	3	4	5	6	7	8	9	10
Belle of Georgia	A	BLS+				•	•	•	•		
Desertgold	A								•	•	•
Early-Red-Fre	A	BLS+				•	•	•	•		
Elberta	A	BLS-				•	•	•	•		
Flordasun	A									•	•[3]
J.H. Hale	B					•	•	•	•		
Madison[2]	A	BLS				•	•	•	•		
Redhaven	A	BLS				•	•	•	•		
Redskin	A	BLS				•	•	•	•		
Reliance[2]	A					•	•	•	•		
Rio-oso-gem	A	BLS-				•	•	•	•		
Sunhaven	A	BLS				•	•	•	•		

[1]Based on USDA Plant Hardiness Zone Map. See page 1020.
[2]Does well in colder areas of Zone 5.
[3]Florida only.

POLLINATION KEY
A Self-fruitful. Requires no pollinator.
B Requires pollinator. Use an A.

DISEASE KEY
BLS+ Resistant to bacterial leaf spot.
BLS Fairly resistant to bacterial leaf spot.
BLS- Susceptible to bacterial leaf spot.

Pears

Variety	Pollination	Disease Resistance	Zone Adaptation[1] 2	3	4	5	6	7	8	9[2]	10
Bartlett	B	FB-				•	•	•		•	
Bosc	B	FB-				•	•	•		•	
Clapp's favorite	B	FB-				•	•	•			
Comice	B	(FB)				•	•	•		•	
D'Anjou	B	FB-				•	•	•			
Kieffer[3]	A	FB			•	•	•	•	•	•	
Moonglow	A	FB+				•	•	•	•		
Orient[3]	A	FB+				•	•	•	•	•	
Seckel	C	FB				•	•	•	•		

[1]Based on USDA Plant Hardiness Zone Map. See page 1020.
[2]California only.
[3]Grown in Florida.

POLLINATION KEY
A Pollinate with another A.
B Pollinate with any B.
C Pollinate with any B except Bartlett.

DISEASE KEY
FB+ Resistant to fireblight.
FB Fairly resistant to fireblight.
(FB) Moderately susceptible to fireblight.
FB- Highly susceptible to fireblight.

Plums

Variety	Type	Pollination	Disease Resistance	Zone Adaptation[1] 4	5	6	7	8	9[2]	10
Blue Damson	E	B	BK-		•	•	•			
Burbank	J	D			•	•	•	•	•	
Ember	J	E		•	•	•	•	•		
Green Gage	E	B				•	•	•		
Italian Prune (Fellenberg)	EPP	F			•	•	•	•		
Methley	J	C	BK		•	•	•	•	•	
Ozark Premier	J	D			•	•	•	•	•	
President	E	A	BK+		•	•	•	•	•	
Santa Rosa	J	C	BK		•	•	•	•	•	
Shiro	J	D	BK		•	•	•	•	•	
Stanley	EPP	F	BK-	•	•	•	•	•		
Underwood	J	E			•	•	•	•	•	

[1]Based on USDA Plant Hardiness Map. See page 1020.
[2]California only.

TYPES
E European blue plum
EPP European prune plum
J Japanese red plum

POLLINATION KEY
A Not self-fruitful, pollinate with a B.
B Self-fruitful, no pollinator necessary.
C Self-fruitful, but crop is improved by a pollinator; use a D.
D Not self-fruitful, pollinate with another D.
E Ember and Underwood cross-pollinate well.
F Self-fruitful, but crop improved by a pollinator; use an F.

DISEASE RESISTANCE
BK+ Resistant to black knot.
BK Fairly resistant to black knot.
BK- Highly susceptible to black knot.

Some bramble varieties, with special regional adaptation and/or disease resistance:

BLACKBERRIES	Disease Resistance	Widely Adapted	North	South	Pacific Coast	California
Black Satin				•		
Darrow		•	•			
Ebony King	OR	•				
Eldorado	OR	•				
Flordagrand*	LS			•		
Lawton	OR, V					
Oklawaha*				•		
RED RASPBERRIES						
August Red			•			
Latham		•	•			
Meeker	PM	•			•	
Southland	LS, A, PM			•		
Sumner	PM	•			•	
Willamette	PM	•			•	
TRAILING BLACKBERRIES						
Boysenberry					•	•
Loganberry					•	
Ollaliberry	V,M					•
Youngberry					•	•

*Need cross-pollination.

DISEASE RESISTANCE KEY

A Resistant to anthracnose.
LS Resistant to leaf spot.
M Resistant to mosaic.
OR Resistant to orange rust.
PM Resistant to powdery mildew.
V Resistant to verticillium wilt.

Sweet cherries

Variety	Pollination	Disease Resistance	Zone Adaptation[1] 2	3	4	5	6	7	8	9[2]	10
Bing	A	BC-				•	•	•	•	•	
Black Tartarian	B					•	•	•	•	•	
Corum	C	BC				•	•	•			
Early Burlat	C	BC+				•	•	•	•	•	
Lambert	A	BC-				•	•	•			
Royal Ann	A	BC-				•	•	•			
Sam	C	BC				•	•	•			
Sue	C	BC				•	•	•			
Van	B	BC-				•	•	•	•	•	

Sour cherries

Meteor	D	CLS			•	•	•	•			
Montmorency	D					•	•	•			
North Star	D	CLS			•	•	•	•	•		

[1]Based on USDA Plant Hardiness Zone Map. See page 1020.
[2]California only.

POLLINATION KEY

A Pollinate with a B.
B Pollinate with an A.
C Pollinate with an A or a B.
D Self-fruitful, needs no pollinator.

DISEASE KEY

BC+ Resistant to bacterial canker.
BC Fairly resistant to bacterial canker.
BC- Susceptible to bacterial canker.
CLS Fairly resistant to cherry leafspot.

Some strawberry varieties—regional adaptation and disease resistance:

Variety	Disease Resistance	Widely Adapted	South	North	California	Northwest
Blakemore	S+, LS, VW+	•				
Catskill	S+, VW+			•		
Darrow	LS, PM, S, RS+, VW	•				
Delite	RS+, VW+	•				
Earlibelle	LS, S		•			
Empire	VW+			•		
Fletcher	S+, VW+			•		
Florida 90*	V		•			
Guardian	RS+, VW+	•				
Hood	RS+, VW+, LS					•
Midway	RS			•		
Northwest	V, LS+					•
Ogallala	LS+	•				
Pocahontas	LS+		•			
Redchief	RS+, S+, VW	•				
Salinas	VW+				•	•
Sequoia					•	
Sparkle	RS+			•		
Surecrop	VW+, RS+	•				
Tioga	V				•	•

*Adapted to extreme southern regions.

DISEASE RESISTANCE KEY

LS	Moderately resistant to leaf spot.
LS+	Resistant to leaf spot.
PM	Moderately resistant to powdery mildew.
RS	Moderately resistant to 1 or more races of red stele.
RS+	Resistant to 1 or more races of red stele.
S	Moderately resistant to scorch
S+	Resistant to scorch
V	Moderately resistant to virus.
VW	Moderately resistant to verticillium wilt.
VW+	Resistant to verticillium wilt.

Some grape varieties, with disease resistance and regional adaptation:

Variety	Disease Resistance	Northeast	Midwest	Pacific Northwest	Southeast	California Arizona
Aurore	DM	•		•		
Beta	BR+	•	•	•		
Campbell's Early	BR+	•		•		
Concord	DM	•	•	•		•
Delaware	PM	•	•	•		
Fredonia	BR+	•		•		
Magnolia					•	
Missouri Reisling	BR+	•				
Niagara	PM	•	•	•		•
Scuppernong*					•	
Thompson Seedless						•
Tokay						•
Worden	BR+	•	•	•		

*Needs pollinator; use Magnolia.

DISEASE RESISTANCE KEY

BR+	Resistant to black rot.
DM	Moderately resistant to downy mildew.
PM	Moderately resistant to powdery mildew.

Earliest dates for safe spring planting of vegetables:

To find the average date of the last freeze, ask at your local nursery or Cooperative Extension office (see page 1029).

Crop	Planting dates for localities in which average date of last freeze is: Feb. 1	Feb. 15	Mar. 1	Mar. 15	Apr. 1	Apr. 15	May 1	May 15	June 1
Asparagus	—	—	—	2/1	2/15	3/15	3/15	4/15	5/1
Bean, lima	2/1	3/1	3/15	4/1	4/15	5/1	5/15	6/1	—
Bean, snap	2/1	3/1	3/15	3/15	4/1	4/15	5/1	5/15	6/1
Beet	1/1	1/15	2/15	2/15	3/1	3/15	4/1	4/15	5/1
Broccoli*	1/1	1/15	2/1	2/15	3/1	3/15	4/1	4/15	5/15
Brussels sprout*	1/1	1/15	2/1	2/15	3/1	3/15	4/1	4/15	5/15
Cabbage*	1/1	1/1	1/15	2/1	2/15	3/1	3/15	4/15	5/15
Carrot	1/1	1/15	2/1	2/15	3/1	3/15	4/1	5/1	5/15
Cauliflower*	1/1	1/15	1/15	2/1	2/15	3/1	4/1	4/15	5/15
Cucumber	2/15	2/15	3/1	4/1	4/15	5/1	5/15	6/1	—
Eggplant*	2/1	2/15	3/15	4/1	4/15	5/1	5/15	6/1	—
Lettuce	1/1	1/1	1/1	2/1	2/15	3/15	4/1	4/15	5/15
Muskmelon	2/15	2/15	3/1	4/1	4/15	5/1	6/1	—	—
Onion	1/1	1/1	1/1	2/1	2/15	3/1	3/15	4/15	5/1
Parsley	1/1	1/1	1/15	2/1	2/15	3/15	4/1	4/15	5/15
Pea	1/1	1/1	1/15	2/1	2/15	3/1	3/15	4/15	5/1
Pepper*	2/1	3/1	3/15	4/1	4/15	5/1	5/15	6/1	6/1
Potato	1/1	1/15	1/15	2/1	3/1	3/15	4/1	4/15	5/1
Radish	1/1	2/2	1/1	1/15	2/15	3/1	3/15	4/1	5/1
Spinach	1/1	1/1	1/1	1/15	2/1	2/15	3/15	4/1	4/15
Squash	2/1	3/1	3/15	4/1	4/15	5/1	5/1	5/15	6/1
Tomato*	2/1	3/1	3/15	4/1	4/15	5/1	5/15	5/15	6/1
Turnip	1/1	1/15	2/1	2/1	2/15	3/1	3/15	4/1	5/1
Watermelon	2/15	2/15	3/1	3/15	4/15	5/1	5/15	6/1	—

* Seeds may be started indoors 4 to 6 weeks before planting date.

Vegetable seed information:

	Optimum germination temperatures	Days to germination
Asparagus	70-75°F	14-21
Bean, lima	70	7-10
Bean, snap	70	6-10
Beet	50-85	10-14
Broccoli	70-75	10-14
Brussels sprout	70-75	10-14
Cabbage	70-75	10-14
Carrot	50-85	14-21
Cauliflower	70-75	8-10
Cucumber	70	7-10
Eggplant	70	10-15
Lettuce	65-70	7-10
Melon	75	5-7
Onion	70-75	10-14
Parsley	70-75	14-21
Pea, garden	40-75	7-10
Pepper	75-80	10
Radish	45-85	4-6
Spinach	70	8-10
Squash	70-75	7-10
Sweet corn	70	5-7
Tomato	70-75	5-8
Turnip	60-85	7-10

Some vegetables that are susceptible to verticillium wilt:

Artichoke
Beet
Brussels sprout
Cabbage
Eggplant
Melon[1]
New Zealand spinach
Okra
Peanut
Pepper
Potato
Pumpkin
Radish
Rhubarb
Spinach
Strawberry[2]
Tomato

[1]Watermelon, cantaloupe, and honeydew become infected, but are not seriously damaged. Persian, casaba, and crenshaw melons are very susceptible.

[2]See page 1024 for strawberry varieties that are resistant to verticillium.

Adapted from "*Plants resistant or susceptible to verticillium wilt,*" University of California Cooperative Extension leaflet 2703.

Regional adaptation of some onion varieties:

FOR THE SOUTH
Excel
Granex
Texas Grano
Tropicana Red
White Granex

FOR THE WEST
California Early Red
Early Yellow Globe
Southport Yellow Globe
Yellow Bermuda

FOR THE NORTH
Downing Yellow Globe
Early Yellow Globe
Empire
Nutmeg
Spartan lines

Some vegetables that are susceptible to fusarium wilt caused by various forms of *Fusarium oxysporum*:

Asparagus
Beans
Brussels sprout
Cabbage
Cauliflower
Celery
Cucumber
Melons
Okra
Onion
Pea
Pepper
Radish
Spinach
Sweet potato
Tomato
Turnip

Some vegetable varieties with resistance to the southern root knot nematode (*Meloidogyne incognita*):

Bean
Bountiful
Brittle Wax
Tender Pod
Wingard Wonder

Corn
Carmel Cross
Golden Beauty Hybrid
Golden Cross Bantam
Span Cross

Pea
Burpeeana Early
Wando

Pepper
All Big
Bontoc Sweet Long
World Beater

Tomato
All Round
Anahu
Anahu-R
Atkinson
Auburn 76
Beefeater
Beefmaster
Big Seven
Calmart
Chicogrande
Coldset
Eurocross
Extase
Monte Carlo
Nemared
Nematex
Patriot
Peto 662 VFN
Ponderosa
VFN-8

Sweet potato
Apache
Carver
Heartogold
Hopi
Jasper
Jewel
Nemagold
Nugget
Ruby
Sunnyside
White Bunch
White Triumph
Whitestar

Some tomato varieties—adaptation and disease resistance:

EARLY SEASON	Disease Resistance	Widely Adapted	For the South	For the North	For the West
Early Cascade	V, F	•			
Jetfire	V, F				•
New Yorker	V			•	
Porter Improved					•
Small Fry	V, F, N	•			
Spring Set	V, F	•			

MIDSEASON	Disease Resistance	Widely Adapted	For the South	For the North	For the West
Ace 55	V, F				•
Atkinson	F, N		•		
Better Boy	V, F, N	•			
Big Girl Hybrid	V, F	•			
Big Set	V, F, N	•			
Bonus	V, F, N	•			
Burpee's VF	V, F	•			
Columbia	V, F, Ct	•			
Floradel	F		•		
Floramerica	V, F	•			
Heinz 1350	V, F	•			
Jet Star	V, F			•	
Marglobe	F	•			
Park's Whopper	V, F, N, T	•			
Roma VF	V, F	•			
Rowpac	V, F, Ct				•
Roza	V, F, Ct				•
Salad Master	V, F, Ct				•
Supersonic	V, F			•	•
Terrific	V, F, N	•			
Tropi-Red	V, F		•		

LATE SEASON	Disease Resistance	Widely Adapted	For the South	For the North	For the West
Beefeater	V, F, N	•			
Beefmaster	V, F, N	•			
Manalucie	F		•		
Ramapo	V, F			•	
Tropic	V, F, T		•		
Wonder Boy	V, F	•			
Vineripe	V, F, N	•			

DISEASE KEY
V Resistant to verticillium wilt.
F Resistant to fusarium wilt.
N Resistant to nematodes.
T Resistant to tobacco mosaic virus.
Ct Resistant to curly top.

Bean varieties resistant to rust:

Cape
Dade
Kentucky Wonder
Resisto

Bean varieties resistant to mosaic:

Aristocrop
Astro
Bonanza Wax
Bush Blue Lake
Bush Blue Lake 47
Bush Blue Lake 274
Cape
Cherokee
Contender
Dade (pole)
Del Rey
Eagle
Early Gallatin
Early Harvest
Flo
Gallatin 50
Gator Green 15
Gold Crop
Golden Rod
Harvester
Improved Tendergreen
M.R.
Peak
Provider
Resistant Cherokee
Resisto
Roma II PVP
Romano
Spartan Arrow
Spurt
Strike
Stringless Blue Lake FM-IK
Sungold
Tendercrop
Tenderlake
Topcrop
Win

Beet varieties that produce round, smooth roots:

Albino White Beet
Detroit Dark Red
Earlisweet Hybrid
Early Wonder, Green Top
Early Wonder, Tall Top
Garnet
Golden Beet
Perfected Detroit
Red Ace Hybrid
Red Ball
Ruby Queen

Corn varieties tolerant of smut (S), bacterial wilt (B), and maize dwarf mosaic (M):

Apache	S, B, M
Aztec	S, B
Bellringer	S, B
Calico	S, B
Calumet	S, B, M
Cherokee	B, M
Comanche	S, B
Comet	S, B
Gold cup	S, B
Merit	S, B, M
Mevak	S, B
Quicksilver	S, B, M
Seneca Sentry	B, M
Silver Queen	B
Sweet Sue	S
Wintergreen	S, B, M

Corn varieties tolerant of or resistant to southern and northern leaf blights:

Apache
Atlantic
BiQueen
Capitan
Cherokee
Comet
Florida Staysweet
Guardian
Wintergreen

Lettuce varieties resistant to or tolerant of tip burn:

Calmar
Climax
Empire
Empress
Fairton
Great Lakes 118, 366, 659, 659-700, and 6238
Green Lake
Ithaca
Merit
Mesa 659
Minetto
Montello
Montemar
New York 515 Improved
Oswego
Parris Island Cos
Pennlake
Salinas
Super 59
Vanguard
Vanguard 75
Vanmax

Onion varieties resistant to or tolerant of pink root:

Autumn Spice
Beltsville Bunching
Brown Beauty
Buccaneer
Collosal
Copper Coast
Danvers
Early Supreme
El Capitan
Evergreen White Bunch
Fiesta
Granada
Granex Yellow
Henry's Special
Majesty
Red Commander
Rialto
Ringer
Spanish Main
White Granex
White Robust
Yellow Globe
Yellow Grano—New Mexico

Potato varieties tolerant of common scab:

Alamo
Cascade
Cherokee
La Rouge
Lemhi
Nooksack
Norchip
Norgold Russet
Norland
Ona
Onaway
Ontario
Plymouth
Pungo
Russet Burbank
Shurchip
Sioux
Superior
Targhee

Spinach varieties resistant to downy mildew:

Aden
Badger Savoy
Basra
Bismark
Bouquet
Califlay
Chesapeake
Chinook
Dixie Market
Duet
Early Smooth
Grandstand
High Pack
Long Standing Savoy
Marathon
Melody
Nares
Salma
Savoy Supreme
Skookum
Vienna
Winter Bloomsdale

CUCUMBER DISEASE RESISTANCE:

Slicing cucumber varieties resistant to or tolerant of common plant diseases:

A & C Hybrid Imp	L+, S+, A+, P+, D+, C+
A & C Hybrid 1810	L+, S+, A+, P+, D+, C+
Cherokee #7	L+, S+, A+, P, D, C+
Dasher	L, S, A, P, D, C
Dasher II	L, S+, A+, P+, D+, C+
Early Triumph	L, S, A, P, D, C
Gemini 7	L, S, A, P, D, C
Medalist	S+, P, D, C+
Poinsett	L+, A+, P+, D+
Poinsett 76	L+, S+, P+, D+
Roadside Fancy	L, S, A, P, D, C
Setter	L, S+, A, P+, D+
Shamrock	L, S, P, D, C
Slicemaster	L, S+, A, P, D, C
Slice-Mor	S+, A+, P, D+, C
Southernsett	L, S+, P, D, C+
Sprint 440	L, S, A, P, D
Sweet-Slice	L, S+, A, P, D, C
Sweet Success	S, P, D, C

Pickling cucumber varieties resistant to or tolerant of common plant diseases:

Addis	A, P, D, C, L
Bounty	S, A, P, D, C, L
Calypso	S, A, P, D, C, L
Carolina	S, A, P, D, C, L
Chipper	A, P, D, C, L
County Fair	S, A, P, D, C
Explorer	P, D, L
Flurry	S, A, P, D, C, L
Liberty	S, D, C, L
Lucky Strike	S, A, P, C
Multipik	S, A, D, C, L
Panorama	S, A, P, D, C, L
Peto Triplemech	S, A, P, D, C, L
Picarow	S, A, P, D, C, L
Premier	S, A, P, D, C, L
Salty	S, P, D, C
Sampson	A, P, D, C, L
Score	S, A, D, C, L
Spear-It	S, A, P, D, C, L
Sumter	S, A, P, D, C, L
Tamor	S, A, P, D, C, L
Triple Crown	S, A, P, C, L
V.I.P.	S, A, P, D, C, L

DISEASE RESISTANCE KEY

A variety's resistance to a disease is indicated by the codes below. If a variety is especially resistant to the disease, the code is followed by a plus (+).

L = angular leaf spot
S = scab
A = anthracnose
P = powdery mildew
D = downy mildew
C = cucumber mosaic virus

Peppers resistant to or tolerant of tobacco mosaic virus:

Ace
Allbig
Annabelle
Argo
Bell Boy
Big Bertha
Burlington
Early Canada Bell
Early Niagara Giant
Early Wonder
Emerald Giant
Gatorbelle
Gypsy
Hybelle
Lady Bell
Liberty Bell
Ma Belle
Merced
Mercury
Midway
Miss Belle
New Ace
Pennwonder
Pimientol
Puerto Rico Perfection
Puerto Rico Wonder
Resistant Florida Giant
Rutgers World Beater
Shamrock
Skipper
Staddon's Select
Thick Walled World Beater
Titan
Valley Giant
Yolo Wonder

Canteloupe and muskmelon varieties resistant to or tolerant of:

DOWNY MILDEW
Ambrosia
Dixie Jumbo
Early Dawn
Summet
Topmark
Topset

ANTHRACNOSE
Samson
Saticoy

POWDERY MILDEW
Ambrosia
Classic
Delicious 51
Early Dawn
Edisto
Saticoy
Summet

Watermelon varieties resistant to or tolerant of anthracnose:

Blackstone
Calhoun
Charleston Gray
Crimson Sweet
Dixielee
Family Fun
Graybelle
Imperial
Madera
Smokylee
Sweet Favorite Hybrid
Verona
You Sweet Thing Hybrid

COUNTY EXTENSION AGENTS

ALABAMA

Autauga	205-365-2243
Baldwin	205-937-7176
Barbour	205-775-3284
Bibb	205-926-4818
Blount	205-274-2129
Bullock	205-738-2580
Butler	205-382-5111
Calhoun	205-237-1621
Chambers	205-864-9373
Cherokee	205-927-3250
Chilton	205-755-3240
Choctaw	205-459-2133
Clarke	205-275-3121
Clay	205-354-2183
Cleburne	205-463-2620
Coffee	205-894-5596
Colbert	205-383-1363
Conecuh	205-578-1311
Coosa	205-377-4713
Covington	205-222-1125
Crenshaw	205-335-6551
Cullman	205-739-3530
Dale	501-774-2329
Dallas	205-875-3200
DeKalb	205-845-3323
Elmore	205-567-6301
Escambia	205-867-6038
Etowah	205-546-2821
Fayette	205-932-8941
Franklin	205-332-2101
Geneva	205-684-2484
Greene	205-372-3401
Hale	205-624-8710
Henry	205-585-6416
Houston	205-794-4108
Jackson	205-574-2143
Jefferson	205-325-5342
Lamar	205-695-7139
Lauderdale	205-766-5180
Lawrence	205-974-1177
Lee	205-749-3353
Limestone	205-232-5510
Lowndes	205-548-2315
Macon	205-727-0340
Madison	205-536-5911
Marengo	205-295-5959
Marion	205-921-3551
Marshall	205-582-2000
Mobile	205-690-8445
Monroe	205-575-3477
Montgomery	205-832-4950
Morgan	205-773-2549
Perry	205-683-6888
Pickens	205-367-8148
Pike	205-566-0985
Randolph	205-357-2841
Russell	205-298-6845
St. Clair	205-338-9416
Shelby	205-669-6763
Sumter	205-652-9501
Talladega	205-362-6187
Tallapoosa	205-825-4228
Tuscaloosa	205-349-3886
Walker	205-221-3392
Washington	205-847-2295
Wilcox	205-682-4289
Winston	205-489-5376

ARIZONA

Apache	602-337-2267
Cochise	602-384-3594
Coconino	602-774-1868
Gila	602-425-7179
Graham	602-428-2611
Greenlee	602-359-2261
Maricopa	602-255-4456
Mohave	602-753-3788
Navajo	602-524-6271
Pima	602-628-5161
Pinal	602-836-5221
Santa Cruz	602-287-4689
Yavapai	602-445-6590
Yuma	602-783-8338

ARKANSAS

Arkansas	501-946-3231
Ashley	501-853-8391
Baxter	501-425-2335
Benton	501-273-3346
Boone	501-741-6168
Bradley	501-226-5813
Calhoun	501-798-2231
Carroll	501-423-2958
Chicot	501-265-5883
Clark	501-246-2281
Clay	501-598-2246
Cleburne	501-362-2524
Cleveland	501-325-6321
Columbia	501-234-1390
Conway	501-354-2494
Craighead	501-932-3621
Crawford	501-474-5286
Crittenden	501-739-3239
Cross	501-238-2335
Dallas	501-352-3505
Desha	501-222-3972
Drew	501-367-3128
Faulkner	501-329-8344
Franklin	501-667-3720
Fulton	501-895-3301
Garland	501-623-6841
Grant	501-942-2231
Greene	501-236-6921
Hempstead	501-777-5771
Hot Spring	501-332-5267
Howard	501-845-2375
Independence	501-793-6826
Izard	501-368-4323
Jackson	501-523-6594
Jefferson	501-534-1033
Johnson	501-754-2240
Lafayette	501-921-4744
Lawrence	501-886-3741
Lee	501-295-5202
Lincoln	501-628-4247
Little River	501-898-3394
Logan	501-963-2360
Lonoke	501-676-3124
Madison	501-738-6826
Marion	501-449-6349
Miller	501-773-4666
Mississippi	501-762-2075
Monroe	501-747-3397
Montgomery	501-867-2311
Nevada	501-887-2818
Newton	501-446-2240
Ouchatia	501-836-6858
Perry	501-889-2661
Phillips	501-338-7447
Pike	501-285-2161
Poinsett	501-578-5496
Polk	501-394-2323
Pope	501-968-7098
Prairie	501-998-2614
Pulaski	501-661-4676
Randolph	501-892-4504
St. Francis	501-633-3034
Saline	501-778-2483
Scott	501-637-2173
Searcy	501-448-3981
Sebastian	501-782-4947
Sevier	501-584-3013
Sharp	501-994-7363
Stone	501-269-3336
Union	501-862-4226
Van Buren	501-745-7117
Washington	501-521-8400
White	501-268-5394
Woodruff	501-347-2556
Yell	501-495-2216

CALIFORNIA

Alameda	415-881-6341
Amador	209-223-3230
Butte	916-534-4201
Calaveras	209-754-4160
Colusa	916-458-2105
Contra Costa	415-944-3540
El Dorado	916-626-2468
Fresno	209-488-3285
Glenn	916-865-4487
Humboldt-Del Norte	707-443-0896
Imperial	619-339-4250
Inyo-Mono	714-873-5891
Kern	805-861-2631
Kings	209-582-3211
Lake	707-263-2281
Lassen	916-257-8311
Los Angeles	213-744-4851
Madera	209-674-4641
Marin	415-499-6352
Mariposa	209-966-2417
Mendocino	707-468-4495
Merced	209-726-7403
Modoc	916-233-2123
Monterey	408-758-4637
Napa	707-253-4221
Orange	714-774-7050
Placer-Nevada	916-823-4691
Plumas-Sierra	916-283-0250
Riverside	714-683-6491
Sacramento	916-366-2013
San Benito	408-637-5346
San Bernardino	714-383-3871
San Diego	714-565-5376
San Joaquin	209-944-3711
San Luis Obispo	805-549-5940
San Mateo-San Francisco	415-726-9059
Santa Barbara	805-968-2149 805-961-3689
Santa Clara	408-299-2635
Santa Cruz	408-724-4734
Shasta	916-246-5621
Siskiyou	916-842-2711
Solano	707-429-6381
Sonoma	707-527-2621
Stanislaus	209-571-6654
Sutter-Yuba	916-673-9645
Tehama	916-527-3101
Trinity	916-624-4000
Tulare	209-733-6363
Tuolumne	209-533-5695
Ventura	805-654-2924
Yolo	916-666-8435

COLORADO

Adams	303-659-4150
Arapahoe	303-795-4670
Archuleta	303-264-5931
Boulder	303-776-4865
Chaffee	303-539-6447
Custer	303-783-2514
Denver	303-575-2716
Dolores	303-677-2283
Douglas	303-688-3096
Eagle	303-328-7311
Elbert	303-541-2361
El Paso	303-471-5764
Fremont	303-275-1514
Garfield	303-945-7437
Grand	303-724-3436
Gunnison	303-641-1260
Huerfano	303-738-2170
Jackson	303-723-4298
Jefferson	303-277-8980
La Plata	303-247-4355
Larimer	303-221-7580
Las Animas	303-846-6881
Lincoln	303-743-2542
Logan	303-522-3200
Moffat	303-824-6673
Montezuma	303-565-3123
Morgan	303-867-2493
Park	303-836-2771
Pitkin	303-925-5185
Pueblo	303-543-3550
Rio Blanco	303-878-4093
Routt	303-879-0825
San Miguel	303-327-4393
Sedgwick	303-474-3479
Summit	303-668-3595
Teller	303-689-2552
Weld	303-356-4000

CONNECTICUT

Fairfield	203-797-4176
Hartford	203-241-4940
Litchfield	203-567-9447
Middlesex	203-345-4511
New Haven	203-789-7865
New London	203-887-1608
Tolland	203-875-3331
Windham	203-774-9600

DELAWARE

Kent	302-736-1448
New Castle	302-738-2506
Sussex	302-856-5250
District of Columbia	202-727-2016

FLORIDA

Alachua	904-377-0400
Baker	904-259-3520
Bay	904-763-5456
Bradford	904-964-6280
Brevard	305-632-9507
Broward	305-475-8450
Calhoun	904-674-8323
Charlotte	813-639-8872
Citrus	904-726-2141
Clay	904-284-6355
Collier	813-774-8370
Columbia	904-752-5247
Dade	305-248-3311
Desoto	813-494-0303
Dixie	904-498-3330
Duval	904-384-2001
Escambia	904-438-1020
Flagler	904-437-3122
Franklin	904-653-9337
Gadsden	904-627-6315
Gilchrist	904-463-2022
Glades	813-946-0244
Gulf	904-229-6123
Hamilton	904-792-1312
Hardee	813-773-2164
Hendry	813-675-2361
Hernando	904-796-9421
Highlands	813-382-5248
Hillsborough	813-621-5605
Holmes	904-547-3602
Indian River	305-567-8000
Jackson	904-482-2064
Jefferson	904-997-3573

COUNTY EXTENSION AGENTS

Lafayette	904-294-1279
Lake	904-343-4101
Lee	813-335-2421
Leon	904-487-3006
Levy	904-486-2165
Liberty	904-643-2478
Madison	904-973-4138
Manatee	813-722-4524
Marion	904-629-8067
Martin	305-283-6760
Monroe	305-294-4641
Nassau	904-845-2121
Okaloosa	904-682-2711
Okeechobee	813-763-6469
Orange	305-420-3265
Osceola	305-846-4181
Palm Beach	305-683-1777
Pasco	904-567-5167
Pinellas	813-586-5477
Polk	813-533-0765
Putnam	904-328-5181
St. Johns	904-824-8131
St. Lucie	305-464-2900
Santa Rosa	904-623-3868
Sarasota	813-955-6239
Seminole	305-323-2500
Sumter	904-793-2728
Suwannee	904-362-2771
Taylor	904-584-4345
Union	904-496-2321
Volusia	904-736-0624
Wakulla	904-926-3931
Walton	904-892-5415
Washington	904-638-0740

GEORGIA

Appling	912-367-2372
Atkinson	912-422-3277
Bacon	912-632-5601
Baker	912-734-5252
Baldwin	912-453-4394
Banks	404-677-2245
Barrow	404-867-7581
Bartow	404-382-2324
Ben Hill	912-423-2360
Berrien	912-686-5431
Bibb	912-744-6338
Bleckley	912-934-6917
Brantley	912-462-5724
Brooks	912-263-4103
Bryan	912-653-2231
Bulloch	912-764-6101
Burke	404-554-2119
Butts	404-775-2601
Calhoun	912-849-2685
Camden	912-576-5465
Candler	912-685-2408
Carroll	404-834-1490
Catoosa	404-935-4211
Charlton	912-496-2040
Chatham	912-944-2291
Chattooga	404-857-1410
Cherokee	404-479-1966
Clarke	404-546-8330
Clay	912-768-2247
Clayton	404-478-9911
Clinch	912-487-2169
Cobb	404-429-3330
Coffee	912-384-1402
Colquitt	912-985-1321
Columbia	404-541-0557
Cook	912-896-4040
Coweta	404-253-2450
Crawford	912-836-3121
Crisp	912-273-1217
Dade	404-657-4116
Dawson	404-265-2442
Decatur	912-246-4528
Dekalb	404-371-2821
Dodge	912-374-4702
Dooly	912-268-4171
Dougherty	912-436-7216
Douglas	404-949-2000
Early	912-723-3072
Echols	912-559-5562
Effingham	912-754-6071
Elbert	404-283-3001
Emanuel	912-237-9933
Evans	912-739-1292
Fannin	404-632-5722
Fayette	404-461-4580
Floyd	404-295-6210
Forsyth	404-887-2418
Franklin	404-384-2843
Fulton	404-572-3261
Gilmer	404-635-4426
Glascock	404-598-2811
Glynn	912-265-0610
Gordon	404-629-8685
Grady	912-377-1312
Greene	404-453-2083
Gwinnett	404-962-1480
Habersham	404-754-2318
Hall	404-536-6681
Hancock	404-444-6596
Haralson	404-646-5288
Harris	404-628-4824
Hart	404-376-3134
Heard	404-675-3513
Henry	404-957-1533
Houston	912-987-2028
Irwin	912-468-7409
Jackson	404-367-8789
Jasper	404-468-6479
Jeff Davis	912-375-5526
Jefferson	912-625-3046
Jenkins	912-982-4408
Johnson	912-864-3373
Jones	912-986-3948
Lamar	404-358-0281
Lanier	912-482-3895
Laurens	912-272-2277
Lee	912-759-6426
Liberty	912-876-2133
Lincoln	404-359-3233
Long	912-545-9549
Lowndes	912-242-1858
Lumpkin	404-864-2275
Macon	912-472-7588
Madison	404-795-2281
Marion	912-649-2625
McDuffie	404-595-1815
McIntosh	912-437-6651
Meriwether	404-672-4235
Miller	912-758-3416
Mitchell	912-336-8464
Monroe	912-994-1118
Montgomery	912-583-2240
Morgan	404-342-2214
Murray	404-695-3031
Muscogee	404-324-7711
Newton	404-786-2574
Oconee	404-769-5207
Oglethorpe	404-743-8341
Paulding	404-445-3885
Peach	912-825-6466
Pickens	404-692-2531
Pierce	912-449-4733
Pike	404-567-8948
Polk	404-748-3051
Pulaski	912-783-1171
Putnam	404-485-4151
Quitman	912-334-4303
Rabun	404-782-3113
Randolph	912-732-2311
Richmond	404-828-6812
Rockdale	404-922-7750
Schley	912-937-2601
Screven	912-564-2064
Seminole	912-524-2326
Spalding	404-228-9900
Stephens	404-886-4046
Stewart	912-838-4908
Sumter	912-924-4476
Talbot	404-665-3230
Tattnall	912-654-2593
Taylor	912-862-5496
Telfair	912-868-6489
Terrell	912-995-2165
Thomas	912-226-3954
Tift	912-382-3600
Toombs	912-526-3101
Towns	404-896-2024
Treutlen	912-529-3766
Troup	404-884-6686
Turner	912-567-3448
Twiggs	912-945-3391
Union	404-745-2524
Upson	404-647-8989
Walker	404-638-2548
Walton	404-267-3101
Ware	912-285-6161
Warren	404-465-2136
Washington	912-552-2011
Wayne	912-427-6865
Webster	912-828-2325
Wheeler	912-568-7138
White	404-865-2832
Whitfield	404-278-8207
Wilcox	912-365-2323
Wilkes	404-678-2332
Wilkinson	912-946-2367
Worth	912-776-2011

HAWAII

Hawaii-Hilo	808-959-9155
Hawaii-Kamuela	808-885-7318
Hawaii-Kona	808-322-2718
Kauai-Lihue	808-245-4471
Maui-Kahului	808-244-3242
Molokai-Kaunakai	808-567-6698
East Oahu-Kaneohe	808-247-0421
South Oahu-Honolulu	808-948-7138
West Oahu-Wahiawa	808-622-4185
Oahu-Pearl City	808-456-9581
Oahu-Waianae	808-696-3908

IDAHO

Ada	208-377-2107
Adams	208-253-4279
Bannock	208-236-7310
Bear Lake	208-945-2266
Benewah	208-245-2422
Bingham	208-785-5005
Blaine	208-788-3451
Bonner	208-263-8511
Bonneville	208-529-1390
Boundary	208-267-3235
Butte	208-527-8587
Camas	208-764-2230
Canyon	208-454-7461
Caribou	208-547-3205
Cassia	208-678-9461
Clark	208-374-5405
Clearwater	208-476-4434
Custer	208-879-2344
Elmore	208-587-4826
Fort Hall Indian Reservation	208-238-3777
Franklin	208-852-1097
Fremont	208-624-3102
Gem	208-365-6363
Gooding	208-934-4401
Idaho	208-983-2667
Jefferson	208-745-6685
Jerome	208-324-7578
Kootenai	208-667-6426
Latah	208-882-8580
Lemhi	208-756-2824
Lewis	208-937-2311
Lincoln	208-886-2406
Madison	208-356-3191
Minidoka	208-436-9331
Nez Perce	208-799-3096
North Idaho Agency	208-843-2267
Oneida	208-766-2243
Owyhee	208-896-4104
Payette	208-642-9397
Power	208-226-2077
Teton	208-354-2961
Twin Falls	208-734-3300
Valley	208-325-8566
Washington	208-549-0415

ILLINOIS

Adams	217-223-8380
Bond	618-664-3665
Boone	815-544-3710
Brown	217-773-3013
Bureau	815-875-2878
Calhoun	618-576-2293
Carroll	815-244-9444
Cass	217-452-3211
Champaign	217-352-3312
Christian	217-287-7246
Clark	217-826-5422
Clay	618-665-3328
Clinton	618-526-4551
Coles	217-345-7034
Cook	312-996-2620
Crawford	618-546-1549
Cumberland	217-849-3931
De Kalb	815-758-8194
De Witt	217-935-5764
Douglas	217-253-2713
Du Page	312-682-7485
Edgar	217-465-8585
Edwards	618-445-2934
Effingham	217-347-7773
Fayette	618-283-2753
Ford	217-388-7791
Franklin	618-439-3178
Fulton	309-547-3711
Gallatin	618-272-4561
Greene	217-942-6996
Grundy	815-942-2725
Hamilton	618-643-3416
Hancock	217-357-2150
Henderson	309-924-1471
Henry	309-937-2424
Iroquois	815-432-5416
Jackson	618-687-1727
Jasper	618-783-2521
Jefferson	618-242-0780
Jersey	618-498-4821
Jo Daviess	815-858-2273
Johnson	618-658-5322
Kane	312-584-6166
Kankakee	815-939-3626
Kendall	312-553-5824
Knox	309-342-5108
Lake	312-223-8627
La Salle	815-433-0707

Lawrence	618-943-5018
Lee	815-857-3525
Livingston	815-844-3622
Logan	217-732-8289
McDonough	309-837-3939
McHenry	815-338-3737
McLean	309-663-8306
Macon	217-877-6042
Macoupin	217-854-9604
Madison	618-656-8400
Marion	618-548-1446
Marshall-Putnam	309-364-2356
Mason	309-543-3308
Massac	618-524-2270
Menard	217-632-7491
Mercer	309-582-5106
Monroe	618-939-6617
Montgomery	217-532-3941
Morgan	217-243-7424
Moultrie	217-728-4318
Ogle	815-732-2191
Peoria	309-686-6033
Perry	618-357-2126
Piatt	217-762-2655
Pike	217-285-5543
Pope-Hardin	618-695-2441
Pulaski-Alexander	618-745-6310
Randolph	618-443-4364
Richland	618-395-2191
Rock Island	309-796-0512
St. Clair	618-233-1047
Saline	618-252-8391
Sangamon	217-782-4617
Schuyler	217-322-6033
Scott	217-742-3172
Shelby	217-774-4321
Stark	309-286-5421
Stephenson	815-235-4125
Tazewell	309-347-6614
Union	618-833-5841
Vermilion	217-442-8615
Wabash	618-262-5725
Warren	309-734-5161
Washington	618-327-8881
Wayne	618-842-3702
White	618-382-2276
Whiteside	815-772-4075
Will	815-727-9296
Williamson	618-993-3304
Winnebago	815-987-7379
Woodford	309-467-3789

INDIANA

Adams	219-724-3000
Allen	219-482-5401
Bartholomew	812-376-9337
Benton	317-884-0140
Blackford	317-348-3213
Boone	317-482-0750
Brown	812-988-4386
Carroll	317-564-3169
Cass	219-722-5050
Clark	812-283-4451
Clay	812-446-2413
Clinton	317-654-8721
Crawford	812-338-2352
Daviess	812-254-2188
Dearborn	812-926-1189
Decatur	812-663-8388
De Kalb	219-925-2562
Delaware	317-747-7732
Dubois	812-482-1782
Elkhart	219-533-0554
Fayette	317-825-8502
Floyd	812-948-5470
Fountain	317-793-2297
Franklin	317-647-6261
Fulton	219-223-3397
Gibson	812-385-3491
Grant	317-668-8871
Greene	812-659-2122
Hamilton	317-776-0854
Hancock	317-462-1113
Harrison	812-738-4236
Hendricks	317-745-9260
Henry	317-529-5002
Howard	317-459-8031
Huntington	219-356-1728
Jackson	812-358-3110
Jasper	219-866-5741
Jay	219-726-4707
Jefferson	812-265-3418
Jennings	812-346-5209
Johnson	317-738-3211
Knox	812-882-6368
Kosciusko	219-267-4444
La Grange	219-463-3512
Lake	219-738-2020
La Porte	219-326-6808
Lawrence	812-275-4623
Madison	317-646-9231
Marion	317-253-0871
Marshall	219-935-8545
Martin	812-247-3041
Miami	317-472-1921
Monroe	812-332-2366
Montgomery	317-362-5940
Morgan	317-342-6679
Newton	219-474-5187
Noble	219-636-2111
Ohio	812-438-3656
Orange	812-723-2439
Owen	312-829-2258
Parke	317-569-3176
Perry	812-547-7084
Pike	812-354-6838
Porter	219-464-8661
Posey	812-838-4449
Pulaski	219-946-3412
Putnam	317-653-8411
Randolph	317-584-2271
Ripley	812-689-6511
Rush	317-932-5974
St. Joseph	219-284-9604
Scott	812-752-2841
Shelby	317-398-4489
Spencer	812-649-2236
Starke	219-772-3553
Steuben	219-665-2189
Sullivan	812-268-4332
Switzerland	812-427-3152
Tippecanoe	317-423-9378
Tipton	317-675-2694
Union	317-458-5055
Vanderburgh	812-426-5287
Vermillion	317-492-3394
Vigo	812-238-8371
Wabash	219-563-8311
Warren	317-762-3231
Warrick	812-897-2500
Washington	812-883-4601
Wayne	317-966-7541
Wells	219-824-0116
White	219-583-7442
Whitley	219-244-7615

IOWA

Adair	515-743-8412
Adams	515-322-3184
Allamakee	319-568-6345
Appanoose	515-856-3885
Audubon	712-563-4239
Benton	319-472-4739
Black Hawk	319-234-6811
Boone	515-432-3882
Bremer	319-882-4275
Buchanan	319-334-7161
Buena Vista	712-732-5056
Butler	319-267-2707
Calhoun	712-297-8611
Carroll	712-792-2364
Cass	712-243-1132
Cedar	319-886-2252
Cerro Gordo	515-423-0844
Cherokee	712-225-6196
Chickasaw	515-394-2174
Clarke	515-342-3316
Clay	712-262-2264
Clayton	319-245-1451
Clinton	319-659-5125
Crawford	712-263-4697
Dallas	515-993-4281
Davis	515-664-2730
Decatur	515-446-4723
Delaware	319-927-4201
Des Moines	319-754-7556
Dickinson	712-336-3488
Dubuque	319-583-6496
Emmet	712-362-3434
Fayette	319-425-3331
Floyd	515-228-1453
Franklin	515-456-4811
Fremont	712-374-2351
Greene	515-386-2138
Grundy	319-824-6315
Guthrie	515-747-2276
Hamilton	515-832-5278
Hancock	515-923-2856
Hardin	515-858-5425
Harrison	712-644-2105
Henry	319-385-8126
Howard	319-547-3001
Humboldt	515-332-2201
Ida	712-364-2820
Iowa	319-642-5504
Jackson	319-652-4923
Jasper	515-792-6433
Jefferson	515-472-4166
Johnson	319-337-2145
Jones	319-462-2791
Keokuk	515-622-2680
Kossuth	515-295-2469
Lee	319-835-5116
Linn	319-377-9839
Louisa	319-523-2371
Lucas	515-774-2016
Lyon	712-472-2146
Madison	515-462-1001
Mahaska	515-673-5841
Marion	515-842-2014
Marshall	515-752-1551
Mills	712-624-8616
Mitchell	515-732-4903
Monona	712-423-2175
Monroe	515-932-5612
Montgomery	712-623-3820
Muscatine	319-263-5701
O'Brien	712-757-5045
Osceola	712-754-3648
Page	712-542-5171
Palo Alto	712-852-2865
Plymouth	712-546-7835
Pocahontas	712-335-3103
Polk	515-284-4158
East Pottawattamie	712-482-6449
West Pottawattamie	712-325-5551
Poweshiek	515-623-5188
Ringgold	515-464-3333
Sac	712-662-7131
Scott	319-359-7577
Shelby	712-755-3104
Sioux	712-737-4230
Story	515-382-6551
Tama	515-484-2703
Taylor	712-523-2137
Union	515-782-8426
Van Buren	319-293-3039
Wapello	515-682-9892
Warren	515-961-6237
Washington	319-653-4811
Wayne	515-872-1755
Webster	515-576-2119
Winnebago	515-584-2261
Winneshiek	319-382-2949
Woodbury	712-276-2157
Worth	515-324-1531
Wright	515-532-3453

KANSAS

Allen	316-365-2242
Anderson	913-448-6826
Atchison	913-883-5450
Barber	316-886-3313
Barton	316-793-3594
Bourbon	316-223-3720
Brown	913-742-2871
Butler	316-321-9660
Chase	316-273-6491
Chautauqua	316-725-3675
Cherokee	316-429-3849
Cheyenne	913-332-3171
Clark	316-635-2811
Clay	913-632-5335
Cloud	913-243-4549
Coffey	316-364-5313
Comanche	316-582-2411
Cowley	316-221-4066
Crawford	316-724-8233
Decatur	913-475-3142
Dickinson	913-263-2001
Doniphan	913-985-3623
Douglas	913-843-7058
Edwards	316-659-2149
Elk	316-374-2320
Ellis	913-625-6571
Ellsworth	913-472-3233
Finney	316-276-3205
Ford	316-227-3159
Franklin	913-242-3166
Geary	913-238-4161
Gove	913-938-4480
Graham	913-674-3411
Grant	316-356-1721
Gray	316-855-3821
Greeley	316-376-4284
Greenwood	316-583-6151
Hamilton	316-384-5225
Harper	316-842-5445
Harvey	316-283-6900
Haskell	316-675-2261
Hodgeman	316-357-6234
Jackson	913-364-4125
Jefferson	913-863-2212
Jewell	913-378-3174
Johnson	913-764-6300
Kearny	316-355-6551
Kingman	316-532-3721
Kiowa	316-723-2156
Labette	316-784-5337
Lane	316-397-5368
Leavenworth	913-682-7611
Lincoln	913-524-4548
Linn	913-795-2829
Logan	913-672-3245
Lyon	316-342-2437
Marion	316-382-2325
Marshall	913-562-3531
McPherson	316-241-1523

COUNTY EXTENSION AGENTS

Meade	316-873-2021
Miami	913-294-4306
Mitchell	913-738-3597
Montgomery	316-331-2690
Morris	316-767-5611
Morton	316-697-2558
Nemaha	913-336-2184
Neosho	316-244-3251
Ness	913-798-3193
Norton	913-877-2173
Osage	913-828-4438
Osborne	913-346-2521
Ottawa	913-392-2147
Pawnee	316-285-6901
Phillips	913-543-2722
Pottawatomie	913-457-3319
Pratt	316-672-6121
Rawlins	913-626-3192
Reno	316-662-2371
Republic	913-527-5084
Rice	316-257-5131
Riley	913-776-4781
Rooks	913-425-6851
Rush	913-222-2710
Russell	913-483-3157
Saline	913-827-3651
Scott	316-872-2930
Sedgwick	316-722-7721
Seward	316-624-5604
Shawnee	913-295-4120
Sheridan	913-675-3268
Sherman	913-899-7110
Smith	913-282-6151
Stafford	316-549-3502
Stanton	316-492-2240
Stevens	316-544-4359
Sumner	316-326-7477
Thomas	913-462-2491
Trego	913-743-6361
Wabaunsee	913-765-3821
Wallace	913-852-4285
Washington	913-325-2121
Wichita	316-375-2724
Wilson	316-378-2167
Woodson	316-625-3113
Wyandotte	913-299-9300

KENTUCKY

Adair	502-384-2317
Allen	502-237-3146
Anderson	502-839-7271
Ballard	502-665-9118
Barren	502-651-3818
Bath	606-674-6121
Bell	606-337-2376
Boone	606-334-2125
Bourbon	606-987-1895
Boyd	606-739-5184
Boyle	606-236-4484
Bracken	606-735-3150
Breathitt	606-666-8812
Breckenridge	502-756-2182
Bullitt	502-543-2257
Butler	502-526-3767
Caldwell	502-365-2787
Calloway	502-753-1452
Campbell	606-635-2116
Carlisle	502-628-5447
Carroll	502-732-4209
Carter	606-474-6686
Casey	606-787-7384
Christian	502-886-6328
Clark	606-744-4682
Clay	606-598-2789
Clinton	606-387-5404
Crittenden	502-965-5236
Cumberland	502-864-2681
Daviess	502-684-5228
Edmonson	502-597-2954
Elliott	606-738-6440
Estill	606-723-4557
Fayette	606-255-5582
Fleming	606-845-4641
Floyd	606-886-2668
Franklin	502-223-7616
Fulton	502-236-2351
Gallatin	502-567-5481
Garrard	606-792-3026
Grant	606-824-3355
Graves	502-247-2334
Grayson	502-259-3492
Green	502-932-5311
Greenup	606-473-9881
Hancock	502-927-6618
Hardin	502-765-4121
Harlan	606-573-4464
Harrison	606-234-5510
Hart	502-524-2451
Henderson	502-826-8387
Henry	502-845-2811
Hickman	502-653-2231
Hopkins	502-821-3650
Jackson	606-287-7693
Jefferson	502-425-4482
Jessamine	606-885-4811
Johnson	606-789-8108
Kenton	606-356-3155
Knott	606-785-5329
Knox	606-546-3447
Larue	502-358-3401
Laurel	606-864-4167
Lawrence	606-638-9495
Lee	606-464-2759
Leslie	606-672-2154
Letcher	606-633-2362
Lewis	606-796-2732
Lincoln	606-365-2459
Livingston	502-928-2168
Logan	502-726-6323
Lyon	502-388-2341
Madison	606-623-4072
Magoffin	606-349-3216
Marion	606-692-2421
Marshall	502-527-3285
Martin	606-298-7742
Mason	606-564-6808
McCracken	502-442-2718
McCreary	606-376-2524
McLean	502-273-3690
Meade	502-422-4958
Menifee	606-768-3866
Mercer	606-734-4378
Metcalfe	502-432-3561
Monroe	502-487-5504
Montgomery	606-498-5856
Morgan	606-743-3292
Muhlenberg	502-338-3124
Nelson	502-348-9204
Nicholas	606-289-2312
Ohio	502-298-7441
Oldham	502-222-9543
Owen	502-484-5703
Owsley	606-593-5109
Pendleton	606-654-3395
Perry	606-436-2044
Pike	606-432-6251
Powell	606-663-2252
Pulaski	606-679-6361
Robertson	606-724-5796
Rockcastle	606-256-2403
Rowan	606-784-5457
Russell	502-343-2161
Scott	502-863-0984
Shelby	502-633-4593
Simpson	502-586-4788
Spencer	502-477-2217
Taylor	502-465-4511
Todd	502-265-5659
Trigg	502-522-3269
Trimble	502-255-7188
Union	502-389-1400
Warren	502-842-1681
Washington	606-336-7741
Wayne	606-348-5686
Webster	502-639-9011
Whitley	606-549-1430
Wolfe	606-668-3712
Woodford	606-873-4601

LOUISIANA

Acadia	318-783-4772
Allen	318-639-4376
Ascension	504-644-8429
Assumption	504-369-6386
Avoyelles	318-253-7526
Beauregard	318-463-7006
Bienville	318-263-2321
Bossier	318-965-2326
Caddo	318-226-6805
Calcasieu	318-433-4671
Caldwell	318-649-2663
Cameron	318-775-5516
Catahoula	318-744-5442
Claiborne	318-927-3110
Concordia	318-336-5315
Desoto	318-872-0533
East Baton Rouge	504-389-3056
East Carroll	318-559-1459
East Felciana	504-683-5456
Evangeline	318-363-5646
Franklin	318-435-7551
Grant	318-627-3675
Iberia	318-367-7768
Iberville	504-687-3540
Jackson	318-259-2452
Jefferson	504-341-7271
Jefferson Davis	318-824-1773
Lafayette	318-233-1770
Lafourche	504-446-1316
Lasalle	318-992-2205
Lincoln	318-255-2580
Livingston	504-686-2593
Madison	318-574-2465
Morehouse	318-281-5741
Natchitoches	318-352-4421
Orleans	504-527-6941
Ouachita	318-323-2251
Plaquemines	504-682-0081
Pointe Coupee	504-638-7115
Rapides	318-445-9313
Red River	318-932-4342
Richland	318-728-3216
Sabine	318-256-3662
St. Bernard	504-279-9402
St. Charles	504-783-6231
St. Helena	504-222-4414
St. James	504-562-7431
St. John	504-497-3261
St. Landry	318-942-5761
St. Martin	318-332-2181
St. Mary	318-828-4100
St. Tammany	504-892-2208
Tangipahoa	504-748-9381
Tensas	318-766-3222
Terrebonne	504-868-3000
Union	318-368-9935
Vermillion	318-893-1356
Vernon	318-239-3231
Washington	504-839-4695
Webster	318-371-1371
West Baton Rouge	504-387-1448
West Caroll	318-428-3571
West Feliciana	504-635-3614
Winn	318-628-4528

MAINE

Androscoggin-Sagadahoc	207-783-8301
Aroostock	207-834-3905
Cumberland	207-780-4205
Franklin	207-778-4650
Hancock	207-667-8212
Kennebec	207-622-7546
Knox-Lincoln	207-594-2104
Oxford	207-743-6329
Penobscot	207-942-7396
Piscataquis	207-564-3301
Somerset	207-474-9622
Waldo	207-338-1650
Washington	207-255-3345
York	207-324-2814

MARYLAND

Allegany	302-724-3320
Anne Arundel	301-787-6755
Baltimore City	301-528-6990
Baltimore	301-666-0445
Calvert	301-535-3662
Caroline	301-479-4619
Carroll	301-848-4611
Cecil	301-398-0200
Charles	301-645-3903
Dorchester	301-228-8800
Frederick	301-694-1599
Garrett	301-334-2145
Harford	301-838-6000
Howard	301-992-2030
Kent	301-778-1661
Montgomery	301-948-9070
Prince George's	301-952-3312
Queen Anne's	301-758-0166
St. Mary's	301-475-5621
Somerset	301-651-1351
Talbot	301-822-1244
Washington	301-791-1304
Wicomico	301-749-6141
Worchester	301-632-1972

MASSACHUSETTS

Barnstable	617-362-2511
Berkshire	413-448-8285
Bristol	617-669-6744
Dukes	617-693-0694
Essex	617-774-0050
Franklin	413-774-2902
Hampden	413-736-7204
Hampshire	413-584-2556
Middlesex	617-369-4845
Norfolk	617-668-0268
Plymouth	617-293-3541
Suffolk	617-482-0395
Worcester	617-853-7317

MICHIGAN

Alcona	517-724-6478
Alger	906-387-2530
Allegan	616-673-8471
Alpena	517-354-3636
Antrim	616-533-8607
Arenac	517-846-4111
Baraga	906-524-6300
Barry	616-948-8039
Bay	517-893-3523
Benzie	616-882-9971
Berrien	616-983-7111
Branch	517-279-8411
Calhoun	616-781-0784
Cass	616-445-8661

Charlevoix	616-582-6232
Cheboygan	616-627-4501
Chippewa	906-632-2871
Clare	517-539-7805
Clinton	517-224-3288
Delta	906-786-3032
Dickinson	906-774-0363
Eaton	517-543-2310
Emmet	616-347-2596
Genesee	313-732-1474
Gladwin	517-426-7741
Gogebic	906-932-1420
Grand Traverse	616-941-2256
Gratiot	517-875-4125
Hillsdale	517-439-9301
Houghton-Keweenaw	906-482-5830
Huron	517-269-9949
Ingham	517-676-5222
Ionia	616-527-1400
Iosco	517-362-3449
Iron	906-875-6642
Isabella	517-772-0911
Jackson	517-788-4292
Kalamazoo	616-383-8830
Kalkaska	616-258-5074
Kent	616-774-3265
Lake	616-745-2721
Lapeer	313-667-0343
Leelanau	616-256-9888
Lenawee	517-263-8831
Livingston	517-546-3950
Luce	906-293-3203
Mackinac	906-643-9570
Macomb	313-469-5180
Manistee	616-889-4277
Marquette	906-228-8500
Mason	616-757-4789
Mecosta	616-796-7637
Menominee	906-753-2209
Midland	517-832-8838
Missaukee	616-839-4667
Monroe	313-243-7113
Montcalm	517-831-5226
Montmorency	517-785-4177
Muskegon	616-724-6361
Newaygo	616-924-0500
Oakland	313-858-0880
Oceana	616-873-2129
Ogemaw	517-345-0692
Ontanagon	906-884-4386
Osceola	616-832-3261
Oscoda	517-826-3241
Otsego	517-732-6484
Ottawa	616-846-8250
Presque Isle	517-734-2168
Roscommon-Crawford	517-275-5043
St. Clair	313-985-7169
St. Joseph	616-467-6361
Saginaw	517-790-5291
Sanilac	313-648-2515
Schoolcraft	906-341-5050
Shiawassee	517-743-3421
Tuscola	517-673-5999
Van Buren	616-657-5564
Washtenaw	313-973-9510
Wayne	313-721-6550
Wexford	616-775-7241

MINNESOTA

Aitkin	218-927-2102
Anoka	612-755-1280
Becker	218-847-7195
Beltrami	218-751-7300
Benton	612-968-7213
Big Stone	612-839-6151
Blue Earth	507-625-3031
Brown	507-794-7993
Carlton	218-384-4281
Carver	612-448-3435
Cass	218-547-3300
Chippewa	612-269-6521
Chisago	612-257-2983
Clay	218-299-5020
Clearwater	218-694-6151
Cook	218-387-2282
Cottonwood	507-831-4022
Crow Wing	218-829-1497
Dakota	612-463-3302
Dodge	507-374-6435
Douglas	612-763-2381
Faribault	507-526-2138
Fillmore	507-765-3896
Freeborn	507-373-1475
Goodhue	612-388-8261
Grant	218-685-4820
Hennepin	612-559-4321
Hennepin	612-872-9441
Houston	507-724-5211
Hubbard	218-732-3391
Isanti	612-689-1810
Itasca	218-326-9466
Jackson	507-662-5293
Kanabec	612-679-3010
Kandiyohi	612-235-1485
Kittson	218-843-3675
Koochiching	218-283-2581
Lac Qui Parle	612-598-3325
Lake	218-834-4395
Lake of the Woods	218-634-1511
Le Sueur	612-357-2251
Lincoln	507-694-1470
Lyon	507-537-6702
Mahnomen	218-935-2226
Marshall	218-745-5232
Martin	507-235-3341
McLeod	612-864-5551
Meeker	612-693-2801
Mille Lacs	612-983-2561
Morrison	612-632-2941
Mower	507-437-6616
Murray	507-836-8551
Nicollet	507-931-6800
Nobles	507-372-7711
Norman	218-784-7183
Olmsted	507-285-8250
E. Otter Tail	218-346-5750
W. Otter Tail	218-739-2271
Pennington	218-681-2116
Pine	612-384-6156
Pipestone	507-825-5416
E. Polk	218-563-2465
W. Polk	218-281-1751
Pope	612-634-5301
Ramsey	612-777-1327
Red Lake	218-253-2895
Red Lake Indian Reservation	218-679-3366
Redwood	507-637-8323
Renville	612-523-2522
Rice	507-334-2281
Rock	507-283-2648
Roseau	218-463-1052
Northern St. Louis	218-749-7120
South St. Louis	218-726-7512
Scott	612-492-2370
Sherburne	612-441-1441
Sibley	612-237-2344
Stearns	612-252-2132
Steele	507-451-8040
Stevens	612-589-4884
Swift	612-843-4796
Todd	612-732-6181
Traverse	612-563-4515
Wabasha	612-565-4509
Wadena	218-631-2332
Waseca	507-835-3610
Washington	612-777-4411
Watonwan	507-375-3341
Wilkin	218-643-5481
Winona	507-454-5101
Wright	612-339-6881
Yellow Medicine	612-669-4825

MISSISSIPPI

Adams	601-445-8201
Alcorn	601-286-5731
Amite	601-657-8902
Attala	601-289-5431
Benton	601-224-6722
Bolivar	601-843-8361
Calhoun	601-628-6671
Carroll	601-237-4413
Chickasaw	601-456-4269
Choctaw	601-285-6337
Claiborne	601-437-5011
Clarke	601-776-3951
Clay	601-494-5371
Coahoma	601-627-5204
Copiah	601-894-4081
Covington	601-765-8252
Desoto	601-368-5011
Forrest	601-545-2412
Franklin	601-384-2349
George	601-947-4223
Greene	601-394-2702
Grenada	601-226-2061
Hancock	601-467-5456
Harrison	601-863-6941
Hinds	601-372-4651
Holmes	601-834-2795
Humphreys	601-247-2915
Issaquena	601-873-2322
Itawamba	601-862-3201
Jackson	601-762-1303
Jasper	601-764-2314
Jefferson	601-786-3131
Jefferson Davis	601-792-5121
Jones	601-428-5201
Kemper	601-743-2837
Lafayette	601-234-4451
Lamar	601-794-8504
Lauderdale	601-482-9776
Lawrence	601-587-2271
Leake	601-267-7301
Lee	601-842-7461
Leflore	601-453-6803
Lincoln	601-833-5711
Lowndes	601-328-2111
Madison	601-859-3842
Marion	601-736-8251
Marshall	601-252-3541
Monroe	601-369-4951
Montgomery	601-283-4133
Neshoba	601-656-4602
Newton	601-635-2267
Noxubee	601-726-4326
Oktibbeha	601-323-5916
Panola	601-487-1725
Pearl River	601-795-4224
Perry	601-964-3668
Pike	601-783-5321
Pontotoc	601-489-4631
Prentiss	601-728-5631
Quitman	601-326-8939
Rankin	601-825-2217
Scott	601-469-4241
Sharkey	601-873-4246
Simpson	601-847-1335
Smith	601-782-4454
Stone	601-928-5286
Sunflower	601-887-4601
Tallahatchie	601-647-8746
Tate	601-562-4274
Tippah	601-837-8184
Tishomingo	601-423-3616
Tunica	601-363-2911
Union	601-534-4146
Walthall	601-876-4021
Warren	601-636-5442
Washington	601-332-0524
Wayne	601-735-2243
Webster	601-258-3971
Wilkinson	601-888-3211
Winston	601-773-3091
Yalobusha	601-675-2730
Yazoo	601-746-2453

MISSOURI

Adair	816-665-9866
Andrew	816-324-3147
Atchison	816-744-2490
Audrain	314-581-3231
Barry	417-847-3161
Barton	417-682-3570
Bates	816-679-4167
Benton	816-438-5012
Bollinger	314-238-2420
Boone	314-449-2541
Buchanan	816-279-1691
Butler	314-785-3634
Caldwell	816-586-2761
Callaway	314-642-5924
Camden	314-346-7214
Cape Girardeau	314-334-5219
Carroll	816-542-1788
Carter	314-323-4418
Cass	816-884-5100
Cedar	417-276-3313
Chariton	816-288-3239
Christian	417-485-2466
Clark	816-727-3330
Clay	816-781-0360
Clinton	816-539-2156
Cole	314-634-2824
Cooper	816-882-5661
Crawford	314-775-2135
Dade	417-637-2112
Dallas	417-345-7551
Daviess	816-663-3232
DeKalb	816-449-5811
Delta Center	314-379-5431
Dent	314-729-3196
Douglas	417-683-4409
Dunklin	314-888-4722
Franklin	314-583-5141
Gasconade	314-437-2165
Gentry	816-726-5610
Greene	417-862-9284
Grundy	816-359-5643
Harrison	816-425-6434
Henry	816-885-5556
Hickory	417-745-6767
Holt	816-446-3724
Howard	816-248-2272
Howell	417-256-2391
Iron	314-546-7515
Jackson	816-373-5500
Jasper	417-358-2158
Jefferson	314-789-2691
Johnson	816-747-3193
Knox	816-397-2179
Laclede	417-532-7126
LaFayette	816-584-3658
Lawrence	417-466-3197
Lewis	314-767-5273
Lincoln	314-528-4613

COUNTY EXTENSION AGENTS

Linn	816-895-5123
Livingston	816-646-0811
Macon	816-385-2173
Madison	314-783-2735
Maries	314-422-3359
Marion	314-769-2177
McDonald	417-223-4775
Mercer	816-748-3315
Miller	314-369-2394
Mississippi	314-683-6129
Moniteau	314-796-3154
Monroe	816-327-4158
Montgomery	314-564-3733
Morgan	314-378-5358
New Madrid	314-748-5531
Newton	417-451-1616
Nodaway	816-582-8101
Oregon	417-778-7490
Osage	314-897-3648
Ozark	417-679-3525
Pemiscot	314-333-0258
Perry	314-547-4504
Pettis	816-827-0591
Phelps	314-364-3147
Pike	314-324-5464
Platte	816-431-2165
Polk	417-326-4916
Pulaski	314-774-2111
Putnam	816-947-2705
Ralls	314-985-3911
Randolph	816-263-3534
Ray	816-776-6961
Reynolds	314-663-2251
Ripley	314-996-2921
St. Charles	314-623-4513
St. Clair	417-646-2419
St. Francois	314-756-4539
St. Genevieve	314-883-3548
St. Louis	314-553-5184
Saline	816-886-6908
Schuyler	816-457-3469
Scotland	816-465-8569
Scott	314-545-3516
Shannon	314-226-3715
Shelby	314-633-2640
Stoddard	314-568-3344
Stone	417-357-6812
Sullivan	816-265-4541
Taney	417-546-2371
Texas	417-967-3862
Vernon	417-667-7203
Warren	314-456-3444
Washington	314-438-2671
Wayne	314-224-3322
Webster	417-468-2044
Worth	816-564-3610
Wright	417-741-6465

MONTANA

Beaverhead	406-683-2842
Big Horn	406-665-1405
Blaine	406-357-3200
Broadwater	406-266-3419
Carbon	406-962-3545
Cascade	406-761-6700
Chouteau	406-622-3751
Custer	406-232-4781
Daniels	406-487-2861
Dawson	406-365-4277
Deer Lodge	406-563-8421
Fallon-Carter	406-778-2891
Fergus	406-538-3919
Flathead	406-755-5300
Gallatin	406-586-0271
Garfield	406-557-2770
Glacier	406-873-2382
Granite	406-859-3292
Hill	406-265-5481
Judith Basin	406-566-2210
Lake	406-676-4271
Lewis & Clark	406-443-1010
Liberty	406-759-5625
Lincoln	406-293-7781
Madison-Jefferson	406-287-3282
McCone	406-485-2605
Mineral	406-822-4561
Missoula	406-721-5700
Musselshell-Golden Valley	406-323-2704
Park	406-222-6120
Phillips	406-654-2543
Pondera	406-278-3121
Powell	406-846-3680
Powder River	406-436-2424
Prairie	406-637-5786
Ravalli	406-363-2044
Richland	406-482-1206
Roosevelt	406-787-5312
Rosebud-Treasure	406-356-7320
Sanders	406-827-3532
Sheridan	406-765-1020
Silver Bow	406-723-8262
Stillwater	406-322-5334
Sweet Grass	406-932-2445
Teton	406-466-2491
Toole	406-434-5351
Valley	406-228-2456
Wibaux	406-795-2432
Yellowstone	406-252-5181

NEBRASKA

Adams	402-463-2491
Antelope	402-887-4122
Boone-Nance	402-395-2158
Box Butte	308-762-5616
Boyd	402-775-2491
Brown, Rock, Keya Paha	402-387-2213
Buffalo	308-237-5966
Burt	402-374-2693
Butler	402-367-3091
Cass	402-267-2205
Cedar	402-254-6821
Chase	308-882-4731
Cherry	402-376-1850
Cheyenne	308-254-4455
Clay	402-762-3644
Colfax	402-352-3821
Cuming	402-372-5356
Custer	308-872-6831
Dakota	402-987-3541
Dawes	308-432-3373
Dawson	308-324-5501
Deuel	308-874-2705
Dixon	402-584-2261
Dodge	402-721-2081
Douglas	402-444-7804
Dundy	308-423-2021
Eureka	702-237-5326
Fillmore	402-759-3712
Franklin	308-425-6277
Frontier	308-367-4424
Furnas	308-268-3105
Gage	402-228-3315
Garden	308-772-3311
Garfield, Loup, Wheeler	308-346-4200
Greeley	308-428-2835
Hall	308-381-5088
Hamilton	402-694-6174
Harlan	308-928-2119
Hayes	308-286-3312
Hitchcock	308-334-5666
Holt	402-336-2760
Howard	308-754-5422
Jefferson	402-729-3487
Johnson	402-335-3669
Kearney	308-832-0430
Keith-Arthur	308-284-6051
Kimball-Banner	308-235-3122
Knox	402-288-4224
Lancaster	402-423-3806
Lander	702-635-5565
Lincoln	308-532-2683
Logan, McPherson	308-636-2332
Madison	402-675-2785
Merrick	308-946-3843
Morrill	308-262-1022
Nemaha	402-274-4959
Nukolls	402-225-2381
Otoe	402-269-2301
Pawnee	402-852-2970
Perkins	308-352-4340
Phelps-Gosper	308-995-4222
Pierce	402-329-4821
Platte	402-564-1311
Polk	402-747-2321
Red Willow	308-345-3390
Richardson	402-245-4324
Saline	402-821-2151
Sarpy	402-339-3225
Saunders	402-443-3522
Scotts Bluff	308-436-6622
Seward	402-643-2981
Sheridan	308-327-2312
Sherman	308-745-1518
Sioux	308-668-2428
Stanton	402-439-2231
Thayer	402-768-7212
Thomas, Blaine, Grant, Hooker	308-546-2247
Thurston	402-846-5656
Valley	308-728-5071
Washington	402-426-9455
Wayne	402-375-3310
Webster	402-746-3417
York	402-362-5508

NEVADA

Carson City, Storey	702-887-2252
Churchill	702-423-5121
Clark	702-731-3130
Douglas	702-782-5176
Or From Reno	702-883-1670, Ext. 278 or 279
Elko	702-738-7291
Eureka/Lander North	702-635-5565
Eureka/Lander South	702-237-5326
Humboldt	702-623-5081, Ext. 295 or 296
Lincoln	702-726-3101
Lyon	702-463-3341, Ext. 236
Nye & Esmeralda	702-482-6794
Pershing	702-273-2922
Washoe	702-784-4848
White Pine	702-289-4459

NEW HAMPSHIRE

Belknap	603-524-1737
Carroll	603-447-5922
Cheshire	603-352-4550
Coos	603-788-4961
Grafton	603-787-6944
Hillsboro	603-673-2510
Merrimack	603-225-5505
Rockingham	603-659-5669
Strafford	603-749-4445
Sullivan	603-543-3181

NEW JERSEY

Atlantic	609-625-7000
Bergen	201-646-2979
Burlington	609-267-3300
Camden	609-784-1001
Cape May	609-465-5115
Cumberland	609-451-2800
Essex	201-239-5213
Gloucester	609-881-1200
Hunterdon	201-788-1340
Jersey City	201-432-0574
Mercer	609-989-6830
Middlesex	201-745-3442
Monmouth	201-431-7260
Morris	201-285-6141
Ocean	201-349-1227
Passaic	201-881-4537
Salem	609-935-7510
Somerset	201-526-6293
Sussex	201-383-3800
Union	201-233-9366
Warren	201-475-5361

NEW MEXICO

Bernalillo	505-243-1386
Catron	505-533-6430
Chaves	505-622-3210
Cibola	505-287-9266
Colfax	505-445-8071
Curry	505-763-6505
De Baca	505-355-2381
Dona Ana	505-523-5618
Eddy	505-887-6595
Grant	505-388-1559
Guadalupe	505-472-3652
Harding	505-673-2341
Hidalgo	505-542-9291
Lea	505-396-3613
Lincoln	505-648-2311
Los Alamos	505-662-2656
Luna	505-546-8806
McKinley	505-863-3432
Mora	505-387-2856
Otero	505-437-0231
Quay	505-461-0562
Rio Arriba	505-753-3405
Roosevelt	505-356-4417
Sandoval	505-867-2582
San Juan	505-334-9496
San Miguel	505-454-1497
Santa Fe	505-471-4711
Sierra	505-894-2375
Socorro	505-835-0610
Taos	505-758-3982
Torrance	505-384-2372
Union	505-374-9361
Valencia	505-865-9561

NEW YORK

Albany	518-765-3635
Allegany	716-268-7644
Broome	607-722-8953
Cattaraugus	716-699-2377
Cayuga	315-255-1183
Chautauqua	716-664-9502
Chemung	607-739-0347
Chenango	607-334-5841
Clinton	518-561-7450
Columbia	518-828-3346
Cortland	607-753-5077
Delaware	607-865-6531
Dutchess	914-677-3489
Erie	716-652-3370
Essex	518-962-4810
Franklin	518-483-6767
Fulton	518-725-6441
Genesee	716-343-3040

Greene	518-622-9820
Hamilton	518-548-6191
Herkimer	315-866-7920
Jefferson	315-788-8450
Lewis	315-376-6551
Livingston	716-658-3250
Madison	315-684-3001
Monroe	716-461-1000
Montgomery	518-853-3471
Nassau	516-454-0900
Niagara	716-433-8839
Oneida	315-732-7131
Onondaga	315-424-9485
Ontario	716-394-3977
Orange	914-343-1105
Orleans	716-589-5561
Oswego	315-963-7286
Otsego	607-547-2536
Putnam	914-628-0454
Rensselaer	518-270-5376
Rockland	914-425-5500
St. Lawrence	315-379-2311
Saratoga	518-885-8995
Schenectady	518-384-0500
Schoharie	518-234-4303
Schuyler	607-535-7466
Seneca	315-539-9252
Steuben	607-776-7666
Suffolk	516-727-7850
Sullivan	914-292-6180
Tioga	607-687-4020
Tompkins	607-272-2292
Ulster	914-331-1680
Warren	518-623-3291
Washington	518-747-2861
Wayne	315-483-6918
Westchester	914-682-3340
Wyoming	716-786-2251
Yates	315-536-3381

NORTH CAROLINA

Alamance	919-227-1482
Alexander	704-632-4451
Alleghany	919-372-5597
Anson	704-694-2415
Ashe	919-246-3021
Avery	704-733-2415
Beaufort	919-946-0111
Bertie	919-794-3194
Bladen	919-862-4591
Brunswick	919-253-4425
Buncombe	704-255-5522
Burke	704-433-4050
Cabarrus	704-782-0212
Caldwell	704-758-8451
Camden	919-338-0171
Carteret	919-728-8421
Caswell	919-694-4158
Catawba	704-464-7880
Chatham	919-542-3974
Cherokee	704-837-2210
Cherokee Reservation	704-497-3521
Chowan	919-482-8431
Clay	704-389-6301
Cleveland	704-482-4365
Columbus	919-642-2788
Craven	919-633-1477
Cumberland	919-484-7156
Currituck	919-232-2261
Dare	919-473-2143
Davidson	704-246-5233
Davie	704-634-6297
Duplin	919-296-1996
Durham	919-688-2240
Edgecombe	919-823-8131
Forsyth	919-767-8213
Franklin	919-496-3344
Gaston	704-866-3002
Gates	919-357-1400
Graham	704-479-3320
Granville	919-693-8806
Greene	919-747-5831
Guilford	919-375-5876
Halifax	919-583-5161
Harnett	919-893-3339
Haywood	704-456-3575
Henderson	704-692-0216
Hertford	919-358-1591
Hoke	919-875-3461
Hyde	919-926-3201
Iredell	704-873-0507
Jackson	704-586-4009
Johnston	919-934-5003
Jones	919-448-9621
Lee	919-775-5624
Lenoir	919-527-2191
Lincoln	704-732-3361
McDowell	704-652-7030
Macon	704-524-6421
Madison	704-649-2411
Martin	919-792-1621
Mecklenburg	704-374-2561
Mitchell	704-688-2172
Montgomery	919-576-6011
Moore	919-947-5800
Nash	919-459-4141
New Hanover	919-762-1848
Northampton	919-534-2711
Onslow	919-455-5873
Orange	919-732-9361
Pamlico	919-745-4121
Pasquotank	919-338-3954
Pender	919-259-2330
Perquimans	919-426-5428
Person	919-599-1195
Pitt	919-752-2934
Polk	704-894-8218
Randolph	919-629-2131
Richmond	919-997-6251
Robeson	919-738-8111
Rockingham	919-349-3371
Rowan	704-633-0571
Rutherford	704-287-2211
Sampson	919-592-7161
Scotland	919-277-0470
Stanly	704-983-2123
Stokes	919-593-8179
Surry	919-386-8265
Swain	704-488-3121
Transylvania	704-884-2112
Tyrrell	919-796-1581
Union	704-289-5511, Ext. 335
Vance	919-438-8188
Wake	919-755-6100
Warren	919-257-3640
Washington	919-793-2163
Watauga	704-264-3061
Wayne	919-735-4331
Wilkes	919-667-5111
Wilson	919-237-0111
Yadkin	919-679-2061
Yancey	704-682-6187

NORTH DAKOTA

Adams	701-567-2735
Barnes	701-845-0931
Benson	701-473-5363
Billings	701-225-6006
Bottineau	701-228-2253
Bowman	701-523-5271
Burke	701-377-2927
Burleigh	701-255-4011
Cass	701-241-5700
Cavalier	701-256-2955
Dickey	701-349-3211
Divide	701-965-6501
Dunn	701-764-5593
Eddy	701-947-2454
Emmons	701-254-4811
Fort Berthold	701-627-3446
Foster	701-652-2581
Golden Valley	701-872-4332
Grand Forks	701-775-2571
Grant	701-622-3470
Griggs	701-797-3312
Hettinger	701-824-2095
Kidder	701-475-2672
LaMoure	701-883-5388
Logan	701-754-2504
McHenry	701-537-5405
McIntosh	701-288-3465
McKenzie	701-842-3451
McLean	701-462-8541
Mercer	701-873-5195
Morton	701-663-4235
Mountrail	701-628-2835
Nelson	701-247-2521
Oliver	701-794-8748
Pembina	701-265-8411
Pierce	701-776-6234
Ramsey	701-662-5354
Ransom	701-683-4175
Renville	701-756-6392
Richland	701-642-8481
Rolette	701-477-5671
Sargent	701-724-3355
Sheridan	701-363-2242
Sioux	701-854-3412
Slope	701-879-6270
Stark	701-225-6006
Steele	701-524-2253
Sutsman	701-252-9030
Towner	701-968-3433
Traill	701-436-5665
Walsh	701-284-6248
Ward	701-839-2412
Wells	701-547-3341
Williams	701-572-6373

OHIO

Adams	513-544-2339
Allen	419-222-9946
Ashland	419-289-0000
Ashtabula	216-576-3866
Athens	614-593-8555
Auglaize	419-738-2219
Belmont	614-695-1455
Brown	513-378-6716
Butler	513-867-5925
Carroll	216-627-4310
Champaign	513-652-2204
Clark	513-324-5791
Clermont	513-732-7195
Clinton	513-382-0901
Columbiana	216-424-7291
Coshocton	614-622-2265
Crawford	419-562-8731
Cuyahoga	216-631-1890
Darke	513-548-5215
Defiance	419-782-4771
Delaware	614-369-8761
Erie	419-627-7631
Fairfield	614-687-7010
Fayette	614-335-1150
Franklin	614-469-5595
Fulton	419-337-5515
Gallia	614-446-7007
Geauga	216-834-4656
Greene	513-372-9971
Guernsey	614-432-2959
Hamilton	513-825-6000
Hancock	419-422-3851
Hardin	419-675-6262
Harrison	614-942-8823
Henry	419-592-0806
Highland	513-393-1918
Hocking	614-385-3222
Holmes	216-674-3015
Huron	419-668-8219
Jackson	614-286-5044
Jefferson	614-283-3757
Knox	614-397-0401
Lake	216-354-3554
Lawrence	614-533-4322
Licking	614-345-6631
Logan	513-599-4227
Lorain	216-322-0127
Lucas	419-259-6364
Madison	614-852-0975
Mahoning	216-533-5538
Marion	614-387-2260
Medina	216-725-4911
Meigs	614-992-6696
Mercer	419-586-2179
Miami	513-335-8341
Monroe	614-472-0810
Montgomery	513-224-9654
Morgan	614-962-4854
Morrow	419-947-1070
Muskingum	614-454-0144
Noble	614-732-5681
Ottawa	419-898-1618
Paulding	419-399-3731
Perry	614-743-1602
Pickaway	614-474-7534
Pike	614-947-2121
Portage	216-296-6432
Preble	513-456-6268
Putnam	419-523-6294
Richland	419-589-2919
Ross	614-775-3200
Sandusky	419-332-5581
Scioto	614-353-5111
Seneca	419-447-9722
Shelby	513-492-9195
Stark	216-489-4488
Summit	216-434-2852
Trumbull	216-394-9246
Tuscarawas	216-364-8811
Union	513-642-1926
Van Wert	419-238-1214
Vinton	614-596-5961
Warren	513-932-1891
Washington	614-373-6623
Wayne	216-264-8722
Williams	419-636-5608
Wood	419-352-6531
Wyandot	419-294-4931

OKLAHOMA

Adair	918-696-2253
Alfalfa	405-596-3131
Atoka	405-889-7337
Beaver	405-625-3464
Beckham	405-928-2139
Blaine	405-623-5195
Bryan	405-924-5312
Caddo	405-247-3376
Canadian	405-262-0155
Carter	405-223-6570
Cherokee	918-456-6163
Chocktaw	405-326-3359
Cimarron	405-544-2562
Cleveland	405-321-4774
Coal	405-927-2262
Comanche	405-355-1176
Cotton	405-875-3136

COUNTY EXTENSION AGENTS

Craig	918-256-7569
Creek	912-224-2192
Custer	405-323-2291
Delaware	918-253-4332
Dewey	405-328-5351
Ellis	405-885-4021
Garfield	405-237-1229
Garvin	405-239-6681
Grady	405-224-5371
Grant	405-395-2134
Greer	405-782-2688
Harmon	405-688-3584
Harper	405-735-2252
Haskell	918-967-4330
Hughes	405-379-5470
Jackson	405-482-0823
Jefferson	405-228-2332
Johnston	405-371-3053
Kay	405-362-3194
Kingfisher	405-375-3822
Kiowa	405-726-3217
Latimer	918-465-3349
LeFlore	918-647-8231
Lincoln	405-258-0560
Logan	405-282-3331
Love	405-276-2110
Major	405-227-3786
Marshall	405-795-3563
Mayes	918-825-3241
McClain	405-527-2174
McCurtain	405-286-7558
McIntosh	918-689-7772
Murray	405-622-3016
Muskogee	918-687-2458
Noble	405-336-4621
Nowata	918-273-3345
Okfuskee	918-623-0641
Oklahoma	405-236-2727, Ext. 256
Okmulgee	918-756-1958
Osage	918-287-4170
Ottawa	918-542-1688
Pawnee	918-762-2735
Payne	405-624-9300 Ext. 24
Pittsburgh	918-423-4120
Pontotoc	405-332-2153
Pottawatomie	405-273-7683
Pushmataha	405-298-5563
Roger Mills	405-497-3339
Rogers	918-341-2736
Seminole	405-257-5433
Sequoyah	918-775-4838
Stephens	405-255-0510
Texas	405-338-7300
Tillman	405-335-2515
Tulsa	918-774-6635
Wagoner	918-485-2412
Washington	918-534-2216
Washita	405-832-3460
Woods	405-327-2786
Woodward	405-254-3391

OREGON

Baker	503-523-6414
Benton	503-757-6750
Clackamas	503-655-8631
Clatsop	503-325-8625
Columbia	503-397-3462
Coos	503-396-3121
Crook	503-447-6228
Curry	503-247-7011
Deschutes	503-548-6088
Douglas	503-672-4461
Gilliam	503-384-2271
Grant	503-575-1911
Harney	503-573-2506
Hood River	503-386-3343
Jackson	503-776-7371
Jefferson	503-475-3808
Josephine	503-476-6613
Klamath	503-883-7131
Lake	503-947-2279
Lane	503-687-4243
Lincoln	503-265-6611
Linn	503-967-3871
Malheur	503-881-1417
Marion	503-588-5301
Morrow	503-676-9642
Multnomah	503-229-4830
Polk	503-623-8395
Sherman	503-565-3230
Tillamook	503-842-5511
Umatilla	503-276-7111
Union	503-963-8686
Wallowa	503-426-3143
Wasco	503-296-5494
Washington	503-648-8771
Wheeler	503-763-4115
Yamhill	503-472-9371

PENNSYLVANIA

Adams	717-334-6271
Allegheny	412-392-8540
Armstrong	412-545-1625
Beaver	412-728-5700
Bedford	814-623-5148
Berks	215-378-1327
Blair	814-695-5541
Bradford	717-265-2896
Bucks	215-343-2800
Butler	412-287-4761
Cambria	814-472-7986
Cameron	814-483-3350
Carbon	717-325-2788
Centre	814-355-4897
Chester	215-696-3500
Clarion	814-226-8230
Clearfield	814-765-7878
Clinton	717-748-3110
Columbia	717-784-6660
Crawford	814-336-1151
Cumberland	717-249-7220
Dauphin	717-652-8460
Delaware	215-565-9070
Elk	814-776-1161
Erie	814-825-0900
Fayette	412-438-0111
Forest	814-755-3544
Franklin	717-263-9226
Fulton	717-485-4111
Greene	412-627-3745
Huntingdon	814-643-1660
Indiana	412-465-2666
Jefferson	814-849-7361
Juniata	717-436-8991
Lackawanna	717-961-4761
Lancaster	717-394-6851
Lawrence	412-658-2541
Lebanon	717-274-2801
Lehigh	215-820-3085
Luzerne	717-825-1701
Lycoming	717-327-2350
McKean	814-887-5613
Mercer	412-622-3800
Mifflin	717-248-9618
Monroe	717-421-6430
Montgomery	215-277-0574
Montour	717-275-3731
Northampton	215-759-6120
Northumberland	717-286-4569
Perry	717-582-2131
Philadelphia	215-276-5167
Pike	717-296-6122
Potter	814-274-8540
Schuylkill	717-385-3431
Snyder	717-837-0691
Somerset	814-445-8911
Sullivan	717-928-9264
Susquehanna	717-278-1158
Tioga	717-724-1906
Union	717-524-4461
Venango	814-437-7607
Warren	814-723-7550
Washington	412-228-6881
Wayne	717-253-5970
Westmoreland	412-837-1402
Wyoming	717-836-3196
York	717-757-9657

RHODE ISLAND

Eastern RI	401-847-0287
Northern RI	401-949-0670
Southern RI	401-277-3982

SOUTH CAROLINA

Abbeville	803-459-4106
Aiken	803-649-6671
Allendale	803-584-4231
Anderson	803-226-1581
Bamberg	803-245-2661
Barnwell	803-259-7141
Beaufort	803-525-7118
Berkeley	803-899-3431
Calhoun	803-874-2354
Charleston	803-724-4226
Cherokee	803-489-3141
Chester	803-385-6181
Chesterfield	803-623-2134
Clarendon	803-435-8429
Colleton	803-549-2596
Darlington	803-393-0481
Dillon	803-774-8218
Dorchester	803-563-3441
Edgefield	803-637-3161
Fairfield	803-635-4722
Florence	803-662-8719
Georgetown	803-546-4481
Greenville	803-232-4431
Greenwood	803-229-6681
Hampton	803-943-3427
Horry	803-248-2267
Jasper	803-726-3470
Kershaw	803-432-9071
Lancaster	803-283-3302
Laurens	803-984-2514
Lee	803-484-5416
Lexington	803-359-4265
McCormick	803-465-2112
Marion	803-423-0891
Marlboro	803-479-6851
Newberry	803-276-1091
Oconee	803-638-5889
Orangeburg	803-534-6280
Pickens	803-868-2810
Richland	803-256-1678
Saluda	803-445-8117
Spartanburg	803-582-6779
Sumter	803-773-5561
Union	803-427-6259
Williamsburg	803-354-6106
York	803-684-9919

SOUTH DAKOTA

Aurora	605-942-6411
Beadle	605-352-8559
Bennett/Shannon	605-685-6972
Bon Homme	605-589-3531
Brookings	605-692-6268
Brown	605-225-2500
Brule	605-734-6589
Butte	605-892-3371
Campbell	605-995-3305
Charles Mix	605-487-7666
Cheyenne	605-964-4955
Clark	605-532-3681
Clay	605-624-2005
Codington	605-886-7100
Corson	605-273-4368
Crow Creek/Lower Brule	605-473-5491
Custer	605-673-2372
Davison	605-996-7536
Day	605-345-4641
Deuel	605-874-2681
Dewey	605-865-3652
Douglas	605-724-2719
Edmunds	605-426-6971
Fall River	605-745-5133
Faulk	605-598-6221
Grant	605-432-9221
Gregory	605-775-2581
Haakon-Jackson	605-859-2840
Hamlin	605-783-3656
Hand	605-853-2738
Hanson	605-239-4542
Harding	605-375-3412
Hughes	605-224-6217
Hutchinson	605-387-2836
Hyde	605-852-2515
Jerauld	605-539-9471
Jones	605-669-2512
Kingsbury	605-854-3851
Lake	605-256-3596
Lawrence	605-642-4696
Lincoln	605-987-2756
Lyman	605-869-2226
McCook	605-425-2242
McPherson	605-439-3331
Marshall	605-448-5171
Meade	605-347-2436
Mellette	605-259-3385
Miner	605-772-4661
Minnehaha	605-334-7700
Moody	605-997-2469
Pennington	605-394-2188
Perkins	605-244-5622
Potter	605-765-9414
Roberts	605-698-7627
Sanborn	605-796-4380
Spink	605-472-2023
Standing Rock	605-823-4204
Stanley	605-223-2812
Sully	605-258-2334
Todd	605-856-4468
Tripp	605-842-2858
Turner	605-297-3112
Union	605-356-2321
Walworth	605-649-7607
Yankton	605-665-3387
Ziebach	605-365-5161

TENNESSEE

Anderson	615-457-5400
Bedford	615-684-5971
Benton	901-584-4601
Bledsoe	615-447-2451
Blount	615-982-6430
Bradley	615-476-4552
Campbell	615-562-9474
Cannon	615-563-2554
Carroll	901-986-3062
Carter	615-542-2641
Cheatham	615-792-4420
Chester	901-989-2461
Claiborne	615-626-3742
Clay	615-243-2311
Cocke	615-623-7531
Coffee	615-728-2612

Crockett	901-696-2412
Cumberland	615-484-6743
Davidson	615-259-6467
Decatur	901-852-2831
DeKalb	615-597-4945
Dickson	615-446-2788
Dyer	901-285-4781
Fayette	901-465-9857
Fentress	615-879-9117
Franklin	615-967-2741
Gibson	901-855-2061
Giles	615-363-3523
Grainger	615-828-3411
Greene	615-638-4196
Grundy	615-592-3971
Hamblen	615-586-6111
Hamilton	615-757-2533
Hancock	615-733-2526
Hardeman	901-658-2421
Hardin	901-925-3441
Hawkins	615-272-7241
Haywood	901-772-2861
Henderson	901-968-5266
Henry	901-642-2941
Hickman	615-729-2404
Houston	615-289-3242
Humphreys	615-296-2543
Jackson	615-268-9437
Jefferson	615-397-2969
Johnson	615-727-8161
Knox	615-521-2340
Lake	901-253-6528
Lauderdale	901-635-9551
Lawrence	615-762-5506
Lewis	615-796-3091
Lincoln	615-433-1582
Loudon	615-458-5612
Macon	615-666-3341
Madison	901-668-8543
Marion	615-942-2656
Marshall	615-359-1929
Maury	615-388-9557
McMinn	615-745-2852
McNairy	901-645-3598
Meigs	615-334-5781
Monroe	615-442-2433
Montgomery	615-647-6514
Moore	615-759-7163
Morgan	615-346-3000
Obion	901-885-3742
Overton	615-823-2735
Perry	615-589-2331
Pickett	615-864-3310
Polk	615-338-2841
Putnam	615-526-4561
Rhea	615-775-9222
Roane	615-376-5558
Robertson	615-384-7936
Rutherford	615-893-5010
Scott	615-663-2003
Sequatchie	615-949-2611
Sevier	615-453-3695
Shelby	901-521-2946
Smith	615-735-2900
Stewart	615-232-5682
Sullivan	615-323-7173
Sumner	615-452-1423
Tipton	901-476-8616
Trousdale	615-374-2421
Unicoi	615-743-9584
Union	615-992-8038
Van Buren	615-946-2435
Warren	615-473-8484
Washington	615-753-3138
Wayne	615-722-3229
Weakley	901-364-3164
White	615-836-3348
Williamson	615-794-8476
Wilson	615-444-9584

TEXAS

Anderson	214-729-5864
Andrews	915-523-2182
Angelina	713-634-3916
Aransas	See San Patricio
Archer	817-574-4914
Armstrong	806-226-3021
Atascosa	512-769-3066
Austin	713-865-2301
Bailey	806-272-4583
Bandera	512-796-3840
Bastrop	512-321-2184
Baylor	817-888-5581
Bee	512-358-4717
Bell	817-939-3521
Bexar	512-220-2774
Blanco	512-868-7167
Borden	915-856-4336
Bosque	817-435-2791
Bowie	214-628-2571
Brazoria	713-849-5711
Brazos	409-775-7400
Brewster-Jeff Davis	915-837-2265
Briscoe	806-823-2343
Brooks	512-325-3681
Brown	915-646-0386
Burleson	713-567-3255
Burnet	512-756-4641
Caldwell	512-398-3122
Calhoun	512-552-9747
Callahan	915-854-1518
Cameron	512-399-2448
Carson	806-537-3882
Camp	214-856-5005
Cass	214-756-5391
Castro	806-647-4115
Chambers	713-267-3185
Cherokee	214-683-4613
Childress	817-937-2351
Clay	817-538-5042
Cochran	806-266-5215
Coke	915-453-2461
Coleman	915-625-4519
Collin	214-542-9441
Collingsworth	806-447-2313
Colorado	713-732-2082
Comal	512-625-9178
Comanche	915-356-2424
Concho	915-732-4351
Cooke	817-665-4931
Coryell	817-865-2414
Cottle	806-492-3151
Crane	915-558-3522
Crockett	915-392-2721
Crosby	806-675-2003
Culberson	915-283-2057
Dallam	806-249-4434
Dallas	214-749-8401
Dawson	806-872-3444
Deaf Smith	806-364-3573
Delta	214-395-4417
Denton	817-566-3607
Dewitt	512-275-5132
Dickens	806-623-5243
Dimmit	512-876-2133
Donley	806-874-2141
Duval and Jim Hogg	512-256-3651
Eastland	817-629-1093
Ector	915-332-3321
Edwards	512-683-4310
El Paso	915-543-7419
Ellis	214-937-4461
Erath	817-965-3510
Falls	817-883-5311
Fannin	214-583-2929
Fayette	713-968-5831
Fisher	915-776-2171
Floyd	806-983-2806
Foard	817-684-1919
Fort Bend	713-342-3034
Franklin	214-537-4017
Freestone	214-389-3436
Frio	512-334-2372
Gaines	915-758-2241
Galveston	713-534-3413
Garza	806-495-2050
Gillespie	512-997-3452
Glasscock	915-354-2381
Goliad	512-645-3353
Gonzales	512-672-3149
Grayson	214-892-6541
Gray	806-669-7429
Gregg	214-758-6181
Grimes	713-825-3495
Guadalupe	512-379-1972
Hale	806-293-8481
Hall	806-259-3015
Hansford	806-659-2030
Hardeman	817-663-6301
Hardin	409-246-3484
Hamilton	817-386-3919
Harris	713-221-5020
Harrison	214-935-5278
Hartley	806-235-3122
Haskell	817-864-2658
Hays	512-392-2453
Hemphill	806-323-9114
Henderson	214-675-6130
Hill	817-582-5222
Hidalgo	512-383-2751
Hockley	806-894-3159
Hood	817-573-2438
Hopkins	214-885-3443
Houston	713-544-2358
Howard	915-267-6671
Hudspeth	915-369-2291
Hunt	214-455-4203
Hutchinson	806-878-2884
Irion	915-835-2711
Jack	817-567-2132
Jackson	512-782-3312
Jasper	713-384-3721
Jeff Davis	See Brewster
Jefferson	713-835-8461
Jim Hogg-Duval	512-527-4748
Jim Wells	512-664-3461
Johnson	817-645-6695
Jones	915-823-2432
Karnes	512-780-3380
Kaufman	214-932-4331
Kendall	512-249-2661
Kenedy	See Kleberg
Kent	806-237-3751
Kerr	512-257-6568
Kimble	915-446-2620
King	806-596-4451
Kinney	512-563-2442
Kleberg-Kenedy	512-592-3316
Knox	817-454-2651
Lamb	806-385-4004
Lampasas	512-556-3191
La Salle	512-879-2213
Lavaca	512-798-2221
Lee	713-542-2753
Leon	214-536-2531
Liberty	409-336-3872
Limestone	817-729-5314
Limpscomb	806-862-4601
Live Oak	512-449-1014
Loving	See Reeves
Lamar	214-785-4513
Llano	915-247-5159
Lubbock	806-741-8084
Lynn	806-998-4650
Madison	713-348-2234
Marion	214-665-2421
Martin	915-756-3316
Mason	915-347-6459
Matagorda	713-245-8415
Maverick	512-773-0258
Medina	512-426-2233
Menard	915-396-4787
McCulloch	915-597-2371
McLennan	817-756-7171
McMullen	512-274-3323
Midland	915-682-9481
Milam	817-697-3382
Mills	915-648-2650
Mitchell	915-728-3111
Montague	817-894-2833
Montgomery	409-539-7824
Moore	806-935-2594
Morris	214-645-3531
Motley	806-347-2733
Nacagdoches	713-564-0427
Newton	713-379-4831
Navarro	214-874-4778
Nolan	915-235-3184
Nueces	512-387-2051
Ochiltree	806-435-3831
Oldham	806-267-2692
Orange	713-883-7740
Palo Pinto	817-659-3651
Panola	214-693-2281
Parker	817-594-6143
Parmer	806-481-3619
Pecos	915-336-2541
Polk	713-327-8811
Potter	806-372-3829
Presidio	915-729-4746
Rains	214-473-2412
Randall	806-655-3371
Reagan	915-884-2335
Real	512-232-6673
Red River	214-427-2493
Reeves-Loving	915-445-2438
Refugio	512-526-2825
Roberts	806-868-3191
Robertson	713-828-4270
Rockwall	214-722-5747
Runnels	915-365-2219
Rusk	214-657-9546
Sabine	713-787-3752
San Augustine	713-275-3644
San Jacinto	713-653-2396
San Patricio-Aransas	512-364-2334
San Saba	915-372-5416
Schleicher	915-853-2610
Scurry	915-573-5423
Shackelford	915-762-2233
Shelby	713-598-3223
Sherman	806-396-2081
Smith	214-595-4861
Somervell	817-897-2289
Starr	512-487-2306
Stephens	817-559-2313
Sterling	915-378-3181
Stonewall	817-989-3510
Sutton	915-387-3604
Swisher	806-995-3726
Tarrant	817-334-1946
Taylor	915-677-1711
Terrell	915-345-2291
Terry	806-637-4060
Throckmorton	817-849-3321
Titus	214-572-5201

COUNTY EXTENSION AGENTS

Tom Green	915-653-2385
Travis	512-473-9600
Trinity	713-642-1421
Tyler	713-283-2482
Upshur	214-843-2511
Upton	915-693-2313
Uvalde	512-278-6661
Val Verde	512-774-3621
Van Zandt	214-567-4149
Victoria	512-575-4581
Walker	713-295-5481
Waller	713-826-3357
Ward	915-943-4112
Washington	713-836-6128
Webb	512-727-7272
Wharton	713-532-3371
Wheeler	806-826-5243
Wichita	817-766-0131
Wilbarger	817-552-2841
Willacy	512-689-2031
Williamson	512-863-2318
Wilson	512-393-2850
Winkler	915-586-2593
Wise	817-627-3341
Wood	214-763-2924
Yoakum	806-456-2263
Young	817-549-0737
Zapata	512-765-4663
Zavala	512-374-2883

UTAH

Beaver	801-438-2252
Box Elder	801-734-2031
Cache	801-752-6263
Carbon	801-637-4700
Davis	801-451-3402
Duchesne	801-738-2437
Emery	801-381-2381
Garfield	801-676-2201
Grand	801-259-7213
Iron	801-586-8132
Juab	801-623-1791
Kane	801-644-2551
Millard	801-743-5412
Morgan	801-829-3472
Piute	801-577-2901
Rich	801-793-2435
Salt Lake	801-533-7757
San Juan	801-587-2231
Sanpete	801-835-2151
Sevier	801-896-4609
Summit	801-336-5921
Tooele	801-882-5550
Uintah	801-789-1542
Utah	801-377-2797
Wasatch	801-654-3211
Washington	801-673-9647
Wayne	801-836-2662
Weber	801-399-5501

VERMONT

Addison	802-388-4969
Bennington	802-447-7582
Caledonia	802-748-8177
Chittenden	802-656-4420
Essex	802-676-3900
Franklin	802-524-6501
Lamoille	802-888-4972
Orange	802-685-4540
Orleans	802-334-7325
Rutland	802-773-3349
Washington	802-223-2380
Windham	802-257-7967
Windsor	802-457-2664

VIRGINIA

Abingdon	703-628-6033
Accomack	804-787-1361
Albemarle	804-296-2191
Alexandria, City of	703-838-4333
Alleghany	703-962-0276
Amelia	804-561-2481
Amherst	804-946-5445
Appomattox	804-352-8244
Arlington	703-558-2475
Augusta	703-885-8931
Bath	703-839-2661
Bedford	703-586-1053
Bland	703-688-3542
Botetourt	703-473-8260
Brunswick	804-848-2151
Buchanan	703-935-4769
Buckingham	804-969-4241
Campbell	804-332-5161
Caroline	804-633-6550
Carroll	703-728-7611
Charles City	804-829-2401
Charlotte	804-542-5884
Charlottesville, City of	804-296-7104
Chesapeake, City of	804-547-6348
Chesterfield	804-271-8989
Clarke	703-955-1131
Craig	703-864-5812
Culpeper	703-825-2233
Cumberland	804-492-4390
Danville, City of	804-799-6558
Dickenson	703-926-4605
Dinwiddie	804-469-3713
Essex	804-443-3551
Fairfax	703-691-3400
Fauquier	703-347-8650
Floyd	703-745-4135
Fluvanna	804-589-8122
Franklin	703-483-5161
Franklin, City of	804-562-4111
Frederick	703-662-8745
Giles	703-921-3455
Gloucester	804-693-2602
Goochland	804-556-3361
Grayson	703-773-2491
Greene	804-985-2510
Greensville	804-348-4233
Halifax	804-476-2147
Hampton	804-772-3791
Hampton, City of	804-727-6403
Hanover	804-798-6081
Henrico	804-264-7224
Henry	703-638-5311
Highland	703-468-2225
Holiday Lake	804-248-5444
Isle of Wight	804-357-4391
James City	804-564-3379
Jamestown	804-229-2571
King George	703-775-3062
King & Queen	804-785-2962
King William	804-769-2884
Lancaster	804-462-5780
Lee	703-346-1522
Loudon	703-777-0373
Louisa	703-967-1222
Lunenburg	804-676-2497
Lynchburg, City of	804-847-9096
Madison	703-948-6881
Mathews	804-725-7196
Mecklenburg	804-738-6133
Middlesex	804-758-4355
Montgomery	703-382-1431
Nelson	804-263-4035
New Kent	804-966-9861
Newport News, City of	804-595-7206
Norfolk, City of	804-446-4816
Norfolk, Navy Ser Project	804-489-8241
Northhampton	804-678-5134
Northern Virginia 4-H Ctr	703-635-7171
Northumberland	804-580-5694
Nottoway	804-645-9315
Orange	703-672-1361
Page	703-743-5794
Patrick	703-694-3341
Petersburg, City of	804-732-2775
Pittsylvania	804-432-2041
Powhatan	804-598-4271
Prince Edward	804-392-4246
Prince George	804-733-4189
Prince William	703-368-8989
Pulaski	703-980-8888
Radford	703-639-9313
Rappahannock	703-675-3619
Richmond	804-333-3420
Richmond, City of	804-786-4150
Richmond-NE	804-257-0027
Roanoke	703-387-6113
Roanoke, City of	703-982-7915
Rockbridge	703-463-4734
Rockingham	703-434-4455
Russell	703-889-1198
Scott	703-386-7574
Shenandoah	703-459-3739
Smyth	703-783-5175
Southampton	804-653-2572
Southeast 4-H Educ Ctr	804-899-4901
Southwest Virginia 4-H Educ Ctr	703-628-7231
Spotsylvania	703-582-6361
Stafford	703-899-4020
Suffolk, City of	804-539-2381
Surry	804-294-3650
Sussex	804-246-5511
Tazewell	703-988-2588
Virginia Beach, City of	804-427-4769
Warren	703-635-4549
Washington	703-628-2161
West Central 4-H Educ Ctr	703-721-2759
Westmoreland	804-493-8911
Windsor	804-242-6195
Wise	703-328-3699
Wythe	703-228-2148
York	804-898-0050

WASHINGTON

Adams	509-659-0090
Asotin	509-243-4118
Benton	509-786-1912
Chelan	509-663-1121
Clallam	206-452-7831
Clark	206-699-2385
Columbia	509-382-4741
Cowlitz	206-577-3014
Douglas	509-745-7411
Ferry	509-775-3161
Franklin	509-545-3511
Garfield	509-843-3701
Grant	509-754-2011
Grays Harbor	206-249-4332
Island	206-678-5111
Jefferson	206-385-3581
King	206-344-2686
Kitsap	206-876-7157
Kittitas	509-925-3157
Klickitat	509-773-5817
Lewis	206-748-9121
Lincoln	509-725-4171
Mason	206-426-4732
Okanogan	509-422-3670
Pacific	206-875-6541
Pend Oreille	509-447-3325
Pierce	206-593-4190
San Juan	206-378-4414
Skagit	206-336-9322
Skamania	509-427-5141
Snohomish	206-259-9422
Spokane	509-456-3651
Stevens	509-684-2588
Thurston	206-753-8056
Wahkiakum	206-795-3278
Walla Walla	509-525-7930
Whatcom	206-676-6736
Whitman	509-397-3401
Yakima	509-575-4218

WEST VIRGINIA

Barbour	304-457-3254
Berkeley	304-263-4901
Boone	304-369-3925
Braxton	304-765-5261
Brooke	304-737-3666
Cabell	304-522-8301
Calhoun	304-354-6332
Clay	304-587-4267
Doddridge	304-873-1801
Fayette	304-574-1200
Gilmer	304-462-7061
Grant	304-257-4688
Greenbrier	304-645-1525
Hampshire	304-822-5013
Hancock	304-564-3311
Hardy	304-538-2373
Harrison	304-624-7431
Jackson	304-372-2011
Jefferson	304-725-9761
Kanawha	304-348-7176
Lewis	304-269-4660
Lincoln	304-824-7472
Logan	304-752-2000
McDowell	304-585-7237
Marion	304-366-3331
Marshall	304-843-1170
Mason	304-675-3710
Mercer	304-487-1439
Mineral	304-788-3621
Mingo	304-235-2175
Monongalia	304-296-6621
Monroe	304-772-3003
Morgan	304-258-1431
Nicholas	304-872-3630
Ohio	304-234-3673
Pendleton	304-358-2286
Pleasants	304-684-3119
Pocahontas	304-799-4852
Preston	304-329-1391
Putnam	304-586-2321
Raleigh	304-255-1401
Randolph	304-636-2455
Ritchie	304-643-2162
Roane	304-927-1930
Summers	304-466-3711
Taylor	304-265-3303
Tucker	304-478-2949
Tyler	304-758-2101
Upshur	304-472-2660
Wayne	304-272-5101
Webster	304-847-2727
Wetzel	304-455-1601
Wirt	304-275-3101
Wood	304-422-6461
Wyoming	304-732-6711

COUNTY EXTENSION AGENTS

WISCONSIN

Adams	608-339-7811
Ashland	715-682-8137
Barron	715-537-3124
Bayfield	715-373-2221
Brown	414-497-3216
Buffalo	608-685-4560
Burnett	715-866-4201
Calumet	414-849-2361
Chippewa	715-723-9195
Clark	715-743-3118
Columbia	608-742-2191
Crawford	608-326-6431
Dane	608-266-4271
Dodge	414-386-4411
Door	414-743-5511
Douglas	715-395-0363
Dunn	715-232-1636
Eau Claire	715-839-4712
Florence	715-528-4480
Fond Du Lac-UW Ctr	414-929-3170
Forest	715-478-2212
Grant	608-723-2125
Green	608-325-5181
Green Lake	414-294-6573
Iowa	608-935-3354
Iron	715-561-2695
Jackson	715-284-7441
Jefferson	414-674-2500
Juneau	608-847-5659
Kenosha	414-656-6793
Kewaunee	414-388-2542
LaCrosse	608-785-9593
Lafayette	608-776-4494
Langlade	715-627-6236
Lincoln	715-536-7151
Manitowoc	414-683-4167
Marathon	715-847-5259
Marinette	715-735-3371
Marquette	414-297-5119
Menominee	715-799-3641
Milwaukee	414-257-5351
Monroe	608-269-8722
Oconto	414-834-5322
Oneida	715-362-6314
Outagamie	414-735-5119
Ozaukee	414-284-9411
Pepin	715-672-5214
Pierce	715-273-4376
Polk	715-485-3136
Portage	715-346-1316
Price	715-339-2555
Racine	414-886-2744
Richland	608-647-6148
Rock	608-755-2196
Rusk	715-532-5539
St. Croix	715-684-3301
Sauk	608-356-5581
Sawyer	715-634-4839
Shawano	715-526-6136
Sheboygan	414-459-3141
Taylor	715-748-3327
Trempealeau	715-538-2311
Vernon	608-637-2165
Vilas	715-479-4797
Walworth	414-723-3838
Washburn	715-635-3192
Washington	414-338-4479
Waukesha	414-544-8080
Waupaca	715-258-7681
Waushara	414-787-4631
Winnebago	414-424-0050
Wood	715-421-8440

WYOMING

Albany	307-742-3749
Big Horn	307-568-2281
Campbell	307-682-7282
Carbon	307-328-2642
Converse	307-358-2417
Crook	307-283-1192
Fremont	307-332-5673
Goshen	307-532-2436
Hot Springs	307-864-3421
Johnson	307-684-7522
Laramie	307-634-4415
Lincoln	307-886-3132
Natrona	307-235-9400
Niobrara	307-334-3534
Park	307-587-2204
Platte	307-322-3667
Sheridan	307-672-2733
Sublette	307-367-4380
Sweetwater	307-362-3461
Teton	307-733-3087
Uinta	307-789-3277
Washakie	307-347-3431
Weston	307-746-3531

U.S. MEASURE AND METRIC MEASURE CONVERSION CHART

Formulas for Exact Measures	Symbol	When you know:	Multiply by	To find:	Rounded Measures for Quick Reference		
Mass (Weight)	oz	ounces	28.35	grams	1 oz		= 30 g
	lb	pounds	0.45	kilograms	4 oz		= 115 g
	g	grams	0.035	ounces	8 oz		= 225 g
	kg	kilograms	2.2	pounds	16 oz	= 1 lb	= 450 kg
					32 oz	= 2 lb	= 900 kg
					36 oz	= 2 1/4 lb	= 1000g (a kg)
Volume	tsp	teaspoons	5.0	milliliters	1/4 tsp	= 1/24 oz	= 1 ml
	tbsp	tablespoons	15.0	milliliters	1/2 tsp	= 1/12 oz	= 2 ml
	fl oz	fluid ounces	29.57	milliliters	1 tsp	= 1/6 oz	= 5 ml
	c	cups	0.24	liters	1 tbsp	= 1/2 oz	= 15 ml
	pt	pints	0.47	liters	1 c	= 8 oz	= 250 ml
	qt	quarts	0.95	liters	2 c (1 pt)	= 16 oz	= 500 ml
	gal	gallons	3.785	liters	4 c (1 qt)	= 32 oz	= 1 l
	ml	milliliters	0.034	fluid ounces	4 qt (1 gal)	= 128 oz	= 3 3/4- l
Length	in.	inches	2.54	centimeters	3/8 in.	= 1 cm	
	ft	feet	30.48	centimeters	1 in.	= 2.5 cm	
	yd	yards	0.9144	meters	2 in.	= 5 cm	
	mi	miles	1.609	kilometers	2-1/2 in.	= 6.5 cm	
	km	kilometers	0.621	miles	12 in. (1 ft)	= 30 cm	
	m	meters	1.094	yards	1 yd	= 90 cm	
	cm	centimeters	0.39	inches	100 ft	= 30 m	
					1 mi	= 1.6 km	
Temperature	°F	Fahrenheit	5/9 (after subtracting 32)	Celsius	32°F	= 0°C	
					68°F	= 20°C	
	°C	Celsius	9/5 (then add 32)	Fahrenheit	212°F	= 100°C	
Area	in.^{2}	square inches	6.452	square centimeters	1 in.^{2}	= 6.5 cm^2	
	ft^2	square feet	929.0	square centimeters	1 ft^2	= 930 cm^2	
	yd^2	square yards	8361.0	square centimeters	1 yd^2	= 8360 cm^2	
	a	acres	0.4047	hectares	1 a	= 4050 m^2	

GENERIC AND TRADE NAMES OF SOME COMMON CHEMICALS

GENERIC NAME	TRADE NAME	ORTHO PRODUCT
Acephate	Orthene®	ORTHENE Systemic Insect Control ORTHENEX Insect & Disease Control Systemic Rose & Floral Spray
Allethrin	Bioallethrin	
Basic Copper Sulfate	Tri-basic Copper Sulfate	
Benomyl	Benlate®	
Bensulide	Betasan®	
Captan	Orthocide®	Home Orchard Spray ORTHOCIDE Garden Fungicide Tomato Vegetable Dust
Carbaryl	Sevin®	Liquid SEVIN Gypsy Moth & Japanese Beetle Killer Rose & Floral Dust SEVIN Garden Dust SEVIN Garden Spray
Chloroneb	Demosan®	
Chlorothalonil	Daconil 2787®	Liquid Lawn Disease Control Vegetable Disease Control
Chlorpyrifos	Dursban®	Lawn Insect Spray ORTHO-KLOR Soil Insect & Termite Killer ORTHO-KLOR Indoor & Outdoor Insect Killer Home Pest Insect Control FLEA-B-GON Flea & Tick Killer
Cycloheximide	Acti-Dione®	
Dalapon	Dowpon®	
DCPA	Dacthal®	Garden Weed Preventer
Diazinon		Diazinon Granules Diazinon Insect Spray Diazinon Soil & Foliage Dust Diazinon Soil & Turf Insect Control Fruit & Vegetable Insect Control Vegetable Guard Insect Killer
Dicamba	Banvel®	Chickweed, Spurge & Oxalis Killer D
Dichlobenil	Casoron®	CASORON Granules
Dicofol	Kelthane®	ISOTOX Insect Killer ORTHENEX Insect & Disease Control Rose & Floral Dust
Dimethoate	Cygon®	
Dinocap	Karathane®	
Diphenamid	Dymid®	
Disulfoton	Di-Syston®	Systemic Rose & Flower Care
Folpet	Phaltan®	PHALTAN Rose & Garden Fungicide Rose & Floral Dust
Glyphosate	Kleenup®	KLEENUP Spot Weed & Grass Killer KLEENUP Ready-To-Use Grass & Weed Killer KLEENUP Systemic Weed & Grass Killer
Iprodione	Rovral®	
Lime Sulfur	Orthorix®	Dormant Disease Control ORTHORIX Spray
Lindane		Lindane Borer & Leafminer Spray
Linuron	Lorox®	
Malathion		Malathion 50 Insect Spray Home Orchard Spray Rose & Floral Dust
Mancozeb	Dithane® M-45	
Maneb	Dithane® M-22	
Mecoprop	MCPP	WEED-B-GON Lawn Weed Killer WEED-B-GON Weed Killer Chickweed & Clover Control WEED-B-GON For Southern Grasses
Methoxychlor		Home Orchard Spray Tomato Vegetable Dust
PCNB	Terrachlor®	
Propoxur	Baygon®	Ant, Roach & Spider Killer Earwig, Roach & Sowbug Bait Hornet & Wasp Killer Mole Cricket Bait PEST-B-GON Roach Bait
Pyrethrins		Indoor Plant Insect Spray Tomato & Vegetable Insect Spray Rose & Flower Insect Killer Tomato & Vegetable Insect Killer
Resmethrin		Systemic Rose & Floral Spray Home & Garden Insect Killer House Plant Insect Control Whitefly & Mealybug Killer
Rotenone		Rotenone Dust or Spray Tomato & Vegetable Insect Spray Tomato Vegetable Dust
Trifluralin	Treflan®	3-Way Rose & Flower Care
Triforine	Funginex®	FUNGINEX Rose Disease Control ORTHENEX Insect & Disease Control Systemic Rose & Floral Spray
Siduron	Tupersan®	
Simazine	Princep®	
Streptomycin	Phytomycin®	
Zineb	Dithane® Z-78	
Ziram	Cumin®	
2,4-D	Weed-B-Gon®	WEED-B-GON Lawn Weed Killer WEED-B-GON Weed Killer Poison Oak & Poison Ivy Killer Chickweed, Spurge & Oxalis Killer D

CHEMICAL TRADEMARK INFORMATION

ISOTOX, KLEENUP, ORTHO, ORTHENE, ORTHENEX, ORTHOCIDE, ORTHO-KLOR, ORTHORIX, PEST-B-GON, PHALTAN, WEED-B-GON—REG. TM OF CHEVRON CHEMICAL CO.; BENLATE, DEMOSAN, LOROX, TUPERSAN, CUMIN—REG. TM OF E.I. DUPONT DE NEMOURS & CO.; BETASAN—REG. TM OF STAUFFER CHEMICAL CO.; SEVIN—REG. TM OF UNION CARBIDE CORP.; DACONIL, DACTHAL—REG. TM OF DIAMOND SHAMROCK CORP.; ACTI-DIONE—REG. TM OF TUCO PRODUCTS COMP., DIVISION OF THE UPJOHN CO.; DOWPON, DURSBAN—REG. TM OF DOW CHEMICAL CO.; BAYGON—REG. TM OF FARBENFABRIKEN BAYER A.G., CHEMARGO CORP. LICENSEE. BANVEL—REG. TM OF VELSICOL CHEMICAL CORP.; CASORON—REG. TM OF DUPHAR B.V. AMSTERDAM, HOLLAND. KELTHANE, KARATHANE, DITHANE—REG. TM OF ROHM & HAAS CHEMICAL CO.; CYGON—REG. TM OF AMERICAN CYNAMID CO.; DYMID, TREFLAN—REG. TM OF ELI LILLY & CO.; ROVRAL—REG. TM OF RHONE-POULENC INC. TERRACLOR—REG. TM OF OLIN MATHIESON CHEMICAL CORP.; FUNGINEX—REG. TM OF CELAMERK G.M.B.H. PRINCEP—REG. TM OF CIBA-GEIGY CORP.; PHYTOMYCIN—REG. TM OF CHARLES PFIZER AND CO.

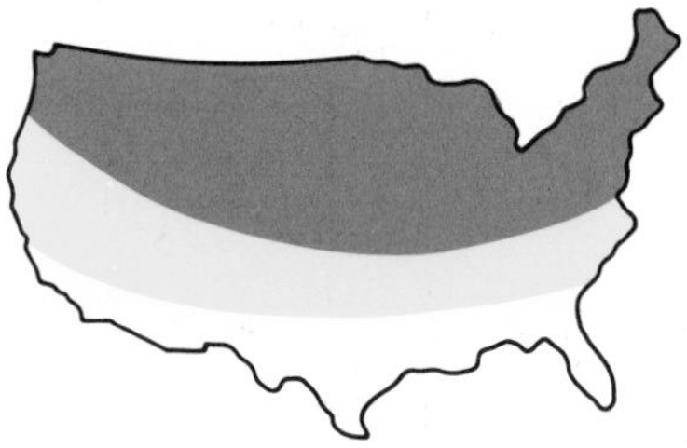

Each problem is accompanied by a map of the United States. In parts of the country that are colored red, the problem is severe or commonplace. In parts of the country that are yellow, the problem is secondary or occasional. In parts of the country that are white, the problem is rare or nonexistent.

HOW TO USE THIS BOOK

1. ■ If you know the name of your plant, the problem it has, or the insect that is bothering it, look up that name in the index beginning on **PAGE 17.**

2. ■ If you don't know the name of your plant, turn to one of these sections:

3. ■ If you have a household pest and don't know its name, turn to **PAGE 785.**

4. ■ If you want to know more about a problem, turn to one of these pages:

5. ■ For a complete description of ORTHO products and a list of the problems each solves, turn to **PAGE 929.**